Discovering Our

Features and Benefits

Dynamic Instructional Strategies

. . . present a clear and comprehensive coverage of history.

- Standards-based instruction offers a comprehensive content base.
- Engaging section introductions include *Guide to Reading; Looking Back, Looking Ahead; Focusing on the Main Ideas;* and *Reading Strategy.*
- Several features allow students to compare primary sources.
- *Big Ideas* are noted throughout the text to alert students to the "big picture."

A Strong Reading Strand

. . . encourages active reading and learning for students of all reading levels.

- A two-page *Get Ready to Read!* reading strategy at the beginning of each chapter reinforces good reading habits.
- *Foldables*™ help students organize and process key concepts as they read.
- *Writing prompts* and activities develop writing and retention skills for students.
- *Reading Checks* help students check their reading comprehension.

Universal Access

. . . makes *Discovering Our Past* accessible to students of all learning levels.

- *Universal Access* activities and strategies are designed for students of differing abilities.
- Glencoe *Booklink CD-Rom* allows teachers to generate reading lists by topic, reading level, or theme.

State Standards Practice

. . . gives students the opportunity to practice for state and national exams.

- Appropriate content standards are listed on pages where students read about them.
- *Section and Chapter Assessments* provide a variety of standards practice opportunities in test question format.
- *At-Home Standards Review* offers additional standards practice.

Intervention

. . . tools help teachers diagnose and prescribe student needs effectively.

- Teacher Wraparound Edition activities scaffold Reading Strategies and Critical Thinking Skills.
- Content *Big Ideas* are presented and reinforced throughout the Student Edition and Teacher Edition.
- Assessment tools—based in print and technology—serve as diagnostic and prescriptive tools.

Teacher Resources and Professional Development

. . . provide convenient strategies to help new and experienced teachers.

- The *Planning Guide* in each unit and chapter provides background information to help you prepare for each unit.
- *Fast File*™ chapter resources contain important reproducible masters.
- *Chapter Videos* offer high interest previews of each chapter.
- Professional Development videos give teaching tips.

Technology

. . . provides time-saving software products to help creatively engage students and reduce your preparation time.

- *Study Central* is an Internet homework helper that makes more content, skills practice, and vocabulary development available.
- *Glencoe Skillbuilder Interactive Workbook, Level 1* offers individual skills practice.
- *TeacherWorks*™ and *ExamView*®*Pro Testmaker CD-ROMs* make lesson preparation and assessment easier.
- Web site ca.hss.glencoe.com holds additional, text-specific resources.

Improving Active Reading and Study Skills

Dinah Zike's FOLDABLES™

Foldables are easy-to-make, three-dimensional, interactive graphic organizers that students create out of plain sheets of paper. The Teacher Classroom Resources includes *Dinah Zike's Reading and Study Skills Foldables*™. This booklet provides you with step-by-step instructions for using Foldables in your classroom. Each Foldable is designed to be used as a study guide for the main ideas and key points presented in a chapter. Foldables can also be used for a more in-depth investigation of a concept, idea, opinion, event, or a person or place studied in a chapter. These unique hands-on tools for studying and reviewing were created exclusively for Glencoe by education specialist Dinah Zike.

Why Use Foldables in Social Studies?

Because they:

- organize, display, and arrange information, making it easier for students to grasp social studies concepts, theories, facts, opinions, questions, research, and ideas.
- are student-made study guides that are compiled as students listen for main ideas, read main ideas, or conduct research.
- integrate language arts, the sciences, and mathematics into the study of social studies.
- provide a multitude of creative formats in which students can present projects, research, interviews, and inquiry-based reports.
- replace teacher-generated writing or photocopied sheets with student-generated print.
- incorporate the use of such skills as comparing and contrasting, recognizing cause-and-effect, and finding similarities and differences.
- continue to immerse students in previously learned vocabulary, concepts, information, generalizations, ideas, and theories, providing them with a strong foundation that they can build upon with new observations, concepts, and knowledge.
- can be used by students or teachers to easily communicate data through graphs, tables, charts, models, and diagrams, including Venn diagrams.
- allow students to make their own journals for recording observations, research information, primary and secondary source data, surveys, and so on.
- can be used as alternative assessment tools by teachers to evaluate student progress or by students to evaluate their own progress.
- provide a sense of student ownership or investiture in the social studies curriculum.

Student Edition ►

FOLDABLES™ Study Organizer

Cause-and-Effect Study Foldable Make this foldable to help you analyze the causes and effects of growth in the East and expansion into the West of the United States.

Step 1 Fold one sheet of paper in half from top to bottom.

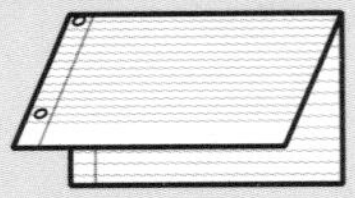

Step 2 Fold it in half again, from side to side.

Step 3 Unfold the paper once. Sketch an outline of the United States across both tabs and label them as shown.

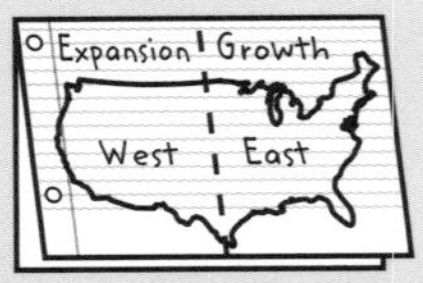

Step 4 Cut up the fold of the top flap only.

Reading and Writing As you read the chapter, list causes and effects of eastern growth and western expansion under the appropriate tabs of your foldable.

TEACHER WRAPAROUND EDITION

8 GLENCOE CALIFORNIA SERIES

DISCOVERING OUR PAST

The American Journey

TO WORLD WAR I

JOYCE APPLEBY, PH.D. ■ ALAN BRINKLEY, PH.D. ■ ALBERT S. BROUSSARD, PH.D.
JAMES M. MCPHERSON, PH.D. ■ DONALD A. RITCHIE, PH.D.

NATIONAL GEOGRAPHIC

McGraw Hill Glencoe

New York, New York   Columbus, Ohio   Chicago, Illinois   Peoria, Illinois   Woodland Hills, California

Authors

Joyce Appleby, Ph.D., is Professor of History at UCLA. Dr. Appleby's published works include *Inheriting the Revolution: The First Generation of Americans; Capitalism and a New Social Order: The Jeffersonian Vision of the 1790s;* and *Ideology and Economic Thought in Seventeenth-Century England,* which won the Berkshire Prize. She served as president of both the Organization of American Historians and the American Historical Association, and chaired the Council of the Institute of Early American History and Culture at Williamsburg. Dr. Appleby has been elected to the American Philosophical Society and the American Academy of Arts and Sciences, and is a Corresponding Fellow of the British Academy.

Alan Brinkley, Ph.D., is University Provost and Allan Nevins Professor of History at Columbia University. His published works include *Voices of Protest: Huey Long, Father Coughlin, and the Great Depression,* which won the 1983 National Book Award; *The End of Reform: New Deal Liberalism in Recession and War; The Unfinished Nation: A Concise History of the American People;* and *Liberalism and its Discontents.* He received the Levenson Memorial Teaching Prize at Harvard University.

Albert S. Broussard, Ph.D., is Professor of History at Texas A&M University. Before joining the Texas A&M faculty, Dr. Broussard was Assistant Professor of History and Director of the African American Studies Program at Southern Methodist University. Among his publications are the books *Black San Francisco: The Struggle for Racial Equality in the West, 1900-1954* and *African American Odyssey: The Stewarts, 1853-1963.* Dr. Broussard has also served as president of the Oral History Association, has chaired the nominating committee of the Organization of American Historians, was the Texas A&M University Distinguished Lecturer for 1999-2000, and received a distinguished teaching award from the College of Liberal Arts.

About the Cover The images on the cover are: the Statue of Liberty, covered wagons beneath Eagle Rock at the Scotts Bluff National Monument in Nebraska, and Independence Hall in Philadelphia.

James M. McPherson, Ph.D., is George Henry Davis Professor Emeritus of American History at Princeton University. Dr. McPherson is the author of 13 books about the Civil War era. These include *Battle Cry of Freedom: The Civil War Era,* for which he won the Pulitzer Prize in 1989, and *For Cause and Comrades: Why Men Fought in the Civil War,* for which he won the 1998 Lincoln Prize. He is a member of many professional historical associations, including the Civil War Preservation Trust.

Donald A. Ritchie, Ph.D., is Associate Historian of the United States Senate Historical Office. Dr. Ritchie received his doctorate in American history from the University of Maryland after service in the U.S. Marine Corps. He has taught American history at various levels, from high school to university. He edited the Executive Sessions of the Senate Permanent Subcommittee on Investigations (the McCarthy hearings) and is the author of several books, including *Doing Oral History; Reporting From Washington: The History of the Washington Press Corps;* and *Press Gallery: Congress and the Washington Correspondents,* which received the Organization of American Historians Richard W. Leopold Prize. Dr. Ritchie has served as president of the Oral History Association and as a council member of the American Historical Association.

The National Geographic Society, founded in 1888 for the increase and diffusion of geographic knowledge, is the world's largest nonprofit scientific and educational organization. Since its earliest days, the Society has used sophisticated communication technologies, from color photography to holography, to convey knowledge to a worldwide membership. The School Publishing Division supports the Society's mission by developing innovative educational programs–ranging from traditional print materials to multimedia programs including CD-ROMs, videodiscs, and software. "National Geographic Geography & History," featured in this textbook, was designed and developed by the National Geographic Society's School Publishing Division.

Glencoe

The McGraw-Hill Companies

Send all inquiries to:
Glencoe/McGraw-Hill, 8787 Orion Place, Columbus, Ohio 43240–4027

ISBN 0-07-869377-2 (Teacher Edition)
ISBN 0-07-869386-1 (Student Edition)
Printed in the United States of America.
3 4 5 6 7 8 9 10 027/043 10 09 08 07 06

Contributing Authors, Consultants, & Reviewers

Contributing Authors

Stephen F. Cunha, Ph.D.
Professor of Geography
Director, California Geographic Alliance
Humboldt State University
Arcata, California

Douglas Fisher, Ph.D.
Professor
San Diego State University
San Diego, California

Nancy Frey, Ph.D.
Assistant Professor
San Diego State University
San Diego, California

Robin C. Scarcella, Ph.D.
Professor and Director
Academic English/ESL
University of California, Irvine
Irvine, California

Emily M. Schell, Ed.D.
Visiting Professor, San Diego State University
Social Studies Education Director
SDSU City Heights Educational Collaborative
San Diego, California

David Vigilante
Associate Director
National Center for History in the Schools
San Diego, California

Ruben Zepeda II, Ed.D.
Adviser, Instructional Support Services
Los Angeles Unified School District
Los Angeles, California

Academic Consultants

Richard G. Boehm, Ph.D.
Professor of Geography
Southwest Texas State University
San Marcos, Texas

Margo J. Byerly, Ph.D.
Assistant Professor of Social Studies Methods
Ball State University
Muncie, Indiana

Maureen D. Danner
Project CRISS
National Training Consultant
Kalispell, Montana

Frank de Varona
Visiting Associate Professor
Department of Curriculum and Instruction
Florida International University
Miami, Florida

Barbara S. Lindemann, Ph.D.
Professor of History and Ethnic Studies
History Department Chair
Santa Barbara City College
Santa Barbara, California

William E. Nelson, Jr., Ph.D.
Research Professor of Black Studies
and Professor of Political Science
The Ohio State University
Columbus, Ohio

Bernard Reich, Ph.D.
Professor of Political Science
and International Affairs
George Washington University
Washington, D.C.

Carol M. Santa, Ph.D.
Director of Education
Montana Academy
CRISS Project Developer
Kalispell, Montana

Elmer Whitcraft
Project CRISS Master Trainer
Kalispell, Montana

FOLDABLES™ **Dinah Zike**
Educational Consultant
Dinah-Might Activities, Inc.
San Antonio, Texas

Reading Consultants

Maureen D. Danner
Project CRISS
National Training Consultant
Kalispell, Montana

ReLeah Cossett Lent
Florida Literacy and Reading Excellence
Project Coordinator
University of Central Florida
Orlando, Florida

Steve Qunell
Social Studies Instructor
Montana Academy
Kalispell, Montana

Carol M. Santa, Ph.D.
CRISS: Project Developer
Director of Education
Montana Academy
Kalispell, Montana

Bonnie Valdes
Project CRISS, Master Trainer
Largo, Florida

Teacher Reviewers

Tabitha Barry
Diegueño Middle School
Encinitas, California

Patrick Bernhardt
John Muir Middle School
San Jose, California

Jennifer Dunlap
Vail Ranch Middle School
Temecula, California

Rob Gaudette
Dale Junior High School
Anaheim, California

Tiffany Gretton
C.A. Jacobs Intermediate
Dixon, California

Brent E. Heath, Ph.D.
De Anza Middle School
Ontario, California

Wayne Osako
Haskell Middle School
Cerritos, California

Andrew Wagoner
Coalinga Middle School
Coalinga, California

California Advisory Board

Eric E. Anderson
American Government Instructor
Pomona Unified School District
Pomona, CA

John Charles Burdick
Social Studies Adviser
Local District H/ Los Angeles Unified School District
Los Angeles, CA

Jan Coleman-Knight
History Department Chair
Thornton Junior High School
Fremont Unified School District
Fremont, CA

Stephen F. Cunha, Ph.D.
Professor of Geography
Director, California Geographic Alliance
Humboldt State University
Arcata, CA

Gail Desler
Social Studies Teacher/Technology Integration Specialist
Elk Grove Unified School District
Elk Grove, CA

Matt Duffy
Social Science Teacher
C.A. Jacobs Intermediate
Dixon Unified School District
Dixon, CA

Douglas Fisher, Ph.D.
Professor
San Diego State University
San Diego, CA

Susan Fisher
Social Studies, English, and Drama Teacher
Los Angeles Unified School District
Los Angeles, CA

Nancy Frey, Ph.D.
Assistant Professor
San Diego State University
San Diego, CA

Brent E. Heath, Ph.D.
Social Studies Chair/GATE Facilitator
De Anza Middle School
Ontario-Montclair School District
Ontario, CA

L. Martha Infante
History and Geography Teacher
Bethune Middle School
Los Angeles Unified School District
Los Angeles, CA

Donna J. Leary
Educational Consultant
University of California, Berkeley
Berkeley, CA

California Advisory Board

Helen Ligh
Social Studies and Language Arts Teacher
Macy Intermediate
Montebello Unified School District
Monterey Park, CA

Barbara S. Lindemann, Ph.D.
Professor of History and Ethnic Studies
History Department Chair
Santa Barbara City College
Santa Barbara, CA

Reynaldo Antonio Macías
World History Teacher
Mark Twain Middle School
Los Angeles Unified School District
Los Angeles, CA

Jennifer Metherd
Program Coordinator
Tehama County Department of Education
Red Bluff, CA

Derrick K. Neal
Social Studies Department Chair
Patrick Henry Middle School
Los Angeles Unified School District
Los Angeles, CA

Robin C. Scarcella, Ph.D.
Professor and Director
Academic English/ESL
University of California, Irvine
Irvine, CA

Emily M. Schell, Ed.D.
Visiting Professor, San Diego State University
Social Studies Education Director
SDSU City Heights Educational Collaborative
San Diego, CA

Dale Steiner, Ph.D.
Professor of History
California State University, Chico
Chico, CA

Roy Sunada
Social Studies Teacher/AP Coordinator
Marshall Fundamental Secondary School
Pasadena Unified School District
Pasadena, CA

David Vigilante
Associate Director
National Center for History in the Schools
San Diego, CA

Ruben Zepeda II, Ed.D.
Adviser, Instructional Support Services
Los Angeles Unified School District
Los Angeles, CA

Contents

Classroom Solutions: Teacher Professional Handbook T24

Emily Schell: Backward Mapping T24
Douglas Fisher: Meeting the Diverse Needs of Our Students T26
Robin Scarcella: Academic Vocabulary T30
Project CRISS T32
Primary Source Strategies T38
Reading in the Content Areas T40
Test-Taking Strategies T42
Alternative Assessment Strategies T44

Teacher Edition Walk-Through T46

Teacher Edition Correlation to the California Standards T62

A Guide to the California Standards........ CA1

Student Edition Correlation to the California Standards....... CA15

At-Home Standards Review CA24

Previewing Your Textbook 1

Scavenger Hunt 13

Reading Skills Handbook 14

NATIONAL GEOGRAPHIC Reference Atlas Maps 24

World: Political 26
North America: Political 28
North America: Physical 29
United States: Political 30
United States: Physical 32
United States: Territorial Growth 34
United States Facts 36

NATIONAL GEOGRAPHIC Geography Handbook 38

How Do I Study Geography? 39
How Do I Use Maps and Globes? 41
Understanding Latitude and Longitude 42
Parts of Maps 43
Types of Maps 44
Geographic Dictionary 46

Tools of the Historian 48

Measuring Time 50
Organizing Time 52
History and Geography 54
What Is a Historical Atlas? 58
How Does a Historian Work? 60
Making Sense of the Past 64
Links Across Time 68

▼ The Golden Gate Bridge

Contents

Revolutionary War drum and fife ▶

Unit 1

A Changing World 72

CHAPTER 1:
Expanding Horizons 76

READING Previewing 78

1 Age of Exploration 80
2 Rise of Modern Capitalism 90
3 The Enlightenment 98

CHAPTER 2:
Road to Independence 112

READING Identifying the Main Idea . . . 114

1 Founding the American Colonies 116
2 Life in Colonial America. 125
3 Trouble in the Colonies 134
4 War of Independence. 149
The Declaration of Independence 164

Unit 2

Creating a Nation. 170

CHAPTER 3:
A More Perfect Union 174

READING Making Connections 176

1 The Articles of Confederation 178
2 Convention and Compromise 193
3 A New Plan of Government 202

CHAPTER 4:
The Constitution 214

READING Summarizing Information . . . 216

1 Goals of the Constitution. 218
2 The Federal Government. 226
3 Citizens' Rights and Responsibilities. 234
The Constitution of the United States 248

Unit 3

Launching the Republic 270

CHAPTER 5:
The Federalist Era 274

READING Recognizing Bias 276

1 The First President 278
2 Early Challenges 285
3 The First Political Parties 290

CHAPTER 6:
The Age of Jefferson. 302

READING Compare and Contrast 304

1 The Republicans Take Power 306
2 The Louisiana Purchase 312
3 Daily Life in Early America 320

CHAPTER 7:
Foreign Affairs in the Early Republic. . . 334

READING Identifying Cause and Effect. 336

1 A Time of Conflict 338
2 The War of 1812. 353
3 Foreign Relations 362

Preparing the Declaration of Independence ▼

Contents

Pioneer chest ▶

Unit 4

The Young Republic 374

CHAPTER 8:
The Northeast: Building Industry 378
READING Problems and Solutions 380
1 Economic Growth 382
2 A System of Transportation 388
3 The North's People 395
4 Reforms and Reformers 402
5 The Women's Movement 408

CHAPTER 9:
The South 418
READING Questioning 420
1 Southern Cotton Kingdom 422
2 Life in the South 427
3 The Peculiar Institution 432

CHAPTER 10:
The Age of Jackson 442
READING Question and Answer Relationships 444
1 Jacksonian Democracy 446
2 The Removal of Native Americans 452
3 Jackson and the Bank 458

CHAPTER 11:
Manifest Destiny 466
READING New Vocabulary 468
1 Westward to the Pacific 470
2 Independence for Texas 480
3 War With Mexico 490
4 New Settlers in California and Utah 500

Unit 5

Civil War and Reconstruction 520

CHAPTER 12:
Road to Civil War 524
READING Making Inferences 526
1 Abolitionists 528
2 Slavery and the West 535
3 A Nation Dividing 543
4 Challenges to Slavery 548
5 Secession and War 554

CHAPTER 13:
The Civil War 566
READING Evaluation 568
1 The Two Sides 570
2 Early Years of the War 576
3 A Call to Freedom 591
4 Life During the Civil War 597
5 The Way to Victory 604

CHAPTER 14:
Reconstruction 620
READING Monitoring and Clarifying 622
1 Reconstruction Plans 624
2 Radicals in Control 629
3 The South During Reconstruction 635
4 Change in the South 640

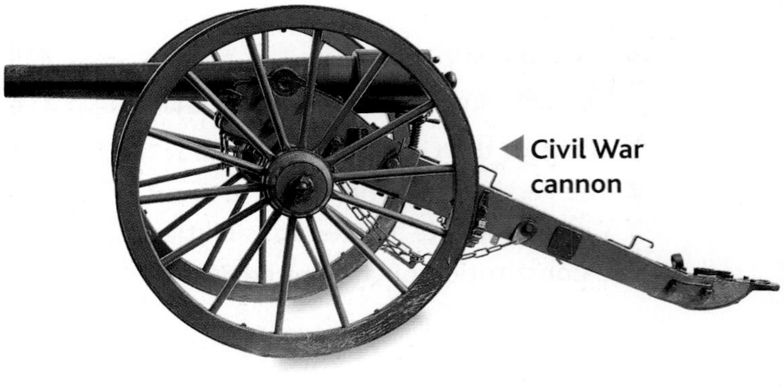

◀ Civil War cannon

Unit 6

Reshaping the Nation 658

CHAPTER 15:
The Western Frontier 662
READING Visualizing 664
1 The Mining Booms 666
2 Ranchers and Farmers 672
3 Native American Struggles 685
4 Farmers in Protest 693

CHAPTER 16:
The Growth of Industry........... 702
READING Predicting Consequences... 704
1 Railroads Lead the Way 706
2 Inventions 712
3 The Age of Big Business 718
4 Industrial Workers 724

CHAPTER 17:
America Enters a New Century 736
READING Visual Literacy 738
1 The New Immigrants 740
2 Moving to the City 750
3 A Changing Culture 757
4 The Progressive Movement 764
5 A Changing Nation 774

Connections to Today 792
1 A Changing Nation in a Changing World ... 794
2 A Changing Society 798
3 New Roles, New Faces 806
4 Rights and Responsibilities 812

Appendix

What is an Appendix? 821
SkillBuilder Handbook 822
Presidents of the United States 840
Honoring America 845
Supreme Court Case Summaries 846
Documents of American History 850
California Standards Handbook 862
English Glossary 885
Spanish Glossary 896
Gazetteer 909
Index 914
Acknowledgements 934

1912 Model T Ford ▲

Features

Analyzing Primary Sources

The Wealth of Nations 94
Guarantees of Rights 106
Columbus Crosses the Atlantic 108
Cortés Encounters the Aztecs 109
The Coming Conflict 139
Penn's Colony 160
The Germantown Protest 160
Poor Richard's Almanack 161
Richard Allen and Absalom Jones 196
The Oneida and the Use of Land 210
What Is an American? 211
Statute for Religious Freedom 235
The Federalist, No. 10 242
Objections to the Constitution 243
On Becoming President 298
Washington's First Inaugural 298
The Great Seal of the United States 299
California in 1804 330
The Explorations of Lewis and Clark 330
Adams's Fourth of July Address 331
Tecumseh's Prediction 342
Treaties with Native Americans 343
"The Star-Spangled Banner" 356
The Battle of Stonington 368
War and Expansion 368
Against the Draft 369
Lowell Girls 385
Newcomers to America 398
On Equality for Women 412
Religious Camp Meeting 414
American Notes 415
Travel on the Erie Canal 415
Working the Cotton Fields 434
A New Invention 438
The Living Conditions of Enslaved Persons 439
News From the South 439
The Inauguration of Andrew Jackson 462
Indian Removal 463
Declaration of War with Mexico 514
The Oregon Trail 514
Petition for Justice 515
Abolishing Slavery 531
The Liberator 562
On the Eve of War 563
"Swing Low, Sweet Chariot" 563
What Was the Reaction to the Gettysburg Address? 607
Early Days of the War 616
Destruction Caused by Troops 616
Barbara Frietchie 617
Jim Crow Laws 647
The South in Ruins 652
On the Plight of African Americans 653
Sarah Winnemucca 691
On the Cattle Trail 698
Winter in Dakota Territory 699
Indian School 699
John Henry 732
The Sweatshop 733
Child Labor 733
George Washington Carver 782
Hull House 786
The Jungle 787

Biography

Lorenzo de' Medici 92
John Locke 104
Junípero Serra 118
Benjamin Franklin 151
James Madison 198
Gouverneur Morris 220
John Marshall 232
Alexander Hamilton 283
Abigail Adams and John Adams 294
Washington Irving and
James Fenimore Cooper 324
Henry Clay and John C. Calhoun 344
Dolley Madison 357
Robert Fulton 391
Henry David Thoreau and
Martin Luther King, Jr. 404
Harriet Tubman 436
Osceola 456
María Amparo Ruiz de Burton 493
John Bidwell and Annie Bidwell 502
Harriet Beecher Stowe 545
Bridget Mason 551
Clara Barton 601
Robert E. Lee and Ulysses S. Grant 611
Charlotte Forten 627
Frederick Douglass 637
The Buffalo Soldiers 677
Chief Joseph 690
Leland Stanford and Charles Crocker 708
Mary Harris Jones and
César Estrada Chávez 728
Jacob Riis 768
Booker T. Washington and
W.E.B. Du Bois 781

TECHNOLOGY & History

Spanish Galleon 85
The *Mayflower* 120
The Conestoga Wagon 314
Textile Mill 384
The *Clermont* 390
How a Canal Works 392
The Cotton Gin 424
Civil War Camera 602
Steam Locomotive 669

◀ Abigail Adams

Frederick Douglass ▶

America's Literature

"Paul Revere's Ride" 142
Second Daughter 186
Crossing the Panther's Path 346
Thunder on the Sierra 507
Rifles for Watie 584
A Lantern in Her Hand 680

Why It Matters

The Great Awakening 128
Surveying the Land 182
The Seneca Falls Convention 410
The Emancipation Proclamation 592
The First Flight at Kitty Hawk 714

Features

History Makers

The Compass, c. 1086 82
The Hispanic Heritage 88
Promoting the General Welfare 219
Roots of the Two-Party System 238
The Capitol 282
Washington Serves Two Terms 291
The American Spelling Book 321
Oberlin and Higher Education 409
Fall Lines 423
Myths and Legends 448
Technology of the Civil War 578
The Impact of the Railroad 707
Standard Time Zones 709
Immigration Stations 744

TIME NOTEBOOK

New Horizons: 1790–1820 360
Looking Westward: 1850–1860 478
Reshaping the Nation: 1885–1914 784

▼ Molly Pitcher at the Battle of Monmouth

More About...

The Boston Tea Party 138
The Alien and Sedition Acts 295
Immigration 399
Living Under Slavery 435
The Oregon Trail 473
Changing the Way We Live 716
Immigration 778

The Way It Was

Home Remedies 195
Working on the Constitution 197
Washington in 1800 308
Moving West 328
One-Room Schoolhouse 406
The California Constitution 504
Agrarians and Industrialists 538
School Days 758

Linking Past & Present

Navigation Tools 83
Women in War 154
Symbols of the Nation 200
The New England Town Meeting 237
The Electoral College 280
Blue Jeans 503

You Decide ...

Independence: Yes or No? 158
Ratifying the Constitution 208
Manifest Destiny: Justified or Not? 476
Union or Confederacy? 560
Should Immigration Be Limited? 748

▼ Immigrant children learn American ways in the classroom.

SkillBuilder Handbook

Taking Notes and Outlining 823
Reading a Time Line 824
Understanding the Parts of a Map 825
Understanding Cause and Effect 826
Making Comparisons 827
Drawing Inferences and Conclusions 828
Predicting Consequences 829
Sequencing and Categorizing Information 830
Writing a Paragraph 831
Analyzing Information 832
Distinguishing Fact from Opinion 833
Recognizing Bias 834
Analyzing Library and Research Resources 835
Analyzing Primary Source Documents 836
Interpreting a Political Cartoon 837
Analyzing News Media 838
Recognizing Economic Indicators 839

Connecting to the Constitution

The Road to Representative Government 132
Freedom of the Press 240
The Supreme Court and the Economy . . . 310
Admission of New States 498
Citizenship 650
Government and Labor 730

NATIONAL GEOGRAPHIC Geography & History

Into the Unknown 318
Vital Resources 488
Antietam: The Bloodiest Day 614
Wild Wonders 772

What If...

The Defenders Had Not Stayed at the Alamo? 482
Lincoln Had Survived? 642

Maps, Charts, and Graphs

Maps

NATIONAL GEOGRAPHIC Reference Atlas Maps 24

World: Political 26
North America: Political 28
North America: Physical 29
United States: Political 30
United States: Physical 32
United States Territorial Growth 34

NATIONAL GEOGRAPHIC Geography Handbook 38

Hemispheres 41
Climate Regions of the United States 43
Thirteen Colonies 44
Population of the United States 45
Election of 1800 45

Tools of the Historian

San Francisco Bay Area 54
LANDSAT of San Francisco Bay 54
The Oregon and California Trails 55
Removal of Native Americans, 1820–1840 56
Cotton Production, 1860 57
Territorial Growth, 1800–1810 58
Major Western Railroads Before 1900 59
The Columbian Exchange 67

Unit 1

European Voyages of Exploration 87
The Columbian Exchange 96
Spread of Christianity 100
The Taino, About 1492 110
European Settlements 119
Thirteen Colonies 122
Proclamation of 1763 135
The Battles of Lexington and Concord 140
The Revolutionary War in the South, 1778–1781 156
National Origin of Colonists, 1760 162

Unit 2

The Northwest Territory 183
Land Claims in North America 212
Emancipation After Independence, 1780–1804 . . . 244
Native American Campaigns 287
Election of 1796 300

Unit 3

The Louisiana Purchase and Western Exploration 316
Washington, D.C. 332
Election of 1800 333
Territorial Growth, 1800–1810 341
The War of 1812 355
Acquisition of Florida, 1819 370

Unit 4

Population of the United States, 1820 386
Population Growth, 1850 416
Cotton Production, 1820–1860 425
Largest Southern Cities, 1850 440
Removal of Native Americans, 1820–1840 454
Election of 1828 464
Oregon Country 474
Texas War for Independence, 1835–1836 485
The War with Mexico, 1846–1848 495
The Oregon and California Trails 516

Unit 5

The Underground Railroad 533
Slavery and Sectionalism 546
Seceding States, 1860–1861 558
Election of 1860 564
Compromise of 1850 565
The Early Battles, 1861–1862 581
Turning Points, 1862–1863 606
The Civil War: Battles and Strategies 608
The Final Battles, 1864–1865 609
Battle of Gettysburg 618
Military Reconstruction Districts, 1867 632
Disputed Election of 1876 644
Congress Before and After Reconstruction 654

Unit 6

Western Land Use, 1890 676
Western Native American Lands, 1860–1890 689
The Cattle Kingdom 700
Major Western Railroads Before 1900 710
Population by State, 1900 734
United States Overseas Possessions, 1900 776
The Panama Canal 788

Charts and Graphs

Agricultural Production in the South 57
Causes and Effects of Political Parties 65
Weaknesses in the Articles of Confederation 181
Powers of the Federal Government 206
Major Principles of the Constitution 221
The Federal System 222
The Bill of Rights 223
How the Constitution is Amended 224
The American System of Checks and Balances ... 228
How a Bill Becomes a Law 229
The Federal Court System 231
Differences Between the First Political Parties ... 292
Imports and Exports, 1800–1820 340
Population Growth, 1800–1840 386
Urban and Rural Population, 1820 386
Annual Immigration, 1820–1860 399
School Enrollment, 1850–2000 417
Southern Population, 1860 428
Election of 1824 447
Comparing Resources 572
Names of Battles 580
Lives Lost 608
Agricultural Production in the South, 1850–1890 645
Native American Population 686
Urban and Rural Population Growth, 1860–1900 751
Voter Registration Before and After the Voting Rights Act 801
Population of the United States by Race and Hispanic/Latino Origin 803
Religious Membership in the United States 805
Poverty in the United States: Total Number and Rate 806
Federal Minimum Wage 807
Number of Employees in Selected Professions, 1910 and 2002 809
High School Enrollment 810
Education and Income 811
Landmark Acts of the Civil Rights Movement 815
Percentage of Voting Age Who Voted 817
Service Learning Facts 818

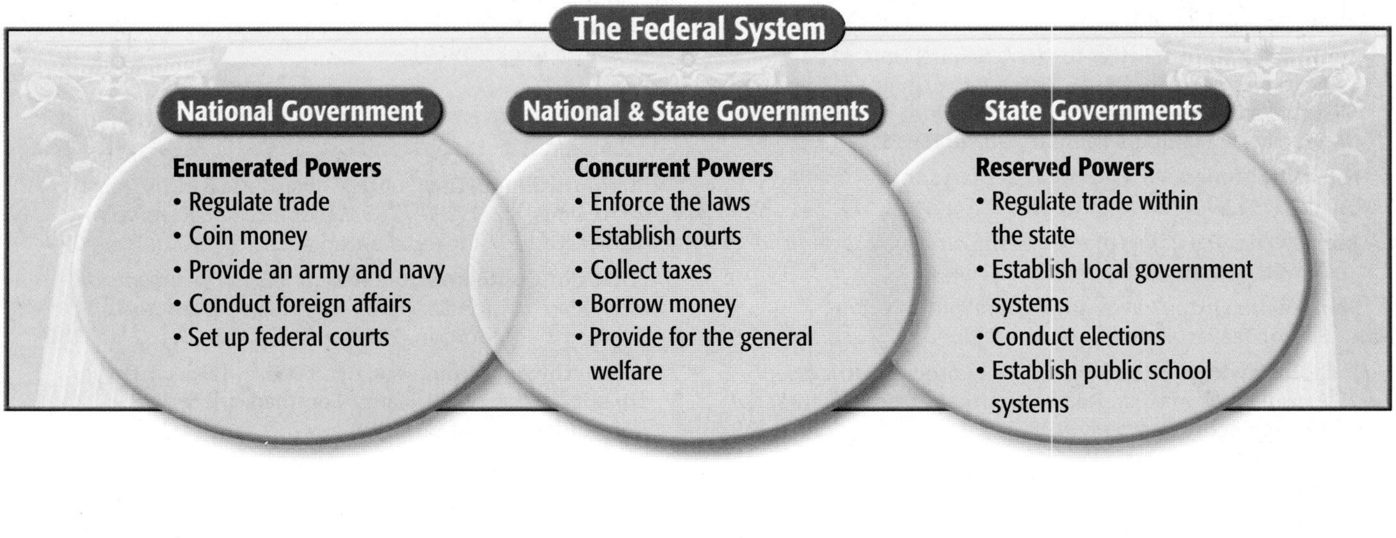

Primary Source Quotes

Chapter 1

Niccolò De Machiavelli. From *Medieval Sourcebook.* http://www.fordham.edu/halsall/source/machiavelli-histflo-lorenzo.html 92

Adam Smith. From *The Wealth of Nations.* Ed. Bruce Mazlish. (Indianapolis: Bobbs-Merrill/Library of Liberal Arts,1983). 94

John Locke. From *Second Treatise of Government.* Ed. C.B. Macpherson. (Indianapolis, Ind.: Hackett Pub. Co., 1980). 104

Magna Carta: Text and Commentary. Ed. A.E. Dick Howard. (Charlottesville: University Press of Virginia,1964). . 106

"The English Bill of Rights." From The Avalon Project at Yale Law School. 1996–2003. http://www.yale.edu/lawweb/avalon/england.htm . . . 106

Christopher Columbus. From *The Log of Christopher Columbus.* Tr. Robert H. Fuson. (Camden, Me.: International Marine Pub. Co., 1987). 108

Bernal Díaz del Castillo. From *The Conquest of New Spain.* Tr. J.M. Cohen. (Harmondsworth: Penguin Books, 1963). 109

John Locke. From *Second Treatise of Civil Government.* Ed. C.B. Macpherson. (Indianapolis, Ind.: Hackett Pub. Co., 1980). 111

Chapter 2

Junípero Serra. http://www.serrainternational.org/serra/bjs.shtml . . . 118

John Winthrop. "A Model of Christian Charity, 1630." In *A Patriot's Handbook.* Selected by Caroline Kennedy. (New York: Hyperion, 2003). 121

William Penn. *Frame of Government of Pennsylvania, 1682.* http://www.constitution.org/bcp/frampenn.htm . . . 122

Olaudah Equiano. *The Interesting Narrative of the Life of Olaudah Equiano.* Ed. Vincent Carretta. (New York: Penguin Books, 1995). 127

Thomas Jefferson. Letter to Pierre Samuel Dupont de Nemours, February 28, 1815. From the Library of Congress http://memory.loc.gov/ Search: De Nemours February 28, 1815 132

Nathaniel Ames. *An Astronomical Diary: or, an Almanack for . . . 1758.* (Portsmouth, NH: D. Fowle, 1757). 135

James Otis. *The Rights of the British Colonies Asserted and Proved.* (Boston: Edes and Gill, 1764). 136

Sam Adams. http://www.americanrevolution.com/BostonTeaParty.htm 138

Joseph Hawley. "Broken Hints." As quoted in *Patrick Henry: Patriot in the Making.* Robert Douthat Meade. (New York: J.B. Lippincott Company, 1957). 139

John Parker. As quoted in *A Book About American History.* George Stimpson. http://www.bartleby.com/73/1940.html 140

Henry Wadsworth Longfellow. "Paul Revere's Ride." In *The Poetical Works of Longfellow.* Cambridge Edition. (Boston: Houghton Mifflin Company, 1975). 142

Colonel William Prescott. From the Boston National Historical Park. http://www.nps.gov/bost/Bunker_Hill.htm 150

Thomas Paine. "Common Sense." In *Collected Writings of Thomas Paine.* (New York: Literary Classics of the United States, Inc., 1995). 150

Benjamin Franklin. *Poor Richard: The Almanacks for the Years 1733–1758.* Ed. Richard Saunders. (New York: Bonanza Books, 1979). 151

"The Declaration of Independence." In *Documents of American History.* Ed. Henry Steele Commager. (New York: Meredith Corporation, 1958). 152

Abigail Adams. Letter to John Adams, May 7, 1776. From *Adams Family Papers: An Electronic Archive.* Massachusetts Historical Society. http://www.masshist.org/digitaladams/ Search: good will to men 155

Thomas Paine. "Common Sense." In *Collected Writings of Thomas Paine.* (New York: Literary Classics of the United States, Inc., 1995). 158

Charles Inglis. *The True Interest of America Impartially Stated, 1776.* (Philadelphia: 1776). 159

William Penn. Letter to John Aubrey, June 13, 1683 and Letter to Lord Halifax, February 9,1683. In *William Penn.* Harry Emerson Wildes (New York: Macmillan Publishing Co., Inc., 1974). 160

Resolutions of the Germantown Mennonites; February 18, 1688. From The Avalon Project at Yale Law School. http://www.yale.edu/lawweb/avalon/amerdoc/men01.htm 160

Benjamin Franklin. *Poor Richard: The Almanacks for the Years 1733–1758.* Ed. Richard Saunders. (New York: Bonanza Books, 1964). 161

Chapter 3

William Cushing. "The Quock Walker Case." In *The Annals of America, V2, 1755–1783, Resistance and Revolution.* (Chicago: Encyclopaedia Britannica, Inc., 1968). 179

"Articles of Confederation. Article II." In *Documents of American History.* Ed. Henry Commager. (New York: Meredith Corporation, 1968). 180

"The Northwest Ordinance, Article 6." In *Documents of American History.* Ed. Henry Commager. (New York: Meredith Corporation, 1968). 182

George Washington. Letter to James McHenry, August 22, 1785. From *The Papers of George Washington, 1748–99, Confederation Series 1784–88.* The University of Virginia Press. http://gwpapers.virginia.edu/constitution/1784/mchenry1.html 185

Mildred Pitts Walter. *Second Daughter: The Story of a Slave Girl.* (New York: Scholastic Inc., 1996). 186

"Bethel Church Resolution." *Bethel AME Church, Philadelphia, January, 15, 1817.* http://www.pbs.org/ Search: Bethel Church Resolution 196

James Madison. *The Federalist*, No. 51. In *The Federalist Papers*. Ed. Clinton Rossiter. (New York: Signet Classic, 2003). 198

Mercy Otis Warren. http://library.thinkquest.org/TQ0312848/mowarren.htm 206

James Wilson. Speech to the Pennsylvania Ratifying Convention: October 6, 1787. In *The Debate on the Constitution*. Ed. Bernard Bailyn. (New York: The Library of America, 1993). 208

Alexander Hamilton. *The Federalist*, No. 70. In *The Federalist Papers*. Ed. Clinton Rossiter. (New York: Signet Classic, 2003). 208

Patrick Henry. Speech to the Virginia Ratifying Convention: June 9, 1788. http://www.constitution.org/rc/rat_va_07.htm 209

George Mason. "Objections to the Proposed Federal Constitution." In *The American Constitution For and Against, The Federalist and Anti-Federalist Papers.* Ed. J.R. Pole. (New York: Hill and Wang, 1987). 209

New York (State) Commissioners of Indian Affairs and Franklin Benjamin Hough. *Proceedings of the Commissioners of Indian Affairs, 1822–1885.* Published from the original manuscript in the library of the Albany Institute. (Albany, N.Y.: J. Munsell, 1861). 210

J. Hector St. John Crèvecoeur. *Letters From an American Farmer, What is an American, Letter III.* (New York: Fox, Duffield, 1904). From the University of Virginia. http://xroads.virginia.edu/ Select: Hypertexts, then select Crèvecoeur 211

CHAPTER 4

"The Preamble of the Constitution." In *Documents of American History*. Ed. Henry Commager. (New York: Meredith Corporation, 1968). 219

"The Preamble of the Constitution." In *Documents of American History*. Ed. Henry Commager. (New York: Meredith Corporation, 1968). 220

Barbara Jordan. Opening Statement to the House Judiciary Committee, July 25, 1974. http://www.utexas.edu/lbj/barbarajordanforum/PDFs/ Select: Opening Statement 225

John Marshall. *Marbury* v. *Madison* (1803). From the National Archives and Records Administration. http://www.ourdocuments.gov/ Select: 100 Milestone Documents 232

"The Declaration of Independence." In *Documents of American History*. Ed. Henry Commager. (New York: Meredith Corporation, 1968). 235

Thomas Jefferson. "Virginia Statute of Religious Liberty, January 16, 1786." In *Documents of American History*. Ed. Henry Commager. (N. Y.: Meredith Corp., 1968). 235

Learned Hand. "The Spirit of Liberty, May 21,1944." In *The Spirit of Liberty: Papers and Addresses of Learned Hand*. Collected by Irving Dilliard. (New York: Knopf, 1963). . . 236

George W. Bush. "State of the Union Address, January 29, 2002." http://www.pbs.org/newshour/bb/white_house/sotu2002/sotu2.html 236

Thomas Jefferson. Letter to Colonel Edward Carrington, January 16, 1787. *The Works of Thomas Jefferson, Federal Edition*. (New York: G.P. Putnam's Sons, 1905). http://memory.loc.gov/ Search: Carrington January 16, 1787 240

James Madison. *The Federalist*, No. 10. In *The Federalist Papers*. Ed. Clinton Rossiter. (New York: Signet Classic, 2003). 242

George Mason. "Objections to the Proposed Federal Constitution." In *The American Constitution For and Against, The Federalist and Anti-Federalist Papers.* Ed. J.R. Pole. (New York: Hill and Wang, 1987). 243

CHAPTER 5

Alexander Hamilton. *The Federalist*, No. 70. In *The Federalist Papers*. Ed. Clinton Rossiter. (New York: Signet Classic, 2003). 283

George Washington. "Farewell Address," In *The Annals of American History, V3, 1784–1796, Organizing the New Nation*. (Chicago: Encyclopaedia Britannica, Inc., 1968). 289

Alexander Hamilton. Speech on the Constitutional Convention on a Plan of Government. In *Selected Writings and Speeches of Alexander Hamilton*. Ed. Morton J. Frisch. (Washington, D.C.: American Enterprise Institute, 1985). 292

Thomas Jefferson. Letter to Samuel Kercheval, 1816. From *The Writings of Thomas Jefferson, Memorial Edition*, V15. Ed. Lipscomb and Bergh. (Washington, D.C., 1903–04). From the University of Virginia. http://etext.virginia.edu/jefferson/quotations/jeff0350.htm 293

Abigail Adams. Letter from Abigail Adams to John Adams, 31 March–5 April 1776. From *Adams Family Papers: An Electronic Archive*. Massachusetts Historical Society. http://www.masshist.org/digitaladams/ Search: Remember the ladies 294

Primary Source Quotes

George Washington. Letter to Henry Knox, April 1, 1789. In *The Writings of George Washington from the Original Manuscript Sources, 1745–1799.* Ed. John C. Fitzpatrick. From the George Washington Papers at the Library of Congress, 1741–1799. http://lcweb2.loc.gov/ Search: Henry Knox April 1, 1789 298

William Maclay. "Chapter 1: On Titles and Ceremonies." In the *Journal of William Maclay, United States Senator from Pennsylvania, 1789–1791.* From the Library of Congress http://memory.loc.gov/ Search: Maclay Chapter I 298

Chapter 6

John Marshall. *McCulloch* v. *Maryland,* 17 U.S. 316 (1819). 310

U.S. Constitution, Article III. 311

Harriet Martineau. *Society in America.* Ed. Seymour Martin Lipset. (Garden City, New York: Anchor Books Doubleday & Company, Inc., 1962). 313

Thomas Jefferson. Letter to Charles Yancey, January 6, 1816. From *The Works of Thomas Jefferson in Twelve Volumes. Federal Edition.* Ed. Paul Leicester Ford. http://memory.loc.gov/ Search: Yancey January 6, 1816 321

Washington Irving. *The Legend of Sleepy Hollow and Other Stories.* (New York: The Modern Library, 2001). 323

James Fenimore Cooper. *The Deerslayer.* (New York: The Modern Library, 2002). 323

James Fenimore Cooper. *The Last of the Mohicans.* (New York: The Modern Library, 2001). 324

William Shaler. *Journal of a Voyage between China and the North-Western Coast of America Made in 1804.* In *The American Register.* (January 1, 1808). 330

Meriwether Lewis. *The Essential Lewis and Clark.* Ed. Landon Y. Jones. (New York: HarperCollins Publisher, Inc., 2000). 330

John Quincy Adams. Fourth of July Address, 1821. In *John Quincy Adams and American Continental Empire.* Ed. Walter LaFeber. (Chicago: Quadrangle Books, 1965). 331

Chapter 7

Thomas Jefferson. First Annual Message, December 8, 1801. *The Works of Thomas Jefferson in Twelve Volumes. Federal Edition.* Ed. Paul Leicester Ford. From The Thomas Jefferson Papers, 1606–1827 at The Library of Congress. http://memory.loc.gov/ Search: Jefferson First Annual Message 339

Tecumseh. As quoted in *The Old Northwest: A Chronicle of the Ohio Valley and Beyond.* Frederic Austin Ogg. (New Haven: Yale University Press, 1919). 342

William Henry Harrison. *Messages and Letters of William Henry Harrison.* Ed. Logan Esarey. (Ayer Company Publishers, Inc., 1975). 342

Tecumseh. As quoted in *William H. Tecumseh, an Indian Moses.* Van Hoose. (Canton, Ohio: Daring Books, 1984). 342

Blue Jacket. *American State Papers, Indian Affairs, March 3, 1789 to March 3, 1815.* http://www.gbl.indiana.edu/ archives/dockett_317/317_36e.html 343

James Madison. War Message, June 1, 1812. http://www.constitution.org/jm/ 18120601_war.htm 345

Elizabeth Alder. *Crossing the Panther's Path.* (New York: Farrar Straus Giroux, 2002). 346

Francis Scott Key. "The Star-Spangled Banner. 1814." From The Library of Congress. http://memory.loc.gov/ Search: Star-Spangled Banner 356

Dolley Payne Madison. Letter to Anna Cutts, August 23, 1814. The *Dolley Madison Digital Edition.* Ed. Holly Shulman. (University of Virginia Press, 2001). From The Library of Congress. http://moderntimes.vcdh.virginia.edu/ madison/exhibit/washington/letters/082314.html . . . 357

James Monroe. First Inaugural Address, March 4, 1817. In *Inaugural Addresses of the Presidents of the United States From George Washington 1789 to George Bush 1989. Bicentennial Edition.* (Washington, D.C.: United States Government Printing Office, 1989). 363

Philip Freneau. "The Battle of Stonington." In *Sound Off: Soldier Songs From The Revolution to World War II.* Ed. Edward Arthur Dolph. (New York: Farrar & Rinehart Inc., 1942). 368

Felix Grundy. "War as a Means of Continental Expansion." In *The Annals of America, V4, 1797–1820, Domestic Expansion and Foreign Entanglements.* (Chicago: Encyclopaedia Britannica, Inc.,1976). 368

Daniel Webster. "Against Conscription." In *The Annals of America, V4, 1797–1820, Domestic Expansion and Foreign Entanglements.* (Chicago: Encyclopedia Britannica, Inc., 1976). 369

Chapter 8

Lucy Larcom. *A New England Girlhood.* (Boston: Houghton Mifflin Company, 1889). 385

Napoleon Bonaparte. "Yes, But Will It Work in Theory?" Norman R. Augustine. 1996 Woodruff Distinguished Lecture. www.me.gatech.edu/me/publicat/ AugTranscript.htm 391

August Blümmer. In *News from the Land of Freedom.* Walter D. Kamphoefner; Wolfgang Johannes Helbich; Ulrike Sommer. (Ithaca: Cornell University Press, 1991) 398

Henry David Thoreau. From "Civil Disobedience." In *The Annals of America, V7, 1841–1849, Manifest Destiny.* (Chicago: Encyclopaedia Britannica, Inc., 1968). 403

Charles Finney. "Directions to Sinners." From *Lectures on Revivals of Religion.* http://www.gospeltruth.net/ Search: Directions to Sinners 403

Emily Dickinson. "Hope." *The Complete Poems of Emily Dickinson.* Ed. R.W. Franklin. (Cambridge, Mass.: The Belknap Press of Harvard University Press, 1999). ... 407

Sarah Grimké. "On the Condition of Women in the United States." *Letters on the Equality of the Sexes, Addressed to Mary S. Parker, President of the Boston Female Anti-Slavery Society, 1837.* http://www.pinn.net/~sunshine/book-sum/grimke3.html 412

James Finley. From the Center for History and New Media, George Mason University. http://www.chnm.gmu.edu/courses/jackson/revival/revival.html 414

Charles Dickens. *American Notes.* Ed. John Lance Griffith. Charlottesville, VA: American Studies, University of Virginia, 1996. http://xroads.virginia.edu/ Select: Hypertexts, then select American Notes 415

Harry Sinclair Drago. *Canal Days in America.* (New York: C. N. Potter; distributed by Crown Publishers, 1972). ... 415

Chapter 9

Alvy L. King. *Louis T. Wigfall: Southern Fire-eater.* (Baton Rouge, LA: Louisiana State University Press, 1970). ... 425

Charles C. Jones. Letter to his wife, Dinah Jones, 1858. In *The Black Family in Slavery and Freedom, 1750–1925.* Herbert G. Gutman. (New York: Pantheon Books, 1976). 433

"Didn't My Lord Deliver Daniel." *Wade in the Water: The Wisdom of the Spirituals.* Arthur C. Jones. (Maryknoll, New York: Orbis Books, 1993). 434

Solomon Northup. *Twelve Years a Slave: Narrative of Solomon Northup, a Citizen of New York, Kidnapped in Washington City in 1841, and Rescued in 1853.* From The Academic Affairs Library, University of North Carolina at Chapel Hill, 1997. http://docsouth.unc.edu/northup/menu.html 434

Harriet Tubman. *Women's Voices: Quotations by Women.* Jone Johnson Lewis, 2003. http://womenshistory.about.com/library/qu/blqulist.htm 436

Eli Whitney. *The World of Eli Whitney.* Jeannette Mirsky and Allan Nevins. (New York: The MacMillan Company, 1952). 438

Josiah Henson. *Uncle Tom's Story of His Life. An Autobiography of the Rev. Josiah Henson.* Ed. John Lobb. (London: "Christian Age" Office, 89, Farringdon Street, 1876). From the Academic Affairs Library, University of North Carolina at Chapel Hill, 2000. 439

Theodore Dwight Weld. *American Slavery As It Is: Testimony of a Thousand Witnesses.* (New York: The American Anti-Slavery Society, Office, No. 143 Nassau Street, 1839). From The Academic Affairs Library, University of North Carolina at Chapel Hill, 2000. http://docsouth.unc.edu/neh/weld/menu.html 439

Alvy L. King. *Louis T. Wigfall: Southern Fire-eater.* (Baton Rouge, LA: Louisiana State University Press, 1970). ... 441

Chapter 10

From *Trail of Tears: The Rise and Fall of the Cherokee Nation.* John Ehle. (New York: Doubleday, 1988). ... 454

Osceola. Letter to General Clinch. In *Osceola: The Unconquered Indian.* William and Ellen Hartley. (New York: Hawthorn Books, Inc., 1973). 456

Black Hawk. Surrender Speech, 1832. http://usinfo.state.gov/usa/infousa/facts/democrac/12.htm 457

Andrew Jackson. "For and Against the Bank Renewal Bill." In *The Annals of America, V5, 1821–1832, Steps Toward Equalitarianism.* (Chicago: Encyclopaedia Britannica, 1976). 459

Margaret Bayard Smith. *The First Forty Years of Washington Society.* Ed. Gaillard Hunt. (New York: C. Scribner's Sons, 1906). From the Library of Congress http://memory.loc.gov/ Search: Bayard Smith Forty Years 462

Andrew Jackson. "On Indian Removal, Message to Congress, December 6, 1830." In *The Annals of America, V5, 1821–1832, Steps Toward Equalitarianism.* (Chicago: Encyclopaedia Britannica, 1976). 463

Chapter 11

Zenas Leonard. Journal of a fur trader clerk. http://www.yosemite.ca.us/history/one_hundred_years_in_yosemite/discovery.html 471

Amelia Stewart Knight. *Women's Diaries of the Westward Journey.* Ed. Lillian Schlissel. (New York: Schocken Books, 1982). 473

Catherine Sager Pringle. *Across the Plains in 1844.* http://www.isu.edu/~trinmich/00.ar.sager1.html 473

Albert Gallatin. As quoted in *The Mission of the United States.* In *The Annals of America, V7, 1841–1849, Manifest Destiny.* (Chicago: Encyclopaedia Britannica, 1976). ... 476

John O'Sullivan. "Annexation." *The United States Democratic Review* V17, no. 085–086 (July–August 1845). 477

William Barret Travis. *Letter from the Alamo, February 24, 1836.* http://www.tsl.state.tx.us/treasures/republic/alamo/travis-03.html 482

Primary Source Quotes

Stephen F. Austin. "The Last Survivor of the Goliad Massacre." In *Southwestern Historical Quarterly* V1, no. 1, (July 1897). http://www.tsha.utexas.edu/publications/journals/shq/Search: Goliad Massacre 482

"Texas Declaration of Independence, March 2, 1836." From http://www.tsl.state.tx.us/treasures/republic/declare-01.html 485

Sam Houston. *Sword of San Jacinto: A Life of Sam Houston.* Marshall De Bruhl. (New York: Random House, 1993). 487

María Amparo Ruiz de Burton. *The Squatter and the Don.* http://www.huntington.org/Education/GoldRush/Lessons/upper.lesson.8.pdf 493

William Marcy. State Paper from the War Department, Washington, June 3, 1846. http://www.californiagenealogy.org/forty_niner/william_l_marcy.htm 494

U.S. Constitution, Amendment 10. In *Documents of American History.* Ed. Henry Steele Commager. (New York: Meredith Corporation, 1968). 498

John Bidwell. *Addresses, reminiscences, etc. of General John Bidwell.* Compiled by C.C. Royce. From the Library of Congress. http://memory.loc.gov/Search: Bidwell Reminiscences 502

George Tinkham. *California Men and Events.* http://www.usgennet.org/usa/ca/state1/tinkhamch11.html 504

Howard Stansbury. *An Expedition to the Valley of the Great Salt Lake of Utah.* (Philadelphia: Lippincott, Grambo & Co., 1855). From the University of Michigan's Digital Library Production Service. http://www.topos.org/Biblio.htm 505

Kathy Balmes. *Thunder on the Sierra.* (New York: Silver Moon Press, 2001). 507

Message of President Polk, May 11, 1846. From the Avalon Project at Yale Law School. http://www.yale.edu/search/search.html Search: Polk May 11, 1846 514

Francis Parkman. *The Oregon Trail.* (New York: Holt, Rinehart and Winston, 1959). 514

William Speer. *The Oldest and the Newest Empire: China and the United States.* (Cincinnati: National Publishing Co., 1870). http://etext.lib.virginia.edu/railton/roughingit/map/chiremon.html 515

Chapter 12

Benjamin Lundy. In *Historical Collections of Ohio.* V1. Ed. Henry Howe. (Norwalk, Ohio: The Laning Printing Co., Public Printers, 1898). 529

Angelina Grimké. Lecture delivered at Pennsylvania Hall. http://www.startribune.com/viewers/story.php?template=print_a&story=646147 530

John Quincy Adams. As quoted in *The President Who Wouldn't Retire.* Leonard Falkner. (New York: Coward-McCann, Inc., 1967). 531

Frederick Douglass. In *Frederick Douglass: Selected Speeches and Writings.* Ed. Philip S. Foner. (Chicago: Lawrence Hill Books, 1999). 532

Nancy Howard. *A North-Side View of Slavery. The Refugee: or the Narratives of Fugitive Slaves in Canada.* Benjamin Drew. From the Academic Affairs Library, University of North Carolina at Chapel Hill, 2000. http://docsouth.unc.edu/neh/drew/menu.html 533

Henry Clay. Speech, 1848. *Familiar Quotations,* 10th Ed. John Bartlett. (1919). http://www.bartleby.com/100/348.3 536

Harriet Beecher Stowe. In *Uncle Tom's Cabin* (Boston: The Jewett Company, 1852). 545

"The Execution of John Brown." *The Anglo-African Magazine,* V1, 1859. Ed. William Loren Katz. (Arno Press, Inc., 1968). 549

Bridget "Biddy" Mason. From the Women's Business Center. www.onlinewbc.gov/ Search: Biddy Mason 551

Abraham Lincoln. From *Following Abraham Lincoln 1809–1865.* Bernhardt Wall. (New York: Wise Parslow Company, 1943). 552

Stephen Douglas. From *Defender of the Union.* Gerald M. Capers. Ed. Oscar Handlin. (Boston: Little, Brown and Company, 1959). 552

Abraham Lincoln. Letter to James T. Hale, January 11, 1861. From the Abraham Lincoln Papers at the Library of Congress. Transcribed and Annotated by the Lincoln Studies Center, Knox College. Galesburg, Illinois. http://lcweb2.loc.gov/ Search: Lincoln Hale January 11 556

Abraham Lincoln. First Inaugural Address, March 4, 1861. In *Inaugural Addresses of the Presidents of the United States from George Washington 1789 to George Bush 1989. Bicentennial Edition.* (Washington, D.C.: United States Government Printing Office, 1989). 557

Abner Doubleday. In *Voices of the Civil War.* Richard Wheeler. (New York: Thomas Y. Crowell Company, 1976). 559

Abraham Lincoln. First Inaugural Address, March 4, 1861. In *Inaugural Addresses of the Presidents of the United States from George Washington 1789 to George Bush 1989. Bicentennial Edition.* (Washington, D.C.: United States Government Printing Office, 1989). 560

Jefferson Davis. Inaugural Address, 18 February 1861. In *Crowned Masterpieces of Eloquence,* Victoria edition, V5. (London: International University Society, 1914). http://douglassarchives.org/davi_b16.htm 561

William Lloyd Garrison. "For Immediate Action." In *The Annals of America, V5, 1821–1832, Steps Toward Equalitarianism.* (Chicago: Encyclopaedia Britannica, Inc., 1968). 562

"Swing Low, Sweet Chariot." In *A Collection of 25 Selected Famous Negro Spirituals.* Ed. Hugo Frey. (Miami, Fla.: Warner Bros., 1999). 563

Mrs. Eugene McLean. *The Women's War in the South.* Ed. Chalres G. Waugh and Martin H. Greenberg. (Nashville: Cumberland House, 1999). 563

CHAPTER 13

Captain D. P. Conyngham. In *A Civil War Treasury of Tales, Legends and Folklore.* Ed. B.A. Botkin. (New York: Random House, 1960). 571

William T. Sherman. http://library.thinkquest.org/3055/netscape/people/sherman.html 575

Mary Ward. In *Voices of the Civil War.* Richard Wheeler. (New York: Thomas Y. Crowell Company, 1976). 577

Samuel J. English. Letter to his mother, July 1861. http://www.eyewitnesstohistory.com/pfbullrun.htm 577

Ulysses S. Grant. In *Voices of the Civil War.* Richard Wheeler. (New York: Thomas Y. Crowell Company, 1976). 579

Joseph Hooker. From *The Eyewitness to the Battle of Antietam.* http://www.nps.gov/anti/eyewitness.htm 582

Harold Keith. *Rifles for Watie.* (New York: Thomas Y. Crowell Company, 1957). 584

Abraham Lincoln. From *Lincoln.* David Herbert Donald. (New York: Simon & Schuster, 1995). 592

Abraham Lincoln. Letter to Horace Greeley, August 22, 1862. *Letters of a Nation: A Collection of Extraordinary American Letters.* Ed. Andrew Carroll. (New York: Kodansha International, 1997). 593

Abraham Lincoln. Cabinet Meeting: September 22, 1862. In *Diary and Correspondence of Salmon P. Chase.* Salmon P. Chase. (New York: Da Capo Press, 1971). 594

Emancipation Proclamation, January 1, 1863. From the National Archives and Records Administration. http://www.ourdocuments.gov/
Select: 100 Milestone Documents 594

Mary Chesnut's Civil War. Ed. C. Vann Woodward. (New Haven: Yale University Press, 1981). 599

Abraham Lincoln. Letter to Erastus Corning and Others, June 1863. *Abraham Lincoln Papers at the Library of Congress.* Transcribed and Annotated by the Lincoln Studies Center, Knox College. Galesburg, Illinois. http://memory.loc.gov/
Search: Lincoln to Corning 600

Clara Barton. Letter to her father, 1861. In *Angel of the Battlefield: the Life of Clara Barton.* (New York: Harper, 1956). 601

Reactions from the *Harrisburg Patriot* and the *Chicago Tribune*. Cornell University Library. http://rmc.library.cornell.edu/gettysburg/
Select: Ideas are always more than battles 607

Abraham Lincoln. Second Inaugural Address, March 4, 1865. In *Inaugural Addresses of the Presidents of the United States from George Washington 1789 to George Bush 1989.* Bicentennial Edition. (Washington, D.C.: United States Government Printing Office, 1989). 610

Robert E. Lee. As quoted in *Voices of the Civil War.* Richard Wheeler. (New York: Thomas Y. Crowell, 1976). 610

Theodore Upson. *With Sherman to the sea; the Civil War letters, diaries & reminiscences of Theodore F. Upson.* (Bloomington: Indiana University Press, 1958). 616

Dolly Lunt Burge. *A Woman's Wartime Journal.* From the Academic Affairs Library, University of North Carolina at Chapel Hill, 1996. http://docsouth.unc.edu/
Search: Dolly Sumner Lunt 616

John Greenleaf Whittier. "Barbara Frietchie." From *Complete Poetical Works,* Cambridge Edition. (Boston: 1894). In *Annals of America,* V9. (Chicago: Encyclopedia Britannica, Inc., 1976). 617

CHAPTER 14

Mary Chesnut. *A Diary from Dixie.* (Gramercy, 1997). . . 625

Thaddeus Stevens. Speech to Congress, December 1865. http://history.furman.edu/~benson/hst41/blue/stevens1.htm 625

Charlotte Forten. From *Life on the Sea Islands.* http://www.pbs.org/onlyateacher/charlotte.html . . . 627

Andrew Jackson. http://www.senate.gov/artandhistory/history/resources/pdf/andrew_johnson.pdf 628

Charles Sumner. "For Conviction." In *The Annals of America,* V10, *1866–1883, Reconstruction and Industrialization.* (Chicago: Encyclopaedia Britannica, 1976). 633

State Convention of the Colored People of South Carolina. *Proceedings of the Colored People's Convention of the State of South Carolina, Held in Zion Church, Charleston, November, 1865.* (Charleston: South Carolina Leader Office, 1865). http://historymatters.gmu.edu/
Search: Charleston's Zion Church 636

Frederick Douglass. *Narrative of the Life of Frederick Douglass. An American Slave.* (Boston: Anti-Slavery Office, 1845). From the Academic Affairs Library, University of North Carolina at Chapel Hill, 1999. http://docsouth.unc.edu/
Search: Douglass Narrative 637

Primary Source Quotes

The Jackson Pilot, October 1875. In *Reconstruction and Redemption in the South.* Ed. Otto H. Olsen. (Baton Rouge: Louisiana State University Press, 1980). 642

Abraham Lincoln. Second Inaugural Address, March 4, 1865. In *Inaugural Addresses of the Presidents of the United States From George Washington 1789 to George Bush 1989. Bicentennial Edition.* (Washington, D.C.: United States Government Printing Office, 1989). 642

Rutherford Hayes. Speech in Atlanta, 1877. In *Rutherford B. Hayes, Warrior and President*. Ari Hoogenboom (Lawrence, Kansas: University Press of Kansas, 1995). 644

John Roy Lynch. Speech before the House of Representatives: February 3, 1875. http://www.law.nyu.edu/davisp/neglectedvoices/LynchFeb031875.html 645

Jim Crow Laws. *Race, Racism, and the Law.* www.udayton.edu 647

W.E.B. Du Bois. *Black Reconstruction in America.* (New York: Atheneum, 1977). 649

John Marshall Harlan. *Plessy* v. *Ferguson* (1896.) National Archives and Records Administration. http://www.ourdocuments.gov/ Search: 100 Milestone Documents 650

Sidney Andrews. *The South since the war, as shown by fourteen weeks of travel and observation in Georgia and the Carolinas.* (Boston: Ticknor and Fields, 1866). http://www.hti.umich.edu/m/moagrp/ Search: The South Since The War 652

Frederick Douglass. "An Appeal to Congress for Impartial Suffrage." *Atlantic Monthly.* (January 1867) 653

CHAPTER 15

Way Out in Idaho. http://www.lib.uidaho.edu/special-collections/ Search: Way Out in Idaho 667

Grenville Dodge. *Mine Eyes Have Seen: a First-Person History of the Events that Shaped America.* Ed. Richard Goldstein. (New York: Touchstone, 1997). 671

E.C. Abbott. *We Pointed Them North.* (Norman: University of Oklahoma Press, 1955). 673

A Nebraska Settler. *The American Story: Settling the West.* Ed. Sarah Brash. (Richmond: Virginia: Time-Life Books, 1996). 676

Senate Resolution 97, 2001. http://thomas.loc.gov/ Search: Resolution 97 Buffalo Soldier 677

Bess Streeter Aldrich. *A Lantern in Her Hand.* (Lincoln: University of Nebraska Press, 1928). 680

Sitting Bull. From http://jaie.asu.edu Search: No White Man Controls Our Footsteps 688

Chief Joseph. Surrender to the U.S. Army, 1877. *A Patriot's Handbook.* Selected by Caroline Kennedy. (New York: Hyperion, 2003). 690

Helen Hunt Jackson. *A Century of Dishonor.* Ed. Andrew F. Rolle. (New York: Harper Torchbooks, 1965). 691

Sarah Winnemucca. *Life Among the Piutes.* (Reno: University of Nevada, 1994). 691

"The Farmer is the Man." *The Annals of America,* V11, *1884–1894, Agrarianism and Urbanization.* (Chicago: Encyclopaedia Britannica, Inc., 1976). 694

Andy Adams. *Trail Drive.* Ed. Glen Rounds. (New York: Holiday House, 1965). 698

Laura Ingalls Wilder. *The Long Winter.* (New York: HarperCollins Publishers, Inc., 1968). 699

Ah-nen-la-de-ni. *Witnessing America.* Ed. Noel Rae. (New York: The Stonesong Press, Inc., 1996). 699

CHAPTER 16

Thomas Casey. "Drill, Ye Tarriers, Drill, 1888." In *Annals of America,* V10, *1866–1883, Reconstruction and Industrialization.* (Chicago: Encyclopaedia Britannica, Inc., 1976). 707

Gus Edwards and Vincent Bryan. "In My Merry Oldsmobile." (New York: M. Witmark & Sons. 1905). http://libraries.mit.edu Search: In My Merry Oldsmobile 713

Herbert Spencer. *First Principles.* 6th Ed. (University Press of the Pacific, 2002). http://www.bartleby.com/100/549.4.html 723

César Chávez. In *Great Labor Quotations.* http://www.afscmeiowa.org/quotations.htm 730

"John Henry." In *Annals of America,* V10, *1866–1883, Reconstruction and Industrialization.* (Chicago: Encyclopaedia Britannica, Inc., 1976). 732

Sadie Frowne. "The Story of a Sweatshop Girl." *Independent,* September 25, 1902. http://www.digitialhistory.uh.edu/social_history/5sweatshop_girl.cfm 733

Labor Standard Newspaper, St. Clair, Pennsylvania, 1877. http://www.snolabor.org/coal.htm 733

CHAPTER 17

Rocco Corresca. "The Biography of a Bootblack." In *The Life Stories of Undistinguished Americans: As Told by Themselves*. Ed. Hamilton Holt. (New York: J. Pott & Co., 1906). http://www.digitalhistory.uh.edu/social_history/1bootblack.cfm 741

Emma Lazarus. "The New Colossus." *A Patriot's Handbook.* Selected by Caroline Kennedy. (New York: Hyperion, 2003). 742

Pauline Newman. Letter to Michael and Hugh Owens, May 1951. http://www.ilr.cornell.edu/trianglefire/texts/ Select: Letter to Michael and Hugh 744

San Francisco Real Estate Circular, September 1874. http://www.sfmuseum.org/hist1/1874.html 748

The Chinese Exclusion Act, 1882. From the Avalon Project at Yale Law School. http://www.yale.edu/lawweb/avalon/statutes/chinese_exclusion_act.htm 748

Constance Gordon-Cumming. From Chinese Immigration to the United States 1851–1900. The Library of Congress. http://lcweb2.loc.gov/learn/ Search: Constance Gordon Cumming 749

Louis Marshall. From *Champion of Liberty: Selected Papers and Addresses.* Ed. Charles Reznikoff. In *The Annals of America,* V14, *1916–1928, World War and Prosperity.* (Chicago: Encyclopaedia Britannica, Inc., 1976). 749

Jacob Riis. *How The Other Half Lives.* (New York: Dover Publications, Inc., 1971) 753

Jane Addams. *Twenty Years at Hull-House with Autobiographical Notes.* (New York: The Macmillan Company, 1912). http://digital.library.upenn.edu/women/addams/hullhouse/hullhouse.html 753

Mark Twain. "The Overgrown Metropolis." San Francisco *Alta California,* March 28, 1867. www.twainquotes.com/18670328.html 755

Mary Antin. *The Promised Land.* (Boston: Houghton Mifflin Company, 1912). 758

Jacob Riis. *The Making of An American.* http://www.gutenberg.org/dirs/etext04/thmkn10.txt 767

Jacob Riis. "The Streets and Alleys of the Poor." From *The Battle With the Slum.* In *The Annals of America,* V12, *1895–1904, Populism, Imperialism, and Reform.* (Chicago: Encyclopaedia Britannica, Inc., 1976). 768

Albert Beveridge. "In Support of an American Empire." http://www.mtholyoke.edu/acad/intrel/ajb72.htm 775

George Washington Carver. From the George Washington Carver National Monument. http://www.nps.gov/gwca/expanded/quotes_2.htm 782

"The Declaration of Independence." In *Documents of American History.* Ed. Henry Steele Commager. (New York: Meredith Corporation, 1968). 783

Jane Addams. *Twenty Years at Hull-House with Autobiographical Notes.* (New York: The Macmillan Company, 1912). http://digital.library.upenn.edu/women/addams/hullhouse/hullhouse.html 786

Upton Sinclair. *The Jungle.* From the American Studies Program at the University of Virginia. http://xroads.virginia.edu/ Select: Hypertexts, then select Upton Sinclair 787

Documents of American History

Magna Carta. http://www.bl.uk/collections/treasures/magnatranslation.html 850

Mayflower Compact. In *Documents of American History.* Ed. Henry Steele Commager. (New York: Appleton-Century-Crofts, 1968). 851

James Madison. *The Federalist,* No. 10. http://www.ourdocuments.gov Select: 100 Milestone Documents 851

Washington's Farewell Address. In *Annals of American History,* V3, *1784–1796, Organizing the New Nation.* (Chicago: Encyclopaedia Britannica, Inc., 1968). 852

"The Star-Spangled Banner." Francis Scott Key. From The Library of Congress. http://memory.loc.gov 852

The Monroe Doctrine. In *Annals of American History,* V5, *1821–1832, Steps Toward Equalitarianism.* (Chicago: Encyclopaedia Britannica, Inc., 1976) 853

The Memorial of the Cherokee Nation. *Native Americans: Opposing Viewpoints.* (San Diego: Greenhaven Press, Inc., 1998). 853

The Seneca Falls Declaration. In *The American Reader.* Ed. Diane Ravitch. (N.Y.: HarperPerennial, 1991). 854

The Emancipation Proclamation, January 1, 1863. From the National Archives and Records Administration. http://www.ourdocuments.gov Select: 100 Milestone Documents 855

Gettysburg Address. In *Documents of American History.* Ed. Henry Steele Commager. (New York: Appleton-Century-Crofts, 1968). 856

Chief Joseph. Surrender to the U.S. Army, 1877. *A Patriot's Handbook.* Ed. Caroline Kennedy. (N.Y.: Hyperion, 2003). 857

The Pledge of Allegiance. Francis Bellamy. From *The Pledge of Allegiance.* Christine Webster. (New York: Children's Press, 2003). 857

American's Creed. William Tyler Page, 1918 http://www.pueblo.gsa.gov/cic_text/misc/ourflag/creed.htm 858

The Fourteen Points. Woodrow Wilson. http://www.ourdocuments.gov Select: 100 Milestone Documents 858

Brown* v. *Board of Education of Topeka, Kansas. http://www.ourdocuments.gov Select: 100 Milestone Documents 859

John F. Kennedy. Inaugural Address, 1961. http://www.ourdocuments.gov Select: 100 Milestone Documents 860

Martin Luther King, Jr. "I Have A Dream," March on Washington, 1963. In *A Patriot's Handbook.* Ed. Caroline Kennedy. (New York: Hyperion, 2003). 861

Classroom Solutions

Backward Mapping

How Can My Instruction Help Students Succeed in a Standards-Based System?

by Emily M. Schell, Ed.D.

Content standards articulate what students should know and be able to do in every social studies classroom. Effective instructional planning based in the standards and maximizing available resources is essential for meaningful teaching and learning of social studies. Planning instruction with educational goals in mind makes for the most effective teaching.

How Do I Map My Curriculum?

Mapping the curriculum from beginning to end, and from the end to the beginning—**backward mapping**—makes for solid instruction.

Mapping out the curriculum allows teachers to achieve several goals. These goals include a better understanding of the standards and content-specific objectives, organization and pacing of the curriculum, and focused assessment related to specific goals and objectives.

- ✔ **Begin the Process of Curriculum Mapping** To begin, teachers analyze the body of content standards for one grade level. They then compare and contrast these standards to additional sources of information that support effective teaching and learning at that grade level and in that subject area. This process works best with same-grade colleagues who bring varying perspectives and expertise to teaching this subject. As a result of this collaboration, strengths and weaknesses of the standards become apparent. Teachers will have a better understanding of the standards and identify concerns and questions for follow-up while mapping.
- ✔ **Analyze the Organization of the Standards-Based Content** Most social studies teachers agree with researchers that history is best taught in chronological order. However, some grade-level standards either do not or cannot present the content in chronological order. Rich discussions about themes and concepts tend to emerge, and teachers identify meaningful methods for presenting complex and overlapping information. In this way students will see the connections that transcend chronology.
- ✔ **Identify the Content and Order of Teaching** A plan is developed to present certain content first, then second, then third and so on. Folding in content that is either missing from the standards or essential in building background knowledge with students enters the curriculum map as well. Outside resources brought into the classroom are good supplements.
- ✔ **Separate Overlapping Units** Identify areas of instruction for the topics, themes, big ideas, or concepts. It is at this stage that backward planning is introduced for the development of instructional units, which will support the grade-level curriculum map. The instruction must support the planned assessment.

Tom & DeeAnn McCarthy/CORBIS STOCK MARKET

- ✔ **Map Curriculum at Each Grade Level** Curriculum planning should be shared among grade levels. Teachers will have a better understanding of what knowledge and skills students bring to their coursework if they take into consideration what has been learned previously.

How Do I Use Backward Mapping?

After a year-long course of study is mapped out, each unit must be further developed through backward mapping. You will start with the end in mind—knowing your curricular goals and objectives at the outset, which are often found in the content standards and articulated in the curriculum maps.

Once goals have been determined, teachers develop assessments that will show progress toward those goals and objectives. In the final step of this backward mapping process, teachers determine meaningful teaching and learning strategies and identify useful resources that support the assessment.

To use backward mapping in developing your units of instruction, consider the following steps:

Step One: Know Your Targets

First, identify exactly what students must know and do in this unit. Analyze content standards and any other resources that support curricular goals and objectives for this unit. As you plan, ask yourself:

- ✔ What do I want my students to know as a result of this unit?
- ✔ What skills will students develop during the course of this unit?
- ✔ How do I describe these goals clearly and concisely to my students so they understand where we should be at the end of this unit?
- ✔ What essential knowledge will students need to access to make sense of this information?
- ✔ Do my instructional goals align with strategies identified in the curriculum map?
- ✔ Have I introduced any Big Ideas that are pertinent to this content?

Step Two: Identify and Develop Assessments

Second, consider the multiple forms of formal and informal assessments that will help you determine to what degree each student has achieved the stated goals and objectives seen in Step One. Some assessments are embedded throughout the instructional unit, while others come at the end of the unit. Some assessments are performance-based, while others are not. Some are authentic applications of information and skills, while others require the formal recall of information. Ask yourself:

- ✔ What do I want to know and see from each student?
- ✔ What are the best methods for students to demonstrate what they know and can do based on the goals and objectives?
- ✔ How many assessments do I need to determine what students know and can do?
- ✔ How will I balance informal and formal assessments?
- ✔ How will I assess students with diverse learning styles, skills, and abilities?
- ✔ How can I prepare and support students?
- ✔ How will these assessments promote student progress in social studies?
- ✔ At what time(s) during the unit will I administer these assessments?

Step Three: Develop Meaningful Instruction

After the assessments for the unit have been determined, consider the meaningful and effective teaching strategies that will support learning and student achievement on assessments. While developing lesson plans for instruction, ask yourself:

- ✔ How will students learn what they are expected to know?
- ✔ How will I engage students in the studies of this unit?
- ✔ In what ways might students relate or connect to this information?
- ✔ What research-based strategies will be most effective with my students and in these studies?
- ✔ How will I differentiate my instruction to meet the diverse needs of my students?
- ✔ How will I scaffold or provide access to the curriculum for my English learners?
- ✔ What vocabulary requires attention in this unit?
- ✔ How much time will I have to effectively teach this unit?
- ✔ How will I use the textbook and other resources to support the goals and objectives for this unit?
- ✔ What lessons will I develop?
- ✔ In what sequence will I teach these lessons during this unit?
- ✔ How will these lessons support the assessments from Step Two?

Step Four: Locate and Manage Resources

Effective teaching and learning of social studies requires the use of multiple forms of text and varied resources. Consider what you have available in your classroom, including your textbook, and identify resources you will add in order to teach this unit successfully. Ask yourself:

- ✔ What parts of the textbook are required for the lessons determined in Step Three?
- ✔ What ancillary materials are needed for the lessons in this unit?
- ✔ What Web sites will I recommend to students to support these lessons?
- ✔ Do I need to contact guest speakers or obtain outside resources?
- ✔ What literature resources are available to support this unit?

Emily Schell is Visiting Professor, San Diego State University; and Social Studies Education Director, SDSU City Heights Educational Collaborative, San Diego, CA

Classroom Solutions

Meeting the Diverse Needs of Our Students

by Douglas Fisher, Ph.D.

Today's classroom contains students from a variety of backgrounds with a variety of learning styles, strengths, and challenges. As teachers we are facing the challenge of helping students reach their educational potential. With careful planning, you can address the needs of all students in the social studies classroom. The basis for this planning is **universal access**. When classrooms are planned with universal access in mind, fewer students require specific accommodations.

What Is a Universal Access Design for Learning?

Universal design was first conceived in architectural studies when business people, engineers, and architects began making considerations for physical access to buildings. The idea was to plan the environment in advance to ensure that everyone had access. As a result, the environment would not have to be changed later for people with physical disabilities, people pushing strollers, workers who had injuries, or others for whom the environment would be difficult to negotiate. The Center for Universal Design at **www.design.ncsu.edu/cud** defines Universal Design as:

The design of products and environments to be usable by all people, to the greatest extent possible, without the need for adaptation or specialized design.

Universal Design and Access in Education

Researchers, teachers, and parents in education have expanded the development of built-in adaptations and inclusive accommodations from architectural space to the educational experience, especially in the area of curriculum.

In 1998, the National Center to Improve the Tools of Educators (NCITE), with the partnership of the Center for Applied Special Technology (CAST), proposed an expanded definition of universal design focused on education:

In terms of learning, universal design means the design of instructional materials and activities that allows the learning goals to be achievable by individuals with wide differences in their abilities to see, hear, speak, move, read, write, understand English, attend, organize, engage, and remember.

How Does Universal Design Work in Education?

Universal design and access, as they apply to education and schooling, suggest the following:

✔ **Inclusive Classroom Participation** Curriculum should be designed with all students and their needs in mind. The Glencoe/McGraw-Hill social studies texts and materials were designed with a wide range of students in mind. For example, understanding that English learners and students who struggle with reading would be using this textbook, vocabulary is specifically taught and

Jonathan Nourok/Photo Edit

reinforced. Similarly, the teacher-support materials provide multiple instructional points to be used depending on the needs of the students in the class. Further, the text is written such that main ideas are identified for all learners. Activating prior knowledge is also taken into consideration by the text. Connections between what students know and think about are made within the text.

- ✔ **Maximum Text Readability** In universally designed classrooms that provide access for all students, texts use direct language, clear noun-verb agreements, and clear construct-based wording. In addition to these factors, the Glencoe Social Studies text uses embedded definitions for difficult terms, provides for specific instruction in reading skills, uses a number of visual representations, and includes note-taking guides.
- ✔ **Adaptable and Accommodating** The content in this textbook can be easily translated, read aloud, or otherwise changed to meet the needs of students in the classroom. The section and end-of-chapter assessments provide students with multiple ways of demonstrating their content knowledge while also ensuring that they have practice with thinking in terms of multiple-choice questions. Critical thinking and analysis skills are also practiced.

How Is Differentiated Instruction the Key to Universal Access?

To differentiate instruction, teachers must acknowledge student differences in background knowledge and current reading, writing, and English language skills. They must also consider student learning styles and preferences, interests, and needs, and react accordingly. There are a number of general guidelines for differentiating instruction in the classroom to reach all students, including:

- ✔ **Link Assessment With Instruction** Assessments should occur before, during, and after instruction to ensure that the curriculum is aligned with what students do and do not know. Using assessments in this way allows you to plan instruction for whole groups, small groups, and individual students. Backward planning, where you establish the assessment before you begin instruction, is also important.
- ✔ **Clarify Key Concepts and Generalizations** Students need to know what is essential and how this information can be used in their future learning. In addition, students need to develop a sense of the **Big Ideas**—ideas that transcend time and place.
- ✔ **Emphasize Critical and Creative Thinking** The content, process, and products used or assigned in the classroom should require that students think about what they are learning. While some students may require support, additional motivation, varied tasks, materials, or equipment, the overall focus on critical and creative thinking allows for all students to participate in the lesson.
- ✔ **Include Teacher- and Student-Selected Tasks** A differentiated classroom includes both teacher- and student-selected activities and tasks. At some points in the lesson or day, the teacher must provide instruction and assign learning activities. In other parts of the lesson, students should be provided choices in how they engage with the content. This balance increases motivation, engagement, and learning.

Classroom Activity	To differentiate this activity:
Display a map of imperialism in Africa around 1914. Be sure your map notes which European powers controlled what countries. Discuss with students the general information on the map. Then have them list each country under the correct European power that controlled it.	• Ask students to imagine they are living at the time of the Boer War. Have students write an editorial to a British newspaper regarding the situation in South Africa. • Have students tabulate the number of countries controlled by each European power. Have them take the data and create a bar graph that shows who were the most active imperialistic powers at the time. • Have students compose a ballad about the presence of the British in India, from an Indian's point of view. • Have students create and present a dialog that might have taken place between a native African and a European during the late 1800s. • Have students create a map—using whatever material they choose—that shows the major physical features of Africa. • Have students choose a country of modern Africa with an unstable government to research. Have them write a three-page paper discussing the potential economic growth that could occur there if a stable government were installed. • Have students list each city they see on the map and write in which country they were located.

Classroom Solutions

How Do I Support Individual Students?

The vast majority of students will thrive in a classroom based on universal access and differentiated instruction. However, wise teachers recognize that no single option will work for all students and that there may be students who require unique systems of support to be successful.

Tips For Instruction

The following tips for instruction can support your efforts to help all students reach their maximum potential.

- ✔ Survey students to discover their individual differences. Use interest inventories of their unique talents so you can encourage contributions in the classroom.
- ✔ Be a model for respecting others. Adolescents crave social acceptance. The student with learning differences is especially sensitive to correction and criticism, particularly when it comes from a teacher. Your behavior will set the tone for how students treat one another.
- ✔ Expand opportunities for success. Provide a variety of instructional activities that reinforce skills and concepts.
- ✔ Establish measurable objectives and decide how you can best help students who meet them.
- ✔ Celebrate successes and make note of and praise "work in progress."
- ✔ Keep it simple. Point out problem areas if doing so can help a student effect change. Avoid overwhelming students with too many goals at one time.
- ✔ Assign cooperative group projects that challenge all students to contribute to solving a problem or creating a product.

How Do I Reach Students With Learning Disabilities?

- ✔ Provide support and structure. Clearly specify rules, assignments, and responsibilities.
- ✔ Practice skills frequently. Use games and drills to help maintain student interest.
- ✔ Incorporate many modalities into the learning process. Provide opportunities to say, hear, write, read, and act out important concepts and information.
- ✔ Link new skills and concepts to those already mastered.
- ✔ If possible, allow students to record answers on audiotape.
- ✔ Allow extra time to complete assessments and assignments.
- ✔ Let students demonstrate proficiency with alternative presentations, including oral reports, role plays, art projects, and musical presentations.
- ✔ Provide outlines, notes, or tape recordings of lecture material.
- ✔ Pair students with peer helpers, and provide class time for pair interaction.

How Do I Reach Students With Behavioral Challenges?

- ✔ Provide a structured environment with clear-cut schedules, rules, seat assignments, and safety procedures.
- ✔ Reinforce appropriate behavior and model it for students.
- ✔ Cue distracted students back to the task through verbal signals and teacher proximity.
- ✔ Set goals that can be achieved in the short term. Work for long-term improvement in the big areas.

How Do I Reach Students With Physical Challenges?

- ✔ Openly discuss with the student any uncertainties you have about when to offer aid.
- ✔ Ask parents or therapists and students what special devices or procedures are needed and whether any special safety precautions need to be taken.
- ✔ Welcome students with physical challenges into all activities, including field trips, special events, and projects.
- ✔ Provide information to assist class members and adults in their understanding of support needed.

How Do I Reach Students with Visual Impairments?

- ✔ Facilitate independence. Modify assignments as needed.
- ✔ Teach classmates how and when to serve as visual guides.
- ✔ Limit unnecessary noise in the classroom if it distracts the student with visual impairments.
- ✔ Provide tactile models whenever possible.
- ✔ Foster a spirit of inclusion. Describe people and events as they occur in the classroom. Remind classmates that the student with visual impairments cannot interpret gestures and other forms of nonverbal communication.

✔ Provide taped lectures and reading assignments for use outside the classroom.
✔ Team the student with a sighted peer for written work.

How Do I Reach Students With Hearing Impairments?

✔ Seat students where they can see your lip movements easily and where they can avoid any visual distractions.
✔ Avoid standing with your back to the window or light source.
✔ Use an overhead projector so you can maintain eye contact while writing information for students.
✔ Seat students where they can see speakers.
✔ Write all assignments on the board, or hand out written instructions.
✔ If the student has a manual interpreter, allow both student and interpreter to select the most favorable seating arrangements.
✔ Teach students to look directly at each other when they speak.

How Do I Reach English Learners?

✔ Remember, students' ability to speak English does not reflect their academic abilities.
✔ Try to incorporate the students' cultural experience into your instruction. The help of a bilingual aide may be effective.
✔ Avoid any references in your instruction that could be construed as cultural stereotypes.
✔ Preteach important vocabulary and concepts.
✔ Encourage students to preview text before they begin reading, noting headings.
✔ Remind students not to ignore graphic organizers, photographs, and maps since there is much information in these visuals.
✔ Use realia and photographs whenever possible to build background knowledge and understanding. Examples of realia would be coins in a foreign currency or a raw cotton boll used to reinforce their importance in history.

How Do I Reach Gifted Students?

✔ Make arrangements for students to take selected subjects early and to work on independent projects.
✔ Ask "what if" questions to develop high-level thinking skills. Establish an environment safe for risk taking in your classroom.
✔ Emphasize concepts, theories, ideas, relationships, and generalizations about the content.
✔ Promote interest in the past by inviting students to make connections to the present.
✔ Let students express themselves in alternate ways such as creative writing, acting, debates, simulations, drawing, or music.
✔ Provide students with a catalog of helpful resources, listing such things as agencies that provide free and inexpensive materials, appropriate community services and programs, and community experts who might be called upon to speak to your students.
✔ Assign extension projects that allow students to solve real-life problems related to their communities.✦

Douglas Fisher is a professor at San Diego State University, San Diego, CA.

Customize Your Classroom!

Advice from L. Martha Infante
Bethune Middle School, LAUSD
Los Angeles, CA

Students respond to a subject better when they can make a personal connection to it. With the growing number of students who are Latino or come from other parts of the world, explaining geography through a worldwide theme such as volcanoes can draw them into an awareness of the world as a whole rather than the region from which they came. To develop this awareness and an understanding of latitude and longitude, first display a large world map. Have students research the longitude and latitude of 15 major volcanoes around the world. The library or Internet can provide this information. Have them pinpoint these locations on the map with markers and answer the following:

- What patterns do you see in volcanic activity?
- What causes volcanic activity?
- Where might more volcanoes appear?
- Where in the world are volcanoes still active?

As a follow-up, suggest students go to http://volcano.und.nodak.edu/vwdocs/kids/legends.html to find legends about the origins of some of these volcanoes. Encourage students to share what they find with the class.

Classroom Solutions

Academic Vocabulary

How Can I Help My Students Learn Academic Vocabulary?

by Robin Scarcella, Ph.D.

What Is Academic English?

Academic English is the language used by the power elite. Academic vocabulary is the basis for academic English. It is the language used in academics, business, and courts of law. It is the type of English used in professional books, including textbooks, and it contains specific linguistic features that are associated with academic disciplines like social studies. Proficiency in reading and using academic English is especially related to long-term success in all parts of life.

By reinforcing academic vocabulary and academic English, teachers can help learners to access authentic, academic texts—not simplified texts that dummy down the content. In this way, they can provide information that will help build their students' background knowledge rapidly.

What Is Academic Vocabulary?

By the time children have completed elementary school, they must have acquired the knowledge needed to understand academic vocabulary. How many words should they acquire to be able to access their textbooks? A basic 2,000-word vocabulary of high-frequency words makes up 87% of the vocabulary of academic texts. Eight hundred other academic words comprise an additional 8% of the words. Three percent of the remaining words are technical words. The remaining 2% are low-frequency words. There may be as many as 123,000 low-frequency words in academic texts.

Why Should Students Learn Academic Vocabulary?

English learners who have mastered a basic 2,000-word vocabulary are ready to acquire the majority of general words found in their academic texts.

Knowledge of academic words combined with continued acquisition of general words can significantly boost an English learner's comprehension level of academic texts. English learners who learn and practice these words before they graduate from high school are likely to be able to master academic material with more confidence and speed. They waste less time and effort in guessing words or consulting dictionaries than those who only know the basic 2,000 words that characterize general conversation.

Also, consider academic success in terms of measurement and assessment—the CAT-6, California's High School Exit Exam, the SAT, the ACT, and the GRE—with regards to word mastery. All demand an understanding of academic vocabulary.

How Do I Include Academic Vocabulary and Academic English in My Teaching?

Teachers can provide their students with rich samples of academic vocabulary and help students understand and attend to the academic English of their text.

To develop academic English, learners must have already acquired a large amount of basic proficiency in the grammar of everyday English.

Will Hart/ PhotoEdit

Academic English should not be taught overtly but rather within contexts that make sense. In terms of instruction, teaching academic English includes providing students with access to core curriculum—in this case Social Studies.

Academic English arises not only from knowledge of a linguistic code and cognition but also from social practices in which academic English is used to accomplish communicative goals. The acquisition of academic vocabulary and grammar is necessary to advance the development of academic English.

Tips for Teaching Academic Vocabulary:

- ✔ **Expose Students to Academic Vocabulary** You do not need to call attention to words students are learning because they will acquire them subconsciously.
- ✔ **Do Not Correct Students' Mistakes When Using the Vocabulary Words** All vocabulary understanding and spelling errors are developmental and will disappear once the student reads more.
- ✔ **Help Students Decode the Words Themselves** Once they learn the alphabet, they should be able to decode words. Decoding each word they don't recognize will help them more than trying to focus on sentence structure. Once they can recognize the words, they can read "authentic" texts.
- ✔ **Do Not Ignore the English Learner in This Process** They can learn academic vocabulary before they are completely fluent in oral English.
- ✔ **Helping Students Build Academic Vocabulary Leads to Broader Learning** Students who have mastered the basic academic vocabulary are ready to continue acquiring words from the rest of the groups. To help determine which words are in the 2,000-word basic group, refer to *West's General Service List of English Words, 1953*. The list is designed to serve as a guide for teachers and as a checklist and goal list for students. For additional information about the list, visit: http://www.vuw.ac.nz/research/awl/info.html or you can check http://www.uni-trier.de/uni/tb2/anglistik/projekte/stubbs/awl.htm

There are a number of guidelines that teachers can follow when teaching academic English and vocabulary:

Guidelines for Teaching Academic Vocabulary
1. Direct and planned instruction
2. Models—that have increasingly difficult language
3. Attention to form—pointing out linguistic features of words
4. Practice
5. Motivation
6. Instructional feedback
7. Assessment—on a regular basis

Robin Scarcella is professor and Director Academic English/ESL, University of California at Irvine, Irvine, CA.

Classroom Activity: Writing About Modern America

Advice from Robin Scarcella

Give students an impromptu writing assignment. Ask them to write a short essay about one of the topics listed below in the left column. Have students use as many of the academic vocabulary words in the right column as they can in their essay. Give students a time limit for their writing. When completed, ask student volunteers to share their writing. Note what academic vocabulary words they use.

Topic	Academic Vocabulary
The challenges of reducing poverty	impoverished
in America	housing
	health insurance
	income
Recent technological advances	computers
	technology
	laptop
	desk station
	compact disc player
	transmit

Classroom Solutions

Project CRISS

How Can I Teach My Students How to Learn Social Studies?

by Carol M. Santa, Ph.D.

We all know that teaching social studies involves far more than teaching just course content. We understand that students need to become engaged, confident learners. Achieving that goal means helping them to understand, organize, and retain information.

Teaching Both Content and Skills

In other words, we want our students to have the skills and confidence to be lifelong learners. With its rich content, social studies offer an ideal arena for teaching both content and skills.

✔ **A Dual Responsibility** Let's take a moment to consider why the dual responsibility of teaching both content and skills is so important. Think back to your own middle and high school years. What do you remember about the content you learned? If I recall my experiences, I find I remember remarkably little content. What did I learn in biology or history? What did my textbooks look like? As the years go by, I don't even remember the names of most of my teachers.

✔ **An Inspiring Teacher** Yet I have vivid memories of my eighth-grade social studies teacher, who came out of retirement to fill in for a history teacher who left on maternity leave. I remember how fascinated I became with ancient history; I recall giving oral reports and how she helped me become comfortable speaking before a group. In fact, I remember more from her class than any other I took during high school.

✔ **Teach How to Learn** More important, I now understand that she taught me how to learn to learn. She showed me how to underline, how to organize information using different note-taking formats, and how to write coherent answers on essay tests. She taught me the need to test myself on what I knew. And during that vulnerable, adolescent year, I went from being a mediocre student to being an excellent one.

This inspirational teacher did something else for me. At some point during that eighth-grade year, I decided to become a teacher. Later I realized that she had launched me on my professional mission—to spread her wisdom to others. Eventually this led to Project CRISS.

What Is CRISS?

CRISS stands for **CR**eating **I**ndependence through **S**tudent-owned **S**trategies. It is a staff development program that I created in collaboration with middle and high school teachers in Kalispell, Montana.

✔ **Origin of CRISS** CRISS had its start 20 years ago in a lunchtime conversation in a teachers' lounge. One of the social studies teachers said, "My students aren't doing a good job of answering chapter questions. In fact, I don't think they even read my assignments. My reading assignments are becoming a waste of time!" His words struck a chord. "My students don't have a clue about how to study, and they don't write very well either," another teacher lamented.

✔ **Evolving Strategies** Supported by a state grant, we started working together to find practical ways to help students read, write, and learn content. We met in teams, read professional literature, and designed studies to test classroom strategies. From these efforts, we evolved a project to help students become better readers, writers, and

Tom & DeeAnn McCarthy/CORBIS STOCK MARKET

learners. Once the project took shape, we shared our discoveries with other teachers by offering a two- or three-day CRISS workshop to schools and districts in the state.

✔ **Constant Growth** Over the last two decades, Project CRISS has spread from teacher to teacher across this country, into Canada, and to several European countries. The project seems to sell itself. Teachers who use CRISS principles and strategies find that their students attain a deeper understanding of course content and become better readers, writers, and learners at the same time. In fact, data from numerous quantitative studies shows that using CRISS strategies improves student learning. (For the most recent data and for information on CRISS workshops, see www.projectcriss.com)

CRISS Strategies in the Teacher Edition

When the editors of Glencoe/McGraw-Hill asked me and my colleagues to help them integrate CRISS strategies into their social studies texts, we welcomed the opportunity. In this teacher wraparound edition, we offer many references to CRISS strategies. We have packed the pages with strategies that help students gain a deeper understanding of specific content.

CRISS Training

We have one word of caution, however: the integration of CRISS strategies within this teacher wraparound edition does not take the place of a Project CRISS workshop, which provides an in-depth knowledge of CRISS. So, if you haven't yet participated in a CRISS workshop, we encourage you to do so. During a workshop, CRISS trainers take you step-by-step through the philosophy and instructional strategies. Participants are actively involved in all aspects of the program—practicing, adapting, and applying strategies to meet teaching needs.

Long-lasting change occurs when teachers and administrators work together to share, extend ideas, and problem solve. The most effective implementations occur when the initial workshop is supported by follow-up sessions, including a specific follow-up day. At this session, teachers bring examples of strategies they have used since the initial training. Part of this time may be spent in review and in learning new strategies. The rest of the time is for sharing applications. Additional ongoing support can occur in teacher planning periods.

In any case, for those of you unfamiliar with Project CRISS, let's begin with a little background knowledge. In this way you will have some context for the various activities suggested throughout the teacher wraparound edition.

The CRISS Philosophy

The first thing to know is that Project CRISS is more than a collection of learning strategies. Its underlying power rests not on the individual strategies but on the teaching philosophy behind them. This philosophy integrates work from cognitive psychology, social learning theory, and neurological research about how the brain learns. It includes these overlapping principles:

- ✔ background knowledge and purposeful reading
- ✔ author's craft
- ✔ active involvement
- ✔ discussion
- ✔ organization
- ✔ writing
- ✔ teacher modeling

Let's look at each of these principles in more detail, along with examples of instructional strategies that illustrate them.

Background knowledge and purposeful reading are powerful determinants of reading comprehension.

Teachers involved in Project CRISS often talk about the importance of background knowledge. Readers are far more likely to learn new information when they have some previous knowledge and have a purpose in mind before they read or listen.

✔ **More Than Simply Reading** We warn students not to simply begin reading. We ask them, *"What might you already know about the topic? What questions do you have about the topic?"* We also remind them to preview the assignment and think about their goals for reading. We often have to be very explicit about the goals. For example, we might tell students, *"After reading this selection, you should be able to . . . ,"* or, *"After viewing the video, you should be able to identify . . ."*

✔ **KWLH** In the teaching strategies included for each chapter in this book, we offer ideas for helping students tap into their background knowledge. For example, we suggest that students preview their reading assignment and consider what they already know about a topic. Or, we might develop a whole-class **KWLH** chart (**K**now, **W**ant to learn, **L**earned, **H**ow to learn more), where students work on this task together. They can generate questions about what they want to learn, and then, after completing the assignment, they can list the new information they have learned and how they can learn more.

What I **Know**	What I **Want** to Find Out	What I **Learned**	**How** I Can Learn More

✔ **Reading Goals** We also suggest ways to make sure your students have clear goals for their reading. Each section opener lists reading strategies and main ideas that outline reading goals. Most students will skip over this material and simply start reading. Teachers need to help students understand that the reading goals are important tools for understanding. We tell students,

(Continued on next page)

Classroom Solutions

Project CRISS

"Don't ignore your purposes for reading. Take time to think about them before delving into your reading." Project CRISS also provides hints about how to get students to use these purpose statements to evaluate whether they have understood their reading.

Reading social studies materials has its own special considerations. CRISS specialist Malla S. Kolhoff shares this advice: "As educators, it is our responsibility to set a purpose for historical reading. Students often must struggle to connect history with their own lives. To compare and contrast, establish cause and effect, and sequence events in chronological order presents a challenge for even the best reader. CRISS strategies allow students to move beyond words to the real significance for their society. With CRISS, my students are able to become engaged in the learning process through:

a. background knowledge
b. active reading, listening, and learning
c. discussion
d. metacognition
e. writing
f. organization
g. understanding

I have found that these strategies help my students attain a higher level of historical thinking and understanding."

Good readers have an intuitive understanding of the author's craft.

When students know how authors craft their writing, they can more readily understand and remember what they read.

✔ **Pay Attention** Good readers and writers know that paying attention to how text is organized—its headings and paragraphs, for example—makes it easier to comprehend its content. Good readers will analyze the author's style of presentation as they read. They might ask themselves, *"What is this author doing to help me learn key concepts? How does the writer lead me from one idea to the next?"* When students become aware of what the author is doing to impart content, they have a clearer idea of what the author is saying.

✔ **The Walk Through** In the sample lesson on the following pages, we offer advice about "walking through" the text to discover the author's style of presentation. Our suggestions go beyond examining the surface structure (headings, bold print, color coding of topical headings, italicized words) to analyzing how the author elaborates on key topics.

Effective learners are actively involved when they listen and read.

We learn best when we act on the information presented. We can do this by using a variety of organizing activities that require us to write, talk, and transform the information we are absorbing. None of us learns much from reading alone—it's far too passive.

CRISS strategies encourage active engagement in learning. We might ask students to read a section and describe what they are learning to a partner, or we might be more elaborate and have students develop concept maps or write summaries.

Students need many opportunities to talk with one another about what they are learning.

Discussion is critical to learning. The discussions we advocate are different from those in which the teacher remains the authority figure, with students simply reciting answers to questions. If discussion becomes mere recitation and there is little interaction among students, little learning occurs. Thus we focus on how to get students to lead their own discussions about a topic. We want them to understand that it is their discussing, their oral grappling with meaning—not ours—that leads to deeper understanding.

(Continued on next page)

Jose L. Pelaez/CORBIS STOCK MARKET

Competent readers know several ways to organize information for learning.

Learning depends on organization. We show students different ways to organize information. They can take notes, underline selectively, develop concept maps, and summarize ideas in charts. Once we have taught students these techniques, we tell them, *"You have to do more than just read this assignment. How are you going to organize the information from this assignment? You have to change it, to transform it so that it becomes your own."*

For each chapter of this text, we offer ideas for assisting students in organizing information. Once students have learned a variety of organizing systems, we suggest ways to help them apply these structures independently.

Students deserve opportunities to write about what they are learning.

Writing is an integral part of the CRISS project. Writing lets us figure out what we know and what we still need to know. We cannot write about something we do not understand. While we teach students how to write expository papers and essay exams, we also encourage students to write more informally by questioning, speculating, and writing explanations in learning logs. We make sure that students are writing continually about what they are learning.

For each chapter of this text, we offer ideas for assisting students in organizing information. Once students have learned a variety of organizing systems, we suggest ways to help them apply these structures independently.

Teaching involves explanation and modeling.

Our final principle has to do with our own teaching. Students learn to think strategically when we use these processes as part of our instruction. Our demonstrations are especially critical for struggling readers. Most have never been taught how to learn. We have to show them how.

✔ **Take Center Stage** When you introduce a new strategy, you should take the center stage: showing, telling, modeling, demonstrating, and explaining not only the content but the process of active reading. As students learn, gradually release responsibility to them. Strategy instruction involves two overlapping steps. First, we explain what the strategy is and why students should use it. If students do not know why they are performing an activity, they will rarely use the activity on their own. Next, we demonstrate and talk about procedures for carrying out the strategy. We discuss, demonstrate, and think aloud while modeling. Then, students practice under our guidance and feedback.

✔ **A Systematic Approach** Project CRISS is a valuable basis for instruction. It provides a systematic approach for using what we now know about teaching and learning. The following chart lists questions we need to continually ask ourselves while we are teaching. Use this chart to monitor your efforts to incorporate CRISS principles into your teaching.

CRISS Principles	The CRISS Philosophy	Yes	No	Somewhat
Background knowledge:	Did I assist students in thinking about what they already knew about the topic before beginning the unit? Did I develop necessary concepts before students read?			
Purpose setting:	Did my students have a clear purpose about what they were going to learn before beginning the lesson?			
Author's craft:	Can my students use the author's style of presentation to facilitate their understanding?			
Active involvement:	Were my students engaged in the topic? Did I help students become actively involved in their learning?			
Discussion:	Did my students have opportunities to talk about what they were learning?			
Organization:	Did my students organize information in a variety of ways?			
Writing:	Did my students write about what they were learning?			
Teacher modeling:	Did I do enough teacher modeling of learning strategies so that students could begin doing them on their own?			

Classroom Solutions

Project CRISS

How Do I Use Project CRISS to Teach Discovering Our Past?

When students know how authors structure their writing, they can more readily understand and remember what they read. For the first several chapters of this book, show students how to analyze the author's craft by "walking through" the chapter, noting text features. Then demonstrate how to use the author's organization to develop two-column notes.

For demonstrating these strategies, make transparencies of the first several pages of Chapter 1. Divide students into small groups.

Introducing the Chapter

Tell students: *"Before reading a text, I take time to figure out how the author has presented the information. If I understand the author's craft, I can do a better job of reading and learning. The authors of this book have a consistent organizational plan for presenting information. Let's discover what they do."*

Ask students to preview the introductory pages of Unit 1: *"Why do you think the authors have included the sections: Why It's Important, the time line, map, Places to Locate, and People to Meet? How might you use these features to gain an overview of what this unit is about?"*

Next ask students to turn to Chapter 1. *"Notice the time line and how it is used to identify key topics included in this chapter. Now look at the chapter Big Ideas. Read the brief summaries of each of the sections. Why do you think the authors have told you information before you read? Notice the foldable activity and the suggestion for using the foldable for taking comparison notes on the three different civilizations. How might you use History Online to expand your understanding of the chapter content?"*

(Ask one or more students to explore what is available online for this chapter and report to the class on ways that this information could be used. It is good to review student online sources before they are presented to the class.)

Ask students to turn to the Get Ready to Read! skill on the next page. Use the ideas described here and "walk" the students through the lesson.

Place a transparency of the first pages of the lesson on the overhead and begin modeling.

Introducing the Section

1. Get Ready to Read!

Ask students to turn to the first page of Section 1. *"Notice how this page is organized."* (It begins with a Guide to Reading that includes: Looking Back, Looking Forward; Focusing on the Main Ideas; Meeting People; Content and Academic Vocabulary; and Reading Strategy.) *"Let's take a moment and talk about how these features might help you."*

Read aloud and point out the Looking Back, Looking Forward introduction. Remind your students: *"Keep this introductory reading purpose in mind as you read."*

- ✔ **Focusing on the Main Ideas:** *"Why has the author included the main ideas at the beginning of the section?"* (helps readers know what they are going to learn; helps readers think about what they might already know about the chapter information; helps set goals for reading)
- ✔ **Meeting People:** *"How might this feature help you prepare to read this section?"* (helps readers build a context for people mentioned in the chapter)
- ✔ **Building Your Vocabulary:** *"Now look at the list of content and academic vocabulary words and skim the first several pages of the chapter. What do you notice about how the vocabulary words are sequenced and highlighted in this chapter?"* (The vocabulary words are highlighted in yellow and presented in the same order in the chapter as listed here.)
- ✔ **Reading Strategy:** *"Why is it important to organize your thinking before you read? How might the strategy suggested here help you?"*

2. Visual Information

"Notice the visuals on the first pages of the chapters. Why do you think the author has included these references? Why should you pay attention to them? It's a good idea to look through these references before reading the chapter." (makes the topics more interesting, provides background knowledge, includes important information for understanding the content, and so on)

Walking Through the Chapter

As you talk aloud, note features on the transparencies for Section 1. *"Now let's see how the authors have helped us figure out the main topics covered in this chapter. Notice the bold print headings.*

The main topics are printed in larger red print, and the subtopics are printed in smaller blue print. Vocabulary terms are noted in yellow. This organization and color coding should help you figure out what is important.

"At the end of each subsection, notice the Reading Check. The Reading Check questions will help you know if you have comprehended each subsection. When you come to a Reading Check, you will stop and try to answer the question. If you can't answer the question, you should reread. You should read through these questions before you begin reading. In this way, you would know what you are supposed to get out of this section. The end-of-section assessment questions will also help you know what you are to learn."

Have students read the topical headings and subheadings for the first section of the chapter and make some predictions about what they will learn. *"Notice how the author has stated some main points as rhetorical questions—that is, questions that do not have a concrete answer."* Explain that good readers take time to preview and to make predictions before reading. Talk about how using the topic headings helps with this process.

Reading the Chapter

Assign students to read the introduction to the chapter, stopping at the first blue header. Have them turn to a partner and retell what they have just read. Explain: *"Good readers are active when they read. They stop and think about what they have just read. If they can't remember the information, they go back and reread."*

Then have students read the rest of Section 1. At the end of each subsection, have them turn to a partner, and, without looking back at the text, retell what they have just read. Also, model how to turn topical headings into questions as a way to evaluate comprehension.

Main Idea-Detail Notes

Ask students to divide their notebook paper into two columns and record key points in the left column and details explaining the key points in the right column. Main points could be questions or key words. Students then use their notes as a study guide, using the key words or questions to quiz themselves.

- ✔ Demonstrate how to use the authors' clues (headings, highlighted vocabulary, Reading Check questions) to develop main idea-detail notes. The authors also might include within this text many rhetorical questions that assist readers in determining main ideas. Talk about how the examples help clarify content, and show students how to include these rhetorical questions and examples within their notes. On a blank transparency, develop two-column notes over the first section of the chapter while students write down their own notes at their desks. Model how to include main topics, rhetorical questions, and vocabulary essential to understanding the content in the left column. In the right column, record details elaborating the main points. Talk about being brief and using your own words. Explain why making the authors' message your own ensures better comprehension and retention.
- ✔ Continue modeling notes over the rest of this section. Then ask students to work in pairs or small groups to develop two-column notes over the rest of the chapter. Ask them to share their notes in a whole-class discussion.

SAMPLE ORGANIZER

Main Ideas	Details
Early Humans **History** **Prehistory** **Archaeologists** **Anthropologists**	 Story of human past Time before people developed writing Uncover clues about early human life—artifacts, fossils Study how humans began and developed—bones, artifacts
Paleolithic or Old Stone Age	Earliest part of Stone Age (2.5 million years ago)
Hunter-Gatherers How did they adapt to the environment?	Moved from place to place finding food—nomads Lived in groups: Men—hunted, clubs; later spears, bows & arrows Women—close to camp Warm climates—few clothes Cold climates—caves Fire—life-changing discovery
Ice Ages What was this time like?	100,000 B.C. to about 8000 B.C. Extreme cold, ice sheets covered parts of Europe, Asia, North America Threatened human life, people built sturdier shelters, changed diet, used animal furs
Major Developments	Fire, language, art, tools (stones, hunting spears—later fishhooks, needles)

Classroom Solutions

Primary Source Strategies

How Do I Use Primary Sources in My Classroom?

PhotoDisc

A primary source is direct evidence of an event, idea, period, or development. It is an oral or written account obtained from actual participants in an event. Examples of primary sources include the following:

- ✔ official documents (records, statistics)
- ✔ political declarations, laws, and rules for governance
- ✔ speeches and interviews
- ✔ diaries, memoirs, and oral histories
- ✔ autobiographies
- ✔ recipes and cookbooks
- ✔ advertisements and posters
- ✔ letters

Physical objects, such as tools and dishes, can be primary sources; so can visual evidence in the form of fine art, photographs, maps, films, and videotapes. Primary sources can also include songs and audio recordings.

Why Use Primary Sources in Your Classroom?

Using primary sources to teach transforms the study of social studies from a passive process to an active one. Students become investigators—finding clues, formulating hypotheses and drawing inferences, making judgments, and reaching conclusions. Bringing primary sources into the classroom stimulates students to think critically about events, issues, and concepts rather than just memorizing dates, names, and generalizations reached by others. Thinking critically then becomes a habit that can help students become good citizens.

Choosing Primary Sources

- ✔ Provide exposure to a variety of source types, including historic photographs, folk or popular music, financial records or household accounts, as well as letters, journals, and historic documents.
- ✔ When choosing print sources, consider the interests and reading levels of your students. Many texts contain challenging vocabulary and unfamiliar sentence structure. You may need to create a reader's guide that defines key vocabulary and paraphrases the main points of the reading.
- ✔ Some documents may be too long. Decide whether using an excerpt will provide enough information for students to draw conclusions.
- ✔ Depending upon the topic and your instructional objectives, you may need to provide several different primary sources to expose students to a variety of perspectives.
- ✔ Decide how students will access the primary sources: through the Internet, the library, a museum, or other print resources. Consider the possibility of an Internet virtual field trip for students. Moving from URL to URL, students can visit museum sites and other Web pages to view artifacts; interpret economic or census data; and read journals, letters, and official documents.

Anthony Redpath/CORBIS STOCK MARKET

How Do I Introduce Students to Primary Sources?

Carefully explain the nature of primary sources when you introduce them to students. Although primary sources contain valuable clues, be sure to alert students that primary sources contain biases and prejudices and must be approached with caution. Every primary source reflects the creator's point of view to some degree. Students must consider the authorship and why the primary source was written.

Using Primary Sources in the Classroom

Primary sources provide a rich source of inspiration for a variety of instructional strategies. They can be used to spark interest in a new topic, foster deeper exploration into a historical era, or assess students' understanding of social studies concepts and facts.

- ✔ **Prereading Activities** Present a primary source for students to study

Aaron Haupt

Interpreting a Primary Source

Before students interpret a primary source, they need to know the context into which the source fits. Then they can use questions and guidelines, such as those below, to help them analyze and interpret the primary source.

Print Sources

- Who created the source, and what was the purpose for doing so?
- Did the writer personally experience or witness the event(s)?
- At what point did the writer record the information—as it happened or afterward? How long after?
- Who was the intended audience?
- Was the writer trying to record facts, express an opinion, or persuade others to take action?
- What is the author's main message?
- What values does the document convey?
- What bias does it reflect?
- What information about the topic can you gather from this document?
- Compare this document with what you know about the topic. Does it confirm those ideas or introduce a new perspective?
- How might other accounts about this topic support or modify the message this source delivers?

Visual Sources

- Who created the source, and what was the purpose for doing so?
- What does the image show?
- What mood does the image convey?
- Who or what dominates the image or catches your eye?
- How does the view impact the message?
- What details can you learn from the image?
- What is excluded from view?
- What bias does the visual reflect?
- What information about the topic can you gather from this visual?
- How might other visuals about this topic support or modify the message this one delivers?

Audio Sources

- Who created the source? What was the purpose for creating this source?
- What is the main idea of the audio?
- What mood does the recorder's voice convey?
- What bias does the audio text reflect?
- What information about the topic can you gather from this audio source?
- Compare the information in this source with what you already know about the topic. Does it confirm those ideas or introduce a new perspective?
- How might other sources about this topic support or modify the message that this one delivers?

at the beginning of a new chapter or topic. Have students analyze the source, using the questions and guidelines presented above. Then have students make predictions about what they might learn in the upcoming lessons.

✔ **Exploring Information** Provide a variety of primary sources related to a topic or time period. Have students compare and contrast the items, analyzing the information, making inferences, and drawing conclusions about the period.

✔ **Evaluation Activities** Have students evaluate a primary source and tell how it supports or refutes what they learned in the textbook, or have students read a primary source document that provides one perspective on a topic and have students write their own account, presenting another perspective or opinion.

Below is a specific, step-by-step activity suggested by educator Leslie Espinosa. This activity is especially beneficial when a less-proficient reader is paired with a more-proficient reader.

1. Before class make a list of student reading partners. Make sure one of the two is a good reader.
2. Have students read a primary source document (or part of a primary source document), taking turns as they go. They should "mark" any words that they do not understand.
3. After each paragraph, the student pair should stop and paraphrase what it says in their own words.
4. Students should look up unfamiliar words they've marked and create an illustrated dictionary entry for each term (over the course of the year or semester).
5. Ask student pairs to present their paraphrased primary source to the rest of the class.✦

Reading in the Content Areas

How Can I Use Jamestown Education Products to Help Struggling Readers?

For over 30 years, Jamestown Education has made its primary focus helping older readers become better readers. The Jamestown products shown on this page support the basic elements of reading cited by the National Reading Panel. Each of them can help your struggling readers become better readers.

Timed Readings Plus in Social Studies

✔ **Reading Levels:** 4–13+

✔ **Benefits:**

This ten-book series will help your students increase both reading rate and comprehension. The nonfiction passages cover current social studies topics and are similar to those found on both state and national tests. Each of the two-part lessons focuses on reading rate, factual recall, comprehension strategies, and higher-level critical thinking skills.

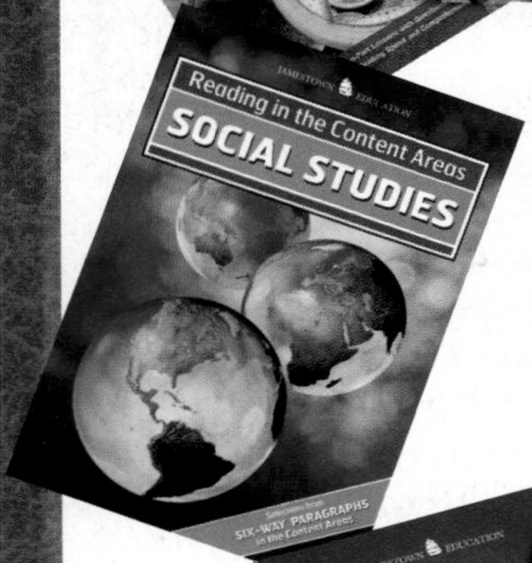

Reading in the Content Areas: Social Studies

✔ **Reading Levels:** 4–12+

✔ **Benefits:**

This book concentrates on six essential reading skills that will help your students better comprehend what they read. Seventy-five high-interest nonfiction passages written at increasing levels of difficulty, followed by consistent, targeted skills, teach the techniques needed to organize, understand, and apply information.

Reading Fluency

✔ **Reading Levels:** 1–10

✔ **Benefits:**

This seven-book series will help your students read smoothly, accurately and expressively. Students work in pairs to provide immediate feedback and self-assessment. Author Camille Blachowicz states that "the ability to read fluently is highly correlated with many other measures of reading competence."

Jamestown's Reading Improvement

✔ **Reading Levels:** 4–10

✔ **Benefits:**

Authored by renowned reading expert Edward Fry, this eight-book series focuses on helping build your students' comprehension, vocabulary, and skimming and scanning skills. Repeated practice with targeted exercises ensures mastery of valuable reading skills.

Critical Reading Series

✔ **Reading Levels:** 2–8

✔ **Benefits:**
This 24-book high-interest series, written at three reading spans, encourages your reluctant readers to build a love for nonfiction while focusing on critical reading skills. Topics ranging from Fateful Journeys to Weird Science to Heroes draw students in, while giving students ample opportunities to master important skills found on both state and national tests.

In addition to the Project CRISS Reading Strategies, you may find it effective to implement some of the following instructional methods. They help *your* struggling students take increasing ownership of the reading process.

Reciprocal Teaching

Reciprocal teaching is characterized by a dialogue between you and your student, and ultimately among students in a group, in which students take the role of dialogue reader. Construction of meaning is built upon four reading strategies:

✔ **Summarizing** Readers identify the most important information in a segment of text and state that information in their own words. Summarizing involves students in recognizing and communicating the significant ideas in a text. Reviewing other reading strategies such as "Finding the Main Idea" might also be helpful.

✔ **Questioning** Readers ask themselves questions about the text segment. These questions should be asked periodically after students have completed "chunks" of the reading. Self-questioning aids comprehension by helping students identify where their understanding of the text has broken down and what they still need to know in order to understand what they have read.

✔ **Clarifying** Readers try to find answers to the questions they have raised and to make sense of parts of the text that have caused confusion. They seek clarification by rereading, reading ahead, or by seeking outside help, such as through a peer or a reference source. Clarifying can work well if students are reading with partners.

✔ **Predicting** Readers tell what they think will happen next, basing their predictions on evidence from the text they have already read. Predicting can take place at the beginning, middle, or end of a reading selection.

✔ **Assessment** The following advice from educator Dr. Sara Wartenberg presents how CRISS strategies can help in assessing student understanding: "Help your students achieve testing success by combining CRISS strategies with the Jamestown Readers. The stories appeal to students of all reading levels. The stories are interesting and informative for students and teachers alike. Implementing CRISS strategies as students read the selections will help them respond with greater success to the questions that accompany each selection. Students will gain confidence and thus work for greater skill in reading comprehension and critical thinking."

Modeling

An important element of strategic instruction is teacher modeling. As a part of the modeling process, think aloud as you apply a strategy to solve a reading problem, putting words to the inner voice that successful readers have with text, and demonstrating the strategy used for understanding. To construct a "think-aloud," read aloud a passage, stopping at pertinent points to talk about what you are thinking. A think-aloud demonstrates the cognitive process and allows students to observe how a proficient reader approaches a problem with reading.

"Fix-Up" Strategies

Explain that readers perform certain tasks. Guide them through these following steps:

✔ **Stop** Tell students to stop and fix the problem when they do not understand.

✔ **Identify the Problem** Have students ask themselves when they stopped understanding and what they do not understand.

✔ **Apply a Fix-Up Strategy** Encourage students to try these strategies:

✔ **Reread**

✔ **Read Ahead**

✔ **Alter** the pace or voice

✔ **Ask** for help

Classroom Solutions

Test-Taking Strategies

How Can I Help My Students Succeed on Tests?

It's not enough for students to learn social studies facts and concepts—they must be able to show what they know in a variety of test-taking situations.

How Can I Help My Students Do Well on Objective Tests?

Objective tests may include multiple choice, true/false, and matching questions. Applying the following strategies can help students do their best on objective tests.

Multiple-Choice Questions

- ✔ Students should read the directions carefully to learn what answer the test requires—the best answer or the right answer. This is especially important when answer choices include "all of the above" or "none of the above."
- ✔ Advise students to watch for negative words in the questions, such as *not, except, unless, never,* and so forth. If the question contains a negative, the correct answer choice is the one that does not fit.
- ✔ Students should try to mentally answer the question before reading the answer choices.
- ✔ Students should read all the answer choices and cross out those that are obviously wrong. Then they should choose an answer from those that remain.

True/False Questions

- ✔ It is important that students read the entire question before answering. For an answer to be true, the entire statement must be true. If one part of a statement is false, the answer should be marked *False.*
- ✔ Remind students to watch for words like *all, never, every,* and *always.* Statements containing these words are often false.

Matching Questions

- ✔ Students should read through both lists before they mark any answers.
- ✔ Unless an answer can be used more than once, students should cross out each choice as they use it.
- ✔ Using what they know about grammar can help students find the right answer. For instance, when matching a word with its definition, the definition is often the same part of speech (noun, verb, adjective, and so forth) as the word.

How Can I Help My Students Do Well on Essay Tests?

Essay tests require students to provide thorough and well-organized written responses, in addition to telling what they know. Help students use the following strategies on essay tests.

Analyze:	To **analyze** means to systematically and critically examine all parts of an issue or event.
Classify or Categorize:	To **classify** or **categorize** means to put people, things, or ideas into groups, based on a common set of characteristics.
Compare and Contrast:	To **compare** is to show how things are similar, or alike. To **contrast** is to show how things are different.
Describe:	To **describe** means to present a sketch or impression. Rich details, especially details that appeal to the senses, flesh out a description.
Discuss:	To **discuss** means to systematically write about all sides of an issue or event.
Evaluate:	To **evaluate** means to make a judgment and support it with evidence.
Explain:	To **explain** means to clarify or make plain.
Illustrate:	To **illustrate** means to provide examples or to show with a picture or other graphic.
Infer:	To **infer** means to read between the lines or to use knowledge and experience to draw conclusions, make a generalization, or form a prediction.
Justify:	To **justify** means to prove or to support a position with specific facts and reasons.
Predict:	To **predict** means to tell what will happen in the future, based on an understanding of prior events and behaviors.
State:	To **state** means to briefly and concisely present information.
Summarize:	To **summarize** means to give a brief overview of the main points of an issue or event.
Trace:	To **trace** means to present the steps or stages in a process or event in sequential or chronological order.

Read the Question

The key to writing successful essay responses lies in reading and interpreting questions correctly. Teach students to identify and underline key words in the questions, and to use these words to guide them in understanding what the question asks. Help students understand the meaning of some of the most common key words, listed in the chart on the previous page.

Plan and Write the Essay

After students understand the question, they should follow the writing process to develop their answer. Encourage students to follow the steps below to plan and write their essays.

1. Map out an answer. Make lists, webs, or an outline to plan the response.
2. Decide on an order in which to present the main points.
3. Write an opening statement that directly responds to the essay question.
4. Write the essay. Expand on the opening statement. Support key points with specific facts, details, and reasons.
5. Write a closing statement that brings the main points together.
6. Proofread to check for spelling, grammar, and punctuation.

How Can I Help My Students Prepare for Standardized Tests?

Students can follow the steps below to prepare for standardized assessments they are required to take.

✔ **Read About the Test** Students can familiarize themselves with the format of the test, the types of questions that will be asked, and the amount of time they will have to complete the test. Emphasize that it is very important for students to budget their time during test-taking.

✔ **Review the Content** Consistent study throughout the school year will help students build social studies knowledge and understanding. If there are specific objectives or standards that are tested on the exam, help students review these facts or skills to be sure they are proficient.

✔ **Practice** Provide practice, ideally with real released tests, to build students' familiarity with the content, format, and timing of the real exam. Students should practice all the types of questions they will encounter on the test—multiple choice, short answer, true or false, and extended response.

✔ **Pace** Students should pace themselves differently depending on how the test is administered. If the test is timed, students should not allow themselves to become stuck on any one question. As students practice, they should try to increase the number of questions they can answer correctly. If the test is untimed, students should work slowly and carefully. If students have trouble with an item, they should mark it and come back to it later.

✔ **Analyze Practice Results** Help students improve test-taking performance by analyzing their test-taking strengths and weaknesses. Spend time discussing students' completed practice tests, explaining why particular answers are right or wrong. Help students identify what kinds of questions they had the most difficulty with. Look for patterns in errors and then tailor instruction to review the appropriate test-taking skills or social studies content.

Bill Aron/PhotoEdit

Below is an example of an activity to incorporate assessment review in the classroom from experienced instructor Tara Musslewhite. Frequently reviewing graded tests is a great way for students to assess their test-taking skills. It also gives teachers the opportunity to teach test-taking strategies and review content. As the class rereads each test question, guide students to think logically about their answer choices. Show students how to:

1. Read each question carefully to determine its meaning.
2. Look for key words in the question to support their answers.
3. Recognize synonyms in the answer choices that may match phrases in the question.
4. Narrow down answer choices by eliminating ones that don't make sense.
5. Anticipate the answer before looking at the answer choices.
6. Circle questions of which they are unsure and go back to them later. Sometimes a clue will be found in another question on the test.✦

Classroom Solutions

Alternative Assessment Strategies

How Can I Go Beyond Tests to Assess Students' Understanding of Social Studies Facts and Concepts?

In response to the growing demand for accountability in the classroom, educators must use multiple assessment measures to accurately gauge student performance. In addition to quizzes, tests, essay exams, and standardized tests, assessment today incorporates a variety of performance-based measures and portfolio opportunities.

Performance assessment is a way of teaching and learning that involves both process and product. It is not just a testing strategy. Performance assessment activities provide hands-on approaches to learning concepts. Through activities students are able to actually experience these concepts rather than just reading and listening about them. These activities also help students become aware of diverse audiences for their work. Students are also involved in developing the process that leads to the finished product.

Performance assessment tasks are based on what is most essential in the curriculum and what is interesting to the student.

What Are Some Typical Performance-Based Assessments?

There are many kinds of performance-based assessments. They all share one common characteristic—they challenge students to create products that demonstrate what they know. One good way to present a performance assessment is in the form of an open-ended question.

Writing

Performance-based writing assessments challenge students to apply their knowledge of social studies concepts and information in a variety of written ways. Writing activities are most often completed by one student, rather than by a group.

Jonathan Nourok/Photo Edit

- ✔ **Journals** Students write from the perspective of a historical character or a citizen of a particular historical era.
- ✔ **Letters** Students write a letter from one historical figure to another or from a historical figure to a family member or other audience.
- ✔ **Position Paper or Editorial** Students explain a controversial issue and present their own opinion and recommendations, supported with strong evidence and convincing reasons.
- ✔ **Newspaper** Students write a variety of stories from the perspective of a reporter living in a particular historical time period. This could also involve the writing of editorials or letters to the editor.
- ✔ **Biographies and Autobiographies** Students write about historical figures either from the third person point of view (biography) or from the first person (autobiography).
- ✔ **Creative Stories** Students integrate historical events into a piece of fiction, incorporating the customs, language, and geography of the period.
- ✔ **Poems and Songs** Students follow the conventions of a particular type of song or poem as they tell about a historical event or person.
- ✔ **Research Reports** Students synthesize information from a variety of sources into a well-developed research report.

Oral Presentations

Oral presentations allow students to demonstrate their social studies literacy before an audience. Oral presentations are often group efforts, although this need not be the case.

✔ **Simulations** Students hold simulations, or reenactments, of actual events, such as trials, acts of civil disobedience, battles, speeches, and so forth.

✔ **Debates** Students debate two or more sides of a historical policy or issue. Students can debate from a contemporary perspective or in a role play in which they assume a viewpoint held by a historical character.

✔ **Interview** Students conduct a mock interview of a historical character or bystander.

✔ **Oral Reports** Students present the results of research efforts in a lively oral report. This report may be accompanied by visuals.

✔ **Skits and Plays** Students use historical events as the basis for a play or skit. Details should accurately reflect customs, language, and the setting of the period.

Visual Presentations

Visual presentations allow students to demonstrate their social studies understandings in a variety of visual formats. Visual presentations can be either group or individual projects.

✔ **Model** Students make a model to demonstrate or represent a process, place, event, battle, artifact, or custom.

✔ **Museum Exhibit** Students create a rich display of materials around a topic. Typical displays might include models, illustrations, photographs, videos, writings, and audiotaped explanations.

✔ **Graph or Chart** Students analyze and represent historical data in a line graph, bar graph, table, or other chart format.

✔ **Drawing** Students represent or interpret a historical event or period through illustration, including political cartoons.

✔ **Posters and Murals** Posters and murals may include maps, time lines, diagrams, illustrations, photographs, and written explanations that reflect students' understandings of historical information.

✔ **Quilt** Students sew or draw a design for a patchwork quilt that shows a variety of perspectives, events, or issues related to a key topic.

✔ **Videotapes** Students film a video to show historical fiction or to preserve a simulation of a historical event.

✔ **Multimedia Presentation or Slide Show** Students create a computer-generated multimedia presentation containing historical information and analysis.

How Are Performance Assessments Scored?

There are a variety of means used to evaluate performance tasks. Some or all of the following methods may be used.

✔ **Scoring Rubrics** A scoring rubric is a set of guidelines for assessing the quality of a process and/or product. It sets out criteria used to distinguish acceptable responses from unacceptable ones, generally along a scale from excellent to poor. Rubrics may be used as guidelines as the students prepare their products. They are also commonly used for self-assessment.

✔ **Models of Excellent Work** Teacher-selected models of excellent work concretely illustrate expectations and help students set goals for their own projects.

✔ **Student Self-Assessment** Common methods of self-assessment include ranking work in relation to the model, using a scoring rubric, and writing their own goals and then evaluating how well they have met the goals they set for themselves. Regardless of which method or methods students use, they should be encouraged to evaluate their behaviors and processes, as well as the finished product.

✔ **Peer or Audience Assessment** Many of the performance tasks target an audience other than the classroom teacher. If possible, the audience of peers should give the student feedback. Have the class create rubrics for specific projects together.

✔ **Observation** As students carry out their performance tasks, you may want to formally observe students at work. Start by developing a checklist, identifying all the specific behaviors and understandings you expect students to demonstrate. Then observe students as they carry out performance tasks and check off the behaviors as you observe them.

✔ **Interviews** As a form of ongoing assessment, you may want to conduct interviews with students, asking them to analyze, explain, and assess their participation in performance tasks. When projects take place over an extended period of time, you can hold periodic interviews as well as exit interviews. In this way the interview process allows you to gauge the status of the project and to guide students' efforts along the way.✦

Teacher Edition Walk-Through

To Teachers:

Welcome to the Teacher Wraparound Edition of *Discovering Our Past: The American Journey to World War I.* We have created this teacher edition based on input from experienced teachers and educational consultants. Our goal is to provide you with standards-driven teaching strategies and activities, which are labeled for you at point-of-use.

Standards-Based Instruction

Point-of-Use
- Strategies and activities apply directly to student content.
- Brackets and guide letters on your reduced student edition pages show you where and when to teach.

Universal Access
- Leveled activities and options for differentiated instruction help meet the needs of all your students, including English learners.

Review and Reinforcement
- Standards learned at the previous grade level are reviewed.
- Scaffolding—the introduction and reinforcement of skills and content—is incorporated throughout the lessons.

Assessment and Intervention
- Lessons provide standards practice.
- Assessments gauge student mastery of standards.
- Additional resources provide intervention options.

Lesson Structure

Each lesson in *Discovering Our Past: The American Journey to World War I* is presented in a structured lesson plan: Focus, Teach, Assess, and Close.

FOCUS

Includes a Bellringer activity to get your class thinking about the lesson topic

GUIDE TO READING

Provides pre-reading strategies to improve content literacy

UNPACKING THE STANDARDS

Assesses student mastery of the California content standards

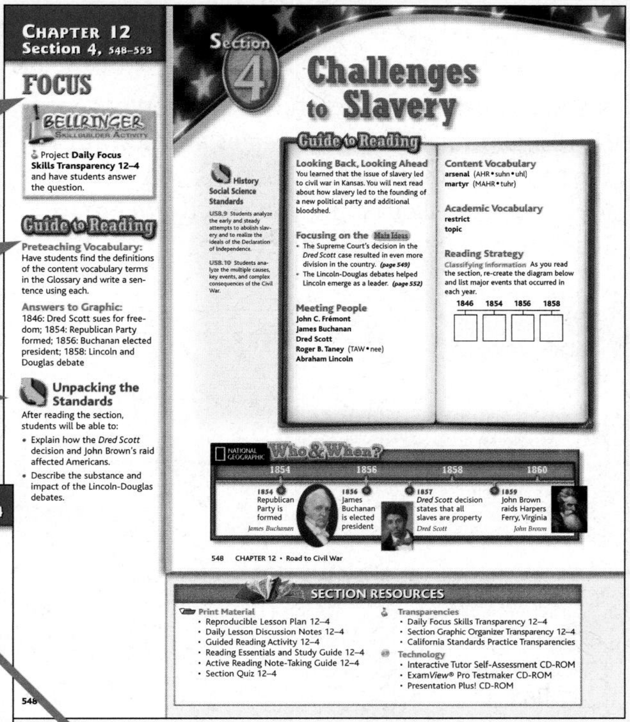

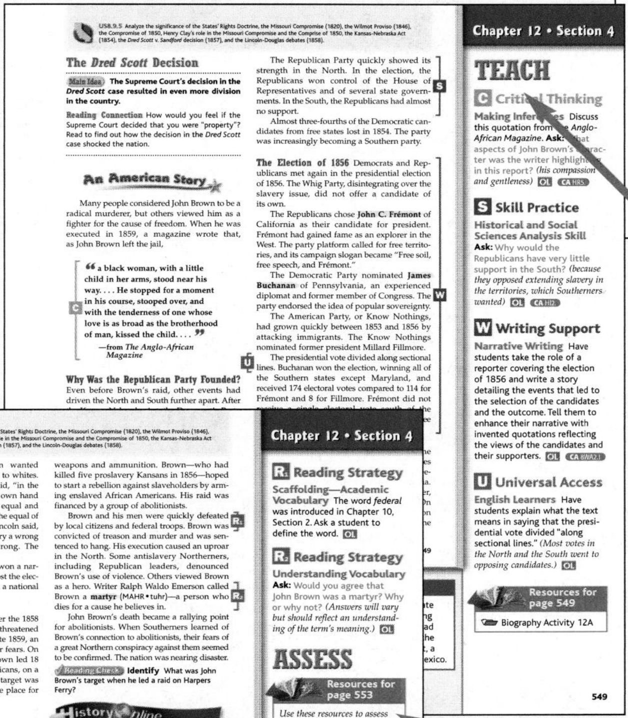

TEACH

Leveled activities to stimulate learning and interest

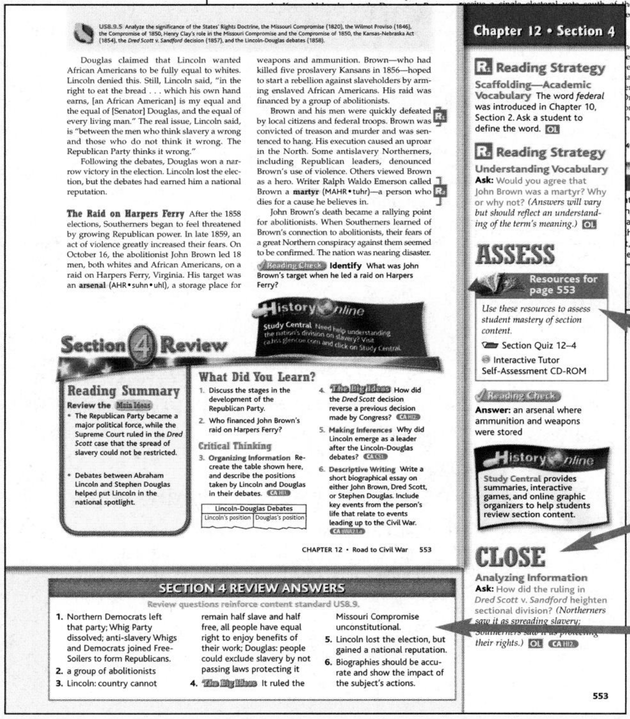

ASSESS

Identifies assessment resources

CLOSE

Gauges comprehension of section content

ANSWERS

Answers to all Student Edition questions

Understanding the Brackets and Letters

Brackets

Brackets on the reduced student edition page correspond to teaching strategies and activities in the teacher wraparound edition. As you teach the lesson, the brackets show you exactly where to teach these strategies and activities.

Letters

The letters on the reduced student edition page identify the type of strategy or activity. See the key below to learn about the different types of strategies and activities.

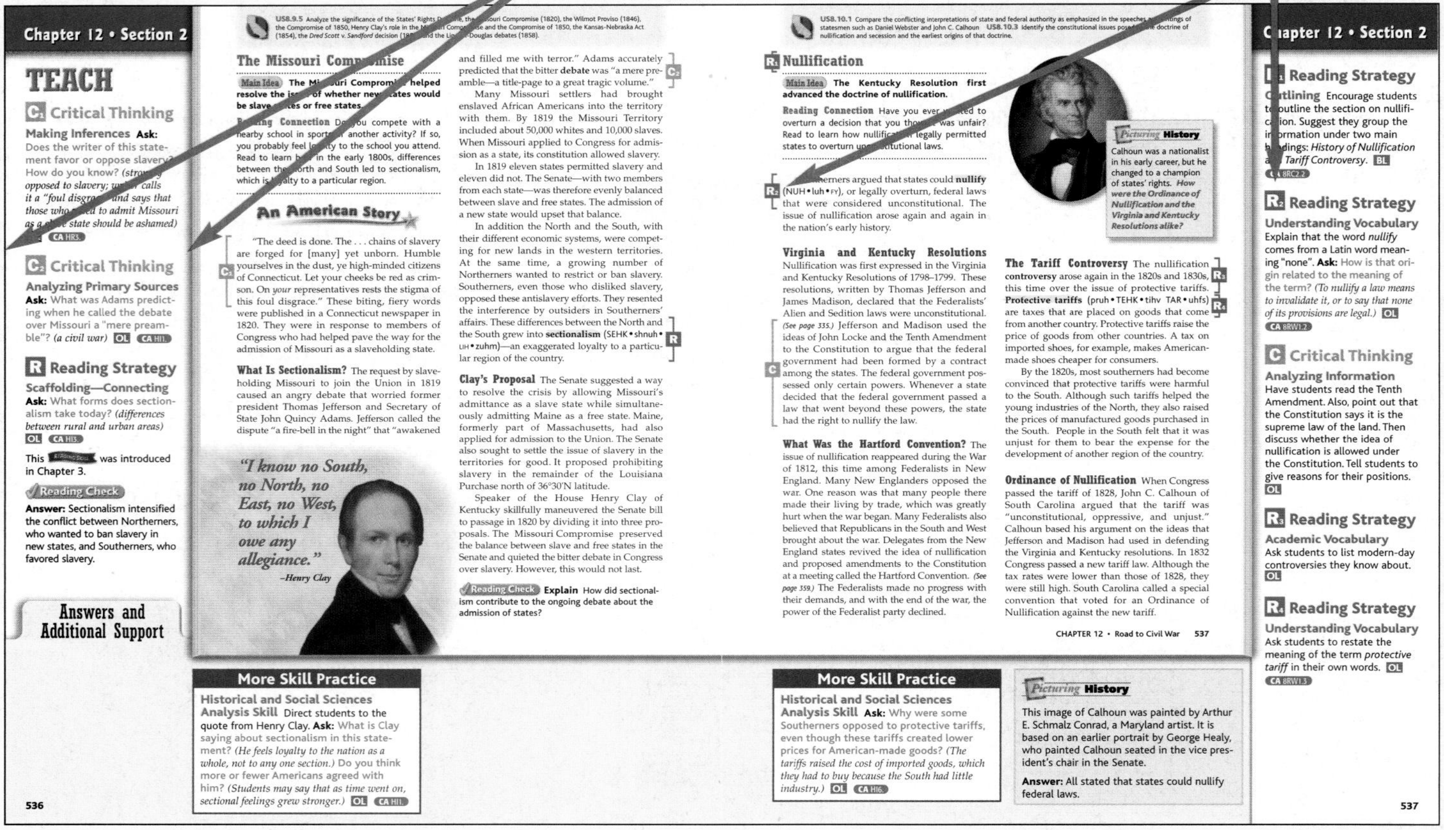

Chapter 12 • Section 2

TEACH

C1 Critical Thinking
Making Inferences Ask: Does the writer of this statement favor or oppose slavery? How do you know? (strongly opposed to slavery; calls it a "foul disgrace" and says that those who voted to admit Missouri as a slave state should be ashamed) CA HR3

C2 Critical Thinking
Analyzing Primary Sources Ask: What was Adams predicting when he called the debate over Missouri a "mere preamble"? (a civil war) OL CA HI1

R Reading Strategy
Scaffolding—Connecting Ask: What forms does sectionalism take today? (differences between rural and urban areas) OL CA HI3

This was introduced in Chapter 3.

Reading Check
Answer: Sectionalism intensified the conflict between Northerners, who wanted to ban slavery in new states, and Southerners, who favored slavery.

Answers and Additional Support

The Missouri Compromise

Main Idea The Missouri Compromise helped resolve the issue of whether new states would be slave states or free states.

Reading Connection Do you compete with a nearby school in sports or another activity? If so, you probably feel loyalty to the school you attend. Read to learn how, in the early 1800s, differences between the North and South led to sectionalism, which is loyalty to a particular region.

An American Story

"The deed is done. The . . . chains of slavery are forged for [many] yet unborn. Humble yourselves in the dust, ye high-minded citizens of Connecticut. Let your cheeks be red as crimson. On your representatives rests the stigma of this foul disgrace." These biting, fiery words were published in a Connecticut newspaper in 1820. They were in response to members of Congress who had helped pave the way for the admission of Missouri as a slaveholding state.

What Is Sectionalism? The request by slaveholding Missouri to join the Union in 1819 caused an angry debate that worried former president Thomas Jefferson and Secretary of State John Quincy Adams. Jefferson called the dispute "a fire-bell in the night" that "awakened and filled me with terror." Adams accurately predicted that the bitter **debate** was "a mere preamble—a title-page to a great tragic volume."

Many Missouri settlers had brought enslaved African Americans into the territory with them. By 1819 the Missouri Territory included about 50,000 whites and 10,000 slaves. When Missouri applied to Congress for admission as a state, its constitution allowed slavery.

In 1819 eleven states permitted slavery and eleven did not. The Senate—with two members from each state—was therefore evenly balanced between slave and free states. The admission of a new state would upset that balance.

In addition the North and the South, with their different economic systems, were competing for new lands in the western territories. At the same time, a growing number of Northerners wanted to restrict or ban slavery. Southerners, even those who disliked slavery, opposed these antislavery efforts. They resented the interference by outsiders in Southerners' affairs. These differences between the North and the South grew into **sectionalism** (SEHK • shnuh • LIH • zuhm)—an exaggerated loyalty to a particular region of the country.

Clay's Proposal The Senate suggested a way to resolve the crisis by allowing Missouri's admittance as a slave state while simultaneously admitting Maine as a free state. Maine, formerly part of Massachusetts, had also applied for admission to the Union. The Senate also sought to settle the issue of slavery in the territories for good. It proposed prohibiting slavery in the remainder of the Louisiana Purchase north of 36°30'N latitude.

Speaker of the House Henry Clay of Kentucky skillfully maneuvered the Senate bill to passage in 1820 by dividing it into three proposals. The Missouri Compromise preserved the balance between slave and free states in the Senate and quieted the bitter debate in Congress over slavery. However, this would not last.

"I know no South, no North, no East, no West, to which I owe any allegiance." –Henry Clay

Reading Check Explain How did sectionalism contribute to the ongoing debate about the admission of states?

536

More Skill Practice
Historical and Social Sciences Analysis Skill Direct students to the quote from Henry Clay. **Ask:** What is Clay saying about sectionalism in this statement? (He feels loyalty to the nation as a whole, not to any one section.) Do you think more or fewer Americans agreed with him? (Students may say that as time went on, sectional feelings grew stronger.) OL CA HI1

R1 Nullification

Main Idea The Kentucky Resolution first advanced the doctrine of nullification.

Reading Connection Have you ever wanted to overturn a decision that you thought was unfair? Read to learn how nullification legally permitted states to overturn unconstitutional laws.

Southerners argued that states could **nullify** (NUH • luh • FY), or legally overturn, federal laws that were considered unconstitutional. The issue of nullification arose again and again in the nation's early history.

Virginia and Kentucky Resolutions Nullification was first expressed in the Virginia and Kentucky Resolutions of 1798–1799. These resolutions, written by Thomas Jefferson and James Madison, declared that the Federalists' Alien and Sedition laws were unconstitutional. (See page 335.) Jefferson and Madison used the ideas of John Locke and the Tenth Amendment to the Constitution to argue that the federal government had been formed by a contract among the states. The federal government possessed only certain powers. Whenever a state decided that the federal government passed a law that went beyond these powers, the state had the right to nullify the law.

What Was the Hartford Convention? The issue of nullification reappeared during the War of 1812, this time among Federalists in New England. Many New Englanders opposed the war. One reason was that many people there made their living by trade, which was greatly hurt when the war began. Many Federalists also believed that Republicans in the South and West brought about the war. Delegates from the New England states revived the idea of nullification and proposed amendments to the Constitution at a meeting called the Hartford Convention. (See page 359.) The Federalists made no progress with their demands, and with the end of the war, the power of the Federalist party declined.

Picturing History Calhoun was a nationalist in his early career, but he changed to a champion of states' rights. *How were the Ordinance of Nullification and the Virginia and Kentucky Resolutions alike?*

The Tariff Controversy The nullification **controversy** arose again in the 1820s and 1830s, this time over the issue of protective tariffs. **Protective tariffs** (pruh • TEHK • tihv TAR • uhfs) are taxes that are placed on goods that come from another country. Protective tariffs raise the price of goods from other countries. A tax on imported shoes, for example, makes American-made shoes cheaper for consumers.

By the 1820s, most southerners had become convinced that protective tariffs were harmful to the South. Although such tariffs helped the young industries of the North, they also raised the prices of manufactured goods purchased in the South. People in the South felt that it was unjust for them to bear the expense for the development of another region of the country.

Ordinance of Nullification When Congress passed the tariff of 1828, John C. Calhoun of South Carolina argued that the tariff was "unconstitutional, oppressive, and unjust." Calhoun based his argument on the ideas that Jefferson and Madison had used in defending the Virginia and Kentucky resolutions. In 1832 Congress passed a new tariff law. Although the tax rates were lower than those of 1828, they were still high. South Carolina called a special convention that voted for an Ordinance of Nullification against the new tariff.

CHAPTER 12 • Road to Civil War 537

Chapter 12 • Section 2

R1 Reading Strategy
Outlining Encourage students to outline the section on nullification. Suggest they group the information under two main headings: *History of Nullification* and *Tariff Controversy.* BL CA 8RC2.2

R2 Reading Strategy
Understanding Vocabulary Explain that the word *nullify* comes from a Latin word meaning "none". **Ask:** How is that origin related to the meaning of the term? (To nullify a law means to invalidate it, or to say that none of its provisions are legal.) OL CA 8RW1.2

C Critical Thinking
Analyzing Information Have students read the Tenth Amendment. Also, point out that the Constitution says it is the supreme law of the land. Then discuss whether the idea of nullification is allowed under the Constitution. Tell students to give reasons for their positions. OL

R3 Reading Strategy
Academic Vocabulary Ask students to list modern-day controversies they know about. OL

R4 Reading Strategy
Understanding Vocabulary Ask students to restate the meaning of the term *protective tariff* in their own words. OL CA 8RW1.3

More Skill Practice
Historical and Social Sciences Analysis Skill Ask: Why were some Southerners opposed to protective tariffs, even though these tariffs created lower prices for American-made goods? (The tariffs raised the cost of imported goods, which they had to buy because the South had little industry.) OL CA HI6

Picturing History
This image of Calhoun was painted by Arthur E. Schmalz Conrad, a Maryland artist. It is based on an earlier portrait by George Healy, who painted Calhoun seated in the vice president's chair in the Senate.
Answer: All stated that states could nullify federal laws.

537

KEY for Using the Teacher Wraparound Edition

R **Reading Strategies** activities help you teach reading skills and vocabulary.

C **Critical Thinking** strategies help students apply and extend what they have learned.

U **Universal Access** activities provide differentiated instruction for students learning to speak English, along with suggestions for teaching various types of learners.

S **Skill Practice** strategies help students practice historical analysis and geography skills.

W **Writing Support** activities provide writing opportunities to help students comprehend the text.

Brackets and Letters

Letters are followed by a number when there is more than one of the same type of strategy or activity on the page.

Chapter 12 • Section 2

R Reading Strategy

Evaluating Ask: How did Webster's view of the Constitution differ from Calhoun's? *(Calhoun believed that individual states had the right to interpret the Constitution, while Webster said that only the Supreme Court could determine a law's constitutionality.)* OL CA HI1.

C Critical Thinking

Identifying Central Issues Tell students that President Jackson was not completely happy with the compromise that ended the tariff controversy, feeling that it simply postponed a conflict with the South over nullification. Organize students into groups to brainstorm ideas for different steps Jackson could have taken. Have the groups present their ideas to the class, and discuss whether any would resolve the nullification issue. AL CA HI1.

Reading Check

Answer: Southerners wanted to overturn a tariff that they considered unfair; people in the Northeast tried to use it when they opposed the War of 1812.

Calhoun had raised an important issue—the supremacy of the national government versus state sovereignty. The states' rights doctrine, first found in the Virginia and Kentucky resolutions, had taken a giant step toward secession. If states were sovereign, they had a right to secede from the Union.

Can a State Nullify a Law? Early in 1830, Calhoun's doctrine of nullification came before the United States Senate during a debate over land policy. People in the West were angry because of a bill that would limit the sale of western lands. Robert Y. Hayne of South Carolina argued that the western states could nullify the bill if it became law.

Daniel Webster of Massachusetts replied to Hayne. Webster denied that the Constitution was just a compact between two states, to be interpreted as each state chose. On the contrary, he said, only the Supreme Court could decide whether a law was constitutional. Webster argued that the federal government was sovereign, that the Union was perpetual, and that any attempt to dismember it was nothing less than treason. Webster closed with this ringing statement: "Liberty and Union, now and forever, one and inseparable." R

In 1833 the nullification crisis was settled by a compromise. The tariff was lowered and, in response, South Carolina withdrew its Ordinance of Nullification. Both sides claimed victory, and the issue was laid to rest—at least temporarily. C

Reading Check **Analyze** Why did the South and the Northeast try to use nullification?

US8.9.5 Analyze the significance of the States' Rights Doctrine, the Missouri Compromise (1820), the Wilmot Proviso (1846), the Compromise of 1850, Henry Clay's role in the Missouri Compromise and the Compromise of 1850, the Kansas-Nebraska Act (1854), the Dred Scott v. *Sandford* decision (1857), and the Lincoln-Douglas debates (1858).

New Western Lands

R1 **Main Idea** **In the 1840s, the issue of slavery in new territories was once again at the forefront.**

Reading Connection Can you think of a debate you have been a part of that turned out to be difficult to resolve? Read to learn how Congress continued to struggle with a solution concerning slavery.

For the next 25 years, Congress managed to avoid the slavery issue. In the 1840s, however, this heated debate moved back into Congress. Once again the cause of the dispute was the issue of slavery in new territories. The territories involved were Texas, which had won its independence from Mexico in 1836, and New Mexico and California, which were still part of Mexico. R2

Many Southerners hoped to see Texas, where slavery already existed, join the Union. As a result, the annexation of Texas became the main issue in the presidential election of 1844. Democrat **James K. Polk** of Tennessee won the election and pressed forward on acquiring Texas. Texas became a state in 1845. At the same time, support for taking over New Mexico and California also grew in the South. The federal government's actions on these lands led to war with Mexico. S

Conflicting Views Just months after the war with Mexico began, Representative David Wilmot of Pennsylvania introduced a proposal in Congress. Called the Wilmot Proviso, it specified that slavery should be prohibited in any lands that might be acquired from Mexico.

The Way It Was

Agrarians and Industrialists

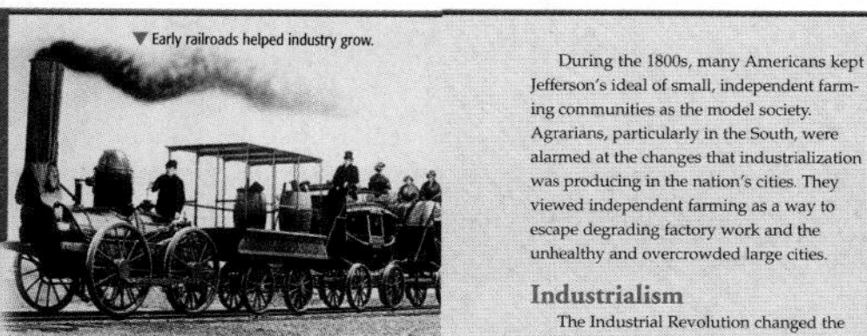

Early railroads helped industry grow.

Sectionalism, the rivalry between one region and another, was based on economic and political interests. One rivalry that developed was between agrarians and industrialists.

Agrarianism

Thomas Jefferson believed that the strength of the United States was its independent farmers. His ideas are sometimes referred to as agrarianism. Jefferson argued that owning land enabled people to be independent. As long as most people owned their own land, they would fight to preserve the Republic.

Jefferson believed that too much of an emphasis on industry and trade would lead to a society that was divided between the rich who owned everything and the poor who worked for wages. He also believed that the wealthy would corrupt the government and threaten the rights and liberties of ordinary people.

538

During the 1800s, many Americans kept Jefferson's ideal of small, independent farming communities as the model society. Agrarians, particularly in the South, were alarmed at the changes that industrialization was producing in the nation's cities. They viewed independent farming as a way to escape degrading factory work and the unhealthy and overcrowded large cities.

Industrialism

The Industrial Revolution changed the Northeast from a region where families lived and worked together at farming, crafts, and home-based businesses to one in which people earned their livings by working for others in industry. Many Americans believed that manufacturing and trade were the basis of national wealth and power. They favored policies that would support these areas of the economy.

Although industrial growth caused problems, economic progress also made life easier in many ways. Improved transportation and mass production meant that more goods were available to more people. American living standards were surpassing those of European countries.

In the cities, people were beginning to enjoy new comforts and conveniences such as gas streetlights and better sewer systems. Some Americans came to believe that they were living in an age of progress. They expected that new inventions, along with America's abundant resources, would improve life for Americans and set an example for other countries of the world.

Many Americans made their living by farming.

Chapter 12 • Section 2

R1 Reading Strategy

Identifying the Main Idea and Supporting Details Have students point out the main idea of this part of the section. **Ask:** What are two details that support this idea? *(Possible answers: Wilmot introduced his proviso to prohibit spread of slavery; Calhoun countered with proslavery proposal; the Free-Soil Party was formed by opponents of slavery.)* OL CA 8RC2.2

R2 Reading Strategy

Activating Prior Knowledge Point out that Texas won its independence in 1836 and applied for annexation right away. **Ask:** Why did the United States not annex Texas in 1836? *(Jackson turned down the request because he did not want to raise the slavery issue.)* OL

S Skill Practice

Historical and Social Science Analysis Skill **Ask:** What area to the north of California and New Mexico, which could be turned into free states, was also added to the United States around this time? *(Oregon)* OL

Answers and Additional Support

The Way It Was

Jefferson laid out his deep belief in the superiority of an agrarian society in his Notes on Virginia, in which he wrote "Generally speaking, the proportion which the aggregate of the other classes of citizens bears in any State to that of its [farmers] is the proportion of its unsound to its healthy parts, and is a good enough barometer whereby to measure its degree of corruption. . . . Those who labor in the earth are the chosen people of God if ever he had a chosen people, whose breasts he has made his peculiar deposit for substantial and genuine virtue

More Skill Practice

Historical and Social Sciences Analysis Skill **Ask:** How did the acquisition of new territory heighten the sectional tensions over slavery? *(Northerners wanted to restrict slavery in the newly acquired territories, while Southerners wanted the right to introduce slavery in the new areas.)* OL

538

539

Answers and Additional Support

Along the bottom of the teacher wraparound edition, you will find student edition answers, more general strategies and activities, and additional content information.

US8.9.1 Describe the leaders of the movement (e.g., John Quincy Adams and his proposed constitutional amendment; John Brown and the armed resistance, Harriet Tubman and the Underground Railroad, Benjamin Franklin, Theodore Weld, William Lloyd Garrison, Frederick Douglass).

The Underground Railroad

S **Main Idea** **Abolitionists established a network of routes and risked their lives to help African Americans escape slavery.**

Reading Connection Can you think of an example in recent times when people fled to avoid oppression? Read and find out about the Underground Railroad.

An American Story

On May 24, 1854, the people of Boston erupted in outrage. Federal officers had seized Anthony Burns, a runaway slave who lived in Boston, to send him back to slavery. Abolitionists tried to rescue Burns from the federal courthouse, and city leaders attempted to buy his freedom. All efforts failed. Local militia units joined the marines and cavalry in Boston to keep order. Federal troops escorted Burns to a ship that would carry him back to Virginia and slavery. In a gesture of bitter protest, Bostonians draped buildings in black and hung the American flag upside down.

The Fugitive Slave Act The Fugitive Slave Act of 1850 required all citizens to help catch runaways. Anyone who aided a fugitive could be fined or imprisoned. People in the South believed the law would force Northerners to recognize the rights of Southerners. Instead, enforcement of the law led to mounting anger in the North, convincing more people of the evils of slavery. After passage of the Fugitive Slave Act, slaveholders stepped up efforts to catch runaway slaves. C1

NATIONAL GEOGRAPHIC **The Underground Railroad**

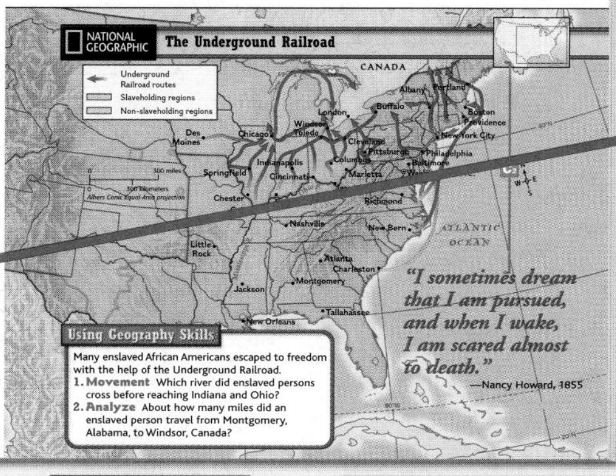

Using Geography Skills

Many enslaved African Americans escaped to freedom with the help of the Underground Railroad.

1. **Movement** Which river did enslaved persons cross before reaching Indiana and Ohio?
2. **Analyze** About how many miles did an enslaved person travel from Montgomery, Alabama, to Windsor, Canada?

Chapter 12 • Section 1

S Skill Practice

Historical and Social Sciences Analysis Skill **Ask:** How would enslaved African Americans see the Underground Railroad? *(as a welcome chance to gain freedom)* How would Southern slave owners see it? *(as taking away their property)* OL CA HI2.

C1 Critical Thinking

Drawing Conclusions Remind students that it was against the law to help enslaved African Americans escape, yet many abolitionists broke the law. **Ask:** Are there some situations in which breaking the law is an acceptable protest? Discuss whether abolitionists were justified in breaking the law. OL CA CS3.

C2 Critical Thinking

Making Inferences **Ask:** Why do many of the routes on the Underground Railroad lead to Canada? *(Students should conclude that Canada did not have slavery and would not return people who escaped from it.)* OL CA CS3.

Using Geography Skills

Answers:

1. Ohio River
2. about 790 miles (1,260 km)

Did You Know?

The story of Henry "Box" Brown is one of the most remarkable in the history of the Underground Railroad. Brown escaped slavery in 1849 by having himself sealed into a small box and shipped from Richmond to Philadelphia. Although "this side up" was marked on the crate, he spent a good part of the trip upside down.

533

Activity Leveling

Teaching strategies and activities have been coded for ability level appropriateness. A competency level is given for each activity using the following code.

- **AL** Activities for students working above grade level
- **OL** Activities for students working on grade level
- **BL** Activities for students working below grade level
- **EL** Activities for English Learners

Planning the Unit

Planning pages appear at the beginning of each unit.

STANDARDS
Use this chart to identify the California standards covered in each chapter.

PREVIEW FROM THE AUTHOR
A personal note from the author tells you about the main themes found in the unit.

Unit 5 Planning Guide

Teaching the Unit

Use the information on these pages to help you teach Unit 5.

History–Social Science Standards Covered in Unit 5

Standard	Chapter 12	13	14
US8.9 Students analyze the early and steady attempts to abolish slavery and to realize the ideals of the Declaration of Independence.	✔		
US8.10 Students analyze the multiple causes, key events, and complex consequences of the Civil War.	✔	✔	
US8.11 Students analyze the character and lasting consequences of Reconstruction.			✔

Pacing Your Lessons

This pacing chart provides time management suggestions for teaching Unit 5.

Unit 5 Civil War and Reconstruction	Days
Unit 5 Introduction	1/2
Chapter 12 • **Reading Skill:** Making Inferences • **Sections 1–5** • **Biography:** Harriet Beecher Stowe, Biddy Mason • **You Decide . . .** • **Analyzing Primary Sources**	7
Chapter 13 • **Reading Skill:** Evaluation • **Sections 1–5** • **Biography:** Clara Barton, Robert E. Lee and Ulysses S. Grant • **America's Literature:** *Rifles for Watie* • **Geography & History** • **Analyzing Primary Sources**	11
Chapter 14 • **Reading Skill:** Monitoring and Clarifying • **Sections 1–4** • **Biography:** Charlotte Forten, Frederick Douglass • **Connecting to the Constitution** • **Analyzing Primary Sources**	7
Unit 5 Review	1/2

Teacher to Teacher

A State of the Union Address on the Fourteenth Amendment—Then and Now

Phil Trotter
San Diego School District
San Diego, CA

Organize the class into an equal number of groups. Have half of the groups research the legal rights of people—particularly African Americans—just prior to the passage of the Fourteenth Amendment. The other half of the class should research how the amendment protects African Americans and other minorities today. Using as many specific examples as they can find, have each group write a State of the Union Address for either "then" or "now." Before having groups present their addresses to the class, ask all students to find articles in newspapers and magazines that deal with the rights and freedoms covered by the Fourteenth Amendment. These articles can be shared during class discussion after each group's State of the Union presentation.

520A

Unit 5 Planning Guide

Previewing the Chapters

Dear American History Teacher:

As you begin to teach this unit, there are themes that reoccur throughout the chapters that you will want to point out to students.

The rising sectional identification of the early 1800s led to sectional conflict and war in the middle decades. Compromises seemed to settle the matter of slavery in the territories, but as the years passed tensions grew sharper and compromise became harder to achieve. Outbreaks of violence in the 1850s led to growing anger and fear and produced all-out war in 1861. The North won that war after Abraham Lincoln set two goals—restoring the Union and finally ending slavery. Years of war and the collapse of its economic and social system required significant rebuilding in the South. At first, Northerners showed interest in protecting the rights of African Americans, but eventually they abandoned Reconstruction. Conservative whites regained control of Southern state governments and put in place new laws that sharply limited the rights of African Americans.

You may want to use the following information at the beginning of each chapter as a lesson launcher to help students begin to focus on what they will be studying.

James M. McPherson

CHAPTER 12: Road to Civil War
(pages 524–565)

A growing number of people began to demand that slavery be ended and worked to help enslaved American Americans escape slavery. The issue of slavery in the western territories became hotly debated. A compromise settled it in 1820 and again in 1850 when California applied for statehood. A new law to organize the territories of Kansas and Nebraska led to violence over the slavery issue. Abraham Lincoln won the presidential election in 1860. Soon after, seven Southern states left the Union and, when Southern forces attacked a Union fort, the Civil War began.

CHAPTER 13: The Civil War
(pages 566–619)

Soldiers in the Civil War came from every region, and each side expected an early victory. The first battle showed that the war would be a long and difficult one. The North blockaded the South's coast, hoping to cut off supplies. The Union won several early victories in the West but had difficulty in the East. In 1863, Lincoln changed the goals of the war by declaring that all slaves in the South would be free. African Americans contributed to the war effort in many different ways, as did women. The Union won key victories in both East and West in 1863, though fighting continued for nearly two more years. Finally, in 1865, the Confederate armies were forced to surrender.

CHAPTER 3: Reconstruction
(pages 620–655)

After Lincoln was assassinated, Andrew Johnson became president and clashed with Congress over policies in the South. Northerners passed new laws aimed at punishing whites and ensuring the rights of African Americans. African Americans had to weather some violence, but they voted, and some won political offices. Meanwhile, the South worked to rebuild the damaged economy. Democrats committed to ending Reconstruction gained control of state governments in the South, and Northerners lost interest in Reconstruction. A disputed presidential election in 1876 led the federal government to withdraw the last troops from the South and end Reconstruction.

520B

PACING CHART
Provides time management suggestions for teaching the unit

TEACHER IDEAS
Activities from the classrooms of successful teachers

LESSON LAUNCHERS
High-interest content helps you launch the lesson.

Teaching the Unit

Connecting to Past Learning

Activates prior knowledge and provides a chronological framework for students

Where in the United States?

Provides opportunities to practice geography skills

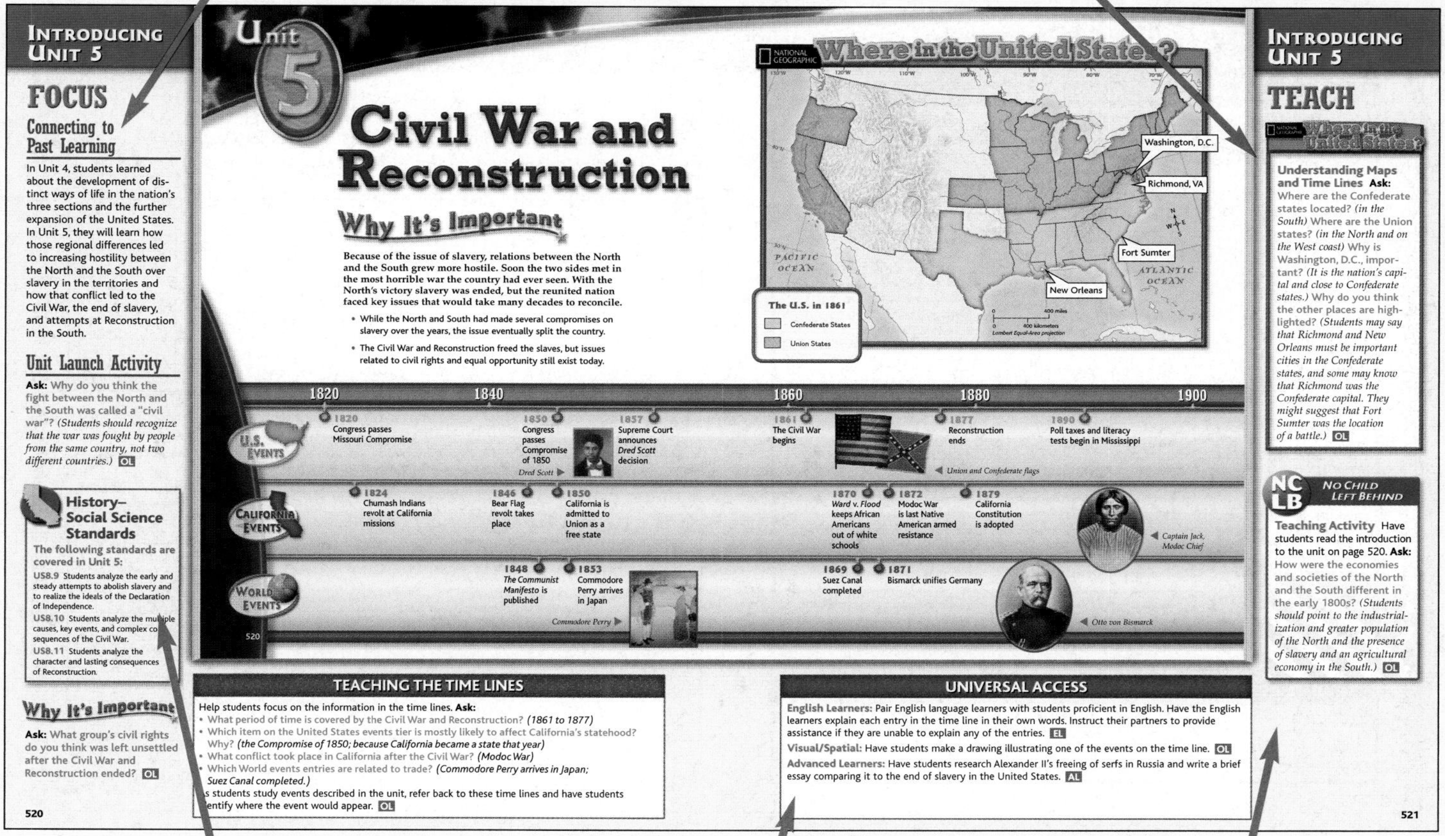

INTRODUCING UNIT 5

FOCUS

Connecting to Past Learning

In Unit 4, students learned about the development of distinct ways of life in the nation's three sections and the further expansion of the United States. In Unit 5, they will learn how those regional differences led to increasing hostility between the North and the South over slavery in the territories and how that conflict led to the Civil War, the end of slavery, and attempts at Reconstruction in the South.

Unit Launch Activity

Ask: Why do you think the fight between the North and the South was called a "civil war"? *(Students should recognize that the war was fought by people from the same country, not two different countries.)* OL

History–Social Science Standards

The following standards are covered in Unit 5:

US8.9 Students analyze the early and steady attempts to abolish slavery and to realize the ideals of the Declaration of Independence.

US8.10 Students analyze the multiple causes, key events, and complex consequences of the Civil War.

US8.11 Students analyze the character and lasting consequences of Reconstruction.

Why It's Important

Ask: What group's civil rights do you think was left unsettled after the Civil War and Reconstruction ended? OL

520

Unit 5

Civil War and Reconstruction

Why It's Important

Because of the issue of slavery, relations between the North and the South grew more hostile. Soon the two sides met in the most horrible war the country had ever seen. With the North's victory slavery was ended, but the reunited nation faced key issues that would take many decades to reconcile.

- While the North and South had made several compromises on slavery over the years, the issue eventually split the country.
- The Civil War and Reconstruction freed the slaves, but issues related to civil rights and equal opportunity still exist today.

TEACHING THE TIME LINES

Help students focus on the information in the time lines. **Ask:**

- What period of time is covered by the Civil War and Reconstruction? *(1861 to 1877)*
- Which item on the United States events tier is mostly likely to affect California's statehood? Why? *(the Compromise of 1850; because California became a state that year)*
- What conflict took place in California after the Civil War? *(Modoc War)*
- Which World events entries are related to trade? *(Commodore Perry arrives in Japan; Suez Canal completed.)*

s students study events described in the unit, refer back to these time lines and have students entify where the event would appear. OL

UNIVERSAL ACCESS

English Learners: Pair English language learners with students proficient in English. Have the English learners explain each entry in the time line in their own words. Instruct their partners to provide assistance if they are unable to explain any of the entries. EL

Visual/Spatial: Have students make a drawing illustrating one of the events on the time line. OL

Advanced Learners: Have students research Alexander II's freeing of serfs in Russia and write a brief essay comparing it to the end of slavery in the United States. AL

INTRODUCING UNIT 5

TEACH

Where in the United States?

Understanding Maps and Time Lines Ask: Where are the Confederate states located? *(in the South)* Where are the Union states? *(in the North and on the West coast)* Why is Washington, D.C., important? *(It is the nation's capital and close to Confederate states.)* Why do you think the other places are highlighted? *(Students may say that Richmond and New Orleans must be important cities in the Confederate states, and some may know that Richmond was the Confederate capital. They might suggest that Fort Sumter was the location of a battle.)* OL

NCLB No Child Left Behind

Teaching Activity Have students read the introduction to the unit on page 520. **Ask:** How were the economies and societies of the North and the South different in the early 1800s? *(Students should point to the industrialization and greater population of the North and the presence of slavery and an agricultural economy in the South.)* OL

521

Standards

The California History–Social Science Standards are listed to help you plan your instruction.

Universal Access

Activities for diverse learners, including English learners

NCLB

Provides suggestions for meeting No Child Left Behind requirements

Planning the Chapter

Planning pages appear at the beginning of each chapter.

Resource List

Resources needed to teach each section

Standards

Use this chart to identify the California standards covered in each section.

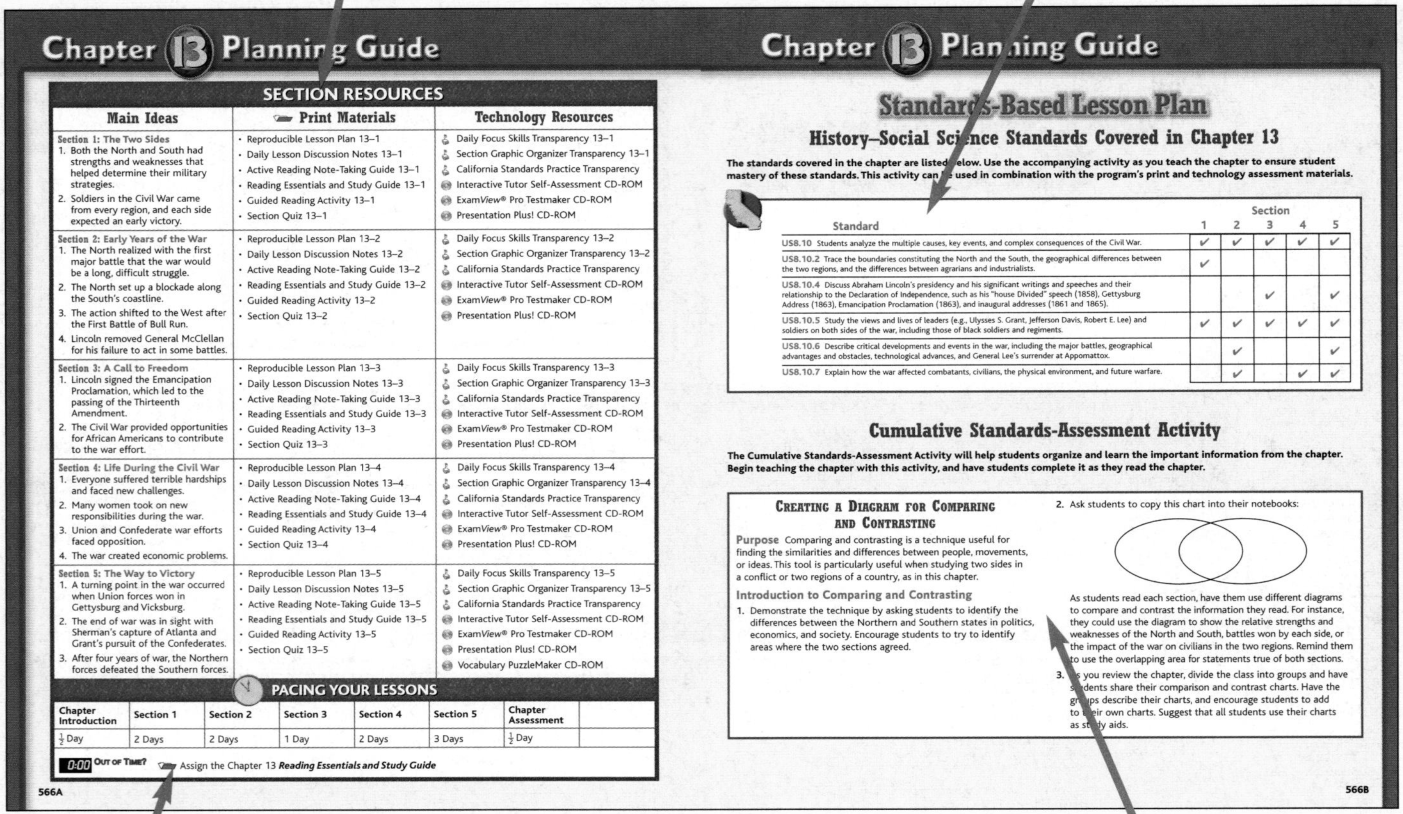

Chapter 13 Planning Guide

SECTION RESOURCES

Main Ideas	Print Materials	Technology Resources
Section 1: The Two Sides 1. Both the North and South had strengths and weaknesses that helped determine their military strategies. 2. Soldiers in the Civil War came from every region, and each side expected an early victory.	• Reproducible Lesson Plan 13–1 • Daily Lesson Discussion Notes 13–1 • Active Reading Note-Taking Guide 13–1 • Reading Essentials and Study Guide 13–1 • Guided Reading Activity 13–1 • Section Quiz 13–1	Daily Focus Skills Transparency 13–1 Section Graphic Organizer Transparency 13–1 California Standards Practice Transparency Interactive Tutor Self-Assessment CD-ROM Exam*View*® Pro Testmaker CD-ROM Presentation Plus! CD-ROM
Section 2: Early Years of the War 1. The North realized with the first major battle that the war would be a long, difficult struggle. 2. The North set up a blockade along the South's coastline. 3. The action shifted to the West after the First Battle of Bull Run. 4. Lincoln removed General McClellan for his failure to act in some battles.	• Reproducible Lesson Plan 13–2 • Daily Lesson Discussion Notes 13–2 • Active Reading Note-Taking Guide 13–2 • Reading Essentials and Study Guide 13–2 • Guided Reading Activity 13–2 • Section Quiz 13–2	Daily Focus Skills Transparency 13–2 Section Graphic Organizer Transparency 13–2 California Standards Practice Transparency Interactive Tutor Self-Assessment CD-ROM Exam*View*® Pro Testmaker CD-ROM Presentation Plus! CD-ROM
Section 3: A Call to Freedom 1. Lincoln signed the Emancipation Proclamation, which led to the passing of the Thirteenth Amendment. 2. The Civil War provided opportunities for African Americans to contribute to the war effort.	• Reproducible Lesson Plan 13–3 • Daily Lesson Discussion Notes 13–3 • Active Reading Note-Taking Guide 13–3 • Reading Essentials and Study Guide 13–3 • Guided Reading Activity 13–3 • Section Quiz 13–3	Daily Focus Skills Transparency 13–3 Section Graphic Organizer Transparency 13–3 California Standards Practice Transparency Interactive Tutor Self-Assessment CD-ROM Exam*View*® Pro Testmaker CD-ROM Presentation Plus! CD-ROM
Section 4: Life During the Civil War 1. Everyone suffered terrible hardships and faced new challenges. 2. Many women took on new responsibilities during the war. 3. Union and Confederate war efforts faced opposition. 4. The war created economic problems.	• Reproducible Lesson Plan 13–4 • Daily Lesson Discussion Notes 13–4 • Active Reading Note-Taking Guide 13–4 • Reading Essentials and Study Guide 13–4 • Guided Reading Activity 13–4 • Section Quiz 13–4	Daily Focus Skills Transparency 13–4 Section Graphic Organizer Transparency 13–4 California Standards Practice Transparency Interactive Tutor Self-Assessment CD-ROM Exam*View*® Pro Testmaker CD-ROM Presentation Plus! CD-ROM
Section 5: The Way to Victory 1. A turning point in the war occurred when Union forces won in Gettysburg and Vicksburg. 2. The end of war was in sight with Sherman's capture of Atlanta and Grant's pursuit of the Confederates. 3. After four years of war, the Northern forces defeated the Southern forces.	• Reproducible Lesson Plan 13–5 • Daily Lesson Discussion Notes 13–5 • Active Reading Note-Taking Guide 13–5 • Reading Essentials and Study Guide 13–5 • Guided Reading Activity 13–5 • Section Quiz 13–5	Daily Focus Skills Transparency 13–5 Section Graphic Organizer Transparency 13–5 California Standards Practice Transparency Interactive Tutor Self-Assessment CD-ROM Exam*View*® Pro Testmaker CD-ROM Presentation Plus! CD-ROM Vocabulary PuzzleMaker CD-ROM

PACING YOUR LESSONS

Chapter Introduction	Section 1	Section 2	Section 3	Section 4	Section 5	Chapter Assessment	
½ Day	2 Days	2 Days	1 Day	2 Days	3 Days	½ Day	

0:00 OUT OF TIME? Assign the Chapter 13 ***Reading Essentials and Study Guide***

566A

Chapter 13 Planning Guide

Standards-Based Lesson Plan

History–Social Science Standards Covered in Chapter 13

The standards covered in the chapter are listed below. Use the accompanying activity as you teach the chapter to ensure student mastery of these standards. This activity can be used in combination with the program's print and technology assessment materials.

Standard	Section 1	2	3	4	5
US8.10 Students analyze the multiple causes, key events, and complex consequences of the Civil War.	✔	✔	✔	✔	✔
US8.10.2 Trace the boundaries constituting the North and the South, the geographical differences between the two regions, and the differences between agrarians and industrialists.	✔				
US8.10.4 Discuss Abraham Lincoln's presidency and his significant writings and speeches and their relationship to the Declaration of Independence, such as his "house Divided" speech (1858), Gettysburg Address (1863), Emancipation Proclamation (1863), and inaugural addresses (1861 and 1865).			✔		✔
US8.10.5 Study the views and lives of leaders (e.g., Ulysses S. Grant, Jefferson Davis, Robert E. Lee) and soldiers on both sides of the war, including those of black soldiers and regiments.	✔	✔	✔	✔	✔
US8.10.6 Describe critical developments and events in the war, including the major battles, geographical advantages and obstacles, technological advances, and General Lee's surrender at Appomattox.		✔			✔
US8.10.7 Explain how the war affected combatants, civilians, the physical environment, and future warfare.		✔		✔	✔

Cumulative Standards-Assessment Activity

The Cumulative Standards-Assessment Activity will help students organize and learn the important information from the chapter. Begin teaching the chapter with this activity, and have students complete it as they read the chapter.

Creating a Diagram for Comparing and Contrasting

Purpose Comparing and contrasting is a technique useful for finding the similarities and differences between people, movements, or ideas. This tool is particularly useful when studying two sides in a conflict or two regions of a country, as in this chapter.

Introduction to Comparing and Contrasting

1. Demonstrate the technique by asking students to identify the differences between the Northern and Southern states in politics, economics, and society. Encourage students to try to identify areas where the two sections agreed.
2. Ask students to copy this chart into their notebooks:

   As students read each section, have them use different diagrams to compare and contrast the information they read. For instance, they could use the diagram to show the relative strengths and weaknesses of the North and South, battles won by each side, or the impact of the war on civilians in the two regions. Remind them to use the overlapping area for statements true of both sections.
3. As you review the chapter, divide the class into groups and have students share their comparison and contrast charts. Have the groups describe their charts, and encourage students to add to their own charts. Suggest that all students use their charts as study aids.

566B

Pacing Chart

Provides time management suggestions for teaching the chapter

Cumulative Standards-Assessment Activity

Front-loaded assessment allows you to monitor student understanding throughout the chapter.

Reading Support
Reading resources for students at all levels

Assessment
Diagnostic and prescriptive resources for identifying standards proficiency

Spanish Resources
Resources for English learners

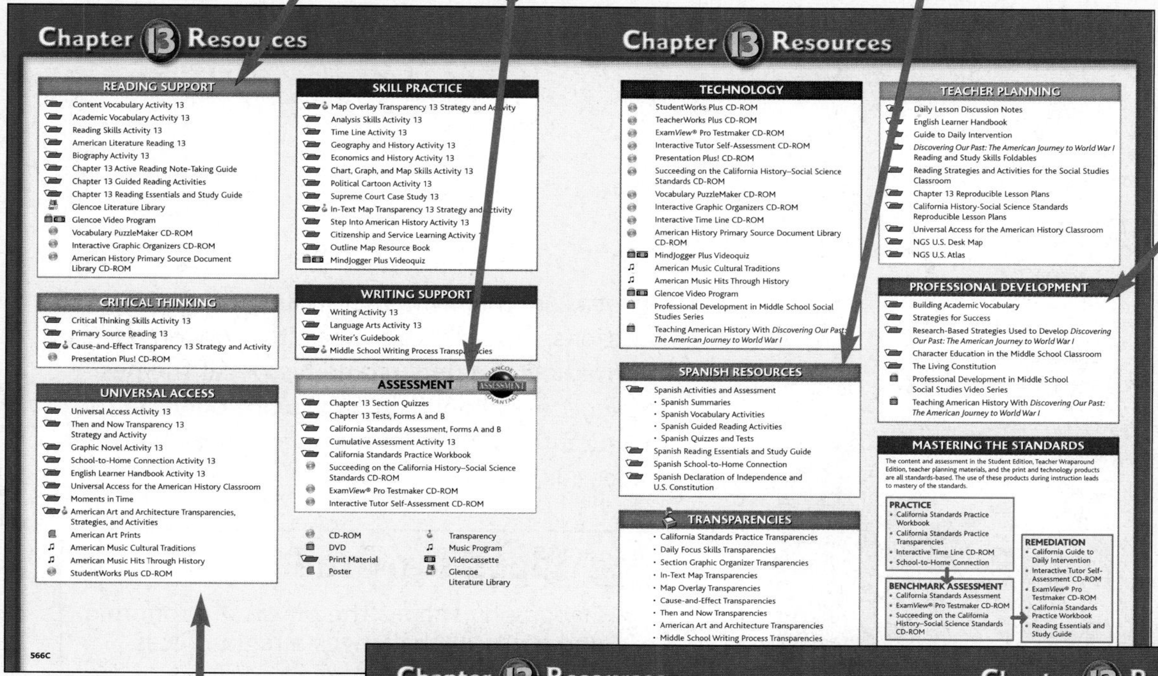

Chapter 13 Resources

READING SUPPORT
- Content Vocabulary Activity 13
- Academic Vocabulary Activity 13
- Reading Skills Activity 13
- American Literature Reading 13
- Biography Activity 13
- Chapter 13 Active Reading Note-Taking Guide
- Chapter 13 Guided Reading Activities
- Chapter 13 Reading Essentials and Study Guide
- Glencoe Literature Library
- Glencoe Video Program
- Vocabulary PuzzleMaker CD-ROM
- Interactive Graphic Organizers CD-ROM
- American History Primary Source Document Library CD-ROM

CRITICAL THINKING
- Critical Thinking Skills Activity 13
- Primary Source Reading 13
- Cause-and-Effect Transparency 13 Strategy and Activity
- Presentation Plus! CD-ROM

UNIVERSAL ACCESS
- Universal Access Activity 13
- Then and Now Transparency 13 Strategy and Activity
- Graphic Novel Activity 13
- School-to-Home Connection Activity 13
- English Learner Handbook Activity 13
- Universal Access for the American History Classroom
- Moments in Time
- American Art and Architecture Transparencies, Strategies, and Activities
- American Art Prints
- American Music Cultural Traditions
- American Music Hits Through History
- StudentWorks Plus CD-ROM

SKILL PRACTICE
- Map Overlay Transparency 13 Strategy and Activity
- Analysis Skills Activity 13
- Time Line Activity 13
- Geography and History Activity 13
- Economics and History Activity 13
- Chart, Graph, and Map Skills Activity 13
- Political Cartoon Activity 13
- Supreme Court Case Study 13
- In-Text Map Transparency 13 Strategy and Activity
- Step Into American History Activity 13
- Citizenship and Service Learning Activity
- Outline Map Resource Book
- MindJogger Plus Videoquiz

WRITING SUPPORT
- Writing Activity 13
- Language Arts Activity 13
- Writer's Guidebook
- Middle School Writing Process Transparencies

ASSESSMENT
- Chapter 13 Section Quizzes
- Chapter 13 Tests, Forms A and B
- California Standards Assessment, Forms A and B
- Cumulative Assessment Activity 13
- California Standards Practice Workbook
- Succeeding on the California History–Social Science Standards CD-ROM
- ExamView® Pro Testmaker CD-ROM
- Interactive Tutor Self-Assessment CD-ROM

CD-ROM · DVD · Print Material · Poster · Transparency · Music Program · Videocassette · Glencoe Literature Library

566C

Chapter 13 Resources

TECHNOLOGY
- StudentWorks Plus CD-ROM
- TeacherWorks Plus CD-ROM
- ExamView® Pro Testmaker CD-ROM
- Interactive Tutor Self-Assessment CD-ROM
- Presentation Plus! CD-ROM
- Succeeding on the California History–Social Science Standards CD-ROM
- Vocabulary PuzzleMaker CD-ROM
- Interactive Graphic Organizers CD-ROM
- Interactive Time Line CD-ROM
- American History Primary Source Document Library CD-ROM
- MindJogger Plus Videoquiz
- American Music Cultural Traditions
- American Music Hits Through History
- Glencoe Video Program
- Professional Development in Middle School Social Studies Series
- Teaching American History With *Discovering Our Past: The American Journey to World War I*

SPANISH RESOURCES
- Spanish Activities and Assessment
  - Spanish Summaries
  - Spanish Vocabulary Activities
  - Spanish Guided Reading Activities
  - Spanish Quizzes and Tests
- Spanish Reading Essentials and Study Guide
- Spanish School-to-Home Connection
- Spanish Declaration of Independence and U.S. Constitution

TRANSPARENCIES
- California Standards Practice Transparencies
- Daily Focus Skills Transparencies
- Section Graphic Organizer Transparencies
- In-Text Map Transparencies
- Map Overlay Transparencies
- Cause-and-Effect Transparencies
- Then and Now Transparencies
- American Art and Architecture Transparencies
- Middle School Writing Process Transparencies

TEACHER PLANNING
- Daily Lesson Discussion Notes
- English Learner Handbook
- Guide to Daily Intervention
- *Discovering Our Past: The American Journey to World War I* Reading and Study Skills Foldables
- Reading Strategies and Activities for the Social Studies Classroom
- Chapter 13 Reproducible Lesson Plans
- California History-Social Science Standards Reproducible Lesson Plans
- Universal Access for the American History Classroom
- NGS U.S. Desk Map
- NGS U.S. Atlas

PROFESSIONAL DEVELOPMENT
- Building Academic Vocabulary
- Strategies for Success
- Research-Based Strategies Used to Develop *Discovering Our Past: The American Journey to World War I*
- Character Education in the Middle School Classroom
- The Living Constitution
- Professional Development in Middle School Social Studies Video Series
- Teaching American History With *Discovering Our Past: The American Journey to World War I*

MASTERING THE STANDARDS

The content and assessment in the Student Edition, Teacher Wraparound Edition, teacher planning materials, and the print and technology products are all standards-based. The use of these products during instruction leads to mastery of the standards.

PRACTICE
- California Standards Practice Workbook
- California Standards Practice Transparencies
- Interactive Time Line CD-ROM
- School-to-Home Connection

BENCHMARK ASSESSMENT
- California Standards Assessment
- ExamView® Pro Testmaker CD-ROM
- Succeeding on the California History-Social Science Standards CD-ROM

REMEDIATION
- California Guide to Daily Intervention
- Interactive Tutor Self-Assessment CD-ROM
- ExamView® Pro Testmaker CD-ROM
- California Standards Practice Workbook
- Reading Essentials and Study Guide

Professional Development
Extra support for beginning and experienced teachers

More Reading Support
Additional resources for intervention and enrichment

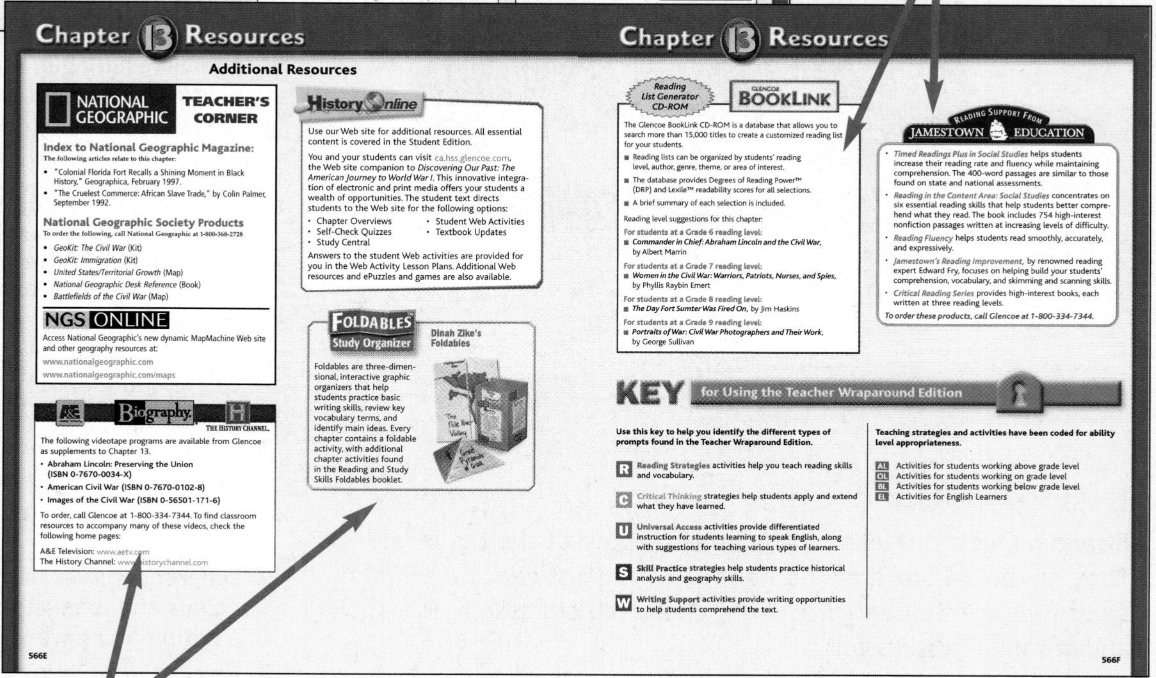

Chapter 13 Resources

Additional Resources

NATIONAL GEOGRAPHIC — TEACHER'S CORNER

Index to National Geographic Magazine:
The following articles relate to this chapter:
- "Colonial Florida Fort Recalls a Shining Moment in Black History," Geographica, February 1997.
- "The Cruelest Commerce: African Slave Trade," by Colin Palmer, September 1992.

National Geographic Society Products
To order the following, call National Geographic at 1-800-368-2728
- *GeoKit: The Civil War* (Kit)
- *GeoKit: Immigration* (Kit)
- *United States/Territorial Growth* (Map)
- *National Geographic Desk Reference* (Book)
- *Battlefields of the Civil War* (Map)

NGS ONLINE
Access National Geographic's new dynamic MapMachine Web site and other geography resources at:
www.nationalgeographic.com
www.nationalgeographic.com/maps

History Online

Use our Web site for additional resources. All essential content is covered in the Student Edition.

You and your students can visit ca.hss.glencoe.com, the Web site companion to *Discovering Our Past: The American Journey to World War I*. This innovative integration of electronic and print media offers your students a wealth of opportunities. The student text directs students to the Web site for the following options:
- Chapter Overviews
- Self-Check Quizzes
- Study Central
- Student Web Activities
- Textbook Updates

Answers to the student Web activities are provided for you in the Web Activity Lesson Plans. Additional Web resources and ePuzzles and games are also available.

A&E Biography — THE HISTORY CHANNEL

The following videotape programs are available from Glencoe as supplements to Chapter 13.
- Abraham Lincoln: Preserving the Union (ISBN 0-7670-0034-X)
- American Civil War (ISBN 0-7670-0102-8)
- Images of the Civil War (ISBN 0-56501-171-6)

To order, call Glencoe at 1-800-334-7344. To find classroom resources to accompany many of these videos, check the following home pages:
A&E Television: www.aetv.com
The History Channel: www.historychannel.com

FOLDABLES Study Organizer — Dinah Zike's Foldables

Foldables are three-dimensional, interactive graphic organizers that help students practice basic writing skills, review key vocabulary terms, and identify main ideas. Every chapter contains a foldable activity, with additional chapter activities found in the Reading and Study Skills Foldables booklet.

566E

Chapter 13 Resources

Reading List Generator CD-ROM — Glencoe BOOKLINK

The Glencoe BookLink CD-ROM is a database that allows you to search more than 15,000 titles to create a customized reading list for your students.
- Reading lists can be organized by students' reading level, author, genre, theme, or area of interest.
- The database provides Degrees of Reading Power™ (DRP) and Lexile™ readability scores for all selections.
- A brief summary of each selection is included.

Reading level suggestions for this chapter:

For students at a Grade 6 reading level:
- *Commander in Chief: Abraham Lincoln and the Civil War*, by Albert Marrin

For students at a Grade 7 reading level:
- *Women in the Civil War: Warriors, Patriots, Nurses, and Spies*, by Phyllis Raybin Emert

For students at a Grade 8 reading level:
- *The Day Fort Sumter Was Fired On*, by Jim Haskins

For students at a Grade 9 reading level:
- *Portraits of War: Civil War Photographers and Their Work*, by George Sullivan

Reading Support From JAMESTOWN EDUCATION
- *Timed Readings Plus in Social Studies* helps students increase their reading rate and fluency while maintaining comprehension. The 400-word passages are similar to those found on state and national assessments.
- *Reading in the Content Area: Social Studies* concentrates on six essential reading skills that help students better comprehend what they read. The book includes 754 high-interest nonfiction passages written at increasing levels of difficulty.
- *Reading Fluency* helps students read smoothly, accurately, and expressively.
- *Jamestown's Reading Improvement*, by renowned reading expert Edward Fry, focuses on helping build your students' comprehension, vocabulary, and skimming and scanning skills.
- *Critical Reading Series* provides high-interest books, each written at three reading levels.

To order these products, call Glencoe at 1-800-334-7344.

KEY for Using the Teacher Wraparound Edition

Use this key to help you identify the different types of prompts found in the Teacher Wraparound Edition.
- R Reading Strategies activities help you teach reading skills and vocabulary.
- C Critical Thinking strategies help students apply and extend what they have learned.
- U Universal Access activities provide differentiated instruction for students learning to speak English, along with suggestions for teaching various types of learners.
- S Skill Practice strategies help students practice historical analysis and geography skills.
- W Writing Support activities provide writing opportunities to help students comprehend the text.

Teaching strategies and activities have been coded for ability level appropriateness.
- AL Activities for students working above grade level
- OL Activities for students working on grade level
- BL Activities for students working below grade level
- EL Activities for English Learners

566F

Universal Access
Resources for differentiated instruction

Additional Resources
Resources for supplementing the chapter

Teaching the Chapter

The Big Ideas and Essential Questions at the beginning of the chapter help you teach the standards.

INTRODUCING CHAPTER 13

FOCUS

History–Social Science Standards

In this chapter, the following standard will be covered:

US8.10 Students analyze the multiple causes, key events, and complex consequences of the Civil War.

More About the Photo

Both sides had leadership problems as they prepared to fight at Gettysburg. General Stonewall Jackson had been mortally wounded at the Battle of Chancellorsville less than two months earlier, taking away Robert E. Lee's most trusted commander. General George Gordon Meade was given command of the Union army less than a week before the battle.

TEACH

The Big Ideas

As you begin teaching each section, use these questions and activities to focus on the Big Ideas.

Section 1

The Two Sides

Essential Question: What things make a country powerful militarily? *(large army, advanced equipment, industrial strength, fighting spirit, effective leaders)* OL

Chapter 13

The Civil War

Gettysburg Battlefield ▶

NATIONAL GEOGRAPHIC Who&When?

1861 · 1863 · 1865

1861 Civil War begins with battle at Fort Sumter

1862 Robert E. Lee commands Confederate army

1863 Emancipation Proclamation issued

1865 War ends; Lincoln assassinated

Section 2

Early Years of the War

Essential Question: How might people's feelings toward a war change as the war continues? *(Some may begin to tire of the sacrifices required; others might grow more determined.)* OL

Section 3

A Call to Freedom

Essential Question: What role did slavery play in the conflict leading up to the Civil War? *(It was a major factor in dividing the North and the South.)* OL

566

Big Ideas

Big Ideas are major themes, issues, concepts, questions, or ideas. They help students organize information and understand historical themes. The *Big Ideas* allow students to not only see the "big picture" but also the relevancy of what they are learning.

Big Ideas for Grade 8:

1. Geography shapes the physical, economic, and political challenges a region faces.
2. Geography influences the divergent paths of people resulting in physical, economic, and political challenges and rewards.
3. Political ideas and major events shape how people form government.
4. A constitution reflects the values and goals of the society that creates it.
5. Citizen participation is essential to the foundation and preservation of the U.S. political system.
6. Political, social, religious, and economic changes influence the way Americans think and act.
7. Economic, social, and political changes create new traditions, values, and beliefs.
8. As a society matures, a distinctive culture can develop.
9. Differences in economic, political, and social beliefs and practices can lead to division within a nation and have lasting consequences.
10. Conflict often brings about great change.
11. Reactions to social injustice can lead to reform movements.
12. Immigration influences a nation's or region's economy and society.
13. Innovations in technology and business help build a nation's industrial power.

Essential Questions

Essential Questions lead to an understanding of the Big Ideas. They are broad and have no right or wrong answers. *Essential Questions* are thought-provoking, challenge old assumptions, and stimulate discussion.

Teaching the Standards

All content and assessment in *Discovering Our Past: The American Journey to World War I* is standards-based. As you develop your lesson plans, you will be able to incorporate the following:

- **California History–Social Science Content Standards**
- **California Historical and Social Sciences Analysis Skills**
- **California English–Language Arts Standards**

A Guide to the California Standards

For Students and Their Families

▼ California state capitol, Sacramento

What are the California History–Social Science Content Standards?

The California Department of Education has developed content standards for every course at every grade level. These standards can be found on the California Department of Education website. The History–Social Science Content Standards for grade 8 are designed to measure a student's knowledge of American history between the founding of our nation and World War I. The content of *Discovering Our Past: The American Journey to World War I* matches these standards.

Why should students be aware of these standards?

In grade 8, students will be tested on what they learn in grades 6 and 7 world history courses and in their United States history course in grade 8.

This Guide Contains:

Historical and Social Sciences Analysis Skills CA1
Mastering these critical thinking, analysis, and research skills will help you in all your classes.

History–Social Science Standards, Grade 8 .... CA2
These standards for grade 8 describe what you will need to learn in your eighth-grade American history course.

English–Language Arts Standards, Grade 8 .... CA10
These standards encourage the development of your reading, writing, and speaking skills.

Correlations to the California Standards CA15

What are the Standards?

A complete list of all the standards is provided on pages CA1–CA14.

Correlation to the California Standards

History–Social Science Content Standards for Grade 8	Student Edition Pages	Teacher Edition Pages
***WH7.11 Students analyze political and economic change in the sixteenth, seventeenth, and eighteenth centuries (the Age of Exploration, the Enlightenment, and the Age of Reason).**	76–77, 80, 90, 98	76, 77, 34–35
WH7.11.1 Know the great voyages of discovery, the locations of the routes, and the influence of cartography in the development of a new European worldview.	81–84, 85, 89, 108–109	81, 84, 85, 108, 109
WH7.11.2 Discuss the exchanges of plants, animals, technology, culture, and ideas among Europe, Africa, Asia, and the Americas in the fifteenth and sixteenth centuries and the major economic and social effects on each continent.	95–97	95, 96
WH7.11.3 Examine the origins of modern capitalism; the influence of mercantilism and cottage industry; the elements and importance of a market economy in seventeenth-century Europe; the changing international trading and marketing patterns, including their locations on a world map; and the influence of explorers and map-makers.	91, 93–95	91, 93, 94, 95
WH7.11.4 Explain how the main ideas of the Enlightenment can be traced back to such movements as the Renaissance, the Reformation, and the Scientific Revolution and to the Greeks, Romans, and Christianity.	92, 99–101	92, 100
WH7.11.5 Describe how democratic thought and institutions were influenced by Enlightenment thinkers (e.g., John Locke, Charles-Louis Montesquieu, American founders).	102–03, 104–107	103, 104, 105, 106, 107
WH7.11.6 Discuss how the principles in the Magna Carta were embodied in such documents as the English Bill of Rights and the American Declaration of Independence.	104–107	106
***Local Options 1 & 2 from Appendix D of the History-Social Science Framework for California Public Schools give schools districts the option of teaching some Grade 7 materials at the Grade 8 level.**		
US8.1 Students understand the major events preceding the founding of the nation and relate their significance to the development of American constitutional democracy.	116–118, 120–141, 149–151, 158–159	121, 124, 128, 129, 133, 132, 150, 151
US8.1.1 Describe the relationship between the moral and political ideas of the Great Awakening and the development of revolutionary fervor.	128–129	128, 129
US8.1.2 Analyze the philosophy of government expressed in the Declaration of Independence, with an emphasis on government as a means of securing individual rights (e.g., key phrases such as "all men are created equal, that they are endowed by their Creator with certain unalienable Rights").	152–157	157

T64 A Guide to the California Standards

Where are the Standards Covered?

Each type of standard is correlated by page number. See pages T62–T73.

Where Are the History–Social Science Standards Found?

CHAPTER STANDARDS

The History–Social Science Content Standards covered in the chapter are listed at the beginning of the chapter.

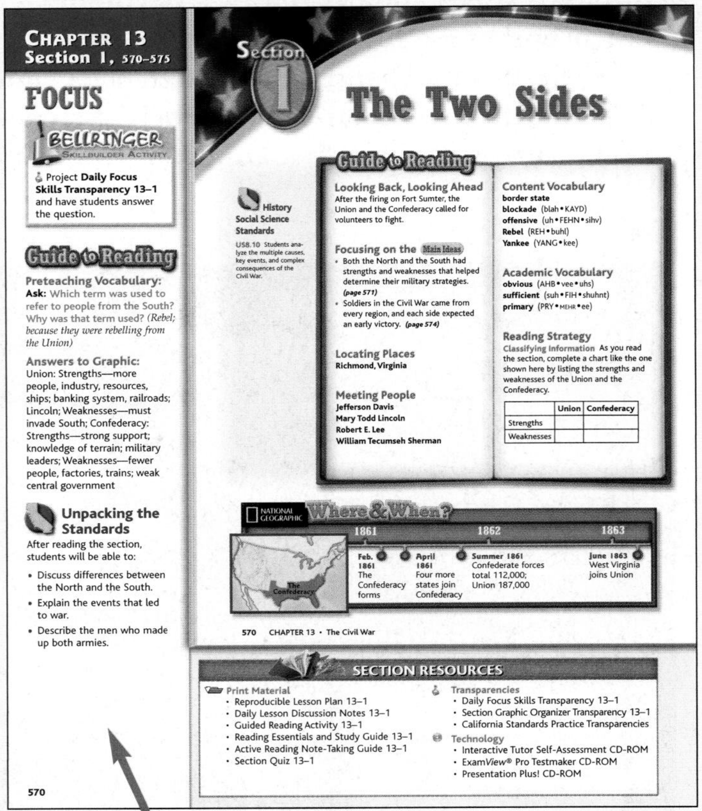

SECTION STANDARDS

The content standards covered in each specific section are listed in the Section Opener.

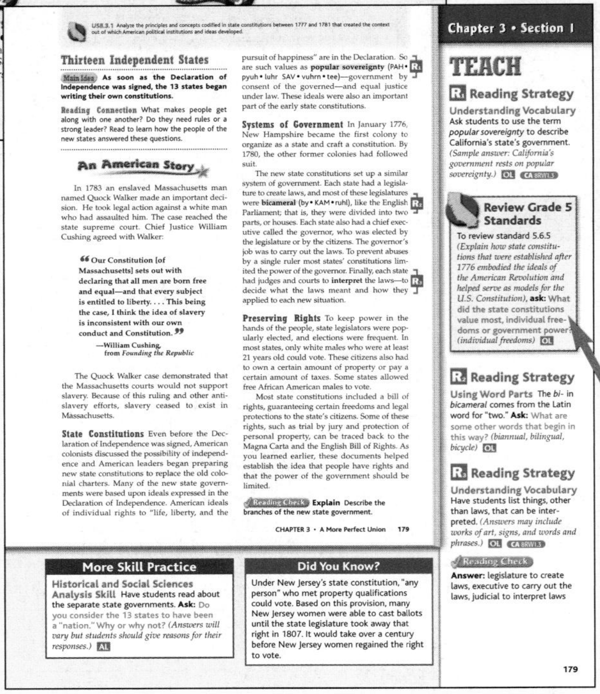

STANDARDS REVIEW

Standards from a previous grade level are reviewed throughout where appropriate.

Where Are the Historical and Social Sciences Analysis Skills Found?

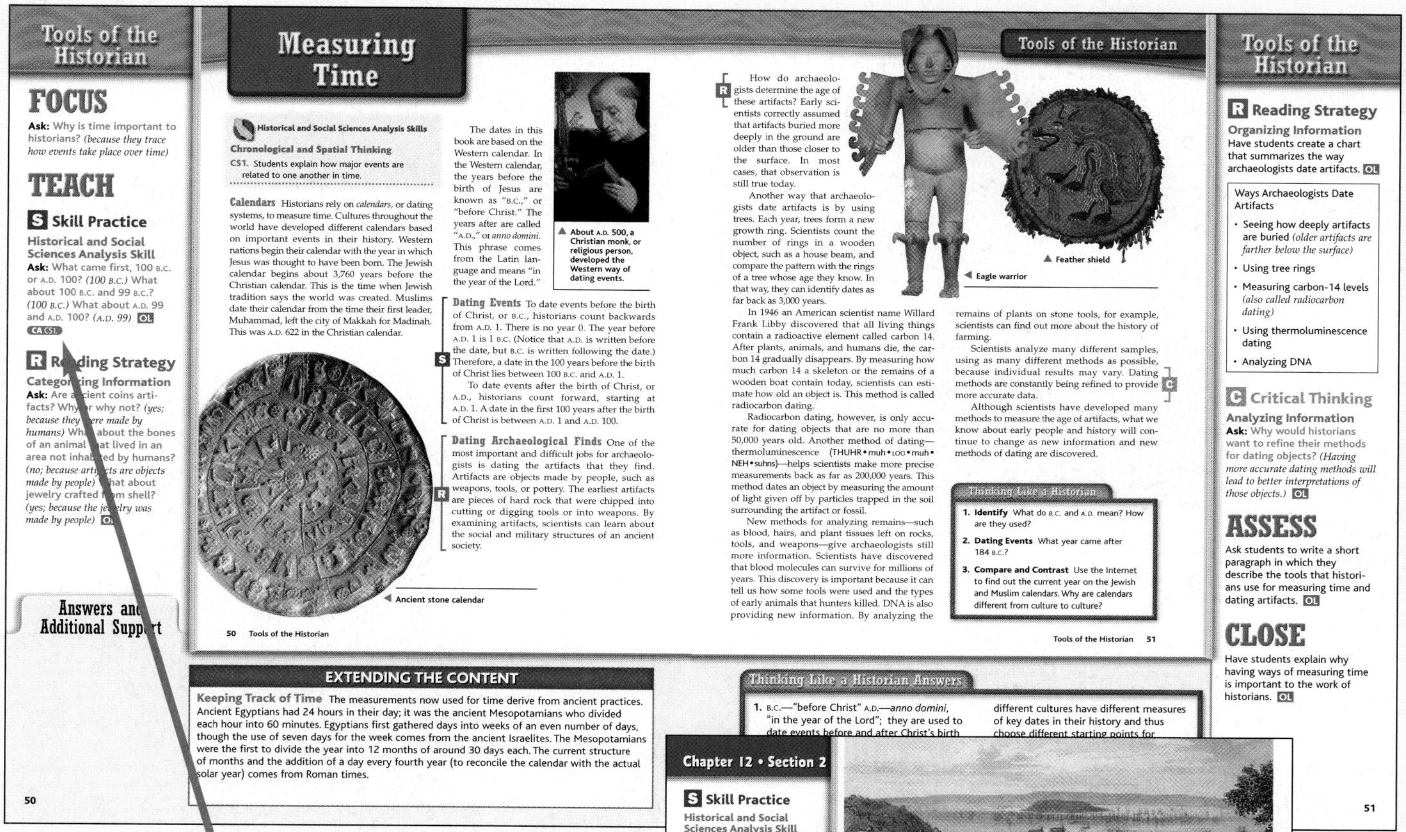
Tools of the Historian

FOCUS

Ask: Why is time important to historians? *(because they trace how events take place over time)*

TEACH

S Skill Practice

Historical and Social Sciences Analysis Skill

Ask: What came first, 100 B.C. or A.D. 100? *(100 B.C.)* What about 100 B.C. and 99 B.C.? *(100 B.C.)* What about A.D. 99 and A.D. 100? *(A.D. 99)* OL CA CS1.

Measuring Time

Historical and Social Sciences Analysis Skills

Chronological and Spatial Thinking

CS1. Students explain how major events are related to one another in time.

Calendars Historians rely on *calendars*, or dating systems, to measure time. Cultures throughout the world have developed different calendars based on important events in their history. Western nations begin their calendar with the year in which Jesus was thought to have been born. The Jewish calendar begins about 3,760 years before the Christian calendar. This is the time when Jewish tradition says the world was created. Muslims date their calendar from the time their first leader, Muhammad, left the city of Makkah for Madinah. This was A.D. 622 in the Christian calendar.

The dates in this book are based on the Western calendar. In the Western calendar, the years before the birth of Jesus are known as "B.C.," or "before Christ." The years after are called "A.D.," or *anno domini*. This phrase comes from the Latin language and means "in the year of the Lord."

About A.D. 500, a Christian monk, or religious person, developed the Western way of dating events.

Dating Events To date events before the birth of Christ, or B.C., historians count backwards from A.D. 1. There is no year 0. The year before A.D. 1 is 1 B.C. (Notice that A.D. is written before the date, but B.C. is written following the date.) Therefore, a date in the 100 years before the birth of Christ lies between 100 B.C. and A.D. 1.

To date events after the birth of Christ, or A.D., historians count forward, starting at A.D. 1. A date in the first 100 years after the birth of Christ is between A.D. 1 and A.D. 100.

Dating Archaeological Finds One of the most important and difficult jobs for archaeologists is dating the artifacts that they find. Artifacts are objects made by people, such as weapons, tools, or pottery. The earliest artifacts are pieces of hard rock that were chipped into cutting or digging tools or into weapons. By examining artifacts, scientists can learn about the social and military structures of an ancient society.

Ancient stone calendar

50 Tools of the Historian

How do archaeologists determine the age of these artifacts? Early scientists correctly assumed that artifacts buried more deeply in the ground are older than those closer to the surface. In most cases, that observation is still true today.

Another way that archaeologists date artifacts is by using trees. Each year, trees form a new growth ring. Scientists count the number of rings in a wooden object, such as a house beam, and compare the pattern with the rings of a tree whose age they know. In that way, they can identify dates as far back as 3,000 years.

In 1946 an American scientist name Willard Frank Libby discovered that all living things contain a radioactive element called carbon 14. After plants, animals, and humans die, the carbon 14 gradually disappears. By measuring how much carbon 14 a skeleton or the remains of a wooden boat contain today, scientists can estimate how old an object is. This method is called radiocarbon dating.

Radiocarbon dating, however, is only accurate for dating objects that are no more than 50,000 years old. Another method of dating—thermoluminescence (THUHR • muh • LOO • muh • NEH • suhns)—helps scientists make more precise measurements back as far as 200,000 years. This method dates an object by measuring the amount of light given off by particles trapped in the soil surrounding the artifact or fossil.

New methods for analyzing remains—such as blood, hairs, and plant tissues left on rocks, tools, and weapons—give archaeologists still more information. Scientists have discovered that blood molecules can survive for millions of years. This discovery is important because it can tell us how some tools were used and the types of early animals that hunters killed. DNA is also providing new information. By analyzing the remains of plants on stone tools, for example, scientists can find out more about the history of farming.

Scientists analyze many different samples, using as many different methods as possible, because individual results may vary. Dating methods are constantly being refined to provide more accurate data.

Although scientists have developed many methods to measure the age of artifacts, what we know about early people and history will continue to change as new information and new methods of dating are discovered.

Eagle warrior

Feather shield

Thinking Like a Historian

1. **Identify** What do B.C. and A.D. mean? How are they used?
2. **Dating Events** What year came after 184 B.C.?
3. **Compare and Contrast** Use the Internet to find out the current year on the Jewish and Muslim calendars. Why are calendars different from culture to culture?

Tools of the Historian 51

Tools of the Historian

R Reading Strategy

Organizing Information Have students create a chart that summarizes the way archaeologists date artifacts. OL

Ways Archaeologists Date Artifacts
- Seeing how deeply artifacts are buried *(older artifacts are farther below the surface)*
- Using tree rings
- Measuring carbon-14 levels *(also called radiocarbon dating)*
- Using thermoluminescence dating
- Analyzing DNA

C Critical Thinking

Analyzing Information Ask: Why would historians want to refine their methods for dating objects? *(Having more accurate dating methods will lead to better interpretations of those objects.)* OL

ASSESS

Ask students to write a short paragraph in which they describe the tools that historians use for measuring time and dating artifacts. OL

CLOSE

Have students explain why having ways of measuring time is important to the work of historians. OL

EXTENDING THE CONTENT

Keeping Track of Time The measurements now used for time derive from ancient practices. Ancient Egyptians had 24 hours in their day; it was the ancient Mesopotamians who divided each hour into 60 minutes. Egyptians first gathered days into weeks of an even number of days, though the use of seven days for the week comes from the ancient Israelites. The Mesopotamians were the first to divide the year into 12 months of around 30 days each. The current structure of months and the addition of a day every fourth year (to reconcile the calendar with the actual solar year) comes from Roman times.

Thinking Like a Historian Answers

1. B.C.—"before Christ" A.D.—*anno domini*, "in the year of the Lord"; they are used to date events before and after Christ's birth ... different cultures have different measures of key dates in their history and thus choose different starting points for ...

50 51

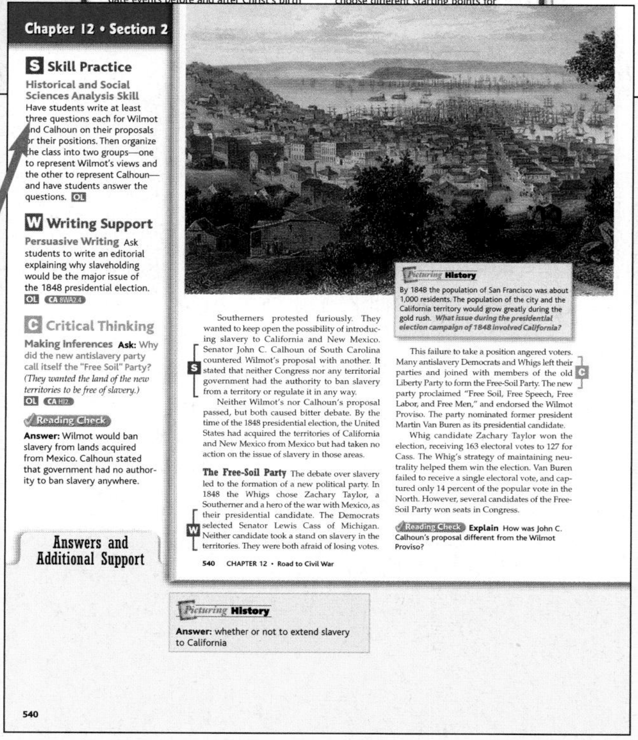
Chapter 12 • Section 2

S Skill Practice

Historical and Social Sciences Analysis Skill Have students write at least three questions each for Wilmot and Calhoun on their proposals or their positions. Then organize the class into two groups—one to represent Wilmot's views and the other to represent Calhoun—and have students answer the questions. OL

W Writing Support

Persuasive Writing Ask students to write an editorial explaining why slaveholding would be the major issue of the 1848 presidential election. OL CA HI...

C Critical Thinking

Making Inferences Ask: Why did the new antislavery party call itself the "Free Soil" Party? *(They wanted the land of the new territories to be free of slavery.)* OL CA HI2.

Reading Check Answer: Wilmot would ban slavery from lands acquired from Mexico. Calhoun stated that neither Congress nor any territorial government had the authority to ban slavery anywhere.

Answers and Additional Support

Picturing History: By 1848 the population of San Francisco was about 1,000 residents. The population of the city and the California territory would grow greatly during the gold rush. *What issue during the presidential election campaign of 1848 involved California?*

Southerners protested furiously. They wanted to keep open the possibility of introducing slavery to California and New Mexico. Senator John C. Calhoun of South Carolina countered Wilmot's proposal with another. It stated that neither Congress nor any territorial government had the authority to ban slavery from a territory or regulate it in any way.

Neither Wilmot's nor Calhoun's proposal passed, but both caused bitter debate. By the time of the 1848 presidential election, the United States had acquired the territories of California and New Mexico from Mexico but had taken no action on the issue of slavery in those areas.

The Free-Soil Party The debate over slavery led to the formation of a new political party. In 1848 the Whigs chose Zachary Taylor, a Southerner and a hero of the war with Mexico, as their presidential candidate. The Democrats selected Senator Lewis Cass of Michigan. Neither candidate took a stand on slavery in the territories. They were both afraid of losing votes.

This failure to take a position angered voters. Many antislavery Democrats and Whigs left their parties and joined with members of the old Liberty Party to form the Free-Soil Party. The new party proclaimed "Free Soil, Free Speech, Free Labor, and Free Men," and endorsed the Wilmot Proviso. The party nominated former president Martin Van Buren as its presidential candidate.

Whig candidate Zachary Taylor won the election, receiving 163 electoral votes to 127 for Cass. The Whig's strategy of maintaining neutrality helped them win the election. Van Buren failed to receive a single electoral vote, and captured only 14 percent of the popular vote in the North. However, several candidates of the Free-Soil Party won seats in Congress.

Reading Check **Explain** How was John C. Calhoun's proposal different from the Wilmot Proviso?

540 CHAPTER 12 • Road to Civil War

Picturing History

Answer: whether or not to extend slavery to California

540

Historical and Social Sciences Analysis Skills

The Historical and Social Sciences Analysis Skills are introduced in **Tools of the Historian,** pages 48–71.

Skills Reinforcement

Opportunities to reinforce the Historical and Social Sciences Analysis Skills are found throughout the lessons.

Where Are the English–Language Arts Standards Found?

STANDARDS-BASED ACTIVITY

The oval shows the English–Language Arts Standard covered by this activity.

Chapter 12 • Section 2

S Skill Practice

Historical and Social Sciences Analysis Skill Have students write at least three questions each for Wilmot and Calhoun on their proposals or their positions. Then organize the class into two groups—one to represent Wilmot's views and the other to represent Calhoun's—and have students answer the questions. OL

W Writing Support

Persuasive Writing Ask students to write an editorial explaining why slaveholding would be the major issue of the 1848 presidential election. OL CA 8WA2.4

C Critical Thinking

Making Inferences **Ask:** Why did the new antislavery party call itself the "Free Soil" Party? *(They wanted the land of the new territories to be free of slavery.)* OL CA HI2

Reading Check

Answer: Wilmot would ban slavery from lands acquired from Mexico. Calhoun stated that government had no authority to ban slavery anywhere.

Answers and Additional Support

Picturing History

By 1848 the population of San Francisco was about 1,000 residents. The population of the city and the California territory would grow greatly during the gold rush. ***What issue during the presidential election campaign of 1848 involved California?***

Southerners protested furiously. They wanted to keep open the possibility of introducing slavery to California and New Mexico. Senator John C. Calhoun of South Carolina countered Wilmot's proposal with another. It stated that neither Congress nor any territorial government had the authority to ban slavery from a territory or regulate it in any way.

Neither Wilmot's nor Calhoun's proposal passed, but both caused bitter debate. By the time of the 1848 presidential election, the United States had acquired the territories of California and New Mexico from Mexico but had taken no action on the issue of slavery in those areas.

The Free-Soil Party The debate over slavery led to the formation of a new political party. In 1848 the Whigs chose Zachary Taylor, a Southerner and a hero of the war with Mexico, as their presidential candidate. The Democrats selected Senator Lewis Cass of Michigan. Neither candidate took a stand on slavery in the territories. They were both afraid of losing votes.

This failure to take a position angered voters. Many antislavery Democrats and Whigs left their parties and joined with members of the old Liberty Party to form the Free-Soil Party. The new party proclaimed "Free Soil, Free Speech, Free Labor, and Free Men," and endorsed the Wilmot Proviso. The party nominated former president Martin Van Buren as its presidential candidate.

Whig candidate Zachary Taylor won the election, receiving 163 electoral votes to 127 for Cass. The Whig's strategy of maintaining neutrality helped them win the election. Van Buren failed to receive a single electoral vote, and captured only 14 percent of the popular vote in the North. However, several candidates of the Free-Soil Party won seats in Congress.

Reading Check **Explain** How was John C. Calhoun's proposal different from the Wilmot Proviso?

540 CHAPTER 12 • Road to Civil War

Picturing History

Answer: whether or not to extend slavery to California

US8.9.4 Discuss the importance of the slavery issue as raised by the annexation of Texas and California's admission to the union as a free state under the Compromise of 1850. US8.9.5 Analyze the significance of the States' Rights Doctrine, the Missouri Compromise (1820), the Wilmot Proviso (1846), the Compromise of 1850, Henry Clay's role in the Missouri Compromise and the Compromise of 1850, the Kansas-Nebraska Act (1854), the *Dred Scott v. Sandford* decision (1857), and the Lincoln-Douglas debates (1858).

The Search [illegible]ompromise

Main Idea **Henry Clay presented a plan [illegible] tle the slavery debate that resulted in the Compromise of 1850.**

Reading Connection Do you remember an argument you have had recently? How did you resolve the argument? Read to learn how Congress settled its dividing issues in 1850.

Once in office, President Zachary Taylor urged leaders in the two territories of California and New Mexico to apply for statehood immediately. After these lands had become states, he [illegible]soned, their citizens could decide whether to allo[illegible] slavery. New Mexico did not apply for stateho[illegible] but California did in 1850.

Taylor's [illegible]lan ran into trouble when California's state[illegible]od became tangled up with other issues before C[illegible]gress. Antislavery forces wanted to abolish sla[illegible] in the District of Columbia, the nation's ca[illegible]l. Southerners wanted a strong national law re[illegible]iring states to return **fugitive** (FYOO • juh • tihv), o[illegible]unaway, slaves to their masters. Another d[illegible]ute involved the New Mexico–Texas border.

The greatest obstacle to Taylor's plan was concern over the balance of power in the Senate. In 1849 the nation included 15 slave states and 15 free states. If California entered as a free state—and New Mexico, Oregon, and Utah followed as free states—which seemed [illegible] South would be hopelessly outvoted in the Se[illegible] As tension grew, some Southerners began talking [illegible]having their states **secede** (sih • SEED) from, or leave, [illegible] United States.

The Debate Begins In January 1850, Henry Clay, now a senator, presented a plan to settle all the issues dividing Congress. First, California would be admitted as a free state. Second, the New Mexico Territory would have no restrictions on slavery. Third, the New Mexico–Texas border dispute would be settled in favor of New Mexico. Fourth, the slave trade, but not slavery itself, would be abolished in the District of Columbia. Finally, Clay pushed for a stronger fugitive slave law.

Clay's proposal launched an emotional debate in Congress that raged for seven months. Senator Calhoun opposed Clay's plan. He believed that the only way to save the Union was to protect slavery. If Congress admitted California as a free state, Calhoun warned, the Southern states would have to leave the Union.

Senator Daniel Webster supported Clay's p[illegible]. He argued that antislavery forces lost little [illegible]agreeing to the compromise.

Picturing History

The Great Debate over the Compromise of 1850 raged for months. ***Why did Daniel Webster favor this compromise?***

Picturing History

This depiction of the Great Debate of 1850 in the U.S. Senate was created by Peter F. Rothermel, a Pennsylvania native who is remembered as one of America's most skillful painters of historical scenes.

Answer: because it would preserve the Union

More Skill Practice

Historical and Social Sciences Analysis Skill **Ask:** Why do you think Henry Clay was called the "Great Compromiser"? *(He played significant roles in the Missouri Compromise, the tariff compromise that ended the nullification crisis of 1833, and the Compromise of 1850.)* OL CA HI1.

Chapter 12 • Section 2

R1 Reading Strategy

Understanding Vocabulary Explain that the word *fugitive* comes from a Latin word meaning *to* "flee". **Ask:** How is that origin related to the meaning [illegible] *(A fugitive is someone who flees.)* [illegible] CA 8RW1.2

R2 Reading Strategy

Organizing Information Have students use a two-column chart to record details about Clay's proposed compromise. Suggest they head the columns *Clay's Proposal* and *Opponents' Response*. Have them record details of each of the proposal's five parts. Students may need to conduct additional research to obtain more information on opponents' responses to Clay's proposal. AL CA HI1.

S Skill Practice

Visual Literacy Have students examine the painting of the Senate Debate of 1850. **Ask:** Who is speaking in this painting? *(Clay)* What aspects of the painting suggest the seriousness of the debate? *(the dignified stance of the speaker, the concentration of all listeners on him, the full gallery)* OL CA 8LS1.9

Review The Big Idea

Review the Big Idea for this section: "Differences in economic, political, and social beliefs and practices can lead to division within a nation and have lasting consequences." Tell students to imagine that they are either Clay, Calhoun, Webster, or Douglas. Ask students to write the text of a speech that tries to convince other Senators to adopt their point of view on the compromise. OL CA 8SA2.4

540

541

Standards Assessment

Student activities and questions throughout the book provide opportunities for standards assessment.

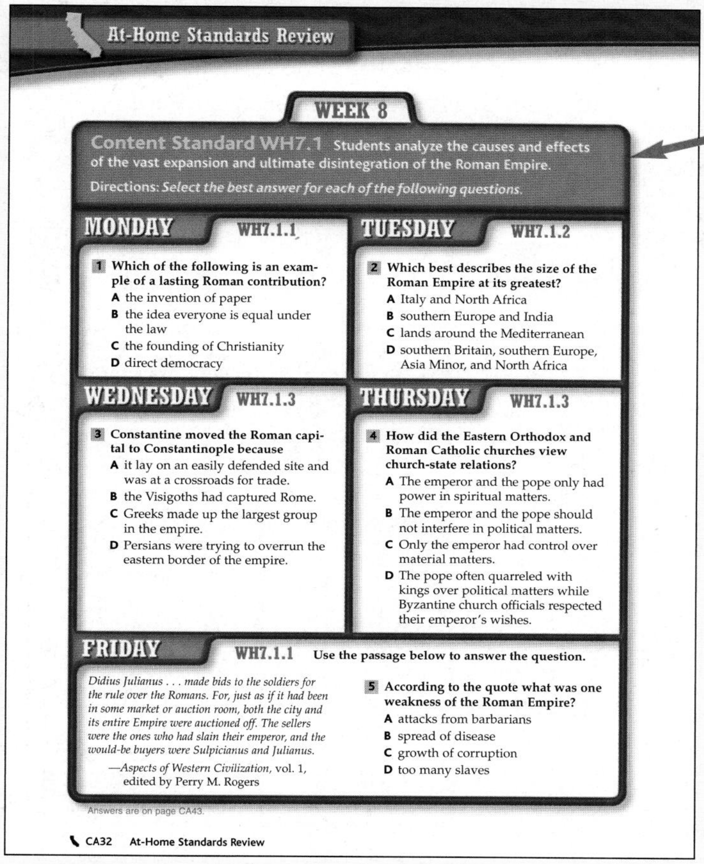

At-Home Standards Review

WEEK 8

Content Standard WH7.1 Students analyze the causes and effects of the vast expansion and ultimate disintegration of the Roman Empire.

Directions: *Select the best answer for each of the following questions.*

MONDAY WH7.1.1

1 Which of the following is an example of a lasting Roman contribution?
- A the invention of paper
- B the idea everyone is equal under the law
- C the founding of Christianity
- D direct democracy

TUESDAY WH7.1.2

2 Which best describes the size of the Roman Empire at its greatest?
- A Italy and North Africa
- B southern Europe and India
- C lands around the Mediterranean
- D southern Britain, southern Europe, Asia Minor, and North Africa

WEDNESDAY WH7.1.3

3 Constantine moved the Roman capital to Constantinople because
- A it lay on an easily defended site and was at a crossroads for trade.
- B the Visigoths had captured Rome.
- C Greeks made up the largest group in the empire.
- D Persians were trying to overrun the eastern border of the empire.

THURSDAY WH7.1.3

4 How did the Eastern Orthodox and Roman Catholic churches view church-state relations?
- A The emperor and the pope only had power in spiritual matters.
- B The emperor and the pope should not interfere in political matters.
- C Only the emperor had control over material matters.
- D The pope often quarreled with kings over political matters while Byzantine church officials respected their emperor's wishes.

FRIDAY WH7.1.1 **Use the passage below to answer the question.**

Didius Julianus . . . made bids to the soldiers for the rule over the Romans. For, just as if it had been in some market or auction room, both the city and its entire Empire were auctioned off. The sellers were the ones who had slain their emperor, and the would-be buyers were Sulpicianus and Julianus.

—*Aspects of Western Civilization*, vol. 1, edited by Perry M. Rogers

5 According to the quote what was one weakness of the Roman Empire?
- A attacks from barbarians
- B spread of disease
- C growth of corruption
- D too many slaves

Answers are on page CA43.

CA32 At-Home Standards Review

STANDARDS REVIEW

Students can work with a learning partner to practice previous grade-level standards found in the At-Home Standards Review section.

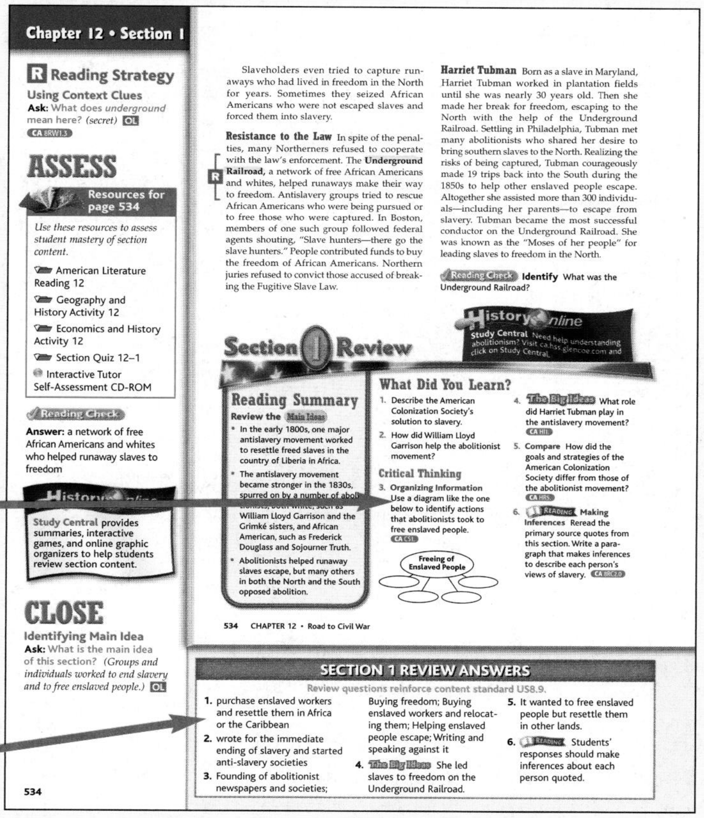

Chapter 12 • Section 1

R Reading Strategy

Using Context Clues

Ask: What does *underground* mean here? *(secret)* OL

CA 8RW1.3

ASSESS

Resources for page 534

Use these resources to assess student mastery of section content.

- American Literature Reading 12
- Geography and History Activity 12
- Economics and History Activity 12
- Section Quiz 12–1
- Interactive Tutor Self-Assessment CD-ROM

Reading Check

Answer: a network of free African Americans and whites who helped runaway slaves to freedom

History Online

Study Central provides summaries, interactive games, and online graphic organizers to help students review section content.

CLOSE

Identifying Main Idea

Ask: What is the main idea of this section? *(Groups and individuals worked to end slavery and to free enslaved people.)* OL

Slaveholders even tried to capture runaways who had lived in freedom in the North for years. Sometimes they seized African Americans who were not escaped slaves and forced them into slavery.

Resistance to the Law In spite of the penalties, many Northerners refused to cooperate with the law's enforcement. The **Underground Railroad,** a network of free African Americans and whites, helped runaways make their way to freedom. Antislavery groups tried to rescue African Americans who were being pursued or to free those who were captured. In Boston, members of one such group followed federal agents shouting, "Slave hunters—there go the slave hunters." People contributed funds to buy the freedom of African Americans. Northern juries refused to convict those accused of breaking the Fugitive Slave Law.

Harriet Tubman Born as a slave in Maryland, Harriet Tubman worked in plantation fields until she was nearly 30 years old. Then she made her break for freedom, escaping to the North with the help of the Underground Railroad. Settling in Philadelphia, Tubman met many abolitionists who shared her desire to bring southern slaves to the North. Realizing the risks of being captured, Tubman courageously made 19 trips back into the South during the 1850s to help other enslaved people escape. Altogether she assisted more than 300 individuals—including her parents—to escape from slavery. Tubman became the most successful conductor on the Underground Railroad. She was known as the "Moses of her people" for leading slaves to freedom in the North.

Reading Check **Identify** What was the Underground Railroad?

History Online

Study Central Need help understanding abolitionism? Visit ca.hss.glencoe.com and click on Study Central.

Section 1 Review

Reading Summary

Review the Main Ideas

- In the early 1800s, one major antislavery movement worked to resettle freed slaves in the country of Liberia in Africa.
- The antislavery movement became stronger in the 1830s, spurred on by a number of abolitionists, both white, such as William Lloyd Garrison and the Grimké sisters, and African American, such as Frederick Douglass and Sojourner Truth.
- Abolitionists helped runaway slaves escape, but many others in both the North and the South opposed abolition.

What Did You Learn?

1. Describe the American Colonization Society's solution to slavery.
2. How did William Lloyd Garrison help the abolitionist movement?

Critical Thinking

3. **Organizing Information** Use a diagram like the one below to identify actions that abolitionists took to free enslaved people. CA CS1.

Freeing of Enslaved People

4. The Big Ideas What role did Harriet Tubman play in the antislavery movement? CA HI1.
5. **Compare** How did the goals and strategies of the American Colonization Society differ from those of the abolitionist movement? CA HR5.
6. Reading **Making Inferences** Reread the primary source quotes from this section. Write a paragraph that makes inferences to describe each person's views of slavery. CA 8RC2.0

534 CHAPTER 12 • Road to Civil War

SECTION 1 REVIEW ANSWERS

Review questions reinforce content standard US8.9.

1. purchase enslaved workers and resettle them in Africa or the Caribbean
2. wrote for the immediate ending of slavery and started anti-slavery societies
3. Founding of abolitionist newspapers and societies; Buying freedom; Buying enslaved workers and relocating them; Helping enslaved people escape; Writing and speaking against it
4. The Big Ideas She led slaves to freedom on the Underground Railroad.
5. It wanted to free enslaved people but resettle them in other lands.
6. Reading Students' responses should make inferences about each person quoted.

534

STUDENT EDITION QUESTIONS AND CORRELATIONS

TEACHER EDITION ANSWERS

Standards Assessment (cont.)

Chapter Assessment
Chapter Assessment pages review the standards covered in the chapter.

Additional Assessment Resources
Additional California standards practice and assessment resources

Analysis Skills
Answers to analysis skills activities are provided in the Teacher Edition.

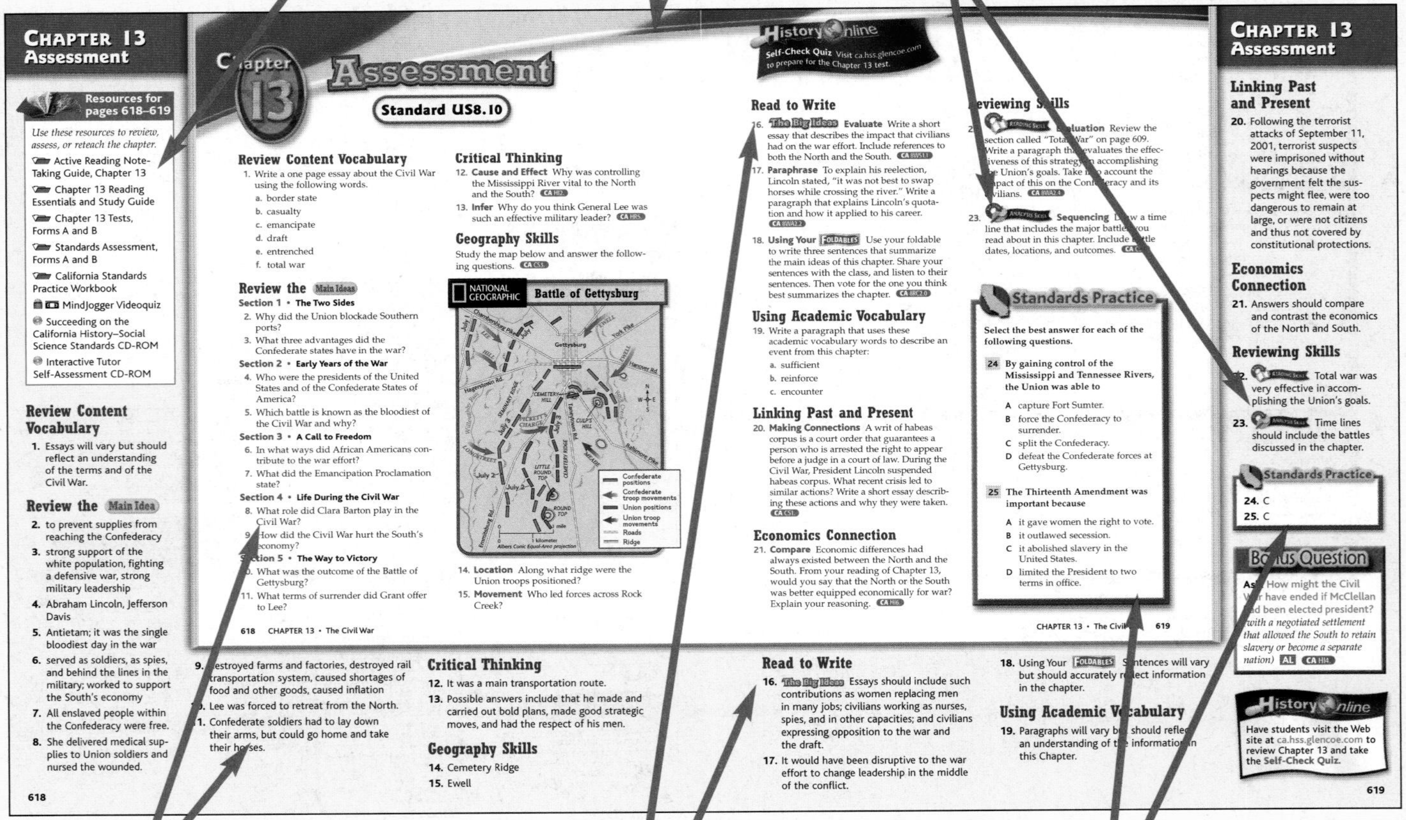

CHAPTER 13 Assessment

Resources for pages 618–619

Use these resources to review, assess, or reteach the chapter.

Active Reading Note-Taking Guide, Chapter 13
Chapter 13 Reading Essentials and Study Guide
Chapter 13 Tests, Forms A and B
Standards Assessment, Forms A and B
California Standards Practice Workbook
MindJogger Videoquiz
Succeeding on the California History–Social Science Standards CD-ROM
Interactive Tutor Self-Assessment CD-ROM

Review Content Vocabulary
1. Essays will vary but should reflect an understanding of the terms and of the Civil War.

Review the Main Idea
2. to prevent supplies from reaching the Confederacy
3. strong support of the white population, fighting a defensive war, strong military leadership
4. Abraham Lincoln, Jefferson Davis
5. Antietam; it was the single bloodiest day in the war
6. served as soldiers, as spies, and behind the lines in the military; worked to support the South's economy
7. All enslaved people within the Confederacy were free.
8. She delivered medical supplies to Union soldiers and nursed the wounded.
9. destroyed farms and factories, destroyed rail transportation system, caused shortages of food and other goods, caused inflation
10. Lee was forced to retreat from the North.
11. Confederate soldiers had to lay down their arms, but could go home and take their horses.

Critical Thinking
12. It was a main transportation route.
13. Possible answers include that he made and carried out bold plans, made good strategic moves, and had the respect of his men.

Geography Skills
14. Cemetery Ridge
15. Ewell

Read to Write
16. The Big Ideas Essays should include such contributions as women replacing men in many jobs; civilians working as nurses, spies, and in other capacities; and civilians expressing opposition to the war and the draft.
17. It would have been disruptive to the war effort to change leadership in the middle of the conflict.
18. Using Your FOLDABLES Sentences will vary but should accurately reflect information in the chapter.

Using Academic Vocabulary
19. Paragraphs will vary but should reflect an understanding of the information in this Chapter.

618

Chapter 13 Assessment

Standard US8.10

Review Content Vocabulary
1. Write a one page essay about the Civil War using the following words.
a. border state
b. casualty
c. emancipate
d. draft
e. entrenched
f. total war

Review the Main Ideas
Section 1 • The Two Sides
2. Why did the Union blockade Southern ports?
3. What three advantages did the Confederate states have in the war?
Section 2 • Early Years of the War
4. Who were the presidents of the United States and of the Confederate States of America?
5. Which battle is known as the bloodiest of the Civil War and why?
Section 3 • A Call to Freedom
6. In what ways did African Americans contribute to the war effort?
7. What did the Emancipation Proclamation state?
Section 4 • Life During the Civil War
8. What role did Clara Barton play in the Civil War?
9. How did the Civil War hurt the South's economy?
Section 5 • The Way to Victory
10. What was the outcome of the Battle of Gettysburg?
11. What terms of surrender did Grant offer to Lee?

Critical Thinking
12. Cause and Effect Why was controlling the Mississippi River vital to the North and the South? CA HI2.
13. Infer Why do you think General Lee was such an effective military leader? CA HR5.

Geography Skills
Study the map below and answer the following questions. CA CS3.

NATIONAL GEOGRAPHIC Battle of Gettysburg

14. Location Along what ridge were the Union troops positioned?
15. Movement Who led forces across Rock Creek?

618 CHAPTER 13 • The Civil War

History Online
Self-Check Quiz Visit ca.hss.glencoe.com to prepare for the Chapter 13 test.

Read to Write
16. The Big Ideas Evaluate Write a short essay that describes the impact that civilians had on the war effort. Include references to both the North and the South. CA 8WS1.1
17. Paraphrase To explain his reelection, Lincoln stated, "it was not best to swap horses while crossing the river." Write a paragraph that explains Lincoln's quotation and how it applied to his career. CA 8WA2.2
18. Using Your FOLDABLES Use your foldable to write three sentences that summarize the main ideas of this chapter. Share your sentences with the class, and listen to their sentences. Then vote for the one you think best summarizes the chapter. CA 8RC2.0

Using Academic Vocabulary
19. Write a paragraph that uses these academic vocabulary words to describe an event from this chapter:
a. sufficient
b. reinforce
c. encounter

Linking Past and Present
20. Making Connections A writ of habeas corpus is a court order that guarantees a person who is arrested the right to appear before a judge in a court of law. During the Civil War, President Lincoln suspended habeas corpus. What recent crisis led to similar actions? Write a short essay describing these actions and why they were taken. CA CS1.

Economics Connection
21. Compare Economic differences had always existed between the North and the South. From your reading of Chapter 13, would you say that the North or the South was better equipped economically for war? Explain your reasoning. CA HI6.

Reviewing Skills
22. Evaluation Review the section called "Total War" on page 609. Write a paragraph that evaluates the effectiveness of this strategy in accomplishing the Union's goals. Take into account the impact of this on the Confederacy and its civilians. CA 8WA2.4
23. Sequencing Draw a time line that includes the major battles you read about in this chapter. Include battle dates, locations, and outcomes. CA CS1.

Standards Practice
Select the best answer for each of the following questions.

24 By gaining control of the Mississippi and Tennessee Rivers, the Union was able to
A capture Fort Sumter.
B force the Confederacy to surrender.
C split the Confederacy.
D defeat the Confederate forces at Gettysburg.

25 The Thirteenth Amendment was important because
A it gave women the right to vote.
B it outlawed secession.
C it abolished slavery in the United States.
D limited the President to two terms in office.

CHAPTER 13 • The Civil War 619

CHAPTER 13 Assessment

Linking Past and Present
20. Following the terrorist attacks of September 11, 2001, terrorist suspects were imprisoned without hearings because the government felt the suspects might flee, were too dangerous to remain at large, or were not citizens and thus not covered by constitutional protections.

Economics Connection
21. Answers should compare and contrast the economics of the North and South.

Reviewing Skills
22. Total war was very effective in accomplishing the Union's goals.
23. Time lines should include the battles discussed in the chapter.

Standards Practice
24. C
25. C

Bonus Question
Ask: How might the Civil War have ended if McClellan had been elected president? *(with a negotiated settlement that allowed the South to retain slavery or become a separate nation)* AL CA HI4.

History Online
Have students visit the Web site at ca.hss.glencoe.com to review Chapter 13 and take the Self-Check Quiz.

619

Content Standards
Answers to content-based questions are provided in the Teacher Edition.

English–Language Arts Standards
Answers to English–Language Arts Activities are provided in the Teacher Edition.

Standards Practice
Questions to help measure standards proficiency are answered in the Teacher Edition.

Standards Reinforcement

Opportunities for intervention are provided to improve standards proficiency.

Scaffolding

Historical and Social Sciences Analysis Skills are reinforced throughout the lessons.

Chapter 13 • Section 5

S1 Skill Practice

Historical and Social Sciences Analysis Skill Have students create a chart that shows the effects of the Union victories in July 1863. *(Gettysburg: drove Lee's army out of the North, and, along with Lincoln's address, gave the Union new inspiration; Vicksburg: split the South, gave the Union control of the Mississippi River)* BL CA HI2.

S2 Skill Practice

Using Geography Skills Have students find Chattanooga, Tennessee, on the map. **Ask:** Why would controlling that city be advantageous for either side? *(Union: controlling it would allow the Union forces to attack into Georgia, further dividing the South. Confederates: Controlling it would allow them to attack into Tennessee and even Kentucky and Ohio.)* OL CA CS3.

W Writing Support

Persuasive Writing Have students write a paragraph explaining which of the two battles fought in July 1863 was the more crucial to the outcome of the war, giving reasons for their choice. OL CA 8WA2.4

Answers and Additional Support

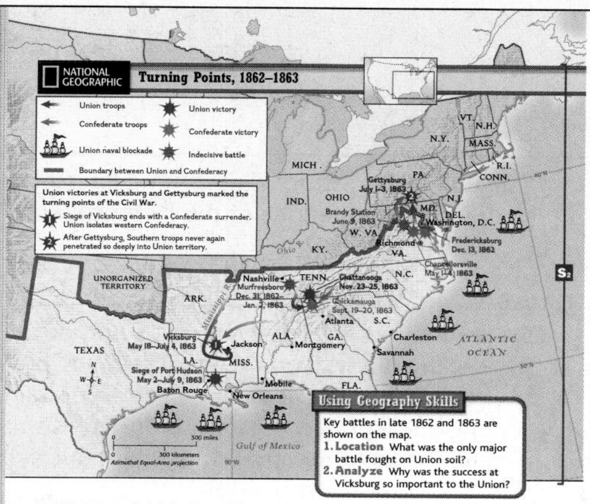

Using Geography Skills

Key battles in late 1862 and 1863 are shown on the map.

1. **Location** What was the only major battle fought on Union soil?
2. **Analyze** Why was the success at Vicksburg so important to the Union?

This last attack, led by General George Pickett, is remembered as Pickett's Charge. About 14,000 Confederate soldiers advanced across about one-half mile of open ground toward the Union lines. They made easy targets for Union fire as they marched. Barely half of the Rebels returned from the charge. Lee knew the battle was lost. "It's all my fault," he told his troops as they retreated to Virginia.

S1 **Victory at Vicksburg** Meanwhile, a great battle was taking place at **Vicksburg, Mississippi.** Vicksburg stood on a high bluff above the Mississippi River. To gain control of the river, one of the North's major war goals, the Union needed to seize Vicksburg. For several months, Union forces under Ulysses S. Grant had laid siege to the town. Finally, on July 4, 1863, Vicksburg surrendered.

With the surrender of Vicksburg and then Port Hudson—a Confederate fort in Louisiana—the Union now held the entire Mississippi River. Texas, Louisiana, and Arkansas were sealed off from the Confederacy.

The Union victories at Gettysburg and Vicksburg marked a turning point in the war. They drove Lee's army out of Pennsylvania, secured the Mississippi as a Union highway, and cut the South in two. **Nevertheless,** the South still had troops and a will to fight. The war would continue for two more terrible years. W

606 CHAPTER 13 • The Civil War

More Skill Practice

Historical and Social Sciences Analysis Skill Ask students to make a list of five questions to ask Ulysses S. Grant about the Union siege and victory at Vicksburg. Then have them research and record the answers that the general might have given. *(Questions will vary; they may focus on the campaign itself, his goals, his worries, his army, or other elements.)* AL CA HR1.

Using Geography Skills

Answers:

1. Gettysburg
2. It gave the Union control of the Mississippi River.

In-Text Map Transparency 13 Ask: From which direction did Grant make his final approach to Vicksburg? *(the southeast)* BL

606

California Standards Handbook

This Handbook, found on pages 862–884, provides content correlations and practice questions for each standard.

California Standards Handbook

US8.6 *cont.*

What Is the Standard?	Where Can I Find It?
US8.6.5 **Trace the development of the American education system from its earliest roots, including the roles of religious and private schools and Horace Mann's campaign for free public education and its assimilating role in American culture.**	**Chapter 8, Section 4** Education played an increasingly important role in the young Republic and took on many different forms, including new colleges and schools for students with disabilities. **(Review page 405.)**
US8.6.6 **Examine the women's suffrage movement (e.g., biographies, writings, and speeches of Elizabeth Cady Stanton, Margaret Fuller, Lucretia Mott, Susan B. Anthony).**	**Chapter 8, Section 5** Women were eager to share in the ideals of the Declaration of Independence, and a movement to give women the right to vote developed. Women also made gains in education and in their legal rights related to marriage and family. **(Review pages 409–413.)**
US8.6.7 **Identify common themes in American art as well as transcendentalism and individualism (e.g., writings about and by Ralph Waldo Emerson, Henry David Thoreau, Herman Melville, Louisa May Alcott, Nathaniel Hawthorne, Henry Wadsworth Longfellow).**	**Chapter 8, Section 4** As American identity evolved, themes in art, writing, and music became distinctive. American authors created and explored new themes like transcendentalism and individualism. **(Review pages 406–407.)**

Standards Practice

1 What was the relationship between the Irish potato famine and the United States in the mid-1800s?

- **A** The famine created a devastating shortage of food, causing more than 1.5 million Irish immigrants to come to the United States.
- **B** The famine limited trade between the United States and Ireland.
- **C** The famine caused a revolt among Irish in New York City.
- **D** The famine inspired new farming technology in the United States.

2 Henry David Thoreau and Ralph Waldo Emerson belonged to a group of writers known as the

- **A** Fundamentalists.
- **B** Constitutionalists.
- **C** Federalists.
- **D** Transcendentalists.

California Standards Handbook 871

Teacher Edition Correlation to the California Standards

Historical and Social Sciences Analysis Skills	Student Edition Pages	Teacher Edition Pages
Chronological and Spatial Thinking		
CS1. Students explain how major events are related to one another in time.	89, 97, 110, 111, 141, 157, 201, 233, 244, 300, 309, 317, 332, 345, 359, 367, 394, 401, 417, 451, 475, 487, 497, 534, 542, 547, 553, 559, 565, 603, 619, 628, 649, 692, 697, 700, 717, 723, 734, 783	50, 84, 86, 120, 135, 174E, 184, 222, 288, 364, 426, 457, 460, 483, 497, 529, 546, 608, 612, 620E, 702E
CS2. Students construct various time lines of key events, people, and periods of the historical eras they are studying.	141, 157, 301, 317, 345, 394, 413, 457, 464, 465, 487, 497, 542, 559, 565, 613, 619, 649, 655, 692, 735	103, 137, 174E, 195, 220, 230, 265, 273, 451, 523, 546, 579, 593, 630, 803, 824
CS3. Students use a variety of maps and documents to identify physical and cultural features of neighborhoods, cities, states, and countries and to explain the historical migration of people, expansion and disintegration of empires, and the growth of economic systems.	110, 111, 131, 162, 212, 244, 289, 300, 332, 370, 416, 431, 440, 464, 497, 499, 516, 564, 583, 618, 654, 700, 734, 756, 788	39, 41, 42, 43, 55, 58, 83, 84, 87, 94, 153, 182, 183, 249, 339, 355, 365, 383, 385, 389, 392, 398, 399, 423, 426, 430, 454, 457, 466E, 471, 474, 491, 495, 496, 533, 546, 555, 572, 581, 606, 608, 614, 615, 668, 670, 673, 676, 678, 689, 702E, 707, 710, 713, 773, 777
Research, Evidence, and Point of View		
HR1. Students frame questions that can be answered by historical study and research.	213, 329, 351, 451, 465, 559, 639	106, 156, 188, 241, 314, 366, 403, 405, 453, 466E, 580, 581, 606, 613, 636, 650, 674, 697
HR2. Students distinguish fact from opinion in historical narratives and stories.	157, 159, 191, 284, 561, 729, 749	299, 328, 429, 501, 653, 708
HR3. Students distinguish relevant from irrelevant information, essential from incidental information, and verifiable from unverifiable information in historical narratives and stories.	107, 124, 131, 133, 162, 185, 201, 207, 209, 297, 301, 309, 317, 333, 351, 387, 413, 416, 437, 461, 477, 497, 547, 564, 575, 613, 639, 653, 671, 749, 756, 763, 783, 788	82, 91, 220, 221, 223, 254, 298, 313, 321, 360, 369, 414, 436, 438, 439, 459, 462, 466E, 482, 514, 530, 536, 551, 552, 561, 574, 607, 616, 688, 689, 694, 699, 744, 745, 752, 768, 775
HR4. Students assess the credibility of primary and secondary sources and draw sound conclusions about them.	162, 213, 300, 369, 371, 465, 723, 771	61, 63, 88, 109, 139, 152, 158, 161, 167, 198, 203, 206, 207, 209, 211, 330, 331, 412, 463, 677, 728, 730, 741, 749, 781, 787
HR5. Students detect the different historical points of view on historical events and determine the context in which the historical statements were made (the questions asked, sources used, author's perspectives).	159, 161, 201, 209, 243, 244, 284, 297, 300, 370, 371, 441, 497, 516, 534, 596, 618, 654, 701, 747, 749	137, 138, 153, 195, 279, 298, 415, 433, 439, 492, 532, 549, 557, 561, 563, 571, 575, 593, 595, 596, 605, 611, 616, 667, 691, 692, 749, 761, 768, 781
Historical Interpretation		
HI1. Students explain the central issues and problems from the past, placing people and events in a matrix of time and place.	97, 110, 124, 225, 241, 329, 332, 359, 367, 370, 407, 413, 426, 437, 440, 457, 464, 506, 515, 534, 542, 547, 553, 583, 596,	86, 88, 92, 100, 101, 104, 117, 130, 135, 150, 166, 180, 181, 186, 199, 200, 201, 203, 213, 252, 258, 269, 282, 283, 296,

Historical and Social Sciences Analysis Skills	Student Edition Pages	Teacher Edition Pages
Historical Interpretation	**Student Edition Pages**	**Teacher Edition Pages**
	603, 634, 639, 649, 651, 679, 692, 697, 711, 729, 763	298, 310, 341, 344, 345, 363, 392, 404, 425, 428, 433, 436, 450, 454, 455, 456, 461, 466E, 485, 495, 529, 530, 531, 533, 536, 538, 541, 542, 545, 547, 550, 551, 552, 553, 556, 558, 572, 573, 580, 583, 592, 599, 600, 620E, 625, 630, 631, 675, 676, 680, 686, 695, 727, 730, 746, 751, 753, 760, 765, 770
HI2. Students understand and distinguish cause, effect, sequence, and correlation in historical events, including the long- and short-term causal relations.	89, 107, 110, 111, 131, 141, 162, 212, 225, 233, 239, 241, 244, 245, 284, 289, 309, 311, 317, 333, 345, 359, 370, 387, 394, 401, 407, 417, 426, 431, 440, 461, 475, 487, 506, 516, 517, 542, 547, 553, 564, 575, 583, 596, 603, 613, 618, 628, 634, 649, 651, 654, 671, 679, 692, 697, 700, 711, 717, 723, 731, 734, 747, 756, 763, 788	40, 82, 83, 86, 91, 96, 97, 108, 117, 126, 132, 137, 139, 160, 164, 180, 184, 185, 195, 196, 199, 200, 201, 206, 223, 236, 238, 259, 286, 292, 293, 308, 313, 317, 322, 326, 328, 336, 337, 340, 356, 358, 359, 363, 365, 367, 371, 383, 396, 423, 426, 435, 447, 449, 450, 451, 453, 454, 459, 461, 465, 474, 473, 481, 484, 485, 491, 495, 503, 514, 532, 533, 540, 544, 545, 549, 552, 553, 555, 572, 573, 574, 575, 577, 580, 583, 592, 594, 595, 596, 598, 600, 601, 606, 608, 609, 610, 611, 612, 620E, 628, 631, 632, 637, 638, 642, 652, 668, 670, 671, 679, 687, 688, 691, 692, 695, 702E, 709, 710, 715, 721, 741, 751, 753, 760, 762, 766, 770, 771, 773, 777, 782, 796, 826
HI3. Students explain the sources of historical continuity and how the combination of ideas and events explains the emergence of new patterns.	107, 111, 157, 163, 207, 211, 225, 245, 332, 437, 451, 457, 517, 628, 634, 711, 717, 747, 756, 771, 783, 788, 789	49, 56, 81, 87, 103, 104, 107, 122, 129, 139, 152, 155, 157, 181, 182, 195, 198, 199, 203, 204, 225, 242, 250, 256, 263, 279, 291, 311, 321, 327, 331, 343, 344, 357, 367, 369, 399, 403, 409, 435, 437, 447, 448, 450, 453, 459, 484, 536, 544, 549, 556, 574, 579, 599, 607, 613, 627, 638, 643, 644, 669, 674, 679, 688, 690, 696, 704, 716, 719, 731, 742, 745, 754, 759, 763, 767, 770, 775, 778, 795, 798, 799, 802, 805, 809, 829
HI4. Students recognize the role of chance, oversight, and error in history.	89, 506, 583	85, 86, 296, 345, 354, 391, 501, 582, 592, 605, 619, 713, 779
HI5. Students recognize that interpretations of history are subject to change as new information is uncovered.	475, 649, 729	87, 198, 221, 224, 324, 484, 530, 562, 577, 772
HI6. Students interpret basic indicators of economic performance and conduct cost-benefit analyses of economic and political issues.	97, 141, 311, 387, 416, 417, 426, 431, 440, 575, 603, 619, 671, 679, 700, 701, 731, 771, 789	131, 139, 183, 385, 393, 396, 429, 504, 537, 646, 673, 675, 677, 720, 722, 728, 761, 839

History–Social Science Content Standards for Grade 8	Student Edition Pages	Teacher Edition Pages
***WH7.11 Students analyze political and economic change in the sixteenth, seventeenth, and eighteenth centuries (the Age of Exploration, the Enlightenment, and the Age of Reason).**	76–77, 80, 90, 98	76, 77, 34–35
WH7.11.1 Know the great voyages of discovery, the locations of the routes, and the influence of cartography in the development of a new European worldview.	81–84, 85, 89, 108–109	81, 84, 85, 108, 109
WH7.11.2 Discuss the exchanges of plants, animals, technology, culture, and ideas among Europe, Africa, Asia, and the Americas in the fifteenth and sixteenth centuries and the major economic and social effects on each continent.	95–97	95, 96
WH7.11.3 Examine the origins of modern capitalism; the influence of mercantilism and cottage industry; the elements and importance of a market economy in seventeenth-century Europe; the changing international trading and marketing patterns, including their locations on a world map; and the influence of explorers and map-makers.	91, 93–95	91, 93, 94, 95
WH7.11.4 Explain how the main ideas of the Enlightenment can be traced back to such movements as the Renaissance, the Reformation, and the Scientific Revolution and to the Greeks, Romans, and Christianity.	92, 99–101	92, 100
WH7.11.5 Describe how democratic thought and institutions were influenced by Enlightenment thinkers (e.g., John Locke, Charles-Louis Montesquieu, American founders).	102–03, 104–107	103, 104, 105, 106, 107
WH7.11.6 Discuss how the principles in the Magna Carta were embodied in such documents as the English Bill of Rights and the American Declaration of Independence.	104–107	106
***Local Options 1 & 2 from Appendix D of the History-Social Science Framework for California Public Schools give school districts the option of teaching some Grade 7 materials at the Grade 8 level.**		
US8.1 Students understand the major events preceding the founding of the nation and relate their significance to the development of American constitutional democracy.	116–118, 120–141, 149–151, 158–159	121, 124, 128, 129, 133, 132, 150, 151
US8.1.1 Describe the relationship between the moral and political ideas of the Great Awakening and the development of revolutionary fervor.	128–129	128, 129
US8.1.2 Analyze the philosophy of government expressed in the Declaration of Independence, with an emphasis on government as a means of securing individual rights (e.g., key phrases such as "all men are created equal, that they are endowed by their Creator with certain unalienable Rights").	152–157	157

History–Social Science Content Standards for Grade 8	Student Edition Pages	Teacher Edition Pages
US8.1.3 Analyze how the American Revolution affected other nations, especially France.	153–157	155
US8.1.4 Describe the nation's blend of civic republicanism, classical liberal principles, and English parliamentary traditions.	119, 130–33, 135–36, 139–41	132, 133
US8.2 Students analyze the political principles underlying the U.S. Constitution and compare the enumerated and implied powers of the federal government.	178, 193, 202, 226, 232	210–211
US8.2.1 Discuss the significance of the Magna Carta, the English Bill of Rights, and the Mayflower Compact.	132–133, 203	132, 133
US8.2.2 Analyze the Articles of Confederation and the Constitution and the success of each in implementing the ideals of the Declaration of Independence.	175, 183–185, 194–196, 206–207, 219, 221–223	184, 221
US8.2.3 Evaluate the major debates that occurred during the development of the Constitution and their ultimate resolutions in such areas as shared power among institutions, divided state-federal power, slavery, the rights of individuals and states (later addressed by the addition of the Bill of Rights), and the status of American Indian nations under the commerce clause.	197, 199–201, 204-05	199, 200, 201, 247
US8.2.4 Describe the political philosophy underpinning the Constitution as specified in the *Federalist Papers* (authored by James Madison, Alexander Hamilton, and John Jay) and the role of such leaders as Madison, George Washington, Roger Sherman, Gouverneur Morris, and James Wilson in the writing and ratification of the Constitution.	198, 206–09, 220, 242–43	206, 207, 208, 220, 242, 243
US8.2.5 Understand the significance of Jefferson's Statute of Religious Freedom as a forerunner of the First Amendment and the origins, purpose, and differing views of the founding fathers on the issue of separation of church and state.	235	235
US8.2.6 Enumerate the powers of government set forth in the Constitution and the fundamental liberties ensured by the Bill of Rights.	224–225, 227–231, 233, 235–236, 240–241	224, 229, 230, 235
US8.2.7 Describe the principles of federalism, dual sovereignty, separation of powers, checks and balances, the nature and purpose of majority rule, and the ways in which the American idea of constitutionalism preserves individual rights.	221–223, 224–225, 235–236	223
US8.3 Students understand the foundation of the American political system and the ways in which citizens participate in it.	178, 193, 202, 210–211, 218, 226, 234, 278, 285, 290	214, 247
US8.3.1 Analyze the principles and concepts codified in state constitutions between 1777 and 1781 that created the context out of which American political institutions and ideas developed.	179	247

History–Social Science Content Standards for Grade 8	Student Edition Pages	Teacher Edition Pages
US8.3.2 Explain how the ordinances of 1785 and 1787 privatized national resources and transferred federally owned lands into private holdings, townships, and states.	180–182	181, 182
US8.3.3 Enumerate the advantages of a common market among the states as foreseen in and protected by the Constitution's clauses on interstate commerce, common coinage, and full-faith and credit.	219, 311	219, 310, 311
US8.3.4 Understand how the conflicts between Thomas Jefferson and Alexander Hamilton resulted in the emergence of two political parties (e.g., view of foreign policy, Alien and Sedition Acts, economic policy, National Bank, funding and assumption of the revolutionary debt).	281, 282, 283, 284, 291, 292, 293, 295, 296, 297	282, 283, 296, 297
US8.3.5 Know the significance of domestic resistance movements and ways in which the central government responded to such movements (e.g., Shays' Rebellion, the Whiskey Rebellion).	194–196, 286	194, 195
US8.3.6 Describe the basic law-making process and how the Constitution provides numerous opportunities for citizens to participate in the political process and to monitor and influence government (e.g., function of elections, political parties, interest groups).	236–239	237, 238
US8.3.7 Understand the functions and responsibilities of a free press.	240–241	240, 241
US8.4 Students analyze the aspirations and ideals of the people of the new nation.	278, 279, 280, 285, 290, 294, 298, 299, 306, 312, 320, 330, 331	330–331, 373
US8.4.1 Describe the country's physical landscapes, political divisions, and territorial expansion during the terms of the first four presidents.	287, 293, 295, 296, 297, 308–309, 313, 314, 315, 316, 317, 318, 319, 328, 329	313, 314, 315, 316, 318, 328, 329
US8.4.2 Explain the policy significance of famous speeches (e.g., Washington's Farewell Address, Jefferson's 1801 Inaugural Address, John Q. Adams's Fourth of July 1821 Address).	288, 289, 307, 330, 331	289, 331
US8.4.3 Analyze the rise of capitalism and the economic problems and conflicts that accompanied it (e.g., Jackson's opposition to the National Bank; early decisions of the U.S. Supreme Court that reinforced the sanctity of contracts and a capitalist economic system of the law).	310, 311	310
US8.4.4 Discuss daily life, including traditions in art, music, and literature, of early national America (e.g., through writings by Washington Irving, James Fenimore Cooper).	321, 322, 323, 324, 325, 326, 327	323, 324
US8.5 Students analyze U.S. foreign policy in the early Republic.	338, 339, 340, 353, 357, 362, 368–369	334–335

History–Social Science Content Standards for Grade 8	Student Edition Pages	Teacher Edition Pages
US8.5.1 Understand the political and economic causes and consequences of the War of 1812 and know the major battles, leaders, and events that led to a final peace.	341, 342, 343, 344, 345, 354, 355 356, 358, 359, 363, 364, 365	334, 354, 355, 358, 359
US8.5.2 Know the changing boundaries of the United States and describe the relationships the country had with its neighbors (current Mexico and Canada) and Europe, including the influence of the Monroe Doctrine, and how those relationships influenced westward expansion and the Mexican-American War.	363, 364, 365, 366, 367	364, 367
US8.5.3 Outline the major treaties with American Indian nations during the administrations of the first four presidents and the varying outcomes of those treaties.	341, 342, 343	343
US8.6 Students analyze the divergent paths of the American people from 1800 to the mid-1800s and the challenges they faced, with emphasis on the Northeast.	382, 388, 395, 402, 408, 414–415	379, 414–415
US8.6.1 Discuss the influences of industrialization and technological developments on the region, including human modification of the landscape and how physical geography shaped human actions (e.g., growth of cities, deforestation, farming, mineral extraction).	383, 384, 385, 386, 387, 396, 397, 502, 668	383, 384, 385
US8.6.2 Outline the physical obstacles to and the economic and political factors involved in building a network of roads, canals, and railroads (e.g., Henry Clay's American System).	389, 390, 391, 392, 393, 394	392, 393
US8.6.3 List the reasons for the wave of immigration from Northern Europe to the United States and describe the growth in the number, size, and spatial arrangements of cities (e.g., Irish immigrants and the Great Irish Famine).	398, 399, 400, 401	398, 399
US8.6.4 Study the lives of black Americans who gained freedom in the North and founded schools and churches to advance their rights and communities.	397	660
US8.6.5 Trace the development of the American education system from its earliest roots, including the roles of religious and private schools and Horace Mann's campaign for free public education and its assimilating role in American culture.	403, 405	405
US8.6.6 Examine the women's suffrage movement (e.g., biographies, writings, and speeches of Elizabeth Cady Stanton, Margaret Fuller, Lucretia Mott, Susan B. Anthony).	409, 410, 411, 4512, 413	409, 410
US8.6.7 Identify common themes in American art as well as transcendentalism and individualism (e.g., writings about and by Ralph Waldo Emerson, Henry David Thoreau, Herman Melville, Louisa May Alcott, Nathaniel Hawthorne, Henry Wadsworth Longfellow).	404, 406, 407	404, 406

History–Social Science Content Standards for Grade 8	Student Edition Pages	Teacher Edition Pages
US8.7 Students analyze the divergent paths of the American people in the South from 1800 to the mid-1800s and the challenges they faced.	422, 427, 432	418–419, 425
US8.7.1 Describe the development of the agrarian economy in the South, identify the locations of the cotton-producing states, and discuss the significance of cotton and the cotton gin.	423, 424, 425, 426	423, 424, 425
US8.7.2 Trace the origins and development of slavery; its effects on black Americans and on the region's political, social, religious, economic, and cultural development; and identify the strategies that were tried to both overturn and preserve it (e.g., through the writings and historical documents on Nat Turner, Denmark Vesey).	433, 434, 435, 437	433, 435
US8.7.3 Examine the characteristics of white Southern society and how the physical environment influenced events and conditions prior to the Civil War.	428, 429, 430, 431	428
US8.7.4 Compare the lives of and opportunities for free blacks in the North with those of free blacks in the South.	430, 431	428
US8.8 Students analyze the divergent paths of the American people in the West from 1800 to the mid-1800s and the challenges they faced.	446, 452, 458, 470, 480, 490, 500, 514–515	442–443
US8.8.1 Discuss the election of Andrew Jackson as president in 1828, the importance of Jacksonian democracy, and his actions as president (e.g., the spoils system, veto of the National Bank, policy of Indian removal, opposition to the Supreme Court).	447–451, 453–457, 459, 460–463	447, 448, 449, 450, 451, 453, 454
US8.8.2 Describe the purpose, challenges, and economic incentives associated with westward expansion, including the concept of Manifest Destiny (e.g., the Lewis and Clark expedition, accounts of the removal of Indians, the Cherokees' "Trail of Tears," settlement of the Great Plains) and the territorial acquisitions that spanned numerous decades.	453–457, 471–477, 501, 503–506	454, 457
US8.8.3 Describe the role of pioneer women and the new status that western women achieved (e.g., Laura Ingalls Wilder, Annie Bidwell; slave women gaining freedom in the West; Wyoming granting suffrage to women in 1869).	412–413, 473–474, 493, 502, 551, 668, 676, 678, 770	412, 770
US8.8.4 Examine the importance of the great rivers and the struggle over water rights.	488–489	489
US8.8.5 Discuss Mexican settlements and their locations, cultural traditions, attitudes toward slavery, land-grant system, and economies.	481–482, 492–494	482, 492

History–Social Science Content Standards for Grade 8	Student Edition Pages	Teacher Edition Pages
US8.8.6 Describe the Texas War for Independence and the Mexican-American War, including territorial settlements, the aftermath of the wars, and the effects the wars had on the lives of Americans, including Mexican Americans today.	483-487, 491, 495-499	483, 485, 486, 496
US8.9 Students analyze the early and steady attempts to abolish slavery and to realize the ideals of the Declaration of Independence.	178, 528–529, 535, 543, 545, 548, 562	562–563
US8.9.1 Describe the leaders of the movement (e.g., John Quincy Adams and his proposed constitutional amendment, John Brown and the armed resistance, Harriet Tubman and the Underground Railroad, Benjamin Franklin, Theodore Weld, William Lloyd Garrison, Frederick Douglass).	436, 530–534, 546–547	531, 533, 547
US8.9.2 Discuss the abolition of slavery in early state constitutions.	195–196	
US8.9.3 Describe the significance of the Northwest Ordinance in education and in the banning of slavery in new states north of the Ohio River.	180, 181, 182	181
US8.9.4 Discuss the importance of the slavery issue as raised by the annexation of Texas and California's admission to the union as a free state under the Compromise of 1850.	539–542	539
US8.9.5 Analyze the significance of the States' Rights Doctrine, the Missouri Compromise (1820), the Wilmot Proviso (1846), the Compromise of 1850, Henry Clay's role in the Missouri Compromise and the Compromise of 1850, the Kansas-Nebraska Act (1854), the *Dred Scott* v. *Sandford* decision (1857), and the Lincoln-Douglas debates (1858).	536, 539–542, 544, 549–550, 553	540, 541, 544, 550, 553
US8.9.6 Describe the lives of free blacks and the laws that limited their freedom and economic opportunities.	397, 430, 551	551
US8.10 Students analyze the multiple causes, key events, and complex consequences of the Civil War.	535, 548, 554, 570, 576, 591, 597, 604	562–563, 567
US8.10.1 Compare the conflicting interpretations of state and federal authority as emphasized in the speeches and writings of statesmen such as Daniel Webster and John C. Calhoun.	537–538	538
US8.10.2 Trace the boundaries constituting the North and the South, the geographical differences between the two regions, and the differences between agrarians and industrialists.	571–573	571
US8.10.3 Identify the constitutional issues posed by the doctrine of nullification and secession and the earliest origins of that doctrine.	537–538, 556–557	537, 538

History–Social Science Content Standards for Grade 8	Student Edition Pages	Teacher Edition Pages
US8.10.4 Discuss Abraham Lincoln's presidency and his significant writings and speeches and their relationship to the Declaration of Independence, such as his "House Divided" speech (1858), Gettysburg Address (1863), Emancipation Proclamation (1863), and inaugural addresses (1861 and 1865).	552, 555–557, 592–594, 605–606	555, 592, 594, 607
US8.10.5 Study the views and lives of leaders (e.g., Ulysses S. Grant, Jefferson Davis, Robert E. Lee) and soldiers on both sides of the war, including those of black soldiers and regiments.	560–561, 574–575, 580–583, 595–596, 598, 607–609, 611	561, 582, 596, 608, 611
US8.10.6 Describe critical developments and events in the war, including the major battles, geographical advantages and obstacles, technological advances, and General Lee's surrender at Appomattox.	558–559, 577–583, 595–596, 605–610, 612–615	559, 577, 579, 581, 605, 614
US8.10.7 Explain how the war affected combatants, civilians, the physical environment, and future warfare.	577–578, 599–603, 610, 612–613, 616–617	577, 599, 610, 617
US8.11 Students analyze the character and lasting consequences of Reconstruction.	624, 627, 629, 635, 637, 652–653	620, 621, 647
US8.11.1 List the original aims of Reconstruction and describe its effects on the political and social structures of different regions.	625–626, 631–634, 638–640, 645–646	626, 631, 632, 636
US8.11.2 Identify the push-pull factors in the movement of former slaves to the cities in the North and to the West and their differing experiences in those regions (e.g. the experiences of the Buffalo Soldiers).	677	677
US8.11.3 Understand the effects of the Freedmen's Bureau and the restrictions placed on the rights and opportunities of freedmen, including racial segregation and "Jim Crow" laws.	625–626, 630–631, 636, 641, 644, 647–649	626, 630, 647
US8.11.4 Trace the rise of the Ku Klux Klan and describe the Klan's effects.	638, 641–644	
US8.11.5 Understand the Thirteenth, Fourteenth, and Fifteenth Amendments to the Constitution and analyze their connection to Reconstruction.	626, 628, 630–631, 634, 647–651	628, 634, 651
US8.12 Students analyze the transformation of the American economy and the changing social and political conditions in the United States in response to the Industrial Revolution.	666, 672, 677, 685, 693, 706, 712, 718, 724, 732–733	662–663, 696, 702–703, 719, 736–737
US8.12.1 Trace patterns of agricultural and industrial development as they relate to climate, use of natural resources, markets, and trade and locate such development on a map.	667–671, 673–676, 678–680, 707, 709–711, 716–717, 719–723	670
US8.12.2 Identify the reasons for the development of federal Indian policy and the wars with American Indians and their relationship to agricultural development and industrialization.	686–692	687, 688, 689, 691

History–Social Science Content Standards for Grade 8	Student Edition Pages	Teacher Edition Pages
US8.12.3 Explain how states and the federal government encouraged business expansion through tariffs, banking, land grants, and subsidies.	669–671	669
US8.12.4 Discuss entrepreneurs, industrialists, and bankers in politics, commerce, and industry (e.g., Andrew Carnegie, John D. Rockefeller, Leland Stanford).	707–708, 719–723	708, 721
US8.12.5 Examine the location and effects of urbanization, renewed immigration, and industrialization (e.g., the effects on social fabric of cities, wealth and economic opportunity, the conservation movement).		736, 744, 747, 751
US8.12.6 Discuss child labor, working conditions, and laissez-faire policies toward big business and examine the labor movement, including its leaders (e.g., Samuel Gompers), its demand for collective bargaining, and its strikes and protests over labor conditions.	725–731	725, 726, 727, 729
US8.12.7 Identify the new sources of large-scale immigration and the contributions of immigrants to the building of cities and the economy; explain the ways in which new social and economic patterns encouraged assimilation of newcomers into the mainstream amidst growing cultural diversity; and discuss the new wave of nativism.		747
US8.12.8 Identify the characteristics and impact of Grangerism and Populism.	694–697	694, 695, 696
US8.12.9 Name the significant inventors and their inventions and identify how they improved the quality of life (e.g., Thomas Edison, Alexander Graham Bell, Orville and Wilbur Wright).	709–711, 713–715	710, 713, 714, 715

English–Language Arts Content Standards for Grade 8	Student Edition Pages	Teacher Edition Pages
8RW1.0 Word Analysis, Fluency, and Systematic Vocabulary Development	191, 475, 517, 729	641, 466E, 620E, 702E
8RW1.1	351, 589, 683	347, 423, 529, 562
8RW1.2		85, 118, 403, 482, 537, 541, 600
8RW1.3	512, 655	94, 102, 123, 127, 179, 180, 181, 185, 187, 194, 199, 203, 204, 205, 206, 288, 295, 339, 363, 384, 409, 428, 430, 434, 447, 449, 455, 472, 473, 476, 481, 497, 529, 534, 537, 544, 546, 556, 573, 574, 578, 579, 594, 603, 639, 645, 667, 668, 673, 677, 678, 687, 695, 710, 721, 732, 766, 771, 778

English–Language Arts Content Standards for Grade 8	Student Edition Pages	Teacher Edition Pages
8RC2.0 Reading Comprehension (Focus on Informational Materials)	124, 163, 185, 213, 233, 239, 245, 329, 345, 371, 415, 426, 441, 534, 565, 575, 619, 628, 655, 701, 789	232, 369, 444, 445, 595, 611, 620E, 689, 694, 696, 698, 701, 702E
8RC2.2		425, 537, 539, 558
8RC2.3	477, 733	
8RC2.4	89, 124, 239	115, 217, 342, 453, 512, 531, 558
8RC2.5		384, 390
8RC2.6		252
8RL3.0 Literary Response and Analysis		381
8RL3.1		368
8RL3.2	512	190, 508, 588
8RL3.3	351, 653	146, 147, 189, 351, 585, 586, 587, 588, 589
8RL3.4		144, 188, 585
8RL3.5		682, 683
8RL3.6	147, 683	349, 582, 587, 787
8RL3.7		143, 147, 324, 348, 363, 612
8WS1.0 Writing Strategies	159, 245, 463, 465, 655	
8WS1.1	111, 163, 211, 213, 225, 301, 333, 439, 441, 451, 517, 565, 619, 655, 701, 735, 783, 789	307, 445, 671, 759, 776
8WS1.3		669
8WS1.4	465, 565	117, 316, 364, 405, 594
8WA2.0 Writing Applications (Genres and Their Characteristics)	89	
8WA2.1	97, 131, 161, 299, 333, 359, 367, 371, 394, 401, 407, 417, 437, 443, 506, 515, 542, 553, 596, 603, 613, 617, 639, 671, 683, 692, 699, 701, 723, 735	85, 117, 145, 220, 288, 319, 342, 356, 404, 411, 436, 478, 479, 483, 549, 551, 563, 571, 577, 601, 609, 623, 668, 678, 697, 698, 743, 754, 803, 816, 818
8WA2.2	111, 147, 512, 589, 619, 735	191, 594, 681, 683, 732
8WA2.3	111, 317, 441, 559, 589, 671, 701, 735, 756, 771	106, 108, 115, 129, 151, 165, 166, 181, 223, 239, 255, 327, 387, 393, 409, 434, 544, 605, 643, 677, 708, 715, 725, 795, 802, 805

English–Language Arts Content Standards for Grade 8	Student Edition Pages	Teacher Edition Pages
8WA2.4	107, 124, 163, 185, 207, 243, 245, 297, 301, 333, 369, 371, 387, 431, 457, 465, 517, 547, 563, 619, 697, 701, 711, 763, 771	96, 103, 123, 132, 137, 138, 155, 167, 195, 207, 224, 237, 255, 267, 277, 291, 342, 355, 366, 391, 397, 424, 448, 456, 472, 477, 482, 495, 496, 498, 531, 540, 546, 557, 560, 592, 602, 606, 649, 650, 653, 675, 691, 713, 722
8WA2.5	233, 284, 461, 603	799, 810, 813
8WA2.6	331	699, 714
8WC1.0 Written and Oral English Language Conventions		
8WC1.1	297	
8LS1.0 Listening and Speaking Strategies	333	
8LS1.1		144, 404, 607
8LS1.2		331, 403, 610
8LS1.3	201, 289, 655	119, 206, 770
8LS1.4	245	
8LS1.9	747, 789	62, 93, 138, 211, 366, 435, 450, 455, 541, 582, 673, 678, 694, 738, 746, 751, 759, 794, 797, 809, 834, 837
2.0 Speaking Applications (Genres and Their Characteristics)		
8SA2.1		411
8SA2.3		550, 775, 800
8SA2.4		138, 259, 397, 541, 607
8SA2.5		368, 775

A Guide to the California Standards

For Students and Their Families

California state capitol, Sacramento

What are the California History–Social Science Content Standards?

The California Department of Education has developed content standards for every course at every grade level. These standards can be found on the California Department of Education website. The History–Social Science Content Standards for grade 8 are designed to measure a student's knowledge of American history between the founding of our nation and World War I. The content of *Discovering Our Past: The American Journey to World War I* matches these standards.

Why should students be aware of these standards?

In grade 8, students will be tested on what they learn in grades 6 and 7 world history courses and in their United States history course in grade 8.

This Guide Contains:

Historical and Social Sciences Analysis Skills CA1

Mastering these critical thinking, analysis, and research skills will help you in all your classes.

History–Social Science Standards, Grade 8 .... CA2

These standards for grade 8 describe what you will need to learn in your eighth-grade American history course.

English–Language Arts Standards, Grade 8 .... CA10

These standards encourage the development of your reading, writing, and speaking skills.

Correlations to the California Standards CA15

Historical and Social Sciences Analysis Skills

To help you learn and understand content standards for any course you take, it is important to master the following skills. These skills focus on critical thinking, analysis, and research and will be represented like this: CA HR1.

Chronological and Spatial Thinking

CS1. Students explain how major events are related to one another in time.

CS2. Students construct various time lines of key events, people, and periods of the historical era they are studying.

CS3. Students use a variety of maps and documents to identify physical and cultural features of neighborhoods, cities, states, and countries and to explain the historical migration of people, expansion and disintegration of empires, and the growth of economic systems.

Research, Evidence, and Point of View

HR1. Students frame questions that can be answered by historical study and research.

HR2. Students distinguish fact from opinion in historical narratives and stories.

HR3. Students distinguish relevant from irrelevant information, essential from incidental information, and verifiable from unverifiable information in historical narratives and stories.

HR4. Students assess the credibility of primary and secondary sources and draw sound conclusions from them.

HR5. Students detect the different historical points of view on historical events and determine the context in which the historical statements were made (the questions asked, sources used, author's perspectives).

Historical Interpretation

HI1. Students explain the central issues and problems from the past, placing people and events in a matrix of time and place.

HI2. Students understand and distinguish cause, effect, sequence, and correlation in historical events, including the long- and short-term causal relations.

HI3. Students explain the sources of historical continuity and how the combination of ideas and events explains the emergence of new patterns.

HI4. Students recognize the role of chance, oversight, and error in history.

HI5. Students recognize that interpretations of history are subject to change as new information is uncovered.

HI6. Students interpret basic indicators of economic performance and conduct cost-benefit analyses of economic and political issues.

History–Social Science Standards

These content standards describe what History–Social Science Standards you should master when you complete this course.

United States History and Geography: Growth and Conflict

Main Standard US8.1 **Students understand the major events preceding the founding of the nation and relate their significance to the development of American constitutional democracy.**

Supporting Standard US8.1.1 Describe the relationship between the moral and political ideas of the Great Awakening and the development of revolutionary fervor.

Supporting Standard US8.1.2 Analyze the philosophy of government expressed in the Declaration of Independence, with an emphasis on government as a means of securing individual rights (e.g., key phrases such as "all men are created equal, that they are endowed by their Creator with certain unalienable Rights").

Supporting Standard US8.1.3 Analyze how the American Revolution affected other nations, especially France.

Supporting Standard US8.1.4 Describe the nation's blend of civic republicanism, classical liberal principles, and English parliamentary traditions.

▼ Windmills

Main Standard US8.2 **Students analyze the political principles underlying the U.S. Constitution and compare the enumerated and implied powers of the federal government.**

Supporting Standard US8.2.1 Discuss the significance of the Magna Carta, the English Bill of Rights, and the Mayflower Compact.

Supporting Standard US8.2.2 Analyze the Articles of Confederation and the Constitution and the success of each in implementing the ideals of the Declaration of Independence.

Supporting Standard US8.2.3 Evaluate the major debates that occurred during the development of the Constitution and their ultimate resolutions in such areas as shared power among institutions, divided state-federal power, slavery, the rights of individuals and states (later addressed by the addition of the Bill of Rights), and the status of American Indian nations under the commerce clause.

Supporting Standard US8.2.4 Describe the political philosophy underpinning the Constitution as specified in the *Federalist Papers* (authored by James Madison, Alexander Hamilton, and John Jay) and the role of such leaders as Madison, George Washington, Roger Sherman, Gouverneur Morris, and James Wilson in the writing and ratification of the Constitution.

Supporting Standard US8.2.5 Understand the significance of Jefferson's Statute for Religious Freedom as a forerunner of the First Amendment and the origins, purpose, and differing views of the founding fathers on the issue of separation of church and state.

Supporting Standard US8.2.6 Enumerate the powers of government set forth in the Constitution and the fundamental liberties ensured by the Bill of Rights.

Supporting Standard US8.2.7 Describe the principles of federalism, dual sovereignty, separation of powers, checks and balances, the nature and purpose of majority rule, and the ways in which the American idea of constitutionalism preserves individual rights.

Main Standard US8.3 **Students understand the foundation of the American political system and the ways in which citizens participate in it.**

Supporting Standard US8.3.1 Analyze the principles and concepts codified in state constitutions between 1777 and 1781 that created the context out of which American political institutions and ideas developed.

Supporting Standard US8.3.2 Explain how the ordinances of 1785 and 1787 privatized national resources and transferred federally owned lands into private holdings, townships, and states.

Supporting Standard US8.3.3 Enumerate the advantages of a common market among the states as foreseen in and protected by the Constitution's clauses on interstate commerce, common coinage, and full-faith and credit.

Supporting Standard US8.3.4 Understand how the conflicts between Thomas Jefferson and Alexander Hamilton resulted in the emergence of two political parties (e.g., view of foreign policy, Alien and Sedition Acts, economic policy, National Bank, funding and assumption of the revolutionary debt).

Supporting Standard US8.3.5 Know the significance of the domestic resistance movements and ways in which the central government responded to such movements (e.g., Shays' Rebellion, the Whiskey Rebellion).

Supporting Standard US8.3.6 Describe the basic law-making process and how the Constitution provides numerous opportunities for citizens to participate in the political process and to monitor and influence government (e.g., function of elections, political parties, interest groups).

Supporting Standard US8.3.7 Understand the functions and responsibilities of a free press.

Main Standard US8.4 **Students analyze the aspirations and ideals of the people of the new nation.**

Supporting Standard US8.4.1 Describe the country's physical landscapes, political divisions, and territorial expansion during the terms of the first four presidents.

Supporting Standard US8.4.2 Explain the policy significance of famous speeches (e.g., Washington's Farewell Address, Jefferson's 1801 Inaugural Address, John Q. Adams' Fourth of July 1821 Address).

Supporting Standard US8.4.3 Analyze the rise of capitalism and the economic problems and conflicts that accompanied it (e.g., Jackson's opposition to the National Bank; early decisions of the U.S. Supreme Court that reinforced the sanctity of contracts and a capitalist economic system of the law).

Supporting Standard US8.4.4 Discuss daily life, including traditions in art, music and literature, of early national American (e.g., through writings by Washington Irving, James Fenimore Cooper).

Main Standard US8.5 **Students analyze U.S. foreign policy in the early Republic.**

Supporting Standard US8.5.1 Understand the political and economic causes and consequences of the War of 1812 and know the major battles, leaders and events that led to a final peace.

Supporting Standard US8.5.2 Know the changing boundaries of the United States and describe the relationships the country had with its neighbors (current Mexico and Canada) and Europe, including the influence of the Monroe Doctrine, and how those relationships influenced westward expansion and the Mexican-American War.

Supporting Standard US8.5.3 Outline the major treaties with American Indian nations during the administrations of the first four presidents and the varying outcomes of those treaties.

Main Standard US8.6 **Students analyze the divergent paths of the American people from 1800 to the mid-1800s and the challenges they faced, with emphasis on the Northeast.**

Supporting Standard US8.6.1 Discuss the influence of industrialization and technological developments on the region, including human modification of the landscape and how physical geography shaped human actions (e.g., growth of cities, deforestation, farming, mineral extraction).

Supporting Standard US8.6.2 Outline the physical obstacles to and the economic and political factors involved in building a network of roads, canals, and railroads (e.g., Henry Clay's American System).

Supporting Standard US8.6.3 List the reasons for the wave of immigration from Northern Europe to the United States and describe the growth in the number, size, and spatial arrangements of cities (e.g., Irish immigrants and the Great Irish Famine).

Supporting Standard US8.6.4 Study the lives of black Americans who gained freedom in the North and founded schools and churches to advance their rights and communities.

Supporting Standard US8.6.5 Trace the development of the American education system from its earliest roots, including the roles of religious and private schools and Horace Mann's campaign for free public education and its assimilating role in American culture.

Supporting Standard US8.6.6 Examine the women's suffrage movement (e.g., biographies, writings, and speeches of Elizabeth Cady Stanton, Margaret Fuller, Lucretia Mott, Susan B. Anthony).

Supporting Standard US8.6.7 Identify common themes in American art as well as transcendentalism and individualism (e.g., writings about and by Ralph Waldo Emerson, Henry David Thoreau, Herman Melville, Louisa May Alcott, Nathaniel Hawthorne, Henry Wadsworth Longfellow).

▼ **White sand dunes, Eureka Valley Dunes, CA**

Main Standard US8.7 Students analyze the divergent paths of the American people in the South from 1800 to the mid-1800s and the challenges they faced.

Supporting Standard US8.7.1 Describe the development of the agrarian economy in the South, identify the locations of the cotton-producing states, and discuss the significance of cotton and the cotton gin.

Supporting Standard US8.7.2 Trace the origins and development of slavery; its effects on black Americans and on the region's political, social, religious, economic, and cultural development; and identify the strategies that were tried to both overturn and preserve it (e.g., through the writings and historical documents on Nat Turner, Denmark Vesey).

Supporting Standard US8.7.3 Examine the characteristics of white southern society and how the physical environment influenced events and conditions prior to the Civil War.

Supporting Standard US8.7.4 Compare the lives of and opportunities for free blacks in the North with those of free blacks in the South.

▼ Golden Gate Bridge

Main Standard US8.8 **Students analyze the divergent paths of the American people in the West from 1800 to the mid-1800s and the challenges they faced.**

Supporting Standard US8.8.1 Discuss the election of Andrew Jackson as president in 1828, the importance of Jacksonian democracy, and his actions as president (e.g., the spoils system, veto of the National Bank, policy of Indian removal, opposition to the Supreme Court).

Supporting Standard US8.8.2 Describe the purpose, challenges, and economic incentives associated with westward expansion, including the concept of Manifest Destiny (e.g., the Lewis and Clark expedition, accounts of the removal of Indians, the Cherokees' "Trail of Tears," settlement of the Great Plains) and the territorial acquisitions that spanned numerous decades.

Supporting Standard US8.8.3 Describe the role of pioneer women and the new status that western women achieved (e.g., Laura Ingalls Wilder, Annie Bidwell; slave women gaining freedom in the West; Wyoming granting suffrage to women in 1869).

Supporting Standard US8.8.4 Examine the importance of the great rivers and the struggle over water rights.

Supporting Standard US8.8.5 Discuss Mexican settlements and their locations, cultural traditions, attitudes toward slavery, land-grant system, and economies.

Supporting Standard US8.8.6 Describe the Texas War for Independence and the Mexican-American War, including territorial settlements, the aftermath of the wars, and the effects the wars had on the lives of Americans including Mexican Americans today.

Main Standard US8.9 **Students analyze the early and steady attempts to abolish slavery and to realize the ideals of the Declaration of Independence.**

Supporting Standard US8.9.1 Describe the leaders of the movement (e.g., John Quincy Adams and his proposed constitutional amendment, John Brown and the armed resistance, Harriet Tubman and the Underground Railroad, Benjamin Franklin, Theodore Weld, William Lloyd Garrison, Frederick Douglass).

Supporting Standard US8.9.2 Discuss the abolition of slavery in early state constitutions.

Supporting Standard US8.9.3 Describe the significance of the Northwest Ordinance in education and in the banning of slavery in new states north of the Ohio River.

Supporting Standard US8.9.4 Discuss the importance of the slavery issue as raised by the annexation of Texas and California's admission to the union as a free state under the Compromise of 1850.

Supporting Standard US8.9.5 Analyze the significance of the States' Rights Doctrine, the Missouri Compromise (1820), the Wilmot Proviso (1846), the Compromise of 1850, Henry Clay's role in the Missouri Compromise and the Compromise of 1850, the Kansas-Nebraska Act (1854), the *Dred Scott* v. *Sandford* decision (1857), and the Lincoln-Douglas debates (1858).

Supporting Standard US8.9.6 Describe the lives of free blacks and the laws that limited their freedom and economic opportunities.

Main Standard US8.10 Students analyze the multiple causes, key events, and complex consequences of the Civil War.

Supporting Standard US8.10.1 Compare the conflicting interpretations of state and federal authority as emphasized in the speeches and writings of statesmen such as Daniel Webster and John C. Calhoun.

Supporting Standard US8.10.2 Trace the boundaries constituting the North and the South, the geographical differences between the two regions, and the differences between agrarians and industrialists.

Supporting Standard US8.10.3 Identify the constitutional issues posed by the doctrine of nullification and secession and the earliest origins of that doctrine.

Supporting Standard US8.10.4 Discuss Abraham Lincoln's presidency and his significant writings and speeches and their relationship to the Declaration of Independence, such as his "House Divided" speech (1858), Gettysburg Address (1863), Emancipation Proclamation (1863), and inaugural addresses (1861 and 1865).

Supporting Standard US8.10.5 Study the views and lives of leaders (e.g., Ulysses S. Grant, Jefferson Davis, Robert E. Lee) and soldiers on both sides of the war, including those of black soldiers and regiments.

Supporting Standard US8.10.6 Describe critical developments and events in the war, including the major battles, geographical advantages and obstacles, technological advances, and General Lee's surrender at Appomattox.

Supporting Standard US8.10.7 Explain how the war affected combatants, civilians, the physical environment and future warfare.

Main Standard US8.11 Students analyze the character and lasting consequences of Reconstruction.

Supporting Standard US8.11.1 List the original aims of Reconstruction and describe its effects on the political and social structures of different regions.

Supporting Standard US8.11.2 Identify the push-pull factors in the movement of former slaves to the cities in the North and to the West and their differing experiences in those regions (e.g. the experiences of the Buffalo Soldiers).

Supporting Standard US8.11.3 Understand the effects of the Freedmen's Bureau and the restrictions placed on the rights and opportunities of freedmen, including racial segregation and "Jim Crow" laws.

Supporting Standard US8.11.4 Trace the rise of the Ku Klux Klan and describe the Klan's effects.

Supporting Standard US8.11.5 Understand the Thirteenth, Fourteenth, and Fifteenth Amendments to the Constitution and analyze their connection to Reconstruction.

Main Standard US8.12 Students analyze the transformation of the American economy and the changing social and political conditions in the United States in response to the Industrial Revolution.

Supporting Standard US8.12.1 Trace patterns of agricultural and industrial development as they relate to climate, use of natural resources, markets, and trade and locate such development on a map.

Supporting Standard US8.12.2 Identify the reasons for the development of federal Indian policy and the wars with American Indians and their relationship to agricultural development and industrialization.

Supporting Standard US8.12.3 Explain how states and the federal government encouraged business expansion through tariffs, banking, land grants, and subsidies.

Supporting Standard US8.12.4 Discuss entrepreneurs, industrialists, and bankers in politics, commerce, and industry (e.g., Andrew Carnegie, John D. Rockefeller, Leland Stanford).

Supporting Standard US8.12.5 Examine the location and effects of urbanization, renewed immigration, and industrialization (e.g., the effects on social fabric of cities, wealth and economic opportunity, the conservation movement).

Supporting Standard US8.12.6 Discuss child labor, working conditions, and laissez-faire policies toward big business and examine the labor movement, including its leaders (e.g., Samuel Gompers), its demand for collective bargaining, and its strikes and protests over labor conditions.

Supporting Standard US8.12.7 Identify the sources of large-scale immigration and the contributions of immigrants to the building of cities and the economy; explain the ways in which new social and economic patterns encouraged assimilation of newcomers into the mainstream amidst growing cultural diversity; and discuss the new wave of nativism.

Supporting Standard US8.12.8 Identify the characteristics and impact of Grangerism and Populism.

Supporting Standard US8.12.9 Name the significant inventors and their inventions and identify how they improved the quality of life (e.g., Thomas Edison, Alexander Graham Bell, Orville and Wilbur Wright).

▼ A street in San Francisco

English–Language Arts Standards

Reading

English–Language Arts Standards are addressed throughout this book in reading and writing skills and activities. Items that relate to an English–Language Arts Standard will be represented like this: CA 8RW1.0 .

8RW1.0 Word Analysis, Fluency, and Systematic Vocabulary Development

Vocabulary and Concept Development

8RW1.1 Analyze idioms, analogies, metaphors, and similes to infer the literal and figurative meanings of phrases.

8RW1.2 Understand the most important points in the history of English language and use common word origins to determine the historical influences on English word meanings.

8RW1.3 Use word meanings within the appropriate context and show ability to verify those meanings by definition, restatement, example, comparison, or contrast.

8RC2.0 Reading Comprehension (Focus on Informational Materials)

Structural Features of Informational Materials

8RC2.1 Compare and contrast the features and elements of consumer materials to gain meaning from documents (e.g., warranties, contracts, product information, instruction manuals).

8RC2.2 Analyze text that uses proposition and support patterns.

Comprehension and Analysis of Grade-Level-Appropriate Text

8RC2.3 Find similarities and differences between texts in the treatment, scope, or organization of ideas.

8RC2.4 Compare the original text to a summary to determine whether the summary accurately captures the main ideas, includes critical details, and conveys the underlying meaning.

8RC2.5 Understand and explain the use of a complex mechanical device by following technical directions.

8RC2.6 Use information from a variety of consumer, workplace, and public documents to explain a situation or decision and to solve a problem.

Expository Critique

8RC2.7 Evaluate the unity, coherence, logic, internal consistency, and structural patterns of text.

California farmland

8RL3.0 Literary Response and Analysis

Structural Features of Literature

8RL3.1 Determine and articulate the relationship between the purposes and characteristics of different forms of poetry (e.g., ballad, lyric, couplet, epic, elegy, ode, sonnet).

Narrative Analysis of Grade-Level-Appropriate Text

8RL3.2 Evaluate the structural elements of the plot (e.g., subplots, parallel episodes, climax), the plot's development, and the way in which conflicts are (or are not) addressed and resolved.

8RL3.3 Compare and contrast motivations and reactions of literary characters from different historical eras confronting similar situations or conflicts.

8RL3.4 Analyze the relevance of the setting (e.g., place, time, customs) to the mood, tone, and meaning of the text.

8RL3.5 Identify and analyze recurring themes (e.g., good versus evil) across traditional and contemporary works.

8RL3.6 Identify significant literary devices (e.g., metaphor, symbolism, dialect, irony) that define a writer's style and use those elements to interpret the work.

Literary Criticism

8RL3.7 Analyze a work of literature, showing how it reflects the heritage, traditions, attitudes, and beliefs of its author. (Biographical approach)

Writing

8WS1.0 Writing Strategies

Organization and Focus

8WS1.1 Create compositions that establish a controlling impression, have a coherent thesis, and end with a clear and well-supported conclusion.

8WS1.2 Establish coherence within and among paragraphs through effective transitions, parallel structures, and similar writing techniques.

8WS1.3 Support theses or conclusions with analogies, paraphrases, quotations, opinions from authorities, comparisons, and similar devices.

Research and Technology

8WS1.4 Plan and conduct multiple-step information searches by using computer networks and modems.

8WS1.5 Achieve an effective balance between researched information and original ideas.

Evaluation and Revision

8WS1.6 Revise writing for word choice; appropriate organization; consistent point of view; and transitions between paragraphs, passages, and ideas.

8WA2.0 Writing Applications (Genres and Their Characteristics)

8WA2.1 Write biographies, autobiographies, short stories, or narratives:

- **a.** Relate a clear, coherent incident, event, or situation by using well-chosen details.
- **b.** Reveal the significance of, or the writer's attitude about, the subject.
- **c.** Employ narrative and descriptive strategies (e.g., relevant dialogue, specific action, physical description, background description, comparison or contrast of characters).

8WA2.2 Write responses to literature:

- **a.** Exhibit careful reading and insight in their interpretations.
- **b.** Connect the student's own responses to the writer's techniques and to specific textual references.
- **c.** Draw supported inferences about the effects of a literary work on its audience.
- **d.** Support judgments through references to the text, other works, other authors, or to personal knowledge.

8WA2.3 Write research reports:

- **a.** Define a thesis.
- **b.** Record important ideas, concepts, and direct quotations from significant information sources and paraphrase and summarize all perspectives on the topic, as appropriate.
- **c.** Use a variety of primary and secondary sources and distinguish the nature and value of each.
- **d.** Organize and display information on charts, maps, and graphs.

8WA2.4 Write persuasive compositions:

- **a.** Include a well-defined thesis (i.e., one that makes a clear and knowledgeable judgment).
- **b.** Present detailed evidence, examples, and reasoning to support arguments, differentiating between facts and opinion.
- **c.** Provide details, reasons, and examples, arranging them effectively by anticipating and answering reader concerns and counter-arguments.

8WA2.5 Write documents related to career development, including simple business letters and job applications:

- **a.** Present information purposefully and succinctly and meet the needs of the intended audience.
- **b.** Follow the conventional format for the type of document (e.g., letter of inquiry, memorandum).

8WA2.6 Write technical documents:

- **a.** Identify the sequence of activities needed to design a system, operate a tool, or explain the bylaws of an organization.
- **b.** Include all the factors and variables that need to be considered.
- **c.** Use formatting techniques (e.g., headings, differing fonts) to aid comprehension.

California's Pacific Coast

Written and Oral English Language Conventions

8WC1.0 Written and Oral English Language Conventions

Sentence Structure

8WC1.1 Use correct and varied sentence types and sentence openings to present a lively and effective personal style.

8WC1.2 Identify and use parallelism, including similar grammatical forms, in all written discourse to present items in a series and items juxtaposed for emphasis.

8WC1.3 Use subordination, coordination, apposition, and other devices to indicate clearly the relationship between ideas.

Grammar

8WC1.4 Edit written manuscripts to ensure that correct grammar is used.

Punctuation and Capitalization

8WC1.5 Use correct punctuation and capitalization.

Spelling

8WC1.6 Use correct spelling conventions.

Listening and Speaking

8LS1.0 Listening and Speaking Strategies

Comprehension

8LS1.1 Analyze oral interpretations of literature, including language choice and delivery, and the effect of the interpretations on the listener.

8LS1.2 Paraphrase a speaker's purpose and point of view and ask relevant questions concerning the speaker's content, delivery, and purpose.

Organization and Delivery of Oral Communication

8LS1.3 Organize information to achieve particular purposes by matching the message, vocabulary, voice modulation, expression, and tone to the audience and purpose.

8LS1.4 Prepare a speech outline based upon a chosen pattern of organization, which generally includes an introduction; transitions, previews, and summaries; a logically developed body; and an effective conclusion.

8LS1.5 Use precise language, action verbs, sensory details, appropriate and colorful modifiers, and the active rather than the passive voice in ways that enliven oral presentations.

8LS1.6 Use appropriate grammar, word choice, enunciation, and pace during formal presentations.

8LS1.7 Use audience feedback (e.g., verbal and nonverbal cues):

a. Reconsider and modify the organizational structure or plan.

b. Rearrange words and sentences to clarify the meaning.

Analysis and Evaluation of Oral and Media Communications

8LS1.8 Evaluate the credibility of a speaker (e.g., hidden agendas, slanted or biased material).

8LS1.9 Interpret and evaluate the various ways in which visual image makers (e.g., graphic artists, illustrators, news photographers) communicate information and affect impressions and opinions.

8SA2.0 Speaking Applications (Genres and Their Characteristics)

8SA2.1 Deliver narrative presentations (e.g., biographical, autobiographical):

- **a.** Relate a clear, coherent incident, event, or situation by using well-chosen details.
- **b.** Reveal the significance of, and the subject's attitude about, the incident, event, or situation.
- **c.** Employ narrative and descriptive strategies (e.g., relevant dialogue, specific action, physical description, background description, comparison or contrast of characters).

8SA2.2 Deliver oral responses to literature:

- **a.** Interpret a reading and provide insight.
- **b.** Connect the students' own responses to the writer's techniques and to specific textual references.
- **c.** Draw supported inferences about the effects of a literary work on its audience.
- **d.** Support judgments through references to the text, other works, other authors, or personal knowledge.

8SA2.3 Deliver research presentations:

- **a.** Define a thesis.
- **b.** Record important ideas, concepts, and direct quotations from significant information sources and paraphrase and summarize all relevant perspectives on the topic, as appropriate.
- **c.** Use a variety of primary and secondary sources and distinguish the nature and value of each.
- **d.** Organize and record information on charts, maps, and graphs.

8SA2.4 Deliver persuasive presentations:

- **a.** Include a well-defined thesis (i.e., one that makes a clear and knowledgeable judgment).
- **b.** Differentiate fact from opinion and support arguments with detailed evidence, examples, and reasoning.
- **c.** Anticipate and answer listener concerns and counterarguments effectively through the inclusion and arrangement of details, reasons, examples, and other elements.
- **d.** Maintain a reasonable tone.

8SA2.5 Recite poems (of four to six stanzas), sections of speeches, or dramatic soliloquies, using voice modulation, tone, and gestures expressively to enhance the meaning.

▼ **California poppies, state flower**

Correlation to the California Standards

Historical and Social Sciences Analysis Skills	Student Edition Pages
Chronological and Spatial Thinking	
CS1. Students explain how major events are related to one another in time.	89, 97, 110, 111, 141, 157, 201, 233, 244, 300, 309, 317, 332, 345, 359, 367, 394, 401, 417, 451, 475, 487, 497, 534, 542, 547, 553, 559, 565, 603, 619, 628, 649, 692, 697, 700, 717, 723, 734, 783
CS2. Students construct various time lines of key events, people, and periods of the historical eras they are studying.	141, 157, 301, 317, 345, 394, 413, 457, 464, 465, 487, 497, 542, 559, 565, 613, 619, 649, 655, 692, 735
CS3. Students use a variety of maps and documents to identify physical and cultural features of neighborhoods, cities, states, and countries and to explain the historical migration of people, expansion and disintegration of empires, and the growth of economic systems.	110, 111, 131, 162, 212, 244, 289, 300, 332, 370, 416, 431, 440, 464, 497, 499, 516, 564, 583, 618, 654, 700, 734, 756, 788
Research, Evidence, and Point of View	
HR1. Students frame questions that can be answered by historical study and research.	213, 329, 351, 451, 465, 559, 639
HR2. Students distinguish fact from opinion in historical narratives and stories.	157, 159, 191, 284, 561, 729, 749
HR3. Students distinguish relevant from irrelevant information, essential from incidental information, and verifiable from unverifiable information in historical narratives and stories.	107, 124, 131, 133, 162, 185, 201, 207, 209, 297, 301, 309, 317, 333, 351, 387, 413, 416, 437, 461, 477, 497, 547, 564, 575, 613, 639, 653, 671, 749, 756, 763, 783, 788
HR4. Students assess the credibility of primary and secondary sources and draw sound conclusions about them.	162, 213, 300, 369, 371, 465, 723, 771
HR5. Students detect the different historical points of view on historical events and determine the context in which the historical statements were made (the questions asked, sources used, author's perspectives).	159, 161, 201, 209, 243, 244, 284, 297, 300, 370, 371, 441, 497, 516, 534, 596, 618, 654, 701, 747, 749
Historical Interpretation	
HI1. Students explain the central issues and problems from the past, placing people and events in a matrix of time and place.	97, 110, 124, 225, 241, 329, 332, 359, 367, 370, 407, 413, 426, 437, 440, 457, 464, 506, 515, 534, 542, 547, 553, 583, 596, 603, 634, 639, 649, 651, 679, 692, 697, 711, 729, 763
HI2. Students understand and distinguish cause, effect, sequence, and correlation in historical events, including the long- and short-term causal relations.	89, 107, 110, 111, 131, 141, 162, 212, 225, 233, 239, 241, 244, 245, 284, 289, 309, 311, 317, 333, 345, 359, 370, 387, 394, 401, 407, 417, 426, 431, 440, 461, 475, 487, 506, 516, 517, 542, 547, 553, 564, 575, 583, 596, 603, 613, 618, 628, 634, 649, 651, 654, 671, 679, 692, 697, 700, 711, 717, 723, 731, 734, 747, 756, 763, 788
HI3. Students explain the sources of historical continuity and how the combination of ideas and events explains the emergence of new patterns.	107, 111, 157, 163, 207, 211, 225, 245, 332, 437, 451, 457, 517, 628, 634, 711, 717, 747, 756, 771, 783, 788, 789

Historical Interpretation (cont.)	Student Edition Pages
HI4. Students recognize the role of chance, oversight, and error in history.	89, 506, 583
HI5. Students recognize that interpretations of history are subject to change as new information is uncovered.	475, 649, 729
HI6. Students interpret basic indicators of economic performance and conduct cost-benefit analyses of economic and political issues.	97, 141, 311, 387, 416, 417, 426, 431, 440, 575, 603, 619, 671, 679, 700, 701, 731, 771, 789

History–Social Science Content Standards for Grade 8	Student Edition Pages
WH7.11 Students analyze political and economic change in the sixteenth, seventeenth, and eighteenth centuries (the Age of Exploration, the Enlightenment, and the Age of Reason). *Local Options 1 & 2 from Appendix D of the History–Social Science Framework for California Public Schools give school districts the option of teaching some Grade 7 materials at the Grade 8 level.	76–77, 80, 90, 98
WH7.11.1 Know the great voyages of discovery, the locations of the routes, and the influence of cartography in the development of a new European worldview.	81–84, 85, 89, 108–109
WH7.11.2 Discuss the exchanges of plants, animals, technology, culture, and ideas among Europe, Africa, Asia, and the Americas in the fifteenth and sixteenth centuries and the major economic and social effects on each continent.	95–97
WH7.11.3 Examine the origins of modern capitalism; the influence of mercantilism and cottage industry; the elements and importance of a market economy in seventeenth-century Europe; the changing international trading and marketing patterns, including their locations on a world map; and the influence of explorers and map-makers.	91, 93–95
WH7.11.4 Explain how the main ideas of the Enlightenment can be traced back to such movements as the Renaissance, the Reformation, and the Scientific Revolution and to the Greeks, Romans, and Christianity.	92, 99–101
WH7.11.5 Describe how democratic thought and institutions were influenced by Enlightenment thinkers (e.g., John Locke, Charles-Louis Montesquieu, American founders).	102–03, 104–107
WH7.11.6 Discuss how the principles in the Magna Carta were embodied in such documents as the English Bill of Rights and the American Declaration of Independence.	104–107
US8.1 Students understand the major events preceding the founding of the nation and relate their significance to the development of American constitutional democracy.	116–118, 120–141, 149–151, 158–159
US8.1.1 Describe the relationship between the moral and political ideas of the Great Awakening and the development of revolutionary fervor.	128–129
US8.1.2 Analyze the philosophy of government expressed in the Declaration of Independence, with an emphasis on government as a means of securing individual rights (e.g., key phrases such as "all men are created equal, that they are endowed by their Creator with certain unalienable Rights").	152–157

History–Social Science Content Standards for Grade 8	Student Edition Pages
US8.1.3 Analyze how the American Revolution affected other nations, especially France.	153–157
US8.1.4 Describe the nation's blend of civic republicanism, classical liberal principles, and English parliamentary traditions.	119, 130–33, 135–36, 139–41
US8.2 Students analyze the political principles underlying the U.S. Constitution and compare the enumerated and implied powers of the federal government.	178, 193, 202, 226, 232
US8.2.1 Discuss the significance of the Magna Carta, the English Bill of Rights, and the Mayflower Compact.	132–133, 203
US8.2.2 Analyze the Articles of Confederation and the Constitution and the success of each in implementing the ideals of the Declaration of Independence.	175, 183–185, 194–196, 206–207, 219, 221–223
US8.2.3 Evaluate the major debates that occurred during the development of the Constitution and their ultimate resolutions in such areas as shared power among institutions, divided state-federal power, slavery, the rights of individuals and states (later addressed by the addition of the Bill of Rights), and the status of American Indian nations under the commerce clause.	197, 199–201, 204–05
US8.2.4 Describe the political philosophy underpinning the Constitution as specified in the *Federalist Papers* (authored by James Madison, Alexander Hamilton, and John Jay) and the role of such leaders as Madison, George Washington, Roger Sherman, Gouverneur Morris, and James Wilson in the writing and ratification of the Constitution.	198, 206–09, 220, 242–43
US8.2.5 Understand the significance of Jefferson's Statute of Religious Freedom as a forerunner of the First Amendment and the origins, purpose, and differing views of the founding fathers on the issue of separation of church and state.	235
US8.2.6 Enumerate the powers of government set forth in the Constitution and the fundamental liberties ensured by the Bill of Rights.	224–225, 227–231, 233, 235–236, 240–241
US8.2.7 Describe the principles of federalism, dual sovereignty, separation of powers, checks and balances, the nature and purpose of majority rule, and the ways in which the American idea of constitutionalism preserves individual rights.	221–223, 224–225, 235–236
US8.3 Students understand the foundation of the American political system and the ways in which citizens participate in it.	178, 193, 202, 210–211, 218, 226, 234, 278, 285, 290
US8.3.1 Analyze the principles and concepts codified in state constitutions between 1777 and 1781 that created the context out of which American political institutions and ideas developed.	179
US8.3.2 Explain how the ordinances of 1785 and 1787 privatized national resources and transferred federally owned lands into private holdings, townships, and states.	181–183
US8.3.3 Enumerate the advantages of a common market among the states as foreseen in and protected by the Constitution's clauses on interstate commerce, common coinage, and full-faith and credit.	219, 311

History–Social Science Content Standards for Grade 8	Student Edition Pages
US8.3.4 Understand how the conflicts between Thomas Jefferson and Alexander Hamilton resulted in the emergence of two political parties (e.g., view of foreign policy, Alien and Sedition Acts, economic policy, National Bank, funding and assumption of the revolutionary debt).	281, 282, 283, 284, 291, 292, 293, 295, 296, 297
US8.3.5 Know the significance of domestic resistance movements and ways in which the central government responded to such movements (e.g., Shays' Rebellion, the Whiskey Rebellion).	194–196, 286
US8.3.6 Describe the basic law-making process and how the Constitution provides numerous opportunities for citizens to participate in the political process and to monitor and influence government (e.g., function of elections, political parties, interest groups).	236–239
US8.3.7 Understand the functions and responsibilities of a free press.	240–241
US8.4 Students analyze the aspirations and ideals of the people of the new nation.	278, 279, 280, 285, 290, 294, 298, 299, 306, 312, 320, 330, 331
US8.4.1 Describe the country's physical landscapes, political divisions, and territorial expansion during the terms of the first four presidents.	287, 293, 295, 296, 297, 308–309, 313, 314, 315, 316, 317, 318, 319, 328, 329
US8.4.2 Explain the policy significance of famous speeches (e.g., Washington's Farewell Address, Jefferson's 1801 Inaugural Address, John Q. Adams's Fourth of July 1821 Address).	288, 289, 307, 330, 331
US8.4.3 Analyze the rise of capitalism and the economic problems and conflicts that accompanied it (e.g., Jackson's opposition to the National Bank; early decisions of the U.S. Supreme Court that reinforced the sanctity of contracts and a capitalist economic system of the law).	310, 311, 459–460
US8.4.4 Discuss daily life, including traditions in art, music, and literature, of early national America (e.g., through writings by Washington Irving, James Fenimore Cooper).	321, 322, 323, 324, 325, 326, 327
US8.5 Students analyze U.S. foreign policy in the early Republic.	338, 339, 340, 353, 357, 362, 368–369
US8.5.1 Understand the political and economic causes and consequences of the War of 1812 and know the major battles, leaders, and events that led to a final peace.	341, 342, 343, 344, 345, 354, 355, 356, 358, 359, 363, 364, 365
US8.5.2 Know the changing boundaries of the United States and describe the relationships the country had with its neighbors (current Mexico and Canada) and Europe, including the influence of the Monroe Doctrine, and how those relationships influenced westward expansion and the Mexican-American War.	363, 364, 365, 366, 367
US8.5.3 Outline the major treaties with American Indian nations during the administrations of the first four presidents and the varying outcomes of those treaties.	341, 342, 343
US8.6 Students analyze the divergent paths of the American people from 1800 to the mid-1800s and the challenges they faced, with emphasis on the Northeast.	382, 388, 395, 402, 408, 414–415
US8.6.1 Discuss the influences of industrialization and technological developments on the region, including human modification of the landscape and how physical geography shaped human actions (e.g., growth of cities, deforestation, farming, mineral extraction).	383, 384, 385, 386, 387, 396, 397, 502, 668

History–Social Science Content Standards for Grade 8	Student Edition Pages
US8.6.2 Outline the physical obstacles to and the economic and political factors involved in building a network of roads, canals, and railroads (e.g., Henry Clay's American System).	389, 390, 391, 392, 393, 394
US8.6.3 List the reasons for the wave of immigration from Northern Europe to the United States and describe the growth in the number, size, and spatial arrangements of cities (e.g., Irish immigrants and the Great Irish Famine).	398, 399, 400, 401
US8.6.4 Study the lives of black Americans who gained freedom in the North and founded schools and churches to advance their rights and communities.	196, 397
US8.6.5 Trace the development of the American education system from its earliest roots, including the roles of religious and private schools and Horace Mann's campaign for free public education and its assimilating role in American culture.	403, 405
US8.6.6 Examine the women's suffrage movement (e.g., biographies, writings, and speeches of Elizabeth Cady Stanton, Margaret Fuller, Lucretia Mott, Susan B. Anthony).	409, 410, 411, 412, 413
US8.6.7 Identify common themes in American art as well as transcendentalism and individualism (e.g., writings about and by Ralph Waldo Emerson, Henry David Thoreau, Herman Melville, Louisa May Alcott, Nathaniel Hawthorne, Henry Wadsworth Longfellow).	404, 406, 407
US8.7 Students analyze the divergent paths of the American people in the South from 1800 to the mid-1800s and the challenges they faced.	422, 427, 432
US8.7.1 Describe the development of the agrarian economy in the South, identify the locations of the cotton-producing states, and discuss the significance of cotton and the cotton gin.	423, 424, 425, 426
US8.7.2 Trace the origins and development of slavery; its effects on black Americans and on the region's political, social, religious, economic, and cultural development; and identify the strategies that were tried to both overturn and preserve it (e.g., through the writings and historical documents on Nat Turner, Denmark Vesey).	433, 434, 435, 437
US8.7.3 Examine the characteristics of white Southern society and how the physical environment influenced events and conditions prior to the Civil War.	428, 429, 430, 431
US8.7.4 Compare the lives of and opportunities for free blacks in the North with those of free blacks in the South.	430, 431
US8.8 Students analyze the divergent paths of the American people in the West from 1800 to the mid-1800s and the challenges they faced.	446, 452, 458, 470, 480, 490, 500, 514–515
US8.8.1 Discuss the election of Andrew Jackson as president in 1828, the importance of Jacksonian democracy, and his actions as president (e.g., the spoils system, veto of the National Bank, policy of Indian removal, opposition to the Supreme Court).	447–451, 453–457, 459, 460–463
US8.8.2 Describe the purpose, challenges, and economic incentives associated with westward expansion, including the concept of Manifest Destiny (e.g., the Lewis and Clark expedition, accounts of the removal of Indians, the Cherokees' "Trail of Tears," settlement of the Great Plains) and the territorial acquisitions that spanned numerous decades.	453–457, 471–477, 501, 503–506

History–Social Science Content Standards for Grade 8	Student Edition Pages
US8.8.3 Describe the role of pioneer women and the new status that western women achieved (e.g., Laura Ingalls Wilder, Annie Bidwell; slave women gaining freedom in the West; Wyoming granting suffrage to women in 1869).	412–413, 473–474, 493, 502, 551, 668, 676, 678, 770
US8.8.4 Examine the importance of the great rivers and the struggle over water rights.	488–489
US8.8.5 Discuss Mexican settlements and their locations, cultural traditions, attitudes toward slavery, land-grant system, and economies.	481–482, 492–494
US8.8.6 Describe the Texas War for Independence and the Mexican-American War, including territorial settlements, the aftermath of the wars, and the effects the wars had on the lives of Americans, including Mexican Americans today.	481–487, 491–497
US8.9 Students analyze the early and steady attempts to abolish slavery and to realize the ideals of the Declaration of Independence.	178, 528–529, 535, 543, 545, 548, 562
US8.9.1 Describe the leaders of the movement (e.g., John Quincy Adams and his proposed constitutional amendment, John Brown and the armed resistance, Harriet Tubman and the Underground Railroad, Benjamin Franklin, Theodore Weld, William Lloyd Garrison, Frederick Douglass).	436, 530–534, 546–547
US8.9.2 Discuss the abolition of slavery in early state constitutions.	195–196
US8.9.3 Describe the significance of the Northwest Ordinance in education and in the banning of slavery in new states north of the Ohio River.	180, 181, 182, 321
US8.9.4 Discuss the importance of the slavery issue as raised by the annexation of Texas and California's admission to the union as a free state under the Compromise of 1850.	539–542
US8.9.5 Analyze the significance of the States' Rights Doctrine, the Missouri Compromise (1820), the Wilmot Proviso (1846), the Compromise of 1850, Henry Clay's role in the Missouri Compromise and the Compromise of 1850, the Kansas-Nebraska Act (1854), the *Dred Scott* v. *Sandford* decision (1857), and the Lincoln-Douglas debates (1858).	536, 539–542, 544, 549–550, 553
US8.9.6 Describe the lives of free blacks and the laws that limited their freedom and economic opportunities.	397, 430, 551
US8.10 Students analyze the multiple causes, key events, and complex consequences of the Civil War.	535, 548, 554, 570, 576, 591, 597, 604
US8.10.1 Compare the conflicting interpretations of state and federal authority as emphasized in the speeches and writings of statesmen such as Daniel Webster and John C. Calhoun.	537–538
US8.10.2 Trace the boundaries constituting the North and the South, the geographical differences between the two regions, and the differences between agrarians and industrialists.	571–573
US8.10.3 Identify the constitutional issues posed by the doctrine of nullification and secession and the earliest origins of that doctrine.	537–538, 556–557

History–Social Science Content Standards for Grade 8	Student Edition Pages
US8.10.4 Discuss Abraham Lincoln's presidency and his significant writings and speeches and their relationship to the Declaration of Independence, such as his "House Divided" speech (1858), Gettysburg Address (1863), Emancipation Proclamation (1863), and inaugural addresses (1861 and 1865).	552, 555–557, 592–594, 605–606
US8.10.5 Study the views and lives of leaders (e.g., Ulysses S. Grant, Jefferson Davis, Robert E. Lee) and soldiers on both sides of the war, including those of black soldiers and regiments.	560–561, 574–575, 580–583, 595–596, 598, 607–609, 611
US8.10.6 Describe critical developments and events in the war, including the major battles, geographical advantages and obstacles, technological advances, and General Lee's surrender at Appomattox.	558–559, 577–583, 595–596, 605–610, 612–615
US8.10.7 Explain how the war affected combatants, civilians, the physical environment, and future warfare.	577–578, 599–603, 610, 612–613, 616–617
US8.11 Students analyze the character and lasting consequences of Reconstruction.	624, 627, 629, 635, 637, 652–653
US8.11.1 List the original aims of Reconstruction and describe its effects on the political and social structures of different regions.	625–626, 631–634, 638–640, 645–646
US8.11.2 Identify the push-pull factors in the movement of former slaves to the cities in the North and to the West and their differing experiences in those regions (e.g. the experiences of the Buffalo Soldiers).	641, 676–677, 751
US8.11.3 Understand the effects of the Freedmen's Bureau and the restrictions placed on the rights and opportunities of freedmen, including racial segregation and "Jim Crow" laws.	625–626, 630–631, 636, 641, 644, 647–649
US8.11.4 Trace the rise of the Ku Klux Klan and describe the Klan's effects.	638, 641–644
US8.11.5 Understand the Thirteenth, Fourteenth, and Fifteenth Amendments to the Constitution and analyze their connection to Reconstruction.	626, 628, 630–631, 634, 647–651
US8.12 Students analyze the transformation of the American economy and the changing social and political conditions in the United States in response to the Industrial Revolution.	666, 672, 677, 685, 693, 706, 712, 718, 724, 732–733
US8.12.1 Trace patterns of agricultural and industrial development as they relate to climate, use of natural resources, markets, and trade and locate such development on a map.	667–671, 673–676, 678–680, 707, 709–711, 716–717, 719–723
US8.12.2 Identify the reasons for the development of federal Indian policy and the wars with American Indians and their relationship to agricultural development and industrialization.	686–692
US8.12.3 Explain how states and the federal government encouraged business expansion through tariffs, banking, land grants, and subsidies.	669–671
US8.12.4 Discuss entrepreneurs, industrialists, and bankers in politics, commerce, and industry (e.g., Andrew Carnegie, John D. Rockefeller, Leland Stanford).	707–708, 719–723
US8.12.5 Examine the location and effects of urbanization, renewed immigration, and industrialization (e.g., the effects on social fabric of cities, wealth and economic opportunity, the conservation movement).	741–747, 751–756, 771–773

History–Social Science Content Standards for Grade 8	Student Edition Pages
US8.12.6 Discuss child labor, working conditions, and laissez-faire policies toward big business and examine the labor movement, including its leaders (e.g., Samuel Gompers), its demand for collective bargaining, and its strikes and protests over labor conditions.	725–731
US8.12.7 Identify the new sources of large-scale immigration and the contributions of immigrants to the building of cities and the economy; explain the ways in which new social and economic patterns encouraged assimilation of newcomers into the mainstream amidst growing cultural diversity; and discuss the new wave of nativism.	741–749, 758–763
US8.12.8 Identify the characteristics and impact of Grangerism and Populism.	694–697
US8.12.9 Name the significant inventors and their inventions and identify how they improved the quality of life (e.g., Thomas Edison, Alexander Graham Bell, Orville and Wilbur Wright).	709–711, 713–715

English–Language Arts Content Standards for Grade 8	Student Edition Pages
8RW1.0 Word Analysis, Fluency, and Systematic Vocabulary Development	191, 475, 517, 729
8RW1.1	351, 589, 683
8RW1.3	512, 655
8RC2.0 Reading Comprehension (Focus on Informational Materials)	124, 163, 185, 213, 233, 239, 245, 329, 345, 371, 415, 426, 441, 534, 565, 575, 619, 628, 655, 701, 789
8RC2.3	477, 733
8RC2.4	89, 124, 239
8RL3.0 Literary Response and Analysis	
8RL3.2	512
8RL3.3	351, 653
8RL3.4	191
8RL3.6	147, 683
8WS1.0 Writing Strategies	159, 245, 463, 465, 655
8WS1.1	111, 163, 211, 213, 225, 301, 333, 439, 441, 451, 517, 565, 619, 655, 701, 735, 783, 789
8WS1.4	465, 565
8WA2.0 Writing Applications (Genres and Their Characteristics)	89
8WA2.1	97, 131, 161, 299, 333, 359, 367, 371, 394, 401, 407, 417, 437, 443, 506, 515, 542, 553, 596, 603, 613, 617, 639, 671, 683, 692, 699, 701, 723, 735

English–Language Arts Content Standards for Grade 8	Student Edition Pages
8WA2.2	111, 147, 512, 589, 619, 735
8WA2.3	111, 317, 441, 559, 589, 671, 701, 735, 756, 771
8WA2.4	107, 124, 163, 185, 207, 243, 245, 297, 301, 333, 369, 371, 387, 431, 457, 465, 517, 547, 563, 619, 697, 701, 711, 763, 771
8WA2.5	233, 284, 461, 603
8WA2.6	331
8WC1.0 Written and Oral English Language Conventions	
8WC1.1	297
8LS1.0 Listening and Speaking Strategies	333
8LS1.3	201, 289, 655
8LS1.4	245
8LS1.9	747, 789

At-Home Standards Review

To Students and Their Families,

Welcome to eighth-grade American history. You will begin your journey with early modern European history and its impact on the Western Hemisphere. Then you will continue with the founding of the United States and its history until 1914.

Take a few moments each day to review what you learned in sixth and seventh grades about world history. By reviewing what you already know, you will gain a better understanding of what you are about to learn. A sample review question is provided for each day of the school week until you have reviewed all the standards for sixth and seventh grades. Try to answer one question each day. **If you want to look back at what you learned in sixth and seventh grade, visit the Online California Standards Review and Practice at ca.hss.glencoe.com.**

WEEK 1

Content Standard WH6.1 Students describe what is known through archaeological studies of the early physical and cultural development of humankind from the Paleolithic era to the agricultural revolution.

Directions: *Select the best answer for each of the following questions.*

MONDAY WH6.1.1

1 The Paleolithic people were able to survive because they learned how to use

A rocks.
B fire.
C water.
D caves.

TUESDAY WH6.1.1

2 One of the most important technologies used by the Paleolithic people was

A tools.
B language.
C art.
D religion.

WEDNESDAY WH6.1.2

3 What are two well-known Neolithic communities?

A Europe and China
B Mexico and Egypt
C Jericho and Çatal Hüyük
D Babylon and Uruk

THURSDAY WH6.1.3

4 What revolutionary change took place during the Neolithic Age?

A building simple shelters
B hunting
C farming
D toolmaking

FRIDAY

5 Because of specialization during the Neolithic Age, people could

A hunt.
B farm.
C set up villages.
D have clothes made of cloth.

Answers are on page CA43.

WEEK 2

Content Standard WH6.2 Students analyze the geographic, political, economic, religious, and social structures of the early civilizations of Mesopotamia, Egypt, and Kush.

Directions: *Select the best answer for each of the following questions.*

MONDAY WH6.2.1

1 Mesopotamia, the cradle of civilization, lay between the

A Nile River and Red Sea.
B Rhine and Rhone rivers.
C Tigris and Euphrates rivers.
D Nile and Niger rivers.

TUESDAY WH6.2.2

2 Using artificial means of bringing water to crops is called

A adulation.
B irrigation.
C initiation.
D inflation.

WEDNESDAY WH6.2.6

3 What did Egyptians trade for in the eastern Mediterranean?

A wheat
B paper
C tools
D wood

THURSDAY WH6.2.7

4 This ruler avoided military conquests and expanded Egypt's economy.

A Hatshepsut
B Nefertiti
C Thutmose III
D Ramses II

FRIDAY WH6.2.8 Read the passage below and answer the question.

We [the Kushite officials] have come to you, O Amon-Re that you might give to us a [new] lord . . . That beneficent office [helpful task] is in your hands—may you give it to your son whom you love!

—*Anonymous*, "The Selection of Aspalta as King of Kush," c. 600 B.C.

5 Both Kushites and Egyptians believed that their rulers were

A ordinary people.
B related to the gods.
C dependent on voters.
D open to criticism.

Answers are on page CA43.

WEEK 3

Content Standard WH6.3 Students analyze the geographic, political, economic, religious, and social structures of the Ancient Hebrews.

Directions: *Select the best answer for each of the following questions.*

MONDAY WH6.3.1

1 Judaism is based on monotheism, or the belief in

A one natural law.
B one God.
C one true faith.
D many gods.

TUESDAY WH6.3.2

2 Which Israelite code of laws shaped the moral laws of many peoples?

A the Code of Hammurabi
B the Sermon on the Mount
C the Ten Commandments
D the Twelve Tables

WEDNESDAY WH6.3.3

3 The Israelites believed they were descended from this man.

A Jacob
B Moses
C Abraham
D Joshua

THURSDAY WH6.3.4

4 The Exodus is the name given to

A the exile of the Jews in Babylon.
B the Israelites' escape from slavery in Egypt.
C Abraham's journey from Mesopotamia to Canaan.
D David's escape from King Saul's soldiers.

FRIDAY WH6.3.5

Read the passage below and answer the question.

One is permitted to remove debris on the Sabbath in order to save a life or to act for the benefit of the community; and we may assemble in the synagogue on the Sabbath to conduct public business.

—*The Talmud for Today,* Rabbi Alexander Feinsilver, trans. and ed.

5 What feature of Jewish life does the Talmud show helped Jews to survive dispersal and persecution?

A religious rituals
B harvest festivals
C a class of priests
D religious laws

Answers are on page CA43.

WEEK 4

Content Standard WH6.4 Students analyze the geographic, political, economic, religious, and social structures of the early civilization of Ancient Greece.

Directions: *Select the best answer for each of the following questions.*

MONDAY WH6.4.4

1 Through mythology, the Greek people expressed their

- **A** religious beliefs.
- **B** love of poetry.
- **C** love of sport.
- **D** political beliefs.

TUESDAY WH6.4.5

2 The Persian king Darius's power depended on his

- **A** nobles.
- **B** tax collectors.
- **C** army.
- **D** chief of police.

WEDNESDAY WH6.4.6

3 The people of Athens prized education, while the people of Sparta valued

- **A** the arts.
- **B** military skills.
- **C** science.
- **D** trade with foreigners.

THURSDAY WH6.4.7

4 A legacy of Alexander the Great was the

- **A** spread of Greek culture to southwest Asia.
- **B** spread of Christianity.
- **C** conquest of Italy and Spain.
- **D** rebuilding of Sparta.

FRIDAY WH6.4.2

Read the passage below and answer the question.

Our constitution is called a democracy because power is in the hands not of a minority but of the whole people. . . . [W]hen it is a question of putting one person before another in positions of public responsibility, what counts is not membership of a particular class, but the actual ability which the man possesses.

—Pericles as recorded by Thucydides, *History of the Peloponnesian War*

5 According to Pericles's Funeral Oration, what standard did the Greeks use to decide who should hold public office?

- **A** royal blood
- **B** ability
- **C** wealth
- **D** class

Answers are on page CA43.

WEEK 5

Content Standard WH6.5 Students analyze the geographic, political, economic, religious, and social structures of the early civilizations of India.

Directions: *Select the best answer for each of the following questions.*

MONDAY WH6.5.1

1 India's earliest civilizations developed

A between the Tigris and Euphrates rivers.
B along the coasts of Southeast Asia.
C in the Indus River valley.
D on the Deccan plateau.

TUESDAY WH6.5.4

2 In early India's social system, the Kshatriyas class contained these people.

A untouchables
B priests
C common people
D warriors

WEDNESDAY WH6.5.5

3 The Buddha believed that the only way to find truth was by

A giving up family and home.
B renouncing all desires.
C praying five times a day.
D worshipping in temples.

THURSDAY WH6.5.6

4 The Indian ruler who became Buddhist, renounced war, and worked for his people's welfare was

A Asoka.
B Sarawati.
C Lakshmi.
D Babur.

FRIDAY WH6.5.7

Read the passage below and answer the question.

Thou grievest where no grief should be! . . .

All, that doth live, lives always! . . .

. . . .

The soul that with a strong and constant calm
Takes sorrow and takes joy indifferently,
Lives in the life undying!

—*Bhagavadgita,* Sir Edwin Arnold, trans.

5 What does Krishna believe about life after death?

A There is no life after death.
B Souls pass through many lives to unite with the universal spirit.
C Souls survive and are later joined to their bodies in heaven.
D Souls pass to a dark underworld of suffering.

Answers are on page CA43.

WEEK 6

Content Standard WH6.6 Students analyze the geographic, political, economic, religious, and social structures of the early civilizations of China.

Directions: *Select the best answer for each of the following questions.*

MONDAY WH6.6.4

1 Confucius believed that peace would come to society if people

A lived in harmony with nature.
B turned to a very strong ruler for protection.
C gave up all concerns about the world.
D put the needs of family and community above personal needs.

TUESDAY WH6.6.6

2 To select the most talented people for government jobs, Han Wudi used

A a council of nobles to make appointments.
B civil service exams.
C educators who named government officials.
D a lottery system.

WEDNESDAY WH6.6.7

3 The Silk Road was significant because it

A brought China into contact with many other civilizations.
B replaced a sea route to Southeast Asia.
C helped link northern and southern parts of China.
D helped Chinese armies conquer the Himalayas.

THURSDAY WH6.6.8

4 What groups brought Buddhism to China?

A merchants and teachers
B warriors and priests
C scientists and prophets
D untouchables and laborers

FRIDAY WH6.6.3 Read the passage below and answer the question.

The sage experiences [life] without abstraction
[being separated from it],
And accomplishes without action;
He accepts the ebb and flow of things,
Nurtures them, but does not own them,
And lives, but does not dwell.

—Laozi, *Dao De Jing*

5 According to Laozi, how should a wise person approach the events of life?

A with energy
B with resistance
C with acceptance
D with self-assertion

Answers are on page CA43.

WEEK 7

Content Standard WH6.7 Students analyze the geographic, political, economic, religious, and social structures during the development of Rome.

Directions: *Select the best answer for each of the following questions.*

MONDAY WH6.7.2

1 The ruling class and top officials of the Roman Republic were the

A Etruscans.
B plebeians.
C patricians.
D consuls.

TUESDAY WH6.7.4

2 Julius Caesar helped end the Roman Republic by

A declaring himself dictator for life.
B becoming part of the First Triumvirate.
C conquering territory for Rome.
D defeating Pompey's forces.

WEDNESDAY WH6.7.6

3 What was one reason why Christianity spread?

A Constantine denied religious freedom to people in the empire.
B Roman peace and order allowed people to travel in safety.
C The teachings of Christianity were all new to most Romans.
D Romans expected everyone to honor the emperor as a god.

THURSDAY WH6.7.8

4 One of Rome's most significant influences on the world is its

A invention of paper.
B creation of democracy.
C establishment of the Silk Road.
D system of law.

FRIDAY WH6.7.1

Read the passage below and answer the question.

Therefore, when I saw that a nefarious [evil] war was waged against the republic, I thought that no delay ought to be interposed to our pursuit of Marcus Antonius; and I gave my vote that we ought to pursue with war that most audacious [bold] man, who . . . was at this moment attacking a general of the Roman people.

—Cicero, "The Sixth Oration of M.T. Cicero Against Marcus Antonius"

5 In giving this speech about the struggle between Octavian and Antony (Marcus Antonius), Cicero was showing that he

A supported talks to end the fighting.
B wanted to help Rome's poor.
C was a defender of Rome's republican institutions.
D supported Rome becoming a monarchy.

Answers are on page CA43.

WEEK 8

Content Standard WH7.1 Students analyze the causes and effects of the vast expansion and ultimate disintegration of the Roman Empire.

Directions: *Select the best answer for each of the following questions.*

MONDAY WH7.1.1

1 Which of the following is an example of a lasting Roman contribution?

- **A** the invention of paper
- **B** the idea everyone is equal under the law
- **C** the founding of Christianity
- **D** direct democracy

TUESDAY WH7.1.2

2 Which best describes the size of the Roman Empire at its greatest?

- **A** Italy and North Africa
- **B** southern Europe and India
- **C** lands around the Mediterranean
- **D** southern Britain, southern Europe, Asia Minor, and North Africa

WEDNESDAY WH7.1.3

3 Constantine moved the Roman capital to Constantinople because

- **A** it lay on an easily defended site and was at a crossroads for trade.
- **B** the Visigoths had captured Rome.
- **C** Greeks made up the largest group in the empire.
- **D** Persians were trying to overrun the eastern border of the empire.

THURSDAY WH7.1.3

4 How did the Eastern Orthodox and Roman Catholic churches view church-state relations?

- **A** The emperor and the pope only had power in spiritual matters.
- **B** The emperor and the pope should not interfere in political matters.
- **C** Only the emperor had control over material matters.
- **D** The pope often quarreled with kings over political matters while Byzantine church officials respected their emperor's wishes.

FRIDAY WH7.1.1

Use the passage below to answer the question.

Didius Julianus . . . made bids to the soldiers for the rule over the Romans. For, just as if it had been in some market or auction room, both the city and its entire Empire were auctioned off. The sellers were the ones who had slain their emperor, and the would-be buyers were Sulpicianus and Julianus.

—*Aspects of Western Civilization*, vol. 1, edited by Perry M. Rogers

5 According to the quote what was one weakness of the Roman Empire?

- **A** attacks from barbarians
- **B** spread of disease
- **C** growth of corruption
- **D** too many slaves

Answers are on page CA43.

WEEK 9

Content Standard WH7.2 Students analyze the geographic, political, economic, religious, and social structures of the civilizations of Islam in the Middle Ages.

Directions: *Select the best answer for each of the following questions.*

MONDAY WH7.2.1

1 What covers most of the Arabian Peninsula?

A mountains
B grassy plains
C desert
D swamp

TUESDAY WH7.2.2

2 What belief do Judaism, Christianity, and Islam have in common?

A A prophet is the son of God.
B There is one God.
C Lying is the greatest wrong.
D Stealing is sometimes allowed.

WEDNESDAY WH7.2.4

3 As the Arab Empire spread,

A Muslims began to believe that Muhammad was a god.
B many conquered peoples converted to Islam and learned Arabic.
C Muslims forced people to become Muslims.
D many Muslims became Catholics.

THURSDAY WH7.2.6

4 Which of the following was a Muslim contribution to learning?

A the philosophy of Stoicism
B the invention of the arch
C the use of aqueducts
D the discovery that blood moves to and from the heart

FRIDAY WH7.2.3

Read the passage below and answer the question.

Serve no other gods besides Allah, lest you incur disgrace and ruin. Your Lord has enjoined [ordered] you to worship none but Him and to show kindness to your parents. . . .
Give to the near of kin [relatives] their due, and also to the destitute and to the wayfarers. Do not squander your substance wastefully, . . .
Keep your promises; you are accountable for all that you promise.
Give full measure, when you measure, and weigh with even scales.

—*The Koran*, N.J. Dawood, trans.

5 Which sentence best describes the contents of the Qu'ran?

A It states a Muslim's responsibilities toward Allah and other people.
B It tells how Muslims should behave in business.
C It explains which countries Muslims should conquer.
D It describes Muhammad's hopes for the people of Arabia.

Answers are on page CA43.

WEEK 10

Content Standard WH7.3 Students analyze the geographic, political, economic, religious, and social structures of the civilizations of China in the Middle Ages.

Directions: *Select the best answer for each of the following questions.*

MONDAY WH7.3.1

1 Buddhism became an important religion in China because

A Buddhism brought peace and comfort in a time of war and famine.
B monks and nuns did not marry.
C missionaries brought it to China.
D the emperors converted people to it.

TUESDAY WH7.3.2

2 Why did farming improve during the Tang dynasty?

A The country was at war.
B The civil system was restored.
C Farmers began to grow tea.
D Farmers developed better kinds of rice.

WEDNESDAY WH7.3.5

3 What did woodblock printing lead to?

A the making of copper coins
B the assessment of taxes
C the introduction of paper money
D the decline of the Chinese economy

THURSDAY WH7.3.6

4 The civil service exam created the scholar-official class because

A men who passed it could appoint relatives to government jobs.
B only men who passed the exam could become government officials.
C the emperor personally chose all the men who would take the test.
D sons could inherit government jobs.

FRIDAY WH7.3.4

Read the passage below and answer the question.

Of late we have dispatched missions to announce our Mandate to foreign nations and during their journeys over the oceans they have been favored with the blessing of Thy beneficent [Buddha's generous] protection. They have escaped disaster or misfortune, . . .

[W]e bestow offerings in recompense [thanks], . . . before the Lord Buddha, . . . of gold and silver.

—Louise Levathes, *When China Ruled the Seas*

5 What indicates if these journeys were important to the Chinese?

A not important because there were no disasters
B not important because Buddha did not pay attention to the journeys
C important because they went to foreign nations
D important because the Chinese are giving gifts of thanks to Buddha

Answers are on page CA43.

WEEK 11

Content Standard WH7.4 Students analyze the geographic, political, economic, religious, and social structures of the sub-Saharan civilizations of Ghana and Mali in Medieval Africa.

Directions: *Select the best answer for each of the following questions.*

MONDAY WH7.4.2

1 The rainforest kingdoms had

A surplus foods that they traded for salt.
B gold that they traded for salt.
C salt that they traded for gold.
D copper and leather goods that they traded for gold.

TUESDAY WH7.4.3

2 Why did some West Africans change from a traditional religion to Islam?

A Muhammad converted them.
B Arab armies forced them to change.
C Being followers of Islam helped them trade with Muslim Arabs.
D Sundiata forced his people to convert to Islam.

WEDNESDAY WH7.4.4

3 Why was there increased use of the Arabic language in West Africa?

A Cordoba was a center of Muslim culture.
B The Bantu gradually settled most of Africa.
C The Spanish extended their control to North and West Africa.
D Arabs traded with the kingdoms of West Africa.

THURSDAY WH7.4.5

4 In West Africa, children were often educated

A in large local schools.
B through oral stories and proverbs.
C by the government.
D after paying a large fee.

FRIDAY WH7.4.1 Read the passage below and answer the question.

The king [of Ghana] exacts the right of one dinar *of gold on each donkey-load of salt that enters his country, and two* dinars *of gold on each load of salt that goes out. A load of copper carries a duty of five* mitqals *and a load of merchandise ten* mitquals.

—Abdullah Abu-Ubayd al Bekri, "Ghana in 1067"

5 According to al Bekri, what is a source of wealth for Ghana?

A a large number of salt and copper mines in the country
B the donkeys that are raised in Ghana
C the taxes charge on goods entering and leaving the country
D the king's gold mines

Answers are on page CA43.

WEEK 12

Content Standard WH7.5 Students analyze the geographic, political, economic, religious, and social structures of the civilizations of Medieval Japan.

Directions: *Select the best answer for each of the following questions.*

MONDAY WH7.5.1

1 Which of the following came to Japan by way of China?

A the model for a shogun style of government

B the religion of Shinto

C tanka and haiku poetry

D a writing system

TUESDAY WH7.5.2

2 What was the goal of Prince Shotoku's reforms?

A to create a strong central government

B to make Japan the strongest country in the area

C to defeat the Chinese

D to divide Japan into a series of provinces

WEDNESDAY WH7.5.5

3 ***The Tale of the Genji***

A recounts the adventures of a Japanese sailor.

B may be the world's first novel.

C is a series of Noh plays.

D contains instructions for how to write poetry.

THURSDAY WH7.5.6

4 A military society developed in twelfth century Japan because

A the Mongols defeated the Japanese.

B the emperor needed an army to attack China.

C the most powerful families were trying to gain more land by fighting each other.

D Buddhism honored a military way of life.

FRIDAY WH7.5.3 Read the passage below and answer the question.

It is further good fortune if . . . [a servant] had wisdom and talent and can use them appropriately. But even a person who is good for nothing . . . will be a reliable retainer [servant] if only he has the determination to think earnestly of [respect and admire] his master. Having only wisdom and talent is the lowest tier [level] of usefulness.

—Yamamoto Tsunetomo, *Hagakure: The Book of the Samurai*

5 According to this excerpt, what should a master most look for in a samurai?

A wisdom that offers good advice

B respect and admiration

C talent in all military things

D willingness to die for his master

Answers are on page CA43.

WEEK 13

Content Standard WH7.6 Students analyze the geographic, political, economic, religious, and social structures of the civilizations of Medieval Europe.

Directions: *Select the best answer for each of the following questions.*

MONDAY WH7.6.3

1 Under feudalism, whose responsibility was it to keep roads repaired and enforce the laws?

A kings
B nobles
C serfs
D priests

TUESDAY WH7.6.4

2 What was the disagreement between Pope Gregory VII and King Henry IV, the Holy Roman Emperor, about?

A the boundaries of the Holy Roman Empire
B the appointment of bishops
C the role of monasteries
D the selection of the next pope

WEDNESDAY WH7.6.5

3 What helped establish the idea that the power of government should be limited?

A the Crusades
B the system of feudalism
C the Battle of Hastings
D the Magna Carta

THURSDAY WH7.6.6

4 Which of the following was a cause of the Crusades?

A the desire to free the Holy Land from the Muslim Turks
B the Inquisition in Spain
C the Muslim conquest of Spain
D the need for trade with China

FRIDAY WH7.6.7

Read the passage below and answer the question.

After the . . . pestilence [disease] many buildings of all sizes in every city fell into total ruin for want of habitants. Likewise, many villages and hamlets were deserted, with no house remaining in them, because everyone who had lived there was dead, and indeed many of these villages were never inhabited again. In the following winter there was such a lack of workers in all areas of activity that it was thought that there had hardly ever been such a shortage before; . . .

—Historian Henry Knighton, c. 1388 in *King Death* by Colin Pratt

5 According to the excerpt, how did the Black Death affect population?

A No workers were needed during the winter.
B There was a shortage of housing.
C All the people who had lived in some villages were dead.
D Inhabitants in different cities destroyed their buildings.

Answers are on page CA43.

WEEK 14

Content Standard WH7.7 Students compare and contrast the geographic, political, economic, religious, and social structures of the Meso-American and Andean civilizations.

Directions: *Select the best answer for each of the following questions.*

MONDAY WH7.7.1

1 Which of the following was used to unite the Inca Empire?

- **A** A system of writing was developed.
- **B** Only government officials were allowed to speak Quechua.
- **C** A network of roads was established.
- **D** Horse-drawn wagons carried goods to different markets.

TUESDAY WH7.7.2

2 Like the Spartans, the Aztec

- **A** believed in human sacrifice.
- **B** celebrated the life and death of a soldier.
- **C** thought that art and poetry were important.
- **D** prized agricultural skills.

WEDNESDAY WH7.7.3

3 How did the Spanish defeat the Aztec?

- **A** The Spanish used horses and guns and were helped by an epidemic.
- **B** The Spanish had a large army of Spanish soldiers.
- **C** The Spanish used bows and arrows.
- **D** The Spanish had better ships.

THURSDAY WH7.7.5

4 Which of the following was a Mayan accomplishment?

- **A** the invention of the gun
- **B** a city built in a desert
- **C** the conquest of Mexico
- **D** the development of a 365-day calendar for planting and harvesting crops

FRIDAY WH7.7.4

Read the passage below and answer the question.

[W]e shall vanquish [conquer] them all,
we shall make them our captives,
and thus our city shall be established.
Mexico Tenochtitlan:
where the eagle screeches,
where he spreads his wings,
where the eagle feeds,
where the fish fly,
and where the serpent is torn apart.

—*The Cronica Mexicayotl* in *A Scattering of Jades*, edited by T.J. Knab

5 What is the writer describing in this excerpt?

- **A** where the Aztec set up a safe place for particular animals
- **B** how the Aztec knew where to set up their capital
- **C** where the Aztec went to hunt for food
- **D** how the Aztec thought they should act in all battles

Answers are on page CA43.

WEEK 15

Content Standard WH7.8 Students analyze the origins, accomplishments, and geographic diffusion of the Renaissance.

Directions: *Select the best answer for each of the following questions.*

MONDAY WH7.8.1

1 Interest in the Romans and Greeks led to humanism because

- **A** Europeans began to think people could make the world better.
- **B** people became more interested in heaven than in life in this world.
- **C** the Black Death became a threat.
- **D** people began to write in the vernacular.

TUESDAY WH7.8.2

2 Why was Florence important in the early days of the Renaissance?

- **A** It had conquered most of the other Italian city-states.
- **B** It controlled trade with the Byzantine and Ottoman empires.
- **C** It was the first wealthy Italian city.
- **D** It had been the capital of the Roman Empire.

WEDNESDAY WH7.8.3

3 After the Silk Road reopened,

- **A** the Mongols came to power.
- **B** Italians could sell spices to the Arabs.
- **C** demand for European wool fell.
- **D** the price of silk fell and the European demand for it increased.

THURSDAY WH7.8.4

4 The invention of the printing press

- **A** encouraged new artistic methods, such as perspective and shadow.
- **B** was based on Greek technology.
- **C** spread humanist ideas.
- **D** discouraged interest in the Bible.

FRIDAY WH7.8.5

Examine the statue below. Answer the question.

◀ *David* by Michelangelo

5 In this statue Michelangelo shows

- **A** the new Renaissance knowledge of human anatomy.
- **B** the Renaissance interest in Roman, Greek, and Jewish history.
- **C** the ability to use perspective.
- **D** the symbolism of medieval artists.

Answers are on page CA43.

WEEK 16

Content Standard WH7.9 Students analyze the historical developments of the Reformation.

Directions: *Select the best answer for each of the following questions.*

MONDAY WH7.9.3

1 The Calvinist practice of congregations choosing their own leaders supported the democratic idea that

- **A** there should be one state-supported religion.
- **B** people should elect their political leaders.
- **C** the king should select all colonial governors.
- **D** government should have three separate branches.

TUESDAY WH7.9.5

2 Which of the following were part of the Counter-Reformation?

- **A** strict rules for the behavior of priests and bishops
- **B** seminaries closing
- **C** an end to the Inquisition
- **D** the disbanding of the Jesuits

WEDNESDAY WH7.9.6

3 European missionaries spread Catholicism to

- **A** Australia
- **B** the Middle East
- **C** the Philippine Islands
- **D** Spain

THURSDAY WH7.9.7

4 In 1492, whom did King Ferdinand and Queen Isabella order to become Catholic or leave Spain?

- **A** Martin Luther
- **B** the Jesuits
- **C** Jews and Muslims
- **D** John Calvin

FRIDAY WH7.9.2

Read the passage below and answer the question.

Those preachers of indulgences are in error, who say that by the pope's indulgences a man is freed from every penalty, and saved; . . .
It must needs be, therefore, that that greater part of the people are deceived by that indiscriminate and high sounding promise of release from penalty.

—Martin Luther, "Disputation of Doctor Martin Luther on the Power and Efficacy of Indulgences" (Ninety-Five Theses)

5 According to the quote, what does Luther think of indulgences?

- **A** They will not help a person avoid punishment.
- **B** The pope should sell more of them.
- **C** They help people get into heaven.
- **D** The pope should give them away.

Answers are on page CA43.

WEEK 17

Content Standard WH7.10 Students analyze the historical developments of the Scientific Revolution and its lasting effect on religious, political, and cultural institutions.

Directions: *Select the best answer for each of the following questions.*

MONDAY WH7.10.1

1 Which of the following revived European interest in science?

A contact with Islamic scientific works
B the introduction of Roman numerals into Europe
C the Catholic Church's desire for more accurate scientific information
D the fall of the Roman Empire

TUESDAY WH7.10.2

2 Unlike Ptolemy, Copernicus believed that

A the planets circled Earth.
B the planets did not follow regular paths.
C the planets were all the same size.
D the planets circled the sun.

WEDNESDAY WH7.10.2

3 Which of the following led to more knowledge about the human body during the Scientific Revolution?

A the barometer
B the microscope
C the telescope
D the caravel

THURSDAY WH7.10.3

4 What idea from the Scientific Revolution developed into a basis for government?

A deism
B absolute monarchy
C natural law
D mercantilism

FRIDAY WH7.10.3 Read the passage below and answer the question.

Now let us review the observations made [with a telescope] during the past two months. . . . I have been led to the opinion and conviction that the surface of the Moon is not smooth, uniform, and precisely spherical [round] as a great number of philosophers believe it and the other heavenly bodies to be, but is uneven, rough, and full of cavities [holes], not unlike the face of . . . Earth, relieved by chains of mountains and deep valleys.

—*Discoveries and Opinions of Galileo* edited by Stillman Drake

5 On what did Galileo base his statements about the moon?

A on opinions of philosophers
B on repeated observations
C on the moon's appearance during one night
D on the appearance of a full moon

Answers are on page CA43.

WEEK 18

Content Standard WH7.11 Students analyze political and economic change in the sixteenth, seventeenth, and eighteenth centuries (the Age of Exploration, the Enlightenment, and the Age of Reason).

Directions: *Select the best answer for each of the following questions.*

MONDAY WH7.11.1

1 Where did the English, the French, and the Dutch send explorers to found colonies?

A Africa
B North America
C South America
D Australia

TUESDAY WH7.11.2

2 Which Asian crop resulted in the enslavement of millions of Africans in the Caribbean?

A sugarcane
B potatoes
C corn
D chocolate

WEDNESDAY WH7.11.3

3 According to mercantilism, a country gains power

A by having an all-powerful king.
B by importing more than it exports.
C by building up its supply of gold and silver.
D by getting rid of colonies.

THURSDAY WH7.11.4

4 In the American Declaration of Independence, King George III is accused of taking away the right to a fair trial which is guaranteed

A in the Ninety-Five Theses.
B in the Magna Carta.
C in the Stamp Act.
D by the Boston Massacre.

FRIDAY WH7.11.5 Read the passage below and answer the question.

Again, there is no liberty, if the judiciary power be not separated from the legislative and executive. Were it joined with the legislative, the life and liberty of the subject would be exposed to arbitrary control; for the judge would be then the legislator. Were it joined to the executive power, the judge might behave with violence and oppression.

—Montesquieu, *The Spirit of Laws*

5 What principle of American democratic government is Montesquieu describing in this excerpt?

A that the executive, legislative, and judicial branches should be separate
B that the president should have the same powers as a king
C that the legislature should be stronger than the president and judges
D that judges are not important

Answers are on page CA43.

The answers for the At-Home Standards Review presented on the previous pages are listed below. Use this answer key to check your understanding of the material covered in the grades 6 and 7 social studies courses.

	WEEK 1 page CA25	WEEK 2 page CA26	WEEK 3 page CA27	WEEK 4 page CA28	WEEK 5 page CA29
1	B	C	B	A	C
2	A	B	C	C	D
3	C	D	C	B	B
4	C	A	B	A	A
5	D	B	D	B	B

	WEEK 6 page CA30	WEEK 7 page CA31	WEEK 8 page CA32	WEEK 9 page CA33	WEEK 10 page CA34
1	D	C	B	C	A
2	B	A	D	B	D
3	A	B	A	B	C
4	A	D	D	D	B
5	C	C	C	A	D

	WEEK 11 page CA35	WEEK 12 page CA36	WEEK 13 page CA37	WEEK 14 page CA38	WEEK 15 page CA39
1	A	D	B	C	A
2	C	A	B	B	C
3	D	B	D	A	D
4	B	C	A	D	C
5	C	B	C	B	A

	WEEK 16 page CA40	WEEK 17 page CA41	WEEK 18 page CA42
1	B	A	B
2	A	D	A
3	C	B	C
4	C	C	B
5	A	B	A

Previewing Your Textbook

Follow the reading road map through the next few pages to learn about using your textbook, *Discovering Our Past: The American Journey to World War I.*

Units

Your textbook is divided into units. Each unit begins with four pages of information to help you begin your study of its topics.

Why It's Important

Each unit begins with a **preview** of important events and **Why It's Important** to read about them.

Where in the United States?

The map shows you **where** the events in this unit happened.

Places to Locate

Look for these important **places** as you read the unit.

Time Line

A time line shows you **when** the events in this unit happened. It also compares events in the United States with events in California and the world.

People to Meet

This list introduces **people** who made an impact on American history during the time period of the unit. They are highlighted throughout your text.

Chapters

Each unit of your textbook is divided into chapters. Each chapter starts by giving you some background information about what you will be reading and help with reading skills.

Chapter Title
The title tells you the **main topic** you will be reading about.

Big Ideas
Throughout your text the important ideas are listed at the beginning of each chapter. These are the **big themes** of history that repeat again and again.

History Online
This tells you where you can go **online** to get more information.

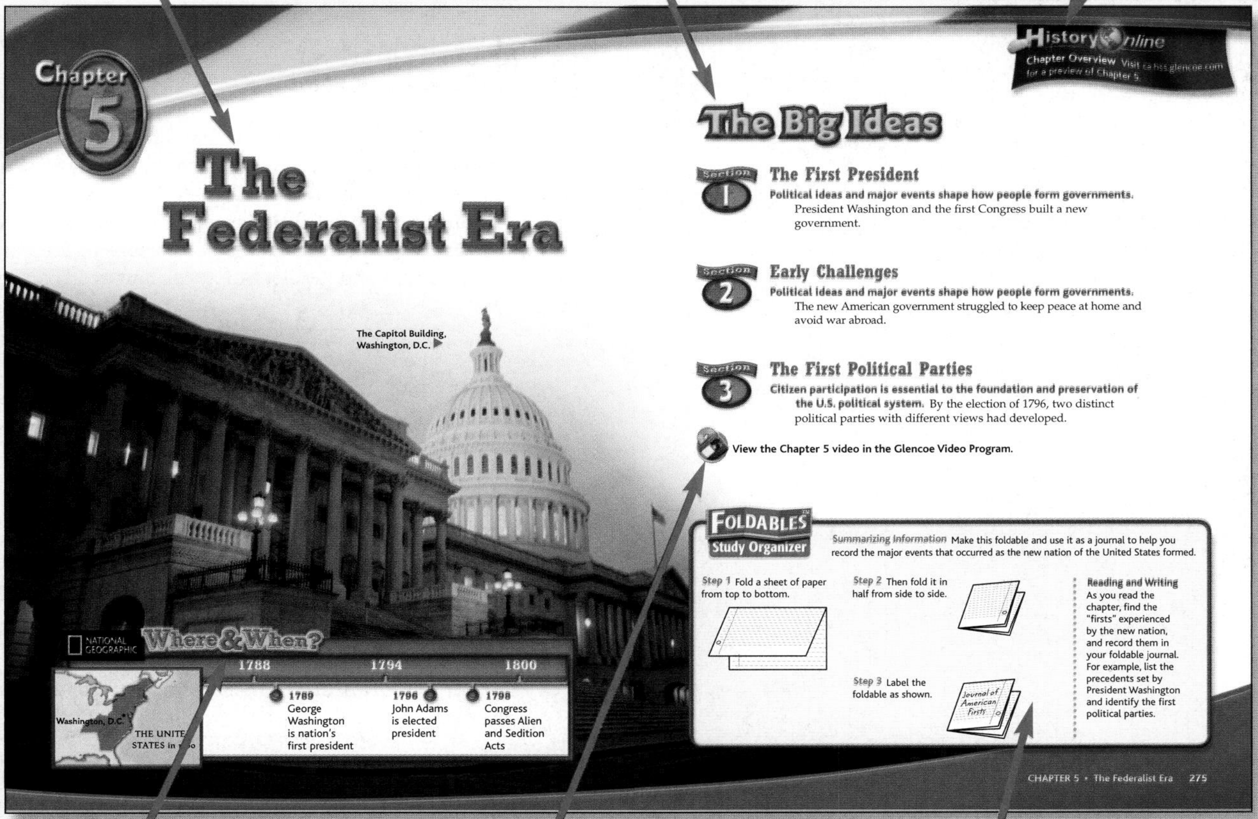

Where & When?
Here you can see **where and when** events in this chapter happened.

Glencoe Video Program
Each **video program** highlights a unique topic in the chapter and has a Viewer's Guide.

Foldables
Every chapter has a **Foldable™** that will help you organize and remember information in the chapter.

Chapter Reading Skill

Because reading about social studies is different than reading a novel or magazine, every chapter offers help with reading skills.

READING SKILL
This shows you what reading skill you will be learning about—**Recognizing Bias.**

LEARN IT!
This explains how the skill applies to the **reading** you do every day.

READING TIP
The Reading Tip tells you more about making **connections** in your reading.

Chapter 5

Get Ready to Read

Recognizing Bias

READING SKILL

1 Learn It!

Most people have feelings and ideas that affect their point of view. This viewpoint, or *bias,* influences the way they interpret events. For this reason, an idea that is stated as a fact may really be only an opinion. Recognizing bias will help you judge the accuracy of what you read. You can look for clues to help uncover bias in written form. Read the list below for hints you can use to identify bias.

- **Identify the author of the statement, and examine his or her views and possible reasons for writing the material.**
- **Look for language that reflects an emotion or opinion—words such as *all, never, best, worst, might,* or *should.***
- **Examine the writing for imbalances—focusing on one viewpoint and failing to discuss other perspectives.**

Reading Tip

One way to identify bias is to find out more about the author. Can you find information about the author that will help you understand opinions he or she may express?

276

PRACTICE IT!

Next comes an easy-to-follow **practice** activity for the reading skill.

2 Practice It!

Look at the two quotes below. Each has a different opinion about "the people." On a separate sheet of paper, restate each opinion in your own words. Discuss your conclusions with a partner.

> "The people are turbulent [disorderly] and changing. . . . They seldom judge or determine right."
>
> —*Alexander Hamilton, Federalist, page 292*

▲ Alexander Hamilton

Read to Write

Write a paragraph describing a person or event about which you feel very strongly. Now try to write a paragraph about the same person or event without including any personal opinion.

READ TO WRITE

Writing about what you read will help you remember the event.

> "I am not among those who fear the people. They, and not the rich, are our dependence [what we depend on] for continued freedom."
>
> —*Thomas Jefferson, Republican, page 293*

▲ Thomas Jefferson

READING SKILLS HANDBOOK

Located on pages 14–23 is a handbook that is full of good **reading strategies** to help you read your text. You can look back at this at any time as you read.

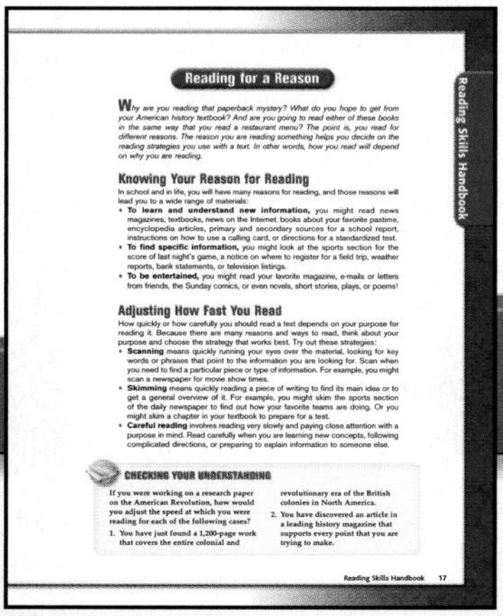

Reading for a Reason

Why are you reading that paperback mystery? What do you hope to get from your American history textbook? And are you going to read either of these books in the same way that you read a restaurant menu? The point is, you read for different reasons. The reason you are reading something helps you decide on the reading strategies you use with a text. In other words, how you read will depend on why you are reading.

Knowing Your Reason for Reading

In school and in life, you will have many reasons for reading, and those reasons will lead you to a wide range of materials:

- **To learn and understand new information,** you might read news magazines, textbooks, news on the Internet, books about your favorite pastime, encyclopedia articles, primary and secondary sources for a school report, instructions on how to use a calling card, or directions for a standardized test.
- **To find specific information,** you might look at the sports section for the score of last night's game, a notice on where to register for a field trip, weather reports, bank statements, or television listings.
- **To be entertained,** you might read your favorite magazine, e-mails or letters from friends, the Sunday comics, or even novels, short stories, plays, or poems!

Adjusting How Fast You Read

How quickly or how carefully you should read a text depends on your purpose for reading it. Because there are many reasons and ways to read, think about your purpose and choose the strategy that works best. Try out these strategies:

- **Scanning** means quickly running your eyes over the material, looking for key words or phrases that point to the information you are looking for. Scan when you need to find a particular piece or type of information. For example, you might scan a newspaper for movie show times.
- **Skimming** means quickly reading a piece of writing to find its main idea or to get a general overview of it. For example, you might skim the sports section of the daily newspaper to find out how your favorite teams are doing. Or you might skim a chapter in your textbook to prepare for a test.
- **Careful reading** involves reading very slowly and paying close attention with a purpose in mind. Read carefully when you are learning new concepts, following complicated directions, or preparing to explain information to someone else.

CHECKING YOUR UNDERSTANDING

If you were working on a research paper on the American Revolution, how would you adjust the speed at which you were reading for each of the following cases?

1. You have just found a 1,200-page work that covers the entire colonial and revolutionary era of the British colonies in North America.
2. You have discovered an article in a leading history magazine that supports every point that you are trying to make.

Reading Skills Handbook 17

Reading Skills Handbook

3 Apply It!

Look for examples of bias in comments made by key figures described in the text.

APPLY IT!

Here is an opportunity to **apply** what you have learned.

CHAPTER 5 • The Federalist Era 277

Sections

A section is a division, or part, of a chapter. The first page of the section, the Section Opener, helps you set a purpose for reading.

Looking Back, Looking Ahead

Read the **connection** between what you already know and what you are about to read.

Content Vocabulary

This list points out important social studies **terms** and their pronunciation.

Academic Vocabulary

This list names other **words** you might not know that will come up in your reading.

Section 2

The Louisiana Purchase

Guide to Reading

History Social Science Standards

US8.4 Students analyze the aspirations and ideals of the people of the new nation.

Looking Back, Looking Ahead
In the early 1800s, the United States experienced rapid growth. The Louisiana Purchase doubled the size of the nation and created remarkable opportunities.

Focusing on the Main Ideas
- As Americans moved west in the early 1800s, Spain and France made a secret agreement about land that affected American trade. *(page 313)*
- The Louisiana Purchase opened a vast area to exploration and settlement. *(page 314)*

Locating Places
Louisiana Territory
New Orleans
St. Louis
Missouri River

Meeting People
Meriwether Lewis
William Clark
Sacagawea (SA • kuh • juh • WEE • uh)
Zebulon Pike

Content Vocabulary
Conestoga wagon (KAH • nuh • STOH • guh)
secede (sih • SEED)

Academic Vocabulary
enormous (in • NAWR • muhs)
generation (JEH • nuh • RAY • shuhn)

Reading Strategy
Classifying Information As you read the section, re-create the diagram below and describe the areas that Lewis and Clark and Zebulon Pike explored.

Explorer	Region explored
Meriwether Lewis and William Clark	
Zebulon Pike	

NATIONAL GEOGRAPHIC Who & When?

1804 1805 1806 1807

Oct. 1803 Senate ratifies Louisiana Purchase treaty

May 1804 Lewis and Clark begin expedition

Sep. 1806 Lewis and Clark return to St. Louis

Nov. 1806 Zebulon Pike reaches Pikes Peak

312 CHAPTER 6 • The Age of Jefferson

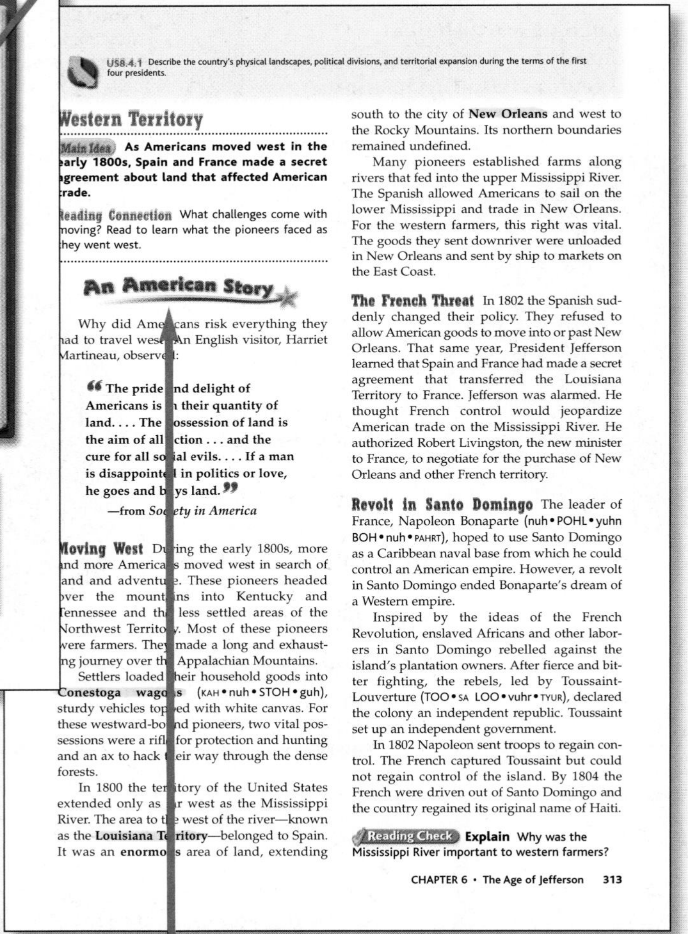

US8.4.1 Describe the country's physical landscapes, political divisions, and territorial expansion during the terms of the first four presidents.

Western Territory

Main Idea As Americans moved west in the early 1800s, Spain and France made a secret agreement about land that affected American trade.

Reading Connection What challenges come with moving? Read to learn what the pioneers faced as they went west.

An American Story

Why did Ame cans risk everything they had to travel wes An English visitor, Harriet Martineau, observe :

> **"The pride nd delight of Americans is their quantity of land. . . . The ossession of land is the aim of all ction . . . and the cure for all so ial evils. . . . If a man is disappoint in politics or love, he goes and b ys land."**
>
> —from *So ety in America*

Moving West Du ing the early 1800s, more and more America s moved west in search of land and adventu e. These pioneers headed over the mount ins into Kentucky and Tennessee and th less settled areas of the Northwest Territo y. Most of these pioneers were farmers. The made a long and exhausting journey over th Appalachian Mountains.

Settlers loaded heir household goods into **Conestoga wago s** (KAH • nuh • STOH • guh), sturdy vehicles top ed with white canvas. For these westward-bo nd pioneers, two vital possessions were a rifl for protection and hunting and an ax to hack eir way through the dense forests.

In 1800 the ter itory of the United States extended only as r west as the Mississippi River. The area to t e west of the river—known as the **Louisiana Te ritory**—belonged to Spain. It was an **enormo s** area of land, extending south to the city of **New Orleans** and west to the Rocky Mountains. Its northern boundaries remained undefined.

Many pioneers established farms along rivers that fed into the upper Mississippi River. The Spanish allowed Americans to sail on the lower Mississippi and trade in New Orleans. For the western farmers, this right was vital. The goods they sent downriver were unloaded in New Orleans and sent by ship to markets on the East Coast.

The French Threat In 1802 the Spanish suddenly changed their policy. They refused to allow American goods to move into or past New Orleans. That same year, President Jefferson learned that Spain and France had made a secret agreement that transferred the Louisiana Territory to France. Jefferson was alarmed. He thought French control would jeopardize American trade on the Mississippi River. He authorized Robert Livingston, the new minister to France, to negotiate for the purchase of New Orleans and other French territory.

Revolt in Santo Domingo The leader of France, Napoleon Bonaparte (nuh • POHL • yuhn BOH • nuh • PAHRT), hoped to use Santo Domingo as a Caribbean naval base from which he could control an American empire. However, a revolt in Santo Domingo ended Bonaparte's dream of a Western empire.

Inspired by the ideas of the French Revolution, enslaved Africans and other laborers in Santo Domingo rebelled against the island's plantation owners. After fierce and bitter fighting, the rebels, led by Toussaint-Louverture (TOO • SA LOO • vuhr • TYUR), declared the colony an independent republic. Toussaint set up an independent government.

In 1802 Napoleon sent troops to regain control. The French captured Toussaint but could not regain control of the island. By 1804 the French were driven out of Santo Domingo and the country regained its original name of Haiti.

Reading Check **Explain** Why was the Mississippi River important to western farmers?

CHAPTER 6 • The Age of Jefferson 313

Focusing on the Main Ideas

Preview the **main ideas** of each section which are repeated in the reading.

An American Story

Read about **real-life** Americans and what they thought and did.

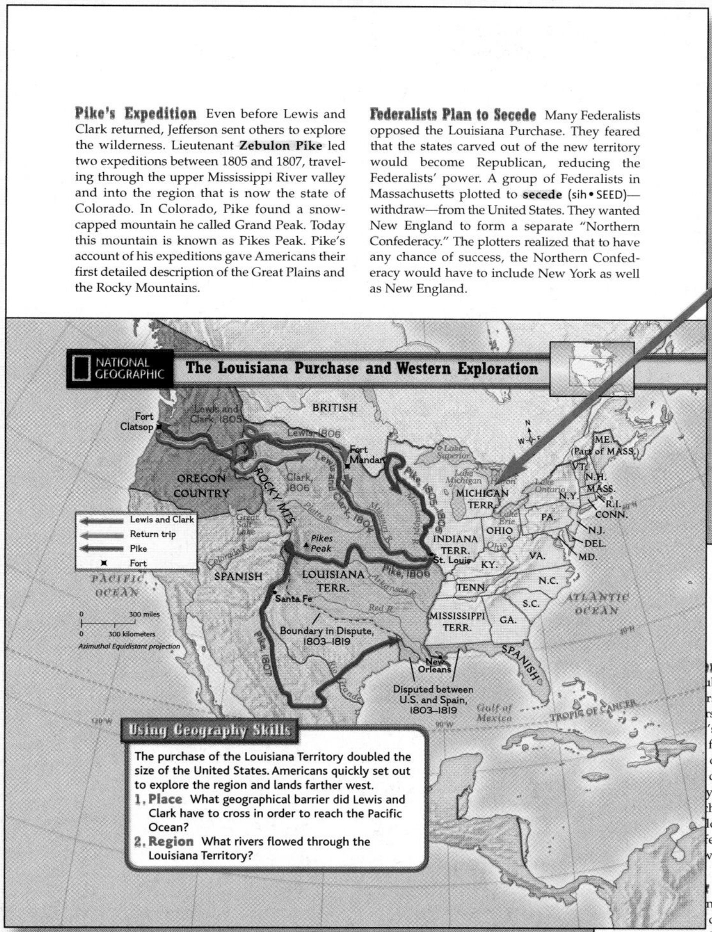

Pike's Expedition Even before Lewis and Clark returned, Jefferson sent others to explore the wilderness. Lieutenant **Zebulon Pike** led two expeditions between 1805 and 1807, traveling through the upper Mississippi River valley and into the region that is now the state of Colorado. In Colorado, Pike found a snow-capped mountain he called Grand Peak. Today this mountain is known as Pikes Peak. Pike's account of his expeditions gave Americans their first detailed description of the Great Plains and the Rocky Mountains.

Federalists Plan to Secede Many Federalists opposed the Louisiana Purchase. They feared that the states carved out of the new territory would become Republican, reducing the Federalists' power. A group of Federalists in Massachusetts plotted to **secede** (sih • SEED)—withdraw—from the United States. They wanted New England to form a separate "Northern Confederacy." The plotters realized that to have any chance of success, the Northern Confederacy would have to include New York as well as New England.

Using Geography Skills

The purchase of the Louisiana Territory doubled the size of the United States. Americans quickly set out to explore the region and lands farther west.

1. **Place** What geographical barrier did Lewis and Clark have to cross in order to reach the Pacific Ocean?
2. **Region** What rivers flowed through the Louisiana Territory?

MAP

Maps help you learn how **geography and history** are related.

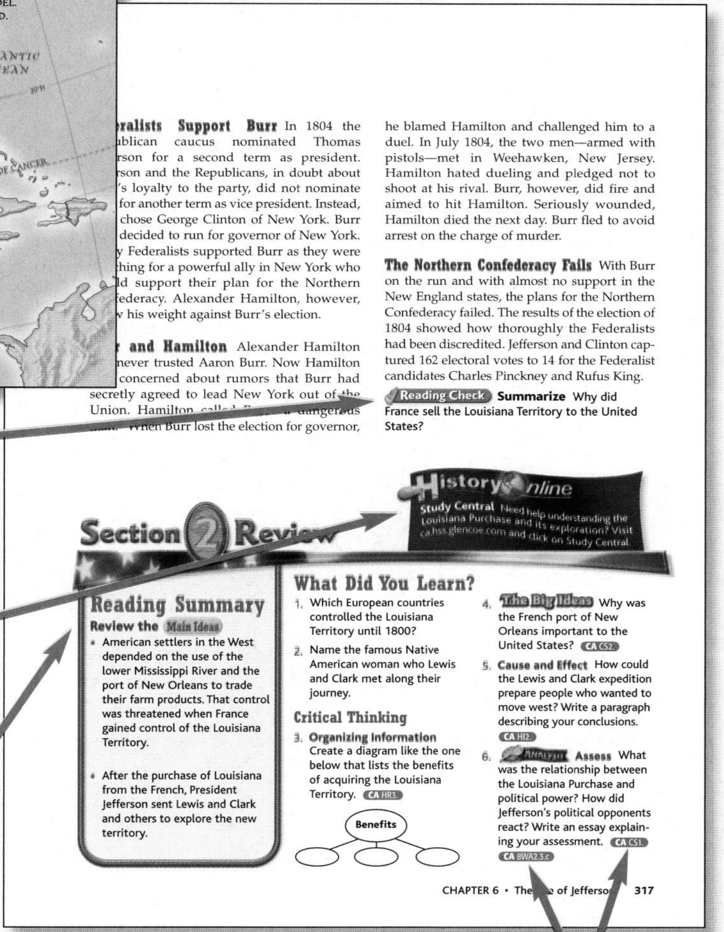

...eralists Support Burr In 1804 the ...ublican caucus nominated Thomas ...rson for a second term as president. ...rson and the Republicans, in doubt about ...'s loyalty to the party, did not nominate ... for another term as vice president. Instead, ... chose George Clinton of New York. Burr ... decided to run for governor of New York. ...y Federalists supported Burr as they were ...hing for a powerful ally in New York who ...ld support their plan for the Northern ...federacy. Alexander Hamilton, however, ...w his weight against Burr's election.

...r and Hamilton Alexander Hamilton ... never trusted Aaron Burr. Now Hamilton ... concerned about rumors that Burr had secretly agreed to lead New York out of the Union. Hamilton called ... a dangerous ... When Burr lost the election for governor, he blamed Hamilton and challenged him to a duel. In July 1804, the two men—armed with pistols—met in Weehawken, New Jersey. Hamilton hated dueling and pledged not to shoot at his rival. Burr, however, did fire and aimed to hit Hamilton. Seriously wounded, Hamilton died the next day. Burr fled to avoid arrest on the charge of murder.

The Northern Confederacy Fails With Burr on the run and with almost no support in the New England states, the plans for the Northern Confederacy failed. The results of the election of 1804 showed how thoroughly the Federalists had been discredited. Jefferson and Clinton captured 162 electoral votes to 14 for the Federalist candidates Charles Pinckney and Rufus King.

Reading Check **Summarize** Why did France sell the Louisiana Territory to the United States?

History Online
Study Central Need help understanding the Louisiana Purchase and its exploration? Visit ca.hss.glencoe.com and click on Study Central.

Section 2 Review

Reading Summary

Review the Main Ideas

- American settlers in the West depended on the use of the lower Mississippi River and the port of New Orleans to trade their farm products. That control was threatened when France gained control of the Louisiana Territory.
- After the purchase of Louisiana from the French, President Jefferson sent Lewis and Clark and others to explore the new territory.

What Did You Learn?

1. Which European countries controlled the Louisiana Territory until 1800?
2. Name the famous Native American woman who Lewis and Clark met along their journey.

Critical Thinking

3. **Organizing Information** Create a diagram like the one below that lists the benefits of acquiring the Louisiana Territory. CA HR3.

Benefits

4. **The Big Ideas** Why was the French port of New Orleans important to the United States? CA CS2.
5. **Cause and Effect** How could the Lewis and Clark expedition prepare people who wanted to move west? Write a paragraph describing your conclusions. CA HI2.
6. **Analysis Assess** What was the relationship between the Louisiana Purchase and political power? How did Jefferson's political opponents react? Write an essay explaining your assessment. CA CS1. CA 8WA2.3.c

CHAPTER 6 • The ... of Jefferso... 317

READING CHECK

This is a **self-check** question to see if you understand the main ideas.

STUDY CENTRAL

Here you can receive **help** with homework.

SECTION REVIEW

Here you can **review** the main topics and answer questions about what you have read.

CALIFORNIA STANDARDS

The California Historical and Social Science Analysis Skills and English–Language Arts **standards** that are covered are shown here.

Chapter Assessment

These pages offer you a chance to check how much you remember after reading the chapter.

Review Content Vocabulary

Content vocabulary is reviewed here.

Review the Main Ideas

Revisit the **Main Ideas** found in your reading.

Read to Write

You are reminded about the chapter **Big Ideas** here.

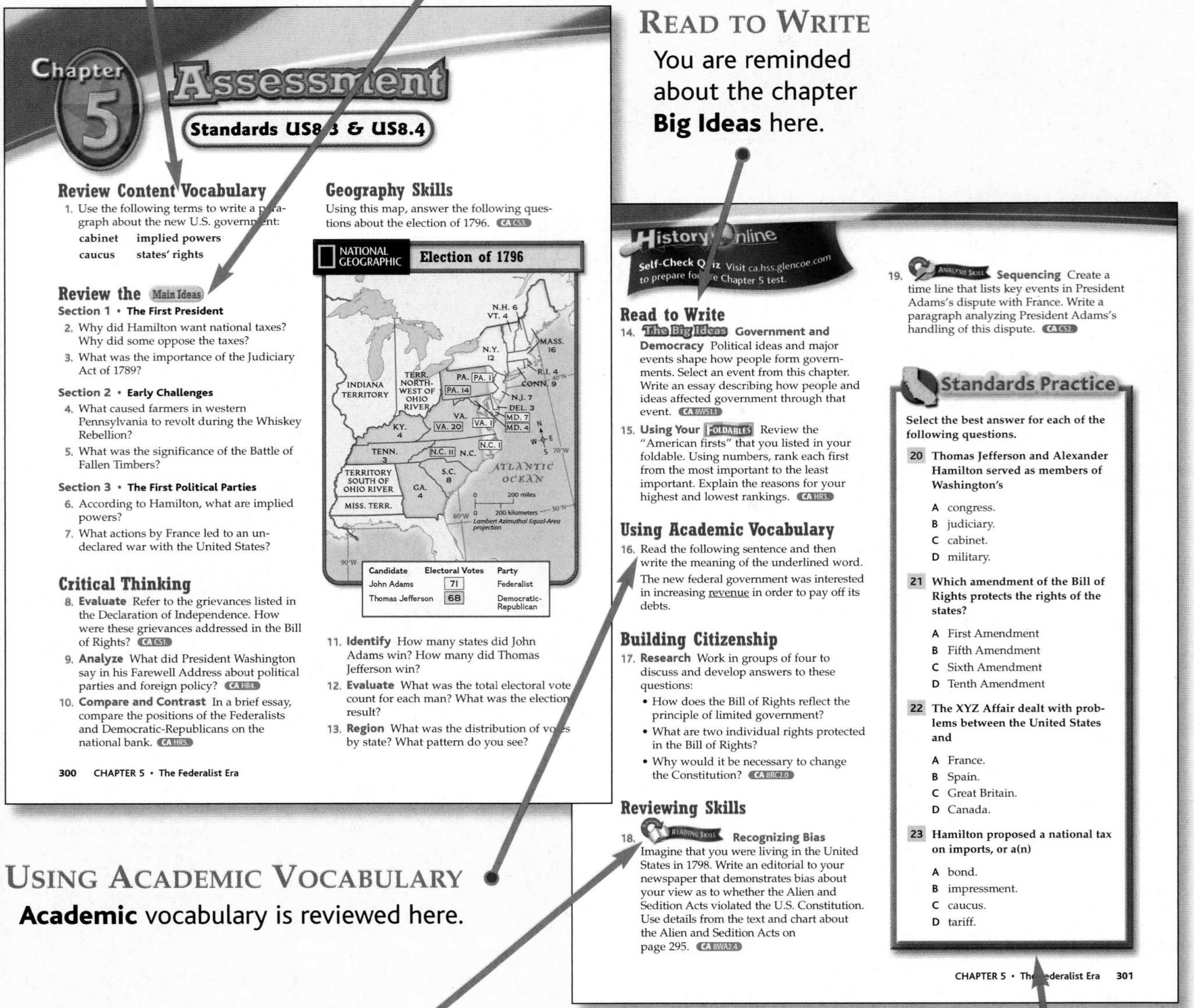

Chapter 5 Assessment

Standards US8.3 & US8.4

Review Content Vocabulary

1. Use the following terms to write a paragraph about the new U.S. government:

cabinet | implied powers
caucus | states' rights

Review the Main Ideas

Section 1 • The First President

2. Why did Hamilton want national taxes? Why did some oppose the taxes?
3. What was the importance of the Judiciary Act of 1789?

Section 2 • Early Challenges

4. What caused farmers in western Pennsylvania to revolt during the Whiskey Rebellion?
5. What was the significance of the Battle of Fallen Timbers?

Section 3 • The First Political Parties

6. According to Hamilton, what are implied powers?
7. What actions by France led to an undeclared war with the United States?

Critical Thinking

8. **Evaluate** Refer to the grievances listed in the Declaration of Independence. How were these grievances addressed in the Bill of Rights? CA CS1.
9. **Analyze** What did President Washington say in his Farewell Address about political parties and foreign policy? CA HR4.
10. **Compare and Contrast** In a brief essay, compare the positions of the Federalists and Democratic-Republicans on the national bank. CA HR5.

Geography Skills

Using this map, answer the following questions about the election of 1796. CA CS3.

National Geographic — Election of 1796

Candidate	Electoral Votes	Party
John Adams	71	Federalist
Thomas Jefferson	68	Democratic-Republican

11. **Identify** How many states did John Adams win? How many did Thomas Jefferson win?
12. **Evaluate** What was the total electoral vote count for each man? What was the election result?
13. **Region** What was the distribution of votes by state? What pattern do you see?

300 CHAPTER 5 • The Federalist Era

History Online — Self-Check Quiz Visit ca.hss.glencoe.com to prepare for the Chapter 5 test.

Read to Write

14. The Big Ideas **Government and Democracy** Political ideas and major events shape how people form governments. Select an event from this chapter. Write an essay describing how people and ideas affected government through that event. CA 8WS1.1
15. **Using Your Foldables** Review the "American firsts" that you listed in your foldable. Using numbers, rank each first from the most important to the least important. Explain the reasons for your highest and lowest rankings. CA HR3.

Using Academic Vocabulary

16. Read the following sentence and then write the meaning of the underlined word. The new federal government was interested in increasing revenue in order to pay off its debts.

Building Citizenship

17. **Research** Work in groups of four to discuss and develop answers to these questions:
- How does the Bill of Rights reflect the principle of limited government?
- What are two individual rights protected in the Bill of Rights?
- Why would it be necessary to change the Constitution? CA 8RC2.0

Reviewing Skills

18. Reading Skill **Recognizing Bias** Imagine that you were living in the United States in 1798. Write an editorial to your newspaper that demonstrates bias about your view as to whether the Alien and Sedition Acts violated the U.S. Constitution. Use details from the text and chart about the Alien and Sedition Acts on page 295. CA 8WA2.4
19. Analysis Skill **Sequencing** Create a time line that lists key events in President Adams's dispute with France. Write a paragraph analyzing President Adams's handling of this dispute. CA CS2.

Standards Practice

Select the best answer for each of the following questions.

20 Thomas Jefferson and Alexander Hamilton served as members of Washington's
- A congress.
- B judiciary.
- C cabinet.
- D military.

21 Which amendment of the Bill of Rights protects the rights of the states?
- A First Amendment
- B Fifth Amendment
- C Sixth Amendment
- D Tenth Amendment

22 The XYZ Affair dealt with problems between the United States and
- A France.
- B Spain.
- C Great Britain.
- D Canada.

23 Hamilton proposed a national tax on imports, or a(n)
- A bond.
- B impressment.
- C caucus.
- D tariff.

CHAPTER 5 • The Federalist Era 301

Using Academic Vocabulary

Academic vocabulary is reviewed here.

Review Arrows

Look for the Review arrows that tell you are **reviewing** material you have learned before.

Standards Practice

Here you get a chance to practice questions related to the **standards.**

California Standards

A Guide to the California Standards appears on pages CA1-CA14 of your textbook. This guide lists all the History–Social Science Standards for grade 8. They are covered in your textbook. In addition, the guide includes the Historical and Social Sciences Analysis Skills and the English-Language Arts Standards, which are addressed throughout the textbook.

FOR STUDENTS AND THEIR FAMILIES

Here is an explanation of what is contained in the **Guide to the California Standards.**

ANALYSIS SKILLS

Here is a list of standards that relate to **thinking and research skills.** You can develop these skills in your history class.

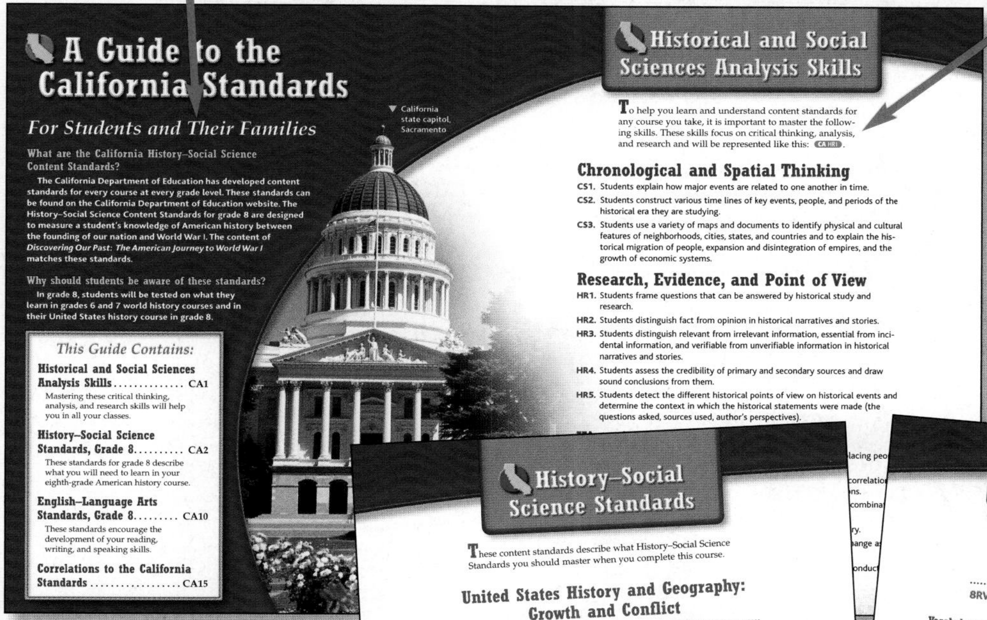

CALIFORNIA HISTORY–SOCIAL SCIENCE STANDARD

This is the **main idea** of the American history content standard.

SUPPORTING STANDARD

Each main standard has **more specific** supporting standards.

CALIFORNIA ENGLISH–LANGUAGE ARTS STANDARDS

These **standards** are for reading, writing, written and oral English language conventions, and listening and speaking. Each **main standard** has one or more **supporting standards.**

California Content Standards

The **standards** covered on a page will be listed at the top of that page.

California Content Standards

You will also find **standards** listed in the side column at the beginning of each section.

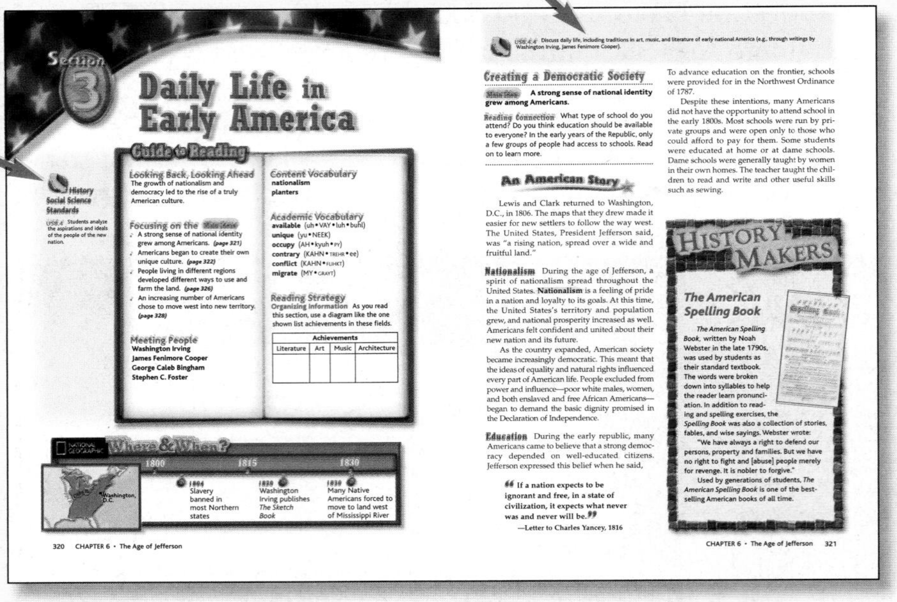

Tools of the Historian

Here is an explanation of how to use the Historical and Social Sciences Analysis Skill for **chronology.**

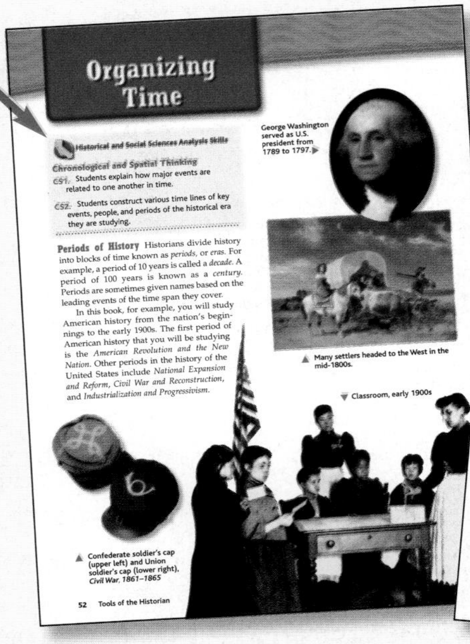

California Standards

The California History–Social Science and English–Language Arts **standards** that are covered are shown here.

California Standards Handbook

This handbook is found on pages 862–884. It gives you another chance to practice your understanding of the **eighth-grade content standards.**

Main Standard

The chart shows the **main standard** of the American history standards.

Where Can I Find It?

Here is more information about the **standard.** The explanations tell **where** in your text this standard and its supporting standards are covered.

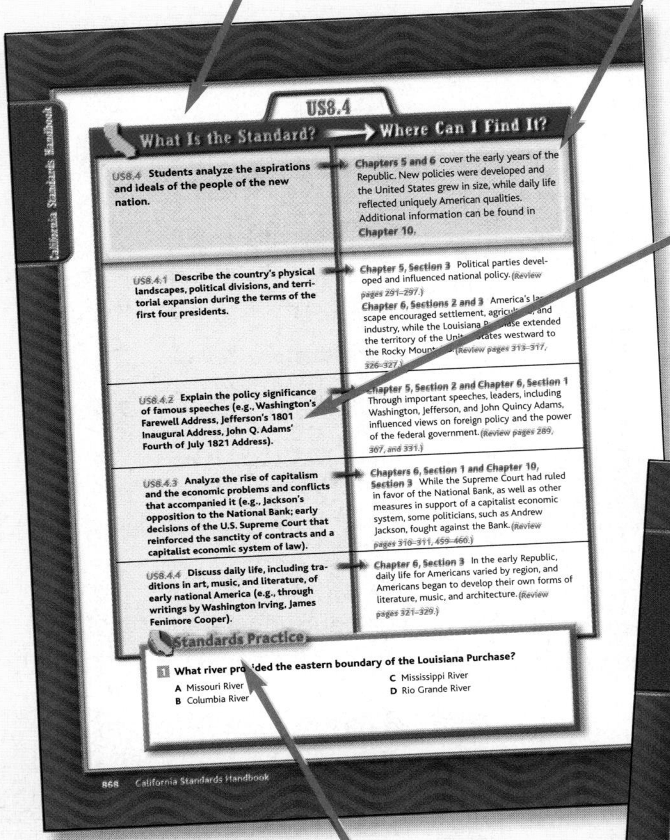

California Standards Handbook

US8.4

What Is the Standard?	Where Can I Find It?
US8.4 Students analyze the aspirations and ideals of the people of the new nation.	Chapters 5 and 6 cover the early years of the Republic. New policies were developed and the United States grew in size, while daily life reflected uniquely American qualities. Additional information can be found in Chapter 10.
US8.4.1 Describe the country's physical landscapes, political divisions, and territorial expansion during the terms of the first four presidents.	Chapter 5, Section 3 Political parties developed and influenced national policy. (Review pages 291–297.) Chapter 6, Sections 2 and 3 America's la[illegible] scape encouraged settlement, agricu[illegible] and industry, while the Louisiana P[illegible]ase extended the territory of the Uni[illegible] States westward to the Rocky Moun[illegible] (Review pages 313–317, 326–327.)
US8.4.2 Explain the policy significance of famous speeches (e.g., Washington's Farewell Address, Jefferson's 1801 Inaugural Address, John Q. Adams' Fourth of July 1821 Address).	Chapter 5, Section 2 and Chapter 6, Section 1 Through important speeches, leaders, including Washington, Jefferson, and John Quincy Adams, influenced views on foreign policy and the power of the federal government. (Review pages 289, 307, and 331.)
US8.4.3 Analyze the rise of capitalism and the economic problems and conflicts that accompanied it (e.g., Jackson's opposition to the National Bank; early decisions of the U.S. Supreme Court that reinforced the sanctity of contracts and a capitalist economic system of law).	Chapters 6, Section 1 and Chapter 10, Section 3 While the Supreme Court had ruled in favor of the National Bank, as well as other measures in support of a capitalist economic system, some politicians, such as Andrew Jackson, fought against the Bank. (Review pages 310–311, 459–460.)
US8.4.4 Discuss daily life, including traditions in art, music, and literature, of early national America (e.g., through writings by Washington Irving, James Fenimore Cooper).	Chapter 6, Section 3 In the early Republic, daily life for Americans varied by region, and Americans began to develop their own forms of literature, music, and architecture. (Review pages 321–329.)

Standards Practice

1 What river pro[illegible]ded the eastern boundary of the Louisiana Purchase?

A Missouri River
B Columbia River
C Mississippi River
D Rio Grande River

868 California Standards Handbook

Supporting Standards

The chart also lists the **supporting standards** for the main standards.

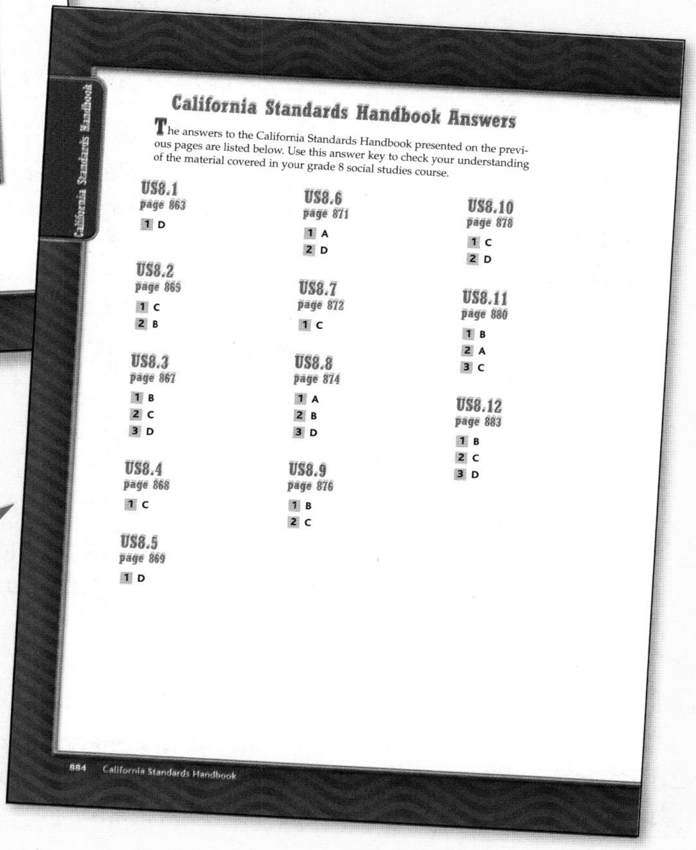

California Standards Handbook

California Standards Handbook Answers

The answers to the California Standards Handbook presented on the previous pages are listed below. Use this answer key to check your understanding of the material covered in your grade 8 social studies course.

US8.1 page 863
1 D

US8.2 page 865
1 C
2 B

US8.3 page 867
1 B
2 C
3 D

US8.4 page 868
1 C

US8.5 page 869
1 D

US8.6 page 871
1 A
2 D

US8.7 page 872
1 C

US8.8 page 874
1 A
2 B
3 D

US8.9 page 876
1 B
2 C

US8.10 page 878
1 C
2 D

US8.11 page 880
1 B
2 A
3 C

US8.12 page 883
1 B
2 C
3 D

884 California Standards Handbook

Standards Practice

Practice questions are written in the same way that you will see them on the standards assessment.

Answers to the Standards Handbook

An **answer key** allows you to check your answers.

Special Features

Special features supply more information about topics in a chapter or unit. They help history come alive.

America's Literature

The literature selection is connected to people or events in the chapter.

Before You Read

Get an idea of what the literature selection is about **before** you start reading.

Vocabulary Preview

Here are words and terms that may be new to you.

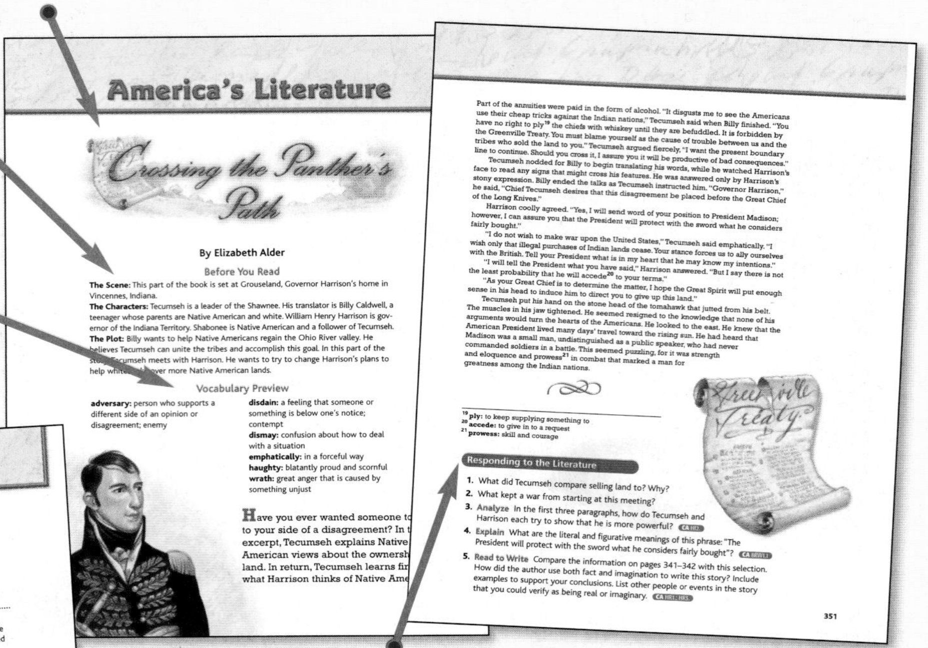

America's Literature

Crossing the Panther's Path

By Elizabeth Alder

Before You Read

The Scene: This part of the book is set at Grouseland, Governor Harrison's home in Vincennes, Indiana.

The Characters: Tecumseh is a leader of the Shawnee. His translator is Billy Caldwell, a teenager whose parents are Native American and white. William Henry Harrison is governor of the Indiana Territory. Shabonee is Native American and a follower of Tecumseh.

The Plot: Billy wants to help Native Americans regain the Ohio River valley. He believes Tecumseh can unite the tribes and accomplish this goal. In this part of the story Tecumseh meets with Harrison. He wants to try to change Harrison's plans to help white [illegible] over more Native American lands.

Vocabulary Preview

adversary: person who supports a different side of an opinion or disagreement; enemy

disdain: a feeling that someone or something is below one's notice; contempt

dismay: confusion about how to deal with a situation

emphatically: in a forceful way

haughty: blatantly proud and scornful

wrath: great anger that is caused by something unjust

Have you ever wanted someone to ... to your side of a disagreement? In t... excerpt, Tecumseh explains Native American views about the ownersh... land. In return, Tecumseh learns fir... what Harrison thinks of Native Ame...

Part of the annuities were paid in the form of alcohol. "It disgusts me to see the Americans use their cheap tricks against the Indian nations," Tecumseh said when Billy finished. "You have no right to ply[19] the chiefs with whiskey until they are befuddled. It is forbidden by the Greenville Treaty. You must blame yourself as the cause of trouble between us and the tribes who sold the land to you." Tecumseh argued fiercely, "I want the present boundary line to continue. Should you cross it, I assure you it will be productive of bad consequences."

Tecumseh nodded for Billy to begin translating his words, while he watched Harrison's face to read any signs that might cross his features. He was answered only by Harrison's stony expression. Billy ended the talks as Tecumseh instructed him. "Governor Harrison," he said, "Chief Tecumseh desires that this disagreement be placed before the Great Chief of the Long Knives."

Harrison coolly agreed. "Yes, I will send word of your position to President Madison; however, I can assure you that the President will protect with the sword what he considers fairly bought."

"I do not wish to make war upon the United States," Tecumseh said emphatically. "I wish only that illegal purchases of Indian lands cease. Your stance forces us to ally ourselves with the British. Tell your President what is in my heart that he may know my intentions."

"I will tell the President what you have said," Harrison answered. "But I say there is not the least probability that he will accede[20] to your terms."

"As your Great Chief is to determine the matter, I hope the Great Spirit will put enough sense in his head to induce him to direct you to give up this land."

Tecumseh put his hand on the stone head of the tomahawk that jutted from his belt. The muscles in his jaw tightened. He seemed resigned to the knowledge that none of his arguments would turn the hearts of the Americans. He looked to the east. He knew that the American President lived many days' travel toward the rising sun. He had heard that Madison was a small man, undistinguished as a public speaker, who had never commanded soldiers in a battle. This seemed puzzling, for it was strength and eloquence and prowess[21] in combat that marked a man for greatness among the Indian nations.

[19] **ply:** to keep supplying something to
[20] **accede:** to give in to a request
[21] **prowess:** skill and courage

Responding to the Literature

1. What did Tecumseh compare selling land to? Why?
2. What kept a war from starting at this meeting?
3. **Analyze** In the first three paragraphs, how do Tecumseh and Harrison each try to show that he is more powerful? CA HI2
4. **Explain** What are the literal and figurative meanings of this phrase: "The President will protect with the sword what he considers fairly bought"? CA 8RW1.1
5. **Read to Write** Compare the information on pages 341–342 with this selection. How did the author use both fact and imagination to write this story? Include examples to support your conclusions. List other people or events in the story that you could verify as being real or imaginary. CA HR1; HR5

351

Responding to the Literature

The questions help you check your understanding of the story. The **writing** activity asks you to analyze the reading.

Reading On Your Own...

From the California Reading List

Do you want to learn more about George Washington, Sacajawea, and the early years of the United States? You might be interested in the following books.

Biography

Founding Father: Rediscovering George Washington by Richard Brookhiser explores Washington as a person, a soldier, and a political leader. He explains why Washington was so important in forming the future of the United States. ***The content of this book is related to*** *History–Social Studies Standard US8.2.*

Nonfiction

Old Ironsides: Americans Build a Fighting Ship by David Weitzman invites readers to see how this great warship was built. As readers follow John Aylwin, a young worker on the ship, they learn what it took to make "Old Ironsides." ***The content of this book is related to*** *History–Social Studies Standard US8.5.*

Historical Fiction

Carry On, Mr. Bowditch by Jean L. Latham tells the amazing tale of Nathaniel Bowditch. Although he had very little education, he mastered sea navigation during his voyages around the world. His book *American Practical Navigator* was used with few changes into the 1900s. ***The content of this book is related to*** *History–Social Studies Standard US8.6.*

Historical Fiction

Sacajawea: The Story of Bird Woman and the Lewis and Clark Expedition by Joseph Bruchac has Sacajawea and Clark taking turns describing events. The story also includes parts of the explorers' journals and Shoshone tales. ***The content of this book is related to*** *History–Social Studies Standard US8.4.*

352

Biography

US8.4 Students analyze the aspirations and ideals of the people of the new nation.

ABIGAIL ADAMS
1744–1818

JOHN ADAMS
1735–1826

John Adams, a young lawyer, and Abigail Smith were married in 1764. The young couple lived on a farm in Braintree, Massachusetts, and had five children. John was one of the leaders of the movement for independence. In late 1774 John Adams went to Philadelphia as a delegate to the Continental Congress, while Abigail Adams remained in Massachusetts to manage their business affairs and take care of the family. During most of the Confederation period, Abigail Adams lived in Europe with John, who was the first American minister to Great Britain. Eventually, when John was elected the second president of the United States, Abigail became the first First Lady to preside over the still unfinished White House.

Although she lacked a formal education, Abigail Adams developed a notable talent as a letter writer. Letter writing, she said, was "a habit, the pleasure of which increases with practice, but becomes irksome by neglect." In one of her most well-known letters, she made the following plea to her husband and his associates in the Continental Congress.

"Remember the Ladies, and be more generous and favourable to them than your ancestors. Do not put such unlimited power into the hands of the Husbands. Remember all Men would be tyrants if they could. If particular care and attention is not paid to the Ladies we are determined to foment a Rebellion, and will not hold ourselves bound by any Laws in which we have no voice."

Despite the hopes of Abigail and many women, they still could not vote or hold office in the years after the American Revolution. Abigail Adams believed strongly in equal rights for women and African Americans at a time in history when such views were not well received.

▲ Abigail Adams

◀ John Adams

Then and Now

How does the role of women in government differ today from their role during Abigail Adams's time?

294

Biography

Read more about important **people** and what they achieved.

Reading On Your Own . . .

These books are suggested readings about topics in the unit.

Then and Now

In the writing activity, you **compare** a similar situation in the past and the present.

Connecting to the Constitution

Here you will learn about how the **Constitution** has been able to respond to challenges that the Framers never imagined.

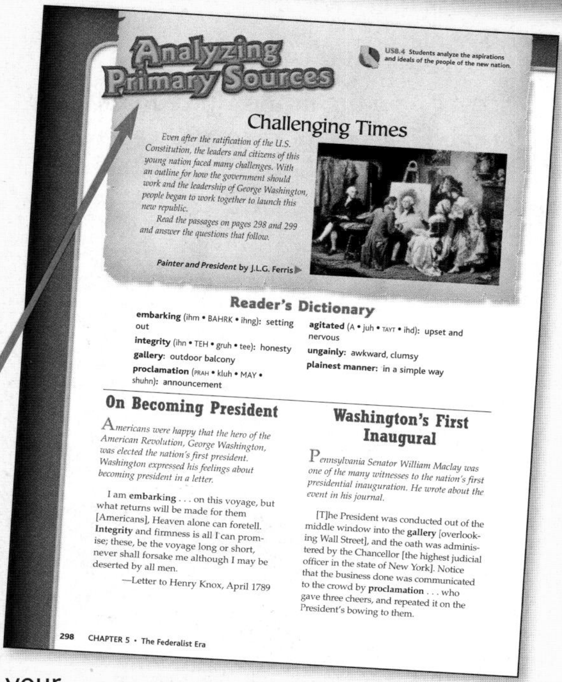

Analyzing Primary Sources

You will check your understanding of the **primary sources** and **write** a response to one or more of them.

You Decide . . .

Imagine that you can give your **opinion** when two opposing views are presented.

You Be the Historian

Give your **opinion** on the issue.

History Makers

Learn how people, decisions, objects, and events **changed history.**

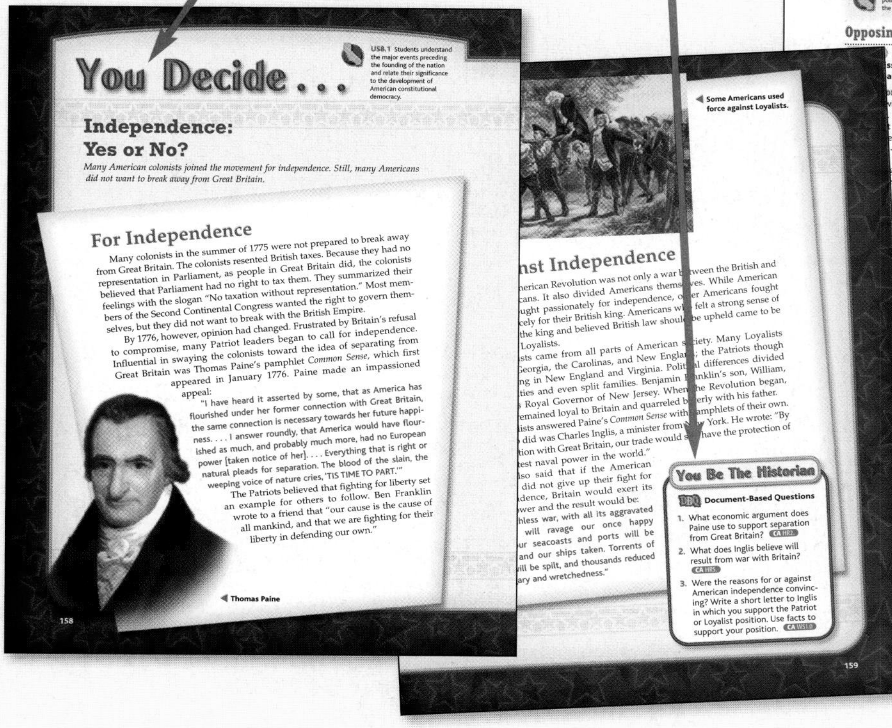

Previewing Your Textbook

The Way It Was

Discover how life in the United States has **changed** over more than 200 years.

Why It Matters

Learn how particular events **influenced** the future.

USS.4.1 Describe the country's physical landscapes, political divisions, and territorial expansion during the terms of the first four presidents.

Jefferson's Policies

Main Idea Jefferson worked to limit the scope of the federal government and shift control of the federal courts away from the Federalists.

Reading Connection How should the federal government balance individual liberty with national interests? Read on to learn of changes Jefferson made to deal with this question.

In 1801, when Jefferson became president, the entire federal government consisted of only a few hundred people. This was exactly how Jefferson thought it should be. (Today nearly 3 million civilians work for the federal government.) In Jefferson's view, the national government should conduct foreign affairs and limit its domestic actions to delivering the mail, collecting customs duties, and taking a census every 10 years.

Jefferson Takes Charge When Jefferson entered office, he surrounded himself with men who shared his Republican principles. His secretary of state was his friend and fellow Virginian, James Madison. For secretary of the treasury, he chose **Albert Gallatin**, a Pennsylvanian with a strong grasp of financial matters.

Jefferson and Gallatin aimed to reduce the national debt that the Federalists had left. They scaled down military expenses by cutting the army by one-third and reducing the navy from 25 to 7 ships. By slashing spending, Jefferson and Gallatin **significantly** lowered the national debt within a few years.

Between the election and Jefferson's inauguration, Federalists in Congress passed the Judiciary Act of 1801. This act increased the number of federal judges. Outgoing President John Adams then filled many positions with Federalists.

The Way It Was

▲ Abigail Adams in the unfinished White House

Washington in 1800

The United States government moved to the new capital city of Washington, D.C., in 1800. Being located along the Potomac River, Washington was expected to emerge as a great trading city, but the plans for a great city had not proceeded very far. The president's house, with laundry sometimes hanging in the unfinished East Room, stood in an open field with two boxlike buildings for executive offices nearby. More than a mile away, across a swamp, stood the partly built Capitol. Members of Congress lived in crowded boardinghouses. The streets were mostly muddy wagon tracks, bordered with the stumps of trees that had been recently cut. Some Americans criticized the choice of Washington as the capital. They believed that the government should move to a larger city.

308

The Women's Rights Movement The Seneca Falls Convention paved the way for the growth of the women's rights movement. During the 1800s, women held several national conventions. Many reformers—male and female—joined the movement.

Susan B. Anthony, the daughter of a Quaker abolitionist in rural New York, worked for women's rights and temperance. She called for equal pay for women, college training for girls, and **coeducation**—the teaching of boys and girls together.

Susan B. Anthony met Elizabeth Cady Stanton at a temperance meeting in 1851. They became lifelong friends and partners in the struggle for women's rights. For the rest of the century, Anthony and Stanton led the women's movement. They worked with other women to win the right to vote, which was granted by several states. It was not until 1920, however, that woman suffrage became a reality everywhere in the United States.

Reading Check **Explain** What is suffrage?

Why It Matters

Photo Gallery

Raising the Status of Women

The Seneca Falls Convention

Throughout the nation's history, women had fought side by side with the men to build a new nation and to ensure freedom. Even though the Declaration of Independence promised equality for all, the promise rang hollow for women.

Female reformers began a campaign for their own rights. In 1848 Lucretia Mott and Elizabeth Cady Stanton organized the Seneca Falls Convention. One of the resolutions demanded suffrage, or the right to vote, for women. This marked the beginning of a long, hard road to gain equal rights.

Lucretia Mott (below) and Susan B. Anthony were leaders in the effort to allow women a greater role in American society.

"We hold these truths to be self-evident: that all men and women are created equal." —*Declaration of the Seneca Falls Convention, 1848*

Gaining the Right to Vote, 1848–1920

The Seneca Falls Convention led to the growth of the woman suffrage movement.

1848	1850	1866	1869	1878	1884
Seneca Falls Convention	First national women's rights convention held in Worcester, Massachusetts	Susan B. Anthony forms Equal Rights Association	Women granted voting rights in Wyoming Territory	Woman suffrage amendment first introduced in U.S. Congress	Belva Lockwood runs for president

410 CHAPTER 8 • The Northeast: Building Industry

Geography & History

Find out how **geography** has affected people and people have affected the environment.

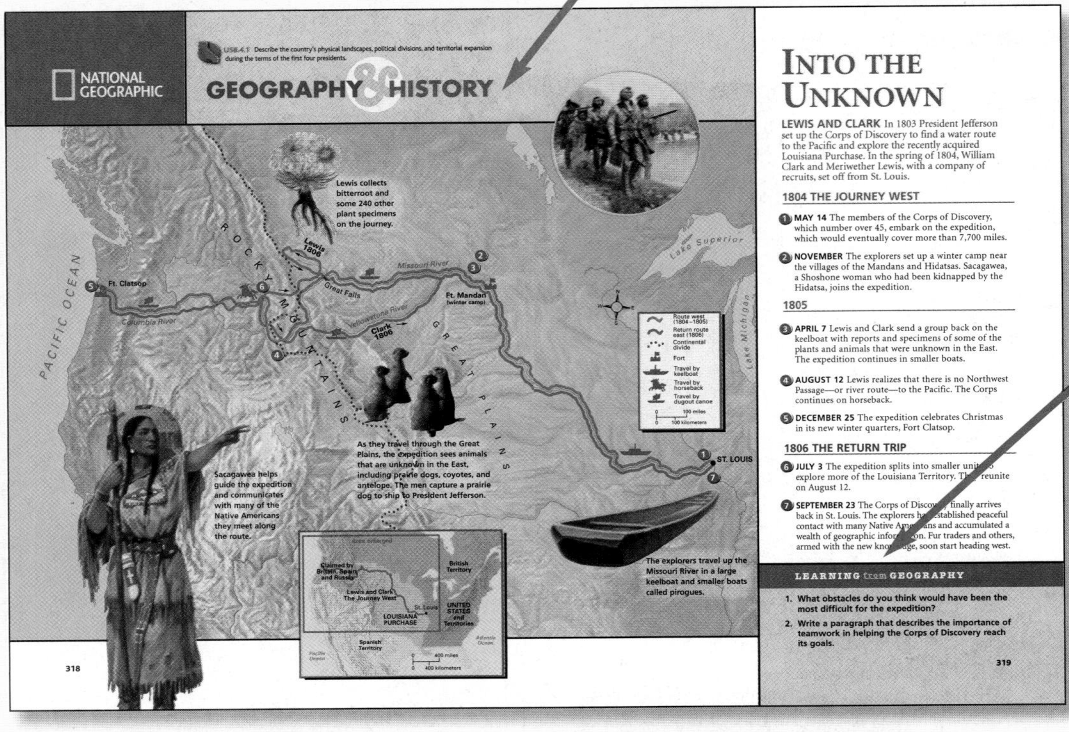

USS.4.1 Describe the country's physical landscapes, political divisions, and territorial expansion during the terms of the first four presidents.

NATIONAL GEOGRAPHIC

GEOGRAPHY & HISTORY

318

INTO THE UNKNOWN

LEWIS AND CLARK In 1803 President Jefferson set up the Corps of Discovery to find a water route to the Pacific and explore the recently acquired Louisiana Purchase. In the spring of 1804, William Clark and Meriwether Lewis, with a company of recruits, set off from St. Louis.

1804 THE JOURNEY WEST

1. **MAY 14** The members of the Corps of Discovery, which number over 45, embark on the expedition, which would eventually cover more than 7,700 miles.
2. **NOVEMBER** The explorers set up a winter camp near the villages of the Mandans and Hidatsas. Sacagawea, a Shoshone woman who had been kidnapped by the Hidatsa, joins the expedition.

1805

3. **APRIL 7** Lewis and Clark send a group back on the keelboat with reports and specimens of some of the plants and animals that were unknown in the East. The expedition continues in smaller boats.
4. **AUGUST 12** Lewis realizes that there is no Northwest Passage—or river route—to the Pacific. The Corps continues on horseback.
5. **DECEMBER 25** The expedition celebrates Christmas in its new winter quarters, Fort Clatsop.

1806 THE RETURN TRIP

6. **JULY 3** The expedition splits into smaller units to explore more of the Louisiana Territory. They reunite on August 12.
7. **SEPTEMBER 23** The Corps of Discovery finally arrives back in St. Louis. The explorers have established peaceful contact with many Native Americans and accumulated a wealth of geographic information. Fur traders and others, armed with the new knowledge, soon start heading west.

LEARNING from GEOGRAPHY

1. What obstacles do you think would have been the most difficult for the expedition?
2. Write a paragraph that describes the importance of teamwork in helping the Corps of Discovery reach its goals.

319

Learning from Geography

Evaluate in **writing** the impact of geography on people and events.

Scavenger Hunt

Discovering Our Past: The American Journey to World War I contains a wealth of information. The trick is to know where to look to access all the information in the book.

If you run through this scavenger hunt exercise with your teacher or parents, you will see how the textbook is organized, and how to get the most out of your reading and study time. Let's get started!

1. How many units and how many chapters are in this book?
   6 units; 17 chapters
2. What is the title of Chapter 4, Section 3?
   Citizens' Rights and Responsibilities
3. You want to quickly find all the maps in the book on the Civil War. Where are they listed?
   in the Table of Contents under Maps, Charts, and Graphs—Maps, Unit 5
4. What time period does Chapter 7, Section 2 cover?
   1800–1830
5. In Chapter 4, what will the *Foldables* activity help you do?
   chart what you know, want to know, and learned about the Constitution
6. What reading skill will you practice in Chapter 1?
   previewing
7. What are the Big, or most important, Ideas in Chapter 2? Where can you find this information? Political ideas and major events shape how people form governments; A constitution reflects the values and goals of a society that creates it; on the second page of the chapter (p. 175)
8. There are six Web sites in Chapter 5. The first one previews the chapter. What do the other five sites do? How are some sites similar?
   Pages 284, 289, and 297 are part of Study Central, which reviews information in a section; page 292 is a web activity based on chapter content; page 301 is a self-check quiz to prepare for the chapter assessment.
9. A primary source is a document or other testimony, dating from the same period as an event. In what part of chapters 1–17 can you always find primary sources?
   just before the Chapter Assessment
10. Where, in the back of the book, can you quickly find the meaning of Content Vocabulary words, such as *confederation*? What is a confederation? in the Glossary or Spanish Glossary; a voluntary association of independent states; una asociación voluntaria de estados independientes

Why Should I Teach Reading to My Social Studies Students?

For many social studies teachers, helping students develop reading skills is a low priority—nice to do if there is time, but not necessary. After all, there is scarcely time to meet many of the state-mandated standards. Why add reading instruction to the list? The answer is that reading skills are essential to the learning of all subjects. In the social studies, students must read to learn. Struggling readers risk learning less than those who are proficient in reading.

Teachers who infuse literacy strategies with social studies content actively engage students in learning. Once students internalize reading strategies such as visualizing, predicting, questioning, and making connections, they inevitably become better social studies students.

Reading Skills Handbook

READING TO LEARN

This handbook focuses on skills and strategies that can help you understand the words you read. The strategies you use to understand whole texts depend on the kind of text you are reading. In other words, you do not read a textbook the way you read a novel. You read a textbook mainly for information; you read a novel for the story and the characters. To get the most out of your reading, you need to choose the right strategy to fit the reason you are reading. This handbook can help you learn about the following reading strategies:

- how to identify new words and build your vocabulary;
- how to adjust the way you read to fit your reason for reading;
- how to use specific reading strategies to better understand what you read;
- how to use critical thinking strategies to think more deeply about what you read; and
- how to understand text structures to identify an author's ideas.

TABLE OF CONTENTS

Identifying Words and Building Vocabulary 15–16
Reading for a Reason 17
Understanding What You Read ... 18–19
Thinking About Your Reading 20–21
Understanding Text Structure 22–23

Professional Development: Teaching Reading

The following sources will help you teach reading skills:

- *Subjects Matter: Every Teacher's Guide to Content-Area Reading,* by Harvey Daniels and Steven Zemelman. Portsmouth, NH: Heinemann, 2004.
- *Improving Adolescent Literacy: Strategies at Work,* by Douglas Fisher and Nancy Frey. Upper Saddle River, NJ: Merrill Education, 2004.
- *I Read It But I Don't Get It: Comprehension Strategies for Adolescent Readers,* by Cris Tovani. Portland, ME: Stenhouse Publishers, 2000.
- *Teaching Reading in the Middle School,* by Laura Robb. New York, NY: Scholastic Professional Books, 2000.

Identifying Words and Building Vocabulary

What do you do when you come across a word you do not know as you read? Do you skip over the word? If you are reading a novel, you use the context to understand the meaning of the word. But if you are reading for information, an unfamiliar word may get in the way of your understanding. When that happens, follow the strategies below to learn how to say the word and what it means.

Reading Unfamiliar Words

Sounding Out the Word One way to figure out how to say a new word is to sound it out, syllable by syllable. Look carefully at the word's beginning, middle, and ending. For example, in the word *coagulate,* what letters make up the beginning sound or beginning syllable of the word? *Co* rhymes with *so.* Inside *coagulate,* do you see a word you already know how to pronounce? The syllable *ag* has the same sound as the *ag* in *bag,* and the syllable *u* is pronounced like the letter *u.* What letters make up the ending sound or syllable? *Late* is a familiar word you already know how to pronounce. Now try pronouncing the whole word: ***co ag u late.***

Determining a Word's Meaning

Using Syntax Like all languages, the English language has rules and patterns for the way words are arranged in sentences. The way a sentence is organized is called the syntax. If English is your first language, you have known this pattern since you started using sentences. If you are learning English now, you may find that the syntax is different from the patterns you know in your first language.

In a simple sentence in English, someone or something (the subject) does something (the predicate or verb) to or with another person or thing (the object): *The soldiers attacked the enemy.* Sometimes adjectives, adverbs, and phrases are added to add details to the sentence: *The courageous young soldiers fearlessly attacked the well-entrenched enemy shortly after dawn.*

Knowing about syntax can help you figure out the meaning of an unfamiliar word. Just look at how syntax can help you figure out the following nonsense sentence: *The blizzy kwarkles sminched the flerky fleans.* Your experience with English syntax tells you that the action word, or verb, in this sentence is *sminched.* Who did the *sminching?* The *kwarkles.* What kind of *kwarkles* were they? *Blizzy.* Whom did they *sminch?* The *fleans.* What kind of *fleans* were they? *Flerky.* Even though you don't know the meaning of the words in the nonsense sentence, you can make some sense of the entire sentence by studying its syntax.

Using Context Clues You can often figure out the meaning of an unfamiliar word by looking at its context, the words and sentences that surround it. To learn new words as you read, follow these steps for using context clues.

- Look before and after the unfamiliar word for a definition or a synonym, a general topic associated with the word, a clue to what the word is similar to or different from, or an action or a description that has something to do with the word.
- Connect what you already know with what the author has written.
- Predict a possible meaning.
- Use the meaning in the sentence.
- Try again if your guess does not make sense.

Identifying Words and Building Vocabulary

Why It's Important

Research documents the relationship between a strong vocabulary and the ability to read and write proficiently. Vocabulary may be the most important factor in comprehension, showing that ongoing, specific vocabulary instruction must be an integral part of every lesson.

Providing instructional support while students are reading is not enough to ensure they are learning the content. For this reason, this handbook provides skills for before reading, during reading, and after reading.

Before Reading

Activating Prior Knowledge

Distribute index cards with a key word from the chapter written on each card. Organize students into groups of four, and give them time to discuss their words. After the group discussion, ask each group to write what they think the word means on the back of the card. Then have groups present the words to the class by writing their words and definitions on the board. Other students should help confirm or revise the definitions. Use pictures or graphs to enhance or correct the students' definitions. **OL**

UNIVERSAL ACCESS

Below Grade Level One way to help students increase their vocabularies is to have them play word games before they read the chapter. Give students a word from the chapter that they do not know, and allow them to ask questions about its definition. When a student correctly guesses its meaning, he or she can then be "it," choosing a new word for the class to question. This type of game demonstrates that there are often many definitions for a word, and it allows students to learn from each other. **BL**

During Reading

Learning Vocabulary Post a chart on the wall listing the steps for learning new vocabulary. Students may refer to the chart as they read. Steps include: sound out the word; look at prefixes, suffixes, and roots; look at how the word is used in the sentence; use context clues in surrounding sentences; use reference materials such as dictionaries and thesauruses; ask someone the meaning of the word. Encourage students to experiment with different steps to find the one that works best for them. OL

After Reading

Understanding Vocabulary Students should use graphic organizers and web diagrams to explain the definition of a word. Have students write the word in the center of a sheet of notebook paper. Then have them write *What it is* at the top left of the page, *What it is like* at the top right, *Examples of its meaning* at the bottom left of the page, and *What it is not* at the bottom right. Have students write the appropriate information under each head. OL

Checking Your Understanding Answers

1. graled
2. shabs
3. the mul-bulowed rotfabs

Using Types of Reference Materials Dictionaries and other reference sources can help you learn new words and how to use them. Check out these reference sources. You can find these in your local public or school library as well as on the Internet.

- A **dictionary** gives the pronunciation, the meaning or multiple meanings, and often examples of how to use the words. Some dictionaries also provide illustrations or diagrams to help define words, other forms of words, their parts of speech, and synonyms. You might also find the historical background of a word, such as its Greek, Latin, or Anglo-Saxon origins.
- A **glossary** is a word list that appears at the end–or Appendix–of a book or other written work and includes only words that are in that work. Like dictionaries, glossaries include the pronunciation and definitions of words.
- A **thesaurus** lists groups of words that have the same, or almost the same, meaning. Words with similar meanings are called synonyms. Seeing the synonyms of words can help you build your vocabulary.

Recognizing Word Meanings Across Subjects

Have you ever learned a new word in one class and then noticed it in your reading for other subjects? The word probably will not mean exactly the same thing in each class. But you can use what you know about the word's meaning to help you understand what it means in a different subject area. Look at the following example from three different subjects:

- **Social studies:** One *product* manufactured in the southern part of the United States is cotton cloth.
- **Math:** After multiplying the numbers five and five, explain how you arrived at the *product*.
- **Science:** One *product* of photosynthesis is oxygen.

CHECKING YOUR UNDERSTANDING

The following sentence does not include real English words, but you can use what you have learned about English syntax to decode the sentence. First read the sentence. Then answer the questions that follow.

The shabs smatously graled the mul-bulowed rotfabs.

1. **What is the verb in the sentence?**
2. **What is the subject?**
3. **What is the object?**

MORE ABOUT THE READING STRATEGY

How can teachers help students understand word concepts instead of just learning simple definitions? One way is to use words often and in a variety of ways. Teams of teachers can choose common vocabulary words which they will present in various content area classes. Teachers should provide opportunities for integrating the words into meaningful contexts. The goal is for students to develop full knowledge of the words so that they become fixed parts of their vocabularies. For example, the word *prime* may mean different things in math, social studies, and science. Students need to understand all of these uses.

Reading for a Reason

Why are you reading that paperback mystery? What do you hope to get from your American history textbook? And are you going to read either of these books in the same way that you read a restaurant menu? The point is, you read for different reasons. The reason you are reading something helps you decide on the reading strategies you use with a text. In other words, how you read will depend on why you are reading.

Knowing Your Reason for Reading

In school and in life, you will have many reasons for reading, and those reasons will lead you to a wide range of materials:

- **To learn and understand new information,** you might read news magazines, textbooks, news on the Internet, books about your favorite pastime, encyclopedia articles, primary and secondary sources for a school report, instructions on how to use a calling card, or directions for a standardized test.
- **To find specific information,** you might look at the sports section for the score of last night's game, a notice on where to register for a field trip, weather reports, bank statements, or television listings.
- **To be entertained,** you might read your favorite magazine, e-mails or letters from friends, the Sunday comics, or even novels, short stories, plays, or poems!

Adjusting How Fast You Read

How quickly or how carefully you should read a text depends on your purpose for reading it. Because there are many reasons and ways to read, think about your purpose and choose the strategy that works best. Try out these strategies:

- **Scanning** means quickly running your eyes over the material, looking for key words or phrases that point to the information you are looking for. Scan when you need to find a particular piece or type of information. For example, you might scan a newspaper for movie show times.
- **Skimming** means quickly reading a piece of writing to find its main idea or to get a general overview of it. For example, you might skim the sports section of the daily newspaper to find out how your favorite teams are doing. Or you might skim a chapter in your textbook to prepare for a test.
- **Careful reading** involves reading very slowly and paying close attention with a purpose in mind. Read carefully when you are learning new concepts, following complicated directions, or preparing to explain information to someone else.

CHECKING YOUR UNDERSTANDING

If you were working on a research paper on the American Revolution, how would you adjust the speed at which you were reading for each of the following cases?

1. **You have just found a 1,200-page work that covers the entire colonial and revolutionary era of the British colonies in North America.**
2. **You have discovered an article in a leading history magazine that supports every point that you are trying to make.**

UNIVERSAL ACCESS

Below Grade Level Students need practice with establishing a reason for reading. Encourage students to read news magazines, newspapers, historical novels, nonfiction books, or Internet articles. Before reading, have students write a rationale for why they have chosen that type of reading. Students should describe what they will do after they read, such as present an oral report or post a response on a discussion board. **BL**

Reading Skills Handbook

Reading for a Reason

Why It's Important

When students have a reason or purpose for reading, the task becomes relevant and meaningful, both of which are necessary for comprehension. Good readers inherently set purposes for themselves, but less-proficient readers might need help finding a reason for reading.

Before Reading

Skimming Help students establish a reason for reading by skimming the text. Point out section headings, illustrations, and boldfaced words. Tell students that these text features can help establish a purpose for reading. **OL**

During Reading

Identifying a Reason for Reading Give students a specific task to perform while they read, such as looking for a specific piece of information, summarizing content, finding details to support a position, or writing a response to what they have read. **BL**

After Reading

Paraphrasing When students finish reading, have them work with a partner to paraphrase what they have read. Encourage them to reread sections of text or share notes and answers to questions in order to clarify the reading. **OL**

Checking Your Understanding Answers

1. scanning
2. careful reading

Understanding What You Read

Why It's Important

Students who read but don't "get it" or who simply will not read at all cannot adequately master the content of their courses. Helping students learn to use a variety of reading strategies as tools for comprehension will lead to long-term benefits in school and everyday life.

Before Reading

Predicting On index cards, write important words from the chapter—one word per card. Place the cards on various desks around the room. Allow students to move from desk to desk until they find a word that they think they may know something about. Have students use the word to make predictions about what they will learn in the chapter. OL

Understanding What You Read

Reading without understanding is like trying to drive a car on an empty gas tank. Fortunately, there are techniques you can use to help you concentrate on and understand what you read. Skilled readers adopt a number of strategies before, during, and after reading to make sure they understand what they read.

Preparing to Read

It is important to set the stage before you read. Following these steps will make the reading process more rewarding.

Previewing If you were making a preview for a movie, you would want to let your audience know what the movie is like. When you preview a piece of writing, you are trying to get an idea about the piece. Follow these steps to preview your reading assignments.

- Look at the title and any illustrations that are included.
- Read the headings, subheadings, and anything in bold letters.
- Skim the passage to see how it is organized.
- Set a purpose for your reading.

Using What You Know You already know quite a bit about what you are going to read. You bring knowledge and personal experience to a selection. Drawing on what you learned in a previous class is called *activating prior knowledge,* and it can help you create meaning in what you read. Ask yourself, *What do I already know about this topic?*

Predicting *Predicting* requires using background and prior knowledge, as well as the ability to make educated guesses. Make educated guesses before you read and while you read to figure out what might happen in the story or article you are reading.

Reading the Text

Following these suggestions while you read will help ensure that you get the most out of your reading.

Visualizing Creating pictures in your mind as you read–called *visualizing*–is a powerful aid to understanding. As you read, set up a movie theater in your imagination. Picture the setting–city streets, the desert, or the moon. If you can visualize, selections will be more vivid, and you will recall them better later on.

Identifying Sequence When you discover the logical order of events or ideas, you are identifying *sequence*. Do you need to understand step-by-step directions? Are you reading a persuasive speech with the reasons listed in order of importance? Look for clues and signal words that will help you find the way information is organized.

Determining the Main Idea When you look for the *main idea* of a selection, you look for the most important idea. The examples, reasons, and details that further explain the main idea are called *supporting details.* Some main ideas are clearly stated within a passage–often in the first sentence of a paragraph, or sometimes in the last sentence of a passage. Other times, however, an author does not directly state the main idea. Instead, he or she provides details that help readers figure out what the main idea is.

MORE ABOUT THE READING STRATEGY

What does it mean to read? What do we know about how the brain processes the written word? Consider forming a study group with other teachers interested in learning more about the process of reading. There are books available through several educational presses that focus on new research about the learning process and comprehension.

Questioning By learning how to analyze questions, you will quickly learn where to look for information as you read. Questions vary in many ways. One of the ways that questions vary is by how explicit or implied the question is compared with the text. These types of questions fall into four categories:

- **Right there** questions can be answered based on a line from the text.
- **Think and search** questions can be answered by looking in a few different places in the text.
- **Author and you** questions can be answered by thinking about the text but that also require your prior knowledge.
- **On your own** questions cannot be answered by the text and rely on the reader.

Clarifying Clear up, or clarify, confusing or difficult passages as you read. When you realize you do not understand something, try these techniques to help you clarify the ideas. *Reread* the confusing parts slowly and carefully. *Look up* unfamiliar words. Simply *talk out* the part to yourself.

Monitoring Your Comprehension As you read, check your understanding by using the following strategies.

- **Summarize** what you read by pausing from time to time and telling yourself the main ideas of what you have just read. Answer the questions *Who? What? Where? When? Why?* and *How?* Summarizing tests your comprehension by encouraging you to clarify key points in your own words.
- **Paraphrase** what you have just read to see whether you really got the point. Paraphrasing is retelling something in your own words. If you cannot explain it clearly, you should probably reread the text.

CHECKING YOUR UNDERSTANDING

1. How does visualizing help you understand what you read in your textbook or when you read for pleasure?
2. How can you determine the main idea of a selection if the author never explicitly explains what it is?
3. Why is clarifying an important skill for you to develop?

Reading Skills Handbook

During Reading

Questioning Encourage students to write questions or mark confusing parts of the text with a sticky note as they read. Organize students into groups and allow them to discuss the comments they made on their notes. Have a member of the group record common difficulties. Discuss as a class the sections of the reading that were difficult or confusing, and help clarify the material for the students. **OL**

After Reading

Reviewing Remind students to use the following strategies after each section or chapter to ensure greater comprehension:

- Readers should summarize the most important parts of the text in their own words.
- Readers should clarify confusing content by rereading, asking questions, or seeking outside help.
- Readers should predict what might happen next.

OL

Checking Your Understanding Answers

1. Visualizing helps make readings more vivid and thus easier to recall later on.
2. Answers will vary, but students should point out that the details in the passage provide a clue about the author's main idea.
3. It helps clear up confusing passages.

UNIVERSAL ACCESS

Below Grade Level Prediction guides (often called anticipation guides) are an effective way of setting a purpose for reading, engaging students during reading, and monitoring comprehension after reading. Create statements related to the upcoming section or chapter. Write some statements that are true, some that are false, and some that are outrageous or funny. Have students write *True* or *False* beside each statement. Students should then check and make corrections to their predictions as they read. **BL**

Thinking About Your Reading

Why It's Important

While many students are capable of reading the text and answering specific comprehension questions about what they have read, understanding subtleties of meaning or thinking critically may be more difficult. Students become better readers, writers, and thinkers when they know how to use critical thinking skills.

Before Reading

Modeling When teaching critical thinking skills, it is best to focus on teaching only one or two skills prior to reading. Explain the skill, and model how you, as a reader, use it to comprehend the reading. OL

Thinking About Your Reading

Sometimes it is important to think more deeply about what you have read so you can get the most out of what the author says. These critical thinking skills will help you go beyond what the words say and get at the important messages of your reading.

Interpreting

When you listen to your best friend talk, you do not just hear the words he or she says. You also watch your friend, listen to the tone of voice, and use what you already know about that person to put meaning to the words. In doing so, you are interpreting what your friend says. Readers do the same thing when they interpret as they read. *Interpreting* is asking yourself *What is the writer really saying here?* and then using what you know about the world to help answer that question.

Inferring

You may not realize it, but you make inferences every day. Here is an example: You run to the bus stop a little later than usual. No one is there. "I have missed the bus," you say to yourself. You might be wrong, but that is the way our minds work. You look at the evidence (you are late; no one is there) and come to a conclusion (you have missed the bus).

When you read, you go through exactly the same process because writers do not always directly state what they want you to understand. They suggest certain information by providing clues and interesting details. Whenever you combine those clues with your own background and knowledge, you are making an inference.

Drawing Conclusions

Skillful readers are always *drawing conclusions,* or figuring out much more than an author says directly. The process is like a detective solving a mystery. You combine information and evidence that the author provides to come up with a statement about the topic. Drawing conclusions helps you find connections between ideas and events and gives you a better understanding of what you are reading.

Making Connections

One way that you can remember what you have read is by making connections with the text. Your teacher often expresses these connections aloud so that you and your classmates have a model. Your teacher may also ask you to make connections with the text and share them with the class. The most common connections include:

MORE ABOUT THE READING STRATEGY

Have students evaluate their proficiency with using different types of critical thinking skills. Draw a continuum on the board for each skill, with 0 representing great difficulty using the skill and 10 indicating mastery of it. Have students rate their abilities by answering questions such as: Am I usually able to infer and understand what the author is suggesting, even if it is not stated? Can I usually draw conclusions when I read? Can I easily tell facts from opinions?

- **Text-to-self** connections, in which you remember something from your own life that serves as a connection with what is being read. *(While reading about the Civil War, you think about a fight you had with a relative.)*
- **Text-to-world** connections, in which you remember something that is happening or has happened in the world that serves as a connection with what is being read. *(While reading about the Civil War, you remember reading a newspaper article about the civil war in Somalia.)*
- **Text-to-text** connections, in which you remember something you have read elsewhere that serves as a connection with what is being read. *(While reading about the Civil War, you recall the novel* Red Badge of Courage.)

Analyzing

Analyzing, or looking at separate parts of something to understand the entire piece, is a way to think critically about written work. In analyzing persuasive *nonfiction,* you might look at the writer's reasons to see if they actually support the main point of the argument. In analyzing *informational text,* you might look at how the ideas are organized to see what is most important.

Distinguishing Fact From Opinion

Distinguishing between fact and opinion is an important reading skill. A *fact* is a statement that can be proved. An *opinion,* on the other hand, is what a writer believes on the basis of his or her personal viewpoint. Writers can support their opinions with facts, but an opinion is something that cannot be proved.

Evaluating

When you form an opinion or make a judgment about something you are reading, you are *evaluating.* If you are reading informational texts or something on the Internet, it is important to evaluate how qualified the author is to be writing about the topic and how reliable the information is that is presented. Ask yourself whether the author seems biased, whether the information is one-sided, and whether the argument presented is logical.

Synthesizing

When you *synthesize,* you combine ideas (maybe even from different sources) to come up with something new. It may be a new understanding of an important idea or a new way of combining and presenting information. For example, you might read a manual on coaching soccer, combine that information with your own experiences playing soccer, and come up with a winning plan for coaching your sister's team this spring.

CHECKING YOUR UNDERSTANDING

1. **How does making connections with what you have read help you remember more?**
2. **How do analyzing and synthesizing differ?**
3. **How do facts and opinions differ? Why is it important to differentiate between the two as you study history?**

UNIVERSAL ACCESS

Below Grade Level When students find connections to their own lives in the text, their ability to comprehend it improves. Offer projects that build upon these connections. Projects may include: debating issues presented in the text; writing articles for the school or local paper; conducting interviews with others who have knowledge of the subject; role playing; finding relevant poetry, art, or music to share with the class; and reading and reporting on books or magazine articles related to the subject. **BL**

During Reading

Thinking Critically Students who interact with the text can think more critically about it. Organize students into small groups, and assign a section of text for each group to read. Have students discuss questions such as, "Why was the *Dred Scott* decision seen differently in the North and the South?" or "Is the reason why this event occurred based on fact or opinion?" Encourage students to examine the questions from different perspectives. Have students share their discussions with the class. **OL**

After Reading

Understanding Question/Answer Relationships Tell students that after they read, they will write one question that reflects each type of the thinking skills described in this handbook. Knowing that they will have to write questions about the text will help students think more about it as they read. **OL**

Checking Your Understanding Answers

1. Relating the reading to prior knowledge or to personal experience helps integrate new learning into what has already been learned.
2. Analyzing involves looking at separate parts of the reading in order to understand the entire text. Synthesizing involves combining ideas to come up with a new conclusion.
3. Facts can be proven; opinions are simply points of view. Differentiating is important in history because you need to separate events that happened from historians' interpretations of them.

Understanding Text Structure

Why It's Important

Students who begin reading without understanding text structures may have difficulty with comprehension and retention. Students can categorize information better and make sense of the text more easily when they learn how authors organize the text.

Before Reading

Skimming Before students read the chapter, walk them through it. For each page, note photos, charts, diagrams, maps, headings, and boldfaced words. Ask students questions such as: Why did the author choose this particular photograph to illustrate this topic? How does this map relate to the topic described in the title? What do you think the author intends for you to learn in the section? **OL**

Understanding Text Structure

Good writers do not just put together sentences and paragraphs in any order. They structure each piece of their writing in a specific way for a specific purpose. That pattern of organization is called text structure. When you know the text structure of a selection, you will find it easier to locate and recall an author's ideas. Here are four ways that writers organize text.

Comparison and Contrast

Comparison-and-contrast structure shows the *similarities* and *differences* among people, things, and ideas. Maybe you have overheard someone at school say something like "He is better at throwing the football, but I can run faster than he can." This student is using comparison-and-contrast structure. When writers use comparison-and-contrast structure, they often want to show you how things that seem alike are different or how things that seem different are alike.
Signal words and phrases: *similarly, on the one hand, on the other hand, in contrast to, but, however*

Cause and Effect

Just about everything that happens in life is the cause or the effect of some other event or action. Sometimes what happens is pretty minor: You do not look when you are pouring milk *(cause);* you spill milk on the table *(effect).* Sometimes it is a little more serious: You do not look at your math book before the big test *(cause);* you mess up on the test *(effect).*

Writers use cause-and-effect structure to explore the reasons for something happening and to examine the results of previous events. This structure helps answer the question that everybody is always asking: *Why?* A historian might tell us why an empire rose and fell. Cause-and-effect structure is all about explaining why things are as they are.
Signal words and phrases: *so, because, as a result, therefore, for the following reasons*

MORE ABOUT THE READING STRATEGY

Why should students understand the different types of text structure? Knowledge about the different types of text structure helps students remember content. It also helps students make sense out of unfamiliar text. Students who internalize the process of cause and effect or problem and solution are developing thinking processes that will serve them for the rest of their lives.

Problem and Solution

How did scientists overcome the difficulty of getting a person to the moon? How will I brush my teeth when I have forgotten my toothpaste? These questions may be very different in importance, but they have one thing in common: Each identifies a problem and asks how to solve it. *Problems and solutions* are part of what makes life interesting. Problems and solutions also occur in fiction and nonfiction writing.

Signal words and phrases: *how, help, problem, obstruction, difficulty, need, attempt, have to, must*

Sequence

Take a look at three common forms of sequencing, the order in which thoughts are arranged.

- **Chronological order** refers to the order in which events take place. First, you wake up; next, you have breakfast; then, you go to school. Those events do not make much sense in any other order.
  Signal words: *first, next, then, later, finally*
- **Spatial order** tells you the order in which to look at objects. For example, consider this description of an ice-cream sundae: *At the bottom of the dish are two scoops of vanilla. The scoops are covered with fudge and topped with whipped cream and a cherry.* Your eyes follow the sundae from the bottom to the top. Spatial order is important in descriptive writing because it helps you as a reader to see an image the way the author does.
  Signal words: *above, below, behind, next to*
- **Order of importance** is going from most important to least important or the other way around. For example, a typical news article has a most important to least important structure.
  Signal words: *principal, central, important, fundamental*

CHECKING YOUR UNDERSTANDING

Read the following paragraph and answer the questions about the selection's text structure below.

The Huntington City Council recently approved an increase in the city sales tax. Recognizing the need to balance the city's budget, the council president Matt Smith noted that the council had no choice. The vote ended more than a year of preparing voters for the bad news. First, the council notified citizens that there would be a public discussion last April. Then, the council issued public statements that the vote would take place in November. Finally, the council approved the increase last week even though many residents opposed it. On one hand, the increase will increase revenues. On the other hand, more taxes could lead to fewer shoppers in the city's struggling retail stores.

1. **How does the writer use comparison and contrast text structure?**
2. **How does the writer use problem and solution text structure?**
3. **What signal words show that the writer is setting the chronological order of events?**

During Reading

Identifying Text Structure
Organize students into groups of four, and assign different sections of the text to each group. Have groups choose a facilitator, a reader, a recorder, and a reporter. As the reader reads a section aloud, have the recorder note all the signal words. The facilitator will help the group identify the section's text structure based on the categories listed in the *Reading Skills Handbook*. The reporter will describe to the class the signal words and the text structure that the group identified. **OL**

After Reading

Organizing Information Graphic organizers help students organize and comprehend ideas and events. Have a variety of blank graphic organizers available for students to choose from to help them organize text information, including flow charts, time lines, and Venn diagrams. **OL**

Checking Your Understanding Answers

1. points out that on one hand the increase will make money but on the other hand it might hurt businesses
2. uses the word *need* when explaining why the council felt it necessary to increase taxes
3. *first, then, finally*

UNIVERSAL ACCESS

Below Grade Level Students who are not proficient readers may get little practice at the skill. As a result, they may be unfamiliar with some of the features of a book that they can use as aids. Review with students how to use the table of contents to locate major divisions in the book, the glossary to find the definitions of new words, and the index to locate the coverage of particular topics. Then review with them the heads within a section so they can see how headings structure the text and provide clues to content. **BL**

Reference Atlas

NATIONAL GEOGRAPHIC

World: Political	26
North America: Political	28
North America: Physical	29
United States: Political	30
United States: Physical	32
United States: Territorial Growth	34

ATLAS KEY

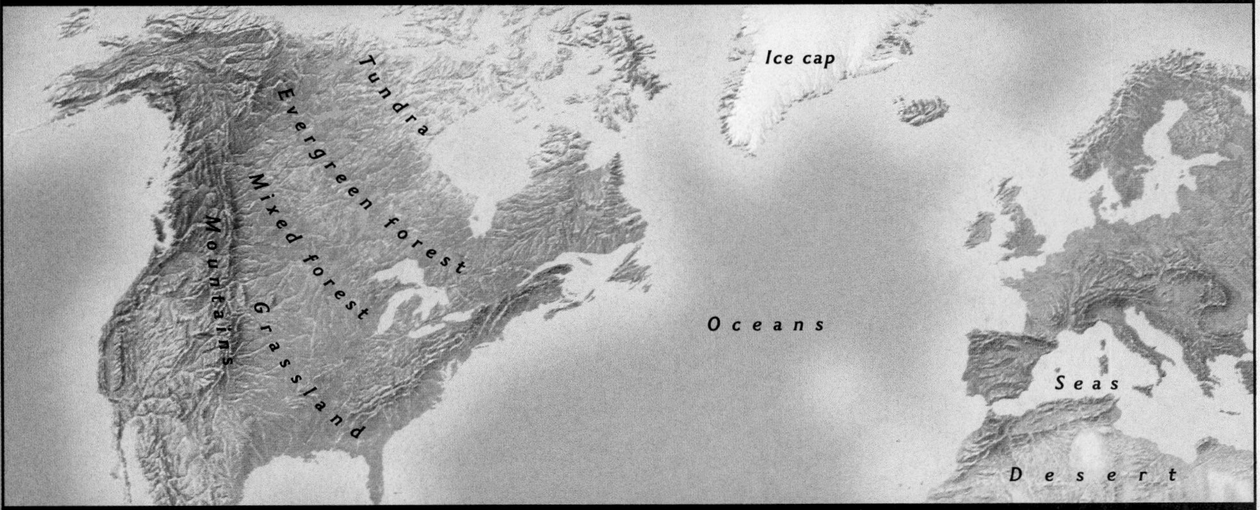

SYMBOL KEY

- Canal
- Claimed boundary
- International boundary
- Depression
- Elevation
- National capital
- Towns
- Below sea level
- Dry salt lake
- Lake
- Rivers
- Lava
- Sand
- Swamp

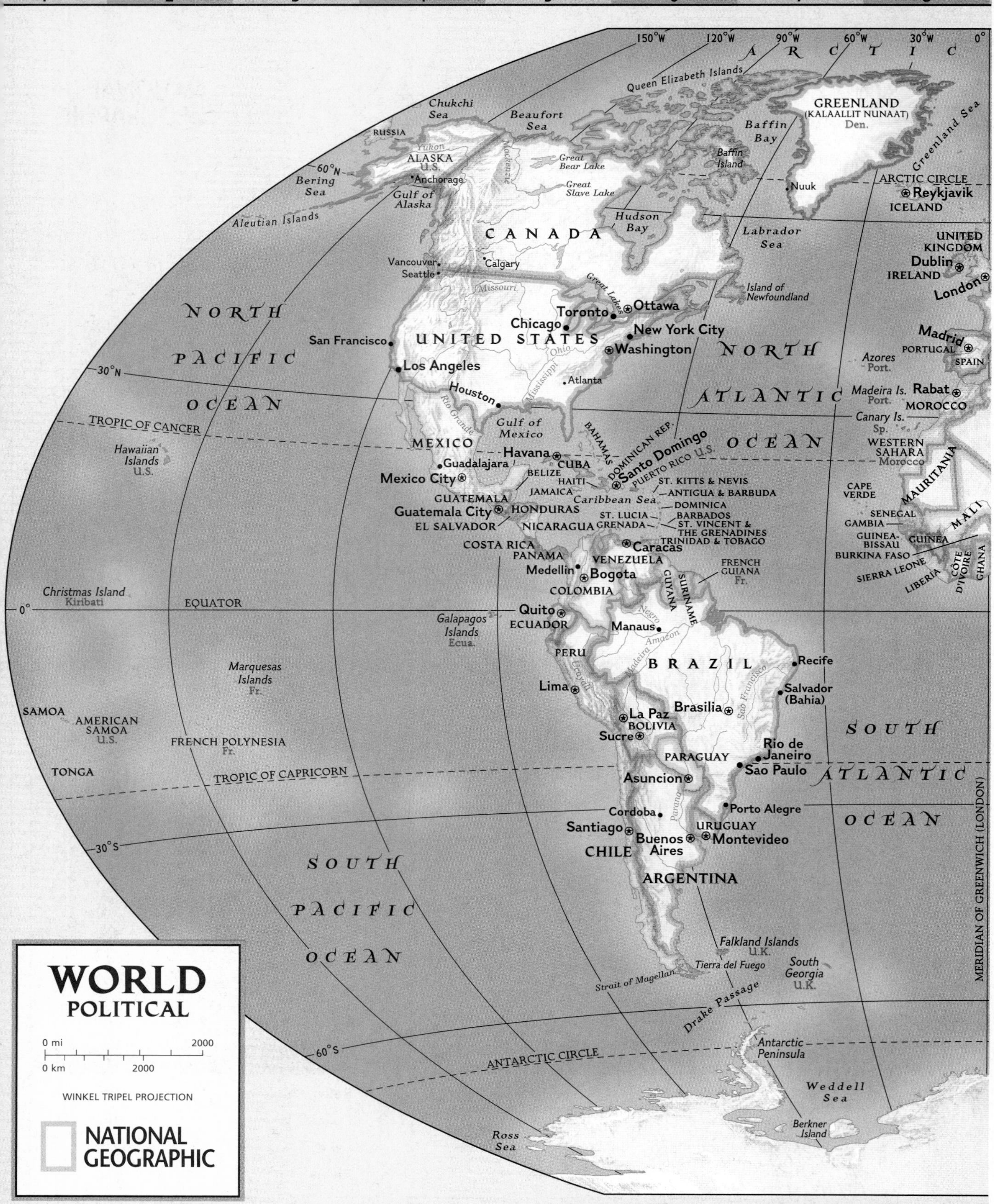
WORLD
POLITICAL
0 mi 2000
0 km 2000
WINKEL TRIPEL PROJECTION
NATIONAL GEOGRAPHIC
1 2 3 4 5 6 7 8
150°W 120°W 90°W 60°W 30°W 0°
ARCTIC
Queen Elizabeth Islands
GREENLAND (KALAALLIT NUNAAT) Den.
Greenland Sea
Baffin Bay
Baffin Island
Chukchi Sea
Beaufort Sea
RUSSIA
Yukon
ALASKA U.S.
Mackenzie
Great Bear Lake
Great Slave Lake
60°N
Bering Sea
Anchorage
Gulf of Alaska
Aleutian Islands
Nuuk
ARCTIC CIRCLE
Reykjavik
ICELAND
Hudson Bay
Labrador Sea
CANADA
UNITED KINGDOM
Dublin
IRELAND
London
Vancouver
Calgary
Seattle
Missouri
Great Lakes
Island of Newfoundland
Ottawa
NORTH PACIFIC OCEAN
Toronto
Chicago
New York City
San Francisco
UNITED STATES
Ohio
Washington
NORTH ATLANTIC OCEAN
Madrid
PORTUGAL
SPAIN
Azores Port.
Los Angeles
30°N
Mississippi
Atlanta
Houston
Madeira Is. Port.
Rabat
MOROCCO
Rio Grande
Canary Is. Sp.
TROPIC OF CANCER
Gulf of Mexico
BAHAMAS
DOMINICAN REP.
Santo Domingo
Hawaiian Islands U.S.
MEXICO
Havana
CUBA
PUERTO RICO U.S.
WESTERN SAHARA Morocco
Guadalajara
BELIZE
MAURITANIA
Mexico City
HAITI
ST. KITTS & NEVIS
JAMAICA
ANTIGUA & BARBUDA
CAPE VERDE
GUATEMALA
Caribbean Sea
DOMINICA
Guatemala City
HONDURAS
ST. LUCIA
BARBADOS
SENEGAL
EL SALVADOR
NICARAGUA
GRENADA
ST. VINCENT & THE GRENADINES
GAMBIA
MALI
TRINIDAD & TOBAGO
GUINEA-BISSAU
GUINEA
COSTA RICA
Caracas
PANAMA
VENEZUELA
FRENCH GUIANA Fr.
BURKINA FASO
Medellin
SIERRA LEONE
Bogota
GUYANA
SURINAME
CÔTE D'IVOIRE
GHANA
LIBERIA
Christmas Island Kiribati
COLOMBIA
EQUATOR
0°
Quito
Galapagos Islands Ecua.
ECUADOR
Manaus
Negro
Amazon
PERU
Madeira
Ucayali
Marquesas Islands Fr.
BRAZIL
Recife
São Francisco
Lima
Salvador (Bahia)
Brasilia
SAMOA
La Paz
AMERICAN SAMOA U.S.
BOLIVIA
Sucre
SOUTH ATLANTIC OCEAN
FRENCH POLYNESIA Fr.
Rio de Janeiro
PARAGUAY
TONGA
Sao Paulo
TROPIC OF CAPRICORN
Asuncion
Parana
Porto Alegre
Cordoba
URUGUAY
Santiago
Buenos Aires
Montevideo
30°S
CHILE
SOUTH PACIFIC OCEAN
ARGENTINA
MERIDIAN OF GREENWICH (LONDON)
Falkland Islands U.K.
Tierra del Fuego
South Georgia U.K.
Strait of Magellan
Drake Passage
60°S
Antarctic Peninsula
ANTARCTIC CIRCLE
Weddell Sea
Berkner Island
Ross Sea

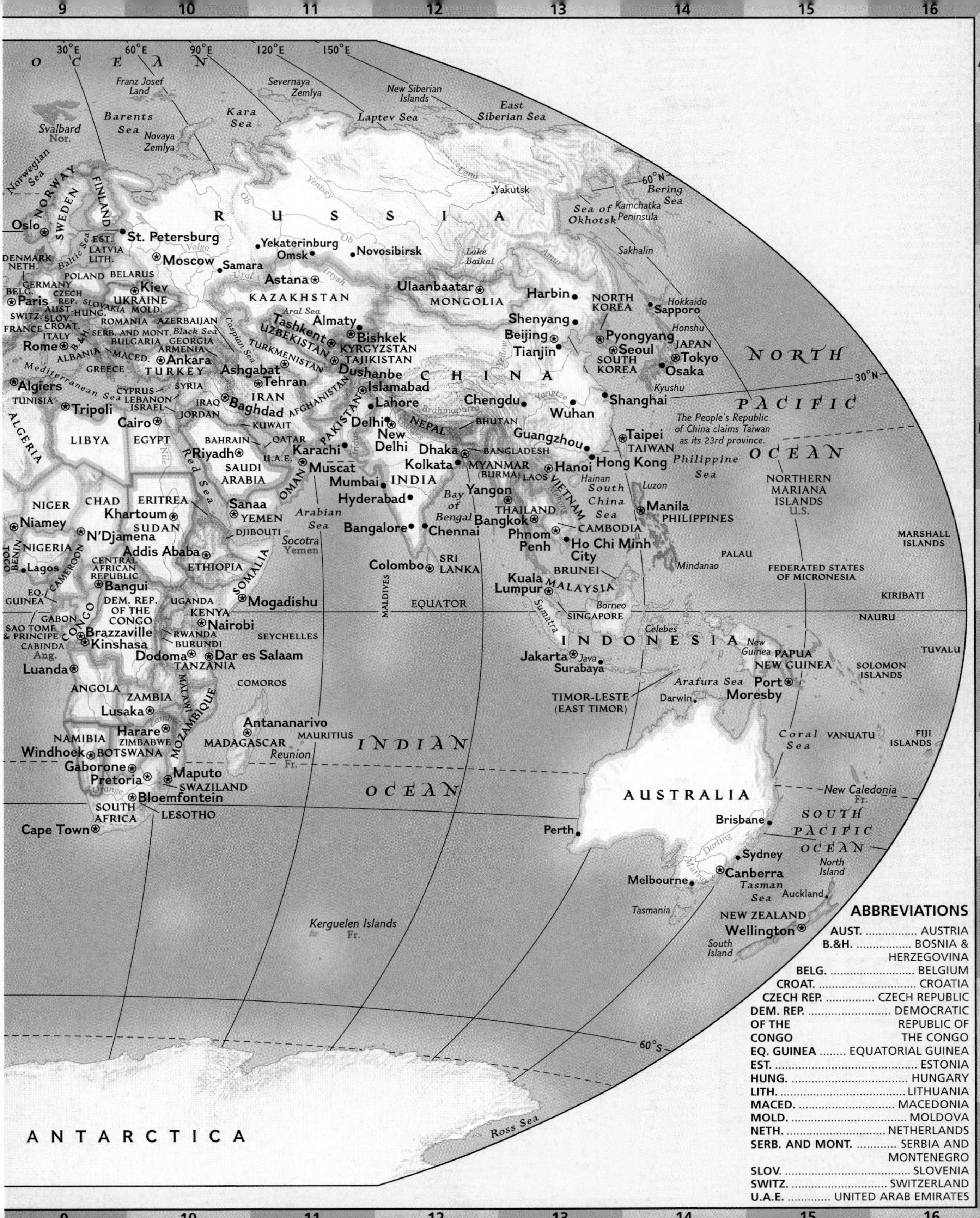

ABBREVIATIONS

AUST. .... AUSTRIA
B.&H. .... BOSNIA & HERZEGOVINA
BELG. .... BELGIUM
CROAT. .... CROATIA
CZECH REP. .... CZECH REPUBLIC
DEM. REP. OF THE CONGO .... DEMOCRATIC REPUBLIC OF THE CONGO
EQ. GUINEA .... EQUATORIAL GUINEA
EST. .... ESTONIA
HUNG. .... HUNGARY
LITH. .... LITHUANIA
MACED. .... MACEDONIA
MOLD. .... MOLDOVA
NETH. .... NETHERLANDS
SERB. AND MONT. .... SERBIA AND MONTENEGRO
SLOV. .... SLOVENIA
SWITZ. .... SWITZERLAND
U.A.E. .... UNITED ARAB EMIRATES

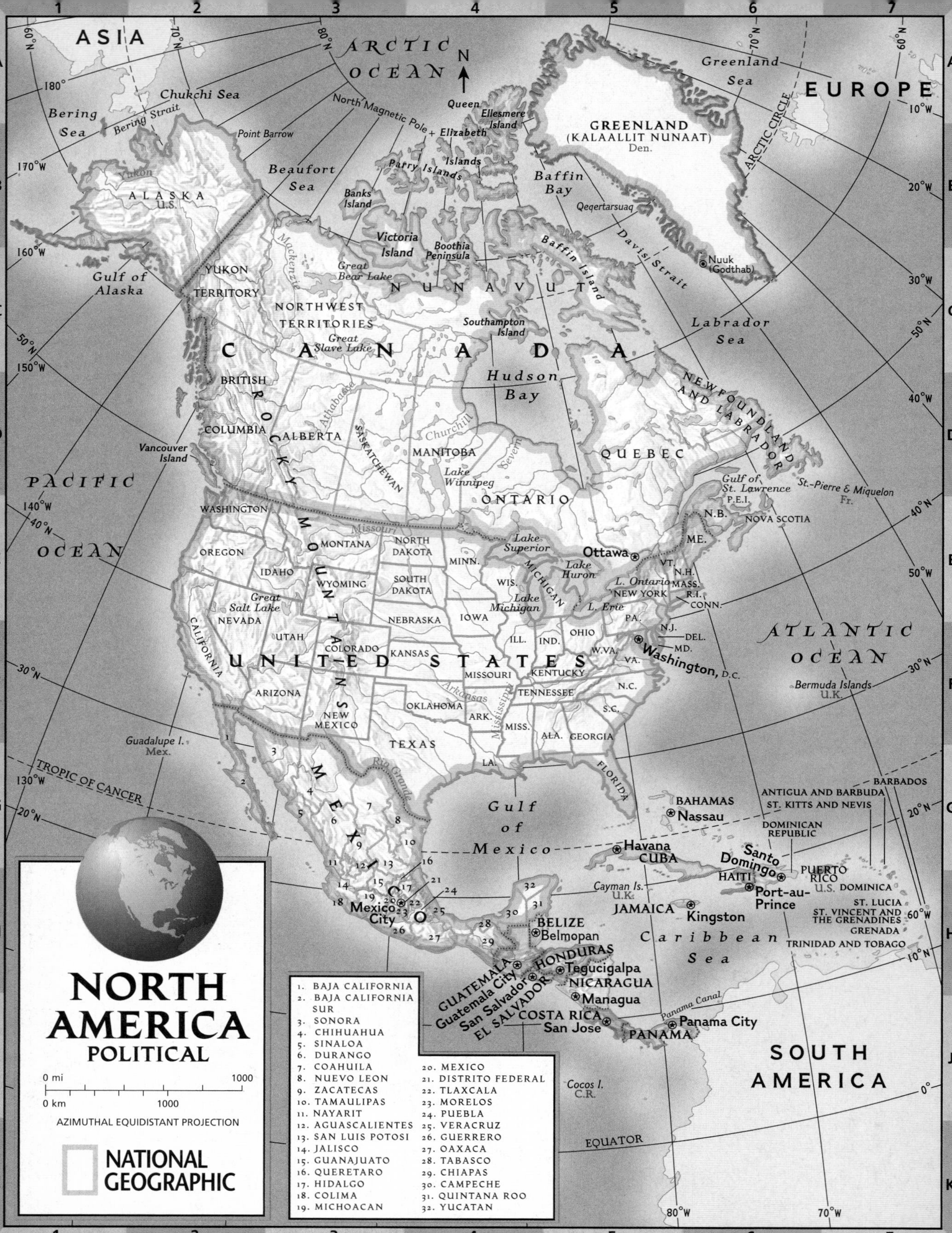

NORTH AMERICA
POLITICAL
0 mi 1000
0 km 1000
AZIMUTHAL EQUIDISTANT PROJECTION
NATIONAL GEOGRAPHIC
1. BAJA CALIFORNIA
2. BAJA CALIFORNIA SUR
3. SONORA
4. CHIHUAHUA
5. SINALOA
6. DURANGO
7. COAHUILA
8. NUEVO LEON
9. ZACATECAS
10. TAMAULIPAS
11. NAYARIT
12. AGUASCALIENTES
13. SAN LUIS POTOSI
14. JALISCO
15. GUANAJUATO
16. QUERETARO
17. HIDALGO
18. COLIMA
19. MICHOACAN
20. MEXICO
21. DISTRITO FEDERAL
22. TLAXCALA
23. MORELOS
24. PUEBLA
25. VERACRUZ
26. GUERRERO
27. OAXACA
28. TABASCO
29. CHIAPAS
30. CAMPECHE
31. QUINTANA ROO
32. YUCATAN
ASIA
ARCTIC OCEAN
EUROPE
GREENLAND (KALAALLIT NUNAAT) Den.
Greenland Sea
ARCTIC CIRCLE
Chukchi Sea
Bering Sea
Bering Strait
Point Barrow
Beaufort Sea
North Magnetic Pole
Queen Elizabeth Islands
Ellesmere Island
Parry Islands
Banks Island
Victoria Island
Boothia Peninsula
Baffin Bay
Qeqertarsuaq
Baffin Island
Davis Strait
Nuuk (Godthab)
ALASKA U.S.
Yukon
Gulf of Alaska
YUKON TERRITORY
Mackenzie
Great Bear Lake
NUNAVUT
NORTHWEST TERRITORIES
Great Slave Lake
Southampton Island
Labrador Sea
CANADA
Hudson Bay
NEWFOUNDLAND AND LABRADOR
BRITISH COLUMBIA
Athabasca
ALBERTA
SASKATCHEWAN
Churchill
MANITOBA
Severn
QUEBEC
Vancouver Island
Lake Winnipeg
ONTARIO
Gulf of St. Lawrence
St.-Pierre & Miquelon Fr.
P.E.I.
N.B.
NOVA SCOTIA
PACIFIC OCEAN
ROCKY MOUNTAINS
WASHINGTON
Missouri
MONTANA
NORTH DAKOTA
MINN.
Lake Superior
Ottawa
ME.
VT.
N.H.
MASS.
R.I.
CONN.
OREGON
IDAHO
WYOMING
SOUTH DAKOTA
WIS.
MICHIGAN
Lake Huron
L. Ontario
NEW YORK
Lake Michigan
L. Erie
Great Salt Lake
NEVADA
UTAH
NEBRASKA
IOWA
PA.
N.J.
DEL.
MD.
CALIFORNIA
COLORADO
KANSAS
ILL.
IND.
OHIO
W.VA.
VA.
Washington, D.C.
UNITED STATES
MISSOURI
KENTUCKY
ATLANTIC OCEAN
ARIZONA
Arkansas
OKLAHOMA
TENNESSEE
N.C.
Bermuda Islands U.K.
NEW MEXICO
ARK.
Mississippi
S.C.
MISS.
ALA.
GEORGIA
Guadalupe I. Mex.
TEXAS
LA.
FLORIDA
TROPIC OF CANCER
Rio Grande
MEXICO
BARBADOS
ANTIGUA AND BARBUDA
ST. KITTS AND NEVIS
BAHAMAS
Nassau
Gulf of Mexico
DOMINICAN REPUBLIC
Havana
CUBA
Santo Domingo
PUERTO RICO U.S.
HAITI
DOMINICA
Port-au-Prince
Cayman Is. U.K.
JAMAICA
Kingston
ST. LUCIA
ST. VINCENT AND THE GRENADINES
GRENADA
Mexico City
BELIZE
Belmopan
Caribbean Sea
TRINIDAD AND TOBAGO
GUATEMALA
Guatemala City
HONDURAS
Tegucigalpa
San Salvador
EL SALVADOR
NICARAGUA
Managua
COSTA RICA
San Jose
Panama Canal
Panama City
PANAMA
SOUTH AMERICA
Cocos I. C.R.
EQUATOR

NORTH AMERICA
PHYSICAL
0 mi
1000
0 km
1000
AZIMUTHAL EQUIDISTANT PROJECTION
NATIONAL GEOGRAPHIC
ASIA
ARCTIC OCEAN
N
Oodaaq Island
Lincoln Sea
Greenland Sea
EUROPE
Chukchi Sea
Bering Sea
St. Lawrence Island
Seward Peninsula
Point Barrow
North Magnetic Pole
Queen Elizabeth Islands
Ellesmere Island
Hayes Peninsula
GREENLAND
Gunnbjorn
12,139 ft
3,700 m
ARCTIC CIRCLE
North Slope
Brooks Range
Yukon
ALASKA
Nunivak Island
Beaufort Sea
Banks Island
Melville Island
Devon I.
Baffin Bay
Mt. McKinley (Denali)
20,320 ft
6,194 m
Kuskokwim
Alaska Range
Bristol Bay
Aleutian Range
Kodiak I.
Kenai Peninsula
Prince of Wales I.
Somerset I.
Victoria Island
Boothia Peninsula
Baffin Island
Davis Strait
Nuuk (Godthab)
Cape Farewell
Gulf of Alaska
19,551 ft
5,959 m
Mt. Logan
Yukon Plateau
Mackenzie Mts.
Mackenzie
Great Bear Lake
Melville Peninsula
Foxe Basin
Southampton Island
Hudson Strait
Labrador Sea
Great Slave Lake
CANADA
Ungava Bay
Alexander Archipelago
Coast Mountains
Peace
Slave
Lake Athabasca
Hudson Bay
Queen Charlotte Islands
Athabasca
CANADIAN SHIELD
Belcher Islands
LABRADOR
Fraser Plateau
Churchill
Nelson
Island of Newfoundland
Avalon Peninsula
Vancouver Island
ROCKY MOUNTAINS
Columbia Mts.
Saskatchewan
Lake Winnipeg
James Bay
Laurentian Mountains
PACIFIC OCEAN
Olympic Peninsula
GREAT PLAINS
Gaspe Pen.
Gulf of St. Lawrence
Cape Breton Island
Prince Edward Island
Nova Scotia
Cascade Range
Missouri
Lake Superior
Ottawa
St. Lawrence
Bay of Fundy
Columbia Plateau
Lake Michigan
Lake Huron
L. Ontario
Gulf of Maine
Cape Mendocino
Coast Ranges
Sierra Nevada
Snake
Great Basin
Great Salt Lake
APPALACHIAN MOUNTAINS
Cape Cod
L. Erie
Long Island
Mt. Whitney
14,494 ft
4,418 m
High Plains
Platte
Missouri
CENTRAL LOWLAND
Ohio
Washington
ATLANTIC OCEAN
Colorado
Chesapeake Bay
Death Valley
-282 ft
-86 m
UNITED STATES
Colorado Plateau
Grand Canyon
Ozark Plateau
Arkansas
Mississippi
Cape Hatteras
Bermuda Islands
Channel Islands
Red
Sonoran Desert
COASTAL PLAIN
Baja California
Gulf of California
Rio Grande
TROPIC OF CANCER
MEXICO
Sierra Madre Occidental
Sierra Madre Oriental
Florida
Gulf of Mexico
BAHAMAS
Florida Keys
Havana
CUBA
WEST INDIES
Virgin Islands
Puerto Rico
Hispaniola
HAITI
DOMINICAN REPUBLIC
Guadeloupe
Martinique
Lesser Antilles
Orizaba
18,855 ft
5,747 m
Yucatan Peninsula
Cozumel Island
Cayman Islands
Greater Antilles
JAMAICA
Kingston
Mexico City
Isthmus of Tehuantepec
BELIZE
Belmopan
Caribbean Sea
Trinidad
Lesser Antilles
Gulf of Tehuantepec
GUATEMALA
Guatemala City
HONDURAS
Tegucigalpa
NICARAGUA
Managua
San Salvador
EL SALVADOR
Lake Nicaragua
Isthmus of Panama
COSTA RICA
San Jose
Panama City
PANAMA
CENTRAL AMERICA
SOUTH AMERICA
EQUATOR
100°W
90°W
80°W
70°W

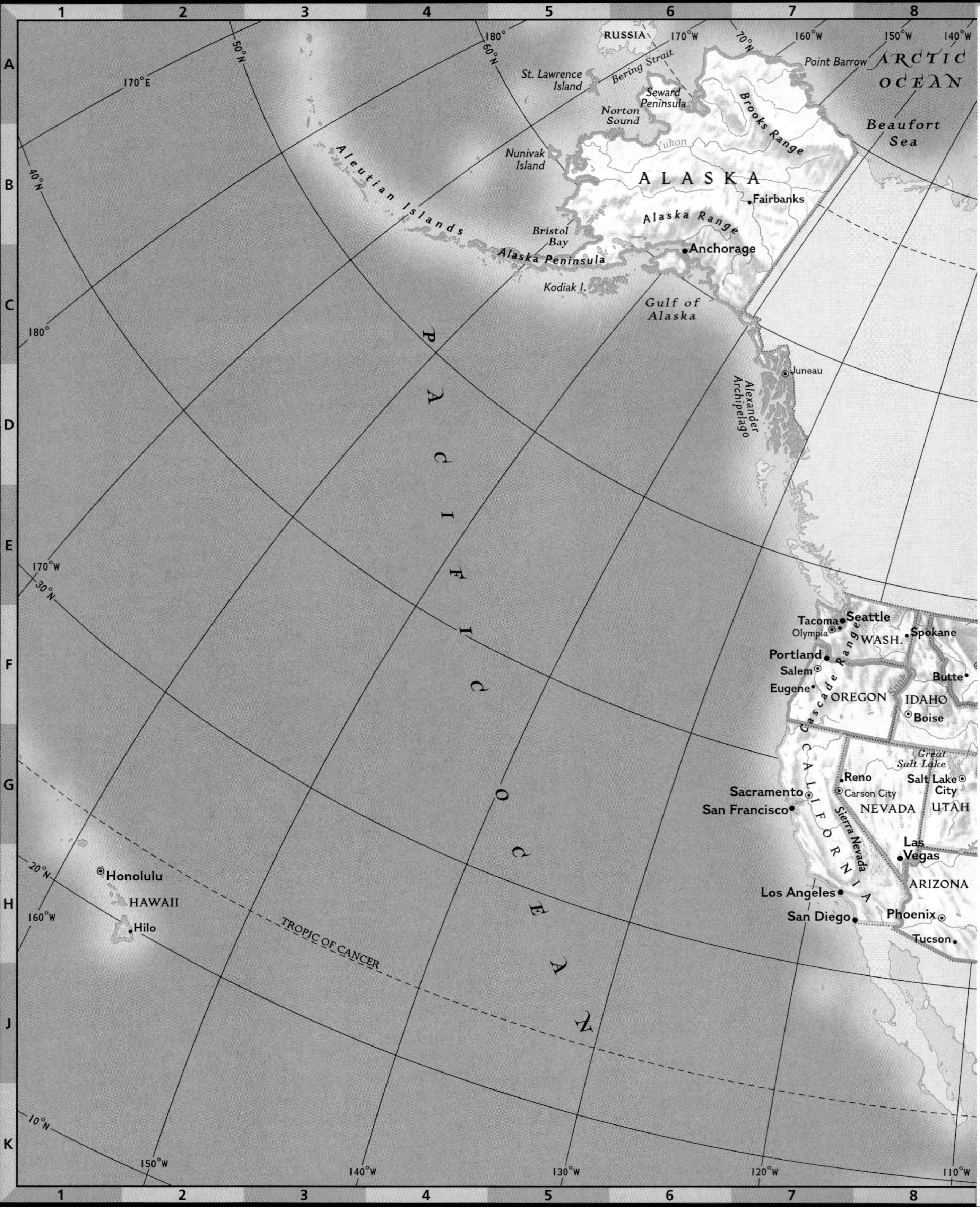
RUSSIA
St. Lawrence Island
Bering Strait
Seward Peninsula
Norton Sound
Point Barrow
ARCTIC OCEAN
Beaufort Sea
Brooks Range
Yukon
Nunivak Island
ALASKA
Fairbanks
Aleutian Islands
Alaska Range
Bristol Bay
Anchorage
Alaska Peninsula
Kodiak I.
Gulf of Alaska
Juneau
Alexander Archipelago
PACIFIC OCEAN
Tacoma
Seattle
Olympia
WASH.
Spokane
Portland
Salem
Cascade Range
Eugene
OREGON
Snake
IDAHO
Butte
Boise
Great Salt Lake
Salt Lake City
CALIFORNIA
Reno
Carson City
Sacramento
San Francisco
NEVADA
UTAH
Sierra Nevada
Las Vegas
ARIZONA
Los Angeles
San Diego
Phoenix
Tucson
Honolulu
HAWAII
Hilo
TROPIC OF CANCER
170°E
180°
170°W
160°W
150°W
140°W
130°W
120°W
110°W
10°N
20°N
30°N
40°N
50°N
60°N
70°N
1 2 3 4 5 6 7 8
A B C D E F G H J K

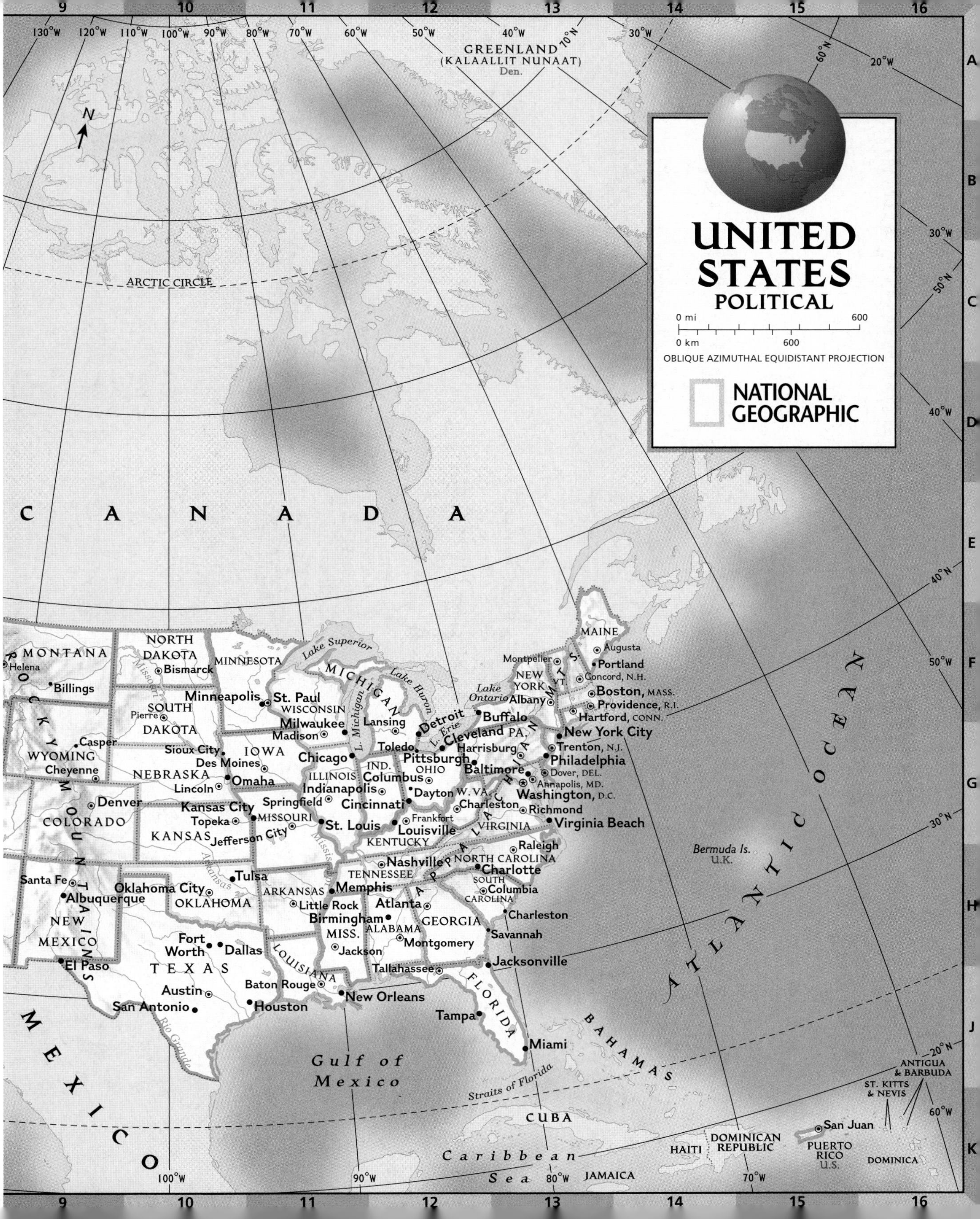
UNITED STATES
POLITICAL
0 mi 600
0 km 600
OBLIQUE AZIMUTHAL EQUIDISTANT PROJECTION
NATIONAL GEOGRAPHIC
9
10
11
12
13
14
15
16
A
B
C
D
E
F
G
H
J
K
130°W
120°W
110°W
100°W
90°W
80°W
70°W
60°W
50°W
40°W
30°W
20°W
70°N
60°N
50°N
40°N
30°N
20°N
GREENLAND
(KALAALLIT NUNAAT)
Den.
ARCTIC CIRCLE
C A N A D A
MONTANA
Helena
Billings
NORTH DAKOTA
Bismarck
MINNESOTA
Minneapolis
St. Paul
SOUTH DAKOTA
Pierre
WYOMING
Casper
Cheyenne
ROCKY MOUNTAINS
NEBRASKA
Lincoln
Omaha
Sioux City
IOWA
Des Moines
COLORADO
Denver
KANSAS
Topeka
Kansas City
MISSOURI
Jefferson City
Springfield
St. Louis
WISCONSIN
Madison
Milwaukee
Chicago
ILLINOIS
IND.
Indianapolis
MICHIGAN
Lansing
Detroit
Lake Superior
Lake Huron
L. Michigan
L. Erie
Lake Ontario
Toledo
Columbus
OHIO
Cleveland
Dayton
Cincinnati
Louisville
Frankfort
KENTUCKY
Pittsburgh
PA.
Harrisburg
Buffalo
NEW YORK
Albany
New York City
Trenton, N.J.
Philadelphia
Dover, DEL.
Annapolis, MD.
Baltimore
Washington, D.C.
W. VA.
Charleston
Richmond
VIRGINIA
Virginia Beach
APPALACHIAN MTS.
Montpelier
VT.
Concord, N.H.
MAINE
Augusta
Portland
Boston, MASS.
Providence, R.I.
Hartford, CONN.
Nashville
TENNESSEE
Memphis
NORTH CAROLINA
Raleigh
Charlotte
SOUTH CAROLINA
Columbia
Charleston
GEORGIA
Atlanta
Savannah
ALABAMA
Birmingham
Montgomery
MISS.
Jackson
ARKANSAS
Little Rock
OKLAHOMA
Oklahoma City
Tulsa
NEW MEXICO
Santa Fe
Albuquerque
El Paso
TEXAS
Fort Worth
Dallas
Austin
San Antonio
Houston
LOUISIANA
Baton Rouge
New Orleans
FLORIDA
Tallahassee
Jacksonville
Tampa
Miami
Missouri
Mississippi
Arkansas
Rio Grande
MEXICO
Gulf of Mexico
Straits of Florida
BAHAMAS
CUBA
Caribbean Sea
JAMAICA
HAITI
DOMINICAN REPUBLIC
PUERTO RICO
U.S.
San Juan
ST. KITTS & NEVIS
ANTIGUA & BARBUDA
DOMINICA
Bermuda Is.
U.K.
ATLANTIC OCEAN
N

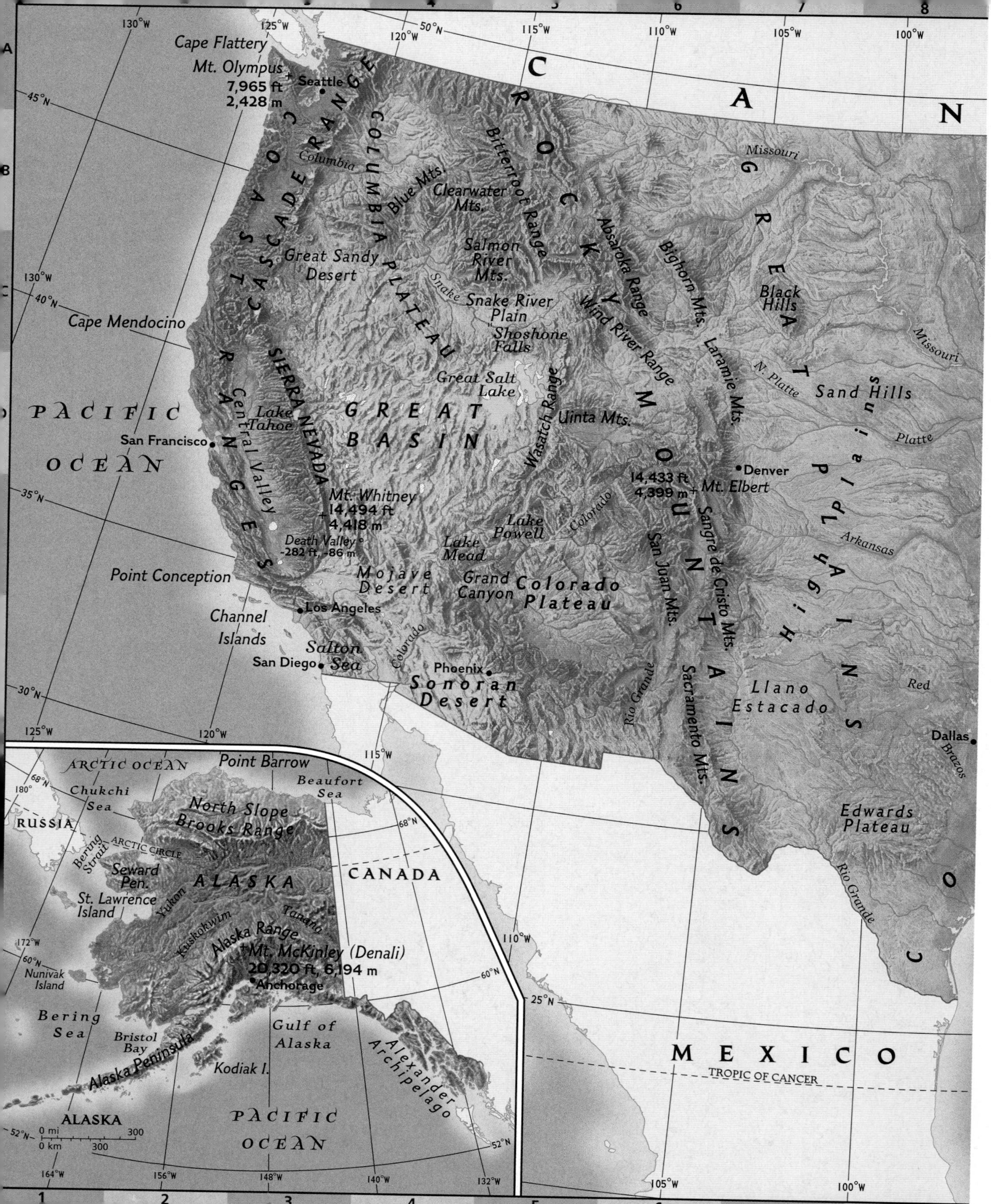

CANADA
PACIFIC OCEAN
Cape Flattery
Mt. Olympus
7,965 ft
2,428 m
Seattle
CASCADE RANGE
COAST RANGES
COLUMBIA PLATEAU
Columbia
Blue Mts.
Clearwater Mts.
Bitterroot Range
ROCKY MOUNTAINS
Salmon River Mts.
Absaroka Range
Bighorn Mts.
Missouri
GREAT PLAINS
Great Sandy Desert
Snake
Snake River Plain
Shoshone Falls
Wind River Range
Black Hills
Cape Mendocino
SIERRA NEVADA
Great Salt Lake
Laramie Mts.
N. Platte
Sand Hills
Lake Tahoe
GREAT BASIN
Wasatch Range
Uinta Mts.
Platte
San Francisco
Central Valley
Denver
14,433 ft
4,399 m
Mt. Elbert
High Plains
Mt. Whitney
14,494 ft
4,418 m
Colorado
Lake Powell
Sangre de Cristo Mts.
San Juan Mts.
Arkansas
Death Valley
-282 ft, -86 m
Lake Mead
Point Conception
Mojave Desert
Grand Canyon
Colorado Plateau
Los Angeles
Channel Islands
Salton Sea
San Diego
Phoenix
Sonoran Desert
Rio Grande
Sacramento Mts.
Llano Estacado
Red
Dallas
Brazos
Edwards Plateau
MEXICO
TROPIC OF CANCER
ARCTIC OCEAN
Point Barrow
Beaufort Sea
Chukchi Sea
RUSSIA
North Slope
Brooks Range
Bering Strait
ARCTIC CIRCLE
Seward Pen.
ALASKA
CANADA
St. Lawrence Island
Yukon
Tanana
Kuskokwim
Alaska Range
Mt. McKinley (Denali)
20,320 ft, 6,194 m
Anchorage
Nunivak Island
Bering Sea
Bristol Bay
Gulf of Alaska
Alexander Archipelago
Alaska Peninsula
Kodiak I.
ALASKA
PACIFIC OCEAN
0 mi 300
0 km 300
130°W
125°W
120°W
115°W
110°W
105°W
100°W
50°N
45°N
40°N
35°N
30°N
25°N
68°N
60°N
52°N
180°
172°W
164°W
156°W
148°W
140°W
132°W

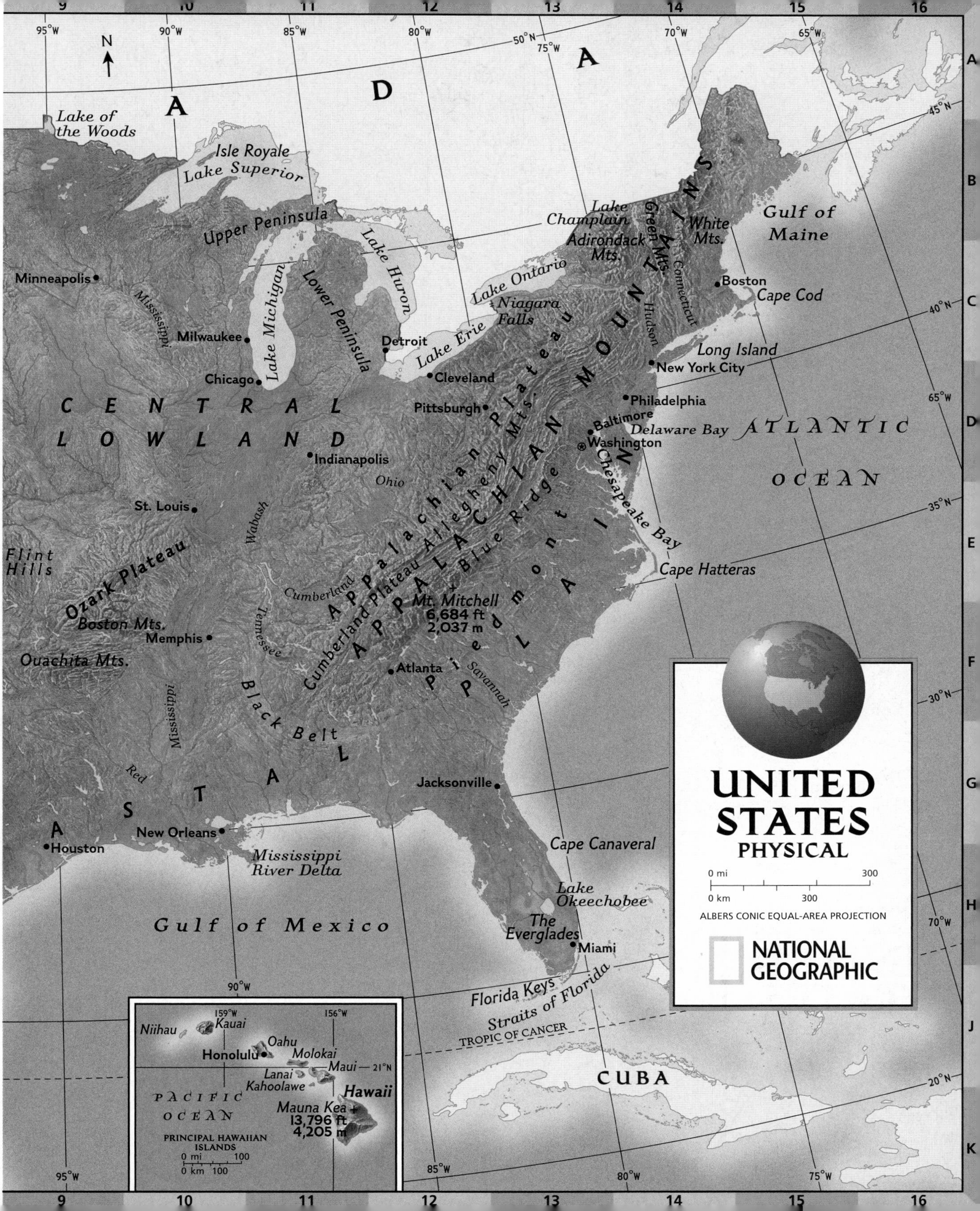

UNITED STATES
PHYSICAL
0 mi 300
0 km 300
ALBERS CONIC EQUAL-AREA PROJECTION
NATIONAL GEOGRAPHIC
CANADA
Lake of the Woods
Isle Royale
Lake Superior
Upper Peninsula
Lake Michigan
Lower Peninsula
Lake Huron
Lake Ontario
Lake Erie
Niagara Falls
Lake Champlain
Adirondack Mts.
Green Mts.
White Mts.
Gulf of Maine
Connecticut
Hudson
Boston
Cape Cod
Long Island
New York City
Philadelphia
Baltimore
Washington
Delaware Bay
Chesapeake Bay
Cape Hatteras
ATLANTIC OCEAN
APPALACHIAN MOUNTAINS
Appalachian Plateau
Allegheny Mts.
Blue Ridge
Cumberland Plateau
Mt. Mitchell
6,684 ft
2,037 m
Piedmont
Minneapolis
Milwaukee
Chicago
Detroit
Cleveland
Pittsburgh
Indianapolis
Ohio
Mississippi
CENTRAL LOWLAND
St. Louis
Wabash
Flint Hills
Ozark Plateau
Boston Mts.
Ouachita Mts.
Memphis
Cumberland
Tennessee
Atlanta
Savannah
Black Belt
Red
COASTAL PLAIN
Jacksonville
New Orleans
Houston
Mississippi River Delta
Cape Canaveral
Lake Okeechobee
The Everglades
Miami
Gulf of Mexico
Florida Keys
Straits of Florida
TROPIC OF CANCER
CUBA
Niihau
Kauai
Oahu
Honolulu
Molokai
Maui
Lanai
Kahoolawe
Hawaii
Mauna Kea
13,796 ft
4,205 m
PACIFIC OCEAN
PRINCIPAL HAWAIIAN ISLANDS
0 mi 100
0 km 100

UNITED STATES TERRITORIAL GROWTH

NATIONAL GEOGRAPHIC

A New Nation, 1787

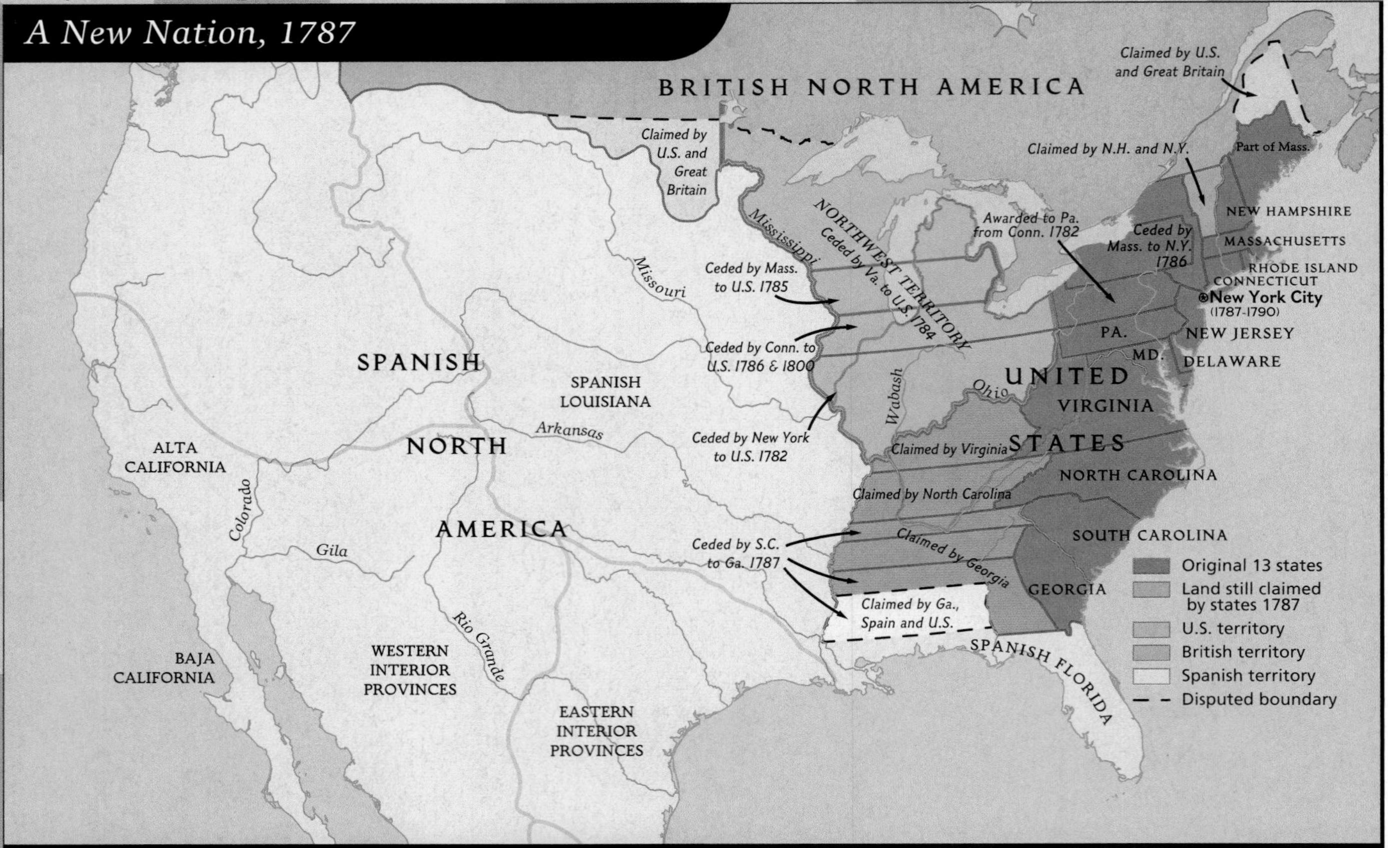

Coming of Age, 1821

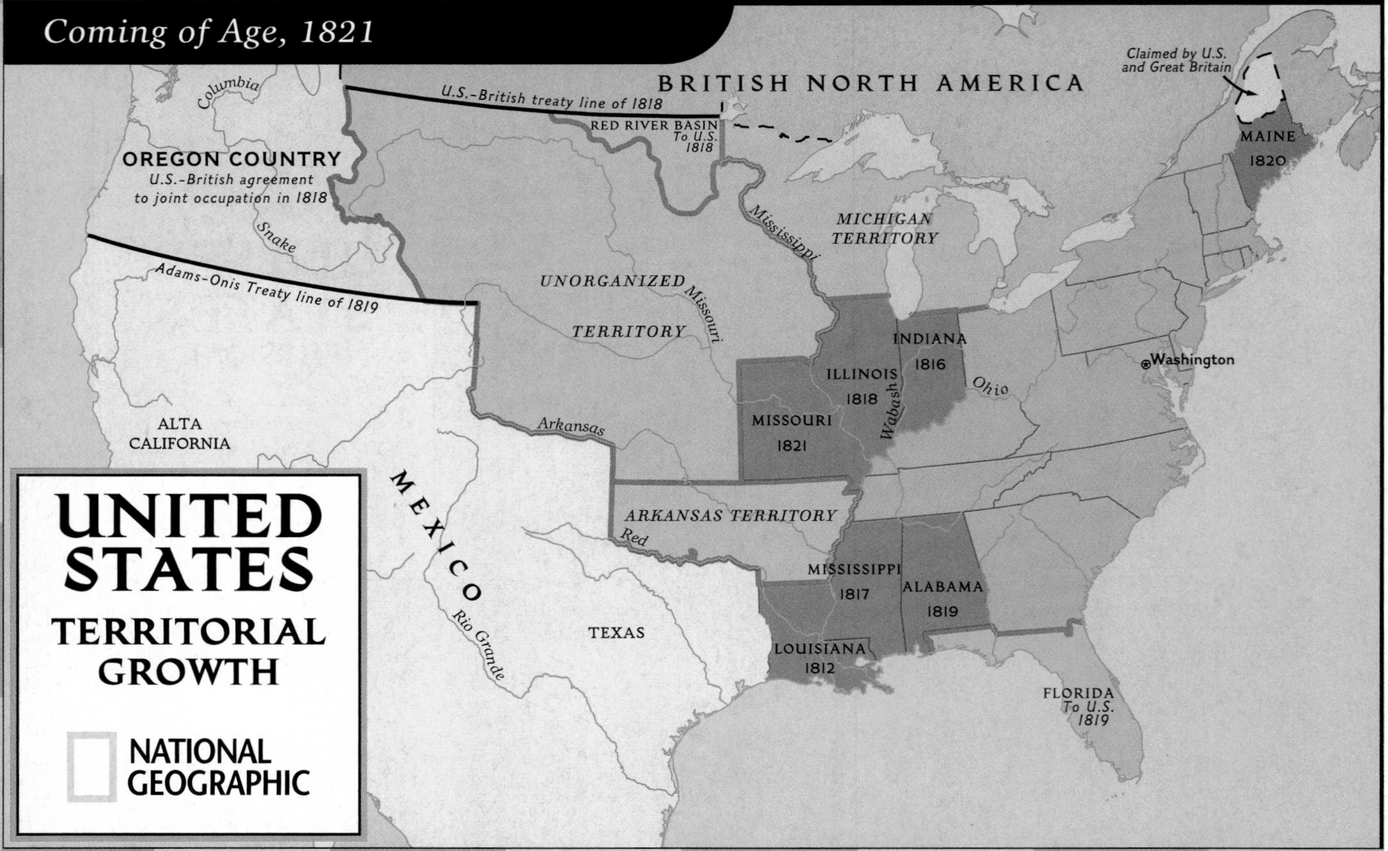

Expanding West of the Mississippi, 1803

Coast to Coast, 1850 and beyond

United States Facts

Washington, D.C.
Population: 572,059
Land area: 61 sq. mi.

U.S. Territories

Puerto Rico
Population: 3,808,610
Land area: 3,425 sq. mi.

Guam
Population: 155,000 (est.)
Land area: 210 sq. mi.

U.S. Virgin Islands
Population: 121,000 (est.)
Land area: 134 sq. mi.

American Samoa
Population: 65,000 (est.)
Land area: 77 sq. mi.

The states are listed in the order they were admitted to the Union.

1 Delaware
Year Admitted: 1787
Population: 783,600
Land area: 1,955 sq. mi.
Representatives: 1

2 Pennsylvania
Year Admitted: 1787
Population: 12,281,054
Land area: 44,820 sq. mi.
Representatives: 19

3 New Jersey
Year Admitted: 1787
Population: 8,414,350
Land area: 7,419 sq. mi.
Representatives: 13

9 New Hampshire
Year Admitted: 1788
Population: 1,235,786
Land area: 8,969 sq. mi.
Representatives: 2

10 Virginia
Year Admitted: 1788
Population: 7,078,515
Land area: 39,598 sq. mi.
Representatives: 11

11 New York
Year Admitted: 1788
Population: 18,976,457
Land area: 47,224 sq. mi.
Representatives: 29

17 Ohio
Year Admitted: 1803
Population: 11,353,140
Land area: 40,953 sq. mi.
Representatives: 18

18 Louisiana
Year Admitted: 1812
Population: 4,468,976
Land area: 43,566 sq. mi.
Representatives: 7

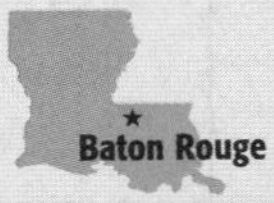

19 Indiana
Year Admitted: 1816
Population: 6,080,485
Land area: 35,870 sq. mi.
Representatives: 9

25 Arkansas
Year Admitted: 1836
Population: 2,673,400
Land area: 52,075 sq. mi.
Representatives: 4

26 Michigan
Year Admitted: 1837
Population: 9,938,444
Land area: 56,809 sq. mi.
Representatives: 15

27 Florida
Year Admitted: 1845
Population: 15,982,378
Land area: 53,997 sq. mi.
Representatives: 25

33 Oregon
Year Admitted: 1859
Population: 3,421,399
Land area: 96,003 sq. mi.
Representatives: 5

34 Kansas
Year Admitted: 1861
Population: 2,688,418
Land area: 81,823 sq. mi.
Representatives: 4

35 West Virginia
Year Admitted: 1863
Population: 1,808,344
Land area: 24,087 sq. mi.
Representatives: 3

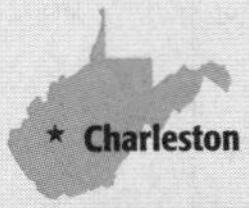

36 Nevada
Year Admitted: 1864
Population: 1,998,257
Land area: 109,806 sq. mi.
Representatives: 3

42 Washington
Year Admitted: 1889
Population: 5,894,121
Land area: 66,582 sq. mi.
Representatives: 9

43 Idaho
Year Admitted: 1890
Population: 1,293,953
Land area: 82,751 sq. mi.
Representatives: 2

44 Wyoming
Year Admitted: 1890
Population: 493,782
Land area: 97,105 sq. mi.
Representatives: 1

45 Utah
Year Admitted: 1896
Population: 2,233,169
Land area: 82,168 sq. mi.
Representatives: 3

Population figures are based on U.S. Bureau of the Census for 2000. House of Representatives figures are from the Clerk of the House of Representatives. States are not drawn to scale.

4 Georgia
Year Admitted: 1788
Population: 8,186,453
Land area: 57,919 sq. mi.
Representatives: 13

5 Connecticut
Year Admitted: 1788
Population: 3,405,565
Land area: 4,845 sq. mi.
Representatives: 5

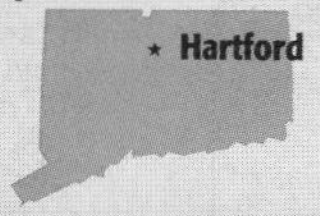

6 Massachusetts
Year Admitted: 1788
Population: 6,349,097
Land area: 7,838 sq. mi.
Representatives: 10

7 Maryland
Year Admitted: 1788
Population: 5,296,486
Land area: 9,775 sq. mi.
Representatives: 8

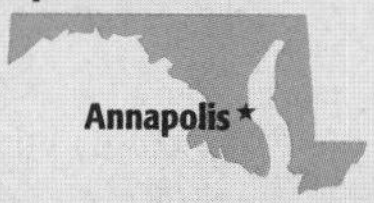

8 South Carolina
Year Admitted: 1788
Population: 4,012,012
Land area: 30,111 sq. mi.
Representatives: 6

12 North Carolina
Year Admitted: 1789
Population: 8,049,313
Land area: 48,718 sq. mi.
Representatives: 13

13 Rhode Island
Year Admitted: 1790
Population: 1,048,319
Land area: 1,045 sq. mi.
Representatives: 2

14 Vermont
Year Admitted: 1791
Population: 608,827
Land area: 9,249 sq. mi.
Representatives: 1

15 Kentucky
Year Admitted: 1792
Population: 4,041,769
Land area: 39,732 sq. mi.
Representatives: 6

16 Tennessee
Year Admitted: 1796
Population: 5,689,283
Land area: 41,220 sq. mi.
Representatives: 9

20 Mississippi
Year Admitted: 1817
Population: 2,844,658
Land area: 46,914 sq. mi.
Representatives: 4

21 Illinois
Year Admitted: 1818
Population: 12,419,293
Land area: 55,593 sq. mi.
Representatives: 19

22 Alabama
Year Admitted: 1819
Population: 4,447,100
Land area: 50,750 sq. mi.
Representatives: 7

23 Maine
Year Admitted: 1820
Population: 1,274,923
Land area: 30,865 sq. mi.
Representatives: 2

24 Missouri
Year Admitted: 1821
Population: 5,595,211
Land area: 68,898 sq. mi.
Representatives: 9

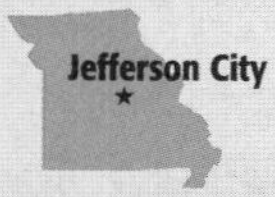

28 Texas
Year Admitted: 1845
Population: 20,851,820
Land area: 261,914 sq. mi.
Representatives: 32

29 Iowa
Year Admitted: 1846
Population: 2,926,324
Land area: 55,875 sq. mi.
Representatives: 5

30 Wisconsin
Year Admitted: 1848
Population: 5,363,675
Land area: 54,314 sq. mi.
Representatives: 8

31 California
Year Admitted: 1850
Population: 33,871,648
Land area: 155,973 sq. mi.
Representatives: 53

32 Minnesota
Year Admitted: 1858
Population: 4,919,479
Land area: 79,617 sq. mi.
Representatives: 8

37 Nebraska
Year Admitted: 1867
Population: 1,711,263
Land area: 76,878 sq. mi.
Representatives: 3

38 Colorado
Year Admitted: 1876
Population: 4,301,261
Land area: 103,730 sq. mi.
Representatives: 7

39 North Dakota
Year Admitted: 1889
Population: 642,200
Land area: 68,994 sq. mi.
Representatives: 1

40 South Dakota
Year Admitted: 1889
Population: 754,844
Land area: 75,898 sq. mi.
Representatives: 1

41 Montana
Year Admitted: 1889
Population: 902,195
Land area: 145,556 sq. mi.
Representatives: 1

46 Oklahoma
Year Admitted: 1907
Population: 3,450,654
Land area: 68,679 sq. mi.
Representatives: 5

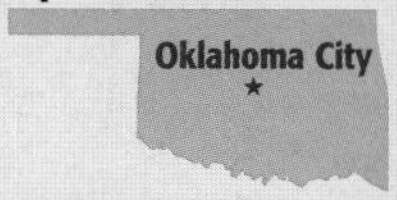

47 New Mexico
Year Admitted: 1912
Population: 1,819,046
Land area: 121,365 sq. mi.
Representatives: 3

48 Arizona
Year Admitted: 1912
Population: 5,130,632
Land area: 113,642 sq. mi.
Representatives: 8

49 Alaska
Year Admitted: 1959
Population: 626,932
Land area: 570,374 sq. mi.
Representatives: 1

50 Hawaii
Year Admitted: 1959
Population: 1,211,537
Land area: 6,423 sq. mi.
Representatives: 2

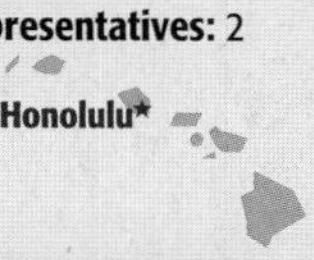

FOCUS

Ask students to list descriptive, colorful terms patterned on those in the song "America, the Beautiful" that describe their region of the United States.

TEACH

R Reading Strategy

Activating Prior Knowledge Before students read the first paragraph, ask volunteers to explain what geography is. Write their ideas on the board. Then have students compare these responses to the explanation in the text. OL

S Skill Practice

Visual Literacy Ask: What differences do you see between Acadia National Park and Monument Valley? *(Acadia National Park has abundant water, grass, and trees while, Monument Valley is located in a dry desert area.)* What differences can you see between Monument Valley and The Tongass National Forest? *(Tongass National Forest has much more vegetation than Monument Valley)* OL

Additional Support

Geography Handbook

R *The story of the world begins with geography–the study of the earth in all of its variety. Geography describes the earth's land, water, and plant and animal life. It is the study of places and the complex relationships between people and their environment.*

The resources in this handbook will help you get the most out of your textbook–and provide you with skills that you will be able to use for the rest of your life.

Acadia National Park, Maine

S

Monument Valley, Utah

The Tongass National Forest in Southeastern Alaska, covering nearly 17 million acres, is the single largest national forest in America.

Did You Know?

The word *geography* comes from the Greek *geo*, or "earth." The suffix *-graphy* comes from a Greek word meaning "to write."

How Do I Study Geography?

Six Essential Elements

Recently, geographers have begun to look at geography in a different way. They do this to understand how our large world is connected. They break down the study of geography into **Six Essential Elements.** You should think of these elements as categories into which to sort information you learn about the world's geography. U1

Being aware of these elements will help you sort what you are learning. Examples of each of the Essential Elements—detailed in maps throughout *Discovering Our Past: The American Journey to World War I*—are explained here.

Element 1

The World in Spatial Terms

Geographers first take a look at where a place is located. **Location** serves as a starting point by asking "Where is it?" Knowing the location of places helps you develop an awareness of the world around you. U2

Element 2

Places and Regions

Place has a special meaning in geography. It means more than where a place is. It also describes what a place is like. It might describe physical characteristics such as landforms, climate, and plant or animal life. Or it might describe human characteristics, including language and way of life.

To help organize their study, geographers often group places into regions. **Regions** are united by one or more common characteristics.

Element 3

Physical Systems

S When studying places and regions, geographers analyze how **physical systems**—such as hurricanes, volcanoes, and glaciers—shape the earth's surface. They also look at communities of plants and animals that depend upon one another and their surroundings for survival.

NATIONAL GEOGRAPHIC

Geography Handbook

U1 Universal Access

English Learners Encourage students to use graphic organizers to help them comprehend the six essential elements of geography. EL

U2 Universal Access

Visual/Spatial Ask students to create a map that shows the route they travel from home to school. Have them consider what major landmarks to include. OL

S Skill Practice

Historical and Social Sciences Analysis Skill
Explain that the physical characteristics of a place help shape its human characteristics. For example, Native Americans living in different regions of California had different lifestyles, housing, and clothing based on the landforms, climate, plants, and animals in their area. Ask students to describe a favorite city, state, or country and explain how its physical characteristics affect the lives of people living there. Have students share their examples with the class. OL CA CS3.

More Skill Practice

Historical and Social Sciences Analysis Skill Ask students to identify the physical systems of their state or region. OL

Did You Know?

The early Inuit labeled distances on their maps with the time it took to travel rather than with miles. The distance between Nome and Point Barrow, then, would be 10 days, rather than 525 miles (845 km).

C1 Critical Thinking

Determining Cause and Effect Call on volunteers to name places from which their family or ancestors moved, either within the United States or from another country. Discuss the different reasons that lead people to leave their homes to live in another place. **OL**

CA HI2.

S Skill Practice

Using Geography Skills

Ask: What are some examples of how humans use the environment in which they live? *(Answers may include such uses as farming or extracting natural resources.)* What are examples of ways they modify environments? *(Answers may include clearing land for houses or building roads, tunnels, or bridges.)* **OL**

C2 Critical Thinking

Analyzing Information Ask students to give examples of ways businesses can use geographic knowledge. *(Examples may include using information about geography to plan where to locate offices or factories or to find efficient routes for shipping goods or moving people.)* **OL**

Additional Support

Element 4

Human Systems

Geographers also examine **human systems,** or how people have shaped our world. They look at political boundary lines and why people settle in certain places. A key theme is the continual **movement** of people, ideas, and goods. C1

Element 5

Environment and Society

What is the relationship between people and their natural surroundings? This is what the theme of **human/environment interaction** investigates. It also shows how people affect the environment. S

Element 6

The Uses of Geography

Knowledge of geography helps us understand people, places, and environments over time. Knowing how to use the tools of geography prepares you for our modern society. C2

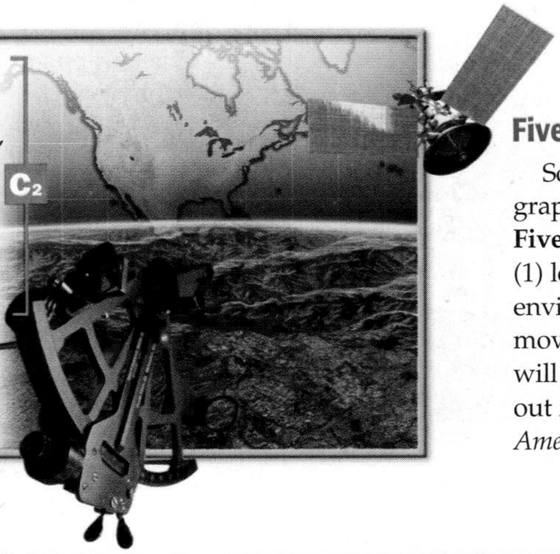

Five Themes

Some geographers study geography through five themes. The **Five Themes of Geography** are (1) location, (2) place, (3) human/environment interaction, (4) movement, and (5) regions. You will see these highlighted throughout *Discovering Our Past: The American Journey to World War I.*

Did You Know?

Geographers distinguish among three types of regions: formal regions, functional regions, and perceptual regions. Formal regions are characterized by a common human property, such as language, religion, or nationality, or a common physical property, such as climate, landforms, or vegetation. Functional regions are areas concentrated on a common node or focal point, such as a transportation hub or economic links. Perceptual regions reflect peoples' feelings or attitudes and are defined by subjective images of an area. Examples of perceptual regions in the United States are the "heartland" and the Midwest.

How Do I Use Maps and Globes?

Hemispheres

To locate a place on the earth, geographers use a system of imaginary lines that crisscross the globe. One of these lines, the **Equator,** circles the middle of the earth like a belt. It divides the earth into "half spheres," or **hemispheres.** Everything north of the Equator is in the Northern Hemisphere. Everything south of the Equator is in the Southern Hemisphere.

Another imaginary line runs from north to south. It helps divide the earth into half spheres in the other direction. Find this line—called the **Prime Meridian**—on a globe. Everything east of the Prime Meridian for 180 degrees is in the Eastern Hemisphere. Everything west of the Prime Meridian is in the Western Hemisphere. U1

NATIONAL GEOGRAPHIC **Hemispheres** R

U2

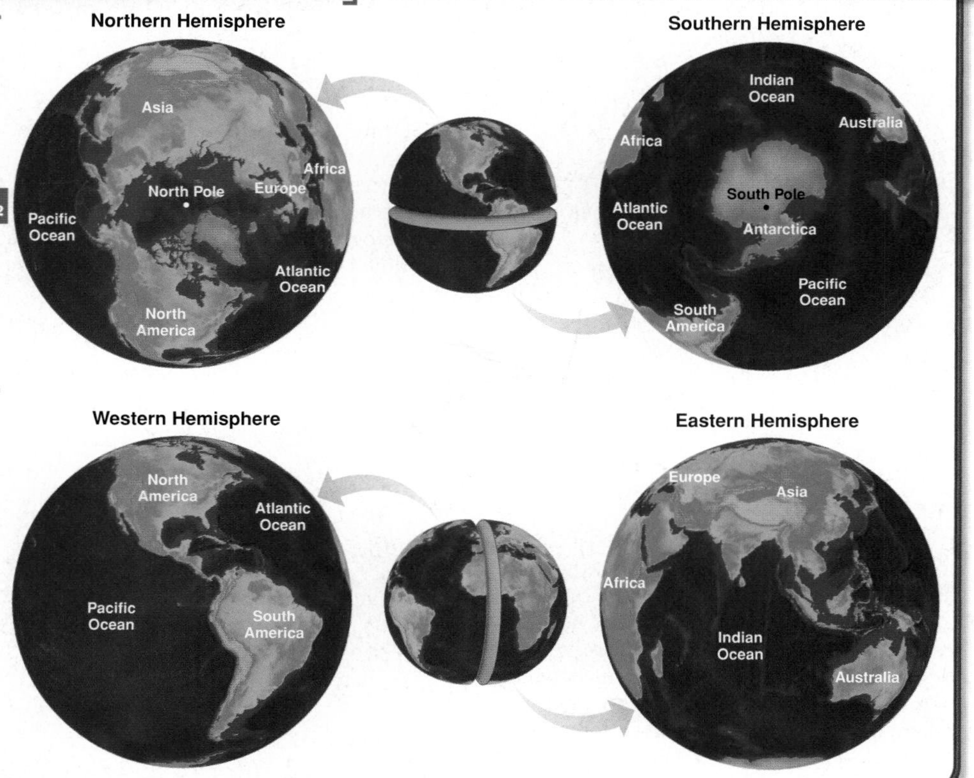

U1 Universal Access

Logical/Mathematical
Ask: How many degrees can a circle be divided into? *(360)* Why is a hemisphere only 180 degrees? *(because it is half a circle)* OL

U2 Universal Access

Kinesthetic Give kinesthetic learners a globe. Have them turn the globe so they look directly down on the North Pole and then compare what they see to the top left image in the "Hemispheres" illustration. Then have them turn the globe upside down to look directly at the South Pole and compare that to the top right image. OL

R Reading Strategy

Reading Maps, Graphs, and Charts Test students' understanding of the idea of four hemispheres by naming cities, countries, or geographic features and having students identify the two hemispheres *(north or south, east or west)* in which each one is found. OL CA CS3.

Did You Know?

There is a place with no latitude and no longitude. The absolute location, or exact point on the earth, where the Equator and the Prime Meridian meet is 0°N 0°S, 0°E 0°W.

R Reading Strategy

Understanding Vocabulary Help students recall the difference between lines of latitude and longitude with this mnemonic device: Parallels of latitude vary in length, with 0° the longest and 89° very short. Lines of *longitude*, however, are all equally *long*.

U Universal Access

Logical/Mathematical Ask students to draw a circle on a piece of paper and draw a line across the center that divides it in half, as the Equator divides the earth. Have them mark the midpoint of that line. Then have them use a protractor to draw lines from the midpoint to the upper right side of the circle at 10°, 30°, and 90°. Explain that the lines of latitude represent the lines made at different degrees of angle from the Equator. OL

S Skill Practice

Using Geography Skills Demonstrate how to use absolute location by giving figures such as 15°S, 135°E or 45°N, 90°E and showing where they appear on this drawing of Earth. OL

Additional Support

Understanding Latitude and Longitude

Lines on globes and maps provide information that can help you easily locate places on the earth. These lines are called ***latitude*** *and* ***longitude.*** *They cross one another, forming a pattern called a grid system.*

Latitude

R Lines of latitude, or **parallels,** circle the earth parallel to the **Equator** and measure the distance north or south of the Equator in degrees. The Equator is at 0° latitude, while the North Pole lies at latitude 90°N (north).

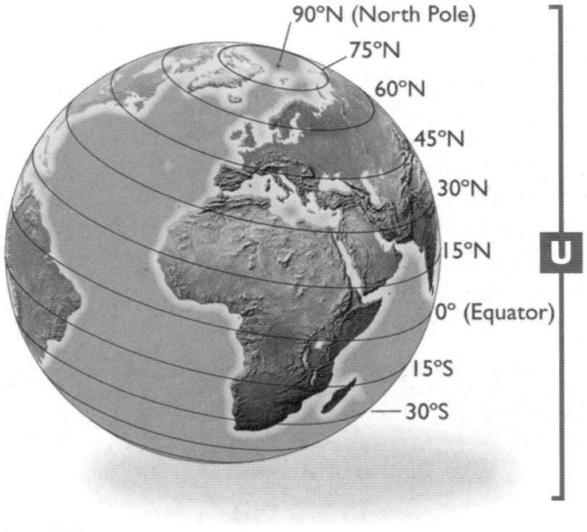

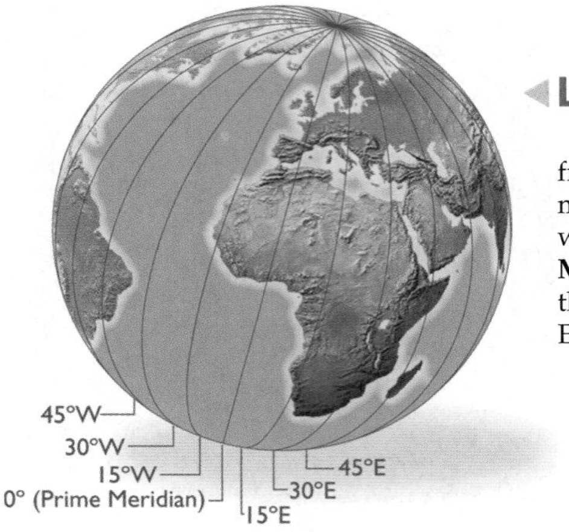

Longitude

Lines of longitude, or **meridians,** circle the earth from the North Pole to the South Pole. These lines measure distances east or west of the starting line, which is at 0° longitude and is called the **Prime Meridian** by geographers. The Prime Meridian runs through the Royal Observatory in Greenwich, England.

Absolute Location

S The grid system formed by lines of latitude and longitude makes it possible to find the absolute location of a place. Only one place can be found at the point where a specific line of latitude crosses a specific line of longitude. By using degrees (°) and minutes (′)—points between degrees—people can pinpoint the precise spot where one line of latitude crosses one line of longitude—an **absolute location.**

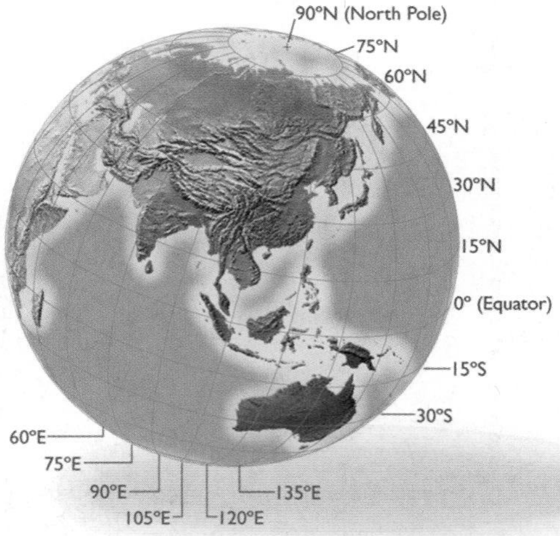

More Skill Practice

Using Geography Skills Organize the class into teams. Give each team a list of 20 different places on the globe, such as cities or physical features, and have them record the absolute location (in degrees of latitude and longitude) of each. Then have teams challenge each other to a contest in which one team gives the absolute location of five of their places, which the other team must locate on a globe. The teams switch roles until all places have been located. The team that uses the least amount of time to find the 20 places wins. OL CA CS3.

Parts of Maps

Map Key An important first step in reading a map is to note the map key. The **map key** explains the lines, symbols, and colors used on a map. For example, the map on this page shows the various climate regions of the United States and the different colors representing them. Cities are usually symbolized by a solid circle (•) and capitals by a star (⊛). On this map, you can see the capital of Texas and the cities of Los Angeles, Seattle, New Orleans, and Chicago.

NATIONAL GEOGRAPHIC **Climate Regions of the United States**

R2 **Scale** A measuring line, often called a **scale bar,** helps you figure distance on the map. The map scale tells you what distance on the earth is represented by the measurement on the scale bar.

R1 **Compass Rose** A map has a symbol that tells you where the **cardinal directions**—north, south, east, and west—are positioned.

NATIONAL GEOGRAPHIC

Geography Handbook

S Skill Practice

Using Geography Skills
Ask: What climate regions are found in California? (*Marine, Mediterranean, Highland; Steppe; Desert)* OL CA CS3.

C Critical Thinking

Analyzing Information
Ask: Why are most of the areas with Highland climate found in the western states? *(That region has the highest mountains.)* OL

R1 Reading Strategy

Reading Maps, Graphs, and Charts Give students practice in determining direction by having volunteers identify the direction from one location on this map to another. OL

R2 Reading Strategy

Reading Maps, Graphs, and Charts Demonstrate how to use a map's scale by transferring the markings onto a piece of paper and then using the marks to measure distance on a map. OL

More Skill Practice

Historical and Social Sciences Analysis Skill On slips of paper, write the page number of a map from the textbook and a question that requires the use of that map's key. Ask volunteers to randomly select a slip of paper, look at the map and its key, and answer the question. OL

C Critical Thinking

Making Inferences Ask: Which type of map do you think changes most frequently, physical or political? Why? *(Students should recognize that political changes happen more often than physical changes.)* OL

S Skill Practice

Using Geography Skills Have students compare this map to the United States physical map on pages 32–33. **Ask:** Which map shows the eastern coastline in greater detail? *(this map)* Why? *(because the map focuses on just this area)* OL

R Reading Strategy

Reading Maps, Graphs, and Charts Point out that the key shows the different colors used for different groups of colonies. **Ask:** What color shows the New England colonies? *(yellow)* Why is there another color below that line? *(The map groups the colonies into regions, and a different region begins there.)* OL

Additional Support

Maps

General Purpose Maps

Geographers use many different types of maps. Maps that show a wide range of general information about an area are called **general purpose maps.** Two of the most common general purpose maps are physical and political maps.

Physical Maps

Physical maps call out landforms and water features. The colors used on physical maps include brown or green for land and blue for water. You may see a physical map of the United States on pages 32–33. In addition, physical maps may use colors to show vegetation and elevation. **Vegetation** refers to the kinds of plant life in an area. **Elevation** is the height of an area above sea level. A key explains what each color and symbol stands for.

A **contour map** is a third kind of physical map. It also shows elevation. A contour map has **contour lines**—one line for each major level of elevation. For example, a low-lying area might have contour lines for 100 feet, 200 feet, and 300 feet above sea level. These lines usually form circles or ovals—one line inside the other. If the lines are spread apart, the land is flat or rises very gradually. If contour lines come very close together, the surface is steep.

Political Maps

Political maps show the names and boundaries of countries, the location of cities and other human-made features of a place, and often identify major physical features. The political map of the thirteen colonies, for example, shows the boundaries of each colony. The map also has their eastern and western boundaries—the Atlantic Ocean and the Appalachian Mountains. In addition, the map shows the three major regions and the largest colonial cities.

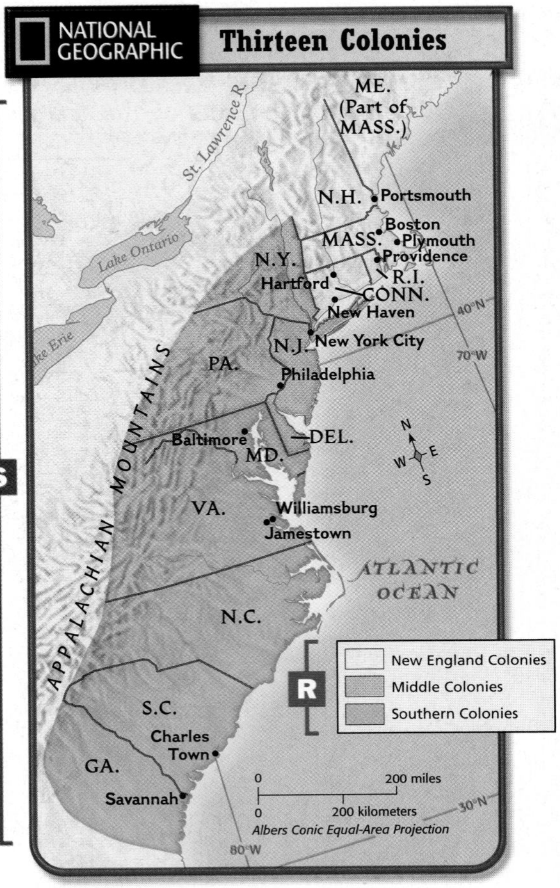

Political Map

Did You Know?

Cartographers, or people who make maps, generally use similar color schemes for physical features. They employ greens and yellows for land at lower elevations; reds, oranges, and browns for mountains; and light blue for water features.

Special Purpose Maps

Some maps are made to present specific kinds of information. These are called **thematic** or **special purpose maps.** They usually show themes or patterns, often emphasizing one subject or theme. Special purpose maps may present climate or natural resources. They may also display historical information, such as battles or territorial changes. The map's title tells what kind of special information it shows. Colors and symbols in the map key are especially important on these types of maps. Special purpose maps are often found in books of maps called atlases.

One type of special purpose map uses colors to show population. Notice the key on the map "Population of the United States, 1820." It indicates that the states with the greatest population are in pink. The map shows these states are along the Atlantic Ocean.

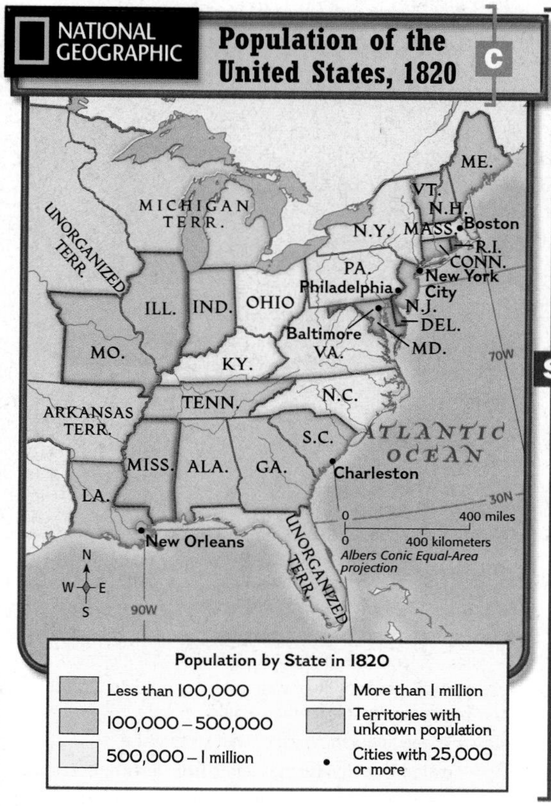

Population of the United States, 1820

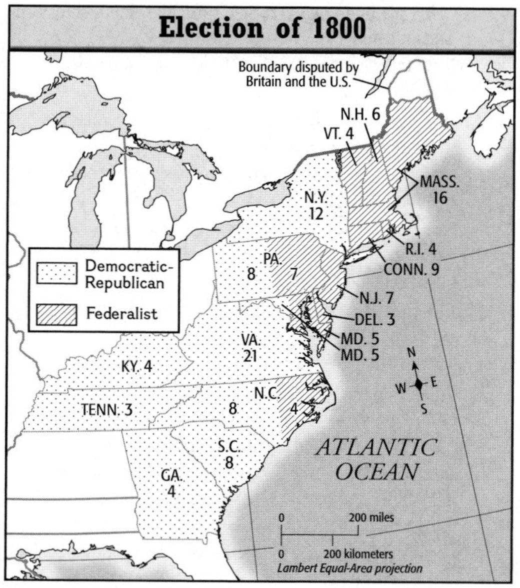

Election of 1800

Some special purpose maps, such as "The Election of 1800," are not in color. This map is an example of what you might find on a standardized test or in a newspaper.

R Reading Strategy

Categorizing Information

Have students work in groups to scan the textbook to find and classify the different maps they see as physical maps, political maps, or special purpose maps. Ask the groups to report their findings to the class. OL

S Skill Practice

Using Geography Skills

Point out that the map shows the population of the United States in 1820. **Ask:** What states had populations greater than 1 million in 1820? *(New York, Pennsylvania, and Virginia)* OL

C Critical Thinking

Analyzing Information

Ask: What political information is given on this map? *(borders of states and the names and locations of cities)* What physical information is provided? *(name and location of the Atlantic Ocean; locations of various rivers)* OL

More Skill Practice

Historical and Social Science Analysis Skill Have students bring to class different kinds of special purpose maps. Examples might include trail maps from a park, road maps, or maps found in works of fiction. Allow time for volunteers to show and display their examples. OL

U Universal Access

Visual/Spatial Have students use clay or other materials to make models of the different landforms identified in the Geographic Dictionary. OL

R Reading Strategy

Categorizing Information Suggest that students categorize the definitions into three groups—landforms (such as basin, canyon, or cape), bodies of water (including bay, channel, and delta), and geographic terms (such as absolute location, latitude, and longitude). OL

C Critical Thinking

Comparing and Contrasting Ask students to find and explain the differences between terms that are similar to each other but describe distinct kinds of forms. For instance, they could contrast *bay* and *gulf* or *canyon* and *valley*. OL

Additional Support

Geographic Dictionary

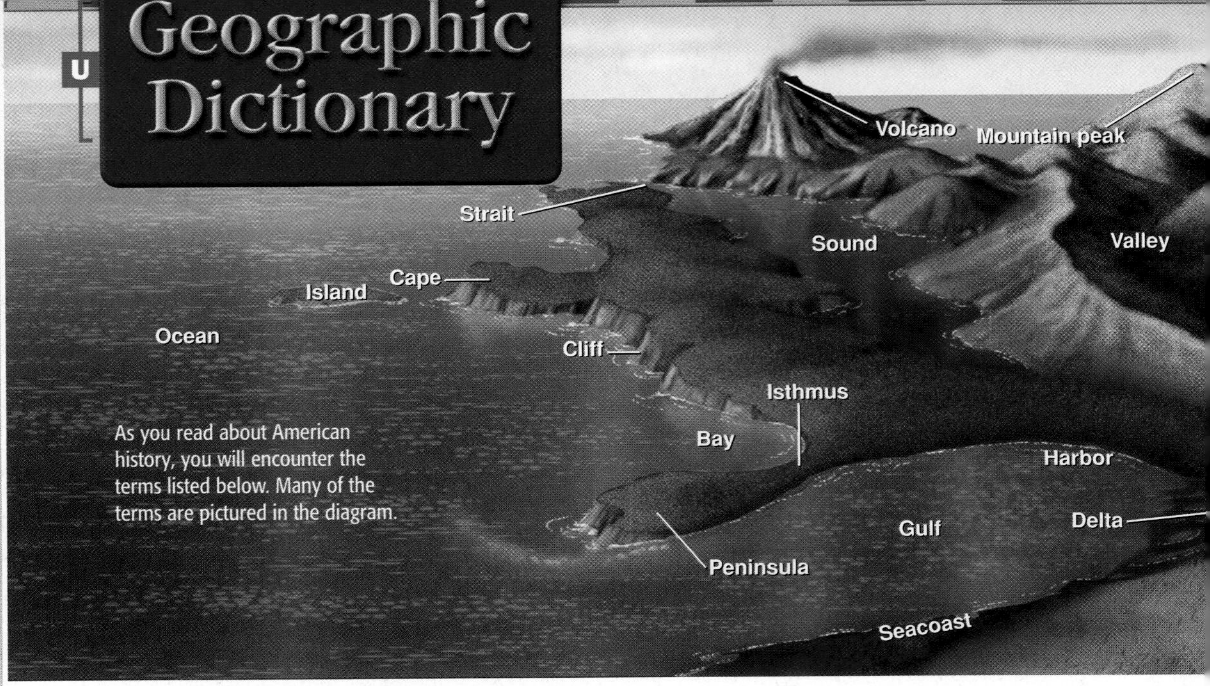

As you read about American history, you will encounter the terms listed below. Many of the terms are pictured in the diagram.

absolute location exact location of a place on the earth described by global coordinates

basin area of land drained by a given river and its branches; area of land surrounded by lands of higher elevation

bay part of a large body of water that extends into a shoreline, generally smaller than a gulf

canyon deep and narrow valley with steep walls

cape point of land that extends into a river, lake, or ocean

channel wide strait or waterway between two landmasses that lie close to each other; deep part of a river or other waterway

cliff steep, high wall of rock, earth, or ice

continent one of the seven large landmasses on the earth

cultural feature characteristic that humans have created in a place, such as language, religion, housing, and settlement pattern

delta flat, low-lying land built up from soil carried downstream by a river and deposited at its mouth

divide stretch of high land that separates river systems

downstream direction in which a river or stream flows from its source to its mouth

elevation height of land above sea level

Equator imaginary line that runs around the earth halfway between the North and South Poles; used as the starting point to measure degrees of north and south latitude

glacier large, thick body of slowly moving ice

gulf part of a large body of water that extends into a shoreline, generally larger and more deeply indented than a bay

harbor a sheltered place along a shoreline where ships can anchor safely

highland elevated land area such as a hill, mountain, or plateau

hill elevated land with sloping sides and rounded summit; generally smaller than a mountain

island land area, smaller than a continent, completely surrounded by water

isthmus narrow stretch of land connecting two larger land areas

lake a sizable inland body of water

latitude distance north or south of the Equator, measured in degrees

longitude distance east or west of the Prime Meridian, measured in degrees

lowland land, usually level, at a low elevation

map drawing of the earth shown on a flat surface

meridian one of many lines on the global grid running from the North Pole to the South Pole; used to measure degrees of longitude

mesa broad, flat-topped landform with steep sides; smaller than a plateau

46 Geography Handbook

Did You Know?

The terms geographers use to describe the earth come from many different languages. For instance, *mesa,* which appears on this page, the Spanish word for "table," is applied to flat-topped, steep-sided hills. Other terms that geographers use include *tsunami,* the Japanese word meaning "overflowing wave," and *fjord,* the Norwegian word meaning "long, narrow bay."

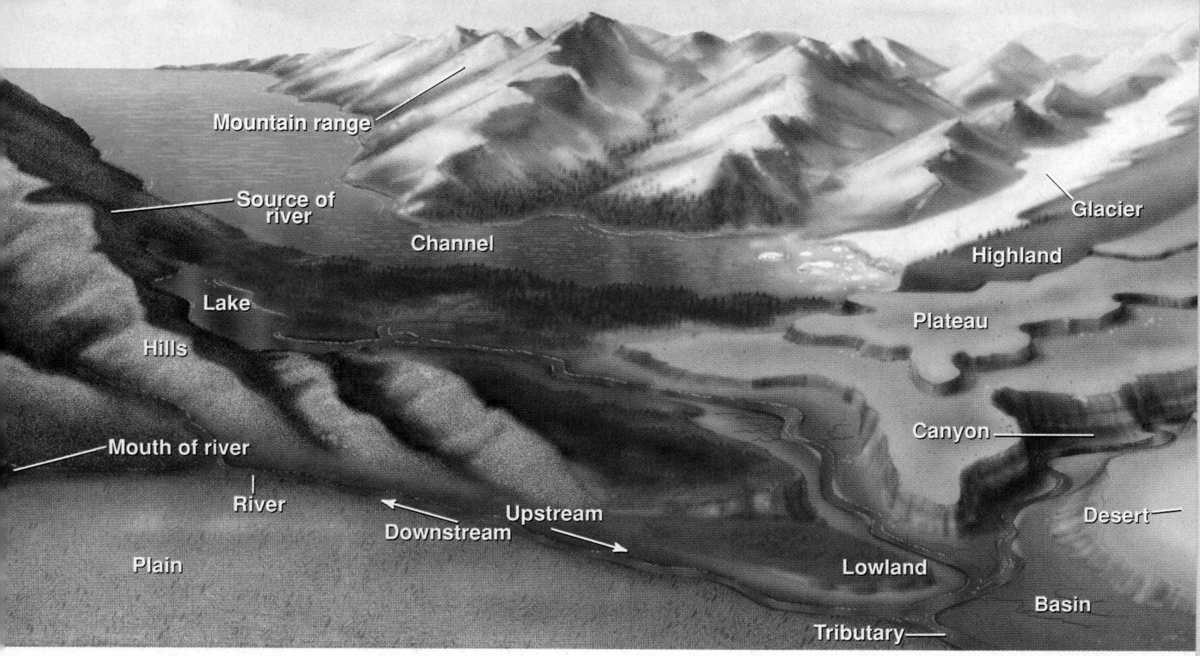

S

mountain land with steep sides that rises sharply (1,000 feet [305 m] or more) from surrounding land; generally larger and more rugged than a hill

mountain peak pointed top of a mountain

mountain range a series of connected mountains

mouth (of a river) place where a stream or river flows into a larger body of water

ocean one of the four major bodies of salt water that surround the continents

ocean current stream of either cold or warm water that moves in a definite direction through an ocean

parallel one of many lines on the global grid that circle the earth north or south of the Equator; used to measure degrees of latitude

peninsula body of land jutting into a lake or ocean, surrounded on three sides by water

physical feature characteristic of a place occurring naturally, such as a landform, body of water, climate pattern, or resource

plain area of level land, usually at a low elevation and often covered with grasses

plateau area of flat or rolling land at a high elevation, about 300–3,000 feet (91–914 m) high

Prime Meridian line of the global grid running from the North Pole to the South Pole through Greenwich, England; starting point for measuring degrees of east and west longitude

relief changes in elevation over a given area of land

river large natural stream of water that runs through the land

sea large body of water completely or partly surrounded by land

seacoast land lying next to a sea or ocean

sea level position on land level with surface of nearby ocean or sea

sound body of water between a coastline and one or more islands off the coast

source (of a river) place where a river or stream begins, often in highlands

strait narrow stretch of water joining two larger bodies of water

tributary small river or stream that flows into a larger river or stream; a branch of the river

upstream direction opposite the flow of a river; toward the source of a river or stream

valley area of low land between hills or mountains

volcano mountain that is created as liquid rock or ash erupts from inside the earth

S Skill Practice

Using Geography Skills Ask students to give examples of the major types of landforms and bodies of water. OL

ASSESS

Provide students with an outline map of the United States and colored pencils. Have students use a different color to label each of the following: Appalachian Mountains, Rocky Mountains, Great Lakes, Great Salt Lake, Mississippi River, Missouri River, Atlantic Ocean, Pacific Ocean, Gulf of Mexico, and Great Plains. Have students choose one of these geographic features and explain how it might have affected American history.

CLOSE

Connecting Have students explain how a region's physical features can influence its economic development. OL

Did You Know?

The Mississippi River is the nineteenth longest river in the world. If you combine the Missouri River with the lower reaches of the Mississippi—from the junction of the two rivers south—the combined river would be the fourth longest in the world.

Tools of the Historian

Objectives

After studying **Tools of the Historian**, students should be able to:

- Demonstrate and apply basic tools of historical research.
- Describe ways of interpreting archaeological evidence.
- Analyze and evaluate historical materials.
- Apply geography to historical research.
- Connect the current world to the early years of American history.

FOCUS

Ask: What do historians do? *(study the past)* What "tools" do historians use to carry out this work? *(books, diaries, and letters written by people who lived in the past; objects they used; buildings they constructed)* OL

TEACH

R Reading Strategy

Analyzing Text Structure
Ask: Which two sections are concerned with time? *(the first two and last two)* Which are concerned with place? *(the third and fourth)* OL

Answers and Additional Support

Tools of the Historian

A historian is a person who studies and writes about people and events of the past. Historians find out how people lived, what happened to them, and what happened around them. They look for the reasons behind events and study the effects of events.

Have you ever wondered if you could be a historian? To answer that question, you will need to find out how history is researched and written. Historians use a number of skills to research and organize information. You can learn about these skills in the next few pages. As you study this textbook, you will see that the sections listed below will help you understand geography and history.

Measuring Time 50
Organizing Time. 52
History and Geography. 54
R What Is a Historical Atlas? . . 58
How Does a Historian Work? . . 60
Making Sense of the Past . . . 64
Links Across Time. 68

Scientists looking for evidence of past civilizations

More Skill Practice

Visual Literacy Have students look at the large photograph at the bottom of the page. **Ask:** What does this photograph show? *(Students should note that the photo shows an archaeological dig site with many people working.)* Ask students to share what they know about archaeology. OL

Digging Up The Past

Historians depend on the work of archaeologists. Archaeologists are scientists who unearth the remains of the past.

What Do Archaeologists Study?

- Human and animal bones, seeds, trees
- Pottery, tools, weapons
- Mounds, pits, canals

▲ Prehistoric pottery

▲ Archaeologist at work

How Do They Gather Data?

- Surveys on foot
- Photographs taken from airplanes or satellites
- Ground-penetrating radar
- Plot locations on maps
- Dig for evidence with heavy equipment as well as shovels
- Sonar scanning to find underwater objects

C

How Do They Interpret Findings?

- Organize artifacts into groups based on similarities
- Compare objects in relation to other objects
- Look for evidence of changes over a period of time
- Date once-living objects by measuring carbon-14 levels
- Use microscopic and biological tests to date objects

S

◀ Carbon-14 dating

Do Your Own Digging

Research the library and Internet to find information on two archaeological diggings, one past and the other recent. Compare and contrast the methods used in each digging. What changes do you notice in the tools that archaeologists have used over time?

Do Your Own Digging Answers

Answer: Encourage students to collect images of the digs that they study and bring them to class. Have students share those images from different periods to see visual evidence of how archaeology has changed.

Tools of the Historian

TEACH

C Critical Thinking

Making Inferences Tell students to suppose archaeologists found two objects similarly made in different regions of the same continent. **Ask:** What might that show? *(It would show that people with the same culture lived in the two regions at the same time, that they moved from one region to the other, or that there was trade between the peoples living in the two regions.)* What would changes over a period of time show? *(the development of new technologies, new uses for objects, new belief systems, or new artistic styles)* OL

CA HI3.

S Skill Practice

Historical and Social Sciences Analysis Skill

Ask: Why would archaeologists want to date objects they found? *(Dating gives archaeologists ways of fixing objects in time so that comparisons over time can be made.)* OL

Tools of the Historian

FOCUS

Ask: Why is time important to historians? *(because they trace how events take place over time)*

TEACH

S Skill Practice

Historical and Social Sciences Analysis Skill

Ask: What came first, 100 B.C. or A.D. 100? *(100 B.C.)* What about 100 B.C. and 99 B.C.? *(100 B.C.)* What about A.D. 99 and A.D. 100? *(A.D. 99)* OL

CA CS1.

R Reading Strategy

Categorizing Information

Ask: Are ancient coins artifacts? Why or why not? *(yes; because they were made by humans)* What about the bones of an animal that lived in an area not inhabited by humans? *(no; because artifacts are objects made by people)* What about jewelry crafted from shell? *(yes; because the jewelry was made by people)* OL

Measuring Time

Historical and Social Sciences Analysis Skills

Chronological and Spatial Thinking

CS1. Students explain how major events are related to one another in time.

Calendars Historians rely on *calendars,* or dating systems, to measure time. Cultures throughout the world have developed different calendars based on important events in their history. Western nations begin their calendar with the year in which Jesus was thought to have been born. The Jewish calendar begins about 3,760 years before the Christian calendar. This is the time when Jewish tradition says the world was created. Muslims date their calendar from the time their first leader, Muhammad, left the city of Makkah for Madinah. This was A.D. 622 in the Christian calendar.

◀ Ancient stone calendar

The dates in this book are based on the Western calendar. In the Western calendar, the years before the birth of Jesus are known as "B.C.," or "before Christ." The years after are called "A.D.," or *anno domini.* This phrase comes from the Latin language and means "in the year of the Lord."

▲ About A.D. 500, a Christian monk, or religious person, developed the Western way of dating events.

Dating Events To date events before the birth of Christ, or B.C., historians count backwards from A.D. 1. There is no year 0. The year before A.D. 1 is 1 B.C. (Notice that A.D. is written before the date, but B.C. is written following the date.) S Therefore, a date in the 100 years before the birth of Christ lies between 100 B.C. and A.D. 1.

To date events after the birth of Christ, or A.D., historians count forward, starting at A.D. 1. A date in the first 100 years after the birth of Christ is between A.D. 1 and A.D. 100.

Dating Archaeological Finds One of the most important and difficult jobs for archaeologists is dating the artifacts that they find. Artifacts are objects made by people, such as weapons, tools, or pottery. The earliest artifacts R are pieces of hard rock that were chipped into cutting or digging tools or into weapons. By examining artifacts, scientists can learn about the social and military structures of an ancient society.

Answers and Additional Support

EXTENDING THE CONTENT

Keeping Track of Time The measurements now used for time derive from ancient practices. Ancient Egyptians had 24 hours in their day; it was the ancient Mesopotamians who divided each hour into 60 minutes. Egyptians first gathered days into weeks of an even number of days, though the use of seven days for the week comes from the ancient Israelites. The Mesopotamians were the first to divide the year into 12 months of around 30 days each. The current structure of months and the addition of a day every fourth year (to reconcile the calendar with the actual solar year) comes from Roman times.

R How do archaeologists determine the age of these artifacts? Early scientists correctly assumed that artifacts buried more deeply in the ground are older than those closer to the surface. In most cases, that observation is still true today.

Another way that archaeologists date artifacts is by using trees. Each year, trees form a new growth ring. Scientists count the number of rings in a wooden object, such as a house beam, and compare the pattern with the rings of a tree whose age they know. In that way, they can identify dates as far back as 3,000 years.

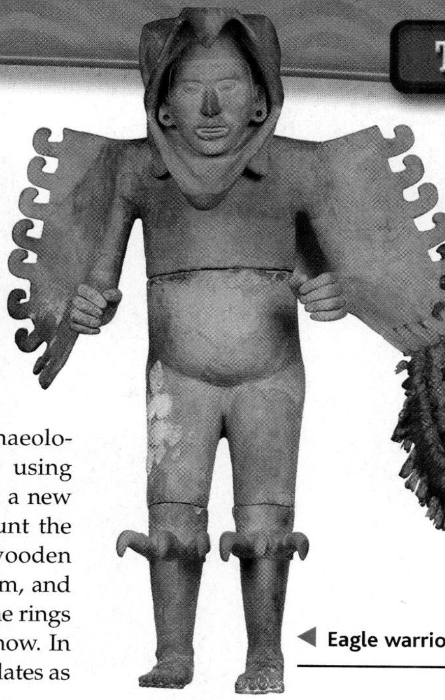

◀ Eagle warrior

▲ Feather shield

In 1946 an American scientist name Willard Frank Libby discovered that all living things contain a radioactive element called carbon 14. After plants, animals, and humans die, the carbon 14 gradually disappears. By measuring how much carbon 14 a skeleton or the remains of a wooden boat contain today, scientists can estimate how old an object is. This method is called radiocarbon dating.

Radiocarbon dating, however, is only accurate for dating objects that are no more than 50,000 years old. Another method of dating—thermoluminescence (THUHR•muh•LOO•muh•NEH•suhns)—helps scientists make more precise measurements back as far as 200,000 years. This method dates an object by measuring the amount of light given off by particles trapped in the soil surrounding the artifact or fossil.

New methods for analyzing remains—such as blood, hairs, and plant tissues left on rocks, tools, and weapons—give archaeologists still more information. Scientists have discovered that blood molecules can survive for millions of years. This discovery is important because it can tell us how some tools were used and the types of early animals that hunters killed. DNA is also providing new information. By analyzing the remains of plants on stone tools, for example, scientists can find out more about the history of farming.

Scientists analyze many different samples, using as many different methods as possible, because individual results may vary. Dating methods are constantly being refined to provide more accurate data. C

Although scientists have developed many methods to measure the age of artifacts, what we know about early people and history will continue to change as new information and new methods of dating are discovered.

Thinking Like a Historian

1. **Identify** What do B.C. and A.D. mean? How are they used?
2. **Dating Events** What year came after 184 B.C.?
3. **Compare and Contrast** Use the Internet to find out the current year on the Jewish and Muslim calendars. Why are calendars different from culture to culture?

Tools of the Historian

R Reading Strategy

Organizing Information
Have students create a chart that summarizes the way archaeologists date artifacts. OL

Ways Archaeologists Date Artifacts

- Seeing how deeply artifacts are buried *(older artifacts are farther below the surface)*
- Using tree rings
- Measuring carbon-14 levels *(also called radiocarbon dating)*
- Using thermoluminescence dating
- Analyzing DNA

C Critical Thinking

Analyzing Information
Ask: Why would historians want to refine their methods for dating objects? *(Having more accurate dating methods will lead to better interpretations of those objects.)* OL

ASSESS

Ask students to write a short paragraph in which they describe the tools that historians use for measuring time and dating artifacts. OL

CLOSE

Have students explain why having ways of measuring time is important to the work of historians. OL

Thinking Like a Historian Answers

1. B.C.—"before Christ" A.D.—*anno domini*, "in the year of the Lord"; they are used to date events before and after Christ's birth
2. 183 B.C.
3. Students should find the appropriate years on the Internet or in an almanac or other reference book. They should note that different cultures have different measures of key dates in their history and thus choose different starting points for their calendars.

FOCUS

Have students recall time periods they have studied in the past. Write the words *ancient times* and *Middle Ages* on the board and ask students to define them. Discuss why historians use labels such as these to characterize a period of time. **OL**

TEACH

C Critical Thinking

Comparing and Contrasting Ask: How are centuries and decades different from periods and eras? *(Decades and centuries are fixed 10-year and 100-year periods of time. Periods and eras are groups of years defined by common historical or cultural characteristics.)* **OL**

U Universal Access

English Learners Ask: What is meant by the term *1900s?* *(The century from 1900 to 1999.)* What about the term *1850s?* *(The decade from 1850 to 1859.)* **EL**

Organizing Time

Historical and Social Sciences Analysis Skills

Chronological and Spatial Thinking

CS1. Students explain how major events are related to one another in time.

CS2. Students construct various time lines of key events, people, and periods of the historical era they are studying.

C **Periods of History** Historians divide history into blocks of time known as *periods,* or *eras.* For example, a period of 10 years is called a *decade.* A period of 100 years is known as a *century.* Periods are sometimes given names based on the leading events of the time span they cover.

U In this book, for example, you will study American history from the nation's beginnings to the early 1900s. The first period of American history that you will be studying is the *American Revolution and the New Nation*. Other periods in the history of the United States include *National Expansion and Reform, Civil War and Reconstruction,* and *Industrialization and Progressivism.*

George Washington served as U.S. president from 1789 to 1797. ▶

▲ Many settlers headed to the West in the mid-1800s.

▲ Confederate soldier's cap (upper left) and Union soldier's cap (lower right), *Civil War, 1861–1865*

▼ Classroom, early 1900s

Answers and Additional Support

More Skill Practice

Historical and Social Sciences Analysis Skill Remind students that centuries can be written in two ways—as an ordinal number and as a number rounded to the hundreds. Write on the board *eighteenth century, nineteenth century, 1700s, 1800s, 1900s.* Have students match the two names for each century. *(eighteenth century—1700s; nineteenth century—1800s)* **OL**

Tools of the Historian

NATIONAL GEOGRAPHIC **Where & When?**

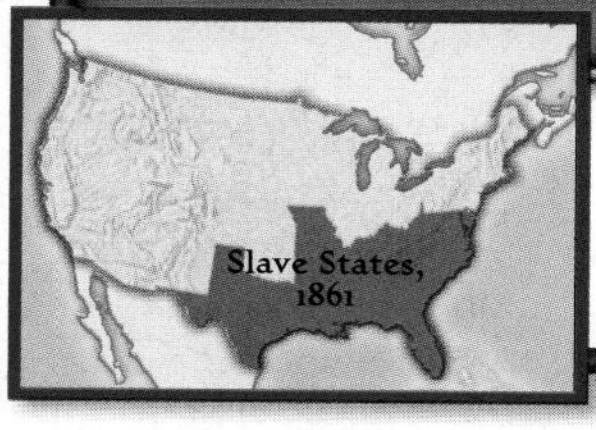

1820 — 1845 — 1870

- **1820** Missouri Compromise is passed
- **1845** Texas becomes a state
- **1860** Abraham Lincoln elected president
- **1861** Civil War begins

S

What Is a Time Line? Which came first: the American Civil War or World War II? Did the train come before or after the invention of the airplane? In studying the past, historians focus on *chronology*, or the order of dates in which events happened.

You might be wondering how to make sense of the flow of dates and events. An easy way is to use or make a time line. A *time line* is a diagram that shows the order of events within a period of time.

Most time lines are divided into sections in which the years are evenly spaced. In some cases, however, a spread of time may be too long to show all of the years in even spaces. To save space, a period of time may be omitted from the time line. Where this happens, a slanted or jagged line appears on the time line to show a break in the even spacing of events.

A time line also labels events. Each event on the time line appears beside the date when the event took place. Sometimes, when the exact date of an event is not known, *c.*, or *circa* (which means "about"), appears before the date. **R**

Events and their dates often are shown on a single time line, as on the time line at the top of this page. In other cases, two or more time lines are stacked one on top of the other. These are called multilevel time lines. They help you compare events in different places at the same time period. For example, the multilevel time line on pages 520–521 shows events in the United States and in other parts of the world from 1820 to 1900.

These dates lead up to and through the Civil War and include the years after the war. The skill lesson "Reading a Time Line" on page 824 will help you learn to work with time lines.

When you read a time line, you see not only when an event took place, but also what events took place before and after it. Some helpful steps will guide you in reading a time line. First, find the dates on the opposite ends of the time line. This tells you the time span. A time line that begins in 1800 and ends in 1860 has a 60-year time span. Second, study the order of events. Finally, analyze relationships among the events on the time line.

Thinking Like a Historian

1. **Reading a Time Line** Look over the time line above to get an idea of what a time line shows. When does it begin and end? What feature makes this time line different from many other time lines? Why was this feature added?
2. **Understanding a Time Line** How many years are included in each section of the time line?
3. **Making a Time Line** Create a time line using the terms B.M.B. (before my birth) and A.M.B. (after my birth). Fill in the time line with five key events that happened before and after you were born. Illustrate the time line with copies of photos from your family album.

Thinking Like a Historian Answers

1. begins in 1820 and ends in 1870; it includes a map; students may suggest that the map was included to show important places mentioned on the time line
2. 25
3. Students' time lines should include ten total events, five before and five after their births; they should also include photographs.

Tools of the Historian

S Skill Practice

Reading a Time Have Have students examine the time line at the top of the page. Have them measure the distance from 1820 to 1845 and from 1845 to 1870. **Ask:** What do you notice about these distances? Why is that the case? *(They are equal; because both show a period of the same number of years.)* **OL**

R Reading Strategy

Questioning **Ask:** What would the date "c. 1850" mean on a time line? *(that something happened around 1850 but not necessarily that specific year)* **OL**

ASSESS

Ask students to create a graphic organizer in which they illustrate how historians organize history. *(Graphic organizers will vary, but should indicate that historians divide history into blocks of time known as periods or eras and they use time lines to show a flow and sequence of dates and events.)* **OL**

CLOSE

Have students work in small groups to create time lines about their community's history. Students may want to focus on specific types of events, such as those of political, economic, or social significance. They might also want to focus on a time period, such as the twentieth century. **OL**

FOCUS

Ask: What does the study of geography involve? *(the study of landforms, bodies of water, climate, and resources; human-environment interaction)* OL

TEACH

C Critical Thinking

Making Generalizations
Ask: What is an example of how geography has shaped history? *(Answers may include the impact of the river and the desert on settlement patterns in Egypt, or Muslim domination of trade routes to Asia as a spur for European exploration.)* AL

S Skill Practice

Visual Literacy Have students compare the map and the LANDSAT image of the San Francisco bay area. **Ask:** What similar information do they provide? *(the shape of the land and bodies of water)* What different information do they show? *(map: names of different features and includes roadways; LANDSAT: contours of the land)* OL

History and Geography

Historical and Social Sciences Analysis Skills

Chronological and Spatial Thinking

CS3. Students use a variety of maps and documents to identify physical and cultural features of neighborhoods, cities, states, and countries and to explain the historical migration of people, expansion and disintegration of empires, and the growth of economic systems.

C *Geography* is the study of the earth and its physical features. In this text, you will discover how geography has shaped the course of events in American history. Sometimes the study of geography is broken down into five themes. *The Five Themes of Geography* are:

- **Location** Where is it?
- **Place** What is it like?
- **Human/Environment Interaction** What is the relationship between people and their surroundings?
- **Movement** How do people in one area relate to people in other areas?
- **Region** What common features bring geographical areas together?

S ▼ LANDSAT satellite map of San Francisco Bay area

Location

"Where is it?" In using geography, historians first look at where a place is located. Every place has an absolute location and a relative location. *Absolute location* refers to the exact spot of a place on the earth's surface. For example, the city of San Francisco, California, is located at one place and one place only. No other place on Earth has exactly the same location.

NATIONAL GEOGRAPHIC **San Francisco Bay Area**

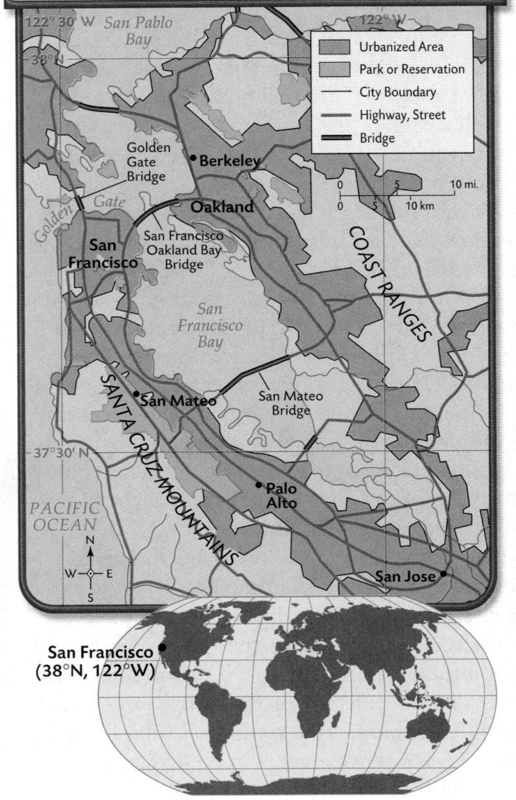

Answers and Additional Support

EXTENDING THE CONTENT

Earth Pictures LANDSAT is the collective name used for seven U.S. satellites, the first of which was launched in 1972 and the most recent of which was sent into space in 1999. (The sixth was launched but malfunctioned.) The satellites have cameras and sensors that enable them to take pictures of Earth and to make other observations. The purpose was to gather information on resources, conditions in the air and water, and pollution. They take images of each spot on Earth at regular intervals. By comparing the pictures, scientists can see changes over time.

▲ Pioneers on the Oregon Trail

Miner seeking gold ▶

Relative location tells where a place is, compared with one or more other places. San Francisco is northwest of Los Angeles and southwest of Seattle. Knowing a place's relative location may help a historian understand how it was settled and how its culture developed. For example, people in California have settled in coastal areas and valleys, because inland areas have many mountains or deserts. They also have turned to the sea for food and trade.

Place

"What is it like?" *Place* describes all of the characteristics that give an area its own special quality. These can be physical features, such as mountains, waterways, climate, and plant or animal life. Places can also be described by human characteristics, such as language, religion, and architecture. For example, pioneers on the Oregon and California Trails crossed vast plains, swift rivers, high mountains, and hot deserts to reach their western destinations. When they arrived, they set up farms, homesteads, and towns.

NATIONAL GEOGRAPHIC **The Oregon and California Trails**

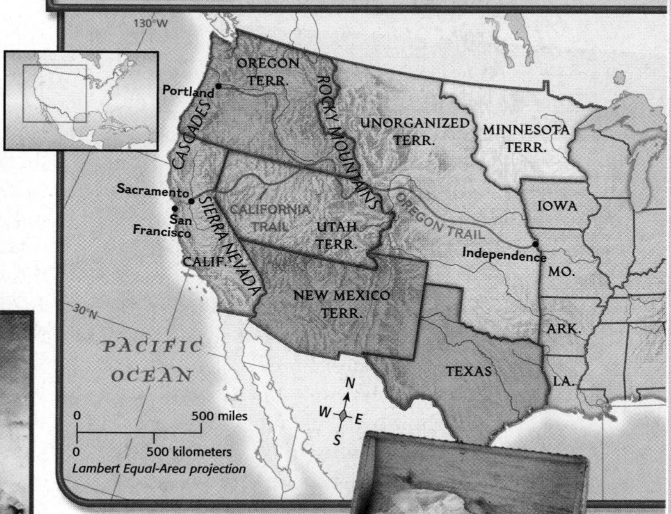

Pioneer chest ▶

Human/Environment Interaction

"What is the relationship between people and their surroundings?" Landforms, waterways, climate, and natural resources all have helped or hindered human activities.

People have responded to their environment, or natural surroundings, in different ways. Sometimes they have adjusted to it. For example, people throughout history have worn light clothing in hot places. At other times, people have changed their environment to meet their needs. For example, some pioneers who went westward set up farms, and others mined for gold and other minerals.

EXTENDING THE CONTENT

Absolute Location Developed by the U.S. Army in the early 1970s, the Global Positioning System (GPS) is a satellite-based system that uses radio signals to pinpoint exact locations on Earth. The system, which became available for civilian use in 1995, uses a network of 24 satellites called Navstars to broadcast radio signals. A computerized receiver receives the radio signal from as few as three satellites or as many as eight. The computerized receiver identifies the location of each satellite sending the signal, notes the time the signal was broadcast, and processes that information to determine the longitude and latitude of the receiver. The GPS generally is accurate to within 33 feet of the receiver's location.

Tools of the Historian

S Skill Practice

Historical and Social Sciences Analysis Skills Explain the ideas of absolute and relative location by pointing to the student in the first seat of the first row. **Ask:** What is that student's absolute location? *(first seat, first row)* What is his or her relative location? *(Answers may include "in front of five students" or "next to Jorge" or "near the door.")* Solicit several responses to the second question. Use the multiple responses to show that relative location changes depending on what the place is being related to. BL

R1 Reading Strategy

Connecting Have students identify at least ten ways to describe the school's relative location. List students' responses on the board. OL CA CS3.

R2 Reading Strategy

Analyzing Information Ask students to identify the physical and human characteristics of place. *(Physical features include mountains, waterways, climate, and plant or animal life. Human characteristics include language, religion, and architecture.)* Have students describe the characteristics of place that distinguish their neighborhood, city, or town from others nearby. OL

U Universal Access

Visual/Spatial Ask students to work in pairs to provide examples of ways in which they and their families adjust to their environment. Then have the pairs share their examples with the class. Discuss the different aspects of life that are influenced by the environment. OL

Tools of the Historian

History and Geography

C1 Critical Thinking

Comparing and Contrasting **Ask:** What is the difference between transportation and communication? *(Transportation is the movement of people or goods. Communication is the exchange of ideas.)* Which can lead to cultural change? Why? *(Either; because ideas brought to a place can change the culture of that place whether communicated from afar or from people who have moved)* OL

CA HI3.

C2 Critical Thinking

Determining Cause and Effect Ask a student to define *migrate*. *(to move from one place to another)* **Ask:** Why do people migrate? *(to escape war, famine, enslavement, economic problems, or other people)* OL

S Skill Practice

Visual Literacy **Ask:** In what direction did Native Americans move? *(from east to west)* Was that movement voluntary? Explain. *(involuntary; the title is "removal," not "movement," which suggests forced movement and the second item in the numbered list says they were forced to move)* OL

Answers and Additional Support

Movement

"How do people in one area affect people in other areas?" Historians answer this question with one word—*movement.* Throughout history, people, ideas, goods, and information have moved from place to place. Movement has brought the world's people closer together.

Transportation—the movement of people and goods—has allowed people to use products that are made thousands of miles away. This has increased the exchange of ideas and cultures. Communication—the movement of ideas and information—has allowed people to find out what is happening in other parts of the world. Unlike in the past, people today receive almost instant communication by radio, television, and the computer.

The movement of people to different places is called migration. Why have people migrated throughout history? Some have chosen to move to seek a better life. Others have been forced to move because of wars, famine, enslavement, or other settlers. For example, many white settlers moved into the southeastern states from the 1820s to the 1840s. They wanted the land held by Native Americans. In 1830 Congress passed the Indian Removal Act to move Native Americans west of the Mississippi River. Under pressure, the Choctaw, Creek, and Chickasaw moved. The Cherokee and the Seminole resisted but in the end many of them were forced to relocate.

NATIONAL GEOGRAPHIC **Removal of Native Americans, 1820–1840**

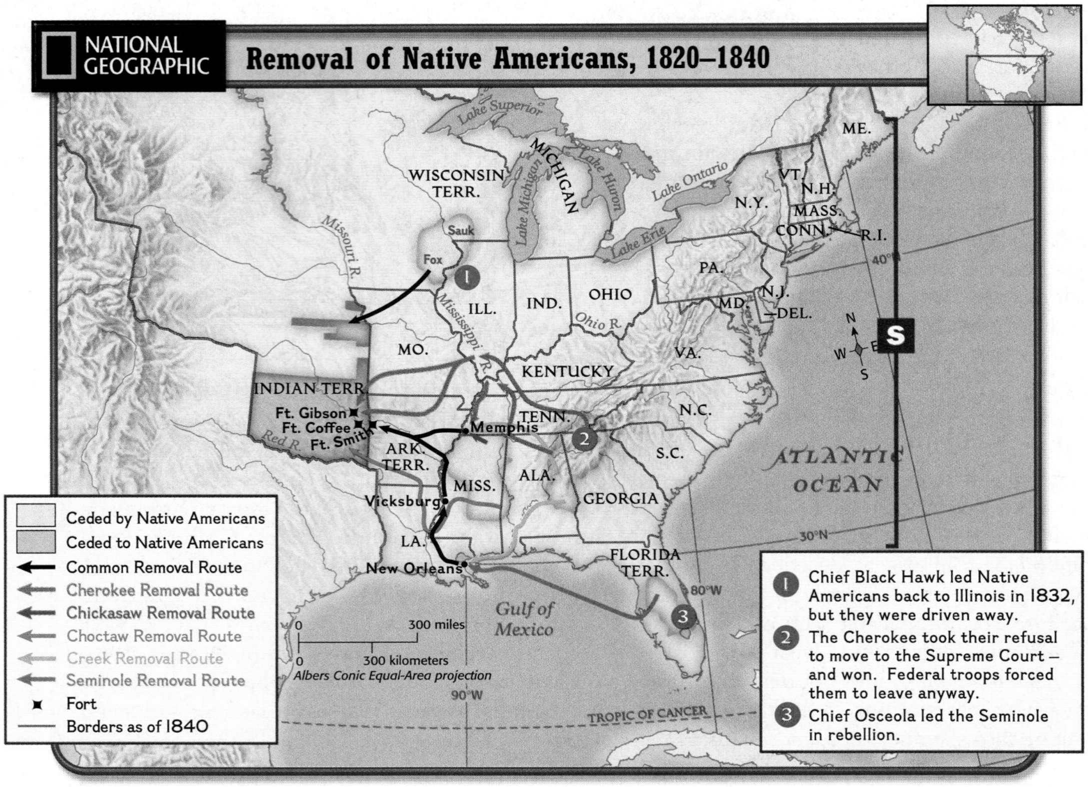

56

More Skill Practice

Using Geography Skills Have students identify these features of the map: the scale *(in the lower left center of the map)*; the key *(there are two—one explains the colors, arrows, and symbols on the map and the other explains what the numbers on the map mean)*. **Ask:** What purpose does the locator map perform? *(It allows you to see the small area of the map in the context of a larger area.)* OL

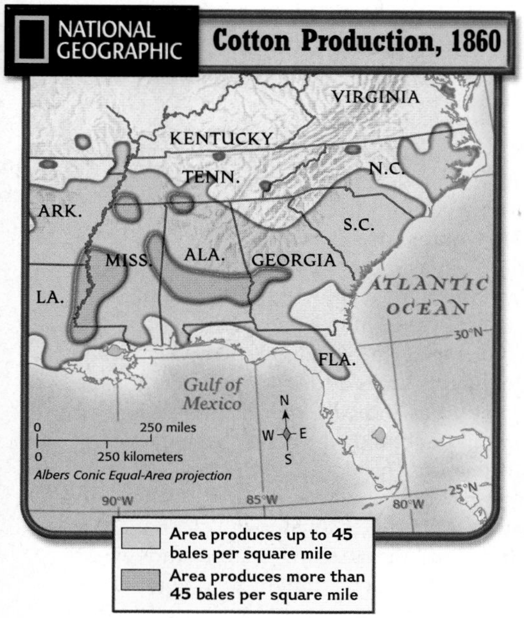

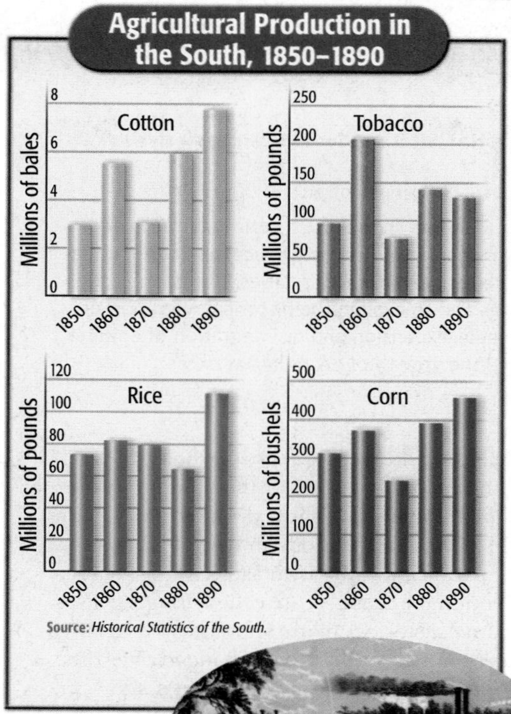

Steamboats on the Mississippi River ▶

Region

"What common characteristics does a certain area share?" Historians often view places or areas as regions. A *region* is an area that is defined by common features. Regions can be defined by physical features, such as mountains and rivers, or by human features, such as religion, language, or livelihood. For example, the South during the 1800s was a largely agricultural region.

C

See the information about the Six Essential Elements in the Geography Handbook on pages 39–40. Knowing these elements will help you in your study of history.

U

Six Essential Elements

Recently geographers have begun to look at geography a different way. They break down the study of geography into *Six Essential Elements.* These elements are:

- The World in Spatial Terms
- Places and Regions
- Physical Systems
- Human Systems
- Environment and Society
- The Uses of Geography

Thinking Like a Historian

1. **Identify** How are absolute location and relative location different?
2. **Analyzing Themes** What characteristics do geographers use to describe a place?
3. **Linking History and Geography** Make a list of the Five Themes of Geography. Under each theme, explain how you think geography has affected the history of your community.

Tools of the Historian

C Critical Thinking

Analyzing Information Challenge students to give examples of regions and to explain what characteristics make the area they identify a region. **AL**

U Universal Access

Below Grade Level Ask: How could you find out where the Geography Handbook is located if the information were not given here? *(by looking in the book's table of contents)* **BL**

ASSESS

Have students work in pairs to review the five themes of geography. Then have them list at least two characteristics describing each theme. **OL**

CLOSE

Ask students to write an essay explaining how using the five themes of geography can help historians understand how a group of people live. **OL**

Thinking Like a Historian Answers

1. Each place has only one absolute location, which is its exact spot on Earth's surface. It can have many relative locations, depending on what other spot it is being compared to.
2. physical features (mountains, waterways, climate, plant or animal life) and human features (language, religion, architecture)
3. Students' answers will vary but should include an example for each theme.

FOCUS

Have students discuss times that they or members of their family have used maps. **Ask:** What were the maps used for? How did they help? *(Students might point to occasions when their family used a road map or a street map to drive to an unfamiliar destination.)* OL

TEACH

S Skill Practice

Using Geography Skills
Direct students' attention to the two maps. **Ask:** Which territory was added to the United States between the date of the first and the second map? *(the Louisiana Territory)* What area or areas became states between the first year and the last one? When did that happen? *(Ohio; in 1803)* OL
CA CS3.

R Reading Strategy

Reading Maps, Charts, and Graphs **Ask:** Why show modern state boundaries on a historical map? *(Students may say that doing so makes it easier for people to identify the area the map shows.)* OL

Answers and Additional Support

What Is a Historical Atlas?

Historical and Social Sciences Analysis Skills

Chronological and Spatial Thinking

CS3. Students should use a variety of maps and documents to identify physical and cultural features of neighborhoods, cities, states, and countries and to explain the historical migration of people, expansion and disintegration of empires, and the growth of economic systems.

Historical Maps An *atlas* is a book of maps that show different parts of the world. A *historical atlas* has maps that show different parts of the world at different periods in history. Maps that show political events, such as invasions, battles, and boundary changes, are called *historical maps.*

Some historical maps show how territories in a certain part of the world changed over time. The maps at the bottom of the page show the territorial size of the United States in 1800 and 1810. By comparing the two maps, you can see how the United States gradually expanded its territory westward from 1800 to 1810.

Both maps use colors to show different political areas: U.S. states, U.S. territories, foreign-ruled areas, and territories claimed but not owned by the United States. Different colored lines indicate territorial boundaries. A heavy blue line highlights areas added to the United States, and gray lines indicate present-day U.S. state boundaries. Labels on the maps present a variety of information. This data includes new states and their dates of admission to the Union, plus recently acquired U.S. territories.

Historical maps show places and events from the past. As you study history, you will use many other kinds of maps. *Thematic maps* deal with specialized information, often on a single topic such as population or land use. A *political map* shows the political boundaries or borders of a state, country, or region.

NATIONAL GEOGRAPHIC **Territorial Growth, 1800–1810**

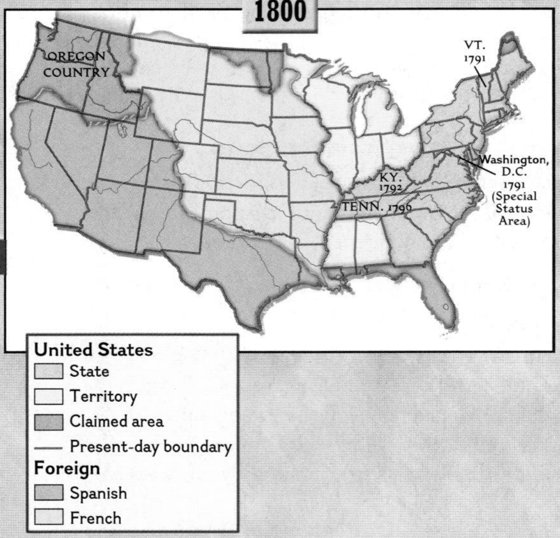

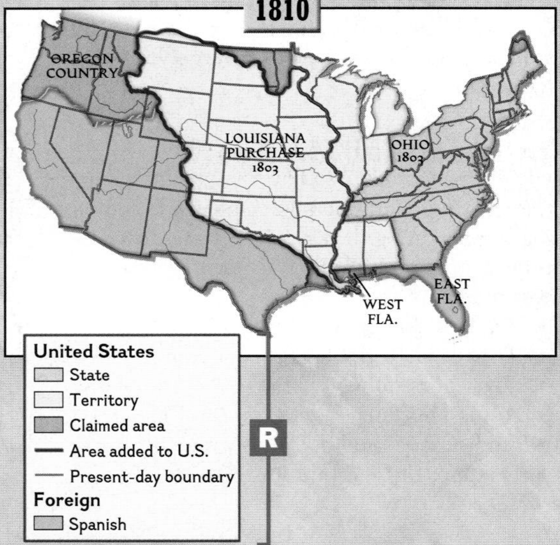

EXTENDING THE CONTENT

Ancient Mapmakers The oldest existing map was made on a clay tablet in Mesopotamia (now part of Iraq) about 2300 B.C. It shows settlements, rivers, and mountains. It was the ancient Greeks, however, who first studied the world in an accurate and systematic way. The most famous geographer of ancient times was Ptolemy, a Greek geographer who worked in Egypt about A.D. 150. His map of the world (as known to Europeans) was the best of its kind in Europe until the time of Christopher Columbus. At about the same time as Ptolemy, a Chinese astronomer named Zhang Heng developed one of the first geographic grid systems for maps.

NATIONAL GEOGRAPHIC

Major Western Railroads Before 1900 **R**

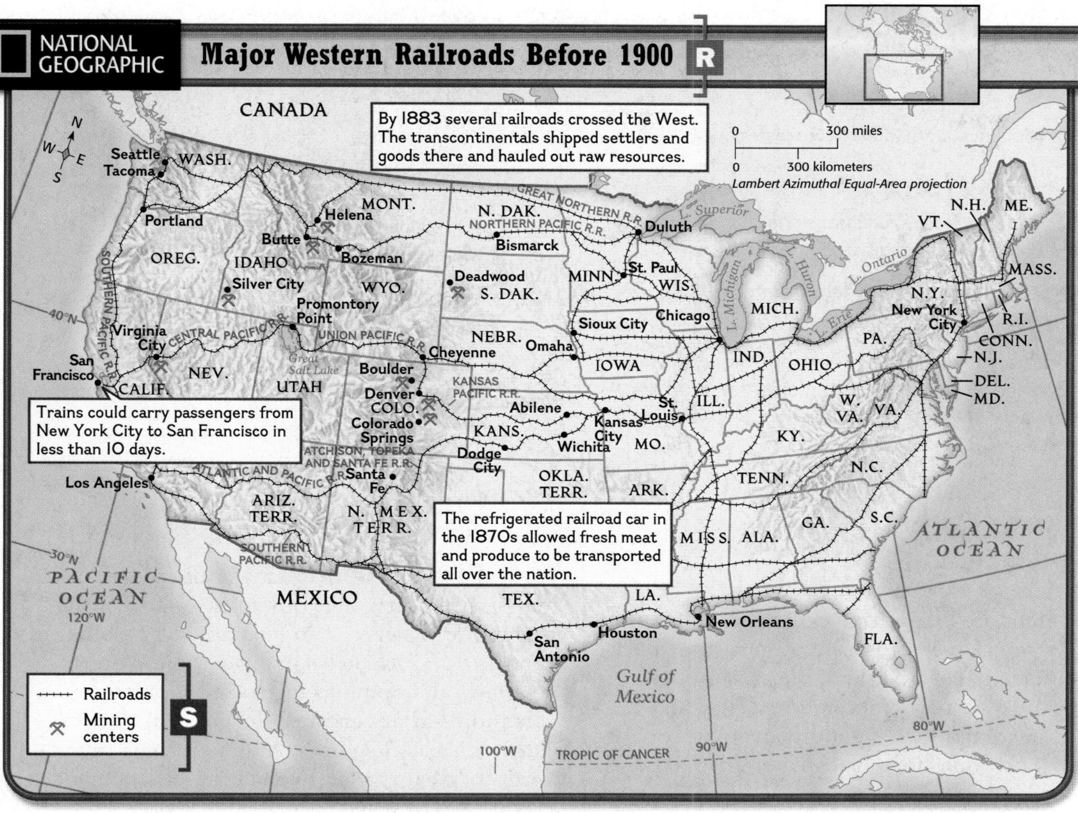

Historical Routes In your study of American history, you will often encounter thematic maps that show movement or routes. On some maps, lines may show *historical routes*. These are roads or courses over which people or goods have traveled all through history. Such routes are often colored or have special markings. On the map above, the black marked lines show major railroad routes in the western United States before 1900.

On maps of historical routes, the key explains what is shown on the maps. This map's key shows railroad routes and mining centers. In addition, boxes on the map provide information about railroad travel during the late 1800s.

Thinking Like a Historian

1. **Analyzing Maps** Look at the map of western railroads. Name one railroad system that extended west to the Pacific Ocean through each of these areas of the country—the North, the central part, and the South.
2. **Reading a Map Key** Look at the map of western railroads. What mining center lay on the Central Pacific Railway?
3. **Analyzing Maps** Select any chapter in your textbook. List the titles of the maps found in that chapter. Beside each map's title, state what kinds of symbols are used in each map key and what they represent.

Tools of the Historian

R Reading Strategy

Reading Maps, Charts, and Graphs **Ask:** Why is there a date in the title? What does it tell you about this map? *(the map shows data for a fixed point in time; the map only shows major railroads to the West present in 1900, not after)* OL

S Skill Practice

Using Geography Skills
Ask: How would you know how long each railroad route ran? *(by using the scale)* OL

ASSESS

Have students summarize the purposes and contents of historical atlases. OL

CLOSE

Ask students to draw a map of an imaginary place using the map details they have learned about on these pages. Have them begin by choosing the type of map they want to create. Then have them make up an imaginary landscape appropriate to their choice of map. If possible, students may use computer-generated graphics to enhance the appeal of their maps. Have volunteers share their maps with the class, explaining the different details they have included. OL

Thinking Like a Historian Answers

1. north—Great Northern or Northern Pacific; central part of the country—Kansas Pacific, Union Pacific, and Central Pacific; south—Atlantic and Pacific or Southern Pacific
2. Virginia City
3. Students' answers should reflect the information on the maps; tell them to identify the page on which each map is found so you can check it.

FOCUS

Bring to class a common object such as a CD or a box of processed food. **Ask:** What does this object show about the people who use it? After students have discussed the question, explain that historians engage in the process of asking and answering such questions to learn about the lives of people from the things they made and used. **OL**

TEACH

C Critical Thinking

Analyzing Information

Ask: What has more weight, any person's opinion or an expert opinion? Why? *(An expert opinion, because the expert has more information on which to base his or her opinion.)* **OL**

R Reading Strategy

Determining Importance

Have students rank the following in order of credibility: opinion supported by facts, opinion not supported by facts, facts alone. *(Facts are the most credible, followed by opinions supported by facts; unsupported opinions are the least credible.)* **OL**

Answers and Additional Support

How Does a Historian Work?

Historical and Social Sciences Analysis Skills

Research, Evidence, and Point of View

HR1. Students frame questions that can be answered by historical study and research.

HR2. Students distinguish fact from opinion in historical narratives and stories.

HR3. Students distinguish relevant from irrelevant information, essential from incidental information, and verifiable from unverifiable information in historical narratives and stories.

▲ Students studying history

Asking Questions About the Past

Historians are like detectives. They look for evidence to solve problems about the past. Historians begin by asking questions, such as: Why did two particular countries go to war? What effect did their fighting have on people's lives? Such questions help historians focus on historical problems. By asking questions, historians can better identify the issues. They also can determine how and why events happened and what the effects of these events were.

R **Is It Fact or Opinion?** Historical sources may contain facts and opinions. A *fact* can be proved, or observed; an *opinion,* on the other hand, is a personal belief or conclusion. We often hear facts and opinions mixed in everyday conversation—in advertising, in political debate, and in historical sources. Although some opinions can be supported by facts, in an argument they do not carry as much weight as facts. C

▲ Civil War quilt

◀ Colonial revenue stamp

▼ Native American cliff dwelling

More Skill Practice

Historical and Social Sciences Analysis Skill The cliff dwelling shows the limits of knowledge that historians sometimes face. Point out that the structures shown here were built hundreds of years ago. **Ask:** Why are they still standing? *(Students may say that they seem to be made of stone or bricks, which can last a long time.)* Ask what would happen to the homes made of wood or of animal hides used by other Native American groups who lived at the same time as the ones who built these structures? *(They would decay and disappear.)* Which group would historians know more about? *(the one that built the stone or brick structures)* **OL**

▲ Enslaved African Americans escaped to the North.

▼ Frederick Douglass

Sources such as letters, diaries, and speeches express personal views. This means they state what a person thinks about another person or an event. As a result, the historian must be able to separate known truth about something from what people say about it. This skill is important because it helps the historian decide whether or not the information is accurate and the historical source can be trusted.

Is It Relevant? Historians often must sift through a lot of information to find what they need. As a result, they must determine whether or not each piece of evidence is *relevant.* This means selecting only the data that helps answer their research questions. Relevant information applies directly to the topic or purpose that the historian has chosen. For example, if you are researching family life in colonial America, information about marriage and children would be relevant information. A description of colonial government or trade would not be relevant because it does not explain the type of families found in colonial America.

Is It Important? In deciding whether information is relevant, historians also must figure out what information is *essential,* or important, and what is incidental, or unimportant. The fact that the writer and speaker Frederick Douglass was married and had four children had little, if any, effect on his political views. However, Douglass's escape from slavery did have a lot to do with his emergence as a leader in the cause to free enslaved African Americans.

Is There Supporting Evidence? Another important task of the historian is to determine whether information in a source is *verifiable.* This means the historian must check to see if the information can be proved by other evidence that is already known to be true.

Thinking Like a Historian

Suppose you were a historian researching Gilbert Stuart and you discovered the following statement about him.

Gilbert Stuart was born in Rhode Island in 1755 and he began painting at age 13. Stuart later trained and worked as an artist in Britain. Back in America, he painted the portraits of leading Americans, including George Washington. Only Stuart could paint a true portrait. He showed the person's character, not just a face.

1. **Recognizing Fact** What in this account is a fact?
2. **Recognizing Opinion** What are opinions?

Tools of the Historian

C Critical Thinking

Drawing Conclusions Tell students that they are historians who come across the diary of a person who lived through a major event, such as the American Revolution. **Ask:** Is the diary useful? Why? *(Students should note that the diary offers valuable eyewitness testimony to events.)* Why might the usefulness be limited? *(The writer might pass on second-hand information of things he or she did not observe directly, and his or her writing could be colored by bias.)* OL

S Skill Practice

Historical and Social Sciences Analysis Skill
Ask: What kinds of documents or artifacts would be relevant to research on education in the 1880s and 1890s? *(Answers might include such items as textbooks, laws about education, recollections of teachers and students about school life, pictures of classrooms, and similar items.)* OL CA HR4.

ASSESS

Ask students to summarize why historians need information that is relevant, important, and reliable. OL

CLOSE

Have students make a checklist of the questions they should ask to evaluate sources. Encourage them to use their checklists as they study history. OL

Thinking Like a Historian Answers

1. Facts: he was born in Rhode Island in 1755; he began painting at age 13; he later trained and worked in Britain; he returned to the United States; he painted the portraits of leading Americans.
2. Opinions: "Only Stuart could paint a true portrait"; "He showed the person's character, not just a face."

FOCUS

Give students the following situation: Two people have an argument. You hear two versions of what happened, one from one of the participants and the other from a friend of the other person involved. **Ask:** Whose version of events would you more likely believe? Why? *(Students are likely to say the version of the participant because he or she had first-hand knowledge.)* Explain that historians also rely on first-hand accounts when they write history. **OL**

TEACH

C Critical Thinking

Drawing Conclusions Tell students that two biographies of a famous person have been written. One was written soon after her death and another more than a century later. The second made use of private letters to a friend that had not been available to the first writer. **Ask:** Which secondary source would be more credible? Why? *(Students should recognize that the later biography would be more credible because it used previously unknown information.)* **OL**

Answers and Additional Support

How Does a Historian Work?

Historical and Social Sciences Analysis Skills

Research, Evidence, and Point of View

HR4. Students assess the credibility of primary and secondary sources and draw sound conclusions from them.

HR5. Students detect the historical points of view on historical events and determine the context in which the historical statements were made (the questions asked, sources used, author's perspectives).

Where Is the Evidence Found? Historians generally find evidence in primary sources and secondary sources. *Primary sources* are firsthand pieces of evidence from people who saw or experienced the events described. They include written documents, such as letters, diaries, and official records. They also include spoken interviews, as well as objects such as photos, paintings, clothing, and tools. The feature Analyzing Primary Sources will give you a chance to work with primary sources throughout the text.

Child's doll made of cornhusks

Secondary sources, on the other hand, often are created long after the events by people who played no part in them. Secondary sources are partially **C** based on primary sources. They include biographies, encyclopedias, and history books—even this textbook!

Historians study secondary sources for background information and for a broader view of an event. However, to get new evidence that advances knowledge, historians must turn to the firsthand information found only in primary sources.

How Are Sources Examined? Historians *analyze,* or examine, primary and secondary sources. First, they determine who the author of a source is and what can be known about the author. Then historians consider *where* and *when* the source was created. Another important question asked by historians is *why* a source was created. Historians also ask: To what audience was the source addressed? What is known about this audience?

William Clark's journal

Glass canteen, 1900

Mexican American cowhands

More Skill Practice

Visual Literacy Have students analyze the five images on these two pages and determine whether they are primary or secondary sources, giving reasons for their classifications. *(cornhusk doll—primary source because it was made by someone; journal—primary source because it is the first-hand account of a person's experiences and ideas; canteen—primary source because it was made at the time of the election; cowhand painting and image of fight at Alamo—depends on whether they were painted based on first-hand observation or came later)* **OL** **CA 8LS1.9**

Can the Sources Be Trusted? Historians examine sources for *credibility,* or truthfulness. This is because each source reflects a *point of view,* or a general attitude about people and life. The creator of a source has a point of view that selects which events are important, which people are key players, and which details are worth recording. A point of view is the particular focus a person takes when considering a problem or situation.

Being Aware of Bias Sometimes a writer's point of view is expressed as a *bias,* or an unreasoned judgment about people and events. A bias is a one-sided, unexamined view. A person who is biased has made a judgment about an event, a person, or a group without C really considering the many parts of the situation. Biased speakers and writers can be detected in various ways. Their statements about certain people or groups are loaded with emotional words like *stupid, ignorant,* and *impossible,* or *great* and *wonderful.* Biased individuals also tend to use words that allow no exceptions, like *always* and *never.*

Finding a Balance Historians seek to uncover point of view and bias in historical documents and articles. They look for the ideas and facts that the author of a source emphasizes. They also think about what ideas and facts the author might be leaving out or touching on only lightly.

To make sense of the past, historians must weigh the known evidence and try to figure out what the facts are. Then they need to bring the facts together to answer the questions that interest them. In doing this, they must use their judgment. This means their own viewpoints come into play.

Historians try to be aware of point of view and bias in their sources and in themselves. Therefore, they check new sources and their own ideas against sources already known to be trustworthy. S To get a balanced picture, historians study documents or articles that develop other points of view about the same situation.

▲ The Battle of the Alamo

Thinking Like a Historian

In 1836 the Texans were fighting the Mexicans to win independence. Outnumbered by the Mexican army, William Travis and about 200 other Texans fought heroically to hold a mission called the Alamo. On February 24, 1836, Travis wrote a message to the people of Texas and the United States asking for their help.

> The enemy is receiving reinforcements daily & will no doubt increase to three or four thousand in four or five days. If this call is neglected I am determined to sustain myself as long as possible & die like a soldier who never forgets what is due to his honor & that of his country.
>
> —William Barret Travis, "Appeal for Aid at the Alamo"

1. **Understand Evidence** William Travis's letter is considered a primary source. Why?
2. **Understand Evidence** Is an account of the stand at the Alamo by a modern historian a primary source? Explain.

Tools of the Historian

C Critical Thinking

Analyzing Information
Ask: How can you tell the bias of a piece of writing if it does not contain any words such as *never* or *always*? *(Students should mention the need to look for emotionally charged words or conclusions that seem unsupported.)* OL

S Skill Practice

Historical and Social Sciences Analysis Skill
Ask: How can historians make the histories that they write—which are secondary sources—more reliable? *(by basing work as much as possible on primary sources; by avoiding his or her own biases)* OL CA HR4.

ASSESS

Ask students to examine the paragraph about William Travis's letter in the "Thinking Like a Historian" feature. Have them determine if there is any bias in the paragraph and explain why they think there is or is not. OL

CLOSE

Have students explain what credibility is and why it is important to histories. OL

Thinking Like a Historian Answers

1. because it is a first-hand piece of evidence created by a participant in an event
2. No; it is a secondary source because it is created after the event by someone who played no part in it.

FOCUS

Ask: What are you doing when you try to analyze a movie or a story to try to understand why characters reacted as they did to the events that took place? Guide students to see that they were interpreting the book or movie—an activity in which historians engage. OL

TEACH

S Skill Practice

Historical and Social Sciences Analysis Skill
Ask: What makes a historian's interpretation of events convincing? *(Students may mention well-supported conclusions that offer plenty of evidence and an absence of bias.)* OL

C Critical Thinking

Making Inferences Ask: What role does technology play in accurately describing setting? *(Students should point out that one cannot have an accurate view of a setting at a particular time period by applying today's technology to a historical setting.)* AL

Answers and Additional Support

Making Sense of the Past

Historical and Social Sciences Analysis Skills

Historical Interpretation

HI1. Students explain the central issues and problems from the past, placing people and events in a matrix of time and place.

HI2. Students understand and distinguish cause, effect, sequence, and correlation in historical events, including the long- and short-term causal relations.

HI3. Students explain the sources of historical continuity and how the combination of ideas and events explains the emergence of new patterns.

Interpreting History By themselves, bits and pieces of information do not reveal the truth. Like pieces of a puzzle, they have to be put together by people using reason.

In the same way, historians must use their knowledge to give historical facts (dates, names, and events) meaning and to put them in an order that people can easily understand. Historians piece together the credible evidence and draw conclusions. They use their own thinking and knowledge of the past to *interpret,* or explain, the meaning of events. Then, they present their findings in a clear, readable, and convincing form. S

Providing a Setting Historians look at people and events of history in the matrix, or setting, of time and place. They also connect historical people and events to central issues. Central issues are main ideas, such as war and peace, the development of scientific inventions, and the forms of governments and societies. Through these links, historians can grasp the whole picture or story. C

Historians also sequence events, or place events in the order in which they occurred. Sequencing helps historians organize information. From the pattern of the data, they can determine how events are related to each other. The relationship among these events can help historians identify other important ideas, such as historical importance and cause and effect.

Cause and Effect Historical events are linked by cause and effect. A *cause* is what makes an event happen. The event that happens as a result

▲ Country school, 1800s

Drafting the Constitution, 1787 ▶

More Skill Practice

Visual Literacy Ask: What do the two paintings on this page reveal about the setting of the time and place that they portray? *(Students should point to details such as dress, the size and condition of the rooms and furniture, and similar details.)* OL

Causes and Effects of Political Parties

Causes
- Different philosophies of government
- Conflicting interpretations of the Constitution
- Different economic and regional interests
- Disagreements over foreign affairs

Effects
- Federalists and Democratic–Republicans propose different solutions
- The two parties nominate candidates
- Political parties become a way of American life

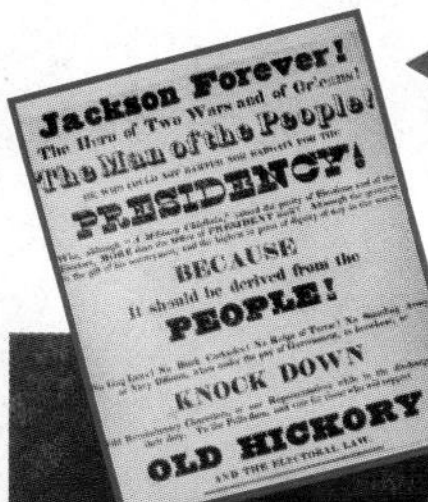

◀ Campaign poster

▼ Candidate appeals for votes

of the cause is known as an *effect*. Historians look for cause-and-effect links to explain why events happen.

Usually, one event is produced by many causes. Similarly, one event often produces several different effects. These cause-and-effect links form what is called a *cause-and-effect chain*. Because so many historical events are related, cause-and-effect chains can become very long and can include events that occur over a long period of time. The chart above shows such a chain of events.

Change and Continuity Historians look at the differences and similarities between events. History is a story of change. Therefore, historians study how events differ greatly from each other. Some historical changes have occurred quickly. For example, in A.D. 1532, Spanish conquerors toppled the vast Inca Empire in Peru, changing South America forever. Other changes take place over centuries, such as the spread of democracy or the changing role of women in many societies.

While looking at historical changes, historians also search for continuity, or the unbroken patterns in history. They study how ongoing traditions and concerns link people across time and place. For example, political actions in the United States today are based on the U.S. Constitution, which is about 220 years old. Also, the goal of passing tests in school was as important to students in America in the 1800s as it is to students today.

Thinking Like a Historian

1. **Recognizing Cause and Effect** Study the cause-and-effect chart on this page. What were some major causes of political parties? What were some important effects of political parties on American life?
2. **Applying Cause and Effect** Read an account of a recent event in your community as reported in a local newspaper. Determine at least one cause and effect of that event. Show the cause-and-effect relationship in a chart.

Tools of the Historian

U Universal Access

English Learners Ask: What is a chain? *(something with interconnected parts)* Why is a set of events with a cause-and-effect relationship called a chain? *(because the events are linked)* EL

C Critical Thinking

Making Inferences Ask: Why do events generally have more than one cause? *(Students should recognize that events are the result of many complex factors and that if many individuals are involved, they might each be driven by different factors.)* OL

ASSESS

Ask students to describe three ways in which historians interpret historical events. *(Answers will vary, but may include that they identify central issues, sequence events and see how they relate, determine cause and effect, see how events are similar and different.)* OL

TEACH

Have students explain how writing history is like putting together a jigsaw puzzle. OL

Thinking Like a Historian Answers

1. Causes: Different philosophies of government, conflicting interpretations of the Constitution, different economic and regional interests, disagreements over foreign affairs; Effects: Federalists and Democratic-Republicans propose different solutions, the two parties nominate candidates, political parties become a way of American life
2. Students' charts might use a format similar to the example shown on this page. Whatever format is chosen, charts should identify both causes and effects.

FOCUS

Ask: Have you ever argued with a friend or family member about why someone acted in a particular way? Point out that historians can have disagreements like this about historical events. OL

TEACH

S Skill Practice

Historical and Social Sciences Analysis Skill Tell students that national leaders must often make decisions based on what their advisors predict about the future. **Ask:** How can that lead to error? *(The predictions could be wrong.)* OL

C Critical Thinking

Making Inferences **Ask:** What had to change before people could interpret the mounds differently? *(They needed additional evidence but they also needed to lose their bias about Native American cultures.)* OL

Answers and Additional Support

Making Sense of the Past

Historical and Social Sciences Analysis Skills

Historical Interpretation

HI4. Students recognize the role of chance, oversight, and error in history.

HI5. Students recognize that interpretations of history are subject to change as new information is uncovered.

HI6. Students interpret basic indicators of economic performance and conduct cost-benefit analyses of economic and political issues.

Error and Chance in History History often has been made by chance, oversight, or error. For example, Christopher Columbus believed that his voyage in 1492 took him to the East Indies, the islands off the coast of Asia. Today the Caribbean islands are often called the West Indies. Also, the Native Americans whom Columbus met came to be called Indians.

Explorations after Columbus, however, made it clear that Columbus had not reached Asia at all. He had found a part of the globe unknown to Europeans, Asians, and Africans. In the following years, the Spanish explored most of the Caribbean region. In time their voyages led to the rise of the Spanish Empire in the Americas.

▲ Columbus reaches land

▼ Great Serpent Mound, Ohio

S Mistakes have not only shaped historical events, they also have influenced people's understanding of the past. For example, C European American settlers moving west in the 1800s discovered large human-made mounds. Biased against Native Americans, many white Americans at that time believed that some other, more advanced and ancient civilization had built the earthworks. Using scientific evidence gathered over the past 100 years, archaeologists have concluded, however, that the mounds were built by early Native American cultures.

Different Interpretations History is often called an ongoing discussion about the past. Historians argue about how to interpret the facts. What causes these differences?

Despite the efforts of the best minds, some facts are ambiguous, or not very clear to interpret. What the facts mean often depends on the historian's judgment. In addition, historians have different values and come to the evidence with different points of view. As a result, historians often arrive at different interpretations of the same event. For example, many historians see the Reformation as a result of religious causes. Others see it as a result of economic demands of a rising middle class in the cities.

EXTENDING THE CONTENT

Cause and Effect Remind students that historians agree that most events have more than one cause. Point out that disagreements such as those discussed here about the causes or meaning of the Reformation tend to be on which cause of several is the most important, not which is the exclusive causative factor.

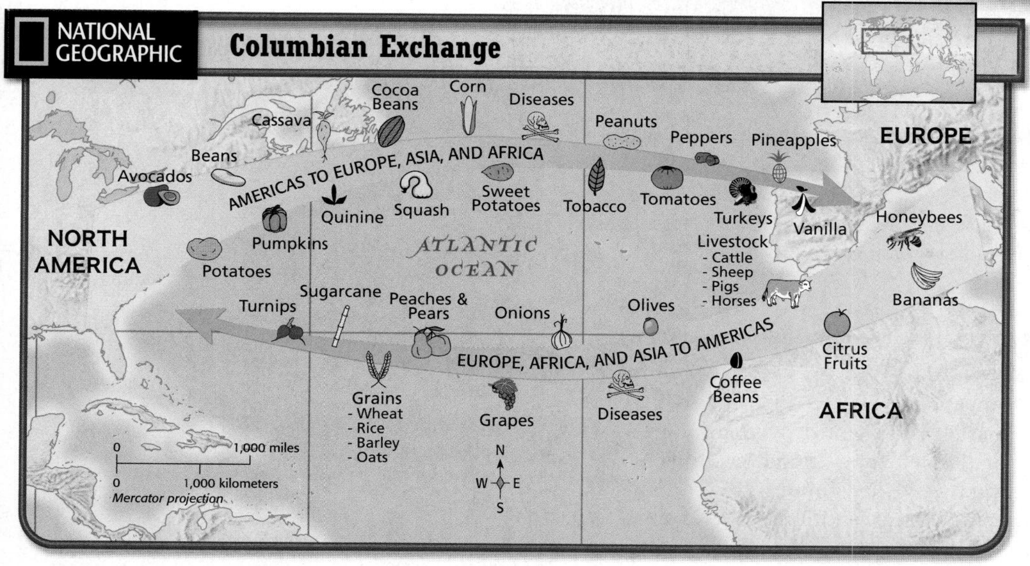

The discussion among historians also continues because historians find new evidence, such as an ancient document. The new evidence leads them to question old interpretations. Sometimes historians take a new look at existing evidence and see things that others have ignored. As they do so, they may correct an earlier historian's mistake or explain events differently.

The questions that historians ask reflect the issues of the times in which they live. As a result, the historian's work is never done. There is never a final, complete version of history.

Economics and History As part of their work, many historians investigate economies, or the ways societies produce, sell, and buy goods. They look at how economies have performed throughout history. Statistics, or mathematical data, are scarce for the economies of long ago. However, statistics for modern economies are abundant and provide historians with a wealth of information. Economists, or scientists who study economies, have developed ways to measure a modern economy's performance. These measurements are called economic indicators.

Economic indicators are statistics that tell how well an economy is doing and how well the economy is expected to do in the future. They include the number of jobless people, the rate at which prices rise and fall over periods of time, and the amount of goods and services that are made and sold.

Historians also analyze the costs and benefits of economic and political issues. This analysis requires figuring out the costs and benefits of any historical action.

Thinking Like a Historian

Christopher Columbus's arrival in the Americas brought together two worlds on opposite sides of the Atlantic Ocean. The resulting trade across the Atlantic became known as the Columbian Exchange.

Study the map of the Columbian Exchange at the top of the page. Then create a table like the one below. Next, list the costs and benefits of that exchange.

Costs	Benefits
1	1
2	2

Tools of the Historian

C Critical Thinking

Analyzing Information

Ask: Why are statistics useful in analyzing a nation's economy? *(because they are facts; because they reveal a nation's overall economic performance and not just the experiences of isolated individuals)* AL

S Skill Practice

Historical and Social Sciences Analysis Skill

Have students look at each of the three economic indicators. **Ask:** For each one, what trends would show positive performance in the economy and what would show negative performance? *(joblessness—more people out of work would be negative, fewer people would be positive; prices rising—prices going up would be negative for consumers, going down would be positive; amount of goods and services made and sold—higher quantity is positive, lower quantity is negative)* AL

ASSESS

Ask students to summarize the factors that affect historians' interpretations of history. OL

CLOSE

Relate to students the common phrase "It is the winners who write history." Have them explain why they agree or disagree with this statement. OL

Thinking Like a Historian Answers

1. Costs: diseases, tobacco
2. Benefits: livestock, tomatoes, and other agricultural products

FOCUS

Ask: What do you think the title of this section means? After students have suggested some possibilities, ask volunteers if they can identify any "links across time." OL

TEACH

R Reading Strategy

Activating Prior Knowledge **Ask:** Where did the explorers come from, and where did they go? *(Students should recall that the explorers sailed from Europe in search of new trade routes to Asia and that they reached Africa, Asia, and the Americas.)* OL

C Critical Thinking

Determining Causes and Effects **Ask:** What have been some impacts of the revolution in communication brought on by the Internet? *(Students may say that people are able to access more information more easily and that people can talk to others around the globe.)* OL

Answers and Additional Support

Links Across Time

Historical and Social Sciences Analysis Skills

Chronological and Spatial Thinking

CS1. Students explain how major events are related to one another in time.

◀ Early compass

▼ European sailing ship

Unit 1 A Changing World

From about 1500 to 1800, people in many parts of the world lived through a time of far-reaching change. Thinkers developed new ideas about government and began to use scientific ideas to explore nature. Explorers traveled to other continents, and an exchange of ideas, peoples, and goods began across the globe. Today, advances in science, transportation, and communication have brought the world's peoples even closer together.

▲ Conestoga wagon

▲ Stock market

Computer and phone ▶

USA–Mexico border ▶

More Skill Practice

Using Geography Skills Remind students of the five themes of geography, which they learned about on pages 54–57 (location, place, human/environment interaction, movement, and region). **Ask:** Which themes are exemplified by the images on this page? *(location, in the top and bottom photos; place in the bottom photo; region in the bottom photo; and movement in all the photos)* OL

Unit 2 Creating a Nation

Adopted in 1788, the Constitution has endured for more than 200 years as the plan of government for the United States. Over the decades, the nation's system of courts has adapted and interpreted the Constitution to deal with the country's most important political and social issues. Many of today's issues, such as privacy rights on the Internet, were never imagined by the Constitution's eighteenth-century writers.

◀ Students viewing the original Constitution

Celebration of the Constitution's first 200 years ▶

S

▲ Framers of the Constitution

Unit 3 Launching the Republic

Although presidents tried to follow Washington's advice to avoid entangling alliances, the country sometimes found itself in conflict with other nations. **R** In today's world, presidents must also decide what to do when the actions of other nations affect the United States. For example, Iraq has large reserves of oil, but it has attacked other countries in the Middle East. Presidents have handled this problem in different ways. President George H.W. Bush led a worldwide group of countries against Iraq to stop its invasion of Kuwait. **C** During his presidency, William Clinton used embargoes. President George W. Bush went to war against Iraq.

▲ Thomas Jefferson was an important leader of the early republic.

Tools of the Historian

S Skill Practice

Visual Literacy **Ask:** What two characteristics do all the framers of the Constitution have in common? *(All are men, and all are white.)* Explain that one change that has taken place since the Constitution was written is that its provisions now extend to all Americans, regardless of gender, race, or any other characteristic. OL

R Reading Strategy

Monitoring **Ask:** Can you think of any foreign conflicts the United States has had? *(Students may mention the War of 1812 with Britain, the war with Mexico in the 1840s, the Spanish-American War, World War I, World War II, the Korean War, the Vietnam War, or the war in Iraq.)* OL

C Critical Thinking

Analyzing Information
Ask: In what ways does the United States cooperate with other nations? *(Students might point to U.S. participation in the United Nations, trade agreements, or formal alliances like NATO; to relations with Mexico and Canada; or to cooperation with other nations on other subjects, such as the war on terrorism.)* OL

EXTENDING THE CONTENT

Washington's Farewell Address Washington delivered his advice to avoid "permanent alliances" in his farewell address, which was drafted for him by Alexander Hamilton. Washington did not speak the address but had it published in a Philadelphia newspaper. In that address, Washington also warned Americans to avoid partisan conflict.

C Critical Thinking

Comparing and Contrasting After students have read this paragraph, **ask:** Would you say that American regions today are different from what they were in the 1800s? If so, how do they differ? How are different regions in the country also the same? Discuss students' responses. OL

S1 Skill Practice

Historical and Social Sciences Analysis Skill
Ask: On what basis are these regions compared? *(Students should see that the main differences being described are the economic foundations of the regions.)* OL

S2 Skill Practice

Using Geography Skills
Ask: What states, other than California, are in the South and the Southwest? *(The South includes the states from Virginia and Kentucky south to Florida and west to Arkansas and Louisiana; the Southwest includes Texas, Oklahoma, New Mexico, Arizona, Nevada, as well as California.)* OL

Answers and Additional Support

Links Across Time

Unit 4 The Young Republic

The new nation had three distinct geographic areas. In the North, the Industrial Revolution began and manufacturing grew increasingly more important. In the South, agriculture and the growing of cotton became king. In the West, the United States kept adding to its territorial size. Low prices for land drew people to these new territories. Settlers there supplied minerals and agricultural products to other parts of the country. Since the 1970s, the fastest-growing areas in the United States have been the South and the Southwest, including California. Industrial growth and a pleasant climate have drawn people to this area known as the Sunbelt.

▼ California Bear Flag

◀ Advertisement, 1800s

▲ Miners searching for gold

Los Angeles skyline ▶

◀ Water power along the Colorado River

More Skill Practice

Visual Literacy Have students explain how each image on the page reveals something about the varied history of California. *(The bear flag represents the California independence movement of 1846; Levi Strauss gained fame selling his jeans to miners in the California Gold Rush, who are evident in the mining photo; parts of California tap into the Colorado River for water; and Los Angeles is now the state's largest city.)* OL

Unit 5 Civil War and Reconstruction

Disputes between the North and the South over slavery led to the Civil War (1861–1865). After the war, the United States ended slavery and gave once-enslaved African Americans citizenship, equal protection under the law, and the right to vote. In practice, however, civil rights were denied to African Americans. Despite obstacles, African Americans pressed for equal rights. In the late 1900s, they made advances in securing their rights under leaders such as Martin Luther King, Jr.

African American voter ▶

▼ Martin Luther King, Jr.

Unit 6 Reshaping the Nation

By the early 1900s, many Americans had moved from farms to the cities, and thousands of immigrants poured into urban areas. A strong spirit of reform swept the country. Farmers and workers organized to improve their lot. During the second half of the 1900s, the drive for equality that had begun with African Americans spread to other groups. Migrant workers and other farm laborers joined the U.S. labor movement during the 1960s. César Chávez, a Mexican American labor leader, founded what is now the United Farm Workers of America (UFW).

Voting rights ▶ poster

◀ Young coal miners, c. 1900

▲ César Chávez

United Farm ▶ Workers

Thinking Like a Historian

As you read *Discovering Our Past: The American Journey to World War I,* notice how the past affects the present. When you begin each unit, collect newspaper or magazine articles about a current event that is related to the period you are studying. Then, after completing each unit, write how you think a past event in that period is related to the current event.

Tools of the Historian

C Critical Thinking

Analyzing Information
Ask: How long did African Americans have to wait before they gained the full rights of Americans? *(more than a hundred years after the Civil War)* OL

S Skill Practice

Historical and Social Sciences Analysis Skill
Ask: Where do most Americans live now—in rural areas or urban areas? *(urban)* OL

ASSESS

Ask students to explain why the present is linked to the past. OL

CLOSE

Have students explain which of the links described in this section is, to them, the most important and why. OL

Thinking Like a Historian Answers

Encourage students to hand in their articles and their reflections on them at the end of each unit. You could also have them share their findings with the rest of the class.

Teaching the Unit

Use the information on these pages to help you teach Unit 1.

History–Social Science Standards Covered in Unit 1

Standard	Chapter 1	Chapter 2
WH7.11 Students analyze political and economic change in the sixteenth, seventeenth, and eighteenth centuries (the Age of Exploration, the Enlightenment, and the Age of Reason).	✓	
US8.1 Students understand the major events preceding the founding of the nation and relate their significance to the development of American constitutional democracy.		✓

Pacing Your Lessons

This pacing chart provides time management suggestions for teaching Unit 1.

Unit 1 A Changing World	Days
Unit 1 Introduction	1/2
Chapter 1 • **Reading Skill:** Previewing • **Sections 1–3** • **Biography:** Lorenzo de' Medici, John Locke • **Analyzing Primary Sources**	6
Chapter 2 • **Reading Skill:** Identifying the Main Idea • **Sections 1–4** • **Biography:** Junípero Serra, Benjamin Franklin • **Connecting to the Constitution** • **America's Literature:** "Paul Revere's Ride" • **You Decide . . .** • **Analyzing Primary Sources**	9
Unit 1 Review	1/2

Teacher to Teacher

Tracing the Road to Revolution

Matt Duffy
C.A. Jacobs Intermediate
Dixon, CA

Help students understand how British actions and colonists' responses led step-by-step to the Revolution by having students describe each action taken by the British, explain why they took that step, and detail the colonists' reaction to it. Focus on key decisions, such as the issuance of the Proclamation of 1763, the passage of the Stamp Act, and the passage of the Intolerable Acts. Have students supplement their answers by creating a map that shows the colonies and the sites of major events, such as the Boston Massacre.

Finally, have students evaluate the impact of all these steps on colonists' thinking. Have them write a paragraph assessing how all these events would affect the relationship between the British and the colonists and predicting what they think will happen as a result of the changing relationship.

Previewing the Chapters

Dear American History Teacher:

As you begin to teach this unit, there are themes that recur throughout the chapters that you will want to point out to students.

Competition with Muslim trade—along with new ideas and new technology—spurred the drive to find new trade routes, and competition between nations led Europeans to explore the Americas and establish colonies there. Religion played a role in exploration as well, and religious differences from Europe were brought to the Americas. Cultural diversity became a hallmark of the lands that developed into the United States, as Europeans, Native Americans, and African Americans all took part in the growing colonies. American political ideas were founded on a base of ancient religious teachings and philosophical ideas and were shaped by the institutions of medieval England, the ideas of the Enlightenment, and the colonists' own experiences with self-government.

You may want to use the following information at the beginning of each chapter as a lesson launcher to help students begin to focus on what they will be studying.

Joyce Appleby

CHAPTER 1: Expanding Horizons

(pages 76–111)

In the Middle Ages, Europeans began to look beyond their own borders in the hopes of increasing their trade with Asia and gathering wealth. Muslims controlled trade routes through the Middle East, which led some nations to search for different routes. After Christopher Columbus landed in North America and conquistadors gained wealth for Spain by conquering Native American empires, other European nations launched expeditions to the Americas. Europeans developed new ways of raising money to finance trade, which were the origins of capitalism. Nations competed to set up colonies in the Americas in the hopes of increasing national wealth. Expanded trade led to a worldwide exchange of products, people, and ideas. At the same time, new ideas were sweeping Europe, which changed religious life there and brought new emphasis on science and reason.

CHAPTER 2: Road to Independence

(pages 112–163)

England had 13 colonies along the east coast of the continent, where colonists established self-government and, in some, religious toleration. Over time, agriculture and trade increased in the colonies, which prospered and grew in population. But while the colonies did enjoy much self-government, the British government controlled trade. After Britain defeated France in the French and Indian War, the government passed several new laws aimed at raising money from the colonists. Many colonists protested these actions, and tension between Britain and the colonists rose. War broke out, and in 1776, colonial leaders declared independence from Britain. The fight took many years, but eventually the British signed a treaty recognizing the independence of the United States. A new nation was born.

FOCUS

Connecting to Past Learning

In earlier grades, students learned about the development of the civilizations of the ancient and medieval worlds. In Unit 1, they will learn how the achievements of those civilizations led to the colonization of the Americas and to the creation of an independent United States.

Unit Launch Activity

Have students suggest ideas explaining why the American colonists might have wanted independence. *(Students might point to the desires of many people to be free and determine their own futures.)* OL

History–Social Science Standards

The following standards are covered in Unit 1:

WH7.11 Students analyze political and economic change in the sixteenth, seventeenth, and eighteenth centuries (the Age of Exploration, the Enlightenment, and the Age of Reason).

US8.1 Students understand the major events preceding the founding of the nation and relate their significance to the development of American constitutional democracy.

Why It's Important

Ask: What ideas affect the world today? How do ideas influence people to act? OL

Unit 1

A Changing World

Why It's Important

For thousands of years, the rich cultures of the Americas had remained virtually unnoticed by the rest of the world. When the Europeans began to explore in the 1400s, they soon conquered the peoples of the Americas and settled on their lands. After facing many challenges, a great new nation emerged in North America.

- New ideas about science, exploration, and trade led Europeans to explore and conquer the Americas.
- Britain's North American colonies fought for and gained their freedom.

1400 — 1500

THE AMERICAS

◀ *Christopher Columbus*

1492 Christopher Columbus reaches Americas

1521 Cortés defeats the Aztec

CALIFORNIA EVENTS

1533 Spanish expedition reaches peninsula of Baja California

1542 Cabrillo expedition reaches San Diego Bay

WORLD EVENTS

◀ *Astrolabe*

1420 Portuguese begin mapping Africa's coast

1517 Martin Luther posts Ninety-Five Theses

1519 Magellan's crew begins voyage around the world

1588 England defeats the Spanish Armada

Defeat of the Spanish Armada ▶

72

TEACHING THE TIME LINES

Help students focus on the information in the time lines. **Ask:**

- What three regions are used to group the information? *(the Americas, California, and the entire world)*
- What time span does the time line cover? *(1400 to 1800)*
- How soon after the conquest of the Aztec did the Spanish reach California? *(12 years)*
- When did the first colonists settle at Jamestown? *(1607)*
- When did Father Serra found the first mission in California? *(1769)*

As students study events described in the unit, refer back to these time lines and have students identify where the event would appear. OL

NATIONAL GEOGRAPHIC

Where in the World?

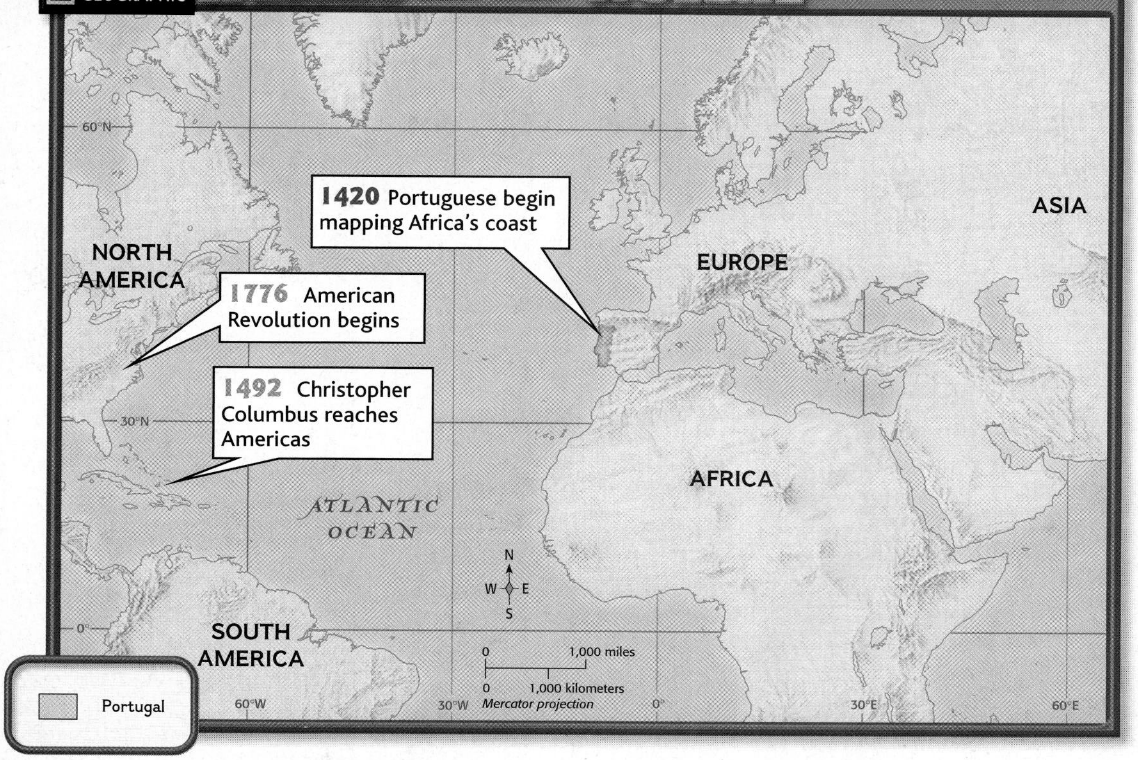

1600 **1700** **1800**

- **1607** Colonists settle at Jamestown
- **1620** Pilgrims found colony in Massachusetts
- **c. 1740** Great Awakening peaks
- **1776** American Revolution begins
- **1781** Americans win independence from Britain

Juan Bautista de Anza ▶

- **1769** Father Serra founds first mission at San Diego
- **1776** De Anza discovers trail from Sonora to San Francisco area

- **1689** English Bill of Rights is signed
- **1690** Locke publishes *Two Treatises of Government*

◀ *John Locke*

UNIVERSAL ACCESS

English Learners: Have students identify the proper nouns in the time lines and categorize them as names of specific people, groups, places, or things. EL

Logical/Mathematical: Have students identify two of the events in one time line and predict why they think these were important enough to include. Tell students to check their answers against the chapter material as they read the textbook. OL

Visual/Spatial: Have students create a collage of images representing one of the events in the time lines. OL

TEACH

NATIONAL GEOGRAPHIC

Where in the World?

Understanding Maps and Time Lines Ask: What continents are shown on this map? *(Asia, Europe, Africa, North America, South America)* What body of water is at the center of the map? *(the Atlantic Ocean)* What transportation routes are likely to be important in this unit? Why do you think so? *(shipping routes connecting Europe and Africa to the Americas; because the Atlantic is at the center of the map and in this period the peoples of these regions did not have air travel)* OL

NCLB No Child Left Behind

Teaching Activity
Organize the class into three groups and assign each group a section of the time line (the Americas, California, or world). Have the groups find out where each event listed on the time line occurred and to find those places on a map. Ask the groups to use a globe or wall map to show their findings. OL

Introducing Unit 1

Unit Objectives

After studying this unit, students should be able to

- Explain the advancements and motivations that encouraged European exploration starting in the late 1400s.
- Describe the development of modern capitalism.
- Discuss major Enlightenment ideas and how they influenced the thinking of American colonists.
- Outline the events that led to the American Revolution.
- Explain how the colonists won independence.

Previewing People to Meet

Have pairs of students write the names of the **People to Meet** on index cards, one to a card. They should write the person's identifying characteristics on another card. Have them mix up all the cards with names and place them facedown in one area and do the same with the characteristics in another area. Then have students take turns turning over one card from each group to match the name and the description. Students should continue the activity until all the cards are correctly matched. OL

Unit 1 Places to Locate

People to Meet

Lorenzo de' Medici
1449–1492
Italian ruler
Chapter 1, page 92

John Locke
1632–1704
English political thinker
Chapter 1, page 104

Junípero Serra
1713–1784
Spanish missionary
Chapter 2, page 118

William Penn
1644–1718
Founder of Pennsylvania
Chapter 2, page 122

74

Previewing Places to Locate

Use the following descriptions to explain the images on the map.

1 Tenochtitlán was originally built on two islands in Lake Texcoco and was connected by causeways to the mainland, where other settlements arose. At the time of the conquest, it held about 400,000 people.

2 Columbus never referred to himself as Columbus, a name found today on cities and buildings across America. Late in life, he preferred to be called Cristóbel Colón.

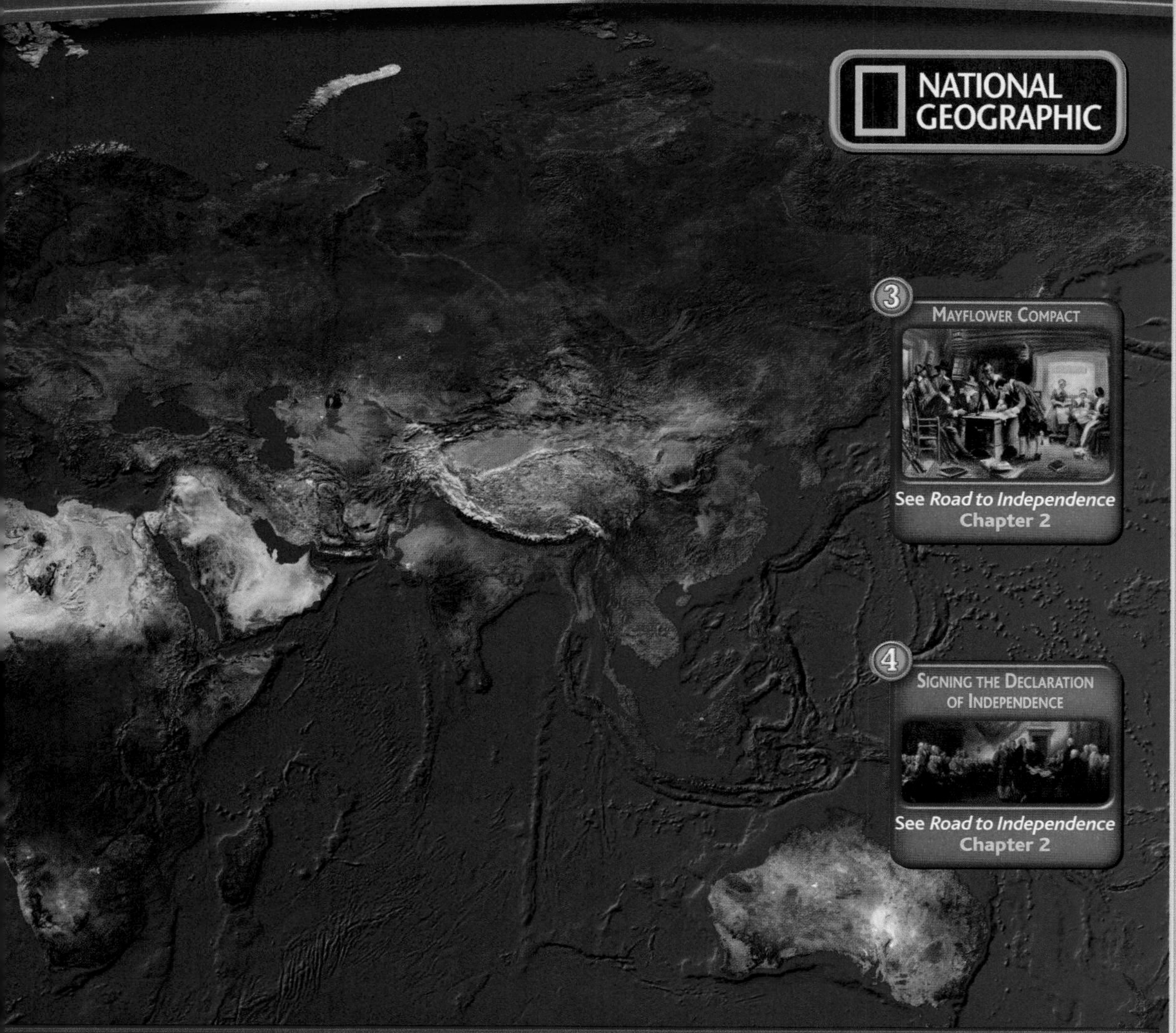

George Washington
1732–1799
Leader of the Patriot army
Chapter 2, page 139

Thomas Jefferson
1743–1826
American political leader
Chapter 2, page 150

Benjamin Franklin
1706–1790
American scientist and patriot
Chapter 2, page 151

Abigail Adams
1744–1818
Patriot and supporter of women's rights
Chapter 2, page 155

Introducing Unit 1

Skill Practice

Using Geography Skills
What areas does this map show? *(the entire world)* Where are most of the places marked on the map found? *(North America)* Which shows where a colony was established in 1620? *(number 3)* **OL**

Skill Practice

Creating a Time Line
Organize students in pairs and have them create a time line that illustrates the dates of the people pictured on these pages. **Ask:** Who was alive during the American Revolution, which lasted from 1776 to 1783? *(Serra, Washington, Jefferson, Franklin, Adams)* **OL**

ASSESS/CLOSE

Have students explain how the winning of American independence is related to European exploration in the 1400s. *(Students should note that when they explored the Americas, European nations established colonies there and that it was the English colonies that fought for and won independence.)* **OL**

3 

Forty-one men who had journeyed to the Americas on the *Mayflower* signed the Compact, in which they pledged to follow the laws created for the colony.

4 

Most Americans believe that the Declaration of Independence was signed on July 4, 1776, but it was only approved that day. Evidence indicates that it was not signed until August, and some names were added even after that.

Chapter 1 Planning Guide

SECTION RESOURCES

Main Ideas	Print Materials	Technology Resources
Section 1 **Age of Exploration** 1. New knowledge and ideas led Europeans to explore overseas. 2. In search of trade routes, Portuguese explorers began an era of overseas exploration. 3. Rivalries between countries led to increased exploration of North America.	• Reproducible Lesson Plan 1–1* • Daily Lesson and Discussion Notes 1–1 • Active Reading Note-Taking Guide 1–1 • Reading Essentials and Study Guide 1–1 • Guided Reading Activity 1–1 • Section Quiz 1–1	Daily Focus Skills Transparency 1–1 Section Graphic Organizer Transparency 1–1 California Standards Practice Transparencies Interactive Tutor Self-Assessment CD-ROM Exam*View*® Pro Testmaker CD-ROM Presentation Plus! CD-ROM
Section 2 **Rise of Modern Capitalism** 1. New ways of doing business developed to raise money to finance trade. 2. Nations competed to establish colonies in the Americas. 3. Exploration and trade led to a worldwide exchange of products, people, and ideas.	• Reproducible Lesson Plan 1–2* • Daily Lesson and Discussion Notes 1–2 • Active Reading Note-Taking Guide 1–2 • Reading Essentials and Study Guide 1–2 • Guided Reading Activity 1–2 • Section Quiz 1–2	Daily Focus Skills Transparency 1–2 Section Graphic Organizer Transparency 1–2 California Standards Practice Transparencies Interactive Tutor Self-Assessment CD-ROM Exam*View*® Pro Testmaker CD-ROM Presentation Plus! CD-ROM
Section 3 **The Enlightenment** 1. Ancient cultures laid the foundation of many modern ideas. 2. Religious and philosophical thinkers changed the way people viewed Christianity and the government. 3. Science and the influence of reason led to new innovations in political thought.	• Reproducible Lesson Plan 1-3* • Daily Lesson and Discussion Notes 1–3 • Active Reading Note-Taking Guide 1–3 • Reading Essentials and Study Guide 1–3 • Guided Reading Activity 1–3 • Section Quiz 1–3	Daily Focus Skills Transparency 1–3 Section Graphic Organizer Transparency 1–3 California Standards Practice Transparencies Interactive Tutor Self-Assessment CD-ROM Exam*View*® Pro Testmaker CD-ROM Presentation Plus! CD-ROM Vocabulary PuzzleMaker CD-ROM

PACING YOUR LESSONS

Unit Introduction	Chapter Introduction	Section 1	Section 2	Section 3	Chapter Assessment
$\frac{1}{2}$ Day	$\frac{1}{2}$ Day	2 Days	1 Day	2 Days	$\frac{1}{2}$ Day

0:00 **OUT OF TIME?** Assign the Chapter 1 ***Reading Essentials and Study Guide***

*Available on TeacherWorks™

Standards-Based Lesson Plan

History–Social Science Standards Covered in Chapter 1

The standards covered in the chapter are listed below. Use the accompanying activity as you teach the chapter to ensure student mastery of these standards. This activity can be used in combination with the program's print and technology assessment materials.

Standard	Section 1	Section 2	Section 3
WH7.11 Students analyze political and economic change in the sixteenth, seventeenth, and eighteenth centuries (the Age of Exploration, the Enlightenment, and the Age of Reason).	✔	✔	✔
WH7.11.1 Know the great voyages of discovery, the locations of the routes, and the influence of cartography in the development of a new European worldview.	✔		
WH7.11.2 Discuss the exchanges of plants, animals, technology, culture, and ideas among Europe, Africa, Asia, and the Americas in the fifteenth and sixteenth centuries and the major economic and social effects on each continent.		✔	
WH7.11.3 Examine the origins of modern capitalism; the influence of mercantilism and cottage industry; the elements and importance of a market economy in seventeenth-century Europe; the changing international trading and marketing patterns, including their locations on a world map; and the influence of explorers and map makers.		✔	
WH7.11.4 Explain how the main ideas of the Enlightenment can be traced back to such movements as the Renaissance, the Reformation, and the Scientific Revolution, and to the Greeks, Romans, and Christianity.		✔	✔
WH7.11.5 Describe how democratic thought and institutions were influenced by Enlightenment thinkers (e.g., John Locke, Charles-Louis Montesquieu, American founders).			✔
WH7.11.6 Discuss how the principles in the Magna Carta were embodied in such documents as the English Bill of Rights and the American Declaration of Independence.			✔

Cumulative Standards-Assessment Activity

he Cumulative Standards-Assessment Activity will help students organize and learn the important information from the chapter. egin teaching the chapter with this activity, and have students complete it as they read the chapter.

Creating a Causes-and-Effects Chart

Purpose Learning how to identify causes and effects is a key to understanding history. This type of organizer helps students see the continuities of history, learning how events develop from prior occurrences and lead to new consequences. Developing this skill helps sharpen students' thinking and can apply to other areas of study as well, including literature and science.

Introduction to Understanding Causes and Effects

1. Begin the discussion by leading students to identify a simple example of a cause-and-effect sequence in daily life. Ask them to explain what happens when a company introduces a new product that becomes very popular. *(The company needs to hire more workers to make more of the product.)* What is the result for those workers? *(Their incomes go up, and they are able to buy more of other products.)*

2. Ask students to copy this chart into their notebooks:

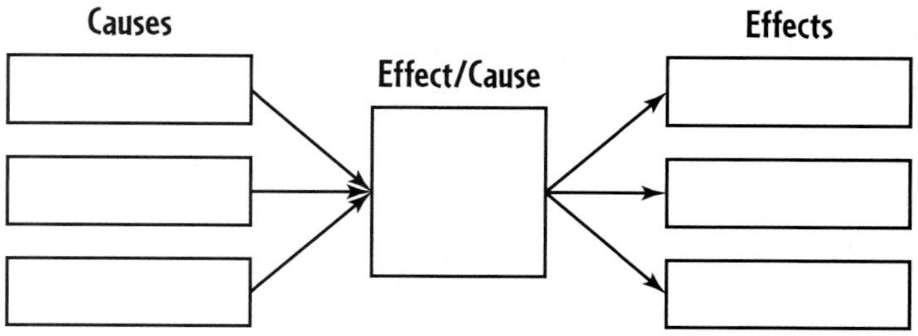

As students read each section, have them search for the causes of events, their effects, and the further effects that flow from the initial effects. Remind them to look for multiple causes and that they might need to add additional boxes to record either more causes or more effects. Tell them to create as many charts as they require to cover all the material in the chapter.

3. As part of your review of the chapter, have students share their charts. Encourage them to use their charts as study aids.

Chapter 1 Resources

READING SUPPORT

- Content Vocabulary Activity 1
- Academic Vocabulary Activity 1
- Reading Skills Activity 1
- American Literature Reading 1
- Biography Activities 1A, 1B
- Chapter 1 Active Reading Note-Taking Guide
- Chapter 1 Guided Reading Activities
- Chapter 1 Reading Essentials and Study Guide
- Glencoe Literature Library
- Glencoe Video Program
- Vocabulary PuzzleMaker CD-ROM
- Interactive Graphic Organizers CD-ROM
- American History Primary Source Document Library CD-ROM

CRITICAL THINKING

- Critical Thinking Skills Activity 1
- Primary Source Reading 1
- Cause-and-Effect Transparency 1, Strategy, and Activity
- Presentation Plus! CD-ROM

UNIVERSAL ACCESS

- Universal Access Activity 1
- Then and Now Transparencies 1A–1B, Strategy, and Activity
- Graphic Novel Activity 1
- School-to-Home Connection Activities 1A–1D
- English Learner Handbook Chapter 1 Activities
- Universal Access for the American History Classroom
- Moments in Time
- American Art and Architecture Transparencies, Strategies, and Activities
- American Art Prints
- American Music Cultural Traditions
- American Music Hits Through History
- StudentWorks Plus CD-ROM

SKILL PRACTICE

- Map Overlay Transparency 1, Strategy, and Activity
- Analysis Skills Activity 1
- Time Line Activity 1
- Geography and History Activity 1
- Economics and History Activity 1
- Chart, Graph, and Map Skills Activity 1
- Political Cartoon Activity 1
- Supreme Court Case Study 1
- In-Text Map Transparency 1, Strategy, and Activity
- Step Into American History Activity 1
- Citizenship and Service Learning Activity 1
- Outline Map Resource Book
- MindJogger Plus Videoquiz

WRITING SUPPORT

- Writing Activity 1
- Language Arts Activity 1
- Writer's Guidebook
- Middle School Writing Process Transparencies

ASSESSMENT

GLENCOE'S ASSESSMENT ADVANTAGE

- Chapter 1 Section Quizzes
- Chapter 1 Tests, Form A and B
- California Standards Assessment, Forms A and B
- Cumulative Assessment Activity WH7.11
- California Standards Practice Workbook
- Succeeding on the California History-Social Science Standards CD-ROM
- *ExamView*® Pro Testmaker CD-ROM
- Interactive Tutor Self-Assessment CD-ROM

CD-ROM
DVD
Print Material
Poster
Transparency
Music Program
Videocassette
Glencoe Literature Library

Chapter 1 Resources

TECHNOLOGY

- StudentWorks Plus CD-ROM
- TeacherWorks Plus CD-ROM
- Exam*View*® Pro Testmaker CD-ROM
- Interactive Tutor Self-Assessment CD-ROM
- Presentation Plus! CD-ROM
- Succeeding on the California History–Social Science Standards CD-ROM
- Vocabulary PuzzleMaker CD-ROM
- Interactive Graphic Organizers CD-ROM
- Interactive Time Line CD-ROM
- American History Primary Source Document Library CD-ROM
- MindJogger Plus Videoquiz
- American Music Cultural Traditions
- American Music Hits Through History
- Glencoe Video Program
- Professional Development in Middle School Social Studies Series
- Teaching American History With *Discovering Our Past: The American Journey to World War I*

SPANISH RESOURCES

- Spanish Activities and Assessment
  - Spanish Content Vocabulary Activities
  - Spanish Guided Reading Activities
  - Spanish Quizzes and Tests
  - Spanish California Standards Assessment
- Spanish Reading Essentials and Study Guide
- Spanish School-to-Home Connection
- Spanish Declaration of Independence and U.S. Constitution

TRANSPARENCIES

- California Standards Practice Transparencies
- Daily Focus Skills Transparencies
- Section Graphic Organizer Transparencies
- In-Text Map Transparencies
- Map Overlay Transparencies
- Cause-and-Effect Transparencies
- Then and Now Transparencies
- American Art and Architecture Transparencies
- Writing Process Transparencies

TEACHER PLANNING

- Daily Lesson and Discussion Notes
- English Learner Handbook
- Guide to Daily Intervention
- *Discovering Our Past: The American Journey to World War I* Reading and Study Skills Foldables
- Reading Strategies and Activities for the Social Studies Classroom
- Chapter 1 Reproducible Lesson Plans (correlated to California History–Social Science Standards)
- Universal Access for the American History Classroom
- NGS U.S. Desk Map
- NGS U.S. Atlas

PROFESSIONAL DEVELOPMENT

- Building Academic Vocabulary
- Strategies for Success
- Research-Based Strategies Used to Develop *Discovering Our Past: The American Journey to World War I*
- Character Education in the Middle School Classroom
- The Living Constitution
- Professional Development in Middle School Social Studies Video Series
- Teaching American History With *Discovering Our Past: The American Journey to World War I*

MASTERING THE STANDARDS

The content and assessment in the Student Edition, Teacher Wraparound Edition, teacher planning materials, and the print and technology products are all standards-based. The use of these products during instruction leads to mastery of the standards.

PRACTICE

- California Standards Practice Workbook
- California Standards Practice Transparencies
- Interactive Time Line CD-ROM
- School-to-Home Connection

BENCHMARK ASSESSMENT

- California Standards Assessment
- Exam*View*® Pro Testmaker CD-ROM
- Succeeding on the California History–Social Science Standards CD-ROM

REMEDIATION

- California Guide to Daily Intervention
- Interactive Tutor Self-Assessment CD-ROM
- Exam*View*® Pro Testmaker CD-ROM
- California Standards Practice Workbook
- Reading Essentials and Study Guide

Additional Resources

NATIONAL GEOGRAPHIC TEACHER'S CORNER

Index to National Geographic Magazine:

The following articles relate to this chapter:

- *The Millennium Series Exploration* (Special Edition) February 1998.
- "Portugal's Sea Road to the East," by Merle Severy, November 1992.
- "The Cruelest Commerce: African Slave Trade," by Colin Palmer, September 1992.

National Geographic Society Products

To order the following, call National Geographic at 1-800-368-2728

- *National Geographic Reading Expeditions, Series Five, Voices From America's Past* (Book)
- *GeoKit: Colonial America* (Kit)
- *Spain in the Americas* (Map)
- *Colonization and Trade in the Americas* (Map)
- *National Geographic Desk Reference* (Book)

NGS ONLINE

Access National Geographic's new dynamic MapMachine Web site and other geography resources at:

www.nationalgeographic.com

www.nationalgeographic.com/maps

A&E HOME VIDEO. Biography® THE HISTORY CHANNEL.

The following videotape programs are available from Glencoe as supplements to Chapter 1.

- **Christopher Columbus: Explorer of the New World (ISBN 1-56501-667-X)**

To order, call Glencoe at 1-800-334-7344. To find classroom resources to accompany many of these videos, check the following home pages:

A&E Television: www.aetv.com
The History Channel: www.historychannel.com

History Online

Use our Web site for additional resources. All essential content is covered in the Student Edition.

You and your students can visit ca.hss.glencoe.com, the Web site companion to *Discovering Our Past: The American Journey to World War I*. This innovative integration of electronic and print media offers your students a wealth of opportunities. The student text directs students to the Web site for the following options:

- Chapter Overviews
- Self-Check Quizzes
- Study Central™
- Student Web Activities
- Textbook Updates
- Multi-Language Glossaries

Answers to the student Web activities are provided for you in the Web Activity Lesson Plans. Additional Web resources and ePuzzles and games are also available.

FOLDABLES™ Study Organizer

Dinah Zike's Foldables

Foldables are three-dimensional, interactive graphic organizers that help students practice basic writing skills, review key vocabulary terms, and identify main ideas. Every chapter contains a foldable activity, with additional chapter activities found in the Reading and Study Skills Foldables booklet.

Reading List Generator CD-ROM

GLENCOE **BOOKLINK**

The Glencoe BookLink CD-ROM is a database that allows you to search more than 15,000 titles to create a customized reading list for your students.

- Reading lists can be organized by students' reading level, author, genre, theme, or area of interest.
- The database provides Degrees of Reading Power™ (DRP) and Lexile™ readability scores for all selections.
- A brief summary of each selection is included.

Reading level suggestions for this chapter:

For students at a Grade 6 reading level:
- ***Indio,*** by Sherry Garland

For students at a Grade 7 reading level:
- ***Exploration and Conquest: The Americas after Columbus: 1500-1620,*** by Betsy Maestro

For students at a Grade 8 reading level:
- ***Ferdinand Magellan and the Discovery of the World Ocean,*** by Rebecca Stefoff

For students at a Grade 9 reading level:
- ***Imperial Rome,*** by Moses Hadas

READING SUPPORT FROM JAMESTOWN EDUCATION

- *Timed Readings Plus in Social Studies* helps students increase their reading rate and fluency while maintaining comprehension. The 400-word passages are similar to those found on state and national assessments.
- *Reading in the Content Area: Social Studies* concentrates on six essential reading skills that help students better comprehend what they read. The book includes 754 high-interest nonfiction passages written at increasing levels of difficulty.
- *Reading Fluency* helps students read smoothly, accurately, and expressively.
- *Jamestown's Reading Improvement,* by renowned reading expert Edward Fry, focuses on helping build your students' comprehension, vocabulary, and skimming and scanning skills.
- *Critical Reading Series* provides high-interest books, each written at three reading levels.

To order these products, call Glencoe at 1-800-334-7344.

KEY for Using the Teacher Wraparound Edition

Use this key to help you identify the different types of prompts found in the Teacher Wraparound Edition.

R **Reading Strategies** activities help you teach reading skills and vocabulary.

C **Critical Thinking** strategies help students apply and extend what they have learned.

U **Universal Access** activities provide differentiated instruction for students learning to speak English, along with suggestions for teaching various types of learners.

S **Skill Practice** strategies help students practice historical analysis and geography skills.

W **Writing Support** activities provide writing opportunities to help students comprehend the text.

Teaching strategies and activities have been coded for ability level appropriateness.

AL Activities for students working above grade level
OL Activities for students working on grade level
BL Activities for students working below grade level
EL Activities for English Learners

FOCUS

History–Social Science Standards

The following option is offered to address the coverage issue at grade seven with additional suggestions for the other grade levels affected:

Move the unit "Early Modern Europe: The Age of Exploration to the Enlightenment" from grade seven to grade eight where it can become the preface to the study of the political ideas and institutions of the United States. The Enlightenment receives further emphasis at grade ten in the unit "Connecting with Past Learnings: The Rise of Democratic Ideas."

In this chapter, the following standard will be covered:

WH7.11 Students analyze political and economic change in the sixteenth, seventeenth and eighteenth centuries (the Age of Exploration, the Enlightenment, and the Age of Reason).

More About the Photo

Founded in 1786, Mission Santa Barbara is also known as "Queen of the Missions." It was the tenth of 21 Franciscan missions in California, and features architecture similar to that of churches built in early 19th century Mexico.

Chapter 1

Expanding Horizons

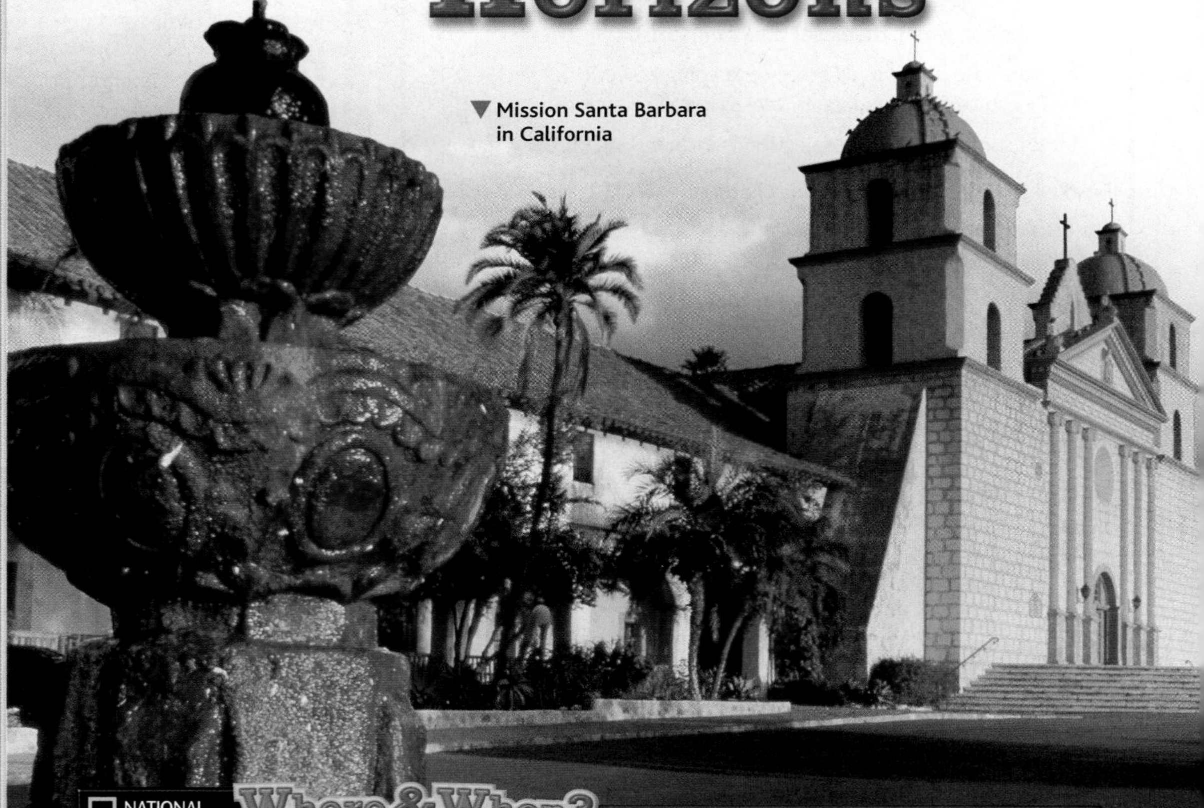

▼ Mission Santa Barbara in California

NATIONAL GEOGRAPHIC Where & When?

1200 — 1450 — 1700

- **1271** Marco Polo travels to China
- **1492** Christopher Columbus sails to the Americas
- **1521** Spanish conquer Aztec Empire
- **1689** English Bill of Rights extends rights

TEACH

The Big Ideas

As you begin teaching each section, use these questions and activities to focus on the Big Ideas.

Section 1

Age of Exploration

Essential Question: How does exploration influence the spread of new ideas? *(As people travel to new places, they bring ideas that are shared with the people living in the new place.)* Point out that in Section 1, students will learn about the Age of Exploration, when Europeans' journeys resulted in the exchange of ideas and goods around the world. **OL**

Section 2

Rise of Modern Capitalism

Essential Question: Why have people created economic systems? *(to buy and sell goods and services and to make money)* Explain that in Section 2, students will learn about the development of the free enterprise system, or capitalism, an economic system that lets business owners make profits from their companies and which leads to many choices for consumers. **BL**

The Big Ideas

History Online
Chapter Overview Visit ca.hss.glencoe.com for a preview of Chapter 1.

Section 1 Age of Exploration

Exploration and trade spread ideas and goods. In the 1400s, Europeans began to explore other areas of the world. Trade increased and goods, technology, and ideas were exchanged around the world.

Section 2 Rise of Modern Capitalism

Humans have created various economic systems. Our economic system is usually referred to as free enterprise, or capitalism. Capitalism is based on individual economic freedom. Capitalism developed gradually from economic and political changes in medieval and early modern Europe over hundreds of years.

Section 3 The Enlightenment

World history has been shaped by significant individuals, groups, ideas, events, eras, and developments. The Scientific Revolution led to new discoveries. Using the scientific method, Europeans of the 1600s and 1700s developed new ideas about society based on reason.

View the Chapter 1 video in the Glencoe Video Program.

FOLDABLES™ Study Organizer

Summarizing Make this foldable to help you learn about European exploration of the Americas.

Step 1 Fold the paper from the top right corner down so the edges line up. Cut off the leftover piece.

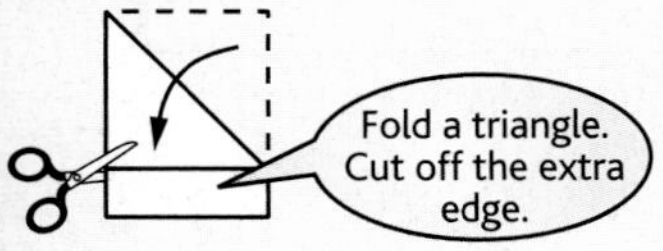

Step 2 Fold the triangle in half. Unfold.

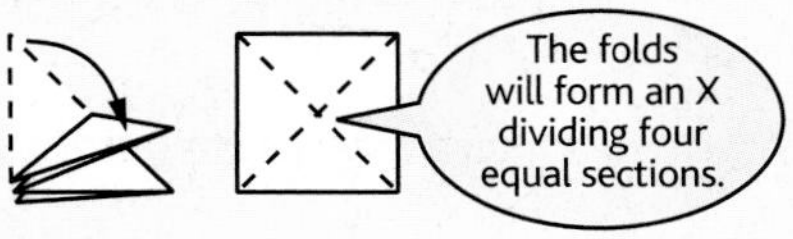

Step 3 Cut up one fold line and stop at the middle. Draw an X on one tab and label the other three.

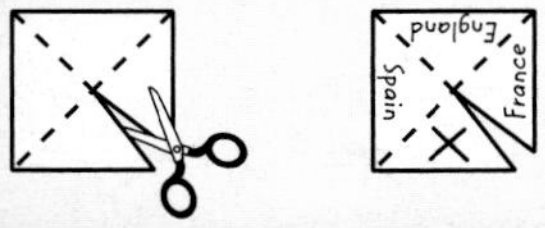

Step 4 Fold the X flap under the other flap and glue together.

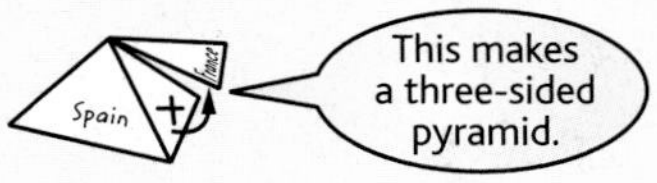

Reading and Writing
As you read, ask yourself why England, France, and Spain were exploring the Americas. Write your questions under each appropriate pyramid wall.

INTRODUCING CHAPTER 1

Section 3

The Enlightenment

Essential Question: What do you think it means to be enlightened? *(Answers will vary. Guide students to see that being enlightened is to be freed from ignorance, or to "see the light.")* Explain that in Section 3, students will learn about the Enlightenment, a period when logic and science led to new ideas about society and government. **OL**

Cultural Perspectives

Ask students to construct a classroom timeline of the founding of American colonies and early U.S. history from the point of view of Native Americans. First, students should provide entries for the time line based on their reading of chapters 1 and 2. Next, students can research other important events to include. Be sure to draw students' attention to the ways that they label each entry on the timeline to reflect a Native American cultural perspective. For example, a 1519 entry should read "Montezuma is captured by invaders from the sea" rather than "Cortes landed in Mexico." Ask students if history can be written in a neutral, balanced way or if it always has a particular perspective.

History Online

Go to ca.hss.glencoe.com for student activities, lesson plans, and links to additional Web resources about the age of exploration.

FOLDABLES™ Study Organizer — Dinah Zike's Foldables

Purpose When making this foldable, students are required to ask themselves questions about the reasons why Europeans explored the Americas. Have students exchange their foldables with a partner and answer the questions on the partner's foldable. **OL**

Why It's Important

Previewing No matter what they are reading—whether a newspaper article, a piece of literature, or a passage on a standardized test—students benefit if they take the time to preview the piece as a whole before reading the text word for word. Previewing gives readers an overview of the material. Remind students that the purpose of previewing is not to master specific content but rather to gain a general idea of what they will be reading.

1 Learn It!

To deepen students' understanding of previewing, encourage them to think about the previews, or "trailers," that are created for feature films. **Ask:** When you see a coming attraction for a new film, what kind of information can you take away from this preview? *(title, main characters, actors' names, director's name, key plot points, what the movie is about)* What impact do these previews have on viewers? *(Answers may include seeing what to look forward to from the movie.)* OL

Chapter 1 Get Ready to Read

Previewing

READING SKILL

1 Learn It!

If you know what to expect before reading, it will be easier to understand ideas and relationships presented in the text. Follow these steps to preview your reading assignments.

1. Look at the title and any illustrations that are included.
2. Read the headings, subheadings, and anything in bold letters.
3. Skim over the passage to see how it is organized. Is it divided into many parts?
4. Look at the graphics—pictures, maps, or diagrams. Read their titles and captions.
5. Set a purpose for your reading. Are you reading to learn something new? Are you reading to find specific information?

Reading Tip

As you preview the chapter, be sure to look over the maps, photographs, and charts.

READING STRATEGY SKIMMING

One valuable tool in previewing a text is skimming. To help students master this skill, you might select a relatively brief portion of text—for example, the first section of Chapter 1—and give students a set amount of time, such as 90 seconds, to skim the section. Encourage students to focus on the headings, subheadings, and first sentences of paragraphs as they skim the material. Then ask students to explain, in their own words, two or three key ideas from the section. OL

2 Practice It!

Take some time to preview this chapter. Skim all the main heads and main ideas. With a partner, discuss your answers to these questions.

- Which part of this chapter looks the most interesting to you?
- What do you think will be covered in the next chapter?
- Are there any words in the Main Ideas that are unfamiliar to you?
- Choose one of the Reading Connection questions to discuss with your partner.

Read to Write
Use the information you have gathered through previewing to write a study outline for the chapter.

Europe Gets Ready to Explore

Main Idea **New knowledge and ideas led Europeans to explore overseas.**

Reading Connection Have you ever done something daring or tried something new not knowing how it would turn out? Read to learn how explorers took chances and went to new places.

Christopher Columbus ▶ in the Americas

3 Apply It!

Now that you have skimmed the chapter, write a short paragraph describing one thing you want to learn from this chapter.

2 Practice It!

Direct students' attention to the Main Idea statements that appear at the beginning of each of the major sections. **Ask:** What does "main idea" mean? *(The main idea is a statement of the central message of a piece of writing.)* How does knowing the main idea help you preview? *(You know what a piece of writing is generally about.)* OL

3 Apply It!

Have students preview a newspaper article or magazine story. After using the previewing techniques described on this page, students should write down three questions that they expect will be answered by the piece. Then have students read the story and check their predictions. OL

READING STRATEGY OUTLINING

To help students learn previewing, tell them how to outline a piece of writing. Explain that outlines use Roman numerals for main sections, capital letters for subsections, and numbers for details. Readers can construct an outline before reading to see the general structure of a piece and then fill in the details as they read. Point out that creating the skeleton of the outline is relatively easy with a textbook chapter, as the headings can be used to generate the first two levels in the outline. OL

Use Reading Skills Activity 1 in the **Chapter 1 Resource Book** for more practice with previewing.

FOCUS

BELLRINGER
SKILLBUILDER ACTIVITY

Project **Daily Focus Skills Transparency 1–1** and have students answer the question.

Guide to Reading

Preteaching Vocabulary: The words *conquistador*, *pueblo*, *presidio*, and *encomienda* are Spanish in origin. **Ask:** Why do those words appear in this section? *(because Spain will be an important topic in the chapter)*

Answers to Graphic: to find new trade routes to Asia; advances in technology; pursuit of new ideas

Unpacking the Standards

After reading the section, students will be able to:

- Discuss Europeans' reasons for exploring.
- Describe the role of Spanish and Portuguese explorers in the Age of Exploration.
- Explain the impact of national rivalries on exploring the Americas.

Section 1

Age of Exploration

History Social Science Standards

WH7.11 Students analyze political and economic change in the sixteenth, seventeenth, and eighteenth centuries (the Age of Exploration, the Enlightenment, and the Age of Reason).

Guide to Reading

Looking Back, Looking Ahead
Europeans risked dangerous ocean voyages to discover new sea routes. Today, people continue to explore the mysteries of Earth and of space.

Focusing on the Main Ideas
- New knowledge and ideas led Europeans to explore overseas. *(page 81)*
- In search of trade routes, Portuguese explorers began an era of overseas exploration. *(page 84)*
- Rivalries between countries led to increased exploration of North America. *(page 86)*

Meeting People
Marco Polo
Bartholomeu Dias (bahr • THAH • luh • MYOO DEE • AHSH)
Vasco da Gama (VAHS • koh dah GA • muh)
Christopher Columbus
Montezuma (MAHN • tuh • ZOO • muh)

Locating Places
Portugal (POHR • chih • guhl)
Tenochtitlán (tay • NAWCH • teet • LAHN)

Content Vocabulary
technology
astrolabe (AS • truh • LAYB)
circumnavigate (SUHR • kuhm • NA • vuh • GAYT)
conquistador (kahn • KEES • tuh • DAWR)
pueblo (PWEH • bloh)
mission
presidio (prih • SEE • dee • OH)
encomienda (ehn • koh • mee • EHN • da)
Northwest Passage

Academic Vocabulary
culture (KUHL • chuhr)
design (dih • ZYN)

Reading Strategy
Determining Cause and Effect Use a diagram like the one below to identify three reasons Europeans increased overseas exploration.

Where & When?
NATIONAL GEOGRAPHIC

1200	1400	1600
1295 Marco Polo returns from China	**1492** Columbus reaches America	**1519** Magellan sails the Pacific Ocean

SECTION RESOURCES

Print Material
- Reproducible Lesson Plan 1–1*
- Daily Lesson and Discussion Notes 1–1
- Guided Reading Activity 1–1
- Reading Essentials and Study Guide 1–1
- Active Reading Note-Taking Guide 1–1
- Section Quiz 1–1

Transparencies
- Daily Focus Skills Transparency 1–1
- Section Graphic Organizer Transparency 1–1
- California Standards Practice Transparencies

Technology
- Interactive Tutor Self-Assessment CD-ROM
- Exam*View*® Pro Testmaker CD-ROM
- Presentation Plus! CD-ROM

*Available on TeacherWorks™

WH7.11.1 Know the great voyages of discovery, the locations of the routes, and the influence of cartography in the development of a new European worldview.

Europe Gets Ready to Explore

Main Idea **New knowledge and ideas led Europeans to explore overseas.**

Reading Connection Have you ever done something daring or tried something new not knowing how it would turn out? Read to learn how explorers took chances and went to new places.

A European Story

In 1271 **Marco Polo** set off from Europe on a great trek across Asia to China. Only 17 years old at the time, Polo journeyed with his father and uncle, both merchants from the Italian city of Venice. Traveling on camels for more than three years, the merchants crossed almost 7,000 miles (11,265 km) of mountains and deserts. Finally they reached the palace of Kublai Khan (KOO•bluh KAHN), the emperor of China. There Marco Polo spent 17 years working for the Khan and learning much about China's advanced **culture.**

When Polo returned from China in 1295, he wrote an account of the marvels of Asia, describing great riches and splendid cities. Polo's *Travels* was eagerly read in Europe and inspired a new age of exploration. Little did Polo realize the effect *Travels* would have. Nearly 200 years later his book about the East would inspire Christopher Columbus and other European explorers to sail in the opposite direction to reach the same destination.

Growth of Trade Marco Polo lived during the Middle Ages, the period in Western Europe that began with the fall of the western Roman Empire and lasted through the 1400s. During this time most Europeans knew little about India, China, or the rest of Asia. They also had no idea that the Western Hemisphere existed. Then, a dramatic series of events occurred that brought Europeans out of their isolation.

From the late 1000s to the early 1300s, Europeans fought a series of crusades, or holy wars, to free the Holy Land where Jesus had lived from the Muslims. The Muslims were followers of Islam, a religion that arose in the Middle East during the A.D. 600s. The Crusades achieved very little for Europeans, but they did increase trade between Europe and the lands to the east. During the time of the Crusades, Marco Polo made his journey. As Polo's story spread and exotic goods from the East appeared in Europe's marketplaces, more people became interested in distant lands. Merchants realized that they could make a fortune selling goods from Asia.

▲ Detail of historic map showing Marco Polo's journey

▲ Kublai Khan presents golden tablets to Marco Polo.

TEACH

R1 Reading Strategy

Categorizing Information Have students create a chart listing the reasons for exploration and categorizing each reason under one of the following headings: *Economic*, *Political*, and *Technological*. OL

R2 Reading Strategy

Academic Vocabulary Have students define the word *culture*. Then ask them to list examples of culture. BL

U Universal Access

Visual/Spatial Using information in this section or outside sources, have students design a book jacket for Marco Polo's *Travels* that has visual appeal and explains the significance of the book. Suggest that students include the book's author and title, an appealing image, and some brief favorable comments from a reviewer. AL

Review Grade 7 Standards

To review Standard **7.4.4** *(Understand the importance of both overland trade and maritime expeditions between China and other civilizations in the Mongol Ascendancy and the Ming Dynasty.)*, **ask:** What impact did Polo's book have on Europeans? *(it inspired Columbus and others to sail west in the effort to go east)* OL

More Skill Practice

Historical and Social Sciences Analysis Skill Ask students to give examples of how one culture can influence and change another culture. *(Answers may include the adoption of foods from other lands by Americans or the spread of American music and movies to other countries.)* OL CA HI3.

Did You Know?

After returning to Venice in 1295, Marco Polo joined the Venetian navy and was taken prisoner in a war between Genoa and Venice. In prison, he dictated a detailed account of his travels to Asia. Though some of the book was inaccurate, it was the basis for some of the earliest accurate maps of Asia. *The Travels of Marco Polo* remains one of the most influential travel books ever written.

Review Grade 5 Standards

To review standard **5.2.1** *Describe the entrepreneurial characteristics of early explorers (e.g., Christopher Columbus, Francisco Vásquez de Coronado) and the technological developments that made sea exploration by latitude and longitude possible (e.g., compass, sextant, astrolabe, seaworthy ships, chronometers, gunpowder)*, have students demonstrate how compasses work and explain why. OL

S Skill Practice

Historical and Social Sciences Analysis Skill

Ask: What role did competition play in causing the Age of Exploration? *(Merchants in western Europe competing with Italian and Muslim merchants wanted to find ways of increasing their share of trade with Asia.)* OL CA HI2.

R Reading Strategy

Understanding Vocabulary

The word *technology* comes from Greek words meaning "skill" and "theory." **Ask:** How is that origin related to the meaning of the term? OL

History Makers

The Compass, c. 1086

European technology improved navigation, but it was the Chinese who invented one of the more important tools for navigation: the compass. Evidence of this technology includes a Chinese document from the year 1086 that tells of sea captains relying on a "south-pointing needle" to help them find their way in foggy weather. The date on the document is more than 100 years earlier than the first recorded use of the compass in Europe.

How does a compass work? It uses a lodestone—a magnetic ore that always points in a north-south direction if allowed to freely rotate. If you know which way is north, you can determine the other directions.

▼ Compasses come in many shapes and sizes.

Centers of Trade Wealthy Europeans clamored for spices, perfumes, silks, and precious stones. Merchants bought goods from Arab traders in the Middle East and sent them overland by caravan to the Mediterranean Sea, then by ship to Italian ports. The cities of Venice, Genoa, and Pisa prospered and became centers of the growing East-West trade. The expansion of trade with Asia made Italian merchants wealthy.

The Rise of Strong Nations During the 1400s, Italian merchants found it harder to get the fabled goods of the East. Political changes in Asia hindered trade between East and West. This made Asian goods more expensive. In areas of western Europe close to the Atlantic Ocean, merchants wanted to expand their businesses through foreign trade. If they could buy spices and silks from the East directly, without going through the Arab and Italian cities, they could earn huge profits. They looked for new routes to East Asia that would bypass the Mediterranean Sea and the Middle East. S

Meanwhile, a new type of centralized state was emerging in western Europe. Strong monarchs had come to power in Spain, Portugal, England, and France. They began to establish national laws, courts, taxes, and armies to replace those of local lords. These ambitious kings and queens sought ways to increase trade and make their countries stronger and wealthier. They played an important role in expanding trade and interest in overseas exploration.

New Technology Advances in **technology**—the use of scientific knowledge for practical purposes—paved the way for European voyages of exploration. Maps were a problem for early navigators. By the 1400s, most educated people in Europe knew the world was round, but they only had maps of Europe and the Mediterranean. Most of these maps were inaccurate because they were drawn from the often-mistaken impressions of traders and travelers. Over time, cartographers, or mapmakers, gradually improved their skills. R

Using the reports of explorers and information from Arab geographers, mapmakers made more accurate land and sea maps. These maps showed the direction of ocean currents and lines of latitude, which measured the distance north and south of the Equator. Only as sailors began to move beyond the coasts of Europe did they gain information about the actual shape of the earth. By 1500, cartography had reached the point where Europeans had fairly accurate maps of the areas they had explored.

Answers and Additional Support

History Makers

Ask: How did the compass further European exploration? *(It helped improve navigation.)* OL CA HR3.

Did You Know?

Silk is spun from the cocoons of the silkworm. The cloth has several desirable qualities—it is light, durable, and holds bright colors when dyed. But silk is very difficult to produce. A single pound of cloth represents the cocoons of about 2,000 silkworms, the worms must be cared for, and many complex tasks are performed to turn the cocoons into thread.

Better Tools and Ships Better instruments were developed for navigating the seas. Sailors could determine their latitude while at sea with an **astrolabe** (AS • truh • LAYB), an instrument that measured the position of the stars. Europeans also improved the magnetic compass, a Chinese invention the Arabs had passed on to Europe in the 1200s. The compass allowed sailors to determine their ship's location when they were far from land.

Advances in ship **design** allowed shipbuilders to build sailing vessels capable of long ocean voyages. The stern rudder and the triangular sail made it possible for ships to sail into the wind. Both of these new features came from the Arabs. In the late 1400s, the Portuguese developed the three-masted caravel. The caravel was a small vessel that sailed faster than earlier ships and carried more cargo and food supplies. It also could float in shallow water, which allowed sailors to explore inlets and to sail their ships up to the beach to make repairs.

Reading Check **Analyze** Why were Marco Polo's travels to China important?

Linking Past & Present

Navigation Tools

Past "Land ho!" The tools that early explorers used to sail the uncharted seas were much different from the instruments used today. One early navigation tool was the astrolabe. A sailor held the astrolabe vertically, located a star through its sights, and measured the star's elevation above the horizon. A ship's approximate location could be identified this way.

▼ Navstar Global Positioning System satellite being launched

▲ Astrolabe

Present Today navigation satellites do the work of an astrolabe—and more! The Navstar Global Positioning System (GPS) is a constellation of orbiting satellites that provides navigation information. Developed by the military, Navstar allows a traveler to find out his or her position anywhere on or above the planet. ***What are some items that help you navigate?***

S Skill Practice

Using Geography Skills To help students see the difficulty of creating maps from secondhand accounts, have them work in pairs, with each writing a description of an area they know. Then have the partners exchange papers and draw maps of the area the other described based on the descriptions. Next have the students check the accuracy of their partners' maps. **Ask:** Were the maps accurate? If not, why not? *(Descriptions may be unclear or incomplete.)* **OL** **CA CS3.**

R Reading Strategy

Understanding Vocabulary *Astrolabe* contains the prefix *astro*, Greek for stars. **Ask:** What are some other words with this prefix? *(astronomy, astronaut, astrology)* **BL**

Reading Check

Answer: because his book about the trip was widely read and spurred an age of exploration

Linking Past & Present

Answers will vary but may include maps, compasses, and global positioning systems.

More Skill Practice

Historical and Social Sciences Analysis Skill Have students select a technological advance of recent times and compare its effects to those of one of the technological advances described in Section 1. Then, in a short persuasive essay, have them explain which has had the greater impact on society. **OL** **CA HI2.**

R Reading Strategy

Taking Notes Suggest that as students read this subsection they take notes by creating a graphic organizer with the following three headings: *Explorer*, *Date(s) of Travel*, and *Region(s) Explored* and filling in the correct information. EL CA CS1.

C1 Critical Thinking

Determining Cause and Effect Ask: What fact of geography forced Portugal to look to the Atlantic Ocean to find trade routes to Asia instead of the Mediterranean Sea? *(It had no port on the Mediterranean.)* BL CA CS3.

C2 Critical Thinking

Analyzing Information Prince Henry brought astronomers, geographers, and mathematicians to work with sailors and shipbuilders. **Ask:** What could each contribute? *(Astronomers could help with navigation because that was done by looking at stars; geographers could help draw maps; mathematicians could help the astronomers and shipbuilders.)* AL CA CS3.

WH7.11.1 Know the great voyages of discovery, the locations of the routes, and the influence of cartography in the development of a new European worldview.

R Exploring the World

Main Idea **In search of trade routes, Portuguese explorers began an era of overseas exploration.**

Reading Connection Do you like traveling to places that you have never been? Read to see why Europeans set off to explore the Americas.

C1 By the mid-1400s, the Italian ports faced increased competition for foreign trade. Powerful countries like **Portugal** (POHR•chih•guhl) and Spain began searching for sea routes to Asia, launching a new era of exploration. These new voyages took sailors down the west coast of Africa, which Europeans had never visited before.

C2 **Portugal Leads the Way** Prince Henry of Portugal laid the groundwork for a new era of exploration. In about 1420, he set up a center for exploration on the southwestern tip of Portugal. Prince Henry brought astronomers, geographers, and mathematicians to share their knowledge with Portuguese sailors and shipbuilders.

***Picturing* History**

Financed by Spain's Queen Isabella, the voyages of Columbus led to an exchange of goods between Europe and the Americas. ***On what island of the Americas did Columbus first land?***

In early 1488, the Portuguese explorer **Bartholomeu Dias** (bahr•THAH•luh•MYOO DEE•AHSH) reached the southern tip of Africa. As Dias approached the area, he ran into a terrible storm that carried him off course and around the southern tip of Africa. Dias wrote that he had been around the "Cape of Storms." On learning of Dias's discovery, King John II renamed this southern tip of land the Cape of Good Hope—he hoped that the passage around Africa might lead to a new route to India.

The first Portuguese voyages to India were made years later. In July 1497, **Vasco da Gama** (VAHS•koh dah GA•muh) set out from Portugal with four ships. Da Gama rounded the Cape of Good Hope and visited cities along the coast of East Africa. In 1498 he reached the port of Calicut, completing the long-awaited eastern sea route to Asia.

Events moved quickly after that. Pedro Alvares Cabral, following Da Gama's route, swung so wide around Africa that he touched Brazil. By claiming land for his king, he gave Portugal a stake in the Americas. Meanwhile, Portuguese ships began to make voyages to India, returning with cargoes of goods.

Columbus Sets Sail While the Portuguese explored Africa, an Italian navigator named **Christopher Columbus** came up with a daring plan to get to Asia. He would sail west across the Atlantic Ocean. At the time, nobody knew that a great landmass blocked the route to Asia.

Desperate for money to make the trip, Columbus obtained support from Queen Isabella of Spain in 1492. The Spanish had been watching the seafaring success of neighboring Portugal with envy. They, too, wanted to share in the riches of Asian trade. Earlier in 1492, the Spanish had driven the Muslims out of Spain. They could now afford to pay for exploration.

Columbus outfitted three ships: the *Niña*, the *Pinta*, and a larger one, the *Santa María*. In 1492 they left Spain and headed west. As the weeks passed, the crew grew desperate. Finally they sighted land—a small island, part of the group now called the Bahamas.

Answers and Additional Support

Did You Know?

Da Gama's voyage to India lasted more than two years and included many hardships. About 170 officers and crew members set out in July 1497; only about a third survived. The rest died in fights or from disease. One of those who died of illness was da Gama's brother. Da Gama profited greatly from the voyage, though.

Picturing History

Columbus made four trips to the Americas, each time bringing back to Europe plants and descriptions he claimed proved that the land he had found was part of Asia.

Answer: a small island in the Bahamas

Columbus went ashore, claimed the island for Spain, and named it San Salvador. Columbus returned to Spain in triumph. Columbus thought he was in Asia. He made three voyages to the region but never realized he had arrived in the Americas. Eventually, Europeans realized they had found two huge continents.

Magellan's Voyage The Spanish wanted to find a sea route through or around South America that would lead them to Asia. In 1519 they employed Ferdinand Magellan, a Portuguese mariner, to lead an expedition. Magellan headed west to sail around the Americas and then all the way to Asia. He sailed south along South America. Finally, he found a way around the continent—a narrow passage that today bears his name: the Strait of Magellan. After passing through the stormy strait, Magellan's expedition entered a vast sea. It was so peaceful, or pacific, that Magellan named the sea the Pacific Ocean. Magellan then headed west. His sailors nearly starved and had to eat leather, sawdust, and rats. Magellan was killed in a skirmish in the Philippines, but some of his crew continued west across the Indian Ocean, around Africa, and back to Spain. Only 18 of the more than 200 crew members completed the difficult journey. These men were the first to **circumnavigate** (SUHR • kuhm • NA • vuh • GAYT), or sail around, the world.

Reading Check **Explain** How did the success of Portugal's voyages of exploration influence Spain?

TECHNOLOGY & History

Spanish Galleon

In the late 1500s and early 1600s, Spanish galleons carried gold and silver from the West Indies to Spain. That is not all these ships carried, however. The threat of pirates prompted the Spanish galleons to carry weapons as part of their cargo. **What powered the Spanish galleons?**

The crow's nest served as a lookout.

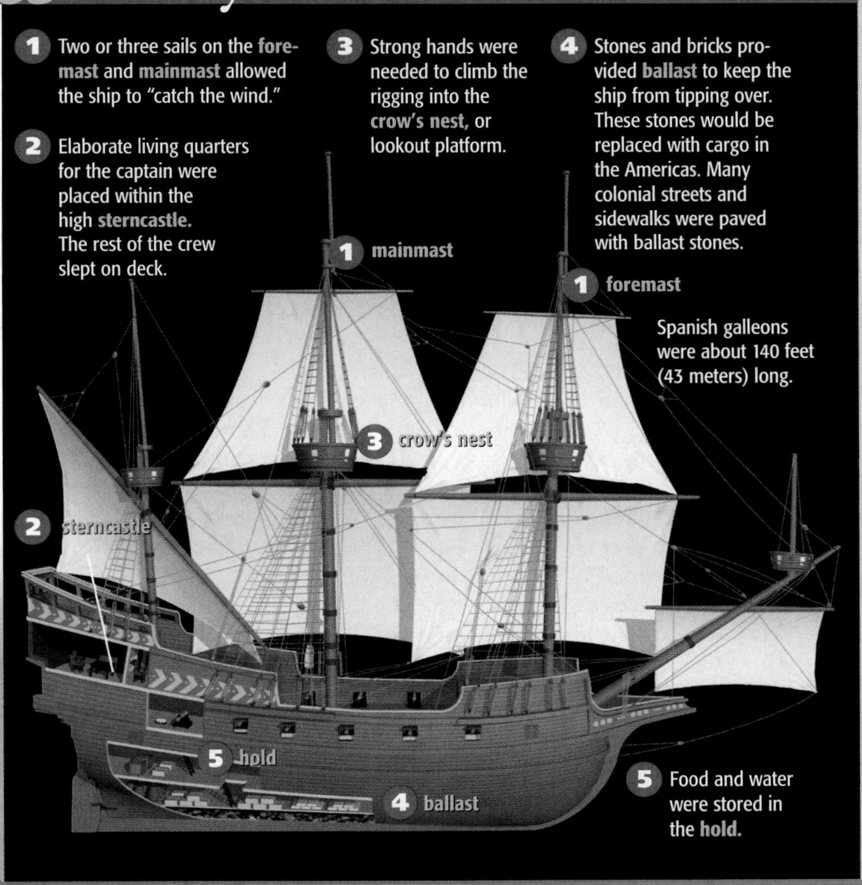

C Critical Thinking

Drawing Conclusions Give students the following statement: "Columbus was a failure because he insisted he had landed in Asia, not the Americas." Have students debate it, giving reasons for why they agree or disagree. OL CA HI4.

W Writing Support

Narrative Writing Have students take the role of Magellan or one of his crew and write a narrative of part of the voyage, detailing the kinds of hardships the crew encountered and what impact those difficulties had on their spirit and determination. OL CA 8WA2.1

R Reading Strategy

Using Word Parts Explain that *circum-* means "around" and comes from a word meaning circle. **Ask:** How does that explain the meaning of *circumnavigate?* *(Magellan sailed around the world, which is round like a circle.)* OL CA 8RW1.2

Reading Check

Answer: Portugal's success made the Spanish become envious and convinced them to back Columbus's voyage.

Did You Know?

Columbus's largest ship, the *Santa Maria*, was destroyed when it hit a reef off the coast of Haiti. Columbus sailed home on the *Niña*, with the *Pinta* following behind. A storm west of the Azores separated the two vessels, and another storm left the *Niña* badly damaged. The *Niña* finally reached its home port of Palos on March 15, 1493. The *Pinta* arrived later that day.

TECHNOLOGY & History

The word *galleon* refers to a specific type of sailing warship introduced in the mid-sixteenth century. Naval architects slimmed down top-heavy sailing ships of the time to produce the new ship. The first galleons were produced in England.

Answer: wind

R Reading Strategy

Understanding Vocabulary
Ask: What word is similar to *conquistador? (conqueror)* OL

C1 Critical Thinking

Determining Cause and Effect Ask: What did the conquistadors gain when they risked their lives in America? *(chance for riches)* What did Spain's rulers gain? *(territory, gold, treasure)* OL CA HI2.

S Skill Practice

Historical and Social Sciences Analysis Skill
Ask: Why did Cortés want to establish alliances with Native Americans? *(to add strength to his small army)* OL CA HI1.

C2 Critical Thinking

Making Inferences Ask: Could the Spanish have predicted that Native Americans would die from diseases brought from Europe? *(No; they brought the diseases unknowingly.)* OL CA HI4.

Resources for page 86

Primary Source Reading 1

Answers and Additional Support

WH7.11.1 Know the great voyages of discovery, the locations of the routes, and the influence of cartography in the development of a new European worldview.

Building Empires

Main Idea **Rivalries between countries led to increased exploration of North America.**

Reading Connection Have you ever competed against someone for something you both wanted? Read to learn how nations competed to claim land in the Americas.

Long before the arrival of Europeans in the early 1500s, several great Native American civilizations, or highly developed societies, arose in present-day Mexico and in Central and South America. Among the largest and most advanced of these civilizations were the Aztec and Inca. Each civilization spread out over hundreds of miles, included millions of people, and established trading networks that linked different parts of the Americas.

Spanish Conquistadors Stories of gold, silver, and kingdoms wealthy beyond belief greeted the early Spanish explorers in the Americas. The reports led them far and wide in search of fabulous riches.

R Known as **conquistadors** (kahn • KEES • tuh • DAWRS), these explorers received grants from the Spanish rulers. C1 They had the right to explore in the Americas. In exchange, they agreed to give the Spanish crown part of any gold or treasure they discovered.

Who Was Cortés? In 1519 the Spanish conquistador Hernán Cortés landed on the east coast of what we now know as Mexico. He came with about 500 soldiers, some horses, and a few cannons. Cortés soon learned about the great Aztec Empire and the capital of **Tenochtitlán** (tay • NAWCH • teet • LAHN).

S Cortés formed alliances with neaby cities against the Aztec. Then he marched into Tenochtitlán with his small army and Native American allies. The emperor **Montezuma** (MAHN • tuh • ZOO • muh)—also spelled Moctezuma—welcomed Cortés and his soldiers. However, Cortés took advantage of the Aztec's hospitality and made Montezuma his prisoner. Cortés attacked and destroyed the Aztec capital in 1521. The Aztec Empire disintegrated, and Spain seized control of the region.

Who Was Pizarro? Another conquistador, Francisco Pizarro, sailed down the Pacific coast of South America with about 180 Spanish soldiers. Pizarro had heard tales of the incredibly wealthy Inca Empire in present-day Peru. In 1532 Pizarro captured the Incan ruler, Atahualpa (ah • tuh • WAHL • puh), and destroyed much of the Incan army. Within a few years, Pizarro controlled most of the Inca Empire.

Why Were the Empires Conquered? The conquistadors' victories in Mexico and Peru were quick and lasting. How could Cortés and Pizarro, with only a few hundred Spanish soldiers, conquer such mighty empires?

First, the Spanish arrived with strange weapons—guns and cannons—and fearsome animals. They rode horses and had huge, ferocious dogs. To the Native Americans, the Spanish seemed almost like gods. Second, many Native Americans hated their Aztec overlords and assisted the conquistadors.

C2 Finally, disease played an extremely important role in the Spanish conquest. Native Americans had no immunity to the diseases the Europeans had unknowingly brought with them. Epidemics of smallpox and other diseases wiped out entire communities in the Americas and did much to weaken the resistance of the Aztec and Inca.

Searching for Gold Mexico and Peru were rich in silver and gold. Hoping to find similar wealth to the north, conquistadors explored the southeastern and southwestern parts of North America. Juan Ponce de León made the first Spanish landing on the mainland of North America, arriving on the east coast of present-day Florida in 1513. Ponce de León failed to find gold and the legendary fountain of youth. However, his exploration led to the first Spanish settlement in what is now the United States. In 1565 the Spanish established a fort at St. Augustine, Florida.

More Skill Practice

Historical and Social Sciences Analysis Skill List the following events and have students put them in the correct sequence:

A. Atahualpa is executed.
B. Pizarro conquers the Incas.
C. Cortés lands on the east coast of the land now known as Mexico.
D. Pizarro sails down the coast of South America with 180 soldiers.
E. Cortés forms alliances with Native American groups.

(C, E, D, A, B) OL CA CS1.

Who Was de Vaca? Many other conquistadors led expeditions to search for quick riches. One who did was Álvar Núñez Cabeza de Vaca (kuh•BAY•zuh day VAH•kuh). De Vaca and his crew were shipwrecked on an island near present-day Texas. Stranded, Cabeza de Vaca and his companions survived by adopting the ways of the Native Americans. After several years, they set off on foot on a great 1,000-mile journey across the Southwest. Arriving in Mexico in 1536, Cabeza de Vaca related tales he had heard of seven cities with walls of emerald and streets of gold.

De Soto and Coronado In search of the cities, Hernando de Soto took a large expedition into the region north of Florida. De Soto's expedition explored parts of what are today North Carolina, Tennessee, Alabama, Arkansas, and Texas. De Soto crossed the Mississippi River in 1541, describing it as "swift, and very deep." The fabled cities of gold, however, were not to be found. Francisco Vásquez de Coronado also wanted to find the legendary "Seven Cities of Gold." After traveling through the present-day southwestern United States, the expedition realized that there was no gold.

NATIONAL GEOGRAPHIC

European Voyages of Exploration

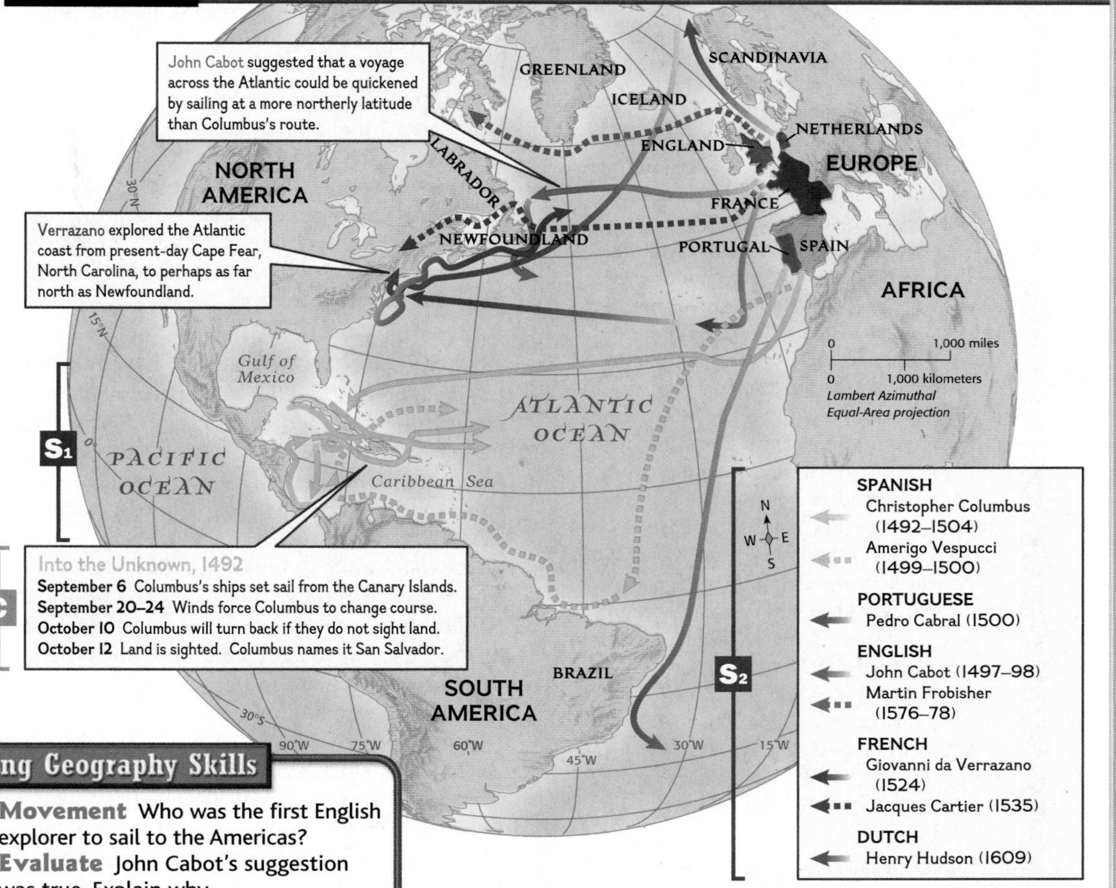

Using Geography Skills

1. **Movement** Who was the first English explorer to sail to the Americas?
2. **Evaluate** John Cabot's suggestion was true. Explain why.

C Critical Thinking

Analyzing Information
Based on information in this section, ask students to draw a map of the world as they think Columbus might have seen it in 1492. *(Students' maps should omit the Americas and the Pacific Ocean. Maps should show Asia about 2,400 miles [3,862 km] directly to the west of Europe.)* AL CA CS3.

S1 Skill Practice

Using Geography Skills
Ask: Which explorer traveled along the coast of Brazil? (*Pedro Cabral*) For which country did he sail? *(Portugal)* How did Cabot's route to the Americas differ from that of Columbus? *(He traveled farther north than Columbus did.)* OL CA CS3.

S2 Skill Practice

Historical and Social Sciences Analysis Skill
Ask: Which of the following explorers does *not* belong in the following group: Cabot, Cartier, Frobisher, Hudson, Vespucci? Why? *(Vespucci; because he did not explore North America)* OL CA HI3.

Resources for page 87

Biography Activity 1A

More Skill Practice

Historical and Social Sciences Analysis Skill For years, many history books claimed that "Columbus discovered America." **Ask:** Why might Native Americans disagree with this use of the word *discovered*? *(Native Americans lived in the Americas before Columbus arrived.)* OL CA HI5.

Using Geography Skills

Answers:

1. John Cabot
2. The earth's greatest circumference is at the Equator, and sailing north or south of the Equator shortens the traveling distance.

Trevor Jenson
Diego

R1 Reading Strategy

Understanding Vocabulary Encourage students to describe Spain's American empire using the terms *pueblo*, *mission*, *presidio*, and *encomienda*. OL

C Critical Thinking

Making Inferences Ask: What motivated Las Casas to protect Native Americans? *(Students may say that Las Casas saw enslavement as a violation of Christian principles.)* OL CA HI1.

R2 Reading Strategy

Understanding Vocabulary Ask: What made the idea of the Northwest Passage important? *(England and France wanted to find a more direct water route to Asia.)* OL

Review The Big Idea

Review the Big Idea for this section: "Exploration and trade spread ideas and goods." **Ask:** Would Europeans have explored the Americas if trade with Asia had been easier? Why or why not? *(Students may say that Europeans would have been content to follow existing trade routes.)* OL

Answers and Additional Support

HISTORY MAKERS

The Hispanic Heritage

▲ St. Augustine, founded in 1565

The Spanish empire in the Americas included more than one-half the continental United States. The oldest surviving building in the United States is located in St. Augustine, Florida.

In what is today the southwestern United States, the Spanish founded the city of Santa Fe at about the same time the English Pilgrims were crossing the Atlantic on the *Mayflower*. By the time the United States won its independence from England, the Spanish had founded Tucson, Albuquerque, San Antonio, and San Diego.

Many elements of the Spanish culture became part of America's heritage. Spanish art forms mixed with Native American cultures to produce new styles in arts and crafts. The architecture of the Spanish missions combined the flat-roofed adobe, or sun-dried mud brick, buildings made by Native Americans with the Spanish designs of open courtyards, covered arcades, and tiled roofs.

Another important element of Spanish culture in the United States is the Spanish language. Spanish is the second most widely spoken language in the country. Many Spanish terms, such as *canyon* and *fiesta*, have been incorporated into the English language. Spanish names—Los Angeles, Mesa Verde, El Paso—fill the maps of the West and Southwest.

The Spanish also introduced horses, sheep, pigs, and beef cattle into the American Southwest. The Spanish were expert ranchers and horse breeders. The first cowboys were Spanish vaqueros.

Spain's American Empire Meanwhile, the Spanish pressed forward with establishing settlements in their new American empire. **Pueblos** (PWEH • bloh), or towns, were established as centers of trade. **Missions** were religious communities that usually included a small town, surrounding farmland, and a church. A **presidio** (prih • SEE • dee • OH), or fort, was usually built near a mission. R1

In the 1500s, the Spanish government granted each conquistador who settled in the Americas an ***encomienda*** (ehn • koh • mee • EHN • da). An *encomienda* is the right to demand taxes or labor from Native Americans living on the land. This system turned the Native Americans into slaves. Grueling labor in the fields and in the gold and silver mines took its toll. Many Native Americans died from malnutrition and disease.

A Spanish priest, Bartolomé de Las Casas, condemned the cruel treatment of the Native Americans. He pleaded for laws to protect them. Because of Las Casas's reports, in 1542 the Spanish government passed the New Laws, which forbade making slaves of Native Americans. Although not always enforced, the laws did correct the worst abuses. C

French, Dutch, and English Explorations England, France, and the Netherlands wanted to profit from trade and colonization. The voyage to Asia—either around the southern tip of Africa or around South America—was long and difficult. For this reason, the three countries hoped to discover a **Northwest Passage** to Asia—a more direct water route through the Americas. R2

In 1497 England hired John Cabot, an Italian-born sailor, to look for a northern route to Asia. Cabot probably landed on the coast of present-day Newfoundland. England used Cabot's voyage as the basis for its claims to North America.

In 1524 France hired an Italian, Giovanni da Verrazano, to map America's coast and find a route to Asia. Verrazano mapped from what is today North Carolina north to Newfoundland but found no path to Asia.

More Skill Practice

Analyzing Primary Sources One conquistador explained, "We came to serve God and the king, and also to get rich." **Ask:** In what way do you think conquistadors planned to "serve God and the king"? *(by converting people to Christianity and claiming land for the king of Spain)* OL CA HR4.

HISTORY MAKERS

Ask: In what ways did Spanish ideas and influences become part of North America? *(Spanish influences can be seen in the architecture, art, and language of North America.)* AL

About ten years later, the French tried again. This time, they sent the French explorer Jacques Cartier (kahr•TYAY). Cartier sailed past Newfoundland and entered the St. Lawrence River. Hoping he had found a passage to Asia, Cartier made two more trips to map the St. Lawrence River. Cartier had heard stories about gold, but he found neither gold nor a sea route to Asia.

The Netherlands also wanted to find a passage through the Americas. They hired Henry Hudson, an English sailor, to explore. In 1609 he found a wide river in present-day New York, today known as the Hudson River. On a second voyage, sponsored by England, Hudson and his crew discovered a huge bay, now called Hudson Bay. However, he found no outlet to the Pacific.

A Trade Rivalry England and Spain also began to compete for trade. Attacks on Spanish ships and ports by such English adventurers as Sir Francis Drake angered King Philip II of Spain. He thought that Queen Elizabeth of England should punish Drake for his raids. Instead, she honored Drake with knighthood. [C] Philip sent the Spanish Armada to conquer England, but it failed completely.

Although war between England and Spain continued until 1604, the defeat of the armada marked the end of Spanish control of the seas. Now the way was clear for England and other nations to start colonies in North America.

Reading Check **Explain** How were the Spanish able to defeat the mighty Aztec and Inca empires?

History Online
Study Central Need help understanding the Age of Exploration? Visit ca.hss.glencoe.com and click on Study Central.

Section 1 Review

Reading Summary

Review the Main Ideas

- By the late 1400s, technological and economic changes in Europe made long sea voyages possible.
- Christopher Columbus sought a sea route to Asia. Instead, he landed in the Americas.
- Spain, England, France, and the Netherlands sent explorers to the Americas in search of trade and colonies.

What Did You Learn?

1. What was the goal of Christopher Columbus's voyage in 1492?
2. What was the purpose of John Cabot's voyage?

Critical Thinking

3. **Taking Notes** Re-create the diagram below. List technological innovations mentioned in this section, and describe the effect of each on exploration.

Technology Innovation	Effect on Exploration

4. **The Big Ideas** Explain why exploration accelerated in the 1400s and 1500s. CA CS1.
5. **Drawing Conclusions** Why do you think the Caribbean islands that Columbus reached are often referred to as the West Indies? CA HI4.
6. **Analyze** Were the French or Spanish explorations more successful? Why? CA HI2.
7. **Descriptive Writing** Take on the role of a sailor on Columbus's first voyage to the Americas. Write a journal entry about the Caribbean islands. CA 8WA2.0
8. **READING** **Previewing** Read the main ideas for Section 2. Write a paragraph describing what you think you will learn. CA 8RC2.3

C Critical Thinking

Drawing Conclusions
Ask: Why do you think Queen Elizabeth honored Sir Francis Drake rather than punish him? *(Drake had weakened the Spanish fleet and strengthened England's position as a naval power.)* OL

ASSESS

Resources for page 89

Use these resources to assess student mastery of section content.

Section Quiz 1–1

Interactive Tutor Self-Assessment CD-ROM

Reading Check

Answer: Answers include the use of guns, cannons, horses, and large dogs, which made the Spanish appear godlike; the help of other Native American groups; and Native Americans' lack of immunity to European diseases.

History Online

Study Central provides summaries, interactive games, and online graphic organizers to help students review section content.

CLOSE

Analyzing Information
Ask students to explain who they think had the most valid claim to the lands described in this section. Remind them to support their argument with evidence. *(Answers will vary but should include facts to support students' arguments.)* OL

SECTION 1 REVIEW ANSWERS

Review questions reinforce content standards WH7.11

1. to reach Asia
2. to show that ships could cross the Atlantic faster by sailing farther north
3. Answers should reflect an understanding of technology and exploration.
4. **The Big Ideas** increased demand for imported goods, a search for new trade routes, and desire to boost strength and wealth
5. because Columbus thought he was reaching Asia, and the Indies are in Asia
6. Spanish; because they gained greater wealth
7. Entries should show awareness of the hardships.
8. **READING** the rise of modern capitalism

FOCUS

BELLRINGER
SKILLBUILDER ACTIVITY

Project **Daily Focus Skills Transparency 1–2** and have students answer the question.

Guide to Reading

Preteaching Vocabulary: Use the **Vocabulary PuzzleMaker CD-ROM** to create crossword and word search puzzles.

Answers to Graphic: Trade: joint-stock companies, governments promote trade; mercantilism; Columbian Exchange; slave trade; Banking: governments charter banks in return for loans; Settlement: overseas colonies

Unpacking the Standards

After reading the section, students will be able to:

- Describe how capitalism and banking helped countries expand wealth through trade and led to colonies.
- Analyze the benefits and drawbacks of the Columbian Exchange.

Section 2

Rise of Modern Capitalism

History Social Science Standards

WH7.11 Students analyze political and economic change in the sixteenth, seventeenth and eighteenth centuries (the Age of Exploration, the Enlightenment, and the Age of Reason).

Guide to Reading

Looking Back, Looking Ahead

You read how the voyages of exploration led to setting up colonies and opening new areas for trade. These changes also led to a new way of doing business and financing expeditions.

Focusing on the Main Ideas

- New ways of doing business developed to raise money to finance trade. *(page 91)*
- Nations competed to establish colonies in the Americas. *(page 94)*
- Exploration and trade led to a worldwide exchange of products, people, and ideas. *(page 95)*

Locating Places

Venice (VEH•nuhs)
Genoa (JEH•noh•uh)

Meeting People

The Medici Family (MEHD•ee•chee)
The Fugger Family (FUG•uhr)
Bartolomé de Las Casas (bahr•TOH•loh•may day lahs KAHS•ahs)

Content Vocabulary

capitalism
joint-stock company
entrepreneur (AHN•truh•pruh•NUHR)
mercantilism (MUHR•kuhn•tuh•LIH•zuhm)
bullion (BUL•yuhn)
colony
Columbian Exchange

Academic Vocabulary

assist
finance (FY•NANTS)
funds
export

Reading Strategy

Summarizing Complete a chart like the one below identifying changes in trade, banking, and settlement that occurred during this period.

Changes
Trade | Banking | Settlement

NATIONAL GEOGRAPHIC Where & When?

1300	1500	1700
Mid-1300s Renaissance begins	**1500s** Columbian Exchange extends trade to new regions	**1600s** Joint-stock companies begin operation

SECTION RESOURCES

Print Material
- Reproducible Lesson Plan 1–2*
- Daily Lesson and Discussion Notes 1–2
- Guided Reading Activity 1–2
- Reading Essentials and Study Guide 1–2
- Active Reading Note-Taking Guide 1–2
- Section Quiz 1–2

Transparencies
- Daily Focus Skills Transparency 1–2
- Section Graphic Organizer Transparency 1–2
- California Standards Practice Transparencies

Technology
- Interactive Tutor Self-Assessment CD-ROM
- Exam*View*® Pro Testmaker CD-ROM
- Presentation Plus! CD-ROM

*Available on TeacherWorks™

WH7.11.3 Examine the origins of modern capitalism; the influence of mercantilism and cottage industry; the elements and importance of a market economy in seventeenth-century Europe; the changing international trading and marketing patterns, including their locations on a world map; and the influence of explorers and map makers.

The Commercial Revolution

Main Idea **New ways of doing business developed to raise money to finance trade.**

Reading Connection Have you ever come up with a plan to raise money when you want to make an expensive purchase? Read on to find out what new ways were developed to raise money for exploration and colonization.

A European Story

In 1587 17-year-old David Baker admired the magnificent view of London from the Thames River. However, he could not begin to take pleasure in the city without walking down its busy streets. No street offered more to delight the eye or tongue than Cheapside, the city's broadest avenue, located north of London Bridge. Cheapside was filled with stalls sheltered by canopies and stocked with a tempting array of local goods as well as exotic imports such as scarves, spices, and even peacocks and apes.

How Did Capitalism Develop? London, England, was among the cities of Europe that grew wealthy as a result of the Age of Exploration. Building empires and overseas trade expanded Europe's economy. Europe's growing population demanded more goods and services. This demand was met by Europe's increasing contacts with the rest of the world. This search for wealth led to the rise of modern **capitalism,** an economic system in which money is invested in business to make profits.

By the 1600s, the nation had replaced the city and village as the basic economic unit in Europe. Nations began competing for markets and trade goods. New business methods were developed to invest money, speed the flow of wealth, and reduce risks in commercial ventures. These changes, which came to be known as the Commercial Revolution, formed the roots of modern financial and business life.

Growth of Banking Launching an overseas trading venture was a major undertaking. To trade goods long distance, merchants needed a lot of money. They had to buy many goods, store them in warehouses, and ship them over land and sea. They had to know what people in distant lands wanted to buy and what prices were like there. Often several years passed before a fleet finished trading overseas and returned home. Only then could the initial investment pay off. Generally, only governments and rich merchants had enough money to back such trading voyages, and even they needed financial **assistance.**

At first, merchants turned to bankers for the money to **finance** their ventures. Families like the **Medici** (MEHD•ee•chee) of Florence, Italy, and the **Fuggers** (FUG•uhrz) of Augsburg, Germany, loaned money as part of their businesses. By the 1500s, these families were so wealthy that they accepted deposits, made loans, and transferred funds over long distances. They set up branches in several European cities and made loans to European monarchs.

▲ European towns and cities grew and prospered during the 1500s and 1600s.

TEACH

U Universal Access

English Learners Write the following phrases on the board: *city where a nation's government is found* and *money and property used to start a business.* **Ask:** Which definition works best for the word *capital* when it is used as the base word for the term *capitalism?* EL

Review The Big Idea

Review the Big Idea for this section: "Humans have created various economic systems." **Ask:** What is the essence of capitalism? *(the idea of profits)* What happens if the business does not succeed? *(loss of investment)* AL

S Skill Practice

Historical and Social Sciences Analysis Skill
Ask: What risks did merchants face when launching an overseas trading venture? *(initial costs; the chance that goods would not be sold or that prices would not be as expected; long lag time between the investment and the profit)* Given these risks, why were they willing to start new businesses? *(They could earn great profits.)* OL

R Reading Strategy

Academic Vocabulary Ask students to read the sentence that contains the word *assistance.* Then ask them to define the word. OL

More Skill Practice

Visual Literacy Have students look at the painting of a European town. **Ask:** What forms of commerce are evident in this image? *(A bustling town square shows vendors offering food, clothing, scarves, and ceramics.)* OL CA HR3.

More Skill Practice

Historical and Social Sciences Analysis Skill **Ask:** How did ordinary citizens like David Baker contribute to the growth of capitalism? *(Citizens' demand for new products and services led merchants to undertake new trading voyages and to seek new ways to profit from investments.)* OL CA HI2.

Resources for page 91

Academic Vocabulary Activity 1

Biography

TEACH

R Reading Strategy

Activating Prior Knowledge **Ask:** What ancient people in Europe had a group of competing city-states? *(ancient Greeks)* Explain that as in Greece, the city-states of Renaissance Italy competed for power, wealth, and influence. OL

S Skill Practice

Historical and Social Sciences Analysis Skill
Ask: Why do you think Lorenzo de' Medici thought it important to support the arts, literature, and learning? *(Students may say that de' Medici wanted to enhance his status or link himself to Florence's reputation for culture.)* OL CA HI1.

C Critical Thinking

Making Inferences Draw students' attention to de' Medici's efforts to create a unified Italy. **Ask:** Why might that effort have failed? *(Milan and Venice probably would not have been willing to be under the power of Florence, and Florence probably would not have been willing to be under their power.)* OL CA HI1.

Answers and Additional Support

Biography

WH7.11.4 Explain how the main ideas of the Enlightenment can be traced back to such movements as the Renaissance, the Reformation, and the Scientific Revolution and to the Greeks, Romans, and Christianity.

LORENZO DE' MEDICI

1449–1492

Renaissance means "rebirth." The years from about 1350 to 1550 in European history are called the Renaissance because a rebirth of interest in art and learning took place.

During the Renaissance, many European nations were ruled by a king or queen. However, Italy did not have a single strong monarch. The lack of a single strong ruler made it possible for a number of city-states in northern and central Italy to remain independent. Three city-states—Milan, Venice, and Florence—expanded and played important roles in Italy's political, economic, and social life. R

The Medici family controlled the city of Florence. The Medicis had acquired great wealth through banking and trade. Using their wealth and personal influence, Cosimo, and later Lorenzo de' Medici, his grandson, dominated the city at a time when Florence was the cultural center of Italy.

Lorenzo de' Medici supported the arts, literature, and learning. Renaissance artists worked at his court, including Leonardo da Vinci and Michelangelo. Lorenzo helped build the Medici Library. He spent huge sums of money to buy Greek and Latin manuscripts and to have them copied. Lorenzo also worked to beautify Florence and the many Medici lands and palaces. S

"Lorenzo took the greatest delight in architecture, music, and poetry."
—Niccolò Machiavelli

In political affairs, Lorenzo tried to maintain a balance of power between the Italian city-states so that no single state became too strong. He also tried to create a more unified Italy, but this effort was not successful. C

Then and Now

Italy's wealth supported new art forms. In what way do bankers and businesspeople support the arts today?

Then and Now

Bankers and businesspeople support contemporary artists by providing funding for museum exhibitions, contributing to arts groups such as symphony orchestras and theaters, and giving the money for radio and television broadcasts of performances, among other actions.

Changes in Banking Meanwhile, many Jews fleeing persecution in Spain settled in port cities in Holland, France, and Germany. There they were granted freedom of worship and offered economic opportunities. Many Jews became financiers and investors as well as importers and shipbuilders.

By the 1600s, governments began to charter, or legally support, banks in return for the banks loaning them money. These government-backed banks accepted deposits of money and charged interest on loans. Before long, the banks began to provide other services. They issued banknotes and checks, making large payments in heavy coins a thing of the past. They acted as money changers, exchanging currencies from other countries.

What Are Joint-Stock Companies? In the 1600s, new ways of doing business developed in Europe. Individual merchants who wanted to invest in exploration often raised money by combining their resources in **joint-stock companies,** organizations that sold stock, or shares, in the venture. This enabled large and small investors to share the profits and risks of a trading voyage. If a loss occurred, investors would lose only the amount they had invested in shares. This sharing of risk provided a stable way of raising **funds** for voyages. R1

A few joint-stock companies became rich and powerful through government support. For example, the Netherlands entered an era of commercial prosperity upon gaining independence from Spain in 1648. Its government gave the Dutch East India Company a monopoly, or the sole right, to carry out Dutch trade with Africa and the East Indies. The Dutch government also gave the company the power to make war, to seize foreign ships, to coin money, and to set up colonies and forts. In return, the government received customs duties, or taxes on imported goods, from the company's trade.

A New Business Class As gold and silver flowed into Europe from abroad, the supply of coined money increased. At the same time, the nature and goals of business changed. It now came to be seen that the goal of business was to make profits. Individuals known as **entrepreneurs** (AHN•truh•pruh•NUHRZ) combined money, ideas, raw materials, and labor to make goods and profits. Profits were then used to expand the business and develop new ventures. R2

An entrepreneur in the cloth industry, for example, would buy wool and employ spinners to make the wool into yarn. Weavers and dyers would then be hired to turn the yarn into cloth. Because these tasks were done in the workers' homes, this system became known as the "cottage industry."

The entrepreneur would then sell the cloth on the open market for a price that brought a profit. Of course, entrepreneurs took risks when they put up capital for businesses. They could lose their investment if prices fell or if workers could not produce goods at a specified time or for a specific market. R3

Picturing History

This picture shows a money changer and his wife at work. Trade often meant the transfer of money from place to place. ***How did banks help finance trading voyages?***

Reading Check **Explain** What was the advantage of investing in a joint-stock company?

R1 Reading Strategy

Understanding Word Parts Explain that *joint-stock* is a compound adjective, formed by joining two words to create a single unit of meaning. **Ask:** What are some other compound adjectives? *(Possible answers include* decision-making, well-known, top-quality, *and* high-level.*)* AL

R2 Reading Strategy

Understanding Vocabulary Have students look up the definitions of *entrepreneur* and *enterprise*. **Ask:** What connection do you see between the origin of these two words? *(They come from the same French root. An enterprise is a business activity; entrepreneurs are the people who have an idea that launches an enterprise.)* OL

R3 Reading Strategy

Connecting Point out that business people today also take risks in the hopes of earning a profit. **Ask:** What happens if a new movie is highly popular? *(The people who made the movie make money.)* What if it is not popular? *(They may lose money.)* BL

Reading Check

Answer: By forming joint-stock companies through the sale of stock shares, investors were able to share both the profits and risks of their business ventures. This meant that if the venture was not profitable, investors' losses would be limited.

More Skill Practice

Visual Literacy Have students examine the painting. **Ask:** What details in the painting provide information on the social status of the money changer and his wife? *(Both are wearing rich clothing and their home is decorated with numerous ornaments, suggesting that they are well-off.)*

OL CA 8LS1.9

Picturing History

This painting is by Quentin Massys, a Flemish painter who lived from c. 1466 to 1530. He is known for placing portrait subjects against a realistic background.

Answer: Bankers loaned money, transferred funds over long distances, and set up branches in various cities.

S Skill Practice

Using Geography Skills
Have students locate Portugal, Spain, England, and Italy on a map of Europe. **Ask:** Which country is farthest from the Atlantic Ocean? *(Italy)* How would this affect Italy's trade with the Americas? *(Italians would be less able to compete with traders from countries like Spain and Portugal.)* BL CA CS3.

R Reading Strategy

Understanding Vocabulary
Have students write a sentence that explains the connection between *mercantilism* and *bullion*. *(Students may say that the goal of mercantilism was to increase a nation's supply of bullion.)* OL CA 8RW1.3

U Universal Access

Below Grade Level Some students may have difficulty understanding the quotation because of the word *sinews*. Explain that the word can mean the power or strength of muscles. **Ask:** What does the quotation mean? *(Bullion drives a nation, just as muscles drive a body.)* BL

Answers and Additional Support

WH7.11.3 Examine the origins of modern capitalism; the influence of mercantilism and cottage industry; the elements and importance of a market economy in seventeenth-century Europe; the changing international trading and marketing patterns, including their locations on a world map; and the influence of explorers and map makers.

Government and Trade

Main Idea **Nations competed to establish colonies in the Americas.**

Reading Connection Suppose your family is thinking about moving to another state. What factors would influence your decision to move? Read on to find out why many Europeans migrated to the Americas.

Governments became closely involved in trade. They believed that a nation's power rested on the wealth obtained from trade. They developed national economic policies to advance trade and become as wealthy as possible.

S In the 1600s, the greatest increase in trade took place in the countries bordering the Atlantic Ocean—Portugal, Spain, England, and the Netherlands—in large part because they had the largest overseas empires. Italian cities, such as **Venice** (VEH • nuhs) and **Genoa** (JEH • noh • uh), formerly the leading trade centers in Europe, found themselves cut out of overseas trade as trade routes and fortunes gradually moved westward toward the Atlantic Ocean and the Americas.

What Is Mercantilism? During the 1600s, Europe's trading nations based their policies on an economic theory known as **mercantilism** (MUHR • kuhn • tuh • LIH • zuhm). This theory held that a nation became powerful by building up its supply of **bullion** (BUL • yuhn), or gold and silver. R One merchant summed up the general feeling about bullion: "[It is] the sinews of all government, it gives it its pulse, its movement. . . ." U Under mercantilism, nations could gain wealth by mining gold or silver at home or overseas.

Primary Sources

The Wealth of Nations

Many nations tried to increase their wealth and power by following the ideas of mercantilism. Putting mercantilism into practice demanded a large amount of government control.

Some economists and writers criticized mercantilism. In his book *The Wealth of Nations* (1776), economist Adam Smith described a system in which government had little to do with a nation's economy. He said individuals left on their own would work for their own self-interest:

> "Every man, as long as he does not violate the laws of justice, is left perfectly free to pursue his own interest his own way, and to bring both his industry and capital into competition with those of any other man, or order of men."

Smith set forth the basic principles of capitalism—that people are free to buy, sell, and produce what they want with little or no government restriction. Smith's ideas influenced the Founders of the United States, who limited the role of government mainly to national defense and keeping the peace.

▲ Gold bullion

DBQ Document-Based Question

Does Smith say that there are no limits on a worker "pursuing his own interest"? Explain.

Primary Sources

Answer: No; he says workers must not "violate the laws of justice."

- What does Smith mean by saying people work for their own self-interest? *(They want to make their lives more comfortable or more enjoyable.)* OL

Resources for page 94

Biography Activity 1B

WH7.11.2 Discuss the exchanges of plants, animals, technology, culture, and ideas among Europe, Africa, Asia, and the Americas in the fifteenth and sixteenth centuries and the major economic and social effects on each continent.

How Did Mercantilism Work? Spain sent conquistadors to the Americas to seize the silver and gold mines of the Aztec and Inca Empires. Nations, however, primarily wanted to gain wealth through trade. They wanted to create a favorable balance of trade by **exporting** more goods than they imported. If a nation exported more goods than it imported, more gold and silver flowed in from other nations than went out. This greater wealth meant greater national power and more influence in the world.

Mercantilism provided great opportunities for individual merchants to make money. To increase national wealth, governments often aided businesses that produced export goods. They sold monopolies, which is the total control of an operation free of competition, to producers in certain key industries. They also set tariffs, or taxes on imported goods, to protect local industries from foreign competition.

Quest for Colonies Mercantilism also led to increased rivalry between nations. Mercantilists believed that nations should set up overseas colonies. A **colony** is a settlement of people living in a new territory controlled by their home country. According to mercantilists, colonies are supposed to produce goods that their home country does not have. That way, the home country will not have to import those goods from other countries.

During the 1600s, several countries in Europe, such as England and Spain, competed for overseas territory that could produce wealth. They wanted to acquire colonies in the Americas that could provide valuable resources, such as gold and silver, or raw materials. The colonies would also serve as a place to sell European products.

Reading Check **Analyze** How did mercantilism increase the wealth of countries like Spain?

History Online

Student Web Activity Visit ca.hss.glencoe.com and click on *Chapter 1—Student Web Activities* for an activity on economic systems.

Global Exchange

Main Idea **Exploration and trade led to a worldwide exchange of products, people, and ideas.**

Reading Connection Think back to the last time you tried a new food or a new way of doing something. Who introduced this new food or idea to you? Read on to find out what happened when new cultures came into contact with one another.

As Europe traded with the world, a global exchange of people, goods, technology, ideas, and even diseases began. We call this transfer the **Columbian Exchange,** after Christopher Columbus.

Trade in Goods This transfer of products from continent to continent brought changes in ways of life throughout the world. Europeans planted many European and Asian grains, such as wheat, oats, barley, rye, and rice, in the Americas. They also brought new animals, such as pigs, sheep, cattle, chickens, and horses. Chickens changed the diet of many people in the Americas, and horses changed the lives of Native Americans. Horses provided a faster way to move from place to place. As a result, Native Americans in North America began hunting buffalo as their main food source.

From Native Americans, Europeans acquired food items such as corn, potatoes, tomatoes, beans, and chocolate, which they brought back to Europe. Corn was used to feed animals. Larger, healthier animals resulted in more meat, leather, and wool. The potato was also important. Europeans discovered that if they planted potatoes instead of grain, about four times as many people could live off the same amount of land.

Other American foods, such as squash, beans, and tomatoes, also made their way to Europe. Tomatoes greatly changed cooking in Italy, where tomato sauces became common. Chocolate was a popular food from Central America. By mixing it with milk and sugar, Europeans created a sweet that is still enjoyed today.

Review Grade 5 Standards

To review standard **5.3.1** *(Describe the competition among the English, French, Spanish, Dutch, and Indian nations for control of North America.)*, have students create a chart summarizing the information from this paragraph under the headings Who? *(Spain and England)*, What? *(acquired colonies)*, Where? *(the Americas)* When? *(in the 1600s)*, and Why? *(to obtain valuable resources or raw materials)* OL

R Reading Strategy

Using Context Clues Point out that the term "Columbian Exchange" is named after Christopher Columbus because his voyages to the Americas led to that exchange. OL

C Critical Thinking

Analyzing Information
Ask: Did the exchange of goods and ideas happen quickly or over a long period of time? *(Since Columbus reached the Americas in 1492 and England and Spain established colonies in the 1600s, the changes probably occurred over many years.)* OL

Reading Check

Answer: by giving them the opportunity to increase their stores of silver and gold from their colonies and having a favorable balance of trade

History Online

Go to ca.hss.glencoe.com for student activities, lesson plans, and links to additional Web resources about economic systems.

More Skill Practice

Historical and Social Sciences Analysis Skill Have students summarize the impact of the Columbian Exchange by creating a two-column chart. In one column students should list the effects on residents of the Americas; in the other column, students should list the effects on Europeans. Remind students that effects can be positive or negative. OL

Did You Know?

As part of the Columbian Exchange, Europeans introduced Native Americans to a range of technologies, including new types of metal-working, new techniques of shipbuilding, and new forms of weapons, including firearms.

W Writing Support

Persuasive Writing Have students write an essay in which they take the position that the Columbian Exchange was, on the whole, good or bad. Students should give reasons for their position. Ask volunteers to state their reasons to the class. After a few students from each side have done so, have the class vote to determine the majority view. OL CA 8WA2.4

R Reading Strategy

Predicting Before students read this paragraph, explain that the Columbian Exchange had some serious unanticipated negative consequences. **Ask:** What do you think some of these were? Why? *(Answers will vary but should be supported by logical reasoning.)* OL

U Universal Access

Naturalist Have students explain how immunity to diseases works and why Native Americans did not have resistance to these diseases that had been common in Europe, Asia, and Africa. AL CA HI2.

NATIONAL GEOGRAPHIC

The Columbian Exchange

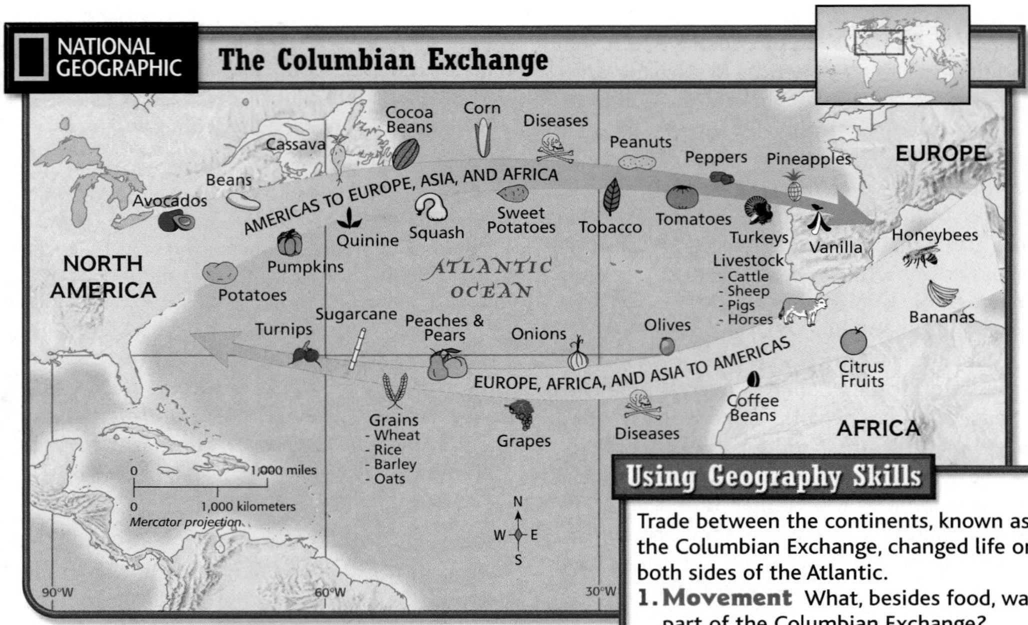

Using Geography Skills

Trade between the continents, known as the Columbian Exchange, changed life on both sides of the Atlantic.

1. **Movement** What, besides food, was part of the Columbian Exchange?
2. **Movement** Which continent do you think benefited the most from the Columbian Exchange? Explain.

Trade Grows The voyages of Columbus and other explorers brought together two parts of the world that previously had no contact: the continents of Europe, Asia, and Africa in one hemisphere and the Americas in the other.

Some American foods, such as chili peppers and peanuts, were taken to Europe, but they also made their way to Asia and Africa where they became popular. Both Europeans and Asians also began smoking tobacco, an American plant.

Foods, such as corn, spread to Asia and Africa, boosting population growth there. From Asia and Africa, Europeans brought to Europe and the Americas tropical products—bananas, coffee, tea, and sugarcane—as well as luxury goods, such as ivory, perfumes, silk, and gems.

Movement of Peoples and Cultures New global trading links increased the movement of people and cultures from continent to continent. Europeans seeking wealth or fleeing economic distress and religious persecution moved to the Americas and other parts of the world. They exchanged food, ideas, and practices with the people living in these areas.

European influences profoundly affected local cultures. European traders spread European languages, and European missionaries taught Christianity and European values. Wealthy Europeans, in turn, developed an interest in the arts, styles, and foods of Asia, especially Chinese porcelain, Indian textiles, and Southeast Asian spices.

With their guns and powerful ships, the Europeans easily defeated Arab fleets and Indian princes. Across Asia, the Europeans forced local rulers to let them set up trading posts. Within a short time, England's East India Company had built an empire in India, and the Dutch East India Company had built an empire in Indonesia.

Not everything exchanged between Europe and America was good. When Europeans arrived in America, they were carrying germs that Native Americans had not previously been exposed to. Many diseases, including smallpox, measles, and malaria, swept across the Americas, killing millions of people.

Answers and Additional Support

Using Geography Skills

Answers:

1. plants, animals, technology, culture, ideas
2. Students may note that Europe reaped the benefits of free land, a cheap labor source, and new foods that helped to feed a growing population

Resources for page 96

Economics and History Activity 1

Beginnings of Slave Trade A huge movement of people also took place after Europeans obtained sugarcane from Asia and began growing it in the Caribbean. To plant and harvest the sugarcane, they enslaved millions of Africans and moved them to the Americas.

Some Spanish settlers made large profits by exporting crops and raw materials back to Spain. In the West Indies, the main exports were tobacco and sugarcane. To raise these crops, the Spanish developed the plantation system. A plantation was a large estate.

C The Spanish used Native Americans to work their plantations. The Spanish priest **Bartolomé de Las Casas** (bahr•TOH•loh•may day lahs KAHS•ahs) suggested replacing them with enslaved Africans—a suggestion he bitterly regretted later. He thought the Africans could endure the labor better than the Native Americans.

By the mid-1500s, the Spanish were bringing thousands from West Africa to the Americas. The Portuguese did the same in Brazil. For enslaved Africans, the voyage to America usually began with a march to a European fort on the West African coast. Tied together with ropes around their necks and hands, they were traded to Europeans, branded, and forced to board a ship. An estimated 10 to 12 million Africans were forcibly transported to the Americas between 1450 and 1870.

The Africans who survived the brutal ocean voyage were sold to plantation owners. By the late 1500s, plantation slave labor was an essential part of the economy of the Spanish colonies.

Reading Check **Describe** How did the slave trade come into being?

History Online
Study Central Need help understanding the rise of modern capitalism? Visit ca.hss.glencoe.com and click on Study Central.

Section 2 Review

Reading Summary

Review the Main Ideas

- The introduction of banking and capitalism allowed countries to increase their wealth by financing trading ventures abroad.
- The growth of mercantilism and trade led to the creation of colonies.
- Trade between Europe and Asia and the Americas led to exchanges of people, ideas, and products.

What Did You Learn?

1. What was the Commercial Revolution?
2. What were some of the things Europeans introduced to Native Americans?

Critical Thinking

3. **Explaining** Draw a chart like the one below and explain how each economic concept or action increased the wealth of European nations. CA CS1.

	Effect on European Wealth
Mercantilism	
Joint-stock company	
Slave trade	

4. **The Big Ideas** Explain how exploration brought about great change in Europe and the Americas.
5. **Creative Writing** Imagine you are a member of a trading company on an expedition to the Americas. Describe the people and things you see when you arrive in the Americas. CA 8WA2.1
6. **Analysis** **Analyzing Economics** Write a brief essay about joint-stock companies. Include a definition and an example from the chapter, as well as a modern-day company. Discuss the strengths and weaknesses of this business model. CA HI6.

C Critical Thinking

Determining Cause and Effect **Ask:** What factors led to the use of millions of Africans as slaves in North America? *(desire of Europeans to grow large amounts of raw materials on plantations; deaths of millions of Native Americans from disease; Las Casas' suggestion that Africans could replace Native Americans to work on the plantations)* OL CA HI2.

ASSESS

Resources for page 97

Use these resources to assess student mastery of section content.

- Universal Access Activity 1
- Section Quiz 1–2
- Interactive Tutor Self-Assessment CD-ROM

Reading Check
Answer: Millions of Africans were enslaved in order to work on plantations in the Americas.

History Online
Study Central provides summaries, interactive games, and online graphic organizers to help students review section content.

CLOSE

Summarizing Why did European countries want colonies in the Americas? *(to obtain valuable resources or raw materials)* OL

SECTION 2 REVIEW ANSWERS

Review questions reinforce content standard WH7.11.

1. new business method that promoted trade
2. several grains, horses and chickens, languages, Christianity, deadly diseases
3. Answers should reflect an understanding of mercantilism, joint stock companies, and the slave trade.
4. **The Big Ideas** Europe: increased trade; colonies; new foods, animals, and customs; Americas: fall of Native American empires; new foods; diseases killed many people
5. Answers will vary.
6. **Analysis** The sale of shares enables investors to share profits and risks; Dutch East India Company and major corporations are examples.

FOCUS

BELLRINGER
Skillbuilder Activity

Project **Daily Focus Skills Transparency 1–3** and have students answer the question.

Guide to Reading

Preteaching Vocabulary: Have students look up the definition of each term in the Glossary before reading the section.

Answers to Graphic: Students' charts should highlight the different influences detailed in the section.

Unpacking the Standards

After reading the section, students will be able to:

- Describe the influence of Greece and Rome on later political thought.
- Explain Renaissance ideas on government and religion.
- Discuss the ideas of Enlightenment thinkers.

Section 3 The Enlightenment

History Social Science Standards

WH7.11 Students analyze political and economic change in the sixteenth, seventeenth, and eighteenth centuries (the Age of Exploration, the Enlightenment and the Age of Reason).

Guide to Reading

Looking Back, Looking Ahead

In Section 2, you learned how Europe gained wealth from overseas territories. In this section, you will learn how past civilizations contributed to our scientific, religious, and political thinking today.

Focusing on the Main Ideas

- Ancient cultures laid the foundation of many modern ideas. *(page 99)*
- Religious and philosophical thinkers changed the way people viewed Christianity and the government. *(page 102)*
- Science and the influence of reason led to new innovations in political thought. *(page 105)*

Meeting People

Thomas Aquinas (uh • KWY • nuhs)
Martin Luther
John Calvin
Thomas Hobbes (HAHBZ)
John Locke
Charles de Montesquieu (MAHN • tuhs • KYOO)

Locating Places

Greece
Rome

Content Vocabulary

rule of law
covenant (KUH • vuh • nuhnt)
theology (thee • AH • luh • jee)
Renaissance (REH • nuh • SAHNTS)
scientific method
philosophe (FEE • luh • ZAWF)

Academic Vocabulary

pursue (puhr • SOO)
document (DAH • kyuh • muhnt)
contract
major

Reading Strategy

Organizing Information Re-create the diagram below. List changes in politics, religion, and science mentioned in this section.

	Changes
Politics	
Religion	
Science	

NATIONAL GEOGRAPHIC Where & When?

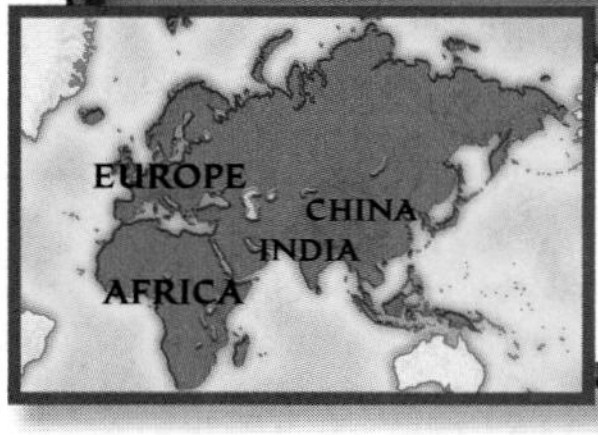

1200 — 1500 — 1800

- **1215** Magna Carta limits power of English king
- **1689** English Bill of Rights guarantees basic rights
- **1748** Montesquieu publishes *Spirit of Laws*

SECTION RESOURCES

Print Material
- Reproducible Lesson Plan 1–3*
- Daily Lesson and Discussion Notes 1–3
- Guided Reading Activity 1–3
- Reading Essentials and Study Guide 1–3
- Active Reading Note-Taking Guide 1–3
- Section Quiz 1–3

Transparencies
- Daily Focus Skills Transparency 1–3
- Section Graphic Organizer Transparency 1–3
- California Standards Practice Transparencies

Technology
- Interactive Tutor Self-Assessment CD-ROM
- Exam*View*® Pro Testmaker CD-ROM
- Presentation Plus! CD-ROM

*Available on TeacherWorks™

WH7.11.4 Explain how the main ideas of the Enlightenment can be traced back to such movements as the Renaissance, the Reformation, and the Scientific Revolution and to the Greeks, Romans, and Christianity.

Europe's Heritage of Ideas

R1 **Main Idea** **Ancient cultures laid the foundation of many modern ideas.**

Reading Connection Do you chew gum, use an alarm clock to get up for school, or carry an umbrella when it rains? All of these things were originally created by ancient peoples. Read on to see which ideas and inventions originated in ancient cultures.

A European Story

Anton van Leeuwenhoek (LAY • vuhn • hook), a Dutch merchant in the late 1600s, had an unusual hobby that unlocked the door to an unknown world. By carefully grinding very small lenses out of clear glass, van Leeuwenhoek discovered that he could make things look much bigger than they appeared to the naked eye. His most remarkable find was a multitude of tiny microorganisms, which he described as "wretched beasties" with "incredibly thin feet" swimming through a tiny universe.

Leeuwenhoek's microscope captured the imagination of Europeans in the 1600s. His invention was part of the rich heritage of ideas that shaped the course of European history since ancient times. These ideas eventually spread to North America, where they helped shape the English colonies that were arising along the Atlantic seaboard.

The Greeks and Romans The ancient Greeks developed philosophy, or "love of wisdom," because they believed the human mind could understand everything. Greek philosophy led to the study of history, mathematics, and political science. During the 400s B.C., the idea of democracy developed in Athens, one of **Greece's** powerful city-states. The Athenians had a direct democracy, in which people gathered at mass meetings to decide government matters. Every citizen could vote firsthand on laws and policies.

Rome was the next important ancient European civilization. Early Rome began as a republic, a form of government in which the citizens elect their leaders to office. In a republic, the citizens have power. The idea of a republic later shaped the founding of the U.S. government. Another of Rome's chief gifts was the idea of the **"rule of law."** This means that the law should apply to everyone equally and that all people should be treated the same. This understanding of justice is at the basis of the American legal system today.

Judaism and Christianity The Jews were a unique group among the peoples who made up Rome's empire. Most religions of the ancient world worshipped many gods, but the Jews gave their allegiance to one God. The Hebrew Bible describes a **covenant** (KUH • vuh • nuhnt), or agreement between the Jews and their God. R2 In the agreement, God promises to protect the Israelites if they follow his laws. The idea of a covenant, or binding agreement, later influenced the American colonists when they set up their societies in North America.

A major Jewish contribution to the West was the Ten Commandments. Jews believed that God revealed the Ten Commandments to a prophet called Moses. These moral principles found in the Hebrew Bible helped shape the moral laws of many nations.

The Torah, the first five books of the Hebrew Bible

TEACH

R1 Reading Strategy

Setting a Purpose Have students use the Main Idea to set themselves a purpose for reading the section. Suggest that they make a two-column chart with the headings *Culture* and *Contribution*. As they read, have them fill out the chart, being sure to include the impact of these contributions today. OL

Review Grade 6 Standards

To review standard **6.4.3**, *(State the key differences between Athenian, or direct, democracy and representative democracy.)*, **ask:** Who made decisions in ancient Athens? *(all citizens who took part)* Who made decisions in the Roman Republic? *(the members of the government elected by Roman citizens)* OL

R2 Reading Strategy

Understanding Vocabulary
Ask: What does it mean to say that a covenant is a "binding agreement"? *(Students may say that the parties to the agreement are required to do what they promised.)* OL

Did You Know?

Romans helped shape the calendar used by much of the world today. August was named for the Roman emperor Augustus Caesar. In voting to name the month for him, the Roman Senate borrowed a day from February, reducing it to 28 days, so that his month would have at least as many days as July, named for Augustus' great-uncle, Julius Caesar.

More About the Art

The six-pointed star, known as the Star of David and depicted twice on the Torah mantle pictured above, was rarely used as a Jewish symbol until the nineteenth century. Today it is widely accepted and appears on the Israeli flag.

S1 Skill Practice

Historical and Social Sciences Analysis Skill
Ask: What do A.D. and B.C. mean when they appear adjacent to dates? *(The time before and after Jesus was born: A.D. comes from the Latin* anno Domini, *meaning "in the year of our Lord"; B.C. stands for "before Christ.")* OL

R Reading Strategy

Using Word Parts Ask: What is the origin of the term *Christianity*? *(It is named for its founder, Jesus Christ.)* EL

S2 Skill Practice

Historical and Social Sciences Analysis Skill
Ask: What are the possible benefits and drawbacks of living in a nation with an official religion? *(possible benefit: government supports religious institutions; possible drawbacks: limited range of views, persecution of those who do not follow the official religion)* OL CA HI1.

Resources for page 100

Geography and History Activity 1

Answers and Additional Support

The Ten Commandments told people not to steal, murder, or tell lies about others. They told people to avoid jealousy and to honor their parents. Like the Roman laws, the Ten Commandments reflect the idea of the "rule of law," that laws should apply to everyone equally.

S1 About the A.D. 30s, a Jewish teacher named Jesus of Nazareth preached to Jews living in the Roman provinces of Judaea and Galilee. His message of love and forgiveness helped shape the values many people hold today. Reports of Jesus' resurrection, or rising from the dead, led R to a new religion called Christianity.

Christianity soon spread to the European part of the Roman Empire. By A.D. 400, S2 Christianity had become Rome's official religion. After the Roman government fell apart, Christianity survived to shape the civilization of the Middle Ages, the period between Rome's fall and the 1500s.

Advance of Learning While Christianity expanded in Europe, the religion of Islam began in the Arabian Peninsula with the preaching of Muhammad. Islam spread throughout the Middle East, North Africa, and Central Asia. Like Jews and Christians, Muslims—the followers of Islam—believe in one God.

During the Middle Ages, Muslim and Jewish scholars in Islamic lands made significant contributions to the culture of Europe. They saved much of the learning of the ancient world. Europeans in the West had lost this knowledge after the western Roman Empire fell.

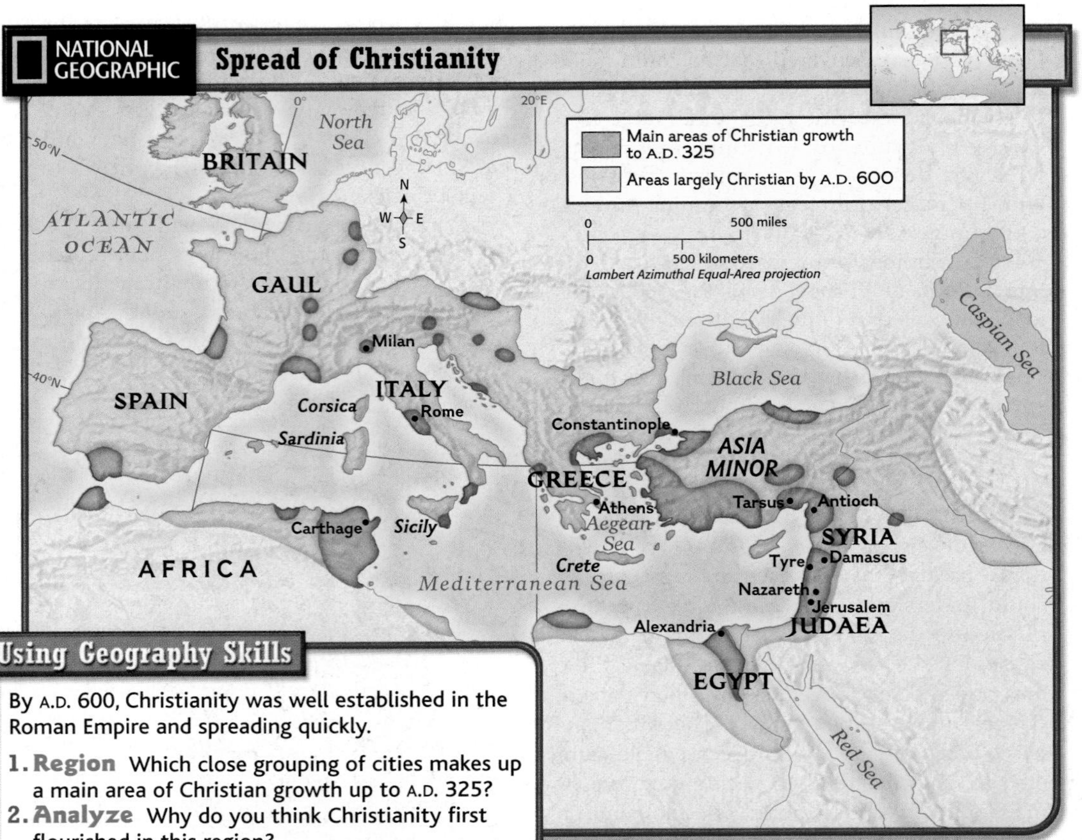

Using Geography Skills

By A.D. 600, Christianity was well established in the Roman Empire and spreading quickly.

1. **Region** Which close grouping of cities makes up a main area of Christian growth up to A.D. 325?
2. **Analyze** Why do you think Christianity first flourished in this region?

100

More Skill Practice

Historical and Social Sciences Analysis Skill Ask: Of the contributions to mankind discussed in this section, which do you consider the most important and long-lasting? Why? Present your answer in a brief essay. *(Answers will vary but should be supported by evidence.)* OL CA HI1.

Using Geography Skills

Answers:

1. Jerusalem, Nazareth, Tyre, Damascus
2. because Jesus was from that area

Picturing History

Muslim doctors' discoveries helped develop European medicine. ***How did Muslim scholars contribute to the culture of Europe?***

Islamic Influence The Muslims also made many advances in the study of mathematics and medicine, and they introduced the system of Arabic numerals that we use today.

Islamic influences were part of a new wave of learning that shaped Europe during the Middle Ages. Another influence came from universities, which first arose in Europe during the 1100s and 1200s. Universities were self-governing groups of scholars who, in turn, educated and trained new scholars. Because universities enjoyed independence from political and church officials, they could freely investigate knowledge in a wide range of fields, such as theology, law, and medicine.

The first European university appeared in Bologna (boh • LOH • nyah), Italy. A great teacher named Inerius, who taught Roman law, attracted students to Bologna from all over Europe. The first university in northern Europe was the University of Paris. In the late 1100s, a number of students and teachers left Paris and started a university at Oxford, England. Kings, popes, and princes thought it honorable to found new universities. By 1500, there were 80 universities in Europe.

Development of Scholasticism Beginning in the 1100s, a new way of thinking called scholasticism began to change **theology** (thee • AH • luh • jee), or the study of religion and God. Its followers used reason to explore questions of faith.

A Catholic priest named **Thomas Aquinas** (uh • KWY • nuhs) was scholasticism's best-known champion. In the 1200s, Aquinas wrote several works explaining that the Greek philosopher Aristotle would have agreed with many Christian teachings.

What Is Natural Law? Aquinas wrote about government as well as theology, with an emphasis on the idea of natural law. People who believe in natural law think there are some laws that are simply part of human nature. These laws do not have to be made by governments.

Aquinas claimed that natural law gave people certain rights that the government should not take away. These included the right to live, to learn, to worship, and to reproduce. Aquinas's writings on natural law have influenced governments to the present day. Our belief that people have rights can partly be traced to the ideas of Aquinas.

The Latin Language Roman writers influenced later writers in Europe and America, but the language of the Romans, Latin, had a great impact on future generations. Latin became Europe's language for government, trade, and learning until about 1500. Latin became the basis of many modern European languages, including Italian, French, and Spanish.

Reading Check **Describe** What was the importance of the Ten Commandments?

C Critical Thinking

Identifying Central Issues
Ask: How did freedom from political or religious officials affect teachers and students in the universities of the Middle Ages? *(They were able to investigate issues freely, without interference.)* OL

R Reading Strategy

Understanding Vocabulary
Explain that *–ology* comes from a Greek word meaning "study of." **Ask:** What other words can you think of with this ending? *(Answers may include biology, geology.)* OL

S Skill Practice

Historical and Social Sciences Analysis Skill
Ask: What did Aquinas mean when he spoke of "natural law"? What are some examples of natural laws? *("Natural law" refers to laws that are not granted by governments, but are an essential part of human nature, such as the right to live and learn.)* OL CA HI1.

Reading Check

Answer: They helped shape the moral laws of many nations.

Picturing History

Much learning came into Western Europe as a result of the recapture of Spain from Muslim hands by Christian kings. An intellectual prize that fell into Christian hands as a result was the library in Toledo, which held the works of Plato, Aristotle, Galen, Hippocrates, Ptolemy, and Euclid. Soon after Christians took the city, scholars began translating these works from Arabic into Latin and spreading them across Europe.

Answer: by saving much of the learning of the ancient world; by making advances in medicine and mathematics, including the system of Arabic numerals

C1 Critical Thinking

Making Inferences **Ask:** What role did economics play in launching the Renaissance? *(Wealthy individuals had the time and money to pursue an interest in classical civilization.)* OL

R1 Reading Strategy

Using Context Clues **Ask:** What are the two "classical civilizations" of Western society? *(ancient Greece and Rome)* BL CA 8RW1.3

R2 Reading Strategy

Understanding Vocabulary **Ask:** During the Renaissance, there was a rebirth of interest in what? *(ideas and learning from ancient Greece and Rome)* OL

C2 Critical Thinking

Comparing and Contrasting **Ask:** How would you compare and contrast the life and work of Luther and Calvin? *(Both led protests against the Catholic Church; both started new forms of Christianity, known as Protestantism; Luther was based in Germany while Calvin was based in France.)* OL

Answers and Additional Support

WH7.11.5 Describe how democratic thought and institutions were influenced by Enlightenment thinkers (e.g., John Locke, Charles-Louis Montesquieu, American founders).

New Ideas

Main Idea **Religious and philosophical thinkers changed the way people viewed Christianity and the government.**

Reading Connection Does your family or someone you know attend a church or other place of worship? Read on to find out how religious sects formed in Christianity.

From the 1400s to the 1700s, Europeans gained new knowledge, explored lands overseas, and spread Christianity. Meanwhile, cultural, religious, and political changes took place in their homeland that would have profound effects on the rest of the world.

The Renaissance From about 1350 to 1550, a powerful new spirit emerged in the city-states of Italy and spread throughout Europe. The development of banking and the expansion of trade with Asia made Italian merchants wealthy. These citizens were able to **pursue** an interest in the region's past and learn more about the glorious civilizations of ancient Rome and Greece. C1

Because they wanted to improve their knowledge of people and the world, Italians studied the classical—ancient Greek and Roman—works with new interest. R1 Scholars translated Greek manuscripts on philosophy, poetry, and science. Influenced by the classical texts, a great many authors began to write about the individual and the universe. Artists studied the sculpture and architecture of the classical world. They especially admired the harmony and balance in Greek art, with its realistic way of portraying people.

This period of intellectual and artistic creativity became known as the **Renaissance** (REH • nuh • SAHNTS). A French word meaning "rebirth," it refers to the renewed interest in classical Greek and Roman learning. R2 Over the next two centuries, the Renaissance spread north, south, and west, reaching Spain and northern Europe in the 1400s.

The Rise of Protestantism Protests against church abuses soon led to a split in western Christianity. In 1517 a German monk named **Martin Luther** criticized the authority of the pope, the leader of the Roman Catholic Church, and many Catholic teachings and practices. Within a few years, Luther had many followers. They broke away from Catholicism to begin their own Christian churches. Martin Luther's protests were the start of a new form of Christianity known as Protestantism.

During the next few years, Luther's religious movement grew. C2 Luther was able to gain the support of many of the German rulers among the numerous states that made up the Holy Roman Empire.

From Germany, Luther's ideas spread rapidly. **John Calvin,** a French religious thinker, also broke away from the Catholic Church. Like Luther, Calvin rejected the idea that good works would ensure a person's salvation. He believed that God had already chosen those who would be saved.

Picturing History

Martin Luther and his followers broke away from Catholicism to begin their own Christian churches. ***What new form of Christianity did Luther and his followers start?***

Picturing History

It has long been accepted as true that Martin Luther first challenged the Roman Catholic Church when he nailed papers containing 95 theses, or statements of issues regarding Church doctrine and practice, to the door of a church in Wittenberg, Germany. In recent years, historians have questioned this idea. They note that the story of the theses did not first appear until 30 years after the event, and Luther himself never said that he had put the papers on a church door.

Answer: Protestantism

To prove they were saved, Calvin's followers worked hard, behaved well, and obeyed the laws of their towns. In this way, Calvin's ideas, which became known as Calvinism, became a powerful tool in society. His ideas encouraged people to work hard at their business and to behave themselves.

Who Were the Puritans? King Henry VIII replaced the pope as head of the Church in England in 1534. His daughter, Queen Elizabeth I, later made this English, or Anglican, Church Protestant with some Catholic features. Some English Protestants, however, were dissatisfied with Elizabeth's reforms. Known as Puritans, they wanted to "purify" the Anglican Church of its remaining Catholic beliefs and rituals.

Queen Elizabeth I tolerated the Puritans, but when James I became king in 1603, the Puritans faced harder times. James I and the king who came after him, Charles I, persecuted the Puritans. They shut down Puritan churches and jailed Puritan leaders. Many Puritans decided to move to America to practice their religion freely. There they founded colonies that eventually became the American states of Massachusetts, Connecticut, New Hampshire, and Rhode Island. **S**

Royal Power and Citizens' Rights During the 1600s and 1700s, powerful kings and queens ruled most of Europe. Under a system known as absolutism, monarchs held absolute, or total, power. They claimed to rule by divine right, or by the will of God. This meant that rulers did not answer to their people but to God alone.

During the late 1600s, however, political changes began that steadily limited the power of monarchs. In 1688 the English Parliament took action. It forced out King James and placed his daughter Mary and her husband William on the throne. This change, which showed the power of the elected representatives over the monarch, came to be known as the Glorious Revolution.

William and Mary signed an English Bill of Rights in 1689 guaranteeing certain basic rights to all citizens. This **document** became part of the heritage of English law that the American colonists would share. It later inspired the American political leaders who created the American Bill of Rights.

Hobbes and Locke During the 1600s, these political changes sparked a great deal of thought and debate about the purpose of government. Two major English thinkers—**Thomas Hobbes** (HAHBZ) and **John Locke**—developed very different ideas about how England's government should work.

In his book, *Leviathan,* Hobbes argued that absolute monarchy was the best form of government. According to Hobbes, humans were naturally selfish and violent. They could not be trusted to make decisions on their own. Left to themselves, people would make life "nasty, brutish, and short." Therefore, Hobbes said, they needed to obey a government that had the power of a leviathan, or sea monster. To Hobbes, that meant the rule of a king, because only a strong ruler could give people direction. **W**

Another English thinker, John Locke, thought differently. He affirmed citizens' rights and stated that government was answerable to the people. In 1690 he explained many of the ideas of the Glorious Revolution in a book called *Two Treatises of Civil Government.* Locke stated that government should be based on natural law. This law, said Locke, gave all people from their birth certain natural rights. Among them were the right to life, the right to liberty, and the right to own property.

Locke believed that the purpose of government was to protect these rights. **R1** All governments, he said, were based on a social **contract,** **R2** or an agreement between rulers and the people. If a ruler took away people's natural rights, the people had a right to revolt and set up a new government.

Reading Check **Explain** How did religious changes affect the governments of Europe?

S Skill Practice

Historical and Social Sciences Analysis Skill
Ask: Why did the Puritans decide to move to America? *(They wanted to escape persecution in England and practice their religion freely.)* OL CA HI3.

W Writing Support

Expository Writing Have students summarize the views of Hobbes and Locke and explain how they differed in their view of the best form of government. AL CA 8WA2.4

R1 Reading Strategy

Connecting Explain that students can better understand the material by linking the ideas of the thinkers covered in this section. **Ask:** What earlier thinker wrote, like Locke, about people's natural rights? *(Aquinas)* Would Locke have agreed with the monarchs who claimed a divine right to rule? Why or why not? *(No; he thought people had the right to revolt against rulers, whose claims to divine right would not have been allowed.)* OL

R2 Reading Strategy

Academic Vocabulary Discuss with students what they know about contracts. Ask them to describe the various kinds of contracts and what they might be used for. OL

Reading Check

Answer: Some countries adopted Protestantism; kings and queens had less power.

More Skill Practice

Historical and Social Sciences Analysis Skill Have students make a graphic organizer that incorporates the information on this page and shows the chronological order in which these events occurred. BL CA CS2.

Did You Know?

By the mid-sixteenth century, Calvinism had replaced Lutheranism as the most important and dynamic form of Protestantism. Calvinism reformed the city of Geneva and Calvinist churches later arose in France, the Netherlands, Scotland, and central and eastern Europe.

Biography

TEACH

C1 Critical Thinking

Identifying Central Issues Ask students to find a sentence that states the central idea of Locke's philosophy of government as they read this biography. *(paragraph 5, sentence 1)* OL

S Skill Practice

Historical and Social Sciences Skill Ask: What did Locke mean by "social contract"? *(an agreement between rulers and the people)* In what ways does our contemporary system of government rely on a social contract? *(American citizens agree to abide by laws and pay taxes; in exchange, the government provides services and protects the people's liberty.)* OL CA HI3.

C2 Critical Thinking

Making Inferences Ask: What do you think Locke meant by this statement? *(that the consent of citizens leads to a peaceful government)* What do you think Locke would say about rule by dictators who seize power? *(Those governments were not properly formed.)* OL CA HI1.

Answers and Additional Support

Biography

WH7.11.5 Describe how democratic thought and institutions were influenced by Enlightenment thinkers (e.g., John Locke, Charles-Louis Montesquieu, American founders).

JOHN LOCKE C1

1632–1704

Born in England, John Locke was a doctor, a philosopher, and a writer. Locke spelled out his political ideas in *Two Treatises of Civil Government,* first published in 1690.

Locke's writings were widely read and discussed in both Europe and America. His ideas deeply influenced the American colonists. Colonial leaders such as Benjamin Franklin, Thomas Jefferson, and James Madison read Locke's writings and discussed his ideas.

Locke and many Enlightenment thinkers believed that God had created an orderly universe governed by established laws. These laws were called natural laws and could be discovered by human reason. By using reason, for example, Sir Isaac Newton, the English physicist, discovered the law of gravity. Natural laws governed not only the physical universe, but also human relations.

The idea that human relations are governed by a set of established laws laid the foundation for the philosophy of natural rights. Locke believed that people in a "state of nature," or a time before the organization of government, had certain basic rights. These included rights to life, liberty, and property.

According to Locke, good government is based on a S social contract between the people and the rulers. The people agree to give up some of their freedom and abide by the decisions of their government. In return, the government promises to protect the lives, property, and liberty of the people.

The American colonists accepted Locke's idea that government was legitimate only as long as people continued to consent to it. Both the Declaration of Independence and the Constitution, written nearly a century after Locke lived, reflect Locke's revolutionary ideas.

"All peaceful beginnings of government have been laid in the consent of the people." C2

—John Locke, *Second Treatise of Civil Government*

Then and Now

Compare the political thought of John Locke to the American form of government. What would Locke support? What would he not support?

104

Then and Now

Locke believed that humans had certain natural rights to life, liberty, and property. This belief is reflected in our belief in the "unalienable rights" to "life, liberty, and the pursuit of happiness." He believed that the government had a duty to protect the rights of the people and, when it fails, that the people have a right to form a new government. This is similar to what happened when the American colonists declared independence from Britain. Locke would probably approve of the American system of government.

WH7.11.5 Describe how democratic thought and institutions were influenced by Enlightenment thinkers (e.g., John Locke, Charles-Louis Montesquieu, American founders). WH7.11.6 Discuss how the principles in the Magna Carta were embodied in such documents as the English Bill of Rights and the American Declaration of Independence.

A New View of the World

Main Idea **Science and the influence of reason led to new innovations in political thought.**

Reading Connection Does your school have a student council? This is usually a group of students who lobby the administration on behalf of the student body. Read on to find out how citizens' rights played a role in governmental reform.

While religious and political changes came to Europe, many European thinkers began to take a more experimental approach to science. They tested new and old theories and evaluated the results. They also began applying reason and scientific ideas to government. They claimed that there was a natural law, or a law that applied to everyone and could be understood by reason. This law was the key to understanding government. R1

Triumph of Reason During the 1500s, European thinkers began to break with old scientific ideas. They increasingly understood that advances in science could come only through mathematics and experimentation. Scientists, such as Nicolaus Copernicus and Galileo Galilei, disagreed with the ancient view that the earth was the center of the universe. Instead, they held to the idea that the sun was the center of the universe and that the planets moved in orbits around the sun.

Sir Isaac Newton further claimed that the physical universe followed natural laws. He believed that the force of gravity held the entire solar system together by keeping the sun and the planets in their orbits.

The Scientific Method Scientific thought was also influenced by the English thinker Francis Bacon, who lived from 1561 to 1626. Bacon believed that ideas based on tradition should be put aside. He developed the **scientific method,** an orderly way of collecting and analyzing evidence. It is still the process used in scientific research today. R2

The scientific method is made up of several steps. First, a scientist begins with careful observation of facts and then tries to find a hypothesis, or explanation of the facts. Through experiments, the scientist tests the hypothesis under all possible conditions to see if it is true. Finally, after repeated experiments show that the hypothesis is true, then it is considered a scientific law.

Enlightenment Thinkers As the Scientific Revolution advanced, many educated Europeans came to believe that reason was a much better guide than faith or tradition. To them, reason was a light that revealed error and showed the way to truth. As a result, the 1700s became known as the Age of Enlightenment.

France was the **major** center of the Enlightenment. As the Enlightenment spread, thinkers in France and elsewhere became known by the French word **philosophe** (FEE • luh • ZAWF), which means "philosopher." Most philosophes were writers, teachers, journalists, and observers of society. R3

The philosophes wanted to use reason to change society. They attacked superstition, or unreasoned beliefs. They also disagreed with Church leaders who opposed new scientific discoveries. The philosophes believed in the individual's right to liberty. They used their skills as writers to spread their ideas across Europe.

Who Were Voltaire and Diderot? One of the greatest thinkers of the Enlightenment was François-Marie Arouet, known as Voltaire (vohl • TAR). Voltaire blamed Catholic Church leaders for keeping knowledge from people in order to maintain the Church's power. Voltaire also opposed the government supporting one religion while forbidding others. He thought people should be free to choose their own beliefs.

Denis Diderot was the French philosophe who did the most to spread Enlightenment ideas. He published a 28-volume encyclopedia. His project, which began in the 1750s, took about 20 years to complete.

R1 Reading Strategy

Activating Prior Knowledge **Ask:** What philosopher promoted the theory that natural law should be applied to government? *(John Locke)* OL

R2 Reading Strategy

Understanding Vocabulary **Ask:** Based on experiments you have conducted in science classes, how would you describe the steps in the scientific method? *(Observation is followed by formation of a hypothesis; the scientist then tests this hypothesis through an experiment. If the hypothesis turns out to be true, it becomes a scientific law.)* OL

R3 Reading Strategy

Understanding Vocabulary Direct students' attention to the pronunciation of this term and point out that the final *e* is silent. OL

Review The Big Idea

Review the Big Idea for this section: "World history has been shaped by significant individuals, groups, ideas, events, eras, and developments." **Ask:** What is the important idea that distinguishes the Enlightenment from earlier eras? *(the belief that reason, not tradition or faith, should be the basis for making decisions about society and government)* OL

Did You Know?

To many thinkers who came after Isaac Newton, the physical world and everything in it was like a giant machine—the Newtonian world-machine. These thinkers reasoned that if Newton could discover the natural laws that governed the physical world, they—by using his methods—could discover the natural laws that governed human society.

W Writing Support

Research Reports Writing Have students do research to learn more about the history and impact of the Magna Carta and the English Bill of Rights. Tell them to frame three questions about the document based on what they read here, such as "Why was it created?" and "Did it solve the intended problem?" Then have them carry out their research and write up their findings. OL CA 8WA2.3 CA HR1.

S Skill Practice

Visual Literacy Tell students that King John signed the Magna Carta in 1215. **Ask:** Based on the illustration, do you think the king signed the document willingly? Why or why not? *(no; he looks unhappy)* OL

C Critical Thinking

Making Inferences **Ask:** How would Locke respond to Rousseau's criticisms of Enlightenment ideas? *(Locke would probably say that reliance on reason is an essential part of government and society.)* OL

Answers and Additional Support

Primary Sources

Guarantees of Rights

The Magna Carta and the English Bill of Rights are two important documents that were integral in forming American political thought. Each contributed an essential building block for the American political principles found in the Declaration of Independence, the Bill of Rights, and the Constitution.

The rights of English citizens, referred to in the Magna Carta, is an important principle of American government. This excerpt from the Magna Carta describes the right to a trial by jury:

> "No free man shall be taken, imprisoned, [seized], outlawed, banished, or in any way destroyed, . . . except by the lawful judgment of his peers and by the law of the land."

The English Bill of Rights assured the people of certain basic rights. Among these are:

> "That the freedom of speech and debates or proceedings in Parliament ought not to be impeached or questioned in any court or place out of Parliament."

The founding documents of our nation express these freedoms and the principle of limited government—a government on which strict limits are placed, usually by a constitution.

King John signs the Magna Carta. ▶

DBQ Document-Based Question

The idea of limited government is an important principle of American government. Why must government be limited?

The *Encyclopedia* included a wide range of topics, such as science, religion, government, and the arts. It became an important weapon in the philosophes' fight against traditional ways.

Who Was Montesquieu? In 1748 Baron **Charles de Montesquieu** (MAHN • tuhs • KYOO) published a book called *Spirit of Laws.* In this book, Montesquieu said that England's government was the best because it had a separation of powers. Separation of powers means that power should be divided equally among the branches of government: executive, legislative, and judicial.

The legislative branch would make the laws, and the executive branch would enforce them. The judicial branch would interpret the laws and judge when they were broken. By separating these powers, government could not become too powerful and threaten people's rights.

Who Was Rousseau? By the late 1700s, some European thinkers were starting to criticize Enlightenment ideas. One of these thinkers was Jean-Jacques Rousseau (zhahn zhak ru • SOH). Rousseau claimed that supporters of the Enlightenment relied too much on reason. Instead, people should pay more attention to their feelings.

What Is a Social Contract? According to Rousseau, human beings were naturally good, but civilized life corrupted them. He thought people could improve themselves by living simpler lives closer to nature. In 1762 Rousseau published a book called *The Social Contract.* In this work, Rousseau wrote that a workable government should be based on a social contract. This is an agreement in which everyone in a society agrees to be governed by the general will, or what the people as a whole want.

Primary Sources

Answer: to preserve the freedoms of citizens

- Is a jury trial preferable to a trial by a judge? Why or why not? *(A single judge could be prejudiced in a case or persuaded by outside influences but a jury can stand together.)* OL
- Name a right established by the English Bill of Rights. *(freedom of speech)* BL
- What American documents were influenced by the Magna Carta and English Bill of Rights? *(Declaration of Independence, Constitution, Bill of Rights)* OL

The Magna Carta In the 1600s and 1700s, ideas of political change spread back and forth across the Atlantic Ocean. The pattern started with the arrival of the first English colonists in North America. They carried with them ideas born of the political struggles in England. By the time the first colonists reached North America, the idea of limited government had become an acceptable part of the English system. The Magna Carta of 1215 had limited royal power and protected nobles from unlawful loss of life, liberty, and property. During the next few centuries, these rights were extended to more and more English people.

The English Bill of Rights In 1689 the English Bill of Rights stated that the monarch could not tax people without Parliament's consent. People had a right to a fair and speedy trial by a jury of their peers. People could also petition the king without fear of being punished. The English colonists in North America shared a belief in these rights with the people of England.

Representative Government From England the American colonists also brought the idea of representative government in which people elect delegates to make laws and conduct government affairs for them. Parliament was a representative assembly that had made laws for England since the mid-1200s. In America colonial legislatures grew directly out of this practice of having representatives pass laws.

For political ideas, the colonists also looked to thinkers of the Enlightenment. John Locke's ideas seemed to fit the colonial experience. Although most had probably never heard of Locke himself, the ideas of natural rights and government responsible to the people became the basis of protest and revolt in the colonies. Colonial leaders, such as Benjamin Franklin, Thomas Jefferson, and James Madison, regarded these ideas as political truths. Locke's ideas became so influential that they have been called the "textbook of the American Revolution." **S**

✓ Reading Check **Summarize** What were the ideas of Charles de Montesquieu?

History Online
Study Central Need help understanding the Enlightenment? Visit ca.hss.glencoe.com and click on Study Central.

Section 3 Review

Reading Summary

Review the Main Ideas

- Rome and Greece became the basis for much political and scientific thought.
- The Renaissance brought about religious and political changes that sought to increase the rights of human beings.
- Political thinkers argued that citizens had religious, political, and social rights.

What Did You Learn?

1. What was the purpose of the English Parliament?
2. What is the Scientific Method?

Critical Thinking

3. **Contrast** How did the ideas of Hobbes and Locke differ? CA HR3.
4. **Identifying** Who were three of the Enlightenment thinkers?

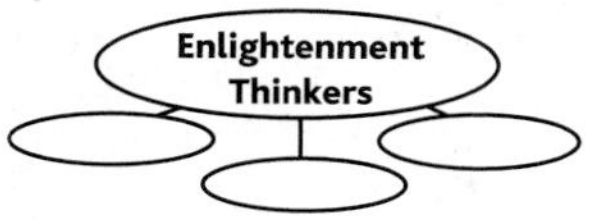

5. **The Big Ideas** How did political, technological, and religious changes affect the formation of the American government? Write a paragraph describing your conclusions. CA HI2.
6. **Persuasive Writing** Imagine you are an English noble in favor of the Magna Carta. Write a letter to the king explaining why he should sign the document. CA 8WA2.4

S Skill Practice

Historical and Social Sciences Analysis Skill
Ask: What does it mean to say that Locke's ideas were the "textbook of the American revolution"? What does this suggest about Locke's impact on America? *(Locke's ideas gave Americans strong ammunition to declare their independence from Britain. He had an enormous impact in the U.S.)* OL CA HI3.

ASSESS

Resources for page 107

Use these resources to assess student mastery of section content.

- Section Quiz 1–3
- Interactive Tutor Self-Assessment CD-ROM

✓ Reading Check

Answer: Citizens' rights are best protected when government powers were separated among the executive, legislative, and judicial branches.

History Online

Study Central provides summaries, interactive games, and online graphic organizers to help students review section content.

CLOSE

Drawing Conclusions
Ask students to imagine how they might have felt in the 1700s when faced with new Enlightenment ideas. Discuss students' responses. OL

SECTION 3 REVIEW ANSWERS

Review questions reinforce content standards WH7.11.

1. to make laws
2. a systemic way of gathering and analyzing evidence and reaching conclusions
3. Hobbes—absolute monarchy; Locke—government based on a social contract
4. Locke, Montesquieu, Rousseau
5. **The Big Ideas** Scientific Revolution promoted reason, which was applied to political ideas; Magna Carta, English Bill of Rights, and Enlightenment addressed people's rights. American colonists brought ideas of representative government, separation of powers, and religious freedom.
6. Students may say the document will protect people's rights.

Analyzing Primary Sources

FOCUS

History–Social Science Standards

The following standard is covered on pages 108–109:

US7.11 Students analyze political and economic change in the sixteenth, seventeenth, and eighteenth centuries (the Age of Exploration, the Enlightenment, and the Age of Reason).

TEACH

W Writing Support

Research Reports Writing Columbus—and other European explorers—brought some Native Americans to Europe on their return voyages. Have students conduct research to learn what happened to these people. OL CA 8WA2.3

R Reading Strategy

Making Inferences Ask: Why would Columbus bother noting all these details about the people he met? *(Europeans had never been in contact with the people before, so everything he could learn about them would be useful.)* OL CA HI2.

Answers and Additional Support

Analyzing Primary Sources

WH7.11.1 Know the great voyages of discovery, the locations of the routes, and the influence of cartography in the development of a new European worldview.

Cultures in Contact

Before the 1400s, Native Americans had little contact with people from other continents. Improved methods of sea travel and the desire for goods led to the growth of overseas trade in the 1400s and 1500s. During this time, people from Europe came into direct contact with people from the Americas.

Read the passages on pages 108 and 109 and answer the questions that follow.

Columbus lands on San Salvador in October 1492. ▶

Reader's Dictionary

reeds: tall grasses with slim stems that grow in wet areas

bear arms: carry or possess weapons

hawks' bells: small, lightweight bells attached to a trained hawk to help an owner find a lost bird

causeway: a raised road across wet ground or water

Mexico: Tenochtitlán

cues (KYOOS)**:** temples

vein (VAYN)**:** way of thinking

Columbus Crosses the Atlantic

Christopher Columbus left Spain in August 1492 with about 90 sailors on three ships. On October 11 he wrote this in his log:

The crew of the *Pinta* spotted some . . . **reeds** and some other plants; they also saw what looked like a small board or plank. A stick was recovered that looks manmade, perhaps carved with an iron tool . . . but even these few [things] made the crew breathe easier; in fact, the men have even become cheerful.

Other entries in Columbus's log describe the islanders that he met.

They are [a] friendly and well-dispositioned people who **[bear]** no **arms** except for small spears, and they have no iron. I showed one my sword, and through ignorance he grabbed it by the blade and cut himself. . . .

They traded and gave everything they had with good will, but it seems to me that they have very little. . . .

[They] came swimming to our ships and in boats made from one log. They brought us parrots, balls of cotton thread, spears, and many other things, . . . For these items we swapped them little glass beads and **hawks' bells.**

—from *The Log of Christopher Columbus*

More Skill Practice

Analyzing Primary Sources Ask: Why did seeing a board and a carved stick make the crew on Columbus's ship more cheerful? *(They were signs that they were nearing land inhabited by people.)* OL CA HR4.

Cortés Encounters the Aztec

The soldier and writer Bernal Díaz de Castillo was part of Hernán Cortés's army. These Spaniards fought their way across the Aztec empire to the capital at Tenochtitlán. Castillo wrote the following about what he saw:

C And when we saw all those cities and villages built in the water, and other great towns on dry land, and that straight and level **causeway** leading to **Mexico,** we were astounded. These great towns and **cues** and buildings rising from the water, all made of stone, seemed like an enchanted vision. . . . Indeed, some of our soldiers asked whether it was not all a dream. It is not surprising therefore that I should write in this **vein.** It was all so wonderful that I do not know how to describe this first glimpse of things never heard of, seen or dreamed of before. . . .

[In the marketplace], we were astounded at the great number of people and the quantities of merchandise, and at the orderliness and good arrangements that prevailed, for we had never seen such a thing before. . . .

[In the market] they have a building there also in which three judges sit, and there are officials like constables who examine the merchandise. . . .

—from *The Conquest of New Spain*

S

▲ **Montezuma and Cortés meet after Cortés entered Tenochtitlán.**

DBQ Document-Based Questions

Columbus Crosses the Atlantic

1. What item did the crew take from the sea and examine?
2. How did Columbus's crew react when they saw the objects in the sea?
3. According to Columbus, why did the islander cut himself on the sword?
4. What items did Columbus and his crew exchange with the islanders?

Cortés Encounters the Aztec

5. What surprised Castillo and Cortés's army about the land of the Aztec?
6. Why did some soldiers compare what they saw with a dream?

Read to Write

7. Imagine you are one of the Native Americans who has just met Columbus or Cortés. What do you notice about him? What do you think of him? How do you feel about this meeting? Write a journal entry describing what you observed and how you reacted to this encounter. CA 8WA2.1

DBQ Document-Based Questions

1. a stick that may have been man-made
2. They were relieved and even became cheerful.
3. He was not familiar with swords and did not know that the blade was sharp.
4. The islanders provided parrots, balls of thread, spears, and other objects; the Spaniards traded glass beads and hawks' bells.
5. the great towns and cities all made of stone
6. because the sights were so spectacular
7. Students' responses should reflect the probable surprise that Native Americans felt at the appearance and behavior of the Spaniards.

C Critical Thinking

Comparing and Contrasting **Ask:** How does the account of Tenochtitlán by Díaz de Castillo contrast with the impressions that Columbus had of the Native Americans he met? How does that contrast explain the Spaniard's reaction to the city? *(The city is much more organized and sophisticated than the lives of the Native Americans Columbus met. If the Spaniards thought of the islanders as being typical Native Americans, their shock at the city is not surprising.)* OL CA HR4.

S Skill Practice

Visual Literacy Have students discuss the impressions they get of Montezuma and Cortés from this illustration. OL

ASSESS

Have students answer the Document-Based Questions.

CLOSE

Comparing and Contrasting Have students contrast the factors that led Europeans to explore with what drove them to place colonies in the Americas. OL

Chapter 1 Assessment

Resources for pages 110–111

Use these resources to review, assess, or reteach the chapter.

- Active Reading Note-Taking Guide, Chapter 1
- Chapter 1 Reading Essentials and Study Guide
- Chapter 1 Tests, Forms A and B
- Standards Assessment, Forms A and B
- California Standards Practice Workbook
- Succeeding on the California History–Social Science Standards CD-ROM
- MindJogger Videoquiz
- Interactive Tutor Self-Assessment CD-ROM

Chapter 1 Assessment

Standard WH7.11

Review Content Vocabulary

Write the vocabulary word that completes each sentence. Write a sentence for each word not used.

a. technology
b. Renaissance
c. Northwest Passage
d. entrepreneur
e. rule of law
f. mercantilism

1. The ___ states that all people are equal under the law and should be treated as such.
2. England, France, and the Netherlands hoped to find a ___ to Asia.
3. During the ___, many political and religious changes took place.
4. The theory of ___ stated that a country could become prosperous by mining silver and gold found in other countries.

Review the Main Ideas

Section 1 • Age of Exploration

5. What led to the European era of exploration?
6. What were English, French, and Dutch explorers searching for while charting the coast of North America?

Section 2 • Rise of Modern Capitalism

7. What made trading ventures in different countries so difficult?
8. What were the benefits of establishing overseas colonies?

Section 3 • The Enlightenment

9. What is the rule of law?
10. How did John Calvin contribute to religious changes in Europe?
11. What did Copernicus and Galileo believe about the universe?

Critical Thinking

12. **Describe** What was the Columbian Exchange? How did it change Europe and the Americas? CA CS1.
13. **Cause and Effect** Re-create the diagram below. Identify three reasons for the voyages of exploration and three effects that resulted from the exploration. CA HI2.

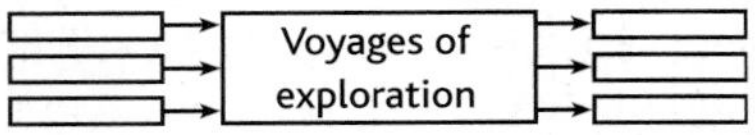

14. **Contrast** How did Judaism differ from most other religions during the Roman era? CA HI2.

Geography Skills

Study the map below and answer the questions that follow. CA CS3.

NATIONAL GEOGRAPHIC **The Taino, About 1492**

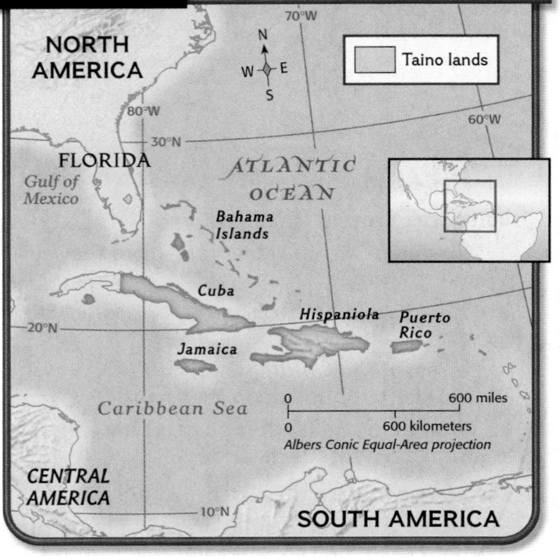

Review Content Vocabulary

1. rule of law
2. Northwest Passage
3. Renaissance
4. mercantilism

Sentences using *technology* and *entrepreneur* should include accurate definitions and use correct grammar.

Review the Main Idea

5. new knowledge and ideas coupled with the desire to expand trade routes and increase wealth
6. a Northwest Passage to Asia
7. large quantities of money were required; many risks were involved.
8. Countries hoped colonies would provide valuable resources and raw materials.
9. the concept that the law should apply equally to everyone
10. He established a form of Protestantism that encouraged people to work hard and behave well.
11. that the sun is the center of the universe

Critical Thinking

12. a global exchange in which people, goods, ideas, technology, and diseases moved around the world; led to growing populations in Asia and Europe, the death of many Native Americans, and the forced relocation of many Africans to the Americas
13. Causes (any three): desire for new trade routes to the East, lure of riches from spices and gold and silver, religion, land acquisition, profits from fur and fish, and the search for a Northwest Passage; Effects (any three): colonization of the Americas, devastation of Native American empires, establishment of missions in North America, economic rivalry between European countries for control of wealth from colonies, religious rivalry

History Online

Self-Check Quiz Visit ca.hss.glencoe.com to prepare for the Chapter 1 test.

15. **Place** What are some of the islands on which the Taino lived?
16. **Location** Between which continents was the Taino homeland located?
17. **Movement** If you traveled from Cuba to Puerto Rico, in what direction would you be going?

Read to Write

18. **The Big Ideas** **Descriptive Writing** Choose an event mentioned in the chapter that had an impact on the Americas. Describe how that event influenced life in the Americas. CA 8WA2.3
19. **Using Your FOLDABLES** Use the information from your completed chapter opener foldable to create a compare-contrast chart of the three countries that were exploring the Americas. Include in the chart their reasons for embarking on explorations, the areas they explored, and the goods and ideas they obtained from the regions. CA CS3.

Using Academic Vocabulary

Read the following sentences and in your own words, write the meaning of the underlined academic vocabulary word.

20. The Magna Carta is an important <u>document</u>.
21. Venice and Genoa became <u>major</u> trading cities.
22. Christopher Columbus hoped that the king and queen of Spain would <u>finance</u> his exploration.
23. Traders wanted to <u>export</u> goods to China and to other areas of the world.

Linking Past and Present

24. **Science Connection** Sir Francis Bacon was the first person to describe the Scientific Method. Describe this method in your own words. Then, describe a modern-day scenario in which scientists are using this method. CA HI3.

Reviewing Skills

25. READING SKILL **Previewing** Take a look at the Big Ideas on page 113. Select one and write a paragraph describing the relationship between that idea and something you learned in this chapter. CA CS1. CA 8WA2.2
26. ANALYSIS SKILL **Summarize** Describe Montesquieu's theories on government. Contrast these with views held by Thomas Hobbes. CA HI2. CA 8WS1.1

Standards Practice

Read the passage below and answer the following questions.

> The *Legislative cannot transfer the Power of Making Laws* to any other hands. For it being but a delegated Power from the People, they who have it, cannot pass it over to others. The People alone can appoint the Form of the Commonwealth, which is by Constituting the Legislative, and appointing in whose hands that shall be.
>
> —*from* Second Treatise of Civil Government *by John Locke*

27 **According to Locke, what branch of government makes the laws?**

A judicial
B executive
C legislative
D state governments

28 **Who gives government its power?**

A the legislature
B the president
C the Supreme Court
D the people

CHAPTER 1 Assessment

Linking Past and Present

24. Answers should reflect the four steps of observation, hypothesis, experiment, and conclusion and refer to a current scenario involving this method.

Reviewing Skills

25. READING SKILL Answers should reflect a clear connection between the Big Idea and a fact presented within the section.

26. ANALYSIS SKILL Montesquieu advocated the separation of government powers, with the executive, judicial, and legislative branch all sharing equal power. Hobbes saw nothing wrong with all power resting in the hands of an absolute monarchy.

Standards Practice

27. C
28. D

Bonus Question

Ask: What was the largest negative effect of the Columbian Exchange? *(Europeans brought new diseases to the Americas, resulting in widespread deaths.)* OL

History Online

Have students visit the Web site at ca.hss.glencoe.com to review Chapter 1 and take the **Self-Check Quiz.**

14. Judaism was based on the belief in one God.

Geography Skills

15. Cuba, the Bahamas, Hispaniola, Puerto Rico
16. North and South America
17. east

Read to Write

18. The Big Ideas Answers will vary, but students should describe the event and its impact in life.

19. Using Your FOLDABLES Answers will vary but should make use of the details that students incorporated in their foldables.

Using Academic Vocabulary

20.–23. Answers should reflect the meaning of the terms as defined in the Glossary.

Chapter 2 Planning Guide

SECTION RESOURCES

Main Ideas	Print Materials	Technology Resources
Section 1: Founding the American Colonies 1. Spain, France, and the Netherlands had settlements in North America. 2. The first permanent English settlement was at Jamestown. 3. The English established 13 colonies along the east coast.	• Reproducible Lesson Plan 2–1* • Daily Lesson and Discussion Notes 2–1 • Active Reading Note-Taking Guide 2–1 • Reading Essentials and Study Guide 2–1 • Guided Reading Activity 2–1 • Section Quiz 2–1	Daily Focus Skills Transparency 2–1 Section Graphic Organizer Transparency 2–1 California Standards Practice Transparencies Interactive Tutor Self-Assessment CD-ROM Exam*View*® Pro Testmaker CD-ROM Presentation Plus! CD-ROM
Section 2: Life in Colonial America 1. As the population of the colonies grew, agriculture and trade increased. 2. American culture, influenced by religion and education, developed. 3. While the American colonies developed some self-government, the British still set many laws.	• Reproducible Lesson Plan 2–2* • Daily Lesson and Discussion Notes 2–2 • Active Reading Note-Taking Guide 2–2 • Reading Essentials and Study Guide 2–2 • Guided Reading Activity 2–2 • Section Quiz 2–2	Daily Focus Skills Transparency 2–2 Section Graphic Organizer Transparency 2–2 California Standards Practice Transparencies Interactive Tutor Self-Assessment CD-ROM Exam*View*® Pro Testmaker CD-ROM Presentation Plus! CD-ROM
Section 3: Trouble in the Colonies 1. Following Britain's victory in the French and Indian War, the British prohibited colonists from moving west of the Appalachians and taxed them to pay for the war. 2. British actions brought strong responses from the colonists. 3. After colonial leaders met with the British, the first shots of the American Revolution were fired.	• Reproducible Lesson Plan 2–3* • Daily Lesson and Discussion Notes 2–3 • Active Reading Note-Taking Guide 2–3 • Reading Essentials and Study Guide 2–3 • Guided Reading Activity 2–3 • Section Quiz 2–3	Daily Focus Skills Transparency 2–3 Section Graphic Organizer Transparency 2–3 California Standards Practice Transparencies Interactive Tutor Self-Assessment CD-ROM Exam*View*® Pro Testmaker CD-ROM Presentation Plus! CD-ROM
Section 4: War of Independence 1. As colonial forces and British troops fought, colonial leaders met to plan their resistance to Britain. 2. The Declaration of Independence used traditional English political rights to call for independence. 3. America's victory and independence led to revolutions in other parts of the world.	• Reproducible Lesson Plan 2–4* • Daily Lesson and Discussion Notes 2–4 • Active Reading Note-Taking Guide 2–4 • Reading Essentials and Study Guide 2–4 • Guided Reading Activity 2–4 • Section Quiz 2–4	Daily Focus Skills Transparency 2–4 Section Graphic Organizer Transparency 2–4 California Standards Practice Transparencies Interactive Tutor Self-Assessment CD-ROM Exam*View*® Pro Testmaker CD-ROM Presentation Plus! CD-ROM

PACING YOUR LESSONS

Chapter Introduction	Section 1	Section 2	Section 3	Section 4	Chapter Assessment	Unit Wrap-Up
½ Day	2 Days	2 Days	2 Days	2 Days	½ Day	½ Day

0:00 **OUT OF TIME?** Assign the Chapter 2 ***Reading Essentials and Study Guide***

*Available on TeacherWorks™

Standards-Based Lesson Plan

History–Social Science Standards Covered in Chapter 2

The standards covered in the chapter are listed below. Use the accompanying activity as you teach the chapter to ensure student mastery of these standards. This activity can be used in combination with the program's print and technology assessment materials.

Standard	Section 1	2	3	4
US8.1 Students understand the major events preceding the founding of the nation and relate their significance to the development of American constitutional democracy.	✔	✔	✔	✔
US8.1.1 Describe the relationship between the moral and political ideas of the Great Awakening and the development of revolutionary fervor.		✔		
US8.1.2 Analyze the philosophy of government expressed in the Declaration of Independence, with an emphasis on government as a means of securing individual rights (e.g., key phrases such as "all men are created equal, that they are endowed by their Creator with certain unalienable rights").				✔
US8.1.3 Analyze how the American Revolution affected other nations, especially France.				✔
US8.1.4 Describe the nation's blend of civic republicanism, classical liberal principles, and English parliamentary traditions.	✔	✔	✔	

Cumulative Standards-Assessment Activity

The Cumulative Standards-Assessment Activity will help students organize and learn the important information from the chapter. Begin teaching the chapter with this activity, and have students complete it as they read the chapter.

Creating a Chart for Organizing Information

Purpose Organizing information is a useful technique for readers to make sense of the mass of details they encounter by helping them establish links between those details. This type of organizer aids students by identifying core concepts and then finding related ideas, which they cluster around the core concepts. It also allows students to identify ideas related to those secondary concepts, showing how concepts branch out.

Introduction to Organizing Information

1. Begin by drawing a large oval on the board and writing the core concept *Columbus's Voyage* inside it. Ask students to name words and phrases related to that event. Write these ideas in new ovals with lines that connect them to the original one. Ask questions to elicit responses connected to at least one of these related ideas and connect it to the smaller oval to show how ideas can branch. For instance, if a student mentions *Columbian Exchange*, a new set of connections could identify the details underlying that concept, such as *new foods in Europe* or *new diseases in the Americas*.
2. Ask students to copy this chart into their notebooks:

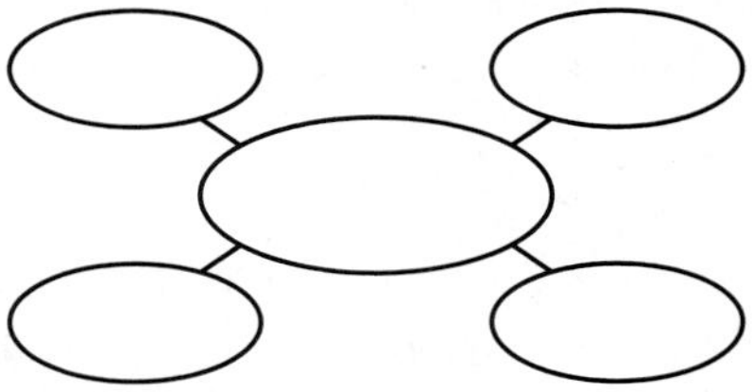

As students read each section, have them search for core concepts and the ideas related to them. Have them create as many concept webs as they need. Encourage them to create more charts as they encounter other core concepts during their reading.

3. As part of your chapter review, have students share their concept webs. Encourage them to use their webs as study aids.

Chapter 2 Resources

READING SUPPORT

- Content Vocabulary Activity 2
- Academic Vocabulary Activity 2
- Reading Skills Activity 2
- American Literature Reading 2
- Biography Activities 2A, 2B
- Chapter 2 Active Reading Note-Taking Guide
- Chapter 2 Guided Reading Activities
- Chapter 2 Reading Essentials and Study Guide
- Glencoe Literature Library
- Glencoe Video Program
- Vocabulary PuzzleMaker CD-ROM
- Interactive Graphic Organizers CD-ROM
- American History Primary Source Document Library CD-ROM

CRITICAL THINKING

- Critical Thinking Skills Activity 2
- Primary Source Reading 2
- Cause-and-Effect Transparency 2, Strategy, and Activity
- Presentation Plus! CD-ROM

UNIVERSAL ACCESS

- Universal Access Activity 2
- Then and Now Transparencies 2A–2B, Strategy, and Activity
- Graphic Novel Activity 2
- School-to-Home Connection Activities 2A–2D
- English Learner Handbook Chapter 2 Activities
- Universal Access for the American History Classroom
- Moments in Time
- American Art and Architecture Transparencies, Strategies, and Activities
- American Art Prints
- American Music Cultural Traditions
- American Music Hits Through History
- StudentWorks Plus CD-ROM

SKILL PRACTICE

- Map Overlay Transparency 2, Strategy, and Activity
- Analysis Skills Activity 2
- Time Line Activity 2
- Geography and History Activity 2
- Economics and History Activity 2
- Chart, Graph, and Map Skills Activity 2
- Political Cartoon Activity 2
- Supreme Court Case Study 2
- In-Text Map Transparency 2, Strategy, and Activity
- Step Into American History Activity 2
- Citizenship and Service Learning Activity 2
- Outline Map Resource Book
- MindJogger Plus Videoquiz

WRITING SUPPORT

- Writing Activity 2
- Language Arts Activity 2
- Writer's Guidebook
- Middle School Writing Process Transparencies

ASSESSMENT

GLENCOE'S ASSESSMENT ADVANTAGE

- Chapter 2 Section Quizzes
- Chapter 2 Tests, Forms A and B
- California Standards Assessment, Forms A and B
- Cumulative Assessment Activity US8.1
- California Standards Practice Workbook
- Succeeding on the California History–Social Science Standards CD-ROM
- Exam*View*® Pro Testmaker CD-ROM
- Interactive Tutor Self-Assessment CD-ROM

CD-ROM	Transparency
DVD	Music Program
Print Material	Videocassette
Poster	Glencoe Literature Library

Chapter 2 Resources

TECHNOLOGY

- StudentWorks Plus CD-ROM
- TeacherWorks Plus CD-ROM
- Exam*View*® Pro Testmaker CD-ROM
- Interactive Tutor Self-Assessment CD-ROM
- Presentation Plus! CD-ROM
- Succeeding on the California History–Social Science Standards CD-ROM
- Vocabulary Puzzlemaker CD-ROM
- Interactive Graphic Organizers CD-ROM
- Interactive Time Line CD-ROM
- American History Primary Source Document Library CD-ROM
- MindJogger Plus Videoquiz
- American Music Cultural Traditions
- American Music Hits Through History
- Glencoe Program
- Professional Development in Middle School Social Studies Series
- Teaching American History With *Discovering Our Past: The American Journey to World War I*

SPANISH RESOURCES

- Spanish Activities and Assessment
  - Spanish Content Vocabulary Activities
  - Spanish Guided Reading Activities
  - Spanish Quizzes and Tests
  - Spanish California Standards Assessment
- Spanish Reading Essentials and Study Guide
- Spanish School-to-Home Connection
- Spanish Declaration of Independence and U.S. Constitution

TRANSPARENCIES

- California Standards Practice Transparencies
- Daily Focus Skills Transparencies
- Section Graphic Organizer Transparencies
- In-Text Map Transparencies
- Map Overlay Transparencies
- Cause-and-Effect Transparencies
- Then and Now Transparencies
- American Art and Architecture Transparencies
- Middle School Writing Process Transparencies

TEACHER PLANNING

- Daily Lesson and Discussion Notes
- English Learner Handbook
- Guide to Daily Intervention
- *Discovering Our Past: The American Journey to World War I* Reading and Study Skills Foldables
- Reading Strategies and Activities for the Social Studies Classroom
- Chapter 2 Reproducible Lesson Plans (correlated to California History–Social Science Standards)
- Universal Access for the American History Classroom
- NGS U.S. Desk Map
- NGS U.S. Atlas

PROFESSIONAL DEVELOPMENT

- Building Academic Vocabulary
- Strategies for Success
- Research-Based Strategies Used to Develop *Discovering Our Past: The American Journey to World War I*
- Character Education in the Middle School Classroom
- The Living Constitution
- Professional Development in Middle School Social Studies Video Series
- Teaching American History With *Discovering Our Past: The American Journey to World War I*

MASTERING THE STANDARDS

The content and assessment in the Student Edition, Teacher Wraparound Edition, teacher planning materials, and the print and technology products are all standards-based. The use of these products during instruction leads to mastery of the standards.

PRACTICE
- California Standards Practice Workbook
- California Standards Practice Transparencies
- Interactive Time Line CD-ROM
- School-to-Home Connection

BENCHMARK ASSESSMENT
- California Standards Assessment
- Exam*View*® Pro Testmaker CD-ROM
- Succeeding on the California History–Social Science Standards CD-ROM

REMEDIATION
- California Guide to Daily Intervention
- Interactive Tutor Self-Assessment CD-ROM
- Exam*View*® Pro Testmaker CD-ROM
- California Standards Practice Workbook
- Reading Essentials and Study Guide

Additional Resources

NATIONAL GEOGRAPHIC TEACHER'S CORNER

Index to National Geographic Magazine:

The following articles relate to this chapter:

- "The Cruelest Commerce: African Slave Trade," by Colin Palmer, September 1992.
- "Two Revolutions," by Charles McCarry, July 1989.
- "Yorktown Shipwreck," by John D. Broadwater, June 1988.
- "Thomas Jefferson: Architect of Freedom," by Mike Edwards, February 1976.

National Geographic Society Products

To order the following, call National Geographic at 1-800-368-2728

- *Colonization and Trade in the Americas* (Book)
- National Geographic Atlas of the World, Seventh Edition (Book)

NGS ONLINE

Access National Geographic's new dynamic MapMachine Web site and other geography resources at:

www.nationalgeographic.com

www.nationalgeographic.com/maps

A&E HOME VIDEO. Biography® THE HISTORY CHANNEL.

The following videotape programs are available from Glencoe as supplements to Chapter 2.

- **Benjamin Franklin: Citizen of the World (ISBN 1-56501-426-X)**
- **George Washington: Founding Father (ISBN 1-56501-377-8)**
- **Thomas Jefferson: Philosopher of Freedom (ISBN 1-56501-502-9)**
- **The American Revolution (six video set) (ISBN 1-56501-436-7)**

To order, call Glencoe at 1-800-334-7344. To find classroom resources to accompany many of these videos, check the following home pages:

A&E Television: www.aetv.com
The History Channel: www.historychannel.com

History Online

Use our Web site for additional resources. All essential content is covered in the Student Edition.

You and your students can visit ca.hss.glencoe.com, the Web site companion to *Discovering Our Past: The American Journey to World War I*. This innovative integration of electronic and print media offers your students a wealth of opportunities. The student text directs students to the Web site for the following options:

- Chapter Overviews
- Self-Check Quizzes
- Study Central™
- Student Web Activities
- Textbook Updates
- Multi-Language Glossaries

Answers to the student Web activities are provided for you in the Web Activity Lesson Plans. Additional Web resources and ePuzzles and games are also available.

FOLDABLES™ Study Organizer

Dinah Zike's Foldables

Foldables are three-dimensional, interactive graphic organizers that help students practice basic writing skills, review key vocabulary terms, and identify main ideas. Every chapter contains a foldable activity, with additional chapter activities found in the Reading and Study Skills Foldables booklet.

Chapter 2 Resources

Reading List Generator CD-ROM

GLENCOE **BOOKLINK**

The Glencoe BookLink CD-ROM is a database that allows you to search more than 15,000 titles to create a customized reading list for your students.

- Reading lists can be organized by students' reading level, author, genre, theme, or area of interest.
- The database provides Degrees of Reading Power™ (DRP) and Lexile™ readability scores for all selections.
- A brief summary of each selection is included.

Reading level suggestions for this chapter:

For students at a Grade 6 reading level:
- ***The Pilgrims of Plimouth,*** by Marcia Sewall

For students at a Grade 7 reading level:
- ***The American Revolution: How We Fought the War of Independence,*** by Edward F. Dolan

For students at a Grade 8 reading level:
- ***Breaking Ground, Breaking Silence,*** by Joyce Hansen and Gary McGowan

For students at a Grade 9 reading level:
- ***Founding Mothers: Women of America in the Revolutionary Era,*** by Linda Grant De Pauw

For students at a Grade 10 reading level:
- ***Junipero Serra,*** by Sean Dolan

Reading Support From JAMESTOWN EDUCATION

- *Timed Readings Plus in Social Studies* helps students increase their reading rate and fluency while maintaining comprehension. The 400-word passages are similar to those found on state and national assessments.
- *Reading in the Content Area: Social Studies* concentrates on six essential reading skills that help students better comprehend what they read. The book includes 754 high-interest nonfiction passages written at increasing levels of difficulty.
- *Reading Fluency* helps students read smoothly, accurately, and expressively.
- *Jamestown's Reading Improvement,* by renowned reading expert Edward Fry, focuses on helping build your students' comprehension, vocabulary, and skimming and scanning skills.
- *Critical Reading Series* provides high-interest books, each written at three reading levels.

To order these products, call Glencoe at 1-800-334-7344.

KEY for Using the Teacher Wraparound Edition

Use this key to help you identify the different types of prompts found in the Teacher Wraparound Edition.

R **Reading Strategies** activities help you teach reading skills and vocabulary.

C **Critical Thinking** strategies help students apply and extend what they have learned.

U **Universal Access** activities provide differentiated instruction for students learning to speak English, along with suggestions for teaching various types of learners.

S **Skill Practice** strategies help students practice historical analysis and geography skills.

W **Writing Support** activities provide writing opportunities to help students comprehend the text.

Teaching strategies and activities have been coded for ability level appropriateness.

AL Activities for students working above grade level
OL Activities for students working on grade level
BL Activities for students working below grade level
EL Activities for English Learners

FOCUS

History–Social Science Standards

In this chapter, the following standard will be covered:

US8.1 Students understand the major events preceding the founding of the nation and relate their significance to the development of American constitutional democracy.

More About the Art

The Old North Bridge was the site of the first American victory in the Revolutionary War. Minutemen from Concord and the surrounding area stopped the British advance at the bridge.

TEACH

The Big Ideas

As you begin teaching each section, use these questions and activities to focus on the Big Ideas.

Section 1

Founding the American Colonies

Essential Question: Why do people leave one country to settle in another? *(Answers may include to escape conflict; to build better lives; for freedom or better economic opportunities.)* Explain that similar reasons compelled Europeans to settle in this country. OL

Chapter 2

Road to Independence

◀ The Old North Bridge, Concord, Massachusetts

NATIONAL GEOGRAPHIC Where & When?

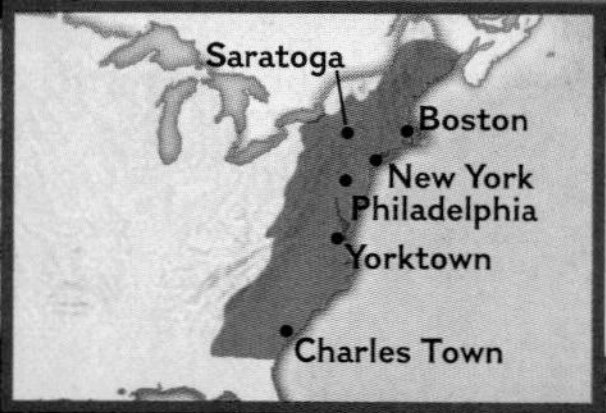

1600 — 1700 — 1800

1620 Mayflower Compact is signed

1682 William Penn plans colony

1775 Boston Tea Party takes place

1781 Americans gain independence with victory at Yorktown

Section 2

Life in Colonial America

Essential Question: What difficulties might settlers face when moving to another country? *(Answers may include different climate; geographical obstacles; encounters with people who speak a different language and who have different customs.)* BL

Section 3

Trouble in the Colonies

Essential Question: What can people do if they feel that their rights are being violated? *(protest; appeal for change; rebel)* Tell students that in this section they will learn how British policies came into conflict with the American colonists' ideas about self-government. OL

The Big Ideas

History Online
Chapter Overview Visit ca.hss.glencoe.com for a preview of Chapter 2.

Section 1 Founding the American Colonies

Geography shapes the physical, economic, and political challenges a region faces. Peoples of various cultures and religions settled the early North American colonies.

Section 2 Life in Colonial America

Geography shapes the physical, economic, and political challenges a region faces. Although the regions of colonial America differed, an American identity was growing.

Section 3 Trouble in the Colonies

Political ideas and major events shape how people form governments. British policies came into conflict with American ideas about self-government.

Section 4 War of Independence

Political ideas and major events shape how people form governments. The United States declared independence in 1776, but it took several years of war and turmoil to earn recognition as a new nation.

View the Chapter 2 video in the Glencoe Video Program.

FOLDABLES™ Study Organizer

Cause and Effect Make this foldable to show the causes and effects of the events that led the Americans to declare independence from Great Britain.

Step 1 Fold one sheet of paper in half from side to side.

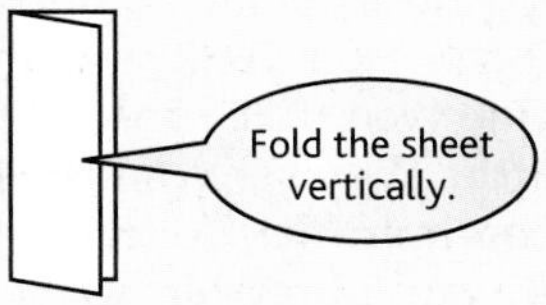

Step 2 Fold again, 1 inch from the top. (Tip: The middle knuckle of your index finger is about 1 inch long.)

Step 3 Open and label as shown.

Reading and Writing As you read this chapter, fill in the causes (British actions) and effects (Colonial reactions) in the correct columns of your foldable.

Section 4

War of Independence

Essential Question: What kind of challenges would a group of people face when claiming independence? *(Possible answers include: difficulty of organizing a new government; need to create a military to fight the ruling government; and the need to find ways of financing the effort.)* Point out that some of these challenges made the American colonists' fight for independence long and difficult. OL

History Online

Go to ca.hss.glencoe.com for student activities, lesson plans, and links to additional Web resources about colonial America.

FOLDABLES™ Study Organizer — Dinah Zike's Foldables

Purpose Have students use their foldables to help them organize the events leading to the Americans' decision to declare independence from Great Britain. Have students discuss their findings at certain points in each section. OL

Why It's Important

Identifying the Main Idea
Locating the main idea and its supporting details is an essential skill for understanding many kinds of writing, from textbooks to essays to news articles. By identifying supporting details, students are better able to remember key information about the content. When they analyze persuasive writing, they can use the skill as a step toward determining whether the details an author provides are adequate to support the author's arguments.

1 Learn It!

Read the following statement aloud: "The weather today is typical for this time of year." Have volunteers provide details that support the statement. Tell students that details can answer such questions as *why*, *when*, and *how*. **OL**

Chapter 2

Get Ready to Read

Identifying the Main Idea

READING SKILL

1 Learn It!

Main ideas are the most important ideas in a paragraph, section, or chapter. Supporting details are facts or examples that explain the main idea. Historical details, such as names, dates, and events, are easier to remember when they are connected to a main idea. Understanding the main idea allows you to grasp the whole picture or story. Read the excerpt below and notice how the author explains the main idea.

Main Idea

Supporting Details

> **The Spanish, however, did not ignore the lands north of Mexico and the Caribbean. During the 1600s, they built settlements and forts along the northern edge of their American empire. These settlements, such as St. Augustine in Florida and Santa Fe in New Mexico, were intended to keep other Europeans out of Spanish territory. Spanish missionary-priests, such as Junípero Serra** (hoo • NEE • puh • ROH SEHR • UH) **and Eusebio Kino** (yoo • SEE • bee • oh)**, also headed north. They set up missions, or religious communities, to teach Christianity and European ways to the Native Americans. Missions were set up in New Mexico, Texas, California, and other areas of North America.**
>
> *—from page 117*

Reading Tip

The main idea is often the first sentence in a paragraph but not always.

114

READING STRATEGY — ORGANIZING INFORMATION

Students can use clues in a written document to help them identify main ideas. Headings and subheadings often provide such clues by indicating a topic or theme that applies to the information grouped under that topic. Remind students that, as in the sample paragraph on this page, the first sentence of a paragraph often—though not always—states the main idea. Ask students to choose a paragraph from one of the sections in Chapter 2 and identify the main idea. **EL**

Practice It!

Read the following paragraph. Draw a graphic organizer like the one below to show the main idea and supporting details.

> The Great Awakening is the name for the powerful religious revival that swept through the colonies beginning in the 1730s. Christian ministers such as George Whitefield and Jonathan Edwards preached throughout the colonies, drawing huge crowds. The Great Awakening had a lasting effect on the way in which the colonists viewed themselves, their relationships with one another, and their faith.
>
> —*from page 128*

Read to Write

Use the main idea that appears under one of the headings in Section 1 of this chapter as the first sentence in a paragraph. As you read, complete the paragraph with supporting details.

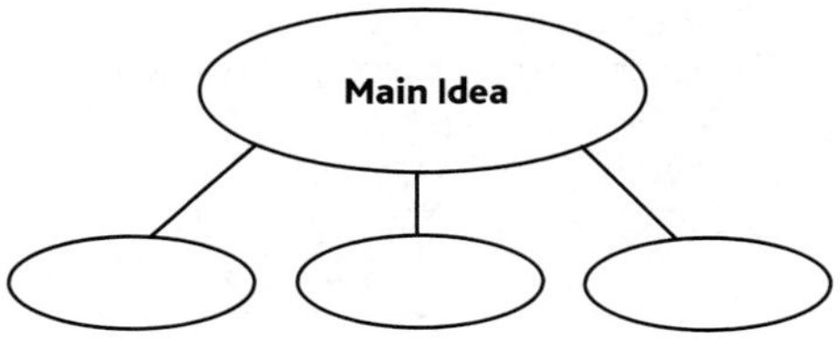

▲ Massachusetts preacher and philosopher Jonathan Edwards

Apply It!

Pick a paragraph from another section of this chapter and diagram the main idea as you did above.

CHAPTER 2 Get Ready to Read

Practice It!

Main idea: The Great Awakening swept through the colonies starting in the 1720s.
Supporting details: Ministers preached throughout the colonies; Ministers drew large crowds; The Great Awakening had lasting effects on the colonists.
Now have students close their books and ask a volunteer to summarize the main idea and details in his or her own words. **OL**

Apply It!

Bring to class a collection of news articles and opinion essays from newspapers and newsmagazines. Divide the class into small groups and have each group analyze a different piece of writing to identify the main idea and supporting details. After they have finished the work, have the class discuss the process. **OL**

READING STRATEGY — SUMMARY WRITING

In writing summaries, students read a text to identify the most important ideas and concepts and only the most essential details. Have students write a brief summary of a subsection of this chapter. Then have students exchange summaries and compare their partners' work to the original. Ask students to comment on whether their partners' writing adequately summarizes the original. **AL**

CA 8WA2.3 **CA** 8RC2.4

Use Reading Skills Activity 2 in the **Chapter 2 Resource Book** for more practice with identifying the main idea.

FOCUS

BELLRINGER
SKILLBUILDER ACTIVITY

Project **Daily Focus Skills Transparency 2–1** and have students answer the question.

Guide to Reading

Preteaching Vocabulary: Have students find the definition of each vocabulary term. Then have students write a sentence that contains two of the terms of their choice.

Answers to Graphic: Reasons might include trade or for religious freedom.

Unpacking the Standards
After reading the section, students will be able to:

- Discuss the first European settlements in North America and the hardships settlers faced.
- Identify the importance of the legislature in Virginia.
- Explain why each of the English colonies was settled.

Section 1

Founding the American Colonies

History Social Science Standards

US8.1 Students understand the major events preceding the founding of the nation and relate their significance to the development of American constitutional democracy.

Guide to Reading

Looking Back, Looking Ahead
You learned that Europeans explored and began to colonize the Americas in the 1400s and 1500s. In North America, early English colonies faced hardships, but in time they began to flourish.

Focusing on the Main Ideas
- Spain, France, and the Netherlands founded colonies in North America. *(page 117)*
- The first permanent English settlement in North America was at Jamestown. *(page 119)*
- The English established 13 colonies along the east coast of North America. *(page 120)*

Locating Places
New England Colonies
Middle Colonies
Southern Colonies

Meeting People
Samuel de Champlain (sham • PLAYN)
Roger Williams
William Penn

Content Vocabulary
charter
burgess (BUHR • juhs)
Mayflower Compact
constitution (KAHN • stuh • TOO • shuhn)
toleration (TAH • luh • RAY • shuhn)
dissenter (dih • SEHN • tuhr)
persecute (PUHR • sih • KYOOT)
diversity (duh • VUHR • suh • TEE)
debtor (DEH • tuhr)

Academic Vocabulary
survive (suhr • VYV)
grant
military (MIH • luh • TEHR • ee)

Reading Strategy
Classifying Information Create a diagram like the one below with a row for each colony studied in the section. Fill in the names of the colonies and details on why or how the colony was settled.

Colony	Reasons the colony was settled

NATIONAL GEOGRAPHIC **Where & When?**

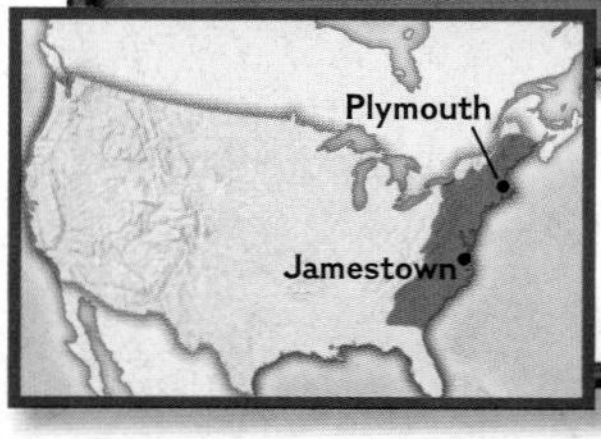

1600	1625	1650
1607 Jamestown colony founded	**1620** Pilgrims land at Plymouth	**1644** Roger Williams founds Rhode Island

SECTION RESOURCES

Print Material
- Reproducible Lesson Plan 2–1*
- Daily Lesson and Discussion Notes 2–1
- Guided Reading Activity 2–1
- Reading Essentials and Study Guide 2–1
- Active Reading Note-Taking Guide 2–1
- Section Quiz 2–1

Transparencies
- Daily Focus Skills Transparency 2–1
- Section Graphic Organizer Transparency 2–1
- California Standards Practice Transparencies

Technology
- Interactive Tutor Self-Assessment CD-ROM
- Exam*View*® Pro Testmaker CD-ROM
- Presentation Plus! CD-ROM

*Available on TeacherWorks™

US8.1 Students understand the major events preceding the founding of the nation and relate their significance to the development of American constitutional democracy.

Settlements in America

Main Idea **Spain, France, and the Netherlands founded colonies in North America.**

Reading Connection How far would you travel to create a new home? What would it be like if you did not know what to expect? How would you plan for it? Read to learn about Europeans who created settlements in North America.

In Chapter 1, you learned that Spain and Portugal built colonies in the Americas during the 1500s. Beginning in the 1600s, France, England, and other European countries began setting up their own colonies in the Americas. Most Spanish colonies were in the Caribbean, Mexico, and Central America, and most French and English colonies were in North America.

The Spanish, however, did not ignore the lands north of Mexico and the Caribbean. During the 1600s, they built settlements and forts along the northern edge of their American empire. These settlements, such as St. Augustine in Florida and Santa Fe in New Mexico, were intended to keep other Europeans out of Spanish territory. Spanish missionary-priests, such as Junípero Serra (hoo • NEE • puh • ROH SEHR • UH) and Eusebio Kino (yoo • SEE • bee • oh), also headed north. They set up missions, or religious communities, to teach Christianity and European ways to the Native Americans. Missions were set up in New Mexico, Texas, California, and other areas of North America.

France's Fur-Trading Empire The French came to North America to make money from fur trading. By the 1600s, beaver fur had become popular in Europe. In 1608 the French explorer **Samuel de Champlain** (sham • PLAYN) set up a trading post named Quebec (kih • BEHK) in what is now Canada. Quebec became the capital of the colony of New France.

From Quebec, French fur trappers, explorers, and missionaries moved into other parts of North America. In 1673 the explorers Louis Joliet and Jacques Marquette discovered the Mississippi River. Then, in 1682, a French explorer named René-Robert Cavalier, Sieur de La Salle followed the Mississippi all the way to the Gulf of Mexico. He named the region Louisiana in honor of France's King Louis XIV. The French settlers in southern Louisiana also began bringing in enslaved Africans to grow sugarcane, rice, and tobacco.

The Dutch in North America The Dutch also founded colonies in North America. Although their country, the Netherlands, was small, its large fleet of sailing ships sailed all over the world. In 1621 the Dutch set up a trading colony—New Netherland—centered in the area of the present-day state of New York. New Amsterdam, the capital, was located on the tip of Manhattan Island where the Hudson River enters New York Harbor. Today, it is known as New York City.

Reading Check **Identify** Name several early Spanish settlements in North America.

Picturing **History**

In the 1600s, French fur traders moved into parts of North America. ***In what areas did the French settle?***

TEACH

C Critical Thinking

Identifying Central Issues
Ask: Based on the information here, what were the reasons that European countries had for founding colonies in the Americas? *(for defense or protection; for religious reasons; for economic reasons)* OL CA HI2.

S Skill Practice

Using Geography Skills
Have students conduct research to identify the places in California where the Spanish set up missions and create a map locating and identifying each mission. Have them use symbols to indicate the missions founded by Serra and by Kino. OL CA CS3. CA 8WS1.4

W Writing Support

Research Reports Writing
Have each student choose one of the Spanish missionaries or French explorers mentioned on this page that he or she would like to learn about. Then have students conduct research to learn about the person's life. Students should use their findings to write a brief biography. OL CA 8WA2.1

Reading Check

Answer: St. Augustine, Santa Fe; missions in New Mexico, Texas, California, and other areas

More Skill Practice

Historical and Social Sciences Analysis Skill European countries believed their power depended on the acquisition of wealth, and considered their colonies sources of raw materials. **Ask:** What does this suggest about the competition among European countries to settle land? *(They tried to claim regions and prevent others from settling nearby.)* AL CA HI1.

Picturing **History**

The French built good relations with Native Americans by sending some fur traders to live with them and adopt their ways. One of the first was Etienne Brulé, who lived among the Algonquin people along the Ottawa River.

Answer: Quebec (or Canada), Great Lakes region, Louisiana

Resources for page 117

Analysis Skills Activity 2

TEACH

R Reading Strategy

Evaluating **Ask:** What does the statement "Always go forward and never turn back," mean to you? *(Don't live in the past, but keep looking toward and working toward the future.)* BL

S1 Skill Practice

Historical and Social Sciences Analysis Skill
Tell students that Father Serra protected the Native Americans living on the missions from mistreatment by members of the Spanish military. **Ask:** Why was he concerned about their leaving the mission to look for food? *(He wanted to convert them to Christianity.)* OL

S2 Skill Practice

Using Geography Skills
Ask: Why would the availability of wood, water, and fields be a factor in determining the location of missions? *(People on the missions needed wood for building and making fires; water for drinking and cooking; fields for growing crops and grazing animals.)* OL CA 8RW1.2

Answers and Additional Support

Biography

US8.1 Students understand the major events preceding the founding of the American nation and relate their significance to the development of American constitutional democracy.

Junípero Serra
1713–1784

The Spanish settlers who came to North America had two aims. They wanted to claim land and to convert the Native Americans to Catholicism. To achieve these goals, the Spaniards set up fortified religious settlements known as missions.

Born in 1713 on an island off the Spanish Coast, Junípero Serra became a Franciscan priest. Because he wanted to work as a missionary among Native Americans, he left Spain in 1749 to travel to Mexico.

At the age of 55, he was sent to take control of Upper California. He established a mission in San Diego in 1769 and later founded eight other missions. By 1820 there were 21 missions stretching up the California coast to San Francisco. Taking as his motto "Always to go forward and never to turn back," Junípero Serra traveled by foot from mission to mission. Despite his crippled leg, Father Serra visited each of his missions regularly.

Father Serra's missions usually were built a day's march from each other. Travelers always had a place to rest after a long day's journey. This also made it easier to trade and sell their food and crafts. The missionaries also built the missions near the coast so that ships could get fresh supplies before heading out to sea.

> ***"Always . . . go forward and never . . . turn back."*** R
> **—Junípero Serra**

Each mission was unique in a few ways, but they all had the same basic plan: a large, four-sided building with a central courtyard. The mission was a bustling world of workshops, storage areas, gardens, and living quarters. Father Serra believed that the Native Americans should "have their own lands and crops so that poverty will not make them [leave the mission]." S1 The location of the mission was often determined by the availability of wood, water, and fields for raising crops and grazing the livestock that the Spanish brought to the Americas. S2

Then and Now

Research the different groups of Native Americans with whom Father Serra came into contact during his explorations and missionary work. Do any of these groups still exist today?

118

Then and Now

Students' research should reveal the groups still in existence.

The Virginia Colony

R1 **Main Idea** **The first permanent English settlement in North America was at Jamestown.**

Reading Connection Would you be willing to stay in a community with few jobs and where many of the residents were starving? Read to find out what happened to the people of Jamestown and what discovery saved the town.

R2 In 1587 a group of English colonists financed by Sir Walter Raleigh sailed for North America. There, they founded a colony on Roanoke (RO•uh•nohk) Island off the coast of present-day North Carolina. After six years, however, the colonists disappeared. No one knows for certain what happened to them. For this reason, Roanoke Island became known as the "Lost Colony."

Virginia For a time, the failure of the Roanoke colony discouraged further plans for English colonies in North America. However, in 1606 the idea emerged again. The Virginia Company, an English joint-stock company, received a R3 **charter,** or the right to organize a settlement. With the backing of the company, more than 100 people braved an Atlantic crossing and set up the first permanent English settlement in North America in 1607. The settlers named it Jamestown after King James I. Jamestown was the first town of a new colony called Virginia.

Life in Virginia was very hard. The colonists had come hoping to find gold or silver. Instead, they could barely find enough to eat. Many settlers died from starvation and the cold winters, and others were killed in clashes with Native Americans. The colony **survived** under the leadership of Captain John Smith, a soldier and explorer. Smith forced the settlers to farm and managed to get corn from the Native Americans.

During those first years, the colony made no money for the merchants who had invested in it. It might have collapsed had not one of its settlers, John Rolfe, discovered that tobacco could grow in Virginia's soil. Tobacco became the first cash crop of the English colonies. A cash crop is grown in large quantities to sell for profit.

NATIONAL GEOGRAPHIC **European Settlements**

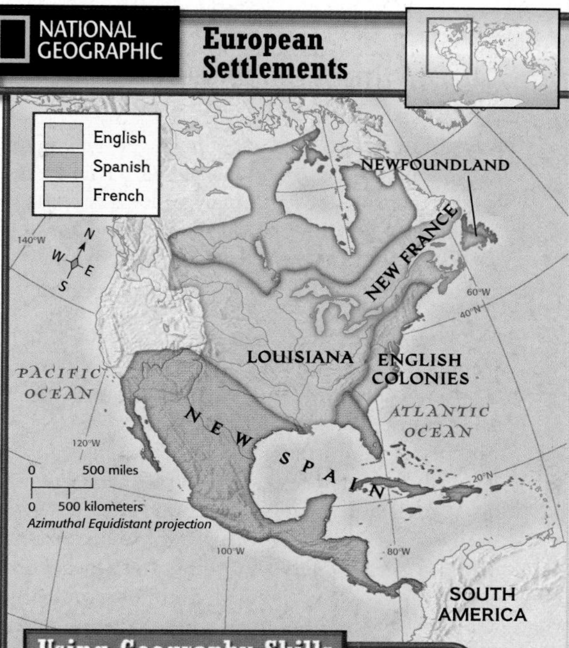

Using Geography Skills

In 1682 Spain, Great Britain, and France claimed land in North America.

1. **Location** Which nations held territory in what is now Canada?
2. **Location** Which nation held territory in what is now Mexico?

Self-Government in Virginia To attract more settlers, the Virginia Company gave the colonists in Virginia the right to elect **burgesses** (BUHR•juhs•ehs), or representatives, from among the men who owned land. The first House of Burgesses met in 1619. It was patterned after the English Parliament and voted on laws for the Virginia Colony. The House of Burgesses set an example for representative government. It was not long before other colonies set up their own legislatures as well. C

Reading Check **Identify** Who was John Smith? How did he help the Virginia settlers?

Using Geography Skills

Answers:

1. France, England
2. Spain

More Skill Practice

Historical and Social Sciences Analysis Skill Tell students that they are to take the role of leaders in colonial times who want to attract settlers to a new colony in the area where they now live. Have them create posters, brochures, or advertisements that promote the advantages of the area. OL CA 8LS1.3

R1 Reading Strategy

Identifying the Main Idea and Supporting Details Point students to the main idea of this part of the section. **Ask:** What are two details that support this idea? *(Possible answers are that charter and backing from the Virginia Company financed the settlement, and that farming for sustenance and cash crops helped settlers survive.)* OL

R2 Reading Strategy

Scaffolding—Academic Vocabulary Students were introduced to the word *finance* in Chapter 1, Section 2. Ask a student to define the word. OL

R3 Reading Strategy

Understanding Vocabulary Have students look at the terms *charter* and *burgess*. **Ask:** How is each related to government? *(Charters were granted by governments to give rights to settle. Burgesses were the elected delegates of the Virginia colonial legislature.)* OL

C Critical Thinking

Analyzing Information **Ask:** What is meant by the phrase "representative government"? *(People are governed by officials whom they elect to represent them.)* What kind of government do we have in the United States today? *(representative government)* OL

Reading Check

Answer: a soldier and explorer who was one of the Jamestown settlers; helped settlers survive by forcing them to farm and get corn from Native Americans

R1 Reading Strategy

Organizing Information Have students create graphic organizers summarizing key facts about each colony. BL

Review The Big Idea

Review the Big Idea for this section: "Geography shapes the physical, economic, and political challenges a region faces." Point out that the Pilgrims at Plymouth had to build their lives from scratch. **Ask:** How important would it be for them to work together? Why? *(very important; might be a matter of survival)* How does the Mayflower Compact reflect this? *(They agreed in it to obey the laws to help the community survive.)* OL

R2 Reading Strategy

Understanding Vocabulary Explain that a *compact* is an agreement. **Ask:** What other documents bind the signers into following the rules? *(contracts and treaties)* OL

Resources for page 120

American Art and Architecture Transparency 3

Answers and Additional Support

US8.1 Students understand the major events preceding the founding of the nation and relate their significance to the development of American constitutional democracy.

R1 The 13 English Colonies

Main Idea **The English established 13 colonies along the east coast of North America.**

Reading Connection Would you be willing to move across the ocean to unexplored, possibly dangerous territory to gain certain freedoms or perhaps just to get a new start on life? Read to find out why English settlers came to North America.

Not all English settlers came to North America in search of wealth. Some came to find religious freedom. In Chapter 1, you learned that many Protestants in England were dissatisfied with the Anglican Church. Some, called Puritans, wanted to stay in the Church but rid it of Catholic rituals and practices. Others, known as Separatists, wanted to leave the Church entirely and set up their own local congregations. King James I and his son King Charles I both believed that Puritans and Separatists were a threat to their authority and persecuted them.

The Pilgrims Arrive in New England In 1620 a group of Separatists called Pilgrims decided to go to America so they could worship freely. They received grants of land from the Virginia Company and sailed for Virginia on the *Mayflower.* Strong winds blew the *Mayflower* off course, causing the Pilgrims to land in New England just north of Cape Cod in present-day Massachusetts. They went ashore on a cold, bleak day in December at a place called Plymouth.

The Mayflower Compact Plymouth was outside the territory of the Virginia Company and its laws. To provide order, the Pilgrims signed a formal document called the **Mayflower Compact,** which set up a civil government. The signers also promised to obey the laws passed "for the general good of the colony." The Mayflower Compact was an important step in the development of democratic government in America. The people of Plymouth governed themselves for 70 years with almost no outside control. Then in 1691, Plymouth became part of a Puritan colony called Massachusetts. R2

TECHNOLOGY & History

The *Mayflower*

In September 1620, 102 passengers set off on the *Mayflower* on the journey across the Atlantic. The 2,750-mile trip took more than two months. In early November, the *Mayflower* reached the shores of America.

More Skill Practice

Historical and Social Sciences Analysis Skill Have students put the following events in the correct sequence:

A. The Pilgrims sail for America.
B. The *Mayflower* lands at Plymouth.
C. Pilgrims sign the Mayflower Compact.
D. Pilgrims receive land grant.

(D, A, B, C) OL CA CS1.

TECHNOLOGY & History

It was impossible for anyone taller than five feet to stand upright below deck on the *Mayflower*. The personal space for each person was smaller than a single size mattress. A person ate, slept, changed clothes, prepared food, and so on, within this small area.

Massachusetts The success of the Pilgrims encouraged persecuted Puritans to begin leaving England for America. In 1629 a group of Puritans formed a company and received a royal charter to settle an area north of Plymouth. Led by John Winthrop, the Puritans landed in America and founded the colony of Massachusetts and its capital, Boston. John Winthrop made their intentions clear:

> **"[W]e shall be as a city upon a hill. The eyes of all people are upon us."**
>
> **—from "A Model of Christian Charity"**

Others soon followed. By 1643 more than 20,000 Puritans had moved to America.

An elected group ran the colony through a General Court owned by the founding company. When the settlers insisted on having a larger role in the government, the company created a colonial legislature. Every adult male who owned property and was a church member could vote for the governor and for representatives to the General Court.

The Puritans came to America to put their religious beliefs into practice. They made the Protestant Congregationalist faith the colony's official religion. However, they barred members of other faiths from practicing their beliefs. Groups of people who disagreed with the Puritan leaders of Massachusetts were expelled and had to form new colonies in neighboring areas.

Connecticut and Rhode Island In the colony of Connecticut, settlers led by Thomas Hooker in 1639 adopted a plan of government called the Fundamental Orders of Connecticut. This was the first written **constitution** (KAHN • stuh • TOO • shuhn), or formal plan of government, in America. It described the organization of representative government in detail. **R1**

Another colony, Rhode Island, was founded by the Puritan minister **Roger Williams.** Williams believed that people should be free to follow their consciences in religious matters. In his view, the church and the government should be completely separate. Williams also believed it was wrong for settlers to take land away from the Native Americans. These ideas caused Massachusetts leaders to banish Williams. In 1644 he set up the Rhode Island colony east of Connecticut. With its policy of religious **toleration** (TAH • luh • RAY • shuhn), the acceptance of different beliefs, Rhode Island became a safe place for **dissenters** (dih • SEHN • tuhrz), or people who disagreed with established views. It was the first place in America where people of all faiths could worship freely. **C** **R2**

The Middle Colonies In 1660 England had two clusters of colonies in what is now the United States—**New England Colonies** such as Massachusetts in the north, and agricultural colonies such as Virginia in the south. Between the two groups of English colonies were lands that the Dutch controlled. During the 1660s, these lands came under English rule and were known as the **Middle Colonies.** They included New York, Pennsylvania, New Jersey, and Delaware.

Key

1. Most of the crew slept in the tiny cabins in the **forecastle,** which also served as the ship's kitchen.
2. The *Mayflower* was a supply ship. It was not built to carry passengers. **'Tween decks** are where the passengers of the *Mayflower* slept and kept their belongings.
3. The **main hold** is the main cargo area. It holds most of the ship's stores of food and supplies and tools.
4. The **helmsman** moves a long lever called the **whipstaff** that moves the rudder and steers the ship.
5. The **great cabin** is the quarters for the commander of the ship.

Review Grade 5 Standards

To review standard 5.4.7 *(Explain the early democratic ideas and practices that emerged during the colonial period, including the significance of representative assemblies and town meetings)*, **ask:** What three steps toward self-government are described in this subsection? *(Massachusetts: signing of Mayflower Compact and creation of colonial legislature; Connecticut: Fundamental Orders as first written constitution in America)* OL

R1 Reading Strategy

Connecting Ask: What is the name of the document that organizes the structure of the U.S. government? *(the Constitution)* OL

C Critical Thinking

Comparing and Contrasting Ask: How did Massachusetts and Rhode Island differ on the issue of religious freedom? *(Massachusetts barred people who were not Congregationalists from practicing their faith; Rhode Island was open to people of all faiths.)* OL

R2 Reading Strategy

Understanding Vocabulary Ask: What does *dissent* mean? *(to disagree with)* What is a *dissenter*? *(someone who disagrees with an established view)* OL

Did You Know?

Roger Williams learned the language of the Narragansett people and was trusted by them. He worked hard for neighboring colonies and Rhode Island as a peacemaker with the local Native Americans.

C1 Critical Thinking

Making Generalizations Have students make two generalizations about each of three regions of colonial America. Ask students to share their generalizations with the class. OL

R1 Reading Strategy

Understanding Vocabulary
Ask: How are *persecute* and *toleration* opposed to each other? *(One means to treat people unfairly because of their beliefs or differences; the other means to accept others regardless of their beliefs or differences.)* OL

C2 Critical Thinking

Analyzing Primary Sources Have students rephrase the quotation from Penn in their own words. **Ask:** What does Penn mean? *(People are free when they play a role in forming the government that makes their laws.)* OL

R2 Reading Strategy

Academic Vocabulary
Discuss with students the use of the word *grant* as both a noun and a verb. EL

New York The desire for wealth drew the English to the area that was to become the colony of New York. Since the 1620s, this area had been ruled by the Dutch as New Netherland. In 1664 an English fleet took control of the prized port of New Amsterdam, and the Dutch quickly surrendered. England's King Charles II then gave New Netherland to his brother, the Duke of York, who renamed it New York. The port of New Amsterdam, later called New York City, became one of the fastest-growing commercial ports in England's American colonies.

A governor and council appointed by the Duke of York directed New York's affairs. The colonists demanded a representative government like the governments of the other English colonies. The duke resisted the ideas, but the people of New York would not give up. Finally, in 1691 the English government allowed New York to elect a legislature.

NATIONAL GEOGRAPHIC **Thirteen Colonies**

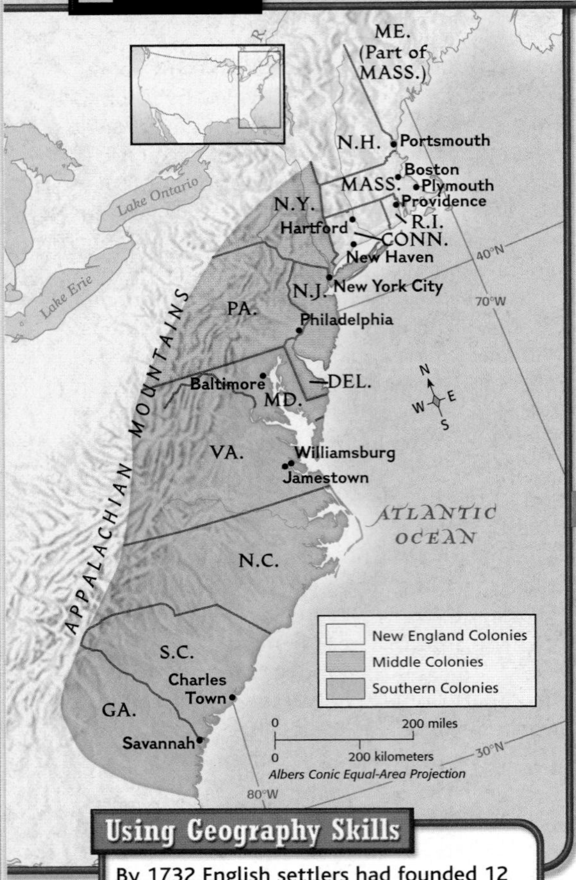

Using Geography Skills

By 1732 English settlers had founded 12 colonies on the eastern coast of what is now the United States.

1. **Region** What five colonies made up the Southern Colonies?
2. **Analyze** What geographic feature made Philadelphia and New York centers for trade?

Pennsylvania The Quakers, a Protestant group that had been **persecuted** (PUHR • sih • KYOOT • ehd), or treated harshly because of their beliefs or differences, in England, founded the colony of Pennsylvania. In 1680 **William Penn,** a wealthy English Quaker, received the land in payment for a debt King Charles II owed Penn's father. Pennsylvania, or "Penn's Woods," extended inland from the Delaware River and was as large as England. R1

William Penn saw Pennsylvania as a "holy experiment," a chance to put in practice the Quaker ideals of toleration and equality. In 1682 he sailed to America to supervise the building of Philadelphia, the "city of brotherly love." Penn believed that C1

> **"Any government is free to the people under it . . . where the laws rule, and the people are a party to those laws."** C2
>
> —from the *Frame of Government of Pennsylvania*

Penn believed that the land belonged to the Native Americans and that settlers should pay for it. Penn advertised his new colony, and by 1683 more than 3,000 English, Welsh, Irish, Dutch, and German settlers had arrived. In 1701 in the Charter of Liberties, Penn **granted** the colonists the right to elect representatives to the legislative assembly. R2

Answers and Additional Support

More Skill Practice

Historical and Social Sciences Analysis Skill Point out that Penn's *Frame of Government* provided for a representative assembly with limited powers. **Ask:** Why would Penn have considered such a document valuable? *(to prevent corrupt government from having too much power over the people; to make his colony attractive)* OL CA H13.

Using Geography Skills

Answers:

1. Maryland, Virginia, North Carolina, South Carolina, and Georgia
2. access to water enabled them to become thriving port cities

W **Virginia and the Southern Colonies** After early hardships, Virginia prospered from growing tobacco. Wealthy planters held the best land near the coast, so new settlers pushed inland. They increasingly began to settle on land belonging to Native Americans. In 1622 a revolt by a Native American group called the Powhatan Confederation nearly destroyed the colony. Following this revolt, the Virginia Company was accused of mismanaging the colony and lost its charter. In 1624 Virginia became a royal colony, with a governor and council appointed by the king. The House of Burgesses was retained, but its laws now had to receive royal approval. In addition, the Anglican Church was made the official religion of the colony. C

Maryland While Virginia struggled and grew, other English colonies were founded in the south. A Catholic noble, George Calvert, who held the title of Lord Baltimore, wanted to set up a safe place for fellow Catholics who faced persecution in England. His dream came true in 1632 when King Charles I gave him a colony north of Virginia. Calvert died before actually receiving the grant. His son Cecilius Calvert, the second Lord Baltimore, took charge of the colony. It was named Maryland after the English queen, Henrietta Maria.

Conflict, however, soon divided Maryland. Protestants as well as Catholics settled in the colony. Soon the Protestants outnumbered the Catholics. To protect Catholics from any attempt to make Maryland a Protestant colony, Lord Baltimore passed a law called the Act of Toleration in 1649. The act granted Protestants and Catholics the right to worship freely. R1 Although the Act initially failed in its goal, it was an early step toward the later acceptance of religious **diversity** (duh • VUHR • suh • TEE), or variety, in the colonies. R2

The Carolinas In the 1660s, King Charles II issued charters creating a large colony south of Virginia called Carolina. The king gave the colony to a group of eight prominent members of his court. The Carolina proprietors carved out large estates for themselves and provided money to bring colonists over from England.

Picturing History

Plantation agriculture became an important part of the economy of the Southern colonies. ***Why did Carolina separate and become two colonies?***

W Writing Support

Persuasive Writing Have students choose the colony in which they would have preferred to live and write a brief, persuasive paper explaining why. OL

CA 8WA2.4

C Critical Thinking

Identifying Central Issues

Ask: How were the rights of Virginians limited when it became a royal colony? *(Laws had to receive royal approval.)* OL

Review Grade 5 Standards

To review standard **5.4.3** *(Describe the religious aspects of the earliest colonies (e.g., Puritanism in Massachusetts, Anglicanism in Virginia, Catholicism in Maryland, Quakerism in Pennsylvania),* **ask:** Why did Lord Baltimore fear an attempt to make Maryland a Protestant colony? *(He was a Catholic and wanted to set up a safe place for Catholics.)* OL

R1 Reading Strategy

Connecting **Ask:** What other colonies tolerated more than one religion? *(Rhode Island, Pennsylvania)* BL

R2 Reading Strategy

Understanding Vocabulary

Ask: What is the opposite of diversity? *(sameness)* OL

CA 8RW1.3

Picturing History

South Carolinians had experimented with growing rice very early in the colony's history. Success came only after 1690, however, when new channels for the supply of enslaved African labor were opened. South Carolina's heavy reliance on enslaved African labor coincided closely with the development of rice as a new and profitable staple.

Answer: The settlers wanted a greater role in its government, so they seized control from its proprietors, leading to its division into two royal colonies.

U Universal Access

English Learners To help students understand debts and debtors, **ask:** What is borrowing? *(being given something for temporary use)* What word refers to money that has been borrowed and has to be repaid? *(debts)* EL

ASSESS

Resources for page 124

Use these resources to assess student mastery of section content.

Section Quiz 2–1

Interactive Tutor Self-Assessment CD-ROM

Reading Check

Answer: a law giving the right to worship; it was a step toward accepting religious diversity

History Online

Study Central provides summaries, interactive games, and online graphic organizers to help students review section content.

CLOSE

Monitoring **Ask:** What documents from this period contributed to the development of fair government? *(Mayflower Compact; Fundamental Orders of Connecticut; Charter of Liberties; Act of Toleration)* OL

Carolina, however, did not develop according to plan. By the early 1700s, Carolina's settlers wanted a greater role in the colony's government. In 1719 the settlers in southern Carolina seized control from its proprietors. In 1729 Carolina became two royal colonies—North and South Carolina.

Georgia Georgia, the last of the English colonies in America to be established, was founded in 1733. A group led by General James Oglethorpe received a charter to create a colony where English **debtors** (DEH • tuhrs)—people who are unable to repay their debts—could make a fresh start. However, most of Georgia's settlers were poor people from the British Isles or religious refugees from Europe's mainland.

The British government had another reason for creating Georgia. This colony could protect the other British colonies from Spanish attack. Great Britain and Spain had been at war in the early 1700s, and new conflicts over territory in North America were always breaking out. Located between Spanish Florida and South Carolina, Georgia could serve as a **military** barrier against Spain.

Many of the new settlers complained about the limits on the size of landholdings and the law banning slave labor. Oglethorpe reluctantly agreed to lift these bans. Frustrated by the colonists' demands and the colony's slow growth, Oglethorpe turned the colony back over to the king in 1751. By that time, British settlers had been in what is now the eastern United States for almost 150 years. They had lined the Atlantic coast with colonies.

Reading Check **Explain** What was Maryland's Act of Toleration, and why was it important?

History Online

Study Central Need help understanding colonial settlements? Visit ca.hss.glencoe.com and click on Study Central.

Section 1 Review

Reading Summary

Review the Main Ideas

- A number of European countries, including England, Spain, France, and the Netherlands, founded colonies in North America.
- The English settlers in Jamestown, Virginia, set up a representative government based on what they had known in England.
- The New England, Middle, and Southern Colonies were settled by the English and other Europeans for a variety of reasons, including religious freedom and financial gain.

What Did You Learn?

1. Why did the French originally come to North America?
2. What was the House of Burgesses?

Critical Thinking

3. **Organizing Information** Draw a table like the one below and fill in details about the New England, Middle, and Southern Colonies. CA HR3.

Region	Information
New England	
Middle Colonies	
Southern Colonies	

4. **Analyze** What was the Mayflower Compact and why was it important? CA HI1.
5. **The Big Idea** What challenges did early English settlers in North America face? Write a short essay that summarizes your conclusions. CA 8RC2.0
6. **Expository Writing** Write a short essay describing the importance of the search for religious freedom in the settling of America. Describe the founding of specific colonies in your essay. CA 8WA2.4
7. **Reading Identifying the Main Idea** Using the essay you wrote on the importance of religious freedom, summarize the main idea and supporting points from your essay. CA 8RC2.4

SECTION 1 REVIEW ANSWERS

Review Questions reinforce content standard US8.1.

1. to profit from fur trading
2. legislature of Virginia
3. Students may note the colonies in each region and the reasons for establishing them.
4. a contract for civil government; it was a crucial step toward the development of democracy in America
5. **The Big Ideas** Students may refer to starvation and clashes with Native Americans.
6. Students should refer to the colonies that were founded for religious reasons.
7. **Reading** Answers will depend on the main idea of the essay.

Section 2

Life in Colonial America

Guide to Reading

Looking Back, Looking Ahead
You read how the 13 English colonies were founded. Those colonies continued to grow and develop their own culture and beliefs about government.

Focusing on the Main Ideas
- As the population of the colonies grew, agriculture and trade increased. *(page 126)*
- An American culture, influenced by religion and education, began to develop. *(page 128)*
- Although the American colonies developed some self-government, the British still set many laws, especially those concerning trade. *(page 130)*

Locating Places
New York City
Philadelphia

Meeting People
Benjamin Franklin

Content Vocabulary
subsistence farming
triangular trade
cash crop
indentured servant (ihn • DEHN • shuhrd)
overseer
charter colony
proprietary colony (pruh • PRY • uh • TERH • ee)
royal colony

Academic Vocabulary
adapt
principle (PRIHN • suh • puhl)

Reading Strategy
Organizing Information Use a chart like the one below to describe the differences in the economies of the New England, Middle, and Southern Colonies.

Economic Development		
New England	Middle Colonies	Southern Colonies

History Social Science Standards

US8.1 Students understand the major events preceding the founding of the nation and relate their significance to the development of American constitutional democracy.

NATIONAL GEOGRAPHIC **Who & When?**

1700 | 1750 | 1800

African drum

1700s Thousands of Africans are brought to America

1730s Great Awakening takes root

George Whitefield

c. 1760 New York City's population reaches 25,000

SECTION RESOURCES

Print Material
- Reproducible Lesson Plan 2–2*
- Daily Lesson and Discussion Notes 2–2
- Guided Reading Activity 2–2
- Reading Essentials and Study Guide 2–2
- Active Reading Note-Taking Guide 2–2
- Section Quiz 2–2

*Available on TeacherWorks™

Transparencies
- Daily Focus Skills Transparency 2–2
- Section Graphic Organizer Transparency 2–2
- California Standards Practice Transparencies

Technology
- Interactive Tutor Self-Assessment CD-ROM
- Exam*View*® Pro Testmaker CD-ROM
- Presentation Plus! CD-ROM

FOCUS

BELLRINGER
SKILLBUILDER ACTIVITY

Project **Daily Focus Skills Transparency 2–2** and have students answer the question.

Guide to Reading

Preteaching Vocabulary:
Have students use the Glossary in the back of their textbooks to help them define each vocabulary word.

Answers to Graphic:
New England: small subsistence farms and businesses, fishing, shipbuilding, trade; Middle Colonies: large farms, cash crops, small-scale manufacturing, lumbering, mining, trade; Southern Colonies: large-scale plantations, use of indentured servants and enslaved Africans

Unpacking the Standards
After reading the section, students will be able to:
- Explain the growth of population, agriculture, and trade in the colonies.
- Describe the economic impact that slavery had in the Southern Colonies.
- Identify the influence of religion and education on American culture.
- Discuss the growing tensions between the colonies and Great Britain over trade.

TEACH

R Reading Strategy

Outlining Have students outline the section, filling in appropriate material under these four main headings: *New England Colonies*, *Middle Colonies*, *Southern Colonies*, and *Slavery*. Students may use their outlines for study before answering section review questions. OL

S Skill Practice

Historical and Social Sciences Analysis Skill
Ask: Why could the Middle Colonies grow larger quantities of crops than the New England Colonies? *(The soil was more fertile and the climate was milder.)* OL CA HI2.

C Critical Thinking

Comparing and Contrasting Ask: What was the difference between slaves and indentured servants? *(Indentured servants came to America willingly and only had to work until they earned back their passage.)* OL

Answers and Additional Support

US8.1 Students understand the major events preceding the founding of the nation and relate their significance to the development of American constitutional democracy.

R The Colonies Grow

Main Idea **As the population of the colonies grew, agriculture and trade increased.**

Reading Connection Is your community or region known for any special product, either agricultural or manufactured? Read to find out how the economies of the New England, Middle, and Southern Colonies differed.

An American Story

In 1760 Englishman Andrew Burnaby traveled throughout the North American colonies, observing American life. He could not imagine that these colonies would ever join in union for they were as different from one another as "fire and water," and each colony was jealous of the other.

Commercial New England Although Burnaby believed that the colonies would never unite, the colonies continued to grow. Economic success and religious and political freedoms drew a steady flow of new settlers.

Long winters and thin, rocky soil in New England made large-scale farming difficult. Farmers there practiced **subsistence farming,** which means that they generally produced just enough to meet the needs of their families, with little left over to sell or exchange.

Shipbuilding was an important New England industry. The lumber for building ships came from the forests of New England and was transported down rivers to the shipyards in coastal towns.

Colonial Trade As the center of the shipping trade in America, New England linked the different English American colonies and linked America to other parts of the world. Some ships followed routes that came to be called the **triangular trade** because the routes formed a triangle. On one leg of such a route, ships brought sugar and molasses from the West Indies to the New England Colonies. In New England, the molasses was made into rum. Next, the rum and other manufactured goods were shipped to West Africa where they were traded for enslaved Africans. On the final leg of the route, the enslaved Africans were taken to the West Indies where they were sold to planters. The profit was used to buy more molasses—and the process started over.

Growth of the Middle Colonies The Middle Colonies enjoyed fertile soil and a slightly milder climate than New England's. Farmers in this region cultivated larger areas of land and produced bigger harvests than did New Englanders. In New York and Pennsylvania, farmers grew large quantities of wheat and other **cash crops**—crops that could be sold easily in markets in the colonies and overseas. S

Farmers sent cargoes of wheat and livestock to **New York City** and **Philadelphia** for shipment, and these cities became busy ports. By the 1760s, New York, with 25,000 people, and Philadelphia, with 30,000 people, were the largest cities in the American colonies.

Like the New England Colonies, the Middle Colonies also had industries. Some were home-based crafts such as carpentry and flour making. Others included larger businesses such as lumbering, mining, and small-scale manufacturing.

The Middle Colonies attracted many German, Dutch, Swedish, and other non-English settlers. They gave the Middle Colonies a cultural diversity, or variety, that was not found in New England. With the diversity came tolerance for religious and cultural differences.

Plantation Life in the South With their rich soil and warm climate, the Southern Colonies were well suited to the growing of cash crops. These included tobacco, rice, and indigo, a blue flowering plant used to dye textiles. Most cash crops were grown on large farms called plantations. At first planters, or plantation owners, used **indentured servants** (ihn•DEHN•shurd) to work in the fields. Indentured servants were laborers who agreed to work without pay for a certain period of time to pay for their passage to America. C

Did You Know?

People in New England also relied on fishing. New Englanders fished for cod, halibut, crabs, oysters, and lobsters. Some ventured far out to sea to hunt whales, which were used for oil and whalebone.

When indentured servants became scarce and expensive, Southern farmers used enslaved Africans instead. Independent small farmers grew corn and tobacco on small farms. They usually worked alone or with their families. Independent small farmers outnumbered the large plantation owners. The plantation owners, however, had greater wealth and more influence. They controlled the economic and political life of the region.

Slavery in the Southern Colonies The slave trade and slavery were major parts of colonial economies. The inhumane part of the triangular trade, shipping enslaved Africans to the Americas, was known as the Middle Passage. Olaudah Equiano, a young African forced onto a ship to the Americas, later described the horror of the voyage across the Atlantic:

> **"We were all put under deck. . . . The stench . . . was so intolerably loathsome, that it was dangerous to remain there for any time. . . . The closeness of the place, and the heat of the climate, added to the number in the ship, which was so crowded that each had scarcely room to turn himself, almost suffocated us. . . ."**
>
> —from *The Interesting Narrative of the Life of Olaudah Equiano*

Most enslaved Africans in the southern colonies lived on plantations. Some of the Africans did housework, but most worked in the fields and often suffered great cruelty. The large plantation owners hired **overseers,** or bosses, to keep the slaves working hard. All the Southern Colonies had slave codes, which were strict rules governing the behavior and punishment of enslaved Africans. All white colonists were encouraged to enforce these laws against enslaved Africans.

African Traditions Although the enslaved Africans had strong family ties, their families were often torn apart. Slaveholders could split up families by selling a spouse, a parent, or a child to another slaveholder. Slaves who worked on plantations found a source of strength in their African roots. They developed a culture that drew on the languages, customs, and religions of their West African homelands.

Some enslaved Africans learned trades such as carpentry, blacksmithing, or weaving. Those lucky enough to be able to buy their freedom joined the small population of free African Americans.

Criticism of Slavery Slavery was one reason for the economic success of the Southern Colonies. That success, however, was built on the idea that one human being could own another. Some colonists did not believe in slavery. Many Puritans refused to hold enslaved people. In Pennsylvania, Quakers and Mennonites condemned slavery. Eventually, the debate over slavery would erupt in a bloody war, pitting North against South.

Reading Check **Explain** Why were the Southern Colonies especially well suited for growing cash crops?

***Picturing* History**

Among the early immigrants to America were some who did not come willingly. Western and Central Africans were taken by force from their homes, shipped across the Atlantic Ocean, and sold as slaves in North and South America. ***What does the term* Middle Passage *refer to?***

U1 Universal Access

Logical/Mathematical To help students comprehend the numbers of enslaved Africans taken from West Africa, provide the following data: British America—427,000; Mexico and Central America—224,000; West Indies—4,040,000; Spanish South America—522,000; Guianas—531,000; Brazil—3,647,000; Europe—175,000. **Ask:** What is the total estimated number of Africans shipped to other countries in the triangular trade? *(9,566,000)* What percentage went to British America? *(4.5 percent)* OL

U2 Universal Access

Intrapersonal Have students take the role of a person who did not own slaves who has read Equiano's account of the Middle Passage. Have them write a letter to the editor of a newspaper explaining what they think of slavery as a result of what they read. OL

R Reading Strategy

Understanding Vocabulary Have students contrast the terms *indentured servant* and *overseer*. **Ask:** Which had more power? *(overseers, who supervised the work of others)* OL

CA 8RW1.3

Reading Check

Answer: They had rich soils and warm climate.

Resources for page 127

Economics and History Activity 2

Did You Know?

Enslaved Africans found ways to express their anger and resentment at their condition. Some might kill an overseer or run away. Some runaways joined bands of other escapees, and some joined Native American groups. Others went to cities and tried to lose themselves in the free African American population.

***Picturing* History**

Between 1761 and 1775, more than 74,000 enslaved people were brought to the colonies. The leading colonies involved were South Carolina, Virginia, and Georgia.

Answer: the leg of the triangular trade in which enslaved Africans were shipped to the West Indies

R Reading Strategy

Academic Vocabulary Ask students to list synonyms for the word *adapt*. OL

Review Grade 5 Standards

To review standard **5.4.4** *(Identify the significance and leaders of the Great Awakening, which marked a shift in religious ideas, practices, and allegiances in the colonial period, the growth of religious toleration, and free exercise of religion.)*, **ask:** In what way did the Great Awakening have a powerful effect on the colonists' religious freedom? *(They came to believe they could choose their own faith.)* OL

Resources for page 128

Universal Access Activity 2

Academic Vocabulary Activity 2

Answers and Additional Support

US8.1 Students understand the major events preceding the founding of the nation and relate their significance to the development of American constitutional democracy. **US8.1.1** Describe the relationship between the moral and political ideas of the Great Awakening and the development of revolutionary fervor.

An Emerging Culture

Main Idea **An American culture, influenced by religion and education, began to develop.**

Reading Connection What are some things you consider truly American? Perhaps baseball or a summer picnic with hamburgers and hot dogs? Read to find out how the colonists began to form a culture that was different from those European cultures.

R Throughout the colonies, people **adapted** their traditions to the new conditions of life in America. Religion, education, and the arts contributed to a new American culture.

The Great Awakening Religion had a strong influence in colonial life. In the 1730s and 1740s, a religious revival called the Great Awakening swept through the colonies. In New England and the Middle Colonies, ministers called for "a new birth," a return to the strong faith of earlier days.

The most important effect of the Great Awakening was greater religious and political freedom in the colonies. More colonists chose their own faith, and the strength of established official churches declined. As a Baptist preacher noted soon after the Great Awakening, "the common people now claim as good a right to judge and act in matters of religion as civil rulers or the learned clergy."

Why It Matters

The Great Awakening

The Great Awakening is the name for the powerful religious revival that swept over the colonies beginning in the 1720s. Christian ministers such as George Whitefield and Jonathan Edwards preached throughout the colonies, drawing huge crowds. The Great Awakening had a lasting effect on the way in which the colonists viewed themselves, their relationships with one another, and their faith.

◀ Jonathan Edwards

Causes and Effects of the Great Awakening

Causes

- Jonathan Edwards, George Whitefield, and others preach of the need for a revival of religious belief.
- Awareness of the importance of religion in people's lives grows.
- A religious revival sweeps through America in the mid-1700s.

Why It Matters

Traveling revivalist ministers toured the colonies, attracting large crowds. They promoted religious zeal, gained converts, and increased church membership. The Great Awakening provided a sense of connection among the colonists, which proved beneficial during the American Revolution. Some members of the established churches rejected the revival because of its emotionalism. Since other members supported the revival, denominations divided into separate churches. **Ask:** How do you think a sense of American nationality affected the colonists? *(A growing sense of being Americans made the colonists feel less loyalty to Britain.)* AL

The Great Awakening also for the first time united colonists from north to south in a common cause. This paved the way for the rapid spread of political ideas and revolutionary fervor during the struggle for independence.

Education in the Colonies Most colonists valued education. Children were often taught to read and write at home by their parents, even though the daily chores left little time for lessons. In 1647 the Massachusetts Puritans passed a public education law. Each community had to have a teacher whose wages would be paid through taxes. Although some communities did not set up schools, most did. In the Middle Colonies, schooling was not as universal as in New England, but it was widespread. In the Southern Colonies, formal education was generally limited to children of large landowners and professionals such as lawyers and doctors. Even where schools were desired, the widely separated plantations and farms of the South made them impractical. Young children were usually educated by their parents or by tutors.

By modern standards, schools in the American colonies were primitive. Schools had few books, and instruction was given only two or three months a year. Only a small percentage of children received education beyond the primary level. Most girls received little formal education. Despite these shortcomings, few regions of the world had such a high proportion of people who could read or write.

Education was closely related to religion. The first colleges—Harvard, William and Mary, and Yale—were established to train ministers. Six colleges were in operation by 1763; all but two were founded by religious groups primarily for the training of ministers.

By the middle of the 1700s, many educated colonists also were influenced by the Enlightenment. This movement, which began in Europe, spread the idea that knowledge, reason, and science could improve society. The best-known scientist in the colonies was **Benjamin Franklin.** Franklin's greatest services to his fellow Americans would come during the 1770s when he would help guide the colonies to freedom.

Effects

- New religious groups such as the Baptists, Methodists, and Presbyterians take root.
- Emphasis on education grows.
- Belief grows that all people are equal before God.
- Makes Americans more willing to challenge authority prior to the American Revolution.

◀ George Whitefield

The Press in America Schools and colleges spread knowledge. So did books, newspapers, and almanacs. Because paper and type were expensive, most books came from Britain. Newspapers, printed weekly, were mostly four pages in length. Almanacs attracted as many readers as newspapers. In addition to a calendar, dates of holidays, times of sunset and sunrise, almanacs published advice on farming, poems, news of the year, and practical advice.

Reading Check **Analyze** What was the Enlightenment, and what effect did it have in the colonies?

S Skill Practice

Historical and Social Sciences Analysis Skill Point out that opposition to taxes for a community service has always existed. **Ask:** How does educating a community's children benefit the entire community? *(Educated people contribute to a community's economic growth.)* OL CA HI3.

W Writing Support

Research Reports Writing Have students work in groups to research the impact of the Great Awakening on the three churches mentioned here (Baptist, Methodist, Presbyterian) and on the other churches important in the colonies (Congregationalist, Anglican, Dutch Reformed, Quaker). Students should present their findings in a brief essay. OL CA 8WA2.3

C Critical Thinking

Determining Cause and Effect **Ask:** How did religion in early America influence education? *(The colonies' early colleges trained ministers.)* OL

Reading Check

Answer: a movement that started in Europe and spread the idea that knowledge, reason, and science could improve society; Ben Franklin's inventions helped improve the lives of many colonists.

Did You Know?

One Enlightenment idea that became popular in the colonies was the belief that the ultimate source of power for a government was the people. This idea was crucial to the formation of democracy in America.

Review The Big Idea

Review the Big Idea for this section: "Geography shapes the physical, economic, and political challenges a region faces." **Ask:** What geographical factors would have influenced the colonies' growing sense of independence? *(the Atlantic Ocean separating the colonies and Great Britain)* OL

R Reading Strategy

Understanding Vocabulary Have students examine the three vocabulary terms on this page. **Ask:** In which of the three types of colonies would the colonists be likely to enjoy the most freedom? *(charter)* Why? *(Because in royal or proprietary colonies, they had to obey the rules of the king or the owner.)* OL

C Critical Thinking

Drawing Conclusions Ask: Were the colonies democratic? Why or why not? *(They were more democratic than any nation in Europe, because a larger share of the population had the right to vote, but they were not completely democratic because many groups did not have that right.)* OL

Answers and Additional Support

US8.1 Students understand the major events preceding the founding of the nation and relate their significance to the development of American constitutional democracy. US8.1.4 Describe the nation's blend of civic republicanism, classical liberal principles, and English parliamentary traditions.

Colonial Government

Main Idea **Although the American colonies developed some self-government, the British still set many laws, especially those concerning trade.**

Reading Connection How would you feel if your parents or teachers told you that you could only trade lunch snacks or baseball cards with certain people, even if someone else had a better card or dessert they were willing to trade? Read to find out how the British attempted to maintain control over colonial trade.

In Chapter 1, you learned that the English colonists brought with them ideas about government that had been developing in England for centuries. At the heart of the English system were two **principles**—limited government and representative government. As the colonies grew, they relied more and more on their own governments to make local laws.

Picturing History

Colonial legislatures gave some Americans a voice in government. ***What groups were not represented?***

Self-Government in America The 13 colonies began either as charter or proprietary colonies. **Charter colonies,** such as Massachusetts, had a charter, or a grant of rights and privileges, granted by the English monarch to stockholders. **Proprietary colonies** (pruh • PRY • uh • TEHR • ee), such as Pennsylvania, were owned by an individual proprietor or by a small group of proprietors. R

Over time, English monarchs began to change colonies into **royal colonies.** Such colonies were under direct English control. In each, Parliament appointed a governor and council, known as the upper house. The colonists selected an assembly, the lower house. The governor and council members usually did what English leaders told them to do. However, this often led to conflicts with the colonists in the assembly, especially when officials tried to enforce tax laws and trade restrictions.

Colonial legislatures gave only some people a voice in government. White men who owned property had the right to vote; however, women, indentured servants, landless poor, and African Americans could not vote. In spite of these limits, a higher proportion of people became involved in government in the colonies than anywhere in the European world. This strong participation gave Americans training that was valuable when the colonies became independent. C

British Colonial Policies During the early 1700s, many changes occurred in England and its overseas colonies. In 1707 England united with Scotland and became the United Kingdom. The term *British* came to mean both the English and the Scots. By 1750 Great Britain had become the world's most powerful trading empire.

More Skill Practice

Historical and Social Sciences Analysis Skill Ask: Why might the colonists' growing amount of self-government lead to conflict with Britain's control over trade in the colonies? *(British control over trade would diminish the colonists' chance to control their own economy.)* AL CA HI1.

Picturing History

This work illustrates Peter Rothermel's technique of combining in a single painting sharp details, such as the figures in the foreground, with shadowy forms, as in the background.

Answer: women, indentured servants, landless poor, and African Americans

For many years, Great Britain had allowed the American colonies the freedom to run their local affairs. However, the British government controlled the colonies' trade according to the ideas of mercantilism. The American colonies produced raw materials such as tobacco, rice, indigo, wheat, lumber, fur, deerskin leather, fish, and whale products. These were shipped to Great Britain and traded for manufactured goods such as clothing, furniture, and goods from Asia, including tea and spices.

S To control this trade, Britain passed a series of laws called Navigation Acts in the 1650s. Under these laws, the colonists had to sell their raw materials to Britain even if they could get a better price elsewhere. Any goods bought by the colonies from other countries in Europe had to go to England first and be taxed before they could be sent to the Americas. The trade laws also said that all trade goods had to be carried on ships built in Britain or the colonies and that the crews had to be British as well.

Colonial Resistance The colonists at first accepted the trade laws because they were guaranteed a place to sell their raw materials. Later, the colonists came to resent British restrictions. With population in the colonies growing, the colonists wanted to make their own manufactured goods. They also wanted to sell their products elsewhere if they could get higher prices. Many colonial merchants began smuggling, or shipping goods in and out of the country without paying taxes or getting government permission. Controls on trade would later cause conflict between the American colonies and England.

Reading Check **Compare** How did charter colonies and proprietary colonies differ?

History Online
Study Central Need help understanding American self-government? Visit ca.hss.glencoe.com and click on Study Central.

Section 2 Review

Reading Summary

Review the Main Ideas

- As the colonies grew, differing economies developed in the New England, Middle, and Southern Colonies.
- In the colonies, family life, education, and religion were important in the emerging American culture.
- Even with British restrictions, especially on trade, the principle of self-government took a strong hold in the colonies.

What Did You Learn?

1. What was the triangular trade?
2. What were some cash crops grown on southern plantations? What crops were grown on smaller independent farms?

Critical Thinking

3. **Compare and Contrast** Draw a chart like the one below. Fill in details comparing farming in the New England and Southern Colonies. CA HR3.

	Similarities	Differences
New England		
Southern Colonies		

4. **Determining Cause and Effect** What effects did the Great Awakening have on the American colonies? CA HI2.
5. **The Big Ideas** How did geography affect the economies of the three colonial regions? CA CS3.
6. **Descriptive Writing** Imagine you live in New England in the mid-1700s and are visiting cousins on a farm in the Carolinas. Write a letter to a friend at home describing your visit to the farm. CA 8WA2.1

S Skill Practice

Historical and Social Sciences Analysis Skill

Ask: How did Britain accumulate great wealth at the expense of the colonies? *(through the requirements of the Navigation Acts)* OL CA HI6.

ASSESS

Resources for page 131

Use these resources to assess student mastery of section content.

- Section Quiz 2–2
- Interactive Tutor Self-Assessment CD-ROM

Reading Check

Answer: Charter colonies were granted rights by the monarch to stockholders; one or a few proprietors owned proprietary colonies.

History Online

Study Central provides summaries, interactive games, and online graphic organizers to help students review section content.

CLOSE

Comparing and Contrasting **Ask:** What was the primary means of economic growth for the New England colonies and for the Southern Colonies? *(New England: trade; Southern: plantations growing cash crops)* OL

SECTION 2 REVIEW ANSWERS

Review questions reinforce content standard US8.1.

1. trade route that linked America to West Africa
2. tobacco, rice, and indigo; corn, tobacco
3. Charts should show subsistence farming in both areas but cash crops in Southern Colonies.
4. revival of religious beliefs; promoted nationality; gave rise to new religions; emphasis on education grew; belief in equality of people grew; Americans more willing to challenge authority
5. **The Big Ideas** Geography affected farming in New England and Southern Colonies.
6. Letters might mention details about servants or slaves, the crops, or the climate.

FOCUS

History–Social Science Standards

The following standard is covered on pages 132–133

US8.1 Students understand the major events preceding the founding of the nation and relate their significance to the development of American constitutional democracy.

TEACH

C Critical Thinking

Making Inferences Ask: Why would the English people have to force King John to sign the Magna Carta? *(He probably did not want to give up any of his power.)* OL

W Writing Support

Persuasive Writing Have students look at the quotation from Thomas Jefferson and write an essay in which they describe what they think are the essential elements of free government. Ask volunteers to present their ideas to the class. AL CA 8WA2.4

Connecting to the Constitution

US8.1.4 Describe the nation's blend of civic republicanism, classical liberal principles, and English parliamentary traditions. **US8.2.1** Discuss the significance of the Magna Carta, the English Bill of Rights, and the Mayflower Compact.

The Road to Representative Government

Why It Matters Many of the rights that American citizens enjoy today can be traced back to the political and legal traditions of England. When English people began settling here in the 1600s, they brought with them a tradition of limited and representative government.

Limited Government By the time the first colonists reached North America, the idea that government was not all-powerful had become an accepted part of the English system. The concept first appeared in the Magna Carta, or Great Charter, that King John was forced to sign in 1215. The Magna Carta established the principle of limited government, in which the power of the **monarch,** or ruler, was limited, not absolute. This document protected the nobles' privileges and upheld their authority. It also granted certain rights to all landholders—rights that eventually came to apply to all English people.

English Parliamentary Traditions The English people had a firm belief in **representative government,** in which people elect delegates to make laws and conduct government. The English Parliament was a representative assembly with the power to make laws. It consisted of two houses, the House of Lords and the House of Commons. American legislatures grew from the English practice of representation.

In the mid-1600s, Parliament and King James II began a struggle for power. In 1688 Parliament removed King James II from the throne and crowned William and Mary to rule.

Thomas Jefferson

"Freedom of religion, freedom of the press, trial by jury, habeas corpus, and a representative legislature . . . I consider as the essentials constituting free government, ..."

—Thomas Jefferson in a letter to Pierre Samuel Dupont de Nemours, 1815

132

Answers and Additional Support

More Skill Practice

Historical and Social Sciences Analysis Skill Tell students that *habeas corpus* means that a person who has been accused of a crime must be brought before the court for a trial. **Ask:** Why would Jefferson have considered habeas corpus an essential right? *(It protects people from being held in prison for no reason.)* OL CA HI2.

Did You Know?

The Glorious Revolution was also called the Bloodless Revolution because the king was replaced without any fighting. King James II had virtually no support. Religious differences were involved in this conflict. James II, a Catholic, wanted to return England to the Catholic Church. The largely Protestant Parliament would not permit that.

▲ By signing the Mayflower Compact, the Pilgrims established a set of rules under which they would govern themselves.

This peaceful transfer of power, known as the Glorious Revolution, changed the idea of government in England. From that time on, no ruler would have more power than the legislature.

R1 **The English Bill of Rights** To set clear limits to what a ruler could and could not do, Parliament drew up the English Bill of Rights in 1689. The document stated that the monarch could not suspend Parliament's laws; the monarch also could not create special courts, impose taxes, or raise an army without Parliament's consent. The Bill of Rights also declared that members of Parliament would be freely elected and be guaranteed free speech during meetings, that every citizen would have the right to a fair trial by jury in court cases, and that cruel and unusual punishments would be banned.

The English Heritage in America English settlers in the American colonies established traditions of representative government that they had learned in England. They believed that the ruler was not above the law. They also expected to have a voice in government and other basic rights. Many of the early state constitutions listed the rights of the citizens.

The Virginia House of Burgesses The first permanent English settlement in North America was Jamestown. At first, the Jamestown colony was managed by a governor and council appointed by the Virginia Company, a group of merchants from London. In 1619, however, the colonists chose two representatives from each community to meet with the governor and his council. These 22 men were called burgesses. They formed the House of Burgesses, which was the first representative assembly, or legislature, in the English colonies. The House of Burgesses had little power, but it marked the beginning of self-government in colonial America.

The Mayflower Compact In 1620, shortly after the House of Burgesses was formed, a new group of colonists, known as the Pilgrims, arrived in America. Even before their ship, the *Mayflower*, reached America, the Pilgrims realized they needed rules to govern themselves if they were to survive in a new land. They drew up a written plan for their government called the Mayflower Compact. R2

The Mayflower Compact stated that the government would make "just and equal laws . . . for the general good of the colony." The compact set up a direct democracy in which all men would vote and the majority would rule. (As was common at this time, only adult males were permitted to vote.)

The Mayflower Compact established a tradition of direct democracy. Throughout the colonial period—and in parts of New England today—citizens meet at town meetings to discuss and vote on important issues.

Checking for Understanding

1. What is the system of representative government? Where did this system come from?
2. What is important about the Virginia House of Burgesses?

Critical Thinking

3. **Evaluate** The idea of limited government, first established in the Magna Carta, is an important principle of the U.S. Constitution. Do you believe governments should be limited? Why or why not?

Connecting to the Constitution

R1 Reading Strategy

Categorizing Information
Ask: Which parts of the Bill of Rights were about the rights and powers of the people as a group, as they were represented in Parliament? *(Monarch cannot suspend Parliament's laws, could not take certain actions without Parliament's consent, and Parliament would be freely elected.)* Which addressed individual rights? *(Members of Parliament could speak freely, all people had the right to a jury trial, and cruel and unusual punishments are banned.)* OL

R2 Reading Strategy

Sequencing Information
Ask: What came first, the Mayflower Compact or the English Bill of Rights? *(Mayflower Compact)* OL

ASSESS

Have students answer the Checking for Understanding and Critical Thinking questions.

CLOSE

Drawing Conclusions Ask: How was the development of limited and representative government in the American colonies a natural progression of the English system of government? *(Colonists were accustomed to such government when they lived in England. Also, the Virginia House of Burgesses and the Mayflower Compact reinforced the ideas.)* OL

Questions reinforce content standard US8.1

Checking for Understanding:

1. a government in which people elect delegates to make laws and conduct government; the English Parliament
2. It was the first representative assembly in the English colonies.

Critical Thinking:

3. Students may say that limiting government power is the best way to ensure people's freedom.

FOCUS

BELLRINGER
SKILLBUILDER ACTIVITY

Project **Daily Focus Skills Transparency 2–3** and have students answer the question.

Guide to Reading

Preteaching Vocabulary: Use the Vocabulary Puzzle-Maker CD-ROM to create crossword and word search puzzles.

Answers to Graphic: prevented the arrival of food and supplies to Boston Harbor; ended town meetings; forced colonists to shelter British soldiers in their homes

Unpacking the Standards

After reading the section, students will be able to:

- Discuss how colonists reacted to British government actions.
- Describe the meeting of the first Continental Congress.
- Explain why the American Revolution broke out.

Section 3

Trouble in the Colonies

Guide to Reading

History Social Science Standards

US8.1 Students understand the major events preceding the founding of the nation and relate their significance to the development of American constitutional democracy.

Looking Back, Looking Ahead

In the last section, you read about the beginnings of colonial resistance to British colonial policies. British attempts to tax the colonists brought the Americans and British to conflict.

Focusing on the Main Ideas

- Following Britain's victory in the French and Indian War, the British prohibited colonists from moving west of the Appalachian Mountains and taxed the colonists to pay for the war. ***(page 135)***
- British actions, including sending more troops to Boston and passing new taxes, brought strong responses from the colonists. ***(page 137)***
- After colonial leaders met to discuss their relations with Britain, the first shots of the American Revolution were fired. ***(page 139)***

Meeting People

Crispus Attucks
Samuel Adams
John Adams
Patrick Henry
George Washington
King George III
Paul Revere

Content Vocabulary

import
smuggling
boycott
repeal (rih • PEEL)
resolution
militia (muh • LIH • shuh)
minutemen

Academic Vocabulary

convince
violate (VY • uh • LAYT)
correspond

Reading Strategy

Organizing Information Use a diagram like the one below to describe how the Intolerable Acts affected Massachusetts colonists.

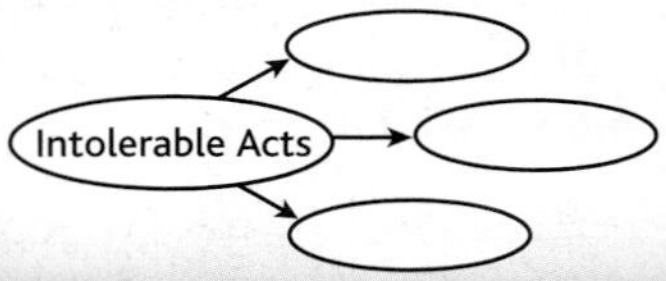

NATIONAL GEOGRAPHIC Where & When?

1760	1770	1780

- **1763** Proclamation of 1763 limits colonial migration
- **1770** Boston Massacre takes place
- **1775** First battles of American Revolution at Lexington and Concord

SECTION RESOURCES

Print Material
- Reproducible Lesson Plan 2–3*
- Daily Lesson and Discussion Notes 2–3
- Guided Reading Activity 2–3
- Reading Essentials and Study Guide 2–3
- Active Reading Note-Taking Guide 2–3
- Section Quiz 2–3

*Available on TeacherWorks™

Transparencies
- Daily Focus Skills Transparency 2–3
- Section Graphic Organizer Transparency 2–3
- California Standards Practice Transparencies

Technology
- Interactive Tutor Self-Assessment CD-ROM
- Exam*View*® Pro Testmaker CD-ROM
- Presentation Plus! CD-ROM

US8.1 Students understand the major events preceding the founding of the nation and relate their significance to the development of American constitutional democracy. US8.1.4 Describe the nation's blend of civic republicanism, classical liberal principles, and English parliamentary traditions.

Chapter 2 • Section 3

R New British Policies

Main Idea **Following Britain's victory in the French and Indian War, the British prohibited colonists from moving west of the Appalachian Mountains and taxed the colonists to pay for the war.**

Reading Connection Have you ever stopped buying a product, perhaps because the manufacturer changed the product or raised its price? Read to find out how the American colonists protested British actions, in part by refusing to buy British products.

An American Story

During the colonial period, Britain and France struggled for control of eastern North America. As their settlements moved inland, both nations claimed the vast territory between the Appalachian Mountains and the Mississippi River. In 1758 writer Nathaniel Ames noted,

S1

> **"The parts of North America which may be claimed by Great Britain or France are of as much worth as either kingdom. That fertile country to the west of the Appalachian Mountains [is the] 'Garden of the World'!"**
>
> —from the *Astronomical Diary and Almanack*, 1758

The French and Indian War In 1754 British-French rivalry led to the outbreak of the French and Indian War. Colonial leaders met in Albany, New York, to find a way for the colonies to defend themselves against the French. The leaders adopted the Albany Plan of Union, calling for "one general government" for 11 of the American colonies. However, the plan was not approved. After Britain won the war in 1763, the colonies began to act together. Their united action, however, was directed against Britain itself. What developments brought about this unusual turn of events?

C

S2

NATIONAL GEOGRAPHIC Proclamation of 1763

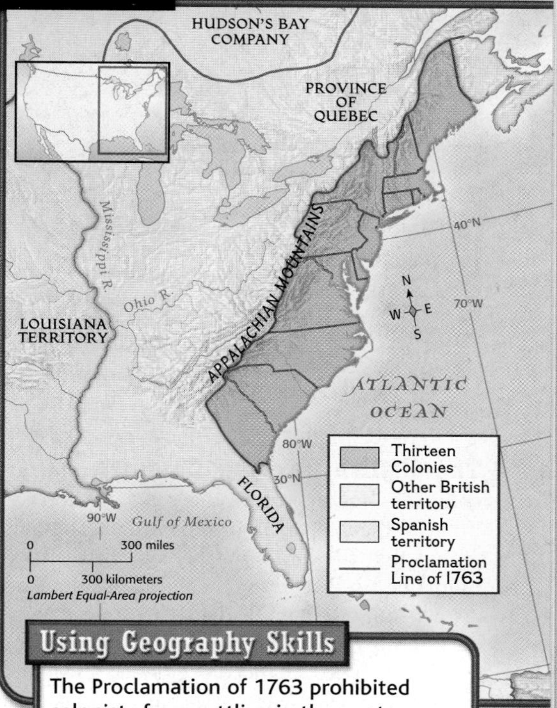

Using Geography Skills

The Proclamation of 1763 prohibited colonists from settling in the west.

1. **Place** What natural feature marked the western boundary of British territory?
2. **Analyze** Who controlled the Louisiana Territory in 1763?

The Proclamation of 1763 Victory in 1763 gained for the British nearly all of France's North American empire. That same year, Britain issued a proclamation that prohibited colonists from moving west of the Appalachian Mountains. Stopping western settlement allowed British officials to control settler movement and avoid a conflict with Native Americans. It also prevented colonists from moving away from the coast—where Britain's important markets and investments were. To protect their interests, the British planned to keep 10,000 troops in America.

TEACH

R Reading Strategy

Taking Notes Encourage students to take notes on the subsection about new British policies. Suggest that they use the five subheadings as ways of organizing their notes. **BL**

S1 Skill Practice

Analyzing Primary Sources Have students read the quotation from Nathaniel Ames. **Ask:** What effect would words like this have on the American colonists? Why? *(make them want to expand to those lands; because the description makes them sound valuable)* **OL**

C Critical Thinking

Drawing Conclusions Ask: Why would it have been easier for a united group of colonies to defend themselves against the French? *(By uniting, the colonies could have pooled their resources to use them more effectively and made plans that could be coordinated.)* **OL**

S2 Skill Practice

Using Geography Skills Refer students to the map on this page. **Ask:** Which group of people lived west of the Proclamation Line of 1763 but are not shown on the map? *(Native Americans)* **OL** **CA CS1.**

More Skill Practice

Historical and Social Sciences Analysis Skill Ask: What did Britain do to let the colonists know it was serious about preventing their westward expansion? *(decided to keep 10,000 troops in America)* **BL** **CA HI1.**

Using Geography Skills

Answers:

1. the Mississippi River
2. Spain

In-Text Map Transparency 2
Ask: What geographic feature bordered the colonies to the east? *(the Atlantic Ocean)* **OL**

R1 Reading Strategy

Understanding Vocabulary Write the phrases "buy goods from foreign countries"; "buy goods illegally"; "refuse to buy"; and "officially cancel a law" on the board in random order. Then write the four terms—*import*, *smuggle*, *boycott*, and *repeal*—to the side. Ask volunteers to match a term with the correct definition. OL

R2 Reading Strategy

Academic Vocabulary Ask students to read the sentence that contains the word *violated*. Then ask them to rewrite the sentence in their own words. OL

C Critical Thinking

Analyzing Information
Ask: What result of the Stamp Act protests was good for the colonists? Why? *(Parliament repealed the tax, which is what the colonists wanted.)* What result was bad for the colonists? Why? *(Parliament passed the Declaratory Act, which rejected Otis's argument.)* OL

Reading Check
Answer: banned colonists from moving west of Appalachians; limited their freedom

Answers and Additional Support

The Stamp Act required colonists to buy revenue stamps for newspapers, licenses, and documents. ▶

▼ The snake on the banner symbolized united American resistance to the British.

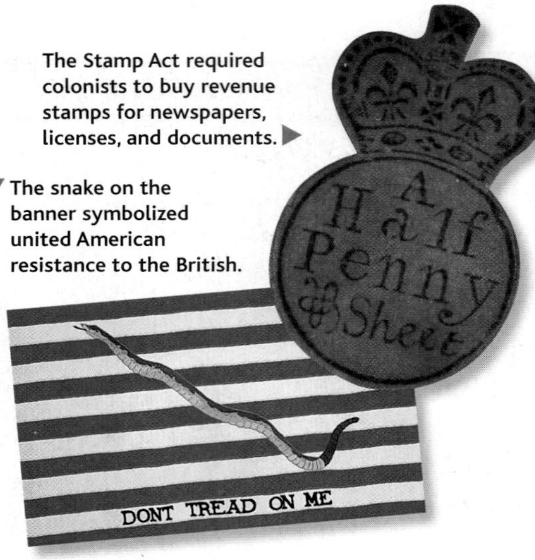

The British Tax the Colonies Alarmed colonists, however, saw the proclamation as a limit on their freedom of movement. They also feared that the large number of British troops might be used to interfere with their liberties. As a result, feelings of distrust began to grow between Britain and its American colonies.

Britain faced financial problems. The French and Indian War was very costly and left the British government deep in debt. Desperate for money, the British made plans to tax the colonies and tighten trade rules.

In 1764 the British Parliament passed the Sugar Act, which lowered the tax on molasses that had been **imported,** or bought from foreign markets, by the colonists. The British government hoped the lower tax would **convince** the colonists to pay the tax instead of **smuggling.** Smuggling means to trade illegally with other nations. The colonists believed their rights as Englishmen were being **violated.** James Otis, a young lawyer in Boston, argued that:

> **"no parts of [England's colonies] can be taxed without their consent . . . every part has a right to be represented."**
>
> —from *The Rights of the British Colonies*

What Was the Stamp Act? In 1765 Parliament passed another law in an effort to raise money. This law, known as the Stamp Act, placed a tax on newspapers and other printed material. All of these items had to bear a stamp showing that the tax was paid. The colonists were outraged. In October, delegates from nine colonies met in New York at the Stamp Act Congress. They sent a letter to the British government stating that the colonies could not be taxed except by their own assemblies. Colonists refused to use the stamps. They also **boycotted,** or refused to buy, British goods.

In February 1766, Parliament gave in to the colonists' demands and **repealed** (rih•PEELD), or cancelled, the Stamp Act. On the same day, however, it passed the Declaratory Act. This law stated that Parliament had the right to tax and make decisions for the British colonies "in all cases." The colonists might have won one battle, but the war over making decisions for the colonies had just begun.

New Taxes In 1767 Parliament passed another set of tax laws known as the Townshend Acts. In these acts, the British leaders tried to avoid some of the problems the Stamp Act caused. They understood that the colonists would not tolerate internal taxes—those levied or paid inside the colonies. As a result, the new taxes applied only to imported goods, with the tax being paid at the port of entry. The taxed goods, however, included basic items—such as glass, tea, paper, and lead—that the colonists had to import because they did not produce them.

The Colonists React By this time, the colonists were outraged by *any* taxes Parliament passed. They believed that only their own representatives had the right to levy taxes on them. The colonists responded by bringing back the boycott that had worked so well against the Stamp Act. The boycott proved to be even more widespread this time.

Reading Check **Explain** What was the Proclamation of 1763, and why did it anger American colonists?

More Skill Practice

Historical and Social Sciences Analysis Skill **Ask:** Which principle of the British government did Otis use as the basis of his argument? *(representative government; he claimed that the colonists had no real representation in Parliament)* OL

Did You Know?

The Stamp Act incited opposition from the vast majority of colonists. In addition to newspapers, the tax was on legal documents, licenses, playing cards, and even dice. It greatly affected the most powerful professionals in colonial society—publishers, lawyers, real estate owners, shipowners, and tavern owners.

US8.1 Students understand the major events preceding the founding of the nation and relate their significance to the development of American constitutional democracy.

Tax Protests Lead to Revolt

Main Idea **British actions, including sending more troops to Boston and passing new taxes, brought strong responses from the colonists.**

Reading Connection How might you protest a new community or school rule that you believed was unfair? Read to find out how American protests to British measures became forceful.

Colonial protests like those related to the Stamp Act made British colonial officials nervous. Worried customs officers sent word back to Britain that the colonies were close to rebellion. Parliament responded by sending two regiments of troops to Boston. As angry Bostonians jeered, the newly arrived "redcoats" set up camp right in the center of the city.

The Boston Massacre On March 5, 1770, tensions between the redcoats and Bostonians reached a peak. That day a crowd of colonists began insulting soldiers and throwing stones, snowballs, oyster shells, and pieces of wood at the soldiers. "Fire, you bloodybacks, you lobsters," the crowd screamed. "You dare not fire."

After one of the soldiers was knocked down, the nervous and confused soldiers did fire. Seven shots rang out, killing five colonists. Among the dead was **Crispus Attucks,** a dockworker who was part African, part Native American. The colonists called the tragic encounter the Boston Massacre.

The Boston Massacre led many colonists to call for stronger boycotts on British goods. Aware of the growing opposition to its policies, Parliament repealed all the Townshend Acts taxes except the one on tea. Many colonists believed they had won another victory. They started to trade with British merchants again.

Some colonial leaders, however, continued to call for resistance to British rule. In 1772 the Massachusetts radical leader **Samuel Adams** revived the Boston committee of **correspondence,** an organization used in earlier protests. The committee circulated writings about colonists' grievances against Britain.

Picturing **History**

The Bloody Massacre (below) is an engraving by Paul Revere. The site of the Boston Massacre in present-day Boston is pictured to the right. ***How did the colonists react to the news of the Boston Massacre?***

Picturing **History**

Redcoats was the name the Patriots used to describe British soldiers. The Patriots also called the British *bloodybacks* and *lobsters* to ridicule their bright red uniforms.

Answer: by calling for stronger boycotts

S Skill Practice

Historical and Social Sciences Analysis Skill Have students construct a time line of events starting with the Stamp Act and leading up to the American Revolution. OL CA CS2.

W Writing Support

Persuasive Writing Use the Boston Massacre to help students understand that every historical event has two points of view. Have each student write an editorial from the point of view of either a British officer or Samuel Adams. Student should incorporate, as well as distinguish between, factual information and opinion in their editorial. Invite students to share their editorials with the class. OL CA HR5. CA 8WA2.4

Review The Big Idea

Review the Big Idea for this section: "Political ideas and major events shape how people form governments." **Ask:** What issues were the colonists most concerned about? *(taxes; Parliament's increasing control over the colonies; their rights as citizens)* OL

C Critical Thinking

Determining Cause and Effect **Ask:** Why would the events of the Boston Massacre raise more opposition to the British among the colonists? *(Students may say that colonists would see the bloodshed as an example of how cruel and oppressive the British were.)* OL CA HR5. CA HI2.

R Reading Strategy

Connecting **Ask:** What similarities to the *Committee of Correspondence* exist today? *(e-mails; telephones)* EL

S Skill Practice

Historical and Social Sciences Analysis Skill Tell students that the tea the colonists threw into Boston Harbor would be worth more than $700,000 today. **Ask:** Why was East India tea cheaper than colonial tea? *(It was not taxed.)* OL

W Writing Support

Persuasive Writing Have students take the role of a member of Parliament giving a speech in support of the Coercive Acts. Tell them to explain why the colonists should be punished. Ask volunteers to deliver their speeches. OL CA 8WA2.4 CA 8SA2.4

Reading Check

Answer: It threatened the livelihood of colonial tea merchants; from the colonists' point of view, it was yet another example of unfair taxing or unfair business practices.

Answers and Additional Support

Soon other committees of correspondence sprang up throughout the colonies, bringing together protesters opposed to British measures.

Crisis Over Tea By the early 1770s, some Americans considered British colonial policy a "conspiracy against liberty." The British government's actions seemed to confirm that view. In 1773 Parliament passed the Tea Act. It allowed the British East India Company to ship tea to the colonies without paying the taxes colonial tea merchants had to pay. This allowed the company to sell its tea very cheaply and threatened to drive the colonial tea merchants out of business.

In Massachusetts, angry colonists decided to take action. A group of protestors dressed as Native Americans boarded several British ships in Boston Harbor and dumped their cargoes of tea overboard, an event that became known as the Boston Tea Party. Word of this act of defiance spread throughout the colonies. Men and women gathered in the streets to celebrate.

To punish the colonists, Parliament in 1774 passed the Coercive Acts, which closed down Boston Harbor and put the government of Massachusetts under military rule. The laws also said that British troops should be quartered, or given a place to live in colonists' homes. The colonists called these the Intolerable Acts, or laws they could not bear. They maintained that the Coercive Acts violated their rights as English citizens.

Reading Check **Analyze** Why were American colonists especially angry with the Tea Act?

MORE ABOUT... The Boston Tea Party

The Boston Tea Party is one of the significant events that ultimately led to American independence.

By 1770, most of the Townshend Acts have been repealed. The tax on tea remains.

In November 1773, the citizens of Boston refuse to allow three British ships to unload 342 chests of tea.

On the evening of December 16, Boston citizens disguised as Native Americans board the ships and empty the tea into Boston Harbor.

King George III and Parliament respond by closing the city port.

"Fellow countrymen, we cannot afford to give a single inch! If we retreat now, everything we have done becomes useless!"

— *Samuel Adams, December 1773*

MORE ABOUT...

Have students draw a political cartoon showing the story of the Boston Tea Party. Tell them to take the perspective of either the colonists or the British government. Have students display their cartoons and discuss how the two sides viewed the event differently. OL CA HR5. CA 8LS1.9

Resources for page 138

- American Literature Reading 2
- Chart, Map, and Graph Skills Activity 2

US8.1 Students understand the major events preceding the founding of the nation and relate their significance to the development of American constitutional democracy. **US8.1.4** Describe the nation's blend of civic republicanism, classical liberal principles, and English parliamentary traditions.

A Call to Arms

Main Idea **After colonial leaders met to discuss their relations with Britain, the first shots of the American Revolution were fired.**

Reading Connection Have you ever served on a student council or another youth group? If so, did that group work together for the benefit of all members? Read to find out how Americans from nearly every colony came together to discuss the colonies' disagreements with Britain.

Colonial leaders realized the colonies had to act together in their opposition to British policies. In September 1774, fifty-six men arrived in the city of Philadelphia. Sent as delegates from all the colonies except Georgia, these men had come to establish a political body to represent American interests and challenge British control. They called the new organization the Continental Congress.

Leaders from all the colonies attended the Continental Congress. Massachusetts sent Samuel Adams and his younger cousin **John Adams,** a successful lawyer. New York sent John Jay, another lawyer. From Virginia came Richard Henry Lee and **Patrick Henry,** two of the most outspoken defenders of colonial rights, as well as **George Washington.** Patrick Henry summarized the meaning of the gathering: "The distinctions between Virginians, Pennsylvanians, New Yorkers, and New Englanders are no more.... I am not a Virginian, but an American."

The delegates were hardly united in their views, but they realized they needed to work together. First they drafted a statement of grievances calling for the repeal of 13 acts of Parliament passed since 1763. They declared that these laws violated the colonists' rights.

The delegates also voted to boycott all British goods and trade. No British products could be brought into or consumed in the colonies, and no colonial goods could be shipped to Britain. The Continental Congress's most important **resolution,** or formal expression of an opinion, concerned the armed forces. After much debate the delegates decided to form militias. A **militia** (muh•LIH•shuh) is a group of citizen soldiers. If fighting broke out, the colonies would be ready with their own armed forces.

Primary Sources

▲ Teapot, c.1770

The Coming Conflict

The American people hoped that the boycott called for by the Continental Congress against British goods and trade would win a quick victory without war. Some members of the Continental Congress believed that economic pressure would force Britain to back down. Richard Henry Lee of Virginia noted that the British "army and fleet will be recalled, and Britain will give up her foolish project."

Other members of the Continental Congress doubted that Great Britain would back down.

In a paper titled "Broken Hints," Joseph Hawley of Massachusetts wrote:

> "We must fight, if we cannot otherwise rid ourselves of British taxation, all revenues, or the constitution or form of government enacted for us by the British Parliament....
>
> Fight we must, finally, unless Britain retreats."

DBQ Document-Based Question

According to Lee, how will Great Britain react? Do Lee or Hawley believe that war is certain to come? Explain your reasoning.

C1 Critical Thinking

Making Inferences Ask: Why did the colonial leaders decide they needed to act together to oppose British policies? *(Students may say that their actions could be more effective if coordinated.)* OL

C2 Critical Thinking

Analyzing Primary Sources Ask: What does Henry mean in this quotation? *(People saw themselves as part of a large group of people with common concerns, not as those from only one colony.)* Why is that attitude significant? *(Students may say that it shows the beginning of a feeling of national identity)* OL CA HR4. CA HI3.

S Skill Practice

Historical and Social Sciences Analysis Skill
Ask: Why would boycotting all British goods lead to a harsh reaction from the British? *(because the British depended on trade from the colonies to build wealth)* OL CA HI2. CA HI6.

R Reading Strategy

Understanding Vocabulary Have students demonstrate their understanding of the vocabulary terms by using each in an original sentence. OL

Resources for page 139

Biography Activity 2A

Primary Sources

Answers: Lee thinks Britain will recall its army and navy and give up. Students may say that Lee seems to believe the British will give up, whereas Hawley seems to think a fight is more likely.

R1 Reading Strategy

Understanding Vocabulary Direct students to the term *minutemen*. **Ask:** What are some examples of similar words? *(fireman, newsman)* OL

C Critical Thinking

Analyzing Primary Sources Tell students that King George III said that "blows must decide" who would control America. **Ask:** What does this statement mean? *(The issue would be settled by fighting.)* OL

R2 Reading Strategy

Inferring Direct students to Paul Revere's warning, "The regulars are out!" **Ask:** What did Paul Revere mean by *regulars*? *(British soldiers)* Point out that Revere is often said to have cried "The British are coming," but those were not the words he used. OL

Preparing for Battle People in the colonies and in Britain wondered whether this meant war. The answer came soon after the Continental Congress adjourned in October.

Colonists expected that if fighting against the British broke out, it would begin in New England. Militia companies in Massachusetts held frequent training sessions, made bullets, and stockpiled rifles and muskets. Some companies, known as **minutemen,** boasted that they would be ready to fight on a minute's notice. R1

The British also prepared for conflict. **King George III** announced to Parliament that the New England colonies were "in a state of rebellion." By April 1775, British general Sir Thomas Gage had 3,000 soldiers under his command in and around Boston. Gage had instructions to take away the weapons of the Massachusetts militia and arrest the leaders. C

Gage learned that the militia was storing arms and ammunition at Concord, a town 20 miles northwest of Boston. He ordered 700 troops to Concord to seize artillery.

Alerting the Colonists On the night of April 18, 1775, the colonists **Paul Revere** and William Dawes rode to Lexington, a town east of Concord, to warn that the British were coming. Revere galloped off across the moonlit countryside, shouting, "The regulars are out!" R2 to the people and houses he passed along the way. When he reached Lexington, he raced to tell Sam Adams and John Hancock his news. Adams could barely control his excitement. "What a glorious morning this is!" Adams was ready to fight for American independence.

Fighting at Lexington and Concord At dawn the redcoats approached Lexington. When they reached the center of the town they discovered a group of about 70 minutemen who had been alerted by Revere and Dawes.

NATIONAL GEOGRAPHIC

The Battles of Lexington and Concord

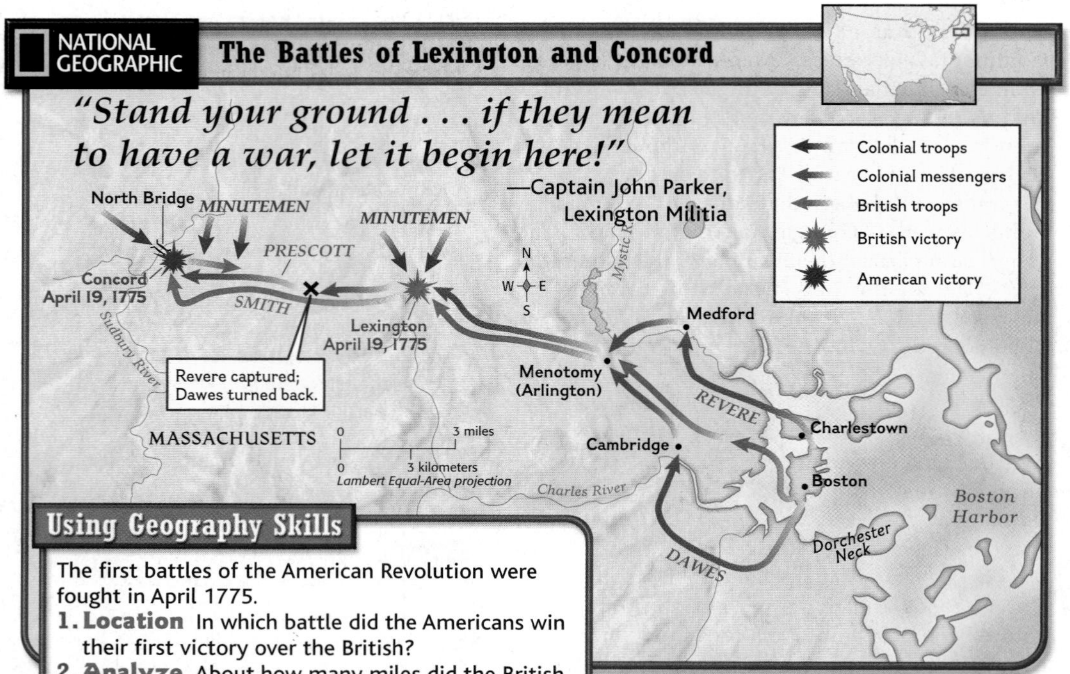

Using Geography Skills

The first battles of the American Revolution were fought in April 1775.

1. **Location** In which battle did the Americans win their first victory over the British?
2. **Analyze** About how many miles did the British troops march from Lexington to Concord?

140

Answers and Additional Support

Using Geography Skills

Answers:

1. Concord
2. about 6 miles.

In-Text Map Transparency 2 Ask: How did the colonists ensure that messengers would reach Menotomy? *(by sending them on two different routes.)* OL

Led by Captain John Parker, the minutemen had positioned themselves on the town common with muskets in hand.

A shot was fired, and then both sides let loose with an exchange of bullets. When the fighting was over, eight minutemen lay dead. The first shots had been fired. But who had fired them? According to one of the minutemen at Lexington, British Major John Pitcairn had given the order to fire. British officers and soldiers told a different story. They claimed that the minutemen had fired first.

C

The British troops continued their march to Concord. When they arrived there, they discovered that most of the militia's gunpowder had already been removed. They destroyed the remaining supplies. At Concord's North Bridge, the minutemen were waiting for them.

Messengers on horseback had spread word of the British movements. All along the road from Concord to Boston, farmers, blacksmiths, saddle makers, and clerks hid behind trees, rocks, and stone fences. As the British marched down the road, the militia fired. By the time the redcoats reached Boston, more than 200 were wounded and 73 were dead. Making matters worse for the British, more than 20,000 militiamen now held Boston under siege.

The Coming Revolution After the bloodshed in Massachusettes, colonial leaders appealed for separation from Great Britain. Many colonists were not ready for independence. As you will see, events during the winter of 1775–1776, however, moved the colonists ever closer to the fight for independence.

Looking back, the poet Ralph Waldo Emerson wrote in "The Concord Hymn" that the Americans at Lexington and Concord had fired the "shot heard 'round the world." The battle for America's independence from Great Britain had begun.

Reading Check **Identify** What is a militia?

History Online
Study Central Need help understanding the road to war? Visit ca.hss.glencoe.com and click on Study Central.

Section 3 Review

Reading Summary

Review the Main Ideas

- American colonists protested restrictive tax laws enacted by the British to help pay for the French and Indian War, such as the Sugar Act and the Stamp Act.
- Events such as the Boston Massacre and the Boston Tea Party demonstrated the growing level of conflict between the British and the Americans.
- Fighting broke out between colonial militia and British troops at Lexington and Concord in Massachusetts in 1775.

What Did You Learn?

1. Why did the British issue the Proclamation of 1763?
2. How did the British punish the colonists for the Boston Tea Party?

Critical Thinking

3. **Sequencing** Re-create the diagram below. Fill in important events with their dates beginning with the Boston Massacre and ending with the fighting at Lexington and Concord. CA CS2.

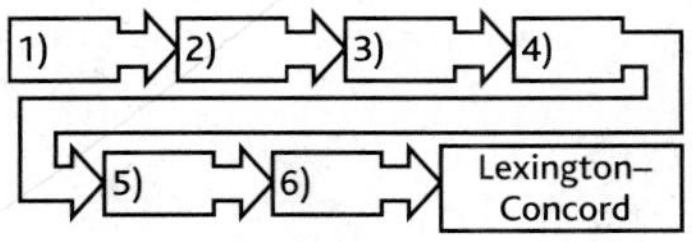

4. **Drawing Conclusions** Do you think the Boston Tea Party was a turning point in the relationship between the British and the colonists? Explain. CA CS1.
5. **The Big Ideas** What political ideas led to the formation of the Continental Congress? CA HI2.
6. **ANALYSIS** **Economics and History** How did laws passed by the British Parliament after 1763 affect American trade and industry? How did the British intend to help their economy through these laws? CA HI6.

SECTION 3 REVIEW ANSWERS

Review questions reinforce content standard US8.1.

1. to ban colonists from moving west of the Appalachians so they could avoid conflict with Native Americans
2. They passed the Coercive Acts.
3. Time lines might include such events as the Boston Tea Party, the Intolerable Acts, and the meeting of the Continental Congress.
4. Students should support their position with reasons.
5. The Big Ideas natural law, the English constitution, and colonies' charters
6. ANALYSIS The laws made the colonists more dependent on British goods. The British hoped to recover funds for the costly French and Indian War.

C Critical Thinking

Comparing and Contrasting **Ask:** How did the American fighters differ from the British fighters? *(The colonists were civilians who came to fight for a cause; the British were professional soldiers who were following orders to fight.)* OL

ASSESS

Resources for page 141

Use these resources to assess student mastery of section content.

Section Quiz 2–3

Interactive Tutor Self-Assessment CD-ROM

Reading Check

Answer: a group of citizen soldiers

History Online

Study Central provides summaries, interactive games, and online graphic organizers to help students review section content.

CLOSE

Sequencing Information
Direct students to the time line in the Section Review. Have them choose the event they believe to be the greatest cause for declaring independence and write a paragraph explaining their choice. OL

FOCUS

Summary

The narrator describes how Paul Revere tells a Patriot friend to watch whether the British soldiers leave Boston to march to Concord by land or by sea and to signal the answer to him. Revere waits across the river, receives the signal, and then rides through the night warning Patriots in many towns to take up their arms and prepare for battle.

Vocabulary Preview Before students begin reading, have them read **Before You Read** and the **Vocabulary Preview**. Point out that difficult words are footnoted throughout the text.

Background Information

This narrative poem by Henry Wadsworth Longfellow evokes the drama and heroism of Revere's ride, but it was meant as a call to arms. Longfellow began writing it in the spring of 1860, as the threat of a civil war grew more likely. It was published in January 1861, as the first wave of Southern states seceded from the Union. The poem aimed to rally the people of the North to the need for new heroism.

Answers and Additional Support

Paul Revere's Ride

By Henry Wadsworth Longfellow

Before You Read

The Scene: A group of friends is gathered around a fire at the Wayside Inn near Boston. Each person in turn tells a story in verse.

The Characters: The landlord is the first storyteller. The patriot Paul Revere is the topic of the landlord's poem.

The Plot: Paul Revere is waiting for a signal. It will be one or two lanterns in the belfry, or bell tower, of the Old North Church in Boston. When Revere sees the signal, he sets off to warn the Patriots. The British troops are on the way to seize the Patriots' guns and gunpowder.

Vocabulary Preview

dread: fear because of evil that is about to occur

gilded: covered with a thin layer of gold

impetuous: acting suddenly without thought

somber: shaded as to be dark and gloomy

stealthy: slow and careful

tranquil: calm

Have you ever wondered what actually happened during an important historical event? In this poem, the landlord at the Wayside Inn is describing what he thinks Paul Revere's ride to Lexington and Concord was like.

◀ *Paul Revere* by John Singleton Copley

Reading Strategy: SETTING A PURPOSE

As students read the poem, have them look for images and phrases that give Paul Revere a heroic quality. Have them begin by thinking about what makes a hero. **Ask:** What kinds of actions are heroic? *(Students may name such actions as fighting for a noble cause, struggling against the odds, and responding to a crisis.)* Have students try to find words, phrases, and actions that show these and other heroic qualities in Revere. **OL**

As You Read

R *Longfellow vividly describes the places in the poem—Boston Harbor, the Old North Church, and the towns—that Revere visits on his ride. These descriptions give the poem a special tone, or feeling. Think about what it might have been like to be a Patriot in Massachusetts at the time of Revere's ride. What do you think it may have been like to make that ride? What kind of person could do such a dangerous thing?*

Listen, my children, and you shall hear
Of the midnight ride of Paul Revere,
On the eighteenth of April, in Seventy-five;
Hardly a man is now alive
Who remembers that famous day and year.

He said to his friend, "If the British march
By land or sea from the town to-night,
Hang a lantern aloft in the belfry arch
Of the North Church tower as a signal light,—
One, if by land, and two, if by sea;
And I on the opposite shore will be,
Ready to ride and spread the alarm
Through every Middlesex[1] village and farm,
For the country folk to be up and to arm."

Then he said, "Good night!" and with muffled[2] oar
Silently rowed to the Charlestown shore,
Just as the moon rose over the bay,
Where swinging wide at her moorings[3] lay
The Somerset, British man-of-war;[4]
A phantom ship, with each mast and spar[5] C
Across the moon like a prison bar,
And a huge black hulk, that was magnified
By its own reflection in the tide.

[1] **Middlesex:** Massachusetts county
[2] **muffled:** wrapped with something to dull the sound
[3] **moorings:** lines or chains holding a ship in place
[4] **man-of-war:** warship
[5] **spar:** strong piece of wood used to support sails

TEACH

R Reading Strategy

Activating Prior Knowledge **Ask:** What do you remember about the battles of Lexington and Concord? *(Students should recall the British mission and the rides of Revere and Dawes.)* OL CA 8RL3.7

C Critical Thinking

Making Inferences Have a student read aloud the lines about the British ship. **Ask:** How does the ship symbolize British colonial rule? *(The shadow cast by its masts on the moon are like prison bars; the colonists felt imprisoned by the actions of the British government.)* OL

Glencoe Literature Library

The following literature from the **Glencoe Literature Library** may enrich the teaching of this chapter:

Johnny Tremain by Esther Forbes

EXTENDING THE CONTENT

Setting the Record Straight Longfellow does not accurately tell the story of Revere's ride. He ignores the role played by others, such as Dr. Joseph Warren, who worked with Revere in planning the ride; William Dawes, who also rode to Lexington; the men who rowed Revere across the Charles River; and the other riders sent out by Patriots in the various towns that Revere reached. Longfellow wrongly places Revere across the river to receive the lantern signals from Old North Church; he only crossed the river *after* they were sent. Finally, Longfellow incorrectly says that the rider reached Concord. Though Revere delivered his warning at Lexington, he was arrested by British patrols before reaching Concord. Another Patriot—Dr. Samuel Prescott—brought word to that town.

R Reading Strategy

Reading Primary Sources
Ask: What is the mood in these seven lines? What words does the poet use to convey this mood? *(tension, quiet, an ominous threat)* OL CA 8RL3.4

U Universal Access

Verbal/Linguistic Have a volunteer read aloud the stanza. Encourage him or her to use expression. Discuss how hearing the poem read aloud increases the feeling of tension it describes. OL CA 8LS1.1

C Critical Thinking

Making Inferences Tell students that all the images in the poem are important. **Ask:** How does the reference to the cemetery fit in? *(A war is about to begin, and people will probably die.)* OL

GLENCOE BOOKLINK

Use **Glencoe BookLink** to create customized reading lists for your students' reading levels, interests, and abilities.

Answers and Additional Support

America's Literature

Meanwhile, his friend, through alley and street,
Wanders and watches with eager ears,
Till in the silence around him he hears
The muster[6] of men at the barrack[7] door,
The sound of arms, and the tramp of feet,
And the measured tread of the grenadiers,[8]
Marching down to their boats on the shore.

Then he climbed the tower of the Old North Church,
By the wooden stairs, with stealthy tread,
To the belfry-chamber overhead,
And startled the pigeons from their perch
On the sombre rafters, that round him made
Masses and moving shapes of shade,—
By the trembling ladder, steep and tall,
To the highest window in the wall,
Where he paused to listen and look down
A moment on the roofs of the town,
And the moonlight flowing over all.

[6] **muster:** an assembling group (of soldiers)
[7] **barrack:** building in which soldiers live
[8] **grenadiers:** soldiers

Beneath, in the churchyard, lay the dead,
In their night-encampment[9] on the hill,
Wrapped in silence so deep and still
That he could hear, like a sentinel's[10] tread,
The watchful night-wind, as it went
Creeping along from tent to tent,
And seeming to whisper, "All is well!"
A moment only he feels the spell
Of the place and the hour, and the secret dread
Of the lonely belfry and the dead;
For suddenly all his thoughts are bent
On a shadowy something far away,
Where the river widens to meet the bay,—
A line of black that bends and floats
On the rising tide, like a bridge of boats.

[9] **encampment:** place where a group is camped
[10] **sentinel:** guard

144

READING STRATEGY VISUALIZING

In these three stanzas, the poet describes the experience of Paul Revere's Patriot colleague moment by moment. Have students describe the pictures that come into their minds as they read the stanzas. Then have them note how Longfellow slows the narrative to focus on this part of the story. **Ask:** What effect does the poet achieve with this focus? *(mood of seriousness, dread; feeling of heightened drama)* OL

Meanwhile, impatient to mount and ride,
Booted and spurred, with a heavy stride
On the opposite shore walked Paul Revere.
Now he patted his horse's side,
Now gazed at the landscape far and near,
Then, impetuous, stamped the earth,
And turned and tightened his saddle-girth,[11]
But mostly he watched with eager search
The belfry-tower of the Old North Church,
As it rose above the graves on the hill,
Lonely and spectral[12] and sombre and still.
And lo! as he looks, on the belfry's height
A glimmer, and then a gleam of light!
He springs to the saddle, the bridle he turns,
But lingers and gazes, till full on his sight
A second lamp in the belfry burns!

A hurry of hoofs in a village street,
A shape in the moonlight, a bulk in the dark,
And beneath, from the pebbles, in passing, a spark
Struck out by a steed[13] flying fearless and fleet;
That was all! And yet, through the gloom and the light,
The fate of a nation was riding that night;
And the spark struck out by that steed, in his flight,
Kindled the land into flame with its heat.

He has left the village and mounted the steep,
And beneath him, tranquil and broad and deep,
Is the Mystic,[14] meeting the ocean tides;
And under the alders[15] that skirt its edge,
Now soft on the sand, now loud on the ledge,
Is heard the tramp of his steed as he rides.

[11] **girth:** strap that goes around the body of an animal
[12] **spectral:** ghostly
[13] **steed:** horse
[14] **Mystic:** river that flows into Boston Harbor
[15] **alders:** type of tree

145

R1 Reading Strategy

Determining Importance
Ask: Why does the poet shift the focus from Revere's colleague to Revere? *(because we want to see Revere's reaction to the lights)* OL

R2 Reading Strategy

Reading Primary Sources
Ask: How does Revere's mood differ in the beginning and end? *(In the beginning Revere is impatient and restless; in the end, he is ready for action.)* OL

U Universal Access

English Learners Explain that the words *booted* and *spurred* are used as adjectives. **Ask:** Who do they describe? *(Revere)* What do they mean? *(He was wearing boots and spurs.)* OL

R3 Reading Strategy

Analyzing Text Structure
Here Longfellow is simply piling one image on top of another; he never includes a verb to turn the collection of phrases into a complete sentence. **Ask:** What is the effect of this rapid sequence of phrases? *(It symbolizes the racing horse and rider, who are never in one spot for long but speed along the road.)* OL

Reading Strategy — SUMMARY WRITING

Have students write a straightforward prose summary of the action of the poem with none of the emotional or figurative language that Longfellow uses. Ask two or three volunteers to read their summaries aloud. Then have a volunteer read two or three stanzas of the poem aloud. **Ask:** How do the rhythm of the language and the images that Longfellow uses create a more dramatic effect while telling the same story? OL CA 8WA2.1

R1 Reading Strategy

Analyzing Text Structure Discuss with students the effect of noting the time that Revere arrives in each town throughout the night. **Ask:** How does noting the time reveal Revere's dedication? *(Students may point out that he must be determined because he rides deep into the night.)* OL CA 8RL3.3

U Universal Access

Advanced Learners Explain that words such as *bleating* and *twitter* are onomatopoeic; that is, the word sounds like what it means. Flocks of sheep make a sound like bleating, and birds make sounds like twittering. Invite students to name other onomatopoeic words. *(Students might suggest such words as hiss and buzz.)* AL

R2 Reading Strategy

Inferring Explain that in foreshadowing, authors hint at events that will take place later in their narratives. **Ask:** What is Longfellow foreshadowing here? *(Some of the Patriots responding to Revere's call will be killed in the fighting.)* OL

Answers and Additional Support

It was twelve by the village clock,
When he crossed the bridge into Medford town.
He heard the crowing of the cock,
And the barking of the farmer's dog,
And felt the damp of the river fog,
That rises after the sun goes down.

It was one by the village clock,
When he galloped into Lexington.
He saw the gilded weathercock[16]
Swim in the moonlight as he passed,
And the meeting-house windows, blank and bare,
Gaze at him with a spectral glare,
As if they already stood aghast[17]
At the bloody work they would look upon.

[16] **weathercock:** a movable device in the shape of a rooster that shows the direction of the wind
[17] **aghast:** shocked

It was two by the village clock,
When he came to the bridge in Concord town.
He heard the bleating of the flock,
And the twitter of birds among the trees,
And felt the breath of the morning breeze
Blowing over the meadows brown.
And one was safe and asleep in his bed
Who at the bridge would be first to fall,
Who that day would be lying dead,
Pierced by a British musket-ball.[18]

[18] **musket-ball:** bullet from a gun

Reading Strategy — READING PRIMARY SOURCES

Words and phrases in a poem help convey certain images and therefore evoke a mood. Words such as "motionless" and "tranquil" create a calm mood. Phrases such as "flying down the hill" evoke speed. Divide the class into groups and assign each group a stanza of the poem. Have them analyze that stanza for the words and images it contains and the mood that they convey. Have the groups share their findings. Discuss how Longfellow uses these images to change mood throughout the poem. OL

You know the rest. In the books you have read,
How the British Regulars fired and fled,—
How the farmers gave them ball for ball,
R1 From behind each fence and farm-yard wall,
Chasing the red-coats down the lane,
Then crossing the fields to emerge again
Under the trees at the turn of the road,
And only pausing to fire and load.

So through the night rode Paul Revere;
And so through the night went his cry of alarm
To every Middlesex village and farm,—
A cry of defiance and not of fear,
R2 A voice in the darkness, a knock at the door,
And a word that shall echo forevermore!
For, borne on the night-wind of the Past,
Through all our history, to the last,
S In the hour of darkness and peril and need,
The people will waken and listen to hear
The hurrying hoof-beats of that steed,
And the midnight message of Paul Revere.

Responding to the Literature

1. According to the speaker in the first stanza, did Revere's ride happen recently or a long time ago? What shows when it took place?
2. What did it mean if Revere saw one lantern in the belfry? What did it mean if he saw two?
3. **Analyze** How did Longfellow use repetition in the poem? Why did he use it? CA 8RL3.6
4. **Explain** What is the meaning of the following lines?

   That he could hear, like a sentinel's tread,
   The watchful night-wind, as it went
   Creeping along from tent to tent,
   And seeming to whisper, "All is well!" CA 8RL3.6
5. **Read to Write** What kind of person do you think Paul Revere was? What actions in the poem show these characteristics? CA 8WA2.2.d

R1 Reading Strategy

Analyzing Text Structure
Ask: Why does Longfellow spend so little time talking about the aftermath of Revere's ride? *(His subject is Revere's heroism.)* OL

R2 Reading Strategy

Analyzing Text Structure
Ask: What does Longfellow mean by "a cry of defiance and not of fear"? *(Revere was not afraid of the British.)* OL CA 8RL3.3

S Skill Practice

Historical and Social Sciences Analysis Skill
Explain to students that Longfellow wrote his poem on the eve of another war. **Ask:** What effect would these words have on Americans? *(Students may say that this stanza will convince Americans to do their part for their country, just as Revere did.)* OL CA 8RL3.7

ASSESS

Have students answer the Responding to the Literature questions.

CLOSE

Connecting Discuss with students how they view Paul Revere after having read this poem. OL

Responding to the Literature Answers

1. a long time ago; the poet gives the date (April 18, 1775), but reveals it was a long time ago by saying that few now living were alive back then
2. one lantern—the British were marching by land; two lanterns—the British were traveling by boat
3. Longfellow repeated words or phrases at the beginning of stanzas; the effect is usually to hurry the pace of the lines.
4. The evening breeze was gentle and reassuring.
5. Possible answers: heroic, brave, committed; he paced impatiently waiting to see the signal and rode with dedication through the night

Reading on Your Own. . .

TEACH

The reading selections for this unit have been chosen to reflect the California History-Social Science Standards. If you assign one of these books, you may want to have students complete the following activity.

Monitoring

Students can monitor their comprehension as they read by asking questions and answering them. They can apply this skill to both fiction and nonfiction. Suggest they follow these steps:

- When reading fiction, ask what relationship the characters have to each other and what events preceded others.
- When reading nonfiction, ask about the sequence of events and the causes and effects of different occurrences.

GLENCOE **BOOKLINK**

Use **Glencoe BookLink** to create customized reading lists for your students' reading levels, interests, and abilities.

Answers and Additional Support

Reading On Your Own...

From the California Reading List

Do you want to learn more about the Age of Exploration and life in the American colonies? You might be interested in the following books.

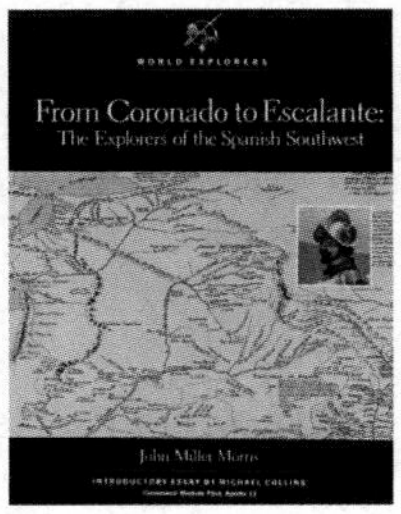

Nonfiction

From Coronado to Escalante: The Explorers of the Spanish Southwest by John M. Morris describes two kinds of searches. Coronado's is for gold and Escalante's is for converts to Catholicism. As readers follow these men, they see the land and Native Americans as the Spanish saw them. ***The content of this book is related to*** *History–Social Science Standard US7.11.*

Historical Fiction

I, Juan de Pareja by Elizabeth Barton de Treviño tells the tale of the African slave Juan and his famous master, the Spanish painter Velasquez. This story describes how Juan becomes an accomplished artist in spite of the laws against slaves learning how to paint. ***The content of this book is related to*** *History–Social Science Standard US7.11.*

Historical Fiction

Maggie's Choice by Norma Jean Lutz takes place during the Great Awakening. When a slave girl dies, Maggie must choose between her conscience, which is supported by the teachings of Jonathan Edwards, and her wealthy friends' way of life. ***The content of this book is related to*** *History–Social Science Standard US8.1.*

Biography

John Peter Zenger by Karen T. Westermann describes Zenger and what happened as the result of his dangerous decision to criticize the colonial government in his newspaper. Zenger's trial was one of the reasons freedom of the press was included in the Bill of Rights. ***The content of this book is related to*** *History–Social Science Standard US8.3.*

READING STRATEGY — TAKING NOTES

To help students practice finding the main idea and supporting details, have them take notes as they read. Taking notes will help them remember important details that support the main idea as well as engage them in the reading. Tell them that writing questions as they read will likewise assist their reading—and that the questions will likely be answered as they read further. **OL**

Section 4 War of Independence

Guide to Reading

Looking Back, Looking Ahead
You learned that American colonists and British troops fired the first shots of the Revolutionary War at Lexington and Concord. It took many battles, fought throughout the colonies, and many casualties before the Americans won their independence.

Focusing on the Main Ideas
- As colonial forces and British troops continued to fight, colonial leaders met again to plan their resistance to Britain. ***(page 150)***
- The Declaration of Independence used traditional English political rights to call for independence for the colonies. ***(page 152)***
- America's victory and independence led to revolutions in other parts of the world. ***(page 153)***

Meeting People
Thomas Paine
Bernardo de Gálvez
Marquis de Lafayette (LAH • fee • EHT)
John Paul Jones

Content Vocabulary
petition (puh • TIH • shuhn)
preamble (PREE • AM • buhl)
Patriots
neutral (NOO • truhl)
Loyalists
guerrilla warfare (guh • RIH • luh)

Academic Vocabulary
challenge
secure (sih • KYUR)
technique (tehk • NEEK)
occupy (AH • kyuh • PY)

Reading Strategy
Organizing Information Draw a diagram like the one below. Use it to list the reasons why the Americans were able to defeat the British in the Revolutionary War.

Reasons for the British defeat

History Social Science Standards

US8.1 Students understand the major events preceding the founding of the nation and relate their significance to the development of American constitutional democracy.

NATIONAL GEOGRAPHIC Where & When?

1776 — 1779 — 1782

1776 American colonies declare independence

1777 American armies victorious at Saratoga

1781 British surrender at Yorktown

CHAPTER 2 Section 4, 149–157

FOCUS

BELLRINGER — Skillbuilder Activity
Project **Daily Focus Skills Transparency 2–4** and have students answer the question.

Guide to Reading
Preteaching Vocabulary: Have students write each term on an index card. When they encounter the term in their reading, they should write the definition and its context on the card.

Answers to Graphic: British were not on their home land; American's victory at Yorktown; other nations helped America

Unpacking the Standards
After reading the section, students will be able to:
- Describe how colonial leaders planned their resistance.
- Outline the ideas behind the Declaration of Independence.
- Identify how American forces won the Revolutionary War.
- Explain how America's Revolutionary War led to revolutions in other parts of the world.

SECTION RESOURCES

Print Material
- Reproducible Lesson Plan 2–4*
- Daily Lesson and Discussion Notes 2–4
- Guided Reading Activity 2–4
- Reading Essentials and Study Guide 2–4
- Active Reading Note-Taking Guide 2–4
- Section Quiz 2–4

*Available on TeacherWorks™

Transparencies
- Daily Focus Skills Transparency 2–4
- Section Graphic Organizer Transparency 2–4
- California Standards Practice Transparencies

Technology
- Interactive Tutor Self-Assessment CD-ROM
- Exam*View*® Pro Testmaker CD-ROM
- Presentation Plus! CD-ROM

TEACH

C Critical Thinking

Drawing Conclusions
Ask: What did Colonel Prescott mean by telling the soldiers not to fire until they could "see the whites of their eyes"? *(to wait until the British were close enough that shots would be sure to hit them)* Why did he say that? *(The Americans were low on ammunition, and he wanted to ensure that their fire would be as damaging as possible.)* OL

R Reading Strategy

Connecting Tell students that petitions are still used to address grievances today. **Ask:** Have you ever seen people collecting signatures on a petition? OL

S Skill Practice

History and Social Sciences Analysis Skills
Common Sense was first published anonymously. **Ask:** Why would Paine do that? *(Paine's words were treasonous.)* OL
CA HI1.

Reading Check
Answer: They realized that defeating the Americans would not be quick or easy.

Answers and Additional Support

US8.1 Students understand the major events preceding the founding of the nation and relate their significance to the development of American constitutional democracy.

Moving Toward Independence

Main Idea **As colonial forces and British troops continued to fight, colonial leaders met again to plan their resistance to Britain.**

Reading Connection Have you ever read a book that was so well written and so powerful that it changed your mind about a subject? Read to find out about a pamphlet that changed many Americans' minds about remaining united with Britain.

An American Story

On June 16, 1775, about 1,200 militiamen under Colonel William Prescott set up fortifications at Bunker Hill and nearby Breed's Hill, across the harbor from Boston. The next day, the British redcoats crossed the harbor and charged up Breed's Hill. With his forces low on ammunition, Colonel Prescott reportedly shouted the order:

C
> **"Don't fire until you see the whites of their eyes."**

The Americans opened fire, forcing the British to retreat. The redcoats charged two more times, receiving furious fire. In the end the Americans ran out of gunpowder and had to withdraw.

The British won the Battle of Bunker Hill but suffered heavy losses. As one British officer wrote in his diary, "A dear bought victory, another such would have ruined us." The British learned that defeating the Americans on the battlefield would not be easy.

The Second Continental Congress As fighting raged in the Boston area, the Second Continental Congress met in Philadelphia. Among its delegates were distinguished colonial leaders such as John and Samuel Adams, Patrick Henry, George Washington, Benjamin Franklin, and Thomas Jefferson.

The Second Continental Congress began to govern the colonies. It immediately created the Continental Army to fight against Britain in a more organized way than the colonial militias could. The Congress unanimously chose George Washington to be the army's commander.

Congress Petitions King George After Washington left to take charge of the colonial forces in Boston, the delegates offered Britain a chance to avoid war. In July, the Continental Congress sent a **petition** (puh•TIH•shuhn), or formal request, to King George III. Called the Olive Branch Petition, it assured the king of the colonists' desire for peace. It asked the king to protect the colonists' rights, which Parliament seemed determined to destroy. George III refused. Instead he prepared for war, hiring more than 30,000 German troops to send to America to fight beside British troops. R

Who Was Thomas Paine? By late 1775 and early 1776, more and more Americans began to think that independence was the only answer. In January 1776, a writer named **Thomas Paine** convinced many when he published a pamphlet called *Common Sense.* Paine used strong language to condemn the king and called for complete separation from Britain. He told the colonists that their cause was not just a squabble over taxes but a struggle for freedom: S

> **"The cause of America is in a great measure the cause of all mankind."**
>
> —*Common Sense*

Common Sense circulated widely and helped convince thousands of American colonists that it was "time to part." At the Second Continental Congress in Philadelphia, delegates appointed a committee to draft a declaration of independence. Thomas Jefferson of Virginia wrote the historic document. After making some changes, the Congress approved the Declaration of Independence on July 4, 1776.

Reading Check **Explain** How did the Battle of Bunker Hill change British expectations about the war?

Resources for page 150
- Biography Activity 2B
- Primary Source Reading 2

Did You Know?

John Adams of Massachusetts nominated George Washington to be commander in chief of the Continental Army, partly for political reasons. Washington came from the highly influential colony of Virginia, and naming him to lead the army would help win Virginia's support for the idea of independence.

Biography

US8.1 Students understand the major events preceding the founding of the nation and relate their significance to the development of American constitutional democracy.

BENJAMIN FRANKLIN

1706–1790

Benjamin Franklin, born in Boston in 1706, was the 15th of 17 children in the Franklin family. Although Franklin loved learning, he left school at the age of 10 to help his father in the candle-making profession. Unsatisfied with this life, Franklin began learning the printer's trade two years later. By the time he was 23, he owned his own newspaper in Philadelphia. Soon afterward, he began publishing *Poor Richard's Almanack*, a calendar filled with advice, philosophy, and wise sayings, such as "Early to bed, early to rise, makes a man healthy, wealthy, and wise." With sales in the thousands every year, it became, next to the Bible, the most widely read publication in the colonies. **R**

> ***"Be civil to all; sociable to many; familiar with few; friend to one; enemy to none."***
>
> **—Benjamin Franklin, *Poor Richard's Almanack***

Franklin was also deeply interested in science. In 1748 he sold his printing business so that he would have time to work on his inventions. He invented the lightning rod, bifocal eyeglasses, and the Franklin stove for heating. Energetic and open-minded, Franklin served in the Pennsylvania Assembly for many years. He founded a hospital, a fire department, America's first lending library, and an academy of higher learning that later became the University of Pennsylvania. **C**

Franklin's greatest services to his fellow Americans came during the 1770s. As a statesman and patriot, Franklin helped guide the colonies toward independence. In 1775, Franklin became a member of the Second Continental Congress and helped draft the Declaration of Independence. In 1776 he traveled to France, seeking the country's support in the fight for independence. Franklin remained an asset to the United States up until his death. After the American Revolution, he served in the Constitutional Convention and later headed an abolition society. **W**

◀ **Poor Richard's Almanack**

Then and Now

Name a person living today who resembles Franklin in either scientific, political, or social endeavors.

Biography

TEACH

R Reading Strategy

Inferring **Ask:** Would Franklin's ideas become influential in the colonies? Why or why not? *(probably; because so many people bought his books)* **OL**

C Critical Thinking

Identifying Central Issues Franklin helped form a group called the Junto, which debated questions of politics and morals. This group led to the ideas for the public library and the volunteer fire department. **Ask:** How did these organizations strengthen colonial society? *(They contributed to colonists' ability to function without aid of British.)* **OL**

W Writing Support

Research Reports Writing Have students research and write about one contribution that Franklin made to independence. Tell students to include details and quotations from the sources and to have a well-defined thesis. **OL** **CA 8WA2.3**

Then and Now

Have students brainstorm people who are in the news because of their contributions in these fields. After students have developed a list of people, discuss whether any have made contributions to American life in as many different areas as Franklin did.

Review The Big Idea

Review the Big Idea for this section: "Political ideas and major events shape how people form governments." **Ask:** How are the ideas inherent in the Declaration of Independence like a contract? *(If a government interferes with people's rights, they have the right to overthrow that government.)* OL CA HI3.

U Universal Access

Below Grade Level Explain that the prefix in preamble, *pre-*, means "before." **Ask:** What are some other words with this prefix? BL

R Reading Support

Reading Primary Sources
Ask: What does this sentence mean? OL CA HR4.

Reading Check
Answer: People who wish to form a new country should explain their reasons for doing so.

History Online
Objectives and answers to the student activity can be found in the **Web Activity Lesson Plan** feature ca.hss.glencoe.com.

Answers and Additional Support

US8.1.2 Analyze the philosophy of government expressed in the Declaration of Independence, with an emphasis on government as a means of securing individual rights (e.g., key phrases such as "all men are created equal, that they are endowed by their Creator with certain unalienable rights").

The Colonies Declare Independence

Main Idea **The Declaration of Independence used traditional English political rights to call for independence for the colonies.**

Reading Connection Why do you think governments are formed? How does the government help you, and what could you do if the government stopped helping you? Read to find out how the writer of the Declaration of Independence addressed these questions.

In the Declaration of Independence, Jefferson explained why the colonies were founding a new nation. To do this, he drew from earlier English documents, such as the Magna Carta and the English Bill of Rights. Both documents established the idea that governments are not all powerful and that rulers had to obey the laws and treat citizens fairly.

Picturing History
Thomas Jefferson prepared the draft of the Declaration, and Benjamin Franklin and John Adams made suggestions. ***Why is July 4, 1776, a historic day?***

Above all, Jefferson drew on the ideas of thinkers such as English philosopher John Locke to set out the colonies' reasons for proclaiming their freedom. Locke wrote that people were born with certain natural rights to life, liberty, and property; that people formed governments to protect these rights; and that a government that interferes with these rights might rightfully be overthrown.

The Declaration has four major sections. The **preamble** (PREE•AM•buhl), or introduction, states that people who wish to form a new country should explain their reasons for doing so. The next two sections list the rights the colonists believed they should have and their complaints against Britain. The final section proclaims the existence of the new nation.

The Declaration of Independence states what Jefferson and many Americans thought were universal principles. It begins with a description of traditional English political rights.

> **"We hold these truths to be self-evident, that all men are created equal, that they are endowed by their Creator with certain unalienable Rights, that among these are Life, Liberty, and the pursuit of Happiness."**

The Declaration ends by announcing America's new status. Now pledging "to each other our Lives, our Fortunes, and our sacred Honor," the Americans declared themselves a new nation. The struggle for American independence—the American Revolution—had begun.

Reading Check **Identify** What does the preamble to the Declaration of Independence state?

History Online
Student Web Activity Visit ca.hss.glencoe.com and click on *Chapter 2—Student Web Activities* for an activity on the Declaration of Independence.

Did You Know?

Congress actually voted in favor of independence on July 2. On July 4, delegates voted to accept Jefferson's statement, the Declaration of Independence, as the explanation of why the colonies wanted independence.

Picturing History

Franklin and Adams served with Jefferson on the committee of five charged with writing the declaration. The other members were Robert Livingston of New York and Roger Sherman of Connecticut.

Answer: that is the day Congress approved the Declaration of Independence

US8.1.2 Analyze the philosophy of government expressed in the Declaration of Independence, with an emphasis on government as a means of securing individual rights (e.g., key phrases such as "all men are created equal, that they are endowed by their Creator with certain unalienable rights"). US8.1.3 Analyze how the American Revolution affected other nations, especially France.

The American Revolution

Main Idea **America's victory and independence led to revolutions in other parts of the world.**

Reading Connection Has someone else's success ever encouraged you to work harder toward a goal? Read to find out how the American victory over the British led to political revolutions in other colonies.

R

After the colonial leaders declared independence in July 1776, the war for freedom was unavoidable. The British planned to crush the rebellion by force. Most of the **Patriots**—Americans who supported independence—believed the British would give up after losing one or two major battles.

Not all Americans, however, supported the struggle for independence. Some people were **neutral** (NOO•truhl), taking neither side in the conflict. Still other Americans—known as **Loyalists**—remained loyal to Great Britain. At least one American in five was a Loyalist—perhaps as many as one in three.

Early Campaigns During the summer of 1776, Britain sent 32,000 troops across the Atlantic to New York. The British hoped the sheer size of their army would convince the Patriots to give up. In late August, British armies defeated George Washington's forces on New York's Long Island. By late November, the Patriots had retreated across New Jersey into Pennsylvania. Meanwhile, the British army settled in New York for the winter of 1776, leaving some troops in New Jersey at Trenton and Princeton.

C

S

Stationed across the Delaware River from the British camp in New Jersey, Washington saw a chance to catch the British off guard. On Christmas night 1776, Washington took 2,400 troops across the icy river and surprised the enemy at Trenton the next day. The British sent reinforcements, but Washington led his troops away from these soldiers. Washington then marched the army to Princeton, where they drove away the British. One discouraged British soldier wrote in his diary that the American victory made the Americans "all liberty mad again."

History *Through Art*

Washington Crossing the Delaware* by Emanuel Leutze** George Washington led his troops across the Delaware River on Christmas night in a surprise attack on British troops at Trenton. ***What effect did the victory at Trenton have on the American cause?

Did You Know?

Just before the victory at Trenton, the American cause was in dire straits. Washington had been thoroughly defeated in several battles around New York, and his army was divided and shrinking, since the terms of enlistment of many soldiers were about to expire. By defeating the British at Trenton and Princeton, Washington revived American hopes.

History *Through Art*

Emanuel Leutze's oil painting shows Washington leading his troops across the ice-clogged Delaware River on Christmas night. The original artwork, painted in 1851, was more than 12 feet high and 21 feet wide.

Answer: encouraged them and boosted their morale

R Reading Strategy

Understanding Vocabulary

Separate the class into three groups, and have each take up the position of Patriots, of neutrality, or of the Loyalists. Have each group state their perspective on the issue of independence using as many reasons as possible to support their case. OL CA HR5.

C Critical Thinking

Making Generalizations

Tell students that George Washington actually lost more battles than he won. However, he met his goal of keeping the army in the field. **Ask:** What qualities do good leaders possess? *(Students may offer such answers as clear idea of the goals, good communication skills, ability to inspire others, and ability to delegate.)* OL

S Skill Practice

Using Geography Skills

Tell students that holding New York City gave Britain an excellent harbor. Have them look at the map of the colonies on page 162. **Ask:** How could they use this base and their naval power to threaten the Americans? *(They could use their ships to move troops anywhere along the coast.)* OL CA CS3.

Resources for page 153

American Art and Architecture Transparency 14

S Skill Practice

Historical and Social Sciences Analysis Skill Work with students to brainstorm a list of reasons why the Patriots might have felt optimistic about the war in the spring of 1778. *(Possible answers: Saratoga had been a major American victory; the army had survived the winter at Valley Forge.)* OL

C Critical Thinking

Identifying Problems and Finding Solutions Have groups of students create a problem/solution chart. In the left-hand column, they should list problems that the Americans faced (such as the need for allies and financing the war); in the right-hand column, they should note how each problem was handled. Have groups share their charts with the class. OL

R Reading Strategy

Academic Vocabulary Ask students to describe a challenge they have encountered. BL

Linking Past & Present

Women in War

Past Molly Pitcher and Deborah Sampson were two of the few women who actually fought in the Revolution. Other colonial women, along with their families, followed the armies to cook and clean for their husbands.

▼ Many women serve in the military today

▲ *Molly Pitcher at the Battle of Monmouth* by Dennis Malone Carter

Present Today women make up about 15 percent of the armed forces in the United States. Women soldiers served in Panama in 1989, the Persian Gulf War of 1991, and the Iraqi conflict that began in 2003. Thousands more have served in peacekeeping missions in Somalia, Bosnia, and Haiti.

The Battle of Saratoga In 1777 the British decided to split New England from the Middle Colonies by taking control of New York's Hudson River valley. The plan called for three British forces to meet at Albany, New York, and destroy the Patriot troops.

A British force under General John Burgoyne advanced southward from Canada. When Burgoyne reached the town of Saratoga in New York, the other two British forces had not arrived. Soon, Burgoyne's forces found themselves surrounded by a larger American army under General Horatio Gates. After a desperate attack, the British realized they were trapped, and Burgoyne surrendered on October 17, 1777. The Battle of Saratoga was the first major American victory in the war.

Winter at Valley Forge As the winter of 1777 approached, other British forces settled in comfort in Philadelphia. Meanwhile, George Washington set up camp at Valley Forge, 20 miles to the west of the British.

Washington and his troops endured a winter of terrible suffering and difficult conditions, lacking decent food, clothing, and shelter. Washington's greatest **challenge** at Valley Forge was keeping the Continental Army together. Yet with strong determination, the Continental Army survived the winter, and conditions gradually improved.

Gaining Allies The victory at Saratoga boosted American spirits. Even more, Saratoga marked a turning point.

Answers and Additional Support

Linking Past & Present

The Women's Army Corps began in 1942 (as the Women's Auxiliary Army Corps), as did its Navy counterpart, Women Accepted for Voluntary Emergency Service. During World War II, there were also women's corps for the Marines and the Coast Guard. Approximately 350,000 women served in the U. S. military during that war.

C1 The European nations, especially France, realized that the United States might actually win its war against Britain. In 1778 the French declared war on Britain and provided aid to the Americans.

Other European nations also helped the Patriots. Spain declared war on Britain in 1779, and the Spanish governor of Louisiana, **Bernardo de Gálvez,** raised an army. Gálvez's army forced British troops from towns and forts along the Gulf of Mexico. His efforts **secured** the southern frontiers of the United States.

Individual foreigners also helped the Americans. One of the hardy soldiers at Valley Forge was a French nobleman, the **Marquis de Lafayette** (LAH • fee • EHT). Dedicated to the ideas of the Declaration of Independence, Lafayette was a trusted aide to Washington. Two Poles—Thaddeus Kosciusko (kawsh • CHUSH • koh), an engineer, and Casimir Pulaski, a cavalry officer—also helped the Americans. Friedrich von Steuben (STOO • buhn), a former army officer from Germany, turned the ragged Continental Army into a more effective fighting force.

Life on the Home Front The war changed the lives of all Americans, even those who C2 stayed at home. With thousands of men away in military service, women took over the duties that had once been the responsibility of their husbands or fathers. Other women ran their husband's or their own businesses.

The ideals of liberty and freedom that inspired the American Revolution caused some women to question their place in society. Abigail Adams was a dedicated champion of women's interests. She wrote to her husband, John Adams, who was a member of the Second Continental Congress:

S
> **"I can not say that I think you very generous to the ladies, for whilst you are proclaiming peace and good will to men, emancipating all nations, you insist upon retaining an absolute power over wives."**
>
> **—Letter, May 7, 1776**

The Revolutionary War ideals of freedom and liberty inspired some white Americans to question slavery. From the beginning of the war, African American soldiers fought for the American cause. To some who were fighting for freedom, both African American and white, the Revolution seemed to bring nearer the day when slavery would be abolished. Vermont, New Hampshire, Massachusetts, and Pennsylvania attempted to end slavery in their states. The issue of slavery would remain unsettled for many years, however.

War in the West and on Sea Along the northwestern frontier, the British and their Native American allies were raiding American settlements. During 1778 and 1779, George Rogers Clark, an officer in the Virginia militia, seized British posts in present-day Illinois and Indiana. Clark's victories strengthened the American position in the West.

Other battles raged at sea. A daring American naval officer, **John Paul Jones,** raided British ports. In September 1779, Jones's ship *Bonhomme Richard* fought the British warship *Serapis.* At one point, Jones's ship was so badly damaged that the British captain asked whether Jones wished to surrender. Jones is said to have answered, "I have not yet begun to fight." In the end the *Serapis* surrendered, making John Paul Jones a naval hero to the American Patriots.

▲ Many soldiers from other countries and about 5,000 African American soldiers fought for American independence.

More About the Art

Francis Marion first won a name for himself for his bravery and skill in fighting in the 1760s in battles against Native Americans. In the Revolution his skill at hiding in the wetlands of the Carolinas earned him the nickname "the Swamp Fox."

Review Grade 5 Standards

To review standard **5.6.7** *(Understand how the ideals set forth in the Declaration of Independence changed the way people viewed slavery.)*, have students take the role of a soldier who fought in the Continental Army. Ask them to write a letter to a member of the state government urging that slavery be ended in their state and explaining why. OL CA 8WA2.4

C1 Critical Thinking

Making Inferences Point out that France would only agree to help the Americans if it believed it could benefit by their winning independence. **Ask:** How would American independence help France? *(by weakening Britain, its rival for power)* OL CA HI3.

S Skill Practice

Historical and Social Sciences Analysis Skill Tell students that Abigail Adams was a strong supporter of women's rights and an opponent of slavery. **Ask:** What did she mean by "retaining an absolute power over wives"? *(Students may point out that laws written by men denied women their rights.)* OL

C2 Critical Thinking

Determining Cause and Effect Ask: Why would women have to take on these additional tasks? *(because men were no longer at home)* OL

Resources for page 155

Geography and History Activity 2

R Reading Strategy

Understanding Vocabulary
The word *guerrilla* comes from the Spanish word for "war." Historically guerrilla warfare has been used by small, independent groups against large, regular forces. OL

W Writing Support

Research Reports Writing
Have students conduct research into British attitudes before and after the Battle of Yorktown. Have them answer the following question: Why did that battle convince the British to negotiate a peace? OL CA HR1.

Struggles in the South By 1778 the British hoped to use sea power and Loyalist support to win victories in the South. By 1780, British forces had seized Savannah and Charles Town. The British, however, could not control their conquered areas. This was due to a new kind of warfare carried out by the Patriots.

As British troops moved through the countryside, small forces of Patriots attacked them. Bands of soldiers suddenly struck and then disappeared. This hit-and-run **technique** of R **guerrilla warfare** (guh • RIH • luh) caught the British off guard.

W **The War Is Won** In 1780 the war was at a critical point. Both armies needed a victory to win. This finally came in 1781 at the Battle of Yorktown on the coast of Virginia. The French navy blocked the British from escaping by sea, while American and French forces surrounded and trapped the British inside Yorktown. Realizing they could not win, the British laid down their weapons.

The Treaty of Paris Britain's defeat at Yorktown did not end the Revolutionary War. The fighting dragged on in some areas for two more years. Peace negotiations, however, began in Paris. Benjamin Franklin, John Adams, and John Jay represented the United States. The final settlement, known as the Treaty of Paris, was signed on September 3, 1783.

The Treaty of Paris was a triumph for the Americans. Great Britain recognized the United States as an independent nation. The territory claimed by the new nation extended from the Atlantic Ocean west to the Mississippi River and from Canada in the north to Spanish Florida in the south. The Revolutionary War was over. The creation of a new nation was about to begin.

NATIONAL GEOGRAPHIC

The Revolutionary War in the South, 1778–1781

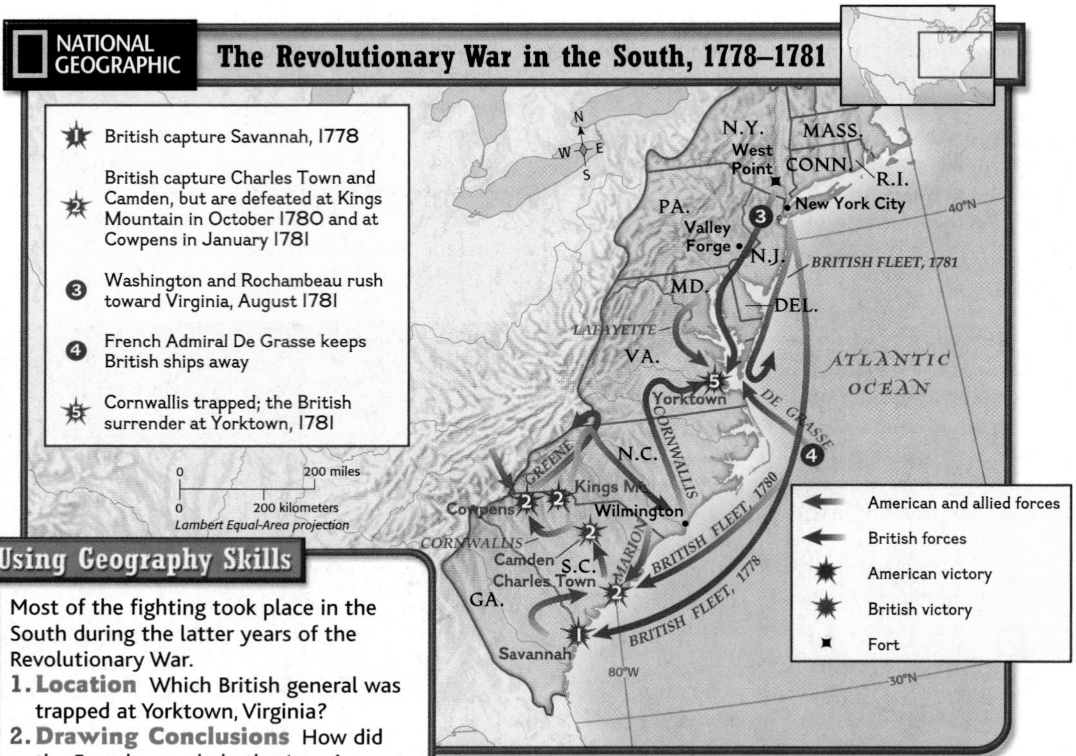

Using Geography Skills

Most of the fighting took place in the South during the latter years of the Revolutionary War.

1. **Location** Which British general was trapped at Yorktown, Virginia?
2. **Drawing Conclusions** How did the French navy help the Americans win the war?

Answers and Additional Support

Using Geography Skills

Answers:

1. Cornwallis
2. It kept British fleets from reaching Yorktown and Cornwallis's troops from escaping by sea; it also cut off supplies and reinforcements.

Why the Americans Won How were the Patriots able to win the Revolutionary War? The Americans had several advantages. They fought on their own land, while the British had to bring troops and supplies from far away. The British succeeded in **occupying** cities but had difficulty controlling the countryside. Help from other nations also contributed to the American victory.

Perhaps most important, the American Revolution was a people's movement. Its outcome depended not on any one battle or event but on the determination and spirit of all the Patriots.

A Model for Others In 1776 the American colonists began a revolution, making clear the principles of freedom and rights outlined in the Declaration of Independence. These ideas bounded back across the Atlantic to influence the French Revolution. French rebels in 1789 fought in defense of "Liberty, Equality, and Fraternity." French revolutionaries repeated the principles of the American Declaration of Independence: "Men are born and remain free and equal in rights."

In 1791 the ideals of the American and French revolutions traveled across the Caribbean and the Atlantic to the French-held island colony of Saint Domingue. Inspired by talk of freedom, enslaved Africans took up arms. Led by Toussaint-Louverture, they rejected French rule. In 1804 Saint Domingue—part of present-day Haiti—became the second nation in the Americas to achieve independence from colonial rule. C

Reading Check **Summarize** Why was the Battle of Saratoga a turning point in the war?

History Online
Study Central Need help understanding the American Revolution? Visit ca.hss.glencoe.com and click on Study Central.

Section 4 Review

Reading Summary

Review the Main Ideas

- The Second Continental Congress met to discuss governing the colonies and to form the Continental Army to fight the British.
- The Declaration of Independence, written by Thomas Jefferson, declared the American colonies to be a new, independent nation.
- The American victory inspired other peoples to seek independence and rebel against their governments.

What Did You Learn?

1. For what did Thomas Paine argue in *Common Sense?*
2. What was guerrilla warfare, and why was it effective?

Critical Thinking

3. **Organizing Information** Draw a chart like the one below. Fill in the names and dates of major Revolutionary War battles and provide details about each battle. CA CS1. CA CS2.

Battle	What Occurred

4. **Predict** What might have happened if the French had not allied with the colonists during the Revolutionary War? CA CS1.
5. **The Big Ideas** On what laws and political ideas did Jefferson draw when writing the Declaration of Independence? CA HI3.
6. **Math Connection** Examine the list of representatives to the Second Continental Congress on page 167 who signed the Declaration of Independence. Draw a bar graph depicting the number of men representing each state. Use the X-axis for the states and the Y-axis for numbers of men.

SECTION 4 REVIEW ANSWERS

Review questions reinforce content standard US8.1.

1. that the colonists' struggle was for freedom
2. hit-and-run fighting; because it caught the British off guard
3. Students should refer to the major battles discussed in the text or on maps.
4. The colonists would likely not have won Yorktown, and the war would have lasted longer.
5. **The Big Ideas** Magna Carta, Bill of Rights, ideas of Locke
6. Students should have the following totals: GA: 3; NC: 3; SC: 4; VA: 7; MD: 4; DE: 3; PA: 9; NJ: 5; NY: 4; CN: 4; RI: 2; MA: 5 (with Hancock); NH: 3.

C Critical Thinking

Making inferences Remind students that European countries wanted colonies to obtain raw materials cheaply so they could build their economies. **Ask:** How might Britain and France have solved their demand for those raw materials once the United States and Saint Domingue won their independence? *(from other colonies or by finding new sources or new colonies)* AL CA HI3.

ASSESS

Resources for page 157

Use these resources to assess student mastery of section content.

- Section Quiz 2–4
- Interactive Tutor Self-Assessment CD-ROM

Reading Check

Answer: It was the first major American victory, and it convinced the French to help the Americans.

History Online

Study Central provides summaries, interactive games, and online graphic organizers to help students review section content.

CLOSE

Making Generalizations

Ask students to explain what the end of the Revolutionary War meant for the British. OL

FOCUS

Remind students of the situation in early 1776. Many Americans were Loyalists, and others were neutral. Fighting had begun, but mainly in Massachusetts. The colonies had never worked together before, had no army or navy, had no money, and were fighting one of the strongest powers in Europe.

TEACH

C Critical Thinking

Identifying Central Issues Discuss the challenges Americans would face in becoming independent. **Ask:** What organizations would they need to form? *(a government, a system of laws, military forces to defend the land, a currency and postal system)* OL

R Reading Strategy

Reading Primary Sources Have students read the excerpt from *Common Sense* and restate Paine's argument in their own words. OL CA HR4.

Answers and Additional Support

You Decide . . .

US8.1 Students understand the major events preceding the founding of the nation and relate their significance to the development of American constitutional democracy.

Independence: Yes or No?

Many American colonists joined the movement for independence. Still, many Americans did not want to break away from Great Britain.

For Independence

Many colonists in the summer of 1775 were not prepared to break away **C** from Great Britain. The colonists resented British taxes. Because they had no representation in Parliament, as people in Great Britain did, the colonists believed that Parliament had no right to tax them. They summarized their feelings with the slogan "No taxation without representation." Most members of the Second Continental Congress wanted the right to govern themselves, but they did not want to break with the British Empire.

By 1776, however, opinion had changed. Frustrated by Britain's refusal to compromise, many Patriot leaders began to call for independence. Influential in swaying the colonists toward the idea of separating from Great Britain was Thomas Paine's pamphlet *Common Sense,* which first appeared in January 1776. Paine made an impassioned appeal:

"I have heard it asserted by some, that as America hath flourished under her former connexion with Great Britain, the same connexion is necessary towards her future happiness. . . . I answer roundly, that America would have flourished as much, and probably much more, had no European power [taken notice of her]. . . . Everything that is right or natural pleads for separation. The blood of the slain, the weeping voice of nature cries, 'TIS TIME TO PART.'" **R**

The Patriots believed that fighting for liberty set an example for others to follow. Ben Franklin wrote to a friend that "our cause is the cause of all mankind, and that we are fighting for their liberty in defending our own."

◀ Thomas Paine

158

Extending the Content

Thomas Paine Thomas Paine was born in England and returned there after the War of Independence. He was welcomed as a celebrity, even after having written the pamphlet that stirred so many to fight for independence. He was, however, later forced to leave England after publishing the *Rights of Man* (1791), which was a defense of the French Revolution. He then moved to France where he became a citizen. He did not return to America until 1802.

Some Americans used force against Loyalists.

Against Independence R

The American Revolution was not only a war between the British and the Americans. It also divided Americans themselves. While American Patriots fought passionately for independence, other Americans fought just as fiercely for their British king. Americans who felt a strong sense of loyalty to the king and believed British law should be upheld came to be known as Loyalists.

Loyalists came from all parts of American society. Many Loyalists lived in Georgia, the Carolinas, and New England; the Patriots though were strong in New England and Virginia. Political differences divided communities and even split families. Benjamin Franklin's son, William, served as Royal Governor of New Jersey. When the Revolution began, William remained loyal to Britain and quarreled bitterly with his father.

Loyalists answered Paine's *Common Sense* with pamphlets of their own. One who did was Charles Inglis, a minister from New York. He wrote: "By a connection with Great Britain, our trade would still have the protection of the greatest naval power in the world." Inglis also said that if the American colonies did not give up their fight for independence, Britain would exert its great power and the result would be:

> "Ruthless war, with all its aggravated horrors, will ravage our once happy land—our seacoasts and ports will be ruined, and our ships taken. Torrents of blood will be spilt, and thousands reduced to beggary and wretchedness."

You Be The Historian

DBQ Document-Based Questions

1. What economic argument does Paine use to support separation from Great Britain?
2. What does Inglis believe will result from war with Britain? CA HR5.
3. Were the reasons for or against American independence convincing? Write a short letter to Inglis in which you support the Patriot or Loyalist position. Use facts to support your position. CA 8WS1.0

You Decide . . .

R Reading Strategy

Organizing Information Have students create a two-column chart. On one side have them write the advantages of the Loyalists' point of view toward independence. On the right, have them list the disadvantages. *(Students might list the following: Advantages—protection of trade; naval support from Britain; no war with Britain; Disadvantages—taxation without representation in British government; lack of compromise from Britain; lack of liberty for basic rights)* OL

ASSESS/CLOSE

Have students answer the You Be The Historian questions. Then, remind students that the colonists had tried for many years leading up to 1776 to push the British to give them their rights. Have students write a one-page essay on what they believe is the strongest reason for a group of people, or colonies, to seek independence from its government. Afterwards, encourage a few volunteers to read their essays to the class. OL

You Be The Historian

1. America would have been better off economically without the British.
2. a ravaged nation with ruined ports and no ships, bloodshed, and poverty
3. Students' letters should contain details to support their position.

Analyzing Primary Sources

FOCUS

History–Social Science Standards

The following standard is covered on pages 160–161.

US8.1 Students understand the major events preceding the founding of the nation and relate their significance to the development of American constitutional democracy.

TEACH

S1 Skill Practice

Historical and Social Sciences Analysis Skill

Ask: How would descriptions like this help Penn if they became public? *(They could help persuade people to move to his colony.)* OL CA HI2.

S2 Skill Practice

Analyzing Primary Sources

Ask: On what grounds do the Mennonites object to slavery—economic, moral, or political? *(moral)* How would they respond to someone who said slavery was too important economically to end? *(They would answer that the moral obligation is too overwhelming to permit slavery.)* OL

Answers and Additional Support

Analyzing Primary Sources

US.8.1 Students understand the major events preceding the founding of the nation and relate their significance to the development of American constitutional democracy.

Life in the American Colonies

Throughout the 1600s and 1700s, more and more English people settled in the 13 colonies along the Atlantic coast of North America. How did these settlers adapt to their new homes? What was their everyday life like? You can get a glimpse of life in colonial America by analyzing letters and published writings from this era.

Read the passages on pages 160 and 161, and answer the questions that follow.

William Penn inspecting deeds during survey expedition of Philadelphia

Reader's Dictionary

tolerable (TAH • luh • ruh • buhl): satisfactory

Languedoc (lahng • DAWK): region in southern France

generation (JEH • nuh • RAY • shuhn): age group

descent (dih • SEHNT): line of ancestors; birth

poultry (POHL • tree): chickens

Penn's Colony

William Penn wrote of the new Pennsylvania colony with pride.

We have laid out a town a mile wide and two miles deep, with 150 very **tolerable** houses. . . . [It is] the largest town south of New York and already the envy of its neighbors.

S1 The air is serene as in **Languedoc,** a most fragrant smell of cedar, pine and sassafras. . . . In short, I am fully satisfied with the country, . . . I must, without vanity, confess that I have led the greatest colony in America. . . .

—Letters to John Aubrey and Lord Halifax, 1683

The Germantown Protest

One of the earliest protests in North America against the enslavement of Africans was this statement written in 1688 by a religious group known as the Mennonites.

Now, though, they are black, we cannot conceive there is more liberty to have them slaves, . . . [than] to have other white ones. There is a saying, that we should do to all men like as we will be done ourselves; making no difference of what **generation, descent,** or color they are. . . . S2

Pray, what thing in the world can be done worse towards us, than if men should rob or steal us away, and sell us for slaves to strange countries; separating husbands from their wives and children. . . .

—Germantown Protest

EXTENDING THE CONTENT

Planned City The city that Penn describes is Philadelphia, bounded on the east by the Delaware River and on the west by the Schuylkill. He created the plan for the city, which called for a grid of streets running north-south and east-west. Penn set aside five square parks, one in the center and the other four at equal distances to the northeast, northwest, southeast, and southwest. The central square is now the home to Philadelphia's City Hall.

Poor Richard's Almanack

Ben Franklin published Poor Richard's Almanack *every year from 1733 to 1758. The almanack included weather forecasts, statistics, and other useful or interesting information.* W *Franklin also included proverbs, or short witty sayings, like those that follow. See if you recognize any of them.*

a. Early to bed and early to rise, makes a man healthy wealthy and wise.

b. Little strokes, fell great oaks.

R1 c. Glass, china, and reputation, are easily crack'd, and never well mended.

d. An open foe may prove a curse; but a pretended friend is worse.

e. One today is worth two tomorrows.

f. Haste makes waste.

R2 g. Beware of little expenses, a small leak will sink a great ship.

h. The sleeping fox catches no **poultry.**

i. A Slip of the Foot you may soon recover: But a Slip of the Tongue you may never get over.

—*Poor Richard's Almanack*

DBQ Document-Based Questions

Penn's Colony

1. How does Penn describe the houses in the colony?
2. Is Penn proud of the colony? How can you tell?

The Germantown Protest

3. What arguments do the writers use as evidence that slavery is evil?
4. What familiar saying is used to make the writers' point about slavery? Why is this saying used?

Poor Richard's Almanack

5. Which of the proverbs have you heard or read? Why do you think Franklin's proverbs are still popular today?
6. Write the meaning of three of the proverbs in your own words.

Read to Write

7. Write a proverb about something that is part of your everyday life. Compare your proverb about life today with one of Franklin's proverbs. What is the same and what is different about the two proverbs? CA 8WA2.1

W Writing Support

Expository Writing Explain that proverbs are supposed to state things that are true about human life. Have students write an essay explaining why one of Franklin's proverbs is true. OL CA HR4.

R1 Reading Strategy

Reading Primary Sources
Ask: Why does Franklin compare reputation to glass and china and not to other objects? *(because they are familiar objects in the home, valuable, and fragile)* OL

R2 Reading Strategy

Reading Primary Sources
Write another proverb on the board: A stitch in time saves nine. **Ask:** Which of Franklin's proverbs is this similar to? Why? *("Beware of little expenses. A small leak will sink a great ship." Both caution that minor problems can become major ones if left unfixed.)* OL

ASSESS

Have students answer the Document-Based Questions.

CLOSE

Analyzing Information
Have students explain how these documents and their authors reflect the influence of religion in the settlement of the United States. OL

DBQ Document-Based Questions

1. he calls them "very tolerable"
2. he says the town is "the envy of the neighbors" and "the greatest colony in America"
3. People would consider it unjust to hold white slaves, so it must be unjust to hold black slaves.
4. Students should note that the statement echoes Jesus' teaching "do unto others as you would have them do unto you."
5. Answers to the first question will vary. For the second, students may suggest that it is because the proverbs state truths about being human.
6. Answers will vary depending on the proverbs chosen.
7. Answers will vary, should include comparison to Franklin's proverbs.

CHAPTER 2 Assessment

Resources for pages 162–163

Use these resources to review, assess, or reteach the chapter.

- Active Reading Note-Taking Guide, Chapter 2
- Chapter 2 Reading Essentials and Study Guide
- Chapter 2 Tests, Forms A and B
- Standards Assessment, Forms A and B
- California Standards Practice Workbook
- Succeeding on the California History–Social Science Standards CD-ROM
- MindJogger Videoquiz
- Interactive Tutor Self-Assessment CD-ROM

Review Content Vocabulary

1. b
2. c
3. a
4. e
5. d

Review the Main Ideas

6. hoping that self-government would attract more settlers
7. Possible answers: Massachusetts: Pilgrims and Puritans sought a place to worship freely; Penn saw Pennsylvania as a place for people of the Quaker religion
8. a period of revival of strong religious beliefs; it helped spread religious and political freedom in the colonies, giving all colonists the opportunity to choose their own faith

Chapter 2 Assessment

Standard US8.1

Review Content Vocabulary

Match the definitions in the second column to the terms in the first column.

1. burgess	a. trading illegally with another country
2. militia	b. representative
3. smuggling	c. group of citizen soldiers
4. boycott	d. acceptance of different beliefs
5. tolerance	e. refuse to buy

Review the Main Ideas

Section 1 • Founding the American Colonies

6. Why did the Virginia Company create the House of Burgesses?
7. Describe the role of religious freedom in the founding of two of the colonies.

Section 2 • Life in Colonial America

8. What was the Great Awakening, and how did it represent the unique American culture that was developing?
9. What was England's reason for the Navigation Acts?

Section 3 • Trouble in the Colonies

10. How did the British government use the colonies to raise revenue?
11. What incident caused the British Parliament to pass the Coercive Acts?

Section 4 • War of Independence

12. According to the Declaration of Independence, if a government does not protect the basic rights of the people it governs, what is the right of the people?
13. What fighting method did the Americans use to keep the British from controlling the Southern Colonies?

Critical Thinking

14. **Predict** What might have happened if Britain had allowed the American colonists more control in creating regulations dealing with colonial trade? CA HI2.
15. **Analyze** What did Patrick Henry mean when he said, "I am not a Virginian, but an American"? CA HR4.
16. **Conclude** Why do you think the British found it easier to capture American cities than to take over the American countryside? CA HR3.

Geography Skills

Study the map below and answer the following questions. CA CS3.

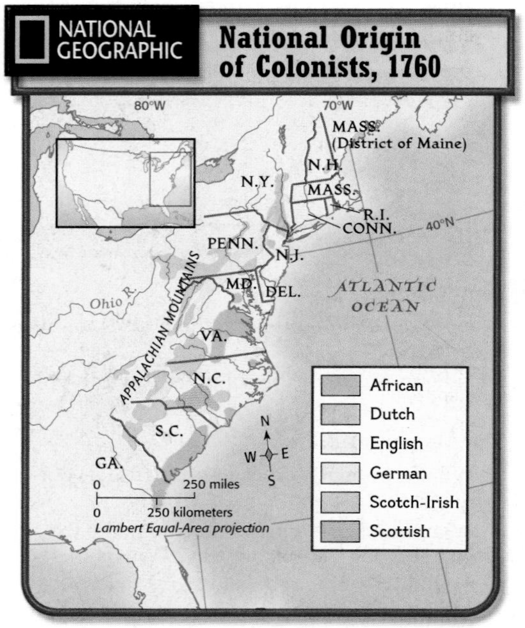

9. to prevent other countries from profiting from trade with the American colonies
10. They taxed the colonies on such things as tea and printed material.
11. the Boston Tea Party
12. overthrow it
13. guerrilla warfare

Critical Thinking

14. Students may say that the colonies would not have declared independence.
15. that he was part of group of colonies instead of merely one independent colony
16. Students may say that the colonists' knowledge of the countryside gave them an advantage outside the cities.

History Online

Self-Check Quiz Visit ca.hss.glencoe.com to prepare for the Chapter 2 test.

17. **Human-Environment Interaction** What geographical feature served as a boundary to westward settlement in 1760?
18. **Location** Which colony had the largest area of Scottish settlement?
19. **Human-Environment Interaction** Describe the location of the colonies' African population. Why was that population found in those colonies?

Read to Write

20. **The Big Ideas** **Evaluate** Write a short essay describing why the American colonists had strong views about self-government. CA 8WS1.1

21. **Using Your FOLDABLES** Draw a graphic organizer that describes the events that led the Americans to declare independence from Great Britain. As you discuss the causes and effects, imagine other possible outcomes to the same situations. Could war have been avoided through diplomacy? Write an essay that summarizes your conclusions. CA 8WS1.1

Using Academic Vocabulary

Choose an academic vocabulary word to complete each sentence. You may need to change the form of the word to provide the best answer.

grant	adapt
secure	violate

22. The Continental Army had to ________ its battle tactics to defeat the highly organized British forces.
23. Colonial leaders believed that British taxation policies ________ their natural rights to representative government.

Building Citizenship

24. **Researching** America's heritage of religious diversity and toleration began in the colonial period. Use the Internet and other sources to research modern laws that are meant to promote religious freedom and toleration. Prepare a report to share with the class. CA 8WS1.4

Reviewing Skills

25. Review READING SKILL **Identifying the Main Idea** Read the "List of Grievances" in the Declaration of Independence. List the main idea and supporting points outlined in that section. Rewrite the grievances in your own words, using the main and supporting points you identified. CA 8RC2.0

26. Review ANALYSIS SKILL **Infer** Why do you think Thomas Jefferson relied so heavily on earlier British documents and on the thoughts of British philosophers as he wrote the Declaration of Independence? Write a short essay explaining your conclusions. CA HI3.

Standards Practice

Read the passage below and answer the following questions.

> An English philosopher named John Locke wrote about his belief that people had natural rights. These included the right to life, liberty, and property. In *Two Treatises of Government,* Locke wrote that people created government to protect natural rights. If a government failed in its basic duty of protecting natural rights, people had the right to overthrow the government.

27 Locke's ideas, as stated in the paragraph above, contributed to the

A Proclamation of 1763.

B Intolerable Acts.

C Declaration of Independence.

D Articles of Confederation.

CHAPTER 2 Assessment

Building Citizenship

24. Students' reports should describe the laws and explain how they support diversity and toleration.

Reviewing Skills

25. Review READING SKILL For the main idea, students may say something like "The King has taken away our rights"; the individual grievances are the supporting details.

26. Review ANALYSIS SKILL Students might point out that these sources would have been part of Jefferson's heritage, so naturally he would draw on them.

Standards Practice

27. C

Bonus Question

Ask: Why did Britain fight to keep the colonies? *(Students may note that Britain had an economic interest in the colonies.)* OL

History Online

Have students visit the Web site at ca.hss.glencoe.com to review Chapter 2 and take the **Self-Check Quiz.**

Geography Skills

17. the Appalachian Mountains
18. North Carolina
19. mostly in the South; they were brought over to work on plantations.

Read to Write

20. **The Big Ideas** Students may mention the English traditions of limited government; the practice of self-government in the colonies; and Enlightenment ideas.
21. Students' essays should highlight the key events in the road to the revolution.

Using Academic Vocabulary

22. adapt
23. violated

FOCUS

The marginal notes explain what each section of the Declaration means and defines difficult words.

TEACH

R1 Reading Strategy

Analyzing Text Structure
Point out that the brackets around the headings indicate that they are not in the original document. **Ask:** Why were these headings added? *(to show how the Declaration is divided)* OL

R2 Reading Strategy

Understanding Vocabulary
Tell students that to impel means to drive something forward. **Ask:** In what ways are the colonists impelled to separate? *(The colonists felt they had no other choice.)* OL

S Skill Practice

Historical and Social Sciences Analysis Skill
Ask: To which government are they referring when they describe "absolute Despotism?" *(Britain)* BL

Answers and Additional Support

The Declaration of Independence

In Congress, July 4, 1776. The unanimous Declaration of the thirteen united States of America,

What It Means
The Preamble The Declaration of Independence has four parts. The Preamble explains why the Continental Congress drew up the Declaration.

R1 ## [Preamble]

When in the Course of human events, it becomes necessary for one people to dissolve the political bands which have connected them with another, and to assume among the Powers of the earth, the separate and equal station to which the Laws of Nature and of Nature's God entitle them, a decent respect to the opinions of mankind requires that they R2 should declare the causes which **impel** them to the separation.

impel *force*

What It Means
Natural Rights The second part, the Declaration of Natural Rights, lists the rights of the citizens. It goes on to explain that, in a republic, people form a government to protect their rights.

[Declaration of Natural Rights]

We hold these truths to be self-evident, that all men are created equal, that they are **endowed** by their Creator with certain unalienable Rights, that among these are Life, Liberty and the pursuit of Happiness.

That to secure these rights, Governments are instituted among Men, deriving their just powers from the consent of the governed,

That whenever any Form of Government becomes destructive of these ends, it is the Right of the People to alter or to abolish it, and to institute new Government, laying its foundation on such principles and organizing its powers in such form, as to them shall seem most likely to effect their Safety and Happiness. Prudence, indeed, will dictate that Governments long established should not be changed for light and transient causes; and accordingly all experience hath shown, that mankind are more disposed to suffer, while evils are sufferable, than to right themselves by abolishing the forms to which they are accustomed. But when a long train of abuses and usurpations, pursuing invariably the same Object evinces a design to reduce them under absolute **Despotism,** it is their right, it is their duty, to throw off such Government, and to provide new Guards for their future security. S

endowed *provided*

despotism *unlimited power*

What It Means
List of Grievances The third part of the Declaration lists the colonists' complaints against the British government. Notice that King George III is singled out for blame.

[List of Grievances]

Such has been the patient sufferance of these Colonies; and such is now the necessity which constrains them to alter their former Systems of Government. The history of the present King of Great Britain is a history of repeated injuries and **usurpations,** all having in direct object the establishment of an absolute Tyranny over these States. To prove this, let Facts be submitted to a candid world.

He has refused his Assent to Laws, the most wholesome and necessary for the public good.

usurpations *unjust uses of power*

More Skill Practice

Historical and Social Sciences Analysis Skill Choose a volunteer to read aloud the first paragraph under the heading "Declaration of Natural Rights." Then have students close their textbooks and write a paraphrase of that paragraph. OL CA HI2.

Did You Know?

The Continental Congress did not accept Jefferson's Declaration as he had written it. The delegates made many changes, cutting about one quarter of the original document, most notably a scathing attack on slaveholding and the slave trade.

He has forbidden his Governors to pass Laws of immediate and pressing importance, unless suspended in their operation till his Assent should be obtained; and when so suspended, he has utterly neglected to attend to them.

W1 He has refused to pass other Laws for the accommodation of large districts of people, unless those people would **relinquish** the right of Representation in the Legislature, a right **inestimable** to them and formidable to tyrants only.

W2 He has called together legislative bodies at places unusual, uncomfortable, and distant from the depository of their Public Records, for the sole purpose of fatiguing them into compliance with his measures.

He has dissolved Representative Houses repeatedly, for opposing with manly firmness his invasions on the rights of the people.

He has refused for a long time, after such dissolutions, to cause others to be elected; whereby the Legislative Powers, incapable of **Annihilation,** have returned to the People at large for their exercise; the State remaining in the mean time exposed to all the dangers of invasion from without, and **convulsions** within.

He has endeavoured to prevent the population of these States; for that purpose obstructing the Laws for **Naturalization of Foreigners;** refusing to pass others to encourage their migrations hither, and raising the conditions of new Appropriations of Lands.

He has obstructed the Administration of Justice, by refusing his Assent to Laws for establishing Judiciary Powers.

He has made Judges dependent on his Will alone, for the **tenure** of their offices, and the amount and payment of their salaries.

He has erected a multitude of New Offices, and sent hither swarms of Officers to harass our people, and eat out their substance.

relinquish *give up*
inestimable *priceless*

R **annihilation** *destruction*

convulsions *violent disturbances*

Naturalization of Foreigners *process by which foreign-born persons become citizens*

tenure *term*

More About the Art

Point out that the calmness of the setting obscures the danger that members of Congress faced. To the British government, these men were guilty of treason. Knowing this, the delegates kept their identities secret until January 1777, when the victories at Trenton and Princeton emboldened them to publish their names.

R Reading Strategy

Evaluating Organize students into small groups, and assign each group several of the grievances. Have the groups find specific events, acts, or statements made by the king or Parliament that relate to at least one of their grievances. Then have the groups present their findings to the class. AL

W1 Writing Support

Research Reports Writing Tell students that the Declaration of Independence had a significant impact on later independence movements. Have each student choose a modern independence movement, such as the Tiananmen Square demonstrations, various movements in Latin America, or the breakup of the Soviet Union. Then have them use library and Internet resources to learn about and report on their assigned movement and the effects that the Declaration of Independence had on it. OL CA 8WA2.3

W2 Writing Support

Research Reports Writing Point out that the Declaration has been a force for change in the United States. People have used its words and ideas to promote such measures as the abolition of slavery and equal rights for women. Divide students into groups and have each group do research to find three examples in which an individual or a group used the words and ideas of the Declaration to promote change or reform. AL

S Skill Practice

Historical and Social Sciences Analysis Skill Have students reread the list of grievances. **Ask:** Is there any one grievance that summarizes the core issue in the Declaration? Support your answer with reasons from the chapter. *(Students might choose the grievance in paragraph three on this page, which refers to the actions of Parliament, the body "foreign to our constitution, and unacklowledged by our laws.")* OL CA HI1.

C Critical Thinking

Making Inferences Have students read this paragraph. **Ask:** What does it mean? *(The colonists have tried to ask for relief from these problems, but those efforts were ignored.)* What is the purpose of making this statement? *(to show that the colonists did not simply jump into a rebellion but had no choice)* OL CA 8WA2.3

Answers and Additional Support

quartering *lodging*

render *make*

abdicated *given up*

perfidy *violation of trust*

insurrections *rebellions*

petitioned for redress *asked formally for a correction of wrongs*

unwarrantable jurisdiction *unjustified authority*

consanguinity *originating from the same ancestor*

He has kept among us, in times of peace, Standing Armies without the Consent of our legislature.

He has affected to render the Military independent of and superior to the Civil Power.

S He has combined with others to subject us to a jurisdiction foreign to our constitution, and unacknowledged by our laws; giving his Assent to their acts of pretended legislation:

For **quartering** large bodies of troops among us:

For protecting them, by a mock Trial, from Punishment for any Murders which they should commit on the Inhabitants of these States:

For cutting off our Trade with all parts of the world:

For imposing taxes on us without our Consent:

For depriving us in many cases, of the benefits of Trial by Jury:

For transporting us beyond Seas to be tried for pretended offences:

For abolishing the free System of English Laws in a neighbouring Province, establishing therein an Arbitrary government, and enlarging its Boundaries so as to **render** it at once an example and fit instrument for introducing the same absolute rule into these Colonies:

For taking away our Charters, abolishing our most valuable Laws, and altering fundamentally the Forms of our Governments:

For suspending our own Legislature, and declaring themselves invested with Power to legislate for us in all cases whatsoever.

He has **abdicated** Government here, by declaring us out of his Protection and waging War against us.

He has plundered our seas, ravaged our Coasts, burnt our towns, and destroyed the lives of our people.

He is at this time transporting large armies of foreign mercenaries to compleat the works of death, desolation and tyranny, already begun with circumstances of Cruelty & **perfidy** scarcely paralleled in the most barbarous ages, and totally unworthy the Head of a civilized nation.

He has constrained our fellow Citizens taken Captive on the high Seas to bear Arms against their Country, to become the executioners of their friends and Brethren, or to fall themselves by their Hands.

He has excited domestic **insurrections** amongst us, and has endeavoured to bring on the inhabitants of our frontiers, the merciless Indian Savages, whose known rule of warfare, is an undistinguished destruction of all ages, sexes and conditions.

In every stage of these Oppressions We have **Petitioned for Redress** in the most humble terms: Our repeated Petitions have been answered only by repeated injury. A Prince, whose character is thus marked by every act which may define a Tyrant, is unfit to be the ruler of a free People.

C Nor have We been wanting in attention to our British brethren. We have warned them from time to time of attempts by their legislature to extend an **unwarrantable jurisdiction** over us. We have reminded them of the circumstances of our emigration and settlement here. We have appealed to their native justice and magnanimity, and we have conjured them by the ties of our common kindred to disavow these usurpations, which, would inevitably interrupt our connections and correspondence. They too have been deaf to the voice of justice and of **consanguinity.** We must, therefore, acquiesce in the necessity, which denounces our Separation, and hold them, as we hold the rest of mankind, Enemies in War, in Peace Friends.

Did You Know?

Although Parliament was the body that drafted the laws that so upset the colonists, Parliament is not mentioned once in the Declaration. All the grievances are aimed at King George III. Still, the third paragraph on this page hints at Parliament in mentioning "others" that the king "combined with" to take away Americans' rights.

[Resolution of Independence by the United States]

We, therefore, the Representatives of the united States of America, in General Congress, Assembled, appealing to the Supreme Judge of the world for the **rectitude** of our intentions, do, in the Name, and by Authority of the good People of these Colonies, solemnly publish and declare, That these United Colonies are, and of Right ought to be Free and Independent States; that they are Absolved from all Allegiance to the British Crown, and that all political connection between them and the State of Great Britain, is and ought to be totally dissolved; and that as Free and Independent States, they have full Power to levy War, conclude Peace, contract Alliances, establish Commerce, and to do all other Acts and Things which Independent States may of right do. **W**

And for the support of this Declaration, with a firm reliance on the Protection of Divine Providence, we mutually pledge to each other our Lives, our Fortunes and our sacred Honor. **S** **C**

John Hancock
President from Massachusetts

Georgia
Button Gwinnett
Lyman Hall
George Walton

North Carolina
William Hooper
Joseph Hewes
John Penn

South Carolina
Edward Rutledge
Thomas Heyward, Jr.
Thomas Lynch, Jr.
Arthur Middleton

Maryland
Samuel Chase
William Paca
Thomas Stone
Charles Carroll of Carrollton

Virginia
George Wythe
Richard Henry Lee
Thomas Jefferson
Benjamin Harrison
Thomas Nelson, Jr.
Francis Lightfoot Lee
Carter Braxton

Pennsylvania
Robert Morris
Benjamin Rush
Benjamin Franklin
John Morton
George Clymer
James Smith
George Taylor
James Wilson
George Ross

Delaware
Caesar Rodney
George Read
Thomas McKean

New York
William Floyd
Philip Livingston
Francis Lewis
Lewis Morris

New Jersey
Richard Stockton
John Witherspoon
Francis Hopkinson
John Hart
Abraham Clark

New Hampshire
Josiah Bartlett
William Whipple
Matthew Thornton

Massachusetts
Samuel Adams
John Adams
Robert Treat Paine
Elbridge Gerry

Rhode Island
Stephen Hopkins
William Ellery

Connecticut
Samuel Huntington
William Williams
Oliver Wolcott
Roger Sherman

What It Means
Resolution of Independence The Final section declares that the colonies are "Free and Independent States" with the full power to make war, to form alliances, and to trade with other countries.

rectitude *rightness*

What It Means
Signers of the Declaration The signers, as representatives of the American people, declared the colonies independent from Great Britain. Most members signed the document on August 2, 1776.

Did You Know?

Richard Henry Lee and Francis Lightfoot Lee were brothers, and John and Samuel Adams were cousins. Roger Sherman was the only person who signed all three of the most important documents of the United States: the Declaration of Independence, the Articles of Confederation, and the Constitution.

W Writing Support

Persuasive Writing Tell students to take the role of a Patriot or Loyalist newspaper editor from 1776 and write an editorial reacting to the Declaration of Independence. OL CA HR4. CA 8WA2.4

S Skill Practice

Historical and Social Sciences Analysis Skill
Ask: What evidence is there in the Resolution that religious beliefs were important to the Declaration? *(appealing to the Supreme Judge; reliance on the Protection of Divine Providence)* OL

C Critical Thinking

Analyzing Primary Sources Ask: What does the closing of the document mean, in which the signers "mutually pledge to each other our Lives, our Fortunes and our sacred Honor"? *(The delegates promise their lives, their wealth, and their good names to each other in a vow to carry out the work of independence.)* OL CA HR4.

ASSESS

Ask students to identify the most important points in the Declaration of Natural Rights and explain why they chose those items. OL

CLOSE

Identifying Central Issues
Have students list the powers the new free and independent states planned to claim. *(to levy war, conclude peace, make alliances, establish commerce, and all other things governments do)* OL

FOCUS

Reviewing Unit Objectives

Having studied this unit, students should be able to

- Explain the motives for and achievements that encouraged European exploration starting in the late 1400s.
- Describe the development of modern capitalism.
- Discuss major Enlightenment ideas and how they influenced the thinking of American colonists.
- Outline the events that led to the American Revolution.
- Explain how the colonists won independence.

TEACH

Have students explain why the focus in this unit shifted from many European countries to primarily Great Britain in this period. *(because the American colonists' main conflict was with Great Britain)* OL

Unit Review Activity

To help students review the unit objectives, ask them to explain how each of the following ideas contributes to the idea of a "changing world": European exploration; the rise of capitalism; the Enlightenment; the road to the Revolution; the American Revolution. OL

Unit 1 REVIEW

A Changing World

Native Americans were the first people to live in the Americas. Europeans and enslaved Africans arrived next. In England new ideas about government evolved. English colonists used those ideas to form the United States of America.

	Chapter 1: Expanding Horizons	Chapter 2: Road to Independence
When	• 1200s–1700s	• 1600s–1700s
Where	• Europe • Asia • Africa • Central America • South America • North America	• New England • West Africa • West Indies • Southern Colonies • Middle Colonies • Great Britain

◀ *Early compass*

▲ First Thanksgiving *by Jennie Browscomb, 1914*

END-OF-UNIT RESOURCES

Use these resources to review and assess unit material.

- Step Into American History Activities
- Cumulative Assessment Activities
- Reading Essentials and Study Guide
- California Standards Practice Workbook
- Interactive Tutor Self-Assessment CD-ROM
- Exam*View*® Pro Testmaker CD-ROM
- Succeeding on the California History–Social Science Standards CD-ROM

	Chapter 1: Expanding Horizons	Chapter 2: Road to Independence
Major Events	• **1215** King John signs Magna Carta • **c. 1400s** Technological advances lead to Age of Exploration and growth of trade • **1492** Columbus reaches the Americas • **1517** Martin Luther's calls for change begin the Reformation • **1521, 1532** Conquistadors conquer Aztec and Inca empires • **1588** English defeat Spanish Armada • **c. 1600s** Governments begin to charter banks • **c. 1600s** Mercantilism becomes basis for national policies • **1689** Bill of Rights guarantees all English people basic rights • **1690** John Locke states that people have rights based on natural law	• **1607** Jamestown is first permanent English colony • **1619** Representatives to House of Burgesses meet • **1620** Pilgrims sign Mayflower Compact • **1730s–1740s** Great Awakening sweeps through English colonies • **1763** Proclamation of 1763 forbids settlement west of Appalachians • **1770** Boston Massacre leads to more boycotts of British goods • **1773** Boston Tea Party protests tax on tea • **1775** First battles of Revolution are fought at Lexington and Concord • **1776** Declaration of Independence is signed • **1781** British surrender at Yorktown
Some Important People	• Christopher Columbus • Queen Elizabeth I • John Locke • Isaac Newton	• Roger Williams • Jonathan Edwards • Benjamin Franklin • George Washington
How do these events and ideas affect our lives today?	• School subjects are rooted in Renaissance learning. • Spanish heritage is an important part of North American culture.	• American Patriots supported rights (free speech, religion, press) that we enjoy today.
What was happening in California at this time?	• **1533** Spanish expedition reaches Baja California peninsula • **1542** Juan Cabrillo reaches San Diego Bay • **1579** Francis Drake encounters Coast Miwok people	• **1769** Father Junípero Serra sets up first mission at San Diego • **1776** Juan Bautista de Anza discovers trail from Sonora to San Francisco area

Christopher Columbus ▶

Revolutionary War drum and fife ▲

Juan Bautista de Anza ▶

UNIT 1 REVIEW

ASSESS/CLOSE

Unit Wrap-Up Activity

Sequencing Information

Have students create graphic organizers that gather key information in the unit on the theme "Road to Independence."

1. Organize students into groups of four. Make sure that each group has writing materials and at least one copy of the textbook.
2. Explain to students that their task is to create a graphic organizer that shows how the British colonies were formed, how they developed institutions that became the basis of self-government, why they came into conflict with Great Britain, and how they won their independence.
3. After groups have completed their graphic organizers, have them share the results with the class. **OL**

PROFESSIONAL DEVELOPMENT: ENGLISH LEARNERS

Use these resources for help teaching English learners.

- Cary, Stephen. *Working with Second Language Learners: Answers to Teachers' Top Ten Questions.* Heinemann, 2000.
- Echevarria, Jana, MaryEllen Vogt, and Deborah J. Short. *Making Content Comprehensible for English Language Learners: The SIOP Model* (Second Edition). Pearson Allyn & Bacon, 2003.
- Jesness, Jerry. *Teaching English Language Learners K Through 12.* Corwin Press, 2004.
- Peregoy, Suzanne, and Owen Boyle. *Reading, Writing, and Learning in ESL: A Resource Book for K–12 Teachers* (Third Edition). Longman, 2001.

Teaching the Unit

Use the information on these pages to help you teach Unit 2.

History–Social Science Standards Covered in Unit 2

Standard	Chapter 3	Chapter 4
US8.2 Students analyze the political principles underlying the U.S. Constitution and compare the enumerated and implied powers of the federal government.	✔	✔
US8.3 Students understand the foundation of the American political system and the ways in which citizens participate in it.	✔	✔

Pacing Your Lessons

This pacing chart provides time management suggestions for teaching Unit 2.

Unit 2 Creating a Nation	Days
Unit 2 Introduction	1/2
Chapter 3 • **Reading Skill:** Making Connections • **Sections 1–3** • **Biography:** James Madison • **America's Literature:** "Second Daughter" • **You Decide . . .** • **Analyzing Primary Sources**	10
Chapter 4 • **Reading Skill:** Summarizing Information • **Sections 1–3** • **Biography:** Gouverneur Morris, John Marshall • **Connecting to the Constitution** • **Analyzing Primary Sources**	6
Unit 1 Review	1/2

Teacher to Teacher

Compromise—My Rights or Yours?

Gary Chinn
Rooftop K-8 School
San Francisco, CA

Have students research both sides of the following debate, which formed the basis of the Federalist and Antifederalist standoff: the United States's, need for a strong central government versus the rights of individual states. After researching, students should choose the side that they support. Then have them produce posters, advertisements, flyers, or political cartoons to promote either the cause of the Federalists or the cause of the Antifederalists. Each student is responsible for a one-minute presentation, explaining his or her artwork and viewpoint. When presentations are completed, have a group of students collate the artwork into a portfolio that can be used during a class discussion or debate concerning the pros and cons of ratifying the Constitution.

Previewing the Chapters

Dear American History Teacher:

As you begin to teach this unit, there are themes that reoccur throughout the chapters that you will want to point out to students.

The states served as proving grounds for representative government, as they developed new constitutions while the fight for independence was going on. The division of power between the states and the national government was a contested issue from the formation of the United States. The first government, under the Articles of Confederation, set up a weak national government, hoping to reserve powers to the states. Its weaknesses led to its replacement by the U.S. Constitution, which gave more power to the federal government. Some Americans worried that this new framework would weaken the states too much and would lead to the loss of individual liberties.

The principle of checks and balances aimed to prevent any branch of the federal government from abusing its power. The fact of popular sovereignty—and the duty of each citizen to meet his or her responsibilities—also help ensure that government will remain limited from arbitrary rule and that individual rights will be protected.

You may want to use the following information at the beginning of each chapter as a lesson launcher to help students begin to focus on what they will be studying.

Donald A. Ritchie

CHAPTER 3: A More Perfect Union
(pages 174–213)

Early in the American Revolution, the states began writing new constitutions, which helped establish many principles of American government. Americans knew that they needed a central government to lead the war effort, and Congress wrote the Articles of Confederation. But the government created under the Articles had weaknesses. When a rebellion broke out, some leaders feared that the nation would be torn apart. They called for a meeting to discuss changes to the Articles government. The Constitutional Convention wrote an entire new plan of government, creating a much stronger central government. Some Americans opposed this plan, but in the end the Constitution was ratified.

CHAPTER 4: The Constitution
(pages 214–245)

The Constitution was written to achieve six goals, which are outlined in the Preamble to the document. In creating a new government, the Framers of the Constitution drew on seven major principles. Those principles—popular sovereignty, republicanism, limited government, federalism, separation of powers, checks and balances, and individual rights—underlie the many provisions of this fundamental law of the land. The Constitution remains a living document, altered by amendments and by the use of implied powers. The federal government has three branches, each of which has a particular role and certain powers and responsibilities. Citizens have rights, duties, and responsibilities as well. By exercising their rights and meeting their responsibilities, they help keep the government strong.

FOCUS

Connecting to Past Learning

In Unit 1, students learned about the Americans' push for independence. In Unit 2, they will explore the way Americans struggled to form a stable government based on the principles set forth in the Declaration of Independence.

Unit Launch Activity

Have students explain why Americans in the 1770s and 1780s would have been worried about having a government that was too powerful. *(Students should recall Americans' complaints about harsh British rule.)* OL

History–Social Science Standards

The following standards are covered in Unit 2:

US8.2 Students analyze the political principles underlying the U.S. Constitution and compare the enumerated and implied powers of the federal government.

US8.3 Students understand the foundation of the American political system and the ways in which citizens participate in it.

Why It's Important

Ask: What is the structure of the American government? When do you think that structure was formed? OL

Unit 2

Creating a Nation

Why It's Important

After the American Revolution, the new nation struggled to draw up a plan of government. Created to meet the needs of a changing nation, the Constitution has been the fundamental law of the United States for more than 200 years. Many developments of this period shape our lives today.

- The Constitution is central to American life and ideals.
- The Constitution has served as a model for many constitutions all over the world.

1775 — 1780 — 1785

U.S. EVENTS

- **1776** U.S. declares independence
- **1783** Peace treaty ends Revolutionary War
- **1785** Northwest Ordinance bans slavery in territory

A reproduction of the Declaration of Independence

CALIFORNIA EVENTS

- **1776** Presidio (fort) established at San Francisco
- **1777** First civic settlement founded at San José
- **1781** New settlement established at Los Angeles
- **1784** Father Junípero Serra dies

Father Junípero Serra

WORLD EVENTS

- **1776** Adam Smith's *Wealth of Nations* published
- **1778** France recognizes American independence
- **1783** Spain regains control of Florida after the American Revolution

170

TEACHING THE TIME LINES

Help students focus on the information in the time lines. **Ask:**

- How many years passed between the colonists declaring independence and the French recognition of that independence? *(two)*
- What kinds of settlements did the Spanish have in California? *(presidio or fort, towns like San José and Los Angeles, missions)*
- What event came first, the beginning of the French Revolution or the ratification of the U.S. Constitution? *(ratification of the U.S. Constitution)*

As students study events described in the unit, refer back to these time lines and have students identify where the event would appear. OL

Where in the United States?

NATIONAL GEOGRAPHIC

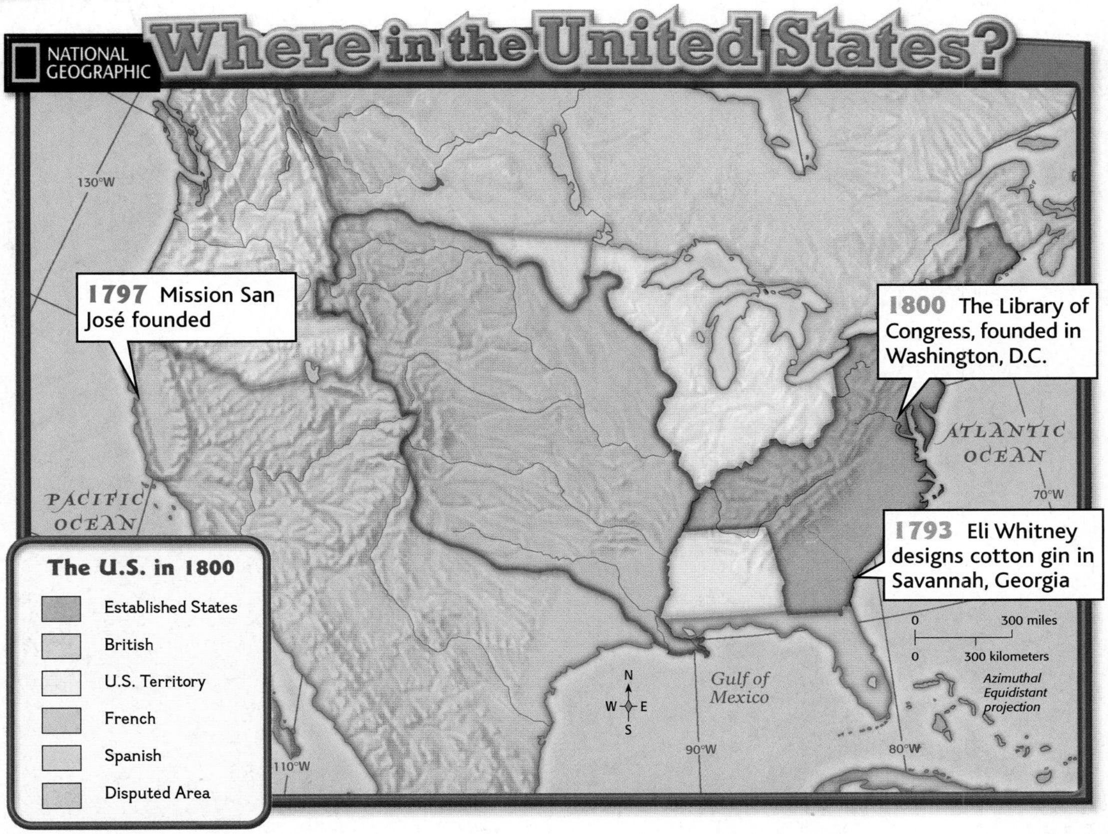

1790 · **1795** · **1800**

1788 U.S. Constitution ratified

◀ *Eli Whitney*

1793 Eli Whitney designs cotton gin in Savannah, Georgia

▼ *The Library of Congress*

1800 The Library of Congress founded in Washington, D.C.

1791 Mission Santa Cruz established

◀ *San Luis Rey Mission*

1797 Mission San José founded

1798 San Luis Rey founded; it is the 18th of 21 California missions

1789 French Revolution begins

1796 English doctor Edward Jenner invents smallpox vaccine

1799 Rosetta Stone discovered

TEACH

NATIONAL GEOGRAPHIC **Where in the United States?**

Understanding Maps and Time Lines **Ask:** What is the difference between the lands in red and those in yellow? *(Both belong to the United States, but the red lands are states and the yellow areas are territories.)* What other nations held land in North America? *(Britain, France, Spain)* What does the map key call the pink areas? *(Disputed Area)* What do you think that means? *(Students may say that the areas were claimed by more than one country but the actual ownership was not settled.)* OL

NCLB *NO CHILD LEFT BEHIND*

Teaching Activity Have students categorize the events on the time line into the categories Government and Culture. *(Government would include the first four entries on the U.S. events time line, the founding of different types of settlements in California, and the middle three events on the World events time line. The other entries would fall into the Culture category.)* OL

UNIVERSAL ACCESS

English Learners: Remind students that some of the names and places on these time lines come from Spanish. Ask volunteers to demonstrate how to pronounce these names and places in Spanish. EL

Below Grade Level: Organize students into pairs. Tell each student to create a five-question quiz on one of the three parts of the time line, with the partners taking different parts. Have them exchange their quizzes and answer the questions. BL

Advanced Learners: Have students research and write a report on one of the Spanish colonies in the present-day United States: California, Arizona, New Mexico, Texas, or Florida. AL

INTRODUCING UNIT 2

Unit Objectives

After studying this unit, students should be able to

- Describe the structure of the national government under the Articles of Confederation.
- Outline the steps that led to the formation of the Constitutional Convention.
- Describe the structure of the national government under the Constitution.
- Give examples of parts of the Constitution that illustrate its underlying principles.

Previewing People to Meet

Have students create the graphic below and complete it as they read the unit. OL
NOTE: Answers are listed in the second column.

Person	Known For
James Madison	*(helped write Constitution)*
Richard Allen	*(argued for rights of African Americans)*
Absalom Jones	*(argued for rights of African Americans)*
Roger Sherman	*(had idea of Great Compromise)*
George Mason	*(opposed Constitution)*
Mercy Otis Warren	*(opposed Constitution)*
Gouverneur Morris	*(writer and editor of the Constitution)*
John Marshall	*(became Chief Justice of the Supreme Court)*

Unit 2 Places to Locate

People to Meet

Richard Allen
1760–1831
Philadelphia preacher
Chapter 3, page 196

Absalom Jones
1746–1818
Philadelphia preacher
Chapter 3, page 196

James Madison
1751–1836
Architect of the Constitution
Chapter 3, page 198

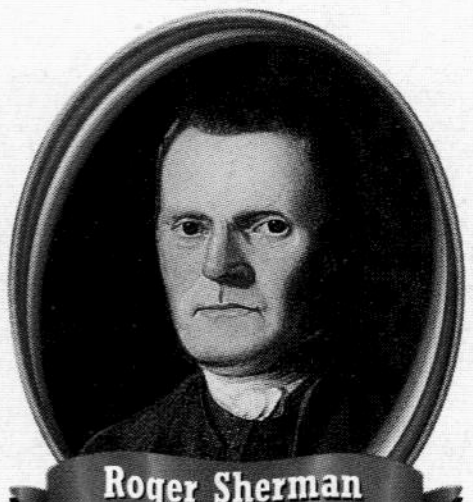

Roger Sherman
1721–1793
Creator of the Great Compromise
Chapter 3, page 199

Previewing Places to Locate

Use the following descriptions to explain the images on the map.

1 
The Northwest Ordinance allowed for three stages of government in the territories: rule by an appointed territorial governor; rule by an elected territorial legislature; and statehood.

2 
Massachusetts state militia troops put down Shays's Rebellion in three towns in the western part of the state. The main force of rebels was driven out of Springfield, where the government had an arsenal.

1725–1792
Political leader
Chapter 3, page 201

1728–1814
Political writer
Chapter 3, page 206

1752–1816
Writer and editor of the Constitution
Chapter 4, page 220

1755–1835
Chief Justice of the Supreme Court
Chapter 4, page 232

INTRODUCING UNIT 2

Skill Practice

Using Geography Skills

Ask: What was the western boundary of the United States during this period? *(the Mississippi River)* What set that boundary? *(the Treaty of Paris of 1783, which ended the Revolutionary War)* **OL**

Skill Practice

Historical and Social Sciences Analysis Skill

Have students conduct research to identify the state where each of the People to Meet came from. Have them list the names by state. **Ask:** What states are represented? *(Massachusetts—Warren; Connecticut—Sherman; Pennsylvania—Allen, Jones, Morris; Virginia—Madison, Mason, Marshall)* **OL**

ASSESS/CLOSE

Have students write a paragraph comparing and contrasting the U.S. events and the California events. *(Students might indicate that the U.S. events show the formation of a new country while the California events suggest the settlement of the area.)* **OL**

Today Independence Hall is part of a national historical park that includes other buildings from the nation's founding. Nearby stands a recently built museum that explores the Constitution.

In 1793, work on building the Capitol began. The building was burned by the British in the War of 1812 and rebuilt and enlarged afterward.

Chapter 3 Planning Guide

SECTION RESOURCES

Main Ideas	Print Materials	Technology Resources
Section 1 **The Articles of Confederation** 1. As soon as the Declaration of Independence was signed, the 13 states began writing their own constitutions. 2. Americans realized the necessity of establishing a central, or national, government for the 13 states 3. The weaknesses of the Articles of Confederation created problems for the new country.	• Reproducible Lesson Plan 3–1* • Daily Lesson and Discussion Notes 3–1 • Active Reading Note-Taking Guide 3–1 • Reading Essentials and Study Guide 3–1 • Guided Reading Activity 3–1 • Section Quiz 3–1	Daily Focus Skills Transparency 3–1 Section Graphic Organizer Transparency 3–1 California Standards Practice Transparencies Interactive Tutor Self-Assessment CD-ROM Exam*View*® Pro Testmaker CD-ROM Presentation Plus! CD-ROM
Section 2 **Convention and Compromise** 1. The government under the Articles of Confederation faced many problems. 2. National leaders worked to produce a new constitution for the United States. 3. The Constitutional Convention broke the deadlock over the form the new government would take.	• Reproducible Lesson Plan 3–2* • Daily Lesson and Discussion Notes 3–2 • Active Reading Note-Taking Guide 3–2 • Reading Essentials and Study Guide 3–2 • Guided Reading Activity 3–2 • Section Quiz 3–2	Daily Focus Skills Transparency 3–2 Section Graphic Organizer Transparency 3–2 California Standards Practice Transparencies Interactive Tutor Self-Assessment CD-ROM Exam*View*® Pro Testmaker CD-ROM Presentation Plus! CD-ROM
Section 3 **A New Plan of Government** 1. Ideas and thinkers of the past influenced the creation of the United States Constitution. 2. The Constitution outlines the responsibilities and the limits of the three branches of government. 3. Americans reacted to the proposed Constitution in different ways.	• Reproducible Lesson Plan 3–3* • Daily Lesson and Discussion Notes 3–3 • Active Reading Note-Taking Guide 3–3 • Reading Essentials and Study Guide 3–3 • Guided Reading Activity 3–3 • Section Quiz 3–3	Daily Focus Skills Transparency 3–3 Section Graphic Organizer Transparency 3–3 California Standards Practice Transparencies Interactive Tutor Self-Assessment CD-ROM Exam*View*® Pro Testmaker CD-ROM Presentation Plus! CD-ROM Vocabulary PuzzleMaker CD-ROM

PACING YOUR LESSONS

Unit Introduction	Chapter Introduction	Section 1	Section 2	Section 3	Chapter Assessment
½ Day	½ Day	3 Days	3 Days	3 Days	½ Day

0:00 **OUT OF TIME?** Assign the Chapter 3 ***Reading Essentials and Study Guide***

*Available on TeacherWorks™

Standards-Based Lesson Plan

History–Social Science Standards Covered in Chapter 3

The standards covered in the chapter are listed below. Use the accompanying activity as you teach the chapter to ensure student mastery of these standards. This activity can be used in combination with the program's print and technology assessment materials.

Standard	Section 1	Section 2	Section 3
US8.2 Students analyze the political principles underlying the U.S. Constitution and compare the enumerated and implied powers of the federal government.	✔	✔	✔
US8.2.1			✔
US8.2.2	✔	✔	✔
US8.2.3		✔	✔
US8.2.4			✔
US8.3 Students understand the foundation of the American political system and the ways in which citizens participate in it.	✔	✔	✔
US8.3.1	✔		
US8.3.2	✔		
US8.3.5		✔	
US8.9 Students analyze the early and steady attempts to abolish slavery and to realize the ideals of the Declaration of Independence.	✔	✔	
US8.9.2		✔	
US8.9.3	✔		

Cumulative Standards-Assessment Activity

The Cumulative Standards-Assessment Activity will help students organize and learn the important information from the chapter. Begin teaching the chapter with this activity, and have students complete it as they read the chapter.

Creating an Outline

Purpose Outlining is a useful way of understanding the structure of a piece of writing and the relationship among the ideas. Readers who develop the skill can apply what they learn about the structure of texts to their own writing.

Introduction to Outlining

1. An outline is like the framework of a house; it provides the overall structure of a text. Write on the board the phrase *Steps Leading to the Revolution* and the numbers *1, 2,* and *3* beneath it. Ask students to identify three events that led to the rebellion by American colonists. Then write *Steps Leading to Declaring Independence* and do the same. Explain that these two lists are outlines for two parts of the previous chapter. The different indents show visually how some information is subordinated to others.
2. Ask students to copy this structure in their notebooks:

   I. ____________________
      A. ____________________
         1. ____________________
         2. ____________________
      B. ____________________
         1. ____________________
         2. ____________________
   II. ____________________

   As students read each section, have them outline the content. Advise them to use as many roman numerals, capital letters, and numbers as they need to cover the section content.
3. Urge students to use their outlines to help them review the chapter.

Chapter 3 Resources

READING SUPPORT

- Content Vocabulary Activity 3
- Academic Vocabulary Activity 3
- Reading Skills Activity 3
- American Literature Reading 3
- Biography Activities 3A–3C
- Chapter 3 Active Reading Note-Taking Guide
- Chapter 3 Guided Reading Activities
- Chapter 3 Reading Essentials and Study Guide
- Glencoe Literature Library
- Glencoe Video Program
- Vocabulary PuzzleMaker CD-ROM
- Interactive Graphic Organizers CD-ROM
- American History Primary Source Document Library CD-ROM

CRITICAL THINKING

- Critical Thinking Skills Activity 3
- Primary Source Reading 3
- Cause-and-Effect Transparency 3, Strategy, and Activity
- Presentation Plus! CD-ROM

UNIVERSAL ACCESS

- Universal Access Activity 3
- Then and Now Transparencies 3A–3B, Strategy, and Activity
- Graphic Novel Activity 3
- School-to-Home Connection Activities 3A–3D
- English Learner Handbook Chapter 3 Activity
- Universal Access for the American History Classroom
- Moments in Time
- American Art and Architecture Transparencies, Strategies, and Activities
- American Art Prints
- American Music Cultural Traditions
- American Music Hits Through History
- StudentWorks Plus CD-ROM

SKILL PRACTICE

- Map Overlay Transparency 3, Strategy, and Activity
- Analysis Skills Activity 3
- Time Line Activity 3
- Geography and History Activity 3
- Economics and History Activity 3
- Chart, Graph, and Map Skills Activity 3
- Political Cartoon Activity 3
- Supreme Court Case Study 3
- In-Text Map Transparency 3, Strategy, and Activity
- Step Into American History Activity 3
- Citizenship and Service Learning Activity 3
- Outline Map Resource Book
- MindJogger Plus Videoquiz

WRITING SUPPORT

- Writing Activity 3
- Language Arts Activity 3
- Writer's Guidebook
- Middle School Writing Process Transparencies

ASSESSMENT

GLENCOE'S ASSESSMENT ADVANTAGE

- Chapter 3 Section Quizzes
- Chapter 3 Tests, Forms A and B
- California Standards Assessment, Forms A and B
- Cumulative Assessment Activity US8.2
- California Standards Practice Workbook
- Succeeding on the California History–Social Science Standards CD-ROM
- Exam*View*® Pro Testmaker CD-ROM
- Interactive Tutor Self-Assessment CD-ROM

CD-ROM | DVD | Print Material | Poster | Transparency | Music Program | Videocassette | Glencoe Literature Library

Chapter 3 Resources

TECHNOLOGY

- StudentWorks Plus CD-ROM
- TeacherWorks Plus CD-ROM
- Exam*View*® Pro Testmaker CD-ROM
- Interactive Tutor Self-Assessment CD-ROM
- Presentation Plus! CD-ROM
- Succeeding on the California History–Social Science Standards CD-ROM
- Vocabulary PuzzleMaker CD-ROM
- Interactive Graphic Organizers CD-ROM
- Interactive Time Line CD-ROM
- American History Primary Source Document Library CD-ROM
- MindJogger Plus Videoquiz
- American Music Cultural Traditions
- American Music Hits Through History
- *Discovering Our Past: The American Journey to World War I* Glencoe Video Program
- Professional Development in Middle School Social Studies Series
- Teaching American History With *Discovering Our Past: The American Journey to World War I*

SPANISH RESOURCES

- Spanish Activities and Assessment
  - Spanish Content Vocabulary Activities
  - Spanish Guided Reading Activities
  - Spanish Quizzes and Tests
  - Spanish California Standards Assessment
- Spanish Reading Essentials and Study Guide
- Spanish School-to-Home Connection
- Spanish Declaration of Independence and U.S. Constitution

TRANSPARENCIES

- California Standards Practice Transparencies
- Daily Focus Skills Transparencies
- Section Graphic Organizer Transparencies
- In-Text Map Transparencies
- Map Overlay Transparencies
- Cause-and-Effect Transparencies
- Then and Now Transparencies
- American Art and Architecture Transparencies
- Middle School Writing Process Transparencies

TEACHER PLANNING

- Daily Lesson and Discussion Notes
- English Learner Handbook
- Guide to Daily Intervention
- *Discovering Our Past: The American Journey to World War I* Reading and Study Skills Foldables
- Reading Strategies and Activities for the Social Studies Classroom
- Chapter 3 Reproducible Lesson Plans (correlated to California History–Social Science Standards)
- Universal Access for the American History Classroom
- NGS U.S. Desk Map
- NGS U.S. Atlas

PROFESSIONAL DEVELOPMENT

- Building Academic Vocabulary
- Strategies for Success
- Research-Based Strategies Used to Develop *Discovering Our Past: The American Journey to World War I*
- Character Education in the Middle School Classroom
- The Living Constitution
- Professional Development in Middle School Social Studies Video Series
- Teaching American History With *Discovering Our Past: The American Journey to World War I*

MASTERING THE STANDARDS

The content and assessment in the Student Edition, Teacher Wraparound Edition, teacher planning materials, and the print and technology products are all standards-based. The use of these products during instruction leads to mastery of the standards.

PRACTICE
- California Standards Practice Workbook
- California Standards Practice Transparencies
- Interactive Time Line CD-ROM
- School-to-Home Connection

BENCHMARK ASSESSMENT
- California Standards Assessment
- Exam*View*® Pro Testmaker CD-ROM
- Succeeding on the California History–Social Science Standards CD-ROM

REMEDIATION
- California Guide to Daily Intervention
- Interactive Tutor Self-Assessment CD-ROM
- Exam*View*® Pro Testmaker CD-ROM
- California Standards Practice Workbook
- Reading Essentials and Study Guide

Additional Resources

NATIONAL GEOGRAPHIC TEACHER'S CORNER

Index to National Geographic Magazine:

The following articles relate to this chapter:

- "L'Enfant's Washington," by Alice H. Hall, August 1991.
- "The Peales: America's First Family of Art," by Otto Friedrich, December 1990.
- "James Madison: Architect of the Constitution," by Alice J. Hall, September 1987.
- "George Washington's Patowmack Canal," by Wilbur E. Garrett, June 1987.

National Geographic Society Products

To order the following, call National Geographic at 1-800-368-2728

- *National Geographic Desk Reference* (Book)
- *National Geographic Atlas of the World, Seventh Edition* (Book)

NGS ONLINE

Access National Geographic's new dynamic MapMachine Web site and other geography resources at:

www.nationalgeographic.com

www.nationalgeographic.com/maps

A&E HOME VIDEO. Biography. THE HISTORY CHANNEL.

The following videotape programs are available from Glencoe as supplements to Chapter 3.

- **George Washington: Founding Father (ISBN 1-56501-377-8)**
- **Thomas Jefferson: Philosopher of Freedom (ISBN 1-56501-502-9)**
- **Benjamin Franklin: Citizen of the World (ISBN 1-56501-426-X)**
- **Patrick Henry: Voice of Liberty (ISBN 1-56501-645-9)**

To order, call Glencoe at 1-800-334-7344. To find classroom resources to accompany many of these videos, check the following home pages:

A&E Television: www.aetv.com
The History Channel: www.historychannel.com

History Online

Use our Web site for additional resources. All essential content is covered in the Student Edition.

You and your students can visit ca.hss.glencoe.com, the Web site companion to *Discovering Our Past: The American Journey to World War I.* This innovative integration of electronic and print media offers your students a wealth of opportunities. The student text directs students to the Web site for the following options:

- Chapter Overviews
- Self-Check Quizzes
- Study Central™
- Student Web Activities
- Textbook Updates
- Multi-Language Glossaries

Answers to the student Web activities are provided for you in the Web Activity Lesson Plans. Additional Web resources and ePuzzles and games are also available.

Glencoe TechCONNECT

Glencoe TechCONNECT™ AC199 "Independence Hall: Birthplace of the United States"

Cumulative Activity Students should understand how structures may have historic significance. They will learn about important events that took place in colonial buildings and then use a spreadsheet application to organize this information. **CA** US8.1.2.; US8.2.3. **CA** HR1.; HR4.; HI1. **CA** 8RW1.0; 8RC2.0; 8RL3.0

You can access this online activity at www.ca.hss.techconnect.glencoe.com Enter the following activation key when prompted: **CONNECTCA.** To access the Teacher Resources for each activity, enter the following password when prompted: **CA123.**

FOLDABLES™ Study Organizer

Dinah Zike's Foldables

Foldables are three-dimensional, interactive graphic organizers that help students practice basic writing skills, review key vocabulary terms, and identify main ideas. Every chapter contains a foldable activity, with additional chapter activities found in the Reading and Study Skills Foldables booklet.

Reading List Generator CD-ROM

GLENCOE BOOKLINK

The Glencoe BookLink CD-ROM is a database that allows you to search more than 15,000 titles to create a customized reading list for your students.

- Reading lists can be organized by students' reading level, author, genre, theme, or area of interest.
- The database provides Degrees of Reading Power™ (DRP) and Lexile™ readability scores for all selections.
- A brief summary of each selection is included.

Reading level suggestions for this chapter:

For students at a Grade 6 reading level:

- ***Thomas Jefferson,*** by T.M. Usel

For students at a Grade 7 reading level:

- ***Dear Benjamin Banneker,*** by Andrea Davis Pinkney

For students at a Grade 9 reading level:

- ***Who Were the Founding Fathers?: Two Hundred Years of Reinventing American History,*** by Steven H. Jaffe

Reading Support From JAMESTOWN EDUCATION

- *Timed Readings Plus in Social Studies* helps students increase their reading rate and fluency while maintaining comprehension. The 400-word passages are similar to those found on state and national assessments.
- *Reading in the Content Areas: Social Studies* concentrates on six essential reading skills that help students better comprehend what they read. The book includes 754 high-interest nonfiction passages written at increasing levels of difficulty.
- *Reading Fluency* helps students read smoothly, accurately, and expressively.
- *Jamestown's Reading Improvement,* by renowned reading expert Edward Fry, focuses on helping build your students' comprehension, vocabulary, and skimming and scanning skills.
- *Critical Reading Series* provides high-interest books, each written at three reading levels.

To order these products, call Glencoe at 1-800-334-7344.

KEY for Using the Teacher Wraparound Edition

Use this key to help you identify the different types of prompts found in the Teacher Wraparound Edition.

R **Reading Strategies** activities help you teach reading skills and vocabulary.

C **Critical Thinking** strategies help students apply and extend what they have learned.

U **Universal Access** activities provide differentiated instruction for students learning to speak English, along with suggestions for teaching various types of learners.

S **Skill Practice** strategies help students practice historical analysis and geography skills.

W **Writing Support** activities provide writing opportunities to help students comprehend the text.

Teaching strategies and activities have been coded for ability level appropriateness.

AL Activities for students working above grade level
OL Activities for students working on grade level
BL Activities for students working below grade level
EL Activities for English Learners

FOCUS

History–Social Science Standards

In this chapter, the following standards will be covered:

US8.2 Students analyze the political principles underlying the U.S. Constitution and compare the enumerated and implied powers of the federal government.

US8.3 Students understand the foundation of the American political system and the ways in which citizens participate in it.

More About the Photo

Independence Hall is also known as the Old State House. It stands a block east of the site of Carpenters' Hall, where the First Continental Congress met in 1774. Independence Hall also housed the Liberty Bell until 1976, when it was moved to a separate pavilion.

TEACH

The Big Ideas

As you begin teaching each section, use these questions and activities to focus on the Big Ideas.

Section 1

The Articles of Confederation

Essential Question: Why is it important what kind of government we live under? *(Government of any kind has a strong effect over almost everything we do.)* BL

Chapter 3

A More Perfect Union

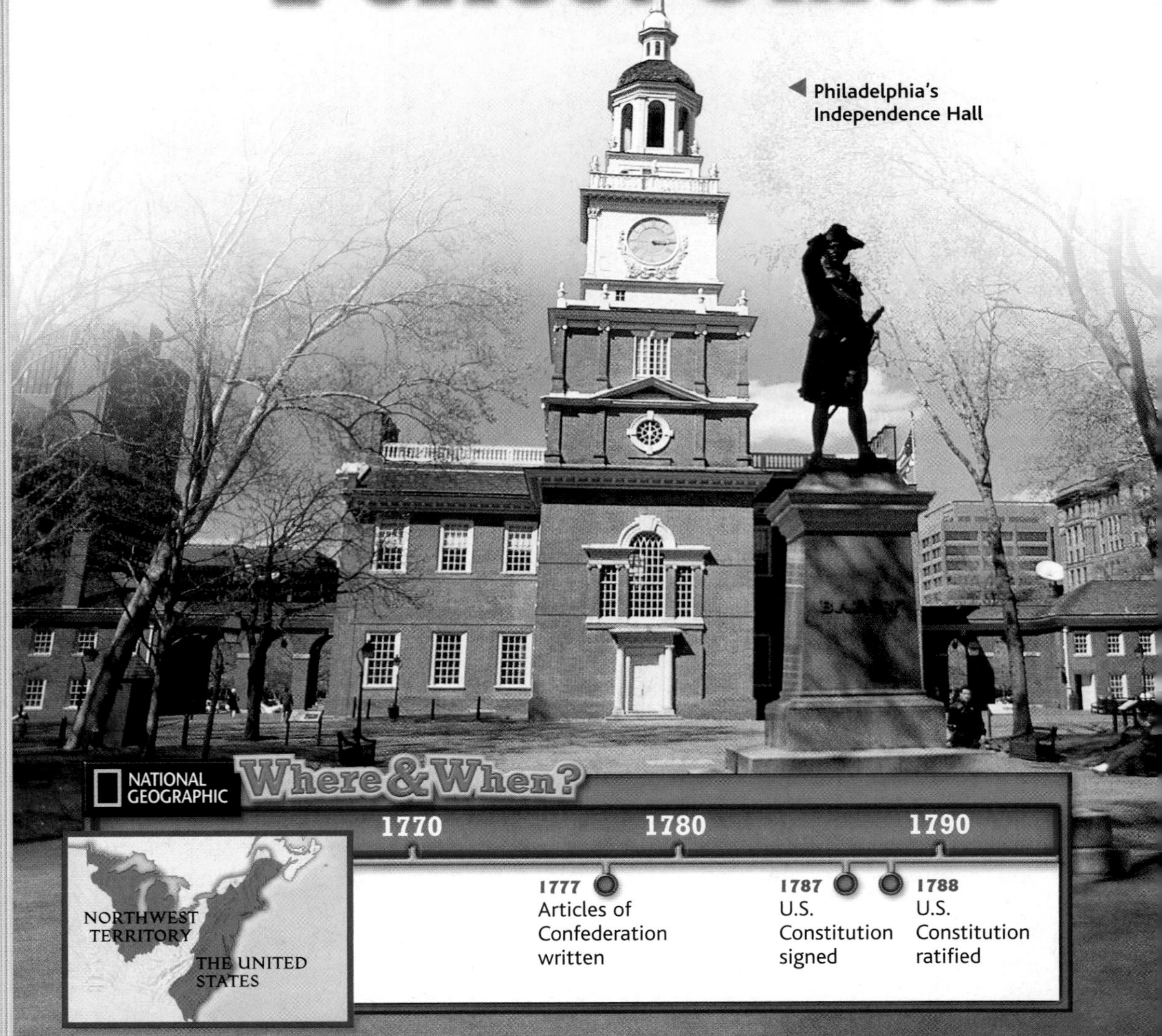

◀ Philadelphia's Independence Hall

NATIONAL GEOGRAPHIC **Where & When?**

1770	1780	1790

1777 Articles of Confederation written

1787 U.S. Constitution signed

1788 U.S. Constitution ratified

Section 2

Convention and Compromise

Essential Question: How does a constitution reflect the values and goals of the society that creates it? *(The most important ideas that people have about government will appear in the constitution.)* OL

Section 3

A New Plan of Government

Essential Question: What ideas and goals are addressed in the U.S. Constitution? *(Answers may include such ideas as it guarantees certain rights to all people and it sets forth the structure of the American government.)* OL

History Online
Chapter Overview Visit ca.hss.glencoe.com for a preview of Chapter 3.

The Big Ideas

Section 1 The Articles of Confederation

Political ideas and major events shape how people form governments. When the American colonies broke their political ties with Great Britain, they faced the task of forming independent governments at both the state and national levels.

Section 2 Convention and Compromise

A constitution reflects the values and goals of a society that creates it. The new Constitution corrected the weaknesses of government under the Articles of Confederation.

Section 3 A New Plan of Government

Political ideas and major events shape how people form governments. The United States system of government rests on the Constitution.

View the Chapter 3 video in the Glencoe Video Program.

FOLDABLES™ Study Organizer

Compare and Contrast Make this foldable to help you compare the Articles of Confederation to the U.S. Constitution.

Step 1 Fold a sheet of paper from side to side, leaving a 2-inch tab uncovered along the side.

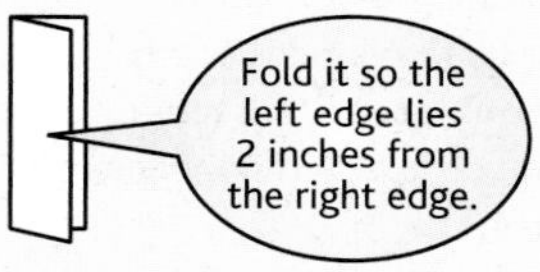

Step 2 Turn the paper and fold it into thirds.

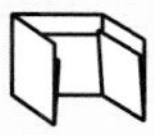

Step 3 Unfold and cut along the two inside fold lines.

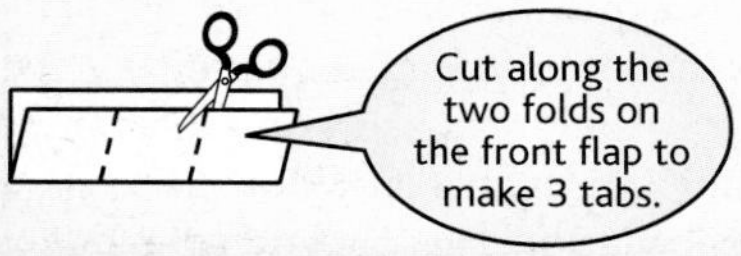

Step 4 Label the foldable as shown.

Reading and Writing As you read the chapter, write what you learn about these documents under the appropriate tabs.

History Online

Go to ca.hss.glencoe.com for student activities, lesson plans, and links to additional Web resources about the creation of the Constitution.

FOLDABLES™ Study Organizer

Dinah Zike's Foldables

Purpose Have students use their foldables to make comparisons between the Articles of Confederation and the Constitution. Encourage them to review their foldables as they prepare for quizzes and answer questions. BL

Why It's Important

Making Connections Making connections enhances students' comprehension and brings text alive for students. Text-to-text connections deepen understanding of history by linking similar events. Text-to-self connections help students place themselves in the historical environment. By examining experiences they have had and feelings they have felt in light of historical events, students gain a better understanding of the dynamics of history. Text-to-world connections help students understand that events in history are linked in many ways with events of the present.

1 Learn It!

Model making connections as you read the excerpt about the Enlightenment. For example, after reading the first sentence, make a text-to-text connection such as, "The Enlightenment led to new ideas about government and society." Then make a text-to-world connection, such as "Enlightenment ideas were put in practice when American leaders formed their new governments. Then ask students to offer their own text-to-self connections. OL

Chapter 3

Get Ready to Read

Making Connections

READING SKILL

1 Learn It!

Good readers make connections between what they are reading and what they know. Some connections are based on personal experiences (text-to-self). Readers also make connections to things they have read in other books (text-to-text). Finally, good readers make connections to things that happen in other places (text-to-world). Making these connections helps you understand words or ideas that are unfamiliar to you and gain knowledge about the world. As you read, ask yourself connecting questions. Are you reminded of something from your life, something you have read, or a person or event in another place or time? Read the paragraph below with these questions in mind.

Text-to-self:
What do you know about how people think and act? What do you think about government?

Framers of the Constitution got many ideas on the nature of people and government from European writers of the Enlightenment. The **Enlightenment** (ihn•LY•tuhn•muhnt) was a movement of the 1700s that promoted knowledge, reason, and science as the means to improve society.

—from page 203

Text-to-text:
What did you read about the Enlightenment in Chapter 1?

Text-to-world:
What other countries have governments based on ideals of the Enlightenment? How do knowledge, reason, and science impact government today?

Reading Tip

Make connections with important ideas, times, and topics in your life. Connecting helps you remember new information.

176

READING STRATEGY **TAKING NOTES**

Remind students that taking notes is a skill that goes hand in hand with making connections. Lead a discussion on tips for taking good notes. Then ask students to follow along as you read a paragraph you select from somewhere in this chapter. Have them take notes on the paragraph. Then ask volunteers to give examples of connections they could make based on their notes. OL

2 Practice It!

Read the following paragraphs. Then make a list of connections you made to the ideas in the reading. Compare your lists and discuss your answers with a partner.

Read to Write

Choose one of the connections you made that was different than your partner's or one that you think was more important. Write a paragraph to explain why you made such a connection. Use vivid details.

> The Northwest Ordinance provided a democratic model for national expansion. When the population of a territory reached 60,000, its people could petition, or apply to Congress, for statehood. Each new state would come into the Union with the same rights and privileges as the original 13 states.
>
> The Northwest Ordinance also guaranteed certain rights to people living in the territory. These rights included freedom of religion, property rights, and the right to trial by jury.
>
> —*from page 181–182*

NATIONAL GEOGRAPHIC **The Northwest Territory**

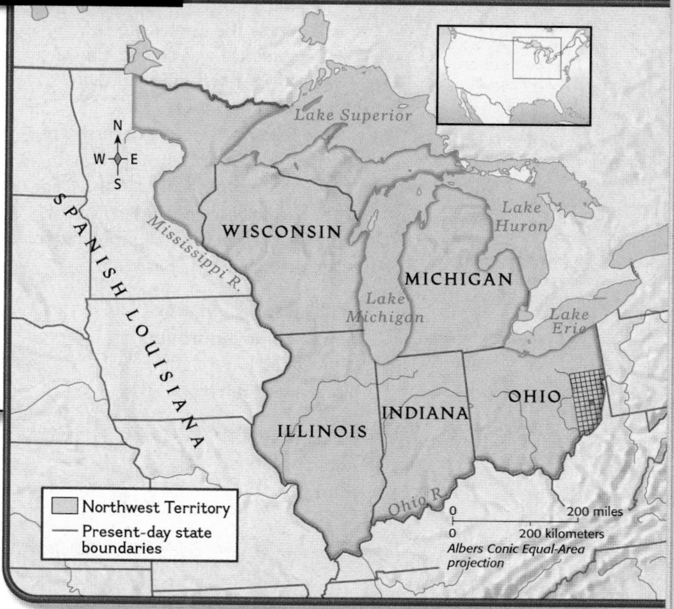

3 Apply It!

As you read this chapter, choose five words or phrases that make a connection to something you already know.

2 Practice It!

Have students repeat the commenting procedure modeled on page 176 with the new excerpt. You may want to have a volunteer read and make connections aloud, as you demonstrated with the passage on the Enlightenment. OL

3 Apply It!

Ask students to keep a list as they read. Have them note the connection, explain what kind it is, and make notes, including questions, to explain the connection. OL

READING STRATEGY — PERSUASIVE WRITING

The reading strategy of questioning can help students make connections to self, text, and world as they read. List some common questions that can be used for identifying connections, such as *Did Americans face a similar problem in another period?* or *What does this idea mean to me?* Have students brainstorm other questions that would often apply to material in their textbook. Suggest that students list the questions and apply them as they read. OL

Use Reading Skills Activity 3 in the **Chapter 3 Resource Book** for more practice with making connections.

FOCUS

BELLRINGER
SKILLBUILDER ACTIVITY

Project **Daily Focus Skills Transparency 3–1** and have students answer the question.

Guide to Reading

Preteaching Vocabulary: Use the Vocabulary PuzzleMaker CD-ROM to create crossword and word search puzzles.

Answers to Graphic: making laws, imposing taxes, issuing currency, conducting foreign relations, raising troops, regulating trade

Unpacking the Standards

After reading the section, students will be able to:

- Explain why the states began writing constitutions in 1776.
- Explain why Americans wanted a stronger central government.
- Discuss the strengths and weaknesses of the Articles of Confederation.

Section 1 The Articles of Confederation

History Social Science Standards

US8.2 Students analyze the political principles underlying the U.S. Constitution and compare the enumerated and implied powers of the federal government.

US8.3 Students understand the foundation of the American political system and the ways in which citizens participate in it.

US8.9 Students analyze the early and steady attempts to abolish slavery and to realize the ideals of the Declaration of Independence.

Guide to Reading

Looking Back, Looking Ahead
In Chapter 2, you learned about the American Revolution. The United States was now independent, but it remained to be seen whether the new nation could survive.

Focusing on the Main Ideas
- As soon as the Declaration of Independence was signed, the 13 states began writing their own constitutions. *(page 179)*
- Americans realized the necessity of establishing a central, or national, government for the 13 states. *(page 180)*
- The weaknesses of the Articles of Confederation created problems for the new country. *(page 183)*

Locating Places
Appalachian Mountains (A • puh • LAY • chuhn)
Northwest Territory

Meeting People
Robert Morris
John Jay

Content Vocabulary
popular sovereignty (PAH • pyuh • luhr SAH • vuhrn • tee)
bicameral (by • KAM • ruhl)
confederation (kuhn • FEH • duh • RAY • shuhn)
sovereignty (SAH • vuhrn • tee)
ratify (RA • tuh • fy)
ordinance (AWR • duhn • uhnts)
right of deposit (di • PAH • zuht)

Academic Vocabulary
interpret (ihn • TUHR • pruht)
authority (uh • THAHR • uh • tee)

Reading Strategy
Organizing Draw a diagram like the one below. In each oval, list a power you think a national government should have.

NATIONAL GEOGRAPHIC Where & When?

1775	1780	1785	1790

- **1777** Articles of Confederation written
- **1781** All states approve Confederation government
- **1787** Northwest Ordinance is passed

SECTION RESOURCES

Print Material
- Reproducible Lesson Plan 3–1*
- Daily Lesson and Discussion Notes 3–1
- Guided Reading Activity 3–1
- Reading Essentials and Study Guide 3–1
- Active Reading Note-Taking Guide 3–1
- Section Quiz 3–1

Transparencies
- Daily Focus Skills Transparency 3–1
- Section Graphic Organizer Transparency 3–1
- California Standards Practice Transparencies

Technology
- Interactive Tutor Self-Assessment CD-ROM
- Exam*View*® Pro Testmaker CD-ROM
- Presentation Plus! CD-ROM

*Available on TeacherWorks™

US8.3.1 Analyze the principles and concepts codified in state constitutions between 1777 and 1781 that created the context out of which American political institutions and ideas developed.

Thirteen Independent States

Main Idea **As soon as the Declaration of Independence was signed, the 13 states began writing their own constitutions.**

Reading Connection What makes people get along with one another? Do they need rules or a strong leader? Read to learn how the people of the new states answered these questions.

An American Story

In 1783 an enslaved Massachusetts man named Quock Walker made an important decision. He took legal action against a white man who had assaulted him. The case reached the state supreme court. Chief Justice William Cushing agreed with Walker:

> **"Our constitution [of Massachusetts] sets out with declaring that all men are born free and equal—and that every subject is entitled to liberty. . . . This being the case, I think the idea of slavery is inconsistent with our own conduct and constitution."**
>
> **—William Cushing, from his private notebook**

The Quock Walker case demonstrated that the Massachusetts courts would not support slavery. Because of this ruling and other antislavery efforts, slavery ceased to exist in Massachusetts.

State Constitutions Even before the Declaration of Independence was signed, American colonists discussed the possibility of independence and American leaders began preparing new state constitutions to replace the old colonial charters. Many of the new state governments were based upon ideals expressed in the Declaration of Independence. American ideals of individual rights to "life, liberty, and the pursuit of happiness" are in the Declaration. So are such values as **popular sovereignty** (PAH • pyuh • luhr SAH • vuhrn • tee)—government by consent of the governed—and equal justice under law. These ideals were also an important part of the early state constitutions. R1

Systems of Government In January 1776, New Hampshire became the first colony to organize as a state and craft a constitution. By 1780, the other former colonies had followed suit.

The new state constitutions set up a similar system of government. Each state had a legislature to create laws, and most of these legislatures were **bicameral** (by • KAM • ruhl), like the English Parliament; that is, they were divided into two parts, or houses. R2 Each state also had a chief executive called the governor, who was elected by the legislature or by the citizens. The governor's job was to carry out the laws. To prevent abuses by a single ruler most states' constitutions limited the power of the governor. Finally, each state had judges and courts to **interpret** the laws—to decide what the laws meant and how they applied to each new situation. R3

Preserving Rights To keep power in the hands of the people, state legislators were popularly elected, and elections were frequent. In most states, only white males who were at least 21 years old could vote. These citizens also had to own a certain amount of property or pay a certain amount of taxes. Some states allowed free African American males to vote.

Most state constitutions included a bill of rights, guaranteeing certain freedoms and legal protections to the state's citizens. Some of these rights, such as trial by jury and protection of personal property, can be traced back to the Magna Carta and the English Bill of Rights. As you learned earlier, these documents helped establish the idea that people have rights and that the power of the government should be limited.

Reading Check **Explain** Describe the branches of the new state government.

TEACH

R1 Reading Strategy

Understanding Vocabulary Ask students to use the term *popular sovereignty* to describe California's state's government. *(Sample answer: California's government rests on popular sovereignty.)* OL CA 8RW1.3

Review Grade 5 Standards

To review standard 5.6.5 *(Explain how state constitutions that were established after 1776 embodied the ideals of the American Revolution and helped serve as models for the U.S. Constitution)*, **ask:** What did the state constitutions value most, individual freedoms or government power? *(individual freedoms)* OL

R2 Reading Strategy

Using Word Parts The *bi-* in *bicameral* comes from the Latin word for "two." **Ask:** What are some other words that begin in this way? *(biannual, bilingual, bicycle)* OL

R3 Reading Strategy

Academic Vocabulary Have students list things, other than laws, that can be interpreted. *(Answers may include works of art, signs, and words and phrases.)* OL CA 8RW1.3

Reading Check

Answer: legislature to create laws, executive to carry out the laws, judicial to interpret laws

More Skill Practice

Historical and Social Sciences Analysis Skill Have students read about the separate state governments. **Ask:** Do you consider the 13 states to have been a "nation." Why or why not? *(Answers will vary but students should give reasons for their responses.)* AL

Did You Know?

Under New Jersey's state constitution, "any person" who met property qualifications could vote. Based on this provision, many New Jersey women were able to cast ballots until the state legislature took away that right in 1807. It would take over a century before New Jersey women regained the right to vote.

R1 Reading Strategy

Understanding Vocabulary

Ask: According to the definition in the text, is the school a confederation? Why or why not? *(no; because the power of the administration does not rest on the agreement of the students)* BL CA 8RW1.3

R2 Reading Strategy

Academic Vocabulary

Ask students to name some people and organizations that have authority over them. *(parents, teachers, governments)* BL CA 8RW1.3

C Critical Thinking

Predicting Consequences

Ask: What do you think will be the result of the Congress not having the power to tax and enforce laws? Ask students to explain their answers. *(Students should see that eventually the government will be too weak and ineffective to be successful, because the two powers it lacked are among the most important of any government.)* OL CA HI2.

Resources for page 180

Economics and History Activity 3

Answers and Additional Support

US8.3.2 Explain how the ordinances of 1785 and 1787 privatized national resources and transferred federally owned lands into private holdings, townships, and states. **US8.9.3** Describe the significance of the Northwest Ordinance in education and in the banning of slavery in new states north of the Ohio River.

Forming the New Government

Main Idea **Americans realized the necessity of establishing a central, or national, government for the 13 states.**

Reading Connection Would you be surprised to learn that the Constitution of the United States was not our nation's first plan of government? Read to find out about the nation's first constitution.

Although each state was well prepared and eager to govern itself when independence was declared, a state could not do some things on its own. It could not raise and maintain a large army, for example, and Americans knew that 13 small, separate forces would be no match for the mighty British army. Americans realized that if they wanted to win the war with Great Britain, they needed a single, strong army under central control. For this and other reasons, the Second Continental Congress made plans for a union of the states.

Picturing **History**

The Second Continental Congress adopted the Articles of Confederation in 1781. ***Why did the Congress form a union of states?***

A Confederation of States At the same time that Jefferson was drafting the Declaration of Independence, members of the Continental Congress were developing a plan for the new government. In 1777 the Congress detailed these plans in a document called the Articles of Confederation, the first constitution of the United States of America.

A confederation is a voluntary association of independent states. In a **confederation** (kuhn • FEH • duh • RAY • shuhn), the member states agree to let the central government undertake a limited number of activities, such as forming an army. R1

The Articles set up a one-house legislature called the Congress. Although the states could send between two and seven delegates to the congress, each state, no matter what the size, had only one vote. The issue of **sovereignty** (SAH • vuhrn • tee), or supreme power, was an important part of the Articles of Confederation:

> **"Each state retains its sovereignty, freedom and independence, and every power, jurisdiction and right, which is not by this Confederation expressly delegated to the United States in Congress assembled."**
>
> **—Article II, Articles of Confederation**

The Powers of Congress Congress had several powers under the Articles of Confederation. Congress had the **authority** to conduct foreign affairs, maintain armed forces, borrow money, and issue currency. These powers of Congress were quite limited, though. R2

As a result of their negative experiences with the British government, the 13 states refused to give the Congress two important powers. It had no power to enforce its laws and no power to tax. The Articles allowed the Congress to ask the states for money but not to demand it. The Congress could not, in fact, require the states to do anything. Without money or real power over the states, the Confederation Congress commanded so little respect that its members often did not bother to attend sessions. C

More Skill Practice

Historical and Social Sciences Analysis Skill Have students create a graphic organizer that shows the powers that the federal government under the Articles did and did not have. *(Graphic organizers should reflect the text information.)* BL CA HI1.

Picturing **History**

The original copy of the Articles of Confederation is held by the National Archives and Records Administration.

Answer: The states needed a central government to form and maintain an army because 13 states could not fight Britain as well as a unified force could.

R1 **Weaknesses of the Articles** By 1781 all 13 states had **ratified** (RA • tuh • fyd), or approved, the Articles of Confederation. Within the next few years, however, it became clear that the Articles had some serious flaws.

To begin with, the Congress could not pass a law unless nine states voted in favor of it. Any attempt to amend, or change, the Articles required a unanimous vote of all 13 states. These strict voting requirements made it difficult for the Congress to accomplish much.

Even when the Congress managed to pass laws, it could not enforce them. Unlike the state constitutions, the Articles did not provide for a chief executive or for courts. If a state decided to ignore a law, the Congress could do nothing.

Despite the weaknesses of the Articles, the Confederation government accomplished some important tasks. Perhaps its greatest achievement was establishing a fair policy for the development of the lands west of the **Appalachian Mountains** (A • puh • LAY • chuhn).

Western Land Policies At the beginning of the Revolutionary War, only a few thousand non-Indian settlers lived west of the Appalachian Mountains. By the 1790s, the number was approaching 120,000. These settlers hoped to organize their lands as states and join the union, but the Articles contained no provision for adding states. Congress knew that it had to extend its authority over the territory.

Lacking the power to tax or regulate trade, the only way for the Confederation Congress to raise money to pay its debts and operate the government was to sell land. To get people to buy land and settle in the western region, the Congress had to establish a system for dividing and selling the land and governing the new settlements. R2

In 1785 Congress passed an **ordinance** (AWR • duhn • uhnts), or law, that established a procedure for surveying and selling the western lands. R3 The new law divided the land into local government units called townships, which are perfectly squared blocks usually six miles wide and six miles long. These townships were to be further divided into 36 sections of 640 acres each that would be sold at public auction for at least a dollar an acre.

The Northwest Ordinance Two years later, Congress passed the Northwest Ordinance, which created a single **Northwest Territory** out of the lands north of the Ohio River and east of the Mississippi River. The lands were to be divided into not fewer than three nor more than five smaller territories.

The Northwest Ordinance provided a democratic model for national expansion. When the population of a territory reached 60,000, its people could petition, or apply to Congress, for statehood. Each new state would come into the Union with the same rights and privileges as the original 13 states. C

Weaknesses in the Articles of Confederation

Weakness	Result
Congress has no power to tax.	It had to rely on the states to collect and forward taxes, which the states were reluctant to do. The central government was always short of money.
Congress has no power to enforce its laws.	Congress depended on the states to enforce its laws, which they rarely did.
There was no executive branch.	Coordinating the work of the national government was almost impossible.
Nine states had to approve any law before it could be passed.	Most laws were difficult, if not impossible, to enact.
Congress could not force the states to meet military quotas.	Congress could not draft soldiers to form a standing army.

U

Understanding Charts

The national government had limited powers. It depended on states for revenue, soldiers, and law enforcement.

Analyze Why did the states approve a government with many weaknesses?

Understanding Charts

Answer: They wanted to retain power themselves.

Did You Know?

Both candidates for the position of national symbol were common in these western territories. The bald eagle became America's national symbol in 1872. Decades earlier, though, Benjamin Franklin had suggested a different bird. He felt the bald eagle was "a bird of bad moral character." He preferred the wild turkey, "a much more respectable bird".

R1 Reading Strategy

Understanding Vocabulary Write on the board other verbs that show acceptance *(such as accept, approve, endorse, OK)*. **Ask:** How does *ratify* differ from these? *(It is more formal; it applies to laws and legal documents.)* EL CA 8RW1.3

R2 Reading Strategy

Connecting **Ask:** How did Congress's need for money lead to laws about the western territories? *(Since it could not tax and there were limits on how much it could borrow, Congress had to sell these western lands to raise the money it needed.)* OL CA HI3.

R3 Reading Strategy

Understanding Vocabulary Have students list and define other words that relate to the law and legal matters. *(court, lawyer, attorney, judge, case, witness, felony, misdemeanor)* BL CA 8RW1.3

C Critical Thinking

Identifying Central Issues **Ask:** Why was it important for Congress to let new states enter the Union with the same rights and powers as the original states? *(it encouraged people to settle in new areas and then join the Union)* OL CA HI1.

U Universal Access

Below Grade Level Have students make a chart listing the key elements of the Ordinance of 1785 and the Northwest Ordinance. *(Charts should reflect the text information.)* BL CA 8WA2.3

C Critical Thinking

Predicting Consequences

Ask: How is this rule different from what had happened in the colonies? *(There was no ban on slavery in the colonies.)* Why might it be important in the future? *(Students may say that it blocked the spread of slavery.)* OL

CA CS3. CA H13.

S Skill Practice

Using Geography Skills

Have students look at the map of the Northwest Territory on page 183. Then ask them to predict which areas of the territory are likely to be settled first. Why? *(Eastern and southern Ohio and southern Indiana because they are easily accessible from the Ohio River and from Pennsylvania and Kentucky, already settled areas)* OL CA CS3.

Reading Check

Answer: to create a single Northwest Territory out of the lands north of the Ohio River and east of the Mississippi River

Resources for page 182

Geography and History Activity 3

Answers and Additional Support

The Northwest Ordinance also guaranteed certain rights to people living in the territory. These rights included freedom of religion, property rights, and the right to trial by jury. The ordinance also included a clause stating,

> C **"There shall be neither slavery nor involuntary servitude in [the] territory."**
>
> —Article 6,
> The Northwest Ordinance

This clause is very important. It marked the United States's first attempt to stop the spread of slavery.

Which States Were Formed? The Confederation's western ordinances had an enormous effect on American expansion and development. The Ordinance of 1785 and the Northwest Ordinance described the steps by which new states would be formed. These policies opened the way for settlement of the Northwest Territory in a clear and orderly manner. S

Ohio was the first state admitted (1803) to the Union from the Northwest Territory. Other states were admitted later. The present-day states of Indiana, Illinois, Michigan, and Wisconsin eventually were formed from the Northwest Territory.

Reading Check **Explain** What was the purpose of the Northwest Ordinance?

Why It Matters

Surveying the Land

When the Revolution began, only a few thousand white settlers lived west of the Appalachian Mountains. By the 1790s their numbers had increased to about 120,000. Through the Ordinance of 1785, Congress created a system for surveying—taking a detailed measurement of an area of land—and selling the western lands.

The Ordinance at first applied only to what was then called the Northwest Territory—present-day Ohio, Indiana, Michigan, Illinois, and Wisconsin. It established a system of land survey and settlement that we still use today.

The Land Ordinance led to the sale of large amounts of land and speeded settlement of the Northwest Territory.

Why It Matters

The administration of public lands later became a responsibility of the United States Department of the Treasury, created in 1789. Congress established the General Land Office within this department in 1812. In 1849, that office was transferred to the Department of the Interior.

Did You Know?

In 1786, a group called the Ohio Company founded the city of Marietta in southeastern Ohio. The group received a grant from Congress for 1.5 million acres (606,000 hectares) of land in the Ohio Valley. They began to sell the wilderness to land-hungry easterners. Marietta later became the capital of the Northwest Territory.

US8.2.2 Analyze the Articles of Confederation and the Constitution and the success of each in implementing the ideals of the Declaration of Independence.

Trouble on Two Fronts

R

Main Idea **The weaknesses of the Articles of Confederation created problems for the new country.**

Reading Connection Imagine paying 10 times the normal price for a gallon of milk or a loaf of bread. Read to find out why the price of goods soared during this era.

Although successful in establishing western land policies, the Confederation government had problems dealing with other important issues. Congress was powerless to regulate trade, so each state passed laws taxing goods from its neighbors. New York taxed firewood from Connecticut and cabbage from New Jersey. New Jersey retaliated by charging New York for a harbor lighthouse on the New Jersey side of the Hudson River. Congress had so little power that it could not deal effectively with the country's economic problems. It also failed to solve trade problems.

W

Economic Problems By 1781 the money printed during the Revolutionary War had depreciated, or fallen in value, so much that it was almost worthless. Unable to collect taxes, both the Congress and the states had printed their own paper money.

U

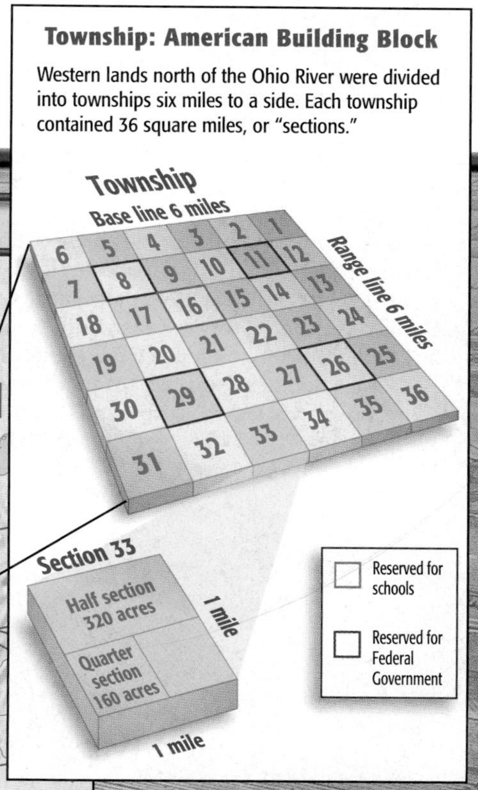

The Northwest Territory was divided into townships, each with 36 sections.

R Reading Strategy

Scaffolding—Previewing Have students identify the major heading on the page. *("Trouble on Two Fronts")* **Ask:** What does this heading signal to you? *(that they are going to read about two different problems facing the nation)* BL

This READING SKILL was introduced in Chapter 1.

W Writing Support

Expository Writing Have students write a paragraph explaining how the weakness of the central government contributed to economic weakness. *(Answers should cite the government's powerlessness to regulate trade, lack of ability to deal with foreign trade problems, worthlessness of currency, and large debt.)* OL CA HI6.

U Universal Access

Verbal/Linguistic Have students write a paragraph that uses words to explain the structure of a township, as shown in the illustration. AL

More Skill Practice

Historical and Social Sciences Analysis Skill Have students use the map of the Northwest Territory to make a three-question quiz about geographical features of the region. For example, they could ask "What is the southern border of the territory?" *(the Ohio River)* Have students exchange quizzes with a partner and complete them. OL CA CS3.

U Universal Access

Kinesthetic Ask students to create a visual display or demonstration that shows how Continental dollars lost much of their value in the 1780s. Have students share their display with the class. OL

Review The Big Idea

Review the Big Idea for this section: "Political ideas and major events shape how people form governments." **Ask:** What events and ideas caused the leaders of the United States to become dissatisfied with the Articles of Confederation? *(central government's lack of power to deal with economic, foreign, and military problems)* OL CA HI2.

C Critical Thinking

Making Inferences Ask: What do you think will happen because of the refusal to allow U.S. traders to use the Mississippi River? *(Students may suggest that the U.S. will try to gain control of the river by diplomacy or war.)* OL CA CS1.

Answers and Additional Support

U The money constantly declined in purchasing power because people feared that it could not be redeemed in gold or silver; if a $10 bill was worth $3 when it came into their hands, it might be worth only $2 or less when they spent it. The value of the money fell, while the price of food and other goods soared. Between 1779 and 1781, the number of Continental dollars required to buy one Spanish silver dollar rose from 40 to 146. In some towns, angry mobs seized overpriced sugar, tea, and bread from storekeepers.

Why Did the Debt Grow? Fighting the war left the Continental Congress with a large debt. Congress had borrowed money from American citizens and foreign governments during the war. It still owed the Revolutionary soldiers their pay for military service. Lacking the power to tax, the Confederation could not pay its debts. It requested funds from the states, but the states contributed only a small portion of the money needed.

Faced with a total collapse of the country's finances, the Confederation created a department of finance under Philadelphia merchant **Robert Morris.** Morris personally pledged large amounts of money for the war effort.

Some members wanted to give Congress some power to tax to raise funds. Although 12 states approved the plan, Rhode Island's opposition killed the measure. A second effort five years later also failed to win unanimous approval. The financial crisis only worsened.

▲ Continental currency

Problems With Britain As the weaknesses of the new American government became clear, the United States had problems with other nations. In the Treaty of Paris of 1783, Britain had promised to withdraw from the lands east of the Mississippi River. Yet British troops continued to occupy several strategic forts in the Great Lakes region. These forts were the centers of a profitable fur trade that Great Britain was determined to keep. The weak Confederation government could do nothing about the presence of foreign troops on American soil.

British trade policy caused other problems. American merchants complained that the British were keeping Americans out of the West Indies and other profitable British markets.

In 1784 Congress sent John Adams to London to discuss these difficulties. The British, however, were not willing to talk. They pointed to the failure of the United States to honor its promises made in the Treaty of Paris. The British claimed that Americans had agreed to pay Loyalists for the property taken from them during the Revolutionary War. The Congress had, in fact, recommended that the states pay the Loyalists, but the states had refused.

Problems With Spain If American relations with Great Britain were poor, affairs with Spain were worse. Spain, which held Florida as well as lands west of the Mississippi River, was anxious to halt American expansion into the territory it claimed. As a result, Spain closed the lower Mississippi River to American shipping in 1784. C Western settlers depended on the Mississippi River for trade. Bulky goods from the West—lumber, grain, and deerskins—could not be carried easily over the mountains to the East, but had to float down the Ohio and Mississippi Rivers on rafts and flatboats. **John Jay,** the American secretary of foreign affairs, noted that Americans accepted the idea that it was their right to use the Mississippi River to transport goods.

More Skill Practice

Historical and Social Sciences Analysis Skill Ask students to describe two examples of the economic weakness of the government under the Articles of Confederation identified on this page. *(inability to get states to approve tax power; inability to force the states to pay Loyalists)* BL CA HI2.

Did You Know?

Robert Morris (1734-1806) was a member of the Continental Congress and signed the Declaration of Independence. During the Revolution, he supervised the nation's finances, using his personal credit. Sadly, Morris lost all of his own money in later land speculation and spent three years in a debtors' prison.

R **What Is the Right of Deposit?** Westerners wanted the **right of deposit** (di • PAH • zuht) at New Orleans—that is, permission to put goods ashore for transfer to ocean going ships. When Spain refused this request, westerners asked Congress for a treaty with Spain that would grant free navigation along the Mississippi River.

In 1786 American diplomats reached an agreement with Spain. The people living in the Southern states, however, blocked the agreement because it did not include the right to use the Mississippi River.

The Government Falters The weakness of the Confederation and its inability to deal with problems worried many leaders. Peace with the British may have been won, but peace within the new nation was hard to find. The states bickered among themselves and refused to support the new central government in almost every way. Each state was beginning to act as an independent country, threatening the unity of the new United States. Some Vermont leaders even considered becoming part of Great Britain again. Only 18 members representing 8 states voted on the Confederation's most important piece of legislation, the Northwest Ordinance.

In a letter to one of George Washington's personal aides during the American Revolution, Washington noted that:

> **"We are one nation today and thirteen tomorrow—Who will treat with us on such terms?"**
>
> **—George Washington, Letter to James McHenry, 22 August 1785**

By the late 1780s, many national leaders had become dissatisfied with the weaknesses of the Confederation.

Reading Check **Analyze** Why did Spain close the lower Mississippi River to American trade?

History Online

Study Central Need help understanding the Articles of Confederation? Visit ca.hss.glencoe.com and click on Study Central.

Section 1 Review

Reading Summary

Review the Main Ideas

- The 13 states began writing their own constitutions.
- Americans knew the importance of establishing a national government for the 13 states.
- Problems arose for the nation because of the weaknesses of the Articles of Confederation.

What Did You Learn?

1. What did the Ordinance of 1785 accomplish?
2. Why was the right of deposit at New Orleans important for western farmers?

Critical Thinking

3. **Organizing** Draw a diagram to summarize the strengths and weaknesses of the Confederation government. CA HR3.

The Articles of Confederation	
Strengths	Weaknesses

4. **Expository Writing** Imagine you are on a committee to write a new state constitution. List three freedoms you want attached to your state's constitution. Explain why you believe it is important to guarantee these rights. CA 8WA2.4.
5. READING **Making Connections** Read the passage called "Problems With Britain." Make three connections with what you read: text-to-text, text-to-self, and text-to-world. Write a sentence describing each connection. CA 8RC2.0

SECTION 1 REVIEW ANSWERS

Review questions reinforce content standards US8.2 and US8.3.

1. established a procedure for surveying and selling western lands
2. allowed them to put goods ashore for transfer to ocean-going ships
3. Strengths: could conduct foreign policy, issue currency, borrow money, maintain armed forces; Weaknesses: needed nine states to pass laws; consent of all states needed to change the Articles; could not regulate trade, force soldiers to join the army, or impose taxes
4. Answers will vary, but students should give reasons for each freedom they list.
5. READING Students should make each kind of connection.

R Reading Strategy

Understanding Vocabulary Ask students to find the definition of *right of deposit* in the text. *(permission to put goods ashore for transfer to ocean-going ships)* Then have them think of and give definitions for other ways the word *deposit* is used. *(money placed in a bank, a supply of a natural resource, a down payment on something)* OL CA 8RW1.3

ASSESS

Resources for page 185

Use these resources to assess student mastery of section content.

- Section Quiz 3–1
- Interactive Tutor Self-Assessment CD-ROM

Reading Check

Answer: to stop American expansion into territory it claimed

History Online

Study Central provides summaries, interactive games, and online graphic organizers to help students review section content.

CLOSE

Identifying Central Issues Ask students to explain why a weak government plan could cause problems for a growing country. OL CA HI2.

FOCUS

Summary

Aissa is the narrator and an enslaved African American. Mistress Ashley testifies that she has always been a good and kind mistress. But Reeve, Bett's lawyer, argues that slavery is wrong. Master Noble, the mistress's lawyer, points out that the Ashleys have been good to Bett. Bett shows the court a bruise. In closing statements, Reeve points out that the Declaration of Independence and the state constitution declare that all people have equal rights. The jury declares that the four siblings should be free and that the Ashleys must pay damages.

Vocabulary Preview Before students begin reading, have them read **Before You Read** and the **Vocabulary Preview**. Point out that difficult words are footnoted throughout the text.

Background Information

The story of Elizabeth Freeman, called Bett in the story, is true. Her husband, a free African American, was killed fighting in the Revolution. Aissa is a fictional character.

Answers and Additional Support

America's Literature

Second Daughter

By Mildred Pitts Walter

Before You Read

The Scene: The events in this part of the story take place in a courtroom in Great Barrington, which is in western Massachusetts. The year is 1781.
The Characters: Judge and Mistress Ashley own several slaves. They include Aissa, her older brother Brom, her older sister Bett, and her sister's daughter Little Bett. Lawyers Noble and Canfield represent the Ashleys. Lawyers Reeve and Sedgwick represent Bett and Brom.
The Plot: Aissa is telling the story. After Mistress Ashley accidentally strikes Bett with a red-hot shovel, Brom and Bett ask the court for their freedom. During the trial, Aissa and Little Bett are in the back of the courtroom.

Vocabulary Preview

bared: uncovered; showed
clammy: cold and damp
folly: lack of good sense or judgment
pity: feeling of sorrow for someone else's suffering
rational: able to think
squared: changed from a slumped over position to a straightened one
title: document that proves that something is lawful
valid: acceptable by law

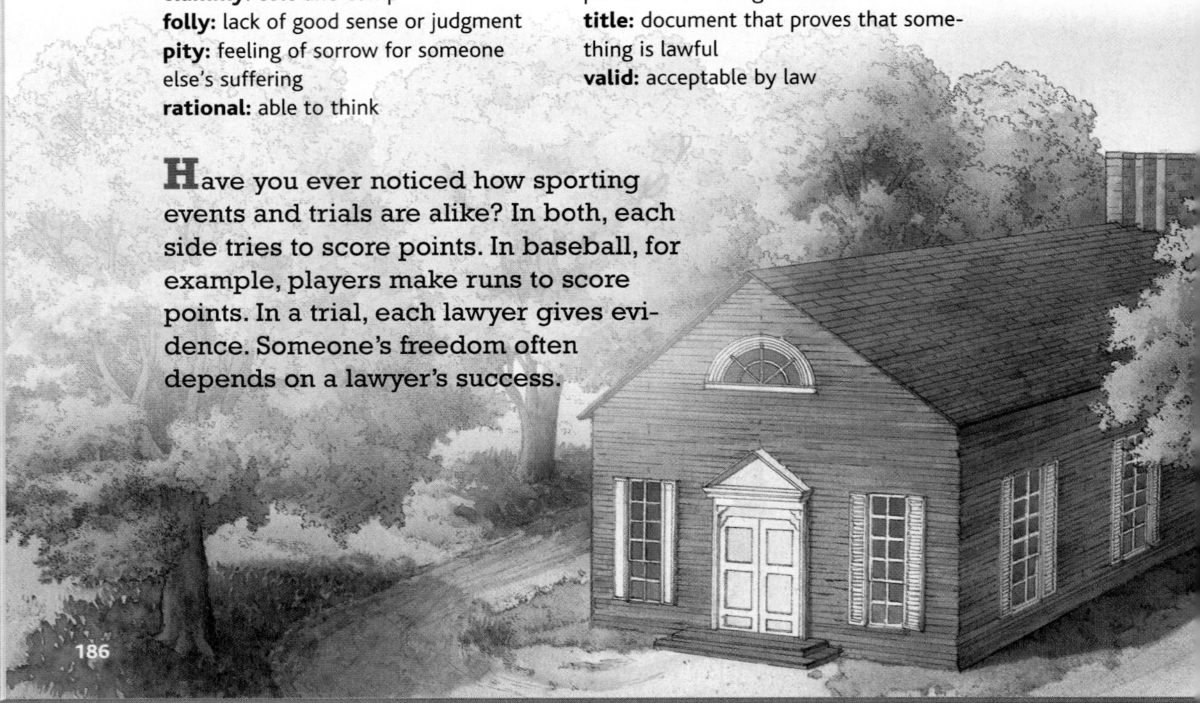

Have you ever noticed how sporting events and trials are alike? In both, each side tries to score points. In baseball, for example, players make runs to score points. In a trial, each lawyer gives evidence. Someone's freedom often depends on a lawyer's success.

READING STRATEGY CONNECTING

Ask students what year the story takes place. *(1781)* Then have them look in their texts to find out what important event happened in the same year as the trial. *(Battle of Yorktown and British surrender there)* BL CA HI1.

As You Read

Earlier in this story, a very emotional scene took place in the Ashleys' kitchen. Bett angrily told Mistress Ashley that she was leaving and not coming back. The mistress got very upset, cried, and apologized to Bett. Then she told Bett that she could not leave, but Bett did. The following scene is also about Bett's freedom, but it takes place in a courtroom. Think about how the setting affects what people say and do. R1

Master Noble called Master Ashley to the stand and questioned him: How had he come to own us? Had he seen to it that we were well fed, clothed, and housed? Had he seen to it that we were changed from heathens[1] to Christians? The master answered, "Yes, I have." When Master Reeve said he had no questions, Master Noble said, "I call Mistress Anna Ashley."

There was a stir in the crowd as she made her way to the stand. As always, when she was in public, she was confident and assured. She seemed not to notice anything around her, except once to raise her eyes to the ceiling. She mopped her brow, suffering from the heat. "Will you describe to the court your relationship with your servant, Bett?" her lawyer asked. R2

"Bett is like one in my family. She was born on my father's land and has been a servant of mine even before I married her master. We have never quarreled, and I have been nothing but kind to her."

I was afraid I was going to start laughing, so I closed my ears and mind to her and held on to keep from being tossed out of the place. How could she sit there pretending that she was a good mistress? I looked at my sister, who sat upright and calm, and I wondered, if asked to disagree with the mistress, would she have the will to do so?

[1] **heathens:** at this time and place, someone who does not believe in the Christian God

TEACH

R1 Reading Strategy

Making Predictions Before reading the story, have students predict what they think will happen. Will Aissa and her family win its suit for freedom? Or will the jury keep them in slavery? *(Predictions will vary, but should be supported by sound reasoning.)* OL

R2 Reading Strategy

Inferring **Ask:** What gesture does Mistress Ashley make as she is sitting on the stand? *(raises her eyes to the ceiling)* What might this gesture mean? *(She may be praying for help in her testimony, or she may be feeling exasperated, angry, or impatient with the trial.)* OL

Glencoe Literature Library

The following literature from the **Glencoe Literature Library** may enrich the teaching of this chapter:

The Autobiography of Miss Jane Pittman by Ernest J. Gaines

READING STRATEGY — UNDERSTANDING VOCABULARY

Explain that words have two kinds of meanings. Denotations are their meaning. Connotations are the positive or negative feelings linked to the word. As an example, point to the word *heathen*, used in this passage. Both *heathen* and *unbeliever* describe people who do not believe in a religion. **Ask:** Which produces negative feelings? *(heathen)* OL CA 8RW1.3

R Reading Strategy

Inferring Ask: How does Aissa know her sister was reluctant to testify? *(Master Reeve had to whisper to her.)* Why do you think Bett was reluctant? *(Students may say she is worried about testifying against Mistress Ashley.)* AL

S Skill Practice

Historical and Social Sciences Analysis Skill Have students use library or Internet sources to compile a bibliography of works on the subject of African Americans in colonial America. *(Bibliographies should include call numbers or URLs.)* OL CA HR1.

U Universal Access

Auditory/Musical Ask students to think of music that could be played as a background to a film of this scene in the story. How would they use music to heighten tension, show the characters' emotions, or add in other ways to the narration? AL

Answers and Additional Support

Master Reeve said he had no questions for the mistress and called Bett. I could tell that Bett was reluctant. He whispered something to her, and finally she came forward and sat in the seat where the mistress had sat. "Your honor," Master Reeve said, "I would like to prove that the mistress Ashley is not the kind mistress she claims." He then turned to the jury. "The issue here is not whether the Ashleys have been kind. The issue is, do they have the right to hold Bett and Brom as slaves for life?" He turned to Bett. "Has Mistress Ashley ever in any way abused you?"

My sister looked at the judge and then at Lawyer Reeve. She did not speak. The courtroom was hushed, waiting. Answer him! I wanted to say. Why didn't she tell them and show the ugly wound on her arm?

Bett looked at the mistress, who was staring Bett in the face. "Yes, Master Reeve, she is not the kind person she wants people to believe she is. I have been in her household many years and was never paid one pence.[2] We work six days a week and sometimes on the seventh. But whether she is kind or not, the constitution says we have rights to our freedom."

"No further questions," Mr. Reeve said.

Master Noble stood and said, "Bett, you sit here well dressed, in good health, with nothing to even hint at your being anything but blessed[3] to be a servant of the Ashleys." There was applause and sounds of "Hear, hear!"

The judge pounded on his desk. "There must be order in this court. Continue, Mr. Noble."

"You know your master and mistress have been good to you, haven't they, Bett?"

"I object," Lawyer Reeve said. "Whether they were good to her is not the question here."

"Objection sustained."

"Your honor, my worthy opponent asked if she had been abused. May I rephrase the question? What proof can you give to this court of Mistress Ashley's abuse?" Lawyer Noble asked.

My sister looked at the mistress, then at the judge. She did not answer. Was she afraid, thinking What if we lost? What would the master and mistress do to us? I felt cold sweat rolling down my sides. In that room that had been almost unbearably warm, I became chilled.

[2] **pence:** a unit of British money that has very little value
[3] **blessed:** bringing pleasure or good luck

READING STRATEGY — ANALYZING TEXT STRUCTURE

Ask: Why does the author describe the reaction of the people in the courtroom? *(Answers may include to let the reader know that the prevailing opinion in the town is in favor of slavery and against Bett in her suit and to create suspense about the eventual outcome of the trial.)* OL CA 8RL3.4

Suddenly Bett squared her shoulders. Without saying a word, she rolled up her sleeve and bared the wound. It was still scarlet with the healing pulling the muscles tight, making the arm twist out of shape, limiting its range of movement.[4] She held her arm so that all could see. There was a gasp in the audience.

Lawyer Noble rushed to the mistress. Lawyer Canfield joined him, and they whispered in conversation with her. The mistress lowered her head when her lawyer said, almost in a whisper, "I have no further questions."

The judge asked if there were other witnesses and questions. Both sides said, "No, your honor." Then the judge gave final instructions to the jury: "You have heard the arguments in this case. You are bound[5] by the law, only by the law, that has been presented here, not by pity and sympathy for either side. It is your duty to determine if the idea of slavery is not in keeping with our own conduct and with our constitution, and that, therefore, there can be no such thing as life servitude[6] of a rational creature." Then he said, "We'll hear your closing statements now." C

In his closing statement, Master Noble reminded the jury of Master Ashley's outstanding citizenship. "He is one who sits in judgment and knows the law. Would he break the laws that he so proudly administers? I say no, he would not." He went on and on.

"Gentlemen of the jury, Master and Mistress Ashley have every right to hold on to their servants, as all of our history declares. The Ashleys along with other great men, Thomas Jefferson, our great General Washington, and many others, hold slaves. W

[4] **range of movement:** ability to move left and right and up and down
[5] **bound:** held to by law or duty
[6] **servitude:** a condition in which one lacks liberty

C Critical Thinking

Drawing Conclusions Have students reread the judge's instructions to the jury. Ask them to summarize the principle on which he says the jury must base its verdict *(Follow the law only, do not be swayed by pity or sympathy.)* Then ask students why the judge gave that direction. *(Students may say that the task of juries is to decide a case based on the laws that exist, not to decide what the law should be.)*
AL CA 8RL3.3

W Writing Support

Persuasive Writing Have students look at Master Noble's question about the Ashleys, Jefferson, and Washington holding slaves: "Are they not good law-abiding citizens?" **Ask:** How have attitudes changed toward the laws that they were obeying? *(Students should point out that modern people do not find slavery to be acceptable.)*
OL CA 8RL3.3

GLENCOE BOOKLINK

Use **Glencoe BookLink** to create customized reading lists for your students' reading levels, interests, and abilities.

READING STRATEGY — SUMMARIZING INFORMATION

Ask students to write a short summary in their own words of this excerpt from *Second Daughter*. Remind them to include only the most important information about the leading characters, the plot events, and other elements of the story. Then have students exchange summaries and critique them.
EL

U Universal Access

Intrapersonal Have students write a poem from the point of view of one of the characters in the story as they await the verdict. Ask them to express the feelings and thoughts of that character about the events that take place. OL

R Reading Strategy

Evaluating Ask students why it was important for the lawyer to mention that Bett was a midwife and Brom was a herdsman. *(This meant that they would be able to earn their own living and not become wards of the state if freed.)* BL CA 8RL3.2

Resources for page 190

Universal Access Activity 3

Are they not good law-abiding[7] citizens? They know that these people are not capable of caring for themselves. If freed, how will they live? Will their freedom make them wards[8] of the state, so that you and I will have to care for them? Let Master Ashley continue to keep his servants, for we all know he is a good kind master. I rest my case."

The applause from the crowd was hammered down by the gavel in the judge's hand. I was so angry and upset that I missed the beginning of Lawyer Reeve's closing.

". . . There are some things in our history that Mr. Noble did not dare talk about that have happened in this very state of Massachusetts and this Berkshire County. Many of you remember the meeting held in the town of Sheffield where even some of you approved without a single 'nay' these words: 'Resolved that Mankind in a State of Nature[9] are equal, free and independent of each other, and have a right to the undisturbed enjoyment of their lives, their liberty and their property.'

"One of those men who hold slaves, Thomas Jefferson, echoed *your* feelings in the Declaration of Independence when he wrote, 'We hold these truths to be self-evident, that all men are created equal, that they are endowed by their Creator with certain unalienable rights, that among these are life, liberty and the pursuit of happiness.' You continued that idea in your state constitution with a bill of rights."

R I was so happy when he told them that Bett was a midwife[10] and Brom a herdsman,[11] who could certainly take care of themselves. There was some laughter when he mentioned how long Bett and Brom had worked and the folly of the idea that they couldn't look after themselves. But the place got real quiet when he came to the end. U

"I say that the city of Sheffield and Berkshire County, the first to have a meeting and a petition on ending slavery and on declaring in favor of independence from the king, is no place where a citizen can be called law abiding if he claims ownership of another human being.

"Gentlemen of the jury, make the Declaration of Independence and your state constitution meaningful in our lives now. Declare that no title to a slave is valid, and grant Brom and Bett their liberty so that they may pursue happiness. I rest my case."

There was no applause, but the silence was complete. The judge waited; no one stirred. "The jury will now convene." He called the bailiff,[12] who escorted the jury to the room where they would decide the verdict.

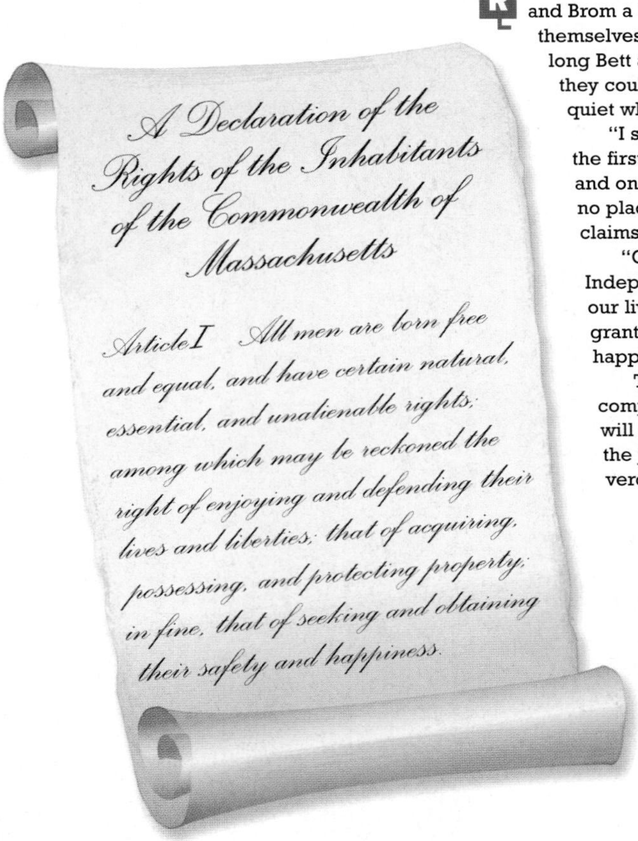

[7] **law-abiding:** obedient to the law
[8] **wards:** people that the court has put under the control of someone other than their parents
[9] **State of Nature:** time before the establishment of government
[10] **midwife:** a woman who helps another woman who is giving birth
[11] **herdsman:** a person who takes care of livestock
[12] **bailiff:** an officer in some U.S. courts who acts as a messenger or usher

Answers and Additional Support

READING STRATEGY CONNECTING

Refer students to Master Noble's defense of Master Ashley, based on the fact that he is an "outstanding citizen." **Ask:** Are prominent or famous people treated more easily when accused of crimes? Why or why not? *(Some students will agree, citing the lenient treatment of white-collar criminals; others may say that defendants in our society are usually treated equally.)* AL

What would happen now? I thought of the applause when Lawyer Noble said that Bett looked anything but mistreated. What if they agree with the master that he has a right to us as his property? I can't go back to that house. But where will I go?

In spite of my worry and fears, time did not drag, and before two hours had passed the bailiff announced that the session would begin again. "All rise." The judge entered.

After we were all seated, the judge asked the jury foreman, "Have you reached a verdict?"

The foreman replied, "We have, Your Honor."

My heartbeat could be seen in my chest and my hands were clammy with sweat. Oh, God, let them. Please let them say we're free.

R "We find for the plaintiffs.[13] The said Brom and Bett are not and were not legally Negro servants of him, the said John Ashley, during life. We further assess thirty shillings, lawful silver money damages."

Did I hear right? I looked at the mistress. Her face was red with anger. Then I looked at my sister, who was smiling and embracing her lawyers. I wanted to join her and Brom up front to share that moment, but the judge was banging his gavel. "Order, order! I adjudge[14] and determine in accordance with the jury's verdict that Brom and Bett are free. I accept the jury's recommendation that the Ashleys pay Brom and Bett thirty shillings damages. In addition, the court assesses the Ashleys the cost of this suit, five pounds, fourteen shillings, and four pence. This court is adjourned."

Finally, the four of us were together. "We are free!" Bett cried. "Can you believe it, *free*." We all four hugged each other and tears of joy flowed.

[13] **plaintiffs:** person who brings a legal action; opposite of *defendant*

[14] **adjudge:** decide or rule upon

Responding to the Literature

1. On what did Bett base her claim to freedom?
2. On what three ideas did Lawyer Noble base the Ashleys' right to keep Brom and Bett as slaves?
3. **Conclude** What is the general meaning of the word *pounds* in "the court assesses the Ashleys the cost of this suit, five pounds, fourteen shillings, and four pence"? Why, do you think, *pounds* means this? CA 8RW1.0
4. **Evaluate** Think about the testimony and the lawyers' arguments during the trial. Choose one fact and one opinion from them. Explain why one is a fact and the other is an opinion. CA HR2.
5. **Read to Write** Use descriptions and details from the scene to show how setting affected its mood and tone. Was the mood mostly angry, funny, or something else? What was the writer's attitude toward the case? CA HR4.

R Reading Strategy

Evaluating **Ask:** Why do you think the jury decided the case in favor of Bett and Brom? Which arguments of their lawyers were the most persuasive? Why? *(Answers will vary. Students may point to the lawyer's several references to the ethical ideas contained in such documents as the Declaration of Independence and state bill of rights and the hypocrisy of not applying these "universal" truths to everyone in society.)* OL CA 8WA2.2

ASSESS

Have students answer the Responding to the Literature questions.

CLOSE

Ask students to predict what the family's life will be like from now on. OL

Responding to the Literature Answers

1. that slavery is wrong according to the Constitution
2. enslaved people cannot take care of themselves; the Ashleys are good masters; other law-abiding people also own slaves
3. some unit of money; because the judge says it in relation to the Ashleys paying costs
4. Sample answer: It is a fact that Washington and Jefferson own slaves because it can be verified. It is an opinion that Bett is blessed to be a servant of the Ashleys; others could think differently.
5. Students may say that the mood is serious.

TEACH

The reading selections for this unit have been chosen to reflect the California History-Social Science Standards. If you assign one of these books, you may want to have students complete the following activity.

Meeting in a Book Club

Group students who read the same book into a book club for discussing the book. Have the group choose a discussion leader. Tell each member to write down one question to discuss or one issue raised by the book. Have the group talk about each suggested topic and others as they arise.

GLENCOE BOOKLINK

Use **Glencoe BookLink** to create customized reading lists for your students' reading levels, interests, and abilities.

Answers and Additional Support

Reading On Your Own...

From the California Reading List

Do you want to learn more about the writing of the Constitution, the Founding Fathers, and Shays's Rebellion? You might be interested in the following books.

Nonfiction

Shays' Rebellion and the Constitution in American History by Mary E. Hull describes Shays's Rebellion and its effects on taxation in the United States. This book explains why people who had just experienced the hardships of one revolution were willing to go through another one. ***The content of this book is related to*** *History–Social Science Standard US8.3.*

Nonfiction

Shh! We're Writing the Constitution by Jean Fritz humorously introduces the people at the Constitutional Convention. She also clearly explains the kinds of choices that these men made as they tried to form a workable government. ***The content of this book is related to*** *History–Social Science Standard US8.2.*

Biography

James Madison: Father of the Constitution by Brent P. Kelley describes Madison's life and his contributions to the United States. These include his work on the Constitution, the Federalist Papers, and the Bill of Rights. ***The content of this book is related to*** *History–Social Science Standard US8.2.*

Nonfiction

Blessings of Liberty: Safeguarding Civil Rights by William C. Lowe explains what civil rights are and why they are important. He also describes six of those rights—freedom of religion, expression, and the press; the right to due process; voting rights; and equality under the law. Interesting parts of this description include how these rights have gradually changed and people who helped win them. ***The content of this book is related to*** *History–Social Science Standard US8.2.*

192

READING STRATEGY: ACTIVATING PRIOR KNOWLEDGE

This activity will help students decide which of the titles for the California Reading List they might want to read. Ask students to read the titles of the books on this page. Then have them brainstorm ideas for what each book's subject is. Write the brainstorming results on the board. For example, the third book, *James Madison: Father of the Constitution*, might elicit responses like married to Dolley, a friend and supporter of Jefferson, the *Federalist Papers*, wrote much of the Constitution, became president, and so on. Suggest that students use these ideas to help them find books they will be interested in. OL

Section 2

Convention and Compromise

Guide to Reading

Looking Back, Looking Ahead

You read about the weaknesses of the Articles of Confederation. Many Americans concluded that the United States needed a new constitution.

Focusing on the Main Ideas

- The government under the Articles of Confederation faced many problems. *(page 194)*
- National leaders worked to produce a new constitution for the United States. *(page 197)*
- The Constitutional Convention broke the deadlock over the form the new government would take. *(page 199)*

Meeting People

Daniel Shays
James Madison
Alexander Hamilton
Gouverneur Morris
Edmund Randolph
Roger Sherman

Content Vocabulary

depression
manumission (MAN • yuh • MIH • shuhn)
proportional (pruh • POHR • shuh • nuhl)
compromise

Academic Vocabulary

participate (pahr • TIH • suh • PAYT)
currency (KUHR • uhn • see)
levy (leh • VEE)
regulate (REH • gyuh • LAYT)
adequate (A • dih • kwuht)

Reading Strategy

Organizing Information Create a diagram like the one below to describe the role each individual played in creating the new plan of government.

Person	Roles
Edmund Randolph	
James Madison	
Roger Sherman	

History Social Science Standards

US8.2 Students analyze the political principles underlying the U.S. Constitution and compare the enumerated and implied powers of the federal government.

US8.3 Students understand the foundation of the American political system and the ways in which citizens participate in it.

US8.9 Students analyze the early and steady attempts to abolish slavery and to realize the ideals of the Declaration of Independence.

NATIONAL GEOGRAPHIC Where & When?

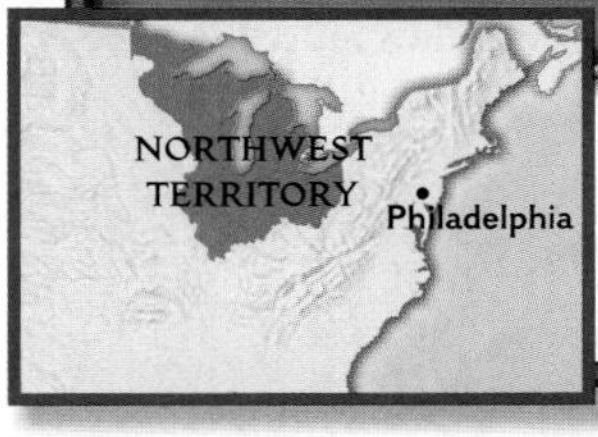

1783 · 1785 · 1787

- **1784** Rhode Island passes plan to end slavery
- **1786** Daniel Shays leads rebellion
- **1787** Delegates sign draft of Constitution

FOCUS

BELLRINGER Skillbuilder Activity

Project **Daily Focus Skills Transparency 3–2** and have students answer the question.

Guide to Reading

Preteaching Vocabulary: Have students look up the definition of each term in the Glossary in the back of the textbook and then use each term in a sentence.

Answers to Graphic: Randolph: introduced the Virginia Plan; Madison: put forth the basic ideas of the Virginia Plan; Sherman: proposed the Great Compromise

Unpacking the Standards

After reading the section, students will be able to:

- Describe the weaknesses of government under the Articles of Confederation.
- Explain how national leaders met to produce a new constitution.
- Discuss how the Constitutional Convention worked to create a new government for the country.

SECTION RESOURCES

Print Material
- Reproducible Lesson Plan 3–2*
- Daily Lesson and Discussion Notes 3–2
- Guided Reading Activity 3–2
- Reading Essentials and Study Guide 3–2
- Active Reading Note-Taking Guide 3–2
- Section Quiz 3–2

Transparencies
- Daily Focus Skills Transparency 3–2
- Section Graphic Organizer Transparency 3–2
- California Standards Practice Transparencies

Technology
- Interactive Tutor Self-Assessment CD-ROM
- Exam*View*® Pro Testmaker CD-ROM
- Presentation Plus! CD-ROM

*Available on TeacherWorks™

TEACH

R1 Reading Strategy

Academic Vocabulary Have students read the sentence that contains the word *participate*. Then ask a student to define the word. OL

R2 Reading Strategy

Understanding Vocabulary Ask students to define the word *depression* as used in the text. *(period when economic activity slows and unemployment rises)* Then ask them for other meanings of this word. *(low place in the ground, weather pattern of low pressure)* Ask them to identify what all the meanings have in common. *(the idea of lowness)* OL CA 8RW1.3

U Universal Access

Visual/Spatial Have students review the text information about Shays's Rebellion. Then have them design a poster that supports or opposes the rebels. *(Posters should be graphically appealing and accurate with regard to details and information.)* EL

US8.2.2 Analyze the Articles of Confederation and the Constitution and the success of each in implementing the ideals of the Declaration of Independence. US8.3.5 Know the significance of domestic resistance movements and ways in which the central government responded to such movements (e.g., Shays' Rebellion, the Whiskey Rebellion). US8.9.2 Discuss the abolition of slavery in early state constitutions.

Troubles Under the Articles

Main Idea **The government under the Articles of Confederation faced many problems.**

Reading Connection You make a plan but the plan is not working—what do you do? Find out how American leaders decided to fix the problems of the Articles of Confederation.

An American Story

By 1786 many Americans observed that the Confederation was not working. George Washington himself agreed that the United States was really "thirteen Sovereignties pulling against each other." In the spring of 1787, Washington joined delegates from Virginia and 11 other states who gathered in Philadelphia to address this problem. Rhode Island decided not to **participate.** The delegates came "for the sole and express purpose of revising the Articles of Confederation."

Picturing History

Only through donations was Massachusetts able to raise a militia to defeat Shays. ***Why did Shays's Rebellion frighten many Americans?***

Economic Depression The call to revise the Articles of Confederation came while the young nation faced difficult problems. Many Americans believed that the Confederation government was too weak to deal with these challenges. After the Revolutionary War ended, the United States went through a **depression,** a period when economic activity slowed and unemployment increased. Southern plantations had been damaged during the war, and rice exports dropped sharply. Trade also fell off when the British closed the profitable West Indies (Caribbean) market to American merchants. What little money there was went to pay foreign debts, and a serious **currency** shortage resulted. Each state printed its own money. The value of the money differed from state to state, and the money often was not accepted outside the states issuing it.

American farmers suffered because they could not sell their goods. They had problems paying the requests for money that the states **levied** to meet Revolutionary War debts. As a result, state officials seized farmers' lands to pay their debts and threw many farmers into jail. Murmurs of protest soon grew into revolt.

Shays's Rebellion Resentment grew especially strong in Massachusetts. Farmers viewed the new government as just another form of tyranny. They wanted the government to issue paper money and make new policies to relieve debtors. In a letter to state officials, some farmers said "many of our good inhabitants are now confined in [jail] for debt and taxes."

In August 1786, a convention of delegates from 50 Massachusetts towns met in Hatfield, Massachusetts. The delegates drew up a petition to the state government protesting the new taxes. State officials replied that the Hatfield convention was against the law and the delegates were rebels.

Answers and Additional Support

Resources for page 194

Biography Activity 3A

Picturing History

The money for the militia formed to put down the rebellion came mostly from Boston merchants, who feared the rebels. Many common people sympathized with the rebels.

Answer: They worried that the government could not control unrest.

C Angry farmers lashed out. Led by **Daniel Shays,** a former Continental Army captain, they forced courts in western Massachusetts to close so judges could not confiscate farmers' lands.

In January 1787, Shays led more than 1,000 farmers toward the federal arsenal in Springfield, Massachusetts, to seize arms and ammunition. The state militia ordered the advancing farmers to halt, then fired over their heads. The farmers did not stop, and the militia fired again, killing four rebels. Shays and his followers scattered, and the uprising was over.

Shays's Rebellion frightened many national leaders. They worried that the government could not control unrest and prevent violence. W On hearing of the rebellion, George Washington wondered whether "mankind, when left to themselves, are unfit for their own government." Thomas Jefferson, minister to France at the time, had a different view. "A little rebellion, now and then," he wrote, "is a good thing."

The Issue of Slavery The Revolutionary War brought attention to the contradiction between the American battle for liberty and the practice of slavery. S The Southern states accepted the institution of slavery. The plantation system of the South had been built on slavery, and many Southerners feared that their economy could not survive without it.

R Although slavery was not a major source of labor in the North, it existed and was legal in all the Northern states. Many individuals and groups began to work to end the institution of slavery. In 1774 Quakers in Pennsylvania organized the first American antislavery society. Six years later, Pennsylvania passed a law that provided for the gradual freeing of enslaved people.

Between 1783 and 1804, Connecticut, Rhode Island, New York, and New Jersey passed laws that gradually ended slavery. Still, free African Americans faced discrimination. They were barred from many public places. Few states gave free African Americans the right to vote.

The Way It Was

The coneflower is a popular Native American plant. As medicine, it is commonly called Echinacea.

Home Remedies

In an age before germs and proper sanitation were understood, home remedies for illnesses became an everyday part of life in early America. While some folk remedies, such as herbal teas, might have had positive effects, other cures could make the patient worse.

For a venomous snakebite, a part of the snake was placed on top of the wound. This, it was thought, would draw out the poison.

Some remedies used by Native Americans were later adopted by Europeans. The Inca, for example, found that boiling a certain kind of tree bark in water eased the symptoms of malaria. But it was not until the 1900s that the ingredient in the tree bark—quinine—was finally isolated.

The Way It Was

During colonial times, doctors were not as rigorously educated and trained as they are today. Although two Philadelphia doctors organized the first medical school in 1765, most physicians received their training by working as apprentices under established doctors.

More Skill Practice

Historical and Social Sciences Analysis Skill Have students make a time line of the events listed in this section that are related to slavery. *(Time lines should include all the events discussed in this section, along with their correct dates.)* BL CA CS2.

C Critical Thinking

Predicting Consequences
Ask: What did Shays and his followers hope to gain by seizing the courts? *(to prevent any more farms from being seized)* Do you think they believed this action would produce a long-term solution? Why or why not? *(Students may say that they probably did not, since eventually the government would reopen the courts. They probably hoped to move the government to some action on their behalf.)* OL CA HR5. CA HI3.

W Writing Support

Persuasive Writing Have students read the statements of Washington and Jefferson about Shays's Rebellion. Then have them write a newspaper editorial supporting or opposing one or the other, giving reasons for their views. AL CA 8WA2.4

S Skill Practice

Historical and Social Sciences Analysis Skill
Have students draw a chart or other graphic that shows the connection between slavery and the economic system of the southern states. *(Graphics should indicate that the plantation system was based on and dependent on the work of enslaved African Americans.)* BL CA HI2.

R Reading Strategy

Scaffolding—Academic Vocabulary Students were introduced to the word *major* in Chapter 1, Section 3. Ask students to name synonyms for the word. OL

R1 Reading Strategy

Understanding Vocabulary
The term *manumission* is based on two Latin words meaning "hand" and "send away." **Ask:** How do the roots combine to explain the meaning of the term? *(It is the act of sending slaves away.)* OL

C Critical Thinking

Drawing Conclusions **Ask:** What does the text mean by saying that the Revolution "had not yet created a nation"? *(people still saw themselves as belonging primarily to their particular state; states competed with each other.)* OL

R2 Reading Strategy

Determining Importance
Ask students why George Washington's opinion about the form of the government might have carried much weight among Americans of the time. *(He had led the battle for independence and was America's most respected leader.)* BL CA HI2.

Reading Check

Answer: to discuss trade issues and address changes to the Articles of Confederation to meet the needs of the Union

Primary Sources

Richard Allen and Absalom Jones

Philadelphia preachers Richard Allen and Absalom Jones founded the Free American Society and later set up the first African American churches.

▲ Richard Allen

Born in slavery, Richard Allen was freed and became a Methodist minister. Allen and Absalom Jones founded an independent Methodist church for black members. In the early 1800s, some African American movements encouraged immigration to Africa. Allen and Jones opposed this idea, stating that since

▲ Absalom Jones

"our ancestors (not of choice) were the first successful cultivators of the wilds of America, we their descendants feel ourselves entitled to participate in the blessings of her luxuriant soil. . . ."

—Bethel Church Resolution

DBQ Document-Based Question

Why did Allen and Jones believe African Americans should stay in America even though they had been brought there against their will?

The children of most free blacks had to attend separate schools. Free African Americans established their own institutions—churches, schools, and mutual-aid societies—to seek opportunity.

An increasing number of slaveholders began freeing the enslaved people that they held after the war. Virginia passed a law that encouraged **manumission** (MAN • yuh • MIH • shuhn), the freeing of individual enslaved persons, and the state's population of free African Americans grew. R1

The abolition of slavery in the North divided the new country on the issue of whether people should be allowed to hold other human beings in bondage. This division came at the time when many American leaders had decided that the Articles of Confederation needed to be strengthened. In the summer of 1787, when state representatives assembled to plan a new government, they compromised on this issue. It would take years of debate, bloodshed, and ultimately a war to settle the slavery question.

A Call for Change The American Revolution had led to a union of 13 states, but it had not yet created a nation. Some leaders believed that a strong national government was the solution to America's problems. They demanded a reform of the Articles of Confederation. C

Two Americans who were active in the movement for change were **James Madison,** a Virginia planter, and **Alexander Hamilton,** a New York lawyer. In September 1786, Hamilton proposed calling a convention in Philadelphia to discuss trade issues. He also suggested that this convention consider what possible changes were needed to make the Articles work.

At first, George Washington was not enthusiastic about the movement to revise the Articles of Confederation. When he heard the news of Shays's Rebellion, Washington changed his mind. After Washington agreed to attend the Philadelphia convention, the meeting took on greater significance. R2

Reading Check **Evaluate** Why did Madison and Hamilton call for a convention in 1787?

Answers and Additional Support

Primary Sources

Answer: because their ancestors had been the first farmers of the American soil

- What challenges would African Americans of the early 1800s have faced if they returned to Africa? *(learning the language, customs, and ways of life; missing relatives back in America; adapting skills to a different climate and lifestyle)* BL
- What are some reasons that African American churches became important early centers of culture? *(There were few other places African Americans could gather in big cities.)* OL

US8.2.3 Evaluate the major debates that occurred during the development of the Constitution and their ultimate resolutions in such areas as shared power among institutions, divided state-federal power, slavery, the rights of individuals and states (later addressed by the addition of the Bill of Rights), and the status of American Indians under the commerce clause.

The Constitutional Convention

Main Idea **National leaders worked to produce a new constitution for the United States.**

Reading Connection Why is it important for a nation to establish a set of laws? Read to find out the issues American leaders faced in organizing a new constitution.

The Philadelphia meeting began in May 1787 and continued through one of the hottest summers on record. The 55 delegates included planters, merchants, lawyers, physicians, generals, governors, and a college president. Three of the delegates were under 30 years of age, and one, Benjamin Franklin, was over 80. Many were well educated. At a time when only one white man in 1,000 went to college, 26 of the delegates had college degrees. Native Americans, African Americans, and women were not considered part of the political process, so none attended.

Several men stood out as leaders. The presence of George Washington and Benjamin Franklin ensured that many people would trust the Convention's work. Two Philadelphians also played key roles. James Wilson often read Franklin's speeches and did important work on the details of the Constitution. **Gouverneur Morris,** a powerful speaker and writer, wrote the final draft of the Constitution.

Two revolutionary leaders who had thought deeply about the best form of government were absent. John Adams of Massachusetts and Thomas Jefferson of Virginia were in Europe serving as ambassadors. From Virginia came **Edmund Randolph** and James Madison. Both were keen supporters of a strong national government. Randolph had served in the Continental Congress and was governor of Virginia. Madison's careful notes are the major source of information about the Convention's work. Madison is often called the Father of the Constitution because he was the author of the basic plan of government that the Convention adopted.

The Way It Was

▲ Delegates to the Constitutional Convention met in this room at Independence Hall.

Working on the Constitution

The delegates to the Constitutional Convention worked for 116 days (of which they actually met on 89) in a room where the windows were usually shut. None of the delegates wanted anybody to hear what they were doing, because they did not want rumors spread about the form of government upon which they would ultimately decide. Besides, if they opened the windows, hordes of flies would descend upon them. The air became humid and hot by noon of each day.

The Way It Was

The Constitutional Convention met in the building now known as Independence Hall, in the same room where the Second Continental Congress had approved the Declaration of Independence.

U Universal Access

Logical/Mathematical Have students calculate the percentage of the country's population that had college degrees in 1787. *(less than 1 percent)* Then have them compute the percentage of the delegates that had college degrees. *(47 percent)* Finally have students draw a conclusion based on these numbers about early American society. *(Possible conclusion: A college education was extremely rare, but those with degrees had a good chance of becoming leaders.)* AL

W Writing Support

Narrative Writing Have students choose one of the men involved in the Constitutional Convention and conduct research to learn more about that person's life. Then have students write a one-page biography describing the person's involvement in government and politics. OL

Resources for page 197

- Biography Activity 3C
- American Art and Architecture Transparency 5

Biography

TEACH

S Skill Practice

Reading Primary Sources
Ask students to paraphrase the quotation. *(A government needs enough power to keep order, but it also needs to allow freedom.)* Discuss whether students agree with Madison. OL CA HR4.

C1 Critical Thinking

Analyzing Information
Tell students to suppose that Madison had not taken notes at the Convention. **Ask:** How would historians be able to judge the goals and thinking of the delegates? *(from the writings of other delegates)* OL CA HI5.

C2 Critical Thinking

Identifying Central Issues
Ask: How does the Bill of Rights help balance the power of government and the rights of people, as Madison wanted? *(The Bill of Rights guarantees people's freedoms, protecting them from the abuse of government power.)* OL CA HI3.

Answers and Additional Support

Biography

US8.2.4 Describe the political philosophy underpinning the Constitution as specified in the Federalist Papers (authored by James Madison, Alexander Hamilton, and John Jay) and the role of such leaders as Madison, George Washington, Roger Sherman, Gouverneur Morris, and James Wilson in the writing and ratification of the Constitution.

JAMES MADISON
c. 1751–1836

Born in 1751, Madison was still a young man at the time of the American Revolution, but his brilliant, incisive mind made him one of the more valuable leaders of the Patriots. After the war, he played a major role at the Constitutional Convention.

As one of the delegates from Virginia, Madison participated in the lengthy, often heated discussions that created a foundation of government. He kept meticulous notes and tried to impress upon the other delegates the need for an effective central government. Power was to be distributed throughout the whole. Every right had to be balanced by a corresponding responsibility.

Madison became the chief architect of the Constitution, and his notes became the best record of what happened at the Convention. There were no official transcripts of the work of the delegates. If Madison had not kept a private diary of the events, historians might know little about what happened in Philadelphia. C1 "Every word *[of the Constitution]*," he later wrote, "decides a question between power and liberty."

After the Constitution went into effect, Madison became a leader of the new national government. In developing the Bill of Rights, he once again was trying to achieve the difficult balance between the rights of the people and the power of government. C2 In 1808 Madison became the fourth president of the United States. Throughout his career, he continued to defend the principle of balance that was built into the Constitution.

"In framing a government . . . you must first enable the government to control the governed; and in the next place, oblige it to control itself." S

—James Madison
***The Federalist*, No. 51**

Then and Now

What qualities did Madison possess that made him a leader and an important part of the constitutional process? Do you think these are important qualities for a political leader today? Explain.

Then and Now

He was intelligent, studious, curious, and well organized. Students may say that these qualities, along with others, are important for leaders at any time.

US8.2.3 Evaluate the major debates that occurred during the development of the Constitution and their ultimate resolutions in such areas as shared power among institutions, divided state-federal power, slavery, the rights of individuals and states (later addressed by the addition of the Bill of Rights), and the status of American Indians under the commerce clause.

Organization The Convention began by unanimously choosing George Washington to preside over the meetings. It was also decided that each state would have one vote on all questions. Decisions would be made by a majority vote of those states present. The delegates decided to keep the sessions secret. This decision made it possible for the delegates to talk freely. C

The Virginia Plan After the rules were adopted, the Convention opened with a surprise. Edmund Randolph proposed that the delegates create a strong national government instead of revising the Articles of Confederation. He introduced the Virginia Plan, which was largely the work of James Madison.

The plan called for a two-house legislature, a chief executive chosen by the legislature, and a court system. The members of the lower house of the legislature would be elected by the people. The members of the upper house would be chosen by the lower house. In both houses, the number of representatives would be **proportional** (pruh • POHR • shuh • nuhl), or corresponding in size, to the population of each state. This would give Virginia many more delegates than Delaware, the smallest state. R1

Delegates from small states objected to the plan. They preferred the Confederation system in which all states were represented equally. On June 15 William Paterson of New Jersey presented an alternative plan that revised the Articles of Confederation, which was all the convention was empowered to do.

The New Jersey Plan The New Jersey Plan kept the Confederation's one-house legislature, with one vote for each state. Congress, however, could set taxes and **regulate** trade—powers it did not have under the Articles. Congress would elect a weak executive branch consisting of more than one person. Paterson argued that the Convention should not deprive the smaller states of the equality they had under the Articles.

Reading Check **Explain** Why did some delegates criticize the Virginia Plan?

Compromise Wins Out

Main Idea **The Constitutional Convention broke the deadlock over the form the new government would take.**

Reading Connection Have you and a rival ever set aside your differences to work for a common cause? This happened when American leaders resolved their differences to create a new constitution.

The convention delegates had to decide whether they were simply revising the Articles of Confederation or writing a constitution for a new national government. On June 19 the states voted to work toward a national government based on the Virginia Plan, but they still had to resolve the thorny issue of representation that divided the large and small states.

As the convention delegates struggled to deal with difficult questions, tempers and temperatures grew hotter. How were the members of Congress to be elected? How would state representation be determined in the upper and lower houses? Were enslaved people to be counted as part of the population on which representation was based? R2

Under Franklin's leadership, the convention appointed a "grand committee" to try to resolve their disagreements. **Roger Sherman** of Connecticut suggested what came to be known as the Great Compromise. A **compromise** is an agreement between two or more sides in which each side gives up some of what it wants. U

Sherman proposed a two-house legislature. In the lower house—the House of Representatives—the number of seats for each state would vary according to the state's population. In the upper house—the Senate—each state would have two members.

Another compromise by the delegates dealt with counting enslaved people. Southern states wanted to include the enslaved in their population counts to gain delegates in the House of Representatives.

C Critical Thinking

Drawing Conclusions Ask students if they agree with the delegates' decision to keep their discussions secret. *(Some will argue that secrecy led to a successful document; others may say it was unnecessary and undemocratic.)* OL CA HI2.

R1 Reading Strategy

Categorizing Information Have students use a Venn diagram to compare the Virginia and New Jersey plans. *(Virginia: executive, court, legislature, bicameral legislature, lower house elected by people, proportional representation, upper house elected by lower house; New Jersey: one-house legislature with one vote for each state, Congress can set taxes and regulate trade, weak executive of more than one person; both: executive(s) elected by legislature)* OL CA HI1.

R2 Reading Strategy

Understanding Vocabulary Have students draw a visual "definition" of the term *proportional*. *(Drawings should communicate the idea of higher population equals greater number of representatives.)* BL CA 8RW1.3

U Universal Access

English Learners Practice pronouncing *compromise* with students, demonstrating how it differs from *promise*. EL

Reading Check

Answer: Representation was proportional and critics wanted all states represented equally.

Resources for page 199

Biography Activity 3B

More Skill Practice

Historical and Social Sciences Analysis Skill Have students explain how the Great Compromise affects how many representatives and senators California has. *(As California's population grows, the number of its representatives also grows, but there will always be only two senators.)* OL CA HI3.

Did You Know?

The city of Philadelphia went to great lengths to make sure the delegates to the Constitutional Convention could work in peace and quiet. The city even covered the paved road outside Independence Hall with dirt so the clatter of carriage wheels on paving stones would be muffled and not disturb the delegates.

C Critical Thinking

Determining Cause and Effect Ask students why the question of slavery was so difficult for the delegates to address. *(Opinions were seriously divided, the South's economic livelihood depended on it, and many in the North hated slavery and wanted to get rid of it.)* OL CA HI1.

Review The Big Idea

Review the Big Idea for this section: "A constitution reflects the values and goals of the society that creates it." Ask students to name one conflict and one compromise that occurred as Americans met to create the Constitution. *(conflicts: revise or replace Articles, small versus large states, one-house or two-house legislature; compromises: Great Compromise, Three-Fifths Compromise, slave trade, add Bill of Rights later)* BL CA HI12.

Linking Past & Present

Symbols of the Nation

Past For Americans, the flag has always had a special meaning. It is a symbol of our nation's freedom and democracy. On June 14, 1777, the Continental Congress designed the first Stars and Stripes. The first flag had 13 stars and 13 stripes. Each star represented a state. Each stripe represented one of the 13 colonies that formed the Union.

▼ The Stars and Stripes today

▲ A legend says that Betsy Ross created the American flag.

Present Many of the symbols through which we express our American identity—heroes, songs, legends, flags, monuments—developed in the early 1800s. Some of our holidays, such as the Fourth of July, and the ways we celebrate them with parades, speeches, and picnics, became established during that time. ***What are other symbols of our nation?***

C **Objections Are Raised** Northern states objected to this idea because enslaved people were legally considered property. Some delegates from Northern states argued that the enslaved, as property, should be counted for the purpose of taxation but not representation. However, neither side considered giving enslaved people the right to vote.

The committee's solution, known as the Three-Fifths Compromise, was to count each enslaved person as three-fifths of a free person for both taxation and representation. In other words, every five enslaved persons would equal three free persons. On July 12, the convention delegates voted to approve the Three-Fifths Compromise. Four days later, they agreed that each state should elect two senators.

Slave Trade The dispute over how to count enslaved people was not the only issue dividing the delegates. The convention needed to resolve another difficult issue that divided the Northern and Southern states. Some Northern delegates wanted to slow the spread of slavery and stop the importation of new slaves. Southern states considered slavery and the slave trade essential to their economies.

Answers and Additional Support

Linking Past & Present

Answer: possible answers include the bald eagle, Uncle Sam, Liberty Bell, Statue of Liberty, Mount Rushmore

More Skill Practice

Making Inferences Ask: Why do you think the Convention agreed that Congress could not interfere with the slave trade until 1808? *(Some students may say the delegates did not want to jeopardize all they had accomplished by disagreeing on this issue.)* OL CA HI2.

To keep the Southern states in the nation, Northerners agreed that the Congress could not interfere with the slave trade until 1808. Beginning that year, Congress could limit the slave trade if it chose to.

Approving the Constitution George Mason of Virginia proposed a bill of rights to be included in the Constitution. Some delegates worried that without the protection of a bill of rights, the new national government might abuse its power. However, most of the delegates believed that the Constitution, with its carefully defined listing of government powers, provided **adequate** protection of individual rights. Mason's proposal was defeated.

The committees finished their work on the Constitution in late summer. On September 17, 1787, the delegates assembled in the Philadelphia State House to sign the document. Franklin made a final plea for approval: "I consent to this Constitution because I expect no better, and because I am not sure, that it is not the best."

History Online
Student Web Activity Visit ca.hss.glencoe.com and click on *Chapter 3—Student Web Activities* for an activity on the Constitutional Convention.

Three delegates refused to sign—Elbridge Gerry of Massachusetts, and Edmund Randolph and George Mason of Virginia. Gerry and Mason would not sign without a bill of rights.

The Confederation Congress then sent the approved draft of the Constitution to the states for consideration. To amend the Articles of Confederation had required unanimous approval of the states. The delegates agreed to change the approval process for the Constitution. When 9 of the 13 states had approved, the new government of the United States would come into existence. R

(See pages 248–269 for the entire text of the Constitution.)

Reading Check **Analyze** Who refused to sign the Constitution? Explain why.

History Online
Study Central Need help understanding the Constitutional Convention? Visit ca.hss.glencoe.com and click on Study Central.

Section 2 Review

Reading Summary

Review the Main Ideas

- The government under the Articles of Confederation faced many problems.
- National leaders worked to produce a new constitution for the United States.
- The Constitutional Convention broke the deadlock over the form the new government would take.

What Did You Learn?

1. Explain what caused Shays's Rebellion. What was one effect?
2. According to the Virginia Plan, who elected the members of the lower house?

Critical Thinking

3. **Analyze Information** Re-create the diagram below and identify arguments for and against approving the Constitution. CA HI1.

Ratification	
Arguments for	Arguments against

4. **The Big Ideas** How did the new Constitution reflect the values of the men who wrote it?
5. **ANALYSIS** How did the Great Compromise satisfy both the small and the large states on the question of representation? Why was this compromise important? Write a paragraph summarizing your conclusions. CA CS1.
6. **Persuasive Writing** Write a short speech in favor of either the Virginia Plan or the New Jersey Plan. CA 8LS1.3

History Online
Objectives and answers to the student activity can be found in the Web Activity Lesson Plan feature at ca.hss.glencoe.com.

R Reading Strategy

Evaluating **Ask:** How did the approval process for adopting the Constitution differ from the process under the Articles of Confederation? *(Under the Articles, changes required unanimous approval; only nine of thirteen states were needed to adopt the new Constitution.)* BL CA HI1.

ASSESS

Resources for page 201

Use these resources to assess student mastery of section content.

- Section Quiz 3–2
- Interactive Tutor Self-Assessment CD-ROM

Reading Check

Answer: Elbridge Gerry, Edmund Randolph, and George Mason; it lacked a bill of rights

History Online
Study Central provides summaries, interactive games, and online graphic organizers to help students review section content.

SECTION 2 REVIEW ANSWERS

Review questions reinforce content standards US8.2 and US8.3.

1. Farmers wanted help with economic problems; effects: some farmers killed, support for revision of Articles grew
2. the people
3. For: strong national government, proportional representation; Against: independent state governments, equal representation
4. **The Big Ideas** The government is based on popular sovereignty and limited power.
5. **ANALYSIS** proportional representation in House for large states; equal in Senate for small states; solved one of the key disagreements
6. Speeches should give reasons for supporting the plan.

CLOSE

Drawing Conclusions Ask students if they think a better national holiday for the United States would be September 17, the day the Constitution was signed. OL CA HI2.

FOCUS

BELLRINGER
SKILLBUILDER ACTIVITY

Project **Daily Focus Skills Transparency 3–3** and have students answer the question.

Guide to Reading

Preteaching Vocabulary: Have students predict which terms will refer to important ideas underlying the Constitution. *(Federalism; checks and balances)*

Answers to Graphic: President: Congress (veto), Supreme Court (appoint justices); Congress: President (override), Supreme Court (approve justices); Supreme Court: Congress and President (rule on laws, actions)

Unpacking the Standards

After reading the section, students will be able to:

- Discuss the ideas and figures that shaped the Constitution.
- Describe the system of checks and balances.
- Explain how Americans reacted to the Constitution.

Section 3

A New Plan of Government

History Social Science Standards

US8.2 Students analyze the political principles underlying the U.S. Constitution and compare the enumerated and implied powers of the federal government.

US8.3 Students understand the foundation of the American political system and the ways in which citizens participate in it.

Guide to Reading

Looking Back, Looking Ahead

You read about the compromises that the delegates made to create a new form of government. The Constitution was based on the political ideals of the people who wrote it.

Focusing on the Main Ideas

- Ideas and thinkers of the past influenced the creation of the United States Constitution. *(page 203)*
- The Constitution outlines the responsibilities and the limits of the three branches of government. *(page 204)*
- Americans reacted to the proposed Constitution in different ways. *(page 206)*

Meeting People

John Jay
Mercy Otis Warren

Content Vocabulary

Enlightenment (ihn • LY • tuhn • muhnt)
federalism
article
legislative branch (LEH • juhs • LAY • tihv)
executive branch (ihg • ZEH • kuh • tihv)
judicial branch (ju • DIH • shuhl)
checks and balances
ratify (RA • tuh • FY)
Federalist
Antifederalist

Academic Vocabulary

promote (pruh • MOHT)
conduct (kuhn • DUHKT)

Reading Strategy

Organizing Information Create a diagram to explain how the system of checks and balances works.

	Has check or balance over:	Example
President		
Congress		
Supreme Court		

NATIONAL GEOGRAPHIC Where & When?

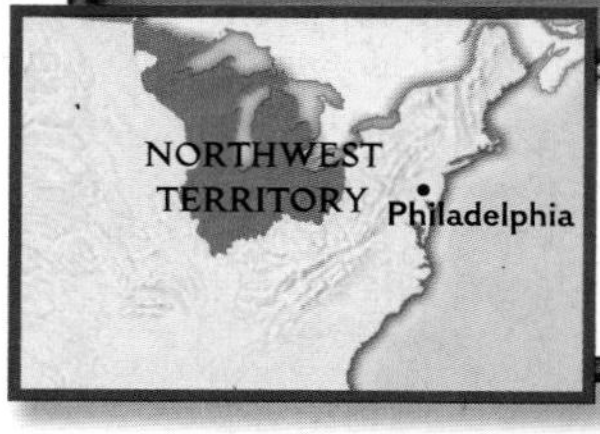

1680 · 1720 · 1760 · 1800

- **1689** English Bill of Rights established
- **1690** Locke publishes *Two Treatises of Civil Government*
- **1748** Montesquieu writes *The Spirit of Laws*
- **1787** The Constitutional Convention meets in Philadelphia

SECTION RESOURCES

Print Material
- Reproducible Lesson Plan 3–3*
- Daily Lesson and Discussion Notes 3–3
- Guided Reading Activity 3–3
- Reading Essentials and Study Guide 3–3
- Active Reading Note-Taking Guide 3–3
- Section Quiz 3–3

Transparencies
- Daily Focus Skills Transparency 3–3
- Section Graphic Organizer Transparency 3–3
- California Standards Practice Transparencies

Technology
- Interactive Tutor Self-Assessment CD-ROM
- Exam*View*® Pro Testmaker CD-ROM
- Presentation Plus! CD-ROM

*Available on TeacherWorks™

Roots of the Constitution

Main Idea **Ideas and thinkers of the past influenced the creation of the United States Constitution.**

Reading Connection Do you have a role model? Has a person you know influenced you to do better in school or take part in a helping activity? Read to learn about the thinkers who influenced the creation of the Constitution.

An American Story

As Benjamin Franklin was leaving the last session of the Constitutional Congress, a woman asked, "What kind of government have you given us, Dr. Franklin? A republic or a monarchy?" Franklin answered, "A republic, Madam, if you can keep it." Franklin's response indicated that a republic—a system of government in which the people elect representatives to exercise power for them—requires citizens to take an active role.

What Ideas Influenced the Framers?

After four long and difficult months, Franklin and the other delegates had produced a new constitution. The document provided the framework for a strong central government for the United States.

Although a uniquely American document, the Constitution has roots in many other civilizations. The delegates had studied and discussed the history of political development at length—starting with ancient Greece—so that their new government could avoid the mistakes of the past.

The Framers who shaped the document were familiar with the parliamentary system of Britain, and many had participated in the colonial assemblies or their state assemblies. They valued the individual rights guaranteed by the British judicial system. Although the Americans had broken away from Britain, they respected many British traditions.

The Magna Carta (1215) had placed limits on the power of the British monarch. England's lawmaking body, which is called Parliament, emerged as a force that the king had to depend on to pay for wars and to finance the royal government. Like Parliament, the assemblies that developed in the Thirteen Colonies controlled their colony's funds. For that reason, the assemblies had some control over colonial governors.

The English Bill of Rights of 1689 provided another important model for Americans. Many Americans believed that the Constitution also needed a bill of rights.

Enlightenment Thinkers Framers of the Constitution got many ideas on the nature of people and government from European writers of the Enlightenment. The **Enlightenment** (ihn • LY • tuhn • muhnt) was a movement of the 1700s that **promoted** knowledge, reason, and science as the means to improve society. James Madison and other architects of the Constitution were familiar with the work of John Locke and Baron de Montesquieu (mahn • tuhs • KYOO), two important philosophers.

▲ John Locke

Locke, an English philosopher, believed that all people have natural rights. These natural rights include the rights to life, liberty, and property. Many Americans interpreted natural rights to mean the rights of Englishmen defined in the Magna Carta and the English Bill of Rights.

In *The Spirit of Laws* (1748), the French writer Montesquieu declared that the powers of government should be separated and balanced against each other. This separation would keep any one person or group from gaining too much power. Following the ideas of Montesquieu, the Framers of the Constitution carefully specified and divided the powers of government.

Reading Check **Identify** What is a republic?

TEACH

R1 Reading Strategy

Activating Prior Knowledge **Ask:** What was the *Enlightenment*? *(movement that emphasized knowledge, reason, and science as ways to improve society)* BL CA 8RW1.3

R2 Reading Strategy

Academic Vocabulary Ask students to write a sentence using the word *promote*. EL

C Critical Thinking

Identifying Central Issues Ask students to discuss what limits should be placed on people's right to the pursuit of life, liberty, and happiness. How should these limits be decided? *(Students may say that these rights should not cause harm to others; some may say that the good of society should prevail over individual happiness.)* OL CA HI3.

R3 Reading Strategy

Summarizing Have students summarize the influence of Locke and Montesquieu on the Framers of the Constitution. OL CA HI1.

Reading Check

Answer: system of government in which people elect representatives to exercise power for them

More Skill Practice

Historical and Social Sciences Analysis Skill Ask students in what ways Locke's ideas could be applied to political and social issues today. *(Possible answers might include questions of individual rights such as freedom of assembly.)* AL CA HR4.

Did You Know?

The English Bill of Rights was adopted in 1689 in connection with the Glorious Revolution. Parliament offered the vacant throne to Mary, daughter of the English king James II and her Dutch husband William, because they were Protestants. In accepting the throne, William and Mary agreed to the Bill of Rights.

R1 Reading Strategy

Connecting Have students give examples of federalism using current events. *(Examples could come from the fields of education, environmental protection, and others.)* OL CA 8RW1.3

U1 Universal Access

Below Grade Level Have students create a table that lists the powers delegated to states and those delegated to the federal government by the Constitution. BL

U2 Universal Access

English Learners Ask: What parts are this textbook divided into? *(units, chapters, sections)* How is that similar to what *articles* are? *(They are part of a document.)* EL CA 8RW1.3

R2 Reading Strategy

Understanding Vocabulary Explain that the root of the word *legislative* is the Latin *lex*, meaning "law." **Ask:** What other words use the same Latin root? *(legal, legitimate)* OL

Answers and Additional Support

US8.2.3 Evaluate the major debates that occurred during the development of the Constitution and their ultimate resolutions in such areas as shared power among institutions, divided state-federal power, slavery, the rights of individuals and states (later addressed by the addition of the Bill of Rights), and the status of American Indians under the commerce clause.

The Federal System

Main Idea **The Constitution outlines the responsibilities and limits of the three branches of government.**

Reading Connection Do you think it is important to identify what leaders can and cannot do? Read to find out why the Constitution limits the government and what those limits are.

The Constitution created a federal system of government that divided powers between the national, or federal, government and the states. Under the Articles of Confederation, the states retained their sovereignty. Under the Constitution, the states gave up some of their powers to the federal government while keeping others.

America's *Architecture*

The Old Senate Chamber The U.S. Senate met in the Old Senate Chamber from 1810 until 1859. The two-story chamber is semicircular in shape and measures 75 feet long and 50 feet wide. Two visitors' galleries overlook the chamber. After the Senate moved to its present location, the room was occupied by the Supreme Court from 1860 until 1935. ***Which branches of government conducted business in the chamber?***

R1 **Shared Powers** **Federalism,** or sharing power between the federal and state governments, is one of the distinctive features of the United States government. Under the Constitution, the federal government gained broad powers to tax, regulate trade, control the currency, raise an army, and declare war. It could also pass laws that were "necessary and proper" for carrying out its responsibilities. U1

However, the Constitution left important powers in the hands of the states. The states had the power to pass and enforce laws and regulate trade within their borders. They could also establish local governments, schools, and other institutions affecting their citizens.

Supreme Law of the Land The Constitution and the laws that Congress passed were to be "the supreme law of the land." No state could make laws or take actions that went against the Constitution. Any dispute between the federal government and the states was to be settled by the federal courts on the basis of the Constitution. Under the new federal system, the Constitution became the final and supreme authority.

The Organization of Government Influenced by Montesquieu's idea of a division of powers, the Framers divided the federal government into three branches—legislative, executive, and judicial. The first three **articles,** or parts, of the Constitution describe the powers and responsibilities of each branch. U2

Article I of the Constitution establishes Congress, the **legislative branch** (LEH • juhs • LAY • tihv), or lawmaking branch, of the government. The Congress of the United States is comprised of the House of Representatives and the Senate. R2

More Skill Practice

Historical and Social Sciences Analysis Skill Brainstorm with students a list of current topics in the national news. Have partners or small groups choose various topics and decide which branch of government is most directly involved in each topic. Discuss the groups' ideas as a class. OL CA HI3.

America's *Architecture*

The Old Senate Chamber was located in the original north wing of the Capitol.

Answer: the legislative and judicial branches

Picturing History

The Supreme Court has the final say in deciding what the Constitution means. ***What types of cases does the Supreme Court hear?***

The powers of Congress include collecting taxes, coining money, and regulating trade. Congress can also declare war and "raise and support armies." Finally, it makes all laws needed to fulfill the functions given to it as stated in the Constitution.

The Executive Branch Memories of King George III's rule made some delegates reluctant to establish a powerful executive, or ruler. Others believed that the Confederation had failed, in part, because it lacked an executive branch or president. They argued that a strong executive would serve as a check, or limit, on Congress.

Article II of the Constitution established the **executive branch** (ihg • ZEH • kuh • tihv), headed by the president, to carry out the nation's laws. The president serves as commander in chief of the armed forces and **conducts** relations with other countries.

The Judicial Branch Article III of the Constitution deals with the **judicial branch** (ju • DIH • shuhl), or court system, of the United States. The nation's judicial power resides in "one supreme Court" and any other lower federal courts that Congress might establish. The Supreme Court and the federal courts hear cases involving the Constitution, laws passed by Congress, and disputes between states.

System of Checks and Balances An important distinctive feature of our government is the separation of powers. The Constitution divides government power among the legislative, executive, and judicial branches. To keep any one branch from gaining too much power, the Framers built in a system of **checks and balances.** The three branches of government have roles that check, or limit, the others so that no single branch can dominate the government.

Both the House and the Senate must pass a bill for it to become law. The president can check Congress by vetoing, or rejecting, the bill. However, Congress can then check the president by overriding, or voting down, the veto. To override a veto, two-thirds of the members of both houses of Congress must vote for the bill.

The system of checks and balances also applies to the Supreme Court. The president appoints Supreme Court justices, and the Senate must approve the appointments.

Over time, the Court became a check on Congress and the president by ruling on the constitutionality of laws and presidential acts. The system has been successful in maintaining a balance of power among the branches of the federal government.

With these revolutionary changes, Americans showed the world that it was possible for a people to change its form of government through discussion and choice—rather than through chaos, force, or war. The rest of the world watched the new nation with interest to see whether its experiment in self-government would really work.

Reading Check **Explain** Why does the Constitution divide government power among the legislative, executive, and judicial branches?

Did You Know?

The Constitution is stored at the National Archives Building in Washington, D.C. During the daytime, pages one and four of the document are displayed in a bullet-proof case. At night the pages are lowered into a vault behind five-ton doors that can withstand a nuclear explosion. The entire Constitution is displayed only one day a year, September 17, which is the anniversary of its signing.

Picturing History

(standing) Ruth Bader Ginsburg, David Souter, Clarence Thomas, and Stephen Breyer; *(sitting)* Antonin Scalia, John Paul Stevens, William Rehnquist, Sandra Day O'Connor and Anthony Kennedy.

Answer: Cases involving the Constitution, laws passed by Congress, and disputes between states.

R1 Reading Strategy

Understanding Vocabulary

Ask: Which branch do you think has the most direct impact on your everyday lives and why? *(Answers will vary but should reflect an understanding of the functions of the three branches.)* OL CA 8RW1.3

R2 Reading Strategy

Understanding Vocabulary

Explain that the word *check* has different meanings. Write the following on the board: *to inspect, to approve, a piece of paper used like money, a pattern on fabric with small squares, to block a player in a contact sport.* **Ask:** Which meaning is closest to the meaning in *checks and balances?* *(to block a player in a contact sport)* Why? *(because it blocks the player from acting)* OL CA 8RW1.3

Reading Check

Answer: to keep any one branch from gaining too much power

Review Grade 5 Standards

To review standard 5.7.4 *(Understand how the Constitution is designed to secure our liberty by both empowering and limiting central government and compare the powers granted to citizens, Congress, the president, and the Supreme Court with those reserved to the states)*, tell students that Supreme Court Justice Charles Evans Hughes once called the judiciary "the safeguard of our liberty." **Ask:** How is Evans's statement true? *(The courts have the final say on whether laws and acts follow the Constitution and can overturn laws that take away people's liberties.)* OL

Review The Big Idea

Review the Big Idea for this section: "Political ideas and major events shape how people form governments." **Ask:** How did the experience of living under British rule affect the kind of government Americans formed? *(Students may say it convinced people to keep one branch from being too powerful and to guarantee individual rights.)* OL CA HI2.

R1 Reading Strategy

Using Word Parts Point out to students that the ending *-ify* or *-fy* makes a word a verb and means "cause to become." Ask them to name other verbs ending in *-fy* or *–ify*. *(identify, magnify)* OL CA 8RW1.3

R2 Reading Strategy

Organizing Information Write a series of statements on the board that are true of either the Federalists or the Antifederalists, such as "wanted a strong central government" or "wanted a Bill of Rights." Have students match each statement with the correct group. OL CA HR4.

Answers and Additional Support

US8.2.2 Analyze the Articles of Confederation and the Constitution and the success of each in implementing the ideals of the Declaration of Independence. US8.2.4 Describe the political philosophy underpinning the Constitution as specified in the *Federalist Papers* (authored by James Madison, Alexander Hamilton, and John Jay) and the role of such leaders as Madison, George Washington, Roger Sherman, Gouverneur Morris, and James Wilson in the writing and ratification of the Constitution.

The Debate Over Ratification

Main Idea **Americans reacted to the proposed Constitution in different ways.**

Reading Connection Have you taken sides on an important issue? What arguments have you used to support your position? Read to learn about the arguments that Americans used to support or oppose ratification of the Constitution.

The delegates at Philadelphia had produced the Constitution, but its acceptance depended upon the will of the people. Gaining approval of the Constitution, with its radical new plan of government, was not going to be easy.

R1 Before the Constitution could go into effect, nine states needed to **ratify** (RA•tuh•FY), or approve, it. State legislatures set up special ratifying conventions to consider the document. By late 1787 these conventions started to meet. Rhode Island stood apart. Its leaders opposed the Constitution from the beginning and therefore did not call a convention to approve it.

Powers of the Federal Government

	Articles of Confederation	United States Constitution
Declare war; make peace	✔	✔
Coin money	✔	✔
Manage foreign affairs	✔	✔
Establish a postal system	✔	✔
Impose taxes		✔
Regulate trade		✔
Organize a court system		✔
Call state militias for service		✔
Protect copyrights		✔
Take other necessary actions to run the federal government		✔

Understanding Charts

The Articles of Confederation and the U.S. Constitution specified certain powers that would be given to the federal government.

1. Which document allowed the government to organize state militias?
2. **Analyze** In what ways are the two documents similar?

Federalists

Supporters of the new Constitution were called **Federalists.** Three of the nation's most gifted political thinkers—James Madison, Alexander Hamilton, and **John Jay**—also backed the Constitution.

Madison, Hamilton, and Jay worked together to write a series of essays explaining and defending the Constitution. These essays appeared in newspapers around the country and were widely read. Called the *Federalist Papers,* they were later published as a book and sent to delegates at the remaining ratifying conventions. Jefferson described the series of essays as "the best commentary on the principles of government which was ever written." R2

Antifederalists

The Federalists called those who opposed ratification **Antifederalists.** Antifederalists criticized the Constitution because it lacked a bill of rights to protect individual freedoms. Antifederalists believed that no government could be trusted to protect the freedom of its citizens. Several state conventions took a stand and announced that they would not ratify the Constitution without the addition of a bill of rights.

Mercy Otis Warren, a Massachusetts opponent of the Constitution, expressed the problem faced by many Antifederalists. She admitted the need for a strong government but feared it.

> **"We have struggled for liberty and made costly sacrifices . . . and there are still many among us who [value liberty] too much to relinquish . . . the rights of man for the dignity of government."**
>
> —Mercy Otis Warren, September 29, 1787

206

Understanding Charts

Answers:

1. Constitution
2. Both give the government the first four powers listed.

Resources for page 206

American Literature Reading 3

In many ways the debate between Federalists and Antifederalists came down to their different fears. Federalists feared disorder without a strong central government. They believed that more uprisings like Shays's Rebellion would occur without a national government capable of maintaining order. The Antifederalists feared oppression more than disorder. They worried about the concentration of power that would result from a strong national government.

Adopting the Constitution With the promise of a bill of rights, many Americans began to favor the Constitution. Many small states ratified it quickly because they were pleased with equal representation in the new Senate. On June 21, 1788, the ninth state—New Hampshire—ratified it. However, without the support of two critical states—New York and Virginia—the future of the new government was not promising. Neither state had ratified yet, and both had strong Antifederalist groups.

In Virginia, George Washington, James Madison, and Edmund Randolph helped swing a close vote on June 25, 1788. In New York, Alexander Hamilton argued for ratification for six weeks. Finally, on July 26, the Federalists in New York won by only three votes. North Carolina ratified in November 1789, and Rhode Island ratified in May 1790.

After ratification came the celebrations. Boston, New York, and Philadelphia held big parades accompanied by cannon salutes and ringing church bells. Smaller celebrations took place in hundreds of American towns.

The task of creating the Constitution had ended. The Federalists promised to add a bill of rights after the new government took office. Now it was time for the nation to elect leaders and begin the work of government.

Reading Check **Explain** According to the Antifederalists, why was a bill of rights important?

History Online
Study Central Need help understanding the development of the Constitution? Visit ca.hss.glencoe.com and click on Study Central.

Section 3 Review

Reading Summary

Review the Main Ideas

- Ideas and thinkers of the past influenced the creation of the United States Constitution.
- The Constitution outlines the responsibilities and the limits of the three branches of government.
- Americans reacted to the proposed Constitution in different ways.

What Did You Learn?

1. What influence did John Locke have on American government?
2. Why was the support of New York and Virginia vital to ratifying the Constitution?

Critical Thinking

3. **Compare** Re-create the diagram below. Describe the differences between Federalist and Antifederalist views on the Constitution. CA HR3.

Views on the Constitution	
Federalist	Antifederalist

4. **The Big Ideas** Why did the Framers of the Constitution believe that a division of powers and a system of checks and balances were necessary in a government?
5. **Persuasive Writing** Search your local newspaper for articles that deal with constitutional issues. Select an issue from one of the articles and write a letter to your senator or representatives expressing your opinion about the issue. CA 8WA2.4

SECTION 3 REVIEW ANSWERS

Review questions reinforce content standards US8.2 and US8.3.

1. Americans agreed with the idea of natural rights.
2. They were the largest states.
3. Federalists: wanted strong national government, feared disorder; Antifederalists: wanted weaker national government, feared oppression
4. **The Big Ideas** to keep any one branch from becoming too powerful
5. Letters should show understanding of the chosen issue and of the constitutional history behind it.

C Critical Thinking

Drawing Conclusions Ask: Do you think the Antifederalists' fears of a too-powerful central government were justified? Why or why not? *(Students may say that most Americans would not have accepted a central government that reminded them of British rule, so that the fears were exaggerated.)* AL CA HR4.

ASSESS

Resources for page 207

Use these resources to assess student mastery of section content.

- Section Quiz 3–3
- Interactive Tutor Self-Assessment CD-ROM

Reading Check

Answer: to protect individual rights and prevent the concentration of too much power in the federal government

History Online

Study Central provides summaries, interactive games, and online graphic organizers to help students review section content.

CLOSE

Identifying Central Issues
Have students take the role of a Federalist or Antifederalist and write a letter to the editor of a newspaper supporting or rejecting ratification of the Constitution. OL CA 8WA2.4

FOCUS

Before reading this feature, have students consider a major political debate occurring today, either locally, in the state, or nationally. Have students identify the issue and the differing positions on it. Then discuss why people differ on issues like this.

TEACH

C1 Critical Thinking

Identifying Central Issues **Ask:** Why does Wilson think the change to amend the Constitution makes it so valuable? *(because problems in it can be fixed)* OL

C2 Critical Thinking

Analyzing Primary Sources **Ask:** Does the argument that a weak president means bad government remove fears that a strong president could be oppressive? Why or why not? *(it does not because the Antifederalists were not worried about a weak executive but an overly strong one)* What argument could Hamilton make about that? *(the system of checks and balances, which places brakes on a president's power)* OL

Answers and Additional Support

You Decide . . .

Ratifying the Constitution

The delegates at Philadelphia had produced the Constitution, but its acceptance depended upon the will of the American people. In each of the 13 states, voters selected delegates to special conventions that would decide whether to accept or reject the new plan of government. Once 9 of the 13 conventions had ratified the Constitution, it could go into effect.

For Ratification

Those who favored the Constitution called themselves Federalists. Federalists wanted a strong government capable of handling the problems facing the United States both at home and abroad. They believed that the new Constitution protected the rights of the states, but gave the central government enough power to function effectively.

James Wilson of Philadelphia was a major force in drafting the Constitution. In a speech to the Pennsylvania Ratifying Convention, Wilson said:

C1 "I am satisfied that anything nearer to perfection could not have been accomplished. If there are errors, it should be remembered, that the seeds of reformation are sown in the work itself, and the concurrence of two thirds of the Congress may at any time introduce alterations and amendments. Regarding it then, in every point of view, with a candid and disinterested mind, I am bold to assert, that it is the best form of government which has ever been offered to the world."

In a series of 85 essays known as *The Federalist Papers*, Alexander Hamilton, James Madison, and John Jay defended the Constitution. In *Federalist*, No. 70, Hamilton argued against the idea of a president with limited or few powers:

C2 "A feeble executive implies a feeble execution of the government. A feeble execution is but another phrase for a bad execution; and a government ill executed, whatever it may be in theory, must be, in practice, a bad government."

Hamilton also believed that a bill of rights would be unnecessary and dangerous. Hamilton wrote that the Constitution gave the national government only limited power. It did not have the power to infringe on the rights of the citizens. Therefore, Hamilton noted, a bill of rights protecting the people's rights is not needed.

Alexander Hamilton ▶

208

Extending the Content

Universal Rights George Mason had written the Virginia Declaration of Rights in 1776—before the Declaration of Independence was written—and it was adopted by the Patriot government of Virginia. In it, Mason declared that "all men are by nature equally free and independent and have certain inherent rights." The document called for freedom of the press and of religion and trial by jury.

US8.2.4 Describe the political philosophy underpinning the Constitution as specified in the *Federalist Papers* (authored by James Madison, Alexander Hamilton, and John Jay) and the role of such leaders as Madison, George Washington, Roger Sherman, Gouverneur Morris, and James Wilson in the writing and ratification of the Constitution.

Against Ratification

Ratification, however, was not a sure thing. Many people who remembered British tyranny were against a powerful national government. Opponents of the Constitution, called Antifederalists, felt that a strong central government was a threat to liberty.

In the Virginia ratification convention of 1788, Patrick Henry spoke out against the adoption of the Constitution:

"I look upon that paper [the Constitution] as the most fatal plan that could be possibly conceived to enslave a free people." **R**

The Antifederalists' strongest argument, however, was that the Constitution lacked a bill of rights. They feared losing the liberties they had gained during the Revolution and wanted to include a guarantee of those liberties in the Constitution. Mercy Otis Warren wrote that "The rights of the individual should be the primary object of all governments." **C**

George Mason of Virginia refused to sign the Constitution because it did not contain a bill of rights. In a letter explaining his objections to the Constitution, Mason stated that the Constitution has

> "no declaration of rights: and the laws of the general government being paramount to the laws and constitutions of the several states, the declarations of rights, in the separate states, are no security. Nor are the people secured even in the enjoyment of the benefit of the common law."

◀ George Mason

You Be The Historian

DBQ Document-Based Questions

1. What group was opposed to ratification of the Constitution? CA HR5.
2. Who argued that the Constitution could be changed if problems arose?
3. What was Hamilton's major argument in *The Federalist*, No. 70? CA HR3.

209

You Decide . . .

R Reading Strategy

Reading Primary Sources
Ask: What does Henry mean by "fatal"? *(dangerous; destructive of freedom)* OL CA HR4.

C Critical Thinking

Identifying Central Issues
Ask: What does Warren mean by "primary object"? *(main goal)* Do you think the Federalists would agree with this view? Why or why not? *(Students may say that the Federalists would be more concerned about order.)* OL

Resources for page 209

Critical Thinking Skills Activity 3

ASSESS/CLOSE

Have students answer the You Be The Historian questions. Then have students identify what they think is the single greatest strength of the Constitution as written in 1787 and its single greatest weakness and explain why. OL

You Be The Historian

Answers

1. Antifederalists
2. James Wilson
3. A weak executive would not be effective, and that means the government would be a bad government.

Analyzing Primary Sources

FOCUS

History–Social Science Standards

The following standards are covered on pages 210–211.

US8.2 Students analyze the political principles underlying the U.S. Constitution and compare the enumerated and implied powers of the federal government.

US8.3 Students understand the foundation of the American political system and the ways in which citizens participate in it.

TEACH

C Critical Thinking

Analyzing Primary Sources Ask: Why do the Oneidas think their plea may succeed? *(They point out that they helped the Americans during the Revolution and that they suffered as a result.)* OL

R Reading Strategy

Reading Primary Sources Ask: Why were the Oneidas disappointed when they met with the "chiefs"? *(They had come to buy the Oneidas' land.)* BL

Answers and Additional Support

Analyzing Primary Sources

US8.3 Students understand the foundation of the American political system and the ways in which citizens participate in it.

Forming a New Nation

Americans fought for their independence from Great Britain between 1776 and 1783. After the Revolutionary War, a great deal of work needed to be done to establish a new nation. Where would they start? How would they form a new government that served the people better than the last government? To understand the people who called themselves Americans, you can look at letters and writings of the eighteenth century.

Read the passages on pages 210 and 211 and answer the questions that follow.

"Ship of State" float parading through New York during the 1788 ratification ▶

Reader's Dictionary

allies (A • LYS): people or groups joined in alliance or agreement

justice: fairness in the way people are treated or decisions are made

acquainted (uh • KWAYNT • ihd): having some knowledge of something

haughty (HAW • tee): behaving in a superior, arrogant way

appellation (A • puh • LAY • shuhn): the name or title of someone or something

perpetual: occurring over and over

contention (kuhn • TEHN • shuhn): disagreement or competition between rivals

The Oneida and the Use of Land

The Oneida Indian Nation fought on the side of the Patriots during the American Revolution. In March 1788, leaders of the Oneida people sent this message to the New York State legislature.

C Brothers. We are your **allies,** we are a free people, our chiefs have directed us to speak to you, as such, therefore, open your ears and hear our words.

Brothers. In your late war with the people on the other side of the great water, . . . we fought by your side, our blood flowed together, and the bones of our warriors mingled with yours; . . .

R [W]e received an invitation to meet some of your chiefs . . . , those chiefs who then met us will doubtless remember how much we were disappointed, when they told us they were only sent to buy our lands. . . .

Brothers. We are determined then never to sell any more; the experience of all the Indian nations to the east and south of us has fully convinced us, that if we follow their example we shall soon share their fate. We wish that our children and grandchildren may derive a comfortable living from the lands which the Great Spirit has given us and our forefathers. . . .

Brothers. We wish you to consider this matter well, and to do us **justice**. . . .

—*Proceedings of the Commissioners of Indian Affairs*

EXTENDING THE CONTENT

Tensions Between the Oneida and the Mohawk The Oneida—part of the Iroquois Confederation—suffered for their support of the American cause during the Revolution. Some of their villages were attacked by the Mohawk people, allies of the British. The American government gave them some funds to help them recover from these losses. By the early 1800s, many Oneida had resettled in Ontario, Canada, or Wisconsin. Only a few remained in the state of New York.

Analyzing Primary Sources

What Is an American?

J. Hector St. John Crèvecoeur of France traveled widely in the American colonies and farmed in New York. His Letters From an American Farmer *was published in 1782.*

I wish I could be **acquainted** with the feelings and thoughts which must . . . present themselves to the mind of an enlightened Englishman, when he first lands on the continent. . . . If he travels through our rural districts he views not the hostile castle, and the **haughty** mansion, contrasted with the clay-built hut and miserable [cabin], where cattle and men help to keep each other warm, and dwell in meanness, smoke, and indigence. A pleasing uniformity of decent competence appears throughout our habitations. The meanest of our log-houses is dry and comfortable. . . . Lawyer or merchant are the fairest titles our towns afford; that of a farmer is the only **appellation** of the rural inhabitants of our country. It must take some time [before] he can reconcile himself to our dictionary, which is but short in words of dignity, and names of honour. . . .

What then is the American, this new man? He is either a European, or the descendant of a European, hence that strange mixture of blood, which you will find in no other country. I could point out to you a family whose grandfather was an Englishman, whose wife was Dutch, and whose son married a French woman, and whose present four sons have now four wives of different nations. . . .

He does not find, as in Europe, a crowded society, where every place is over-stocked; he does not feel that **perpetual** collision of parties, that difficulty of beginning, that **contention** which oversets so many. There is room for everybody in America; has he particular talent, or industry? He exerts it in order to produce a livelihood, and it succeeds. . . .

—Letters From an American Farmer

S

▲ ***The Peale Family*** **by Charles Willson Peale, c. 1770–1773** American artists favored informal scenes over the more formal European styles.

C

DBQ Document-Based Questions

The Oneida and the Use of Land

1. Who are the "Brothers" that the Oneida leaders address? Why would the Oneida address legislators in this way?
2. What are the Oneida asking for?
3. What do the Oneida pledge to never do? Why did they make this decision and statement?

What Is an American?

4. How does de Crèvecoeur describe the typical home in the colonies?
5. Why might de Crèvecoeur refer to the American as a "new man"?
6. How are Americans described in comparison to Europeans?
7. What is meant by "there is room for everybody in America"? Is this still true today?

Read to Write

8. What does it mean to have justice in America? What would it look like? How would it work? How would the authors of these documents define justice in their time? How would you define justice in America today? Compare and contrast the ideas from different eras. CA HI3. CA 8WS1.1

S Skill Practice

Visual Literacy **Ask:** What impressions do you get of the family shown in this painting? *(Students may say that it seems like a large family; that some people are happy though others look quite serious; and that they seem to have comfortable lives.)* OL CA 8LS1.9

C Critical Thinking

Analyzing Primary Sources Explain that in this passage, Crèvecoeur is criticizing conditions in Europe. **Ask:** What groups of society does he have in mind when writing about the "haughty mansion" and the "miserable cabin"? *(powerful, wealthy nobles and poor people)* How does this contrast make his point that Americans are "new men"? *(He is saying that the poor in America are not as miserable as those in Europe.)* AL CA HR4.

ASSESS

Have students answer the Document-Based Questions.

CLOSE

Summarizing Have students summarize what these documents say about life in America in the 1780s. OL

DBQ Document-Based Questions

1. the New York state legislature; to establish unity
2. to be allowed to remain on the land
3. never to sell their land; they fear they will disappear as a people
4. dry, comfortable log-built houses
5. because Americans were unlike other people
6. They have more room, and they are not always fighting with each other.
7. The country is large and has plenty of land for everybody; some areas are congested.
8. Justice for the Native Americans would have meant being left alone, but white Americans did not recognize that they had the same rights. Now, though, most Americans agree that all people should be treated the same.

CHAPTER 3 Assessment

Resources for pages 212–213

Use these resources to review, assess, or reteach the chapter.

- Active Reading Note-Taking Guide, Chapter 3
- Chapter 3 Reading Essentials and Study Guide
- Chapter 3 Tests, Forms A and B
- Standards Assessment, Forms A and B
- California Standards Practice Workbook
- Succeeding on the California History–Social Science Standards CD-ROM
- MindJogger Videoquiz
- Interactive Tutor Self-Assessment CD-ROM

Review Content Vocabulary

1. c
2. a
3. b
4. d

Sentences should accurately define *bicameral* and *executive branch*.

Review the Main Idea

5. to set up a government, or "league of friendship," for the 13 independent states
6. It created a single territory for lands north of the Ohio River and east of the Mississippi River and provided for how areas within that territory, once they had enough people, could become states.
7. two houses with proportional representation; members of the lower house were elected by the people and those of the upper house were chosen by the lower house

Chapter 3 Assessment

Standards US8.2 & US8.3

Review Content Vocabulary

Write the vocabulary word that completes each sentence. Write a sentence for each word that is not used.

a. bicameral
b. ratify
c. compromise
d. republic
e. executive branch

1. To resolve their differences, the delegates used ______, with each side giving up something but gaining something else.
2. A legislature divided into two parts, or houses, is called ______.
3. On June 21, 1788, New Hampshire became the ninth state to ______ the Constitution.
4. A(n) ______ is a system of government in which the people elect representatives to exercise power for them.

Review the Main Ideas

Section 1 • The Articles of Confederation

5. What was the purpose of the Articles of Confederation?
6. How did the Northwest Ordinance provide for the country's expansion?

Section 2 • Convention and Compromise

7. According to the Virginia Plan, how was the legislature to be set up?
8. How did the Great Compromise address the issue of representation in Congress?

Section 3 • A New Plan of Government

9. Why did some Americans want a bill of rights added to the Constitution?
10. Why is it important that the powers of government are separated?

Critical Thinking

11. **Identify** What was the purpose of holding secret sessions at the Constitutional Convention? If you had been a delegate, would you have been in favor of secret sessions? Why or why not? CA HI2.
12. **Analyze** Why was a system of checks and balances built into the Constitution? CA HI2.

Geography Skills

Study the map below and answer the following questions. CA CS3.

NATIONAL GEOGRAPHIC **Land Claims in North America, 1783**

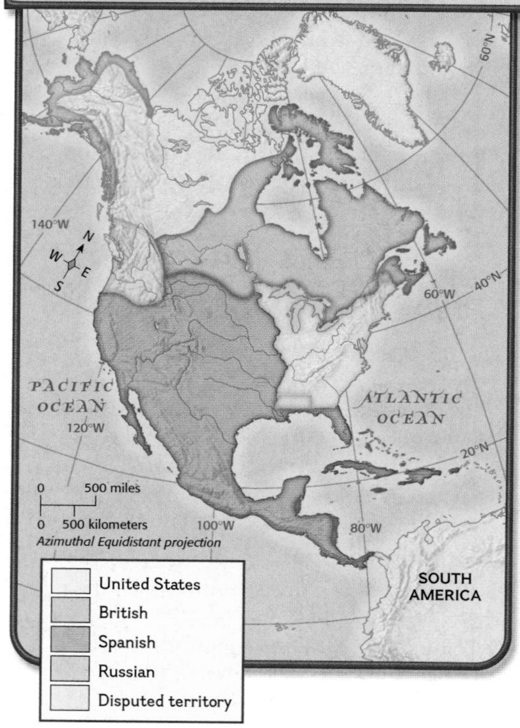

8. It had a proportional number of seats for each state in the lower house but an equal number in the upper house, the Senate.
9. to protect individual rights
10. so that no branch or single person can become too powerful

Critical Thinking

11. to allow delegates to speak freely; answers will vary but should be supported with reasons
12. to prevent any one branch of the government from gaining too much power

Geography Skills

13. Answers will vary, but should accurately reflect the map.
14. Spain

History Online

Self-Check Quiz Visit ca.hss.glencoe.com to prepare for the Chapter 3 test.

13. **Place** Who controlled the area in which you live today?
14. **Region** What country held territory directly west of the United States?

Read to Write

15. **The Big Ideas Government and Democracy** Write a short essay discussing the many compromises that are reflected in the final version of the U.S. Constitution. CA 8WS1.1

16. **Using Your FOLDABLES** Use the information you wrote in your foldable to create a fill-in-the blank quiz for a classmate. Write a paragraph about one of the sections, leaving blanks for your classmates to fill in. Also write an answer key. CA 8RC2.0

Using Academic Vocabulary

17. Write two words that are related to the academic vocabulary word *currency*.

Building Citizenship

18. **Interviewing** Interview students from your school and adults from your community to find out what they know about the powers of government specified in the Constitution. Prepare a list of questions to use in your interviews. Compile the answers and present a report to your class. CA HR1.

Reviewing Skills

19. Review READING SKILL **Making Connections** Review the literature excerpt called "Second Daughter." Write a paragraph describing the connections you made while reading. Be sure to include text-to-self, text-to-text, and text-to-world connections. CA 8RC2.0

20. Review ANALYSIS SKILL **Paraphrasing** Select a quotation or primary source from one of the sections in this chapter. Reread it and then paraphrase what you have read. CA HR4.

Standards Practice

Read the passage below and answer the following questions.

> The Senate of the United States shall be composed of two Senators from each State, chosen by the Legislature thereof, for six Years; and each Senator shall have one vote.
>
> —U.S. Constitution, Article I, Section 3.1

21 According to the above excerpt from the U.S. Constitution, by whom were Senators originally chosen?

- A other Senators
- B members of the U.S. House of Representatives
- C the voters of the state
- D the state's legislature

22 Each of the states enacted state constitutions in the late 1700s. All state constitutions

- A established equal rights for all persons living in the state.
- B set up legislative and executive branches of state government.
- C granted women the right to vote.
- D agreed that states would be supervised by the federal government.

23 The law that established a procedure for surveying and selling the western lands north of the Ohio River was the

- A Ordinance of 1785.
- B Virginia Plan.
- C New Jersey Plan.
- D Bill of Rights.

CHAPTER 3 Assessment

Reviewing Skills

19. Review READING SKILL Connections should be appropriate for the excerpt; students should be sure to include all three kinds of connections.

20. Review ANALYSIS SKILL Paraphrases should be grammatically correct and accurately reflect the meaning of the quotation.

Standards Practice

21. D
22. B
23. A

Bonus Question

Ask: What was the goal of the *Federalist Papers*? *(convince people to ratify the Constitution)* OL CA HI1.

History Online

Have students visit the Web site at ca.hss.glencoe.com to review Chapter 3 and take the Self-Check Quiz.

Read to Write

15. The Big Ideas Essays should include the Great Compromise (a proportional lower house and equal upper house) and the Three-Fifths Compromise (regarding the counting of enslaved persons for purposes of representation).

16. Using Your FOLDABLES Quizzes and paragraphs should reflect information in the chapter.

Using Academic Vocabulary

17. Answers will vary.

Building Citizenship

18. Questions should accurately reflect information in the chapter; reports should reflect the results of the survey and include a conclusion about how much or little Americans know about the Constitution.

Chapter 4 Planning Guide

SECTION RESOURCES

Main Ideas	Print Materials	Technology Resources
Section 1 **Goals of the Constitution** 1. The Preamble to the Constitution describes six goals for the United States government. 2. The Constitution is based on seven major principles. 3. The Framers wrote the Constitution so that it could be altered or adapted to meet changing needs.	• Reproducible Lesson Plan 4–1* • Daily Lesson and Discussion Notes 4–1 • Active Reading Note-Taking Guide 4–1 • Reading Essentials and Study Guide 4–1 • Guided Reading Activity 4–1 • Section Quiz 4–1	Daily Focus Skills Transparency 4–1 Section Graphic Organizer Transparency 4–1 California Standards Practice Transparencies Interactive Tutor Self-Assessment CD-ROM Exam*View*® Pro Testmaker CD-ROM Presentation Plus! CD-ROM
Section 2 **The Federal Government** 1. The legislative branch is responsible for making the nation's laws. 2. The executive branch carries out the laws made by the legislative branch. 3. The Supreme Court and a number of lesser courts make up the judicial branch.	• Reproducible Lesson Plan 4–2* • Daily Lesson and Discussion Notes 4–2 • Active Reading Note-Taking Guide 4–2 • Reading Essentials and Study Guide 4–2 • Guided Reading Activity 4–2 • Section Quiz 4–2	Daily Focus Skills Transparency 4–2 Section Graphic Organizer Transparency 4–2 California Standards Practice Transparencies Interactive Tutor Self-Assessment CD-ROM Exam*View*® Pro Testmaker CD-ROM Presentation Plus! CD-ROM
Section 3 **Citizens' Rights and Responsibilities** 1. Americans have certain rights that are protected in the Constitution. 2. American citizens are expected to carry out certain duties and responsibilities.	• Reproducible Lesson Plan 4–3* • Daily Lesson and Discussion Notes 4–3 • Active Reading Note-Taking Guide 4–3 • Reading Essentials and Study Guide 4–3 • Guided Reading Activity 4–3 • Section Quiz 4–3	Daily Focus Skills Transparency 4–3 Section Graphic Organizer Transparency 4–3 California Standards Practice Transparencies Interactive Tutor Self-Assessment CD-ROM Exam*View*® Pro Testmaker CD-ROM Presentation Plus! CD-ROM Vocabulary PuzzleMaker CD-ROM

PACING YOUR LESSONS

Chapter Introduction	Section 1	Section 2	Section 3	Chapter Assessment	Unit Wrap-Up
$\frac{1}{2}$ Day	2 Days	2 Days	2 Days	$\frac{1}{2}$ Day	$\frac{1}{2}$ Day

0:00 **OUT OF TIME?** Assign the Chapter 4 ***Reading Essentials and Study Guide***

*Available on TeacherWorks™

Standards-Based Lesson Plan

History–Social Science Standards Covered in Chapter 4

The standards covered in the chapter are listed below. Use the accompanying activity as you teach the chapter to ensure student mastery of these standards. This activity can be used in combination with the program's print and technology assessment materials.

Standard	Section 1	Section 2	Section 3
US8.2 Students analyze the political principles underlying the U.S. Constitution and compare the enumerated and implied powers of the federal government.	✔	✔	✔
US8.2.2	✔		
US8.2.4	✔		
US8.2.5			✔
US8.2.6	✔	✔	✔
US8.2.7	✔		
US8.3 Students understand the foundation of the American political system and the ways in which citizens participate in it.	✔		✔
US8.3.3	✔		
US8.3.6			✔
US8.3.7			✔

Cumulative Standards-Assessment Activity

The Cumulative Standards-Assessment Activity will help students organize and learn the important information from the chapter. Begin teaching the chapter with this activity, and have students complete it as they read the chapter.

Creating a Chart for Categorizing Information

Purpose Categorizing information is a useful skill because it helps students see the relationship between different details. By linking related events, people, and trends, students can better grasp how these details unite to describe life in a particular era.

Introduction to Categorizing Information

1. Begin the discussion by writing on the board the following phrases related to the last chapter: *Northwest Ordinance; inability to tax; mounting debt; Shays's Rebellion; Land Ordinance*. Ask students to think of ways to link these phrases into two categories. Explain that linking ideas will help them grasp the connections between the information they read.
2. Ask students to copy this chart into their notebooks:

Topic 1	Topic 2

As students read each section, have them use different charts that follow this format to categorize the information they read. In the first section, they might chart the seven principles underlying the Constitution and give examples of each. In others, they could list the three branches of the government and the powers they possess.

3. As part of your review of the chapter, have students share their charts. Encourage them to use their charts as study aids.

Chapter 4 Resources

READING SUPPORT

- Content Vocabulary Activity 4
- Academic Vocabulary Activity 4
- Reading Skills Activity 4
- American Literature Reading 4
- Biography Activity 4A
- Chapter 4 Active Reading Note-Taking Guide
- Chapter 4 Guided Reading Activities
- Chapter 4 Reading Essentials and Study Guide
- Glencoe Literature Library
- Glencoe Video Program
- Vocabulary PuzzleMaker CD-ROM
- Interactive Graphic Organizers CD-ROM
- American History Primary Source Document Library CD-ROM

SKILL PRACTICE

- Map Overlay Transparency 4, Strategy, and Activity
- Analysis Skills Activity 4
- Time Line Activity 4
- Geography and History Activity 4
- Economics and History Activity 4
- Chart, Graph, and Map Skills Activity 4
- Political Cartoon Activity 4
- Supreme Court Case Study 4
- In-Text Map Transparency 4, Strategy, and Activity
- Step Into American History Activity 4
- Citizenship and Service Learning Activity 4
- Activity Workbook
- Outline Map Resource Book
- MindJogger Plus Videoquiz

CRITICAL THINKING

- Critical Thinking Skills Activity 4
- Primary Source Reading 4
- Cause-and-Effect Transparency 4, Strategy, and Activity
- Presentation Plus! CD-ROM

WRITING SUPPORT

- Writing Activity 4
- Language Arts Activity 4
- Writer's Guidebook
- Middle School Writing Process Transparencies

UNIVERSAL ACCESS

- Universal Access Activity 4
- Then and Now Transparencies 4A–4B, Strategy, and Activity
- Graphic Novel Activity 4
- School-to-Home Connection Activities 4A–4D
- English Learner Handbook Chapter 4 Activities
- Universal Access for the American History Classroom
- American Art and Architecture Transparencies, Strategies, and Activities
- American Art Prints
- American Music Cultural Traditions
- American Music Hits Through History
- StudentWorks Plus CD-ROM

ASSESSMENT

GLENCOE'S ASSESSMENT ADVANTAGE

- Chapter 4 Section Quizzes
- Chapter 4 Tests, Forms A and B
- California Standard Assessment, Forms A and B
- Cumulative Assessment Activity US8.3
- California Standards Practice Workbook
- Succeeding on the California History–Social Science Standards CD-ROM
- Exam*View*® Pro Testmaker CD-ROM
- Interactive Tutor Self-Assessment CD-ROM

CD-ROM
DVD
Print Material
Poster
Transparency
Music Program
Videocassette
Glencoe Literature Library

Chapter 4 Resources

TECHNOLOGY

- StudentWorks Plus CD-ROM
- TeacherWorks Plus CD-ROM
- Exam*View*® Pro Testmaker CD-ROM
- Interactive Tutor Self-Assessment CD-ROM
- Presentation Plus! CD-ROM
- Succeeding on the California History–Social Science Standards CD-ROM
- Vocabulary PuzzleMaker CD-ROM
- Interactive Graphic Organizers CD-ROM
- Interactive Time Line CD-ROM
- American History Primary Source Document Library CD-ROM
- MindJogger Plus Videoquiz
- American Music Cultural Traditions
- American Music Hits Through History
- Glencoe Video Program
- Professional Development in Middle School Social Studies Series
- Teaching American History With *Discovering Our Past: The American Journey to World War I*

SPANISH RESOURCES

- Spanish Activities and Assessment
  - Spanish Content Vocabulary Activities
  - Spanish Guided Reading Activities
  - Spanish Quizzes and Tests
  - Spanish California Standards Assessment
- Spanish Reading Essentials and Study Guide
- Spanish School-to-Home Connection
- Spanish Declaration of Independence and U.S. Constitution

TRANSPARENCIES

- California Standards Practice Transparencies
- Daily Focus Skills Transparencies
- Section Graphic Organizer Transparencies
- In-Text Map Transparencies
- Map Overlay Transparencies
- Cause-and-Effect Transparencies
- Then and Now Transparencies
- American Art and Architecture Transparencies
- Middle School Writing Process Transparencies

TEACHER PLANNING

- Daily Lesson and Discussion Notes
- English Learner Handbook
- Guide to Daily Intervention
- *Discovering Our Past: The American Journey to World War I* Reading and Study Skills Foldables
- Reading Strategies and Activities for the Social Studies Classroom
- Chapter 4 Reproducible Lesson Plans (correlated to California History–Social Science Standards)
- Universal Access for the American History Classroom
- NGS U.S. Desk Map
- NGS U.S. Atlas

PROFESSIONAL DEVELOPMENT

- Building Academic Vocabulary
- Strategies for Success
- Research-Based Strategies Used to Develop *Discovering Our Past: The American Journey to World War I*
- Character Education in the Middle School Classroom
- The Living Constitution
- Professional Development in Middle School Social Studies Video Series
- Teaching American History With *Discovering Our Past: The American Journey to World War I*

MASTERING THE STANDARDS

The content and assessment in the Student Edition, Teacher Wraparound Edition, teacher planning materials, and the print and technology products are all standards-based. The use of these products during instruction leads to mastery of the standards.

PRACTICE
- California Standards Practice Workbook
- California Standards Practice Transparencies
- Interactive Time Line CD-ROM
- School-to-Home Connection

BENCHMARK ASSESSMENT
- California Standards Assessment
- Exam*View*® Pro Testmaker CD-ROM
- Succeeding on the California History–Social Science Standards CD-ROM

REMEDIATION
- California Guide to Daily Intervention
- Interactive Tutor Self-Assessment CD-ROM
- Exam*View*® Pro Testmaker CD-ROM
- California Standards Practice Workbook
- Reading Essentials and Study Guide

Additional Resources

NATIONAL GEOGRAPHIC **TEACHER'S CORNER**

Index to National Geographic Magazine:

The following articles relate to this chapter:

- "L'Enfant's Washington," by Alice J. Hall, August 1991.
- "James Madison, Architect of the Constitution," by Alice J. Hall, September 1987.

National Geographic Society Products

To order the following, call National Geographic at 1-800-368-2728

- *National Geographic Desk Reference* (Book)
- *Democratic Government Series, "The United States"* (Video)
- *Branches of Government Series* (Video)
- *Washington, D.C.* (Video)

NGS ONLINE

Access National Geographic's new dynamic MapMachine Web site and other geography resources at:

www.nationalgeographic.com

www.nationalgeographic.com/maps

A&E HOME VIDEO · Biography® · THE HISTORY CHANNEL®

The following videotape programs are available from Glencoe as supplements to Chapter 4.

- **George Washington: Founding Father (ISBN 1-56501-377-8)**
- **Thomas Jefferson: Philosopher of Freedom (ISBN 1-56501-502-9)**

To order, call Glencoe at 1-800-334-7344. To find classroom resources to accompany many of these videos, check the following home pages:

A&E Television: www.aetv.com
The History Channel: www.historychannel.com

History Online

Use our Web site for additional resources. All essential content is covered in the Student Edition.

You and your students can visit ca.hss.glencoe.com, the Web site companion to *Discovering Our Past: The American Journey to World War I*. This innovative integration of electronic and print media offers your students a wealth of opportunities. The student text directs students to the Web site for the following options:

- Chapter Overviews
- Self-Check Quizzes
- Study Central™
- Student Web Activities
- Textbook Updates
- Multi-Language Glossaries

Answers to the student Web activities are provided for you in the Web Activity Lesson Plans. Additional Web resources and ePuzzles and games are also available.

FOLDABLES™ Study Organizer

Dinah Zike's Foldables

Foldables are three-dimensional, interactive graphic organizers that help students practice basic writing skills, review key vocabulary terms, and identify main ideas. Every chapter contains a foldable activity, with additional chapter activities found in the Reading and Study Skills Foldables booklet.

Chapter 4 Resources

Reading List Generator CD-ROM

GLENCOE **BOOKLINK**

The Glencoe BookLink CD-ROM is a database that allows you to search more than 15,000 titles to create a customized reading list for your students.

- Reading lists can be organized by students' reading level, author, genre, theme, or area of interest.
- The database provides Degrees of Reading Power™ (DRP) and Lexile™ readability scores for all selections.
- A brief summary of each selection is included.

Reading level suggestions for this chapter:

For students at a Grade 6 reading level:
- ***A More Perfect Union: The Story of Our Constitution,*** by Betsy Maestro

For students at a Grade 7 reading level:
- ***The Supreme Court of the United States,*** by David Heath

For students at a Grade 8 reading level:
- ***Our Congress,*** by Michael Weber

For students at a Grade 9 reading level:
- ***Washington: The Indispensable Man,*** by James Thomas Flexner

READING SUPPORT FROM JAMESTOWN EDUCATION

- *Timed Readings Plus in Social Studies* helps students increase their reading rate and fluency while maintaining comprehension. The 400-word passages are similar to those found on state and national assessments.
- *Reading in the Content Area: Social Studies* concentrates on six essential reading skills that help students better comprehend what they read. The book includes 754 high-interest nonfiction passages written at increasing levels of difficulty.
- *Reading Fluency* helps students read smoothly, accurately, and expressively.
- *Jamestown's Reading Improvement,* by renowned reading expert Edward Fry, focuses on helping build your students' comprehension, vocabulary, and skimming and scanning skills.
- *Critical Reading Series* provides high-interest books, each written at three reading levels.

To order these products, call Glencoe at 1-800-334-7344.

KEY for Using the Teacher Wraparound Edition

Use this key to help you identify the different types of prompts found in the Teacher Wraparound Edition.

R **Reading Strategies** activities help you teach reading skills and vocabulary.

C **Critical Thinking** strategies help students apply and extend what they have learned.

U **Universal Access** activities provide differentiated instruction for students learning to speak English, along with suggestions for teaching various types of learners.

S **Skill Practice** strategies help students practice historical analysis and geography skills.

W **Writing Support** activities provide writing opportunities to help students comprehend the text.

Teaching strategies and activities have been coded for ability level appropriateness.

AL Activities for students working above grade level
OL Activities for students working on grade level
BL Activities for students working below grade level
EL Activities for English Learners

FOCUS

History–Social Science Standards

In this chapter, the following standards will be covered:

US8.2 Students analyze the political principles underlying the U.S. Constitution and compare the enumerated and implied powers of the federal government.

US8.3 Students understand the foundation of the American political system and the ways in which citizens participate in it.

More About the Photo

The National Archives and Records Administration is a federal agency that helps preserve the nation's history by overseeing the management of all federal records. The documents of our government—the Declaration of Independence, the Constitution, and the Bill of Rights—are housed in the original building in Washington, D.C.

TEACH

The Big Ideas

As you begin teaching each section, use these questions and activities to focus on the Big Ideas.

Chapter 4 The Constitution

▼ The National Archives, Washington, D.C.

NATIONAL GEOGRAPHIC **Where & When?**

1785 — 1790 — 1795

1787 The Constitution is signed

1789 John Jay becomes first Supreme Court Chief Justice

1792 President Washington vetoes a bill from Congress for first time

Section 1

Goals of the Constitution

Essential Question: How does the U.S. Constitution reflect the goals of American society? *(Students may say that it describes the basic rights of U.S. citizens and outlines the goals of the U.S. government.)* Tell students that this section discusses the importance of the U.S. Constitution. OL

Section 2

The Federal Government

Essential Question: What was the structure of the national government under the Articles of Confederation? *(it had only a legislature, the Congress)* How did that national government perform after the Revolution? *(Many leaders thought it was too weak.)* Explain that in this section students will learn how the organization

History Online

Chapter Overview Visit ca.hss.glencoe.com for a preview of Chapter 4.

The Big Ideas

Section 1 Goals of the Constitution

A constitution reflects the values and goals of the society that creates it. For more than 200 years, the Constitution has provided the framework for the United States government and has helped preserve the basic rights of American citizens.

Section 2 The Federal Government

Political ideas and major events shape how people form governments. The Constitution provided for a United States government that was set up as three equal branches with different responsibilities.

Section 3 Citizens' Rights and Responsibilities

Citizen participation is essential to the foundation and preservation of the U.S. political system. Citizens of the United States have certain duties and responsibilities that help maintain our form of government.

View the Chapter 4 video in the Glencoe Video Program.

FOLDABLES™ Study Organizer

Know-Want-Learn Make this foldable to determine what you already know, to identify what you want to know, and to record what you learn about the Constitution of the United States.

Step 1 Fold a sheet of paper into thirds from top to bottom.

Step 2 Turn the paper horizontally, unfold, and label the three columns as shown.

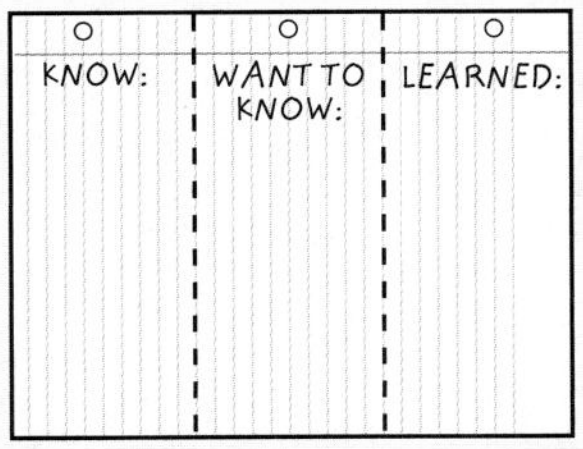

Reading and Writing Before you read the chapter, write what you already know about the Constitution in the "Know" column. Write what you want to know about the Constitution in the "Want to Know" column. Then, as you read the chapter, write what you learn in the "Learned" column. Check to see if you have learned what you wanted to know (from the second column).

and function of the federal government is influenced by political ideas and events. **AL**

Section 3

Citizens' Rights and Responsibilities

Essential Question: What is one way that citizens can participate in government? *(Answers may include voting, taking part in political campaigns, and working for particular causes.)* Tell students that in this section they will read about certain rights and responsibilities that U.S. citizens have that help maintain our form of government. **OL**

Cultural Perspectives

The Framers of the Constitution extended citizenship rights only to white male landowners. Discuss with students the reasons the Framers did not extend citizenship rights to other groups such as colonial women, Native Americans, and African Americans. Ask students: what might members of these groups have felt or said about the new Constitution? Next, organize students into small groups and have them list ways that some of the specific citizens' rights in the Bill of Rights were not extended to these categories of people. Students may wish to use a three-column table to arrange their examples. Then have students read the Constitution (pages 246–267) and include in their tables the amendments to the Constitution that rectify these situations.

History Online

Go to ca.hss.glencoe.com for student activities, lesson plans, and links to additional Web resources about the Constitution.

FOLDABLES™ Study Organizer — Dinah Zike's Foldables

Purpose Have students use their foldables to assess what they have learned about the Constitution. If they have learning goals in the "Want to Know" column that were not met, encourage them to research the answers. **OL**

Why It's Important

Summarizing Information The ability to accurately and concisely summarize information is a valuable learning skill. Workers frequently have to use the skill in many different situations; for example, they may need to recount an incident to a supervisor or summarize the findings of a report. Point out to students that in school, writing summaries can be an effective way of reviewing content.

1 Learn It!

Two keys to writing summaries are to identify the essential details and to ignore the nonessential ones. Give students this situation: You are working on a computer, but the program has frozen. You call a customer support number to ask for help. **Ask:** **Which of the following details are essential to tell the support worker and which are not:**

- Computer type and operating system *(essential)*
- Program you were using *(essential)*
- Picture used for wallpaper *(not essential)*
- What you were doing when the computer froze *(essential)*
- Your password to use a Web browser *(not essential)* OL

CA 8LS1.3

Chapter 4

Get Ready to Read

Summarizing Information

READING SKILL

1 Learn It!

Summarizing helps you clarify key points in your own words. You can summarize what you have read by pausing and restating the main ideas of the text. Then answer the key questions *Who? What? Where? When? Why?* and *How?* Read the information under "Major Principles" on page 221. Work with a partner to summarize the main points of what you read.

Did your summary include some of these details?

- **The Constitution rests on seven major principles.**
- **Those principles are: popular sovereignty, republicanism, limited government, federalism, separation of powers, checks and balances, and individual rights.**

Reading Tip

As you read, take note of the sections that you may want to go over again.

216

READING STRATEGY — MODELING

Help students learn how to summarize information by modeling the skill for them. Take a passage from the chapter, such as the material on checks and balances on page 223 and demonstrate how to summarize it by breaking it down into the essential parts:

- Definition of checks and balances
- Goal of checks and balances
- Examples: veto and override; judicial review; power of appointment BL

Practice It!

With a partner, read the paragraph below. Then read the sections titled "Rights of American Citizens" on page 235 and "Citizen Participation" on page 236. Work together to make a list summarizing what you read. As you discuss your conclusions, see if you can answer the questions that follow.

It is the combination of rights, responsibilities, and duties that characterize what it means to be a citizen of a free democratic society. As citizens, we are free to exercise our rights. In return we are expected to fulfill certain duties and responsibilities.

Read to Write

Choose two editorials in your local newspaper. Read them carefully and then summarize each writer's main point.

- **What is a citizen?**
- **What are the rights citizens hold?**
- **What is the difference between duty and responsibility?**
- **What is one of the most important responsibilities of citizens?**

Citizens take part in a town hall meeting. ▶

Apply It!

As you read this chapter, keep track of the main ideas of each section.

CHAPTER 4 Get Ready to Read

Practice It!

Have students apply the skill by writing a summary of a section in a chapter they studied earlier. Remind them to include essential details only. OL

Apply It!

Tell students to write a summary of a movie or television show that they saw recently. Have them exchange summaries with someone not familiar with the movie or show. After partners read the summaries, have the summary writers ask them one or two questions about key features of the movie or show that they think are answerable and record whether the reader answered them correctly. If the respondent could not answer correctly, have students check their own summary to see if the information is missing and, if so, revise the summary. OL

READING STRATEGY — MONITORING COMPREHENSION

Writing summaries and then comparing them to the original is an excellent way for students to monitor their comprehension of content. Have students summarize a subsection of the chapter and hand their summary to a partner. Ask each student to compare the partner's summary to the original text, noting any main ideas or key details that are missing and any nonessential details that are included. Then have the two partners review their findings so they can see how accurate their summaries were. OL CA 8RC2.4

Use Reading Skills Activity 4 in the **Chapter 4 Resource Book** for more practice with summarizing information.

FOCUS

BELLRINGER
SKILLBUILDER ACTIVITY

Project **Daily Focus Skills Transparency 4–1** and have students answer the question.

Guide to Reading

Preteaching Vocabulary: Use the Vocabulary PuzzleMaker CD-ROM to create crossword and word search puzzles.

Answers to Graphic: popular sovereignty, republicanism, limited government, federalism, separation of powers, checks and balances, individual rights

Unpacking the Standards

After reading the section, students will be able to:

- Identify the goals of the Constitution as set out in the Preamble.
- Explain each of the seven principles of the Constitution.
- Discuss how the Constitution is still alive today.

Section 1

Goals of the Constitution

Guide to Reading

History Social Science Standards

US8.2 Students analyze the political principles underlying the U.S. Constitution and compare the enumerated and implied powers of the federal government.

US8.3 Students understand the foundation of the American political system and the ways in which citizens participate in it.

Looking Back, Looking Ahead

You read that the last of the 13 states ratified the Constitution in 1790. The ratifying states had closely examined the goals of and the principles behind the document creating the new government.

Focusing on the Main Ideas

- The Preamble to the Constitution describes six goals for the United States government. *(page 219)*
- The Constitution is based on seven major principles. *(page 221)*
- The Framers wrote the Constitution so that it could be altered or adapted to meet changing needs. *(page 224)*

Content Vocabulary

Preamble
popular sovereignty (SAH • vuhrn • tee)
republicanism
federalism
enumerated powers (ih • NYOO • muh • RAYT • ehd)
reserved powers
concurrent powers (kuhn • KUHR • uhnt)
amendment
implied powers (ihm • PLYD)
judicial review

Academic Vocabulary

function (FUHNG • shuhn)
cooperate (koh • AH • puh • RAYT)
anticipate (an • TIH • suh • PAYT)

Reading Strategy

Organizing Information Use a diagram like the one below to list the seven major principles on which the Constitution is based.

NATIONAL GEOGRAPHIC Who & When?

1785 | 1795 | 1805

1786 Shays's Rebellion causes concerns with "domestic tranquility"

1787 Gouverneur Morris writes the Preamble to the Constitution

1803 President Thomas Jefferson increases powers of the presidency

Thomas Jefferson

SECTION RESOURCES

Print Material
- Reproducible Lesson Plan 4–1*
- Daily Lesson and Discussion Notes 4–1
- Guided Reading Activity 4–1
- Reading Essentials and Study Guide 4–1
- Active Reading Note-Taking Guide 4–1
- Section Quiz 4–1

Transparencies
- Daily Focus Skills Transparency 4–1
- Section Graphic Organizer Transparency 4–1
- California Standards Practice Transparencies

Technology
- Interactive Tutor Self-Assessment CD-ROM
- Exam*View*® Pro Testmaker CD-ROM
- Presentation Plus! CD-ROM

*Available on TeacherWorks™

US8.2.2 Analyze the Articles of Confederation and the Constitution and the success of each in implementing the ideals of the Declaration of Independence. US8.3.3 Enumerate the advantages of a common market among the states as foreseen in and protected by the Constitution's clauses on interstate commerce, common coinage, and full-faith and credit.

Goals of the Constitution

R1 **Main Idea** **The Preamble to the Constitution describes six goals for the United States government.**

Reading Connection Just as you often determine goals when working on a project, the creators of the Constitution thought about what they wanted the new government to do for the nation's people. Read to find out the goals set by the Constitution's Framers for the United States government.

An American Story

On September 17, 1787, the delegates to the Constitutional Convention signed the document. When it came Benjamin Franklin's turn to sign, the elderly leader had to be helped forward in order to write his name on the parchment. Tears streamed down his face as he signed. He looked at the carving of the sun on the back of George Washington's chair. "I have often looked at that sun behind the president of the convention without being able to tell whether it was rising or setting," he said, "but now, I have the happiness to know that it is a rising and not a setting sun." C

The rising sun that Franklin spoke of was the new government of a very young country, the United States of America.

R2 **The Preamble** The **Preamble,** or introduction, to the Constitution, written by Gouverneur Morris, begins "We the People." It reflects the basic principle of the new American government—the right of the people to govern themselves. The Preamble also lists six goals for the United States government:

> **"... to form a more perfect Union, establish Justice, insure domestic Tranquility, provide for the common defence [defense], promote the general Welfare, and secure the Blessings of Liberty to ourselves and our Posterity..."**

These goals guided the Constitution's Framers as they created the new government. They remain as important today as they were when the Constitution was written.

History Makers

Promoting the General Welfare

Under the Articles of Confederation, the United States had faced difficulties with trade and commerce. Trying to gain an economic advantage, states interfered with one another's trade through tariffs and other means. Under the goal of promoting the general welfare, the Constitution allowed the new government to regulate commerce. The United States became a large common market in which trade barriers between the states were eliminated, and individual states were prohibited from acting as separate nations.

According to the Constitution, the states were required to respect the laws and regulations of all the other states, a concept known as full faith and credit. They could in no way impede trade and commerce between one another. The national government could also develop a common currency to encourage trade. This clause led to the monetary system you use today. The paper bills and coins you carry can be used anywhere in the United States without question.

TEACH

R1 Reading Strategy

Setting a Purpose Advise students to turn the Main Idea into a question to give themselves a purpose for reading this subsection. BL

C Critical Thinking

Analyzing Information
Ask: Which kind of sun do people see as a symbol of hope and promise, a rising or setting one? Why? *(rising; because it is the beginning of a new day, which can bring a solution to problems)* How does that connect to Franklin's statement? *(He's saying that he sees the new Constitution as a hopeful thing for the country.)* OL

R2 Reading Strategy

Using Word Parts
Ask: What words do you know that use the word part *pre-*? *(predict, prepare, preview)* What does it mean? *(to come before)* What does that suggest about a preamble? *(It comes at the beginning of the Constitution)* OL

Resources for page 219

Refer to ***The Living Constitution*** for student activities and information related to the Constitution.

Economics and History Activity 4

History Makers

Ask volunteers who have traveled from one state to another to raise their hands. **Ask:** How difficult was it to cross state lines? *(Students should describe no difficulties.)* Did you or your parents buy anything in the other state? Were there any difficulties in doing so? *(There should be no difficulties.)* Would the situation have been different if each state had its own money? Why or why not? *(Students should see that it would be more difficult to make purchases because money would have to be converted to a different currency.)* OL

Biography

TEACH

R Reading Strategy

Sequencing Information Have students make a time line that includes both milestones in Morris's life and important events in American history. OL CA CS2.

U Universal Access

Intrapersonal Have students take the role of Morris as he tried to decide whether to support the Revolution. Mention that some of his family did join the revolutionary cause with him; half-brother Lewis Morris was one of the signers of the Declaration of Independence. Have students write a diary entry in which Morris explains his reasons for backing the Revolution. AL CA 8WA2.1

W Writing Support

Expository Writing Inform students that when prominent people die, newspapers publish obituaries summarizing the person's life and achievements. Have students work in pairs to write a brief obituary of Morris. OL CA 8WA2.1

Biography

US8.2.4 Describe the political philosophy underpinning the Constitution as specified in the *Federalist Papers* (authored by James Madison, Alexander Hamilton, and John Jay) and the role of such leaders as Madison, George Washington, Roger Sherman, Gouverneur Morris, and James Wilson in the writing and ratification of the Constitution.

GOUVERNEUR MORRIS

1752–1816 R

A brilliant speaker and writer, Gouverneur Morris was a leader during the American Revolution and the Constitutional Convention. As a young man, Morris devoted himself to education, graduating from King's College in 1768, at the age of 16, and earning a degree in law in 1771.

Morris joined the struggle for American independence although his family supported the Loyalist cause. While his brother served as an officer in the British army, Morris joined the American military despite a physical handicap that left him without the full use of his right arm. Later he lost his left leg in an accident. U

In 1778 Morris became one of the youngest delegates to the Continental Congress. At Valley Forge, he had seen "an army of skeletons . . . naked, starved, sick, discouraged," and worked to improve conditions for the soldiers. In 1781 Morris served as an assistant to the Minister of Finance. He developed the system of decimal coinage, or the addition of pennies, nickels, dimes, and quarters to the American dollar.

"We the people of the United States . . ."

—from the ***Preamble to the U.S. Constitution***

W In 1787 Morris joined the Constitutional Convention as a delegate from Pennsylvania. He was an opponent of slavery and tried to get the Constitutional Convention to ban it. He wrote the inspiring Preamble to the Constitution and helped write and edit much of the rest of the document. Because of his belief in nationalism, Morris changed the first line of the Constitution from "We the people of the states of New Hampshire, Massachusetts, . . ." with all 13 states listed, to "We the people of the United States." James Madison said of Morris: "A better choice [to rework the Constitution] could not have been made."

Then and Now

Although physically impaired, Morris made a significant impact on American history. Can you identify other local or national leaders like him?

Answers and Additional Support

Then and Now

Have students verify their answers by conducting research on the persons they name. Prominent national leaders who have had handicaps include President Franklin Delano Roosevelt, who was paralyzed by polio and former Senator Bob Dole of Kansas, who lost the use of one arm due to wounds suffered in World War II.

More Skill Practice

Analyzing Primary Sources Ask: What is the significance of the change Morris made to the opening sentence? *(The change to the opening sentence demonstrates Morris's belief in the dominance of the national government over the state governments.)* AL CA HR3.

US8.2.2 Analyze the Articles of Confederation and the Constitution and the success of each in implementing the ideals of the Declaration of Independence. US8.2.7 Describe the principles of federalism, dual sovereignty, separation of powers, checks and balances, the nature and purpose of majority rule, and the ways in which the American idea of constitutionalism preserves individual rights.

To Form a More Perfect Union Under the Articles of Confederation, the states **functioned** like independent nations, often disagreeing on defense and finances. To form "a more perfect Union," the Framers believed the states needed to agree to operate as a single country and **cooperate** on major issues.

To Establish Justice For the Framers, treating each citizen equally was a fundamental principle. The Constitution provides a national system of courts to protect the people's rights and to hear cases involving violations of federal law and disputes among the states.

R1 **To Insure Domestic Tranquility** The violent protests of Shays's Rebellion in 1786 shocked Americans. The Constitution seeks to "insure domestic Tranquility"—that is, to keep peace among the people.

To Provide for the Common Defense Under the Articles of Confederation, the nation's defense depended on state militias. The Constitution gives the federal government the power to maintain armed forces to protect the country and its citizens from attack.

To Promote the General Welfare The Declaration of Independence states that the purpose of government is to promote "Life, Liberty, and the pursuit of Happiness" for the people of the nation. The Constitution includes ways to "promote the general Welfare"—or well-being—of the people by maintaining order, protecting individual liberties, regulating commerce and bankruptcies, and promoting science and technology by granting patents.

R2 **To Secure the Blessings of Liberty** The Framers believed that preserving liberty should be a major goal of the Constitution. The Constitution guarantees that no American's basic rights will be taken away now or for posterity (generations not yet born).

Reading Check **Analyze** What is the purpose of the Preamble?

Major Principles

Main Idea **The Constitution is based on seven major principles.**

Reading Connection What are principles? What principles do you live by? Read to discover how the basic principles of the Constitution have remained the same for more than 200 years.

The principles outlined in the Constitution were the Framers' solution to the problems of a representative government. The Constitution rests on seven major principles: (1) popular sovereignty, (2) republicanism, (3) limited government, (4) federalism, (5) separation of powers, (6) checks and balances, and (7) individual rights. C

Major Principles of the Constitution

Popular Sovereignty	People are the source of the government's power.
Republicanism	People elect their political representatives.
Limited Government	The Constitution limits the actions of government by specifically listing powers it does and does not have.
Federalism	In this government system, power is divided between national and state governments.
Separation of Powers	Each of the three branches of government has its own responsibilities.
Checks and Balances	Each branch of government holds some control over the other two branches.
Individual Rights	Basic liberties and rights of all citizens are guaranteed in the Bill of Rights.

U

Understanding Charts

The principles outlined in the Constitution were the Framers' solution to the complex problems presented by a representative government.

Analyze What is the relationship between checks and balances and separation of powers?

R1 Reading Strategy

Understanding Vocabulary Help students learn the term by understanding each word in the compound. **Ask:** What does *domestic* mean? *(within a country; not foreign)* What does *tranquil* mean? *(peaceful)* OL

R2 Reading Strategy

Scaffolding—Connecting **Ask:** What are the "blessings of liberty" to you? Discuss what students treasure about the freedoms Americans enjoy. OL

This READING SKILL was introduced in Chapter 3.

C Critical Thinking

Analyzing Primary Sources Organize the class into seven groups, and assign each group one of the principles of the Constitution. Have them locate a part of the Constitution that demonstrates the principle. Ask each group to report their findings to the class, explaining how the section they identified shows the principle at work. OL CA HR3.

U Universal Access

Special Education Pair children with visual disabilities with sighted students. Ask the latter to describe the chart on this page and others in the chapter to their partner. OL

Reading Check

Answer: to list six goals for the new U.S. government

Resources for page 221

Academic Vocabulary Activity 4

More Skill Practice

Historical and Social Sciences Analysis Skill **Ask:** Are there any other goals you think the Framers of the Constitution should have included? Why? Would the Framers have agreed with that goal, or is the need for it a result of changing interpretation of history? AL CA HI5.

Understanding Charts

Answer: Although each government branch has its own responsibilities, a system of checks and balances keeps the legislative, executive, and judicial branches from becoming too powerful.

R1 Reading Strategy

Taking Notes Point out that this page has several key terms. Suggest that to remember their meanings, students take notes on each one. BL

R2 Reading Strategy

Categorizing Information
Ask: Does the power to take each action belong to the federal or state government or is it shared?

- Make a treaty with another country *(federal)*
- Stage a vote for members of Congress *(state)*
- Create taxes *(shared)* OL

Review The Big Idea

Review the Big Idea for this section, "A constitution reflects the values and goals of the society that creates it." **Ask:** How does the division of powers between the states and the federal government reflect compromise? *(Some people wanted a very strong central government; others wanted very strong state governments. This compromise gave some powers to each.)* OL

Answers and Additional Support

Popular Sovereignty The Declaration of Independence states that governments derive their powers from "the consent of the governed." The opening words of the Constitution, "We the people," reinforce this idea of **popular sovereignty**—or authority of the people. R1

Republicanism Under **republicanism**, voters hold sovereign power. The people choose their representatives in government. Today, the terms *republic* and *representative democracy* mean the same thing: a system of limited government where the people are the ultimate source of governmental power.

Limited Government The Framers agreed that the nation needed strong central authority but feared misuse of power. By creating a limited government, they made certain the government would have only those powers granted by the people.

Article I of the Constitution states the powers that the government has as well as the powers that it does not have. Other limits on government appear in the Bill of Rights, which guarantees certain rights and liberties to the people. Limited government can be described as the "rule of law." No people or groups are above the law.

Federalism Under the Constitution, states gave up some independence. They could no longer print their own money or tax imports from other states. Nevertheless, each state governed itself much as it had in the past. This system, in which the power to govern is shared between the national government and the states, is called the federal system, or **federalism**. This system allows each state to deal with its needs in its own way. At the same time, it lets the states act together to deal with matters that affect all Americans.

The Constitution defines three types of government powers. **Enumerated powers** (ih • NYOO • muh • RAYT • ehd) belong only to the federal government. These include the power to coin money, regulate interstate and foreign trade, maintain the armed forces, and create federal courts. The powers retained by the states are known as **reserved powers**. They include such rights as the power to establish schools, pass marriage laws, and regulate trade within a state. Although reserved powers are not listed specifically in the Constitution, the Tenth Amendment says that all powers not specifically granted to the federal government "are reserved to the States." R2

The third set of powers defined by the Constitution are **concurrent powers** (kuhn • KUHR • uhnt)—powers shared by the state and federal governments. Among these powers are the right to raise taxes, borrow money, and provide for public welfare.

When conflicts arise between state law and federal law, the Constitution declares that the Constitution is "the supreme Law of the Land." Conflicts between state law and federal law must be settled in a federal court.

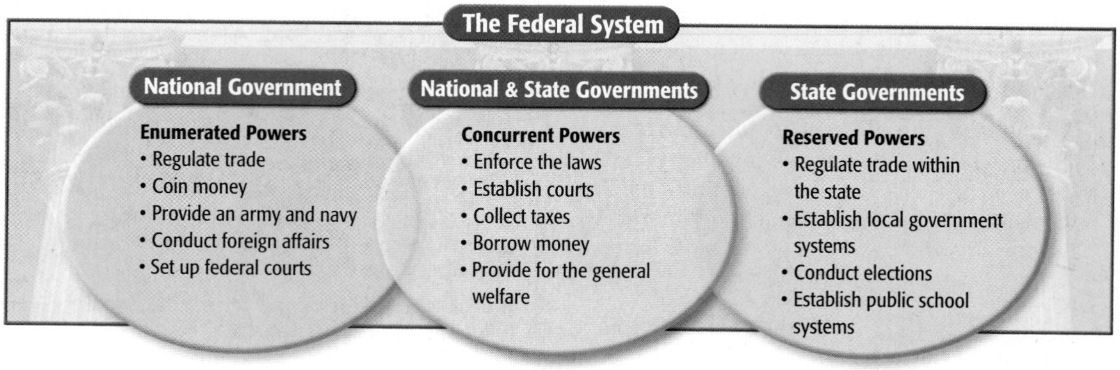

More Skill Practice

Historical and Social Sciences Analysis Skill **Ask:** Why were the Framers concerned about government abuse of power? *(They believed that King George III had abused his power to take away their rights before the Revolution.)* OL

CA CS1.

R1 **Separation of Powers** To prevent any single group or institution in government from gaining too much authority, the Framers divided the federal government into three branches. The three branches are the legislative, the executive, and the judicial. Each branch has its own functions and powers. The legislative branch, Congress, makes the laws. The executive branch, headed by the president, carries out the laws. The judicial branch, consisting of the Supreme Court and other federal courts, interprets and applies the laws.

Checks and Balances As an additional safeguard, the Framers established a system of R2 checks and balances. Under this system, each branch of government can check, or limit, the power of the other branches. For example, the legislative branch, Congress, can pass a law. Then the executive branch, headed by the president, can reject the law by vetoing it. However, Congress can override, or reverse, the president's veto if two-thirds of the members of both houses vote again to approve the law.

Over the years, the Supreme Court has acquired the power to determine the meaning of the Constitution. The Supreme Court can also declare that a law or a government policy U goes against the Constitution. In doing so, the Court provides a check on the powers of Congress and the president. Judicial decisions—those made by the courts—can be overruled by amending the Constitution. The president and the Senate provide a check on the judicial branch through their power to appoint and approve federal judges. Congress can also change a law so that it no longer conflicts with the Constitution, or it can amend the Constitution.

Individual Rights The Bill of Rights became part of the Constitution in 1791. These first 10 **amendments,** or changes to the Constitution, protect basic liberties and rights that you may W take for granted—including freedom of speech, freedom of the press, freedom of assembly, and freedom of religion.

The 17 amendments that follow the Bill of Rights expand the rights of Americans and adjust certain provisions of the Constitution. Included among them are amendments that abolish slavery, define citizenship, guarantee the right to vote to all citizens, authorize an income tax, and set a two-term limit on the presidency.

Reading Check **Explain** What is popular sovereignty?

The Bill of Rights

1	Guarantees freedom of religion, speech, assembly, and press, and the right of people to petition the government
2	Protects the rights of states to maintain a militia and of citizens to bear arms
3	Restricts quartering of troops in private homes
4	Protects against "unreasonable searches and seizures"
5	Assures the right not to be deprived of "life, liberty, or property, without due process of law"
6	Guarantees the right to a speedy and public trial by an impartial jury
7	Assures the right to a jury trial in cases involving the common law (the law established by previous court decisions)
8	Protects against excessive bail, or cruel and unusual punishment
9	Provides that people's rights are not restricted to those specified in the first eight amendments
10	Restates the Constitution's principle of federalism by providing that powers not granted to the national government nor prohibited to the states are reserved to the states and to the people

Understanding Charts

The Bill of Rights protects many of the basic liberties we expect as Americans today.

Analyze Which of these amendments appear to be responses to British abuses before the Revolution?

R1 Reading Strategy

Understanding Vocabulary Give students the following memory aid to help them learn the responsibilities of the three branches:

- The *legislative* branch makes laws
- The *executive* branch *executes* laws
- The *judicial* branch *judges* laws BL

R2 Reading Strategy

Understanding Vocabulary The word *check* comes from the Persian language, and is related to the word *shah*, the name for the ruler of Persia. BL

U Universal Access

Visual/Spatial Have students create a graphic organizer to show how the three powers of government are separated and how each can use the system of checks and balances to limit the power of another. AL

W Writing Support

Research Reports Writing Have students read on page 235 about the Virginia Statute for Religious Freedom written by Thomas Jefferson. Students should find out when, where, and why it was written and what influence it had on the First Amendment. Have them write an essay reporting their findings. AL CA H12.

CA 8WA2.3

Reading Check

Answer: the idea that the people have the ultimate authority

More Skill Practice

Historical and Social Sciences Analysis Skill **Ask:** How many amendments in the Bill of Rights have to do with citizens' rights in court? Which are they? *(five of the ten; Fourth, Fifth, Sixth, Seventh, Eighth)* Why are there so many on this issue? *(The Framers were very concerned about having a just court system.)* OL

CA HR3.

Understanding Charts

Answer: Students may answer the First through the Seventh.

R1 Reading Strategy

Academic Vocabulary Have students read the sentence containing the word *anticipated.* Then ask a student to define the word. OL

W Writing Support

Expository Writing Have students choose one of the approved amendments to the Constitution and learn about why it was proposed and ratified. Then have them take the role of a citizen living at the time it was being debated. Ask students to write a brief speech arguing in favor of the amendment. AL CA 8WA2.4

R2 Reading Strategy

Reading Primary Sources
Ask: How does the wording of this clause lead to differences in how the Constitution is interpreted? *(People can disagree over what is "necessary and proper.")* AL CA H15.

U Universal Access

English Learners Explain that things that are implied are not directly stated but suggested. EL

US8.2.6 Enumerate the powers of government set forth in the Constitution and the fundamental liberties ensured by the Bill of Rights. **US8.2.7** Describe the principles of federalism, dual sovereignty, separation of powers, checks and balances, the nature and purpose of majority rule, and the ways in which the American idea of constitutionalism preserves individual rights.

A Living Constitution

Main Idea **The Framers wrote the Constitution so that it could be altered or adapted to meet changing needs.**

Reading Connection How do you think the Constitution and our government have changed in the 200 years since they were created? Read to find out how the Framers planned for changes to be possible.

Two years after the Constitutional Convention, Benjamin Franklin wrote, "Our Constitution is in actual operation; everything appears to promise that it will last; but in this world nothing is certain but death and taxes."

Despite Franklin's uncertainty about the future of the nation's Constitution, it is still very much alive today. The Constitution has survived because it allows the government to deal with matters the Framers never **anticipated**—such as regulating nuclear power plants. In addition the Constitution contains a provision for amending—changing or adding to—the document.

Amending the Constitution The Framers intentionally made the amendment process difficult to discourage minor or frequent changes being made. Although more than 9,000 amendments have been proposed since 1788, only 27 of them have become part of the Constitution.

An amendment may be proposed in two ways: by the vote of two-thirds of both houses of Congress or by two-thirds of the state legislatures asking for a special convention on the amendment. Ratification of an amendment requires approval by three-fourths of the states.

Interpreting the Constitution The Constitution includes two provisions that give Congress the power to act as needed to meet changing conditions. The first of these provisions is what is known as the "elastic clause" (Article I, Section 8). It directs Congress to "make all Laws which shall be necessary and proper" for executing all the powers of government. Congress has interpreted this clause to mean that it has certain **implied powers** (ihm • PLYD), meaning powers not specifically defined in the Constitution.

How the Constitution is Amended

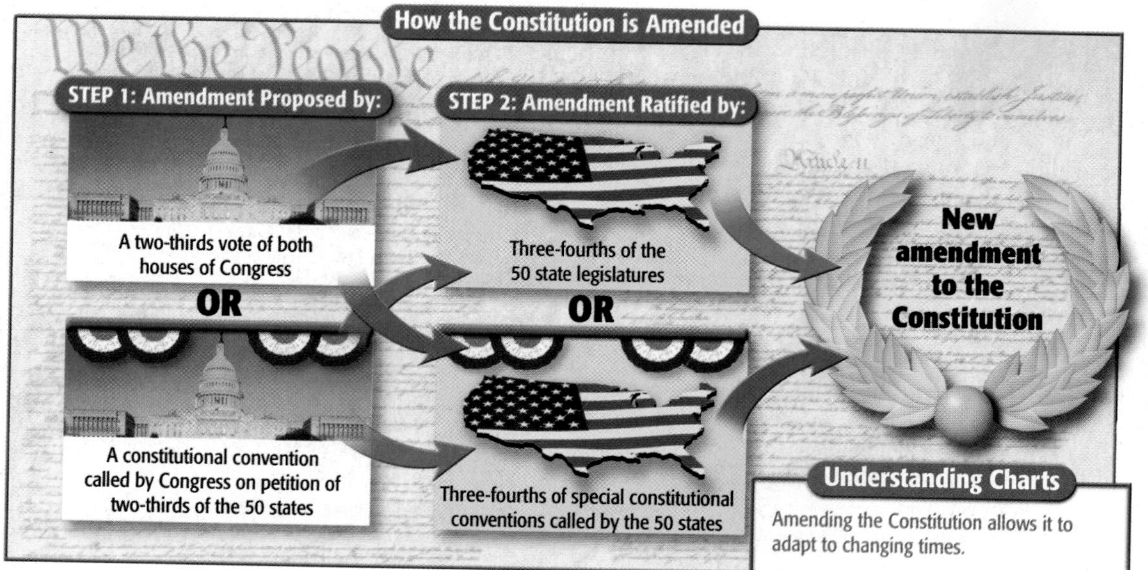

Understanding Charts

Amending the Constitution allows it to adapt to changing times.

Analyze What role do the states play in the amendment process?

Answers and Additional Support

Resources for page 224

Universal Access Activity 4

Understanding Charts

Answer: The approval of three-fourths of the states, either through their legislatures or special conventions, are needed for an amendment to become final.

The second provision used to expand congressional authority, the "commerce clause" (Article I, Section 8), gives Congress the power to "regulate Commerce with foreign Nations, and among the several States." Congress has used this clause to expand its powers into a number of areas, including regulation of the airline industry, radio and television, and nuclear energy.

Powers of the Presidency The Constitution describes the role and the powers of the president in general terms. This has allowed the executive branch to extend its powers. In 1803, for example, President Thomas Jefferson approved a treaty with France that enabled the United States to buy an enormous tract of land.

The Courts The role of the judicial branch has also grown as powers implied in the Constitution have been put into practice. In 1803 Chief Justice John Marshall expanded the powers of the Supreme Court by striking down an act of Congress in the case of *Marbury* v. *Madison*. In that decision, the Court defined its right to determine whether a law violates the Constitution. Although not mentioned in the Constitution, **judicial review** has become a major power of the judicial branch.

The process of amending the Constitution and applying its principles in new areas helps keep our government strong and functioning well. In 1974 Barbara Jordan, an African American member of Congress and a constitutional scholar, spoke in ringing tones of her faith in the Constitution:

C

> **"But through the process of amendment, interpretation, and court decision I have finally been included in 'We, the people.'"**
>
> —Barbara Jordan, *Opening Statement to the House Judiciary Committee*

Reading Check **Explain** What are implied powers?

History Online
Study Central Need help understanding the goals of the Constitution? Visit ca.hss.glencoe.com and click on Study Central.

Section 1 Review

Reading Summary

Review the Main Ideas

- The six goals of the Constitution include providing for the common defense and promoting the general welfare of the people.
- The seven principles outlined in the Constitution were meant as solutions to the problems of a representative government.
- The amendment process allows for changes to the Constitution.

What Did You Learn?

1. What does *domestic tranquility* mean?
2. Explain the origin of judicial review.

Critical Thinking

3. **Compare** Re-create the diagram below and describe how each branch of government has power over another branch. CA HI2.

Branch	Power
Legislative	
Executive	
Judicial	

4. **Evaluate** What is the importance of federalism in the Constitution?
5. **The Big Ideas** How does the ability to interpret and amend the Constitution represent a compromise? CA HI1.
6. **Reading Summarizing Information** Write a short essay summarizing the major principles found in the Preamble. CA 8WS1.1

C Critical Thinking

Analyzing Primary Sources Explain that the word *amendment* comes from a Latin word meaning "to correct a fault." **Ask:** How does that origin connect to the point Jordan makes in this quotation? *(She believes that the Constitution needed to be fixed through amendments to include all Americans, regardless of race or gender.)* OL CA HI3.

ASSESS

Resources for pages 225

Use these resources to assess student mastery of section content.

- Section Quiz 4–1
- Interactive Tutor Self-Assessment CD-ROM

Reading Check

Answer: powers not specifically defined in the Constitution

History Online
Study Central provides summaries, interactive games, and online graphic organizers to help students review section content.

CLOSE

Summarizing Have students explain what features of the Constitution help make it a living document. OL

SECTION 1 REVIEW ANSWERS

Review questions reinforce content standards US8.2 and US8.3.

1. keeping peace among people
2. The Supreme Court, *Marbury* v. *Madison*, declared its right to determine whether a law violates the Constitution.
3. *legislative*—can override president's veto, approves appointments of judges; *executive*—can veto laws; appoints judges; *judiciary*—power of judicial review
4. Power is shared by federal and state governments
5. **The Big Ideas** Students may say that the Framers left the Constitution vague on some points so that they could agree on the document.
6. **Reading** Students' essays should explain each of the seven principles.

FOCUS

BELLRINGER
SKILLBUILDER ACTIVITY

Project **Daily Focus Skills Transparency 4–2** and have students answer the question.

Guide to Reading

Preteaching Vocabulary: Have students use the Glossary in the back of the book to find the definitions of each content vocabulary term.

Answers to Graphic: Responsibilities of Congress: make laws, control spending; Powers: can impeach officials; Senate acts as court of impeachment, ratifies treaties, approves appointments

Unpacking the Standards

After reading the section, students will be able to:

- Explain the powers of Congress and how Congress works.
- Discuss the roles of the President and how the executive branch works.
- Outline the structure of the courts and their role.

Section 2

The Federal Government

History Social Science Standards

US8.2 Students analyze the political principles underlying the U.S. Constitution and compare the enumerated and implied powers of the federal government.

Guide to Reading

Looking Back, Looking Ahead
You learned that separation of powers and checks and balances are important principles behind the Constitution. These principles are apparent in the organization of the federal government.

Focusing on the Main Ideas
- The legislative branch is responsible for making the nation's laws. *(page 227)*
- The executive branch carries out the laws made by the legislative branch. *(page 229)*
- The Supreme Court and a number of lesser courts make up the judicial branch. *(page 230)*

Content Vocabulary
appropriate (uh • PROH • pree • AYT)
impeach (ihm • PEECH)
constituent (kuhn • STIHCH • wuhnt)

Academic Vocabulary
monitor (MAH • nuh • tuhr)
intervene (IHN • tuhr • VEEN)
assume (uh • SOOM)

Reading Strategy
Summarizing Information Draw a diagram like the one below and list some of the responsibilities and powers of Congress.

NATIONAL GEOGRAPHIC Who & When?

1785 · 1795 · 1805

1789 John Jay becomes first chief justice

John Jay

1792 George Washington uses the first presidential veto

George Washington

1801 John Marshall becomes chief justice of the Supreme Court

John Marshall

SECTION RESOURCES

Print Material
- Reproducible Lesson Plan 4–2*
- Daily Lesson and Discussion Notes 4–2
- Guided Reading Activity 4–2
- Reading Essentials and Study Guide 4–2
- Active Reading Note-Taking Guide 4–2
- Section Quiz 4–2

Transparencies
- Daily Focus Skills Transparency 4–2
- Section Graphic Organizer Transparency 4–2
- California Standards Practice Transparencies

Technology
- Interactive Tutor Self-Assessment CD-ROM
- Exam*View*® Pro Testmaker CD-ROM
- Presentation Plus! CD-ROM

*Available on TeacherWorks™

US8.2.6 Enumerate the powers of government set forth in the Constitution and the fundamental liberties ensured by the Bill of Rights.

The Legislative Branch

R1 **Main Idea** **The legislative branch is responsible for making the nation's laws.**

Reading Connection Have you ever considered how important our country's laws are to the success of our nation? Read to find out about the branch of government that creates the laws for the United States.

Congress, the legislative branch of the government, makes the nation's laws. It also has the power to "lay and collect taxes" and to declare war. Congress has two houses, the House of Representatives and the Senate.

The House and Senate Today The House of Representatives has 435 voting members and five nonvoting delegates from the District of Columbia, Puerto Rico, Guam, American Samoa, and the Virgin Islands. The number of representatives from each state is determined by the state's population. Representatives, who must be at least 25 years old, serve 2-year terms.

The Senate consists of 100 senators, 2 from each state. Senators, who must be at least 30 years old, serve 6-year terms. The senators' terms are staggered, which means that one-third of the Senate seats come up for election every 2 years.

The Role of Congress Congress has two primary functions: to make the nation's laws and to control government spending. The government cannot spend any money unless Congress **appropriates** (uh • PROH • pree • AYTS), or sets aside, funds. R2 All tax and spending bills must originate in the House of Representatives and gain approval in both the House and the Senate before moving on to the president for signature.

Congress also serves as a watchdog over the executive branch, **monitoring** its actions and investigating possible abuses of power. The House of Representatives can **impeach** (ihm • PEECH), or bring formal charges against, any federal official it suspects of wrongdoing. R3 If an official is impeached, the Senate acts as a court and tries the accused official. Officials who are found guilty may be removed from office.

The Senate also holds certain special powers. Only the Senate can ratify treaties made by the president and confirm presidential appointments of federal officials, such as department heads, ambassadors, and federal judges.

All members of Congress have the responsibility of representing their **constituents** (kuhn • STIHCH • wuhntz), the people of their home states and districts. R4 As a constituent, you can expect your senators and representatives to promote and protect your state's interests as well as those of the nation.

Congress at Work Thousands of bills, or proposed laws, are introduced in Congress every year. Because individual members of Congress cannot possibly study all these bills carefully, both houses use committees of selected members to evaluate proposed legislation.

Standing committees are permanent committees in both the House and the Senate that specialize in a particular topic, such as agriculture, commerce, or veterans' affairs. These committees usually are broken down into subcommittees that focus on a particular aspect of a problem or issue. The House and the Senate sometimes form temporary select committees to deal with issues requiring special attention.

▲ Seal of the U.S. Congress

TEACH

R1 Reading Strategy

Organizing Information Have students create a chart of the section with the headings *Branch, Parts, Roles, How It Works*. Then, as they read, have them fill out the chart with information from the section. BL

R2 Reading Strategy

Scaffolding—Academic Vocabulary The word *funds* was introduced in Chapter 1, Section 2. Ask students to write a sentence using the word. OL

R3 Reading Strategy

Understanding Vocabulary Make sure students understand that to *impeach* is simply to levy charges. A Senate vote determines whether the person is guilty or acquitted. OL

R4 Reading Strategy

Understanding Vocabulary The word *constituents* is also used to refer to the parts that make up a whole. **Ask:** How is that meaning related to the meaning here? *(Each constituent is one among many people that a member of Congress represents.)* OL

Resources for page 227

Refer to ***The Living Constitution*** for student activities and information related to the Constitution.

Did You Know?

The office of Speaker of the House—the presiding officer for that chamber—appeared in the first Congress, which met in 1789. The first Speaker was Frederick Muhlenberg of Pennsylvania, who served in the post for just one Congress. The longest-serving speaker was Thomas P. "Tip" O'Neill, Jr., who was Speaker for ten years. One future president—James Knox Polk—served as Speaker.

R Reading Strategy

Categorizing Information

Ask: What is the difference between a joint committee and a conference committee? *(Joint committees are set up to address special issues. Conference committees are used to write compromise bills acceptable to both houses)* How are they similar? *(Both have members from both the House and the Senate.)* OL

C Critical Thinking

Comparing and Contrasting **Ask:** Why do you think the Framers wanted more than a simple majority to override a veto? *(Students may say to give the president an effective check on Congress.)* AL

Reading Check

Answer: A member of Congress proposes the bill; a committee studies it and prepares it for consideration by the full House and Senate; it is debated and approved in both houses; and the president signs it, or the president vetoes the bill and both House and Senate vote to override the veto.

Answers and Additional Support

The Lawmaking Process Occasionally the House and the Senate form joint committees with members from both houses. These committees meet to consider specific issues, such as the system of federal taxation. One type of joint committee, a conference committee, has a special function. If the House and the Senate pass different versions of a bill, a conference committee tries to work out a compromise bill that is acceptable to both houses. R

Committee Action When it receives a bill, a committee can reject it outright, "pigeonhole" it by setting it aside without reviewing it, or prepare it for consideration by the full House or Senate. While preparing bills, committees hold public hearings at which citizens can present arguments and documents supporting or opposing the bills.

Once a bill is approved by a committee in either house of Congress, it is sent to the full Senate or House for debate. After debate the bill may be passed, rejected, or returned to committee for further changes.

When both houses pass a bill, the bill goes to the president. If the president approves the bill and signs it, it becomes law. If the president vetoes the bill, it does not become law, unless Congress overrides (cancels) the presidential veto by a vote of two-thirds of the members in each house. The first congressional bill to be vetoed was in 1792 by President George Washington. It concerned the reassignment of districts for U.S. Representatives and was not overridden. C

Reading Check **Sequence** List the basic steps of how a bill becomes a law.

The American System of Checks and Balances

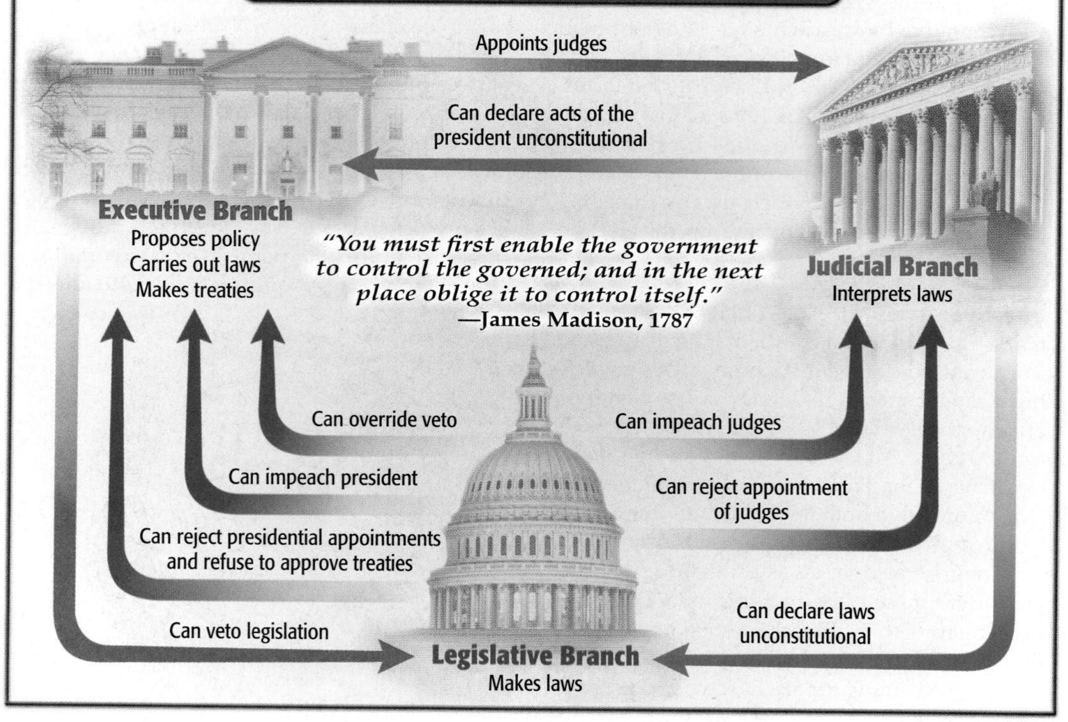

Did You Know?

George Washington vetoed two bills in his presidency. The record for presidential vetoes is held by Franklin D. Roosevelt, with 635. Second is Grover Cleveland, with 584 vetoes. Andrew Johnson had the highest proportion of his vetoes overridden (15 of 29).

US8.2.6 Enumerate the powers of government set forth in the Constitution and the fundamental liberties ensured by the Bill of Rights.

The Executive Branch

Main Idea **The executive branch carries out the laws made by the legislative branch.**

Reading Connection How important is the leader of a club or the captain of a team? What duties does he or she carry out? Read to find out the many duties held by the president of the United States.

The executive branch of government includes the president; the vice president; and various executive offices, departments, and agencies. The executive branch carries out the laws that Congress passes.

Chief Executive The president plays a number of different roles in government, each of which has specific powers and responsibilities. These roles include the nation's chief executive, chief diplomat, commander in chief, chief of state, and legislative leader.

As chief executive, the president is responsible for carrying out the nation's laws. Many executive departments and agencies assist the president in this job.

Chief Diplomat As chief diplomat, the president directs foreign policy, appoints ambassadors, and negotiates treaties with other nations. Treaties must be approved by a two-thirds vote of the Senate before they go into effect.

Commander in Chief As commander in chief of the armed forces, the president can use the military to **intervene** or offer assistance in crisis situations at home and around the world. The president cannot declare war; only Congress holds this power. The president can send troops to other parts of the world for up to 60 days but must notify Congress when doing so. The troops may remain longer only if Congress gives approval or declares war. The president may also use the military to control serious disorders in the nation.

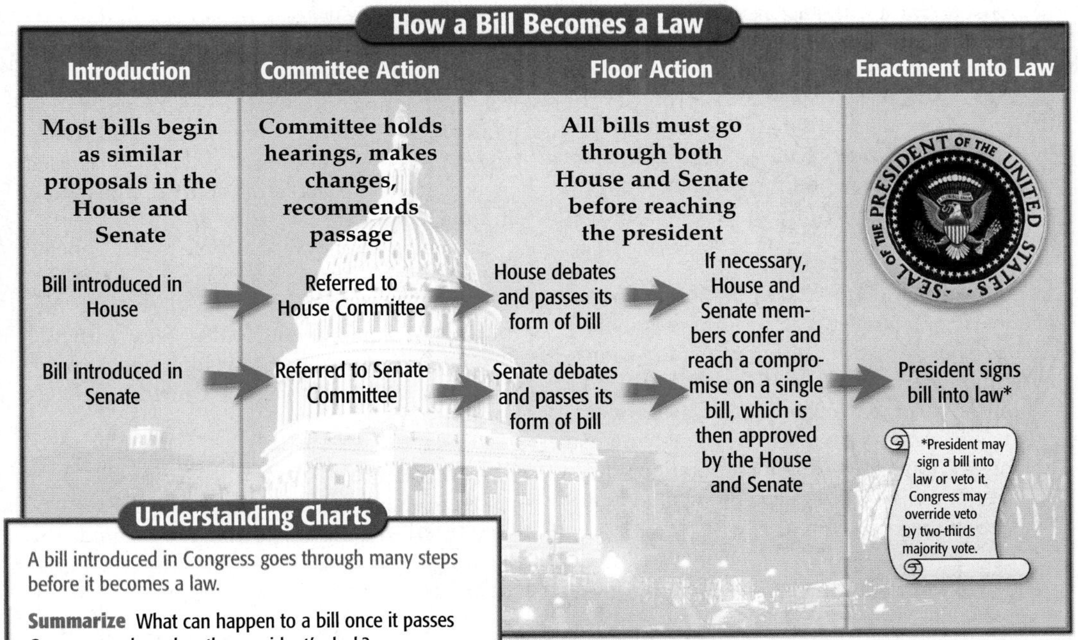

Understanding Charts

A bill introduced in Congress goes through many steps before it becomes a law.

Summarize What can happen to a bill once it passes Congress and reaches the president's desk?

U Universal Access

Below Grade Level Ask: What personal qualities does the head of a club or a team captain need to be an effective leader? *(Students may say good judgment, ability to communicate, ability to motivate others, ability to organize.)* Which of those personal qualities would a president need? What others would a president need? *(Students may say a president would also need the ability to understand complex issues and make decisions.)* BL

R Reading Strategy

Scaffolding—Previewing
Have students preview the headings before reading the section to determine what roles the president plays. Ask them to write down each role and then, as they read, write descriptions of that role. BL

This READING SKILL was introduced in Chapter 1.

C Critical Thinking

Identifying Central Issues
Ask: Why did the Framers give only to Congress, not the president, the power to declare war? *(So the representatives of the people make this important decision.)* Why do presidents have the power to commit troops for at least 60 days? *(to allow the president to act in an emergency)* AL

Understanding Charts

Answers: The president must sign the bill for it to become law and can veto it if he or she decides it is undesirable.

Ask: What happens if one chamber approves a bill but the other does not? *(It does not go to the president for signing.)* OL

More Skill Practice

Historical and Social Sciences Analysis Skill Ask: How many people does a member of the House represent? *(all those in one district)* How many people does a senator represent? *(all those in a state)* How many does the president represent? *(everyone in the country)* OL

U Universal Access

English Learners The word *lesser* may confuse some English learners, who are accustomed to *less* meaning "fewer than." Explain that the word can also be used to describe a person or object at a lower level than another person or object. EL

R Reading Strategy

Sequencing Information Have students create a brief time line highlighting the three steps in the development of the federal court system. BL

CA CS2.

C Critical Thinking

Making Inferences Ask: Why are there fewer appeals courts than district courts in the federal judicial system? *(Students may suggest that fewer are needed because all cases are not appealed or that appeals cases take less time to handle.)* OL

Reading Check

Answer: the heads of the executive branch departments, who help the president make decisions and set government policies

Answers and Additional Support

US8.2.6 Enumerate the powers of government set forth in the Constitution and the fundamental liberties ensured by the Bill of Rights.

Chief of State As chief of state, the president serves a symbolic role as the representative of all Americans. The president fulfills this role when receiving foreign ambassadors or heads of state, visiting foreign nations, or bestowing honors on Americans.

Legislative Leader The president serves as a legislative leader by proposing laws to Congress and working for their passage. In the annual State of the Union address, the president presents goals for legislation.

The Executive Branch at Work Many executive offices, departments, and independent agencies help the president carry out and enforce the nation's laws. The Executive Office of the President (EOP) is made up of individuals and agencies that directly assist the president. Presidents rely heavily on the EOP for advice and for gathering information.

What Is the Cabinet? The executive branch also includes executive departments, each responsible for a different area of government. For example, the Department of State plans and carries out foreign policy, and the Department of the Interior manages and protects the nation's public lands and natural resources. The heads, or secretaries, of these departments are members of the president's cabinet, a group that helps the president make decisions and set government policy.

Independent Agencies The independent agencies manage federal programs in many fields. These include aeronautics and space, banking, communications, farm credit, and trade. Government corporations are government agencies that are run like privately owned businesses. One government corporation whose services you may often use is the United States Postal Service.

Reading Check **Describe** What is the president's cabinet?

The Judicial Branch

Main Idea **The Supreme Court and a number of lesser courts make up the judicial branch.** U

Reading Connection Do you think a society could exist without a court system that determines in a fair manner if laws have been broken? Read to find out about the powers of the courts as established in the Constitution.

Article III of the Constitution called for the creation of a Supreme Court and "such inferior [lower] courts as Congress may from time to time ordain and establish." In 1789 Congress passed a Judiciary Act, which added a series of district courts to the federal court system. Congress added appeals courts, sometimes called circuit courts, in 1891 to ease the workload of the Supreme Court. R

Lower Federal Courts At the lowest level of the federal court system are the United States district courts. These courts consider criminal and civil cases that come under federal, rather than state, authority. The criminal cases include such offenses as kidnapping and federal tax evasion. Civil cases cover claims against the federal government and cases involving constitutional rights, such as free speech. There are 94 district courts in the nation and the territories.

The next level of federal courts, the appeals courts, reviews district court decisions in which the losing side has asked for a review of the verdict. If an appeals court disagrees with the lower court's decision, it can either overturn the verdict or order a retrial. The United States has 14 appeals courts. C

The Supreme Court The Supreme Court stands at the top of the American legal system. Article III of the Constitution created the Supreme Court as one of three coequal branches of the national government, along with Congress and the president.

Did You Know?

Nations distinguish between the head of state—a symbol of the country as a whole—and the head of government—who simply leads the government. In Mexico and Brazil, as in the United States, those roles are combined in one person, the president. The same is true in some monarchies, such as Saudi Arabia, where the king fills both roles. In constitutional monarchies like Belgium, Spain, and the United Kingdom, the monarch is the head of state and the prime minister is head of government. France and Russia are among the countries with a president serving as head of state and a prime minister acting as head of government.

The Supreme Court is led by a chief justice. John Jay became the first chief justice in 1789. Congress sets the number of associate justices and has the power to change that number. Over the years it has varied from four to nine, but it has been nine since 1869.

The Constitution does not describe the duties of the chief justice or the associate justices. Instead, the duties have developed from laws, through tradition, and as the needs and circumstances of the nation have developed. The main duty of the justices is to hear and rule on cases. This duty involves them in three decision-making tasks: deciding which cases to hear from among the thousands appealed to the Court each year; deciding the case itself; and determining an explanation for the decision, called the Court's opinion.

Judicial Review As you have read, the Supreme Court's power to examine the laws and actions of local, state, and national governments and to cancel them if they violate the Constitution is called judicial review. The Supreme Court, under Chief Justice John Marshall, first **assumed** the power of judicial review in the case of *Marbury* v. *Madison* (1803). Since then, the Court has invalidated, or canceled, nearly 200 provisions of federal law.

The Supreme Court may also review presidential policies. In the case of *Ex parte Milligan* (1866), the Court ruled that President Lincoln's suspension of certain civil rights during the Civil War was unconstitutional. In its decision, the Court noted that the "Constitution of the United States is a law for rulers and people, equally in war and in peace."

The Federal Court System

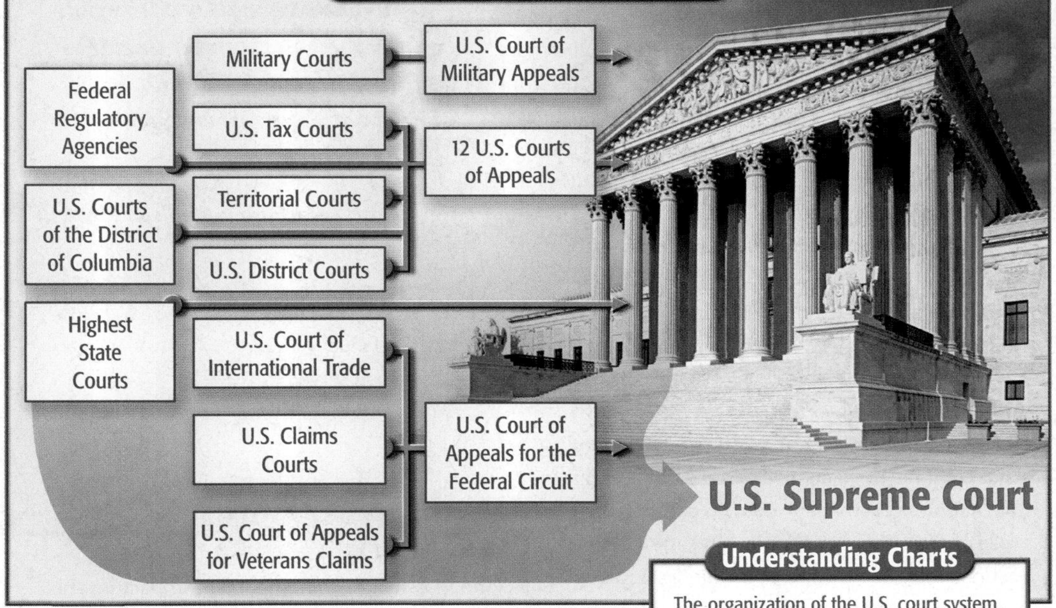

Understanding Charts

The organization of the U.S. court system is based on the U.S. Constitution and federal laws.

Interpret What is the last court in which a case may be appealed?

Understanding Charts

Answer: the Supreme Court

U Universal Access

Logical/Mathematical
Supreme Court decisions are made on the principle that the majority rules. **Ask:** What problem might arise if the court had an even number of justices? *(There could be a tie, which would mean no decision.)* OL

R1 Reading Strategy

Evaluating Ask: Can Congress or the president force the Supreme Court to hear a particular case? Why or why not? *(no; because the court alone decides which cases it will hear)* OL

C Critical Thinking

Making Inferences Ask: Why would Supreme Court justices need to have good writing skills? *(to write clear and convincing opinions)* OL

Review The Big Idea

Review the Big Idea for this section, "Political ideas and major events shape how people form governments." **Ask:** What principle of the Constitution is shown by the Supreme Court's power of judicial review? *(checks and balances)* How does that principle reflect the experiences that the Framers lived through? *(It reflects their concern that one branch of government could abuse its power, as they felt the king had done.)* OL

R2 Reading Strategy

Academic Vocabulary
Discuss with students the meaning of the word *assume*. Ask students to write sentences using the word in different ways. AL

Biography

TEACH

R Reading Strategy

Determining Importance
Explain that a biography includes information about a person's life and achievements. Have students look at the first sentences of each of the four paragraphs in this biography.
Ask: Which is the most important statement about Marshall? Why? *(first sentence of last paragraph; because it describes why Marshall is significant)* Why does the biography include other information, such as his family background and the other positions he held? *(to give a sense of Marshall as a person)* **OL** CA 8RC2.0

W Writing Support

Expository Writing Have students write a tombstone for Marshall that pays tribute to his accomplishments. **OL**

Answers and Additional Support

Biography

US8.2 Students analyze the political principles underlying the U.S. Constitution and compare the enumerated and implied powers of the federal government.

JOHN MARSHALL R

1755–1835

John Marshall is the only individual to serve in the House of Representatives, the Senate, the president's cabinet, as governor of a state, and as Supreme Court chief justice. John Adams once said that his greatest act as president was "the gift of John Marshall to the people." Marshall, the fourth chief justice of the United States, hardly looked like the head of the Supreme Court. He often wore mismatched clothes and an old floppy hat. He rejected the gold-braided robes worn by justices at the time in favor of the simple black robes worn by justices today.

Marshall, the oldest of 15 children, grew up on the Virginia frontier. At the outbreak of the Revolutionary War, Marshall joined a Virginia regiment. He never forgot the reasons for which he joined the American Revolution. As a soldier, he once sewed the words "Liberty or Death" onto his shirt. He brought those same principles to his tenure as chief justice and supported both the national government and the new Constitution.

"If two laws conflict with each other, the courts must decide on the operation of each. . . . This is of the very essence of judicial duty."

—**John Marshall, *Marbury* v. *Madison* (1803)**

Marshall served in the Virginia legislature and supported the Federalist party. In 1800 President John Adams appointed him secretary of state. In January 1801, Adams appointed Marshall chief justice of the United States. Marshall served in that position 34 years.

W Marshall heard cases and made landmark rulings that continue to guide the Supreme Court and the nation's government today. In deciding the case of *Marbury* v. *Madison* in 1803, the Marshall court established the principle of judicial review of acts of Congress. Marshall reinforced the ideas that the Supreme Court is the final authority to interpret the Constitution and that the Constitution truly was the "supreme law of the land."

Then and Now

John Marshall had an important impact on the position of the Supreme Court in the country's government. Research a current Supreme Court justice and describe the impact he or she has had upon the court or upon the nation.

Then and Now

Students' responses should clearly describe what the justice did and why it was significant.

More Skill Practice

Historical and Social Sciences Analysis Skill **Ask:** What effect do you think Marshall's army service had on his commitment to the government? *(Students may say that having fought for independence, he was deeply committed to making the government work.)* **AL**

Reviewing State Laws Judicial review of state laws and actions may have as much significance as the Court's activities at the federal level. One important case involved segregation in schools. Many cities had segregated schools: white students attended one school and black students attended a different school. In 1896 the Supreme Court had ruled in *Plessy* v. *Ferguson* that segregation was constitutional as long as equal facilities were provided for both races.

One important case involved a young African American girl named Linda Brown, who was not allowed to attend her neighborhood school in Topeka, Kansas, because of her race. She was told to attend an all-black school across town. Her parents then sued the Topeka school board, arguing that black children were not getting the same quality of education as white children.

On May 17, 1954, the Supreme Court ruled unanimously in the case of *Brown* v. *Board of Education of Topeka, Kansas*, that segregation in public schools was unconstitutional. The *Brown* decision overturned the *Plessy* decision. The *Brown* decision also cleared the way for the end of segregated schools throughout the nation.

Reading Check

Describe How was the court system set up?

Linda Brown was at the center of the important Supreme Court case, *Brown* v. *Board of Education of Topeka, Kansas*.

History Online

Study Central Need help understanding the branches of federal government? Visit ca.hss.glencoe.com and click on Study Central.

Section 2 Review

Reading Summary

Review the Main Ideas

- Congress works to make the nation's laws and to control government spending.
- Many executive departments and agencies assist the president in carrying out the nation's laws.
- The judicial branch settles disputes and interprets the meaning of laws.

What Did You Learn?

1. List three responsibilities of the president.
2. Does the Constitution describe the duties of the Supreme Court? How have these duties developed?

Critical Thinking

3. **Organizing Information** Re-create the diagram below and provide five different kinds of congressional committees. CA 8RC2.0

4. **The Big Ideas** How does politics affect Supreme Court decisions? Give one example from 1803 and one from modern history. CA CS1.
5. **Creative Writing** Write a help-wanted ad for the position of president of the United States. Describe the various responsibilities and what skills might be needed to fulfill those duties. CA 8WA2.5
6. **Analysis** Describe the role of the legislative branch in government spending and how that role relates to legislators' constituencies. CA HI2.

U Universal Access

English Learners Explain what *overturned* means. By its decision in the *Brown* case, the court ruled that its earlier decision was no longer correct law. EL

ASSESS

Resources for pages 233

Use these resources to assess student mastery of section content.

Section Quiz 4–2

Interactive Tutor Self-Assessment CD-ROM

Reading Check

Answer: by the Judiciary Act of 1789 and another act of Congress passed in 1891

History Online

Study Central provides summaries, interactive games, and online graphic organizers to help students review section content.

CLOSE

Monitoring Have students identify a situation in which all three branches of government become involved in a law about education. OL

SECTION 2 REVIEW ANSWERS

Review questions reinforce content standards US8.2 and US8.3.

1. *any three*: carrying out the nation's law; directing foreign policy; acting as commander in chief; representing all Americans as chief of state; proposing goals to Congress
2. no; developed from laws, through tradition, and as country's needs, circumstances have changed
3. standing committees; subcommittees; select committees; joint committees; conference committees
4. **The Big Ideas** Students should give reasons for their choices.
5. Answers should describe responsibilities and skills.
6. **Analysis** Only Congress can appropriate money which keeps treasury closer to voters' control

FOCUS

BELLRINGER
SKILLBUILDER ACTIVITY

Project **Daily Focus Skills Transparency 4–3** and have students answer the question.

Guide to Reading

Preteaching Vocabulary
Have students look up the terms in the Glossary at the back of the book and use in a sentence.

Answers to Graphic:
Rights: due process, protection, basic freedoms; Duties: obey law, pay taxes, defend nation, serve on juries; Responsibilities: keep informed; voice opinion, exercise rights, vote, communicate with officials

Unpacking the Standards
After reading the section, students will be able to:
- name Americans' basic rights.
- describe the requirements for becoming a citizen.
- discuss the duties and responsibilities of citizens.

Section 3

Citizens' Rights and Responsibilities

Guide to Reading

History Social Science Standards

US8.2 Students analyze the political principles underlying the U.S. Constitution and compare the enumerated and implied powers of the federal government.

US8.3 Students understand the foundation of the American political system and the ways in which citizens participate in it.

Looking Back, Looking Ahead
You learned about the three branches of the federal government and the people who make up those branches. American citizens must also actively participate to make the government work.

Focusing on the Main Ideas
- Americans have certain rights that are protected in the Constitution. *(page 235)*
- American citizens are expected to carry out certain duties and responsibilities. *(page 236)*

Content Vocabulary
due process of law
citizen (SIH•tuh•zuhn)
naturalization (NA•chuh•ruh•luh•ZAY•shuhn)

Academic Vocabulary
involve (ihn•VAHLV)
diminish (duh•MIH•nihsh)
environment (ihn•VY•ruhn•muhnt)

Reading Strategy
Summarizing Information Draw a chart like the one below and fill in some of the rights, duties, and responsibilities of American citizens.

Rights	Duties	Responsibilities

NATIONAL GEOGRAPHIC **Who & When?**

1780 | 1790 | 1800

Thomas Jefferson

1786 Thomas Jefferson's Virginia Statute for Religious Freedom is adopted

John Adams

1796 John Adams wins presidential election

SECTION RESOURCES

Print Material
- Reproducible Lesson Plan 4–3*
- Daily Lesson and Discussion Notes 4–3
- Guided Reading Activity 4–3
- Reading Essentials and Study Guide 4–3
- Active Reading Note-Taking Guide 4–3
- Section Quiz 4–3

*Available on TeacherWorks™

Transparencies
- Daily Focus Skills Transparency 4–3
- Section Graphic Organizer Transparency 4–3
- California Standards Practice Transparencies

Technology
- Interactive Tutor Self-Assessment CD-ROM
- Exam*View*® Pro Testmaker CD-ROM
- Presentation Plus! CD-ROM

US8.2.5 Understand the significance of Jefferson's Statute for Religious Freedom as a forerunner of the First Amendment and the origins, purpose, and differing views of the founding fathers on the issue of the separation of church and state.

Rights of American Citizens

Main Idea **Americans have certain rights that are protected in the Constitution.**

Reading Connection What do you consider to be some of your basic rights as an American? Freedom of speech? Freedom of religion? Read to find out where these rights are guaranteed in the Constitution.

An American Story

> **"We hold these truths to be self-evident, that all men are created equal, that they are endowed by their Creator with certain unalienable Rights, that among these are Life, Liberty and the pursuit of Happiness."**

These words from the Declaration of Independence continue to inspire Americans. They have encouraged Americans to pursue the ideals expressed in the Declaration and to create a Constitution and a Bill of Rights that protect these rights. The rights of Americans fall into three broad categories: the right to be protected from unfair actions of the government, to have equal treatment under the law, and to have basic freedoms.

R1 **Due Process** The Fifth Amendment states that no person shall "be deprived of life, liberty, or property, without due process of law." **Due process of law** means that the government must follow certain procedures that have been established by law and are guaranteed in the Constitution. All people must be treated according to these principles. R2

Equal Protection All Americans, regardless of race, religious beliefs, or political beliefs, have the right to be treated the same under the law. The Fourteenth Amendment requires every state to grant its citizens "equal protection of the laws."

Primary Sources

Statute for Religious Freedom

▲ Thomas Jefferson

Many people came to America in search of religious freedom. In 1777 Thomas Jefferson wrote a resolution on religious freedom that was adopted by the Virginia state legislature in 1786. Commonly known as the Statute for Religious Freedom, the resolution said:

R3
> "No man shall be compelled to frequent or support any religious worship, place or ministry whatsoever, nor shall be enforced, restrained, molested, or [burdened] in his body or goods, nor shall otherwise suffer on account of his religious opinions or belief; but that all men shall be free to profess, and by argument to maintain, their opinion in matters of religion, and that the same shall in no wise diminish, enlarge or affect their civil capacities."
>
> —Thomas Jefferson, "Virginia Statute of Religious Liberty"

A few years after this resolution was adopted, the United States became an independent country, and freedom of religion was one of the principles upon which the nation was founded.

DBQ Document-Based Question

Jefferson wrote that "no man shall be compelled to frequent or support any religious worship." Write a sentence in your own words that expresses this statement.

TEACH

R1 Reading Strategy

Evaluating **Ask:** What parts of the Constitution provide the rights that Americans enjoy as individuals? *(amendments such as the First, Fifth, and Fourteenth)* OL

R2 Reading Strategy

Understanding Vocabulary
Ask: What does the word *process* mean in this term? *(legal procedures)* OL

R3 Reading Strategy

Organizing Information
Help students understand the passage from Jefferson's Statute for Religious Freedom by breaking it into sections. The first part (lines 1–3) blocks the government from forcing people to attend church or support a particular church. The second part (lines 3–7) prohibits the government from punishing an individual, either personally or in terms of property, as a result of the person's religion. The last section (lines 7–12) declares that people have the right to their religious beliefs. BL

Resources for page 235

Refer to ***The Living Constitution*** for student activities and information related to the Constitution.

Primary Sources

Answer: The government cannot force a person to attend a particular church or pay taxes to support that church.

- What did Jefferson mean by "burdened in his body or goods"? *(People cannot be punished physically or lose property for religious reasons.)* AL
- What is meant by the words *diminish* and *enlarge*? *(to diminish is to make smaller; to enlarge is to make greater)* What is Jefferson saying by using these words? *(People cannot lose some rights or gain others because of their religion.)* OL

U Universal Access

English Learners Have students show their understanding of the First Amendment by giving an example of a way citizens can exercise each right. EL

C Critical Thinking

Drawing Conclusions
Ask: Why must limits on rights apply to everyone? *(because of the principle of equal protection of the laws)* OL

R Reading Strategy

Understanding Vocabulary
Have students write a sentence explaining how the terms *citizen* and *naturalization* are connected. *(Naturalization is the process that makes someone born in another country a citizen.)* OL

Reading Check
Answer: the idea that the government must follow procedures established by law and guaranteed by the Constitution

Resources for page 236

Biography Activity 4

Answers and Additional Support

US8.3.6 Describe the basic law-making process and how the Constitution provides numerous opportunities for citizens to participate in the political process and to monitor and influence government (e.g., function of elections, political parties, interest groups).

Basic Freedoms The basic freedoms **involve** the liberties outlined in the First Amendment—freedom of speech, freedom of religion, freedom of the press, freedom of assembly, and the right to petition. In a democratic society such as ours, power exists in the hands of the people. Therefore, its citizens must be able to exchange ideas freely.

The First Amendment, part of the Bill of Rights, which was added to the Constitution in 1791, allows citizens to criticize the government, in speech or in the press, without fear of punishment. It also states that the government cannot endorse a religion, nor can it prohibit citizens from practicing a religion if they choose to do so. In addition, the Ninth Amendment states that the rights of Americans are not limited to those mentioned in the Constitution. This has allowed our basic freedoms to continue to grow. The Twenty-sixth Amendment, for example, extends the right to vote to American citizens who are 18 years of age. U

The ultimate responsibility to protect these rights lies with the American people. Voting and expressing our opinions to our elected representatives help uphold our rights. Judge Learned Hand expressed:

> **"Liberty lies in the hearts of men and women; when it dies there, . . . no constitution, no law, no court can even do much to help it."**
>
> —Learned Hand, *The Spirit of Liberty*

Limits on Rights Our rights are not unlimited. The government can establish laws or rules to restrict certain standards to protect the health, safety, security, and moral standards of a community. Moreover, rights may be limited to prevent one person's rights from interfering with the rights of others. The restrictions of rights, however, must be reasonable and must apply to everyone equally. C

Reading Check **Summarize** What is due process of law?

Citizen Participation

Main Idea **American citizens are expected to carry out certain duties and responsibilities.**

Reading Connection Would a democracy be effective if few of the citizens voted? Read to find out what it means to be a good citizen.

An American Story

On September 11, 2001, terrorist attacks killed thousands of Americans. President George W. Bush led the nation during the troubled times. He said:

> **"[A]fter America was attacked, it was as if our entire country looked into a mirror, and saw our better selves. We were reminded that we are citizens, with obligations to each other, to our country, and to history."**

What Is a Citizen? A **citizen** (SIH • tuh • zuhn) is a person who owes loyalty to and is entitled to the protection of a state or nation. How do you become an American citizen? Generally, citizenship is granted to anyone born within the borders of the United States. Citizenship is also granted to anyone born outside the United States if one parent is a United States citizen. A person of foreign birth can also become a citizen through the process of **naturalization** (NA • chuh • ruh • luh • ZAY • shuhn). R

To qualify, applicants must be at least 18 years old. They must have been lawfully admitted for permanent residence and have lived in the United States for at least five years. They must possess good moral character and accept the principles of the Constitution. Applicants must also understand English and demonstrate an understanding of U.S. history and government. Before being granted citizenship, applicants must be willing to give up any foreign allegiance and must promise to obey the Constitution and the laws of the United States.

EXTENDING THE CONTENT

Separation of Church and State Some American leaders such as William Williams of Connecticut thought that the Preamble to the Constitution should express "a firm belief of the being and perfections of the one living and true God, the creator and supreme Governour of the world." At that time, many state constitutions included a religious test for officeholders. Thomas Jefferson and others, however, believed that the First Amendment builds "a wall of separation between Church and State." **Ask:** Which of these views has the U.S. government held? What are some recent controversies related to this subject? *(The government has mostly upheld a separation of church and state. Students may recall the controversy surrounding the line "One nation under God" in the Pledge of Allegiance.)* AL CA HI2.

As citizens of the United States, we are expected to carry out certain duties and responsibilities. Duties are things we are required to do by law. Responsibilities are things we should do. Fulfilling both our duties and our responsibilities helps ensure that we have a good government and that we continue to enjoy the rights that the Framers set forth.

W **Duties** One of the duties of all Americans is to obey the law. Laws serve three important functions. They help maintain order; they protect the health, safety, and property of all citizens; and they make it possible for people to live together peacefully. If you disobey laws, for example, you may endanger others and interfere with the smooth functioning of society. If you believe a law needs to be changed, you can work through your elected representatives to improve it.

Americans also have a duty to pay taxes. The government uses tax money to defend the nation, provide health insurance for people over age 65, and build roads and bridges. Americans benefit from services provided by the government.

Linking Past & Present

The New England Town Meeting

Past In colonial times, New England citizens practiced a form of direct democracy called the town meeting. Any citizen who could vote could attend these meetings and decide upon the important issues of the town such as taxes, laws, and monetary expenditures. Every person's vote counted, and every voter's voice could be heard.

▼ Town meeting today

▲ Colonial town meeting

Present Today similar meetings still take place in some of the smaller New England towns. These meetings are usually held once a year to determine such issues as local laws, taxes, and the town budget. In larger communities, however, town meetings are often impractical. ***What are some other ways that citizens can participate in government?***

C

W Writing Support

Persuasive Writing Have students write a public service announcement that encourages people to obey the law. OL

CA 8WA2.4

C Critical Thinking

Comparing and Contrasting Have students compare the pictures of the colonial town meeting and the town meeting today.

Ask: How are the meetings alike and how are they different? What else do you think has changed about the meetings? *(Students may note that at both meetings, only one person is speaking at a time. Also, while the colonial meeting has only men in attendance, the modern meeting also includes women. Students may suggest that modern town meetings may have more people in attendance if they are held only once a year.)* OL

Linking Past & Present

Answer: Answers may include voting, communicating with representatives on issues, working on political campaigns, doing volunteer work to make the community better and stronger, testifying before congressional committees, and joining an interest group or political party.

Review The Big Idea

Review the Big Idea for this section, "Citizen participation is essential to the foundation and preservation of the U.S. political system." Explain that some people can be excused from jury duty, though they have to meet specific requirements that courts set. **Ask:** What would happen if not enough people met their responsibility to serve on juries? *(People who were accused of crimes would be denied their rights to a trial by jury.)* OL

R1 Reading Strategy

Taking Notes Have students take notes on the responsibilities of citizens. Encourage them to use the notes to guide their actions in the future, when they have these responsibilities. OL

R2 Reading Strategy

Academic Vocabulary Ask students to read the sentence that contains the word *diminish*. Have students list synonyms and antonyms for the word. OL

Resources for page 238

Geography and History Activity 4

Answers and Additional Support

Another duty of citizens is to defend the nation. All males aged 18 and older must register with the government in case they are needed for military service. The nation no longer has a draft, or required military service, but a war could make the draft necessary again.

The Constitution guarantees all Americans the right to a trial by a jury of their peers (equals). For this reason, you should be prepared to serve on a jury when you become eligible at the age of 18. Having a large group of jurors on hand is necessary to guarantee the right to a fair and speedy trial.

Responsibilities All citizens have responsibilities. However, the responsibilities of citizens are not as clear-cut as their duties. Because responsibilities are voluntary, people are not arrested or punished if they do not fulfill these obligations. The quality of our government and R2 of our lives will **diminish,** however, if our responsibilities are not carried out.

Civic Republicanism Keep in mind that one of your responsibilities as a citizen is to know what the government is doing and to voice your opinion when you feel strongly about R1 something the government has done or has failed to do. You can let your representatives know how you feel about issues through letters, telephone calls, and petitions. When the government learns that most people favor or oppose an action, it usually follows their wishes.

You also need to be informed about your rights and to exercise them when necessary. Knowing your rights helps preserve them. Other responsibilities include respecting diversity, accepting responsibility for your actions, supporting your family, and volunteering within your community.

History Online

Student Web Activity Visit ca.hss.glencoe.com and click on *Chapter 4—Student Web Activities* for an activity on volunteering opportunities.

History Makers

Roots of the Two-Party System

Americans have not always had political parties to choose between. In fact, in his Farewell Address of 1796, President George Washington warned against the harmful effects of the "spirit of party." Even so, by the end of President Washington's second term, two political parties had organized in opposition to one another. The Federalist Party supported Alexander Hamilton's policies that encouraged a strong national government. Those who distrusted a strong national government formed their own party, the Democratic-Republicans, led by James Madison and Thomas Jefferson. In the election of 1796, the Federalist candidate, John Adams, was elected president. Four years later, Democratic-Republican Thomas Jefferson was elected.

Other Ways to Participate Perhaps your most important responsibility as an American citizen will be to vote when you reach the age of 18. Voting allows you to participate in government and guide its direction. If you disapprove of the job your representatives are doing, it will be your responsibility to help elect others.

While not everyone holds public office, everyone can participate in government in other ways. Working on a political campaign, volunteering to help in a hospital or a library, and participating in a local park cleanup are all ways to take responsibility and to make a contribution to good government and a well-run community.

History Makers

Encourage students to visit the Web sites of the modern Democratic and Republican parties to learn what ideas each party supports. Organize the class into groups and have each group find both parties' positions on a particular issue. Have the groups report to the class.

More Skill Practice

Historical and Social Sciences Analysis Skill Divide students into groups and assign each a presidential election. Have groups find out what percentage of voters turned out in each election. Then construct a class chart or graph to display each group's findings. **Ask:** How has turnout changed over the years? Why do you think it has changed? OL CA HI2.

You read earlier that when a bill is in a House or Senate committee for discussion, citizens are sometimes allowed to present arguments supporting or opposing the bill. The people making the arguments often work for special interest groups. Belonging or contributing to a special interest group is another way citizens can participate in government and the making of laws. Through interest groups, citizens communicate their "wants," or policy goals, to government leaders—the president, Congress, state legislators, the mayor, or city council.

Interest groups represent a variety of causes. Many groups deal with economic interests, including groups like the National Association of Manufacturers and powerful labor organizations. Other interest groups deal with more specific causes. The Sierra Club supports issues to protect the **environment,** and MADD works to prevent drunken driving.

U Another way for citizens to be involved in the political process is to join a political party. Political parties choose candidates to run for the various political offices. Political parties also present voters with views on a wide variety of issues. They consider conflicting issues and problems that affect all Americans, not just certain groups. Political parties keep citizens informed about these issues, as well as about how party members and members of the opposition are performing in office. Belonging to a party involves no obligations or duties besides voting, although party members can also volunteer during campaigns.

Respecting Others' Rights To enjoy your rights to the fullest, you must be prepared to respect the rights of others. Respecting the rights of others also means respecting the rights of people with whom you may disagree. Respecting and accepting others regardless of race, religion, beliefs, or other differences is essential to the success of a democracy. All Americans are entitled to the same respect and good treatment.

Reading Check **Identify** What is naturalization?

History Online **Study Central** Need help understanding citizens' rights and responsibilities? Visit ca.hss.glencoe.com and click on Study Central.

Section 3 Review

Reading Summary

Review the Main Ideas

- Americans have the right to be protected from unfair actions of the government, to be treated equally under the law, and to have basic freedoms.
- Americans have certain duties, such as obeying the laws, and responsibilities, such as staying informed about one's rights, that they must carry out.

What Did You Learn?

1. Are the rights of American citizens unlimited? Explain.
2. Why are personal responsibilities important?

Critical Thinking

3. **Organizing Information** Re-create the diagram below and provide the three categories of American rights. CA 8RC2.0

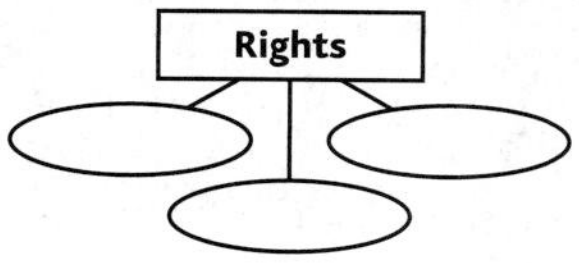

4. **The Big Ideas** How does citizen participation, as described in this section, help preserve the American political system? CA HI2.
5. **Creative Writing** One responsibility of being an American citizen is to become involved in the democratic system. Make a poster showing how students can get involved in their community's democracy. Display your poster in a prominent place in school. CA 8RC2.4

History Online

Objectives and answers to the students activity can be found in the Web Activity Lesson Plan feature at ca.hss.glencoe.com.

U Universal Access

Advanced Learners Have students research the role that third-party candidates played in one of the following presidential elections: 1848; 1856; 1892; 1912; 1924; 1948; 1968; 1992. AL CA 8WA2.3

ASSESS

Resources for page 239

Use these resources to assess student mastery of section content.

Section Quiz 4–3

Interactive Tutor Self-Assessment CD-ROM

Reading Check

Answer: the process by which someone born in another country becomes a citizen

History Online

Study Central provides summaries, interactive games, and online graphic organizers to help students review section content.

CLOSE

Determining Cause and Effect Have students explain how citizens can protect their rights by exercising their responsibilities. OL

SECTION 3 REVIEW ANSWERS

Review questions reinforce content standard US8.3.

1. no; government can make laws that set certain standards people need to meet, and people cannot interfere with others' rights
2. They help ensure quality of government.
3. the right to be protected from unfair actions of the government; the right to equal treatment under the law; basic freedoms
4. **The Big Ideas** by making sure that representatives are responsive to citizens' wishes
5. Review students' posters before displaying them to ensure that they are appropriate.

Connecting to the Constitution

FOCUS

History–Social Science Standards

The following standards are covered on pages 240–241.

US8.2.6 Enumerate the powers of government set forth in the Constitution and the fundamental liberties ensured by the Bill of Rights.

US8.3.7 Understand the functions and responsibilities of a free press.

TEACH

R Reading Strategy

Understanding Vocabulary Explain that libel is not any criticism but unfair attacks that damage a person's reputation or harms his or her career. **Ask:** Is it fair to criticize someone for something they did? Is it fair to say something untrue about someone to make others turn against him or her? OL

C Critical Thinking

Analyzing Primary Sources Ask: Why does Jefferson think that newspapers are so important? *(They help people become informed.)* OL

Connecting to the Constitution

US8.2.6 Enumerate the powers of government set forth in the Constitution and the fundamental liberties ensured by the Bill of Rights. **US8.3.7** Understand the functions and responsibilities of a free press.

Freedom of the Press

Why It Matters Freedom of the press means the right to publish facts, ideas, and opinions without interference from the government or private groups. This right applies to printed materials, including books and newspapers, and to electronic communications, including radio, television, movies, and computer networks. Such a free flow of materials allows the people in a democracy to receive the information they need to make informed decisions.

The First Amendment In the United States, freedom of the press is guaranteed by the First Amendment to the Constitution, which says in part that "Congress shall make no law . . . abridging [limiting] the freedom . . . of the press." Because of this guarantee, writers, editors, and journalists have the freedom to decide what goes in or stays out of their publications. This independence has led many to call the press a "watchdog" over government. This means that the press watches government actions and helps keep the government responsible to the people.

The mass media—newspapers, magazines, television, radio, and the Internet—however, are not totally free of government regulation. Many reasonable restrictions can be placed on rights of the media. For example, no person has the right to libel, or use printed words to injure another person's character or reputation. Laws also prohibit the printing and distribution of obscene materials. R

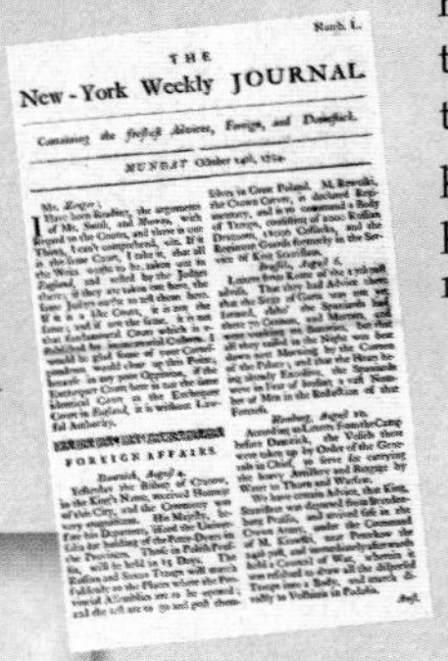
THE New-York Weekly JOURNAL

John Peter Zenger's *New York Weekly Journal*

> *"[W]ere it left to me to decide whether we should have a government without newspapers or newspapers without a government, I should not hesitate a moment to prefer the latter."* C
>
> —*Thomas Jefferson, Letter to Colonel Edward Carrington, January 16, 1787*

Printing press

Answers and Additional Support

Did You Know?

Andrew Hamilton—Zenger's lawyer—gave a powerful speech that persuaded the jury. It included the following words: "The question before the court and you, gentlemen of the jury, is not of small nor private concern, it is not the cause of a poor printer, nor of New-York alone, which you are now trying. No! It may in its consequence affect every freeman that lives under a British government [in] America. It is the best cause. It is the cause of liberty."

▲ *Press coverage can be limited by order of the judge. Here, members of the press, barred from the courtroom, wait for a chance to interview participants.*

The Zenger Case Freedom of the press was an important issue in colonial America. Newspapers in colonial cities, such as Boston and Philadelphia, carried political news and often faced government censorship. Censorship is the banning of printed materials because they contain unpopular or offensive ideas. In 1733 publisher John Peter Zenger, in his paper the *New-York Weekly Journal*, accused New York's royal governor of corruption. Zenger was arrested and put on trial. His lawyer argued that free speech was a basic right of the British people. The jury found Zenger not guilty.

The Government and the Press After the American Revolution, several states provided for freedom of the press in their state constitutions. Later, the First Amendment of the U.S. Constitution provided for a free press in American society as a whole. At times, however, the government, in the name of public interest, has attempted to regulate the press.

Supreme Court rulings allowed the press to be limited when the printed materials might threaten national security. During World War I, publishing materials that were critical of the government was considered a crime. A 1931 Supreme Court ruling, however, struck down a Minnesota state law that banned publication of magazine or newspaper articles that were critical of public officials. Although censorship occurred during World War II, it was a voluntary system with which most newspapers and magazines cooperated. **C** A Supreme Court ruling in the 1970s allowed the publication of a secret government report about the Vietnam War. The government could not prove that publishing it endangered national security.

Free Press and Trials In some trials, reporters have refused to testify in order to protect confidential, or secret, sources. Although the Supreme Court has ruled that reporters must cooperate during trials, many states have enacted so-called shield laws. These laws provide reporters with some protection against having to reveal confidential information.

Another issue deals with gag orders. Such orders were given to prevent information about a criminal case from being published, especially if that information might violate a defendant's **R** right to a fair trial. The Supreme Court ruled that gag orders are unconstitutional except in extraordinary circumstances.

Radio, Television, and the Internet **U** Today, First Amendment rights must be considered for the many new forms of media that have developed since the Framers first discussed freedom of the press. The Federal Communications Commission (FCC) is the government agency that regulates radio and television. The FCC cannot censor materials before they are broadcast, but it does prohibit the use of indecent language.

In the 1990s, Congress passed legislation to prevent children from accessing indecent materials on the Internet. The Supreme Court, however, struck down the law, ruling that speech on the Internet was entitled to First Amendment protection.

Checking for Understanding

1. Why is freedom of the press important in a democracy? What guarantees freedom of the press in the United States?
2. When can the United States government censor information before it is published?

Critical Thinking

3. **Conclude** What responsibilities should the press have toward the American people? CA HI2.

Connecting to the Constitution

C Critical Thinking

Identifying Central Issues
Ask: Why is censorship more likely to be a problem during wartime? What kind of information might the government not want newspapers to publish? *(Students might mention specific information about troop movements or future plans.)* OL

R Reading Strategy

Understanding Vocabulary
Explain what a *gag* is. **Ask:** How does this explain the meaning of *gag order*? *(A gag order prevents the press from printing information just as a gag stops someone from speaking.)* OL

U Universal Access

Verbal/Linguistic Have students look up and report to class on the legal difference between broadcast television and radio and cable television. They should explain why the first two kinds of media are regulated and the other is not. AL CA HR1.

ASSESS

Have students answer the Checking for Understanding and Critical Thinking questions.

CLOSE

Evaluating Ask: Why is censorship a problem? *(Students answers will vary but should be supported with reasons and examples.)* OL

Questions reinforce content standard US8.2.6 and US8.3.7.

Checking for Understanding:

1. because words have great power to influence people; the First Amendment
2. when what may be printed will threaten national security

Critical Thinking:

3. Answers will vary but may include the responsibility of reporting truthfully and fairly.

Analyzing Primary Sources

FOCUS

History–Social Science Standards

The following standard is covered on pages 242–243.

US8.2 Students analyze the political principles underlying the U.S. Constitution and compare the enumerated and implied powers of the federal government.

TEACH

C1 Critical Thinking

Analyzing Primary Sources Ask: What are some examples of what Madison would call *factions* active in society today? *(political parties or interest groups)* OL CA HI3.

C2 Critical Thinking

Identifying Central Issues Explain that *adverse* means "against" or "in opposition to." **Ask:** Why does Madison say that factions are by definition adverse to other groups? *(Madison thinks that each group competes for advantage against other groups; what helps one will hurt another.)* OL

Answers and Additional Support

Analyzing Primary Sources

US8.2.4 Describe the political philosophy underpinning the Constitution as specified in the Federalist Papers (authored by James Madison, Alexander Hamilton, and John Jay) and the role of leaders such as Madison, George Washington, Roger Sherman, Gouverneur Morris, and James Wilson in the writing and ratification of the Constitution.

A New Constitution

Throughout the new nation, people discussed a Constitution for America. Many people supported ideas for a stronger central government, but many others did not. People worried about the protection of individual rights for all citizens. How would Americans settle their differences of opinion and reach an agreement on governing the nation?

Read the passages on pages 242 and 243, then answer the questions that follow.

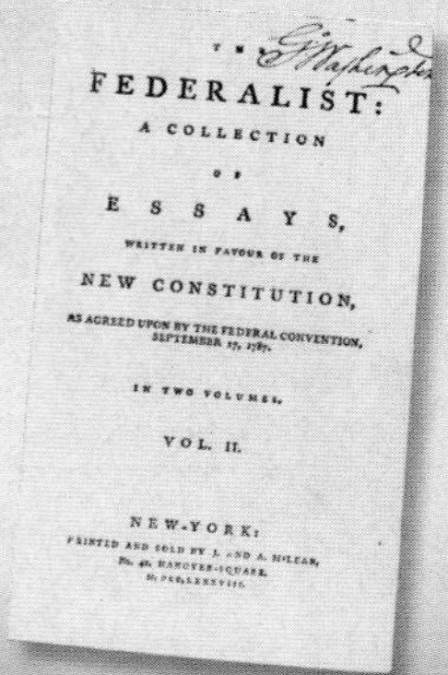
FEDERALIST: A COLLECTION OF ESSAYS, WRITTEN IN FAVOUR OF THE NEW CONSTITUTION, AS AGREED UPON BY THE FEDERAL CONVENTION, SEPTEMBER 17, 1787. IN TWO VOLUMES. VOL. II. NEW-YORK:

The Federalist Papers **supported ratification of the Constitution.** ▶

Reader's Dictionary

enumerated (ih • NOO • muh • RAYT • ehd): a number of named things on a list

monopolies (muh • NAH • puh • lees): situations in which a single company controls an industry

aristocracy (AR • uh • STAH • kruh • see): governing by a small group of people, particularly nobility

latent (LAY • tuhnt): underlying

faction (FAK • shuhn): a group that has specific interests or beliefs that are in conflict with the larger group

actuated (AK • chuh • WAYT • ehd): moved to action

annihilation (uh • NY • uh • LAY • shuhn): the complete destruction of something

fallible (FA • luh • buhl) : liable to be wrong or make mistakes

The Federalist, No.10

In 1787 and 1788, James Madison, Alexander Hamilton, and John Jay wrote 85 anonymous articles for the New York Journal. *The purpose of these articles was to persuade the people of New York to ratify the proposed Constitution. These articles became known as* The Federalist Papers. *This article focused on divisions, or factions, among people:*

Among the numerous advantages promised by a well-constructed Union, none deserves to be more accurately developed than its tendency to break and control the violence of **faction**. . . .

By a faction, I understand a number of citizens, whether amounting to a majority or minority of the whole, who are united and **actuated** by some common impulse of passion, or of interest, adverse to the rights of other citizens, or to the permanent and aggregate [collected] interests of the community. . . . C1 C2

There are . . . two methods of removing the causes of faction: the one, by destroying the liberty which is essential to its existence; the other, by giving to every citizen the same opinions, the same passions, and the same interests.

EXTENDING THE CONTENT

The Federalist Papers The *Federalist Papers* have been called by historian Clinton Rossiter "the one product of the American mind that is rightly counted among the classics of political theory." What makes their achievement even more impressive is that they were written quickly. Alexander Hamilton had the idea of writing the pieces, and he contributed most of the essays.

It could never be more truly said than of the first remedy that it was worse than the disease. Liberty is to faction what air is to fire, [a fuel] without which it instantly expires. But it could not be a less folly to abolish liberty, which is essential to political life, because it nourishes faction than it would be to wish the **annihilation** of air, which is essential to animal life, because it imparts to fire its destructive agency.

▲ James Madison

The second [remedy] is as impracticable as the first would be unwise. As long as the reason of man continues **fallible**, and he is at liberty to exercise it, different opinions will be formed. . . .

The **latent** causes of faction are thus sown in the nature of man; and we see them everywhere brought into different degrees of activity, according to the different circumstances of civil society. . . . But the most common and durable source of factions has been the various and unequal distribution of property. Those who hold and those who are without property have ever formed distinct interests in society. C1

— James Madison

Objections to the Constitution

George Mason served as a state leader in Virginia in the 1780s. Mason opposed the Constitution and wrote pamphlets to express his concerns:

Under their own construction of the general clause at the end of the **enumerated** powers, the Congress may grant **monopolies** in trade and commerce, constitute new crimes, inflict unusual and severe punishments, and extend their power as far as they shall think proper; so that the state legislatures have no security for the powers now presumed to remain to them; or the people for their rights. C2 There is no declaration of any kind for preserving the liberty of the press, the trial by jury in civil cases, nor against the danger of standing armies in time of peace. . . . C3

This government will commence in a moderate **aristocracy;** it is at present impossible to foresee whether it will, in its operation, produce a monarchy, or a corrupt oppressive aristocracy; it will most probably vibrate some years between the two, and then terminate in the one or the other.

▲ George Mason

DBQ Document-Based Questions

The Federalist, No. 10

1. How does Madison describe factions?
2. What is identified as a main source of factions?
3. What two ways are proposed to eliminate factions?
4. What would be lost if factions were eliminated in the Union?

Objections to the Constitution

5. What were Mason's concerns about the U.S. Constitution?
6. What did Mason suggest would happen to the government?
7. Was Mason correct in his predictions about America's government?

Read to Write

8. Imagine that you are a New York delegate trying to decide whether or not to ratify the U.S. Constitution. Write a response to the article and pamphlet that you just read. Explain your decision to ratify or not using information from the above texts. Try to persuade others to follow your decision. CA 8WA2.4 CA HR5.

C1 Critical Thinking

Identifying Central Issues
Ask: Do you agree with Madison that the unequal distribution of property is the "most common and durable source of factions"? Why or why not? *(Students may agree or may point to other causes, such as disagreements over rights or principles.)* OL

C2 Critical Thinking

Analyzing Primary Sources Why did Mason and others think that the Constitution needed to have an explicit defense of peoples' rights? *(Students may say they were afraid of how governments could abuse power based on their experience with Britain.)* OL

C3 Critical Thinking

Predicting Consequences
Ask: If a Bill of Rights had been included in the Constitution, would that have been enough to persuade Mason to support it? Why or why not? *(Students may suggest that he had other objections, including the potential loss of state power, and might thus still have rejected the Constitution.)* OL

ASSESS

Have students answer the Document-Based Questions.

CLOSE

Summarizing Have students explain what values Madison and Mason both shared, even though they disagreed on the Constitution. *(Students should see that both valued liberty but saw different ways of preserving it.)* OL

DBQ Document-Based Questions

1. a group of citizens united by a common passion or interest that goes against the interest of other groups or the community
2. the unequal distribution of property
3. to destroy liberty or to make sure everyone thinks the same way
4. liberty
5. the apparently unlimited powers of Congress, which can take away the rights of the states and the people
6. It would become either an oppressive aristocracy or an oppressive monarchy.
7. Students should recognize that Americans still enjoy democratic rule by elected representatives.
8. Students should give reasons for their support of ratification or their opposition to it.

CHAPTER 4 Assessment

Resources for pages 244–245

Use these resources to review, assess, or reteach the chapter.

- Active Reading Note-Taking Guide, Chapter 4
- Chapter 4 Reading Essentials and Study Guide
- Chapter 4 Tests, Forms A and B
- California Standards Assessment, Forms A and B
- California Standards Practice Workbook
- Succeeding on the California History-Social Science Standards CD-ROM
- MindJogger Videoquiz
- Interactive Tutor Self-Assessment CD-ROM

Chapter 4 Assessment

Standards US8.2 & US8.3

Review Content Vocabulary

1. On a sheet of paper, use all of the following terms in a short paragraph related to the Constitution.

a. popular sovereignty	d. implied powers
b. reserved powers	e. judicial review
c. amendment	f. enumerated powers

Review the Main Ideas

Section 1 • Goals of the Constitution

2. List the six goals of government stated in the Preamble.
3. Explain why the amendment process is so difficult.

Section 2 • The Federal Government

4. Why does Congress use committees to evaluate proposed legislation?
5. Describe the main duty of the justices of the Supreme Court, along with the tasks involved.

Section 3 • Citizens' Rights and Responsibilities

6. Why is responsible citizenship important? Provide examples of responsible citizenship.
7. What are the basic freedoms outlined in the First Amendment?

Critical Thinking

8. **Analyze** Describe why limited government, republicanism, and popular sovereignty are important parts of the Constitution. CA CS1.
9. **Compare** Some people argue that there should be a limit on the number of terms a senator or representative can serve. Compare the advantages and the disadvantages of the present system, which does not limit these terms. CA HR5.
10. **Predict** Predict what might have happened to the United States if the Framers had not provided for a system of checks and balances. CA HI2.

Geography Skills

Study the map below and answer the following questions. CA CS3.

NATIONAL GEOGRAPHIC **Emancipation After Independence, 1780–1804**

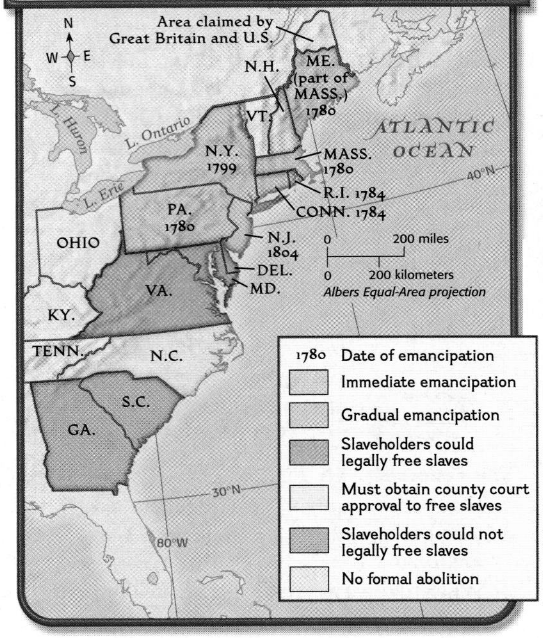

11. **Place** Which state freed enslaved people in 1780?
12. **Place** Which states required court approval to free enslaved people?

Review Content Vocabulary

1. Paragraphs will vary but should reflect information in the chapter.

Review the Main Ideas

2. to form a more perfect union; to establish justice; to insure domestic tranquility; to provide for the common defense; to promote the general welfare; to secure the blessings of liberty
3. to discourage minor or frequent changes
4. because individual members of Congress cannot carefully study all the bills that are proposed every year
5. to hear and rule on cases; that involves three tasks—deciding which cases to hear each year; deciding the case; writing opinions explaining the decision
6. It helps ensure that we have a good government and continue to enjoy our rights. Examples include obeying the laws, paying taxes, defending the nation, serving on juries, expressing your opinion on policy issues, voting.
7. freedom of speech, religion, the press, and assembly and the right to petition the government

Critical Thinking

8. Popular sovereignty means that the people hold the ultimate power, which is demonstrated in republican government by their power to elect government officials, whose powers are limited by the Constitution.
9. Answers will vary. Students might say that an advantage of no term limits is that it results in having more experienced lawmakers; a disadvantage is that they can grow less responsive to voters.

History Online

Self-Check Quiz Visit ca.hss.glencoe.com to prepare for the Chapter 4 test.

Read to Write

13. **Speech Writing** Part of your responsibility as an American citizen is to be informed about what the government is doing and to voice your opinion about its actions. Draft a speech you would give at a school-wide meeting outlining your views on issues your school or community is currently facing. CA 8LS1.4

14. **The Big Ideas** **Citizen Participation** In an essay, discuss why citizen participation is essential to preserving the American political system and how the basic freedoms outlined in the Constitution allow for that participation. CA 8WA2.4

15. **Using Your FOLDABLES** Write a short essay that describes what you have learned about the Constitution. Include a summary of what you already knew and what you wanted to learn. CA 8RC2.0

Using Academic Vocabulary

16. Use each of the following academic vocabulary words in a separate sentence:

function	grant
intervene	diminish

Building Citizenship

17. **Researching Local Government** Contact a local government official to find out about the basic plan, or constitution, of your city or town. Share your findings with the class. CA 8WS1.0

Reviewing Skills

18. Review READING SKILL **Summarizing Information** Read the summary of *Marbury* v. *Madison* on page 225. Summarize the important parts of the passage. CA 8RC2.0

19. Review ANALYSIS SKILL **Evaluating** Reread the Bill of Rights, and identify one freedom that is protected there. Then review your local newspapers for an article relating to that freedom. Based on the article you read, is that freedom being protected or threatened? CA HI2.

Standards Practice

Select the best answer for each of the following questions.

20 **Under the Constitution, the president chooses judges to serve on the Supreme Court, but each choice must be approved by the Senate. This is an example of what principle of government?**

A checks and balances
B federalism
C separation of powers
D judicial review

21 **The highest level of the American judicial system is the**

A appeals court.
B president's cabinet.
C Supreme Court.
D House of Representatives.

22 **The government powers that are shared between the federal and state governments are known as**

A enumerated powers.
B popular powers.
C reserved powers.
D concurrent powers.

CHAPTER 4 Assessment

Using Academic Vocabulary

16. Students' sentences will vary but should reflect an understanding of each term.

Building Citizenship

17. Students' plans should outline the branches of local government and the responsibilities of each branch.

Reviewing Skills

18. Review READING SKILL Summaries will vary but should include the issue raised by the case, the Court's decision, and the establishment of the principle of judicial review.

19. Review ANALYSIS SKILL Students' answers will vary but should include sound reasoning for their position.

Standards Practice

20. A
21. C
22. D

Bonus Question

Ask: What is a citizens' most important responsibility? Why? (*voting; because it exercises the right of self-government*) OL

History Online

Have students visit the Web site at ca.hss.glencoe.com to review Chapter 4 and take the **Self-Check Quiz.**

10. Answers may include the domination of the government by one branch.

Geography Skills

11. Massachusetts
12. North Carolina

Read to Write

13. Students' speeches should have a clear pattern of organization with an introduction, transitions, previews, summaries, a logically developed body, and an effective conclusion.

14. **The Big Ideas** Students' essays should include a well-defined thesis; present detailed evidence, examples, and reasoning as support; and arrange details, reasons, and examples effectively to answer reader concerns and counterarguments.

15. Answers will vary.

UNIT 2 REVIEW

FOCUS

Reviewing Unit Objectives

Having studied this unit, students should be able to

- Describe the structure of the national government under the Articles of Confederation.
- Explain what the Confederation Congress achieved and what problems it encountered.
- Outline the steps that led to the formation of the Constitutional Convention.
- Describe the structure of the national government under the U.S. Constitution.
- Identify the compromises needed to finish the U.S. Constitution and explain why they were required.
- Give examples of parts of the U.S. Constitution that illustrate its underlying principles.

TEACH

Have students explain how British traditions, American experience, and Enlightenment ideas all contributed to the U.S. Constitution. OL

Unit Review Activity

To help students review the unit objectives, have them compare and contrast the government under the Articles of Confederation and under the Constitution and explain the process by which the Constitution was written and approved. OL

Unit 2 REVIEW

Creating a Nation

Government under the Articles of Confederation was weak. When the Founders wrote a new constitution, they created a strong government. It was based on British traditions and the ideas of the Enlightenment.

	Chapter 3 A More Perfect Union	Chapter 4 The Constitution
When	• 1777–1790	• 1787–present
Where	• The Northeast • The Northwest Territory • The South	• Philadelphia, Pennsylvania

▲ *The Articles of Confederation*

▲ *Seal of Congress*

END-OF-UNIT RESOURCES

Use these resources to review and assess unit material.

- Step Into American History Activities
- Cumulative Assessment Activities
- Reading Essentials and Study Guide
- California Standards Practice Workbook
- Interactive Tutor Self-Assessment CD-ROM
- Exam*View*® Pro Testmaker CD-ROM
- Succeeding on the California History–Social Science Standards CD-ROM

Unit 2 Review

	Chapter 3: A More Perfect Union	Chapter 4: The Constitution
Major Events	• **1776–1780** Colonies become states with written constitutions • **1777** The Articles of Confederation are the first constitution of the United States of America • **1785** Ordinance of 1785 provides way to survey and sell western lands • **1786–1787** Shays's Rebellion challenges national government • **1787** Northwest Ordinance sets up system under which western lands may become states • **1787** Constitutional Convention meets • **1787** Three-fifths Compromise is temporary solution to slavery issue • **1787–1790** Federalists work for ratification of the Constitution and Antifederalists work for its defeat	• **1791** Bill of Rights added to Constitution • **1803** *Marbury* v. *Madison* establishes Supreme Court's power of judicial review • **1866** *Ex parte Milligan* demonstrates Supreme Court's power to review presidential policies • **1954** *Brown* v. *Board of Education* demonstrates Supreme Court's right to review state laws
Some Important People	• Daniel Shays • James Madison • Edmund Randolph • Roger Sherman • Alexander Hamilton	• Gouverneur Morris • John Marshall
How do these events and ideas affect our lives today?	• Since the Articles of Confederation could not solve serious problems, the Founders developed a new constitution. We live under that constitution today.	• The Bill of Rights guarantees certain rights and freedoms to all U.S. citizens. The government may not make laws that take them away.
What was happening in California at this time?	• **1777** Spanish establish town of San José • **1781** Spanish found Los Angeles • **1784** Father Junípero Serra dies	• **1824** A new constitution establishes the Federal Republic of Mexico, which includes the province of California

Linda Brown ▶

James Madison ▶

Gouverneur Morris ▶

ASSESS/CLOSE

Unit Wrap-Up Activity

Creating Slide Presentations Have students work collaboratively to create slide presentations that focus on one of the following topics: the writing of state constitutions and the Articles of Confederation; weaknesses of the Articles government; achievements of that government; the writing of the Constitution; or the debate over ratification.

1. Organize students into groups of equal size and assign each group one of the topics.
2. Tell students to create a slide show that uses text and visuals to summarize all they know about their topic.
3. Have each group present its slide show to the class. OL

PROFESSIONAL DEVELOPMENT: TEACHING READING

Use these resources for help teaching reading skills.

- Beers, G. Kylene. *When Kids Can't Read, What Teachers Can Do: A Guide for Teachers, 6–12.* Heinemann, 2003.
- Daniels, Harvey, and Steven Zemelman. *Subjects Matter: Every Teacher's Guide to Content-Area Reading.* Heinemann, 2004.
- Robb, Laura. *Teaching Reading in the Middle School.* Scholastic Professional Books, 2000.
- Tovani, Cris. *I Read It But I Don't Get It: Comprehension Strategies for Adolescent Readers.* Stenhouse Publishers, 2000.

FOCUS

BELLRINGER
SKILLBUILDER ACTIVITY

Ask students to read the Preamble to the Constitution. Have them identify which purpose of the Constitution is the most important to them personally.

TEACH

U Universal Access

English Learners The Constitution is reproduced in its original language, some of which can be difficult due to complex sentence structure. The explanatory notes should help students grasp the purpose of major sections. Many of its difficult words are defined in marginal notes on the page where they appear. Suggest that students substitute the definitions for the original words to help them understand the point of the document. EL

Answers and Additional Support

The Constitution of the United States

The Constitution of the United States is truly a remarkable document. It was one of the first written constitutions in modern history. The Framers wanted to devise a plan for a strong central government that would unify the country, as well as preserve the ideals of the Declaration of Independence. The document they wrote created a representative legislature, the office of president, a system of courts, and a process for adding amendments. For over 200 years, the flexibility and strength of the Constitution has guided the nation's political leaders. The document has become a symbol of pride and a force for national unity.

U The entire text of the Constitution and its amendments follows. Those passages that have been set aside, outdated by the passage of time, or changed by the adoption of amendments are printed in blue. Also included are explanatory notes that will help clarify the meaning of each article and section.

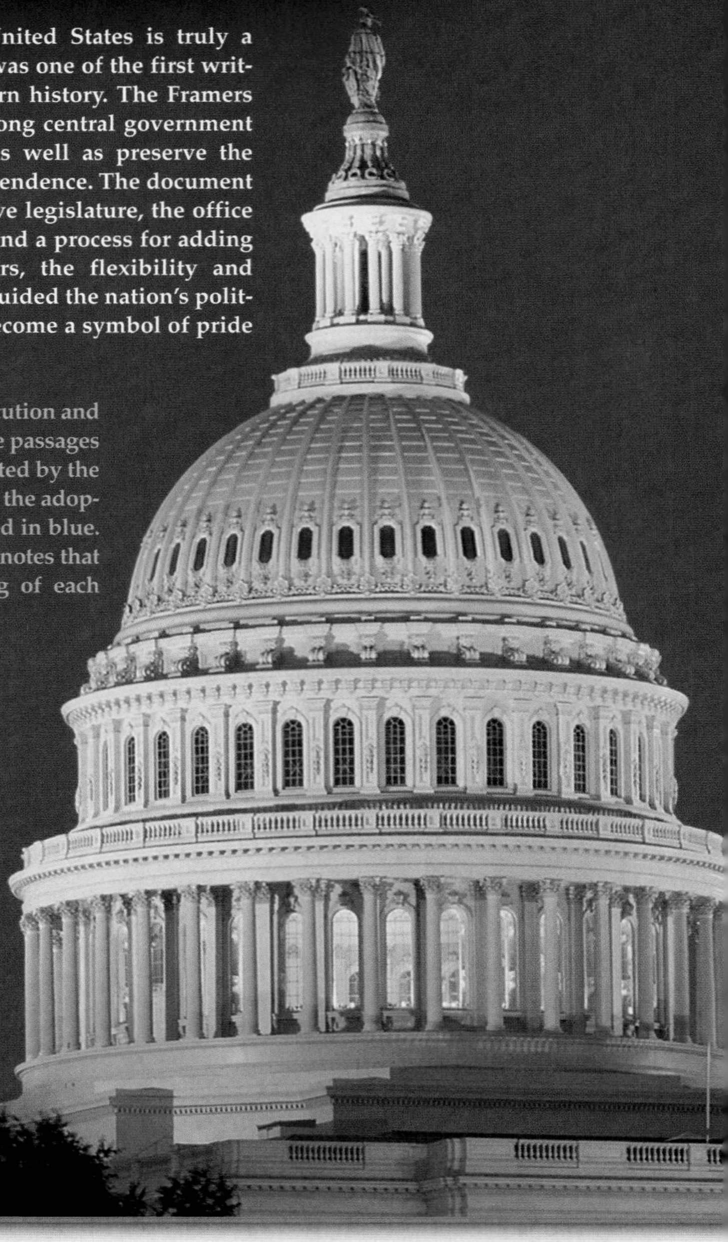

James Madison, author of the Constitution

Did You Know?

The final draft of the Constitution was prepared by a group of five delegates called the Committee of Style. Chaired by William Samuel Johnson of Connecticut, the committee included Alexander Hamilton of New York, Rufus King of Massachusetts, James Madison of Virginia, and Gouverneur Morris of Pennsylvania. It worked for five days, completing its task on September 12. Morris did most of the work of styling the document.

United States Constitution

Preamble

U1 We the People of the United States, in Order to form a more perfect Union, establish Justice, insure domestic Tranquility, provide for the common defence, promote the general Welfare, and secure the Blessings of Liberty to ourselves and our Posterity, do ordain and establish this Constitution for the United States of America.

The Preamble introduces the Constitution and sets forth the general purposes for which the government was established. The Preamble also declares that the power of the government comes from the people.

The printed text of the document shows the spelling and punctuation of the parchment original.

Article I

Section 1

All legislative Powers herein granted shall be vested in a Congress of the United States, which shall consist of a Senate and House of Representatives.

Section 2

[1.] The House of Representatives shall be composed of Members chosen every second Year by the People of the several States, and the Electors in each State shall have the Qualifications requisite for Electors of the most numerous Branch of the State Legislature.

[2.] No person shall be a Representative who shall not have attained to the Age of twenty five Years, and been seven Years a Citizen of the United States, and who shall not, when elected, be an Inhabitant of that State in which he shall be chosen.

U2 [3.] Representatives and direct Taxes shall be apportioned among the several States which may be included within this Union, according to their respective Numbers, which shall be determined by adding to the whole Number of free Persons, including those bound to Service for a Term of Years, and excluding Indians not taxed, three fifths of all other Persons. The actual Enumeration shall be made within three Years after the first Meeting of the Congress of the United States, and within every subsequent Term of ten Years, in such Manner as they shall by Law direct. The Number of Representatives shall not exceed one for every thirty Thousand, but each State shall have at Least one Representative; and until such enumeration shall be made, the State of New Hampshire shall be entitled to chuse three; Massachusetts eight, Rhode-Island and Providence Plantations one, Connecticut five, New-York six, New Jersey four, Pennsylvania eight, Delaware one, Maryland six, Virginia ten, North Carolina five, South Carolina five, and Georgia three.

[4.] When vacancies happen in the Representation from any State, the Executive Authority thereof shall issue Writs of Election to fill such Vacancies.

[5.] The House of Representatives shall chuse their Speaker and other Officers; and shall have the sole Power of Impeachment.

Article I. The Legislative Branch C

R The Constitution contains seven divisions called articles. Each article covers a general topic. For example, Articles I, II, and III create the three branches of the national government—the legislative, executive, and judicial branches. Most of the articles are divided into sections.

Section 2. House of Representatives

Division of Representatives Among the States The number of representatives from each state is based on the size of the state's population. Each state is entitled to at least one representative. *What are the qualifications for members of the House of Representatives?*

Vocabulary

preamble: *introduction*
constitution: *principles and laws of a nation*
enumeration: *census or population count*
impeachment: *bringing charges against an official*

Did You Know?

The opening phrase "We the People of the United States" was written by the Committee of Style. The previous draft had listed each of the thirteen states. The change emphasized the sovereignty of the people. Also, the Committee did not think it was proper to list New York and Rhode Island, which did not have delegates at the Convention.

Section 2.
House of Representatives

Answer: A member of the House must be at least 25 years old, be a United States citizen for at least seven years, and be an inhabitant of the state from which he or she was elected.

U1 Universal Access

English Learners Point out that the use of capitalization in the Constitution does not follow modern rules. **Ask:** What examples of unusual capitalization do you see in the Preamble? *(People, Order, Union, Justice, Tranquility, Welfare, Blessings, Liberty, Posterity)* EL

C Critical Thinking

Making Inferences Ask: What is the significance of discussing the legislative branch first? *(Answers may include the idea that the lawmaking power is the most important or that the lawmaking power logically comes first because Congress must pass laws before the president can execute them or judges interpret them.)* AL

R Reading Strategy

Analyzing Text Structure Each article is divided into sections. **Ask:** What is the subject of Article I? *(the legislative branch, or Congress)* Have students look over the next few pages to see the subjects of the different sections of this article. **Ask:** What is the subject of Article I, Section 2? *(the Senate)* BL

U2 Universal Access

Visual/Spatial Have students carry out research to identify the number of representatives in each state in 1992 and 2002. They should determine which states gained and which lost representatives. Have them create two maps comparing the two years and highlighting the differences. OL CA CS3.

S Skill Practice

Historical and Social Sciences Analysis Skill
Ask: How many votes does each state get in the Senate? *(two)* How many votes did each state have under the Articles of Confederation? *(one)* AL

CA HI3.

C Critical Thinking

Comparing and Contrasting Ask: How much of the Senate is the subject of an election every two years? *(one third)* How many seats in the House of Representatives are subject to an election every two years? *(all)* Which house is likely to be more responsive to voters' wishes? Why? *(the House; because members who want to be re-elected must face voters more often)* OL

R Reading Strategy

Monitoring Comprehension Ask: What happens if the Senate ties when holding a vote? *(the Vice President has the right to cast the deciding vote)* OL

Section 3. The Senate
Number of Members, Terms of Office, and Voting Procedure Originally, senators were chosen by the state legislators of their own states. The Seventeenth Amendment changed this, so that senators are now elected by the people. There are 100 senators, 2 from each state. The vice president serves as president of the Senate.

John Adams, the first vice president

Section 3. The Senate
Trial of Impeachment One of Congress's powers is the power to impeach—to accuse government officials of wrongdoing, put them on trial, and if necessary remove them from office. *Which body has the power to decide the official's guilt or innocence?*

Vocabulary

president pro tempore: *presiding officer of Senate who serves when the vice president is absent*
indictment: *charging a person with an offense*
quorum: *minimum number of members that must be present to conduct sessions*
adjourn: *to suspend a session*
immunity privilege: *members cannot be sued or prosecuted for anything they say in Congress*
emoluments: *salaries*
bill: *draft of a proposed law*
revenue: *income raised by government*

Section 3

[1.] The Senate of the United States shall be composed of two Senators from each State, chosen by the Legislature thereof, for six Years; and each Senator shall have one Vote. S

[2.] Immediately after they shall be assembled in Consequence of the first Election, they shall be divided as equally as may be into three Classes. The Seats of the Senators of the first Class shall be vacated at the Expiration of the second Year, of the second Class at the Expiration of the fourth Year, and of the third Class at the Expiration of the sixth Year, so that one third may be chosen every second Year; and if Vacancies happen by Resignation, or otherwise, during the Recess of the Legislature of any State, the Executive thereof may make temporary Appointments until the next Meeting of the Legislature, which shall then fill such Vacancies. C

[3.] No Person shall be a Senator who shall not have attained to the Age of thirty Years, and been nine Years a Citizen of the United States, and who shall not, when elected, be an Inhabitant of that State for which he shall be chosen.

[4.] The Vice President of the United States shall be President of the Senate, but shall have no Vote, unless they be equally divided. R

[5.] The Senate shall chuse their other Officers, and also a President pro tempore, in the Absence of the Vice President, or when he shall exercise the Office of the President of the United States.

[6.] The Senate shall have the sole Power to try all Impeachments. When sitting for that Purpose, they shall be on Oath or Affirmation. When the President of the United States is tried, the Chief Justice shall preside: And no Person shall be convicted without the Concurrence of two thirds of the Members present.

[7.] Judgment in Cases of Impeachment shall not extend further than to removal from Office, and disqualification to hold and enjoy any Office of honor, Trust or Profit under the United States: but the Party convicted shall nevertheless be liable and subject to Indictment, Trial, Judgment and Punishment, according to Law.

Section 4

[1.] The Times, Places and Manner of holding Elections for Senators and Representatives, shall be prescribed in each State by the Legislature thereof; but the Congress may at any time by Law make or alter such Regulations, except as to the Places of chusing Senators.

[2.] The Congress shall assemble at least once in every Year, and such Meeting shall be on the first Monday in December, unless they shall by Law appoint a different Day.

Answers and Additional Support

Did You Know?

Each state has a senior senator and a junior senator. The senior senator is not the older of the two, but the one who has served in the Senate the longest.

Section 3. The Senate
Answer: the Senate

Section 5

[1.] Each House shall be the Judge of the Elections, Returns and Qualifications of its own Members, and a Majority of each shall constitute a Quorum to do Business; but a smaller Number may adjourn from day to day, and may be authorized to compel the Attendance of absent Members, in such Manner, and under such Penalties as each House may provide.

[2.] Each House may determine the Rules of its Proceedings, punish its Members for disorderly Behaviour, and, with the Concurrence of two thirds, expel a Member.

[3.] Each House shall keep a Journal of its Proceedings, and from time to time publish the same, excepting such Parts as may in their Judgment require Secrecy; and the Yeas and Nays of the Members of either House on any question shall, at the Desire of one fifth of those Present, be entered on the Journal.

[4.] Neither House, during the Session of Congress, shall, without the Consent of the other, adjourn for more than three days, nor to any other Place than that in which the two Houses shall be sitting.

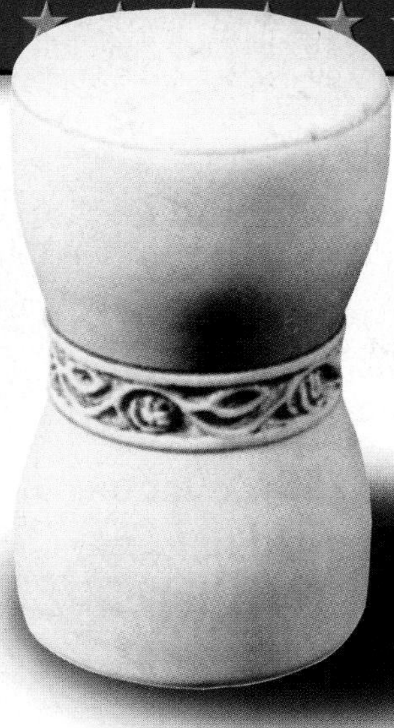

Senate gavel

Section 6

[1.] The Senators and Representatives shall receive a Compensation for their Services, to be ascertained by Law, and paid out of the Treasury of the United States. They shall in all Cases, except Treason, Felony and Breach of the Peace, be privileged from Arrest during their Attendance at the Session of their respective Houses, and in going to and returning from the same; and for any Speech or Debate in either House, they shall not be questioned in any other Place.

[2.] No Senator or Representative shall, during the Time for which he was elected, be appointed to any civil Office under the Authority of the United States, which shall have been created, or the Emoluments whereof shall have been encreased during such time; and no Person holding any Office under the United States, shall be a Member of either House during his Continuance in Office.

Section 6. Privileges and Restrictions
Pay and Privileges To strengthen the federal government, the Founders set congressional salaries to be paid by the United States Treasury rather than by members' respective states. Originally, members were paid $6 per day. In 2002, all members of Congress received a base salary of $150,000.

Section 7

[1.] All Bills for raising Revenue shall originate in the House of Representatives; but the Senate may propose or concur with Amendments as on other Bills.

[2.] Every Bill which shall have passed the House of Representatives and the Senate, shall, before it become a Law, be presented to the President of the United States; If he approve he shall sign it, but if not he shall return it, with his Objections to that House in which it shall have originated, who shall enter the Objections at large on their Journal, and proceed to reconsider it. If after such Reconsideration two thirds of that House shall agree to pass the Bill, it shall be sent, together with the Objections, to the other House, by which it shall likewise be reconsidered, and if approved by two thirds

Section 7. Passing Laws
Revenue Bills All tax laws must originate in the House of Representatives. This ensures that the branch of Congress that is elected by the people every two years has the major role in determining taxes.

Section 7. Passing Laws
How Bills Become Laws A bill may become a law only by passing both houses of Congress and by being signed by the president. The president can check Congress by rejecting—vetoing—its legislation. *How can Congress override the president's veto?*

R Reading Strategy

Understanding Vocabulary
Direct students' attention to the bottom of the previous page for a definition of *quorum*. **Ask:** How many members of the 100-person Senate are needed for a quorum? *(51)* OL

C Critical Thinking

Drawing Conclusions Ask: Why is Congress required to make its proceedings public? *(to let people know what members said on particular issues)* Why is Congress allowed to keep some discussions secret? *(Answers may include need to maintain security on defense matters.)* OL

S Skill Practice

Historical and Social Sciences Analysis Skill
Ask: What is meant by the "Yeas and Nays"? *(the yes and no votes that members of Congress register on a bill)* AL

Did You Know?

When the first Congress met in New York City in 1789, it took nearly a month for enough members to arrive to make a quorum.

Section 7. Passing Laws

Answer: A bill can become a law, despite not being signed by the president, if two-thirds of the House of Representatives and two-thirds of the Senate approve it a second time.

S Skill Practice

Historical and Social Sciences Analysis Skill

Both houses of Congress have several committees that oversee all bills in certain areas, such as banking, defense, or agriculture. Those committees are often divided further into subcommittees that focus on specific parts of that broader area. Have students conduct research to find out what committees and subcommittees the representative from your district and the two senators from your state serve on and whether those members have leadership roles on the committees or subcommittees. OL CA 8RC2.6

C Critical Thinking

Identifying Central Issues

Both the first clause and the fourth clause in this section point out that laws Congress passes on particular subjects should be "uniform." **Ask:** What problem with the Articles of Confederation were the Framers trying to solve by using this word? *(difficulty caused by having different laws from state to state)* OL CA HI1.

Answers and Additional Support

Civil War money

Section 8. Powers Granted to Congress

Expressed Powers Expressed powers are those powers directly stated in the Constitution. Most of the expressed powers of Congress are listed in Article I, Section 8. These powers are also called enumerated powers because they are numbered 1–18. *Which clause gives Congress the power to declare war?*

Section 8. Powers Granted to Congress

The Commerce Clause Congress has the power to make laws that control trade, or commerce. This trade may be with other countries, among the states, or with Native Americans. During the 1800s, the Supreme Court ruled that the tribes were independent nations. Congress may limit their independence, however, because they are inside the United States. The Constitution does not state how Congress may limit the tribes. As a result, the tribes have had changing amounts of independence over the years.

Vocabulary

resolution: *legislature's formal expression of opinion*
naturalization: *procedure by which a citizen of a foreign nation becomes a citizen of the United States*
tribunal: *a court*
letter of marque: *authority given to a citizen to outfit an armed ship and use it to attack enemy ships in time of war*
reprisal: *taking by force property or territory belonging to another country or to its citizens*
insurrection: *rebellion*

of that House, it shall become a Law. But in all such Cases the Votes of both Houses shall be determined by yeas and Nays, and the Names of the Persons voting for and against the Bill shall be entered on the Journal of each House respectively. If any Bill shall not be returned by the President within ten Days (Sundays excepted) after it shall have been presented to him, the Same shall be a Law, in like Manner as if he had signed it, unless the Congress by their Adjournment prevent its Return, in which Case it shall not be a Law.

[3.] Every Order, Resolution, or Vote to which the Concurrence of the Senate and House of Representatives may be necessary (except on a question of Adjournment) shall be presented to the President of the United States; and before the Same shall take Effect, shall be approved by him, or being disapproved by him, shall be repassed by two thirds of the Senate and House of Representatives, according to the Rules and Limitations prescribed in the Case of a Bill.

Section 8

[1.] The Congress shall have the Power To lay and collect Taxes, Duties, Imposts and Excises, to pay the Debts and provide for the common Defence and general Welfare of the United States; but all Duties, Imposts and Excises shall be uniform throughout the United States;
[2.] To borrow Money on the credit of the United States;
[3.] To regulate Commerce with foreign Nations, and among the several States, and with the Indian Tribes;
[4.] To establish an uniform Rule of Naturalization, and uniform Laws on the subject of Bankruptcies throughout the United States;
[5.] To coin Money, regulate the Value thereof, and of foreign Coin, and fix the Standard of Weights and Measures;
[6.] To provide for the Punishment of counterfeiting the Securities and current Coin of the United States;
[7.] To establish Post Offices and post Roads;
[8.] To promote the Progress of Science and useful Arts, by securing for limited Times to Authors and Inventors the exclusive Right to their respective Writings and Discoveries;
[9.] To constitute Tribunals inferior to the supreme Court;
[10.] To define and punish Piracies and Felonies committed on the high Seas, and Offences against the Law of Nations;
[11.] To declare War, grant Letters of Marque and Reprisal, and make Rules concerning Captures on Land and Water;

Did You Know?

Though Congress has the sole power to declare war, the government sent troops into battle several times in the twentieth century without a declaration of war. Two major examples are the Korean War of the 1950s and the Vietnam War of the 1960s and 1970s. Both wars were fought on the president's authority to support governments against external aggression.

Section 8. Powers Granted to Congress

Answer: Article 1, Section 8, Clause 11

[12.] To raise and support Armies, but no Appropriation of Money to that Use shall be for a longer Term than two Years;
[13.] To provide and maintain a Navy;
[14.] To make Rules for the Government and Regulation of the land and naval Forces;
[15.] To provide for calling forth the Militia to execute the Laws of the Union, suppress Insurrections and repel Invasions;
[16.] To provide for organizing, arming, and disciplining, the Militia, and for governing such Part of them as may be employed in the Service of the United States, reserving to the States respectively, the Appointment of the Officers, and the Authority of training the Militia according to the discipline prescribed by Congress;
R [17.] To exercise exclusive Legislation in all Cases whatsoever, over such District (not exceeding ten Miles square) as may, by Cession of particular States, and the Acceptance of Congress, become the Seat of Government of the United States, and to exercise like Authority over all Places purchased by the Consent of the Legislature of the State in which the Same shall be, for the Erection of Forts, Magazines, Arsenals, dock-Yards, and other needful Buildings;—And
C [18.] To make all Laws which shall be necessary and proper for carrying into Execution the foregoing Powers, and all other Powers vested by this Constitution in the Government of the United States, or in any Department or Officer thereof.

Section 9

S [1]. The Migration or Importation of such Persons as any of the States now existing shall think proper to admit, shall not be prohibited by the Congress prior to the Year one thousand eight hundred and eight, but a Tax or duty may be imposed on such Importation, not exceeding ten dollars for each Person.
[2.] The Privilege of the Writ of Habeas Corpus shall not be suspended, unless when in Cases of Rebellion or Invasion the public Safety may require it.
[3.] No Bill of Attainder or ex post facto Law shall be passed.
[4.] No Capitation, or other direct, Tax shall be laid, unless in Proportion to the Census or Enumeration herein before directed to be taken.
[5.] No Tax or Duty shall be laid on Articles exported from any State.
[6.] No Preference shall be given by any Regulation of Commerce or Revenue to the Ports of one State over those of another: nor shall Vessels bound to, or from, one State, be obliged to enter, clear, or pay Duties in another.

Seal of the U.S. Navy

Section 8. Powers Granted to Congress

Elastic Clause The final enumerated power is often called the "elastic clause." This clause gives Congress the right to make all laws "necessary and proper" to carry out the powers expressed in the other clauses of Article I. It is called the elastic clause because it lets Congress "stretch" its powers to meet situations the Founders could never have anticipated.

What does the phrase "necessary and proper" in the elastic clause mean? Almost from the beginning, this phrase was a subject of dispute. The issue was whether a strict or a broad interpretation of the Constitution should be applied. The dispute was first addressed in 1819, in the case of *McCulloch* v. *Maryland*, when the Supreme Court ruled in favor of a broad interpretation.

Section 9. Powers Denied to the Federal Government

Habeas Corpus A writ of habeas corpus issued by a judge requires a law official to bring a prisoner to court and show cause for holding the prisoner. A bill of attainder is a bill that punished a person without a jury trial. An "ex post facto" law is one that makes an act a crime after the act has been committed. *What does the Constitution say about bills of attainder?*

R Reading Strategy

Evaluating Text Remind students that Washington, D.C., is the nation's capital. **Ask:** What body has authority over that city? Why? *(Congress; the Constitution grants the power in Section 8, Clause 17)* OL

C Critical Thinking

Analyzing Information
Ask: Is the term "elastic clause" appropriate for Section 8, Clause 18? Why or why not? *(Students may say that it is appropriate because Congress can stretch the clause to cover many actions.)* OL

S Skill Practice

Historical and Social Sciences Analysis Skill
Explain that this clause prevented Congress from passing any law banning the importation of Africans as slaves before 1808. This language was a compromise between delegates who wanted to ban the importation of slaves and those who wished to keep the practice open. **Ask:** Which part of the country was represented by the delegates who supported slavery? *(the South)* OL

Did You Know?

Habeas corpus was suspended by President Abraham Lincoln during the Civil War on the grounds that the Constitution allowed suspension in the case of rebellion. The Supreme Court ruled in *Ex parte Merryman* that Lincoln's move violated the Constitution because only Congress had the power to suspend habeus corpus.

Section 9.
Powers Denied to the Federal Government

Answer: Congress cannot pass such bills.

R1 Reading Strategy

Reading Primary Sources **Ask:** What limits does this clause (Section 9, Clause 7) place on the federal government? *(prevents it from spending any money unless authorized by Congress)* OL CA HR3.

R2 Reading Strategy

Taking Notes Have students create a chart in which they list the powers denied the states in one column and, in another, specify the clause in which that power is granted to Congress. OL

R3 Reading Strategy

Monitoring Comprehension **Ask:** Who are the only two members of the executive branch specified in the Constitution? *(president and vice president)* OL

Answers and Additional Support

R1 [7.] No Money shall be drawn from the Treasury, but in Consequence of Appropriations made by Law; and a regular Statement and Account of the Receipts and Expenditures of all public Money shall be published from time to time.

[8.] No Title of Nobility shall be granted by the United States: And no Person holding any Office of Profit or Trust under them, shall, without the Consent of the Congress, accept of any present, Emolument, Office, or Title, of any kind whatever, from any King, Prince, or foreign State.

R2 **Section 10. Powers Denied to the States**

Limitations on Power Section 10 lists limits on the states. These restrictions were designed, in part, to prevent an overlapping in functions and authority with the federal government.

Section 10

[1.] No State shall enter into any Treaty, Alliance, or Confederation; grant Letters of Marque and Reprisal; coin Money; emit Bills of Credit; make any Thing but gold and silver Coin a Tender in Payment of Debts; pass any Bill of Attainder, ex post facto Law, or Law impairing the Obligation of Contracts, or grant any Title of Nobility.

[2.] No State shall, without the Consent of the Congress, lay any Imposts or Duties on Imports or Exports, except what may be absolutely necessary for executing it's inspection Laws: and the net Produce of all Duties and Imposts, laid by any State on Imports and Exports, shall be for the Use of the Treasury of the United States; and all such Laws shall be subject to the Revision and Controul of the Congress.

[3.] No State shall, without the Consent of Congress, lay any Duty of Tonnage, keep Troops, or Ships of War in time of Peace, enter into any Agreement or Compact with another State, or with a foreign Power, or engage in War, unless actually invaded, or in such imminent Danger as will not admit of delay.

United States coins

Article II. The Executive Branch

Article II creates an executive branch to carry out laws passed by Congress. Article II lists the powers and duties of the presidency, describes qualifications for office and procedures for electing the president, and provides for a vice president.

Article II

Section 1

R3 [1.] The executive Power shall be vested in a President of the United States of America. He shall hold his Office during the Term of four Years, and, together with the Vice President, chosen for the same Term, be elected, as follows

[2.] Each State shall appoint, in such Manner as the Legislature thereof may direct, a Number of Electors, equal to the whole Number of Senators and Representatives to which the State may be entitled in the Congress: but no Senator or Representative, or Person holding an Office of Trust or Profit under the United States, shall be appointed an Elector.

[3.] The Electors shall meet in their respective States, and vote by Ballot for two Persons, of whom one at least shall not be an Inhabitant of the same State with

Vocabulary

appropriations: *funds set aside for a specific use*
emolument: *payment*
impost: *tax*
duty: *tax*

Did You Know?

The Constitution placed no limits on the number of terms a president could serve. When George Washington retired after two terms, that set a precedent that all presidents followed until 1940, when Franklin Delano Roosevelt ran for—and won—re-election to a third term. (He won a fourth in 1944.) Many people opposed Roosevelt's actions, and in 1951 the Twenty-first Amendment was ratified to put an official two-term limit on all future presidents.

themselves. And they shall make a List of all the Persons voted for, and of the Number of Votes for each; which List they shall sign and certify, and transmit sealed to the Seat of the Government of the United States, directed to the President of the Senate. The President of the Senate shall, in the Presence of the Senate and House of Representatives, open all the Certificates, and the Votes shall then be counted. The Person having the greatest Number of Votes shall be the President, if such Number be a Majority of the whole Number of Electors appointed; and if there be more than one who have such Majority, and have an equal Number of Votes, then the House of Representatives shall immediately chuse by Ballot one of them for President; and if no person have a Majority, then from the five highest on the List the said House shall in like Manner chuse the President. But in chusing the President, the Votes shall be taken by States, the Representation from each State having one Vote; A quorum for this Purpose shall consist of a Member or Members from two thirds of the States, and a Majority of all the States shall be necessary to a Choice. In every Case, after the Choice of the President, the Person having the greatest Number of Votes of the Electors shall be the Vice President. But if there should remain two or more who have equal Votes, the Senate shall chuse from them by Ballot the Vice President.

[4.] The Congress may determine the Time of chusing the Electors, and the Day on which they shall give their Votes; which Day shall be the same throughout the United States.

W1 **[5.]** No Person except a natural born Citizen, or a Citizen of the United States, at the time of the Adoption of this Constitution, shall be eligible to the Office of President; neither shall any Person be eligible to that Office who shall not have attained to the Age of thirty five Years, and been fourteen Years a Resident within the United States.

W2 **[6.]** In Case of the Removal of the President from Office, or of his Death, Resignation, or Inability to discharge the Powers and Duties of the said Office, the Same shall devolve on the Vice President, and the Congress may by Law provide for the Case of Removal, Death, Resignation or Inability, both of the President and Vice President, declaring what Officer shall then act as President, and such Officer shall act accordingly, until the Disability be removed, or a President shall be elected.

[7.] The President shall, at stated Times, receive for his Services, a Compensation, which shall neither be encreased nor diminished during the Period for which he shall have been elected, and he shall not receive within that Period any other Emolument from the United States, or any of them.

S **[8.]** Before he enter on the Execution of his Office, he shall take the following Oath or Affirmation:—"I do solemnly swear (or affirm) that I will faithfully execute the Office of President of the United States, and will to the best of my Ability, preserve, protect and defend the Constitution of the United States."

Section 1. President and Vice President

Former Method of Election The Twelfth Amendment, added in 1804, changed the method of electing the president stated in Article II, Section 1, paragraph 3. The Twelfth Amendment requires that the electors cast separate ballots for president and vice president.

George Washington, the first president

Section 1. President and Vice President

Qualifications The president must be a citizen of the United States by birth, at least 35 years of age, and a resident of the United States for 14 years.

Section 1. President and Vice President

Vacancies If the president dies, resigns, is removed from office by impeachment, or is unable to carry out the duties of the office, the vice president assumes the duties of the president. The Twenty-fifth Amendment sets procedures for presidential succession.

Section 1. President and Vice President

Salary Originally, the president's salary was $25,000 per year. The president's current salary is $400,000 plus a $50,000 nontaxable expense account per year. The president also receives living accommodations in two residences—the White House and Camp David.

W1 Writing Support

Persuasive Writing Have students write an essay in which they argue whether, in modern times, a person who is 35 is or is not adequately prepared for the complex demands of serving as president of the United States. If they believe the age is not enough, tell them to specify what minimum age they would set. OL CA 8WA2.4

W2 Writing Support

Research Reports Writing Have students research and prepare an oral presentation on the vice presidents who became president. Have them explain why he was chosen as vice president, how he became president, and whether or not he won election as president in his own right. OL CA 8SA2.3

S Skill Practice

Analyzing Primary Sources **Ask:** What pledge does the president make when taking the oath of office? *(to preserve, protect, and defend the Constitution)* What does that pledge mean? *(Answers may include acting only so as to uphold the Constitution and not to undermine it.)* OL

Did You Know?

Electors almost always vote in accordance with the state's popular vote. Exceptions are rare, but some have occurred. There have been nine cases of "faithless electors" in American history. In 1988, Democratic presidential candidate Michael Dukakis was denied an electoral vote in West Virginia. One elector voted for running mate Lloyd Bentsen for president and gave Dukakis the vice presidential vote.

R1 Reading Strategy

Organizing Information
Have students read Article II to find the powers of the president. Suggest that they classify those powers under the headings *Executive, Legislative, Diplomatic, Military, and Judicial*. OL

C Critical Thinking

Identifying Central Issues
Ask: What was the purpose of making the president commander in chief of the armed forces? *(to create civilian control of the military)* Why not put Congress in charge of the military? (*Students may say that in time of war there needs to be one person in charge.*) AL

R2 Reading Strategy

Questioning **Ask:** What does the Constitution mean by saying that judges "hold their Offices during good Behaviour"? If students are unable to answer, explain that this means federal judges hold office for life unless they retire, resign, or are impeached and removed from office. OL

Answers and Additional Support

Section 2. Powers of the President
Military, Cabinet, Pardons Mention of "the principal officer in each of the executive departments" is the only suggestion of the president's cabinet to be found in the Constitution. The cabinet is an advisory body, and its power depends on the president. Section 2, Clause 1 also makes the president—a civilian—the head of the armed services. This established the principle of civilian control of the military.

Section 2. Powers of the President
Treaties and Appointments An executive order is a command issued by a president to exercise a power which he has been given by the U.S. Constitution or by a federal statute. In times of emergency, presidents sometimes have used the executive order to override the Constitution of the United States and the Congress. During the Civil War, President Lincoln suspended many fundamental rights guaranteed in the Constitution and the Bill of Rights. He closed down newspapers that opposed his policies and imprisoned some who disagreed with him. Lincoln said that these actions were justified to preserve the Union.

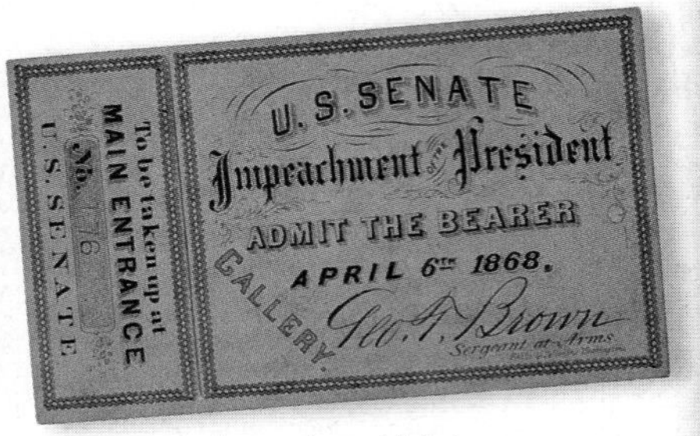

Impeachment ticket

Article III. The Judicial Branch

The term *judicial* refers to courts. The Constitution set up only the Supreme Court but provided for the establishment of other federal courts. The judiciary of the United States has two different systems of courts. One system consists of the federal courts, whose powers derive from the Constitution and federal laws. The other includes the courts of each of the 50 states, whose powers derive from state constitutions and laws.

Section 2
[1.] The President shall be Commander in Chief of the Army and Navy of the United States, and of the Militia of the several States, when called into the actual Service of the United States; he may require the Opinion, in writing, of the principal Officer in each of the executive Departments, upon any Subject relating to the Duties of their respective Offices, and he shall have Power to grant Reprieves and Pardons for Offences against the United States, except in Cases of Impeachment.
[2.] He shall have Power, by and with the Advice and Consent of the Senate, to make Treaties, provided two thirds of the Senators present concur; and he shall nominate, and by and with the Advice and Consent of the Senate, shall appoint Ambassadors, other public Ministers and Consuls, Judges of the supreme Court, and all other Officers of the United States, whose Appointments are not herein otherwise provided for, and which shall be established by Law: but the Congress may by Law vest the Appointment of such inferior Officers, as they think proper, in the President alone, in the Courts of Law, or in the Heads of Departments.
[3.] The President shall have Power to fill up all Vacancies that may happen during the Recess of the Senate, by granting Commissions which shall expire at the End of their next Session.

Section 3
He shall from time to time give to the Congress Information of the State of the Union, and recommend to their Consideration such Measures as he shall judge necessary and expedient; he may, on extraordinary Occasions, convene both Houses, or either of them, and in Case of Disagreement between them, with Respect to the Time of Adjournment, he may adjourn them to such Time as he shall think proper; he shall receive Ambassadors and other public Ministers; he shall take Care that the Laws be faithfully executed, and shall Commission all the Officers of the United States.

Section 4
The President, Vice President and all civil Officers of the United States, shall be removed from Office on Impeachment for, and Conviction of, Treason, Bribery, or other high Crimes and Misdemeanors.

Article III

Section 1
The judicial Power of the United States, shall be vested in one supreme Court, and in such inferior Courts as the Congress may from time to time ordain and establish. The Judges, both of the supreme and inferior Courts, shall hold their Offices during good Behaviour, and shall, at stated Times, receive for their Services, a Compensation, which shall not be diminished during their Continuance in Office.

More Skill Practice

Historical and Social Sciences Analysis Skill One of the most difficult questions for the Framers of the Constitution to resolve concerned the powers of the president. **Ask:** Why did the Framers place limits on those powers? *(They feared the results if they concentrated too much power in one person's hands.)* OL CA HI3.

Did You Know?

The provision in Article II, Section 3, that the president "shall take Care that the Laws be faithfully executed" has been used by presidents as the basis for the power of issuing executive orders, which have the force of law. By expanding the scope of executive orders, presidents over the years have increased the power of the office.

Section 2

[1.] The judicial Power shall extend to all Cases, in Law and Equity, arising under this Constitution, the Laws of the United States, and Treaties made, or which shall be made, under their Authority;—to all Cases affecting Ambassadors, other public Ministers and Consuls;—to all Cases of admiralty and maritime Jurisdiction;—to Controversies to which the United States shall be a Party;—to Controversies between two or more States;—between a State and Citizens of another State;—between Citizens of different States,—between Citizens of the same State claiming Lands under Grants of different States, and between a State, or the Citizens thereof, and foreign States, Citizens or Subjects. R2

[2.] In all Cases affecting Ambassadors, other public Ministers and Consuls, and those in which a State shall be Party, the supreme Court shall have original Jurisdiction. In all the other Cases before mentioned, the R1 supreme Court shall have appellate Jurisdiction, both as to Law and Fact, with such Exceptions, and under such Regulations as the Congress shall make.

[3.] The Trial of all Crimes, except in Cases of Impeachment, shall be by Jury; and such Trial shall be held in the State where the said Crimes shall have been committed; but when not committed within any State, the Trial shall be at such Place or Places as the Congress may by Law have directed.

Section 3

[1.] Treason against the United States, shall consist only in levying War against them, or in adhering to their Enemies, giving them Aid and Comfort. No Person shall be convicted of Treason unless on the Testimony of two Witnesses to the same overt Act, or on Confession in open Court.

[2.] The Congress shall have Power to declare the Punishment of Treason, but no Attainder of Treason shall work Corruption of Blood, or Forfeiture except during the Life of the Person attainted.

Article IV

Section 1

Full Faith and Credit shall be given in each State to the public Acts, Records, and judicial Proceedings of every other State. And the Congress may by general Laws prescribe the Manner in which such Acts, Records and Proceedings shall be proved, and the Effect thereof.

Section 2. Jurisdiction

Statute Law Federal courts deal mostly with "statute law," or laws passed by Congress, treaties, and cases involving the Constitution itself.

Section 2. Jurisdiction

The Supreme Court A Court with "original jurisdiction" has the authority to be the first court to hear a case. The Supreme Court primarily has "appellate jurisdiction" and mostly hears cases appealed from lower courts.

Article IV. Relations Among the States

Article IV explains the relationship of the states to one another and to the national government. This article requires each state to give citizens of other states the same rights as its own citizens, addresses admitting new states, and guarantees that the national government will protect the states.

Vocabulary

original jurisdiction: *authority to be the first court to hear a case*
appellate jurisdiction: *authority to hear cases that have been appealed from lower courts*
treason: *violation of the allegiance owed by a person to his or her own country, for example, by aiding an enemy*

R1 Reading Strategy

Analyzing Text Structure
Ask: Which branch of the government is described in more detail in the Constitution, the legislative or the judiciary? *(legislative)* Explain that as a result, Congress had to pass laws, starting with the Judiciary Act of 1789, to set up the federal courts. OL

R2 Reading Strategy

Summarizing Ask: What kinds of cases are heard in federal courts? *(disputes involving officials of the federal government; cases about ships; when the government is involved; cases that involve two state governments, a citizen of one state and the government of another state, or citizens of different states; cases involving land grants by different states; cases between a citizen or state and a foreign person or government)* AL

Did You Know?

As an appellate court, the U.S. Supreme Court hears two types of cases, appeals and cases entered on a basis called certiorari. The Court *must* hear the appeals but has the discretion to choose whether or not to hear certiorari cases. This distinction was created by Congress at the Court's request so it could cut down on and manage its workload. Most cases are certiorari ones, giving the Court great control over its workload—and over the content of the cases it hears.

S Skill Practice

Analyzing Primary Sources Ask: Why is this material in blue type? *(because it is no longer valid)* What is meant by a "Person held to Service of Labour"? *(an enslaved person; this clause blocked states from keeping African Americans who had fled slavery)* AL

CA HI1.

R Reading Strategy

Activating Prior Knowledge Ask: How many states were needed to approve an amendment to the Articles of Confederation? *(all of them)* How many are needed to amend the Constitution? *(two-thirds of the states in Congress and in the state legislatures for proposing amendments; three-fourths for approving one)* Why did the Convention make it easier? *(because they had seen problems arise from the need for unanimous approval)* OL

Section 3. New States and Territories

New States Congress has the power to admit new states. It also determines the basic guidelines for applying for statehood. Two states, Maine and West Virginia, were created within the boundaries of another state. In the case of West Virginia, President Lincoln recognized the West Virginia government as the legal government of Virginia during the Civil War. This allowed West Virginia to secede from Virginia without obtaining approval from the Virginia legislature.

Section 4. Federal Protection for States

Republic Government can be classified in many different ways. The ancient Greek philosopher Aristotle classified government based on the question: Who governs? According to Aristotle, all governments belong to one of three major groups: (1) autocracy—rule by one person; (2) oligarchy—rule by a few persons; or (3) democracy—rule by many persons. A republic is a form of democracy in which the people elect representatives to make laws and conduct government.

Article V. The Amendment Process

Article V spells out the ways that the Constitution can be amended, or changed. All of the 27 amendments were proposed by a two-thirds vote of both houses of Congress. Only the Twenty-first Amendment was ratified by constitutional conventions of the states. All other amendments have been ratified by state legislatures. *What is an amendment?*

Vocabulary

extradition: *surrender of a criminal to another authority*
amendment: *a change to the Constitution*
ratification: *process by which an amendment is approved*

Section 2

[1.] The Citizens of each State shall be entitled to all Privileges and Immunities of Citizens in the several States.
[2.] A Person charged in any State with Treason, Felony, or other Crime, who shall flee from Justice, and be found in another State, shall on Demand of the executive Authority of the State from which he fled, be delivered up, to be removed to the State having Jurisdiction of the Crime.
[3.] No Person held to Service of Labour in one State, under the Laws thereof, escaping into another, shall, in Consequence of any Law or Regulation therein, be discharged from such Service or Labour, but shall be delivered up on Claim of the Party to whom such Service or Labour may be due. S

Section 3

[1.] New States may be admitted by the Congress into this Union; but no new State shall be formed or erected within the Jurisdiction of any other State; nor any State be formed by the Junction of two or more States, or Parts of States, without the Consent of the Legislatures of the States concerned as well as of the Congress.
[2.] The Congress shall have Power to dispose of and make all needful Rules and Regulations respecting the Territory or other Property belonging to the United States; and nothing in this Constitution shall be so construed as to Prejudice any Claims of the United States, or of any particular State.

Section 4

The United States shall guarantee to every State in this Union a Republican Form of Government, and shall protect each of them against Invasion; and on Application of the Legislature, or of the Executive (when the Legislature cannot be convened) against domestic Violence.

Article V

The Congress, whenever two thirds of both Houses shall deem it necessary, shall propose Amendments to this Constitution, or, on the Application of the Legislatures of two thirds of the several States, shall call a Convention for proposing Amendments, which, in either Case, shall be valid to all Intents and Purposes, as Part of this Constitution, when ratified by the Legislatures of three fourths of the several States, or by Conventions in three fourths thereof, as the one or the other Mode of Ratification may be proposed by the Congress; Provided that no Amendment which may be made prior to the Year One thousand eight hundred and eight shall in any Manner affect the first and fourth Clauses in the Ninth Section of the first Article; and that no State, without its Consent, shall be deprived of its equal Suffrage in the Senate. R

Answers and Additional Support

Article V. The Amendment Process
Answer: a change to the Constitution

Article VI

[1.] All Debts contracted and Engagements entered into, before the Adoption of this Constitution, shall be as valid against the United States under this Constitution, as under the Confederation.

C [2.] This Constitution, and the Laws of the United States which shall be made in Pursuance thereof; and all Treaties made, or which shall be made, under the Authority of the United States, shall be the supreme Law of the Land; and the Judges in every State shall be bound thereby, any Thing in the Constitution or Laws of any State to the Contrary notwithstanding.

[3.] The Senators and Representatives before mentioned, and the Members of the several State Legislatures, and all executive and judicial Officers, both of the United States and of the several States, shall be bound by Oath or Affirmation, to support this Constitution; but no religious Test shall ever be required as a Qualification to any Office or public Trust under the United States.

Article VI. National Supremacy

Article VI contains the "supremacy clause." This clause establishes that the Constitution, laws passed by Congress, and treaties of the United States "shall be the supreme Law of the Land." The "supremacy clause" recognized the Constitution and federal laws as supreme when in conflict with those of the states.

Article VII

The Ratification of the Conventions of nine States, shall be sufficient for the Establishment of this Constitution between the States so ratifying the Same.

Done in Convention by the Unanimous Consent of the States present the Seventeenth Day of September in the Year of our Lord one thousand seven hundred and Eighty seven and of the Independence of the United States of America the Twelfth. In witness whereof We have hereunto subscribed our Names,

Article VII. Ratification

Article VII addresses ratification and declares that the Constitution would take effect after it was ratified by nine states.

W1 **Signers**

George Washington, ***President and Deputy from Virginia***

New Hampshire
John Langdon
Nicholas Gilman

Massachusetts
Nathaniel Gorham
Rufus King

Connecticut
William Samuel Johnson
Roger Sherman

New York
Alexander Hamilton

New Jersey
William Livingston
David Brearley
William Paterson
Jonathan Dayton

Pennsylvania
Benjamin Franklin
Thomas Mifflin
Robert Morris
George Clymer
Thomas FitzSimons
Jared Ingersoll
James Wilson
Gouverneur Morris

Delaware
George Read
Gunning Bedford, Jr.
John Dickinson
Richard Bassett
Jacob Broom

Maryland
James McHenry
Daniel of St. Thomas Jenifer
Daniel Carroll

Virginia
John Blair
James Madison, Jr.

North Carolina
William Blount
Richard Dobbs Spaight
Hugh Williamson

South Carolina
John Rutledge
Charles Cotesworth Pinckney
Charles Pinckney
Pierce Butler

Georgia
William Few
Abraham Baldwin

Attest: *William Jackson,* ***Secretary*** W2

C Critical Thinking

Drawing Conclusions A political scientist once named the supremacy clause as "the most important single provision of the Constitution." **Ask:** Do you agree or disagree? Why or why not? Discuss students' answers as a class. OL CA HI2.

W1 Writing Support

Persuasive Writing Explain that three members of the Convention did not sign the Constitution because they objected to the lack of a Bill of Rights. Have students write an essay in which they explain why they would have signed the document or not signed it. OL

W2 Writing Support

Research Reports Writing Have each student write a brief biography of one of the signers of the Constitution and present their findings orally. OL CA 8SA2.4

Did You Know?

Of the 55 delegates who attended the Constitutional Convention, only 38 signed. A thirty-ninth signature, that of John Dickinson, was added at his request by George Read of Delaware. Three members—Elbridge Gerry of Massachusetts and Edmund Randolph and George Mason of Virginia—refused to sign the document. Another 13 left the Convention before it finished writing the document.

Did You Know?

Alexander Hamilton could not officially sign the Constitution as a representative of New York. He was one of three New Yorkers sent as delegates to the Convention, but two left early in the proceedings. Since New York was not represented by a majority of its delegates, the rules of the Convention said that the state was not officially part of the proceedings.

S Skill Practice

Historical and Social Sciences Analysis Skill Give students the following situation and have them identify which part of the First Amendment applies:

- A magazine column criticizes the president *(freedom of the press)*
- Protestors gather outside a city hall *(right of assembly)*
- People call a radio show to express their thoughts on a public issue *(freedom of speech)*
- Muslims go to a mosque without being bothered *(freedom of religion)*
- Citizens ask the government to change a tax law *(right of petition)* OL

C Critical Thinking

Identifying Central Issues Explain that the Fourth Amendment is aimed at protecting the rights of a person accused of a crime. **Ask:** What limits does this place on law enforcement officials? *(They cannot search a person or his or her property without having a reason.)* OL

Bill of Rights

The first 10 amendments are known as the Bill of Rights (1791). These amendments limit the powers of government. The First Amendment protects the civil liberties of individuals in the United States. The amendment freedoms are not absolute, however. They are limited by the rights of other individuals. *What freedoms does the First Amendment protect?*

Amendment I

Congress shall make no law respecting an establishment of religion, or prohibiting the free exercise thereof; or abridging the freedom of speech, or of the press; or the right of the people peaceably to assemble, and to petition the Government for a redress of grievances. S

Amendment 2

Right to Bear Arms This amendment is often debated. Originally, it was intended to prevent the national government from repeating the actions of the British, who tried to take weapons away from the colonial militia, or armed forces of citizens. This amendment seems to support the right of citizens to own firearms, but the Supreme Court has ruled that it does not prevent Congress from regulating the interstate sale of weapons. *Why is the Second Amendment's meaning debated?*

Amendment II

A well regulated Militia, being necessary to the security of a free State, the right of the people to keep and bear Arms, shall not be infringed.

Amendment III

No Soldier shall, in time of peace be quartered in any house, without the consent of the Owner, nor in time of war, but in a manner to be prescribed by law.

Amendment IV

The right of the people to be secure in their persons, houses, papers, and effects, against unreasonable searches and seizures, shall not be violated, and no Warrants shall issue, but upon probable cause, supported by Oath or affirmation, and particularly describing the place to be searched, and the persons or things to be seized. C

Amendment 5

Rights of Accused Persons This amendment contains important protections for people accused of crimes. One of the protections is that government may not deprive any person of life, liberty, or property without due process of law. This means that the government must follow proper constitutional procedures in trials and in other actions it takes against individuals. *According to Amendment V, what is the function of a grand jury?*

Amendment V

No person shall be held to answer for a capital, or otherwise infamous crime, unless on a presentment or indictment of a Grand Jury, except in cases arising in the land or naval forces, or in the Militia, when in actual service in time of War or public danger; nor shall any person be subject for the same offence to be twice put in jeopardy of life or limb; nor shall be compelled in any criminal case to be a witness against himself, nor be deprived of life, liberty, or property, without due process of law; nor shall private property be taken for public use without just compensation.

Vocabulary

quarter: *to provide living accommodations*
probable cause: *police must have a reasonable basis to believe a person is linked to a crime*
warrant: *document that gives police particular rights or powers*
common law: *law established by previous court decisions*
bail: *money that an accused person provides to the court as a guarantee that he or she will be present for a trial*

Answers and Additional Support

Bill of Rights and Amendments

Answer (First Amendment): freedom of religion, freedom of speech, freedom of the press, freedom to peaceably assemble, and freedom to petition the government for a redress of grievances

Answer (Second Amendment): Students may say that the amendment is debated because it is vague.

Answer (Fifth Amendment): "Presentment" or "indictment" means to formally charge a person with committing a crime. The grand jury evaluates whether there is enough evidence to bring the accused person to trial.

Amendment VI

R In all criminal prosecutions, the accused shall enjoy the right to a speedy and public trial, by an impartial jury of the State and district wherein the crime shall have been committed, which district shall have been previously ascertained by law, and to be informed of the nature and cause of the accusation; to be confronted with the witnesses against him; to have compulsory process for obtaining Witnesses in his favor, and to have the assistance of counsel for his defence.

W **Amendment 6**
Right to a Speedy, Fair Trial A basic protection is the right to a speedy, public trial. The jury must hear witnesses and evidence on both sides before deciding the guilt or innocence of a person charged with a crime. This amendment also provides that legal counsel must be provided to a defendant. In 1963, the Supreme Court ruled, in *Gideon* v. *Wainwright*, that if a defendant cannot afford a lawyer, the government must provide one to defend him or her. *Why is the right to a "speedy" trial important?*

Amendment VII

In Suits at common law, where the value in controversy shall exceed twenty dollars, the right of trial by jury shall be preserved, and no fact tried by a jury, shall be otherwise reexamined in any Court of the United States, than according to the rules of common law.

Amendment VIII

Excessive bail shall not be required, nor excessive fines imposed, nor cruel and unusual punishments inflicted.

Amendment IX

The enumeration in the Constitution, of certain rights, shall not be construed to deny or disparage others retained by the people.

Amendment 9
Powers Reserved to the People This amendment prevents government from claiming that the only rights people have are those listed in the Bill of Rights.

Amendment X

The powers not delegated to the United States by the Constitution, nor prohibited by it to the States, are reserved to the States respectively, or to the people.

Amendment 10
Powers Reserved to the States The final amendment of the Bill of Rights protects the states and the people from an all-powerful federal government. It establishes that powers not given to the national government—or denied to the states—by the Constitution belong to the states or to the people.

Amendment XI

The Judicial power of the United States shall not be construed to extend to any suit in law or equity, commenced or prosecuted against one of the United States by Citizens of another State, or by Citizens or Subjects of any Foreign State.

Amendment 11
Suits Against States The Eleventh Amendment (1795) limits the jurisdiction of the federal courts. The Supreme Court had ruled that a federal court could try a lawsuit brought by citizens of South Carolina against the state of Georgia. This case, *Chisholm* v. *Georgia*, decided in 1793, raised a storm of protest, leading to passage of the Eleventh Amendment.

W Writing Support

Persuasive Writing Some defense lawyers say that the large amount of coverage of some trials in the mass media threatens the accused person's Sixth Amendment rights. Have students write an essay explaining why they agree or disagree. OL

R Reading Strategy

Monitoring Make sure that students understand the protections granted in the Sixth Amendment. Write the four phrases from "to be informed of the nature and cause of the accusation" to the end on the board. Then read each of the following rewordings and ask which phrase it applies to:

- A person accused of a crime has the right to be represented by a lawyer. *(to have the assistance of counsel for his defence)*
- A person must be able to hear the words of anyone who testifies against him to a court. *(to be confronted with the witnesses against him)*
- An accused person must be told what crime he or she is accused of. *(to be informed of the nature and cause of the accusation)*
- The court can order people to appear as witnesses for an accused person. *(to have compulsory process for obtaining Witnesses)* OL

Amendment 6.
Answer: The requirement to a "speedy" trial ensures than an accused person will not be held in jail for a lengthy period as a means of punishing the accused without a trial.

C Critical Thinking

Identifying Central Issues
Ask students to identify a particular problem that they think could be addressed by an amendment to the Constitution. Write their ideas on the board and discuss them as a class. Have them consider whether the matter is best addressed by an amendment or a law passed by Congress. OL

S Skill Practice

Historical and Social Sciences Analysis Skill
Point out that the Electoral College has been criticized as being obsolete, and various ideas have been suggested for changing it or abolishing it altogether. Have students debate the question: Should the Electoral College be abolished and the president elected by popular vote? Point out that those in favor must address the concern of small states that they would have no voice in such a system. OL

Amendment 12
Election of President and Vice President The Twelfth Amendment (1804) corrects a problem that had arisen in the method of electing the president and vice president. This amendment provides for the Electoral College to use separate ballots in voting for president and vice president. *If no candidate receives a majority of the electoral votes, who elects the president?*

S

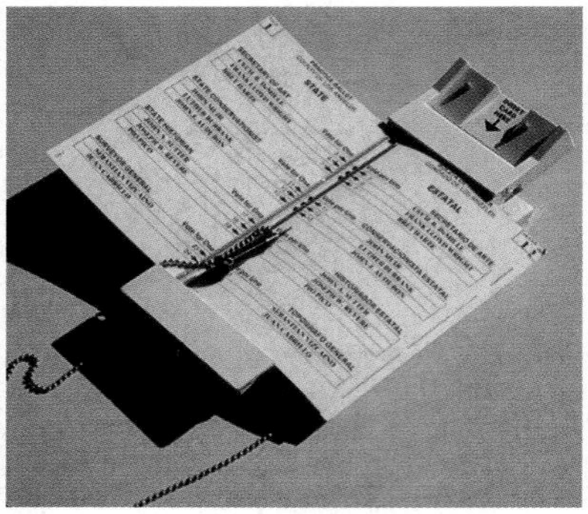

Ballot and ballot marker

Amendment XII C

The electors shall meet in their respective states and vote by ballot for President and Vice-President, one of whom, at least, shall not be an inhabitant of the same state with themselves; they shall name in their ballots the person voted for as President, and in distinct ballots the person voted for as Vice-President, and they shall make distinct lists of all persons voted for as President, and of all persons voted for as Vice-President, and of the number of votes for each, which lists they shall sign and certify, and transmit sealed to the seat of the government of the United States, directed to the President of the Senate;—The President of the Senate shall, in the presence of the Senate and House of Representatives, open all the certificates and the votes shall then be counted;—The person having the greatest number of votes for President, shall be the President, if such number be a majority of the whole number of Electors appointed; and if no person have such majority, then from the persons having the highest numbers not exceeding three on the list of those voted for as President, the House of Representatives shall choose immediately, by ballot, the President. But in choosing the President, the votes shall be taken by states, the representation from each state having one vote; a quorum for this purpose shall consist of a member or members from two-thirds of the states, and a majority of all the states shall be necessary to a choice. And if the House of Representatives shall not choose a President whenever the right of choice shall devolve upon them, before the fourth day of March next following, then the Vice-President shall act as President, as in the case of the death or other constitutional disability of the President. The person having the greatest number of votes as Vice-President, shall be the Vice-President, if such number be a majority of the whole number of Electors appointed, and if no person have a majority, then from the two highest numbers on the list, the Senate shall choose the Vice-President; a quorum for the purpose shall consist of two-thirds of the whole number of Senators, and a majority of the whole number shall be necessary to a choice. But no person constitutionally ineligible to the office of President shall be eligible to that of Vice-President of the United States.

Amendment 13
Abolition of Slavery Amendments Thirteen (1865), Fourteen (1868), and Fifteen (1870) often are called the Civil War amendments because they grew out of that great conflict. The Thirteenth Amendment outlaws slavery.

Amendment XIII

Section 1

Neither slavery nor involuntary servitude, except as a punishment for crime whereof the party shall have been duly convicted, shall exist within the United States, or any place subject to their jurisdiction.

Section 2

Congress shall have power to enforce this article by appropriate legislation.

Vocabulary

majority: *more than half*
devolve: *to pass on*
abridge: *to reduce*
insurrection: *rebellion against the government*
emancipation: *freedom from slavery*

Answers and Additional Support

Amendment 12.
Answer: the House of Representatives
Ask: If no candidate for vice president receives a majority of electoral votes, who chooses the new vice president? *(the Senate)* OL

More Skill Practice

Analyzing Primary Sources Ask: What is the significance of Section 2 of the Thirteenth Amendment? *(Students may say that it takes away any question about the power of Congress to act further on the matter addressed by the amendment.)* AL

Amendment XIV

Section 1

R1 All persons born or naturalized in the United States, and subject to the jurisdiction thereof, are citizens of the United States and of the State wherein they reside. No State shall make or enforce any law which shall abridge the privileges or immunities of citizens of the United States; nor shall any State deprive any person of life, liberty, or property, without due process of law; nor deny to any person within its jurisdiction the equal protection of the laws.

Section 2

Representatives shall be apportioned among the several States according to their respective numbers, counting the whole number of persons in each State, excluding Indians not taxed. But when the right to vote at any election for the choice of electors for President and Vice President of the United States, Representatives in Congress, the Executive and Judicial officers of a State, or the members of the Legislature thereof, is denied to any of the male inhabitants of such State, being twenty-one years of age, and citizens of the United States, or in any way abridged, except for participation in rebellion, or other crime, the basis of representation therein shall be reduced in the proportion which the number of such male citizens shall bear to the whole number of male citizens twenty-one years of age in such State.

Section 3

No person shall be a Senator or Representative in Congress, or elector of President and Vice President, or hold any office, civil or military, under the United States, or under any State, who, having previously taken an oath, as a member of Congress, or as an officer of the United States, or as a member of any State legislature, or as an executive or judicial officer of any State, to support the Constitution of the United States, shall have engaged in insurrection or rebellion against the same, or given aid or comfort to the enemies thereof. But Congress may by a vote of two-thirds of each House, remove such disability.

Section 4

The validity of the public debt of the United States, authorized by law, including debts incurred for payment of pensions and bounties for service in suppressing insurrection or rebellion, shall not be questioned. But neither the United States nor any State shall assume or pay any debt or obligation incurred in aid of insurrection or rebellion against the United States, or any claim for the loss or emancipation of any slave; but all such debts, obligations and claims shall be held illegal and void.

Amendment 14

Rights of Citizens The Fourteenth Amendment (1868) originally was intended to protect the legal rights of the freed slaves. Today it protects the rights of citizenship in general by prohibiting a state from depriving any person of life, liberty, or property without "due process of law." In addition, it states that all citizens have the right to equal protection of the law in all states.

Amendment 14. Section 2

Representation in Congress This section reduced the number of members a state had in the House of Representatives if it denied its citizens the right to vote. Later civil rights laws and the Twenty-fourth Amendment guaranteed the vote to African Americans.

R2

Amendment 14. Section 3

Penalty for Engaging in Insurrection The leaders of the Confederacy were barred from state or federal offices unless Congress agreed to remove this ban. By the end of Reconstruction all but a few Confederate leaders were allowed to return to public life.

Amendment 14. Section 4

Public Debt The public debt acquired by the federal government during the Civil War was valid and could not be questioned by the South. However, the debts of the Confederacy were declared to be illegal. *Could former slaveholders collect payment for the loss of their slaves?*

R1 Reading Strategy

Activating Prior Knowledge What two principles of the Constitution are stated in Section 1 of the Fourteenth Amendment? *(due process of law; equal protection of the laws)* OL CA HI3.

R2 Reading Strategy

Previewing Suggest that students use the brief description of each section of this amendment as a tool for previewing. OL

Did You Know?

Both the Fifth and the Fourteenth Amendments refer to "due process of law." Supreme Court decisions have established two types of due process. Procedural due process requires that government use fair procedures in enforcing the law. Substantive due process requires that the laws under which the government acts be fair.

Amendment 14, Section 4

Answer: no, they could not

C Critical Thinking

Comparing and Contrasting **Ask:** Did the Seventeenth Amendment make the Senate more or less democratic? Why? *(more; because all the voters in a state could choose senators)* OL

U Universal Access

Verbal/Linguistic Have students rephrase the Seventeenth Amendment, Section 3, in their own words. *(Senators elected under the old system will continue to serve their terms.)* AL

Amendment 15
Right to Vote The Fifteenth Amendment (1870) prohibits the government from denying a person's right to vote on the basis of race. Despite the law, many states denied African Americans the right to vote by such means as poll taxes, literacy tests, and white primaries. During the 1950s and 1960s, Congress passed successively stronger laws to end racial discrimination in voting rights.

Internal Revenue Service

Amendment 17
Direct Election of Senators The Seventeenth Amendment (1913) states that the people, instead of state legislatures, elect United States senators. *How many years are in a Senate term?*

Section 5
The Congress shall have power to enforce, by appropriate legislation, the provisions of this article.

Amendment XV

Section 1
The right of citizens of the United States to vote shall not be denied or abridged by the United States or by any State on account of race, color, or previous condition of servitude.

Section 2
The Congress shall have power to enforce this article by appropriate legislation.

Amendment XVI
The Congress shall have power to lay and collect taxes on incomes, from whatever source derived, without apportionment among the several States and without regard to any census or enumeration.

Amendment XVII

Section 1
C The Senate of the United States shall be composed of two Senators from each State, elected by the people thereof, for six years; and each Senator shall have one vote. The electors in each State shall have the qualifications requisite for electors of the most numerous branch of the State legislatures.

Section 2
When vacancies happen in the representation of any State in the Senate, the executive authority of such State shall issue writs of election to fill such vacancies: *Provided,* That the legislature of any State may empower the executive thereof to make temporary appointments until the people fill the vacancies by election as the legislature may direct.

Section 3
U This amendment shall not be so construed as to affect the election or term of any Senator chosen before it becomes valid as part of the Constitution.

Vocabulary
apportionment: *distribution of seats in House based on population*
vacancy: *an office or position that is unfilled or unoccupied*

Answers and Additional Support

Did You Know?
The Fifteenth Amendment was meant to guarantee voting rights for African Americans, including those freed from slavery by the Thirteenth Amendment. Not until the 1960s, did Congress take firm action to enforce this guarantee.

Amendment 17
Answer: six years

Amendment XVIII

Section 1
After one year from ratification of this article, the manufacture, sale, or transportation of intoxicating liquors within, the importation thereof into, or the exportation thereof from the United States and all territory subject to the jurisdiction thereof for beverage purposes is hereby prohibited.

Section 2
The Congress and the several States shall have concurrent power to enforce this article by appropriate legislation.

Section 3
This article shall be inoperative unless it shall have been ratified as an amendment to the Constitution by the legislatures of the several States, as provided in the Constitution, within seven years from the date of the submission hereof to the States by the Congress.

Amendment 18
Prohibition of Alcoholic Beverages The Eighteenth Amendment (1919) prohibited the production, sale, or transportation of alcoholic beverages in the United States. Prohibition proved to be difficult to enforce. This amendment was later repealed by the Twenty-first Amendment.

Amendment XIX

Section 1
The right of citizens of the United States to vote shall not be denied or abridged by the United States or by any State on account of sex.

Section 2
Congress shall have power by appropriate legislation to enforce the provisions of this article.

Amendment 19
Woman Suffrage The Nineteenth Amendment (1920) guaranteed women the right to vote. By then women had already won the right to vote in many state elections, but the amendment put their right to vote in all state and national elections on a constitutional basis.

S

Amendment XX

Section 1
The terms of the President and Vice President shall end at noon on the 20th day of January, and the terms of the Senators and Representatives at noon on the 3d day of January, of the years in which such terms would have ended if this article had not been ratified; and the terms of their successors shall then begin.

Section 2
The Congress shall assemble at least once in every year, and such meeting shall begin at noon on the 3d day of January, unless they shall by law appoint a different day.

Amendment 20
"Lame-Duck" Amendment The Twentieth Amendment (1933) sets new dates for Congress to begin its term and for the inauguration of the president and vice president. Under the original Constitution, elected officials who retired or who had been defeated remained in office for several months. For the outgoing president, this period ran from November until March. Such outgoing officials had little influence and accomplished little, and they were called lame ducks because they were so inactive. *What date was fixed as Inauguration Day?*

U

S Skill Practice

Historical and Social Sciences Analysis Skill
Point out that several states gave women the right to vote before the federal government did. Have students research the matter and create a time line showing when women gained suffrage in different states. OL
CA CS2.

U Universal Access

English Learners Students learning the English language are probably not familiar with the expression "lame duck." Explain that it refers to people who had announced they would retire or who had lost re-election but whose original term of office still had time left. They were called "lame ducks" because—like ducks who were injured and could not fly—they were not very active. EL

Did You Know?

Prohibition, enacted by the Eighteenth Amendment, led to many problems in American society. It did succeed, however, in reducing the consumption of alcohol in the country. As a result, the United States saw a decrease in the number of alcohol-related deaths and accidents while it was in force.

Amendment 20
Answer: January 20

U Universal Access

Below Grade Level Direct students' attention to the bottom of the page, where "president elect" is defined. **Ask:** What does "vice president elect" mean? *(a vice president who was elected but had not yet begun serving his or her term)* BL

C Critical Thinking

Predicting Consequences This is the first amendment that was ratified that put a time limit on the time of ratification. **Ask:** Do you expect later amendments to include this language? Why or why not? *(Students are likely to answer yes because once the idea was introduced people would probably want to repeat it.)* OL

R Reading Strategy

Using Context Clues Have students read the note explaining the Twenty-First Amendment. **Ask:** What does "repeal" mean? *(to cancel an earlier law)* OL

Answers and Additional Support

Amendment 20. Section 3
Succession of President and Vice President This section provides that if the president-elect dies before taking office, the vice president-elect becomes president.

John Tyler was the first vice president to become president when a chief executive died.

Amendment 21
Repeal of Prohibition Amendment The Twenty-first Amendment (1933) repeals the Eighteenth Amendment. It is the only amendment ever passed to overturn an earlier amendment. It is also the only amendment ratified by special state conventions instead of state legislatures.

Vocabulary

president-elect: *individual who is elected president but has not yet begun serving his or her term*
District of Columbia: *site of nation's capital, occupying an area between Maryland and Virginia*

Section 3
If, at the time fixed for the beginning of the term of the President, the President elect shall have died, the Vice President elect shall become President. If a President shall not have been chosen before the time fixed for the beginning of his term, or if the President elect shall have failed to qualify, then the Vice President elect shall act as President until a President shall have qualified; and the Congress may by law provide for the case wherein neither a President elect nor a Vice President elect shall have qualified, declaring who shall then act as President, or the manner in which one who is to act shall be selected, and such person shall act accordingly until a President or Vice President shall have qualified.

Section 4
The Congress may by law provide for the case of the death of any of the persons from whom the House of Representatives may choose a President whenever the right of choice shall have devolved upon them, and for the case of the death of any of the persons from whom the Senate may choose a Vice President whenever the right of choice shall have devolved upon them.

Section 5
Sections 1 and 2 shall take effect on the 15th day of October following the ratification of this article.

Section 6
This article shall be inoperative unless it shall have been ratified as an amendment to the Constitution by the legislatures of three-fourths of the several States within seven years from the date of its submission.

Amendment XXI

Section 1
The eighteenth article of amendment to the Constitution of the United States is hereby repealed.

Section 2
The transportation or importation into any State, Territory, or possession of the United States for delivery or use therein of intoxicating liquors, in violation of the laws thereof, is hereby prohibited.

Section 3
This article shall be inoperative unless it shall have been ratified as an amendment to the Constitution by conventions in the several States, as provided in the Constitution, within seven years from the date of the submission hereof to the States by the Congress.

Did You Know?

The Constitution had no provision for filling the office of Vice-President once that official had to assume the presidency. That problem was rectified with ratification of the Twenty-Fifth Amendment in 1967.

Amendment XXII

Section 1

R No person shall be elected to the office of the President more than twice, and no person who had held the office of President, or acted as President, for more than two years of a term to which some other person was elected President shall be elected to the office of the President more than once. But this Article shall not apply to any person holding the office of President when this Article was proposed by the Congress, and shall not prevent any person who may be holding the office of President, or acting as President, during the term within which this Article becomes operative from holding the office of President or acting as President during the remainder of such term. W

Section 2

This article shall be inoperative unless it shall have been ratified as an amendment to the Constitution by the legislatures of three-fourths of the several States within seven years from the date of its submission to the States by the Congress.

Amendment 22

Limit on Presidential Terms The Twenty-second Amendment (1951) limits presidents to a maximum of two elected terms. It was passed largely as a reaction to Franklin D. Roosevelt's election to four terms between 1933 and 1945.

Presidential campaign buttons

Amendment XXIII

Section 1

The District constituting the seat of Government of the United States shall appoint in such manner as the Congress may direct:

A number of electors of President and Vice President equal to the whole number of Senators and Representatives in Congress to which the District would be entitled if it were a State, but in no event more than the least populous State; they shall be in addition to those appointed by the States, but they shall be considered, for the purposes of the election of President and Vice President, to be electors appointed by a State; and they shall meet in the District and perform such duties as provided by the twelfth article of amendment.

Section 2

The Congress shall have power to enforce this article by appropriate legislation.

Amendment 23

Presidential Electors for the District of Columbia The Twenty-third Amendment (1961) allows citizens living in Washington, D.C., to vote for president and vice president, a right previously denied residents of the nation's capital. The District of Columbia now has three presidential electors, the number to which it would be entitled if it were a state. C

R Reading Strategy

Monitoring Make sure that students understand the differences in the limits. **Ask:** How many times can someone be elected as president? *(two)* How many times can someone be elected as president if he or she first is a vice president who succeeds to the presidency and serves two or more years? *(one)* OL

W Writing Support

Persuasive Writing Have students write a persuasive essay in which they argue that the two-term limit on presidents is a good or bad idea. Remind them to write a coherent statement of their thesis and have a well-supported conclusion. OL

CA 8WA2.4

C Critical Thinking

Analyzing Information Point out that though the people of the District of Columbia have presidential electors, they do not have members with full voting rights in the House or Senate. Have students discuss the issue of whether or not this situation is fair for the people of the District. OL

Did You Know?

In the 1960 census, the District of Columbia had more people than 15 states. Since then, the District's population has fallen slightly, and the populations of various states have risen. In the 2000 census, the District had more people than only one state—Wyoming.

R Reading Strategy

Activating Prior Knowledge **Ask:** What earlier amendment is related to the Twenty-Fourth Amendment? *(Fifteenth)* OL

C Critical Thinking

Making Inferences **Ask:** Why does Section 4 of the Twenty-Fifth Amendment provide a way for someone other than the president to declare that the president cannot serve? *(in case the president is too ill to be able to make the declaration)* OL

Answers and Additional Support

Amendment 24

Abolition of Poll Tax The Twenty-fourth Amendment (1964) prohibits poll taxes in federal elections. Prior to the passage of this amendment, some states had used such taxes to keep low-income African Americans from voting. In 1966 the Supreme Court banned poll taxes in state elections as well.

Amendment XXIV

Section 1

The right of citizens of the United States to vote in any primary or other election for President or Vice-President, for electors for President or Vice President, or for Senator or Representative in Congress, shall not be denied or abridged by the United States or any State by reason of failure to pay any poll tax or other tax. R

Section 2

The Congress shall have power to enforce this article by appropriate legislation.

Amendment 25

Presidential Disability and Succession The Twenty-fifth Amendment (1967) established a process for the vice president to take over leadership of the nation when a president is disabled. It also set procedures for filling a vacancy in the office of vice president.

This amendment was used in 1973, when Vice President Spiro Agnew resigned from office after being charged with accepting bribes. President Richard Nixon then appointed Gerald R. Ford as vice president in accordance with the provisions of the 25th Amendment. A year later, President Nixon resigned during the Watergate scandal and Ford became president. President Ford then had to fill the vice presidency, which he had left vacant upon assuming the presidency. He named Nelson A. Rockefeller as vice president. Thus individuals who had not been elected held both the presidency and the vice presidency. *Whom does the president inform if he or she cannot carry out the duties of the office?*

Amendment XXV

Section 1

In case of the removal of the President from office or his death or resignation, the Vice President shall become President.

Section 2

Whenever there is a vacancy in the office of the Vice President, the President shall nominate a Vice President who shall take the office upon confirmation by a majority vote of both Houses of Congress.

Section 3

Whenever the President transmits to the President pro tempore of the Senate and the Speaker of the House of Representatives his written declaration that he is unable to discharge the powers and duties of his office, and until he transmits to them a written declaration to the contrary, such powers and duties shall be discharged by the Vice President as Acting President.

Section 4

Whenever the Vice President and a majority of either the principal officers of the executive departments or of such other body as Congress may by law provide, transmit to the President pro tempore of the Senate and the Speaker of the House of Representatives their written declaration that the President is unable to discharge the powers and duties of his office, the Vice President shall immediately assume the power and duties of the office of Acting President. C

Thereafter, when the President transmits to the President pro tempore of the Senate and the Speaker of the House of Representatives his written declaration that no inability exists, he shall resume the powers and duties of his office unless the Vice President and a majority of either the principal officers of the executive department or of such other body as Congress may by law provide, transmit within four days to the President pro tempore of the Senate and the Speaker of the House of Representatives their written declaration that the President is unable to discharge the powers and duties of his office.

President Gerald Ford

Did You Know?

The United States has had a disabled president several times in its history. In the 1880s James Garfield remained bedridden for 79 days before dying from injuries sustained by an assassin's bullet. In the twentieth century, Woodrow Wilson had a stroke and was incapacitated for the last several months of his presidency.

Amendment 25

Answer: the president pro tempore of the Senate *(the vice president)* and the Speaker of the House

Thereupon Congress shall decide the issue, assembling within forty-eight hours for that purpose if not in session. If the Congress, within twenty-one days after receipt of the latter written declaration, or, if Congress is not in session, within twenty-one days after Congress is required to assemble, determines by two-thirds vote of both Houses that the President is unable to discharge the powers and duties of his office, the Vice President shall continue to discharge the same as Acting President; otherwise, the President shall resume the power and duties of his office.

W Amendment XXVI

Section 1

C The right of citizens of the United States, who are eighteen years of age or older, to vote shall not be denied or abridged by the United States or by any State on account of age.

Section 2

The Congress shall have power to enforce this article by appropriate legislation.

Amendment 26

Eighteen-Year-Old Vote The Twenty-sixth Amendment (1971) guarantees the right to vote to all citizens 18 years of age and older.

Amendment XXVII

No law, varying the compensation for the services of Senators and Representatives, shall take effect, until an election of representatives shall have intervened.

Amendment 27

Restraint on Congressional Salaries The Twenty-seventh Amendment (1992) makes congressional pay raises effective during the term following their passage. James Madison offered the amendment in 1789, but it was never adopted. In 1982 Gregory Watson, then a student at the University of Texas, discovered the forgotten amendment while doing research for a school paper. Watson made the amendment's passage his crusade.

Joint meeting of Congress

W Writing Support

Research Reports Writing

Have students look up the history of the Twenty-Sixth Amendment. Tell them to find out what major issue facing the nation led to its approval. OL CA HI1.

C Critical Thinking

Analyzing Information

Point out that turnout in elections among people 18 to 21 tends to be low. **Ask:** If so few young people vote in elections, should they lose the right to vote? Have students debate the issue. OL

Did You Know?

Not all citizens over the age of 18 are allowed to vote. Forty-six states and the District of Columbia prohibit prison inmates from voting while serving a felony sentence. Ten prohibit all ex-offenders from voting for the rest of their lives, while five others ban only some ex-offenders.

Teaching the Unit

Use the information on these pages to help you teach Unit 3.

History–Social Science Standards Covered in Unit 3

Standard	Chapter 5	Chapter 6	Chapter 7
US8.3 Students understand the foundation of the American political system and the ways in which citizens participate in it.	✓		
US8.4 Students analyze the aspirations and ideals of the people of the new nation.	✓	✓	
US8.5 Students analyze U.S. foreign policy in the early Republic.			✓

Pacing Your Lessons

This pacing chart provides time management suggestions for teaching Unit 3.

Unit 3 Launching the Republic	Days
Unit 3 Introduction	1/2
Chapter 5 • **Reading Skill:** Recognizing Bias • **Sections 1–3** • **Biography:** Alexander Hamilton, Abigail Adams and John Adams • **Analyzing Primary Sources**	5
Chapter 6 • **Reading Skill:** Compare and Contrast • **Sections 1–3** • **Biography:** Washington Irving and James Fenimore Cooper • **Connecting to the Constitution** • **Geography & History** • **Analyzing Primary Sources**	5
Chapter 7 • **Reading Skill:** Identifying Cause and Effect • **Sections 1–3** • **Biography:** Henry Clay and John C. Calhoun, Dolley Madison • **America's Literature:** *Crossing the Panther's Path* • **Time Notebook** • **Analyzing Primary Sources**	8
Unit 3 Review	1/2

Teacher to Teacher

Lewis & Clark Reader's Theater

Robert Gaudette
Dale Junior High School
Anaheim, CA

A reader's theater is a fantastic way to bring history alive for students, and the Lewis and Clark expedition is the perfect opportunity to introduce this powerful learning strategy.

After students have studied the expedition, divide the class into eight teams of five to six students. Divide the journey into eight parts—Preparation, Up the Missouri, Winter at Fort Mandan, Toward the Headwaters, Over the Mountains, Down the Clearwater, Winter on the Pacific, and Return Journey. Have each team randomly select part of the journey. Provide them with appropriate expository text and access to the Internet.

Tell students they need to write a play and recreate at least three pivotal scenes that took place in their part of the expedition. Tell them to create props and perform their scenes in front of their classmates. If possible, videotape their performances and watch the highlights the following day.

Previewing the Chapters

Dear American History Teacher:

As you begin to teach this unit, there are themes that reoccur throughout the chapters that you will want to point out to students.

The nation began to take shape under the first five presidents, as government institutions were set up and the nation grew in size and population. Differences over policy and principle led to the formation of the first political parties in this era, and party leaders argued bitterly over several issues. George Washington set many precedents, including the policy of steering clear of foreign entanglements. The other presidents continued this policy. Also under James Madison, anger at British actions grew so strong that the country declared war. The war's outcome led to a surge of national unity that ushered in the 1820s.

You may want to use the following information at the beginning of each chapter as a lesson launcher to help students begin to focus on what they will be studying.

CHAPTER 5: The Federalist Era
(pages 274–301)

George Washington worked with Congress to set up the new government and add the Bill of Rights. Alexander Hamilton developed plans to fix financial problems. A revolt against a tax on whiskey was swiftly put down by Washington, showing that protest had to be peaceful. Washington took steps to settle conflicts with Britain, Spain, and Native Americans and left office urging Americans to avoid European affairs. Disagreements on many issues led to the development of political parties. John Adams, the next president, avoided a war with France, but Congress passed tough laws that many Americans thought took away people's rights.

CHAPTER 6: The Age of Jefferson
(pages 302–333)

Thomas Jefferson defeated Adams for the presidency in 1800, demonstrating that power could be transferred peacefully even when political parties disagree. Jefferson limited the scope of the federal government, though the Supreme Court issued a ruling that established its power of judicial review. Jefferson bought the vast Louisiana Territory, doubling the country's size. He sent an expedition led by Lewis and Clark to explore the new region. Americans developed a strong sense of national identity in the early 1800s and began to create their own unique culture. Distinct ways of life developed in the country's different sections.

CHAPTER 7: Foreign Affairs in the Early Republic **(pages 334–371)**

Trade was an important part of the American economy in the early 1800s, but Britain and France both tried to block U.S. trade. President James Madison also faced conflict on the western frontier, where Native Americans tried to resist American expansion. Some Americans called for a war against Britain to stop its practices of impressing American sailors and of helping the Native Americans. Congress finally declared war in 1812, but the country was ill prepared. Eventually, the two sides tired of the war and reached a peace agreement. A final victory on the battlefield helped stir strong national feeling among Americans. After the War of 1812, the United States used diplomacy to settle several border disputes with other countries, and President James Monroe issued his Monroe Doctrine.

FOCUS

Connecting to Past Learning

In Unit 2, students learned about the writing and ratification of the U.S. Constitution. In Unit 3, they will study the challenges—domestic and foreign—that faced the first presidents who held office and read about the nation's expansion.

Unit Launch Activity

Have students explain why they think the unit is called "Launching the Republic." **Ask:** How was the new government like a ship being launched on its first voyage? *(Students might say that, like a ship on a first voyage, the government's functioning and stability were unknown.)* OL

History–Social Science Standards

The following standards are covered in Unit 3:

US8.3 Students understand the foundation of the American political system and the ways in which citizens participate in it.

US8.4 Students understand the aspirations and ideals of the people of the new nation.

US8.5 Students analyze U.S. foreign policy in the early Republic.

Why It's Important

Ask: Which other nations or groups might the United States come into conflict with between 1790 and 1820? Why? OL

Unit 3

Launching the Republic

Why It's Important

With the Constitution in place, the newly chosen government began to set procedures and customs for the country. The nation continued to gain new territory and grow, but faced challenges from other countries, including its old foe, Great Britain. The United States also set foreign policy that would guide its actions for many years.

- The American political process took shape during the country's early years.
- The United States began to establish its place in the world as it gained territory and fought wars with foreign powers.

1780 — 1790 — 1800

U.S. EVENTS

◀ *Washington banner*

1789 Washington becomes first president

1791 Bill of Rights is added to Constitution

1798 Alien and Sedition Acts are passed

1804 Lewis and Clark begin expedition

CALIFORNIA EVENTS

1796 American ship opens up trade with California

1800 Strong earthquake hits San Diego region

WORLD EVENTS

1789 The French Revolution begins

◀ *Storming of the Bastille*

1804 Napoleon crowns himself emperor of France

270

TEACHING THE TIME LINES

Help students focus on the information in the time lines. **Ask:**

- What two national leaders are mentioned on the time line? What nations did they lead? *(Washington and Napoleon; United States and France)*
- When did people from the United States first come in contact with Californians? How did that happen? *(1796; when an American ship opened up trade with California)*
- What two events on the California and world time lines are related? *(California becomes Mexican province; Mexico wins independence from Spain.)*

As students study events described in the unit, refer back to these time lines and have students identify where the event would appear. OL

TEACH

NATIONAL GEOGRAPHIC **Where in the United States?**

Understanding Maps and Time Lines **Ask:** What modern state was partly, but not completely, in the United States in 1830? *(Maine)* What area of the current United States was part of Mexico in 1830? *(the southwestern states from Texas to California)* OL

NCLB No Child Left Behind

Teaching Activity Have students read the events in the time line and the **Where in the United States?** map. **Ask:** What wars will appear in this unit? How do you think they will affect the people of the United States? *(Students should name a war against France and another between the United States and Britain.)* OL

NATIONAL GEOGRAPHIC

Where in the United States?

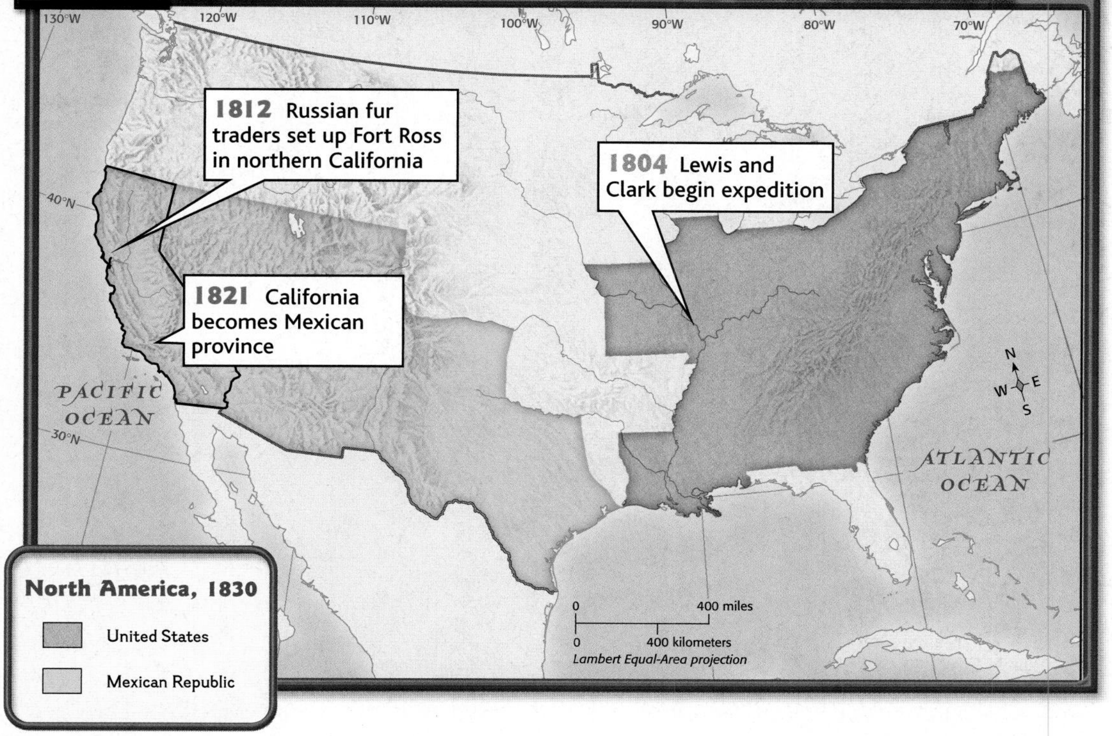

1810 **1820** **1830**

1812 U.S. declares war on Britain

American sailors

1823 Monroe Doctrine is declared

1812 Russian fur traders set up Fort Ross in northern California

Fort Ross

1819 Northern California border is set at 42nd parallel

1821 California becomes Mexican province

1824 Rancho economy begins

Mexican flag

1815 Allies defeat Napoleon at Waterloo

1821 Mexico wins its independence from Spain

1824 Mexico offers land grants to Mexicans and immigrants

UNIVERSAL ACCESS

English Learners: Pair students learning English with those strong in English language skills. Have the stronger students review difficult vocabulary or concepts in the time lines with the English learners to make sure the latter understand what took place in each event. EL

Below Grade Level: Have students demonstrate their comprehension by rewriting the time line entries in their own words. BL

Musical/Auditory: Pair auditory learners with students who can read aloud smoothly. Have the latter students read the different events on the time line and then quiz the auditory learners to make sure they understand what was described. OL

Introducing Unit 3

Unit Objectives

After studying this unit, students should be able to

- Explain the decisions of the first presidents and the Congresses of the early republic.
- Describe the policies and principles that led to the formation of the first political parties.
- Identify the Louisiana Purchase and describe its effects.
- Describe daily life in the early republic.
- Discuss what actions and attitudes led to the War of 1812 and the effects of that war.
- Outline how the United States settled differences with other nations or groups over territory.

Previewing People to Meet

Have students categorize the People to Meet as *Political Leader* or *Other* and record an achievement for each person in the *Other* category. OL
NOTE: Answers are listed in the second column.

Person	Known For
Sacagawea	*(served as guide on Lewis and Clark expedition)*
James Fenimore Cooper	*(novelist; wrote books about the pioneer spirit)*
Washington Irving	*(novelist; wrote books on American life)*
Dolley Madison	*(saved important papers during War of 1812)*

Unit 3 Places to Locate

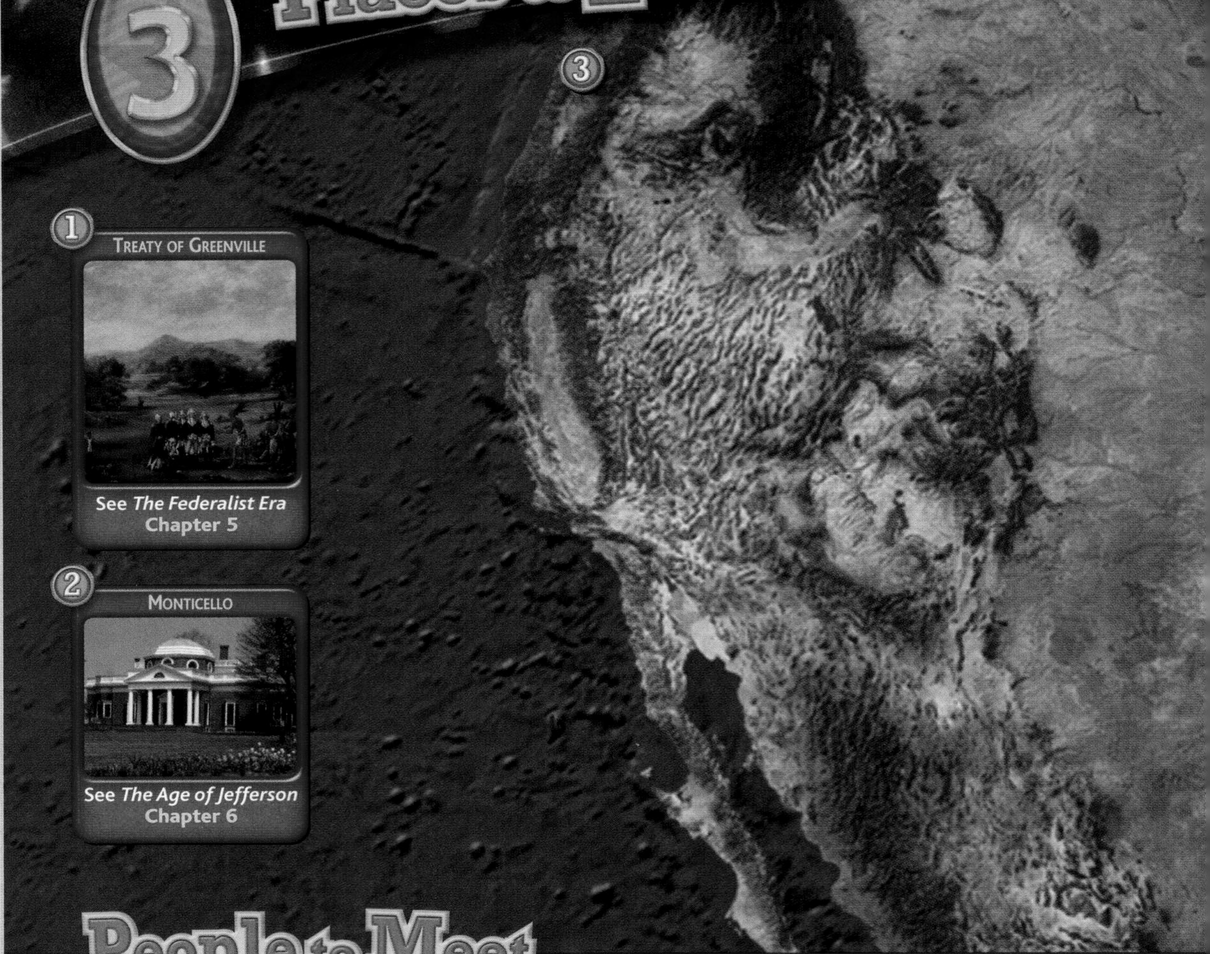

People to Meet

Alexander Hamilton
1755–1804
First Secretary of the Treasury
Chapter 5, page 283

John Adams
1735–1826
First vice president and second president
Chapter 5, page 294

Toussaint Louverture
c. 1743–1804
Haitian revolutionary
Chapter 6, page 313

Sacagawea
c. 1787–1812
Shoshone guide for Lewis and Clark
Chapter 6, page 315

272

Previewing Places to Locate

Use the following descriptions to explain the images on the map.

1 
Greenville took its name from Fort Greene, named for a Revolutionary War general. Sharpshooter Annie Oakley, who starred in Wild West shows in the late 1800s, was born near the fort.

2 
Thomas Jefferson's Monticello was the first building he designed, and was built before the Revolutionary War. He retired to this home in 1809 and lived there the rest of his life.

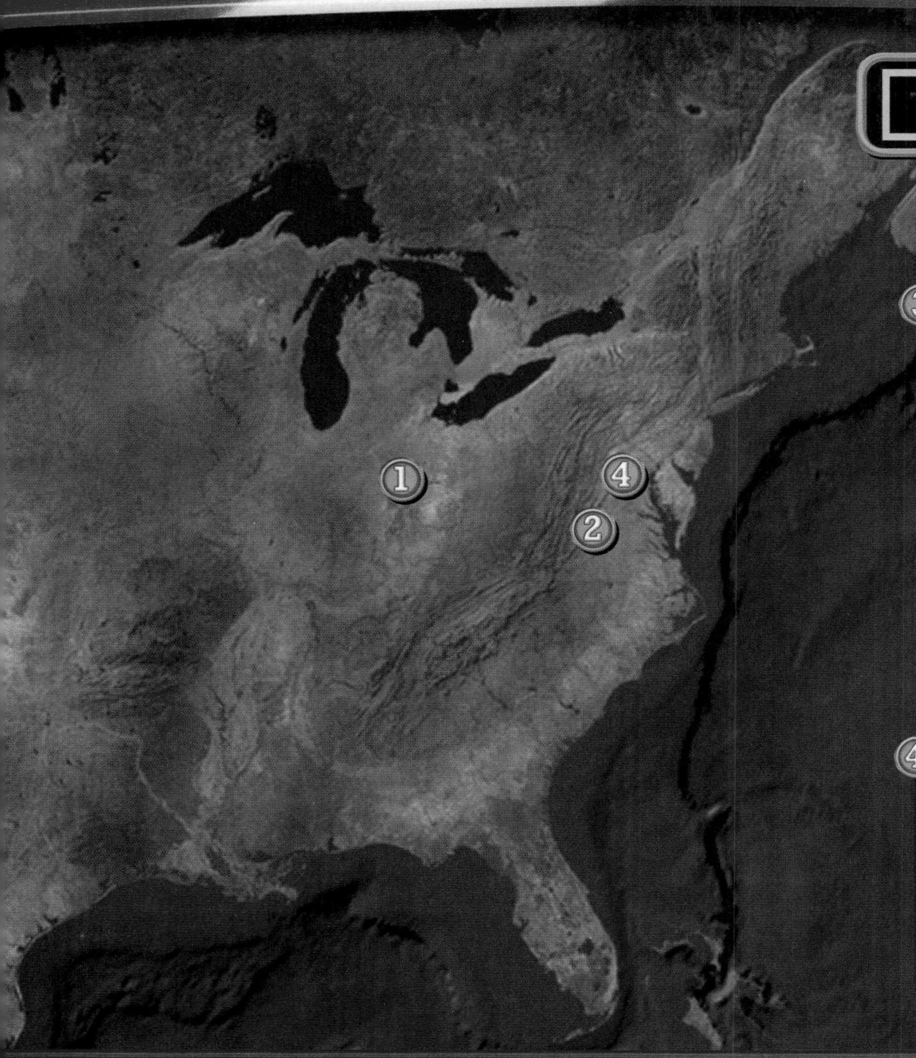

3 LEWIS AND CLARK

See *The Age of Jefferson* Chapter 6

4 BATTLE OF NORTH POINT

See *Foreign Affairs in the Early Republic* Chapter 7

James Fenimore Cooper
1789–1851
American writer
Chapter 6, page 324

Washington Irving
1783–1859
American writer
Chapter 6, page 324

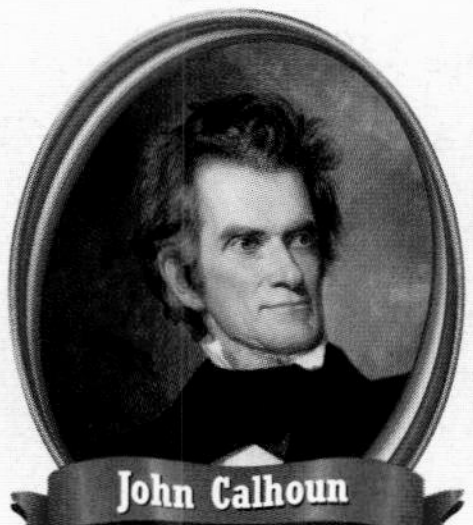

John Calhoun
1782–1850
Political leader
Chapter 7, page 344

Dolley Madison
1768–1849
First lady
Chapter 7, page 357

Meriwether Lewis had been President Thomas Jefferson's personal secretary before his selection as head of the western expedition. Clark's older brother was George Rogers Clark, who won several battles west of the Appalachians during the Revolutionary War.

The Battle of North Point was part of the defense of Baltimore during the War of 1812, shortly after the British had burned Washington, D.C. Their failure to take Baltimore gave American diplomats a stronger hand in negotiating the peace treaty that ended the war.

INTRODUCING UNIT 3

Skill Practice

Using Geography Skills
Ask: In what area was the United States confined after the American Revolution? *(the area east of the Mississippi River)* Where did Lewis and Clark travel? *(to the Pacific Ocean)* What impact is that likely to have on American history after this period? *(Students should recognize that this marked the beginning of a continental perspective among Americans.)* **OL**

Skill Practice

Creating a Time Line Have students create a time line plotting the lives of the People to Meet listed on these two pages. As they read the unit, have them identify other people to add to their time line. Students should research the dates of those individuals and add them. **OL**

ASSESS/CLOSE

Explain that the conclusion of the War of 1812 allowed the United States to enjoy new standing among leading nations of the world and ushered in an era of nationalism known as the "Era of Good Feelings". Have students identify the events on the time line that are the result of this nationalism and infer why that was the case. *(Students should be able to infer that the United States survived the war, since the Monroe Doctrine was issued afterward.)* **OL**

Chapter 5 Planning Guide

SECTION RESOURCES

Main Ideas	Print Materials	Technology Resources
Section 1 **The First President** 1. President Washington and the new Congress established the departments in the executive branch, set up the nation's court system, and added the Bill of rights to the Constitution. 2. Alexander Hamilton, the secretary of the treasury under Washington, worked to fix financial problems and strengthen the economy.	• Reproducible Lesson Plan 5–1* • Daily Lesson and Discussion Notes 5–1 • Active Reading Note-Taking Guide 5–1 • Reading Essentials and Study Guide 5–1 • Guided Reading Activity 5–1 • Section Quiz 5–1	Daily Focus Skills Transparency 5–1 Section Graphic Organizer Transparency 5–1 California Standards Practice Transparencies Interactive Tutor Self-Assessment CD-ROM Exam*View*® Pro Testmaker CD-ROM Presentation Plus! CD-ROM
Section 2 **Early Challenges** 1. Hamilton's taxes led to rebellion in western Pennsylvania and changed the way the government handled protestors. 2. The new government faced difficult problems in the West. 3. President Washington wanted the nation to remain neutral in foreign conflicts.	• Reproducible Lesson Plan 5–2* • Daily Lesson and Discussion Notes 5–2 • Active Reading Note-Taking Guide 5–2 • Reading Essentials and Study Guide 5–2 • Guided Reading Activity 5–2 • Section Quiz 5–2	Daily Focus Skills Transparency 5–2 Section Graphic Organizer Transparency 5–2 California Standards Practice Transparencies Interactive Tutor Self-Assessment CD-ROM Exam*View*® Pro Testmaker CD-ROM Presentation Plus! CD-ROM
Section 3 **The First Political Parties** 1. Americans began taking opposing sides on issues by 1796, and as a result, two political parties emerged. 2. John Adams dealt with many things in office, including the dispute with France, which led to a series of measures called the Alien and Sedition Acts.	• Reproducible Lesson Plan 5–3* • Daily Lesson and Discussion Notes 5–3 • Active Reading Note-Taking Guide 5–3 • Reading Essentials and Study Guide 5–3 • Guided Reading Activity 5–3 • Section Quiz 5–3	Daily Focus Skills Transparency 5–3 Section Graphic Organizer Transparency 5–3 California Standards Practice Transparencies Interactive Tutor Self-Assessment CD-ROM Exam*View*® Pro Testmaker CD-ROM Presentation Plus! CD-ROM Vocabulary PuzzleMaker CD-ROM

PACING YOUR LESSONS

Unit Introduction	Chapter Introduction	Section 1	Section 2	Section 3	Chapter Assessment
$\frac{1}{2}$ Day	$\frac{1}{2}$ Day	1 Day	1 Day	2 Days	$\frac{1}{2}$ Day

0:00 **OUT OF TIME?** Assign the Chapter 5 ***Reading Essentials and Study Guide***

*Available on TeacherWorks™

Standards-Based Lesson Plan

History–Social Science Standards Covered in Chapter 5

The standards covered in the chapter are listed below. Use the accompanying activity as you teach the chapter to ensure student mastery of these standards. This activity can be used in combination with the program's print and technology assessment materials.

Standard	Section 1	Section 2	Section 3
US8.3 Students understand the foundation of the American political system and the ways in which citizens participate in it.	✔	✔	✔
US8.3.4 Understand how the conflicts between Thomas Jefferson and Alexander Hamilton resulted in the emergence of two political parties (e.g., view of foreign policy, Alien and Sedition Acts, economic policy, National Bank, funding and assumption of the revolutionary debt).	✔		✔
US8.3.5 Know the significance of domestic resistance movements and ways in which the central government responded to such movements (e.g., Shays's Rebellion, the Whiskey Rebellion).		✔	
US8.4 Students analyze the aspirations and ideals of the people of the new nation.	✔	✔	✔
US8.4.1 Describe the country's physical landscapes, political divisions, and territorial expansion during the terms of the first four presidents.		✔	✔
US8.4.2 Explain the policy significance of famous speeches (e.g., Washington's Farewell Address, Jefferson's 1801 Inaugural Address, John Q. Adams's Fourth of July 1821 Address).		✔	

Cumulative Standards-Assessment Activity

The Cumulative Standards-Assessment Activity will help students organize and learn the important information from the chapter. Begin teaching the chapter with this activity, and have students complete it as they read the chapter.

Creating a Diagram for Comparing and Contrasting

Purpose Comparing and contrasting is a technique useful for finding the similarities and differences between people, movements, or ideas. This tool is particularly useful when studying two sides in a conflict or two regions of a country.

Introduction to Comparing and Contrasting

1. Demonstrate the technique by asking students to identify the different positions of the Federalists and the Antifederalists discussed in the previous chapter. Encourage students to not only identify areas where the two groups differed but also to name issues on which they agreed.
2. Ask students to copy this chart into their notebooks:

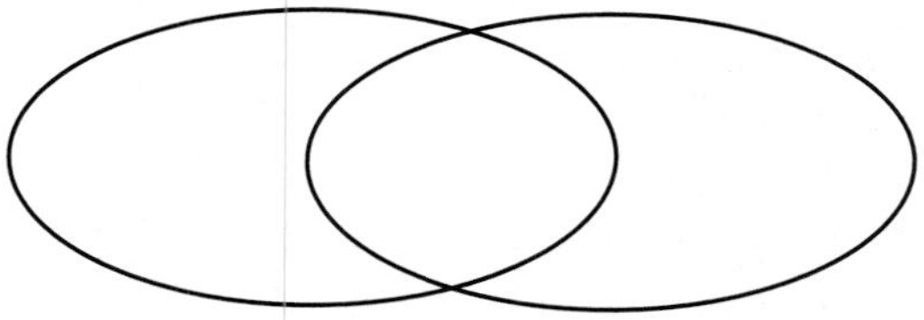

   As students read each section, have them use different diagrams to compare and contrast the information they read. In the first section, they might compare and contrast the different actions of the first president and Congress. In the last, they might compare the positions of the two early political parties.
3. As you review the chapter, divide the class into groups and have students share their comparison and contrast charts. Have the groups describe their charts, and encourage students to add to their own charts. Encourage them to use their charts as study aids.

Chapter 5 Resources

READING SUPPORT

- Content Vocabulary Activity 5
- Academic Vocabulary Activity 5
- Reading Skills Activity 5
- American Literature Reading 5
- Biography Activities 5A, 5B
- Chapter 5 Active Reading Note-Taking Guide
- Chapter 5 Guided Reading Activities
- Chapter 5 Reading Essentials and Study Guide
- Glencoe Literature Library
- Glencoe Video Program
- Vocabulary PuzzleMaker CD-ROM
- Interactive Graphic Organizers CD-ROM
- American History Primary Source Document Library CD-ROM

CRITICAL THINKING

- Critical Thinking Skills Activity 5
- Primary Source Reading 5
- Cause-and-Effect Transparency 5, Strategy, and Activity
- Presentation Plus! CD-ROM

UNIVERSAL ACCESS

- Universal Access Activity 5
- Then and Now Transparencies 5A–5B, Strategy, and Activity
- Graphic Novel Activity 5
- School-to-Home Connection Activities 5A–5D
- English Learner Handbook Chapter 5 Activities
- Universal Access for the American History Classroom
- Moments in Time
- American Art and Architecture Transparencies, Strategies, and Activities
- American Art Prints
- American Music Cultural Traditions
- American Music Hits Through History
- StudentWorks Plus CD-ROM

SKILL PRACTICE

- Map Overlay Transparency 5, Strategy, and Activity
- Analysis Skills Activity 5
- Time Line Activity 5
- Geography and History Activity 5
- Economics and History Activity 5
- Chart, Graph, and Map Skills Activity 5
- Political Cartoon Activity 5
- Supreme Court Case Study 5
- In-Text Map Transparency 5, Strategy, and Activity
- Step Into American History Activity 5
- Citizenship and Service Learning Activity 5
- Activity Workbook
- Outline Map Resource Book
- MindJogger Plus Videoquiz

WRITING SUPPORT

- Writing Activity 5
- Language Arts Activity 5
- Writer's Guidebook
- Middle School Writing Process Transparencies

ASSESSMENT

GLENCOE'S ASSESSMENT ADVANTAGE

- Chapter 5 Section Quizzes
- Chapter Tests, Forms A and B
- California Standards Assessment, Forms A and B
- Cumulative Assessment Activities US8.3, US8.4
- California Standards Practice Workbook
- Succeeding on the California History–Social Science Standards CD-ROM
- Exam*View*® Pro Testmaker CD-ROM
- Interactive Tutor Self-Assessment CD-ROM

CD-ROM
DVD
Print Material
Poster
Transparency
Music Program
Videocassette
Glencoe Literature Library

Chapter 5 Resources

TECHNOLOGY

- StudentWorks Plus CD-ROM
- TeacherWorks CD-ROM
- Exam*View*® Pro Testmaker CD-ROM
- Interactive Tutor Self-Assessment CD-ROM
- Presentation Plus! CD-ROM
- Succeeding on the California History–Social Science Standards CD-ROM
- Vocabulary PuzzleMaker CD-ROM
- Interactive Graphic Organizers CD-ROM
- Interactive Time Line CD-ROM
- American History Primary Source Document Library CD-ROM
- MindJogger Plus Videoquiz
- American Music Cultural Traditions
- American Music Hits Through History
- Glencoe Video Program
- Professional Development in Middle School Social Studies Series
- Teaching American History With *Discovering Our Past: The American Journey to World War I*

SPANISH RESOURCES

- Spanish Activities and Assessment
  - Spanish Content Vocabulary Activities
  - Spanish Guided Reading Activities
  - Spanish Quizzes and Tests
  - Spanish California Standards Assessment
- Spanish Reading Essentials and Study Guide
- Spanish School-to-Home Connection
- Spanish Declaration of Independence and U.S. Constitution

TRANSPARENCIES

- California Standards Practice Transparencies
- Daily Focus Skills Transparencies
- Section Graphic Organizer Transparencies
- In-Text Map Transparencies
- Map Overlay Transparencies
- Cause-and-Effect Transparencies
- Then and Now Transparencies
- American Art and Architecture Transparencies
- Middle School Writing Process Transparencies

TEACHER PLANNING

- Daily Lesson and Discussion Notes
- English Learner Handbook
- Guide to Daily Intervention
- *Discovering Our Past: The American Journey to World War I* Reading and Study Skills Foldables
- Reading Strategies and Activities for the Social Studies Classroom
- Chapter 5 Reproducible Lesson Plans (correlated to California History–Social Science Standards)
- Universal Access for the American History Classroom
- NGS U.S. Desk Map
- NGS U.S. Atlas

PROFESSIONAL DEVELOPMENT

- Building Academic Vocabulary
- Strategies for Success
- Research-Based Strategies Used to Develop *Discovering Our Past: The American Journey to World War I*
- Character Education in the Middle School Classroom
- The Living Constitution
- Professional Development in Middle School Social Studies Video Series
- Teaching American History With *Discovering Our Past: The American Journey to World War I*

MASTERING THE STANDARDS

The content and assessment in the Student Edition, Teacher Wraparound Edition, teacher planning materials, and the print and technology products are all standards-based. The use of these products during instruction leads to mastery of the standards.

PRACTICE
- California Standards Practice Workbook
- California Standards Practice Transparencies
- Interactive Time Line CD-ROM
- School-to-Home Connection

BENCHMARK ASSESSMENT
- California Standards Assessment
- Exam*View*® Pro Testmaker CD-ROM
- Succeeding on the California History–Social Science Standards CD-ROM

REMEDIATION
- California Guide to Daily Intervention
- Interactive Tutor Self-Assessment CD-ROM
- Exam*View*® Pro Testmaker CD-ROM
- California Standards Practice Workbook
- Reading Essentials and Study Guide

Additional Resources

NATIONAL GEOGRAPHIC TEACHER'S CORNER

Index to National Geographic Magazine:

The following articles relate to this chapter:

- "L'Enfant's Washington," by Alice J. Hall, August 1991.
- "The Peales: America's First Family of Art," by Otto Friedrich, December 1990.
- "James Madison, Architect of the Constitution," by Alice J. Hall, September 1987.
- "George Washington's Patowmack Canal," by Wilbur E. Garrett, June 1987.

National Geographic Society Products:

To order the following, call national Geographic at 1-800-368-2728

- *National Geographic Desk Reference* (Book)
- *National Geographic Atlas of the World, Seventh Edition* (Book)

NGS ONLINE

Access National Geographics' new dynamic MapMachine Web site and other geography resources at:

www.nationalgeographic.com

www.nationalgeographic.com/maps

A&E Biography — THE HISTORY CHANNEL.

The following videotape programs are available from Glencoe as supplements to Chapter 5.

- **George Washington: Founding Father (ISBN 1-56501-377-8)**
- **Thomas Jefferson: Philosopher of Freedom (ISBN 1-56501-502-9)**

To order, call Glencoe at 1-800-334-7344. To find classroom resources to accompany many of these videos, check the following home pages:

A&E Television: www.aetv.com
The History Channel: www.historychannel.com

MOMENTS IN TIME DBQ

The following resource can help you teach the content of this chapter.

Unit 1 George Washington

History Online

Use our Web site for additional resources. All essential content is covered in the Student Edition.

You and your students can visit ca.hss.glencoe.com, the Web site companion to *Discovering Our Past: The American Journey to World War I*. This innovative integration of electronic and print media offers your students a wealth of opportunities. The student text directs students to the Web site for the following options:

- Chapter Overviews
- Self-Check Quizzes
- Study Central™
- Student Web Activities
- Textbook Updates
- Multi-Language Glossaries

Answers to the student Web activities are provided for you in the Web Activity Lesson Plans. Additional Web resources and ePuzzles and games are also available.

FOLDABLES™ Study Organizer

Dinah Zike's Foldables

Foldables are three-dimensional, interactive graphic organizers that help students practice basic writing skills, review key vocabulary terms, and identify main ideas. Every chapter contains a foldable activity, with additional chapter activities found in the Reading and Study Skills Foldables booklet.

Chapter 5 Resources

Reading List Generator CD-ROM

GLENCOE BOOKLINK

The Glencoe BookLink CD-ROM is a database that allows you to search more than 15,000 titles to create a customized reading list for your students.

- Reading lists can be organized by students' reading level, author, genre, theme, or area of interest.
- The database provides Degrees of Reading Power™ (DRP) and Lexile™ readability scores for all selections.
- A brief summary of each selection is included.

Reading level suggestions for this chapter:

For students at a Grade 6 reading level:
- ***Abigail Adams: Witness to a Revolution,*** by Natalie S. Bober

For students at a Grade 7 reading level:
- ***John Adams: 2nd President of the United States,*** by Rebecca Stefoff

For students at a Grade 8 reading level:
- ***George Washington: 1st President of the United States,*** by Lucille Falkof

For students at a Grade 9 reading level:
- ***The Bill of Rights: How We Got It and What It Means,*** by Milton Meltzer

READING SUPPORT FROM JAMESTOWN EDUCATION

- *Timed Readings Plus in Social Studies* helps students increase their reading rate and fluency while maintaining comprehension. The 400-word passages are similar to those found on state and national assessments.
- *Reading in the Content Area: Social Studies* concentrates on six essential reading skills that help students better comprehend what they read. The book includes 754 high-interest nonfiction passages written at increasing levels of difficulty.
- *Reading Fluency* helps students read smoothly, accurately, and expressively.
- *Jamestown's Reading Improvement,* by renowned reading expert Edward Fry, focuses on helping build your students' comprehension, vocabulary, and skimming and scanning skills.
- *Critical Reading Series* provides high-interest books, each written at three reading levels.

To order these products, call Glencoe at 1-800-334-7344.

KEY for Using the Teacher Wraparound Edition

Use this key to help you identify the different types of prompts found in the Teacher Wraparound Edition.

R **Reading Strategies** activities help you teach reading skills and vocabulary.

C **Critical Thinking** strategies help students apply and extend what they have learned.

U **Universal Access** activities provide differentiated instruction for students learning to speak English, along with suggestions for teaching various types of learners.

S **Skill Practice** strategies help students practice historical analysis and geography skills.

W **Writing Support** activities provide writing opportunities to help students comprehend the text.

Teaching strategies and activities have been coded for ability level appropriateness.

AL Activities for students working above grade level
OL Activities for students working on grade level
BL Activities for students working below grade level
EL Activities for English Learners

FOCUS

History–Social Science Standards

In this chapter, the following standards will be covered:

US8.3 Students understand the foundation of the American political system and the ways in which citizens participate in it.

US8.4 Students analyze the aspirations and ideals of the people of the new nation.

More About the Photo

Today's dome is actually the second to sit atop the Capitol building. When the Capitol was expanded in the 1850s by adding the current Senate and House chambers, the old dome was judged too small for the enlarged building. A new cast-iron dome with columns, scores of windows, and a crowning statue was constructed between 1855 and 1866.

Chapter 5

The Federalist Era

The Capitol Building, Washington, D.C. ▶

NATIONAL GEOGRAPHIC **Where & When?**

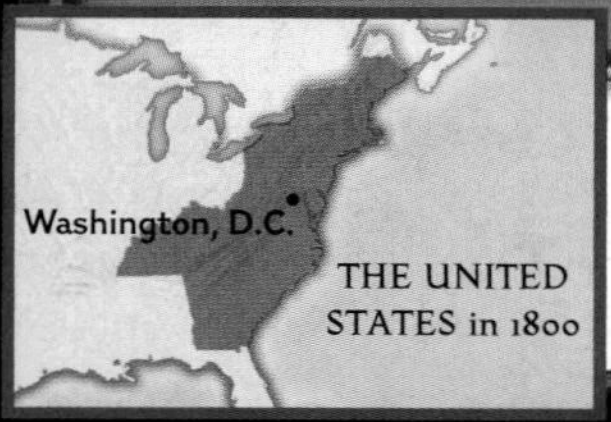

1788	1794	1800

- **1789** George Washington is nation's first president
- **1796** John Adams is elected president
- **1798** Congress passes Alien and Sedition Acts

TEACH

The Big Ideas

As you begin teaching each section, use these questions and activities to focus on the Big Ideas.

Section 1

The First President

Essential Question: What major events have had an impact on the officials leading the government of the nation or your state in recent years? *(Students might point to the terrorist attacks of September 11, 2001, which led the federal and state governments to pay more attention to the issue of homeland security.)* After students discuss the question, point out that this section discusses the important events that influenced George Washington's service as the first president. **OL**

Section 2

Early Challenges

Essential Question: What kinds of challenges might a newly independant nation face as its leaders try to set up the government? Explain that in this section students will learn how Americans used their rights to make decisions about the country's future. **OL**

History Online
Chapter Overview Visit ca.hss.glencoe.com for a preview of Chapter 5.

The Big Ideas

Section 1 The First President

Political ideas and major events shape how people form governments. President Washington and the first Congress built a new government.

Section 2 Early Challenges

Political ideas and major events shape how people form governments. The new American government struggled to keep peace at home and avoid war abroad.

Section 3 The First Political Parties

Citizen participation is essential to the foundation and preservation of the U.S. political system. By the election of 1796, two distinct political parties with different views had developed.

View the Chapter 5 video in the Glencoe Video Program.

FOLDABLES™ Study Organizer

Summarizing Information Make this foldable and use it as a journal to help you record the major events that occurred as the new nation of the United States formed.

Step 1 Fold a sheet of paper from top to bottom.

Step 2 Then fold it in half from side to side.

Step 3 Label the foldable as shown.

Reading and Writing As you read the chapter, find the "firsts" experienced by the new nation, and record them in your foldable journal. For example, list the precedents set by President Washington and identify the first political parties.

Section 3

The First Political Parties

Essential Question: What parties dominate national politics today? *(Democratic, Republican)* What differences define the parties? *(differences on foreign policy, taxes, role of national government)* Tell students that this section discusses similar differences that began to divide political leaders in the early years of the country. **OL**

History Online

Go to ca.hss.glencoe.com for student activities, lesson plans, and links to additional Web resources about the Federalist era.

FOLDABLES™ Study Organizer Dinah Zike's Foldables

Purpose Have students use their foldables to identify important "firsts" experienced by the new nation, such as precedents set by President Washington. Have students share their journal entries and expand their lists. **OL**

Why It's Important

Recognizing Bias The ability to recognize bias has become increasingly important with the prevalence of unfiltered information on the Internet. Of course, Web sites can show bias in the opinions they state or point of view they reflect. They can also reflect bias in the information they choose to include and exclude. The ability to detect bias can help students as they choose how to use the information they find when conducting research on the Internet.

1 Learn It!

Read the following statements aloud. Have the class determine by a show of hands whether each reflects bias or not. *(The first, third, and fourth statements do.)* Remind students of the differences between bias, often based on generalizations, and informed judgments.

- "His movies are always dull."
- "The goalie made several big saves in the shutout."
- "That group makes the best music videos."
- "I never believe anything she says."
- "The consumer magazine rated that camera as the most reliable." OL

Chapter 5 Get Ready to Read

Recognizing Bias

READING SKILL

1 Learn It!

Most people have feelings and ideas that affect their point of view. This viewpoint, or *bias,* influences the way they interpret events. For this reason, an idea that is stated as a fact may really be only an opinion. Recognizing bias will help you judge the accuracy of what you read. You can look for clues to help uncover bias in written form. Read the list below for hints you can use to identify bias.

- **Identify the author of the statement, and examine his or her views and possible reasons for writing the material.**
- **Look for language that reflects an emotion or opinion—words such as *all, never, best, worst, might,* or *should.***
- **Examine the writing for imbalances—focusing on one viewpoint and failing to discuss other perspectives.**

Reading Tip

One way to identify bias is to find out more about the author. Can you find information about the author that will help you understand opinions he or she may express?

276

READING STRATEGY **QUESTIONING**

Identifying bias is often a matter of asking questions like the following as you read a text:

- Who wrote the piece? Is this person especially knowledgeable on the subject?
- Does the author have a personal stake in the subject? That is, will he or she benefit in some way by having more people agree with him or her?
- Does the author support his or her claims with facts, statistics, and expert opinions? Is such supporting evidence believable?
- Does the author present other points of view? Are those positions presented fairly, and are the arguments against them reasonable?

Suggest that students make a checklist of these questions and use them when they analyze texts. OL

2 Practice It!

Look at the two quotes below. Each has a different opinion about "the people." On a separate sheet of paper, restate each opinion in your own words. Discuss your conclusions with a partner.

"The people are turbulent [disorderly] and changing. . . . They seldom judge or determine right."

—*Alexander Hamilton, Federalist, page 292*

▲ Alexander Hamilton

Read to Write

Write a paragraph describing a person or event about which you feel very strongly. Now try to write a paragraph about the same person or event without including any personal opinion.

"I am not among those who fear the people. They, and not the rich, are our dependence [what we depend on] for continued freedom."

—*Thomas Jefferson, Republican, page 293*

▲ Thomas Jefferson

3 Apply It!

Look for examples of bias in comments made by key figures described in the text.

CHAPTER 5 Get Ready to Read

2 Practice It!

Have students work in pairs to read the excerpt from an Abigail Adams letter on page 294 and analyze it for bias. Instruct them to look for words and phrases that indicate the author's point of view. *(Phrases include "be more generous and favourable" and "all Men would be tyrants if they could.")* Have the pairs explain Adams's point of view. *(She believes that all women have been denied their rights by men.)* OL

3 Apply It!

Have students find a news story in a newspaper, magazine, or news organization's Web site. Caution them to choose a report and not an opinion piece. Have them analyze the story for bias and identify the elements that reveal what the bias is. OL

READING STRATEGY **PERSUASIVE WRITING**

In persuasive writing, a writer attempts to win support for his or her point of view on a particular topic. One important technique that persuasive writers use is to present objections to their own argument and answer them. Have students write a brief essay in which they argue that a particular amendment to the Constitution is the most important of all these additions to the document. Remind them to use part of their essay to mention another amendment that some people might find more important and explain why it is not. AL CA 8WA2.4

Use Reading Skills Activity 5 in the **Chapter 5 Resource Book** for more practice with recognizing bias.

FOCUS

BELLRINGER
SKILLBUILDER ACTIVITY

Project **Daily Focus Skills Transparency 5–1** and have students answer the question.

Guide to Reading

Preteaching Vocabulary: Have students find the definitions of each term. Then quiz them on those definitions.

Answers to Graphic: Washington: named cabinet heads, chief justice; supported Hamilton's policies; Congress: created executive departments, judiciary; chose site of new capital; approved debt plan, national bank

Unpacking the Standards

After reading the section, students will be able to:

- Identify the actions taken to launch the new government.
- List some principles of the Bill of Rights.

Section 1

The First President

History Social Science Standards

US8.3 Students understand the foundation of the American political system and the ways in which citizens participate in it.

US8.4 Students analyze the aspirations and ideals of the people of the new nation.

Guide to Reading

Looking Back, Looking Ahead

American leaders faced a great challenge. Nobody knew if the political system laid out by the Constitution would work. Many people wondered: Could this new kind of government last?

Focusing on the Main Ideas

- President Washington and the new Congress established the departments in the executive branch, set up the nation's court system, and added the Bill of Rights to the Constitution. *(page 279)*
- Alexander Hamilton, the secretary of the treasury under Washington, worked to fix financial problems and strengthen the economy. *(page 281)*

Locating Places

Washington, D.C.

Meeting People

Thomas Jefferson
Alexander Hamilton
Henry Knox
Edmund Randolph
John Jay

Content Vocabulary

precedent (PREH • suh • duhnt)
cabinet
national debt (DEHT)
bond (BAHND)
speculator (SPEH • kyuh • LAY • tuhr)
unconstitutional
tariff (TAR • uhf)

Academic Vocabulary

ultimate (UHL • tuh • muht)
structure
confirm
revenue (REH • vuh • NOO)

Reading Strategy

Classifying Information Use a diagram like the one below to list the actions taken by Congress and Washington's first administration.

Actions	
Washington's First Administration	Congress

NATIONAL GEOGRAPHIC **Who & When?**

1789 — 1790 — 1791 — 1792

Apr. 30, 1789 Washington takes the oath of office

George Washington

Sep. 1789 Judiciary Act sets up federal court system

John Jay

Dec. 1791 Bill of Rights added to the Constitution

James Madison

SECTION RESOURCES

Print Material
- Reproducible Lesson Plan 5–1*
- Daily Lesson and Discussion Notes 5–1
- Guided Reading Activity 5–1
- Reading Essentials and Study Guide 5–1
- Active Reading Note-Taking Guide 5–1
- Section Quiz 5–1

Transparencies
- Daily Focus Skills Transparency 5–1
- Section Graphic Organizer Transparency 5–1
- California Standards Practice Transparencies

Technology
- Interactive Tutor Self-Assessment CD-ROM
- Exam*View*® Pro Testmaker CD-ROM
- Presentation Plus! CD-ROM

*Available on TeacherWorks™

President Washington

Main Idea **President Washington and the new Congress established the departments in the executive branch, set up the nation's court system, and added the Bill of Rights to the Constitution.**

Reading Connection If you were founding our nation's government, what do you think would be most important? As you read this section, think about the choices that Washington and the new Congress had to make.

An American Story

Celebrations erupted in the streets of Philadelphia, New York, Boston, and Charleston in 1789. News of the Constitution's ratification was greeted with relief and enthusiasm. All that was needed now was a leader to guide the new nation.

On April 6, the new Senate counted the presidential ballots. To no one's surprise, the votes were unanimous. Senator John Langdon wrote to General George Washington: "Sir, I have the honor to transmit to Your Excellency the information of your unanimous election to the office of President of the United States of America." Washington was ready to begin the difficult task of leading the country.

The Nation's First President The 57-year-old president-elect made his way slowly toward New York City, then the nation's capital. After the Constitutional Convention, George Washington had looked forward to a quiet retirement. Instead his fellow citizens elected him to the highest office in the land. On April 30, 1789, Washington took the oath of office as the first president of the United States under the federal Constitution. John Adams became vice president.

Perhaps no office in the new government created more suspicion among the people than the office of president. Many Americans feared that a president would try to become king, but Americans trusted Washington and they believed that it was his leadership that brought them victory in the Revolutionary War. Equally important, he had willingly given up his military power as soon as the war was over to return to his civilian life tending his plantation.

Washington was aware of the difficulties he faced. He knew that the **precedents** (PREH • suh • duhnts), or traditions, he established as the nation's first president would shape the future of the United States. "No slip will pass unnoticed," he remarked. One precedent he established concerned the way people should address him. Vice President Adams supported "His Highness the President of the United States," but **ultimately** it was decided that "Mr. President" would be more appropriate.

Washington and the new Congress also had many decisions to make about the **structure** of government. For example, the Constitution gave Congress the power to establish executive departments, but it did not state whether the department heads would report to the president or to Congress.

The First Congress During the summer of 1789, Congress established three executive departments: a Department of State to take charge of foreign affairs, a Department of the Treasury to handle the nation's finances, and a Department of War to manage the military.

▲ Banner celebrating George Washington

Chapter 5 • Section 1

TEACH

R1 Reading Strategy

Categorizing Information Point out to students that the subsection on George Washington's presidency begins with a statement of its main idea. The information in the sentence can be split into two categories—who acted? *(Washington and the Congress)* What did they do? *(established the departments of the executive branch; set up the nation's courts; passed the Bill of Rights).* BL

Review The Big Idea

Review the Big Idea for this section: "Political ideas and major events shape how people form governments." **Ask:** Why did Americans fear the power of a king? *(Americans believed that George III had abused his power as king and taken away some of their rights.)* OL CA H13.

R2 Reading Strategy

Understanding Vocabulary Pronounce *president* and *precedent* distinctly so students hear the differences. To help them distinguish between the terms, give them this memory aid: A *president presides* over the government. A *precedent precedes* a later event. EL

R3 Reading Strategy

Understanding Vocabulary Have students read the sentence that contains the word *ultimately*. Then ask a student to define the word. OL

More Skill Practice

Historical and Social Sciences Analysis Skill Read aloud Washington's statement "No slip will pass unnoticed." **Ask:** What does that suggest about Washington as he took office? *(Possible answer: He was concerned about how people would view his actions.)* OL CA HR5.

Resources for page 279

American Art and Architecture Transparency 5

R1 Reading Strategy

Organizing Informaton Students can use a three-column chart to record details about the first cabinet. Suggest they head the columns *Person; Office;* and *Responsibility.* Charts like this can be valuable study aids when preparing for exams. OL

R2 Reading Strategy

Using Context Clues Help students learn how to use context clues by pointing to the sentence that introduces the term *cabinet*. Have a volunteer read the sentence aloud. **Ask:** Based on this sentence, how would you define the president's cabinet? *(It includes the heads of the executive departments and the attorney general.)* BL

C Critical Thinking

Identifying Central Issues **Ask:** Why would it weaken the president if he or she could not remove a cabinet official from office? *(Students may point out that a cabinet officer could disobey a president's orders, blocking his or her chance to put desired policies into action.)* AL

Congress also created the office of attorney general to handle the government's legal affairs and the office of postmaster general to direct the postal service. To head the departments, Washington chose prominent political figures of the day—**Thomas Jefferson** as secretary of state, **Alexander Hamilton** as secretary of the treasury, and **Henry Knox** as secretary of war. He appointed **Edmund Randolph** as attorney general. Washington met regularly with the three department heads and the attorney general, who together became known as the **cabinet.**

According to the Constitution, the Senate must approve presidential appointments to many important positions. However, other issues arose. For example, should the president be able to replace an official that he had appointed and the Senate had **confirmed?** Senators were evenly divided when they voted on the issue.

Vice President Adams broke the tie by voting to allow the president the authority to dismiss cabinet officers without the Senate's approval. This decision strengthened the president's position. It also helped establish the president's authority over the executive branch.

Linking Past & Present

The Electoral College

Past The presidents are not elected directly by the voters, but by a body of representatives called the Electoral College. The Constitution left it up to the states to determine how the electors of the Electoral College are chosen. In the first few presidential elections, the state legislatures chose the electors in many states.

▼ Billboard advertises new voting system

▲ George Washington

Present Today, the voters choose the members of the Electoral College in all the states. Although the ballot shows the names of the presidential candidates, voters are actually voting for a list of presidential electors pledged to that candidate. ***Why do you think voters choose the members of the Electoral College?***

Answers and Additional Support

Linking Past & Present

Answer: So that they can have a voice in who becomes president

Did You Know?

The Constitution gives the vice president only two official duties. One is to act as presiding officer of the Senate when it is in session. The other is to cast a vote in the Senate when the senators' votes are tied. John Adams had more than thirty opportunities to cast tie-breaking votes. No later vice president has voted as often.

US8.3.4 Understand how the conflicts between Thomas Jefferson and Alexander Hamilton resulted in the emergence of two political parties (e.g., view of foreign policy, Alien and Sedition Acts, economic policy, National Bank, funding and assumption of the revolutionary debt).

What Did the Judiciary Act Do? The first Congress also had to decide how to set up the nation's court system. The Constitution briefly mentioned a supreme court but did not provide details about the court system. This became a job for Congress.

In the Judiciary Act of 1789, Congress established the Supreme Court and the lower federal courts: district courts and courts of appeals. The Supreme Court would be the final authority on many issues. Washington nominated **John Jay** to lead the Supreme Court as chief justice, and the Senate approved Jay's nomination. With the Judiciary Act, Congress had taken the first steps toward creating a strong and independent national judiciary.

C **The Bill of Rights** Americans mistrusted strong central governments. They had fought a revolution to throw off one and did not want to replace it with another. Many people insisted that the Constitution needed to include guarantees of personal liberties. Some states had supported the Constitution on the condition that a bill of rights be added to protect individual rights.

James Madison introduced a set of amendments during the first session of Congress. Congress passed 12 amendments, and the states ratified 10 of them. In December 1791, these 10 amendments were added to the Constitution and became known as the Bill of Rights.

The Bill of Rights protects our individual liberties. Government may not interfere with freedom of speech, press, or religion and must provide a fair and speedy trial for those accused of crimes. The Tenth Amendment protects the rights of states and individuals by saying that powers not specifically given to the federal government "are reserved to the States respectively, or to the people." With the Tenth Amendment, Madison hoped to use the states as an important line of defense against a too-powerful national government. *(See pages 260–261 for the entire text of the Bill of Rights.)*

Reading Check **Describe** Why was the Bill of Rights created?

Strengthening the Economy

Main Idea **Alexander Hamilton, the secretary of the treasury under Washington, worked to fix financial problems and strengthen the economy.**

Reading Connection Have you ever borrowed money from a family member or one of your friends? By doing so, you acquired a debt and had to figure out how and when to pay it back. Hamilton faced a similar challenge with the nation's debt.

Washington himself rarely proposed laws, and he almost always approved the bills that were passed by Congress. The first president concentrated on foreign affairs and military matters and left the government's economic policies to his secretary of the treasury, Alexander Hamilton.

The new nation faced serious financial problems. The **national debt** (DEHT)—the amount the nation's government owed—was growing. The United States owed millions of dollars to France and the Netherlands for loans made during and after the Revolutionary War. The Continental Congress also had borrowed millions of dollars from American citizens. U

What Was Hamilton's Plan? In 1790 Hamilton proposed that the new government pay off the millions of dollars in debts owed by the Confederation government to other countries and to individual American citizens. The states had fought for the nation's independence, Hamilton argued, so the national government should pay for the cost of their help. Hamilton also believed that federal payment of state debts would give the states a strong interest in the success of the national government.

Opposition to the Plan Congress readily agreed to pay the money owed to other nations, but Hamilton's plan to pay off the debt to American citizens unleashed a storm of protest. When the government borrowed money during the American Revolution, it issued **bonds** (BAHNDZ)—paper notes promising to repay the money in a certain length of time. R

C Critical Thinking

Analyzing Information Have students read the first ten amendments to the Constitution (see pages 260–261). Then organize students into teams. State a right guaranteed by the Bill of Rights and ask a team to identify the amendment. Take turns addressing the questions to each team. If a team cannot answer or answers incorrectly, give the question to another team. OL

U Universal Access

English Learners Point out to students that as in *doubt*, the *b* in *debt* is silent. Have them practice pronouncing the term *national debt* to become familiar with it. EL

R Reading Strategy

Scaffolding—Connecting Explain that a *bond* is also an agreement between two people. **Ask:** How does this meaning connect to the meaning of the term *bond?* *(Bonds are agreements between a government and the person who bought them.)* EL

This READING SKILL was introduced in Chapter 3.

Reading Check

Answer: to guarantee personal liberties; because some states had supported the Constitution on the condition that a Bill of Rights would be added

Did You Know?

The First Congress actually passed twelve amendments to the Constitution and sent them to the states. Only ten were approved at the time. These amendments never had a time limit placed on their ratification, so more than 200 years later, in 1992, one of the two unratified amendments was finally approved by two-thirds of the states. It became the Twenty-Seventh Amendment to the Constitution, which says that when Congress votes a pay increase for itself, the new rate of pay will become effective only after a new congressional election has taken place.

R1 Reading Strategy

Understanding Vocabulary Have students look at the term *speculator.* Explain that in the American economic system, all businesspeople risk money in the hope of making a profit. Speculators make investments with higher than normal risk in the hope of making higher than normal profits. OL

R2 Reading Strategy

Understanding Word Parts To clarify the meaning of the prefix *un-*, **ask:** What do *unjust* and *unfair* mean? *(not just; not fair)* What does *unconstitutional* mean? *(not according to the Constitution)* OL

R3 Reading Strategy

Activating Prior Knowledge Ask: What actions from before the Revolution are *tariffs* similar to? *(the taxes on imported goods approved by Parliament)* OL

Resources for page 282

Economics and History Activity 5

Answers and Additional Support

While waiting for the payment, many original bond owners—shopkeepers, farmers, and soldiers—had sold the bonds for less than their value. They were purchased by **speculators** (SPEH • kyuh • LAY • tuhrz), people who take risks with their money in order to make a larger profit. Hamilton proposed that these bonds be paid off at their original value. Opponents believed that Hamilton's plan would make speculators rich. R1

The original bond owners felt betrayed by Hamilton's proposal. They had lost money on the bonds they had bought in support of the war effort while new bond owners would profit. Opponents in Congress argued that the proposal was contrary to "national justice, gratitude, and humanity."

Even stronger opposition came from the Southern states, which had accumulated much less debt than the Northern states. Southern states complained that they would have to pay more than their share under Hamilton's plan.

Compromise Results in a Capital To win support for his plan, Hamilton worked out a compromise with Southern leaders. They voted for his plan to pay off the state debts, and in return he supported locating the permanent capital in the South. A special district was laid out between Virginia and Maryland along the banks of the Potomac River. This district became **Washington, D.C.** While workers prepared the new city for the federal government, the nation's capital was moved from New York to Philadelphia.

The Fight Over the Bank Hamilton made other proposals for building a strong national economy. He asked Congress to create a national bank, the Bank of the United States. The bank would be a place for the federal government to deposit money raised from taxes. The bank could also provide loans to government and to businesses.

Madison and Jefferson opposed the idea of a national bank. They believed it would give the wealthy too much power over national finances. They also charged that the Bank was **unconstitutional**—that it was inconsistent with the Constitution. R2 Hamilton argued that although the Constitution did not specifically say that Congress could create a bank, Congress still had the power to do so. In the end, the president agreed with Hamilton and signed the bill creating the national bank.

What Is a Tariff? Although most Americans earned their living by farming, Hamilton thought the development of manufacturing would make America's economy stronger. He proposed a **tariff** (TAR • uhf)—a tax on imports—to encourage people to buy American products. R3

History Makers

The Capitol

The Capitol is the seat of the United States Congress in Washington, D.C. Built on a hill popularly called Capitol Hill, the Capitol contains floor space equivalent to more than 16 acres. The dome of the United States Capitol, finished in 1863, is one of the most famous landmarks in the United States. Other important parts of the Capitol include the Rotunda directly under the dome, the Senate Chamber in the north wing, the House chamber in the south wing, and the National Statuary Hall.

▲ The Capitol

More Skill Practice

Historical and Social Sciences Analysis Skill Direct students' attention to the quote reflecting objections to Hamilton's debt plan. **Ask:** What did opponents mean by saying the plan was contrary to "justice" and "gratitude"? *(because the speculators would make more money than the people who had originally bought the bonds to support the country during the Revolution)* AL CA HI1.

History Makers

The room now used as National Statuary Hall was originally the chamber used by the House of Representatives. The original Senate chamber was on the other side of the Rotunda. The Capitol was enlarged, with the present House and Senate chambers added, in the 1850s.

Biography

US8.3.4 Understand how the conflicts between Thomas Jefferson and Alexander Hamilton resulted in the emergence of two political parties (e.g., view of foreign policy, Alien and Sedition Acts, economic policy, National Bank, funding and assumption of the revolutionary debt).

ALEXANDER HAMILTON

1755–1804

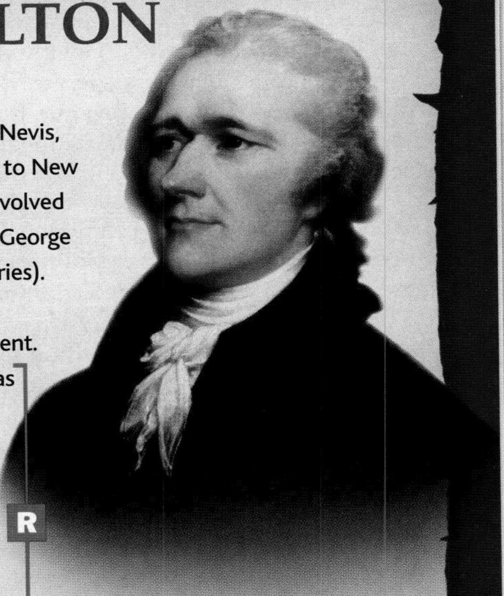

Alexander Hamilton was born on the West Indies island of Nevis, where he worked as a clerk as a young man. In 1773 he moved to New York and studied at King's College. Hamilton quickly became involved in the fight for American independence. He impressed General George Washington, who made him one of his aides-de-camp (secretaries). Hamilton and Washington established a strong friendship and Hamilton served his country on the battlefield and in government.

Hamilton was elected to the Continental Congress and was a driving force in the ratification of the Constitution. Hamilton, James Madison, and John Jay wrote a series of essays called *The Federalist Papers* that explained how the new Constitution worked and why it was needed. **S** Hamilton became the nation's first Secretary of the Treasury. He believed that manufacturing and trade were the basis of national wealth and power. He favored policies that would support these areas of the economy. **R**

During Washington's presidency, Hamilton and Secretary of State Thomas Jefferson had some major differences. They disagreed strongly about how the U.S. government should operate. Hamilton was the leader of the Federalist Party, and Jefferson led the Democratic-Republican Party. These two men became, in essence, the founders of today's political parties.

When Jefferson and Aaron Burr tied with 73 electoral votes in the presidential election of 1800, the Federalist-controlled House of Representatives had to choose a president. Hamilton urged his followers to support Jefferson, and Jefferson became the new president. After Burr failed in his bid to become president, he campaigned to become governor of New York in 1804. **C** Hamilton worked actively against Burr. When Burr lost, he blamed his defeat on Hamilton and challenged him to a duel. Hamilton was fatally wounded and died on July 12, 1804, ending the life of one of the nation's most influential leaders.

"A feeble executive implies a feeble execution of the government."

—Alexander Hamilton, The Federalist, No. 70

Then and Now

Which of Hamilton's actions do you think most influenced the nation's government? Explain your reasoning.

Biography

TEACH

R Reading Strategy

Scaffolding—Summarizing
Ask: What ideas did Hamilton support? Have students write a paragraph summarizing Hamilton's beliefs. *(Support for the Constitution; belief that manufacturing and trade were the basis of national wealth)* **OL**

This READING SKILL was introduced in Chapter 4.

S Skill Practice

Historical and Social Sciences Analysis Skill In one *Federalist* essay, Hamilton explains that the president has more limited power than the British king. **Ask:** Why would Hamilton make this comparison? *(To show that the president could not commit the kinds of abuses that George III was accused of in the Declaration.)* **AL** **CA HI1.**

C Critical Thinking

Making Inferences Ask: Why could Hamilton play a key role in deciding the election of 1800? *(Because of a tie in electoral votes, the election was being decided in the House of Representatives. The Federalists had a majority there, and Hamilton was head of the Federalist Party.)* **OL**

Then and Now

Students may point to Hamilton's role in writing *The Federalist Papers*; his work as Secretary of the Treasury; his role in forming the first political parties; or his part in deciding the election of 1800.

ASSESS

Resources for page 284

Use these resources to assess student mastery of section content.

Section Quiz 5–1

Interactive Tutor Self-Assessment CD-ROM

Reading Check

Answer: For: encourage people to buy American products, raise revenue for government, protect American companies; Against: would not help the South

History Online

Study Central provides summaries, interactive games, and online graphic organizers to help students review section content.

CLOSE

Making Inferences A member of the first Congress said "We are in a wilderness." **Ask:** What did the representative mean? *(Launching the new government would be like traveling through unmapped land.)* OL

Answers and Additional Support

Opposition to the Tariff This protective tariff would not only raise revenue for the new national government, but also protect American industry from foreign competition. However, many Americans were against the tariff.

The South, having little industry to protect, opposed protective tariffs. Congress rejected protective tariffs but did pass low tariffs to raise money. By the 1790s, the **revenue** from tariffs provided 90 percent of the national government's income.

Taxes The final part of Hamilton's economic program concerned the creation of national taxes. The government needed additional funds to operate and to make interest payments on the national debt. At Hamilton's request, Congress approved a variety of taxes, including one on whiskey distilled in the United States.

Hamilton and Jefferson Under Alexander Hamilton's economic program, the national government exercised new financial powers. Soon, however, well-organized opposition to Hamilton's political and economic beliefs grew.

The opposition to Hamilton was led by Thomas Jefferson and James Madison. Where Hamilton's policies favored merchants, bankers, and speculators, his opponents spoke for the interests of the farmers and laborers. When Hamilton favored increasing the power of the federal government, Jefferson wanted to limit it. They had a very different vision of what America should become.

Reading Check **Compare** Summarize the arguments for and against protective tariffs.

History Online

Study Central Need help understanding Washington's presidency? Visit ca.hss.glencoe.com and click on Study Central.

Section 1 Review

Reading Summary

Review the Main Ideas

- President Washington and the first Congress established the cabinet and a federal court system. The first 10 amendments to the Constitution, the Bill of Rights, were introduced during the first session of Congress.
- Under Secretary of the Treasury Alexander Hamilton, the national government agreed to pay off states' debts, created a national bank, and put in place a number of tariffs and taxes.

What Did You Learn?

1. What challenges did Washington face as the nation's first president?
2. Name one thing Hamilton wanted to do to create a stable economic system and strengthen the economy.

Critical Thinking

3. **Comparing** Re-create the diagram below. Compare the views of Hamilton and Jefferson. In the boxes, write "for" or "against" for each issue. CA HR5.

Issue	Hamilton	Jefferson
National bank		
Protective tariff		
National taxes		

4. **The Big Ideas** What compromise led to acceptance of Hamilton's plan for reducing the national debt? CA HI2.
5. **Expository Writing** Imagine you are choosing the first cabinet members. Write job descriptions for the secretaries of state, treasury, and war. CA 8WA2.5
6. **READING** **Recognizing Bias** Read Hamilton's quote. Explain in writing why it does or does not contain bias.

"Can a democratic assembly. . . steadily pursue the public good? Nothing but a permanent body can check the imprudence [disregard of others] of democracy." CA HR2.

SECTION 1 REVIEW ANSWERS

Review questions reinforce content standards US8.3 and US8.4.

1. importance of precedent, the difficulty of starting a new government, need to solve the problem of the national debt
2. Any one: pay off debt, create national bank, enact tariff, impose taxes
3. Hamilton: for all three; Jefferson: against all three
4. **The Big Ideas** Hamilton agreed to having the new national capital placed in the South in return for votes by Southerners for his plan.
5. Students' job descriptions should outline the responsibilities of each secretary.
6. **READING** Students should recognize that Hamilton's use of the word imprudence reveals his bias against a truly democratic assembly.

Section 2

Early Challenges

Guide to Reading

Looking Back, Looking Ahead

The United States needed money to pay its war debts and to finance national growth. Although located an ocean away from Europe, the United States could not hope to exist in isolation. The nation had to respond to overseas pressures.

Focusing on the Main Ideas

- Hamilton's taxes led to rebellion in western Pennsylvania and changed the way the government handled protesters. *(page 286)*
- The new government faced difficult problems in the West. *(page 287)*
- President Washington wanted the nation to remain neutral in foreign conflicts. *(page 288)*

Locating Places

Fallen Timbers
New Orleans

Meeting People

Anthony Wayne
Edmond Genêt (zhuh • NAY)
Thomas Pinckney (PINGK • nee)

Content Vocabulary

neutrality (noo • TRA • luh • tee)
impressment (ihm • PREHS • muhnt)

Academic Vocabulary

transport
maintain

Reading Strategy

Classifying Information As you read the section, re-create the diagram below and list results of government actions during the early Republic.

Government action	Results
Treaty of Greenville	
Proclamation of Neutrality	
Jay's Treaty	
Pinckney's Treaty	

History Social Science Standards

US8.3 Students understand the foundation of the American political system and the ways in which citizens participate in it.

US8.4 Students analyze the aspirations and ideals of the people of the new nation.

NATIONAL GEOGRAPHIC Where & When?

1791 — 1793 — 1795

- **Nov. 1791** Little Turtle defeats St. Clair's forces
- **July 1794** Whiskey Rebellion
- **Aug. 1794** Battle of Fallen Timbers
- **Oct. 1795** Spain opens Mississippi River to American shipping

FOCUS

BELLRINGER
Skillbuilder Activity

Project **Daily Focus Skills Transparency 5–2** and have students answer the question.

Guide to Reading

Preteaching Vocabulary: Have students locate the two content vocabulary terms in the textbook's Glossary and write a sentence using each.

Answers to Graphic: Treaty of Greenville: Native Americans surrendered most of their land in present-day Ohio; Proclamation of Neutrality: kept the U.S. out of war between Britain and France; Jay's Treaty: British agreed to withdraw from American soil, open trade; Pinckney's Treaty: Americans gained right to navigate Mississippi River

Unpacking the Standards

After reading the section, students will be able to:

- Explain the causes and effects of the Whiskey Rebellion.
- Describe the struggle with Native Americans over present-day Ohio.
- Discuss why Washington issued the Neutrality Proclamation.
- Outline the results of Jay's Treaty and Pinckney's Treaty.

SECTION RESOURCES

Print Material
- Reproducible Lesson Plan 5–2*
- Daily Lesson and Discussion Notes 5–2
- Guided Reading Activity 5–2
- Reading Essentials and Study Guide 5–2
- Active Reading Note-Taking Guide 5–2
- Section Quiz 5–2

Transparencies
- Daily Focus Skills Transparency 5–2
- Section Graphic Organizer Transparency 5–2
- California Standards Practice Transparencies

Technology
- Interactive Tutor Self-Assessment CD-ROM
- Exam*View*® Pro Testmaker CD-ROM
- Presentation Plus! CD-ROM

*Available on TeacherWorks™

TEACH

R Reading Strategy

Outlining Encourage students to outline the section on the Whiskey Rebellion. Tell them they should have four main headings: Cause of the rebellion; Farmers' actions; Washington's response; Effects. BL CA 6RC2.4

Review The Big Idea

Review the Big Idea for this section: "Political ideas and major events shape how people form governments." Have students review the events of Shays's Rebellion on pages 194–195. **Ask:** How were Shays's Rebellion and the Whiskey Rebellion similar and how did they differ? *(Similarities—arose in western parts of states; involved economic issues; armies were sent to restore order; Differences—Shays's Rebellion showed the weakness of the Confederation government, but Whiskey Rebellion resulted in a stronger government)* OL

Reading Check

Answer: It set a precedent for government to use force when necessary to maintain social order.

Answers and Additional Support

US8.3.5 Know the significance of domestic resistance movements and ways in which the central government responded to such movements (e.g., Shays' Rebellion, the Whiskey Rebellion).

R The Whiskey Rebellion

Main Idea **Hamilton's taxes led to rebellion in western Pennsylvania and changed the way the government handled protesters.**

Reading Connection Is there a recent government action that you have opposed? What actions did you take? Read to learn what actions the farmers took in regards to the whiskey tax.

An American Story

Far removed from the bustle of trade and shipping along the Atlantic coast, farmers on the western frontier lived quite differently. In fact, western ways seemed almost primitive to travelers from the East. Easterners seemed to notice only the poor roads and the plain diet of corn and salted pork. Living in scattered, isolated homesteads, frontier farmers were proud of their self-reliance. They wanted no "eastern" tax collectors heading their way.

Life in the West In the days before canals and railroads, the Western farmers did not ship their grain east of the Appalachian Mountains because **transporting** the grain was expensive. A wagonload of whiskey was worth much more than a wagonload of grain, so Western farmers distilled their grain into whiskey before they shipped it to market.

The farmers rarely had cash. As a result, most lived on a system of bartering—exchanging whiskey and other items they produced for goods they needed.

The Tax Leads to Protests In 1791 both houses of Congress approved a bill that placed a special tax on whiskey and other alcoholic beverages. Secretary of the Treasury Alexander Hamilton wanted the tax to help prevent the national debt from growing.

The farmers' resistance was mostly peaceful—until July 1794, when federal officers stepped up efforts to collect the tax. Then a large mob of farmers armed with swords, guns, and pitchforks attacked tax collectors and burned down buildings.

The armed protest, called the Whiskey Rebellion, alarmed government leaders as had Shays's Rebellion in 1786. *(See Chapter 3, pages 194–195.)* Now, however, the national government had the taxing and military power that it lacked in 1786. The secretary of the treasury, Alexander Hamilton, urged President Washington to use the full power of the federal government to crush the challenge. The president sent an army of 15,000 across the Appalachian Mountains, only to find that the rebels had already disbanded.

By his action, Washington sent a clear message to those who opposed government actions. If citizens wished to change the law, they had to do so peacefully, through constitutional means such as proposing legislation or using the courts. Otherwise, government would use force when necessary to **maintain** order.

Picturing History

In 1794 President Washington sent nearly 15,000 troops to crush the Whiskey Rebellion. ***What did Washington's action say about the government use of force?***

Reading Check **Explain** How did the Whiskey Rebellion affect the way government handled protesters?

More Skill Practice

Historical and Social Sciences Analysis Skill To help students see the long-term and immediate causes of the Whiskey Rebellion, **ask:** What issue angered the western farmers? *(the tax on whiskey)* What specific action led them to rebel? *(Federal officers stepped up efforts to collect the tax.)* OL CA HI2.

Picturing History

This image of Washington reviewing the troops was painted by Frederick Kemmelmeyer, who had been born in Germany but settled in Baltimore, Maryland, in the 1780s.

Answer: The government was willing to use force to enforce the laws.

US8.4.1 Describe the country's physical landscapes, political divisions, and territorial expansion during the terms of the first four presidents.

Struggle Over the West

Main Idea **The new government faced difficult problems in the West.**

Reading Connection Imagine you are a member of George Washington's government in 1791. Could you balance the interests of settlers who are moving into the Northwest Territory with the interests of the Native American nations who live there? Read on to see how President Washington handled a similar challenge.

The Native Americans who lived between the Appalachian Mountains and the Mississippi River insisted that the United States had no authority over them.

NATIONAL GEOGRAPHIC **Native American Campaigns**

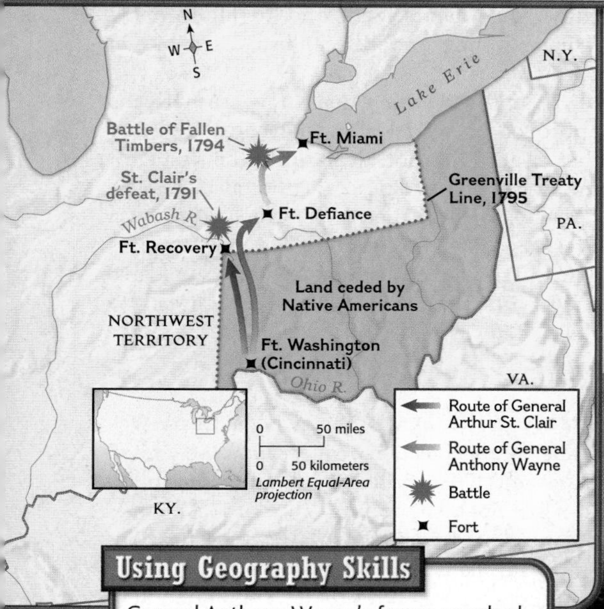

Using Geography Skills

General Anthony Wayne's forces marched north from Fort Washington to fight the Shawnee chief Blue Jacket.

1. **Location** When and where was St. Clair defeated?
2. **Location** On what lake was Fort Miami located?

Armed to defend their lands and encouraged by the British and the Spanish, Native Americans battled settlers over frontier land. Hundreds of people were killed.

Washington sent an army under the command of General Arthur St. Clair to restore order in the Northwest Territory. In November 1791, St. Clair's forces were defeated by Little Turtle, chief of the Miami people. More than 600 American soldiers died in a battle by the Wabash River.

Battle of Fallen Timbers The Native Americans demanded that all settlers north of the Ohio River leave the territory. Washington sent another army headed by **Anthony Wayne,** a former Revolutionary War general, to challenge their demands. In August 1794, his army defeated more than 1,000 Native Americans who fought under Shawnee chief Blue Jacket at the Battle of **Fallen Timbers** (near present-day Toledo, Ohio). The Battle of Fallen Timbers crushed the Native Americans' hopes of keeping their land. In the Treaty of Greenville (1795), the Native Americans agreed to surrender most of their land in present-day Ohio.

Reading Check **Explain** Why did President Washington send troops to the Northwest Territory?

Picturing History

Upon signing the Treaty of Greenville, 12 Native American nations received $20,000 worth of goods to share. ***How did the treaty affect white settlement?***

Using Geography Skills

Answers:

1. In 1791; by the Wabash River near Ft. Recovery
2. Lake Erie

In-Text Map Transparency 5 Ask: What modern city is on the site of Ft. Washington? *(Cincinnati)* OL

Picturing History

The painting shows the Miami chief Little Turtle gesturing as he speaks to American officers. The officer standing in the center is General Wayne. One of the figures on his right is William Henry Harrison.

Caption Answer: It opened most of present-day Ohio to settlers.

R1 Reading Strategy

Scaffolding—Identifying the Main Idea and Supporting Details Point students to the Main Idea of this part of the section. **Ask:** What are two details that support this idea? *(Possible answers: Conflict with Native Americans over settling present-day Ohio; British and Spanish actions to encourage Native Americans to fight)* OL

This READING SKILL was introduced in Chapter 2.

Review Grade 5 Standards

To review standard 5.3.4 *(Discuss the role of broken treaties and massacres and the factors that led to the Indians' defeat, including the resistance of Indian nations to encroachments and assimilation (e.g., the story of Trail of Tears)),* **ask:** What consequences do you see for Native Americans once they give up their claims to Ohio? *(Answers may include a stream of settlers into the area and conflict between whites and Native Americans over other lands.)* OL

R2 Reading Strategy

Scaffolding—Academic Vocabulary The word *challenge* was introduced in Chapter 2, Section 4. Tell students that *challenge* can be used as a noun or a verb. Have students write sentences using the word as both parts of speech. OL

Reading Check

Answer: in 1791, to restore order in the Northwest Territory; in 1794, to challenge the Native Americans' demands that all white settlers leave the area

W Writing Support

Narrative Writing Have students write a narrative summary of the section "Problems With Europe". OL CA 8WA2.1

R1 Reading Strategy

Understanding Vocabulary Explain that the word *neutrality* comes from a Latin word meaning "neither." **Ask:** How is that origin related to the meaning of the term? *(Neutrality means choosing neither side in a dispute.)* OL

U Universal Access

Visual/Spatial Encourage students to draw a political cartoon showing George Washington working to keep the country neutral during the war between Britain and France. OL

R2 Reading Strategy

Understanding Vocabulary Have students restate the meaning of the term *impressment* in their own words. Ask a few volunteers to read their versions aloud. OL CA 8RW1.3

Answers and Additional Support

US8.4.2 Explain the policy significance of famous speeches (e.g., Washington's Farewell Address, Jefferson's 1801 Inaugural Address, John Q. Adams's Fourth of July 1821 Address).

Problems With Europe

Main Idea **President Washington wanted the nation to remain neutral in foreign conflicts.**

Reading Connection Have you ever felt like you were in the middle of a disagreement between two other people? Read on to see how President Washington looked for middle ground in a war between Great Britain and France.

Shortly after Washington was inaugurated in 1789, the French Revolution began. At first most Americans cheered upon hearing the news. The French people had helped the Americans in their struggle for independence, and their revolution seemed to reflect many of the ideals of the American Revolution.

By 1793 the French Revolution had turned bloody. The leaders had executed the king and queen of France and thousands of French citizens. Public opinion in the United States started to divide. The violence of the French Revolution offended many Americans. Others hailed the new republic as a copy of the United States.

When Britain and France went to war in 1793, Washington hoped that the nation could maintain its **neutrality** (noo • TRA • luh • tee)—that is, that it would not take sides in the conflict between France and Britain. As time went on, however, remaining neutral became increasingly difficult.

Washington Proclaims Neutrality The French wanted the help of the United States. In April 1793, they sent diplomat **Edmond Genêt** (zhuh • NAY) to the United States. His mission was to recruit American volunteers to attack British ships.

President Washington took action to discourage American involvement. On April 22, he issued a Proclamation of Neutrality. It prohibited American citizens from fighting in the war and barred French and British warships from American ports. Genêt's plans eventually failed, but he did manage to sign up a few hundred Americans to serve on French ships. These ships seized British vessels and stole their cargoes.

Outraged by the French attacks at sea, the British began capturing American ships that traded with the French. The British also stopped American merchant ships and forced their crews into the British navy. This practice, known as **impressment** (ihm • PREHS • muhnt), infuriated the Americans. British attacks on American ships and sailors pushed the nation close to war with Great Britain.

A Controversial Treaty President Washington decided to make one last effort to come to a peaceful solution with Britain. He sent John Jay, chief justice of the Supreme Court, to negotiate.

The British were willing to listen to Jay's proposals. War with the United States would only make it harder to carry on the war with France. In addition, Britain did not want to lose its profitable trade with the United States.

In Jay's Treaty the British agreed to evacuate their forts on American soil, to pay damages for ships they had seized, and to allow some American ships to trade with British colonies in the Caribbean.

Despite these gains, few Americans approved of Jay's Treaty. They protested that the treaty did not deal with the issue of impressment and did not mention British interference with American trade. Although President Washington found fault with Jay's Treaty, he realized it would end an explosive crisis with Great Britain. He sent the treaty to the Senate, which approved it after a fierce debate.

Treaty With Spain When Jay's Treaty was made, Spanish leaders realized that the United States and Great Britain might now join forces to seize Spanish territory in North America. Spain wanted to establish a positive relationship with the United States and was willing to offer concessions. President Washington sent **Thomas Pinckney** (PINGK • nee) to Spain to try to settle the differences between the two nations. In 1795 Pinckney's Treaty gave the Americans free navigation of the Mississippi River and the right to trade at **New Orleans.**

More Skill Practice

Historical and Social Sciences Analysis Skill Give students the following events and have them put them in the correct sequence:

A. British begin impressing American sailors.
B. Britain and France declare war.
C. French ships seize British ships and steal their cargoes.
D. Washington declares neutrality.
E. French Revolution breaks out.

(E, B, D, C, A) OL CA CS1.

R **Washington's Farewell** In September 1796, after serving two four-year terms as president, Washington announced he would not seek a third term. By choosing to serve only two terms, Washington had set a precedent that later presidents would follow.

Plagued with a variety of ailments, the 64-year-old president looked forward to retirement. He also felt troubled over the divisions that had developed in American politics and with what he considered a grave danger to the new nation—the growth of political parties.

Washington's "Farewell Address" was published in a Philadelphia newspaper. In it he attacked the evils of political parties and entanglement in foreign affairs. He urged citizens to

> **"Observe good faith and justice toward all nations. . . . It is our true policy to steer clear of permanent alliances."**
>
> —George Washington

Washington's "Farewell Address" included his explanation for not seeking a third term as president. Even more important, he gave the young republic his best advice on the conduct of politics and foreign affairs.

Washington's parting words influenced the nation's foreign policy for more than 100 years. The text of his address is still read aloud in the United States Senate each year on Washington's birthday. *(See page 852 of the Appendix for an excerpt from Washington's Farewell Address.)*

Upon returning to Mount Vernon, Washington had every reason to feel proud of his administration's achievements. Most of the difficulties of the Confederation period had been overcome. In the difficult situation presented by war between France and Britain, Washington had steered a course that kept the United States prosperous and at peace.

Reading Check **Explain** What was the impact of Washington's Farewell Address?

History Online
Study Central Need help understanding the government's early challenges? Visit ca.hss.glencoe.com and click on Study Central.

Section 2 Review

Reading Summary

Review the Main Ideas

- On the western frontier, protests against new taxes led to the Whiskey Rebellion, which collapsed when President Washington sent troops to the area.
- Following their defeat at the Battle of Fallen Timbers, Native Americans gave up their claims to lands in Ohio.
- A number of treaties and a policy of neutrality helped the United States remain at peace with the European powers.

What Did You Learn?

1. What message was Washington sending to the American people when he used force to stop the Whiskey Rebellion?
2. What precedent did George Washington set for future presidents?

Critical Thinking

3. **Determining Cause and Effect** Re-create the diagram below. In the boxes, list the cause and effects of the Whiskey Rebellion. CA HI2.

Cause → Cause/Effect: Whiskey Rebellion → Effects

4. **The Big Ideas** How did the Treaty of Greenville affect the land claims of Native Americans in the Northwest Territory? CA CS3.
5. **Creative Writing** Imagine you are a Shawnee following chief Blue Jacket. Write a speech you could give to the Shawnee about the implications of giving up your lands. CA 8LS1.3
6. **Analysis** **Evaluate** What did the United States have to gain by remaining neutral in foreign affairs? Write a short essay describing your conclusions. CA HI3.

R Reading Strategy

Setting a Purpose
Encourage students to set a purpose for themselves when they read. For the material on Washington's Farewell Address, for example, their purpose could be to answer the question "What did Washington say about foreign relations before leaving office?" **BL**

ASSESS

Resources for page 289

Use these resources to assess student mastery of section content.

- Section Quiz 5–2
- Interactive Tutor Self-Assessment CD-ROM

Reading Check
Answer: It influenced American leaders to avoid foreign alliances for more than 100 years.

History Online
Study Central provides summaries, interactive games, and online graphic organizers to help students review section content.

CLOSE

Analyzing Information
Ask: Was Washington's foreign policy effective? Why or why not? *(effective; he gained most of Ohio; maintained neutrality; and won important treaties with Britain and Spain)* **OL**

SECTION 2 REVIEW ANSWERS

Review questions reinforce content standards US8.3 and US8.4.

1. The government would not tolerate violent protests. Laws had to be changed peacefully.
2. He served only two terms.
3. Cause: farmers' resistance to tax on whiskey; Effects: mob attacked tax collectors and burned buildings; Washington sent an army to stop rebellion; people learned that government will vigorously enforce laws
4. **The Big Ideas** Native Americas were forced to give up claims to much of present-day Ohio.
5. Speeches should point to negative effects.
6. **Analysis** Students may mention that Americans would not die in battle and that the country would suffer less financially.

FOCUS

BELLRINGER
SKILLBUILDER ACTIVITY

Project **Daily Focus Skills Transparency 5–3** and have students answer the question.

Guide to Reading

Preteaching Vocabulary: Have students write each term and its definition on an index card.

Answers to Graphic: Federalists: strong federal government, loose interpretation; Republicans: weak federal government, strong state governments, strict interpretation

Unpacking the Standards

After reading the section, students will be able to:

- Explain why the first political parties were formed.
- Describe the foreign policy of John Adams.
- Explain the debate over the Alien and Sedition Acts.

Section 3

The First Political Parties

History Social Science Standards

US8.3 Students understand the foundation of the American political system and the ways in which citizens participate in it.

US8.4 Students analyze the aspirations and ideals of the people of the new nation.

Guide to Reading

Looking Back, Looking Ahead

Today the United States has two major political parties. The origins of the nation's two-party political system are found in the conflicts between the followers of Alexander Hamilton and Thomas Jefferson.

Focusing on the Main Ideas

- Americans began to take opposing sides on issues by 1796, and, as a result, two political parties emerged. *(page 291)*
- John Adams dealt with many things in office, including a dispute with France, which led to a group of measures called the Alien and Sedition Acts. *(page 293)*

Meeting People

Philip Freneau (frih • NOH)
Charles de Talleyrand (TA • lee • RAND)

Content Vocabulary

partisan (PAHR • tuh • zuhn)
implied powers
caucus (KAW • kuhs)
alien (AY • lee • uhn)
sedition (sih • DIH • shuhn)
nullify (NUH • luh • FY)
states' rights

Academic Vocabulary

distinct
contrast
accompany (uh • KUHM • puh • nee)
assign (uh • SYN)

Reading Strategy

Classifying Information As you read Section 3, create a diagram like the one below and list the differences between the Federalists and the Democratic-Republicans.

Issue	Federalists	Democratic-Republicans
Role of federal government		

NATIONAL GEOGRAPHIC Where & When?

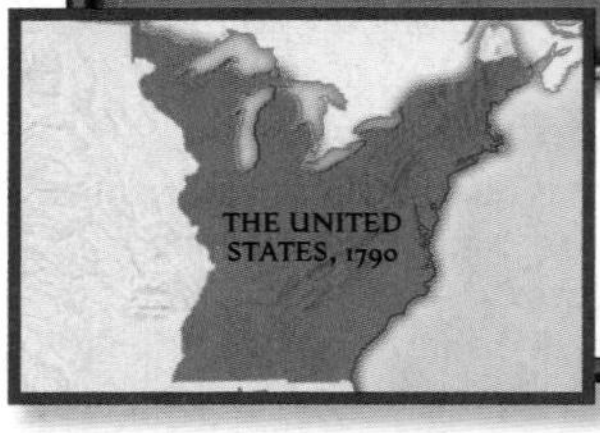

1796 | **1798** | **1800**

- **1796** Adams and Jefferson run for president
- **1797** John Adams becomes president
- **1798** Congress passes Alien and Sedition Acts
- **1800** Convention of 1800

SECTION RESOURCES

Print Material
- Reproducible Lesson Plan 5–3*
- Daily Lesson and Discussion Notes 5–3
- Guided Reading Activity 5–3
- Reading Essentials and Study Guide 5–3
- Active Reading Note-Taking Guide 5–3
- Section Quiz 5–3

Transparencies
- Daily Focus Skills Transparency 5–3
- Section Graphic Organizer Transparency 5–3
- California Standards Practice Transparencies

Technology
- Interactive Tutor Self-Assessment CD-ROM
- Exam*View*® Pro Testmaker CD-ROM
- Presentation Plus! CD-ROM

*Available on TeacherWorks™

US8.3.4 Understand how the conflicts between Thomas Jefferson and Alexander Hamilton resulted in the emergence of two political parties (e.g., view of foreign policy, Alien and Sedition Acts, economic policy, National Bank, funding and assumption of the revolutionary debt).

Opposing Views

Main Idea **Americans began to take opposing sides on issues by 1796, and, as a result, two political parties emerged.**

U

Reading Connection Think about a time when you disagreed with something that one of your classmates said. Did you voice your opinion? Read to learn what happened when conflict occurred between the supporters of Hamilton and Jefferson.

Although hailed by Americans as the nation's greatest leader, George Washington did not escape criticism during his two terms as president. From time to time, harsh attacks on his policies and on his personality appeared in newspapers. One paper even called Washington "the misfortune of his country."

How Did Americans View the President?

Most attacks on Washington came from supporters of Thomas Jefferson. They were trying to discredit the policies of Washington and Hamilton by attacking the president. By 1796 Americans were beginning to divide into opposing groups and to form political parties.

W

In Washington's cabinet, Hamilton and Jefferson often took opposing sides. They disagreed on economic policy and foreign relations, on the power of the federal government, and on interpretations of the Constitution. Even R1 Washington was sometimes **partisan** (PAHR•tuh•zuhn)—favoring one side of an issue. Although he believed he stood above politics, Washington usually supported Hamilton's positions.

Political Parties Emerge Like Hamilton R2 and Jefferson, Congress and the nation at large also had differences. By the mid-1790s, two **distinct** political parties had taken shape.

The name *Federalist* had first described someone who supported ratification of the Constitution. By the 1790s the word was applied to the group of people who supported the policies of the Washington administration.

Generally, Federalists stood for a strong federal government. They admired Britain because of its stability and distrusted France because of the violent changes following the French Revolution. Federalist policies tended to favor banking and business. Federalists received the strongest support in the Northeast and from wealthy plantation owners in the South.

Efforts to turn opinion against the Federalists began seriously in late 1791 when **Philip Freneau** (frih•NOH) began publishing the *National Gazette.* Jefferson, then secretary of state, helped the newspaper get started. Later he and Madison organized people who disagreed with Hamilton.

HISTORY MAKERS

Washington Serves Two Terms

Washington was elected president in 1789 and reelected in 1792—both times unanimously. Although many Americans encouraged Washington to seek a third term, he refused nomination and retired from public life. Stepping down after two terms was one of Washington's most important acts and established a precedent that lasted until Franklin Roosevelt was elected for a third term in 1940 and later a fourth term in 1944.

George Washington ▶

More Skill Practice

Historical and Social Sciences Analysis Skill Point out that George Washington had twice been elected to the presidency unanimously. **Ask:** Why did he then suffer such harsh criticism? *(Opponents of Hamilton's ideas wanted to discredit them, and Washington generally supported Hamilton's plans.)* OL CA H13.

HISTORY MAKERS

As a general and commander-in-chief of the revolutionary army, George Washington is one of the most important figures in American history. He is the only U.S. president to date to ever be chosen unanimously by the electoral college—a feat he accomplished twice.

TEACH

U Universal Access

English Learners Encourage English language learners to note material they have difficulty understanding. Then divide the class into groups and have group members share their lists. Students who understand a particular section can help the others understand the concept. EL

W Writing Support

Persuasive Writing Have students take the position of a citizen from the 1790s who supports either Jefferson or Hamilton and write a paragraph arguing whether Washington was a good or bad president based on that perspective. AL CA 8WA2.4

R1 Reading Strategy

Understanding Vocabulary Explain that a *partisan* is someone who supports a political *party.* BL

R2 Reading Strategy

Scaffolding—Identifying the Main Idea and Supporting Details On this and the following pages, the text indicates four broad areas where Hamilton and Jefferson disagreed—economic policy, foreign policy, the power of the government, and interpretation of the Constitution. Have students find evidence of political differences in each of those areas. OL

This READING SKILL was introduced in Chapter 2.

C Critical Thinking

Comparing and Contrasting **Ask:** Did Jefferson and Madison believe that the federal government had *no* implied powers? *(No)* How did their position differ from Hamilton's? *(They believed that the implied powers were limited by necessity; Hamilton believed the government had more flexibility.)* OL

R Reading Strategy

Understanding Vocabulary Explain that to *imply* something is to hint at it. Have students explain the connection of this to the term *implied powers.* *(These powers are suggested but not directly stated.)* OL

W Writing Support

Expository Writing Divide students into groups and assign each group to one of the two emerging political parties. Have the groups work together to write a party platform. OL

History Online

Objectives and answers to the Student Web Activity can be found in the Web Activity Lesson Plan feature at ca.hss.glencoe.com.

Answers and Additional Support

History Online

Student Web Activity Visit ca.hss.glencoe.com and click on *Chapter 5—Student Web Activities* for an activity on the first political parties.

The followers of Jefferson and Madison called their party the Republicans, or the Democratic-Republicans. The Republicans wanted to limit government. They feared that a strong government would endanger people's liberties. They supported the French and condemned what they regarded as the Washington administration's pro-British policies. Republican policies appealed to small farmers and urban workers, especially in the Middle Atlantic states and the South.

Views of the Constitution One difference between Federalists and Republicans concerned the basis of government power. In Hamilton's view, the federal government had **implied powers,** powers that were suggested but not directly stated in the Constitution.

Hamilton used the idea of implied powers to justify a national bank. He argued that the Constitution gave Congress the power to issue money and regulate trade, and a national bank would clearly help the government carry out these responsibilities. Therefore, he believed that creating a bank was within the constitutional power of Congress.

Jefferson and Madison, however, believed in a strict interpretation of the Constitution. They accepted the idea of implied powers, but in a much more limited sense than Hamilton did. They believed that implied powers are those powers that are "absolutely necessary" for Congress to exercise its stated powers.

The People's Role The differences between the parties, however, went even deeper. Federalists and Republicans had sharply opposing views on the role ordinary people should play in government.

Federalists supported representative government, in which elected officials ruled in the people's name. They did not believe that it was wise to let the public become too involved in politics. Hamilton said:

> **"The people are turbulent [disorderly] and changing; they seldom judge or determine right."**
>
> **—Alexander Hamilton, Speech on the Constitutional Convention**

Public office, Federalists thought, should be held by honest and educated men who own property and would protect everyone's rights. In **contrast,** the Republicans feared a strong central government controlled by a few people.

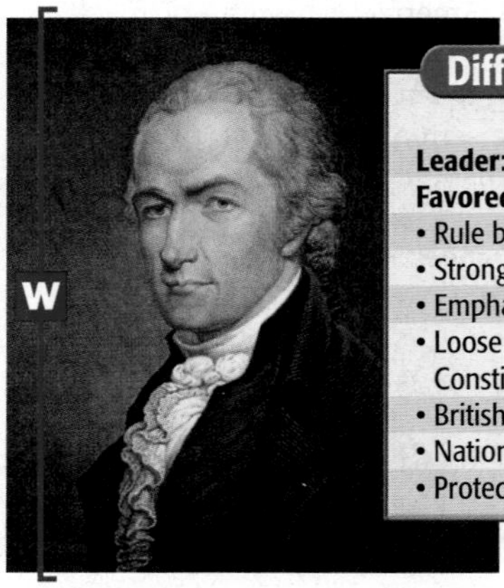

Differences Between the First Political Parties

Federalists	Democratic-Republicans
Leader: Alexander Hamilton	**Leader:** Thomas Jefferson
Favored:	**Favored:**
• Rule by the wealthy class	• Rule by the people
• Strong federal government	• Strong state governments
• Emphasis on manufacturing	• Emphasis on agriculture
• Loose interpretation of the Constitution	• Strict interpretation of the Constitution
• British alliance	• French alliance
• National bank	• State banks
• Protective tariffs	• Free trade

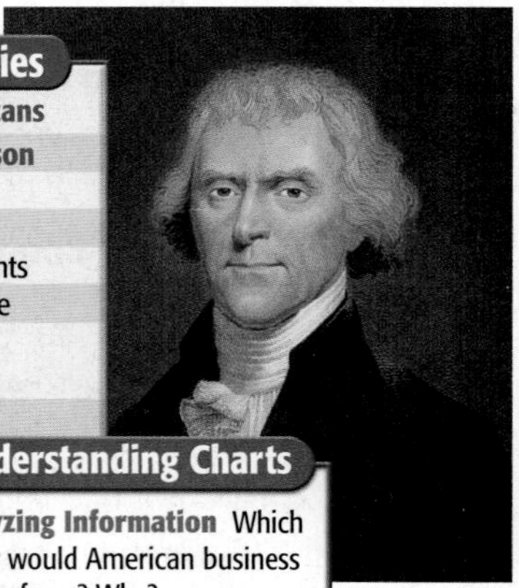

Understanding Charts

Analyzing Information Which leader would American business owners favor? Why?

Understanding Charts

Answer: Hamilton; because he favored rule by the wealthy, emphasized manufacturing, believed in strong tariffs to help build American industry, and favored a national bank

More Skill Practice

Historical and Social Sciences Analysis Skill Explain that the Constitution is sometimes vague. The "elastic clause" grants Congress the power "to make all laws which shall be necessary and proper for carrying" out its powers. **Ask:** What laws are "necessary and proper" to defend the country? *(Answers will vary, but should reveal how broad the elastic clause is.)* OL CA HI2.

US8.3.4 Understand how the conflicts between Thomas Jefferson and Alexander Hamilton resulted in the emergence of two political parties (e.g., view of foreign policy, Alien and Sedition Acts, economic policy, National Bank, funding and assumption of the revolutionary debt). US8.4.1 Describe the country's physical landscapes, political divisions, and territorial expansion during the terms of the first four presidents.

R1 The Republicans believed that liberty would be safe only if ordinary people participated in government. As Jefferson explained:

> "I am not among those who fear the people. They, and not the rich, are our dependence [what we depend on] for continued freedom."
>
> —Letter to Samuel Kercheval

Washington tried to get his two advisers to work out their differences. Nevertheless, by 1793 Jefferson was so unhappy that he resigned as secretary of state. In 1795 Hamilton resigned, too, as secretary of the treasury. The rival political parties moved further apart.

The Election of 1796 In the presidential election of 1796, candidates sought office for the first time as members of a party. R2 To prepare for the election, the Federalists and the Republicans held meetings called **caucuses** (KAW•kuhs•ihz). At the caucuses, members of Congress and other leaders chose their party's candidates for office.

The Federalists nominated Vice President John Adams for president and Charles Pinckney for vice president. The Republicans nominated Jefferson for president and Aaron Burr for vice president. Adams and Jefferson, who had been good friends, became rivals. The Federalists expected to carry New England. The Republicans' strength lay in the South, which would give most of its votes to Jefferson.

C In the end, Adams received 71 electoral votes, winning the election. Jefferson finished second with 68 votes. According to the Constitution at that time, the person with the second-highest number of electoral votes became vice president. Jefferson therefore became the new vice president. The administration that took office on March 4, 1797, had a Federalist president and a Republican vice president.

Reading Check **Explain** Which political party would a Boston factory owner most likely support?

President John Adams

Main Idea **John Adams dealt with many things in office, including a dispute with France, which led to a group of measures called the Alien and Sedition Acts.**

Reading Connection Do you think you should be free to say or write anything you want about the government? Do you think the government has the right to send you to jail if you criticize its policies? The Federalists passed laws restricting freedom of speech. Read on to find out why.

John Adams had spent much of his life in government. One of Massachusetts's most active patriots, he later became ambassador to France and to Great Britain. He helped negotiate the Treaty of Paris that ended the Revolution. Under Washington, he served two terms as vice president.

John's wife, Abigail, actively supported the American cause and raised their sons and daughter while John was away on government business. Abigail also capably managed their family farm in Braintree, Massachusetts.

The XYZ Affair When Adams took office, the nation faced a crisis with France. The French regarded Jay's Treaty, signed in 1794, as an American attempt to help the British in their war with France. To punish the United States, the French seized American ships that carried cargo to Britain.

Adams wanted to avoid war with France. In the fall of 1797, he sent a delegation to Paris to try to resolve the dispute. French foreign minister **Charles de Talleyrand** (TA•lee•RAND), however, refused to meet with the Americans. Instead, Talleyrand sent three agents who demanded a bribe and a loan for France from the Americans. "Not a sixpence," the Americans replied and sent a report of the incident to the United States. Adams was furious. Referring to the three French agents as X, Y, and Z, the president urged Congress to prepare for war. The incident became known as the XYZ affair.

R1 Reading Strategy

Scaffolding—Academic Vocabulary The word *participate* was introduced in Chapter 3, Section 2. Ask students to list synonyms for the word. OL

R2 Reading Strategy

Understanding Vocabulary Explain that the term *caucus* is used to refer only to political meetings. OL

C Critical Thinking

Drawing Conclusions Have students review the paragraph stating the results of the 1796 election. **Ask:** Do you think the country was closely divided? Why or why not? *(yes; because the electoral vote for Adams and Jefferson was so close)* OL

Review The Big Idea

Review the Big Idea for this section: "Citizen participation is essential to the foundation and preservation of the U.S. political system." **Ask:** What roles did political parties play in the election of 1796? *(They held meetings to choose candidates for office.)* OL

Reading Check
Answer: the Federalist Party

More Skill Practice

Historical and Social Sciences Analysis Skill **Ask:** Why was Washington unable to convince Jefferson and Hamilton to work together? *(They disagreed on both principles and policies.)* OL CA HI2.

Resources for page 293

♫ American Music; Hits Through History, "College Hornpipe/Belle Catherine"

Biography

TEACH

R Reading Strategy

Sequencing Information Check students' comprehension of the sequence of events in the Adams's lives by giving them pairs of events and asking which came first. OL

C1 Critical Thinking

Predicting Consequences During the Revolutionary War, many women took responsibility for family farms or businesses while their husbands served in the army. **Ask:** What impact might that have on their attitudes towards women's rights? Why? *(make them more likely to push for equal rights)* OL

C2 Critical Thinking

Drawing Conclusions **Ask:** Why would frequent separations from John contribute to Abigail's skill in writing letters? *(Answers may include the desire to communicate with her husband and the absence of other means of communication, such as telephone, in the 1700s.)* AL

Answers and Additional Support

Biography

US8.4 Students analyze the aspirations and ideals of the people of the new nation.

ABIGAIL ADAMS
1744–1818

JOHN ADAMS
1735–1826

R

▲ Abigail Adams

John Adams, a young lawyer, and Abigail Smith were married in 1764. The young couple lived on a farm in Braintree, Massachusetts, and had five children. John was one of the leaders of the movement for independence. In late 1774 John Adams went to Philadelphia as a delegate to the Continental Congress, while Abigail Adams remained in Massachusetts to manage their business affairs and take care of the family. During most of the Confederation period, Abigail Adams lived in Europe with John, who was the first American minister to Great Britain. Eventually, when John was elected the second president of the United States, Abigail became the first First Lady to preside over the still unfinished White House. C1

Although she lacked a formal education, Abigail Adams developed a notable talent as a letter writer. Letter writing, she said, was "a habit, the pleasure of which increases with practice, but becomes irksome by neglect." In one of her most well-known letters, she made the following plea to her husband and his associates in the Continental Congress. C2

"Remember the Ladies, and be more generous and favourable to them than your ancestors. Do not put such unlimited power into the hands of the Husbands. Remember all Men would be tyrants if they could. If [particular] care and attention is not paid to the Ladies we are determined to foment a Rebellion, and will not hold ourselves bound by any Laws in which we have no voice."

Despite the hopes of Abigail and many women, they still could not vote or hold office in the years after the American Revolution. Abigail Adams believed strongly in equal rights for women and African Americans at a time in history when such views were not well received.

◀ John Adams

Then and Now

How does the role of women in government differ today from their role during Abigail Adams's time?

Then and Now

Answers may include the fact that many women serve in government positions, including several women in Congress, two who have sat on the bench of the Supreme Court, some who have been state governors, and many who have served in state, local, and city governments.

Undeclared War With France Congress responded with a program to strengthen the armed forces. It established the Navy Department in April 1798 and set aside money for building warships. Congress also increased the size of the army. George Washington was appointed commanding general.

Between 1798 and 1800, United States and French naval vessels clashed on a number of occasions, although war was not formally declared. Adams's representatives negotiated an agreement with France in September 1800 that ensured peace.

In the view of most Americans, France had become an enemy. The Republican Party, friendly toward France in the past, hesitated to turn around and condemn France. As a result, in the 1798 elections, Americans voted some Republicans out of office.

Alien and Sedition Acts The threat of war with France made Americans more suspicious of **aliens** (AY • lee • uhnz)—immigrants who were not citizens but were living in the nation. Many Europeans who came to the United States in the 1790s supported the ideals of the French Revolution. Some Americans questioned whether these aliens would remain loyal if the United States went to war with France. Because many of the newcomers to the nation were anti-British, many of them tended to support the Republican Party.

Federalists in Congress responded with strict laws to protect the nation's security. In 1798 they passed a group of measures known as the Alien and Sedition Acts. **Sedition** (sih • DIH • shuhn) refers to activities aimed at weakening established government. Many Federalists believed that the laws would weaken the Republican Party.

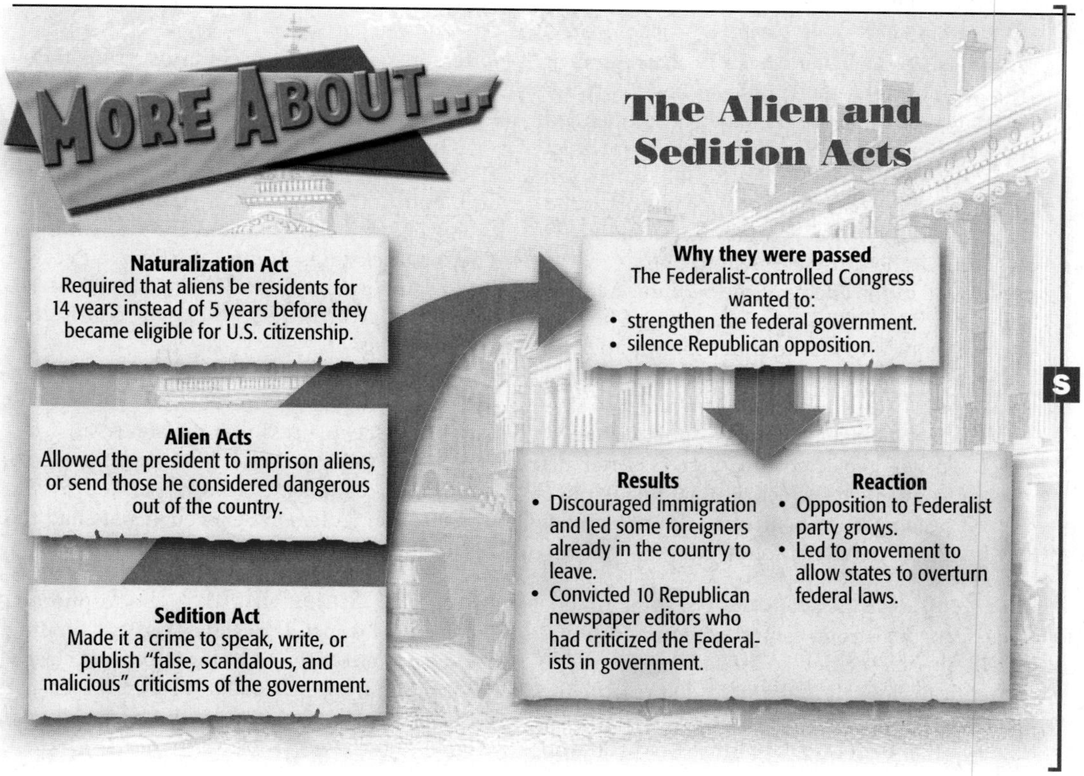

R1 Reading Strategy

Understanding Vocabulary Explain that the origin of the term *alien* is a Latin word meaning "other." **Ask:** How does that origin relate to the meaning of the term? *(An alien is someone from a different country.)* OL

R2 Reading Strategy

Understanding Vocabulary Explain that *treason* is a matter of hurting the security or defenses of one's own country by helping an enemy. **Ask:** How does *sedition* differ? *(It does not necessarily involve an enemy but could include inciting people to a revolt.)* OL CA 8RW1.3

S Skill Practice

Visual Literacy Write the following three headings on the board: *Causes, Actions, Effects.* Then point to each section of the chart about the Alien and Sedition Acts and ask volunteers to identify the heading under which it should be placed. *(the three boxes identifying the acts: causes; the box with "Results": actions; the box "Why they were passed" and "Reaction": effects)* OL

MORE ABOUT...

When Congress passed the Alien and Sedition Acts, Philadelphia still served as the nation's capital. The city was full of people who had left France and Ireland at the time. A French diplomat guessed that as many as 25,000 French people could be found in the city. There was great concern among the Federalists that such a sizable number of people could be a danger in the event of a war between the United States and France. The Irish immigrants were mistrusted as well. Many of them had fled the island after a 1798 rebellion against British rule had failed. In the end, the Alien and Sedition Acts were little used.

R1 Reading Strategy

Academic Vocabulary
Ask students to write a sentence using the word *accompanied*. **EL**

R2 Reading Strategy

Understanding Vocabulary
Explain that in mathematics the word *null* refers to something that has the value of zero. **Ask:** How does that help clarify the meaning of the term *nullify*? **OL**

C Critical Thinking

Identifying Central Issues
Remind students of the issues and principles on which Hamilton and Jefferson disagreed. **Ask:** Which of those disagreements is related to Jefferson's idea of a state's power to nullify an act of Congress? *(limits to federal power)* **AL** CA HI1.

Answers and Additional Support

Analyzing *Political Cartoons*

Fighting in Congress The Sedition Act led to hard feelings, even violence. This cartoon provides a humorous look at a fight in Congress. Federalist Roger Griswold attacks Republican Matthew Lyon with a cane. Lyon seizes a pair of fire tongs and fights back. On the wall is a painting named "Royal Sport" showing animals fighting. ***How are the other members of Congress reacting to the fight?***

1 Matthew Lyon 2 Roger Griswold 3 painting

What Effects Did the Acts Have? As it turned out, the anti-Republican laws hurt the Federalist Party more. The Alien Acts offended new immigrants and drove them more than ever to the support of the Republicans. Ten Republicans, mostly newspaper editors, who were jailed under the Sedition Act were hailed as heroes in the cause of freedom of the press.

Typical of the effects of the Sedition Act was the case of Matthew Lyon of Vermont, who was the editor of an Antifederalist newspaper. In 1798 he was convicted under the Sedition Act for the publication in the *Vermont Journal* of a letter criticizing President John Adams. While in jail, Lyon was reelected to Congress. After his release from prison he set off for Philadelphia. R1 He was **accompanied** on the first day of his journey by a long parade of followers.

The Republicans Respond For some Americans, fears of a strong central government abusing its power seemed to be coming true. The Republicans looked to the states to preserve the people's liberties and stand up to what they regarded as Federalist tyranny. Madison and Jefferson drafted documents of protest that were passed by the Virginia and Kentucky legislatures.

The Virginia and Kentucky Resolutions of 1798 and 1799 claimed that the Alien and Sedition Acts could not be put into action because they violated the Constitution. The Kentucky Resolutions further suggested that states might **nullify** (NUH • luh • FY)—legally overturn—federal laws considered unconstitutional. R2

What does nullification mean? Thomas Jefferson, who authored the Kentucky Resolutions, explained that the states are "sovereign and independent." If an act of the government exceeded the powers granted by the Constitution, Jefferson believed, a state had the right to refuse to obey.

What Are States' Rights? The resolutions affirmed the principle of **states' rights**—limiting the federal government to those powers clearly **assigned** to it by the Constitution and reserving to the states all other powers not expressly forbidden to them. C

Analyzing *Political Cartoons*

Answer: They are amused by the fight.

More Skill Practice

Analyzing Primary Sources The Sedition Act made it illegal to publish "false, scandalous, and malicious" criticisms of the government. Have a volunteer read aloud the First Amendment on page 260. **Ask:** Was the Sedition Act constitutional? Did the Federalists make an error when they passed it? *(Students should support answers with reasons.)* **AL** CA HI4.

To phrase it differently, the state had the right to assert its power to protect its citizens from the misuse of federal power. The issue of states' rights would arise again and again in the nation's early history.

Federalists criticized the Kentucky and Virginia Resolutions as a step toward the breakup of the Union. They argued that if any state could nullify any federal law it considered unconstitutional, the power of the federal government would cease.

C **Making Peace With France** As the election of 1800 approached, the Federalists found themselves under attack. They urged Adams to step up the war with France. If war continued, the Federalists expected to win reelection. They believed Americans would be reluctant to elect a new president in wartime. Adams refused to rush to war, especially for his own political gain. Instead he appointed a new commission to seek peace with France.

In 1800 the French agreed to a treaty and stopped attacks on American ships. Although the agreement with France was in the best interest of the United States, it hurt Adams's chance for reelection. Rather than applauding the agreement, Hamilton and his supporters now opposed their own president. Federalist leaders were furious, but they could not long oppose an effort to make peace. By the end of Adams's presidency, peace with France had been restored.

Adams's action in making peace against the wishes of most of his party was a courageous act. Proud of his nonpartisan action, Adams wrote that on his gravestone he wanted written "Here lies John Adams who took upon himself the responsibility of the peace with France in the year 1800."

With the Federalists split, the Republican prospects for capturing the presidency improved. The way was prepared for Thomas Jefferson in the election of 1800.

Reading Check **Summarize** How did the peace agreement with France affect the Federalists?

History Online
Study Central Need help understanding the origins of political parties? Visit ca.hss.glencoe.com and click on Study Central.

Section 3 Review

Reading Summary

Review the Main Ideas

- By the election of 1796, the political parties known as the Federalists and the Republicans had developed.
- During President John Adams's term, the threat of war with France led to the passage of the Alien and Sedition Acts, which were greatly opposed by the Republicans.

What Did You Learn?

1. Who was elected president in 1796, and who became vice president?
2. What does "sedition" refer to in the Alien and Sedition Acts?

Critical Thinking

3. **Classifying Information** Re-create the diagram below. Provide information about the election of 1796 in the spaces provided. CA HR3.

Presidential Election of 1796		
Candidate		
Electoral votes		
Elected position		

4. **The Big Ideas** How were the Federalists different from the Republicans in how they viewed the Constitution? CA HR5.
5. **Drawing Conclusions** Do you think the development of political parties was necessary? Why or why not? Write a short essay justifying your conclusion. CA 8WA2.4
6. **Persuasive Writing** Design a campaign poster or button for the presidential candidate you would have chosen in 1796. Write a short paragraph that summarizes your reasons for your choice. CA 8WC1.1

C Critical Thinking

Drawing Conclusions
Ask: Based on Adams's actions regarding the war with France and the election, what kind of character did he have? *(Answers may include cautious, honorable, principled.)* AL

ASSESS

Resources for page 297

Use these resources to assess student mastery of section content.

- Section Quiz 5–3
- Interactive Tutor Self-Assessment CD-ROM

Reading Check

Answer: It split the party, giving Republican Jefferson a better chance of winning the 1800 election.

History Online
Study Central provides summaries, interactive games, and online graphic organizers to help students review section content.

CLOSE

Drawing Conclusions **Ask:** What impact did foreign relations have on domestic politics during Adams's presidency? OL

SECTION 3 REVIEW ANSWERS

Review questions reinforce content standards US8.3 and US8.4.

1. John Adams; Thomas Jefferson
2. activities aimed at weakening the government
3. Adams, 71, president; Jefferson, 68, vice president
4. **The Big Ideas** Federalists: loose interpretation with broad federal powers; Republicans: strict interpretation with limited federal powers
5. Some students may say yes because people will always disagree on some issues and seek out allies. Others may say no because parties divide the nation.
6. Students' paragraphs should give reasons for supporting the candidate they chose.

Analyzing Primary Sources

FOCUS

History–Social Science Standards

The following standards are covered on pages 298–299:

US8.3 Students understand the foundation of the American political system and the ways in which citizens participate in it.

US8.4 Students analyze the aspirations and ideals of the people of the new nation.

TEACH

C Critical Thinking

Analyzing Primary Sources Ask: Was Washington more concerned about the impact of the presidency on himself or on the people? Explain. *(the impact on the people, he wonders what the result of the voyage will be for them)* OL CA HR3.

R Reading Strategy

Inferring Ask: What does Washington mean by saying that he is setting out on a voyage? *(He and the nation are doing something new.)* OL CA HI1.

Answers and Additional Support

US8.4 Students analyze the aspirations and ideals of the people of the new nation.

Analyzing Primary Sources

Challenging Times

Even after the ratification of the U.S. Constitution, the leaders and citizens of this young nation faced many challenges. With an outline for how the government should work and the leadership of George Washington, people began to work together to launch this new republic.

Read the passages on pages 298 and 299 and answer the questions that follow.

Painter and President **by J.L.G. Ferris**

Reader's Dictionary

embarking (ihm • BAHRK • ihng): setting out

integrity (ihn • TEH • gruh • tee): honesty

gallery: outdoor balcony

proclamation (PRAH • kluh • MAY • shuhn): announcement

agitated (A • juh • TAYT • ihd): upset and nervous

ungainly: awkward, clumsy

plainest manner: in a simple way

On Becoming President

Americans were happy that the hero of the American Revolution, George Washington, was elected the nation's first president. Washington expressed his feelings about becoming president in a letter.

> I am **embarking** . . . on this voyage, but what returns will be made for them [Americans], Heaven alone can foretell. **Integrity** and firmness is all I can promise; these, be the voyage long or short, never shall forsake me although I may be deserted by all men.
>
> —Letter to Henry Knox, April 1789

Washington's First Inaugural

Pennsylvania Senator William Maclay was one of the many witnesses to the nation's first presidential inauguration. He wrote about the event in his journal.

> [T]he President was conducted out of the middle window into the **gallery** [overlooking Wall Street], and the oath was administered by the Chancellor [the highest judicial officer in the state of New York]. Notice that the business done was communicated to the crowd by **proclamation** . . . who gave three cheers, and repeated it on the President's bowing to them.

More Skill Practice

Analyzing Information Ask: Should you believe the statements made by Maclay? Why or why not? *(Students may say that he was a witness to the events, so he saw what he wrote, but should also point out that he had biases and opinions that shaped how he saw events.)* OL CA HR5.

As the company returned into the Senate chamber, the President took the chair and the Senators and Representatives their seats. He rose, and all arose also and [he] addressed them. This great man was **agitated** and embarrassed more than ever he was by the leveled cannon or pointed musket. He trembled, and several times could scarce make out to read, though it must be supposed he had often read **R** it before.... When he came to the words *all the world,* he made a flourish with his right hand, which left rather an **ungainly** impression. I sincerely, for my part, wished all set ceremony in the hands of the dancing-masters, and that this first of men had read off his address in the **plainest manner,** without ever taking his eyes from the paper, for I felt hurt that he was not first in everything.

—from the Journal of William Maclay

The face of the seal shows an American eagle with its wings spread. The seal also includes the motto *E pluribus unum* ("From many, one"). Most Americans may not know it, but they often carry around the seal. The one-dollar bill shows both sides of the Great Seal.

The seal's reverse side shows a 13-step pyramid with the year 1776 in Roman numerals at the base. Below the pyramid, a scroll reads, *Novus Ordo Seclorum,* meaning "New Order of the Ages." It refers to the year 1776 as the beginning of a new era.

The number 13 is featured prominently on the Great Seal. There are 13 stars in the crest above the eagle, 13 stripes on the eagle's shield, 13 arrows in the eagle's left claw, and 13 olives and leaves in the eagle's right claw. Why thirteen? The number represents the original 13 states of the nation.

The Great Seal of the United States

The Great Seal of the United States is the official seal of the United States government. The seal appears on important government documents. First adopted in 1782, it remains in use today.

The Great Seal ▶

DBQ Document-Based Questions

On Becoming President

1. What promise did Washington make?
2. How would you describe Washington's feelings about becoming president? Explain your answer.

Washington's First Inaugural

3. What events at Washington's inaugural did Maclay seem to like?
4. What was it about Washington's public speaking manner that troubled Maclay?

The Great Seal of the United States

5. What image on the Great Seal is one of the nation's symbols?

Read to Write

6. Choose a U.S. president that has been in office during the last 50 years. Do research to find out how that president might have viewed his role. Playing the role of this president, write a letter similar to George Washington's letter. Then design a symbol that would have been appropriate for the nation under that president's leadership. CA 8WA2.1

R Reading Strategy

Evaluating **Ask:** Which statements made by Maclay are facts? Which are opinions? *(Facts include the description of Washington's actions and statements about what people did in response. Opinions include Maclay's guess on how Washington's nervousness compared to other times in his life and his feeling about speaking style.)* **OL** CA HR2.

Resources for page 299

Primary Source Reading 5

ASSESS

Have students answer the Document-Based Questions.

CLOSE

Evaluating **Ask:** Should Washington have been nervous on taking the oath as president? Why or why not? *(Students' answers should be supported by logical reasons.)*

DBQ Document-Based Questions

1. that he would act with integrity and firmness
2. Students may say that, based on his letter to Knox, Washington was concerned about the burdens of the office but determined to act on behalf of the country.
3. Students may say that Maclay liked the part where Washington took the oath of office, as he noted the three cheers from the crowd.
4. the gestures he made with his hand
5. the eagle
6. Answers will vary but should include specific references to a U.S. President.

Chapter 5 Assessment

Resources for pages 300–301

Use these resources to review, assess, or reteach the chapter.

- Active Reading Note-Taking Guide, Chapter 5
- Chapter 5 Reading Essentials and Study Guide
- Chapter 5 Tests, Forms A and B
- California Standards Assessment, Forms A and B
- California Standards Practice Workbook
- Succeeding on the California History–Social Science Standards CD-ROM
- MindJogger Videoquiz
- Interactive Tutor Self-Assessment CD-ROM

Review Content Vocabulary

1. Paragraphs will vary but should reflect information in the chapter.

Review the Main Ideas

2. to have the funds for the government to operate and to make interest payments on the national debt; some feared a national government with strong economic powers
3. It marked the first steps toward creating a strong and independent national judiciary.
4. They opposed the whiskey tax.
5. It crushed Native Americans' hope of keeping their land in Ohio.
6. powers that were suggested but not directly stated in the Constitution
7. They were seizing American cargo ships headed for Britain.

Chapter 5 Assessment

Standards US8.3 & US8.4

Review Content Vocabulary

1. Use the following terms to write a paragraph about the new U.S. government:

cabinet	**implied powers**
caucus	**states' rights**

Review the Main Ideas

Section 1 • The First President

2. Why did Hamilton want national taxes? Why did some oppose the taxes?
3. What was the importance of the Judiciary Act of 1789?

Section 2 • Early Challenges

4. What caused farmers in western Pennsylvania to revolt during the Whiskey Rebellion?
5. What was the significance of the Battle of Fallen Timbers?

Section 3 • The First Political Parties

6. According to Hamilton, what are implied powers?
7. What actions by France led to an undeclared war with the United States?

Critical Thinking

8. **Evaluate** Refer to the grievances listed in the Declaration of Independence. How were these grievances addressed in the Bill of Rights? CA CS1.
9. **Analyze** What did President Washington say in his Farewell Address about political parties and foreign policy? CA HR4.
10. **Compare and Contrast** In a brief essay, compare the positions of the Federalists and Democratic-Republicans on the national bank. CA HR5.

Geography Skills

Using this map, answer the following questions about the election of 1796. CA CS3.

NATIONAL GEOGRAPHIC Election of 1796

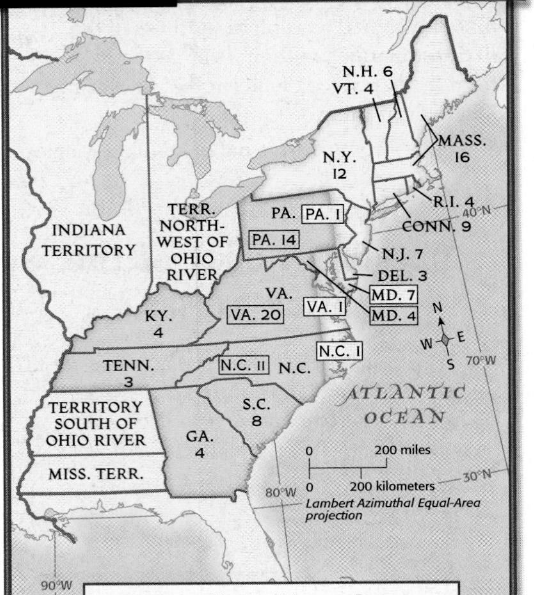

Candidate	Electoral Votes	Party
John Adams	71	Federalist
Thomas Jefferson	68	Democratic-Republican

11. **Identify** How many states did John Adams win? How many did Thomas Jefferson win?
12. **Evaluate** What was the total electoral vote count for each man? What was the election result?
13. **Region** What was the distribution of votes by state? What pattern do you see?

Critical Thinking

8. Students might say that the Bill of Rights guaranteed the freedom of speech, the press, and religion; ensured a fair and speedy trial; and reserved to the states and the people those powers not specifically given to the federal government.
9. He said that political parties were evil and warned against entangling alliances with foreign countries.
10. Hamilton believed the bank would help the government carry out its responsibilities of issuing money and regulating trade. Democratic-Republicans believed the Constitution did not give Congress the power to create a national bank.

Geography Skills

11. Adams: 9; Jefferson: 7
12. Adams: 71; Jefferson: 68; Adams won

History Online

Self-Check Quiz Visit ca.hss.glencoe.com to prepare for the Chapter 5 test.

Read to Write

14. **The Big Ideas** **Government and Democracy** Political ideas and major events shape how people form governments. Select an event from this chapter. Write an essay describing how people and ideas affected government through that event. CA 8WS1.1

15. **Using Your FOLDABLES** Review the "American firsts" that you listed in your foldable. Using numbers, rank each first from the most important to the least important. Explain the reasons for your highest and lowest rankings. CA HR3.

Using Academic Vocabulary

16. Read the following sentence and then write the meaning of the underlined word.

    The new federal government was interested in increasing <u>revenue</u> in order to pay off its debts.

Building Citizenship

17. **Research** Work in groups of four to discuss and develop answers to these questions:
    - How does the Bill of Rights reflect the principle of limited government?
    - What are two individual rights protected in the Bill of Rights?
    - Why would it be necessary to change the Constitution? CA 8RC2.0

Reviewing Skills

18. **Review READING SKILL** **Recognizing Bias** Imagine that you were living in the United States in 1798. Write an editorial to your newspaper that demonstrates bias about your view as to whether the Alien and Sedition Acts violated the U.S. Constitution. Use details from the text and chart about the Alien and Sedition Acts on page 295. CA 8WA2.4

19. **Review ANALYSIS SKILL** **Sequencing** Create a time line that lists key events in President Adams's dispute with France. Write a paragraph analyzing President Adams's handling of this dispute. CA CS2.

Standards Practice

Select the best answer for each of the following questions.

20 Thomas Jefferson and Alexander Hamilton served as members of Washington's

A congress.
B judiciary.
C cabinet.
D military.

21 Which amendment of the Bill of Rights protects the rights of the states?

A First Amendment
B Fifth Amendment
C Sixth Amendment
D Tenth Amendment

22 The XYZ Affair dealt with problems between the United States and

A France.
B Spain.
C Great Britain.
D Canada.

23 Hamilton proposed a national tax on imports, or a(n)

A bond.
B impressment.
C caucus.
D tariff.

CHAPTER 5 Assessment

the election.

13. Adams won mainly in the northern states, and Jefferson in the southern ones.

Read to Write

14. **The Big Ideas** Answers will vary, but students should describe the event and explain how people's behavior affected government policy.

15. Using Your **FOLDABLES** Rankings will vary, but the top and bottom rankings should be explained.

Using Academic Vocabulary

16. the income collected by the government

Building Citizenship

17. Answers might include: the Bill of Rights protects individual liberty and limits the role of government in citizens' lives; freedom of speech and religion; to meet the changing needs of the country

Reviewing Skills

18. **Review READING SKILL** Students should address either the need for the Alien and Sedition Acts or the reasons they violate citizens' rights.

19. **Review ANALYSIS SKILL** Events might include the following: 1794: Jay's Treaty leads to French seizure of American ships; 1797: XYZ Affair; 1798: Congress establishes Navy; 1800: Adams negotiates treaty with France. Students' paragraphs should explain that Adams was hesitant to enter a war with France.

Standards Practice

20. C
21. D
22. A
23. D

Bonus Question

Ask: Why did many Americans worry about the office of president? *(They feared that a president would try to become king.)* OL

History Online

Have students visit the Web site at ca.hss.glencoe.com to review Chapter 5 and take the **Self-Check Quiz.**

Chapter 6 Planning Guide

SECTION RESOURCES

Main Ideas	Print Materials	Technology Resources
Section 1 **The Republicans Take Power** 1. The election of 1800 showed that power in the United States could be peacefully transferred even when political parties are in disagreement. 2. Jefferson worked to limit the scope of the federal government and shift control of the federal courts away from the Federalists.	• Reproducible Lesson Plan 6–1* • Daily Lesson and Discussion Notes 6–1 • Active Reading Note-Taking Guide 6–1 • Reading Essentials and Study Guide 6–1 • Guided Reading Activity 6–1 • Section Quiz 6–1	Daily Focus Skills Transparency 6–1 Section Graphic Organizer Transparency 6–1 California Standards Practice Transparencies Interactive Tutor Self-Assessment CD-ROM Exam*View*® Pro Testmaker CD-ROM Presentation Plus! CD-ROM
Section 2 **The Louisiana Purchase** 1. As Americans moved west in the early 1800s, Spain and France made a secret agreement about land that affected American trade. 2. The Louisiana Purchase opened a vast area to exploration and settlement.	• Reproducible Lesson Plan 6–2* • Daily Lesson and Discussion Notes 6–2 • Active Reading Note-Taking Guide 6–2 • Reading Essentials and Study Guide 6–2 • Guided Reading Activity 6–2 • Section Quiz 6–2	Daily Focus Skills Transparency 6–2 Section Graphic Organizer Transparency 6–2 California Standards Practice Transparencies Interactive Tutor Self-Assessment CD-ROM Exam*View*® Pro Testmaker CD-ROM Presentation Plus! CD-ROM
Section 3 **Daily Life in Early America** 1. A strong sense of national identity grows among Americans. 2. Americans begin to create their own unique culture. 3. People living in different regions developed different ways to use and farm the land. 4. An increasing number of Americans chose to move West into new territory.	• Reproducible Lesson Plan 6–3* • Daily Lesson and Discussion Notes 6–3 • Active Reading Note-Taking Guide 6–3 • Reading Essentials and Study Guide 6–3 • Guided Reading Activity 6–3 • Section Quiz 6–3	Daily Focus Skills Transparency 6–3 Section Graphic Organizer Transparency 6–3 California Standards Practice Transparencies Interactive Tutor Self-Assessment CD-ROM Exam*View*® Pro Testmaker CD-ROM Presentation Plus! CD-ROM Vocabulary PuzzleMaker CD-ROM

PACING YOUR LESSONS

Chapter Introduction	Section 1	Section 2	Section 3	Chapter Assessment
½ Day	1 Day	1 Day	1 Day	½ Day

0:00 **OUT OF TIME?** Assign the Chapter 6 ***Reading Essentials and Study Guide***

*Available on TeacherWorks™

Standards-Based Lesson Plan

History–Social Science Standards Covered in Chapter 6

The standards covered in the chapter are listed below. Use the accompanying activity as you teach the chapter to ensure student mastery of these standards. This activity can be used in combination with the program's print and technology assessment materials.

Standard	Section 1	Section 2	Section 3
US8.4 Students analyze the aspirations and ideals of the people of the new nation.	✔	✔	✔
US8.4.1 Describe the country's physical landscapes, political divisions, and territorial expansion during the terms of the first four presidents.	✔	✔	✔
US8.4.2 Explain the policy significance of famous speeches (e.g., Washington's Farewell Address, Jefferson's 1801 Inaugural Address, John Q. Adams's Fourth of July 1821 Address)	✔		
US8.4.3 Analyze the rise of capitalism and the economic problems and conflicts that accompanied it (e.g., Jackson's opposition to the National Bank; early decisions of the U.S. Supreme Court that reinforced the sanctity of contracts and a capitalist economic system of law).	✔		
US8.4.4 Discuss daily life, including traditions in art, music, and literature, of early national America (e.g., through writings by Washington Irving, James Fenimore Cooper).			✔

Cumulative Standards-Assessment Activity

The Cumulative Standards-Assessment Activity will help students organize and learn the important information from the chapter. Begin teaching the chapter with this activity and have students complete it as they read the chapter.

Creating a Main Idea and Supporting Details Chart

Purpose Reviewing how to locate main ideas throughout the chapter will help students continue to refine their reading skills. This type of organizer aids students in identifying main ideas of sections and the supporting details. It helps them develop the skill of knowing what is important and what facts support those important points. Identifying main ideas and details can give students practice in logical and systematic thinking.

Introduction to Main Ideas and Supporting Details

1. Begin the discussion with a brainstorming session. Ask students to list what they know or believe they know about the Federalist era. Write the information on an overhead transparency. Guide them to identify some key main ideas about this period. You may also want to model how certain comments are, in fact, details that support the main ideas.
2. Ask students to copy this chart into their notebooks:

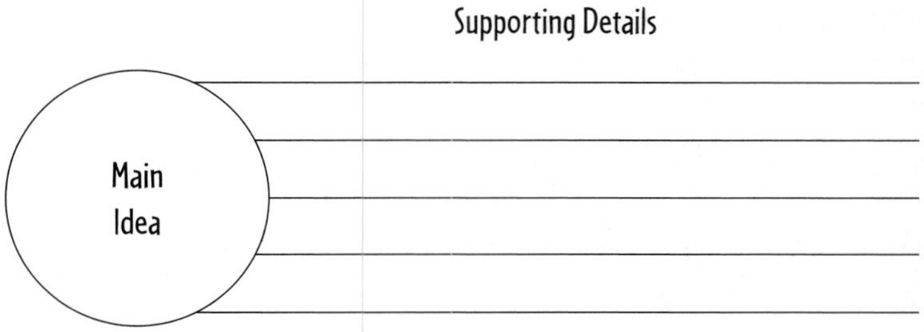

As students read each section, have them search for a main idea and details that support it. Have them fill in the chart with as many supporting details as necessary, adding lines as needed. Encourage them to create more charts as they encounter important concepts during their reading.

3. As part of your chapter review, have students share their main idea and supporting details charts. Consider asking them to do a final chart with a single main idea for the entire chapter. Encourage them to use their charts as study aids.

Chapter 6 Resources

READING SUPPORT

- Content Vocabulary Activity 6
- Academic Vocabulary Activity 6
- Reading Skills Activity 6
- American Literature Reading 6
- Biography Activities 6A–6C
- Chapter 6 Active Reading Note-Taking Guide
- Chapter 6 Guided Reading Activities
- Chapter 6 Reading Essentials and Study Guide
- Glencoe Literature Library
- Glencoe Video Program
- Vocabulary PuzzleMaker CD-ROM
- Interactive Graphic Organizers CD-ROM
- American History Primary Source Document Library CD-ROM

SKILL PRACTICE

- Map Overlay Transparency 6, Strategy, and Activity
- Analysis Skills Activity 6
- Time Line Activity 6
- Geography and History Activity 6
- Economics and History Activity 6
- Chart, Graph, and Map Skills Activity 6
- Political Cartoon Activity 6
- Supreme Court Case Study 6
- In-Text Map Transparency 6, Strategy, and Activity
- Step Into American History Activity 6
- Citizenship and Service Learning Activity 6
- Activity Workbook
- Outline Map Resource Book
- MindJogger Plus Videoquiz

CRITICAL THINKING

- Critical Thinking Skills Activity 6
- Primary Source Reading 6
- Cause-and-Effect Transparency 6, Strategy, and Activity
- Presentation Plus! CD-ROM

WRITING SUPPORT

- Writing Activity 6
- Language Arts Activity 6
- Writer's Guidebook
- Middle School Writing Process Transparencies

UNIVERSAL ACCESS

- Universal Access Activity 6
- Then and Now Transparencies 6A–6B, Strategy, and Activity
- Graphic Novel Activity 6
- School-to-Home Connection Activities 6A–6D
- English Learner Handbook Chapter 6 Activities
- Universal Access for the American History Classroom
- American Art and Architecture Transparencies, Strategies, and Activities
- American Art Prints
- American Music Cultural Traditions
- American Music Hits Through History
- StudentWorks Plus CD-ROM

ASSESSMENT

GLENCOE'S ASSESSMENT ADVANTAGE

- Chapter 6 Section Quizzes
- Chapter 6 Tests, Forms A and B
- California Standards Assessment, Forms A and B
- Cumulative Assessment Activity US8.4
- California Standards Practice Workbook
- Succeeding on the California History–Social Science Standards CD-ROM
- Exam*View*® Pro Testmaker CD-ROM
- Interactive Tutor Self-Assessment CD-ROM

CD-ROM
DVD
Print Material
Poster
Transparency
Music Program
Videocassette
Glencoe Literature Library

Chapter 6 Resources

TECHNOLOGY

- StudentWorks Plus CD-ROM
- TeacherWorks CD-ROM
- Exam*View*® Pro Testmaker CD-ROM
- Interactive Tutor Self-Assessment CD-ROM
- Presentation Plus! CD-ROM
- Succeeding on the California History–Social Science Standards CD-ROM
- Vocabulary PuzzleMaker CD-ROM
- Interactive Graphic Organizers CD-ROM
- Interactive Time Line CD-ROM
- American History Primary Source Document Library CD-ROM
- MindJogger Plus Videoquiz
- American Music Cultural Traditions
- American Music Hits Through History
- Glencoe Video Program
- Professional Development in Middle School Social Studies Series
- Teaching American History With *Discovering Our Past: The American Journey to World War I*

SPANISH RESOURCES

- Spanish Activities and Assessment
  - Spanish Content Vocabulary Activities
  - Spanish Guided Reading Activities
  - Spanish Quizzes and Tests
  - Spanish California Standards Assessment
- Spanish Reading Essentials and Study Guide
- Spanish School-to-Home Connection
- Spanish Declaration of Independence and U.S. Constitution

TRANSPARENCIES

- California Standards Practice Transparencies
- Daily Focus Skills Transparencies
- Section Graphic Organizer Transparencies
- In-Text Map Transparencies
- Map Overlay Transparencies
- Cause-and-Effect Transparencies
- Then and Now Transparencies
- American Art and Architecture Transparencies
- Middle School Writing Process Transparencies

TEACHER PLANNING

- Daily Lesson and Discussion Notes
- English Learner Handbook
- Guide to Daily Intervention
- *Discovering Our Past: The American Journey to World War I* Reading and Study Skills Foldables
- Reading Strategies and Activities for the Social Studies Classroom
- Chapter 6 Reproducible Lesson Plans (correlated to California History–Social Science Standards)
- Universal Access for the American History Classroom
- NGS U.S. Desk Map
- NGS U.S. Atlas

PROFESSIONAL DEVELOPMENT

- Building Academic Vocabulary
- Strategies for Success
- Research-Based Strategies Used to Develop *Discovering Our Past: The American Journey to World War I*
- Character Education in the Middle School Classroom
- The Living Constitution
- Professional Development in Middle School Social Studies Video Series
- Teaching American History With *Discovering Our Past: The American Journey to World War I*

MASTERING THE STANDARDS

The content and assessment in the Student Edition, Teacher Wraparound Edition, teacher planning materials, and the print and technology products are all standards-based. The use of these products during instruction leads to mastery of the standards.

PRACTICE
- California Standards Practice Workbook
- California Standards Practice Transparencies
- Interactive Time Line CD-ROM
- School-to-Home Connection

BENCHMARK ASSESSMENT
- California Standards Assessment
- Exam*View*® Pro Testmaker CD-ROM
- Succeeding on the California History–Social Science Standards CD-ROM

REMEDIATION
- California Guide to Daily Intervention
- Interactive Tutor Self-Assessment CD-ROM
- Exam*View*® Pro Testmaker CD-ROM
- California Standards Practice Workbook
- Reading Essentials and Study Guide

Additional Resources

NATIONAL GEOGRAPHIC TEACHER'S CORNER

Index to National Geographic Magazine:

The following articles relate to this chapter:

- "The Way West," by John G. Mitchell, September 2000.
- "Lewis and Clark: Naturalist-Explorers," by Ron Fisher, October 1998.
- "L'Enfant's Washington," by Alice J. Hall, August 1991.
- "Thomas Jefferson: Architect of Freedom," by Mike Edwards, February 1976.

National Geographic Society Products

To order the following, call National Geographic at 1-800-368-2728

- *GeoKit: Lewis and Clark* (Kit)
- *GeoKit: Westward Movement* (Kit)
- *The West That Was* (Video)
- *United States/Territorial Growth* (Map)
- *National Geographic Atlas of the World, Seventh Edition* (Book)
- *Washington, D.C.* (Video)

NGS ONLINE

Access National Geographic's new dynamic MapMachine Web site and other geography resources at:

www.nationalgeographic.com

www.nationalgeographic.com/maps

A&E Home Video · Biography® · The History Channel®

The following videotape programs are available from Glencoe as supplements to Chapter 6.

- **Lewis and Clark (ISBN 1-56501-592-4)**

To order, call Glencoe at 1-800-334-7344. To find classroom resources to accompany many of these videos, check the following home pages:

A&E Television: www.aetv.com
The History Channel: www.historychannel.com

MOMENTS IN TIME DBQ

The following resource can help you teach the content of this chapter.

Unit 2 Territorial Expansion (1834–1859)

History Online

Use our Web site for additional resources. All essential content is covered in the Student Edition.

You and your students can visit ca.hss.glencoe.com, the Web site companion to *Discovering Our Past: The American Journey to World War I*. This innovative integration of electronic and print media offers your students a wealth of opportunities. The student text directs students to the Web site for the following options:

- Chapter Overviews
- Self-Check Quizzes
- Study Central™
- Student Web Activities
- Textbook Updates
- Multi-Language Glossaries

Answers to the student Web activities are provided for you in the Web Activity Lesson Plans. Additional Web resources and ePuzzles and games are also available.

FOLDABLES™ Study Organizer

Dinah Zike's Foldables

Foldables are three-dimensional, interactive graphic organizers that help students practice basic writing skills, review key vocabulary terms, and identify main ideas. Every chapter contains a foldable activity, with additional chapter activities found in the Reading and Study Skills Foldables booklet.

Reading List Generator CD-ROM

GLENCOE BOOKLINK

The Glencoe BookLink CD-ROM is a database that allows you to search more than 15,000 titles to create a customized reading list for your students.

- Reading lists can be organized by students' reading level, author, genre, theme, or area of interest.
- The database provides Degrees of Reading Power™ (DRP) and Lexile™ readability scores for all selections.
- A brief summary of each selection is included.

Reading level suggestions for this chapter:

For students at a Grade 6 reading level:

- ***Sacajawea: Shoshone Trailblazer,*** by Diane Shaughnessy and Jack Carpenter

For students at a Grade 7 reading level:

- ***The Saga of Lewis and Clark: Into the Uncharted West,*** by Thomas Schmidt and Jeremy Schmidt

For students at a Grade 8 reading level:

- ***Beyond the Mississippi: Early Westward Expansion of the United States,*** by Angela M. Herb

For students at a Grade 9 reading level:

- ***The Last of the Mohicans,*** by James Fenimore Cooper

For students at a Grade 10 reading level:

- ***American Sphinx: The Character of Thomas Jefferson,*** by Joseph J. Ellis

READING SUPPORT FROM JAMESTOWN EDUCATION

- *Timed Readings Plus in Social Studies* helps students increase their reading rate and fluency while maintaining comprehension. The 400-word passages are similar to those found on state and national assessments.
- *Reading in the Content Area: Social Studies* concentrates on six essential reading skills that help students better comprehend what they read. The book includes 754 high-interest nonfiction passages written at increasing levels of difficulty.
- *Reading Fluency* helps students read smoothly, accurately, and expressively.
- *Jamestown's Reading Improvement,* by renowned reading expert Edward Fry, focuses on helping build your students' comprehension, vocabulary, and skimming and scanning skills.
- *Critical Reading Series* provides high-interest books, each written at three reading levels.

To order these products, call Glencoe at 1-800-334-7344.

KEY for Using the Teacher Wraparound Edition

Use this key to help you identify the different types of prompts found in the Teacher Wraparound Edition.

R **Reading Strategies** activities help you teach reading skills and vocabulary.

C **Critical Thinking** strategies help students apply and extend what they have learned.

U **Universal Access** activities provide differentiated instruction for students learning to speak English, along with suggestions for teaching various types of learners.

S **Skill Practice** strategies help students practice historical analysis and geography skills.

W **Writing Support** activities provide writing opportunities to help students comprehend the text.

Teaching strategies and activities have been coded for ability level appropriateness.

AL Activities for students working above grade level
OL Activities for students working on grade level
BL Activities for students working below grade level
EL Activities for English Learners

FOCUS

History–Social Science Standards

In this chapter, the following standard will be covered:

US8.4 Students analyze the aspirations and ideals of the people of the new nation.

More About the Photo

Monticello, located in central Virginia, was the home of Thomas Jefferson for 56 years. Jefferson designed the mansion, which is one of the earliest examples of American classic revival. The building materials—stone, brick, lumber, and nails—were prepared on the estate.

TEACH

The Big Ideas

As you begin teaching each section, use these questions and activities to focus on the Big Ideas.

Section 1

The Republicans Take Power

Have students recall what they learned about the Federalists and Republicans in the previous chapter. **Essential Question:** What do you expect the Republicans to do if they win control of the federal government? *(Answers may include cutting the power of the government; undoing the Alien Act and the Sedition Act.)* Explain that in this section students will learn about how the election of 1800 marked the transfer of power from one potitical party to another. OL

Section 2

The Louisiana Purchase

Remind students that the United States was not always the same size it is today. **Essential Question:** How did the United States increase its land area to its current size? *(through wars and treaties to gain land; through the purchase of land)* What was the western boundary of the United States in 1800? *(the Mississippi River)* Tell students that this section discusses the Louisiana Purchase and its impact on the growth of the United States. BL

Chapter 6

The Age of Jefferson

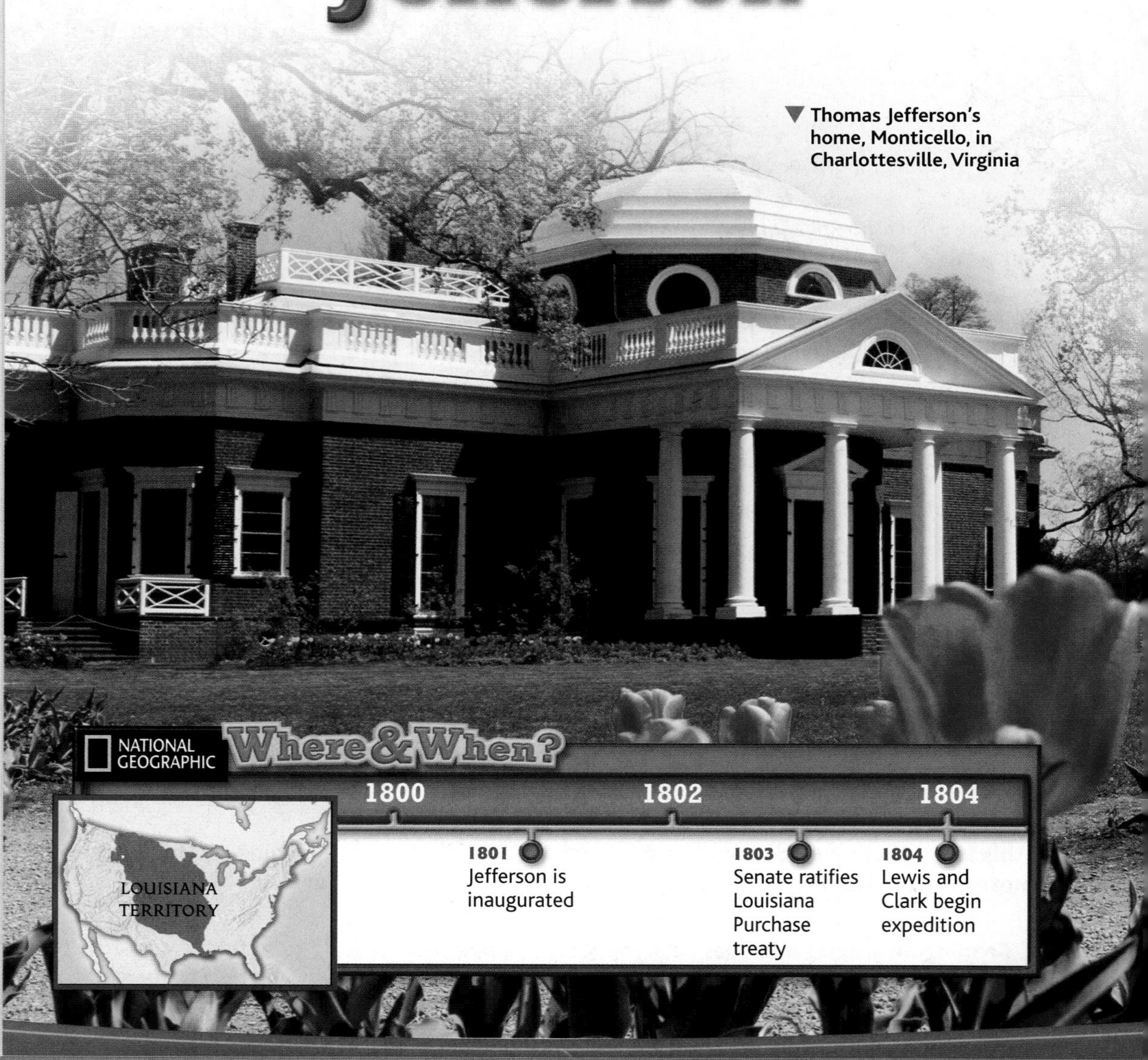

▼ Thomas Jefferson's home, Monticello, in Charlottesville, Virginia

NATIONAL GEOGRAPHIC **Where & When?**

LOUISIANA TERRITORY

1800 — 1802 — 1804

- **1801** Jefferson is inaugurated
- **1803** Senate ratifies Louisiana Purchase treaty
- **1804** Lewis and Clark begin expedition

History Online

Chapter Overview Visit ca.hss.glencoe.com for a preview of Chapter 6.

The Big Ideas

Section 1

The Republicans Take Power

Political ideas and major events shape how people form governments. The election of 1800 marked the transfer of power from one political party to another through a democratic election.

Section 2

The Louisiana Purchase

Geography shapes the physical, economic, and political challenges a region faces. The Louisiana Purchase opened a vast area to exploration and settlement.

Section 3

Daily Life in Early America

Political, social, religious, and economic changes influence the way Americans think and act. A powerful wave of nationalism swept through American life. Americans began to create a distinct culture.

View the Chapter 6 video in the Glencoe Video Program.

FOLDABLES™ Study Organizer

Organizing Information Make this foldable to organize information and sequence events about the Jefferson era into a flowchart.

Step 1 Fold a sheet of paper in half from side to side.

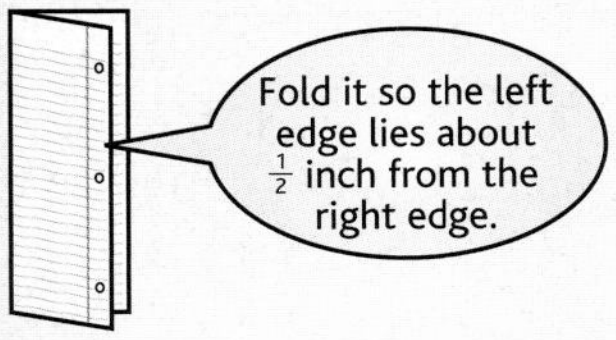

Step 2 Cut the top layer only to make five tabs.

Step 3 Label your foldable as shown.

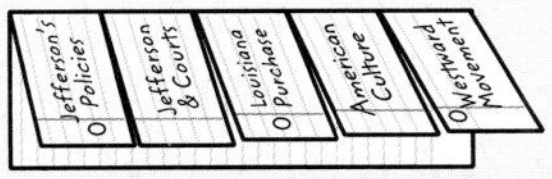

Reading and Writing As you read, select key facts about the events of the Jefferson era and write them under the tabs of your foldable.

History Online

Go to ca.hss.glencoe.com for student activities, lesson plans, and links to additional Web resources about the Jefferson presidency.

FOLDABLES™ Study Organizer **Dinah Zike's Foldables**

Purpose Have students use their foldables to summarize the Jefferson era in a paragraph. OL

Section 3

Daily Life in Early America

Essential Question: How do people in a nation define themselves? *(Answers may include the type of government; shared culture, beliefs; and type of economic system.)* How does the variety of cultures in the United States contribute to its national identity? *(Answers may include the increasing number of minorities in political roles, in movies, and in music.)* Tell students that this section describes how nationalism fueled the creation of a distinct American culture. OL

Cultural Perspectives

Remind students of the words in the Declaration of Independence: "We hold these truths to be self-evident, that all men are created equal ...." Inform students that Thomas Jefferson, the author, was born into a slaveholding family and as an adult owned slaves. Assign students to read the narratives of enslaved people collected by the Federal Writers Project in the 1930s, which are housed at the Library of Congress. How were individual rights denied by the early American government? Have students summarize one person's story. Compile these into a volume to copy and distribute to the class. Refer to the stories throughout this unit and the next two to provide more perspective on these periods. Ask students: would the same events be important to enslaved persons?

Why It's Important

Compare and Contrast

Comparing and contrasting is an organizational structure that students can use often for improving their comprehension. Point out that the structure is particularly valuable when studying individuals or groups who oppose each other in politics, some kind of contest, or war. The structure can be used to define the positions of competing groups and also to analyze their relative advantages and disadvantages.

1 Learn It!

Draw a Venn diagram like the one below on the board.

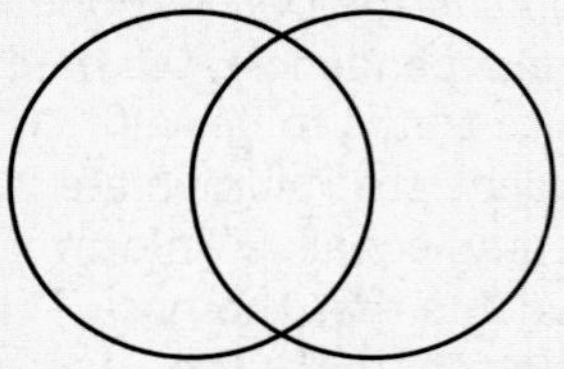

Explain that such diagrams can be used when comparing two things. Characteristics of each object of comparison are listed in the circle belonging to it. Those it shares with the other object are listed in the area where the two circles overlap. Those not shared are written in the outer area. Demonstrate the technique with an example. **Ask:** What are the similarities between riding in a car and flying in a plane? *(Both are methods of transportation; both can be used for long distance travel.)* How are they different? *(cars—travel on ground; tend to have few riders; mostly used by owners; typically used for shorter distances; planes—travel in air; have more passengers; people need to buy tickets)* **OL**

Chapter 6

Get Ready to Read

Compare and Contrast

READING SKILL

1 Learn It!

Good readers compare and contrast information as they read. This means they look for similarities and differences. They compare the ways in which people, places, or ideas are the same or different in order to understand how each is unique. Look for signal words in the text to let you know when the author is giving information for comparing or contrasting. Some comparison signal words are *similarly, at the same time,* and *likewise.* Contrast signal words include *however, rather, on the other hand, yet, but,* and *or.* Read the excerpt below and notice how the author uses contrast to discuss conflicting opinions.

> **Federalists charged the Republican Jefferson, who believed in freedom of religion, with being "godless." Republicans warned that the Federalists would bring back monarchy. Federalists, they claimed, only represented the interests of wealthy people with property.**
>
> *—from page 307*

Reading Tip

As you read, use other skills, such as summarizing and connecting, to help you understand comparisons and contrasts.

304

READING STRATEGY — ACTIVATING PRIOR KNOWLEDGE

To help students build on and connect knowledge from earlier chapters, have them recall the events that led to the developments of the Federalist and the Republican parties. Remind them that the issues of taxation and a strong national government were also two important concerns that led the colonies to separate from Great Britain. This connection should help students understand that the issues dividing Federalists and Republicans were very important to many Americans. Indeed, they continue to be important issues today. **OL**

2 Practice It!

Read the section called "Conflict in the West" on page 329. Use the questions below to help you identify the different responses of Native American groups to white settlers who moved into their lands. Create a graphic organizer to record your answers.

- **What did the Native Americans have in common?**
- **How were their reactions to white settlement different?**
- **What results did Native Americans experience?**

Read to Write

Make a graphic organizer to record differences between living today and in 1803. Then, write a short paragraph summarizing your thoughts.

Sequoyah developed the alphabet for the Cherokee language. ▶

3 Apply It!

Compare and contrast political parties today and political parties at the time of Jefferson.

CHAPTER 6 Get Ready to Read

2 Practice It!

Have students read the passage on pages 315–316 about the expeditions of Lewis and Clark and Pike. Then ask them to compare and contrast the two expeditions. Suggest that students use a table or a Venn diagram to list the similarities and differences. **OL**

3 Apply It!

Have students find a magazine or newspaper article that compares today's political parties or two candidates for office. Ask students to use a graphic organizer like a Venn diagram to find the similarities and differences. Students should also highlight the signal words used in the article. **OL**

READING STRATEGY — EXPOSITORY WRITING

Comparing and contrasting can be used to structure essays, which can follow one of two formats. One is to describe one subject completely before moving to the other. For instance, a writer could present the positions of the Republicans first and the Federalists second. The other approach is to look at both subjects one characteristic at a time, such as examining the two parties' positions on different issues, taking up one issue at a time. Have students use the notes they made in the "Apply It!" activity to compare and contrast political parties today to those in the 1800s. **AL**

Use Reading Skills Activity 6 in the **Chapter 6 Resource Book** for more practice with comparing and contrasting.

FOCUS

BELLRINGER
SKILLBUILDER ACTIVITY

Project **Daily Focus Skills Transparency 6–1** and have students answer the question.

Guide to Reading

Preteaching Vocabulary: Have students develop questions for each content vocabulary word. Then have students trade questions with a partner and answer their partner's questions.

Answers to Graphic: allowed the Alien and Sedition Acts to expire; repealed the Naturalization Act; reduced the national debt by cutting military expenses

Unpacking the Standards

After reading the section, students will be able to:

- Describe how Jefferson won the 1800 election.
- Outline the goals Jefferson set in his inaugural address.
- Explain how Jefferson reduced the role of government.
- Discuss the *Marbury v. Madison* decision and its impact.

Section 1

The Republicans Take Power

History Social Science Standards

US8.4 Students analyze the aspirations and ideals of the people of the new nation.

Guide to Reading

Looking Back, Looking Ahead
The presidency of Thomas Jefferson launched a new era, a time of many changes and rapid growth for the new nation.

Focusing on the Main Ideas

- The election of 1800 showed that power in the United States could be peacefully transferred even when political parties are in disagreement. *(page 307)*
- Jefferson worked to limit the scope of the federal government and shift control of the federal courts away from the Federalists. *(page 308)*

Locating Places
Washington, D.C.
Potomac River (puh • TOH • mihk)

Meeting People
Thomas Jefferson
Aaron Burr
Albert Gallatin
John Marshall

Content Vocabulary
laissez-faire (LEH • ZAY FEHR)
judicial review

Academic Vocabulary
require (rih • KWYR)
philosophy (fuh • LAH • suh • fee)
significant (sig • NIH • fih • kuhnt)
ensure (ihn • SHUR)

Reading Strategy
Organizing Information As you read the section, use a diagram like the one shown here to identify ways Republicans tried to reduce the role of government.

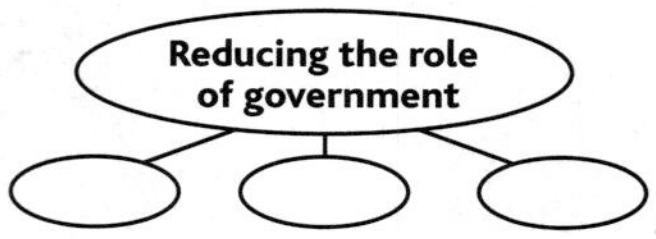

NATIONAL GEOGRAPHIC **Who & When?**

1800	1801	1802	1803

Thomas Jefferson

1800 Jefferson and Adams contend for presidency

Feb. 1801 Judiciary Act expands court system

March 1801 Jefferson is inaugurated

John Marshall

1803 *Marbury* v. *Madison* sets precedent for judicial review

SECTION RESOURCES

Print Material
- Reproducible Lesson Plan 6–1*
- Daily Lesson and Discussion Notes 6–1
- Guided Reading Activity 6–1
- Reading Essentials and Study Guide 6–1
- Active Reading Note-Taking Guide 6–1
- Section Quiz 6–1

Transparencies
- Daily Focus Skills Transparency 6–1
- Section Graphic Organizer Transparency 6–1
- California Standards Practice Transparencies

Technology
- Interactive Tutor Self-Assessment CD-ROM
- Exam*View*® Pro Testmaker CD-ROM
- Presentation Plus! CD-ROM

*Available on TeacherWorks™

US8.4.2 Explain the policy significance of famous speeches (e.g., Washington's Farewell Address, Jefferson's 1801 Inaugural Address, John Q. Adams's Fourth of July 1821 Address).

Jefferson Becomes President

Main Idea **The election of 1800 showed that power in the United States could be peacefully transferred even when political parties are in disagreement.**

Reading Connection Do you think it is more important for the president to dress formally or casually? Why? Read to learn what changed when Jefferson became president.

An American Story

In 1801 **Washington, D.C.,** was slowly rising from a swampy site on the **Potomac River** (puh • TOH • mihk). The nation's new capital had only two prominent buildings—the president's mansion (later called the White House) and the still-unfinished Capitol. Between them stretched about two miles of muddy streets on which pigs and chickens roamed freely.

Very few people liked being in Washington. It was hot and humid in the summer, and the river and swamps were a breeding ground for mosquitoes. Abigail Adams, the wife of John Adams, called the new capital "the very dirtiest Hole."

The Election of 1800 In 1800 Federalists supported President Adams for a second term and Charles Pinckney of South Carolina for vice president. Republicans nominated **Thomas Jefferson** for president and **Aaron Burr** of New York for vice president.

The election campaign of 1800 differed greatly from campaigns of today. Neither Adams nor Jefferson traveled around the country making speeches. Instead the candidates and their followers wrote letters to leading citizens and newspapers to publicize their views. The letter-writing campaign, however, was not polite.

W Federalists charged the Republican Jefferson, who believed in freedom of religion, with being "godless." Republicans warned that the Federalists would bring back monarchy. Federalists, they claimed, only represented the interests of wealthy people with property.

Election Deadlock When members of the Electoral College voted, Jefferson and Burr each received 73 votes. Because of this tie, the House of Representatives had to decide the election. At the time, the electors voted for each presidential and vice-presidential candidate individually rather than voting for a party's candidates as a team.

In the House, Federalists saw a chance to prevent the election of Jefferson by supporting Burr. For 35 ballots, the election remained tied. Finally, at Alexander Hamilton's urging, one Federalist decided not to vote for Burr. Jefferson became president, and Burr became vice president.

To prevent another tie between a presidential and a vice-presidential candidate, Congress passed the Twelfth Amendment to the Constitution in 1803. This amendment, ratified in 1804, **requires** electors to vote for the president and vice president on separate ballots. R1 *(See page 262 for the entire text of the Twelfth Amendment.)*

Jefferson's Inauguration On March 4, 1801, the day of the presidential inauguration, Jefferson dressed in everyday clothes. He left his boardinghouse and walked to the Senate to be sworn in as president. President Adams had slipped out of the presidential mansion and left the city so he would not have to watch Jefferson become president.

In his Inaugural Address, Jefferson tried to reach out to Federalists: "We are all Republicans, we are all Federalists," he said. Then he outlined some of his goals, which included maintaining "a wise and frugal [economical] government" and "the support of state governments in all their rights." He believed that a large federal government threatened liberty and that the states could best protect freedom.

Jefferson believed in reducing the power and size of the federal government. These ideas were similar to the French **philosophy** of **laissez-faire** (LEH • ZAY FEHR), which means "let (people) do (as they choose)." R2

Reading Check **Describe** What does the Twelfth Amendment to the Constitution require?

Did You Know?

Adams and Jefferson had worked closely together during the American Revolution, not only in the Continental Congress but in Europe, where both represented the nation to the governments of other nations. Jefferson had a special regard for Abigail Adams as well. The political fights of the 1790s led to bitter feelings and seriously damaged the friendship between the two men. After Jefferson left the presidency, mutual friend Dr. Benjamin Rush convinced the two former presidents to resume their friendship by writing letters to each other. The two continued a correspondence for the rest of their lives.

TEACH

Review The Big Idea

Review the Big Idea for this section: "Political ideas and major events shape how people form governments." Link it to the letter-writing campaign before the election of 1800. **Ask:** How would such a campaign have an impact on election results? *(by giving voters more information on candidates' positions)* OL

W Writing Support

Persuasive Writing Ask students to consider which view they would have supported during the election of 1800. Then have each student write a letter to the editor of a newspaper that aims to persuade readers to vote for Adams or Jefferson. Remind students to have a well-defined thesis and detailed evidence. *(Letters might include information about the size of government, taxes, or a discussion of Adams's record as president.)* OL CA 8WS1.1

R1 Reading Strategy

Academic Vocabulary Have students read the sentence that includes the word *requires*. Then ask students to use context clues to determine the meaning of the word. OL

R2 Reading Strategy

Understanding Vocabulary Suggest that students use the first letters in *laissez-faire* as the first letters in a phrase that will help them remember its meaning—*"Leave [people] free."* EL

Reading Check

Answer: electors to vote for the president and vice president on separate tickets

R1 Reading Strategy

Inferring Ask: Why would Jefferson surround himself with men who shared the same principles? *(He wanted people who would support his policies and carry them out.)* OL

U Universal Access

Below Grade Level Explain that the phrase "cutting the army by one-third" means that the army would lose one-third of its men. Write the number *9,000* on the board. **Ask:** What is one-third of 9,000? *(3,000)* What would be the result if 9,000 were cut by one-third? *(6,000, which is achieved by subtracting 3,000 from 9,000)* BL

R2 Reading Strategy

Predicting Ask: How is Jefferson likely to respond to Adams's appointments? Why? *(Jefferson will be angry because he would prefer to appoint judges who agree with his views.)* OL CA HI2.

Resources for page 308

- Biography Activity 6A
- Primary Source Reading 6
- Economics and History Activity 6

US8.4.1 Describe the country's physical landscapes, political divisions, and territorial expansion during the terms of the first four presidents.

Jefferson's Policies

Main Idea **Jefferson worked to limit the scope of the federal government and shift control of the federal courts away from the Federalists.**

Reading Connection How should the federal government balance individual liberty with national interests? Read on to learn of changes Jefferson made to deal with this question.

In 1801, when Jefferson became president, the entire federal government consisted of only a few hundred people. This was exactly how Jefferson thought it should be. (Today nearly 3 million civilians work for the federal government.) In Jefferson's view, the national government should conduct foreign affairs and limit its domestic actions to delivering the mail, collecting customs duties, and taking a census every 10 years.

Jefferson Takes Charge When Jefferson entered office, he surrounded himself with men who shared his Republican principles. His secretary of state was his friend and fellow Virginian, James Madison. For secretary of the treasury, he chose **Albert Gallatin,** a Pennsylvanian with a strong grasp of financial matters. R1

Jefferson and Gallatin aimed to reduce the national debt that the Federalists had left. They scaled down military expenses by cutting the army by one-third and reducing the navy from 25 to 7 ships. By slashing spending, Jefferson and Gallatin **significantly** lowered the national debt within a few years. U

Between the election and Jefferson's inauguration, Federalists in Congress passed the Judiciary Act of 1801. This act increased the number of federal judges. Outgoing President John Adams then filled many positions with Federalists. R2

The Way It Was

▲ Abigail Adams in the unfinished White House

Washington in 1800

The United States government moved to the new capital city of Washington, D.C., in 1800. Being located along the Potomac River, Washington was expected to emerge as a great trading city, but the plans for a great city had not proceeded very far. The president's house, with laundry sometimes hanging in the unfinished East Room, stood in an open field with two boxlike buildings for executive offices nearby. More than a mile away, across a swamp, stood the partly built Capitol. Members of Congress lived in crowded boardinghouses. The streets were mostly muddy wagon tracks, bordered with the stumps of trees that had been recently cut. Some Americans criticized the choice of Washington as the capital. They believed that the government should move to a larger city.

308

The Way It Was

George Washington personally chose the spot for the new capital city. The land was surveyed by Benjamin Banneker, a free African American from Maryland who had considerable skill in mathematics. He was recommended for the job by Thomas Jefferson. Pierre Charles L'Enfant planned the layout of the new city and chose the spot now called Capitol Hill where the new Capitol building would be placed. Arguments led to L'Enfant's dismissal from the project. The project seemed doomed when he left and took all his maps with him. Banneker, however, was able to redraw all the maps from memory, and work was able to proceed.

The judges that President Adams appointed were known as "midnight judges" because Adams supposedly signed appointments for judges until midnight on his last day in office. Through these appointments Adams **ensured** that Federalists would control the courts.

Marbury* v. *Madison The appointments could not take effect, however, until the legal papers (commissions) for these last-minute "midnight judges" were delivered. When Jefferson became president on March 4, a few of the commissions had not yet been delivered. He told Secretary of State Madison not to deliver them. One commission was addressed to William Marbury.

To force the delivery of his commission, Marbury took his case directly to the Supreme Court. Chief Justice **John Marshall** turned down Marbury's claim. Marshall noted that the Constitution did not give the Court jurisdiction to decide Marbury's case.

R In his opinion, Marshall set out three principles of **judicial review:** (a) The Constitution is the supreme law of the land. (b) When a conflict arises between the Constitution and any other law, the Constitution must be followed. (c) The judicial branch has a duty to uphold the Constitution. The courts must be able to determine when a federal law conflicts with the Constitution and to nullify, or cancel, unconstitutional laws.

Marshall not only extended the power of the Court, he also broadened federal power at the expense of the states. In *McCulloch* v. *Maryland* (1819), the Court held that the elastic clause allows Congress to do more than the Constitution expressly authorizes it to do. In *Gibbons* v. *Ogden* (1824) the Court held that federal law takes precedence over state law in interstate transportation. *(See the Supreme Court Case Summaries beginning on page 846 for more on these cases.)*

History Online

Student Web Activity Visit ca.hss.glencoe.com and click on *Chapter 6—Student Web Activities* for an activity on the history of the Supreme Court.

Reading Check **Explain** How did the changes that Jefferson made reflect his views about government?

History Online

Study Central Need help understanding Jefferson's election and his policies? Visit ca.hss.glencoe.com and click on Study Central.

Section 1 Review

Reading Summary

Review the Main Ideas

- In the presidential election of 1800, Republican Thomas Jefferson defeated Federalist John Adams.
- After taking office as the first Republican president, Jefferson began to implement his party's ideas on how the government should function.

What Did You Learn?

1. Explain how Jefferson cut government spending.
2. Name the court case that established judicial review.

Critical Thinking

3. **Cause and Effect** Re-create the diagram below and list the effects caused by the appointment of the "midnight judges." CA HI2.

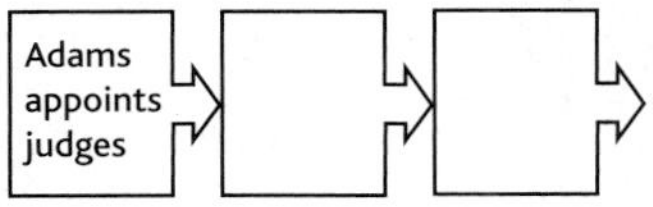

4. **The Big Ideas** How did Jefferson try to calm Federalist fears of Republican rule? CA HI2.
5. **READING Compare and Contrast** Election campaigns have changed since 1800. Write an essay that compares and contrasts current campaigns with those of Jefferson's time. CA CS1.

SECTION 1 REVIEW ANSWERS

Review questions reinforce content standard US8.4.

1. He made the army and navy smaller and reduced the national debt.
2. *Marbury* v. *Madison*
3. Jefferson tells Secretary of State Madison not to send out commissions appointing some judges; Marbury takes his case to the Supreme Court to force delivery of his commission; Court decides *Marbury* v. *Madison*
4. **The Big Ideas** With the establishment of judicial review, the Supreme Court could review and rule on acts of the other branches of government.
5. **READING** Students should identify two issues and include both principles and actions that reveal differences.

History Online

Go to ca.hss.glencoe.com for student activities, lesson plans, and links to additional Web resources about the Supreme Court.

R Reading Strategy

Understanding Vocabulary
Ask: What does the word *judge* mean? *(to act as a judge of a legal case)* What, then, does *judicial* mean? *(relating to a judge)* OL

ASSESS

Resources for page 309

Use these resources to assess student mastery of section content.

Section Quiz 6–1

Interactive Tutor Self-Assessment CD-ROM

Reading Check

Answer: They revealed his belief in small, non-intrusive government.

History Online

Study Central provides summaries, interactive games, and online graphic organizers to help students review section content.

CLOSE

Evaluating **Ask:** How did *Marbury* v. *Madison* counter the goals of the Republican government? *(It broadened federal power at the expense of the states.)* OL

FOCUS

History–Social Science Standards

The following standard is covered on pages 310–311.

US8.4 Students analyze the aspirations and ideals of the people of the new nation.

TEACH

R1 Reading Strategy

Setting a Purpose Have students consider the importance of profit in capitalism. **Ask:** Why are people willing to risk their money to start a business? *(because they can keep the profits if they succeed)* BL

R2 Reading Strategy

Scaffolding—Connecting Explain that the government regulates many aspects of the economy. **Ask:** What are some examples? *(food labeling requirements; safety requirements for new medicines; minimum wage laws)* OL

The READING SKILL was introduced in Chapter 3.

Answers and Additional Support

Connecting to the Constitution

US8.4.3 Analyze the rise of capitalism and the economic problems and conflicts that accompanied it (e.g., Jackson's opposition to the National Bank; early decisions of the U.S. Supreme Court that reinforced the sanctity of contracts and a capitalist economic system of law).

The Supreme Court and the Economy

R1 ***Why It Matters*** People in the United States are free to own property; to make a profit; and to make their own choices about what to produce, buy, and sell. The Framers of the U.S. Constitution believed that economic freedom is a basic right of citizens. As a result, the Constitution laid the basis for an economy based on capitalism, or free enterprise.

Although capitalism is the basis of the American economic system, ours is a mixed economy—a system in which the government both supports and regulates private enterprise. Over the years, the American judicial system—headed by the Supreme Court—has made decisions that have encouraged business competition and private property ownership. R2 However, the Court also has expanded the power of the government to regulate, or lay down rules for, the economy as a whole.

The Commerce Power Article I, Section 8 of the Constitution gives Congress the authority to regulate commerce. It is known as the commerce clause. Under the Articles of Confederation, each state jealously guarded its own commerce. Trade barriers among the states restricted commerce and stood in the way of a strong national economy. The Framers of the U.S. Constitution sought to avoid state rivalries by giving Congress the power to regulate all forms of commerce among the states. It also affirmed Congress's right to regulate trade with foreign nations.

"An unlimited power to tax involves, necessarily, a power to destroy; because there is a limit beyond which no institution and no property can bear taxation."

—John Marshall, *McCulloch* v. *Maryland*, 1819

◀ John Marshall

310

More Skill Practice

Historical and Social Sciences Analysis Skill Consider the possible effects of having trade barriers among the states. **Ask:** How would such trade barriers discourage a strong national economy? *(Inconsistent practices and barriers among states would prevent a uniform, cost-efficient system that can benefit the entire nation.)* AL CA HI1.

Did You Know?

Though *Marbury* v. *Madison* established the authority of the Supreme Court to override an act of Congress, the Court did not do so until the *Dred Scott* decision in 1857 in which the Court ruled that African Americans were property and not citizens.

▲ The young nation's growing trade meant new laws were needed to regulate commerce.

Over the years, the Supreme Court has expanded this commerce power to include a wide range of economic activities. The judiciary today consistently interprets *commerce* to mean nearly all activities concerned with the production, buying, selling, and transporting of goods. Appealing to the commerce clause, and with the Court's backing, Congress has passed many laws that prohibit, promote, and establish rules for many areas of business activity.

Judicial Review In exercising its authority, the Supreme Court has a major tool: the power of **judicial review.** This is the right to examine government laws and actions and to cancel them if they violate the Constitution. Article III of the Constitution states that the

> ***"judicial power shall extend to all cases . . . arising under this Constitution."***

The Founders, however, did not clearly give the power of judicial review to the Court. In fact, the Supreme Court in its early days had a minor role in the federal government compared with the Congress and the Presidency. You might ask: How did the Supreme Court acquire the power to influence the economy as well as other areas of American society?

The Marshall Court The Court's role began to change when John Marshall was appointed Chief Justice of the Supreme Court in 1801. Marshall headed the Court until 1835 and helped increase its power. In the case *Marbury* v. *Madison* (1803), the Supreme Court first established the power of judicial review and ruled an act of Congress unconstitutional. By doing this, the Court defined its role as the final authority on what the Constitution means.

In other important decisions, Marshall used federal power to overturn state restrictions on the economy. In this way, the Marshall Court gave legal support to free enterprise ideas and practices. In *Fletcher* v. *Peck* (1810) the Court declared a Georgia law unconstitutional because it broke the **sanctity of contracts**—the idea that such written agreements are legally binding. The Supreme Court ruled that a land grant was a valid contract and could not be repealed even if corruption was involved. In *Dartmouth College* v. *Woodward* (1819), the Court again upheld the sanctity of contracts. In this case, the Court found it unconstitutional for New Hampshire's legislature to change the Dartmouth College charter and to change the college from a private school into a state university.

Finally, in *Gibbons* v. *Ogden* (1824), the Supreme Court struck down a New York law that gave a company the sole right to operate steamboats on New York waters. In taking this step, Marshall stated that federal power was superior to state power in all matters of **interstate commerce,** or trade among states. New York argued that the states had the right to control commerce involving only products. The Court, however, ruled that *all* forms of business across state lines came under the Constitution's commerce clause. This decision opened the way for Congress to involve itself in nearly all areas of the national economy.

Checking for Understanding

1. What is the commerce clause?
2. Why was *Gibbons* v. *Ogden* an important case?

Critical Thinking

3. **Conclude** Why is the idea of sanctity of contracts necessary to a capitalist economic system? CA HI6.
4. **Analyze** Why did the Supreme Court extend the commerce clause to include a wide range of economic activities? CA HI2.

Connecting to the Constitution

C Critical Thinking

Determining Cause and Effect Explain that business throughout the United States would be very different today without federal power over all commerce. **Ask:** What would happen to national companies if they had to meet different state rules to sell their products or services? *(The businesses would be hurt; they would suffer higher costs.)* BL

R Reading Strategy

Activating Prior Knowledge Ask: What principle of the Constitution is carried out in the Supreme Court's power of judicial review? *(checks and balances)* BL CA HI3.

ASSESS

Have students answer the Checking for Understanding and Critical Thinking questions.

CLOSE

Summarizing Ask: What Supreme Court decisions ended state restrictions on the economy? *(*Fletcher *v.* Peck *and* Dartmouth College *v.* Woodward *upheld the sanctity of contracts;* Gibbons *v.* Ogden *said that federal power over interstate commerce was superior to state power.)* OL

CONNECTING TO THE CONSTITUTION ANSWERS

Questions reinforce content standard US8.4.

Checking for Understanding

1. Article 1, Section 8, which gives Congress the authority to regulate commerce
2. It made the powers of the federal government superior to those of the states in matters of interstate commerce. It allowed the government to play a role in regulating the economy.

Critical Thinking

3. Businessmen were guaranteed that the agreements they made would be enforced, which would make the economy work smoothly.
4. Answers may include the desires to promote economic growth and to ensure fair business practices.

FOCUS

BELLRINGER
SKILLBUILDER ACTIVITY

Project **Daily Focus Skills Transparency 6–2** and have students answer the question.

Guide to Reading

Preteaching Vocabulary:
Read each content vocabulary word, its definition, and a false definition to the class. Have students vote for the definition they think is correct.

Answers to Graphic:
Louisiana Territory; upper Mississippi Valley and present-day Colorado

Unpacking the Standards
After reading the section, students will be able to:

- Explain the challenges to American expansion and importance of the Louisiana Purchase.
- Discuss the expeditions of Lewis and Clark and of Pike.
- Describe tensions between Federalists and Republicans.

Section 2

The Louisiana Purchase

History Social Science Standards

US8.4 Students analyze the aspirations and ideals of the people of the new nation.

Guide to Reading

Looking Back, Looking Ahead
In the early 1800s, the United States experienced rapid growth. The Louisiana Purchase doubled the size of the nation and created remarkable opportunities.

Focusing on the Main Ideas
- As Americans moved west in the early 1800s, Spain and France made a secret agreement about land that affected American trade. ***(page 313)***
- The Louisiana Purchase opened a vast area to exploration and settlement. ***(page 314)***

Locating Places
Louisiana Territory
New Orleans
St. Louis
Missouri River

Meeting People
Meriwether Lewis
William Clark
Sacagawea (SA • kuh • juh • WEE • uh)
Zebulon Pike

Content Vocabulary
Conestoga wagon (KAH • nuh • STOH • guh)
secede (sih • SEED)

Academic Vocabulary
enormous (in • NAWR • muhs)
generation (JEH • nuh • RAY • shuhn)

Reading Strategy
Classifying Information As you read the section, re-create the diagram below and describe the areas that Lewis and Clark and Zebulon Pike explored.

Explorer	Region explored
Meriwether Lewis and William Clark	
Zebulon Pike	

NATIONAL GEOGRAPHIC Who & When?

1804 | 1805 | 1806 | 1807

Oct. 1803 Senate ratifies Louisiana Purchase treaty

May 1804 Lewis and Clark begin expedition

Sep. 1806 Lewis and Clark return to St. Louis

Nov. 1806 Zebulon Pike reaches Pikes Peak

SECTION RESOURCES

Print Material
- Reproducible Lesson Plan 6–2*
- Daily Lesson and Discussion Notes 6–2
- Guided Reading Activity 6–2
- Reading Essentials and Study Guide 6–2
- Active Reading Note-Taking Guide 6–2
- Section Quiz 6–2

Transparencies
- Daily Focus Skills Transparency 6–2
- Section Graphic Organizer Transparency 6–2
- California Standards Practice Transparencies

Technology
- Interactive Tutor Self-Assessment CD-ROM
- Exam*View*® Pro Testmaker CD-ROM
- Presentation Plus! CD-ROM

*Available on TeacherWorks™

US8.4.1 Describe the country's physical landscapes, political divisions, and territorial expansion during the terms of the first four presidents.

Western Territory

Main Idea **As Americans moved west in the early 1800s, Spain and France made a secret agreement about land that affected American trade.**

Reading Connection What challenges come with moving? Read to learn what the pioneers faced as they went west.

An American Story

Why did Americans risk everything they had to travel west? An English visitor, Harriet Martineau, observed:

R1

> **"The pride and delight of Americans is in their quantity of land. . . . The possession of land is the aim of all action . . . and the cure for all social evils. . . . If a man is disappointed in politics or love, he goes and buys land."**
>
> —from *Society in America*

Moving West During the early 1800s, more and more Americans moved west in search of land and adventure. These pioneers headed over the mountains into Kentucky and Tennessee and the less settled areas of the Northwest Territory. Most of these pioneers were farmers. They made a long and exhausting journey over the Appalachian Mountains.

R2 Settlers loaded their household goods into **Conestoga wagons** (KAH • nuh • STOH • guh), sturdy vehicles topped with white canvas. For these westward-bound pioneers, two vital possessions were a rifle for protection and hunting and an ax to hack their way through the dense forests.

In 1800 the territory of the United States extended only as far west as the Mississippi River. The area to the west of the river—known as the **Louisiana Territory**—belonged to Spain. R3 It was an **enormous** area of land, extending south to the city of **New Orleans** and west to the Rocky Mountains. Its northern boundaries remained undefined.

Many pioneers established farms along rivers that fed into the upper Mississippi River. The Spanish allowed Americans to sail on the lower Mississippi and trade in New Orleans. For the western farmers, this right was vital. The goods they sent downriver were unloaded in New Orleans and sent by ship to markets on the East Coast.

The French Threat In 1802 the Spanish suddenly changed their policy. They refused to allow American goods to move into or past New Orleans. That same year, President Jefferson learned that Spain and France had made a secret agreement that transferred the Louisiana Territory to France. Jefferson was alarmed. He thought French control would jeopardize American trade on the Mississippi River. He authorized Robert Livingston, the new minister to France, to negotiate for the purchase of New Orleans and other French territory. U

Revolt in Santo Domingo The leader of France, Napoleon Bonaparte (nuh • POHL • yuhn BOH • nuh • PAHRT), hoped to use Santo Domingo as a Caribbean naval base from which he could control an American empire. However, a revolt in Santo Domingo ended Bonaparte's dream of a Western empire.

Inspired by the ideas of the French Revolution, enslaved Africans and other laborers in Santo Domingo rebelled against the island's plantation owners. After fierce and bitter fighting, the rebels, led by Toussaint-Louverture (TOO • SA LOO • vuhr • TYUR), declared the colony an independent republic. Toussaint set up an independent government.

In 1802 Napoleon sent troops to regain control. The French captured Toussaint but could not regain control of the island. By 1804 the French were driven out of Santo Domingo and the country regained its original name of Haiti.

Reading Check **Explain** Why was the Mississippi River important to western farmers?

TEACH

R1 Reading Strategy

Reading Primary Sources Point out to students that a person's observation of an event can be a primary source. Explain that historians study accounts such as Harriet Martineau's to understand an event or an era. **Ask:** What do you learn from Martineau's observations? *(Americans were eager to own land and proud to do so.)* OL

CA HR3.

R2 Reading Strategy

Understanding Vocabulary Have students research the origin of the name for the Conestoga wagon. *(The wagon originated in the Conestoga region of Pennsylvania.)* OL

R3 Reading Strategy

Academic Vocabulary Have students rewrite the sentence using a synonym for the word *enormous*. OL

U Universal Access

English Learners Have a volunteer read the sentence with the word *jeopardize*. Have students use context clues to try to devise a definition for the word. Then read the correct definition. Ask two or three volunteers to use the word in a sentence to demonstrate mastery of its meaning. EL

Reading Check

Answer: They needed the river to ship their crops to market.

Resources for page 313

Universal Access Activity 6

More Skill Practice

Historical and Social Sciences Analysis Skill Have students identify the ways in which farmers in the early 1800s could ship goods to market. *(by wagon; by animal; by carrying it; by boat)* **Ask:** Why did farmers use the Mississippi River to ship goods to the east coast? *(Moving goods by water would be easier and faster than doing it by land.)* OL CA HI2.

Did You Know?

Toussaint-Louverture led the rebellion that created the first independent nation, now called Haiti, in Latin America. He added Louverture to his name, which is a French term for "opening," because he was good at finding openings in enemy lines.

R1 Reading Strategy

Identifying the Main Idea and Supporting Details Direct students to the main idea of this part of the section. Tell them, as they read, to find two details that support this idea. *(Possible answers: The new territory would provide cheap and abundant land for farmers; The journey of Lewis and Clark inspired people to move west.)* OL

C Critical Thinking

Making Inferences Ask: Why were Livingston and Monroe taken by surprise at the French offer to sell the entire Louisiana Territory? *(They assumed that the French would want to continue holding the region.)* AL

R2 Reading Strategy

Evaluating Ask: What risk did President Jefferson face in purchasing the Louisiana Territory? *(The purchase might not have been legal.)* OL

US8.4.1 Describe the country's physical landscapes, political divisions, and territorial expansion during the terms of the first four presidents.

The Nation Expands

R1 **Main Idea** **The Louisiana Purchase opened a vast area to exploration and settlement.**

Reading Connection Imagine you are preparing to lead an expedition to explore new lands. Who would you travel with? What research would you do? Read on to learn about Lewis and Clark's travels in the Louisiana Territory.

Without Santo Domingo, Napoleon had little use for Louisiana. The French believed they had something to sell that the United States might want to buy. French foreign minister Charles de Talleyrand informed American diplomats that the entire Louisiana Territory was for sale. Livingston and James Monroe, Jefferson's new special representative, were taken completely by surprise. Accepting the offer went far beyond what they were authorized to do, but the deal was too good to pass up. C After a few days of negotiation, the parties agreed on a price of $15 million.

The Louisiana Purchase pleased Jefferson. The new territory would provide cheap and abundant land for farmers for **generations** to come. He worried, however, whether the purchase was legal. R2 The Constitution said nothing about acquiring new territory. By what authority could he justify the purchase? Livingston wrote from Paris, urging Jefferson to accept the deal before Napoleon changed his mind. Jefferson decided the government's treaty-making powers allowed the purchase of the new territory. The Senate gave its approval in October 1803. With the ratification of the treaty, the size of the United States doubled.

TECHNOLOGY & History

The Conestoga Wagon

By the mid-1700s, sturdy Conestoga wagons transported settlers and their freight over the Appalachian Mountains. These wagons were first built in the Conestoga Creek region of Lancaster, Pennsylvania. As people pushed even farther westward, the Conestoga was seen rolling across the plains toward Oregon and California. **Why did Conestoga wagons have a high front and back?**

1. Six to eight draft horses or a dozen oxen pull the wagon. The driver rides or walks beside the animals.
2. The boat-shaped wagon's high front and back keep goods from falling out on steep mountain trails.
3. A **toolbox** attached to the side of the wagon holds spare parts for needed repairs.
4. A white canvas cloth stretches over the hoops, or **wagon bows**. This cover protects passengers and cargo from heat, rain, and snow.
5. Broad **wheels** help keep the heavy wagon from being mired in the mud.

The average Conestoga wagon was 21 feet long, 11 feet high, and 4 feet in width and depth. It could carry up to 12,000 pounds of cargo.

Answers and Additional Support

TECHNOLOGY & History

Conestoga wagons were later known as prairie schooners because, when seen from a distance on the Great Plains, their white canvas covers resembled sails.

Answer: to keep goods from falling out when the wagon was going uphill or downhill

More Skill Practice

Historical and Social Sciences Analysis Skill Challenge students to frame questions that can be answered by further research. **Ask:** What are two questions you would ask to learn more about the information on this page? *(Possible answers: What were Napoleon's plans? What were the negotiations like between the Americans and the French?)* OL CA HR1.

The Expedition West Very little was known about the area west of the Mississippi, and it excited Jefferson's curiosity. Even before the Louisiana Purchase was complete, he persuaded Congress to sponsor an expedition to explore the new territory. Jefferson was particularly interested in the expedition as a scientific venture. Congress was interested in the natural resources in the territory and in sites for military forts.

Who Were Lewis and Clark? To head the expedition, Jefferson chose his private secretary, 28-year-old **Meriwether Lewis.** Lewis was well qualified to lead this journey of exploration. He had joined the militia during the Whiskey Rebellion and had been in the army since that time. The expedition's co-leader was **William Clark,** 32, a friend of Lewis's from military service. Both Lewis and Clark were knowledgeable amateur scientists. Together they assembled a crew that included expert gunsmiths, carpenters, scouts, and a cook. Two men of mixed Native American and French heritage served as interpreters. Clark's servant, an African American named York, rounded out the group. York's skills in hunting and fishing made him a valuable member of the expedition. He was particularly successful in making friends with the Native Americans they met along the way.

The expedition left **St. Louis** in the spring of 1804 and slowly worked its way up the **Missouri River.** Lewis and Clark kept a journal of their voyage and made notes on what they saw and did.

Along their journey they encountered Native American groups. One young Shoshone woman named **Sacagawea** (SA • kuh • juh • WEE • uh) joined their group as a guide. After 18 months and nearly 4,000 miles, Lewis and Clark reached the Pacific Ocean. After spending the winter there, both explorers headed back east along separate routes.

When the expedition returned in September 1806, they had collected and recorded valuable information on people, plants, animals, and the geography of the West. The expedition also helped the United States lay claim to the northern region between the Rocky Mountains and the Pacific Ocean known as Oregon. Within a few years, fur traders based in St. Louis were traveling to and settling in the Rockies. Perhaps most important, the journey provided inspiration to a nation of people eager to move westward.

Picturing History

Soldiers fire a salute during ceremonies in which Louisiana was officially transferred to the United States. ***How did the Louisiana Purchase change the size of the United States?***

Review The Big Idea

Review the Big Idea for this section: "Geography shapes the physical, economic, and political challenges a region faces." **Ask:** What goals did Jefferson and Congress have when sending explorers into the Louisiana Territory? *(Jefferson was interested in the science, and Congress wanted to find natural resources in the area and identify sites for military forts.)* BL

C1 Critical Thinking

Analyzing Information Lewis and Clark were amateur scientists. **Ask:** Why would this help the expedition? *(Jefferson had scientific goals for the expedition.)* Why would it help that Lewis and Clark had military experience? *(Students may say that they would have discipline and be trained to face difficult situations.)* OL

R Reading Strategy

Scaffolding—Academic Vocabulary Students were introduced to the word *interpreter* in Chapter 3, Section 1. Have a student define the word by using it in a sentence. OL

C2 Critical Thinking

Drawing Conclusions **Ask:** Why would Sacagawea have been helpful to Lewis and Clark? *(Students may say that she could communicate with other Native Americans.)* AL

Did You Know?

Though few facts are known about Sacagawea, many believe her Shoshone name was Boinaiv, which means "grass maiden." Before she helped guide Lewis and Clark she had been captured by the Hidatsa people, who had given her the name Sacagawea, which comes from the Hidasta words for "bird" and "woman."

Picturing History

Though France had received Louisiana by treaty from Spain in 1800, it had never formally taken possession. On November 30, 1803, then, Spain officially gave the land to France. Almost three weeks later, on December 20, France formally gave it to the United States.

Answer: It doubled its size.

Resources for page 315

- Biography Activity 6B
- Biography Activity 6C

W Writing Support

Research Reports Writing
Have students research to find five Web sites with information on Zebulon Pike's expedition. Ask them to prepare a chart evaluating the credibility of each source. Remind students to give reasons for their evaluations.
OL CA 8WS1.4

R Reading Strategy

Understanding Vocabulary
The term *secede* comes from a Latin word meaning "to go away." Encourage volunteers to use *secede* correctly in a sentence. OL

Review Grade 5 Standards

To review standard **5.8.3** *(Demonstrate knowledge of the explorations of the trans-Mississippi West following the Louisiana Purchase (e.g., Meriwether Lewis and William Clark, Zebulon Pike, John Frémont.)*, **ask:** Which expedition took the longest route outside the Louisiana Territory, Lewis and Clark's or Pike's? *(Pike's)* OL

Answers and Additional Support

W **Pike's Expedition** Even before Lewis and Clark returned, Jefferson sent others to explore the wilderness. Lieutenant **Zebulon Pike** led two expeditions between 1805 and 1807, traveling through the upper Mississippi River valley and into the region that is now the state of Colorado. In Colorado, Pike found a snow-capped mountain he called Grand Peak. Today this mountain is known as Pikes Peak. Pike's account of his expeditions gave Americans their first detailed description of the Great Plains and the Rocky Mountains.

Federalists Plan to Secede Many Federalists opposed the Louisiana Purchase. They feared that the states carved out of the new territory would become Republican, reducing the Federalists' power. A group of Federalists in Massachusetts plotted to **secede** (sih • SEED)—withdraw—from the United States. They wanted New England to form a separate "Northern Confederacy." The plotters realized that to have any chance of success, the Northern Confederacy would have to include New York as well as New England. R

NATIONAL GEOGRAPHIC **The Louisiana Purchase and Western Exploration**

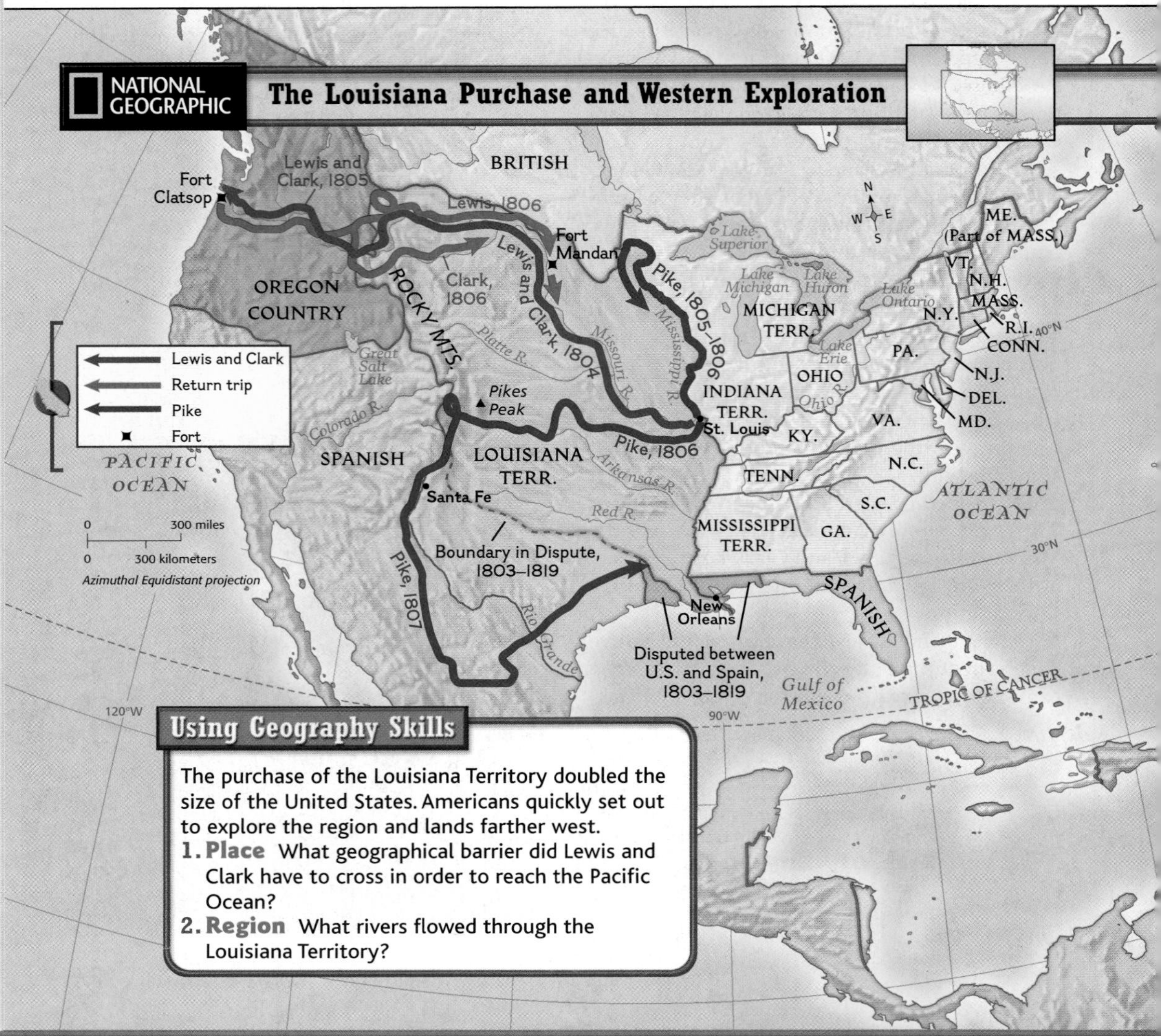

Using Geography Skills

The purchase of the Louisiana Territory doubled the size of the United States. Americans quickly set out to explore the region and lands farther west.

1. **Place** What geographical barrier did Lewis and Clark have to cross in order to reach the Pacific Ocean?
2. **Region** What rivers flowed through the Louisiana Territory?

Resources for page 316

- Analysis Skills Activity 6
- Geography and History Activity 6

Using Geography Skills

Answers:

1. the Rocky Mountains
2. the Missouri River, the Platte River, the Mississippi River, the Arkansas River, the Red River (with the Mississippi River serving as a border)

R

Federalists Support Burr In 1804 the Republican caucus nominated Thomas Jefferson for a second term as president. Jefferson and the Republicans, in doubt about Burr's loyalty to the party, did not nominate Burr for another term as vice president. Instead, they chose George Clinton of New York. Burr then decided to run for governor of New York. Many Federalists supported Burr as they were searching for a powerful ally in New York who would support their plan for the Northern Confederacy. Alexander Hamilton, however, threw his weight against Burr's election.

Burr and Hamilton Alexander Hamilton had never trusted Aaron Burr. Now Hamilton was concerned about rumors that Burr had secretly agreed to lead New York out of the Union. Hamilton called Burr "a dangerous man." When Burr lost the election for governor, he blamed Hamilton and challenged him to a duel. In July 1804, the two men—armed with pistols—met in Weehawken, New Jersey. Hamilton hated dueling and pledged not to shoot at his rival. Burr, however, did fire and aimed to hit Hamilton. Seriously wounded, Hamilton died the next day. Burr fled to avoid arrest on the charge of murder.

The Northern Confederacy Fails With Burr on the run and with almost no support in the New England states, the plans for the Northern Confederacy failed. The results of the election of 1804 showed how thoroughly the Federalists had been discredited. Jefferson and Clinton captured 162 electoral votes to 14 for the Federalist candidates Charles Pinckney and Rufus King.

Reading Check **Summarize** Why did France sell the Louisiana Territory to the United States?

History Online

Study Central Need help understanding the Louisiana Purchase and its exploration? Visit ca.hss.glencoe.com and click on Study Central.

Section 2 Review

Reading Summary

Review the Main Ideas

- American settlers in the West depended on the use of the lower Mississippi River and the port of New Orleans to trade their farm products. That control was threatened when France gained control of the Louisiana Territory.
- After the purchase of Louisiana from the French, President Jefferson sent Lewis and Clark and others to explore the new territory.

What Did You Learn?

1. Which European countries controlled the Louisiana Territory until 1800?
2. Name the famous Native American woman who Lewis and Clark met along their journey.

Critical Thinking

3. **Organizing Information** Create a diagram like the one below that lists the benefits of acquiring the Louisiana Territory. CA HR3.

4. **The Big Ideas** Why was the French port of New Orleans important to the United States? CA CS2.
5. **Cause and Effect** How could the Lewis and Clark expedition prepare people who wanted to move west? Write a paragraph describing your conclusions. CA HI2.
6. **ANALYSIS Assess** What was the relationship between the Louisiana Purchase and political power? How did Jefferson's political opponents react? Write an essay explaining your assessment. CA CS1. CA 8WA2.3.c

SECTION 2 REVIEW ANSWERS

Review questions reinforce content standard US8.4.

1. Spain
2. Sacagawea
3. cheap and abundant land for farmers; control of the Mississippi River; control of port of New Orleans.
4. **The Big Ideas** Farmer shipped their goods down the river to New Orleans to get them to markets.
5. Students may suggest that the expedition provided maps; information about Native American groups and distribution of animals and plants.
6. **ANALYSIS** Students may say that the purchase gave potential power to the Republicans. Some Federalists threatened to secede.

TEACH

R Reading Strategy

Activating Prior Knowledge **Ask:** What action had Hamilton taken to oppose Burr in the 1800 election? *(After Jefferson and Burr finished the presidential election tied in electoral votes, he had convinced Federalists in the House to vote for Jefferson instead of Burr.)* How might Burr have felt as a result? *(angry, bitter)* OL CA HI2.

ASSESS

Resources for page 317

Use these resources to assess student mastery of section content.

Section Quiz 6–2

Interactive Tutor Self-Assessment CD-ROM

Reading Check

Answer: The French needed money to finance Napoleon's plans for war against Britain.

History Online

Study Central provides summaries, interactive games, and online graphic organizers to help students review section content.

CLOSE

Drawing Conclusions Ask students whether they consider Jefferson's purchase of the Louisiana Territory his greatest accomplishment and explain why. *(Students should give reasons to support their answers.)* OL

FOCUS

History–Social Science Standards

The following standard is covered on pages 318–319.

US8.4.1 Students describe the country's physical landscapes, political divisions, and territorial expansion during the terms of the first four presidents.

TEACH

R Reading Strategy

Reading Maps, Graphs, and Charts **Ask:** What geographic features would have helped or hindered Lewis and Clark as they traveled through the Louisiana Territory? *(The Missouri, Yellowstone, and Columbia Rivers would have made traveling easier, but crossing through the Rocky Mountains could have been difficult.)* OL

C Critical Thinking

Making Inferences Have students identify the three methods of transportation shown on the map. *(travel by keel boat, horseback, and dugout canoe)* OL

Answers and Additional Support

NATIONAL GEOGRAPHIC

US8.4.1 Describe the country's physical landscapes, political divisions, and territorial expansion during the terms of the first four presidents.

GEOGRAPHY & HISTORY

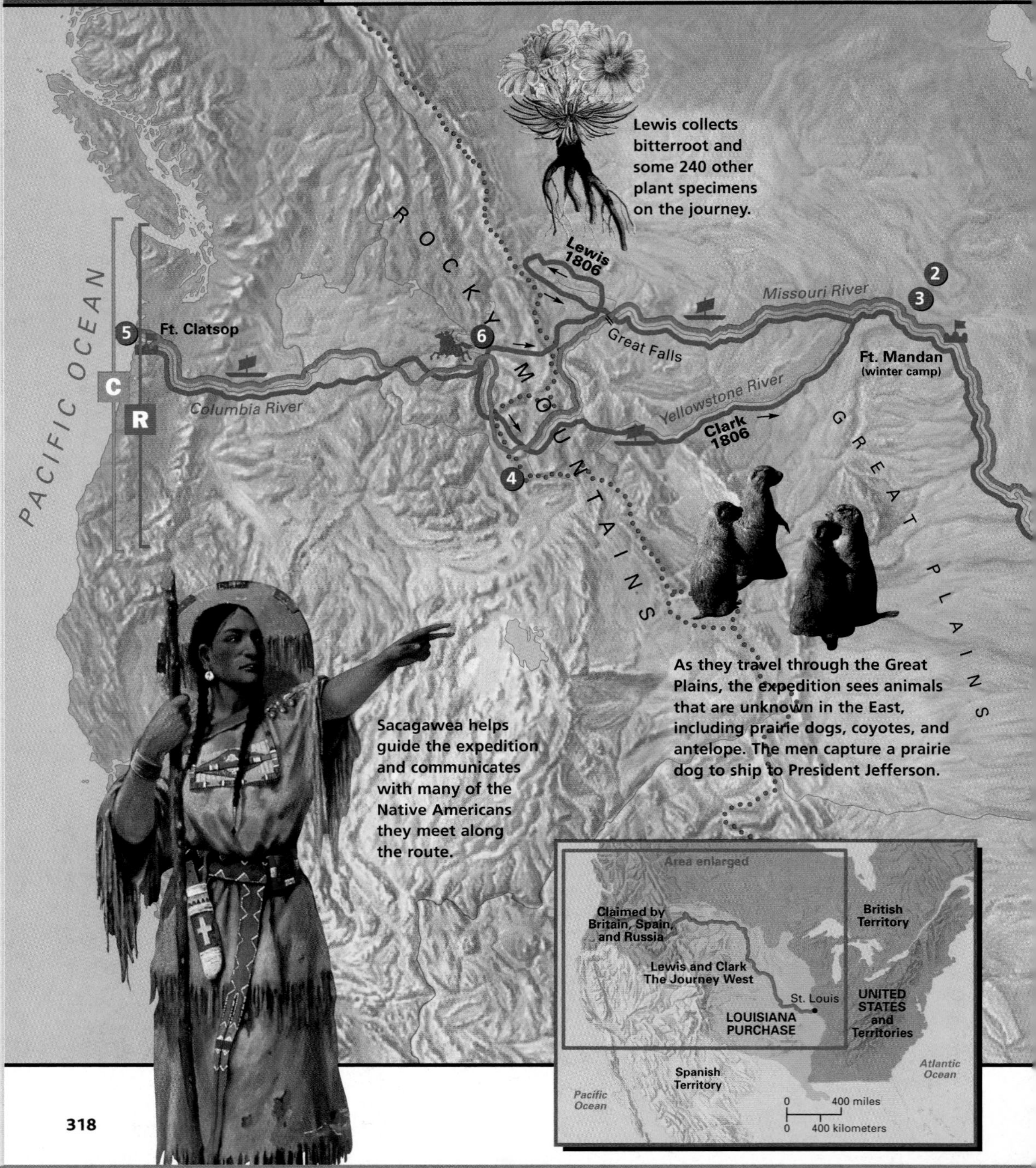

318

Did You Know?

On his last official ceremony in the White House, President Bill Clinton awarded a posthumous promotion to William Clark to the rank of army captain and gave the title of honorary army sergeant to Sacagawea and to Clark's enslaved African, York.

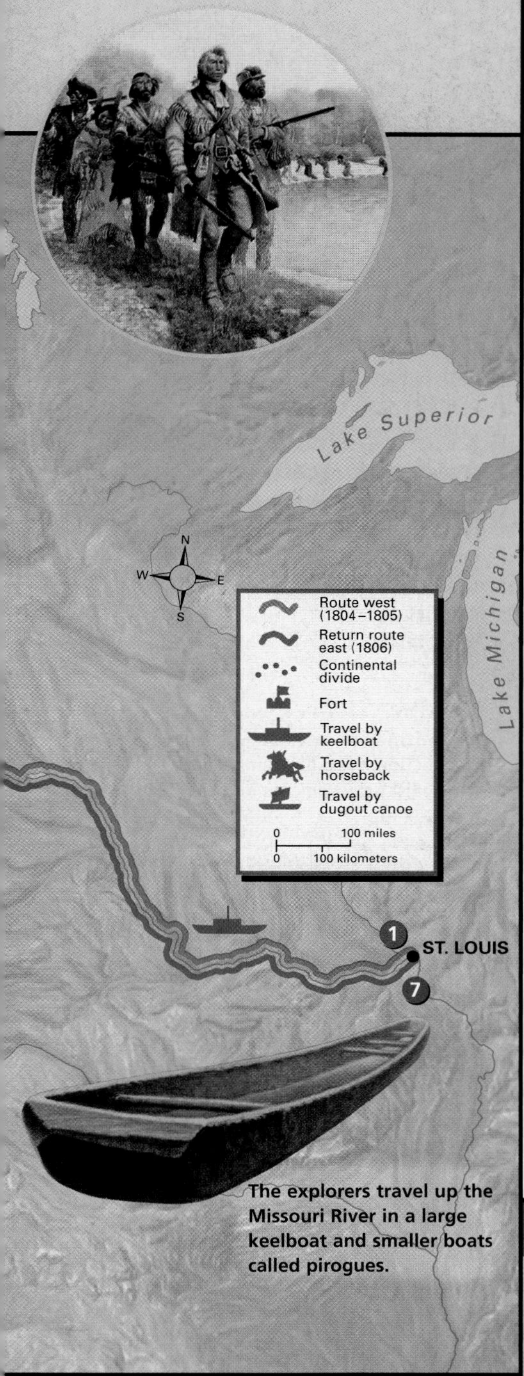

The explorers travel up the Missouri River in a large keelboat and smaller boats called pirogues.

INTO THE UNKNOWN

LEWIS AND CLARK In 1803 President Jefferson set up the Corps of Discovery to find a water route to the Pacific and explore the recently acquired Louisiana Purchase. In the spring of 1804, William Clark and Meriwether Lewis, with a company of recruits, set off from St. Louis.

1804 THE JOURNEY WEST

1 **MAY 14** The members of the Corps of Discovery, which number over 45, embark on the expedition, which would eventually cover more than 7,700 miles. **W**

2 **NOVEMBER** The explorers set up a winter camp near the villages of the Mandans and Hidatsas. Sacagawea, a Shoshone woman who had been kidnapped by the Hidatsa, joins the expedition.

1805

3 **APRIL 7** Lewis and Clark send a group back on the keelboat with reports and specimens of some of the plants and animals that were unknown in the East. The expedition continues in smaller boats.

4 **AUGUST 12** Lewis realizes that there is no Northwest Passage—or river route—to the Pacific. The Corps continues on horseback.

5 **DECEMBER 25** The expedition celebrates Christmas in its new winter quarters, Fort Clatsop.

1806 THE RETURN TRIP

6 **JULY 3** The expedition splits into smaller units to explore more of the Louisiana Territory. They reunite on August 12.

7 **SEPTEMBER 23** The Corps of Discovery finally arrives back in St. Louis. The explorers had established peaceful contact with many Native Americans and accumulated a wealth of geographic information. Fur traders and others, armed with the new knowledge, soon start heading west.

LEARNING from GEOGRAPHY

1. **What obstacles do you think would have been the most difficult for the expedition?**
2. **Write a paragraph that describes the importance of teamwork in helping the Corps of Discovery reach its goals.**

NATIONAL GEOGRAPHIC

GEOGRAPHY & HISTORY

W Writing Support

Narrative Writing Have students take the role of a member of the Corps of Discovery and write three or four diary entries reflecting how the explorers would have felt when they finally reached the Pacific Ocean. Ask volunteers to share their passages with the class. OL CA 8WA2.1

ASSESS

Have students answer the **Learning from Geography** questions.

NGS ONLINE

Access National Geographic's Web site for current events, atlas updates, activities, links, interactive features, and archives at www.nationalgeographic.com.

CLOSE

Determining Cause and Effect Have students create a graphic organizer that shows the causes and effects of the Lewis and Clark expedition. OL

LEARNING from GEOGRAPHY

Answers:

1. Answers will vary but may include navigating the terrain, maintaining a food supply, and communicating with different Native American groups.
2. Students may point out that by working together, the members of the Corps of Discovery could overcome obstacles they faced.

FOCUS

BELLRINGER
SKILLBUILDER ACTIVITY

Project **Daily Focus Skills Transparency 6–3** and have students answer the question.

Guide to Reading

Preteaching Vocabulary:
Have students find the definition of each content vocabulary term in the Glossary in the back of their textbook. Then ask them to write a sentence using the term.

Answers to Graphic:
Literature: Irving and Cooper novels; Bryant poetry; Art: Bingham, Caitlin, and Doughty paintings; Music: Foster's melodies; Architecture: Greek Revival

Unpacking the Standards
After reading the section, students will be able to:

- Identify major figures in the arts in early America.
- Compare rural life in the North and South.
- Discuss the growth of industries in the North.
- Explain what attracted Americans to settle in the West.

Section 3 Daily Life in Early America

Guide to Reading

History Social Science Standards

US8.4 Students analyze the aspirations and ideals of the people of the new nation.

Looking Back, Looking Ahead
The growth of nationalism and democracy led to the rise of a truly American culture.

Focusing on the Main Ideas
- A strong sense of national identity grew among Americans. ***(page 321)***
- Americans began to create their own unique culture. ***(page 322)***
- People living in different regions developed different ways to use and farm the land. ***(page 326)***
- An increasing number of Americans chose to move west into new territory. ***(page 328)***

Meeting People
Washington Irving
James Fenimore Cooper
George Caleb Bingham
Stephen C. Foster

Content Vocabulary
nationalism
planters

Academic Vocabulary
available (uh • VAY • luh • buhl)
unique (yu • NEEK)
occupy (AH • kyuh • PY)
contrary (KAHN • TREHR • ee)
conflict (KAHN • FLIHKT)
migrate (MY • GRAYT)

Reading Strategy
Organizing Information As you read this section, use a diagram like the one shown list achievements in these fields.

Achievements			
Literature	Art	Music	Architecture

NATIONAL GEOGRAPHIC Where & When?

1800 — 1815 — 1830

1804 Slavery banned in most Northern states

1820 Washington Irving publishes *The Sketch Book*

1830 Many Native Americans forced to move to land west of Mississippi River

SECTION RESOURCES

Print Material
- Reproducible Lesson Plan 6–3*
- Daily Lesson and Discussion Notes 6–3
- Guided Reading Activity 6–3
- Reading Essentials and Study Guide 6–3
- Active Reading Note-Taking Guide 6–3
- Section Quiz 6–3

Transparencies
- Daily Focus Skills Transparency 6–3
- Section Graphic Organizer Transparency 6–3
- California Standards Practice Transparencies

Technology
- Interactive Tutor Self-Assessment CD-ROM
- Exam*View*® Pro Testmaker CD-ROM
- Presentation Plus! CD-ROM

*Available on TeacherWorks™

Creating a Democratic Society

Main Idea **A strong sense of national identity grew among Americans.**

Reading Connection What type of school do you attend? Do you think education should be available to everyone? In the early years of the Republic, only a few groups of people had access to schools. Read on to learn more.

An American Story

Lewis and Clark returned to Washington, D.C., in 1806. The maps that they drew made it easier for new settlers to follow the way west. The United States, President Jefferson said, was "a rising nation, spread over a wide and fruitful land."

R

Nationalism During the age of Jefferson, a spirit of nationalism spread throughout the United States. **Nationalism** is a feeling of pride in a nation and loyalty to its goals. At this time, the United States's territory and population grew, and national prosperity increased as well. Americans felt confident and united about their new nation and its future.

S

As the country expanded, American society became increasingly democratic. This meant that the ideas of equality and natural rights influenced every part of American life. People excluded from power and influence—poor white males, women, and both enslaved and free African Americans—began to demand the basic dignity promised in the Declaration of Independence.

Education During the early republic, many Americans came to believe that a strong democracy depended on well-educated citizens. Jefferson expressed this belief when he said,

C

> **"If a nation expects to be ignorant and free, in a state of civilization, it expects what never was and never will be."**
>
> **—Letter to Charles Yancey, 1816**

To advance education on the frontier, schools were provided for in the Northwest Ordinance of 1787.

Despite these intentions, many Americans did not have the opportunity to attend school in the early 1800s. Most schools were run by private groups and were open only to those who could afford to pay for them. Some students were educated at home or at dame schools. Dame schools were generally taught by women in their own homes. The teacher taught the children to read and write and other useful skills such as sewing.

HISTORY MAKERS

The American Spelling Book

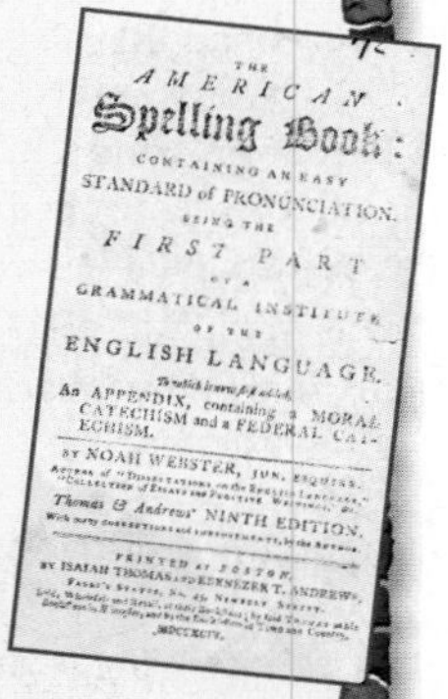
THE
AMERICAN
Spelling Book:
CONTAINING AN EASY
STANDARD of PRONUNCIATION.
BEING THE
FIRST PART
OF A
GRAMMATICAL INSTITUTE
OF THE
ENGLISH LANGUAGE.
An APPENDIX, containing a MORAL CATECHISM and a FEDERAL CATECHISM.
BY NOAH WEBSTER, JUN. ESQUIRE.
Thomas & Andrews' NINTH EDITION.
PRINTED AT BOSTON,
BY ISAIAH THOMAS AND EBENEZER T. ANDREWS.

The American Spelling Book, written by Noah Webster in the late 1790s, was used by students as their standard textbook. The words were broken down into syllables to help the reader learn pronunciation. In addition to reading and spelling exercises, the *Spelling Book* was also a collection of stories, fables, and wise sayings. Webster wrote:

"We have always a right to defend our persons, property and families. But we have no right to fight and [abuse] people merely for revenge. It is nobler to forgive."

Used by generations of students, *The American Spelling Book* is one of the best-selling American books of all time.

TEACH

R Reading Strategy

Activating Prior Knowledge Tell students that words that end with the suffix *-ism*, like *nationalism*, involve a movement or a system of belief. **Ask:** What other words with this ending do you know? *(Possible answers: federalism, mercantilism, capitalism)* OL

S Skill Practice

Historical and Social Sciences Analysis Skill **Ask:** To whom did early Americans believe that equality and natural rights belonged? *(the individual)* What effect would this belief have on how people treated each other? *(People would treat each other as equals.)* OL

C Critical Thinking

Analyzing Primary Sources Refer students to the quotation by Jefferson. **Ask:** What does Jefferson mean by "a state of civilization." *(Answers may include people following laws; a fair system of courts; people taking responsibility for their actions.)* Why does Jefferson say that people living in civilization cannot be ignorant and free? *(People need to have knowledge to act responsibly as citizens.)* AL CA HR3.

More Skill Practice

Historical and Social Sciences Analysis Skill Have students discuss the description of *The American Spelling Book*. **Ask:** Based on the description, what similarities are there between *The American Spelling Book* and textbooks used today? *(words broken down into syllables; reading and spelling exercises; both contain stories and wise sayings, or quotes)* OL CA HI3.

HISTORY MAKERS

The American Spelling Book has sold an estimated 100,000,000 copies. The book remained in print throughout Webster's life and provided him with a great deal of income.

R1 Reading Strategy

Academic Vocabulary Ask a volunteer to read the sentence that includes the word *available*. Then ask students to define the word. BL

R2 Reading Strategy

Evaluating Ask: How was the Second Great Awakening an influence on the growth of democracy? *(by stressing the equality of all believers before God; because the message was simple, and all believers could grasp it)* OL

C Critical Thinking

Determining Cause and Effect Have small groups of students discuss the possible reasons that people influenced by the Awakening were moved to end slavery, curb drinking, and advance education. *(heightened awareness of the morality of these issues)* AL CA HI2.

Reading Check

Answer: the equality of all believers before God and the promise of salvation for all who believed

Answers and Additional Support

US8.4.4 Discuss daily life, including traditions in art, music, and literature of early national America (e.g., through writings by Washington Irving, James Fenimore Cooper).

Massachusetts and Philadelphia, however, had public schools that provided free education. R1 Their success increased demands for a nationwide system of public schools that would make education **available** to all citizens.

Religion A powerful influence on the growth of democracy was religion. During the early 1800s, a religious revival known as the Second Great Awakening swept the nation. At gatherings known as camp meetings, preachers R2 offered a simple message that ordinary people could grasp. They stressed the equality of all believers before God and the promise of salvation for all who believed.

The Second Great Awakening had an important effect on the young republic. It gave people the determination to better their lives C and improve society as a whole. Many Americans influenced by the Awakening joined movements to end slavery, curb drinking, and advance education.

Many African Americans were won to Christianity at this time. Inspired by the message of equality, they formed their own denominations and churches, including independent Baptist churches and the first African Methodist Episcopal Church.

Reading Check **Explain** What message was stressed by preachers during the Second Great Awakening?

An American Culture

Main Idea **Americans began to create their own unique culture.**

Reading Connection What kinds of music do you like? What do you enjoy reading? Read on to learn more about the music and literature of the early Republic.

The growth of nationalism and democracy in the early republic led to the rise of a truly American culture. Since colonial times, cultural life in the United States had been strongly influenced by Europe, chiefly Great Britain. During the first decade of the 1800s, Americans began to create their own art forms, including literature, painting, music, and architecture.

Literature During the early 1800s, American writers started to turn away from European influences. They began using settings and characters that were typically American. In 1820 **Washington Irving** wrote *The Sketch Book*, a collection of short stories that were mostly set in rural New York. One story, "Rip Van Winkle," tells about a man who falls asleep in the woods for 20 years. Another story, "The Legend of Sleepy Hollow," describes the schoolteacher Ichabod Crane's encounter with a headless horseman.

History *Through Art*

Religious Camp Meeting* by J. Maze Burbank** A powerful influence on the growth of democracy was religion. At gatherings called camp meetings, preachers revived America's commitment to religion. ***What was this religious revival called?

History *Through Art*

Religious camp meetings often lasted many days during the summer months. Huge crowds came to these meetings, and they brought supplies to last for the duration of the event. Numerous preachers directed a meeting, often preaching at the same time in different locations of the camp.

Answer: the Second Great Awakening

Picturing History

Like other artists of the Hudson River School, Frederic Edwin Church showed scenes of nature untouched by settlement. ***How was American art and literature changing during the early 1800s?***

In this passage, Irving describes the terror that Ichabod Crane felt as he came upon the headless horseman late at night:

> **"Mounting a rising ground, which brought the figure of his fellow traveller in relief against the sky, gigantic in height, and muffled in a cloak, Ichabod was horror struck, on perceiving that [the rider] was headless! but his horror was still more increased, on observing, that the head, which should have rested on his shoulders, was carried before him on the pommel of the saddle! His terror rose to desperation; he rained a shower of kicks and blows upon [his horse] Gunpowder, hoping, by a sudden movement, to give his companion the slip—but the spectre started full jump with him. Away, then, they dashed, through thick and thin; stones flying, and sparks flashing, at every bound."**
>
> **—"The Legend of Sleepy Hollow"**

Another New York author, **James Fenimore Cooper,** wrote novels such as *The Last of the Mohicans* and *The Deerslayer.* In these novels, a trapper folk hero of many names—Natty Bumppo, Leatherstocking, Deerslayer, and Pathfinder—is portrayed as strong, brave, resourceful, and honorable. When asked if he had ever shot an enemy that was capable of killing him, Deerslayer responded:

> **"To own the truth, I never did," answered Deerslayer, "seeing that a fitting occasion never offered. The Delawares [a Native American group] have been peaceable since my sojourn with 'em, and I hold it to be [wrong] to take the life of a man, except in open and [generous] warfare."**
>
> **—from *The Deerslayer***

U Universal Access

Verbal/Linguistic Ask a volunteer to read the passage from "The Legend of Sleepy Hollow" aloud with expression. **Ask:** What impression does the author give of Ichabod Crane? *(Answers may include that he is tall and poorly dressed; his reaction to the rider is somewhat comic.)* EL

S Skill Practice

Visual Literacy Have students study the painting. **Ask:** What impression does this painting give of the landscape? *(Answers may include the power of nature or the majesty of western scenery.)* OL

C Critical Thinking

Making Inferences

Ask: What do the names *Leatherstocking*, *Deerslayer*, and *Pathfinder* refer to? What do they say about how Natty Bumppo lived? *(Leatherstocking—leather clothing; Deerslayer—hunting; Pathfinder—exploring; reveal that he lived in the wilderness)* AL

Resources for page 323

American Literature Reading 6

Did You Know?

Samuel B. Morse, the well-known American inventor of the Morse Code, was also a painter. His paintings of historical events showed romantic, idealized viewpoints, similar to those of the Hudson School paintings.

Picturing History

The Hudson River School was the first school of painting in the United States. One of its goals was to establish a distinct type of painting that separated it from any of the European schools of painting.

Answer: It was becoming less European and more distinctly American.

Biography

TEACH

C Critical Thinking

Making Generalizations Review the characteristics that Cooper and Irving considered essentially American—the spirit of the frontier and possibilities of improvement and change. **Ask:** What qualities are part of the American national character today? Discuss students' answers. AL

R Reading Strategy

Inferring Ask: What do you think Cooper means by the quote? *(He is suggesting that people should avoid prejudice against other groups.)* OL

S Skill Practice

Historical and Social Sciences Analysis Skill
Ask: What problem might arise if Cooper's writings were the only information that readers had about the American frontier? *(Reader's view of the frontier would be distorted because Cooper's was only one perspective.)* What other sources could people read? *(first-person accounts of life on the frontier; the words of Native Americans)* AL CA HI5.

Answers and Additional Support

Biography

US8.4.4 Discuss daily life, including traditions in art, music, and literature of early national America (e.g., through writings by Washington Irving, James Fenimore Cooper).

WASHINGTON IRVING
1783–1859
JAMES FENIMORE COOPER
1789–1851

C In the 1800s, American literature became more "American." Writers, reflecting a sense of national pride, were turning away from European influences and writing about America. Authors such as James Fenimore Cooper and Washington Irving reveal the spirit of the expanding American frontier and of the possibilities for improvement and change.

James Fenimore Cooper ▶

Washington Irving was the first American writer to win international fame. *The Sketch Book* (1820), a collection of stories admired throughout Europe, included Irving's two most famous tales, "Rip Van Winkle" and "The Legend of Sleepy Hollow."

Irving was a born wanderer, even as a child. He later wrote, "I began my travels, and made many tours into foreign parts and unknown regions of my native city, to the frequent alarm of my parents."

R ***"Should we distrust the man, because his manners are not our manners, and that his skin is dark!"***
—from ***The Last of the Mohicans***

Although he wrote many works, Cooper is best known for his novels about Natty Bumppo's frontier life. *The Leatherstocking Tales* is set in the huge expanse of the New York State frontier. Natty Bumppo is a trapper who is forced westward by the movement of settlers into his beloved frontier. Cooper is the first American writer to draw greatly from American history for his setting and characterization. S As a result of reading Cooper's novels, generations of children—not only here but in France and Great Britain—gloried in the drama of Native Americans and pioneers on the frontier.

◀ Washington Irving

Then and Now

Why do you think works by Irving and Cooper are still popular today?

Then and Now

Answers will vary but may include reasons such as the spirit of exploring new lands and characters that have courage, honor, and resourcefulness.

More Skill Practice

Historical and Social Sciences Analysis Skill Help students understand how the ideals of a nation are represented in its literature. **Ask:** What does the subject matter of Cooper's novels tell about the ideals of Americans in this period? *(They believed in characteristics like those of the strong, brave, resourceful, and honorable folk hero.)* OL CA 8RL3.7

Other writers, such as William Cullen Bryant of Massachusetts, wrote poetry. Bryant expressed a love for natural beauty. His poem "Thanatopsis" appeared in 1817. In it, he suggested that by studying nature, people could better understand life and death.

Art During the early 1800s, American artists turned their attention to American people and landscapes. **George Caleb Bingham** painted fur traders, riverboat workers, and political speakers.

Another artist, George Catlin, was one of several artists who lived among the Native Americans and painted scenes of their daily life. Thomas Doughty was one of the first successful landscape painters and a leader of the Hudson River School of painting. This school was made up of artists who liked to paint views of the Catskill Mountains and the Hudson River in New York.

Music In the early 1800s, Americans developed their own forms of music. Instruments such as banjos and pianos were used to play American tunes. Musicals filled with American songs were performed in large cities and in barns, tents, or log cabins throughout the country.

U One of the most successful American songwriters was **Stephen C. Foster.** Although born in Pennsylvania, Foster combined African and European music to create **uniquely** American melodies about life in the South, such as "My Old Kentucky Home" and "Swanee River."

Architecture American architects of the early 1800s developed their own forms of building based on the classical styles of ancient Greece and Rome. R Classical designs became the model for public buildings all over the country, including the Capitol in Washington, D.C. Thomas Jefferson used classical styles when he planned his home, Monticello, and buildings for the University of Virginia. A style known as Greek Revival also was used for private homes, such as plantation houses in the South.

Reading Check **Describe** What qualities did James Fenimore Cooper give his main character?

America's *Architecture*

University of Virginia Thomas Jefferson founded the University of Virginia to provide educational opportunity for all. Jefferson planned and supervised the construction, including a central domed round building called the Rotunda.

America's *Architecture*

The Rotunda, a half-scale interpretation of the Roman Pantheon, was created by Thomas Jefferson to symbolize the enlightened human mind. The building originally housed the university's library.

Review The Big Idea

Review the Big Idea for this section: "Political, social, religious, and economic changes influence the way Americans think and act." **Ask:** How did the vast spaces of the Louisiana Territory influence the art of the early 1800s? *(Students may say that the huge amount of space and the impressive physical features of the landscape inspired painters.)* AL

U Universal Access

Auditory/Musical Play for the class a recording of one or two of Foster's songs. Then discuss as a class how the tunes differ from the music of today. OL

R Reading Strategy

Scaffolding—Academic Vocabulary Students were introduced to the word *design* in Chapter 1, Section 1. Discuss how the word can be used as both a noun and a verb. OL

Reading Check

Answer: strong, brave, resourceful, and honorable

Resources for page 325

American Art and Architecture, Transparency 9

R1 Reading Strategy

Questioning Have each student write on a sheet of paper two questions based on the Main Idea statement. Then tell them to try to find the answers as they read. EL

W Writing Support

Summary Writing Have each student write a brief summary of the differences between the Northern and Southern lifestyles. OL

C Critical Thinking

Determining Cause and Effect **Ask:** What factors contributed to the growth of plantation culture in the South? *(growth of cotton as cash crop; transfer of slave labor from tobacco to cotton; growth of planters as economic leaders)* OL

R2 Reading Strategy

Categorizing Information Explain that *plan*ters owned *plan*tations; *farm*ers worked *farms*. BL

Answers and Additional Support

US8.4.4 Discuss daily life, including traditions in art, music, and literature, of early national America (e.g., through writings by Washington Irving, James Fenimore Cooper).

A Rural Nation

Main Idea **People living in different regions developed different ways to use and farm the land.**

Reading Connection Do you live in a neighborhood that works together? Read on to see how people in the early years of the Republic experienced work and community.

During the early 1800s, most Americans lived in rural areas and made their living on the land. People, however, **occupied** the land in very different ways in different regions of the country.

Farm Life in the North During the early years of the republic, people in the North tended to cluster in villages and towns made up of neat rows of wooden frame houses, churches, and stores. Beyond these settlements were farm communities located within a relatively short traveling distance of each other. Northern farmers cut down forests and created fields marked by hedges or stone walls. They produced enough crops and livestock to sell or exchange in nearby marketplaces for teas, sugar, window glass, and tools.

Farming was the North's major economic activity, but not all rural people in the North worked on the land. Some labored in the small workshops, grain and sawmills, and iron forges that dotted the rural landscape. Others worked as craftspeople or day laborers in nearby towns.

Picturing History

Some people in the North lived in villages, but many lived and worked in rural areas. ***What was the major economic activity in the North?***

The South's Plantation Culture While Northerners lived close together, Southerners lived on small farms or large plantations that were widely separated from each other. The South's economy depended on slavery and growing cash crops.

Beginning in the 1790s, the growth at home and in Great Britain of the textile industry turned cotton into a major cash crop throughout the South. Cotton production boomed, leading to an increase in demand for enslaved labor.

Because of their wealth from agriculture, **planters**, or large landowners, became the South's economic and social leaders. However, the planters were few in number. About three out of every four white Southerners was a small farmer who worked a small plot of land and had no enslaved workers.

Southern Slavery In time, slavery became "the peculiar institution" that set the South apart from the rest of the country. Most enslaved people in the South worked on farms and plantations. They labored together from dawn to dusk and were closely supervised. While enslaved men generally worked the fields, enslaved women cooked, cleaned, did laundry, sewed, and cared for the plantation's children.

Still, many enslaved people never saw a farm or plantation. They lived and worked in the South's towns and small cities. Enslaved people also carried out tasks other than farming. Some were coach drivers, household servants, and artisans. Others worked at ironworks or mined gold, coal, or salt.

More Skill Practice

Historical and Social Sciences Analysis Skill **Ask:** Why would slavery be called "the peculiar institution" in the South? *("peculiar" because by this period it was unique to the South; "institution" because it was an important social structure)*

AL CA HI2.

Picturing History

Log cabins were ideal for the frontier. Trees were plentiful, and had to be cut down anyway to clear the land for planting. The idea of the log cabin was introduced to North America by Swedish settlers who lived along the Delaware River in the 1600s.

Answer: farming

Picturing **History**

The South developed an economy based on commercial agriculture. ***What became the major cash crop of the South?***

W Wherever they lived, enslaved people formed their own communities. During the evenings, they often shared in song, prayer, and dancing. As one slave recalled, "From sunup to sundown, we belonged to the master; but from sundown to sunup we were our own."

R **The Rise of Urban Life** Most Americans were rural dwellers, but an increasing number of them were living in cities. In the North, cities such as Boston, New York City, and Philadelphia were thriving Atlantic seaports that exported American farm products and imported European manufactured goods. The South had fewer towns and cities than the North. From ports such as New Orleans, Charleston, and Savannah, Southern agricultural goods were shipped to Northern and European markets.

Life in Northern Cities During the early 1800s, America's cities had only a few small industries that made products, such as textiles, C shoes, and metal goods. In the North, mills and factories grew and drew in workers from the farms or from overseas. Children also went to work in these industries.

With the rise of industries in the North, the gap between richer and poorer city residents widened. Prosperous merchants and businesspeople controlled urban economic and social life. A middle class of artisans, shopkeepers, and professionals shared modestly in the general prosperity. At the bottom was a growing working class, many of whose members had to struggle to survive. During the early 1800s, rising land values forced the lower classes into increasingly crowded tenements, or rented row houses. Meanwhile, more prosperous urban dwellers stayed in their own detached dwellings in fashionable neighborhoods.

Free African Americans Northern cities attracted many free African Americans during the early 1800s. After the American Revolution, slavery in the North declined. Why did this happen? Farming in the North came to depend on families and paid workers, not enslaved labor. Many northerners came to believe that slavery was **contrary** to the nation's ideals of equality and justice. By 1804 most northern states had passed laws ending slavery.

S Still, free African Americans faced many obstacles to full equality. Only a few had voting rights. A small number owned their own homes or businesses. They were excluded from white churches and schools and increasingly from skilled jobs. African Americans responded by building their own churches, schools, newspapers, and charitable and social organizations. They used these institutions to develop their own culture and eventually to demand full freedom and equality.

Reading Check **Identify** What group made up the South's political leaders?

W Writing Support

Research Report Writing
Divide students into five groups and have each group research and write a brief report on an aspect of the lives of enslaved African Americans. Assign the following topics: food, clothing, and housing; work performed; family life; culture and customs; and resistance and rebellion. Have each group report its findings to the class. Remind the groups to begin by framing some questions to be answered by their historical study and research. **OL** CA 8WA2.3

R Reading Strategy

Connecting **Ask:** What connections, if any, are there between urban life in the early 1800s and urban life today? *(Answers may include wealthy people controlling businesses and living in own neighborhoods; difficult conditions for the poor.)* **AL** CA HI3.

C Critical Thinking

Predicting Consequences
Ask: What difficulties do you think children faced from working in factories? *(Answers may include poor health, lack of education.)* **OL**

S Skill Practice

Historical and Social Sciences Analysis Skill
Ask: How were freed African Americans able to participate in Northern cities? *(formed own churches, schools, newspapers, and charitable and social organizations)* What rights did they not enjoy? *(voting rights; were excluded from white churches, schools, good jobs)* **BL**

Reading Check
Answer: the planters, or large landowners

Did You Know?

Even though most Northern states had ended slavery by 1804, freed African American men could not vote until the Fifteenth Amendment was passed in 1868.

Picturing **History**

The South had several cash crops. Kentucky and Missouri grew hemp, and Virginia and Kentucky produced tobacco. Rice was important in South Carolina, and Louisiana had a thriving sugar industry. Cotton, though, dominated the region's economy.
Answer: cotton

S1 Skill Practice

Historical and Social Sciences Analysis Skill

Ask: Why did settlers risk rough or extreme conditions to move west? *(opportunities for land; to escape laws and growing populations)* BL CA HI2.

S2 Skill Practice

Using Geography Skills

Ask: Why did Southern farmers not develop an economy based on growing cotton in the Northwest? *(climate was not suitable; Northwest Ordinance banned slavery, and slave labor was needed for widespread cotton farming)* AL CA HI2.

Review Grade 5 Standards

To review standard **5.8.4** *(Discuss the experience of settlers on the overland trails to the West (e.g., location of the routes; purpose of the journeys; the influence of the terrain, rivers, vegetation, and climate; life in the territories at the end of those trails))*, have students imagine they are one of the early settlers to the West and describe their family's typical day. OL

Answers and Additional Support

US8.4.1 Describe the country's physical landscapes, political divisions, and territorial expansion during the terms of the first four presidents.

Westward Movement

Main Idea **An increasing number of Americans chose to move west into new territory.**

Reading Connection If you could move somewhere new, where would you go? Would you drive, take a train, or fly to get there? Read to see how Americans in the early Republic realized their dreams on a new frontier.

S1 While the North and South developed different ways of life, Americans in ever larger numbers pushed westward beyond the Appalachian Mountains. They were eager to claim new land and establish farms in the West. They also wanted to escape the growing population and restricting laws and taxes of the East.

How Did the Settlers Travel? Some settlers came to the West by horseback or wagon along difficult overland routes. Others traveled on boats that floated down waterways, such as the Ohio River and the Mississippi River. Upon arrival, settlers had to provide themselves with shelter, food, and clothing. They cut down trees, built log cabins, and cleared the land for farming. As expanding areas of land came under the farmers' plows, forests and wildlife increasingly gave way to human settlement.

What Was Life Like in the West? Living on the frontier was very rigorous. Pioneers wrestled with uncertain climate, limited supplies, and sometimes failing crops. Life could be lonesome. Settlements were far apart and often hard to reach. The few roads that existed were poor, and westerners found it difficult to transport goods and produce to eastern markets.

Despite hardships, pioneers still enjoyed themselves. Weddings, for example, were major events that drew people from the surrounding area. A short ceremony was followed by eating and dancing that lasted for days. The food was usually simple—bread and butter, fried pork, and wild fruits.

The Way It Was

Moving West

S2 Rich soil and cheap land drew many farmers to the Northwest. Between 1800 and 1840, thousands of settlers poured into the region.

Once the pioneers arrived, their survival depended upon the long-handled axe and the rifle. With the axe, the farmer cleared trees from the land and fashioned the wood from those trees into cabins and crude furniture.

▲ Life in the West meant work for every member of a pioneer family.

A good rifle was also essential. It was used for defense from enemies—human and otherwise—and for shooting game for food. Until the 1840s, the weapon most settlers chose was the "Kentucky Rifle."

The Way It Was

Read the following excerpt from a letter written to a brother in Britain by a settler who had left that country for the Northwest:

"There is enough to spare of everything a person can desire. . . . The poorest families adorn the table three times a day like a wedding dinner. . . . If you knew the difference between this country and England you would need no persuading to leave it.

Ask: Which statements are facts? *(statements about abundance and food)* Which are opinions? *(conclusion that people would move to America if they knew what the situation was like)* OL CA HR2.

R **Conflict in the West** As the settlers moved farther and farther west; they came into **conflict** with Native American groups that controlled the vast areas of land beyond the Appalachian Mountains. Native Americans were angry that land-hungry settlers began creating farms on tribal hunting grounds. As the pressures of settler expansion increased, Native Americans developed ways of resistance and survival.

Some Native American groups, like the Cherokee, tried to adjust peacefully to American settler ways. To defend their freedom and prevent further loss of land, the Cherokee adopted written laws and a constitution patterned after those of American states. Many Cherokee accepted Christianity and settled down as farmers, mill owners, and shopkeepers. Cherokee culture continued to flourish with the invention of a Cherokee alphabet by Sequoya in 1821. Sequoya developed symbols to represent all syllables in Cherokee speech. Many Cherokee learned how to read and write. Sequoya even published a Cherokee newspaper and translated parts of the Bible into Cherokee. As Cherokee self-confidence grew, so did the hostility of their settler neighbors.

Meanwhile, other Native American groups were opposed to accepting settler ways. Wanting to preserve their traditional culture, the Shawnee and the Creek prepared for armed resistance. In the end, neither peaceful adaptation nor armed resistance was successful. By 1830, Native Americans faced cultural loss, military defeat, or forced **migration** to lands west of the Mississippi River.

Reading Check **Explain** Why were people eager to move west?

History Online
Study Central Need help understanding daily life in early America? Visit ca.hss.glencoe.com and click on Study Central.

Section 3 Review

Reading Summary

Review the Main Ideas

- During Jefferson's presidency, Americans developed a sense of pride, or nationalism.
- Literature, music, art, and architecture began to reflect distinctly American themes.
- Daily life in the young Republic was varied, based on regional differences and ethnicity.
- People were eager to take advantage of new land opportunities in the Louisiana Purchase.

What Did You Learn?

1. What was Jefferson's view of the relationship between education and democracy?
2. What institutions set the South apart from the rest of the country?

Critical Thinking

3. **Comparing** Create a table to describe economic activities and regional distinctions that developed in each area during this period. CA HI1.

	Urban	Rural
North		
South		

4. **The Big Ideas** Describe how a distinct American identity and culture grew during this period. Be sure to include references to literature, art, music, and architecture. CA 8RC2.0
5. **Creative Writing** Imagine you can travel back in time. You are a newspaper reporter sent to write a story on either farming life in the South or the Native American experience after the Louisiana Purchase. Choose a topic and then identify people of the time to interview. Make a list of questions you would ask them and responses they might give you. CA HR1.

R Reading Strategy

Outlining Have students outline the information about Native Americans. OL

ASSESS

Resources for page 329

Use these resources to assess student mastery of section content.

Section Quiz 6–3

Interactive Tutor Self-Assessment CD-ROM

Reading Check

Answer: There was rich soil and cheap land, and they wanted to escape restricting laws and population growth in the East.

History Online

Study Central provides summaries, interactive games, and online graphic organizers to help students review section content.

CLOSE

Summarizing **Ask:** Which populations generally benefited and which did not during the early years of westward expansion? *(benefited: white settlers; did not benefit: Native Americans, African American slaves)* OL

SECTION 3 REVIEW ANSWERS

Review questions reinforce content standard US8.4.

1. It is important for all people in a democracy to be educated in order to remain free.
2. slavery and cash crop farming
3. North: Urban—growth of industries, growing gap between rich and poor; Rural—small family farms; South: Urban—ports used for shipping crops; Rural—many small farms and some large plantations
4. **The Big Ideas** Answers may include Irving and Cooper's works, Hudson River School's paintings, Foster's uniquely American melodies, and new forms of building.
5. Students should identify a topic, a list of interviewees, and questions.

Analyzing Primary Sources

FOCUS

History–Social Science Standards

The following standards are covered on pages 330–331.

US8.4 Students analyze the aspirations and ideals of the people of the new nation.

US8.4.2 Explain the policy significance of famous speeches (e.g., Washington's Farewell Address, Jefferson's 1801 Inaugural Address, John Q. Adams's Fourth of July 1821 Address).

TEACH

R Reading Strategy

Reading Primary Sources

Ask: What evidence is there in these primary sources that Americans were looking beyond their own shores to foreign lands? *(Shaler traded with China and wrote about Spanish California; Adams spoke about American relations with other countries.)* OL CA HR4.

Answers and Additional Support

Analyzing Primary Sources

US8.4 Students analyze the aspirations and ideals of the people of the new nation. **US8.4.2** Explain the policy significance of famous speeches (e.g., Washington's Farewell Address, Jefferson's 1801 Inaugural Address, John Q. Adams's Fourth of July 1821 Address).

Looking Westward

R *The early 1800s was an important time in America. For the first time in modern history, the political power of a country transferred peacefully from one political party to another. It also marked a time of great expansion and change for the United States. The United States looked westward, and also began to look beyond its borders. As you read these primary source selections, think about why this was a time of such rapid growth for the nation.*

Meriwether Lewis views the Rocky Mountains. ▶

Reader's Dictionary

maritime (MAR • uh • TYM): bordering on the ocean

garrison (GAR • uh • suhn): fort

pirogue (PEE • ROHG): dugout boat resembling canoes

trodden (TRAH • duhn): stepped

esteem (ihs • TEEM): value

benediction (BEH • nuh • dihk • shuhn): blessing

avarice (A • vuh • ruhs): greed

maxim (MAK • suhm): rule of conduct

California in 1804

Sea captain William Shaler visited the coast of California while engaged in trade with China and recorded his observations.

[The Spanish are] masters of the **maritime** part of the country only. Beyond that range of mountains [the Sierra Madre] the country is remarkably fine, well watered, and covered with forests: these they have not as yet been able to penetrate, on account of their being thickly inhabited by warlike tribes of Indians. I am informed that the government [aims] to establish lines of missions and **garrisons** from San Francisco to New Mexico, and by the country of the Colorado Indians to the same place, and by these means to complete the conquest of the country. But that is a project that does not seem likely to be very soon realized.

—*from Shaler's Journal*

The Explorations of Lewis and Clark

From 1804 to 1806, Meriwether Lewis and William Clark explored and mapped the Louisiana Territory.

Our vessels consisted of six small canoes, and two large [**pirogues**]. This little fleet, altho' not quite so respectable as those of Columbus or Capt. Cook, were still viewed by us with as much pleasure. . . .

EXTENDING THE CONTENT

Trade with China In July 1783, the British government banned American ships from trading in the British islands of the West Indies. American merchants began looking for new markets for their goods. Early the following year, a merchant ship named the *Empress of China* left New York City for China carrying more than 40 tons of ginseng, a plant consumed in China to extend one's life. Fifteen months later, it returned with profits from selling the ginseng and with silk, tea, and other goods that brought even more profits. This voyage launched the lucrative China trade.

We were now about to penetrate a country at least two thousand miles in width, on which the foot of civilized man had never **trodden.** The good or evil it had in store . . . was for experiment yet to determine. . . . [T]he picture which now presented itself to me was a most pleasing one. . . . I could but **esteem** this moment of my departure as among the most happy of my life.

—*from an April 1805 entry in the journal of Meriwether Lewis, as he prepares to leave Fort Mandan on the upper Missouri River*

U

▼ William Clark's log book

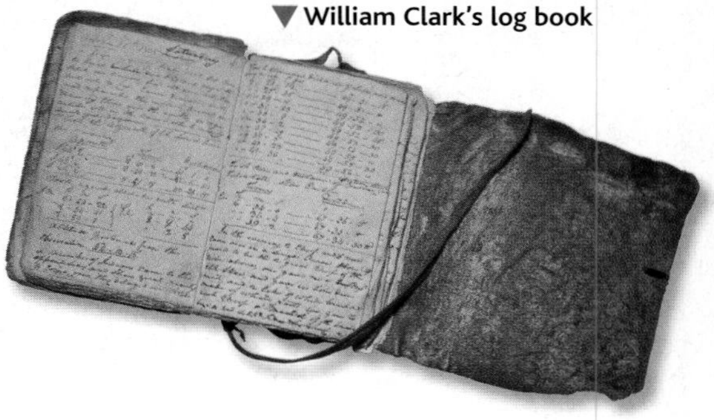

Adams's Fourth of July Address

On July 4, 1821, Secretary of State John Quincy Adams took part in a ceremony held at the Capitol. Adams reads an original copy of the Declaration of Independence. He then gives a speech on American freedom and foreign policy.

C

Wherever the standard of freedom and Independence has been or shall be unfurled, there will her [America's] heart, her **benedictions** and her prayers be. But she goes not abroad, in search of monsters to destroy. She is the well-wisher to the freedom and independence of all. . . . [But if the United States involves itself in the affairs of other nations, even those fighting for freedom, the nation would become involved] in all the wars of interest and intrigue, of individual **avarice,** envy, and ambition, which assume the colors and usurp the standard of freedom. The fundamental **maxims** of her policy would insensibly change from *liberty* to *force*. . . . She might become the dictatress [ruler] of the world. She would be no longer the ruler of her own spirit.

DBQ Document-Based Questions

California in 1804

1. What area of California do the Spanish control?
2. Does Shaler think it will take a long time for the Spanish to settle California? Why or why not?

The Explorations of Lewis and Clark

3. Is Lewis looking forward to the exploration? How can you tell?
4. At the start of their expedition, how many boats did Lewis and Clark have?

Adams's Fourth of July Address

5. Was Adams calling for a stronger U.S. role in other countries' affairs? Explain.

Read to Write

6. Imagine the land that was soon to be settled by American pioneers. What would people need in the 1800s to settle and develop the land? What tools would be required? What skills? How would settlers deal with Native Americans who were already living there? Write a list of things that early settlers would need to bring with them, as well as recommendations for what to do once they arrived. CA 8WA2.6

U Universal Access

Visual/Spatial Have students use Lewis's journal entry to create a drawing of what the expedition looked like as it set off from Fort Mandan. EL

C Critical Thinking

Analyzing Primary Sources **Ask:** Why did Adams read the Declaration of Independence before making his speech? *(The occasion is the Fourth of July, the anniversary of that document.)* How is that document related to his words? *(Adams talks about freedom and independence as American ideals.)* OL CA HI3. CA 8LS1.2

ASSESS

Have students answer the Document-Based Questions.

CLOSE

Making Inferences Have students explain how each of these primary sources shows a growing confidence among Americans. OL CA HR4.

DBQ Document-Based Questions

1. The Spanish control the maritime, or coastal regions of California.
2. yes; Shaler believes that the Spanish will have difficulty settling the rest of California because of the Native Americans.
3. Lewis's journal entry indicates that the departure from Fort Mandan was among the happiest moments in his life.
4. 8; six canoes and 2 pirogues.
5. no; he wants the United States to stay uninvolved with other countries.
6. Students' lists might include tools like axes and saws to cut trees; plows and other farming tools for farming; clothing, furniture, and cooking equipment. They might suggest that settlers had to be willing to cooperate with Native Americans.

CHAPTER 6 Assessment

Resources for pages 332–333

Use these resources to review, assess, or reteach the chapter.

- Active Reading Note-Taking Guide, Chapter 6
- Chapter 6 Reading Essentials and Study Guide
- Chapter 6 Tests, Forms A and B
- Standards Assessment, Forms A and B
- California Standards Practice Workbook
- Succeeding on the California History–Social Science Standards CD-ROM
- MindJogger Videoquiz
- Interactive Tutor Self-Assessment CD-ROM

Chapter 6 Assessment

Standard US8.4

Review Content Vocabulary

Define each of the terms below. Use them in a paragraph that discusses government in the early Republic.

1. laissez-faire
2. judicial review

Review the Main Ideas

Section 1 • The Republicans Take Power

3. What was the outcome of the election of 1800?
4. What Federalist measures were ended under Jefferson soon after he took office?

Section 2 • The Louisiana Purchase

5. How far west did U.S. territory extend in 1800?
6. Who sold the Louisiana Territory to the United States? How much did the United States pay for it?
7. How long did Lewis and Clark explore the Louisiana Territory?

Section 3 • Daily Life in Early America

8. What caused the surge of nationalism in the early Republic?
9. What effects did the Second Great Awakening have on American culture?
10. What land-use strategies were practiced by people in the North region?

Critical Thinking

11. **Analyze** Explain the significance of the *Marbury* v. *Madison* decision. Discuss why judicial review is important. CA HI1.
12. **Explore** What was the relationship between the revolt in Santo Domingo and France's interests in North America? How did these events affect U.S. territorial expansion? CA CS1.
13. **Explain** What was the Federalist response to the Louisiana Purchase? What outcomes resulted from this political disagreement? How do you think this might affect future disagreements in the Republic? CA HI3.

Geography Skills

Study the map and answer the questions that follow. CA CS3.

NATIONAL GEOGRAPHIC **Washington, D.C.**

14. **Location** Along what two state borders is Washington, D.C., located?
15. **Location** What city on the map is located approximately 40 miles northeast of Washington, D.C.?

Review Content Vocabulary

1. policy of letting people do as they choose
2. power of Supreme Court to rule that acts of Congress or the executive branch are unconstitutional

Paragraphs will vary but should reflect information in the chapter.

Review the Main Ideas

3. Jefferson and Burr received the same number of the electoral votes, the House had to decide and elected Jefferson.
4. the Alien and Sedition Acts and the Naturalization Act
5. to the Mississippi River
6. Napoleon Bonaparte; $15 million
7. about two and a half years
8. confidence about the new nation and its future
9. gave people determination to improve their lives and society
10. villages and towns surrounded by felled forests on which crops were grown and livestock raised to sell or exchange nearby for needed goods

Critical Thinking

11. It set the precedent that the Constitution is the supreme law of the land; judicial review gives prominence to the Supreme Court to review laws and determine when they conflict with the Constitution.
12. The revolt against French control in Santo Domingo convinced Napoleon to give up the idea of controlling an American empire, which led to the Louisiana Purchase.
13. The Federalists feared that the Louisiana Territory would become Republican, and a Federalist plot developed to secede from the United States. Aaron Burr took part in the effort, which failed. Answers about future effects may suggest that the success of the Louisiana Purchase ended all opposition to such increases in land.

History Online
Self-Check Quiz Visit ca.hss.glencoe.com to prepare for the Chapter 6 test.

Read to Write

16. **The Big Ideas** **Evaluate** Write an essay highlighting the impact of Jefferson's decision to buy the Louisiana Territory. Be sure to include references to politics, geography, trade, and migration. CA 8WS2.4
17. **Narrative Writing** Imagine you were selected to travel with Lewis and Clark. Use the information in this chapter as well as other sources to write letters to your family to describe what you are seeing. CA 8WA2.1
18. **Using Your FOLDABLES** You have been asked to give a speech to a large audience in Washington, D.C. Use the information from your completed chapter opener foldable to write a speech reviewing Jefferson's presidency. CA HR3. CA LS1.0

Using Academic Vocabulary

Synonyms are words that have the same or nearly the same meaning. Choose the synonym that best matches each term's precise meaning.

19. **ensure**
    a. open b. deliver c. guarantee
20. **unique**
    a. ordinary b. huge c. rare
21. **migrate**
    a. travel b. inhabit c. distribute

Reviewing Skills

22. READING SKILL **Compare and Contrast** Review the descriptions of rural life in Section 3. Write an essay describing how people lived off the land in the North, South, and West. Note similarities and differences among the regions. CA HR3.
23. ANALYSIS SKILL **Predict** How would the Louisiana Purchase affect U.S. relationships with Native American cultures? Make three predictions based on what you've learned about their interactions from colonization through 1803. CA HI2.

Standards Practice

Use the map below to answer the following questions.

Election of 1800

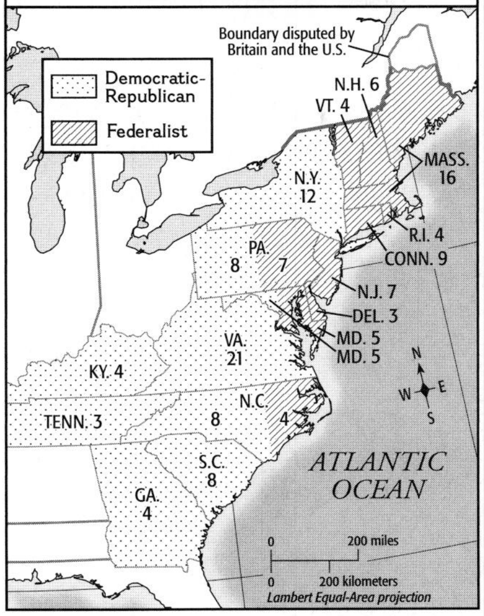

24 Which of the following statements about the election of 1800 is true?

A Federalists won Georgia's electoral votes.
B New Hampshire supported the Democratic-Republican ticket.
C Connecticut had seven electoral votes.
D Pennsylvania was one of the states that split its votes.

25 Which states split their electoral votes between Jefferson and Adams?

A Pennsylvania and Georgia
B Tennessee and New Hampshire
C North Carolina, New York, and Delaware
D Pennsylvania, Maryland, and North Carolina

CHAPTER 6 Assessment

Using Academic Vocabulary

19. c
20. c
21. a

Reviewing Skills

22. READING SKILL Answers will vary but should contrast the mix of farming and village life in the North with cash-crop plantation agriculture in the South and settlement patterns in the West.
23. ANALYSIS SKILL Answers may include the idea that conflict will likely arise.

Standards Practice

24. D
25. D

Bonus Question

Ask: What group made up the largest share of the white population in the South? What group of whites was small in number? *(farmers who worked small plots of land and had no slaves; planters with large plantations and many slaves)* OL

History Online

Have students visit the Web site at ca.hss.glencoe.com to review Chapter 6 and take the **Self-Check Quiz.**

Geography Skills

14. Maryland, Virginia
15. Baltimore

Read to Write

16. **The Big Ideas** Students should cite the decline of the Federalists as a result, the doubling of the nation's size, the fact that movement along the Mississippi River for trade was no longer an issue, and the growing stream of settlers moving to the West after Lewis and Clark's expedition.
17. Letters might include details from Section 2 and the National Geographic Geography & History spread.
18. **Using Your FOLDABLES** Speeches should include information in the chapter about Jefferson's presidency. Encourage students to take a position approving or disapproving Jefferson's actions.

Chapter 7 Planning Guide

SECTION RESOURCES

Main Ideas	Print Materials	Technology Resources
Section 1 **A Time of Conflict** 1. In the early 1800s, the livelihoods of many Americans depended on foreign trade, but a war between Great Britain and France threatened U.S. shipping and trade. 2. President James Madison struggled with trade issues with France and Britain, as well as with tensions between Native Americans and white settlers.	• Reproducible Lesson Plan 7–1* • Daily Lesson and Discussion Notes 7–1 • Active Reading Note-Taking Guide 7–1 • Reading Essentials and Study Guide 7–1 • Guided Reading Activity 7–1 • Section Quiz 7–1	Daily Focus Skills Transparency 7–1 Section Graphic Organizer Transparency 7–1 California Standards Practice Transparencies Interactive Tutor Self-Assessment CD-ROM Exam*View*® Pro Testmaker CD-ROM Presentation Plus! CD-ROM
Section 2 **The War of 1812** 1. In 1812 the United States was at war with Britain and was unprepared from the onset. 2. Even though the last battle of the war, the Battle of New Orleans, took place two weeks after the war had officially ended, the American victory there instilled a strong sense of national pride.	• Reproducible Lesson Plan 7–2* • Daily Lesson and Discussion Notes 7–2 • Active Reading Note-Taking Guide 7–2 • Reading Essentials and Study Guide 7–2 • Guided Reading Activity 7–2 • Section Quiz 7–2	Daily Focus Skills Transparency 7–2 Section Graphic Organizer Transparency 7–2 California Standards Practice Transparencies Interactive Tutor Self-Assessment CD-ROM Exam*View*® Pro Testmaker CD-ROM Presentation Plus! CD-ROM
Section 3 **Foreign Relations** 1. After the War of 1812, a new spirit of nationalism took hold in American society. 2. In 1823, the United States proclaimed its dominant role in the Americas with the Monroe Doctrine.	• Reproducible Lesson Plan 7–3* • Daily Lesson and Discussion Notes 7–3 • Active Reading Note-Taking Guide 7–3 • Reading Essentials and Study Guide 7–3 • Guided Reading Activity 7–3 • Section Quiz 7–3	Daily Focus Skills Transparency 7–3 Section Graphic Organizer Transparency 7–3 California Standards Practice Transparencies Interactive Tutor Self-Assessment CD-ROM Exam*View*® Pro Testmaker CD-ROM Presentation Plus! CD-ROM Vocabulary PuzzleMaker CD-ROM

PACING YOUR LESSONS

Chapter Introduction	Section 1	Section 2	Section 3	Chapter Assessment	Unit Wrap-Up
$\frac{1}{2}$ Day	3 Days	2 Days	2 Days	$\frac{1}{2}$ Day	$\frac{1}{2}$ Day

0:00 **OUT OF TIME?** Assign the Chapter 7 ***Reading Essentials and Study Guide***

*Available on TeacherWorks™

Standards-Based Lesson Plan

History–Social Science Standards Covered in Chapter 7

The standards covered in the chapter are listed below. Use the accompanying activity as you teach the chapter to ensure student mastery of these standards. This activity can be used in combination with the program's print and technology assessment materials.

Standard	Section 1	Section 2	Section 3
US8.5 Students analyze U.S. foreign policy in the early Republic.	✔	✔	✔
US8.5.1 Understand the political and economic causes and consequences of the War of 1812 and know the major battles, leaders, and events that led to a final peace.	✔	✔	✔
US8.5.2 Know the changing boundaries of the United States and describe the relationships the country had with its neighbors (current Mexico and Canada) and Europe, including the influence of the Monroe Doctrine, and how those relationships influenced westward expansion and the Mexican-American War.			✔
US8.5.3 Outline the major treaties with American Indian nations during the administrations of the first four presidents and the varying outcomes of those treaties.	✔		

Cumulative Standards-Assessment Activity

The Cumulative Standards-Assessment Activity will help students organize and learn the important information from the chapter. Begin teaching the chapter with this activity, and have students complete it as they read the chapter.

Creating a Chart for Questioning

Purpose Questioning is a skill that can be used to monitor comprehension as students work their way through a text. By asking themselves questions on a particular section, answering the questions, and checking the answers, they can make sure that they are absorbing the material and are ready to move on to the next segment of text.

Introduction to Categorizing Information

1. Model the skill by directing students to any page of the previous chapter that is full of text. Have the students read the section and, while they do so, write a question on the board aimed at a key concept. After students have completed their reading, ask volunteers to answer the question. Then have students check the answers against the text to see if they are correct.
2. Ask students to copy this chart into their notebooks:

   Question: ____________________

   Answer: ____________________

   ☐ Correct ☐ Incorrect

   Correction: ____________________

   As students read each section, have them use the format to ask questions and answer them. Remind them to check the questions and answers against the text to ensure that they are correct. Instruct them that if they find an answer that is not correct they should use the Correction line to fix the problem. Remind students that their questions should focus on key concepts in the text, not less important material.
3. As you review the chapter, ask volunteers to share their questions, and discuss which ones successfully identified key concepts. Encourage them to use their questions as study aids.

Chapter 7 Resources

READING SUPPORT

- Content Vocabulary Activity 7
- Academic Vocabulary Activity 7
- Reading Skills Activity 7
- American Literature Reading 7
- Biography Activities 7A, 7B
- Chapter 7 Active Reading Note-Taking Guide
- Chapter 7 Guided Reading Activities
- Chapter 7 Reading Essentials and Study Guide
- Glencoe Literature Library
- Glencoe Video Program
- Vocabulary PuzzleMaker CD-ROM
- Interactive Graphic Organizers CD-ROM
- American History Primary Source Document Library CD-ROM

CRITICAL THINKING

- Critical Thinking Skills Activity 7
- Primary Source Reading 7
- Cause-and-Effect Transparency 7 Strategy and Activity
- Presentation Plus! CD-ROM

UNIVERSAL ACCESS

- Universal Access Activity 7
- Then and Now Transparencies 7A–7B, Strategy and Activity
- Graphic Novel Activity 7
- School-to-Home Connection Activities 7A–7D
- English Learner Handbook Chapter 7 Activities
- Universal Access for the American History Classroom
- American Art and Architecture Transparencies, Strategies, and Activities
- American Art Prints
- American Music Cultural Traditions
- American Music Hits Through History
- StudentWorks Plus CD-ROM

SKILL PRACTICE

- Map Overlay Transparency 7, Strategy, and Activity
- Analysis Skills Activity 7
- Time Line Activity 7
- Geography and History Activity 7
- Economics and History Activity 7
- Chart, Graph, and Map Skills Activity 7
- Political Cartoon Activity 7
- Supreme Court Case Study 7
- In-Text Map Transparency 7, Strategy, and Activity
- Step Into American History Activity 7
- Citizenship and Service Learning Activity 7
- Outline Map Resource Book
- MindJogger Plus Videoquiz

WRITING SUPPORT

- Writing Activity 7
- Language Arts Activity 7
- Writer's Guidebook
- Middle School Writing Process Transparencies

ASSESSMENT

GLENCOE'S ASSESSMENT ADVANTAGE

- Chapter 7 Section Quizzes
- Chapter 7 Tests, Forms A and B
- California Standards Assessment, Forms A and B
- Cumulative Assessment Activity US8.5
- California Standards Practice Workbook
- Succeeding on the California History–Social Science Standards CD-ROM
- Exam*View*® Pro Testmaker CD-ROM
- Interactive Tutor Self-Assessment CD-ROM

CD-ROM
DVD
Print Material
Poster
Transparency
Music Program
Videocassette
Glencoe Literature Library

Chapter 7 Resources

TECHNOLOGY

- StudentWorks Plus CD-ROM
- TeacherWorks Plus CD-ROM
- Exam*View*® Pro Testmaker CD-ROM
- Interactive Tutor Self-Assessment CD-ROM
- Presentation Plus! CD-ROM
- Succeeding on the California History–Social Science Standards CD-ROM
- Vocabulary PuzzleMaker CD-ROM
- Interactive Graphic Organizers CD-ROM
- Interactive Time Line CD-ROM
- American History Primary Source Document Library CD-ROM
- MindJogger Plus Videoquiz
- American Music Cultural Traditions
- American Music Hits Through History
- Glencoe Video Program
- Professional Development in Middle School Social Studies Series
- Teaching American History With *Discovering Our Past: The American Journey to World War I*

SPANISH RESOURCES

- Spanish Activities and Assessment
  - Spanish Content Vocabulary Activities
  - Spanish Guided Reading Activities
  - Spanish Quizzes and Tests
  - Spanish California Standards Assessment
- Spanish Reading Essentials and Study Guide
- Spanish School-to-Home Connection
- Spanish Declaration of Independence and U.S. Constitution

TRANSPARENCIES

- California Standards Practice Transparencies
- Daily Focus Skills Transparencies
- Section Graphic Organizer Transparencies
- In-Text Map Transparencies
- Map Overlay Transparencies
- Cause-and-Effect Transparencies
- Then and Now Transparencies
- American Art and Architecture Transparencies
- Middle School Writing Process Transparencies

TEACHER PLANNING

- Daily Lesson and Discussion Notes
- English Learner Handbook
- Guide to Daily Intervention
- *Discovering Our Past: The American Journey to World War I* Reading and Study Skills Foldables
- Reading Strategies and Activities for the Social Studies Classroom
- Chapter 7 Reproducible Lesson Plans (correlated to California History–Social Science Standards)
- Universal Access for the American History Classroom
- NGS U.S. Desk Map
- NGS U.S. Atlas

PROFESSIONAL DEVELOPMENT

- Building Academic Vocabulary
- Strategies for Success
- Research-Based Strategies Used to Develop *Discovering Our Past: The American Journey to World War I*
- Character Education in the Middle School Classroom
- The Living Constitution
- Professional Development in Middle School Social Studies Video Series
- Teaching American History With *Discovering Our Past: The American Journey to World War I*

MASTERING THE STANDARDS

The content and assessment in the Student Edition, Teacher Wraparound Edition, teacher planning materials, and the print and technology products are all standards-based. The use of these products during instruction leads to mastery of the standards.

PRACTICE

- California Standards Practice Workbook
- California Standards Practice Transparencies
- Interactive Time Line CD-ROM
- School-to-Home Connection

BENCHMARK ASSESSMENT

- California Standards Assessment
- Exam*View*® Pro Testmaker CD-ROM
- Succeeding on the California History–Social Science Standards CD-ROM

REMEDIATION

- California Guide to Daily Intervention
- Interactive Tutor Self-Assessment CD-ROM
- Exam*View*® Pro Testmaker CD-ROM
- California Standards Practice Workbook
- Reading Essentials and Study Guide

Additional Resources

NATIONAL GEOGRAPHIC TEACHER'S CORNER

Index to National Geographic Magazine:

The following articles relate to this chapter:

- "The Way West," by John G. Mitchell, September 2000.
- "The Peales: America's First Family of Art," by Otto Friedrich, December 1990.
- "Thomas Jefferson: Architect of Freedom," by Mike Edwards, February 1976.

National Geographic Society Products

To order the following, call National Geographic at 1-800-368-2728

- *GeoKit: Westward Movement* (Kit)
- *United States/Territorial Growth* (Map)
- *National Geographic Desk Reference* (Book)

NGS ONLINE

Access National Geographics' new dynamic MapMachine Web site and other geography resources at:

www.nationalgeographic.com

www.nationalgeographic.com/maps

A&E Home Video · Biography · The History Channel

The following videotape programs are available from Glencoe as supplements to Chapter 7.

- **The Best of the Real West (five video set) (ISBN 1-56501-352-2)**
- **Tecumseh: The Dream of a Confederacy (ISBN 1-56501-1247-X)**

To order, call Glencoe at 1-800-334-7344. To find classroom resources to accompany many of these videos, check the following home pages:

A&E Television: www.aetv.com
The History Channel: www.historychannel.com

History Online

Use our Web site for additional resources. All essential content is covered in the Student Edition.

You and your students can visit ca.hss.glencoe.com, the Web site companion to *Discovering Our Past: The American Journey to World War I.* This innovative integration of electronic and print media offers your students a wealth of opportunities. The student text directs students to the Web site for the following options:

- Chapter Overviews
- Self-Check Quizzes
- Study Central™
- Student Web Activities
- Textbook Updates
- Multi-Language Glossaries

Answers to the student Web activities are provided for you in the Web Activity Lesson Plans. Additional Web resources and ePuzzles and games are also available.

FOLDABLES™ Study Organizer

Dinah Zike's Foldables

Foldables are three-dimensional, interactive graphic organizers that help students practice basic writing skills, review key vocabulary terms, and identify main ideas. Every chapter contains a foldable activity, with additional chapter activities found in the Reading and Study Skills Foldables booklet.

Chapter 7 Resources

Reading List Generator CD-ROM

GLENCOE **BOOKLINK**

The Glencoe BookLink CD-ROM is a database that allows you to search more than 15,000 titles to create a customized reading list for your students.

- Reading lists can be organized by students' reading level, author, genre, theme, or area of interest.
- The database provides Degrees of Reading Power™ (DRP) and Lexile™ readability scores for all selections.
- A brief summary of each selection is included.

Reading level suggestions for this chapter:

For students at a Grade 6 reading level:
- ***Simon Bolivar: Latin American Liberator,*** by Frank De Varona

For students at a Grade 7 reading level:
- ***The Great Little Madison,*** by Jean Fritz

For students at a Grade 8 reading level:
- ***James Monroe: 5th President of the United States,*** by Rebecca Stefoff

Reading Support From JAMESTOWN EDUCATION

- *Timed Readings Plus in Social Studies* helps students increase their reading rate and fluency while maintaining comprehension. The 400-word passages are similar to those found on state and national assessments.
- *Reading in the Content Area: Social Studies* concentrates on six essential reading skills that help students better comprehend what they read. The book includes 754 high-interest nonfiction passages written at increasing levels of difficulty.
- *Reading Fluency* helps students read smoothly, accurately, and expressively.
- *Jamestown's Reading Improvement,* by renowned reading expert Edward Fry, focuses on helping build your students' comprehension, vocabulary, and skimming and scanning skills.
- *Critical Reading Series* provides high-interest books, each written at three reading levels.

To order these products, call Glencoe at 1-800-334-7344.

KEY for Using the Teacher Wraparound Edition

Use this key to help you identify the different types of prompts found in the Teacher Wraparound Edition.

R **Reading Strategies** activities help you teach reading skills and vocabulary.

C **Critical Thinking** strategies help students apply and extend what they have learned.

U **Universal Access** activities provide differentiated instruction for students learning to speak English, along with suggestions for teaching various types of learners.

S **Skill Practice** strategies help students practice historical analysis and geography skills.

W **Writing Support** activities provide writing opportunities to help students comprehend the text.

Teaching strategies and activities have been coded for ability level appropriateness.

AL Activities for students working above grade level
OL Activities for students working on grade level
BL Activities for students working below grade level
EL Activities for English Learners

FOCUS

History–Social Science Standards

In this chapter, the following standard is covered:

US8.5 Students analyze U.S. foreign policy in the early Republic.

More About the Photo

Fort Niagara, located on the southern shore of Lake Ontario, was originally constructed by France in 1726. The fort was captured by the British during the French and Indian War, and later turned over to the United States by Jay's Treaty. Fort Niagara remained a U.S. military post until 1946. Today it is a New York state park.

TEACH

The Big Ideas

As you begin teaching each section, use these questions and activities to focus on the Big Ideas.

Chapter 7

Foreign Affairs in the Early Republic

Fort Niagara in New York ▶

NATIONAL GEOGRAPHIC **Where & When?**

1810 — 1820 — 1830

1812 War with Great Britain begins

1814 The British burn Washington, D.C.

1823 Monroe Doctrine is issued

Section 1

A Time of Conflict

Essential Question: How might relationships with other countries influence a country's economy? *(Students' answers will vary, but may include problems with foreign trade; getting the necessary goods and services; and incurring debt.)* Tell students that in this section they will learn about U.S. trade around the world. OL

Section 2

The War of 1812

Essential Question: How would a country's victory in a war influence the feelings and actions of its citizens? *(happiness; feeling of pride in the country)* Ask students to look for signs of Americans' reaction to the War of 1812 as they read this section. BL

History Online
Chapter Overview Visit ca.hss.glencoe.com for a preview of Chapter 7.

The Big Ideas

Section 1 A Time of Conflict

Political ideas and major events shape how people form governments. As the United States expanded its trade around the world, it faced a number of foreign challenges.

Section 2 The War of 1812

Political ideas and major events shape how people form governments. Although the United States gained no territory from its victory in the War of 1812, American self-confidence increased greatly.

Section 3 Foreign Relations

Political ideas and major events shape how people form governments. The wave of nationalism in Congress and among the American people influenced the nation's foreign affairs.

View the Chapter 7 video in the Glencoe Video Program.

FOLDABLES™ Study Organizer

Identifying Make this foldable to help you identify and learn key terms.

Step 1 Stack four sheets of paper, one on top of the other. On the top sheet of paper, draw a large circle.

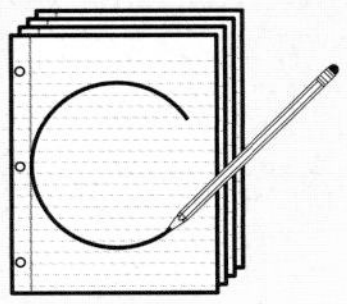

Step 2 With the papers still stacked, cut out all four circles at the same time.

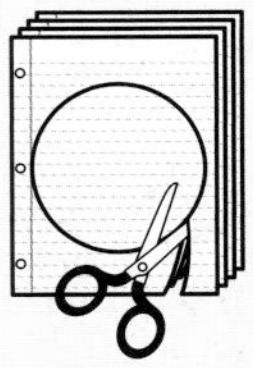

Step 3 Staple the paper circles together at one point around the edge.

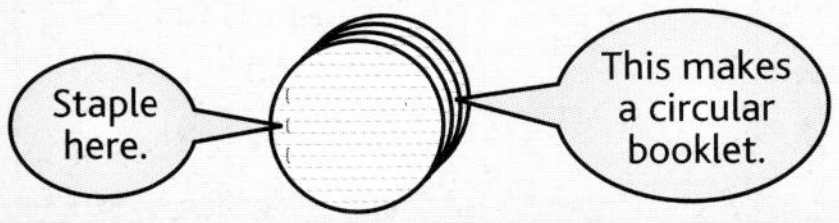

Step 4 Label the front circle as shown and take notes on the pages that open to the right.

Reading and Writing As you read the chapter, write the Content Vocabulary terms for each section in your foldable. Write a definition for each term. Then turn your foldable over (upside down) and write a short sentence using each term on the other side of the pages.

INTRODUCING CHAPTER 7

Section 3 Foreign Relations

Essential Question: What techniques might a country use to settle differences with other countries? *(Answers may include compromise, agreements, doing favors for others.)* Have students look for evidence of these same techniques in the relations between the United States and other countries after the War of 1812. OL

History Online

Go to ca.hss.glencoe.com for student activities, lesson plans, and links to additional Web resources about the Federalist era.

FOLDABLES™ Study Organizer Dinah Zike's Foldables

Purpose Have students use their foldables to identify and record vocabulary terms. Students should use their foldables as they prepare to answer the section and chapter review questions. BL

Why It's Important

Identifying Cause and Effect Spotting causes and effects is a vital skill for understanding history. Events do not happen randomly but as the result of trends, ideas, or actions that develop over time. Grasping the connections between events helps deepen the understanding of history. Point out that historical movements and events typically have more than one cause, and that their results can themselves become causes for later events.

1 Learn It!

Tell students that some words such as *because* and *as a result* are clear signs that the text is identifying causes and effects. **Ask:** What are some other signal words? *(since, consequently, thus)* Often, though, students will have to use context to identify causes and effects. **Ask:** How can you tell that the two sentences about the actions of Britain and France are describing effects? *(The sentences directly follow a statement that the countries adopted a new strategy, so they must be describing the impact of the strategy.)* OL

Chapter 7 Get Ready to Read

READING SKILL

Identifying Cause and Effect

1 Learn It!

Learning to identify causes and effects helps you understand how and why things happen in history. A *cause* is any person, event, or condition that makes something happen. What happens as a result is the *effect*. Use graphic organizers to help you sort and understand causes and effects in your reading. Read the following passage, and see how the information can be sorted.

CAUSE

The warring nations enforced a new strategy.

> For two years, American shipping continued to prosper. By 1805, however, the warring nations enforced a new strategy. Britain blockaded the French coast and threatened to search all ships trading with France. France later announced that it would search and seize ships caught trading with Britain.
>
> —*from page 339*

EFFECTS

Britain blockaded the French coast, threatening to search all ships.

France announced it will search and seize all ships trading with Britain.

Reading Tip

To help you make sense of what you read, create different types of graphic organizers that suit your own learning style.

READING STRATEGY **SEQUENCING INFORMATION**

Remind students that sequencing information correctly can be a helpful step when trying to identify causes and effects. Create a flow chart on the board by drawing a row of boxes connected by arrows pointing in the same direction. Explain that a flow chart shows the sequence of events or the order in which they occurred. Then model how to use the chart. As you read aloud "Baltimore Holds Firm" in Section 2, have students raise their hand when an event is mentioned that should be placed in the flow chart and identify where in the chart it should go. Ask a volunteer to add it to the chart. When the chart is complete, have students write a statement identifying a cause and its effects. *(Baltimore's defenders were ready. As a result, British attack was blocked and subsequent bombardment led to the writing of "The Star-Spangled Banner.")* OL CA HI2.

2 Practice It!

History is often a chain of causes and effects. The result, or effect, of one event can also be the cause of another effect. Read the passage called "Frontier Conflicts" from Section 1 on page 341. Then use the graphic organizer below, or create your own to show the chain of causes and effects explained in the passage.

CAUSE → EFFECT

CAUSE → EFFECT

CAUSE → EFFECT

CAUSE → EFFECT

CAUSE → EFFECT

Read to Write

Choose a major event from the chapter. Then write a brief paragraph explaining what caused this event.

▼ American merchant ships

3 Apply It!

Identify causes and effects in the War of 1812 as you read the chapter. Find at least five causes and their effects, and create a graphic organizer to record them.

Chapter 7 Get Ready to Read

2 Practice It!

Remind students that they already have some experience with this skill. **Ask:** What were the causes of the American Revolution? *(Americans' growing feelings of distance from Britain; ideas of Enlightenment about natural rights and self-government; protests over British taxation and anger over harsh British response to those protests)* What were the effects? *(American independence; formation of new American government)* **OL**

3 Apply It!

Have students find a passage from a book, magazine, or newspaper article, read it, and identify the causes and effects described in the piece. Ask students to share their findings with the class, and discuss what signal words and context clues they used to identify the causes and effects in their passage. **AL**

Reading Strategy — Categorizing Information

Explain that events can have effects immediately after they take place. These are called short-term effects. Those effects that occur much later or continue to shape the lives of a group of people much later are called long-term effects. Help students see the difference between short-term and long-term effects by having them consider the events in the preceding chapter. **Ask:** What happened as a result of the presidential election of 1800? *(Jefferson became president.)* What change to America's geography happened as a result and still affects the country today? *(the Louisiana Purchase)* **OL** **CA HI2.**

Use Reading Skills Activity 7 in the **Chapter 7 Resource Book** for more practice with identifying cause and effect.

FOCUS

BELLRINGER
SKILLBUILDER ACTIVITY

Project **Daily Focus Skills Transparency 7–1** and have students answer the question.

Guide to Reading

Preteaching Vocabulary:
Use the **Vocabulary PuzzleMaker CD-ROM** to create crossword and word search puzzles.

Answers to Graphic:
Negotiations lead to agreement to end conflict; U.S. passes Embargo Act; Harrison defeated confederation at Tippecanoe

Unpacking the Standards

After reading the section, students will be able to:

- Outline the conflict with the Barbary Coast states.
- Discuss how tensions with Great Britain and France threatened the nation with war.
- Describe the conflict with Native Americans on the frontier and how it led to clashes.

Section 1
A Time of Conflict

History Social Science Standards

US8.5 Students analyze U.S. foreign policy in the early Republic.

Guide to Reading

Looking Back, Looking Ahead
As the United States began to take a stronger role in world affairs, the new nation faced challenges.

Focusing on the Main Ideas
- In the early 1800s, the livelihoods of many Americans depended on foreign trade, but a war between Great Britain and France threatened U.S. shipping and trade. ***(page 339)***
- President James Madison struggled with trade issues with France and Britain, as well as with tensions between Native Americans and white settlers. ***(page 341)***

Meeting People
Stephen Decatur (dih • KAY • tuhr)
Tecumseh (tuh • KUHM • suh)
The Prophet
William Henry Harrison
Henry Clay
John Calhoun (kahl • HOON)

Locating Places
Barbary Coast states
Virginia
Ohio

Content Vocabulary
tribute (TRIH • byoot)
neutral rights
impressment
embargo (ihm • BAHR • goh)
War Hawks
nationalism

Academic Vocabulary
resolve
guarantee (GAR • uhn • TEE)
strategy
conclude

Reading Strategy
Classifying Information As you read the section, re-create the diagram below and describe in the box the actions the United States took in each of these situations.

U.S. actions	
	Demand for tribute
	Attack on *Chesapeake*
	Tecumseh's confederation

NATIONAL GEOGRAPHIC Where & When?

1804 — 1808 — 1812

1804 Barbary pirates seize the U.S. warship *Philadelphia*

1807 The British navy attacks the American vessel *Chesapeake*

1811 Harrison defeats the Prophet at Tippecanoe

1812 Madison asks Congress to declare war on Britain

SECTION RESOURCES

Print Material
- Reproducible Lesson Plan 7–1*
- Daily Lesson and Discussion Notes 7–1
- Guided Reading Activity 7–1
- Reading Essentials and Study Guide 7–1
- Active Reading Note-Taking Guide 7–1
- Section Quiz 7–1

Transparencies
- Daily Focus Skills Transparency 7–1
- Section Graphic Organizer Transparency 7–1
- California Standards Practice Transparencies

Technology
- Interactive Tutor Self-Assessment CD-ROM
- Exam*View*® Pro Testmaker CD-ROM
- Presentation Plus! CD-ROM

*Available on TeacherWorks™

Freedom of the Seas

Main Idea **In the early 1800s, the livelihoods of many Americans depended on foreign trade, but a war between Great Britain and France threatened U.S. shipping and trade.**

Reading Connection Have you ever traveled by boat? If so, describe the experience. Read to learn what sailors on American merchant ships experienced in foreign seas.

An American Story

By the late 1700s, America faced challenges to its growing trade. In an address to Congress, President Thomas Jefferson described a problem with a country that was raiding American ships, as well as his response to that country.

> **"Tripoli, the least considerable of the Barbary States, had come forward with demands unfounded. . . . The . . . demand admitted but one answer. I sent a small squadron of frigates [warships] into the Mediterranean."**
>
> —Thomas Jefferson, "First Annual Message to Congress, 1801"

U **Barbary Pirates** Sailing in foreign seas was dangerous. In the Mediterranean, for example, ships had to be on guard for pirates from Tripoli and the other **Barbary Coast states** of North Africa. For years these Barbary pirates had raided ships in the area. They demanded **tribute** (TRIH • byoot), or protection money, from European governments to let their ships pass safely.

C In 1804 the pirates seized the U.S. warship *Philadelphia* and towed it into Tripoli Harbor. They threw the captain and crew into jail. **Stephen Decatur** (dih • KAY • tuhr), a 25-year-old U.S. Navy captain, took action. Slipping into the heavily guarded harbor with a small raiding party, Decatur burned the captured ship to prevent the pirates from using it. A British admiral praised the deed as the "most bold and daring act of the age." Negotiations finally ended the conflict with Tripoli in June 1805. Tripoli agreed to stop demanding tribute, but the United States had to pay a ransom of $60,000 for the release of the American prisoners. R1

Although the United States had resolved the threat from the Barbary pirates, Americans faced other challenges on the seas. U.S. foreign trade depended on being able to sail the seas freely. By the time Jefferson won reelection in 1804, two powerful European nations were already involved in a war that threatened to interfere with American trade.

Neutral Rights Violated When Britain and France went to war in 1803, America enjoyed a profitable trade with both countries. As long as the United States remained neutral during the war, shippers could continue doing business. A nation not involved in a conflict had **neutral rights**—the right to sail the seas and not take sides. R2

For two years, American shipping continued to prosper. By 1805 however, the warring nations enforced a new strategy. Britain blockaded the French coast and threatened to search all ships trading with France. France later announced that it would search and seize ships caught trading with Britain.

American Sailors Kidnapped The British needed sailors for their naval war against France. Conditions in the British Royal Navy were terrible. British sailors were poorly paid and fed, and badly treated. Many of them deserted, or ran away. Desperately in need of sailors, the British often used force to get them. British naval patrols claimed the right to stop American ships at sea and search for any sailors on board suspected of being deserters from the British navy.

The British would force sailors on these ships to serve in the British navy. This practice was called **impressment.** Although some of those taken were deserters from the British navy, thousands of native-born and naturalized American citizens were also impressed. R3

Did You Know?

The war between Britain and France that raged for most of this period is known as the Napoleonic War. The French dictator Napoleon Bonaparte fought and defeated most of the other countries in Europe. However, he never attained his goal of invading Britain and conquering that island nation. In 1815, Napoleon was finally defeated by a coalition of Britain, Prussia, Austria, and Russia.

TEACH

U Universal Access

Visual/Spatial Explain that the Barbary Coast was the part of North Africa from Egypt west to modern Morocco. Have students locate the region on a world map. Then have them identify a major problem the United States would have in fighting the pirates. *(Since the area is thousands of miles away, sailing ships would have needed weeks to reach it.)* OL CA CS3.

C Critical Thinking

Identifying Central Issues Have students compose headlines for Stephen Decatur's raid or other major events described in this section. BL CA 7WA2.5

R1 Reading Strategy

Scaffolding—Academic Vocabulary Students were introduced to the word *conflict* in Chapter 6, Section 3. Ask students to list synonyms for the word. OL

R2 Reading Strategy

Understanding Vocabulary Ask students to define *neutral.* *(not taking sides)* Then have them use the word to explain why referees or umpires should be neutral when officiating athletic contests. OL CA 8RW1.3

R3 Reading Strategy

Activating Prior Knowledge Remind students that they learned about the problem of *impressment* of American sailors in Chapter 5. **Ask:** Which country carried out this action during Washington's presidency? *(Britain)* OL

R Reading Strategy

Understanding Vocabulary The word *embargo* comes from the Spanish, meaning "to barricade or impede." Ask students to think of other English words that have come from Spanish. *(fiesta, bronco, mosquito, patio)* OL

C Critical Thinking

Determining Cause and Effect Ask students to create a graphic that shows the effects of the embargo. Remind them that a cause, such as the embargo, can have several effects. *(Students should show two effects: severe damage to American commerce; more British trade with Latin America.)* OL CA HI2.

Reading Check

Answer: ineffective, because American trade with other countries was wiped out and Britain traded with South America for agricultural products it needed; probably not, because other countries would trade with the embargoed country

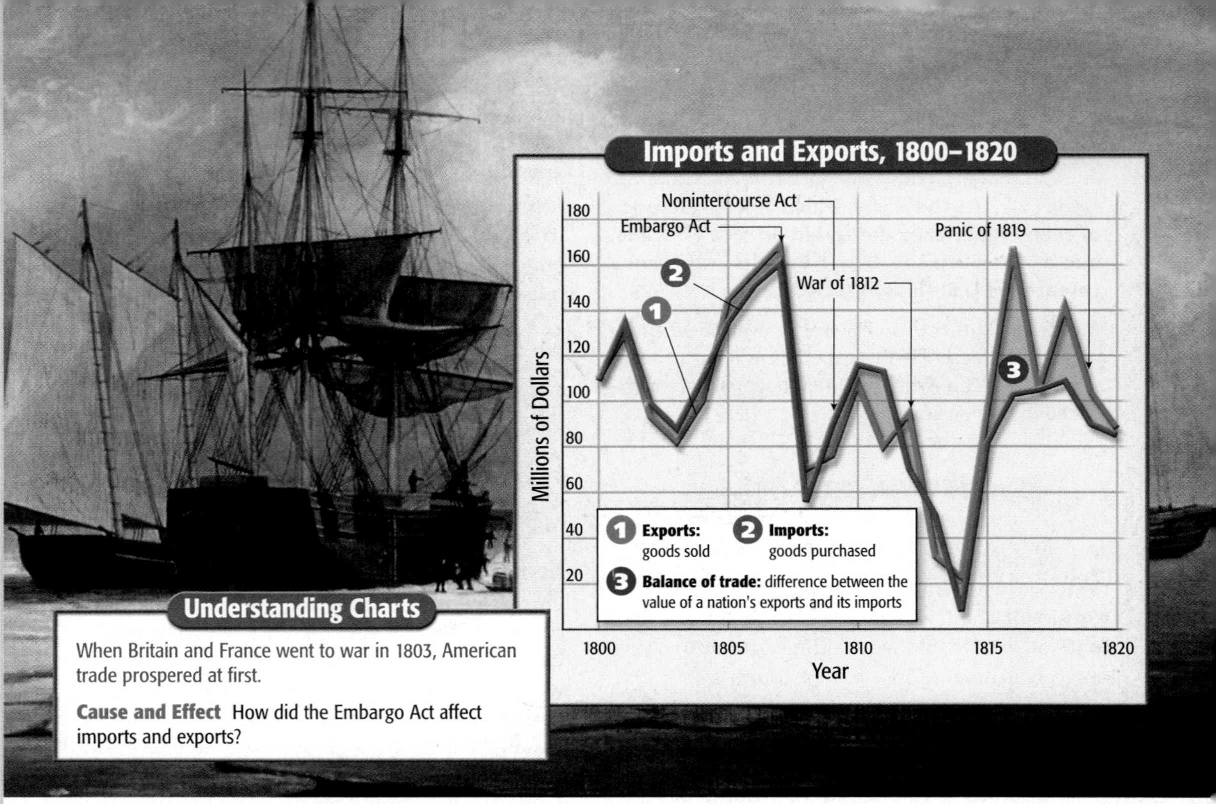

Understanding Charts

When Britain and France went to war in 1803, American trade prospered at first.

Cause and Effect How did the Embargo Act affect imports and exports?

Often the British would wait for American ships outside an American harbor. This happened in June 1807 off the coast of **Virginia.** A British warship, the *Leopard,* intercepted the American vessel *Chesapeake,* and the British demanded to search the ship for British deserters. When the *Chesapeake's* captain refused, the British opened fire, killing 3 and wounding 18.

A Disastrous Trade Ban Britain's practice of impressment and its violation of America's neutral rights led Jefferson to stop some trade with Britain. The attack on the *Chesapeake* triggered even stronger measures. In December 1807, the Republican Congress passed the Embargo Act. An **embargo** (ihm • BAHR • goh) prohibits trade with another country. The embargo banned imports from and exports to all foreign countries. R

With the embargo, Jefferson and Madison hoped to hurt Britain but avoid war. They believed the British depended on American agricultural products. As it turned out, the embargo of 1807 was a disaster. The measure wiped out American trade with other nations. Worse, it proved ineffective against Britain. The British simply traded with Latin America for its agricultural goods. C

Jefferson Leaves Office Following Washington's precedent, Jefferson made it clear in mid-1808 that he would not be a candidate for a third term. With Jefferson's approval, the Republicans chose James Madison as their candidate for president.

The Federalists again nominated Charles Pinckney and hoped that anger over the embargo would help their party. Pinckney won most of New England, but the Federalist party had little support in other regions. Madison won with 122 electoral votes to Pinckney's 47 votes.

Reading Check **Evaluate** How effective was the Embargo Act? Would such an act work today?

Answers and Additional Support

Understanding Charts

1. Both imports and exports significantly decreased.

Resources for page 340

- Economics and History Activity 7
- Primary Source Reading 7
- Biography Activity 7A

US8.5.1 Understand the political and economic causes and consequences of the War of 1812 and know the major battles, leaders, and events that led to a final peace. US8.5.3 Outline the major treaties with American Indian nations during the administrations of the first four presidents and the varying outcomes of those treaties.

War Fever

Main Idea **President James Madison struggled with trade issues with France and Britain, as well as with tensions between Native Americans and white settlers.**

Reading Connection Why does tension between different groups occur? Think about this as you read about the conflicts among the various groups in this section.

R James Madison became president during a difficult time. At home and abroad, the nation was involved in the embargo crisis. Meanwhile, Britain continued to claim the right to halt American ships, and cries for war with Britain grew stronger.

Closer to War In 1810 Congress passed a law permitting direct trade with either France or Britain, depending on which country first lifted its trade restrictions against America. France's leader Napoleon Bonaparte seized the opportunity and promised to end France's trade restrictions.

Unfortunately for Madison, Napoleon had tricked the American administration. The French continued to seize American ships. Americans were deeply divided. To some it seemed as if the nation was on the verge of war—but it was hard to decide if the enemy should be Britain or France. Madison knew that France had tricked him, but he continued to see Britain as the bigger threat to the United States.

Frontier Conflicts While Madison was trying to decide how to **resolve** the difficulties with European powers, news arrived about problems in the West. **Ohio** had become a state in 1803. Between 1801 and 1810, white settlers continued to press for more land in the Ohio Valley. Now the settlers were moving onto lands that had been **guaranteed** to Native Americans by treaty.

As tensions increased, some Native Americans began renewing their contacts with British agents and fur traders in Canada. Others pursued a new **strategy.** A powerful Shawnee chief named **Tecumseh** (tuh • KUHM • suh) built a confederacy, or union, among Native American nations in the Northwest. Tecumseh believed that a strong confederacy—with the backing of the British in Canada—could put a halt to white movement onto Native American lands. Many Native Americans were ready to follow Tecumseh.

NATIONAL GEOGRAPHIC Territorial Growth 1800–1810

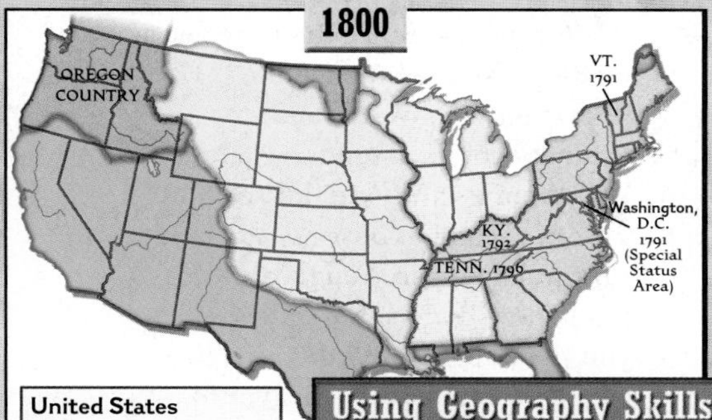

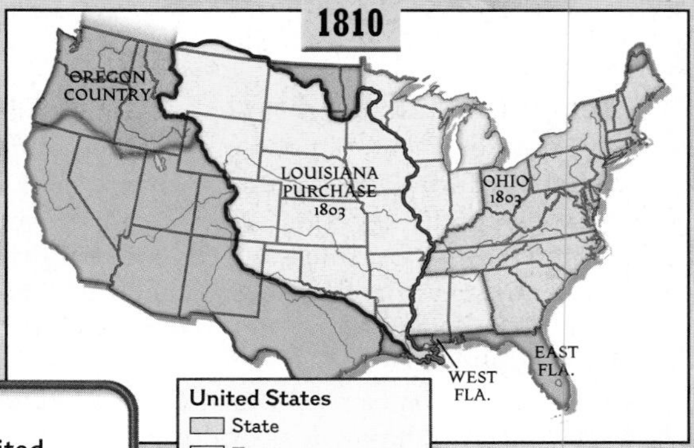

Using Geography Skills

Between 1790 and 1810, the United States doubled its size.

1. **Place** When did Ohio become part of the United States?
2. **Region** Describe the changes in French territory between 1800 and 1810.

Using Geography Skills

Answers:

1. 1803
2. France owned the vast Louisiana Territory in 1800. With its sale to the United States in 1803, France no longer owned any territory in the present-day United States.

Did You Know?

Tecumseh is the English version of the Shawnee name *Tek-am-thi*, which means "Panther Passing Across." Tecumseh's father chose this name because, at the moment his son was born, a shooting star of great brightness passed overhead. According to Shawnee legend, shooting stars were panthers looking for a cave in which to sleep.

R Reading Strategy

Activating Prior Knowledge Ask students what they already know about James Madison. *(Students should recall his key role in creating the U.S. Constitution and in the Washington administration, covered in Chapters 4 and 5.)* BL

Review The Big Idea

Review the Big Idea for this section: "Political ideas and major events shape how people form governments." **Ask:** Which of the challenges that the United States faced in this period do you feel was the most serious? Why? *(Students should choose either the trade conflicts with France and Britain or the conflict on the frontier with Tecumseh's confederacy. Students should support their choice with reasons from the text.)* OL CA HI1.

Review Grade 5 Standards

To review standard **5.3.4** *(Discuss the role of broken treaties and massacres and the factors that led to the Indians' defeat, including the resistance of Indian nations to encroachments and assimilation (e.g., the story of the Trail of Tears))*, **ask:** Was the settlers' takeover of Native American lands in the Northwest inevitable? Why or why not? *(Students may say it was inevitable because a growing population would always need more land since most people lived by farming.)* OL

W1 Writing Support

Summary Writing Ask students to summarize in one paragraph the information in this section about the relations between the Native Americans and white settlers on the western frontier. Then have students exchange paragraphs with a partner and check them for completeness and accuracy. **BL** CA 8RC2.4

U Universal Access

Intrapersonal Have students write an imaginary dialogue between Tecumseh and the Prophet. Ask them to consider how each man felt about the challenges facing the Native American people and how they should respond. **AL** CA 8WA2.1

W2 Writing Support

Persuasive Writing Have students write memos to President Madison on what he should do about the problems on the frontier and Canadian border. Students should address the conflicts with the British and the Native Americans and support their suggestions with reasons. **AL** CA 8WS2.4

Primary Sources

Tecumseh's Prediction

When William Henry Harrison was serving as governor of Indiana, he told Tecumseh that only the president had the authority to return disputed lands to the Native Americans. Tecumseh replied:

> "As the great chief [President Madison] is to determine the matter, . . . I hope the Great Spirit will put sense enough into his head to induce [make] him to direct you to give up this land. It is true he is so far off he will not be injured by the war . . . while you and I will have to fight it out."
>
> —quoted in *The Old Northwest: A Chronicle of the Ohio Valley and Beyond*

Tecumseh's prediction came true.

DBQ Document-Based Question

Do Tecumseh's words show respect for President Madison? For Harrison? Explain.

Tecumseh and the Prophet A commanding speaker, Tecumseh possessed great political skills. In his view, the U.S. government's treaties with separate Native American nations were worthless. "The Great Spirit gave this great [land] to his red children," he said. Tecumseh felt no one nation had the right to give it away.

Tecumseh had a powerful ally—his brother, Tenskwatawa, known as **the Prophet.** The Prophet urged Native Americans everywhere to return to the customs of their ancestors. They should, he said, give up practices learned from the white invaders—wearing western dress, using plows and firearms, and especially drinking alcohol. The Prophet attracted a huge following among Native Americans. He founded a village at a site in northern Indiana, near present-day Lafayette, where the Tippecanoe and Wabash Rivers meet. It was called Prophetstown.

A Meeting With Harrison The American governor of the Indiana Territory, General **William Henry Harrison,** became alarmed by the growing power of the two Shawnee brothers. He feared they would form an alliance with the British.

In a letter to Tecumseh, Harrison warned that the United States had many more warriors than all the Indian nations could put together.

> **"Do not think that the redcoats can protect you, they are not able to protect themselves."**
>
> —*Messages and Letters of William Henry Harrison*

Tecumseh sent word that he would reply in person.

A few weeks later, Tecumseh came to Harrison and spoke to the white people assembled there:

> **"Brother, . . . Since the peace was made, you have killed some Shawnees, Delawares and Winnebagoes . . . You have taken land from us and I do not see how we can remain at peace if you continue to do so. You try to force red people to do some injury. It is you that are pushing them on to some mischief. You endeavor to make distinctions. You try to prevent the Indians from doing as they wish—to unite."**
>
> —from *Tecumseh, an Indian Moses*

Answers and Additional Support

Primary Sources

Answer: Answers will vary. Students may say that Tecumseh doubts if Madison has enough sense to make a good decision. He does, however, seem to respect Harrison as a fellow warrior.

- **What evidence can you find in the quotation that Tecumseh is shrewd?** *(He realizes that, although Madison makes the key decisions about war and peace, he is remote from the conflict.)* **OL**

The Battle of Tippecanoe In 1811 while Tecumseh was in the South trying to expand his confederacy, Harrison decided to attack Prophetstown on the Tippecanoe River. After more than two hours of battle, the Prophet's forces fled the area in defeat. The Battle of Tippecanoe was proclaimed a glorious victory for the Americans. Harrison acquired the nickname "Tippecanoe" and his supporters used it as a patriotic rallying cry when he ran for president in 1840.

The Battle of Tippecanoe left about one fourth of Harrison's troops dead or wounded, but the impact on the Native Americans was far greater. Prophetstown was destroyed. The clash also shattered Native American confidence in the Prophet's leadership. Many, including Tecumseh, fled to Canada.

Tecumseh's flight to British-held Canada seemed to prove that the British were supporting and arming the Native Americans. To Harrison and to many white people who settled in the West, there seemed only one way to make the region secure from attack—to drive the British out of Canada and take over the province.

Who Were the War Hawks? Back in the nation's capital, President Madison faced demands for a more aggressive policy toward the British. The most insistent voices came from a group of young Republicans elected to Congress in 1810. Known as the **War Hawks,** they came from the South and the West. The War Hawks pressured the president to declare war against Britain.

Primary Sources

Treaties with Native Americans

Many treaties between Native Americans and the U.S. government were signed during the early years of the new nation. These agreements included treaties with the Creeks (1790 and 1814); the Cherokee (1791 and 1794); the Oneida, Tuscarora, and Stockbridge (1794); and the Chickasaw (1805, 1816, and 1818).

Some treaties, like the Treaty of Greenville (1795), were signed to end conflicts. Other treaties ceded Indian land to the United States. White leaders and Indian leaders rarely trusted one another. Shawnee leader Blue Jacket is quoted as saying:

> "From all quarters, we receive speeches from the Americans, and not one is alike. We suppose that they intend to deceive us."
>
> —*American State Papers, Indian Affairs*

Blue Jacket ▶

The treaties often proved impossible to enforce. Often, white settlers and soldiers crossed into territory and took land that was reserved for Native Americans. Some Native American chiefs were forced to sign a treaty under threat of military force, but they had no intention of abiding by the terms of the treaty. Some chiefs signed only to obtain badly needed items such as food, ammunition, and clothing. In addition, even if a Native American chief signed a treaty, that did not mean that the action was binding on anyone else in the tribe. Other members of the tribe could choose to ignore it.

DBQ Document-Based Question

How would you describe Blue Jacket's view of the white leaders?

S Skill Practice

Historical and Social Sciences Analysis Skill

Direct students' attention to the statement that Harrison ran for president in 1840. **Ask:** Do you think his victory at Tippecanoe helped him in that campaign? Why or why not? *(Some students may say that victory in battle helped Harrison by making him seem a strong and successful leader. Others may say that being president demands other skills than good generalship.)* OL CA HI3.

R Reading Strategy

Understanding Vocabulary

Ask students to explain why a hawk is a good animal to represent leaders like Clay and Calhoun. *(A hawk is a fierce hunter.)* EL

Primary Sources

Answer: He does not trust them.

- Why would the government need to sign more than one treaty with a Native American group? *(A first treaty might have allowed Native Americans to stay in an area that, later, white settlers wanted for themselves.)* AL
- Imagine a group of Native Americans signed a treaty granting them the right to stay in a certain area but white settlers came into that area nevertheless. How would those Native Americans react? *(with anger or frustration; with unwillingness to sign other treaties)* BL

Biography

TEACH

C Critical Thinking

Comparing and Contrasting Ask students to list the ways in which Clay and Calhoun were similar and the ways in which they were different. *(Similar: both war hawks, supported strong military, were nationalists; Different: Clay remained a nationalist, Calhoun later backed states' rights)* BL

S Skill Practice

Using Geography Skills Have students locate Kentucky on a map. **Ask:** Why would a politician from this state become known as an advocate of compromise between different regions? *(In the early 1800s, Kentucky was probably influenced by all three regions.)* OL CA HI1.

U Universal Access

Advanced Learners Ask students to discuss whether nationalism and sectionalism are in conflict in our country today. *(Students may point to some water rights, air pollution, or border security as issues with sectional interest.)* AL CA HI3

Biography

US8.5.1 Understand the political and economic causes and consequences of the War of 1812 and know the major battles, leaders, and events that led to a final peace.

HENRY CLAY
1777–1852

JOHN C. CALHOUN
1782–1850

C

▲ Henry Clay

During their early years in Congress, Henry Clay and John C. Calhoun often joined in support of the young federal government. They were known as War Hawks because of the position they took on the War of 1812. Each argued in stirring speeches the need for a strong army and navy and for the establishment of a national bank.

Both Clay and Calhoun had long, distinguished careers in government. The careers of these two men reflected the conflict between nationalism and sectionalism in the early 1800s.

S

Born in Virginia, Clay moved to Kentucky, a state that kept him in Congress—and in the center of the political scene—for nearly 50 years. Clay was known as the Great Compromiser for his role in working out various agreements between leaders of the North and South. He served as a Kentucky state legislator, speaker of the U.S. House of Representatives, U.S. senator, and secretary of state.

U

Clay was a consistent champion of nationalism and devoted his career to strengthening the Union. Although nominated for president three times, the popularity of his opponents and weakness of his political party, the Whigs, kept him from achieving his lifelong goal of winning the presidency.

Calhoun represented South Carolina. He was an influential member of Congress and, at least for a time, a close friend of Henry Clay. Calhoun supported states' rights and the interests of the South. Fearing that the North intended to dominate the South, Calhoun spent the rest of his career trying to prevent the federal government from weakening states' rights and from interfering with the Southern way of life.

◀ John C. Calhoun

Then and Now

What political leaders represent the region in which you live? Do you think leaders should represent the views of the citizens who elected them?

344

Answers and Additional Support

Then and Now

Students should be able to name notable regional leaders (representatives, senators, and state officials). Some students may agree that leaders should represent the views of their constituents. Others may say that leaders have more information than most people and need to take that into account in making decisions.

Did You Know?

Henry Clay was first elected to the House of Representatives in 1811. Even though he lacked experience as a congressman, his colleagues elected him Speaker of the House on the first day of the session.

The Push for War The War Hawks wanted revenge for British actions against Americans, and they were also eager to expand the nation's power. Their **nationalism,** or loyalty to their country, appealed to a renewed sense of American patriotism.

The leading War Hawks were **Henry Clay** from Kentucky and **John Calhoun** (kahl • HOON) from South Carolina, both in their 30s. Hunger for land heightened war fever. Westerners wanted to move north into the fertile forests of southern Canada. A war with Britain might make Canadian land available. Southerners wanted Spanish Florida.

The War Hawks urged major military spending. Through their efforts Congress quadrupled the army's size. The Federalists in the Northeast, however, remained strongly opposed to the war.

Declaring War By the spring of 1812, Madison **concluded** that war with Britain was inevitable. In a message to Congress in early June of 1812, Madison asked for a declaration of war. His message emphasized national honor and the abuses suffered at the hands of the British.

> **"[T]housands of American citizens . . . have been torn from their country and from everything dear to them [and] have been dragged on board ships of war of a foreign nation."**
>
> **—from Madison's "War Message to Congress"**

In the meantime, the British had decided to end their policy of search and seizure of American ships. Unfortunately, because of the amount of time it took for news to travel across the Atlantic, this change in policy was not known in Washington. Word of the breakthrough arrived too late. Once set in motion, the war machine could not be stopped. **C**

Reading Check **Explain** Why did the War Hawks call for war with Britain?

History Online

Study Central Need help understanding U.S. foreign conflicts in the early 1800s? Visit ca.hss.glencoe.com and click on Study Central.

Section 1 Review

Reading Summary

Review the Main Ideas

- In the early 1800s, American merchant ships were threatened by pirates and the British navy. Great Britain's violation of America's neutral rights led to the passage of the Embargo Act, which greatly hurt American trade.
- The War Hawks in Congress pressured President Madison to go to war as conflicts with Native Americans in the West arose and the conflict with Britain at sea continued.

What Did You Learn?

1. Describe the negotiations that ended the conflict between the United States and Tripoli.
2. Who were the leading War Hawks?

Critical Thinking

3. **Sequencing Information** Re-create the time line below and list key events in the nation's effort to remain neutral in the war between France and Britain. CA CS2.

   1805 — June 1807 — Dec. 1807 — 1810

4. **The Big Ideas** How did the conflict in Europe help the American shipping industry prosper? CA CS1.
5. **Analyze** How did frontier battles with Native Americans intensify Americans' anti-British feelings? CA HI2.
6. **READING** **Cause and Effect** Write a short essay that identifies causes and effects in foreign affairs and the road to war during this period. CA 8RC2.0

SECTION 1 REVIEW ANSWERS

Review questions reinforce content standards US8.5.

1. Tripoli agreed to stop demanding tribute in return for a $60,000 ransom for American prisoners.
2. Henry Clay and John Calhoun
3. 1805: U.S. neutral in war between Britain and France; June 1807: Britain's attack on the *Chesapeake* does not result in war; Dec. 1807: Congress passes Embargo Act; 1810: Congress allows trade with either Britain or France
4. **The Big Ideas** by allowing trade with both France and Britain
5. because the British sided with Native Americans
6. **READING** Answers should reflect conflicts between France, Britain and the United States.

C Critical Thinking

Predicting Consequences Ask students to discuss what they think would have happened if word of the change in British policy had reached Washington before war was declared. Have them offer reasons for their answers. *(Students may argue that, because war fever was so widespread, conflict may have broken out anyway.)* OL CA HI4.

ASSESS

Resources for page 345

Use these resources to assess student mastery of section content.

- Section Quiz 7–1
- Interactive Tutor Self-Assessment CD-ROM

Reading Check

Answer: They wanted to expand the nation's power while gaining revenge for British actions against Americans.

History Online

Study Central provides summaries, interactive games, and online graphic organizers to help students review section content.

CLOSE

Making Inferences When Thomas Jefferson left the White House in 1809, he wrote, "Never did a prisoner, released from his chains, feel such relief as I on shaking off the shackles of power." Have students explain what they think Jefferson meant. OL CA HI1.

FOCUS

Summary

Billy Caldwell accompanies Tecumseh to a meeting with William Henry Harrison, the governor of the Indiana Territory. Tecumseh tells Harrison that the Americans have no right to the land that some Native Americans sold them. If the Americans continue to drive the Shawnee and others off their ancestral lands, Tecumseh warns, trouble will follow. Harrison disagrees, and as the men lose their tempers, violence almost breaks out. The two leaders end the meeting before fighting begins.

Vocabulary Preview Before students begin reading, have them read **Before You Read** and the **Vocabulary Preview**. Point out that difficult words are footnoted throughout the text.

Background Information

This excerpt is based on a real event, which took place in the Indiana wilderness in the early 1800s. While Tecumseh and Harrison are real and their words are part of history, the character of Billy is made up by the author.

Answers and Additional Support

America's Literature

Crossing the Panther's Path

By Elizabeth Alder

Before You Read

The Scene: This part of the book is set at Grouseland, Governor Harrison's home in Vincennes, Indiana.
The Characters: Tecumseh is a leader of the Shawnee. His translator is Billy Caldwell, a teenager whose parents are Native American and white. William Henry Harrison is governor of the Indiana Territory. Shabonee is Native American and a follower of Tecumseh.
The Plot: Billy wants to help Native Americans regain the Ohio River valley. He believes Tecumseh can unite the tribes and accomplish this goal. In this part of the story, Tecumseh meets with Harrison. He wants to try to change Harrison's plans to help whites take over more Native American lands.

Vocabulary Preview

adversary: person who supports a different side of an opinion or disagreement; enemy
disdain: a feeling that someone or something is below one's notice; contempt
dismay: confusion about how to deal with a situation
emphatically: in a forceful way
haughty: blatantly proud and scornful
wrath: great anger that is caused by something unjust

Have you ever wanted someone to listen to your side of a disagreement? In this excerpt, Tecumseh explains Native American views about the ownership of land. In return, Tecumseh learns firsthand what Harrison thinks of Native Americans.

◀ William Henry Harrison

346

Reading Strategy: CONNECTING

Ask students to explain what happens when William Henry Harrison and Tecumseh first meet. Explain that similar situations often arise between two people who insist on having their status recognized by another and are unwilling to yield. Ask volunteers to describe similar standoffs they have seen. Have them describe why the situation arose and how it was resolved. OL

As You Read

Sometimes many people witness an event. Some of them record what they saw and heard. In such cases, the authors of historical novels may use that information in their stories. At other times, there are few or no records of what happened. Then authors imagine what people said and did. As you read, think about how the author may have used facts and imagination in this story.

Tecumseh halted a stone's throw from the porch steps, pausing in a small grove of trees. William Henry Harrison came out and waited for Tecumseh. It was clear that he wanted the Shawnee to come to him. But Tecumseh was satisfied where he was. Harrison paced. Finally, he sent an emissary[1] to invite the Indian forward.

"I do not care to talk with a roof above us," Tecumseh answered the man. "Tell your chief I prefer the council to be held here where I stand."

When he received the message, Harrison uncrossed his arms and angrily pointed his finger in his emissary's face. Then he pointed to Tecumseh emphatically. It was clear that the governor of the Indiana Territory was not pleased. Other advisers intervened,[2] perhaps suggesting a conciliatory[3] approach, and finally Harrison instructed men to carry out a table and chairs from the porch and set them at the edge of the grove.

Harrison strode forward then, followed by his advisers. The armed guard was close behind. Flipping his coattails out behind him, Harrison sat in one of the chairs provided. Tecumseh remained standing but signaled for his men to be seated in a semicircle behind him.

"Listen to me well," Tecumseh explained in English. His voice carried to the edge of the crowd that had gathered. He stood tall, his shoulders squared. A pair of eagle feathers adorned his hair and bands of silver encircled his wrists. It was a hot day, and his light brown skin glistened with sweat.

"I am a Shawnee. My forefathers were warriors. Their son is a warrior."

He spoke in measured[4] tones. He would not rush through what he had come to say.

"From them I take my only existence. From my tribe I take nothing. I have made myself what I am. And I would that I could make the red people as great as the conceptions of my own mind, when I think of the Great Spirit[5] that rules over us all," he said, shaking his head slowly. "I would not then come to Governor Harrison to ask him to tear up the treaty. But I would say to him, 'Brother, you have the liberty to return to your own country.'"

Harrison bristled[6] when Tecumseh addressed him as "Brother."

[1] **emissary:** agent, representative
[2] **intervened:** came between as a way of changing something
[3] **conciliatory:** way of gaining goodwill or calm
[4] **measured:** slow, unhurried, and careful
[5] **Great Spirit:** God
[6] **bristled:** swelled up and took on an angry appearance

Tecumseh ▶

347

TEACH

U1 Universal Access

Visual/Spatial Ask students to make a drawing of a scene in the story. Have them include details from the text to include in their drawings. BL

U2 Universal Access

Verbal/Linguistic and Kinesthetic Ask volunteers to read the words of Tecumseh and Harrison aloud and with expression. AL

R1 Reading Strategy

Visualizing Ask students to visualize, or create a mental picture of, Tecumseh. Ask students what details the author gives that make it easier to picture the chief. *(his clothing, the sound of his voice, the words he chooses)* Have students suggest words that describe Tecumseh's character. *(Answers may include dignity, power, anger, and pride.)* Encourage them to read on to see if their mental pictures prove accurate. OL CA 8RW1.1

R2 Reading Strategy

Inferring **Ask:** Why does Harrison bristle when Tecumseh calls him "Brother"? *(He does not consider Tecumseh a brother.)* OL

READING STRATEGY — MAKING PREDICTIONS

Predicting what will happen in a story helps students' comprehension in several ways. It forces them to read actively and carefully to look for clues. It also helps them analyze characters' words and actions so they can identify hints about what events might result from what they do and say and how they might respond to those events. Ask students to predict how the encounter will end based on the men's first meeting. Have them explain their predictions. OL

R1 Reading Strategy

Inferring **Ask:** What do you think is the author's attitude toward Harrison's values? How do you know? *(She seems to disapprove of Harrison, as his actions are described less favorably than Tecumseh's.)* AL CA 8RL3.7

R2 Reading Strategy

Using Context Clues **Ask:** How does Harrison feel when Tecumseh accuses him of wanting to drive Native Americans into the Great Lake? What clues tell you his feelings? *(He is becoming quite angry; his face reddens and he grips the arms of his chair.)* BL

Answers and Additional Support

Tecumseh paced across the open ground, sometimes facing Harrison, sometimes facing his own men. "You wish," he said in a richly modulated[7] voice, "to prevent the Indians from doing as we wish, to unite and let them consider their lands as the common property of the whole. You take the tribes aside and advise them not to come into this measure. You want by your distinctions of tribes, in allotting to each a particular tract of land, to make them war with each other. You never see an Indian endeavor to make the white people do this. You are continually driving the red people; at last you will drive them into the Great Lake,[8] where they can neither stand nor walk." R1

The governor's long face had reddened. He clasped the arms of his chair. Close by, his soldiers stood at attention, ready and menacing. R2

"Since my residence at Tippecanoe," Tecumseh continued, "we have endeavored to level all distinctions, to remove village chiefs, by whom all mischiefs are done. It is they who sell the land to the Americans.

"Brother," Tecumseh said accusingly, "these lands that were sold, and the goods that were given for them, were done by only a few. In the future, we are prepared to punish those who propose to sell land to the Americans. If you continue to purchase from them, it will make war among the different tribes, and I do not know what will be the consequences among the white people. Brother, I wish you would take pity on the red people and do as I have requested. If you will not give up the land and do cross the boundary of our present settlement, it will be very hard, and produce great trouble between us."

Tecumseh listed all the grievances the Indians held against the Americans. He protested the many treaties gained by guile[9] and the use of alcohol. He spoke of treaties broken by settlers and soldiers alike and of outrageous massacres against peaceful Indians. He spoke of Chief Cornstalk and the betrayal that had embittered[10] Indians throughout the Ohio Valley.

"The way," he said, nearly overcome with emotion, "the only way, to stop this evil is for the red men to unite in claiming a common and equal right in the land, as it was at first, and should be now—for it was never divided but belongs to all. No tribe has the right to sell, even to each other, much less to strangers."

Here Tecumseh chuckled bitterly, for the notion was preposterous to him. "Sell a country! Why not sell the air, the great sea, as well as the earth? Did not the Great Spirit make them all for the use of his children?"

The Americans murmured among themselves. Many were impressed by his eloquence.

"Everything I have told you is the truth," Tecumseh said. "The Great Spirit has inspired me.

[7] **modulated:** varied speed and loudness
[8] **Great Lake:** Lake Michigan
[9] **guile:** deceit; trickery
[10] **embittered:** badly disappointed

EXTENDING THE CONTENT

A Great Speaker Tecumseh was so eloquent that white settlers who heard him speak compared him to Henry Clay of Kentucky, who was widely admired for his speaking ability. Tecumseh spent much time studying treaties and speaking to other Native Americans at councils.

"Brother, I hope you will confess that you ought not to have listened to those bad birds who bring you ill news," he admonished,[11] referring to the spies Harrison had sent to Tippecanoe.

Satisfied then that he had said what he had come to say, he concluded with the words many Indian statesmen used to close their arguments: "I have spoken."

He sat down between Billy and Shabonee.

Harrison unfolded his long legs and rose to his full height. His father had been one of the signers of the Declaration of Independence, and the son's demeanor[12] was haughty. Blue steel flashed from his eyes. "It is ridiculous," he began contemptuously,[13] "for you to declare that the Indians are all one people. Why then do you speak in different tongues? The land along the Wabash[14] belongs to the Miami tribe. They decided to sell it, and they have been well paid. Tecumseh, you and your Shawnee have no business on that land—"

Before Harrison could finish, Tecumseh sprang to his feet shouting, "*You are a liar!* Everything you have said is false! The Indians have been cheated and imposed upon by you and the Seventeen Fires.[15] Nothing you have said—before, or now at this council—can be trusted. You lie and you cheat!"

In his wrath, Tecumseh had spoken in the Shawnee language. Billy froze with horror. He felt the blood drain from his face. He had, after all, been introduced as the translator should the need arise, and in the first rush of Tecumseh's words, Harrison had glanced toward him, silently demanding an answer. Did he dare translate this into English—before the governor of the territory, before his armed soldiers? A second wave of dismay washed over him as he saw Harrison turn back to Tecumseh. The American had stiffened, his nostrils flared, and Billy saw that there was no need for a translator. It was clear to everyone present what Tecumseh thought of his adversary.

One of the officers shouted, "Bring up the guard!"

Shabonee and the other chiefs leaped to their feet and drew their weapons. They encircled Tecumseh, shielding him with their bodies. As Harrison drew his sword from its scabbard,[16] Tecumseh shouted orders to his men hidden in the woods. They burst forward, many with their knives and tomahawks in their hands. Others were already taking up positions at the edge of the trees, aiming their rifles.

American soldiers were raising their rifles, too. Billy's heart hammered in his chest. His breathing was ragged—swift and shallow. He watched the two leaders glare at each other. It would take only the order "Fire!" on the American side, or for Tecumseh to shout the war cry, for Grouseland's lawn to explode in a violent bloodletting. Tecumseh had not come for this. He had come to speak to this man, to change his heart as he had so many others. He had not expected to be treated with such disdain. It was true, Billy imagined, that Tecumseh hated Harrison and all that he represented. But he had not come here today to make war.

[11] **admonished:** expressed warning or disapproval in a gentle or earnest way
[12] **demeanor:** one's attitude toward others as shown in how one behaves
[13] **contemptuously:** in a way showing disdain, disrespect, or scorn
[14] **Wabash:** river that begins in western Ohio and flows west across Indiana
[15] **Seventeen Fires:** the United States
[16] **scabbard:** a case in which to carry a knife, sword, or bayonet

R Reading Strategy

Evaluating A metaphor is a figure of speech in which a person, place, or object, is described by a word normally used in another way, such as "a cold stare." **Ask:** What metaphor on this page describes Harrison's response to Tecumseh's speech? *(Blue steel flashed from his eyes.)* What comparison is the author making? *(to steel used to make sword blades)* **OL**

CA 8RL3.6

C Critical Thinking

Making Inferences **Ask:** Do you think it is a good idea for Tecumseh to call Harrison a liar, even in Shawnee? What does his action tell you about Tecumseh? *(Some may argue that Tecumseh angered Harrison on purpose; others may say that Tecumseh's own anger got the better of him.)* **AL**

W Writing Support

Response to Literature Writing **Ask:** According to Billy, why had Tecumseh come to the meeting? *(to change Harrison's heart)* Ask students to write a paragraph explaining why this was a realistic or unrealistic goal. Have them support their answers with evidence from the story. *(Some students may argue that the goal was unrealistic, given the state of American-Native American relations; others may say it was worth trying.)* **OL**

EXTENDING THE CONTENT

We Are Family Tecumseh's father was a Shawnee and his mother a Muskogee. His father was killed by whites when the boy was only six; his mother moved with part of the Shawnee tribe to another area the following year. Tecumseh was raised by a sister and then later adopted by a Shawnee chief named Blackfish. In Blackfish's family were several white boys who had been kidnapped from their families by the Shawnee.

349

R Reading Strategy

Understanding Vocabulary Ask students to use context clues to understand the definition of *scoff.* Model this strategy for students. Ask questions aloud such as: What do I know about Harrison's views toward the Native Americans? Did he believe in working with the Native Americans for a fair settlement? How might he respond to requests by them for a fair settlement? Based on what I know, if Harrison had to respond to the Native Americans, would he speak with respect or disrespect? Then, ask students to find the definition of *scoff* in the dictionary to see if their reasoning was correct. OL

W Writing Support

Response to Literature Writing Have students write one paragraph that describes what they think Billy might have been feeling as he met with Tecumseh and Harrison. *(Students might describe feelings of tension and fear.)* OL

Answers and Additional Support

Billy felt certain that Harrison also regretted what had happened. A council must never be allowed to degenerate[17] into a skirmish. It would be a terrible blot on his career.

With a few curt words, Harrison asked Tecumseh to leave. "We shall speak tomorrow when our tempers have cooled," he said.

That evening, in the camp the Indians had made on the far side of the river, Tecumseh drew his inner circle together. "I should not have allowed my anger to drive me to speak as I did," he admitted. "The time for war has not yet come."

Billy slept little that night. He tossed and turned restlessly in his blanket. During the lonely hours of the night, he heard an owl call, and now and then the splash of a fish in the river. He had come to this council only because Tecumseh wouldn't listen to his protests. R The youth had suspected from the beginning that Harrison would scoff at their entreaties[18] and speak to them with contempt. Billy was now very certain that the American would be satisfied with nothing less than driving the Indians from their land. There would be no compromises. War would come.

"Shabonee...are you awake?" Billy whispered to the gigantic figure stretched out next to him.

Light from the dying fire glinted in Shabonee's eyes as he woke. "Mmmm," he answered.

"Will Tecumseh go to war soon?"

Shabonee moaned. He raised himself up and leaned on one elbow. "What?"

Billy repeated his question.

Shabonee rubbed his eyes. "He will pick up the tomahawk when he is ready."

"Do you think he'll include me among his men?" Billy asked.

"I think he likes you. You stood like a straight tree before the Long Knives today."

Billy chuckled. He had told Shabonee his Mohawk name. "Inside, I was quivering like the leaves of the cottonwood tree," he admitted. "There were so many rifles pointed at us." He rolled over on his back and stared up at the stars. "I *do* want to be a warrior for my people."

"Which people?" Shabonee asked. He knew the British wanted the fur trade.

"The Indians."

"Stay among us, then," Shabonee said in way of invitation, "and learn our ways."

Billy nodded thoughtfully. It was true. He still had so much to learn. Eight moons ago, when he had argued with his father, he had thought himself very wise. Since then, he had slowly come to know how little wisdom he truly possessed.

W The next afternoon, Tecumseh met with Harrison again. Billy was not surprised to see that the American soldiers were heavily armed and tense, their numbers doubled. This time Tecumseh went forward alone with only Billy to help interpret. He had said he was sometimes unsure of his English, and there must be no misunderstanding today.

The Shawnee leader was most anxious to speak of the borders between his people and the Americans.

"This new boundary you have drawn will cause trouble between our peoples," Tecumseh said as soon as Billy concluded translating the formal opening statements. "The old line must remain," he insisted.

Billy had heard the talk in Detroit. He had read the newspaper articles. He knew that Harrison was determined to enlarge American territory by crossing into Indian lands. Now it became clear from the governor's speech that as long as the Americans felt themselves to be numerically superior and better armed, they would not hesitate to take what they wanted.

"The tribes will lose their annuities if they follow you," Harrison threatened.

Tecumseh scowled as Billy finished translating it into Shawnee. He asked that the term *annuities* be explained further. These were gifts of goods or money, Billy explained.

---

17 **degenerate:** break or sink down

18 **entreaties:** requests

EXTENDING THE CONTENT

The End of a Dream Harrison and Tecumseh would meet on the battlefield a few years after this encounter. In 1813, Harrison led U.S. troops into Canada, where they defeated a British and Native American force at the Battle of the Thames. Tecumseh, who led the Native American forces, was killed in the battle. He was buried in an unmarked grave, which has never been discovered. His dream of a great Native American confederacy was buried with him.

Part of the annuities were paid in the form of alcohol. "It disgusts me to see the Americans use their cheap tricks against the Indian nations," Tecumseh said when Billy finished. "You have no right to ply[19] the chiefs with whiskey until they are befuddled. It is forbidden by the Greenville Treaty. You must blame yourself as the cause of trouble between us and the tribes who sold the land to you." Tecumseh argued fiercely, "I want the present boundary line to continue. Should you cross it, I assure you it will be productive of bad consequences." R

Tecumseh nodded for Billy to begin translating his words, while he watched Harrison's face to read any signs that might cross his features. He was answered only by Harrison's stony expression. Billy ended the talks as Tecumseh instructed him. "Governor Harrison," he said, "Chief Tecumseh desires that this disagreement be placed before the Great Chief of the Long Knives."

Harrison coolly agreed. "Yes, I will send word of your position to President Madison; however, I can assure you that the President will protect with the sword what he considers fairly bought."

"I do not wish to make war upon the United States," Tecumseh said emphatically. "I wish only that illegal purchases of Indian lands cease. Your stance forces us to ally ourselves with the British. Tell your President what is in my heart that he may know my intentions."

"I will tell the President what you have said," Harrison answered. "But I say there is not the least probability that he will accede[20] to your terms."

"As your Great Chief is to determine the matter, I hope the Great Spirit will put enough sense in his head to induce him to direct you to give up this land."

C Tecumseh put his hand on the stone head of the tomahawk that jutted from his belt. The muscles in his jaw tightened. He seemed resigned to the knowledge that none of his arguments would turn the hearts of the Americans. He looked to the east. He knew that the American President lived many days' travel toward the rising sun. He had heard that Madison was a small man, undistinguished as a public speaker, who had never commanded soldiers in a battle. This seemed puzzling, for it was strength and eloquence and prowess[21] in combat that marked a man for greatness among the Indian nations.

[19] **ply:** to keep supplying something to
[20] **accede:** to give in to a request
[21] **prowess:** skill and courage

Responding to the Literature

1. What did Tecumseh compare selling land to? Why?
2. What kept a war from starting at this meeting?
3. **Analyze** In the first three paragraphs, how do Tecumseh and Harrison each try to show that he is more powerful? CA HI2.
4. **Explain** What are the literal and figurative meanings of this phrase: "The President will protect with the sword what he considers fairly bought"? CA 8RW1.1
5. **Read to Write** Compare the information on pages 341–342 with this selection. How did the author use both fact and imagination to write this story? Include examples to support your conclusions. List other people or events in the story that you could verify as being real or imaginary. CA HR1.; HR3.

R Reading Strategy

Activating Prior Knowledge Ask: What is the significance of the Greenville Treaty, which you learned about in Chapter 5? *(In 1795, Native Americans gave up control of much of Ohio.)* OL

C Critical Thinking

Drawing Conclusions Have students discuss what each man is thinking and feeling at the end of the story. Ask students to support their answers with evidence from the text. *(Answers will vary; for example, some students may say that both men leave expecting war, because they have taken irreconcilable positions and have left no room for compromise.)* AL

ASSESS

Have students answer the **Responding to the Literature** questions.

Resources for page 351

American Literature Reading 7

CLOSE

Ask students to describe characters from other novels they have read that remind them of Tecumseh and Governor Harrison in this story. OL CA 8RL3.3

Responding to the Literature Answers

1. selling the air or the sea, because the Great Spirit had given the land to all people
2. Harrison suggested they talk again tomorrow when they were less angry.
3. Neither will come to where the other man is.
4. literal: Madison will use a sword to defend the land; figurative: Madison will order his men to fight for the land
5. Students may say that the conflict between Native Americans and whites was real but that the reactions of characters to each others' words are imaginary. Students could do research into the meeting to see if the words attributed to Harrison and Tecumseh are accurate.

TEACH

The reading selections for this unit have been chosen to reflect the California History-Social Science Standards. If you assign one of these books, you may want to have students complete the following activity.

SUMMARIZING

Have students write brief summaries of the books they read. They should write the summaries in such a way as to help other students decide whether they find the book interesting to read for themselves. Students should follow these guidelines in writing their summaries:

- Avoid giving away the ending.
- Do not try to include every detail.
- Describe things you liked about the book and things you did not like.

GLENCOE BOOKLINK

Use **Glencoe BookLink** to create customized reading lists for your students' reading levels, interests, and abilities.

Answers and Additional Support

Reading On Your Own...

From the California Reading List

Do you want to learn more about George Washington, Sacajawea, and the early years of the United States? You might be interested in the following books.

Biography

Founding Father: Rediscovering George Washington by Richard Brookhiser explores Washington as a person, a soldier, and a political leader. He explains why Washington was so important in forming the future of the United States. ***The content of this book is related to*** *History–Social Studies Standard US8.2.*

Nonfiction

Old Ironsides: Americans Build a Fighting Ship by David Weitzman invites readers to see how this great warship was built. As readers follow John Aylwin, a young worker on the ship, they learn what it took to make "Old Ironsides." ***The content of this book is related to*** *History–Social Studies Standard US8.5.*

Historical Fiction

Carry On, Mr. Bowditch by Jean L. Latham tells the amazing tale of Nathaniel Bowditch. Although he had very little education, he mastered sea navigation during his voyages around the world. His book *American Practical Navigator* was used with few changes into the 1900s. ***The content of this book is related to*** *History–Social Studies Standard US8.6.*

Historical Fiction

Sacajawea: The Story of Bird Woman and the Lewis and Clark Expedition by Joseph Bruchac has Sacajawea and Clark taking turns describing events. The story also includes parts of the explorers' journals and Shoshone tales. ***The content of this book is related to*** *History–Social Studies Standard US8.4.*

352

READING STRATEGY SKIMMING

Suggest that students use the strategy of skimming to get an overview of the book before deciding whether or not to read it. They can look at the table of contents, preface or introduction, and notes on the jacket or cover to see if the book seems interesting. They might also read the first page or two to see if they like the author's writing style and find the subject matter engaging. BL

Section 2: The War of 1812

Guide to Reading

Looking Back, Looking Ahead
Beginning in 1812, the United States went to war with Britain. Fighting took place in the United States, in Canada, and at sea.

Focusing on the Main Ideas
- In 1812 the United States was at war with Britain and was unprepared from the onset. *(page 354)*
- Even though the last battle of the war, the Battle of New Orleans, took place two weeks after the war had officially ended, the American victory there instilled a strong sense of national pride. *(page 356)*

Locating Places
Detroit
Lake Erie

Meeting People
William Hull
Oliver Hazard Perry
Andrew Jackson
Francis Scott Key

Content Vocabulary
frigate (FRIH • guht)
privateer (PRY • vuh • TIHR)

Academic Vocabulary
consist (kuhn • SIHST)
assemble (uh • SEHM • buhl)
economy (ih • KAH • nuh • mee)

Reading Strategy
Taking Notes As you read this section, re-create the diagram below and describe each battle's outcome.

Battle	Outcome
Lake Erie	
Washington, D.C.	
New Orleans	

History Social Science Standards

US8.5 Students analyze U.S. foreign policy in the early Republic.

NATIONAL GEOGRAPHIC Where & When?

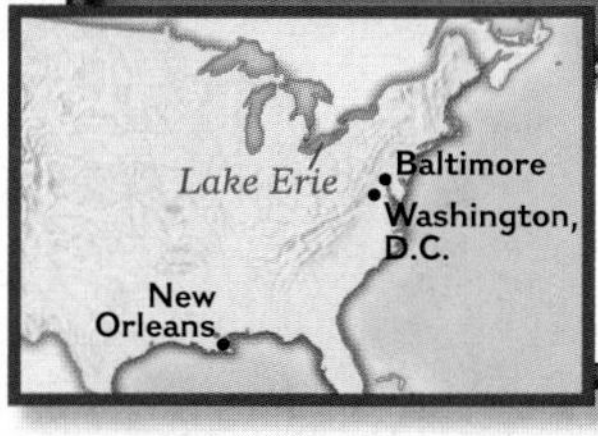

1812 — 1813 — 1814 — 1815

June 1812 United States declares war on Britain

Sep. 1813 Perry defeats the British navy on Lake Erie

Aug. 1814 The British burn Washington, D.C.

Jan. 1815 American forces win the Battle of New Orleans

FOCUS

BELLRINGER
SKILLBUILDER ACTIVITY

Project **Daily Focus Skills Transparency 7–2** and have students answer the question.

Guide to Reading

Preteaching Vocabulary: Tell students that the ending on *privateer* comes from a French ending, *-ier*, and refers to a person associated with an activity. Ask students to name and define other words that have the same ending. *(buccaneer, musketeer, pamphleteer, sloganeer)*

Answers to Graphic: Lake Erie: American naval forces destroy British naval forces; Washington, D.C.: British burn government buildings; New Orleans: British defeated

Unpacking the Standards
After reading the section, students will be able to:
- Describe the major events of the War of 1812.
- Outline the agreements made in the peace treaty that ended the war.
- Explain why the American victory led to an increase in nationalism and pride.

SECTION RESOURCES

Print Material
- Reproducible Lesson Plan 7–2*
- Daily Lesson and Discussion Notes 7–2
- Guided Reading Activity 7–2
- Reading Essentials and Study Guide 7–2
- Active Reading Note-Taking Guide 7–2
- Section Quiz 7–2

Transparencies
- Daily Focus Skills Transparency 7–2
- Section Graphic Organizer Transparency 7–2
- California Standards Practice Transparencies

Technology
- Interactive Tutor Self-Assessment CD-ROM
- Exam*View*® Pro Testmaker CD-ROM
- Presentation Plus! CD-ROM

*Available on TeacherWorks™

TEACH

R Reading Strategy

Academic Vocabulary Ask students to use the Glossary in the back of their textbook to look up the meaning of *consisted*. Then have them use the word in a sentence. OL

C Critical Thinking

Predicting Consequences
Ask: What evidence is there that the United States was unprepared for the war? *(The army was small; the state militias were untrained.)* What might result from these mistakes? *(early defeats)* AL CA HI4.

U Universal Access

Below Grade Level Have students improve their comprehension of the material by preparing an outline as they read. Use the board to show how an outline is structured, using roman numerals for main headings (such as "War Begins"); capital letters for subsections ("Naval Battles"); and numbers for specific points. BL

Answers and Additional Support

US8.5.1 Understand the political and economic causes and consequences of the War of 1812 and know the major battles, leaders, and events that led to a final peace.

War Begins

Main Idea **In 1812 the United States was at war with Britain and was unprepared from the onset.**

Reading Connection Have you ever been unprepared for a quiz or test? Read to learn what happened when the United States was unprepared in the beginning of the War of 1812.

At the beginning of the war, the U.S. army **consisted** of fewer than 7,000 troops. The states had between 50,000 and 100,000 militia, but the units were poorly trained. Additionally, many states opposed "Mr. Madison's war." The Americans also underestimated the strength of the British and their Native American allies.

Fighting began in July 1812, when General **William Hull** led the American army from **Detroit** into Canada. Hull was met by Tecumseh and his warriors. Fearing a massacre by the Native Americans, Hull surrendered Detroit to a small British force in August. Another attempt by General William Henry Harrison was unsuccessful as well. Harrison realized that British control of Lake Erie prevented an American victory.

Naval Battles **Oliver Hazard Perry,** commander of the **Lake Erie** naval forces, had his orders. He was to **assemble** a fleet and seize the lake from the British. From his headquarters in Put-in-Bay, Ohio, Perry could watch the movements of the enemy ships. The showdown came on September 10, 1813, when the British ships sailed out to face the Americans. In the bloody battle that followed, Perry and his ships defeated the British naval force. After the battle, Perry sent General William Henry Harrison the message, "We have met the enemy and they are ours."

With Lake Erie in American hands, the British and their Native American allies tried to pull back from the Detroit area. Harrison and his troops cut them off. In the fierce Battle of the Thames on October 5, the great leader Tecumseh was killed.

A John Bull represents Britain. B Brother Jonathan represents the United States.

Analyzing Political Cartoons

The cartoon shows Brother Jonathan forcing John Bull to drink a tankard of American medicine. Brother Jonathan was used to represent Americans in many cartoons, beginning with the American Revolution. ***Why is the name "Perry" on the tankard?***

Analyzing Political Cartoons

The figure of Brother Jonathan was one of the models for a later—and better known—symbol of the United States, Uncle Sam. Though the exact origin of Uncle Sam is unknown, that character is generally linked to a New York businessman who provided American armies with food during the War of 1812. The business owner, Samuel Wilson, was often called "Uncle Sam."

Answer: because Americans under the command of Perry defeated British naval forces at the Battle of Lake Erie

W The Americans also attacked the town of York (present-day Toronto, Canada), burning the parliament buildings. Canada remained unconquered, but by the end of 1813 the Americans had won some victories on land and at sea.

R Republicans had reduced the size of the navy to help lower the national debt. However, the navy still boasted three of the fastest **frigates** (FRIH • guhts), or warships, afloat. Americans exulted when the *Constitution*, one of these frigates, destroyed two British vessels—the *Guerrière* in August 1812 and the *Java* four months later. After seeing a shot bounce off the *Constitution's* hull during battle, a sailor nicknamed the ship "Old Ironsides."

American **privateers** (PRY • vuh • TIHRZ), armed private ships, also staged spectacular attacks on British ships and captured numerous vessels. These victories were important for American morale.

Setback for Native Americans In March 1814, a lanky Tennessee planter named **Andrew Jackson** led an attack against the Creeks in present-day Alabama. Jackson's forces slaughtered more than 550 of the Creek people. Known as the Battle of Horseshoe Bend, the defeat broke the Creeks' resistance and forced them to give up most of their lands to the United States.

Reading Check **Evaluate** Do you think the United States was prepared to wage war? Explain.

NATIONAL GEOGRAPHIC **The War of 1812**

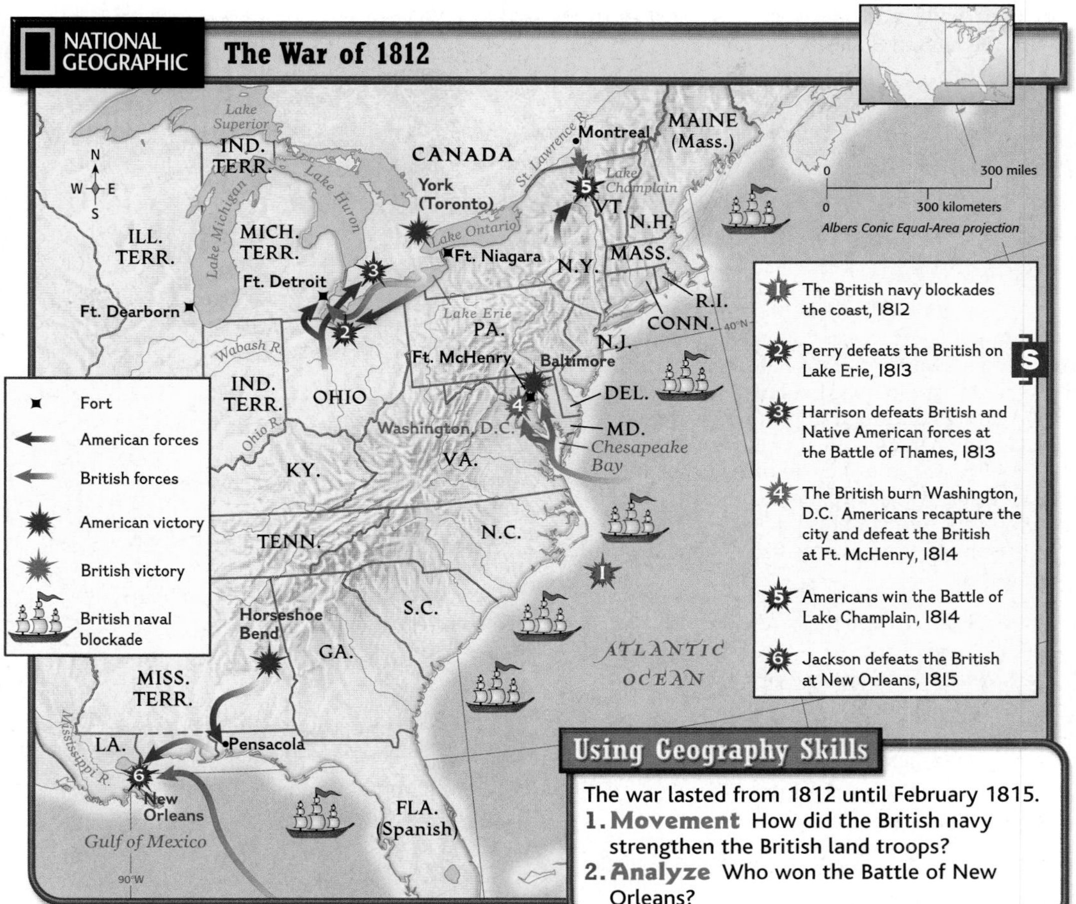

S

Using Geography Skills

The war lasted from 1812 until February 1815.

1. **Movement** How did the British navy strengthen the British land troops?
2. **Analyze** Who won the Battle of New Orleans?

W Writing Support

Persuasive Writing Have students write a short essay on how the war would have turned out differently if the Americans had conquered Canada. Students should include evidence from the text in their essays. *(Students may say that if the United States had won it might have incorporated parts of Canada into the country.)* AL CA 8WA2.4

R Reading Strategy

Understanding Vocabulary Point out the terms *frigates* and *privateers*. Have students work with a partner to make a list of as many different names for kinds of ships as they can. Have pairs share their list, using a dictionary to define their words. OL

S Skill Practice

Using Geography Skills Have students study the map. **Ask:** Why was the area around Lake Erie the site of several important battles? *(The lake lay between the United States and British-controlled Canada; control of the lake would mean control of the West.)* OL CA CS3.

Reading Check

Answer: Students may note that the United States was unprepared because its forces were small, and many Americans opposed the war.

Resources for page 355

Chart, Map, and Graph Skills Activity 7

Using Geography Skills

Answers:

1. by blockading the coast
2. the Americans

Did You Know?

One of the most famous ships in American history, the *U.S.S. Constitution* can still be visited in Boston and is still a commissioned ship of the U.S. Navy. Launched in 1797, the ship was slated for destruction in 1828, when Oliver Wendell Holmes, Sr., wrote a poem about it that generated public support for keeping the ship afloat.

W Writing Support

Narrative Writing Ask students to take the role of a person who saw the burning of Washington in 1814 and write an eyewitness account. OL
CA 8WA2.1

C Critical Thinking

Drawing Conclusions Ask: How much damage would it do to a country at war to have its capital city burned? *(Most students will conclude that it would be a severe psychological blow, as well as a damaging logistical blow; the government could, however, move and continue its operations.)* BL CA HI2.

U Universal Access

Auditory/Musical Have students research and play recordings of other songs that have been suggested as replacements for "The Star Spangled Banner" as our national anthem, such as "America, the Beautiful." Then poll the class on whether the country should replace the current anthem with another song and, if so, with which song. OL

Answers and Additional Support

US8.5.1 Understand the political and economic causes and consequences of the War of 1812 and know the major battles, leaders, and events that led to a final peace.

The British Offensive

Main Idea **Even though the last battle of the war, the Battle of New Orleans, took place two weeks after the war had officially ended, the American victory there instilled a strong sense of national pride.**

Reading Connection When was the last time you were moved by patriotic feelings? What did you feel? Read to learn how the national anthem was inspired by the War of 1812.

British fortunes improved in the spring of 1814. They had been fighting a war with Napoleon and had won. With the war against France over, the British were able to send much of their navy and many more troops to deal with the United States.

Attack on Washington, D.C. In August 1814, the British sailed into Chesapeake Bay. Their destination was Washington, D.C. On the outskirts of Washington, D.C., the British troops quickly overpowered the American militia and then marched into the city. "They proceeded, without a moment's delay, to burn and destroy everything in the most distant degree connected with government," reported a British officer. W

The Capitol and the president's mansion were among the buildings burned. Watching from outside the city, President Madison, his wife Dolley Madison, and the cabinet saw the night sky turn orange. Fortunately, a violent thunderstorm put out the fires before they could do more damage. August 24, 1814, was a low point for the Americans. C

Primary Sources

"The Star-Spangled Banner"

U On the night of September 13, 1814, Francis Scott Key, a young Maryland lawyer, watched from Baltimore Harbor as the British bombarded Fort McHenry. The shelling continued into the morning hours. A huge American flag waved over the fort. As the sun rose, Key strained to see if the flag still waved. To his great joy, it did. He took a letter from his pocket and began scribbling these words for a poem on the back:

"O! say can you see by the dawn's
early light,
What so proudly we hail'd at the
twilight's last gleaming;
Whose broad stripes and bright stars,
through the perilous fight,
O'er the ramparts we watch'd
were so gallantly streaming;

▲ The first Star-Spangled Banner, 1779–1818

And the rocket's red glare, the bombs
bursting in air,
Gave proof through the night that our
flag was still there;
O! say does that star spangled banner
yet wave,
O'er the land of the free, and the home
of the brave."

DBQ Document-Based Question

Why was it important to Key that the flag still waved over the fort?

Primary Sources

Answer: It showed that the fort had not surrendered.

- Whom do you think Key is talking to in his poem? *(possibly a fellow American, or to Americans in general)* OL
- What features of the flag does Key describe? *(its stripes and stars)* BL
- What kinds of weapons threatened the fort and the flag? *(rockets and bombs)* BL

Biography

US8.5 Students analyze U.S. foreign policy in the early Republic.

W DOLLEY MADISON

1768–1849

Born in North Carolina, Dolley Payne grew up in Virginia under the strict influence of her Quaker family and neighborhood. While still heeding the requirements of the Quaker lifestyle, Dolley's jubilant and warm personality greeted everyone she met. At age 15, her family moved to Philadelphia, and there she married John Todd, Jr. As Dolley Todd, she gave birth to two children. Later, Dolley lost her husband and one child during a yellow fever epidemic in 1793.

The following year she married James Madison. While her husband was secretary of state, Dolley Madison served as unofficial first lady for the widower president, Thomas Jefferson. She became the nation's official first lady when C James Madison was elected president in 1808.

Dolley's tenure as first lady was punctuated by social gatherings and Wednesday evening "drawing rooms" attended by the time's most important citizens and politicians. Her charac- R ter made even the most ill-at-ease feel at home in the White House, and her insight into political matters was well regarded and well used by her husband.

During the War of 1812 she showed remarkable bravery. In 1814 as the British approached the capital, she refused to leave the executive mansion until she had packed up many valuable government documents, a painting of George Washington, and other priceless valuables.

"I must leave [the White House] or the retreating army will make me a prisoner in it, by filling up the road I am directed to take. When I shall again write you, or where I shall be tomorrow, I cannot tell!!"

—Dolley Madison, letter to her sister Anna Cutts, August 23, 1814

Then and Now

Compare Dolley Madison to the present first lady. How are they similar? How are they different?

357

Biography

TEACH

W Writing Support

Research Reports Writing

After reading the biography, have students write two questions they want answered about Dolley Madison. Then have them conduct some basic research to answer those questions. BL

C Critical Thinking

Analyzing Information

Ask: What kind of person was Dolley Madison? How do you know? *(Using details in the biography, students may say that Madison was courageous, helpful, resourceful, intelligent, and cheerful even though her life was touched by tragedy.)* BL

R Reading Strategy

Scaffolding—Connecting

Point out that important people are invited to social gatherings at the White House today, as during Dolley Madison's time. Divide students into groups and have each group create a guest list of ten people they would invite to such a gathering today if they lived in the White House. Ask students to explain their choices. OL CA HI3.

This READING SKILL was introduced in Chapter 3.

Then and Now

Students' answers should show knowledge of the interests and personality of the current first lady and incorporate details from the biography of Dolley Madison.

U Universal Access

Visual/Spatial Have students make a drawing, painting, mural, or other visual representation of the War of 1812. Display the works around the classroom as you study this section. OL

W Writing Support

Summary Writing Have students write a summary of the reasons the War of 1812 ended when it did. *(Summaries should include the most important facts from the text.)* BL

Review The Big Idea

Review the Big Idea for this section: "Political ideas and major events shape how people form governments."

Ask: What events from the war probably helped increase Americans' self-confidence? *(Students may point out that American troops fought well against the world's leading power, they bounced back from defeats, their navy enjoyed many successes, and they had ended the threat posed by Tecumseh.)* OL CA HI2.

History *Through Art*

Battle of North Point* by Don Troiani** At North Point, Americans soldiers battled British forces advancing on Baltimore. The clash slowed the British advance, giving the Americans time to reinforce their defenses around the city. ***What happened when the British tried to enter Baltimore?

Baltimore Holds Firm Much to everyone's surprise, the British did not try to hold Washington. They left the city and sailed north to Baltimore. Baltimore, however, was ready and waiting—with barricaded roads, a blocked harbor, and some 13,000 militiamen. The British attacked in mid-September. They were kept from entering the town by a determined defense and ferocious bombardment from Fort McHenry in the harbor.

U During the night of September 13–14, a young attorney named **Francis Scott Key** watched as the bombs burst over Fort McHenry. Finally, "by the dawn's early light," Key was able to see that the American flag still flew over the fort. Deeply moved by patriotic feeling, Key wrote a poem called "The Star-Spangled Banner." In 1931 Congress designated "The Star-Spangled Banner" as the national anthem.

Defeat at Plattsburgh Meanwhile, in the north, General Sir George Prevost led more than 10,000 British troops into New York State from Canada. The first British goal was to capture Plattsburgh, a key city on the shore of Lake Champlain. The invasion was stopped when an American naval force on Lake Champlain defeated the British fleet in September 1814. Knowing the American ships could use their control of the lake to bombard them and land troops behind them, the British retreated to Canada.

After the Battle of Lake Champlain, the British decided the war in North America was too costly and unnecessary. Napoleon had been defeated in Europe. To keep fighting the United States would gain little and was not worth the effort.

The War Ends American and British representatives signed a peace agreement on December 24, 1814, in Ghent, Belgium. The Treaty of Ghent did not change any existing borders. Nothing was mentioned about the impressment of sailors, but with Napoleon's defeat, neutral rights was no longer an issue. W

Answers and Additional Support

Did You Know?

Officially known as the president's or executive mansion, the White House got its current name because its light gray sandstone contrasted strongly with the other red brick buildings in the capital. It officially became known as the White House in 1902.

History *Through Art*

Answer: The Americans prevented them from doing so.

Before word of the treaty had reached the United States, one final—and ferocious—battle occurred at New Orleans. In December 1814, British army troops moved toward New Orleans. Awaiting them behind earthen fortifications was an American army led by Andrew Jackson.

On January 8, 1815, the British troops advanced. The redcoats were no match for Jackson's soldiers, who shot from behind bales of cotton. In a short but gruesome battle, hundreds of British soldiers were killed. At the Battle of New Orleans, Americans achieved a decisive victory. Andrew Jackson became a hero, and his fame helped him win the presidency in 1828.

American Nationalism Most New England Federalists had opposed "Mr. Madison's war" from the start. In December 1814, unhappy New England Federalists gathered in Connecticut at the Hartford Convention. A few favored secession. Most wanted to remain within the Union, however. To protect their interests, they drew up a list of proposed amendments to the Constitution.

After the convention broke up, word came of Jackson's spectacular victory at New Orleans, followed by news of the peace treaty. In this moment of triumph, the Federalist grievances seemed unpatriotic. The party lost respect in the eyes of the public. Most Americans felt proud and self-confident at the end of the War of 1812. The young nation had gained new respect from other nations in the world. Americans felt a renewed sense of patriotism and a strong national identity.

Although the Federalist Party weakened, its philosophy of strong national government was carried on by the War Hawks, who were part of the Republican Party. They favored trade, western expansion, the energetic development of the **economy,** and a strong army and navy. **R**

Reading Check **Analyze** Did the Treaty of Ghent resolve any major issues? Explain.

History Online
Study Central Need help understanding the War of 1812? Visit ca.hss.glencoe.com and click on Study Central.

Section 2 Review

Reading Summary

Review the Main Ideas

- While at first unprepared and experiencing setbacks on the battlefield, American forces soon began to gain victories on land and at sea in the War of 1812.
- In 1814 the British succeeded in capturing Washington, D.C., but they lost a number of other important battles, including the one at New Orleans.

What Did You Learn?

1. Who won the Battle of Lake Champlain? Why was it an important victory?
2. What were the effects of the Battle of New Orleans?

Critical Thinking

3. **Determining Cause and Effect** Re-create the diagram below. In the ovals, list four effects that the War of 1812 had on the United States. CA HI2.

4. **The Big Ideas** Why did the Federalist Party lose support after the War of 1812? CA CS1.
5. **Creative Writing** Imagine if Francis Scott Key had been at the Battle of New Orleans instead of in Baltimore. Rewrite "The Star-Spangled Banner" based on what occurred in that battle. CA 8WA2.1
6. **Analysis** **Making Connections** Explain the relationship between Britain's war with France and the War of 1812 and the Treaty of Ghent. CA CS1.

R Reading Strategy

Scaffolding—Academic Vocabulary Students were introduced to the word *philosophy* in Chapter 6, Section 1. Ask a student to define the word, and then discuss other situations in which students might have encountered the word. OL

ASSESS

Resources for page 359

Use these resources to assess student mastery of section content.

- Section Quiz 7–2
- Interactive Tutor Self-Assessment CD-ROM

Reading Check

Answer: No, it did not change existing borders and it did not address the impressment of sailors.

History Online

Study Central provides summaries, interactive games, and online graphic organizers to help students review section content.

CLOSE

Identifying Central Issues
Ask students to identify problems the United States would have to address now that the War of 1812 was over. Ask students to suggest solutions to the problems. OL CA HI2.

SECTION 2 REVIEW ANSWERS

Review questions reinforce content standard US8.5.

1. U.S.; convinced Britain to end war
2. The Federalists lost support because of their opposition to the war; the nation gained self-confidence.
3. Federalists lost power; Nationalism; Americans felt themselves as equals of other countries; Strong government
4. **The Big Ideas** It looked unpatriotic.
5. Students' songs should reflect what happened at the battle.
6. **Analysis** After Napoleon's defeat and the Battle of Lake Champlain, Britain no longer wanted to pursue war with the U.S.; the Treaty of Ghent didn't change any borders or address impressment.

FOCUS

Ask students to brainstorm what they already know about how people lived in the early 1800s. Write the following headings on the board ands have students suggest statements that fit in each category: *Food, Daily Life, Work, Interests,* and *Religion.* OL

TEACH

R Reading Strategy

Reading Primary Sources

Have students read Sagoyewatha's speech. **Ask:** What two things does Sagoyewatha say that whites have done to his people? *(took their land; now trying to force them to accept their religion)* Why does Sagoyewatha think that the whites are hypocritical about religion? *(He says the whites tell Native Americans there is just one way to worship God, but the whites have many different religions.)* What is Sagoyewatha's tone in his speech? *(Students may say he is angry and critical of whites, but his tone is respectful and controlled.)* OL CA HR3.

Answers and Additional Support

What were people's lives like in the past?

What—and who—were people talking about? What did they eat? What did they do for fun? These two pages will give you some clues to everyday life in the U.S. as you step back in time with TIME Notebook.

Profile

SAGOYEWATHA *is the great Iroquois leader some call Red Jacket. Why? Because he fought with the British in the Revolutionary War. Sagoyewatha means "He Causes Them to Be Awake." Below is part of a speech Sagoyewatha delivered in 1805 to a group of religious leaders from Boston:*

R

"BROTHERS, OUR (*NATIVE AMERICAN*) SEATS were once large and yours (colonists) were small. You have now become a great people, and we have scarcely a place left to spread our blankets. You have got our country but are not satisfied; you want to force your religion upon us. . . .

Brothers, continue to listen. You say there is but one way to worship and serve the Great Spirit. If there is but one religion, why do you white people differ so much about it?. . .

Brothers, we . . . also have a religion which was given to our forefathers and has been handed down to us, their children. . . ."

Sagoyewatha

VERBATIM

WHAT PEOPLE ARE SAYING

"We are one."

"Mind your business."

FIRST OFFICIAL U.S. COIN, *sayings are on the front and back of the coin minted in 1787*

"I die hard, but I am not afraid to go."

GEORGE WASHINGTON, *on his deathbed in 1799*

"My mother and myself begged Mr. Carter not to sell this child out of Fredg [*plantation*], he gave us his word and honor that he would not, but as soon as we left him, he sold the child."

JAMES CARTER, *African American slave of Landon Carter, writing around 1790 about his sister, whom he never saw again*

"May the Lord bless King George, convert him, and take him to heaven, as we want no more of him."

REVEREND JOHN GRUBER, *to his Baltimore congregation during the War of 1812*

1790s WORD PLAY

Ahoy There!

The U.S.S. *Constitution,* a powerful frigate, or warship, was launched in 1797 with a crew of 450 and 54 cannons. Want to join the crew? First, you must prove you can understand a sailor's vocabulary. Match each word or phrase in the first column with its original meaning.

1. Keel over
2. Try a new tack
3. Let the cat out of the bag
4. Mind your p's and q's
5. Shipshape

a. Sailors who do wrong are disciplined with a cat-o'-nine-tails whip that's kept in a red sack

b. Putting a ship in for repair

c. Bartenders keep track of what sailors drink and owe by marking numbers under "pints" and "quarts"

d. The course or direction boats take into the wind

e. Good condition

answers: 1. b; 2. d; 3. a; 4. c; 5. e

History Online

Visit the TIME Web site at www.time.com for up-to-date news, weekly magazine articles, editorials, online polls, and an archive of past magazine and Web articles.

Did You Know?

Sagoyewatha was a chief of the Seneca, one of the nations that formed the Iroquois Confederacy. By the early 1600s, five once-warring nations in northern New York had formed a union. The five were the Mohawk, Oneida, Onondaga, Cayuga, and Seneca. In 1722, the Tuscorora joined.

NATIVE AMERICAN LIFE

Sports Story

GEORGE CATLIN *is a white man with a strong interest in Native American life. This lawyer has made a name for himself as an artist, painting portraits of Native American leaders, families, and everyday Western life. Here he paints with words, telling us about a game (one the French call lacrosse) played by Choctaw men:*

R

"EACH PARTY (TEAM) HAD THEIR GOAL MADE WITH TWO UPRIGHT POSTS, about 25 feet high and six feet apart, set firm in the ground, with a pole across at the top. These goals were about 40 to 50 rods (660–825 feet) apart. At a point just halfway between was another small stake, driven down, where the ball was to be thrown up at the firing of a gun, to be struggled for by the players ... who were some 600 or 700 in numbers, and were (trying) to catch the ball in their sticks, and throw it home and between their respective stakes.... For each time that the ball was passed between the stakes of either party, one was counted for their game... until the successful party arrived to 100, which was the limit of the game, and accomplished at an hour's sun."

RIGHT: George Catlin *painted this picture of a 15-year-old Native American girl. Her name, Ka-te-qua, means "female eagle."*

BELOW: *Painting by* **George Catlin** *of* **Choctaw athletes** *playing their version of lacrosse.*

NUMBERS

U.S. AT THE TIME

30 Number of treaties that took away Native American land or moved their borders. The treaties were between the U.S. and the Creeks, Choctaws, and Chickasaws between 1789 and 1825

$158 million The price the U.S. spent to fight the War of 1812

First Elizabeth Seton founds the Sisters of Charity, a Roman Catholic order, in 1809

First Mary Kies becomes the first woman to receive a U.S. patent in 1809 for a method of weaving straw with silk

$3,820.33 Amount paid to Paul Revere for providing the U.S.S. *Constitution* with copper parts and a ship's bell in 1797

45 feet Length of the dinosaur dug up by Lewis and Clark on their 1804 expedition

R Reading Strategy

Scaffolding—Connecting
Have students read Catlin's account of a lacrosse game and try to describe the rules of the game. Then have them compare this game to popular sports played today. OL

This READING SKILL was introduced in Chapter 3.

ASSESS

Point out to students that Native Americans were a minority living in the United States in the early 1800s. Have students compare and contrast the situation of Native Americans in the early 1800s with minorities currently living in the United States. Use a class chart to keep track of similarities and differences. OL CA HI2.

CLOSE

Ask students to brainstorm the names of other famous Native American leaders they know of (such as Pontiac, Crazy Horse, Sitting Bull, Geronimo). As students call out the names, have the class give one reason for that leader's fame. BL

EXTENDING THE CONTENT

Native American Life George Catlin made more than 500 paintings and drawings of Native American subjects, mostly of Great Plains people. His goal was to observe and record their way of life before it disappeared under the wave of American settlement in the West. He published most of his art in *Letters and Notes on the Manners, Customs, and Condition of the North American Indians* in 1841. Most of his paintings and drawings are now in the Smithsonian Institution in Washington, D.C.

FOCUS

BELLRINGER
SKILLBUILDER ACTIVITY

Project **Daily Focus Skills Transparency 7–3** and have students answer the question.

Guide to Reading

Preteaching Vocabulary: Point out that two terms use common prefixes, or word beginnings *(disarmament and demilitarized)*. Explain that both have the meaning of "not," or "the oppposite of." Ask volunteers to name other words using the same prefixes. *(discolor, disconnect, declaw, deflate)*

Answers to Graphic: Oregon, Florida, Texas

Unpacking the Standards

After reading the section, students will be able to:

- Describe the national pride and self-confidence of the Era of Good Feelings.
- Explain how disputes with other countries over territories were resolved.
- Discuss how Latin American countries fought for and won independence.

Section 3

Foreign Relations

History Social Science Standards

US8.5 Students analyze U.S. foreign policy in the early Republic.

Guide to Reading

Looking Back, Looking Ahead
In Section 2, you learned about the War of 1812. In this section you will read about the United States's relations with foreign countries in the postwar period.

Focusing on the Main Ideas
- After the War of 1812, a new spirit of nationalism took hold in American society. ***(page 363)***
- In 1823 the United States proclaimed its dominant role in the Americas with the Monroe Doctrine. ***(page 366)***

Locating Places
Louisiana Territory
Oregon Country
Spanish East Florida
Mexico

Meeting People
James Monroe
John Quincy Adams
Andrew Jackson
Miguel Hidalgo (ee • DAHL • goh)
Simón Bolívar (see • MOHN buh • LEE • VAHR)
José de San Martín (hoh • ZAY day SAHN mahr • TEEN)

Content Vocabulary
disarmament (dih • SAHR • muh • muhnt)
demilitarize (dee • MIH • luh • tuh • RYZ)
court-martial

Academic Vocabulary
establish (ihs • TA • blihsh)
demonstrate (DEH • muhn • STRAYT)
policy (PAH • luh • see)

Reading Strategy
Organizing Information Create a diagram like the one below to list three disputed territories in North America.

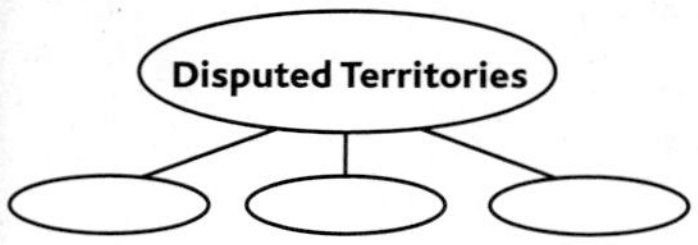

NATIONAL GEOGRAPHIC Where & When?

1817		1820		1823
1818 U.S. and Britain agree to occupy Oregon jointly	**1819** Spain cedes East Florida to U.S.	**1821** Mexico declares independence from Spain	**1823** Monroe Doctrine issued	

SECTION RESOURCES

Print Material
- Reproducible Lesson Plan 7–3*
- Daily Lesson and Discussion Notes 7–3
- Guided Reading Activity 7–3
- Reading Essentials and Study Guide 7–3
- Active Reading Note-Taking Guide 7–3
- Section Quiz 7–3

Transparencies
- Daily Focus Skills Transparency 7–3
- Section Graphic Organizer Transparency 7–3
- California Standards Practice Transparencies

Technology
- Interactive Tutor Self-Assessment CD-ROM
- Exam*View*® Pro Testmaker CD-ROM
- Presentation Plus! CD-ROM

*Available on TeacherWorks™

US8.5.1 Understand the political and economic causes and consequences of the War of 1812 and know the major battles, leaders, and events that led to a final peace. **US8.5.2** Know the changing boundaries of the United States and describe the relationships the country had with its neighbors (current Mexico and Canada) and Europe, including the influence of the Monroe Doctrine, and how those relationships influenced westward expansion and the Mexican-American War.

Relations With European Powers

Main Idea **After the War of 1812, a new spirit of nationalism took hold in American society.**

Reading Connection Think about your favorite sports team. Do you feel they are better than or superior to any other team? Read on to find out about the feeling of national pride many Americans felt.

An American Story

Following the War of 1812, Americans felt buoyed by a new sense of pride and faith in the United States. In his Inaugural Address on March 4, 1817, President **James Monroe** expressed feelings of hope and optimism for the country.

> **"Never did a government commence under auspices so favorable. . . . If we look to the history of other nations, ancient or modern, we find no example of a growth so rapid, so gigantic, of a people so prosperous and happy. . . . If we persevere . . . we can not fail . . . to attain the high destiny which seems to await us."**
>
> **—from James Monroe's Inaugural Address, 1817**

Era of Good Feelings The absence of major political divisions after the War of 1812 helped forge this sense of national unity. As political differences seemed to fade away, a Boston newspaper called these years the Era of Good Feelings. The president himself symbolized these good feelings. Monroe had been involved in national politics since the American Revolution. He wore breeches and powdered wigs—a style no longer in fashion. With his sense of dignity, Monroe represented a united America free of political strife.

Early in his presidency, Monroe toured the nation. No president since George Washington had done this. He paid his own expenses and tried to travel without an official escort. Everywhere Monroe went, local officials greeted him, and local people celebrated his visit. However, Monroe did not think this outpouring of support was meant for him personally. He wrote former President Madison that they revealed "a desire in the body of the people to show their attachment to the union." During this time, Americans began to think of themselves as equal, or even superior, to Europeans. Abigail Adams, wife of the second president John Adams, wrote from England to her sister back in Massachusetts: "Do you know that European birds have not half the melody of ours? Nor is their fruit half so sweet, nor their flowers half so fragrant, nor their manners half so pure, nor their people half so virtuous." C1

Despite such boasting, many Americans realized that the United States needed peaceful relations with the European powers to grow and develop. The young American republic had to put differences aside and **establish** a new relationship with the "Old World." C2

Relations With Britain In the years after the War of 1812, President Monroe and his secretary of state, **John Quincy Adams,** moved to resolve long-standing disputes with Great Britain. In 1817, in the Rush-Bagot Treaty, the United States and Britain agreed to set limits on the number of naval vessels each could have on the Great Lakes. The treaty provided for the **disarmament** (dih • SAHR • muh • muhnt)—the removal of weapons—along an important part of the border between the United States and British Canada. R1

Setting a Northern Boundary The United States also worked with Britain to establish the American-Canadian boundary farther west. A second agreement with Britain, the Convention of 1818, set the boundary of the **Louisiana Territory** between the United States and Canada at the 49th parallel. The convention created a secure and **demilitarized** (dee • MIH • luh • tuh • RYZD) border—a border without armed forces. R2

TEACH

C1 Critical Thinking

Analyzing Primary Sources Read Abigail Adams' statement to students. **Ask:** Why did she feel this way? *(Students may say that her national pride and patriotism led her to express these thoughts.)* **OL** **CA 8RL3.7**

C2 Critical Thinking

Making Inferences Ask: Why was it in the best interests of the United States to have good relations with European powers? *(Answers may include a greater chance to grow economically through increased trade with Europe, avoiding cost and trauma of war, and opportunity to agree on new territorial acquisitions.)* **AL** **CA HI2**

R1 Reading Strategy

Understanding Vocabulary **Ask:** What does disarmament mean? *(removal of weapons)* Have students identify current issues in which they have heard the term. *(Examples may include disarmament in Iraq or Afghanistan or talks on nuclear disarmament)* **OL** **CA 8RW1.3**

R2 Reading Strategy

Understanding Vocabulary **Ask:** What does *demilitarized* mean? *(without armed forces)* What are some other terms that use the suffix *–ize*? *(hospitalize, jeopardize)* **OL**

More Skill Practice

Historical and Social Sciences Analysis Skill Ask: How is the name "Era of Good Feelings" appropriate for this period? *(People were unified politically.)* How is the name not accurate? *(Students may point out that there were disputes with other countries that needed to be settled.)* **OL** **CA HI1.**

Did You Know?

In an amazing coincidence, three of the first five U.S. presidents died on Independence Day during this period. John Adams and Thomas Jefferson, died within hours of each other, on July 4, 1826—the fiftieth anniversary of the approval of the Declaration of Independence. James Monroe died five years later on July 4, 1831.

Resources for page 363

- Biography Activity 7B
- Geography and History Activity 7

W Writing Support

Research Reports Writing Have students conduct a search on the Internet to find information they could use to write a report on the Convention of 1818, the Adams-Onís Treaty of 1819, or the introduction of American settlers in Texas. Have them create a bibliography of five sources. OL CA 8WS1.4

R Reading Strategy

Categorizing Information Have students make graphic organizers for the information in the text about the territorial disputes in Oregon, Florida, and Texas. Suggest they use charts, outlines, or other forms to group statements about each border dispute. Have pairs of students exchange organizers and review the statements. *(Statements should be categorized accurately based on the text discussion.)* BL

Analyzing Political Cartoons

English cartoonist James Gillray shows European leaders carving up the world (above). American cartoonist David Claypoole Johnston portrays Andrew Jackson as a ruthless general (right). ***What opinions are the cartoonists expressing?***

Decades later, after lingering tensions had settled, the American-Canadian boundary became known as the longest unguarded border in the world. Through Adams's efforts, Americans also gained the right to settle in the **Oregon Country,** a vast area extending from California to Alaska.

W **Oregon** Many Americans wanted control of the Oregon Country so they could gain access to the Pacific Ocean. In the early 1800s, four countries—Britain, Spain, Russia, and the United States—claimed this vast, rugged land. Spain and Russia eventually gave up their claims, leaving control of Oregon to Britain and the United States.

Both countries based their claims to the Oregon on the explorations of American and British fur trappers and traders. To prevent a war over Oregon, British and American diplomats worked to settle the dispute peacefully. R In the Convention of 1818, Britain and the United States agreed to jointly occupy Oregon. This meant that people from both the nations could settle there.

In the following years, thousands of Americans streamed into the Oregon Country. The number of British settlers remained small, however. As the American presence grew, the question of who should own Oregon arose again. In the Treaty of 1846, Britain and the United States compromised by dividing Oregon into American and British portions at latitude 49°N.

Relations With Spain The United States also worked to settle border disputes with Spain. In the early 1800s, Spain owned East Florida and also claimed West Florida. The United States contended that West Florida was part of the Louisiana Purchase. In 1810 and 1812, Americans simply added parts of West Florida to Louisiana and Mississippi. Spain objected but took no action.

In April 1818, General **Andrew Jackson** invaded **Spanish East Florida,** seizing control of two Spanish forts. Jackson had been ordered to stop Seminole raids on American territory from Florida. In capturing the Spanish forts, however, Jackson went beyond his instructions.

Answers and Additional Support

More Skill Practice

Historical and Social Sciences Analysis Skill Have students construct time lines of the important events regarding one of the disputed territories discussed in "Relations with European Powers." OL CA CS1.

Analyzing Political Cartoons

James Gillray's 1805 cartoon is called "The Plum Pudding in Danger." The figure on the left is British prime minister William Pitt; on the right is French dictator Napoleon.

Answer: left—Great Britain and France were dividing up control of the world; right—Jackson was harsh and difficult

Adams-Onís Treaty Luis de Onís, the Spanish minister to the United States, protested forcefully and demanded the punishment of Jackson and his officers. Secretary of War John Calhoun said that Jackson should be **court-martialed**—tried by a military court—for overstepping instructions. Secretary of State John Quincy Adams disagreed.

R1

Although Secretary of State Adams had not authorized Jackson's raid, he did nothing to stop it. Adams guessed that the Spanish did not want war and that they might be ready to settle the Florida dispute. He was right. For the Spanish, the raid had **demonstrated** the military strength of the United States. Already troubled by rebellions in Mexico and South America, Spain signed the Adams-Onís Treaty in 1819. Spain gave East Florida to the United States and abandoned all claims to West Florida.

R2

The two countries also agreed on a border between the United States and Spanish possessions in the West. These lands had been in dispute since 1803, when the United States received the Louisiana Territory. In the Adams-Onís Treaty, the United States gave up its claims to Spanish Texas and took over responsibility for paying the $5 million that American citizens claimed Spain owed them for damages. The treaty also extended the border northwest from the Gulf of Mexico to the 42nd parallel and then west to the Pacific, recognizing the United States's claim to the Oregon Country. America had become a transcontinental power.

C

The Struggle for Frontier Lands In the early 1800s, Spain held most of the land west of the Mississippi River, with the exception of Oregon and the Louisiana Territory. Spanish officials tried to keep Americans and other foreigners out of this frontier area. However, they found it increasingly difficult to enforce this policy. When Mexico won its freedom from Spain in 1821, it gained control of this vast area of 75,000 Spanish-speaking inhabitants and 150,000 Native Americans. The Mexicans also faced the American push for expansion that Spain had tried to block.

R3

Why Did Mexico Change Its Policy? Economics finally won out over politics. In 1823 the Mexican government decided to welcome American traders and settlers into its frontier lands. It hoped that increased trade and population would boost the region's economy. Shortly, Americans began arriving in the region to settle.

Mexican officials soon questioned the wisdom of their invitation. Most of the new settlers remained American, and many disliked and even resisted Mexican laws and customs. At the same time, in the United States, an increasing number of Americans were accepting the idea that the United States had a right to expand its territory from the Atlantic Ocean to the Pacific Ocean. This expansion, it was believed, would make the young country rich and more powerful. It would also provide security, because an enlarged United States would be bordered by the sea instead of by foreign powers. As a result, many Americans saw the advantage of obtaining Mexico's frontier lands and extending United States territory to the Pacific.

Conflict With Mexico The United States tried to buy territory from **Mexico**, but the Mexicans refused. Relations between the two countries worsened when American settlers in Texas revolted against Mexican rule. Texas gained its independence in 1836 and U.S. statehood in 1845. These events greatly angered Mexico, which broke diplomatic ties with the United States. A dispute over the Texas-Mexico border caused more trouble. By the following year, Mexico and the United States were at war. Mexico was defeated and lost almost half of its territory to the United States. In 1848 the peace treaty ending the war gave the United States the area that today includes California, New Mexico, Arizona, and a number of other western states.

Reading Check **Explain** Why was Andrew Jackson's action considered by some to be unlawful?

R1 Reading Strategy

Understanding Vocabulary Explain that *martial*—from Mars, the Greek god of war—refers to things related to the military or to war. Ask a volunteer to connect this to the meaning of *court-martial*. OL

R2 Reading Strategy

Academic Vocabulary Have students read the sentence that contains the word *demonstrated*. Then discuss other forms of *demonstrate*, such as *demonstration*. Point out the different types of speech of each form.

C Critical Thinking

Making Generalizations Explain that a generalization is a broad statement put together from several pieces of information. Ask students to make a generalization, based on their reading of this subsection, about how the United States settled its border disputes. Have students share and support their generalizations. *(Example: The United States successfully settled its border disputes, using military action only as a last resort.)* OL

CA HI2.

R3 Reading Strategy

Reading Maps, Graphs, and Charts Have students work in pairs. Ask one student in each pair to read about one border dispute. Have the other student use a map of the United States to identify the area in question. Then have students switch roles until all the disputes in this section have been covered. EL

CA CS3.

Reading Check

Answer: He had been ordered only to stop Seminole raids, but he disobeyed orders and seized Spanish forts, too.

EXTENDING THE CONTENT

Splitting Texas and Mexico At first, the new independent government of Mexico welcomed American settlers into its northern frontier areas, including Texas. However, when the number of American settlers became so great and the number of migrants from southern Mexico into the area proved smaller than expected, Mexico decided to stop this migration in 1830. Americans continued to arrive. These Americana settlers became a driving force in splitting Texas from the rest of Mexico in the 1830s.

S Skill Practice

Visual Literacy Ask students to examine the portrait of Hidalgo. Have them find visual evidence for each of the following points: (1) Hidalgo's campaign was based on religion. *(his clerical collar, the cross on the left side)* (2) His supporters were poor people. *(peasant clothes of people at the bottom)* (3) The rebellion was violent. *(his bloody knife and clenched fist)* AL CA 8LS1.9

W Writing Support

Persuasive Writing Have students write a newspaper editorial giving reasons why the United States should support or not support independence movements in Latin America. OL CA 8WA2.4

History Online

Objectives and answers to the **Student Web Activity** can be found in the Web Activity Lesson Plan feature at ca.hss.glencoe.com.

Answers and Additional Support

U.S. 8.5.2 Know the changing boundaries of the United States and describe the relationships the country had with its neighbors (current Mexico and Canada) and Europe, including the influence of the Monroe Doctrine, and how those relationships influenced westward expansion and the Mexican-American War.

The United States and Latin America

Main Idea **In 1823 the United States proclaimed its dominant role in the Americas with the Monroe Doctrine.**

Reading Connection You recall how the American colonies felt about throwing off British rule. Read on to find out how many Latin American countries gained independence from Spain.

While working out its relations with Europe after the War of 1812, the United States pursued new policies with Latin America. These policies would guide the nation's relations in the Western Hemisphere for years to come.

During the early 1800s, Spain controlled a vast colonial empire that included what is now the southwestern United States, Mexico, Central America, and all of South America except Portuguese-ruled Brazil. At this time, the Spanish and Portuguese faced a series of challenges within their empires. Although the United States had given little thought to Europe's Latin American colonies before 1800, it voiced support when those colonies began their struggles for independence from Spain and Portugal. W

S

▲ Miguel Hidalgo

Mexico In the fall of 1810, a priest, **Miguel Hidalgo** (ee•DAHL•goh), led a rebellion against the Spanish government of Mexico. Hidalgo called for racial equality and the redistribution of land. The Spanish defeated the revolutionary forces and executed Hidalgo. Mexico finally gained its independence in 1821. Along with independence, Mexico also gained control of the northern frontier lands that included present-day Texas, Arizona, New Mexico, Nevada, Utah, western Colorado, California, and small parts of Wyoming, Kansas, and Oklahoma.

Bolívar and San Martín In South America, independence came largely as a result of the efforts of two men. **Simón Bolívar** (see•MOHN buh•LEE•VAHR), also known as "the Liberator," led the movement that won freedom for the present-day countries of Venezuela, Colombia, Panama, Bolivia, and Ecuador. **José de San Martín** (hoh•ZAY day SAHN mahr•TEEN) successfully achieved independence for Chile and Peru. By 1824 the revolutionaries' military victory was complete, and most of South America had liberated itself from Spain. Portugal's large colony of Brazil gained its independence peacefully in 1822.

In working for independence, Simón Bolívar and other Latin American leaders were inspired by the example of the United States. Americans, in turn, were glad to see European empires further weakened. They looked forward to increased trade between the United States and Latin America and to the spread of American ideals within the region.

History Online

Student Web Activity Visit ca.hss.glencoe.com and click on *Chapter 7—Student Web Activities* for an activity on democratic movements in the Americas.

More Skill Practice

Historical and Social Sciences Analysis Skill Ask students to write three questions they would like to have answered about the United States and its relations with Latin American countries in the early 1800s. Then have them exchange lists with a partner and write suggestions on where the answers could be found. OL CA HR1

More About the Art

The painting of Father Hidalgo is a fresco (paint applied to wet plaster) by Mexican artist José Clemente Orozco. It is in the Governor's Mansion in Guadalajara, Mexico.

On July 4, 1821, Secretary of State John Quincy Adams gave a speech to Congress. He said: "Wherever the standard of freedom and Independence has been or shall be unfurled, there will her heart, her benedictions, her prayers be." Adams meant that the United States should support colonies that wanted to gain their freedom. To demonstrate this support, President Monroe quickly recognized the independence of the Latin American republics.

The Monroe Doctrine In 1822 the Quadruple Alliance—France, Austria, Russia, and Prussia—discussed a plan to help Spain regain its American holdings. The possibility of increased European involvement in North America led President Monroe to consider action.

President Monroe declared in 1823 that the American continents were "not to be considered as subjects for future colonization by any European powers." Any foreign military expeditions sent to the Western Hemisphere would be seen as a threat to the United States, Monroe warned. No European country should interfere in United States affairs, at home or abroad.

The president's proclamation, later called the Monroe Doctrine, was a bold act. The United States might not have been able to back up its new **policy** if challenged. The Monroe Doctrine marked the beginning of a long-term American policy of preventing other great powers from interfering in Latin American political affairs. By keeping the European powers out of the Americas, the Monroe Doctrine upheld George Washington's policy of avoiding entangling alliances in European power struggles.

Reading Check **Identify** What event led to the creation of the Monroe Doctrine?

History Online
Study Central Need help understanding independence movements in the Americas? Visit ca.hss.glencoe.com and click on Study Central.

Section 3 Review

Reading Summary

Review the Main Ideas

- Following the War of 1812, Americans entered into a period known as the Era of Good Feelings in which they felt politically and economically secure.
- Latin American countries, inspired by the American Revolution, fought for independence from Spain.

What Did You Learn?

1. Why did America support the Latin American countries in their fight for independence?
2. What were the provisions of the Monroe Doctrine?

Critical Thinking

3. **Summarize** Draw a table like the one below and summarize what happened in each territorial dispute. CA CS1.

Territory	Action
Oregon Country	
Louisiana Territory	
Spanish East Florida	
Texas	

4. **The Big Ideas** Why do you think the United States wanted dominance over most of the territories in North America? CA HI1.
5. **Persuasive Writing** Reread the section on the seizure of Spanish forts in Florida by Andrew Jackson. Choose a side either for or against Andrew Jackson's actions, and write a letter to the president stating why you feel Jackson either should or should not be court-martialed. CA 8WA2.1

SECTION 3 REVIEW ANSWERS

Review questions reinforce content standard US8.5.

1. to weaken European empires, gain trading partners, and spread democracy
2. Americas were not subjects for colonization by Europe, military expeditions to the Americas would be considered a threat to the U.S.; no country should interfere with U.S. affairs at home or abroad
3. Oregon: U.S., Britain split it equally; Louisiana: border fixed by treaty; Florida: Spain gives it up; Texas: Texans revolt, gain independence and join U.S.
4. **The Big Ideas** for growth, security
5. Students should support their positions with reasons.

Review The Big Idea

Review the Big Idea for this section: "Political ideas and major events shape how people form governments." **Ask:** How did the Monroe Doctrine reflect the wave of nationalism that followed the War of 1812? *(It revealed America's growing confidence, which led the government to stand up to European powers.)* OL CA HI3

ASSESS

Resources for page 367

Use these resources to assess student mastery of section content.

- Universal Access Activity 7
- Section Quiz 7–3
- Interactive Tutor Self-Assessment CD-ROM

Reading Check

Answer: the decision by the Quadruple Alliance to discuss helping Spain regain its holdings in Latin America.

History Online

Study Central provides summaries, interactive games, and online graphic organizers to help students review section content.

CLOSE

Drawing Conclusions Ask: Why do you think the United States was able to expand so quickly in the first half of the 1800s? OL CA HI2.

Analyzing Primary Sources

FOCUS

History–Social Science Standards

The following standard is covered on pages 368–369.

US8.5 Students analyze U.S. foreign policy in the early Republic.

TEACH

U Universal Access

Verbal/Linguistic Invite a student to read the poem with enthusiastic expression. **Ask:** How does hearing the poem compare to reading it silently? OL CA 8SA2.5

R Reading Strategy

Paraphrasing To verify that students understand the poem, have them paraphrase each stanza of the poem using a complete sentence. OL CA 8RL3.4

Answers and Additional Support

US8.5 Students analyze U.S. foreign policy in the early Republic.

Analyzing Primary Sources

Nationalism in the United States

In the early 1800s, the idea of being an American and part of a country called the "United States" was still new. If the United States was going to succeed as a country, people would need to think of themselves as being Americans. Feelings of nationalism—loyalty to a nation and the promotion of its interests above all others—began to grow. Some Americans expressed pride in their new nation in songs and poems. The War of 1812 helped bring about even stronger feelings of nationalism.

Read the passages on pages 368 and 369 and answer the questions that follow.

Flag flown at Fort McHenry ▶ during the War of 1812

Reader's Dictionary

Ramilies, Nimrod: British ships

valor (VA • luhr): courage, bravery

maritime (MAR • uh • TYM): relating to ships and the sea

submission (suhb • MIH • shuhn): giving in to the will or power of another

intriguing (ihn • TREE • gihng): making secret plans

diminished (duh • MIH • nihshd): made less

strife (STRYF): conflict, struggle

prosecute (PRAH • sih • KYOOT): carry out

The Battle of Stonington

This excerpt is from a song by Philip Freneau that describes the British attack on Stonington, Connecticut, in 1814.

Three gallant ships from England came,
Freighted deep with fire and flame,
And other things we need not name,
To have a dash at Stonington. . . .

The **Ramilies** first began the attack,
And **Nimrod** made a mighty crack,
And none can tell what kept them back
From setting fire to Stonington. . . .

To have a turn we thought but fair.
We Yankees brought two guns to bear,
And, sir, it would have made you stare
To have seen the smoke at Stonington. . . .

The Ramilies then gave up the fray [fight],
And with her comrades sneaked away;
Such was the **valor** on that day
Of British [sailors] at Stonington. . . .

—Philip Freneau

War and Expansion

A number of young War Hawks were elected to Congress in 1810. In this speech, War Hawk Felix Grundy explains why the United States should go to war with Great Britain.

What, Mr. Speaker, are we now called on to decide? It is whether we will resist by force the attempt made by that government to subject our **maritime** rights to . . . her will; . . . Sir, I prefer war to **submission**. . . .

EXTENDING THE CONTENT

Great Speaker Daniel Webster, one of the leading figures in the early 1800s, was well respected for his speaking ability. As a lawyer, Webster argued and won several important cases before the Supreme Court. One of his most famous speeches came against the idea of nullification. Webster finished his speech with the words "Liberty and Union, now and forever, one and inseparable!" In his career, he served in the U.S. House and Senate and was also secretary of state.

This war, if carried on successfully, will have its advantages. We shall drive the British from our continent—they will no longer have an opportunity of **intriguing** with our Indian neighbors. . . . That nation will lose her Canadian trade, and, by having no resting place in this country, her means of annoying us will be **diminished**. . . . I am willing to receive the Canadians as adopted brethren; . . . [I] therefore feel anxious not only to add the Floridas to the South, but the Canadas to the North of this empire.

—from a speech in the House of Representatives, December 1811

Against the Draft

In 1813 President Madison proposed a bill that would draft, or force, men into the army. Representative Daniel Webster of New Hampshire spoke against this bill. At the same time, he criticized the war.

Is this, sir, consistent with the character of a free government? Is this civil liberty? Is this the real character of our Constitution? No, sir, indeed it is not. . . .

If, sir, in this **strife** he [the draftee] fall; if, while ready to obey every rightful command of government, he is forced from his home against right, not to contend for the defense of his country but to **prosecute** a miserable and detestable project of invasion, and in that strife he fall, 'tis murder.

—from a speech in the House of Representatives, December 9, 1814

▲ Daniel Webster

DBQ Document-Based Questions

The Battle of Stonington

1. How was the Battle of Stonington fought?
2. Who won the battle? How?

War and Expansion

3. What government is Grundy referring to in the first paragraph?
4. Whose empire does Grundy want the Floridas and the Canadas to belong to?

Against the Draft

5. What is a military draft?
6. How does Webster object to the draft?

Read to Write

7. Evaluate Grundy's and Webster's arguments about the War of 1812. What arguments does each man use to support his beliefs about the war? What do you think of each argument? Write a short essay on the topic. CA 8WA2.4 CA HR4.

C Critical Thinking

Comparing and Contrasting **Ask:** How are Grundy's arguments similar to those made at the time of the American Revolution? *(He says Britain has violated Americans' rights; he says the British have acted unjustly.)* OL CA HI3.

R Reading Strategy

Reading Primary Sources **Ask:** What grounds does Webster give for his position that a draft is wrong? *(It is unconstitutional.)* Does he believe that any forced military service is wrong? *(possibly acceptable in time of national danger)* OL CA 8RC2.0

ASSESS

Have students answer the Document-Based Questions.

CLOSE

Connecting **Ask:** Though he is critical of the government, how is Webster's attitude toward the United States similar to those of the poet and of Grundy? *(Students may note that Webster feels the government is not living up to American ideals.)* OL CA HR3.

DBQ Document-Based Questions

1. 3 British ships attacked the town.
2. The Yankees; they used two guns to drive off the ships.
3. the British
4. the United States
5. forcing men to join the army
6. Webster says that draftees should not be forced to fight in a war that is wrong.
7. Students may note that Grundy thinks the war is in the nation's interest because it will drive the British out of North America and may gain territory; Webster believes it to be unnecessary and unwise.

Resources for pages 370–371

Use these resources to review, assess, or reteach the chapter.

- Active Reading Note-Taking Guide, Chapter 7
- Chapter 7 Reading Essentials and Study Guide
- Chapter 7 Tests, Forms A and B
- Standards Assessment, Forms A and B
- California Standards Practice Workbook
- Succeeding on the California History–Social Science Standards CD-ROM
- MindJogger Videoquiz
- Interactive Tutor Self-Assessment CD-ROM

Chapter 7 Assessment

Standard US8.5

Review Content Vocabulary

Match each word with the correct definition below.

1. tribute	5. nationalism
2. frigate	6. privateer
3. disarmament	7. embargo
4. demilitarized	8. neutral rights

a. armed private ship
b. the removal of weapons
c. money paid to gain protection from someone or something
d. an order that prohibits trade with other countries
e. without military occupation
f. the ability to sail the seas and not take sides in a conflict
g. a warship
h. loyalty to one's country

Review the Main Ideas

Section 1 • A Time of Conflict

9. How did the Embargo Act of 1807 hurt the United States?
10. Who were the War Hawks?

Section 2 • The War of 1812

11. What were the important naval victories early in the War of 1812?
12. What battle occurred after the Treaty of Ghent was signed? What was its significance?

Section 3 • Foreign Relations

13. Which nations signed the Rush-Bagot Treaty?
14. What line of latitude did the United States and Great Britain agree upon as the border of the Oregon Territory?

Critical Thinking

15. **Evaluate** Why was the Florida territory so important to Spain and the United States? CA HI2.
16. **Analyze** When was the Battle of Horseshoe Bend? Why was it important? CA HI1.
17. **Compare** Describe the differences between the War Hawks and the Federalists in their views of the War of 1812. CA HR5.

Geography Skills

In 1819 Spain ceded Florida to the United States in the Adams-Onís Treaty. Study the map and answer the questions that follow. CA CS3.

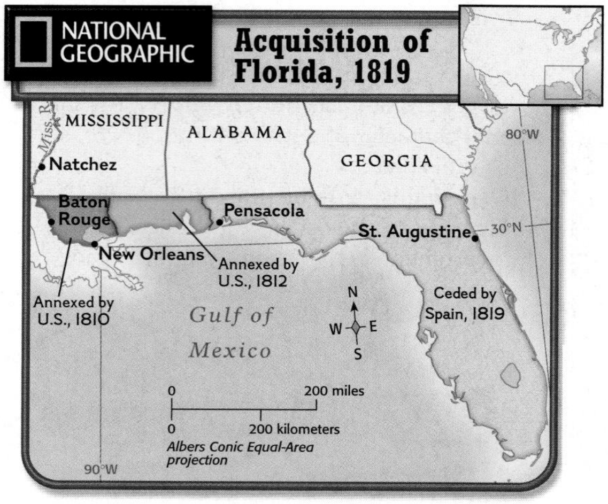

18. **Region** When was the largest portion of Florida acquired from Spain?
19. **Location** What body of water blocked further expansion of Florida to the west?
20. **Movement** In what direction did the United States acquire the various parts of Florida?

Review Content Vocabulary

1. c
2. g
3. b
4. e
5. h
6. a
7. d
8. f

Review the Main Ideas

9. It stopped American trade with other nations.
10. a group of Republicans in Congress from the South and West who urged war with Great Britain
11. Lake Erie, Lake Champlain, victories by the *Constitution* and privateers
12. Battle of New Orleans; gave Americans new self-confidence and sense of national identity, weakened the Federalist Party, and gave the U.S. new respect in foreign eyes
13. the United States and Great Britain
14. the 49°N

Critical Thinking

15. The area controlled the east bank of the Mississippi River and, in another country's hands, could threaten several southern states.
16. March 1814; with his victory Jackson forced the Creeks to give up most of their lands to the U.S.
17. War Hawks supported war against Britain; Federalists opposed it

Geography Skills

18. 1819
19. Mississippi River
20. west to east

History Online

Self-Check Quiz Visit ca.hss.glencoe.com to prepare for the Chapter 7 test.

Read to Write

21. **The Big Ideas** **Expository Writing** Using library or Internet resources, research the American Revolution and one of the Latin American wars for independence mentioned in Section 3. Compare and contrast the two wars for independence in a brief essay. CA 8WA2.4

22. **Creative Writing** Imagine you are a soldier during the War of 1812. Write a letter home to your family describing the things you see and how you feel about your place in the war. CA 8WA2.1

23. **Using Your FOLDABLES** Use the information from your completed chapter foldable to create a brief study guide for the chapter. Your study guide should include at least five questions for each section. Questions should focus on the main ideas. Exchange your study guide with a partner and answer each of the questions. CA 8RC2.0

Using Academic Vocabulary

24. Use each of the following academic vocabulary words in a sentence.

strategy	**establish**
conclude	**policy**

Building Citizenship

25. **Analyzing Current Events** With a partner, choose a recent event for which you will be able to locate primary and secondary sources of information. Compare the primary source with one secondary source. Prepare a report for the class in which you describe the event and compare the information in the primary and secondary sources. CA HR4.

Reviewing Skills

26. Review READING SKILL **Cause and Effect** What were the effects of Jackson's invasion of Spanish East Florida in 1818? Write a paragraph discussing the impact on U.S. territorial expansion. CA 8RC2.0

27. Review ANALYSIS SKILL **Compare and Contrast** Reread the sections in this chapter on Tecumseh. Summarize his point of view on American settlement of Native American lands and contrast that with what Harrison's view would have been. CA HR5.

Standards Practice

Read the passage below and answer the following questions.

> The American continents, by the free and independent condition which they have assumed and maintain, are henceforth not to be considered as subjects for future colonization by any European powers.
>
> We . . . should consider any attempt on their part to extend their system to any portion of this hemisphere as dangerous to our peace and safety.
>
> —The Monroe Doctrine

28 To what nations did Monroe direct his statements?

A Russia
B Central America
C South America
D European nations

29 The Monroe Doctrine sent a clear message from the United States. The doctrine was designed to

A preserve the United States's trade routes with Europe.
B prevent Central American countries from declaring war against the United States.
C prohibit European nations from colonizing any lands in the Western Hemisphere.
D protect the United States from invasion by European nations.

CHAPTER 7 Assessment

Reviewing Skills

26. Review READING SKILL The invasion led Spain to take notice of American military strength and agree to cede Florida to the U.S.

27. Review ANALYSIS SKILL Essays should point out that Tecumseh was opposed to further expansion of white settlements whereas Harrison supported that expansion.

Standards Practice

28. D
29. C

Bonus Question

Ask: Was the War of 1812 necessary? Why or why not? *(Answers will vary, but students should have relevant and informed reasons for their answers.)* OL CA HI2.

History Online

Have students visit the Web site at ca.hss.glencoe.com to review Chapter 7 and take the **Self-Check Quiz.**

Read to Write

21. The Big Ideas Essays should accurately describe some similarities and differences.

22. Letters should reflect details in the text about the war and offer reasonable contemporary opinions about them.

23. Using Your FOLDABLES Students' study guides should include relevant questions related to the main ideas and concepts in each section.

Using Academic Vocabulary

24. Students' sentences will vary but should reflect an understanding of each term.

Building Citizenship

25. Students may point out that a single primary source reflects only the perspective of one writer, while the secondary source can take more information into account.

FOCUS

Reviewing Unit Objectives

Having studied this unit, students should be able to

- Explain the decisions of the first presidents and the Congresses of the early republic.
- Describe the policies and principles that led to the formation of the first political parties.
- Identify the Louisiana Purchase and describe its effects.
- Describe daily life in the early republic.
- Discuss what actions and attitudes led to the War of 1812 and the effects of that war.
- Outline how the United States settled differences with other nations over territory.

TEACH

Have students cite two details on each of the following main ideas: the new nation struggled to survive; the United States expanded westward; a unique American culture began to develop; and slavery began to divide the country. OL

Unit Review Activity

To help students review the unit objectives, ask them to create a quiz of 10 to 15 questions focusing on the points addressed in the objectives. Students should write the questions and provide the answers as well. OL

Unit 3 REVIEW

Launching the Republic

The early years of the United States saw the nation struggling to survive and expanding westward. A unique American culture continued to develop. Even in these early days, the issue of slavery divided the country.

	Chapter 5 The Federalist Era	Chapter 6 The Age of Jefferson	Chapter 7 Foreign Affairs in the Early Republic
When	• 1789–1800	• 1800–1812	• 1812–1830
Where	• New York • Northwest Territory • Great Britain • Spain • France	• Washington, D.C. • Louisiana Territory • Mississippi River • France • Santo Domingo • Colorado • the North • the South	• Mediterranean Sea • Ohio • Washington, D.C. • Baltimore, Maryland • Oregon • Florida • Mexico • Texas • Latin America

Pitcher honoring Washington's inauguration, 1789 ▶

Lewis and Clark ▶

END-OF-UNIT RESOURCES

Use these resources to review and assess unit material.

- Step Into American History Activities
- Cumulative Assessment Activities
- Reading Essentials and Study Guide
- California Standards Practice Workbook
- Interactive Tutor Self-Assessment CD-ROM
- Exam*View*® Pro Testmaker CD-ROM
- Succeeding on the California History–Social Science Standards CD-ROM

Unit 3 Review

	Chapter 5: The Federalist Era	Chapter 6: The Age of Jefferson	Chapter 7: Foreign Affairs in the Early Republic
Major Events	• **1789** Judiciary Act • **1790s** Emergence of political parties • **1791** Bill of Rights • **1791** National Bank • **1793** Proclamation of Neutrality • **1794** Whiskey Rebellion • **1794** Battle of Fallen Timbers • **1794** Jay's Treaty • **1796** Washington's Farewell Address • **1796** XYZ Affair • **1798** Alien and Sedition Acts • **1798–1799** Virginia and Kentucky Resolutions	• **1801** Judiciary Act • **1801** Jefferson's Inaugural Address • **1803** *Marbury* v. *Madison* • **1803** Louisiana Purchase ratified • **1804–1806** Lewis and Clark expedition • **early 1800s** Second Great Awakening	• **1807** Embargo Act • **1809** Nonintercourse Act • **1811** Battle of Tippecanoe • **1812–1814** War of 1812 • **1814** British burn government buildings in Washington, D.C. • **1815** Battle of New Orleans • **1817** Rush-Bagot Treaty • **1819** Adams-Onís Treaty • **1821** Mexican independence • **1823** Monroe Doctrine • **1824** Most South American countries independent
Some Important People	• George Washington • Thomas Jefferson • Alexander Hamilton • John Jay • Edmond Genêt • John Adams • Charles de Talleyrand	• Thomas Jefferson • Albert Gallatin • John Marshall • Napoleon Bonaparte • Toussaint-Louverture • Meriwether Lewis • William Clark • Sacagawea • Zebulon Pike	• Thomas Jefferson • James Madison • Tecumseh • William Henry Harrison • Henry Clay • John Calhoun • Andrew Jackson • James Monroe
How do these events and ideas affect our lives today?	• Most candidates for office today belong to a political party. They run on the policies supported by their party.	• Lands that were part of the Louisiana Purchase are now part of the United States.	• The Monroe Doctrine set the tone for future relations between the United States and Latin America.
What was happening in California at this time?	• **1796** First American ship sails into California waters	• **1812** Russian fur traders establish Fort Ross	• **1821** California becomes part of Mexico

William Clark's journal ▼

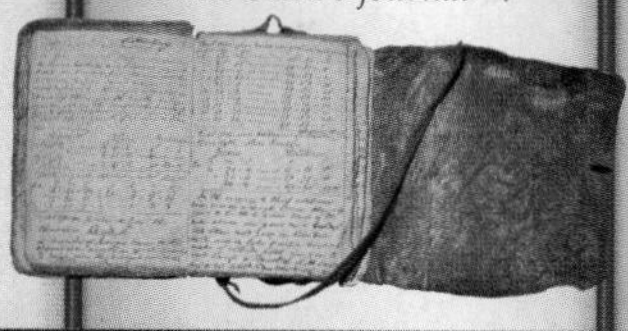

Tecumseh ▲

Fort Ross ▶

ASSESS/CLOSE

Unit Wrap-Up Activity

Making a Newspaper Have students work in groups to make a newspaper that focuses on events during the presidency of Washington, Adams, Jefferson, Madison, or Monroe.

1. Organize students into groups of equal size and assign each group one presidency.
2. Tell groups that their newspapers should include information on politics, economics, society, and culture. Remind them to include both news stories reporting events and features that focus on special issues. Point out that both types of articles will be more effective if they include quotations, which students can take from the text or other sources. Urge them to include pictures as well as words. Set a limit on the number of pages that each group should produce.
3. Have each group display its newspaper for the class. **OL**

PROFESSIONAL DEVELOPMENT: TEACHING WRITING

Use these resources for help teaching writing skills.

- Fleming, Gerald. *Rain, Steam, and Speed: Building Fluency in Adolescent Writers.* Jossey-Bass, 2004.
- Robb, Laura. *Nonfiction Writing: From the Inside Out.* Teaching Resources, 2004.
- Schrecengost, Maity. *Writing Whizardry: 60 Mini-Lessons to Teach Elaboration and Writer's Craft.* Maupin House Publishing, 2001.
- Spandel, Vicki. *Creating Writers Through 6-Trait Writing Assessment and Instruction* (Third Edition). Allyn & Bacon, 2000.

Teaching the Unit

Use the information on these pages to help you teach Unit 4.

History–Social Science Standards Covered in Unit 4

Standard	Chapter 8	Chapter 9	Chapter 10	Chapter 11
US8.6 Students analyze the divergent paths of the American people from 1800 to the mid-1800s and the challenges they faced, with emphasis on the Northeast.	✔			
US8.7 Students analyze the divergent paths of the American people in the South from 1800 to the mid-1800s and the challenges they faced.		✔		
US8.8 Students analyze the divergent paths of the American people in the West from 1800 to the mid-1800s and the challenges they faced.			✔	✔

Pacing Your Lessons

This pacing chart provides time management suggestions for teaching Unit 4.

Unit 4 Divergent Paths of the American People	Days
Unit 4 Introduction	1/2
Chapter 8 • **Reading Skill:** Problems and Solutions • **Sections 1–5** • **Biography:** Robert Fulton, Henry David Thoreau and Martin Luther King, Jr. • **Analyzing Primary Sources**	12
Chapter 9 • **Reading Skill:** Questioning • **Sections 1–3** • **Biography:** Harriet Tubman • **Analyzing Primary Sources**	6
Chapter 10 • **Reading Skill:** Question and Answer Relationships • **Sections 1–3** • **Biography:** Osceola • **Analyzing Primary Sources**	6
Chapter 11 • **Reading Skill:** New Vocabulary • **Sections 1–4** • **Biography:** María Amparo Ruiz de Burton, John Bidwell and Annie Bidwell • **You Decide . . .** • **Geography & History** • **Connecting to the Constitution** • **America's Literature:** *Thunder on the Sierra* • **Analyzing Primary Sources**	9
Unit 4 Review	1/2

Teacher to Teacher

Songs About Westward Expansion

Dr. Brent E. Heath
De Anza Middle School
Ontario, CA

Ask students if they have ever heard or know anything about the songs "Oh! Susanna" by Sephen Foster, "On Top of Old Smokey," "Home on the Range," or "I've Been Working on the Railroad." Encourage sharing to lay a foundation of prior knowledge. Then discuss how these songs might reflect westward expansion and the concept of Manifest Destiny.

Play a recording of the song "Oh! Susanna." After students listen to the song once, discuss what they learned by listening to it and how it connects to the concepts of westward expansion and Manifest Destiny. Do the same with the other songs. Complete the lesson by having students write their own lyrics for a song reflecting these concepts. Students could use the melodies of one of the four songs studied as a model for developing their lyrics. Encourage students to share their lyrics and even sing the song for the rest of the class.

Previewing the Chapters

Dear American History Teacher:

As you begin to teach this unit, there are themes that reoccur throughout the chapters that you will want to point out to students.

Regional distinctiveness continued to evolve and was evident in the societies and economies that developed. While the sections differed in their economic foundations, North, South, and West all experienced booming growth, and the nation was in the midst of a period of economic and geographical expansion. The prospect of future sectional conflict loomed as disagreement over slavery and States' rights grew.

You may want to use the following information at the beginning of each chapter as a lesson launcher to help students begin to focus on what they will be studying.

Albert S. Broussard

CHAPTER 8: The Northeast: Building America (pages 378–417)

In the North, business people invested in new industries, which led to the development of factories and encouraged the growth of cities. The nation built new transportation systems, which helped settlers move west, improved the movement of goods, and linked the eastern and western parts of the country together. As northern cities grew, so did the number of immigrants. Some people reacted to these changes by calling for reforms to solve social problems. One of those reform movements aimed to bring women more equality.

CHAPTER 9: The South (pages 418–441)

The South developed a different culture, which emphasized agriculture. Most farmers in the South did not own slaves and were poor. Plantations held by slave-owners varied in size and wealth and held different numbers of slaves, but the large slaveowners dominated Southern society and politics. Enslaved African Americans led difficult lives, but they managed to create a unique culture and family life that blended African and American elements. Many of them resisted slavery, and some ran away or fought for their freedom.

CHAPTER 10: The Age of Jackson (pages 442–465)

The presidential elections of 1824 and 1828 introduced new ways of campaigning, and states gave suffrage to more people, making the country more democratic, though some groups were still excluded. A new tariff law split the North and South; though a compromise was reached, it signaled growing sectionalism. President Andrew Jackson got Congress to pass a law that forced Native Americans in the southeastern states to give up their lands and move west. Jackson forced the National Bank to close. Economic problems allowed the Whig Party to rise in power, but after 1844 it lost the presidency.

CHAPTER 11: Manifest Destiny (pages 466–517)

Thousands of Americans began moving to Oregon to settle there, and the United States and Britain eventually agreed to divide the region. Many Americans moved to Texas and disputes with the Mexican government led Texans to declare independence. Many Americans called for the nation to expand to the Pacific Ocean. This feeling helped produce a war with Mexico that gained the United States large amounts of land. California's population grew rapidly when gold was discovered there, and Mormons settled in Utah.

FOCUS

Connecting to Past Learning

In Unit 3, students learned how the nation responded to various domestic and foreign challenges and grew in size. In Unit 4, they will read about the development of distinct ways of life in the nation's three sections, efforts to improve American society, and the further expansion of the United States.

Unit Launch Activity

Ask: Do you think relations with European countries would be a major concern of Americans in the time period covered in this unit? Why or why not? *(Students might answer no, since the events on the time line refer to domestic issues.)* OL

History–Social Science Standards

The following standards are covered in Unit 4:

US8.6 Students analyze the divergent paths of the American people from 1800 to the mid-1800s and the challenges they faced, with emphasis on the Northeast.

US8.7 Students analyze the divergent paths of the American people in the South from 1800 to the mid-1800s and the challenges they faced.

US8.8 Students analyze the divergent paths of the American people in the West from 1800 to the mid-1800s and the challenges they faced.

Why It's Important

Ask: What conflicts are hinted at by the introduction to this unit? OL

Unit 4

The Young Republic

Why It's Important

The United States continued to grow, both geographically and economically. Industry boomed in the North, and cotton became a major crop in the South. At the same time, settlers streamed to newly opened territories in the West. Certain groups of Americans, such as women and African Americans, pursued freedoms that would take many years to achieve.

- The United States grew greatly in size and wealth.
- More Americans gained the right to vote, and reform movements took root.

1790 — 1805 — 1820

U.S. EVENTS

1793 Whitney invents the cotton gin

◀ *Cotton gin*

Erie Canal barrel ▶

1825 Erie Canal is completed

CALIFORNIA EVENTS

Jedediah Smith ▶

1824 Jedediah Smith makes first U.S. trip by land to California

WORLD EVENTS

1804 Haiti wins independence from France

1814 Congress of Vienna meets to restore Europe's balance of power

◀ *Congress of Vienna*

374

TEACHING THE TIME LINES

Help students focus on the information in the time lines. **Ask:**

- Which events in the U.S. time line had to do with economics? *(Whitney invents cotton gin; Erie Canal is completed; Jackson challenges the Bank of the United States.)*
- Which events had to do with the rights of groups of people? *(Congress creates the Indian Territory; Seneca Falls Convention backs women's suffrage.)*
- What three major changes take place in California in this period? *(It changes from being part of Mexico to joining the United States; Gold is discovered; It becomes a U.S. state.)*

As students study events described in the unit, refer back to these time lines and have students identify where the event would appear. OL

Where in the United States?

NATIONAL GEOGRAPHIC

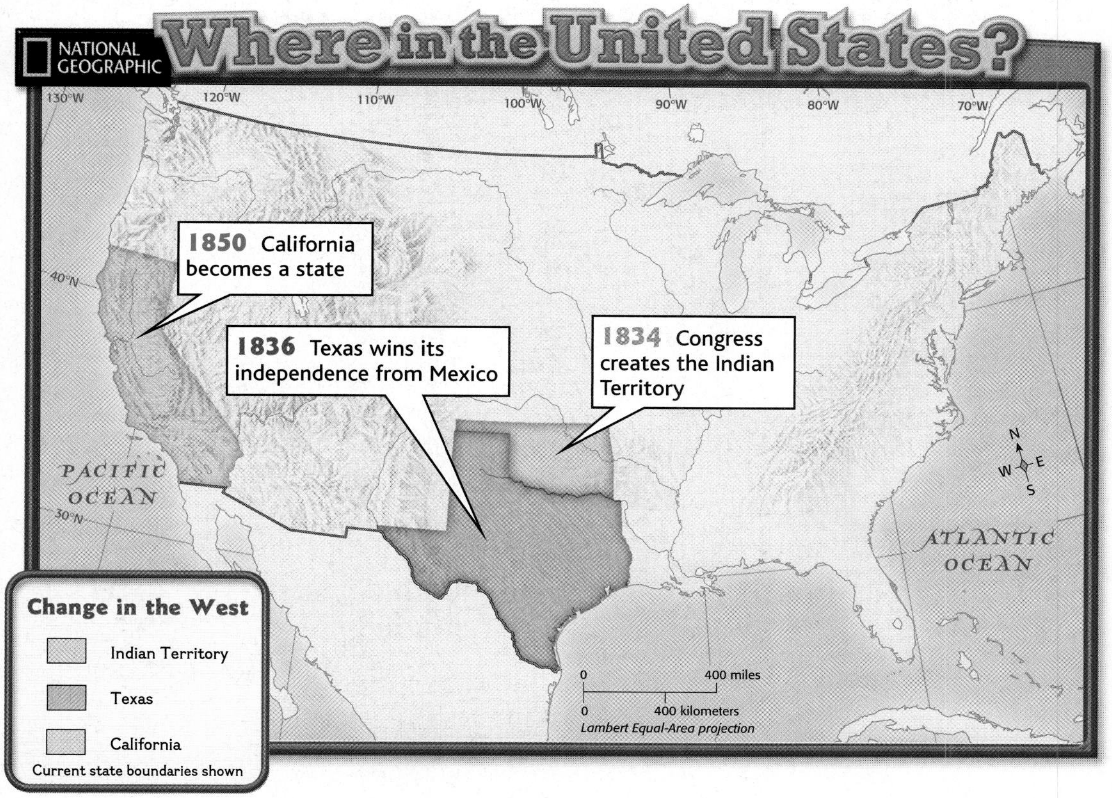

1835 — **1850** — **1865**

1832 Jackson challenges the Bank of the United States

1834 Congress creates the Indian Territory

1846 Congress declares war on Mexico

1848 Seneca Falls Convention backs woman suffrage

Lucretia Mott

1834 Mexico begins to break up missions

California Bear flag

1846 Americans declare California an independent nation

1850 California becomes a state

1833 Great Britain abolishes slavery in its colonies

1836 Texas wins its independence from Mexico

1848 Revolutions sweep through Europe

1850 Tai Ping Rebellion begins in China

Tai Ping Rebellion

TEACH

NATIONAL GEOGRAPHIC Where in the United States?

Understanding Maps and Time Lines **Ask:** What states are highlighted on this map? *(present-day Oklahoma, Texas, and California)* How does this map differ from the map on page 171? *(It does not show any countries with claims on land within the present-day United States.)* OL

NCLB No Child Left Behind

Teaching Activity Have students read the events in the time line. **Ask:** Which of the entries on the world events time line do you think will have the most effect on the United States? Why? *(Students may answer the independence of Texas, since that area is now a state.)* OL

UNIVERSAL ACCESS

English Learners: Have students write down unfamiliar words from the time line on separate index cards. Then have them look the words up in the Glossary or in a dictionary and write down the definitions. EL

Visual/Spatial: Have students draw two maps of North America, one showing the United States and Mexico in 1821 and the other showing those two nations in 1850. OL

Advanced Learners: Have students conduct research to learn why there were so many rebellions and independence movements during this period. Students should write an essay answering the question, "What were people trying to gain by these steps?" AL

Unit Objectives

After studying this unit, students should be able to

- Describe the growth of industry and transportation in the North and its impact on society.
- Describe the growth of cotton growing in the South and its impact on society.
- Discuss expanded settlements in the West and how the settlers lived.
- Explain why reform movements arose and what the reformers achieved.
- Discuss political changes during the period.
- Outline how the nation expanded its territory.

Previewing People to Meet

Have students read the descriptions of the **People to Meet** on pages 376 and 377. Then have them close their books and organize into teams. Play a "Who Am I?" game by giving clues to an individual's identity and asking students to identify the person from those clues. Award three points for answering correctly on one clue, two points for using two clues, and one point for answering after three clues. **OL**

Unit 4 Places to Locate

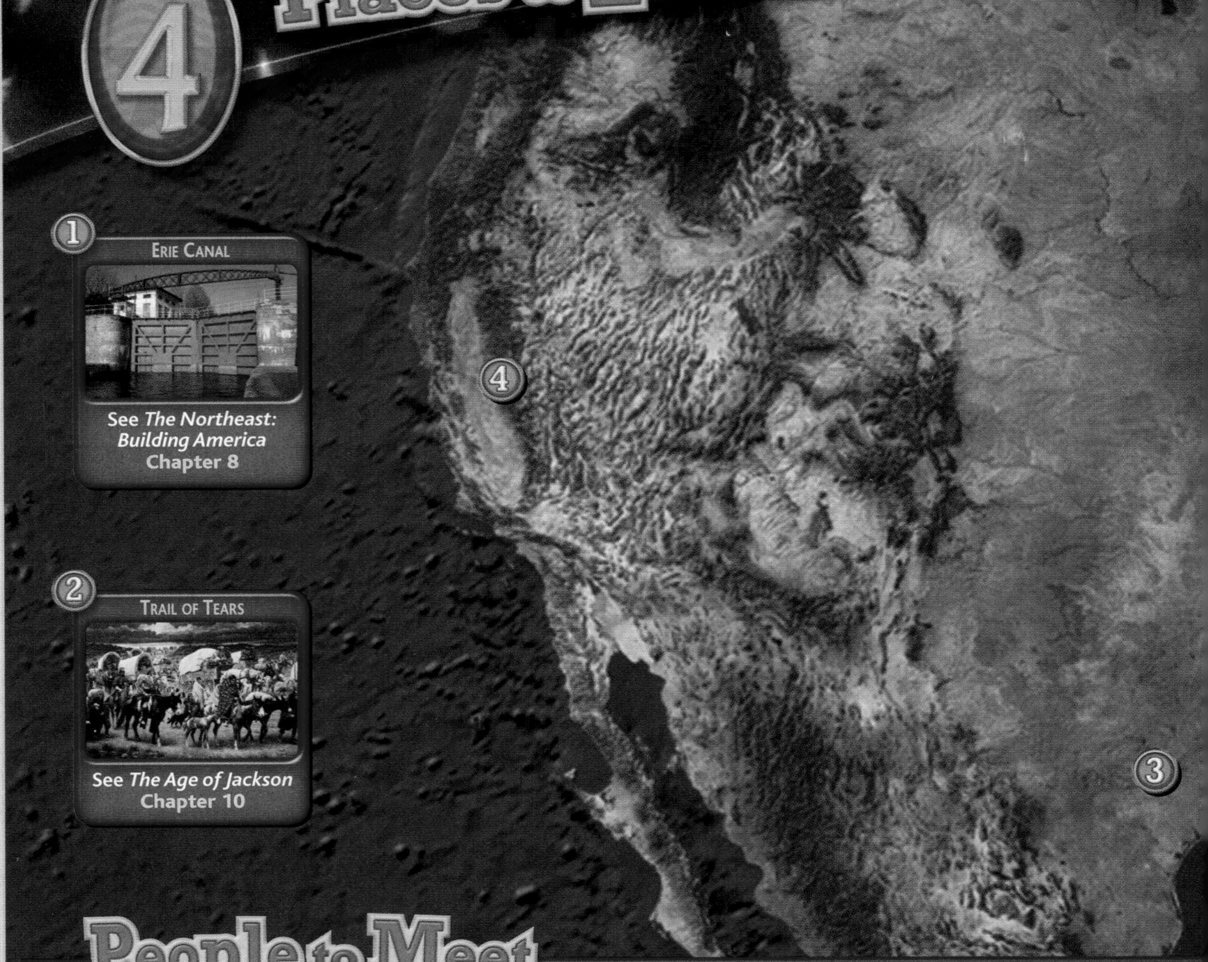

People to Meet

Eli Whitney
1765–1825
American inventor
Chapter 8, page 384

Dorothea Dix
1802–1887
Prison reformer
Chapter 8, page 405

Elizabeth Cady Stanton
1815–1902
Women's rights activist
Chapter 8, page 409

Harriet Tubman
c. 1820–1913
African American leader
Chapter 9, page 436

376

Previewing Places to Locate

Use the following descriptions to explain the images on the map.

1 
The Erie Canal helped make New York City the most important port in the country. It also contributed to the growth of Utica, Rochester, and Buffalo, all towns along the canal.

2 
A Cherokee described his people as "my poor and unhappy countrymen, driven by brutal power from all they loved and cherished in the land of their fathers."

Andrew Jackson
1767–1845
Seventh president of the United States
Chapter 10, page 447

Sequoya
c. 1760–1845
Inventor of Cherokee alphabet
Chapter 10, page 453

Osceola
c. 1804–1838
Seminole leader
Chapter 10, page 456

John C. Frémont
1813–1890
American explorer of California
Chapter 11, page 494

INTRODUCING UNIT 4

Skill Practice

Using Geography Skills

Write the words *location, place, human/environment interaction, movement,* and *regions* on the board. Explain that these are themes of geography that geographers have identified. **Ask:** Which theme or themes are represented by the events shown in these images? *(All—location and place; Erie Canal—human/environment interaction, movement, regions; Trail of Tears—movement; Alamo—regions; Gold Rush—human/environment interaction, movement, regions)* **OL**

Skill Practice

Historical and Social Sciences Analysis Skill

Tell students to write down the items in the United States events tier of the time line on pages 374–375. As they read the unit, have them explain the significance of each event. **OL**

ASSESS/CLOSE

Explain that in this period, the nation could be divided into three sections—North, South, and West. Ask students to predict which areas belonged to each of those sections. Then have them check their predictions as they read the unit. **OL**

The Alamo was originally one of several missions the Spanish established in Texas. Named San Antonio de Valero, it was founded in 1718 but was abandoned by 1793. The name Alamo probably comes from cottonwood trees that grew nearby.

The first reports of gold in California did not appear on the East Coast until August, more than half a year after the discovery. In February of 1849—more than a year after gold had been found—a ship reached Sacramento with the first of 80,000 forty-niners.

Chapter 8 Planning Guide

SECTION RESOURCES

Main Ideas	Print Materials	Technology Resources
Section 1 **Economic Growth** 1. The rise of industry and trade led to the growth of cities. 2. The growth of factories and trade led to the growth of cities.	• Reproducible Lesson Plan 8–1* • Daily Lesson and Discussion Notes 8–1 • Active Reading Note-Taking Guide 8–1 • Reading Essentials and Study Guide 8–1 • Guided Reading Activity 8–1 • Section Quiz 8–1	Daily Focus Skills Transparency 8–1 Section Graphic Organizer Transparency 8–1 California Standards Practice Transparencies Interactive Tutor Self-Assessment CD-ROM Exam*View*® Pro Testmaker CD-ROM Presentation Plus! CD-ROM
Section 2 **A System of Transportation** 1. Transportation routes improved, while steamboats improved the transport of goods along rivers. 2. Business and government officials planned to build a canal linking the country together. 3. Americans continued to move westward and settled near rivers.	• Reproducible Lesson Plan 8–2* • Daily Lesson and Discussion Notes 8–2 • Active Reading Note-Taking Guide 8–2 • Reading Essentials and Study Guide 8–2 • Guided Reading Activity 8–2 • Section Quiz 8–2	Daily Focus Skills Transparency 8–2 Section Graphic Organizer Transparency 8–2 California Standards Practice Transparencies Interactive Tutor Self-Assessment CD-ROM Exam*View*® Pro Testmaker CD-ROM Presentation Plus! CD-ROM
Section 3 **The North's People** 1. As industrialism grew in the North, many saw the need for reforms in working conditions. 2. As cities grew, so did the number of immigrants.	• Reproducible Lesson Plan 8–3* • Daily Lesson and Discussion Notes 8–3 • Active Reading Note-Taking Guide 8–3 • Reading Essentials and Study Guide 8–3 • Guided Reading Activity 8–3 • Section Quiz 8–3	Daily Focus Skills Transparency 8–3 Section Graphic Organizer Transparency 8–3 California Standards Practice Transparencies Interactive Tutor Self-Assessment CD-ROM Exam*View*® Pro Testmaker CD-ROM Presentation Plus! CD-ROM
Section 4 **Reforms and Reformers** 1. Religious and philosophical ideas inspired various reform movements. 2. Reformers wanted to make education accessible to all citizens. 3. A new wave of literature swept the U. S. that was distinctly American.	• Reproducible Lesson Plan 8–4* • Daily Lesson and Discussion Notes 8–4 • Active Reading Note-Taking Guide 8–4 • Reading Essentials and Study Guide 8–4 • Guided Reading Activity 8–4 • Section Quiz 8–4	Daily Focus Skills Transparency 8–4 Section Graphic Organizer Transparency 8–4 California Standards Practice Transparencies Interactive Tutor Self-Assessment CD-ROM Exam*View*® Pro Testmaker CD-ROM Presentation Plus! CD-ROM
Section 5 **The Women's Movement** 1. Many women wanted the same opportunities as men, and they organized to gain these rights. 2. Women made progress in education, marriage laws, and in the professional sector.	• Reproducible Lesson Plan 8–5* • Daily Lesson and Discussion Notes 8–5 • Active Reading Note-Taking Guide 8–5 • Reading Essentials and Study Guide 8–5 • Guided Reading Activity 8–5 • Section Quiz 8–5	Daily Focus Skills Transparency 8–5 Section Graphic Organizer Transparency 8–5 California Standards Practice Transparencies Interactive Tutor Self-Assessment CD-ROM Exam*View*® Pro Testmaker CD-ROM Presentation Plus! CD-ROM Vocabulary PuzzleMaker CD-ROM

PACING YOUR LESSONS

Unit Introduction	Chapter Introduction	Section 1	Section 2	Section 3	Section 4	Section 5	Chapter Assessment
$\frac{1}{2}$ Day	$\frac{1}{2}$ Day	3 Days	2 Days	3 Days	2 Days	1 Day	$\frac{1}{2}$ Day

0:00 **OUT OF TIME?** Assign the Chapter 8 ***Reading Essentials and Study Guide***

*Available on TeacherWorks™

Chapter 8 Planning Guide

Standards-Based Lesson Plan

History–Social Science Standards Covered in Chapter 8

The standards covered in the chapter are listed below. Use the accompanying activity as you teach the chapter to ensure student mastery of these standards. This activity can be used in combination with the program's print and technology assessment materials.

Standard	Section 1	2	3	4	5
US8.6 Students analyze the divergent paths of the American people from 1800 to the mid-1800s and the challenges they faced, with emphasis on the Northeast.	✔	✔	✔	✔	✔
US8.6.1 Discuss the influence of industrialization and technological developments on the region, including human modification of the landscape and how physical geography shaped human actions (e.g., growth of cities, deforestation, farming, mineral extraction).	✔		✔		
US8.6.2 Outline the physical obstacles to and the economic and political factors involved in building a network of roads, canals, and railroads (e.g., Henry Clay's American System).		✔			
US8.6.3 List the reasons for the wave of immigration from Northern Europe to the United States and describe the growth in number, size, and spatial arrangement of cities (e.g., Irish immigrants and the Great Irish Famine).			✔		
US8.6.4 Study the lives of black Americans who gained freedom in the North and founded schools and churches to advance their rights and communities.			✔		
US8.6.5 Trace the development of the American education system from its earliest roots, including the roles of religious and private schools and Horace Mann's campaign for free public education and its assimilating role in American culture.				✔	✔
US8.6.6 Examine the women's suffrage movement (e.g., biographies, writings, and speeches of Elizabeth Cady Stanton, Margaret Fuller, Lucretia Mott, Susan B. Anthony).					✔
US8.6.7 Identify common themes in American art as well as transcendentalism and individualism (e.g., writings about and by Ralph Waldo Emerson, Henry David Thoreau, Herman Melville, Louisa May Alcott, Nathaniel Hawthorne, Henry Wadsworth Longfellow).				✔	

Cumulative Standards-Assessment Activity

The Cumulative Standards-Assessment Activity will help students organize and learn the important information from the chapter. Begin teaching the chapter with this activity, and have students complete it as they read the chapter.

Creating a Chart for Making Generalizations

Purpose When they make generalizations, students study many particular details and then make broader statements about them that reveal links between them. This skill allows students to think creatively about what they read and develop their own ideas about the material.

Introduction to Making Generalizations

1. Begin by showing how to make valid generalizations. Ask students to identify some of the effects of the War of 1812. Ask volunteers to connect these effects into a general statement. Students might conclude that the war led to a wave of nationalist feeling. Ask: Does this idea seem reasonable? If not, what generalization would be better?
2. Ask students to copy this chart into their notebooks:

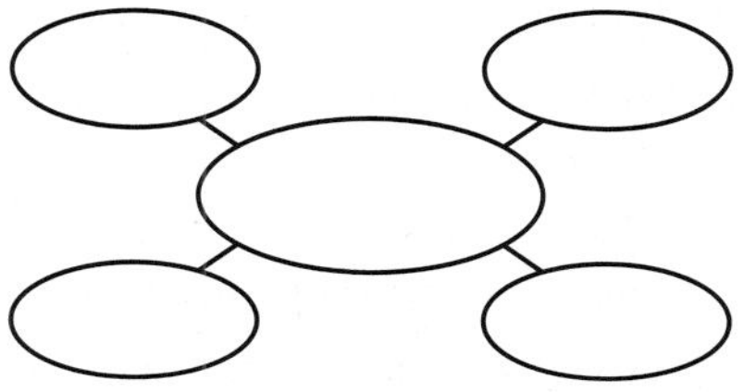

Generalization: ______________________________

As students read each section, have them use different charts to categorize the facts they read. Then have them write valid generalizations that link those facts together.

3. As part of the chapter review, have students share their generalizations. Remind students to use their charts as study aids.

Chapter 8 Resources

READING SUPPORT

- Content Vocabulary Activity 8
- Academic Vocabulary Activity 8
- Reading Skills Activity 8
- American Literature Reading 8
- Biography Activities 8A–8K
- Chapter 8 Active Reading Note-Taking Guide
- Chapter 8 Guided Reading Activities
- Chapter 8 Reading Essentials and Study Guide
- Glencoe Literature Library
- Glencoe Video Program
- Vocabulary PuzzleMaker CD-ROM
- Interactive Graphic Organizers CD-ROM
- American History Primary Source Document Library CD-ROM

CRITICAL THINKING

- Critical Thinking Skills Activity 8
- Primary Source Reading 8
- Cause-and-Effect Transparency 8, Strategy, and Activity
- Presentation Plus! CD-ROM

UNIVERSAL ACCESS

- Universal Access Activity 8
- Then and Now Transparencies 8A–8B, Strategy, and Activity
- Graphic Novel Activity 8
- School-to-Home Connection Activities 8A–8D
- English Learner Handbook Chapter 8 Activities
- Universal Access for the American History Classroom
- Moments in Time
- American Art and Architecture Transparencies, Strategies, and Activities
- American Art Prints
- American Music Cultural Traditions
- American Music Hits Through History
- StudentWorks Plus CD-ROM

SKILL PRACTICE

- Map Overlay Transparency 8, Strategy, and Activity
- Analysis Skills Activity 8
- Time Line Activity 8
- Geography and History Activity 8
- Economics and History Activity 8
- Chart, Graph, and Map Skills Activity 8
- Political Cartoon Activity 8
- Supreme Court Case Study 8
- In-Text Map Transparency 8, Strategy, and Activity
- Step Into American History Activity 8
- Citizenship and Service Learning Activity 8
- Outline Map Resource Book
- MindJogger Plus Videoquiz

WRITING SUPPORT

- Writing Activity 8
- Language Arts Activity 8
- Writer's Guidebook
- Middle School Writing Process Transparencies

ASSESSMENT

GLENCOE'S ASSESSMENT ADVANTAGE

- Chapter 8 Section Quizzes
- Chapter 8 Tests, Forms A and B
- California Standards Assessment, Forms A and B
- Cumulative Assessment Activity US8.6
- California Standards Practice Workbook
- Succeeding on the California History–Social Science Standards CD-ROM
- Exam*View*® Pro Testmaker CD-ROM
- Interactive Tutor Self-Assessment CD-ROM

CD-ROM · DVD · Print Material · Poster · Transparency · Music Program · Videocassette · Glencoe Literature Library

Chapter 8 Resources

TECHNOLOGY

- StudentWorks Plus CD-ROM
- TeacherWorks CD-ROM
- Exam*View*® Pro Testmaker CD-ROM
- Interactive Tutor Self-Assessment CD-ROM
- Presentation Plus! CD-ROM
- Succeeding on the California History–Social Science Standards CD-ROM
- Vocabulary PuzzleMaker CD-ROM
- Interactive Graphic Organizers CD-ROM
- Interactive Time Line CD-ROM
- American History Primary Source Document Library CD-ROM
- MindJogger Plus Videoquiz
- American Music Cultural Traditions
- American Music Hits Through History
- Glencoe Video Program
- Professional Development in Middle School Social Studies Series
- Teaching American History With *Discovering Our Past: The American Journey to World War I*

SPANISH RESOURCES

- Spanish Activities and Assessment
  - Spanish Content Vocabulary Activities
  - Spanish Guided Reading Activities
  - Spanish Quizzes and Tests
  - Spanish California Standards Assessment
- Spanish Reading Essentials and Study Guide
- Spanish School-to-Home Connection
- Spanish Declaration of Independence and U.S. Constitution

TRANSPARENCIES

- California Standards Practice Transparencies
- Daily Focus Skills Transparencies
- Section Graphic Organizer Transparencies
- In-Text Map Transparencies
- Map Overlay Transparencies
- Cause-and-Effect Transparencies
- Then and Now Transparencies
- American Art and Architecture Transparencies
- Middle School Writing Process Transparencies

TEACHER PLANNING

- Daily Lesson and Discussion Notes
- English Learner Handbook
- Guide to Daily Intervention
- *Discovering Our Past: The American Journey to World War I* Reading and Study Skills Foldables
- Reading Strategies and Activities for the Social Studies Classroom
- Chapter 8 Reproducible Lesson Plans (correlated to California History–Social Science Standards)
- Universal Access for the American History Classroom
- NGS U.S. Desk Map
- NGS U.S. Atlas

PROFESSIONAL DEVELOPMENT

- Building Academic Vocabulary
- Strategies for Success
- Research-Based Strategies Used to Develop *Discovering Our Past: The American Journey to World War I*
- Character Education in the Middle School Classroom
- The Living Constitution
- Professional Development in Middle School Social Studies Video Series
- Teaching American History With *Discovering Our Past: The American Journey to World War I*

MASTERING THE STANDARDS

The content and assessment in the Student Edition, Teacher Wraparound Edition, teacher planning materials, and the print and technology products are all standards-based. The use of these products during instruction leads to mastery of the standards.

PRACTICE
- California Standards Practice Workbook
- California Standards Practice Transparencies
- Interactive Time Line CD-ROM
- School-to-Home Connection

BENCHMARK ASSESSMENT
- California Standards Assessment
- Exam*View*® Pro Testmaker CD-ROM
- Succeeding on the California History–Social Science Standards CD-ROM

REMEDIATION
- California Guide to Daily Intervention
- Interactive Tutor Self-Assessment CD-ROM
- Exam*View*® Pro Testmaker CD-ROM
- California Standards Practice Workbook
- Reading Essentials and Study Guide

Chapter 8 Resources

Additional Resources

NATIONAL GEOGRAPHIC TEACHER'S CORNER

Index to National Geographic Magazine:

The following articles relate to this chapter:

- "The Way West," by John G. Mitchell, September 2000.
- "America's Poet: Walt Whitman," by Max Guerout, December 1994.
- "The Cruelest Commerce: African Slave Trade," by Colin Palmer, September 1992.

National Geographic Society Products

To order the following, call National Geographic at 1-800-368-2728

- *GeoKit: Westward Movement* (Kit)
- *GeoKit: Immigration* (Kit)
- *The West That Was* (Video)
- *United States/Territorial Growth* (Map)
- *National Geographic Desk Reference* (Book)
- *Immigration: The Triumph of Hope* (Video)

NGS ONLINE

Access National Geographic's new dynamic MapMachine Web site and other geography resources at:

www.nationalgeographic.com

www.nationalgeographic.com/maps

A&E HOME VIDEO · Biography · THE HISTORY CHANNEL

The following videotape programs are available from Glencoe as supplements to Chapter 8.

- **The Best of the Real West (ISBN 1-56501-352-2)**
- **The Mighty Mississippi (ISBN 1-56501-1090-6)**
- **Textiles: Birth of an American Industry (ISBN 1-56501-0624-0)**
- **Susan B. Anthony: Rebel for the Cause (ISBN 1-56501-646-7)**

To order, call Glencoe at 1-800-334-7344. To find classroom resources to accompany many of these videos, check the following home pages:

A&E Television: www.aetv.com

The History Channel: www.historychannel.com

MOMENTS IN TIME DBQ

The following resource can help you teach the content of this chapter.

Unit 2 Territorial Expansion (1834–1859)

History Online

Use our Web site for additional resources. All essential content is covered in the Student Edition.

You and your students can visit ca.hss.glencoe.com, the Web site companion to *Discovering Our Past: The American Journey to World War I.* This innovative integration of electronic and print media offers your students a wealth of opportunities. The student text directs students to the Web site for the following options:

- Chapter Overviews
- Self-Check Quizzes
- Study Central™
- Student Web Activities
- Textbook Updates
- Multi-Language Glossaries

Answers to the student Web activities are provided for you in the Web Activity Lesson Plans. Additional Web resources and ePuzzles and games are also available.

FOLDABLES™ Study Organizer

Dinah Zike's Foldables

Foldables are three-dimensional, interactive graphic organizers that help students practice basic writing skills, review key vocabulary terms, and identify main ideas. Every chapter contains a foldable activity, with additional chapter activities found in the Reading and Study Skills Foldables booklet.

Chapter 8 Resources

Reading List Generator CD-ROM

GLENCOE BOOKLINK

The Glencoe BookLink CD-ROM is a database that allows you to search more than 15,000 titles to create a customized reading list for your students.

- Reading lists can be organized by students' reading level, author, genre, theme, or area of interest.
- The database provides Degrees of Reading Power™ (DRP) and Lexile™ readability scores for all selections.
- A brief summary of each selection is included.

Reading level suggestions for this chapter:

For students at a Grade 6 reading level:
- ***Erie Canal: Creating America's Great Waterway,*** by Peter Lourie

For students at a Grade 7 reading level:
- ***The Lowell Mill Girls: Life in the Factory,*** by JoAnne B. Weisman

For students at a Grade 8 reading level:
- ***Not for Ourselves Alone: The Story of Elizabeth Cady Stanton,*** by Geoffrey C. Ward and Ken Burns

For students at a Grade 9 reading level:
- ***Industrial Revolution,*** by John D. Clare

Reading Support From JAMESTOWN EDUCATION

- *Timed Readings Plus in Social Studies* helps students increase their reading rate and fluency while maintaining comprehension. The 400-word passages are similar to those found on state and national assessments.
- *Reading in the Content Area: Social Studies* concentrates on six essential reading skills that help students better comprehend what they read. The book includes 754 high-interest nonfiction passages written at increasing levels of difficulty.
- *Reading Fluency* helps students read smoothly, accurately, and expressively.
- *Jamestown's Reading Improvement,* by renowned reading expert Edward Fry, focuses on helping build your students' comprehension, vocabulary, and skimming and scanning skills.
- *Critical Reading Series* provides high-interest books, each written at three reading levels.

To order these products, call Glencoe at 1-800-334-7344.

KEY for Using the Teacher Wraparound Edition

Use this key to help you identify the different types of prompts found in the Teacher Wraparound Edition.

R **Reading Strategies** activities help you teach reading skills and vocabulary.

C **Critical Thinking** strategies help students apply and extend what they have learned.

U **Universal Access** activities provide differentiated instruction for students learning to speak English, along with suggestions for teaching various types of learners.

S **Skill Practice** strategies help students practice historical analysis and geography skills.

W **Writing Support** activities provide writing opportunities to help students comprehend the text.

Teaching strategies and activities have been coded for ability level appropriateness.

AL Activities for students working above grade level
OL Activities for students working on grade level
BL Activities for students working below grade level
EL Activities for English Learners

FOCUS

History–Social Science Standards

In this chapter, the following standard will be covered:

US8.6 Students analyze the divergent paths of the American people from 1800 to the mid-1800s and the challenges they faced, with emphasis on the Northeast.

More About the Photo

Many Europeans praised the new factories of New England built in the early 1800s. Like this mill in Plymouth, Massachusetts, they ran on clean water power, unlike the smoky coal-burning factories of the Industrial Revolution in Britain.

TEACH

The Big Ideas

As you begin teaching each section, use these questions and activities to focus on the Big Ideas.

Section 1

Economic Growth

Essential Question: What are some effects that geography might have on a society? *(Answers may include land and climate that is good or poor for agriculture, the availability of resources, and relative distance to other areas.)* Explain that in this section, students will learn how geography and new technology led to the Industrial Revolution. OL

Chapter 8

The Northeast: Building Industry

◀ Mill in Plymouth, Massachusetts

NATIONAL GEOGRAPHIC

Where & When?

1805 — 1820 — 1835 — 1850

1806 Congress approves funds for the National Road

1825 Erie Canal is completed

1833 Oberlin College admits women and African Americans

1848 First women's rights convention held

Section 2

A System of Transportation

Essential Question: Why is improved transportation important? *(Answers may include making it easier for people to move themselves, as well as goods and services.)* Tell students that in this section they will read about how advances in transportation led to Western settlement. OL

Section 3

The North's People

Essential Question: What happens if two areas of a nation develop separate ways of life? *(Students may say that they will develop different values or grow to mistrust each other.)* Explain that this section discusses how differences between the North and the South led to varying levels of development. OL

History Online

Chapter Overview Visit ca.hss.glencoe.com for a preview of Chapter 8.

The Big Ideas

Section 1 Economic Growth

Geography shapes the physical, economic, and political challenges a region faces. New technology produced the Industrial Revolution.

Section 2 A System of Transportation

Geography shapes the physical, economic, and political challenges a region faces. Improvements in transportation led to Western settlement.

Section 3 The North's People

Differences in economic, political, and social beliefs and practices can lead to division within a nation and have lasting consequences. The North saw an increase in industrialism and the growth of cities.

Section 4 Reforms and Reformers

Reactions to social injustice can lead to reform movements. Many Americans worked for reform in education and other areas.

Section 5 The Women's Movement

Reactions to social injustice can lead to reform movements. Women lobbied for increased rights and an equal status with men in America.

View the Chapter 8 video in the Glencoe Video Program.

FOLDABLES™ Study Organizer

Organizing Make this foldable to organize information from the chapter to help you learn more about the changes in the North.

Step 1 Collect three sheets of paper and place them on top of one another about 1 inch apart.

Step 2 Fold up the bottom edges of the paper to form 6 tabs.

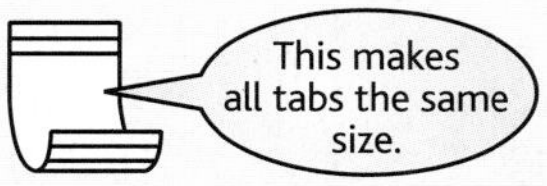

Step 3 When all the tabs are the same size, fold the paper to hold the tabs in place and staple the sheets together. Turn the paper and label each tab as shown.

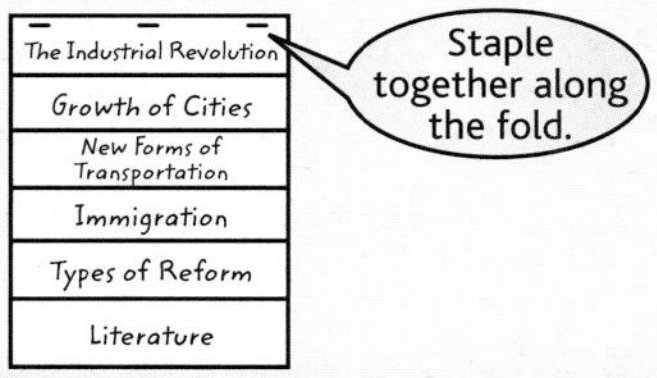

Reading and Writing As you read, use your foldable to write under each appropriate tab what you learned about the people, the economy, and the culture of the North.

INTRODUCING CHAPTER 8

Section 4

Reforms and Reformers

Essential Question: How can social injustice lead to reform movements? *(Some people see or experience unfair treatment and move to change such situations.)* Tell students that in this section they will learn about reform movements to improve education. **OL**

Section 5

The Women's Movement

Essential Question: What do you think was the status of women in the early 1800s? *(Students may suggest that women had fewer opportunities than men.)* Explain that this section discusses how women lobbied for equal rights during this period. **OL**

History Online

Go to ca.hss.glencoe.com for student activities, lesson plans, and links to additional Web resources about the Northeast in the early 1800s.

FOLDABLES™ Study Organizer Dinah Zike's Foldables

Purpose Have students use their foldables to record key facts about different topics covered in the chapter. Suggest that they use these facts to help them review the chapter content. **BL**

Why It's Important

Problems and Solutions History is often the story of people or leaders facing difficult situations that they want to improve. Remind students that in both analyzing problems and developing solutions, people act without perfect knowledge. In addition, the solutions that people develop are based on what they perceive the problem to be. Historians who view the situation later might have more background information or perceive the problem differently. Both this greater knowledge or different perspective can sometimes help historians explain why particular solutions do not work.

1 Learn It!

Work with volunteers to apply the three questions to these two paragraphs. Point out that sometimes the problem is not directly stated but implied.

Ask: What was the problem that Gallaudet perceived? *(Students may say that there were no adequate methods for educating people who are hearing impaired.)* **OL**

Chapter 8

Get Ready to Read

Problems and Solutions

READING SKILL

1 Learn It!

To explain how and why a person, society, or government made a particular decision in history, authors sometimes use a problem/solution approach in their writing. You can recognize a problem/solution structure by asking three questions. What was the problem? What was the solution? What were the results of that solution? As you read the text below, notice how the author used a problem/solution approach to explain how reformers developed methods to teach people with disabilities.

Some reformers focused on teaching people with disabilities. Thomas Gallaudet (GA • luh • DEHT), who developed a method to educate people who were hearing impaired, opened the Hartford School for the Deaf in Connecticut in 1817.

At about the same time, Dr. Samuel Gridley Howe advanced the cause of those who were visually impaired. He developed books with large raised letters that people with sight impairments could "read" with their fingers. Howe headed the Perkins Institute, a school for the blind, in Boston.

—from page 405

Reading Tip

As you read, make a chart listing problems and solutions that are described in the text.

READING STRATEGY **VISUALIZING**

Visualizing is a useful technique to help students understand how people in the past defined problems and developed solutions to address those problems. When reading about problems and solutions from the past, students need to bear in mind the circumstances of people's lives at the time. For instance, those people could not solve their problems by using technology unavailable to them. By visualizing what life was like in the past, students will be better able to understand how people of that time saw the world. **OL**

2 Practice It!

As you read this chapter, complete a chart like the one below to show how Americans solved problems by inventing new machines.

Problem		Solution
Need more thread to make cloth	→	Spinning jenny
Cotton bolls difficult to clean	→	
Machine parts are hard to find	→	

Read to Write

Understanding problems and creating solutions is part of everyday life. Can you think of a challenge you have had this week? How have you found solutions? Write a short paragraph describing one of your own problem/solution situations.

▲ Eli Whitney

Cotton gin ▶

3 Apply It!

As you read this chapter, watch for ways that everyday people met the challenges they faced.

2 Practice It!

Have students practice the skill by considering the situation that confronted the new nation in the 1780s. **Ask:** What problem did American leaders see with the Articles of Confederation? *(It created a central government that was too weak to do much to meet the nation's challenges.)* What solution did they undertake? *(They wrote a new Constitution.)* What were the results of that solution? *(Answers may include that the new national government was stronger and more stable and that the country's financial situation improved.)* **OL**

3 Apply It!

Have students apply the skill by looking at an issue currently facing the nation. Ask them to create a chart that identifies the problem and more than one potential solution. If a solution was attempted, have students describe what the solution was and how it worked. If the problem still exists, have them describe at least two solutions that have been proposed and the possible effects of each one.
OL **CA** 8RC2.6

READING STRATEGY **PERSUASIVE WRITING**

Persuasive essays are often the product of a process of identifying problems and finding solutions. These essays should follow a clear structure, in which the problem is described and the solution presented. Such essays are strongest when the writer considers other possible solutions and explains why they are undesirable. Writers should also address potential objections to the solution they propose and explain how those objections are not important or can be overcome. **AL**

Use Reading Skills Activity 8 in the **Chapter 8 Resource Book** for more practice with identifying problems and finding solutions.

FOCUS

BELLRINGER
SKILLBUILDER ACTIVITY

Project **Daily Focus Skills Transparency 8–1** and have students answer the question.

Guide to Reading

Preteaching Vocabulary: Organize students into groups and have each group look up the meaning of one of the content vocabulary terms and find a way of teaching that term to the rest of the class.

Answers to Graphic: New ways of manufacturing goods; Factory system; Growth of agriculture; Cities grew larger

Unpacking the Standards

After reading the section, students will be able to:

- Describe how manufacturing changed and why it happened first in New England.
- Discuss the impact of the Industrial Revolution on the nation's economy.
- List ways that cities changed in the early 1800s.

Section 1 Economic Growth

History Social Science Standards

US8.6 Students analyze the divergent paths of the American people from 1800 to the mid-1800s and the challenges they faced, with emphasis on the Northeast.

Guide to Reading

Looking Back, Looking Ahead
Beginning in the early 1800s, revolutions in industry brought great changes to the North.

Focusing on the Main Ideas
- New technology led to changes in the way things are made. *(page 383)*
- The growth of factories and trade led to the growth of cities. *(page 386)*

Meeting People
Eli Whitney
Samuel Slater
Francis Cabot Lowell

Content Vocabulary
Industrial Revolution (ihn • DUHS • tree • uhl REH • vuh • LOO • shuhn)
capitalism
capital (KA • puh • tuhl)
free enterprise (EHN • tuhr • PRYZ)
technology (tehk • NAH • luh • jee)
cotton gin
patent (PA • tuhnt)
factory system
interchangeable parts (IHN • tuhr • CHAYN • juh • buhl)

Academic Vocabulary
percent
expand
concentrate (KAHN • suhn • TRAYT)

Reading Strategy
Organizing Information As you read the section, re-create the diagram below and describe in the ovals changes brought about by the Industrial Revolution.

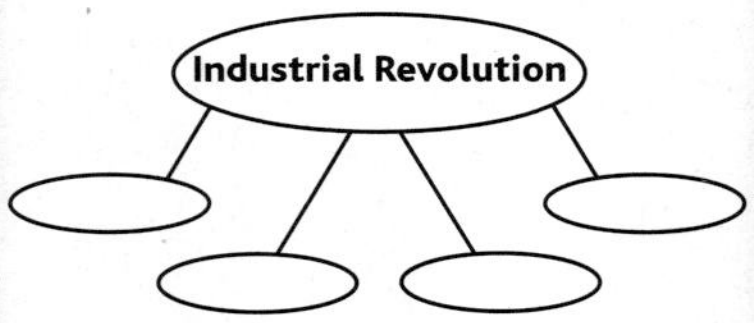

NATIONAL GEOGRAPHIC Who & When?

1780 — 1800 — 1820

Velocipede patent

1790 Congress passes patent law

1793 Samuel Slater starts cotton mill

Samuel Slater

1814 Textile plant opens in Waltham, Massachusetts

SECTION RESOURCES

Print Material
- Reproducible Lesson Plan 8–1*
- Daily Lesson and Discussion Notes 8–1
- Guided Reading Activity 8–1
- Reading Essentials and Study Guide 8–1
- Active Reading Note-Taking Guide 8–1
- Section Quiz 8–1

Transparencies
- Daily Focus Skills Transparency 8–1
- Section Graphic Organizer Transparency 8–1
- California Standards Practice Transparencies

Technology
- Interactive Tutor Self-Assessment CD-ROM
- Exam*View*® Pro Testmaker CD-ROM
- Presentation Plus! CD-ROM

*Available on TeacherWorks™

US8.6.1 Discuss the influence of industrialization and technological developments on the region, including human modification of the landscape and how physical geography shaped human actions (e.g., growth of cities, deforestation, farming, mineral extraction).

The Growth of Industry

Main Idea **New technology led to changes in the way things are made.**

Reading Connection Do you know someone who works in a factory? What is his or her job like? Read to learn how new technology spurred the Industrial Revolution in New England and what working in mills or factories was like.

From colonial times, most of the people of New England had lived and worked on farms. Work on a new farm was difficult. Eager to plant crops, the farmers first cleared the land. The trees were felled for building materials, fences, and firewood. People believed that trees grew on the most fertile land. As a result, they often cut down all the trees in an area. This created problems. Often the soil eroded without the protection of trees and tree roots.

A New Way of Working During the colonial era, workers were in short supply. Americans learned to develop tools that made work easier and more efficient.

People working in their homes or in workshops made cloth and most other goods. Using hand tools, they produced furniture, farm equipment, household items, and clothing.

R1 In the mid-1700s, however, the way goods were made began to change. These changes appeared first in Great Britain. British inventors created machinery to perform some of the work involved in cloth making, such as spinning. The machines ran on waterpower, so British cloth makers built mills along rivers and installed the machines in these mills. People left their homes and farms to work in the mills and earn wages. U The changes this system brought about were so great that this historic development is known as the **Industrial Revolution** (ihn • DUHS • tree • uhl REH • vuh • LOO • shuhn).

The Industrial Revolution The Industrial Revolution began to take root in the United States around 1800, appearing first in New England—Massachusetts, Rhode Island, Connecticut, Vermont, and New Hampshire. New England's soil was poor, and farming was difficult. As a result, some people were willing to leave their farms to find work elsewhere. Also, New England had many rushing rivers and streams. These provided the waterpower necessary to run the machinery in the new factories.

New England's Geography New England's geographic location also proved to be an advantage. It was close to other resources, including coal and iron from nearby Pennsylvania. New England also had many ports. Through these ports passed the cotton shipped from Southern states to New England factories, as well as the finished cloth produced in the North and bound for markets throughout the nation.

A Changing Economy The economic system of the United States is called **capitalism.** Under capitalism, individuals put their **capital** (KA • puh • tuhl), or money, into a business in hopes of making a profit. R2

Free enterprise (EHN • tuhr • PRYZ) is another term used to describe the American economy. In a system of free enterprise, people are free to buy, sell, and produce whatever they want. They can also work wherever they wish. The major elements of free enterprise are competition, profit, private property, and economic freedom. Business owners have the freedom to produce the products that they think will be the most profitable. Buyers also compete to find the best products at the lowest prices.

▲ American blacksmith, early 1800s woodcut

TEACH

R1 Reading Strategy

Scaffolding—Identifying the Main Idea and Supporting Details Write the word *change* on the board and have students copy it on a piece of paper. Tell them, as they read the section, to write down every example of change they can identify. BL

This READING SKILL was introduced in Chapter 2.

U Universal Access

English Learners Tell students that a word similar in meaning to *revolution* is *change*. **Ask:** How is a revolution different from normal changes that society goes through? *(Students may say that revolutions are deeper and longer-lasting changes.)* EL

R2 Reading Strategy

Activating Prior Knowledge Remind students that they studied the term *capitalism* in an earlier chapter. Have them explain its relation to *capital* and *free enterprise*. *(Capital is the money that people invest to start businesses. They can keep their profits under capitalism. Free enterprise is another name for capitalism.)* OL

Resources for page 383

Geography and History Activity 8

More Skill Practice

Using Geography Skills Explain that the Industrial Revolution spread within a few decades from Great Britain to the United States. **Ask:** Would Americans have adopted this revolution as quickly if it had developed in another European country, such as Spain or Italy? Why or why not? *(probably not; the United States had closer ties to Britain because the states had once been British colonies)* Why did this revolution not reach the United States as early as the 1770s or 1780s? *(Those were the years of the Revolutionary War, when people were more concerned about winning independence.)* OL CA CS3. CA HI2.

R1 Reading Strategy

Understanding Vocabulary Have students give examples of technology commonly used today. *(cars, televisions, cell phones, computers, CD players)* EL CA 8RW1.3

R2 Reading Strategy

Understanding Vocabulary Explain that *gin* is short for *engine*. OL

R3 Reading Strategy

Understanding Vocabulary **Ask:** Have you ever seen a patent number on an appliance or other good? Why would the government give numbers to patents? *(to keep track of them)* OL

U Universal Access

Visual/Spatial Have students use diagrams and technical directions to explain how the waterwheels and gear systems work to power the different machines in the factory. OL CA 8RC2.5

New Technology Workers, waterpower, location, and capital were key factors in New England's Industrial Revolution. Yet without the invention of new machines and **technology** (tehk • NAH • luh • jee)—scientific discoveries that simplify work—the Industrial Revolution could not have taken place.

Inventions such as the spinning jenny and the water frame, which spun thread, and the power loom, which wove the thread into cloth, made it possible to perform many steps in making cloth by machine, saving time and money. Because these new machines ran on waterpower, most mills were built near rivers.

Another invention greatly increased the production of cotton. In 1793 **Eli Whitney** of Massachusetts invented the **cotton gin,** a simple machine that quickly and efficiently removed seeds from cotton fiber. The cotton gin enabled one worker, usually a slave, to clean cotton as fast as 50 people working by hand.

In 1790 Congress passed a patent law to protect the rights of those who developed "useful and important inventions." A **patent** (PA • tuhnt) gives an inventor the sole legal right to the invention and its profits for a certain period of time. One of the first patents went to Jacob Perkins for a machine to make nails.

TECHNOLOGY & History

Textile Mill

The Lowell factory system was designed to bring work and workers together. A typical Lowell textile mill in 1830 housed 4,500 spindles, 120 power looms, and more than 200 employees under one roof. ***What type of energy powered the mills?***

Gears

1. The first steps in textile production clean the raw cotton and turn loose cotton into crude yarn.
2. The spinning process transforms the yarn into thread.
3. At the weaving stage, power looms interlace the threads into coarse cloth or fabric.
4. Fabric is measured and batched for dyeing. Vegetable dyes were the earliest known dyes.

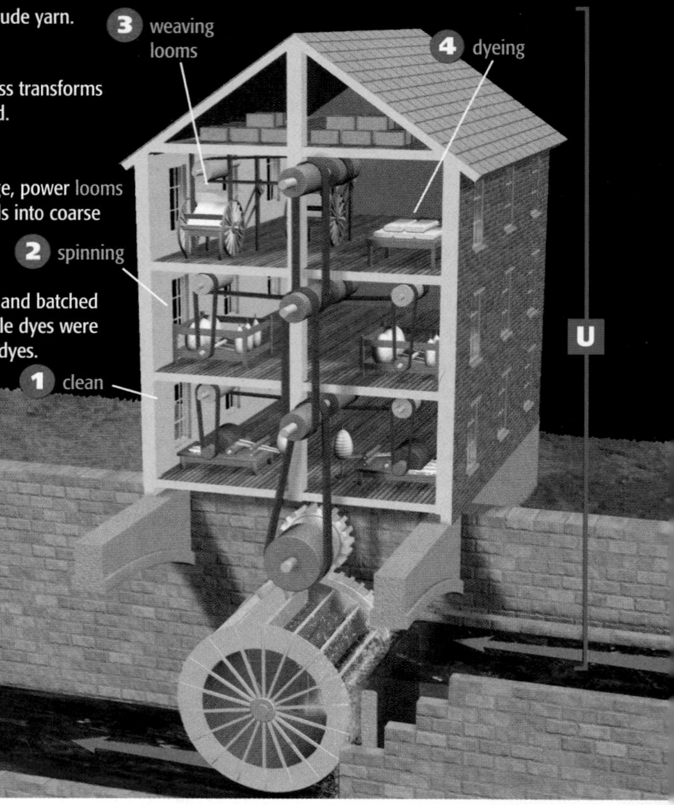

Answers and Additional Support

TECHNOLOGY & History

Factory jobs were hazardous. Some workers lost their hearing from the loud noise of the machinery. Tiny particles of fiber filled the air people breathed, causing respiratory diseases.

Answer: water power

Did You Know?

The War of 1812 played an important role in the coming of the Industrial Revolution to the United States. The war kept Americans from buying British goods and encouraged American companies to increase their output to meet demand.

S **New England Factories** The British tried to keep their new industrial technology a secret. Great Britain even passed laws prohibiting their machinery as well as their skilled mechanics from leaving the country. However, a few enterprising workers managed to slip away to the United States.

In Britain **Samuel Slater** had worked in a factory that used machines invented by Richard Arkwright for spinning cotton thread. Slater memorized the design of Arkwright's machines and slipped out of Britain. Once in the United States, Slater operated a cotton mill in Pawtucket, Rhode Island, in 1793. There he duplicated all of Arkwright's machines. Using these machines, the mill produced cotton thread. Slater's mill marked an important step in the Industrial Revolution in America.

In 1814 **Francis Cabot Lowell** opened a textile plant in Waltham, Massachusetts. The plan he implemented went several steps beyond Slater's mill. For the first time, all the stages of cloth making were performed under one roof. Lowell's mill launched the **factory system,** a system that brought manufacturing steps together in one place to increase efficiency. The factory system was a significant development in the way goods were made and another important part of the Industrial Revolution. By 1840 many textile mills were operating in the Northeast. Industrialists soon applied factory techniques to the production of lumber, shoes, leather, and other products.

R

Interchangeable Parts The inventor Eli Whitney started the use of **interchangeable parts** (IHN • tuhr • CHAYN • juh • buhl). These were identical machine parts that could be put together quickly to make a complete product. Because all the parts were alike, they could be manufactured with less-skilled labor and they made machine repair easier. Interchangeable parts opened the way for producing many different kinds of goods on a mass scale and for reducing the price of the goods.

Reading Check **Analyze** Why were the first mills in Great Britain built near rivers?

Primary Sources

Lowell Girls

Many of the workers in the mills in Lowell, Massachusetts, were young girls. Lucy Larcom started working in the mills when she was 11 years old. She later recalled her life at the factory:

> "At this time I had learned to do a spinner's work, and I obtained permission to tend some frames that stood directly in front of the river-windows, with only them and the wall behind me, extending half the length of the mill,—and one young woman beside me, at the farther end of the row. She was a sober, mature person, who scarcely thought it worth her while to speak often to a child like me; and I was, when with strangers, rather a reserved girl; so I kept myself occupied with the river, my work, and my thoughts. . . .
>
> Still, we did not call ourselves ladies. We did not forget that we were working-girls, wearing coarse aprons suitable to our work, and that there was some danger of our becoming drudges."
>
> —Lucy Larcom, *A New England Girlhood*

DBQ Document-Based Question

What "danger" does Lucy foresee?

Review The Big Idea

Review the Big Idea for this section: "Geography shapes the physical, economic, and political challenges a region faces." **Ask:** Would the Industrial Revolution have been as likely to develop in New England if it had had better soil for farming? Why or why not? *(Some students may say no because New Englanders would have been less willing to leave their farms, providing the work force needed for factories.)* OL CA CS3.

S Skill Practice

Historical and Social Sciences Analysis Skill

Ask: Why would the British want to keep their new industrial technology a secret? What would they hope to gain? *(to prevent other countries from developing factories as well; to develop a better position in world trade by producing goods more cheaply than in other countries)* OL CA HI6.

R Reading Strategy

Categorizing Information

Write definitions of the terms *factory system* and *interchangeable parts*—on the board. Have students choose the correct definition. BL

Reading Check

Answer: because they ran on water power

Primary Sources

The women who worked in the Lowell mills stayed in well-kept, supervised company-owned boardinghouses. Women living in these homes were required to be in bed by ten o'clock and to attend church on Sunday. They were encouraged to read books, write letters, and listen to lectures. They were not allowed to drink or play cards. Lowell girls received wages of about $3.00 a week, about half of which went for room and board.

Answer: becoming drudges (people who do boring work)

C Critical Thinking

Comparing and Contrasting Have students create a chart with three columns labeled *North*, *South*, and *West* and list characteristics of the farms in each region. Then have them write a few sentences in which they describe the similarities and differences among farms in these three regions. OL

R Reading Strategy

Academic Vocabulary Ask students to list synonyms and antonyms for the word *expand*. OL

U Universal Access

Logical/Mathematical Give students the following population figures for the United States at five different points in the early 1800s: 1800: 5.3 million; 1810: 7.2 million; 1820: 9.6 million; 1830: 12.9 million; 1840: 17.1 million. Have them calculate the rate at which the country's population increased from each year to the next. *(1800 to 1810: 35.8 percent; 1810 to 1820: 33.3 percent; 1820 to 1830: 34.4 percent; 1830 to 1840: 32.6 percent)* AL

Answers and Additional Support

US8.6.1 Discuss the influence of industrialization and technological developments on the region, including human modification of the landscape and how physical geography shaped human actions (e.g., growth of cities, deforestation, farming, mineral extraction).

A Changing Economy

Main Ideas **The growth of factories and trade led to the growth of cities.**

Reading Connection Do you think you would rather work on a farm or in a factory? Read to learn what caused agriculture to expand at the same time that factories and towns were growing.

C Although many New Englanders went to work in factories, most Americans still lived and worked on farms. In the 1820s, more than 65 **percent** of Americans were farmers.

In the Northeast, farms tended to be small, and the produce was usually marketed locally. In the South, cotton production increased dramatically. The demand for cotton had grown steadily with the development of the textile industries of New England and Europe. Southern plantation owners used enslaved workers to plant, tend, and pick the cotton. The cotton gin—which made it possible to clean the cotton faster and less expensively than by hand—encouraged the planters to raise larger crops. Between 1790 and 1820, cotton production soared from 3,000 to more than 300,000 bales a year.

There were also changes in the West. Agriculture in that region **expanded.** Southern farmers seeking new land moved west to plant cotton. Western farmers north of the Ohio River **concentrated** on raising pork and cash crops such as corn and wheat. R

NATIONAL GEOGRAPHIC Population of the United States, 1820

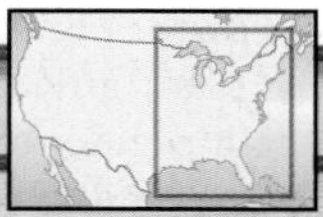

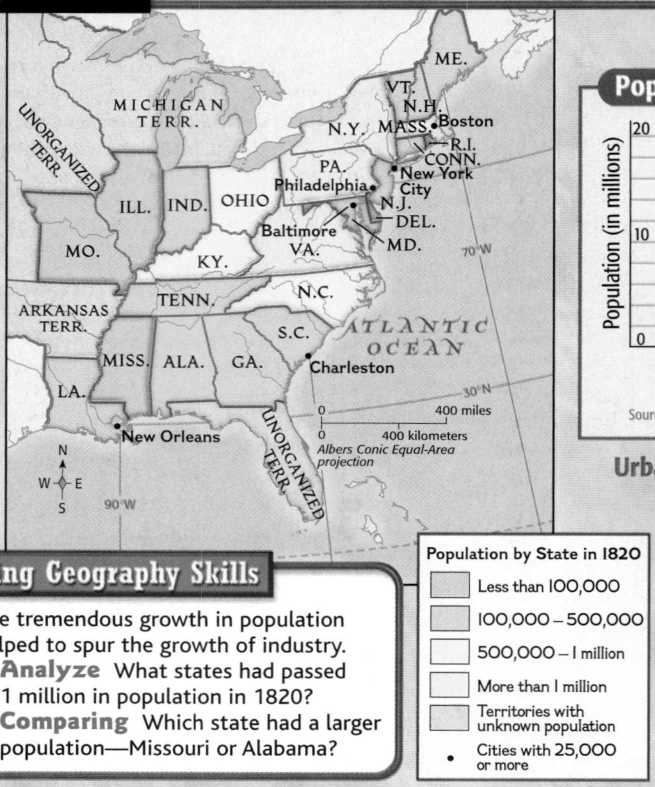

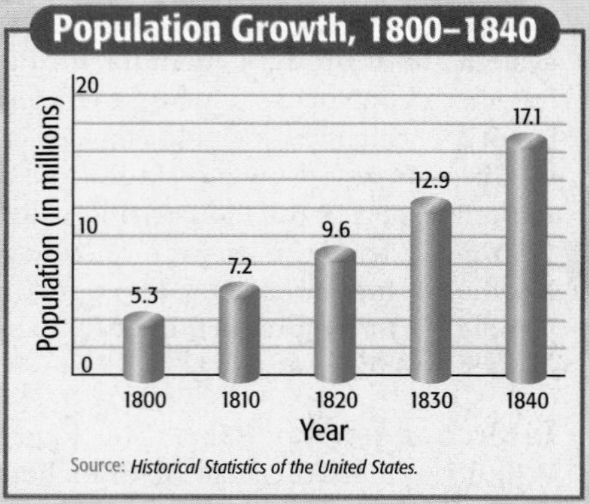

Source: *Historical Statistics of the United States.*

U

Urban and Rural Population, 1820

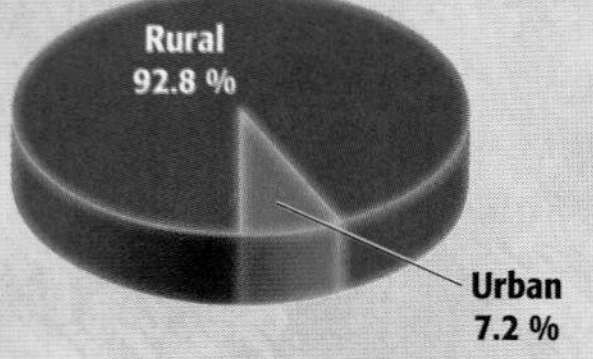

Using Geography Skills

The tremendous growth in population helped to spur the growth of industry.

1. **Analyze** What states had passed 1 million in population in 1820?
2. **Comparing** Which state had a larger population—Missouri or Alabama?

Using Geography Skills

Answers:

1. New York, Pennsylvania, and Virginia
2. Alabama

Resources for page 386

Academic Vocabulary Activity 8

Economic Independence Most new industries were financed by small investors—merchants, shopkeepers, and farmers. These people invested some of their money in the hope of earning profits if the new businesses succeeded. Low taxes, few government regulations, and competition encouraged people to invest in new industries.

Cities Come of Age The growth of factories and trade spurred the growth of towns and cities. The new industrial towns grew quickest. Many developed along rivers and streams to take advantage of the waterpower. Older cities such as New York, Boston, and Baltimore also grew as centers of commerce and trade. To the west, towns like Pittsburgh, Cincinnati, and Louisville profited from their locations on major rivers. As nearby farmers shipped more and more of their products by water, these towns grew rapidly.

Cities and towns looked different from modern urban areas. Buildings were made of wood or brick. Streets and sidewalks were unpaved, and barnyard animals often roamed freely. No sewers existed to carry waste and dirty water away, so the danger of diseases such as cholera and yellow fever was very real. In 1793, for example, a yellow fever epidemic in Philadelphia killed thousands of people. U

Fire posed another threat to cities. Sparks from a fireplace or chimney could easily ignite a wooden building and spread to others. Few towns or cities had organized fire companies, so fires could be disastrous.

Cities and towns of the period also had advantages, however. Some people left farming because cities and towns offered a variety of jobs and steady wages. As cities grew, they added libraries, museums, and shops that were unavailable in the countryside. For many, the jobs and attractions of city life outweighed any of the dangers.

Reading Check **Analyze** Why did cities such as Pittsburgh and Louisville grow?

History Online
Study Central Need help understanding the growth of industry in cities? Visit ca.hss.glencoe.com and click on Study Central.

Section 1 Review

Reading Summary

Review the Main Ideas

- The Industrial Revolution first began in the United States in New England, thanks to new technology, local resources, and the capitalist economic system.
- As large businesses continued to grow in the East, so did towns and cities. Further west, agriculture expanded, along with towns such as Cincinnati and Louisville.

What Did You Learn?

1. Describe the reasons New England was ideal for the development of factories.
2. How did farming in the Northeast differ from that in the South?

Critical Thinking

3. **Classifying Information** Re-create the diagram below and describe the major elements of the free enterprise system. CA HR3.

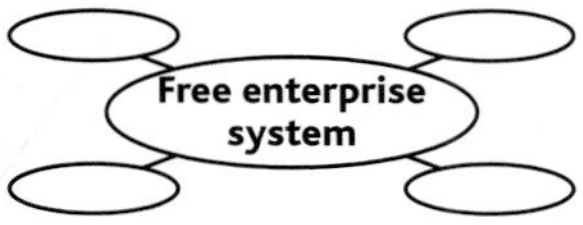

4. **The Big Ideas** Was new technology necessary for the Industrial Revolution? Explain. CA HI2.
5. **Economic Factors** How did the cotton gin affect cotton production? CA HI6.
6. **Reading Problems and Solutions** Write a paragraph describing the relationship between the quality of farmland and the growth of new industry in New England using a problem/solution structure. CA 8WA2.4

U Universal Access

Naturalist Have students research and report on the causes of cholera and yellow fever and explain why those diseases were particular problems in this period. OL CA 8WA2.3

ASSESS

Resources for page 387

Use these resources to assess student mastery of section content.

Section Quiz 8–1

Interactive Tutor Self-Assessment CD-ROM

Reading Check

Answer: As more settlers moved West, those farmers increasingly sent their crops to those cities, which were built along rivers, to get them to markets.

History Online

Study Central provides summaries, interactive games, and online graphic organizers to help students review section content.

CLOSE

Connecting Have students say whether they would have stayed on a family farm or moved to a city to work in a factory if they had lived in the early 1800s. Tell them to give reasons for their choices. OL

SECTION 1 REVIEW ANSWERS

Review questions reinforce content standard US8.6.

1. soil poor for farming; fast rivers and streams could provide power; deposits of coal and iron; ports
2. Northeast: farms small, grew crops for local markets; South: farms could be large, grew cotton for export
3. competition, profit, private property, economic freedom
4. **The Big Ideas** New technology made it possible to produce more goods more cheaply.
5. It made it faster to clean cotton, which spurred increased cotton production.
6. **Reading** Students might say that adoption of industry was a solution applied to the problem of poor farmland.

FOCUS

BELLRINGER
SKILLBUILDER ACTIVITY

Project **Daily Focus Skills Transparency 8–2** and have students answer the question.

Guide to Reading

Preteaching Vocabulary: Have students identify the three content vocabulary terms that have to do with transportation. *(turnpike, canal, lock)*

Answers to Graphic: National Road: connected Midwest to East; Fitch: helped develop the steamboat; Erie Canal: linked New York City to Great Lakes; Each led to better transportation, increased settlement.

Unpacking the Standards

After reading the section, students will be able to:

- Discuss how transportation improvements helped settlers to move west.
- Describe the Erie Canal and its impact on the nation.
- Outline changes in western settlement in the early 1800s.

Section 2

A System of Transportation

History Social Science Standards

US8.6 Students analyze the divergent paths of the American people from 1800 to the mid-1800s and the challenges they faced, with emphasis on the Northeast.

Guide to Reading

Looking Back, Looking Ahead
In the last section, you learned how the Industrial Revolution changed the American economy. In this section, you will learn how changes in transportation helped the nation expand.

Focusing on the Main Ideas
- Transportation routes such as roads improved as settlers moved west, and steamboats greatly improved the transport of goods along rivers. *(page 389)*
- Business and government officials came up with a plan to build a canal to link the eastern and western parts of the country. *(page 392)*
- Americans continued to move westward, settling near rivers so they could ship their crops to market. *(page 393)*

Locating Places
Hudson River
Albany
Lake Erie
Erie Canal

Meeting People
Robert Fulton

Content Vocabulary
census (SEHN • suhs)
turnpike
canal (kuh • NAL)
lock

Academic Vocabulary
undertake (UHN • duhr • TAYK)
equip (ih • KWIHP)

Reading Strategy
Taking Notes As you read the section, re-create the diagram below and describe why each was important to the nation's growth.

	Significance
National Road	
John Fitch	
Erie Canal	

NATIONAL GEOGRAPHIC Who & When?

1800 — 1815 — 1830

1806 Congress approves funds for National Road

1807 Fulton's *Clermont* steams to Albany, New York

Robert Fulton

1825 Erie Canal is completed

Erie Canal barrel

SECTION RESOURCES

Print Material
- Reproducible Lesson Plan 8–2*
- Daily Lesson and Discussion Notes 8–2
- Guided Reading Activity 8–2
- Reading Essentials and Study Guide 8–2
- Active Reading Note-Taking Guide 8–2
- Section Quiz 8–2

Transparencies
- Daily Focus Skills Transparency 8–2
- Section Graphic Organizer Transparency 8–2
- California Standards Practice Transparencies

Technology
- Interactive Tutor Self-Assessment CD-ROM
- Exam*View*® Pro Testmaker CD-ROM
- Presentation Plus! CD-ROM

*Available on TeacherWorks™

US8.6.2 Outline the physical obstacles to and the economic and political factors involved in building a network of roads, canals, and railroads (e.g., Henry Clay's American System).

Moving West

R1 **Main Idea** **Transportation routes such as roads improved as settlers moved west, and steamboats greatly improved the transport of goods along rivers.**

Reading Connection Have you ever gone on a trip to another state? Read to learn how transportation was different in the 1800s and how the new network of roads connected the country.

An American Story

In the 1820s Congressman Henry Clay of Kentucky prepared an ambitious program to improve transportation and strengthen the nation's economy called the American System. The American System included building canals and roads to link the South, Northeast, and West together. The American System, Clay believed, would bring the United States "to that height to which God and nature had destined it." Even before Clay's plans, Americans were working to improve transportation.

R2 **Growth and Movement** The first **census** (SEHN•suhs)—the official count of a population—of the nation in 1790 revealed a population of nearly 4 million. Most Americans counted lived east of the Appalachian Mountains and within a few hundred miles of the Atlantic coast.

Within a few decades this changed. The number of settlers heading west increased greatly. In 1811 a Pennsylvania resident reported seeing 236 wagons filled with people and their possessions on the road to Pittsburgh. In 1820, just 30 years after the first census, the population of the United States had more than doubled to about 10 million people, with nearly 2 million living west of the Appalachians.

Traveling west was not easy in the late 1790s and early 1800s. The 363-mile trip from New York City to Buffalo could take as long as three weeks. A pioneer family heading west with a wagonload of household goods faced hardship and danger along the way.

Roads and Turnpikes The nation needed good inland roads for travel and for the shipment of goods. Private companies built many **turnpikes**, or toll roads. The fees travelers paid to use those roads helped pay for construction. R3 Many of the roads had a base of crushed stone. In areas where the land was often muddy, companies built "corduroy roads," which consisted of logs laid side by side like the ridges of corduroy cloth.

When Ohio joined the Union in 1803, the new state asked the federal government to build a road to connect it with the East. In 1806 Congress approved funds for a National Road to the West and five years later agreed on the route. Because work on the road stopped during the War of 1812, the first section, from Maryland to western Virginia, did not open until 1818. In later years, the National Road reached Ohio and continued on to Vandalia, Illinois. Congress viewed the National Road as a military necessity, but it did not **undertake** other road-building projects.

River Travel River travel had definite advantages over wagon and horse travel. It was far more comfortable than travel over the bumpy roads, and pioneers could load all their goods on river barges—if they were heading downstream in the direction of the current.

River travel had two problems, however. The first related to the geography of the eastern United States. Most major rivers in the region flowed in a north-south direction, not east to west, where most people and goods were headed. Second, traveling upstream by barge against the current was an extremely difficult and slow way to travel.

History Online

Student Web Activity Visit ca.hss.glencoe.com and click on *Chapter 8—Student Web Activities* for an activity on the National Road.

TEACH

R1 Reading Strategy

Organizing Information As students read the section, have them create a graphic organizer summarizing the information in each subsection. For instance, for this first subsection, they should draw an oval and label it "Growth and Movement." Then they can connect smaller ovals to it with the words *population growth; increased westward movement;* and *transportation difficulties*. Have students continue with the rest of the section. BL

R2 Reading Strategy

Scaffolding—Connecting Point out that the census is still carried out today. OL

This READING SKILL was introduced in Chapter 3.

R3 Reading Strategy

Activating Prior Knowledge Several states today have turnpikes. **Ask:** Have you ever ridden on a turnpike or any other toll road? EL

History Online

Objectives and answers to the student activity can be found in the Web Activity Lesson Plan feature at ca.hss.glencoe.com.

More Skill Practice

Historical and Social Sciences Analysis Skill The government counts the number of people in the country every ten years. People also answer questions about their gender, age, education, and so on. **Ask:** Why would historians view each census as a valuable tool? *(They can identify changes over time)* AL CA CS3.

Did You Know?

The government spent nearly $7 million on the National Road, which was also called the Cumberland Road. In the twentieth century, U.S. Highway 40 was built largely following its path. There are now plans to restore a part of the original National Road to its early nineteenth-century condition as a historical landmark.

U Universal Access

Below Grade Level Remind students that traveling *downstream* means going *with* the current; *upstream* is *against* the current. **Ask:** Which direction is faster? Why? *(downstream; because the current can help carry the vessel)* OL

C Critical Thinking

Identifying Central Issues
Ask: What were two problems with river travel? How did the steamboat solve those problems? *(problems: most major rivers flowed north-south and not east-west; traveling upstream by barge was difficult and slow; solution: made upstream travel faster but could not solve the east-west problem)* OL

W Writing Support

Expository Writing Have students convert the captions in the drawing into a one or two paragraph description of how a steamboat worked. OL
CA 8RC2.5

Reading Check

Answer: It was cheaper and faster to move people and goods, and the ride on a steamboat was more comfortable

Answers and Additional Support

The Era of the Steamboat Steam engines were already being used in the 1780s and 1790s to power boats in quiet waters. Inventor James Rumsey **equipped** a small boat on the Potomac River with a steam engine. John Fitch, another inventor, built a steamboat that navigated the Delaware River. Neither boat, however, had enough power to withstand the strong currents and winds found in large rivers or open bodies of water.

In 1802 Robert Livingston, a political and business leader, hired **Robert Fulton** to develop a steamboat with a powerful engine. Livingston wanted the steamboat to carry cargo and passengers up the **Hudson River** from New York City to **Albany.**

In 1807 Fulton had his steamboat, the *Clermont*, ready for a trial. Powered by a newly designed engine, the *Clermont* made the 150-mile trip from New York to Albany in the unheard-of time of 32 hours. Using only sails, the trip would have taken four days. About 140 feet long and 14 feet wide, the *Clermont* offered great comforts to its passengers. They could sit or stroll about on deck, and at night they could relax in the sleeping compartments below deck. The engine was noisy, but its power provided a fairly smooth ride.

Steamboats ushered in a new age in river travel. They greatly improved the transport of goods and passengers along major inland rivers. Shipping goods became cheaper and faster. Steamboats also played an important role in the growth of river cities such as Cincinnati and St. Louis. By 1850 more than 700 steamboats traveled along the nation's waterways.

Reading Check **Compare** What advantages did steamboat travel have over wagon and horse travel?

TECHNOLOGY & History

The Clermont

On August 17, 1807, the *Clermont* steamed up the Hudson River from New York City on its way to Albany, New York. The trip took only 32 hours—a commercial success. **What type of energy was used to power this ship?**

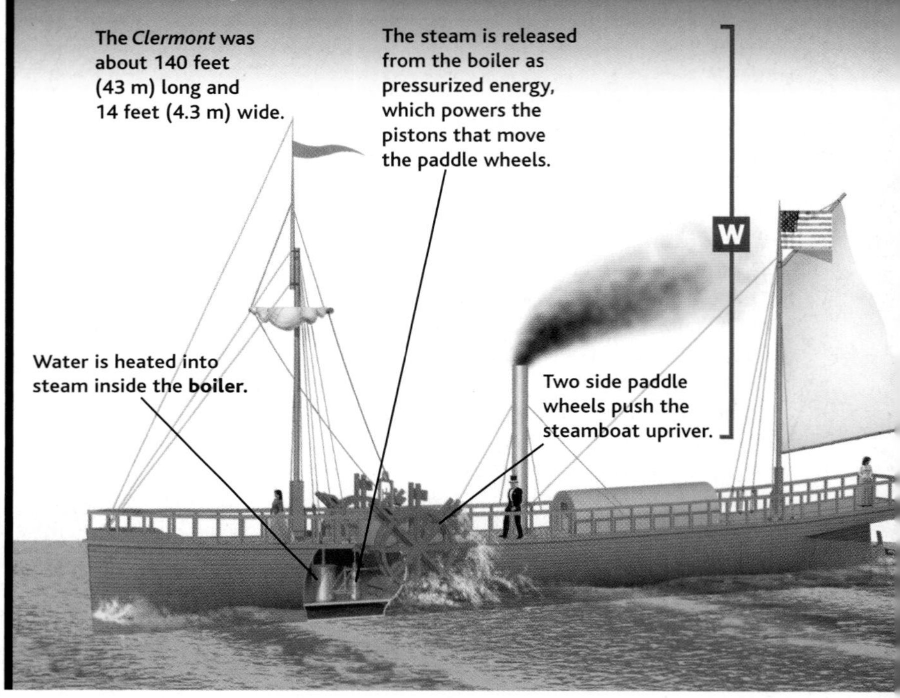

TECHNOLOGY & History

An eyewitness to the first voyage of the *Clermont* described the scene many years later: "The whole country talked of nothing but the sea monster belching forth fire and smoke. The fishermen became terrified and rowed homewards, and they saw nothing but destruction devastating their fishing grounds, while the wreaths of black vapor and the rushing noise of the paddlewheels, foaming with the stirred up waters, produced great excitement among the boatmen."

Answer: Steam was used to power the *Clermont*.

Biography

US8.6.2 Outline the physical obstacles to and the economic and political factors involved in building a network of roads, canals, and railroads (e.g., Henry Clay's American System).

ROBERT FULTON

1765–1815

Robert Fulton grew up in Lancaster, Pennsylvania. At an early age he created his own lead pencils and rockets. While living in Europe in the late 1790s, Fulton designed and built a submarine called the *Nautilus* to be used in France's war against Britain. Submarine warfare became common later. **W**

Fulton returned to the United States and developed a steamboat engine that was more powerful and provided a smoother ride than previous engines. On August 18, 1807, Fulton's *Clermont* made its first successful run. The *Clermont* made its first voyages on the Hudson River, chugging the 150 miles from New York City to Albany at about five miles per hour.

By demonstrating the usefulness of two-way river travel, Fulton launched the steamboat era. In the years between 1830 and 1850, the steamboat became the most important means of transportation on major rivers.

"I have no time to listen to such nonsense."

—Napoleon Bonaparte about Fulton's plans for a steam-powered engine **C1**

Steamboats cruised in and out of the Great Lakes, as well as up and down the Mississippi River and its tributaries. By 1850 more than 700 steamboats, also called riverboats, traveled along the nation's waterways.

Fulton designed many other devices such as submarines and steam warships. He also engineered canal systems. Thomas Jefferson and James Madison considered him a mechanical genius with many talents. When the United States went to war with Great Britain in the War of 1812, President Madison said, "I have been asked, on a number of occasions, how the United States could conceivably defeat England, with the resources of its vast empire. I invariably reply, 'The United States has Robert Fulton, and he is all the empire we need.'" **C2**

Then and Now

What modern inventions have changed the way we travel?

Then and Now

Students might mention jet planes, high-speed trains, and cars and buses.

Did You Know?

Designing steamboats was Robert Fulton's second career. He began as an artist who painted miniature portraits of people such as Benjamin Franklin. After several years, Fulton abandoned the fine arts to work in what he called the "useful arts." Fulton worked on canals, then on designing experimental submarines, called "plunging boats."

Biography

TEACH

W Writing Support

Research Reports Writing Have students find out what happened to Napoleon and his plans for a European empire. Then have them write an essay arguing that Napoleon would or would not have benefited from having steamboats at his disposal. AL CA HI4. CA 8WA2.4

C1 Critical Thinking

Comparing and Contrasting Have students read the quotations from Napoleon and James Madison.

Ask: Which leader was more open to new ideas? Why? *(Madison, since he gave great credit to Fulton's talents, whereas Napoleon rejected the idea of steamboats.)* OL

C2 Critical Thinking

Analyzing Primary Sources Thomas Jefferson and James Madison considered Fulton a "mechanical genius."

Ask: Does the quotation from Madison support this conclusion? Why or why not? *(It does, since Madison praises Fulton so highly.)* OL CA HR5.

Resources for page 391

Economics and History Activity 8

C Critical Thinking

Identifying Central Issues Encourage students to take notes on this subsection by writing down the problem that Americans faced, the solution some attempted, and whether it worked. *(problem: western and eastern regions still not linked by water; solution: build a canal; effectiveness: succeeded very well)* OL CA HI1.

R Reading Strategy

Understanding Vocabulary Have students write a sentence explaining the connection between canals and locks. BL

U Universal Access

Interpersonal Organize students into groups and have each group research and report on the effect of the canal on the development of one city along the routes. Encourage students to create visual aids to supplement their reports. OL CA 8WA2.3 CACS3.

Answers and Additional Support

US8.6.2 Outline the physical obstacles to and the economic and political factors involved in building a network of roads, canals, and railroads (e.g., Henry Clay's American System).

Canals

C **Main Idea** **Business and government officials came up with a plan to build a canal to link the eastern and western parts of the country.**

Reading Connection Have you ever worked long and hard to build something? Did you feel a sense of accomplishment when you finished? Read to learn the accomplishment of thousands of laborers who worked on the construction of the 363-mile Erie Canal.

Although steamboats represented a great improvement in transportation, their routes depended on the existing river system. Steamboats could not effectively tie the eastern and western parts of the country together.

In New York, business and government officials led by De Witt Clinton came up with a plan to link New York City with the Great Lakes region. They would build a **canal** (kuh•NAL)—an artificial waterway—across New York State, connecting Albany on the Hudson River with Buffalo on **Lake Erie.**

Building the Erie Canal Thousands of laborers, many of them Irish immigrants, worked on the construction of the 363-mile **Erie Canal.** Along the canal, they built a series of **locks**—separate compartments where water levels were raised or lowered. Locks provided a way to raise and lower boats at places where canal levels changed. R

After more than two years of digging, the Erie Canal opened on October 26, 1825. Clinton boarded a barge in Buffalo and journeyed on the canal to New York City. As crowds cheered in New York, the officials poured water from Lake Erie into the Atlantic. The East and Midwest were joined. U

TECHNOLOGY & History

How a Canal Works

A ship traveling downstream enters a lock and remains there while a gate is closed behind it, creating a watertight chamber. Water is slowly released through the downstream gate to lower the water level in the lock. The downstream gate is then opened, and the ship continues on its way at a lower elevation. To raise a ship, water is added to the lock through the upstream gate. **What happens as a boat travels through each lock of the canal?**

"Get up there mule, here comes a lock
We'll make Rome 'fore 6 'clock
And back we'll go to our home dock
Right back home to Buffalo"

The "lock" in the song verse refers to the Erie Canal. Locks are chambers, with gates at each end, that raise and lower ships to compensate for elevation changes along a waterway.

TECHNOLOGY & History

In 1815, goods needed 52 days to travel by land from Cincinnati to New York City. By the 1840s, after the Erie Canal had been built, goods could be shipped on an all-water route using the Erie Canal in just 18 to 20 days.

Answer: The boat changes the elevation at which it travels.

More Skill Practice

Historical and Social Sciences Analysis Skill Suggest that students write five headlines that summarize stages in the building of the Erie Canal. Tell them to make at least one headline describe the idea to build a canal and another to mark its opening. The other headlines can come from any time during the building or use of the canal. OL

US8.6.2 Outline the physical obstacles to and the economic and political factors involved in building a network of roads, canals, and railroads (e.g., Henry Clay's American System).

In its early years, the canal did not allow steamboats because their powerful engines could damage the earthen embankments along the canal. Instead, teams of mules or horses hauled the boats and barges. In the 1840s, the canal banks were reinforced to accommodate steam tugboats pulling barges.

The success of the Erie Canal led to an explosion in canal building. By 1850 the United States had more than 3,600 miles of canals. Canals lowered the cost of shipping goods and brought prosperity to the towns along their routes. Canals also created opportunities for new businesses to supply food, shelter, and other necessities to workers—and later to travelers on the canals. Perhaps most important, they helped unite the growing country.

Reading Check **Identify** What two cities did the Erie Canal connect?

Western Settlement

Main Idea **Americans continued to move westward, settling near rivers so they could ship their crops to market.**

Reading Connection What do you do when you get together with your friends? Do you watch a movie or play soccer? Read to learn what kinds of social events western families had in the early 1800s.

Americans moved westward in waves. The first wave began before the 1790s and led to the admission of four new states between 1791 and 1803—Vermont, Kentucky, Tennessee, and Ohio. A second wave of westward growth began between 1816 and 1821. Five new western states were created—Indiana, Illinois, Mississippi, Alabama, and Missouri.

S Skill Practice

Historical and Social Sciences Analysis Skill
Before the Erie Canal was built, it cost $100 to ship a ton of goods from the Great Lakes to the east. With the canal, the cost dropped to $9 a ton. **Ask:** How would this affect consumers who bought those goods? *(They would pay less because producers could lower prices since their costs were lower.)* OL CA HI6.

C Critical Thinking

Analyzing Information
Before the canal was built, De Witt Clinton and others predicted that the canal would make New York City the center of trade in the United States. Within a few years, more than twice as many goods shipped through New York as moved through New Orleans, and New York City had grown much larger. **Ask:** Were predictions about the canal correct or incorrect? *(correct; because the amount of shipping and the city's population increased)* OL

Reading Check
Answer: Buffalo and Albany

Did You Know?

When the canal officially opened, New York City staged a huge celebration. Seven thousand people marched along many of the city's streets to City Hall. An estimated one hundred thousand people—about two-thirds of all the city's population—watched them proceed. At night, public buildings and private homes were lit up with candles and oil lamps. The celebration ended with a massive fireworks display.

W Writing Support

Letter Writing Ask students to imagine that they are some of the many Americans that lived in rural areas of Ohio, Kentucky, and Tennessee. Have them write a letter to friends living in New York City describing how changes and improvements in transportation have affected their daily life. OL

ASSESS

Resources for page 394

Use these resources to assess student mastery of section content.

Section Quiz 8–2

Interactive Tutor Self-Assessment CD-ROM

Reading Check

Answer: Vermont, Kentucky, Tennessee, Ohio

History Online

Study Central provides summaries, interactive games, and online graphic organizers to help students review section content.

CLOSE

Summarizing Have students take the role of a government worker who oversees the country's transportation network. Ask them to write a report from the year 1840 that summarizes the advances in transportation that have taken place in the last two decades. OL

The new states reflected the dramatic growth of the region west of the Appalachians. Ohio, for example, had only 45,000 settlers in 1800. By 1820 it had 581,000.

Pioneer families tended to settle in communities along the great rivers, such as the Ohio and the Mississippi, so that they could ship their crops to market. The expansion of canals, which crisscrossed the land in the 1820s and 1830s, allowed people to live farther away from the rivers.

Pioneer families often gathered together for social events. Men took part in sports such as wrestling. Women met for quilting and sewing parties. Both men and women participated in cornhuskings—gatherings where farm families shared the work of stripping the husks from ears of corn.

Their lives did not include the conveniences of Eastern town life, but the pioneers had not moved to be pampered. They wanted to make a new life for themselves and their families.

Transportation and Daily Life Improved transportation meant that people could now buy goods produced in distant places. Rural Americans could hang curtains sewn from cloth manufactured in the mills of New England. Citizens of Illinois could enjoy the same foods, fashions, and household furnishings as residents of Vermont. W

The new transportation changed America in other ways as well. In 1825 Congress established home delivery of letters by mail, and in 1847 the first national postage stamps were created. With the mail came newspapers, which brought national issues to the attention of remote rural communities.

Reading Check **Identify** Which states were formed between 1791 and 1803?

History Online

Study Central Need help understanding the effects of changes in transportation? Visit ca.hss.glencoe.com and click on Study Central.

Section 2 Review

Reading Summary

Review the Main Ideas

- Settlers used new roads and turnpikes to move west of the Appalachians, and steamboats opened a new era of river travel.
- The success of the Erie Canal led to the building of other canals to link the East and Midwest.
- Although life west of the Appalachian Mountains was often difficult, the population there grew tremendously in the early 1800s.

What Did You Learn?

1. Describe the improvements in transportation during the westward expansion in the early 1800s.
2. What were the benefits of canals in the mid-1800s?

Critical Thinking

3. **Comparing** What forms of communication and transportation linked East to West in the early 1800s? What links exist today? Re-create the diagram below and compare the links. CA CS1.

Links	
Early 1800s	Today

4. **The Big Ideas** How did better transportation affect westward expansion? CA HI2.
5. **Descriptive Writing** Write a newspaper headline along with a brief article describing one of the events discussed in this section, such as a trip on an early steamboat or the opening of the Erie Canal. CA 8WA2.1
6. **Analysis** **Sequencing** Draw a time line identifying major developments in transportation during this period. CA CS2.

SECTION 2 REVIEW ANSWERS

Review questions reinforce content standard US8.6.

1. steamboats, canals, Erie Canal, the National Road
2. lowered cost of shipping helped towns grow.
3. early 1800s: letters, turnpikes, roads, canals, steamboats, barges, wagons; today: email, telephone, fax, highways, planes, trains, cars, trucks, ships
4. **The Big Ideas** shortened travel time; allowed people to live farther from rivers
5. Students should convey excitement.
6. **Analysis** 1807—first voyage of *Clermont*; 1818—National Road opens; 1825—Erie Canal opens; 1850—U.S. has more than 3,600 miles of canals

The North's People

Guide to Reading

Looking Back, Looking Ahead

In Section 2, you learned how advances in transportation changed the geography of America. In Section 3, you will learn about the people and the economy of the North.

Focusing on the Main Ideas

- As industrialism grew in the North, many saw the need for reforms in working conditions. ***(page 396)***
- Immigrants entered northern cities from many parts of Europe. They often faced hardships and discrimination upon arriving in America. ***(page 398)***

Meeting People

Henry Boyd
Samuel Cornish
John B. Russwurm
Sarah G. Bagley

Content Vocabulary

trade union
strike
prejudice (PREH • juh • duhs)
discrimination (dis • KRIH • muh • NAY • shuhn)
famine (FA • muhn)
nativist (NAY • tih • VIHST)

Academic Vocabulary

shift
manual

Reading Strategy

Determining Cause and Effect As you read the section, re-create the diagram below and list two reasons for the growth of cities.

Growth of Cities

History Social Science Standards

US8.6 Students analyze the divergent paths of the American people from 1800 to the mid-1800s and the challenges they faced, with emphasis on the Northeast.

NATIONAL GEOGRAPHIC Who & When?

1820 — 1840 — 1860

- **1827** *Freedom's Journal*, first African American newspaper, is published
- **1833** The General Trades Union of New York is formed
- **1840s** Potato famine in Ireland leads to great emigration
- **1854** American Party (Know Nothings) becomes a political force

FOCUS

BELLRINGER
SKILLBUILDER ACTIVITY

Project **Daily Focus Skills Transparency 8–3** and have students answer the question.

Guide to Reading

Preteaching Vocabulary: Use the Vocabulary PuzzleMaker CD-ROM to create crossword and word search puzzles.

Answers to Graphic: any two: growth of factories, growth of trade and shipping, increased immigration

Unpacking the Standards

After reading the section, students will be able to:

- describe working conditions in the North's factories and problems workers faced.
- discuss the special concerns of African American and women workers.
- explain why immigration rose in the early 1800s and how the immigrants lived after they reached the United States.
- discuss the reaction to these immigrants and problems they faced.

SECTION RESOURCES

Print Material
- Reproducible Lesson Plan 8–3*
- Daily Lesson and Discussion Notes 8–3
- Guided Reading Activity 8–3
- Reading Essentials and Study Guide 8–3
- Active Reading Note-Taking Guide 8–3
- Section Quiz 8–3

Transparencies
- Daily Focus Skills Transparency 8–3
- Section Graphic Organizer Transparency 8–3
- California Standards Practice Transparencies

Technology
- Interactive Tutor Self-Assessment CD-ROM
- Exam*View*® Pro Testmaker CD-ROM
- Presentation Plus! CD-ROM

*Available on TeacherWorks™

TEACH

S Skill Practice

Historical and Social Sciences Analysis Skill
Ask: Why did business owners who produced goods other than textiles, such as shoes, watches, and guns, adopt the factory system? *(they wanted to achieve the same success as owners of textile mills)* OL CA HI6.

C Critical Thinking

Determining Cause and Effect **Ask:** Why did the number of accidents go up as workdays grew longer? *(Students may say that since workers were in the factory longer, they had more opportunities to have accidents; also the later they worked, the more tired and accident-prone they probably became.)* OL CA HI2.

U Universal Access

Auditory/Musical Have students write a song that workers might sing to help them get through the long, difficult days. Suggest that they set their words to an existing tune. Invite students to share their songs with the class. OL

US8.6.1 Discuss the influence of industrialization and technological developments in the region, including human modification of the landscape and how physical geography shaped human actions. US8.6.4 Study the lives of black Americans who gained freedom in the North and founded schools and churches to advance their rights and communities.

Northern Factories

Main Idea **As industrialism grew in the North, many saw the need for reforms in working conditions.**

Reading Connection Do you baby-sit or mow lawns to earn money? Do you think the money you earn is fair for the job you perform? Read on to learn about how workers organized to receive better pay and improve working conditions.

An American Story

"At first the hours seemed very long, but I was so interested in learning that I endured it very well; when I went out at night the sound of the mill was in my ears," a Northern mill worker wrote in 1844.

The worker compared the noise of the cotton mill to the deafening roar of Niagara Falls. The roar of machinery was only one of the features of factory life that these workers had to adjust to. Industrialization created new challenges for the men, women, and children who worked in the nation's factories.

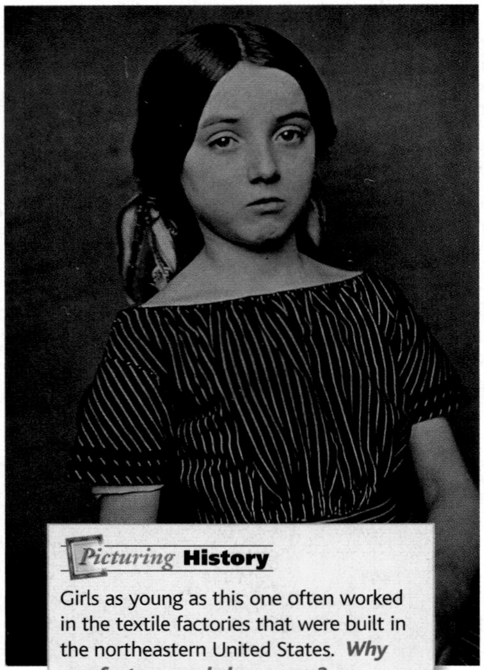

Picturing History

Girls as young as this one often worked in the textile factories that were built in the northeastern United States. ***Why was factory work dangerous?***

What Were Working Conditions Like?

Between 1820 and 1860, more and more of America's manufacturing **shifted** to mills and factories. Machines took over many of the production tasks.

In the early 1800s, in the mills established in Lowell, Massachusetts, the entire production process was brought together under one roof, setting up the factory system. In addition to textiles and clothing, factories now produced such items as shoes, watches, guns, sewing machines, and agricultural machinery. S

As the factory system developed, working conditions worsened. Factory owners wanted their employees to work longer hours to produce more goods. By 1840 factory employees worked an average of 11.4 hours per day. As the workday grew longer, on-the-job accidents became more common. C

Factory work was often dangerous. For example, the long leather belts that connected the machines to the factory's water-powered driveshaft had no protective shields. Workers often suffered injuries such as lost fingers and broken bones from the rapidly spinning belts. Young children working on machines with powerful moving parts were especially at risk.

Workers often labored under unpleasant conditions. In the summer, factories were miserably hot and stifling. The machines gave off heat, and air-conditioning had not yet been invented. In the winter, workers suffered because most factories had no heating.

Factory owners often showed more concern for profits than for the comfort and safety of their employees. Employers knew they could easily replace an unhappy worker with someone else who was eager for a job. No laws existed to regulate working conditions or to protect workers. U

Answers and Additional Support

More Skill Practice

Historical and Social Sciences Analysis Skill Tell students that workers in this period were sometimes called "wage slaves." **Ask:** Is the name appropriate? Why or why not? *(Some students will say it is appropriate because the workers had few rights; others will say that while they suffered, their lives were not as difficult as those of slaves.)* OL

Picturing History

Answer: Accidents involving the machines could cause serious injuries.

Attempts to Organize By the 1830s, workers began organizing to improve working conditions. Skilled workers formed **trade unions**—organizations of workers with the same trade, or skill. Steadily deteriorating working conditions led unskilled workers to organize as well.

In the mid-1830s, skilled workers in New York City staged a series of **strikes,** refusing to work in order to put pressure on employers. Workers wanted higher wages and to limit their workday to 10 hours. Groups of skilled workers formed the General Trades Union of New York.

In the early 1800s, going on strike was illegal. Striking workers could be punished by the law, or they could be fired from their jobs. In 1842 a Massachusetts court ruled that workers did have the right to strike. In other cities and states, workers won some protections. However, it would be many years before workers received federal protection of their right to strike.

African American Workers Slavery had largely disappeared from the North by 1820. However, racial **prejudice** (PREH•juh•duhs)—an unfair opinion that is not based on facts—and **discrimination** (dis•KRIH•muh•NAY•shuhn)—unfair treatment of a group—remained in Northern states. For example, both Rhode Island and Pennsylvania passed laws prohibiting free African Americans from voting.

Most communities would not allow free African Americans to attend public schools and barred them from public facilities, as well. Often African Americans were forced into segregated, or separate, schools and hospitals.

Some African Americans found success in business. **Henry Boyd** owned a furniture manufacturing company in Cincinnati, Ohio. In 1827 **Samuel Cornish** and **John B. Russwurm** founded *Freedom's Journal*, the nation's first African American newspaper. In 1845 Macon B. Allen became the first African American licensed to practice law in the United States.

Women Workers Women took jobs in the developing mills and factories. However, employers discriminated against women, paying them less than male workers. When men began to form unions, they excluded women. Male workers wanted women kept out of the workplace so that more jobs would be available for men.

Some female workers attempted to organize in the 1830s and 1840s. In Massachusetts the Lowell Female Labor Reform Organization, founded by a weaver named **Sarah G. Bagley,** petitioned the state legislature for a 10-hour day in 1845. Because most of the petition's signers were women, the legislature did not discuss the petition.

Most of the early efforts by women to achieve equality and justice in the workplace failed. They led, however, to later movements to correct the injustices against female workers.

History *Through Art*

Young Man in White Apron* by John Mackie Falconer** The artist of this painting was known for his watercolors depicting New York City workers such as this African American clerk. ***How did prejudice affect the lives of African Americans in the North?

Reading Check **Describe** How did conditions for workers change as the factory system developed?

R1 Reading Strategy

Connecting **Ask:** What groups today form unions? *(Answers may include auto workers, athletes, or teachers, among others.)* OL

R2 Reading Strategy

Understanding Vocabulary The term *strike* was first used in a labor context in 1768 when British sailors protested by striking, or taking down, their ship's sails. **Ask:** What is a strike? *(workers refusing to work to protest pay, benefits, or working conditions)* OL

R3 Reading Strategy

Understanding Vocabulary Invite students to suggest a sentence that explains the link between *prejudice* and *discrimination*. OL

R4 Reading Strategy

Scaffolding—Academic Vocabulary The word *available* was introduced in Chapter 6, Section 3. Ask students why male workers wanted women kept out of the workplace. OL

W Writing Support

Persuasive Writing Have students work in groups to draft a petition that women factory owners could have sent to the state government. Have one member of each group read its petition aloud, and ask the class to determine which arguments and which delivery were most effective. OL CA 8WA2.4 CA 8SA2.4

Reading Check

Answer: Conditions worsened as factory owners pushed employees to work longer days and as machines became more dangerous.

More Skill Practice

Historical and Social Sciences Analysis Skill Pay depended not on the job but on gender and age. Lowell girls made from $2.50 to $3.00 per week, less than the $4.00 a week that males earned doing the same job. Have students research the current average wages of male and female workers and prepare a graph comparing them. AL

History *Through Art*

John Mackie Falconer was born in Scotland in 1820 and came to the United States at age 16. He settled in Brooklyn, New York, and is known for his etchings as well as his watercolors.

Answer: They did not have all the rights that whites did.

S Skill Practice

Using Geography Skills
Ask: How did geography shape these cities? *(Proximity to major rivers or lakes—and thus transportation—helped them grow.)* Is such a location as important a factor for modern cities to grow? Why or why not? *(Students may say no since people and goods can be moved over highways and by air.)* AL
CA CS3.

U Universal Access

English Learners Remind students that when words like *Great Lakes* are capitalized, they refer to specific lakes. Have students find out which lakes have this name and locate them on a map. EL

R Reading Strategy

Connecting Explain that famines are food shortages that are widespread, affecting large areas or entire countries. BL

US8.6.3 List the reasons for the wave of immigration from Northern Europe to the United States and describe the growth in number, size, and spatial arrangement of cities (e.g., Irish immigrants and the Great Irish Famine).

The Rise of Cities

Main Idea **Immigrants entered northern cities from many parts of Europe. They often faced hardships and discrimination upon arriving in America.**

Reading Connection Did you know that the tradition of decorating a tree at Christmas comes from a German tradition? Many of our foods, words, and traditions originated in other countries. Read on to find out how immigrants influenced Northern cities.

The growth of factories helped Northern cities grow. People looking for work moved to the cities, where most of the factories were located. The population of New York City, the nation's largest city, reached 800,000, and Philadelphia's population was more than 500,000 in 1860.

Between 1820 and 1840, communities that had been small villages became major cities, including St. Louis, Pittsburgh, Cincinnati, and Louisville. All of them profited from their location on the Mississippi River or one of the river's branches. These cities became centers of the growing trade that connected the farmers of the Midwest with the cities of the Northeast. After 1830 the Great Lakes became a center for shipping, creating major new urban centers. These centers included Buffalo, Detroit, Milwaukee, and Chicago.

Immigration Immigration, which is the movement of people into a country, increased dramatically between 1840 and 1860. American manufacturers welcomed immigrants, many of whom were willing to work for low pay.

The largest group of immigrants to the United States at this time traveled across the Atlantic from Ireland. Between 1846 and 1860, more than 1.5 million Irish immigrants arrived in the United States, settling mostly in the Northeast. Today, more people of Irish descent live in the United States than in Ireland.

The Irish migration to the United States was brought on by the Great Irish Famine. A **famine** (FA•muhn) is an extreme shortage of food. Potatoes were the main staple of the Irish diet. When a devastating blight, or disease, destroyed Irish potato crops in the 1840s, starvation struck the country. More than 1 million people died from the lack of food and from diseases.

Primary Sources

Newcomers to America

For many immigrants to America, their new home meant freedom and liberty. German immigrant August Blümmer expressed this idea in a letter he wrote in 1838:

> "Over there [Germany] common sense and free speech lie in shackles. . . . I invite you to come over here, should you want to obtain a clear notion of genuine public life, freedom of the people, and sense of being a nation. . . . I have never regretted that I came here, and never! never! again shall I bow my head under the yoke of despotism and folly."
>
> — quoted in *News from the Land of Freedom*

▲ Traveler's trunk

DBQ Document-Based Question

Explain what the writer means by "a sense of being a nation."

Answers and Additional Support

Primary Sources

Answer: Blümmer found the strong American national spirit appealing.

- What impact do you think letters like this had on the people in Europe? *(Answers may include that they persuaded many to come to America.)* OL
- Was Blümmer appealing to Germans' political goals or economic goals? *(political)* OL

Although most of the immigrants had been farmers in Ireland, they were too poor to buy land in the United States. For this reason, many Irish immigrants took low-paying factory jobs in Northern cities. The men who came from Ireland worked in factories or performed **manual** labor, such as working on the railroads. The women became servants and factory workers.

The second-largest group of immigrants in the United States between 1820 and 1860 came from Germany. Some sought work and opportunity. Others had left their homes because of the failure of a democratic revolution in Germany in 1848. During this time, many German Jews came to the United States seeking religious freedom.

MORE ABOUT... Immigration

Newcomers came to America from many different countries in the mid-1800s, but the overwhelming majority came from Ireland and Germany.

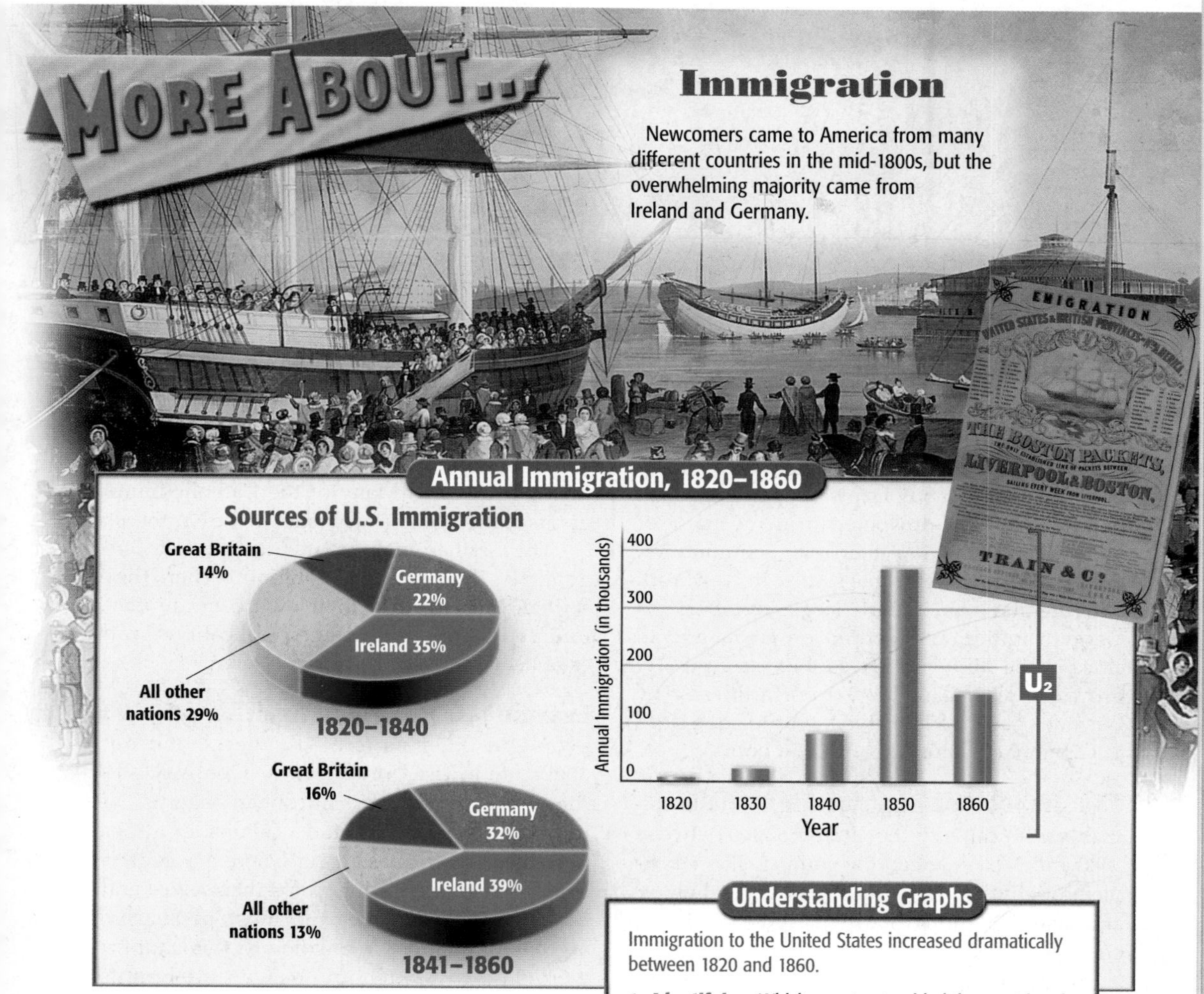

Understanding Graphs

Immigration to the United States increased dramatically between 1820 and 1860.

1. **Identifying** Which country provided the most immigrants between 1840 and 1860?
2. **Analyze** From the graph, in which years did immigration surpass 100,000?

R Reading Strategy

Academic Vocabulary

Discuss with students the use of the word *manual* to describe physical, hands-on work. EL

U1 Universal Access

Logical/Mathematical

Have students create Venn diagrams to find the similarities and differences between Irish and German immigration in this period. OL CA HI3.

C Critical Thinking

Identifying Central Issues

Historians speak of "push" and "pull" factors that influence immigration. "Push" factors persuade people to leave their home country. "Pull" factors attract them to a particular new country. **Ask:** What were the "push" and "pull" factors for German immigrants in this period? *(Push: failed democratic revolution; Pull: economic opportunity, freedom in U.S.)* OL CA HI3.

U2 Universal Access

Visual/Spatial Have students research three periods of high immigration to the United States: 1840 to 1860; 1890 to 1910; and 1970 to the present. Have them create charts or graphs that compare the numbers of people who came in these three periods and the areas where they originated. OL CA CS3. CA HI3.

Understanding Graphs

Answers:

1. Ireland
2. 1850 and 1860.

Did You Know?

So many Irish people stayed in New York City after immigrating that it soon became the city with the largest Irish population in the world. In just a few decades, there were more Irish living in the United States than in Ireland.

U Universal Access

Intrapersonal Ask: Do you think it would have been easier or more difficult for German immigrants to adjust compared to Irish immigrants? Why? *(Students may say the Germans would have more difficulty because of language differences; others may say the Irish would have had a harder time because of their poverty.)* OL

History *Through Art*

Boston Harbor as Seen from Constitution Wharf* by Robert Salmon** In the 1820s and 1830s, artist Robert Salmon recorded the emerging cities and scenic harbors of the young nation. ***What urban centers developed because of their location near the Great Lakes?

Between 1848 and 1860, more than 1 million German immigrants settled in the United States. Many German immigrants arrived with enough money to buy farms or open their own businesses. They prospered in many parts of the country, founding their own communities. Some German immigrants settled in New York and Pennsylvania, but large numbers of German immigrants settled on farms and in cities in the Midwest—areas that were rapidly growing and had job opportunities. The Germans gave a distinctive flavor to such cities as Cincinnati, Milwaukee, and St. Louis.

The Impact of Immigration The immigrants who came to the United States between 1820 and 1860 changed the country. These people brought their languages, customs, religions, and ways of life with them, some of which became part of American culture. U

Before the early 1800s, the majority of immigrants to America had been either Protestants from Great Britain or Africans brought forcibly to America as slaves. At the time, the country had relatively few Catholics, and most of them lived around Baltimore, New Orleans, and St. Augustine. Most of the Irish immigrants and about half of the German immigrants were Roman Catholics. Many of the Catholic immigrants of this era settled in cities in the Northeast.

The German immigrants brought their language as well as their religion. When they settled, they lived in their own communities, founded German-language publications, and established musical societies.

Learning About Life in America How did people in other parts of the world find out about life in the United States? One way was through advertising. European agents of railroad companies and steamship lines described America as a land where newcomers could make a better living for themselves and their families. Perhaps the most persuasive arguments for others to come to this country were letters written by recent immigrants to their family and friends. "If you wish to be happy and independent, then come here," wrote a German farmer from his new home in Missouri.

Answers and Additional Support

More Skill Practice

Historical and Social Sciences Analysis Skill Ask: How do you think Americans who were already here reacted to the rise in Irish and German immigrants? Why? *(Students may say that employers would welcome them since they provided low-cost labor, but others would object to them because of cultural differences.)* OL

History *Through Art*

Robert Salmon came to the United States in 1828 and remained for 14 years before returning to Britain. In that period, though, he was the best painter in the country of scenes of ships and the sea.

Answer: Buffalo, Milwaukee, Detroit, and Chicago

Immigrants Face Prejudice During the colonial period, workers were badly needed in all the colonies and immigrants had been readily accepted in many communities. In the 1830s and 1840s, however, some native-born Americans began to resent the newcomers, especially the Irish immigrants. Some Americans resented them because they dressed and sounded "different" and because they were Catholics.

R People who were opposed to immigration were known as **nativists** (NAY•tih•VIHSTS) because they believed that immigration threatened the future of "native"—American-born—citizens. Some nativists accused immigrants of taking jobs from "real" Americans and were angry that immigrants would work for lower wages. Others accused the newcomers of bringing crime and disease to American cities. Immigrants who lived in crowded slums were often targets of this kind of prejudice.

The Know-Nothing Party The nativists formed secret anti-Catholic societies, and in the 1850s they joined to form a new political party: the American Party. By 1854 the party had become a force in American politics. Because members of nativist groups often answered questions about their organization with the statement "I know nothing," their party came to be known as the Know-Nothing Party. They did this to protect the secrecy of their organization.

The Know-Nothings called for stricter citizenship laws—extending the immigrants' waiting period for citizenship from 5 to 14 years—and wanted to ban foreign-born citizens from holding office.

In the mid-1850s, the Know-Nothing movement split into a Northern branch and a Southern branch over the question of slavery. At this time, the slavery issue was also dividing the Northern and Southern states of the nation. C

Reading Check **Identify** Which two nations provided the largest number of immigrants to the United States during this era?

History Online **Study Central** Need help understanding the people and economy of the North? Visit ca.hss.glencoe.com and click on Study Central.

Section 3 Review

Reading Summary

Review the Main Ideas

- Northern factories grew in the mid-1800s and many workers faced discrimination and unsafe working conditions.
- Immigrants flooded into the North seeking better opportunities than existed in their own countries.

What Did You Learn?

1. What was the nation's largest city in 1860?
2. How did German and Irish immigrants differ in where they settled?

Critical Thinking

3. **Determining Cause and Effect** Re-create the diagram below and list reasons workers formed labor unions. CA HI2.

Cause
Cause
Cause
→ Effect: Workers organize

4. **The Big Ideas** Study the graphs on page 399. Did immigration from Ireland increase or decrease after 1840? How did immigration from Germany change? CA CS1.
5. **Expository Writing** Write two paragraphs on being an American: one to defend the nativist point of view and the other to appreciate the value of diversity in immigration. Look through your local newspaper for examples of each point of view. CA 8WA2.1

R Reading Strategy

Using Word Parts Remind students that the word ending *-ist* shows that people belong to a particular group or perform a particular action. **Ask:** What are other words with this ending? *(artist, dentist)* BL

C Critical Thinking

Determining Cause and Effect **Ask:** Why did the Know-Nothing party break apart? What impact would that have on the party's ability to win elections? Why? *(disagreements between Northern and Southern members over slavery; make it ineffective because it could not command wide support)* OL

ASSESS

Resources for page 401

Use these resources to assess student mastery of section content.

Section Quiz 8–3
Interactive Tutor Self-Assessment CD-ROM

Reading Check

Answer: Ireland, Germany

History Online

Study Central provides summaries, interactive games, and online graphic organizers to help students review section content.

CLOSE

Questioning Have students write a five-question quiz about the section and then exchange papers with a partner and answer those questions. OL

SECTION 3 REVIEW ANSWERS

Review questions reinforce content standard US8.6.

1. New York City
2. Irish immigrants settled mostly in the cities of the Northeast. German immigrants settled in New York, Pennsylvania, and the Midwest, and many bought their own farms.
3. Worsening working conditions; Low wages; Long workdays; Fear of growing factory system
4. **The Big Ideas** Irish immigration, as a share of all immigration, went up. German immigration rose more.
5. Students should give reasons for both positions.

FOCUS

BELLRINGER
SKILLBUILDER ACTIVITY

Project **Daily Focus Skills Transparency 8–4** and have students answer the question.

Guide to Reading

Preteaching Vocabulary:
Have students find the definitions of each content vocabulary term and write the definition in their own words.

Answers to Graphic:
Mann: reformed public schools in Massachusetts; Gallaudet: developed method for educating the hearing impaired; Dix: pushed for better treatment of prisoners, the mentally ill

Unpacking the Standards
After reading the section, students will be able to:

- explain the impact of the Second Great Awakening.
- identify the principal leaders of various reform movements.
- describe changing American culture in the early 1800s and name some important writers.

Section 4

Reforms and Reformers

History Social Science Standards

US8.6 Students analyze the divergent paths of the American people from 1800 to the mid-1800s and the challenges they faced, with emphasis on the Northeast.

Guide to Reading

Looking Back, Looking Ahead
In the last section, you learned about what life was like in the Northern cities. In Section 4, you will learn about how reformers worked to make life better for many Americans.

Focusing on the Main Ideas
- Religious and philosophical ideas inspired various reform movements. *(page 403)*
- Reformers wanted to make education accessible to all citizens. *(page 405)*
- A new wave of literature that was distinctly American swept the United States. *(page 406)*

Meeting People
Henry David Thoreau (thuh • ROH)
Ralph Waldo Emerson
Horace Mann
Thomas Gallaudet (GA • luh • DEHT)
Dr. Samuel Gridley Howe
Dorothea Dix
Margaret Fuller
Emily Dickinson

Content Vocabulary
utopia (yu • TOH • pee • uh)
revival
temperance (TEHM • puh • ruhns)
normal school
transcendentalist (TRAN • sehn • DEHN • tuhl • ihst)

Academic Vocabulary
founded
focus
publish

Reading Strategy
Taking Notes Re-create the diagram below and identify these reformers' contributions as you read Section 4.

	Contributions
Horace Mann	
Thomas Gallaudet	
Dorothea Dix	

NATIONAL GEOGRAPHIC Who & When?

1820 — 1835 — 1850

1825 Robert Owen establishes New Harmony, Indiana

Horace Mann

1837 Horace Mann initiates education reform

1843 Dorothea Dix reveals abuses of mentally ill

Dorothea Dix

SECTION RESOURCES

Print Material
- Reproducible Lesson Plan 8–4*
- Daily Lesson and Discussion Notes 8–4
- Guided Reading Activity 8–4
- Reading Essentials and Study Guide 8–4
- Active Reading Note-Taking Guide 8–4
- Section Quiz 8–4

Transparencies
- Daily Focus Skills Transparency 8–4
- Section Graphic Organizer Transparency 8–4
- California Standards Practice Transparencies

Technology
- Interactive Tutor Self-Assessment CD-ROM
- Exam*View*® Pro Testmaker CD-ROM
- Presentation Plus! CD-ROM

*Available on TeacherWorks™

US8.6.5 Trace the development of the American education system from its earliest roots, including the roles of religious and private schools and Horace Mann's campaign for free public education and its assimilating role in American culture.

The Reforming Spirit

Main Idea **Religious and philosophical ideas inspired various reform movements.**

Reading Connection Do your parents set limits on how much junk food you can consume? Read on to find out how reformers sought to place limits on the consumption of alcohol.

An American Story

Because he had refused to pay a one-dollar tax to vote, **Henry David Thoreau** (thuh•ROH) sat on a hard, wooden bench in a jail cell. He did not want his money to support the Mexican War. As he looked through the cell bars, he heard a voice. "Why are you here?" asked his friend **Ralph Waldo Emerson.** Thoreau replied, "Why are you *not* here?" Thoreau would later write:

> **"Under a government which imprisons any unjustly, the true place for a just man is also a prison."**
>
> —from "Civil Disobedience"

Utopias Thoreau represented a new spirit of reform in America. The men and women who led the reform movement wanted to extend the nation's ideals of liberty and equality to all Americans. They believed the nation should live up to the noble goals stated in the Declaration of Independence and the Constitution.

The spirit of reform brought changes to American religion, politics, education, art, and literature. Some reformers sought to improve society by forming **utopias** (yu•TOH•pee•uhs), communities based on a vision of a perfect society. In 1825 Robert Owen established New Harmony, Indiana, a village dedicated to cooperation rather than competition among its members. **Founded** on high hopes and sometimes impractical ideas, few of the utopian communities lasted more than a few years.

The Second Great Awakening In the early 1800s, a wave of religious fervor—known as the Second Great Awakening—stirred the nation. The movement began with frontier camp meetings called **revivals.** People came from miles around to hear eloquent preachers such as Charles Finney. The experience often made men and women eager to reform both their own lives and the world. The Second Great Awakening increased church membership and inspired many to do missionary work and take part in reform movements.

What Was the Temperance Movement? Religious leaders led a war against alcohol. Alcohol abuse was common in the early 1800s, especially in the West and among urban workers. Reformers blamed alcohol for poverty, the breakup of families, and crime. They called for **temperance** (TEHM•puh•ruhns), drinking little or no alcohol.

Temperance crusaders used lectures, pamphlets, and revival-style rallies to warn people of the dangers of liquor. The temperance movement gained a major victory in 1851, when Maine passed a law banning the manufacture and sale of alcoholic beverages. Other states passed similar laws, but most were repealed within several years.

Reading Check **Analyze** What were the effects of the Second Great Awakening?

"Repentance is a change of willing, of feeling, and of life, in respect to God."
—*Charles Finney*

TEACH

C Critical Thinking

Making Inferences The term *utopia* comes from Greek word parts that mean "nowhere." **Ask:** Why are these perfect communities called "nowhere"? *(because perfect societies do not exist)* OL

R1 Reading Strategy

Scaffolding—Academic Vocabulary The word *cooperate* was introduced in Chapter 4, Section 1. Ask a student to define the word. OL

R2 Reading Strategy

Understanding Vocabulary *Revival* comes from Latin words meaning "again" and "to live." Have students explain how this meaning links to the purpose of revival meetings. *(Students may say that the meetings aimed at giving people new life through religion.)* OL CA 8RW1.2

S Skill Practice

Historical and Social Sciences Analysis Skill Have students research the result of the Eighteenth Amendment, which enacted Prohibition. Have them compare the results then to the results when temperance laws were passed in the 1800s. AL CA HR1. CA HI3.

Reading Check

Answer: Church membership increased; people were inspired to become involved in missionary work and social reform movements.

Resources for page 403

Biography Activity 8K

More Skill Practice

Analyzing Primary Sources Have students read the quotation from Charles Finney. **Ask:** What does *repentance* mean? *(to feel sorry for having committed sins)* What does Finney mean by saying that repentance is a change "of living, with respect to God"? *(People who feel repentance need to change the way they act and follow God's rules in the future.)* AL CA 8LS1.2

Biography

TEACH

C Critical Thinking

Identifying Central Issues
Ask: Why are these two men, who lived nearly a century apart, discussed together? *(Thoreau first described the idea of civil disobedience to unjust laws, a technique that Dr. King used.)* OL CA HI1.

R Reading Strategy

Connecting Remind students of what they read about the works of John Locke in Chapters 1 and 3. **Ask:** How are Thoreau's ideas similar to Locke's? How are they different? *(Locke said that all the people had the right to form a new government if the current one took away their rights; Thoreau gives the power of protesting unjust laws to each individual.)* OL

W Writing Support

Research Reports Writing
Have students look up the text of Dr. King's "I have a dream" speech from the 1963 march on Washington. Ask them to write a report analyzing the language of the speech to explain why it became so important. AL
CA 8LS1.1

Answers and Additional Support

Biography

US8.6.7 Identify the common themes in American art as well as transcendentalism and individualism (e.g., writings about and by Ralph Waldo Emerson, Henry David Thoreau, Herman Melville, Louisa May Alcott, Nathaniel Hawthorne, Henry Wadsworth Longfellow).

HENRY DAVID THOREAU
1817–1862

MARTIN LUTHER KING, JR.
1929–1968

C

▲ Henry David Thoreau

R Henry David Thoreau believed strongly in personal freedom. He thought that if a government or society interfered with a person's life, that person had the right to protest. When Thoreau saw something in society that he thought was unjust, he spoke out.

In his 1849 essay "Civil Disobedience," Thoreau supported the peaceful protest of unfair laws. "Unjust laws exist," he wrote, "shall we be content to obey them, or shall we endeavor to amend them . . . ?"

Many of Thoreau's ideas had a far-reaching impact. In India during the mid-twentieth century, the leader Mohandas Gandhi used Thoreau's ideas of civil disobedience through nonviolence to win eventual freedom for his nation. The nonviolent protests of Dr. Martin Luther King, Jr., in the civil rights movement of the 1950s and 1960s were also based, in part, on ideas expressed by Thoreau and Gandhi.

Dr. King grew up in Atlanta, Georgia. Both his father and his mother's father were Baptist ministers. When King became a minister, he used his position to fight racial inequality.

In the 1950s, Dr. Martin Luther King, Jr., became one of the main leaders of the civil rights movement. A Baptist minister and stirring speaker, King believed in nonviolent resistance—the peaceful protest of unfair laws. He told people to disobey unjust laws, but asked them to love their oppressors and never fight with them even if provoked. King organized marches, boycotts, and demonstrations that opened many people's eyes to the need for change.

King is probably most famous for the march he led on Washington to support a civil rights bill. On August 28, 1963, Dr. King delivered a powerful speech outlining his dream of freedom and equality. W

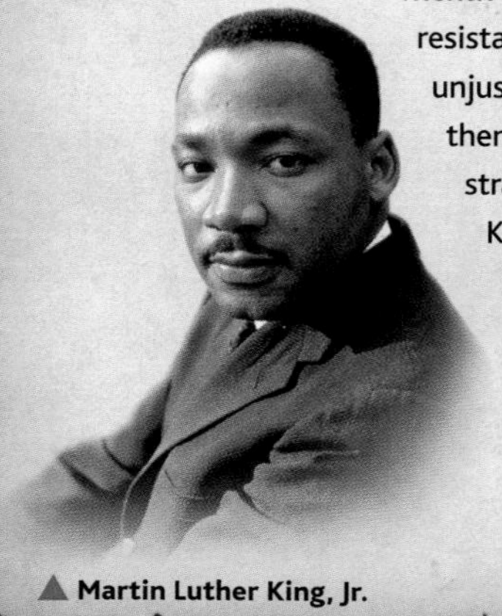
▲ Martin Luther King, Jr.

Then and Now

Give examples of how civil disobedience could be used today to help remedy society's ills.

404

Then and Now

Answers: Students might point to citizen action on national issues such as economic and environmental issues or local issues that they know of.

More Skill Practice

Historical and Social Sciences Analysis Skill Have students research the career of Dr. Martin Luther King, Jr., and write a brief biography outlining his life and achievements. OL CA 8WA2.1

US8.6.5 Trace the development of the American education system from its earliest roots, including the roles of religious and private schools and Horace Mann's campaign for free public education and its assimilating role in American culture.

R

Reforming Education

Main Idea **Reformers wanted to make education accessible to all citizens.**

Reading Connection Do you know of any students with visual or hearing impairments who attend your school? Most likely your school has resources to help these students learn. Read on to find out how reformers opened education to those it had previously been unable to reach.

In the early 1800s, only New England provided free elementary education. In other areas, parents had to pay fees or send their children to schools for the poor—a choice some parents refused out of pride. Some communities had no schools at all.

In the early 1800s, many reformers began to push for a system of public education—government-funded schools that were open to all citizens. The leader of educational reform was **Horace Mann,** a lawyer who became the head of the Massachusetts Board of Education in 1837. Mann lengthened the school year to six months, made improvements in the school curriculum, doubled teachers' salaries, and developed better ways of training teachers.

U

Partly due to Mann's effort, Massachusetts in 1839 founded the nation's first state-supported **normal school,** a school for training high school graduates as teachers. Other states soon adopted Mann's reforms.

C

How Did Education Change? By the 1850s, most states had accepted three basic principles of public education: that schools should be free and supported by taxes, that teachers should be trained, and that children should be required to attend school. These principles did not go into effect immediately though. Schools were poorly funded, and many teachers lacked training. In addition, some people opposed compulsory, or required, education.

Most females received a limited education. Parents often kept their daughters from school because of the belief that a woman's role was to become a wife and mother and that this role did not require an education. When girls did go to school, they often studied music or needlework rather than science, mathematics, and history, which were considered "men's" subjects.

Higher Education Dozens of new colleges were created during the age of reform. Most admitted only men. Religious groups founded many colleges between 1820 and 1850, including Trinity and Wesleyan in Connecticut.

Slowly, higher education became available to groups that were previously denied the opportunity. Oberlin College of Ohio, founded in 1833, admitted both women and African Americans. In 1837 a teacher named Mary Lyon in Massachusetts opened Mount Holyoke, the nation's first permanent women's college. The first college for African Americans, Ashmun Institute, opened in Pennsylvania in 1854.

People With Special Needs Some reformers **focused** on teaching people with disabilities. **Thomas Gallaudet** (GA • luh • DEHT), who developed a method to educate people who were hearing impaired, opened the Hartford School for the Deaf in Connecticut in 1817.

At about the same time, **Dr. Samuel Gridley Howe** advanced the cause of those who were visually impaired. He developed books with large raised letters that people with sight impairments could "read" with their fingers. Howe headed the Perkins Institute, a school for the blind, in Boston.

When schoolteacher **Dorothea Dix** began visiting prisons in 1841, she found that the prisoners were often living in inhumane conditions—chained to the walls with little or no clothing, often in unheated cells. To her further horror, she learned that some of the inmates were guilty of no crime—they were mentally ill persons. Dix made it her life's work to educate the public about the poor conditions for both the mentally ill and for prisoners.

Reading Check **Identify** How did Dr. Samuel Howe help the visually impaired?

R Reading Strategy

Taking Notes Encourage students to take notes of the reforms discussed in this subsection by creating a chart with the headings *Public Schools*, *Higher Education*, and *Education for People with Special Needs*. Students should add details on the advances made in each area. BL

U Universal Access

English Learners Remind students that in this term, *normal* does not have its usual meaning of things that are typical or usual. EL

C Critical Thinking

Making Inferences **Ask:** Why do you think people of the early 1800s opposed making children attend school? *(Students may say that many people did not believe children needed an education since most would be farmers.)* How do you think Horace Mann responded to those people? *(Mann would argue that children needed an education to be good citizens.)* OL

Reading Check

Answer: He developed books with raised letters that people with sight impairments could "read" with their fingers.

Resources for page 405

Biography Activity 8A

More Skill Practice

Historical and Social Sciences Analysis Skill Have students research the founding of one of the schools mentioned on this page—the Hartford School for the Deaf, Mount Holyoke, Oberlin, the Perkins Institute, Trinity, or Wesleyan—or others that were founded in the period, such as Amherst and Holy Cross. Have them write three questions they want to see answered by their research and then use reliable library or Internet sources to find the answers. OL

CA HR1. CA 8WS1.4

R1 Reading Strategy

Using Word Parts Help students master the term by pulling out the root *transcend*, which means "to go beyond human limits." Explain that these writers hoped to break past the limits of human knowledge. **OL**

C Critical Thinking

Analyzing Information
Ask: What does Emerson mean by the "inner voice of conscience"? *(he means people should base their actions on morality)* How does that relate to Thoreau's call for "civil disobedience"? *(Thoreau wants people to use their conscience in deciding what laws to follow.)* **OL**

R2 Reading Strategy

Visualizing Encourage students to use the photograph and the text description to visualize what one-room schools were like. Invite them to offer their ideas. **OL**

Resources for page 406

- Biography Activity 8E
- Biography Activity 8F

Answers and Additional Support

US8.6.7 Identify common themes in American art as well as transcendentalism and individualism (e.g., writings about and by Ralph Waldo Emerson, Henry David Thoreau, Herman Melville, Louisa May Alcott, Nathaniel Hawthorne, Henry Wadsworth Longfellow).

Cultural Trends

Main Idea **A new wave of literature that was distinctly American swept the United States.**

Reading Connection Have you read Henry David Thoreau, Ralph Waldo Emerson, or Emily Dickinson for any of your English classes? Read on to find out how these writers changed literature in America in the 1800s.

The changes in American society influenced art and literature. Earlier generations of American painters and writers looked to Europe for their inspiration and models. Beginning in the 1820s, American writers and artists developed their own style and explored uniquely American themes.

Who Were the Transcendentalists? The American spirit of reform influenced **transcendentalists** (TRAN • sehn • DEHN • tuhl • ihsts). Transcendentalists stressed the relationship between humans and nature, as well as the importance of the individual conscience. Writers such as **Margaret Fuller,** Ralph Waldo Emerson, and Henry David Thoreau were leading transcendentalists. Through her writings, Fuller supported rights for women. In his poems and essays, Emerson urged people to listen to the inner voice of conscience and to break the bonds of prejudice.

Thoreau put his beliefs into practice through civil disobedience—refusing to obey laws he thought were unjust. In 1846 Thoreau went to jail rather than pay a tax to support the Mexican War.

The Way It Was

The Country School by Winslow Homer

One-Room Schoolhouse

Until education became widespread, many children learned to read and write in one-room schoolhouses. Students of all ages learned mostly by rote—one group recited while the rest studied their lessons. Two popular schoolbooks of the 1800s were the *McGuffey Readers* and the *Columbian Orator.* Both of these schoolbooks provided moral lessons as well as lessons in reading and grammar. Excerpts in these readers came from well-known speeches and works of literature, as well as passages from the Bible and other religious texts.

Hornbook, left
Lunch pail, center,
Page from *McGuffey's Readers*, right

406

The Way It Was

School attendance often depended on the needs of the farm where most students lived.
Ask: Why would attendance go down during planting and harvesting seasons? *(Many students would be needed to help on the family farm.)* **BL**

Answers:

1. Modern books do not provide moral lessons.
2. Students might mention technological tools, such as computers and CD-ROMs, or the use of standardized tests.

American Writers Emerge The transcendentalists were not the only important writers of this time. Many poets created impressive works about American subjects during this period. Henry Wadsworth Longfellow wrote narrative, or story, poems, such as the "Song of Hiawatha." John Greenleaf Whittier in "Snow-Bound" described winter on a New England farm. Edgar Allan Poe, a poet and short-story writer, told tales involving the terrors that lurk in the world of imagination and dreams.

Perhaps the most important poet of the era was Walt Whitman, who **published** a volume of poetry in 1855 called *Leaves of Grass*. Whitman loved nature, the common people, and American democracy, and his famous work reflects these passions. The best-remembered woman poet of the era was **Emily Dickinson,** who wrote simple, personal, deeply emotional poetry.

In a poem called "Hope," Dickinson compares hope with a bird:

> **"'Hope' is the thing with feathers—**
> **That perches in the soul—**
> **And sings the tune without the words—**
> **And never stops–at all—"**
>
> —Emily Dickinson, "Hope"

U

Women writers of the period were generally not taken seriously, yet they were the authors of the most popular fiction. Harriet Beecher Stowe wrote the most successful best-seller of the mid-1800s, *Uncle Tom's Cabin*. Stowe's novel explores the injustice of slavery—an issue that took on new urgency during the age of reform.

Reading Check **Describe** What was one of the subjects that Margaret Fuller wrote about?

History Online
Study Central Need help understanding American literature? Visit ca.hss.glencoe.com and click on Study Central.

Section 4 Review

Reading Summary

Review the Main Ideas

- Reformers attempted to make the United States a better place for its citizens.
- Reforms in secondary and higher education allowed more Americans to become educated.
- American literature gained a new voice through the writings of Thoreau, Emerson, Dickinson, and others.

What Did You Learn?

1. What did Horace Mann accomplish?
2. How did Thoreau act on his beliefs? What impact might such acts have had on the government?

Critical Thinking

3. **Determining Cause and Effect** Re-create the diagram below and describe two ways the religious movement influenced reform. CA HI2.

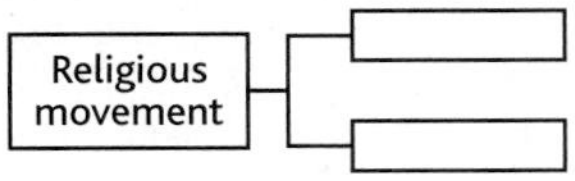

4. **The Big Ideas** Who was Horace Mann, and what was his contribution to public education? How were women and African Americans able to have access to education? Summarize your conclusions in a short essay. CA HI1.
5. **Biography** Using your textbook, the library, and the Internet, learn more about Thomas Gallaudet, Dorothea Dix, or Samuel Gridley Howe. Write a short biography of the person you chose. Include key events in his or her life and the person's impact on the world. CA 8WA2.1

SECTION 4 REVIEW ANSWERS

Review questions reinforce content standards US8.6.

1. Schools should be free and supported by taxes; teachers should be trained; and children should be required to attend school.
2. He went to jail rather than pay a tax to support a war he opposed. Answers will vary.
3. People wanted to reform their own lives; and to improve society.
4. **The Big Ideas** head of Massachusetts Board of Education; enacted several reforms of education that were adopted in other states. Some educators opened schools for them.
5. Students' biographies should include key events and explain the subject's impact.

U Universal Access

Verbal/Linguistic Ask: What does Dickinson mean in the last line of the poem, when she says that the bird "never stops at all"? *(Students may say that it means people always have hope.)* OL

ASSESS

Resources for page 407

Use these resources to assess student mastery of section content.

- American Literature Reading 8
- Biography Activity 8G
- Biography Activity 8H
- Section Quiz 8–4
- Interactive Tutor Self-Assessment CD-ROM

Reading Check
Answer: rights for women

History Online
Study Central provides summaries, interactive games, and online graphic organizers to help students review section content.

CLOSE

Organizing Information Have students create graphic organizers with three columns labeled *Reform Movement*, *Goal*, and *Steps Taken*. Then have them fill in the details on the reform movements of this period. OL

FOCUS

BELLRINGER
SKILLBUILDER ACTIVITY

Project **Daily Focus Skills Transparency 8–5** and have students answer the question.

Guide to Reading

Preteaching Vocabulary: Have students look up the definition of each content vocabulary term in their Glossary in the back of the textbook and then use each term in a sentence.

Answers to Graphic: Mott: gave lectures on reform topics, helped organize first meeting for women's rights; Stanton: won demand for women's suffrage at Seneca Falls meeting; Anthony: worked for women's rights and temperance

Unpacking the Standards

After reading the section, students will be able to:

- describe what happened at the Seneca Falls Convention.
- explain how the women's rights movement changed.
- outline how American women progressed in the 1800s.

Section 5

The Women's Movement

History Social Science Standards

US8.6 Students analyze the divergent paths of the American people from 1800 to the mid-1800s and the challenges they faced, with emphasis on the Northeast.

Guide to Reading

Looking Back, Looking Ahead

In Section 4, you learned about the reform movement that swept America in the 1800s. In Section 5, you will learn about how that movement influenced women to lobby for increased rights.

Focusing on the Main Ideas

- Many women believed they should have the same opportunities as men, and they organized to gain these rights. *(page 409)*
- Women made progress in gaining equality in education, marriage laws, and the professional sector. *(page 411)*

Meeting People

Lucretia Mott
Elizabeth Cady Stanton
Susan B. Anthony
Mary Lyon
Elizabeth Blackwell

Content Vocabulary

suffrage (SUH • frihj)
coeducation

Academic Vocabulary

ministry (MIH • nuh • stree)
goal

Reading Strategy

Taking Notes As you read the section, use a chart like the one below to identify the contributions these individuals made to women's rights.

	Contributions
Lucretia Mott	
Elizabeth Cady Stanton	
Susan B. Anthony	

NATIONAL GEOGRAPHIC Who & When?

1830 — 1845 — 1860

Mary Lyon

1837 Mary Lyon establishes Mount Holyoke Female Seminary

1848 First women's rights convention held in Seneca Falls, New York

Lucretia Mott

1857 Elizabeth Blackwell founds New York Infirmary for Women and Children

SECTION RESOURCES

Print Material
- Reproducible Lesson Plan 8–5*
- Daily Lesson and Discussion Notes 8–5
- Guided Reading Activity 8–5
- Reading Essentials and Study Guide 8–5
- Active Reading Note-Taking Guide 8–5
- Section Quiz 8–5

Transparencies
- Daily Focus Skills Transparency 8–5
- Section Graphic Organizer Transparency 8–5
- California Standards Practice Transparencies

Technology
- Interactive Tutor Self-Assessment CD-ROM
- Exam*View*® Pro Testmaker CD-ROM
- Presentation Plus! CD-ROM

*Available on TeacherWorks™

US8.6.6 Examine the women's suffrage movement (e.g., biographies, writings, and speeches of Elizabeth Cady Stanton, Margaret Fuller, Lucretia Mott, Susan B. Anthony).

Women and Reform

Main Idea **Many women believed they should have the same opportunities as men, and they organized to gain these rights.**

Reading Connection Can you imagine a time when women were not allowed to vote and had limited access to education and jobs? Read on to see how women worked to change their status in America.

An American Story

Women who fought to end slavery began to recognize their own bondage. On April 19, 1850, about 400 women met at a Quaker meeting-house in the small town of Salem, Ohio. They came together "to assert their rights as independent human beings." One speaker stated: "[W]e should demand our recognition as equal members of the human family."

The Seneca Falls Convention Many women abolitionists also worked for women's rights. Like many of the women reformers, **Lucretia Mott** was a Quaker. Quaker women enjoyed a certain amount of equality in their own communities. Mott gave lectures in Philadelphia calling for temperance, peace, workers' rights, and abolition. Mott also helped fugitive slaves and organized the Philadelphia Female Anti-Slavery Society. At the world antislavery convention in London, Mott met **Elizabeth Cady Stanton.** There the two female abolitionists joined forces to work for women's rights.

In July 1848, Elizabeth Cady Stanton, Lucretia Mott, and a few other women organized the first women's rights convention in Seneca Falls, New York. About 200 women and 40 men attended.

The convention issued a Declaration of Sentiments and Resolutions modeled on the Declaration of Independence. The women's document declared: "We hold these truths to be self-evident: that all men and women are created equal."

The women's declaration called for an end to all laws that discriminated against women. It demanded that women be allowed to enter the all-male world of trades, professions, and businesses. The most controversial issue at the Seneca Falls Convention concerned **suffrage** (SUH • frihj), or the right to vote.

Elizabeth Stanton insisted that the declaration include a demand for woman suffrage, but delegates thought the idea of women voting was too radical. After much debate, the demand for woman suffrage in the United States was included. *(See page 854 of the Appendix for excerpts of the Seneca Falls Declaration.)*

HISTORY MAKERS

Oberlin and Higher Education

Most women had less access to education than men, a situation that survived into the mid-1800s. Oberlin College in Ohio became the first college in America to accept women students. It permitted four women to enroll in 1837. Few other colleges shared Oberlin's views, however. Colleges that admitted women remained extraordinarily rare until long after the Civil War. Oberlin College was also one of the first institutions of higher education to admit African Americans.

Women's rights activist Lucy Stone graduated from Oberlin in 1847 ▶

TEACH

U Universal Access

English Learners Give students the following synonyms for *assert: declare*, *state*, and *claim*. Then have them rewrite the quotation in their own words. *(Students may say that the people in the meeting were "claiming their equal rights as people.")* EL

W Writing Support

Research Reports Writing Have students conduct research to find information about the Society of Friends, or Quakers, in the United States in the early 1800s. Have them find out what core beliefs of the Quakers led many to take part in reform movements. Students should summarize their findings in a written report. OL CA 8WA2.3

C Critical Thinking

Making Inferences **Ask:** Why did the women at the Seneca Falls Convention make their declaration echo the words of the Declaration of Independence? *(Students may say that they hoped to win more support by using a document that was popular, or that those words meant a lot to the women.)* OL CA HI3.

R Reading Strategy

Understanding Vocabulary Have students define the term *suffrage* in their own words. OL CA 8RW1.3

HISTORY MAKERS

Lucy Stone began working as a teacher at age sixteen and used her earnings to pay for her own education. She was 25 before being accepted at Oberlin. After graduation, she spoke often—and forcefully—against slavery and for women's rights.

Resources for page 409

- American Art and Architecture Transparencies
- Biography Activity 8B
- Biography Activity 8C
- Biography Activity 8D

R1 Reading Strategy

Connecting Tell students that in 1872, Susan B. Anthony was arrested for trying to vote. Tried and convicted, she was ordered to pay a fine, but she refused to pay it. **Ask:** What act studied in Section 4 does Anthony's behavior remind you of? *(Thoreau's civil disobedience)* OL

R2 Reading Strategy

Using Word Parts **Ask:** What other words can you think of that begin with *co-*? *(cooperation, co-captain)* OL

U Universal Access

Intrapersonal Women who worked for their rights suffered ridicule, taunting, and other abuse. Have students write a brief essay explaining what led the women to continue to push for reform despite these attacks. OL

Reading Check

Answer: the right to vote

Answers and Additional Support

The Women's Rights Movement The Seneca Falls Convention paved the way for the growth of the women's rights movement. During the 1800s, women held several national conventions. Many reformers—male and female—joined the movement.

R1 **Susan B. Anthony,** the daughter of a Quaker abolitionist in rural New York, worked for women's rights and temperance. She called for equal pay for women, college training for girls, and R2 **coeducation**—the teaching of boys and girls together.

Susan B. Anthony met Elizabeth Cady Stanton at a temperance meeting in 1851. They became lifelong friends and partners in the struggle for women's rights. For the rest of the century, Anthony and Stanton led the women's movement. They worked with other women to win the right to vote, which was granted by several states. It was not until 1920, however, that woman suffrage became a reality everywhere in the United States. U

Reading Check **Explain** What is suffrage?

Why It Matters

Photo Gallery

Raising the Status of Women

The Seneca Falls Convention

Throughout the nation's history, women had fought side by side with the men to build a new nation and to ensure freedom. Even though the Declaration of Independence promised equality for all, the promise rang hollow for women.

Female reformers began a campaign for their own rights. In 1848 Lucretia Mott and Elizabeth Cady Stanton organized the Seneca Falls Convention. One of the resolutions demanded suffrage, or the right to vote, for women. This marked the beginning of a long, hard road to gain equal rights.

Lucretia Mott (below) and Susan B. Anthony were leaders in the effort to allow women a greater role in American society.

"We hold these truths to be self-evident: that all men and women are created equal."
—***Declaration of the Seneca Falls Convention, 1848***

Gaining the Right to Vote, 1848–1920

The Seneca Falls Convention led to the growth of the woman suffrage movement.

- **1848** Seneca Falls Convention
- **1850** First national women's rights convention held in Worcester, Massachusetts
- **1866** Susan B. Anthony forms Equal Rights Association
- **1869** Women granted voting rights in Wyoming Territory
- **1878** Woman suffrage amendment first introduced in U.S. Congress
- **1884** Belva Lockwood runs for president

Why It Matters

All the resolutions passed by the Seneca Falls Convention were approved unanimously except one—the one demanding suffrage. Lucretia Mott told Elizabeth Cady Stanton that that demand would make the convention "look ridiculous." But Stanton insisted on keeping it.

More Skill Practice

Reading a Time Line **Ask:** What happened in Worcester, Massachusetts, in 1850? *(the first national meeting for women's rights)* In what way did that meeting probably differ from the Seneca Falls Convention? *(Students may say it had people from many different states, since it is called a "national" meeting.)* OL

US8.6.5 Trace the development of the American education system from its earliest roots, including the roles of religious and private schools and Horace Mann's campaign for free public education and its assimilating role in American culture. **US8.6.6** Examine the women's suffrage movement (e.g., biographies, writings, and speeches of Elizabeth Cady Stanton, Margaret Fuller, Lucretia Mott, Susan B. Anthony).

Progress by American Women

Main Idea **Women made progress in gaining equality in education, marriage laws, and the professional sector.**

Reading Connection Laws are often put in place to protect individuals and society—for example, laws against speeding or stealing. How would you feel about laws that barred women from the same privileges as men? Is that fair or discriminatory? Read on to find out how women worked for change.

In the early 1800s, the Industrial Revolution began to change the economic roles of men and women. In the 1700s, most economic activity took place in or near the home because a great many Americans lived and worked in a rural farm setting. Although husbands and wives had separate chores, their main effort was maintaining the farm. By the mid-1800s, these circumstances had started to change, especially in the northeastern states.

Maria Mitchell gained world renown when she discovered a comet in 1847. She became a professor of astronomy and the first woman elected to the American Academy of Arts and Sciences.

Mary Ann Shadd Cary was the first African American woman in the nation to earn a law degree.

Elizabeth Blackwell was the first woman to receive a medical degree in the United States.

Helen Keller overcame the challenges of an illness that left her deaf, blind, and mute to help others with similar disabilities.

Susette La Flesche was a member of the Omaha tribe and campaigned for Native American rights.

1893 → Colorado adopts woman suffrage

1896 → Utah joins the Union, granting women full suffrage

1910–1918 → States including Washington, Kansas, and Michigan adopt woman suffrage

1919 → House and Senate pass the federal woman suffrage amendment

1920 → Tennessee ratifies the Nineteenth Amendment, called the Susan B. Anthony Amendment. It becomes law on August 26, 1920.

U Universal Access

Below Grade Level Have students outline the subsection to help them see how women gained in many areas. BL

W Writing Support

Narrative Writing Have students research and report on the lives of any of the women discussed in this subsection or in the **Why It Matters** feature. Encourage them to focus on the difficulties these women encountered and how they worked to overcome them. Have students present their findings orally. OL CA 8WA2.1 CA 8SA2.1

R Reading Strategy

Scaffolding—Academic Vocabulary The word *maintain* was introduced in Chapter 5, Section 2. Ask students to write a sentence using the word. BL

Did You Know?

Maria Mitchell was only 19 when she discovered her comet; the discovery won her a prize. She was one of only two female professors when Vassar College—a college for women—was launched in 1865. She remained at Vassar for most of the rest of her life, though she was active in both science and efforts to improve the education of women. One of her students at Vassar was Harriot Stanton, daughter of Elizabeth Cady Stanton.

S Skill Practice

Historical and Social Sciences Analysis Skill

Ask: What does Grimké mean by referring to jobs "peculiar to women"? *(jobs that only women do)* What is her point about these jobs? *(Women who do this work receive lower wages than men who do work that is comparable.)* OL CA HR4.

R Reading Strategy

Questioning Develop a set of questions regarding the women who made accomplishments in this period. Organize the class into teams and ask them the questions, taking turns with the different teams. Give a point when a team gives a correct answers. If any team cannot answer a question, give the other teams the opportunity to do so. OL

Resources for page 412

- Universal Access Activity 8
- Primary Source Reading 8

Primary Sources

On Equality for Women

Sarah and Angeline Grimké were daughters of a wealthy South Carolina judge and plantation owner. The sisters fought against the institution of slavery. They also spoke out for women's rights. In this passage, Sarah Grimké writes about the differences in pay for men and women.

"There is another way in which the general opinion, that women are inferior to men, is manifested [shown], that bears with tremendous effect on the laboring class, and indeed on almost all who are [obliged] to earn a subsistence [living], whether it be by mental or physical exertion. I allude [refer] to the [unequal] value set on the time and labor of men and of women. A man who is engaged in teaching, can always, I believe, command a higher price . . . than a woman—even when he teaches the same branches [subjects], and is not in any respect superior to the woman. . . . In tailoring, a man [earns] twice or three times as much for making a waistcoat or pantaloons as a woman, although the work done by each may be equally good. In those employments [jobs] which are peculiar to women, their time is estimated at only half the value of that of men. A woman who goes out to wash, works as hard in proportion as a wood sawyer, or a coal heaver, but she is not generally able to make more than half as much by a day's work."

—*Letters on the Equality of the Sexes*

Sarah Grimké ▶

DBQ Document-Based Question

What point is Sarah Grimké making about women and men workers in the same occupation?

The development of factories separated the home from the workplace. Men now often left home to go to work, while women tended the house and children.

As the nature of work changed, many Americans began to divide life into two areas of activities—the home and the workplace. Many believed the home to be the proper area for women, partly because of popular ideas about the family. Some also believed that women belonged in the home because the outside world was seen as dangerous and corrupt.

The Great Awakening greatly influenced the American family. For many parents, raising children was a serious responsibility because it prepared young people for a disciplined Christian life. Women often were viewed as kinder and more moral than men, and they were expected to be models of goodness for their children and husbands.

The idea grew that women should be homemakers and should take the main responsibility for raising the sons and daughters. Magazine articles and novels aimed at women supported the value of their role at home.

Opportunities for Education Pioneers in women's education began to call for more opportunity. Early pioneers such as Catherine Beecher and Emma Hart Willard believed that women should be educated for their traditional roles in life. They also thought that women could be capable teachers. Beecher, the daughter of a minister and reformer, wrote a book called *A Treatise on Domestic Economy*. It gave instructions on children, cooking, and health matters. The Milwaukee College for Women set up courses based on Beecher's ideas "to train women to be healthful, intelligent, and successful wives, mothers, and housekeepers."

Answers and Additional Support

Primary Sources

Answer: that women receive less pay than men for the same work

After her marriage, Emma Willard educated herself in subjects considered suitable only for boys, such as science and mathematics. In 1821 Willard established the Troy Female Seminary in New York. The school taught mathematics, history, geography, and physics, as well as the usual homemaking subjects.

Mary Lyon established Mount Holyoke Female Seminary in Massachusetts in 1837. It was the first institution of higher education for women only. Lyon modeled its curriculum on that of nearby Amherst College.

Marriage and Family Laws During the 1800s, women made some gains in the area of marriage and property laws. New York, Pennsylvania, Indiana, Wisconsin, Mississippi, and the new state of California recognized the right of women to own property after their marriage.

Some states passed laws permitting women to share the guardianship of their children jointly with their husbands. Indiana was the first of several states that allowed women to seek divorce if their husbands were chronic abusers of alcohol.

Breaking Barriers In the 1800s, women had few career choices. They could become elementary school teachers—although school boards often paid lower salaries to women than to men. Breaking into fields such as medicine and the **ministry** was more difficult. Some determined women, however, succeeded in entering these all-male professions.

Hoping to study medicine, **Elizabeth Blackwell** was turned down by more than 20 schools. Finally accepted by Geneva College in New York, Blackwell graduated at the head of her class. She went on to win acceptance and fame as a doctor.

C Despite the accomplishments of notable women, gains in education, and changes in state laws, women in the 1800s remained limited by social customs and expectations. The early feminists—like the abolitionists, temperance workers, and other activists of the age of reform—had just begun the long struggle to achieve their **goals.**

Reading Check **Identify** Who established the Troy Female Seminary?

History Online
Study Central Need help understanding the women's movement? Visit ca.hss.glencoe.com and click on Study Central.

Section 5 Review

Reading Summary

Review the Main Ideas

- The abolitionist movement helped women see the discrimination they encountered in their own lives, and they organized to end this discrimination.
- Women created their own schools and colleges, increased their legal standing in their families, and gained more professional choices.

What Did You Learn?

1. How did the fight to end slavery help spark the women's movement?
2. Discuss three goals of the women's rights movement.

Critical Thinking

3. **Organizing Information** Re-create the diagram below and list the areas where women gained rights.

4. **The Big Ideas** What qualities do you think women such as Susan B. Anthony, Elizabeth Cady Stanton, and Elizabeth Blackwell shared? CA HR3.
5. **Sequencing Information** Study the information on the feature on the Seneca Falls Convention on pages 410–411. When did Wyoming women gain the right to vote? What "first" did Elizabeth Blackwell accomplish? CA CS2.

SECTION 5 REVIEW ANSWERS

Review questions reinforce content standard US8.6.

1. Many women in the women's movement had also worked to end slavery.
2. any three: an end to laws that discriminate; chance to work in the same careers as men; suffrage; equal pay; college training; coeducation
3. opening of women's colleges; recognition of property rights after marriage; laws allowing shared guardianship of children; laws allowing divorce; breaking into some new careers
4. **The Big Ideas** Answers may include perseverance, dedication, strong will.
5. 1869; first woman to receive a medical degree

C Critical Thinking

Drawing Conclusions Ask: What does the textbook mean by the statement in the first sentence of the last paragraph? *(Some women had made gains, and some laws giving women rights had been passed, but women as a whole still did not enjoy equal rights with men.)* OL

ASSESS

Resources for page 413

Use these resources to assess student mastery of section content.

- Biography Activity 8I
- Biography Activity 8J
- Section Quiz 8–5
- Interactive Tutor Self-Assessment CD-ROM

Reading Check

Answer: Emma Willard

History Online

Study Central provides summaries, interactive games, and online graphic organizers to help students review section content.

CLOSE

Sequencing Information Have students make a time line of key dates in women's struggle for equal rights in the 1800s. OL

FOCUS

History–Social Science Standards

The following standard is covered on pages 414–415:
US8.6 Students analyze the divergent paths of the American people from 1800 to the mid-1800s and the challenges they faced, with emphasis on the Northeast.

TEACH

S Skill Practice

Historical and Social Sciences Analysis Skill
Explain that revivals like the one Finley described would include many hundreds of people. **Ask:** Would a meeting that large today include seven ministers speaking at the same time? Why might that have been necessary in the 1830s? *(no; because people did not have microphones and speakers back then, so one preacher might not necessarily be able to be heard by an entire crowd of that size)* OL CA HR3.

Answers and Additional Support

Analyzing Primary Sources

US8.6 Students analyze the divergent paths of the American people from 1800 to the mid-1800s and the challenges they faced, with emphasis on the Northeast.

Life in the North

In the early 1800s, the northeast United States underwent rapid change. The Industrial Revolution led to new jobs, and new forms of transportation, such as canals and railroads, developed. A Second Great Awakening led to a renewed interest in religion and reform.

Read the passages on pages 414 and 415 and answer the questions that follow.

This scene shows Lockport on the Erie Canal near Buffalo, New York.

Reader's Dictionary

exempted (ihg • ZEHMPT • ihd): excused from something that others must do

pervading (puhr • VAYD • ihng): spreading throughout all parts

melodious (muh • LOH • dee • uhs): having a pleasant sound

tumultuously (tu • MUHL • chuh • wuhs • lee): violently and in confusion

quivered: shook, shivered, trembled

occupation (AH • kyuh • PAY • shuhn): job

station: position in society

packet: passenger boat that usually carries mail and cargo

salons (suh • LAHNZ): sitting rooms

ventilators (VEHN • tuhl • AY • tuhrz): air vents

Religious Camp Meeting

By the 1830s, the Second Great Awakening was in full swing. One revivalist, James Finley, described a revival meeting:

S The noise was like the roar of Niagara [Falls]. . . . I counted seven ministers, all preaching at one time, some on stumps, others on wagons . . . no sex nor color, class nor description, were **exempted** from the **pervading** influence of the spirit; even from the age of 8 months to 60 years . . . some of the people were singing, others praying, some crying for mercy . . . some struck with terror . . . others surrounding them with **melodious** song. A peculiar sensation came over me. My heart beat **tumultuously,** my knees trembled, my lips **quivered,** and I felt as though I must fall to the ground.

—James Finley

Camp meetings could attract thousands of people for days of prayer, song, and expressions of faith.

EXTENDING THE CONTENT

Alexis de Tocqueville Dickens was not the only European who traveled to the United States in the early 1800s to observe and write about American society. The French writer Alexis de Tocqueville did so as well. De Tocqueville introduced his masterwork, *Democracy in America*, with this observation: "Amongst the novel objects that attracted my attention during my stay in the Unites States, nothing struck me more forcibly than the general equality of condition among the people. . . . This equality of condition is the fundamental fact from which all others seem to be derived."

American Notes

British writer Charles Dickens traveled to America in 1842. After returning to England, he published American Notes, *a book about what he had seen in America. In this excerpt, Dickens describes his visit to a factory in Lowell, Massachusetts.*

C The rooms in which they worked were as well ordered as themselves. In the windows of some there were green plants, which were trained to shade the glass; in all, there was as much fresh air, cleanliness, and comfort as the nature of the **occupation** would possibly admit of. . . .

They have got up among themselves a periodical called THE LOWELL OFFERING, "a repository of original articles, written exclusively by females actively employed in the mills,"—which is duly printed, published, and sold; and whereof I brought away from Lowell four hundred good solid pages, which I have read from beginning to end. . . .

It is their **station** to work. And they *do* work. They labour in these mills, upon an average, twelve hours a day, which is unquestionably work, and pretty tight work too.

—from *American Notes* by Charles Dickens

Travel on the Erie Canal

This is an 1843 advertisement for traveling on the canal.

S

—from *Canal Days in America: The History and Romance of Old Towpaths and Waterways*

DBQ Document-Based Questions

Religious Camp Meeting

1. Finley says that the camp meeting is like the roar of Niagara. What is he comparing?
2. Who does the preaching affect?

American Notes

3. According to Dickens, what are conditions in the factory like?
4. How long is the workday?

Travel on the Erie Canal

5. According to the poster, how long does it take to travel from Niagara Falls to Albany if people take a packet boat?
6. What new conveniences do these packet boats have?

Read to Write

7. Review the readings looking for three sentences that are complicated or confusing. Work through each sentence to clarify the meaning for yourself, and then restate that meaning on your paper. CA 8RC2.0

C Critical Thinking

Analyzing Primary Sources Ask: What attitude does Dickens have toward the factory? *(seems to present it in a positive way)* What attitude does he take towards the work that the Lowell girls had to do? *(He thinks it was very hard work.)* Do you think he would have supported calls for greater workers' rights? Why or why not? *(Students may say that it is too difficult to determine from this brief excerpt.)* OL CA HR5.

S Skill Practice

Visual Literacy Ask: How appealing does the poster make travel by packet boat appear? OL

ASSESS

Have students answer the Document-Based Questions.

CLOSE

Evaluating Have students explain how each of these primary sources reveals the changes that were taking place in the Northeast. OL

DBQ Document-Based Questions

1. the sound of the crowd at the meeting to the sound of the water rushing over the falls
2. all the people who were there
3. well ordered, clean, and comfortable, with fresh air
4. 12 hours
5. a day and a half; passengers left Niagara Falls in the afternoon and arrived in Albany the next evening.
6. sitting rooms, ventilators, and accomodations for sleeping
7. Students' answers will vary.

Resources for pages 416–417

Use these resources to review, assess, or reteach the chapter.

- Active Reading Note-Taking Guide, Chapter 8
- Chapter 8 Reading Essentials and Study Guide
- Chapter 8 Tests, Forms A and B
- Standards Assessment, Forms A and B
- California Standards Practice Workbook
- Succeeding on the California History-Social Science Standards CD-ROM
- MindJogger Videoquiz
- Interactive Tutor Self-Assessment CD-ROM

Review Content Vocabulary

1. Paragraphs will vary but should reflect information in the chapter.

Review the Main Ideas

2. Poor soil made farming difficult and people ready to move off farms; new factories were built along rushing waters and rivers, which led to growing towns.
3. Inventions such as the spinning jenny, water frame, and power loom and the cotton gin made it possible to process cotton and make and weave large amounts of thread very quickly, which spurred industrial growth.
4. Canals allowed people to live farther from rivers but still ship their crops to market.
5. to provide a way to raise and lower boats at places where canal levels changed

Chapter 8 Assessment

Standard US8.6

Review Content Vocabulary

1. Use the following words in a paragraph about the Industrial Revolution.

capital	free enterprise
technology	factory system

Review the Main Ideas

Section 1 • Economic Growth

2. How did the landscape of New England affect how and where people lived in the late 1700s and early 1800s?
3. How did new technology contribute to the growth of the Industrial Revolution?

Section 2 • A System of Transportation

4. How did canals boost the economy of the Great Lakes region?
5. What was the purpose of canal locks?

Section 3 • The North's People

6. Give three reasons why cities grew in the early 1800s.
7. In what ways were women in the work-force discriminated against?
8. Why did immigration from Germany increase after 1848?

Section 4 • Reforms and Reformers

9. What were the founders of utopias hoping to achieve?
10. What problems in society did reformers in the temperance movement blame on alcohol?
11. What were the basic principles of public education?

Section 5 • The Women's Movement

12. What role did Catherine Beecher play in education for women?
13. What was the significance of the Seneca Falls convention?

Critical Thinking

14. **Compare** Discuss an advantage and a disadvantage of city life in the North. CA HR3.
15. **Explain** How did the Industrial Revolution make the United States more economically independent in the early 1800s? CA HI6.

Geography Skills

Study the map below and answer the following questions. CA CS3.

NATIONAL GEOGRAPHIC **Population Growth, 1850**

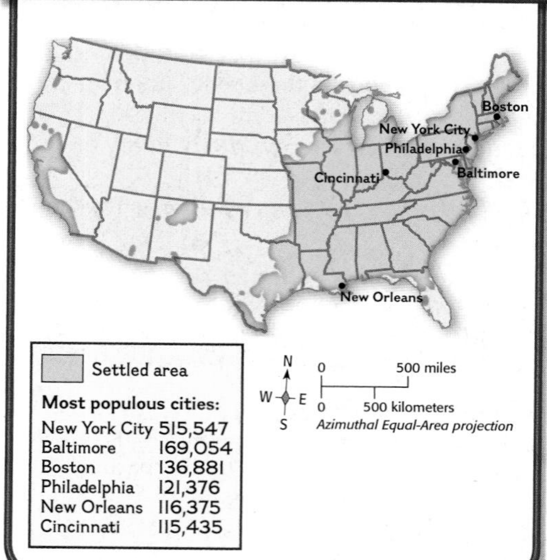

16. **Location** Which city had the largest population in 1850?
17. **Region** Which area of the country was most heavily settled?

6. the growth of factories; the creation of transportation networks such as roads and canals; and the surge in immigration
7. They were paid less than male workers, and when male workers formed unions they blocked women from joining.
8. because of the failure of a democratic revolution in Germany
9. improve society
10. poverty, breakup of families, crime, and insanity
11. schools should be free and supported by taxes, teachers should be trained, and children should be required to attend school
12. Her ideas for educating women became the basis for the Milwaukee College for Women.
13. It issued the first call for equal rights for women, including voting rights.

History Online

Self-Check Quiz Visit ca.hss.glencoe.com to prepare for the Chapter 8 test.

Read to Write

18. **The Big Ideas** **Descriptive Writing** Review Section 2 of the chapter for information about what it was like to live in the Midwest in the early 1800s. Using the information you find, write a postcard to a friend describing your social life. CA 8WA2.1

19. **Using Your FOLDABLES** Use the information you collected in your foldable to create a compare-contrast chart. In your chart, you will assess the roots, goals, and achievements of social reform, educational reform, and the women's rights movement. How are these movements similar? How do they differ? CA HI2.

Using Academic Vocabulary

20. Use two of the following academic vocabulary words to complete the sentence.

focus	expand
manual	goal

As the U.S. economy continued to ___, immigrants provided much of the ___ labor.

Building Citizenship Skills

21. **Explore** Working with two other students, contact a local historical society to learn about your community's history. Prepare a list of questions to ask your historical society. Then interview people in your neighborhood to learn about their roots in the community. Find out when their families first settled there. Write a history of the community and give a copy of it to the historical society. CA CS1.

Reviewing Skills

22. **Review READING SKILL** **Problems and Solutions** This chapter highlighted various problems, or challenges, that groups of people faced. Choose one group and describe their unique challenges and the ways in which people attempted to face those challenges. CA HI2.

23. **Review ANALYSIS SKILL** **Describe** Identify and describe the economic impact of canals on the Northeast. CA HI6.

Standards Practice

Use the graph below to answer the following questions.

School Enrollment, 1850–2000

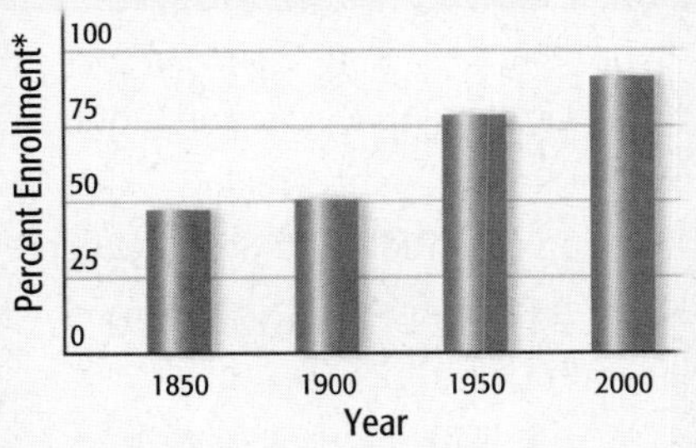

*In percent of persons of elementary and high school age

Source: *Historical Statistics of the United States; Statistical Abstract.*

24 **According to the graph above, the greatest increase in the percentage of school enrollment occurred between**

A 1850 and 1880.
B 1850 and 1900.
C 1900 and 1950.
D 1950 and 2000.

25 **Labor unions were formed for all of the following reasons EXCEPT**

A to improve workers' wages.
B to protect factory owners from being sued.
C to make factories safer.
D to prevent children from working long hours.

CHAPTER 8 Assessment

Critical Thinking

14. Disadvantage (any one): threat of illness, destructive fires; Advantage (any one): variety of jobs and steady wages, cultural opportunities, and growing number of shops

15. Low taxes, few government regulations, and competition encouraged many people to open their own businesses.

Geography Skills

16. New York City

17. entire area east of the Mississippi River was settled, but northeast also had the most large cities

Read to Write

18. **The Big Ideas** Students' postcards should reflect the fact that life in the West was full of work although there were community activities for having fun.

19. Using Your **FOLDABLES** Students might say that all three movements came from similar impulses but that the education reform movement enjoyed the most success in this period.

Using Academic Vocabulary

20. expand; manual

Building Citizenship

21. Students' projects should include a history of the community and information from two interviews.

Reviewing Skills

22. **Review READING SKILL** Answers will vary but should include facts about the difficulties faced by a particular group.

23. **Review ANALYSIS SKILL** All these improvements in travel and the transport of goods helped promote economic growth.

Standards Practice

24. C
25. B

Bonus Question

Ask: Why did large numbers of immigrants come to the United States from Ireland between 1846 and 1860? *(to escape a famine caused by failure of the potato crop)* **OL**

History Online

Have students visit the Web site at ca.hss.glencoe.com to review Chapter 8 and take the **Self-Check Quiz.**

Chapter 9 Planning Guide

SECTION RESOURCES

Main Ideas	Print Materials	Technology Resources
Section 1 **Southern Cotton Kingdom** 1. Unlike the North, the Southern economy remained mainly agrarian. 2. For many reasons, industry developed slowly in the South.	• Reproducible Lesson Plan 9–1* • Daily Lesson and Discussion Notes 9–1 • Active Reading Note-Taking Guide 9–1 • Reading Essentials and Study Guide 9–1 • Guided Reading Activity 9–1 • Section Quiz 9–1	Daily Focus Skills Transparency 9–1 Section Graphic Organizer Transparency 9–1 California Standards Practice Transparencies Interactive Tutor Self-Assessment CD-ROM Exam*View*® Pro Testmaker CD-ROM Presentation Plus! CD-ROM
Section 2 **Life in the South** 1. Most farmers in the South did not own slaves and lived in poor rural areas. 2. Plantations varied in size and wealth and contained varying numbers of slaves. 3. The South contained large cities, and education began to grow in the mid-1800s.	• Reproducible Lesson Plan 9–2* • Daily Lesson and Discussion Notes 9–2 • Active Reading Note-Taking Guide 9–2 • Reading Essentials and Study Guide 9–2 • Guided Reading Activity 9–2 • Section Quiz 9–2	Daily Focus Skills Transparency 9–2 Section Graphic Organizer Transparency 9–2 California Standards Practice Transparencies Interactive Tutor Self-Assessment CD-ROM Exam*View*® Pro Testmaker CD-ROM Presentation Plus! CD-ROM
Section 3 **The Peculiar Institution** 1. Enslaved African Americans faced many hardships but were able to create family lives, religious beliefs, and a distinct culture. 2. Many enslaved people fought against slavery.	• Reproducible Lesson Plan 9–3* • Daily Lesson and Discussion Notes 9–3 • Active Reading Note-Taking Guide 9–3 • Reading Essentials and Study Guide 9–3 • Guided Reading Activity 9–3 • Section Quiz 9–3	Daily Focus Skills Transparency 9–3 Section Graphic Organizer Transparency 9–3 California Standards Practice Transparencies Interactive Tutor Self-Assessment CD-ROM Exam*View*® Pro Testmaker CD-ROM Presentation Plus! CD-ROM Vocabulary PuzzleMaker CD-ROM

PACING YOUR LESSONS

Chapter Introduction	Section 1	Section 2	Section 3	Chapter Assessment
$\frac{1}{2}$ Day	1 Day	2 Days	2 Days	$\frac{1}{2}$ Day

0:00 **OUT OF TIME?** Assign the Chapter 9 ***Reading Essentials and Study Guide***

*Available on TeacherWorks™

Standards-Based Lesson Plan

History–Social Science Standards Covered in Chapter 9

The standards covered in the chapter are listed below. Use the accompanying activity as you teach the chapter to ensure student mastery of these standards. This activity can be used in combination with the program's print and technology assessment materials.

Standard	Section 1	Section 2	Section 3
US8.7 Students analyze the divergent paths of the American people in the South from 1800 to the mid-1800s and the challenges they faced.	✔	✔	✔
US8.7.1 Describe the development of the agrarian economy in the South, identify the locations of the cotton-producing states, and discuss the significance of cotton and the cotton gin.	✔		
US8.7.2 Trace the origins and development of slavery; its effects on black Americans and on the region's political, social, religious, economic, and cultural development; and identify the strategies that were tried to both overturn and preserve it (e.g., through the writings and historical documents on Nat Turner, Denmark Vesey).			✔
US8.7.3 Examine the characteristics of white Southern society and how the physical environment influenced events and conditions prior to the Civil War.		✔	
US8.7.4 Compare the lives of and opportunities for free blacks in the North with those of free blacks in the South.		✔	
US8.9 Students analyze the early and steady attempts to abolish slavery and to realize the ideals of the Declaration of Independence.			✔
US8.9.1 Describe the leaders of the movement (e.g., John Quincy Adams and the proposed constitutional amendment, John Brown and the armed resistance, Harriet Tubman and the Underground Railroad, Benjamin Franklin, Theodore Weld, William Lloyd Garrison, Frederick Douglass).			✔

Cumulative Standards-Assessment Activity

The Cumulative Standards-Assessment Activity will help students organize and learn the important information from the chapter. Begin teaching the chapter with this activity, and have students complete it as they read the chapter.

Creating an Outline

Purpose Remind students that outlining is a useful way of understanding the structure of a piece of writing and the relationship among the ideas. Seeing how ideas relate to each other makes them easier to remember and to manipulate.

Introduction to Outlining

1. Model outline writing by writing on the board the roman numeral *I*, the capital letters *A* and *B*, and the numbers *1*, *2*, and *3* under each of the letters. Have the class turn to a part of the previous chapter and ask volunteers to identify text to place in each of the levels of the outline shown on the board. Remind students that outlines use words and phrases, not complete sentences.
2. Ask students to copy this structure in their notebooks:

I. ______________________
  A. ______________________
    1. ______________________
    2. ______________________
  B. ______________________
    1. ______________________
    2. ______________________
II. ______________________

Have students outline the content of each section as they read. Suggest that as they complete their outlines, they write a brief summary of the main idea or ideas of the section to help them pull together the different details they have outlined.

3. Urge students to use their outlines to help them review the chapter.

Chapter 9 Resources

READING SUPPORT

- Content Vocabulary Activity 9
- Academic Vocabulary Activity 9
- Reading Skills Activity 9
- American Literature Reading 9
- Biography Activities 9A, 9B
- Chapter 9 Active Reading Note-Taking Guide
- Chapter 9 Guided Reading Activities
- Chapter 9 Reading Essentials and Study Guide
- Glencoe Literature Library
- Glencoe Video Program
- Vocabulary PuzzleMaker CD-ROM
- Interactive Graphic Organizers CD-ROM
- American History Primary Source Document Library CD-ROM

SKILL PRACTICE

- Map Overlay Transparency 9, Strategy, and Activity
- Analysis Skills Activity 9
- Time Line Activity 9
- Geography and History Activity 9
- Economics and History Activity 9
- Chart, Graph, and Map Skills Activity 9
- Political Cartoon Activity 9
- Supreme Court Case Study 9
- In-Text Map Transparency 9, Strategy, and Activity
- Step Into World History Activity 9
- Citizenship and Service Learning Activity 9
- Outline Map Resource Book
- MindJogger Plus Videoquiz

CRITICAL THINKING

- Critical Thinking Skills Activity 9
- Primary Source Reading 9
- Cause-and-Effect Transparency 9, Strategy, and Activity
- Presentation Plus! CD-ROM

WRITING SUPPORT

- Writing Activity 9
- Language Arts Activity 9
- Writer's Guidebook
- Middle School Writing Process Transparencies

UNIVERSAL ACCESS

- Universal Access Activity 9
- Then and Now Transparencies 9A–9B, Strategy, and Activity
- Graphic Novel Activity 9
- School-to-Home Connection Activities 9A–9D
- English Learner Handbook Chapter 9 Activities
- Universal Access for the American History Classroom
- Moments in Time
- American Art and Architecture Transparencies, Strategies, and Activities
- American Art Prints
- American Music Cultural Traditions
- American Music Hits Through History
- StudentWorks Plus CD-ROM

ASSESSMENT

Glencoe's Assessment Advantage

- Chapter 9 Section Quizzes
- Chapter 9 Tests, Forms A and B
- California Standards Assessment, Forms A and B
- Cumulative Assessment Activity US8.7
- California Standards Practice Workbook
- Succeeding on the California History–Social Science Standards CD-ROM
- Exam*View*® Pro Testmaker CD-ROM
- Interactive Tutor Self-Assessment CD-ROM

CD-ROM
DVD
Print Material
Poster
Transparency
Music Program
Videocassette
Glencoe Literature Library

Chapter 9 Resources

TECHNOLOGY

- StudentWorks Plus CD-ROM
- TeacherWorks Plus CD-ROM
- Exam*View*® Pro Testmaker CD-ROM
- Interactive Tutor Self-Assessment CD-ROM
- Presentation Plus CD-ROM
- Succeeding on the California History–Social Science Standards CD-ROM
- Vocabulary PuzzleMaker CD-ROM
- Interactive Graphic Organizers CD-ROM
- Interactive Time Line CD-ROM
- American History Primary Source Document Library CD-ROM
- MindJogger Plus Videoquiz
- American Music Cultural Traditions
- American Music Hits Through History
- Glencoe Video Program
- Professional Development in Middle School Social Studies Series
- Teaching American History With *Discovering Our Past: The American Journey to World War I*

SPANISH RESOURCES

- Spanish Activities and Assessment
  - Spanish Content Vocabulary Activities
  - Spanish Guided Reading Activities
  - Spanish Quizzes and Tests
  - Spanish California Standards Assessment
- Spanish Reading Essentials and Study Guide
- Spanish School-to-Home Connection
- Spanish Declaration of Independence and U.S. Constitution

TRANSPARENCIES

- California Standards Practice Transparencies
- Daily Focus Skills Transparencies
- Section Graphic Organizer Transparencies
- In-Text Map Transparencies
- Map Overlay Transparencies
- Cause-and-Effect Transparencies
- Then and Now Transparencies
- American Art and Architecture Transparencies
- Middle School Writing Process Transparencies

TEACHER PLANNING

- Daily Lesson and Discussion Notes
- English Learner Handbook
- Guide to Daily Intervention
- *Discovering Our Past: The American Journey to World War I* Reading and Study Skills Foldables
- Reading Strategies and Activities for the Social Studies Classroom
- Chapter 9 Reproducible Lesson Plans (correlated to California History–Social Science Standards)
- Universal Access for the American History Classroom
- NGS U.S. Desk Map
- NGS U.S. Atlas

PROFESSIONAL DEVELOPMENT

- Building Academic Vocabulary
- Strategies for Success
- Research-Based Strategies Used to Develop *Discovering Our Past: The American Journey to World War I*
- Character Education in the Middle School Classroom
- The Living Constitution
- Professional Development in Middle School Social Studies Video Series
- Teaching American History With *Discovering Our Past: The American Journey to World War I*

MASTERING THE STANDARDS

The content and assessment in the Student Edition, Teacher Wraparound Edition, teacher planning materials, and the print and technology products are all standards-based. The use of these products during instruction leads to mastery of the standards.

PRACTICE

- California Standards Practice Workbook
- California Standards Practice Transparencies
- Interactive Time Line CD-ROM
- School-to-Home Connection

BENCHMARK ASSESSMENT

- California Standards Assessment
- Exam*View*® Pro Testmaker CD-ROM
- Succeeding on the California History–Social Science Standards CD-ROM

REMEDIATION

- California Guide to Daily Intervention
- Interactive Tutor Self-Assessment CD-ROM
- Exam*View*® Pro Testmaker CD-ROM
- California Standards Practice Workbook
- Reading Essentials and Study Guide

Additional Resources

NATIONAL GEOGRAPHIC TEACHER'S CORNER

Index to National Geographic Magazine:

The following articles relate to this chapter:

- "The Cruelest Commerce: African Slave Trade," by Colin Palmer, September 1992.

National Geographic Society Products

To order the following, call National Geographic at 1-800-368-2728

- *GeoKit: The Civil War* (Kit)
- *National Geographic Desk Reference* (Book)
- *Steal Away: The Harriet Tubman Story* (Video)

NGS ONLINE

Access National Geographic's new dynamic MapMachine Web site and other geography resources at:

www.nationalgeographic.com

www.nationalgeographic.com/maps

A&E Home Video · Biography® · The History Channel®

The following videotape programs are available from Glencoe as supplements to Chapter 9.

- **Civil War Journal (Set 1) (ISBN 1-56501-200-3)**
- **Underground Railroad (ISBN 1-56501-1679-3)**

To order, call Glencoe at 1-800-334-7344. To find classroom resources to accompany many of these videos, check the following home pages:

A&E Television: www.aetv.com
The History Channel: www.historychannel.com

MOMENTS IN TIME DBQ

The following resource can help you teach the content of this chapter.

Unit 3 The Road to Civil War (1850–1860)

History Online

Use our Web site for additional resources. All essential content is covered in the Student Edition.

You and your students can visit ca.hss.glencoe.com, the Web site companion to *Discovering Our Past: The American Journey to World War I.* This innovative integration of electronic and print media offers your students a wealth of opportunities. The student text directs students to the Web site for the following options:

- Chapter Overviews
- Self-Check Quizzes
- Study Central™
- Student Web Activities
- Textbook Updates
- Multi-Language Glossaries

Answers to the student Web activities are provided for you in the Web Activity Lesson Plans. Additional Web resources and ePuzzles and games are also available.

FOLDABLES™ Study Organizer

Dinah Zike's Foldables

Foldables are three-dimensional, interactive graphic organizers that help students practice basic writing skills, review key vocabulary terms, and identify main ideas. Every chapter contains a foldable activity, with additional chapter activities found in the Reading and Study Skills Foldables booklet.

Reading List Generator CD-ROM — Glencoe BookLink

The Glencoe BookLink CD-ROM is a database that allows you to search more than 15,000 titles to create a customized reading list for your students.

- Reading lists can be organized by students' reading level, author, genre, theme, or area of interest.
- The database provides Degrees of Reading Power™ (DRP) and Lexile™ readability scores for all selections.
- A brief summary of each selection is included.

Reading level suggestions for this chapter:

For students at a Grade 6 reading level:
- ***Harriet Tubman: Conductor on the Underground Railroad,*** by Ann Petry

For students at a Grade 7 reading level:
- ***Our Song: Our Toil: The Story of American Slavery as Told by Slaves,*** by Michele Stepto

For students at a Grade 8 reading level:
- ***Rebels Against Slavery,*** by Patricia C. McKissack and Fredrick L. McKissack

For students at a Grade 9 reading level:
- ***Cotton,*** by Lewis Miles

Reading Support From Jamestown Education

- *Timed Readings Plus in Social Studies* helps students increase their reading rate and fluency while maintaining comprehension. The 400-word passages are similar to those found on state and national assessments.
- *Reading in the Content Areas: Social Studies* concentrates on six essential reading skills that help students better comprehend what they read. The book includes 754 high-interest nonfiction passages written at increasing levels of difficulty.
- *Reading Fluency* helps students read smoothly, accurately, and expressively.
- *Jamestown's Reading Improvement,* by renowned reading expert Edward Fry, focuses on helping build your students' comprehension, vocabulary, and skimming and scanning skills.
- *Critical Reading Series* provides high-interest books, each written at three reading levels.

To order these products, call Glencoe at 1-800-334-7344.

KEY for Using the Teacher Wraparound Edition

Use this key to help you identify the different types of prompts found in the Teacher Wraparound Edition.

R **Reading Strategies** activities help you teach reading skills and vocabulary.

C **Critical Thinking** strategies help students apply and extend what they have learned.

U **Universal Access** activities provide differentiated instruction for students learning to speak English, along with suggestions for teaching various types of learners.

S **Skill Practice** strategies help students practice historical analysis and geography skills.

W **Writing Support** activities provide writing opportunities to help students comprehend the text.

Teaching strategies and activities have been coded for ability level appropriateness.

AL Activities for students working above grade level
OL Activities for students working on grade level
BL Activities for students working below grade level
EL Activities for English Learners

FOCUS

History–Social Science Standards

In this chapter, the following standard will be covered:

US8.7 Students analyze the divergent paths of the American people in the South from 1800 to the mid-1800s and the challenges they faced.

More About the Photo

Drayton Hall, a plantation house located on the Ashley River, was constructed over four years begining in 1738. Its Georgian-Palladian architecture represents the oldest surving example of its kind in the American South.

TEACH

The Big Ideas

As you begin teaching each section, use these questions and activities to focus on the Big Ideas.

Section 1

Southern Cotton Kingdom

Essential Question: What geographic features set where we live apart from other areas of the country? How do these features affect daily life? After students discuss these questions, explain that geography—including the widespread planting of cotton crops—played a vital role in shaping the South during the early and mid 1800s. OL

Chapter 9

The South

▼ Drayton Hall Plantation, near Charleston, South Carolina

NATIONAL GEOGRAPHIC **Where & When?**

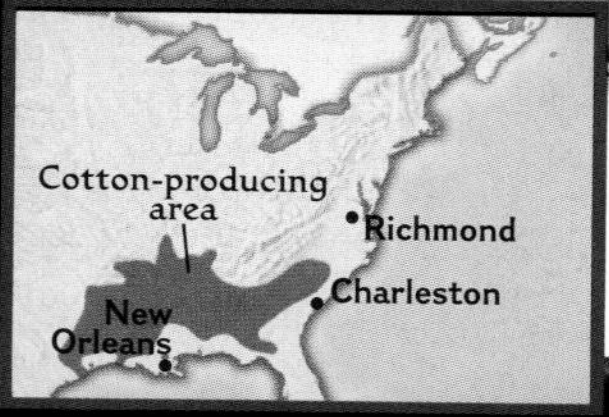

1790 | 1825 | 1860

1793 The cotton gin is invented

1831 Nat Turner's slave revolt strikes fear in Southerners

1860 Baltimore's population is over 200,000

Section 2

Life in the South

Essential Question: What films or books have you seen or read that depict the life in the South before the Civil War? What impressions have they given you of life for Southern whites and African Americans? Explain that this section will dispel some popular myths about Southern history and describe how geography helped shape life in the South. OL

Section 3

The Peculiar Institution

Essential Question: What kinds of issues divide Americans today? *(the role of government, foreign policy decisions, social questions)* Point out that in the mid-1800s, the expansion of slavery led to increasing polarization between the North and the South. OL

History Online
Chapter Overview Visit ca.hss.glencoe.com for a preview of Chapter 9.

The Big Ideas

Section 1
Southern Cotton Kingdom
Geography shapes the physical, economic, and political challenges a region faces. Cotton was vital to the economy of the South.

Section 2
Life in the South
Geography shapes the physical, economic, and political challenges a region faces. Most of the people in the South worked in agriculture in the first half of the 1800s.

Section 3
The Peculiar Institution
Differences in economic, political, and social beliefs and practices can lead to division within a nation and have lasting consequences. Enslaved African Americans developed a unique culture and fought against slavery.

View the Chapter 9 video in the Glencoe Video Program.

FOLDABLES™ Study Organizer

Summarizing Make this foldable and use it as a journal to help you take notes about the South during the period from 1800 to 1850.

Step 1 Stack four sheets of paper, one on top of the other. On the top sheet of paper, trace a large circle.

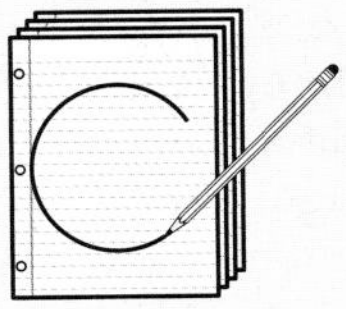

Step 2 With the papers still stacked, cut out all four circles at the same time.

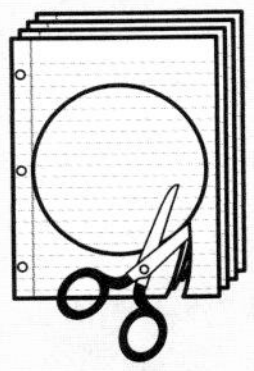

Step 3 Staple the paper circles together at one point around the edge.

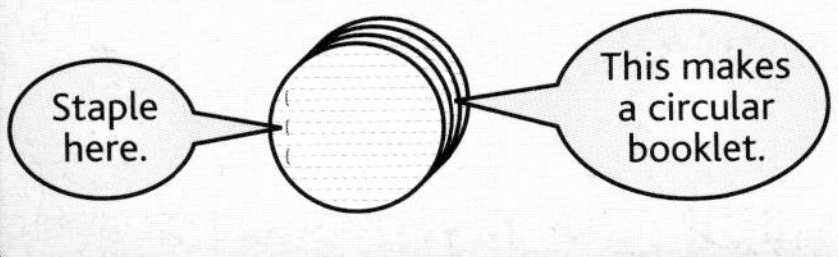

Step 4 Label the front cover as shown and take notes on the pages that open to the right.

Reading and Writing
As you read the chapter, write what you learn about the South in your foldable.

History Online

Go to ca.hss.glencoe.com for student activities, lesson plans, and links to additional Web resources about the South before the Civil War.

FOLDABLES™ Study Organizer
Dinah Zike's Foldables

Purpose Have students use their foldables to identify aspects of daily life in the South during the early and mid 1800s. Encourage students to share their journals with the class. **OL**

Why It's Important

Questioning Reading is not a passive activity. Readers who interact with a text take away more information and a deeper understanding of what they have read. One powerful technique for encouraging students to become actively engaged with a text is to encourage them to ask questions as they read. These questions can address content, the author's point of view, or topics suggested by, but not directly covered, in the text.

1 Learn It!

Read aloud the following newspaper headlines. Have students come up with questions raised by each headline and list them on the board. Remind students that multiple questions can be based on a single sentence:

- "Vaccine Shortage Points to Global Risk"
- "Good News: Jobless Rate Falls"
- "Deadly Explosion Rips Through Marketplace"
- "Senate to Take Crucial Vote" OL

Chapter 9

Get Ready to Read

Questioning

READING SKILL

1 Learn It!

One way to understand what you are reading is to interact with the text by asking questions. What questions would you like answered? What are you curious about? As you read, you may be able to locate the answer in the next paragraph or section. Practice asking questions by turning headings into questions. For instance, a heading that reads "Life Under Slavery" can be turned into the question "What was life like under slavery?" Read this selection from Chapter 9. What questions do you have?

> **Enslaved people faced constant uncertainty and danger. American law in the early 1800s did not protect enslaved families. At any time, a husband or wife could be sold to a different owner, or a slaveholder's death could lead to the breakup of an enslaved family. Although marriage between enslaved people was not recognized by law, many couples did marry. Their marriage ceremonies included the phrase "until death or separation do us part"—recognizing the possibility that their life together might end with the sale of one spouse.**
>
> — *from page 433*

Reading Tip

Good questions start with key words such as *who*, *what*, *when*, *where*, *why*, and *how*.

READING STRATEGY — SETTING A PURPOSE

Asking effective questions can help students set a purpose before they begin to read. Just as students can turn headings into questions, they can do the same with the Main Ideas statements at the beginnings of major subsections. Direct students' attention to the Main Idea statement on page 423. Have them generate two or three questions from that heading and use those questions to guide their reading of the section. OL

2 Practice It!

Read the following paragraph, and answer this question with a partner: What were the economic goals of a plantation owner?

> The main economic goal for large plantation owners was to earn profits. Such plantations had fixed costs—regular expenses such as housing and feeding workers and maintaining cotton gins and other equipment. Fixed costs remained about the same year after year.
>
> Cotton prices, however, varied from season to season, depending on the market. To receive the best prices, planters sold their cotton to agents in cities such as New Orleans, Charleston, Mobile, and Savannah. The cotton exchanges, or trade centers, in Southern cities were of vital importance to those involved in the cotton economy. The agents of the exchanges extended credit—a form of loan—to the planters and held the cotton for several months until the price rose. Then the agents sold the cotton. This system kept the planters always in debt because they did not receive payment for their cotton until the agents sold it.
>
> *—from page 429*

Read to Write

Write a *What If* paragraph based on what you read in this chapter. For example, *what if* the South had become industrialized like the North? Your paragraph should answer your *What If* question.

▲ Plantation in the South

3 Apply It!

As you read the chapter, look for answers to section headings that are in the form of questions. For the other sections, turn the headings into questions that you can answer as you read.

2 Practice It!

After students carry out the Practice It! activity on the student page, ask volunteers to state other questions they could ask about plantations in the South. **Ask:** Where could you get these questions answered? *(possibly in other sections of the chapter; by consulting other sources of information)* **OL**

3 Apply It!

Point out to students that anything they read (or view or listen to) can help them practice their question-asking skills. Have students look beyond the textbook and select a passage from another book, a magazine story, a television report, or some other communication. Ask students to use this as the basis for a series of questions. **Ask:** What generalizations can you make about forming effective questions? What words work best when phrasing questions? *(Students might suggest such words as* what, why, *or* how.*)* **OL**

READING STRATEGY **READING PRIMARY SOURCES**

Have students locate a published interview in a newspaper or magazine that follows a question-and-answer format. After students read the interview, have them come up with three additional questions that address areas not covered in the interview or that were raised by the answers given. **OL**

Use Reading Skills Activity 9 in the **Chapter 9 Resource Book** for more practice with questioning.

FOCUS

BELLRINGER
SKILLBUILDER ACTIVITY

Project **Daily Focus Skills Transparency 9–1** and have students answer the question.

Guide to Reading

Preteaching Vocabulary:
Have students use the Glossary in the back of their textbooks to find definition of each term. Then ask students to write sentences using each term.

Answers to Graphic:
Cotton production: cotton gin cut processing time, farmers grew more cotton; Industry: farming very profitable so no new businesses started, lack of capital

Unpacking the Standards

After reading the section, students will be able to:

- Explain the role of cotton production in the South and why the economy there relied on agriculture.
- Discuss why industry did not develop as widely in the South as in the North.

Section 1 Southern Cotton Kingdom

Guide to Reading

History Social Science Standards

US8.7 Students analyze the divergent paths of the American people in the South from 1800 to the mid-1800s and the challenges they faced.

Looking Back, Looking Ahead

In the last chapter, you learned about life in and the economy of the Northeastern states. In this section, you will learn about the economy of the South.

Focusing on the Main Ideas

- Unlike the North, the Southern economy remained mainly agrarian. *(page 423)*
- For many reasons, industry developed slowly in the South. *(page 424)*

Locating Places

Upper South
Deep South

Meeting People

Eli Whitney
William Gregg
Joseph Reid Anderson

Content Vocabulary

cotton gin
capital (KA • puh • tuhl)

Academic Vocabulary

predominant (prih • DAH • muh • nuhnt)
sum

Reading Strategy

Comparing As you read the section, re-create the diagram below. In the ovals, give reasons why cotton production grew but industrial growth was slower.

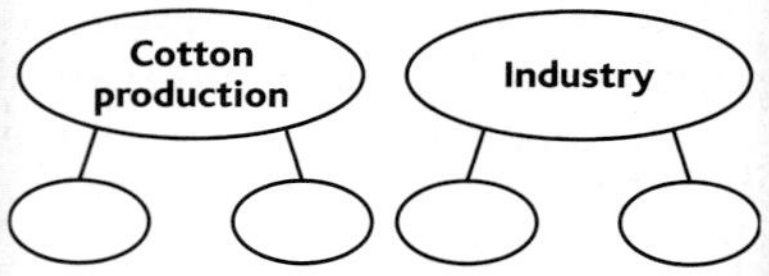

NATIONAL GEOGRAPHIC Who & When?

1780 | 1800 | 1820 | 1840

Cotton gin

1793 Eli Whitney invents cotton gin

1820 Cotton makes up one-third of all U.S. exports

1840s Joseph Reid Anderson's Tredegar Iron Works is a leading iron producer

422

SECTION RESOURCES

Print Material
- Reproducible Lesson Plan 9–1*
- Daily Lesson and Discussion Notes 9–1
- Guided Reading Activity 9–1
- Reading Essentials and Study Guide 9–1
- Active Reading Note-Taking Guide 9–1
- Section Quiz 9–1

Transparencies
- Daily Focus Skills Transparency 9–1
- Section Graphic Organizer Transparency 9–1
- California Standards Practice Transparencies

Technology
- Interactive Tutor Self-Assessment CD-ROM
- Exam*View*® Pro Testmaker CD-ROM
- Presentation Plus! CD-ROM

*Available on TeacherWorks™

US8.7.1 Describe the development of the agrarian economy in the South, identify the locations of the cotton-producing states, and discuss the significance of cotton and the cotton gin.

Rise of the Cotton Kingdom

Main Idea **Unlike the North, the Southern economy remained mainly agrarian.**

Reading Connection Check the label on your pants or shirt. What materials are found in the fabric? Chances are you wear something at least partly made of cotton. Read on to find out how cotton was a major economic asset to the Deep South.

An American Story

Cotton was not the only crop grown in the South, but it was the crop that fueled the Southern economy. Southerners began saying, rightly, "Cotton is king." "Look which way you will, you see it; and see [cotton] moving," wrote a visitor to Mobile, Alabama. "Keel boats, ships, brigs, schooners, wharves, stores, and press-houses, all appeared to be full."

Cotton Rules the Deep South Most Southerners lived along the Atlantic coast in Maryland, Virginia, Tennessee, and North Carolina in what came to be known as the **Upper South.** By 1850 the South had changed. Its population had spread inland to the states of the **Deep South**—Georgia, South Carolina, Alabama, Mississippi, Louisiana, Florida, Arkansas, and Texas.

In colonial times, rice, indigo (a plant used to make blue dye), and tobacco made up the South's main crops. After the American Revolution, demand for these crops decreased. European mills, however, wanted Southern cotton to make into cloth. But cotton was difficult to produce. After cotton was harvested, workers had to painstakingly separate the plant's sticky seeds from the cotton fibers.

In 1793 **Eli Whitney** invented the cotton gin. The **cotton gin** was a compact machine that removed seeds from cotton fibers much more quickly than could be done by hand. Because cotton could be processed more easily, Southern planters wanted to grow more. As a result, they depended on slave labor to plant and pick cotton.

By 1860 the economies of the Deep South and the Upper South had developed in different ways. Both parts of the South were agricultural, but the Upper South still produced tobacco, hemp, wheat, and vegetables. The Deep South was committed to cotton and, in some areas, to rice and sugarcane.

The value of enslaved people increased because of their key role in producing cotton and sugar. In time, the Upper South became a center for the sale of enslaved people.

Reading Check **Describe** What effect did the cotton gin have on the South's economy?

History Makers

Fall Lines

▲ Waterfall in central Georgia

In the eastern United States, many cities developed along fall lines. A "fall line" is the boundary between an upland region and a lower region where rivers and streams move down over rapids or waterfalls to the lower region. Cities sprang up along fall lines for a number of reasons. Boats could not travel beyond the fall line, so travelers and merchants had to transfer their goods to other forms of transportation there. Early manufacturers also took advantage of the falls to power their mills. Cities in the South that grew along fall lines include Richmond, Virginia, and Augusta, Georgia.

TEACH

U Universal Access

English Learners The phrase "cotton is king" contains a metaphor, an expression that compares two objects that are different from one another. **Ask:** What is cotton compared to? *(a king)* What does this say about the role of cotton in the South? *(It was extremely important and powerful, like a king.)* EL

R Reading Strategy

Using Context Clues Point out to students that the word "gin" is taken from a longer word. **Ask:** Using context clues, can you guess what that longer word is? *(engine)* OL

Review The Big Idea

Review the Big Idea for this section: "Geography shapes the physical, economic, and political challenges a region faces." **Ask:** How did fall lines affect the development of the South? *(by influencing where major cities arose)* OL CA CS3.

Reading Check

Answer: It increased the demand for enslaved African Americans and kept the South committed to cotton production.

More Skill Practice

Historical and Social Sciences Analysis Skill **Ask:** What were the positive and negative effects of the invention of the cotton gin? *(Positive: increased cotton production and enriched the South; Negative: increased reliance on slave labor)* OL CA HI2.

History Makers

Other fall line cities include Trenton, Philadelphia, Baltimore, and Washington, D.C. The upland region to the west of the fall line is called the Piedmont. In some parts of the South, the lowland region to the east is called the Tidewater.

R1 Reading Strategy

Questioning Ask: Based on statements in this paragraph, what questions do you have about the economy of the South? *(Questions may include: Why did the South remain rural? Why did manufacturing take root in the North but not in the South?)* Tell students to read on to see if their questions are answered in the text. OL

R2 Reading Strategy

Academic Vocabulary Have students read the sentence containing the word *predominantly*. Then ask a student to use context clues to define the word. OL

W Writing Support

Persuasive Writing Have students imagine they are the editors of a Southern newspaper. Ask them to write an editorial in which they support or oppose Southerners' decision to expand cotton farming instead of launching new businesses. Remind students to give reasons for their arguments. OL

CA 8WA2.4

US8.7.1 Describe the development of the agrarian economy in the South, identify the locations of the cotton-producing states, and discuss the significance of cotton and the cotton gin.

Industry in the South

Main Idea **For many reasons, industry developed slowly in the South.**

Reading Connection How do you get to school each morning? Do you take the bus or ride in a car, or do you walk to school? Read on to find out what modes of transportation transported people and goods in the South.

The economy of the South prospered between 1820 and 1860. Unlike the industrial North, however, the South remained **predominantly** rural, and its economy became increasingly different from the Northern economy. The South accounted for only a small percentage of the nation's manufacturing in the 1850s. In fact, the entire South produced fewer manufactured goods than the state of Massachusetts.

Barriers to Industry Why was there little industry in the South? One reason was the boom in cotton sales. Because agriculture was so profitable, Southerners remained committed to farming rather than starting new businesses.

Another reason was the lack of **capital** (KA • puh • tuhl)—money to invest in businesses—in the South. To develop industries required money, but many Southerners had their wealth invested in land and slaves. Planters would have had to sell slaves to raise the money to build factories. Most wealthy Southerners were unwilling to do this. They believed that an economy based on cotton and slavery would continue to prosper.

In addition, the market for manufactured goods in the South was smaller than it was in the North. A large portion of the Southern population consisted of enslaved people with no money to buy merchandise. So the limited local market discouraged industries from developing.

TECHNOLOGY & History

The Cotton Gin

In 1793 Eli Whitney visited Catherine Greene, a Georgia plantation owner. She asked him to build a device that removed the seeds from cotton pods. Whitney called the machine the cotton gin—*gin* being short for "engine".

How did the invention of the cotton gin affect slavery?

Eli Whitney

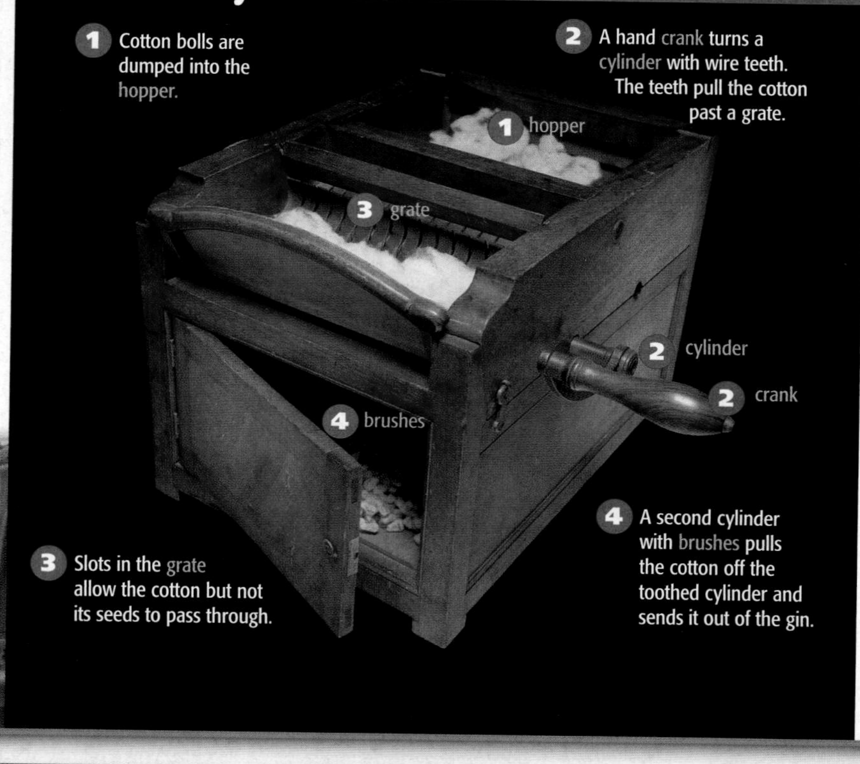

Answers and Additional Support

Did You Know?

Historians estimate that between 1820 and 1860, 50 percent of the African Americans living in the Upper South were taken by slaveholders to new cotton fields in the states along the Gulf of Mexico and the Mississippi River.

TECHNOLOGY & History

Answer: It increased the amount of cotton that could be processed in the same amount of time. Since more cotton could be processed, planters grew more, which increased the need for enslaved people to plant and harvest it.

NATIONAL GEOGRAPHIC Cotton Production, 1820–1860

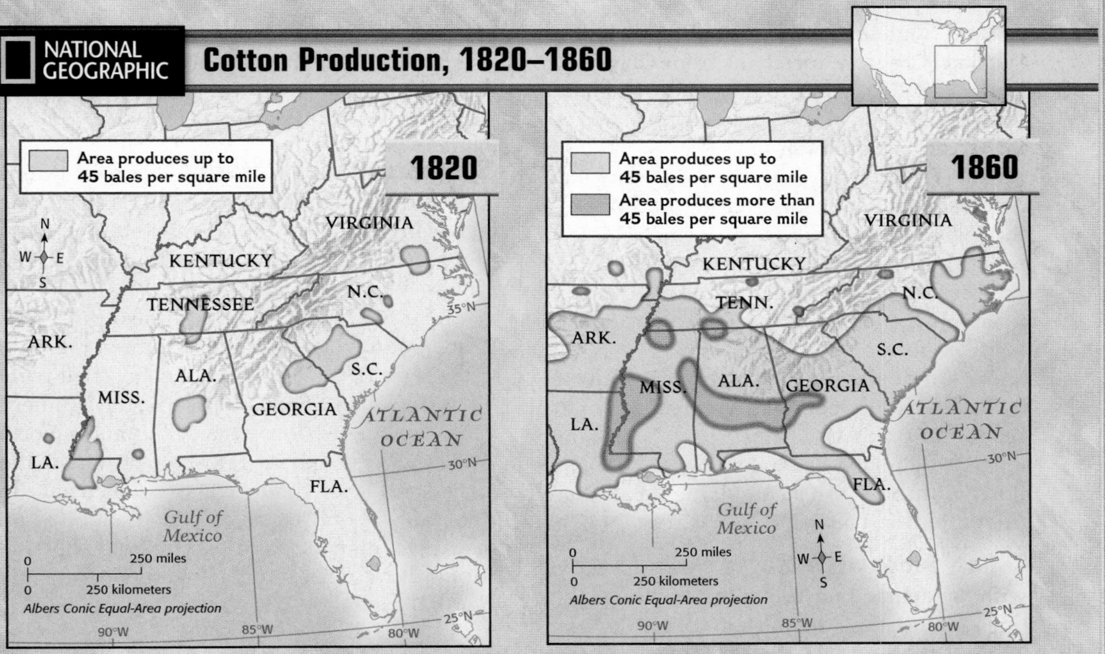

Cotton production as a percentage of U.S. exports

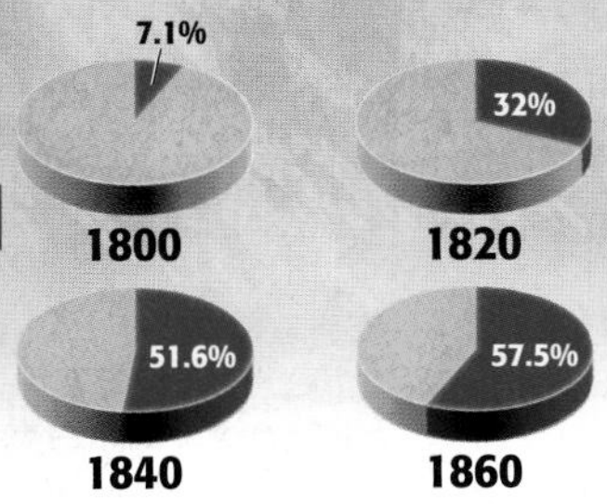

Source: *Historical Statistics of the United States.*

Using Geography Skills

Cotton was the nation's top export in the mid-1800s.

1. **Human-Environment Interaction** What states included areas that produced more than 45 bales of cotton per square mile in 1860?
2. **Human-Environment Interaction** Describe the changes in South Carolina's areas of cotton production from 1820 to 1860.

Another reason for the lack of industry is that some Southerners did not want industry to flourish there. One political leader **summed** up the Southerners' point of view this way:

> **"As long as we have our rice, our sugar, our tobacco, and our cotton, we can command wealth to purchase all we want."**
>
> —quoted in *Louis T. Wigfall, Southern Fire-Eater*

Southern Factories While most Southerners felt confident about the future of the cotton economy, some leaders wanted to develop industry in the region. These leaders argued that by remaining committed to cotton production, the South was becoming dependent on the North for manufactured goods. These Southerners also argued that factories and workshops would revive the economy of the Upper South, which was less prosperous than the cotton states.

Using Geography Skills

Answers:

1. Arkansas, Louisiana, Mississippi, Alabama, Tennessee, Georgia
2. Cotton production spread to most areas of the state.

Resources for page 425

- Economics and History Activity 9
- Chart, Graph, and Map Skills Activity 9

S Skill Practice

Visual Literacy Ask: What do these four graphs tell you about cotton production from 1800 to 1860? *(Cotton made up a growing share of overall American exports in that period.)* What do they *not* tell you about cotton production in that period? *(exactly how much cotton was grown or exported)* **OL** CA 8RC2.2

C Critical Thinking

Predicting Consequences
Ask: What could result from the South's decision to build up the cotton economy while discouraging industry? *(Positive: profits from farming will increase as long as cotton is in demand; Negative: dependence on a single crop could lead to problems during poor growing seasons; the South might become dependent on other areas for manufactured goods)* **AL** CAHI1.

R1 Reading Strategy

Academic Vocabulary Tell students that the word *sum* can be used as a noun or a verb. Ask students to describe how it is used here. **BL**

R2 Reading Strategy

Scaffolding—Identifying the Main Idea and Supporting Details Have students read all the material under this heading and find the main idea. (*Some Southerners wanted to develop industry.*)
Ask: What are two details that support this main idea? *(Details: Gregg opened a textile factory; Tredegar Iron Works became a leading iron producer.)* **OL** CA 8RW1.2

This READING SKILL was introduced in Chapter 2.

S Skill Practice

Using Geography Skills

Ask: What role did geography play in the spread of cotton? *(Cotton moved into western areas that had soil suitable to growing it.)* Would cotton growing necessarily spread to all areas? Why or why not? *(no; because they might not have the right soil for growing it)* OL CA CS3. CA HI2.

ASSESS

Resources for page 426

Use these resources to assess student mastery of section content.

- Geography and History Activity 9
- Section Quiz 9–1
- Interactive Tutor Self-Assessment CD-ROM

Reading Check

Answer: money to invest in business; more available capital allows for more investment in businesses, which results in economic growth

History Online

Study Central provides summaries, interactive games, and online graphic organizers to help students review section content.

CLOSE

Predicting Consequences

Ask: How do you think the growth and production of cotton, along with Southern resistance to industrial growth, became critical issues in the debate about slavery? OL CA CS1.

One Southerner who shared this view was **William Gregg,** a merchant from Charleston, South Carolina. After touring New England's textile mills in 1844, Gregg opened his own textile factory in South Carolina.

In Richmond, Virginia, **Joseph Reid Anderson** took over the Tredegar Iron Works in the 1840s and made it one of the nation's leading producers of iron. Years later, during the Civil War, Tredegar provided artillery (weapons) and other iron products for the Southern forces.

The industries that Gregg and Anderson built were the exception rather than the rule in the South. For the most part, the South remained a region of rural villages and plantations with only three large cities: Baltimore, Charleston, and New Orleans.

Cotton Production Moves West To keep up with the demand for raw cotton, cotton plantations sprang up to the west, in the fertile "black belt" (so called for its rich, black soil) of Mississippi and Alabama, and in the rich bottomlands along the Mississippi River and its tributaries. The growing population in these areas led to statehood for Mississippi in 1817, for Alabama in 1819, and for Arkansas in 1836.

Southern Transportation Natural waterways provided the chief means for transporting goods in the South. Most towns were located on the seacoast or along rivers. There were few canals, and roads were poor.

Like the North, the South also built railroads but to a lesser extent. Southern rail lines were short, local, and did not connect all parts of the region in a network. As a result, Southern cities grew more slowly than cities in the North and Midwest, where railways provided the major routes for commerce and settlement. By 1860 only about one-third of the nation's rail lines lay within the South. The railway shortage would have devastating consequences for the South during the Civil War.

Reading Check **Explain** What is capital? Why is it important for economic growth?

History Online

Study Central Need help understanding the economy of the South? Visit ca.hss.glencoe.com and click on Study Central.

Section 1 Review

Reading Summary

Review the Main Ideas

- The success of cotton production in the South kept it an agrarian region.
- Lack of capital, a small market for manufactured goods, and a desire to remain agrarian hindered the growth of industry in the South.

What Did You Learn?

1. What were the major crops in the Deep South?
2. Why did the invention of the cotton gin increase the demand for enslaved people?

Critical Thinking

3. **Compare** How did agriculture in the Upper South differ from agriculture in the Deep South? Re-create the diagram below and describe the differences.

Agriculture	
Upper South	Deep South

4. **The Big Ideas** How might the banning of slavery have affected the South's economy? CA HI6.
5. **Cause and Effect** Describe transportation in the South during this period. How did transportation affect or limit other areas of Southern life? CA HI2.
6. **READING Asking Questions** Turn the two Main Ideas listed in the Reading Summary into questions and then answer them. CA 8RC2.0

SECTION 1 REVIEW ANSWERS

Review questions reinforce content standard US8.7.

1. cotton, rice, sugarcane
2. Because farmers could process their cotton more quickly, they wanted to grow more and thus needed more enslaved people.
3. Upper South: tobacco, hemp, wheat, vegetables; Deep South: mostly cotton, some rice and sugarcane
4. **The Big Ideas** increased the price of cotton, or lowered the profits; economy might have become more diverse
5. transportation was poor; cities grew slowly
6. **READING** Why did the South remain an agrarian region? What factors prevented industry from growing in the South?

Section 2

Life in the South

Guide to Reading

Looking Back, Looking Ahead

In the last section, you learned about the economy of the South. In this section, you will read about the way of life of the Southern people.

Focusing on the Main Ideas

- Most farmers in the South did not own slaves and lived in poor rural areas. *(page 428)*
- Plantations varied in size and wealth and contained varying numbers of enslaved people. *(page 429)*
- The South was home to several large cities, and education began to grow in the mid-1800s. *(page 430)*

Locating Places

New Orleans
Charleston
Mobile
Savannah
Columbia
Chattanooga
Montgomery
Atlanta

Content Vocabulary

yeoman (YOH • muhn)
tenant farmer (TEH • nuhnt)
fixed cost
credit
overseer (OH • vuhr • SEE • uhr)

Academic Vocabulary

purchase
exceed (ihk • SEED)

Reading Strategy

Organizing Information As you read the section, re-create the diagram below and describe the work that was done on Southern plantations.

History Social Science Standards

US8.7 Students analyze the divergent paths of the American people in the South from 1800 to the mid-1800s and the challenges they faced.

NATIONAL GEOGRAPHIC Where & When?

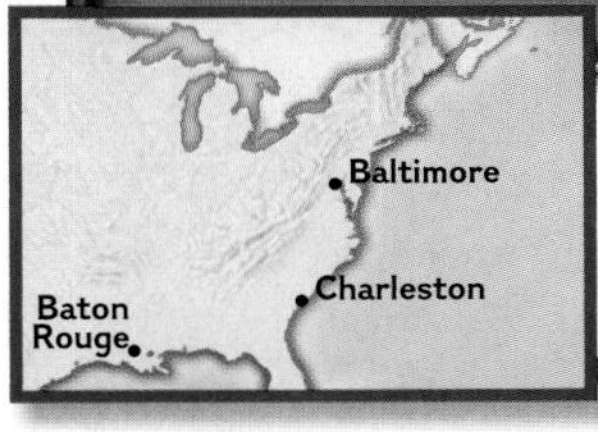

1800 | 1830 | 1860

1800 Charleston, South Carolina, is nation's fifth-largest city

1830s Southern states pass laws to limit rights of free African Americans

1860 Population of Baltimore reaches 212,000

FOCUS

BELLRINGER Skillbuilder Activity

Project **Daily Focus Skills Transparency 9–2** and have students answer the question.

Guide to Reading

Preteaching Vocabulary: Use the **Vocabulary PuzzleMaker CD-ROM** to create crossword and word search puzzles.

Answers to Graphic: domestic work; skilled labor; care of farm animals; fieldwork

Unpacking the Standards

After reading the section, students will be able to:

- Describe life on Southern farms and plantations during the early and mid-1800s.
- Identify the economic groups in the South during that period.
- Explain what led to the growth in education for Southern whites.

SECTION RESOURCES

Print Material
- Reproducible Lesson Plan 9–2*
- Daily Lesson and Discussion Notes 9–2
- Guided Reading Activity 9–2
- Reading Essentials and Study Guide 9–2
- Active Reading Note-Taking Guide 9–2
- Section Quiz 9–2

Transparencies
- Daily Focus Skills Transparency 9–2
- Section Graphic Organizer Transparency 9–2
- California Standards Practice Transparencies

Technology
- Interactive Tutor Self-Assessment CD-ROM
- Exam*View*® Pro Testmaker CD-ROM
- Presentation Plus! CD-ROM

*Available on TeacherWorks™

TEACH

R1 Reading Strategy

Categorizing Information
Encourage students to create charts to categorize the information under this heading. For instance, they might give one chart the headings *Myth* and *Reality* and for another use *Yeomen* and *Tenant Farmers*. BL

R2 Reading Strategy

Understanding Vocabulary
Have students explain the differences between *yeomen* and *tenant farmers*. *(Yeomen owned the land they farmed; tenant farmers rented it.)* OL CA 8RW1.3

S Skill Practice

Historical and Social Sciences Analysis Skill
Ask: How did the position of poor whites in the South compare to that of factory workers in the North? *(Students may say that they were more independent though they may not have been better off economically.)* OL

Reading Check
Answer: yeomen

Answers and Additional Support

US8.7.3 Examine the characteristics of white Southern society and how the physical environment influenced events and conditions prior to the Civil War.

R1 Life on the Small Farms

Main Idea **Most farmers in the South did not own slaves and lived in poor rural areas.**

Reading Connection When you think about the South during the height of slavery, what images come to mind? Read on to find out what the South was really like during the 1800s.

Popular novels and films often portray the South before 1860 as a land of stately plantations owned by rich white slaveholders. In reality, most white Southerners were either small farmers without slaves or planters with a handful of slaves. Only a few planters could afford the many enslaved people and the lavish mansions shown in fictional accounts of the Old South. Most white Southerners fit into one of four categories: yeomen, tenant farmers, the rural poor, or plantation owners.

Small Farmers and the Rural Poor The farmers who did not have slaves—**yeomen** (YOH • muhn)—made up the largest group of whites in the South. R2 Most yeomen owned land. Although they lived throughout the region, they were most numerous in the Upper South and in the hilly rural areas of the Deep South, where the land was unsuited to large plantations.

A yeoman's farm usually ranged from 50 to 200 acres. Yeomen grew crops both for their own use and to sell, and they often traded their produce to local merchants and workers for goods and services.

Most Southern whites did not live in elegant mansions or on large plantations. They lived in far simpler homes, though the structure of their homes changed over time. In the early 1800s, many lived in cottages built of wood and plaster with thatched roofs. Later many lived in one-story frame houses or log cabins.

Not all Southern whites owned land. Some rented land or worked as **tenant farmers** (TEH • nuhnt) on landlords' estates. Others—the rural poor—lived in crude cabins in wooded areas where they could clear a few trees, plant some corn, and keep a hog or a cow. They also fished and hunted for food.

The poor people of the rural South were fiercely independent. They refused to take any job that resembled the work of enslaved people. S Although looked down on by other whites, the rural poor were proud of being self-sufficient.

Reading Check **Identify** What group made up the largest number of whites in the South?

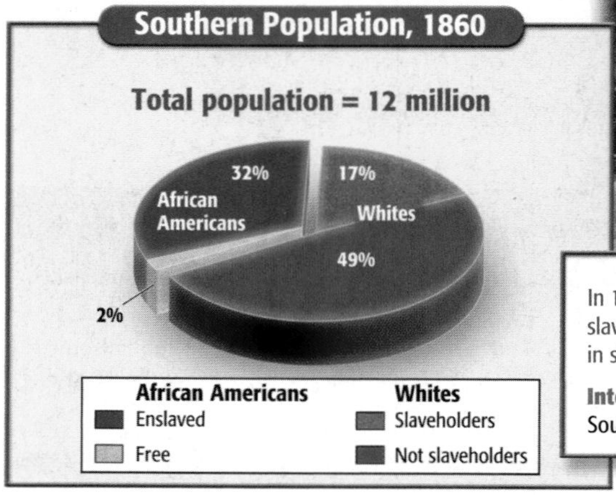

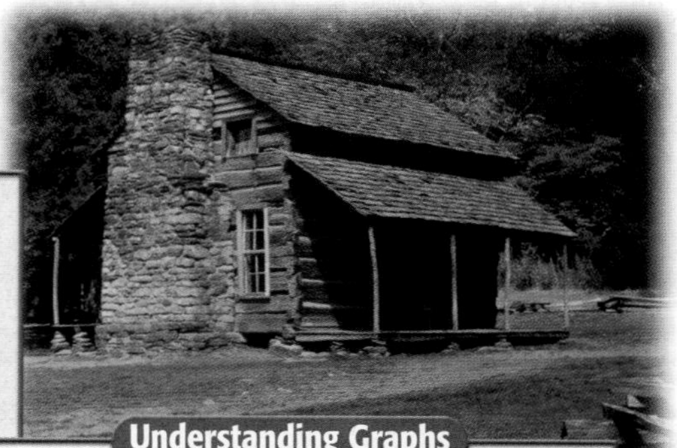

Understanding Graphs

In 1860 about 400,000 households in the South held slaves. Nearly 4 million African Americans remained in slavery.

Interpreting a Graph What total percentage of the Southern population did whites make up?

Understanding Graphs
Answer: 66 percent

More Skill Practice

Historical and Social Sciences Analysis Skill Have students create a chart in which they compare and contrast the daily lives of the various types of Southerners: plantation owners, yeomen, tenant farmers, rural poor, enslaved African Americans, and free African Americans. OL CA HI1.

US8.7.3 Examine the characteristics of white Southern society and how the physical environment influenced events and conditions prior to the Civil War.

Plantations

Main Idea **Plantations varied in size and wealth and contained varying numbers of enslaved people.**

Reading Connection Imagine that you want to open your own business. What things do you need to get your business started? Read on to find out what plantation owners needed to keep their plantations running.

A large plantation might cover several thousand acres. Well-to-do plantation owners usually lived in comfortable but not luxurious farmhouses. They measured their wealth partly by the number of enslaved people they controlled and partly by such possessions as homes, furnishings, and clothing. A small group of plantation owners in the South—about 12 percent of the population—held more than half of the slaves. About half of the planters held fewer than five enslaved workers.

A few free African Americans possessed slaves. The Metoyer family of Louisiana owned thousands of acres of land and more than 400 slaves. Most often, these slaveholders were free African Americans who **purchased** their own family members in order to free them.

Plantation Owners The main economic goal for large plantation owners was to earn profits. R1 Such plantations had **fixed costs**—regular expenses such as housing and feeding workers and maintaining cotton gins and other equipment. Fixed costs remained about the same year after year.

Cotton prices, however, varied from season to season, depending on the market. To receive the best prices, planters sold their cotton to agents in cities such as **New Orleans, Charleston, Mobile,** and **Savannah.** The cotton exchanges, or trade centers, in Southern cities were of vital importance to those involved in the cotton economy. The agents of the exchanges extended **credit**—a form of loan—to the planters and held the cotton for several months until the price rose. Then the agents sold the cotton. This system kept the planters always in debt because they did not receive payment for their cotton until the agents sold it. S R2

History Online
Student Web Activity Visit ca.hss.glencoe.com and click on *Chapter 9—Student Web Activities* for an activity on family life in the South.

Picturing **History**
Although wealthy planters were not numerous, they dominated the economy and political system of the South. ***What were the duties of the wife of a plantation owner?***

Plantation Wives The wife of a plantation owner generally was in charge of watching over the enslaved workers who toiled in her home and tending to them when they became ill. Her responsibilities also included supervising the plantation's buildings and the fruit and vegetable gardens. Some wives served as accountants, keeping the plantation's financial records.

Women often led a difficult and lonely life on the plantation. When plantation agriculture spread westward into Alabama and Mississippi, many planters' wives felt they were moving into a hostile, uncivilized region. Planters traveled frequently to look at new land or to deal with agents in New Orleans or Memphis, so their wives spent long periods alone at the plantation.

R1 Reading Strategy

Scaffolding—Connecting
Ask: What is a synonym for *fixed* in the phrase *fixed costs?* *(unchanging, constant)* OL

This READING SKILL was introduced in Chapter 3.

R2 Reading Strategy

Understanding Vocabulary
Ask: What does it mean to buy something "on credit"? *(the seller agrees to let the buyer pay for the item at a later date, and usually charges interest)* OL

S Skill Practice

Historical and Social Sciences Analysis Skill
Ask: Why did the agents want to hold the cotton before selling it? *(to wait for the price to rise)* OL CA HI6.

History Online
Objectives and answers to the student activity can be found in the Web Activity Lesson Plan feature at ca.hss.glencoe.com.

Resources for page 429
- Universal Access Activity 9
- American Literature Reading 9
- Academic Vocabulary Activity 9

More Skill Practice

Historical and Social Sciences Analysis Skill Have students evaluate the depiction of plantations in film or literary works, such as *Gone With the Wind* or *Uncle Tom's Cabin*. Ask students to identify ways in which plantation life is portrayed both accurately and inaccurately in the work. Have them share their findings with classmates.
OL CA HR2.

Picturing **History**

Plantations were far apart and travel was slow, so when a planter held a party, most guests stayed at the host's home for several days or even weeks.

Answer: overseeing enslaved domestic workers; supervising buildings and gardens; sometimes serving as accountant

US8.7.3 Examine the characteristics of white Southern society and how the physical environment influenced events and conditions prior to the Civil War. US8.7.4 Compare the lives of and opportunities for free blacks in the North with those of free blacks in the South.

R Reading Strategy

Understanding Vocabulary Have students restate the meaning of *overseer* in their own words. OL CA 8RW1.3

U Universal Access

English Learners Encourage English learners to note material they have difficulty understanding. Then form the class into small groups and have students who understand that material help the others understand the concept. EL

Review The Big Idea

Review the Big Idea for this section: "Geography shapes the physical, economic, and political challenges a region faces." **Ask:** Why do you think the ten largest cities in the South were ports? *(They grew as centers of shipping for cotton.)* OL CA CS3.

Reading Check

Answer: There were many jobs to keep the plantation running, including tending to animals, planting, cultivating, and doing housework.

Work on the Plantation Large plantations needed many different kinds of workers. Some enslaved people worked in the house, cleaning, cooking, doing laundry, sewing, and serving meals. They were called domestic slaves. Other enslaved people were trained as blacksmiths, carpenters, shoemakers, or weavers. Still others worked in the pastures, tending the horses, cows, sheep, and pigs. Most of the enslaved African Americans, however, were field hands. They worked from sunrise to sunset planting, cultivating, and picking cotton and other crops. R They were supervised by an **overseer** (OH • vuhr • SEE • uhr)—a plantation manager.

Reading Check **Explain** Why were so many slaves needed on a plantation?

Picturing **History**

This photo shows businesses along a street in Atlanta, Georgia, around 1860. ***Why did cities such as Atlanta and Columbia, South Carolina, grow as centers of trade?***

City Life and Education

Main Idea **The South was home to several large cities, and education began to grow in the mid-1800s.** U

Reading Connection Imagine living in a town of only a few hundred people. The closest school is miles away—too far to walk—and transportation is not readily accessible. Read on to find out why it was hard for many families to send their children to school in the South.

Although the South was primarily an agricultural region, it was the site of several large cities by the mid-1800s. By 1860 the population of Baltimore had reached 212,000 and the population of New Orleans **exceeded** 165,000. The ten largest cities in the South were either seaports or river ports.

With the coming of the railroad, many other cities began to grow as centers of trade. Among the cities located at the crossroads of the railways were **Columbia,** South Carolina; **Chattanooga,** Tennessee; **Montgomery,** Alabama; Jackson, Mississippi; and **Atlanta,** Georgia. The population of Southern cities included white city dwellers, some enslaved workers, and many of the South's free African Americans.

The cities provided free African Americans with opportunities to form their own communities. African American barbers, carpenters, and small traders offered their services throughout their communities. Free African Americans also founded their own churches and institutions. In New Orleans, many of them were well-educated and prosperous. They used their resources to form an opera company.

Although some free African Americans prospered in the cities, their lives were far from secure. Between 1830 and 1860, Southern states passed laws that limited the rights of free African Americans. Most states would not allow them to migrate from other states. Although spared the horrors of slavery, free African Americans were denied an equal share in economic and political life.

Answers and Additional Support

Picturing **History**

Answer: They were located at the crossroads of railways.

Did You Know?

In the early 1850s, Indiana, Iowa, and Illinois bordered slave states. All three had laws that banned African Americans, free or enslaved, from entering their states.

Education Plantation owners and those who could afford to do so often sent their children to private schools. One of the best known was the academy operated by Moses Waddel in Willington, South Carolina. Students attended six days a week. The Bible and classical literature were stressed, but the courses also included mathematics, religion, Greek, Latin, and public speaking.

In many smaller rural areas, classes met in small schoolhouses or in church buildings. School terms lasted only three to four months. Due to poverty, few books were available for study.

C

During this era, no statewide public school system existed. However, cities such as Charleston, Louisville, and Mobile did establish excellent public schools.

By the mid-1800s, education was growing. Hundreds of public schools were operating in North Carolina by 1860. Even before that, the Kentucky legislature set up a funding system for public schools. Many states in the South also had charity schools. There are schools for students whose parents could not afford to pay.

Although the number of schools and teachers in the South grew, the South lagged behind other areas of the country in literacy, the number of people who can read or write. One reason for this was the geography of the South. Even in the more heavily populated Southern states there were few people per square mile. Virginia and North Carolina had fewer than 15 white inhabitants per square mile. In contrast, Massachusetts had 127 inhabitants per square mile.

It was too great a hardship for many Southern families to send their children great distances to attend school. In addition, many Southerners believed education was a private matter, not a state function; therefore, the state should not spend money on education.

Reading Check **Identify** What Southern city had surpassed 200,000 in population by the year 1860?

History Online
Study Central Need help understanding Southern life in the mid-1800s? Visit ca.hss.glencoe.com and click on Study Central.

Section 2 Review

Reading Summary

Review the Main Ideas

- Many farmers in the South were yeomen who lived on small farms.
- Many plantations were small and had relatively few slaves.
- By the mid-1800s, the number of cities in the South was increasing, and education was growing.

What Did You Learn?

1. List two differences between yeoman and plantation owners.
2. Explain why some free African Americans might own slaves.

Critical Thinking

3. **Compare** Create a chart like the one below and compare the life of a plantation owner to that of a small farmer. CA HI2.

Plantation Owner	Small Farmer

4. **The Big Ideas** Describe the life of free African Americans in Southern cities. CA CS3.
5. **Descriptive Writing** Study the pictures on pages 429 and 430. Write a paragraph explaining what you think the pictures portray about life in the South. CA 8WA2.4
6. **ANALYSIS** **Explain** Write a short paragraph explaining the relationship between the plantation owner and the cotton exchange. Then, discuss which job you would choose. CA HI6.

C Critical Thinking

Analyzing Information
Ask: Do you believe public funds should be spent on education? Why or why not? *(Answers will vary but should include reasons to support students' arguments.)* OL

ASSESS

Resources for page 431

Use these resources to assess student mastery of section content.

- Section Quiz 9–2
- Interactive Tutor Self-Assessment CD-ROM

Reading Check
Answer: Baltimore

History Online
Study Central provides summaries, interactive games, and online graphic organizers to help students review section content.

CLOSE

Connecting **Ask:** Did the information in this chapter change your perceptions about life in the South before the Civil War? If so, explain in a summary. If not, write a summary of what you consider the most important fact presented in this section. OL

SECTION 2 REVIEW ANSWERS

Review questions reinforce content standard 8.7.

1. Yeomen: had smaller farms, no slaves; Plantation owners: had slaves, larger farms, were wealthier
2. Students may say they did so in order to free them.
3. Plantation Owners: had many slaves, grew cotton, lived in debt; Small Farmer: grew different crops, did own farm work
4. could own businesses and join groups but did not enjoy security or many rights
5. Answers should reflect the photographs and section content.
6. ANALYSIS Answers should reflect section content; students should give reasons for their choice.

CHAPTER 9
Section 3, 431–436

FOCUS

BELLRINGER
SKILLBUILDER ACTIVITY

Project **Daily Focus Skills Transparency 9–3** and have students answer the question.

Guide to Reading

Preteaching Vocabulary: Have students write each term on an index card and record the definition of each term as they read the text.

Answers to Graphic: Family life: many couples married; families could be separated; extended family networks provided stability; Culture: African dance, music, and folk stories; Religion: many enslaved people accepted Christianity but also followed African religious practices

Unpacking the Standards

After reading the section, students will be able to:

- Describe the hardships that enslaved African Americans endured.
- Identify elements of the distinct culture that enslaved African Americans created.
- Explain how enslaved African Americans resisted slavery.

Section 3

The Peculiar Institution

History Social Science Standards

US8.7 Students analyze the divergent paths of the American people in the South from 1800 to the mid-1800s and the challenges they faced.

US8.9 Students analyze the early and steady attempts to abolish slavery and to realize the ideals of the Declaration of Independence.

Guide to Reading

Looking Back, Looking Ahead

In Section 2, you learned about the life of Southern whites in the country, as well as about life in Southern cities. In this section, you will learn about slavery and the lives of African Americans in the South.

Focusing on the Main Ideas

- Enslaved African Americans faced many hardships but were able to create family lives, religious beliefs, and a distinct culture. *(page 433)*
- Many enslaved people fought against slavery. *(page 434)*

Meeting People

Nat Turner
Harriet Tubman
Frederick Douglass

Content Vocabulary

spiritual (SPIHR • ih • chuh • wuhl)
slave codes

Academic Vocabulary

constant
communicate

Reading Strategy

Organizing Information Create a chart like the one below to list aspects of African American life in the South.

Way of Life	Aspects
Family Life	
Culture	
Religion	

NATIONAL GEOGRAPHIC **Who & When?**

1820 — 1840 — 1860

1821 Denmark Vesey plots uprising in South Carolina

1831 Nat Turner leads slave revolt

1850s Harriet Tubman helps enslaved people escape

SECTION RESOURCES

Print Material
- Reproducible Lesson Plan 9–3*
- Daily Lesson and Discussion Notes 9–3
- Guided Reading Activity 9–3
- Reading Essentials and Study Guide 9–3
- Active Reading Note-Taking Guide 9–3
- Section Quiz 9–3

Transparencies
- Daily Focus Skills Transparency 9–3
- Section Graphic Organizer Transparency 9–3
- California Standards Practice Transparencies

Technology
- Interactive Tutor Self-Assessment CD-ROM
- Exam*View*® Pro Testmaker CD-ROM
- Presentation Plus! CD-ROM

*Available on TeacherWorks™

US8.7.2 Trace the origins and development of slavery; its effects on black Americans and on the region's political, social, religious, economic, and cultural development; and identify the strategies that were tried to both overturn and preserve it (e.g., through the writings and historical documents on Nat Turner, Denmark Vesey).

Life Under Slavery

R1 **Main Idea** **Enslaved African Americans faced many hardships but were able to create family lives, religious beliefs, and a distinct culture.**

Reading Connection Imagine being taken to a foreign land where you do not speak the language and do not understand the customs. How would you adapt to such a situation? Read on to find out how enslaved Southerners developed family and social ties to cope with their situation.

An American Story

Planters gathered in the bright Savannah sunshine. They were there to bid on a strong slave who could plow their fields. Fear and grief clouded the enslaved man's face because he had been forced to leave his wife and children. Later, he wrote this letter:

C1

> **"My Dear wife I [write] . . . with much regret to inform you that I am Sold to a man by the name of Peterson. . . . Give my love to my father and mother and tell them good Bye for me. And if we Shall not meet in this world, I hope to meet in heaven. My Dear wife for you and my Children my pen cannot Express the [grief] I feel to be parted from you all."**
>
> —as quoted in *The Black Family in Slavery and Freedom, 1750–1925*

C2 **Family Life** Enslaved people faced constant uncertainty and danger. American law in the early 1800s did not protect enslaved families. At any time, a husband or wife could be sold to a different owner, or a slaveholder's death could lead to the breakup of an enslaved family. Although marriage between enslaved people was not recognized by law, many couples did marry. Their marriage ceremonies included the phrase "until death or separation do us part"—recognizing the possibility that their life together might end with the sale of one spouse.

To provide some measure of stability in their lives, enslaved African Americans established a network of relatives and friends, who made up their extended family. If a father or mother were sold away, an aunt, uncle, or close friend could raise the children left behind. Large, close-knit extended families became a vital feature of African American culture.

African American Culture Enslaved African Americans endured their hardships by extending their own culture, fellowship, and community. They fused African and American elements into a new culture.

The growth of the African American population came mainly from children born in the United States. In 1808 Congress had outlawed the slave trade. Although slavery remained legal in the Southern States, no new slaves could enter the United States. By 1860 almost all the enslaved people in the South had been born there.

These native-born African Americans practiced their African customs. They continued to enjoy African music and dance. They passed traditional African folk stories to their children. Some wrapped colored cloths around their heads in the African style. Although a large number of enslaved African Americans accepted Christianity, they often followed the religious beliefs and practices of their African ancestors as well.

African American Christianity For many enslaved African Americans, Christianity became a religion of hope and resistance. They prayed fervently for the day when they would be free from bondage.

R2 The passionate beliefs of the Southern slaves found expression in the **spiritual** (SPIHR • ih • chuh • wuhl), an African American religious folk song. The song "Didn't My Lord Deliver Daniel," for example, refers to the biblical story of Daniel, who was saved from the lions' den.

More Skill Practice

Historical and Social Sciences Analysis Skill **Ask:** How did enslaved people cope with the injustices that they faced? *(They developed their own culture, established extended family networks, and turned to religion as a source of hope and resistance.)* OL CA HI1.

TEACH

R1 Reading Strategy

Scaffolding—Previewing **Ask:** Based on the main idea, what four aspects of slavery will be addressed in this section? *(hardships, family life, African American culture, and African American Christianity)* OL

This READING SKILL was introduced in Chapter 1.

C1 Critical Thinking

Analyzing Primary Sources Have one student read the quotation aloud. **Ask:** What can you say about the man's family and future from this quote? *(He is married and the father of children, and his parents are both alive. He is despondent about being sold and believes he may never see his family again.)* OL CA HR5.

C2 Critical Thinking

Making Inferences Given that marriages between enslaved people were not recognized by law, why do you think many couples chose to marry anyway? *(Students may suggest they wanted to establish family units for raising children or they believed marriages would be recognized by God even if not by the government.)* OL CA HI1.

R2 Reading Strategy

Using Word Parts **Ask:** What shorter word is contained within *spiritual*? *(spirit)* What connection do you see between the two words? *(a spiritual is a sacred song with themes related to the spirit or soul)* OL

R1 Reading Strategy

Academic Vocabulary Ask students to describe the different ways in which they communicate with their friends and family. OL

W Writing Support

Research Reports Writing Encourage students to learn more about spirituals and write a report on what they discover. OL CA 8RWA2.3

R2 Reading Strategy

Using Context Clues
Ask: What is another word for *codes* as used in this term? *(laws)* OL CA 8RW1.3

Reading Check

Answer: as a way for African Americans to communicate secretly and express their beliefs

Resources for page 434

- American Music: Hits Through History, "Joshua Fit the Battle of Jericho"
- Critical Thinking Skills Activity 9

US8.7.2 Trace the origins and development of slavery; its effects on black Americans and on the region's political, social, religious, economic, and cultural development; and identify the strategies that were tried to both overturn and preserve it (e.g., through the writings and historical documents on Nat Turner, Denmark Vesey.)

"Didn't my Lord deliver Daniel, deliver Daniel, deliver Daniel? Didn't my Lord deliver Daniel, And why [not] every man?"

— from *Wade in the Water*

R1 Spirituals provided a way for the enslaved African Americans to **communicate** secretly with one another. The spirituals often reflected the connection African American enslaved people felt to enslaved people who were depicted in the Bible. Passed down through the oral tradition, spirituals helped form an African American culture. They also became one of the best-known forms of American music. W

Reading Check **Explain** How did the African American spiritual develop?

Resisting Slavery

Main Idea **Many enslaved people fought against slavery.**

Reading Connection How do you react when someone treats you unfairly? Read on to find out how enslaved people resisted.

Enslaved people had few legal rights. Between 1830 and 1860, life under slavery became even more difficult because the **slave codes**—the laws in the Southern states that controlled enslaved people—became more severe. R2 In existence since the 1700s, slave codes were written to prevent the event white Southerners dreaded most—the slave rebellion. For this reason slave codes prohibited slaves from assembling in large groups and from leaving their master's property without a written pass.

Primary Sources

Working the Cotton Fields

Solomon Northup was a free black who was kidnapped and sold into slavery. He picked cotton on a Louisiana plantation for 12 years before winning his freedom. His description of picking cotton follows.

> When a new hand, one unaccustomed to the business, is sent for the first time into the field, he is whipped up smartly, and made for that day to pick as fast as he can possibly. At night it is weighed, so that his capability in cotton picking is known. He must bring in the same weight each night following. If it falls short, it is considered evidence that he has been laggard, and a greater or less number of lashes is the penalty. . . . The hands are required to be in the cotton field as soon as it is light in the morning, and, with the exception of ten or fifteen minutes, which is given them at noon to swallow their allowance of cold bacon, they are not permitted to be a moment idle until it is too dark to see, and when the moon is full, they often times labor till the middle of the night. They do not dare to stop even at dinner time, nor return to the quarters, however late it be, until the order to halt is given by the driver. . . .

—from *Twelve Years a Slave* by Solomon Northup

▲ Solomon Northup

DBQ Document-Based Question

Why do you think it seems like Northup's perspective is that of an outsider?

Answers and Additional Support

Primary Sources

Answer: He uses the third person to create a sense of objectivity and to show that he is referring to an entire system.

- How did overseers determine the amount of cotton a new hand would be required to pick each day? *(by forcing new hands to work as quickly as possible on the first day, then requiring them to match this level of productivity)* OL
- What were working conditions like for people who picked cotton? *(work from dawn to dark, only a few minutes for lunch, and no dinner break)* OL

More About...

Living Under Slavery

Enslaved workers reached the fields before the sun came up, and they stayed there until sundown. Planters wanted to keep the slaves busy all the time, which meant long and grueling days in the fields. Enslaved women as well as men were required to do heavy fieldwork. Young children carried buckets of water. By the age of 10, they were considered ready for fieldwork.

Cabins were usually made of small logs, about 10 to 20 feet square. Often, two or three families shared a cabin.

Heavy iron leg shackles were used to punish workers, especially those who tried to run away.

When rented to other masters, enslaved people wore identification tags.

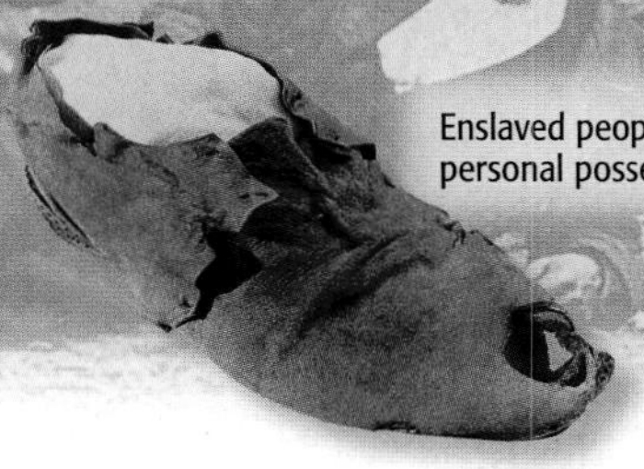

Enslaved people had few personal possessions.

Slave codes also made it a crime to teach enslaved people to read or write. White Southerners believed a slave who did not know how to read and write was less likely to rebel.

Rebellions Some enslaved African Americans did rebel openly against their masters. One was **Nat Turner,** a popular religious leader among his fellow slaves. Turner had taught himself to read and write. In 1831 Turner led a group of followers on a brief, violent rampage in Southhampton County, Virginia, that resulted in the death of at least 55 whites. Nat Turner was hanged, but his rebellion frightened whites and led to more severe slave codes.

Even before the rebellion led by Nat Turner, other enslaved persons had plotted uprisings. In 1800 Gabriel Prosser planned a rebellion to capture Richmond, Virginia, and massacre whites. An informer gave the plot away, and Prosser and 35 others were convicted and executed.

Denmark Vesey, a Charleston, South Carolina, carpenter, who had earlier purchased his freedom, was outraged by the existence of slavery. His reading of the Bible and the Declaration of Independence fueled his hatred of slavery. His 1821 plan for a slave revolt failed when it was betrayed at the last moment by some of his followers.

C Critical Thinking

Determining Cause and Effect **Ask:** Why did Southern slaveholders respond as they did to revolts by enslaved people? *(Students may suggest they feared similar uprisings.)* OL CA HI2.

S Skill Practice

Visual Literacy Have students study the images in the More About feature. Lead a discussion in which students pose questions raised by these images. *(Questions might include: Were all enslaved people given identification numbers, or only those rented to other masters? Who built the cabins that housed enslaved people? If one enslaved person ran away, would members of his or her family be punished?)* AL CA 8LS1.9

R Reading Strategy

Activating Prior Knowledge **Ask:** What ideas in the Declaration of Independence could Vesey have used to support his opposition to slavery? *(idea that all men are created equal and that they have inalienable rights to "life, liberty, and the pursuit of happiness")* BL CA HI3.

Resources for page 435

- Biography Activity 9A
- Biography Activity 9B

More About...

One study of life under slavery analyzed the census of 1850 to determine life expectancy. It found that at birth enslaved people could expect to live 36 years, compared to 40 years for whites.

Did You Know?

Southern whites attempted to wipe out African culture. Slaveholders deliberately mixed Africans of different ethnic groups. By mixing Africans who had different languages and customs, the slaveholders hoped to prevent a sense of ethnic identity from fostering a unified rebellion.

Biography

TEACH

S Skill Practice

Historical and Social Sciences Analysis Skill

Ask: Why was Harriet Tubman unhappy even after she escaped from slavery? *(She was free but the other members of her family were still enslaved.)* BL CA HI1.

W Writing Support

Narrative Writing Have students write a diary entry from the point of view of Tubman as she prepares for another journey to the South. OL CA 8WA2.1

C Critical Thinking

Drawing Conclusions

Discuss the quotation from Harriet Tubman. **Ask:** Who were Tubman's "passengers"? *(enslaved people seeking freedom)* What were her duties as "conductor"? *(guiding enslaved people to freedom)* What emotion does she express here? *(pride)* OL CA HR3.

Biography

US8.9.1 Describe the leaders of the movement (e.g., John Quincy Adams and his proposed constitutional amendment, John Brown and the armed resistance, Harriet Tubman and the Underground Railroad, Benjamin Franklin, Theodore Weld, William Lloyd Garrison, Frederick Douglass).

HARRIET TUBMAN

1820–1913

Born a slave in Maryland, Harriet Tubman worked in plantation fields until she was nearly 30 years old. Then she made her break for freedom, escaping to the North with the help of the Underground Railroad. While jubilant over the success of her escape when she crossed the line from Delaware into Pennsylvania, Tubman's happiness was short-lived. She explained, "I was *free*, but there was no one to welcome me to the land of freedom. . . . [M]y home, after all, was down in Maryland, because my father, my mother, my brothers, my sisters, and friends were there. But I was free and *they should be free!*" S

Settling in Philadelphia, Tubman met many abolitionists who shared her desire to bring Southern slaves to the North. Realizing the risks of being captured, Tubman courageously made 19 trips back into the South during the 1850s to help other enslaved people escape. Altogether she assisted about 70 individuals—including her parents—to escape from slavery.

Tubman did not establish the Underground Railroad, but she certainly became its most famous and successful conductor. Tubman was known as the "Moses of her people" for leading slaves to freedom in the North. Despite huge rewards offered in the South for her capture and arrest, Tubman always managed to elude her enemies. W

During the Civil War, Tubman assisted the Union army as a nurse and a spy, caring for the sick and wounded and making trips behind enemy lines to scout out Confederate troops. Tubman continued to experience discrimination at the end of the war and was never paid for her services in the army. Despite financial difficulties, Tubman opened her home in New York to African Americans journeying North after the war. Many were sick or near starvation, and she fed them, clothed them, and cared for them. In 1896 Tubman opened a center for the sick and needy on land across from her home. Until her death in 1913, Tubman continued to help those in need and continued to support civil and women's rights.

"I was the conductor of the Underground Railroad for eight years, and . . . I never ran my train off the track and I never lost a passenger." C

—Harriet Tubman, from *Women's Voices: Quotations by Women*

Then and Now

Many African Americans relied on Tubman and other abolitionists to survive in the North. If a present-day family moved to a new city, what resources could they use to help them find work, shelter, and other necessities?

436

Answers and Additional Support

Then and Now

Students may suggest agencies of the city, state, and federal governments; relatives and friends living in the area; real estate brokers and newspaper listings to find housing; employment agencies and newspaper listings to find jobs; religious institutions; national organizations that the family belongs to; and neighborhood associations.

Other Forms of Resistance Armed rebellions were rare, however. African Americans in the South knew that they would only lose in an armed uprising. For the most part enslaved people resisted slavery by working slowly or by pretending to be ill. Occasionally resistance took more active forms, such as setting fire to a plantation building or breaking tools. Resistance helped enslaved African Americans endure their lives by striking back at white masters—and perhaps establishing boundaries that white people would respect.

Escaping Slavery Some enslaved African Americans tried to run away to the free states in the North. A few succeeded. **Harriet Tubman** and **Frederick Douglass,** two African American leaders who were born into slavery, gained their freedom when they fled to the North.

Yet for most enslaved people, getting to the North was almost impossible, especially from the Deep South. Most slaves who succeeded in running away escaped from the Upper South. The Underground Railroad—a network of "safe houses" owned by free blacks and whites who opposed slavery—offered assistance to runaway slaves. Some slaves ran away to find relatives on nearby plantations or to escape punishment.

Most runaways were captured and returned to their owners. Discipline was usually severe. The most common punishment for captured runaways was whipping.

Even if an enslaved man or woman escaped to the free states in the North, they were not always safe there. In some Northern communities, fugitive slaves were captured and returned to the South. This prevented many slaves from settling in free states and forced them to escape to Canada, where slavery was banned in 1834.

Reading Check **Summarize** Besides rebellions, what other forms did resistance to slavery take?

History Online
Study Central Need help understanding how African Americans in the South lived? Visit ca.hss.glencoe.com and click on Study Central.

Section 3 Review

Reading Summary

Review the Main Ideas

- Enslaved Southerners developed a culture and religion that had both African and American elements.
- While some enslaved people attempted to rebel openly against slavery, others resisted by running away, refusing to work, or destroying farm tools.

What Did You Learn?

1. Why were extended families vital to African American culture?
2. What was the Underground Railroad?

Critical Thinking

3. **Classify** Re-create the diagram below. In the boxes, briefly explain how the slave codes operated. CA HR3.

Slave Codes	
Education	Assembly

4. **The Big Ideas** Trace the development of the unique elements of African American slave culture in the South. CA HI3.
5. **Summarize** Who were Denmark Vesey and Nat Turner? Write a short paragraph about their efforts against slavery. CA HI1.
6. **Creative Writing** Imagine you are enslaved on a Southern plantation. Write a description of a typical day that you might experience. CA 8WA2.1

SECTION 3 REVIEW ANSWERS

Review questions reinforce content standard US8.7.

1. could care for children if a husband or wife was sold
2. a network of "safe houses" that offered help to runaway slaves
3. Education: crime to teach enslaved people to read or write; Assembly: banned slaves from gathering in large groups, moving without a pass
4. **The Big Ideas** Enslaved people told traditional African folk stories, combined African religious practices with Christian traditions, and developed spirituals.
5. Students should describe Turner and Vesey's revolts and their outcomes.
6. Answers should reflect section content.

Review The Big Idea

Review the Big Idea for this section: "Differences in economic, political, and social beliefs and practices can lead to division within a nation and have lasting consequences." **Ask:** How would Southerners react to Northerners who helped enslaved people escape? *(anger; frustration)* OL

ASSESS

Resources for page 436

Use these resources to assess student mastery of section content.

Section Quiz 9–3

Interactive Tutor Self-Assessment CD-ROM

Reading Check

Answer: working slowly, pretending to be ill, escaping

History Online

Study Central provides summaries, interactive games, and online graphic organizers to help students review section content.

CLOSE

Drawing Conclusions Ask: What were the short-term and long-term consequences of rebellions by enslaved people? *(short term: harsher slave codes; long term: signaling to both whites and African Americans that many viewed slavery as unjust)* OL CA HI3.

Analyzing Primary Sources

FOCUS

History–Social Science Standards

The following standard is covered on pages 438–439.

US8.7 Students analyze the divergent paths of the American people in the South from 1800 to the mid-1800s and the challenges they faced.

TEACH

R Reading Strategy

Reading Primary Sources
Ask: What is the tone of Whitney's letter? How does he feel about the future? *(pleased by getting the patent and by hearing his machine praised; he also seems preoccupied and excited about his upcoming trip to the South; optimistic about the future)* OL

C Critical Thinking

Making Inferences Ask: What do you think Whitney will do when he goes to the South? *(Students should infer that he is going to the South to try to sell cotton gins to plantation owners.)* OL CA HR3.

Answers and Additional Support

Analyzing Primary Sources

US8.7 Analyze the divergent paths of the American people in the South from 1800 to the mid-1800s and the challenges they faced.

Cotton and Slavery in the South

Industry boomed in the North, but agriculture reigned in the South. Cotton was the South's most important crop. The production of cotton depended on a large supply of cheap labor. In the South, enslaved African Americans supplied that labor.

Read the passages on pages 438 and 439 and answer the questions that follow.

Many people copied Eli Whitney's cotton gin and ignored his patent because the gin was so easy to make. ▶

Reader's Dictionary

patent: a document that gives the inventor the sole legal right to an invention for a period of time

miry (MYR • ee)**:** muddy

pigsty: enclosed area where pigs live

speculator (SPEH • kyuh • LAY • tuhr)**:** an individual who buys or sells land in hopes of making a profit

A New Invention

Eli Whitney had invented a workable cotton gin by 1793. One of his next steps was to apply for a patent for the machine. In the following letter, Whitney tells his family, who live in Westboro, Massachusetts, about the progress he is making and his plans.

March 30, 1794

R It is with no small satisfaction that I have in my power to inform you I am in good health. I have just returned from Philadelphia. My business there was to lodge a Model of my machine and receive a **Patent** for it. I accomplished everything agreeable to my wishes. I had the satisfaction to hear it declared by a number of the first men in America that my machine is the most perfect & the most valuable invention that has ever appeared in this Country. I have received my Patent. . . .

I wish very much to see you before I go. But should I come to Westboro' now I must neglect my business so much as to lose several Hundred Dollars. If you come [here] I shall be able to show you my machine. I have six of them nearly complete which I expect to carry to the Southward with me. I shall leave this place for Georgia in about twelve or fourteen days at the farthest. . . . Though I have as yet expended much more money than profits of the machine have been heretofore, and am at present a little pressed for money, I am by no means in the least discouraged. And I shall probably gain some honour as well as some profit by the Invention. . . . C

—from *The World of Eli Whitney*

EXTENDING THE CONTENT

The Inspiration for *Uncle Tom's Cabin* Josiah Henson's 1849 autobiography inspired the character of Uncle Tom in *Uncle Tom's Cabin,* Harriet Beecher Stowe's best-selling antislavery novel. Born in Maryland in 1789, Henson was sold three times before he was 18. He managed to save $350 to buy his freedom, but when he gave the money to his master, he was told that the price had gone up to $1,000. Henson escaped with his wife and four children to Canada, where he became a preacher, abolitionist, farmer, and teacher. He lived to the age of 94.

The Living Conditions of Enslaved Persons

Josiah Henson was an enslaved person. He escaped and later wrote about his life. In this excerpt, he describes the area where the slaves lived.

C1 We lodged in log huts, and on the bare ground. Wooden floors were an unknown luxury. In a single room were huddled, like cattle, ten or a dozen persons, men, women, and children. . . . Our beds were collections of straw and old rags, thrown down in the corners and boxed in with boards; a single blanket the only covering. . . . The wind whistled and the rain and snow blew in through the cracks, and the damp earth soaked in the moisture till the floor was **miry** as a **pigsty.**

—from *Uncle Tom's Story of His Life. An Autobiography of the Rev. Josiah Henson*

▲ Slave quarters were usually gathered together in one area of a plantation.

News From the South

The American Anti-Slavery Society published American Slavery As It Is *by Sarah and Angelina Grimké and Angelina's husband Theodore Weld in 1839. For this book, Weld gathered newspaper ads from Southern papers to show the effects of slavery.*

From the "Richmond (Va.) Compiler," Sept. 8, 1837. Ranaway from the subscriber, Ben. He ran off without any known cause, and *I suppose he is aiming to go to his wife, who was carried from the neighborhood last winter.*

JOHN HUNT.

From the "Jackson (Tenn.) Telegraph," Sept. 14, 1838. Committed to the jail of Madison county, a negro woman, who calls her name Fanny, and says she belongs to William Miller, of Mobile. She formerly belonged to John Givins, of this county, who now owns *several of her children.* C2

DAVID SHROPSHIRE, Jailor.

From the "Richmond (Va.) Enquirer," Feb. 20, 1838. Stop the Runaway!!!—$25 Reward. Ranaway from the Eagle Tavern, a negro fellow, named Nat. He is no doubt attempting to *follow his wife, who was lately sold to a* ***speculator*** named Redmond. The above reward will be paid by Mrs. Lucy M. Downman, of Sussex county, Va.

DBQ Document-Based Questions

A New Invention

1. What has Whitney recently obtained?
2. How successful has Whitney been in making money from the cotton gin?

The Living Conditions of Enslaved Persons

3. How weatherproof are the cabins? Why do you think that?

News From the South

4. According to the ads, why do slaves run away?

Read to Write

5. Imagine that you are living in the early 1800s. You know nothing about slavery. Then you read "The Living Conditions of Enslaved Persons" and "News from the South." Write an editorial to your local newspaper about slavery. What do you think about the fact that there is slavery in the United States? CA 8WS1.1

C1 Critical Thinking

Analyzing Primary Sources Ask: What words and phrases in Henson's account reveal his point of view on life in the slave cabins? *(He says enslaved people lived "like cattle" and compares the cabin to "a pigsty." These details convey his anger.)* OL CA HR5.

C2 Critical Thinking

Making Inferences Ask: What situation is common to all the enslaved people described in these ads? *(All are separated from members of their families.)* Why would Weld include examples like this in his book? *(to try to gain sympathy for enslaved people by showing how slavery hurt families)* OL CA HR3.

Resources for page 439

- Analysis Skills Activity 9
- Primary Source Reading 9

ASSESS

Have students answer the Document-Based Questions.

CLOSE

Summarizing Have students use these quotations and information in the text to explain why cotton growing and slavery spread in the South. OL

DBQ Document-Based Questions

1. a patent for the cotton gin
2. Up to the time of the letter, not very successful—he has had more expenses than income.
3. not very; because wind, snow, and rain come in through cracks in the wall
4. These examples are all cases of enslaved persons apparently trying to rejoin families.
5. Students' editorials will vary but should be supported by reasons and reflect correct grammar and usage.

Resources for pages 440–441

Use these resources to review, assess, or reteach the chapter.

- Active Reading Note-Taking Guide, Chapter 9
- Chapter 9 Reading Essentials and Study Guide
- Chapter 9 Tests, Forms A and B
- Standards Assessment, Forms A and B
- California Standards Practice Workbook
- Succeeding on the California History–Social Science Standards CD-ROM
- MindJogger Videoquiz
- Interactive Tutor Self-Assessment CD-ROM

Review Content Vocabulary

1. b
2. a
3. f
4. d

Sentences using the terms *cotton gin* and *tenant farmers* should include accurate definitions and use correct grammar.

Review the Main Ideas

5. dramatically increased it
6. agriculture was very profitable, lack of capital to invest in businesses, small market for manufactured goods
7. to watch over enslaved workers and supervise buildings on the plantation
8. No statewide public school system existed; many white Southerners lived far from schools; some whites thought the government should not be involved in education. African Americans were banned from learning to read and write.
9. Some were captured and returned to the South.
10. to prevent slave rebellions and to control slaves

Critical Thinking

11. They merged African and American elements into a new culture, practiced African music and dance, passed African folk stories and proverbs on to their children, and followed traditional religious beliefs.
12. Cotton was in high demand, and with the cotton gin, harvests could be processed quickly.
13. Religion provided a source of hope and resistance.
14. Students should explain that their lives varied depending on whether they lived on plantations or were yeomen or tenant farmers.

Chapter 9 Assessment

Standard US8.7

Review Content Vocabulary

Write the vocabulary word that best completes each sentence. Write a sentence for each word not used.

a. yeomen
b. capital
c. cotton gin
d. slave codes
e. tenant farmers
f. spiritual

1. The South lacked the ___ needed to develop industries.
2. ___ farmers owned land and lived mostly in the Upper South.
3. A(n) ___ is an African religious folk song.
4. The South's ___ made it difficult for enslaved African Americans to gain an education.

Review the Main Ideas

Section 1 • Southern Cotton Kingdom

5. How did the cotton gin affect cotton production?
6. Why was there little industry in the South?

Section 2 • Life in the South

7. What were the main duties of plantation wives?
8. What obstacles existed to gaining an education in the South?

Section 3 • The Peculiar Institution

9. Why were escaped slaves not always safe in the North?
10. What was the purpose of the slave codes?

Critical Thinking

11. **Analyze** How did enslaved African Americans hold on to their African customs? CA HI1.
12. **Conclude** Why was the production of cotton so lucrative in the South? CA HI6.
13. **Explain** How did African Christianity help slaves cope with their situation? CA HI2.
14. **Summarize** What was life like for most whites in the South? CA HI1.

Geography Skills

The map shows Southern cities with more than 10,000 people in 1850. Study the map and answer the following questions. CA CS3.

NATIONAL GEOGRAPHIC **Largest Southern Cities, 1850**

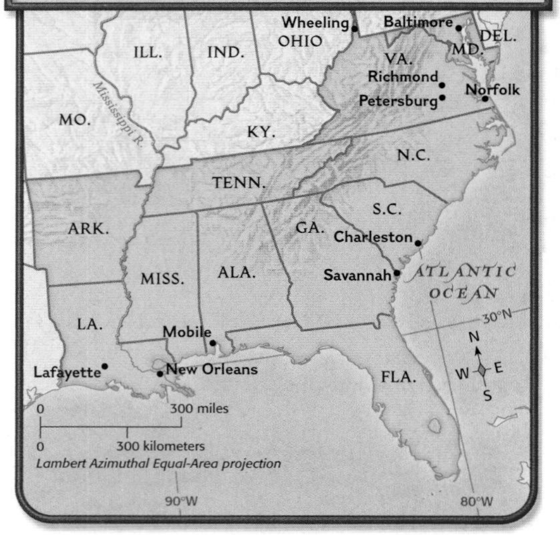

15. **Location** Which state had four of the South's major cities?
16. **Region** Which of the major cities shown were in the Deep South?
17. **Human-Environment Interaction** What do the locations of many of the Southern cities have in common? Why is that significant?

History Online

Self-Check Quiz Visit ca.hss.glencoe.com to prepare for the Chapter 9 test.

Read to Write

18. **The Big Ideas** **Expository Writing** Use the Internet or library resources to identify arguments Southerners used to defend slavery. Write a short paper in which you explain why these arguments may have found support in the South. CA 8WA2.3

19. **Narrative Writing** Imagine that you are a slave who has been sold away from your family to another plantation. Write a letter to your family telling them how you feel about your separation. CA 8WA2.1

20. **Using Your FOLDABLES** Use the information you created in your foldable to create a summary of the chapter. In your summary, be sure to cover the main ideas and events that were discussed. CA 8RC1.0

Using Academic Vocabulary

Read the following sentences. Then, in your own words, write the meaning of the underlined academic vocabulary word.

21. The doctor's patients were predominantly elderly.

22. The estimate noted that the cost was not to exceed $75.

Building Citizenship

23. **Explain** Choose an issue you think is important to your community or the nation today. Explain why you think it is important and how you would take steps to resolve that issue. Compare your solutions with steps government officials are taking to address the issue. CA 8WS1.1

Reviewing Skills

24. Review READING SKILL **Asking Questions** Using your local newspaper or an Internet news site, find an article about human rights. Write questions about any elements of the story you do not understand. Then describe how you could get your questions answered. CA 8RC2.0

25. Review ANALYSIS SKILL **Inferring** Read the following quote, then identify the region you think the speaker might be from and explain your answer:

"We are an agricultural people. . . . We have no cities—we don't want them. . . . We want no manufactures: we desire no trading, no mechanical or manufacturing classes. As long as we have our rice, our sugar, our tobacco, and our cotton, we can command wealth to purchase all we want." CA HR5

Standards Practice

Select the best answer for each of the following questions.

26 **The economy of the Deep South was based on**

A growing cotton.
B growing tobacco.
C manufacturing.
D growing vegetables.

27 **The white supervisor of enslaved workers on a plantation was known as a(n)**

A blacksmith.
B yeoman.
C overseer.
D tenant.

28 **The Southern laws that controlled enslaved people were called**

A spirituals.
B overseers.
C credits.
D slave codes.

CHAPTER 9 Assessment

Building Citizenship

23. Answers will vary but should indicate why the issue is important and how the student proposes to address it.

Reviewing Skills

24. Review READING SKILL Questions will vary but should relate directly to passages in the article that the student seeks to clarify.

25. Review ANALYSIS SKILL Students should identify the quote as coming from a Southerner because some Southern leaders did not want industry.

Standards Practice

26. A
27. C
28. D

Bonus Question

Ask: What historical American document inspired Denmark Vesey to plan a rebellion against slave owners? *(the Declaration of Independence)* OL

History Online

Have students visit the Web site at ca.hss.glencoe.com to review Chapter 9 and take the **Self-Check Quiz.**

Geography Skills

15. Virginia
16. Savannah, Charleston, Mobile, New Orleans, and Lafayette.
17. on the coast; centers of trade

Read to Write

18. **The Big Ideas** Answers will vary, but students should quote the arguments and analyze reasons for their support by Southerners.

19. Students' letters might reflect anger and sorrow at the separation.

20. Using Your FOLDABLES Summaries will vary but should refer to the three main topics in the chapter: the Southern cotton kingdom, daily life in the South, and life under slavery.

Using Academic Vocabulary

21. overwhelmingly
22. go over

Chapter 10 Planning Guide

SECTION RESOURCES

Main Ideas	Print Materials	Technology Resources
Section 1 **Jacksonian Democracy** 1. Adams and Jackson introduced new ways of campaigning in the elections of 1824 and 1828. 2. The United States's political system changed under Andrew Jackson, becoming more democratic. 3. The fight over tariffs divided the nation and raised the question of states' rights versus the rights of the federal government.	• Reproducible Lesson Plan 10–1* • Daily Lesson and Discussion Notes 10–1 • Active Reading Note-Taking Guide 10–1 • Reading Essentials and Study Guide 10–1 • Guided Reading Activity 10–1 • Section Quiz 10–1	Daily Focus Skills Transparency 10–1 Section Graphic Organizer Transparency 10–1 California Standards Practice Transparecies Interactive Tutor Self-Assessment CD-ROM Exam*View*® Pro Testmaker CD-ROM Presentation Plus! CD-ROM
Section 2 **The Removal of Native Americans** 1. As settlements spread westward, many Native Americans were forced off their lands. 2. Some groups of Native Americans attempted to resist relocation. Most were eventually taken from their lands by force.	• Reproducible Lesson Plan 10–2* • Daily Lesson and Discussion Notes 10–2 • Active Reading Note-Taking Guide 10–2 • Reading Essentials and Study Guide 10–2 • Guided Reading Activity 10–2 • Section Quiz 10–2	Daily Focus Skills Transparency 10–2 Section Graphic Organizer Transparency 10–2 California Standards Practice Transparecies Interactive Tutor Self-Assessment CD-ROM Exam*View*® Pro Testmaker CD-ROM Presentation Plus! CD-ROM
Section 3 **Jackson and the Bank** 1. President Jackson forced the National Bank to close, and the Panic of 1837 caused economic problems that split the Democratic Party. 2. After Harrison's death, Tyler took the presidency in a direction opposed to the Whigs' goals and the Whigs lost power after 1844.	• Reproducible Lesson Plan 10–3* • Daily Lesson and Discussion Notes 10–3 • Active Reading Note-Taking Guide 10–3 • Reading Essentials and Study Guide 10–3 • Guided Reading Activity 10–3 • Section Quiz 10–3	Daily Focus Skills Transparency 10–3 Section Graphic Organizer Transparency 10–3 California Standards Practice Transparecies Interactive Tutor Self-Assessment CD-ROM Exam*View*® Pro Testmaker CD-ROM Presentation Plus! CD-ROM Vocabulary PuzzleMaker CD-ROM

PACING YOUR LESSONS

Chapter Introduction	Section 1	Section 2	Section 3	Chapter Assessment
½ Day	2 Days	2 Days	1 Day	½ Day

0:00 **OUT OF TIME?** Assign the Chapter 10 ***Reading Essentials and Study Guide***

*Available on TeacherWorks™

Standards-Based Lesson Plan

History–Social Science Standards Covered in Chapter 10

The standards covered in the chapter are listed below. Use the accompanying activity as you teach the chapter to ensure student mastery of these standards. This activity can be used in combination with the program's print and technology assessment materials.

Standard	Section 1	Section 2	Section 3
US8.8 Students analyze the divergent paths of the American people in the West from 1800 to the mid-1800s and the challenges they faced.	✔	✔	✔
US8.8.1 Discuss the election of Andrew Jackson as president in 1828, the importance of Jacksonian democracy, and his actions as president (e.g., the spoils system, veto of the National bank, policy of Indian removal, opposition to the Supreme Court).	✔		✔
US8.8.2 Describe the purpose, challenges, and economic incentives associated with westward expansion, including the concept of Manifest Destiny (e.g, the Lewis and Clark expedition, accounts of the removal of Indians, the Cherokees' "Trail of Tears," settlement of the Great Plains) and the territorial acquisitions that spanned numerous decades.		✔	

Cumulative Standards-Assessment Activity

The Cumulative Standards-Assessment Activity will help students organize and learn the important information from the chapter. Begin teaching the chapter with this activity, and have students complete it as they read the chapter.

Creating a Main Idea and Supporting Details Chart

Purpose Reviewing how to locate main ideas throughout the chapter will help students continue to refine their reading skills. This type of organizer aids students in identifying main ideas of sections and the supporting details. It helps them develop the skill of knowing what is important and the facts that support those key points. Students can apply their skill in identifying main ideas and supporting details not only in social studies but in many other academic disciplines.

Introduction to Main Ideas and Supporting Details

1. Review with students how to identify main ideas and supporting details. Identify the main idea from a section in the previous chapter, and ask volunteers to name details that support it. Ask them to name details, and challenge the class to determine if those facts do indeed support the main idea or are extraneous to it.
2. Ask students to copy this chart into their notebooks:

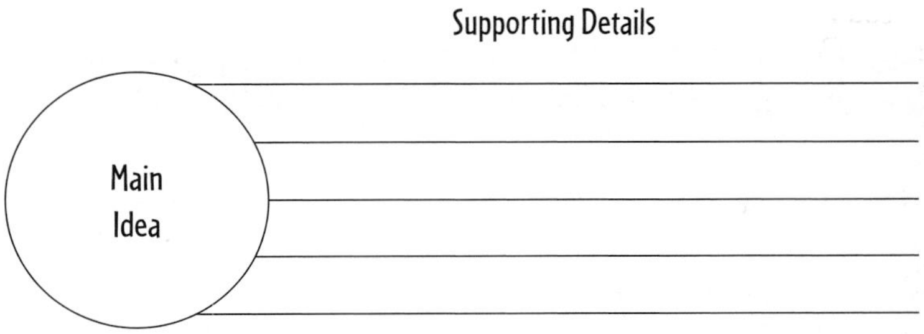

As students read each section, have them complete the charts for each main idea. Tell them to create as many charts as they need to cover all the main ideas in the chapter.

3. As part of your chapter review, have students share their charts. Encourage them to use their charts as study aids.

Chapter 10 Resources

READING SUPPORT

- Content Vocabulary Activity 10
- Academic Vocabulary Activity 10
- Reading Skills Activity 10
- American Literature Reading 10
- Biography Activities 10A, 10B
- Chapter 10 Active Reading Note-Taking Guide
- Chapter 10 Guided Reading Activities
- Chapter 10 Reading Essentials and Study Guide
- Glencoe Literature Library
- Glencoe Video Program
- Vocabulary PuzzleMaker CD-ROM
- Interactive Graphic Organizers CD-ROM
- American History Primary Source Document Library CD-ROM

CRITICAL THINKING

- Critical Thinking Skills Activity 10
- Primary Source Reading 10
- Cause-and-Effect Transparency 10, Strategy, and Activity
- Presentation Plus CD-ROM

UNIVERSAL ACCESS

- Universal Access Activity 10
- Then and Now Transparencies 10A–10B, Strategy, and Activity
- Graphic Novel Activity 10
- School-to-Home Connection Activities 10A–10D
- English Learner Handbook Chapter 10 Activities
- Universal Access for the American History Classroom
- Moments in Time
- American Art and Architecture Transparencies, Strategies, and Activities
- American Art Prints
- American Music Cultural Traditions
- American Music Hits Through History
- StudentWorks Plus CD-ROM

SKILL PRACTICE

- Map Overlay Transparency 10, Strategy, and Activity
- Analysis Skills Activity 10
- Time Line Activity 10
- Geography and History Activity 10
- Economics and History Activity 10
- Chart, Graph, and Map Skills Activity 10
- Political Cartoon Activity 10
- Supreme Court Case Study 10
- In-Text Map Transparency 10, Strategy, and Activity
- Step Into American History Activity 10
- Citizenship and Service Learning Activity 10
- Outline Map Resource Book
- MindJogger Plus Videoquiz

WRITING SUPPORT

- Writing Activity 10
- Language Arts Activity 10
- Writer's Guidebook
- Middle School Writing Process Transparencies

ASSESSMENT

GLENCOE'S ASSESSMENT ADVANTAGE

- Chapter 10 Section Quizzes
- Chapter 10 Tests, Forms A and B
- California Standards Assessment, Forms A and B
- Cumulative Assessment Activity US8.8
- California Standards Practice Workbook
- Succeeding on the California History–Social Science Standards CD-ROM
- Exam*View*® Pro Testmaker CD-ROM
- Interactive Tutor Self-Assessment CD-ROM

CD-ROM · DVD · Print Material · Poster · Transparency · Music Program · Videocassette · Glencoe Literature Library

Chapter 10 Resources

TECHNOLOGY

- StudentWorks Plus CD-ROM
- TeacherWorks Plus CD-ROM
- Exam*View*® Pro Testmaker CD-ROM
- Interactive Tutor Self-Assessment CD-ROM
- Presentation Plus! CD-ROM
- Succeeding on the California History–Social Science Standards CD-ROM
- Vocabulary PuzzleMaker CD-ROM
- Interactive Graphic Organizers CD-ROM
- Interactive Time Line CD-ROM
- American History Primary Source Document Library CD-ROM
- MindJogger Plus Videoquiz
- American Music Cultural Traditions
- American Music Hits Through History
- Glencoe Video Program
- Professional Development in Middle School Social Studies Series
- Teaching American History With *Discovering Our Past: The American Journey to World War I*

SPANISH RESOURCES

- Spanish Activities and Assessment
  - Spanish Content Vocabulary Activities
  - Spanish Guided Reading Activities
  - Spanish Quizzes and Tests
  - Spanish California Standards Assessment
- Spanish Reading Essentials and Study Guide
- Spanish School-to-Home Connection
- Spanish Declaration of Independence and U.S. Constitution

TRANSPARENCIES

- California Standards Practice Transparencies
- Daily Focus Skills Transparencies
- Section Graphic Organizer Transparencies
- In-Text Map Transparencies
- Map Overlay Transparencies
- Cause-and-Effect Transparencies
- Then and Now Transparencies
- American Art and Architecture Transparencies
- Middle School Writing Process Transparencies

TEACHER PLANNING

- Daily Lesson and Discussion Notes
- English Learner Handbook
- Guide to Daily Intervention
- *Discovering Our Past: The American Journey to World War I* Reading and Study Skills Foldables
- Reading Strategies and Activities for the Social Studies Classroom
- Chapter 10 Reproducible Lesson Plans (correlated to California History–Social Science Standards)
- Universal Access for the American History Classroom
- NGS U.S. Desk Map
- NGS U.S. Atlas

PROFESSIONAL DEVELOPMENT

- Building Academic Vocabulary
- Strategies for Success
- Research-Based Strategies Used to Develop *Discovering Our Past: The American Journey to World War I*
- Character Education in the Middle School Classroom
- The Living Constitution
- Professional Development in Middle School Social Studies Video Series
- Teaching American History With *Discovering Our Past: The American Journey to World War I*

MASTERING THE STANDARDS

The content and assessment in the Student Edition, Teacher Wraparound Edition, teacher planning materials, and the print and technology products are all standards-based. The use of these products during instruction leads to mastery of the standards.

PRACTICE
- California Standards Practice Workbook
- California Standards Practice Transparencies
- Interactive Time Line CD-ROM
- School-to-Home Connection

BENCHMARK ASSESSMENT
- California Standards Assessment
- Exam*View*® Pro Testmaker CD-ROM
- Succeeding on the California History–Social Science Standards CD-ROM

REMEDIATION
- California Guide to Daily Intervention
- Interactive Tutor Self-Assessment CD-ROM
- Exam*View*® Pro Testmaker CD-ROM
- California Standards Practice Workbook
- Reading Essentials and Study Guide

Additional Resources

NATIONAL GEOGRAPHIC TEACHER'S CORNER

Index to National Geographic Magazine:

The following articles relate to this chapter:

- "The Way West," by John G. Mitchell, September 2000.
- "The Cherokee," by Geoffrey Norman, May 1995.
- "Powwow," by Michael Parfit, June 1994.
- "The Cruelest Commerce: African Slave Trade," by Colin Palmer, September 1992.
- "Philadelphia's African Americans," by Ronald L. Freeman, August 1990.

National Geographic Society Products

To order the following, call National Geographic at 1-800-368-2728

- *GeoKit: Westward Movement* (Kit)
- *The West That Was* (Video)
- *United States/Territorial Growth* (Map)
- *National Geographic Desk Reference* (Book)

NGS ONLINE

Access National Geographics' new dynamic MapMachine Web site and other geography resources at:

www.nationalgeographic.com

www.nationalgeographic.com/maps

A&E HOME VIDEO. Biography® THE HISTORY CHANNEL.

The following videotape programs are available from Glencoe as supplements to Chapter 10.

- **Andrew Jackson: A Man for the People (ISBN 1-56501-647-5)**

To order, call Glencoe at 1-800-334-7344. To find classroom resources to accompany many of these videos, check the following home pages:

A&E Television: www.aetv.com
The History Channel: www.historychannel.com

MOMENTS IN TIME DBQ

The following resource can help you teach the content of this chapter.

Unit 2 Territorial Expansion (1834–1859)

History Online

Use our Web site for additional resources. All essential content is covered in the Student Edition.

You and your students can visit ca.hss.glencoe.com, the Web site companion to *Discovering Our Past: The American Journey to World War I*. This innovative integration of electronic and print media offers your students a wealth of opportunities. The student text directs students to the Web site for the following options:

- Chapter Overviews
- Self-Check Quizzes
- Study Central™
- Student Web Activities
- Textbook Updates
- Multi-Language Glossaries

Answers to the student Web activities are provided for you in the Web Activity Lesson Plans. Additional Web resources and ePuzzles and games are also available.

FOLDABLES™ Study Organizer

Dinah Zike's Foldables

Foldables are three-dimensional, interactive graphic organizers that help students practice basic writing skills, review key vocabulary terms, and identify main ideas. Every chapter contains a foldable activity, with additional chapter activities found in the Reading and Study Skills Foldables booklet.

Chapter 10 Resources

Reading List Generator CD-ROM

GLENCOE BOOKLINK

The Glencoe BookLink CD-ROM is a database that allows you to search more than 15,000 titles to create a customized reading list for your students.

- Reading lists can be organized by students' reading level, author, genre, theme, or area of interest.
- The database provides Degrees of Reading Power™ (DRP) and Lexile™ readability scores for all selections.
- A brief summary of each selection is included.

Reading level suggestions for this chapter:

For students at a Grade 6 reading level:

- ***The Cherokee Nation: Life Before the Tears,*** by Madeleine Meyers

For students at a Grade 7 reading level:

- ***The Seminoles,*** by Virginia Sneve

For students at a Grade 8 reading level:

- ***Andrew Jackson: 7th President of the United States,*** by Rebecca Stefoff

READING SUPPORT FROM JAMESTOWN EDUCATION

- *Timed Readings Plus in Social Studies* helps students increase their reading rate and fluency while maintaining comprehension. The 400-word passages are similar to those found on state and national assessments.
- *Reading in the Content Areas: Social Studies* concentrates on six essential reading skills that help students better comprehend what they read. The book includes 754 high-interest nonfiction passages written at increasing levels of difficulty.
- *Reading Fluency* helps students read smoothly, accurately, and expressively.
- *Jamestown's Reading Improvement,* by renowned reading expert Edward Fry, focuses on helping build your students' comprehension, vocabulary, and skimming and scanning skills.
- *Critical Reading Series* provides high-interest books, each written at three reading levels.

To order these products, call Glencoe at 1-800-334-7344.

KEY for Using the Teacher Wraparound Edition

Use this key to help you identify the different types of prompts found in the Teacher Wraparound Edition.

R **Reading Strategies** activities help you teach reading skills and vocabulary.

C **Critical Thinking** strategies help students apply and extend what they have learned.

U **Universal Access** activities provide differentiated instruction for students learning to speak English, along with suggestions for teaching various types of learners.

S **Skill Practice** strategies help students practice historical analysis and geography skills.

W **Writing Support** activities provide writing opportunities to help students comprehend the text.

Teaching strategies and activities have been coded for ability level appropriateness.

AL Activities for students working above grade level
OL Activities for students working on grade level
BL Activities for students working below grade level
EL Activities for English Learners

FOCUS

History–Social Science Standards

In this chapter, the following standard will be covered:

US8.8 Students analyze the divergent paths of the American people in the West from 1800 to the mid-1800s and the challenges they faced.

More About the Photo

The White House had a troubled beginning. In 1800, when John and Abigail Adams moved in, the house was not yet completed. By 1803, Thomas Jefferson had to repair the ceiling of the East Room, which had been destroyed by a leaking roof. And, of course, the building was burned by the British in 1814.

Chapter 10

The Age of Jackson

▼ The White House, Washington, D.C.

NATIONAL GEOGRAPHIC **Who & When?**

1825 | 1835 | 1845

1828 Andrew Jackson elected president

1838 Cherokee begin Trail of Tears

1841 President William Henry Harrison dies in office

TEACH

The Big Ideas

As you begin teaching each section, use these questions and activities to focus on the Big Ideas.

Section 1

Jacksonian Democracy

Essential Question: Ask students to name a major event of their lifetime and explain how it has shaped today's government. *(Students may mention the terrorist attacks of September 11, 2001, which moved the government to fight terrorism.)* Tell students that this section describes the changes Andrew Jackson brought to the U.S. political system. **OL**

Section 2

The Removal of Native Americans

Essential Question: Do you think Native Americans are better off today than they were in the 1830s? Explain your answer. *(Students may take either position, arguing that Native Americans would be happier if they could live on their traditional lands or that they have adapted to modern life while maintaining the traditions that they can.)* Explain that in this section, students will learn how some Native American groups were moved from one part of the country to another. **AL**

History Online

Chapter Overview Visit ca.hss.glencoe.com for a preview of Chapter 10.

The Big Ideas

Section 1

Jacksonian Democracy

Political ideas and major events shape how people form governments. President Andrew Jackson brought many changes to the American political system.

Section 2

The Removal of Native Americans

Differences in economic, political, and social beliefs and practices can lead to division within a nation and have lasting consequences. Many Native Americans were forced off their lands in the Southeast.

Section 3

Jackson and the Bank

Differences in economic, political, and social beliefs and practices can lead to division within a nation and have lasting consequences. Economic issues had a strong effect on politics and government in the mid-1800s.

View the Chapter 10 video in the Glencoe Video Program.

FOLDABLES™ Study Organizer

Evaluating Information Make this foldable to help you ask and answer questions about the Jackson era.

Step 1 Fold a sheet of paper in half from side to side, leaving a $\frac{1}{2}$-inch tab along the side.

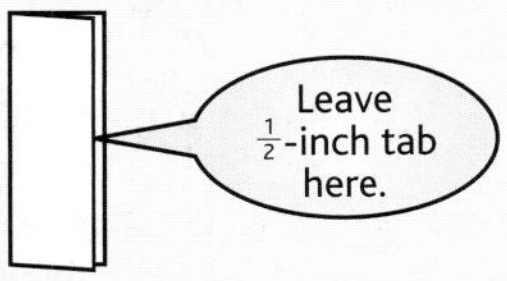

Step 2 Turn the paper and fold it into fourths.

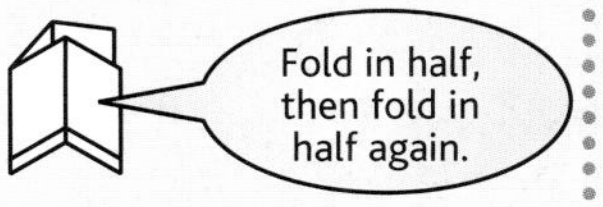

Step 3 Unfold and cut up along the three fold lines.

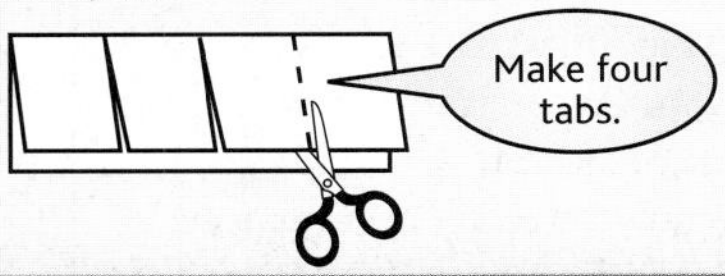

Step 4 Label your foldable as shown.

Reading and Writing
As you read, ask yourself "who" Andrew Jackson was, "what" he did, "when" he did it, and "why" it happened. Write your thoughts and facts under each appropriate tab.

INTRODUCING CHAPTER 10

Section 3

Jackson and the Bank

Essential Question: Which economic, political, and social beliefs and practices of today do you think are the most divisive? Will they have long-lasting consequences for our nation? Why? *(Answers will vary, but students should explain why the beliefs and practices they identify are divisive and how they affect the nation, both now and in the future.)* Tell students that in this chapter they will learn about the economic issues that affected politics and government in the mid-1800s. **OL**

History Online

Go to ca.hss.glencoe.com for student activities, lesson plans, and links to additional Web resources about the age of Jackson.

FOLDABLES™ Study Organizer

Dinah Zike's Foldables

Purpose Have students use their foldables to write questions about Andrew Jackson, the Native American removals, and other key events and people covered in this chapter. Have students exchange their quizzes with a partner and answer the questions. **OL**

Why It's Important

Question and Answer Relationships Finding answers to the questions they formulate as they read requires students to read actively. First, they need to process the information they read to generate questions. Then they need to pay attention to the text to find the answers to their questions or to determine if they must search for answers elsewhere. Determining where to find that information builds critical thinking and research skills. By promoting active reading, this skill helps students build comprehension.

1 Learn It!

Model other questions and answers using the sample passage. **Ask:** Where did the African Americans the Seminole joined with come from? *(The text states that they had run away from slavery.)* Why did the Seminole and African Americans retreat back into the forests and swamps? *(Readers can infer that doing so made it hard for soldiers to pursue them.)* Remind students to use the common question words *who*, *what*, *when*, *where*, *why*, and *how* as they formulate their questions. OL

Chapter 10 Get Ready to Read

READING SKILL

Question-and-Answer Relationships

1 Learn It!

Knowing how to find answers to questions will help you on reviews and tests. Some answers can be found in the textbook, while other answers require you to go beyond the text. These answers might be based on knowledge you already have or things you have personally experienced.

How were the Seminole able to resist removal?

They joined forces with a group of African Americans and used guerrilla tactics.

This answer comes directly from the text.

> **The Seminole people of Florida were the only Native Americans who successfully resisted their removal. . . . The Seminole decided to go to war against the United States instead.**
>
> **In 1835 the Seminole joined forces with a group of African Americans who had run away to escape slavery. . . . They used guerrilla tactics (guh • RIH • luh), making surprise attacks and then retreating back into the forests and swamps.**
>
> —*from page 455*

What are guerrilla tactics? This answer is not directly stated. You need to rely on information you already know or draw conclusions based on how this term is used in the text.

Reading Tip

As you read, keep track of questions you answer in the chapter. This will help you remember what you have read.

444

READING STRATEGY — ACTIVATING PRIOR KNOWLEDGE

Point out that students can draw on knowledge they already possess to answer some of the questions they raise. For instance, the text passage on this page mentions the guerrilla tactics used by the Seminoles and their African American allies. Students can understand this statement by recalling what they learned about guerrilla fighting in Chapter 2, where the guerrilla tactics used in the American Revolution were discussed. OL CA 8RC2.0

Practice It!

Read the excerpt below. Answer the following questions and discuss them with a partner.

> Two months after Van Buren took office, the country entered a severe economic depression, a period in which business and employment fall to a very low level. The depression began with the Panic of 1837, a time when land values dropped sharply, investments declined suddenly, and banks failed.
>
> Within a few weeks, thousands of businesses had closed and hundreds of thousands of people had lost their jobs. Many Americans could not afford food or rent.
>
> —*from page 460*

Read to Write

Pick three Content Vocabulary terms from Section 1 and write a question about each one. As you read the section, write a sentence or two answering each question based on what you learned.

- What is a depression?
- What started the depression of 1837?
- Do you think people who lived on farms or people who lived in cities were more deeply affected by the depression of 1837?

▲ Martin Van Buren

Apply It!

Look closely at the Reading Check questions throughout the chapter. Which questions can be answered with information directly from the text? Which require you to go beyond the text?

Practice It!

Have students answer the questions and explain how they found the answers. **Ask:** What is a depression? *(a period in which business and employment fall to a very low level; defined in the text)* What started the depression of 1837? *(a panic in which land values dropped, investments, declined, and banks failed; stated in the text)* Who suffered more deeply, people who lived on farms or people who lived in cities? *(This question is not directly answered in the text, though the problems of business owners and workers are mentioned but those of farmers are not; students may conclude that farmers did not suffer.)* OL CA 8RC2.0

Apply It!

Have students apply the skill to other sources of information. Assign pairs of students readings from outside sources. Ask the pairs to develop questions from their reading and attempt to answer them. Have the pairs report to the class on what they found. **Ask:** Is there a connection between how many questions are answered and how clear a piece of writing is? OL

READING STRATEGY **EXPOSITORY WRITING**

Students can use question and answer relationships to improve their own writing. After they have written a draft, they can review their work with an eye to asking questions that a reader might pose. The goal is to make sure that their writing provides needed answers. Questions that cannot be answered may reveal unstated assumptions, unsupported assertions, or steps omitted from the description of a process. Students can use question and answer relationships for revising and strengthening their writing. OL CA 8WS1.1

Use Reading Skills Activity 10 in the **Chapter 10 Resource Book** for more practice with question and answer relationships.

FOCUS

BELLRINGER
SKILLBUILDER ACTIVITY

Project **Daily Focus Skills Transparency 10–1** and have students answer the question.

Guide to Reading

Preteaching Vocabulary:
Ask: What terms have you already seen? *(caucus, tariff, nullify, secede)*

Answers to Graphic:
Democratic-Republicans: Jackson; states' rights; National Republicans: Adams; strong central government

Unpacking the Standards

After reading the section, students will be able to:

- Discuss new ways of campaigning used in 1824 and 1828.
- Describe how the nation became more democratic under Jackson.
- Explain how political fights over several issues resulted in changes.

Section 1 Jacksonian Democracy

History Social Science Standards

US8.8 Students analyze the divergent paths of the American people in the West from 1800 to the mid-1800s and the challenges they faced.

Guide to Reading

Looking Back, Looking Ahead

In the last chapter, you learned about the people and economy of the South. In this section, you will learn about the Jackson presidency.

Focusing on the Main Ideas

- Adams and Jackson introduced new ways of campaigning in the elections of 1824 and 1828. *(page 447)*
- The United States's political system changed under Andrew Jackson, becoming more democratic. *(page 448)*
- The fight over tariffs divided the nation and raised the question of states' rights versus the rights of the federal government. *(page 450)*

Meeting People

Henry Clay
Andrew Jackson
John Quincy Adams
John C. Calhoun (kal • HOON)
Daniel Webster
Robert Hayne (HAYN)

Content Vocabulary

favorite son
plurality (plu • RA • luh • tee)
mudslinging
landslide
suffrage
bureaucracy (byu • RAH • kruh • see)
spoils system
caucus (KAW • kuhs)
tariff (TAR • uhf)
nullify
secede (sih • SEED)

Academic Vocabulary

role (ROHL)
issue (IH • SHOO)

Reading Strategy

Organizing Information As you read Section 1, create a chart to describe the political parties in 1828.

	Candidate	Views
Democratic-Republicans		
National Republicans		

NATIONAL GEOGRAPHIC Who & When?

1824 — 1828 — 1832

1825 John Quincy Adams wins presidency in House election

1828 Andrew Jackson elected president

1830 Webster and Hayne debate

SECTION RESOURCES

Print Material
- Reproducible Lesson Plan 10–1*
- Daily Lesson and Discussion Notes 10–1
- Guided Reading Activity 10–1
- Reading Essentials and Study Guide 10–1
- Active Reading Note-Taking Guide 10–1
- Section Quiz 10–1

Transparencies
- Daily Focus Skills Transparency 10–1
- Section Graphic Organizer Transparency 10–1
- California Standards Practice Transparencies

Technology
- Interactive Tutor Self-Assessment CD-ROM
- Exam*View*® Pro Testmaker CD-ROM
- Presentation Plus! CD-ROM

*Available on TeacherWorks™

US8.8.1 Discuss the election of Andrew Jackson as president in 1828, the importance of Jacksonian democracy, and his actions as president (e.g., the spoils system, veto of the National Bank, policy of Indian removal, opposition to the Supreme Court).

The Elections of 1824 and 1828

Main Idea **Adams and Jackson introduced new ways of campaigning in the elections of 1824 and 1828.**

Reading Connection Think of the ways that presidential candidates campaign in current times. What methods do they use? Read on to find out how Adams and Jackson brought about new ways of campaigning.

The Election of 1824 In 1824 several candidates competed for the presidency. Three of them were **favorite sons,** meaning their home states supported them rather than the national party. They were **Henry Clay** of Kentucky, **Andrew Jackson** of Tennessee, and **John Quincy Adams** of Massachusetts, son of the former president.

In the election Jackson won the most popular votes. However, no candidate received a majority, or more than half, of the electoral votes. Jackson won 99 electoral votes, giving him a **plurality** (plu•RA•luh•tee), or largest single share. Under the Twelfth Amendment, when no candidate gets a majority of electoral votes, the House of Representatives selects the president.

While the House prepared to vote, Clay and Adams made an agreement. Clay would use his influence as Speaker of the House to defeat Jackson. In return, Clay may have hoped to become secretary of state. With Clay's help, Adams was elected president. Adams then named Clay as secretary of state. Jackson's followers accused the two men of making a "corrupt bargain" and stealing the election.

The "corrupt bargain," as well as unpopular policies, cast a shadow over Adams's presidency. Adams favored a stronger navy and federal government direction of the economy. Such ideas horrified people who wanted a more limited federal **role.** Congress turned down many of Adams's proposals.

The Election of 1828 By 1828 there were two political parties: the Democratic-Republicans, who supported Jackson, and the National Republicans, who backed Adams. The Democratic-Republicans favored states' rights and mistrusted strong central government. Many Democrats were frontier people, immigrants, or city workers. The National Republicans wanted a strong central government. They supported federal measures, such as road building and a national bank, that would help the economy. Many were merchants or farmers.

During the campaign, both parties resorted to **mudslinging,** attempts to ruin their opponent's reputation with insults. Supporters of John Quincy Adams passed out a pamphlet attacking Jackson. One of the illustrations showed Jackson plunging his sword through the body of a helpless civilian. Meanwhile, Jackson's supporters accused Adams of kidnapping a young American girl and selling her to the ruler of Russia.

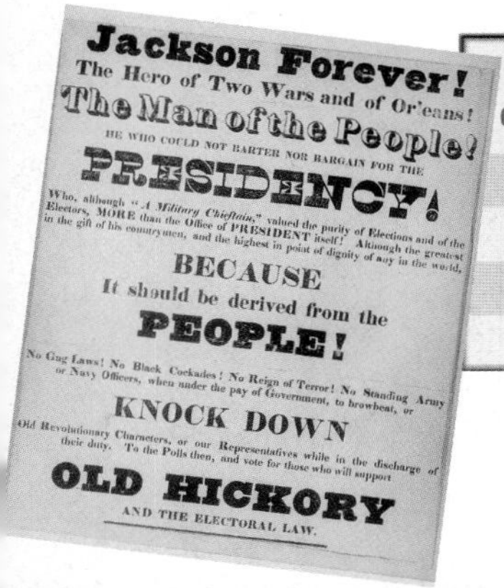

Election of 1824

Candidate	Electoral Vote	Popular Vote	House Vote
Jackson	99	153,544	7
Adams	84	108,740	13
Crawford	41	46,618	4
Clay	37	47,136	–

Understanding Charts

The presidential election of 1824 was decided in the House of Representatives.

Analyze Which candidate received the most electoral votes?

TEACH

R1 Reading Strategy

Understanding Vocabulary **Ask:** Who might be a favorite son or daughter presidential candidate from California or another state today? *(Answers will vary.)* BL CA HI3.

R2 Reading Strategy

Understanding Vocabulary Have students use the words *plurality* and *majority* in a sentence about your class. BL CA 8RW1.3

C Critical Thinking

Drawing Conclusions **Ask:** Why were Jackson's supporters so angry about the "corrupt bargain"? *(They felt Jackson deserved to become president because he had won a plurality of the votes.)* Was such a bargain between Adams and Clay unethical, or simply an ordinary political agreement? AL CA HI3.

R3 Reading Strategy

Understanding Vocabulary Have students explain the metaphor *mudslinging.* *(Criticism can stain a candidate's reputation, just as mud can stain a clean shirt.)* OL

U Universal Access

Logical/Mathematical Have students calculate the percentage of electoral votes and popular votes won by each candidate. *(Electoral vote: Jackson—37.9%; Adams—32.2%; Crawford—15.7%; Clay—14.2%; Popular vote: Jackson—43.1%; Adams—30.5%; Crawford—13.1%; Clay—13.2%)* OL

More Skill Practice

Historical and Social Sciences Analysis Skill Have students debate whether having the House of Representatives decide an inconclusive election is the best solution, or if there is another way that would work better. Ask students to explain why they support either option. AL CA HI3.

Understanding Charts

Answer: Jackson

Ask: How many votes did that candidate receive in the House? *(7)* How many did the winning candidate receive? *(13)*

R1 Reading Strategy

Connecting Ask students to give examples of political slogans they have heard. Discuss the suggested slogans. **Ask:** What do they mean? Are they effective? Why or why not? OL CA HI3.

R2 Reading Strategy

Understanding Vocabulary Have students explain the metaphor *landslide*. *(A political landslide is powerful and overwhelming, like a real rush of earth and rock.)* EL

W Writing Support

Persuasive Writing Ask students to write a paragraph comparing Andrew Jackson to a current political figure in the United States they feel most resembles him and justify the comparison. OL CA 8WA2.4

Reading Check

Answer: After Adams won the 1824 election in the House, he named Clay secretary of state.

Answers and Additional Support

US8.8.1 Discuss the election of Andrew Jackson as president in 1828, the importance of Jacksonian democracy, and his actions as president (e.g., the spoils system, veto of the National Bank, policy of Indian removal, opposition to the Supreme Court).

R1 The parties also aroused enthusiasm with slogans, rallies, and buttons. These new strategies became a permanent part of American political life. In the election, Jackson won the votes of frontier people. He also did well in the South, which liked his call for states' rights. South Carolina's **John C. Calhoun** (kal•HOON) of South Carolina, who had served as Adams's vice president, switched parties to run with Jackson. R2 Jackson won in a **landslide,** an overwhelming victory, with 56 percent of the popular vote and 178 electoral votes.

Reading Check **Describe** Why were Adams and Clay accused of making a "corrupt bargain"?

HISTORY MAKERS

Myths and Legends

▲ John Henry

In the early 1800s, as the West was opened for settlement, the folklore of rugged individualism began to sweep the country. This was the idea that brave and resourceful pioneers paved the way west for later settlers. Stories such as the legends of Paul Bunyan, John Henry, and Davy Crockett were loaded with feats of strength and daring. These myths, which sometimes had a basis in fact, contributed to the image of America as a country of strong, innovative, and talented citizens. They established America as a country based on individualism in politics, economics, and society.

Jackson as President

Main Idea **The United States's political system changed under Andrew Jackson, becoming more democratic.**

Reading Connection What are the requirements for today's citizens to be eligible to vote? Read on to find out how President Jackson expanded suffrage to include a larger number of people.

Andrew Jackson was a man most Americans admired—a patriot, a self-made man, and a war hero. W On March 4, 1829, thousands of farmers, craft workers, and other ordinary Americans crowded into the nation's capital to hear Jackson's Inaugural Address. After Jackson's speech, a crowd joined him at a White House reception. They filled the elegant rooms of the mansion, trampling on the carpets with muddy shoes, spilling food on sofas and chairs. They were there to shake the hand of the new president who seemed just like them.

Why Was Jackson Popular? Jackson gained fame during the War of 1812. He led the troops that defeated the Creek Nation in the Battle of Horseshoe Bend and defeated the British at the Battle of New Orleans. His troops called him "Old Hickory" because he was as tough as a hickory—a hardwood tree.

Small farmers, craft workers, and others who felt left out of the expanding American economy admired Jackson. They felt that his rise from poverty to the White House demonstrated the American success story. His popularity with the common man changed politics in Washington, D.C.

How Did Voting Rights Change? President Andrew Jackson promised "equal protection and equal benefits" for all Americans—at least for all white American men. During his first term, a spirit of equality spread through American politics. In the nation's early years, most states had limited **suffrage,** or the right to vote, for men who owned property or paid taxes.

HISTORY MAKERS

Ask students to identify modern examples of American individualism. **Ask:** Do Americans still value individualism? Why or why not? AL CA HI3.

Did You Know?

During his presidency, Andrew Jackson surrounded himself with a group of trusted advisors. Because they met in the White House kitchen, his critics called them the "kitchen cabinet." This term has continued to mean an unofficial, but trusted, group of advisors to a president.

Analyzing *Political Cartoons*

A Political Card Game Andrew Jackson plays a card game with his political enemies. ***Why did Jackson's opponents criticize the spoils system?***

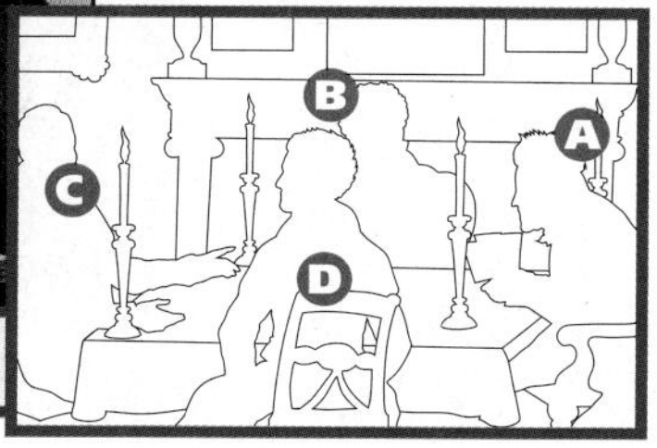

A Andrew Jackson B Nicholas Biddle C Henry Clay D John C. Calhoun

Starting in 1815 Western and Eastern states alike relaxed the property requirements for voting. In the 1820s, people who had not been allowed to vote—white male sharecroppers, factory workers, and many others—voted for the first time. However, women still could not vote, and African Americans and Native Americans had few rights of any kind.

Another change was in the selection of presidential electors. By 1828, 22 of the 24 states changed their constitutions to allow the people, rather than the state legislatures, to choose presidential electors.

What Is the Spoils System? Democrats carried the spirit of democracy into government. Their goal was to shake up the federal **bureaucracy** (byu • RAH • kruh • see), a system in which nonelected officials carry out laws. Democrats argued that ordinary citizens could handle any government job. President Jackson replaced many federal workers with his supporters. The fired employees charged that Jackson was acting like a tyrant. Jackson responded that a new set of federal employees would be good for democracy.

One Jackson supporter explained it another way: "To the victors belong the spoils." In other words, because the Jacksonians had won the presidential election, they had the right to the spoils—benefits of victory—such as handing out government jobs to supporters. The practice of replacing government employees with the winning candidate's supporters became known as the **spoils system.**

What Electoral Changes Occurred? Jackson's supporters worked to make the political system more democratic as well. They abandoned the unpopular **caucus** (KAW • kuhs) system. In this system, major political candidates were chosen by committees made up of members of Congress. The caucuses were replaced by nominating conventions in which delegates from the states selected the party's presidential candidate.

The Democrats held their first national party convention in 1832 in Baltimore, Maryland. The convention drew delegates from each state in the Union. The delegates decided to nominate the candidate who could gather two-thirds of the vote, and Jackson won the nomination. This system allowed many people to participate in the selection of political candidates.

Reading Check **Compare** Compare the caucus system and nominating conventions. Why was the new system more popular with the people?

C Critical Thinking

Predicting Consequences
Have students discuss the likely results of expanding suffrage by reducing property requirements. *(Possible answers include election of fewer upper-class candidates and more of those who share beliefs with middle-class voters.)* OL CA HI2.

R Reading Strategy

Understanding Vocabulary
Have students use each term in a sentence about Jackson's presidency. BL CA 8RW1.3

S Skill Practice

Historical and Social Sciences Analysis Skill
Ask students to make a list of the positive and negative aspects of the spoils system. *(Positive: helps president to have loyal workers; builds strong parties to reward loyalty, hard work; Negative: people may not be qualified for jobs; experienced people would be replaced with inexperienced ones)* AL CA HI2.

Reading Check

Answer: caucus—political leaders pick candidates; nominating conventions—delegates chose them; because more people could take part

Analyzing *Political Cartoons*

Answer: They felt he was acting like a tyrant by hiring and firing people at will.

Review The Big Idea

Review the Big Idea for this section: "Political ideas and events shape how people form governments." **Ask:** How did the political system change under Jackson? *(more people with right to vote; voters given power to choose presidential electors in most states; spoils system and nominating conventions introduced)* OL CA HI2.

R1 Reading Strategy

Understanding Vocabulary
Have students make flash cards using the terms on this page. Students should write the definition on the back and then quiz a partner. BL

R2 Reading Strategy

Activating Prior Knowledge
Ask: When was the idea of nullifying a national law first used? *(in the 1790s)* What was the issue then? *(Jefferson and Madison opposed the Alien and Sedition Acts.)* OL CA HI3.

Resources for page 450

- Academic Vocabulary Activity 10
- Biography Activity 10A

Answers and Additional Support

US8.8.1 Discuss the election of Andrew Jackson as president in 1828, the importance of Jacksonian democracy, and his actions as president (e.g., the spoils system, veto of the National Bank, policy of Indian removal, opposition to the Supreme Court).

R1 The Tariff Debate

Main Idea **The fight over tariffs divided the nation and raised the question of states' rights versus the rights of the federal government.**

Reading Connection What items do you own that were made in the United States? What items of yours were manufactured overseas? Read on to learn how foreign imports led to protests in the South.

Americans from different parts of the country disagreed strongly on some **issues.** One such issue was the **tariff** (TAR•uhf), a fee paid by merchants who imported goods. While president, Jackson faced a tariff crisis that tested the national government's powers.

In 1828 Congress passed a law that placed a very high tariff on manufactured goods from Europe. Manufacturers in the United States—mostly in the Northeast—welcomed the tariff. Because tariffs made European goods more expensive, American consumers were more likely to buy American-made goods.

Analyzing *Political Cartoons*

King Andrew Some people called Andrew Jackson "a man of the people." Others called him a power-hungry ruler. ***What symbols does the cartoonist use to suggest items of royalty?***

Southerners, however, despised the new tariff. There were fewer manufacturers in the South so they did not benefit from increased sales. They called it the Tariff of Abominations—something hateful. These critics argued that although tariffs forced consumers to buy American goods, tariffs also meant higher prices.

How Did the South Protest the Tariff?

Southern politicians were ready to act. Vice President John C. Calhoun argued that a state or group of states had the right to **nullify,** or cancel, a federal law it considered against state interests. Some Southerners called for the Southern states to **secede** (sih•SEED), or break away, from the United States and form their own government. When Calhoun explored this idea, troubling questions arose. The United States had been a nation for nearly 50 years. What if a state disagreed with the federal government? Did a state have the right to go its own way? This debate would continue for decades and eventually lead to civil war. R2

Calhoun drew from ideas in the Virginia and Kentucky Resolutions of 1798–1799. Calhoun argued that since the federal government was a creation of the states, the states have the power to decide whether federal laws are constitutional. The alternative to state sovereignty, Calhoun pointed out, is to allow the Supreme Court or Congress to tell the people what our Constitution means and what laws we must obey.

The Webster-Hayne Debate In January 1830, Senator **Daniel Webster** of Massachusetts delivered a stinging attack on nullification. Webster stood on the floor of the Senate to challenge a speech given by **Robert Hayne** (HAYN), a young senator from South Carolina. Hayne had defended the idea that the states had a right to nullify acts of the federal government and even to secede.

In his response, Webster defended the Constitution and the Union. He argued that nullification could only mean the end of the Union. Webster closed with the ringing statement, "Liberty and Union, now and forever, one and inseparable!"

Did You Know?

When Andrew Jackson finally won election to the presidency in November 1828, his triumph was marred by a personal tragedy. His wife, Rachel Donelson Jackson, died in December and never saw her husband become president.

Analyzing *Political Cartoons*

Ask: Jackson's right foot is standing on the Constitution. What is the artist indicating with this image? *(Jackson has taken more power than the Constitution gives the president.)* OL CA HI1. CA 8LS1.9

Answer: crown with jewels, scepter, throne, robe

Jackson Takes a Stand Nobody knew Jackson's thoughts about nullification. In 1830 Jackson made his position clear at a dinner given by supporters of states' rights. In a toast, Jackson said: "Our federal union . . . must be preserved!" The audience was stunned, but Calhoun quickly responded, "The Union—next to our liberty, most dear." He meant that the Union's fate must take second place to a state's liberty to overrule the Constitution if its interests were threatened.

Calhoun realized that Jackson would not change his views. Wanting to speak for the South in Congress, Calhoun won election to the Senate in December 1832. Two weeks later, he resigned the vice presidency.

What Was the Nullification Crisis? Anger over the tariff continued to build in the South. The Union seemed on the verge of splitting apart. In 1832 Congress passed a new, lower tariff, hoping that the protest in the South would die down. Southern leaders continued their protests, however. The South Carolina legislature passed the Nullification Act, refusing to pay the "illegal" tariffs of 1828 and 1832. It threatened secession if the federal government interfered.

To ease the crisis, President Jackson supported a compromise bill by Henry Clay to lower the tariff. To make sure that the South would accept the compromise, he had Congress pass a Force Bill, allowing military action to enforce acts of Congress. In response, South Carolina nullified the Force Act. Calhoun and his supporters claimed victory because they believed they had forced a revision of the tariff. However, they also had to recognize that a state could not leave the Union without a fight. C

Reading Check **Summarize** Why did South Carolina pass the Nullification Act?

History Online
Study Central Need help understanding Jackson's presidency? Visit ca.hss.glencoe.com and click on Study Central.

Section 1 Review

Reading Summary

Review the Main Ideas

- The election of 1824 was widely seen as corrupt, and the election of 1828 ushered a president to power who identified with much of the American public.
- Elections became more democratic as caucuses were eradicated and suffrage was extended to more voters.
- The introduction of a tariff on imported goods caused many Southerners to turn against the government and lobby for state rights.

What Did You Learn?

1. Why did the House of Representatives select the president in the 1824 presidential election?
2. What election practices used in the 1828 presidential campaign are still used today?

Critical Thinking

3. **Organize Information** Recreate the diagram below and describe the changes that took place in the political system under Andrew Jackson. CA CS1.

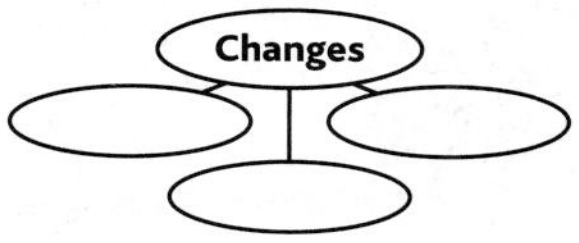

4. **The Big Ideas** What was the main reason President Adams was not popular with the Democratic-Republicans?
5. **Expository Writing** Prepare a list of five questions that you might have asked President Jackson if you had interviewed him. CA 8WS1.1
6. **READING Question and Answer Relationships** Look at questions 1 and 2 above. Will the answers come directly from the text or do they require you to draw on other information as well? Explain. CA HR1.

C Critical Thinking

Predicting Consequences Ask students whether they think the problem of nullification was solved by Jackson's actions, or if it could reemerge as a national issue. *(Students may see that this conflict would lead eventually to the Civil War.)* AL CA HI2.

ASSESS

Resources for page 451

Use these resources to assess student mastery of section content.

Section Quiz 10–1

Interactive Tutor Self-Assessment CD-ROM

Reading Check

Answer: to protest the tariffs of 1828 and 1832

History Online

Study Central provides summaries, interactive games, and online graphic organizers to help students review section content.

CLOSE

Summarizing Have students make a time line of the key events in the nullification crisis. OL CA CS2.

SECTION 1 REVIEW ANSWERS

Review questions reinforce content standard US8.8.

1. No candidate received a majority of electoral votes.
2. mudslinging, slogans, rallies, buttons, staged events
3. More democratic process for nominating political candidates; Expansion of suffrage; Introduction of spoils system
4. **The Big Ideas** He tried to make the federal government more powerful.
5. Questions should show understanding of the issues discussed in the section.
6. **READING** The answers to both can be found in the text.

FOCUS

BELLRINGER
SKILLBUILDER ACTIVITY

Project **Daily Focus Skills Transparency 10–2** and have students answer the question.

Guide to Reading

Preteaching Vocabulary: Have students guess the meaning of *relocate* and predict what group will be relocated.

Answers to Graphic: Cherokee: won legal challenge to removal but forced to move anyway; Sauk/Fox: driven off when tried to reclaim land; Seminole: fought to win right to remain in Florida

Unpacking the Standards

After reading the section, students will be able to:

- Discuss why and how Native Americans were relocated from eastern states to western areas.
- Explain why some Native Americans resisted relocation and the outcomes of their resistance.

Section 2

The Removal of Native Americans

History Social Science Standards

US8.8 Students analyze the divergent paths of the American people in the West from 1800 to the mid-1800s and the challenges they faced.

Guide to Reading

Looking Back, Looking Ahead

In Section 1, you learned about some of the actions Andrew Jackson took as president. In Section 2, you will learn about his policies toward Native Americans.

Focusing on the Main Ideas

- As settlements spread westward, many Native Americans were forced off their lands. *(page 453)*
- Some groups of Native Americans attempted to resist relocation. Most were eventually taken from their lands by force. *(page 455)*

Meeting People

Black Hawk
Osceola (AH • see • OH • luh)

Content Vocabulary

relocate
guerrilla tactics (guh • RIH • luh)

Academic Vocabulary

federal (FEH • duh • ruhl)
remove (rih • MOOV)

Reading Strategy

Taking Notes As you read Section 2, create a chart like the one below that describes what happened to each group of Native Americans as the United States expanded.

	Description
Cherokee	
Sauk/Fox	
Seminole	

NATIONAL GEOGRAPHIC Who & When?

1830 | 1835 | 1840

1830 Congress passes the Indian Removal Act

Osceola

1835 Seminole refuse to leave Florida

1838 Cherokee driven from their homelands on the Trail of Tears

SECTION RESOURCES

Print Material
- Reproducible Lesson Plan 10–2*
- Daily Lesson and Discussion Notes 10–2
- Guided Reading Activity 10–2
- Reading Essentials and Study Guide 10–2
- Active Reading Note-Taking Guide 10–2
- Section Quiz 10–2

Transparencies
- Daily Focus Skills Transparency 10–2
- Section Graphic Organizer Transparency 10–2
- California Standards Practice Transparencies

Technology
- Interactive Tutor Self-Assessment CD-ROM
- Exam*View*® Pro Testmaker CD-ROM
- Presentation Plus! CD-ROM

*Available on TeacherWorks™

US8.8.2 Describe the purpose, challenges, and economic incentives associated with westward expansion, including the concept of Manifest Destiny (e.g., the Lewis and Clark expedition, accounts of the removal of Indians, the Cherokees' "Trail of Tears," settlement of the Great Plains) and the territorial acquisitions that spanned numerous decades.

Moving Native Americans

W **Main Idea** **As settlements spread westward, many Native Americans were forced off their lands.**

Reading Connection How long have you lived in your community? Can you imagine being forced to leave and settle elsewhere? Read on to find out how many Native Americans were forced onto reservations in the West.

The Cherokee held their land long before European settlers arrived. Through treaties with the United States government, the Cherokee became a separate nation within Georgia. By the early 1800s, the Cherokee had their own schools, their own newspaper, and their own C written constitution. Sequoya's invention of a Cherokee alphabet enabled many of the Cherokee to read and write in their own language. The Cherokee farmed some of Georgia's richest land, and in 1829 gold was discovered there. White Americans began trespassing on Cherokee territory in pursuit of riches.

What Is Relocation? While the United States had expanded westward by the 1830s, large numbers of Native Americans still lived in the eastern part of the country. In Georgia, Alabama, Mississippi, and Florida lived the "Five Civilized Tribes"—the Cherokee, Creek, Seminole, Chickasaw, and Choctaw. These tribes had established successful farming societies.

Because the area west of the Mississippi River was dry and seemed unsuitable for farming, few white Americans lived there. Many settlers R wanted the **federal** government to **relocate** Native Americans living in the Southeast. They wanted to force the Native Americans to leave their land and move west of the Mississippi River. President Andrew Jackson, a man of the frontier himself, supported the settlers' demand for Native American land.

What Was the Indian Removal Act? In 1830 Congress passed the Indian Removal Act. It allowed the federal government to pay Native Americans to move west. Jackson then sent officials to negotiate treaties with Native Americans of the Southeast. In 1834 Congress created the Indian Territory, an area in present-day Oklahoma, for these Native Americans.

Picturing **History**

Sequoya holds a sample of the Cherokee alphabet. ***What happened to the Cherokee people in the 1830s?***

The Cherokee Nation The Cherokee Nation, however, refused to give up its land. In treaties of the 1790s, the federal government had recognized the Cherokee people as a separate nation with their own laws. Georgia, however, refused to recognize Cherokee laws.

The Cherokee sued the state and eventually took their case to the Supreme Court. In *Worcester* v. *Georgia* (1832), Chief Justice John Marshall ruled that Georgia had no right to interfere with the Cherokee. The Native Americans, he said, were protected by the federal government and the Constitution. *(See page 849 of the Appendix for a summary of* Worcester v. Georgia.*)*

President Jackson had supported Georgia's efforts to **remove** the Cherokee. He vowed to ignore the Supreme Court's ruling. "John Marshall has made his decision," Jackson reportedly said. "Now let him enforce it."

TEACH

W Writing Support

Summary Writing Have students write a summary of the ways Native Americans responded to the Indian Removal Act and the outcomes of those responses. Ask students to exchange their summaries with another student and review the accuracy of their partner's summary. BL CA 8RC2.4

C Critical Thinking

Predicting Consequences Ask students how having a written language might change Cherokee culture. *(Their culture could be handed down in written, rather than oral, form; information could be spread much more widely; the language could be standardized.)* AL CA HI2.

R Reading Strategy

Academic Vocabulary Discuss with students the meaning of the word *federal* and point out the differences between federal, state, and local governments. OL

Review The Big Idea

Review the Big Idea for this section: "Differences in economic, political, and social beliefs and practices can lead to division within a nation and have lasting consequences." **Ask:** Should Native American groups have their own laws applying to the lands they occupy? Why or why not? *(Students should give reasons for their answers.)* OL CA HI3.

More Skill Practice

Historical and Social Sciences Analysis Skill Have students imagine that they are members of the Cherokee tribal council and must decide how to respond to Jackson's refusal to honor the Supreme Court decision. Have students debate their options. OL CA HR1.

Picturing **History**

Though Sequoyah invented an alphabet for the Cherokee language, he never learned to read or write English. His alphabet had more than 80 characters based on letters in ancient Greek, Hebrew, and English.

Answer: They were forced to relocate to the new Indian Territory.

C Critical Thinking

Making Inferences Ask: Why did the Cherokee feel that fighting against removal would lead to their doom? *(Students may suggest that they felt tied to the land where they had traditionally lived and to the homes they had built there.)* BL CA HI2.

U Universal Access

Visual/Spatial and Verbal/Linguistic Have students respond artistically to the Trail of Tears with a drawing or painting or a story, poem, or dialogue. OL CA HI1.

Reading Check

Answer: to resettle Native Americans west of the Mississippi River

Resources for page 454

- Universal Access Activity 10
- Biography Activity 10B
- Primary Source Reading 10

Answers and Additional Support

NATIONAL GEOGRAPHIC

Removal of Native Americans, 1820–1840

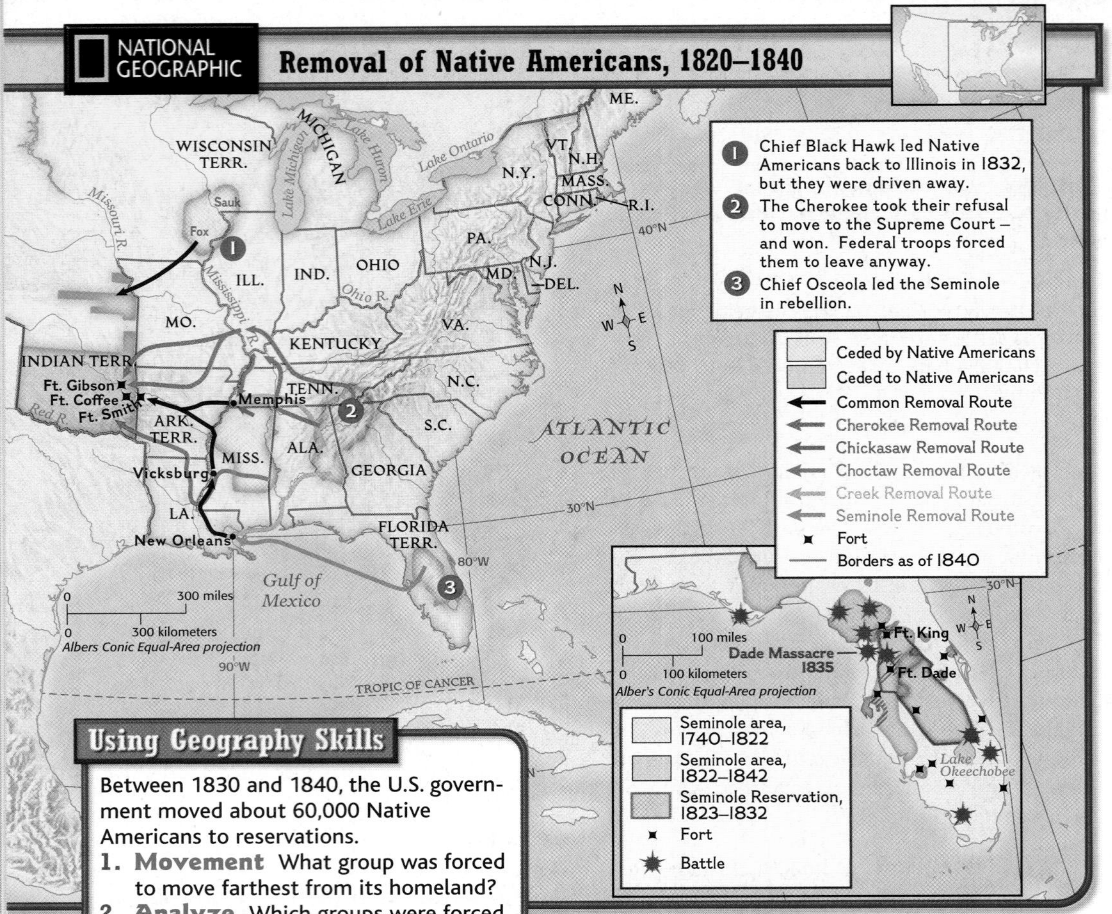

Using Geography Skills

Between 1830 and 1840, the U.S. government moved about 60,000 Native Americans to reservations.

1. **Movement** What group was forced to move farthest from its homeland?
2. **Analyze** Which groups were forced to move from Mississippi?

What Was the Trail of Tears? In 1835 the federal government persuaded a few Cherokee to sign a treaty giving up their people's land. Yet most of the Cherokee refused to honor the treaty. They wrote a protest letter to the government and people of the United States pleading for understanding. It did not soften the resolve of President Jackson or the area's white settlers. In 1838 federal troops under General Winfield Scott came to remove the Cherokee from their homes and lead them west. *(See page 853 of the Appendix for the text of the Cherokee protest.)*

C Scott threatened force if the Cherokee did not leave. The Cherokee knew that fighting would only lead to their doom. Filled with sadness and anger, their leaders yielded, and then the long march to the West began. One man in Kentucky wrote of seeing hundreds of Cherokee marching by:

> **"Even [the] aged . . . were traveling with heavy burdens attached to the back. . . ."**
>
> —from *The Trail of Tears*

U Brutal weather along the way claimed thousands of Cherokee lives. Their forced journey west became known to Cherokee people as the Trail Where They Cried. Historians call it the Trail of Tears.

Reading Check **Explain** What was the purpose of the Indian Removal Act?

Using Geography Skills

Answers:

1. Seminole
2. Choctaw, Chickasaw

In-Text Map Transparency 10 Ask: Why are there so many forts in the Indian Territory? *(possibly due to fear of attacks by relocated Native Americans)* OL CA CS3.

Did You Know?

By the end of the twentieth century, about 47,000 descendants of those who made the Trail of Tears march still lived in northeastern Oklahoma. Of these, about 15,000 are full Cherokee. About 3,000 Cherokee, descended from those who escaped into the Smoky Mountains in 1838, now live in western North Carolina.

US8.8.2 Describe the purpose, challenges, and economic incentives associated with westward expansion, including the concept of Manifest Destiny (e.g., the Lewis and Clark expedition, accounts of the removal of Indians, the Cherokees' "Trail of Tears," settlement of the Great Plains) and the territorial acquisitions that spanned numerous decades.

Native American Resistance

Main Idea **Some groups of Native Americans attempted to resist relocation. Most were eventually taken from their lands by force.**

Reading Connection Have you ever been told to do something you thought was wrong? Did you attempt to resist? Read on to find out how some Native Americans resisted relocation.

An American Story

In 1832 the Sauk chieftain, **Black Hawk**, led a force of Sauk and Fox people back to Illinois, their homeland. They wanted to recapture this area, which had been given up in a treaty. The state militia and federal troops responded with force, killing hundreds of Sauk and Fox and chasing the survivors into present-day Iowa. The troops pursued the people and slaughtered most of them.

The Seminole The Seminole people of Florida were the only Native Americans who successfully resisted their removal. Although they were pressured in the early 1830s to sign treaties giving up their land, the Seminole chief, **Osceola** (AH • see • OH • luh), and some of his people refused to leave Florida. The Seminole decided to go to war against the United States instead.

History Online
Student Web Activity Visit ca.hss.glencoe.com and click on *Chapter 10—Student Web Activities* for an activity on the Trail of Tears.

In 1835 the Seminole joined forces with a group of African Americans who had run away to escape slavery. Together they attacked white settlements along the Florida coast. They used **guerrilla tactics** (guh • RIH • luh), making surprise attacks and then retreating back into the forests and swamps. In December 1835, Seminole ambushed soldiers under the command of Major Francis Dade. Only a few of the 110 soldiers survived the attack. The Dade Massacre led to sending more troops and equipment to fight the Seminole.

By 1842 more than 1,500 American soldiers had died in the Seminole wars. The government gave up and allowed the Seminole to remain in Florida. Many Seminole, however, had died in the long war, and many more were captured and forced to move westward. After 1842 only a few scattered groups of Native Americans lived east of the Mississippi. Most had been removed to the West.

Native Americans had given up more than 100 million acres of eastern land to the federal government. They had received in return about $68 million and 32 million acres in lands west of the Mississippi River.

History *Through Art*

Trail of Tears* by Robert Lindneux** Native Americans who were forced from their land traveled west in the 1830s. ***Why was the forced march called the Trail of Tears?

Did You Know?

The Sauk's resistance to removal in Illinois in 1832 is known as the Black Hawk War. Abraham Lincoln served as a militia captain in that war, though he later wrote that while he had seen not a single "live, fighting Indian" he did have "a good many bloody struggles with the mosquitoes."

History *Through Art*

Although created a century after the event, Robert Lindeaux's painting captures the defeat and sadness of the Cherokee people.

Answer: because the Cherokee were sad to be forced from their homes and because thousands died on the march

C Critical Thinking

Comparing and Contrasting Ask students to list the ways in which the Seminoles and escaped African Americans were similar and the ways in which they were different. *(Similar: fighting for freedom, knew the swamps and forests; Different: Seminoles were native to the region, African Americans had escaped to that area)* OL CA HI1.

R1 Reading Strategy

Understanding Vocabulary Tell students that the word *guerrilla* comes from Spanish. **Ask:** What are other wars in which guerrilla tactics have been used? *(American Revolution, Civil War, Vietnam War, wars in Afghanistan and Iraq)* OL CA 8RW1.3

R2 Reading Strategy

Scaffolding—Academic Vocabulary The word *equipment* was introduced in Chapter 8, Section 2. Ask a student to define the word. OL

S Skill Practice

Visual Literacy Ask students to find evidence in the painting that the march is an unhappy one. *(Many of the people are grim, hunched over with their burdens, and downcast, the sky is dark and stormy.)* OL CA 8LS1.9

History Online

Objectives and answers to the student activity can be found in the Web Activity Lesson Plan feature at ca.hss.glencoe.com.

Biography

TEACH

S Skill Practice

Historical and Social Sciences Analysis Skill
Ask: If you were a Seminole, would you have fought with Osceola or agreed to move to the Indian Territory? Why? *(Answers will vary but should be supported with sound reasons that show an understanding of the historical reality of the situation.)* OL CA HI1.

W Writing Support

Persuasive Writing Have students write a paragraph that takes and supports a position on this question: Did the United States deal honorably with Osceola and the Seminole? Why or why not? OL
CA 8WA2.4

C Critical Thinking

Identifying Central Issues
Ask students what they would have done to resolve the conflict between the Seminole and the United States in Florida and explain why they think it would have worked. *(Solutions will vary.)*
AL CA HI1.

Biography

US8.8.2 Describe the purpose, challenges, and economic incentives associated with westward expansion, including the concept of Manifest Destiny (e.g., the Lewis and Clark expedition, accounts of the removal of Indians, the Cherokees' "Trail of Tears," settlement of the Great Plains) and the territorial acquisitions that spanned numerous decades.

OSCEOLA

c. 1804–1838

Osceola was born in 1804. His ancestors were Creek, African American, British, Irish, and Scottish. After President Jackson signed the Indian Removal Act in 1830, Osceola became the leader of the Seminoles and led successful attacks on United States forts. He was much revered among the Seminole for his ability as a warrior and his refusal to yield to the government's demands. S

The Seminoles hid in the swampy lands of the Everglades throughout 1836 and continued to carry out attacks on U.S. soldiers, as well as on local farms and businesses. However, as food became scarce, the Seminoles grew tired, sick, and hungry. A group of Seminole chiefs negotiated peace with the soldiers and offered to move to a reservation in Arkansas. In exchange, they requested that the many runaway slaves who had found refuge with them be allowed to remain with the Seminoles and not be returned to slavery. The army agreed but later broke the promise and declared that those slaves who had joined the Seminoles after the start of the war would be taken back to their owners. Angered over this violation of the new treaty, the Seminoles again moved into the swamps and the war resumed.

W

The U.S. Army captured one of the Seminole leaders. It offered to release him if Osceola agreed to talks. Osceola tried to surrender but was captured. He and his family were imprisoned, and he died of a throat infection in 1838. Most of the Seminoles were removed from Florida to the Oklahoma Territory. Some Seminoles remained in Florida and settled in reservations there. Although Osceola had fought against the United States, he was respected as a hero and given a funeral with full military honors. C

"You have guns, and so do we; . . . You have men and so have we; Your men will fight, and so will ours until the last drop of the Seminoles' blood has moistened the dust of his hunting grounds."

—Osceola in a letter to General Clinch

Then and Now

Osceola and his men had many advantages during the Seminole wars. His men knew the terrain and had superior fighting skills. Research to find information about a recent or current war. Describe the advantages and disadvantages each side possessed.

Answers and Additional Support

Then and Now

Students may look at such issues as relative size and strength of the military forces on the two sides; the degree of unity of the people behind the war effort; how achievable the goals of the two sides were; the quality of leaders; and so on.

"We told them to let us alone, and keep away from us; but they followed on."

—Black Hawk, Sauk leader (left), pictured here with his son, Whirling Thunder

S **The Five Civilized Tribes** The Five Civilized Tribes were relocated in present-day Oklahoma on lands claimed by several Plains groups, including the Osage, Comanche, and Kiowa. The Plains groups agreed to let the Five Civilized Tribes live in peace. Settled in their new homes, the Five Tribes developed their governments, improved their farms, and built schools.

Reading Check **Compare** How was the response of the Seminoles different from that of the Cherokee when they were removed from their lands?

History Online

Study Central Need help understanding the removal of Native Americans? Visit ca.hss.glencoe.com and click on Study Central.

Section 2 Review

Reading Summary

Review the Main Ideas

- Native Americans' requests to remain on their lands were refused, and they were often forcibly removed.
- Native Americans often resisted, waging war against the United States in an attempt to keep their land.

What Did You Learn?

1. Describe how President Jackson reacted to the Supreme Court decision supporting the Cherokees' rights.
2. How were the Seminole able to resist relocation?

Critical Thinking

3. **Organize Information** Re-create the diagram below to show how the Cherokee were eventually removed from their land. CA HI1.

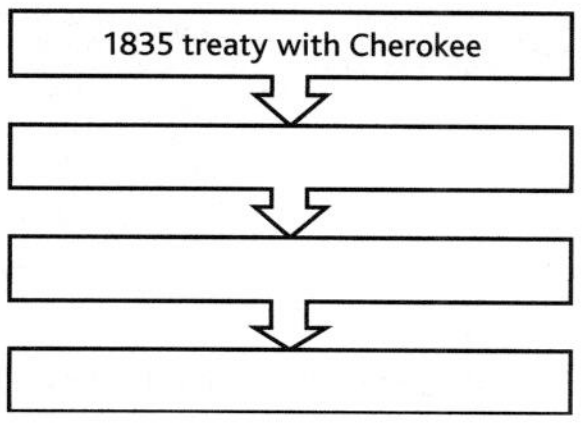

4. **The Big Ideas** How was Georgia's policy toward the Cherokee different from previous federal policy? CA HI3.
5. **Persuasive Writing** Write a letter to Andrew Jackson telling him why the Native Americans should or should not be allowed to stay in their homelands. CA 8WA2.4
6. **Analysis** **Time Line** Create a time line of John Marshall's career as a Supreme Court Justice. Use the index of your book to find other references to him. On your time line, note which decisions brought him into conflict with the president of the time. CA CS2.

SECTION 2 REVIEW ANSWERS

Review questions reinforce content standard US8.8.

1. He challenged Marshall to enforce the ruling; then he disregarded it.
2. by waging a guerrilla war
3. Most Cherokee refused to sign; Cherokee protested to federal government; Federal troops removed the Cherokee
4. **The Big Ideas** Previous federal policy had recognized the Cherokee as a separate nation with its own laws.
5. Letters should offer reasons supporting the position taken.
6. **Analysis** Time lines should cite *Worcester* v. *Georgia* as an instance of conflict.

S Skill Practice

Using Geography Skills

Have students look up the land, climate, and resources of Oklahoma in the early 1800s and use their findings to explain what challenges the Five Civilized Tribes would face in their new homes. *Native Americans would find it difficult in the new area to continue their way of life.)* AL

CA CS3.

ASSESS

Resources for page 457

Use these resources to assess student mastery of section content.

- American Literature Reading 10
- Section Quiz 10–2
- Interactive Tutor Self-Assessment CD-ROM

Reading Check

Answer: They responded by attacking the white settlements on their land; the Cherokee tried to use the court system to block their removal.

History Online

Study Central provides summaries, interactive games, and online graphic organizers to help students review section content.

CLOSE

Sequencing Information

Have students list the important events of this section in chronological order and explain the significance of each. OL

CA CS1.

FOCUS

BELLRINGER
SKILLBUILDER ACTIVITY

Project **Daily Focus Skills Transparency 10–3** and have students answer the question.

Guide to Reading

Preteaching Vocabulary: Have students find the definitions of the terms in the Glossary in the back of their textbooks and use each in a sentence.

Answers to Graphic: Jackson vetoes bill to renew Bank's charter; Jackson orders all government deposits taken out of Bank

Unpacking the Standards

After reading the section, students will be able to:

- Discuss the fight over the Bank of the United States.
- Describe the Panic of 1837 and the economic hardships it caused.
- Explain why the Whig Party grew in power.

Section 3

Jackson and the Bank

Guide to Reading

History Social Science Standards

US8.8 Students analyze the divergent paths of the American people in the West from 1800 to the mid-1800s and the challenges they faced.

Looking Back, Looking Ahead

In Section 2, you learned about the removal of Native Americans to Western lands. In this section, you will learn about Jackson's fight with the National Bank and the election of the Whigs to power.

Focusing on the Main Ideas

- President Jackson forced the National Bank to close, and the Panic of 1837 caused economic problems that split the Democratic Party. *(page 459)*
- After Harrison's death, Tyler took the presidency in a direction opposed to the Whigs' goals, and the Whigs lost power after 1844. *(page 461)*

Meeting People

Nicholas Biddle
Martin Van Buren
William Henry Harrison
John Tyler

Content Vocabulary

veto
depression
laissez-faire (LEH • SAY • FEHR)

Academic Vocabulary

contribute (kuhn • TRIH • byuht)
symbol (SIHM • buhl)

Reading Strategy

Sequencing Information As you read the section, re-create the diagram below. In the spaces provided, describe the steps Andrew Jackson took that put the Bank of the United States out of business.

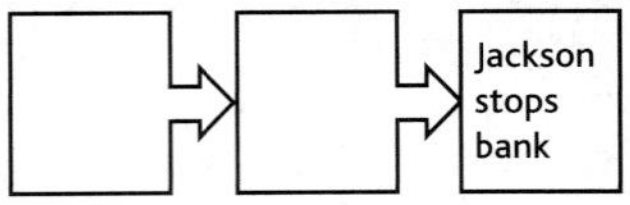

NATIONAL GEOGRAPHIC Who & When?

1830 — 1836 — 1842

Bank note

1832 Andrew Jackson challenges the Bank of the United States

1837 Economic depression strikes the nation

1841 President William Henry Harrison dies in office

William Henry Harrison

SECTION RESOURCES

Print Material
- Reproducible Lesson Plan 10–3*
- Daily Lesson and Discussion Notes 10–3
- Guided Reading Activity 10–3
- Reading Essentials and Study Guide 10–3
- Active Reading Note-Taking Guide 10–3
- Section Quiz 10–3

Transparencies
- Daily Focus Skills Transparency 10–3
- Section Graphic Organizer Transparency 10–3
- California Standards Practice Transparencies

Technology
- Interactive Tutor Self-Assessment CD-ROM
- Exam*View*® Pro Testmaker CD-ROM
- Presentation Plus! CD-ROM

*Available on TeacherWorks™

US8.8.1 Discuss the election of Andrew Jackson as president in 1828, the importance of Jacksonian democracy, and his actions as president (e.g., the spoils system, veto of the National Bank, policy of Indian removal, opposition to the Supreme Court).

R1 War Against the Bank

Main Idea **President Jackson forced the National Bank to close, and the Panic of 1837 caused economic problems that split the Democratic Party.**

Reading Connection Do you have a bank account? Do you know what would happen to your money if an economic crisis occurred? Read on to find out what happened to banks during the Panic of 1837.

Jackson had another great struggle during his presidency. For years, he had criticized the Bank of the United States as being an organization of wealthy Easterners over which ordinary citizens had no control. The Bank of the United States was a powerful institution. It held the federal government's money and controlled much of the country's money supply. Although the Bank had been chartered by Congress, it was run by private bankers rather than elected officials.

C1

The Bank's president, **Nicholas Biddle**, represented everything Jackson disliked. Jackson prided himself on being a self-made man who started with nothing. Biddle, on the other hand, came from a wealthy family.

In 1832 Jackson's opponents gave him the chance to take action against the Bank. Senators Henry Clay and Daniel Webster, friends of Biddle, planned to use the Bank to defeat Jackson in the 1832 presidential election. They persuaded Biddle to apply early for a new charter—a government permit to operate the Bank—even though the Bank's current charter did not expire until 1836.

Clay and Webster believed the Bank had popular support. They thought that an attempt by Jackson to take away its charter would lead to his defeat and allow Henry Clay to be elected president. When the bill to renew the Bank's charter came to Jackson for signature, he was sick in bed. Jackson told his friend **Martin Van Buren**, "The bank, Mr. Van Buren, is trying to kill me. But I will kill it!" Jackson **vetoed**, or rejected, the bill.

R2

▼ Paper money issued in mid-1800s

Jackson, like many others, believed the Bank was unconstitutional despite the Supreme Court's decision to the contrary in *McCulloch* v. *Maryland* (1819). In a message to Congress, Jackson denounced the Bank arguing that:

> **"when the laws ... make the rich richer and the potent more powerful, the humble members of society—the farmers, mechanics, and laborers—who have neither the time nor the means of securing like favors to themselves, have a right to complain of the injustice of their Government."**
>
> —**Andrew Jackson, as quoted in *The Annals of America***

C2

Once again, Jackson was publicly opposing a ruling by the Supreme Court, as he had in *Worcester* v. *Georgia*.

The Election of 1832 Webster and Clay were right about one thing. The Bank of the United States did play a large part in the campaign of 1832. Their strategy for gaining support for Clay as president, however, backfired. Most people supported Jackson's veto of the bank charter bill. Jackson was reelected, receiving 55 percent of the popular vote and collecting 219 electoral votes to Clay's 49. Martin Van Buren was elected vice president.

Once reelected, Jackson decided on a plan to "kill" the Bank. He ordered the withdrawal of all government deposits from the Bank and placed the funds in smaller state banks.

TEACH

R1 Reading Strategy

Organizing Information Have students make a chart that shows the sequence of events leading to Jackson's veto of the Bank bill and the result of that action. OL CA HI2.

C1 Critical Thinking

Drawing Conclusions
Ask: Why did Jackson hate the Bank? *(Answers should include his feeling that it was dominated by Easterners; that ordinary people had no control over it; and that it was unconstitutional.)* OL CA HR3.

R2 Reading Strategy

Understanding Vocabulary
Ask: What are some synonyms and antonyms for *veto?* *(Synonyms: reject, disapprove; Antonyms: approve, OK, accept)* EL

C2 Critical Thinking

Analyzing Primary Sources Have students write a paraphrase of the quotation on this page. *(Possible answer: When laws favor the rich and powerful, common people, who do not have the same advantages, have the right to ask the government for help.)* OL

Resources for page 459

- Geography and History Activity 10
- Economics and History Activity 10

More Skill Practice

Historical and Social Sciences Analysis Skill Ask students if they can name agencies or organizations of today that, like the Bank, are chartered by the federal government yet run by private officials. *(Answers may include the Public Broadcasting System and the Federal National Mortgage Association, or Fannie Mae.)* AL CA HI3.

Review The Big Idea

Review the Big Idea for this section: "Differences in economic, political, and social beliefs and practices can lead to division within a nation and have lasting consequences."
Ask: What economic issue played a role in the 1832 election? *(the Bank)* **BL**
CA CS1.

R1 Reading Strategy

Understanding Vocabulary
Ask: What is the cause and effect relationship between the Panic of 1837 and the depression? *(The Panic caused land and investment values to drop and banks to fail, which led to the collapse of many businesses and loss of jobs—the depression.)*

R2 Reading Strategy

Understanding Vocabulary
Have students explain how "hands off" is a good restatement of *laissez-faire*. *(The term refers to a government policy of not interfering with the economy, or keeping its hands off.)* **BL**

Reading Check
Answer: other bank crises

Analyzing Political Cartoons

Many cartoons from the period depicted Jackson's battle against the Second Bank of the United States. ***Does this cartoon support the president or the Bank? Explain.***

A The Bank B President Jackson C American people

Without those government deposits, the National Bank could not do business. By putting an end to the Bank, Jackson had won a political victory. Later, however, critics charged that the end of the National Bank **contributed** to the economic problems that the nation faced in the years ahead.

What Caused Economic Problems? When Jackson decided not to run for a third term in 1836, the Democrats selected Martin Van Buren of New York, Jackson's vice president, as their candidate. Van Buren faced bitter opposition from the Whigs, a new political party that included former National Republicans and other anti-Jackson forces. Jackson's great popularity and his personal support helped Van Buren easily defeat several Whig opponents. Van Buren was inaugurated in 1837.

R1 Two months after Van Buren took office, the country entered a severe economic **depression,** a period in which business and employment fall to a very low level. The depression began with the Panic of 1837, a time when land values dropped sharply, investments declined suddenly, and banks failed.

Within a few weeks, thousands of businesses had closed and hundreds of thousands of people had lost their jobs. Many Americans could not afford food or rent. In February 1837, people in New York put up signs voicing their anger: "Bread, Meat, Rent, and Fuel! Their prices must come down!"

President Van Buren believed in the principle of **laissez-faire** (LEH • SAY • FEHR)—that government should interfere as little as possible in the nation's economy. R2 However, Van Buren believed that some actions were necessary. Van Buren persuaded Congress to establish an independent federal treasury in 1840. The government would no longer deposit its money with private individual banks as it had started to do during President Jackson's war with the Bank of the United States. Instead, the government would store its money in the federal treasury. The new system, Van Buren believed, would guard against bank crises.

Van Buren called the new law a "second declaration of independence" because it separated government finances from those of the nation's banks. However, criticism of the act came from members of Van Buren's own Democratic Party as well as from Whigs. The split in the Democratic Party meant the Whigs had a chance to win the presidency in 1840.

Reading Check **Explain** What was the new treasury system supposed to prevent?

Answers and Additional Support

Analyzing Political Cartoons

The Bank is portrayed as an ancient Greek mythological monster called the hydra. "Until I can strangle the hydra," Jackson vowed, "I will not shrink from my duty."

Answer: supports Jackson; the Bank is shown as a monster attacking Americans

Did You Know?

There are many different theories about the origin of the expression "OK." One of the most popular revolves around Martin Van Buren. His home in New York was called Old Kinderhook. His supporters in the election of 1840 formed Old Kinderhook, or OK, Clubs, and cried "OK!" at rallies

US8.8.1 Discuss the election of Andrew Jackson as president in 1828, the importance of Jacksonian democracy, and his actions as president (e.g., the spoils system, veto of the National Bank, policy of Indian removal, opposition to the Supreme Court).

The Whigs Come to Power

Main Idea **After Harrison's death, Tyler took the presidency in a direction opposed to the Whigs' goals, and the Whigs lost power after 1844.**

Reading Connection What kind of political disagreements take place in your community? Read on to find out how the Whig Party lost the election of 1844 due to internal disputes.

With the country still in a depression, the Whigs hoped to beat Van Buren in the election of 1840. Their candidates were the military hero **William Henry Harrison** and his running mate **John Tyler.** Because Harrison had won fame in the Battle of Tippecanoe, the Whigs' campaign slogan was "Tippecanoe and Tyler Too."

C Harrison sought the votes of laborers and farmers. Harrison was portrayed as a "man of the people." Whig cartoons showed him in front of a log cabin, the Whigs' campaign **symbol.** The log cabin campaign worked, and Harrison won easily. Four weeks after his inauguration in 1841, Harrison died of pneumonia. John Tyler became the first vice president to gain the presidency because the elected president died in office.

Although Tyler had been elected as a Whig, he had once been a Democrat. As president, Tyler backed states' rights and vetoed several Whig-sponsored bills. This lack of party loyalty angered Whigs. Most of the cabinet resigned, and Whig leaders in Congress expelled Tyler from the party.

Whig leaders, however, could not agree on policies. This division partly explains why the Whig candidate, Henry Clay, lost the election of 1844 to Democratic candidate Polk. After only four years, the Whigs were out of power again. R

Reading Check **Describe** How did John Tyler become president?

History Online

Study Central Need help understanding Jackson and the Bank? Visit ca.hss.glencoe.com and click on Study Central.

Section 3 Review

Reading Summary

Review the Main Ideas

- Jackson waged a war against the bank and won not only his side of the war but the election of 1832 as well.
- Criticism over Van Buren's response to the Panic of 1837 brought the Whigs to power, but dissension among members of the party helped a Democrat to win the next election.

What Did You Learn?

1. List Jackson's reasons for wanting to "kill" the Bank of the United States.
2. What tactics did the Whigs borrow from Jackson's campaign to win the election of 1840?

Critical Thinking

3. **Organize Information** Re-create the diagram below to show how the Panic of 1837 affected the presidency of Martin Van Buren. CA HI2.

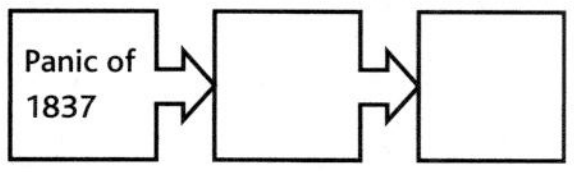

4. **The Big Ideas** Why did President Van Buren do little to solve the nation's economic problems during the depression?
5. **Creative Writing** Write a campaign slogan for Van Buren or Harrison in the election of 1840. Then design a campaign button that incorporates your slogan. CA 8WA2.5.a

SECTION 3 REVIEW ANSWERS

Review questions reinforce content standard US8.8.

1. He believed it favored the rich and hurt the poor and that it was unconstitutional.
2. trying to appeal to the "common man"; ridiculing Van Buren
3. Supporters turned against him; He loses 1840 election, ending his presidency.
4. **The Big Ideas** He believed in laissez-faire, the idea that government should not interfere in the nation's economy.
5. Slogans and buttons will vary but should accurately reflect section content.

C Critical Thinking

Making Inferences **Ask:** Why do you think the Whigs portrayed Harrison as a "man of the people," even though he was rich? *(Students may suggest they hoped to win support of common people or take that support away from the Democrats.)* OL CA HI2.

R Reading Strategy

Scaffolding—Academic Vocabulary The word *policy* was introduced in Chapter 7, Section 3. Have students write a sentence using the word. OL

ASSESS

Resources for page 461

Use these resources to assess student mastery of section content.

Section Quiz 10–3

Interactive Tutor Self-Assessment CD-ROM

Reading Check

Answer: He was vice president when President Harrison died.

History Online

Study Central provides summaries, interactive games, and online graphic organizers to help students review section content.

CLOSE

Evaluating Have students decide which of Jackson's nicknames is more fitting: "King Andrew" or "Old Hickory" and explain why. OL CA HI1.

Analyzing Primary Sources

FOCUS

History–Social Science Standards

The following standards are covered on pages 462–463.

US8.8 Students analyze the divergent paths of the American people in the West from 1800 to the mid-1800s and the challenges they faced.

TEACH

R Reading Strategy

Visualizing Suggest that students visualize the scene as they read the account. **Ask:** What impression do you get from the words "silent, orderly, and tranquil"? *(that the crowd is well behaved)* OL

C Critical Thinking

Analyzing Primary Sources Ask: What point is Mrs. Smith making about Jackson and the United States in this last paragraph? *(She is very favorable to Jackson for paying respect—through bowing—to the people and that she sees the people as the source of power in the U.S.)* OL CA HR3.

Answers and Additional Support

Analyzing Primary Sources

US8.8.1 Discuss the election of Andrew Jackson as president in 1828, the importance of Jacksonian democracy, and his actions as president (e.g., the spoils system, veto of the National Bank, policy of Indian removal, opposition to the Supreme Court).

Jacksonian Democracy

The spirit of Jacksonian democracy was seen in the 1829 inauguration of America's new president, Andrew Jackson. Unlike previous presidents, Jackson invited "common people" to his inauguration and presented himself as one of them. Called "the people's choice," Jackson responded to the wishes of ordinary Americans who wanted changes in their government's leadership.

Jackson is sworn in as president. ▶

Reader's Dictionary

tranquil (TRAN • kwuhl)**:** free of disturbance or commotion

edifice (EH • duh • fuhs)**:** a building, especially one that is large or impressive

portico (POHR • tih • KOH)**:** a covered entrance or walkway

rotunda (roh • TUHN • duh)**:** a large round room or hall

rends: disturbs the silence or pierces the air with a loud sound

reverberate: to echo repeatedly

sublime (suh • BLYM)**:** awe-inspiringly beautiful

pecuniary (pih • KYOO • nee • EHR • ee)**:** relating to or involving money

incalculably (ihn • KAL • kyuh • luh • buh • lee)**:** too great or numerous to be measured

solicitude (suh • LIH • suh • TOOD)**:** concern and consideration

The Inauguration of Andrew Jackson

R *In 1829 Andrew Jackson became president. A Washington resident, Mrs. Samuel Harrison Smith, wrote about Jackson's inauguration in a letter:*

Thousands and thousands of people, without distinction of rank, collected in an immense mass round the Capitol, silent, orderly and **tranquil,** with their eyes fixed on the front of that **edifice,** waiting the appearance of the President in the **portico.** The door from the **Rotunda** opens, preceded by the marshals, surrounded by the Judges of the Supreme Court, the old man with his gray locks, that crown of glory, advances, bows to the people, who greet him with a shout that **rends** the air, the Cannons from the heights around, . . . proclaim the oath he has taken and all the hills **reverberate** the sound. It was grand,—it was **sublime!** An almost breathless silence, succeeded and the multitude was still,—listening to catch the sound of his voice, [though] it was so low, as to be heard only by those nearest to him. After reading his speech, the oath was administered to him by the Chief Justice. The Marshal presented the Bible. The President took it from his hands, pressed his lips to it, laid it reverently down, then bowed again to the people—Yes, to the people in all their majesty. C

—from *The First Forty Years of Washington Society*

EXTENDING THE CONTENT

Outdoor Inaugurations In 1828 Andrew Jackson became the first president to take his oath of office on the portico on the east side of the Capitol, though four years later, his second inaugural took place in the chamber of the House of Representatives. His was not the first outdoor inauguration; that distinction belongs to James Monroe in 1817, when the Capitol was still being rebuilt after being burned down in the War of 1812.

Indian Removal

In 1830 President Andrew Jackson delivered a message to Congress describing his plans for removing Native Americans from their lands by forcing them west to an area beyond the Mississippi River.

The consequences of a speedy removal will be important to the United States, to individual states, and to the Indians themselves. The **pecuniary** advantages which it promises to the government are the least of its recommendations. It puts an end to all possible danger of collision between the authorities of the general and state governments on account of the Indians. It will place a dense and civilized population in large tracts of country now occupied by a few savage hunters. By opening the whole territory between Tennessee on the north and Louisiana on the south to the settlement of the whites it will **incalculably** strengthen the southwestern frontier and render the adjacent states strong enough to repel future invasions without remote aid. It will relieve the whole state of Mississippi and the western part of Alabama of Indian occupancy, and enable those states to advance rapidly in population, wealth, and power.

It will separate the Indians from immediate contact with settlements of whites; free them from the power of the states; enable them to pursue happiness in their own way and under their own rude institutions; will retard the progress of decay, which is lessening their numbers, and perhaps cause them gradually, under the protection of the government and through the influence of good counsels, to cast off their savage habits and become an interesting, civilized, and Christian community. These consequences, some of them so certain and the rest so probable, make the complete execution of the plan sanctioned by Congress at their last session an object of much **solicitude.**

—Message to Congress, December 6, 1830

▲ **John Ross (left), the principal chief of the Cherokee, opposed the removal of his people. Rebecca Neugin (right) was one of the Cherokee forced to march west to Oklahoma. In this 1931 photograph, Neugin is 96 years old.**

DBQ Document-Based Questions

The Inauguration of Andrew Jackson

1. How do you think Mrs. Smith's account of this event might be different from a news reporter's account?

Indian Removal

2. What does President Jackson state is the best reason for the removal of Native Americans?
3. How will the Native Americans benefit from this plan, according to President Jackson?

Read to Write

4. President Jackson was known as a "man of the people." Is this perception apparent in these documents? Do you see any inconsistencies? Summarize your conclusions. Next, identify a political leader that has an image in popular culture and contrast that with policy decisions made by that leader. Compare the contemporary leader you chose with Andrew Jackson. CA 8WS1.0

DBQ Document-Based Questions

1. A news reporter would convey the same information but not inject as much opinion.
2. Students may say that Jackson does not directly state which reason is the most important.
3. They will be free of conflict with whites and state governments, the move may halt the decline in their numbers, and they will eventually become civilized.
4. Students' responses should give reasons for their statements.

R Reading Strategy

Reading Primary Sources

Ask: What does Jackson mean when he says that the "pecuniary advantages" are "the least of its recommendations"? *(that the financial gains are not the most important reason to favor the idea)* OL

C Critical Thinking

Analyzing Primary Sources **Ask:** What does Jackson call the Native Americans when he contrasts them to the "few savage hunters" who now live where they will be relocated? *("a dense and civilized population")* What future benefit does he suggest for the Native Americans being relocated? *(They may "cast off their savage habits and become an interesting, civilized, and Christian community.")* How do these statements contradict each other? *(Jackson first says the Native Americans are civilized and then says they are not.)* OL CA HR4

Resources for page 463

- Analysis Skills Activity 10
- Critical Thinking Skills Activity 10

ASSESS

Have students answer the Document-Based Questions.

CLOSE

Analyzing Information

Have students use these quotations to discuss Andrew Jackson's presidency in terms of majority rule and minority rights. OL

CHAPTER 10 Assessment

Resources for pages 464–465

Use these resources to review, assess, or reteach the chapter.

- Active Reading Note-Taking Guide, Chapter 10
- Chapter 10 Reading Essentials and Study Guide
- Chapter 10 Tests, Forms A and B
- Standards Assessment, Forms A and B
- California Standards Practice Workbook
- MindJogger Videoquiz
- Succeeding on the California History–Social Science Standards CD-ROM
- Interactive Tutor Self-Assessment CD-ROM

Review Content Vocabulary

1. g
2. c
3. d
4. a
5. e
6. b
7. f

Review the Main Ideas

8. Jackson's supporters favored states' rights; Adams's favored a strong central government and supported measures such as road building and a national bank.
9. mudslinging, slogans, rallies, buttons, staged events
10. women, African Americans, Native Americans
11. escaped enslaved African Americans
12. Supreme Court ruled that the state of Georgia had no right to interfere with the Cherokee, but Jackson ignored the decision.
13. Land values dropped, investments declined, and banks failed.
14. By appealing to the same voters who had been attracted to Jackson.

Critical Thinking

15. No, he supported their relocation, showing that he did not consider them to have the same rights as other Americans.
16. Federal employees: fired many, replaced them with supporters; Electoral change: replaced caucuses with nominating conventions; Nullification: opposed it; Removal: ordered relocation by force when Native Americans did not leave voluntarily; National Bank: ordered all government deposits to be removed from Bank, placed money in state banks, vetoed Bank renewal

Chapter 10 Assessment

Standard US8.8

Reviewing Content Vocabulary

Match each word below to the correct definition.

a. plurality
b. suffrage
c. majority
d. nullify
e. landslide
f. secede
g. depression

___ 1. a period in which business and employment fall to very low levels
___ 2. a portion that is more than half
___ 3. to cancel
___ 4. the largest single share of something
___ 5. an overwhelming victory
___ 6. the right to vote
___ 7. to break away

Review the Main Ideas

Section 1 • Jacksonian Democracy

8. How did the supporters of Jackson and Adams differ in their beliefs?
9. What were some of the political tactics used by Democratic-Republicans and the National Republicans in the election of 1828?
10. Which Americans were prohibited from voting in most states before the 1800s?

Section 2 • The Removal of Native Americans

11. Who did the Seminoles join forces with as they fought against forced removal from their land?
12. What was the outcome of *Worcester* v. *Georgia?*

Section 3 • Jackson and the Bank

13. How did the Panic of 1837 affect the nation's economy?
14. Why was Harrison's log cabin campaign successful?

Critical Thinking

15. **Conclude** President Andrew Jackson promised "equal protection and equal benefits" for all Americans. Do you think he included Native Americans in his promise? Why or why not? CA HI1.
16. **Organize Information** Re-create the chart below. List the issues that Jackson dealt with during his presidency. Then describe how he responded to each issue. CA CS2.

Issues	Jackson's response

Geography Skills

The issue of states' rights was debated in the election of 1828. Study the map below and answer the questions that follow. CA CS3.

NATIONAL GEOGRAPHIC **Election of 1828**

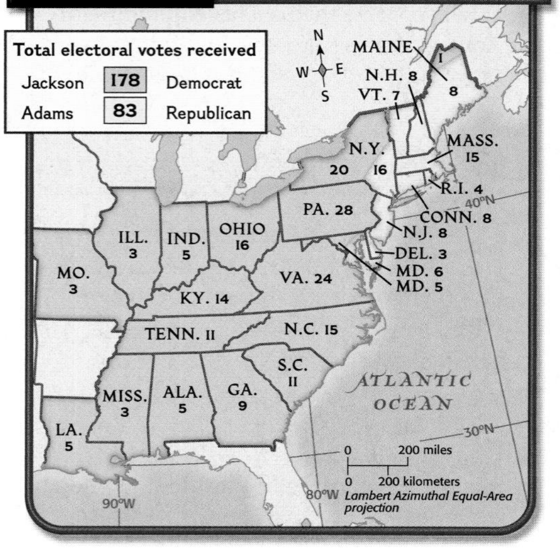

History Online

Self-Check Quiz Visit ca.hss.glencoe.com to prepare for the Chapter 10 test.

17. **Region** Which general areas of the United States voted for Andrew Jackson in the election of 1828?
18. **Location** Which candidate won more votes in Adams's home state of Massachusetts?

Read to Write

19. **The Big Ideas** **Persuasive Writing** Choose one of the events in this chapter over which Americans were divided in opinion. Choose one side or the other and write a short essay arguing why you think your view is correct. CA 8WA2.4

20. **Using Your FOLDABLES** Use the information you gathered in your foldable to create a time line of Andrew Jackson's presidency. Illustrate your time line with drawings or pictures. CA CS2.

Using Academic Vocabulary

Some words like *issue* have multiple meanings. Find definitions of the word *issue*. It can be a noun or a verb. Write T for True or F for False to indicate whether the following statements use the correct meaning of the word *issue*.

21. An important issue during Andrew Jackson's presidency was the National Bank.
22. The Five Civilized Tribes issued farming societies with successful economies.

Building Citizenship

23. **Become an Informed Voter** With a partner, choose an election in your community. Outline how you would become informed on the candidates and/or the issues. Share your outline and your findings with the class. CA 8WS1.4

Economics Connection

24. **Predict** How would an economic recession or depression affect your life today? Write a few paragraphs describing your ideas. CA 8WS1.0 CA HI6.

Reviewing Skills

25. **Review READING SKILL** **Question and Answer Relationships** Write your own review questions and answers. Write two that are directly from the text and two that require other information. CA HR1.

26. **Review ANALYSIS SKILL** **Compare and Contrast** Read the primary source document on the Cherokee removal on page 853. Then reread the passage on page 454 that deals with this event. Write a summary paragraph comparing the primary and secondary sources. CA HR4.

Standards Practice

Select the best answer to each of the following questions.

27 **In *Worcester* v. *Georgia*, Chief Justice John Marshall ruled that the state of Georgia**

- A must adopt the spoils system.
- B had no right to interfere with the Cherokee.
- C could limit suffrage.
- D must support the National Bank.

28 **Which of the following statements expresses an opinion about Andrew Jackson?**

- A Jackson served two terms as president.
- B He spoke out against South Carolina's Nullification Act.
- C Jackson created the best system of filling government positions.
- D Jackson supported the Indian Removal Act.

CHAPTER 10 Assessment

Building Citizenship Skills

23. Students' outlines should show organized planning and evidence of research.

Economics Connection

24. Answers should show understanding of the effects of high unemployment, low level of business activity, and other effects associated with economic slumps.

Reviewing Skills

25. **Review READING SKILL** Questions and answers should accurately reflect chapter content.

26. **Review ANALYSIS SKILL** Comparisons should explain why the Cherokee felt as they did.

Standards Practice

27. B
28. C

Bonus Question

Ask: Was Andrew Jackson's influence on the U.S. political system positive or negative? Why? *(Answers will vary but students should be able to support their opinions.)* OL CA HI2.

History Online

Have students visit the Web site at ca.hss.glencoe.com to review Chapter 10 and take the **Self-Check Quiz.**

Geography Skills

17. the West and the South
18. Adams

Read to Write

19. **The Big Ideas** Possible events include the different elections, any of Jackson's reforms, the Bank, nullification, the tariff, sectionalism and states' rights, the Native American removals, and how to address the Panic and depression. Essays should accurately reflect chapter content.

20. Using Your **FOLDABLES** Time lines should accurately reflect chapter content.

Using Academic Vocabulary

21. True
22. False

Chapter 11 Planning Guide

SECTION RESOURCES

Main Ideas	Print Materials	Technology Resources
Section 1 **Westward to the Pacific** 1. Many Americans wanted control of the Oregon country to gain access to the Pacific Ocean. 2. Increased American settlement led the United States and Britain to divide Oregon.	• Reproducible Lesson Plan 11–1* • Daily Lesson and Discussion Notes 11–1 • Active Reading Note-Taking Guide 11–1 • Reading Essentials and Study Guide 11–1 • Guided Reading Activity 11–1 • Section Quiz 11–1	Daily Focus Skills Transparency 11–1 Section Graphic Organizer Transparency 11–1 California Standards Practice Transparencies Interactive Tutor Self-Assessment CD-ROM Exam*View*® Pro Testmaker CD-ROM Presentation Plus! CD-ROM
Section 2 **Independence for Texas** 1. Texas was settled by people from Mexico and the United States, creating cultural tension. 2. Texans wanted to be a nation separate from Mexico.	• Reproducible Lesson Plan 11–2* • Daily Lesson and Discussion Notes 11–2 • Active Reading Note-Taking Guide 11–2 • Reading Essentials and Study Guide 11–2 • Guided Reading Activity 11–2 • Section Quiz 11–2	Daily Focus Skills Transparency 11–2 Section Graphic Organizer Transparency 11–2 California Standards Practice Transparencies Interactive Tutor Self-Assessment CD-ROM Exam*View*® Pro Testmaker CD-ROM Presentation Plus! CD-ROM
Section 3 **War With Mexico** 1. The Santa Fe Trail was a busy trade route through New Mexico, a large region governed by Mexico. 2. California was settled and populated by diverse cultures. 3. Strained relations between the U.S. and Mexico resulted in war.	• Reproducible Lesson Plan 11–3* • Daily Lesson and Discussion Notes 11–3 • Active Reading Note-Taking Guide 11–3 • Reading Essentials and Study Guide 11–3 • Guided Reading Activity 11–3 • Section Quiz 11–3	Daily Focus Skills Transparency 11–3 Section Graphic Organizer Transparency 11–3 California Standards Practice Transparencies Interactive Tutor Self-Assessment CD-ROM Exam*View*® Pro Testmaker CD-ROM Presentation Plus! CD-ROM
Section 4 **New Settlers in California and Utah** 1. The discovery of gold in California had a significant impact on the settlement and economy of the region. 2. Utah was settled by Mormons, a religious group looking for safe haven.	• Reproducible Lesson Plan 11–4* • Daily Lesson and Discussion Notes 11–4 • Active Reading Note-Taking Guide 11–4 • Reading Essentials and Study Guide 11–4 • Guided Reading Activity 11–4 • Section Quiz 11–4	Daily Focus Skills Transparency 11–4 Section Graphic Organizer Transparency 11–4 California Standards Practice Transparencies Interactive Tutor Self-Assessment CD-ROM Exam*View*® Pro Testmaker CD-ROM Presentation Plus! CD-ROM Vocabulary PuzzleMaker CD-ROM

PACING YOUR LESSONS

Chapter Introduction	Section 1	Section 2	Section 3	Section 4	Chapter Assessment	Unit Wrap-Up
½ Day	2 Days	2 Days	2 Days	2 Days	½ Day	½ Day

0:00 **OUT OF TIME?** Assign the Chapter 11 ***Reading Essentials and Study Guide***

*Available on TeacherWorks™

Standards-Based Lesson Plan

History–Social Science Standards Covered in Chapter 11

The standards covered in the chapter are listed below. Use the accompanying activity as you teach the chapter to ensure student mastery of these standards. This activity can be used in combination with the program's print and technology assessment materials.

Standard	Section 1	2	3	4
US8.8 Students analyze the divergent paths of the American people in the West from 1800 to the mid-1800s and the challenges they faced.	✔	✔	✔	✔
US8.8.2 Describe the purpose, challenges, and economic incentives associated with westward expansion, including the concept of Manifest Destiny (e.g., the Lewis and Clark expedition, accounts of the removal of Indians, the Cherokees' "Trail of Tears," settlement of the Great Plains) and the territorial acquisitions that spanned numerous decades.	✔		✔	✔
US8.8.3 Describe the role of pioneer women and the new status that western women achieved (e.g. Laura Ingalls Wilder, Annie Bidwell; slave women gaining freedom in the west; Wyoming granting suffrage to women in 1869).				✔
US8.8.4 Examine the importance of the great rivers and the struggle over water rights.		✔		
US8.8.5 Discuss Mexican settlements and their locations, cultural traditions, attitudes toward slavery, land-grant system, and economies.		✔	✔	
US8.8.6 Describe the Texas War for Independence and the Mexican-American War, including territorial settlements, the aftermath of the wars, and the effects the wars had on the lives of Americans, including Mexican-Americans today.		✔	✔	

Cumulative Standards-Assessment Activity

The Cumulative Standards-Assessment Activity will help students organize and learn the important information from the chapter. Begin teaching the chapter with this activity, and have students complete it as they read the chapter.

Creating a Sequencing Chart

Purpose Sequencing events is a vital skill when studying history. Understanding the proper sequence of events helps students when they carry out critical thinking tasks such as identifying cause-and-effect relationships and generalizing about trends or developments. Using graphic organizers like time lines to record events also helps students see how material that they study in two different parts of a chapter are related in time, preventing the misconception that content presented later necessarily occurred later in time.

Introduction to Sequencing

1. Model how to construct a time line by asking students to identify key dates in the previous chapter and briefly state what happened and why it was important. Write students' suggestions on the board, not necessarily in chronological order. After you have four or five dates, show how to sequence them properly in a time line.
2. Ask students to copy this chart into their notebooks:

Date	Event and Significance

Explain that students should collect all the dates and events from the chapter before constructing their time lines. If not, the result could become messy if they have to add dates encountered in a later section between two dates identified earlier and there is not sufficient room. Tell them when they have finished taking notes, they should make their time lines.

3. As you review the chapter, ask volunteers to name some of the key dates they identified. Encourage them to use their time lines as study aids.

Chapter 11 Resources

READING SUPPORT

- Content Vocabulary Activity 11
- Academic Vocabulary Activity 11
- Reading Skills Activity 11
- American Literature Reading 11
- Biography Activities 11A, 11B
- Chapter 11 Active Reading Note-Taking Guide
- Chapter 11 Guided Reading Activities
- Chapter 11 Reading Essentials and Study Guide
- Glencoe Literature Library
- Glencoe Video Program
- Vocabulary PuzzleMaker CD-ROM
- Interactive Graphic Organizers CD-ROM
- American History Primary Source Document Library CD-ROM

CRITICAL THINKING

- Critical Thinking Skills Activity 11
- Primary Source Reading 11
- Cause-and-Effect Transparency 11, Strategy, and Activity
- Presentation Plus! CD-ROM

UNIVERSAL ACCESS

- Universal Access Activity 11
- Then and Now Transparencies 11A–11B, Strategy, and Activity
- Graphic Novel Activity 11
- School-to-Home Connection Activities 11A–11D
- English Learner Handbook Chapter 11 Activities
- Universal Access for the American History Classroom
- Moments in Time
- American Art and Architecture Transparencies, Strategies, and Activities
- American Art Prints
- American Music Cultural Traditions
- American Music Hits Through History
- StudentWorks Plus CD-ROM

SKILL PRACTICE

- Map Overlay Transparency 11, Strategy, and Activity
- Analysis Skills Activity 11
- Time Line Activity 11
- Geography and History Activity 11
- Economics and History Activity 11
- Chart, Graph, and Map Skills Activity 11
- Political Cartoon Activity 11
- Supreme Court Case Study 11
- In-Text Map Transparency 11, Strategy, and Activity
- Step Into American History Activity 11
- Citizenship and Service Learning Activity 11
- Outline Map Resource Book
- MindJogger Plus Videoquiz

WRITING SUPPORT

- Writing Activity 11
- Language Arts Activity 11
- Writer's Guidebook
- Middle School Writing Process Transparencies

ASSESSMENT

GLENCOE'S ASSESSMENT ADVANTAGE

- Chapter 11 Section Quizzes
- Chapter 11 Tests, Forms A and B
- California Standards Assessment, Forms A and B
- Cumulative Assessment Activity US8.8
- California Standards Practice Workbook
- Succeeding on the California History–Social Science Standards CD-ROM
- Exam*View*® Pro Testmaker CD-ROM
- Interactive Tutor Self-Assessment CD-ROM

CD-ROM	Transparency
DVD	Music Program
Print Material	Videocassette
Poster	Glencoe Literature Library

Chapter 11 Resources

TECHNOLOGY

- StudentWorks Plus CD-ROM
- TeacherWorks Plus CD-ROM
- Exam*View*® Pro Testmaker CD-ROM
- Interactive Tutor Self-Assessment CD-ROM
- Presentation Plus! CD-ROM
- Succeeding on the California History–Social Science Standards CD-ROM
- Vocabulary PuzzleMaker CD-ROM
- Interactive Graphic Organizers CD-ROM
- Interactive Time Line CD-ROM
- American History Primary Source Document Library CD-ROM
- MindJogger Plus Videoquiz
- American Music Cultural Traditions
- American Music Hits Through History
- Glencoe Video Program
- Professional Development in Middle School Social Studies Series
- Teaching American History With *Discovering Our Past: The American Journey to World War I*

SPANISH RESOURCES

- Spanish Activities and Assessment
  - Spanish Content Vocabulary Activities
  - Spanish Guided Reading Activities
  - Spanish Quizzes and Tests
  - Spanish California Standards Assessment
- Spanish Reading Essentials and Study Guide
- Spanish School-to-Home Connection
- Spanish Declaration of Independence and U.S. Constitution

TRANSPARENCIES

- California Standards Practice Transparencies
- Daily Focus Skills Transparencies
- Section Graphic Organizer Transparencies
- In-Text Map Transparencies
- Map Overlay Transparencies
- Cause-and-Effect Transparencies
- Then and Now Transparencies
- American Art and Architecture Transparencies
- Middle School Writing Process Transparencies

TEACHER PLANNING

- Daily Lesson and Discussion Notes
- English Learner Handbook
- Guide to Daily Intervention
- *Discovering Our Past: The American Journey to World War I* Reading and Study Skills Foldables
- Reading Strategies and Activities for the Social Studies Classroom
- Chapter 11 Reproducible Lesson Plans (correlated to California History–Social Science Standards)
- Universal Access for the American History Classroom
- NGS U.S. Desk Map
- NGS U.S. Atlas

PROFESSIONAL DEVELOPMENT

- Building Academic Vocabulary
- Strategies for Success
- Research-Based Strategies Used to Develop *Discovering Our Past: The American Journey to World War I*
- Character Education in the Middle School Classroom
- The Living Constitution
- Professional Development in Middle School Social Studies Video Series
- Teaching American History With *Discovering Our Past: The American Journey to World War I*

MASTERING THE STANDARDS

The content and assessment in the Student Edition, Teacher Wraparound Edition, teacher planning materials, and the print and technology products are all standards-based. The use of these products during instruction leads to mastery of the standards.

PRACTICE
- California Standards Practice Workbook
- California Standards Practice Transparencies
- Interactive Time Line CD-ROM
- School-to-Home Connection

BENCHMARK ASSESSMENT
- California Standards Assessment
- Exam*View*® Pro Testmaker CD-ROM
- Succeeding on the California History–Social Science Standards CD-ROM

REMEDIATION
- California Guide to Daily Intervention
- Interactive Tutor Self-Assessment CD-ROM
- Exam*View*® Pro Testmaker CD-ROM
- California Standards Practice Workbook
- Reading Essentials and Study Guide

Additional Resources

NATIONAL GEOGRAPHIC TEACHER'S CORNER

Index to National Geographic Magazine:

The following articles relate to this chapter:

- "The Way West," by John G. Mitchell, September 2000.
- "Tex-Mex Border," by Richard Conniff, February 1996.
- "Powwow," by Michael Parfit, June 1994.
- "The American Prairie: Roots of the Sky," by Douglas H. Chadwick, October 1993.
- "Along the Santa Fe Trail," by Rowe Findley, February 1989.
- "Life and Death on the Oregon Trail: The Itch to Move West," by Boyd Gibbons, August 1986

National Geographic Society Products

To order the following, call National Geographic at 1-800-368-2728

- *GeoKit: Westward Movement* (Kit)
- *The West That Was* (Video)
- *United States Territorial Growth* (Map)
- *National Geographic Desk Reference* (Book)
- *American Indians: A Brief History* (Video)

NGS ONLINE

Access National Geographic's new dynamic MapMachine Web site and other geography resources at:

www.nationalgeographic.com

www.nationalgeographic.com/maps

A&E Home Video · Biography® · The History Channel®

The following videotape programs are available from Glencoe as supplements to Chapter 11.

- **The Alamo (ISBN 1-56501-784-6)**
- **The Best of the Real West (ISBN 1-56501-352-2)**
- **California and the Dream Seekers (2 Pack) (ISBN 1-56501-0555-4)**

To order, call Glencoe at 1-800-334-7344. To find classroom resources to accompany many of these videos, check the following home pages:

A&E Television: www.aetv.com

The History Channel: www.historychannel.com

History Online

Use our Web site for additional resources. All essential content is covered in the Student Edition.

You and your students can visit ca.hss.glencoe.com, the Web site companion to *Discovering Our Past: The American Journey to World War I*. This innovative integration of electronic and print media offers your students a wealth of opportunities. The student text directs students to the Web site for the following options:

- Chapter Overviews
- Self-Check Quizzes
- Study Central™
- Student Web Activities
- Textbook Updates
- Multi-Language Glossaries

Answers to the student Web activities are provided for you in the Web Activity Lesson Plans. Additional Web resources and ePuzzles and games are also available.

Glencoe TechCONNECT

Glencoe TechCONNECT™ AC200 "Women of the Frontier"

Cumulative Activity Students should understand the role of women in the westward movement by reading first-hand accounts and then using a word processing application to write a fictional journal entry by a pioneer woman or girl. **CA** US8.8.3 **CA** CS3.; HR3.; HI1. **CA** 8RW1.0

You can access this online activity at www.ca.hss.techconnect.glencoe.com. Enter the following activation key when prompted: **CONNECTCA.** To access the Teacher Resources for each activity, enter the following password when prompted: **CA123.**

FOLDABLES™ Study Organizer

Dinah Zike's Foldables

Foldables are three-dimensional, interactive graphic organizers that help students practice basic writing skills, review key vocabulary terms, and identify main ideas. Every chapter contains a foldable activity, with additional chapter activities found in the Reading and Study Skills Foldables booklet.

Reading List Generator CD-ROM

GLENCOE BOOKLINK

The Glencoe BookLink CD-ROM is a database that allows you to search more than 15,000 titles to create a customized reading list for your students.

- Reading lists can be organized by students' reading level, author, genre, theme, or area of interest.
- The database provides Degrees of Reading Power™ (DRP) and Lexile™ readability scores for all selections.
- A brief summary of each selection is included.

Reading level suggestions for this chapter:

For students at a Grade 6 reading level:

- ***Across the Wide and Lonesome Prairie: The Oregon Trail Diary of Hattie Campbell,*** by Kristiana Gregory

For students at a Grade 7 reading level:

- ***The Great American Gold Rush,*** by Rhonda Blumberg

For students at a Grade 8 reading level:

- ***Una Linda Raza: Cultural and Artistic Traditions of the Spanish Southwest,*** by Angel Vigil

For students at a Grade 9 reading level:

- ***Hunter's Stew and Hangtown Fry: What Pioneer America Ate and Why,*** by Lila Perl

READING SUPPORT FROM JAMESTOWN EDUCATION

- *Timed Readings Plus in Social Studies* helps students increase their reading rate and fluency while maintaining comprehension. The 400-word passages are similar to those found on state and national assessments.
- *Reading in the Content Area: Social Studies* concentrates on six essential reading skills that help students better comprehend what they read. The book includes 754 high-interest nonfiction passages written at increasing levels of difficulty.
- *Reading Fluency* helps students read smoothly, accurately, and expressively.
- *Jamestown's Reading Improvement,* by renowned reading expert Edward Fry, focuses on helping build your students' comprehension, vocabulary, and skimming and scanning skills.
- *Critical Reading Series* provides high-interest books, each written at three reading levels.

To order these products, call Glencoe at 1-800-334-7344.

KEY for Using the Teacher Wraparound Edition

Use this key to help you identify the different types of prompts found in the Teacher Wraparound Edition.

R **Reading Strategies** activities help you teach reading skills and vocabulary.

C **Critical Thinking** strategies help students apply and extend what they have learned.

U **Universal Access** activities provide differentiated instruction for students learning to speak English, along with suggestions for teaching various types of learners.

S **Skill Practice** strategies help students practice historical analysis and geography skills.

W **Writing Support** activities provide writing opportunities to help students comprehend the text.

Teaching strategies and activities have been coded for ability level appropriateness.

AL Activities for students working above grade level
OL Activities for students working on grade level
BL Activities for students working below grade level
EL Activities for English Learners

FOCUS

History–Social Science Standards

In this chapter, the following standard will be covered:

US8.8 Students analyze the divergent paths of the American people in the West from 1800 to the mid-1800s and the challenges they faced.

More About the Photo

By the time of the Texas War for Independence, the Alamo had long been abandoned. Texans captured it in late 1835, soon after the war broke out. Sam Houston urged that they give it up since the defenders were so few, but they decided to stay.

TEACH

The Big Ideas

As you begin teaching each section, use these questions and activities to focus on the Big Ideas.

Section 1

Westward to the Pacific

Essential Question: What ideas cause people to come to the United States from other lands today? *(freedom; economic opportunity)* Explain that in this section, students will learn what led people to move west in the early 1800s. OL

Chapter 11

Manifest Destiny

▼ The Alamo, San Antonio, Texas

NATIONAL GEOGRAPHIC Where & When?

1820 — 1835 — 1850

- **1821** California becomes a state of Mexico
- **1836** Whitmans build mission in Oregon country
- **1845** The United States annexes Texas
- **1850** California becomes a state

Section 2

Independence for Texas

Essential Question: How do people of different cultures and backgrounds get along in the United States today? *(Students may point to some examples of tolerance or some of conflict.)* Point out that in this section, they will learn how differences led to conflict. OL

Section 3

War With Mexico

Essential Question: What examples in American history can you think of in which conflict led to important changes? *(Students may point to the American Revolution, which produced American independence.)* OL

The Big Ideas

History Online
Chapter Overview Visit ca.hss.glencoe.com for a preview of Chapter 11.

Section 1 Westward to the Pacific

Geography influences the divergent paths of people resulting in physical, economic, and political challenges and rewards. Manifest Destiny is the idea that it was inevitable that the United States would extend its borders from the Atlantic Ocean to the Pacific Ocean.

Section 2 Independence for Texas

Immigration influences a nation's or region's economy and society. American settlers began moving into the part of Mexico called Texas in the 1820s. Conflict forced Mexico to grant Texas its independence.

Section 3 War With Mexico

Conflict often brings about great change. Through war with Mexico and diplomatic negotiations with Great Britain, the United States acquired Texas, Oregon, California, Utah, and the remainder of the Southwest.

Section 4 New Settlers in California and Utah

Immigration influences a nation's or region's economy and society. By 1850, thousands of American settlers had crossed the Great Plains for new homes.

View the Chapter 11 video in the Glencoe Video Program.

FOLDABLES™ Study Organizer

Organizing Information Make this foldable to organize information from the chapter to help you learn more about how Manifest Destiny led to western expansion.

Step 1 Collect three sheets of paper and place them on top of one another about 1 inch apart.

Step 2 Fold up the bottom edges of the paper to form 6 tabs.

Step 3 When all the tabs are the same size, fold the paper to hold the tabs in place and staple the sheets together along the fold. Turn the paper and label each tab as shown.

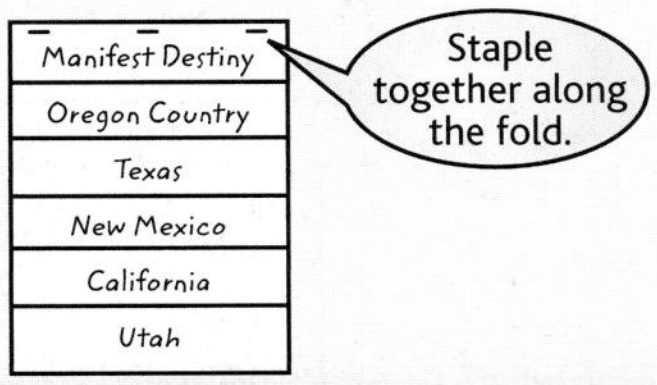

Reading and Writing As you read, use your foldable to write under each appropriate tab what you learn about Manifest Destiny and how it affected the borders of the United States.

INTRODUCING CHAPTER 11

Section 4

New Settlers in California and Utah

Essential Question: Why do areas with growing economies attract people? *(Students may point out that many people are always looking for ways to better their lives.)* **OL**

Cultural Perspectives

The idea that Americans had a higher calling to expand westward to the natural border of the Pacific Ocean is known as Manifest Destiny. During this expansion, several countries lost territories to the Americans, including Mexico. Have students investigate the Mexican perspective on the effects of this expansion and the Mexican-American War. Ask students to write about one event or situation as though they were writing an article for a Mexican newspaper for its local readers. Remind students that newspaper writing is presumed to be factual and non-biased, but point out that their choice of what details are included and emphasized can convey a distinct perspective. How is this also true for the writing of history?

History Online

Go to ca.hss.glencoe.com for student activities, lesson plans, and links to additional Web resources about westward expansion.

FOLDABLES™ Study Organizer — Dinah Zike's Foldables

Purpose Have students use their foldables to write a brief summary of the changes that affected the United States in this period. **OL**

Why It's Important

New Vocabulary Learning new vocabulary is a vital skill in reading in general and in content areas as well. Readers at all ability levels encounter new and challenging words. More effective readers have developed their skills at understanding the new words that they find. Point out to students that learning vocabulary can be similar to exercising—the more they do it, the easier it becomes.

1 Learn It!

Review with students what each of the techniques described in the feature means. Ask volunteers to explain each technique—using context clues; using word parts; getting help; guessing at meaning; and looking the word up. Ask if students can give examples of times when they have applied each of those methods. For those that students cannot, provide your own examples. Ask students if they can think of any other techniques. OL

Chapter 11

Get Ready to Read

READING SKILL

New Vocabulary

1 Learn It!

What should you do if you find a word you don't know or understand? Here are some suggested strategies:

1. Use context clues (from the sentence or paragraph) to help you define it.
2. Look for prefixes, suffixes, or root words that you already know.
3. Write it down and ask for help with the meaning.
4. Guess at its meaning.
5. Look it up in the glossary or a dictionary.

Look at the word boomtowns in the following passage. See how context clues can help you understand its meaning:

Context Clue
Boomtowns were new communities.

Context Clue
They were built almost overnight.

> **As people rushed to a new area to look for gold, they built new communities, called boomtowns, almost overnight. At one site on the Yuba River where only two houses stood in September 1849, a miner arrived the next year to find a town of 1,000 people "with a large number of hotels, stores, groceries, bakeries and . . . gambling houses." The miners gave some of the boomtowns colorful names such as Shinbone Peak and You Bet.**
>
> —*from page 503*

Context Clue
They had characteristics similar to other towns.

Reading Tip

To use context to help you define a word, read the sentences before and after the word.

READING STRATEGY — USING WORD PARTS

Point out that some common prefixes and suffixes are used often and can provide clues to the meaning of a new word. Challenge students to define the following and give examples of their use:

- co- *(with; examples—cooperate; copresident)*
- ex- *(out of, from; examples—export, exit, exceed)*
- im- *(into; examples—import, immigrate)*
- re- *(to do again or repeat; examples—restate, review)*
- -logy *(study of; examples—biology, geology)*
- -tion *(a process; examples—absorption, initiation)* OL

2 Practice It!

List three things in these paragraphs that help you understand the term *rendezvous* (RAHN•dih•VOO). Write a sentence defining the word.

Read to Write

Write a paragraph about a *rendezvous* you could have with your friends.

Some mountain men worked for fur-trading companies, but others sold their furs to the highest bidder. Throughout the spring and early summer, they traveled across the mountains, setting traps and then collecting the beaver pelts. In late summer, they gathered for a rendezvous (RAHN • dih • VOO), or meeting.

For the mountain men, the annual rendezvous was the high point of the year. They met with trading companies to exchange their beaver skins for traps, guns, coffee, and other goods. They met old friends and exchanged news. They swapped stories about who had been on the most exciting adventures.

—*from page* 472

◀ Mountain man

3 Apply It!

Make a vocabulary bookmark with a 2-inch-wide strip of paper. As you read the chapter, keep track of the words you do not know or want to learn more about.

2 Practice It!

Give students the following paragraph. Have them define the boldfaced word:

When families prepared to move to Oregon, they packed everything they owned into covered wagons. Many families traveled together in caravans called ***wagon trains****. The wagons formed into long lines, one family following another. Oxen slowly pulled each wagon across the Great Plains while some emigrants walked alongside. To guide them along the correct route and to lead them through the dangers, they hired experienced* ***wagon masters****. (wagon trains: long lines of wagons carrying emigrants to Oregon; wagon masters: experienced guides and leaders)* OL

3 Apply It!

Encourage students to follow up on the activity by learning the definitions of the words that they identify and track what techniques they used. Take a poll in the class to see which techniques appear most often. Ask volunteers to describe how they used particular approaches and why they found them effective. OL

READING STRATEGY — MONITORING

Have students monitor their understanding of new vocabulary. First, have students write sentences using the new words that they identified. Then have them turn those sentences into completion tests, substituting blank spaces for the terms. Have them exchange their papers with a partner and take the vocabulary quizzes. OL

Use Reading Skills Activity 11 in the **Chapter 11 Resource Book** for more practice with learning new vocabulary.

FOCUS

BELLRINGER
SKILLBUILDER ACTIVITY

Project **Daily Focus Skills Transparency 11–1** and have students answer the question.

Guide to Reading

Preteaching Vocabulary: Call on volunteers to define each of the content vocabulary terms and then have students use the Glossary to check those definitions.

Answers to Graphic: 1819: Adams-Onís Treaty; 1825: Adams becomes President; 1836: Whitman builds mission in Oregon; 1846: U.S. and Britain settle Oregon's boundary

Unpacking the Standards

After reading the section, students will be able to:

- Describe the lives of the mountain men.
- Explain how and why Americans settled Oregon.
- Discuss how the U.S. and Britain settled the dispute over Oregon.

Section 1

Westward to the Pacific

History Social Science Standards

US8.8 Students analyze the divergent paths of the American people in the West from 1800 to the mid-1800s and the challenges they faced.

Guide to Reading

Looking Back, Looking Ahead
Americans had begun moving to Texas in the 1820s. By the 1830s and 1840s, they were making their way to Oregon.

Focusing on the Main Ideas
- Many Americans wanted control of the Oregon country to gain access to the Pacific Ocean. *(page 471)*
- Increased American settlement led the United States and Britain to divide Oregon. *(page 473)*

Locating Places
Oregon Country
Columbia River
Oregon Trail

Meeting People
John Jacob Astor
Jim Beckwourth
Jedediah Smith
Marcus Whitman
Narcissa Whitman
James K. Polk

Content Vocabulary
joint occupation
mountain man
rendezvous (RAHN • dih • voo)
emigrant (EH • mih • gruhnt)
Manifest Destiny

Academic Vocabulary
access (AK • sehs)
annual (AN • yuh • wuhl)
route (ROWT)
sole (SOHL)

Reading Strategy
Sequencing Information As you read Section 1, re-create the diagram below and in the boxes list key events that occurred.

1819	1825	1836	1846

NATIONAL GEOGRAPHIC Who & When?

1810 — 1830 — 1850

1819 Adams-Onís Treaty is signed

1840s Great migration to Oregon

1844 James K. Polk elected president

James K. Polk

SECTION RESOURCES

Print Material
- Reproducible Lesson Plan 11–1*
- Daily Lesson and Discussion Notes 11–1
- Guided Reading Activity 11–1
- Reading Essentials and Study Guide 11–1
- Active Reading Note-Taking Guide 11–1
- Section Quiz 11–1

Transparencies
- Daily Focus Skills Transparency 11–1
- Section Graphic Organizer Transparency 11–1
- California Standards Practice Transparencies

Technology
- Interactive Tutor Self-Assessment CD-ROM
- Exam*View*® Pro Testmaker CD-ROM
- Presentation Plus! CD-ROM

*Available on TeacherWorks™

US8.8.2 Describe the purpose, challenges, and economic incentives associated with westward expansion, including the concept of Manifest Destiny (e.g., the Lewis and Clark expedition, accounts of the removal of Indians, the Cherokees' "Trail of Tears," settlement of the Great Plains) and the territorial acquisitions that spanned numerous decades.

Rivalry in the Northwest

Main Idea **Many Americans wanted control of the Oregon Country to gain access to the Pacific Ocean.**

Reading Connection Have you ever moved to a new city or town? Saying good-bye can be difficult, but the possibilities are exciting. Read to find out about people who moved to new lands.

An American Story

On an April morning in 1851, 13-year-old Martha Gay said good-bye to her friends, her home, and the familiar world of Springfield, Missouri. She and her family were beginning a long, hazardous journey. The townsfolk watched as the family left in four big wagons pulled by teams of oxen. "Farewell sermons were preached and prayers offered for our safety," Martha wrote years later. "All places of business and the school were closed . . . and everybody came to say good-bye to us." This same scene occurred many times in the 1840s and 1850s as thousands of families set out for the Oregon Country.

What Was Oregon Country? The **Oregon Country** was the huge area that lay between the Pacific Ocean and the Rocky Mountains north of California. It included all of what is now Oregon, Washington, and Idaho plus parts of Montana and Wyoming. The region also contained about half of what is now the Canadian province of British Columbia.

In the early 1800s, four nations claimed the vast, rugged land known as the Oregon Country. The United States based its claim on Robert Gray's exploration of the **Columbia River** in 1792 and on the Lewis and Clark expedition. Great Britain based its claim on British explorations of the Columbia River. Spain, which controlled California to the south, claimed a share of Oregon. Russia had settlements that stretched south from Alaska into California. Fort Ross in California was the Russians' southernmost settlement.

Adams-Onís Treaty Many Americans wanted control of the Oregon country and its **access** to the Pacific Ocean to build trade. Secretary of State John Quincy Adams played a key role in promoting this goal. In 1819 he negotiated a treaty with Spanish foreign minister Louis de Onís. In the Adams-Onís Treaty, the Spanish agreed to set the limits of their territory at what is now California's northern border and gave up any claim to Oregon. In 1824 Russia also surrendered its claim. Only Britain remained to challenge American control of Oregon.

In 1818 Adams had worked out an agreement with Britain for **joint occupation** of the area. This meant that people from both the United States and Great Britain could settle in Oregon. When Adams became president in 1825, he proposed that the two nations divide Oregon along the 49°N line of latitude.

"To explore unknown regions . . . was his chief delight."

—Clerk in a fur trade company describing Joseph Walker, an early explorer of Yosemite

TEACH

Review Grade 5 Standards

To review standard **5.8.4** *(Discuss the experiences of settlers on the overland trails to the West (e.g., location of the routes; purpose of the journeys; the influence of the terrain, rivers, vegetation, and climate; life in the territories at the end of these trails,)* have students write a continuation of Martha Gay's memory about departing Missouri for the Oregon country, elaborating on how she and her family members felt as they looked ahead to their long journey. OL

S Skill Practice

Using Geography Skills Have students use the political map of the United States on pages 30–31 to locate the areas that were part of the Oregon Country. OL CA CS3.

R1 Reading Strategy

Scaffolding—Academic Vocabulary The word *ministry* is introduced in Chapter 8, Section 5. Ask a student to define *ministry*. OL

R2 Reading Strategy

Understanding Vocabulary
Ask: What does *joint* mean? *(shared by two people)* What about *occupation*? *(having people living in an area)* OL

More Skill Practice

Using Geography Skills Have a volunteer read aloud the Main Idea. **Ask:** Why would Americans want access to the Pacific Ocean? *(Answers may include for protection and for trade opportunities with Asia.)* OL

More About the Art

Fur traders placed ads in newspapers to recruit men to work in the fur trade. One ad called for a hundred men to work for one, two, or three years under the leadership of an army major.

R Reading Strategy

Using Vocabulary Have students write a short paragraph using the terms *mountain men* and *rendezvous*. OL CA 8RW1.3

Review The Big Idea

Review the Big Idea for this section "Geography influences the divergent paths of people resulting in physical, economic, and political challenges and rewards." Have students research the life of one of the mountain men and prepare a report on the work he did, the dangers he faced, and the contributions, if any, he made to knowledge of the West. OL CA 8WA2.4

C Critical Thinking

Making Inferences Ask: Why did the mountain men need to be resourceful? *(to survive in the wilderness)* OL

Reading Check

Answer: Natural resources (furs) were plentiful and, once collected, they could be easily transported on the Pacific Ocean.

Answers and Additional Support

Britain refused Adams's proposal, insisting on a larger share of the territory. Unable to resolve their dispute, the two countries agreed to allow both British and Americans to settle there.

Who Were the Mountain Men? The first Americans to reach the Oregon Country were not farmers but fur traders. They had come to trap beaver, whose skins were in great demand in the eastern United States and in Europe. The beaver skins were used to make hats, which were very popular at that time. The British established several trading posts in the region, as did American merchant **John Jacob Astor** of New York. In 1808 Astor organized the American Fur Company. It soon became the largest of the fur companies in America, allowing Astor to build up trade with the East Coast, the Pacific Northwest, and China. Astor and his family later became one of the wealthiest families in America.

R Fur companies hired trappers, who over time became known as **mountain men.** Many mountain men had Native American wives and adopted Native American ways. They lived in lodges and dressed in fringed buckskin pants, moccasins, and beads.

Some mountain men worked for fur-trading companies, but others sold their furs to the highest bidder. Throughout the spring and early summer, they traveled across the mountains, setting traps and then collecting the beaver pelts. In late summer, they gathered for a **rendezvous** (RAHN • dih • voo), or meeting.

For the mountain men, the **annual** rendezvous was the high point of the year. They met with the trading companies to exchange their beaver skins for traps, guns, coffee, and other goods. They met old friends and exchanged news. They swapped stories about who had been on the most exciting adventures.

As they roamed the region searching for beaver, the mountain men explored the mountains, valleys, and trails of the West. **Jim Beckwourth,** an African American mountain man from Virginia, explored Wyoming's Green River. Robert Stuart and **Jedediah Smith** both found the South Pass, a broad break through the Rockies. South Pass later became the main **route** that settlers took to Oregon.

To survive in the wilderness, a mountain man had to be skillful and resourceful. C Trapper Joe Meek told how, when faced with starvation, he once held his hands "in an anthill until they were covered with ants, then greedily licked them off." The mountain men took pride in joking about the dangers they faced.

In time, the mountain men killed off most of the beaver and could no longer trap the once plentiful animals. Some went to settle on farms in Oregon. With their knowledge of the western lands, though, some mountain men found new work. Jim Bridger, Kit Carson, and others acted as guides to lead the parties of settlers now streaming west.

Reading Check **Explain** Why did trading posts develop in the Oregon Country?

Picturing History

Jim Beckwourth (right) explored many parts of the West, including the Green River area of Wyoming (left). ***How did mountain men make their living?***

Picturing History

Jim Beckwourth also found a pass through California's Sierra Nevada mountains, which was often used by forty-niners during the Gold Rush. The pass and a valley in California where he later settled are both named for him. Beckwourth was not the only African American mountain man. One trapper recalled that these adventurers liked to bring along African Americans, who got along better with Native Americans.

Answer: by trapping beavers and collecting their pelts; some worked for companies, though others were independent

US8.8.2 Describe the purpose, challenges, and economic incentives associated with westward expansion, including the concept of Manifest Destiny (e.g., the Lewis and Clark expedition, accounts of the removal of Indians, the Cherokees' "Trail of Tears," settlement of the Great Plains) and the territorial acquisitions that spanned numerous decades.

R1

Settling Oregon

Main Idea **Increased American settlement led the United States and Britain to divide Oregon.**

Reading Connection If you could travel across the United States, where would you go? Read on to learn more about the settlement of the Oregon Country.

Americans began settling the Oregon Country in the 1830s. Reports of the fertile land and economic troubles in the East made the West look attractive.

R2

The Whitman Mission Among the first settlers of the Oregon Country were missionaries who wanted to bring Christianity to the Native Americans. **Dr. Marcus Whitman** and his wife **Narcissa** went to Oregon in 1836 and built a mission among the Cayuse people near the present site of Walla Walla, Washington.

New settlers unknowingly brought measles to the mission. An epidemic killed many of the Native American children. Blaming the Whitmans for the sickness, the Cayuse attacked the mission in November 1847.

MORE ABOUT...

The Oregon Trail

The Importance of the Trail The Oregon Trail was much more than just a trail to Oregon. It served as the most practical route to the western United States. The pioneers traveled in large groups, often of related families. Some went all the way to Oregon in search of farmland. Many others split off for California in search of gold.

The Journey The trip west lasted five or six months. The pioneers had to start in the spring and complete the trip before winter snows blocked the mountain passes. The trail crossed difficult terrain. The pioneers walked across seemingly endless plains, forded swift rivers, and labored up high mountains.

Problems Along the Way Although the pioneers feared attacks by Native Americans, such attacks did not often occur. More often Native Americans assisted the pioneers, serving as guides and trading necessary food and supplies. About 1 in 10 of the pioneers died on the trail, perishing from disease, overwork, hunger, or accidents.

C

When did use of the trail stop? With the building of a transcontinental railroad in 1869, the days of using the Oregon Trail as a corridor to the West were over.

"We are creeping along slowly, one wagon after another, the same old gait, and the same thing over, out of one mud hole into another all day."

—Amelia Stewart Knight, 1853

"After Laramie we entered the great American desert, which was hard on the teams. Sickness became common. . . ."

—Catherine Sager Pringle, 1844

R1 Reading Strategy

Outlining Suggest that students outline the section to record details about the settling of Oregon and the resolving of the U.S. and British dispute over ownership. OL

R2 Reading Strategy

Inferring **Ask:** Based on this information here, what is a *missionary*? *(someone who travels to a land that is not his or her home to try to convert people to a religion)* OL CA 8RW1.3

C Critical Thinking

Determining Cause and Effect **Ask:** What change in technology brought about the end of the Oregon Trail? *(spread of railroads)* Why would it have that effect? *(people could travel faster using trains)* OL CA HI2.

Resources for page 473

♫ American Music: Hits Through History, "Nabucca's Quick Step"

Economics and History Activity 11

MORE ABOUT...

One of the many stories of endurance along the Oregon Trail is Janette Riker's. In Montana in September 1849, her father and two brothers went hunting but never came back. To survive the winter, Riker built a hut and chopped firewood, and killed one of the family's oxen for food.

Did You Know?

The following quote from a Missouri farmer gives one person's reason for moving to Oregon: "Dad burn me, I am done with this country. Winters it's frost and snow to freeze a body; summers the overflow from Old Muddy drowns half my acres; taxes take the yield of them that are left."

R1 Reading Strategy

Understanding Vocabulary Explain that *emigrants* and *immigrants* can refer to the same people depending on the perspective of the person speaking. Someone in the place they left would call them *emigrants*. To a person living in the place where they arrived, those people are *immigrants*.

U Universal Access

Visual/Spatial Travel on the 2,000-mile (3,200-km) Oregon Trail was slow. Wagons went about 1 to 2 miles an hour (1.6 to 3.2 kph). Today the same trip could be completed by car at an average of 60 miles per hour (97 kph). Have students create a pictograph comparing the pioneer trip to the modern trip. OL

R2 Reading Strategy

Understanding Vocabulary Point out that *manifest* means "evident" or "obvious." **Ask:** Why did O'Sullivan use the word *manifest*? *(to make it clear that this destiny could not be argued with or denied)* OL

NATIONAL GEOGRAPHIC **Oregon Country**

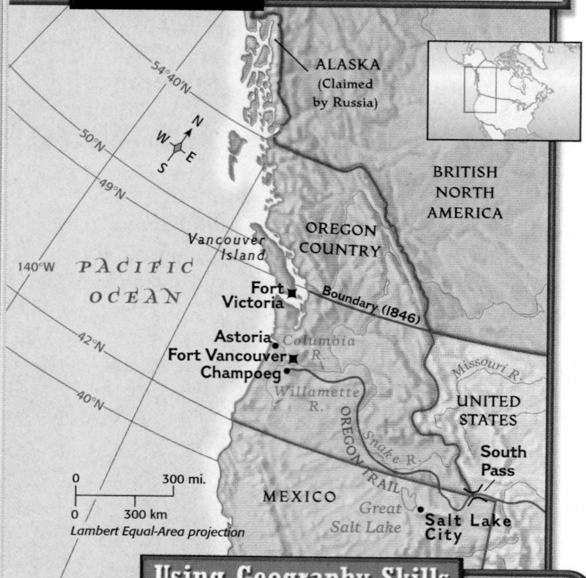

Using Geography Skills

Oregon Country included parts of several present-day states, including Oregon, Washington, and Idaho.

1. **Place** What major city is located between 40°N and 42°N?
2. **Location** At what line of latitude was the Oregon country divided between the United States and Britain?

The Cayuse killed the Whitmans and 11 others. Despite this tragedy, the flood of new settlers into Oregon continued.

The Oregon Trail In the early 1840s, "Oregon fever"—a desire to follow others to Oregon—began to sweep through the towns of the Mississippi Valley. People formed societies to gather information about Oregon and to plan and make the long journey. The "great migration" had begun. Tens of thousands of Americans made the trip. These pioneers were called **emigrants** (EH•mih•gruhnts) because they left the United States to go to Oregon, which was not yet a state. R1

Before the difficult 2,000-mile journey, these pioneers stuffed their canvas-covered wagons, called prairie schooners, with supplies. From a distance, these wagons looked like schooners (ships) at sea. Gathering in Independence or other towns in Missouri, they followed the **Oregon Trail** across the Great Plains, along the Platte River, and through the South Pass of the Rocky Mountains. On the other side, they took the trail north and west along the Snake and Columbia Rivers into Oregon Country. U

Most American pioneers headed for the fertile Willamette Valley south of the Columbia River. Between 1840 and 1845, the number of American settlers in the area increased from 500 to 5,000, while the British population remained at about 700. The question of ownership of Oregon arose again.

What Is Manifest Destiny? Many Americans thought their nation had a special role to fulfill. In the 1800s, many believed that the United States's mission was to occupy the entire continent. In 1819 John Quincy Adams expressed what many Americans were thinking when he said expansion to the Pacific was as inevitable "as that the Mississippi should flow to the sea."

In the 1840s, newspaper editor John O'Sullivan put the idea of a national mission in more specific words. O'Sullivan declared it was America's "**Manifest Destiny** to overspread and to possess the whole of the continent which Providence has given us." O'Sullivan meant that the United States was clearly destined—set apart for a special purpose—to extend its boundaries all the way to the Pacific. R2

"Fifty-four Forty or Fight" The settlers in Oregon insisted that the United States should have **sole** ownership of the area. More and more Americans agreed. In Congress, Tennessee representative Davy Crockett compared joint occupancy—shared ownership—to the time he shared a tree with a panther. "The place [was] big enough for us both," said Crockett, "but we couldn't agree to stay there together." As pressure mounted, Oregon became a major issue in the 1844 presidential election.

Answers and Additional Support

Using Geography Skills

Answers:

1. Salt Lake City
2. 49°N

More Skill Practice

Using Geography Skills Direct students' attention to the path taken by the Oregon Trail after it crosses South Pass. **Ask:** Why would the trail not turn immediately to the west? *(Students may say that the trail probably continues southwest because of mountains)* OL CA CS3. CA HI2.

In 1844 the Democrats were expected to nominate former president Martin Van Buren for president. Then the unexpected happened. The Democratic Party nominated **James K. Polk,** a former Congressman and governor of Tennessee for president. Polk supported American claims for sole ownership of Oregon. Democrats campaigned using the slogan "Fifty-four Forty or Fight." The slogan referred to the line of latitude that Democrats believed should be the nation's northern border in Oregon. Polk's campaign slogan captured the imagination of the voters.

R Henry Clay of the Whig Party, Polk's principal opponent, did not take a strong position on the Oregon issue. Polk won 50 percent of the popular vote and 170 electoral votes to Clay's 48 percent and 105 electoral votes.

Reaching a Settlement Filled with the spirit of Manifest Destiny, President Polk was determined to make Oregon part of the United States. Britain would not accept a border at "Fifty-four Forty," however, because this would have meant giving up its claim entirely. Instead, in June 1846, the two countries compromised, setting the boundary between the American and British portions of Oregon at latitude 49°N. The two nations had finally resolved the Oregon issue.

During the 1830s, Americans sought to fulfill their Manifest Destiny by looking at other regions as well as Oregon. At that time, much attention was also focused on Texas.

Reading Check **Explain** What did some Americans see as the purpose of Manifest Destiny?

History Online

Study Central Need help understanding Manifest Destiny? Visit ca.hss.glencoe.com and click on Study Central.

Section 1 Review

Reading Summary

Review the Main Ideas

- Oregon Country was the key element to the United States gaining access to the Pacific Ocean, and the government negotiated agreements with other nations toward accomplishing that goal.
- Many Americans made plans to settle in Oregon Territory, while ownership of the land drove political decisions.

What Did You Learn?

1. Which four countries claimed parts of the Oregon Country?
2. What mission does Manifest Destiny express?

Critical Thinking

3. **Determining Cause and Effect** Re-create the diagram below. In the box, describe how the fur trade led to interest in Oregon. CA HI2.

Cause	→	Effect
The fur trade develops		

4. **The Big Ideas** How did the idea of Manifest Destiny help Americans justify their desire to extend the United States to the Pacific Ocean? CA CS1.
5. **Picturing History** Study the painting on page 473. Do you think it provides a realistic portrayal of the journey west? Why or why not? CA HI5.
6. **Reading New Vocabulary** Write a paragraph using the following vocabulary terms: mountain man, rendezvous, and Manifest Destiny. Provide context clues, assuming that your readers will not know the meaning of these words. CA 8RW1.0

SECTION 1 REVIEW ANSWERS

Review questions reinforce content standard US8.8.

1. U.S., Britain, Spain, Russia
2. the American mission to occupy land from coast to coast
3. Fur traders were the first whites to settle in Oregon; Some fur trappers helped guide settlers to the area.
4. That idea said that Americans had the right to settle the whole continent, including Oregon.
5. Answers will vary; students may say that a family was unlikely to travel alone, as this one seems to be doing.
6. **Reading** Paragraphs will vary but should reflect information in the text.

R Reading Practice

Activating Prior Knowledge **Ask:** What do you know about Henry Clay? *(Students may recall that he was one of the War Hawks who were influential leading up to the War of 1812 and that he was charged with making a "corrupt bargain" along with John Quincy Adams after the 1824 presidential election.)* OL

ASSESS

Resources for page 475

Use these resources to assess student mastery of section content.

Section Quiz 11–1

Interactive Tutor Self-Assessment CD-ROM

Reading Check

Answer: to settle and possess all of North America

History Online

Study Central provides summaries, interactive games, and online graphic organizers to help students review section content.

CLOSE

Evaluating Text Have students evaluate John Quincy Adams's statement that American expansion to the Pacific was a "law of nature." OL

FOCUS

Point out to students that many issues invite opposing viewpoints. Sometimes those viewpoints are based on different principles. Sometimes they arise from the same shared principles that are applied in different ways. This feature poses a question and offers evidence on two sides of the matter. Students' task is to bring an open mind to the issue and read and evaluate the evidence provided.

TEACH

R1 Reading Strategy

Setting a Purpose **Ask:** What is the issue being debated in this feature? *(Whether Manifest Destiny contradicted the spirit of equality important to many Americans.)* OL

R2 Reading Strategy

Understanding Vocabulary Explain that *usurpation* means illegal seizure of control. **Ask:** Why did Gallatin use this word and not just say *seizure*? *(to emphasize that the seizure was illegal and thus not justified)* OL CA 8RW1.3

Answers and Additional Support

You Decide . . .

Manifest Destiny: Justified or Not? R1

Did Manifest Destiny contradict the spirit of equality important to so many Americans?

▲ Albert Gallatin

Not Justified

Albert Gallatin was one of many Americans who opposed Manifest Destiny. At the age of 86, after a distinguished career in public service, Gallatin became president of the New York Historical Society. The war against Mexico revived his interest in politics:

"It is said that the people of the United States have a hereditary superiority of race over the Mexicans, which gives them the right to subjugate and keep in bondage the inferior nation. . . . Is it compatible with the principle of democracy, which rejects every hereditary claim of individuals, to admit a hereditary superiority of races? . . . Can you for a moment suppose that a very doubtful descent from men who lived 1,000 years ago has transmitted to you a superiority over your fellow men?

. . . At this time the claim is but a pretext for covering and justifying unjust usurpation and unbounded ambition. R2

. . . Among ourselves the most ignorant, the most inferior, either in physical or mental faculties, is recognized as having equal rights, and he has an equal vote with anyone, however, superior to him in all those respects. This is founded on the immutable principle that no one man is born with the right of governing another man."

—quoted in *The Annals of America*

Extending the Content

Thoreau and the Mexican War Henry David Thoreau opposed the Mexican War. Like many abolitionists, he believed that the war was simply an excuse to expand the land available to slavery. When the federal government passed a law requiring citizens to pay a poll tax to fund the war, Thoreau refused to pay it and spent a night in jail. He later wrote the essay "Civil Disobedience" to express his thoughts on the need to stand against unjust laws.

Justified

John L. O'Sullivan first used the phrase Manifest Destiny in a July 1845 edition of the *United States Magazine and Democratic Review.* In the following article, he promotes the spread of democracy: O'Sullivan supported Manifest Destiny. **W**

"Texas is now ours. Already, before these words are written, her Convention has undoubtedly ratified the acceptance by her Congress, of our proffered invitation into the Union.... Her star and her stripe may already be said to have taken their place in the glorious blazon of our common nationality....

... The next session of Congress will see the representatives of the new young state in their places in both our halls of national legislation, side by side with those of the old Thirteen.

C Why ... [have] other nations ... undertaken to intrude themselves into [the question of Texas?] between us and the proper parties to the case, in a spirit of hostile interference against us, for the avowed object of thwarting our policy and hampering our power, limiting our greatness and checking the **R** fulfillment of our manifest destiny to overspread the continent allotted by Providence for the free development of our yearly multiplying millions."

—quoted in *Annexation*

▲ ***Spirit of the Frontier*** by John Gast

US8.8.2 Describe the purpose, challenges, and economic incentives associated with westward expansion, including the concept of Manifest Destiny (e.g., the Lewis and Clark expedition, accounts of the removal of Indians, the Cherokees' "Trail of Tears," settlement of the Great Plains) and the territorial acquisitions that spanned numerous decades.

You Be The Historian

DBQ Document-Based Questions

1. What does Albert Gallatin think is the real motivation underlying the idea of Manifest Destiny? CA HR3.
2. Imagine you could interview Gallatin and O'Sullivan. Write a list of three questions you could ask each man about his views on Manifest Destiny. CA HR3. CA 8RC2.3

You Decide...

W Writing Support

Persuasive Writing Have students write a response to either Gallatin's or O'Sullivan's positions. OL CA 8WA2.4

C Critical Thinking

Making Inferences Ask: What country is O'Sullivan thinking of when he mentions "other nations"? Why might that country have an interest in whether Texas became part of the United States? *(Mexico; because it is near Texas and because it still claimed that area)* OL

R Reading Strategy

Activating Prior Knowledge Ask: What does O'Sullivan mean by "Providence"? *(God)* How is this claim similar to that of the Spanish conquistadors of the 1500s? *(They also thought they were conquering in the name of God.)* OL

ASSESS/CLOSE

Have your students answer the You Be the Historian questions. Then, have them evaluate the two arguments. **Ask:** What flaws do you see in each position? Which writer argues his position most effectively? Have students discuss their conclusions. OL

You Be The Historian

1. greed and ambition
2. Students' questions will vary but should address the key points of each writer.

FOCUS

Write the following words on the board: *cell phone*, *pizza box*, *pair of jeans*, *newspaper sports section*, and *car*. Have students discuss what these objects reveal about people's lives in America today. Explain that in this feature they will read words and see images from life in the early 1800s.

TEACH

R Reading Strategy

Monitoring Discuss the details in the excerpt that show how difficult travel on the Oregon Trail was. **Ask:** What other problems do you think travelers faced in their journey to Oregon? *(Answers may include diseases; traveling through mountains; bad weather; and lack of food.)* OL

W Writing Support

Narrative Writing After reading Amelia Stewart's writing, have students write their own diary entries describing life along the Oregon Trail. OL

CA 8WA2.1

Answers and Additional Support

What were people's lives like in the past?

What—and who—were people talking about? What did they eat? What did they do for fun? These two pages will give you some clues to everyday life in the U.S. as you step back in time with TIME Notebook.

Profile

It's 1853, and **AMELIA STEWART** *is heading west to Oregon with her husband and seven children in a covered wagon. How hard can the five-month trip be? Here are two entries from her diary:* R

MONDAY, AUGUST 8 We have to make a drive of 22 miles without water today. Have our cans filled to drink. Here we left, unknowingly, our [daughter] Lucy behind, not a soul had missed her until we had gone some miles, when we stopped a while to rest the cattle; just then another train drove up behind us, with Lucy. She was terribly frightened and said she was sitting under the bank of the river when we started, busy watching some wagons cross, and did not know that we were ready. . . .It was a lesson for all of us.

FRIDAY, AUGUST 12 Lost one of our oxen. We were traveling slowly along, when he dropped dead in the yoke. . . .I could hardly help shedding tears, when we drove round this poor ox who had helped us along thus far, and had given us his very last step. W

BROWN BROTHERS

MILESTONES

EVENTS OF THE TIME

CLOTHED. Hundreds of miners in 1850 by **LEVI STRAUSS**. Using canvas he originally intended to make into tents, Levi made sturdy, tough pants with lots of pockets—perfect clothing for the rough work of mining. Can you imagine anyone in the city ever wearing them?

BETTMANN/CORBIS

MARCHED. Just under 100 camels in 1857, from San Antonio to Los Angeles, led by hired Turkish, Greek, and Armenian camel drivers. It is hoped the desert beasts will help the U.S. Army open the West.

MAILED. Thousands of letters carried by **PONY EXPRESS** in 1860 from Missouri to California in an extremely short time—only 10 days! Riders switch to fresh horses every 10 or 15 miles and continue through the night, blizzards, and attacks by outlaws.

FRONTIER FOOD

Trail Mix

Hard Tack for a Hard Trip

INGREDIENTS: 3 cups flour • 3 tsp. salt • 1 cup water

Mix all ingredients and stir until it becomes too difficult. Knead the dough; add more flour until mixture is very dry. Roll to 1/2-inch thickness and cut into 3" squares, poke with a skewer [pin] to make several holes in each piece (for easy breaking). Bake 30 minutes in a hot oven until hard. Store for up to 10 years.

History Online

Visit the TIME Web site at www.time.com for up-to-date news, weekly magazine articles, editorials, online polls, and an archive of past magazine and Web articles.

WESTERN WORD PLAY

Word Watch

Can you talk "Western"? Match the words below to their meaning.

1. maverick
2. Hangtown fry
3. grubstake
4. bonanza
5. palo alto
6. pard or rawwheel

a. gold rush favorite, made of eggs, bacon, and oysters
b. inexperienced '49er; eastern type not used to wearing boots
c. a lucky discovery of gold; a source of sudden wealth
d. a style of hat worn by gold rush miners
e. an individual who takes an independent stand, from the name of a Texas cattleman who left his herd unbranded
f. food provided by an investor to a gold prospector in exchange for a share of whatever gold the prospector finds

answers: 1. e; 2. a; 3. f; 4. c; 5. d; 6. b

The Price of a Life

This notice appeared in 1852.

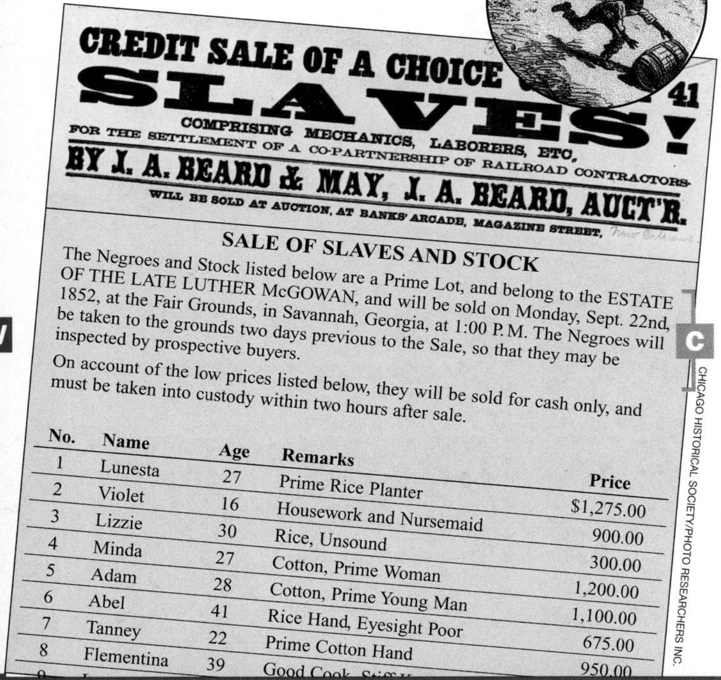

CREDIT SALE OF A CHOICE ... 41

SLAVES!

COMPRISING MECHANICS, LABORERS, ETC,

FOR THE SETTLEMENT OF A CO-PARTNERSHIP OF RAILROAD CONTRACTORS.

BY J. A. BEARD & MAY, J. A. BEARD, AUCT'R.

WILL BE SOLD AT AUCTION, AT BANKS' ARCADE, MAGAZINE STREET,

SALE OF SLAVES AND STOCK

The Negroes and Stock listed below are a Prime Lot, and belong to the ESTATE OF THE LATE LUTHER McGOWAN, and will be sold on Monday, Sept. 22nd, 1852, at the Fair Grounds, in Savannah, Georgia, at 1:00 P.M. The Negroes will be taken to the grounds two days previous to the Sale, so that they may be inspected by prospective buyers.

On account of the low prices listed below, they will be sold for cash only, and must be taken into custody within two hours after sale.

No.	Name	Age	Remarks	Price
1	Lunesta	27	Prime Rice Planter	$1,275.00
2	Violet	16	Housework and Nursemaid	900.00
3	Lizzie	30	Rice, Unsound	300.00
4	Minda	27	Cotton, Prime Woman	1,200.00
5	Adam	28	Cotton, Prime Young Man	1,100.00
6	Abel	41	Rice Hand, Eyesight Poor	675.00
7	Tanney	22	Prime Cotton Hand	950.00
8	Flementina	39	Good Cook, Stiff ...	

CHICAGO HISTORICAL SOCIETY/PHOTO RESEARCHERS INC.

NUMBERS

U.S. AT THE TIME

$81,249,700 Estimated value of gold mined in 1852

BROWN BROTHERS

89 Days it takes the American clipper ship, the *Flying Cloud,* to go from Boston around Cape Horn to San Francisco in 1851—a trip that normally takes eight or nine months

12 Poems included in Walt Whitman's new collection, called *Leaves of Grass* (1855)

33 Number of states in 1859 after Oregon enters the union

100 Seats in Congress won by the Republicans in 1854, the year the party was created

300,000 Copies of Harriet Beecher Stowe's novel, *Uncle Tom's Cabin,* sold in 1852

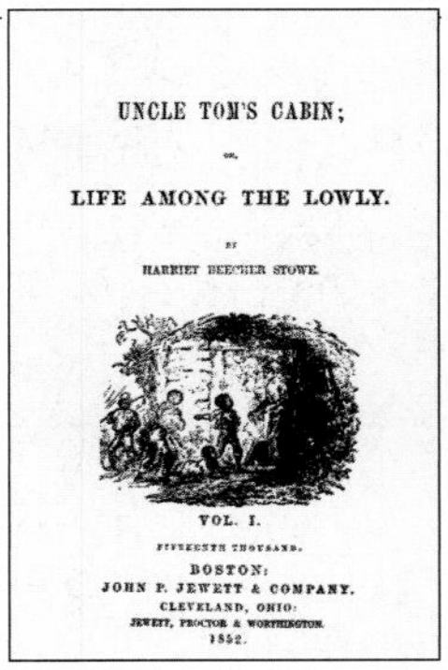

UNCLE TOM'S CABIN;

OR,

LIFE AMONG THE LOWLY.

BY

HARRIET BEECHER STOWE.

VOL. I.

FIFTEENTH THOUSAND.

BOSTON:

JOHN P. JEWETT & COMPANY.

CLEVELAND, OHIO:

JEWETT, PROCTOR & WORTHINGTON.

1852.

NORTH WIND PICTURE ARCHIVES

W Writing Support

Expository Writing Have students write a description of this sale from the perspective of one of the enslaved African Americans. OL CA 8WA2.1.

C Critical Thinking

Making Inferences Ask: Why were these enslaved people being sold? Why did the sellers insist on cash payment? *(the owner—"the late Luther McGowan"—had died; the family probably wanted to have cash so they could immediately take care of their needs)* OL

ASSESS

Have students identify which section of the feature they think tells most about life in the early 1800s and explain why. OL

CLOSE

Analyzing Information
Have students analyze the information on these pages to answer the question: "Did Americans live more challenging lives in the early 1800s than we do today"? Have them include details from the feature to support their argument.

EXTENDING THE CONTENT

The Oregon Trail Life along the Oregon Trail was long, extremely difficult, and sometimes tragic. Though often starting as part of a wagon train, individual families would be left behind to care for a sick family member or repair a wagon. Tolls were charged to ferry wagons across rivers or to travel along sections of the trail. Treasured family items and furniture were sometimes left behind as oxen labored to pull heavy wagons up steep embankments and mountains.

FOCUS

BELLRINGER
SKILLBUILDER ACTIVITY

Project **Daily Focus Skills Transparency 11–2** and have students answer the questions.

Guide to Reading

Preteaching Vocabulary: Have students find each content vocabulary term in the section, read it in context, and write a definition of it.

Answers to Graphic: Oct. 1835: Battle at Gonzales; Dec. 1835: Texans take San Antonio; Feb. 1836: siege of Alamo begins; Mar. 1836: Texans declare independence; Apr. 1836: Battle of San Jacinto; May 1836: Santa Anna signs treaty; Sept. 1836: Houston elected president of Texas

Unpacking the Standards

After reading the section, students will be able to:

- Discuss how and why Americans settled Texas.
- Explain why Texans declared independence.
- Describe how Texans won independence.

Section 2: Independence for Texas

Guide to Reading

History Social Science Standards

US8.8 Students analyze the divergent paths of the American people in the West from 1800 to the mid-1800s and the challenges they faced.

Looking Back, Looking Ahead
In the last section, you read about new settlements in Oregon country and the annexation of that land to the United States. In this section, you will learn about settlement in Texas.

Focusing on the Main Ideas
- Texas was settled by people from Mexico and the United States, creating cultural tension. *(page 481)*
- Texans wanted to be a nation separate from Mexico. *(page 483)*

Locating Places
Texas
Mexico
Alamo

Meeting People
Davy Crockett
Stephen F. Austin
General Antonio López de Santa Anna

Content Vocabulary
Tejano (teh • HAH • noh)
empresario (ehm • pray • SAR • ih • oh)
decree (dih • KREE)
annex (A • nehks)

Academic Vocabulary
status
similar

Reading Strategy
Sequencing Information As you read Section 2, re-create the diagram below. In the boxes, list key events that occurred in Texas.

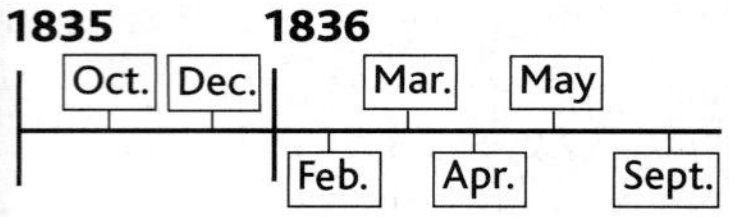

NATIONAL GEOGRAPHIC Who&When?

1830 — 1835 — 1840

1830 Mexico halts U.S. immigration into Texas

1833 Santa Anna becomes president of Mexico

March 1836 The Alamo falls

September 1836 Sam Houston is elected president of Texas

SECTION RESOURCES

Print Material
- Reproducible Lesson Plan 11–2*
- Daily Lesson and Discussion Notes 11–2
- Guided Reading Activity 11–2
- Reading Essentials and Study Guide 11–2
- Active Reading Note-Taking Guide 11–2
- Section Quiz 11–2

Transparencies
- Daily Focus Skills Transparency 11–2
- Section Graphic Organizer Transparency 11–2
- California Standards Practice Transparencies

Technology
- Interactive Tutor Self-Assessment CD-ROM
- Exam*View*® Pro Testmaker CD-ROM
- Presentation Plus! CD-ROM

*Available on TeacherWorks™

A Clash of Cultures

Main Idea **Texas was settled by people from Mexico and the United States, creating cultural tension.**

Reading Connection Did you know that Texas was not always part of the United States? Read to find out how this important region was the scene of international conflict.

An American Story

U Davy Crockett's skill as a hunter and storyteller helped get him elected to three terms in Congress representing Tennessee. But when he started his first political campaign, Crockett was doubtful about his chances of winning. "The thought of having to make a speech made my knees feel mighty weak and set my heart to fluttering." Fortunately for Crockett, the other candidates spoke all day and tired out the audience. "When they were all done," Crockett boasted, "I got up and told some laughable story, and quit. . . . I went home, and didn't go back again till after the election was over." In the end, Crockett won the election by a wide margin.

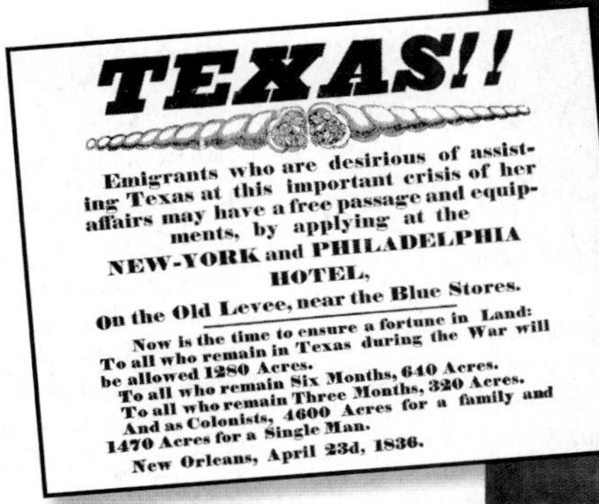
TEXAS!!

Emigrants who are desirious of assist-
ing Texas at this important crisis of her
affairs may have a free passage and equip-
ments, by applying at the
NEW-YORK and PHILADELPHIA
HOTEL,
On the Old Levee, near the Blue Stores.

Now is the time to ensure a fortune in Land:
To all who remain in Texas during the War will
be allowed 1280 Acres.
To all who remain Six Months, 640 Acres.
To all who remain Three Months, 320 Acres.
And as Colonists, 4600 Acres for a family and
1470 Acres for a Single Man.
New Orleans, April 23d, 1836.

Picturing History

This April 1836 poster from New Orleans asked for volunteers during the Texas War for Independence. Tennessee frontiersman Davy Crockett was one of the many who came to Texas. ***Why did Crockett go to Texas?***

Conflict Over Texas In 1835 **Davy Crockett** lost his seat in Congress. He then left Tennessee and headed southwest to **Texas.** Crockett thought he could make a new start there. Little did he know his deeds in Texas would bring him greater fame than his adventures on the frontier or his years in Congress.

R1 In 1803 the United States laid claim to Texas as part of the Louisiana Purchase. Spain protested, and in 1819 the United States agreed to drop its claim. At that time, most of Texas's 3,000 residents were ***Tejanos*** (teh • HAH • nohs), or Mexicans who claimed Texas as their home. R2 Native Americans, such as the Comanches, Apaches, and Kiowas, also lived in the area.

Wanting to promote Texas's growth, the Spanish offered vast tracts of land to people who agreed to bring families to settle on the land. The people who obtained these grants and recruited settlers were called ***empresarios*** (ehm • pray • SAR • ih • ohs). Moses Austin of Missouri received the first land grant in 1821. Before Austin set up his colony, **Mexico** declared its independence from Spain. Austin died soon afterward, and the land passed to his son, **Stephen F. Austin.** The younger Austin recruited 300 American families to settle the fertile land along the Brazos and Colorado Rivers of Texas. Austin's success made him a leader among the American settlers in Texas.

Chapter 11 • Section 2

TEACH

U Universal Access

Intrapersonal Point out that as a hunter and fighter, Davy Crockett had to be a brave man. **Ask:** Why was he so afraid about speaking in public? *(Students may say that public speaking called on skills he was not used to demonstrating.)* OL

R1 Reading Strategy

Activating Prior Knowledge **Ask:** Do you think the agreement about American claims to Texas took place in the Adams-Onís Treaty? Why or why not? *(Students are likely to say yes since that treaty was signed in 1819 and settled other land disputes between the U.S. and Spain.)* OL

R2 Reading Strategy

Understanding Vocabulary Have students write sentences using each term. *(Answers will vary but should demonstrate correct use of each term.)* OL CA 8RW1.3

Review The Big Idea

Review the Big Idea for this section "Immigration influences a nation's or region's economy and society." **Ask:** What geographical feature helped Foster's colonies on the Brazos and Colorado rivers gain success? *(The land was fertile.)* OL CA HI2.

Did You Know?

Born in Austinville, Virginia, Stephen F. Austin lived in Missouri, where he served in the territorial legislature. The economic panic of 1819 persuaded his father to abandon his Missouri lead-mining business and colonize Texas.

Picturing History

Ask: What in addition to free land does the poster use to encourage men to join the fight for Texas? *(By describing Texas's situation as a "crisis," those who created the poster hope to win support.)*

Answer: out of a desire to start a new life

W Writing Support

Persuasive Writing Have students take the role of a Mexican and write a letter to a local newspaper taking a position on the growing tension in Texas. OL CA 8WA2.4

R Reading Strategy

Understanding Vocabulary Point out that *decree* comes from a French word meaning "to decide." **Ask:** How is that origin connected to the meaning of the term? *(A decree is something that a ruler decides and then makes public.)* OL CA 8RW1.2

C Critical Thinking

Analyzing Information **Ask:** If Santa Anna agreed to allow Americans to settle in Texas once again, why were the Texans upset? *(because he would not change the status of Texas and because he overthrew the constitution of Mexico, which took away their legal protections)* OL

Reading Check

Answer: American settlers did not adopt Mexican ways, and the Mexican government viewed growing American influence with alarm.

Why Did Tension Grow? By 1830 Americans in Texas far outnumbered Mexicans and the American settlers had not adopted Mexican ways. In 1830 Mexico issued a **decree** (dih•KREE), or official order, that stopped all immigration from the United States. A tax was also placed on American goods entering Texas. These new policies angered the Texans. Many depended on trade with the United States and hoped for more Americans to settle in Texas. Those colonists who held slaves also feared that Mexico would try to end slavery in the territory.

Why Did Hopes for Reconciliation Fade? Some of the American settlers called for independence. Others hoped to stay within Mexico, but on better terms. In 1833 the Mexican president, **General Antonio López de Santa Anna,** agreed to remove the ban on American settlers. However, he refused to change Texas's political **status.** When Austin began making plans for independence, the Mexican government arrested him. Meanwhile, Santa Anna became a dictator and overthrew Mexico's constitution. Without a constitution to protect their rights, Texans felt betrayed. Austin believed the time had come to act. He urged the people to unite:

> **"War is our only recourse. There is no other remedy. We must defend our rights . . . by the force of arms."**
>
> —quoted in *Southwestern Historical Quarterly*

Reading Check **Explain** Why was colonization of Americans into Texas failing?

What If...

The Defenders Had Not Stayed at the Alamo?

William Travis and almost 200 other defenders were determined to hold the Alamo. Travis wrote several messages to the people of Texas and the United States asking them for assistance. Travis's appeal was unsuccessful. Texas military forces were not yet well organized and were badly scattered. Travis's letter of February 24, 1836, is one of the finest statements of courage in American history.

The defenders—mostly volunteers—were free to leave whenever they chose. But they decided to defend the Alamo for a cause in which they believed.

Santa Anna hoped the fall of the Alamo would convince other Texans that it was useless to resist his armies. Instead, the heroism of those in the Alamo inspired other Texans to carry on the struggle. "Remember the Alamo!" became the battle cry of Texas's army.

Travis's Appeal for Aid at the Alamo, February 24, 1836

To the People of Texas
and All Americans in the World–

Fellow Citizens and Compatriots:

I am besieged by a thousand or more of the Mexicans under Santa Anna. I have sustained a continual Bombardment & cannonade for 24 hours & have not lost a man. The enemy has demanded a surrender at discretion, otherwise the garrison are to be put to the sword if the fort is taken. I have answered the demand with a cannon shot, and our flag still waves proudly from the walls. I shall never surrender or retreat.

Then, I call on you in the name of Liberty, of patriotism, & of everything dear to the American character, to come to our aid with all dispatch. The enemy is receiving reinforcements daily & will no doubt increase to three or four thousand in four or five days. If this call is neglected I am determined to sustain myself as long as possible & die like a soldier who never forgets what is due to his honor & that of his country.

Victory or Death
William Barret Travis
Lt. Col. Comdt.

Answers and Additional Support

More Skill Practice

Analyzing Primary Sources Have students analyze Travis's letter to identify key words and phrases that might work in convincing others to come to the aid of the Alamo and of Texas in general. *(many possible answers, including "compatriots," the cannon shot fired in defiance of the demand to surrender, the words "I shall never surrender or retreat," and so on)* OL CA HR3.

US8.8.6 Describe the Texas War for Independence and the Mexican-American War, including territorial settlements, the aftermath of the wars, and the effects the wars had on the lives of Americans, including Mexican Americans today.

The Struggle for Independence

Main Idea **Texans wanted to be a nation separate from Mexico.**

Reading Connection Would you have the courage to stand up to a huge army for something you believed in? Read on to see how the soldiers at the Alamo defended their beliefs.

During 1835 unrest grew among Texans and occasionally resulted in open conflict. Santa Anna sent an army into Texas late that year to punish the rebels. In October some Mexican troops tried to seize a cannon held by Texans at the town of Gonzales. During the battle, the Texans taunted the Mexican troops, decorating the front of the cannon with a white flag that bore the words "Come and Take It." After a brief struggle, the Texans drove back the Mexican troops. Texans considered this to be the first fight of the Texan Revolution. **R**

The Texans called on volunteers to join their fight. They offered free land to anyone who would help. Davy Crockett and many others—including a number of African Americans and Tejanos—answered that call.

In December 1835, the Texans scored an important victory. They liberated the city of San Antonio from the control of a larger Mexican force. The Texas army at San Antonio included more than 100 Tejanos. Many of them served in a scouting company commanded by Captain Juan Seguín. Born in San Antonio, Seguín was an outspoken champion of the Texans' demand for independence. **U**

Despite these victories, the Texans encountered problems. With the Mexican withdrawal, some Texans left San Antonio, thinking the war was won. Various groups argued over what course of action to follow. In early 1836, when Texas should have been making preparations to face Santa Anna, little was being done. **C**

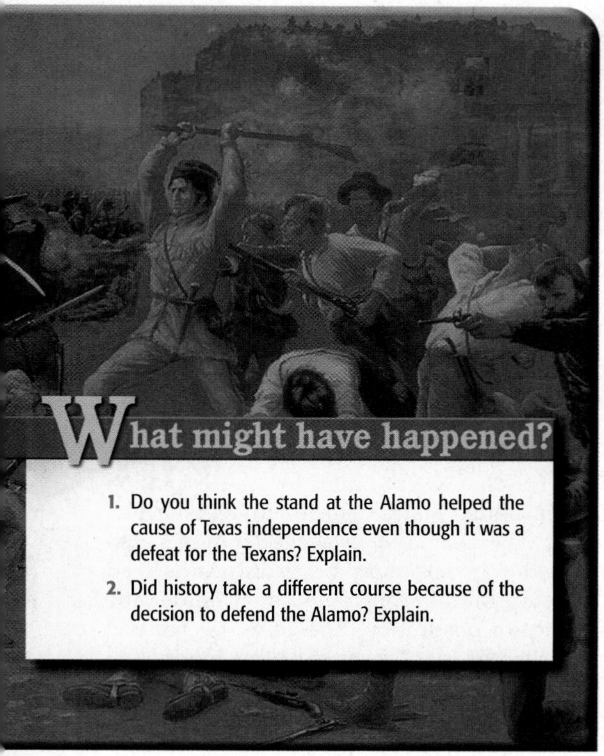

What might have happened?

1. Do you think the stand at the Alamo helped the cause of Texas independence even though it was a defeat for the Texans? Explain.
2. Did history take a different course because of the decision to defend the Alamo? Explain.

What Happened at the Alamo? Santa Anna marched north, furious about the loss of San Antonio. When his army reached San Antonio in late February 1836, it found a small Texan force barricaded inside a nearby mission called the **Alamo.**

Although the Texans had cannons, they lacked gunpowder. Worse, they had only about 160 soldiers to face Santa Anna's army of several thousand. The Texans did have brave leaders, though, including Davy Crockett, who had arrived with a band of sharpshooters from Tennessee, and a tough Texan named Jim Bowie. The American commander, William B. Travis, was only 26 years old, but he was determined to hold the mission. Travis managed to send messengers through the Mexican lines. He wrote several messages asking others to come to the aid of his soldiers. In his last message, Travis described the fighting that had already taken place and repeated his request for assistance. **W**

R Reading Strategy

Using Context Clues **Ask:** What does the phrase "Texas Revolution" mean? *(Texans' fight for independence from Mexico)* OL

U Universal Access

Below Grade Level Remind students that the Tejanos were people who lived in Texas but had come originally from Mexico, not the United States. BL

C Critical Thinking

Drawing Conclusions
Ask: Why did the Texans not use the time after winning San Antonio to better prepare for war? *(Students may suggest they were overconfident or disorganized.)* OL

W Writing Support

Expository Writing Have students write a newspaper story that explains what happened at the Alamo. OL CA 8WA2.1

What If...

Answers:

1. Answers will vary but students should note that the stand at the Alamo encouraged Texans to continue to fight for independence.
2. If the defenders of the Alamo had surrendered, Texas leaders might not have had time to declare independence.

More Skill Practice

Reading a Time Line Have students work together to make a large, illustrated time line of the events leading to Texas independence. Assign each student one event or one section of the line, and have them contribute text or images to highlight that event or section. OL CA CS1.

C1 Critical Thinking

Comparing and Contrasting **Ask:** How was the Alamo similar to the Battles of Lexington and Concord in the American Revolution? How was it different? *(similar: both fought early in the war; Americans and Texans were civilian fighters outnumbered by professional soldiers; both inspired others to fight; differences: Alamo and Lexington were defeats for the militia, while Concord was a victory)* OL CA HI2.

C2 Critical Thinking

Drawing Conclusions
Ask: Why is the survival of these people important to historians? *(Students may note that the accounts they could give of what happened would provide historians with the only chance to see what took place among the Alamo's defenders.)* OL CA HI5.

History Online

Objectives and answers to the student activity can be found in the Web Activity Lesson Plan feature at ca.hss.glencoe.com.

Answers and Additional Support

Picturing **History**

Susanna Dickinson was allowed by Santa Anna to leave the Alamo. She helped spread news of the Alamo defeat to the other Texas forces. ***What is the significance of the Battle of the Alamo?***

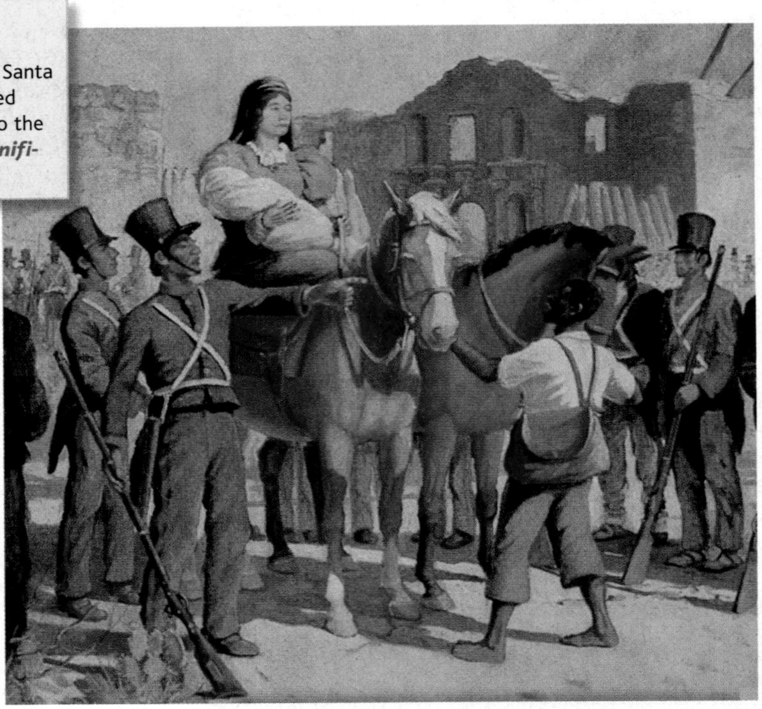

Travis warned that "the power of Santa Anna is to be met here, or in the colonies; we had better meet them here than to suffer a war of devastation to rage in our settlements."

Travis concluded with the statement that he and his troops were determined to hold the Alamo. For 13 long days, the defenders of the Alamo kept Santa Anna's army at bay with rifle fire. During the siege, 32 volunteers from Gonzales slipped through the Mexican lines to join the Alamo's defenders.

On March 6, 1836, Mexican cannon fire smashed the Alamo's walls, and the Mexicans launched an all-out attack. The Alamo defenders killed many Mexican soldiers, but the Mexicans were too numerous to hold back. They finally entered the fortress, killing William Travis, Davy Crockett, Jim Bowie, and all the other defenders. Only a few women and children and some servants survived to tell of the battle.

In the words of Santa Anna's aide, "The Texans fought more like devils than like men." The defenders of the Alamo had killed hundreds of Mexican soldiers. But more important, they had bought Texans some much needed time.

History Online

Student Web Activity Visit ca.hss.glencoe.com and click on *Chapter 11—Student Web Activities* for an activity on the fight for Texas independence.

Texas Declares Its Independence During the siege of the Alamo, Texan leaders were meeting at Washington-on-the-Brazos, where they were drawing up a new constitution. There, on March 2, 1836—four days before the fall of the Alamo—American settlers and Tejanos firmly declared independence from Mexico and established the Republic of Texas. Thus, Texas became a country and a neighbor to the United States.

The Texas Declaration of Independence was in some ways **similar** to the Declaration of the United States, which had been written 60 years earlier. The Texas Declaration stated that the government of Santa Anna had violated the liberties guaranteed under the Mexican Constitution. The Texas Declaration also charged that Texans had been deprived of freedom of religion, the right to trial by jury, the right to bear arms, and the right to petition.

More Skill Practice

Analyzing Primary Sources Have students conduct research to find the text of the Texas Declaration of Independence. Have them compare and contrast it to the American Declaration of Independence of 1776. AL CA HI2. CA HI3.

Picturing **History**

Dickinson was the wife of Captain Almeron Dickinson, who was in charge of the artillery that the Alamo defenders had.

Answer: Texans might not have gained independence without the battle. News of the defeat led to support for the struggle.

The Declaration stated that the Texans' protests against these policies were met with force. The Mexican government had sent a large army to drive Texans from their homes. Because of these grievances, the declaration proclaimed the following:

> **"The people of Texas. . . . do now constitute a free, sovereign, and independent republic. . . . "**
>
> **—from the Texas Declaration of Independence**

With Mexican troops in Texas, it was not possible to hold elections to ratify the constitution and vote for leaders of the new republic. Texas leaders set up a temporary government. They selected officers to serve until regular elections could be held.

David G. Burnet, an early pioneer in Texas, was chosen president and Lorenzo de Zavala, vice president. De Zavala had worked to establish a democratic government in Mexico. He moved to Texas when it became clear that Santa Anna would not make reforms.

The government named Sam Houston as commander in chief of the Texas forces. Houston had come to Texas in 1833. Raised among the Cherokee people, he became a soldier, fighting with Andrew Jackson against the Creek people in the Creek Wars (1813–1814). A politician as well, Houston had served in Congress and as governor of Tennessee.

Houston wanted to prevent areas from being overrun by the Mexican troops. He ordered the troops at the city of Goliad to abandon their position. As they retreated, however, they came face to face with Mexican troops. After a fierce fight, several hundred Texans surrendered. On Santa Anna's orders, the Texans were executed a few days later.

The Battle of San Jacinto Houston moved his small army eastward about 100 miles, watching the movements of Santa Anna and waiting for a chance to strike. Six weeks after the Alamo, he found the opportunity.

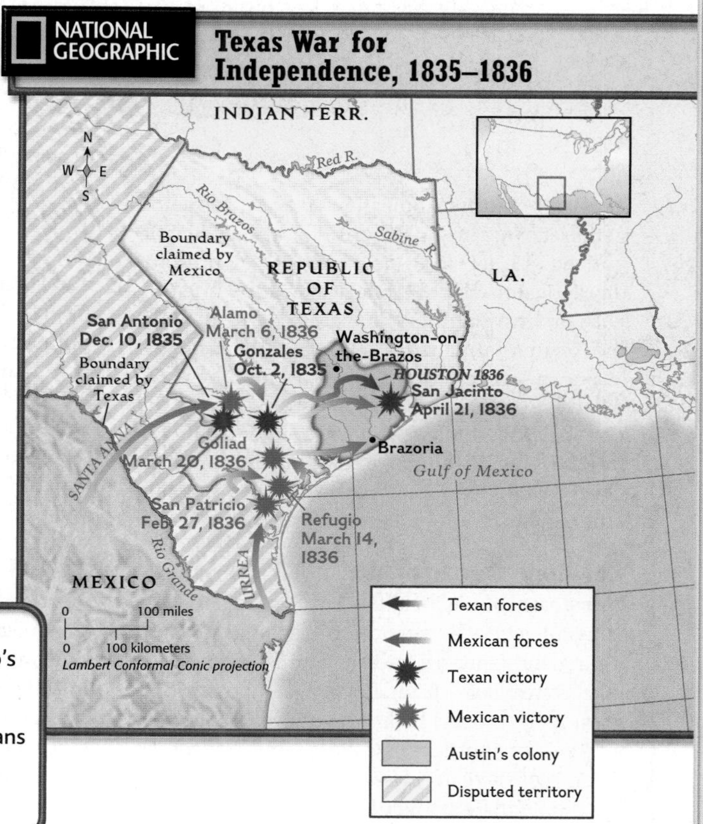

Using Geography Skills

In 1836 General Santa Anna led Mexico's main forces across the Rio Grande into Texas.

1. **Location** At which battles did Texans win victories?
2. **Analyze** What battle immediately followed the Alamo?

C1 Critical Thinking

Analyzing Primary Sources
Ask: Why did the Texans make these statements in their Declaration of Independence? *(to explain why they were driven to declare independence; to give reasons for their actions)* OL CA HI1.

R Reading Strategy

Monitoring Ask: Why did the Texans have to set up a temporary government? *(They could not hold elections with Mexican troops in their midst.)* OL

C2 Critical Thinking

Predicting Consequences
Ask: What effect do you think the Goliad massacre will have on Texans in future battles in this war? *(Students may say that the outraged Texans would be more likely to fight with determination.)* OL

C3 Critical Thinking

Determining Cause and Effect Ask: What disadvantage did Houston face at the Battle of San Jacinto? *(Santa Anna's army outnumbered his.)* How would launching a surprise attack help overcome that disadvantage? *(He might catch the Mexicans unprepared and disorganized.)* OL CA HI2.

Using Geography Skills

Answers:

1. San Antonio, Gonzales, San Jacinto
2. Refugio

Ask: What was the date of the last battle shown on the map? *(April 21, 1836)*

Did You Know?

Santa Anna tried to escape after his defeat at San Jacinto by dressing in an ordinary soldier's uniform and hiding in a marsh. He was captured the day after the battle by Texan soldiers who did not recognize him. His identity was revealed when he was brought into the Texans' camp and other captured Mexican soldiers saluted him.

Review Grade 5 Standards

To review standard **5.8.6** *(Relate how and when California, Texas, Oregon, and other western lands became part of the United States, including the significance of the Texas War for Independence and the Mexican-American War.),* **ask:** Why was independent Texas called "the Lone Star Republic"? *(Each state in the United States is represented on the flag by a star, but since Texas was its own country, its flag had only one star.)* OL

R Reading Strategy

Understanding Vocabulary

Have students define the term *annex*. *(to take control of an area)* **Ask:** What is annexation? *(the act of annexing an area)* OL

Picturing **History**

The painting (above) and the monument (left) commemorate the Battle of San Jacinto. ***Why was the battle a pivotal battle?***

After adding some new troops, Houston gathered an army of about 900 at San Jacinto (SAN huh • SIHN • toh), near the site of present-day Houston. Santa Anna was camped nearby with an army of more than 1,300. On April 21, the Texans launched a surprise attack on the Mexican camp, shouting, "Remember the Alamo! Remember Goliad!"

They killed more than 600 soldiers and captured about 700 more—including Santa Anna. On May 14, 1836, Santa Anna signed a treaty that recognized the independence of Texas.

The Lone Star Republic Texans elected Sam Houston as their president, in September 1836. Houston sent a delegation to Washington, D.C., asking the United States to **annex** (A • nehks)—take control of—Texas. However, the nation's president, Andrew Jackson, refused because the addition of another slave state would upset the balance of slave and free states in Congress. For the moment, Texas would remain an independent country.

The Question of Annexation Despite rapid population growth, the new republic faced political and financial difficulties. The Mexican government refused to honor Santa Anna's recognition of independence, and fighting continued between Texas and Mexico.

Many Texans still hoped to join the United States. Southerners favored the annexation of Texas, but Northerners objected that Texas would add another slave state to the Union. President Martin Van Buren, like Jackson, did not want to inflame the slavery issue. He put off the question of annexing Texas.

John Tyler, who became the nation's president in 1841, was the first vice president to become president upon the death of a chief executive. He succeeded William Henry Harrison, who died in April, just one month after taking office. He became ill after spending his inauguration day outdoors in bad weather.

Answers and Additional Support

Picturing **History**

The painting, by J.A. McArdle, shows the Texan forces charging from the left. Sam Houston, the Texan commander, stands just to the left of center waving a hat to urge his troops forward.

Answer: The Texan victory forced Santa Anna to sign a treaty that recognized the independence of Texas.

C Once he became president, Tyler supported adding Texas to the Union and persuaded Texas to reapply for annexation. However, the U.S. Senate was divided over slavery and failed to ratify the annexation treaty.

Texas Becomes a State The situation changed with the 1844 presidential campaign. The feeling of Manifest Destiny was growing throughout the country. The South favored annexation of Texas. The North demanded that the United States gain control of the Oregon country from Britain. The Democratic candidate, James K. Polk, supported both actions. The Whig candidate, Henry Clay, initially opposed adding Texas to the Union. When he finally supported annexation, it lost him votes in the North—and the election.

After Polk's victory, supporters of annexation pressed the issue in Congress. They proposed and passed a resolution to annex Texas. On December 29, 1845, Texas officially became a state of the United States.

Reading Check **Analyze** How has early Texas history influenced its reputation as a land of rugged individualists?

"We must now act or abandon all hope!"

—Sam Houston, before the Battle of San Jacinto

History Online

Study Central Need help understanding Texas's battle for independence? Visit ca.hss.glencoe.com and click on Study Central.

Section 2 Review

Reading Summary

Review the Main Ideas

- The majority of settlers in Texas were from the United States. American influence in the territory caused concern among Mexicans in Texas and Mexico.
- Texans struggled to create a state independent from Mexico, eventually achieving that goal in May 1836.

What Did You Learn?

1. What did the Spanish do to promote the growth of Texas?
2. Which leader of Mexico fought against the Texans?

Critical Thinking

3. **Categorizing Information** Re-create the diagram below. In the boxes, describe two causes of the war between Mexico and Americans in Texas. CA HI2.

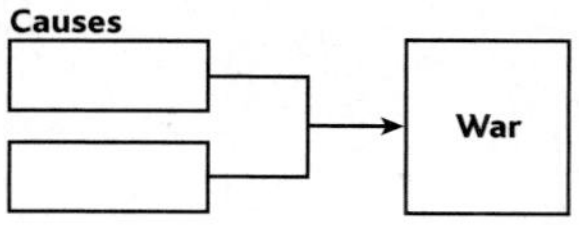

4. **The Big Ideas** Why did Northerners and Southerners disagree on the annexation of Texas? Explain. CA CS1.
5. **Analyze** How did the fall of the Alamo help the cause of Texas independence, even though it was a defeat for the Texans? CA CS1.
6. **Analysis Sequencing** Study the map on page 485. Place these battles in order on a time line, starting with the earliest: Gonzalez, San Jacinto, the Alamo, Goliad. CA CS2.

C Critical Thinking

Identifying Central Issues
Ask: Why was Texas not annexed by the United States after it won independence, when the government of Texas asked to be annexed? *(because of disputes in the U.S. over slavery)* How did that issue affect Texas when a president who favored annexation finally took office? *(The U.S. finally annexed it.)* OL

ASSESS

Resources for page 487

Use these resources to assess student mastery of section content.

- Section Quiz 11–2
- Interactive Tutor Self-Assessment CD-ROM

Reading Check

Answer: Many individuals fought against difficult odds to help Texas win independence.

History Online

Study Central provides summaries, interactive games, and online graphic organizers to help students review section content.

CLOSE

Monitoring **Ask:** Why did Houston's troops at San Jacinto shout "Remember the Alamo" and "Remember Goliad"? *(They wanted to avenge the deaths of the Texans who had fought there.)* OL

SECTION 2 REVIEW ANSWERS

Review questions reinforce content standard US8.8.

1. offered land to people who agreed to settle it
2. Antonio López de Santa Anna
3. Mexican government alarmed at growing American settlement; Mexican laws block more American settlers; Texans upset over change in status of Texas
4. **The Big Ideas** Texas had slavery; Northerners were opposed to bringing in another slave state, but Southerners favored it.
5. It bought Texans needed time to declare independence and form an army.
6. **Analysis** Oct. 2, 1835: Gonzales; Mar. 6, 1836: Alamo; Mar. 20, 1836: Goliad; Apr. 21, 1836: San Jacinto

NATIONAL GEOGRAPHIC

GEOGRAPHY & HISTORY

FOCUS

History–Social Science Standards

The following standard is covered on pages 488–489.

US8.8.4 Examine the importance of the great rivers and the struggle over water rights.

TEACH

R Reading Strategy

Understanding Vocabulary

Ask: What is a *tributary*?

(a stream or river that feeds into a larger river) **OL**

Answers and Additional Support

NATIONAL GEOGRAPHIC

GEOGRAPHY & HISTORY

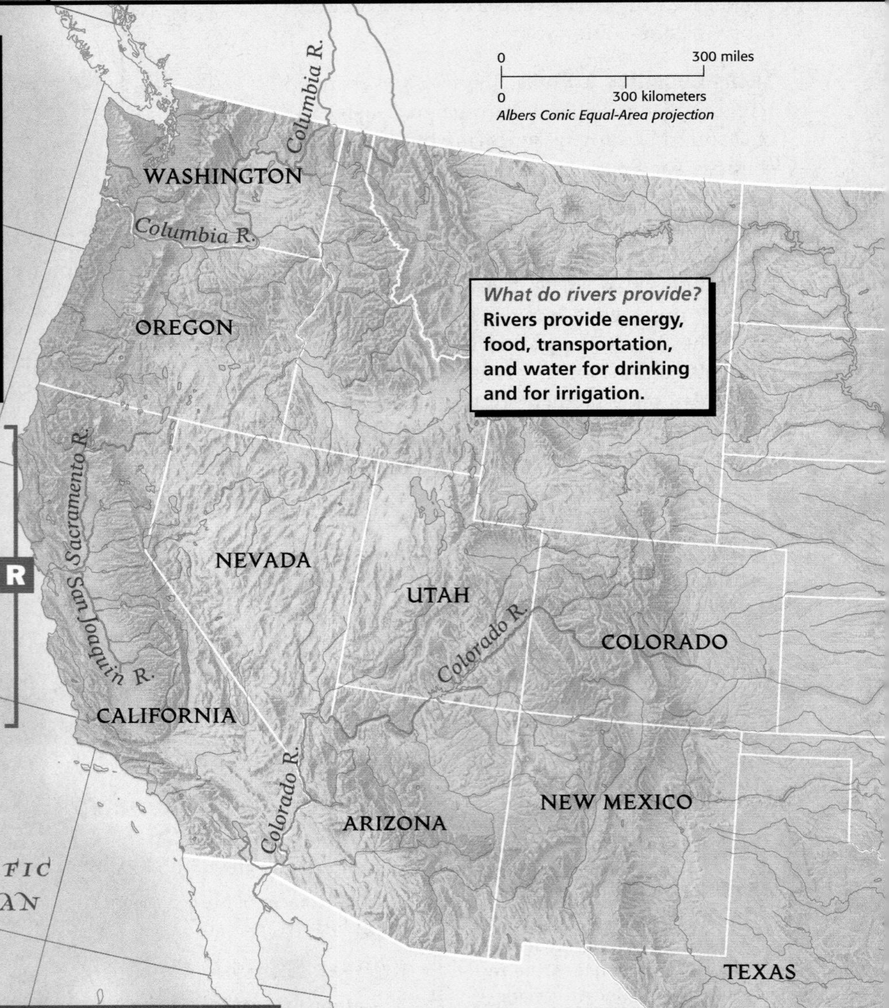

What do rivers provide? **Rivers provide energy, food, transportation, and water for drinking and for irrigation.**

What is a river? **A river is freshwater flowing across the surface of the land, usually to the sea. Rivers are formed when one stream meets another and they come together. These smaller streams are called tributaries.** **R**

What is the Colorado River Basin? **The Colorado River and its tributaries are called the Colorado River Basin. A basin is an area of land drained by a river and its tributaries. The Colorado River and its tributaries drain more than 240,000 square miles in the United States.**

Did You Know?

John Wesley Powell was a Civil War major who explored the uncharted territories of the Colorado River. In a series of daring river runs, Powell and a group of men canoed the length of the river from the Green River to the Gulf of California. Along the way, they collected specimens of plant and animal life, studied local Native American tribes, and drew maps of the river. Powell's findings were important to the many settlers who inhabited the region as well as to scientists interested in the area.

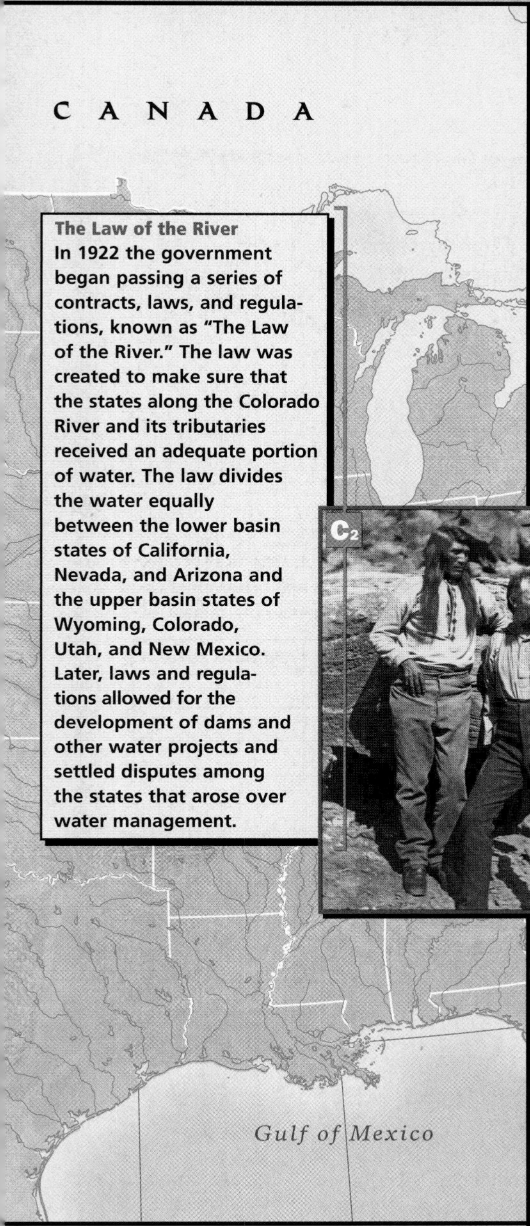

The Law of the River
In 1922 the government began passing a series of contracts, laws, and regulations, known as "The Law of the River." The law was created to make sure that the states along the Colorado River and its tributaries received an adequate portion of water. The law divides the water equally between the lower basin states of California, Nevada, and Arizona and the upper basin states of Wyoming, Colorado, Utah, and New Mexico. Later, laws and regulations allowed for the development of dams and other water projects and settled disputes among the states that arose over water management.

VITAL RESOURCES

Water—or rather the scarcity of it—defines the western states where precipitation averages just half that of the eastern states. In 1879 explorer John Wesley Powell correctly predicted that the ability to determine water rights and manage rivers was the key to settling this arid land. C1

COLORADO RIVER The Colorado River plunges 1,450 miles from the Rocky Mountains to the Gulf of California, through several states and two countries. Early settlers complained that its silt-laden waters were "too thick to drink, and too thin to plow." Today, a complex system of dams and canals controls and disperses the water to thirsty fields and cities from Colorado to Mexico. In the 1920s, the "Law of the River" apportioned the water between the seven Colorado River Basin states.

C2

▲ John Wesley Powell (right) and Paiute Chief Tau-gu during an expedition to the Grand Canyon

COLUMBIA RIVER This clear water once flowed unimpeded 1,243 miles from Canada to the Pacific Northwest. Today, 14 dams block the main course but provide cheap electricity, irrigation, drinking water, and flood control for millions of people. The human-caused changes reduced both salmon runs and the traditional jobs tied to them, prompting a new look at how humans use this vital waterway. R

SACRAMENTO/SAN JOAQUIN RIVERS Fed by winter snows in the lofty Sierra Nevada and Cascade Mountains, these rivers and a dozen tributaries drain California's vast interior. Complicated laws and a scheme of dams, reservoirs, and aqueducts channel this precious water to immense farmlands and densely populated cities throughout California.

LEARNING from GEOGRAPHY

1. What changes helped bring water to many regions? What problems did these changes cause?
2. What regulations did "The Law of the River" establish?

C1 Critical Thinking

Determining Cause and Effect Ask: Why is water availability more of a problem in the West than in the East? *(The West gets half the rainfall of the East.)* OL

R Reading Strategy

Sequencing Information Have students rank the three rivers—the Columbia, Sacramento, and Colorado—in size from longest to shortest. *(Colorado, Columbia, Sacramento)* OL

C2 Critical Thinking

Analyzing Information Ask: Why would states farther down a river want a law regulating the use of the river's water? *(to prevent states upriver from drawing off large amounts of water)* OL

ASSESS

Have students answer the **Learning from Geography** questions.

NGS ONLINE

Access National Geographic's Web site for current events, atlas updates, activities, links, interactive features, and archives at www.nationalgeographic.com.

CLOSE

Evaluating Have students explain the different uses that people have for rivers and why managing river water is important. OL

LEARNING from GEOGRAPHY

Answers to Learning from Geography

1. dams, canals, reservoirs, and aqueducts; the changes affected fish and people who depended on fish for their livelihood
2. division of water between the seven states; development of dams and other water projects and settlement of disputes among the states

FOCUS

BELLRINGER
SKILLBUILDER ACTIVITY

Project **Daily Focus Skills Transparency 11–3** and have students answer the question.

Guide to Reading

Preteaching Vocabulary: Have students identify which of the content vocabulary words came from Spanish. *(ranchero, rancho, Californios)*

Answers to Graphic: Becknell: blazed Santa Fe Trail; Smith: visited, wrote about San Gabriel Mission; Frémont: visited, wrote about California

Unpacking the Standards

After reading the section, students will be able to:

- Explain the importance of New Mexico Territory and the Santa Fe Trail.
- Describe California's Spanish culture.
- Discuss the causes and effects of the war with Mexico.

Section 3 War With Mexico

History Social Science Standards

US8.8 Students analyze the divergent paths of the American people in the West from 1800 to the mid-1800s and the challenges they faced.

Guide to Reading

Looking Back, Looking Ahead
You read about the Texans' brave struggle for independence. This section will focus on the war with Mexico over the California and New Mexico provinces.

Focusing on the Main Ideas
- The Santa Fe Trail was a busy trade route through New Mexico, a large region governed by Mexico. *(page 491)*
- California was settled and populated by diverse cultures. *(page 492)*
- Strained relations between the United States and Mexico resulted in war. *(page 495)*

Locating Places
Santa Fe (SAN • tuh FAY)
El Camino Real (kah • MEE • noh RAY • ahl)
Nueces River (nu • AY • suhs)
Bear Flag Republic

Meeting People
William Becknell
Jedediah Smith
María Amparo Ruiz de Burton
John C. Frémont

Content Vocabulary
ranchero (ran • CHEHR • oh)
rancho (RAN • choh)
Californio (ka • luh • FAWR • nee • OH)
cede (SEED)

Academic Vocabulary
concept
devote

Reading Strategy
Taking Notes As you read the section, describe the actions and achievements of each of the individuals in the table.

	Actions taken
William Becknell	
Jedediah Smith	
John C. Frémont	

NATIONAL GEOGRAPHIC Who & When?

1844 — 1846 — 1848

1845 American forces led by General Zachary Taylor fight Mexican forces

1846 Bear Flag Republic is proclaimed

1848 Treaty of Guadalupe Hidalgo is signed

SECTION RESOURCES

Print Material
- Reproducible Lesson Plan 11–3*
- Daily Lesson and Discussion Notes 11–3
- Guided Reading Activity 11–3
- Reading Essentials and Study Guide 11–3
- Active Reading Note-Taking Guide 11–3
- Section Quiz 11–3

Transparencies
- Daily Focus Skills Transparency 11–3
- Section Graphic Organizer Transparency 11–3
- California Standards Practice Transparencies

Technology
- Interactive Tutor Self-Assessment CD-ROM
- Exam*View*® Pro Testmaker CD-ROM
- Presentation Plus! CD-ROM

*Available on TeacherWorks™

US8.8.6 Describe the Texas War for Independence and the Mexican-American War, including territorial settlements, the aftermath of the wars, and the effects the wars had on the lives of Americans, including Mexican Americans today.

The New Mexico Territory

Main Idea **The Santa Fe Trail was a busy trade route through New Mexico, a large region governed by Mexico.**

Reading Connection Can you imagine walking from Missouri to Arizona, or beyond? Read on to see how traders did just that.

An American Story

Long lines of covered wagons stretched as far as the eye could see. "All's set!" a driver called out. "All's set!" everyone shouted in reply.

"Then the 'Heps!' of drivers—the cracking of whips—the trampling of feet—the occasional creak of wheels—the rumbling of wagons—form a new scene of [intense] confusion," reported Josiah Gregg. Gregg was one of the traders who traveled west on the Santa Fe Trail in the 1830s to sell cloth, knives, and other goods in New Mexico.

What Areas Did New Mexico Include? In the early 1800s, New Mexico was the name of a vast region sandwiched between the Texas and California territories. It included all of present-day New Mexico, Arizona, and Nevada, and parts of Colorado and Utah.

Native American peoples had lived in the area for thousands of years. Spanish conquistadors began exploring the region in the late 1500s and made it part of Spain's colony of Mexico. In 1610 the Spanish founded the settlement of **Santa Fe** (SAN•tuh FAY). When Mexico won its independence from Spain in 1821, it inherited the New Mexico province.

The Spanish had tried to keep Americans away from Santa Fe, fearing that Americans would want to take over the area. The Mexican government changed this policy, welcoming American traders into New Mexico. It hoped that trade would boost the economy of the province.

How Was the Santa Fe Trail Used? **William Becknell,** the first American trader to reach Santa Fe, arrived in 1821 with a pack of mules loaded with manufactured goods to exchange for furs.

Becknell's route into New Mexico came to be known as the Santa Fe Trail. The trail left the Missouri River near Independence, Missouri, and crossed the prairies to the Arkansas River. It followed the river west toward the Rocky Mountains before turning south into New Mexico. Because the trail was mostly flat, on later trips Becknell used wagons to carry his merchandise.

Other traders followed Becknell, and the Santa Fe Trail became a busy trade route for hundreds of wagons. Americans brought cloth and firearms, which they exchanged in Santa Fe for silver, furs, and mules. The trail remained in use until the arrival of the railroad in 1880.

As trade with New Mexico increased, Americans began settling in the region. In the United States, the **concept** of Manifest Destiny became popular, and many people saw New Mexico as territory worth acquiring. At the same time, they eyed another prize—the Mexican territory of California, which would provide access to the Pacific.

Reading Check **Identify** Where did the Santa Fe Trail end? What was it used for?

▲ Santa Fe Trail marker

TEACH

R Reading Strategy

Connecting **Ask:** How does the New Mexico Territory of the 1800s compare to the state of New Mexico today? *(much larger; included present-day states of Arizona and Nevada and parts of Utah and Colorado as well as New Mexico)* OL CA CS3.

Review Grade 7 Standards

To review standard **7.9.4** *(Identify and locate the European regions that remained Catholic and those that became Protestant and explain how the division affected the distribution of religions in the New World),* **ask:** Did the people who lived in the New Mexico Territory share the same culture, language, and religion as Americans? Explain why or why not. *(Students should infer that since the region was settled by Spain, the people had Spanish culture, spoke Spanish, and were Catholics.)* OL

Reading Check

Answer: Santa Fe, New Mexico; to carry out trade between the U.S. and Mexico

More Skill Practice

Historical and Social Science Analysis Skill Why did Mexico have a different policy toward American traders in New Mexico than Spain had had? *(It wanted to encourage trade to build up the economy.)*
OL CA HI2.

R1 Reading Strategy

Categorizing Information Have students take notes on this subsection under three headings: *Spanish California; Mexican California;* and *Americans and California.* OL

C Critical Thinking

Analyzing Primary Sources **Ask:** What did the American in Smith's party mean by this statement? *(Students may say that, like slaves, the Native Americans on missions had no control over their own lives.)* OL

CA HR5.

R2 Reading Strategy

Academic Vocabulary Ask students to list synonyms for the word *devoted.* OL

R3 Reading Strategy

Understanding Vocabulary **Ask:** What is the difference between a *rancho* and a *ranchero*? *(Rancho is a ranch; ranchero is a person who owns a ranch.)* OL

Resources for page 492

Geography and History Activity 11

US8.8.5 Discuss Mexican settlements and their locations, cultural traditions, attitudes toward slavery, land-grant system, and economies.

R1 California's Spanish Culture

Main Idea **California was settled and populated by diverse cultures.**

Reading Connection Imagine you lived in California in the mid-1800s. Would you like to have been a Native American, a rancher, or a settler from the East?

Spanish explorers and missionaries from Mexico had been the first Europeans to settle in California. Explorer Juan Bautista de Anza opened the overland route from Mexico to California and established the first settlement at San Francisco in 1776. Seven years earlier, Captain Gaspar de Portolá and Father Junípero Serra began building a string of missions that eventually extended from San Diego to Sonoma. These missions were connected along a route known as ***El Camino Real*** (kah • MEE • noh RAY • ahl), "the King's Highway," named for the king of Spain who ordered the missions built.

The mission system was a key part of Spain's plan to colonize California. The Spanish used the missions to convert Native Americans to Christianity. By 1820 California had 21 missions, with about 20,000 Native Americans living in them. In 1820 American mountain man **Jedediah Smith** visited the San Gabriel Mission east of present-day Los Angeles. Smith reported that the Native Americans farmed thousands of acres and worked at weaving and other crafts. He described the missions as "large farming and grazing establishments." Another American in Smith's party called the Native Americans "slaves in every sense of the word." C

California After 1821 After Mexico gained its independence from Spain in 1821, California became a state of Mexico. At the time only a few hundred Spanish settlers lived in California, but emigrants began arriving from Mexico. The wealthier settlers lived on ranches **devoted** to raising cattle and horses. R2

In 1833 the Mexican government passed a law abolishing the Spanish missions. The government gave some of the lands to Native Americans and sold the remainder. Mexican settlers called **rancheros** (ran • CHEHR • ohs)—ranch owners—bought these lands and built huge properties called **ranchos** (RAN • chohs). R3

History *Through Art*

Vaqueros in a Horse Corral **by James Walker** Mexican American cowhands, or vaqueros, work on a ranch in the Southwest. ***Why did the number of ranchos grow in the 1820s and 1830s?***

Answers and Additional Support

More Skill Practice

Comparing and Contrasting Have students create a chart showing the similarities and differences between the New Mexico Territory and California. OL

History *Through Art*

Many words in English come from the work of the vaqueros, including *bronco*, *corral*, and *rodeo*.

Answer: In 1833 the Mexican government abolished the missions and sold some of the land to people, who established ranchos.

Biography

US8.8.5 Discuss Mexican settlements and their locations, cultural traditions, attitudes toward slavery, land-grant system, and economies.

María Amparo Ruiz de Burton

1832–1895

María Amparo Ruiz de Burton was the first Mexican American to publish a novel in English in the United States. Born into a wealthy family in Baja California in 1832, she stood to inherit the vast landholdings of her grandfather. She would eventually learn, however, that though the treaty of Guadalupe Hidalgo ensured the land rights of Mexican American citizens, these rights would not be enforced.

After the war with Mexico, María married Colonel Henry Burton, an officer in the U.S. army. In 1859 the Burton family moved to Rhode Island, and María did not return to California until 1869 after the death of her husband. When she returned, she found that much of the land she and her husband owned had been sold and that the rest was inhabited by American squatters. **R** In 1851 the California Land Act made all land owned by Mexicans public domain and available for settlement until the land titles of the original owners could be verified. Burton began a lengthy and expensive legal battle that would continue until her death in 1895. She died destitute and landless.

"I think but few Americans know or believe to what extent we have been wronged by Congressional action." **C2**
—from ***The Squatter and the Don***

Burton wrote two novels during her battles with the government over her land. Her first novel, *Who Would Have Thought It?*, challenges the idea of American supremacy by claiming that Mexicans are as white by blood as Americans. Although this argument maintains a social hierarchy of certain races over others, her statements on the treatment of Mexicans and on U.S. political corruption were important to the time period. **C1** Her second novel, *The Squatter and the Don*, again deals with the problems of corruption and racism by focusing on land battles in California. Burton's legacy impacted both literature and Mexican American history. Her fight for her land, though unsuccessful, exposed the discriminatory actions by many Americans against Mexican citizens.

Then and Now

Burton fought for most of her life for her land. Find someone today who similarly has fought for his or her rights.

Biography

TEACH

R Reading Strategy

Using Context Clues **Ask:** Based on the text, what is a *squatter*? *(Students should determine that squatters are people who occupy and lay claim to another person's land or empty land.)* OL

Review The Big Ideas

Review the Big Idea for this section "Conflict often brings about great change." **Ask:** What changes did Burton and others like her face? *(the loss of their land)* OL

C1 Critical Thinking

Identifying Central Issues **Ask:** What would Burton hope to gain by publishing novels with these themes? *(Students may say that she hoped to win wider support for Mexican Americans and herself.)* OL

C2 Critical Thinking

Analyzing Primary Sources **Ask:** Do you agree with Burton that only a few Americans knew of the problem? Why or why not? *(Answers will vary but should be supported by reasons.)* OL

Then and Now

Answers will vary, but students should give reasons for the person or persons they identify.

Review Grade 5 Standards

To review standard **5.8.3** *(Demonstrate knowledge of the explorations of the trans-Mississippi West following the Louisiana Purchase (e.g., Meriwether Lewis and William Clark, Zebulon Pike, John Frémont.),* **ask:** How would American readers respond to Frémont's description of California? Why? *(Students should note that they would be likely to find the area appealing.)* OL

C Critical Thinking

Drawing Conclusions

Ask: Why do you think Mexico refused to sell New Mexico and California? *(Students may suggest that Mexico wanted to keep these valuable lands and to protect the Mexican people who lived in those territories.)* OL

Reading Check

Answer: its location; also, Frémont wrote of the region's mild climate, scenic beauty, and abundant natural resources

Answers and Additional Support

Picturing History

Established in 1826, Monterey was the capital of California until 1847. ***When did California become a state of Mexico?***

Manifest Destiny and California Americans had been visiting California for years. Most arrived on trading or whaling ships, although a few hardy travelers like Jedediah Smith came overland from the East. Soon more began to arrive by land and sea.

At first, the Mexican authorities welcomed Americans in California. In 1839 they granted land in the Sacramento Valley to John Sutter, a German immigrant. There Sutter built a trading post that became one of the first stopping points for Americans reaching California.

The newcomers included agents for American shipping companies, fur traders from Oregon, and merchants from New Mexico. In the 1840s, families began to arrive in California to settle. They made the long journey from Missouri on the Oregon Trail and then turned south after crossing the Rocky Mountains. Still, by 1845 the American population of California numbered only about 700. Most Americans lived in the Sacramento River valley.

Some American travelers wrote glowing reports of California. **John C. Frémont,** an army officer who made several trips through California in the 1840s, wrote of the region's mild climate, scenic beauty, and abundance of natural resources.

Americans began to talk about adding California to the nation. Shippers and manufacturers hoped to build ports on the Pacific coast for trade with China and Japan. Many Americans saw the advantage of extending United States territory to the Pacific. That way, the nation would be safely bordered by the sea instead of by a foreign power, namely Mexico. William Marcy, U.S. Secretary of War, wrote:

> **"It is the wish. . . of the United States to provide for [California] a free government with the least possible delay, similar to that which exists in our territories."**
>
> **—letter to Colonel Stevenson**

President James Polk twice offered to buy California and New Mexico from Mexico, but Mexico refused. Soon, the United States would take over both regions by force. C

Reading Check **Examine** What made California attractive for U.S. expansion?

Did You Know?

John C. Frémont had two valuable allies. His father-in-law was Thomas Hart Benton of Missouri, a powerful member of the Senate and a supporter of Manifest Destiny. Frémont's wife, Jessie Benton Frémont, was a skillful writer who helped craft Frémont's reports, which were well received.

Picturing History

The first settlement at Monterey was a presidio, or fort, founded by the Spanish in 1770. Today that presidio is home to the Defense Language Institute.

Answer: in 1821

War With Mexico

C1

Main Idea **Strained relations between the United States and Mexico resulted in war.**

Reading Connection How much would you pay for California and New Mexico? Read to learn what President Polk offered and how his offer was received.

President James K. Polk was determined to get the California and New Mexico territories from Mexico. Their possession would guarantee that the United States had clear passage to the Pacific Ocean—an important consideration because the British still occupied part of Oregon. Polk's main reason, though, involved fulfilling the nation's Manifest Destiny. Like many Americans, Polk believed California and New Mexico belonged to the United States.

C2

After Mexico refused to sell California and New Mexico, President Polk plotted to pull the Mexican provinces into the Union through war. He wanted, however, to provoke Mexico into taking military action first. This way Polk could justify the war to Congress and the American people.

Relations between Mexico and the United States had been strained for some years. When the United States annexed Texas in 1845, the situation worsened. Mexico, which had never recognized the independence of Texas, charged that the annexation was illegal.

Another dispute concerned the Texas-Mexico border. The United States insisted that the Rio Grande formed the border. Mexico claimed that the border lay along the **Nueces River** (nu • AY • suhs), 150 miles farther north. Because of this dispute, Mexico had stopped payments to American citizens for losses suffered during Mexico's war for independence.

Polk sent an agent, John Slidell, to Mexico City to propose a deal. Slidell was authorized to offer $30 million for California and New Mexico in return for Mexico's acceptance of the Rio Grande as the Texas boundary. In addition, the United States would take over payment of Mexico's debts to American citizens.

How Did Conflict Begin? Mexican officials refused to meet with Slidell and stated their plan to reclaim Texas. Polk then ordered General Zachary Taylor to march his soldiers across the Nueces River into the disputed border area. R

NATIONAL GEOGRAPHIC

The War With Mexico, 1846–1848

Using Geography Skills

War between the United States and Mexico broke out in 1846 near the Rio Grande.

1. **Location** Which battle occurred farthest north?
2. **Infer** What information on the map can you use to infer which side won the war?

R Reading Strategy

Understanding Question and Answer Relationships Suggest that students use the questions in this and other headings in this subsection to guide their reading. **Ask:** How did the conflict begin? *(Polk ordered American troops into the disputed area, and they were attacked by Mexican forces.)* OL

C1 Critical Thinking

Identifying Central Issues Have students take the role of a Mexican government official and write a memo to the country's president in which they outline the problem with the United States and recommend what steps to take. AL CA HI1. CA 8WA2.4

C2 Critical Thinking

Determining Cause and Effect **Ask:** Why did Polk want to provoke Mexico? *(so it would attack first and he could more easily justify a war)* OL CA HI2.

S Skill Practice

Using Geography Skills **Ask:** Why is part of Texas labeled "disputed territory"? *(Mexico and the U.S. disagreed on the location of the border between Texas and Mexico.)* OL CA CS3.

Using Geography Skills

Answers:

1. Bear Flag Revolt
2. There are many more blue symbols indicating American victories than green symbols that show Mexican victories.

W Writing Support

Persuasive Writing Have students take the role of a Northern political leader who opposes the war with Mexico. Have them draft a speech explaining why they oppose the war. OL CA 8WA2.4

S Skill Practice

Using Geography Skills Suggest that students refer to the map on page 495 as they read about battles in the war to locate where they took place. OL CA CS3.

C Critical Thinking

Making Inferences Ask: Did Mexico have strong military forces in New Mexico? Explain why you think it did or did not. *(Students may say that Mexico did not have strong forces since the area was given up to Kearny's force without a fight.)* OL

R Reading Strategy

Monitoring Ask: What was the Bear Flag Republic? *(new republic proclaimed in June 1846 by some Americans in California)* OL

Answers and Additional Support

Taylor followed the order and built a fort there. In April 1846, Mexican soldiers attacked a small force of Taylor's soldiers. Taylor quickly notified Polk. On May 9, Polk told Congress that "Mexico has . . . shed blood on American soil." Congress passed a declaration of war against Mexico.

How Was News of the War Received? The war with Mexico divided Americans. Polk's party, the Democrats, generally backed it. Many Whigs believed the war was aggressive and unjust. Northerners accused the Democrats of waging war to spread slavery. W

Illinois congressman Abraham Lincoln demanded to know the exact spot where the first attack on American troops had occurred. He claimed that the spot was clearly in Mexico and that Polk had no reason for blaming Mexico.

Frederick Douglass, an African American leader, called the war "disgraceful." He believed that the Southern states would bring slavery to any new territories won in the war. Newspapers mostly backed the war, and volunteers rushed to join the military.

Picturing History

In June 1846, settlers in northern California declared California independent of Mexico and renamed the region the Bear Flag Republic. ***What was John C. Frémont's role in the uprising?***

Polk's War Plan President Polk planned for American forces to drive Mexico out of the disputed border region in Texas. Then, the forces would move into New Mexico and California. Finally, Mexico City, the capital of Mexico, would be taken.

In September 1846, General Taylor's forces crossed the Rio Grande and captured the town of Monterrey. About five months later, he defeated the Mexicans again at Buena Vista. The Texas border was secure. S

While Taylor advanced in northern Mexico, General Stephen Watts Kearney led his troops to California and New Mexico. In the summer of 1846, Kearny led about 1,500 cavalry soldiers along the Santa Fe Trail from Missouri to New Mexico. The Americans captured New Mexico's capital, Sante Fe, without firing a shot. Kearny and his forces then moved westward across the deserts to California. C

What Was the Bear Flag Republic? In June 1846, a small group of Americans had seized the town of Sonoma north of San Francisco and proclaimed the independent Republic of California. They called the new country the **Bear Flag Republic** because their flag showed a bear and star on a white background. John C. Frémont and mountain man Kit Carson joined the Americans in Sonoma. R

Though unaware of the outbreak of war with Mexico, Frémont declared he would seize California. Frémont's actions outraged many **Californios** (ka•luh•FAWR•nee•OHS), the Mexicans who lived in California. They might have supported a revolt for local control of government, but they opposed what looked like an attempt by a band of Americans to seize land.

Naval Intervention In July 1846, U.S. naval forces under Commodore John Sloat captured the ports of Monterey and San Francisco. Sloat declared California annexed to the United States. Sloat's fleet then sailed for San Diego, carrying Frémont and Carson. The Americans captured San Diego and moved north toward Los Angeles.

More Skill Practice

Historical and Social Science Analysis Skill Ask: Why did the war with Mexico increase tensions between sections in the United States? *(Most Southerners supported it, but many in the North thought it was part of a plan to extend slavery and opposed it.)* OL

Picturing History

Frémont's explorations of California gained him the nickname "Pathfinder." Portraits like this one helped project his image as a romantic hero.

Answer: He moved to seize the region.

Carson headed east with the news of California's annexation. On the way, he joined Kearny's force, marching west from Santa Fe.

After Sloat's ships left, many Californios in San Diego rose up against the Americans controlling the city. General Kearny's troops arrived in the midst of the uprising. They faced a stiff fight but finally won. By January 1847, California was under American control.

The Capture of Mexico City After these victories, American forces set out to take Mexico City. In March 1847, troops under General Winfield Scott landed on the coast of Mexico, near the port of Veracruz. Scott captured the city and then began a 300-mile march to Mexico City. On the way, the Americans battled Mexican soldiers and armed citizens. By mid-September, Mexico City had been taken, and the Mexican government surrendered.

What Were the Terms of the Peace Treaty?

Peace talks began in January 1848. A month later, the Treaty of Guadalupe Hidalgo (GWAH • duhl • OOP hih • DAL • goh) was signed. In the treaty, Mexico gave up all claims to Texas and agreed to the Rio Grande as the border between Texas and Mexico. Also, in what was called the Mexican Cession, Mexico **ceded** (SEED • uhd)—gave—California and New Mexico to the United States. In return, the United States gave Mexico $15 million. **R**

In 1853 the United States paid Mexico another $10 million for the Gadsden Purchase, a strip of land along the southern edge of present-day Arizona and New Mexico. With this purchase, the United States mainland reached its present size. All that remained was to settle the newly won territories.

Reading Check **Describe** What lands did Mexico cede to the United States?

History Online
Study Central Need help understanding the war with Mexico? Visit ca.hss.glencoe.com and click on Study Central.

Section 3 Review

Reading Summary

Review the Main Ideas

- Americans established a busy trade route called the Santa Fe Trail through a large region governed by Mexico, called New Mexico.
- The cultures of Mexicans, Native Americans, and white Americans intermingled in California.
- The United States continued to pursue annexing California and the rest of the New Mexico region, which eventually resulted in war between the United States and Mexico.

What Did You Learn?

1. According to the Mexican government, where was the border between Texas and Mexico?
2. How much did the United States pay for New Mexico and California?

Critical Thinking

3. **Categorizing Information** Re-create the diagram below and describe the three parts of Polk's strategy to extend U.S. territory. CA CS1.

4. **The Big Ideas** Why did the Spanish establish missions? What happened to the mission land after Mexico gained its independence? CA HR3.
5. **Analyzing Literature** Explain the meaning of this statement from page 493: "I think but few Americans know or believe to what extent we have been wronged by Congressional action." CA HR5.
6. **Geography Skills** List the battles that appear on the map on page 495 in order from first to last. Identify each as a Mexican victory or a U.S. victory. CA CS2. CA CS3.

R Reading Strategy

Understanding Vocabulary
Ask: How does the meaning of *cede* differ from the meaning of *annex*? *(ceding is giving up control of land; annexing is claiming control of land)* OL
CA 8RW1.3

ASSESS

Resources for page 497

Use these resources to assess student mastery of section content.

- Section Quiz 11–3
- Interactive Tutor Self-Assessment CD-ROM

Reading Check
Answer: California and New Mexico

History Online
Study Central provides summaries, interactive games, and online graphic organizers to help students review section content.

CLOSE

Sequencing Information
Have students devise a time line of the events leading up to the war with Mexico, the war itself, and after the war. OL CA CS1.

SECTION 3 REVIEW ANSWERS

Review questions reinforce content standards US8.5 and US8.8.

1. the Nueces River
2. $15 million
3. Drive Mexican forces out of disputed area in Texas; Move into New Mexico and California; Take Mexico City
4. **The Big Ideas** to convert Native Americans; lands became ranchos
5. The writer felt that she and others had been betrayed by the California Land Act.
6. *U.S. victories*—Matamoros; Bear Flag Revolt; Monterey; Santa Fe; Monterrey; Tampico; El Brazito; San Gabriel; Buena Vista, Sacramento; Cerro Gordo; Mexico City; *Mexican victory*—San Pascual

FOCUS

History–Social Science Standards

The following standard is covered on pages 498–499

US8.8.2 Describe the purpose, challenges, and economic incentives associated with westward expansion, including the concept of Manifest Destiny (e.g., the Lewis and Clark expedition, accounts of the removal of Indians, the Cherokees' "Trail of Tears," settlements of the Great Plains) and the territorial acquisitions that spanned numerous decades.

US8.8.6 Describe the Texas War for Independence and the Mexican-American War, including territorial settlements, the aftermath of the wars, and the effects the wars had on the lives of Americans, including Mexican Americans today.

TEACH

R Reading Strategy

Activating Prior Knowledge Remind students that they learned the meaning of this word in Chapter 2. **Ask:** What does *petition* mean? *(to formally request something)* OL

CA 8WA2.4

Answers and Additional Support

Connecting to the Constitution

US8.8.6 Describe the Texas War for Independence and the Mexican-American War, including territorial settlements, the aftermath of the wars, and the effects the wars had on the lives of Americans, including Mexican Americans today.

Admission of New States

Why It Matters In 1783 the United States was made up of 13 states. It also included lands that stretched west to the Mississippi River. In the years that followed, the United States added more territory by buying lands, fighting wars, and signing treaties. In these ways, the territory of the United States has gradually spread to form the 50 states that we know today.

Joining the Union The U.S. Constitution gives Congress the power to admit new states to the Union. Once admitted to the Union, each state is equal to every other state and has the right to control its internal affairs. No state has more privileges or fewer responsibilities than any other. All states in the Union are bound to support the Constitution.

Thirty-seven states have been admitted to the Union since the Constitution was ratified. Of these 37 states, 30 were admitted after often lengthy periods as United States territories. However, some states—Vermont, Kentucky, Tennessee, and Maine—were formed from existing states with the approval of those states and Congress.

R To become a state, a territory usually **petitions,** or asks, Congress to be admitted into the Union. If the petition is approved, Congress passes an enabling act. When signed by the president, an enabling act allows the people of the territory to prepare a constitution setting up a representative, republican government. Next, the territory elects delegates to draft a constitution. If approved by the residents of the territory, the document is sent to Congress for approval. Once approved, Congress then passes an act of admission—a law that makes the territory a state.

▲ California state seal

◀ California's State Capitol in Sacramento

"The powers not delegated [given] to the United States by the Constitution, nor prohibited by it to the States, are reserved to the States respectively, or to the people."

—*10th Amendment,* U.S. Constitution

498

More Skill Practice

Historical and Social Sciences Analysis Skill Have students investigate and report on the status of those areas that belong to the United States today but are not states, such as Puerto Rico, Guam, Wake, and American Samoa. OL

Alaska state flag ▼

The Northwest Ordinance of 1787

The Northwest Ordinance of 1787 set up the Northwest Territory, the first territorial government in the United States. At the same time, the ordinance laid down a plan for eventually dividing the territory into states to be admitted into the Union. By 1850 six states—Ohio, Indiana, Illinois, Michigan, Wisconsin, and Minnesota—had been formed from the old Northwest Territory. From the early 1800s, to the present day, this plan with only minor changes has served as the model for admitting new states into the Union.

Westward Expansion During the 1840s, many Americans believed in **Manifest Destiny,** the idea that the United States should stretch from the Atlantic Ocean to the Pacific Ocean. Conflict soon arose between the United States and Mexico over Mexican-ruled lands in the West. In 1836 Texas had broken away from Mexico and became a republic. Its largely American-born leaders sought **annexation,** or admission, to the United States. In 1845 Congress passed a joint resolution to annex Texas. Bypassing becoming a territory, Texas was immediately admitted into the Union as a state.

Texas's annexation and border disputes led to war between the United States and Mexico in 1846. After Mexico's defeat, the Treaty of Guadalupe Hidalgo in 1848 gave the United States the area that today includes California, Nevada, Arizona, New Mexico, Utah, and western Colorado. In 1854 the United States bought the remaining portions of present-day Arizona and New Mexico from Mexico. With this land purchase, the general boundaries of the mainland United States reached their final form.

Slavery and New States After the Mexican War, Northerners wanted to ban slavery in the new territories gained from Mexico. Southerners claimed that the territories belonged to the entire nation. Therefore, all Americans had equal rights in them, including the right to bring in slavery. A crisis erupted in 1849 when California sought admission to the Union as a free state. Again, the balance between North and South was threatened, this time in the North's favor. In the Compromise of 1850, Congress finally decided that California would be admitted as a free state. In the other lands gained from Mexico, however, territorial governments would allow slavery.

Toward 50 States In the late 1800s, the country entered a period of industrial growth. Railroads finally spanned the continent, and waves of settlers moved to the West. One by one, the western territories became states of the United States. In 1912 New Mexico and Arizona became the 47th and 48th—and final—states on the U.S. mainland.

C The most recent states to be admitted are Alaska and Hawaii. Both lie outside the mainland United States. The United States bought Alaska from Russia in 1867 for $7.2 million in gold. Hawaii, once an independent kingdom, was annexed to the United States in 1898. In joining the Union, both territories shortened the statehood admissions process. They each adopted a proposed constitution without waiting for an enabling act. Both were admitted as states in 1959.

Checking for Understanding

1. How are states usually admitted to the Union?
2. What issue caused difficulties concerning the admission of states during much of the 1800s?

Critical Thinking

3. **Connect** How was the creation of new territories and states related to westward expansion? CA CS3.

Connecting to the Constitution

Review Grade 5 Standards

To review standard **5.8.2** *(Name the states and territories that existed in 1850 and identify their locations and major geographical features (e.g., mountain ranges, principal rivers, dominant plant regions.),* have students create a map of the United States in 1850, showing and labeling all the states and territories of the time. OL

C Critical Thinking

Comparing and Contrasting **Ask:** How is Hawaii similar to Texas? *(Both were once independent countries before becoming states.)* OL

ASSESS

Have students answer the Checking for Understanding and Critical Thinking questions.

CLOSE

Identifying Central Issues
Ask: Why is it important for new states to have the same powers as existing states? *(Students may say that this rule helped encourage people to settle new areas because they knew they would have equal rights.)* OL

Questions reinforce content standard US8.8.2 and US8.8.6.

Checking for Understanding

1. The Constitution gives Congress the right to admit new states. The process followed is for Congress to approve a petition for statehood from the people of the territory, who then write and approve a state constitution, after which Congress passes an act of admission.
2. slavery

Critical Thinking

3. Students may mention the migration of settlers westward and the need to organize them into territories to establish law and order and the eventual desire of the people in the territories to become states.

FOCUS

BELLRINGER
Skillbuilder Activity

Project **Daily Focus Skills Transparency 11–4** and have students answer the questions.

Guide to Reading

Preteaching Vocabulary: Use the Vocabulary PuzzleMaker CD-ROM to create crossword and word search puzzles.

Answers to Graphic: Forty-niners: people who came to California to get rich by finding gold; Mormons: religious group who moved to present-day Utah; Young: Mormon leader, governor of Utah Territory

Unpacking the Standards

After reading the section, students will be able to:

- Discuss the differences between forty-niners and Californios.
- Explain how the gold rush changed California.
- Describe why the Mormons came to Utah and the community they built there.

Section 4 New Settlers in California and Utah

Guide to Reading

History Social Science Standards

US8.8 Students analyze the divergent paths of the American people in the West from 1800 to the mid-1800s and the challenges they faced.

Looking Back, Looking Ahead

California and the New Mexico provinces became part of the United States in 1846. Many American settlers were eager to move there for a variety of reasons.

Focusing on the Main Ideas

- The discovery of gold in California had a significant impact on the settlement and economy of the region. *(page 501)*
- Utah was settled by Mormons, a religious group looking for safe haven. *(page 505)*

Meeting People

James Marshall
Joseph Smith
Brigham Young

Content Vocabulary

forty-niner
boomtown
vigilante (VIH • juh • LAN • tee)

Academic Vocabulary

range
community
item
pose
vision (VIH • zhuhn)

Reading Strategy

Organizing Information As you read this section, re-create the diagram below. In the boxes, describe who these groups and individuals were and what their role was in the settlement of California and Utah.

	What was their role?
Forty-niners	
Mormons	
Brigham Young	

NATIONAL GEOGRAPHIC Who & When?

1846 — 1848 — 1850

1846 Mormons migrate to the Great Salt Lake area

1849 California gold rush begins

1850 California applies for statehood

SECTION RESOURCES

Print Material
- Reproducible Lesson Plan 11–4*
- Daily Lesson and Discussion Notes 11–4
- Guided Reading Activity 11–4
- Reading Essentials and Study Guide 11–4
- Active Reading Note-Taking Guide 11–4
- Section Quiz 11–4

Transparencies
- Daily Focus Skills Transparency 11–4
- Section Graphic Organizer Transparency 11–4
- California Standards Practice Transparencies

Technology
- Interactive Tutor Self-Assessment CD-ROM
- Exam*View*® Pro Testmaker CD-ROM
- Presentation Plus! CD-ROM

*Available on TeacherWorks™

US8.8.2 Describe the purpose, challenges, and economic incentives associated with westward expansion, including the concept of Manifest Destiny (e.g., the Lewis and Clark expedition, accounts of the removal of Indians, the Cherokees' "Trail of Tears," settlement of the Great Plains) and the territorial acquisitions that spanned numerous decades.

The California Gold Rush

Main Idea **The discovery of gold in California had a significant impact on the settlement and economy of the region.**

Reading Connection Have you ever found money on the street? Imagine how exciting it would be to find a place where you could pick up money off the ground. Read to find out how dreams of easy gold brought many people to California.

An American Story

James Marshall was building a sawmill on the South Fork of the American River in California. He worked for John Sutter, who owned a vast tract of land about 40 miles from present-day Sacramento. On January 24, 1848, Marshall saw something shining in a ditch. "I reached my hand down and picked it up," he wrote later. "It made my heart thump, for I was certain it was gold." Looking around, he found other shiny pieces. Marshall rushed to show the glittering pieces to Sutter, who determined that they were gold. Sutter tried to keep the discovery a secret, but word soon leaked out. The great California Gold Rush was under way!

Who Were the Forty-Niners? People from all over the world flocked to California in search of quick riches. Nearly 100,000 people came to California looking for gold in 1848 and 1849. Those who arrived in 1849 were called **forty-niners.** An official in Monterey reported that "the farmers have thrown aside their plows, the lawyers their briefs [statement of a client's case], the doctors their pills, the priests their prayer books, and all are now digging gold." By the end of 1848, they had taken $6 million in gold from the American River. In modern-day value, the gold would be worth more than $100 million.

Many of the gold seekers came to California by sea. Thousands of forty-niners sailed to San Francisco from New York, Boston, and Galveston. Most traveled around the southern tip of South America. By far the greatest number of gold seekers came overland, traveling on the Oregon Trail or Santa Fe Trail and then pushing westward through California's Sierra Nevada mountain **range.**

Americans made up more than half of the forty-niners. Others came from Mexico, South America, Europe, and Australia. About 300 men arrived from China, the first large group of Asian immigrants to come to America. Although some eventually returned to China, many remained, establishing California's Chinese American **community.**

Land Rights The Treaty of Guadalupe Hidalgo ending the war with Mexico made Californios (Hispanic Californians) citizens of the United States. The treaty also guaranteed them the rights to their lands. But these rights would soon be weakened.

The Land Law of 1851 set up a group of people to review the Californios' land rights. The Californios had to prove what land they owned. When a new settler claimed the rights to a Californio's land, the two parties would go to court. Some Californios were able to prove their claims by providing official documents. Many, however, lost their land.

Picturing History

Many miners used a device like this to pan for gold. It is sometimes called a rocking cradle. ***Why do you think it is known as a cradle?***

TEACH

R1 Reading Strategy

Connecting **Ask:** What similar names for a group of people can you think of? *(baby boomers)* OL

C1 Critical Thinking

Analyzing Primary Sources **Ask:** Is this quotation literally true or figuratively true? If the latter, what is the speaker actually saying? *(probably only figuratively true; Many people from many walks of life gave up their work in the hopes of finding gold.)* OL CA HR2.

R2 Reading Strategy

Determining Importance **Ask:** What is important about this group of Chinese immigrants? *(They were the first large number of Asians to come to the United States; they established the Chinese American community of California.)* OL

R3 Reading Strategy

Academic Vocabulary Ask students to describe their community. Then explain how the word *community* is used here to describe an ethnic population. OL

C2 Critical Thinking

Identifying Central Issues Have students discuss whether the Land Law of 1851 was a fair way of handling the issue of Californios' land ownership. If not, what alternative approach would they suggest? OL CA HI4.

Did You Know?

Sutter had been a successful businessman up until 1848. When Marshall discovered gold on his land, most of Sutter's workers abandoned their jobs to look for the precious metal. Within just a few years, Sutter fell into poverty that lasted the rest of his life.

Picturing History

Point students to the tray at the left end of the rocking cradle. The piece would hold the gold nuggets as water flowed through the holes and down the chute.

Answer: because it looks somewhat like a cradle

Biography

TEACH

R Reading Strategy

Setting a Purpose Have students read the biography of the Bidwells with the aim of finding out why they are thought of as reformers. *(Annie taught Native Americans; both worked in the temperance movement; Annie supported woman suffrage; John worked to end hydraulic mining; both promoted the spread of agriculture.)* OL

S Skill Practice

Using Geography Skills Have students locate Chico on a map. **Ask:** In what region of the state does it sit? *(northern California; the Sacramento Valley)* OL

C Critical Thinking

Making Inferences Ask: What would mining companies think of the Bidwells? Why? *(They probably were upset at John's testimony that ended hydraulic mining because they would have to find new ways to extract ore.)* OL

Answers and Additional Support

Biography

US8.8.3 Describe the role of pioneer women and the new status that western women achieved (e.g., Laura Ingalls Wilder, Annie Bidwell; slave women gaining freedom in the West; Wyoming granting suffrage to women in 1869).

JOHN BIDWELL
1819–1900

ANNIE BIDWELL
1839–1918

R

The Bidwell mansion in Chico, California, stands as a monument to two pioneers who dedicated their lives to agricultural and social reform. John Bidwell set out from Missouri in 1841 on an overland journey to California. The expedition set out with not much more than the vague knowledge that California lay somewhere to the west. S

Upon arriving in California, John Bidwell befriended John Sutter and was able to make a large fortune mining gold. Bidwell soon turned to agricultural endeavors, introducing Bermuda grass and the casaba melon to California. In 1868 John married Annie Ellicott Kennedy, a young woman from Washington, D.C. The construction of the Bidwell mansion had begun three years before. Upon its completion, Annie used its various rooms to educate the Mechoopda, a tribe of Native Americans who lived on the land surrounding the mansion.

Both John and Annie joined the Temperance movement. John ran unsuccessfully for president on the prohibition ticket in 1892, and Annie joined the Woman's Christian Temperance Union. Annie also championed women's rights and joined the woman suffrage movement, at which time she met and befriended Susan B. Anthony.

As the Gold Rush boomed in California, John noticed the effects hydraulic mining had on the California environment. This process of mining caused silt to sift down upon farms and streams and eroded the Sierra hillsides. John testified in *Woodruff* v. *North Bloomfield*, an environmental case that ended hydraulic mining in the United States. C The Bidwells left an unforgettable impact on the Chico region of California. They aided the development of agriculture in the region, and their mansion still stands today as a historic park under the direction of the Department of Parks and Recreation of California.

"Our ignorance of the route was complete. We knew that California lay west, and that was the extent of our knowledge. . . ."

—John Bidwell

Then and Now

The Bidwells were dedicated to environmental causes. Research a current environmentalist and explain how his or her actions are similar to the Bidwells'.

Then and Now

Answers will vary, but students should give reasons to support their choices.

Life in California As people rushed to a new area to look for gold, they built new communities, called **boomtowns,** almost overnight. At one site on the Yuba River where only two houses stood in September 1849, a miner arrived the next year to find a town of 1,000 people "with a large number of hotels, stores, groceries, bakeries, and . . . gambling houses." The miners gave some of the boomtowns colorful names such as Shinbone Peak and You Bet. Cities also flourished during the Gold Rush. As ships arrived daily with gold seekers and adventurers, San Francisco quickly grew from a tiny village to a city of about 20,000 people. By 1860 the city had 57,000 residents, making it the fifteenth largest American city and the largest city west of the Mississippi River.

Most of the hopeful forty-niners had no experience in mining. Rushing furiously from place to place, they attacked hillsides with pickaxes and shovels and spent hours bent over streambeds, "washing" or "panning" the water to seek gold dust and nuggets.

Linking Past & Present

Blue Jeans

Past In 1873 Levi Strauss, a dry goods merchant living in San Francisco, and Jacob Davis, a Nevada tailor, developed and began to market denim pants reinforced with small copper tacks called rivets.

▼ Jeans are popular everyday wear.

▲ Early Levi ads were aimed at miners and farmers.

Present At one time, jeans were associated exclusively with hard work. Now they're worn everywhere. Levi's popular denims—called blue jeans today—are known for their durability and quality. ***Why do you think miners and farmers were among the first to wear Levi's denims?***

U Universal Access

English Learners Explain that "almost overnight" is an idiomatic expression that is not meant literally. **Ask:** What is the text trying to say? *(Boomtowns grew very rapidly.)* EL

S Skill Practice

Historical and Social Sciences Analysis Skill Have students conduct research to find population figures for the ten most populous cities in the United States in 1860. Have them create a bar graph showing the number of people in those ten cities and in San Francisco. AL

C Critical Thinking

Predicting Consequences **Ask:** What impact would all this gold seeking have on the environment? Why? *(Students may suggest that the rapid increase in people and the aggressive search for gold will hurt the environment as miners cut down trees and do other damage.)* OL CA HI2.

More Skill Practice

Historical and Social Science Analysis Skill **Ask:** What effect did the Gold Rush have on the Native Americans and Californios? Why? *(Students may say that growing numbers of people took away Native Americans' land and threaten the position of Californios because the new arrivals were eager for gold and not concerned with the rights of these groups.)* OL

Linking Past & Present

In May 2001 the oldest known pair of Levi's jeans, dating back to the 1880s, was sold to Levi Strauss & Co. for $46,532, the highest price ever paid for a pair of denim jeans.

Answer: because they needed rugged, durable clothing

S Skill Practice

Historical and Social Sciences Analysis Skill Explain that as the supply of a good increases, price goes down, and as it decreases, price goes up. Demand works the opposite way—high demand means high prices, while low demand leads to lower prices. **Ask:** What was pushing up the prices forty-niners had to pay for goods? *(both high demand and limited supply)* OL CA HI6.

C Critical Thinking

Identifying Problems and Finding Solutions Have students discuss the problem of law and order in the boomtowns to determine if vigilance committees were the best solution or if they can identify other alternatives. OL

R Reading Strategy

Understanding Vocabulary Explain that the term comes from a Latin word mean "watchful" or "on the watch." **Ask:** How does that origin explain the meaning of the term? *(Vigilantes watched their communities for people committing crimes.)* OL

Answers and Additional Support

The Way It Was

▼ Peter H. Burnett

▲ Pablo de la Guerra

The California Constitution

Forty-eight delegates met in Monterey to draw up a constitution in September of 1849. Eight delegates were Californios. A declaration of rights guaranteed freedom of assembly, religion, and speech. The first section of the California Declaration of Rights begins:

> **"All men are by nature free and independent, and have certain inalienable rights, among which are those of enjoying and defending life and liberty, acquiring, possessing, and protecting property: and pursuing and obtaining safety and happiness."**

The right to vote was extended to all white males over the age of 21 who had been residents of California for 30 days. Pablo de la Guerra of Santa Barbara led other Hispanic delegates to the convention in arguing for the right to vote for Native Americans, African Americans, and mestizos. The delegates agreed to recognize any man who had been a Mexican citizen, regardless of race, as a citizen of California. However, African Americans and Native Americans who were not of Mexican descent would not be included.

Californians approved the constitution in November 1849 by a vote of more than 12,000 to 811. Voters elected Peter H. Burnett governor and chose members of the state legislature and a representative to the United States Congress.

The California Gold Rush more than doubled the world's supply of gold. For all their effort, however, very few of the forty-niners achieved lasting wealth. Most of the miners found little or no gold. Many of those who did find gold lost their riches through gambling or wild spending.

S Merchants, however, made huge profits. They could charge whatever they liked because the miners had no place else to go to buy food and other essential **items.** Eggs sold for $10 a dozen. Mining tools were expensive too, and the price of a burro went from $15 to $40.

C **Gold Rush Society** Very few women lived in the mining camps, which were filled with men of all backgrounds. Lonely and suffering from the hardships of mining, many men spent their free hours drinking, gambling, and fighting.

Mining towns had no police or prisons, so lawbreakers **posed** a real threat to business owners and miners. One miner wrote:

> **"Robberies and murders were almost of daily occurrence. Threats had been made to burn down the town."**
>
> —from *California Men and Events*

R Concerned citizens formed vigilance committees to protect themselves. The **vigilantes** (VIH • juh • LAN • tees) took the law into their own hands, acting as police, judge, jury, and sometimes executioner.

The Way It Was

Ask: What American document does the Declaration of Rights resemble? How? *(the Declaration of Independence; its statement that "all men are by nature free," the mention of "inalienable rights," which include "life and liberty" and "pursuing . . . happiness")* AL

Resources for page 504

- Academic Vocabulary Activity 11

US8.8.2 Describe the purposes, challenges, and economic incentives associated with westward expansion, including the concept of Manifest Destiny (e.g., the Lewis and Clark expedition, accounts of removal of Indians, the Cherokees' "Trail of Tears," settlement of the Great Plains) and the territorial acquisitions that spanned numerous decades.

Economic and Political Progress The Gold Rush ended within a few years but had lasting effects on California's economy. Agriculture, shipping, and trade expanded to meet the miners' needs for food and other goods. Many people who had come looking for gold stayed to farm or run a business. California's population soared, rising from about 20,000 in 1848 to more than 220,000 only four years later.

Such rapid growth brought the need for more effective government. In March 1850, California applied for statehood. Because California's new constitution banned slavery, however, the request caused a crisis in Congress. The South opposed making California a state because it would upset the balance of free and slave states. California did not become a state until Congress worked out a compromise six months later. R1

Reading Check **Explain** Why did the forty-niners come to California?

A Religious Refuge in Utah

Main Idea **Utah was settled by Mormons, a religious group looking for safe haven.**

Reading Connection If you were building a new home what would you do first? Read on to see how the Mormons made the most of the harsh terrain they settled.

In 1855, a visitor to the Utah Territory wrote admiringly of:

> **"[The] indomitable energy . . . which seems to possess the entire Mormon community."**
>
> —Howard Stansbury

This account described the Mormons, or members of the Church of Jesus Christ of Latter-day Saints. Mormons had come to Utah to fulfill their **vision** of the godly life. R2

Picturing **History**

Several thousand Mormons forged their way west along a path that became known as the Mormon Trail. ***Where did the Mormons settle?***

R1 Reading Strategy

Activating Prior Knowledge **Ask:** How was the debate over California statehood the reverse of the situation that had delayed the statehood of Texas? *(With Texas, it was Northerners who blocked statehood because Texas did have slavery and Southerners wanted statehood.)* OL

Review The Big Ideas

Review the Big Idea for this section "Immigration influences a nation's or region's economy and society." **Ask:** What reasons led the Mormons to settle in Utah? *(to fulfill their vision of a godly life)* How did their motivation differ from that of the forty-niners? *(The forty-niners hoped to get rich; the Mormons wanted to live a godly life.)*

R2 Reading Strategy

Academic Vocabulary Explain that the word *vision* can be used to refer to a persons's or group's plan or goals for the future. Ask students to write a sentence using the word. OL

Reading Check

Answer: in the hopes of winning a fortune by finding gold

Did You Know?

Though Utah is far inland, its state bird is the seagull. In 1848, Mormons' crops were being attacked by crickets. When seagulls arrived, they ate the crickets and saved the crops.

Picturing **History**

Answer: Utah

C Critical Thinking

Analyzing Information Have the class brainstorm the issues the Mormons had to address in planning this trip. OL

R Reading Strategy

Scaffolding—Academic Vocabulary The word *migrate* was introduced in Chapter 6, Section 3. Ask a student to define the word *migration*. OL

ASSESS

Resources for page 506

Use these resources to assess student mastery of section content.

- Biography Activity 11B
- Section Quiz 11–4
- Interactive Tutor Self-Assessment CD-ROM

Reading Check

Answer: Mormons worked hard.

History Online

Study Central provides summaries, interactive games, and online graphic organizers to help students review section content.

CLOSE

Summarizing Have students write a summary of how California became a state. OL

How Was the Mormon Religion Founded?

In 1830 **Joseph Smith** of New York State had visions that led him to found the Mormon **R** church. The visions also inspired him to build an ideal society.

Smith believed that property should be held in common. He also favored polygamy, the idea that a man could have more than one wife. This angered many people, so the Mormons eventually gave up this practice.

Smith formed a community in New York, but neighbors disapproved of the Mormons' religion. They forced the Mormons to move on. From New York, the Mormons went to Ohio, then to Missouri, and then to Illinois.

In 1844 a mob in Illinois killed Smith, and **Brigham Young** took over as the Mormon leader. Young decided that the Mormons should move again, this time near the Great Salt Lake in present-day Utah. Although part of Mexico at that time, no Mexicans had settled in the area because of its harsh terrain.

A Haven in the Desert About 12,000 Mormons **C** made the trek to the Great Salt Lake area. It was the largest single migration in American history. The hard-working Mormons made their new home, Deseret, flourish. They planned their towns carefully and built irrigation canals to water their farms. They also set up industries so they could be self-sufficient. Mormon merchants sold supplies to forty-niners who were headed westward.

In 1848 the United States acquired the Great Salt Lake area from Mexico. Two years later Congress set up the Utah Territory, and Brigham Young became its governor. Utah did not easily become part of the United States, however. The Mormons wanted to be left alone and resisted federal authority. In the late 1850s, war almost broke out between the Mormons and the United States Army. Utah did not become a state until 1896.

Reading Check **Explain** Why was Deseret able to grow economically?

History Online

Study Central Need help understanding the settlement of California and Utah? Visit ca.hss.glencoe.com and click on Study Central.

Section 4 Review

Reading Summary

Review the Main Ideas

- Settlement of California was significantly impacted by the discovery of gold in 1849.
- Joseph Smith and Brigham Young led the Mormons on a cross-country journey to find a safe haven for settlement. Eventually, they chose present-day Utah to establish their community.

What Did You Learn?

1. Why was California's entry into the Union delayed?
2. What is another name for the Mormons?

Critical Thinking

3. **Organizing Information** Re-create the diagram below. In the boxes, describe how the Gold Rush helped California's economy grow. CA HI2.

Growth in California

4. **The Big Ideas** What steps did Californians take to apply for statehood? When was California admitted? CA HI1.
5. **Predicting Consequences** How might the history of California be different if the Gold Rush had not happened? CA HI4.
6. **Creative Writing** You are living in a boomtown in California in the mid-1800s. Write a week's worth of journal entries, recording what your life is like. CA 8WA2.1

SECTION 4 REVIEW ANSWERS

Review questions reinforce content standard US8.8.

1. The South opposed letting it into the Union because that would upset the balance between free and slave states.
2. members of the Church of Jesus Christ of Latter-Day Saints
3. Increased population; Expanded agriculture, shipping, trade
4. **The Big Ideas** applied for statehood in March 1850; admitted in September
5. Students may say that the population would not have grown as rapidly but that California's climate and resources still would have attracted settlers.
6. Students' entries should reflect text information.

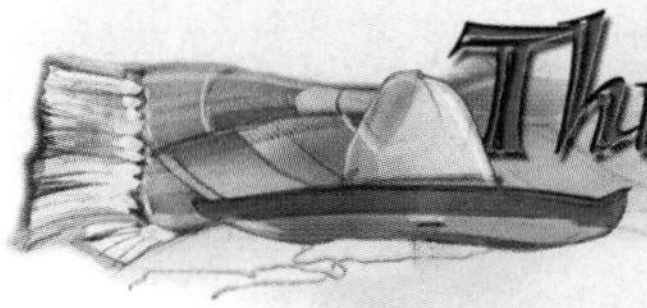

Thunder on the Sierra

By Kathy Balmes

Before You Read

The Scene: This part of the story takes place at Señor Sosa's gold claim in the Sierra in 1852.

The Characters: Mateo is a 13-year-old boy who trades with miners in the California gold camps. His pack animals are mules with names, such as Fabio and Cisco. Señor Sosa has a gold claim in the mountains somewhere between the mining camps of Indian Gulch and Poverty Hill.

The Plot: While restocking supplies that he will sell to the gold miners, Mateo agrees to deliver a letter to a Señor Sosa if he can find the man.

Vocabulary Preview

decaying: rotting
ghastly: scary like a ghost or corpse
glossy: shiny on the surface
hue (HYOO): color or shade of color
moan: long, low sound of pain, sorrow, or grief
nauseating (NAW • zhee • AYT • ihng): causing a strong sick feeling in the stomach
stench: strong, bad smell

Has a promise ever led you into an unexpected situation? That's what happened to Mateo.

507

FOCUS

Summary

In this excerpt from the novel *Thunder on the Sierra*, young Mateo looks for Señor Sosa, a miner for whom he is carrying a letter. Finding Sosa nearly dead of scurvy, he nurses him back to better health. Mateo then reads Sosa the letter, written by a lawyer colleague who asks Sosa—also a lawyer—to return to San Francisco to help defend the land claims of rancheros.

Vocabulary Preview Before students begin reading, have them read **Before You Read** and the **Vocabulary Preview**. Point out that difficult words are foot-noted throughout the text.

Background Information

The first Spanish land grants were made in they 1700s by Spain's king to soldiers who had come to California to staff the forts built there. Once Mexico gained its independence from Spain and took control of California, it, too, issued land grants. According to the Land Act of 1851, rancheros had two years to prove that they owned their land.

Reading Strategy: ACTIVATING PRIOR KNOWLEDGE

When students approach historical fiction, like *Thunder on the Sierra*, it can help their understanding and appreciation of the book to first take stock of what they know about the time and place being depicted. In this case, they can use the information under the heading "Before You Read" as clues. For instance, the fact that this story takes place in 1852 tells them that the story takes place after California has become a state. Ask volunteers to name other facts about California in this period that might be relevant to the story. OL

TEACH

R1 Reading Strategy

Connecting Have students give examples of main plots and subplots that they know of from other books or from movies or plays. OL CA 8RL3.2

R2 Reading Strategy

Understanding Vocabulary
Ask: Why did the author not use the word *smell* instead of *stench*? *(Stench is a strong, unpleasant smell; the word is more vivid.)* OL

C Critical Thinking

Determine Cause and Effect **Ask:** Why does Mateo hesitate to enter? *(He is afraid that he might catch one of these serious diseases from Sosa.)* OL

Answers and Additional Support

As You Read

R1 *A novel has a main plot that relates to the action in all or almost all of the book. The main plot in* Thunder on the Sierra *concerns Mateo's desire to get back his stolen horse. This novel also has subplots, or shorter plots, that occur in part of the story. As you read, think about the subplot that takes place in this excerpt. What is the problem or conflict? How is it resolved? Or is it solved?*

When I first came across Señor Sosa's camp, I thought it was deserted. I had crossed between Indian Gulch and Poverty Hill twice, looking for the man. I was ready to give up when a downpour started, and I saw a broken down shack. As I hobbled[1] and unloaded the mules a short distance away, I heard a low moan. I pushed the door of the shack open. Inside was dark. R2 A nauseating stench, like a decaying corpse, almost knocked me backwards.

"Hello? Who are you?" a weak voice asked in Spanish.

"My name is Mateo."

"You must be an angel. Good. I'm finally dying."

"No. I'm not an angel. I'm an arriero,"[2] I replied.

"My name is Sebástiano Sosa."

I had found my man.

"Are you sick or hurt?" I asked, knowing it must be one or the other.

"Sick."

C Even though it was pouring rain, I hesitated to enter the shack.

"Do you have cholera[3] or dysentery[4] or malaria?[5] I have quinine. It can ease malaria."

"I don't have malaria."

---

[1] **hobbled:** tied a rope or strap around two legs
[2] **arriero:** a person who drives mules
[3] **cholera:** very severe diarrhea that can kill the patient
[4] **dysentery:** severe diarrhea
[5] **malaria:** severe chills and fever

EXTENDING THE CONTENT

Connecting the Story This subplot—as in many novels—also connects to the main plot, which is Mateo's story. Before the events recounted here, Mateo lived on a rancho with his father, who later died. The land law described in the letter to Sosa at the end of this excerpt, then, also affects Mateo.

R1 I pushed down my fear of the deadly cholera and entered the shack. He had not been able to get up from his bed. His shack smelled of vomit, urine, and diarrhea. I breathed through my mouth to avoid the overwhelming odors.

I had never seen anyone in such awful condition. His bleeding gums made his attempt to smile ghastly. His skin had a purple hue. His arms were swollen to double their normal size. They were black where his blood vessels had broken. He was hideous. But as I moved closer, I could see what was wrong with him.

"What have you been eating?" I asked.

"Nothing lately. Before that only spoiled salt pork and flour fried in grease," he said weakly. C

"For how long?" I asked.

"Months," he said.

"Were you always alone?" I said.

"No. I had a partner. We had studied law together before the gold rush. We met again in the diggings.[6] But he gave up this summer. We hadn't found any gold, and our food was running out. He left for San Francisco to start a law firm. I planned to follow him back in a few weeks to become his law partner."

"Why didn't you?" I asked.

R2 "I found gold. Not much. But enough to keep me here panning. After a few months I got sick. My arms and legs swelled. Now it hurts me to move," he said.

"You have scurvy. I've seen it in other camps where the miners don't have good food. You're the worst case I've ever seen."

The watery brown eyes pleaded, "Can you help me?"

"Yes. You need fruits and vegetables. I have some in my packs. I'll stay until you are strong enough to take care of yourself."

The sick man lay back and closed his eyes. "God bless you. You are an angel," he murmured.

I brought him raisins and dried apples from Fabio's pack. I filled his cup with water and fed him. His breath stunk like an animal that had been dead for a month. He could barely chew and swallow. Was I too late?

[6] **diggings:** area where people are looking for gold

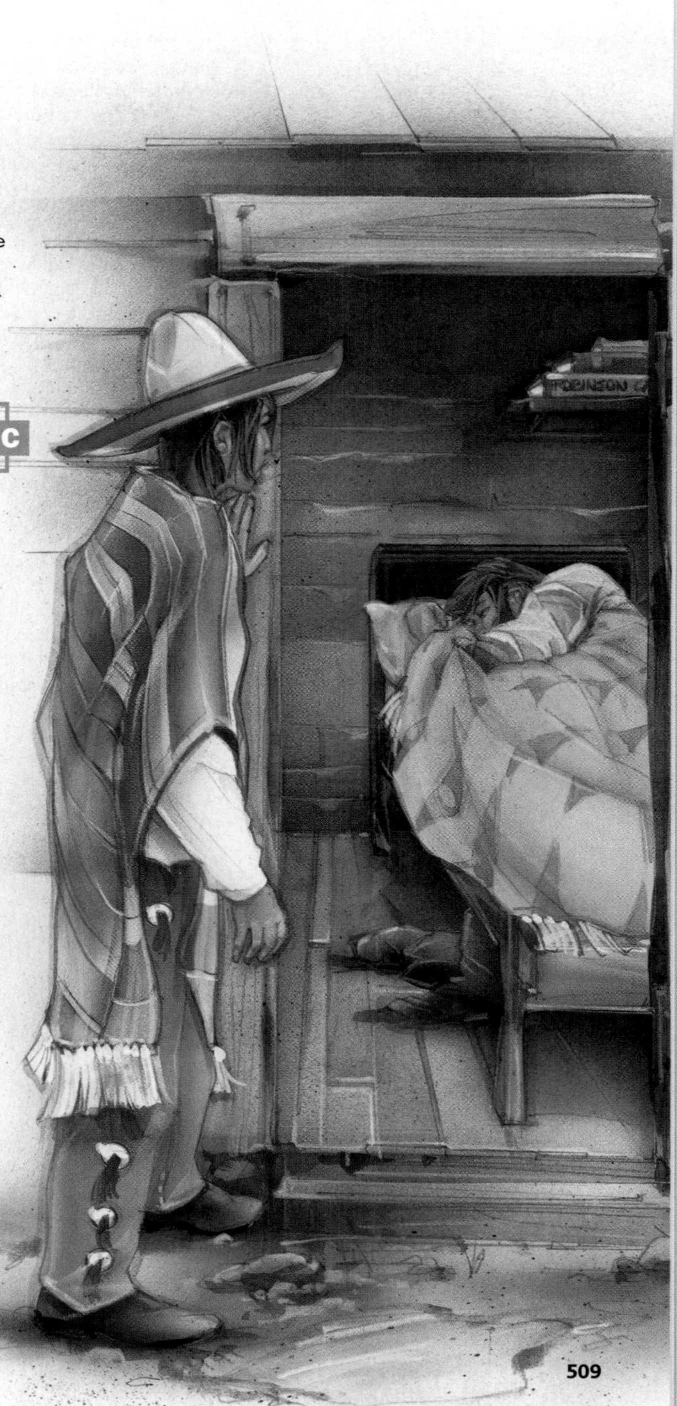

R1 Reading Strategy

Analyzing Text Structure
Ask: Who is the person narrating the story? *(Mateo)* How do we know what he is thinking? *(He describes his thoughts.)* How do we know what Sosa is thinking? *(only from the words he says)* OL

C Critical Thinking

Predicting Consequences
Ask: Is this a healthful diet? If not, what is wrong with it? *(Students should note that the diet is not varied enough and lacks fresh fruits and vegetables, which means that Sosa is not getting enough nutrients.)* OL

R2 Reading Strategy

Monitoring **Ask:** What are the two reasons Sosa did not leave his camp? *(first because he found some gold and wanted to stay in the hopes he would find more; second because he became too sick to leave)* OL

Glencoe Literature Library

The following literature from the **Glencoe Literature Library** may enrich the teaching of this chapter: *The Call of The Wild* by Jack London.

EXTENDING THE CONTENT

Vitamin Deficiencies Scurvy is a vitamin-deficiency disease caused by the lack of vitamin C. The symptoms described here are the classic problems associated with the disease. Sailors on long ocean voyages often suffered from it due to the lack of fresh fruit and vegetables. A doctor in the British navy linked the disease to a lack of vitamin C in 1753 and soon began urging that British sailors be given citrus fruits. When the Royal Navy finally agreed in the 1790s, the disease quickly disappeared from British fleets. The slang name *limey* for a British sailor stemmed from the new diet of oranges, lemons, and limes.

S Skill Practice

Historical and Social Sciences Analysis Skill

Ask: How would Native Americans come to know what plants were good for treating specific diseases? *(Students may note that traditional societies typically develop such knowledge as they do not have manufactured medicines.)* OL

R Reading Strategy

Connecting Ask volunteers who have eaten dried fruit to explain why Sosa, with his swollen gums and difficulty chewing, would have difficulty eating it if it had not been put in water. *(Students should note that dried fruit can be tough.)* OL

C Critical Thinking

Making Inferences Ask: What kind of a person do you think Mateo is? How would you describe him? Challenge students to offer evidence from the story to support their ideas. *(Students may say that he's kind because he is willing to help Sosa and that he's competent since he can do so many things.)* OL

Answers and Additional Support

America's Literature

"I can't make a fire to cook potatoes and onions for you until the rain stops. I'm going to hike around and see if I can find some wild greens. An old Indian showed me which plants cure scurvy."

I looked around for the plants. But I found nothing.

The rain had stopped by the time I returned. I took dry wood from inside the shack and built a fire outside. I fried a pan full of onions and potatoes. The wonderful aroma floated into the shack.

I brought a plate of vegetables to his bed.

"Smells good," said the grateful man.

"Eat as much as you can. It will make you better."

I fed him. But he wasn't able to chew much.

I noticed a copy of *Robinson Crusoe*[7] and three law books on a crude wooden shelf. The law books reminded me of the letter. *I'll wait until he's stronger,* I thought. *It might be bad news.*

I slept outside the door. I couldn't stand the smell in the shack.

The sick man seemed a little better in the morning and ate more of the onions and potatoes. I heated the dried fruit in water until it became plump and easier for him to swallow.

After breakfast I moved the mules to a new place to graze and informed them that they had the rest of the week off. I returned to the shack.

"Can you walk outside so I can clean your cabin? You can lean on me."

"I'll try," Señor Sosa replied weakly.

After I settled him in the sunshine, I cleaned his shack. Señor Sosa looked spent[8] when I helped him back inside and settled him in his clean bed. He slept all afternoon.

The next morning I helped him peel off his dirty clothes, wash, and put on clean ones. After I fed him lunch I asked, "Would you like me to read you *Robinson Crusoe?*"

"That would ease my suffering, Mateo, my angel."

[7] ***Robinson Crusoe:*** story about a man who is marooned on a desert island for many years

[8] **spent:** exhausted

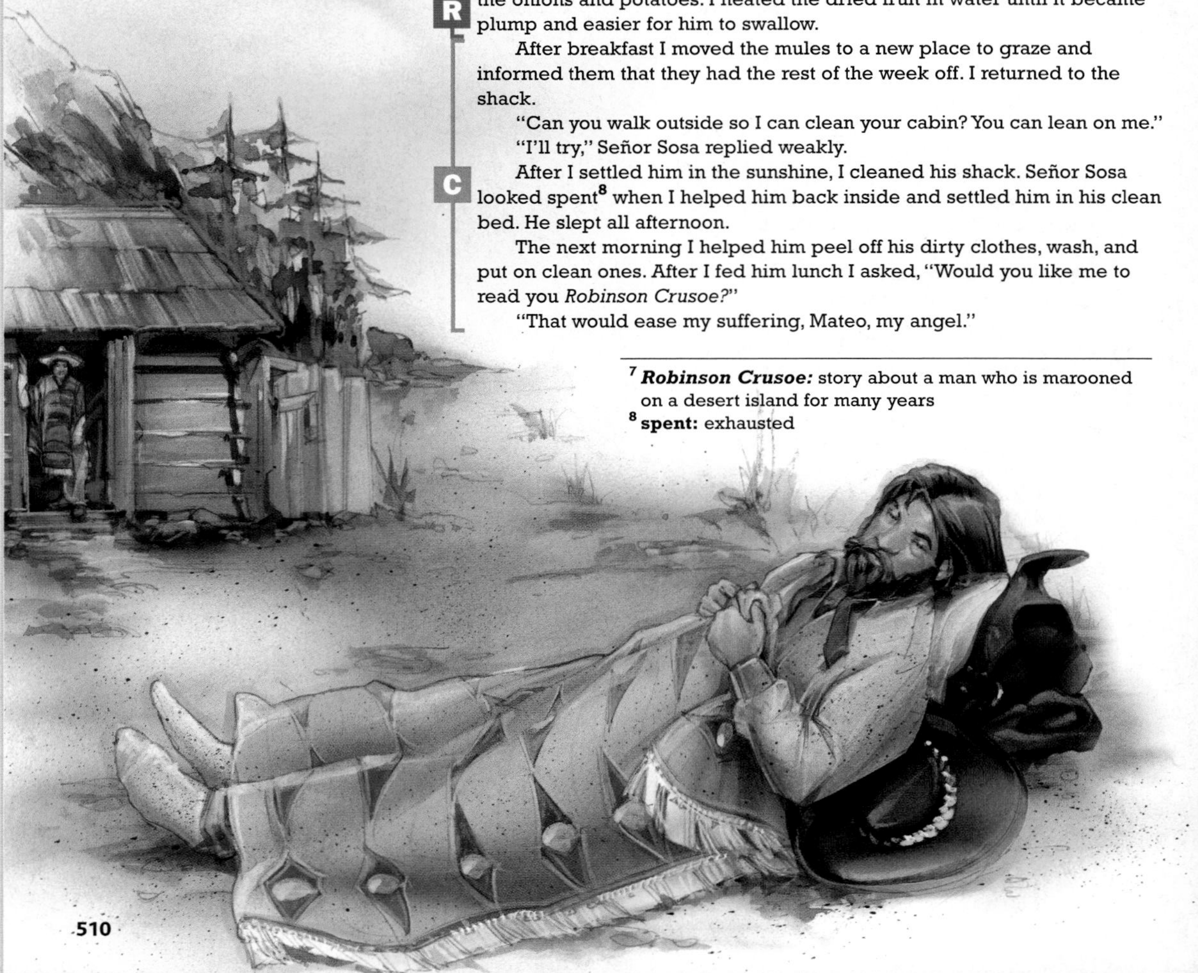

READING STRATEGY VISUALIZING

Have students close their eyes and visualize what Sosa's shack must have looked like. Prompt their responses by asking questions such as: How large is it? Does it have windows? What furniture is there? What condition is it in? Have them compare their ideas about the shack with the illustrations. **Ask:** Do these pictures look right to you? Why or why not? OL

After I had read for about an hour, a movement in a shadowy corner of the cabin caught my eye. I saw a small, sleek[9] animal slink out of a hole under the crude boards and bound gracefully onto Señor Sosa's bed.

"Is that supposed to be in here?" I asked, pointing to the small animal with round, bright eyes. It looked like a tiny raccoon, only cuter, and its coat was softer.

Señor Sosa smiled. "She's my pet," he said as he stroked her velvet fur. "Madalena was my only companion before you came. She's a ringtail. They're so good at catching rats and mice that they're often called miner's cats. This cabin would be overrun with rodents if she didn't eat them."

"She's pretty," I said.

"Madalena has been a great comfort. I figured she'd keep the rodents off my corpse. I'd been warned that one in five miners died in the first year of the gold rush. I didn't believe it. Now I wonder how so many survived."

I reached out a hand to pet the glossy fur. But Madalena darted off the bed and down the hole.

The next morning the lawyer was noticeably healthier. *He's a young man,* I realized with amazement. *It's time,* I decided.

"I have a letter for you," I announced after he fed himself breakfast.

Señor Sosa stared at me in surprise.

"It's from your partner in San Francisco. He said it's important. I kept it until you were strong, in case it's bad news."

"Read it to me, Mateo. I am still weak."

"Yes, señor. The letter is dated September 15, 1852."

"What month is it now, Mateo?"

"December, señor."

"Continue."

I read: " *'My Friend, I hope this letter finds you in good health.'* "

The lawyer snorted. "Go on," he urged.

[9] **sleek:** smooth and glossy

R Reading Strategy

Inferring Ask: Why does Sosa say that he now is surprised that only one in five gold miners died? *(He has seen how close he himself came to dying and how only the chance appearance of Mateo saved him.)* OL

C1 Critical Thinking

Drawing Conclusions Ask: What is a sign that Sosa is feeling better? *(He was well enough to feed himself breakfast.)* OL

C2 Critical Thinking

Analyzing Information
Before reading the letter, **ask:** Do you think Mateo was right to read the letter to Sosa so soon? Why or why not? *(Answers will vary but should be supported with sound reasoning.)* OL

EXTENDING THE CONTENT

Ringtails Ringtails, sometimes called miner's cats or ringtailed cats, are not cats but similar to raccoons. They are about two to three feet long, with half of that length coming from their tails. They are carnivores, though they also eat plant food, and are indeed known for their ability to catch mice. Ringtails are found in the American Southwest and in Mexico.

R Reading Strategy

Evaluating Text **Ask:** Why would the lawyers benefit from knowing both Spanish and English? *(because they could talk to both Californios and to Americans; because they can understand documents written in either language)* OL

ASSESS

Have students answer the Responding to the Literature questions.

CLOSE

Summarizing Have students write a brief summary of this excerpt. Then have students exchange papers and read their partner's summary. Tell them to comment on whether the summary misses any important details. Finally, have them revise their summaries as needed. OL
CA 8RC2.4

Answers and Additional Support

America's Literature

R *Please join me in San Francisco immediately. Because we are Spanish-speaking lawyers, who also speak English, we are needed to help rancheros to prove in court that they own the land they live on.*

Disappointed Yankee miners often want land in California. They have pressured the American government to issue the Land Act of 1851. It requires all rancheros to submit proof, within two years, that their land was given to them by the Spanish or Mexican governments. Often the land grants are not well documented so lawyers and courts find it easy to detect some flaw in the titles. Many Californios have already lost part or all of their ranchos. Others don't realize that their ranchos are in danger.

The court's deadline is approaching. I have too much business to handle by myself. It cannot wait. I need your help. Please join me in San Francisco. I anxiously await you.

Sincerely,
Your Partner,
Manuel Torres Vargas

After I finished reading him the letter, we sat in stunned silence. . . .

"I'm leaving here as soon as I'm able. Will you sell me a mule? I have gold. I'll pay you twice what it is worth. That should satisfy its owner. Please?"

"Yes, señor. And I'll sell you the food you will need. Tomorrow I must be on my way. There are miners waiting for supplies."

Responding to the Literature

1. How did Mateo find Señor Sosa?
2. Why did Mateo wait to read the letter to Señor Sosa?
3. **Synthesize** Use the word *scurvy* in a sentence that shows its meaning. You may define scurvy, use it as an example, or compare or contrast it. CA 8RW1.3
4. **Infer** What country were Mateo and Señor Sosa originally citizens of? Give examples from the selection of how the author established this fact. CA 8RC2.0
5. **Read to Write** This excerpt contains one of the subplots in *Thunder on the Sierra*. Describe the subplot. What is the conflict? Is the conflict resolved? Explain. What new conflict does the letter raise? CA 8RL3.2

Responding to the Literature Answers

1. He found him in a broken-down shack when seeking shelter from the rain.
2. for Sosa to feel better
3. Answers will vary, but students should reveal understanding that scurvy is a vitamin-deficiency disease.
4. Spain or Mexico; the author has them using Spanish words, and Mateo calls Sosa "señor"
5. Students may identify the conflict as the need to find and then help Sosa, which Mateo achieves by locating him and then cooking, cleaning, and caring for him.

Reading On Your Own...

From the California Reading List

Do you want to learn more about Andrew Jackson and the new groups of people who became part of the United States? You might be interested in the following books.

Biography

Andrew Jackson: Frontier President by Nancy Whitelaw describes the life of this colorful frontiersman who became president. She includes his two terms as president and his many firsts in that position. ***The content of this book is related to** History–Social Science Standard US8.4.*

Nonfiction

Black Potatoes: The Story of the Great Irish Famine, 1845–1850 by Susan Campbell Bartoletti leads readers through five years of failed potato crops in Ireland. The story of millions of Irish dying and emigrating is told in first-person accounts, news reports, and sketches. ***The content of this book is related to** History–Social Science Standard US8.6.*

Nonfiction

In the Days of the Vaqueros: America's First True Cowboys by Russell Freedman tracks the origins of the cowboy back to Spanish Mexico in the 1500s. Freedman describes the equipment and techniques that they developed, their migration to California, and the debt that American settlers owed the vaqueros. ***The content of this book is related to** History–Social Science Standard US8.8.*

Historical Fiction

The Journal of Wong Ming-Chung by Laurence Yep recounts the experiences of a Chinese immigrant, nicknamed "Runt," and his uncle during the California Gold Rush. When it becomes clear that there is no Golden Mountain, they develop other ingenious ways to find opportunity in the United States. ***The content of this book is related to** History–Social Science Standard US8.8.*

America's Literature

TEACH

The reading selections for this unit have been chosen to reflect the California History-Social Science Standards. If you assign one of these books, you may want to have students complete the following activity.

Analyzing Characters

One of the keys to understanding a book is to analyze the main and most important minor characters. This applies to biographies and some other nonfiction as much as it does to fiction. Give students a list of questions they can use to get a better understanding of characters they encounter in their reading. Questions might begin with the following:

- What is the person's background?
- What are his or her goals?
- How does he or she plan to accomplish those goals?
- How do other characters react to the person?

Brainstorm more questions with the class, and encourage students to use them as they read.

GLENCOE BOOKLINK

Use **Glencoe BookLink** to create customized reading lists for your students' reading levels, interests, and abilities.

READING STRATEGY — ORGANIZING INFORMATION

Have students create a concept web for the books they read in their additional reading. Have them place each book's title in an oval in the center of a web. Then have them branch to three connecting ovals that focus on specific aspects of the book: *Basic information; Subject; Recommendation*. They can branch from those to provide details about the book, its content, and their evaluation of it. Have students share their concept webs so other students can use the information to help them make their own book selections. OL

Analyzing Primary Sources

FOCUS

History–Social Science Standards

The following standard is covered on pages 514–515.

US8.8 Students analyze the divergent paths of the American people in the West from 1800 to the mid-1800s and the challenges they faced.

TEACH

R Reading Strategy

Reading Primary Sources

Ask: What does Polk mean by saying that "the cup of forbearance" was already "exhausted"? *(that the American government had lost patience with Mexico before)* OL CA HR3.

S Skill Practice

Historical and Social Sciences Analysis Skill

Ask: How does this paragraph reflect Polk's plans for handling the dispute with Mexico? *(Students should recall from the textbook that Polk wanted to provoke Mexico to open hostilities.)* OL CA HI2.

Answers and Additional Support

Analyzing Primary Sources

US8.8 Students analyze the divergent paths of the American people in the West from 1800 to the mid-1800s and the challenges they faced.

Going to War With Mexico

The war with Mexico (1846–1848) was supported by President James K. Polk and those who believed in Manifest Destiny. This war was fought to settle the border dispute between the United States and Mexico after Texas declared independence from Mexico. When the Mexican War was over, the United States had gained the vast California and New Mexico territories.

Read the passages on pages 514 and 515 and answer the questions that follow.

Mormons heading west in Conestoga wagon trains ▶

Reader's Dictionary

forbearance (fawr • BAR • uhns): patience, tolerance, or self control

vindicate (VIHN • duh • KAYT): to free from blame or guilt

declivity (dih • KLIHV • uht • ee): a descending slope

lauded (LAWD • ihd): celebrated

extolled (ihk • STOHLD): praised highly

Declaration of War With Mexico

On May 9, 1846, after several Americans were killed by Mexican troops in the borderlands between Texas and Mexico, President James Polk declared to Congress that the United States and Mexico were at war.

R The cup of **forbearance** had been exhausted even before the recent information from the frontier of the Del Norte. But now, after reiterated menaces, Mexico has passed the boundary of the United States, has invaded our territory and shed American blood upon the American soil. She has proclaimed that hostilities have commenced, and that the two nations are now at war.

S As war exists, and, notwithstanding, all our efforts to avoid it, exists by the act of Mexico herself, we are called upon by every consideration of duty and patriotism to **vindicate** with decision the honor, the rights, and the interests of our country. . . .

The Oregon Trail

In The Oregon Trail, *historian Francis Parkman tells of his encounters during an 1845 journey through the West.*

When we came to the descent of the broad shallow valley . . . an unlooked for sight awaited us. The stream glistened at the bottom, and along its banks were pitched a multitude of tents, while hundreds of cattle were feeding over the meadows. Bodies of troops, both horse and foot, and long trains of wagons, with men, women, and children, were moving over the opposite ridge and descending the broad **declivity** before us. These were the

EXTENDING THE CONTENT

Parkman and the Oregon Trail Francis Parkman was at home studying archives and historical records and experiencing life in the outdoors. He spent the summer of 1846 along the Oregon Trail and turned the experiences into several magazine articles before penning his book. Its first title was *The California and Oregon Trail*. The publisher added "California" to try to spur sales for the book, published in 1849 in the middle of Gold Rush fever. Since Parkman had not been near that area, the decision irked him.

Mormon battalion in the service of government, together with a considerable number of Missouri Volunteers. The Mormons were to be paid off in California, and they were allowed to bring with them their families and property. . . . to found, it might be, a Mormon empire in California.

Petition for Justice

The Chinese immigrants who came to California during the Gold Rush suffered much prejudice and violence. Chinese merchant Pun Chi describes the discrimination in a petition for justice from Congress.

When your honorable government threw open the territory of California, the people of other lands were welcomed here to search for gold and to engage in trade. The shipmasters of your respected nation came over to our country, **lauded** the equality of your laws, **extolled** the beauty of your manners and customs, and made it known that your officers and people were extremely cordial toward the Chinese. . . . we trusted in your sincerity. Not deterred by the long voyage, we came here presuming that our arrival would be hailed with cordiality and favor. But, alas! what times are these! —when former kind relations are forgotten, when we Chinese are viewed like thieves and enemies, when in the administration of justice our testimony is not received, when in the legal collection of the licenses we are injured and plundered, and villains of other nations are encouraged to rob and do violence to us! Our numberless wrongs it is most painful even to recite.

▲ Engraving of Chinese miners in California

DBQ Document-Based Questions

Declaration of War With Mexico

1. Who does Polk blame for causing the war?
2. Why does Polk believe the United States should go to war with Mexico?

The Oregon Trail

3. What does Parkman see in the valley that is so surprising?
4. Who was working for the government?

Petition for Justice

5. According to Pun Chi, how did Chinese immigrants expect to be treated in America?
6. What injustices were being committed against the Chinese in California?

Read to Write

7. Suppose the United States still had much unsettled western land, with no claims on it and little government or population. Imagine that you are preparing to move to this new territory. Write a letter to your family explaining your reasons and your plans. Use references to the primary sources you just read. CA HI1. CA 8WA2.1

Analyzing Primary Sources

C Critical Thinking

Analyzing Primary Sources Ask: Why did the Chinese decide to come to the United States? *(They were convinced by the statements made by ship captains about how wonderful the country was.)* OL

ASSESS

Have students answer the Document-Based Questions.

CLOSE

Connecting Have students explain how each of these primary sources raises issues about conflict between groups that took place as a result of Manifest Destiny. OL

DBQ Document-Based Questions

1. Mexico
2. because, he says, Mexican forces killed Americans on American soil
3. many tents and cattle
4. Mormons and Missouri volunteers
5. with fairness and kindness
6. They are viewed as thieves and enemies, not allowed to testify in court, cheated, robbed, and hurt physically.
7. Students' letters may refer to the opportunities available in such a situation.

CHAPTER 11 Assessment

Resources for pages 516–517

Use these resources to review, assess, or reteach the chapter.

- Active Reading Note-Taking Guide, Chapter 11
- Reading Essentials and Study Guide
- Chapter 11 Tests, Forms A and B
- Standards Assessment, Forms A and B
- California Standards Practice Workbook
- Succeeding on the California History–Social Science Standards CD-ROM
- MindJogger Videoquiz
- Interactive Tutor Self-Assessment CD-ROM

Chapter 11 Assessment

Standard US8.8

Review Content Vocabulary

Use the following vocabulary terms to create a newspaper article in which you describe events in the Southwest during this era.

1. emigrant
2. *Tejano*
3. *empresario*
4. ranchero
5. forty-niner

Review the Main Ideas

Section 1 • Westward to the Pacific

6. What agreement did the United States and Great Britain reach about the Oregon Territory?
7. What was Manifest Destiny?

Section 2 • Independence for Texas

8. Who was Stephen Austin? What was his role in early Texas history?
9. What was the outcome of the Battle of San Jacinto?

Section 3 • War With Mexico

10. Some Americans believed that annexing California would benefit national security. Why?
11. Identify the two main causes of the United States's war with Mexico.

Section 4 • New Settlers in California and Utah

12. What started the California Gold Rush?
13. Why did Mormons emigrate to Utah?

Critical Thinking

14. **Determining Cause and Effect** How did economic troubles in the East affect settlement in the Oregon area? CA HI2.
15. **Conclude** How did the war with Mexico change the U.S. border and its land holdings? CA CS3.
16. **Drawing Conclusions** How do you think the government of Mexico reacted to the American idea of Manifest Destiny? CA HR5.
17. **Compare** How did the negotiations between the United States and Britain over the Oregon Territory differ from those between the United States and Mexico over the Southwest? CA HI2.

Geography Skills

Study the routes of the western trails shown on the map. Then answer the questions that follow. CA CS3.

NATIONAL GEOGRAPHIC **The Oregon and California Trails**

18. **Region** Which mountains did settlers have to cross to reach Oregon's Pacific coast? California's Pacific coast?
19. **Location** In what city did the Oregon Trail begin? In what city did it end?

Review Vocabulary

Articles will vary but should reflect information in the chapter.

Review the Main Ideas

6. to divide Oregon at latitude 49°N
7. the belief that the United States had a right to extend its control over much of North America
8. He was an empresario who settled American families in parts of Texas and became a leader in the Texan community.
9. The Texans won and captured Santa Anna. They got him to agree to a treaty granting them independence.
10. because the nation would be bordered by seas on east and west and not by a foreign power
11. annexation of Texas; location of Texas-Mexican border
12. the discovery of gold on Sutter's land
13. to find a safe haven

Critical Thinking

14. Economic troubles made moving to the West look attractive.
15. settled the border between Texas and Mexico at the Rio Grande; added large area in the West, including the Mexican provinces of New Mexico and California
16. Students are likely to say that Britain and Mexico did not approve of the idea.
17. Control of Oregon was settled peaceably; conflict with Mexico was only settled by war.

Geography Skills

18. Cascades; Sierra Nevada
19. Independence, Missouri; Portland, Oregon

History Online

Self-Check Quiz Visit ca.hss.glencoe.com to prepare for the Chapter 11 test.

Read to Write

20. **The Big Ideas** **Evaluate** How did immigration impact the economy and society of Texas, California, and Utah? Write an essay summarizing your conclusions. CA 8WS1.1

21. **Using Your FOLDABLES** Manifest Destiny was a term first used by a reporter in 1845. Was he introducing a new concept for Americans or describing something that settlers had believed since colonial times? Does Manifest Destiny have any modern forms? Explain your conclusions in a short essay. CA 8WA2.4 CA HI3.

Academic Vocabulary

Choose an academic vocabulary word to complete each sentence.

a. range
b. access
c. route
d. vision

22. The United States government was eager to have ___ to the Pacific Ocean.
23. Political leaders had a clear ___ of Manifest Destiny and pursued acquiring new territory for Americans to settle.

Building Citizenship

24. **Analyze** According to the Constitution of the United States, what steps need to be taken in order for new states to enter the Union? Why was Texas admitted by a joint resolution of the Senate rather than by treaty? Explain. CA HI2.

Reviewing Skills

25. Review READING SKILL **New Vocabulary** Write definitions for the words *emigrant* and *immigrant*. Clearly explain what each term means. Then use each of these words in a sentence. CA 8RW1.0

26. Review ANALYSIS SKILL **Predicting** Write a paragraph predicting how Manifest Destiny will affect relationships with Native Americans. CA HI2.

Standards Practice

Select the best answer for the following questions.

27 The discovery of gold in California led to which of the following?

A discovery of gold in the Black Hills of the Dakotas
B increased western expansion and foreign immigration
C annexation of California as a slave state
D war with Mexico over the independence of California

28 The Mormons immigrated to the West to

A mine for gold.
B settle Texas.
C escape further religious persecution.
D purchase California from Mexico.

29 Some Northern leaders opposed admitting Texas to the United States because

A Texas was part of Mexico.
B they feared Texas would become a slave state.
C Texans did not want to join the Union.
D they feared Texas would become a free state.

Read to Write

20. **The Big Ideas** Students' essays should point out that the immigration of Americans into all three areas changed the economies and societies. They may also mention the immigration of Chinese to California and point out that the Mormons who settled in Utah had a particular religion that they practiced.

21. Using Your FOLDABLES Students should support their conclusions with reasons.

Using Academic Vocabulary

22. b.
23. d.

CHAPTER 11 Assessment

Building Citizenship

24. a territory must petition Congress to be admitted; Congress passes an enabling act, which allows the people to set up a constitution, which Congress approves and then passes an act of admission; because it bypassed first becoming a territory

Reviewing Skills

25. Review READING SKILL Sentences will vary but should reflect information in the chapter.

26. Review ANALYSIS SKILL Students should predict that expansion of white settlement in the West will lead to renewed conflict with Native Americans there.

Standards Practice

27. B
28. C
29. B

Bonus Question

Ask: What did the defenders of the Alamo achieve? *(They bought the Texans time to declare independence and form an army.)* OL

History Online

Have students visit the Web site at ca.hss.glencoe.com to review Chapter 11 and take the Self-Check Quiz.

FOCUS

Reviewing Unit Objectives

Having studied this unit, students should be able to

- Describe the growth of industry and transportation in the North and its impact on society.
- Describe the growth of cotton growing in the South and its impact on society.
- Discuss expanded settlements in the West and how the settlers lived.
- Explain why reform movements arose and what the reformers achieved.
- Discuss political changes in the period.
- Outline how the nation expanded its territory.

TEACH

Have students explain how the nation was both stronger and more divided in 1850 than it had been in 1820. OL

Unit Review Activity

To help students review the unit objectives, create a question-and-answer game show with six categories of information—one for each objective—and five questions in each category. The questions in each category should increase in both difficulty and point values. Form the class into teams and have them compete to answer the questions. OL

Unit 4 REVIEW

The Young Republic

Between 1800 and 1860, the United States grew stronger as it expanded to the Pacific Ocean. At the same time, the North, the South, and the West developed sectional differences that would affect the country's future.

	Chapter 8: The Northeast: Building Industry	Chapter 9: The South	Chapter 10: The Age of Jackson	Chapter 11: Manifest Destiny
When	• 1790–1850	• 1820–1860	• 1815–1848	• 1819–1858
Where	• New England • the South • the West • New York • the North	• the South • Upper South • Deep South	• the South • the Northeast • Georgia • Alabama • Mississippi • Florida • Indian Territory	• Oregon Country • Texas • Mexico • New Mexico Territory • California • Utah

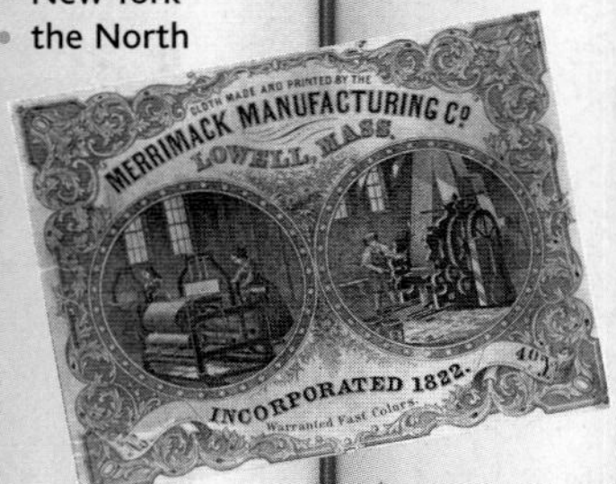

▲ *The textile mills in Lowell, Massachusetts, employed many young women.*

◀ *Goblet showing Andrew Jackson's log cabin*

518

END-OF-UNIT RESOURCES

Use these resources to review and assess unit material.

- Step Into American History Activities
- Cumulative Assessment Activities
- Reading Essentials and Study Guide
- California Standards Practice Workbook
- Interactive Tutor Self-Assessment CD-ROM
- Exam*View*® Pro Testmaker CD-ROM
- Succeeding on the California History–Social Science Standards CD-ROM

	Chapter 8: The Northeast: Building Industry	Chapter 9: The South	Chapter 10: The Age of Jackson	Chapter 11: Manifest Destiny
Major Events	• c.1800 Industrial Revolution • 1807 Steamboat *Clermont* • c. 1820s on Changes in art and literature • 1825 Erie Canal • 1840s–1860s Millions of new immigrants • 1848 Seneca Falls Convention	• **1793** Cotton gin • **1808** End of importing slaves • **1830–1860** More severe slave codes • **1831** Nat Turner's rebellion • **1840s** Tredegar Iron Works is a leading iron producer • **1860** South has only one-third of nation's rail lines • **1860** New Orleans has 168,000 people	• **1820s** Expansion of voting rights • **1830** Webster-Hayne Debate • **1830** Indian Removal Act • **1832** Nullification Act • **1832** Veto of National Bank • **1835–1842** Seminole wars • **1837** Panic of 1837 • **1838** Trail of Tears	• 1830–1840s American settlers in Oregon • 1835–1836 Texas War for Independence • 1845 Texas statehood • 1846–1847 Mexican War • 1846 Bear Flag Republic • 1846 Mormons migrate to Utah • 1848 California gold rush • 1853 Gadsden Purchase
Some Important People	• Samuel Slater • Francis Cabot Lowell • Robert Fulton • Horace Mann • Henry David Thoreau • Henry Wadsworth Longfellow • Elizabeth Cady Stanton • Susan B. Anthony	• Eli Whitney • William Gregg • Joseph Reid Anderson • Nat Turner • Harriet Tubman • Frederick Douglass	• Andrew Jackson • Henry Clay • John Q. Adams • John C. Calhoun • Daniel Webster • Black Hawk • Osceola • Martin Van Buren	• William Henry Harrison • John Q. Adams • James Polk • Henry Clay • Stephen Austin • Santa Anna • Sam Houston • John Frémont • Zachary Taylor • Joseph Smith • Brigham Young
How do these events and ideas affect our lives today?	• The United States began to emerge as an industrial giant during this period.	• The heritage of discrimination and unequal rights created by slavery still poses problems today.	• Many Native Americans still live on reservations.	• The United States grew from coast to coast during this period.
What was happening in California at this time?	• 1820s Beginning of rancho economy • 1834 Break up of missions starts	• **1846** Bear Flag Revolt	• **1848** Territorial transfer to U.S. • **1848** Discovery of gold	• 1850 California statehood • 1851 Land Law of 1851

◄ *Erie Canal barrel*

◄ *Harriet Tubman*

◄ *Gold nuggets*

Unit 4 Review

ASSESS/CLOSE

Unit Wrap-Up Activity

Creating a Display Have students work in groups to develop a display that focuses on one of the three sections of the country in this period or on national politics.

1. Organize students into groups of equal size and assign each group the North, the South, the West, or the national government.
2. Tell groups that their displays should include text and graphics that detail what life was like in their section of the country, including economics, society, culture, and politics. Students might reproduce primary source documents and images or write their own descriptions and draw their own pictures. Tell the group assigned to the topic of national politics that they should similarly use text and visuals to highlight the issues and the leaders important to the country in this period.
3. Have each group present its display to the class. **OL**

PROFESSIONAL DEVELOPMENT: MULTICULTURAL CLASSROOM

Use these resources for help teaching a culturally diverse classroom.

- Banks, James A. and Cherry A. McGee Banks. *Multicultural Education: Issues and Perspectives.* Jossey-Bass, 2003.
- Gay, Geneva, ed. *Becoming Multicultural Educators: Personal Journey Toward Professional Agency.* Jossey-Bass, 2003.
- Nieto, Sonia. *Affirming Diversity: The Sociopolitical Context of Multicultural Education* (Fourth Edition). Allyn & Bacon, 2003.

Unit 5 Planning Guide

Teaching the Unit

Use the information on these pages to help you teach Unit 5.

History–Social Science Standards Covered in Unit 5

Standard	Chapter 12	Chapter 13	Chapter 14
US8.9 Students analyze the early and steady attempts to abolish slavery and to realize the ideals of the Declaration of Independence.	✔		
US8.10 Students analyze the multiple causes, key events, and complex consequences of the Civil War.	✔	✔	
US8.11 Students analyze the character and lasting consequences of Reconstruction.			✔

Pacing Your Lessons

This pacing chart provides time management suggestions for teaching Unit 5.

Unit 5 Civil War and Reconstruction	Days
Unit 5 Introduction	1/2
Chapter 12 • **Reading Skill:** Making Inferences • **Sections 1–5** • **Biography:** Harriet Beecher Stowe, Biddy Mason • **You Decide . . .** • **Analyzing Primary Sources**	7
Chapter 13 • **Reading Skill:** Evaluation • **Sections 1–5** • **Biography:** Clara Barton, Robert E. Lee and Ulysses S. Grant • **America's Literature:** *Rifles for Watie* • **Geography & History** • **Analyzing Primary Sources**	11
Chapter 14 • **Reading Skill:** Monitoring and Clarifying • **Sections 1–4** • **Biography:** Charlotte Forten, Frederick Douglass • **Connecting to the Constitution** • **Analyzing Primary Sources**	7
Unit 5 Review	1/2

Teacher to Teacher

A State of the Union Address on the Fourteenth Amendment—Then and Now

Phil Trotter
San Diego School District
San Diego, CA

Organize the class into an equal number of groups. Have half of the groups research the legal rights of people—particularly African Americans—just prior to the passage of the Fourteenth Amendment. The other half of the class should research how the amendment protects African Americans and other minorities today. Using as many specific examples as they can find, have each group write a State of the Union Address for either "then" or "now." Before having groups present their addresses to the class, ask all students to find articles in newspapers and magazines that deal with the rights and freedoms covered by the Fourteenth Amendment. These articles can be shared during class discussion after each group's State of the Union presentation.

Previewing the Chapters

Dear American History Teacher:

As you begin to teach this unit, there are themes that reoccur throughout the chapters that you will want to point out to students.

The rising sectional identification of the early 1800s led to sectional conflict and war in the middle decades. Compromises seemed to settle the matter of slavery in the territories, but as the years passed tensions grew sharper and compromise became harder to achieve. Outbreaks of violence in the 1850s led to growing anger and fear and produced all-out war in 1861. The North won that war after Abraham Lincoln set two goals—restoring the Union and finally ending slavery. Years of war and the collapse of its economic and social system required significant rebuilding in the South. At first, Northerners showed interest in protecting the rights of African Americans, but eventually they abandoned Reconstruction. Conservative whites regained control of Southern state governments and put in place new laws that sharply limited the rights of African Americans.

You may want to use the following information at the beginning of each chapter as a lesson launcher to help students begin to focus on what they will be studying.

James M. McPherson

CHAPTER 12: Road to Civil War
(pages 524–565)

A growing number of people began to demand that slavery be ended and worked to help enslaved African Americans escape slavery. The issue of slavery in the western territories became hotly debated. A compromise settled it in 1820 and again in 1850 when California applied for statehood. A new law to organize the territories of Kansas and Nebraska led to violence over the slavery issue. Abraham Lincoln won the presidential election in 1860. Soon after, seven Southern states left the Union, and when Southern forces attacked a Union fort, the Civil War began.

CHAPTER 13: The Civil War
(pages 566–619)

Soldiers in the Civil War came from every region, and each side expected an early victory. The first battle showed that the war would be a long and difficult one. The North blockaded the South's coast, hoping to cut off supplies. The Union won several early victories in the West but had difficulty in the East. In 1863, Lincoln changed the goals of the war by declaring that all slaves in the South would be free. African Americans contributed to the war effort in many different ways, as did women. The Union won key victories in both East and West in 1863, though fighting continued for nearly two more years. Finally, in 1865, the Confederate armies were forced to surrender.

CHAPTER 14: Reconstruction
(pages 620–655)

After Lincoln was assassinated, Andrew Johnson became president and clashed with Congress over policies in the South. Northerners passed new laws aimed at punishing whites and ensuring the rights of African Americans. African Americans had to weather some violence, but they voted, and some won political offices. Meanwhile, the South worked to rebuild the damaged economy. Democrats committed to ending Reconstruction gained control of state governments in the South, and Northerners lost interest in Reconstruction. A disputed presidential election in 1876 led the federal government to withdraw the last troops from the South and end Reconstruction.

FOCUS

Connecting to Past Learning

In Unit 4, students learned about the development of distinct ways of life in the nation's three sections and the further expansion of the United States. In Unit 5, they will learn how those regional differences led to increasing hostility between the North and the South over slavery in the territories and how that conflict led to the Civil War, the end of slavery, and attempts at Reconstruction in the South.

Unit Launch Activity

Ask: Why do you think the fight between the North and the South was called a "civil war"? *(Students should recognize that the war was fought by people from the same country, not two different countries.)* **OL**

History–Social Science Standards

The following standards are covered in Unit 5:

US8.9 Students analyze the early and steady attempts to abolish slavery and to realize the ideals of the Declaration of Independence.

US8.10 Students analyze the multiple causes, key events, and complex consequences of the Civil War.

US8.11 Students analyze the character and lasting consequences of Reconstruction.

Why It's Important

Ask: What group's civil rights do you think were left unsettled after the Civil War and Reconstruction ended? **OL**

Unit 5

Civil War and Reconstruction

Why It's Important

Because of the issue of slavery, relations between the North and the South grew more hostile. Soon the two sides met in the most horrible war the country had ever seen. With the North's victory slavery was ended, but the reunited nation faced key issues that would take many decades to reconcile.

- While the North and South had made several compromises on slavery over the years, the issue eventually split the country.
- The Civil War and Reconstruction freed the slaves, but issues related to civil rights and equal opportunity still exist today.

1820 **1840**

U.S. Events

- **1820** Congress passes Missouri Compromise
- **1850** Congress passes Compromise of 1850
- **1857** Supreme Court announces *Dred Scott* decision

Dred Scott ▶

California Events

- **1824** Chumash Indians revolt at California missions
- **1846** Bear Flag revolt takes place
- **1850** California is admitted to Union as a free state

World Events

- **1848** *The Communist Manifesto* is published
- **1853** Commodore Perry arrives in Japan

Commodore Perry ▶

520

TEACHING THE TIME LINES

Help students focus on the information in the time lines. **Ask:**

- What period of time is covered by the Civil War and Reconstruction? *(1861 to 1877)*
- Which item on the United States events tier is mostly likely to affect California's statehood? Why? *(the Compromise of 1850; because California became a state that year)*
- What conflict took place in California after the Civil War? *(Modoc War)*
- Which World events entries are related to trade? *(Commodore Perry arrives in Japan; Suez Canal completed.)*

As students study events described in the unit, refer back to these time lines and have students identify where the event would appear. **OL**

NATIONAL GEOGRAPHIC

Where in the United States?

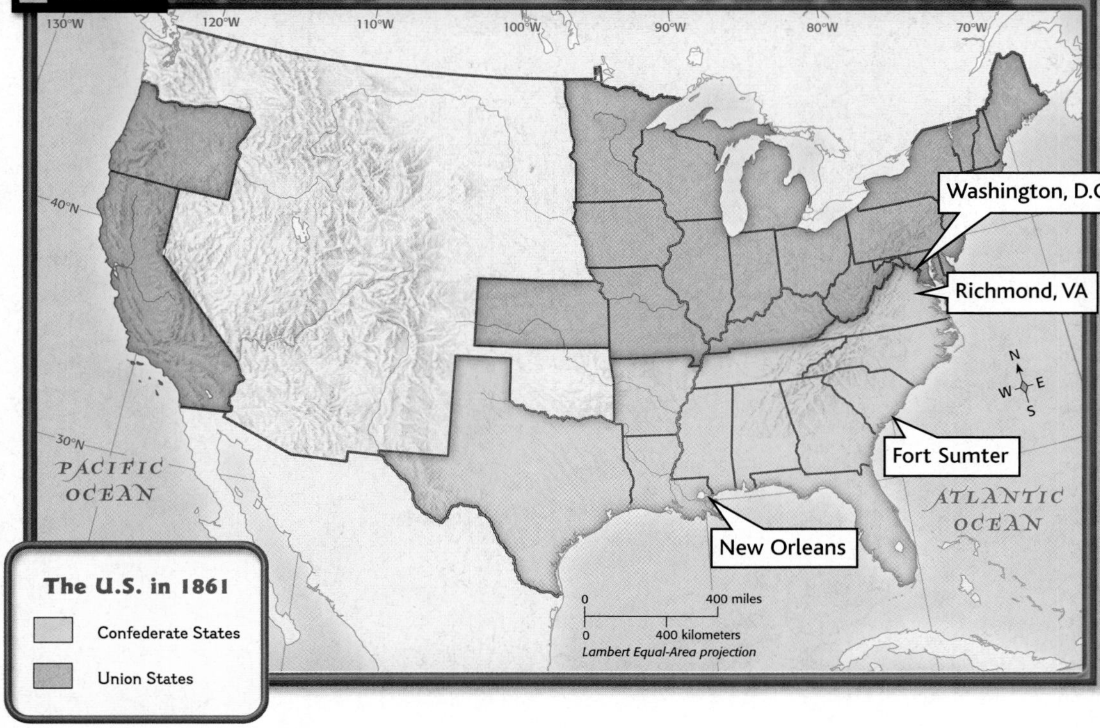

1860 **1880** **1900**

1861 The Civil War begins

Union and Confederate flags

1877 Reconstruction ends

1890 Poll taxes and literacy tests begin in Mississippi

1870 *Ward* v. *Flood* keeps African Americans out of white schools

1872 Modoc War is last Native American armed resistance

1879 New California Constitution is adopted

Captain Jack, Modoc Chief

1869 Suez Canal completed

1871 Bismarck unifies Germany

Otto von Bismarck

UNIVERSAL ACCESS

English Learners: Pair English language learners with students proficient in English. Have the English learners explain each entry in the time line in their own words. Instruct their partners to provide assistance if they are unable to explain any of the entries. EL

Visual/Spatial: Have students make a drawing illustrating one of the events on the time line. OL

Advanced Learners: Have students research Alexander II's freeing of serfs in Russia and write a brief essay comparing it to the end of slavery in the United States. AL

TEACH

NATIONAL GEOGRAPHIC **Where in the United States?**

Understanding Maps and Time Lines Ask: Where are the Confederate states located? *(in the South)* Where are the Union states? *(in the North and on the West coast)* Why is Washington, D.C., important? *(It is the nation's capital and close to Confederate states.)* Why do you think the other places are highlighted? *(Students may say that Richmond and New Orleans must be important cities in the Confederate states, and some may know that Richmond was the Confederate capital. They might suggest that Fort Sumter was the location of a battle.)* OL

NCLB *No Child Left Behind*

Teaching Activity Have students read the introduction to the unit on page 520. **Ask:** How were the economies and societies of the North and the South different in the early 1800s? *(Students should point to the industrialization and greater population of the North and the presence of slavery and an agricultural economy in the South.)* OL

INTRODUCING UNIT 5

Unit Objectives

After studying this unit, students should be able to

- Outline the events that led to the Civil War and explain why people in the North and the South reacted to each event as they did.
- Discuss the election of 1860 and why it led to secession.
- Compare the strengths, weaknesses, and strategies of the North and the South at the beginning of the war.
- Identify key battles in the war and explain their significance.
- Discuss how life changed for African Americans during the war.
- Compare the different plans for Reconstruction of the South and explain why Congress came to control this process.
- Describe changes in the South as a result of Reconstruction and explain why Reconstruction ended.

Previewing People to Meet

Have pairs of students write the names of the **People to Meet** on index cards, one to a card. They should write the person's identifying characteristics on another card. Have them mix up all the cards with names and place them face down in one area and do the same with the characteristics in another area. Then have students take turns turning over one card from each group to match the name and the description. Students should continue the activity until all the cards are correctly matched. OL

Unit 5 Places to Locate

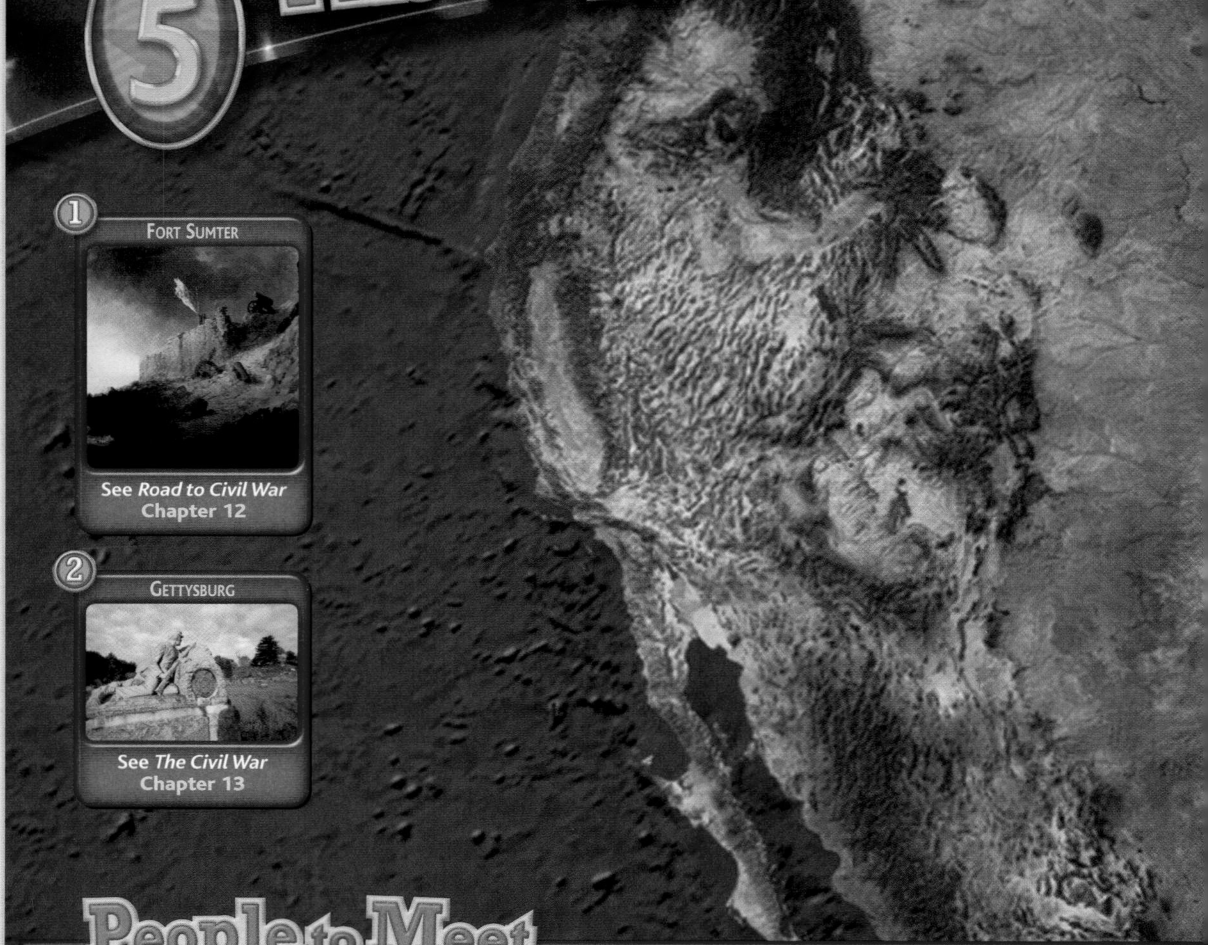

1 FORT SUMTER

See *Road to Civil War* Chapter 12

2 GETTYSBURG

See *The Civil War* Chapter 13

People to Meet

Frederick Douglass
c. 1817–1895
African American leader
Chapter 12, page 532

Sojourner Truth
c. 1797–1883
African American leader
Chapter 12, page 532

Dred Scott
c. 1800–1857
Subject of Supreme Court case on slavery
Chapter 12, page 549

Abraham Lincoln
1809–1865
Sixteenth president of the United States
Chapter 12, page 552

522

Previewing Places to Locate

Use the following descriptions to explain the images on the map.

1 

Confederate soldiers bombed Fort Sumter with about 4,000 shells. The tiny Union garrison—fewer than 80 men—surrendered after 33 hours of attack.

2 

Gettysburg was the site of a bloody and decisive three-day battle and the spot where President Abraham Lincoln delivered his famous address that tried to explain the meaning of the war.

Ulysses S. Grant
1822–1885
Union general
Chapter 13, page 611

Robert E. Lee
1807–1870
Confederate general
Chapter 13, page 611

Clara Barton
1821–1912
Civil War nurse
Chapter 13, page 601

Andrew Johnson
1808–1875
Seventeenth president of the United States
Chapter 14, page 628

INTRODUCING UNIT 5

Skill Practice

Using Geography Skills

Explain that three of these places represent the sites of important events during the Civil War. **Ask:** Why are they all clustered in the eastern part of the country? *(Students should recognize that the centers of population were in the east.)* **OL**

Skill Practice

Creating a Time Line

Have students create a time line for the period from 1861 to 1865. Tell them that as they read the unit, they should fill in important dates from the Civil War. **OL**

ASSESS/CLOSE

Have students explain why Grant and Lee were likely to play much more important roles during the Civil War than before it. *(They were generals, and the war would involve armies led by generals.)* **OL**

Grant and Lee signed the formal surrender agreement in the home of Wilmer McLean, an Appomattox resident. McLean had originally lived in the area of Manassas, but moved to southern Virginia after the First Battle of Bull Run was fought near his property.

President Abraham Lincoln and his wife were attending a play at Ford's Theater when John Wilkes Booth assassinated him. Lincoln died just a few hours later.

Chapter 12 Planning Guide

SECTION RESOURCES

Main Ideas	Print Materials	Technology Resources
Section 1: Abolitionists 1. By the early 1800s, Americans began to demand an end to slavery. 2. Slavery became an important social issue in the 1830s. 3. Abolitionists established the Underground Railroad.	• Reproducible Lesson Plan 12–1* • Daily Lesson and Discussion Notes 12–1 • Active Reading Note-Taking Guide 12–1 • Reading Essentials and Study Guide 12–1 • Guided Reading Activity 12–1 • Section Quiz 12–1	Daily Focus Skills Transparency 12–1 Section Graphic Organizer Transparency 12–1 California Standards Practice Transparencies Interactive Tutor Self-Assessment CD-ROM Exam*View*® Pro Testmaker CD-ROM Presentation Plus! CD-ROM
Section 2: Slavery and the West 1. The Missouri Compromise resolved the issue of slave states. 2. The Kentucky Resolution advanced the doctrine of nullification. 3. The issue of slavery in new territories was at the forefront. 4. Henry Clay's plan resulted in the Compromise of 1850.	• Reproducible Lesson Plan 12–2* • Daily Lesson and Discussion Notes 12–2 • Active Reading Note-Taking Guide 12–2 • Reading Essentials and Study Guide 12–2 • Guided Reading Activity 12–2 • Section Quiz 12–2	Daily Focus Skills Transparency 12–2 Section Graphic Organizer Transparency 12–2 California Standards Practice Transparencies Interactive Tutor Self-Assessment CD-ROM Exam*View*® Pro Testmaker CD-ROM Presentation Plus! CD-ROM
Section 3: A Nation Dividing 1. The Kansas-Nebraska Act resulted from another dispute over slavery. 2. Violence erupted as the proslavery Kansas legislature was elected.	• Reproducible Lesson Plan 12–3* • Daily Lesson and Discussion Notes 12–3 • Active Reading Note-Taking Guide 12–3 • Reading Essentials and Study Guide 12–3 • Guided Reading Activity 12–3 • Section Quiz 12–3	Daily Focus Skills Transparency 12–3 Section Graphic Organizer Transparency 12–3 California Standards Practice Transparencies Interactive Tutor Self-Assessment CD-ROM Exam*View*® Pro Testmaker CD-ROM Presentation Plus! CD-ROM
Section 4: Challenges to Slavery 1. The Supreme Court's decision in the *Dred Scott* case resulted in even more division in the country. 2. The Lincoln-Douglas debates helped Lincoln emerge as a leader.	• Reproducible Lesson Plan 12–4* • Daily Lesson and Discussion Notes 12–4 • Active Reading Note-Taking Guide 12–4 • Reading Essentials and Study Guide 12–4 • Guided Reading Activity 12–4 • Section Quiz 12–4	Daily Focus Skills Transparency 12–4 Section Graphic Organizer Transparency 12–4 California Standards Practice Transparencies Interactive Tutor Self-Assessment CD-ROM Exam*View*® Pro Testmaker CD-ROM Presentation Plus! CD-ROM
Section 5: Secession and War 1. A split occurred in the Democratic Party, allowing Lincoln to win. 2. South Carolina led other southern states in seceding from the Union. 3. The Civil War began when Fort Sumter was attacked.	• Reproducible Lesson Plan 12–5* • Daily Lesson and Discussion Notes 12–5 • Active Reading Note-Taking Guide 12–5 • Reading Essentials and Study Guide 12–5 • Guided Reading Activity 12–5 • Section Quiz 12–5	Daily Focus Skills Transparency 12–5 Section Graphic Organizer Transparency 12–5 California Standards Practice Transparencies Interactive Tutor Self-Assessment CD-ROM Exam*View*® Pro Testmaker CD-ROM Presentation Plus! CD-ROM Vocabulary PuzzleMaker CD-ROM

PACING YOUR LESSONS

Unit Introduction	Chapter Introduction	Section 1	Section 2	Section 3	Section 4	Section 5	Chapter Assessment
$\frac{1}{2}$ Day	$\frac{1}{2}$ Day	2 Days	1 Day	1 Day	1 Day	1 Day	$\frac{1}{2}$ Day

0:00 **OUT OF TIME?** Assign the Chapter 12 ***Reading Essentials and Study Guide***

*Available on TeacherWorks™

Standards-Based Lesson Plan

History–Social Science Standards Covered in Chapter 12

The standards covered in the chapter are listed below. Use the accompanying activity as you teach the chapter to ensure student mastery of these standards. This activity can be used in combination with the program's print and technology assessment materials.

Standard	Section 1	2	3	4	5
US8.9 Students analyze the early and steady attempts to abolish slavery and to realize the ideals of the Declaration of Independence.	✔	✔	✔	✔	
US8.9.1 Describe the leaders of the movement (e.g., John Quincy Adams and his proposed constitutional amendment; John Brown and the armed resistance, Harriet Tubman and the Underground Railroad, Benjamin Franklin, Theodore Weld, William Lloyd Garrison, Frederick Douglass).	✔		✔		
US8.9.4 Discuss the importance of the slavery issue as raised by the annexation of Texas and California's admission to the union as a free state under the Compromise of 1850.		✔			
US8.9.5 Analyze the significance of the States' Rights doctrine, the Missouri Compromise (1820), the Wilmot Proviso (1846), the Compromise of 1850, Henry Clay's role in the Missouri Compromise and the Compromise of 1850, the Kansas-Nebraska Act (1854), the *Dred Scott* v. *Sandford* decision (1857), and the Lincoln-Douglas debates (1858).		✔	✔	✔	
US8.9.6 Describe the lives of free blacks and the laws that limited their freedom and economic opportunities.				✔	
US8.10 Students analyze the multiple causes, key events, and complex consequences of the Civil War.		✔		✔	✔
US8.10.1 Compare the conflicting interpretations of state and federal authority as emphasized in the speeches and writings of statesmen such as Daniel Webster and John C. Calhoun.		✔			
US8.10.3 Identify the constitutional issues posed by the doctrine of nullification and secession and the earliest origins of that doctrine.		✔			✔
US8.10.4 Discuss Abraham Lincoln's presidency and his significant writings and speeches and their relationship to the Declaration of Independence, such as his "House Divided" speech (1858), Gettysburg Address (1863), Emancipation Proclamation (1863), and inaugural addresses (1861 and 1865).				✔	✔
US8.10.5 Study the views and lives of leaders (e.g., Ulysses S. Grant, Jefferson Davis, Robert E. Lee) and soldiers on both sides of the war, including those of black soldiers and regiments.					✔
US8.10.6 Describe critical developments and events in the war, including the major battles, geographical advantages and obstacles, technological advances, and General Lee's surrender at Appomattox.					✔

Cumulative Standards-Assessment Activity

The Cumulative Standards-Assessment Activity will help students organize and learn the important information from the chapter. Begin teaching the chapter with this activity, and have students complete it as they read the chapter.

Creating a Causes-and-Effects Chart

Purpose This type of organizer helps students see how events develop from prior occurrences and lead to new consequences.

Introduction to Understanding Causes and Effects

1. Remind students that key events are not only the result of effects but the causes of other effects.
2. Ask students to copy a chart like the one on page 76B into their notebooks. As students read each section, have them search for the causes of events, their effects, and the further effects that flow from the initial effects. Tell them to create as many charts as they require to cover all the material in the chapter.
3. As part of your review of the chapter, have students share their charts. Suggest that students supplement their own charts with the ideas that they hear from other students. Encourage them to use their charts as study aids.

Chapter 12 Resources

READING SUPPORT

- Content Vocabulary Activity 12
- Academic Vocabulary Activity 12
- Reading Skills Activity 12
- American Literature Reading 12
- Biography Activities 12A–12H
- Chapter 12 Active Reading Note-Taking Guide
- Chapter 12 Guided Reading Activities
- Chapter 12 Reading Essentials and Study Guide
- Glencoe Literature Library
- Glencoe Video Program
- Vocabulary PuzzleMaker CD-ROM
- Interactive Graphic Organizers CD-ROM
- American History Primary Source Document Library CD-ROM

CRITICAL THINKING

- Critical Thinking Skills Activity 12
- Primary Source Reading 12
- Cause-and-Effect Transparency 12, Strategy, and Activity
- Presentation Plus! CD-ROM

UNIVERSAL ACCESS

- Universal Access Activity 12
- Then and Now Transparencies 12A–12B, Strategy, and Activity
- Graphic Novel Activity 12
- School-to-Home Connection Activities 12A–12D
- English Learner Handbook Chapter 12 Activities
- Universal Access for the American History Classroom
- Moments in Time
- American Art and Architecture Transparencies, Strategies, and Activities
- American Art Prints
- American Music Cultural Traditions
- American Music Hits Through History
- StudentWorks Plus CD-ROM

SKILL PRACTICE

- Map Overlay Transparency 12, Strategy, and Activity
- Analysis Skills Activity 12
- Time Line Activity 12
- Geography and History Activity 12
- Economics and History Activity 12
- Chart, Graph, and Map Skills Activity 12
- Political Cartoon Activity 12
- Supreme Court Case Study 12
- In-Text Map Transparency 12, Strategy, and Activity
- Step Into American History Activity 12
- Citizenship and Service Learning Activity 12
- Outline Map Resource Book
- MindJogger Plus Videoquiz

WRITING SUPPORT

- Writing Activity 12
- Language Arts Activity 12
- Writer's Guidebook
- Middle School Writing Process Transparencies

ASSESSMENT

GLENCOE'S ASSESSMENT ADVANTAGE

- Chapter 12 Section Quizzes
- Chapter 12 Tests, Forms A and B
- California Standards Assessment, Forms A and B
- Cumulative Assessment Activity US8.9
- California Standards Practice Workbook
- Succeeding on the California History–Social Science Standards CD-ROM
- Exam*View*® Pro Testmaker CD-ROM
- Interactive Tutor Self-Assessment CD-ROM

CD-ROM
DVD
Print Material
Poster
Transparency
Music Program
Videocassette
Glencoe Literature Library

Chapter 12 Resources

TECHNOLOGY

- StudentWorks Plus CD-ROM
- TeacherWorks Plus CD-ROM
- Exam*View*® Testmaker CD-ROM
- Interactive Tutor Self-Assessment CD-ROM
- Presentation Plus! CD-ROM
- Succeeding on the California History–Social Science Standards CD-ROM
- Vocabulary PuzzleMaker CD-ROM
- Interactive Graphic Organizers CD-ROM
- Interactive Time Line CD-ROM
- American History Primary Source Document Library CD-ROM
- MindJogger Plus Videoquiz
- American Music Cultural Traditions
- American Music Hits Through History
- Glencoe Video Program
- Professional Development in Middle School Social Studies Series
- Teaching American History With *Discovering Our Past: The American Journey to World War I*

SPANISH RESOURCES

- Spanish Activities and Assessment
  - Spanish Content Vocabulary Activities
  - Spanish Guided Reading Activities
  - Spanish Quizzes and Tests
  - Spanish California Standards Assessment
- Spanish Reading Essentials and Study Guide
- Spanish School-to-Home Connection
- Spanish Declaration of Independence and U.S. Constitution

TRANSPARENCIES

- California Standards Practice Transparencies
- Daily Focus Skills Transparencies
- Section Graphic Organizer Transparencies
- In-Text Map Transparencies
- Map Overlay Transparencies
- Cause-and-Effect Transparencies
- Then and Now Transparencies
- American Art and Architecture Transparencies
- Middle School Writing Process Transparencies

TEACHER PLANNING

- Daily Lesson and Discussion Notes
- English Learner Handbook
- Guide to Daily Intervention
- *Discovering Our Past: The American Journey to World War I* Reading and Study Skills Foldables
- Reading Strategies and Activities for the Social Studies Classroom
- Chapter 12 Reproducible Lesson Plans (correlated to California History–Social Science Standards)
- Universal Access for the American History Classroom
- NGS U.S. Desk Map
- NGS U.S. Atlas

PROFESSIONAL DEVELOPMENT

- Building Academic Vocabulary
- Strategies for Success
- Research-Based Strategies Used to Develop *Discovering Our Past: The American Journey to World War I*
- Character Education in the Middle School Classroom
- The Living Constitution
- Professional Development in Middle School Social Studies Video Series
- Teaching American History With *Discovering Our Past: The American Journey to World War I*

MASTERING THE STANDARDS

The content and assessment in the Student Edition, Teacher Wraparound Edition, teacher planning materials, and the print and technology products are all standards-based. The use of these products during instruction leads to mastery of the standards.

PRACTICE

- California Standards Practice Workbook
- California Standards Practice Transparencies
- Interactive Time Line CD-ROM
- School-to-Home Connection

BENCHMARK ASSESSMENT

- California Standards Assessment
- Exam*View*® Pro Testmaker CD-ROM
- Succeeding on the California History–Social Science Standards CD-ROM

REMEDIATION

- California Guide to Daily Intervention
- Interactive Tutor Self-Assessment CD-ROM
- Exam*View*® Pro Testmaker CD-ROM
- California Standards Practice Workbook
- Reading Essentials and Study Guide

Additional Resources

NATIONAL GEOGRAPHIC TEACHER'S CORNER

Index to National Geographic Magazine:
The following articles relate to this chapter:

- "African Rituals in Colonial America," Geographica, February 1997.
- "The Cruelest Commerce: African Slave Trade," by Colin Palmer, September 1992.

National Geographic Society Products
To order the following, call National Geographic at 1-800-368-2728

- *GeoKit: The Civil War* (Kit)
- *GeoKit: Immigration* (Kit)
- *United States: Territorial Growth* (Map)
- *National Geographic Desk Reference* (Book)
- *Steal Away: The Harriet Tubman Story* (Video)

NGS ONLINE

Access National Geographic's new dynamic MapMachine Web site and other geography resources at:

www.nationalgeographic.com
www.nationalgeographic.com/maps

A&E Home Video · Biography · The History Channel

The following videotape programs are available from Glencoe as supplements to Chapter 12.

- **American Civil War (ISBN 1-56501-0102-8)**
- **Images of the Civil War (ISBN 1-56501-171-6)**

To order, call Glencoe at 1-800-334-7344. To find classroom resources to accompany many of these videos, check the following home pages:

A&E Television: www.aetv.com
The History Channel: www.historychannel.com

MOMENTS IN TIME DBQ

The following resource can help you teach the content of this chapter.

Unit 4 Division Within (1876–1901)

History Online

Use our Web site for additional resources. All essential content is covered in the Student Edition.

You and your students can visit ca.hss.glencoe.com, the Web site companion to *Discovering Our Past: The American Journey to World War I*. This innovative integration of electronic and print media offers your students a wealth of opportunities. The student text directs students to the Web site for the following options:

- Chapter Overviews
- Self-Check Quizzes
- Study Central™
- Student Web Activities
- Textbook Updates
- Multi-Language Glossaries

Answers to the student Web activities are provided for you in the Web Activity Lesson Plans. Additional Web resources and ePuzzles and games are also available.

FOLDABLES™ Study Organizer

Dinah Zike's Foldables

Foldables are three-dimensional, interactive graphic organizers that help students practice basic writing skills, review key vocabulary terms, and identify main ideas. Every chapter contains a foldable activity, with additional chapter activities found in the Reading and Study Skills Foldables booklet.

Chapter 12 Resources

Reading List Generator CD-ROM

GLENCOE BOOKLINK

The Glencoe BookLink CD-ROM is a database that allows you to search more than 15,000 titles to create a customized reading list for your students.

- Reading lists can be organized by students' reading level, author, genre, theme, or area of interest.
- The database provides Degrees of Reading Power™ (DRP) and Lexile™ readability scores for all selections.
- A brief summary of each selection is included.

Reading level suggestions for this chapter:

For students at a Grade 6 reading level:

- ***Sojourner Truth and the Struggle for Freedom,*** by Edward Beecher Claflin

For students at a Grade 7 reading level:

- from ***My Bondage and My Freedom,*** by Frederick Douglass

For students at a Grade 8 reading level:

- ***James Buchanan: 15th President of the United States,*** by David R. Collins

For students at a Grade 9 reading level:

- ***Been in the Storm So Long: The Aftermath of Slavery,*** by Leon F. Litwack

READING SUPPORT FROM JAMESTOWN EDUCATION

- *Timed Readings Plus in Social Studies* helps students increase their reading rate and fluency while maintaining comprehension. The 400-word passages are similar to those found on state and national assessments.
- *Reading in the Content Area: Social Studies* concentrates on six essential reading skills that help students better comprehend what they read. The book includes 754 high-interest nonfiction passages written at increasing levels of difficulty.
- *Reading Fluency* helps students read smoothly, accurately, and expressively.
- *Jamestown's Reading Improvement,* by renowned reading expert Edward Fry, focuses on helping build your students' comprehension, vocabulary, and skimming and scanning skills.
- *Critical Reading Series* provides high-interest books, each written at three reading levels.

To order these products, call Glencoe at 1-800-334-7344.

KEY for Using the Teacher Wraparound Edition

Use this key to help you identify the different types of prompts found in the Teacher Wraparound Edition.

R **Reading Strategies** activities help you teach reading skills and vocabulary.

C **Critical Thinking** strategies help students apply and extend what they have learned.

U **Universal Access** activities provide differentiated instruction for students learning to speak English, along with suggestions for teaching various types of learners.

S **Skill Practice** strategies help students practice historical analysis and geography skills.

W **Writing Support** activities provide writing opportunities to help students comprehend the text.

Teaching strategies and activities have been coded for ability level appropriateness.

AL Activities for students working above grade level

OL Activities for students working on grade level

BL Activities for students working below grade level

EL Activities for English Learners

FOCUS

History–Social Science Standards

In this chapter, the following standards will be covered:

US8.9 Students analyze the early and steady attempts to abolish slavery and to realize the ideals of the Declaration of Independence.

US8.10 Students analyze the multiple causes, key events, and complex consequences of the Civil War.

More About the Photo

Fort Sumter, Located in Charleston, South Carolina harbor, was built between 1829 and 1860 on a man-made island of sea shells and granite. The fort has a pentagonal shape, with walls that are fifty feet high, and eight to twelve feet thick. It was named after General Thomas Sumter, a hero of the American Revolution.

Chapter 12

Road to Civil War

▼ Fort Sumter is where the Civil War began.

NATIONAL GEOGRAPHIC Where & When?

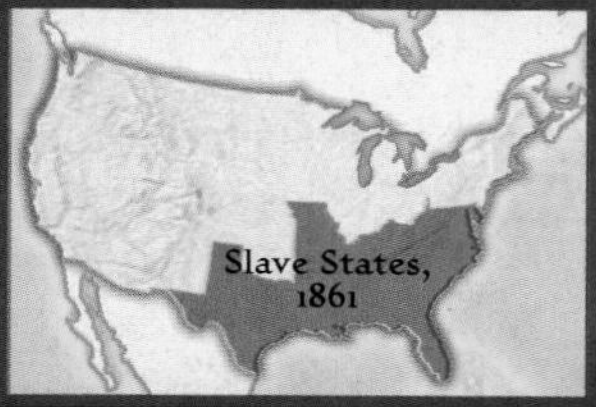

1820 — 1845 — 1870

- **1820** Missouri Compromise is passed
- **1845** Texas becomes a state
- **1860** Abraham Lincoln elected president
- **1861** Civil War begins

TEACH

The Big Ideas

As you begin teaching each section, use these questions and activities to focus on the Big Ideas.

Section 1

Abolitionists

Essential Question: What injustices do you see in today's world? What reform movements address them? After students discuss these questions, explain that in the early and middle 1800s, thousands of Americans considered slavery to be unjust and crusaded to end it. OL

Section 2

Slavery and the West

Essential Question: What might have influenced people's opinions on the issue of slavery in the western territories? *(differences in economic, political, and social beliefs and practices)* Tell students that when California wanted to become a state, it made national headlines because of the fierce debate over whether or not it would allow slavery. OL

Section 3

A Nation Dividing

Essential Question: Do Americans disagree over any issues today? How do today's issues compare to those of the 1800s? After students have discussed these questions, point out that in the 1800s, divisions between North and South were so extreme that people fought over them. Section 3 discusses the growing tensions over slavery that led to violence. OL

The Big Ideas

History Online **Chapter Overview** Visit ca.hss.glencoe.com for a preview of Chapter 12.

Section 1 Abolitionists

Reactions to social injustice can lead to reform movements. Many reformers turned their attention to eliminating slavery.

Section 2 Slavery and the West

Differences in economic, political, and social beliefs and practices can lead to division within a nation and have lasting consequences. The question of whether to admit new states as free states or slave states arose.

Section 3 A Nation Dividing

Differences in economic, political, and social beliefs and practices can lead to division within a nation and have lasting consequences. Growing tensions over slavery eventually led to violence in the new territories.

Section 4 Challenges to Slavery

Conflict often brings about great change. A new antislavery party and a Supreme Court decision divided the nation further on slavery.

Section 5 Secession and War

Conflict often brings about great change. In response to Lincoln's election as president, most Southern states left the Union.

View the Chapter 12 video in the Glencoe Video Program.

FOLDABLES™ Study Organizer

Sequencing Events Make and use this foldable to sequence some of the key events that led to the Civil War.

Step 1 Fold a sheet of paper in half from side to side, leaving a $\frac{1}{2}$ inch tab along the side.

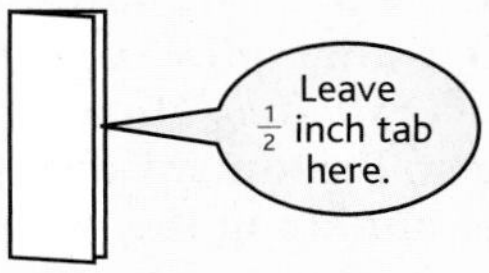

Step 2 Cut the top flap to make 5 tabs.

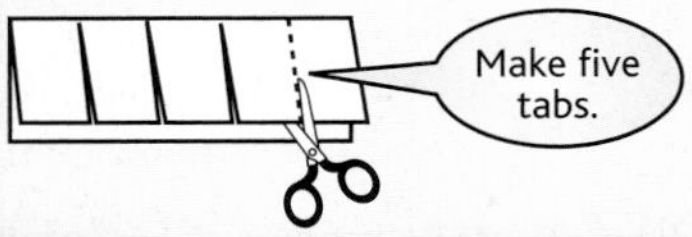

Step 3 Label your foldable as shown.

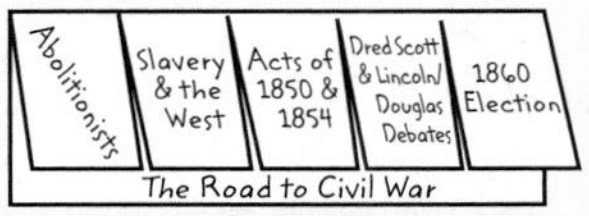

Reading and Writing As you read, write facts about the events under each appropriate tab of your foldable. How did these events lead to the Civil War?

INTRODUCING CHAPTER 12

Section 4

Challenges to Slavery

Essential Question: How do civil rights groups respond to discrimination today? Explain that before the Civil War, a new political party was formed to block the spread of slavery. **OL**

Section 5

Secession and War

Essential Question: What reactions do you see from those who opposed the winning candidates in elections today? After students respond, explain that after Abraham Lincoln was elected in 1860, many Southerners were so upset that they tried to form a new nation. **OL**

History Online

Go to ca.hss.glencoe.com for student activities, lesson plans, and links to additional Web resources about the growing sectional conflict.

FOLDABLES™ Study Organizer — Dinah Zike's Foldables

Purpose Have students use their foldables to organize events leading up to the Civil War. When students have completed the activity, they should have an outline of the key events leading up to the Civil War. **OL**

Why It's Important

Making Inferences Good readers are like good detectives: they use clues to help them uncover meaning. The ability to make inferences is a critical reading skill. It enables students to develop a richer understanding of what they read.

1 Learn It!

Explain to students that this skill is one that they use in their daily lives. **Ask:** Suppose you came into a room decorated with balloons and streamers and saw a birthday cake on the table. What occasion is being celebrated? *(someone's birthday)* How did you know even though no one told you? *(from the appearance of the room)* Explain that making inferences when reading is similar—by paying attention to details, readers infer additional meaning in what they read. OL

Chapter 12 Get Ready to Read

Making Inferences

READING SKILL

1 Learn It!

Good readers make inferences to help them understand text. Another way to describe this skill is "reading between the lines." Use this skill to look for clues that might explain what is occurring in the passage even though it may not be explicitly stated. Think about what you already know and draw conclusions based on this knowledge. Because it is impossible to include every detail, the author relies on a reader's ability to infer. Making inferences will draw on many of the other reading strategies you have been using in this book, including recognizing bias and questioning. When you read the paragraph below, answer the question "What did the people in Boston think of slavery?"

> **On May 24, 1854, the people of Boston erupted in outrage. Federal officers had seized Anthony Burns, a runaway slave who lived in Boston, to send him back to slavery. Abolitionists tried to rescue Burns from the federal courthouse, and city leaders attempted to buy his freedom. All efforts failed. . . . In a gesture of bitter protest, Bostonians draped buildings in black and hung the American flag upside down.**
>
> —*from page 533*

Reading Tip

As you read, ask yourself "What facts or information does the author expect me to already know about this topic?"

526

READING STRATEGY — USING CONTEXT CLUES

Making sound inferences depends on the ability to use context clues. Explain that by looking carefully at what the author *does* say, students can make more accurate inferences about what is not said. For instance, they can use details about people's actions to determine their attitudes or underlying thinking. Read students the following sentence: "Before leaving the house, Rosa put on her raincoat and grabbed her umbrella." **Ask:** What kind of weather does Rosa expect? *(rain)* Ask students to write similar sentences that state actions but reflect a person's thoughts or feelings. Then have them exchange their sentences with a partner, who should try to infer the correct thought or feeling. OL

2 Practice It!

With a partner, discuss these questions to make more inferences from the passage about Anthony Burns. Be sure to discuss why this account may have been included by the author.

- **What was the opinion of the Boston public? The city leaders?**
- **What message did they want to send to the federal government?**
- **A flag flown upside down is a naval distress signal. Why did they choose this signal?**
- **The issue of slavery divided Americans in the 1850s. What are some issues today that divide Americans? What distinguishes a divisive issue from one that can be solved through compromise?**

Read to Write

Can you rewrite the passage about Anthony Burns from his perspective? Use the same facts but convey a different impression.

◀ Pamphlet, 1854

3 Apply It!

As you read this chapter, practice your skill at making inferences by making connections and asking questions. Try to think about the information "between the lines."

Chapter 12 Get Ready to Read

2 Practice It!

Point out to students that they can also make inferences from titles and headings. Have them go back to pages 524 and 525 and look at the titles of the chapter and the five sections. **Ask:** What do you think this chapter will be about? What were the clues for that inference? *(Students should be able to see that the chapter will discuss growing tensions between the North and the South over the issue of slavery that will lead to war. The chapter title and the last section title suggest that war will result; "a nation dividing" and "secession" say there is a split; and the Section 1 and Section 4 titles identify the issue in dispute as slavery.)* **OL**

3 Apply It!

Ask each student to select a short piece of text (one-page maximum) from a book, newspaper, magazine, or Web site. Explain that they may choose an opinion column, news report, or piece of narrative writing. Have students read the piece of writing and make as many inferences as they can. **OL**

Reading Strategy — RECOGNIZING BIAS

Explain that the ability to make inferences enables readers to recognize bias. By looking at the words used to describe a person, action, or problem, they can infer the writer's point of view. Writers may use positive words to describe people or ideas they favor and negative ones for those they do not. Have students read the quotation from Frederick Douglass on page 532. Tell them not to look at any other information on the page. Then have them state what position they think the writer has on slavery and cite the clues for that inference. **OL**

Use Reading Skills Activity 12 in the **Chapter 12 Resource Book** for more practice with making inferences.

FOCUS

BELLRINGER
SKILLBUILDER ACTIVITY

Project **Daily Focus Skills Transparency 12–1** and have students answer the question.

Guide to Reading

Preteaching Vocabulary: Have students develop questions for each content vocabulary term. Then have students trade questions with a partner and answer their partner's questions.

Answers to Graphic: Garrison: founded *The Liberator* and two antislavery societies; Cornish and Russwurm: started *Freedom's Journal;* Grimkés: freed some of family's slaves; Douglass: spoke, wrote against slavery; Truth: part of abolitionist, women's rights movements

Unpacking the Standards

After reading the section, students will be able to:

- Explain how abolitionists campaigned against slavery.
- Discuss why many people opposed ending slavery.
- Describe how the Underground Railroad enabled some African Americans to escape slavery.

Section 1

Abolitionists

History Social Science Standards

US8.9 Students analyze the early and steady attempts to abolish slavery and to realize the ideals of the Declaration of Independence.

Guide to Reading

Looking Back, Looking Ahead
You learned earlier that slave labor was important to the South. You will now read about how groups and individuals worked to end slavery and to free individual enslaved people.

Focusing on the Main Ideas
- By the early 1800s, a growing number of Americans had begun to demand an immediate end to slavery in the South. ***(page 529)***
- The issue of slavery became the most pressing social issue for reformers, beginning in the 1830s. ***(page 530)***
- Abolitionists established a network of routes and risked their lives to help African Americans escape slavery. ***(page 533)***

Meeting People
William Lloyd Garrison
Sarah and Angelina Grimké
David Walker
Frederick Douglass
Sojourner Truth

Content Vocabulary
abolitionist (A • buh • LIH • shuhn • ihst)
Underground Railroad (UHN • duhr • GROWND RAYUHL • ROHD)

Academic Vocabulary
notion (NOH • shuhn)
publication (PUH • bluh • KAY • shuhn)

Reading Strategy
Organizing Information Create a diagram like the one below. As you read the section, identify five abolitionists. Below each name, write a sentence describing his or her role in the movement.

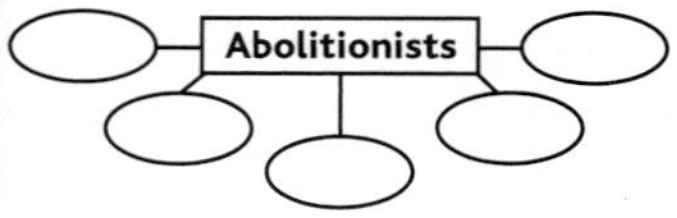

NATIONAL GEOGRAPHIC Where & When?

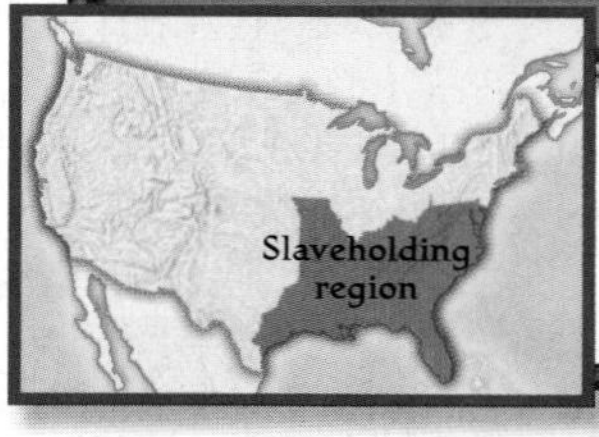

1815	1830	1845	1860

- **1816** American Colonization Society is formed
- **1822** First African Americans settle in Liberia
- **1831** William Lloyd Garrison founds *The Liberator*
- **1847** Liberia becomes an independent country

SECTION RESOURCES

Print Material
- Reproducible Lesson Plan 12–1*
- Daily Lesson and Discussion Notes 12–1
- Guided Reading Activity 12–1
- Reading Essentials and Study Guide 12–1
- Active Reading Note-Taking Guide 12–1
- Section Quiz 12–1

Transparencies
- Daily Focus Skills Transparency 12–1
- Section Graphic Organizer Transparency 12–1
- California Standards Practice Transparencies

Technology
- Interactive Tutor Self-Assessment CD-ROM
- Exam*View*® Pro Testmaker CD-ROM
- Presentation Plus! CD-ROM

*Available on TeacherWorks™

Early Efforts to End Slavery

Main Idea **By the early 1800s, a growing number of Americans had begun to demand an immediate end to slavery in the South.**

Reading Connection Can you think of an issue that caused disagreement in your family or group of friends? Read to learn how divisive the issue of slavery was to the nation.

An American Story

William Lloyd Garrison, a dramatic and spirited man, fought strongly for the right of African Americans to be free. On one occasion, Garrison was present when Frederick Douglass, an African American who had escaped from slavery, spoke to a white audience about life as a slave. Douglass electrified his listeners with a powerful speech. Suddenly, Garrison leaped to his feet. "Is this a man," he demanded of the audience, "or a thing?" R1 Garrison shared Douglass's outrage at the **notion** that people could be bought and sold like objects.

The spirit of reform that swept the United States in the early 1800s was not limited to R2 improving education and expanding the arts. It also included the efforts of **abolitionists** (A•buh•LIH•shuhn•ihsts) like Garrison and Douglass—members of the growing band of reformers who worked to abolish, or end, slavery.

R3 Even before the American Revolution, some Americans had tried to limit or end slavery. At the Constitutional Convention in 1787, the delegates had reached a compromise on the difficult issue, agreeing to let each state decide whether to allow slavery. By the early 1800s, Northern states had ended slavery, but it continued in the South.

The religious revival and the reform movement of the early and mid-1800s gave new life to the antislavery movement. Many Americans came to believe that slavery was wrong. Yet not all Northerners shared this view. The conflict over slavery continued to build.

Many of the men and women who led the antislavery movement came from the Quaker faith. One Quaker, Benjamin Lundy, wrote:

> **"I heard the wail of the captive; I felt his pang of distress, and the iron entered my soul."**
>
> —from *Historical Collections of Ohio*

Lundy founded a newspaper in 1821 to spread the abolitionist message.

American Colonization Society The first large-scale antislavery effort was aimed at resettling African Americans in Africa or the Caribbean. The American Colonization Society, formed in 1816 by a group of white Virginians, attempted to free enslaved workers gradually by buying them from slaveholders and sending them abroad to start new lives.

The society raised enough money from private donors, Congress, and a few state legislatures to send several groups of African Americans out of the country. Some went to the west coast of Africa, where the society had acquired land for a colony. In 1822 the first African American settlers arrived in this colony, called Liberia, Latin for "place of freedom."

In 1847 Liberia became an independent country. American emigration to Liberia continued until the Civil War. Some 12,000 to 20,000 African Americans settled in the new country between 1822 and 1865.

S The American Colonization Society did not halt the growth of slavery. The number of enslaved people continued to increase at a steady pace, and the society could only resettle a small number of African Americans. Furthermore, most African Americans regarded the United States as their home and were not prepared to migrate to another continent. Many were from families that had lived in America for several generations. They simply wanted to be free in American society.

Reading Check **Explain** How did the American Colonization Society fight slavery?

TEACH

R1 Reading Strategy

Academic Vocabulary Have students read the sentence that contains the word *notion*. Then ask students to list synonyms for the word. OL

R2 Reading Strategy

Using Word Parts Explain that the term *abolitionist* comes from the word *abolish*. **Ask:** What does that word mean? *(bring something to an end)* What were abolitionists trying to end? *(slavery)* OL CA 8RW1.3

R3 Reading Strategy

Activating Prior Knowledge **Ask:** Why did delegates at the Constitutional Convention agree to let states decide whether to allow slavery? *(To win the approval of the Southern states for the Constitution.)* OL CA CS1.

S Skill Practice

Historical and Social Sciences Analysis Skill
Ask: Imagine that you are an enslaved African American and that you have an opportunity to emigrate to Liberia. Would you go? Why or why not? *(Answers will vary but should be supported by reasons.)* OL CA HI1.

Reading Check
Answer: by buying enslaved people and sending them abroad to live in freedom

More Skill Practice

Analyzing Primary Sources Direct students to the quotation from Lundy. **Ask:** What is Lundy referring to when he mentions "iron"? *(the shackles and chains that held the captive in slavery)* What did he mean by the words "the iron entered my soul"? *(the enslavement of anyone pains him)* OL CA 8RW1.1

U Universal Access

Visual/Spatial Have students choose a reformer or event discussed in this subsection and create a monument highlighting the importance of that person or event. OL CA HI1.

C Critical Thinking

Determining Cause and Effect Ask: What content in the book *American Slavery As It Is* made it so influential? *(true stories about the lives of enslaved people)* OL CA HI5.

Resources for page 530

- Biography Activity 12C
- Biography Activity 12D
- Biography Activity 12F
- Biography Activity 12G

US8.9.1 Describe the leaders of the movement (e.g., John Quincy Adams and his proposed constitutional amendment; John Brown and the armed resistance, Harriet Tubman and the Underground Railroad, Benjamin Franklin, Theodore Weld, William Lloyd Garrison, Frederick Douglass).

The New Abolitionists

Main Idea **The issue of slavery became the most pressing social issue for reformers, beginning in the 1830s.**

Reading Connection Think of a person or a leader whom you admire. Does he or she stand up for others? Read to learn how abolitionists worked to end slavery.

The Movement Changes Reformers realized that the gradual approach to ending slavery had failed. Moreover, the numbers of enslaved persons had sharply increased because the cotton boom in the Deep South made planters increasingly dependent on slave labor. Beginning in about 1830, the American antislavery movement took on new life. Soon it became the most pressing social issue for reformers.

***Picturing* History**

In 1831 William Lloyd Garrison began publishing a newspaper called *The Liberator.* ***What was Garrison's position regarding slavery?***

William Lloyd Garrison An abolitionist named **William Lloyd Garrison** stimulated the growth of the antislavery movement. In 1829 Garrison left Massachusetts to work for the country's leading antislavery newspaper in Baltimore. Impatient with the paper's moderate position, Garrison returned to Boston in 1831 to found his own newspaper, *The Liberator.*

Garrison was one of the first white abolitionists to call for the "immediate and complete emancipation [freeing]" of enslaved people. In the first issue of his paper, he wrote: "I will not retreat a single inch—AND I WILL BE HEARD."

Garrison *was* heard. He attracted enough followers to start the New England Anti-Slavery Society in 1832 and the American Anti-Slavery Society the next year. The abolitionist movement grew rapidly. By 1838 the antislavery societies Garrison started had more than 1,000 chapters, or local branches.

The Grimké Sisters Among the first women who spoke out publicly against slavery were **Sarah and Angelina Grimké.** Born in South Carolina to a wealthy slaveholding family, the sisters moved to Philadelphia in 1832.

In the North, the Grimké sisters lectured and wrote against slavery. At one antislavery meeting, Angelina Grimké exclaimed:

> **"As a Southerner, I feel that it is my duty to stand up . . . against slavery. I have seen it—I have seen it."**
>
> **—Angelina Grimké, lecture, 1838**

The Grimkés persuaded their mother to give them their share of the family inheritance. Instead of money or land, the sisters asked for several of the enslaved workers, whom they immediately freed.

The Grimkés and Angelina's husband, abolitionist Theodore Weld, wrote *American Slavery As It Is* in 1839. This collection of firsthand accounts of life under slavery was an influential abolitionist **publication,** selling more than 100,000 copies in its first year.

Answers and Additional Support

More Skill Practice

Historical and Social Sciences Analysis Skill Ask: What strategy did Angelina Grimké use when she tried to persuade Northerners to oppose slavery? *(She stressed her position as an eyewitness who had lived in the South and seen slavery's impact.)* OL CA HR3.

***Picturing* History**

Answer: He believed it should be abolished immediately.

African American Abolitionists White abolitionists drew public attention to the cause, but African Americans played a major role in the abolitionist movement from the start. The abolition of slavery was an especially important goal to the free African Americans of the North.

Many African Americans in the North lived in poverty in cities. Although they were excluded from most jobs and were often attacked by white mobs, a great many of these African Americans were intensely proud of their freedom and wanted to help those who were still enslaved.

African Americans took an active part in organizing and directing the American Anti-Slavery Society, and they subscribed in large numbers to William Lloyd Garrison's *The Liberator.* In 1827 Samuel Cornish and John Russwurm started the country's first African American newspaper, *Freedom's Journal.* Most of the other newspapers that African Americans founded before the Civil War also promoted abolition.

Born a free man in North Carolina, writer **David Walker** of Boston published an impassioned argument against slavery, challenging African Americans to rebel and overthrow slavery by force. "America is more our country than it is the whites'—we have enriched it with our blood and tears," he wrote.

In 1830 free African American leaders held their first convention in Philadelphia. Delegates met "to devise ways and means for the bettering of our condition." They discussed starting an African American college and encouraging free African Americans to emigrate to Canada.

Primary Sources

Abolishing Slavery

While serving in the House of Representatives, former President John Quincy Adams battled slavery. In 1839 he proposed a constitutional amendment that provided for the abolition of slavery. Its three provisions follow.

◀ John Quincy Adams

1st From and after the 4th of July, 1842, there shall be, throughout the United States, no hereditary slavery; but on and after that day every child born within the United States, their Territories or jurisdiction, shall be born free.

2d. With the exception of the Territory of Florida, there shall henceforth never be admitted into this Union any State, the constitution of which shall tolerate within the same the existence of slavery.

3d. From and after the 4th of July, 1845, there shall be neither slavery nor slave trade at the seat of Government of the United States.

DBQ Document-Based Questions

1. How would each part of the amendment bring about the end of slavery?
2. Was Adams providing for its immediate or gradual end? Why do you think he chose this method?

R Reading Strategy

Scaffolding—Summarizing Organize students into pairs and have each student write a one-sentence summary of each African American abolitionist discussed in this section. Then have members of each pair compare and combine their drafts to create a final version that summarizes the text as accurately as possible. OL CA 8RC2.4

This READING SKILL was introduced in Chapter 4.

C Critical Thinking

Comparing and Contrasting **Ask:** In what ways was life similar for enslaved African Americans in the South and free African Americans in the North? *(Both faced discrimination and sometimes violence from whites; both lived in poor conditions.)* OL CA HI1.

W Writing Support

Persuasive Writing Have students adopt the point of view of Cornish and Russwurm and write an essay intended to persuade whites in the North to join in the struggle to end slavery. OL CA 8WA2.4

Resources for page 531

Universal Access Activity 12

Primary Sources

1. Children born to enslaved parents would be free as of 1842; no new slave states (except Florida) could join the Union; slavery would be outlawed in the District of Columbia as of 1845.
2. Gradual; to allow time for Southerners to adjust

- Why do you think Adams chose July 4 as the date for two of the provisions to take effect? *(for symbolic value—July 4 reminds Americans of the ideal of freedom)* OL
- How do you think people reacted to Adams's proposal? *(Slaveholders objected; enslaved people and abolitionists approved.)* OL

C Critical Thinking

Analyzing Primary Sources
Ask: What can you infer about the audience for Douglass's speech? *(He was speaking to white listeners: he refers to "your" Fourth of July.)* OL CA HR5.

Review The Big Idea

Review the Big Idea for this section: "Reactions to social injustice can lead to reform movements." **Ask:** Why would African Americans who escaped slavery risk being recaptured by speaking and writing against it? *(because they felt so strongly about the need to end slavery)* OL CA HI2.

R Reading Strategy

Understanding Vocabulary
Explain that to *sojourn* is to travel **Ask:** How does that explain Sojourner Truth's statement quoted here? *(When she says she will "walk in the light of [God's] truth," she means she will journey in truth.)* OL

Reading Check

Answer: He thought he had to fight slavery at its source.

Answers and Additional Support

Frederick Douglass **Frederick Douglass,** the most widely known African American abolitionist, was born enslaved in Maryland. After teaching himself to read and write, he escaped from slavery in Maryland in 1838 and settled first in Massachusetts and then in New York.

As a runaway, Douglass could have been captured and returned to slavery. Still, he joined the Massachusetts Anti-Slavery Society and traveled widely to address abolitionist meetings. A powerful speaker, Douglass often moved listeners to tears with his message. At an Independence Day gathering, he told the audience:

> **"What, to the American slave, is your [Fourth] of July? I answer; a day that reveals to him, more than all other days in the year, the gross injustice and cruelty to which he is the constant victim. To him, your celebration is a sham . . . your national greatness, swelling vanity; your sounds of rejoicing are empty and heartless . . . your shouts of liberty and equality, hollow mockery."**
>
> —from *Frederick Douglass: Selected Speeches and Writings*

C

For 16 years, Douglass edited an antislavery newspaper called the *North Star.* Douglass won admiration as a powerful and influential speaker and writer. He traveled abroad, speaking to huge antislavery audiences in London and the West Indies.

Douglass returned to the United States because he believed abolitionists must fight slavery at its source. He insisted that African Americans receive not only their freedom but full equality with whites as well. In 1847 friends helped Douglass purchase his freedom from the slaveholder in Maryland from whom he had fled.

Sojourner Truth "I was born a slave in Ulster County, New York," Isabella Baumfree began when she told her story to audiences. Called "Belle," she lived in the cellar of a slaveholder's house. She escaped in 1826 and gained official freedom in 1827 when New York banned slavery. Quaker friends then helped her recover one son who had been sold as a slave. She eventually settled in New York City with her two youngest children. She supported her family by doing domestic work. During this time, she began preaching in the streets.

In 1843 Belle chose a new name. "**Sojourner Truth** is my name," she said, "because from this day I will walk in the light of [God's] truth." She dedicated her life to the movements for abolition and for women's rights. R

Picturing History

Sojourner Truth learned about abolition in 1843 when she was preaching in Massachusetts. ***How did Sojourner Truth get and keep her freedom?***

Reading Check **Explain** Why did Frederick Douglass return to the United States?

Resources for page 532

- Biography Activity 12E
- Biography Activity 12H

Picturing History

Like many abolitionists, Sojourner Truth became a fervent advocate for women's rights. In 1851, she delivered her classic "Ain't I a Woman?" speech at a women's rights convention in Ohio.

Answer: She escaped in 1826 and became officially free the next year, when New York outlawed slavery.

US8.9.1 Describe the leaders of the movement (e.g., John Quincy Adams and his proposed constitutional amendment; John Brown and the armed resistance, Harriet Tubman and the Underground Railroad, Benjamin Franklin, Theodore Weld, William Lloyd Garrison, Frederick Douglass).

The Underground Railroad

S **Main Idea** **Abolitionists established a network of routes and risked their lives to help African Americans escape slavery.**

Reading Connection Can you think of an example in recent times when people fled to avoid oppression? Read and find out about the Underground Railroad.

An American Story

On May 24, 1854, the people of Boston erupted in outrage. Federal officers had seized Anthony Burns, a runaway slave who lived in Boston, to send him back to slavery. Abolitionists tried to rescue Burns from the federal courthouse, and city leaders attempted to buy his freedom. All efforts failed. Local militia units joined the marines and cavalry in Boston to keep order. Federal troops escorted Burns to a ship that would carry him back to Virginia and slavery. In a gesture of bitter protest, Bostonians draped buildings in black and hung the American flag upside down.

The Fugitive Slave Act The Fugitive Slave Act of 1850 required all citizens to help catch runaways. Anyone who aided a fugitive could be fined or imprisoned. People in the South believed the law would force Northerners to recognize the rights of Southerners. Instead, enforcement of the law led to mounting anger in the North, convincing more people of the evils of slavery. After passage of the Fugitive Slave Act, slaveholders stepped up efforts to catch runaway slaves. C1

S Skill Practice

Historical and Social Sciences Analysis Skill

Ask: How would enslaved African Americans see the Underground Railroad? *(as a welcome chance to gain freedom)* How would Southern slave owners see it? *(as taking away their property)* OL CA HI2.

C1 Critical Thinking

Drawing Conclusions Remind students that it was against the law to help enslaved African Americans escape, yet many abolitionists broke the law. **Ask:** Are there some situations in which breaking the law is an acceptable protest? Discuss whether abolitionists were justified in breaking the law. OL CA CS3.

C2 Critical Thinking

Making Inferences Ask: Why do many of the routes on the Underground Railroad lead to Canada? *(Students should conclude that Canada did not have slavery and would not return people who escaped from it.)* OL CA CS3.

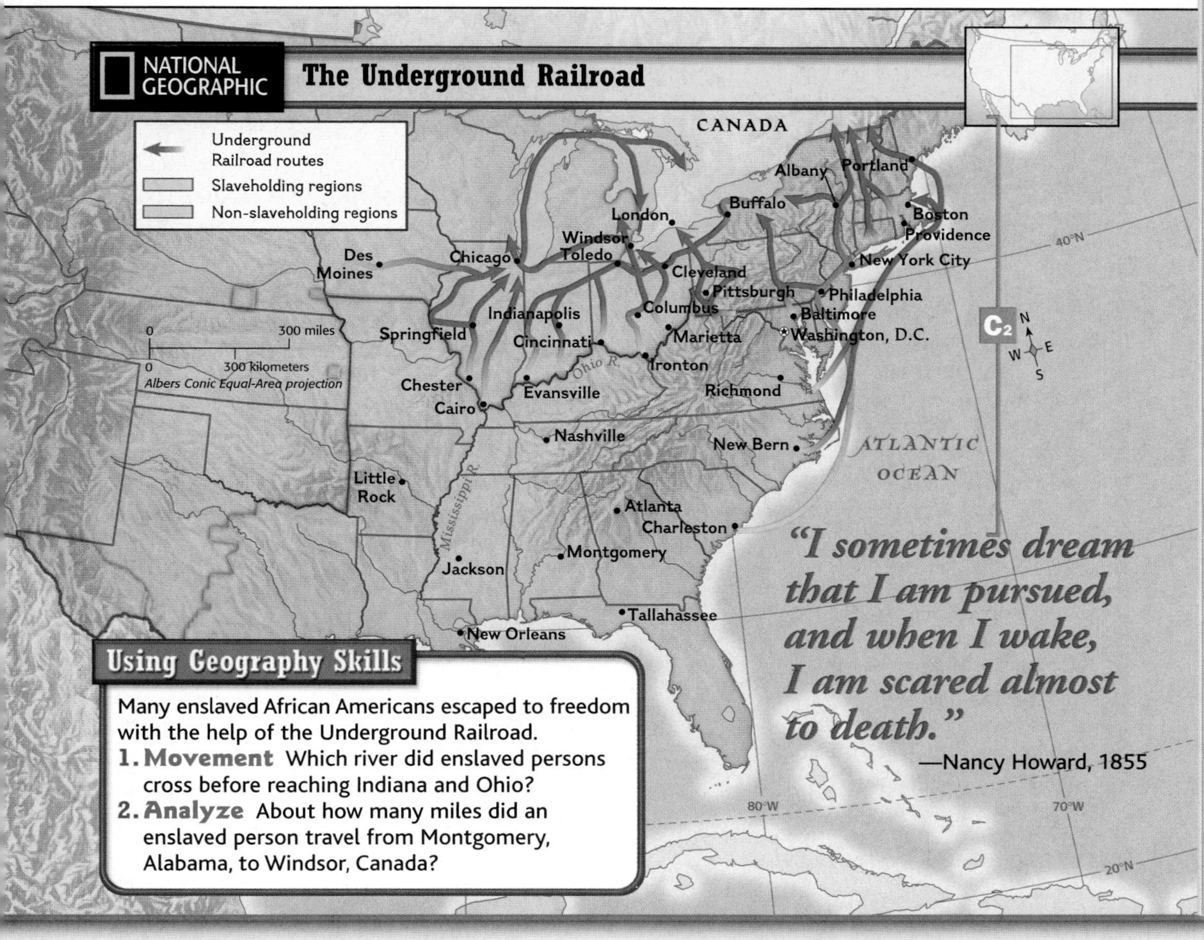

Using Geography Skills

Many enslaved African Americans escaped to freedom with the help of the Underground Railroad.

1. **Movement** Which river did enslaved persons cross before reaching Indiana and Ohio?
2. **Analyze** About how many miles did an enslaved person travel from Montgomery, Alabama, to Windsor, Canada?

Using Geography Skills

Answers:

1. Ohio River
2. about 790 miles (1,260 km)

Did You Know?

The story of Henry "Box" Brown is one of the most remarkable in the history of the Underground Railroad. Brown escaped slavery in 1849 by having himself sealed into a small box and shipped from Richmond to Philadelphia. Although "this side up" was marked on the crate, he spent a good part of the trip upside down.

R Reading Strategy

Using Context Clues

Ask: What does *underground* mean here? *(secret)* OL

CA 8RW1.3

ASSESS

Resources for page 534

Use these resources to assess student mastery of section content.

- American Literature Reading 12
- Geography and History Activity 12
- Economics and History Activity 12
- Section Quiz 12–1
- Interactive Tutor Self-Assessment CD-ROM

Reading Check

Answer: a network of free African Americans and whites who helped runaway slaves to freedom

History Online

Study Central provides summaries, interactive games, and online graphic organizers to help students review section content.

CLOSE

Identifying Main Idea

Ask: What is the main idea of this section? *(Groups and individuals worked to end slavery and to free enslaved people.)* OL

Slaveholders even tried to capture runaways who had lived in freedom in the North for years. Sometimes they seized African Americans who were not escaped slaves and forced them into slavery.

Resistance to the Law In spite of the penalties, many Northerners refused to cooperate with the law's enforcement. The **Underground Railroad,** a network of free African Americans and whites, helped runaways make their way to freedom. Antislavery groups tried to rescue African Americans who were being pursued or to free those who were captured. In Boston, members of one such group followed federal agents shouting, "Slave hunters—there go the slave hunters." People contributed funds to buy the freedom of African Americans. Northern juries refused to convict those accused of breaking the Fugitive Slave Law.

Harriet Tubman Born as a slave in Maryland, Harriet Tubman worked in plantation fields until she was nearly 30 years old. Then she made her break for freedom, escaping to the North with the help of the Underground Railroad. Settling in Philadelphia, Tubman met many abolitionists who shared her desire to bring Southern slaves to the North. Realizing the risks of being captured, Tubman courageously made 19 trips back into the South during the 1850s to help other enslaved people escape. Altogether she assisted about 70 individuals—including her parents—to escape from slavery. Tubman became the most successful conductor on the Underground Railroad. She was known as the "Moses of her people" for leading slaves to freedom in the North.

Reading Check **Identify** What was the Underground Railroad?

History Online

Study Central Need help understanding abolitionism? Visit ca.hss.glencoe.com and click on Study Central.

Section 1 Review

Reading Summary

Review the Main Ideas

- In the early 1800s, one major antislavery movement worked to resettle freed slaves in the country of Liberia in Africa.
- The antislavery movement became stronger in the 1830s, spurred on by a number of abolitionists, both white, such as William Lloyd Garrison and the Grimké sisters, and African American, such as Frederick Douglass and Sojourner Truth.
- Abolitionists helped runaway slaves escape, but many others in both the North and the South opposed abolition.

What Did You Learn?

1. Describe the American Colonization Society's solution to slavery.
2. How did William Lloyd Garrison help the abolitionist movement?

Critical Thinking

3. **Organizing Information** Use a diagram like the one below to identify actions that abolitionists took to free enslaved people. CA CS1.

4. **The Big Ideas** What role did Harriet Tubman play in the antislavery movement? CA HI1.
5. **Compare** How did the goals and strategies of the American Colonization Society differ from those of the abolitionist movement? CA HR5.
6. **Reading Making Inferences** Reread the primary source quotes from this section. Write a paragraph that makes inferences to describe each person's views of slavery. CA 8RC2.0

SECTION 1 REVIEW ANSWERS

Review questions reinforce content standard US8.9.

1. purchase enslaved workers and resettle them in Africa or the Caribbean
2. wrote for the immediate ending of slavery and started anti-slavery societies
3. Founding of abolitionist newspapers and societies; Buying freedom; Buying enslaved workers and relocating them; Helping enslaved people escape; Writing and speaking against it
4. **The Big Ideas** She led slaves to freedom on the Underground Railroad.
5. It wanted to free enslaved people but resettle them in other lands.
6. **Reading** Students' responses should make inferences about each person quoted.

Section 2

Slavery and the West

Guide to Reading

Looking Back, Looking Ahead

As you know, abolitionists tried to end slavery. At the same time, the possible spread of slavery into the West was an issue that repeatedly divided the nation.

Focusing on the Main Ideas

- The Missouri Compromise helped resolve the issue of whether new states would be slave states or free states. *(page 536)*
- The Kentucky Resolution first advanced the doctrine of nullification. *(page 537)*
- In the 1840s, the issue of slavery in new territories was once again at the forefront. *(page 539)*
- Henry Clay presented a plan to settle the slavery debate that resulted in the Compromise of 1850. *(page 541)*

Meeting People

James K. Polk
Millard Fillmore
Stephen A. Douglas

Content Vocabulary

sectionalism (SEHK • shnuh • LIH • zuhm)
nullify (NUH • luh • FY)
protective tariff (pruh • TEHK • tihv TAR • uhf)
fugitive (FYOO • juh • tihv)
secede (sih • SEED)
abstain (uhb • STAYN)

Academic Vocabulary

debate
controversy (KAHN • truh • VUHR • see)
collapse

Reading Strategy

Organizing Information As you read the section, describe how these compromises dealt with the admission of new states.

Admission of New States	
The Missouri Compromise	The Compromise of 1850

History Social Science Standards

US8.9 Students analyze the early and steady attempts to abolish slavery and to realize the ideals of the Declaration of Independence.

US8.10 Students analyze the multiple causes, key events, and complex consequences of the Civil War.

NATIONAL GEOGRAPHIC Where & When?

1820 | 1840 | 1860

1820 Missouri Compromise is passed

1845 Texas becomes a state

1848 Free-Soil Party nominates Van Buren

1850 Compromise of 1850 diverts war

FOCUS

BELLRINGER
SKILLBUILDER ACTIVITY

Project **Daily Focus Skills Transparency 12–2** and have students answer the question.

Guide to Reading

Preteaching Vocabulary: Quiz students on the meaning of each content vocabulary term.

Answers to Graphic: Missouri: admit Missouri (slave state) and Maine (free state), ban slavery from other areas of Louisiana Purchase north of 36°30′; 1850: admit California (free state), no limits on slavery in New Mexico, end slave trade in D.C.

Unpacking the Standards

After reading the section, students will be able to:

- Describe the features of the Missouri Compromise.
- Explain the meaning of nullification.
- Analyze how the government dealt with slavery in new lands acquired from Mexico.
- Outline the central aspects of the Compromise of 1850.

SECTION RESOURCES

Print Material
- Reproducible Lesson Plan 12–2*
- Daily Lesson and Discussion Notes 12–2
- Guided Reading Activity 12–2
- Reading Essentials and Study Guide 12–2
- Active Reading Note-Taking Guide 12–2
- Section Quiz 12–2

Transparencies
- Daily Focus Skills Transparency 12–2
- Section Graphic Organizer Transparency 12–2
- California Standards Practice Transparencies

Technology
- Interactive Tutor Self-Assessment CD-ROM
- Exam*View*® Pro Testmaker CD-ROM
- Presentation Plus! CD-ROM

*Available on TeacherWorks™

TEACH

C1 Critical Thinking

Making Inferences Ask: Does the writer of this statement favor or oppose slavery? How do you know? *(strongly opposed to slavery; writer calls it a "foul disgrace" and says that those who voted to admit Missouri as a slave state should be ashamed)* OL CA HR3.

C2 Critical Thinking

Analyzing Primary Sources Ask: What was Adams predicting when he called the debate over Missouri a "mere preamble"? *(a civil war)* OL CA HI1.

R Reading Strategy

Scaffolding—Connecting Ask: What forms does sectionalism take today? *(differences between rural and urban areas)* OL CA HI3.

This READING SKILL was introduced in Chapter 3.

Reading Check

Answer: Sectionalism intensified the conflict between Northerners, who wanted to ban slavery in new states, and Southerners, who favored slavery.

Answers and Additional Support

US8.9.5 Analyze the significance of the States' Rights Doctrine, the Missouri Compromise (1820), the Wilmot Proviso (1846), the Compromise of 1850, Henry Clay's role in the Missouri Compromise and the Compromise of 1850, the Kansas-Nebraska Act (1854), the *Dred Scott* v. *Sandford* decision (1857), and the Lincoln-Douglas debates (1858).

The Missouri Compromise

Main Idea **The Missouri Compromise helped resolve the issue of whether new states would be slave states or free states.**

Reading Connection Do you compete with a nearby school in sports or another activity? If so, you probably feel loyalty to the school you attend. Read to learn how in the early 1800s, differences between the North and South led to sectionalism, which is loyalty to a particular region.

An American Story

C1 "The deed is done. The . . . chains of slavery are forged for [many] yet unborn. Humble yourselves in the dust, ye high-minded citizens of Connecticut. Let your cheeks be red as crimson. On *your* representatives rests the stigma of this foul disgrace." These biting, fiery words were published in a Connecticut newspaper in 1820. They were in response to members of Congress who had helped pave the way for the admission of Missouri as a slaveholding state.

What Is Sectionalism? The request by slaveholding Missouri to join the Union in 1819 caused an angry debate that worried former president Thomas Jefferson and Secretary of State John Quincy Adams. Jefferson called the dispute "a fire-bell in the night" that "awakened and filled me with terror." Adams accurately predicted that the bitter **debate** was "a mere preamble—a title-page to a great tragic volume." C2

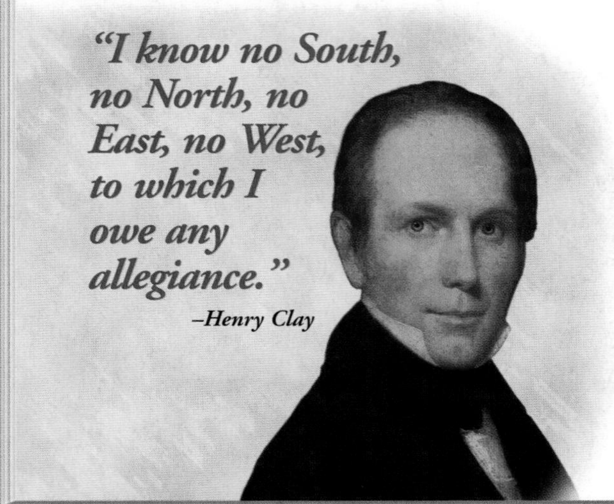

Many Missouri settlers had brought enslaved African Americans into the territory with them. By 1819 the Missouri Territory included about 50,000 whites and 10,000 slaves. When Missouri applied to Congress for admission as a state, its constitution allowed slavery.

In 1819 eleven states permitted slavery and eleven did not. The Senate—with two members from each state—was therefore evenly balanced between slave and free states. The admission of a new state would upset that balance.

In addition the North and the South, with their different economic systems, were competing for new lands in the western territories. At the same time, a growing number of Northerners wanted to restrict or ban slavery. Southerners, even those who disliked slavery, opposed these antislavery efforts. They resented the interference by outsiders in Southerners' affairs. These differences between the North and the South grew into **sectionalism** (SEHK • shnuh • LIH • zuhm)—an exaggerated loyalty to a particular region of the country. R

Clay's Proposal The Senate suggested a way to resolve the crisis by allowing Missouri's admittance as a slave state while simultaneously admitting Maine as a free state. Maine, formerly part of Massachusetts, had also applied for admission to the Union. The Senate also sought to settle the issue of slavery in the territories for good. It proposed prohibiting slavery in the remainder of the Louisiana Purchase north of 36°30'N latitude.

Speaker of the House Henry Clay of Kentucky skillfully maneuvered the Senate bill to passage in 1820 by dividing it into three proposals. The Missouri Compromise preserved the balance between slave and free states in the Senate and quieted the bitter debate in Congress over slavery. However, this would not last.

Reading Check **Explain** How did sectionalism contribute to the ongoing debate about the admission of states?

More Skill Practice

Historical and Social Sciences Analysis Skill Direct students to the quote from Henry Clay. **Ask:** What is Clay saying about sectionalism in this statement? *(He feels loyalty to the nation as a whole, not to any one section.)* Do you think more or fewer Americans agreed with him? *(Students may say that as time went on, sectional feelings grew stronger.)* OL CA HI1.

US8.10.1 Compare the conflicting interpretations of state and federal authority as emphasized in the speeches and writings of statesmen such as Daniel Webster and John C. Calhoun US8.10.3 Identify the constitutional issues posed by the doctrine of nullification and secession and the earliest origins of that doctrine.

R1 Nullification

Main Idea **The Kentucky Resolution first advanced the doctrine of nullification.**

Reading Connection Have you ever wanted to overturn a decision that you thought was unfair? Read to learn how nullification legally permitted states to overturn unconstitutional laws.

R2 Southerners argued that states could **nullify** (NUH • luh • FY), or legally overturn, federal laws that they considered unconstitutional. The issue of nullification arose again and again in the nation's early history.

Virginia and Kentucky Resolutions Nullification was first expressed in the Virginia and Kentucky Resolutions of 1798–1799. These resolutions, written by Thomas Jefferson and James Madison, declared that the Federalists' Alien and Sedition laws were unconstitutional. *(See page 295-96.)* C Jefferson and Madison used the ideas of John Locke and the Tenth Amendment to the Constitution to argue that the federal government had been formed by a contract among the states. The federal government possessed only certain powers. Whenever a state decided that the federal government passed a law that went beyond these powers, the state had the right to nullify the law.

What Was the Hartford Convention? The issue of nullification reappeared during the War of 1812, this time among Federalists in New England. Many New Englanders opposed the war. One reason was that many people there made their living by trade, which was greatly hurt when the war began. Many Federalists also believed that Republicans in the South and West brought about the war. Delegates from the New England states revived the idea of nullification and proposed amendments to the Constitution at a meeting called the Hartford Convention. *(See page 359.)* The Federalists made no progress with their demands, and with the end of the war, the power of the Federalist party declined.

***Picturing* History**

Calhoun was a nationalist in his early career, but he changed to a champion of states' rights. ***How were the Ordinance of Nullification and the Virginia and Kentucky Resolutions alike?***

The Tariff Controversy The nullification **controversy** arose again in the 1820s and 1830s, R3 this time over the issue of protective tariffs. **Protective tariffs** (pruh • TEHK • tihv TAR • uhfs) R4 are taxes that are placed on goods that come from another country. Protective tariffs raise the price of goods from other countries. A tax on imported shoes, for example, makes American-made shoes more attractive to consumers.

By the 1820s, most Southerners had become convinced that protective tariffs were harmful to the South. Although such tariffs helped the young industries of the North, they also raised the prices of manufactured goods purchased in the South. People in the South felt that it was unjust for them to bear the expense for the development of another region of the country.

Ordinance of Nullification When Congress passed the tariff of 1828, John C. Calhoun of South Carolina argued that the tariff was "unconstitutional, oppressive, and unjust." Calhoun based his argument on the ideas that Jefferson and Madison had used in defending the Virginia and Kentucky Resolutions. In 1832 Congress passed a new tariff law. Although the tax rates were lower than those of 1828, they were still high. South Carolina called a special convention that voted for an Ordinance of Nullification against the new tariff.

R1 Reading Strategy

Outlining Encourage students to outline the section on nullification. Suggest they group the information under two main headings: *History of Nullification* and *Tariff Controversy*. BL CA 8RC2.2

R2 Reading Strategy

Understanding Vocabulary Explain that the word *nullify* comes from a Latin word meaning "none". **Ask:** How is that origin related to the meaning of the term? *(To nullify a law means to invalidate it, or to say that none of its provisions are legal.)* OL CA 8RW1.2

C Critical Thinking

Analyzing Information Have students read the Tenth Amendment. Also, point out that the Constitution says it is the supreme law of the land. Then discuss whether the idea of nullification is allowed under the Constitution. Tell students to give reasons for their positions. OL

R3 Reading Strategy

Academic Vocabulary Ask students to list modern-day controversies they know about. OL

R4 Reading Strategy

Understanding Vocabulary Ask students to restate the meaning of the term *protective tariff* in their own words. OL CA 8RW1.3

More Skill Practice

Historical and Social Sciences Analysis Skill **Ask:** Why were some Southerners opposed to protective tariffs, even though these tariffs created lower prices for American-made goods? *(The tariffs raised the cost of imported goods, which they had to buy because the South had little industry.)* OL CA HI6.

***Picturing* History**

This image of Calhoun was painted by Arthur E. Schmalz Conrad, a Maryland artist. It is based on an earlier portrait by George Healy, who painted Calhoun seated in the vice president's chair in the Senate.

Answer: All stated that states could nullify federal laws.

R Reading Strategy

Evaluating Ask: How did Webster's view of the Constitution differ from Calhoun's? *(Calhoun believed that individual states had the right to interpret the Constitution, while Webster said that only the Supreme Court could determine a law's constitutionality.)* OL CA HI1.

C Critical Thinking

Identifying Central Issues Tell students that President Jackson was not completely happy with the compromise that ended the tariff controversy, feeling that it simply postponed a conflict with the South over nullification. Organize students into groups to brainstorm ideas for different steps Jackson could have taken. Have the groups present their ideas to the class, and discuss whether any would resolve the nullification issue. AL CA HI1.

Reading Check

Answer: Southerners wanted to overturn a tariff that they considered unfair; people in the Northeast tried to use it when they opposed the War of 1812.

Answers and Additional Support

Calhoun had raised an important issue—the supremacy of the national government versus state sovereignty. The states' rights doctrine, first found in the Virginia and Kentucky Resolutions, had taken a giant step toward secession. If states were sovereign, they had a right to secede from the Union.

Can a State Nullify a Law? Early in 1830, Calhoun's doctrine of nullification came before the United States Senate during a debate over land policy. People in the West were angry because of a bill that would limit the sale of western lands. Robert Y. Hayne of South Carolina argued that the western states could nullify the bill if it became law.

Daniel Webster of Massachusetts replied to Hayne. Webster denied that the Constitution was just a compact between the states, to be interpreted as each state chose. On the contrary, he said, only the Supreme Court could decide whether a law was constitutional. Webster argued that the federal government was sovereign, that the Union was perpetual, and that any attempt to dismember it was nothing less than treason. Webster closed with this ringing statement: "Liberty and Union, now and forever, one and inseparable." **R**

In 1833 the nullification crisis was settled by a compromise. The tariff was lowered and, in response, South Carolina withdrew its Ordinance of Nullification. Both sides claimed victory, and the issue was laid to rest—at least temporarily. **C**

Reading Check **Analyze** Why did the South and the Northeast try to use nullification?

The Way It Was

▼ Early railroads helped industry grow.

Agrarians and Industrialists

Sectionalism, the rivalry between one region and another, was based on economic and political interests. One rivalry that developed was between agrarians and industrialists.

Agrarianism

Thomas Jefferson believed that the strength of the United States was its independent farmers. His ideas are sometimes referred to as agrarianism. Jefferson argued that owning land enabled people to be independent. As long as most people owned their own land, they would fight to preserve the Republic.

Jefferson believed that too much of an emphasis on industry and trade would lead to a society that was divided between the rich who owned everything and the poor who worked for wages. He also believed that the wealthy would corrupt the government and threaten the rights and liberties of ordinary people.

538

The Way It Was

Jefferson laid out his deep belief in the superiority of an agrarian society in his Notes on Virginia, in which he wrote "Generally speaking, the proportion which the aggregate of the other classes of citizens bears in any State to that of its [farmers] is the proportion of its unsound to its healthy parts, and is a good enough barometer whereby to measure its degree of corruption. . . . Those who labor in the earth are the chosen people of God if ever he had a chosen people, whose breasts he has made his peculiar deposit for substantial and genuine virtue."

US8.9.5 Analyze the significance of the States' Rights Doctrine, the Missouri Compromise (1820), the Wilmot Proviso (1846), the Compromise of 1850, Henry Clay's role in the Missouri Compromise and the Compromise of 1850, the Kansas-Nebraska Act (1854), the *Dred Scott* v. *Sandford* decision (1857), and the Lincoln-Douglas debates (1858).

New Western Lands

R1

Main Idea **In the 1840s, the issue of slavery in new territories was once again at the forefront.**

Reading Connection Can you think of a debate you have been a part of that turned out to be difficult to resolve? Read to learn how Congress continued to struggle with a solution concerning slavery.

For the next 25 years, Congress avoided the issue of slavery's expansion. In the 1840s, however, this heated debate moved back into Congress. Again, the dispute was over slavery in new territories. The territories involved were Texas, which had won its independence from Mexico in 1836, and New Mexico and California, which were still part of Mexico.

R2

Many Southerners hoped to see Texas, where slavery already existed, join the Union. As a result, the annexation of Texas became the main issue in the presidential election of 1844. Democrat **James K. Polk** of Tennessee won the election and pressed forward on acquiring Texas. Texas became a state in 1845. At the same time, support for taking over New Mexico and California also grew in the South. The federal government's actions on these lands led to war with Mexico.

S

Conflicting Views Just months after the war with Mexico began, Representative David Wilmot of Pennsylvania introduced a proposal in Congress. Called the Wilmot Proviso, it specified that slavery should be prohibited in any lands that might be acquired from Mexico.

During the 1800s, many Americans kept Jefferson's ideal of small, independent farming communities as the model society. Agrarians, particularly in the South, were alarmed at the changes that industrialization was producing in the nation's cities. They viewed independent farming as a way to escape degrading factory work and the unhealthy and overcrowded large cities.

Industrialism

The Industrial Revolution changed the Northeast from a region where families lived and worked together at farming, crafts, and home-based businesses to one in which people earned their livings by working for others in industry. Many Americans believed that manufacturing and trade were the basis of national wealth and power. They favored policies that would support these areas of the economy.

Although industrial growth caused problems, economic progress also made life easier in many ways. Improved transportation and mass production meant that more goods were available to more people. American living standards were surpassing those of European countries.

In the cities, people were beginning to enjoy new comforts and conveniences such as gas streetlights and better sewer systems. Some Americans came to believe that they were living in an age of progress. They expected that new inventions, along with America's abundant resources, would improve life for Americans and set an example for other countries of the world.

▼ Many Americans made their living by farming.

R1 Reading Strategy

Identifying the Main Idea and Supporting Details Have students point out the main idea of this part of the section. **Ask:** What are two details that support this idea? *(Possible answers: Wilmot introduced his proviso to prohibit spread of slavery; Calhoun countered with proslavery proposal; the Free-Soil Party was formed by opponents of slavery.)* OL

CA 8RC2.2

R2 Reading Strategy

Activating Prior Knowledge Point out that Texas won its independence in 1836 and applied for annexation right away. **Ask:** Why did the United States not annex Texas in 1836? *(Jackson turned down the request because he did not want to raise the slavery issue.)* OL

S Skill Practice

Historical and Social Science Analysis Skill
Ask: What area to the north of California and New Mexico, which could be turned into free states, was also added to the United States around this time? *(Oregon)* OL

More Skill Practice

Historical and Social Sciences Analysis Skill **Ask:** How did the acquisition of new territory heighten the sectional tensions over slavery? *(Northerners wanted to restrict slavery in the newly acquired territories, while Southerners wanted the right to introduce slavery in the new areas.)* OL

S **Skill Practice**

Historical and Social Sciences Analysis Skill Have students write at least three questions each for Wilmot and Calhoun on their proposals or their positions. Then organize the class into two groups—one to represent Wilmot's views and the other to represent Calhoun—and have students answer the questions. OL

W **Writing Support**

Persuasive Writing Ask students to write an editorial explaining why slaveholding would be the major issue of the 1848 presidential election. OL CA 8WA2.4

C **Critical Thinking**

Making Inferences **Ask:** Why did the new antislavery party call itself the "Free Soil" Party? *(They wanted the land of the new territories to be free of slavery.)* OL CA HI2.

Reading Check

Answer: Wilmot would ban slavery from lands acquired from Mexico. Calhoun stated that government had no authority to ban slavery anywhere.

Answers and Additional Support

Picturing **History**

By 1848 the population of San Francisco was about 1,000 residents. The population of the city and the California territory would grow greatly during the gold rush. ***What issue during the presidential election campaign of 1848 involved California?***

Southerners protested furiously. They wanted to keep open the possibility of introducing slavery to California and New Mexico. **S** Senator John C. Calhoun of South Carolina countered Wilmot's proposal with another. It stated that neither Congress nor any territorial government had the authority to ban slavery from a territory or regulate it in any way.

Neither Wilmot's nor Calhoun's proposal passed, but both caused bitter debate. By the time of the 1848 presidential election, the United States had acquired the territories of California and New Mexico from Mexico but had taken no action on the issue of slavery in those areas.

The Free-Soil Party The debate over slavery led to the formation of a new political party. In 1848 the Whigs chose Zachary Taylor, a Southerner and a hero of the war with Mexico, as **W** their presidential candidate. The Democrats selected Senator Lewis Cass of Michigan. Neither candidate took a stand on slavery in the territories. They were both afraid of losing votes.

This failure to take a position angered voters. Many antislavery Democrats and Whigs left their parties and joined with members of the old **C** Liberty Party to form the Free-Soil Party. The new party proclaimed "Free Soil, Free Speech, Free Labor, and Free Men," and endorsed the Wilmot Proviso. The party nominated former president Martin Van Buren as its presidential candidate.

Whig candidate Zachary Taylor won the election, receiving 163 electoral votes to 127 for Cass. The Whig's strategy of maintaining neutrality helped them win the election. Van Buren failed to receive a single electoral vote, and captured only 14 percent of the popular vote in the North. However, several candidates of the Free-Soil Party won seats in Congress.

Reading Check **Explain** How was John C. Calhoun's proposal different from the Wilmot Proviso?

Picturing **History**

Answer: whether or not to extend slavery to California

US8.9.4 Discuss the importance of the slavery issue as raised by the annexation of Texas and California's admission to the union as a free state under the Compromise of 1850. **US8.9.5** Analyze the significance of the States' Rights Doctrine, the Missouri Compromise (1820), the Wilmot Proviso (1846), the Compromise of 1850, Henry Clay's role in the Missouri Compromise and the Compromise of 1850, the Kansas-Nebraska Act (1854), the *Dred Scott* v. *Sandford* decision (1857), and the Lincoln-Douglas debates (1858).

The Search for Compromise

Main Idea **Henry Clay presented a plan to settle the slavery debate that resulted in the Compromise of 1850.**

Reading Connection Do you remember an argument you have had recently? How did you resolve the argument? Read to learn how Congress settled its dividing issues in 1850.

Once in office, President Zachary Taylor urged leaders in the two territories of California and New Mexico to apply for statehood immediately. After these lands had become states, he reasoned, their citizens could decide whether to allow slavery. New Mexico did not apply for statehood, but California did in 1850.

Taylor's plan ran into trouble when California's statehood became tangled up with other issues before Congress. Antislavery forces wanted to abolish slavery in the District of Columbia, the nation's capital. Southerners wanted a strong national law requiring states to return **fugitive** (FYOO • juh • tihv), or runaway, slaves to their masters. Another dispute involved the New Mexico–Texas border.

The greatest obstacle to Taylor's plan was concern over the balance of power in the Senate. In 1849 the nation included 15 slave states and 15 free states. If California entered as a free state—and New Mexico, Oregon, and Utah followed as free states—which seemed likely—the South would be hopelessly outvoted in the Senate. As tension grew, some Southerners began talking about having their states **secede** (sih • SEED) from, or leave, the United States.

The Debate Begins In January 1850, Henry Clay, now a senator, presented a plan to settle all the issues dividing Congress. First, California would be admitted as a free state. Second, the New Mexico Territory would have no restrictions on slavery. Third, the New Mexico–Texas border dispute would be settled in favor of New Mexico. Fourth, the slave trade, but not slavery itself, would be abolished in the District of Columbia. Finally, Clay pushed for a stronger fugitive slave law.

Clay's proposal launched an emotional debate in Congress that raged for seven months. Senator Calhoun opposed Clay's plan. He believed that the only way to save the Union was to protect slavery. If Congress admitted California as a free state, Calhoun warned, the Southern states would have to leave the Union.

Senator Daniel Webster supported Clay's plan. He argued that antislavery forces lost little in agreeing to the compromise.

Picturing **History**

The Great Debate over the Compromise of 1850 raged for months. ***Why did Daniel Webster favor this compromise?***

R1 Reading Strategy

Understanding Vocabulary Explain that the word *fugitive* comes from a Latin word meaning *to* "flee". **Ask:** How is that origin related to the meaning of the term? *(A fugitive is someone who flees.)* BL CA 8RW1.2

R2 Reading Strategy

Organizing Information Have students use a two-column chart to record details about Clay's proposed compromise. Suggest they head the columns *Clay's Proposal* and *Opponents' Response*. Have them record details of each of the proposal's five parts. Students may need to conduct additional research to obtain more information on opponents' responses to Clay's proposal. AL CA HI1.

S Skill Practice

Visual Literacy Have students examine the painting of the Senate Debate of 1850. **Ask:** Who is speaking in this painting? *(Clay)* What aspects of the painting suggest the seriousness of the debate? *(the dignified stance of the speaker, the concentration of all listeners on him, the full gallery)* OL CA 8LS1.9

Review The Big Idea

Review the Big Idea for this section: "Differences in economic, political, and social beliefs and practices can lead to division within a nation and have lasting consequences." Tell students to imagine that they are either Clay, Calhoun, Webster, or Douglas. Ask students to write the text of a speech that tries to convince other Senators to adopt their point of view on the compromise. OL CA 8SA2.4

Picturing **History**

This depiction of the Great Debate of 1850 in the U.S. Senate was created by Peter F. Rothermel, a Pennsylvania native who is remembered as one of America's most skillful painters of historical scenes.

Answer: because it would preserve the Union

More Skill Practice

Historical and Social Sciences Analysis Skill **Ask:** Why do you think Henry Clay was called the "Great Compromiser"? *(He played significant roles in the Missouri Compromise, the tariff compromise that ended the nullification crisis of 1833, and the Compromise of 1850.)* OL CA HI1.

R1 Reading Strategy

Academic Vocabulary Have students write a sentence using the word *collapse*. BL

R2 Reading Strategy

Understanding Vocabulary Have students define *abstain* in their own words. OL

ASSESS

Resources for page 542

Use these resources to assess student mastery of section content.

- Section Quiz 12–2
- Interactive Tutor Self-Assessment CD-ROM

Reading Check

Answer: no restrictions on slavery for New Mexico Territory; California entered as free state

History Online

Study Central provides summaries, interactive games, and online graphic organizers to help students review section content.

CLOSE

Predicting Consequences Have students explain how the events discussed in this section led the nation closer to a war. OL

Webster reasoned that geography would prevent slavery from taking root in the new territories, because most of the land was not suited for plantations. What was most important was to preserve the Union.

The Compromise of 1850 Clay's plan could not pass as a complete package. Too many members of Congress objected to one part of it or another. On July 4, 1850, before the issue R1 could be decided, President Taylor **collapsed** with a severe stomach illness. He died five days later, having served just 16 months as president. The new president, **Millard Fillmore,** supported some form of compromise. At the same time, **Stephen A. Douglas,** a young senator from Illinois, took charge of efforts to resolve the crisis. Douglas divided Clay's plan into a series of measures that Congress could vote on separately. In this way, members of Congress would not have to support proposals they opposed.

President Fillmore persuaded several Whig representatives to **abstain** (uhb • STAYN)—not to cast votes—on measures they opposed. R2 Congress finally passed a series of five separate bills in August and September of 1850. Taken together these laws, known as the Compromise of 1850, contained the five main points of Clay's original plan. Fillmore believed they settled the conflict between North and South. The president would soon be proved wrong.

Reading Check **Explain** How did the Compromise of 1850 affect the New Mexico Territory? What role did California play in this?

History Online

Study Central Need help understanding the issue of slavery in the West? Visit ca.hss.glencoe.com and click on Study Central.

Section 2 Review

Reading Summary

Review the Main Ideas

- The Missouri Compromise allowed both Missouri and Maine to enter the Union in order to maintain the balance between slave and free states.
- In the 1820s and 1830s, South Carolina threatened to nullify federal tariff laws.
- The acquisition of new territories in the West—Texas, New Mexico, and California—created more conflicts over slavery.
- The Compromise of 1850, developed by Henry Clay, included a number of provisions dealing with slavery that temporarily resolved the debate between the North and South.

What Did You Learn?

1. List the provisions of the Missouri Compromise.
2. Why did it matter if California entered as a slave state or a free state?

Critical Thinking

3. **Comparing** Re-create the table below and describe what the North and South each gained from the Compromise of 1850. CA HI1.

Compromise of 1850	
Northern gains	Southern gains

4. **The Big Ideas** Why was the Free-Soil Party created? CA HI2.
5. **Analyze** What was the Wilmot Proviso? Why was it controversial? CA CS1.
6. **Persuasive Writing** Create a poster for the Free-Soil Party presidential candidate. Include slogans and symbols to gain popular support. CA 8WA2.1.C
7. **Analysis** **Making Connections** Make a time line highlighting key issues of federal sovereignty versus states' rights. Include the Virginia-Kentucky Resolutions of 1798–99 and the Compromise of 1850. CA CS2.

SECTION 2 REVIEW ANSWERS

Review questions reinforce content standards US8.9 and US8.10.

1. Missouri admitted as slave state and Maine as free state; slavery banned from Louisiana Purchase north of 36°30′ N latitude.
2. The Senate was evenly divided.
3. North: California admitted as free state, slave trade banned in D.C.; South: no restrictions on slavery in New Mexico, slavery still allowed in D.C., stronger fugitive slave law
4. **The Big Ideas** to oppose extending slavery
5. proposal to ban slavery from any lands acquired from Mexico; Southerners opposed it
6. Posters should address the slavery issue.
7. **Analysis** Entries should reflect key issues.

Section 3 A Nation Dividing

Guide to Reading

Looking Back, Looking Ahead
The Compromise of 1850 seemed to have settled the problem of slavery in new states. When statehood for Kansas and Nebraska drew near, however, slavery again divided the nation.

Focusing on the Main Ideas
- The Kansas-Nebraska Act resulted from another dispute over slavery in Congress. ***(page 544)***
- Violence erupted as proslavery and antislavery forces came to arms when the new proslavery Kansas legislature was elected. ***(page 546)***

Locating Places
Kansas
Nebraska

Meeting People
Harriet Beecher Stowe
John Brown
Charles Sumner
Preston Brooks

Content Vocabulary
popular sovereignty (SAH • vruhn • tee)
border ruffians (RUH • fee • uhns)
civil war

Academic Vocabulary
reveal
inevitable (ih • NEH • vuh • tuh • buhl)

Reading Strategy
Taking Notes As you read the section, re-create the table below and describe how Southerners and Northerners reacted to the Kansas-Nebraska Act.

Kansas-Nebraska Act	
Southern reaction	Northern reaction

History Social Science Standards

US8.9 Students analyze the early and steady attempts to abolish slavery and to realize the ideals of the Declaration of Independence.

NATIONAL GEOGRAPHIC Where & When?

1850 — 1853 — 1856

- **1850** Fugitive Slave Act is passed
- **1852** *Uncle Tom's Cabin* is published
- **1854** Kansas-Nebraska Act is passed
- **1856** Charles Sumner is attacked in Senate

FOCUS

BELLRINGER Skillbuilder Activity
Project **Daily Focus Skills Transparency 12–3** and have students answer the question.

Guide to Reading

Preteaching Vocabulary: Help students learn the content vocabulary word by using a dictionary to define each term, and then the overall concept, in these compound words.

Answers to Graphic: Southern reaction: Supported bill; Northern reaction: Opposed bill

Unpacking the Standards
After reading the section, students will be able to:
- Explain how the Kansas-Nebraska Act further divided the North and the South.
- Describe how popular sovereignty led to violence.

SECTION RESOURCES

Print Material
- Reproducible Lesson Plan 12–3*
- Daily Lesson and Discussion Notes 12–3
- Guided Reading Activity 12–3
- Reading Essentials and Study Guide 12–3
- Active Reading Note-Taking Guide 12–3
- Section Quiz 12–3

Transparencies
- Daily Focus Skills Transparency 12–3
- Section Graphic Organizer Transparency 12–3
- California Standards Practice Transparencies

Technology
- Interactive Tutor Self-Assessment CD-ROM
- Exam*View*® Pro Testmaker CD-ROM
- Presentation Plus! CD-ROM

*Available on TeacherWorks™

TEACH

C Critical Thinking

Determining Cause and Effect Ask: Why did Douglas want to organize the territories of Kansas and Nebraska? *(to encourage settlement and open them for the development of a transcontinental railroad)* OL CA HI2.

R Reading Strategy

Activating Prior Knowledge
Students encountered the term *popular sovereignty* in discussing the Constitution. **Ask:** What does the concept mean? *(that all the power rests with the people)* OL CA 8RW1.3

W Writing Support

Research Reports Writing
Have students pose a question about the debate over the Kansas-Nebraska Act, such as "Why did Pierce, a Northern Democrat, support the bill?" and carry out research to find the answer. Have students write a report presenting their question and the answer. OL CA 8WA2.3

Reading Check

Answer: Answers will vary, but should show an understanding of *popular sovereignty*.

Answers and Additional Support

US8.9.5 Analyze the significance of the States' Rights Doctrine, the Missouri Compromise (1820), the Wilmot Proviso (1846), the Compromise of 1850, Henry Clay's role in the Missouri Compromise and the Compromise of 1850, the Kansas-Nebraska Act (1854), the *Dred Scott* v. *Sandford* decision (1857), and the Lincoln-Douglas debates (1858).

The Kansas-Nebraska Act

Main Idea **The Kansas-Nebraska Act resulted from another dispute over slavery in Congress.**

Reading Connection Do you know where the present-day states of Kansas and Nebraska are located? Find them on the Reference Atlas maps in the front of your book. Read to learn what happened in this part of the country in the mid-1850s.

Franklin Pierce, a New Hampshire Democrat who supported the Fugitive Slave Act, became president in 1853. Pierce intended to enforce the Fugitive Slave Act, and his actions hardened the opposition to slavery. **Harriet Beecher Stowe's** popular book *Uncle Tom's Cabin* added fuel to antislavery feelings with its description of slavery as a cruel and inhuman system.

In 1854 the dispute over slavery erupted in Congress again. The cause was a bill introduced by Stephen A. Douglas, the Illinois senator who had forged the Compromise of 1850. Hoping to encourage settlement of the West and open the way for a transcontinental railroad, Douglas proposed organizing the region west of Missouri and Iowa as the territories of **Kansas** and **Nebraska.** Douglas was developing a plan for the nation to expand that both the North and the South would accept. Instead his bill reopened the conflict about slavery in the territories.

Picturing History
Stephen Douglas enthusiastically supported national expansion. ***Why did the Kansas-Nebraska Act reopen the question of whether slavery should be allowed in the territories?***

Geography of Slavery Because of their location, Kansas and Nebraska seemed likely to become free states. Both lay north of 36°30′N latitude, the line established in the Missouri Compromise as the boundary of slavery. Douglas knew that Southerners would object to having Kansas and Nebraska become free states because it would give the North more members in the Senate. As a result, Douglas proposed abandoning the Missouri Compromise and letting the settlers in each territory vote on whether to allow slavery. He called this **popular sovereignty** (SAH • vruhn • tee)—allowing the people to decide.

Passage of the Act Many Northerners protested strongly. Douglas's plan to repeal the Missouri Compromise would allow slavery into areas that had been free for more than 30 years. Opponents of the bill demanded that Congress vote down the bill.

Southerners in Congress, however, provided solid support for the bill. They expected that Kansas would be settled in large part by slaveholders from Missouri who would vote to keep slavery legal. With some support from Northern Democrats and the backing of President Pierce, Congress passed the Kansas-Nebraska Act in May 1854.

Division Grows Northern Democrats in the House split almost evenly on the vote, **revealing** deep divisions in the party. Many Northerners became convinced that compromise with the South was no longer possible. Sam Houston, senator from Texas, predicted that the bill "will convulse [upset] the country from Maine to the Rio Grande."

Reading Check **Describe** Write a definition of *popular sovereignty* in your own words.

More Skill Practice

Historical and Social Sciences Analysis Skill Ask: Why does control of the Senate matter? What is the current balance of power between Democrats and Republicans in the Senate? *(The majority party has a greater chance of passing legislation.)* OL CA HI3.

Picturing History

Douglas defeated Abraham Lincoln for the Illinois Senate seat in 1858 but lost to him in the 1860 presidential election.

Answer: because it called for the repeal of the Missouri Compromise and therefore would allow slavery into areas that had been free since 1820

Biography

US8.9 Students analyze the early and steady attempts to abolish slavery and to realize the ideals of the Declaration of Independence.

Harriet Beecher Stowe

1811–1896

Writer Harriet Beecher Stowe called the Fugitive Slave Act a "nightmare abomination." Stowe, born Harriet Elizabeth Beecher to a New England minister, moved to Cincinnati with her family when she was 21. There, on the banks of the Ohio River, she saw enslaved people being loaded onto ships to be taken to slave markets. Stowe was introduced to many abolitionists, some of whom owned safe houses along the Underground Railroad. Stowe strongly opposed slavery, but for some time, she did not know how she could help end it. With the help of her children and husband, Stowe developed an antislavery story called *Uncle Tom's Cabin*. Packed with dramatic incidents and vivid characters, the novel shows slavery as a cruel and brutal system.

Published in 1852, *Uncle Tom's Cabin* quickly became a sensation, selling more than 300,000 copies in the first year. Some people, however, strongly opposed the book. Its sales were banned in the South, **C** and many slaveholders said the book unfairly and inaccurately represented their way of life. To counter these accusations, Stowe published *A Key to Uncle Tom's Cabin; Presenting the Original Facts and Documents Upon Which It Is Based.* This book detailed Stowe's extensive research into slavery in the South. The book had such an impact on public feelings about slavery that when **S** Abraham Lincoln was introduced to Stowe during the Civil War, he said, "so you're the little woman who wrote the book that started this great war."

After the Civil War, Stowe continued to write. She began to speak publicly and gave readings of *Uncle Tom's Cabin* to many large audiences. In 1896, at the age of 85, Stowe died. Her famous book has since been adapted into plays and songs, and remains a much-read novel from the Civil War era.

"[I hope these writings] awaken sympathy and feeling for the African race, as they exist among us; to show their wrongs and sorrows. . ."

—Harriet Beecher Stowe

Then and Now

Write a short story similar to *Uncle Tom's Cabin* about a group of people who are unfairly treated in today's world. Be sure to research the topic so that your story remains as factual as possible.

Biography

TEACH

Review The Big Idea

Review the Big Idea for this section: "Differences in economic, political, and social beliefs and practices can lead to division within a nation and have lasting consequences." **Ask:** Why would the Southern states ban the book? *(Answers will vary but students should recognize that Southerners did not want Stowe's anti-slavery views to be spread.)* **OL** **CA HI2.**

C Critical Thinking

Making Inferences **Ask:** If *Uncle Tom's Cabin* was banned in many Southern states, how could it become a bestseller? *(Students should conclude that it sold most of its copies in the North.)* **OL** **CA HI2.**

S Skill Practice

Historical and Social Sciences Analysis Skill
Ask: How did Stowe respond to critics who said her novel was inaccurate? Why do you think she responded this way? *(By publishing a book citing historical evidence and documents, she offered support for the events in the novel. She responded that way to convince people that though her book was fictional, it was based on fact.)* **OL** **CA HI1.**

Then and Now

Students' stories will vary. Allow them time to conduct their research as well as write their story.

R1 Reading Strategy

Sequencing Information Have students construct a time line to show the events in Kansas. OL CA CS1.

R2 Reading Strategy

Using Context Clues
Ask: Based on this sentence, which side in the conflict called these people *ruffians*? Why do you say so? *(anti-slavery people; because ruffian is a negative word)* OL CA 8RW1.3

W Writing Support

Persuasive Writing Have students take the role of a citizen for or against slavery in Kansas. Ask them to write a letter to their senator urging recognition of the appropriate territorial government and giving reasons why. OL CA 8WA2.4

S Skill Practice

Historical and Social Sciences Analysis Skill
Ask: Why did Minnesota, Washington, or Oregon not become open to slavery? *(They were organized as territories earlier.)* OL CA CS3.

Answers and Additional Support

US8.9.1 Describe the leaders of the movement (e.g., John Quincy Adams and his proposed constitutional amendment, John Brown and the armed resistance, Harriet Tubman and the Underground Railroad, Benjamin Franklin, Theodore Weld, William Lloyd Garrison, Frederick Douglass.)

Conflict in Kansas

R1 **Main Idea** **Violence erupted as proslavery and antislavery forces came to arms when the new proslavery Kansas legislature was elected.**

Reading Connection Think of an issue that is important to you. What would you be willing to do to stand up for that issue? Read to learn how the rival groups in Kansas clashed in the mid-1800s over slavery.

Right after passage of the Kansas-Nebraska Act, proslavery and antislavery groups rushed supporters into Kansas. In the spring of 1855, when elections took place in Kansas, a proslavery legislature was elected.

Although only about 1,500 voters lived in Kansas at the time, more than 6,000 people cast ballots in the elections. Thousands of proslavery supporters from Missouri had crossed the border just to vote in the election. These Missourians traveled in armed groups and became known as **border ruffians** (RUH • fee • uhns). R2 Soon after the election, the new Kansas legislature passed laws supporting slavery. One law even restricted political office to only those candidates who supported slavery.

The antislavery people refused to accept these laws. Instead they armed themselves, held their own elections, and adopted a constitution that banned slavery. By January 1856, rival governments existed in Kansas, one for and one against slavery. Each asked Congress for recognition. To confuse matters further, President Pierce and the U.S. Senate favored the proslavery government, and the U.S. House of Representatives backed the forces that were opposed to slavery. W

With proslavery and antislavery forces in Kansas arming themselves, the outbreak of violence became **inevitable.** In May 1856, about 800 slavery supporters attacked the town of Lawrence, the antislavery capital.

NATIONAL GEOGRAPHIC **Slavery and Sectionalism**

The Compromise of 1850

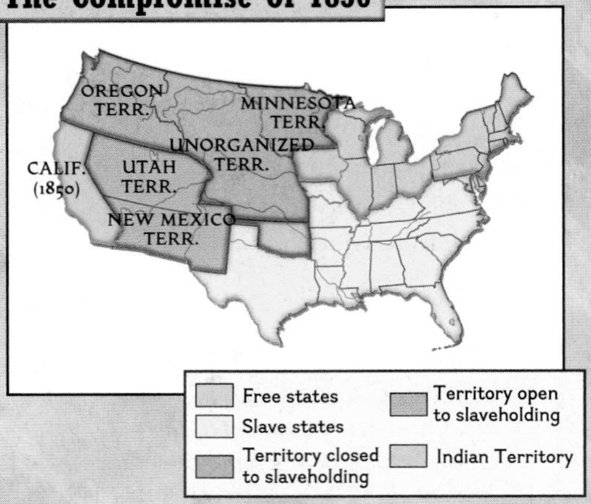

Kansas-Nebraska Act, 1854

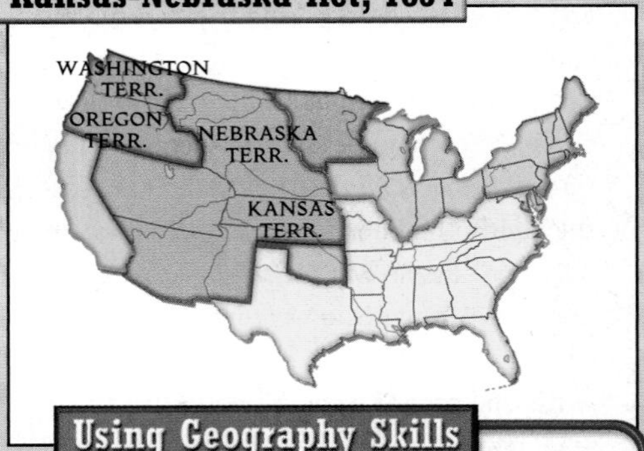

S

Using Geography Skills

1. **Region** How did the Kansas-Nebraska Act change the amount of territory that was open to slaveholding?
2. **Analyze** Which territories were nonslaveholding in 1854?

Using Geography Skills

Answers:

1. It more than doubled the territories open to slavery.
2. Washington, Oregon, Minnesota

Did You Know?

The term "Bleeding Kansas" was coined by Horace Greeley, founder of the *New York Tribune* and an outspoken abolitionist. In 1872 Greeley received the presidential nomination of both the Democratic and Liberal Republican parties, but he was defeated by Republican Ulysses S. Grant.

The slavery supporters destroyed the town, burned the hotel and the home of the governor, and tore down two newspaper offices. Soon after, forces opposed to slavery retaliated.

"Bleeding Kansas" **John Brown,** a fervent abolitionist, believed God had chosen him to end slavery. When he heard of the attack on Lawrence, Brown went into a rage. He vowed to "strike terror in the hearts of the proslavery people." One night, Brown led four of his sons and two other men along Pottawatomie Creek, where they seized and killed five supporters of slavery.

More violence followed as armed bands roamed the territory. Newspapers began referring to "Bleeding Kansas" and "the Civil War in Kansas." A **civil war** is a conflict between citizens of the same country. Not until October of 1856 did John Geary, the newly appointed territorial governor, stop the bloodshed in Kansas. Geary ordered 1,300 federal troops to suppress the guerrilla forces.

Violence in Congress The violence that erupted in Kansas spilled over to the halls of the U.S. Congress as well. Abolitionist senator **Charles Sumner** of Massachusetts delivered a speech entitled "The Crime Against Kansas." Sumner lashed out against proslavery forces in Kansas. He also criticized proslavery senators, repeatedly attacking Andrew P. Butler of South Carolina.

Two days after the speech, Butler's distant cousin, Representative **Preston Brooks,** walked into the Senate chamber. He hit Sumner again and again over the head and shoulders with a cane. Sumner fell to the floor, unconscious and bleeding. He suffered injuries so severe that he did not return to the Senate for several years. The Brooks-Sumner incident and the fighting in "Bleeding Kansas" revealed the rising level of hostility between North and South.

Reading Check **Predict** Who do you predict will be the combatants if the United States is torn apart by Civil War?

History Online
Study Central Need help understanding the Kansas-Nebraska Act and its effects? Visit ca.hss.glencoe.com and click on Study Central.

Section 3 Review

Reading Summary

Review the Main Ideas

- The Kansas-Nebraska Act abandoned the provisions of the Missouri Compromise and put in place the doctrine of popular sovereignty to decide the issue of slavery in new territories.
- In Kansas antislavery and proslavery forces came into violent conflict.

What Did You Learn?

1. Who were the border ruffians?
2. How many cast votes in the Kansas elections? How did that compare with the population at the time?

Critical Thinking

3. **Organizing Information** Re-create the diagram below and list the steps that led to bloodshed in Kansas. CA CS1.

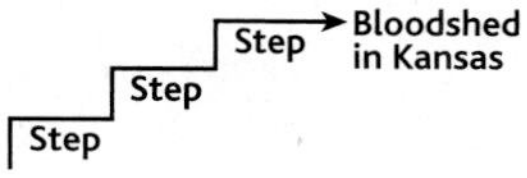

4. **The Big Ideas** How did popular sovereignty lead to violence in Kansas? CA HI2.
5. **Predicting Consequences** Could the violence in Kansas have been prevented if Congress had not abandoned the Missouri Compromise? Explain. CA HR3.
6. **Persuasive Writing** Decide whether you would have been for or against the Kansas-Nebraska Act and the concept of popular sovereignty. Then write a newspaper editorial arguing your position. CA 8WA2.4

U Universal Access

Visual/Spatial Encourage students to draw a political cartoon that expresses a point of view on one of the following topics: the violence in Kansas, John Brown's attack at Pottawatomie, or the caning of Sumner. OL CA HI1.

R Reading Strategy

Understanding Vocabulary
Ask: What element needs to be included in a conflict to make it qualify as a civil war? *(fighting)* OL CA HI1.

ASSESS

Resources for page 547

Use these resources to assess student mastery of section content.

- Biography Activity 12B
- Section Quiz 12–3
- Interactive Tutor Self-Assessment CD-ROM

Reading Check
Answer: Northerners vs. Southerners

History Online
Study Central provides summaries, interactive games, and online graphic organizers to help students review section content.

SECTION 3 REVIEW ANSWERS

Review questions reinforce content standard US8.9.

1. Missouri residents who crossed into Kansas to cast proslavery ballots in the elections of 1855
2. more than 6,000 ballots were cast, about four times the actual Kansas population
3. Answers should reflect information in the section.
4. **The Big Ideas** Outsiders corrupted the election, and fighting broke out over the results.
5. Students should give evidence to support their answers.
6. Answers will vary but should reflect an understanding of the concept of popular sovereignty and the effects it might have on the nation.

CLOSE

Drawing Conclusions
Ask students to speculate about what the federal government could have done, if anything, to prevent the violence that erupted over the Kansas-Nebraska Act. OL

FOCUS

BELLRINGER
SKILLBUILDER ACTIVITY

Project **Daily Focus Skills Transparency 12–4** and have students answer the question.

Guide to Reading

Preteaching Vocabulary: Have students find the definitions of the content vocabulary terms in the Glossary and write a sentence using each.

Answers to Graphic: 1846: Dred Scott sues for freedom; 1854: Republican Party formed; 1856: Buchanan elected president; 1858: Lincoln and Douglas debate

Unpacking the Standards

After reading the section, students will be able to:

- Explain how the *Dred Scott* decision and John Brown's raid affected Americans.
- Describe the substance and impact of the Lincoln-Douglas debates.

Section 4

Challenges to Slavery

History Social Science Standards

US8.9 Students analyze the early and steady attempts to abolish slavery and to realize the ideals of the Declaration of Independence.

US8.10 Students analyze the multiple causes, key events, and complex consequences of the Civil War.

Guide to Reading

Looking Back, Looking Ahead
You learned that the issue of slavery led to civil war in Kansas. You will next read about how slavery led to the founding of a new political party and additional bloodshed.

Focusing on the Main Ideas
- The Supreme Court's decision in the *Dred Scott* case resulted in even more division in the country. ***(page 549)***
- The Lincoln-Douglas debates helped Lincoln emerge as a leader. ***(page 552)***

Meeting People
John C. Frémont
James Buchanan
Dred Scott
Roger B. Taney (TAW•nee)
Abraham Lincoln

Content Vocabulary
arsenal (AHR•suhn•uhl)
martyr (MAHR•tuhr)

Academic Vocabulary
restrict
topic

Reading Strategy
Classifying Information As you read the section, re-create the diagram below and list major events that occurred in each year.

1846	1854	1856	1858

NATIONAL GEOGRAPHIC Who & When?

1854 — 1856 — 1858 — 1860

1854 Republican Party is formed

James Buchanan

1856 James Buchanan is elected president

Dred Scott

1857 *Dred Scott* decision states that all slaves are property

1859 John Brown raids Harpers Ferry, Virginia

John Brown

SECTION RESOURCES

Print Material
- Reproducible Lesson Plan 12–4*
- Daily Lesson and Discussion Notes 12–4
- Guided Reading Activity 12–4
- Reading Essentials and Study Guide 12–4
- Active Reading Note-Taking Guide 12–4
- Section Quiz 12–4

Transparencies
- Daily Focus Skills Transparency 12–4
- Section Graphic Organizer Transparency 12–4
- California Standards Practice Transparencies

Technology
- Interactive Tutor Self-Assessment CD-ROM
- Exam*View*® Pro Testmaker CD-ROM
- Presentation Plus! CD-ROM

*Available on TeacherWorks™

US8.9.5 Analyze the significance of the States' Rights Doctrine, the Missouri Compromise (1820), the Wilmot Proviso (1846), the Compromise of 1850, Henry Clay's role in the Missouri Compromise and the Comprise of 1850, the Kansas-Nebraska Act (1854), the *Dred Scott* v. *Sandford* decision (1857), and the Lincoln-Douglas debates (1858).

The *Dred Scott* Decision

Main Idea **The Supreme Court's decision in the *Dred Scott* case resulted in even more division in the country.**

Reading Connection How would you feel if the Supreme Court decided that you were "property"? Read to find out how the decision in the *Dred Scott* case shocked the nation.

An American Story

Many people considered John Brown to be a radical murderer, but others viewed him as a fighter for the cause of freedom. When he was executed in 1859, a magazine published this imaginative account of Brown's exit from the jail,

> **"a black woman, with her little child in arms, stood near his way. . . . He stopped. . . and with the tenderness of one whose love is as broad as the brotherhood of man, kissed the child. . . . "**
>
> —from *The Anglo-African Magazine*

Why Was the Republican Party Founded?

Even before Brown's raid, other events had driven the North and South further apart. After the Kansas-Nebraska Act, the Democratic Party began to divide along sectional lines, with Northern Democrats leaving the party. Differing views over the slavery issue destroyed the Whig Party.

In 1854 antislavery Whigs and Democrats joined forces with Free-Soilers to form the Republican Party. The Republicans challenged the proslavery Whigs and Democrats, choosing candidates to run in the state and congressional elections of 1854. Their main message was that the government should ban slavery from new territories.

The Republican Party quickly showed its strength in the North. In the election, the Republicans won control of the House of Representatives and of several state governments. In the South, the Republicans had almost no support.

Almost three-fourths of the Democratic candidates from free states lost in 1854. The party was increasingly becoming a Southern party.

The Election of 1856 Democrats and Republicans met again in the presidential election of 1856. The Whig Party, disintegrating over the slavery issue, did not offer a candidate of its own.

The Republicans chose **John C. Frémont** of California as their candidate for president. Frémont had gained fame as an explorer in the West. The party platform called for free territories, and its campaign slogan became "Free soil, free speech, and Frémont."

The Democratic Party nominated **James Buchanan** of Pennsylvania, an experienced diplomat and former member of Congress. The party endorsed the idea of popular sovereignty.

The American Party, or Know-Nothings, had grown quickly between 1853 and 1856 by attacking immigrants. The Know-Nothings nominated former president Millard Fillmore.

The presidential vote divided along sectional lines. Buchanan won the election, winning all of the Southern states except Maryland, and received 174 electoral votes compared to 114 for Frémont and 8 for Fillmore. Frémont did not receive a single electoral vote south of the Mason-Dixon line, but he carried 11 of the 16 free states.

The *Dred Scott* Decision Until 1857 some slaves who had lived in free states or territories were successful when they sued for their freedom. Biddy Mason had done this in California. The case of another slave, Dred Scott, however, went all the way to the Supreme Court. On March 6, 1857, the Court announced a decision about slavery and the territories that shook the nation.

TEACH

C Critical Thinking

Making Inferences Discuss this quotation from the *Anglo-African Magazine*. **Ask:** What aspects of John Brown's character was the writer highlighting in this report? *(his compassion and gentleness)* OL CA HR5.

S Skill Practice

Historical and Social Sciences Analysis Skill
Ask: Why would the Republicans have very little support in the South? *(because they opposed extending slavery in the territories, which Southerners wanted)* OL CA HI2.

W Writing Support

Narrative Writing Have students take the role of a reporter covering the election of 1856 and write a story detailing the events that led to the selection of the candidates and the outcome. Tell them to enhance their narrative with invented quotations reflecting the views of the candidates and their supporters. OL CA 8WA2.1

U Universal Access

English Learners Have students explain what the text means in saying that the presidential vote divided "along sectional lines." *(Most votes in the North and the South went to opposing candidates.)* OL

More Skill Practice

Historical and Social Sciences Analysis Skill **Ask:** Why did the Whigs not last as a political party? *(split over slavery caused such dissension among them that the party collapsed)* Will the same problem affect the Democrats during the 1850s and 1860s? Why or why not? *(Answers will vary but students should give reasons.)* OL CA HI3.

Did You Know?

In 1852 the Whigs chose not to nominate incumbent Millard Fillmore, whose strong enforcement of the Fugitive Slave Act had alienated many Northern members of the party, but instead named Winfield Scott, a successful general from the war with Mexico.

Resources for page 549

Biography Activity 12A

Dred Scott was an enslaved African American who was bought by an army doctor in Missouri, a slave state. In the 1830s, the doctor moved his household to Illinois, a free state, and then to the Wisconsin Territory, where slavery was banned by the Northwest Ordinance of 1787. Later the family returned to Missouri, where the doctor died.

R In 1846 with the help of antislavery lawyers, Scott sued for his freedom. He claimed he should be free because he had once lived on free soil. Eleven years later, in the midst of growing anger over the slavery issue, the case reached the Supreme Court.

U **The Court's Decision** The case attracted enormous attention. Although the immediate issue was Dred Scott's status, the Court also had the opportunity to rule on the question of slavery in territories. Many Americans hoped that the Court would resolve the issue for good.

The Court's decision electrified the nation. Chief Justice **Roger B. Taney** (TAW•nee) said that Dred Scott was still a slave. As a slave, Scott was not a citizen and had no right to bring a lawsuit. Taney could have stopped there, but he decided to address the broader issues.

Taney wrote that Scott's residence on free soil did not make him free. An enslaved person was property, and the Fifth Amendment prohibits Congress from taking away property without "due process of law."

Finally, Taney wrote that Congress had no power to prohibit slavery in any territory. The Missouri Compromise—which had banned slavery north of 36°30′N latitude—was unconstitutional. For that matter, so was popular sovereignty. Not even the voters in a territory could prohibit slavery because that would amount to taking away a person's property. In effect, the decision meant that the Constitution protected slavery. *(See page 846 of the Appendix for a summary of the Dred Scott decision.)*

Reaction to the Decision Rather than settling the issue, the Supreme Court's decision divided the country even more. Many Southerners were elated. The Court had reaffirmed what many in the South had always maintained: Nothing could legally prevent the spread of slavery. Northern Democrats were pleased that the Republicans' main issue—**restricting** the spread of slavery—had been ruled unconstitutional.

Republicans and other antislavery groups were outraged, calling the *Dred Scott* decision "the greatest crime" ever committed in the nation's courts.

Reading Check **Explain** How did the *Dred Scott* decision regulate the spread of slavery?

***Picturing* History**

Chief Justice Roger B. Taney (above right) delivered the Supreme Court's ruling in the *Dred Scott* case. The decision made Scott a topic for the nation's press. ***What impression of Scott's family do you get from the engravings shown here?***

R Reading Strategy

Scaffolding—Summarizing

Ask: What was Dred Scott's argument? *(He should be free because he had lived in a free state.)* OL

This READING SKILL was introduced in Chapter 4.

Review The Big Idea

Review the Big Idea for this section: "Differences in economic, political, and social beliefs and practices can lead to division within a nation and have lasting consequences."

Ask: What different beliefs are seen in Dred Scott's argument and the Court's ruling? *(Scott argued that African Americans had a right to freedom and to be treated as citizens; Taney said African Americans are property and have no rights.)* OL CA HI1.

U Universal Access

Verbal/Linguistic Have students write a script for a radio program on the reaction to the *Dred Scott* decision. AL CA 8SA2.3

Reading Check

Answer: It said that neither Congress nor voters could ban slavery in any territory.

Answers and Additional Support

Resources for page 550

Academic Vocabulary Activity 12

***Picturing* History**

Frank Leslie's Illustrated Newspaper began publication in 1855 and appeared in various forms until 1922.

Answer: They appear to be respectable people whose formal clothing suggests a middle-class status.

Biography

US8.9.6 Describe the lives of free blacks and the laws that limited their freedom and economic opportunities.

BRIDGET MASON

1818–1891

Born a slave in 1818, Bridget Mason had worked on plantations in Georgia and Mississippi. In 1851 slaveholder Robert Smith moved his family and their 12 slaves to California. Among the slaves were Bridget —or Biddy as she was usually called—and her three children. Smith's plan to start a ranch and mine for gold did not work. In the autumn of 1855, Smith made plans to move to Texas.

Before Smith could leave, charges were filed against him for planning to move enslaved people from California, a free state, to Texas, a slave state. In court, Smith's attorney argued that Biddy and the other slaves had agreed to come to California and were willing to go to Texas.

C Before Judge Benjamin Hayes issued his verdict, he wanted to hear how Biddy felt about moving to Texas. Biddy told the judge, "Mr. Smith told me I would be just as free in Texas as here." S But she admitted she "always feared this trip to Texas since I first heard of it." In his decision, Hayes said that Biddy and the others were "entitled to their freedom and cannot be held in slavery or involuntary servitude . . . [they] are free forever." W

"If you hold your hand closed, nothing good can come in. The open hand is blessed, for it gives in abundance, even as it receives."
—Bridget Mason

In 1856 when Biddy was declared free, she and her family decided to settle in Los Angeles. Biddy first worked as a servant, then was hired by Dr. John Strother Griffin to help care for his patients. Saving her money, she purchased her first home in 1866. Biddy soon bought and sold more property, making money during the mid-1870s when property in Los Angeles was in demand.

Biddy devoted her life to helping others. She helped form the First African Methodist Episcopal Church in 1872, visited jail inmates, and provided food and shelter for the poor. When floods struck the Los Angeles area in the 1880s, Biddy paid to feed the flood victims.

Then and Now

Read the quote above. Can you think of anyone today who lives by that motto? Explain.

Biography

C Critical Thinking

Comparing and Contrasting **Ask:** What similarities and differences do you see between the cases of Biddy Mason and Dred Scott? *(similarities: both cases involve African Americans who were enslaved and then moved to a free state; differences: Mason's case took place in California while Scott's went to the Supreme Court; the California judge granted Mason her freedom, while Taney denied that Scott was entitled to freedom.)* OL CA HI1.

S Skill Practice

Historical and Social Sciences Analysis Skill
Ask: Was Smith speaking the truth when he told Biddy Mason she would be "just as free" in Texas as in California? *(No; Texas was a slave state while California was a free state.)* OL CA HR3.

W Writing Support

Narrative Writing Ask students to imagine they are Biddy Mason on the day that she was granted her freedom. Have them write a journal entry from her point of view. Then have them write a second journal entry, also from Mason's point of view, but dated fifteen years later. Have her views of freedom changed? If so, how? OL CA 8WA2.1

Then and Now

nswers will vary, but might include missionaries who work with the poor; philanthropists who onate money to improve society; or ordinary citizens who volunteer their time to work at soup tchens, hospitals, schools, and in groups such as the Red Cross.

R Reading Strategy

Academic Vocabulary Ask students to list important topics in a congressional election today. AL

C Critical Thinking

Identifying Central Issues Remind students that the Lincoln-Douglas debates took place after the Dred Scott decision had been issued. **Ask:** Why would Douglas's answer cost him support in the South? *(It seemed to go against the* Dred Scott *decision, which said the Constitution protected slavery.)* OL CA HR3.

S Skill Practice

Visual Literacy **Ask:** From the painting, what similarities and differences do you see between this debate and modern political debates? *(similarities: both candidates are well dressed, patriotic trappings surround them; differences: today only candidates are allowed on the stage)* OL

Resources for page 552

Primary Source Reading 12

Answers and Additional Support

US8.10.4 Discuss Abraham Lincoln's presidency and his significant writings and speeches and their relationship to the Declaration of Independence, such as his "House Divided" speech (1858), Gettysburg Address (1863), Emancipation Proclamation (1863), and inaugural addresses (1861 and 1865).

Lincoln and Douglas

Main Idea **The Lincoln-Douglas debates helped Lincoln emerge as a leader.**

Reading Connection If you really wanted something, what risks would you be willing to take? Read to learn how Lincoln, who was nearly unknown, challenged Douglas to a series of debates and emerged as a leader.

In the congressional election of 1858, the Senate race in Illinois was the center of national attention. The current senator, Democrat Stephen A. Douglas, ran against Republican challenger **Abraham Lincoln.** People considered Douglas a likely candidate for president in 1860. Lincoln was nearly an unknown.

Short and powerful, Douglas was called "the Little Giant." He disliked slavery but thought that the controversy over it would interfere with the nation's growth. He believed the issue could be resolved through popular sovereignty.

Born in the poor backcountry of Kentucky, Abraham Lincoln moved to Indiana as a child, and later to Illinois. Like Douglas, Lincoln was intelligent, ambitious, and a successful lawyer. Lincoln started his campaign with a memorable speech, in which he declared:

> **"A house divided against itself cannot stand. I believe this government cannot endure permanently half slave and half free. I do not expect the Union to be dissolved—I do not expect the house to fall—but I do expect it will cease to be divided. It will become all one thing or all the other."**

The Lincoln-Douglas Debates Not as well known as Douglas, Lincoln challenged the senator to a series of debates. Douglas reluctantly agreed. The two met seven times in August, September, and October of 1858 in towns throughout Illinois. Thousands came to these debates. The main **topic,** of course, was slavery. R

During the debate at Freeport, Lincoln questioned Douglas about his views on popular sovereignty. Could the people of a territory legally exclude slavery before achieving statehood? Douglas replied that the people could exclude slavery by refusing to pass laws protecting slaveholders' rights. Douglas's response, which satisfied antislavery followers but lost him support in the South, became known as the Freeport Doctrine. C

S

More Skill Practice

Making Inferences Have students read the quotes from Lincoln and Douglas. Then have them continue the dialogue by coming up with Douglas's response to Lincoln's statement, and vice versa. OL CA HI1.

More About the Art

This image, of the 1858 Lincoln-Douglas debate held in Charleston, was painted by Robert Marshall Root, an Illinois artist who lived from 1863 to 1937. The painting hangs in the Illinois governor's office; a copy is also displayed at the Lincoln-Douglas Debate Museum in Charleston.

US8.9.5 Analyze the significance of the States' Rights Doctrine, the Missouri Compromise (1820), the Wilmot Proviso (1846), the Compromise of 1850, Henry Clay's role in the Missouri Compromise and the Compromise of 1850, the Kansas-Nebraska Act (1854), the *Dred Scott* v. *Sandford* decision (1857), and the Lincoln-Douglas debates (1858).

Douglas claimed that Lincoln wanted African Americans to be fully equal to whites. Lincoln denied this. Still, Lincoln said, "in the right to eat the bread . . . which his own hand earns, [an African American] is my equal and the equal of [Senator] Douglas, and the equal of every living man." The real issue, Lincoln said, is "between the men who think slavery a wrong and those who do not think it wrong. The Republican Party thinks it wrong."

Following the debates, Douglas won a narrow victory in the election. Lincoln lost the election, but the debates had earned him a national reputation.

The Raid on Harpers Ferry After the 1858 elections, Southerners began to feel threatened by growing Republican power. In late 1859, an act of violence greatly increased their fears. On October 16, the abolitionist John Brown led 18 men, both whites and African Americans, on a raid on Harpers Ferry, Virginia. His target was an **arsenal** (AHR•suhn•uhl), a storage place for weapons and ammunition. Brown—who had killed five proslavery Kansans in 1856—hoped to start a rebellion against slaveholders by arming enslaved African Americans. His raid was financed by a group of abolitionists.

Brown and his men were quickly defeated by local citizens and federal troops. Brown was convicted of treason and murder and was sentenced to hang. His execution caused an uproar in the North. Some antislavery Northerners, including Republican leaders, denounced Brown's use of violence. Others viewed Brown as a hero. Writer Ralph Waldo Emerson called Brown a **martyr** (MAHR•tuhr)—a person who dies for a cause he believes in. R1 R2

John Brown's death became a rallying point for abolitionists. When Southerners learned of Brown's connection to abolitionists, their fears of a great Northern conspiracy against them seemed to be confirmed. The nation was nearing disaster.

Reading Check **Identify** What was John Brown's target when he led a raid on Harpers Ferry?

History Online
Study Central Need help understanding the nation's division on slavery? Visit ca.hss.glencoe.com and click on Study Central.

Section 4 Review

Reading Summary

Review the Main Ideas

- The Republican Party became a major political force, while the Supreme Court ruled in the *Dred Scott* case that the spread of slavery could not be restricted.
- Debates between Abraham Lincoln and Stephen Douglas helped put Lincoln in the national spotlight.

What Did You Learn?

1. Discuss the stages in the development of the Republican Party.
2. Who financed John Brown's raid on Harpers Ferry?

Critical Thinking

3. **Organizing Information** Re-create the table shown here, and describe the positions taken by Lincoln and Douglas in their debates. CA HI1.

Lincoln-Douglas Debates	
Lincoln's position	Douglas's position

4. **The Big Ideas** How did the *Dred Scott* decision reverse an earlier ruling made by Congress? CA HI2.
5. **Making Inferences** Why did Lincoln emerge as a leader after the Lincoln-Douglas debates? CA CS1.
6. **Descriptive Writing** Write a short biographical essay on either John Brown, Dred Scott, or Stephen Douglas. Include key events from the person's life that relate to events leading up to the Civil War. CA 8WA2.1.a

SECTION 4 REVIEW ANSWERS

Review questions reinforce content standard US8.9.

1. Northern Democrats left that party; Whig Party dissolved; anti-slavery Whigs and Democrats joined Free-Soilers to form Republicans.
2. a group of abolitionists
3. Lincoln: country cannot remain half slave and half free, all people have equal right to enjoy benefits of their work; Douglas: people could exclude slavery by not passing laws protecting it
4. **The Big Ideas** It ruled the Missouri Compromise unconstitutional.
5. Lincoln lost the election, but gained a national reputation.
6. Biographies should be accurate and show the impact of the subject's actions.

R1 Reading Strategy

Scaffolding—Academic Vocabulary The word *federal* was introduced in Chapter 10, Section 2. Ask a student to define the word. OL

R2 Reading Strategy

Understanding Vocabulary
Ask: Would you agree that John Brown was a martyr? Why or why not? *(Answers will vary but should reflect an understanding of the term's meaning.)* OL

ASSESS

Resources for page 553

Use these resources to assess student mastery of section content.

- Section Quiz 12–4
- Interactive Tutor Self-Assessment CD-ROM

Reading Check
Answer: an arsenal where ammunition and weapons were stored

History Online
Study Central provides summaries, interactive games, and online graphic organizers to help students review section content.

CLOSE

Analyzing Information
Ask: How did the ruling in *Dred Scott* v. *Sandford* heighten sectional division? *(Northerners saw it as spreading slavery; Southerners saw it as protecting their rights.)* OL CA HI2.

FOCUS

BELLRINGER
SKILLBUILDER ACTIVITY

Project **Daily Focus Skills Transparency 12–5** and have students answer the question.

Guide to Reading

Preteaching Vocabulary: Use the Vocabulary PuzzleMaker CD-ROM to create crossword and word search puzzles.

Answers to Graphic: Nov. 1860: Lincoln elected president; Dec. 1860: S.C. secedes; Feb. 1861: Confederacy formed; March 1861: Lincoln's inaugural; April 1861: attack on Fort Sumter begins Civil War

Unpacking the Standards

After reading the section, students will be able to:

- Describe how Abraham Lincoln won the election of 1860.
- Explain why South Carolina and other states seceded.
- Identify the significance of the Confederate attack on Fort Sumter.

Section 5

Secession and War

History Social Science Standards

US8.10 Students analyze the multiple causes, key events, and complex consequences of the Civil War.

Guide to Reading

Looking Back, Looking Ahead

As you know, the *Dred Scott* decision and John Brown's raid further divided the nation. Read to learn how the election of 1860 affected the possible disaster that faced the country.

Focusing on the Main Ideas

- A split occurred in the Democratic Party, which allowed Lincoln to win the election of 1860. *(page 555)*
- South Carolina led other Southern states in seceding from the Union. *(page 556)*
- The Civil War began when Confederate forces attacked Fort Sumter in South Carolina. *(page 558)*

Locating Places

South Carolina
Fort Sumter

Meeting People

John Crittenden
Jefferson Davis

Content Vocabulary

border states
secession (sih•SEH•shuhn)
states' rights

Academic Vocabulary

eventual (ih•VEHNT•shuh•wuhl)
justify
theory

Reading Strategy

Classifying Information As you read the section, re-create the time line below and list the major events at each time.

Nov. 1860 | Dec. 1860 | Feb. 1861 | Mar. 1861 | Apr. 1861

NATIONAL GEOGRAPHIC Where & When?

1860 — 1861 — 1862

Nov. 1860 Abraham Lincoln is elected president

Dec. 1860 South Carolina secedes

Feb. 1861 Southern states form the Confederate States of America

April 1861 Confederate forces attack Fort Sumter; Civil War begins

SECTION RESOURCES

Print Material
- Reproducible Lesson Plan 12–5*
- Daily Lesson and Discussion Notes 12–5
- Guided Reading Activity 12–5
- Reading Essentials and Study Guide 12–5
- Active Reading Note-Taking Guide 12–5
- Section Quiz 12–5

Transparencies
- Daily Focus Skills Transparency 12–5
- Section Graphic Organizer Transparency 12–5
- California Standards Practice Transparencies

Technology
- Interactive Tutor Self-Assessment CD-ROM
- Exam*View*® Pro Testmaker CD-ROM
- Presentation Plus! CD-ROM

*Available on TeacherWorks™

US8.10.4 Discuss Abraham Lincoln's presidency and his significant writings and speeches and their relationship to the Declaration of Independence, such as his "House Divided" speech (1858), Gettysburg Address (1863), Emancipation Proclamation (1863), and inaugural addresses (1861 and 1865).

The Election of 1860

Main Idea **A split occurred in the Democratic Party, which allowed Lincoln to win the election of 1860.**

Reading Connection Think of an issue that you feel strongly about. Do you think your views would affect your choice for president? Read to learn how the slavery issue affected the election of 1860.

An American Story

After John Brown's raid on Harpers Ferry, calls for secession grew. South Carolina's *Charleston Mercury* declared "The day of compromise is passed . . . [T]here is no peace for the South in the Union." The *Nashville Union and American* said, "The South will hold the whole party of Republicans responsible for the bloodshed at Harpers Ferry."

Republicans argued that secession was only a scare tactic, aimed at frightening voters from casting their ballot for Abraham Lincoln. To many Southerners, however, Lincoln's election would be a signal that their position in the Union was hopeless.

Many Parties Would the Union break up? That was the burning question in the months before the presidential election of 1860. The issue of slavery **eventually** caused a break in the Democratic Party. Northern Democrats nominated Stephen Douglas for the presidency and supported popular sovereignty. Southern Democrats—vowing to uphold slavery—nominated John C. Breckinridge of Kentucky and supported the *Dred Scott* decision. Southern Democrats denounced John Brown's raid as "among the gravest of crimes." Northern and Southern moderates formed the Constitutional Union Party and nominated John Bell of Tennessee. This party took no position on slavery. However, voters in the North and South would no longer tolerate neutrality on this important issue.

Lincoln Nominated The Republicans nominated Abraham Lincoln. Their platform, designed to attract voters from many quarters, was that slavery should be left undisturbed where it existed, but that it should be excluded from the territories. Many Southerners feared, however, that a Republican victory would encourage slave revolts.

Lincoln Elected Lincoln won a clear majority of the electoral votes—180 out of 303. He received 40 percent of the popular vote. Douglas was second with 30 percent of the vote.

The vote was along purely sectional lines. Lincoln's name did not even appear on the ballot in most Southern states, but he won every Northern state. Breckinridge swept the South, and Bell took most **border states.** These states were located between the North and the South. They were divided over whether to stay in the Union or join the Confederacy. Douglas won only the state of Missouri and three of New Jersey's seven electoral votes.

Reading Check **Examine** What caused the split in the Democratic Party in 1860?

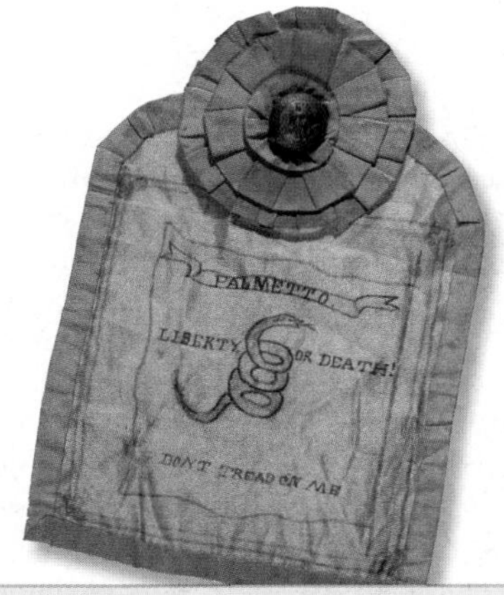

Picturing History

Patriots used these mottos on this secessionist ribbon during the American Revolution. ***What did they mean during the Revolution? Why do you think secessionists used these mottos?***

TEACH

C Critical Thinking

Making Inferences **Ask:** Given that the raid on Harpers Ferry did not succeed, and that it ended with John Brown's execution, why do you think this event led increasing numbers of Southerners to favor secession? *(They feared the raid signaled that the North was going to be more active against slavery.)* OL CA HI2.

R1 Reading Strategy

Organizing Information Have students use a two-column chart to record details about the political parties' stance on slavery prior to the 1860 election. Suggest they label the columns *Party* and *Stance on Slavery*. OL

U Universal Access

Logical/Mathematical **Ask:** How many electoral votes did a candidate need to win to win the election of 1860? *(152)* How many more than that did Lincoln win? *(28)* What percentage of the electoral votes did he win? *(59.4%)* OL

R2 Reading Strategy

Understanding Vocabulary Direct students to turn to the map on page 558. **Ask:** Which are the border states? *(Missouri, Kentucky, Maryland, and Delaware)* OL CA CS3.

Did You Know?

In April, 1860 delegates to the Democratic convention in Charleston cast 57 ballots without selecting a candidate before they decided to adjourn. They reconvened six weeks later in Baltimore.

Picturing History

Answer: During the Revolution, it meant that if colonists could not win freedom from Great Britain, then they would welcome death. On the secessionist ribbon, the motto meant that Southerners demanded freedom from what they saw as oppression by the Union.

Resources for page 555

♫ American Music: Hits Through History: "John Brown's Dream"

Reading Check

Answer: the issue of slavery

R1 Reading Strategy

Understanding Vocabulary Have students relate the term *seccession* to *secede.* *(Secession is the act of seceding.)* OL CA 8RW1.3

C Critical Thinking

Comparing and Contrasting Ask: How did Lincoln's response to Crittenden's plan differ from southern leaders' reaction? *(Both rejected the plan, though for different reasons.)* OL CA HI1.

R2 Reading Strategy

Activating Prior Knowledge Ask: What are earlier instances of the doctrine of states' rights? *(Kentucky and Virginia resolutions; nullification crisis)* OL CA HI3.

History Online

Objectives and answers to the student activity can be found in the Web Activity Lesson Plan feature at ca.hss.glencoe.com.

Answers and Additional Support

US8.10.3 Identify the constitutional issues posed by the doctrine of nullification and secession and the earliest origins of that doctrine. **US8.10.4** Discuss Abraham Lincoln's presidency and his significant writings and speeches and their relationship to the Declaration of Independence, such as his "House Divided" speech (1858), Gettysburg Address (1863), Emancipation Proclamation (1863), and inaugural addresses (1861 and 1865).

The South Secedes

Main Idea **South Carolina led other Southern states in seceding from the Union.**

Reading Connection Have you ever been so angry that you needed to leave a room? Read to find out about the South's decision to leave the Union.

In the election of 1860, the more populous North had outvoted the South. The victory for Lincoln was a short-lived one, however, for the nation Lincoln was to lead would soon disintegrate.

Lincoln and the Republicans had promised not to disturb slavery where it already existed. Many people in the South, however, did not trust the party, fearing that the Republican administration would not protect Southern rights. On December 20, 1860, the South's long-standing threat to leave the Union became a reality when **South Carolina** held a special convention and voted to secede.

Attempt at Compromise Even after South Carolina's action, many people still wished to preserve the Union. The question was *how.* As other Southern states debated **secession** (sih • SEH • shuhn)—withdrawal from the Union—leaders in Washington, D.C., worked frantically to fashion a last-minute compromise. On December 18, 1860, Senator **John Crittenden** of Kentucky proposed a series of amendments to the Constitution. Central to Crittenden's plan was a provision to protect slavery south of 36°30'N latitude—the line set by the Missouri Compromise—in all territories "now held or hereafter acquired."

Republicans considered this unacceptable. They had just won an election on the principle that slavery would not be extended in any territories. "Now we are told. . . ," Lincoln wrote,

> **"the government shall be broken up, unless we surrender to those we have beaten."**
>
> —*letter to James T. Hale, January 11, 1861*

Leaders in the South also rejected the plan. "We spit upon every plan to compromise," exclaimed one Southern leader. "No human power can save the Union," wrote another.

The Confederacy By February 1861, Texas, Louisiana, Mississippi, Alabama, Florida, and Georgia had joined South Carolina and also seceded. Delegates from these states and South Carolina met in Montgomery, Alabama, on February 4 to form a new nation and government. Calling themselves the Confederate States of America, or the Confederacy, they chose **Jefferson Davis,** a senator from Mississippi, as their president.

Southerners **justified** secession with the **theory** of **states' rights.** The states, they argued, had voluntarily chosen to enter the Union. They defined the Constitution as a contract among the independent states. Now because the national government had violated that contract—by refusing to enforce the Fugitive Slave Act and by denying the Southern states equal rights in the territories—the states felt justified in leaving the Union.

Reactions to Secession Many Southerners welcomed secession. Senator Albert Brown of Mississippi said in a speech to a Southern audience "disunion is a fearful thing, but emancipation is worse." In Charleston, South Carolina, people rang church bells, fired cannons, and celebrated in the streets. A newspaper in Atlanta, Georgia, said the South "will never submit" and would defend its liberties no matter what the cost.

Other Southerners, however, were alarmed. A South Carolinian wrote, "My heart has been rent [torn] by . . . the destruction of my country—the dismemberment of that great and glorious Union."

History Online

Student Web Activity Visit ca.hss.glencoe.com and click on *Chapter 12—Student Web Activities* for an activity on the period leading up to the Civil War.

Did You Know?

States seceded in this order: South Carolina, December 20, 1860; Mississippi, January 9, 1861; Florida, January 10, 1861; Alabama, January 11, 1861; Georgia, January 19, 1861; Louisiana, January 26, 1861; Texas, February 1, 1861; Virginia, April 17, 1861; Arkansas, May 6, 1861; North Carolina, May 20, 1861.

The Tennessee legislature adopted a "Declaration of Independence" on May 7, 1861—effectively breaking with the Union. Convention delegates did not formally accept secession until a referendum was passed on June 8, 1861.

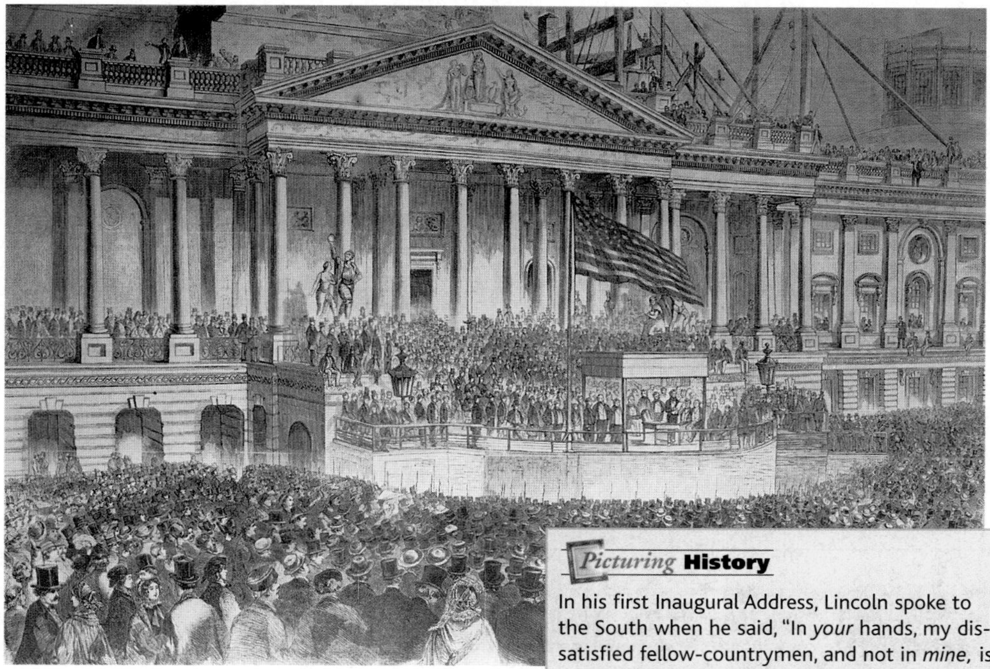

Picturing **History**

In his first Inaugural Address, Lincoln spoke to the South when he said, "In *your* hands, my dissatisfied fellow-countrymen, and not in *mine*, is the momentous issue of civil war." ***How did Southerners feel about secession?***

C1 Virginian Robert E. Lee expressed concern about the future. "I see only that a fearful calamity is upon us," he wrote.

W In the North, some abolitionists preferred to allow the Southern states to leave. If the Union could be kept together only by compromising on slavery, they declared, then let the Union be destroyed. Most Northerners, however, believed that the Union must be preserved. For Lincoln the issue was "whether in a free government the minority have the right to break up the government whenever they choose."

Presidential Responses Lincoln had won the election, but he was not yet president. James Buchanan's term ran until March 4, 1861. In December 1860, Buchanan sent a message to Congress saying that the Southern states had no right to secede. Then he added that he had no power to stop them from doing so.

As Lincoln prepared for his inauguration on March 4, 1861, people in both the North and the South wondered what he would say and do. They wondered, too, what would happen in Virginia, Maryland, North Carolina, Kentucky, Tennessee, Missouri, and Arkansas. These slave states had chosen to remain in the Union, but the decision was not final. If the United States used force against the Confederate States of America, the remaining slave states also might secede. In his Inaugural Address, the new president mixed toughness and words of peace. He said that secession would not be permitted, vowing to hold federal property in the South and to enforce the laws of the United States. At the same time, Lincoln pleaded with the people of the South for reconciliation:

> **"We are not enemies, but friends. We must not be enemies. Though passion may have strained, it must not break our bonds of affection."** C2
>
> —from *Inaugural Addresses of the Presidents*

Reading Check **Explain** How did the seceding states justify their right to leave the Union?

C1 Critical Thinking

Analyzing Primary Sources **Ask:** What do you think Lee was worried about? *(Students may say that he feared that the secession conflict would lead to war.)* OL CA HR5.

W Writing Support

Persuasive Writing Tell students to imagine they are a close advisor to President Lincoln. Have them write a letter to the president explaining why he should or should not let the Southern states leave the Union. OL CA 8WA2.4

C2 Critical Thinking

Analyzing Primary Sources Direct students to Lincoln's quote. **Ask:** What did Lincoln mean when he said that passion "must not break our bonds of affection"? *(that political differences should not destroy the Union)* How do you think Southerners would react to those words? *(Students should see that by this point Southerners would not respond to the message.)* OL CA HR5.

Reading Check

Answer: They believed their states' rights had been violated by the federal government, nullifying the contract between the states and the Union.

Did You Know?

Lincoln rejected the counsel of advisors and rode to his inauguration in an open carriage, where he was accompanied by President Buchanan. Roger Taney, Chief Justice of the Supreme Court, administered the oath of office for Lincoln—the seventh time Taney had performed this function.

Picturing **History**

Ask: What did Lincoln mean by saying that the issue lay in "your hands"? *(Students may say that he was telling the South that their actions would drive his response.)* OL

Answer: Some welcomed it, but others were alarmed.

R Reading Strategy

Identifying the Main Idea and Supporting Details Point students to the main idea of this part of the section. **Ask:** What are two details that support this idea? *(Davis ordered Confederate troops to attack Fort Sumter on April 12, 1861, before Union supplies arrived; thousands of Northerners volunteered to fight for the Union as a result; several more states then seceded.)* **OL** **CA 8RC2.2**

S Skill Practice

Historical and Social Sciences Analysis Skill **Ask:** Why did Lincoln vow to protect federal property in the South? *(That property belonged to the federal govenment, not to the individual states.)* **OL** **CA HI1.**

C Critical Thinking

Determining Cause and Effect **Ask:** Why do you think Lincoln decided to send only supplies rather than more soldiers? *(Students may say he was simply trying to give the soldiers in the fort what they needed or that he was trying to put the burden for starting the war on the South.)* **OL**

Answers and Additional Support

US8.10.6 Describe critical developments and events in the war, including the major battles, geographical advantages and obstacles, technological advances, and General Lee's surrender at Appomattox.

Fort Sumter

Main Idea **The Civil War began when Confederate forces attacked Fort Sumter in South Carolina.**

Reading Connection Have you ever been startled by a loud noise? Read to learn how Fort Sumter was attacked on April 12, 1861, and what it was like from inside the fort.

The South soon tested President Lincoln's vow to hold federal property. Confederate forces had already seized some United States forts within their states. Although Lincoln did not want to start a war by trying to take the forts back, allowing the Confederates to keep them would amount to admitting their right to secede.

On the day after his inauguration, Lincoln received a dispatch from Major Robert Anderson, the commander of **Fort Sumter,** a United States fort on an island guarding Charleston Harbor. The message warned that the fort was low on supplies and that the Confederates demanded its surrender.

The War Begins Lincoln responded by sending a message to Governor Francis Pickens of South Carolina. He informed Pickens that he was sending an unarmed expedition with supplies to Fort Sumter.

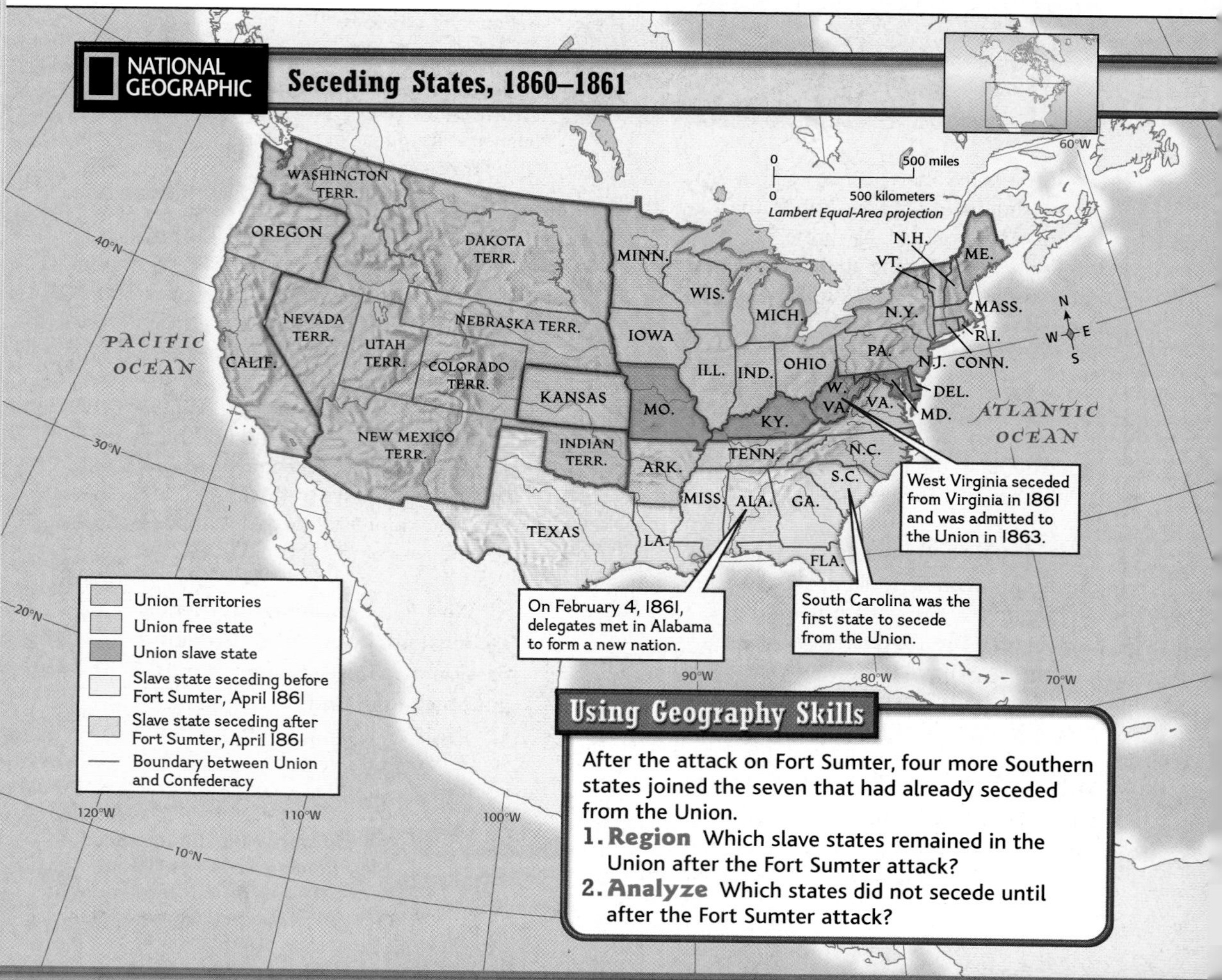

Using Geography Skills

After the attack on Fort Sumter, four more Southern states joined the seven that had already seceded from the Union.

1. **Region** Which slave states remained in the Union after the Fort Sumter attack?
2. **Analyze** Which states did not secede until after the Fort Sumter attack?

Using Geography Skills

Answers:

1. Missouri, Kentucky, Maryland, Delaware
2. Virginia, North Carolina, Tennessee, Arkansas

In-Text Map Transparency 12 Ask: What Union states had slavery? *(Missouri, Kentucky, West Virginia, Delaware, Maryland)* **OL**

Lincoln promised that Union forces would not "throw in men, arms, or ammunition" unless they were fired upon. The president thus left the decision to start shooting up to the Confederates.

Confederate president Jefferson Davis and his advisers made a fateful choice. They ordered their forces to attack Fort Sumter before the Union supplies could arrive. Confederate guns opened fire on the fort early on April 12, 1861. Union captain Abner Doubleday witnessed the attack from inside the fort:

> **"Showers of balls . . . and shells . . . poured into the fort in one incessant stream, causing great flakes of masonry to fall in all directions."**
>
> —as quoted in *Voices of the Civil War*

High seas had prevented Union relief ships from reaching the fort. The Union garrison held out for 33 hours before surrendering on April 14. Thousands of shots were exchanged during the siege, but no lives were lost on either side. The Confederates hoisted their flag over the fort, and all the guns in the harbor sounded a triumphant salute.

Once Fort Sumter was attacked, both the North and South took action. President Lincoln issued a call for 75,000 troops to fight to save the Union, and volunteers quickly signed up. Meanwhile, volunteers signed up to fight for the South, and Virginia, North Carolina, Tennessee, and Arkansas voted to join the Confederacy. The Civil War had begun.

Reading Check **Explain** What action did Lincoln take after the attack on Fort Sumter?

History Online
Study Central Need help understanding the election of 1860, secession, and war? Visit ca.hss.glencoe.com and click on Study Central.

Section 5 Review

Reading Summary

Review the Main Ideas

- In a contest in which votes were split between four candidates, Abraham Lincoln came out the winner of the 1860 presidential election.
- Following Lincoln's election, a number of Southern states seceded from the Union and formed the Confederate States of America.
- The Confederate attack on Fort Sumter in the harbor of Charleston, South Carolina, marked the beginning of the Civil War.

What Did You Learn?

1. What was Senator John Crittenden's last-minute proposal to save the Union?
2. Who served as the president of the Confederate States of America?

Critical Thinking

3. **Sequencing Events** Re-create the diagram below. Fill in the events leading up to the surrender of Fort Sumter and the start of the Civil War. CA CS2.

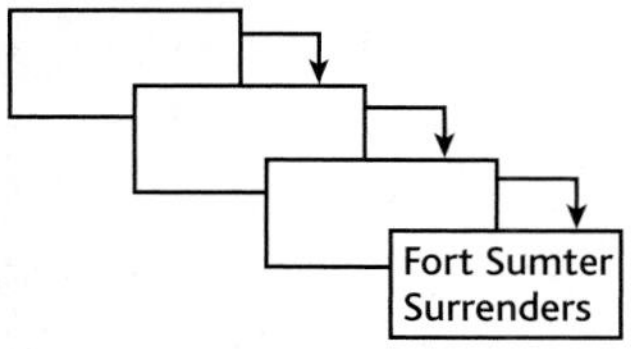

4. **The Big Ideas** What role did sectionalism play in Lincoln's victory in the 1860 election? CA CS1.
5. **Drawing Conclusions** Based on what you read, how would you describe President Lincoln's priorities as he took office in March 1861?
6. **Expository Writing** Write a paragraph describing what you consider to be key reasons for the Civil War. CA 8WA2.3

SECTION 5 REVIEW ANSWERS

Review questions reinforce content standard US8.10.

1. to allow slavery in current and future territories south of 36°30'N latitude
2. Jefferson Davis
3. Confederate troops demand surrender of Fort Sumter; Lincoln sends unarmed expedition to the fort; Confederates bombard the fort.
4. **The Big Ideas** Lincoln won in every Northern state; votes in the South were divided among three other candidates.
5. He was determined to preserve the Union by opposing secession and enforcing U.S. laws, and he hoped to prevent war from breaking out.
6. Paragraphs will vary but should reflect information in the chapter.

Review The Big Idea

Review the Big Idea for this section: "Differences in economic, political, and social beliefs and practices can lead to division within a nation and have lasting consequences." **Ask:** What differences led to the clash at Fort Sumter? *(Lincoln's vow to defend federal property; the South's resolve to oust the federal government from its land)* OL

ASSESS

Resources for page 559

Use these resources to assess student mastery of section content.

Section Quiz 12–5

Interactive Tutor Self-Assessment CD-ROM

Reading Check

Answer: called for 75,000 soldiers to fight to save the Union

History Online

Study Central provides summaries, interactive games, and online graphic organizers to help students review section content.

CLOSE

Drawing Conclusions

Although Confederates fired the first shots of the Civil War, Jefferson Davis argued that the North was to blame for having provoked the attack at Fort Sumter. **Ask:** In your opinion, which side began the war? Explain. *(Answers will vary, but should be supported with reasons.)* OL

FOCUS

Before reading the two passages, have students predict what they think the two presidents' main arguments will be. Then have them compare their predictions to the actual speeches.

TEACH

C Critical Thinking

Analyzing Primary Sources Point out that Lincoln makes two arguments—that the Southern states cannot secede because the Union is permanent and that the two sections cannot be separated for practical reasons. Have students write a response to the second position—do they think Lincoln was right or wrong? Why or why not? OL CA 8WA2.4

Answers and Additional Support

You Decide . . .

US8.10.5 Study the views and lives of leaders (e.g., Ulysses S. Grant, Jefferson Davis, Robert E. Lee) and soldiers on both sides of the war, including those of black soldiers and regiments.

Union or Confederacy?

President Abraham Lincoln and Jefferson Davis, president of the Confederacy, were inaugurated just several weeks apart. These excerpts from their Inaugural Addresses will help you understand differing points of view about secession from the United States in 1861.

Abraham Lincoln—Union

I hold, that . . . the Union of these States is perpetual [forever]. Perpetuity is implied, if not expressed, in the fundamental law of all national governments.

One section of our country believes slavery is right, and ought to be extended, while the other believes it is wrong, and ought not to be extended. This is the only substantial dispute. . . .

C Physically speaking, we cannot separate. We cannot remove our respective sections from each other, nor build an impassable wall between them. A husband and wife may be divorced, and go out of the presence, and beyond the reach of each other; but the different parts of our country cannot do this. . . .

In your hands, my dissatisfied fellow countrymen, and not in mine, is the momentous issue of civil war.

—from Abraham Lincoln's First Inaugural Address, March 4, 1861

Abraham Lincoln ▶

560

Extending the Content

The Confederate Constitution Delegates from the seven states that had seceded met in Montgomery, Alabama, on February 4, 1861, to draft a constitution for their newly formed nation. The next month, the delegates adopted the Confederate Constitution, which bears many similarities to the U.S. Constitution. Among the key differences: It stipulates that slavery would be permitted in states and territories; it bans protective tariffs; and it grants the president only one six-year term (along with a line-item veto).

Jefferson Davis—Confederacy

Our present condition [as a new confederacy] . . . illustrates the American idea that governments rest upon the consent of the governed, and that it is the right of the people to alter or abolish governments whenever they become destructive of the ends for which they were established. . . . In this they [the people of the Confederacy] merely asserted a right which the Declaration of Independence of 1776 had defined to be inalienable. . . . [I]t is by abuse of language that their act has been denominated [called] a revolution. They formed a new alliance, but within each State its government has remained, the rights of person and property have not been disturbed. . . . C1

As a necessity, not a choice, we have resorted to the remedy of separation; and henceforth our energies must be directed to the conduct of our own affairs, and the [continuation] of the Confederacy which we have formed. If a just perception of mutual interest shall permit us peaceably to pursue our separate political career, my most earnest desire will have been fulfilled. But if this be denied to us . . . [we will be forced] to appeal to arms. . . . C2

—from Jefferson Davis's Inaugural Address, February 18, 1861

◀ Jefferson Davis

You Be The Historian

DBQ Document-Based Questions

1. According to Lincoln, what was the major disagreement between the North and South?
2. What did Lincoln compare the United States to? CA HR3.
3. Did Lincoln and Davis say anything in their addresses that was similar? Explain. CA HR3.

You Decide . . .

C1 Critical Thinking

Analyzing Primary Sources
Ask: What fact does Davis state here? *(The Declaration of Independence said that people have the right to abolish their government when it abuses their rights.)* What opinion does he state? *(that the South faces a similar situation as that which led to the American Revolution)* **OL** CA HR5.

C2 Critical Thinking

Comparing and Contrasting Ask: According to Davis, why might armed conflict be necessary? *(if the North refuses to allow the Confederacy to exist in peace as a separate country)* How does Lincoln answer the same question? *(War will occur if the South pursues secession rather than returning to the Union.)* **OL** CA HR3.

ASSESS/CLOSE

Have students answer the You Be the Historian questions. Then organize a class debate on whether secession was legal or a violation of the Constitution. Following the debate, students may want to vote to decide which argument was more persuasive. **OL**

You Be The Historian

1. the issue of whether slavery was right and should be extended or wrong and should not be extended
2. a husband and wife who divorce
3. Both hinted that war might be necessary to resolve the issue.

Analyzing Primary Sources

FOCUS

History–Social Science Standards

The following standards are covered on pages 562–563.

US8.9 Students analyze the early and steady attempts to abolish slavery and to realize the ideals of the Declaration of Independence.

US8.10 Students analyze the multiple causes, key events, and complex consequences of the Civil War.

TEACH

C1 Critical Thinking

Historical and Social Sciences Analysis Skill
Ask: Did Garrison's "severity" help produce the Civil War? *(Answers should be supported by reasons.)* OL CA HI5.

C2 Critical Thinking

Analyzing Primary Sources Ask: Why does Garrison choose the examples he uses to explain why he will not "write with moderation"? *(to underscore his belief that the situation with slavery is an emergency)* OL CA 8RW1.1

Answers and Additional Support

Analyzing Primary Sources

US8.9 Students analyze the early and steady attempts to abolish slavery and to realize the ideals of the Declaration of Independence.

Challenging Slavery

In the days leading up to the Civil War, people throughout the United States debated about economics, states' rights, and the institution of slavery. Antislavery society and religious group members were vocal, as were politicians, businesspeople, and plantation owners. In some cases, the voices of both free and enslaved African Americans could be heard.

Read the passages on pages 562 and 563 and answer the questions that follow.

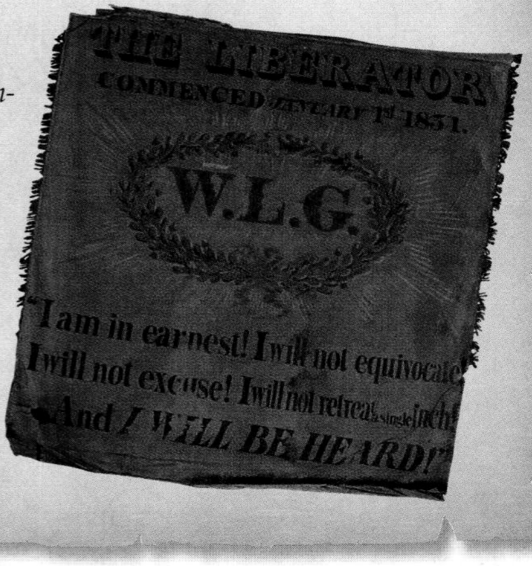

Banner celebrating Garrison's abolitionist newspaper, *The Liberator* ▶

Reader's Dictionary

severity (suh • VEHR • uh • tee): being strict, stern, or harsh

moderation (MAH • duh • RAY • shuhn): limiting or controlling something so as not to be extreme or excessive

ravisher: one who carries somebody or something off by violent force

extricate (EHK • struh • KAYT): to release somebody or something with difficulty from being constrained

equivocate (ih • KWIH • vuh • KAYT): to speak vaguely, especially in order to mislead

dissolution (DIH • suh • LOO • shun): the act or process of dissolving

atone (uh • TOHN): to make amends

The Liberator

Through his newspaper, The Liberator, *abolitionist William Lloyd Garrison demanded the immediate emancipation of all slaves. Founded in 1831 in Boston,* The Liberator *continued publishing antislavery messages under Garrison's leadership for 35 years. In one edition, he wrote:*

C1 [I support] the "self-evident truth" . . . that all men are created equal, and endowed by their Creator with certain inalienable rights. . . .

I am aware that many object to the **severity** of my language; but is there not cause for severity? I *will be* as harsh as truth and as uncompromising as justice. On this subject I do not wish to think or speak, or write with **moderation.** No! No! Tell a man whose house is on fire to give a moderate alarm; tell him to moderately rescue his wife from the hands of a **ravisher;** tell the mother to gradually **extricate** her babe from the fire into which it has fallen—but urge me not to use moderation in a cause like the present. I am in earnest; I will not **equivocate;** I will not excuse; I will not retreat a single inch—AND I WILL BE HEARD. . . . C2

EXTENDING THE CONTENT

Challenging Slavery After fugitive Anthony Burns was captured in Boston and returned South, Garrison made a dramatic gesture to show his anger. On the Fourth of July, little over a month after Burns's capture, Garrison burned copies of the Fugitive Slave Law and the Constitution itself. "So perish all compromises with tyranny," he said, "and let the people say Amen!"

On the Eve of War

Mrs. Eugene McLean kept a diary of her experiences as an Army officer's wife during the Civil War. This passage describes her thoughts after the fall of Fort Sumter. Her husband joined the Confederate Army.

Strange, strange, strange, how we have accustomed ourselves to the thought, and accept the **dissolution** of the Union as a natural consequence! Whom have we to blame for bringing us to this state . . . ? Wherever the fault lies, I do not envy them their feelings in this hour, and fear both sections will **atone** in mourning and ashes for the crime.

Swing Low, Sweet Chariot

Spirituals—songs of salvation—provided the enslaved African Americans who wrote and sang them with not only a measure of comfort in bleak times but with a means for communicating secretly among themselves. Here is an example of a popular song that was sung by enslaved African Americans at work:

Swing low, sweet chariot,
Coming for to carry me home,
Swing low, sweet chariot,
Coming for to carry me home.
I looked over Jordan, and what did I see,
Coming for to carry me home;
A band of angels coming after me,
Coming for to carry me home.
If you get there before I do,
Coming for to carry me home;
Tell all my friends I'm coming too,
Coming for to carry me home.
Swing low, sweet chariot,
Coming for to carry me home,
Swing low, sweet chariot,
Coming for to carry me home.

—*Selected Famous Negro Spirituals*

▲ The spiritual is a unique and important part of African American history.

DBQ Document-Based Questions

The Liberator

1. Who do you think Garrison is referring to when he states that he is aware that many object to the severity of his language?
2. What analogies does Garrison use to make his point about the need for severity over moderation?

On the Eve of War

3. How does the author feel about secession?
4. Does she blame either the Union or the Confederacy for the war? Explain.

Swing Low, Sweet Chariot

5. What does the phrase "swing low, sweet chariot" mean? What is meant by the lines "If you get there before I do . . . Tell all my friends I'm coming too"?
6. Why do you think enslaved African Americans sang this song?

Read to Write

7. Review each of the readings. Do you think these were written to inform, to entertain, to tell a story, or to persuade the reader? Write a one-page paper and give reasons for your answer. CA 8WA2.4

Analyzing Primary Sources

C Critical Thinking

Analyzing Primary Sources
Ask: How do the writer's views compare with Jefferson Davis's in his inaugural address? *(Students should see that Davis would agree with the writer that the Union, if it uses force, is guilty of coercion.)* OL CA HR5.

R Reading Strategy

Connecting Explain that the song refers to the Jordan River, which was in the land of Canaan that the ancient Israelites called the Promised Land. The Israelites believed that they were saved by God from slavery in Egypt. **Ask:** Why would enslaved African Americans refer to that river? *(Students should see that they saw the Israelites' situation as similar to their own and prayed for their own release from slavery.)* What other meaning could the river have? OL

ASSESS

Have students answer the Document-Based Questions.

CLOSE

Summarizing Have students write a brief description of the anti-slavery movement or the events that led up to and immediately followed Fort Sumter that incorporates quotations from at least two of the sources in this feature. OL CA 8WA2.1

DBQ Document-Based Questions

1. proslavery people, but also probably some anti-slavery people
2. to a person whose house is on fire; someone whose spouse is being attacked; and a parent whose child is in a fire
3. her feelings seem negative
4. both; she says "wherever the fault lies"
5. Students may suggest it refers to death, since angels await the chariot, or that it is a symbol for freedom.
6. Students may suggest that death would represent a release from slavery or that the chariot is the vehicle that will carry them to freedom on earth.
7. Answers will vary.

CHAPTER 12 Assessment

Resources for pages 564–565

Use these resources to review, assess, or reteach the chapter.

- Active Reading Note-Taking Guide, Chapter 12
- Chapter 12 Reading Essentials and Study Guide
- Chapter 12 Tests, Forms A and B
- Standards Assessment, Forms A and B
- California Standards Practice Workbook
- Succeeding on the California History-Social Science Standards CD-ROM
- MindJogger Videoquiz
- Interactive Tutor Self-Assessment CD-ROM

Review Content Vocabulary

1. Paragraphs will vary but should reflect information in the chapter.

Review the Main Ideas

2. He attracted thousands to join anti-slavery groups he had founded; he also started his own newspaper.
3. to resettle African Americans in Africa or the Caribbean
4. to ease tension between the North and South by preserving the balance between slave and free states in Congress
5. California admitted as a free state; no restrictions on slavery in New Mexico Territory; border dispute between New Mexico and Texas settled in favor of New Mexico; slave trade, but not slavery, abolished in D.C.; fugitive slave law strengthened

Chapter 12 Assessment

Standards US8.9 & US8.10

Review Content Vocabulary

1. Use the following terms to write a brief paragraph describing events in the United States just prior to 1860.

   secede
   fugitive
   civil war
   abolitionist

Review the Main Ideas

Section 1 • Abolitionists

2. How was William Lloyd Garrison effective in the antislavery movement?
3. What was the purpose of the American Colonization Society?

Section 2 • Slavery and the West

4. What was the purpose of the Missouri Compromise?
5. List the five parts of the Compromise of 1850.

Section 3 • A Nation Dividing

6. What was Stephen Douglas's solution to the slavery issue in the Kansas and Nebraska territories?
7. How did abolitionists and African Americans resist the Fugitive Slave Act?

Section 4 • Challenges to Slavery

8. How did Abraham Lincoln become a national figure in politics?
9. What was the *Dred Scott* decision? What did it mean for those opposed to slavery?

Section 5 • Secession and War

10. Why were there four parties and candidates in the presidential election of 1860?
11. How did Lincoln plan to prevent secession?

Critical Thinking

12. **Evaluate** Why was the balance of free and slave states in the Senate such an important issue? CA HR3.
13. **Analyze** What contributions did Frederick Douglass make to the abolitionist movement? Was he successful? Describe your conclusions in a paragraph. CA HI2.

Geography Skills

Study the map below and answer the following questions. CA CS3.

NATIONAL GEOGRAPHIC **Election of 1860**

Candidate	Electoral Vote	Popular Vote	Political Party
Lincoln	180	1,865,593	Republican
Breckinridge	72	848,356	Southern Democrat
Bell	39	592,906	Constitutional Union
Douglas	12	1,382,713	Northern Democrat

14. **Location** Which states supported Douglas?
15. **Region** In what region(s) was the Republican Party strongest?
16. **Region** In what region did Breckinridge find support?

6. the Kansas-Nebraska Act, which abandoned the Missouri Compromise and used popular sovereignty to determine if slavery would be allowed in Kansas and Nebraska
7. by helping them escape via the Underground Railroad
8. through a series of debates with Stephen Douglas in the 1858 Senate campaign
9. a Supreme Court ruling that declared that enslaved African Americans were property, stated that neither Congress nor voters could prohibit slavery; and ruled that the Constitution protected slavery; it meant they had no hope of ending it without amending the Constitution
10. The issue of slavery divided the Democratic Party into three factions, and the Republican Party provided the fourth candidate.
11. He vowed to hold federal property in the South and enforce U.S. laws.

History Online

Self-Check Quiz Visit ca.hss.glencoe.com to prepare for the Chapter 12 test.

Read to Write

17. **The Big Ideas** **Conflict and War** Make a list of 10 important events that you read about in this chapter. Select the two events that you think did the most to create conflict between the North and South. Write a one-page essay in which you explain how these events led to war. CA 8WS1.1

18. **Using Your FOLDABLES** Use the information you listed in your foldable to create a brief study guide for the chapter. For each section, your study guide should include at least five questions that focus on the main ideas. CA 8RC2.0

Using Academic Vocabulary

19. Write two words that are related to each of the following academic vocabulary words.

publication **controversy** **inevitable**

Building Citizenship

20. **Making Compromises** With a partner, think of a controversial issue that is a source of disagreement today. Take opposite sides on the issue; then work together to come up with a list of three compromises that would make the solution to this problem acceptable to both sides. CA CS1.

Linking Past and Present

21. **Political Parties** Search the Internet for a list of political parties in existence today. Research to find the date that the party was founded and its current goals. Create a table that briefly summarizes this information. Then compare your table to the political parties discussed in Chapter 12. CA 8WS1.4

Reviewing Skills

22. **Review READING SKILL** **Making Inferences** Reread Jefferson Davis's Inaugural Address on page 561. How do you think Davis feels about his new role? How does he feel about the prospect of war? Write a paragraph explaining your conclusions. CA 8RC2.0

23. **Review ANALYSIS SKILL** **Sequencing Information** Draw two time lines highlighting key figures, dates, and milestones in the abolitionist movement and the political battle over slavery. CA CS2.

Standards Practice

Use the map below to answer the following question.

The Compromise of 1850

24 **Which of the following statements is true?**

A The Compromise of 1850 allowed the Oregon Territory to be open to slaveholding.

B The Compromise of 1850 did not make any land on the Pacific Ocean open to slaveholding.

C The Compromise of 1850 made every state touching the southern border of the United States open to slaveholding.

D The Compromise of 1850 gave the Minnesota Territory the authority to choose whether it would allow slaveholding.

CHAPTER 12 Assessment

Using Academic Vocabulary

19. publication, publisher; controversial, uncontroversial; evitable, inevitability

Building Citizenship

20. Students should choose a controversial issue and identify three compromises that would be acceptable to both sides.

Linking Past and Present

21. Tables should reflect text information.

Reviewing Skills

22. **Review READING SKILL** Davis says that the South did not choose to secede and suggests that he wants to avoid war.

23. **Review ANALYSIS SKILL** Time lines should reflect text information.

Standards Practice

24. B

Bonus Question

Ask: When did the Republican Party first field a presidential candidate? *(1856)* **OL**

Critical Thinking

12. If the balance was upset, one section of the country would have more decision-making power than the other.

13. Douglass was an effective speaker who often moved listeners to tears and edited the *North Star*.

Geography Skills

14. Missouri. (He also received three of New Jersey's seven electoral votes.)

15. Northeast, upper Midwest, and West Coast

16. South

Read to Write

17. **The Big Ideas** Answers should be supported by reasons.

18. Using Your **FOLDABLES** Questions will vary but should be related directly to the main ideas.

History Online

Have students visit the Web site at ca.hss.glencoe.com to review Chapter 12 and take the **Self-Check Quiz.**

Chapter 13 Planning Guide

SECTION RESOURCES

Main Ideas	Print Materials	Technology Resources
Section 1: The Two Sides 1. Both the North and South had strengths and weaknesses that helped determine their military strategies. 2. Soldiers in the Civil War came from every region, and each side expected an early victory.	• Reproducible Lesson Plan 13–1* • Daily Lesson and Discussion Notes 13–1 • Active Reading Note-Taking Guide 13–1 • Reading Essentials and Study Guide 13–1 • Guided Reading Activity 13–1 • Section Quiz 13–1	Daily Focus Skills Transparency 13–1 Section Graphic Organizer Transparency 13–1 California Standards Practice Transparency Interactive Tutor Self-Assessment CD-ROM Exam*View*® Pro Testmaker CD-ROM Presentation Plus! CD-ROM
Section 2: Early Years of the War 1. The North realized with the first major battle that the war would be a long, difficult struggle. 2. The North set up a blockade along the South's coastline. 3. The action shifted to the West after the First Battle of Bull Run. 4. Lincoln removed General McClellan for his failure to act in some battles.	• Reproducible Lesson Plan 13–2* • Daily Lesson and Discussion Notes 13–2 • Active Reading Note-Taking Guide 13–2 • Reading Essentials and Study Guide 13–2 • Guided Reading Activity 13–2 • Section Quiz 13–2	Daily Focus Skills Transparency 13–2 Section Graphic Organizer Transparency 13–2 California Standards Practice Transparency Interactive Tutor Self-Assessment CD-ROM Exam*View*® Pro Testmaker CD-ROM Presentation Plus! CD-ROM
Section 3: A Call to Freedom 1. Lincoln signed the Emancipation Proclamation, which led to the passing of the Thirteenth Amendment. 2. The Civil War provided opportunities for African Americans to contribute to the war effort.	• Reproducible Lesson Plan 13–3* • Daily Lesson and Discussion Notes 13–3 • Active Reading Note-Taking Guide 13–3 • Reading Essentials and Study Guide 13–3 • Guided Reading Activity 13–3 • Section Quiz 13–3	Daily Focus Skills Transparency 13–3 Section Graphic Organizer Transparency 13–3 California Standards Practice Transparency Interactive Tutor Self-Assessment CD-ROM Exam*View*® Pro Testmaker CD-ROM Presentation Plus! CD-ROM
Section 4: Life During the Civil War 1. Everyone suffered terrible hardships and faced new challenges. 2. Many women took on new responsibilities during the war. 3. Union and Confederate war efforts faced opposition. 4. The war created economic problems.	• Reproducible Lesson Plan 13–4* • Daily Lesson and Discussion Notes 13–4 • Active Reading Note-Taking Guide 13–4 • Reading Essentials and Study Guide 13–4 • Guided Reading Activity 13–4 • Section Quiz 13–4	Daily Focus Skills Transparency 13–4 Section Graphic Organizer Transparency 13–4 California Standards Practice Transparency Interactive Tutor Self-Assessment CD-ROM Exam*View*® Pro Testmaker CD-ROM Presentation Plus! CD-ROM
Section 5: The Way to Victory 1. A turning point in the war occurred when Union forces won in Gettysburg and Vicksburg. 2. The end of war was in sight with Sherman's capture of Atlanta and Grant's pursuit of the Confederates. 3. After four years of war, the Northern forces defeated the Southern forces.	• Reproducible Lesson Plan 13–5* • Daily Lesson and Discussion Notes 13–5 • Active Reading Note-Taking Guide 13–5 • Reading Essentials and Study Guide 13–5 • Guided Reading Activity 13–5 • Section Quiz 13–5	Daily Focus Skills Transparency 13–5 Section Graphic Organizer Transparency 13–5 California Standards Practice Transparency Interactive Tutor Self-Assessment CD-ROM Exam*View*® Pro Testmaker CD-ROM Presentation Plus! CD-ROM Vocabulary PuzzleMaker CD-ROM

PACING YOUR LESSONS

Chapter Introduction	Section 1	Section 2	Section 3	Section 4	Section 5	Chapter Assessment	
$\frac{1}{2}$ Day	2 Days	2 Days	1 Day	2 Days	3 Days	$\frac{1}{2}$ Day	

0:00 **OUT OF TIME?** Assign the Chapter 13 ***Reading Essentials and Study Guide***

*Available on TeacherWorks™

Standards-Based Lesson Plan

History–Social Science Standards Covered in Chapter 13

The standards covered in the chapter are listed below. Use the accompanying activity as you teach the chapter to ensure student mastery of these standards. This activity can be used in combination with the program's print and technology assessment materials.

Standard	Section 1	2	3	4	5
US8.10 Students analyze the multiple causes, key events, and complex consequences of the Civil War.	✔	✔	✔	✔	✔
US8.10.2 Trace the boundaries constituting the North and the South, the geographical differences between the two regions, and the differences between agrarians and industrialists.	✔				
US8.10.4 Discuss Abraham Lincoln's presidency and his significant writings and speeches and their relationship to the Declaration of Independence, such as his "house Divided" speech (1858), Gettysburg Address (1863), Emancipation Proclamation (1863), and inaugural addresses (1861 and 1865).			✔		✔
US8.10.5 Study the views and lives of leaders (e.g., Ulysses S. Grant, Jefferson Davis, Robert E. Lee) and soldiers on both sides of the war, including those of black soldiers and regiments.	✔	✔	✔	✔	✔
US8.10.6 Describe critical developments and events in the war, including the major battles, geographical advantages and obstacles, technological advances, and General Lee's surrender at Appomattox.		✔	✔		✔
US8.10.7 Explain how the war affected combatants, civilians, the physical environment, and future warfare.		✔		✔	✔

Cumulative Standards-Assessment Activity

The Cumulative Standards-Assessment Activity will help students organize and learn the important information from the chapter. Begin teaching the chapter with this activity, and have students complete it as they read the chapter.

Creating a Diagram for Comparing and Contrasting

Purpose Comparing and contrasting is a technique useful for finding the similarities and differences between people, movements, or ideas. This tool is particularly useful when studying two sides in a conflict or two regions of a country, as in this chapter.

Introduction to Comparing and Contrasting

1. Demonstrate the technique by asking students to identify the differences between the Northern and Southern states in politics, economics, and society. Encourage students to try to identify areas where the two sections agreed.
2. Ask students to copy this chart into their notebooks:

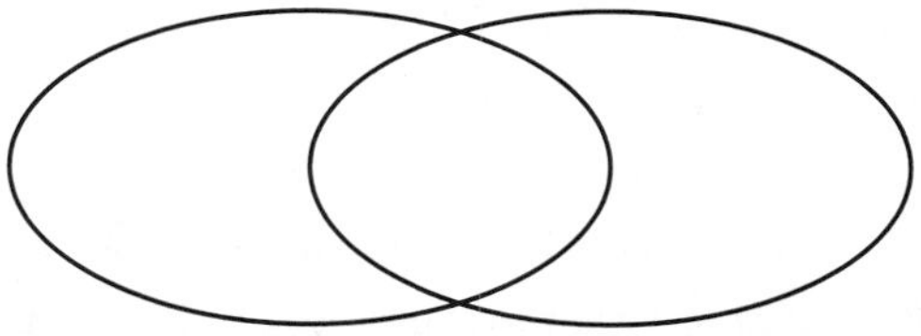

As students read each section, have them use different diagrams to compare and contrast the information they read. For instance, they could use the diagram to show the relative strengths and weaknesses of the North and South, battles won by each side, or the impact of the war on civilians in the two regions. Remind them to use the overlapping area for statements true of both sections.

3. As you review the chapter, divide the class into groups and have students share their comparison and contrast charts. Have the groups describe their charts, and encourage students to add to their own charts. Suggest that all students use their charts as study aids.

Chapter 13 Resources

READING SUPPORT

- Content Vocabulary Activity 13
- Academic Vocabulary Activity 13
- Reading Skills Activity 13
- American Literature Reading 13
- Biography Activities 13A–13C
- Chapter 13 Active Reading Note-Taking Guide
- Chapter 13 Guided Reading Activities
- Chapter 13 Reading Essentials and Study Guide
- Glencoe Literature Library
- Glencoe Video Program
- Vocabulary PuzzleMaker CD-ROM
- Interactive Graphic Organizers CD-ROM
- American History Primary Source Document Library CD-ROM

CRITICAL THINKING

- Critical Thinking Skills Activity 13
- Primary Source Reading 13
- Cause-and-Effect Transparency 13, Strategy, and Activity
- Presentation Plus! CD-ROM

UNIVERSAL ACCESS

- Universal Access Activity 13
- Then and Now Transparencies 13A–13B, Strategy, and Activity
- Graphic Novel Activity 13
- School-to-Home Connection Activities 13A–13D
- English Learner Handbook Chapter 13 Activities
- Universal Access for the American History Classroom
- Moments in Time
- American Art and Architecture Transparencies, Strategies, and Activities
- American Art Prints
- American Music Cultural Traditions
- American Music Hits Through History
- StudentWorks Plus CD-ROM

SKILL PRACTICE

- Map Overlay Transparency 13, Strategy, and Activity
- Analysis Skills Activity 13
- Time Line Activity 13
- Geography and History Activity 13
- Economics and History Activity 13
- Chart, Graph, and Map Skills Activity 13
- Political Cartoon Activity 13
- Supreme Court Case Study 13
- In-Text Map Transparency 13, Strategy, and Activity
- Step Into American History Activity 13
- Citizenship and Service Learning Activity 13
- Outline Map Resource Book
- MindJogger Plus Videoquiz

WRITING SUPPORT

- Writing Activity 13
- Language Arts Activity 13
- Writer's Guidebook
- Middle School Writing Process Transparencies

ASSESSMENT

Glencoe's Assessment Advantage

- Chapter 13 Section Quizzes
- Chapter 13 Tests, Forms A and B
- California Standards Assessment, Forms A and B
- Cumulative Assessment Activity US8.10
- California Standards Practice Workbook
- Succeeding on the California History–Social Science Standards CD-ROM
- Exam*View*® Pro Testmaker CD-ROM
- Interactive Tutor Self-Assessment CD-ROM

CD-ROM	Transparency
DVD	Music Program
Print Material	Videocassette
Poster	Glencoe Literature Library

Chapter 13 Resources

TECHNOLOGY

- StudentWorks Plus CD-ROM
- TeacherWorks Plus CD-ROM
- Exam*View*® Pro Testmaker CD-ROM
- Interactive Tutor Self-Assessment CD-ROM
- Presentation Plus! CD-ROM
- Succeeding on the California History–Social Science Standards CD-ROM
- Vocabulary PuzzleMaker CD-ROM
- Interactive Graphic Organizers CD-ROM
- Interactive Time Line CD-ROM
- American History Primary Source Document Library CD-ROM
- MindJogger Plus Videoquiz
- American Music Cultural Traditions
- American Music Hits Through History
- Glencoe Video Program
- Professional Development in Middle School Social Studies Series
- Teaching American History With *Discovering Our Past: The American Journey to World War I*

SPANISH RESOURCES

- Spanish Activities and Assessment
  - Spanish Content Vocabulary Activities
  - Spanish Guided Reading Activities
  - Spanish Quizzes and Tests
  - Spanish California Standards Assessment
- Spanish Reading Essentials and Study Guide
- Spanish School-to-Home Connection
- Spanish Declaration of Independence and U.S. Constitution

TRANSPARENCIES

- California Standards Practice Transparencies
- Daily Focus Skills Transparencies
- Section Graphic Organizer Transparencies
- In-Text Map Transparencies
- Map Overlay Transparencies
- Cause-and-Effect Transparencies
- Then and Now Transparencies
- American Art and Architecture Transparencies
- Middle School Writing Process Transparencies

TEACHER PLANNING

- Daily Lesson and Discussion Notes
- English Learner Handbook
- Guide to Daily Intervention
- *Discovering Our Past: The American Journey to World War I* Reading and Study Skills Foldables
- Reading Strategies and Activities for the Social Studies Classroom
- Chapter 13 Reproducible Lesson Plans (correlated to California History-Social Science Standards)
- Universal Access for the American History Classroom
- NGS U.S. Desk Map
- NGS U.S. Atlas

PROFESSIONAL DEVELOPMENT

- Building Academic Vocabulary
- Strategies for Success
- Research-Based Strategies Used to Develop *Discovering Our Past: The American Journey to World War I*
- Character Education in the Middle School Classroom
- The Living Constitution
- Professional Development in Middle School Social Studies Video Series
- Teaching American History With *Discovering Our Past: The American Journey to World War I*

MASTERING THE STANDARDS

The content and assessment in the Student Edition, Teacher Wraparound Edition, teacher planning materials, and the print and technology products are all standards-based. The use of these products during instruction leads to mastery of the standards.

PRACTICE
- California Standards Practice Workbook
- California Standards Practice Transparencies
- Interactive Time Line CD-ROM
- School-to-Home Connection

BENCHMARK ASSESSMENT
- California Standards Assessment
- Exam*View*® Pro Testmaker CD-ROM
- Succeeding on the California History–Social Science Standards CD-ROM

REMEDIATION
- California Guide to Daily Intervention
- Interactive Tutor Self-Assessment CD-ROM
- Exam*View*® Pro Testmaker CD-ROM
- California Standards Practice Workbook
- Reading Essentials and Study Guide

Additional Resources

NATIONAL GEOGRAPHIC TEACHER'S CORNER

Index to National Geographic Magazine:
The following articles relate to this chapter:

- "Colonial Florida Fort Recalls a Shining Moment in Black History," Geographica, February 1997.
- "The Cruelest Commerce: African Slave Trade," by Colin Palmer, September 1992.

National Geographic Society Products
To order the following, call National Geographic at 1-800-368-2728

- *GeoKit: The Civil War* (Kit)
- *GeoKit: Immigration* (Kit)
- *United States/Territorial Growth* (Map)
- *National Geographic Desk Reference* (Book)
- *Battlefields of the Civil War* (Map)

NGS ONLINE

Access National Geographic's new dynamic MapMachine Web site and other geography resources at:

www.nationalgeographic.com
www.nationalgeographic.com/maps

A&E HOME VIDEO. Biography. THE HISTORY CHANNEL.

The following videotape programs are available from Glencoe as supplements to Chapter 13.

- **Abraham Lincoln: Preserving the Union (ISBN 0-7670-0034-X)**
- **American Civil War (ISBN 0-7670-0102-8)**
- **Images of the Civil War (ISBN 0-56501-171-6)**

To order, call Glencoe at 1-800-334-7344. To find classroom resources to accompany many of these videos, check the following home pages:

A&E Television: www.aetv.com
The History Channel: www.historychannel.com

History Online

Use our Web site for additional resources. All essential content is covered in the Student Edition.

You and your students can visit ca.hss.glencoe.com, the Web site companion to *Discovering Our Past: The American Journey to World War I*. This innovative integration of electronic and print media offers your students a wealth of opportunities. The student text directs students to the Web site for the following options:

- Chapter Overviews
- Self-Check Quizzes
- Study Central™
- Student Web Activities
- Textbook Updates
- Multi-Language Glossaries

Answers to the student Web activities are provided for you in the Web Activity Lesson Plans. Additional Web resources and ePuzzles and games are also available.

FOLDABLES™ Study Organizer

Dinah Zike's Foldables

Foldables are three-dimensional, interactive graphic organizers that help students practice basic writing skills, review key vocabulary terms, and identify main ideas. Every chapter contains a foldable activity, with additional chapter activities found in the Reading and Study Skills Foldables booklet.

Chapter 13 Resources

Reading List Generator CD-ROM

GLENCOE **BOOKLINK**

The Glencoe BookLink CD-ROM is a database that allows you to search more than 15,000 titles to create a customized reading list for your students.

- Reading lists can be organized by students' reading level, author, genre, theme, or area of interest.
- The database provides Degrees of Reading Power™ (DRP) and Lexile™ readability scores for all selections.
- A brief summary of each selection is included.

Reading level suggestions for this chapter:

For students at a Grade 6 reading level:
- ***Commander in Chief: Abraham Lincoln and the Civil War,*** by Albert Marrin

For students at a Grade 7 reading level:
- ***Women in the Civil War: Warriors, Patriots, Nurses, and Spies,*** by Phyllis Raybin Emert

For students at a Grade 8 reading level:
- ***The Day Fort Sumter Was Fired On,*** by Jim Haskins

For students at a Grade 9 reading level:
- ***Portraits of War: Civil War Photographers and Their Work,*** by George Sullivan

READING SUPPORT FROM JAMESTOWN EDUCATION

- *Timed Readings Plus in Social Studies* helps students increase their reading rate and fluency while maintaining comprehension. The 400-word passages are similar to those found on state and national assessments.
- *Reading in the Content Area: Social Studies* concentrates on six essential reading skills that help students better comprehend what they read. The book includes 754 high-interest nonfiction passages written at increasing levels of difficulty.
- *Reading Fluency* helps students read smoothly, accurately, and expressively.
- *Jamestown's Reading Improvement,* by renowned reading expert Edward Fry, focuses on helping build your students' comprehension, vocabulary, and skimming and scanning skills.
- *Critical Reading Series* provides high-interest books, each written at three reading levels.

To order these products, call Glencoe at 1-800-334-7344.

KEY for Using the Teacher Wraparound Edition

Use this key to help you identify the different types of prompts found in the Teacher Wraparound Edition.

R **Reading Strategies** activities help you teach reading skills and vocabulary.

C **Critical Thinking** strategies help students apply and extend what they have learned.

U **Universal Access** activities provide differentiated instruction for students learning to speak English, along with suggestions for teaching various types of learners.

S **Skill Practice** strategies help students practice historical analysis and geography skills.

W **Writing Support** activities provide writing opportunities to help students comprehend the text.

Teaching strategies and activities have been coded for ability level appropriateness.

AL Activities for students working above grade level
OL Activities for students working on grade level
BL Activities for students working below grade level
EL Activities for English Learners

FOCUS

History–Social Science Standards

In this chapter, the following standard will be covered:

US8.10 Students analyze the multiple causes, key events, and complex consequences of the Civil War.

More About the Photo

Both sides had leadership problems as they prepared to fight at Gettysburg. General Stonewall Jackson had been mortally wounded at the Battle of Chancellorsville less than two months earlier, taking away Robert E. Lee's most trusted commander. General George Gordon Meade was given command of the Union army less than a week before the battle.

Chapter 13

The Civil War

Gettysburg Battlefield ▶

NATIONAL GEOGRAPHIC **Who & When?**

1861 | 1863 | 1865

1861 Civil War begins with battle at Fort Sumter

1862 Robert E. Lee commands Confederate army

1863 Emancipation Proclamation issued

1865 War ends; Lincoln assassinated

TEACH

The Big Ideas

As you begin teaching each section, use these questions and activities to focus on the Big Ideas.

Section 1

The Two Sides

Essential Question: What things make a country powerful militarily? *(large army, advanced equipment, industrial strength, fighting spirit, effective leaders)* OL

Section 2

Early Years of the War

Essential Question: How might people's feelings toward a war change as the war continues? *(Some may begin to tire of the sacrifices required; others might grow more determined.)* OL

Section 3

A Call to Freedom

Essential Question: What role did slavery play in the conflict leading up to the Civil War? *(It was a major factor in dividing the North and the South.)* OL

The Big Ideas

History Online
Chapter Overview Visit ca.hss.glencoe.com for a preview of Chapter 13.

Section 1 The Two Sides

Differences in economic, political, and social beliefs and practices can lead to division within a nation and have lasting consequences. The Union and the Confederacy prepared for war.

Section 2 Early Years of the War

Conflict often brings about great change. Neither the Union nor the Confederate forces gained a strong early advantage.

Section 3 A Call to Freedom

Reactions to social injustice can lead to reform movements. African Americans struggled for their civil rights.

Section 4 Life During the Civil War

Citizen participation is essential to the foundation and preservation of the U.S. political system. Civilians as well as soldiers had an impact on the war effort.

Section 5 The Way to Victory

Conflict often brings about great change. Aggressive offensives resulted in a victory for the Union.

View the Chapter 13 video in the Glencoe Video Program.

FOLDABLES™ Study Organizer

Organizing Information Make this foldable to help you organize what you learn about the Civil War.

Step 1 Fold a sheet of paper in half from side to side.

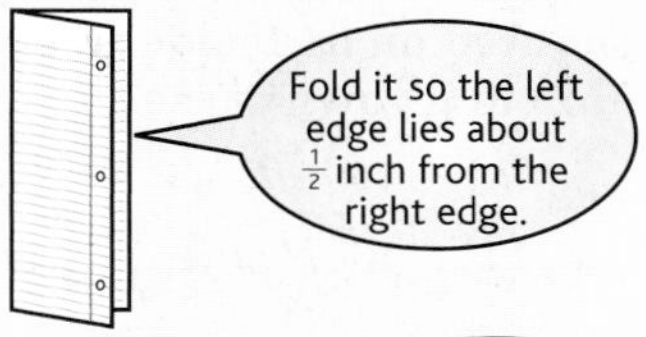

Step 2 Turn the paper and fold it into thirds.

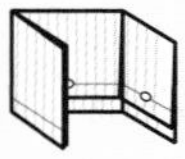

Step 3 Unfold and cut the top layer only along both folds.

Step 4 Label your foldable as shown.

Reading and Writing As you read the chapter, list events that occurred before, during, and after the Civil War under the appropriate tabs of your foldable.

INTRODUCING CHAPTER 13

Section 4 Life During the Civil War

Essential Question: How do citizens contribute to the effort of a nation at war? *(by joining the armed forces; by helping produce supplies and equipment needed by those armed forces; by paying taxes)* OL

Section 5 The Way to Victory

Essential Question: How do wars bring about change? *(loss of life; victory for aggressors; new government or laws)* OL

History Online

Go to ca.hss.glencoe.com for student activities, lesson plans, and links to additional Web resources about the Civil War.

FOLDABLES™ Study Organizer Dinah Zike's Foldables

Purpose Have students use their foldables to arrange important Civil War events chronologically under tabs labeled *Before*, *During*, and *After*. Students should use their Foldables to prepare quizzes for a partner. BL

Why It's Important

Evaluation Evaluating text is a way of reading actively. Like other strategies, such as monitoring and questioning, evaluating increases students' engagement with the text and deepens their comprehension.

1 Learn It!

Have students define the word *value* *(the worth of something)* and explain that evaluating is a way of determining the worth, value, or importance of a piece of information. Ask them what techniques they use to determine the value of a TV commercial. *(Answers may include asking if the claim makes sense or what the product resembles, referring to their own experiences with the product or one similar to it, and applying their own common sense.)* Tell students they can use similar techniques when reading and evaluating informational text. OL

Chapter 13 Get Ready to Read

Evaluation

READING SKILL

1 Learn It!

Good readers evaluate information as they read. That means they draw conclusions and determine the significance of events, ideas, and people that they read about. As you read history, ask yourself such questions as:

- What caused this person or group of people to react that way? In the same situation, how did other people in history react?
- What words has the author chosen to describe this event or person? How do these words help me form an opinion?
- Is the information that I'm reading based on fact or opinion?

Keep these questions in mind as you read the excerpt below.

> **Gone were the parades and masses of volunteers, the fancy uniforms, and the optimism of the first years of the war. From 1862 until 1865, the soldiers and civilians faced a grim conflict marked by death, destruction, and wrenching change. What endured on each side was a fierce dedication to its own cause.**
>
> *—from page 605*

Reading Tip

As you read, write down some of your conclusions or opinions in your notebook. When you finish the chapter, go back and review them. Did your conclusions and opinions change?

568

READING STRATEGY **DETERMINING IMPORTANCE**

One goal of evaluating text is to identify the material that is most important and pay particular attention to that. Give students some guidance on how to spot such information:
- Use the Main Idea statements in the text to focus on key concepts.
- Use headings and subheadings to identify common themes in a particular discussion.
- Look for key words such as *because*, *since*, or *as a result* to signal discussion of causes and effects.
- Focus on sentences that use *important*, *significant*, *vital*, or related words. OL

Practice It!

Turn to page 600 and read the passage called "Treating the Sick and Wounded." Then, use the questions below to evaluate what you read.

- Were women well received as nurses in Civil War hospitals?
- What did doctors and other men initially think about women assisting in hospitals?
- How do you feel about this? Do you agree?
- How did some women respond to being discouraged from nursing?
- What word did the author use to describe women who disregarded the objections of men? Does that word give you a clue to the author's opinions?
- Do you think that you would be able to work in a battlefield hospital? Why or why not?

Read to Write

You can also use your evaluation skills when you observe images. Select a painting or photograph in this chapter depicting a war scene and describe what you see and how you would evaluate it.

Image of nurse with soldier ▶

Apply It!

Choose one paragraph in Section 1 to evaluate. Write a list of five questions that you would ask as a part of that evaluation.

CHAPTER 13 Get Ready to Read

Practice It!

Before assigning the Practice It! activity in the Student Edition, have students practice the skill using the brief paragraph on page 568. **Ask:** What other questions could you ask about this paragraph? *(What happened to take away the optimism? What kinds of changes took place? What were the causes the two sides were fighting for?)* Point out that sometimes answers to the questions they raise cannot be found in the same passage but are addressed in later material. OL

Apply It!

Divide students into groups, and assign each group a different topic, such as African American soldiers, military leaders of both sides, the role of women in the war, Civil War medicine, or others. Have them locate information on the Internet about their topic. Ask each group to evaluate the information they find to determine its credibility. OL

READING STRATEGY — READING MAPS, GRAPHS, AND CHARTS

Students' success at evaluating parts of this chapter, especially discussions of war aims and strategies, battles, and troop movements, depends on their ability to read and understand maps. Before beginning the chapter, have students examine each map. Discuss the different colors and symbols to make sure that students understand how they are used to present information. OL

Use Reading Skills Activity 13 in the **Chapter 13 Resource Book** for more practice with evaluating text.

FOCUS

BELLRINGER
Skillbuilder Activity

Project **Daily Focus Skills Transparency 13–1** and have students answer the question.

Guide to Reading

Preteaching Vocabulary:
Ask: Which term was used to refer to people from the South? Why was that term used? *(Rebel; because they were rebelling from the Union)*

Answers to Graphic:
Union: Strengths—more people, industry, resources, ships; banking system, railroads; Lincoln; Weaknesses—must invade South; Confederacy: Strengths—strong support; knowledge of terrain; military leaders; Weaknesses—fewer people, factories, trains; weak central government

Unpacking the Standards

After reading the section, students will be able to:

- Discuss differences between the North and the South.
- Explain the events that led to war.
- Describe the men who made up both armies.

Section 1

The Two Sides

History Social Science Standards

US8.10 Students analyze the multiple causes, key events, and complex consequences of the Civil War.

Guide to Reading

Looking Back, Looking Ahead
After the firing on Fort Sumter, the Union and the Confederacy called for volunteers to fight.

Focusing on the Main Ideas
- Both the North and the South had strengths and weaknesses that helped determine their military strategies. *(page 571)*
- Soldiers in the Civil War came from every region, and each side expected an early victory. *(page 574)*

Locating Places
Richmond, Virginia

Meeting People
Jefferson Davis
Mary Todd Lincoln
Robert E. Lee
William Tecumseh Sherman

Content Vocabulary
border state
blockade (blah • KAYD)
offensive (uh • FEHN • sihv)
Rebel (REH • buhl)
Yankee (YANG • kee)

Academic Vocabulary
obvious (AHB • vee • uhs)
sufficient (suh • FIH • shuhnt)
primary (PRY • MEHR • ee)

Reading Strategy
Classifying Information As you read the section, complete a chart like the one shown here by listing the strengths and weaknesses of the Union and the Confederacy.

	Union	Confederacy
Strengths		
Weaknesses		

NATIONAL GEOGRAPHIC Where & When?

1861 — 1862 — 1863

Feb. 1861 The Confederacy forms

April 1861 Four more states join Confederacy

Summer 1861 Confederate forces total 112,000; Union 187,000

June 1863 West Virginia joins Union

SECTION RESOURCES

Print Material
- Reproducible Lesson Plan 13–1*
- Daily Lesson and Discussion Notes 13–1
- Guided Reading Activity 13–1
- Reading Essentials and Study Guide 13–1
- Active Reading Note-Taking Guide 13–1
- Section Quiz 13–1

Transparencies
- Daily Focus Skills Transparency 13–1
- Section Graphic Organizer Transparency 13–1
- California Standards Practice Transparencies

Technology
- Interactive Tutor Self-Assessment CD-ROM
- Exam*View*® Pro Testmaker CD-ROM
- Presentation Plus! CD-ROM

*Available on TeacherWorks™

US8.10.2 Trace the boundaries constituting the North and the South, the geographical differences between the two regions, and the differences between agrarians and industrialists.

Comparing North and South

Main Idea **Both the North and the South had strengths and weaknesses that helped determine their military strategies.**

Reading Connection Which do you think would be more important to a country at war: an army with experienced leaders or a large number of factories? Read to find out the advantages held by both the North and the South at the beginning of the war.

An American Story

U

Union sergeant Driscoll directed his troops at Malvern Hill on July 1, 1862. The enemy fought fiercely, especially one young Confederate soldier. Driscoll raised his rifle, took aim, and shot the boy. As he passed the spot where the boy had fallen, Driscoll turned the daring soldier over to see what he looked like. The boy opened his eyes and faintly murmured "Father," then his eyes fluttered shut, never to open again. A Union captain, D.P. Conyngham, later wrote,

> **"I will forever recollect the frantic grief of Driscoll; it was harrowing to witness. He [had killed] his son, who had gone South before the war."**
>
> —as quoted in *A Civil War Treasury of Tales, Legends and Folklore*

Like the Driscolls, many families were divided by the war. Neither side imagined, however, that the war would cost such a terrible price in human life. During the four years of fighting, hundreds of thousands of Americans were killed in battle.

The Border States By February 1861, seven states had left the Union and formed the Confederacy. After the Confederate bombardment of Fort Sumter, President Abraham Lincoln issued a call for troops to save the Union. His action caused Virginia, North Carolina, Tennessee, and Arkansas to join the Confederacy. These four states brought needed soldiers and supplies to the Confederacy. For its capital, the Confederacy chose **Richmond, Virginia,** a city located only about 100 miles from the Union capital of Washington, D.C. W

Four states that allowed slavery—Missouri, Kentucky, Maryland, and Delaware—remained in the Union. The people of these **border states** were divided over which side to support. R Missouri, Kentucky, and Maryland had such strong support for the South that the three states teetered on the brink of secession. Losing the border states would seriously damage the North. Each of the four states had strategic locations.

History *Through Art*

7th New York Militia at Jersey City on April 19, 1861* by E.L. Henry** The 7th New York Militia was one of the first fully equipped and trained units at the outbreak of the war. ***Why were troops ordered to the nation's capital in early 1861?

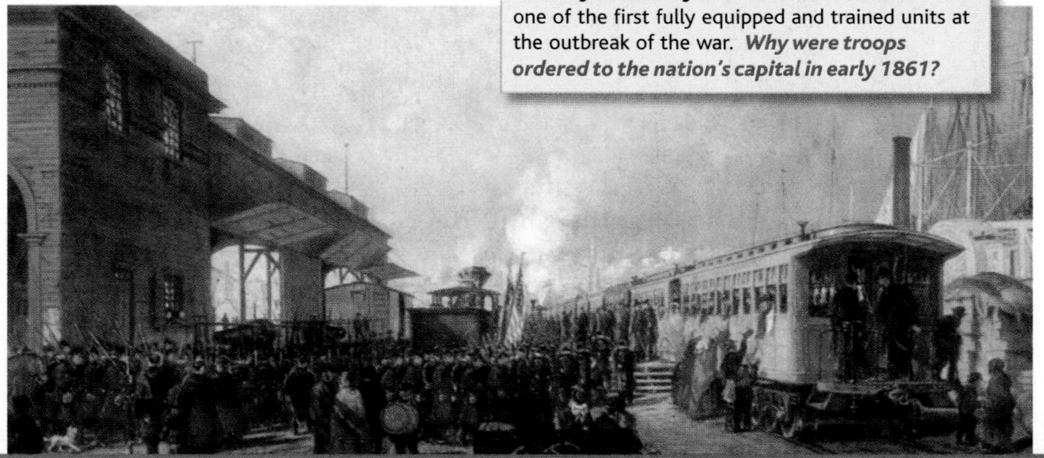

TEACH

U Universal Access

Linguistic/Verbal Ask students to write a poem about the death of Sergeant Driscoll's son. Have them choose a point of view and express the emotions surrounding the incident. *(Poems might address the tragic coincidence or the father's grief.)* OL CA HR5.

W Writing Support

Narrative Writing Divide students into groups and have each group design and create the front page of a newspaper announcing the beginning of the Civil War. Recommend that groups include a banner headline, an illustration, a story with eyewitness accounts, and announcements from Union and Confederate governments about the outbreak of war. AL CA 8WA2.1

R Reading Strategy

Understanding Vocabulary Have students locate the four border states on a map of the United States. **Ask:** Why were they called border states? *(They were on the border between the North and the South.)* BL

History *Through Art*

The vast railroad network of the North, here used to transport troops, was a significant advantage during the war.

Answer: to protect Washington, D.C., and vital railroad lines passing through Maryland, and to prevent Maryland from leaving the Union

U Universal Access

Below Grade Level Pair two English learners for this activity. Have them use a map to take turns explaining the strategic importance of each border state. *(Students should point out the natural features, such as rivers, that made the states important.)* **BL** CA CS3.

R Reading Strategy

Evaluating Ask students if they think Lincoln's handling of the border states was a success. Why or why not? *(Because the states did not secede, even though many people from them fought for the South, most students will say that Lincoln was successful.)* **OL** CA HI2.

S Skill Practice

Historical and Social Sciences Analysis Skill Have students choose an advantage of the North or South and explain in their own words how it helped the war effort. *(For example, the North's banking advantage helped it borrow money to pay for the war.)* **OL** CA HI1.

Answers and Additional Support

Missouri could control parts of the Mississippi River and major routes to the West. Kentucky controlled the Ohio River. Delaware was close to the important Northern city of Philadelphia.

Maryland, perhaps the most important of the border states, was close to Richmond. Vital railroad lines passed through Maryland. Most importantly, Washington, D.C., lay within the state. If Maryland seceded, the North's government would be surrounded.

U Maryland's key role became clear in April 1861. A mob in Baltimore attacked Northern troops; Confederate sympathizers burned railroad bridges and cut the telegraph line to Washington, isolating the capital from the rest of the North. Northern troops soon arrived and restored order, but the nation's capital had suffered some anxious days.

Remaining With the Union Lincoln had to move cautiously to avoid upsetting people in the border states. If he announced that he aimed to end slavery, groups supporting the Confederacy R might take their states out of the Union. If he ordered Northern troops into Kentucky, its citizens could decide to support the South.

In some ways, Lincoln acted boldly. He suspended some constitutional rights and used his power to arrest people who supported secession. In the end, Lincoln's approach worked. The border states stayed in the Union, but many of their citizens joined armies of the South.

Strengths and Weaknesses When the war began, both sides had advantages and disadvantages. How they would use those strengths and weaknesses would determine the war's outcome.

The North enjoyed the advantages of a larger population, more industry, and more S abundant resources than the South. It had a better banking system, which helped raise money for the war. The North also possessed more ships and had a larger and more efficient railway network.

The North also faced disadvantages. Bringing the Southern states back into the Union would be difficult. The North would have to invade the South—a large area filled with a hostile population. To win the war, the North had to occupy the Confederacy's territory and subdue a population of millions. In addition, the Southern people's support for the war remained strong. Recalling the example of the American Revolution, when the smaller, weaker colonies had won independence from wealthy Great Britain, many believed the South had a good chance of winning.

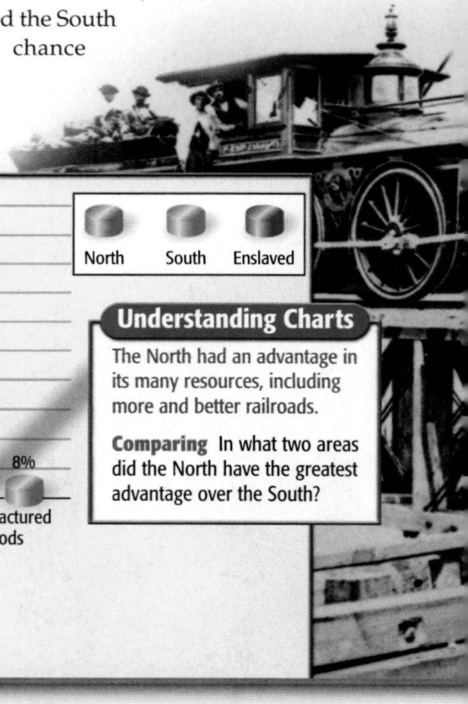

Comparing Resources

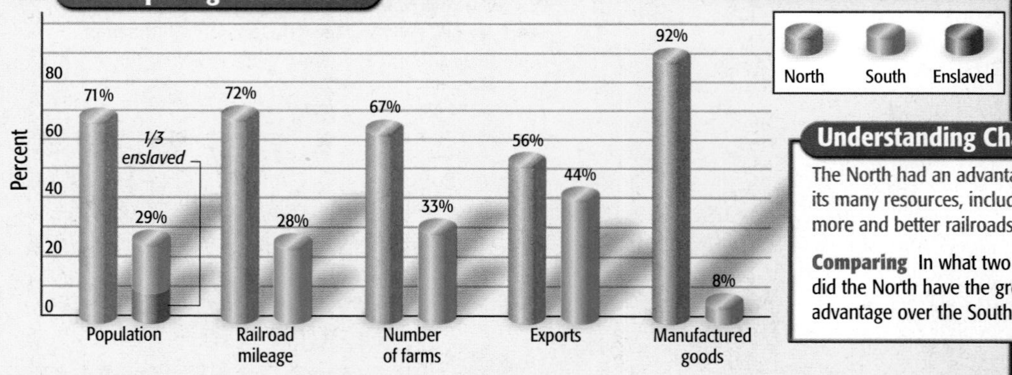

Source: *Historical Statistics of the United States: Colonial Times to 1970.*

Understanding Charts

The North had an advantage in its many resources, including more and better railroads.

Comparing In what two areas did the North have the greatest advantage over the South?

Understanding Graphs

Answer: manufactured goods and population (since one-third of the South's population was enslaved)

More Skill Practice

Historical and Social Sciences Analysis Skill Have students create a graphic organizer about the strengths and weaknesses of the North and South. Ask them to scan the section for information and then categorize the strengths and weaknesses as cultural, social, economic, or political. Students should decide on the form of their graphic organizer. **OL** CA HI1.

One Northern advantage was not **obvious** until later. Both sides greatly underestimated Abraham Lincoln. His dedication and intelligence would lead the North to victory.

One of the main advantages for Southerners was fighting in familiar territory—defending their land, their homes, and their way of life.

The military leadership of the South, at least at first, was superior to the North's. Southern families had a strong tradition of military training and service, and military college graduates provided the South with a large pool of officers. Overseeing the Southern effort was Confederate president **Jefferson Davis,** a West Point graduate and an experienced soldier.

The South also faced some disadvantages. It had a smaller population of free men to draw upon in building an army. It also possessed very few factories to manufacture weapons and other supplies, and it produced less than half as much food as the North. With less than half the miles of railroad tracks and vastly fewer trains than the North, the Confederate government had difficulty delivering food, weapons, and other supplies to its troops.

The belief in states' rights—a founding principle of the Confederacy—also hampered the South's efforts. The individual states refused to give the Confederate government **sufficient** power. As a result, the government found it difficult to fight the war effectively.

War Aims and Strategy The North and the South entered the Civil War with different goals. The main goal of the North was to bring the Southern states back into the Union. Ending slavery was not a major Northern goal at first, but this changed as the war continued.

The Union's plan for winning the war included three main strategies. First, the North would **blockade** (blah • KAYD), or close, Southern ports to prevent supplies from reaching the South—and to prevent the South from earning money by exporting cotton. Second, the Union intended to gain control of the Mississippi River to cut Southern supply lines and to divide the Confederacy. Third, the North planned to take control of Richmond, Virginia, the Confederate capital.

For the South, the **primary** aim of the war was to win recognition as an independent nation. Independence would allow Southerners to preserve their traditional way of life—a way of life that included slavery.

To achieve this goal, the South worked out a defensive strategy. It planned to defend its homeland, holding on to as much territory as possible until the North tired of fighting. The South expected that Britain and France, which imported large quantities of Southern cotton, would pressure the North to end the war to restore their cotton supplies.

During the war, Southern leaders sometimes changed strategy and took the **offensive** (uh • FEHN • sihv)—went on the attack. They moved their armies northward to threaten Washington, D.C., and other Northern cities, hoping to persuade the North that it could not win the war.

Reading Check **Compare** What advantages and disadvantages did each side possess?

C1 Critical Thinking

Drawing Conclusions Ask students to decide which of the North's advantages and which of the South's was the most important. Discuss students' choices. **AL** CA HI2.

R1 Reading Strategy

Scaffolding—Academic Vocabulary The word *strategy* was introduced in Chapter 7, Section 1. Ask a student to define the word. **OL**

C2 Critical Thinking

Predicting Consequences
Ask: How successful do you think each side will be in attaining its war aims? Have students give reasons for their predictions. **OL** CA HI1.

R2 Reading Strategy

Understanding Vocabulary
Ask: What does *offensive* mean here? *(on the attack)* What are some similar uses of the word in other topics? *(in sports, it refers to efforts by a team to score points)* **OL** CA 8RW1.3

Reading Check

Answer: Union: Advantages—more people, industry, resources, ships; banking system, railroads; Lincoln; Disadvantages—must invade South; Confederacy: Advantages—strong support; knowledge of terrain; military leaders; Disadvantages—fewer people, factories, trains; weak central government

More Skill Practice

Historical and Social Sciences Analysis Skill **Ask:** Which side had the more easily achievable war aims? Why? *(Some students may say the South because it had only to avoid giving up until the North grew tired of fighting. Some may say the North because of its many material advantages over the South.)* **AL** CA HI2.

Did You Know?

The presidents of the Union and Confederacy had different ideas about the coming war. Lincoln, in his inaugural address, said, "We are not enemies, but friends. We must not be enemies." Jefferson Davis, however, had other thoughts. "The time for compromise has now passed," he announced.

Resources for page 573

- Biography Activity 13 B
- Biography Activity 13 C

Review The Big Idea

Review the Big Idea for this section: "Differences in economic, political, and social beliefs and practices can led to division within a nation and have lasting consequences."
Ask: Which difference between the North and the South was the greatest? Why? *(Students may suggest slavery, because the entire social and economic system in the South was based on this institution.)*
AL CA HI3.

C Critical Thinking

Making Inferences Ask: What advantages might soldiers who grew up on farms have over those who grew up in the city? *(experienced with firearms, used to living and working outdoors, strong from physical work)*
OL CA HR3.

R Reading Strategy

Understanding Vocabulary
Ask: How did use of the term *Yankee* change since the American Revolution? *(Earlier, it had been used as a term for all Americans by the British.)* **EL**
CA 8RW1.3

US8.10.5 Study the views and lives of leaders (e.g., Ulysses S. Grant, Jefferson Davis, Robert E. Lee) and soldiers on both sides of the war, including those of black soldiers and regiments.

American People at War

Main Idea **Soldiers in the Civil War came from every region, and each side expected an early victory.**

Reading Connection What motivates men and women to join the armed forces today? Read to find out about the backgrounds of the soldiers in the Union and Confederate armies.

The Civil War was more than a war between the states. It often pitted brother against brother, parents against their children, and neighbor against neighbor.

American Against American The leaders from both North and South—and their families—felt these divisions. President Lincoln's wife, **Mary Todd Lincoln,** had several relatives who fought in the Confederate army. John Crittenden, a senator from Kentucky, had two sons who became generals in the war—one for the Confederacy and one for the Union. Officers on both sides—including Confederate general **Robert E. Lee,** and Union generals George McClellan and **William Tecumseh Sherman**—had attended the United States Military Academy at West Point, never dreaming that they would one day command forces fighting against each other.

Who Were the Soldiers? Most of the soldiers were young. The average recruit was 25 years old, but about 40 percent were 21 or younger. Ted Upson of Indiana was only 16 when he begged his father to let him join the Union army. His father replied, "This Union your ancestors and mine helped to make must be saved from destruction."

William Stone from Louisiana rushed to join the Confederate army after the attack on Fort Sumter. His sister Kate wrote that he was "wild to be off to Virginia. He so fears that the fighting will be over before he can get there."

Soldiers came from every region and all walks of life. Most, though, came from farms. Almost half of the North's troops and more than 60 percent of the South's had owned or worked on farms. The Union army did not permit African Americans to join at first, but they did serve later. Lincoln's early terms of enlistment asked governors to supply soldiers for 90 days. When the conflict did not end quickly, soldiers' terms became longer. **C**

By the summer of 1861, the Confederate army had about 112,000 soldiers, who were sometimes called **Rebels** (REH•buhlz). The Union had about 187,000 soldiers, or **Yankees** (YANG•keez), as they were also known. By the end of the war, about 850,000 men fought for the Confederacy and about 2.1 million men fought for the Union. **R**

Picturing **History**

The Civil War divided the nation, but it also divided families. ***What did the soldiers from the Union and the Confederacy have in common?***

Answers and Additional Support

More Skill Practice

Historical and Social Sciences Analysis Skill Ask: How could the large African American population in the South be seen as both an advantage and a disadvantage for the Confederacy? *(Advantage: enslaved workers would maintain the South's economy and allow whites to serve in the army; Disadvantage: they might revolt)* **AL** CA HI2.

Picturing **History**

Answer: The great majority of soldiers on both sides were volunteers. Units were formed by local and state leaders, and companies often included men from one town or a particular part of a city. When units suffered heavy losses in battle, this could devastate those communities.

The Union number included just under 200,000 African Americans. About 10,000 Hispanic soldiers fought in the conflict.

False Hopes When the war began, each side expected an early victory. A Confederate soldier from a town in Alabama expected the war to be over well within a year because "we are going to kill the last Yankee before that time if there is any fight in them still." Northerners were just as confident that they would beat the South quickly.

Some leaders saw the situation more clearly. Northern general William Tecumseh Sherman wrote, "I think it is to be a long war—very long—much longer than any politician thinks." The first spring of the war proved that Sherman's prediction was accurate. From the first battle, both sides learned there would be no quick victory.

Reading Check **Compare** Which side had the larger fighting force?

"I think it is to be a long war. . . ."
—General William Tecumseh Sherman

C

History Online
Study Central Need help understanding the start of the Civil War? Visit ca.hss.glencoe.com and click on Study Central.

Section 1 Review

Reading Summary

Review the Main Ideas

- The North hoped to use its large number of soldiers and industry to cut off supplies to the South, and the South planned to fight defensively and win foreign recognition.
- Many of the soldiers from both North and South were young, had come from farms, and mistakenly expected a short war.

What Did You Learn?

1. Why were the border states important to the North and the South?
2. Why was the Civil War especially difficult for families?

Critical Thinking

3. **Comparing** Create a diagram to compare Northern and Southern aims and strategies. CA HR3.

	North	South
Aims		
Strategies		

4. **Analyze** How did a strong belief in states' rights affect the South during the war? CA HI2.
5. **The Big Ideas** How did the South's economy differ from that of the North, and how did it place the South at a disadvantage during the war? CA HI6.
6. **Reading** **Evaluating Text** Reread the passage at the beginning of Section 1 about Union sergeant Driscoll. Using your evaluation skills, write a short paragraph that explains why the author chose to include this account. How does it relate to what you read in that section? CA 8RC2.0

C Critical Thinking

Analyzing Information
Ask: Why would Sherman's statement have surprised many people in the North and the South? *(They expected a short war.)* OL CA HR5.

ASSESS

Resources for page 575

Use these resources to assess student mastery of section content.

- Analysis Skills Activity 13
- Section Quiz 13–1
- Interactive Tutor Self-Assessment CD-ROM

Reading Check
Answer: the Union

History Online
Study Central provides summaries, interactive games, and online graphic organizers to help students review section content.

CLOSE

Historical and Social Sciences Analysis Skill
Ask students if they think the Civil War could have been avoided. Why or why not? OL CA HI2.

SECTION 1 REVIEW ANSWERS

Review questions reinforce content standard US8.10.

1. controlled land, water routes; near capital
2. Many had family members fighting for each side.
3. North: Aims—bring South back into Union; Strategies—blockade, control Mississippi, capture Richmond; South: Aims—independence and slavery; Strategies—fight until North gives up, gain foreign support
4. State governments refused to give enough power to Confederacy central government.
5. **The Big Ideas** fewer factories, resources, ships; inferior banking system, rail network; it could not maintain as large an army
6. **Reading** It shows how the war divided families.

FOCUS

BELLRINGER
SKILLBUILDER ACTIVITY

Project **Daily Focus Skills Transparency 13–2** and have students answer the question.

Guide to Reading

Preteaching Vocabulary: Have students use the Glossary in the back of their textbooks to find the definitions of the terms. Then have students write sentences using the terms.

Answers to Graphic: First Bull Run (Manassas): Confederate victory; *Monitor* v. *Merrimack*: neither ship sank, but the Union stopped *Merrimack*'s attacks on its ships; Antietam: Union victory

Unpacking the Standards

After reading the section, students will be able to:

- Explain why both sides expected a short war.
- Describe the successes and failures of each side in the war's early years.
- Discuss the Union's problems with finding effective generals.

Section 2 Early Years of the War

History Social Science Standards

US8.10 Students analyze the multiple causes, key events, and complex consequences of the Civil War.

Guide to Reading

Looking Back, Looking Ahead
In 1861, the Union and Confederacy expected a brief war and early victory.

Focusing on the Main Ideas
- The North realized with the first major battle that the war would be a long, difficult struggle. *(page 577)*
- The North set up a blockade along the South's coastline, which caused serious problems for the South. *(page 578)*
- The action shifted to the West after the First Battle of Bull Run as each side reorganized its forces. *(page 579)*
- Battles continued, and after several Southern victories, Lincoln removed General McClellan for his failure to act in these battles. *(page 580)*

Locating Places
Norfolk, Virginia

Meeting People
"Stonewall" Jackson
George B. McClellan
Ulysses S. Grant
David Farragut (FAR • uh • guht)

Content Vocabulary
ironclad
casualty (KAZH • wuhl • tee)

Academic Vocabulary
reinforce (REE • uhn • FOHRS)
abandon (uh • BAN • duhn)
prospect (PRAH • spehkt)
evaluate (ih • VAL • yuh • WAYT)
encounter (ihn • KOWN • tuhr)

Reading Strategy
Classifying Information As you read, describe the outcome of each of these battles on a chart like the one shown.

Battle	Outcome
First Battle of Bull Run (Manassas)	
Monitor v. *Merrimack*	
Antietam	

NATIONAL GEOGRAPHIC Where & When?

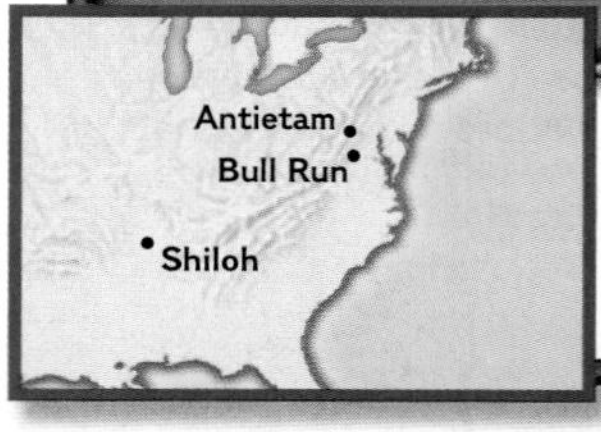

1861 — 1862 — 1863

- **July 1861** First Battle of Bull Run (Manassas)
- **Feb. 1862** Grant captures Fort Henry and Fort Donelson
- **Apr. 1862** Battle of Shiloh
- **Sept. 1862** Battle of Antietam

SECTION RESOURCES

Print Material
- Reproducible Lesson Plan 13–2*
- Daily Lesson and Discussion Notes 13–2
- Guided Reading Activity 13–2
- Reading Essentials and Study Guide 13–2
- Active Reading Note-Taking Guide 13–2
- Section Quiz 13–2

Transparencies
- Daily Focus Skills Transparency 13–2
- Section Graphic Organizer Transparency 13–2
- California Standards Practice Transparencies

Technology
- Interactive Tutor Self-Assessment CD-ROM
- Exam*View*® Pro Testmaker CD-ROM
- Presentation Plus! CD-ROM

*Available on TeacherWorks™

US8.10.6 Describe critical developments and events in the war, including the major battles, geographical advantages and obstacles, technological advances, and General Lee's surrender at Appomattox. **US8.10.7** Explain how the war affected combatants, civilians, the physical environment, and future warfare.

The First Battle

Main Idea **The North realized with the first major battle that the war would be a long, difficult struggle.**

Reading Connection What goes through the mind of a soldier in battle for the first time? Read to learn about the Battle of Bull Run and the soldiers involved.

An American Story

Sunday, July 21, 1861, was a pleasant, sunny day in Washington, D.C. Hundreds of cheerful residents left the city and planned to picnic while watching the first battle between the Union and the Confederate armies. Expecting to see Union troops crush the Rebels, they looked forward to a quick victory. The Confederate soldiers also expected a quick victory.

> **"[The soldiers] carried dress suits with them, and any quantity of fine linen. . . . Every soldier, nearly, had a servant with him, and a whole lot of spoons and forks, so as to live comfortably and elegantly in camp. . . ."**
>
> **—Mary A. Ward,** ***Voices of the Civil War***

First Battle of Bull Run This first major battle of the Civil War was fought in northern Virginia, about five miles from a town called Manassas Junction near Bull Run—a small river in the area. Usually called the First Battle of Bull Run, it began when about 30,000 inexperienced Union troops attacked a smaller, equally inexperienced Confederate force.

The Yankees drove the Confederates back at first. Then the Rebels rallied, inspired by **reinforcements** under General Thomas Jackson. Jackson, who fought the enemy heroically "like a stone wall," became known thereafter as **"Stonewall" Jackson.**

The Confederates surged forward with a strange, unearthly scream that came to be known as the Rebel yell. Terrified, the Northern soldiers began to drop their guns and packs and run. One Union soldier wrote:

> **"As we gained the cover of the woods the stampede became even more frightful, for the baggage wagons and ambulances became entangled with the artillery and rendered the scene even more dreadful than the battle. . . ."**
>
> **—Corporal Samuel J. English, letter to his mother, July 1861**

The Union army began an orderly retreat that quickly became a mad stampede when the retreating Union troops collided with the civilians, fleeing in panic back to Washington, D.C.

A Shock for the North The outcome of the battle shocked the North, but President Abraham Lincoln was ready to act. He issued a call for more volunteers for the army. He signed two bills requesting a total of 1 million soldiers, who would serve for three years. Volunteers soon crowded into recruiting offices. Lincoln also appointed a new general, **George B. McClellan,** to head the Union army of the East—called the Army of the Potomac—and to organize the troops.

Reading Check **Explain** How did the First Battle of Bull Run change expectations about the war?

Civil War cannon

Did You Know?

Before the war, Confederate General Thomas "Stonewall" Jackson was a teacher at the Virginia Military Institute (V.M.I.), the state's military college. In 1859, he commanded a squad of V.M.I. cadets serving as guards at the execution of John Brown. Robert E. Lee had commanded the troops that defeated and captured Brown.

More About the Art

Artillery first became an important weapon of war in the 1400s. The deadly combination of gunpowder, iron barrel, and shot allowed attackers to breach the walls of previously unconquerable castles and fortresses.

TEACH

C1 Critical Thinking

Comparing and Contrasting Have students look at two quotations on this page. **Ask:** How does this description of Union troops fleeing the battle contrast with the soldiers' behavior before the battle? *(The first quotation shows the glamorous side of war, whereas the battle revealed the frightful reality of combat.)* **OL** **CA HI5.**

R Reading Strategy

Academic Vocabulary Discuss with students the verb *reinforce*. Explain that *reinforcements*, a different form of the word is used as a noun. **EL**

C2 Critical Thinking

Determining Cause and Effect **Ask:** What role do you think inexperience played in the battle? Why? *(It was an important factor, since strong attacks, first by the Union and then by the Confederates, were able to drive back defending troops, suggesting they were unable to keep their discipline.)* **OL** **CA HI2.**

W Writing Support

Narrative Writing Have students take the part of either a Union or Confederate soldier at the First Battle of Bull Run and write a letter home after the battle. Ask students to describe their feelings about the action and outcome of the battle. **OL** **CA 8WA2.1**

Reading Check

Answer: Because of the Southern victory, Northerners began to realize that the war could be long, difficult, and costly.

R1 Reading Strategy

Reading Secondary Sources Ask students to review the text about the Union blockade. Then have them explain what the Union was trying to accomplish with this strategy. *(to prevent supplies from reaching the Confederacy)* BL

R2 Reading Strategy

Understanding Vocabulary Explain that the word *clad* is related to the word *clothing*. Have them explain why it is used to refer to these ships. *(Both were covered in iron, as clothing covers a person's body.)* EL CA 8RW1.3

U Universal Access

Visual/Spatial Have students make detailed drawings or models of the *Monitor*, *Merrimack*, or *Hunley*. Students should research the designs of the ships, choose appropriate media, and share their model or drawing with the class. AL

Reading Check

Answer: It was the first battle in world history between two metal-covered ships.

Answers and Additional Support

US8.10.6 Describe critical developments and events in the war, including the major battles, geographical advantages and obstacles, technological advances, and General Lee's surrender at Appomattox. **US8.10.7** Explain how the war affected combatants, civilians, the physical environment, and future warfare.

War at Sea

Main Idea **The North set up a blockade along the South's coastline, which caused serious problems for the South.**

Reading Connection Have you ever toured an old warship? Read to learn about the first battle between metal-covered ships.

Even before Bull Run, Lincoln had ordered a naval blockade of Southern ports. An effective blockade would prevent the South from exporting its cotton and from importing the supplies necessary to continue the war. R1

The blockade caused serious problems for the South. Goods such as coffee, shoes, nails, and salt—as well as guns and ammunition—were in short supply in the South throughout the war.

The *Monitor* Versus the *Merrimack* The South did not intend to let the blockade go unchallenged. Southerners salvaged the *Merrimack*, a Union warship that Northern forces had **abandoned** when Confederate forces seized the naval shipyard in **Norfolk, Virginia.** The Confederates rebuilt the wooden ship, covered it with thick iron plates, and renamed it the *Virginia*.

R2 On March 8, 1862, this **ironclad,** or warship, attacked a group of Union ships off the coast of Virginia. The North's wooden warships could not damage the Confederate ship—shells simply bounced off its sides.

The North sent an iron-clad ship of its own, the *Monitor,* to engage the Confederate ship in battle. On March 9, the two ironclads exchanged fire, but neither ship could sink the other. The Union succeeded in keeping the *Merrimack* in the harbor, so it never again threatened Northern ships. The battle marked a new age in naval warfare—the first battle between two metal-covered ships. Both the North and the South used these ships as models to build more iron-clad ships.

Reading Check **Explain** What was the significance of the battle of the ironclads?

HISTORY MAKERS

Technology of the Civil War U

Some historians call the Civil War the first modern war. The Civil War was the first war that featured widespread use of mechanical and electrical equipment. For the first time, troops traveled by railroad. Messages were sent by telegraph. Railroads and telegraphs changed how generals made battlefield decisions. At sea, the battle of ironclad ships changed naval warfare. The *Merrimack* and the *Monitor,* in their famous battle, proved the sturdiness of these metal-covered ships.

In February 1864, the *H.L. Hunley* became the first submarine to sink an enemy warship in combat. *The Hunley,* however, never returned to port. For more than 130 years, the disappearance of the submarine remained a mystery. In August 2000, a team of divers located the long-lost ship, and the *H.L. Hunley* was raised from the waters of Charleston Harbor in South Carolina.

▲ Ironclads marked the beginning of the modern, armored, self-propelled warship.

HISTORY MAKERS

The *Monitor*, invented by Swedish born engineer John Ericsson, had two guns, compared to ten for the *Merrimack*. However, the *Monitor's* guns were mounted on a revolving turret, so it could shoot in any direction. Following the battle, the Union built sixty more *Monitor*-inspired ironclads.

US8.10.6 Describe critical developments and events in the war, including the major battles, geographical advantages and obstacles, technological advances, and General Lee's surrender at Appomattox.

War in the West

Main Idea **The action shifted to the West after the First Battle of Bull Run as each side reorganized its forces.**

Reading Connection Do you have a nickname, or know someone who does? Read to find out how General Ulysses S. Grant earned his unusual nickname.

After the First Battle of Bull Run in July 1861, the war in the East settled into a stalemate as each side built its strength. Generals focused on training raw recruits, turning civilians into soldiers. For a while, the action shifted to the West.

Early Victories for the North One of the North's primary goals in the West was to gain control of the Mississippi and Tennessee Rivers. This would split the Confederacy and hinder Southern efforts to transport goods.

The Union launched its operations in the West from Cairo, Illinois. The Union commander at Cairo was **Ulysses S. Grant.** Early in 1862, Grant was ordered to move against Confederate forces in Kentucky and Tennessee. On February 6, with the aid of a fleet of newly made ironclads, Grant captured Fort Henry on the Tennessee River. Ten days later, Grant captured Fort Donelson on the Cumberland. When the Confederate commander at Fort Donelson realized he was trapped, he asked Grant for his terms. Grant's reply was:

> **"No terms except an unconditional and immediate surrender can be accepted."**
>
> **—Ulysses S. Grant, note to General Simon Buckner**

"Unconditional Surrender" Grant became the North's new hero. Ulysses S. Grant had earned a new nickname. Grant's victories helped secure the lower Tennessee River. They also opened a path for Union troops to march into Tennessee, Mississippi, and Alabama.

The Battle of Shiloh General Grant and about 40,000 troops then headed south along the Tennessee River toward Corinth, Mississippi, an important railroad junction. In early April 1862, the Union army camped at Pittsburg Landing, 20 miles from Corinth. Nearby was a church named Shiloh. Additional Union forces came from Nashville to join Grant.

Early on the morning of April 6, Confederate forces launched a surprise attack on the Union troops. The Battle of Shiloh lasted two days, with some of the most bitter, bloody fighting of the war. The first day, the Confederates drove Grant and his troops back to the Tennessee River. The second day, the Union forces recovered. Aided by the 25,000 troops from Nashville and shelling by gunboats on the river, they defeated the Confederates, who withdrew to Corinth. **C**

R The losses in the Battle of Shiloh were enormous. Together the two armies suffered more than 20,000 **casualties** (KAZH•wuhl•teez)—people who are killed or wounded. Confederate general Johnston also died in the bloodbath.

After their narrow victory at Shiloh, Union forces gained control of Corinth on May 30. Memphis, Tennessee, fell to Union armies on June 6. The North seemed well on its way to controlling the Mississippi River.

New Orleans Falls A few weeks after Shiloh, the North won another important victory. On April 25, 1862, Union naval forces under **David Farragut** (FAR•uh•guht) captured New Orleans, Louisiana, the South's largest city. Farragut, who was of Spanish descent, had grown up in the South but remained loyal to the Union. His capture of New Orleans, near the mouth of the Mississippi River, meant that the Confederacy could no longer use the river to carry its goods to sea. Together with Grant's victories to the north, Farragut's capture of New Orleans gave the Union control of almost the entire Mississippi River.

Reading Check **Analyze** Why was control of the Mississippi River important to the North and to the South?

C Critical Thinking

Making Generalizations Have students read the account of the Battle of Shiloh. Then ask them to make some generalizations about battle strategy. *(Students might suggest that striking first is a good tactic because it can surprise the enemy; reinforcements can change a battle's outcome; naval bombardment can influence land battles.)* AL CA HI3.

R Reading Strategy

Understanding Vocabulary Make sure students understand that a casualty is a person either killed or wounded. All of the 20,000 casualties at Shiloh were not killed. OL CA 8RW1.3

Resources for page 579

- Universal Access Activity 13
- American Music: Hits Through History, "Johnny Comes Marching Home" and "Battle Hymn of the Republic" medley

Reading Check

Answer: Control of the Mississippi River would split the Confederacy and hinder Southern efforts to transport goods and troops.

More Skill Practice

Reading a Time Line Give students the following information about a day in the life of a Civil War soldier when not engaged in battle. Have them create a time line from it: 5:00 A.M.—reveille played; 5:15 A.M.—roll call and special orders; 5:30 to 8:00 A.M.— breakfast, tend horses, infirmary calls, cleanup duty, and necessary chores; 8:00 A.M. to 2:00 P.M.—two hours of sentry duty out of six hours; 8:00 A.M. to 12:00 P.M.—drill if not on sentry duty; 12:00 P.M.—dinner followed by more drill; 4:30 P.M.—polish weapons and care for uniforms; 5:45 P.M.—retreat ceremony with roll call, inspection, and dress parade; 7:30 P.M.—supper; 8:30 P.M.— assembly and last roll call; 9:00 P.M.—taps sounded and lights out. OL CA CS2.

U Universal Access

Interpersonal Have students script a dialogue between President Lincoln and General McClellan on the subject of engaging the enemy. Ask them to scan the text for details to include in their dialogues. *(Dialogues should reflect Lincoln's growing impatience and McClellan's caution.)* OL CA HI1.

C1 Critical Thinking

Analyzing Information
Ask: Was McClellan's caution good for the Union or a problem? Why? *(a problem; because his delays allowed the South to strengthen its defenses)* AL CA HI2.

C2 Critical Thinking

Determining Cause and Effect Ask: Why would Stuart's ride around the Union army boost Southern morale? *(because it was bold and daring; because he suffered so few casualties; because it happened at a time when the capital, Richmond, was threatened by a large army)* OL CA HI2.

US8.10.5 Study the views and lives of leaders (e.g., Ulysses S. Grant, Jefferson Davis, Robert E. Lee) and soldiers on both sides of the war, including those of black soldiers and regiments. **US8.10.6** Describe critical developments and events in the war, including the major battles, geographical advantages and obstacles, technological advances, and General Lee's surrender at Appomattox.

War in the East

Main Idea **Battles continued, and after several Southern victories, Lincoln removed General McClellan for his failure to act in these battles.**

Reading Connection Have you heard the expression "he who hesitates is lost"? Read and find out about a Union general whose hesitancy cost many lives.

While Union and Confederate troops were struggling for control of Tennessee and the Mississippi River, another major military campaign was being waged in the east. General George B. McClellan led the Union army in the east.

McClellan Hesitates In the East, General McClellan was training the Army of the Potomac to be an effective fighting force. An expert at training soldiers, McClellan reorganized and drilled the Army of the Potomac.

U However, when faced with the **prospect** of battle, McClellan was cautious and worried that his troops were not ready. He hesitated to fight because of reports that overestimated the size of the Rebel forces. Finally, in March 1862, the Army of the Potomac was ready for action. Its goal was to capture Richmond, the Confederate capital.

Instead of advancing directly overland to Richmond as Lincoln wished, McClellan moved his huge army by ship to a peninsula between the York and the James Rivers southeast of the city. From there he began a major offensive known as the Peninsular Campaign. The operation took many weeks.

Time passed and opportunities to attack slipped away as General McClellan readied his troops and tried to **evaluate** the enemy's strength. Lincoln, constantly prodding McClellan to fight, ended one message with an urgent plea: "You must act." McClellan did not act. His delays allowed the Confederates to prepare their defense of Richmond. At the end of June, the Union forces finally met the C1 Confederates in a series of **encounters** known as the Seven Days' Battles.

In these battles, Confederate general Robert E. Lee took command of the army opposing McClellan. Before the battles began, Lee's cavalry leader, James E.B. (J.E.B.) Stuart, performed a daring tactic. He led his 1,200 troops in a circle around the Union army, gathering vital information about Union positions and boosting Southern morale. Lee's forces eventually drove the Yankees back. The Union troops had failed to capture Richmond. C2

Gloom in the North Reports from Richmond disheartened the North. Another call was made for volunteers—300,000 this time—but the response was slow. The Southern strategy of making the North weary of war seemed to be working. The defeat had not been complete, however. McClellan's army had been pushed back, but it was larger than Lee's and still only 25 miles from Richmond. President Lincoln ordered him to move his army back to northern Virginia and join the troops led by Major General John Pope.

Names of Battles

Bull Run	Manassas
Antietam	Sharpsburg
Stone's River	Murfreesboro
Pittsburg Landing	Shiloh

Understanding Charts

Many Civil War battles have two names. The Union mostly named battles after the nearest body of water. The Confederacy often named them after the nearest town or city. Here are some battles with two names.

Answers and Additional Support

More About the Art

The Confederate flag shown here was the South's battle flag. Another flag, the official flag of the Confederacy, was called the Stars and Bars. It had a blue box with a circle of stars in the upper left and a red field with a large white stripe. A third flag, the Stainless Banner, had a white field with the battle flag reduced in the upper left.

C Stonewall Jackson's forces moved north to attack Pope's supply base at Manassas. Jackson's troops marched 50 miles in two days and were then joined by the rest of Lee's army. On August 29, 1862, Pope attacked the approaching Confederates and started the Second Battle of Bull Run. The battle ended in a Confederate victory. Richmond was no longer threatened. Instead, the situation of the two sides was completely reversed. Lee and the Confederates now stood only 20 miles from Washington, D.C.

History Online

Student Web Activity Visit ca.hss.glencoe.com and click on *Chapter 13—Student Web Activities* for an activity on the Second Battle of Bull Run.

The Early Battles, 1861–1862

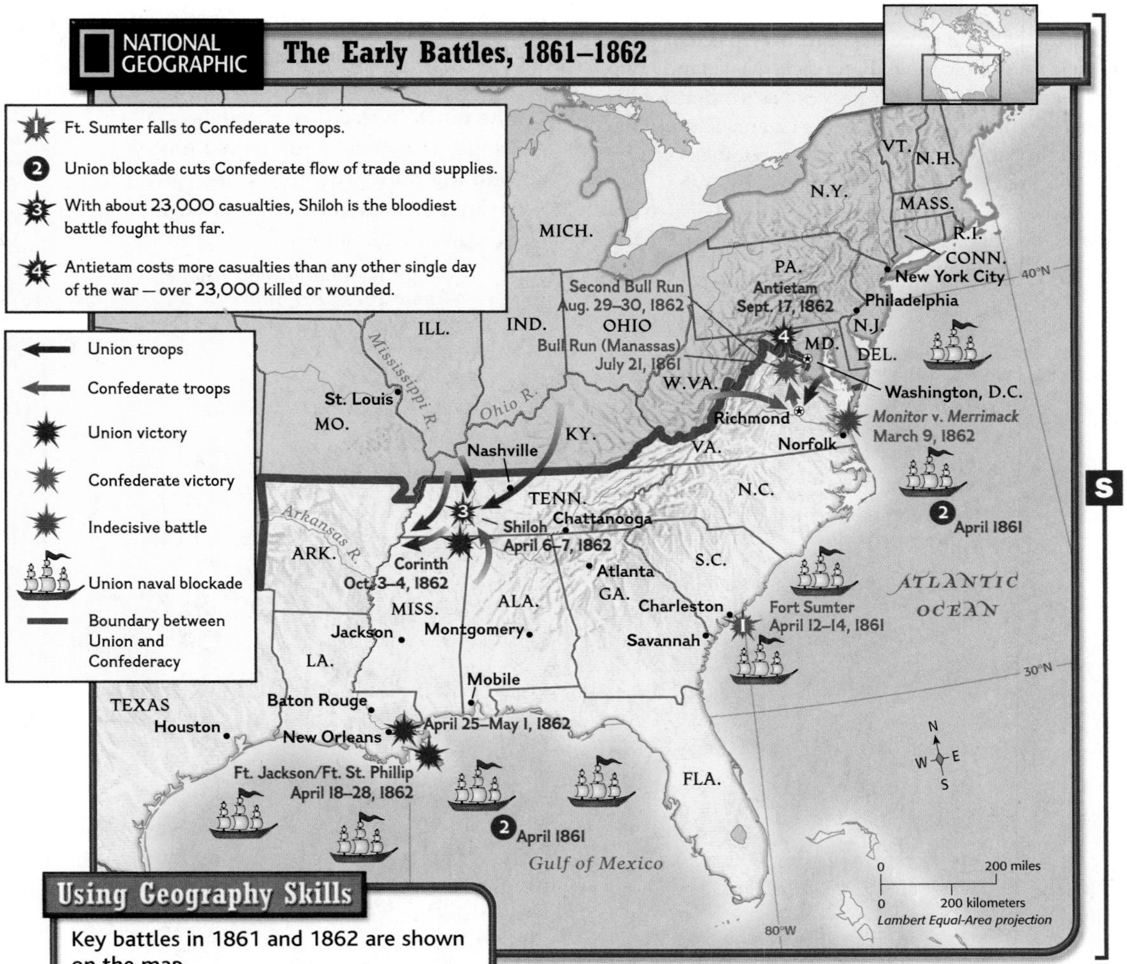

Using Geography Skills

Key battles in 1861 and 1862 are shown on the map.

1. **Location** In what state was the Battle of Shiloh fought?
2. **Summarize** In what battles were Confederate forces victorious?

C Critical Thinking

Analyzing Information
Explain that Jackson moved toward Manassas on Lee's orders. **Ask:** Based on the actions described here, how would you describe Lee as a general? Why? *(Students may say that Lee was bold and skillful since he attacked larger forces and defeated them.)* AL CA HR1.

S Skill Practice

Using Geography Skills
Have students refer to the map to explain why the Union victory at New Orleans was important. *(gave the Union control of the mouth of the Mississippi River; allowed the Union to send ships up the river to attack other Confederate strong points along it)* AL CA CS3.

History Online

Objectives and answers to the student activity can be found in the Web Activity Lesson Plan feature at ca.hss.glencoe.com.

Resources for page 581

Chart, Graph, and Map Skills Activity 13

Using Geography Skills

Answers:

1. Tennessee
2. Fort Sumter; Bull Run (Manassas); Second Bull Run

In-Text Map Transparency 13 Ask: What battle took place in September 1862? *(Antietam)* BL

More Skill Practice

Using Geography Skills Organize students into pairs and have the partners take turns describing the movements of various armies. Remind students to indicate which side they are describing, where the units began, how they moved, and where they ended up. BL CA CS3.

S1 Skill Practice

Historical and Social Sciences Analysis Skill Ask students what might have happened if Lee's orders had not been found by the two Union soldiers. *(McClellan would not have known Lee's plans and that his army was split; given his earlier behavior, he might not have attacked Lee.)* OL CA HI4.

C Critical Thinking

Analyzing Primary Sources Ask students why the description of the cut stalks of corn can be seen as a symbolic reference to the battle itself. *(Like the corn, the thousands of dead at the battle were cut down where they had stood.)* AL CA 8RL3.6

S2 Skill Practice

Visual Literacy Ask students to describe the hospital ward in the photograph. What were conditions there? *(The ward seems reasonably clean, bright, and cheerful, although it is crowded. Many of the soldiers are able to sit up and move around.)* OL CA 8LS1.9

Answers and Additional Support

Lee Enters Maryland Following these Southern victories, Confederate president Jefferson Davis ordered Lee to launch an offensive into Maryland, northwest of Washington. He hoped another victory would win aid from Great Britain and France. Lee also issued a proclamation urging the people of Maryland to join the Confederacy.

As Lee's army marched into Maryland in September 1862, McClellan and 80,000 Union troops moved slowly after them. On September 13, the North had an extraordinary piece of good luck. In a field near Frederick, Maryland, two Union soldiers found a copy of Lee's orders for his army wrapped around three cigars. The bundle had probably been dropped by a Southern officer.

Now McClellan knew exactly what Lee planned to do. He also learned that Lee's army was divided into four parts. This provided McClellan with an opportunity to overwhelm Lee's army one piece at a time.

The Battle of Antietam Once again, McClellan was overly cautious. He waited four days before he decided to attack the Confederates. This enabled Lee to gather most of his forces together near Sharpsburg, Maryland, along the Antietam Creek.

The Union and the Confederate armies clashed on September 17 in the Battle of Antietam. It was the single bloodiest day of the entire war. A Union officer wrote that

> **"In the time that I am writing every stalk of corn in [cornfields to the north] was cut as closely as could have been done with a knife, and the slain lay in rows precisely as they had stood in their ranks a few moments before."**
>
> —Major General Joseph Hooker, *Eyewitness Accounts*

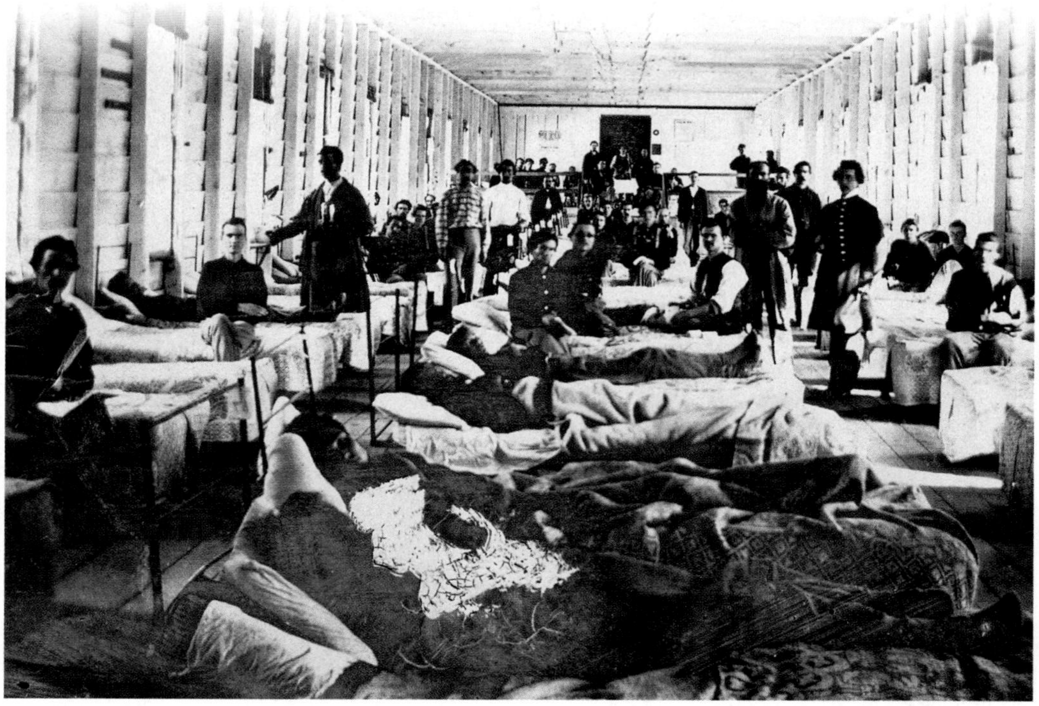

▲ Wounded soldiers at a military hospital at Alexandria, Virginia

Did You Know?

Although McClellan has gone down in history as a failure, he had remarkable skills in rebuilding, training, and reorganizing the Union army after its defeat at First Bull Run (Manassas). His early successes in securing western Virginia for the Union earned him the nickname "the Young Napoleon of the West," although his soldiers called him "Little Mac."

By the time the fighting ended, close to 6,000 Union and Confederate soldiers lay dead or dying, and another 17,000 were seriously wounded. Although both armies suffered heavy losses, neither was destroyed.

The day after the battle, Lee withdrew to Virginia. The Confederate retreat allowed the Union troops to claim victory. However, McClellan, who had been ordered by President Lincoln to "destroy the rebel army," did not pursue the Confederate troops. The president, disgusted with McClellan's failure to follow up his victory, removed McClellan from his command in November. Lincoln placed General Ambrose Burnside in command.

The Battle of Antietam was a crucial victory for the Union. The British government had been ready to intervene in the war as a mediator if Lee's invasion had succeeded. It had also begun making plans to recognize the Confederacy in the event the North rejected mediation. With Lee's defeat, the British decided to withhold its support, and the South lost its best chance at gaining international recognition and support.

Antietam had a profound impact on the war. The Army of the Potomac finally gained some confidence, having forced Lee and his soldiers back south. More important, the battle marked a major change in Northern war aims. President Lincoln used the battle to take action against slavery.

Reading Check **Summarize** What was the outcome of the Seven Days' Battles?

History Online
Study Central Need help understanding early battles of the Civil War? Visit ca.hss.glencoe.com and click on Study Central.

Section 2 Review

Reading Summary

Review the Main Ideas

- Following the first major battle of the war, the Battle of Bull Run, which ended in a Confederate victory, the Union called for more troops and planned for a long war.
- A new era in naval warfare emerged as ironclad ships, belonging to the Union and Confederacy, fought for the first time.
- The Union gained a number of victories in the West as the North and South fought for control of the Mississippi River.
- In the East, the Union faced defeat, although a Confederate invasion of Maryland was turned back at the Battle of Antietam.

What Did You Learn?

1. Explain why the North wanted to blockade the South.
2. Which general won victories for the Union at Fort Henry and Fort Donelson? What nickname did he earn at the second battle?

Critical Thinking

3. **Drawing Conclusions** Why was control of the Mississippi River important? Use a diagram like the one shown here. CA CS3.

4. **Analyze** Why was Union general McClellan not effective as a military commander? CA HI2.
5. **The Big Ideas** What was the importance of the Union victory at the Battle of Antietam?
6. **ANALYSIS** **Analyze** You read about General Lee's battle orders that were dropped and found by a Union soldier. Write a short paragraph explaining the role of chance and error in this discovery and McClellan's use of the information. CA HI4.

Review The Big Idea

Review the Big Idea for this section: "Political ideas and major events shape how people form governments." **Ask:** What event convinced Lincoln that the time was right to move against slavery? *(the withdrawal of Lee's troops from Maryland)* OL CA HI2.

ASSESS

Resources for page 583

Use these resources to assess student mastery of section content.

Section Quiz 13–2

Interactive Tutor Self-Assessment CD-ROM

Reading Check

Answer: Northern forces were driven back to the James River, failing to capture Richmond.

History Online

Study Central provides summaries, interactive games, and online graphic organizers to help students review section content.

CLOSE

Drawing Conclusions
Have students decide if they think Lincoln was right to fire McClellan and explain why or why not. OL CA HI1.

SECTION 2 REVIEW ANSWERS

Review questions reinforce content standard US8.10.

1. to prevent imports of supplies needed to fight the war
2. General Ulysses S. Grant; "Unconditional Surrender"
3. The river joined the Confederacy geographically and was a transportation route.
4. He was too cautious, moved too slowly, and gave his opponents time to strengthen.
5. **The Big Ideas** The Union army gained confidence; Lee moved south; it gave Lincoln the chance to act against slavery.
6. **ANALYSIS** It was pure chance, although McClellan did not make the best use of the surprise information, delaying for four days.

FOCUS

Summary

Jeff and his fellow soldiers are advancing into their first battle. As the line moves forward, the soldiers hear bullets whizzing around them. Jeff feels fear, but moves forward, comforted and strengthened by the nearness of the other soldiers. They fix their bayonets. Strangely, Jeff's thoughts return to his home, and he prays to be safe. Suddenly, the Union artillery behind them begins firing, and then the order to charge is given. Yelling and sprinting, Jeff stops to fire several times. Convinced he is about to die, he wants to get the worst over with.

Vocabulary Preview Before students begin reading, have them read **Before You Read** and the **Vocabulary Preview**. Point out that difficult words are footnoted throughout the text.

Background Information

The Battle of Prairie Grove was part of the Union attempt to control the West and the Mississippi River. It resulted in a Union victory, and led to the Union capture of Little Rock, Arkansas, the next year.

Answers and Additional Support

America's Literature

Rifles for Watie

By Harold Keith

Before You Read

The Scene: This selection takes place at the Battle of Prairie Grove in northwest Arkansas. The date is December 7, 1862.

The Characters: Jeff Bussey is a private in the First Kansas Regiment of Infantry. His best friends, Noah Babbitt, Bill Earie, and Big Jake Lonegan are all in the same company, and Captain Clardy commands it. Mary and Bess are his sisters, and Ring is his dog. The Union army is under General Blunt.

The Plot: Jeff joined the army to defend his home from Confederate raiders. They were destroying the homes and farms of Union supporters in Kansas. Jeff has wanted to be in a battle since he joined the army.

Vocabulary Preview

acrid: smelling or tasting bitter
din: loud or confused sound
doleful: expressing grief; sad
gaunt: very thin and bony
ominously: in a way that is a sign of future trouble or evil
perplexed: puzzled
ricocheting: hitting a hard surface lightly and bouncing back
sheepishly: acting in an embarrassed way after becoming aware of a mistake

Have you ever wanted to do something because it seemed exciting? Was it as you imagined it would be, or was it different? Jeff is about to have his wish to be in a battle fulfilled. What will it be like?

584

READING STRATEGY MODELING

As students read, they should adjust their reading strategies to clarify the ideas or events. Model how this is done by reading the passage on page 585 aloud. As you read, model these strategies:

- Inferring: "Bill Earlie makes a joke from the bottom of the pile. He's probably feeling nervous."
- Drawing conclusions: "Why is Jeff's breath quickening? It's fear, isn't it?"
- Connecting: "How do I feel when I'm afraid? Like Jeff, my throat gets dry and I feel my heart beating extra fast."

This modeling will help students see how to employ various strategies as they read independently. OL

As You Read

Writers may choose words and events to state an opinion. For example, Jeff lives with Confederates in another part of Rifles for Watie. *During this experience, he discovers that they are no different than any other people. As you read this selection, notice the kinds of words and events the author used. Think about what the writer may be saying concerning war.* R1

Jeff saw a tiny, circular puff of white smoke blossom above the trees. Then suddenly on the prairie some fifty yards in front of their line, a dash of dust, and something whizzed noisily over their heads, buzzing like a monster bee.

"Blam!"

Jeff dove flat on his stomach. He felt a painful jar as several of his comrades jumped in on top of him to escape the glancing rebel cannon ball.

"Boys, if I ain't flat enough, won't some o' you please jump on me and mash me flatter?" Bill Earie said weakly from the bottom of the pile.

U "Git back into line!" Clardy roared sternly. "Eyes front! Stop your cowardly dodging! Any man leaving his station again will be shot!" With the flat[1] of his sword, Clardy spanked a timid recruit in the seat of his pants and pushed another roughly into position. R2

Sheepishly they re-formed their line. Jeff felt his breathing quicken. He saw another tiny spiral of smoke appear above the tops of the trees. This time a charge of grape[2] came flying overhead, screeching like forty locomotives. Again the men ducked instinctively, but this time only a few left the line.

"It's all right, boys," Jeff heard Bill giggle in his nervous tenor.[3] "Just dodge the biggest of 'em."

[1] **flat:** side
[2] **grape:** short for grape shot, which is a group of small iron balls shot from a cannon
[3] **tenor:** a man's singing voice with the highest natural range

EXTENDING THE CONTENT

A Confederate Leader The title figure of this Newbery Award–winning novel is Stand Watie (1806–1871), a feared Cherokee leader who led cavalry troops in the Confederate army. Eventually rising to the rank of brigadier-general, Watie was known for devastating raids behind Union lines that destroyed crops and settlements. He was among the last Confederates to surrender, not giving up until June 23, 1865, more than two months after Robert E. Lee surrendered his army at Appomattox.

TEACH

R1 Reading Strategy

Scaffolding—Connecting **Ask:** Think about a time you faced a major challenge. How did you approach it? What did you do to get ready? *(Students' answers will probably describe a variety of approaches to facing a challenge.)* OL

This READING SKILL was introduced in Chapter 3.

U Universal Access

Naturalistic **Ask:** What does the battlefield look like? How do you know? *(It is a wide flat prairie with trees on one side, where the Confederates are; the author describes the battlefield as he tells what happens.)* BL CA 8RL3.4

R2 Reading Strategy

Inferring **Ask:** Do you think Clardy is serious that anyone who leaves his station again will be shot? Why or why not? *(He is probably serious; discipline in the military is critical, especially with inexperienced troops.)* OL CA 8RL3.3

Glencoe Literature Library

The following literature from the **Glencoe Literature Library** may enrich the teaching of this chapter:

The Red Badge of Courage by Stephen Crane

W Writing Support

Response to Literature Writing Have students write a paragraph describing how the author uses sensory details (sight, smell, sound) to describe the battle and how that enhances readers' understanding of the characters' emotions. *(sights: puffs of smoke; smell: the gunpowder; sounds: beating of the drums and the crackle of rifle fire; all make the scene real and show how Jeff's senses are heightened by his fear)* OL

R1 Reading Strategy

Inferring Ask: The author talks about Jeff's odd behavior. What is this odd behavior? What is the reason for it? *(His throat is dry, his palms itch, his heart is pounding, he feels hysterical, his legs refuse to move, his chest feels heavy, it is hard to breathe. He is probably afraid.)* OL CA 8RL3.3

R2 Reading Strategy

Inferring Ask: Why does Jeff feel comforted by the presence of Noah? *(Students may say that the other soldier makes him feel less alone or isolated or that Noah's calmness is reassuring.)* OL CA 8RL3.3

Answers and Additional Support

America's Literature

Jeff felt a hysterical urge to laugh but discovered that he couldn't. For some strange reason, his throat had gone dry as a bone. The insides of his palms itched, and he could hear his pulse pounding. Again he checked the load in his rifle and was angry at himself. He knew there was nothing wrong with the rifle load.

R1 Furious because he couldn't control his odd behavior, he clenched his jaws and shook his head vigorously. He had looked forward so long to his first battle. And now that the long-awaited moment had finally come, he discovered that some queer species of paralysis[4] had gripped his legs. His chest felt heavy, as if a blacksmith's anvil[5] was weighing it down. It was hard for him to breathe.

Noah looked at him anxiously. "What's the matter, youngster?"

Jeff licked his lips and swallowed once. Perplexed, he shook his brown head. "I don't know. My stomach feels bashful." Embarrassed, he looked around, hoping nobody would get the wrong idea and impute[6] this accursed nervousness to cowardice. He was fiercely determined not to disgrace his family or his county.

Suddenly the Union drums began to roll, loudly and ominously. . . .

"Fall in!"

W Obediently Jeff backed into line, dressing up[7] on Noah's tall form next to him. A spiteful[8] crackle of rifle fire, punctuated by the deeper roar of cannon, broke suddenly from the woods. Now the stinking, acrid odor of gunpowder was on the air. A rebel bombshell screeched over their heads, hunting for them. Jeff imagined he could hear it say, "Where-is-yuh, where-is-yuh, where-is-yuh—boooom!"

He began to hear tiny thuds here and there in the ground. They reminded him of the first, isolated dropping of hailstones during a spring storm on the Kansas prairies. Tardily he realized they were rebel rifle bullets.

R2 "Fix bayonets!" Mechanically Jeff groped for the scabbard at his belt. Fingers shaking, he managed to clamp the long knife over the muzzle of his rifle. He shot a quick look at Noah. It was good to have Noah next to him.

"Be ready, youngster! We're goin' in after 'em!" Noah yelled. Jeff pulled a couple of long breaths and felt the goose bumps rising on his arms.

He heard Clardy cursing. Big Jake Lonegan had thrown down his musket and run in terror to the rear. Jeff felt a powerful urge to follow him. He could hear the officers shouting threats, too, but they failed to stop the big sergeant or even to slow him down.

[4] **paralysis:** loss of ability to feel or move a body part or parts
[5] **anvil:** heavy metal block that has a flat top on which heated metal objects are hammered into shape
[6] **impute:** to falsely put the responsibility on
[7] **dressing up:** standing in a straight line and at the correct distance
[8] **spiteful:** annoying

586

EXTENDING THE CONTENT

Soldier Boys Boys under the age of 16 served in both Union and Confederate armies. Many began as musicians, playing drums and bugles, which told soldiers how and when to maneuver in battle. For this reason, the boys were often targeted by the enemy. One of the most famous of these soldier boys was John Lincoln Clem. He joined the 22nd Michigan Infantry. His drum was destroyed at Shiloh, and, at Chickamauga, he killed a Confederate colonel. He earned the nickname "The Drummer Boy of Chickamauga."

"Eyes front!" bellowed Clardy. "Any man leaving his position will be shot!"

Swallowing nervously, Jeff found he could not keep his thoughts on the coming battle. Oddly, they kept wandering back to Linn County. It was a Sunday afternoon, and his family had probably just returned from church in the rock mission at Sugar Mound. He could see his mother, busy over her fireplace ovens, cooking the Sunday dinner, with Bess and Mary both helping, each careful not to soil the Sunday dresses they had not yet taken off. He could see his father unhitching Jack and Beck from the buckboard and Ring crouching mischievously by the gooseberry bushes, waiting to give the mules a run when they were liberated through the corral gate.

Tears stung Jeff's eyes. Angry at himself for showing emotion, he winked them off. What in the world was the matter with him? The rebel fire grew hotter. What funny music the rebel Minie balls[9] made. Some of them mewed like kittens. Others hummed like angry hornets or whined like ricocheting nails.

A soldier on Jeff's right went down with a strangled moan, clutching and raking at his stomach. Jeff began to pray hard, straight from the heart. He hadn't dreamed that war was anything like this. He vowed[10] that if by some miracle he came out alive, he would always go to church thereafter.

"Forward march!" Jeff barely heard the command above the battle's din. But every man obeyed. Bayoneted muskets carried at the ready, they strode blindly forward to whatever fate awaited them. . . .

Bullets zipped all about them. Jeff wondered how it felt to be hit by a musket ball; whether it stung or whether it burned. He wondered why their own artillery hadn't begun shooting.

[9] **Minie balls:** rifle bullets with cone-shaped heads that were used in muzzle-loading guns
[10] **vowed:** promised seriously; pledged

C1 Critical Thinking

Making Generalizations Ask students if they think Jeff's reaction to his first battle is typical for young soldiers. Why or why not? *(Some students will agree, since going into battle is undoubtedly a difficult action to take.)* OL CA 8RL3.3

C2 Critical Thinking

Making Inferences Ask students why Jeff's thoughts return to his home as the troops get ready to attack. *(Students may suggest he cannot stand to think about what he is about to do or that his mind is seeking comfort in a familiar activity that seems far away and safe.)* OL

R Reading Strategy

Evaluating Remind students that figurative language is language meant to be understood imaginatively rather than literally. Ask students to find examples of figurative language on this page. *(the minié balls making music, mewing like kittens, humming like hornets, or whining like ricocheting nails)* OL CA 8RL3.6

GLENCOE BOOKLINK

Use **Glencoe BookLink** to create customized reading lists for your students' reading levels, interests, and abilities.

EXTENDING THE CONTENT

Advances in Ammunition The minié ball was the invention of Claude-Etienne Minié, a French army officer. In 1849, he designed a cylindrical bullet. On its bottom was an iron cup. When the musket was fired, the iron cup pushed into the bullet and expanded its base. This expanded bullet fit snugly into grooves in the barrel. The spin that the grooves gave to the minié ball made it much more accurate—and deadly. The minié ball was used extensively by both sides. Minié himself retired from the French army in 1858 and worked at the Remington Arms Company in the United States.

C Critical Thinking

Analyzing Information Have students describe how Jeff's attitude changes on this page. *(In the first paragraph he is resigned to being killed. He throws away his coat because he won't need it. His feelings change halfway through the page, when he finds a new determination to live. His mind is clearer and he understands what he has to do.)* **AL** CA 8RL3.3

U Universal Access

Auditory/Musical Ask students to find examples of sounds being spelled out on this page. *(Flam-a-dee rattled the drums; Ba-loom is the sound the cannons make.)* Ask them to make up and write other sounds for things that happen in the story. *(Students should use their imaginations to make up new sounds.)* **OL**

R Reading Strategy

Inferring Ask: What happens during the battle to lift Jeff's spirits? *(The Union artillery begins shelling the enemy, which helps Jeff realize that the Union artillery and infantry are working well together.)* **OL** CA 8RL3.2

Answers and Additional Support

Looking to both right and left, he found himself part of a long blue line of soldiers moving at a quick walk toward the woods ahead. Men all around him were taking off their coats and dropping them on the prairie. Jeff peeled off his, flung it to the ground and felt a little better. He wouldn't need it anyhow because he expected to be killed.

"Flam-a-dee! Flam-a-dee! Flam-a-dee-dee!" rattled the drums, sounding their doleful call to death. They entered the woods. A wounded horse screamed in agony.[11] Stifling an impulse to turn and run, he clenched his teeth and kept advancing, dreading what lay ahead because he couldn't see it, nor imagine what it was like.

Although it was December, sweat ran down the tip of his nose. The winter sun gleamed brightly off his steel bayonet.

Noah, tall, gaunt, looking grim as death, was walking in a low crouch, his bayonet-tipped musket held in front of him. Jeff felt a little better. Just being close to Noah helped. The presence of the other men helped, too.

U He stumbled over a fallen log but kept going. His mind was sharp now. He began to recall all the mean things he had ever done and how he might never have time to atone[12] for them. Life was running out on him. He wasn't ready to die. He didn't want to be rushed into it. He needed more time to think about it. After all, a person died just once. Anybody who let himself get killed was just plain stupid. The world was a wonderful place to live. No matter how revered he was in life, a dead person was so completely out of things. Even his own relatives soon forgot him and quickly reshaped their lives without him.

"Ba-loom! Ba-loom!"

A sudden rush of air passed overhead, and Jeff's heart leaped thankfully. Casting a startled look back over his shoulder, he saw streaks of orange-gold flame burst from Blunt's forward guns as the Union batteries,[13] elevating their cannon, fired over the heads of their infantry, using two-second fuses. For the first time he appreciated how dependent the infantry and artillery were upon each other. R

"Charge bayonets!"

With a wild yell the long blue line leaped forward. Sprinting at breakneck speed, Jeff yelled at the top of his lungs, too. Their little red and white striped flag with the blue patch in the corner was going along with them at a jerky motion. There was a steady rattle of musket fire ahead. Gaps were torn in the line by the rebel volleys.[14] They began to run through clouds of sulphurous[15] smoke. It stank and made his eyes smart. . . .

[11] **agony:** extreme pain for a long time
[12] **atone:** make up for
[13] **batteries:** groupings of similar things so that they can be used together
[14] **volleys:** firings of many guns or other weapons at the same time
[15] **sulphurous:** made from sulphur, one of the chemicals in gunpowder and matches

Reading Strategy: CONNECTING

Point out that Jeff feels better just knowing the other men are with him. Have students think about an experience in which having another person or persons around made a difficult experience easier to handle. Ask them to write a paragraph about the experience and how other people helped them through it. *(Students' paragraphs should describe the situation and how the presence of other people helped.)* **OL**

A rebel bullet sheared off a branch a yard away. Jeff dove to his knees, furious at the stupidity of both armies standing in line and shooting at one another like duelists at ten paces. On his right, he saw Noah firing carefully off one knee. That still wasn't low enough for Jeff.

Flat on his belly, he began firing as fast as he could. Loading a single-shot musket was an intricate operation. Rolling over on his back, he bit off the end of the paper cartridge, thrust it in the gun, poured powder into the muzzle, withdrew his iron ramrod from the groove beneath the barrel, and rammed the charge and the bullet down the barrel. Then he pulled the hammer back with his thumb and stuck [on] a percussion cap.[16] . . . After that, all he had to do was draw a bead on the enemy and press the trigger. With the firing of the shot, smoke and fire from the black gunpowder belched into his face, and then he had the whole thing to do over.

Each time he fired, Jeff scrambled to his feet, ran forward a few steps, then dropped again to reload. He bit the cartridges off so fast that he swallowed some of the spilled powder. It tasted bitter. He wanted to rinse his mouth. But he couldn't. His canteen had been full of good, cold Arkansas spring water but he had foolishly thrown it away with his coat. Hot with battle now, he felt only that he wanted to encounter the worst and get it over as quickly as possible.

[16] **percussion cap:** a thin container that holds material that will explode when hit

Responding to the Literature

1. Onomatopoeia is the use of a word or words to imitate the sound that something makes. Write two examples of onomatopoeia in this selection.
2. What would happen to a soldier if he left his unit before the battle?
3. **Analyze** What are the literal and figurative meanings of this phrase: "a charge of grape came flying overhead, screeching like forty locomotives"? CA 8RW1.1
4. **Compare and Contrast** Describe Jeff's opinion of what being in a battle is like. Include examples to show how his opinion changed during the story. CA 8WA2.2.a, d
5. **Read to Write** Write a report of 500 to 700 words on one of these battles: Chickamauga, Chancellorsville, or Shiloh. Include the reason for the battle, what happened, and its casualties. Include a map of the area and at least one quotation. Explain how the battle is or is not similar to the one in the story. CA 8WA2.3b, d

C Critical Thinking

Analyzing Information
Have a volunteer read aloud the paragraph describing the actions needed to fire a gun during the Civil War. **Ask:** Do you think those actions are easy or difficult to do during a battle? Why? What does that tell you about the soldiers? *(Students may say that the actions are difficult because there are many steps, which would be challenging to do while under fire. They may conclude that the soldiers were very disciplined and determined.)* OL CA 8RL3.3

R Reading Strategy

Predicting **Ask:** What do you think will happen next in the book? Why? Discuss students' responses. OL

Resources for page 589

American Literature Reading 13

ASSESS

Assign the Responding to the Reading Questions as an in-class activity or as homework.

CLOSE

Summarizing **Ask:** What did Jeff learn about himself and about life during the battle? OL

Responding to the Literature Answers

1. "flam-a-dee" (the drums) "ba-loom" and "blam" (the cannons)
2. Clardy and other officers said he would be shot.
3. literal: grapeshot fired from a cannon flew over their heads; figurative: the sound it made seemed extremely loud to the frightened soldiers
4. He is frightened at the beginning, as shown by his "odd behavior" as the battle begins, however, he regains a clear head and new purpose, does what he has been trained to do, and goes into battle grimly and with acceptance of what might happen.
5. Reports should be accurate and use correct grammar and spelling.

TEACH

The reading selections for this unit have been chosen to reflect the California History-Social Science Standards. If you assign one of these books, you may want to have students complete the following activity.

Setting a Purpose

Have students set a purpose to help them choose which book to read. For instance, they might want to know about some aspect of the war, such as life on the home front or the traits of the leaders. For those topics, students may be better off reading a nonfiction book. If they want to know more about how Americans experienced the war and felt about it, they might prefer a fictional account. Have students develop a list of questions they would like to see answered and identify book titles that might provide those answers.

GLENCOE **BOOKLINK**

Use **Glencoe BookLink** to create customized reading lists for your students' reading levels, interests, and abilities.

Answers and Additional Support

Reading On Your Own...

From the California Reading List

Do you want to learn more about people who experienced the Civil War? If so, check out the following books:

Historical Fiction

Across Five Aprils by Irene Hunt recounts what happens to Jethro Creighton during the Civil War. When his older brothers and teacher join the Union and Confederate armies, Jethro must run the family farm. He experiences the hopes and fears of a land at war and struggles to understand what is happening. ***The content of this book is related to*** *History–Social Science Standard US8.10.*

Historical Fiction

The Bravest Girl in Sharpsburg by Kathleen Ernst tells the story of two girls whose friendship is ended by their differing loyalties to the North and the South. When Confederate troops march into their hometown, the girls are thrown into the middle of a battle. After many hardships, their friendship is restored. ***The content of this book is related to*** *History–Social Science Standard US8.10.*

Nonfiction

Those Courageous Women of the Civil War by Karen Zeinert describes the many roles that women played during the war. In addition to keeping farms, businesses, and homes functioning, they were doctors, nurses, spies, and soldiers. ***The content of this book is related to*** *History–Social Science Standard US8.10.*

Biography

Lincoln: A Photobiography by Russell Freedman describes the private and public life of Abraham Lincoln. In this description, the author traces how Lincoln reached the decision to emancipate the slaves. There is also a generous presentation of pictures of Lincoln, his family, and his associates throughout the book. ***The content of this book is related to*** *History–Social Science Standard US8.10.*

590

READING STRATEGY — ANALYZING TEXT STRUCTURE

Students can analyze the structure of books they are considering to see whether the book is likely to meet the purpose they set for their reading. The table of contents and preface or introduction of a nonfiction book should provide a good idea of the book's scope. Leafing through the book to look at illustrations, if there are any, will also help. For works of fiction, reviews or descriptions on the cover can provide hints. With works of either type, they may wish to read a few early pages to see if they like the author's writing style. OL

Section 3

A Call to Freedom

Guide to Reading

Looking Back, Looking Ahead
As the war continued, African Americans gained opportunities to contribute to the war effort. The Emancipation Proclamation officially permitted African Americans to enlist in the Union army and navy.

Focusing on the Main Ideas
- Lincoln signed the Emancipation Proclamation, which led to the passing of the Thirteenth Amendment freeing enslaved Americans. *(page 592)*
- The Civil War provided opportunities for African Americans to contribute to the war effort. *(page 595)*

Meeting People
Harriet Tubman

Content Vocabulary
emancipate (ih • MAN • suh • PAYT)
ratify (RA • tuh • FY)

Academic Vocabulary
reluctance (rih • LUHK • tuhns)
area

Reading Strategy
Taking Notes As you read the section, complete a table like the one shown describing what the Emancipation Proclamation and the Thirteenth Amendment to the Constitution were meant to accomplish.

	Accomplishments
Emancipation Proclamation	
Thirteenth Amendment	

History Social Science Standards

US8.10 Students analyze the multiple causes, key events, and complex consequences of the Civil War.

NATIONAL GEOGRAPHIC Who & When?

1862 | 1863 | 1864 | 1865

1862 African Americans begin to serve in Union army

Jan. 1863 Lincoln signs the Emancipation Proclamation

July 1863 Nearly half of the 54th Massachusetts Regiment is wiped out

1865 Thirteenth Amendment is ratified

SECTION RESOURCES

Print Material
- Reproducible Lesson Plan 13–3*
- Daily Lesson and Discussion Notes 13–3
- Guided Reading Activity 13–3
- Reading Essentials and Study Guide 13–3
- Active Reading Note-Taking Guide 13–3
- Section Quiz 13–3

Transparencies
- Daily Focus Skills Transparency 13–3
- Section Graphic Organizer Transparency 13–3
- California Standards Practice Transparencies

Technology
- Interactive Tutor Self-Assessment CD-ROM
- Exam*View*® Pro Testmaker CD-ROM
- Presentation Plus! CD-ROM

*Available on TeacherWorks™

FOCUS

BELLRINGER
SKILLBUILDER ACTIVITY

Project **Daily Focus Skills Transparency 13–3** and have students answer the question.

Guide to Reading

Preteaching Vocabulary: Explain that *emancipate* means "to free." Have students speculate on the purpose of the Emancipation Proclamation. *(to free enslaved people)*

Answers to Graphic: Emancipation Proclamation: end slavery in the South, cause Britain and France to be less likely to aid the South, decrease number of enslaved workers in the South; Thirteenth Amendment: abolish slavery throughout the U.S.

Unpacking the Standards
After reading the section, students will be able to:
- Explain why Lincoln issued the Emancipation Proclamation.
- Discuss the contributions of African Americans to the war.

TEACH

Review The Big Idea

Review the Big Idea for this section: "Reactions to social injustice can lead to reform movements." Have students work in small groups to create a story map detailing the story of the war leading up to the Emancipation Proclamation. Explain that story maps have four sections: (1) introduction of the problem; (2) roadblocks; (3) climax or high point; and (4) solution. Groups should present their completed story maps to the class. OL CA HI1.

W Writing Support

Persuasive Writing Tell students to imagine that they are advisors to President Lincoln, and he has asked them to write a memo advising him on whether or not to issue the Emancipation Proclamation. The memo should give political, diplomatic, and ethical reasons for the recommendation. AL CA HI1. CA HI2. CA 8LA2.4

Resources for page 592

Critical Thinking Skills Activity 13

Answers and Additional Support

US8.10.4 Discuss Abraham Lincoln's presidency and his significant writings and speeches and their relationship to the Declaration of Independence, such as his "House Divided" speech (1858), Gettysburg Address (1863), Emancipation Proclamation (1863), and inaugural addresses (1861 and 1865).

Emancipation

Main Idea **Lincoln signed the Emancipation Proclamation, which led to the passing of the Thirteenth Amendment, freeing enslaved Americans.**

Reading Connection Do you recall a time when an announcement had everyone talking? Read and find out about an announcement by Lincoln that changed lives forever.

W President Lincoln shook many hands on New Year's Day of 1863, as a reception was held to commemorate the official signing of the Emancipation Proclamation. Diplomats, cabinet members, and army officers filed past the president, and when he finally left the reception, he noted that his arm was very stiff. As the document was presented, Lincoln remarked:

> **"Now, this signature is one that will be closely examined and if they find my hand trembled, they will say 'he had some compunctions [second thoughts].' But, any way, it is going to be done!"**
>
> —from *Lincoln*

Why It Matters

The Emancipation Proclamation

On January 1, 1863, President Lincoln issued the Emancipation Proclamation to a nation divided by war. The proclamation stated that all enslaved people in the states controlled by the Confederacy were free.

"If my name ever goes into history, it will be for this act."
—Abraham Lincoln, 1863

"The Emancipation Proclamation is the greatest event of our nation's history."
—Frederick Douglass, 1864

The Legacy of Freedom

Where America stands today on the issues of human freedom was fueled by the Emancipation Proclamation.

- **1863** → Emancipation Proclamation issued
- **1865** → Thirteenth Amendment abolishes slavery
- **1868** → Fourteenth Amendment guarantees citizens equal protection
- **1870** → Fifteenth Amendment strengthens voting rights
- **1954** → *Brown* v. *Board of Education of Topeka, Kansas* ruling outlaws school segregation

Why It Matters

Lincoln's preliminary Emancipation Proclamation gave the Confederate states three months to end the war without losing their enslaved workers. He offered this as a means of providing a more peaceful and gradual way of ending slavery. **Ask:** How do you think history might have been changed if the Confederacy had accepted Lincoln's first proposal and ended the war? *(Slavery might have continued and the sectional problems would not have been solved.)* AL CA HI4.

From the start of the war through the brutal Battle of Antietam, the Northerners' main goal was to preserve the Union rather than to destroy slavery. Abolitionists did not control the North, or even the Republican Party. Abraham Lincoln and other Republican leaders insisted on many occasions that they would act only to prevent the expansion of slavery.

R1 Although Lincoln considered slavery immoral, he showed **reluctance** to move against slavery because of the border states. Lincoln R2 knew that making an issue of slavery would divide the people and make the war less popular. In August 1862, Abraham Lincoln responded to pressure to declare an end to slavery.

C **"If I could save the Union without freeing any slave, I would do it; if I could save it by freeing all the slaves, I would do it; and if I could save it by freeing some and leaving others alone, I would also do that. What I do about slavery, . . . I do because I believe it helps to save the Union."**

—Letter to Horace Greeley, August 22, 1862

That was his official position. His personal wish was "that all men everywhere could be free."

As news of the proclamation spread throughout the Confederacy, thousands of enslaved people fled to freedom. About 200,000 freed African Americans served as soldiers, sailors, and laborers for the Union forces.

Union Forces

More than 2 million soldiers served in the Union army, and more than 100,000 sailors served in the Union navy. About 200,000 African Americans served with the Union.

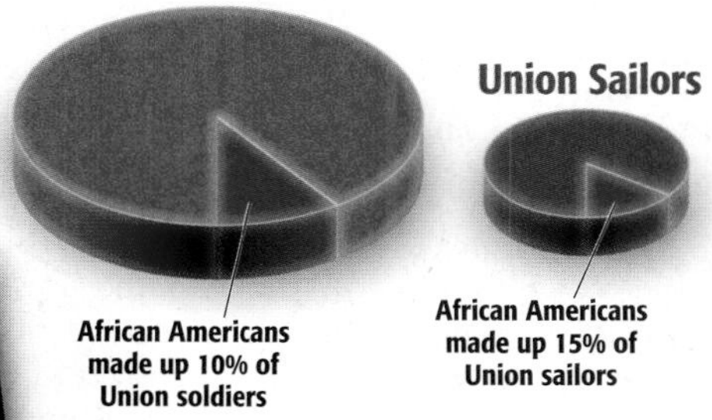

The proclamation established that the war was being fought not only to preserve the Union, but to end slavery. Few enslaved people were freed by the action, however.

S

- **1955** Rosa Parks refuses to give up her bus seat; Montgomery, Alabama
- **1963** March on Washington
- **1964** Twenty-fourth Amendment ends use of poll tax; Civil Rights Act passed
- **2001** Colin Powell named secretary of state
- **2003** Scheduled work on national monument to Martin Luther King, Jr., begins

R1 Reading Strategy

Academic Vocabulary Ask students to list synonyms for the word *reluctant*. OL

R2 Reading Strategy

Scaffolding—Academic Vocabulary The word *issue* was introduced in Chapter 10, Section 1. Ask a student to define the word as it is used here. OL

C Critical Thinking

Drawing Conclusions Point out to students the conflict between Lincoln's public attitude towards slavery and his personal wish. **Ask:** Is it wrong for a political leader to have different public and private views on an issue? Why or why not? *(Answers will vary, but students should support their opinions and cite examples.)* AL CA HR5.

S Skill Practice

Reading a Time Line Ask students to make a three-item quiz using the time line in **Why It Matters**. Have them write a true/false question, a fill-in-the-blank question, and a short answer question. Ask them to write answers and exchange quizzes with a partner. BL CA CS2.

Did You Know?

Lincoln's famous declaration about saving the Union was made in a letter to the editor of the *New York Tribune*, Horace Greeley. It was at the end of this letter that Lincoln revealed his personal feelings on the matter: "I have here stated my purpose according to my view of *official* duty; and I intend no modification of the oft-expressed *personal* wish that all men everywhere could be free."

R Reading Strategy

Understanding Vocabulary Have students identify words that are either synonyms (words that have the same meaning) or antonyms (words that have the opposite meaning) of *emancipate*. *(synonyms: free, liberate, release, set free; antonyms: capture, enslave, imprison)* EL CA 8RW1.3

W Writing Support

Summary Writing Have students read the Emancipation Proclamation in the Appendix of this textbook. Then have them summarize a section in their own words. AL

S Skill Practice

Historical and Social Sciences Analysis Skill Have students take and support a position on this statement: Because it freed almost no enslaved people, the Emancipation Proclamation was a waste of time. *(Students' positions should be supported with evidence of its effects from the text and by sound reasoning.)* OL CA HI2.

Reading Check

Answer: abolished slavery in the United States

Answers and Additional Support

Changing Attitudes As the war went on, attitudes toward slavery began to change. More Northerners believed that slavery was helping the war effort in the South. Enslaved people in the Confederacy raised crops used to feed the armies and did the heavy work in the trenches at the army camps. In the North's view, anything that weakened slavery struck a blow against the Confederacy.

As early as May 1861, some African Americans in the South escaped slavery by going into territory held by the Union army. In 1861 and 1862, Congress passed laws that freed enslaved people who were held by those active in the rebellion against the Union.

Antietam and the Proclamation Lincoln was keenly aware of the shift in public opinion. He also knew that striking a blow against slavery would make Britain and France less likely to aid the South. Moreover, Lincoln became convinced that slavery helped the South continue fighting. Every enslaved person who worked enabled a white Southerner to fight in the Confederate army.

Lincoln also had political reasons for taking action on slavery. He believed it was important that the president rather than the antislavery Republicans in Congress make the decision on ending slavery. Lincoln told the members of his cabinet:

> **"I must do the best I can, and bear the responsibility."**

R By the summer of 1862, Lincoln had decided to **emancipate** (ih • MAN • suh • PAYT)—or free—all enslaved African Americans in the South. He waited for the right moment so that he would not appear to be acting in desperation when the North seemed to be losing the war.

On September 22, 1862, five days after the Union forces turned back the Confederate troops at the Battle of Antietam, Lincoln announced his plan to issue an order freeing all enslaved people in the Confederacy. On January 1, 1863, Lincoln signed the Emancipation Proclamation, which said:

> **". . . all persons held as slaves within any state . . . in rebellion against the United States, shall be then, thenceforward, and forever free."** W
>
> **—The Emancipation Proclamation**

Effects of the Proclamation The Emancipation Proclamation applied only to **areas** that the Confederacy controlled. Lincoln knew, however, that many enslaved people would hear about the proclamation. He hoped that knowledge of it would encourage them to run away from their slaveholders. Even before the Emancipation Proclamation, some 100,000 African Americans had left slavery for the safety of the Union. *(See page 855 of the Appendix for the text of the Emancipation Proclamation.)*

Despite the limitations of the Emancipation Proclamation, African Americans in the North greeted it joyfully. On the day it was signed, a crowd of African Americans gathered at the White House to cheer the president. Frederick Douglass wrote, "We shout for joy that we live to record this righteous decree." S

The proclamation had the desired effect in Europe as well. The Confederacy had been seeking support from its trading partners, Britain and France. However, the British took a strong position against slavery. Once Lincoln proclaimed emancipation, Britain and France decided to withhold recognition of the Confederacy.

In 1864 Republican leaders in Congress prepared a constitutional amendment to abolish slavery in the United States. In 1865 Congress passed the Thirteenth Amendment, which was **ratified** (RA • tuh • FYD), or approved, the same year by states loyal to the Union. It was this amendment that truly freed enslaved Americans. *(See page 262 for the complete text of the Thirteenth Amendment.)*

Reading Check **Explain** What did the Thirteenth Amendment do that the Emancipation Proclamation did not do?

More Skill Practice

Historical and Social Sciences Analysis Skill Ask students to use library or Internet sources to find two contemporary responses to the Emancipation Proclamation. Have students read the responses and report on what position they took and what reasons they gave for that stand. OL CA 8WS1.4 CA 8WA2.2

US8.10.5 Study the views and lives of leaders (e.g., Ulysses S. Grant, Jefferson Davis, Robert E. Lee) and soldiers on both sides of the war, including those of black soldiers and regiments. US8.10.6 Describe critical developments and events in the war, including the major battles, geographical advantages and obstacles, technological advances, and General Lee's surrender at Appomattox.

U African Americans in the War

Main Idea **The Civil War provided opportunities for African Americans to contribute to the war effort.**

Reading Connection How do you think freed African Americans affected the Union war effort? Read to find out how many formerly enslaved people fought against the South during the Civil War.

C1 The Emancipation Proclamation announced Lincoln's decision to permit African Americans to join the Union army. In the South, as well as in the North, the Civil War was changing the lives of all African Americans.

In the South When the war began, more than 3.5 million enslaved people lived in the Confederacy. Making up more than 30 percent of the region's population and the bulk of its workforce, enslaved workers labored on plantations and in vital iron, salt, and lead mines. Some worked as nurses in military hospitals and cooks in the army. By the end of the war, about one-sixth of the enslaved population had fled to areas controlled by Union armies.

The possibility of a slave rebellion terrified white Southerners. For this reason, most Southerners refused to use African Americans as soldiers—for then they would be given weapons.

Near the end of the war, however, the Confederate military became desperate. Robert E. Lee and some others supported using African Americans as soldiers and believed that those who fought should be freed. The Confederate Congress passed a law in 1865 to enlist enslaved people. The war ended before any regiments could be organized.

Helping the North The story was different in the North. At the start of the war, African Americans were not permitted to serve as soldiers in the Union army. This disappointed many free African Americans who had volunteered to fight for the Union. C2

Yet African Americans who wished to help the war effort found ways to do so. Although the army would not accept them, the Union navy did. African Americans who had escaped slavery often proved to be useful as guides and spies because of their knowledge of the South. Some women, such as **Harriet Tubman,** who had helped dozens escape slavery by way of the Underground Railroad, repeatedly spied behind Confederate lines.

▲ Nearly 200,000 African Americans joined Union forces.

U Universal Access

Below Grade Level Ask students to make a word web with the words "How African Americans helped win the Civil War" in the center. Have them add ways that African Americans served in the war. *(fought as soldiers and sailors, served as work and supply units, were spies and guides)* BL CA 8RC2.0.

C1 Critical Thinking

Making Inferences Explain that Lincoln opposed having African American soldiers at first. **Ask:** Why do you think Lincoln changed his mind? *(Possible answers include lack of success and need for more men, the ideas expressed in the Emancipation Proclamation, and arguments from people like Frederick Douglass)* OL CA HI2.

C2 Critical Thinking

Analyzing Primary Sources Write on the board and have students discuss this quotation from March 5, 1863, by abolitionist leader Frederick Douglass: "The arm of the slave is the best defense against the arm of the slaveholder. Who would be free themselves must strike the blow." **Ask:** What does Douglass mean? *(He believes that African Americans should be allowed to fight, that they are a tremendous resource for the North)* OL CA HR5.

Resources for page 595

Primary Source Reading 13

More Skill Practice

Historical and Social Sciences Analysis Skill **Ask:** Would using enslaved African Americans as soldiers have helped the Confederacy win the war? Why or why not? *(Students may cite the doubtful loyalty of enslaved African Americans to the Confederate cause and the lack of weapons and supplies of the Confederate army.)* AL CA HI2.

Did You Know?

Even when African Americans were finally allowed to become soldiers, they were not immediately allowed into combat. At first, African American units were used as labor battalions and supply troops.

C Critical Thinking

Comparing and Contrasting Ask students why whites and African Americans of the South reacted differently to the North's use of African American soldiers. *(Students may say that whites felt threatened while African Americans felt inspired.)* OL CA HI2.

ASSESS

Resources for page 596

Use these resources to assess student mastery of section content.

- Section Quiz 13–3
- Interactive Tutor Self-Assessment CD-ROM

Reading Check

Answer: They were organized into separate units, commanded by white officers, and received lower pay.

History Online

Study Central provides summaries, interactive games, and online graphic organizers to help students review section content.

CLOSE

Analyzing Primary Sources
Have students discuss this quotation by Henry Adams, who was living in London during the Civil War: "The Emancipation Proclamation has done more for us here than all our former victories and our diplomacy. It is creating an almost convulsive reaction in our favor." OL CA HR5.

African American Soldiers In 1862 Congress passed a law allowing African Americans to serve in the Union army. By the end of the war, African American volunteers made up nearly 10 percent of the Union army and about 15 percent of the navy. In all, nearly 200,000 African Americans served. About 37,000 lost their lives defending the Union. By becoming soldiers, African Americans were taking an important step toward securing civil rights.

African American soldiers were organized into regiments separate from the rest of the Union army. Most commanding officers of these regiments were white. African Americans received lower pay than white soldiers at first, but protests led to equal pay in 1864.

One of the most famous African American regiments was the 54th Massachusetts, led by white abolitionists. On July 18, 1863, the 54th spearheaded an attack on a Confederate fortification near Charleston, South Carolina. Under heavy fire, the troops battled their way to the top of the fort. The Confederates drove them back with heavy fire. Nearly half of the 54th were wounded, captured, or killed. Their bravery won respect for African American troops.

Many white Southerners, outraged that African American soldiers were fighting for the Union, threatened to execute any they captured. In a few instances, this threat was carried out. However, enslaved workers were overjoyed when they saw that the Union army included African American soldiers. As one African American regiment entered Wilmington, North Carolina, young and old ran through the streets, shouting and praising God. One of the soldiers said, "We could then truly see what we have been fighting for." C

Reading Check **Compare** How were African American soldiers treated differently than white soldiers?

History Online
Study Central Need help understanding life for African Americans during the war? Visit ca.hss.glencoe.com and click on Study Central.

Section 3 Review

Reading Summary

Review the Main Ideas

- The Emancipation Proclamation freed all enslaved African Americans who were living in Confederate states.
- Many free African Americans and African Americans who had escaped from slavery enlisted with the Union army and fought in the war.

What Did You Learn?

1. Summarize President Lincoln's reasons for issuing the Emancipation Proclamation.
2. How did Harriet Tubman help the North?

Critical Thinking

3. **Determining Cause and Effect** Re-create the diagram below and list the factors that caused Lincoln to change his war goals to include freeing enslaved persons. CA HI2.

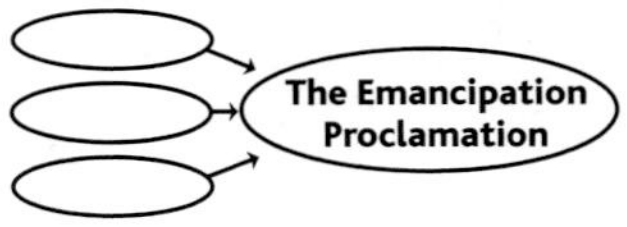

4. **Compare** How did President Lincoln's political stand on slavery differ from his personal stand? CA HR5.
5. **The Big Ideas** Describe the role of African Americans in the Union army. How were they treated, and how did President Lincoln justify their role? CA HI1.
6. **Creative Writing** Write the dialogue for a short play in which enslaved African Americans on a Southern plantation learn of the Emancipation Proclamation and discuss what it means to them. CA 8WA2.1C

SECTION 3 REVIEW ANSWERS

Review questions reinforce content standard US8.10.

1. to weaken the South; to prevent British and French support of South; to earn public support
2. as a spy in the South
3. public opinion changed; goal of blocking British and French aid to South; idea that slavery helped the South
4. political: first priority was to restore the Union; personal: opposed slavery
5. **The Big Ideas** They were organized into separate units, commanded by white officers, and received lower pay; Lincoln believed that their use weakened the South and strengthened the North.
6. Plays may reflect joy.

Section 4 Life During the Civil War

Guide to Reading

Looking Back, Looking Ahead
The Civil War affected civilians as well as soldiers. Civilians had an important impact on the war effort.

Focusing on the Main Ideas
- In both the North and the South, civilians and soldiers suffered terrible hardships and faced new challenges. *(page 598)*
- Many Northern and Southern women took on new responsibilities during the war. *(page 599)*
- The war efforts of the Union and the Confederate governments faced opposition. *(page 600)*
- The war created economic problems in the North and in the South. *(page 603)*

Meeting People
Mary Chesnut
Rose O'Neal Greenhow
Belle Boyd
Loretta Janeta Velázquez (vuh • LAS • kwihz)
Dorothea Dix
Clara Barton
Sally Tompkins

Content Vocabulary
habeas corpus (HAY • bee • uhs KAWR • puhs)
draft
bounty
inflation (ihn • FLAY • shuhn)

Academic Vocabulary
distribute (dih • STRIH • byuht)
substitute
occur (uh • KUHR)

Reading Strategy
Classifying Information As you read the section, complete a table like the one shown by describing the roles of these individuals during the war.

Person	Role
Loretta Janeta Velázquez	
Dorothea Dix	
Clara Barton	

History Social Science Standards

US8.10 Students analyze the multiple causes, key events, and complex consequences of the Civil War.

NATIONAL GEOGRAPHIC Who & When?

1861 1862 1863 1864

Union soldier

1861 Union Congress passes income tax

Confederate soldier

Apr. 1862 Confederate Congress passes draft

Mar. 1863 Union passes draft law

July 1863 Angry mobs oppose the draft in New York City

FOCUS

BELLRINGER Skillbuilder Activity
Project **Daily Focus Skills Transparency 13–4** and have students answer the question.

Guide to Reading

Preteaching Vocabulary: Write the entries listed under Key Terms on the board. Have volunteers skim the section to find each term and paraphrase its meaning to the class.

Answers to Graphic: Velázquez: Confederate spy and soldier; Dix: organized Union nurses; Barton: treated wounded Union soldiers

Unpacking the Standards
After reading the section, students will be able to:
- Outline the hardships suffered by soldiers and civilians during the war.
- Identify the responsibilities women in the North and South took on.
- Describe the opposition to the war in the North and the South.
- Discuss the impact of the war on the economies of the North and the South.

SECTION RESOURCES

Print Material
- Reproducible Lesson Plan 13–4*
- Daily Lesson and Discussion Notes 13–4
- Guided Reading Activity 13–4
- Reading Essentials and Study Guide 13–4
- Active Reading Note-Taking Guide 13–4
- Section Quiz 13–4

Transparencies
- Daily Focus Skills Transparency 13–4
- Section Graphic Organizer Transparency 13–4
- California Standards Practice Transparencies

Technology
- Interactive Tutor Self-Assessment CD-ROM
- Exam*View*® Pro Testmaker CD-ROM
- Presentation Plus! CD-ROM

*Available on TeacherWorks™

TEACH

U Universal Access

Logical/Mathematical

Write the following organizational structure of Civil War armies on the board:

- Company = 100 soldiers
- Regiment = 10 companies
- Brigade = 5 regiments
- Division = 3 brigades
- Corps = 3 divisions

Have students calculate and record how many soldiers made up each unit using the company as a base. *(regiment: 1,000; brigade: 5,000; division: 15,000; corps: 45,000)* OL

R Reading Strategy

Inferring Ask: Why were the soldiers at Shiloh allowed to lie dying for so long in the rain? *(Students may suggest enemy fire and limited medical care.)* OL

CA HI2.

Reading Check

Answer: because of fear, hunger, and sickness

Answers and Additional Support

US8.10.5 Study the views and lives of leaders (e.g., Ulysses S. Grant, Jefferson Davis, Robert E. Lee) and soldiers on both sides of the war, including those of black soldiers and regiments.

The Lives of Soldiers

Main Idea **In both the North and the South, civilians and soldiers suffered terrible hardships and faced new challenges.**

U **Reading Connection** How do most movies portray the life of a soldier? Do they make the military life seem exciting and filled with action? Read to find out what life was really like for a Civil War soldier.

A soldier's life was not easy. In touching letters to their families and friends at home, soldiers described what they saw and how they felt—their boredom, discomfort, sickness, fear, and horror.

At the start of the war, men in both the North and the South rushed to volunteer for the armies. Their enthusiasm did not last.

Most of the time, the soldiers lived in camps. Camp life had its pleasant moments of songs, stories, letters from home, and baseball games. Often, however, a soldier's life was dull, a routine of drills, bad food, marches, and rain.

The Reality of War In spite of some moments of calm, the reality of war was never far away. Both sides suffered terrible losses. The new rifles used during the Civil War fired with greater accuracy than the muskets of earlier wars.

R Medical facilities were overwhelmed by the thousands of casualties in each battle. After the Battle of Shiloh, many wounded soldiers lay in the rain for more than 24 hours waiting for medical treatment. A Union soldier recalled, "Many had died there, and others were in the last agonies as we passed. Their groans and cries were heart-rending."

Faced with such horrors, many men deserted. About 1 of every 11 Union soldiers and 1 of every 8 Confederates ran away because of fear, hunger, or sickness.

Rebel soldiers suffered from a lack of food and supplies. One reason for Lee's invasion of Maryland in 1862 was to allow his army to feed off Maryland crops. A woman who saw the Confederates march to Antietam recalled the "gaunt starvation that looked from their cavernous eyes."

Reading Check **Explain** Why did many soldiers desert from the armies?

Picturing **History**

Some paintings offered an idealized picture of the Civil War. Photographs provided a chilling account of life—and death—at the front lines. ***In what ways might photographs have affected Americans' view of the war in a way that paintings did not?***

More Skill Practice

Historical and Social Sciences Analysis Skill Ask students to give reasons why the soldiers' initial enthusiasm for the war may have disappeared. *(boredom, homesickness, hard work, bad food, uncomfortable conditions, lack of supplies, bad medical care)*

OL CA HI2.

Picturing **History**

Answer: Photographs, especially of dead and wounded soldiers on the battlefield, would have shown civilians the real horrors of war, while paintings like the one on this page projected a more romantic view. Photographs might also have made people more horrified by the war and more eager to see it end.

US8.10.7 Explain how the war affected combatants, civilians, the physical environment, and future warfare.

Women and the War

Main Idea **Many Northern and Southern women took on new responsibilities during the war.**

Reading Connection Think of ways the women in your family would be affected by a war in their own backyards. Read to learn the many ways women were affected by the Civil War.

In times of war, people often fill new roles. Women in the North and the South became teachers and office workers, and they managed farms. They also suffered the loss of husbands, fathers, sons, and brothers. As **Mary Chesnut** of South Carolina wrote:

> **"Does anyone wonder [why] so many women die? Grief and constant anxiety kill nearly as many women at home as men are killed on the battle-field."**
>
> —from *Mary Chesnut's Civil War*

Women performed many jobs that helped the soldiers and the armies. They rolled bandages, wove blankets, and made ammunition. Many women collected food, clothing, and medicine to **distribute** to the troops. They also raised money for supplies. S

Life at Home For the most part, Northerners saw the war from a distance, since most of the battles took place in the South. News from the battlefront and letters home from the soldiers kept the war in people's minds.

Almost every woman who stayed at home was touched in some way by the war. But while everyday life in the North suffered little disruption, life in the South was dramatically changed. C

Those who lived in the paths of marching armies lost crops and homes. As one Southerner noted: the South had depended upon the outside world "for everything from a hairpin to a toothpick, and from a cradle to a coffin." As the war dragged on, shortages became more commonplace.

Picturing **History**

This 1862 photo shows a Union soldier with his family at the front near Washington, D.C. Most soldiers on both sides, however, faced long separations from their families. ***What other hardships did Civil War soldiers face?***

Review The Big Idea

Review the Big Idea for this section: "Citizen participation is essential to the foundation and preservation of the U.S. political system." Ask students to outline the subsection "Women and the War" to identify ways women participated in the war effort. Have them use their outline to contribute to a class outline on the board. BL CA HI1.

S Skill Practice

Historical and Social Sciences Analysis Skill Have students discuss whether it would be possible and a good idea for soldiers' families to accompany them to the front-lines of a battle today. *(Most will say no, citing the danger, great distances, lack of facilities, and other reasons.)* OL CA HI3.

C Critical Thinking

Comparing and Contrasting **Ask:** Why was life disrupted more in the South than in the North? *(Most Northerners were far from the fighting, but many battles took place in the South.)* How did Southern civilians suffer from the war? *(lost homes and other property; shortages of goods; loss of family members)* OL CA HI3.

Resources for page 599

- American Art and Architecture Transparency 15
- American Art Print, *Matthew Brady*

More Skill Practice

Historical and Social Sciences Analysis Skill **Ask:** How are the lives of military spouses affected today when their husbands or wives are away on active duty? Are the challenges they face similar to or different from those of Civil War women? Discuss students' answers. AL CA HI3.

Picturing **History**

The army hired its own photographers to produce pictures of such things as field fortifications, bridges, and major buildings. Civilian photographers also photographed the war.

Answer: lack of food and supplies, boredom, sickness, discomfort, fear, horror, bad weather.

C Critical Thinking

Determining Cause and Effect Ask: How did the South's economy of the pre-war period help cause severe shortages during the war? *(The South's dependence on cotton for export before the war meant that it had little industry to produce needed goods for the war.)* OL CA HI2.

W Writing Support

Narrative Writing Ask students to choose one of the women spies or nurses discussed in this section. Have them write a journal entry that one of the women could have written about her activities. OL CA HI1.

R Reading Strategy

Understanding Vocabulary *Habeas corpus* is a Latin phrase that means "you should have the body." The phrase comes from the opening words of a court order that required law enforcement officials to produce a person they had arrested. AL CA 8RW1.2

Reading Check

Answer: established a hospital for soldiers in Richmond, Virginia; Dorothea Dix and Clara Barton

Answers and Additional Support

US8.10.7 Explain how the war affected combatants, civilians, the physical environment, and future warfare.

C The South ran out of almost everything. Shortages in feed for animals and salt for curing meant that little meat was available. Shortages of meat were matched by shortages of clothing, medicine, and even shelter.

Women as Spies Some women served as spies. Harriet Tubman spied for the North. **Rose O'Neal Greenhow** entertained Union leaders in Washington, D.C., picking up information about Union plans that she passed to the South. Greenhow was caught and exiled to the South.

Belle Boyd, of Virginia, informed Confederate generals of Union army movements in the Shenandoah Valley. Some women disguised themselves as men and became soldiers. A Cuban native, **Loretta Janeta Velázquez** (vuh•LAS•kwihz), of New Orleans, reportedly fought for the South at the First Battle of Bull Run and at Shiloh.

Treating the Sick and Wounded In the Civil War, thousands of women served as W nurses. At first many doctors did not want women nurses because they felt that women were too delicate for such work. Men disapproved of women doing what was considered men's work. Also, it was thought improper for women to tend the bodies of unknown men.

Strong-minded women disregarded these objections. In the North, **Dorothea Dix,** the reformer for conditions of prisoners and people with disabilities, organized large numbers of women to serve as military nurses. Another Northerner, **Clara Barton,** became famous for her work with wounded soldiers. In the South, **Sally Tompkins** established a hospital for soldiers in Richmond, Virginia.

Nursing was hard work. Kate Cummings of Alabama, who nursed the wounded in Corinth after the Battle of Shiloh, wrote, "Nothing that I had ever heard or read had given me the faintest idea of the horrors witnessed here."

Reading Check **Describe** What role did Sally Tompkins play in the war effort? Which other women played a similar role in the North?

Opposition to the War

Main Idea **The war efforts of the Union and the Confederate governments faced opposition.**

Reading Connection Can you think of a time when you disagreed or opposed something? Did you take action? Read to learn how various people opposed the Civil War and why.

Both the Union and the Confederate governments faced opposition. Politicians objected to war policies, and ordinary citizens protested the way the war affected their lives.

When the war began, Northern Democrats split into two groups. One group supported most of Lincoln's wartime policies. The other, the "Peace Democrats," favored negotiating with the Confederacy. The Peace Democrats warned that continuing the war would lead to "terrible social change and revolution."

Conflict With the Copperheads Republicans called the Peace Democrats "Copperheads" after a poisonous snake that strikes without warning. When Union armies lost battles, support for the Copperheads rose.

Some Republicans suspected Copperheads of aiding the Confederates. The president ordered the arrest of anyone interfering with the war effort, such as discouraging men from enlisting in the army. Several times Lincoln suspended the right of **habeas corpus** (HAY•bee•uhs KAWR•puhs), which guarantees accused individuals the right to a hearing before being jailed. Lincoln defended his actions, asking: R

> **"Must I shoot a simple-minded soldier boy who deserts, while I must not touch a hair of a wily agitator who induces him to desert?"**
>
> **—Letter to Erastus Corning, June 12, 1863**

Enlistments Decline As the war dragged on, fewer men volunteered to serve. Enlisting enough soldiers became a problem, so the Confederacy and the Union tried new measures.

More Skill Practice

Historical and Social Sciences Analysis Skill Have students draw a political cartoon based on some information in these two sections. Suggest they consider such topics as Lincoln and the Copperheads, opposition to the war, hardships at home and in the battlefield, spies, nurses, buying one's way out of the draft, or the payment of bounties. AL CA HI1.

Did You Know?

Some women disguised themselves as men and enlisted in the Confederate and Union armies. One woman, Jennie Hodgers, signed on with an Illinois regiment under the name of Albert Cashier.

Biography

US8.10.7 Explain how the war affected combatants, civilians, the physical environment, and future warfare.

Clara Barton

1821–1912

When the Civil War began, Clara Barton, a U.S. Patent Office clerk, began collecting provisions for the Union army. In 1862 she began to deliver supplies directly to the front and to tend to the wounded and dying during battle. **S**

The youngest of five children, Barton often felt out of place among her successful older brothers and sisters. When her brother, David, suffered a work-related accident, Barton found her place in the family as David's nurse and caregiver. Her talent for nursing led her into a life in which she was satisfied only when helping and caring for others.

Arriving at the Battle of Antietam to deliver supplies, Barton watched as surgeons dressed the soldiers' wounds with corn husks because they did not have bandages. As the battle raged around her, Barton comforted the wounded and helped the doctors with their work. For her courage, Barton became known as "the angel of the battlefield."

As the Civil War drew to a close, Barton set up an office to assist families and friends looking for missing soldiers and prisoners of war. Thousands of letters came flooding in written by mothers looking for sons and wives looking for husbands. Barton began to publish advertisements in newspapers asking readers to send information on the whereabouts of any soldier listed in the ad. By 1868 she had identified 22,000 missing men. **W** **C**

". . . I shall remain here while anyone remains, and do whatever comes to my hand. I may be compelled to face danger, but never fear it, and while our soldiers can stand and fight, I can stand and feed and nurse them."

—Letter to her father, 1861

Then and Now

Look online or in the phone book to find your local chapter of the Red Cross. Call or e-mail your local office and find out the following information: What kind of work has the chapter recently done? How can volunteers aid the organization?

601

Biography

TEACH

S Skill Practice

Historical and Social Sciences Analysis Skill

Clara Barton often ran into conflicts with other nurses and doctors over her nursing methods and ideas. **Ask:** Why might Barton have met opposition from nurses and doctors who had been working in the field longer than she had? *(They might have resented the newcomer or felt that her methods were unproven, they might have been offended by her strong personality and determination.)* OL CA HI2.

W Writing Support

Research Reports Writing

Have students research the life of Clara Barton following the Civil War and prepare a presentation summarizing their findings. OL CA 8WA2.1

C Critical Thinking

Drawing Conclusions

Ask: If you were helping Clara Barton's office look for missing persons after the Civil War, how would you do it? *(asking other members of a missing soldier's unit, posting flyers in public places, or publishing newspaper ads)* AL

Did You Know?

Heavy death tolls in battle led Civil War soldiers to create the first dog tags for identification. Soldiers printed their names on handkerchiefs or paper, which they pinned to their clothing before going into battle.

Then and Now

Answers will vary, but should accurately describe the activities of the local chapter (such as providing help in natural disasters and maintaining a safe blood supply) and identify volunteer opportunities at the Red Cross.

R Reading Strategy

Scaffolding—Connecting
Ask: What other situations can you think of that are like bounties? *(bonuses paid by employers to workers)* OL

This READING SKILL was introduced in Chapter 3.

W Writing Support

Persuasive Writing Have students write a newspaper editorial supporting or opposing the draft during the Civil War. Students should provide reasons for their positions. OL CA 8WA2.4

Reading Check

Answer: The number of volunteers declined as the war continued; due to opposition to the draft and to fighting to free African Americans

Answers and Additional Support

Draft Laws In April 1862, the Confederate Congress passed a **draft** law that required men between ages 18 and 35 to serve in the army for three years. A person could avoid the draft by hiring a **substitute** to serve in his place.

R Union states encouraged enlistment by offering **bounties**—payments to encourage volunteers. In March 1863, when this system failed, W the North turned to a draft. All men from age 20 to 45 had to register, and the army drew the soldiers it needed from this pool of names. A person could avoid the draft by hiring a substitute or by paying the government $300.

Protests against the draft erupted in several Northern cities. The worst disturbance took place in New York City in July 1863. Angry mobs, opposed to the draft and to fighting to free African Americans, went on a rampage of burning, looting, and killing. After four days of terror, more than 100 people were dead.

No disturbance as severe took place in the South, but many opposed the draft. The strong opposition led Jefferson Davis, the president of the Confederacy, to proclaim military law and suspend habeas corpus as Lincoln had done early in the war. Davis's action outraged Southerners, who feared that they would lose the liberties for which they had gone to war.

Reading Check **Examine** Why did the governments institute a draft? Why did protests occur in some places?

TECHNOLOGY & History

Civil War Camera

Photographer Mathew Brady and his many assistants recorded the camps, lives, and deaths of soldiers in more than 10,000 photos. **What is the biggest difference between this camera and a more modern one?**

1. The photographer looks at the subject through a **glass plate.**
2. A **plate holder** is inserted into the back panel.
3. The photographer opens the **lens.** The lens creates a reversed, upside-down image on the "wet" plate.
4. The **body** of the camera protects the wet plate.

The plate holder and the exposed wet plate are removed from the back panel, then developed into a negative in the photographer's "traveling" **darkroom.**

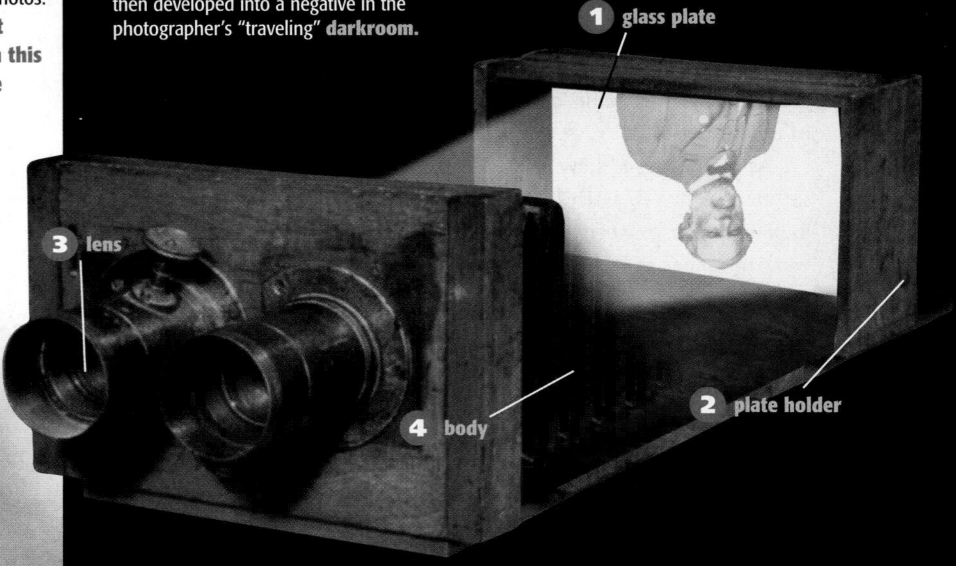

Photographer Mathew Brady

TECHNOLOGY & History

Photographic methods were first invented in 1839 in England and France. Americans produced some of the first war photographs during the Mexican War.

Answer: Answers will vary, but students should note the changes in technology such as size, automation, film processing, and the introduction of digital cameras.

Did You Know?

Civil War photography pioneer Matthew Brady learned to make daguerreotypes, a kind of early photograph, from Samuel F.B. Morse, inventor of the telegraph. In addition to his Civil War work, Brady decided to photograph as many famous Americans of his day as he could. His subjects included Daniel Webster, Edgar Allan Poe, and James Fenimore Cooper, in addition to nineteen U.S. presidents.

US8.10.7 Explain how the war affected combatants, civilians, the physical environment, and future warfare.

War and the Economy

Main Idea **The war created economic problems in the North and in the South.**

Reading Connection If you had to choose a side to fight for in the Civil War, which side would you choose? Read to learn the effects the war economy had on both the North and South.

The Civil War is often called the first "modern" war because it required the total commitment of resources. Such a war has an impact on every part of life. However, the impact was more devastating on the South than on the North.

The South struggled to carry out its war effort. Its government encouraged factories to supply arms and ammunition, but the South lacked the industry to provide necessities for civilians and for the military.

The economy of the South suffered far more than that of the North. Because most fighting **occurred** in the South, Southern farmland was overrun and rail lines were torn up.

The North's blockade of Southern ports caused severe shortages of essential goods. A scarcity of food led to riots in Atlanta, Richmond, and other cities. **Inflation** (ihn • FLAY • shuhn)—a general increase in the level of prices—was much worse in the South. R

These conditions affected soldiers. Worries about their families caused many men to desert. A Mississippi soldier who overstayed his leave to help his family wrote the governor: "We are poor men and are willing to defend our country but our families [come] first."

Reading Check **Explain** What is inflation? What hardships did inflation cause in the South?

History Online
Study Central Need help understanding how the war affected daily life? Visit ca.hss.glencoe.com and click on Study Central.

Section 4 Review

Reading Summary

Review the Main Ideas

- Civil War soldiers faced boredom in camp and terrible horrors on the battlefield.
- During the Civil War, women took over men's jobs on farms and in factories. They also served as nurses and spies.
- Opposition to the war was especially strong in the North, and as the war dragged on, both the North and the South faced declining enlistments.
- During the war, the North's economy suffered some, but the South's economy faced ruin as the fighting devastated farmland and rail lines.

What Did You Learn?

1. Why was life on the home front more difficult for Southerners?
2. What do Rose O'Neal Greenhow, Belle Boyd, and Loretta Janeta Velázquez have in common with Harriet Tubman?

Critical Thinking

3. **Analyze** Describe three ways that women in the North and South contributed to the war effort. CA HI1.

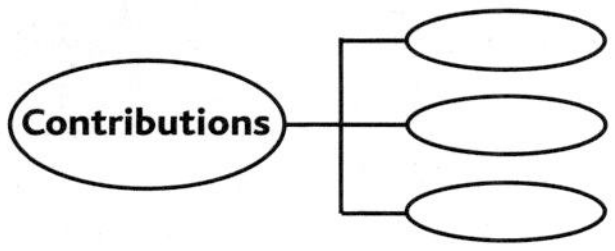

4. **Evaluate** Why do you think President Lincoln believed the Copperheads were a threat to the Union war effort? CA HI2.
5. **The Big Ideas** Describe the methods used by both the North and the South to enlist men into the army in the later years of the war. CA CS1.
6. **Economics** List three sectors of the economy that welcomed women during the Civil War. Describe the jobs women held and contributions they made. CA HI6. CA 8WA2.5

R Reading Strategy

Understanding Vocabulary
Ask: What does it mean to inflate a basketball? *(to pump it up or fill it up with air)* Have students connect that meaning to the definition of *inflation*. *(inflation is an increase in prices.)* EL CA 8RW1.3

ASSESS

Resources for page 603

Use these resources to assess student mastery of section content.

- Economics and History Activity 13
- Section Quiz 13–4
- Interactive Tutor Self-Assessment CD-ROM

Reading Check
Answer: a general increase in the level of prices; made it difficult to buy food

History Online
Study Central provides summaries, interactive games, and online graphic organizers to help students review section content.

CLOSE

Analyzing Primary Sources Write this quotation from a New York colonel on the board and ask students to explain it: "We started out in the spring . . . smart, well provided with everything. . . . And we were returning before the autumn, sad, weary, covered with mud, with uniforms in rags." OL CA HR5.

SECTION 4 REVIEW ANSWERS

Review questions reinforce content standard US8.10.

1. because most of the fighting took place in the South, which led to great damage to Southern property
2. They were all spies.
3. Answers may include: started hospitals, cared for wounded, maintained family business or farm.
4. because they discouraged men from enlisting in the army
5. **The Big Ideas** Both resorted to a draft, though men could hire substitutes; the Union also paid bounties to convince soldiers to reenlist.
6. Responses may include education, government, industry, and agriculture.

FOCUS

BELLRINGER
SKILLBUILDER ACTIVITY

Project **Daily Focus Skills Transparency 13–5** and have students answer the question.

Guide to Reading

Preteaching Vocabulary: Ask students to list synonyms for *total* (complete, 100 percent) and speculate on the meaning of the term *total war*.

Answers to Graphic: Seize Vicksburg to control the Mississippi River; Crush Lee's army in Virginia; Advance to Atlanta and crush Confederate forces in the Deep South

Unpacking the Standards

After reading the section, students will be able to:

- Discuss how the Confederacy gained the upper hand by 1863.
- Describe the Civil War battles that turned the tide.
- Explain what led to the South's surrender in 1865.

Section 5

The Way to Victory

History Social Science Standards

US8.10 Students analyze the multiple causes, key events, and complex consequences of the Civil War.

Guide to Reading

Looking Back, Looking Ahead

The Civil War continued with the Confederacy gaining the upper hand by 1863. However, victories at Gettysburg and Vicksburg turned the tide in favor of the Union.

Focusing on the Main Ideas

- After Confederate victories in Fredericksburg and Chancellorsville, a turning point occurred when Union forces won in Gettysburg and Vicksburg. *(page 605)*
- The end of the war was in sight with Sherman's capture of Atlanta and Grant's pursuit of the Confederates in Virginia. *(page 607)*
- After four years of war that claimed the lives of more than 600,000 Americans, the Northern forces defeated the Southern forces. *(page 610)*

Locating Places

Chancellorsville, Virginia
Vicksburg, Mississippi
Petersburg, Virginia
Mobile Bay
Savannah, Georgia
Appomattox Court House

Meeting People

Ambrose Burnside
Joseph Hooker
George Meade
William Tecumseh Sherman

Content Vocabulary

entrench (ihn • TREHNCH)
total war

Academic Vocabulary

outcome
nevertheless (NEH • vuhr • thuh • LEHS)

Reading Strategy

Organizing Information Use a web like the one shown to describe the strategy Grant adopted to defeat the Confederacy.

NATIONAL GEOGRAPHIC Where & When?

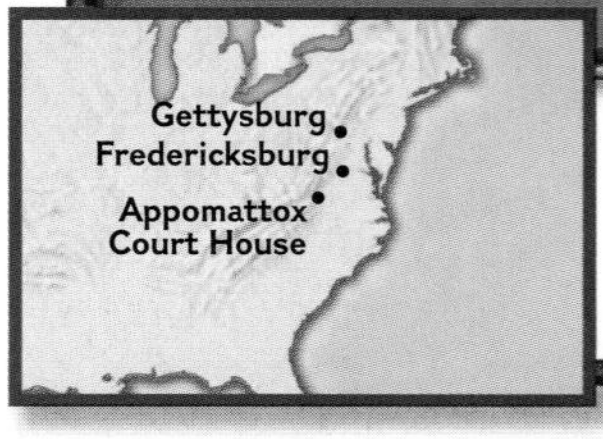

1862	1863	1864	1865
Dec. 1862 Lee wins the Battle of Fredericksburg	**July 1863** Battle of Gettysburg	**Mar. 1864** Grant takes over Union command	**Apr. 1865** Lee surrenders to Grant

SECTION RESOURCES

Print Material
- Reproducible Lesson Plan 13–5*
- Daily Lesson and Discussion Notes 13–5
- Guided Reading Activity 13–5
- Reading Essentials and Study Guide 13–5
- Active Reading Note-Taking Guide 13–5
- Section Quiz 13–5

Transparencies
- Daily Focus Skills Transparency 13–5
- Section Graphic Organizer Transparency 13–5
- California Standards Practice Transparencies

Technology
- Interactive Tutor Self-Assessment CD-ROM
- Exam*View*® Pro Testmaker CD-ROM
- Presentation Plus! CD-ROM

*Available on TeacherWorks™

US8.10.4 Discuss Abraham Lincoln's presidency and his significant writings and speeches and their relationship to the Declaration of Independence, such as his "House Divided" speech (1858), Gettysburg Address (1863), Emancipation Proclamation (1863), and inaugural addresses (1861 and 1865). US8.10.6 Describe critical developments and events in the war, including the major battles, geographical advantages and obstacles, technological advances, and General Lee's surrender at Appomattox.

The Tide of War Turns

Main Ideas **After Confederate victories in Fredericksburg and Chancellorsville, a turning point occurred when Union forces won in Gettysburg and Vicksburg.**

Reading Connection Why was the small Pennsylvania town of Gettysburg so important that Lincoln gave one of his most famous speeches there? Read to find out how Gettysburg came to be at the center of the Civil War's greatest battle.

An American Story

"My shoes are gone; my clothes are almost gone. I'm weary, I'm sick, I'm hungry. My family have been killed or scattered, and may be now wandering helpless and unprotected in a strange country. And I have suffered all this for my country. I love my country. I would die—yes, I would die willingly because I love my country. But if this war is ever over, I'll . . . [n]ever love another country!" A Confederate soldier expressed these thoughts during difficult times in 1863.

The Reality of War Gone were the parades and masses of volunteers, the fancy uniforms, and the optimism of the first years of the war. From 1862 until 1865, the soldiers and civilians faced a grim conflict marked by death, destruction, and wrenching change. What endured on each side was a fierce dedication to its own cause.

The winter of 1862–1863 saw gloom in the North and hope in the South. Robert E. Lee's Army of Northern Virginia seemed unbeatable. Lee's grasp of strategy made him more than a match for weak Union generals.

W **Fredericksburg and Chancellorsville** Lee needed little skill to win the Battle of Fredericksburg. On December 13, 1862, Union general **Ambrose Burnside** clashed with Lee near the Virginia town. Burnside had the larger R1 army, but the Confederates were **entrenched,** or set up in a strong position, on a number of hills south of the town. Repeated attacks failed to overcome Lee's troops as thousands of Union soldiers fell on the hillside. Devastated by his failure, Burnside resigned his command and was replaced by General **Joseph Hooker.**

Hooker rebuilt the army and in early May 1863, launched a campaign against Lee. Before Hooker could mount a major attack, Lee struck at **Chancellorsville, Virginia,** a few miles west of Fredericksburg. Boldly dividing his troops for an assault on the Union forces, Lee won another victory—but the **outcome** proved R2 costly. The battle's heavy casualties included General Stonewall Jackson.

S On May 2, Jackson and his troops attacked Union troops at dusk. One of the Confederate companies fired on Jackson's party by mistake, wounding the general in the left arm. Jackson's arm had to be amputated, and he died a week later.

The Battle of Gettysburg Despite heavy losses, Lee began moving north in June with an army of 75,000. Another victory—one on Northern soil—might persuade Britain and France to aid the Confederacy. Union general Hooker wanted to advance against Richmond, but Lincoln told him to attack Lee's army. When Hooker failed to do this, Lincoln replaced him with General **George Meade.** Meade's mission was to find and fight Lee's forces and to protect Washington and Baltimore from Confederate attack.

The two armies met on July 1, 1863, near the small town of Gettysburg, Pennsylvania. The three-day Battle of Gettysburg began when Union cavalry surprised Rebel infantry, who were looking for shoes. Outnumbered, the Northerners fought desperately to hold the town before retreating to Cemetery Ridge, a line of hills south of Gettysburg. The next day, the Rebels launched another assault, but a counterattack saved the Union position.

On the third and final day of battle, Lee decided to launch an attack, determined to "create a panic and virtually destroy the [Union] army."

TEACH

W Writing Support

Expository Writing
Have students write a paragraph explaining why the Confederates won the Battle of Fredericksburg. *(Answers should point out that the Confederates were well entrenched on high ground, making a successful attack difficult.)* BL

CA 8WA2.3

R1 Reading Strategy

Understanding Vocabulary
Ask students to find the definition of *entrenched*. *(set up in a strong position)* Then have them speculate on the connection of this word to *trench*. *(Trenches are one way an army has of setting up in a strong position.)* OL

R2 Reading Strategy

Academic Vocabulary Ask students to write a sentence using the word *outcome*. EL

S Skill Practice

Historical and Social Sciences Analysis Skill
Have students consider how the outcome of the Civil War might have been different if Stonewall Jackson had not been killed at Chancellorsville. **Ask:** Could he have helped the Confederacy and Lee win the war? *(Students may say that though Jackson could have helped the South win more battles, the South still lacked the resources to defeat the North unless the North gave up.)* AL CA HI4.

Resources for page 605

Geography and History Activity 13

More Skill Practice

Analyzing Primary Sources Direct students to the quotation at the beginning of the section. **Ask:** Do you agree that love of one's country should be avoided? Have students discuss whether the soldier really meant what he said. *(Students may say he was temporarily disheartened by his circumstances and did not really mean what he said.)* OL

CA HR5.

Did You Know?

Sideburns are named after Union general Ambrose E. Burnside. His distinctive mutton-chop whiskers inspired a fashion, which became known as burnsides. Before long, the two syllables were transposed and the term was applied to all styles of sideburns.

S1 Skill Practice

Historical and Social Sciences Analysis Skill
Have students create a chart that shows the effects of the Union victories in July 1863. *(Gettysburg: drove Lee's army out of the North, and, along with Lincoln's address, gave the Union new inspiration; Vicksburg: split the South, gave the Union control of the Mississippi River)* BL
CA HI2.

S2 Skill Practice

Using Geography Skills
Have students find Chattanooga, Tennessee, on the map. **Ask:** Why would controlling that city be advantageous for either side? *(Union: controlling it would allow the Union forces to attack into Georgia, further dividing the South. Confederates: Controlling it would allow them to attack into Tennessee and even Kentucky and Ohio.)*
OL CA CS3.

W Writing Support

Persuasive Writing Have students write a paragraph explaining which of the two battles fought in July 1863 was the more crucial to the outcome of the war, giving reasons for their choice. OL CA 8WA2.4

Answers and Additional Support

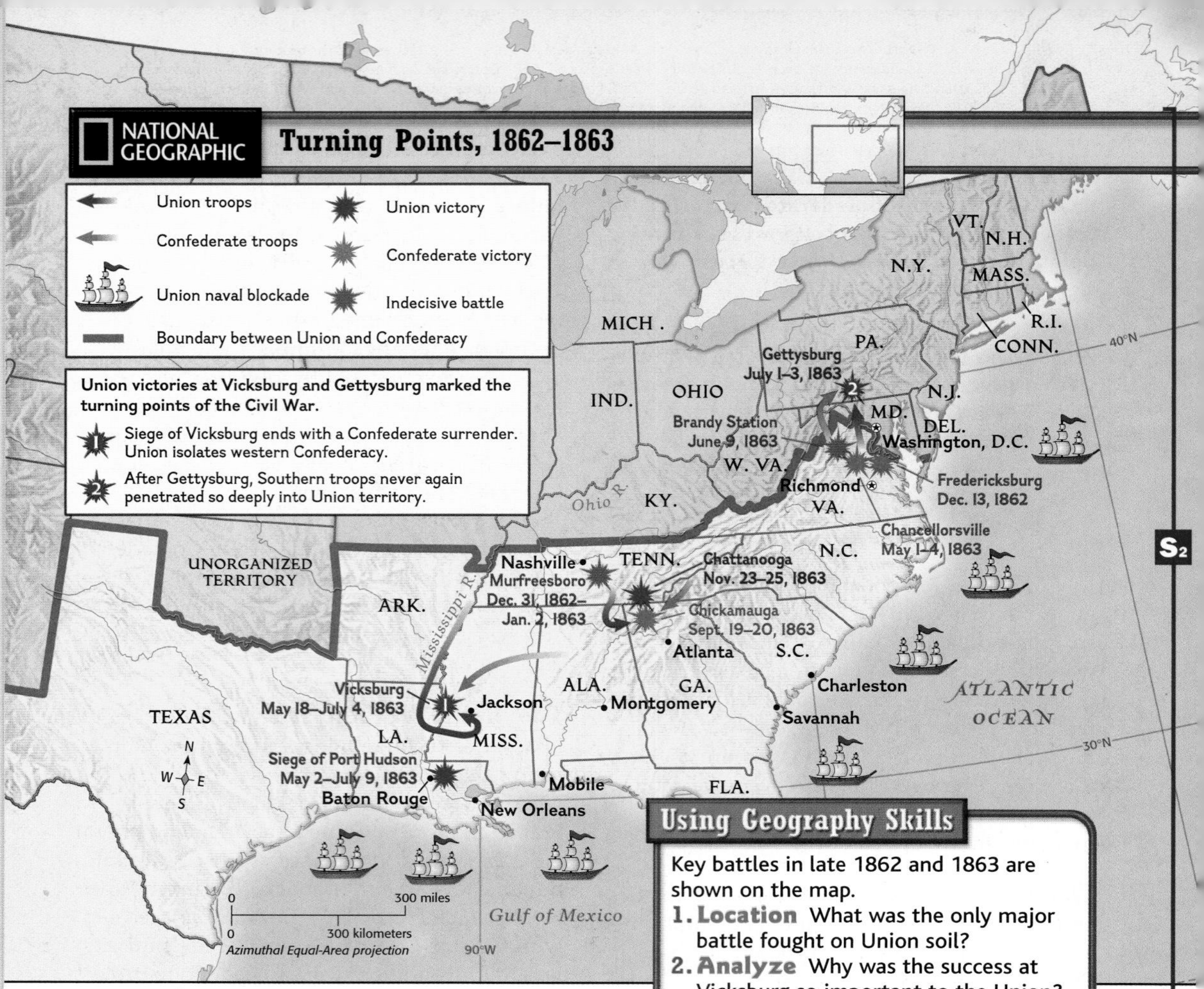

Using Geography Skills

Key battles in late 1862 and 1863 are shown on the map.

1. **Location** What was the only major battle fought on Union soil?
2. **Analyze** Why was the success at Vicksburg so important to the Union?

This last attack, led by General George Pickett, is remembered as Pickett's Charge. About 14,000 Confederate soldiers advanced across about one-half mile of open ground toward the Union lines. They made easy targets for Union fire as they marched. Barely half of the Rebels returned from the charge. Lee knew the battle was lost. "It's all my fault," he told his troops as they retreated to Virginia.

Victory at Vicksburg Meanwhile, a great Union victory took place at **Vicksburg, Mississippi.** Vicksburg stood on a high bluff above the Mississippi River. To gain control of the river, one of the North's major war goals, the Union needed to seize Vicksburg. For several weeks, Union forces under Ulysses S. Grant had laid siege to the town. Finally, on July 4, 1863, Vicksburg surrendered.

With the surrender of Vicksburg and then Port Hudson in Louisiana, the Union now held the entire Mississippi River. Texas, Louisiana, and Arkansas were sealed off from the rest of the Confederacy.

The Union victories at Gettysburg and Vicksburg marked a turning point in the war. They drove Lee's army out of Pennsylvania, secured the Mississippi as a Union highway, and cut the South in two. **Nevertheless,** the South still had troops and a will to fight. The war would continue for two more terrible years.

More Skill Practice

Historical and Social Sciences Analysis Skill Ask students to make a list of five questions to ask Ulysses S. Grant about the Union siege and victory at Vicksburg. Then have them research and record the answers that the general might have given. *(Questions will vary; they may focus on the campaign itself, his goals, his worries, his army, or other elements.)* AL CA HR1.

Using Geography Skills

Answers:

1. Gettysburg
2. It gave the Union control of the Mississippi River.

In-Text Map Transparency 13 Ask: From which direction did Grant make his final approach to Vicksburg? *(the southeast)* BL

US8.10.5 Study the views and lives of leaders (e.g., Ulysses S. Grant, Jefferson Davis, Robert E. Lee) and soldiers on both sides of the war, including those of black soldiers and regiments. US8.10.6 Describe critical developments and events in the war, including the major battles, geographical advantages and obstacles, technological advances, and General Lee's surrender at Appomattox.

U **Lincoln at Gettysburg** On November 19, 1863, at a ceremony dedicating a cemetery at Gettysburg, President Lincoln beautifully expressed what the war had come to mean: "It is for us the living . . . to be here dedicated to the great task remaining before us . . . that these dead shall not have died in vain—that this nation shall have a new birth of freedom; and that this government, of the people, by the people, for the people, shall not perish from the earth." C

The speech went beyond the immediacy of the battlefield horrors and instead emphasized Americans' shared ideals. *(See page 856 of the Appendix for the entire text of the Gettysburg Address.)*

Reading Check **Identify** What battle victories gave the Union control of the Mississippi River?

Final Phases of the War

Main Ideas **The end of the war was in sight with Sherman's capture of Atlanta and Grant's pursuit of the Confederates in Virginia.**

Reading Connection Do you think an army should attack an enemy's civilian population? Read to find out why General Sherman waged "total war" as his army marched through Georgia.

In November 1863, Grant, General **William Tecumseh Sherman**, and another general won an important victory at Chattanooga, Tennessee. Following the Northern triumphs at Vicksburg and Gettysburg, Chattanooga further weakened the Confederates. The following March, President Lincoln turned to Grant for help.

Primary Sources

R What Was the Reaction to the Gettysburg Address?

President Abraham Lincoln delivered the Gettysburg Address on November 19, 1863, during the dedication of the Gettysburg National Cemetery. The dedication was in honor of the more than 7,000 Union and Confederate soldiers who died in the Battle of Gettysburg earlier that year. Lincoln's brief speech is often recognized as one of the finest speeches in the English language. It is also one of the most moving speeches in the nation's history.

On the day following the Gettysburg dedication, many of the nation's newspapers reprinted the speech. Some newspapers praised the speech. The *Chicago Tribune* noted that:

> "The dedicatory remarks by President Lincoln will live among the annals of man."

▲ Gettysburg Cemetery

Other newspapers did not think it was a worthy address by a president. *The Harrisburg* (Pennsylvania) *Patriot* criticized the speech, noting:

> "We pass over the silly remarks of the President; for the credit of the Nation we are willing that the veil of oblivion shall be dropped over them and that they shall no more be repeated or thought of."

DBQ Document-Based Question

The Gettysburg Address is considered one of the great speeches. Why do you think some Americans were critical of the address?

Primary Sources

Answer: Students may suggest that Lincoln's speech was so brief that all listeners did not understand its significance right away or that those who objected to it were opposed to the war or his presidency.

- What state was Lincoln from? *(Illinois)* Might that have affected the opinion of the *Chicago Tribune* writer? *(The writer may have been biased in favor of Lincoln.)* OL

U Universal Access

Auditory/Musical Have students practice speaking the Gettysburg Address and then read it for the class. Have them make a copy of the speech and mark it up to note points of emphasis, where to slow down, and other techniques to enhance their reading. Have the class comment on which techniques were most effective. OL

CA 8SA2.4 CA 8LS1.1

C Critical Thinking

Analyzing Primary Sources **Ask:** What does Lincoln say is the main task of those living on after the battle? *(to make sure that the dead did not die in vain, to bring about a new birth of freedom, and ensure that democracy shall not perish)* To whom do they have a responsibility? *(those who died)* OL CA HR3.

R Reading Strategy

Reading Primary Sources Have students list some of the shared ideals that Americans became more aware of thanks to Lincoln's speech at Gettysburg. *(Possible answers include belief in democracy, feeling of responsibility for the nation, connection between emancipation and early history of the country.)* AL CA HI3.

Reading Check

Answer: Vicksburg and Port Hudson

U Universal Access

Visual/Spatial Have students make a diagram of how Grant planned to crush the Confederate armies. Then have them summarize the strategy. *(Diagrams and summaries should emphasize launching multiple attacks and putting pressure on the South.)* BL CA CS1.

C Critical Thinking

Comparing and Contrasting Have students compare Grant's actions following the battles at Wilderness, Spotsylvania, and Cold Harbor with McClellan's actions after Antietam. Contrast President Lincoln's reactions to both generals' decision making. *(Grant resumed the attack, while McClellan refused to follow Lee's army into Virginia. Lincoln approved of Grant's aggressiveness, while he eventually fired McClellan for his caution.)* OL CA HI2.

Answers and Additional Support

Ulysses S. Grant was average and unimpressive in appearance. His early army career was not impressive either, and in 1854 he had been forced to resign because of a drinking problem. When the war began, he rejoined the army. His victories in the West and his willingness to attack hard impressed President Lincoln. "I can't spare this man," the president said. "He fights." After the victory at Chattanooga, Lincoln named Grant commander of all the Union armies.

U Grant devised a plan to attack the Confederacy on all fronts. The Army of the Potomac would try to crush Lee's army in Virginia. The western army, under Sherman, would advance to Atlanta, Georgia, and crush the Confederate forces in the Deep South. If the plan succeeded, they would destroy the Confederacy.

C Grant soon put his strategy into effect. In May and June of 1864, Grant's army of 115,000 men smashed into Lee's 64,000 troops in a series of three battles near Richmond, Virginia—the Battles of the Wilderness, Spotsylvania Courthouse, and Cold Harbor. Each time, Confederate lines held, but each time Grant quickly resumed the attack.

The battles cost the North thousands of men. Critics called Grant a butcher, but he said, "I propose to fight it out on this line if it takes all summer." Lincoln supported Grant.

After Cold Harbor, Grant swung south of Richmond to attack **Petersburg, Virginia,** an important railroad center. If it fell, Richmond would be cut off from the rest of the Confederacy. Grant's assault turned into a nine-month siege.

NATIONAL GEOGRAPHIC

The Civil War: Battles and Strategies

Confederate Control
Union Control
Union naval blockade

The Anaconda Plan From the beginning, the Northern war strategy was to invade the South and divide it. As the plan—called the Anaconda Plan—progressed, the North blocked Southern supply lines and isolated Confederate troops.

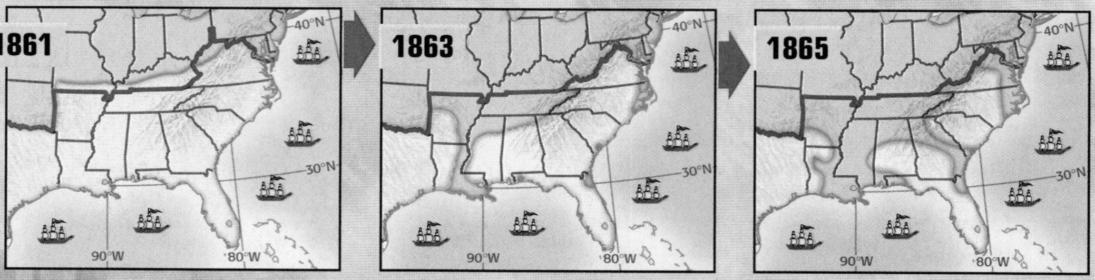

Early Stages Confederate troops won most of the battles in the first year of the Civil War.

Union Gains Union control of the Mississippi River cut off Texas and Arkansas, the South's leading food producers, from the Confederacy.

Final Stages By 1865 the Union controlled large parts of the Confederacy.

Lives Lost
More lives were lost in the Civil War than in any other major American conflict. Deadly weapons, poor medical practices, infection, and disease contributed to this.

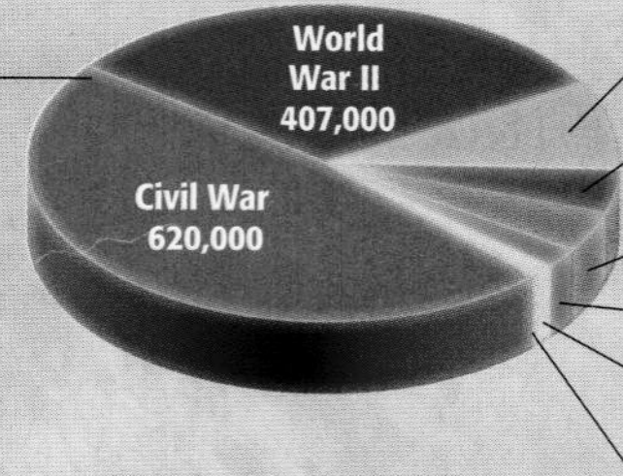

608

More Skill Practice

Using Geography Skills Ask: Which side was in the best position to win in 1861? Why? *(Students might say either side.)* Which side was in the best position to win in 1863? Why? *(the North; because it had captured Tennessee, much of Arkansas and Louisiana, and controlled the Mississippi River.)* BL CA CS3.

The Election of 1864 To the war-weary North, the events of the first half of 1864 were discouraging. Grant was stuck outside Richmond and Petersburg, and Sherman was stuck outside Atlanta. In the summer of 1864, Lincoln's chances for reelection did not look good. "I am going to be beaten and unless some great change takes place, badly beaten," he said.

Great changes did take place. In August, David Farragut led a Union fleet into **Mobile Bay.** The Union now controlled the Gulf of Mexico. In September, news arrived that Sherman had captured Atlanta. With these victories, the end of the war was in sight. Lincoln easily won reelection, taking 55 percent of the popular vote.

Total War Leaving Atlanta in ruins, Sherman convinced Grant to let him try a bold plan. Sherman's army began a "march to the sea" to **Savannah, Georgia.** As the army advanced, it lived off the land. Union troops took what food they needed and tore up railroad lines and fields in an effort to destroy anything useful to the South. They cut a path of destruction sometimes 50 miles wide. This method of waging war was known as **total war.** W C

After capturing Savannah in December, Sherman turned north. The army marched through South Carolina, devastating the state. Sherman planned to join Grant's forces in Virginia.

Reading Check **Describe** What was the "march to the sea"?

NATIONAL GEOGRAPHIC **The Final Battles, 1864–1865**

Review The Big Idea

Review the Big Idea for this section: "Political ideas and major events shape how people form governments." **Ask:** How did events influence the election of 1864? *(Several major Union victories helped Lincoln win reelection.)* BL CA HI2.

W Writing Support

Narrative Writing Have students write a letter from a resident of Georgia to a friend in another part of the Confederacy describing what it was like to be in the path of Sherman's march to the sea. *(Letters may stress the hardships, chaos, and fear people experienced.)* OL CA 8WA2.1

C Critical Thinking

Drawing Conclusions
Ask: Was Sherman's total war justified? Why or why not? *(Those feeling it was may say that civilians were contributing to the Confederate war effort; those saying it was not may say it is immoral to harm civilians.)* AL CA HI2.

Reading Check
Answer: Sherman and his troops marched from Atlanta to Savannah, destroying anything that could be of use to the Confederacy.

Did You Know?

Lincoln's Democratic opponent in the election of 1864 was former general George McClellan. McClellan was nominated by the Democrats on a peace platform. The Union victories late in the year helped Lincoln win a landslide victory in the electoral college, 212 to 21.

R1 Reading Strategy

Reading Primary Sources
Have students paraphrase in their own words the excerpt from Lincoln's second Inaugural Address. *(Paraphrases should be accurate and complete.)* EL
CA 8LS1.2

R2 Reading Strategy

Reading Primary Sources
Ask: What does Lincoln ask his listeners to do? *(have no hard feelings, heal the nation's wounds, do everything they can to make and keep peace)* Would those attitudes be easy for Americans to adopt at the time or difficult? Why? *(Students may say that the long, bloody years of war would make it difficult.)* OL

C Critical Thinking

Identifying Central Issues
Remind students that capturing Richmond had been a key goal of the Union at the beginning of the war. **Ask:** Why did the war not end when Richmond fell? *(because there were still Southern armies in the field; because the Confederate government leaders had fled the city)* OL CA HI2.

US8.10.6 Describe critical developments and events in the war, including the major battles, geographical advantages and obstacles, technological advances, and General Lee's surrender at Appomattox. US8.10.7 Explain how the war affected combatants, civilians, the physical environment, and future warfare.

Victory for the North

Main Ideas **After four years of war that claimed the lives of more than 600,000 Americans, the Northern forces defeated the Southern forces.**

Reading Connection After several years of terrible fighting and death, do you think a victorious general might want to punish the soldiers of the defeated army? Read to find out how General Grant treated the defeated Confederate soldiers after General Lee's surrender.

R1 In his second Inaugural Address on March 4, 1865, Lincoln spoke of the coming peace:

> **"With malice toward none, with charity for all . . . let us strive on to finish the work we are in, to bind R2 up the nation's wounds . . . to do all which may achieve and cherish a just and lasting peace among ourselves and with all nations."**

Throughout the fall and winter of 1864, Grant continued the siege of Petersburg. Lee and his troops defended the town, but sickness, hunger, casualties, and desertion weakened them. Finally, on April 2, 1865, the Confederate lines broke and Lee withdrew his troops.

C Richmond fell the same day. Rebel troops, government officials, and many residents fled the Confederate capital. As they left, they set fire to much of the city to keep it from falling into Union hands.

On April 4, Lincoln visited Richmond and walked its streets. One elderly African American man approached the president, took off his hat, and bowed. Tearfully, he said, "May God bless you." Lincoln removed his own hat and bowed in return.

Surrender at Appomattox Lee moved his army west of Richmond, hoping to link up with the small Confederate force that was trying to stop Sherman's advance. But the Union army blocked his escape route. Realizing the situation was hopeless, Lee said:

> **"There is nothing left [for] me but to go and see General Grant, and I [would] rather die a thousand deaths."**
>
> —as quoted in *Voices of the Civil War*

On April 9, 1865, Lee and his troops surrendered to Grant in a small Virginia village called **Appomattox Court House.**

Picturing **History**
After Robert E. Lee surrendered to Ulysses S. Grant, Grant ordered Union troops not to celebrate. "The war is over," he said, "the rebels are our countrymen again." ***Where did Lee surrender?***

Answers and Additional Support

Did You Know?

Many historians believe that baseball was invented by Union General Abner Doubleday, who called it "base ball." The sport spread during the Civil War because Union soldiers played it between battles. Confederate prisoners and other troops watched the game and learned it too. Before long, people were playing in all parts of the country.

Picturing **History**

Answer: a small Virginia village called Appomattox Court House

Biography

US8.10.5 Study the views and lives of leaders (e.g., Ulysses S. Grant, Jefferson Davis, Robert E. Lee) and soldiers on both sides of the war, including those of black soldiers and regiments.

ROBERT E. LEE
1807–1870

ULYSSES S. GRANT
1822–1885

▲ Robert E. Lee

The two outstanding generals of the Civil War, Robert E. Lee and Ulysses S. Grant, were both excellent leaders. But only one could emerge the victor. At the beginning of the war, most people would have guessed that Lee would be the winner.

Lee was born to a prominent Virginia family. In 1828 he graduated from West Point at the top of his class. During the war with Mexico, he proved his skill and daring as a soldier.

When the Civil War broke out, Lincoln asked Lee to take command of the Union forces. Lee was torn, because he did not believe in slavery or secession. But when Virginia seceded, he felt that his loyalty had to lie with his home state. Instead of fighting for the Union, he became the South's most brilliant strategist. C

R When Lee surrendered at Appomattox, he surrendered to a general who was almost his complete opposite. Grant was the son of a farmer and a tanner. Although he went to West Point, he was only an average student. He distinguished himself in the war with Mexico but later resigned from the army. During the next few years, he failed repeatedly in farming and in business.

When the Civil War started, Grant volunteered his services. At first he had trouble being accepted into the Union army. Once accepted, however, he impressed Lincoln with his ability. In 1864 Grant was given command of the Union armies. His abilities to plan and make decisions, backed by the North's superior resources, changed the strategy—and the outcome—of the Civil War.

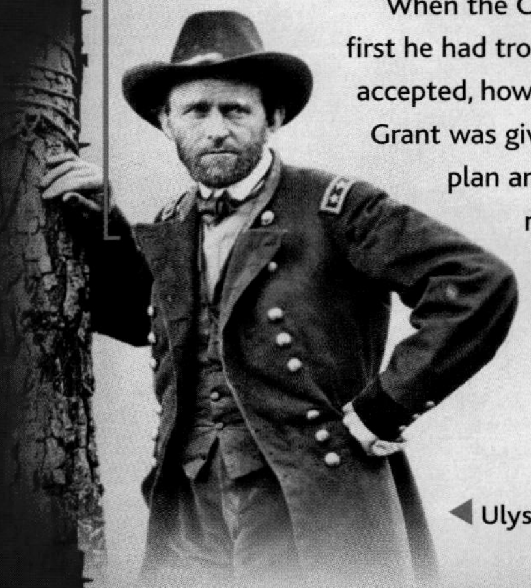

◀ Ulysses S. Grant

Then and Now

Can you think of any military leaders today who have the qualities that made Grant and Lee great generals?

611

Biography

TEACH

R Reading Strategy

Categorizing Information Have students describe the ways in which Grant and Lee were similar and the ways in which they were different. *(Similar: West Point graduates, against slavery and secession, excellent leaders; different: Lee well off, Grant poor; Lee a good student, Grant mediocre, Lee successful before the war, Grant unsuccessful)* **OL** CA 8RC2.0

C Critical Thinking

Predicting Consequences Tell students that, after the war, Lee pledged his allegiance to the United States once again. Ask students how his example may have smoothed relations between former enemies. *(Seeing their beloved general swear loyalty to the Union probably made many other Confederates feel it was all right for them to do the same.)* **OL** CA HI2.

Then and Now

Answers will vary but should reflect an understanding of those qualities that made Grant and Lee such great military leaders.

More Skill Practice

Historical and Social Sciences Analysis Skill Lee said of Grant: "I doubt his superior can be found in all history." **Ask:** What things might have influenced Lee to say this about his enemy? *(his determination, strategic skill, leadership qualities, generosity at the surrender)* **AL** CA HR5.

Terms of Surrender Grant's terms were generous. The Confederate soldiers had to lay down their arms but then were free to go home. Grant allowed them to keep their horses so that they could, as he said, "put in a crop to carry themselves and their families through the next winter." Grant also ordered three days' worth of food sent to Lee's hungry troops.

Several days after Lee's surrender, the Confederate forces in North Carolina surrendered. Jefferson Davis, the president of the Confederacy, was captured in Georgia on May 10. The Civil War was over at last.

A New President President Lincoln did not live to see the end of the war, however. On April 14, 1865, just five days after Lee's surrender, Lincoln was assassinated by John Wilkes Booth, a fanatical Confederate sympathizer. Booth's deed was a tragedy for both North and South, for it removed the one person who could best "bind up the nation's wounds." C

A Richmond, Virginia, newspaper called Lincoln's death "the heaviest blow which has ever fallen upon the people of the South." A young Southern woman wrote in her diary, "The most terrible part of the war is now to come." W

Picturing **History**

By April 1865, many major cities of the Confederacy, including Atlanta, had felt the full force of war. ***What is total war?***

C Critical Thinking

Making Inferences Ask: Why do you think many people in the South were gloomy about Lincoln's death? *(Students may say that they knew he would treat the South generously, whereas others in the North would seek revenge.)* OL CA CS1.

W Writing Support

Response to Literature Writing Have students read one of Walt Whitman's poems about the death of Abraham Lincoln ("Memories of President Lincoln: When Lilacs Last in the Dooryard Bloom'd" or "O Captain! My Captain!") and write an essay explaining how Whitman felt about Lincoln's death. AL CA RL3.7

Answers and Additional Support

More Skill Practice

Historical and Social Sciences Analysis Skill Ask students what would be the likely reaction of Confederate soldiers to Grant's peace terms. *(They would likely be grateful that Grant allowed them to keep their horses and go home, as well as for the food.)* OL CA HI2.

Picturing **History**

Answer: destruction of anything, from fields, to towns, to transportation routes, that could help the enemy

Lincoln's vice president, Andrew Johnson, became president. Johnson had been a Democrat living in Tennessee before the Civil War. He had served as a mayor and state legislator before being elected to the United States Senate. When Tennessee seceded from the Union, Johnson remained loyal and stayed in the U.S. Senate, making him a hero in the North.

Results of the War The Civil War was the most devastating conflict in American history. More than 600,000 soldiers died, and the war caused billions of dollars of damage, most of it in the South. The devastation had left the South's economy in a state of collapse. Roughly two thirds of the transportation system lay in ruins, with many bridges destroyed and miles of railroad twisted and rendered useless. The war also created bitter feelings among defeated Southerners that lasted for generations.

The war had other consequences as well. The North's victory saved the Union. The federal government was strengthened and was now clearly more powerful than the states. Finally, the war freed millions of African Americans. The end of slavery, however, did not solve the problems that the newly freed African Americans were to face.

R Following the war, many questions remained. No one yet knew how to bring the Southern states back into the Union, nor what the status of African Americans would be in Southern society. Americans from the North and the South tried to answer these questions in the years following the Civil War—an era known as Reconstruction.

Reading Check **Identify** Where did General Lee surrender?

History Online

Study Central Need help understanding the conclusion of the war? Visit ca.hss.glencoe.com and click on Study Central.

Section 5 Review

Reading Summary

Review the Main Ideas

- The Confederate army seemed unbeatable after the Battles of Fredericksburg and Chancellorsville, but Northern victories at Gettysburg and Vicksburg turned the tide of the war for the Union.
- In the West, Sherman's army captured Atlanta and marched to the Atlantic coast. In the East, Grant's army maintained a strong offensive against the Confederate army under General Lee.
- In early April 1865, Grant's forces captured Richmond, and Lee's Confederate army surrendered soon after.

What Did You Learn?

1. Identify the reasons that Gettysburg and Vicksburg were important battles.
2. At what Virginia town did Lee defeat Burnside's forces?

Critical Thinking

3. **Analyze** Use a chart like the one shown to explain the significance of each battle listed. CA CS2.

Battle	Importance
Gettysburg	
Vicksburg	
Mobile Bay	
Richmond	

4. **Math Connection** Using the chart on page 608, create two new charts or graphs that communicate the same information in different ways. CA HR3.
5. **The Big Ideas** How did battlefield events affect Lincoln's reelection? CA HI2.
6. **Expository Writing** Refer to Lincoln's Gettysburg Address on page 856. Write an essay discussing Lincoln's ideas on freedom and the importance of saving the Union. CA 8WA2.4

R Reading Strategy

Scaffolding—Questioning
Have students write five questions they would like to know about the United States at the end of the Civil War. Have them keep the lists to guide their reading of the next chapter. BL CA HR1.

This READING SKILL was introduced in Chapter 9.

ASSESS

Resources for pages 613

Use these resources to assess student mastery of section content.

Section Quiz 13–5

Interactive Tutor Self-Assessment CD-ROM

Reading Check

Answer: Appomattox Court House, Virginia

History Online

Study Central provides summaries, interactive games, and online graphic organizers to help students review section content.

CLOSE

Analyzing Information
Have students explain what events led to the final outcome of the war. *(several Northern victories; Lincoln's reelection)* OL CA HI3.

SECTION 5 REVIEW ANSWERS

Review questions reinforce content standard US8.10.

1. At Gettysburg, Lee's army was driven from Pennsylvania; at Vicksburg, the North secured the Mississippi.
2. Fredericksburg
3. Gettysburg: Lee's invasion ended; Vicksburg: Union gained control of Mississippi; Mobile Bay: Union gained control of Gulf of Mexico; Richmond: Union captured Confederate capital
4. Options could include bar graph, line graph.
5. **The Big Ideas** Until Union victories at Mobile Bay, Atlanta, and the Shenandoah Valley, Lincoln's reelection looked doubtful.
6. Students should give reasons for their answers.

NATIONAL GEOGRAPHIC

GEOGRAPHY & HISTORY

FOCUS

History–Social Science Standards

The following standard is covered on pages 614–615.

US8.10 Students analyze the multiple causes, key events, and complex consequences of the Civil War.

TEACH

R Reading Strategy

Reading Maps, Graphs, and Charts Ask students to describe how soldiers for both sides used the area around Sharpsburg before and during the battle. *(used local roads to transport people and equipment; took positions along roads or in woods; took some areas for headquarters)* OL CA CS3.

U Universal Access

Visual/Spatial Have students use the scale on the inset map to determine the distance between Union headquarters and Confederate headquarters. *(about 3 miles)* OL

Answers and Additional Support

US8.10.6 Describe critical developments and events in the war, including the major battles, geographical advantages and obstacles, technological advances, and General Lee's surrender at Appomattox.

NATIONAL GEOGRAPHIC

GEOGRAPHY & HISTORY

614

More Skill Practice

Historical and Social Sciences Analysis Skill Point out that the Civil War was fought entirely on American soil. **Ask:** How does a war differ if a nation fights on its own soil, as opposed to another country's soil? *(Students should note that wars fought on one's own soil create more damage for the nation.)* OL

Did You Know?

Each year, on the first Saturday in December, the Antietam National Battlefield in Sharpsburg, Maryland, is illuminated by thousands of candles placed in paper bags weighted by sand to keep them stationary. Each candle honors one of the Union or Confederate casualties from the 1862 battle.

ANTIETAM: THE BLOODIEST DAY

FOUGHT ON SEPTEMBER 17, 1862, the Battle of Antietam, or Sharpsburg, was the bloodiest day in American history, with more than 23,000 soldiers killed or wounded. Antietam changed the course of the Civil War. McClellan's Union forces stopped Lee's invasion of the North and forced him on the defensive. This strategic victory encouraged Lincoln to issue the Emancipation Proclamation.

MORNING

The battle began at dawn when Union artillery fired on Stonewall Jackson's forces in Miller Cornfield north of town. Union troops attacked the Confederates north of Dunker Church. For three hours, the battle lines swept back and forth along the West and East Woods, the Cornfield, and along Hagerstown Pike.

MIDDAY

Union soldiers emerged from the East Woods and were turned back by the Confederates in the West Woods. Later, the Yankees advanced toward "Bloody Lane," a sunken farm road held by the Confederates just south of Dunker Church. The Confederates held their line until midday, when the fighting stopped briefly.

AFTERNOON

After much fighting, the Union troops crossed Antietam Creek and slowly drove the Confederate forces back toward Sharpsburg. Just when all hope seemed lost, Confederate forces arrived from Harpers Ferry and stopped the Union advance. The day ended in a standoff that halted Lee's march northward. The next day, Lee began his retreat along the Potomac River.

LEARNING from GEOGRAPHY

1. **How do you think Bloody Lane got its name?**
2. **Why do you think Lee retreated after the Battle of Antietam?**

NATIONAL GEOGRAPHIC

GEOGRAPHY & HISTORY

S Skill Practice

Using Geography Skills

Have students locate Harpers Ferry on the inset map. **Ask:** How far is it from Sharpsburg? *(about 10 miles)* OL CA CS3.

C Critical Thinking

Analyzing Information

Direct students' attention to the groups of Union troops moving south from the Miller Cornfield. **Ask:** How are they moving? *(in lines a few soldiers deep)* Why would that be difficult for soldiers in the middle of a battle? *(Students may point out that they are out in the open, exposed to cannon fire and bullets, with no protection.)* OL

ASSESS

Have students answer the **Learning from Geography** questions.

NGS ONLINE

Access National Geographic's Web site for current events, atlas updates, activities, links, interactive features, and archives at www.nationalgeographic.com.

CLOSE

Summarizing Have students create a flow chart that shows the main sequence of events in the Battle of Antietam. OL

LEARNING from GEOGRAPHY

Answers to Learning from Geography:

1. Students may suggest that particularly fierce fighting took place there.
2. Students may suggest that Lee retreated because he lost a large number of men or that he was short of ammunition or supplies.

Analyzing Primary Sources

FOCUS

History–Social Science Standards

The following standard is covered on pages 616–617:

US8.10 Students analyze the multiple causes, key events, and complex consequences of the Civil War.

TEACH

C1 Critical Thinking

Analyzing Primary Sources
Ask: Whose attitude toward the South is more realistic, Upson's or those of other people in the town? Why? *(Upson's; because he is skeptical that the South will not fight hard)* OL

CA HR5.

C2 Critical Thinking

Making Inferences **Ask:** Does Upson know the Hale family? How can you tell? *(apparently so, since his family received a letter from a member of that family and he refers to the children by name)* OL

Answers and Additional Support

Analyzing Primary Sources

US8.10.7 Explain how the war affected combatants, civilians, the physical environment, and future warfare.

A Nation Divided By War

Between 1861 and 1865, a Civil War divided the people of the United States. The South wanted to become an independent nation, upholding its rights to enslave African Americans, protect its economy, and retain states' rights. The North refused to allow the South to break away from the Union.

Read the passages on pages 616 and 617 and answer the questions that follow.

General Sherman led Union troops through Georgia in 1864. ▶

Reader's Dictionary

enlist: join the armed forces
apparel (uh • PAR • uhl): clothing
deprived (dih • PRYVD): taken away from
spires (SPYRZ): church steeples
horde: a large group or crowd
crimson (KRIHM • zuhn): red
fourscore: 80

Early Days of the War

Theodore Upson, a 17 year-old Indiana boy, writes about his feelings during the first days of the Civil War.

We had another meeting at the school house last night; we are raising money to take care of the families of those who **enlist**. . . . I said I would go but they laughed at me and said they wanted men not boys for this job; that it would all be over soon; that those fellows down South are big bluffers and would rather talk than fight. I am not so sure about that. . . . Mother had a letter from the Hales. Charlie and his Father are in their army and Dayton wanted to go but was too young. I wonder if I were in our army and they should meet me would they shoot me. I suppose they would.

—*With Sherman to the Sea*

Destruction Caused by Troops

In 1864, Union troops march through Georgia, destroying everything in their path. One Southerner, Dolly Sumner Lunt, describes the situation in her diary.

July 29, 1864—Sleepless nights. . . . They robbed every house on the road of its provisions, sometimes taking every piece of meat, blankets and wearing **apparel,** silver and arms of every description. . . . Is this the way to make us love them and their Union? Let the poor people answer [those] whom they have **deprived** of every mouthful of meat and of their livestock to make any!

—*A Woman's Wartime Journal*

EXTENDING THE CONTENT

Setting It Straight Whittier's famous poem is compelling, but misleading. There was a woman named Barbara Frietchie who lived in Frederick around the time of the battle of Antietam. And the ninety-five-year old woman did indeed wave an American flag at an army marching through the town. But the army she waved at not Jackson's force. In fact, it was not even Confederates. She waved the flag at a Union army.

Barbara Frietchie

John Greenleaf Whittier stated that this poem is based on a real incident in Frederick, Maryland. Barbara Frietchie was intensely loyal to the Union.

Up from the meadows rich with corn,
Clear in the cool September morn,

The cluster **spires** of Frederick stand
Green-walled by the hills of Maryland.

C Round about them orchards sweep,
Apple and peach tree fruited deep,

Fair as the garden of the Lord
To the eyes of the famished rebel **horde,**

On that pleasant morn of the early fall
When Lee marched over the mountain wall;

Over the mountains winding down,
Horse and foot, into Frederick town.

Forty flags with their silver stars,
Forty flags with their **crimson** bars,

Flapped in the morning wind: the sun
R Of noon looked down, and saw not one.

Up rose old Barbara Frietchie then,
Bowed with her **fourscore** years and ten;

Bravest of all in Frederick town,
She took up the flag the men hauled down;

In her attic window the staff she set,
To show that one heart was loyal yet.

Up the street came the rebel tread,
Stonewall Jackson riding ahead.

Under his slouched hat left and right
He glanced; the old flag met his sight.

"Halt!"—the dust-brown ranks stood fast.
"Fire!"—out blazed the rifle-blast.

It shivered the window, pane and sash;
It rent the banner with seam and gash,

Quick, as it fell, from the broken staff
Dame Barbara snatched the silken scarf.

She leaned far out on the window-sill,
And shook it forth with a royal will.

"Shoot, if you must, this old gray head,
But spare your country's flag," she said.

—excerpted from "Barbara Frietchie"
by John Greenleaf Whittier
in *The Annals of America*, vol. 9

◀ Confederate battle flag

DBQ Document-Based Questions

Early Days of the War

1. Why was money being raised?
2. What does Theodore think might happen if he were in the Union army and ran into the Hales?

Destruction Caused by Troops

3. According to Lunt, what did the Yankees do?
4. What is the situation of poor people because of these Yankee actions?

Barbara Frietchie

5. Who came marching into Frederick?
6. What did Barbara Frietchie do that was so unusual?

Read to Write

7. The lives of the people in these readings changed because of the experience of war. Write about an experience that completely changed your attitude toward something. Explain how your outlook changed. CA 8WA2.1

C Critical Thinking

Analyzing Primary Sources Ask: What contrast does Whittier make between the Confederate army and the surroundings? *(The countryside is described as lush and green and full of ripening fruit; the army is a "horde," which sounds menacing, and is full of hungry, or "famished," men.)* OL CA HR3.

R Reading Strategy

Visualizing Have students visualize the scene. **Ask:** How does the use of numbers to describe the Confederate and Union flags add to the drama? *(Frietchie's single flag is overwhelmingly outnumbered by the 40 Confederate flags, making her lonely stand more brave.)* OL

ASSESS

Have students answer the Document-Based Questions.

CLOSE

Evaluating Have students explain how each of these primary sources reveals the divisions in the nation. OL

DBQ Document-Based Questions

1. to help the families of people who enlisted
2. They would shoot him.
3. took any food or possessions that they could from people's homes
4. They are hungry and without animals.
5. Confederate forces under Stonewall Jackson.
6. She displayed the American flag.
7. Students' answers will vary. Ask volunteers to share their experiences with the class.

CHAPTER 13 Assessment

Resources for pages 618–619

Use these resources to review, assess, or reteach the chapter.

- Active Reading Note-Taking Guide, Chapter 13
- Chapter 13 Reading Essentials and Study Guide
- Chapter 13 Tests, Forms A and B
- Standards Assessment, Forms A and B
- California Standards Practice Workbook
- MindJogger Videoquiz
- Succeeding on the California History–Social Science Standards CD-ROM
- Interactive Tutor Self-Assessment CD-ROM

Chapter 13 Assessment

Standard US8.10

Review Content Vocabulary

1. Write a one page essay about the Civil War using the following words.
   a. border state
   b. casualty
   c. emancipate
   d. draft
   e. entrenched
   f. total war

Review the Main Ideas

Section 1 • The Two Sides

2. Why did the Union blockade Southern ports?
3. What three advantages did the Confederate states have in the war?

Section 2 • Early Years of the War

4. Who were the presidents of the United States and of the Confederate States of America?
5. Which battle is known as the bloodiest of the Civil War and why?

Section 3 • A Call to Freedom

6. In what ways did African Americans contribute to the war effort?
7. What did the Emancipation Proclamation state?

Section 4 • Life During the Civil War

8. What role did Clara Barton play in the Civil War?
9. How did the Civil War hurt the South's economy?

Section 5 • The Way to Victory

10. What was the outcome of the Battle of Gettysburg?
11. What terms of surrender did Grant offer to Lee?

Critical Thinking

12. **Cause and Effect** Why was controlling the Mississippi River vital to the North and the South? CA HI2.
13. **Infer** Why do you think General Lee was such an effective military leader? CA HR3.

Geography Skills

Study the map below and answer the following questions. CA CS3.

NATIONAL GEOGRAPHIC **Battle of Gettysburg**

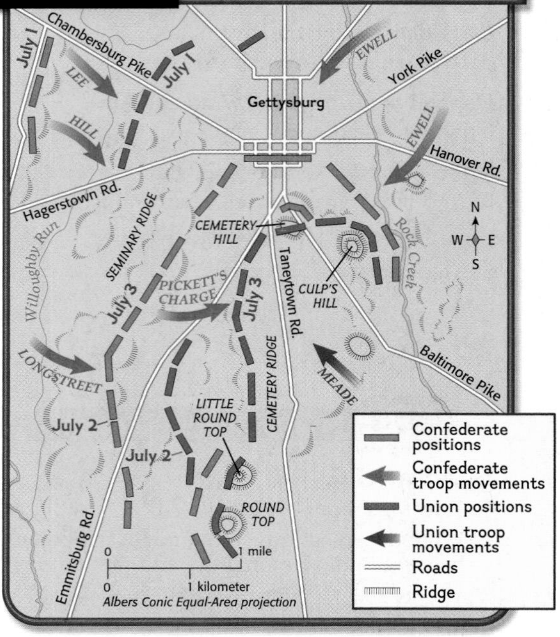

14. **Location** Along what ridge were the Union troops positioned?
15. **Movement** Who led forces across Rock Creek?

Review Content Vocabulary

1. Essays will vary but should reflect an understanding of the terms and of the Civil War.

Review the Main Idea

2. to prevent supplies from reaching the Confederacy
3. strong support of the white population, fighting a defensive war, strong military leadership
4. Abraham Lincoln, Jefferson Davis
5. Antietam; it was the single bloodiest day in the war
6. served as soldiers, as spies, and behind the lines in the military; worked to support the South's economy
7. All enslaved people within the Confederacy were free.
8. She delivered medical supplies to Union soldiers and nursed the wounded.
9. destroyed farms and factories, destroyed rail transportation system, caused shortages of food and other goods, caused inflation
10. Lee was forced to retreat from the North.
11. Confederate soldiers had to lay down their arms, but could go home and take their horses.

Critical Thinking

12. It was a main transportation route.
13. Possible answers include that he made and carried out bold plans, made good strategic moves, and had the respect of his men.

Geography Skills

14. Cemetery Ridge
15. Ewell

History Online

Self-Check Quiz Visit ca.hss.glencoe.com to prepare for the Chapter 13 test.

Read to Write

16. The Big Ideas **Evaluate** Write a short essay that describes the impact that civilians had on the war effort. Include references to both the North and the South. CA 8WS1.1

17. **Paraphrase** To explain his reelection, Lincoln stated, "it was not best to swap horses while crossing the river." Write a paragraph that explains Lincoln's quotation and how it applied to his career. CA 8WA2.2

18. **Using Your FOLDABLES** Use your foldable to write three sentences that summarize the main ideas of this chapter. Share your sentences with the class, and listen to their sentences. Then vote for the one you think best summarizes the chapter. CA 8RC2.0

Using Academic Vocabulary

19. Write a paragraph that uses these academic vocabulary words to describe an event from this chapter:
    a. sufficient
    b. reinforce
    c. encounter

Linking Past and Present

20. **Making Connections** A writ of habeas corpus is a court order that guarantees a person who is arrested the right to appear before a judge in a court of law. During the Civil War, President Lincoln suspended habeas corpus. What recent crisis led to similar actions? Write a short essay describing these actions and why they were taken. CA CS1.

Economics Connection

21. **Compare** Economic differences had always existed between the North and the South. From your reading of Chapter 13, would you say that the North or the South was better equipped economically for war? Explain your reasoning. CA HI6.

Reviewing Skills

22. Review READING SKILL **Evaluation** Review the section called "Total War" on page 609. Write a paragraph that evaluates the effectiveness of this strategy in accomplishing the Union's goals. Take into account the impact of this on the Confederacy and its civilians. CA 8WA2.4

23. Review ANALYSIS SKILL **Sequencing** Draw a time line that includes the major battles you read about in this chapter. Include battle dates, locations, and outcomes. CA CS2.

Standards Practice

Select the best answer for each of the following questions.

24 By gaining control of the Mississippi and Tennessee Rivers, the Union was able to

A capture Fort Sumter.
B force the Confederacy to surrender.
C split the Confederacy.
D defeat the Confederate forces at Gettysburg.

25 The Thirteenth Amendment was important because

A it gave women the right to vote.
B it outlawed secession.
C it abolished slavery in the United States.
D limited the President to two terms in office.

Read to Write

16. The Big Ideas Essays should include such contributions as women replacing men in many jobs; civilians working as nurses, spies, and in other capacities; and civilians expressing opposition to the war and the draft.

17. It would have been disruptive to the war effort to change leadership in the middle of the conflict.

18. Using Your FOLDABLES Sentences will vary but should accurately reflect information in the chapter.

Using Academic Vocabulary

19. Paragraphs will vary but should reflect an understanding of the information in this Chapter.

CHAPTER 13 Assessment

Linking Past and Present

20. Following the terrorist attacks of September 11, 2001, terrorist suspects were imprisoned without hearings because the government felt the suspects might flee, were too dangerous to remain at large, or were not citizens and thus not covered by constitutional protections.

Economics Connection

21. Answers should compare and contrast the economics of the North and South.

Reviewing Skills

22. Review READING SKILL Total war was very effective in accomplishing the Union's goals.

23. Review ANALYSIS SKILL Time lines should include the battles discussed in the chapter.

Standards Practice

24. C
25. C

Bonus Question

Ask: How might the Civil War have ended if McClellan had been elected president? *(with a negotiated settlement that allowed the South to retain slavery or become a separate nation)* AL CA HI4.

History Online

Have students visit the Web site at ca.hss.glencoe.com to review Chapter 13 and take the **Self-Check Quiz.**

Chapter 14 Planning Guide

SECTION RESOURCES

Main Ideas	Print Materials	Technology Resources
Section 1 **Reconstruction Plans** 1. Differences over how Reconstruction after the Civil War should be carried out divided the government. 2. After Abraham Lincoln was assassinated, Johnson became president and announced his plan of "Restoration."	• Reproducible Lesson Plan 14–1* • Daily Lesson and Discussion Notes 14–1 • Active Reading Note-Taking Guide 14–1 • Reading Essentials and Study Guide 14–1 • Guided Reading Activity 14–1 • Section Quiz 14–1	Daily Focus Skills Transparency 14–1 Section Graphic Organizer Transparency 14–1 California Standards Practice Transparency Interactive Tutor Self-Assessment CD-ROM ExamView® Pro Testmaker CD-ROM Presentation Plus! CD-ROM
Section 2 **Radicals in Control** 1. When Northerners realized that African Americans in the South were still being mistreated, Congress worked to find a solution. 2. Radical Republicans were able to put their version of Reconstruction into action.	• Reproducible Lesson Plan 14–2* • Daily Lesson and Discussion Notes 14–2 • Active Reading Note-Taking Guide 14–2 • Reading Essentials and Study Guide 14–2 • Guided Reading Activity 14–2 • Section Quiz 14–2	Daily Focus Skills Transparency 14–2 Section Graphic Organizer Transparency 14–2 California Standards Practice Transparency Interactive Tutor Self-Assessment CD-ROM ExamView® Pro Testmaker CD-ROM Presentation Plus! CD-ROM
Section 3 **The South During Reconstruction** 1. Violence against African Americans and their white supporters took place during Reconstruction. 2. After the Civil War, the South had to rebuild not only its farms and roads, but its social and political structures as well.	• Reproducible Lesson Plan 14–3* • Daily Lesson and Discussion Notes 14–3 • Active Reading Note-Taking Guide 14–3 • Reading Essentials and Study Guide 14–3 • Guided Reading Activity 14–3 • Section Quiz 14–3	Daily Focus Skills Transparency 14–3 Section Graphic Organizer Transparency 14–3 California Standards Practice Transparency Interactive Tutor Self-Assessment CD-ROM ExamView® Pro Testmaker CD-ROM Presentation Plus! CD-ROM
Section 4 **Change in the South** 1. Democrats steadily regained control of Southern governments as support for Radical Reconstruction policies decreased. 2. When Reconstruction ended, many changes took place in the South including a political shift and growth in industry. 3. As Reconstruction ended, true freedom for African Americans became a distant dream.	• Reproducible Lesson Plan 14–4* • Daily Lesson and Discussion Notes 14–4 • Active Reading Note-Taking Guide 14–4 • Reading Essentials and Study Guide 14–4 • Guided Reading Activity 14–4 • Section Quiz 14–4	Daily Focus Skills Transparency 14–4 Section Graphic Organizer Transparency 14–4 California Standards Practice Transparency Interactive Tutor Self-Assessment CD-ROM ExamView® Pro Testmaker CD-ROM Presentation Plus! CD-ROM Vocabulary PuzzleMaker CD-ROM

PACING YOUR LESSONS

Chapter Introduction	Section 1	Section 2	Section 3	Section 4	Chapter Assessment
$\frac{1}{2}$ Day	1 Day	2 Days	2 Days	1 Day	$\frac{1}{2}$ Day

0:00 **OUT OF TIME?** Assign the Chapter 14 ***Reading Essentials and Study Guide***

*Available on TeacherWorks™

Standards-Based Lesson Plan

History–Social Science Standards Covered in Chapter 14

The standards covered in the chapter are listed below. Use the accompanying activity as you teach the chapter to ensure student mastery of these standards. This activity can be used in combination with the program's print and technology assessment materials.

Standard	Section 1	Section 2	Section 3	Section 4
US8.11 Students analyze the character and lasting consequences of Reconstruction.	✔	✔	✔	✔
US8.11.1 List the original aims of Reconstruction and describe its effects on the political and social structures of different regions.	✔	✔	✔	✔
US8.11.2 Identify the push-pull factors in the movement of former slaves to the cities in the North and to the West and their differing experiences in those regions (e.g., the experiences of Buffalo Soldiers).				✔
US8.11.3 Understand the effects of the Freedmen's Bureau and the restrictions placed on the rights and opportunities of freedmen, including racial segregation and "Jim Crow" laws.	✔	✔	✔	✔
US8.11.4 Trace the rise of the Ku Klux Klan and describe the Klan's effects.			✔	
US8.11.5 Understand the Thirteenth, Fourteenth, and Fifteenth Amendments to the Constitution and analyze their connection to Reconstruction.	✔	✔		✔

Cumulative Standards-Assessment Activity

The Cumulative Standards-Assessment Activity will help students organize and learn the important information from the chapter. Begin teaching the chapter with this activity, and have students complete it as they read the chapter.

Creating a Sequencing Chart

Purpose Sequencing events is a vital skill when studying history. Understanding the proper sequence of events helps students when they carry out critical thinking tasks such as identifying cause-and-effect relationships and generalizing about trends or developments. Using graphic organizers like time lines to record events also helps students see how material that they study in two different parts of a chapter are related in time, preventing the misconception that content presented later necessarily occurred later in time.

Introduction to Sequencing

1. Model how to construct a time line by asking students to identify key dates in the previous chapter and briefly state what happened and why it was important. Write students' suggestions on the board, not necessarily in chronological order. After you have four or five dates, show how to sequence them properly in a time line.
2. Ask students to copy this chart into their notebooks:

Date	Event and Significance

Explain that students should collect all the dates and events from the chapter before constructing their time lines. If not, the result could become messy if they have to add dates encountered in a later section between two dates identified earlier and there is not sufficient room. Tell them when they have finished taking notes, they should make their time lines. Remind students to record the months and days of key events, if those are provided, since many events happened in the same year.

3. As you review the chapter, ask volunteers to name some of the key dates they identified. Encourage them to use their time lines as study aids.

Chapter 14 Resources

READING SUPPORT

- Content Vocabulary Activity 14
- Academic Vocabulary Activity 14
- Reading Skills Activity 14
- American Literature Reading 14
- Biography Activities 14A, 14B
- Chapter 14 Active Reading Note-Taking Guide
- Chapter 14 Guided Reading Activities
- Chapter 14 Reading Essentials and Study Guide
- Glencoe Literature Library
- Glencoe Video Program
- Vocabulary PuzzleMaker CD-ROM
- Interactive Graphic Organizers CD-ROM
- American History Primary Source Document Library CD-ROM

SKILL PRACTICE

- Map Overlay Transparency 14, Strategy, and Activity
- Analysis Skills Activity 14
- Time Line Activity 14
- Geography and History Activity 14
- Economics and History Activity 14
- Chart, Graph, and Map Skills Activity 14
- Political Cartoon Activity 14
- Supreme Court Case Study 14
- In-Text Map Transparency 14, Strategy, and Activity
- Step Into World History Activity 14
- Citizenship and Service Learning Activity 14
- Outline Map Resource Book
- MindJogger Plus Videoquiz

CRITICAL THINKING

- Critical Thinking Skills Activity 14
- Primary Source Reading 14
- Cause-and-Effect Transparency 14, Strategy, and Activity
- Presentation Plus! CD-ROM

WRITING SUPPORT

- Writing Activity 14
- Language Arts Activity 14
- Writer's Guidebook
- Middle School Writing Process Transparencies

UNIVERSAL ACCESS

- Universal Access Activity 14
- Then and Now Transparencies 14A–14B, Strategy, and Activity
- Graphic Novel Activity 14
- School-to-Home Connection Activities 14A–14D
- English Learner Handbook Chapter 14 Activities
- Universal Access for the American History Classroom
- Moments in Time
- American Art and Architecture Transparencies 14, Strategies, and Activities
- American Art Prints
- American Music Cultural Traditions
- American Music Hits Through History
- StudentWorks Plus CD-ROM

ASSESSMENT

Glencoe's Assessment Advantage

- Chapter 14 Section Quizzes
- Chapter 14 Tests, Forms A and B
- California Standards Assessment, Forms A and B
- Cumulative Assessment Activity US8.11
- California Standards Practice Workbook
- Succeeding on the California History–Social Science Standards CD-ROM
- Exam*View*® Pro Testmaker CD-ROM
- Interactive Tutor Self-Assessment CD-ROM

CD-ROM
DVD
Print Material
Poster
Transparency
Music Program
Videocassette
Glencoe Literature Library

Chapter 14 Resources

TECHNOLOGY

- StudentWorks Plus CD-ROM
- TeacherWorks CD-ROM
- Exam*View*® Pro Testmaker CD-ROM
- Interactive Tutor Self-Assessment CD-ROM
- Presentation Plus! CD-ROM
- Succeeding on the California History–Social Science Standards CD-ROM
- Vocabulary PuzzleMaker CD-ROM
- Interactive Graphic Organizers CD-ROM
- Interactive Time Line CD-ROM
- American History Primary Source Document Library CD-ROM
- MindJogger Plus Videoquiz
- American Music Cultural Traditions
- American Music Hits Through History
- Glencoe Program
- Professional Development in Middle School Social Studies Series
- Teaching American History With *Discovering Our Past: The American Journey to World War I*

SPANISH RESOURCES

- Spanish Activities and Assessment
  - Spanish Content Vocabulary Activities
  - Spanish Guided Reading Activities
  - Spanish Quizzes and Tests
  - Spanish California Standards Assessment
- Spanish Reading Essentials and Study Guide
- Spanish School-to-Home Connection
- Spanish Declaration of Independence and U.S. Constitution

TRANSPARENCIES

- California Standards Practice Transparencies
- Daily Focus Skills Transparencies
- Section Graphic Organizer Transparencies
- In-Text Map Transparencies
- Map Overlay Transparencies
- Cause-and-Effect Transparencies
- Then and Now Transparencies
- American Art and Architecture Transparencies
- Middle School Writing Process Transparencies

TEACHER PLANNING

- Daily Lesson and Discussion Notes
- English Learner Handbook
- Guide to Daily Intervention
- *Discovering Our Past: The American Journey to World War I* Reading and Study Skills Foldables
- Reading Strategies for the Social Studies Classroom
- Chapter 14 Reproducible Lesson Plans (correlated to California History–Social Science Standards)
- Universal Access for the American History Classroom
- NGS U.S. Desk Map
- NGS U.S. Atlas

PROFESSIONAL DEVELOPMENT

- Building Academic Vocabulary
- Strategies for Success
- Research-Based Strategies Used to Develop *Discovering Our Past: The American Journey to World War I*
- Character Education in the Middle School Classroom
- The Living Constitution
- Professional Development in Middle School Social Studies Video Series
- Teaching American History With *Discovering Our Past: The American Journey to World War I*

MASTERING THE STANDARDS

The content and assessment in the Student Edition, Teacher Wraparound Edition, teacher planning materials, and the print and technology products are all standards-based. The use of these products during instruction leads to mastery of the standards.

PRACTICE

- California Standards Practice Workbook
- California Standards Practice Transparencies
- Interactive Time Line CD-ROM
- School-to-Home Connection

BENCHMARK ASSESSMENT

- California Standards Assessment
- Exam*View*® Pro Testmaker CD-ROM
- Succeeding on the California History–Social Science Standards CD-ROM

REMEDIATION

- California Guide to Daily Intervention
- Interactive Tutor Self-Assessment CD-ROM
- Exam*View*® Pro Testmaker CD-ROM
- California Standards Practice Workbook
- Reading Essentials and Study Guide

Additional Resources

NATIONAL GEOGRAPHIC **TEACHER'S CORNER**

Index to National Geographic Magazine:

The following articles relate to this chapter:

- "The Cruelest Commerce: African Slave Trade," September 1992

National Geographic Society Products

To order the following, call National Geographic at 1-800-368-2728

- *GeoKit: The Civil War* (Kit)
- *GeoKit: Immigration* (Kit)
- *United States/Territorial Growth* (Map)
- *National Geographic Desk Reference* (Book)

NGS ONLINE

Access National Geographic's new dynamic MapMachine Web site and other geography resources at:

www.nationalgeographic.com

www.nationalgeographic.com/maps

A&E HOME VIDEO. Biography. THE HISTORY CHANNEL.

The following videotape programs are available from Glencoe as supplements to Chapter 14.

- **The Lincoln Assassination Set (ISBN 1-56501-568-1)**
- **John Wilkes Booth (ISBN 1-56501-715-3)**

To order, call Glencoe at 1-800-334-7344. To find classroom resources to accompany many of these videos, check the following home pages:

A&E Television: www.aetv.com
The History Channel: www.historychannel.com

History Online

Use our Web site for additional resources. All essential content is covered in the Student Edition.

You and your students can visit ca.hss.glencoe.com, the Web site companion to *Discovering Our Past: The American Journey to World War I*. This innovative integration of electronic and print media offers your students a wealth of opportunities. The student text directs students to the Web site for the following options:

- Chapter Overviews
- Self-Check Quizzes
- Study Central™
- Student Web Activities
- Textbook Updates
- Multi-Language Glossaries

Answers to the student Web activities are provided for you in the Web Activity Lesson Plans. Additional Web resources and ePuzzles and games are also available.

Glencoe TechCONNECT

Glencoe TechCONNECT™ AC201 "Freedmen's Education During Reconstruction"

Cumulative Activity Students should understand how the Freedmen's schools led to a public school system in the South, by examining the education of African Americans during Reconstruction and then creating a slide show of what they've learned. **CA** US8.11.3. **CA** CS1.; HI1.; HI2. **CA** 8RW1.0; 8RC2.0

You can access this online activity at www.ca.hss techconnect.glencoe.com. Enter the following activation key when prompted: **CONNECTCA.** To access the Teacher Resources for each activity, enter the following password when prompted: **CA123.**

FOLDABLES™ Study Organizer

Dinah Zike's Foldables

Foldables are three-dimensional, interactive graphic organizers that help students practice basic writing skills, review key vocabulary terms, and identify main ideas. Every chapter contains a foldable activity, with additional chapter activities found in the Reading and Study Skills Foldables booklet.

Reading List Generator CD-ROM — GLENCOE BOOKLINK

The Glencoe BookLink CD-ROM is a database that allows you to search more than 15,000 titles to create a customized reading list for your students.

- Reading lists can be organized by students' reading level, author, genre, theme, or area of interest.
- The database provides Degrees of Reading Power™ (DRP) and Lexile™ readability scores for all selections.
- A brief summary of each selection is included.

Reading level suggestions for this chapter:

For students at a Grade 6 reading level:
- ***Tancy,*** by Belinda Hurmence

For students at a Grade 7 reading level:
- ***Now Is Your Time!: The African-American Struggle for Freedom,*** by Walter Dean Myers

For students at a Grade 8 reading level:
- ***Going Home to Nicodemus,*** by Daniel Chu and Bill Shaw

For students at a Grade 9 reading level:
- ***Separate But Not Equal: The Dream and the Struggle,*** by Jim Haskins

For students at a Grade 10 reading level:
- ***Been in the Storm So Long: The Aftermath of Slavery,*** by Leon F. Litwack

Reading Support From JAMESTOWN EDUCATION

- *Timed Readings Plus in Social Studies* helps students increase their reading rate and fluency while maintaining comprehension. The 400-word passages are similar to those found on state and national assessments.
- *Reading in the Content Area: Social Studies* concentrates on six essential reading skills that help students better comprehend what they read. The book includes 754 high-interest nonfiction passages written at increasing levels of difficulty.
- *Reading Fluency* helps students read smoothly, accurately, and expressively.
- *Jamestown's Reading Improvement,* by renowned reading expert Edward Fry, focuses on helping build your students' comprehension, vocabulary, and skimming and scanning skills.
- *Critical Reading Series* provides high-interest books, each written at three reading levels.

To order these products, call Glencoe at 1-800-334-7344.

KEY for Using the Teacher Wraparound Edition

Use this key to help you identify the different types of prompts found in the Teacher Wraparound Edition.

R **Reading Strategies** activities help you teach reading skills and vocabulary.

C **Critical Thinking** strategies help students apply and extend what they have learned.

U **Universal Access** activities provide differentiated instruction for students learning to speak English, along with suggestions for teaching various types of learners.

S **Skill Practice** strategies help students practice historical analysis and geography skills.

W **Writing Support** activities provide writing opportunities to help students comprehend the text.

Teaching strategies and activities have been coded for ability level appropriateness.

AL Activities for students working above grade level
OL Activities for students working on grade level
BL Activities for students working below grade level
EL Activities for English Learners

FOCUS

History–Social Science Standards

In this chapter, the following standard will be covered:

US8.11 Students analyze the character and lasting consequences of Reconstruction.

More About the Photo

At least a dozen towns were partially or totally burned during Sherman's march through South Carolina. Countless homes and farms were destroyed, as well as significant portions of the state's railroads.

TEACH

The Big Ideas

As you begin teaching each section, use these questions and activities to focus on the Big Ideas.

Section 1

Reconstruction Plans

Essential Question: What challenges might two groups who sharply disagree over an important issue face as they try to resolve their differences? After students discuss the challenges, explain that in this section they will read about the disagreements among Northern politicians as they tried to find ways to bring the Southern states back into the Union. OL

Chapter 14

Reconstruction

◀ Ruins of a railroad depot, Charleston, South Carolina

NATIONAL GEOGRAPHIC **Who & When?**

1860 — 1870 — 1880

1865 President Lincoln is assassinated

1870 Fifteenth Amendment extends voting rights

1877 Reconstruction ends

Members of Congress

Section 2

Radicals in Control

Discuss the basic rights that citizens have in the United States. **Essential Question:** How are those rights guaranteed? *(by the Constitution, the courts, the government)* Explain that in the early years of Reconstruction, Congress acted to ensure that African Americans had the rights of citizens. OL

Section 3

The South During Reconstruction

Essential Question: How does extending basic rights to all populations help the entire nation? After discussing the question, explain that even though African Americans won some crucial rights during Reconstruction, it took many years before most white Southerners recognized these rights. OL

History Online
Chapter Overview Visit ca.hss.glencoe.com for a preview of Chapter 14.

The Big Ideas

Section 1
Reconstruction Plans
Political ideas and major events shape how people form governments. Northern politicians disagreed on how to bring the southern states back into the Union.

Section 2
Radicals in Control
A constitution reflects the values and goals of the society that creates it. The Radical Republicans in Congress worked to ensure the rights of the newly freed African Americans in the South.

Section 3
The South During Reconstruction
Political ideas and major events shape how people form governments. African Americans in the South made some gains in government and education, but many white Southerners attempted to limit their rights.

Section 4
Change in the South
Economic, social, and political changes create new traditions, values, and beliefs. As Reconstruction ended, white Southerners attempted to make economic changes in the South, while restricting the rights of African Americans.

View the Chapter 14 video in the Glencoe Video Program.

FOLDABLES™ Study Organizer

Comparison Make this foldable to help you compare and contrast Reconstruction in the Northen and Southern states.

Step 1 Mark the midpoint of the side edge of a sheet of paper.

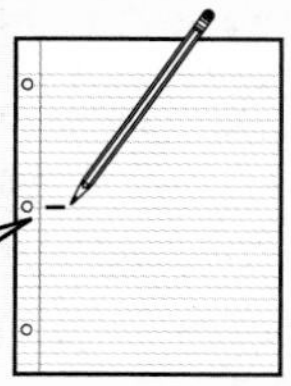

Step 2 Turn the paper and fold the edges in to touch at the midpoint.

Step 3 Turn and label your foldable as shown.

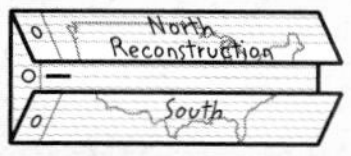

Reading and Writing As you read the chapter, write facts that show how Reconstruction differed and was the same in the Northern states and Southern states. Write the facts in the appropriate places inside your foldable.

Section 4
Change in the South
Essential Question: How do economic, social, and political changes create new values and beliefs? After discussing the question, explain that after Reconstruction ended changes to the economy and to African American rights. OL

Cultural Perspectives
During the Civil War, many Northern and Southern white women took on new responsibilities. Yet while everyday life for women in the North did not change much, Southern women endured tremendous disruptions because of the war. Similarly, white women and African American women in the South had very different experiences of Reconstruction. Organize students into groups to research and compare the experiences of one of these pairs of women. They should create presentations that compare the daily lives and activities of their groups and draw conclusions about the women's perspective on the events surrounding them. Ask students, is someone's knowledge and experience of historical events determined by their gender? Which group of women do they think was more likely to learn about the existence of women's rights activities, for example, and why?

History Online
Go to ca.hss.glencoe.com for student activities, lesson plans, and links to additional Web resources about Reconstruction.

FOLDABLES™ Study Organizer
Dinah Zike's Foldables
Purpose Have students use their foldables to write summaries of the similarities and differences in how the Northern and Southern states experienced Reconstruction. OL

Why It's Important

Monitoring and Clarifying
By monitoring their understanding of a text and clarifying its meaning, students build comprehension. When students fail to comprehend the meaning of a word or passage, that can hamper their ability to understand later material on which it builds. By making the effort to clarify the meaning of a text, students develop a solid foundation of knowledge on which they can build.

1 Learn It!

Ask: What do you do when someone gives you a direction and you do not understand it? *(Students are likely to say that they ask for clarification)* Explain that monitoring and clarifying is a similar process. If you have difficulty clarifying a passage of text, to whom can you turn for help? *(a teacher; other students)* OL

Chapter 14 Get Ready to Read

Monitoring and Clarifying

READING SKILL

1 Learn It!

Good readers monitor their understanding of text. When a portion of the reading is confusing, good readers use strategies to understand, such as looking up new words, rereading, and reading a bit farther to locate more information. This is called clarifying. As you read, stop and determine which parts were unclear. Identify unfamiliar words, and look on the page for supporting diagrams, maps, or pictures that might help you. Read the following paragraph using these techniques.

What is a reconstruction government? Was it explained earlier in the chapter?

> In the 1870s, Reconstruction governments began creating public school systems for both races, which had not existed in the South before the war. Within a few years, more than 50 percent of the white children and about 40 percent of African American children in the South were enrolled in public schools. Northern missionary societies also established academies offering advanced education for African Americans.
>
> —*from page 638*

What were the children doing who weren't enrolled in public schools?

What is a missionary society? Is it defined in the glossary?

Reading Tip

As you read, make a list of words you don't know. Look them up in the dictionary. Practice using them and your vocabulary words in sentences.

READING STRATEGY **QUESTIONING**

Asking and answering questions is basic to monitoring comprehension. Suggest that students develop a checklist of general questions they can ask themselves when they are reading:

- Who did what, and why?
- What were the actual results, and how did they respond to those results?
- How did others respond to their actions and the results?
- Do these events connect to events that happened earlier? How?
- Are there any clues that these events may have an impact on future events?
- What is the main idea of the paragraph or section, and what details support that idea? OL

Chapter 14
Get Ready to Read

2 Practice It!

Read the passage on the Freedmen's Bureau from Section 1. With a partner, see if you can answer the questions below:

> More progress was made in helping freed African Americans. In March 1865, Congress and the president set up a new government agency to help former enslaved persons, or freedmen. It was known as the Freedmen's Bureau.
>
> After the war, the Freedmen's Bureau helped African Americans adjust to freedom. The agency distributed food and clothing, and provided medical services that lowered the death rate among freed African Americans. It also set up schools staffed by Northern teachers such as Charlotte Forten and gave aid to new African American schools of high learning, such as Atlanta University, Howard University, and Fisk University. The bureau helped freed people acquire land or work with fair wages. Although the main goal of the bureau was to aid African Americans, it also helped pro-Union Southerners.
>
> —*from page 626*

Read to Write

Look in your local newspaper or a magazine for an interview with a famous person. Based on what you read, what additional questions would you ask?

▼ Mother and daughter reading

Monitor	Clarify
Were there any unfamiliar words?	Look in a glossary or dictionary
Do you know what the Freedmen's Bureau was?	
Who created the new agency?	Reread selection

3 Apply It!

As you read this chapter, identify one topic or event that you would like explained more fully. Then, do research to find answers to the questions you have. Use your answers to write a paragraph of explanation.

2 Practice It!

Have students turn to page 626 in Section 1 and read the information up to the subhead, "A Nation Mourns." When they have finished, ask volunteers to answer the following questions:

- How did people greet the news of Lincoln's death? *(shock, sadness, mourning, grief)*
- Where did the funeral train go? *(from Washington, D.C. to Springfield, Illinois)*
- Why did people respond as they did to the train? *(to pay tribute to Lincoln; to show their grief)*
- What message was spoken at Lincoln's funeral? *(words of peace from his second Inaugural Address)*

Tell students that these are just some examples of the kinds of questions they can use to monitor their comprehension. OL

3 Apply It!

Have students locate a newspaper article or Web site. Ask them to read the article and practice their monitoring and clarifying skills. Discuss what kinds of questions helped them understand what they read. Challenge students to identify sources they could use for any material they did not understand. OL

Reading Strategy — Narrative Writing

Students can make use of these strategies to improve their own writing. Have students write a narrative about an event or situation, using details to make clear exactly what happened and why. Have them write five questions that they think reflect the main elements of the narrative. Then have them trade their narratives with a partner. Tell the partners to read the narratives and answer the questions. Have students look at their partners' answers to see if they are correct. If they are not, have them review their narratives to see if they need to make the writing more clear. OL CA 8WA2.1

Use Reading Skills Activity 14 in the **Chapter 14 Resource Book** for more practice with monitoring and clarifying.

FOCUS

BELLRINGER
SKILLBUILDER ACTIVITY

Project **Daily Focus Skills Transparency 14–1** and have students answer the question.

Guide to Reading

Preteaching Vocabulary: Have students use the Glossary in the back of their textbook to find the definition of each term. Then have them write a sentence using each term.

Answers to Graphic: Ten Percent Plan: 10 percent swear loyalty, ban slavery; Wade-Davis Plan: 50 percent swear loyalty, ban slavery, no Confederates can hold office; Restoration: most Southerners could receive amnesty, officials and landowners apply to president, denounce secession, ratify Thirteenth Amendment

Unpacking the Standards

After reading the section, students will be able to:

- Explain how differences over the issue of Reconstruction divided the government.
- Describe why President Lincoln was assassinated.
- Discuss ideas for Reconstruction by President Johnson and Congress.

Section 1

Reconstruction Plans

History Social Science Standards

US8.11 Students analyze the character and lasting consequences of Reconstruction.

Guide to Reading

Looking Back, Looking Ahead

You learned that the Civil War ended in a Northern victory but at terrible costs to both sides. Northern politicians needed to figure out how to return the Southern states to the Union and what rights to allow the newly freed African Americans.

Focusing on the Main Ideas

- Differences over how Reconstruction after the Civil War should be carried out divided the government. *(page 625)*
- After Lincoln was assassinated, Johnson became president and announced his plan of "Restoration." *(page 626)*

Meeting People

Thaddeus Stevens
Charlotte Forten
John Wilkes Booth
Andrew Johnson

Content Vocabulary

Reconstruction (REE • kuhn • STRUHK • shuhn)
amnesty (AM • nuh • stee)
radical (RA • dih • kuhl)
freedmen

Academic Vocabulary

period
approach (uh • PROHCH)
deny (dih • NY)
aid

Reading Strategy

Taking Notes As you read the section, re-create the diagram below and describe each of the Reconstruction plans.

Plan	Description
Ten Percent Plan	
Wade-Davis Plan	
Restoration	

NATIONAL GEOGRAPHIC Who & When?

1864 — 1865

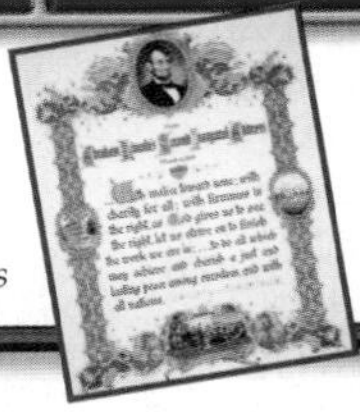

Lincoln's second Inaugural Address

Nov. 1864 Lincoln is elected to second term

March 1865 Freedmen's Bureau is established

Apr. 9, 1865 Lee surrenders

Apr. 14, 1865 President Lincoln is assassinated

Freedmen's School

SECTION RESOURCES

Print Material
- Reproducible Lesson Plan 14–1*
- Daily Lesson and Discussion Notes 14–1
- Guided Reading Activity 14–1
- Reading Essentials and Study Guide 14–1
- Active Reading Note-Taking Guide 14–1
- Section Quiz 14–1

Transparencies
- Daily Focus Skills Transparency 14–1
- Section Graphic Organizer Transparency 14–1
- California Standards Practice Transparencies

Technology
- Interactive Tutor Self-Assessment CD-ROM
- Exam*View*® Pro Testmaker CD-ROM
- Presentation Plus! CD-ROM

*Available on TeacherWorks™

US8.11.1 List the original aims of Reconstruction and describe its effects on the political and social structures of different regions. US8.11.3 Understand the effects of the Freedmen's Bureau and the restrictions placed on the rights and opportunities of freedmen, including racial segregation and "Jim Crow" laws.

Reconstruction Debate

Main Idea **Differences over how Reconstruction after the Civil War should be carried out divided the government.**

Reading Connection How would you have established terms of peace and rebuilding following the Civil War? Read to find out how President Lincoln and the Republicans in Congress disagreed about the treatment of the Southern states as they returned to the Union.

An American Story

When Confederate soldiers—tired, ragged, and hungry—went home at the end of the war, they often returned to a ruined land. Mary Chesnut of South Carolina wrote about what she saw and felt when she traveled:

> **"CAMDEN, S. C., *May 2, 1865.* Since we left Chester nothing but solitude, nothing but tall blackened chimneys, to show that any man has ever trod this road before. This is Sherman's track. It is hard not to curse him. I wept incessantly at first. The roses of the gardens are already hiding the ruins."**
>
> —Mary Chesnut, *A Diary From Dixie*

Destruction in the South The war saved the Union but left the South devastated. Cities and plantations were in ruin, and roads, bridges and railroads were destroyed. More than 258,000 Confederate soldiers had died in the war, and illness and injuries weakened thousands more. Americans everywhere agreed that the South needed to be rebuilt, but they disagreed bitterly over how to accomplish it. This R1 period of rebuilding is called **Reconstruction** (REE • kuhn • STRUHK • shuhn). This term also refers to the various plans for carrying out the rebuilding.

"We have turned. . . loose four million slaves without a hut to shelter them or a cent in their pockets." R2

—Thaddeus Stevens in a speech to Congress, December 1865

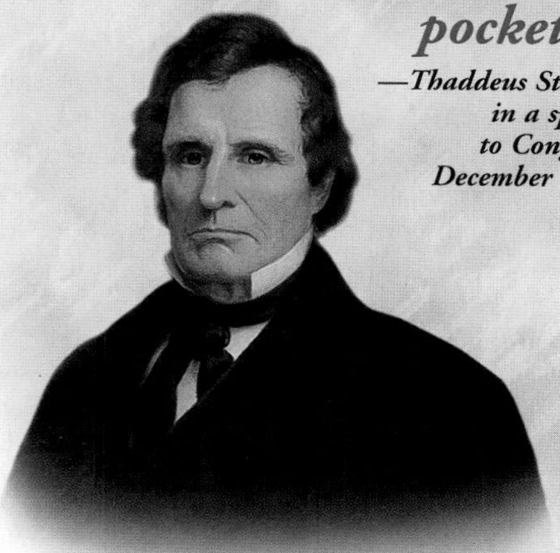

Lincoln's Plan President Lincoln offered the first plan for accepting the South back into the Union. In December 1863, during the Civil War, the president announced the Ten Percent Plan. When 10 percent of the voters of a state took an oath of loyalty to the Union, the State could form a government and adopt a new constitution that banned slavery.

Lincoln wanted to encourage pro-Union Southerners to run the state governments. He believed that punishing the South would only delay healing the torn nation. The president offered **amnesty** (AM • nuh • stee)—immunity from prosecution—to all white Southerners, except Confederate leaders, who gave loyalty to the Union. R3 In 1864 three states under Union occupation—Louisiana, Arkansas, and Tennessee—set up governments under Lincoln's plan. Some Republicans considered Lincoln's plan too mild. Favoring a more **radical,** or extreme, **approach,** they were called Radical Republicans.

TEACH

R1 Reading Strategy

Understanding Vocabulary Point out that *Reconstruction* means both the plans to rebuild the South and the period during which this took place. OL

R2 Reading Strategy

Reading Primary Sources **Ask:** What difficulties does Stevens say African Americans will face in the South? What others can you think of? *(need to find housing, earn money; need for schooling, medical care, and new relations with whites in the South)* OL

R3 Reading Strategy

Understanding Vocabulary Explain that the word *amnesty* comes from a Greek word meaning "forgetfulness." **Ask:** How does this relate to the meaning of the term? *(Amnesty represents forgetting the past by not punishing people for actions they have taken.)* BL

Resources for page 625

- Universal Access Activity 14
- Language Arts Activity 14

More Skill Practice

Historical and Social Sciences Analysis Skill **Ask:** How do you think Northerners responded to Lincoln's plan? Why? *(Students may say that many in the North would find it too lenient and want to punish the South because of the suffering brought on by the war.)* OL CA HI1.

C Critical Thinking

Analyzing Primary Sources Have students paraphrase Stevens's quote. *(The South has to be completely changed or all the lives lost and money spent in the war were wasted.)* OL

U Universal Access

English Learners Explain that the term *freedmen* applied to all African Americans freed from slavery, not just men. EL

Review The Big Idea

Review the Big Idea for this section: "Political ideas and major events shape how people form governments." **Ask:** How did Northerners' views differ about how to bring Southern states back into the Union? *(Lincoln believed that harsh policies were unwise, but the Radical Republicans in Congress wanted to punish the South.)* OL

Reading Check

Answer: plan that would allow states back into the Union if only 10 percent of their voters swore loyalty to the government and if they adopted new constitutions that banned slavery

Answers and Additional Support

US8.11.5 Understand the Thirteenth, Fourteenth, and Fifteenth Amendments to the Constitution and analyze their connection to Reconstruction.

The Radicals' Plan A leading Radical Republican, **Thaddeus Stevens,** declared that the foundations of the South "must be broken up and relaid, or all our blood and treasure have been spent in vain." Controlled by Radical Republicans, Congress voted to **deny** seats to representatives from any state reconstructed under Lincoln's plan. Then it began to create its own more radical plan.

In July 1864, Congress passed the Wade-Davis Bill. First, most white males in a state had to swear loyalty to the Union. Second, only white males who swore they had not fought the Union could vote for delegates to a constitutional convention. Former Confederates were barred from public office. Finally, any new state constitution had to end slavery. Only then could a state rejoin the Union.

Lincoln refused to sign the bill into law. He did, however, want new state governments that would restore order quickly. He realized that he would have to compromise with the Radical Republicans.

The Freedmen's Bureau More progress was made in helping freed African Americans. In March 1865, Congress and the president set up a new government agency to help former enslaved persons, or **freedmen.** It was known as the Freedmen's Bureau.

After the war, the Freedmen's Bureau helped African Americans adjust to freedom. The agency distributed food and clothing, and provided medical services that lowered the death rate among freed African Americans. It also set up schools staffed by Northern teachers such as **Charlotte Forten** and gave **aid** to new African American schools of higher learning, such as Atlanta University, Howard University, and Fisk University. The bureau helped freed people acquire land or work with fair wages. Although the main goal of the bureau was to aid African Americans, it also helped pro-Union Southerners.

Reading Check **Explain** What was Lincoln's Ten Percent Plan?

Lincoln Is Assassinated

Main Idea **After Lincoln was assassinated, Johnson became president and announced his plan of "Restoration."**

Reading Connection How do you think the loss of a strong leader might impact a nation during a difficult time? Read to find out how the death of Lincoln affected the course of Reconstruction.

A terrible event soon threw the debates over Reconstruction into confusion. On the evening of April 14, 1865, President and Mrs. Lincoln attended a play at Ford's Theater in Washington, D.C. As the Lincolns watched the play from a private box in the balcony, **John Wilkes Booth,** a pro-Confederate actor, entered the box and shot the president in the head. He then leaped to the stage and escaped from the theater. The wounded president died a few hours later.

After fleeing Ford's Theater, Booth rode on horseback to Virginia. There, Union troops tracked him down and cornered him in a barn. When Booth refused to give up, he was shot to death. Booth was part of a small group that had plotted to kill several government officials.

A Nation Mourns News of Lincoln's death shocked the nation. African Americans mourned the death of the man who had helped them win their freedom. Northern whites grieved for the leader who had saved the Union.

A funeral train carried Lincoln's body on a 1,700-mile journey from Washington, D.C., to his home town of Springfield, Illinois. Thousands of people lined the route. At night, bonfires and torches lit the way. By day, bells tolled and cannons fired.

Lincoln's second Inaugural Address, read at the cemetery, reminded Americans of his plan "to do all which may achieve and cherish a just, and a lasting peace, among ourselves, and with all nations." The future, however, was in the hands of those who favored harsher measures against the former Confederacy.

More Skill Practice

Historical and Social Sciences Analysis Skill Tell students that the Freedmen's Bureau also helped found and construct numerous churches for African Americans. **Ask:** How might churches have aided the freed African Americans? *(Possible answers: helped provide social connections, spiritual advice, and strength)* OL

Did You Know?

When Booth leapt from the balcony onto the stage he shouted, *"Sic semper tyrannis!"* The Latin phrase means "Thus always to tyrants!" and is the state motto of Virginia. The assassination plot also included Vice President Andrew Johnson and Secretary of State William H. Seward. Johnson was unharmed, but Seward was stabbed, though he survived.

Biography

US8.11 Students analyze the character and lasting consequences of Reconstruction.

CHARLOTTE FORTEN

1837–1914

Charlotte Forten was the first northern African American schoolteacher to go south to teach former slaves. **R** In late 1861, Union army forces captured a group of islands off the coast of South Carolina and Georgia. Thousands of enslaved people had been left there as their owners fled from the northern soldiers. Many government leaders and abolitionists saw this as a chance to show that former slaves could live successfully as free citizens. The Port Royal Experiment gave educational and medical aid to the freed slaves on the islands. Charlotte Forten was one of the teachers who volunteered to help. **S** She taught there from 1862 to 1864.

Forten was born in Philadelphia. She studied in Salem, Massachusetts, from 1854 to 1856. For two years, she taught elementary school there. However, she wanted to be part of a larger cause. The Port Royal Experiment gave her the opportunity to help others.

Forten kept a journal of her years on the Sea Islands. In it she expressed her commitment to help the former slaves. She also revealed her own feelings **W** as a young African American woman growing up in a mostly white country.

"[T]he eyes of these freed children see no clouds in it."

—from *Life on the Sea Islands* by Charlotte Forten

"This morning a large number—superintendents, teachers, and freed people, assembled in the little Baptist church. It was a sight that I shall not soon forget—that crowd of eager, happy black faces from which the shadow of slavery had forever passed. 'Forever free!' 'Forever free!' Those magical words were all the time singing themselves in my soul. . . ."

Later, she lived in Washington, D.C., and continued to support equal rights for African Americans.

Then and Now

Through her work in education, Charlotte Forten influenced many people. What teachers have influenced you and helped you learn?

Biography

TEACH

R Reading Strategy

Scaffolding—Connecting

Ask: Do you know of people acting similarly to Forten today? What kinds of actions do they take? *(Students may point to people who work actively for many different causes or who dedicate themselves to helping others.)* BL CA HI3.

This READING SKILL was introduced in Chapter 3.

S Skill Practice

Historical and Social Sciences Analysis Skill

Ask: What barriers did the freedmen face during the first stages of the Port Royal Experiment? *(Possible answers: barriers to education, employment, integrating into society)* OL

W Writing Support

Narrative Writing Have students imagine they are in Charlotte's place and write a journal entry from what might be considered a typical day in her life in the South. BL

Then and Now

Answer: Suggest that students explain the reason for their choices. Accept any answer that is written grammatically and clearly explained.

Did You Know?

When Forten arrived in South Carolina, she experienced culture shock. The freedmen she met had lived a very different life than she had experienced in the North. Although her purpose in South Carolina was to teach the freedmen, they taught her as well. By the time she left the area in 1864, she had new insights into both the culture and the sufferings of the freedmen in the South.

S Skill Practice

Historical and Social Sciences Analysis Skill Tell students that President Johnson had declared that "Restoration" was almost complete. **Ask:** What did he mean? *(Nearly all the states had new governments and ratified the Thirteenth Amendment.)* OL CA HI2.

ASSESS

Resources for page 628

Use these resources to assess student mastery of section content.

- Biography Activity 14A
- Section Quiz 14–1
- Interactive Tutor Self-Assessment CD-ROM

Reading Check

Answer: Johnson's plan gave the states control over many decisions and offered no help to African Americans.

History Online

Study Central provides summaries, interactive games, and online graphic organizers to help students review section content.

CLOSE

Summarizing Have students summarize the three Reconstruction plans described in this section. OL

A New President When Lincoln died, Vice President **Andrew Johnson** became president. Johnson was Southern born but pro Union. When Johnson's state (Tennessee) seceded in 1861, Johnson rejected its action and remained in his Senate seat.

In 1864 the Republicans nominated him for vice president. As Lincoln's running mate, Johnson had sharply attacked southern leaders. He once said:

> **"Treason, must be made odious [hateful] and Traitors punished."**
>
> **—as Tennessee war governor, 1862**

The Radical Republicans were pleased with Johnson's statements and expected him to be harsher than Lincoln toward the South. Johnson announced his own Reconstruction plan, which he called "Restoration," in May 1865. Under his plan, most Southerners would be granted amnesty once they swore loyalty to the Union. High-ranking or wealthy Confederates could be pardoned by appealing to the president. This provision revealed Johnson's desire to humiliate the wealthy leaders who he believed had tricked the South's people into seceding.

Johnson also allowed only loyal, pardoned whites to vote for delegates to the state constitutional conventions. Stating that "white men alone must manage the South," Johnson opposed African Africans having equal rights or the vote.

The Thirteenth Amendment Before entering the Union, a state had to denounce secession and end slavery. States also had to ratify the Thirteenth Amendment to the Constitution, which Congress had passed in January 1865. The amendment abolished slavery in all of the United States. By the end of 1865, all the former Confederate states except Texas had new governments and were ready to rejoin the Union. S

Reading Check **Compare** How did President Johnson's plan for Reconstruction differ from that of the Radical Republicans?

History Online

Study Central Need help understanding Reconstruction? Visit ca.hss.glencoe.com and click on Study Central.

Section 1 Review

Reading Summary

Review the Main Ideas

- The plan for Reconstruction developed by the Radical Republicans was much harsher than that proposed by President Lincoln.
- Following the assassination of President Lincoln, President Andrew Johnson took office and announced his plan for the "Restoration" of the South.

What Did You Learn?

1. What did the Thirteenth Amendment provide?
2. What was the Freedmen's Bureau, and what was its goal?

Critical Thinking

3. **Comparing** Re-create the diagram below and compare Lincoln's Ten Percent Plan to the Radical Republicans' Wade-Davis Bill. CA HI2.

Reconstruction Plans	
Ten Percent Plan	Wade-Davis Bill

4. **Drawing Conclusions** Do you think President Johnson's early ties to the South influenced his Reconstruction plans? Explain your answer. CA CS1.
5. **The Big Ideas** How did Lincoln's and the Radical Republicans' ideas about Reconstruction differ? CA HI2.
6. **READING Monitoring and Clarifying** Reread the passage called "Lincoln's Plan" on page 625. What words were new to you? List words you did not know and define them. CA 8RC2.0

SECTION 1 REVIEW ANSWERS

Review questions reinforce content standard US8.11.

1. It ended slavery.
2. government agency; helped freedmen with food, clothing, schooling, getting jobs
3. Ten Percent Plan: 10 percent swear loyalty, ban slavery, amnesty; Wade-Davis Bill: 50 percent swear loyalty, ban slavery, limited voting rights
4. Students may say his attitudes were like those of many Southerners.
5. **The Big Ideas** Differ: Lincoln had smaller percentage of voters needed to form a new government and offered amnesty; Radicals said new state constitutions had to ban slavery; Alike: excluded former Confederate officers
6. **READING** Answers will vary.

Section 2

Radicals in Control

Guide to Reading

Looking Back, Looking Ahead

You learned that after Lincoln was assassinated, Andrew Johnson became president and proposed his own plan for restoring the Southern states into the Union. The Radical Republicans in Congress, however, had very different ideas about how the Southern states should be allowed to rejoin the North.

Focusing on the Main Ideas

- When Northerners realized that African Americans in the South were still being mistreated, Congress worked to find a solution. ***(page 630)***
- Radical Republicans were able to put their version of Reconstruction into action. ***(page 631)***

Meeting People

Edwin Stanton
Ulysses S. Grant

Content Vocabulary

black codes
override
impeach (ihm • PEECH)

Academic Vocabulary

prohibit (proh • HIH • buht)
enable (ih • NAY • buhl)

Reading Strategy

Organizing Information As you read the section, re-create the diagram below and provide information about impeachment.

Impeachment	
What is it?	
Who was impeached?	
Outcome of the trial?	

History Social Science Standards

US8.11 Students analyze the character and lasting consequences of Reconstruction.

NATIONAL GEOGRAPHIC **Who & When?**

1865 1867 1869 1871

1865 Andrew Johnson becomes president

Andrew Johnson

1867 Radical Reconstruction begins

1868 Ulysses S. Grant elected president

Ulysses S. Grant

1870 Fifteenth Amendment extends voting rights

FOCUS

BELLRINGER SKILLBUILDER ACTIVITY

Project **Daily Focus Skills Transparency 14–2** and have students answer the question.

Guide to Reading

Preteaching Vocabulary: Have students predict what each term means and then use the Glossary in the back of their textbook to look up the definitions and check their predictions.

Answers to Graphic: What: formal charging of wrongdoing; Who: President Andrew Johnson; Outcome: Senate vote one short of majority required to remove Johnson from office

Unpacking the Standards

After reading the section, students will be able to:

- Describe the mistreatment of freedmen and how Congress tried to stop it.
- Identify how the black codes blocked the rights of African Americans.
- Explain how Radical Republicans helped Reconstruction efforts.
- Discuss the impeachment of President Johnson.

SECTION RESOURCES

Print Material

- Reproducible Lesson Plan 14–2*
- Daily Lesson and Discussion Notes 14–2
- Guided Reading Activity 14–2
- Reading Essentials and Study Guide 14–2
- Active Reading Note-Taking Guide 14–2
- Section Quiz 14–2

Transparencies

- Daily Focus Skills Transparency 14–2
- Section Graphic Organizer Transparency 14–2
- California Standards Practice Transparencies

Technology

- Interactive Tutor Self-Assessment CD-ROM
- Exam*View*® Pro Testmaker CD-ROM
- Presentation Plus! CD-ROM

*Available on TeacherWorks™

TEACH

S Skill Practice

Reading a Time Line
Have students create a time line of the important events of Reconstruction detailed in this subsection. OL CA CS2.

R1 Reading Strategy

Understanding Vocabulary
Ask: What was the purpose of the black codes? *(to limit African Americans' freedoms)* OL

R2 Reading Strategy

Scaffolding—Understanding Question-Answer Relationships
Ask: Why did Congress pass a civil rights bill making the freedmen citizens? *(to combat the black codes)* OL

This READING SKILL was introduced in Chapter 10.

R3 Reading Strategy

Understanding Vocabulary
Ask: How does the term *override* signify the power that Congress has over a President's veto? *(Congress's action is superior to the President's.)* OL

Answers and Additional Support

US8.11.3 Understand the effects of the Freedmen's Bureau and the restrictions placed on the rights and opportunities of freedmen, including racial segregation and "Jim Crow" laws. **US8.11.5** Understand the Thirteenth, Fourteenth, and Fifteenth Amendments to the Constitution and analyze their connection to Reconstruction.

African Americans' Rights

S **Main Idea** **When Northerners realized that African Americans in the South were still being mistreated, Congress worked to find a solution.**

Reading Connection Do you know the requirements for being a United States citizen? Is being born in this country enough to make a person a citizen? Read to find out how Congress made sure that the African Americans freed after the Civil War became citizens.

An American Story

In May 1866, white mobs in Memphis, Tennessee, burned African American churches, schools, and homes. Close to 50 people, nearly all of them African American, died. Many Northerners saw the violence as an attempt by whites to keep African Americans from exercising their rights. This and similar riots in the South made Radical Republicans realize that the Johnson Reconstruction plan was not strong enough.

Southern Representatives During the fall of 1865, Southerners created new state governments based on the Johnson plan. They also elected to Congress new representatives, some of whom had been leading Confederate officials. When the Southern representatives arrived in Washington, D.C., Congress refused to seat them. Many Republicans opposed readmitting the South on such easy terms.

▲ As early as 1865, groups were forming to commit violence against African Americans. This flag is the symbol for one such group, the Ku Klux Klan.

To many Northerners, Johnson's plan was robbing the Union of its hard-won victory. Northerners also realized that the treatment of African Americans in the South was not improving.

Black Codes By the spring of 1866, Southern states had passed **black codes,** or laws that aimed to control freed men and women. The black codes trampled the rights of African Americans. They permitted plantation owners to exploit African American workers and allowed officials to arrest and fine jobless African Americans. The black codes also banned African Americans from owning or renting farms. To freed men and women and many Northerners, the black codes brought back slavery in disguise. R1

Challenging the Codes In early 1866, Congress gave the Freedmen's Bureau new powers. The agency now was able to set up special courts to try individuals charged with violating the rights of African Americans. African Americans could serve on juries in these courts. This gave them the opportunity to play a new role in pursuing justice.

Congress also passed a civil rights bill that overturned the black codes. This measure made African Americans full citizens and gave the federal government power to intervene in state affairs to protect African American rights. R2

President Johnson vetoed both bills, arguing that the federal government was going beyond its proper authority. He also said that the measures were unconstitutional because they were passed by a Congress that did not include representation from all the states. By raising the issue of representation, Johnson indirectly threatened to veto any bill passed by this Congress.

Republicans in Congress had enough votes to **override,** or defeat, both vetoes, and the bills became law. R3 As the split between the president and Congress grew, the chances of them working together faded. The Radical Republicans rejected any compromise and drafted a new Reconstruction plan—one led by Congress.

More Skill Practice

Historical and Social Sciences Analysis Skill Have students create a chart that outlines the Reconstruction goals of the following groups: Radical Republicans, freed African Americans, white Southerners, white Northerners. Have the class discuss the similarities and differences among these goals. OL CA HI1.

More About the Art

The Ku Klux Klan was formed in December, 1865 with the purpose of terrorizing African Americans. This group eventually focused on the issue of white supremacy along with the repression of African American freedoms throughout the twentieth century.

US8.11.1 List the original aims of Reconstruction and describe its effects on the political and social structures of different regions.

The Fourteenth Amendment Although the Thirteenth Amendment ensured the freedom of African Americans, it did not guarantee them full rights. After the Civil War, many Southern states passed laws that kept African Americans from holding certain jobs, limited their property rights, and restricted them in other ways. S1

To remedy this situation, Congress passed the Fourteenth Amendment to the Constitution in 1866. The Fourteenth Amendment was enacted in 1868. This new amendment gave full citizenship to all people born in the United States. Because most African Americans were American born, they became full citizens. The amendment also required every state to grant its citizens "equal protection of the laws."

This clause has been extremely important. In recent years, it has been used to benefit women, people with disabilities, and other groups whose rights have not always been protected fairly. The amendment also stated that no state could take away a citizen's life, liberty, and property "without due process of law." States that kept any adult male citizen from voting could lose part of their representation in Congress. Finally, the amendment barred leading former Confederates from holding national or state office unless pardoned by Congress. R1 *(See pages 263–264 for the entire text of the Fourteenth Amendment.)*

Congress declared that Southern states had to ratify the amendment to rejoin the Union. Of the 11 Southern states, the only state to ratify was Tennessee. The refusal of the other Southern states delayed the adoption of the amendment until 1868.

Republican Victory In the congressional elections of 1866, President Johnson campaigned vigorously against the Fourteenth Amendment and its supporters. Many Northerners objected to the nasty tone of Johnson's campaign. The Republicans won a solid victory, giving Congress the signal to take Reconstruction into its own hands. S2

Reading Check **Describe** What does the Fourteenth Amendment provide?

Radical Reconstruction

Main Idea **Radical Republicans were able to put their version of Reconstruction into action.**

Reading Connection If you were a member of Congress during this time, what do you think would be most important to include in Reconstruction plans? Read to learn some of the plans that Congress passed.

The Republicans in Congress quickly took charge of Reconstruction. President Johnson could do little to stop them because Congress could easily override his vetoes. Thus began a period known as Radical Reconstruction. R2

History *Through Art*

His First Vote **by Thomas Waterman Wood**
Wood's oil painting emphasized the importance of the ballot to African American voters. ***How did African American males gain the right to vote?***

S1 Skill Practice

Historical and Social Sciences Analysis Skill
Ask: Why did Congress pass the Fourteenth Amendment? *(to block the actions of white Southerners aimed at limiting African Americans' rights)* **OL**
CA HI1.

R1 Reading Strategy

Scaffolding—Evaluating
Discuss whether students think Congress was right to ban former Confederates from holding public office. **OL**

This READING SKILL was introduced in Chapter 13.

S2 Skill Practice

Historical and Social Sciences Analysis Skill
Ask: Why did the 1866 congressional elections strengthen the hand of the Radical Republicans in Congress? *(because voters gave them a solid majority in Congress; because voters rejected Johnson's campaign against them)* **OL**
CA HI2.

R2 Reading Strategy

Monitoring **Ask:** Why is the period in which Congress controlled Reconstruction policy called "Radical Reconstruction"? *(because Radical Republicans dominated Congress)* **BL**

Reading Check
Answer: full citizenship to all people born in the United States; protection from states taking away a citizen's life, liberty, and property without due process; equal protection of the laws to all citizens

History *Through Art*

The Fifteenth Amendment is the last of three Reconstruction amendments. The Thirteenth and the Fifteenth Amendments were meant to guard the people against the misuse of state power.

Answer: The passage of the Fifteenth Amendment gave African American males the right to vote.

Review The Big Idea

Review the Big Idea for this section: "A constitution reflects the values and goals of the society that creates it." **Ask:** What conflict led to the passage of the Reconstruction Act of 1867? *(Radical Republicans' objections to how Southern whites treated the freedmen.)* BL CA HI2.

U Universal Access

Below Grade Level Suggest that students use a chart to take notes on the different steps in Reconstruction. Students should list the names and dates of the two Reconstruction acts and the key provisions of each. BL

C Critical Thinking

Determining Cause and Effect **Ask:** Why did Republicans gain control of the new state governments after the two Reconstruction acts of 1867? *(white Southerners did not take part in the process; African Americans who did apparently supported Republicans)* OL CA HI2.

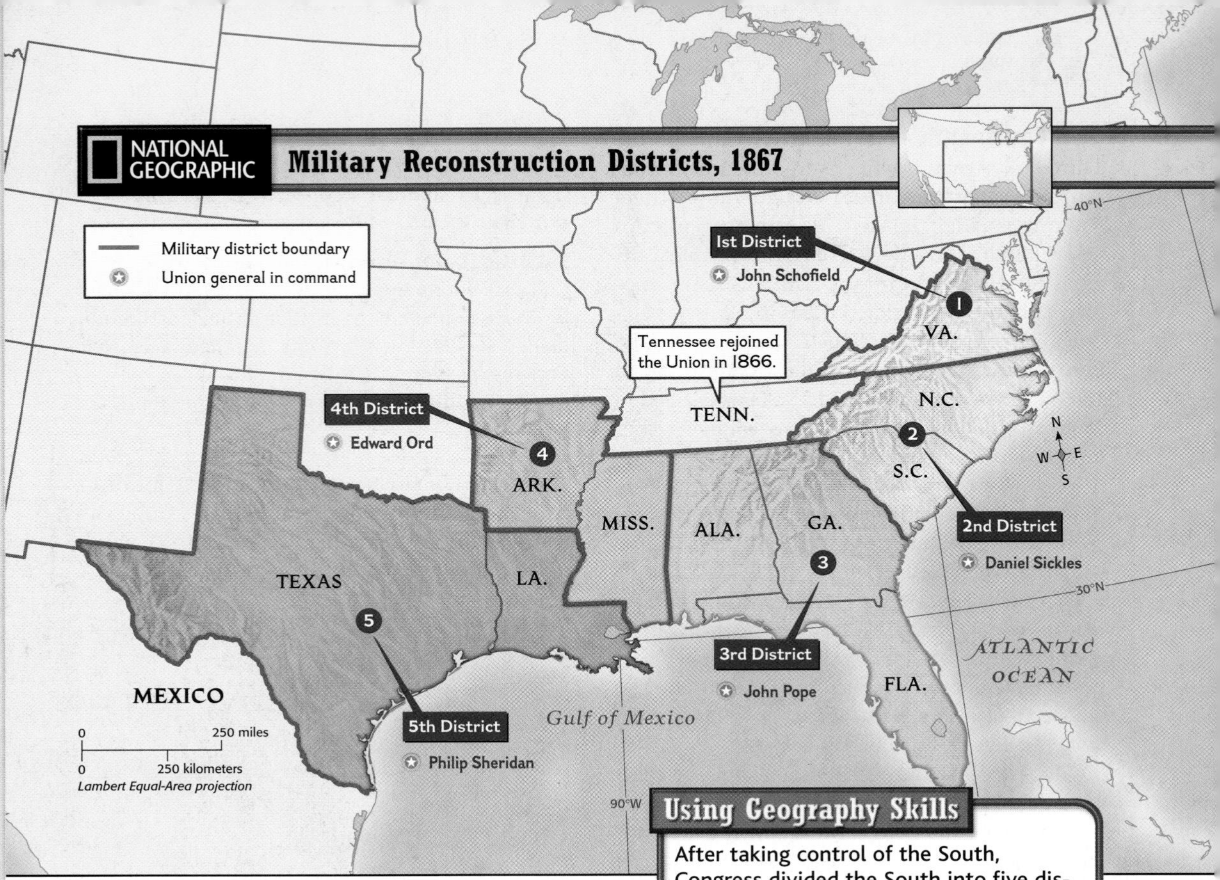

Using Geography Skills

After taking control of the South, Congress divided the South into five districts under the command of military officers.

1. **Region** Which two states made up the largest district?
2. **Analyze** Why did no Union troops occupy Tennessee?

Reconstruction Act of 1867 In March 1867 Congress passed the Reconstruction Act. It called for the creation of new governments in the 10 Southern states that had not ratified the Fourteenth Amendment. Tennessee, which had ratified the amendment, kept its government, and the state rejoined the Union.

U The act divided the 10 Southern states into five military districts and placed each under the authority of a military commander until new governments were formed. The act also guaranteed African American males the right to vote in state elections, and it prevented former Confederate leaders from holding political office.

To rejoin the Union, the states had to ratify the Fourteenth Amendment and submit new state constitutions to Congress for approval. A Second Reconstruction Act required the military commanders to register voters and prepare for state constitutional conventions.

The Readmission of States Many white Southerners refused to take part in the elections for constitutional conventions and state governments. Thousands of newly registered African American voters did use their right to vote. In the elections, Republicans gained control of Southern state governments. By 1868 seven Southern states—Alabama, Arkansas, Florida, Georgia, Louisiana, North Carolina, and South Carolina—had established new governments C and met the conditions for readmission to the Union. By 1870 Mississippi, Virginia, and Texas were restored to the Union.

Answers and Additional Support

More Skill Practice

Historical and Social Sciences Analysis Skill **Ask:** What situations might military control over the Southern states create? *(Possible answers: resentment and further resistance among whites; relief among freedmen)* OL

Using Geography Skills

Answers:

1. Texas and Louisiana
2. because it had already rejoined the Union

In-Text Map Transparency 14
Ask: Which district did John Pope command? *(3rd)* OL

Challenge to Johnson Strongly opposed to Radical Reconstruction, President Johnson had the power as commander in chief of the army to direct the actions of the military governors. For this reason, Congress passed several laws to limit the president's power.

R1 R2 One of these laws, the Tenure of Office Act of March 1867, was a deliberate challenge. It **prohibited** the president from removing government officials, including members of his own cabinet, without the Senate's approval. The act violated the tradition that presidents controlled their cabinets, and it threatened presidential power.

W **Impeaching the President** The conflict between Johnson and the Radicals grew more intense. In August 1867—when Congress was not in session—Johnson suspended Secretary of War **Edwin Stanton** without the Senate's approval.

When the Senate met again and refused to approve the suspension, Johnson removed Stanton from office—a deliberate violation of the Tenure of Office Act. Johnson angered the Republicans further by appointing some generals the Radicals opposed as commanders of Southern military districts.

R3 Outraged by Johnson's actions, the House of Representatives voted to **impeach** (ihm•PEECH)—formally charge with wrongdoing—the president. The House accused Johnson of misconduct and sent the case to the Senate for trial.

The Constitution allows Congress to remove from office any federal official who has committed serious wrongdoing. If a majority of the House votes to impeach a public official, the Senate acts as jury and decides by a two-thirds vote whether to convict and remove the person from office.

The Impeachment Trial The trial began in March 1868 and lasted almost three months. Johnson's defenders claimed that the president was exercising his right to challenge laws he considered unconstitutional. The impeachment, they argued, was politically motivated and thus contrary to the spirit of the Constitution.

Picturing **History**

President Johnson's attempt to dismiss his secretary of war gave Radical Republicans the opportunity to impeach him. ***Who can impeach the president?***

Samuel J. Tilden, a Democrat from New York, claimed that Congress was trying to remove the president from office without accusing him of a crime "or anything more than a mere difference of opinion."

Johnson's accusers argued that Congress should retain the supreme power to make the laws. Senator Charles Sumner of Massachusetts declared that Johnson had turned

> **"the veto power conferred by the Constitution as a remedy for ill-considered legislation . . . into a weapon of offense against Congress."**
>
> —**Charles Sumner**, speech at Johnson's impeachment trial

S In May the senators cast two votes. In both instances, the result was 35 to 19 votes to convict the president—one vote short of the two-thirds majority required by the Constitution for conviction. Several moderate Republicans voted for a verdict of not guilty because they did not believe a president should be removed from office for political differences. As a result, Johnson stayed in office until the end of his term in March 1869.

R1 Reading Strategy

Monitoring **Ask:** Did the Tenure of Office Act violate the Constitution? Why or why not? *(No; it only violated a tradition that presidents control their cabinets.)* EL

R2 Reading Strategy

Academic Vocabulary Have students read the sentence that contains the word *prohibited*. Then ask students to list synonyms for the word. OL

W Writing Support

Summary Writing Have students write a summary describing why Johnson was impeached, what the outcome was, and why. OL

R3 Reading Strategy

Understanding Vocabulary
Ask: When someone is accused of a crime, does that mean they are guilty? Why or why not? *(no; it only means that they must stand trial; they are only guilty if they plead guilty or are found to be so by a jury)* How does that compare to being impeached? *(the same; to impeach is simply to charge an officeholder with wrongdoing)* OL

S Skill Practice

Historical and Social Sciences Analysis Skill Have students debate whether Johnson was guilty of "high crimes and misdemeanors" or should have been acquitted. AL

More Skill Practice

Historical and Social Sciences Analysis Skill **Ask:** What was Senator Sumner referring to when he commented that President Johnson tried to turn veto power "into a weapon of offense against Congress"? *(After Congress challenged the black codes, Johnson had indirectly threatened to veto any bill passed by Congress.)* OL

Picturing **History**

Answer: The House of Representatives votes to impeach the president, and the Senate votes to convict him or her based on the evidence.

S Skill Practice

Historical and Social Sciences Analysis Skill

Ask: Which part of the population was still denied the right to vote after approval of the Fifteenth Amendment? *(women; Native Americans)* OL

ASSESS

Resources for page 634

Use these resources to assess student mastery of section content.

Section Quiz 14–2

Interactive Tutor Self-Assessment CD-ROM

Reading Check

Answer: The Senate was one vote short of the number needed to convict Johnson and remove him from office so he remained president until 1869.

History Online

Study Central provides summaries, interactive games, and online graphic organizers to help students review section content.

CLOSE

Summarizing Explain why the Thirteenth, Fourteenth, and Fifteenth Amendments were passed. OL

Only two presidents have been impeached: Johnson in 1868 and Bill Clinton in 1998. Both presidents were tried by the Senate and acquitted (they were not removed from office).

Election of 1868 By the presidential election of 1868, most Southern states had rejoined the Union. Many Americans hoped that conflicts over Reconstruction and sectional divisions were behind them.

Abandoning Johnson, the Republicans chose General **Ulysses S. Grant,** the Civil War hero, as their presidential candidate. The Democrats nominated Horatio Seymour, a former governor of New York.

Grant won the election, gaining 214 of 294 electoral votes. He also received most of the votes of African Americans in the South. The 1868 election was a vote on Reconstruction, and the voters supported the Republican approach to the issue.

The Fifteenth Amendment The election of 1868 made some Republicans realize that if African Americans could vote throughout the country, they could help Republicans win elections. After the election, Republicans developed their last major piece of Reconstruction legislation. In February 1869, Congress passed the Fifteenth Amendment. It prohibited the state and federal governments from denying the right to vote to any male citizen because of "race, color, or previous condition of servitude."

African American men won the right to vote when the Fifteenth Amendment was ratified and became law in February 1870. Republicans thought that the power of the ballot would **enable** African Americans to protect themselves. That belief, it turned out, was too optimistic. S

(See page 264 for the entire text of the Fifteenth Amendment.)

Reading Check **Explain** What two presidents have been impeached by Congress?

History Online

Study Central Need help understanding Radical Reconstruction? Visit ca.hss.glencoe.com and click on Study Central.

Section 2 Review

Reading Summary

Review the Main Ideas

- To challenge the South's black codes, which limited the rights of newly freed African Americans, the Republicans in Congress passed legislation addressing civil rights and creating the Freedmen's Bureau.
- President Johnson's opposition to the Reconstruction plans of the Radical Republicans led to his impeachment trial.

What Did You Learn?

1. Discuss two ways Southerners violated Lincoln's plan for Reconstruction.
2. What is impeachment? Was President Johnson impeached?

Critical Thinking

3. **Summarizing Information** Re-create the diagram below and answer the questions about these amendments. CA HI2.

	Date ratified	Impact on life
Fourteenth Amendment		
Fifteenth Amendment		

4. **The Big Ideas** Why did the Radical Republicans in Congress turn to constitutional amendments to guarantee the rights of African Americans?
5. **ANALYSIS** How did disagreement over states' rights and federal sovereignty affect Reconstruction plans? What examples of the "balance of power" and the system of checks and balances established by the Constitution can you find in this section? Write an essay summarizing your conclusion. CA HI1.

SECTION 2 REVIEW ANSWERS

Review questions reinforce content standard US8.11.

1. Former Confederate officials were elected to Congress, and treatment of African Americans did not improve.
2. formally charging an official with misconduct.; yes
3. Fourteenth: June 1866, most African Americans became citizens; Fifteenth: Feb. 1869, no male citizen could be denied right to vote
4. **The Big Ideas** Acts of Congress can be ruled unconstitutional.
5. **ANALYSIS** Students may conclude that the federal government had more power.

Section 3

The South During Reconstruction

Guide to Reading

Looking Back, Looking Ahead

You learned that Congress passed the Fourteenth and Fifteenth Amendments to help African Americans gain equal rights. Although African Americans made some gains, most white Southerners refused to recognize their rights.

Focusing on the Main Ideas

- Violence against African Americans and their white supporters took place during Reconstruction. *(page 636)*
- After the Civil War, the South had to rebuild not only its farms and roads, but its social and political structures as well. *(page 638)*

Meeting People

Hiram Revels
Frederick Douglass
Blanche K. Bruce

Content Vocabulary

scalawag (SKA • lih • WAG)
carpetbagger (KAHR • puht • BA • guhr)
corruption (kuh • RUHP • shuhn)
integrate (IN • tuh • GRAYT)
sharecropping (SHEHR • KRAHP • ihng)

Academic Vocabulary

dominate (DAH • muh • NAYT)
brief (BREEF)
region (REE • juhn)
create (kree • AYT)

Reading Strategy

Organizing Information As you read the section, re-create the diagram below and describe improvements in the South in education.

History Social Science Standards

US8.11 Students analyze the character and lasting consequences of Reconstruction.

NATIONAL GEOGRAPHIC Who & When?

1865 | 1867 | 1869 | 1871

- **1865** Freedmen's Bank is established
- **1866** Ku Klux Klan is formed
- **1869** African Americans serve in House of Representatives
- **1870** First African American is elected to the Senate

Hiram Revels

CHAPTER 14 Section 3, 635–639

FOCUS

BELLRINGER Skillbuilder Activity

Project **Daily Focus Skills Transparency 14–3** and have students answer the question.

Guide to Reading

Preteaching Vocabulary: Have students demonstrate their understanding of the vocabulary terms by using each in an original sentence.

Answers to Graphic: new public schools created; several schools offering advanced education to African Americans opened

Unpacking the Standards

After reading the section, students will be able to:

- Discuss advances by African Americans in government.
- Detail the violence against African Americans during Reconstruction.
- Explain how the South rebuilt social and political structures.

SECTION RESOURCES

Print Material
- Reproducible Lesson Plan 14–3*
- Daily Lesson and Discussion Notes 14–3
- Guided Reading Activity 14–3
- Reading Essentials and Study Guide 14–3
- Active Reading Note-Taking Guide 14–3
- Section Quiz 14–3

Transparencies
- Daily Focus Skills Transparency 14–3
- Section Graphic Organizer Transparency 14–3
- California Standards Practice Transparencies

Technology
- Interactive Tutor Self-Assessment CD-ROM
- Exam*View*® Pro Testmaker CD-ROM
- Presentation Plus! CD-ROM

*Available on TeacherWorks™

TEACH

R1 Reading Strategy

Organizing Information Have students create a two-column chart. One column should list how the South changed during Reconstruction, and the other should list how it stayed the same. *(Changed: African Americans' rights increased, improvements in education; Same: many whites resisted Reconstruction, continued violence towards African Americans)* OL

Review The Big Idea

Review the Big Idea for this section: "Political ideas and major events shape how people form governments." **Ask:** What ideas inspired the Colored State Convention of South Carolina? *(Students might refer to the opening of the Declaration of Independence and the idea that "all men are created equal.")* OL

R2 Reading Strategy

Scaffolding—Academic Vocabulary This word was introduced in Chapter 10, Section 1. Ask students to define the word *role* and then use it in a sentence of their own. OL

Answers and Additional Support

US8.11.3 Understand the effects of the Freedmen's Bureau and the restrictions placed on the rights and opportunities of freedmen, including racial segregation and "Jim Crow" laws. US8.11.4 Trace the rise of the Ku Klux Klan and describe the Klan's effects.

New Groups Take Charge

R1

Main Idea **Violence against African Americans and their white supporters took place during Reconstruction.**

Reading Connection How might you feel if someone tried to take away your rights through threats and violence? Read to find out how some white Southerners attempted to intimidate African Americans and keep them from voting and exercising their rights.

An American Story

"The dust of our fathers mingles with yours in the same graveyards. . . . This is your country, but it is ours too." So spoke an emancipated African American after the Civil War. Most formerly enslaved people did not seek revenge or power over whites, only respect and equality. The petition of an African American convention in 1865 stated:

Picturing **History**

In 1870 Hiram Revels was elected to the Senate. ***What state did he represent?***

"We simply desire that we shall be recognized as men; . . . that the same laws which govern *white men* shall direct colored men; . . . that we be dealt with as others, in equity [fairness] and justice."

—Address of the Colored State Convention to the People of the State of South Carolina

Republicans Take Charge During Reconstruction, the Republicans came to **dominate** Southern politics. Support for the Republican party came from African Americans, white Southerners who backed Republican goals, and white settlers from the North. These groups ran state governments.

African Americans in Government R2 African Americans played an important role both as voters and as officials. In some states, they contributed heavily to Republican victories. African Americans did not control the government of any state, although they **briefly** had a majority in the lower house of the South Carolina legislature. In other Southern states, they held major positions but never in proportion to their numbers.

At the national level, 16 African Americans served in the House of Representatives and 2 in the Senate between 1869 and 1880. **Hiram Revels,** one of the African American senators, was an ordained minister who had recruited African Americans for the Union army. He also started a school for freed African Americans in Missouri and served as a chaplain of an African American regiment in Mississippi. Revels remained in Mississippi after the war and was elected to the Senate in 1870. **Frederick Douglass** was also an important leader who insisted on full equality for African Americans.

Blanche K. Bruce, the other African American senator, also came from Mississippi. A former runaway slave, Bruce taught in an African American school in Missouri when the war began. In 1869 he went to Mississippi and entered politics. He was elected to the Senate in 1874.

Picturing **History**

Hiram Revels took the Senate seat that had once been held by Jefferson Davis, who left it to become president of the Confederacy.

Answer: Mississippi

More Skill Practice

Historical and Social Sciences Analysis Skill Have students write three to five questions about the first African Americans elected in the United States that would require historical research to answer. OL CA HR1.

Biography

US8.11 Students analyze the character and lasting consequences of Reconstruction.

FREDERICK DOUGLASS

1817–1895

Frederick Douglass lived as a slave for 21 years before he escaped to the North in 1838. He was born on a Maryland plantation in 1817, and his early years were characterized by beatings, poor living conditions, and constant shuffling from one plantation to another. The wife of one of his masters, Sophia Auld, took a liking to **R** Douglass and began to teach him to read and write. Her efforts stopped after her husband learned of her teachings, and Douglass took it upon himself to continue where she had left off.

The more Douglass read, the more he felt the injustice of slavery. In 1838 Douglass made his way north by disguising himself as a free African American sailor. In Massachusetts, he quickly emerged as a leader of the movement for liberty **C** for African Americans. In 1841 Douglass became a well-known speaker for the American Anti-Slavery Society. Douglass traveled through the Northern states speaking against slavery and for the equality of African Americans. When the Civil War began, Douglass urged President Lincoln to free the enslaved people, and he helped organize African American troops to fight for freedom.

After Lincoln was assassinated, Douglass opposed President Johnson's Reconstruction program. Instead he supported the Radical Republican plan. A skilled and powerful speaker, Douglass traveled throughout the nation insisting on full equality for African Americans. He was particularly outspoken in support of the Fifteenth Amendment, guaranteeing African American men the right to vote.

"Whenever my condition was improved, instead of its increasing my contentment, it only increased my desire to be free."

—from ***Narrative of the Life of Frederick Douglass, an American Slave***

Douglass continued to support civil rights **S** causes late into his life. He also wrote, started his own newspaper, and gave lectures. On January 20, 1895, he gave a speech at a meeting **W** of women's rights advocates in Washington, D.C. Later that night, he died of a heart attack.

Then and Now

Frederick Douglass overcame many obstacles to be a leader in the fight for freedom. Can you think of any present-day individuals who overcame obstacles to excel at something? Explain.

Then and Now

Students' answers will vary, but they should give reasons for their position.

Did You Know?

Tell students that before emancipation, Frederick Douglass had become so famous from his lectures he was afraid he would be captured and returned to Maryland as a fugitive slave. He left for England to raise money to buy his own freedom.

Biography

TEACH

R Reading Strategy

Activating Prior Knowledge Ask: How did white Southerners view the education of African Americans before the Civil War? *(They passed laws against it.)* **OL**

C Critical Thinking

Drawing Conclusions
Ask: Why do you think that extensive reading increased Douglass's belief in the injustice of slavery? *(Students may suggest he found more arguments that slavery was immoral.)* **OL** **CA HI2.**

S Skill Analysis

Historical and Social Sciences Analysis Skill Point out that in 1848 Douglass spoke at the Seneca Falls Convention in favor of women having the right to vote. **Ask:** Why do you think Douglass would take this position? *(Students may say that since he was denied his rights, he did not want others to be denied theirs.)* **OL**

W Writing Support

Expository Writing After reading this biography, have students write an epitaph for Frederick Douglass. Ask them to share their epitaphs with the class. **OL**

C Critical Thinking

Comparing and Contrasting Have students contrast the terms *scalawags* and *carpetbaggers*. *(scalawags—Southern whites who supported the Republicans; carpetbaggers—Northerners who came to the South)* OL

R1 Reading Strategy

Understanding Vocabulary **Ask:** What is an example of corrupt actions by public officials? *(taking money in exchange for a vote on a bill)* OL CA HI3.

R2 Reading Strategy

Understanding Vocabulary **Ask:** What is the opposite of *integrated*? *(separated, segregated)* OL

History Online

Objectives and answers to the students activity can be found in the Web Activity Lesson Plan feature at ca.hss.glencoe.com.

Reading Check

Answer: Most white Southerners refused to testify against them.

Answers and Additional Support

US8.11.1 List the original aims of Reconstruction and describe its effects on the political and social structures of different regions.

Scalawags and Carpetbaggers Some Southern whites—for example, non-slaveholding farmers and pro-Union business leaders—backed the Republicans. Former Confederates called them **scalawags** (SKA • lih • WAGZ), a term meaning "worthless rascals." Also, many Northern whites living in the South, such as Union army veterans and Freedmen's Bureau members, were Republican supporters. Critics called them **carpetbaggers** (KAHR • puht • BA • guhrz) because some arrived with their belongings in cheap suitcases made of carpet fabric.

Many Southerners accused Reconstruction governments of **corruption** (kuh • RUHP • shuhn), or dishonest or illegal actions. Although some officials made money illegally, probably less corruption occurred in the South than in the North.

Resistance to Reconstruction Most Southern whites opposed efforts to expand African Americans' rights. Life soon became difficult for African Americans. Most white landowners refused to rent land to freedmen. Store owners refused African Americans credit, and employers would not hire them.

Secret societies, such as the Ku Klux Klan, used fear and violence to deny rights to freed men and women. Wearing white sheets and hoods, Klan members killed many African Americans and their white friends. They beat and wounded many more and burned African American homes, schools, and churches. Many Southerners, especially planters and Democrats, backed the Klan and other violent groups. These Southerners, who had the most to gain from the return of white supremacy, saw violence as a defense against Republican rule.

Reading Check **Explain** Why did laws to control the Ku Klux Klan have little effect?

History Online

Student Web Activity Visit ca.hss.glencoe.com and click on Chapter 14—*Student Web Activities* for an activity on the first African American members of Congress.

Some Improvements

Main Idea **After the Civil War, the South had to rebuild not only its farms and roads, but its social and political structures as well.**

Reading Connection How important is education to a person's ability to function as a citizen and to protect his or her rights? Read to find out about the improvements Reconstruction brought to education for African Americans in the South.

Despite the violence, Reconstruction brought important changes throughout the South. This was especially true in education.

Education improved for both African Americans and whites. African Americans saw education as an important step to a better life. In many **regions,** they created their own schools, contributing both labor and money to build the schools.

The Freedmen's Bureau and private charities played a major role in spreading education. Northern women and free African Americans came South to teach in these schools. By 1870 about 4,000 schools had been established, with 200,000 students. More than half the teachers in these schools were African American.

Public Schools In the 1870s, Reconstruction governments began **creating** public school systems for both races, which had not existed in the South before the war. Within a few years, more than 50 percent of the white children and about 40 percent of African American children in the South were enrolled in public schools. Northern missionary societies also established academies offering advanced education for African Americans. Some academies developed into colleges and universities, such as Morehouse College and Atlanta University.

Generally, African American and white students attended different schools. Only Louisiana, South Carolina, and Florida required that schools be **integrated** (IN • tuh • GRAYT • ihd)—include both whites and African Americans—but the laws were not enforced.

More Skill Practice

Historical and Social Sciences Analysis Skill **Ask:** Why did white Southerners oppose the expansion of African Americans' rights? *(Students might suggest that whites resented the overturning of their society by the North, that they feared the loss of political power, or that they were prejudiced.)* AL CA HI2.

Farming the Land Along with education, most freed people wanted land. Some African Americans were able to buy land with the assistance of the Freedmen's Bank, established in 1865. Most, however, failed to get their own land.

R The most common form of farmwork for freed individuals was **sharecropping** (SHEHR • KRAHP • ihng). In this system, a landowner rented a plot of land to a sharecropper, or farmer, along with a crude shack, some seeds and tools, and perhaps a mule. Sharecroppers did not pay their rent in cash. Instead, they paid a share of their crops—often as much as one-half to two-thirds—to cover their rent as well as the cost of the seed, fertilizer, tools, and animals they needed.

After paying the landowners, sharecroppers often had little left to sell. Sometimes they had barely enough to feed their families. For many, sharecropping was little better than slavery.

Reading Check **Explain** How did sharecroppers get land to farm?

▲ Mother and daughter reading

History Online

Study Central Need help understanding life in the South during Reconstruction? Visit ca.hss.glencoe.com and click on Study Central.

Section 3 Review

Reading Summary

Review the Main Ideas

- Some African Americans, along with white Northerners and white Southerners who had opposed the Confederacy, served in government; other Southerners used violence to prevent African Americans from exercising their rights.
- New schools in the South helped African Americans gain an education, but most African Americans were denied the opportunity to own land.

What Did You Learn?

1. How did some Southerners try to maintain control over freed people?
2. What role did scalawags and carpetbaggers play in Reconstruction?

Critical Thinking

3. **Organizing Information** Re-create the diagram below and identify the three groups that made up the Southern Republican Party.

4. **The Big Ideas** Why were the political ideas of the Radical Republicans difficult to carry out in the South? CA HR3.
5. **Persuasive Writing** Imagine you are a newspaper journalist in 1869 and have set up interviews with an African American senator from Mississippi, a carpetbagger living in Georgia, and a white plantation owner from South Carolina. List questions you could ask about Reconstruction. Imagine how each would respond, and write a newspaper article detailing your interview. CA HR1. CA 8WA2.1.c

R Reading Strategy

Understanding Vocabulary Have volunteers restate the meaning of *sharecropping* in their own words. OL CA 8RW1.3

ASSESS

Resources for page 639

Use these resources to assess student mastery of section content.

- Section Quiz 14–3
- Interactive Tutor Self-Assessment CD-ROM

Reading Check

Answer: They rented a plot from landowners.

History Online

Study Central provides summaries, interactive games, and online graphic organizers to help students review section content.

CLOSE

Identifying Central Issues Have students list the problems that the South faced and suggest what they would have done to solve them. OL

SECTION 3 REVIEW ANSWERS

Review questions reinforce content standard US8.11.

1. by refusing to rent land to them or hire them; by denying them store credit; by using violence to intimidate them
2. voting for Republican candidates; serving in government
3. African Americans; some white Southerners; whites from the North
4. **The Big Ideas** Many white Southerners opposed freedom for African Americans or expansion of their rights.
5. Students' questions and articles should show understanding of the different goals of the groups represented by these individuals.

FOCUS

BELLRINGER
Skillbuilder Activity

Project **Daily Focus Skills Transparency 14–4** and have students answer the question.

Guide to Reading

Preteaching Vocabulary:
Use the Vocabulary PuzzleMaker CD-ROM to make crossword and word search puzzles.

Answers to Graphic:
Advantages: region can feed itself, land owners have financial independence; Disadvantages: depend on other areas for manufactured goods, farming may not be profitable, reliance on one cash crop can hurt economy

Unpacking the Standards

After reading the section, students will be able to:

- Describe how Democrats regained control of Southern state governments.
- Explain the results of the election of 1876.
- Identify changes in the South when Reconstruction ended, including restrictions on African Americans.

Section 4 Change in the South

History Social Science Standards

US8.11 Students analyze the character and lasting consequences of Reconstruction.

Guide to Reading

Looking Back, Looking Ahead

You read earlier that Reconstruction met resistance in the South, and African Americans made few real economic gains there. By the mid-1870s, Reconstruction was coming to an end, and the South was undergoing even more changes.

Focusing on the Main Ideas

- Democrats steadily regained control of Southern governments as support for Radical Reconstruction policies decreased. *(page 641)*
- When Reconstruction ended, many changes took place in the South including a political shift and growth in industry. *(page 645)*
- As Reconstruction ended, true freedom for African Americans became a distant dream. *(page 647)*

Meeting People

Horace Greeley
Rutherford B. Hayes
Samuel Tilden
Henry Grady
James Duke
W.E.B. Du Bois (doo BAWIHS)

Content Vocabulary

reconciliation (REH • kuhn • SIH • lee • AY • shuhn)
commission
cash crop
poll tax
literacy test (LIH • tuh • ruh • see)
grandfather clause
segregation (SEH • grih • GAY • shuhn)
lynching (LIHNCH • ihng)

Academic Vocabulary

exploit (EHK • SPLOYT)
enforce (ihn • FOHRS)
eliminate (ih • LIH • muh • NAYT)
commit

Reading Strategy

Comparing As you read the section, re-create the diagram below and list the advantages and disadvantages of an agricultural economy.

Agricultural Economy

Advantages	Disadvantages

NATIONAL GEOGRAPHIC Who & When?

1870 — 1885 — 1900

Rutherford B. Hayes

1877 Hayes wins presidency; Reconstruction ends

1890 Poll taxes and literacy tests begin in Mississippi

1896 *Plessy* v. *Ferguson* rules segregation constitutional

SECTION RESOURCES

Print Material
- Reproducible Lesson Plan 14–4*
- Daily Lesson and Discussion Notes 14–4
- Guided Reading Activity 14–4
- Reading Essentials and Study Guide 14–4
- Active Reading Note-Taking Guide 14–4
- Section Quiz 14–4

Transparencies
- Daily Focus Skills Transparency 14–4
- Section Graphic Organizer Transparency 14–4
- California Standards Practice Transparencies

Technology
- Interactive Tutor Self-Assessment CD-ROM
- Exam*View*® Pro Testmaker CD-ROM
- Presentation Plus! CD-ROM

*Available on TeacherWorks™

US8.11.2 Identify the push-pull factors in the movement of former slaves to the cities in the North and to the West and their differing experiences in those regions (e.g., the experiences of Buffalo Soldiers). US8.11.3 Understand the effects of the Freedmen's Bureau and the restrictions placed on the rights and opportunities of freedmen, including racial segregation and "Jim Crow" laws.

Reconstruction Ends

Main Idea **Democrats steadily regained control of Southern governments as support for Radical Reconstruction policies decreased.**

Reading Connection How does politics affect your local community? Do you think issues like equality and fair treatment for African Americans should be influenced by politics? Read on to see how the changing political landscape dramatically affected Reconstruction in the 1870s.

An American Story

Before and during Reconstruction, freed African Americans began moving to Northern cities and to the West in hopes of a better life. Often they faced hostility. One example is the Cox family. Freed by slaveholder John Randolph in Virginia, the Cox family purchased a tract of land in Mercer County, Ohio. When they arrived in their new home, white settlers "came out in force, with their muskets patrolled the banks of the canal and refused to let them settle on their own purchased land." Yet many freed families continued to try to find a new life for themselves.

These reasons for leaving one area and going to another are called push-pull factors. Push factors (racial segregation, Jim Crow laws) drive people away from an area. Pull factors (the opportunity to own land) attract people towards an area.

Loss of Support During the Grant administration, Northerners began losing interest in Reconstruction. Many believed it was time for the South to solve its own problems.

C Reconstruction declined for other reasons. The old Radical leaders began to disappear from the political scene. Thaddeus Stevens died in 1868, and others retired or lost elections.

S Another factor that weakened enthusiasm for Reconstruction was racial prejudice in the North. This prejudice was **exploited** by opponents of Reconstruction. They argued that only Southerners really knew how to deal with African Americans and that the fate of the freed people should be left to the South. Southerners protested what they called "bayonet rule"—the use of federal troops to support Reconstruction governments. President Grant had sent federal troops to the South to stop violence or to **enforce** the law only when absolutely necessary. Generally, though, he tried to avoid any clashes with the South.

Republican Revolt In the early 1870s, reports of corruption in Grant's administration and in Reconstruction governments spread throughout the nation. Some Republicans split with the party over the issue of corruption. Another group of Republicans broke with the party over Reconstruction, proposing peaceful **reconciliation** (REH • kuhn • SIH • lee • AY • shuhn)—coming together again—with Southern whites. Calling themselves Liberal Republicans, these two groups nominated **Horace Greeley,** a newspaper editor from New York, to run against Grant in the 1872 presidential election. R

Analyzing *Political Cartoons*

Problems in the Grant administration hurt the Republican Party. ***Who does the woman at the far right represent? Why is she turning away?***

TEACH

C Critical Thinking

Making Generalizations
Ask: How would you describe the overall changes taking place as Reconstruction winds down? *(Possible answers: Southerners have tired of the continual pressure; Northerners have tired of continued conflict.)* OL

S Skill Practice

Historical and Social Sciences Analysis Skill
Ask: What is prejudice? *(feelings against people of a particular group)* OL CA 8RW1.0

R Reading Strategy

Using Word Parts Tell students that the *con-* in *reconciliation* means "together." **Ask:** What other words use *con-* to express joining or bringing together? *(convene, concur, concentrate, confluence)* OL CA 8RW1.0

Analyzing *Political Cartoons*

Answer: Students may say that the woman represents liberty, and she is turning away in shame or disappointment because of the scandals of the Grant administration.

Did You Know?

Horace Greeley was a prominent newspaper editor whose editorials against the spread of slavery into the Western territories before the war helped shape public opinion in the North. Greeley popularized the expression, "Go west, young man." He died one month after the 1872 election, in which he unsuccessfully challenged Grant's bid for a second term as president.

C1 Critical Thinking

Determining Cause and Effect **Ask:** How did the Amnesty Act change the balance of politics in the South? *(By allowing former Confederates to vote and hold office again, it opened the way to their domination over Republicans.)* OL CA HI2.

R Reading Strategy

Outlining Have students outline the successes of the Democrats and the failures of the Republicans that led to increased popularity of the Democratic Party. OL CA HI2.

C2 Critical Thinking

Analyzing Primary Sources **Ask:** What does the speaker mean by these words? *(African Americans should vote regardless of threats by Democrats. African American leaders feared that a win by the Democrats would mean a step backward for the status of African Americans).* AL

Resources for page 642

Analysis Skills Activity 14

The Democrats also supported Greeley for president because he offered a chance to defeat the Republicans. Despite the division in the Republican ranks, however, Grant was reelected.

C1 **The Amnesty Act** During the 1872 election campaign, Liberal Republicans called for expanded amnesty for white Southerners. In May 1872, Congress passed the Amnesty Act, which pardoned most former Confederates. Nearly all white Southerners could vote and hold office again. The amnesty changed the political balance in the South by restoring full rights to people who supported the Democratic Party.

R **Democrats Regain Power** In Southern states such as Virginia and North Carolina, where a majority of voters were white, Democrats soon regained control of state governments. In states where African Americans held a majority or where white and African American populations were nearly equal, the Ku Klux Klan and other violent groups helped the Democrats take power by terrorizing Republican voters.

By the election of 1875, Republican political power in Mississippi was quickly eroding. African American leaders urged voters to go to the polls on election day in spite of threats of violence by Democrats. In a Mississippi newspaper, fourteen African American leaders claimed:

> **"The success of the Democratic Party will, to all intents and purposes, sound the death knell of all the hopes that the colored man has indulged of educating, elevating and improving his race in this State . . ."** C2
>
> **—from the *Jackson Pilot*, October 4, 1875**

What If...

Lincoln Had Survived?

Lincoln's main goal had been to preserve the Union. In his second Inaugural Address, he indicated that he would deal compassionately with the South after the war ended:

> **"With malice toward none; with charity for all, with firmness in the right as God gives us to see the right, let us strive on to finish the work we are in, to bind up the nation's wounds, to care for him who shall have borne the battle and for his widow and his orphan. . . ."**
>
> –Abraham Lincoln, Second Inaugural Address, March 1865

President Lincoln did not live to carry out his plan. On April 14, 1865, just five days after Lee's surrender, he was assassinated.

Andrew Johnson, who succeeded to the presidency, attempted to carry out Lincoln's Reconstruction policies. He was hampered in this effort because as an unelected president he had little popular following. In addition, as a former Democrat, he could not command the support of the Republican majority in Congress. As a Tennessean and former slaveholder, he offended the Radicals. If these handicaps were not enough, his critics viewed Johnson as self-righteous, hot-tempered, stubborn, and crude.

In March 1868, the House adopted 11 articles of impeachment against Johnson. Although Johnson was acquitted and served out his term, any influence he might have had on Reconstruction was lost.

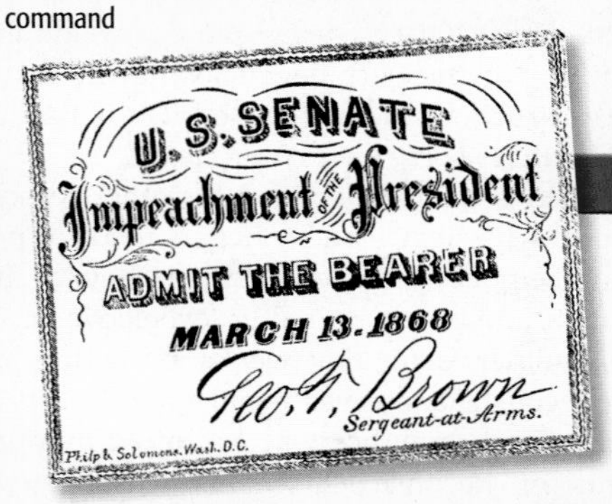

Ticket to Johnson's impeachment trial ▶

Answers and Additional Support

What If...

1. Answers should note the powerful leadership of Lincoln and give examples of personality traits for both Lincoln and Johnson.
2. Answers will vary, but students should use their knowledge of Lincoln, Johnson, and the Radical Republicans to answer the question.

By 1876 Republicans held a majority in Congress in only three Southern states—Florida, South Carolina, and Louisiana. During these years, the Republicans had other problems they could not blame on the Democrats. In 1873 a series of political scandals came to light. Investigations uncovered top government officials making unfair business deals, scheming to withhold public tax money, and accepting bribes. One scandal involved the vice president, and another the secretary of war. These scandals further damaged the Grant administration and the Republicans. At the same time, the nation suffered an economic depression. Blame for the hard times fell on the Republicans.

By the time of the congressional elections in 1874, charges of corruption and economic mismanagement had badly weakened the Republican Party. Democrats gained seats in the Senate and won control of the House. For the first time since the Civil War, the Democratic Party controlled a part of the federal government. This situation further weakened Congress's commitment to Reconstruction and protecting the rights of newly freed African Americans.

The Election of 1876 President Grant considered running for a third term in 1876. Most Republican leaders preferred a new candidate—one who could win back the Liberal Republicans and unite the party.

The Republicans nominated **Rutherford B. Hayes,** governor of Ohio, for president. A champion of political reform, Hayes had a reputation for honesty, and he held moderate views on Reconstruction. The Democrats nominated New York governor **Samuel Tilden.** Tilden had gained national fame for fighting political corruption in New York City.

After the election, Tilden appeared to be the winner, receiving almost 250,000 more votes than Hayes. However, disputed returns from Florida, Louisiana, South Carolina, and Oregon—representing 20 electoral votes—kept the outcome in doubt. Tilden had 184 electoral votes, only one short of what he needed to win. Yet if Hayes received all 20 of the disputed votes, he would have the 185 electoral votes required for victory.

In January Congress created a special **commission,** or group, of seven Republicans, seven Democrats, and one independent to review the election results. But the independent resigned, and a Republican took his place. After examining the reports of state review boards, the commission voted 8 to 7 to award all 20 disputed votes, and the election, to Hayes. The vote followed party lines.

Democrats in Congress threatened to fight the decision to award the presidency to Hayes. Inauguration Day approached, yet the country still had no new president. Finally, Republican and Southern Democratic leaders met secretly to work out an agreement.

▼ *Lincoln's funeral carriage*

What might have happened?

1. How did Lincoln and Johnson differ in qualities of leadership? In personality? Do you think these qualities made a difference in the way political leaders responded to the two presidents?
2. Would Reconstruction have taken a different course if Lincoln had not been assassinated? Explain.

S Skill Practice

Historical and Social Sciences Analysis Skill
Ask: Why did voters blame the Republicans for the country's economic problems in the 1870s? *(because the Republicans had controlled the presidency and Congress for many years)* OL
CA HI3.

R1 Reading Strategy

Scaffolding—Academic Vocabulary This word was introduced in Chapter 7, Section 2. Discuss the meaning of *economy* with students and explain the use of the adjective *economic.* BL

C Critical Thinking

Analyzing Information
Ask: Why did both parties nominate candidates for president in 1876 who had reputations of being against corruption? *(because corruption was a major issue that year)* OL

R2 Reading Strategy

Understanding Vocabulary
Explain that a *commission* is a group authorized to carry out a specific task. BL

U Universal Access

English Learners Ask: What does "The vote followed party lines" mean? *(All members of the same political party voted the same way.)* EL

More Skill Practice

Historical and Social Sciences Analysis Skill Remind students of the role of the electoral college in presidential elections. Have them conduct research to find out why the Framers of the Constitution set up this system and write an explanation. OL
CA 8WA2.3

Did You Know?

Republicans held a private swearing in for Hayes on the evening before the official inauguration ceremony.

S Skill Practice

Historical and Social Sciences Analysis Skill
Ask: Why was the outcome of the 1876 election in dispute? *(Neither candidate won a majority of electoral votes because of disputed votes.)* OL

R Reading Strategy

Scaffolding—Summarizing
Ask: What was the agreement to settle the 1876 election? *(Hayes became president, gave more aid to the South, and withdrew remaining troops. Southerners respected African Americans' rights.)* OL

This READING SKILL was introduced in Chapter 4.

C Critical Thinking

Predicting Consequences
Ask: Do you think Southern whites kept this promise? Why or why not? *(probably not; they had shown they were willing to persecute African Americans and deny them their rights whenever they had a chance)* OL CA HI3.

Reading Check

Answer: It effectively ended Reconstruction.

Answers and Additional Support

NATIONAL GEOGRAPHIC **Disputed Election of 1876**

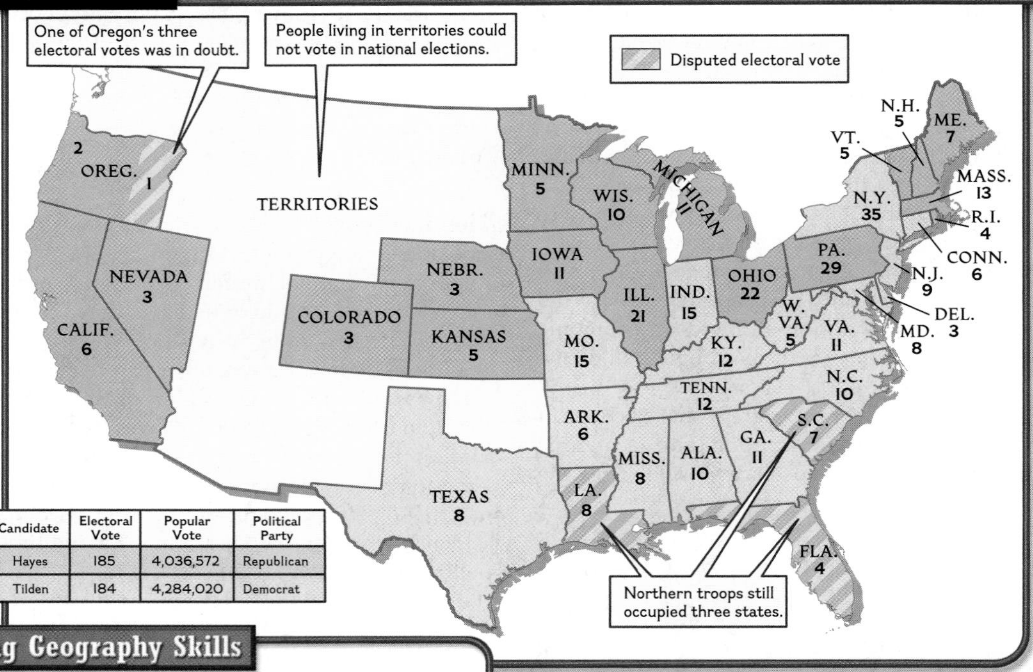

Candidate	Electoral Vote	Popular Vote	Political Party
Hayes	185	4,036,572	Republican
Tilden	184	4,284,020	Democrat

Using Geography Skills

Because of some conflicting results, a committee of 15 members from Congress and the Supreme Court decided the final count in the 1876 election.

1. **Location** Which Southern states sent in election returns that were disputed?
2. **Analyze** By how many electoral votes did Hayes finally win?

Compromise of 1877 Southern Democratic leaders agreed to accept Hayes as president. On March 2, 1877—almost four months after the election—Congress confirmed the verdict of the commission and declared Hayes the winner. He was inaugurated president two days later.

The deal congressional leaders made to settle the election dispute, the Compromise of 1877, included various favors to the South. The new government would give more aid to the region and withdraw all remaining troops from Southern states. The Democrats, in turn, promised to maintain African Americans' rights.

In his Inaugural Address, Hayes declared that what the South needed most was the restoration of "wise, honest, and peaceful local self-government." During a goodwill trip to the South, Hayes announced his intention of letting Southerners handle racial issues. In Atlanta he told an African American audience:

> **"... [your] rights and interests would be safer if this great mass of intelligent white men were let alone by the general Government."**

Hayes's message was clear. The federal government would no longer attempt to reshape Southern society or help Southern African Americans. Reconstruction was over.

Reading Check **Summarize** What effect did the Compromise of 1877 have on Reconstruction?

Using Geography Skills

Answers:

1. Louisiana, Florida, South Carolina
2. 185

In-Text Map Transparency 14 Ask: What region showed the most support for Tilden? *(South)* OL

Did You Know?

There were also voting irregularities in Mississippi, where the electoral votes went to the Democratic candidate, Tilden. But there is evidence that Republican voters, many who were African American, were threatened and assaulted as they tried to vote.

US8.11.1 List the original aims of Reconstruction and describe its effects on the political and social structures of different regions.

The South After Reconstruction

R1 **Main Idea** **When Reconstruction ended, many changes took place in the South including a political shift and growth in industry.**

Reading Connection How difficult do you think it would be for an area to change its economy from agricultural to industrial? Read to find out how Southern leaders attempted to create a "New South" with strong industries that could compete with those in the North.

An American Story

John Lynch, a member of Congress who had once been enslaved, spoke these words:

> **"I am treated, not as an American citizen, but as a brute. . . . [A]nd for what? Not that I am unable to or unwilling to pay my way; not that I am obnoxious in my personal appearance or disrespectful in my conduct; but simply because I happen to be of a darker complexion."**
>
> —quoted in "John Roy Lynch"

At the end of Reconstruction, many African Americans faced lives of poverty, indignity, and despair.

A New Ruling Party Many Southern whites hated Republicans because of their role in the Civil War and during Reconstruction. When Reconstruction ended, political power in the South shifted from the Republicans to the Democrats.

In some regions, the ruling Democrats were the large landowners and other groups that had held power before the Civil War. In most areas, however, a new ruling class took charge. Among their ranks were merchants, bankers, industrialists, and other business leaders who supported economic development and opposed Northern interference. These Democrats called themselves "Redeemers" because they had "redeemed," or saved, the South from Republican rule.

The Redeemers adopted conservative policies such as lower taxes, less public spending, and reduced government services. They drastically cut, or even **eliminated,** many social services started during Reconstruction, including public education. R2 Their one-party rule and conservative policies dominated Southern politics well into the 1900s. U

Rise of the "New South" By the 1880s, forward-looking Southerners were convinced that their region must develop a strong industrial economy. They argued that the South had lost the Civil War because its industry and manufacturing did not match the North's.

Agricultural Production in the South, 1850–1890

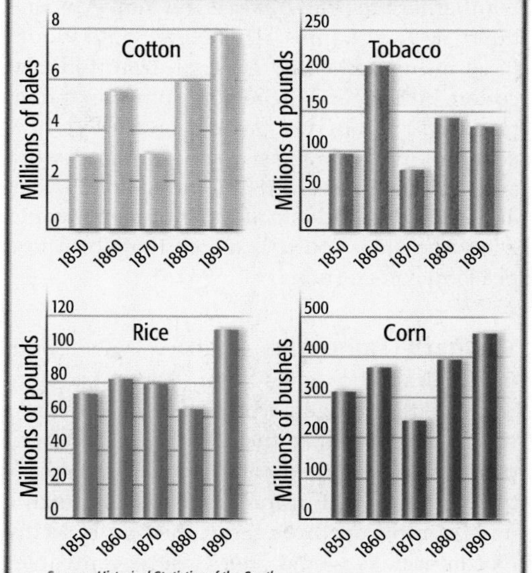

Source: *Historical Statistics of the South.*

S

Understanding Charts

Southern farm production decreased during the war years of the 1860s.

Compare By what year did cotton production levels again equal levels of 1860?

R1 Reading Strategy

Scaffolding—Identifying the Main Idea and Supporting Details Have students identify at least four details that support this main idea. *(Answers may include switch to Democratic control; decline of African Americans' voting power; growth of industry; renewed growth of agriculture)* OL

This READING SKILL was introduced in Chapter 2.

R2 Reading Strategy

Academic Vocabulary
Ask students to list antonyms for the word *eliminate.* OL

U Universal Access

English Learners Ask: What does "one-party rule" mean? *(only one party was legal or one party dominated so much that the other party was almost powerless)* EL CA 8RW1.3

S Skill Practice

Visual Literacy Ask: In what year would you say that Southern agriculture fully regained prewar success? *(In 1880, production of cotton and corn passed prewar levels, and those were the two main crops; Some students might say 1890, when rice also passed prewar levels.)* OL

Did You Know?

Today the South still leads the nation in the production of cotton and tobacco. But the region also leads the United States in the production of foods such as chickens, hogs, turkeys, shrimp, peanuts, pecans, sweet potatoes, and peaches.

Understanding Graphs

Answer: 1880

Ask: About how many bushels of corn were produced in 1890? *(about 450 million)*

R Reading Strategy

Taking Notes Have students take notes on changes in the South's economy after the Civil War. Suggest that they organize their information under two headings—*Industry* and *Agriculture*. BL

S Skill Practice

Historical and Social Sciences Analysis Skill Explain that economists would say the cotton prices were following the law of supply and demand. **Ask:** Based on the description here, how would you describe that law? *(When there is an oversupply of an item, the price will fall.)* AL CA HI6.

C Critical Thinking

Determining Cause and Effect **Ask:** What happened to farmers when cotton prices fell? *(They lost money and tried to grow more cotton to recover their losses.)* What effect would that have on prices? *(Prices would continue to fall.)* OL CA HI6.

Reading Check

Answer: Prices were forced down.

Answers and Additional Support

Picturing **History**

During this era, iron and steel industries developed in the South. ***How did the Bessemer process help these industries grow?***

Henry Grady, editor of the *Atlanta Constitution,* headed a group that urged Southerners to "out-Yankee the Yankees" and build a "New South." This New South would have industries based on coal, iron, tobacco, cotton, lumber, and the region's other abundant resources. Southerners would create this new economy by embracing a spirit of hard work and regional pride. In 1886 Grady told a Boston audience that industrial development would allow the New South to match the North in a peaceful competition.

Southern Industries Industry in the South made dramatic gains after Reconstruction. Some of the strongest advances were in the textile industry. Before the Civil War, Southern planters had shipped cotton to textile mills in the North or in Europe. In the 1880s, textile mills sprang up throughout the South. Many Northern mills would later close as companies built new plants in the South.

Other important industries were lumbering and tobacco processing. The tobacco industry was developed largely through the efforts of **James Duke** of North Carolina. Duke's American Tobacco Company eventually controlled almost all tobacco manufacturing.

The iron and steel industry also grew rapidly. In the mid-1800s, William Kelly, an American ironworker, and Henry Bessemer, a British engineer, had developed methods—called the Bessemer process—to inexpensively produce steel from iron. Steel answered industry's need for a sturdy, workable metal. By 1890 Southern mills produced nearly 20 percent of the nation's iron and steel. Much of the industry was in Alabama near deposits of iron ore.

A cheap and reliable workforce helped the South's industry grow. Most factory workers put in long hours for low wages. Sometimes whole families, including children, worked in factories. African Americans worked in the lowest-paying jobs.

More railroads aided the rise of industry. By 1870 the South's war-damaged railroads were largely rebuilt and expanded. Still, the South was not as industrialized as the North. It remained primarily agricultural.

Rural Economy Supporters of the New South also hoped to change Southern agriculture. Their goal was small, profitable farms raising many crops rather than plantations devoted to cotton. A different economy emerged, however. Some plantations were broken up, but large landowners held on to their land. When estates were divided, much of the land went to sharecropping and tenant farming, neither of which was profitable.

Debt also caused problems. Poor farmers used credit to get food and supplies. Merchants who sold on credit charged high prices, and farmers' debts rose. To repay debts, farmers grew **cash crops**—crops that could be sold for money.

Too much cotton, a major cash crop, forced prices down, however. Farmers then had to grow even more cotton to recover their losses. Sharecropping and reliance on one cash crop kept Southern agriculture from advancing. The rural South sank deeper into poverty and debt.

Reading Check **Describe** What happened to prices when too much cotton was produced?

Resources for page 646

- Geography and History Activity 14
- Economics and History Activity 14

Picturing **History**

Answer: The Bessemer process inexpensively produced steel from iron. Steel was used in various industries.

US8.11.3 Understand the effects of the Freedmen's Bureau and the restrictions placed on the rights and opportunities of freedmen, including racial segregation and "Jim Crow" laws. **US8.11.5** Understand the Thirteenth, Fourteenth, and Fifteenth Amendments to the Constitution and analyze their connection to Reconstruction.

A Divided Society

R **Main Idea** **As Reconstruction ended, true freedom for African Americans became a distant dream.**

Reading Connection What might it be like to be forced to pass an impossibly difficult test in order to earn a basic right, when others do not have to take the test at all? Read to find out how white Southerners attempted to prevent African Americans from voting.

As Reconstruction ended, African Americans' dreams for justice faded. In the last 20 years of the 1800s, racism became firmly entrenched, and individuals took steps to keep African Americans separated from whites and to deny them basic rights.

Voting Restrictions The Fifteenth Amendment prohibited any state from denying an individual the right to vote because of race. Southern leaders, however, found ways to get around the amendment and prevent African Americans from voting.

Many Southern states required a **poll tax,** a fee that people had to pay before voting. Because many African Americans could not afford the tax, they could not vote. The tax also prevented many poor whites from voting.

What Is a Literacy Test? Another approach was to make prospective voters take a **literacy test** (LIH • tuh • ruh • see) in which they had to read and explain difficult parts of state constitutions or the federal Constitution. Because most African Americans had little education, literacy tests prevented many from voting. C

Primary Sources

Jim Crow Laws

Southern communities and states passed laws that enforced segregation between the black and white races.

Railroads The conductor of each passenger train is authorized and required to assign each passenger to the car or the division of the car, when it is divided by a partition, designated for the race to which such passenger belongs. (Alabama)

Restaurants All persons licensed to conduct a restaurant, shall serve either white people exclusively or colored people exclusively and shall not sell to the two races within the same room or serve the two races anywhere under the same license. (Georgia)

Education The schools for white children and the schools for Negro children shall be conducted separately. (Florida)

▲ Business sign of the era

Libraries The state librarian is directed to fit up and maintain a separate place for the use of the colored people who may come to the library for the purpose of reading books or periodicals. (North Carolina)

—*Race, Racism, and the Law*

DBQ Document-Based Question

What do these laws have in common?

R Reading Strategy

Organizing Information Suggest that students take notes on the different steps taken by Southern whites to limit African Americans' rights by listing them in a two-column chart with the headings *Action* and *Effect*. Point out that some of these actions had unexpected effects. Suggest that students find a way of distinguishing between the intended and unintended consequences. OL

C Critical Thinking

Comparing and Contrasting **Ask:** How were poll taxes and literacy tests different? *(poll taxes levied a tax on voters; literacy tests forced them to show they could read)* How were they similar? *(both were aimed at limiting the voting rights of African Americans; both also blocked some poor whites from voting)* OL

Review The Big Idea

Review the Big Idea for this section: "Economic, social, and political changes create new traditions, values, and beliefs." **Ask:** What did Southern whites intend to achieve by limiting the rights of African Americans? *(to prevent African Americans from having any political or economic power)* OL

Primary Sources

Answer: the segregation of African Americans from whites

- Who makes seating arrangements on trains? *(conductor)* BL
- Why might a restaurant owner choose to serve white people instead of African Americans? *(could make more money since African Americans were generally poor)* OL

R1 Reading Strategy

Questioning **Ask:** Why did white governments in the South need to pass laws with grandfather clauses? *(to prevent the literacy test from blocking poor whites from voting)* OL

C Critical Thinking

Determining Cause and Effect **Ask:** Why did these barriers to voting not appear in most Southern states until after 1889? *(The federal government protected African Americans' rights up until 1876.)* OL

R2 Reading Strategy

Predicting **Ask:** What does *segregation* mean? *(separation of people into different groups, in this case, separation by race)* OL

R3 Reading Strategy

Understanding Vocabulary
Tell students that *lynching* comes from an eighteenth–century Virginia man named William Lynch, who hanged people for supposed crimes without waiting for them to be tried.

Analyzing *Political Cartoons*

African Americans were often barred from voting. ***What do the people in the cartoon represent?***

Literacy tests could also keep some whites from voting. For this reason, some states passed **grandfather clauses.** These laws allowed individuals who did not pass the literacy test to vote if their fathers or grandfathers had voted before Reconstruction. Because African Americans could not vote until 1867, they were excluded. Georgia enacted a poll tax and other limits as early as 1870. Such laws, however, did not become widespread until after 1889. African Americans continued to vote in some states until the end of the 1800s. Then, voting laws and the constant threat of violence caused African American voting to decline drastically.

Jim Crow Laws Another set of laws hurt African Americans. By the 1890s, **segregation** (SEH • grih • GAY • shuhn), or the separation of the races, was a prominent feature of life in the South.

The Southern states formed a segregated society by passing so-called Jim Crow laws. Taking their name from a character in a song, Jim Crow laws required African Americans and whites to be separated in almost every public place where they might come in contact with each other.

In 1896 the Supreme Court upheld Jim Crow laws and segregation in *Plessy* v. *Ferguson.* The case involved a Louisiana law requiring separate sections on trains for African Americans. The Court ruled that segregation was legal as long as African Americans had access to public facilities or accommodations equal to those of whites. *(See page 849 of the Appendix for a summary of* Plessy v. Ferguson.*)*

One problem, however, was that the facilities were separate but in no way equal. Southern states spent much more money on schools and other facilities for whites than on those for African Americans. This "separate but equal" doctrine provided a legal foundation for segregation in the South that lasted more than 50 years.

Along with restrictions on voting rights and laws passed to segregate society, white violence against African Americans increased. This violence took many terrible forms, including **lynching** (LIHNCH • ihng), in which an angry mob killed a person by hanging. African Americans were lynched because they were suspected of **committing** crimes—or because they did not behave as whites thought they should behave.

Reconstruction's Impact Reconstruction was both a success and a failure. It helped the South recover from the Civil War and begin rebuilding its battered economy. Yet economic recovery was far from complete. Although Southern agriculture took a new form, the South was still a rural economy, and that economy was still very poor.

Under Reconstruction, African Americans gained greater equality and began creating their own institutions. They joined with whites in new governments, fairer and more democratic than the South had ever seen. This improvement for African Americans did not last long, however.

Answers and Additional Support

Analyzing *Political Cartoons*

The hooded men represent the Ku Klux Klan. The large cannon shows the physical power in the form of arms over the African Americans.

Answer: The African American man represents the right to vote; the group stands for those opposed to African American voting.

In the words of African American writer and civil rights leader **W.E.B. Du Bois** (doo BAWIHS),

> **"The slave went free; stood a brief moment in the sun; then moved back again toward slavery."**
>
> —from *Black Reconstruction*

The biggest disappointment of Reconstruction was that it did not make good on the promise of true freedom for freed African Americans. With troop withdrawals and the end of Reconstruction, African Americans lost most of the gains they had made. The South soon created a segregated society.

W The Civil War had ended slavery, but the failure of Reconstruction left many African Americans trapped in economic, political, and social circumstances whereby they lost most of their newly gained freedom.

Reading Check **Describe** What is segregation? How was segregation carried out?

▲ W.E.B. Du Bois demanded full political rights for African Americans.

History Online
Study Central Need help understanding the end of Reconstruction? Visit ca.hss.glencoe.com and click on Study Central.

Section 4 Review

Reading Summary

Review the Main Ideas

- As support for Reconstruction weakened, Democrats regained power in the South. Reconstruction ended because of a political compromise that allowed Rutherford B. Hayes to become president.
- A number of industries, such as textiles and steel, developed in the South, but agriculture also remained important.
- Following the end of Reconstruction, African Americans in the South lost many of the rights they had briefly gained.

What Did You Learn?

1. Why was the presidential election of 1876 controversial?
2. Who was reelected president in 1872?

Critical Thinking

3. **Organizing Information** Re-create the diagram below and describe how the poll tax and literacy tests restricted voting rights. CA CS1.

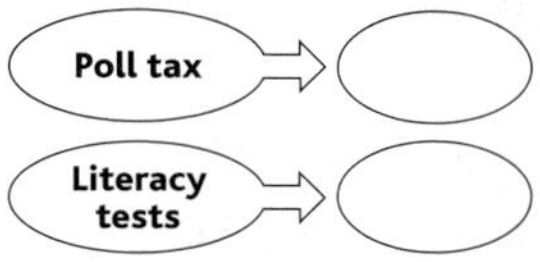

4. **Determining Cause and Effect** Explain how the Amnesty Act helped the Democratic Party regain its strength. CA HI2.
5. **The Big Ideas** What ideas led to political changes in the South beginning in the early 1870s? CA CS2.
6. **Analyze** Find two secondary sources that discuss Reconstruction—one from the 1800s and one written in the past 20 years. Identify how the views expressed in the later source are based on new historical information or research. CA HI5.

W Writing Support

Persuasive Writing Have students write an essay in which they state whether they think Reconstruction was largely a success or largely a failure and explain why. OL CA 8WA2.4

ASSESS

Resources for page 649

Use these resources to assess student mastery of section content.

- Section Quiz 14–4
- Interactive Tutor Self-Assessment CD-ROM

Reading Check

Answer: the separation of the races; via laws

History Online

Study Central provides summaries, interactive games, and online graphic organizers to help students review section content.

CLOSE

Summarizing Have students summarize the political, economic, and social changes in the South after the election of 1876. OL

SECTION 4 REVIEW ANSWERS

Review questions reinforce content standard US8.11.

1. Disputed returns from three states left the electoral count in doubt, and the election was settled by a deal.
2. Ulysses S. Grant
3. Poll tax: blocked African Americans and poor whites from voting; Literacy tests: blocked most African Americans from voting because they had little education
4. by allowing most white Southerners to vote and hold office again
5. **The Big Ideas** Amnesty Act, rise of Ku Klux Klan, growing power of Democrats, loss of power by Republicans
6. Answers will vary.

FOCUS

History–Social Science Standards

The following standard is covered on pages 650–651:

US8.11.5 Understand the Thirteenth, Fourteenth, and Fifteenth Amendments to the Constitution and analyze their connection to Reconstruction.

TEACH

W Writing Support

Persuasive Writing Discuss the various rights and duties of citizens. Have students write a persuasive paper describing the importance of having these rights and of fulfilling these duties by starting their papers with the statement, "Democracy requires participation." OL CA 8WA2.4

C Critical Thinking

Analyzing Information Have the class debate whether naturalized citizens should be allowed to be president or vice-president. Ask those in favor if they would place any limits on the right, such as a residency requirement. AL

Answers and Additional Support

Connecting to the Constitution

US8.11.5 Understand the Thirteenth, Fourteenth, and Fifteenth Amendments to the Constitution and analyze their connection to Reconstruction.

Citizenship

Why It Matters Today, most people are citizens of the country in which they live. They are community members who owe loyalty to that country. They also expect to be protected by it. Citizens may share a common history, common customs, or common values. They agree to follow the laws and to accept the government's authority.

Who Are U.S. Citizens? Every country has rules about how people gain citizenship. In the United States, a citizen is a person who by birth or by choice owes loyalty to this nation. In the Fourteenth Amendment, the U.S. Constitution states that anyone "born or naturalized in the United States" is a citizen. If you were born in the United States and its territories, you automatically are an American citizen by birth. Foreigners who choose to become U.S. citizens do so through naturalization. **Naturalization** is the legal process by which a person becomes a citizen. Naturalized citizens have all the rights and duties of citizens by birth except the right to be president or vice president.

National and State Citizenship Over the years, the basis of citizenship has changed greatly in the United States. Today, citizenship relates both to the nation as a whole and to the states. This was not always so, however.

The Articles of the Constitution mention citizenship only as a qualification for holding office in the federal government. The Constitution's writers assumed that the states would decide who was or was not a citizen. Their citizens were also citizens of the United States. The exceptions were African Americans and immigrants who became citizens through naturalization.

◀ New American citizens pledging allegiance

"Our Constitution is color-blind, and neither knows nor tolerates classes among citizens. In respect of civil rights, all citizens are equal before the law."

—Justice John Marshall Harlan, 1896

650

More Skill Practice

Historical and Social Sciences Analysis Skill Have students write three or four questions about the process of becoming a naturalized citizen. Then have them research the process to find the answers to their questions. OL CA HR1.

Did You Know?

The concept of citizenship comes from ancient Greece, where women, poor community members, and slaves were not considered citizens. Ancient Rome was where citizenship was first used to separate the Romans from the people of other territories Rome had conquered and brought under its rule.

The basis of state citizenship became an issue in the *Dred Scott* v. *Sandford* case in 1857. The Supreme Court, led by Chief Justice Roger Taney, ruled that Dred Scott, an enslaved African American, could not bring a legal suit in a federal court. Taney reasoned that African Americans, whether enslaved or free, were not United States citizens at the time the Constitution was adopted. Therefore, they could not claim citizenship. Only descendants of people who were state citizens at that time, or immigrants who became citizens through naturalization, were U.S. citizens.

The Fourteenth Amendment The *Dred Scott* decision caused great outrage and protest in the North. It added to the tensions that led to the Civil War. After the war ended, many Southern states passed laws that kept African Americans from holding certain jobs, limited their property rights, and restricted them in other ways. To remedy this situation, the Fourteenth Amendment was enacted in 1868.

The new amendment clearly stated what citizenship is at both the national and state levels of government. Overruling the *Dred Scott* decision, the Fourteenth Amendment stated that a United States citizen is anyone "born or naturalized in the United States." This definition included most African Americans. It guaranteed that people of all races born in the United States are citizens, making state citizenship an automatic result of national citizenship.

Denial of Citizens' Rights The Fourteenth Amendment granted citizenship to former enslaved African Americans and their descendants. It also guaranteed their rights as citizens. The amendment did this by requiring every state to grant citizens equal protection under the laws.

C

Despite this guarantee, African Americans routinely faced **discrimination,** or unfair treatment based on prejudice against a certain group. In the late 1800s, Southern states, for example, passed so-called Jim Crow laws requiring African Americans and whites to be separated in most public places, such as schools. Later, African Americans had to ride in the back of buses and sit in separate sections of restaurants and theaters.

The Supreme Court supported Jim Crow laws in *Plessy* v. *Ferguson* (1896). The Court said the Fourteenth Amendment allowed separate facilities for different races as long as those facilities were equal. For the next 50 years, this decision was used to justify segregation in the United States.

Extension of Citizens' Rights By the 1950s, society's views on racial segregation were beginning to change. In 1954 in the case of *Brown* v. *Board of Education of Topeka*, the Court overturned the ruling of "separate but equal." The justices ruled that racially separate schools are unequal simply because they are separate. The unanimous opinion of the Court found that segregation was a violation of the Fourteenth Amendment's principle of equal protection under the law.

S

Linda Brown was able to attend the school of her choice after the *Brown* decision. ▶

Checking for Understanding

1. How do people become citizens in the United States?
2. Why did the Supreme Court overturn the "separate but equal" idea in *Brown* v. *Board of Education of Topeka*?

Critical Thinking

3. Why do you think the writers of the Constitution assumed that the states would decide who was or who was not a citizen? CA HI1.
4. How was the promise of the Fourteenth Amendment fulfilled in the mid-twentieth century? CA HI2.

Connecting to the Constitution

C Critical Thinking

Identifying Central Issues
Inform students that, at times, the constitutional provisions protecting personal liberties have been tested. One such test occurred during World War II, when more than 100,000 Japanese Americans were considered security risks and put into relocation camps. Discuss whether, in times of crisis, the government is justified in suspending personal liberties. Have students give reasons to support their positions. OL

S Skill Practice

Historical and Social Sciences Analysis Skill
Ask: What impact can the Supreme Court have on basic human rights in the United States? *(Students should note that the impact can be substantial.)* OL

ASSESS

Have students answer the Checking for Understanding and Critical Thinking questions.

CLOSE

Identifying Central Issues
Ask: Why is the inclusion of states' rights part of the Fourteenth Amendment? *(because states have passed laws protecting a variety of minorities, and because the Constitution guarantees due process of law, then states' citizens are equally protected)* OL

Questions reinforce content standard US8.11.5.

Checking for Understanding:

1. by birth or through naturalization
2. because it violated the Fourteenth Amendment principle of equal protection for all citizens under the law

Critical Thinking:

3. because state governments already had rules about citizenship and that powers not given to the federal government remained with the states
4. by the Supreme Court overruling segregation laws as a violation of the Fourteenth Amendment principle of equal protection under the laws for all citizens

Analyzing Primary Sources

FOCUS

History–Social Science Standards

The following standard is covered on pages 652–653:

US8.11 Students analyze the character and lasting consequences of Reconstruction.

TEACH

S Skill Practice

Historical and Social Sciences Analysis Skill

Some Northerners felt the South should be punished after the Civil War. **Ask:** If Northerners had suffered destruction like this, would they have felt differently about the South? Why or why not? *(Students may say they would have been more sympathetic or more embittered.)* OL CA HI2.

Resources for page 652

American Literature Reading 14

Answers and Additional Support

US8.11 Students analyze the character and lasting consequences of Reconstruction.

Analyzing Primary Sources

Reconstruction

Most of the Civil War was waged in the South. After the war, the South faced the huge task of rebuilding. In addition, freed African Americans had to make a new life for themselves. There was also the difficult problem of how to make the former Confederacy and the Union into one nation again.

Read the passages on pages 652 and 653 and answer the questions that follow.

The head of the Freedmen's Bureau (seated at the far right) is pictured with students in a Freedmen's school. ▶

Reader's Dictionary

charge: blame

exterminating (ihk • STUHR • muh • NAYT • ihng)**:** getting rid of completely

emerged: have risen from a low condition

bondage (BAHN • dihj)**:** slavery

plea (PLEE)**:** serious or sincere call for help

quarters: places

The South in Ruins

Newspaper reporter Sidney Andrews toured major Southern cities in the fall of 1865. He wrote the following account about Columbia, South Carolina.

S Columbia was doubtless once the gem of the state. . . . What with its broad streets, beautiful shade trees, handsome lawns . . . I can easily see that it must have been a delightful place of residence. No South Carolinian with whom I have spoken hesitates an instant in declaring that [Columbia] was the most beautiful city on the continent; and, as already mentioned, they **charge** its destruction directly to General Sherman.

[Columbia] is now a wilderness of ruins. Its heart is but a mass of blackened chimneys and crumbling walls. Two thirds of the buildings in the place were burned, including, without exception, everything in the business portion. Not a store, office, or shop escaped; and for a distance of three fourths of a mile on each of twelve streets there was not a building left. . . .

The work of clearing away the ruins is going on, not rapidly or extensively, to be sure, but something is doing, and many small houses of the cheaper sort are going up. Yet, at the best, this generation will not ever again see the beautiful city of a year ago.

—from *The South Since the War*

EXTENDING THE CONTENT

Reconnecting with Family After the war ended, many African Americans placed ads in newspapers hoping to learn the whereabouts of family members. One such letter reveals the kind of information they gave and the deep feeling behind the ads:

"Lewis Wade wishes to learn the whereabouts of his wife, Lucy, and three children, named respectively, Benjamin, Harriet and Charlotte. He left them in 1850, they then being in Rockbridge county, Virginia. He belonged to Wm. Thompson, while his wife and children belonged to James Watts. . . . Heaven bless the hand that guides the wanderers home."

On the Plight of African Americans

In 1867 Frederick Douglass appealed to Congress on behalf of African Americans.

Yet the negroes have marvelously survived all the **exterminating** forces of slavery, and have **emerged** at the end of two hundred and fifty years of **bondage,** not [sad and hateful], but cheerful, hopeful, and forgiving. They now stand before Congress and the country, not complaining of the past, but simply asking for a better future. . . .

S It is true that a strong **plea** for equal suffrage might be addressed to the national sense of honor. Something, too, might be said of national gratitude. A nation might well hesitate before the temptation to betray its allies. There is something . . . mean, to say nothing of the cruelty, in placing the loyal negroes of the South under the political power of their Rebel masters. . . . We asked the negroes to [support] our cause, to be our friends, to fight for us, and against their masters; and now, after they have done all that we asked them to do, . . . it is proposed in some **quarters** to turn them over to the political control of the common enemy of the government and of the negro. . . .

▼ Douglass fought for civil rights for newly freed slaves and was active in the women's movement.

C What, then, is the work before Congress? . . . In a word, it must [allow African Americans to vote], and by means of the loyal negroes and the loyal white men of the South build up a national party there, and in time bridge the [gap] between North and South, so that our country may have a common liberty and a common civilization.

—*An Appeal to Congress for Impartial Suffrage*

DBQ Document-Based Questions

The South in Ruins

1. To what does Andrews compare Columbia? Why?
2. What does Andrews mean when he writes that "Not a store, office, or shop escaped"?

On the Plight of African Americans

3. According to Douglass, why does the United States owe a debt of gratitude to African Americans?
4. How did Douglass think that Congress could ensure the nation a common liberty and civilization for whites and African Americans?

Read to Write

5. During Reconstruction, some people worked to get African Americans the same rights as whites. List the rights that these primary sources include and others that you know about. Then research the civil rights movement of the 1960s. What right or rights were African Americans seeking at that time? Compare and contrast the rights and the methods used to gain them in the two time periods. CA HR3. CA 8RL3.3

S Skill Practice

Analyzing Primary Sources

Ask: Why does Douglass say that denying African Americans the right to vote is "mean"? *(It shows ingratitude.)* Why does it show "cruelty"? *(He expects that they will suffer if white Southerners can vote and they cannot.)* OL CA HR2.

C Critical Thinking

Analyzing Information

Ask: How does Douglass say people in the North will benefit from giving African Americans the right to vote? *(Blacks in the South can join with pro-Union whites to build a strong party and help unify the country.)* OL CA HI1.

ASSESS

Have students answer the Document-Based Questions.

CLOSE

Have students take the role of one of the Radical Republicans and write a brief speech calling for passage of the Fourteenth Amendment. Their speeches might cite some of the information in these primary source documents to support the need for such an amendment. OL CA 8WA2.4

DBQ Document-Based Questions

1. a wilderness
2. All were destroyed.
3. because they had supported the Union cause and fought for it
4. give African Americans the right to vote
5. Students might note that the rights include the right to vote, to marry, and to have access to jobs, public places, and schools. The civil rights movement aimed to gain many of the same rights, which still had been denied to African Americans.

Resources for pages 654–655

Use these resources to review, assess, or reteach the chapter.

- Active Reading Note-Taking Guide, Chapter 14
- Chapter 14 Reading Essentials and Study Guide
- Chapter 14 Tests, Forms A and B
- Standards Assessment, Forms A and B
- California Standards Practice Workbook
- Succeeding on the California History–Social Science Standards CD-ROM
- MindJogger Videoquiz
- Interactive Tutor Self-Assessment CD-ROM

Chapter 14 Assessment

Standard US8.11

Review Content Vocabulary

Each of the following statements is false. Replace each word in italics with a content vocabulary word that makes the statement true. Write the correct words on a separate sheet of paper.

___ 1. The reorganization of the Southern states after the war was called *integration*.

___ 2. *Carpetbaggers* were Southern whites who sided with Republicans.

___ 3. To *grant amnesty* is to formally charge with a crime.

___ 4. Fees called *grandfather clauses* were often required before voters could cast their ballots in the south.

Review the Main Ideas

Section 1 • Reconstruction Plans

5. What services did the Freedmen's Bureau provide?
6. Who succeeded Lincoln as president?

Section 2 • Radicals in Control

7. How was the Fourteenth Amendment supposed to help African Americans?
8. What verdict did the Senate reach in the trial of President Johnson?

Section 3 • The South During Reconstruction

9. What role did African Americans play in early Reconstruction politics in the South?
10. What tactic did the Ku Klux Klan use to influence elections in the South?

Section 4 • Change in the South

11. Why was a special commission needed to decide the presidential election of 1876?
12. What Supreme Court decision upheld the legality of segregation so long as "separate but equal" facilities were provided?

Critical Thinking

13. **Analyze** How did the black codes deny rights? CA HI2.
14. **Evaluate** Explain the following quote as it applies to Reconstruction: "The slave went free; stood a brief moment in the sun; then moved back again toward slavery." CA HR5.

Geography Skills

Study the map below and answer the question that follows. CA CS3.

NATIONAL GEOGRAPHIC **Congress During and After Reconstruction**

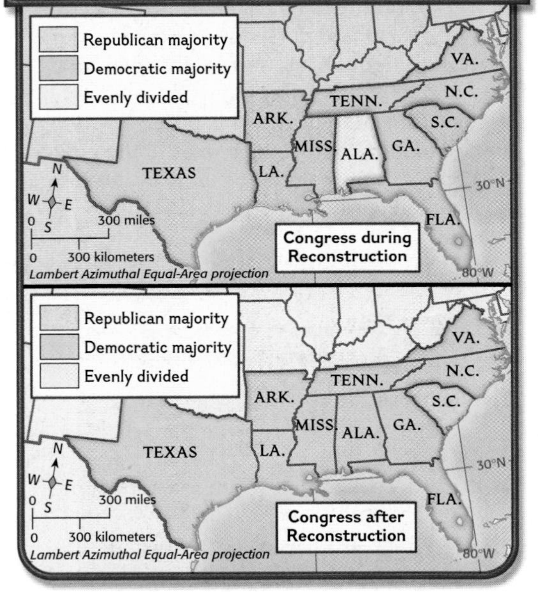

15. **Summarize** Write a paragraph summarizing the changes in congressional representation during and after Reconstruction.

Review Content Vocabulary

1. Reconstruction
2. Scalawags
3. impeach
4. poll taxes

Review the Main Ideas

5. distributed food, clothing; provided medical services; set up schools; helped people get land; provided transportation to jobs; helped workers obtain fair wages
6. Andrew Johnson
7. by granting full citizenship to all people born in the U.S. and prohibiting states from denying citizens their rights without due process
8. not guilty
9. They voted and won elective office in some states.
10. terrorized African Americans and other Republican voters to keep them from voting
11. because ballots from three states were disputed and thus the winner was not decided
12. *Plessy* v. *Ferguson*

Critical Thinking

13. They restricted the rights of freedmen and allowed whites to exploit African American workers.
14. African Americans were freed from slavery and briefly enjoyed some rights in the South, but when whites regained control of state governments, those rights were taken away.

Geography Skills

15. Answers should reflect data on the map.

History Online

Self-Check Quiz Visit ca.hss.glencoe.com to prepare for the Chapter 14 test.

Read to Write

16. **The Big Ideas** **Expository Writing** Review the chapter to make a list of specific ways that Southern states tried to deny equal rights to African Americans after the war. Then decide which amendment(s)—Thirteenth, Fourteenth, or Fifteenth—should have prevented each action. Include this information in an essay. CA 8WS1.0

17. **Using Your FOLDABLES** Use the information you wrote in your foldable to create a fill-in-the-blank quiz for a classmate. Write a paragraph about one of the sections, leaving blanks for your classmate to fill in. Leave blanks for vocabulary words or significant places and people. CA 8RW1.3

Using Academic Vocabulary

Choose the academic vocabulary word that best completes each sentence. You may need to change the form of the word to provide the best answer (for example, "create" becomes "creating").

create **enable** **dominate**
exploit **eliminate**

18. Many Americans thought the poll tax was unfair and sought to ____ it.
19. Republicans in the South thought that the power of the ballot would ____ African Americans to protect themselves.
20. In the 1870s, Reconstruction governments began ____ public school systems.
21. The Radical Republicans began to ____ the Reconstruction process.

Building Citizenship

22. **Registering to Vote** Laws about voter registration vary from place to place. Working with a partner, contact your local election board to find out what the requirements for voter registration are in your community. Then design a brochure that encourages citizens to register to vote. CA 8LS1.3

Reviewing Skills

23. **Review READING SKILL** **Monitoring and Clarifying** Turn to pages 263–264 and read the Fourteenth and Fifteenth Amendments to the U.S. Constitution. Write down concepts that are unfamiliar to you and what you will do to understand them. Then, write a paragraph summarizing the amendments in your own words. CA 8RC2.0

24. **Review ANALYSIS SKILL** **Sequencing Events** Review this chapter and draw a time line of key events during Reconstruction. Identify the event that you believe had the most impact and write a short essay justifying your conclusions. CA CS2. CA 8WS1.1

Standards Practice

Read the passage below and answer the following question.

> The right of citizens of the United States to vote shall not be denied or abridged by the United States or any State on account of race, color, or previous condition of servitude.
>
> —*excerpt from the Fifteenth Amendment to the Constitution*

25 The main idea of the Fifteenth Amendment is that

A enslaved people convicted of crimes had the right to a fair trial.

B slavery was made illegal in every state of the Union.

C the government was not allowed to deny a person's right to vote on the basis of race.

D Congress had the right to set voting restrictions in whatever state it chose.

CHAPTER 14 Assessment

Building Citizenship

22. Students' brochures should include information and messages aimed at encouraging voting.

Reviewing Skills

23. Review READING SKILL The concepts students note will vary. To understand them, they might look them up in the book's Glossary, a dictionary, or an encyclopedia or ask a teacher what they mean.

24. Review ANALYSIS SKILL Timelines should reflect information from the chapter, and students should give reasons for the event they chose.

Standards Practice

25. C

Bonus Question

Ask: For what group was the Fifteenth Amendment written? *(African Americans)* OL

History Online

Have students visit the Web site at ca.hss.glencoe.com to review Chapter 14 and take the **Self-Check Quiz.**

Read to Write

16. The Big Ideas Students' essays should include the actions taken in Southern states to limit African Americans' freedoms and should note whether the Thirteenth, Fourteenth, or Fifteenth Amendment was passed to prevent these types of actions.

17. Using Your FOLDABLES Quiz questions will vary but should reflect information in the chapter.

Using Academic Vocabulary

18. eliminate
19. enable
20. creating
21. dominate

FOCUS

Reviewing Unit Objectives

Having studied this unit, students should be able to

- Outline the events that led to the Civil War and explain why people in the North and the South reacted to each event as they did.
- Discuss the election of 1860 and why it led to secession.
- Compare the strengths, weaknesses, and strategies of the North and the South at the beginning of the war.
- Identify key battles in the war and explain their significance.
- Discuss how life changed for African Americans during the war.
- Compare the different plans for Reconstruction of the South and explain why Congress came to control this process.
- Describe changes in the South as a result of Reconstruction and explain why Reconstruction ended.

TEACH

Have students explain why the Civil War took place and name three challenges the nation faced during Reconstruction. OL

Unit Review Activity

To help students review the unit objectives, have them write two or three questions on each objective, exchange questions, and answer their partner's questions. OL

Unit 5 Review

Civil War and Reconstruction

In Unit 5 you learned how social, economic, and political differences between the North and South grew. As compromises failed, the country plunged into civil war. Following the North's victory, bringing the country back together also proved challenging.

	Chapter 12: Road to Civil War	Chapter 13: Civil War	Chapter 14: Reconstruction
When	• 1820–1861	• 1861–1865	• 1865–1896
Where	• New Western lands: Texas, New Mexico, California • Kansas and Nebraska Territories	• Bull Run • Shiloh • Antietam • Vicksburg • Gettysburg • Atlanta • Savannah • Appomattox Court House	• Military Reconstruction Districts in the South

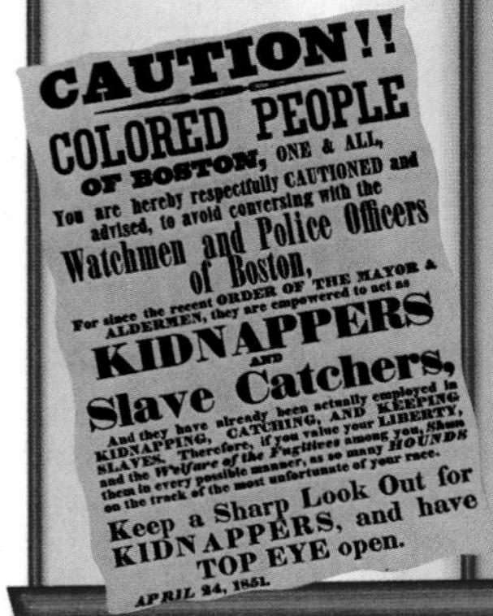

CAUTION!!
COLORED PEOPLE
OF BOSTON, ONE & ALL,
You are hereby respectfully CAUTIONED and advised, to avoid conversing with the
Watchmen and Police Officers of Boston,
For since the recent ORDER OF THE MAYOR & ALDERMEN, they are empowered to act as
KIDNAPPERS
AND
Slave Catchers,
And they have already been actually employed in KIDNAPPING, CATCHING, AND KEEPING SLAVES. Therefore, if you value your LIBERTY, and the Welfare of the Fugitives among you, Shun them in every possible manner, as so many HOUNDS on the track of the most unfortunate of your race.
Keep a Sharp Look Out for KIDNAPPERS, and have TOP EYE open.
APRIL 24, 1851.

◀ *Poster warning African Americans*

Confederate soldier ▶

END-OF-UNIT RESOURCES

Use these resources to review and assess unit material.

- Step Into American History Activities
- Cumulative Assessment Activities
- Reading Essentials and Study Guide
- California Standards Practice Workbook
- Interactive Tutor Self-Assessment CD-ROM
- Exam*View*® Pro Testmaker CD-ROM
- Succeeding on the California History–Social Science Standards CD-ROM

	Chapter 12 Road to Civil War	Chapter 13 Civil War	Chapter 14 Reconstruction
Major Events	• **1820** Missouri Compromise • **1857** *Dred Scott* decision • **1860** Lincoln elected • **1861** Confederate States of America formed • **1861** Fort Sumter attacked	• **1861** First Battle of Bull Run • **1862** *Monitor* versus *Merrimack* • **1863** Emancipation Proclamation • **1863** Battles of Gettysburg and Vicksburg • **1864** Grant leads the Union army • **1865** Lee surrenders	• **1864** Wade-Davis Bill • **1865** Thirteenth Amendment passes • **1865** Lincoln assassinated • **1866–1870** Southern states readmitted to Union • **1866** Ku Klux Klan formed • **1868** President Andrew Johnson impeached • **1877** Reconstruction ends • **1896** *Plessy* v. *Ferguson*
Some Important People	• Henry Clay • Stephen Douglas • Harriet Beecher Stowe • Abraham Lincoln • John Brown • Dred Scott	• Jefferson Davis • Abraham Lincoln • "Stonewall" Jackson • Ulysses S. Grant • Robert E. Lee	• John Wilkes Booth • Andrew Johnson • Frederick Douglass • Rutherford B. Hayes
How do these events and ideas affect our lives today?	• The events discussed in this chapter led up to the Civil War, which forever changed relations within our country.	• The Union victory established the power of the federal government over the states.	• The passage of the Fourteenth and Fifteenth Amendments established rights for all citizens.
What was happening in California at this time?	• **1821** Mexico wins independence from Spain; gains control of California • **1846** Bear Flag Revolt • **1848** U.S. gains California Territory • **1848** Gold Rush begins	• **1861** First telegram sent from California to the East • **1862** Leland Stanford becomes governor • **1863** Work begins on Central Pacific Railroad	• **1869** Rail service links California to the rest of the nation • **1869** State capitol built • **1879** California Constitution revised

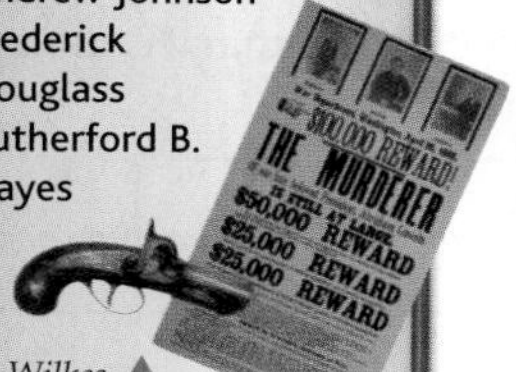

John Wilkes Booth pistol and poster

Secessionist ribbon

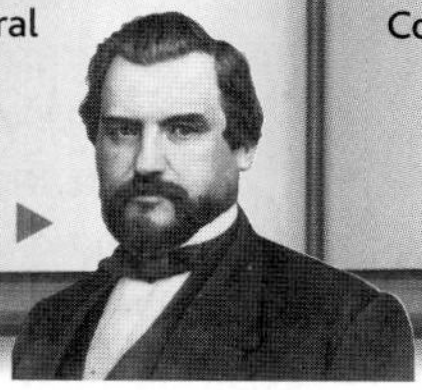
Leland Stanford

ASSESS/CLOSE

Unit Wrap-Up Activity

Creating an Annotated Map Have students work in groups to create annotated maps that tell the story of the events leading up to the Civil War, the war itself, or the period of Reconstruction.

1. Organize students into three groups and assign each group a period, either before the war, during the war, or after the war.
2. Tell groups that their task is to use a map of the United States to highlight key events and people in their assigned period by using text and images tied to the places where those events took place or where those individuals were active. The group with the period during the war, for instance, could use their map to show the states that fought with the North and the South, the sites of the two capitals, the location of key battles, and the Union blockade of the South, among other aspects of the war.
3. Have each group present its map to the class. **OL**

PROFESSIONAL DEVELOPMENT: DIFFERENTIATED INSTRUCTION

Use these resources for help teaching students with different learning styles.

- Benjamin, Amy. *Differentiated Instruction: A Guide for Middle and High School Teachers.* Eye on Education, 2002.
- Gregory, Gayle H. *Differentiated Instructional Strategies: One Size Doesn't Fit All.* Corwin Press, 2002.
- Heacox, Diane. *Differentiating Instruction in the Regular Classroom: How to Reach and Teach All Learners, Grades 3–12.* Free Spirit, 2002.
- Tomlinson, Carol Ann. *How to Differentiate Instruction in Mixed-Ability Classrooms.* ASCD, 2001.

Teaching the Unit

Use the information on these pages to help you teach Unit 6.

History–Social Science Standards Covered in Unit 6

Standard	Chapter 15	Chapter 16	Chapter 17
US8.12 Students analyze the transformation of the American economy and the changing social and political conditions in the United States in response to the Industrial Revolution.	✔	✔	✔

Pacing Your Lessons

This pacing chart provides time management suggestions for teaching Unit 6.

Unit 6 Reshaping the Nation	Days
Unit 6 Introduction	1/2
Chapter 15 • **Reading Skill:** Visualizing • **Sections 1–4** • **Biography:** The Buffalo Soldiers, Chief Joseph • **America's Literature:** "A Lantern in Her Hand" • **Analyzing Primary Sources**	7
Chapter 16 • **Reading Skill:** Predicting Consequences • **Sections 1–4** • **Biography:** Leland Stanford and Charles Crocker, Mary Harris Jones and César Estrada Chávez • **Connecting to the Constitution** • **Analyzing Primary Sources**	7
Chapter 17 • **Reading Skill:** Visual Literacy • **Sections 1–5** • **Biography:** Jacob Riis, Booker T. Washington and W.E.B. Du Bois • **You Decide . . .** • **Geography & History** • **Time Notebook** • **Analyzing Primary Sources**	9
Unit 6 Review	1/2

Teacher *to* Teacher

In-Class Pen Pals

Katherine Sweet
Rooftop K-8 School
San Francisco, CA

Create in-class pen pals by first organizing the class into pairs representing pen pals. One student will write a letter as an immigrant who has recently arrived in the United States. The other student will write a response letter, playing the role of someone still living in the immigrant's home country. The initial letter writer could write about topics such as poverty, crime, inadequate housing, and poor working conditions that are encountered in the new country. The responder could provide sympathy, understanding, and advice to the immigrant friend on how to cope with the situation. The letter exchanges should be shared with the rest of the class. Some students may want to do additional research before composing their letters. Photocopies of pictures from research materials could also be included to illustrate conditions in early urban America.

Previewing the Chapters

Dear American History Teacher:

As you begin to teach this unit, there are themes that reoccur throughout the chapters that you will want to point out to students.

The late nineteenth and early twentieth centuries were a time of remarkable growth in the United States. Population grew rapidly, and with it cultural diversity, as millions of immigrants from many areas of the world streamed into the country. The economy grew as well, propelled by railroad expansion, mining, new industries, and important inventions. New settlers moved west, contributing to the destruction of the traditional way of life of Native American groups. Some American leaders began looking beyond the United States and successfully promoted the acquisition of colonies overseas. Growth and change created both progress and instability. Reformers, who called themselves Progressives, worried about the growing power of large corporations and about political corruption. They enacted some important reforms, but many problems remained, including racial segregation in the South and other patterns of discrimination and oppression of minorities throughout the country.

You may want to use the following information at the beginning of each chapter as a lesson launcher to help students begin to focus on what they will be studying.

CHAPTER 15: The Western Frontier (pages 662–701)

Discoveries of gold and silver brought thousands of miners to many areas in the West and led to the growth of boomtowns. Railroads grew rapidly in the period after the Civil War and spurred the growth of cattle drives. Free land and new farming methods attracted thousands to settle on the Great Plains, though they found difficult lives there. The increase in white settlement of the West caused problems for Native Americans, who were forced to live on reservations. Some resisted, but they met defeat. Farmers tried to organize to find ways to solve their problems, but the party they formed could not win the presidency.

CHAPTER 16: The Growth of Industry (pages 702–735)

The growth of railroads helped spur the economy, and new innovations made travel by railroad faster and more efficient. Other new inventions improved communications and made life more pleasant and enjoyable. Some business leaders enjoyed great success and built large, powerful corporations. Abuses of that power led the government to regulate business. Industrialization led to very harsh and hazardous working conditions for workers. People tried to organize unions to change conditions and win higher wages, but some violent strikes caused the nation to turn against unions.

CHAPTER 17: America Enters a New Century (pages 736–789)

Millions of immigrants came to the United States in the late 1800s and early 1900s, bringing new cultures to the country. Some Americans tried to limit immigration, fearing the loss of jobs. Cities grew very large, with great contrast between the very rich, the middle class, and the poor. The expanding education system brought new opportunities for learning, and a more educated public began to enjoy more reading and leisure activities. Problems in the cities, in business, and in government led to calls for reforms. Progressive reformers achieved many successes. The United States also looked abroad, hoping to expand its power. Back home, though, many members of minority groups suffered discrimination, and they worked to try to win equal rights.

FOCUS

Connecting to Past Learning

In Unit 5, students learned about the events leading up to the Civil War, the course and effects of that conflict, and Reconstruction in the South. In Unit 6, they will read about the Industrial Revolution in the United States, expansion to the West, and the social and political changes that took place in the late 1800s.

Unit Launch Activity

Ask: What ideas spurred reform in the early 1800s? *(Students should point to the religious or moral principles underlying the reform movements of the early 1800s.)* Based on the introduction to the unit, what ideas do you think will drive reform in this period? *(economic inequality)* OL

History–Social Science Standards

The following standard is covered in Unit 6:

US8.12 Students analyze the transformation of the American economy and the changing social and political conditions in the United States in response to the Industrial Revolution.

Why It's Important

Ask: What group do you think will be hurt by expanded white settlements on the Great Plains? Why? OL

Unit 6

Reshaping the Nation

Why It's Important

Following the Civil War, the United States grew at an even greater rate. Settlers flocked to the West and immigrants came to the great eastern cities to work in new factories. While the nation's economy grew strong, not everyone shared equally in the wealth, and reformers worked for equal rights and equal opportunity for all citizens.

- The settling of the Plains and the growth of industry helped the United States become an agricultural and industrial leader.
- America's tremendous growth also led to problems within society, which a number of reformers attempted to resolve.

1860 — 1870 — 1880

U.S. EVENTS

1862 Congress passes the Homestead Act

1869 Transcontinental railroad links the East and West

Golden railroad spike

1879 Edison invents the electric lightbulb

1882 Congress passes the Chinese Exclusion Act

CALIFORNIA EVENTS

1861 Transcontinental telegraph line is completed

1863 Construction begins on the Central Pacific Railway

Leland Stanford

WORLD EVENTS

1861 Giuseppe Garibaldi helps unite Italy

Giuseppe Garibaldi

1876 Queen Victoria becomes "Empress of India"

Queen Victoria

1884 European powers partition Africa

TEACHING THE TIME LINES

Help students focus on the information in the time lines. **Ask:**

- What changes in transportation and communication are described on these time lines? *(transcontinental telegraph; transcontinental railroad)*
- What event in California history is linked to the 1869 event in the United States events tier? *(beginning of construction on Central Pacific Railway in 1863)*
- What disaster struck California? When? *(San Francisco earthquake and fire; 1906)*
- What book is cited as important in one of the time lines? (The Jungle)

As students study events described in the unit, refer back to these time lines and have students identify where the event would appear. OL

NATIONAL GEOGRAPHIC Where in the United States?

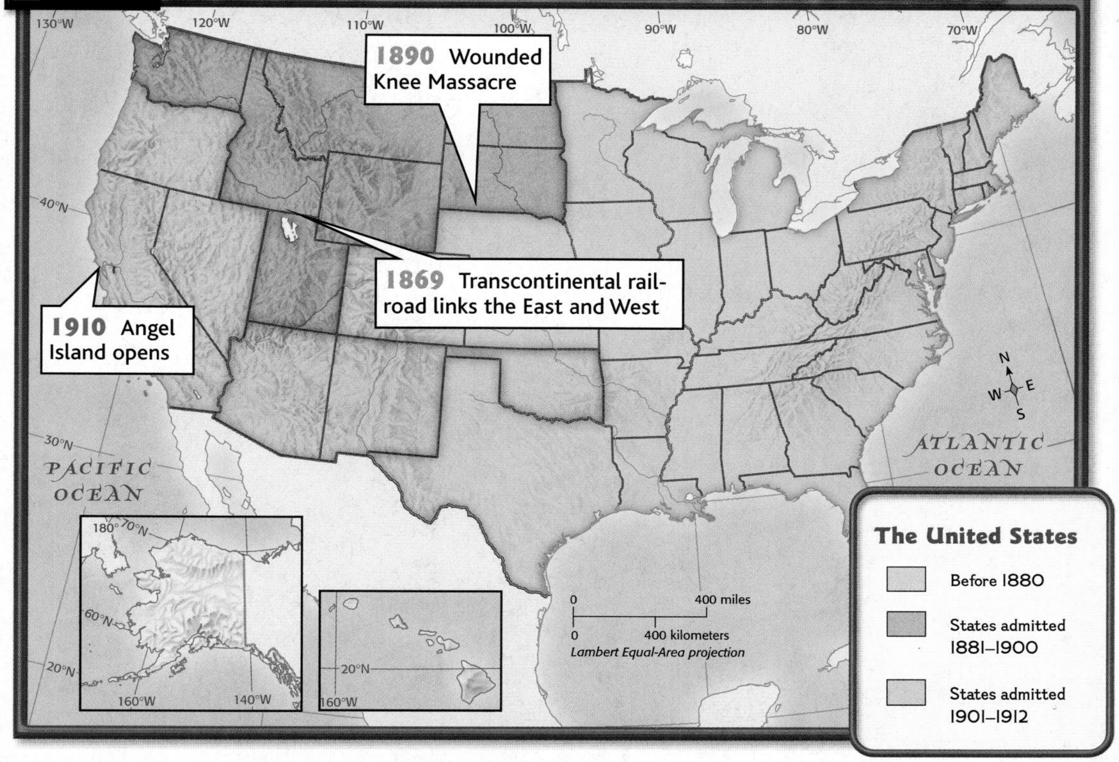

1890 | **1900** | **1910**

1890 Wounded Knee Massacre

◀ The Jungle

1906 Upton Sinclair publishes *The Jungle*

1913 Seventeenth Amendment is ratified

Devastation following the San Francisco earthquake ▶

1906 San Francisco earthquake and fire occurs

1910 Angel Island opens

1911 Women gain the right to vote in some state elections

1895 Lumière brothers show first projected motion picture films

◀ *Emiliano Zapata*

1911 Zapata leads demand for land reform in Mexico

1914 World War I begins

UNIVERSAL ACCESS

Below Grade Level: Have students organize into pairs. Tell each student to create a five-question quiz on one of the three parts of the time line, with the partners taking different parts. Have them exchange their quizzes and answer the questions. BL

Musical/Auditory: Pair auditory learners with students who can read aloud smoothly. Have the latter students read the different events on the time line and then quiz the auditory learners to make sure they understand what was described. OL

Advanced Learners: Have students research and write a report on one of the events listed on the time line. AL

TEACH

NATIONAL GEOGRAPHIC Where in the United States?

Understanding Maps and Time Lines Ask: Why are the states newly added in this period all located in the West? *(because they became part of the United States and were settled later than the eastern states)* Which present-day states still do not appear as states on this map? *(Alaska and Hawaii)* OL

NCLB No Child Left Behind

Teaching Activity Have students read the introduction to the unit on page 658 and the time line on both pages. **Ask:** Do you think the unit will be mostly about domestic issues or foreign issues? Why? *(domestic; because the introduction speaks of economic growth and reform)* What event comes at the end of this period that will involve foreign affairs? *(World War I)* OL

INTRODUCING UNIT 6

Unit Objectives

After studying this unit, students should be able to

- Explain how businesses changed and grew and why some had great power.
- Discuss the impact of immigration and how immigrants were treated.
- Describe the groups that settled in the West and the impact of that settlement.
- Identify how cities changed and the problems that arose from these changes.
- Explain how the United States took a greater role in the world.

Previewing People to Meet

Have students create the graphic below and complete it as they read the unit. OL **NOTE:** Answers are listed in the second column.

Person	Known For
Chief Joseph	*(tried to lead Nez Perce to Canada)*
Thomas Edison	*(invented many new machines)*
Mother Jones	*(campaigned for workers' rights)*
Jane Addams	*(founded a settlement house)*
Booker T. Washingon	*(worked to better African Americans' lives)*
Jacob Riis	*(exposed problems of urban poor)*
Ida Wells	*(campaigned against lynching)*
W.E.B. Du Bois	*(worked to better African Americans' lives)*

Unit 6 Places to Locate

1 PROMONTORY SUMMIT

See *The Western Frontier* Chapter 15

2 THE BROOKLYN BRIDGE

See *America Enters a New Century* Chapter 17

People to Meet

Chief Joseph
1840–1904
Nez Perce leader
Chapter 15, page 690

Thomas Edison
1847–1931
Inventor
Chapter 16, page 714

Mother Jones
1830–1930
Worker's rights leader
Chapter 16, page 728

Jane Addams
1860–1935
Founder of Chicago's Hull House
Chapter 17, page 753

660

Previewing Places to Locate

Use the following descriptions to explain the images on the map.

1 

Leland Stanford was the first dignitary to try to drive the final spike, though he missed on the first try. The same happened to T.C. Durant of the Union Pacific. The head engineers of the two railroads completed driving that spike.

2 

John Roebling, designer of the Brooklyn Bridge, died during work on that bridge. His son directed the rest of the project.

Booker T. Washington
1856–1915
Equal rights advocate
Chapter 17, page 781

Jacob Riis
1849–1914
Journalist
Chapter 17, page 768

Ida Wells
1862–1931
Journalist
Chapter 17, page 780

W.E.B. Du Bois
1868–1963
Equal rights advocate
Chapter 17, page 781

The first skyscrapers appeared in Chicago in the 1880s, where architects experimented with using iron or steel to form the skeleton of a building. Daniel Burnham and Louis Sullivan were the pioneers in the new form of construction.

The beauty of Yosemite's landscape attracted tourists as early as 1855. The national park—established in 1890—has 760,000 acres and contains more than a thousand varieties of flowering plants as well as the country's highest waterfall.

Skill Practice

Historical and Social Sciences Analysis Skill

Ask: Based on the images on this map, how important do you think technology will be in this unit? Why? *(Students should indicate that the presence of the railroads, the bridge, and the skyscraper all show that technology was very important and was changing Americans' lives.)* **OL**

Skill Practice

Creating a Time Line

Have students copy the three-tiered structure of the time line on pages 658 and 659 on a piece of paper. Have them label the three levels *Economy*, *Society and Culture*, and *Government*. As they read the chapters in the unit, have them fill in key dates on the appropriate section of the time line. **OL**

ASSESS/CLOSE

Have students explain how the people and events listed on these pages are linked to the government's announcement in 1890 of the end of the frontier. **OL**

Chapter 15 Planning Guide

SECTION RESOURCES

Main Ideas	Print Materials	Technology Resources
Section 1 **The Mining Booms** 1. In the late 1850s, discoveries of gold and silver sent miners flocking to the American West. 2. A number of boomtowns grew quickly in the mining areas of the West. 3. Railroads grew rapidly in the period following the Civil War.	• Reproducible Lesson Plan 15–1* • Daily Lesson and Discussion Notes 15–1 • Active Reading Note-Taking Guide 15–1 • Reading Essentials and Study Guide 15–1 • Guided Reading Activity 15–1 • Section Quiz 15–1	Daily Focus Skills Transparency 15–1 Section Graphic Organizer Transparency 15–1 California Standards Practice Transparency Interactive Tutor Self-Assessment CD-ROM Exam*View*® Pro Testmaker CD-ROM Presentation Plus! CD-ROM
Section 2 **Ranchers and Farmers** 1. Cattle ranching in Texas became a profitable business once the new railroad reached the Great Plains. 2. The work of the cowhands who drove the cattle north from Texas to the railroads was both difficult and dangerous. 3. Free land and new farming methods brought many settlers to the Great Plains.	• Reproducible Lesson Plan 15–2* • Daily Lesson and Discussion Notes 15–2 • Active Reading Note-Taking Guide 15–2 • Reading Essentials and Study Guide 15–2 • Guided Reading Activity 15–2 • Section Quiz 15–2	Daily Focus Skills Transparency 15–2 Section Graphic Organizer Transparency 15–2 California Standards Practice Transparency Interactive Tutor Self-Assessment CD-ROM Exam*View*® Pro Testmaker CD-ROM Presentation Plus! CD-ROM
Section 3 **Native American Struggles** 1. The Native Americans of the Great Plains lived a nomadic lifestyle while following the great herds of buffalo. 2. During the late 1800s, whites and Native Americans fought while Native Americans tried to preserve their civilizations.	• Reproducible Lesson Plan 15–3* • Daily Lesson and Discussion Notes 15–3 • Active Reading Note-Taking Guide 15–3 • Reading Essentials and Study Guide 15–3 • Guided Reading Activity 15–3 • Section Quiz 15–3	Daily Focus Skills Transparency 15–3 Section Graphic Organizer Transparency 15–3 California Standards Practice Transparency Interactive Tutor Self-Assessment CD-ROM Exam*View*® Pro Testmaker CD-ROM Presentation Plus! CD-ROM Vocabulary PuzzleMaker CD-ROM
Section 4 **Farmers in Protest** 1. When crop prices fell in the late 1800s, farmers began to organize politically. 2. In the 1890s, a political party supporting the views of farmers and the common people arose.	• Reproducible Lesson Plan 15–4* • Daily Lesson and Discussion Notes 15–4 • Active Reading Note-Taking Guide 15–4 • Reading Essentials and Study Guide 15–4 • Guided Reading Activity 15–4 • Section Quiz 15–4	Daily Focus Skills Transparency 15–4 Section Graphic Organizer Transparency 15–4 California Standards Practice Transparency Interactive Tutor Self-Assessment CD-ROM Exam*View*® Pro Testmaker CD-ROM Presentation Plus! CD-ROM Vocabulary PuzzleMaker CD-ROM

PACING YOUR LESSONS

Unit Introduction	Chapter Introduction	Section 1	Section 2	Section 3	Section 4	Chapter Assessment
½ Day	½ Day	1 Day	2 Days	2 Days	1 Day	½ Day

0:00 **OUT OF TIME?** Assign the Chapter 15 ***Reading Essentials and Study Guide***

*Available on TeacherWorks™

Standards-Based Lesson Plan

History–Social Science Standards Covered in Chapter 15

The standards covered in the chapter are listed below. Use the accompanying activity as you teach the chapter to ensure student mastery of these standards. This activity can be used in combination with the program's print and technology assessment materials.

Standard	Section 1	Section 2	Section 3	Section 4
US8.11 Students analyze the character and lasting consequences of Reconstruction.		✓		
US8.11.2 Identify the push-pull factors in the movement of former slaves to the cities in the North and to the West and their differing experiences in those regions (e.g., the experiences of Buffalo Soldiers).		✓		
US8.12 Students analyze the transformation of the American economy and the changing social and political conditions in the United States in response to the Industrial Revolution.	✓	✓	✓	✓
US8.12.1 Trace patterns of agricultural and industrial development as they relate to climate, use of natural resources, markets, and trade and locate such development on a map.	✓	✓		
US8.12.2 Identify the reasons for the development of the federal Indian policy and the wars with American Indians and their relationship to agricultural development and industrialization.			✓	
US8.12.3 Explain how states and the federal government encouraged business expansion through tariffs, banking, land grants, and subsidies.	✓			
US8.12.8 Identify the characteristics and impact of Grangerism and Populism.				✓

Cumulative Standards-Assessment Activity

The Cumulative Standards-Assessment Activity will help students organize and learn the important information from the chapter. Begin teaching the chapter with this activity, and have students complete it as they read the chapter.

Creating a Summary

Purpose Summarizing is an important reading skill. By writing effective summaries, students demonstrate that they have identified the key points in a text and that they can distill the most important information related to those points.

Introduction to Summarizing

1. Model how to summarize by reading the material under the first subheadings of Section 1 and helping students see how to boil it down to a few sentences that convey the most important information. You could ask for volunteers to summarize each paragraph, so students become accustomed to the process.
2. Ask students to copy this chart into their notebooks:

   Section 1 Summary

   ____

   ____

   ____

   ____

   Explain that students should use a similar structure for the other sections in the chapter. Suggest that after students summarize one part of a section, they review their summaries and then reread the text to make sure their summaries are accurate. They can take the time to revise their summaries at this point.
3. As you review the chapter, ask volunteers to read from their summaries. Encourage students to use their summaries as study aids.

Chapter 15 Resources

READING SUPPORT

- Content Vocabulary Activity 15
- Academic Vocabulary Activity 15
- Reading Skills Activity 15
- American Literature Reading 15
- Biography Activities 15A, 15B
- Chapter 15 Active Reading Note-Taking Guide
- Chapter 15 Guided Reading Activities
- Chapter 15 Reading Essentials and Study Guide
- Glencoe Literature Library
- Glencoe Video Program
- Vocabulary PuzzleMaker CD-ROM
- Interactive Graphic Organizers CD-ROM
- American History Primary Source Document Library CD-ROM

CRITICAL THINKING

- Critical Thinking Skills Activity 15
- Primary Source Reading 15
- Cause-and-Effect Transparency 15, Strategy, and Activity
- Presentation Plus CD-ROM

UNIVERSAL ACCESS

- Universal Access Activity 15
- Then and Now Transparencies 15A–15B, Strategy, and Activity
- Graphic Novel Activity 15
- School-to-Home Connection Activities 15A–15D
- English Learner Handbook Chapter 15 Activities
- Universal Access for the American History Classroom
- Moments in Time
- American Art and Architecture Transparencies, Strategies, and Activities
- American Art Prints
- American Music Cultural Traditions
- American Music Hits Through History
- StudentWorks Plus CD-ROM

SKILL PRACTICE

- Map Overlay Transparency 15, Strategy, and Activity
- Analysis Skills Activity 15
- Time Line Activity 15
- Geography and History Activity 15
- Economics and History Activity 15
- Chart, Graph, and Map Skills Activity 15
- Political Cartoon Activity 15
- Supreme Court Case Study 15
- In-Text Map Transparency 15, Strategy, and Activity
- Step Into American History Activity 15
- Citizenship and Service Learning Activity 15
- Outline Map Resource Book
- MindJogger Plus Videoquiz

WRITING SUPPORT

- Writing Activity 15
- Language Arts Activity 15
- Writer's Guidebook
- Middle School Writing Process Transparencies

ASSESSMENT

GLENCOE'S ASSESSMENT ADVANTAGE

- Chapter 15 Section Quizzes
- Chapter 15 Tests, Forms A and B
- California Standards Assessment, Forms A and B
- Cumulative Assessment Activity US8.12
- California Standards Practice Workbook
- Succeeding on the California History–Social Science Standards CD-ROM
- Exam*View*® Pro Testmaker CD-ROM
- Interactive Tutor Self-Assessment CD-ROM

CD-ROM
DVD
Print Material
Poster
Transparency
Music Program
Videocassette
Glencoe Literature Library

Chapter 15 Resources

TECHNOLOGY

- StudentWorks Plus CD-ROM
- TeacherWorks CD-ROM
- Exam*View*® Pro Testmaker CD-ROM
- Interactive Tutor Self-Assessment CD-ROM
- Presentation Plus! CD-ROM
- Succeeding on the California History–Social Science Standards CD-ROM
- Vocabulary PuzzleMaker CD-ROM
- Interactive Graphic Organizers CD-ROM
- Interactive Time Line CD-ROM
- American History Primary Source Document Library CD-ROM
- MindJogger Plus Videoquiz
- American Music Cultural Traditions
- American Music Hits Through History
- Glencoe Video Program
- Professional Development in Middle School Social Studies Series
- Teaching American History With *Discovering Our Past: The American Journey to World War I*

SPANISH RESOURCES

- Spanish Activities and Assessment
  - Spanish Content Vocabulary Activities
  - Spanish Guided Reading Activities
  - Spanish Quizzes and Tests
  - Spanish California Standards Assessment
- Spanish Reading Essentials and Study Guide
- Spanish School-to-Home Connection
- Spanish Declaration of Independence and U.S. Constitution

TRANSPARENCIES

- California Standards Practice Transparencies
- Daily Focus Skills Transparencies
- Section Graphic Organizer Transparencies
- In-Text Map Transparencies
- Map Overlay Transparencies
- Cause-and-Effect Transparencies
- Then and Now Transparencies
- American Art and Architecture Transparencies
- Middle School Writing Process Transparencies

TEACHER PLANNING

- Daily Lesson and Discussion Notes
- English Learner Handbook
- Guide to Daily Intervention
- *Discovering Our Past: The American Journey to World War I* Reading and Study Skills Foldables
- Reading Strategies for the Social Studies Classroom
- Chapter 15 Reproducible Lesson Plans (correlated to California History–Social Science Standards)
- Universal Access for the American History Classroom
- NGS U.S. Desk Map
- NGS U.S. Atlas

PROFESSIONAL DEVELOPMENT

- Building Academic Vocabulary
- Strategies for Success
- Research-Based Strategies Used to Develop *Discovering Our Past: The American Journey to World War I*
- Character Education in the Middle School Classroom
- The Living Constitution
- Professional Development in Middle School Social Studies Video Series
- Teaching American History With *Discovering Our Past: The American Journey to World War I*

MASTERING THE STANDARDS

The content and assessment in the Student Edition, Teacher Wraparound Edition, teacher planning materials, and the print and technology products are all standards-based. The use of these products during instruction leads to mastery of the standards.

PRACTICE
- California Standards Practice Workbook
- California Standards Practice Transparencies
- Interactive Time Line CD-ROM
- School-to-Home Connection

BENCHMARK ASSESSMENT
- California Standards Assessment
- Exam*View*® Pro Testmaker CD-ROM
- Succeeding on the California History–Social Science Standards CD-ROM

REMEDIATION
- California Guide to Daily Intervention
- Interactive Tutor Self-Assessment CD-ROM
- Exam*View*® Pro Testmaker CD-ROM
- California Standards Practice Workbook
- Reading Essentials and Study Guide

Additional Resources

NATIONAL GEOGRAPHIC **TEACHER'S CORNER**

Index to National Geographic Magazine:

The following articles relate to this chapter:

- "The Way West," by John G. Mitchell, September 2000.
- "Buffalo: Back Home on the Range," by Bryan Hodgson, November 1994.
- "John Wesley Powell," by Peter Miller, April 1994.
- "Federal Lands," by Richard Conniff, February 1994.
- "The American Prairie: Roots of the Sky," by Douglas H. Chadwick, October 1993.

National Geographic Society Products

To order the following, call National Geographic at 1-800-368-2728

- *NGS Reading Expeditions, Series Six, Seeds of Change in American History* (Kit)
- *GeoKit: Westward Movement* (Video)
- *The West That Was* (Video)
- *United States/Territorial Growth* (Map)
- *Heritage of the Black West* (Video)
- *American Indians: A Brief History* (Video)

NGS ONLINE

Access National Geographics' new dynamic MapMachine Web site and other geography resources at:

www.nationalgeographic.com

www.nationalgeographic.com/maps

A&E HOME VIDEO. Biography® THE HISTORY CHANNEL®

The following videotape programs are available from Glencoe as supplements to Chapter 15.

- **George Custer: Showdown at Little Bighorn (ISBN 1-56501-583-1)**
- **The Best of the Real West (Set) (ISBN 1-56501-352-2)**
- **Geronimo (ISBN 1-56501-939-3)**
- **The Transcontinental Railroad (ISBN 1-56501-731-5)**

To order, call Glencoe at 1-800-334-7344. To find classroom resources to accompany many of these videos, check the following home pages:

A&E Television: www.aetv.com
The History Channel: www.historychannel.com

History Online

Use our Web site for additional resources. All essential content is covered in the Student Edition.

You and your students can visit ca.hss.glencoe.com, the Web site companion to *Discovering Our Past: The American Journey to World War I.* This innovative integration of electronic and print media offers your students a wealth of opportunities. The student text directs students to the Web site for the following options:

- Chapter Overviews
- Self-Check Quizzes
- Study Central™
- Student Web Activities
- Textbook Updates
- Multi-Language Glossaries

Answers to the student Web activities are provided for you in the Web Activity Lesson Plans. Additional Web resources and ePuzzles and games are also available.

FOLDABLES™ Study Organizer

Dinah Zike's Foldables

Foldables are three-dimensional, interactive graphic organizers that help students practice basic writing skills, review key vocabulary terms, and identify main ideas. Every chapter contains a foldable activity, with additional chapter activities found in the Reading and Study Skills Foldables booklet.

Chapter 15 Resources

Reading List Generator CD-ROM

Glencoe BookLink

The Glencoe BookLink CD-ROM is a database that allows you to search more than 15,000 titles to create a customized reading list for your students.

- Reading lists can be organized by students' reading level, author, genre, theme, or area of interest.
- The database provides Degrees of Reading Power™ (DRP) and Lexile™ readability scores for all selections.
- A brief summary of each selection is included.

Reading level suggestions for this chapter:

For students at a Grade 6 reading level:

- ***Chief Joseph: Nez Perce Peacekeeper,*** by Diane Shaughnessy and Jack Carpenter

For students at a Grade 7 reading level:

- ***Sitting Bull and His World,*** by Albert Marrion

For students at a Grade 8 reading level:

- ***The Forgotten Heroes: The Story of the Buffalo Soldiers,*** by Clinton Cox

For students at a Grade 9 reading level:

- ***A Strange and Distant Shore: Indians of the Great Plains in Exile,*** by Brent Ashabranner

Reading Support From Jamestown Education

- *Timed Readings Plus in Social Studies* helps students increase their reading rate and fluency while maintaining comprehension. The 400-word passages are similar to those found on state and national assessments.
- *Reading in the Content Area: Social Studies* concentrates on six essential reading skills that help students better comprehend what they read. The book includes 754 high-interest nonfiction passages written at increasing levels of difficulty.
- *Reading Fluency* helps students read smoothly, accurately, and expressively.
- *Jamestown's Reading Improvement,* by renowned reading expert Edward Fry, focuses on helping build your students' comprehension, vocabulary, and skimming and scanning skills.
- *Critical Reading Series* provides high-interest books, each written at three reading levels.

To order these products, call Glencoe at 1-800-334-7344.

KEY for Using the Teacher Wraparound Edition

Use this key to help you identify the different types of prompts found in the Teacher Wraparound Edition.

R **Reading Strategies** activities help you teach reading skills and vocabulary.

C **Critical Thinking** strategies help students apply and extend what they have learned.

U **Universal Access** activities provide differentiated instruction for students learning to speak English, along with suggestions for teaching various types of learners.

S **Skill Practice** strategies help students practice historical analysis and geography skills.

W **Writing Support** activities provide writing opportunities to help students comprehend the text.

Teaching strategies and activities have been coded for ability level appropriateness.

AL Activities for students working above grade level
OL Activities for students working on grade level
BL Activities for students working below grade level
EL Activities for English Learners

FOCUS

History–Social Science Standards

In this chapter, the following standard will be covered:

US8.12 Students analyze the transformation of the American economy and the changing social and political conditions in the United States in response to the Industrial Revolution.

More About the Photo

As part of the Great Plains, Wyoming was an ideal place for cattle ranches. Other pioneers established homesteads and made their living by growing wheat and other crops. Farmers used dry farming methods to take advantage of the water from rain and snow during the wet season.

Chapter 15

The Western Frontier

◀ Mother and child in a Wyoming wheat field

NATIONAL GEOGRAPHIC Who & When?

1860 | 1875 | 1890

1862 Homestead Act gives free land to settlers

1869 Transcontinental railroad links East and West

Populist Party banner

1890 Battle at Wounded Knee; Populist Party forms

TEACH

The Big Ideas

As you begin teaching each section, use these questions and activities to focus on the Big Ideas.

Section 1

The Mining Booms

Essential Question: What are the biggest geographic challenges we face in our area? How have people addressed them? After students have named challenges, such as climate, terrain, or others, explain that they will read about how people in one part of the United States faced and overcame serious geographic challenges. **OL**

Section 2

Ranchers and Farmers

Essential Question: What geographical factors might determine if someone becomes a crop farmer or a rancher? *(fertility of soil, terrain, climate, availability of water for irrigation, amount of land available)* Tell students that in this section they will learn about ranching and farming in the Great Plains and the West. **OL**

Section 3

Native American Struggles

Essential Question: What are some examples of differences in beliefs that can lead to division within a nation? *(Possible answers include political disagreements, regional differences, or cultural differences.)* Explain that in this section, students will learn about conflict between white settlers and Native Americans over land. **OL**

The Big Ideas

History Online

Chapter Overview Visit ca.hss.glencoe.com for a preview of Chapter 15.

Section 1 The Mining Booms

Geography shapes the physical, economic, and political challenges a region faces. Rail lines and mining speeded the flow of settlers to the West.

Section 2 Ranchers and Farmers

Geography shapes the physical, economic, and political challenges a region faces. Following the Civil War, settlers began to move west in great numbers.

Section 3 Native American Struggles

Differences in economic, political, and social beliefs and practices can lead to division within a nation and have lasting consequences. The settlement of white people in the West forced change on the Native Americans of the Plains.

Section 4 Farmers in Protest

Reactions to social injustice can lead to reform movements. In the late 1800s, farmers began to band together in groups and associations to fight their problems.

View the Chapter 15 video in the Glencoe Video Program.

FOLDABLES™ Study Organizer

Evaluating Information Make this foldable to organize information and ask yourself questions as you read about the western frontier of the United States.

Step 1 Fold a sheet of paper in half from side to side, leaving a $\frac{1}{2}$-inch tab along the side.

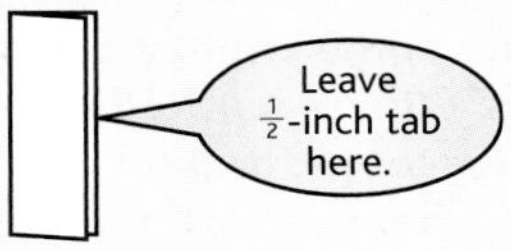

Step 2 Turn the paper and fold it into fourths.

Step 3 Unfold and cut along the three fold lines.

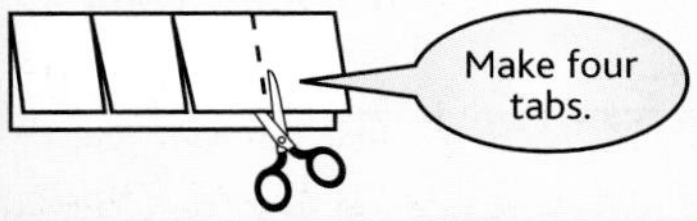

Step 4 Label your foldable as shown.

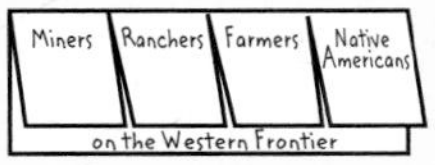

Reading and Writing As you read the chapter, ask yourself and write down questions (under each appropriate tab) about the tragedies and triumphs these four groups of people experienced during the expansion of the western frontier.

Section 4 Farmers in Protest

Have students think of a reform movement that has arisen in the nation, either in the past or currently. **Essential Question:** What events or conditions led to the movement's formation? After students answer the question, tell them that in this section they will read about reform that arose over economic issues. **OL**

History Online

Go to ca.hss.glencoe.com for student activities, lesson plans, and links to additional Web resources about the opening of the West.

FOLDABLES™ Study Organizer Dinah Zike's Foldables

Purpose Have students use their foldables to ask themselves questions about the experiences of Americans on the western frontier. Students might also quiz each other to review. **OL**

Why It's Important

Visualizing Many students, not only visual learners, will benefit from visualizing the events, places, and people they read about in the text. Looking for descriptive words that aid visualizing will also help them become more attentive readers.

1 Learn It!

Ask students to visualize a place they know well, such as a room at home. Have them write down 10 words that describe this place. Then ask them to show the words to a partner and have the partner try to describe the place. After both partners have tried to describe the place using the words, have them discuss which words were most helpful in visualizing the unfamiliar place. Then have them read the paragraph on page 664 and point out words and phrases that help them visualize the scene described. OL

Chapter 15 Get Ready to Read

Visualizing

READING SKILL

1 Learn It!

Creating pictures in your mind as you read—called visualizing—is a powerful aid to understanding. If you can visualize what you read, selections will be more vivid, and you will recall them better later. Authors use descriptive language to create a picture of a person, location, time, or event. These words appeal to the senses and may evoke sights, sounds, or smells. Authors also use words to describe feelings and emotions to make the text come alive to the reader. Good readers take the time to visualize people, places, and events. As you read the following paragraphs, make a picture in your mind of life in a boomtown.

Boomtowns were largely men's towns in the early days. Men outnumbered women by two to one in Virginia City, and children made up less than 10 percent of the population.

Eager to share in the riches of the boomtowns, some women opened businesses. Others worked as laundresses, cooks, or dance-hall entertainers. Women often added stability to the boomtowns, founding schools and churches and working to make the communities safer.

—from page 668

Reading Tip

Look for descriptive words or images in the text to help you form a visual image of what you read.

664

READING STRATEGY **ACTIVATING PRIOR KNOWLEDGE**

Writers do not always provide every detail in descriptions of people or places. Students can use prior knowledge to help themselves fill in the gaps. **Ask:** When you visualized boomtowns, what material did you think people used to make the town buildings? Why? *(Students are likely to say wood because they know that this was a common building material at the time.)* Encourage students to continue to apply their prior knowledge to other readings. OL

2 Practice It!

Now read the section below about cowhands. Discuss your impressions with a partner and then reread the selection. Did your visual image change at all?

Read to Write

Think about your favorite place. In writing, describe the picture you have in your mind. Use vivid language and descriptive details.

Many cowhands were veterans of the Confederate army. Some were African Americans who moved west in search of a better life after the Civil War. Others were Hispanics. In fact, the traditions of cattle herding began with Hispanic ranch hands in the Spanish Southwest. These vaqueros (vah • KEHR • ohs) developed many of the skills—riding, roping, and branding—that cowhands used on the drives. Much of the language of the rancher today is derived from Spanish words used by vaqueros for centuries. Even the word *ranch* comes from the Spanish word *rancho.*

The cowhand's equipment was based on the vaquero's equipment too. Cowhands wore wide-brimmed hats to protect themselves from the sun and leather leggings, called chaps, to shield their legs from brush and mishaps with cattle. They used ropes called lariats to lasso cattle that strayed from the herd.

—from page 674

Cowhand Nat Love

3 Apply It!

Before you begin reading this chapter, look at all the photographs, maps, and illustrations to help you visualize what you are about to read.

2 Practice It!

Have students read the passage on page 665. After they have discussed their impressions with a partner, ask volunteers to describe such items as chaps and lariats and such procedures as roping and branding. Discuss whether students developed similar images of these objects and practices and what words provided clues to how they looked. OL

3 Apply It!

Have students read a passage from a history book or historical novel that describes a person, group of people, or place in history. Ask them to write a brief description of how that person, group, or place looks to them. You may wish to allow students to draw or paint the image if they wish. OL

READING STRATEGY MONITORING

Remind students that they can use their ability to visualize to monitor the clarity and effectiveness of their own writing. When they are writing a description of something or a narrative of an event, they should carefully read what they have written and try to visualize it. As they do so, they should ask themselves whether the picture that they develop is an accurate one. If not, they will know that they need to revise their writing. Have students use this technique to evaluate what they write for the Apply It! activity suggested above. OL

Use Reading Skills Activity 15 in the **Chapter 15 Resource Book** for more practice with visualizing.

FOCUS

BELLRINGER
SKILLBUILDER ACTIVITY

Project **Daily Focus Skills Transparency 15–1** and have students answer the question.

Guide to Reading

Preteaching Vocabulary: Have students look up unfamiliar vocabulary words using the Glossary in the back of their textbook. Then have them use each term in a sentence.

Answers to Graphic: Pikes Peak: Discovery of gold started rush to Colorado; Comstock Lode: Discovery of silver started rush to Nevada, gave birth to Virginia City; Promontory Summit: Transcontinental railroad completed

Unpacking the Standards

After reading the section, students will be able to:

- Discuss the discoveries of gold and silver that sent miners west.
- Explain how boomtowns grew and describe them.
- Identify ways that the transcontinental railroad changed life in the West.

Section 1: The Mining Booms

Guide to Reading

History Social Science Standards

US8.12 Students analyze the transformation of the American economy and the changing social and political conditions in the United States in response to the Industrial Revolution.

Looking Back, Looking Ahead
You read earlier about how the California Gold Rush brought thousands of people to California to try to make their fortunes. In the late 1850s, many more miners headed west as more precious metals were discovered.

Focusing on the Main Ideas
- In the late 1850s, discoveries of gold and silver sent miners flocking to the American West. *(page 667)*
- A number of boomtowns grew quickly in the mining areas of the West. *(page 668)*
- Railroads grew rapidly in the period following the Civil War. *(page 669)*

Locating Places
Pikes Peak
Virginia City, Nevada
Promontory Summit

Meeting People
Leland Stanford

Content Vocabulary
lode (LOHD)
ore
boomtown
vigilante (VIH • juh • LAN • tee)
subsidy (SUHB • suh • dee)
transcontinental (TRANS • kahn • tuhn • EHN • tuhl)

Academic Vocabulary
extract (ihk • STRAKT)
obtain (uhb • TAYN)

Reading Strategy
Analyzing Information As you read the section, re-create the diagram below and explain why these places were significant to the mining boom.

	Significance
Pikes Peak	
Comstock Lode	
Promontory Summit	

Where & When?
NATIONAL GEOGRAPHIC

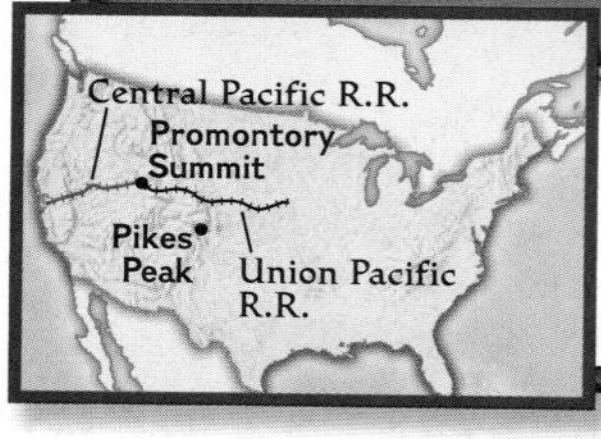

1855		1865		1875
	1858 Gold is discovered at Pikes Peak		**1869** Transcontinental railroad links East and West	**1876** Colorado joins the Union

SECTION RESOURCES

Print Material
- Reproducible Lesson Plan 15–1*
- Daily Lesson and Discussion Notes 15–1
- Guided Reading Activity 15–1
- Reading Essentials and Study Guide 15–1
- Active Reading Note-Taking Guide 15–1
- Section Quiz 15–1

Transparencies
- Daily Focus Skills Transparency 15–1
- Section Graphic Organizer Transparency 15–1
- California Standards Practice Transparencies

Technology
- Interactive Tutor Self-Assessment CD-ROM
- Exam*View*® Pro Testmaker CD-ROM
- Presentation Plus! CD-ROM

*Available on TeacherWorks™

US8.12.1 Trace patterns of agricultural and industrial development as they relate to climate, use of natural resources, markets, and trade and locate such development on a map.

Mining Is Big Business

Main Idea **In the late 1850s, discoveries of gold and silver sent miners flocking to the American West.**

Reading Connection Have you ever wanted to take part in a great adventure? Read to find out about the gold and silver rushes that lured thousands of Americans into the West.

An American Story

C1

"We'll need no pick or spade, no shovel, pan, or hoe, the largest chunks are 'top of ground. . . . We'll see hard times no more, and want [we'll] never know, when once we've filled our sacks with gold, Way out in Idaho."

—from *Way Out in Idaho*

Miners sang this hopeful song as they headed for new places where gold had been discovered.

Picturing **History**

A miner works the Comstock Lode.
Where was the Comstock Lode located?

Searching for Gold and Silver By the mid-1850s, the California Gold Rush had ended. R1 Miners, still hoping to strike it rich, began prospecting in other parts of the West.

In 1858 a mining expedition found gold on the slopes of **Pikes Peak** in the Colorado Rockies. C2 Newspapers claimed that miners were making $20 a day panning for gold—a large sum at a time when servants made less than a dollar a day. By the spring of 1859, about 50,000 prospectors had flocked to Colorado. Their slogan was "Pikes Peak or Bust."

Prospectors skimmed gold dust from streams or scratched particles of gold from the surface of the land. R2 Most of the gold, however, was deep in underground **lodes** (LOHDZ), rich streaks of ore sandwiched between layers of rock. Mining this rock, or **ore,** and then **extracting** the gold required expensive machinery, many workers, and an organized business. Companies made up of several investors had a better chance of getting rich in the goldfields than individual miners did. Mining companies soon replaced the lone miner.

The Comstock Lode In 1859 several prospectors found a rich lode of silver-bearing ore on the banks of the Carson River in Nevada. The discovery was called the Comstock Lode after Henry Comstock, who owned a share of the claim.

Thousands of mines opened near the site, but only a few were profitable. Mining companies reaped the largest share of the profits. When Comstock sold his share of the claim, he received $11,000 and two mules—a huge sum at the time. It was, however, just a tiny fraction of the hundreds of millions of dollars worth of gold and silver pulled from the Comstock Lode strike.

Reading Check **Describe** What was the Comstock Lode?

Did You Know?

Many prospectors mistook pyrite, also known as "fool's gold," for the real thing. Although it closely resembles gold, it behaves differently when subjected to tests. Gold does not break when hammered, as pyrite does. Gold will not melt when held in a campfire on a shovel. Gold also is not affected by cold or acid.

Picturing **History**

Answer: on the banks of the Carson River in Nevada

TEACH

C1 Critical Thinking

Analyzing Primary Sources
Ask: What is the general tone of the song? How do you know? What might account for this tone? *(The general tone is excited and optimistic; the reason is their hope to strike it rich.)* OL
CA HR5.

R1 Reading Strategy

Scaffolding—Academic Vocabulary The word *prospect* was introduced in Chapter 13, Section 2. Ask students how the meaning of *prospect* relates to the meaning of *prospecting*. OL

C2 Critical Thinking

Making Generalizations
To test students' ability to generalize from details, **ask:** Did only servants leave their jobs to try to find gold at Pikes Peak? *(Students should recognize that, although servants' wages are mentioned, that is just an example of how low wages were at the time and not meant to suggest that all miners were former servants.)*
OL CA 8RC2.4

R2 Reading Strategy

Understanding Vocabulary
Ask students to use the words *lode* and *ore* in a sentence that explains how they are related.
BL CA 8RW1.3

Reading Check

Answer: rich lode of silver ore discovered in 1859 in Nevada

W Writing Support

Expository Writing Have students write a letter to a friend back east about what it was like to live in a boomtown. AL CA 8WA2.1

R Reading Strategy

Understanding Vocabulary Have students use the two terms on this page in answering this question: Who was responsible for law and order in the new mining towns? *(Citizens known as vigilantes often took the job of enforcing justice in boomtowns.)* OL CA 8RW1.3

Review The Big Idea

Review the Big Idea for this section: "Geography shapes the physical, economic, and political challenges a region faces." **Ask:** How did the geography of the West lead to a boom and bust cycle in some areas? *(Rich lodes of ore attracted many people, but when the mines ran out most people left.)* OL CA CS3.

Reading Check

Answer: Prospectors deserted many boomtowns when the mines no longer had ore.

Answers and Additional Support

US8.12.1 Trace patterns of agricultural and industrial development as they relate to climate, use of natural resources, markets, and trade and locate such development on a map.

The Mining Frontier

W

Main Idea **A number of boomtowns grew quickly in the mining areas of the West.**

Reading Connection Have you ever seen a deserted section of a city where a factory has closed? Read to find out what happened to many mining towns in the West after the gold or silver in nearby mines was gone.

The gold strikes created **boomtowns**—towns that grew up almost overnight around mining sites. The Comstock boomtown was **Virginia City, Nevada.** In 1859 the town was a mining camp. Two years later, it had a stock exchange, hotels, banks, an opera company, and five newspapers.

Boomtowns were lively, and often lawless, places. Money came quickly—and was often spent just as quickly through extravagant living and gambling. A fortunate miner could earn as much as $2,000 a year, about four times the annual salary of a teacher at that time. Still food, lodging, clothing, and other goods were expensive in the boomtowns, draining miners' earnings.

R

Violence was part of everyday life in boomtowns. Few boomtowns had police or prisons, so citizens sometimes took the law into their own hands. These **vigilantes** (VIH • juh • LAN • tees) dealt out their own brand of justice without benefit of judge or jury, often hanging the accused person from the nearest tree.

Women in the Boomtowns Boomtowns were largely men's towns in the early days. Men outnumbered women by two to one in Virginia City, and children made up less than 10 percent of the population.

Eager to share in the riches of the boomtowns, some women opened businesses. Others worked as laundresses, cooks, or dance-hall entertainers. Women often added stability to the boomtowns, founding schools and churches and working to make the communities safer.

Changing Industry Many mining "booms" were followed by "busts." When the mines no longer yielded ore, people left the towns, and the deserted mine towns became known as ghost towns. At its peak in the 1870s, Virginia City had about 30,000 inhabitants. By 1900 its population had dropped to fewer than 4,000. Toward the end of the rush, gold and silver mining in some places gave way to the mining of other metals. Copper became the key metal found in Montana, New Mexico, and Arizona in the 1870s.

Mining helped the economy, but it hurt the environment. Wildlife was hunted to provide meat for the miners. Mining led to high levels of arsenic and mercury in the ground that contaminated land, lakes, and rivers.

What Were the New States? Frontier areas around the boomtowns eventually became states. Colorado joined the United States in 1876. North Dakota, South Dakota, Washington, and Montana became states in 1889. Wyoming and Idaho were admitted to the Union in 1890.

Reading Check **Explain** Why did the population drop in many boomtowns?

Picturing History

The boomtown of Leadville, Colorado, surrounds a settler's cabin that sits in the middle of the main street. ***What happened to many boomtowns when the mines closed?***

668

More Skill Practice

Historical and Social Sciences Analysis Skill Have students write a paragraph describing the life cycle of a boomtown. Have them start with the beginnings of the mining activities and then describe subsequent steps in the rise and fall of the towns. OL CA HI2.

Picturing History

The area around Leadville yielded both gold and silver. At the town's height in the 1880s, 30,000 people lived there. At the end of the twentieth century, Leadville was home to about 3,000 people.

Answer: Many lost most or all of their population.

US8.12.1 Trace patterns of agricultural and industrial development as they relate to climate, use of natural resources, markets, and trade and locate such development on a map. **US8.12.3** Explain how states and the federal government encouraged business expansion through tariffs, banking, land grants, and subsidies.

Railroads Connect East to West

Main Idea **Railroads grew rapidly in the period following the Civil War.**

Reading Connection Would you like to travel across the country by train? Read to find out how the first railroad to connect the east and west coasts was completed in 1869.

The western mines operated far from the industrial centers of the East and Midwest. For this reason, transportation played a vital role in the survival of mining communities. Gold and silver had little value unless they could reach factories, ports, and markets. At the same time, the miners and others in the boomtowns needed shipments of food and other supplies.

Wagon trains and stagecoach lines could not move people and goods fast enough to meet these demands. Railroads could—and did. The nation's railroad network expanded rapidly between 1865 and 1890. During that period, the number of miles of track in the United States grew from about 35,000 to more than 150,000.

Railroad construction was often supported by large government **subsidies** (SUHB•suh•dees)—financial aid and land grants from the government. Railroad executives pushed for free public land on which to lay track because a rail network would benefit the entire nation. The national government and states agreed. In all, the federal government granted more than 130 million acres of land to the railroad companies. Much of the land was purchased or **obtained** by treaties from Native Americans. The government grants included the land for the tracks plus strips of land along the railway, 20 to 80 miles wide. Railroad companies sold those strips of land to raise additional money for construction costs.

TECHNOLOGY & History

Steam Locomotive

Since 1825, when the first steam locomotive was built in the United States, trains have crisscrossed the country. As America's transportation needs increased, so did the miles of railroad track linking its people. **Why do you think steam power was the first power source for locomotives?**

1. The **firebox** burns coal, wood, or sometimes oil.
2. Water in the **boiler,** heated by gases from the firebox, creates steam.
3. The **smokebox** draws hot gases from the firebox and keeps an even fire.
4. In the **steam header tank,** the heated steam expands and creates great pressure.
5. Hot steam is piped to the **pistons.** The pistons power the **drive rods,** which in turn push the **drive wheels.**

More Skill Practice

Visual Literacy Give students these figures for the number of miles of railroad track in the U.S.—1860: 31,000 miles; 1870: 53,000 miles; 1880: 93,000 miles; 1890: 150,000 miles; and 1900: 193,000 miles.
Ask: What kind of graph would be best for showing this data? Why? *(Bar graph; because you can compare the years)* **OL**

TECHNOLOGY & History

The first public railroad in the world opened in Great Britain in 1825 and ran for 25 miles (32 km). The first public railroad in the United States opened in 1830. Railroads remained the nation's chief form of long-distance transportation until passenger airplanes took over in the late twentieth century.

Answer: Students may say that fuel (wood or coal) was readily available.

R1 Reading Strategy

Scaffolding—Identifying the Main Idea and Supporting Details **Ask:** What is the main idea of this paragraph? *(Railroads were better than other methods for meeting the transportation needs of the West.)* **OL**

This READING SKILL was introduced in Chapter 2.

R2 Reading Strategy

Connecting **Ask:** What kinds of subsidies does the government give today? *(Answers may include subsidies to farmers or tax breaks to businesses.)* **OL** **CA HI3.**

C Critical Thinking

Drawing Conclusions Ask students to write a paragraph either supporting or opposing the railroad executives' argument that they should be given free land because the railroads benefit the entire nation. *(Those supporting the argument may cite the benefits of a rail network and the economic growth railroads brought. Those opposed may claim that in a free market economy, it is wrong for some businesses to receive government subsidies while others do not.)* **AL** **CA 8WS1.3**

W Writing Support

Narrative Writing Have students write a narrative describing how the steam engine of a locomotive works to power a train. **OL** **CA 8WA2.6**

R1 Reading Strategy

Using Word Parts Remind students that the Latin prefix *trans-* means "across." **Ask:** What are some other words using that prefix? *(transportation, transfer, transatlantic)* OL

C Critical Thinking

Identifying Central Issues Ask students to list specific problems in laying track in different types of terrain, such as mountains, plains, and deserts. *(Mountains: blasting through rock, building tunnels; Plains: attacks from Native Americans, heat, storms, cold in winter; Deserts: extreme heat, sandstorms, lack of water, hard to lay track in shifting sands)* OL CA HI2.

U Universal Access

Auditory/Musical Have students compose a team song, rap, or cheer for one of the companies building the transcontinental railroad. Ask volunteers to share their creations with the class. AL

Answers and Additional Support

History *Through Art*

The Race* by Mort Kunstler** The artist is well-known for his realistic paintings about dramatic events in American history. ***What does the painting express about the American West?

States and local communities also helped the railroads. Towns offered cash subsidies to make sure that railroads came to their communities. For example, Los Angeles gave the Southern Pacific Railroad money and paid for a passenger terminal to ensure that the railroad would pass through its town.

R1 **Spanning the Continent** The search for a route for a **transcontinental** (TRANS • kahn • tuhn • EHN • tuhl) rail line—one that would span the continent and connect the Atlantic and Pacific coasts—began in the 1850s. During the Civil War, the Union government chose a northerly route for the line. The government offered land grants to railroad companies that were willing to build the transcontinental railroad.

C The challenge was enormous—laying track for more than 1,700 miles across hot plains and through rugged mountains. Two companies accepted the challenge. The Union Pacific Company began laying track westward from Omaha, Nebraska, while the Central Pacific Company worked eastward from Sacramento, California. The two companies competed fiercely. Each wanted to cover a greater distance in order to receive more of the government subsidies.

U The Central Pacific hired about 10,000 Chinese laborers to work on its tracks. The first Chinese were hired in 1865 at about $28 per month. The Union Pacific relied on Irish and African American workers. All workers toiled for low wages in harsh conditions. In the choking heat of summer and the icy winds of winter, they cleared forests, blasted tunnels through mountains, and laid hundreds of miles of track. In the end, the Union Pacific workers laid 1,038 miles of track; Central Pacific workers laid 742 miles over a much harsher terrain.

The Transcontinental Railway On May 10, 1869, construction was completed. A Chinese crew was chosen to lay the final 10 miles of track, which was completed in only 12 hours. The two sets of track met at **Promontory Summit** in Utah Territory.

History *Through Art*

Have students discuss which aspects of the painting would require historical research to ensure their accuracy. *(Answers may include the look of the train and stagecoach and the number of horses drawing the coach.)*

Answer: wide open spaces, exciting lives, an attitude of adventure

More Skill Practice

Using Geography Skills Have students look at a physical map of the United States and follow the route of the transcontinental railroad from Omaha to Sacramento. **Ask:** Which company had a more difficult job, the Union Pacific or the Central Pacific? Why? *(Students may say the Central Pacific because it had to cross more mountains.)* OL CA CS3.

W Leland Stanford, governor of California, drove a final golden spike into a tie to join the two railroads. According to Grenville Dodge, chief engineer for the Union Pacific:

> "Prayer was offered; a number of spikes were driven in the two adjoining rails. . . . The engineers ran up their locomotives until they touched . . . and thus the two roads were welded into one great trunk line from the Atlantic to the Pacific."
>
> —from *Mine Eyes Have Seen*

What Effects Did Railroads Have? By 1883 two more transcontinental lines and dozens of shorter lines connected cities in the West with the rest of the nation. The railroads brought thousands of workers to the West. Trains carried metals and produce east and manufactured goods west. As more tracks were laid, more steel was needed, and the demand boosted the nation's steel industry. Coal producers, railroad car manufacturers, and construction companies also thrived as the railroads spread across the West.

Towns sprang up along the rail lines that carried farm goods to market. Some of these towns eventually grew into large cities such as Denver, Colorado. The railroads also brought the next wave of new settlers to the West—cattle ranchers and farmers.

C Railroads even changed how people measured time. Before railroads, each community kept its own time. Clocks in Boston, for example, were 11 minutes ahead of clocks in New York. The demand for sensible train schedules, however, changed that. In 1883 the railroad companies divided the country into four time zones. All communities in each zone would share the same time, and each zone was exactly one hour apart from the zones on either side of it. Congress passed a law making this practice official in 1918.

Reading Check **Identify** To what California city did the transcontinental railroad extend?

History Online **Study Central** Need help understanding how mining affected railroad growth? Visit ca.hss.glencoe.com and click on Study Central.

Section 1 Review

Reading Summary

Review the Main Ideas

- New discoveries of gold and silver, such as those at the Comstock Lode, brought thousands of miners to the West.
- Many of the boomtowns that developed as miners rushed to the West became ghost towns as the mines became depleted.
- The transcontinental railway connecting the East and West coasts was completed in 1869.

What Did You Learn?

1. Describe life in a boomtown.
2. What are subsidies, and why did the railroads receive them?

Critical Thinking

3. **Determining Cause and Effect** Re-create the diagram below and explain how railroads helped open the West to settlement. CA HI2.

Coming of the railroad
Effect | Effect

4. **The Big Ideas** What were the economic effects of building railroads? CA HI6.
5. **Drawing Conclusions** Some boomtowns thrived after the mining boom, but others became ghost towns. Why do you think some towns survived and others did not? CA HR3.
6. **READING Visualizing** Imagine you are a prospector. Write a short paragraph describing what it was like to arrive at Pikes Peak in early summer 1859. Use strong, descriptive language so that your reader can visualize the scene. CA 8WA2.1

W Writing Support

Expository Writing Have students take the role of one of the officials at Promontory Summit and write a brief speech celebrating the completion of the railroad. Remind students to have a clear thesis and supporting details. OL CA 8WS1.1

C Critical Thinking

Determining Cause and Effect **Ask:** Why did the railroads want to standardize how time was measured? *(to make it easier to schedule trains)* OL

ASSESS

Resources for page 671

Use these resources to assess student mastery of section content.

- Analysis Skills Activity 15
- Section Quiz 15–1
- Interactive Tutor Self-Assessment CD-ROM

Reading Check

Answer: Sacramento

History Online

Study Central provides summaries, interactive games, and online graphic organizers to help students review section content.

CLOSE

Evaluating **Ask:** Which do you think was more important for the development of the West, mines or railroads? Why? OL CA HI2.

SECTION 1 REVIEW ANSWERS

Review questions reinforce content standard US8.12.

1. lively, violent, often lawless
2. financial aid and land grants from the government; to encourage them to build more railroads
3. Brought workers to the West; Transported goods; Boosted new industries; Encouraged growth of towns
4. **The Big Ideas** They brought thousands of new workers to the West, boosted other industries, made it easier and cheaper to ship manufactured goods and crops
5. Factors may include location and availability of other ways to make a living.
6. **READING** Answers will vary but should use strong descriptive language.

FOCUS

BELLRINGER
SKILLBUILDER ACTIVITY

Project **Daily Focus Skills Transparency 15–2** and have students answer the question.

Guide to Reading

Preteaching Vocabulary: Use the Vocabulary PuzzleMaker CD-ROM to create crossword and word search puzzles.

Answers to Graphic: Weather, Separation from other families, New farming methods, Debt

Unpacking the Standards

After reading the section, students will be able to:

- Explain how railroads made ranching profitable on the Great Plains.
- Describe the difficult work of cowhands.
- Discuss why thousands of settlers moved to the Great Plains.

Section 2

Ranchers and Farmers

History Social Science Standards

US8.11 Students analyze the character and lasting consequences of Reconstruction.

US8.12 Students analyze the transformation of the American economy and the changing social and political conditions in the United States in response to the Industrial Revolution.

Guide to Reading

Looking Back, Looking Ahead

You learned that the transcontinental railroad linked the East and the West in 1869. The new railroads promoted ranching and farming in the Great Plains and the West.

Focusing on the Main Ideas

- Cattle ranching in Texas became a profitable business once the new railroad reached the Great Plains. *(page 673)*
- The work of the cowhands who drove the cattle north from Texas to the railroads was both difficult and dangerous. *(page 674)*
- Free land and new farming methods brought many settlers to the Great Plains. *(page 676)*

Locating Places

Sedalia, Missouri
Abilene, Kansas
Dodge City, Kansas
Cheyenne, Wyoming

Content Vocabulary

open range
brand
vaquero (vah • KEHR • oh)
homestead (HOHM • STEHD)
sodbuster (SAHD • BUHS • tuhr)
dry farming

Academic Vocabulary

derive (dih • RYV)
acquire (uh • KWYR)

Reading Strategy

Taking Notes As you read the section, re-create the diagram below and list the challenges settlers faced on the Great Plains.

NATIONAL GEOGRAPHIC **Where & When?**

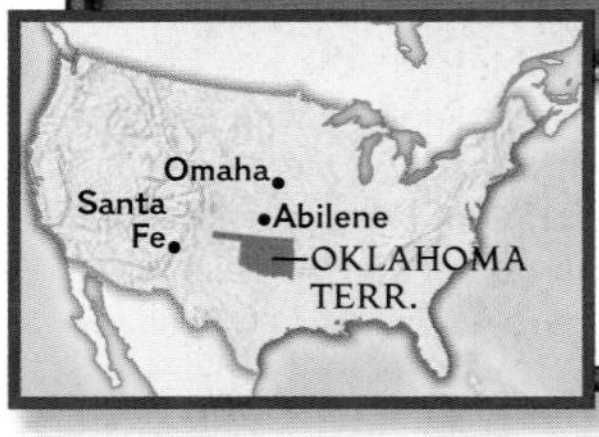

1860	1875	1890
1862 Homestead Act gives free land to settlers	**1867** Town of Abilene founded	**1889** Oklahoma land rush takes place

SECTION RESOURCES

Print Material
- Reproducible Lesson Plan 15–2*
- Daily Lesson and Discussion Notes 15–2
- Guided Reading Activity 15–2
- Reading Essentials and Study Guide 15–2
- Active Reading Note-Taking Guide 15–2
- Section Quiz 15–2

Transparencies
- Daily Focus Skills Transparency 15–2
- Section Graphic Organizer Transparency 15–2
- California Standards Practice Transparencies

Technology
- Interactive Tutor Self-Assessment CD-ROM
- Exam*View*® Pro Testmaker CD-ROM
- Presentation Plus! CD-ROM

*Available on TeacherWorks™

Cattle on the Plains

Main Idea **Cattle ranching in Texas became a profitable business once the new railroad reached the Great Plains.**

Reading Connection Have you seen large trucks on highways carrying food and supplies to stores? Read to find out about the long, difficult journey that cowhands had to make in order for America's eastern cities to get beef in the mid-1800s.

An American Story

An old Texas cowhand, E.C. Abbott, recalled the early days of riding the trail:

> **"Here [were] all these cheap long-horned steers overrunning Texas; here was the rest of the country crying for beef—and no railroads to get them out. So they trailed them out, across hundreds of miles of wild country that was thick with Indians. . . . In 1867 the town of Abilene was founded at the end of the Kansas Pacific Railroad and that was when the trail really started."**
>
> —from *We Pointed Them North*

The Texas Open Range When the Spanish settled Mexico and Texas, they brought a tough breed of cattle with them. Called longhorns because of their prominent horns, these cattle gradually spread across Texas.

R1 At this time, much of Texas was **open range**—not fenced or divided into lots. Huge ranches covered other areas of the state. Ranchers added to their own herds by rounding up wild cattle. The ranchers burned a U **brand,** or symbol, into the animals' hides to show who owned the cattle.

Railroads and Cow Towns Although Texas ranchers had plenty of cattle, the markets for beef were in the North and the East. In 1866 the Missouri Pacific Railroad reached Missouri, and Texas cattle suddenly increased in value. The cattle could be loaded onto trains in Missouri for shipment north and east. R2 Some Texans drove their combined herds—sometimes 260,000 head of cattle—north to **Sedalia, Missouri,** the nearest rail point. Longhorns that had formerly been worth $3 each quickly rose in value to $40.

Cattle drives to cow towns—towns located near railroads to market and ship cattle—turned into a yearly event. Over the next decade, cow towns such as **Abilene, Kansas, Dodge City, Kansas,** and **Cheyenne, Wyoming,** became important rail stations.

What was the Long Drive? The sudden increase in the longhorns' value began what became known as the Long Drive—the herding of cattle 1,000 miles or more to meet the railroads. The drives left Texas in the spring, when there was enough grass along the way to feed the cattle. During the heyday of the "Cattle Kingdom," from the late 1860s to the mid-1880s, the trails carried more than 5 million cattle north.

Reading Check **Explain** Why did the value of cattle increase in the mid-1860s?

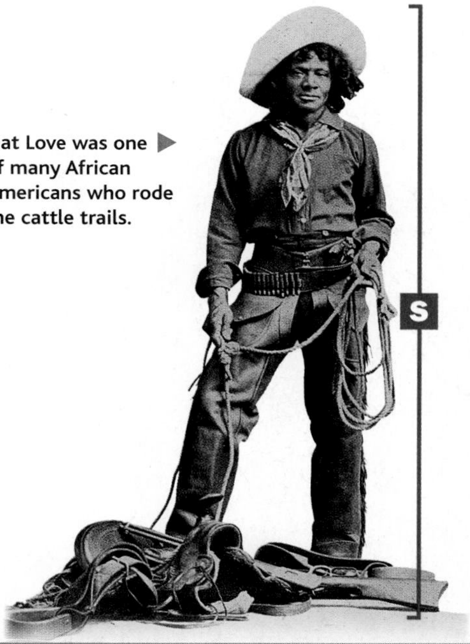

S

Nat Love was one of many African Americans who rode the cattle trails.

Chapter 15 • Section 2

TEACH

R1 Reading Strategy

Understanding Vocabulary **Ask:** Why was the range called open? *(because it was unfenced)* OL CA 8RW1.3

U Universal Access

Below Grade Level **Ask:** How is the word *brand* used today? *(a trademarked name for a product)* How is that similar to the use here? *(both uses express ownership)* BL

R2 Reading Strategy

Reading Maps, Graphs, and Charts Have students find the named cow towns on a map of the United States. Ask them to trace the routes of cattle drives, starting in Texas. *(Routes ran north from central and southern Texas.)* OL CA CS3.

S Skill Practice

Visual Literacy Ask students to look for details in the photograph that show Nat Love was a cowboy. Have them explain why each element was important for a cowboy. *(Lariat—used to rope cattle; Hat—to shade the sun; Bandana—protect mouth from dust; Saddle—for riding; Guns—for protection; Chaps—for protecting legs)* OL CA 8LS1.9

Reading Check

Answer: Completion of the railroads made it easier to ship cattle to the North and East, the major markets for beef.

More Skill Practice

Historical and Social Sciences Analysis Skill Have students write a paragraph about the cause-and-effect relationship of cattle prices and the railroads. *(Paragraphs should describe the great rise in cattle value when it became possible to ship them to eastern markets by train.)* BL CA HI6.

Did You Know?

At roundup time there were usually some motherless calves who came to be called *dough-guts*. That name came from the fact that the calves were weaned prematurely, which left their stomachs underdeveloped and unable to digest grass, which made their stomachs swell like rising dough when they ate. The name was later shortened to *dogies*.

R1 Reading Strategy

Questioning Ask students to write five questions, with answers, about the content of the subsection "Life on the Trail." Have them write each question on a strip of paper, with the answer on the reverse side. Then put all the questions in a hat. Have one student act as quizmaster, drawing a slip and asking the question to the class. OL

CA HR1.

S Skill Practice

Historical and Social Sciences Analysis Skill Have students create a diagram showing the influence of vaqueros on the cowboy of the West. *(Diagrams should include the influences discussed in the text.)* BL CA HI3.

R2 Reading Strategy

Understanding Vocabulary Remind students that English has many loan words from other languages. Have students look for other English words on this page that they suspect come from Spanish. *(Possible answers include* ranch, chaps, lariat, stampede, *and* lassoing.*)* EL

US8.12.1 Trace patterns of agricultural and industrial development as they relate to climate, use of natural resources, markets, and trade and locate such development on a map.

Life on the Trail

R1 **Main Idea** **The work of the cowhands who drove the cattle north from Texas to the railroads was both difficult and dangerous.**

Reading Connection What do you know about cowhands in the old West based on the movies you have seen? Read to find out about the hazards faced by cowhands on the trail and what life in the "Wild West" was really like.

The cattle drives and the cowhands who worked on them captured the imagination of the nation. Cattle driving, however, was hard work. Cowhands rode in the saddle for up to 15 hours every day, in driving rain, dust storms, and blazing sun. Life on the trail was lonely too. Cowhands saw few outsiders.

Spanish Influence Many cowhands were veterans of the Confederate army. Some were African Americans who moved west in search of a better life after the Civil War. Others were S Hispanics. In fact, the traditions of cattle herding began with Hispanic ranch hands in the Spanish Southwest. These **vaqueros** (vah•KEHR•ohs) developed many of the skills—riding, roping, and branding—that cowhands used on the drives. Much of the language of the rancher today is **derived** from Spanish words used by vaqueros for centuries. Even the word *ranch* comes from the Spanish word *rancho*. R2

The cowhand's equipment was based on the vaquero's equipment too. Cowhands wore wide-brimmed hats to protect themselves from the sun and leather leggings, called chaps, to shield their legs from brush and mishaps with cattle. They used ropes called lariats to lasso cattle that strayed from the herd.

Hazards on the Trail During the months on the trail, the cowhands faced violent storms, rustlers who tried to steal cattle, and many other dangers. They had to drive the herds across swift-flowing rivers, where cattle could be lost. One of the greatest dangers on the trail was the stampede, when thousands of cattle ran in panic.

History *Through Art*

Jerked Down* by Charles Russell** Celebrated for his detailed and dramatic scenes of Western life, Charles Russell depicts cowhands on their horses lassoing cattle. ***Where did the traditions of cattle herding begin?

Answers and Additional Support

History *Through Art*

Charles Russell (1864–1926) was a self-taught painter, sculptor, illustrator, and writer. He produced more than 100 bronze sculptures and thousands of paintings.

Answer: with Hispanic ranch hands in the Spanish Southwest

Resources for page 674

- American Literature Reading 15
- American Art And Architecture Transparency 23

Any sudden sound—a roar of thunder or the crack of a gunshot—could set off the cattle. Then the cowhands had to race on horseback with the stampeding cattle and bring them under control.

African American, Native American, Hispanic, and Anglo cowhands met and worked together. Yet discrimination existed in the West just as it did elsewhere in the nation. Non-Anglo cowhands rarely became trail bosses and often received less pay for their work. Some towns discriminated against Hispanics, segregated African Americans, and excluded Chinese cowhands altogether.

C After many tiring weeks on the trail, the cowhands delivered their cattle and enjoyed some time off in cow towns. Cowhands drank and gambled, and got involved in fistfights and gunplay. Some towns, such as Dodge City and Abilene, were rowdy, lawless, and often violent. Eventually, though, they grew into settled, businesslike communities.

Ranching Becomes Big Business Ranchers were building herds in Wyoming, Montana, and other territories. At the same time, sheep ranchers were moving their flocks across the range, and farmers were trying to cultivate crops. Competition over land use and access resulted U in range wars. After much loss of life, the range was fenced off with a new invention—barbed wire—which enabled hundreds of square miles to be fenced off cheaply and easily.

At first, ranchers saw barbed wire as more of a threat than an opportunity. They did not want to abandon open grazing and complained when farmers put up barriers that prevented livestock from roaming freely. Soon, however, ranchers used barbed wire to shut out those competing with them for land and to keep their animals closer to sources of food and water. For cowhands, barbed wire ended the excitement of long cattle drives. Ranch hands replaced cowboys.

S **The Cattle Kingdom Ends** As profits from cattle increased, cattle ranching spread north from Texas. On the northern Plains, ranchers crossbred the longhorns with fatter Hereford and Angus cattle to produce hardy, plumper new breeds.

The sturdy crossbred cattle multiplied on open-range ranches. When cattle prices boomed in the early 1880s, ranchers became rich. The boom, however, was soon followed by a bust. Overgrazing depleted the grasslands. In addition, too many cattle glutted the beef market and prices fell. The bitterly cold winters of 1885 and 1886 killed large numbers of cattle.

The price collapse of the mid-1880s marked the end of the "Cattle Kingdom." The cattle industry survived, but was changed forever. Another type of life would rise on the Plains—farming.

Reading Check **Describe** How did the Hispanics influence life in the West?

Picturing **History**

Books like *The Beef Bonanza* by General Brisbin helped fuel the cattle boom. ***Why did the cattle boom collapse?***

C Critical Thinking

Identifying Central Issues Ask students to imagine they are the mayor of a cow town in the "Wild West." Have them write a list of dos and don'ts for cowhands who are staying in their town at the end of a cattle drive. Have "mayors" read their lists to the class. *(Answers should reflect the information in the text about the rowdiness of cow towns during drives.)* OL CA HI1.

U Universal Access

Advanced Learners Have students design a newspaper ad for barbed wire. Begin by having them brainstorm uses of the product, the problem it is intended to solve, and other elements that could go into a marketing campaign. Encourage students to use computer graphics in creating their ads. *(Ads should be creative and incorporate details from the text discussion.)* AL CA 8WA2.4

S Skill Practice

Historical and Social Sciences Analysis Skill Have students explain the role of competition in the falling price of beef. *(Prices fell because there were many different ranch owners selling their beef; meat companies could pick and choose the ranchers willing to take low prices.)* OL CA HI6.

Reading Check

Answer: Hispanic ranch hands in the Spanish Southwest developed the traditions and skills of cattle herding.

Did You Know?

The popular image of the "Wild West" was fueled by dime novels—exaggerated tales of daring that sold for a dime. One author, Edward Wheeler, wrote a series of books about Deadwood Dick, a cowhand. Dick was based on Nat Love.

Picturing **History**

Answer: Overgrazing depleted grasslands, an oversupply of cattle resulted in falling prices; and bitterly cold winters in 1885 and 1886 killed large numbers of cattle.

R Reading Strategy

Understanding Vocabulary

Ask students to define *homestead.* *(earning ownership of land by settling on it)* OL

S Skill Practice

Using Geography Skills

Ask: Which areas in the West were not yet states in 1890? *(present-day states of Utah, Arizona, New Mexico, and Oklahoma)* OL CA CS3.

C Critical Thinking

Making Inferences Ask: Why would homesteading have been especially appealing to recent immigrants? *(They may have had little or no money and could go anywhere because they did not yet have a permanent home in this country.)* OL CA HI1.

Resources for page 676

- Biography Activity 15A
- Biography Activity 15B

US8.12.1 Trace patterns of agricultural and industrial development as they relate to climate, use of natural resources, markets, and trade and locate such development on a map.

Farmers Settle the Plains

Main Idea **Free land and new farming methods brought many settlers to the Great Plains.**

Reading Connection Have you ever experienced a drought or flood? Read on to learn about what farmers faced on the Great Plains, including droughts, flooding, plagues of insects, and harsh winters.

The early pioneers who reached the Great Plains did not believe they could farm the dry, treeless area. In the late 1860s, however, farmers began settling there and planting crops. Before long, much of the Plains became farmland. In 1872 a Nebraska settler wrote,

> **"One year ago this was a vast houseless, uninhabited prairie. . . . Today I can see more than thirty dwellings from my door."**
>
> —from *Settling the West*

Several factors brought settlers to the Plains. The railroads made the journey west easier and cheaper. Above-average rainfall in the late 1870s made the Plains better suited to farming. Finally, new laws offered free land.

In 1862 Congress passed the Homestead Act, which gave 160 free acres of land to a settler who paid a filing fee and lived on the land for five years. This federal land policy brought farmers to the Plains to **homestead** (HOHM • STEHD)—earn ownership of land by settling on it. R

Homesteading lured thousands of new settlers. Some were immigrants who had begun the process of becoming American citizens and were eligible to file for land. C Others were women. Although married women could not claim land, single women and widows had the same rights as men—and they used the Homestead Act to **acquire** property.

Steamship companies went to great lengths to advertise the American Plains in Scandinavia. By 1880 more than 100,000 Swedes and Norwegians had settled in the northern Plains—Minnesota and the Dakotas. The Scandinavian influence remains strong in this region today.

Soon after the Civil War ended, many African American soldiers, called "Buffalo Soldiers," served in the West. Thousands of African Americans also migrated from the Southern states into Kansas in the late 1870s. They called themselves "Exodusters," from the biblical book of Exodus, which describes the Jews' escape from slavery in Egypt.

NATIONAL GEOGRAPHIC **Western Land Use, 1890**

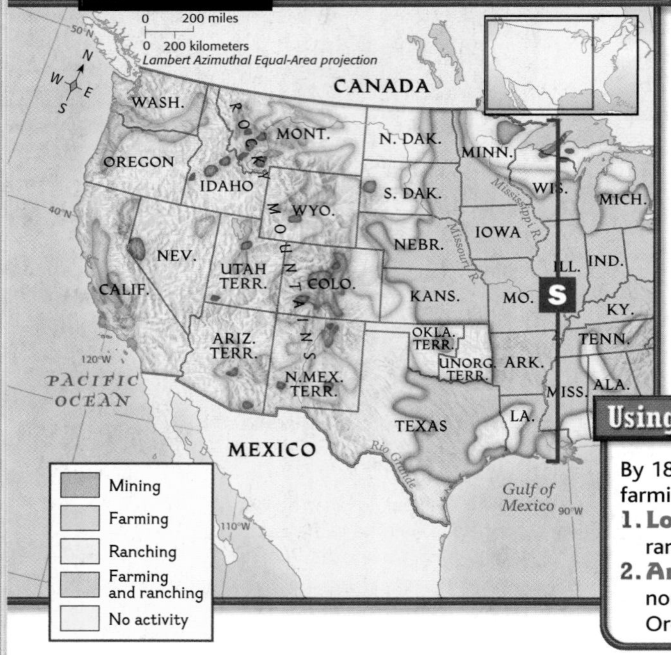

Using Geography Skills

By 1890, nearly every state had developed farming, ranching, and mining regions.

1. **Location** In what region of Texas was ranching concentrated?
2. **Analyze** What was the main economic activity in Washington and Oregon?

Answers and Additional Support

Using Geography Skills

Answers:

1. western half
2. farming

Did You Know?

Place names offer a clue to the original settlers of a town or village. For example, many places in the Great Plains have Scandinavian names, named by the original settlers from Sweden and Norway. Swedeburg and Gothenburg, Nebraska; Lindstrom, Minnesota; Norway, Iowa; Baltic, South Dakota; and Scandia, Kansas, are just a few.

Biography

US8.12 Students analyze the transformation of the American economy and the changing social and political conditions in the United States in response to the Industrial Revolution. US8.11.2 Identify the push-pull factors in the movement of former slaves to the cities in the North and to the West and their differing experiences in those regions (e.g., the experiences of the Buffalo Soldiers).

THE BUFFALO SOLDIERS S1

African Americans had fought in military conflicts since colonial times. Many had served and died during the Civil War.

When Congress set up the peacetime army after the Civil War, it also organized four segregated regiments of African American soldiers and cavalry, the 9th Cavalry, 10th Cavalry, 24th Infantry, and 25th Infantry. Many African Americans joined because of the opportunity for steady pay and a pension. These soldiers first served on the western frontier. R S2

These segregated units answered the nation's call to arms not only in the West, but also in Cuba, the Philippines, Hawaii, and Mexico. They fought in the Indian Wars and served in the western United States from 1867 until 1896. According to legend, the men were called "Buffalo Soldiers" by the Apache and Cheyenne. The name was adopted by the African American soldiers as a sign of honor and respect.

The Buffalo Soldiers did not, however, receive equal treatment from the Anglo American settlers or soldiers. The Buffalo Soldiers were sometimes harassed and abused. Despite being mistreated, these regiments overcame hardships to become among the most decorated military units in the United States Army.

W The army, recognizing the courage of the Buffalo Soldiers, presented the Medal of Honor to at least 20 Buffalo Soldiers for service during the wars in the American West. The Buffalo Soldiers also received commendations for their bravery in other wars and conflicts, including the Spanish-American War, World War I, and World War II.

In 1992 Colin Powell, who then served as chairman of the Joint Chiefs of Staff, dedicated a memorial to the Buffalo Soldiers in Fort Leavenworth, Kansas. In recognition, Powell noted that "since 1641 there has never been a time in this country when Blacks were unwilling to serve and sacrifice for America."

▲ Charles M. Young

"Colonel Charles Young . . . stands out as a shining example of the dedication, service, and commitment of the Buffalo Soldiers."

—quoted in Senate Resolution 97, 2001

Then and Now

Research the careers of some of the high-ranking African American officers in today's armed forces.

Then and Now

Reports should summarize the life and achievements of the subject person.

Did You Know?

John J. Pershing—who headed the American forces in France in World War I—commanded the 10th Cavalry for a while. During that time, he was a strong supporter of his African American troops, earning him the nickname "Black Jack."

Biography

TEACH

S1 Skill Practice

Historical and Social Sciences Analysis Skill

Have students conduct an Internet search for the term *Buffalo Soldier* and compile a list of sites they feel would be appropriate for a class report on them. Ask them to evaluate the reliability and suitability of the sites. AL CA HR4.

R Reading Strategy

Activating Prior Knowledge

Ask: What does *segregated* mean? *(divided according to race)* What does the word tell you about these army units? *(They only had African American soldiers.)* OL CA 8RW1.3

S2 Skill Practice

Historical and Social Sciences Analysis Skill

Ask: Why would African Americans in the late 1800s have found a soldier's pay so appealing? *(Students may note that they often suffered job discrimination and probably had difficulty earning a living otherwise.)* OL CA HI6.

W Writing Support

Research Reports Writing

Have students use library or Internet sources to learn more about the history of one of the Medal of Honor winners from among the Buffalo Soldiers. Ask students to write a report describing what he did to earn the medal. OL CA 8WA2.3

Review The Big Idea

Review the Big Idea for this section: "Geography shapes the physical, economic, and political challenges a region faces." Ask students to make a list of ways their lives would be different if they had lived on a homestead farm on the Great Plains in the 1870s. Then have them combine lists with a partner and discuss which difference would be the most important and why. OL CA CS3.

U Universal Access

Intrapersonal Have students write two or three journal entries by a young person in a homesteading family describing life on a homestead. OL CA 8WA2.1

R Reading Strategy

Understanding Vocabulary Have students use *sodbuster* and *dry farming* in a sentence. OL CA 8RW1.3

Picturing History

To survive on the treeless Plains, settlers had to build houses that did not require lumber. A Plains family's first home was usually made of sod, which are rectangular pieces of soil and grass. ***Why did many homesteaders settle in the Plains?***

The Farmers' Frontier The climate of the Plains presented farmers with a great challenge. Generally there was little rainfall, but in some years rain came down in torrents, destroying crops and flooding homesteads. The other extreme—drought—also threatened crops and lives. Fire was another enemy. In times of drought, brushfires swept rapidly through a region, destroying crops, livestock, and homes.

Several times during the 1870s, swarms of grasshoppers swept over the Plains. Thousands of the insects would land on a field of corn. When they left, not a stalk remained.

In winters winds howled across the open Plains, and deep snow could bury animals and trap families in their homes. Families had to plan ahead and store food for the winter.

Farm Families Farming on the Great Plains was a family affair. Men labored hard in the fields. Women often did the same work, but they also cared for the children. A farm wife sewed clothing, made candles, and cooked and preserved food. She often also tended to the children's health and education. When her husband was away—taking the harvest to town or buying supplies—she was responsible for keeping the farm running.

When children grew old enough, they helped in the fields, tended animals, and did chores around the house. Farmwork often kept children from attending school.

Although separated by great distances, people took much pleasure in getting together for weddings, church services, picnics, and other occasions. As communities grew, schools and churches began to dot the rural landscape. U

New Farming Methods The Plains could not be farmed by the usual methods of the 1860s. Most parts of the region had little rainfall and too few streams for irrigation. The Plains farmers, known as **sodbusters** (SAHD • BUHS • tuhrs), needed new methods and tools.

One approach, called **dry farming**, was to plant seeds deep in the ground where there was some moisture. Wooden plows could not penetrate the tough layer of sod, but in the late 1870s farmers could use the newly invented, lightweight steel plows to do the job. R

Answers and Additional Support

Picturing History

Charley O'Kieffe of Nebraska expressed the self-reliance necessary for homesteaders: "After all, we said to each other, this was a new country and folks had to learn to look after themselves."

Answer: Homesteading land was available there.

More Skill Practice

Visual Literacy Have students examine the photos on this page and identify elements that show that life on the Great Plains required a lot of work. *(Windmill pumped water from a well, the horse and wagon needed to be looked after, the sod house needed maintenance, the woman is washing clothes by hand.)* OL CA 8LS1.9

The sodbusters had other tools to help them cultivate the Plains—windmills to pump water from deep in the ground and barbed wire fencing. With no wood to build fences, farmers used these wire fences to protect their land.

C Dry farming, however, did not produce large crop yields, and the 160-acre grants were too small to make a living. Most farmers needed at least 300 acres, as well as advanced machinery, to make a farm profitable. Many farmers went into debt. Others lost ownership of their farms and then had to rent the land.

What Was the Oklahoma Land Rush? The last part of the Plains to be settled was the Oklahoma Territory, designated by Congress as Indian Territory in the 1830s. After years of pressure from land dealers and settlers' groups, the federal government opened Oklahoma to homesteaders in 1889. Settlers were eager to receive title to 160 acres of land. Their only condition was to remain on, improve, and develop the property for five years.

On the morning of April 22, 1889—the official opening day—more than 10,000 people lined up on the edge of this land. At the sound of a bugle, the homesteaders charged across the border to stake their claims. The eager settlers discovered that some people had already slipped into Oklahoma. These so-called "sooners" had claimed most of the best land. Within a few years, all of Oklahoma was opened to settlement.

Closing the Frontier Not long after the Oklahoma land rush, the government announced in the 1890 census that the frontier no longer existed. Settlement had changed the Plains dramatically. No one felt these changes more keenly than the Native Americans who had lived on the Plains for centuries.

Reading Check **Explain** Why was the Homestead Act important to settlers?

History Online
Study Central Need help understanding ranching and farming on the Great Plains? Visit ca.hss.glencoe.com and click on Study Central.

Section 2 Review

Reading Summary

Review the Main Ideas

- Cattle raised on the open range in Texas were driven north to railroad lines and shipped to eastern markets.
- Cowhands in the American West, who included African Americans, Native Americans, Hispanics, and whites, faced many dangers during cattle drives.
- The Homestead Act helped bring many settlers to the Great Plains.

What Did You Learn?

1. Explain why cow towns developed.
2. What new methods and tools helped settlers successfully farm the Great Plains?

Critical Thinking

3. **Determining Cause and Effect** Re-create the diagram below and explain how the Homestead Act encouraged settlement of the Great Plains. CA HI2.

4. **Analyze** What opportunities did settlement on the Plains provide for women and African Americans? CA HI1.
5. **The Big Ideas** How did geography influence the settlement and economic growth of the Great Plains and American West? CA HI6.
6. **Analysis** In an essay, discuss the growth, life, and decline of the Wild West in American history. Be sure to mention the geographical, economic, and social factors involved in that period in history. CA 8WA2.3

SECTION 2 REVIEW ANSWERS

Review questions reinforce content standard US8.12.

1. Ranchers drove cattle to places where they could be loaded onto trains. Towns grew up around these cattle-shipping centers.
2. sod houses, dry farming, steel plows, windmills, barbed wire
3. Free land attracted settlers.
4. Both groups could own land.
5. **The Big Ideas** It allowed cattle drives and ranching and the availability of vast amounts of land through the Homestead Act.
6. **Analysis** Essays should reflect accurately the information in the section.

C Critical Thinking

Determining Cause and Effect **Ask:** Why did many homesteads fail? *(Dry farming did not produce large crop yields, and expensive machinery was needed to farm the large acreage required to make a living.)* OL CA HI2.

ASSESS

Resources for page 679

Use these resources to assess student mastery of section content.

- Geography and History Activity 15
- Section Quiz 15–2
- Interactive Tutor Self-Assessment CD-ROM

Reading Check

Answer: By providing free land, it made land ownership possible for many who could not afford it any other way.

History Online

Study Central provides summaries, interactive games, and online graphic organizers to help students review section content.

CLOSE

Predicting Consequences Ask students to predict what happened to the sodbusters of the Great Plains in the following decades. AL CA HI3.

FOCUS

Summary

The Deals, a homesteading family in eastern Nebraska, have worked hard. This year the harvest looks promising after several years of disappointments. However, a huge swarm of grasshoppers arrives to devour all their crops and shatter their dreams.

Vocabulary Preview Before students begin reading, have them read **Before You Read** and the **Vocabulary Preview**. Point out that difficult words are footnoted throughout the text.

Background Information

The story is told as a series of memories by Abbie when she is an old woman, looking back on her family's difficult life on the Great Plains. Born in Iowa, author Bess Streeter Aldrich lived most of her life in the small Nebraska town of Elmwood.

Answers and Additional Support

A Lantern in Her Hand

By Bess Streeter Aldrich

Before You Read

The Scene: The homestead in this story is in eastern Nebraska. It is 1874.
The Characters: Will and Abbie Deal set up their homestead in 1868. Mack is their seven-year-old son. The Lutzes are their closest neighbors. The Reinmuellers live a little farther away.
The Plot: Will and his family went to Nebraska because they could own land there. Until this year, they have not had good crops because there has not been enough rain. They have also lived through a prairie fire and blizzards. Will and Abbie still believe, however, that the land is their fortune.

Vocabulary Preview

billowing: bulging or swelling out in the wind
colossal: huge, enormous
diabolical: like a devil; very evil
hazy: unclear because of smoke, dust, or clouds
incredulously: in a way that is unbelieving
perforations: holes
raw: not prepared for use; natural
uncanny: beyond ordinary human means or ability

Have you ever worked hard to make a wish come true? Were you able to reach your goal? Farming is an uncertain business, but it seems that Will and Abbie's hopes may soon be realized.

READING STRATEGY **PREDICTING**

Remind students that they have read about some of the challenges facing farm families on the Great Plains in the late 1800s. Ask them to use this information, along with what they know about the kinds of problems that farmers face today, to make a list of challenges the family in this excerpt may have to address. Have students check their predictions after reading the story. OL CA HI1.

As You Read

Contrast and vivid description are two tools that writers use to emphasize the importance of an event. As you begin reading this selection, imagine what the homestead looks like. As you continue, pay close attention to the pictures the writer is painting with words. What changes do you see? R1

The crop of 1874 was the sixth crop and it seemed to give a little more promise than the previous ones. By the twentieth of July, Will had laid by all his corn. Most of his small grain[1] was in the shocks,[2] but one oat field of a few acres was still uncut. Standing there under the July sun, its ripened surface seemed to reflect back the yellow rays. In the afternoon Abbie went out to pick a mess[3] of beans. The garden had come to be Abbie's care. Aside from the potato crop, to which Will attended, she looked after the entire garden. It was quite generally so,—the men bending all their energies to bigger things, the corn and wheat and the stock, with the chickens and the gardens falling to the lot of the wives. Some of the women went into the fields. Christine Reinmueller was out beside Gus many days. Will drew the line at that. "When you have to do that, we'll quit," he said.

R2 Abbie, in her starched[4] sunbonnet, began picking beans for supper. She could see Will and Henry Lutz working together, shocking the last of Henry's oats. To-morrow the two would work together on Will's last stand. It was nice for the men to be so neighborly.

It seemed hazy in the west. By the time she had finished the long rows, a big panful of the yellow pods in her arms, Will had come home from the Lutzes'. In the welcome shade of the house Abbie took off her bonnet, wiped her flushed perspiring face and waited for Will to come up.

"My...it's a scorcher." She looked hot and tired.

In a moment of tenderness, more to be desired because of its rarity, Will picked up Abbie's hands. The slender nails were stubbed and broken,—the grime of the garden was on her tapering fingers. He lifted her hand suddenly and kissed the hollow of it. As his lips touched the calloused palms, his eyes filled with rare tears. He uttered a short swift oath, "I wish you didn't have to, Abbie-girl. It's tough for you. Some day...in a few years...we'll pull out. Weather conditions may change... the land will be high....You can have better things...and your organ. That singing and painting of yours...maybe we can get to a teacher then...."

[1] **small grain:** grains, such as oat, rye, wheat; any grain that is not corn
[2] **in the shocks:** grain stacked in a standing position in a field to dry
[3] **mess:** enough food of one kind to serve as a meal or a dish
[4] **starched:** clothing that has been made stiff

TEACH

R1 Reading Strategy

Scaffolding—Monitoring Remind students before they read that they should ask questions about what they read. In fiction, they can use questions to evaluate characters, actions, and events. Write the following questions on the board as suggestions: What is the writer describing? What is the writer's attitude about the events or characters? How do I know? Would real people behave this way? Why or why not? OL

This READING SKILL was introduced in Chapter 14.

R2 Reading Strategy

Using Context Clues Ask: What do you learn about Abbie and Will's work habits? How do you know? *(They are hard-working, as shown by the chores they complete and have planned for the coming days.)* BL

Glencoe Literature Library

The following literature from the **Glencoe Literature Library** may enrich the teaching of this chapter:

My Ántonia by Willa Cather.

READING STRATEGY VISUALIZING

Challenge students to visualize the Deal family farm. What does the farmhouse look like? What about the fields? How does the area in general look? Encourage them to visualize how the sights change during the course of the story. Have students write a brief essay comparing the look of the farm at the beginning of the story and at the end. OL CA 8WA2.2

W Writing Support

Response to Literature Writing Have students write a paragraph describing how Abbie or Will felt as they watched their crops being eaten by the grasshoppers. *(Paragraphs should conclude that they were very unhappy about the waste of all their hard work; they may also have considered giving up.)* OL

C Critical Thinking

Analyzing Information
Ask: Are the grasshoppers an evil force, or only a natural phenomenon? Explain your answer. *(Students may point out that the author describes them as "fiends" and destroyers of dreams because this is how the settlers view them; however, grasshoppers are not evil in themselves, merely animals looking for food.)* AL
CA 8RL3.5

GLENCOE BOOKLINK

Use **Glencoe BookLink** to create customized reading lists for your students' reading levels, interests, and abilities.

Answers and Additional Support

America's Literature

It affected Abbie as it always did. In a moment like that it seemed the end and aim of everything...the family. All her dreams for herself were as nothing. In her own moment of emotion she returned, "We'll make it, Will...don't worry!"

For a moment they stood together looking out over the raw rolling acreage. Even as they looked, the sun darkened and the day took on a grayness. They looked for the storm, and heard it as soon as they saw it,—a great black cloud roar out of the west, with a million little hissing vibrations.[5] Their eyes on the sky, neither moved. Then there was a cessation[6] of the roaring, a soft thud of dropping things, and the cloud of a billion wings lay on the fields.

"Grasshoppers," they said simultaneously, incredulously.

The grasshoppers swarmed over the young waist-high corn and the pasture and the garden. By evening the long rows of sweet corn had been eaten to the plowed ground. The tender vines of the tomatoes were stripped down to the stalk. The buds of the fruit trees were gone. Part of the garden was a memory. The chickens had feasted themselves to the bursting point. Gus Reinmueller, driving up to the door, could hardly control his raring horses, so irritated were they by the bouncing, thumping pests. The farm was a squirming, greenish-gray mass of them. W

All evening Will sat by the stove with his head in his hands. It was the first time he had visibly lost his grit. Abbie went over to him and ran her hand through his hair. She tried to think of something to console him. "Don't, Will.... There's one thing we can do. There's the string of pearls. We can always fall back on it. There must be jewelry stores in Omaha that would take it and pay well. You can take the team and make the drive.... You can do it in three days,...and I'll look after things here. When Mother gave the pearls to me, she said 'You'll ne'er starve with them' ...and we won't, Will. We'll sell them for the children's sake."

Will threw her hands away from his hair roughly and stood up. "Hell...no!" He yelled it at her. "I've taken your music away from you and your painting and your teaching and some of your health. But, *by God,*...I won't take your mother's present to you."

He slammed the rough soddie door and went out to the barn.

By the next night the stalks of field corn were skeletons, a few delicate veins of leaves left, like so many white bones bleaching on the desert of the fields. At the end of three days the oat field was stripped almost as bare as the day the plow had finished its work. The young orchard was a graveyard of hopes. Some of the small grain previously harvested had been saved, and luckily, one digging of early potatoes was in the hole in the ground in which Will always kept them. But everything else went through the crunching incisors[7] of the horde. It was as though the little grayish-green fiends[8] became a composite whole,—one colossal insect into whose grinding maw[9] went all the green of the fields and the gardens, all the leaves and tender twigs of the young fruit trees, all the dreams and the hopes of the settlers. C

The pests were everywhere. With nightmarish persistence, they appeared in everything. As tightly as Will kept the well covered, he drew them up in the bucket, so that he began

[5] **vibrations:** quick movements back and forth
[6] **cessation:** ending
[7] **incisors:** front teeth that are particularly good for cutting
[8] **fiends:** evil spirits
[9] **maw:** the jaws of an animal that has a huge appetite

READING STRATEGY — ANALYZING TEXT STRUCTURE

Ask students to discuss this question: Why did the author describe how the grasshoppers ate each kind of crop, rather than just saying that they ate everything in sight? *(Describing each plant and what the insects did increases the horror and disappointment of the characters; it is as if the reader were watching the grasshoppers move from one crop to another. Also, the specific details make the information more vivid and meaningful.)* OL going back to the old spring for water. Abbie caught them eating the curtains of the little half-windows and sent them to a fiery death. She was forced to dry the weekly wash around the cook stove, her one attempt to hang it in the sun ending speedily with a dozen perforations in the first billowing garment.

The garden was a total loss. They had tried to save some of the beans by putting gunny-sacks[10] over them and weighting them down with stones from the creek bed. The grasshoppers, after eating the beans, had begun on the gunny-sacks.

"Will they eat the stones, too, Mother?" Mack wanted to know. And they could not laugh at him.

Abbie wrote a letter to her sister Mary, telling of this last hard piece of luck. Even letters were expensive luxuries so that one was made to do for the entire group of relatives back in eastern Iowa. She gave the letter to Will, who said that he would ride over to the little post office in the Lutz store as soon as he had finished caring for the stock. In an hour Will came in holding the letter by a corner. The edges of the envelope had been eaten all the way around with little neat flutings so that the two sides fell apart and the letter fluttered to the floor. The pocket of his old denim coat, where the letter had lain, was flapping down, cut on two sides by the same diabolical jaws.

What could you do? You could not fight them. You could not kill them. They were an army with an uncanny and unnatural power. Abbie looked out upon the devastation[11] of the fields and the garden upon which they both had worked so hard. The hot wind blew over the ruins with Mephistophelean[12] laughter. She looked up at the cloudless blue,—huge cruel, sardonic.[13]

[10] **gunny-sacks:** a bag made from coarse heavy material, such as burlap

[11] **devastation:** destruction

[12] **Mephistophelean:** like the proud fallen angel Mephistopheles who is cold-hearted, funny, and sardonic

[13] **sardonic:** making fun in a way that shows someone or something is not important

Responding to the Literature

1. What was Abbie doing when the selection started? What was Will doing?
2. How did Abbie and Will try to save the beans? What happened next?
3. **Analyze** In **foreshadowing** a writer gives clues to prepare readers for what will happen. What did the author foreshadow in this selection? How did she do it? CA 8RL3.6
4. **Explain** What are the literal and figurative meanings of the following sentence? "The young orchard was a graveyard of hopes." CA 8RW1.1
5. **Read to Write** In 500 to 700 words, write a story or describe an incident in your life. Base the narrative on an event related to your local weather, such as a hurricane or blizzard. As an alternative, you may use an environmental issue, such as water pollution or an endangered species. What was life like before and during this incident? Why was the event important? What was your attitude about it? Be sure to include dialogue in the narrative. CA 8WA2.1a,b,c

ASSESS

Assign the Responding to the Literature questions as an in-class activity or as homework. In addition or as an alternative assessment, ask students to write an essay on the role of nature in the lives of homesteaders. OL CA 8WA2.2

CLOSE

Ask students to name other books that have similar themes, characters, or settings. OL CA 8RL3.5

Responding to the Literature Answers

1. Abbie was picking beans, while Will was helping a neighbor shock his oats.
2. They put cloth sacks over them and weighted them with stones, but the grasshoppers ate the sacks too.
3. Some may say that the word *seemed* in the first sentence may be foreshadowing a catastrophe. Another instance may be the haziness in the distant sky, which turns out to be the insects.
4. The literal meaning is that hopes are buried there. The figurative meaning is that the family lost hope when the garden was destroyed.
5. Responses should discuss an appropriate incident or address a suitable subject and use correct grammar and spelling.

TEACH

The reading selections for this unit have been chosen to reflect the California History-Social Science Standards. If you assign one of these books, you may want to have students complete the following activity.

Using Free-Form Maps

Free-form mapping and sequence mapping are tools that can be used for reviewing textbook material and literature readings. Have students who have read the same book create a free-form map. After the groups have made their presentations, ask the class to discuss themes or concepts common to all of the maps. Display the free-form maps around the classroom so that students who are interested in reading the other selections can review the maps to find which books interest them.

GLENCOE BOOKLINK

Use **Glencoe BookLink** to create customized reading lists for your students' reading levels, interests, and abilities.

Answers and Additional Support

Reading On Your Own...

From the California Reading List

Do you want to learn more about life and inventions in the years between the Civil War and 1914? You might be interested in the following books.

Nonfiction

Native Americans and the Reservation in American History by Anita Louise McCormick recounts the history of relations between whites and Native Americans, beginning in the 1600s. McCormick also explains the historical and cultural beliefs that led members of each ethnic group to act as they did. ***The content of this book is related to*** *History–Social Science Standard US8.12.*

Biography

The Wright Brothers: How They Invented the Airplane by Russell Freedman does more than simply describe the brothers' experiments. Freedman has included portions of their journals and letters, plus photos that the brothers took as they documented their experiments. ***The content of this book is related to*** *History–Social Science Standard US8.12.*

Historical Fiction

Dreams in the Golden Country: The Diary of Zipporah Feldman, a Jewish Immigrant Girl by Kathryn Lasky begins by describing the Feldmans' experience on Ellis Island. As the diary continues, Zipporah tells about their life in New York City in the early 1900s and her hopes for the future. ***The content of this book is related to*** *History–Social Science Standard US8.12.*

Nonfiction

McGuffey's Fourth Eclectic Reader by William McGuffey starts with directions to the teacher, followed by poetry and prose reading selections for students. This book gives the reader an interesting insight into what students read in the 1800s and why particular pieces were chosen. ***The content of this book is related to*** *History–Social Science Standard US8.12.*

684

READING STRATEGY PREVIEWING

Remind students that there are many different ways to decide if they want to read a book. Other people's recommendations are one way. Choosing a book by an author they already know and like is another. A third way is previewing a book. Ask students to identify ways they can preview a book to help them decide whether to read it. *(Possible answers include reading the jacket, looking at the cover picture, skimming the table of contents, looking through the book to see the pictures and read at random, reading the first few pages or the first chapter, finding a book review in a magazine or online, and asking a librarian.)* **OL**

Section 3

Native American Struggles

Guide to Reading

Looking Back, Looking Ahead

You learned that following the Civil War, many whites moved to the Great Plains and the American West to mine, ranch, and farm. Many Native American groups, however, already lived in those areas, and the two peoples came into conflict.

Focusing on the Main Ideas

- The Native Americans of the Great Plains lived a nomadic lifestyle while following the great herds of buffalo. ***(page 686)***
- During the late 1800s, whites and Native Americans fought while Native Americans tried to preserve their civilizations. ***(page 687)***

Locating Places

Oklahoma
Dakota Territory
Black Hills
Little Bighorn River
Wounded Knee

Meeting People

Red Cloud
William Cody
Crazy Horse
Black Kettle
Sitting Bull
George Custer
Geronimo (juh • RAH • nuh • MOH)
Helen Hunt Jackson

Content Vocabulary

nomadic (noh • MA • dihk)
reservation

Academic Vocabulary

despite (di • SPYT)
achieve

Reading Strategy

Determining Cause and Effect As you read the section, re-create the diagram below and describe how Western settlement affected Native Americans.

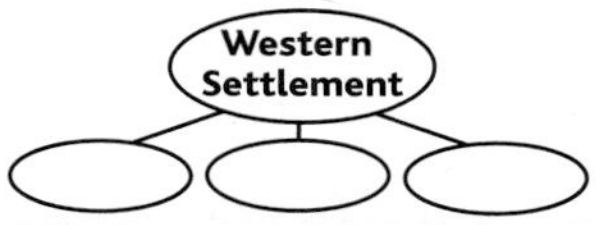

History Social Science Standards

US8.12 Students analyze the transformation of the American economy and the changing social and political conditions in the United States in response to the Industrial Revolution.

NATIONAL GEOGRAPHIC Where & When?

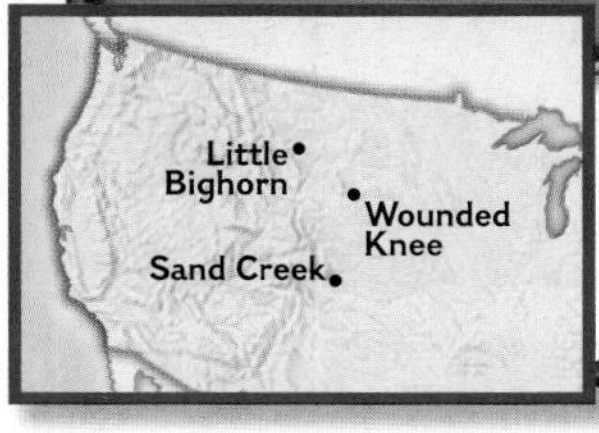

1860	1875	1890
1864 Cheyenne attacked at Sand Creek	**1876** Sioux victorious at Little Bighorn	**1890** Battle at Wounded Knee

FOCUS

BELLRINGER Skillbuilder Activity

Project **Daily Focus Skills Transparency 15–3** and have students answer the question.

Guide to Reading

Preteaching Vocabulary: Ask students to predict how the two terms will be used in this section. Have them check the accuracy of their predictions as they read.

Answers to Graphic: Buffalo were killed, destroying their means of support and nomadic lifestyle; Forced to relocate onto reservations; Increased armed clashes with whites

Unpacking the Standards

After reading the section, students will be able to:

- Describe the nomadic lifestyle of the Native Americans of the Great Plains and how it was based on the buffalo.
- Explain why there was growing conflict between Native Americans and whites in the West in the late 1800s.

SECTION RESOURCES

Print Material
- Reproducible Lesson Plan 15–3*
- Daily Lesson and Discussion Notes 15–3
- Guided Reading Activity 15–3
- Reading Essentials and Study Guide 15–3
- Active Reading Note-Taking Guide 15–3
- Section Quiz 15–3

Transparencies
- Daily Focus Skills Transparency 15–3
- Section Graphic Organizer Transparency 15–3
- California Standards Practice Transparencies

Technology
- Interactive Tutor Self-Assessment CD-ROM
- Exam*View*® Pro Testmaker CD-ROM
- Presentation Plus! CD-ROM

*Available on TeacherWorks™

TEACH

C Critical Thinking

Comparing and Contrasting **Ask:** How did the lifestyle of the Osage and Omaha differ from that of the Sioux, Comanche, and Blackfeet? *(The first pair were farmers and hunters living in one place; the last three were nomads who followed buffalo herds.)* OL CA HI1.

U Universal Access

Logical/Mathematical Ask students to use their math skills to compute the percentage of Native American population loss from 1850 to 1900, using the figures 410,000 (1850) and 245,000 (1900). *(40%)* OL

S Skill Practice

Visual Literacy Ask students to describe some of the activities shown in the painting. *(Three people are working with buffalo skins; others are talking in a group; still others are riding horses.)* OL

Reading Check

Answer: settling in one place for only part of the year, traveling for the rest

Answers and Additional Support

US8.12.2 Identify the reasons for the development of federal Indian policy and the wars with American Indians and their relationship to agricultural development and industrialization.

Following the Buffalo

Main Idea **The Native Americans of the Great Plains lived a nomadic lifestyle while following the great herds of buffalo.**

Reading Connection What might it be like to move from place to place throughout the year, following a large herd of animals so that your people could hunt and eat? Read to find out about the lifestyle of the Native Americans of the Great Plains.

In the mid-1850s, miners, railroads, cattle drivers, and farmers came to the Plains. Each new group threatened Native American culture. The Sioux chief **Red Cloud** lamented, "The white children [settlers] have surrounded me and left me nothing but an island."

For centuries the Great Plains was home to many Native American nations. The Omaha and the Osage nations lived in communities as farmers and hunters. The Sioux, the Comanche, and the Blackfeet lived a **nomadic** (noh • MA • dihk) life. They traveled vast distances following their main source of food—the great herds of buffalo that roamed the Great Plains.

Despite their differences, the people of the Plains were similar in many ways. Plains Indian nations, sometimes numbering several thousand people, were divided into bands consisting of up to 500 people each. A governing council headed each band, but most members participated in making decisions.

The women reared the children, cooked, and prepared hides. The men hunted, traded, and supervised the military life of the band. Most Plains Indians practiced a religion based on a belief in the spiritual power of the natural world.

Threats to the Buffalo At one time, the Plains Indians had millions of buffalo to supply their needs. After the Civil War, though, American hunters hired by the railroads began slaughtering the animals to feed the crews building the railroad. The railroad companies also wanted to prevent huge herds of buffalo from blocking the trains. **William Cody,** hired by the Kansas Pacific Railroad, once claimed that he had killed more than 4,000 buffalo in less than 18 months. He became known as Buffalo Bill. Starting in 1872, hunters targeted buffalo to sell the hides to the East, where tanneries made them into leather goods.

Reading Check **Describe** What is a nomadic way of life?

Native American Population

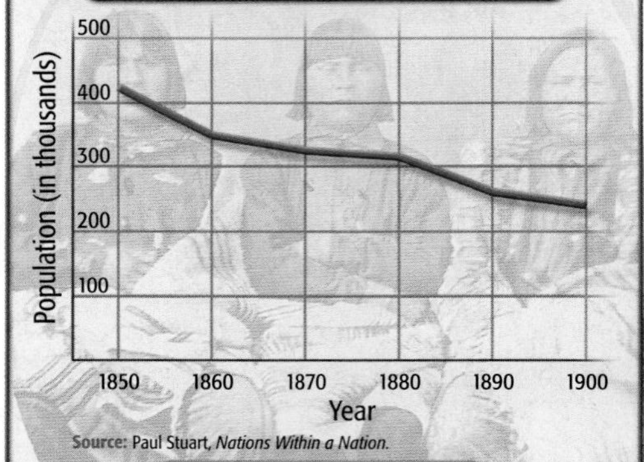

Source: Paul Stuart, *Nations Within a Nation.*

Understanding Charts

Census figures show a declining Native American population before 1900.

Analyze During what 10-year period did the Native American population decline the least?

▲ Native Americans of the Great Plains settled in one place for only part of the year.

Understanding Charts

Answer: 1870 to 1880

Ask: About how many Native Americans were there in 1870? *(about 330,000)* In 1900? *(about 250,000)* OL

Resources for page 686

Chart, Graph, and Map Skills Activity 15

US8.12.2 Identify the reasons for the development of federal Indian policy and the wars with American Indians and their relationship to agricultural development and industrialization.

Conflict

Main Idea **During the late 1800s, whites and Native Americans fought while Native Americans tried to preserve their civilizations.**

Reading Connection How would you react if the government suddenly forced you to move from your home? Read to find out how Native Americans reacted when settlers moved into their lands and attempted to change the way they lived.

As ranchers, miners, and farmers moved onto the Plains, they deprived Native Americans of their hunting grounds, broke treaties guaranteeing certain lands to the Plains Indians, and often forced them to relocate to new territory. Native Americans resisted by attacking wagon trains, stagecoaches, and ranches. Occasionally, an entire group would go to war against nearby settlers and troops. In the late 1860s, the government pursued a new Indian policy to deal with these challenges.

Reservation Policy In 1867 the federal government appointed the Indian Peace Commission to set policies for Native Americans. The commission recommended moving the Native Americans to a few large **reservations**—tracts of land set aside for them.

One large reservation was in **Oklahoma,** the "Indian Territory" that Congress had created in the 1830s for Native Americans who were relocated from the Southeast. Another one, meant for the Sioux people, was in the **Dakota Territory.** Managing the reservations would be the job of the federal Bureau of Indian Affairs.

Government agents often used trickery to persuade Native American nations to move to the reservations. Many reservations were located on poor land. In addition the government often failed to deliver promised food and supplies, and the goods that were delivered were of poor quality.

A great many Native Americans accepted the reservation policy at first. Many southern Kiowa, Comanche, Cheyenne, and Arapaho agreed to stay on the Oklahoma reservation. Thousands of Sioux agreed to move onto the Dakota reservation in the North.

Pockets of resistance remained, however. Some Native Americans refused to make the move, and some who tried reservation life abandoned it. The stage was set for trouble.

Conflict on the Plains During the 1860s, many armed clashes between Native Americans and whites took place. Minnesota Territory was the site of one especially bloody confrontation. Resentful of the settlers, Sioux warriors, led by Red Cloud, burned and looted white settlers' homes in the summer of 1862. Hundreds died before troops arrived from St. Paul and ended the uprising.

Following the Minnesota uprising, the army sent patrols far out onto the northern Great Plains. This action brought troops into contact with another branch of the Sioux—the nomadic Lakota. The Lakota fought hard to keep control of their hunting grounds, which extended from the Black Hills and the surrounding Badlands—rocky and barren terrain in the western parts of the Dakotas and northwestern Nebraska—westward to the Bighorn Mountains.

▲ Native American buffalo shield

R Reading Strategy

Understanding Vocabulary Ask students to explain the link between the term *reservation* and the verb *reserve*. *(Reserve means to set aside, and a reservation is land set aside for Native Americans.)* EL CA 8RW1.3

S Skill Practice

Historical and Social Sciences Analysis Skill Have students write a paragraph describing the adjustments that Native Americans had to make when they moved onto a reservation. Note that not only did their way of life change, but they came into contact with different kinds of people. OL CA HI2.

Review The Big Idea

Review the Big Idea for this section: "Differences in economic, political, and social beliefs can lead to division within a nation and have lasting consequences." **Ask:** How did the reservation policy of the federal government set the stage for conflict between whites and Native Americans? *(Because the reservation policy was not carried out honestly, with poor land, shoddy supplies, and broken promises, and because the policy required Native Americans to change how they lived.)* AL CA HI2.

Did You Know?

Today's nearly 275 Native American reservations vary widely in size. The largest is the 16-million-acre Navajo reservation in Arizona, New Mexico, and Utah. The smallest reservations are less than 100 acres.

C Critical Thinking

Drawing Conclusions Ask students to describe the Native Americans' battle strategy against the United States and explain why they chose this strategy. *(They usually used guerrilla tactics like ambushes, small raids, and isolated attacks rather than major battles. They probably felt they could not defeat the numerically superior U.S. Army.)* OL CA HI2.

R1 Reading Strategy

Connecting Ask: How is the situation in the Black Hills similar to the situation of another Native American group earlier in history? What happened then? *(similar to situation of Cherokees in Georgia, who were driven off their land when gold was found on it)* OL CA HI3.

R2 Reading Strategy

Setting a Purpose Before reading about the Battle of Little Bighorn, ask students to share what they already know about it. Make a class list of statements. Then have students look for information in the text that supports or disproves each one. OL CA HR3.

Answers and Additional Support

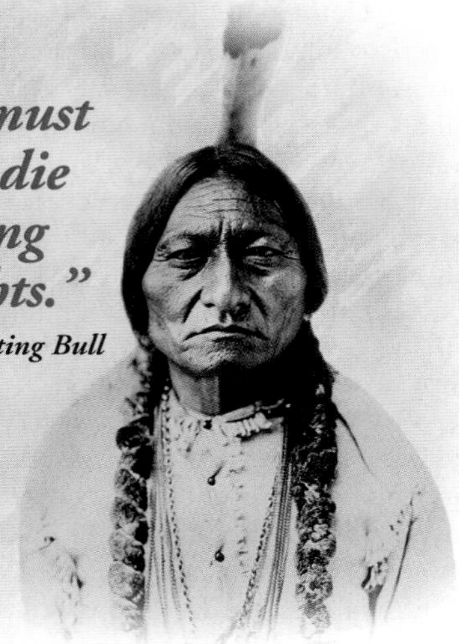

The Sioux, along with Cheyenne and Arapaho warriors, staged a series of attacks from 1865 to 1867. The bloodiest incident occurred on December 21, 1866. Army troops, led by Captain William J. Fetterman, were manning a fort on the Bozeman Trail, used by prospectors to reach gold mines in Montana. A Sioux military leader, **Crazy Horse,** acted as a decoy and lured the troops into a deadly trap. He tricked the fort's commander into sending a detachment of about 80 soldiers in pursuit. Hundreds of warriors were waiting in ambush and wiped out the entire detachment. This incident came to be known as the Fetterman Massacre.

Colorado was another site of conflict. The number of miners who had flocked to Colorado in search of gold and silver grew. Bands of Cheyenne and Arapaho began raiding wagon trains and stealing cattle and horses from ranches. By the summer of 1864, travelers heading to Denver or the mining camps were no longer safe. Dozens of ranches had been burned, and an estimated 200 settlers had been killed. The territorial governor of Colorado ordered the Native Americans to surrender at Fort Lyon, where he said they would be given food and protection.

Although several hundred Native Americans surrendered at the fort, many others did not. In November 1864, Chief **Black Kettle** brought several hundred Cheyenne to negotiate a peace deal. They camped at Sand Creek. Shortly after, Colonel John Chivington led the Colorado Volunteers on an attack on the unsuspecting Cheyenne. Fourteen volunteers and hundreds of Cheyenne died. Retaliation by the Cheyenne was swift, causing widespread uprisings before some of the Cheyenne and Arapaho leaders agreed to stop the fighting in October 1865.

What Occurred at Little Bighorn? Treaties were supposed to bring peace, but tensions remained and erupted in more fighting a few years later. This time the conflict arose over the **Black Hills** of the Dakotas. The government had promised that "No white person or persons shall be permitted to settle upon or occupy" or even "to pass through" these hills. However, the hills were rumored to contain gold. Prospectors swarmed into the area.

The Sioux protested against the trespassers. Instead of protecting the Sioux's rights, the government tried to buy the hills. **Sitting Bull,** an important leader of the Lakota Sioux, refused. "I do not want to sell any land. Not even this much," he said, holding a pinch of dust.

Sitting Bull gathered Sioux and Cheyenne warriors along the **Little Bighorn River** in present-day Montana. They were joined by Crazy Horse, another Sioux chief, and his forces. The United States Army was ordered to round up the warriors and move them to reservations. The Seventh Cavalry, led by Lieutenant Colonel **George Custer,** was ordered to scout the Native American encampment.

Custer wanted the glory of leading a major victory. He divided his regiment and attacked the Native Americans on June 25, 1876. He had seriously underestimated their strength, however. With about 250 soldiers, Custer faced a Sioux and Cheyenne force of thousands. Custer and his entire command lost their lives. News of the army's defeat shocked the nation.

More Skill Practice

Analyzing Primary Sources Share with students this quotation from Sitting Bull: "If we must die, we die defending our rights." **Ask:** Why would Native Americans feel that way? *(Students may point out that Native Americans would feel that they were being pushed too hard.)* OL CA HI3.

Did You Know?

Sitting Bull said he had a vision that foretold the defeat of Custer's troops. In the spring of 1876 at a war council, Sitting Bull saw U.S. soldiers falling upside down from the sky into the Lakota camp like grasshoppers. Later in his life, another vision foretold his own death at the hands of his fellow Lakota.

The Native American triumph at Little Bighorn was short-lived. The army soon crushed the uprising, sending most of the Native Americans to reservations. Sitting Bull and his followers fled north to Canada. By 1881, exhausted and starving, the Lakota and Cheyenne agreed to live on a reservation.

C

Who Were the Nez Perce? Farther west, members of the Nez Perce, led by Chief Joseph, refused to be moved to a smaller reservation in Idaho in 1877. When the army came to relocate them, they fled their homes and traveled more than 1,000 miles. After a remarkable flight to Canada, Chief Joseph realized that resistance was hopeless. Finally, in October 1877, Chief Joseph surrendered, and his followers were moved to reservations.

The Apache Wars Trouble also broke out in the Southwest. The Chiracahua Apache had been moved from their homeland in present-day New Mexico and Arizona to the San Carlos reservation in Arizona in the mid-1870s. Many Apache resented confinement to this reservation. The Apache leader, **Geronimo** (juh • RAH • nuh • MOH), escaped from San Carlos and fled to Mexico with a small band of followers. During the 1880s, he led raids against settlers and the army in Arizona. Army troops pursued Geronimo and his warriors. Several times Geronimo went back to the reservation only to leave again. Geronimo said, "Once I moved about like the wind. Now I surrender to you." In 1886 the Apache leader finally gave up—the last Native American to surrender formally to the United States. R

NATIONAL GEOGRAPHIC

Western Native American Lands, 1860–1890

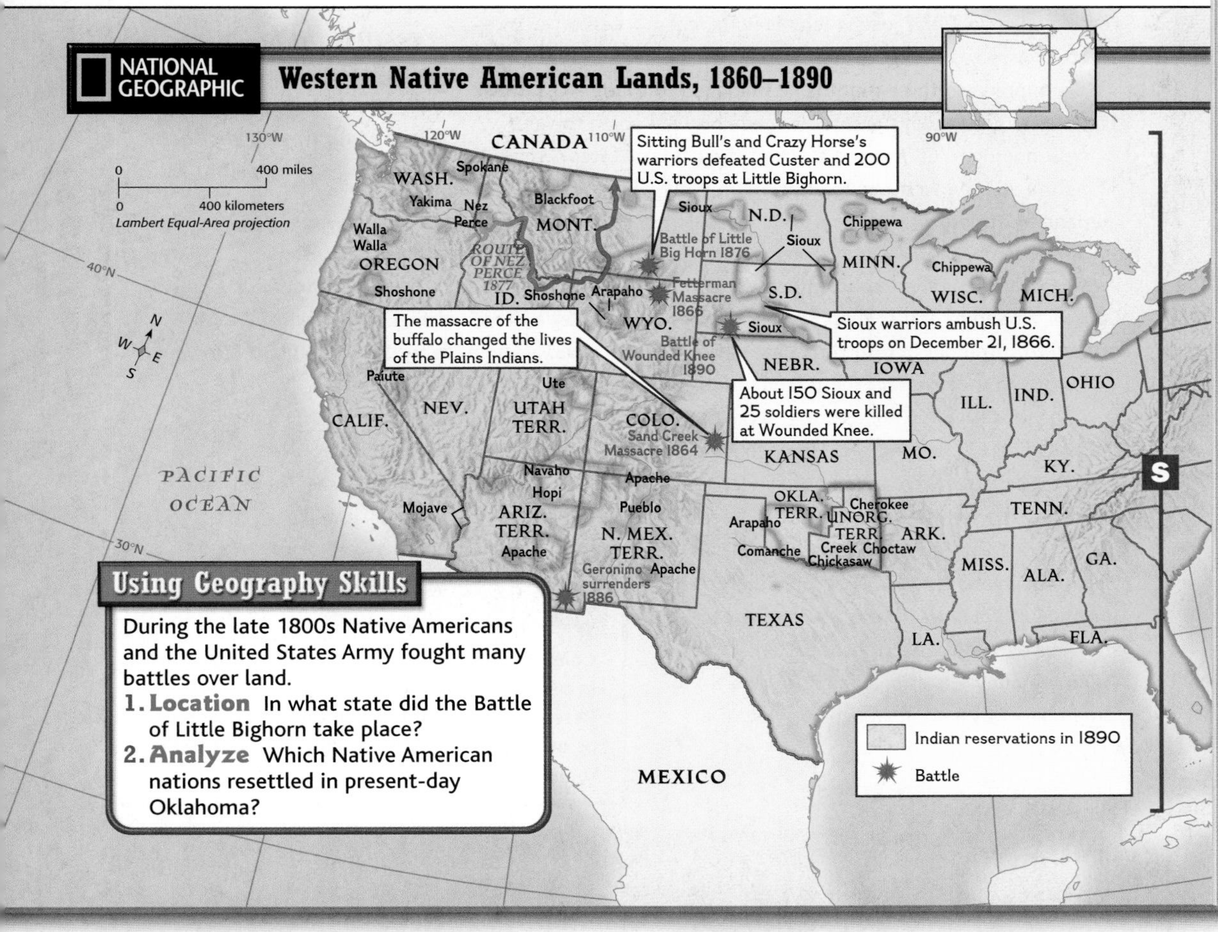

Using Geography Skills

During the late 1800s Native Americans and the United States Army fought many battles over land.

1. **Location** In what state did the Battle of Little Bighorn take place?
2. **Analyze** Which Native American nations resettled in present-day Oklahoma?

S

C Critical Thinking

Making Generalizations

Ask students to make generalizations about the content of the subsection titled "Conflict", which begins on page 687. Then have them identify the details they used to make their generalizations. *(Generalizations may include: Native American groups that resisted being placed on reservations were eventually defeated and confined to reservations; the United States usually broke agreements with Native Americans; and the way of life of the Plains people was doomed.)* **OL** CA 8RC2.0 CA HR3.

R Reading Strategy

Determining Importance

Ask: Why is Geronimo's surrender significant? *(He was the last Native American to surrender to the U.S.)* **BL**

S Skill Practice

Using Geography Skills

Have pairs of students find on this map the names of places mentioned in this subsection. Ask one student to find place names in the text and have the other find the location on the map. *(Student pairs should find states and territories, battles, and reservations.)* Then have them switch tasks and repeat the exercise. **BL** CA CS3.

Using Geography Skills

Answers:

1. Montana
2. Cherokee, Choctaw, Creek, Chickasaw, Comanche, Arapaho

In-Text Map Transparency 15
Ask: In what year was the Sand Creek Massacre? *(1864)* **BL**

Did You Know?

Nez Perce is French for "pierced nose." The name was given to the group by an interpreter who saw some native people with decorative shells in their noses. The words have been anglicized but were originally pronounced NAY PURSAY.

Biography

TEACH

S Skill Practice

Historical and Social Sciences Analysis Skill Ask students to use the map on page 689 to trace the route of the Nez Perce in 1877 under Chief Joseph's leadership. Have them describe the different directions the group traveled as it tried to reach Canada. *(It traveled east, then south, then east, then north.)* BL CA HI3.

R Reading Strategy

Scaffolding—Questioning **Ask:** Why did many whites admire Chief Joseph? *(He treated prisoners humanely and was concerned for women, children, and the elderly.)* OL

This READING SKILL was introduced in Chapter 9.

U Universal Access

Auditory/Musical Ask students to identify music appropriate for Chief Joseph's words. Have them bring a recording of their choices and play them for the class. *(Compositions will probably reflect the melancholy tone of the speech.)* AL

Answers and Additional Support

Biography

US8.12.2 Identify the reasons for the development of federal Indian policy and the wars with American Indians and their relationship to agricultural development and industrialization.

Chief Joseph

1840–1904

Chief Joseph was born in 1840 as Hin ma to yah lat k'it, which means Thunder Emerging from the Mountains. He grew up in the Wallowa Valley, located in present-day Oregon. In 1860, when gold was found on Nez Perce land, white settlers flooded into the region. In 1877 the United States government demanded that the Nez Perce give up their lands and move onto a reservation in Idaho. Chief Joseph, hoping to avoid violence, prepared his people for the move. He learned, however, that several young braves had attacked a group of white settlers. Fearing revenge, Chief Joseph led his followers more than 1,000 miles across Oregon, Washington, Idaho, and Montana. **S**

R For more than three months he managed to evade a U.S. force 10 times larger than his group. He made his way north toward Canada, hoping to escape the reach of the United States Army. Along the way, he won the admiration of many whites for his humane treatment of prisoners and for his concern for women, children, and the elderly.

In September 1877, the Nez Perce had reached the Bear Paw Mountains in Montana, just 40 miles from the Canadian border. As the Nez Perce rested before their move into Canada, a band of 400 soldiers surrounded the camp. After a fierce battle, Chief Joseph offered to surrender in return for safe passage to the reservation in Idaho. Chief Joseph's words of surrender reflect the tragedy of his people:

"The little children are freezing to death. My people . . . have no blankets, no food. . . . I am tired; my heart is sick and sad. From where the sun now stands I will fight no more forever." **U**

The Nez Perce were taken not to Idaho, but to a swampy tract of land in Kansas. There, unused to the weather and the environment, many fell ill and died. Eventually, the Nez Perce were scattered among reservations in Oklahoma, Idaho, and Washington. Chief Joseph continued to plead with the government to allow his people to return to their land in the Wallowa Valley. His efforts failed, but he is remembered as a great warrior, as well as a man of peace.

> ***"I will fight no more forever."***
>
> **—Chief Joseph, from *A Patriot's Handbook***

Then and Now

Chief Joseph's reputation as a great leader arose in part from his ability and dignity in battle. Research to find at least three U.S. presidents or other government officials who built their reputations in the military.

690

Then and Now

Possible suggestions include George Washington, Andrew Jackson, William Henry Harrison, Zachary Taylor, and Ulysses Grant; other leaders are possible.

Resources for page 690

- American Art and Architecture Transparency 17
- Critical Thinking Skills Activity 15

A Changing Culture Many things contributed to changing the traditional way of life of Native Americans—the movement of whites onto their lands, the slaughter of the buffalo, United States Army attacks, and the reservation policy. More change came from well-meaning reformers who wanted to abolish reservations and absorb the Native Americans into white American culture.

American reformers such as **Helen Hunt Jackson** were horrified by the massacres of Native Americans and by the cruelty of the reservation system. Describing the whites' treatment of Native Americans in her 1881 book, *A Century of Dishonor*, Jackson wrote:

> **"It makes little difference . . . where one opens the record of the history of the Indians; every page and every year has its dark stain. The story of one tribe is the story of all, varied only by differences of time and place."**
>
> —Helen Hunt Jackson, *A Century of Dishonor*

Congress changed government policy with the Dawes Act in 1887. The law aimed to eliminate what white Americans regarded as the two weaknesses of Native American life: the lack of private property and the nomadic tradition.

The Dawes Act proposed to break up the reservations and to end identification with a tribal group. Each Native American would receive a plot of reservation land. The goal was to encourage native peoples to become farmers and, eventually, American citizens. Native American children would be sent to white-run boarding schools. Some of the reservation lands would be sold to support this schooling.

Over the next 50 years, the government divided up the reservations. Speculators acquired most of the valuable land. Native Americans often received dry, gravelly plots that were not suited to farming.

Primary Sources

Sarah Winnemucca

Sarah Winnemucca was the daughter of a Northern Paiute chief in western Nevada. She learned to speak English and Spanish, and she traveled widely to tell others about the plight of the Paiute. In her autobiography, she wrote:

> "I have been sincere with my own people . . . as well as with my white brothers. Alas, how truly our women prophesied when they told my dear old grandfather that his white brothers, whom he loved so much, had brought sorrow to his people."
>
> —Sara Winnemucca, *Life Among the Piutes*

DBQ Document-Based Question

Why do you think Winnemucca wrote that she was "sincere" with both the Paiutes and the white settlers?

Cultural Impact This plan failed to **achieve** its goals. Some Native Americans succeeded as farmers or ranchers, but many had little training or enthusiasm for either pursuit. Their land allotments were too small to be profitable. Some Native Americans had adapted to life on reservations and did not want to see it transformed into homesteads. In the end, the Dawes Act did not benefit Native American nations. The culture of the Plains Indians was doomed because it was dependent on buffalo. Once the buffalo were wiped out, Native Americans on the Plains had no means to sustain their way of life and little interest in adopting white American culture in place of their own.

Primary Sources

Answer: Answers will vary; students may suggest she said it to reinforce the idea that she was telling the truth.

- **Why do you think Sarah Winnemucca learned to speak Spanish?** *(Many people spoke Spanish in the West and Southwest.)* OL
- **What prophecy does Sarah Winnemucca refer to? Who made it?** *(Paiute women prophesied to her grandfather that the whites would bring sorrow to the Paiute.)* OL
- **What was Sarah's grandfather's attitude towards the whites?** *(Sarah says he loved them.)* BL

R1 Reading Strategy

Taking Notes Have students make a list of the causes that contributed to changing the traditional way of life of Native Americans. BL

C1 Critical Thinking

Analyzing Primary Sources Ask students what Helen Hunt Jackson meant by the words "dark stain." *(broken treaties, cruelty, massacres, and other harsh and unfair treatment of Native Americans by whites)* Have the class debate whether Jackson's words are fair or unfair. OL CA HR5.

C2 Critical Thinking

Predicting Consequences Before students read on, poll the class to determine how many think Native Americans will benefit from the Dawes Act and how many think they will not. After reading the rest of this subsection, have students discuss what happened and why. OL CA HI2.

W Writing Support

Persuasive Writing Have students imagine they have been asked to write a recommendation to a member of Congress about how to vote on the Dawes Act of 1877. Ask them to write a memo detailing that recommendation and support it with reasons. AL CA 8WA2.4

R2 Reading Strategy

Scaffolding—Academic Vocabulary The word *adapted* was introduced in Chapter 2, Section 2. Ask students to list synonyms for the word. OL

C Critical Thinking

Drawing Conclusions Ask students to discuss why the Ghost Dance became such a source of hope for the Sioux. *(Students may say the Sioux were desperate to save their culture.)* AL CA HI2.

ASSESS

Resources for page 692

Use these resources to assess student mastery of section content.

Section Quiz 15–3

Interactive Tutor Self-Assessment CD-ROM

Reading Check

Answer: to eliminate what Americans regarded as weaknesses of Native American life

History Online

Study Central provides summaries, interactive games, and online graphic organizers to help students review section content.

CLOSE

Evaluating Historian Dee Brown wrote a famous book called *Bury My Heart at Wounded Knee*. Ask students how that title accurately summarizes the fate of the Plains peoples. OL CA HR5.

What Was the Battle at Wounded Knee?

The Dawes Act changed forever the Native American way of life and undermined their cultural traditions. In their despair, the Sioux turned in 1890 to Wovoka, a prophet. Wovoka claimed that the Sioux could regain their former greatness if they performed a ritual known as the Ghost Dance.

C This ritual celebrated a hoped-for day of reckoning when settlers would disappear, the buffalo would return, and Native Americans would reunite with their deceased ancestors. As the ritual spread, reservation officials became alarmed and decided to ban the dance. Believing that the Sioux chief, Sitting Bull, was the leader of the movement, police went to his camp to arrest him. During a scuffle, they shot and killed Sitting Bull.

Several hundred Lakota Sioux fled in fear after Sitting Bull's death. They gathered at a creek called **Wounded Knee** in southwestern South Dakota. On December 29, 1890, the army went there to collect the Sioux's weapons. No one knows how the fighting started, but when a pistol shot rang out, the army responded with fire. More than 200 Sioux and 25 soldiers were killed.

Wounded Knee marked the end of armed conflict between whites and Native Americans. The Native Americans of the Plains had fought hundreds of battles from 1860 to 1890, but they could fight no more. They depended on the buffalo for food, clothing, fuel, and shelter. When the herds were wiped out, resistance became impossible. The Native Americans had lost their long struggle.

Reading Check **Describe** What was the purpose of the Dawes Act?

History Online

Study Central Need help understanding Native American struggles? Visit ca.hss.glencoe.com and click on Study Central.

Section 3 Review

Reading Summary

Review the Main Ideas

- For centuries, Native Americans lived on the Great Plains. Some were farmers and others were nomadic. The buffalo supplied most of their needs.
- As white settlers continued to migrate and settle the West, Native American civilization was continually threatened. Conflict between the whites and the Native Americans persisted through the late 1800s.

What Did You Learn?

1. Who were Geronimo and Chief Joseph?
2. What was the Ghost Dance?

Critical Thinking

3. **Identifying Central Issues** Re-create the diagram below and identify ways the government reservation policy ignored the needs of Native Americans. CA CS1.

4. **The Big Ideas** How did differences in social beliefs between the white settlers and the Native Americans lead to the conflict that occurred in the West? CA HI1.
5. **Analyze** What two aspects of Native American life was the Dawes Act supposed to eliminate? CA HI2.
6. **Sequence** Draw a time line that lists key developments between the U.S. government and Native American nations from 1860 to 1890. CA CS2.
7. **Creative Writing** From the point of view of a Native American, write a poem describing the Plains Indians' lifestyle or a battle or event that occurred on the Plains. CA 8WA2.1

SECTION 3 REVIEW ANSWERS

Review questions reinforce content standard US8.12.

1. Geronimo: Apache chief who led raids to avoid reservation; Chief Joseph: Nez Perce chief who fled to escape reservation
2. Sioux ritual thought to bring about disappearance of whites and return of traditional life
3. Prevented them from following buffalo herds; Located reservations on poor land; Failed to deliver supplies
4. **The Big Ideas** Whites tried to change Native Americans' way of life, which many Native Americans resisted.
5. lack of private property, nomadic tradition
6. Time lines should reflect information in the text.
7. Poems should reflect section information.

Section 4

Farmers in Protest

Guide to Reading

Looking Back, Looking Ahead

You learned that new farming methods and the defeat of the Native Americans allowed settlers to farm the Great Plains. In time, farmers began to organize to solve problems, such as falling crop prices.

Focusing on the Main Ideas

- When crop prices fell in the late 1800s, farmers began to organize politically. *(page 694)*
- In the 1890s, a political party developed supporting the views of farmers and the common people. *(page 695)*

Locating Places

Omaha, Nebraska

Meeting People

James B. Weaver
Grover Cleveland
William Jennings Bryan
William McKinley

Content Vocabulary

National Grange
cooperative (koh • AH • puh • ruh • tiv)
Populist Party (PAH • pyuh • lihst)
free silver

Academic Vocabulary

decline
dynamic (dy • NA • mihk)

Reading Strategy

Identifying Central Issues As you read the section, re-create the diagram below and identify the problems farmers faced in the late 1800s.

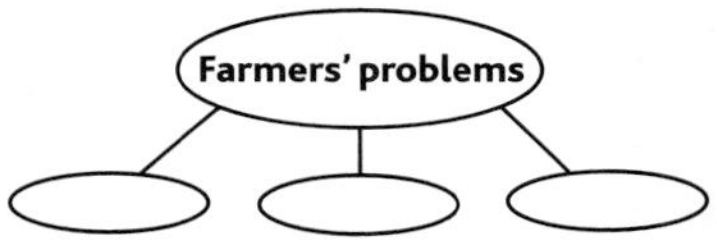

History Social Science Standards

US8.12 Students analyze the transformation of the American economy and the changing social and political conditions in the United States in response to the Industrial Revolution.

NATIONAL GEOGRAPHIC Who & When?

1880 — 1890 — 1900

1880s Farmers' Alliances form

Populist Party banner

1890 Populist Party forms

1892 Populist candidate James Weaver receives 1 million votes for president

1896 William McKinley elected president

William McKinley

FOCUS

BELLRINGER
SKILLBUILDER ACTIVITY

Project **Daily Focus Skills Transparency 15–4** and have students answer the question.

Guide to Reading

Preteaching Vocabulary:
Ask: Which terms are the names of groups? How do you know? *(National Grange and Populist Party; because they are capitalized)*

Answers to Graphic:
falling prices; high expenses and shipping costs; high interest rates

Unpacking the Standards

After reading the section, students will be able to:

- Describe the problems of farmers in the late 1800s.
- Discuss the rise of the Populist Party and other responses to these problems.

SECTION RESOURCES

Print Material
- Reproducible Lesson Plan 15–4*
- Daily Lesson and Discussion Notes 15–4
- Guided Reading Activity 15–4
- Reading Essentials and Study Guide 15–4
- Active Reading Note-Taking Guide 15–4
- Section Quiz 15–4

Transparencies
- Daily Focus Skills Transparency 15–4
- Section Graphic Organizer Transparency 15–4
- California Standards Practice Transparencies

Technology
- Interactive Tutor Self-Assessment CD-ROM
- Exam*View*® Pro Testmaker CD-ROM
- Presentation Plus! CD-ROM

*Available on TeacherWorks™

C Critical Thinking

Drawing Conclusions Ask students what the main idea of the song is. *(Farmers are the most important element of society but others take advantage of them.)* Was that true? Why or why not? *(Students may say that farmers were very important but that by the late 1800s industry was driving the country's economy.)* OL CA 8RC2.0 CA HR3.

W Writing Support

Summary Writing Ask students to summarize the position of farmers after the Civil War. OL

R1 Reading Strategy

Understanding Vocabulary **Ask:** Why did the organization call itself the *National* Grange? *(to appear widespread)* OL

R2 Reading Strategy

Connecting **Ask:** What does *cooperate* mean? *(work together effectively)* How is that meaning related to the term? *(In a cooperative, farmers worked together.)* OL

Answers and Additional Support

US8.12.8 Identify the characteristics and impact of Grangerism and Populism.

The Farmers Organize

Main Idea **When crop prices fell in the late 1800s, farmers began to organize politically.**

Reading Connection Have you heard the expression "strength in numbers"? Read to find out how farmers organized in groups in the late 1800s to help solve the challenges they faced.

An American Story

In the last decades of the 1800s, farmers suffered from falling prices and rising costs. They expressed their frustration in a popular song:

> **"When the banker says he's broke,**
> **And the merchant's up in smoke,**
> **They forget that it's the farmer**
> **feeds them all. . . .**
> **The farmer is the man,**
> **Lives on credit till the fall;**
> **With the interest rates so high,**
> **It's a wonder he don't die,**
> **For the mortgage man's the one**
> **who gets it all."**
>
> **—from "The Farmer Is the Man"**

▲ Honoring the Farmer, 1870s poster

Crop Prices Fall After the Civil War, farming expanded in the West and the South, and more land came under cultivation. The supply of crops grew faster than the demand for them, however, and prices fell steadily. In 1866 a bushel of wheat sold for $1.45. By the mid-1880s, the price had dropped to 80 cents, and by the mid-1890s to 49 cents. At the same time, farmers' expenses—for transporting their goods to market, for seed, and for equipment and other manufactured goods—remained high.

Farmers blamed their troubles on three groups in particular. They resented the railroad companies, which charged farmers high rates to ship their crops. They were angry at the Eastern manufacturers, who charged high prices for their products. They also had problems with bankers.

Farmers needed to borrow money to buy seed, equipment, and other goods. After they sold their crops, they had to pay the high interest rates set by bankers. If crops failed and farmers could not repay the loans, they were in danger of losing their farms.

Farmers with small and middle-sized holdings struggled to survive. Senator William A. Peffer of Kansas summed up the farmers' plight when he noted that the railroad companies "took possession of the land" and the bankers "took possession of the farmer."

What Did the Grange Do? Farmers began to organize in an effort to solve their problems. Within a short time, they created a mass political movement. The first farmers' organization of this period was a network of local organizations that came to be called the **National Grange.** The Grange offered farmers education, fellowship, and support.

Above all, the Grange tried to encourage economic self-sufficiency. It set up "cash-only" **cooperatives** (koh • AH • puh • ruh • tivz), stores where farmers bought products from each other. The cooperatives charged lower prices than regular stores and provided an outlet for farmers' crops. The purpose of the "cash-only" policy was to remove the burden of credit buying that threatened farmers.

More Skill Practice

Visual Literacy Ask students to identify elements in the pictures that may present an idealized or romanticized image of the farmer and farming. *(The horses, farmer, and plow are very clean, not covered with dirt or mud; the horses are sleek, more like races horses than plough horses; the home on the hill is large and tidy, not like a sod house of the Plains.)* OL CA 8LS1.9

US8.12.8 Identify the characteristics and impact of Grangerism and Populism.

In the 1870s, the Grange tried to cut farmers' costs by asking state legislatures to place a limit on railroad shipping rates. Many Midwestern states did pass such laws. By 1878 however, the railroads had put so much pressure on state legislatures that these states repealed the rate regulations.

Adding to the problems of the Grange, the cooperatives also began to fail. Farmers were often short of cash and had to borrow money until their next crop was sold. The cash-only cooperative could not work if borrowing was necessary. By the late 1870s, the Grange had **declined.** Rural reformers then tried to help farmers through the Farmers' Alliances.

What Were Farmers' Alliances? The Farmers' Alliances were networks of organizations that sprang up in the West and the South in the 1880s. Alliance leaders extended the movement to other states. By 1890 the Southern Alliance had more than 3 million members, and the Colored Farmers' National Alliance, a separate organization of African American farmers, had 1 million members.

Like the Grange, the Farmers' Alliances sponsored education and cooperative buying and selling. The Alliances also proposed a plan in which the federal government would store farmers' crops in warehouses and lend money to the farmers. When the stored crops were sold, the farmers would pay back the loans. Such a plan would reduce the power that railroads, banks, and merchants had over farmers and would offer farmers some federal protection. Regional differences and personality clashes impacted the effectiveness of the Alliances, even as they moved into politics.

Reading Check **Describe** What is the purpose of a cooperative?

History Online

Student Web Activity Visit ca.hss.glencoe.com and click on Chapter 15—*Student Web Activities* for an activity on the life of a farmer in the late 1800s.

A Party of the People

Main Idea **In the 1890s, a political party developed supporting the views of farmers and the common people.**

Reading Connection What beliefs and ideas do you think a political party today would have to support in order to be considered a party of the common people? Read to find out about the beginnings of the People's, or Populist, Party in the late 1800s.

In 1890 members of the Farmers' Alliance identified candidates who supported the cause of the farmer. That year, four governors in the South were elected after promising to support the Alliance program. Several Southern legislatures now had pro-Alliance majorities, and more than 40 Democrats who supported the Alliance program were elected to Congress. Alliance candidates in the West did equally well.

The Populist Party Pleased with such successes, Alliance leaders worked to turn the movement into a national political party. In February 1890, Alliance members formed the People's Party of the U.S.A., also known as the **Populist Party** (PAH•pyuh•lihst). The goals of this new party were rooted in populism, or appeal to the common people.

▲ Populist farmers gather in Dickinson County, Kansas

C Critical Thinking

Making Generalizations Have students make generalizations about the successes and failures of the two farm organizations discussed in this section. Ask them to explain the evidence they used to make their generalizations. *(Answers may include that farmers had difficulty staying organized and working together; that economic forces proved too powerful for the organizations; or that regional differences were difficult to overcome.)* AL CA HI1.

R1 Reading Strategy

Academic Vocabulary Have students read the sentence containing the word *declined*. Then ask them to write a sentence using the word. EL

R2 Reading Strategy

Scaffolding—Connecting Point out to students the root of the word *Populist* is the same as for *people* and *popular*. Have them speculate on the beliefs of the Populist Party in the late 1800s. OL CA 8RW1.3

This READING SKILL was introduced in Chapter 3.

History Online

Objectives and answers to the student activity can be found in the Web Activity Lesson Plan feature at ca.hss.glencoe.com.

Reading Check

Answer: to provide farmers with a way to achieve economic self-sufficiency by providing them with stores that charged lower prices and gave them an outlet for crops

More Skill Practice

Historical and Social Sciences Analysis Skill Have students make a Venn diagram comparing and contrasting the Grange and the Farmers Alliances. If necessary, provide them with a labeled Venn diagram to serve as a model. OL CA HI2.

R Reading Strategy

Understanding Vocabulary

Have students explain why Populists wanted the unlimited coinage of silver money. *(They believed it would give farmers more money to pay their debts.)* EL CA 8RC2.0

Review The Big Idea

Review the Big Idea for this section: "Reactions to social injustice can lead to reform movements." Have students find out which Populist reforms were eventually adopted and which were not. *(Adopted: direct election of senators, secret ballot, shorter working hours, national income tax, government ownership of some railroads; Not adopted: free silver, government ownership of telegraph lines, single term for president and vice president)* OL CA HI3.

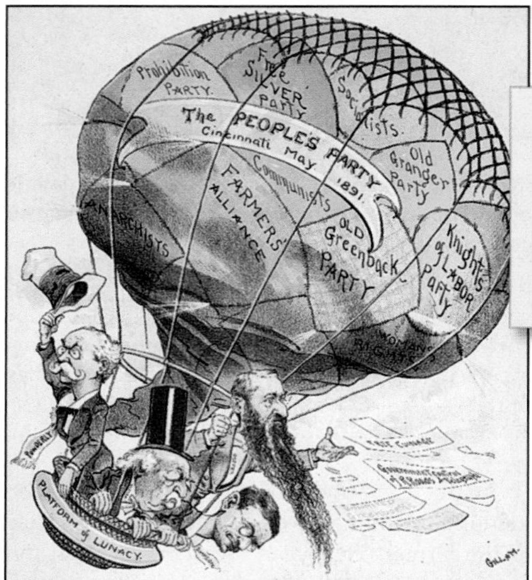

A PARTY OF PATCHES.
Grand Balloon Ascension—Cincinnati, May 20th, 1891.

Analyzing *Political Cartoons*

Party of Patches The cartoonist shows the Populist Party as a collection of special interest groups and minor political parties. ***Does the cartoon support or ridicule the Populist Party? Explain.***

The new party claimed that the government, not private companies, should own the railroads and telegraph lines. The Populists also wanted to replace the country's gold-based currency system with a flexible currency system that was based on **free silver**—the unlimited production of silver coins. They believed that putting more silver coins into the economy would give farmers more money to pay their debts.

The Populist Party supported a number of political and labor reforms. The party wanted election reforms such as limiting the president and vice president to a single term, electing senators directly, and introducing the use of secret ballots. The Populist Party also called for shorter hours for workers and the creation of a national income tax.

Populist Gains and Problems At a convention in **Omaha, Nebraska,** in July 1892, the Populist Party nominated **James B. Weaver** of Iowa to run for president. In the election, Weaver received more than 1 million votes—8.5 percent of the total—and 22 electoral votes. **Grover Cleveland,** the Democratic candidate, won the election, but the Populists had done well for a third party.

The Populists made a strong showing in the state and local elections of 1894 and had hopes for building even stronger support in the presidential election of 1896. The party nominated a number of energetic candidates, but lacked money and organization.

Another blow against populism was struck by the Democratic Party in the South. In the 1890s, Democrat-controlled Southern state legislatures placed strict limits on the rights of African Americans to vote. Many freedmen—who might have supported the Populists—were unable to vote.

The Populist crusade for free silver and against the "money power" continued, however. Banking and business interests warned that coining unlimited amounts of new currency would lead to inflation and ruin the economy.

Farmers were joined by debtors in supporting free silver, hoping that loans could be repaid more cheaply. Silver-mining companies in the West also supported the cause. If the government coined large quantities of silver, they had a place to sell their metal.

In the mid-1890s, Democrats from farm and silver-producing states took up the free silver issue. This created a problem for Populists. Should they ally themselves with these Democrats? Or should they remain a separate party and risk dividing the free-silver vote?

The Election of 1896 President Grover Cleveland, a Democrat, opposed free silver. At their 1896 convention, however, the Democrats chose a candidate for president who supported free silver and other Populist goals.

The Democratic Party's candidate was 36-year-old **William Jennings Bryan**, known as the Great Commoner because of his appeal to average Americans. Bryan passionately believed in the farmers' causes.

Answers and Additional Support

Analyzing *Political Cartoons*

The four men in the balloon basket are recognizable leaders of the Populist Party.

Answer: ridicules it; the term "Party of Patches" is negative, the cartoon shows the party as a fragmented collection of special interests, and the basket is labeled "Platform of Lunacy."

Did You Know?

A scholar has argued that the popular children's classic *The Wizard of Oz*, published in 1900, contained numerous symbols of the Populist Party. The Yellow Brick Road was the gold standard. Dorothy's slippers, silver in the book, represent free silver. The Wicked Witch of the East symbolized Eastern bankers who controlled the people, the Munchkins.

The Populists decided to endorse Bryan as their candidate for president and to nominate their own candidate, Tom Watson of Georgia, for vice president. The Republicans nominated **William McKinley** of Ohio for president. A former representative and governor of Ohio, McKinley was a shrewd politician who opposed free silver.

A fiery and popular speaker, Bryan proved to be an outstanding campaigner. He crossed the nation giving one **dynamic** speech after another, attacking bankers and other money interests.

Bryan's strenuous campaigning did not produce an election victory. By the time of the election, an economic depression was nearly over, and voters believed that good times were returning. They put their trust in the Republican candidate McKinley, who represented stability. Even the economic situation of the farmers was improving. The Populists' message no longer W seemed urgent. McKinley won 271 electoral votes to Bryan's 176. McKinley received 7.1 million popular votes to 6.5 million for Bryan. The Populist ticket did poorly, receiving only 222,600 popular votes and no electoral votes.

The Populist Legacy The Populist Party had an impact on politics and government far beyond its showing in national elections. R Minor parties have often promoted reform by taking clear-cut stands on controversial issues and proposing bold and original solutions. Reformers adopted many Populist ideas and succeeded in getting many new laws passed. Among the Populist proposals that were adopted and are still in place today are the federal income tax (Sixteenth Amendment, 1913), direct election of U.S. senators (Seventeenth Amendment, 1913), the secret ballot (late 1890s), and primary elections (Wisconsin, 1903). In the 1900s, the United States adopted an eight-hour workday.

Reading Check **Examine** Why did the Republican candidate win the presidential election of 1896?

History Online
Study Central Need help understanding why farmers organized to protest? Visit ca.hss.glencoe.com and click on Study Central.

Section 4 Review

Reading Summary

Review the Main Ideas

- To help solve their economic problems, farmers formed organizations such as the National Grange and Farmers' Alliances.
- In time the farm organizations developed into a national political party, the Populist Party.

What Did You Learn?

1. Which three groups did farmers blame for their problems? Why?
2. Who were the presidential candidates in the election of 1896?

Critical Thinking

3. **Analyzing Information** Re-create the diagram below and explain what actions farmers took to address their problems. CA HI2.

Farmers' problems
Action: | Action: | Action:

4. **Analyze** Why were granges and alliances formed? CA HI1.
5. **Infer** Why do you think the Populists considered themselves to be a party of the people? CA CS1.
6. **The Big Ideas** What reforms eventually resulted from the Populist campaign? CA HI2.
7. **Persuasive Writing** Write a campaign slogan for a Populist candidate who is running for office, and design a bumper sticker displaying your slogan. CA 8WA2.4

SECTION 4 REVIEW ANSWERS

Review questions reinforce content standards US8.2 and US8.3.

1. railroad companies, manufacturers, bankers
2. Democrat and Populist William Jennings Bryan, Republican William McKinley
3. Formed groups like Grange and Farmers' Alliances; Set up cooperatives; Pushed legislatures to limit railroad rates; Backed Populists
4. to help farmers
5. They endorsed policies that favored common people.
6. The Big Ideas national income tax, direct election of senators, secret ballot, primary elections, shorter working hours
7. Answers will vary but should reflect understanding of the Populist program.

W Writing Support

Narrative Writing Have students write a newspaper article about the election of 1896, using details from the text. OL CA 8WA2.1

R Reading Strategy

Scaffolding—Academic Vocabulary The word *controversy* was introduced in Chapter 12, Section 2. Ask a student to define the word *controversial*. OL

ASSESS

Resources for page 697

Use these resources to assess student mastery of section content.

- Section Quiz 15–4
- Interactive Tutor Self-Assessment CD-ROM

Reading Check

Answer: The economic slowdown ended, and voters put their trust in McKinley, who represented stability.

History Online

Study Central provides summaries, interactive games, and online graphic organizers to help students review section content.

CLOSE

Drawing Conclusions
Ask students if they consider the Populist Party to be a success. Why or why not? OL CA HR1.

Analyzing Primary Sources

FOCUS

History–Social Science Standards

The following standard is covered on pages 698–699.

US8.12 Students analyze the transformation of the American economy and the changing social and political conditions in the United States in response to the Industrial Revolution.

TEACH

R Reading Strategy

Visualizing Ask: What sights and sounds do you think are part of Adams's cattle drive? How many cattle are being herded? How many cowhands are leading them? What does the land look like? Discuss students' responses. OL CA 8RC2.0

W Writing Support

Narrative Writing Have students continue Adams's journal by writing entries for their arrival in Iowa. Students' writings should reflect the cowhands' feelings as well as the kind of work they think would be necessary. OL CA 8WA2.1

Answers and Additional Support

Analyzing Primary Sources

US8.12 Students analyze the transformation of the American economy and the changing social and political conditions in the United States in response to the Industrial Revolution.

On the Western Frontier

Following the Civil War, many settlers headed West to build new lives. Some of them raised cattle, others farmed the land. These settlers affected the people who had lived there for generations—the Native Americans. The government's plans for accommodating this expansion included moving Native Americans to reservations and schooling their children.

Read the passages on pages 698 and 699 and answer the questions that follow.

This painting by Charles M. Russell shows cowboys breaking camp while on a long drive. ▶

Reader's Dictionary

loaf: to spend time in idleness

afoot: on foot

blueing (BLOO • ing): a preparation used in laundering to counteract yellowing of white fabrics

abide (uh • BYD): to endure or withstand something

dumb (DUHM): not able to speak

detected: discovered, found out

On the Cattle Trail

R *Cowboy Andy Adams describes the start of his first cattle drive and the instructions given by the trail boss.*

Flood seldom gave orders; but, as a number of us had never worked on the trail before, at breakfast on the morning of our start he gave in substance these general directions:

"Boys, the secret of trailing cattle is never to let your herd know that they are under restraint. Let everything that is done be done voluntarily by the cattle. From the moment you let them off the bed ground in the morning until they are bedded at night, never let a cow take a step, except in the direction of its destination. In this manner you can **loaf** away the day, and cover from fifteen to twenty miles, and the herd in the meantime will enjoy all the freedom of an open range. Of course, it's long, tiresome hours to the men; but the condition of the herd and saddle stock demands sacrifices on our part, if any have to be made. And I want to caution you younger boys about your horses. . . . Accidents will happen to horses, but don't let it be your fault; keep your saddle blankets dry and clean, for no better word can be spoken of a man than that he is careful with his horses . . . we have not a horse to spare, and a man **afoot** is useless."

—from *Trail Drive: A True Narrative of Cowboy Life from Andy Adams' Log of a Cowboy* W

EXTENDING THE CONTENT

Cattle Drives Ten to twelve people led a herd that could number 3,000 cattle on a long drive. The trail boss led the team, assisted by a cook and a ramrod. The group included a few wranglers, who led spare horses, and several cowhands, called "waddies." Typically two waddies rode on point, leading the herd. Two more rode alongside on the flank. Another pair trailed behind the herd, which was called riding drag. This dusty position was undesirable and was given either to inexperienced hands or to those who were being punished.

Winter in Dakota Territory

Settlers endured challenging living conditions. Laura Ingalls Wilder wrote of her family's experiences during the bitter winter of 1880–81.

Ma said " . . . We must get out the washing while the weather's clear so we can."

All that day Laura and Carrie and Mary looked forward to the [magazine] *Youth's Companions* and often they spoke of them. But the bright day was short. They stirred and punched the clothes boiling on the stove; they lifted them on the broom handle into the tub where Ma soaped them and rubbed them. Laura rinsed them, Carrie stirred the **blueing** bag in the second rinse-water until it was blue enough. Laura made the boiled starch. And when for the last time Ma went out into the cold to hang the freezing wash on the line, Pa had come for dinner.

Then they washed the dishes, they scrubbed the floor and blacked the stove, and washed the inside of the windowpanes. Ma brought in the frozen-dry clothes and they sorted them and sprinkled them and rolled them tightly, ready for ironing. Twilight had come. It was too late to read that day and after supper there was no lamplight because they must save the last of the kerosene.

—from *The Long Winter*

◀ This shirt was part of the Ghost Dance in which the Sioux tried to preserve their way of life.

Indian School

In attempts to "civilize" Native American children, Indian schools were created in several parts of the country. In this passage, Ah-nen-la-de-ni of the Mohawk people describes his first experience in such a school.

After the almost complete freedom of reservation life the cramped quarters and the dull routine of the school were maddening to all us strangers. There were endless rules for us to study and **abide** by, and hardest of all was the rule against speaking to each other in our own language. We must speak English or remain silent, and those who knew no English were forced to be **dumb** or else break the rules in secret. This last we did quite frequently, and were punished, when **detected,** by being made to stand in the "public hall" for a long time or to march about the yard while the other boys were at play. [R] [C]

—from *Witnessing America*

DBQ Document-Based Questions

On the Cattle Trail

1. What seems to be the cowhand's biggest secret?
2. According to the foreman, what is worth the sacrifice of the cowboys' comfort?

Winter in Dakota Territory

3. How many steps were involved in washing the clothes for Laura's family?
4. What activity did Laura and her sisters look forward to doing once their chores were done?

Indian School

5. How does Ah-nen-la-de-ni describe school?
6. What is the hardest rule for the children to follow?

Read to Write

7. Reread the documents to find evidence that shows how each author needed to adapt to a new environment or circumstance. What adjustments did they make? Do they explain why? Write an essay explaining your conclusions. CA 8WA1.1

R Reading Strategy

Evaluating Ask: How did Ah-nen-la-de-ni describe his earlier life compared to living at the school? *(a life of complete freedom)* OL

C Critical Thinking

Analyzing Information
Ask: Why did the school have the rule that the children could not speak Mohawk? *(to force the children to use English)* If you were in charge of the school, would you have had the same rule? Why or why not? *(Students should give reasons for their response.)* OL CA HR3.

ASSESS

Have students answer the Document-Based Questions.

CLOSE

Comparing and Contrasting Ask: What similarities can you see among the lives of these three writers? How were they different? *(Students should note that all three traveled to new places, though Duffield probably returned to Texas after the cattle drive.)* OL

DBQ Document-Based Questions

1. never to let your herd know they are under restraint
2. the condition of the herd was more important than their comfort.
3. about eleven steps
4. reading *Youth's Companion's*
5. cramped living conditions, boring routine, endless rules
6. the one requiring them not to speak to each other in their own language but only to use English
7. Students should list those things they would want to continue and give reasons for each item on the list.

CHAPTER 15 Assessment

Resources for pages 700–701

Use these resources to review, assess, or reteach the chapter.

- Active Reading Note-Taking Guide, Chapter 15
- Chapter 15 Reading Essentials and Study Guide
- Chapter 15 Tests, Forms A and B
- Standards Assessment, Forms A and B
- California Standards Practice Workbook
- Succeeding on the California History–Social Science Standards CD-ROM
- MindJogger Videoquiz
- Interactive Tutor Self-Assessment CD-ROM

Review Content Vocabulary

Sample clues:

1. land set aside for Native Americans
2. stores where farmers bought products from one another
3. citizens who took the law into their own hands
4. Hispanic ranch hands
5. streaks of ore underground
6. when cattle run in a panic

Review the Main Idea

7. a rich lode of silver-bearing ore on the Carson River in Nevada discovered in 1859
8. brought workers to the West; transported goods to and from the East; gave boost to steel and other industries; supported the growth of towns around the railroad; attracted settlers
9. Hispanic ranch hand

Chapter 15 Assessment

Standard US8.12

Review Content Vocabulary

On a sheet of paper, create a crossword puzzle using the following terms. Use the terms' definitions as your crossword clues.

1. reservations
2. cooperatives
3. vigilantes
4. vaqueros
5. lodes
6. stampedes

Review the Main Ideas

Section 1 • The Mining Booms

7. What was the Comstock Lode?
8. In what ways did the railroads boost the American economy?

Section 2 • Ranchers and Farmers

9. What is a vaquero?
10. What attracted farmers to the Great Plains?

Section 3 • Native American Struggles

11. What actions by whites destroyed the buffalo population?
12. In what present-day state was the Indian Territory located?

Section 4 • Farmers in Protest

13. How did the Grange help farmers?
14. What political reforms did the Populists support?

Critical Thinking

15. **Analyze** How did the rush to find gold and silver spark the creation of new communities in the West? CA CS1.
16. **Economics Link** Why was the Cattle Kingdom dependent on the railroads? CA HI6.
17. **Cause and Effect** Describe the problems that led farmers to organize granges and alliances. CA HI2.

Geography Skills

Study the map below and answer the following questions. CA CS3.

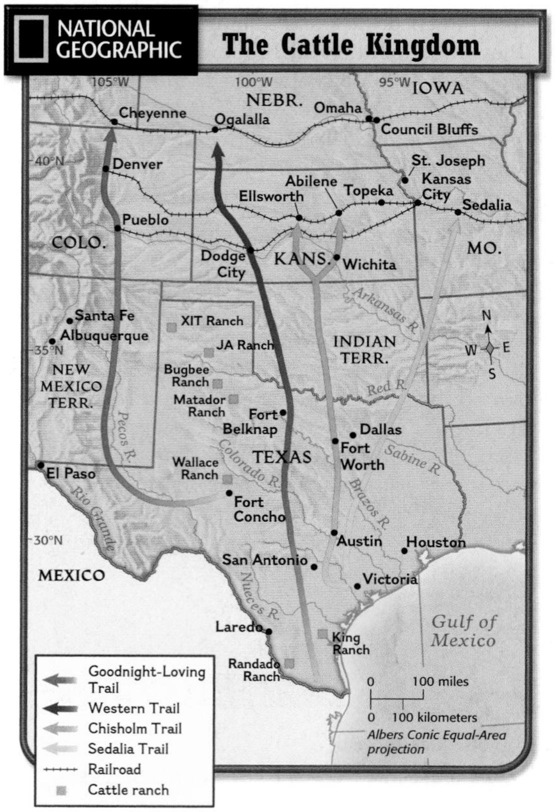

18. **Location** In what part of Texas were most of the large cattle ranches located?
19. **Movement** To which railroad towns did the Goodnight-Loving Trail run?
20. **Movement** Which cattle trails ran though Indian Territory?

10. railroad made journey easier and cheaper; Homestead Act offered free land; above average rainfall in late 1870s promised good harvests; advertising
11. hiring of hunters by railroads to kill buffalo for food and to prevent animals from blocking tracks; hunting for sport; selling hides for profit
12. Oklahoma
13. encouraged them to organize and solve their problems; offered education, fellowship, and support; encouraged self-sufficiency; influenced political and labor policies
14. limiting presidential and vice-presidential terms; electing senators directly; using secret ballots

Critical Thinking

15. Communities were formed to serve the needs of miners. It motivated timely

History Online

Self-Check Quiz Visit ca.hss.glencoe.com to prepare for the Chapter 15 test.

Read to Write

21. **The Big Ideas** **Analyze** Briefly discuss the geographic challenges faced by settlers and Native Americans in the American West and Great Plains. How did they overcome the challenges? CA 8WA2.4

22. **Expository Writing** Reread and take notes on the section of the chapter that discusses the chores of a farm woman. Use your notes to create an hour-by-hour schedule to show one day's typical activities for a farm wife living on the Great Plains. CA 8RC2.0

23. **Using Your FOLDABLES** Choose one of the four groups of people you learned about in this chapter. Describe that groups' triumphs and tragedies in a newspaper article you could have written in the late 1800s. CA WS1.1

Using Academic Vocabulary

24. Read the following sentences and write the meaning of the underlined academic vocabulary word.

    Power in a republic is <u>derived</u> from the people.

    New machinery was developed to <u>extract</u> ore from the earth's crust.

Economics Connection

25. **Researching** Research to find information about a Native American reservation in the United States today. Write a report describing one of the major businesses on that reservation. CA HI6. CA 8WA2.3

Reviewing Skills

26. Review READING SKILL **Visualizing** If you lived on the frontier in the late 1800s, would you have been a miner, a rancher, a Native American, or a farmer? Select one and write an essay describing a day in your life. Use clear descriptive language so that your readers have a good visual sense of what your life was like. CA 8WA2.1

27. Review ANALYSIS SKILL **Composing** Reread the quote from the farmer's song on page 694. Write a song or poem that a banker or merchant might write. CA HR5.

Standards Practice

Read the passage below and answer the following question.

> Having behind us the producing masses of this nation and the world, supported by the commercial interests, the laboring interests and the toilers everywhere, we will answer their demand for a gold standard by saying to them: You shall not press down upon the brow of labor this crown of thorns, you shall not crucify mankind upon a cross of gold.
>
> —William Jennings Bryan, "Cross of Gold" Speech, 1896

28 By speaking against the gold standard, Bryan was showing his support for the Populist goal of

A an eight-hour workday.

B a currency system based on free silver.

C farmers' cooperatives.

D an income tax.

29 When Bryan refers to "the producing masses of this nation," he most likely is including

A farmers.

B political leaders.

C manufacturers.

D Republicans.

completion of the transcontinental railroad, which led to further settlement and growth.

16. Ranchers used railroads to ship cattle to Eastern markets.

17. falling prices, rising costs, debt problems, loneliness on the frontier

Geography Skills

18. west central and northwest

19. Pueblo, Denver, Cheyenne

20. Western, Chisholm, Sedalia

Read to Write

21. **The Big Ideas** Geographic challenges included hard-to-plow ground, dry climate, treeless terrain, fire, insects, and cold snowy winters; methods to address these challenges included dry farming, steel plows, windmills, and barbed wire.

22. Students' schedules should reflect the description of the lives of women on the Great Plains.

23. Using Your FOLDABLES Articles should reflect an understanding of the text information.

Using Academic Vocabulary

24. received; take out

Economics Connection

25. Reports should describe a major business operated on the chosen reservation.

Reviewing Skills

26. Review READING SKILL Students' descriptions should reflect the information in the text.

27. Review ANALYSIS SKILL Students' songs should reflect the bankers' and merchants' views of their own importance.

Standards Practice

28. B

29. A

Bonus Question

Ask: What was the most important piece of legislation you read about in this chapter? *(Answers may include the Homestead Act or the Dawes Act.)* OL CA 8RC2.0

History Online

Have students visit the Web site at ca.hss.glencoe.com to review Chapter 15 and take the **Self-Check Quiz.**

Chapter 16 Planning Guide

SECTION RESOURCES

Main Ideas	Print Materials	Technology Resources
Section 1: Railroads Lead the Way 1. Railroad barons used consolidation to expand their companies and create a growing system of railroads throughout the United States. 2. Railroad growth stimulated the economy, and innovations made railroad travel more efficient and profitable.	• Reproducible Lesson Plan 16–1* • Daily Lesson and Discussion Notes 16–1 • Active Reading Note-Taking Guide 16–1 • Reading Essentials and Study Guide 16–1 • Guided Reading Activity 16–1 • Section Quiz 16–1	Daily Focus Skills Transparency 16–1 Section Graphic Organizer Transparency 16–1 California Standards Practice Transparencies Interactive Tutor Self-Assessment CD-ROM Exam*View*® Pro Testmaker CD-ROM Presentation Plus! CD-ROM
Section 2: Inventions 1. New inventions improved communication and allowed Americans to contact one another over long distances. 2. The invention of electricity gave America a new source of power. 3. Improvements in transportation made travel easier and helped industries make their goods available to a wider audience.	• Reproducible Lesson Plan 16–2* • Daily Lesson and Discussion Notes 16–2 • Active Reading Note-Taking Guide 16–2 • Reading Essentials and Study Guide 16–2 • Guided Reading Activity 16–2 • Section Quiz 16–2	Daily Focus Skills Transparency 16–2 Section Graphic Organizer Transparency 16–2 California Standards Practice Transparencies Interactive Tutor Self-Assessment CD-ROM Exam*View*® Pro Testmaker CD-ROM Presentation Plus! CD-ROM
Section 3: The Age of Big Business 1. The American economy grew because the country contained abundant land, labor, and capital. 2. The development of the oil industry created one of the first monopolies. 3. Monopolies in the steel business and other industries created the need for governmental regulation.	• Reproducible Lesson Plan 16–3* • Daily Lesson and Discussion Notes 16–3 • Active Reading Note-Taking Guide 16–3 • Reading Essentials and Study Guide 16–3 • Guided Reading Activity 16–3 • Section Quiz 16–3	Daily Focus Skills Transparency 16–3 Section Graphic Organizer Transparency 16–3 California Standards Practice Transparencies Interactive Tutor Self-Assessment CD-ROM Exam*View*® Pro Testmaker CD-ROM Presentation Plus! CD-ROM
Section 4: Industrial Workers 1. Industrialization created many jobs, but it also created hazardous working conditions. 2. Workers created labor unions to combat unsafe working conditions in many of the nation's industries. 3. Strikes often ended in violence, causing many people to turn against labor unions.	• Reproducible Lesson Plan 16–4* • Daily Lesson and Discussion Notes 16–4 • Active Reading Note-Taking Guide 16–4 • Reading Essentials and Study Guide 16–4 • Guided Reading Activity 16–4 • Section Quiz 16–4	Daily Focus Skills Transparency 16–4 Section Graphic Organizer Transparency 16–4 California Standards Practice Transparencies Interactive Tutor Self-Assessment CD-ROM Exam*View*® Pro Testmaker CD-ROM Presentation Plus! CD-ROM Vocabulary PuzzleMaker CD-ROM

PACING YOUR LESSONS

Chapter Introduction	Section 1	Section 2	Section 3	Section 4	Chapter Assessment
$\frac{1}{2}$ Day	1 Day	2 Days	2 Days	1 Day	$\frac{1}{2}$ Day

0:00 **OUT OF TIME?** Assign the Chapter 16 ***Reading Essentials and Study Guide***

*Available on TeacherWorks™

Standards-Based Lesson Plan

History–Social Science Standards Covered in Chapter 16

The standards covered in the chapter are listed below. Use the accompanying activity as you teach the chapter to ensure student mastery of these standards. This activity can be used in combination with the program's print and technology assessment materials.

Standard	Section 1	Section 2	Section 3	Section 4
US8.12 Students analyze the transformation of the American economy and the changing social and political conditions in the United States in response to the Industrial Revolution.	✔	✔	✔	✔
US8.12.1 Trace patterns of agricultural and industrial development as they relate to climate, use of natural resources, markets, and trade and locate such development on a map.	✔	✔	✔	
US8.12.4 Discuss entrepreneurs, industrialists, and bankers in politics, commerce, and industry (e.g., Andrew Carnegie, John D. Rockefeller, Leland Stanford).	✔		✔	
US8.12.6 Discuss child labor, working conditions, and laissez-faire policies toward big business and examine the labor movement, including its leaders (e.g., Samuel Gompers), its demand for collective bargaining, and its strikes and protests over labor conditions.				✔
US8.12.9 Name the significant inventors and their inventions and identify how they improved the quality of life (e.g., Thomas Edison, Alexander Graham Bell, Orville and Wilbur Wright).	✔	✔		

Cumulative Standards-Assessment Activity

The Cumulative Standards-Assessment Activity will help students organize and learn the important information from the chapter. Begin teaching the chapter with this activity, and have students complete it as they read the chapter.

Creating a Chart for Activating Prior Knowledge

Purpose By activating prior knowledge, students relate new content to information they already know. This process helps them see connections between events and trends. They can also use the exercise to set a purpose for their reading.

Introduction to Activating Prior Knowledge

1. Write on the board one of the topics of this chapter, such as railroads or inventions. Have the class brainstorm facts that they already know about that topic. **Ask:** What would you like to learn further about the topic?
2. Ask students to copy this chart into their notebooks:

What I Know	What I Want to Learn	What I Learned

Explain that students should first scan each section's headings and subheadings and develop a list of topics covered in the chapter. They should create a chart for each of those topics. Before reading each section, they should complete the first two columns of the chart, identifying what they already know and would like to learn. As they read, they can complete the third column. Caution students to read carefully to see if they identify any statements in the "What I Know" column that are not accurate, and revise them if needed.

3. As you review the chapter, ask volunteers to name some of the new information they acquired. Encourage them to do further research if there are any questions that they still have on a topic that was not addressed in the text.

Chapter 16 Resources

READING SUPPORT

- Content Vocabulary Activity 16
- Academic Vocabulary Activity 16
- Reading Skills Activity 16
- American Literature Reading 16
- Biography Activities 16A–16C
- Chapter 16 Active Reading Note-Taking Guide
- Chapter 16 Guided Reading Activities
- Chapter 16 Reading Essentials and Study Guide
- Glencoe Literature Library
- Glencoe Video Program
- Vocabulary PuzzleMaker CD-ROM
- Interactive Graphic Organizers CD-ROM
- American History Primary Source Document Library CD-ROM

CRITICAL THINKING

- Critical Thinking Skills Activity 16
- Primary Source Reading 16
- Cause-and-Effect Transparency 16, Strategy, and Activity
- Presentation Plus! CD-ROM

UNIVERSAL ACCESS

- Universal Access Activity 16
- Then and Now Transparencies 16A–16B, Strategy, and Activity
- Graphic Novel Activity 16
- School-to-Home Connection Activities 16A–16D
- English Learner Handbook Chapter 16 Activities
- Universal Access for the American History Classroom
- Moments in Time
- American Art and Architecture Transparencies, Strategies, and Activities
- American Art Prints
- American Music Cultural Traditions
- American Music Hits Through History
- StudentWorks Plus CD-ROM

SKILL PRACTICE

- Map Overlay Transparency 16, Strategy, and Activity
- Analysis Skills Activity 16
- Time Line Activity 16
- Geography and History Activity 16
- Economics and History Activity 16
- Chart, Graph, and Map Skills Activity 16
- Political Cartoon Activity 16
- Supreme Court Case Study 16
- In-Text Map Transparency 16, Strategy, and Activity
- Step Into American History Activity 16
- Citizenship and Service Learning Activity 16
- Outline Map Resource Book
- MindJogger Plus Videoquiz

WRITING SUPPORT

- Writing Activity 16
- Language Arts Activity 16
- Writer's Guidebook
- Middle School Writing Process Transparencies

ASSESSMENT

GLENCOE'S ASSESSMENT ADVANTAGE

- Chapter 16 Section Quizzes
- Chapter 16 Tests, Forms A and B
- California Standards Assessment, Forms A and B
- Cumulative Assessment Activity US8.12
- California Standards Practice Workbook
- Succeeding on the California History–Social Science Standards CD-ROM
- Exam*View*® Pro Testmaker CD-ROM
- Interactive Tutor Self-Assessment CD-ROM

CD-ROM
DVD
Print Material
Poster
Transparency
Music Program
Videocassette
Glencoe Literature Library

Chapter 16 Resources

TECHNOLOGY

- StudentWorks Plus CD-ROM
- TeacherWorks Plus CD-ROM
- Exam*View*® Pro Testmaker CD-ROM
- Interactive Tutor Self-Assessment CD-ROM
- Presentation Plus! CD-ROM
- Succeeding on the California History–Social Science Standards CD-ROM
- Vocabulary PuzzleMaker CD-ROM
- Interactive Graphic Organizers CD-ROM
- Interactive Time Line CD-ROM
- American History Primary Source Document Library CD-ROM
- MindJogger Plus Videoquiz
- American Music Cultural Traditions
- American Music Hits Through History
- Glencoe Video Program
- Professional Development in Middle School Social Studies Series
- Teaching American History With *Discovering Our Past: The American Journey to World War I*

SPANISH RESOURCES

- Spanish Activities and Assessment
  - Spanish Content Vocabulary Activities
  - Spanish Guided Reading Activities
  - Spanish Quizzes and Tests
  - Spanish California Standards Assessment
- Spanish Reading Essentials and Study Guide
- Spanish School-to-Home Connection
- Spanish Declaration of Independence and U.S. Constitution

TRANSPARENCIES

- California Standards Practice Transparencies
- Daily Focus Skills Transparencies
- Section Graphic Organizer Transparencies
- In-Text Map Transparencies
- Map Overlay Transparencies
- Cause-and-Effect Transparencies
- Then and Now Transparencies
- American Art and Architecture Transparencies
- Middle School Writing Process Transparencies

TEACHER PLANNING

- Daily Lesson and Discussion Notes
- English Learner Handbook
- Guide to Daily Intervention
- *Discovering Our Past: The American Journey to World War I* Reading and Study Skills Foldables
- Reading Strategies and Activities for the Social Studies Classroom
- Chapter 16 Reproducible Lesson Plans (correlated to California History–Social Studies Standards)
- Universal Access for the American History Classroom
- NGS U.S. Desk Map
- NGS U.S. Atlas

PROFESSIONAL DEVELOPMENT

- Building Academic Vocabulary
- Strategies for Success
- Research-Based Strategies Used to Develop *Discovering Our Past: The American Journey to World War I*
- Character Education in the Middle School Classroom
- The Living Constitution
- Professional Development in Middle School Social Studies Video Series
- Teaching American History With *Discovering Our Past: The American Journey to World War I*

MASTERING THE STANDARDS

The content and assessment in the Student Edition, Teacher Wraparound Edition, teacher planning materials, and the print and technology products are all standards-based. The use of these products during instruction leads to mastery of the standards.

PRACTICE

- California Standards Practice Workbook
- California Standards Practice Transparencies
- Interactive Time Line CD-ROM
- School-to-Home Connection

BENCHMARK ASSESSMENT

- California Standards Assessment
- Exam*View*® Pro Testmaker CD-ROM
- Succeeding on the California History–Social Science Standards CD-ROM

REMEDIATION

- California Guide to Daily Intervention
- Interactive Tutor Self-Assessment CD-ROM
- Exam*View*® Pro Testmaker CD-ROM
- California Standards Practice Workbook
- Reading Essentials and Study Guide

Additional Resources

NATIONAL GEOGRAPHIC TEACHER'S CORNER

Index to National Geographic Magazine:

The following articles relate to this chapter:

- "The Way West," by John G. Mitchell, September 2000.
- "Buffalo: Back Home on the Range," by Bryan Hodgson, November 1994.
- "The American Prairie: Roots of the Sky," by Douglas H. Chadwick, October 1993.

National Geographic Society Products

To order the following, call National Geographic at 1-800-368-2728

- *GeoKit: Immigration* (Kit)
- *United States/Territorial Growth* (Map)
- *National Geographic Desk Reference* (Book)
- *Full Steam Ahead: The Race to Build a Transcontinental Railroad* (Book)

NGS ONLINE

Access National Geographic's new dynamic MapMachine Web site and other geography resources at:

www.nationalgeographic.com

www.nationalgeographic.com/maps

A&E HOME VIDEO · Biography · THE HISTORY CHANNEL

The following videotape programs are available from Glencoe as supplements to Chapter 16.

- **Andrew Carnegie: Prince of Steel (ISBN 1-56501-741-2)**
- **Henry Ford: Tin Lizzy Tycoon (ISBN 1-56501-380-8)**
- **Wilbur & Orville Wright: Dreams of Flying (ISBN 1-56501-386-7)**

To order, call Glencoe at 1-800-334-7344. To find classroom resources to accompany many of these videos, check the following home pages:

A&E Television: www.aetv.com
The History Channel: www.historychannel.com

MOMENTS IN TIME DBQ

The following resource can help you teach the content of this chapter.

Unit 5 The Progressive Era (1890–1919)

History Online

Use our Web site for additional resources. All essential content is covered in the Student Edition.

You and your students can visit ca.hss.glencoe.com, the Web site companion to *Discovering Our Past: The American Journey to World War I*. This innovative integration of electronic and print media offers your students a wealth of opportunities. The student text directs students to the Web site for the following options:

- Chapter Overviews
- Self-Check Quizzes
- Study Central™
- Student Web Activities
- Textbook Updates
- Multi-Language Glossaries

Answers to the student Web activities are provided for you in the Web Activity Lesson Plans. Additional Web resources and ePuzzles and games are also available.

Glencoe TechCONNECT

Glencoe TechCONNECT™ AC202 "The Railroad Era: Rise of Industries"

Cumulative Activity Students should understand how the transcontinental railroads spurred economic growth by exploring the railroads' effects on various industries and then creating a slide show of what they've learned.

CA US8.12.1. CA CS1.; CS3.; HI2. CA 8RW1.0; 8RC2.0

You can access this online activity at www.ca.hss.techconnect.glencoe.com Enter the following activation key when prompted: **CONNECTCA.** To access the Teacher Resources for each activity, enter the following password when prompted: **CA123.**

FOLDABLES™ Study Organizer

Dinah Zike's Foldables

Foldables are three-dimensional, interactive graphic organizers that help students practice basic writing skills, review key vocabulary terms, and identify main ideas. Every chapter contains a foldable activity, with additional chapter activities found in the Reading and Study Skills Foldables booklet.

Chapter 16 Resources

Reading List Generator CD-ROM — GLENCOE BOOKLINK

The Glencoe BookLink CD-ROM is a database that allows you to search more than 15,000 titles to create a customized reading list for your students.

- Reading lists can be organized by students' reading level, author, genre, theme, or area of interest.
- The database provides Degrees of Reading Power™ (DRP) and Lexile™ readability scores for all selections.
- A brief summary of each selection is included.

Reading level suggestions for this chapter:

For students at a Grade 6 reading level:
- ***The Jungle***, by Upton Sinclair

For students at a Grade 7 reading level:
- ***Mother Jones: One Woman's Fight for Labor***, by Betsy Harvey Kraft

For students at a Grade 8 reading level:
- ***Inventors***, by Martin W. Sandler

For students at a Grade 9 reading level:
- ***Full Steam Ahead: The Race to Build a Transcontinental Railroad***, by Rhonda Blumberg

Reading Support From JAMESTOWN EDUCATION

- *Timed Readings Plus in Social Studies* helps students increase their reading rate and fluency while maintaining comprehension. The 400-word passages are similar to those found on state and national assessments.
- *Reading in the Content Area: Social Studies* concentrates on six essential reading skills that help students better comprehend what they read. The book includes 754 high-interest nonfiction passages written at increasing levels of difficulty.
- *Reading Fluency* helps students read smoothly, accurately, and expressively.
- *Jamestown's Reading Improvement,* by renowned reading expert Edward Fry, focuses on helping build your students' comprehension, vocabulary, and skimming and scanning skills.
- *Critical Reading Series* provides high-interest books, each written at three reading levels.

To order these products, call Glencoe at 1-800-334-7344.

KEY for Using the Teacher Wraparound Edition

Use this key to help you identify the different types of prompts found in the Teacher Wraparound Edition.

R **Reading Strategies** activities help you teach reading skills and vocabulary.

C **Critical Thinking** strategies help students apply and extend what they have learned.

U **Universal Access** activities provide differentiated instruction for students learning to speak English, along with suggestions for teaching various types of learners.

S **Skill Practice** strategies help students practice historical analysis and geography skills.

W **Writing Support** activities provide writing opportunities to help students comprehend the text.

Teaching strategies and activities have been coded for ability level appropriateness.

- **AL** Activities for students working above grade level
- **OL** Activities for students working on grade level
- **BL** Activities for students working below grade level
- **EL** Activities for English Learners

FOCUS

History–Social Science Standards

In this chapter, the following standards will be covered:

US8.12 Students analyze the transformation of the American economy and the changing social and political conditions in the United States in response to the Industrial Revolution.

More About the Photo

This surging locomotive is a fitting symbol for the growing industrial power of the American economy in the late 1800s. Have students think about what industry or industries are important to the American economy today.

Chapter 16

The Growth of Industry

▲ Railroads sped industrialization in the late 1800s.

NATIONAL GEOGRAPHIC Who & When?

1870 — 1890 — 1910

1870 Rockefeller organizes Standard Oil Company

1876 Bell patents the telephone

1886 Trade unions form AFL

1903 Wright brothers fly first motorized airplane

TEACH

The Big Ideas

As you begin teaching each section, use these questions and activities to focus on the Big Ideas.

Section 1

Railroads Lead the Way

Essential Question: How did people travel over land up until the 1800s? *(on foot, by horseback, wagon or carriage)* How do you think the building of the railroads changed life? *(People were able to travel and transport goods over longer distances.)* This section describes how connecting cities and states by railroad opened up vast possibilities for industry and growth. **OL**

Section 2

Inventions

Essential Question: What inventions have made life today easier? How has life changed as a result of modern inventions? After students discuss various inventions, tell them that during the late 1800s, numerous important inventions helped the nation grow. **OL**

Section 3

The Age of Big Business

Essential Question: What do you think of when you hear the term "big business"? *(Students may give such answers as large corporations or Wall Street.)* Tell them that in this section, they will learn about the growth of the country's first big corporations. **OL**

History Online

Chapter Overview Visit ca.hss.glencoe.com for a preview of Chapter 16.

The Big Ideas

Section 1 Railroads Lead the Way

Geography shapes the physical, economic, and political challenges a region faces. The spread of railroads across the country encouraged America's expanding economy.

Section 2 Inventions

Innovations in technology and business help build a nation's industrial power. Inventions improved the transportation and communication networks that were vital to the nation's industrial growth.

Section 3 The Age of Big Business

Innovations in technology and business help build a nation's industrial power. Corporations changed the American economy of the late 1800s.

Section 4 Industrial Workers

Reactions to social injustice can lead to reform movements. Workers organized to demand better pay and working conditions.

View the Chapter 16 video in the Glencoe Video Program.

FOLDABLES™ Study Organizer

Identifying Main Ideas Make this foldable to describe the growth of industry in the United States in the late 1800s.

Step 1 Fold two sheets of paper in half from top to bottom. Cut the papers in half along the folds.

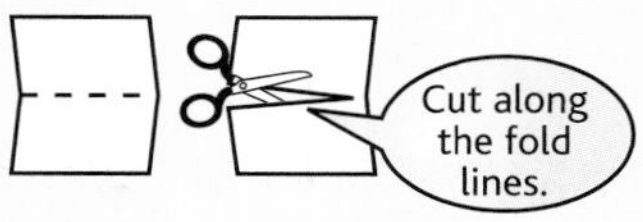

Step 2 Fold each of the four papers in half from top to bottom.

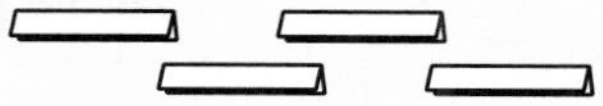

Step 3 On each folded paper, make a cut 1 inch from the side on the top flap.

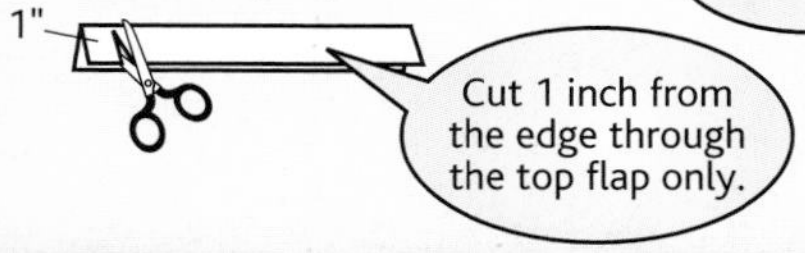

Step 4 Place the folded papers one on top of the other. Staple the four sections together and label each of the tabs **Railroads, Inventions, Big Business,** and **Industrial Workers.**

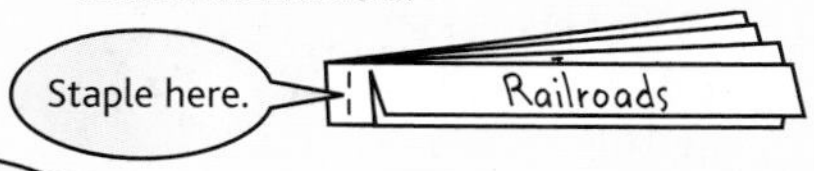

Reading and Writing As you read, write what you learn about the developments of industry under each appropriate tab.

Section 4

Industrial Workers

Essential Question: What have workers done to address injustice on the job? *(Answers may include unions that oversee workers' rights, minimum wage laws, and safety and health laws.)* Explain that the regulations that exist to protect workers today have not always existed. **OL**

History Online

Go to ca.hss.glencoe.com for student activities, lesson plans, and links to additional Web resources about industrial growth in the late 1800s.

FOLDABLES™ Study Organizer Dinah Zike's Foldables

Purpose Have students use their foldables to connect supporting details to the main ideas about the growth of industry. Students should consider the questions, *how*, *why*, *for whom*, and *when* to help them locate details. **OL**

Why It's Important

Predicting Consequences

The ability to predict consequences is evidence of a student's growing understanding of history. By successfully predicting how people or groups will react or what effects may flow from a particular change, students show they understand the ideas, social structures, and economic circumstances of a person, group, or society.

1 Learn It!

Explain that finding patterns is something detectives do when trying to identify an unknown criminal. Have students think about mystery novels they have read or movies they have seen. **Ask:** What types of questions do detectives ask to find patterns in a series of crimes? *(Questions may include such issues as whether the crimes take place at a similar time of day or night, in places that have something in common, or using the same weapon.)* OL

Chapter 16 Get Ready to Read

Predicting Consequences

READING SKILL

1 Learn It!

Did you ever wish you could see into the future? Although it is impossible to predict future events, you can develop skills to help you identify the consequences of decisions or actions. Follow these steps to help you thoughtfully predict consequences:

- **Review what you already know about a situation by listing facts, events, and people's responses. The list will help you recall events and how they affected people.**
- **Use your knowledge and observations of similar situations. In other words, ask yourself, "What were the consequences of a similar decision or action that occurred in the past?"**
- **Look for patterns. Try to determine what the patterns show. Are some consequences more likely to occur than others?**
- **Make a prediction.**

Reading Tip

Read the first two pages of a chapter to get an overview of its contents. Next, reflect on what you have already studied. Last, make some educated guesses about what you might learn in the chapter.

READING STRATEGY — CONNECTING

A useful tool for predicting consequences is to make connections. Text-to-text connections help students activate prior knowledge about a situation or about similar circumstances in the past. Text-to-self and text-to-world connections can help them understand how people facing a particular situation might feel and, as a result, how they might react. Suggest that students practice the skill by making connections to the information in the left column of the chart on page 705. OL CA HI3.

2 Practice It!

You have already learned about some of the changes in transportation, trade, and settlement between 1800 and 1869. You learned that inland roads, along with the steamboat and the canal system, stimulated trade and settlement. Railroads spanning the continent took settlers and entrepreneurs into new regions of the United States. In this chapter, you will read more about how the railroad impacted life and industry, setting the stage for a new Industrial Revolution. Practice making some predictions about what you might learn. Complete the chart below, then discuss your predictions with a partner.

Event	Predicted results
Railroads made new regions accessible	New areas were settled by farmers, miners, and ranchers
Transcontinental railroad completed	Thousands of workers brought West
Several railroads connected East and West	
Railroads offered employment opportunities	
Railroad companies consolidated	

Read to Write

Based on what you read about labor conditions during the building of the transcontinental railroad, write a short paragraph predicting what labor conditions might have been like in other industries at that time.

European immigrants on a railroad flatcar view land open for settlement on the Great Plains.

3 Apply It!

Read the main ideas for this chapter. Take notes predicting what you'll discover. Monitor your progress to see if your expectations were accurate.

CHAPTER 16 Get Ready to Read

2 Practice It!

Have students read the information at the beginning of Section 1 on page 707 through the end of the material under the heading "Growth of the Rail System." Tell students to think about three groups of people—railroad owners, railroad workers, and people who travel on railroads. **Ask:** What do you think will happen to each of these groups as a result of railroad consolidation? Why? Discuss students' responses. OL

3 Apply It!

Explain that historians sometimes ask "What if?" questions, in which they explore the consequences of events *not* happening as they did. These speculations are the results of predictions. **Ask:** What would have happened if the government had not passed the Homestead Act opening the Great Plains to settlement? How would the West have changed? Have students write a brief essay explaining their predictions. OL

Reading Strategy: QUESTIONING

Even incorrect predictions can be useful learning tools by revealing to students influences they had not expected would affect people. Suggest that students evaluate incorrect predictions by asking the following questions: What factors led the person or group to act in the unexpected way? Had I not identified those factors, or had I thought them less important? Why were they more important to the decision than I had expected? Have students use these questions to analyze an incorrect prediction they make while reading this chapter. OL

Use Reading Skills Activity 16 in the **Chapter 16 Resource Book** for more practice with predicting consequences.

FOCUS

BELLRINGER
SKILLBUILDER ACTIVITY

Project **Daily Focus Skills Transparency 16–1** and have students answer the question.

Guide to Reading

Preteaching Vocabulary: Have students find each term in the section and then use it in a sentence.

Answers to Graphic: Use of steel track expanded steel industry; Use of lumber for track expanded lumber industry; Use of coal to fuel locomotives expanded coal industry

Unpacking the Standards

After reading the section, students will be able to:

- Explain how railroad barons consolidated their companies.
- Describe how railroad growth stimulated the economy.
- List the innovations that helped railroad travel.

Section 1
Railroads Lead the Way

History Social Science Standards

US8.12 Students analyze the transformation of the American economy and the changing social and political conditions in the United States in response to the Industrial Revolution.

Guide to Reading

Looking Back, Looking Ahead

In the last chapter, you read about the expansion of the nation into the West. In this chapter, you will read about America's economic expansion and the shift from an agricultural economy to an industrial nation.

Focusing on the Main Ideas

- Railroad barons used consolidation to expand their companies and create a growing system of railroads throughout the United States. *(page 707)*
- Railroad growth stimulated the economy, and innovations made railroad travel more efficient and profitable. *(page 709)*

Meeting People

Cornelius Vanderbilt
James J. Hill
Collis P. Huntington
Leland Stanford
George Westinghouse
Eli H. Janney
Gustavus Swift (guh • STAHV • uhs)
George M. Pullman

Content Vocabulary

consolidation (kuhn • SAH • luh • DAY • shuhn)
standard gauge (GAYJ)
rebate
pool

Academic Vocabulary

technology (tehk • NAH • luh • jee)
convert (kuhn • VUHRT)
network

Reading Strategy

Analyze As you read the section, complete a diagram like the one shown by describing the contributions of the railroad to the growth of industry.

The role of the railroad → [ ] [ ] [ ]

NATIONAL GEOGRAPHIC Where & When?

1860	1875	1890

- **1869** First transcontinental railroad is completed
- **1880s** Standard width for railroad tracks is adopted
- **1883** Northern Pacific Railroad opens

SECTION RESOURCES

Print Material
- Reproducible Lesson Plan 16–1*
- Daily Lesson and Discussion Notes 16–1
- Guided Reading Activity 16–1
- Reading Essentials and Study Guide 16–1
- Active Reading Note-Taking 16–1
- Section Quiz 16–1

Transparencies
- Daily Focus Skills Transparency 16–1
- Section Graphic Organizer Transparency 16–1
- California Standards Practice Transparencies

Technology
- Interactive Tutor Self-Assessment CD–ROM
- Exam*View*® Pro Testmaker CD–ROM
- Presentation Plus! CD–ROM

*Available on TeacherWorks™

US8.12.1 Trace patterns of agricultural and industrial development as they relate to climate, use of natural resources, markets, and trade and locate such development on a map. **US8.12.4** Discuss entrepreneurs, industrialists, and bankers in politics, commerce, and industry (e.g., Andrew Carnegie, John D. Rockefeller, Leland Stanford).

Railroad Expansion

Main Idea **Railroad barons used consolidation to expand their companies and create a growing system of railroads throughout the United States.**

Reading Connection What methods do companies today use to expand their businesses? Read on to find out how railroads grew after the Civil War.

An American Story

Rugged construction gangs labored on the Union Pacific and other railways during the transportation boom of the late 1800s. The chorus of a favorite song told of the hard work of the tarriers, or drillers:

> *"And drill, ye tarriers, drill!*
> *Drill, ye tarriers, drill!*
> *For its work all day for sugar in your tay,*
> *Down behind of the railway and,*
> *Drill, ye tarriers, drill!*
> *And blast!*
> *And fire!"*
>
> —Thomas Casey, 1888

Growth of the Rail System In the decades after the Civil War, railroads became a driving force behind America's economic growth. The first transcontinental railroad, completed in 1869, was soon followed by others. By the 1890s, five railway lines crossed the country, and hundreds of smaller lines branched off from them.

R The expansion of the railroad system was accompanied by **consolidation** (kuhn • SAH • luh • DAY • shuhn)—the practice of combining separate companies—in the industry. Large railroad companies expanded by buying smaller companies or by driving them out of business. Consolidation made the large companies more efficient. After consolidation, a few powerful individuals known as railroad barons controlled the nation's rail traffic.

Railroad Barons New Yorker **Cornelius Vanderbilt,** one of the first railroad barons, gained control of the New York Central line and then other lines. His railroad empire stretched from New York City to the Great Lakes.

James J. Hill built the Great Northern line between Minnesota and Washington State. Until his death in 1916, Hill continued building and directing his ever-growing business empire. **Collis P. Huntington, Leland Stanford,** and two other partners founded the Central Pacific, which connected California and Utah.

C The railroad barons were aggressive and competitive. They lived in an age when few laws had been passed to regulate business, and some of their methods were highly questionable. Nevertheless, the railroad barons played an important part in building the nation's transportation system.

Reading Check **Analyze** What did consolidation mean for many small companies?

HISTORY MAKERS

The Impact of the Railroad

S By 1860 there were about 30,000 miles (48,270 km) of railroad track in the nation—almost as much as in the rest of the world combined. By 1900 the nation had nearly 250,000 miles (402,250 km) of track. An average of 15 new miles (24 km) of track were laid each day. By the late 1800s, the railroad industry passed all other industries as a buyer of iron, steel, and coal and became the nation's largest employer.

TEACH

R Reading Strategy

Understanding Vocabulary Have students think of synonyms for *consolidate*. (*merge, combine, join*) OL

C Critical Thinking

Predicting Consequences **Ask:** What might result from such aggressive business practices with little regulation? *(Students should see that the railroad barons will be able to act as they wish regarding their workers, their customers, and businesses.)* OL

S Skill Practice

Using Geography Skills Have students look at the world map on pages 37–38 and compare the size of the United States to that of the countries in western Europe. Point out that these were the industrialized countries in the late 1800s. **Ask:** What geographic fact explains why the United States had so many more miles of railroad track than other industrialized countries of the time? *(It is much larger and needed more track.)* OL CA CS3.

Reading Check

Answer: Smaller companies were bought up by larger ones or were driven out of business.

Resources for page 707

American Art Prints: William Henry Jackson

HISTORY MAKERS

In 1870, the nation had 53,000 miles of railroad track. **Ask:** How much did the amount of track increase from 1860 to 1870? *(23,000 miles)* How much was that per year? *(2,300 miles)* How much did the amount of track increase from 1870 to 1900? *(197,000 miles)* How much was that per year? *(6,555 miles)* What can you conclude from this? *(the rate of railroad building was much higher after 1870)* OL

Biography

TEACH

C1 Critical Thinking

Determining Cause and Effect Ask: Why did Judah go to these men who already had businesses? *(Students should recognize that he needed to approach men who had the money to invest in the company.)* OL

W Writing Support

Research Reports Writing Have students choose one of "The Big Four" and research his and his family's contributions and donations to the community. Tell students to write several specific questions about the person before beginning their research and then try to find the answers to those questions. OL CA 8WA2.3

C2 Writing Support

Analyzing Information Ask: Is the statement that Crocker fought against racial prejudice a fact or an opinion? Why? *(Fact—he criticized unfair treatment of members of some minorities)* OL CA HR2.

Biography

US8.12.4 Discuss entrepreneurs, indust alists, and bankers in politics, commerce, industry (e.g., Andrew Carnegie, John D. Rockefeller, Leland Stanford).

LELAND STANFORD
1824–1893

CHARLES CROCKER
1822–1888

▲ Leland Stanford

The Central Pacific Railroad began as the dream of engineer Theodore Judah. He sold stock in the new company to four Sacramento merchants: grocer Leland Stanford, shop C1 owner Charles Crocker, and hardware store owners Mark Hopkins and Collis P. Huntington. The four men became known as "The Big Four" for their role in California's economic development. W

In the early 1860s, these men managed the construction of the Central Pacific railroad. Eventually, they controlled a large railroad network that gave them great wealth and political power. Although some of their methods were questioned, the four business partners and their families donated land and money for the building of parks, churches, and libraries. Their donations either founded or helped fund art museums, including the Crocker Art Museum in Sacramento, the San Francisco Art Institute, and the Huntington Library and Art Gallery in San Marino.

Leland Stanford and his wife, Jane, donated land and money to create Stanford University. Leland Stanford became governor of California and later served as a United States senator.

C2 Crocker fought against racial prejudice. He criticized unfair treatment of Native Americans and of Chinese and Japanese immigrants. Crocker believed that if "we deny to the individual, no matter what his creed, his color, or his nationality, the right to justice, which every man possesses . . . there will be no enduring prosperity and [the nation's] decline will surely follow."

Crocker gave money to support African American churches in California. He also supported African American schools and colleges in the southern United States.

▲ Charles Crocker

Then and Now

Is it important for people to donate to the arts and education? Why or why not?

708

Answers and Additional Support

Then and Now

Students should recognize that many cultural, artistic, and educational organizations require the donations of individuals or foundations to survive, as is the case with many charities and religious groups. **Ask:** What are other ways people can contribute to these groups besides giving money? *(Answers may include volunteering to help and working on fund raisers.)* OL

US8.12.1 Trace patterns of agricultural and industrial development as they relate to climate, use of natural resources, markets, and trade and locate such development on a map. **US8.12.9** Name the significant inventors and their inventions and identify how they improved the quality of life (e.g., Thomas Edison, Alexander Graham Bell, Orville and Wilbur Wright).

Railroads Spur the Economy

Main Idea **Railroad growth stimulated the economy, and innovations made railroad travel more efficient and profitable.**

Reading Connection Can you think of a recent invention that has significantly changed the way in which you live? Read on to find out how railroads changed America in economic and social ways.

The fast-growing national rail system created new economic links in the country. The railroads carried raw materials such as iron ore, coal, and timber to factories. They also carried manufactured goods from factories to markets and transported produce from farming areas to the cities.

The national railroad system encouraged the expanding economy in many other ways. At first the demand for iron tracks and locomotives helped the iron mining and processing industries grow. Around 1880 railroad companies began using steel tracks. Steel is a metal made stronger by adding carbon and other elements to refined iron. The use of steel in railroad tracks stimulated America's steel industry.

S

The railroads also helped other industries thrive. The lumber industry, which supplied wood for railway ties, and the coal industry, which provided fuel for locomotives, saw extraordinary growth. In addition, railroad companies provided work for thousands of people who laid tracks and built stations and for those who manufactured railway cars and equipment.

Improving the Railroads Increased use made it necessary for railroads to expand and unify their systems. Railroads were being built across the country, but different lines used rails of different gauges, or widths. As a result, trains of one line could not use another line's tracks. Many early local lines carried goods for short distances and did not even connect with other lines. The gaps in service between the various lines made long-distance railroad travel slow and inefficient.

HISTORY MAKERS

Standard Time Zones

Throughout much of the 1800s, few Americans could agree on the time of day because every community determined its own time by the position of the sun. When it was noon in New York City, for example, it was 11:55 A.M. in Philadelphia and 11:47 in Washington, D.C. Local time interfered with train scheduling and at times even threatened passenger safety. When two trains traveled on the same track, collisions could result from scheduling errors caused by time differences.

To make rail service safer and more reliable, in 1883 the American Railway Association agreed to use four time zones for the continental United States: Eastern, Central, Mountain, and Pacific.

▼ Time zones

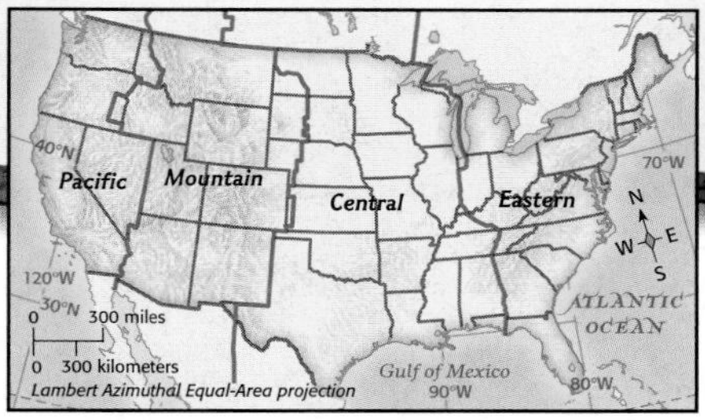

As the railroad companies consolidated, railroad barons saw the advantages of being part of a national railroad network. During the late 1880s, almost all companies adopted a **standard gauge** (GAYJ) of 4 feet, 8.5 inches as the width of the railroad track. A standard gauge allowed faster shipment of goods at a reduced cost. It was no longer necessary to load and unload goods from one train to another. One train could make the entire journey.

R

S Skill Practice

Historical and Social Sciences Analysis Skill
Ask: How did the railroad industry contribute to the growth of other industries in the country? *(Iron mining and processing—through need for tracks and locomotives; Lumber industry—through need for ties; Coal—through need for fuel; Steel—through need for track; Manufacturing industries—through need for railroad cars)* OL

R Reading Strategy

Understanding Vocabulary
Explain that a railroad's gauge is the width from one rail to the other. **Ask:** What would happen if a train built to one gauge tried to run on a wider gauge track? *(Students should recognize that the train would not stay on the track.)* OL

Review The Big Idea

Review the Big Idea for this section: "Geography shapes the physical, economic, and political challenges a region faces." Discuss with students the challenges and opportunities the railroads posed to and provided for late nineteenth-century Americans. **Ask:** How did the railroads help create standards across the country? *(They set standard gauges and standardized time.)* OL

More Skill Practice

Historical and Social Sciences Analysis Skill **Ask:** What would happen to the industries that grew along with railroads if railroad companies had a bad year, with low demand? *(They would suffer.)*
OL CA HI2.

HISTORY MAKERS

Each of the time zones is 15 degrees of longitude wide. **Ask:** When it is 4:00 P.M. in California, what time is it in St. Louis, Missouri? *(6:00 P.M.)* What time is it in Miami, Florida? *(7:00 P.M.)* BL

C Critical Thinking

Analyzing Information Have students create a chart that links the inventor to the invention. The charts should include a column that explains why each invention would be significant. **OL**

U Universal Access

Visual/Spatial Invite students to create an ad with words and pictures to announce the development of the Pullman sleeping car. **OL**

R Reading Strategy

Summarizing Have students explain what a *rebate* is in their own words. *(money you get back from a company after buying their product)* **BL** **CA 8RW1.3**

S Skill Practice

Historical and Social Sciences Analysis Skill Have students locate the city of Chicago, Illinois, on this map. **Ask:** What do you think happened to the economy of Chicago in this period? Why? *(Students should see that the economy would grow since the city was an important center of railroads and rail travel.)* **OL**

CA CS3. **CA HI2.**

Answers and Additional Support

Railroad Technology Railway transportation also improved with the introduction of new **technology.** Four developments were particularly important. Inventor **George Westinghouse** devised air brakes that improved the system for stopping trains, making train travel safer. Janney car couplers, named after inventor **Eli H. Janney,** made it easier for railroad workers to link cars. Shortly after the Civil War, Thaddeus Lowe invented the ice machine, the basis of the refrigerator.

In the early 1870s, **Gustavus Swift** (guh • STAHV • uhs) hired an engineer to develop a refrigerated railroad car. In 1877 Swift shipped the first refrigerated load of fresh meat. The widespread use of refrigeration kept food fresh longer and reduced the risk of food poisoning. Finally, **George M. Pullman** developed the Pullman sleeping car—a luxury railway car with seats that **converted** into beds for overnight journeys. Pullman also introduced improved dining cars, raising train travel to a new level of comfort.

Competing for Customers As the railroad network continued to grow, the railroad companies competed fiercely with one another to keep old customers and to win new ones. Large railroads offered secret discounts called **rebates** to their biggest customers. Smaller railroads that could not match these rebates were sometimes forced out of business. Giving discounts to big customers raised freight rates for farmers and other customers who shipped small amounts of goods.

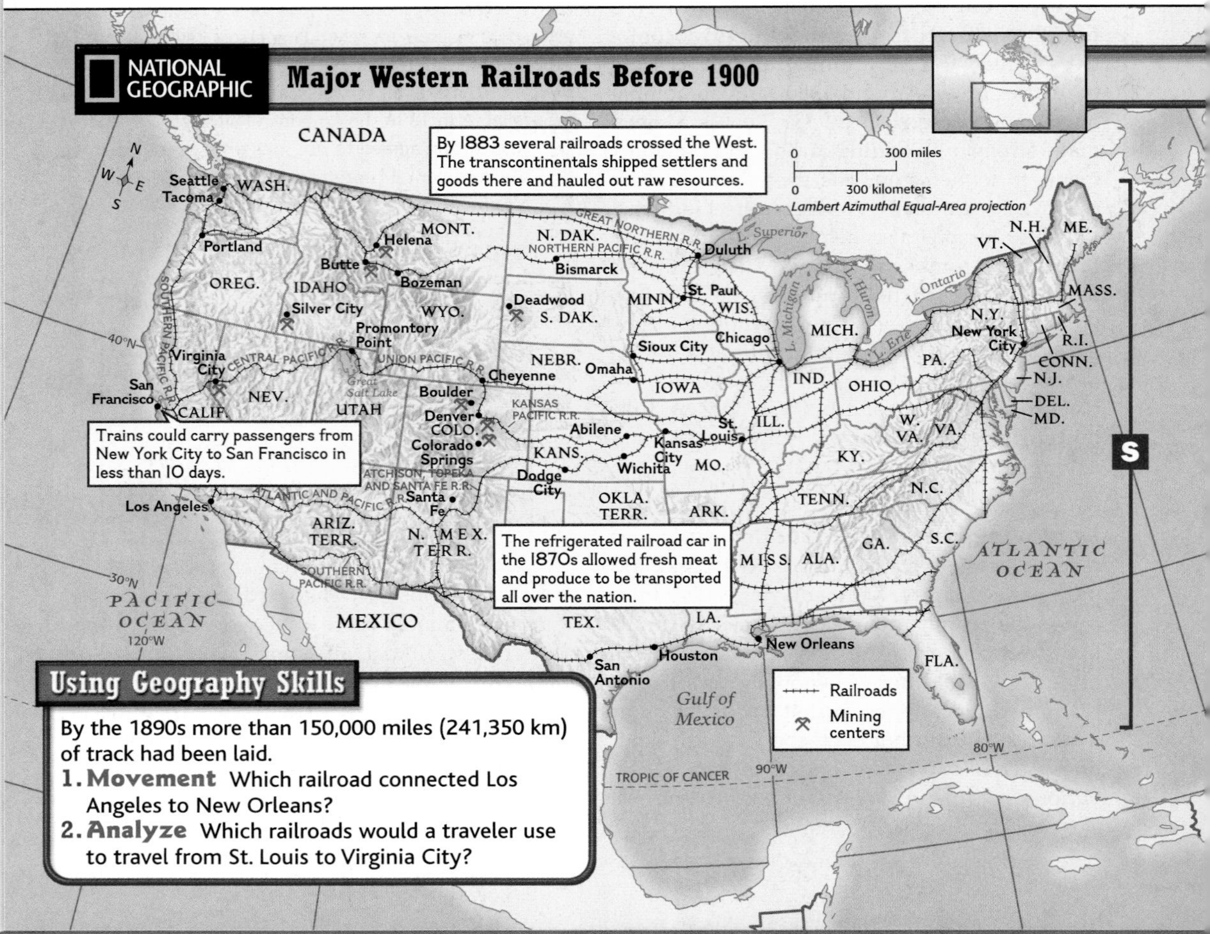

Using Geography Skills

By the 1890s more than 150,000 miles (241,350 km) of track had been laid.

1. **Movement** Which railroad connected Los Angeles to New Orleans?
2. **Analyze** Which railroads would a traveler use to travel from St. Louis to Virginia City?

Did You Know?

The growth of Gustavus Swift's company reflects the great wealth businesses could amass in the late 1800s. In 1878, Swift and his brother became partners in a new meatpacking company. Seven years later, when they made Swift & Company a corporation, it was worth $300,000. When Swift died in 1903, the company was valued at $25 million.

Using Geography Skills

Answers:

1. Southern Pacific
2. Kansas Pacific, Union Pacific, Central Pacific

R The railroad barons also made secret agreements among themselves, known as **pools.** They divided the railway business among their companies and set rates for a region. With no other competition in its region, a railroad could charge higher rates and earn greater profits. Although Congress and some states passed laws to regulate the railroads, these laws did little to curb the railroad barons.

How Did Railroads Change America? The growing railroad network paved the way for American industry to expand into the West. The center of the flour milling industry, for example, shifted westward in the 1800s, moving from the East Coast to Ohio, to Minneapolis, and finally to Kansas City.

Other industries followed the same pattern. As farmers settled the Great Plains, the manufacturing center for agricultural equipment moved from central New York State to Illinois and Wisconsin.

Railroads also touched the lives of thousands of Americans. Trains redistributed the population. They carried homesteaders into the Great Plains and the West. Trains also made it easy for people to move from rural areas to the cities.

As you have learned, railroads affected the way Americans thought about time as well. As train travel became more common, people began measuring distances by how many hours the trip would take rather than by the number of miles traveled. The spread of the railroad system led to a national system of time with four time zones.

The railroads opened the entire United States to settlement and economic growth and united the different regions of the country into a single **network.** At the same time, inventions that revolutionized transportation and communication brought Americans together in new ways.

Reading Check **Explain** Why was adopting standard-gauge tracks important for the railroad industry?

History Online

Study Central Need help understanding how railroad growth stimulated the economy? Visit ca.hss.glencoe.com and click on Study Central.

Section 1 Review

Reading Summary

Review the Main Ideas

- After the Civil War, railroads continued to grow, allowing the faster transportation of goods and people.
- Railroads stimulated the American economy and resulted in many changes to the way Americans lived and traveled.

What Did You Learn?

1. How did railroad barons drive smaller companies out of business?
2. How did the railroads pave the way for the expansion of industry in the West?

Critical Thinking

3. **Organizing Information** Re-create the diagram below and identify the developments in technology that improved railroad transportation. CA H12.

4. **The Big Ideas** Explain how railroads changed the American economy.
5. **Expository Writing** Should the U.S. government have intervened to regulate unfair practices of the railroad barons? Explain your position in a short essay. CA 8WA2.4
6. **READING** **Predict** Many innovations were made to improve railroad transportation. Write a short paragraph predicting the impact on the development of cities and regions. CA H13.

R Reading Strategy

Understanding Vocabulary
Ask: What does the expression *pool your resources* mean? (sharing) How does that relate to this term? *(Rail owners shared information about customers and then benefited from how they used it.)* OL

ASSESS

Resources for page 711

Use these resources to assess student mastery of section content.

Section Quiz 16–1

Interactive Tutor Self-Assessment CD-ROM

Reading Check

Answer: It allowed trains from different railroads to use the same rails, eliminating the transfer of goods from one train to another.

History Online

Study Central provides summaries, interactive games, and online graphic organizers to help students review section content.

CLOSE

Drawing Conclusions Explain that in medieval Europe, barons were nobles who dominated society and had large estates with many peasants working for them. **Ask:** Why were men such as Hill and Vanderbilt called "railroad barons"? *(Students should point to similarities in the power of rail barons.)* OL

SECTION 1 REVIEW ANSWERS

Review questions reinforce content standard US8.12.

1. bought up some and used rebates, pools, and other practices to compete against others
2. by making it easier to transport raw materials to factories and manufactured goods to markets
3. air brakes, Janney car couplers, refrigerated cars, sleeping car
4. **The Big Ideas** contributed to development of iron, steel, lumber, coal industries; business practices rail companies developed changed way business was done; helped growth of economy in West
5. Answers should be well supported.
6. **READING** Answers should be well supported.

FOCUS

BELLRINGER
SKILLBUILDER ACTIVITY

Project **Daily Focus Skills Transparency 16–2** and have students answer the question.

Guide to Reading

Preteaching Vocabulary: Have students explain the relationship between the terms *assembly line* and *mass production*.

Answers to Graphic: Morse: telegraph and Morse Code; made distance communication easier; Bell: telephone; allowed for vocal communication; Edison: many inventions, including lightbulb, phonograph; provided light, improved communications, provided entertainment

Unpacking the Standards

After reading the section, students will be able to:

- Explain how inventions improved communications.
- Identify how electricity changed people's lives.
- Describe how transportation improvements helped commercial industries.

Section 2

Inventions

History Social Science Standards

US8.12 Students analyze the transformation of the American economy and the changing social and political conditions in the United States in response to the Industrial Revolution.

Guide to Reading

Looking Back, Looking Ahead

In the last section, you read about how the expansion of railroads stimulated various sectors of the economy. In this section, you will learn how inventions changed the lives of the American people.

Focusing on the Main Ideas

- New inventions improved communication and allowed Americans to contact one another over long distances. *(page 713)*
- The harnessing of electricity gave America a new source of power. *(page 714)*
- Improvements in transportation made travel easier and helped industries make their goods available to a wider audience. *(page 716)*

Meeting People

Samuel Morse
Alexander Graham Bell
Thomas Edison
Lewis Howard Latimer
Granville Woods
Henry Ford

Locating Places

Menlo Park, New Jersey
Detroit, Michigan

Content Vocabulary

assembly line
mass production

Academic Vocabulary

unify (YOO • nuh • FY)
transmit
device (dih • VYS)

Reading Strategy

Organizing Information As you read the section, re-create the diagram below to list each person's invention and to explain the significance of each invention to industrial growth.

	Invention	Significance
Samuel Morse		
Alexander Bell		
Thomas Edison		

NATIONAL GEOGRAPHIC **Who & When?**

1870 — 1890 — 1910

1876 Alexander Graham Bell develops the telephone

1903 The Wright brothers fly at Kitty Hawk

1908 Henry Ford introduces the Model T

SECTION RESOURCES

Print Material
- Reproducible Lesson Plan 16–2*
- Daily Lesson and Discussion Notes 16–2
- Guided Reading Activity 16–2
- Reading Essentials and Study Guide 16–2
- Active Reading Note-Taking Guide 16–2
- Section Quiz 16–2

Transparencies
- Daily Focus Skills Transparency 16–2
- Section Graphic Organizer Transparency 16–2
- California Standards Practice Transparencies

Technology
- Interactive Tutor Self-Assessment CD-ROM
- Exam*View*® Pro Testmaker CD-ROM
- Presentation Plus! CD-ROM

*Available on TeacherWorks™

US8.12.9 Name the significant inventors and their inventions and identify how they improved the quality of life (e.g., Thomas Edison, Alexander Graham Bell, Orville and Wilbur Wright).

C Communication Changes

Main Idea **New inventions improved communication and allowed Americans to contact one another over long distances.**

Reading Connection Do you use a cell phone or a computer to communicate with your friends? These are relatively new methods of communication. Read on to find out about the new methods of communication developed in the mid-1800s.

An American Story

In the early 1900s, American songwriters were caught up in the public fascination with new inventions. One of the most popular songs of 1905, "In My Merry Oldsmobile," celebrated the automobile:

> **"Come away with me Lucile,**
> **In my merry Oldsmobile.**
> **Down the road of life we'll fly,**
> **Automobubbling you and I.**
> **To the church we'll swiftly steal,**
> **Then our wedding bells will peal;**
> **You can go as far as you like . . . ,**
> **In my merry Oldsmobile."**
>
> **—by Vincent Bryan and Gus Edwards**

How Did Life Change After 1870? By 1910 Americans in cities drove cars through streets lit with electric lights. They went to department stores where they bought everything from kitchen sinks to shoes. Americans could also do their shopping by mail—or pick up the telephone and order groceries from the local store. U The automobile, the electric light, and the telephone were all invented after 1870. Within a generation, they had become part of everyday life for millions of people. New inventions helped people communicate more quickly over long distances. Improvements in communication helped **unify** the regions of the country and promoted economic growth.

The Telegraph **Samuel Morse** had introduced the telegraph in 1844. By 1860 the United States had thousands of miles of telegraph lines, which were controlled for the most part by the Western Union Telegraph Company. At telegraph offices, trained operators transmitted messages called telegrams in Morse code. Telegrams offered almost instant communication. Shopkeepers relied on telegrams to order goods, and reporters used them to **transmit** stories to their newspapers. Americans also began sending personal messages by telegram.

The telegraph soon linked the United States and Europe. In the 1860s news from Europe traveled to this country by ship and took several weeks. Cyrus Field wanted to speed up the process. After several unsuccessful attempts, in 1866 Field managed to lay a telegraph cable across the Atlantic Ocean. The new transatlantic telegraph carried messages in a matter of seconds, bringing the United States and Europe closer together.

The Telephone Rings **Alexander Graham Bell** invented a **device** that revolutionized communications even more than Morse's telegraph. Born and educated in Scotland, Bell moved to the United States, where he studied ways of teaching people with hearing loss to speak. At the same time, he experimented with sending voices through electrical wires.

By 1876 Bell developed a device that transmitted speech—the telephone. While Bell was preparing to test the device, he accidentally spilled some battery acid on his clothes. In panic, Bell called out to his assistant in another room: "Mr. Watson, come here. I want you!" Watson heard Bell's voice coming through the telephone. The invention was a success. R

Bell formed the Bell Telephone Company in 1877. By the 1890s, he had sold hundreds of thousands of phones. Most early telephone customers were businesses. Before long, though, telephones became common in homes.

Reading Check **Explain** How did the telegraph affect communication?

TEACH

C Critical Thinking

Analyzing Information Have students choose from the inventions described in this section and rank them in importance. Ask volunteers to read their lists aloud and explain why they ranked them as they did. OL

U Universal Access

Intrapersonal Ask students to write a description of an ordinary day in the life of a person before the invention of the car, telephone, and electric light. Then have them describe that same day using those inventions. Have them describe how differently the person would feel as a result of using the inventions. OL CA 8WA2.4

R Reading Strategy

Scaffolding—Monitoring
Ask: Was Bell ready to test his device when he found out it worked? How did he discover that it was ready to use? *(no; by accident)* OL CA H14.

This READING SKILL was introduced in Chapter 14.

Reading Check
Answer: allowed for faster communication; improved communication between businesses and individuals and across the Atlantic Ocean

More Skill Practice

Historical and Social Sciences Analysis Skill Have students use a world map to estimate the miles of telegraph cable that stretched from New York to London. *(about 4,400 to 4,500 miles)* OL CA CS3.

Did You Know?

The first connection through the transatlantic telegraph cable was from Queen Victoria of Britain to U.S. President James Buchanan. Fields's cable broke shortly thereafter, however, and his project was not successful until 1866.

Resources for page 713

- Academic Vocabulary Activity 16
- Biography Activity 16B

R Reading Support

Categorizing Information Have students make a chart of the inventions discussed in the entire section and categorize each as first used mainly for business, for personal use, or both. With personal items, have students rate them as primarily useful for recreation or as inventions that would save time and labor. OL

W Writing Support

Expository Writing Have students choose one of the inventions discussed in the section and read about how it works. Then have them write a description of it—without mentioning its name. Have students exchange descriptions with a partner and try to identify the invention the other student described. OL CA 8WA2.6

Review The Big Idea

Review the Big Idea for this section: "Innovations in technology and business help build a nation's industrial power."
Ask: How did nineteenth-century inventions change industry? *(They made it more efficient and more productive.)* OL

US8.12.9 Name the significant inventors and their inventions and identify how they improved the quality of life (e.g., Thomas Edison, Alexander Graham Bell, Orville and Wilbur Wright).

R The Genius of Invention

Main Idea **The harnessing of electricity gave America a new source of power.**

Reading Connection As you get ready for school in the morning, think about all the ways that you use electricity. Do you need lights to shower and dress? Do you blow-dry your hair or make your breakfast in the microwave? Read on to find out how electricity improved the lives of people living in the late 1800s.

W The late 1800s saw a burst of inventiveness in the United States. Between 1860 and 1890, the United States government granted more than 400,000 patents for new inventions.

Many of the inventions helped businesses operate more efficiently. Among these were Christopher Sholes's typewriter (1868) and William Burroughs's adding machine (1888).

Other inventions affected everyday life. In 1888 George Eastman invented a small box camera—the Kodak—that made it easier and less costly to take photographs. John Thurman developed a vacuum cleaner in 1899 that simplified housework.

The Wizard of Menlo Park **Thomas Edison** was called "dull" by his teachers. Because of poor hearing, he had trouble in school and often didn't attend. His mother finally removed him from school and taught him at home.

Why It Matters

The First Flight at Kitty Hawk

A small crowd of people assembled on the sand dunes at Kitty Hawk, North Carolina, to test the Wrights' Flyer. Covering a few hundred feet in 12 seconds, the flight came to a halt when the Flyer's wing caught on one of the dunes. It was enough to encourage the Wrights to try further flights though. They would soon have a practical aircraft, and the world would have a new form of transportation.

The Beginning of Controlled, Powered Flight
Inventors experimented with engine-powered aircraft in the 1800s, but the age of air travel did not begin until 1903 at Kitty Hawk, North Carolina. Orville and Wilbur Wright, brothers and bicycle mechanics, built a wood-and-canvas plane with a 12-horsepower engine. On the morning of December 17, Orville Wright took off in their plane and flew a distance of 120 feet.

Firsts in Aviation History

In less than 100 years, aviators advanced from making the first flight in a glider to breaking the speed of sound.

- **1853** → Human-carrying flight in a glider built by Sir George Cayley takes place
- **1874** → Steam-powered monoplane is briefly airborne
- **1903** → Wright brothers take flight at Kitty Hawk
- **1914** → Scheduled airline service opens between St. Petersburg and Tampa, Florida
- **1919** → First nonstop flight across the Atlantic Ocean

Answers and Additional Support

Why It Matters

The flight of the Wright brothers in 1903 marked the beginning of modern aviation. History was made in 1909 when the U.S. military purchased a Wright-designed airplane for $30,000; that plane was the world's first military aircraft. Soon after, the Wright brothers began their first manufacturing firm, the Wright Company, in Dayton, Ohio. Firms such as the Wright Company and others continued to produce thousands of planes by the end of World War I. **Ask:** In what year did Charles Lindbergh complete the first nonstop solo transatlantic flight? *(1927)* OL

Edison loved anything related to science. His mother allowed him to set up a chemistry lab in the family's basement. When he was 12, he got a job working for the railroad, where he set up a new lab in an empty freight car. One day, Edison saved the life of a child who had fallen onto the tracks of an oncoming train. The child's father took an interest in Edison and taught him to use the telegraph. Edison's first invention was a gadget that sent automatic telegraph signals—which he invented so he could sleep on the job.

While still in his 20s, Thomas Edison decided to go into the "invention business." In 1876 Edison set up a workshop in **Menlo Park, New Jersey.** Out of this famous laboratory

History Online
Student Web Activity Visit ca.hss.glencoe.com and click on *Chapter 16—Student Web Activities* for an activity on inventions.

came the phonograph, the motion picture projector, the telephone transmitter, and the storage battery. But Edison's most important invention was the electric lightbulb.

Edison developed the first workable lightbulb in 1879. He then designed power plants that could produce electric power and distribute it to lightbulbs. For Christmas in 1880, Edison used 40 bulbs to light up Menlo Park. Visitors came to see the "light of the future." He built the first central electric power plant in 1882 in New York City—illuminating 85 buildings! C1

Inventor George Westinghouse took Edison's work with electricity even further. In 1885 Westinghouse developed and built transformers that could send electric power more cheaply over longer distances. Soon electricity powered factories, trolleys, streetlights, and lamps all over America. Westinghouse also developed a system for transporting natural gas and invented many safety devices. C2

African American Inventors A number of African Americans contributed to the era of invention. **Lewis Howard Latimer,** an engineer, developed an improved filament for the lightbulb and joined Thomas Edison's company. **Granville Woods,** an electrical and mechanical engineer from Ohio, patented dozens of inventions. Among them were an electric incubator and railroad improvements such as an electromagnetic brake and an automatic circuit breaker. Elijah McCoy invented a mechanism for oiling machinery. W

Jan E. Matzeliger, another African American inventor, developed a shoe-making machine that performed many steps that were previously done by hand. His device, which revolutionized the shoe industry, was adopted in shoe factories in the United States and overseas.

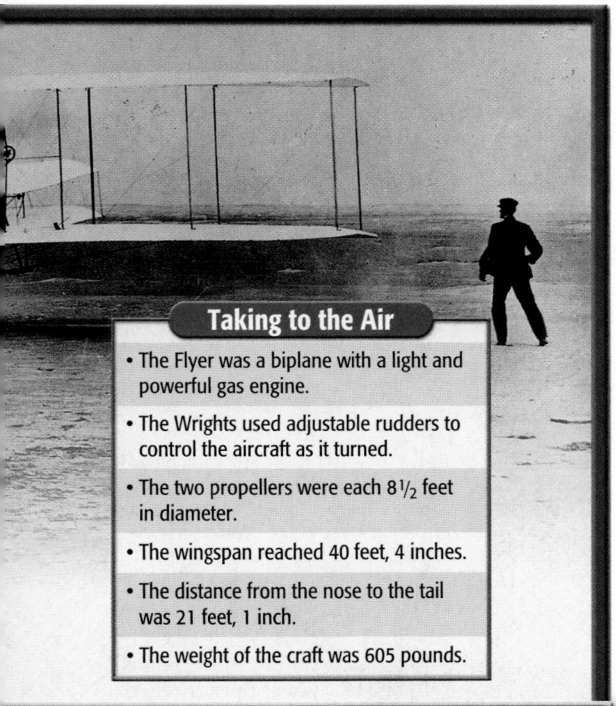

Taking to the Air

- The Flyer was a biplane with a light and powerful gas engine.
- The Wrights used adjustable rudders to control the aircraft as it turned.
- The two propellers were each 8 1/2 feet in diameter.
- The wingspan reached 40 feet, 4 inches.
- The distance from the nose to the tail was 21 feet, 1 inch.
- The weight of the craft was 605 pounds.

1927 → Lindbergh completes first nonstop solo transatlantic flight

1947 → Chuck Yeager is first to fly faster than the speed of sound

Reading Check **Evaluate** Which of Edison's inventions do you think is the most valuable to our world? Explain your reasoning.

C1 Critical Thinking

Making Inferences Explain that many of Edison's—and others'—inventions took many years to develop. **Ask:** Why would that be true? *(Students may suggest because of trial and error or lack of sufficient funds.)* AL CA H12.

C2 Critical Thinking

Drawing Conclusions **Ask:** How was Westinghouse's work vital to the success and spread of Edison's inventions? *(because he made transmission of electricity possible, and electricity powered Edison's inventions)* OL

W Writing Support

Research Reports Writing Have students conduct research to find out why the government gives patents, what is required to qualify for a patent, how inventors file for one, and what rights a patent grants. Students should present their findings in a report. AL CA 8WA2.3

History Online
Objectives and answers to the student activity can be found in the Web Activity Lesson Plan feature at ca.hss.glencoe.com.

Reading Check
Answer: Answers will vary, but students should support their opinions.

Did You Know?

In the 1920s, Henry Ford moved Edison's original lab in Menlo Park to Greenfield Village, a large museum site that the automobile tycoon built in Dearborn, Michigan. On the 50-year anniversary of the invention of the lightbulb, Edison, 82 years old at the time, was on hand to re-create his original experiment.

Resources for page 715

- American Art Prints: Thomas Eakins
- Biography Activity 16A
- Biography Activity 16C

R1 Reading Strategy

Scaffolding—Identifying the Main Idea and Supporting Details Have students identify the details that support this main idea. *(reduced cost of automobile made it more affordable for more people; improved techniques for selling brought goods to more people)* OL

This READING SKILL was introduced in Chapter 2.

R2 Reading Strategy

Connecting **Ask:** What is an example of an improvement that we now enjoy on the inventions described here? *(Lightbulb—long-lasting bulbs; Camera—digital cameras; Phonograph—CD or MP3 players; Telephone—cell phones)* OL

C Critical Thinking

Determining Cause and Effect **Ask:** What impact would street lights have on a city? *(Students may suggest that lights would make streets safer by providing more light; create more nightlife and give an economic boost to businesses that provide food and entertainment.)* OL

CA HI3.

Answers and Additional Support

US8.12.1 Trace patterns of agricultural and industrial development as they relate to climate, use of natural resources, markets, and trade and locate such development on a map.

A Changing Society

Main Idea **Improvements in transportation made travel easier and helped industries make their goods available to a wider audience.** R1

Reading Connection When your family takes a trip, how do you travel? Read on to find out how the automobile changed transportation.

In the 1900s, improvements ushered in a new era of transportation. After a period of experimentation, the automobile became a practical method of getting from place to place.

Henry Ford's Automobiles Henry Ford wanted to build an inexpensive car that would last a lifetime. While working as an engineer in **Detroit, Michigan,** in the 1890s, Ford had experimented with an automobile engine powered by gasoline. In 1903 he began designing cars at his automaking company.

In 1906 Ford told Charles Sorenson, later Ford's general superintendent, "We're going to get a car now that we can make in great volume and get the prices way down." For the next year, Ford and Sorenson worked on the Model T, building the car and testing it on rough roads. In 1908 Ford introduced the Model T to the public.

MORE ABOUT...

Changing the Way We Live

R2 **Inventions** American ingenuity, innovation, and imagination led to the inventions that changed the way we live and how we communicate.

The Telephone Alexander Graham Bell demonstrated the telephone in 1876. The telephone soon became a necessity. By 1900 there were 2 million in use.

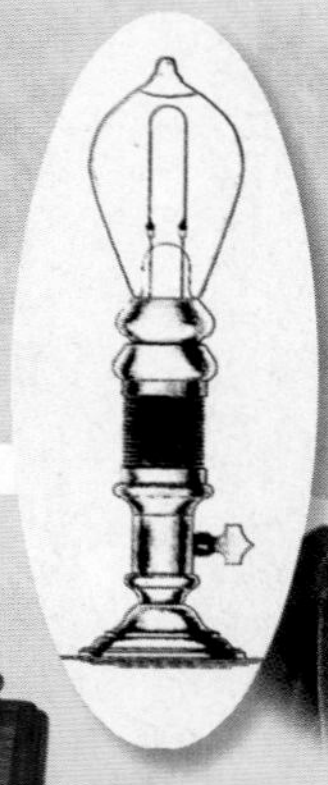

Lighting the World Lewis Latimer improved on Edison's version, creating a bulb that lasted much longer, and developed the threaded socket. Latimer directed the installation of electric streetlights in New York City, Philadelphia, Montreal, and London. C

Phonograph The first practical phonograph was built by Thomas Edison in 1877.

Kodak Camera In 1888 George Eastman invented a small camera that made it easier and less costly to take photographs.

More Skill Practice

Analyzing Primary Sources Read Edison's famous statement to students: "genius is one percent inspiration and ninety-nine percent perspiration." **Ask:** What did Edison mean by that? *(Students may say that coming up with an idea for an invention is easier than the effort required to figure out how to make it work.)* OL

MORE ABOUT...

Lewis Latimer worked in a law firm that specialized in patent law, where he drew schematics. He did such work for Alexander Graham Bell before joining Edison's company.

Sorenson described the sturdy black vehicle as ". . . a car which anyone could afford to buy, which anyone could drive anywhere, and which almost anyone could keep in repair."

The Model T became immensely popular. During the next 18 years, Ford's company sold 15 million Model T's. Henry Ford also pioneered a less expensive way to manufacture cars—the moving **assembly line.** On the line, each worker performed an assigned task again and again at a certain stage in the production of the automobile. The assembly line revolutionized industry, enabling manufacturers to produce large quantities of goods more quickly. This **mass production** of goods decreased manufacturing costs, so products could be sold more cheaply.

R

In 1908 the Model T's first year, it sold for $850. In 1914 mass production reduced the price to $490. By 1924 Model Ts were selling for $295. Ford's business philosophy was simple. "Every time I reduce the charge for our car by one dollar," he said, "I get a thousand new buyers. In this way, Ford made the automobile affordable for millions of Americans.

Selling Goods With factories churning out more and more products, merchants looked for better ways to sell their goods. One way was through the mail. In 1863 mail delivery to homes began—up to then, service was only to post offices. By the 1890s, the U.S. Post Office had expanded its delivery service in rural areas.

Some firms developed mail order businesses, receiving and shipping orders by mail. Companies such as Montgomery Ward and Sears Roebuck published catalogs that offered a wide range of goods from shoes to farm equipment. Catalogs introduced rural families to a wide assortment of goods not found in country stores.

Chain stores—stores with identical branches in many places—grew rapidly. F.W. Woolworth's chain of "five-and-ten-cent stores" specialized in everyday household and personal items at bargain prices. By 1911, more than a thousand Woolworth stores were in operation.

Reading Check **Describe** What qualities made the Model T popular?

History Online
Study Central Need help understanding how inventions changed peoples lives? Visit ca.hss.glencoe.com and click on Study Central.

Section 2 Review

Reading Summary

Review the Main Ideas

- The telegraph and the telephone changed the way Americans communicated.
- Electricity and other inventions lit up the world in a new way.
- The introduction of the automobile made it easier for people to travel and helped businesses bring their goods to new areas.

What Did You Learn?

1. Name and describe two inventions that changed the way Americans communicated.
2. How was transportation improved during the 1800s?

Critical Thinking

3. **Organizing Information** Re-create the diagram below, and classify each invention described in this section in one of the categories. CA HI2.

Mostly rural use	Mostly urban use	Both urban and rural	Mostly used by business and industry

4. **The Big Ideas** Which of the inventions discussed do you think had the greatest impact on the economy of the United States? Why? CA CS1.
5. **ANALYSIS** **Compare and Contrast** Study the photographs of the inventions and products that appear in this section. Which have undergone the greatest change? Why do you think this is so? CA HI3.

SECTION 2 REVIEW ANSWERS

Review questions reinforce content standard US8.12.

1. any two of the following: telegraph, telephone, typewriter, phonograph, camera
2. by the development of the electromagnetic train brake and automatic circuit breaker for railroads, and the gasoline-powered auto engine
3. Rural: electric incubator; Urban: telegraph; Both: telephone, vacuum cleaner, camera, lightbulb, auto; Business/Industry: typewriter, adding machine, shoe-making machine
4. **The Big Ideas** Answers will vary but should be supported by reasons.
5. **ANALYSIS** Answers will vary but should be supported by reasons.

R Reading Strategy

Understanding Vocabulary Have students describe the relevance of both assembly lines and mass production to the country's growing economy. *(Both made it possible to sell products more cheaply, making them more widely available.)* OL

ASSESS

Resources for page 717

Use these resources to assess student mastery of section content.

- Section Quiz 16–2
- Interactive Tutor Self-Assessment CD-ROM

Reading Check

Answer: It was affordable, could be driven anywhere, and could be easily repaired.

History Online

Study Central provides summaries, interactive games, and online graphic organizers to help students review section content.

CLOSE

Evaluating In 1878 a newspaper printed this headline: "Edison Invents a Machine That Will Feed the Human Race—Manufacturing Biscuits, Meat, Vegetables, and Wine out of Air, Water, and Common Earth." **Ask:** What does this joking headline suggest about Edison? OL

FOCUS

BELLRINGER
Skillbuilder Activity

Project **Daily Focus Skills Transparency 16–3** and have students answer the question.

Guide to Reading

Preteaching Vocabulary: Quiz students on the meaning of the content vocabulary words. Have them look up unfamiliar terms in the Glossary.

Answers to Graphic: Shareholders: Corporations made it possible for many people to invest in a business; Stock exchanges: Where people buy and sell stocks; Mergers: Corporations combined to form giant businesses that drove economic growth

Unpacking the Standards

After reading the section, students will be able to:

- Explain how economic growth results from abundant land, labor, and capital.
- Describe the growth of monopolies in oil and steel.
- Explain why government decided to regulate business.

Section 3

The Age of Big Business

Guide to Reading

History Social Science Standards

US8.12 Students analyze the transformation of the American economy and the changing social and political conditions in the United States in response to the Industrial Revolution.

Looking Back, Looking Ahead

You have learned how inventions helped the American economy grow. In Section 3, you will learn how entrepreneurs gained control of various industries and turned them into successful businesses.

Focusing on the Main Ideas

- The American economy grew because the country contained abundant land, labor, and capital. ***(page 719)***
- The development of the oil industry created one of the first monopolies. ***(page 720)***
- Monopolies in the steel business and other industries created the need for government regulation. ***(page 721)***

Locating Places

Pittsburgh, Pennsylvania (PIHTS • BUHRG)
Cleveland, Ohio
Chicago, Illinois
Birmingham, Alabama

Meeting People

John D. Rockefeller
Andrew Carnegie (KAHR • nuh • gee)
J. Pierpont Morgan

Content Vocabulary

corporation (KAWR • puh • RAY • shuhn)
stock
shareholder
dividend (DIH • vuh • DEHND)
horizontal integration (HAWR • uh • ZAHN • tuhl IHN • tuh • GRAY • shuhn)
trust
monopoly
vertical integration (VUHR • tih • kuhl)
philanthropy (fuh • LAN • thruh • pee)
merger (MUHR • juhr)

Academic Vocabulary

resource
invest

Reading Strategy

Analyze Re-create the diagram below and explain the significance of each term in business in the late 1800s.

	Significance
Shareholders	
Stock exchanges	
Mergers	

NATIONAL GEOGRAPHIC **Who & When?**

1870 — 1885 — 1900

1870 Rockefeller organizes the Standard Oil Company

John D. Rockefeller

1882 Rockefeller organizes trust

1890 Andrew Carnegie dominates the steel industry

Andrew Carnegie

SECTION RESOURCES

Print Material
- Reproducible Lesson Plan 16–3*
- Daily Lesson and Discussion Notes 16–3
- Guided Reading Activity 16–3
- Reading Essentials and Study Guide 16–3
- Active Reading Note-Taking Guide 16–3
- Section Quiz 16–3

Transparencies
- Daily Focus Skills Transparency 16–3
- Section Graphic Organizer Transparency 16–3
- California Standards Practice Transparencies

Technology
- Interactive Tutor Self-Assessment CD–ROM
- Exam*View*® Pro Testmaker CD–ROM
- Presentation Plus! CD-ROM

*Available on TeacherWorks™

US8.12.1 Trace patterns of agricultural and industrial development as they relate to climate, use of natural resources, markets, and trade and locate such development on a map. US8.12.4 Discuss entrepreneurs, industrialists, and bankers in politics, commerce, and industry (e.g., Andrew Carnegie, John D. Rockefeller, Leland Stanford).

Foundations for Growth

Main Idea **The American economy grew because the country contained abundant land, labor, and capital.**

Reading Connection Imagine you want to start your own business. What is needed to get that business up and running? Read on to find out how industries in America gained the resources they needed to succeed.

The period from the end of the Civil War to 1900 was an era of unmatched economic growth in the United States. New methods in technology and business allowed the country to tap its rich supply of natural **resources,** increase its production, and raise the money needed for growth. The growing transportation system made it easier for merchants to reach distant markets.

What Are the Factors of Production? The change from an agricultural economy to an industrial one was possible because the United States had the resources needed for a growing economy. Among these resources were what economists call the factors of production: land, labor, and capital.

The first factor of production, land, means not just the land itself but all natural resources. The United States held a variety of natural resources that had industrial uses.

The second production factor is labor. Large numbers of workers were needed to turn raw materials into goods. This need was met by the rapid growth of population. Between 1860 and 1900, the population of the country more than doubled.

The third production factor, capital, is the equipment—buildings, machinery, and tools—used in production. Land and labor are needed to produce capital goods. These goods, in turn, are essential for the production of consumer goods. The term *capital* is also used to mean money for investment. Huge amounts of money were needed to finance industrial growth. One source of money was the selling of stock by corporations. Another was corporate savings, or businesses investing a portion of their earnings in better equipment.

Raising Capital With the economy growing after the Civil War, many businesses looked for ways to expand. To do so, they had to raise capital. They needed capital to buy raw materials and equipment, to pay workers, and to cover shipping and advertising costs.

One way a company could raise capital was by becoming a **corporation** (KAWR • puh • RAY • shuhn). A corporation is a company that sells **stock,** or shares, of its business to the public. The people who **invest** in the corporation by buying stock are its **shareholders,** or partial owners.

In good times, shareholders earn **dividends** (DIH • vuh • DEHNDZ)—cash payments from the corporation's profits—on the stock they own. If the company prospers, its stock rises in value, and the shareholders can sell it for a profit. If the company fails, however, the shareholders lose their investment. In the late 1800s, hundreds of thousands of people shared in corporate profits by buying and selling stocks in special markets known as stock exchanges.

Growth of Corporations The nation's early corporations were created only for specific public benefits, such as the building of a highway. Soon many manufacturing and business firms were incorporating. Big corporations had several advantages over small manufacturing companies. Big corporations could produce goods more cheaply and efficiently. They could continue to operate in poor economic times by cutting prices to increase sales. Many were also able to negotiate refunds from the railroads, which lowered their operating costs further.

Banks played a major role in this period of economic growth. Businesses borrowed money from banks to start or expand their operations. The banks, in turn, made profits on the loans.

Reading Check **Explain** What happens to dividends when a company does well?

More Skill Practice

Historical and Social Sciences Analysis Skill **Ask:** What business form used in early modern times led to the development of corporations? *(joint-stock companies)* How are they similar to corporations? *(in both, investors pool their resources and, by doing so, limit their risk)* OL CA HI3.

TEACH

R1 Reading Strategy

Categorizing Information Ask students to give an example of each factor of production. *(Possible answers: Land—farmland, water, oil, coal; Labor—workers, business owners; Capital—machinery, tools, factories)* BL

R2 Reading Strategy

Scaffolding—Summarizing Have students write a paragraph explaining how the terms *corporation*, *stock*, *shareholder*, and *dividends* are related. OL

This READING SKILL was introduced in Chapter 4.

R3 Reading Strategy

Academic Vocabulary Ask students to share what they know about the meaning of the word *invest*. Then have students use the Glossary to look up the definition of the word. EL

Review The Big Idea

Review the Big Idea for this section: "Innovations in technology and business help build a nation's industrial power."
Ask: How would the initial growth of corporations help feed the country's economic growth? *(As corporations grow, the businesses they buy from would also grow, and both they and those business would hire more workers, who would have more money to spend.)* AL

Reading Check
Answer: They go up.

R1 Reading Strategy

Visualizing Help students visualize the meaning of the term *horizontal integration* by drawing sketches of four buildings on the board in a row. Label them *Cleveland Oil*, *Penn Oil*, *Great Lakes Oil*, and *Central Oil*. Draw an oval around the first three and change their names to *Standard Oil*. OL

C Critical Thinking

Analyzing Information
Have students recall what *rebates* are from Section 1 of this chapter. *(discounts)* **Ask:** How would Rockefeller benefit if he was getting rebates and competitors were not? *(by having lower costs, which he could either use to lower his own prices or to increase his profits)* OL

CA H16.

R2 Reading Strategy

Understanding Vocabulary
Have students explain how the terms *trust* and *monopoly* differ as a matter of what is being controlled. *(Trust: matter of who controls the corporation; Monopoly: the business controls an industry)* OL

Reading Check

Answer: horizontal integration, combining competing firms into one corporation

Answers and Additional Support

US8.12.1 Trace patterns of agricultural and industrial development as they relate to climate, use of natural resources, markets, and trade and locate such development on a map. **US8.12.4** Discuss entrepreneurs, industrialists, and bankers in politics, commerce, and industry (e.g., Andrew Carnegie, John D. Rockefeller, Leland Stanford).

The Oil Business

Main Idea **The development of the oil industry created one of the first monopolies.**

Reading Connection Is there someone in your town who has started a successful business? What type of business is it? Read on to find out how John D. Rockefeller created an empire in the oil industry.

In 1870 **John D. Rockefeller** organized the Standard Oil Company of Ohio and set out to dominate the oil industry. One method Rockefeller used to build his empire was **R1** **horizontal integration** (HAWR • uh • ZAHN • tuhl IHN • tuh • GRAY • shuhn)—combining two or more firms producing the same kind of product. The corporation produced and used its own tank cars, pipelines, and even its own wooden barrels—made from forests owned by Standard Oil. Standard Oil grew in wealth and power, becoming the most famous corporate empire of the day.

To strengthen Standard Oil's position in the oil industry, Rockefeller lowered his prices to drive his competitors out of business. In addition, he pressured customers not to deal with rival oil companies, and he persuaded the railroads to grant him rebates in exchange for his business. **C**

Rockefeller increased his control of the oil industry in 1882 by forming a **trust,** a group of companies managed by the same board of directors. First he acquired stock in many different oil companies. Then the shareholders of these companies traded their stock for Standard Oil stock, which paid higher dividends. This gave Standard Oil's board of directors ownership of the other companies' stock and the right to manage those companies. Rockefeller had created a **monopoly**—almost total control by a single producer—of the oil industry. **R2**

Reading Check **Explain** What method did Rockefeller use to build his oil empire?

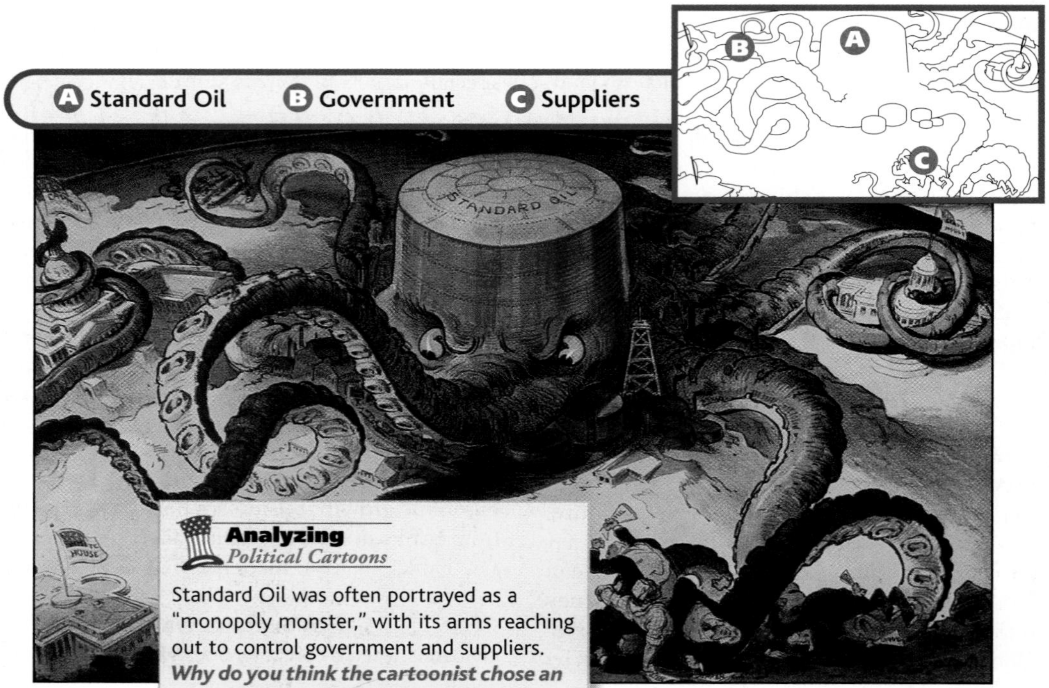

Analyzing *Political Cartoons*

Standard Oil was often portrayed as a "monopoly monster," with its arms reaching out to control government and suppliers. ***Why do you think the cartoonist chose an octopus to represent Standard Oil?***

Resources for page 720

- Art and Architecture Transparency 18
- Geography and History Activity 16
- American Art Prints: Richard Morris Hunt

Analyzing *Political Cartoons*

The head of the octopus is a giant oil tank.

Answer: The use of an octopus depicts Standard Oil's ability to control several levels of the market at once.

US8.12.1 Trace patterns of agricultural and industrial development as they relate to climate, use of natural resources, markets, and trade and locate such development on a map. **US8.12.4** Discuss entrepreneurs, industrialists, and bankers in politics, commerce, and industry (e.g., Andrew Carnegie, John D. Rockefeller, Leland Stanford).

The Steel Business

Main Idea **Monopolies in the steel business and other industries created the need for government regulation.**

Reading Connection What kinds of cars do people drive in your neighborhood? Chances are they do not all drive the same type of car. That is because car companies compete with each other to get people to buy their products. Read on to find out how monopolies came to dominate certain industries.

Steel also became a huge business in the late 1800s. Steel is a strong and long-lasting form of iron treated with carbon—the ideal material for railroad tracks, bridges, and many other products. Before the 1860s, however, steel was not widely used because it was expensive to manufacture. The development of new manufacturing techniques helped overcome this problem.

Steel Industry Growth Two new methods of making steel—the Bessemer process, which was developed by Henry Bessemer of England, and the open-hearth process—changed the industry. With these new methods, mills could produce steel at affordable prices and in large quantities. In the 1870s, large steel mills were built close to sources of iron ore in western Pennsylvania and eastern Ohio. **Pittsburgh, Pennsylvania** (PIHTS • BUHRG), became the steel capital of the United States. Cities located near the mines and close to waterways like **Cleveland, Ohio; Chicago, Illinois; Birmingham, Alabama;** and Detroit, Michigan, also became centers of steel production.

Andrew Carnegie The leading figure in the early years of the American steel industry was **Andrew Carnegie** (KAHR • nuh • gee), son of a Scottish immigrant. Starting as a telegraph operator, Carnegie worked his way up to become manager of the Pennsylvania Railroad. While in that job, he introduced the first successful sleeping car. In 1865 he left the railroad to invest in the growing iron industry.

Carnegie soon realized that steel would have an enormous market. After learning about the Bessemer process, he built a steel plant near Pittsburgh that used the new process. Carnegie named the plant the J. Edgar Thompson Steel Works, after the president of the Pennsylvania Railroad—his biggest customer.

Vertical Integration By 1890 Andrew Carnegie dominated the steel industry. His company became powerful through **vertical integration** (VUHR • tih • kuhl), combining firms involved in different steps of manufacturing. Carnegie bought iron and coal mines, warehouses, ore ships, and railroads to gain control of all parts of the business of making and selling steel.

Analyzing Political Cartoons

Andrew Carnegie is shown (right) as a mason. The blocks are the libraries to which he has donated money. ***What point do you think the cartoonist is making?***

Analyzing Political Cartoons

Answer: that Carnegie is buildiing something valuable or useful

C1 Critical Thinking

Determining Cause and Effect **Ask:** What made steel a valuable material? *(It is strong and long-lasting.)* What made it possible for the steel industry to grow? *(development of new manufacturing processes)* OL CA HI2.

S Skill Practice

Using Geography Skills **Ask:** Why was it beneficial for these cities to be close to sources of iron ore? *(Students should note that it would be cheaper to transport the ore short distances.)* OL CA HI2.

C2 Critical Thinking

Making Inferences **Ask:** What kind of a person do you think Carnegie was? Why? *(Students may say that Andrew Carnegie must have been hard-working, since he rose from being a telegraph operator to president of a railroad, and shrewd because he spotted the benefits of making steel.)* OL

R Reading Strategy

Scaffolding—Questioning To help students understand vertical integration, write the following on the board: *Meatpacker*; *Bakery*; *Soft drinks*; *Publishing*. **Ask:** Suppose a fast-food company bought companies in each of those areas. Which would represent vertical integration? *(all but the publishing company)* OL CA 8RW1.3

This READING SKILL was introduced in Chapter 9.

R1 Reading Strategy

Using Word Parts Explain that the term comes from words meaning "love" and "humankind." **Ask:** How do those origins relate to the meaning of the term? *(Students may say that only someone who loved humankind would give money to help people.)* OL

W Writing Support

Persuasive Writing Have students take the role of a newspaper editor and write an editorial encouraging wealthy people to perform acts of philanthropy. Remind students to give reasons for their position. OL CA 8WA2.4

R2 Reading Strategy

Understanding Vocabulary Have students give a synonym (word meaning the same thing) and antonym (word meaning the opposite) for *merger*. *(joining, union, fusion; breaking apart, dividing, splitting)* OL

Resources for page 722

Primary Source Reading 16

Answers and Additional Support

▲ John D. Rockefeller

When Carnegie combined all his holdings into the Carnegie Steel Company in 1900, he was producing one-third of the nation's steel. In 1901 Carnegie sold his steel company to banker **J. Pierpont Morgan.** Morgan combined the Carnegie company with other businesses to form the United States Steel Corporation, the world's first billion-dollar corporation.

Philanthropists Andrew Carnegie, John D. Rockefeller, and other industrial millionaires of the time grew interested in **philanthropy** (fuh • LAN • thruh • pee)—the use of money to benefit the community. The philanthropists founded schools, universities, and other civic institutions across the United States.

Carnegie donated $350 million to various organizations. He built Carnegie Hall in New York City, one of the world's most famous concert halls; the Carnegie Foundation for the Advancement of Teaching; and more than 2,000 libraries worldwide. Carnegie often wrote about social and political issues. He felt that a person who has great wealth also has a duty to use the surplus to help humankind. He stated that a "man who dies rich dies disgraced." Rockefeller used his fortune to establish the University of Chicago in 1890 and New York's Rockefeller Institute for Medical Research.

Corporations Grow Larger In 1889 New Jersey encouraged the trend toward business monopolies by allowing holding companies to obtain charters, a practice that some states prohibited. A holding company would buy controlling interests in the stock of other companies instead of purchasing the companies outright. Rockefeller formed Standard Oil of New Jersey so that the corporation could expand its holdings. Other states also passed laws that made corporate **mergers** (MUHR • juhrz)—the combining of companies—easier.

Mergers concentrated economic power in a few giant corporations and a few powerful individuals, such as Rockefeller and banker J. Pierpont Morgan. By 1900 one-third of all American manufacturing was controlled by just 1 percent of the country's corporations. These giant corporations were the driving force behind the great economic growth of the period, but they also posed problems. On the one hand, many Americans admired the efficiencies that large businesses provided. On the other hand, some argued that a lack of competition hurt consumers. Without competition, corporations had no reason to keep their prices low or to improve their goods and services.

Big Business and Social Science Some business practices in the late 1800s were based on a scientific idea known as social Darwinism. Charles Darwin, a British scientist, had published a theory in 1859 that all plants and animals evolved over long periods of time by a process known as natural selection. According to the theory, organisms competed for survival, and those animals best adapted to the environment survived, while the others did not.

More Skill Practice

Historical and Social Sciences Analysis Skill Ask: How would a state benefit by granting charters to holding companies? *(Students may suggest that taxes from the company would go to the state rather than another state or that the company would move to the state and thus create jobs.)* AL CA HI6.

More Skill Practice

Historical and Social Sciences Analysis Skill Ask: Why would market domination by one or two companies hurt the economy? *(Students may say that the economy could become dependent on the controlling companies or that they could raise prices.)* OL

Later thinkers applied Darwin's biological theory to human society and business. Some industrial leaders, such as John D. Rockefeller, argued that "survival of the fittest" helped explain the growth of huge companies. As one supporter of social Darwinism put it,

> **C** **"We have unmistakable proof that throughout all past time, there has been a ceaseless devouring of the weak by the strong."**
>
> **—from *First Principles* by Herbert Spencer**

Carnegie argued that big companies like his own were beneficial to society. The revolution in productivity enabled "the poor to enjoy what the rich could not before afford." Companies that grew and thrived raised their workers' standard of living.

Government Regulation Due to increasing pressure from the public, government stepped in to regulate business. During the 1880s, several states passed laws restricting business mergers. Corporations, however, avoided these laws by doing business in states that had no such laws.

Public pressure for a federal law to prohibit trusts and monopolies led Congress to pass the Sherman Antitrust Act in 1890. The law sought "to protect trade and commerce against unlawful restraint and monopoly." The act did not clearly define either "trusts" or "monopolies," however.

In its early years, the Sherman Antitrust Act did little to curb the power of big business. By contrast, in the 1890s the government did use the act to stop a strike by railroad workers that threatened to slow the nation's mail delivery.

Reading Check **Compare** How does vertical integration differ from horizontal integration?

History Online

Study Central Need help understanding how industries grew and became monopolies? Visit ca.hss.glencoe.com and click on Study Central.

Section 3 Review

Reading Summary

Review the Main Ideas

- The American economy shifted from agriculture to industry as the nation realized it had the necessary materials for industrial growth.
- As oil was discovered, boomtowns sprang up around centers of oil and Rockefeller created his oil monopoly.
- Carnegie dominated the steel industry and as competing companies were driven out of business, the government attempted to regulate industrial growth.

What Did You Learn?

1. Which cities became centers of steel production in the late 1800s?
2. How did state and federal governments respond to the growth of trusts and monopolies?

Critical Thinking

3. **Determining Cause and Effect** Re-create the diagram below and list the benefits of competition to consumers. CA CS1.

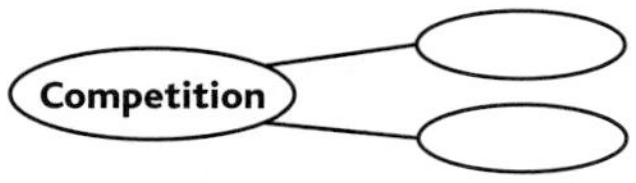

4. **The Big Ideas** Compare methods used by Rockefeller and Carnegie to build their industrial empires. Describe any differences between the two. CA HI2.
5. **Analyze** Study the cartoon on page 720. Whom do the figures represent? What is the cartoon saying about the Standard Oil Company? CA HR4.
6. **Expository Writing** Research to find a philanthropist who has supported the community in which you live. Write a short essay describing his or her contributions. CA 8WA2.1

SECTION 3 REVIEW ANSWERS

Review questions reinforce content standard US8.12.

1. Pittsburgh, Cleveland, Chicago, Detroit, Birmingham
2. by passing laws restricting mergers and banning trusts and monopolies
3. keeps prices low; improves quality of goods and services
4. **The Big Ideas** Rockefeller used horizontal integration to develop his oil monopoly. Carnegie used vertical integration to develop his steel monopoly.
5. The figures represent government, Standard Oil, and suppliers. The cartoon says that Standard Oil had the power to control government and suppliers.
6. Students' essays should describe the person's contributions

C Critical Thinking

Analyzing Information
Ask: Does Social Darwinism, as described in this quotation, justify the harsh business practices carried out during the late 1800s? Have students debate the point. AL

ASSESS

Resources for page 723

Use these resources to assess student mastery of section content.

Section Quiz 16–3

Interactive Tutor Self-Assessment CD-ROM

Reading Check

Answer: Vertical integration combines companies at all levels of manufacturing into one corporation; horizontal integration combines competing firms into one corporation.

History Online

Study Central provides summaries, interactive games, and online graphic organizers to help students review section content.

CLOSE

Making inferences John D. Rockefeller claimed that consolidation protected business from "wasteful conditions." **Ask:** What did he mean by this statement? *(Consolidation helped companies operate more efficiently.)* OL

FOCUS

BELLRINGER
SKILLBUILDER ACTIVITY

Project **Daily Focus Skills Transparency 16–4** and have students answer the question.

Guide to Reading

Preteaching Vocabulary: Use the Vocabulary Puzzle-Maker CD-ROM to create crossword and word search puzzles.

Answers to Graphic: Organized nationally; Recruited African Americans, immigrants, women, and unskilled laborers; Made use of collective bargaining; Organized strikes

Unpacking the Standards

After reading the section, students will be able to:

- Describe the harsh working conditions in the late 1800s.
- Explain how workers combated unsafe working conditions.
- Discuss the development of the strike.

Section 4

Industrial Workers

Guide to Reading

History Social Science Standards

US8.12 Students analyze the transformation of the American economy and the changing social and political conditions in the United States in response to the Industrial Revolution.

Looking Back, Looking Ahead

In the last section, you read about how industries were able to grow and expand. In this section, you will read about the workers in these industries and the conditions in which they worked.

Focusing on the Main Ideas

- Industrialization created many jobs, but it also created hazardous working conditions. *(page 725)*
- Workers created labor unions to combat unsafe working conditions in many of the nation's industries. *(page 726)*
- Strikes often ended in violence, causing many people to turn against labor unions. *(page 727)*

Meeting People

Terence V. Powderly
Samuel Gompers
Mary Harris Jones
Eugene V. Debs (yoo • JEEN DEHBZ)
Grover Cleveland

Locating Places

Philadelphia, Pennsylvania (FIH • luh • DEHL • fee • uh)
New York City, New York
Homestead, Pennsylvania

Content Vocabulary

sweatshop
trade union
collective bargaining
strikebreaker
injunction (ihn • JUHNK • shuhn)

Academic Vocabulary

job
labor

Reading Strategy

Organizing Information As you read the section, re-create the diagram below and list actions labor unions took to improve working conditions.

NATIONAL GEOGRAPHIC **Who & When?**

1885 | 1890 | 1895

Samuel Gompers

1886 American Federation of Labor forms; Haymarket Riot

Haymarket news report

1892 Homestead Strike

1894 Pullman Strike

SECTION RESOURCES

Print Material
- Reproducible Lesson Plan 16–4*
- Daily Lesson and Discussion Notes 16–4
- Guided Reading Activity 16–4
- Reading Essentials and Study Guide 16–4
- Active Reading Note-Taking Guide 16–4
- Section Quiz 16–4

Transparencies
- Daily Focus Skills Transparency 16–4
- Section Graphic Organizer Transparency 16–4
- California Standards Practice Transparencies

Technology
- Interactive Tutor Self-Assessment CD–ROM
- ExamView® Pro Testmaker CD–ROM
- Presentation Plus! CD–ROM

*Available on TeacherWorks™

US8.12.6 Discuss child labor, working conditions, and laissez-faire policies toward big business and examine the labor movement, including its leaders (e.g., Samuel Gompers), its demand for collective bargaining, and its strikes and protests over labor conditions.

Working Conditions

Main Idea **Industrialization created many jobs, but it also created hazardous working conditions.**

Reading Connection What do your parents or guardians do for a living? What safeguards are in place to protect them from getting hurt at their jobs or to help them if they do? Read on to find out about the working conditions in the late 1800s.

The industrial growth of the late 1800s created new **jobs.** Growth also raised the standard of living for many American workers. That is, necessities and luxuries were more available and affordable. Yet workers paid a price for economic progress. Factories had once been small workplaces where employers and employees knew one another and often worked side by side. As mass production spread, however, factories became larger and less personal.

Industrial laborers worked for 10 or 12 hours a day, six days a week. They could be fired at any time for any reason. Many lost their jobs during business downturns or were replaced by immigrants who were willing to work for lower pay.

Factories and mines were noisy, unhealthy, and unsafe. Accidents were common. Steel workers suffered burns from spills of hot steel. Coal miners died in cave-ins and from the effects of gas and coal dust. Textile workers' lungs were damaged by airborne lint. Garment workers toiled in crowded urban factories called **sweatshops,** where their eyesight was ruined by sewing for hours in poor light. Filled with flammable materials, the sweatshops were also terrible firetraps.

Women Workers Although the majority of working women in the late 1800s had jobs as domestic servants, women also joined the industrial workforce, especially the textile industry. By 1900 more than one million women worked in industry. However, because no laws regulated workers' salaries, women generally received about half of what men earned for the same work. In addition, it was assumed that a woman had a man to support her—either her father or her husband. A man, therefore, needed higher wages because he was supporting a family.

Child Labor Industries also hired children. In 1900 hundreds of thousands of children under 16 years of age worked in factories. Concerned groups brought child **labor** to the attention of their state legislatures. As a result, many states passed child labor laws. These laws stated that children working in factories had to be at least 12 years old and should not work more than 10 hours a day. Employers widely ignored child labor laws, however. Also, the laws did not apply to agriculture, which employed about one million children.

Reading Check **Examine** How did mass production change the size of factories?

Picturing History

Young boys worked long hours in the mines to earn \$1 to \$3 a week. By 1900, many states had passed child labor laws. ***Were the child labor laws effective? Why or why not?***

TEACH

W Writing Support

Research Report Writing Have students work in groups to investigate labor laws that exist today. You might assign each group a topic, such as health and safety laws; length of workday and workweek; discrimination in hiring; equal pay; child labor laws; minimum wage; and so on. Each group should report its findings to the class. OL CA 8WA2.3

R1 Reading Strategy

Scaffolding—Academic Vocabulary The word *available* was introduced in Chapter 6, Section 3. Ask a student to define the word. OL

R2 Reading Strategy

Understanding Vocabulary Have students take turns describing the images conjured up by the word *sweatshop.* *(dirty, loud, bad air, people of all ages working very hard)* OL

C Critical Thinking

Recognizing Bias **Ask:** What bias is evident in the reasons that women were paid less than men? *(assumption that women had men to support them)* OL

Reading Check

Answer: Factories became larger and more impersonal; they also became noisy, unhealthy, and unsafe.

More Skill Practice

Historical and Social Sciences Analysis Skill Tell students that workplace dangers led to various disasters, which led governments to pass workplace safety laws. **Ask:** Should governments pass such laws before disasters occur or wait until after? Have students explain their answers. OL

Picturing History

The young boys in this photo were coal miners in Kingston, Pennsylvania, around 1900.

Answer: They were ineffective because they were widely ignored and because they did not apply to agriculture, where many children worked.

R Reading Strategy

Using Context Clues Ask: What do you think a trade is? *(a profession or craft, such as carpentry or plumbing)* OL

S Skill Practice

Historical and Social Sciences Analysis Skill

Ask: Why would employers fire workers who joined labor organizations? *(because the organizations pressured employers to pay laborers more money and improve working conditions)* OL

Review The Big Idea

Review the Big Idea for this section: "Reactions to social injustice can lead to reform movements." **Ask:** What problems might the Knights of Labor have tried to fight against? *(Students may cite such problems as long workdays and workweeks; low wages; poor, hazardous, or unhealthy working conditions.)* Why did they have to meet in secret? *(because employers fired workers who openly took part in unions)* OL

Answers and Additional Support

US8.12.6 Discuss child labor, working conditions, and laissez-faire policies toward big business and examine the labor movement, including its leaders (e.g., Samuel Gompers), its demand for collective bargaining, and its strikes and protests over labor conditions.

Labor Unions Form

Main Idea **Workers created labor unions to combat unsafe working conditions in many of the nation's industries.**

Reading Connection What do you think should be done about unsafe conditions at businesses and factories? Read on to learn about how employees attempted to change the conditions in which they worked.

Dissatisfied workers organized into groups—labor unions—to demand better pay and working conditions from their employers. Earlier in the 1800s, skilled workers had formed unions to represent workers in certain crafts or trades, such as carpentry. These **trade unions** had little influence because each represented only one trade. By the mid-1800s, labor leaders looked to expand their unions. R

Noble and Holy Order Knights of Labor

In 1869 garment cutters in **Philadelphia, Pennsylvania** (FIH • luh • DEHL • fee • uh), founded the Noble and Holy Order of the Knights of Labor. Employers fired workers who joined labor organizations, so the Knights met secretly and used special handshakes to identify each other. Under the leadership of **Terence V. Powderly,** the Knights of Labor became a national labor organization in the 1880s. S

History *Through Art*

The Ironworkers' Noontime **by Thomas Pollock Anshutz** Factory workers in Wheeling, West Virginia, take their noontime break. ***What national trade union represented skilled workers?***

Resources for page 726

- Universal Access Activity 16
- Economics and History Activity 16

History *Through Art*

In this small factory, painted by Thomas Pollock Anshutz, workers made iron nails by melting the ingredients for iron in large cauldrons and pouring the liquid into molds.

Answer: American Federation of Labor

US8.12.6 Discuss child labor, working conditions, and laissez-faire policies toward big business and examine the labor movement, including its leaders (e.g., Samuel Gompers), its demand for collective bargaining, and its strikes and protests over labor conditions.

Unlike most unions, the Knights recruited people who had been kept out of trade unions, including women, African Americans, immigrants, and unskilled laborers. The Knights of Labor grew rapidly to more than 700,000 members by 1886. However, setbacks in many strikes weakened the unions and resulted in the loss of members and power in the 1890s.

American Federation of Labor In 1881 a group of national trade unions formed a federation that five years later became known as the American Federation of Labor (AFL). The AFL represented skilled workers in various crafts.

The AFL was led by **Samuel Gompers,** the tough, practical-minded president of the Cigar Makers' Union. The organization pressed for higher wages, shorter working hours, better working conditions, and the right to bargain collectively with employers. In the process of **R** **collective bargaining,** unions represent workers in bargaining with management.

Although violent strikes turned some people against workers and unions in the late **S** 1880s, the AFL survived and grew. By 1904 the AFL was able to claim more than 1.6 million members.

Women and the Unions Many unions would not admit women workers, so some women formed their own unions. **Mary Harris Jones,** better known as Mother Jones, spent 50 years fighting for workers' rights.

In 1911 a fire broke out at the Triangle Shirtwaist Company factory, a crowded sweatshop in **New York City, New York.** The workers, mostly young immigrant women, could not escape from the building because the company had locked the doors to prevent employees from leaving early. Nearly 150 workers died in the fire. The disaster led the International Ladies' Garment Workers Union (ILGWU) to push for a safer working environment.

Reading Check **Compare** Who was eligible for membership in the AFL? In the Knights of Labor?

The Unions Act

Main Idea **Strikes often ended in violence, causing some people to turn against labor unions.** **C**

Reading Connection Do you know anyone who was laid off from a job or whose wages were lowered due to economic downturns? How did these people cope with their loss of wages? Read on to find out about the conflict between employers and labor unions as an economic depression set in during the late 1800s.

An American Story

On a spring day in 1886, about 12,000 workers in Chicago's Haymarket Square manufacturing district were on strike. At 2 o'clock, a man climbed up on an empty freight car near the crowd. He moved to the edge of the roof and waved frantically at the crowd below. "Stand firm," he yelled. "Let every man stand shoulder to shoulder and we will win this fight. We must have our rights. Strike while the iron is hot." The events at Haymarket Square soon turned violent, as did many other strikes.

Strikes and Strikebreakers Economic depressions in the 1870s and the 1890s led companies to fire workers and lower wages. Unions responded with large strikes that sometimes sparked violence.

Economic depression hit the nation following a financial panic in 1873. To cut costs, companies forced their workers to take pay cuts. In July 1877, as the depression continued, several railroads announced another round of wage cuts. This triggered the first nationwide labor protest. Angry strikers smashed equipment; tore up tracks; and blocked rail service in New York, Baltimore, Pittsburgh, Chicago, and other cities. The companies hired **strikebreakers** to replace the striking workers. State militia or federal **U** troops restored order in different places. By the time the strike ended, however, more than 100 people lay dead, and millions of dollars of property had been destroyed.

R Reading Strategy

Understanding Vocabulary **Ask:** Why would workers want to bargain *collectively*? *(Students should recognize that by joining together, all workers had more power than individual workers had separately.)* OL

S Skill Practice

Historical and Social Sciences Analysis Skill **Ask:** Why would strikes turn some people against a union? *(Possible answer: People fear violence; striking workers do not produce goods.)* AL CA HI1.

C Critical Thinking

Determining Cause and Effect Ask students to create a chart outlining the cause of labor strife in the late 1800s and its resulting effects. OL

U Universal Access

English Learners **Ask:** What two individual words are put together to form the term *strikebreakers*? *(strike* and *breakers)* EL

Reading Check

Answer: AFL: skilled workers in various crafts; Knights of Labor: laborers turned away from other unions, including African Americans, women, immigrants, and unskilled laborers

Did You Know?

A Triangle Shirtwaist Company worker who survived the fire described what it was like: "The door was locked. We were about a hundred people. We were hollering and crying 'Open the door!' Banging and banging quite a long time. . . . We waited a long time. We didn't feel any of the flames, but it was getting warm. The fires went to the windows. I thought about my mother and father. What would they do if I died? Then all of a sudden we all fell over. Somebody [had] opened the door. 'Thank God!' We were all crying and yelling."

Biography

TEACH

C1 Critical Thinking

Comparing and Contrasting **Ask:** How were the lives of Mary Harris Jones and César Estrada Chávez similar? *(both knew suffering—Jones from losing her husband and children and being forced to earn a living, Chávez from working in the fields; both campaigned for workers' rights)* **OL**

C2 Critical Thinking

Analyzing Primary Sources **Ask:** What did Mother Jones mean when she said "I abide where there is a fight against wrong"? *(Students may say she meant that she feels called to work wherever there is injustice.)* **OL** **CA HR4.**

C3 Critical Thinking

Making Inferences **Ask:** Why would a boycott be a powerful weapon against a company? *(A company being boycotted cannot make any money because it is selling less of its goods.)* **OL** **CA HI6.**

Answers and Additional Support

Biography

US8.12.6 Discuss child labor, working conditions, and laissez-faire policies toward big business and examine the labor movement, including its leaders (e.g., Samuel Gompers), its demand for collective bargaining, and its strikes and protests over labor conditions.

MARY HARRIS JONES

1830–1930

▲ Mary Harris Jones

Mary Harris "Mother" Jones was born in Ireland and moved to the United States with her family. In 1867 her husband George and their four children died from yellow fever. Widowed and childless, Jones moved to Chicago and opened a dressmaker's shop.

By the 1880s, Jones was fully involved in the union movement and became one of its most important leaders. For the next 50 years, she traveled around the country speaking to workers and promoting unions. She said, "My address is like my shoes: it travels with me. I abide where there is a fight against wrong." C2

She told her listeners to "look on yourselves, and upon each other. Let us consider this together for I am one of you, and I know what it is to suffer."

CÉSAR ESTRADA CHÁVEZ

1927–1993

C1

▲ César Estrada Chávez

César Chávez knew the suffering of farmworkers. He had labored in the fields since age 10, when his family lost their Arizona farm during the Great Depression. Like thousands of other farmers, the Chávez family became migrant workers. Chávez attended some 65 schools before dropping out at the end of eighth grade.

After serving in World War II, Chávez took a paid job to win greater rights for Mexican Americans. In 1962 with the support of his wife Helen Fabela Chávez, he returned to the fields and his dream of organizing farmworkers into a union.

In 1965 Chávez launched La Huelga—"the strike." He asked Americans to boycott grapes until growers in the San Joaquin Valley signed union contracts. C3 Some 17 million Americans responded. "For the first time," Chávez said, "the farmworker got some power." The power came from the United Farm Workers, the first successful farmworkers union in the nation's history.

Then and Now

Mary Harris Jones and César Chávez both worked to better the lives of workers. Who might they choose to represent today? Why?

728

Then and Now

Answers will vary but students should give reasons for their responses.

More Skill Practice

Historical and Social Sciences Analysis Skill Tell students that when a judge asked Mother Jones who had given her a permit to speak on the streets, she replied, "Patrick Henry, Thomas Jefferson, and John Adams." **Ask:** What did she mean? *(The founders of the country gave all Americans the right to free speech.)* **OL** **CA HR4.**

Major Strikes Antilabor feeling grew stronger after events in Chicago's Haymarket Square in May 1886. Striking workers from the McCormick Harvester Company gathered to protest the killings of four strikers the previous day. When police ordered the crowd to break up, an unidentified person threw a bomb that killed a police officer. Several more were killed in a riot that followed. Following the Haymarket Riot, some Americans associated the labor movement with violence and disorder.

In 1892 workers went on strike at Andrew Carnegie's steel plant in **Homestead, Pennsylvania.** Homestead managers hired nonunion workers and brought in 300 armed guards to protect them. A fierce battle left at least 10 people dead. The plant reopened with nonunion workers, protected by the troops. After the failure of the Homestead Strike, the steelworkers' union dwindled.

After employees of George Pullman's railway-car plant near Chicago went on strike in May 1894, Pullman closed the plant. One month later, workers in the American Railway Union supported the strikers by refusing to handle Pullman cars, paralyzing rail traffic.

Pullman and the railroad owners fought back. They persuaded U.S. Attorney General Richard Olney to obtain an **injunction** (ihn • JUHNK • shuhn), or court order, to stop the union from "obstructing the railways and holding up the mails." The workers and their leader, **Eugene V. Debs** (yoo • JEEN DEHBZ), refused to end the strike. Debs was arrested for interfering with the mail. **R**

President **Grover Cleveland** sent federal troops to Chicago, and soon the strike was over. The failure of the Pullman Strike dealt another blow to the union movement. Despite these setbacks, workers continued to organize to work for better wages and working conditions.

Reading Check **Describe** Why did many railroad workers go on strike in 1877?

History Online
Study Central Need help understanding the labor movement? Visit ca.hss.glencoe.com and click on Study Central.

Section 4 Review

Reading Summary

Review the Main Ideas

- Industrial workers labored long hours for low pay, often in unsafe conditions.
- Labor unions helped workers gain economic and political power.
- Strikes ending in violence and deaths caused labor unions to lose much of their power.

What Did You Learn?

1. What role did Samuel Gompers play in union growth?
2. What were the goals of the American Federation of Labor when it was founded?

Critical Thinking

3. **Organizing Information** Re-create the diagram below and describe the roles each person played in labor-management issues. CA HI1.

Individual	Role
Terence Powderly	
Mary Harris Jones	
George Pullman	

4. **Analyze** Explain how the separate words in the term *sweatshop* can help you determine its meaning. CA 8RW1.0
5. **The Big Ideas** Why do you think many Americans did or did not support the labor unions?
6. **Analyze** Find two sources that discuss unions—one from the early 20th century and one modern source. Identify how the authors view unions. How has new historical information impacted the views of the modern author? CA HI5.

SECTION 4 REVIEW ANSWERS

Review questions reinforce content standards US8.12.

1. headed the AFL
2. higher wages, shorter hours, improved working conditions, and right to collective bargaining
3. Powderly: helped the Knights of Labor grow; Jones: fought for workers' rights; Pullman: obtained court order to stop strike; Cleveland: sent troops to Chicago to end Pullman strike
4. *Sweat* describes the hard work people did; *shop* shows the link to business.
5. **The Big Ideas** did support: supported workers' rights; did not support: deplored violence
6. Diary entries should reveal long hours and poor working conditions.

R Reading Strategy

Understanding Vocabulary
Tell students that an injunction is often used to block a person, company, or group from taking an action before they do it. **Ask:** What synonyms could be used in place of the word *injunction*? *(ban, forbid, prohibit)* OL

ASSESS

Resources for page 729

Use these resources to assess student mastery of section content.

Section Quiz 16–4

Interactive Tutor Self-Assessment CD-ROM

Reading Check

Answer: The company cut workers' wages.

History Online

Study Central provides summaries, interactive games, and online graphic organizers to help students review section content.

CLOSE

Analyzing Information
Ask: How did the efforts of people such as Terence Powderly, Samuel Gompers, Mother Jones, and César Chávez help workers? *(They formed unions that could campaign for workers' rights and wages.)* OL

FOCUS

History–Social Science Standards

The following standards are covered on pages 730–731.

US8.12.6 Discuss child labor, working conditions, and laissez-faire policies toward big business and examine the labor movement, including its leaders (e.g. Samuel Gompers), its demand for collective bargaining, and its strikes and protests over labor conditions.

TEACH

C1 Critical Thinking

Making Inferences Ask: Why do unions today include airline workers and teachers? *(because service workers like them are an increasingly large part of the economy)* AL

C2 Critical Thinking

Analyzing Primary Sources Ask: What does Chávez mean by these words? *(The effort of unions is not about the products people make or work on, but the people who do the work.)* OL CA HR4.

Answers and Additional Support

Connecting to the Constitution

US8.12.6 Discuss child labor, working conditions, and laissez-faire policies toward big business and examine the labor movement, including its leaders (e.g., Samuel Gompers), its demand for collective bargaining, and its strikes and protests over labor conditions.

Government and Labor

Why It Matters Labor unions are an important part of the American society. They present the concerns of many workers to businesses and to the U.S. government at all levels. Through unions, workers try to improve their wages and working conditions. They also can gain a voice in almost all matters relating to their jobs. Unions have helped unite workers and provide a source of pride and a sense of dignity to workers.

In the past, unions were formed mainly by workers in heavy industries that produce goods such as machines, mining equipment, and steel. Today, however, people in jobs as different as airline workers, teachers, and professional athletes also belong to unions. Although only a small number of American workers are union members, the influence of unions is powerfully felt, especially on issues such as job safety, working conditions, and workers' grievances. In national, state, and local government, labor unions are active in backing candidates and laws favorable to their interests.

César Chávez

Government, Business, and Labor

During the late 1800s, some unions won recognition from employers and influenced local and state laws. However, many federal and state governments favored big business over labor unions. Many states passed laws to restrict union activities. On the national level, the Sherman Antitrust Act of 1890—passed to break up large companies that hindered trade—was used mostly against labor. The courts found union leaders guilty of breaking the law, stating that unions interfered with commerce. Judges often issued **injunctions**, or court orders, banning strikes.

During the early 1900s, the political climate changed. An increasing number of Americans began to call for limits on big business and more rights for workers. As a result, government attitudes toward labor began to change. Most of the larger cities and more than half the states placed limits on working hours for employees on public works.

> ***"The fight is never about grapes or lettuce. It is always about people."***
>
> —César Chávez, quoted in *Great Labor Quotations*

730

More Skill Practice

Historical and Social Sciences Analysis Skill Read the following quotation by Chief Justice Charles Evans Hughes to students: "The exploitation [unjust use] of a class of workers. . . casts a direct burden for their support upon the community. . . . The community may direct its lawmaking power to correct the abuse." **Ask:** What did Hughes mean by the community's "lawmaking power"? *(the legislature)* OL CA HI1.

▲ *Union strikes, such as the Pullman strike of 1894, sometimes turned violent.*

The courts, however, supported employers who challenged state laws that tried to regulate wages and working conditions. In 1905, for example, the Supreme Court ruled in the case *Lochner* v. *New York* that states could not set limits on the working hours of bakery workers. The Court reasoned that the New York law was unconstitutional because it interfered with the right of employers and employees to make contracts, or agreements, about working hours. The Court's reasoning was based on the principle that individuals have "liberty of contract" based on the Fourteenth Amendment.

Protecting Unions and Workers The Great Depression of the 1930s left many American workers without jobs. President Franklin D. Roosevelt's effort to end the Depression included helping labor. One of the most important laws passed by Congress during Roosevelt's administration was the Wagner Act C in 1935. This law sought to protect the right of workers to organize and to bargain collectively, or hold contract talks with employers. Under the Wagner Act, companies could not punish a worker because of union activities. Another measure was the Fair Labor Standards Act of 1938. It set the first minimum wage for workers and banned child labor.

Many employers believed that the Wagner Act was unconstitutional, but the Supreme Court upheld the act. In the case *National Labor Relations Board* v. *Jones & Laughlin Steel Corporation* (1937), the Court ruled that local activities of trade unions may affect commerce. Because Congress had the constitutional power to regulate commerce, it could also regulate relations between business and labor. This meant that the National Labor Relations Board created by Congress had the authority to punish businesses involved in interstate commerce that discriminated against union members.

Unions Today During the 1960s and 1970s, several groups, such as government workers and farmworkers, formed new unions. For example, César E. Chávez, a Mexican American labor leader, began to organize farmworkers in California. Chávez founded what is now the United Farm Workers of America (UFW), a union of migrant workers and other farm laborers. Union membership among other Hispanic Americans, African Americans, and women also increased during this period.

Over the years, labor unions—as well as economic prosperity—have raised workers' standards of living. However, as a result of political and economic changes, the number of S workers belonging to unions has declined sharply in recent years. Unions face other challenges too. One is defending workers' interests in declining industries that have fewer jobs. Another is protecting the jobs and wages of workers affected by **automation,** or the use of R machines to do tasks once performed by people. Despite these difficulties, labor unions remain a powerful force in American life.

Checking for Understanding

1. What reason did the courts of the late 1800s give for finding union leaders guilty of breaking the law?
2. How did the federal government help labor during the Great Depression?

Critical Thinking

3. **Evaluate** Why did the Supreme Court adjust its view on labor in *NLRB* v. *Jones & Laughlin Steel Company*? CA HI2.
4. **Analyze** Restate the Court's reasoning in *Lochner* v. *New York* and predict the ruling's impact on other industries. CA HI6.

Questions reinforce content standard US8.12.6

Checking for Understanding:

1. Unions interfered with commerce.
2. Wagner Act helped workers organize and bargain collectively. Fair Labor Standards Act of 1938 set the first minimum wage for workers and banned child labor.

Critical Thinking:

3. Students may say that the Court was more sympathetic to help workers hurt by the Great Depression.
4. States cannot pass laws regulating working conditions. Students should recognize that the ruling would block laws affecting workers in other industries as well.

Connecting to the Constitution

C Critical Thinking

Determining Cause and Effect Ask: What event favored the rights of workers? *(the Great Depression)* Why might this event have changed people's and Congress's views toward workers? *(Although the Depression affected everyone, workers were hit hard.)* OL

S Skill Practice

Visual Literacy Have students conduct research to learn what percentage of non-farm workers belonged to unions in the following years: 1900, 1920, 1940, 1960, 1980, and 2000. Then have them prepare a graph showing their findings and write a paragraph analyzing what they found. OL CA HI3.

R Reading Strategy

Scaffolding—Questioning Ask: What difficulties confront labor unions today? *(the problem of how to represent workers in declining industries and in the face of automation)* OL

This READING SKILL was introduced in Chapter 9.

ASSESS

Have students answer the Checking for Understanding and Critical Thinking questions.

CLOSE

Predicting Consequences Ask students to predict the future of unions based on the paths that they have taken and their current status and effectiveness. OL

FOCUS

History–Social Science Standards

The following standard is covered on pages 732–733.

US8.12 Students analyze the transformation of the American economy and the changing social and political conditions in the United States in response to the Industrial Revolution.

TEACH

W Writing Support

Response to Literature Writing Have students write a brief essay explaining what they think about the story of John Henry and why railroad workers would enjoy singing it. OL

CA 8WA2.2

R Reading Strategy

Using Context Clues Ask: What do you think a "steam drill" is? *(Students should infer that it is a drill driven by steam power.)* What challenge does John Henry take on? *(a drilling contest against the steam drill)*

OL CA 8RW1.3

Answers and Additional Support

Analyzing Primary Sources

US8.12 Students analyze the transformation of the American economy and the changing social and political conditions in the United States in response to the Industrial Revolution.

The Growth of Industry in America

Following the Civil War, the railroads expanded throughout the country. The railroads and inventions created the chance for other industries to grow. Many companies in these industries had long working hours, paid minimal salaries, and provided unsafe working conditions.

Read the passages on pages 732 and 733 and answer the questions that follow.

These women are working on the cloth after it has been woven. ▶

Reader's Dictionary

shaker: person who shook and turned the drill after each blow to keep the drill from getting caught in the rock or the rock dust

haste (HAYST)**:** hurrying too fast

garments (GAHR • muhnts)**:** pieces of clothing

inclined plane: slanted surface

slate: type of rock that is used for chalkboards and roof tiles

John Henry

W *"John Henry" is a song that railroad men sang as they worked. John Henry hand drilled holes into stone to place dynamite.*

When John Henry was a little baby,
Sitting on his pappy's knee,
He grabbed a hammer and a little piece of steel,
Said, "This hammer'll be the death of me,
Lord, Lord,
This hammer'll be the death of me. . . ."

John Henry told his captain,
"A man ain't nothing but a man,
R But before I'll let that steam drill beat me down
I'll die with my hammer in my hand,
Lord, Lord,
I'll die with my hammer in my hand."

John Henry said to his **shaker,**
"Now shaker, why don't you sing?
'Cause I'm throwing twelve pounds from my hips on down,
Just listen to that cold steel ring,
Lord, Lord,
Just listen to that cold steel ring."

The man that invented the steam drill,
He thought he was mighty fine,
But John Henry he made fourteen feet
While the steam drill only made nine,
Lord, Lord,
The steam drill only made nine.

John Henry hammered on the mountain
Till his hammer was striking fire,
He drove so hard he broke his poor heart,
Then he laid down his hammer and he died, Lord, Lord,
He laid down his hammer and he died.

EXTENDING THE CONTENT

John Henry The ballad of John Henry has some connection to fact. The Chesapeake and Ohio Railroad started to dig a tunnel through the Allegheny Mountains to extend its line. The railroad hired mostly former slaves for the work, some of which involved digging holes for the placement of dynamite. That work was done by hand until a steam driller was introduced. Whether an actual driller challenged the machine to a contest is lost in history, but the legendary John Henry became a symbol for the competition of man against machine—and of the African American man against the power of white society.

They took John Henry to the graveyard,
And they buried him in the sand,
And every locomotive comes rolling by
Says, "There lies a steel-driving man,
Lord, Lord,
There lays a steel-driving man."

—Anonymous in *Annals of America*

The Sweatshop

In factories, people had to work very quickly. In this passage, a young woman described her day in a factory where clothing was made.

At seven o'clock we all sit down to our machines and the boss brings to each one the pile of work that he or she is to finish during the day. . . . This pile is put down beside the machine and as soon as a skirt is done it is laid on the other side of the machine. . . .

S

The machines go like mad all day, because the faster you work, the more money you get. Sometimes in my **haste** I get my finger caught and the needle goes right through it. . . . We all have accidents like that. . . . Sometimes a finger has to come off. . . .

R

All the time we are working the boss walks about examining the finished **garments** and making us do them over again if they are not just right. So we have to be careful as well as swift.

—Sadie Frowne, "The Story of a Sweatshop Girl"

Child Labor

Laws forbidding children to work did not exist or were not enforced at this time.

In a little room in this big, black shed—a room not twenty feet square—forty boys are picking their lives away. The floor of this room is an **inclined plane**, and a stream of coal pours constantly in. They work here, in this little black hole, all day and every day, . . . picking their way among the black coals, bending over till their little spines are curved. . . .

C

Not three boys in this roomful could read or write. Shut out from everything that is pleasant, with no chance to learn, with no knowledge of what is going on about them. . . .

They know nothing but the difference between **slate** and coal.

—from a local Labor Standard Newspaper, St. Clair, Pennsylvania

▲ Young coal miners

DBQ Document-Based Questions

John Henry

1. What does John Henry predict in the first stanza?
2. Who won the contest? How do you know?

The Sweatshop

3. Why do people work quickly at the factory?
4. Why do people have to work carefully?

Child Labor

5. Where do the boys work?
6. What is their job?

Read to Write

7. Make two lists—one labeled Working Conditions and the other Effects of Working Conditions. Use the information in "The Sweatshop," "Child Labor," and what you already know about working conditions at this time to complete the lists. Write a paragraph explaining how you feel about these conditions. Include ideas for how they could be improved. CA 8RC2.3

DBQ Document-Based Questions

1. that he will die with a hammer in his hand
2. John Henry; because he drilled deeper, but the effort killed him
3. the more they finish, the more they are paid
4. So they don't get hurt in machines.
5. an enclosed room smaller than 20 feet square
6. sort coal from slate
7. Students' paragraphs should draw on information in these sources and from the text to identify the problems and then propose some solutions.

S Skill Practice

Historical and Social Sciences Analysis Skill
Ask: What health and safety problems are evident in these two accounts? *(Workers in the sweatshop sometimes put needles through their fingers and sometimes lose their fingers. The coal sorters are probably breathing large amounts of coal dust, and their work makes their spines curved.)* OL

R Reading Strategy

Scaffolding—Monitoring
Ask: Why must the workers make sure they sew correctly as well as quickly? *(The boss walks around as they work and if anything is incorrectly done, he makes them do it over.)* OL

This READING SKILL was introduced in Chapter 14.

C Critical Thinking

Recognizing Bias **Ask:** What bias does the writer show? How can you tell? *(sympathy for the child workers; the description of their working conditions is very negative)* AL

ASSESS

Ask students to answer the Document-Based Questions.

CLOSE

Inferring Ask students to infer how the workers described in these selections would see themselves, their coworkers, their bosses, and their work. Have them write a brief essay explaining their inferences. OL

Resources for pages 734–735

Use these resources to review, assess, or reteach the chapter.

- Active Reading Note-Taking Guide, Chapter 16
- Chapter 16 Reading Essentials and Study Guide
- Chapter 16 Tests, Forms A and B
- Standards Assessment, Forms A and B
- California Standards Practice Workbook
- Succeeding on the California History–Social Science Standards CD-ROM
- MindJogger Videoquiz
- Interactive Tutor Self-Assessment CD-ROM

Review Content Vocabulary

1. rebates
2. standard gauge
3. trade union

Review the Main Ideas

4. air brakes, car couplers, refrigerated cars, sleeping cars, dining cars
5. to make it easier to schedule trains
6. telegraph, telephone, typewriter
7. assembly line to produce large quantities of automobiles more quickly; mass production to cut manufacturing costs
8. acquiring companies that provide the equipment and services needed by a single company
9. passed the Sherman Antitrust Act
10. Unions that represent all a company's workers bargain with management for improved working conditions, hours, and pay on behalf of those workers.
11. Its violence turned public opinion against the labor movement.

Critical Thinking

12. By uniting, they had a better chance of being heard.
13. Railroads connected previously unconnected industries, markets, and cities, thereby creating national markets and industries, which relied on all sizes of businesses for growth.

Chapter 16 Assessment

Standard US8.12

Review Content Vocabulary

Write the key term that completes each sentence.

a. standard gauge
b. assembly line
c. horizontal integration
d. trade union
e. rebates

1. Railroads offered ___, or discounts, to their largest customers.
2. Railroad companies adopted 4 feet, 8.5 inches as the width of the railroad track, also known as the ___.
3. The Knights of Labor was a ___ of garment workers.

Review the Main Ideas

Section 1 • Railroads Lead the Way

4. What improvements in railway transportation were brought about by new technology?
5. Why did the American Railway Association divide the country into four time zones?

Section 2 • Inventions

6. What inventions improved communications in the late 1800s?
7. What manufacturing methods did Henry Ford use to make his new automobile affordable?

Section 3 • The Age of Big Business

8. What is vertical integration?
9. What action did Congress take to control trusts and monopolies in response to pressure from the American people?

Section 4 • Industrial Workers

10. What is collective bargaining?
11. How did the Haymarket Riot of 1886 affect public opinion about the labor movement?

Critical Thinking

12. **Conclude** Why did workers think that forming organized labor unions would help them get what they wanted from employers? CA CS1.
13. **Analyze** How did American industry benefit from the growing railroad network in the late 1800s? CA HI2.

Geography Skills

A cartogram is a kind of map used to present statistical information. On a population cartogram the sizes of the states appear in proportion to their populations. Study the population cartogram below and answer the following questions. CA CS3.

NATIONAL GEOGRAPHIC **Population by State, 1900**

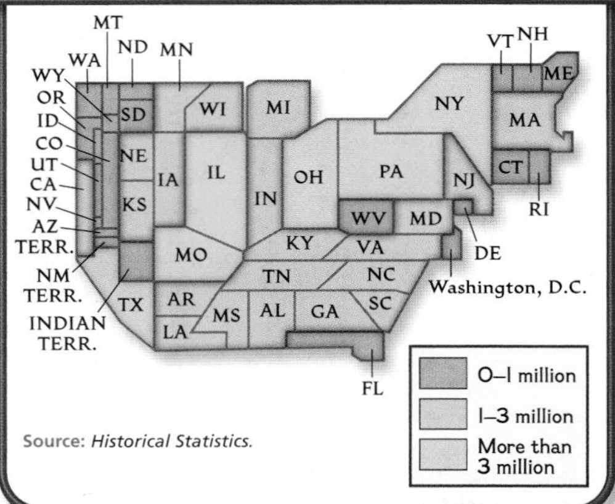

14. **Location** Did Florida or Illinois have a larger population 1900?
15. **Location** Did North Dakota have more or fewer people than South Dakota?

History Online

Self-Check Quiz Visit ca.hss.glencoe.com to prepare for the Chapter 16 test.

Read to Write

16. **The Big Ideas Evaluate** In a short essay, describe how the increasing size of corporations was both beneficial and harmful to American business. CA 8WA2.3

17. **Summarize** Review the chapter for information about the four major union strikes between 1877 and 1894. Write a headline for each that might have appeared in newspapers following the strike. CA 8WA2.2

18. **Using Your FOLDABLES** Write a poem, series of journal entries, or short story using the main ideas and supporting details from your completed foldable. CA 8WA2.1

Using Academic Vocabulary

Identify the correct form of the academic vocabulary word to complete each sentence.

technology technological technologically

19. The computer is an example of a ___ advance.

transmit transmits transmitted

20. The reporter used the telegraph to ___ the story to the newspaper.

Building Citizenship

21. **Evaluate** With another student, write a short essay in which you support or criticize labor unions from the point of view of a young person who has just entered the workforce. Note how you think a union could or could not improve your life. Share your essay with the class. CA 8WS1.1

Reviewing Skills

22. Review READING SKILL **Predicting Consequences** How would the growth of industry and new innovations in technology impact preparations for a war? Write a short essay predicting the potential effect. CA 8WA2.3

23. Review ANALYSIS SKILL **Organizing Information** Do research to find the dates when the inventions described in this chapter were first created. Also find other inventions created by the inventors mentioned in the chapter, along with their dates of creation. Draw an annotated time line with the information you have found. Be sure to include the importance of each invention. CA CS2.

Standards Practice

Select the best answer for each of the following questions.

24 The development of the transformers that Westinghouse built led to an increase in

A the price of electricity.
B the use of gas to heat homes.
C the use of electricity to power factories.
D imported goods.

25 John D. Rockefeller was the founder of the

A Pennsylvania Railroad.
B United States Steel Corporation.
C Titusville oil well.
D Standard Oil Company of Ohio.

26 The process in which a union represents its workers when negotiating with management is known as

A collective bargaining.
B strikebreaking.
C vertical integration.
D philanthropy.

Chapter 16 Assessment

Geography Skills

14. Illinois

15. fewer

Read to Write

16. The Big Ideas Students may say that corporate growth created jobs and made products cheaper and more widely available but that many smaller companies were driven out of business and workers suffered.

17. Headlines should address the rail strike of 1877; the McCormick strike of 1886 that led to the Haymarket Riot; the 1892 Homestead strike; and the 1894 Pullman strike.

18. Using Your FOLDABLES Students' writing should reflect information in the chapter.

Using Academic Vocabulary

19. technological

20. transmit

Building Citizenship

21. Students should provide examples, evidence, or reasonable explanations for their positions.

Reviewing Skills

22. READING SKILL Students might suggest that the presence of industry would make it possible to produce war goods more quickly.

23. ANALYSIS SKILL Time lines should include more inventions that those outlined in the chapter.

Standards Practice

24. C

25. D

26. A

Bonus Question

Ask: Why did several major strikes in the late 1800s involve railroads or companies that supplied materials to railroads? *(because these were among the nation's leading industries)* OL

History Online

Have students visit the Web site at ca.hss.glencoe.com to review Chapter 16 and take the **Self-Check Quiz.**

Chapter 17 Planning Guide

SECTION RESOURCES

Main Ideas	Print Materials	Technology Resources
Section 1: The New Immigrants 1. Immigrants came from many different countries. 2. Many immigrants faced harsh working conditions. 3. Many native-born Americans resented the immigrants.	• Reproducible Lesson Plan 17–1* • Daily Lesson and Discussion Notes 17–1 • Active Reading Note-Taking Guide 17–1 • Reading Essentials and Study Guide 17–1 • Guided Reading Activity 17–1 • Section Quiz 17–1	Daily Focus Skills Transparency 17–1 Section Graphic Organizer Transparency 17–1 California Standards Practice Transparencies Interactive Tutor Self-Assessment CD-ROM Exam*View*® Pro Testmaker CD-ROM Presentation Plus! CD-ROM
Section 2: Moving to the City 1. As Americans crowded into cities, strong contrasts emerged between the lives of the rich and the poor. 2. Growing cities faced problems. 3. Americans created new styles of buildings and improved transportation.	• Reproducible Lesson Plan 17–2* • Daily Lesson and Discussion Notes 17–2 • Active Reading Note-Taking Guide 17–2 • Reading Essentials and Study Guide 17–2 • Guided Reading Activity 17–2 • Section Quiz 17–2	Daily Focus Skills Transparency 17–2 Section Graphic Organizer Transparency 17–2 California Standards Practice Transparencies Interactive Tutor Self-Assessment CD-ROM Exam*View*® Pro Testmaker CD-ROM Presentation Plus! CD-ROM
Section 3: A Changing Culture 1. The expanding education system provided many opportunities. 2. Reading grew popular as education and leisure time increased. 3. American art, music, and leisure activities developed their own style.	• Reproducible Lesson Plan 17–3* • Daily Lesson and Discussion Notes 17–3 • Active Reading Note-Taking Guide 17–3 • Reading Essentials and Study Guide 17–3 • Guided Reading Activity 17–3 • Section Quiz 17–3	Daily Focus Skills Transparency 17–3 Section Graphic Organizer Transparency 17–3 California Standards Practice Transparencies Interactive Tutor Self-Assessment CD-ROM Exam*View*® Pro Testmaker CD-ROM Presentation Plus! CD-ROM
Section 4: The Progressive Movement 1. Americans took action against corruption in business and government. 2. New calls for reform were aided by writers who exposed corruption. 3. More people received the right to vote, and the government began to regulate industry.	• Reproducible Lesson Plan 17–4* • Daily Lesson and Discussion Notes 17–4 • Active Reading Note-Taking Guide 17–4 • Reading Essentials and Study Guide 17–4 • Guided Reading Activity 17–4 • Section Quiz 17–4	Daily Focus Skills Transparency 17–4 Section Graphic Organizer Transparency 17–4 California Standards Practice Transparencies Interactive Tutor Self-Assessment CD-ROM Exam*View*® Pro Testmaker CD-ROM Presentation Plus! CD-ROM
Section 5: A Changing Nation 1. The U.S. demonstrated its power in Latin America and the Pacific. 2. Ethnic and religious minorities faced discrimination and violence. 3. Minority groups sought to end discrimination and gain equal rights.	• Reproducible Lesson Plan 17–5* • Daily Lesson and Discussion Notes 17–5 • Active Reading Note-Taking Guide 17–5 • Reading Essentials and Study Guide 17–5 • Guided Reading Activity 17–5 • Section Quiz 17–5	Daily Focus Skills Transparency 17–5 Section Graphic Organizer Transparency 17–5 California Standards Practice Transparencies Interactive Tutor Self-Assessment CD-ROM Exam*View*® Pro Testmaker CD-ROM Presentation Plus! CD-ROM Vocabulary Puzzle Maker CD-ROM

PACING YOUR LESSONS

Chapter Introduction	Section 1	Section 2	Section 3	Section 4	Section 5	Chapter Assessment	Unit Wrap-Up
$\frac{1}{2}$ Day	1 Day	2 Days	1 Day	2 Days	2 Days	$\frac{1}{2}$ Day	$\frac{1}{2}$ Day

0:00 **OUT OF TIME?** Assign the Chapter 17 ***Reading Essentials and Study Guide***

*Available on TeacherWorks™

Chapter 17 Planning Guide

Standards-Based Lesson Plan

History–Social Science Standards Covered in Chapter 17

The standards covered in the chapter are listed below. Use the accompanying activity as you teach the chapter to ensure student mastery of these standards. This activity can be used in combination with the program's print and technology assessment materials.

Standard	Section 1	2	3	4	5
US8.12 Students analyze the transformation of the American economy and the changing social and political conditions in the United States in response to the Industrial Revolution.	✔	✔	✔	✔	✔
US8.12.5 Examine the location and effects of urbanization, renewed immigration, and industrialization (e.g., the effects on social fabric of cities, wealth and economic opportunity, the conservation movement).		✔		✔	
US8.12.6 Discuss child labor, working conditions, and laissez-faire policies toward big business and examine the labor movement, including its leaders (e.g., Samuel Gompers), its demand for collective bargaining, and its strikes and protests over labor conditions.				✔	
US8.12.7 Identify the new sources of large-scale immigration and the contributions of immigrants to the building of cities and the economy; explain the ways in which new social and economic patterns encouraged assimilation of newcomers into the mainstream amidst growing cultural diversity; and discuss the new wave of nativism.	✔		✔		✔

Cumulative Standards-Assessment Activity

The Cumulative Standards-Assessment Activity will help students organize and learn the important information from the chapter. Begin teaching the chapter with this activity, and have students complete it as they read the chapter.

Creating a Chart for Questioning

Purpose When they make generalizations, students study many particular details and then make broader statements about them that reveal links between them. This valuable skill allows students to think creatively about what they read and develop their own ideas about the material. Well-supported generalizations demonstrate mastery of the content and can be used as an important step in prewriting.

Creating a Chart for Making Generalizations

1. Begin the discussion by showing how to make valid generalizations. Ask students to identify some of the effects of the industrial growth. After writing their ideas on the board, ask volunteers to connect these effects into a general statement. Students might conclude that industrialization helped contribute to growing urbanization. Ask: Do enough details support the idea to make it seem reasonable? If not, what generalization would be better?
2. Point out to students that facts and details are the building blocks of generalizations. Ask students to copy this chart into their notebooks:

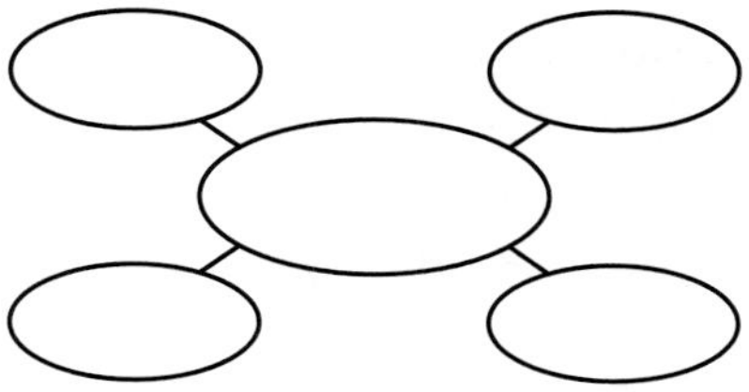

As students read each section, have them use different charts to categorize the facts they read. Then have them write valid generalizations that link those facts together.

3. As part of your review of the chapter, ask volunteers to state their generalizations for each section. Discuss as a class whether those generalizations are valid and, if not, which would be better. Remind students that they can use their charts as study aids.

Chapter 17 Resources

READING SUPPORT

- Content Vocabulary Activity 17
- Academic Vocabulary Activity 17
- Reading Skills Activity 17
- American Literature Reading 17
- Biography Activities 17A–17C
- Chapter 17 Active Reading Note-Taking Guide
- Chapter 17 Guided Reading Activities
- Chapter 17 Reading Essentials and Study Guide
- Glencoe Literature Library
- Glencoe Video Program
- Vocabulary PuzzleMaker CD-ROM
- Interactive Graphic Organizers CD-ROM
- American History Primary Source Document Library CD-ROM

CRITICAL THINKING

- Critical Thinking Skills Activity 17
- Primary Source Reading 17
- Cause-and-Effect Transparency 17, Strategy, and Activity
- Presentation Plus CD-ROM

UNIVERSAL ACCESS

- Universal Access Activity 17
- Then and Now Transparencies 17A–17B, Strategy, and Activity
- Graphic Novel Activity 17
- School-to-Home Connection Activities 17A–17D
- English Learner Handbook Chapter 17 Activities
- Universal Access Activities for the American History Classroom
- Moments in Time
- American Art and Architecture Transparencies, Strategies, and Activities
- American Art Prints
- American Music Cultural Traditions
- American Music Hits Through History
- StudentWorks Plus CD-ROM

SKILL PRACTICE

- Map Overlay Transparency 17, Strategy, and Activity
- Analysis Skills Activity 17
- Time Line Activity 17
- Geography and History Activity 17
- Economics and History Activity 17
- Chart, Graph, and Map Skills Activity 17
- Political Cartoon Activity 17
- Supreme Court Case Study 17
- In-Text Map Transparency 17, Strategy, and Activity
- Step Into American History Activity 17
- Citizenship and Service Learning Activity 17
- Outline Map Resource Book
- MindJogger Plus Videoquiz

WRITING SUPPORT

- Writing Activity 17
- Language Arts Activity 17
- Writer's Guidebook
- Middle School Writing Process Transparencies

ASSESSMENT

GLENCOE'S ASSESSMENT ADVANTAGE

- Chapter 17 Section Quizzes
- Chapter 17 Tests, Forms A and B
- California Standards Assessment, Forms A and B
- Cumulative Assessment Activity US8.12
- California Standards Practice Workbook
- Succeeding on the California History–Social Science Standards CD-ROM
- Exam*View*® Pro Testmaker CD-ROM
- Interactive Tutor Self-Assessment CD-ROM

CD-ROM
DVD
Print Material
Poster
Transparency
Music Program
Videocassette
Glencoe Literature Library

Chapter 17 Resources

TECHNOLOGY

- StudentWorks Plus CD-ROM
- TeacherWorks Plus CD-ROM
- Exam*View*® Pro Testmaker CD-ROM
- Interactive Tutor Self-Assessment CD-ROM
- Presentation Plus! CD-ROM
- Succeeding on the California History–Social Science Standards CD-ROM
- Vocabulary PuzzleMaker CD-ROM
- Interactive Graphic Organizers CD-ROM
- Interactive Time Line CD-ROM
- American History Primary Source Document Library CD-ROM
- MindJogger Plus Videoquiz
- American Music Cultural Traditions
- American Music Hits Through History
- Glencoe Video Program
- Professional Development in Middle School Social Studies Series
- Teaching American History With *Discovering Our Past: The American Journey to World War I*

SPANISH RESOURCES

- Spanish Activities and Assessment
  - Spanish Guided Reading Activities
  - Spanish Content Vocabulary Activities
  - Spanish Quizzes and Tests
  - Spanish California Standards Assessment
- Spanish Reading Essentials and Study Guide
- Spanish School-to-Home Connection
- Spanish Declaration of Independence and U.S. Constitution

TRANSPARENCIES

- California Standards Practice Transparencies
- Daily Focus Skills Transparencies
- Section Graphic Organizer Transparencies
- In-Text Map Transparencies
- Map Overlay Transparencies
- Cause-and-Effect Transparencies
- Then and Now Transparencies
- American Art and Architecture Transparencies
- Middle School Writing Process Transparencies

TEACHER PLANNING

- Daily Lesson and Discussion Notes
- English Learner Handbook
- Guide to Daily Intervention
- *Discovering Our Past: The American Journey to World War I* Reading and Study Skills Foldables
- Reading Strategies and Activities for the Social Studies Classroom
- Chapter 17 Reproducible Lesson Plans (correlated to California History–Social Studies Standards)
- Universal Access for the American History Classroom
- NGS U.S. Desk Map
- NGS U.S. Atlas

PROFESSIONAL DEVELOPMENT

- Building Academic Vocabulary
- Strategies for Success
- Research-Based Strategies Used to Develop *Discovering Our Past: The American Journey to World War I*
- Character Education in the Middle School Classroom
- The Living Constitution
- Professional Development in Middle School Social Studies Video Series
- Teaching American History With *Discovering Our Past: The American Journey to World War I*

MASTERING THE STANDARDS

The content and assessment in the Student Edition, Teacher Wraparound Edition, teacher planning materials, and the print and technology products are all standards-based. The use of these products during instruction leads to mastery of the standards.

PRACTICE
- California Standards Practice Workbook
- California Standards Practice Transparencies
- Interactive Time Line CD-ROM
- School-to-Home Connection

BENCHMARK ASSESSMENT
- California Standards Assessment
- Exam*View*® Pro Testmaker CD-ROM
- Succeeding on the California History–Social Science Standards CD-ROM

REMEDIATION
- California Guide to Daily Intervention
- Interactive Tutor Self-Assessment CD-ROM
- Exam*View*® Pro Testmaker CD-ROM
- California Standards Practice Workbook
- Reading Essentials and Study Guide

Additional Resources

NATIONAL GEOGRAPHIC TEACHER'S CORNER

Index to National Geographic Magazine:

The following articles relate to this chapter:

- "New York's Chinatown," by Joel L. Swerdlow, August 1998.
- "Chicago: Welcome to the Neighborhood," by Richard Conniff, May 1991.
- "New Life for Ellis Island," by Alice J. Hall, September 1990.

National Geographic Society Products

To order the following, call National Geographic at 1-800-368-2728

- *GeoKit: Immigration* (Kit)
- *GeoKit: 20th Century: 1910–1945* (Kit)
- *Eyewitness to the 20th Century* (Book)
- *Immigration: The Triumph of Hope* (Video)

NGS ONLINE

Access National Geographic's new dynamic MapMachine Web site and other geography resources at:

www.nationalgeographic.com

www.nationalgeographic.com/maps

A&E HOME VIDEO · Biography · THE HISTORY CHANNEL

The following videotape programs are available from Glencoe as supplements to Chapter 17.

- **Ellis Island (3 Pack) (ISBN 0-7670-005-6)**
- **The Panama Canal (ISBN 1-56501-468-5)**
- **The U.S. in Latin America: Yankee Go Home (ISBN 0-7670-0816-2)**

To order, call Glencoe at 1-800-334-7344. To find classroom resources to accompany many of these videos, check the following home pages:

A&E Television: www.aetv.com
The History Channel: www.historychannel.com

MOMENTS IN TIME DBQ

The following resource can help you teach the content of this chapter.

Unit 5 The Progressive Era (1890–1919)

History Online

Use our Web site for additional resources. All essential content is covered in the Student Edition.

You and your students can visit ca.hss.glencoe.com, the Web site companion to *Discovering Our Past: The American Journey to World War I*. This innovative integration of electronic and print media offers your students a wealth of opportunities. The student text directs students to the Web site for the following options:

- Chapter Overviews
- Self-Check Quizzes
- Study Central™
- Student Web Activities
- Textbook Updates
- Multi-Language Glossaries

Answers to the student Web activities are provided for you in the Web Activity Lesson Plans. Additional Web resources and ePuzzles and games are also available.

FOLDABLES™ Study Organizer

Dinah Zike's Foldables

Foldables are three-dimensional, interactive graphic organizers that help students practice basic writing skills, review key vocabulary terms, and identify main ideas. Every chapter contains a foldable activity, with additional chapter activities found in the Reading and Study Skills Foldables booklet.

Chapter 17 Resources

Reading List Generator CD-ROM — GLENCOE BOOKLINK

The Glencoe BookLink CD-ROM is a database that allows you to search more than 15,000 titles to create a customized reading list for your students.

- Reading lists can be organized by students' reading level, author, genre, theme, or area of interest.
- The database provides Degrees of Reading Power™ (DRP) and Lexile™ readability scores for all selections.
- A brief summary of each selection is included.

Reading level suggestions for this chapter:

For students at a Grade 6 reading level:
- ***Kaiulani: The People's Princess,*** by Ellen Emerson White

For students at a Grade 7 reading level:
- ***Immigrants,*** by Martin W. Sandler

For students at a Grade 8 reading level:
- ***The Path Between the Seas: The Creation of the Panama Canal,*** by David McCullough

For students at a Grade 9 reading level:
- ***The Souls of Black Folk,*** by W.E.B. Du Bois

Reading Support From JAMESTOWN EDUCATION

- *Timed Readings Plus in Social Studies* helps students increase their reading rate and fluency while maintaining comprehension. The 400-word passages are similar to those found on state and national assessments.
- *Reading in the Content Area: Social Studies* concentrates on six essential reading skills that help students better comprehend what they read. The book includes 754 high-interest nonfiction passages written at increasing levels of difficulty.
- *Reading Fluency* helps students read smoothly, accurately, and expressively.
- *Jamestown's Reading Improvement,* by renowned reading expert Edward Fry, focuses on helping build your students' comprehension, vocabulary, and skimming and scanning skills.
- *Critical Reading Series* provides high-interest books, each written at three reading levels.

To order these products, call Glencoe at 1-800-334-7344.

KEY for Using the Teacher Wraparound Edition

Use this key to help you identify the different types of prompts found in the Teacher Wraparound Edition.

R **Reading Strategies** activities help you teach reading skills and vocabulary.

C **Critical Thinking** strategies help students apply and extend what they have learned.

U **Universal Access** activities provide differentiated instruction for students learning to speak English, along with suggestions for teaching various types of learners.

S **Skill Practice** strategies help students practice historical analysis and geography skills.

W **Writing Support** activities provide writing opportunities to help students comprehend the text.

Teaching strategies and activities have been coded for ability level appropriateness.

AL Activities for students working above grade level
OL Activities for students working on grade level
BL Activities for students working below grade level
EL Activities for English Learners

FOCUS

History–Social Science Standards

In this chapter, the following standard will be covered:

US8.12 Students analyze the transformation of the American economy and the changing social and political conditions in the United States in response to the Industrial Revolution.

More About the Photo

This scene is of a set of Victorian houses in San Francisco called "postcard row" for their attractive look. The homes are among the nearly 50,000 houses built in the late 1800s.

TEACH

The Big Ideas

As you begin teaching each section, use these questions and activities to focus on the Big Ideas.

Section 1

The New Immigrants

Ask students to think about periods in U.S. history when people worried about how immigrants might affect American society. **Essential Question:** How do you think Americans reacted to the arrival of large numbers of immigrants in the late 1800s? *(Some people would feel threatened by many new people with a different culture needing jobs; others might be glad to have more workers for the new industries.)* OL

Chapter 17

America Enters a New Century

▼ The growth of American cities continued throughout the twentieth century.

NATIONAL GEOGRAPHIC **Who & When?**

1880 — 1895 — 1910

1882 Chinese Exclusion Act passed

1884 First sky-scraper constructed in Chicago

1892 Ellis Island admits immigrants

1909 The NAACP is formed

W.E.B. Du Bois

Section 2

Moving to the City

Essential Question: How did the influx of immigrants affect cities in the late 1800s? *(rapid population increase)* What problems do you think the rapid increase in population created in cities? *(Students may suggest shortages in housing, transportation, food and other needed supplies, and health services.)* OL

Section 3

A Changing Culture

Essential Question: How did immigrants influence existing culture in America? *(they brought new ideas, music, books, and art)* Where do you think immigrant children and adults learned how to be a part of American society? *(schools and workplaces)* OL

The Big Ideas

History Online
Chapter Overview Visit ca.hss.glencoe.com for a preview of Chapter 17.

Section 1
The New Immigrants
Immigration influences a nation's or region's economy and society. In the late 1800s and early 1900s, the pattern of immigration was changing.

Section 2
Moving to the City
Immigration influences a nation's or region's economy and society. Cities in the United States expanded rapidly in the late 1800s.

Section 3
A Changing Culture
As a society matures, a distinctive culture can develop. A unique American culture was developing that affected many parts of American life.

Section 4
The Progressive Movement
Reactions to social injustice can lead to reform movements. Many men and women became part of a widespread movement to bring about reform.

Section 5
A Changing Nation
Political ideas and major events shape how people form governments. In the new century, the United States began to expand outwardly while still facing problems at home.

View the Chapter 17 video in the Glencoe Video Program.

FOLDABLES™ Study Organizer

Analyzing Make this foldable to help you analyze information about the United States's people and policies as the country entered a new century.

Step 1 Fold a sheet of paper in half from side to side, leaving a $\frac{1}{2}$-inch tab along the side.

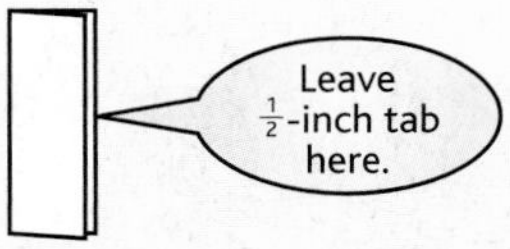

Step 2 Turn the paper and fold into fourths.

Step 3 Unfold and cut up along the three fold lines.

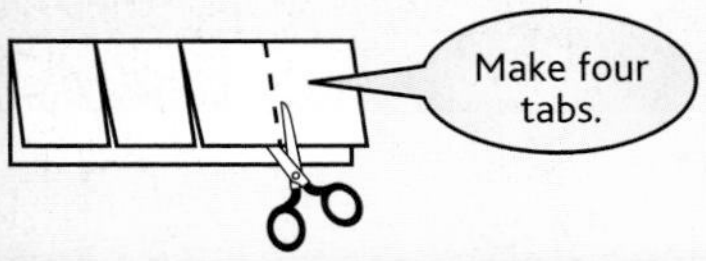

Step 4 Label your foldable as shown.

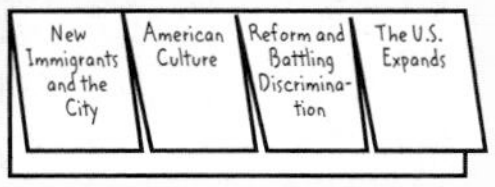

Reading and Writing As you read the chapter, write information about each topic under the appropriate tab.

INTRODUCING CHAPTER 17

Section 4
The Progressive Movement
Essential Question: What are some goals of reformers today? *(protecting the environment, ensuring equal opportunities for minorities, monitoring business practices, election reform)* Explain that some of the important reform movements of today—such as the environmental movement—began about 100 years ago. **OL**

Section 5
A Changing Nation
Essential Question: What does it mean to be a world power? *(Students might say the ability to control other countries or to influence their politics and economy or to do business in many parts of the world.)* Tell students that they will read about how the United States first became a world power. **OL**

Cultural Perspectives
During the late 1800s and early 1900s, most European immigrants entered America through Ellis Island, while Asian immigrants most often entered America at San Francisco Bay's Angel Island. An estimated 175,000 Chinese, along with Filipinos, Indians, Japanese, Koreans, and Russians, passed through here between 1910 and 1940. Poetry written by these immigrants on the walls of the detention center was discovered during restoration in the late 1990s. Bring in or ask students to find examples of this poetry. What perspective on immigration do they provide?

History Online
Go to ca.hss.glencoe.com for student activities, lesson plans, and links to additional Web resources about life in the late 1800s and early 1900s.

FOLDABLES™ Study Organizer — Dinah Zike's Foldables
Purpose Have students use their foldables to take notes about people and policies in the late 1800s and early 1900s. Then have students use their notes to write a five-question quiz and exchange their quizzes with a partner. **OL**

Why It's Important

Visual Literacy People today—particularly young people—are bombarded by visual media. Still images in magazine articles and advertising can portray a subject as more or less attractive, thus influencing the viewer's attitude towards it. Moving pictures on television, films, the Internet, and other media can change so quickly that they manipulate emotions without giving the viewer time to think. Students need to learn to analyze visual media as critically as they would written works to make good decisions for themselves.

1 Learn It!

Have students examine the photograph on page 741. **Ask:** What impression of immigration to the United States does it give? How? *(The large crowd of people on deck implies that large numbers must have been coming.)* What does the photograph imply about conditions aboard ship? How? *(Conditions must have been crowded given how tightly packed people are on deck.)* OL

Chapter 17

Get Ready to Read

Visual Literacy

READING SKILL

1 Learn It!

As you read and evaluate text, you are evaluating images as well. Painters and photographers use their craft to intentionally communicate ideas to the observer, in much the same way as authors use text.

Carefully study the image below. Then try to answer the following questions. What can you learn about the subject and the photographer?

- Why is this image here? What is it telling me?
- Is the image communicating facts or opinions?
- How does the image compare with what I already know?

Students at Tuskegee Institute ▶

Reading Tip

When taking notes, be sure to include references to images. These will help you understand and remember important points in the text.

READING STRATEGY **INFERRING**

Explain that visual literacy is often a matter of inferring meaning. People who interpret visual information must use clues to understand the purposes of the person who created the visual. Ask students to bring in an advertisement they have cut out of a newspaper or magazine. Have students answer the three questions on page 739 about the image in the ad. Tell them to explain why the image was used in connection with the product being advertised. Then have students show their ads to the class and explain their analyses to the class. OL CA 8LS1.9

2 Practice It!

Political cartoons are another kind of image you will see. Political cartoons often appear on the editorial page of the newspaper. These cartoons express opinions on political issues. Political cartoons are good sources of historical information because they reflect opinions on current events.

Review this political cartoon. Its topic is immigration. Write three questions you could ask about this visual information. Then answer your questions with a short paragraph describing what you see. Check your conclusions as you read through the chapter.

Read to Write

Select two Internet news sites, one American and one from another country. Identify an image from each and describe the assumptions that went into placing the image on the Web site. Write an essay describing what you saw and interpreted.

3 Apply It!

Review the images on page 736. Why were these images selected for the chapter opener? What do you think the author is trying to communicate with them?

CHAPTER 17 Get Ready to Read

2 Practice It!

Have students look at the photograph on page 754. Discuss the impression that it conveys. *(great height; danger)* Ask a volunteer to read aloud the headings on the page. Talk about how the photograph illustrates those ideas. OL

3 Apply It!

Have students read the chapter title, the section titles, and the Big Ideas. Then tell them to look closely at the chapter opener images on pages 736–737. Discuss how the images fit the chapter content and what ideas they communicate. OL

READING STRATEGY ANALYZING INFORMATION

Ask students to choose an image from an earlier chapter in the textbook that strongly communicates an idea. Have them write a short essay explaining the first impression the image makes on the viewer and the idea it communicates. Remind them to discuss how specific details from the image communicate the idea. Tell them to explain whether the idea is a fact or an opinion. OL

Use Reading Skills Activity 17 in the **Chapter 17 Resource Book** for more practice with visual literacy.

FOCUS

BELLRINGER
SKILLBUILDER ACTIVITY

Project **Daily Focus Skills Transparency 17–1** and have students answer the question.

Guide to Reading

Preteaching Vocabulary: Have students find the meaning of each content vocabulary word and then use each word in a sentence.

Answers to Graphic: Economic problems; Ethnic discrimination and persecution; Image of America as a land of opportunity

Unpacking the Standards

After reading the section, students will be able to:

- Identify who emigrated to the United States in the late 1800s and early 1900s.
- Explain why immigrants came to the United States.
- Describe how immigrants adjusted to life in America.
- Explain how native-born Americans reacted to the new immigrants.

Section 1: The New Immigrants

Guide to Reading

History Social Science Standards

US8.12 Students analyze the transformation of the American economy and the changing social and political conditions in the United States in response to the Industrial Revolution.

Looking Back, Looking Ahead

You read about the tremendous growth in industry in the United States in the late 1800s. Large numbers of immigrants came to America in search of jobs.

Focusing on the Main Ideas

- The immigrants who arrived in America in the late 1800s came from many different countries. *(page 741)*
- After a difficult journey to America, many immigrants faced harsh working conditions. *(page 742)*
- Many native-born Americans resented the immigrants and pushed for laws to control their numbers. *(page 746)*

Locating Places

New York City
Ellis Island
Angel Island

Meeting People

Emma Lazarus
Grace Abbott
Julia Clifford Lathrop

Content Vocabulary

emigrate (EH • muh • GRAYT)
ethnic group
steerage (STIHR • ihj)
sweatshop
assimilate (uh • SIH • muh • LAYT)
nativist (NAY • tuh • vihst)

Academic Vocabulary

register (REH • juh • stuhr)
process
aspect (AS • PEHKT)

Reading Strategy

Analyzing Information As you study Section 1, re-create the diagram below and write the reasons immigrants came to America.

NATIONAL GEOGRAPHIC Where & When?

1880 · 1900 · 1920

- **1882** Chinese Exclusion Act is passed
- **1886** Statue of Liberty is erected
- **1892** Ellis Island starts processing immigrants
- **1917** Immigration Act of 1917 requires literacy

SECTION RESOURCES

Print Material
- Reproducible Lesson Plan 17–1*
- Daily Lesson and Discussion Notes 17–1
- Guided Reading Activity 17–1
- Reading Essentials and Study Guide 17–1
- Active Reading Note-Taking Guide 17–1
- Section Quiz 17–1

Transparencies
- Daily Focus Skills Transparency 17–1
- Section Graphic Organizer Transparency 17–1
- California Standards Practice Transparencies

Technology
- Interactive Tutor Self-Assessment CD-ROM
- ExamView® Pro Testmaker CD-ROM
- Presentation Plus! CD-ROM

*Available on TeacherWorks™

US8.12.7 Identify the new sources of large-scale immigration and the contributions of immigrants to the building of cities and the economy; explain the ways in which new social and economic patterns encouraged assimilation of newcomers into the mainstream amidst growing cultural diversity; and discuss the new wave of nativism.

A Flood of Immigrants

Main Idea **The immigrants who arrived in America in the late 1800s came from many different countries.**

Reading Connection Have you known anyone who has moved away because a parent or family member found a better job in another part of the country? Read to find out why immigrants to America in the late 1800s left Europe.

An American Story

In the 1870s, two young brothers left Italy for America.

R

> **"We were so long on the water that we began to think we should never get to America. . . . We were all landed on an island and the bosses there said that Francisco and I must go back because we had not enough money, but a man named Bartolo came up and told them that . . . he was our uncle and would take care of us. . . . We came to Brooklyn to a wooden house on Adams Street that was full of Italians from Naples. Bartolo had a room on the third floor and there were fifteen men in the room, all boarding with Bartolo. . . . It was very hot in the room, but we were soon asleep, for we were very tired."**
>
> —from "Biography of a Bootblack"

Who Were the "New" Immigrants? Before 1865 most immigrants to the United States—except for the enslaved—came from northern and western Europe. The greater part of these "old" immigrants were Protestant, spoke English, and blended easily into American society. After the Civil War, even greater numbers of immigrants made the journey to the United States. The tide of newcomers reached a peak in 1907 when nearly 1.3 million people came to America.

C

Picturing **History**

Immigrants arrive in New York Harbor from Hamburg, Germany, in 1906. ***Where did most immigrants to America come from after 1880?***

TEACH

R Reading Strategy

Scaffolding—Inferring

Ask: How much did the brothers know about America before coming? How prepared were they for life in the United States? *(They seem to have known little about America, not even how long the journey would be. They were not prepared to find a job or a place to live, and went off with a complete stranger)* OL CA HR4.

This READING SKILL was introduced in Chapter 12.

C Critical Thinking

Determining Cause and Effect **Ask:** Why were the "old" immigrants able to blend easily into American society? *(Most already spoke English and were Protestants like most Americans, so they did not have to make as many adjustments. Those who came from the British Isles probably had other cultural similarities, such as customs and diet.)* OL CA HI2.

Picturing **History**

Steamship companies made a fabulous profit from transporting immigrants. The cost of a steerage ticket was just $30, but many ships could carry well over 1,500 people in steerage. Conditions below deck were so bad that during the early years 10 percent of the passengers died during the crossing. Hundreds of people would be crammed into low-ceilinged rooms filled with bunks separated by aisles. They sat on benches or stood by shelves along the sides to eat. Toilet and washing facilities were inadequate, and ventilation was extremely poor.

Answer: eastern and southern Europe, Mexico, China, and Japan

Review The Big Idea

Review the Big Idea for this section: "Immigration influences a nation's or region's economy and society." **Ask**: How did the new immigrants differ from native-born Americans? *(Many were Catholic or Jewish; few spoke English.)* How did these differences affect the cities where they went to live? *(cities became more diverse.)* OL

R1 Reading Strategy

Activating Prior Knowledge Remind students that they learned this word once before, when they studied the Oregon Trail. **Ask:** What word is it based on? *(migrate)* OL

R2 Reading Strategy

Understanding Vocabulary Review the meaning of the terms *ethnic groups* and *steerage*. Then tell students to define the terms in their own words. OL

Reading Check

Answer: immigrants from eastern and southern Europe, Mexico, and Asia

Answers and Additional Support

US8.12.7 Identify the new sources of large-scale immigration and the contributions of immigrants to the building of cities and the economy; explain the ways in which new social and economic patterns encouraged assimilation of newcomers into the mainstream amidst growing cultural diversity; and discuss the new wave of nativism.

In the mid-1880s, the pattern of immigration started to change. Large groups of "new" immigrants arrived from eastern and southern Europe. Greeks, Russians, Hungarians, Italians, Turks, and Poles were among the newcomers. At the same time, the number of "old" immigrants started to decrease. By 1907 only about 20 percent of the immigrants came from northern and western Europe, while 80 percent came from southern and eastern Europe.

Many of the newcomers from eastern and southern Europe were Catholics or Jews. Few spoke English. Because of this, they did not blend into American society as easily as the "old" immigrants had. Many newcomers felt like outsiders, and they clustered together in urban neighborhoods made up of people of the same nationality.

Reasons for Emigrating Why did so many people leave their homelands for the United States in the late 1800s and early 1900s? They were "pushed" away by difficult conditions at home and "pulled" to the United States by new opportunities.

R1 Many people **emigrated** (EH • muh • GRAY • tuhd), or left their homelands, because of economic troubles. In Italy and Hungary, overcrowding and poverty made jobs scarce. Farmers in Croatia and Serbia could not own enough land to support their families. New machines such as looms put many craft workers out of work.

Persecution also drove people from their homelands. In some countries, the government passed laws or followed policies against certain R2 **ethnic groups**—minorities that spoke different languages or followed different customs from those of most people in a country. Members of these ethnic groups often emigrated to escape discrimination or unfair laws. Many Jews fled persecution in Russia in the 1880s and came to the United States.

Immigrants saw the United States as a land of jobs, plentiful and affordable land, and opportunities for a better life. Although some immigrants returned to their homelands, ultimately, most decided to stay.

The Journey to America

Main Idea **After a difficult journey to America, many immigrants faced harsh working conditions.**

Reading Connection What would it be like to move to a place across an ocean, thousands of miles from home, where most people did not speak your language? Read to find out how immigrants to America in the late 1800s adjusted to their new lives.

Immigrants often had a difficult journey to America. Many had to first travel to a seaport to board a ship. Often they traveled for hundreds of miles to get to the port cities.

Then came the long ocean voyage to America—12 days across the Atlantic or several weeks across the Pacific. Immigrants usually could afford only the cheapest tickets, and they traveled in **steerage** (STIHR • ihj)—cramped, noisy quarters on the lower decks. One writer noted, "Crowds everywhere, ill smelling bunks, uninviting washrooms—this is steerage."

The Statue of Liberty Most European immigrants landed at **New York City.** After 1886 the magnificent sight of the Statue of Liberty, standing 300 feet above the ground, greeted the immigrants as they sailed into New York Harbor. The statue, a gift from France, seemed to promise hope for a better life in the new country. On the base of the statue, the stirring words of **Emma Lazarus**, an American poet, welcomed immigrants from Europe:

> **"Give me your tired, your poor, Your huddled masses yearning to breathe free, The wretched refuse of your teeming shore. Send these, the homeless, tempest-tossed to me, I lift my lamp beside the golden door!"**
>
> —from "The New Colossus"

Reading Check **Describe** Who were the "new" immigrants?

More Skill Practice

Historical and Social Sciences Analysis Skill Tell students to interview a person who immigrated to the United States or someone who remembers a friend or family member who did so. Suggest that students ask about reasons for emigrating; reasons for choosing the United States; a description of the journey; feelings upon entering the United States; and problems or cultural differences experienced. As a class, discuss the similarities and differences in the experiences of the people interviewed and compare them to those of the immigrants described in Section 1. OL CA HI3.

An American Story

Sailing from Ireland, a 15-year-old girl, Annie Moore, arrived in America on January 1, 1892. Accompanying her were her two brothers. Their parents had come to America two years earlier, leaving Annie and her brothers under the care of their aunt. The parents had finally made enough money to bring the children to America.

When Annie stepped off the gangplank, to her surprise, city and state leaders and immigration officials greeted her. Annie was the first of about 12 million people to enter the United States through Ellis Island, the new immigration processing center. Today, a statue of Annie Moore stands in the Ellis Island Museum in New York.

Entering America Before the new arrivals could actually pass through the "golden door" to America, they had to **register** at government reception centers. In the East, immigrants were U1 **processed** at Castle Garden, a former fort on Manhattan Island, and after 1892 at **Ellis Island** in New York Harbor. Most Asian immigrants arrived in America on the West Coast and went through the processing center on **Angel Island** in San Francisco Bay. Examiners at the centers U2 recorded the immigrants' names—sometimes shortening or simplifying a name they found too difficult to write. The examiners asked the immigrants where they came from, their occupation, and whether they had relatives in the United States. The examiners also gave health examinations. Immigrants with contagious illnesses could be refused permission to enter the United States. C

Where Did Immigrants Find Work? After passing through the reception centers, most immigrants entered the United States. Where would they go? How would they live? Some had relatives or friends to stay with and to help them find jobs. Others knew no one and would have to strike out on their own.

An immigrant's greatest challenge was finding work. Sometimes organizations in his or her homeland recruited workers for jobs in the United States. The organization supplied American employers with unskilled workers who unloaded cargo or dug ditches.

Some of America's fastest-growing industries hired immigrant workers. In the steel mills of Pittsburgh, for example, most of the common laborers in the early 1900s were immigrant men. They might work 12 hours a day, seven days a week.

Picturing **History**

Immigrant children learned the English language and American customs in neighborhood schools. ***How did language highlight the differences between generations of immigrants?***

U1 Universal Access

Advanced Learners Have students use the Internet to conduct research on the number of immigrants who came to the United States between 1880 and 1920. Tell students to create a double line graph tracking the numbers of people who entered at Ellis Island and Angel Island. **AL**

U2 Universal Access

Intrapersonal Ask students to write a diary or journal entry reflecting how the immigrants might have felt when going through the processing at Ellis Island or Angel Island. **OL** CA 8WA2.1

C Critical Thinking

Making Inferences Ask: Why might immigrants with contagious diseases not be allowed to enter the United States? *(out of concern that they will spread the disease and create a health problem)* Explain to students that there were no vaccines for diseases like the measles, polio, or the flu at the time. **OL**

Resources for page 743

Academic Vocabulary Activity 17

Did You Know?

Ellis Island was abandoned in 1954 and fell into total disrepair. Efforts to restore it began in the early 1970s. The Main Building, which includes the Registry Room where immigrants waited to be processed, was restored. Walls where immigrants inscribed their names or messages have been carefully protected for visitors to read.

Picturing **History**

Answer: Immigrants who learned English as children could speak it fluently and adapt to American customs more easily. Adult immigrants who were more accustomed to the traditions of their native land and learned English while working probably had more difficulty adapting.

R1 Reading Strategy

Using Context Clues **Ask:** Why were the workshops called *sweatshops?* *(People worked hard for long hours, so they probably sweated a lot.)* OL

C Critical Thinking

Analyzing Primary Sources Have students read the quotation. **Ask:** What details from the quotation show how workers were taken advantage of? *(Workers were not paid for overtime, and they were given only a piece of apple pie to keep them going.)* OL CA HR3.

R2 Reading Strategy

Understanding Vocabulary Explain that the term *assimilate* and *similar* share the same Latin root, which means "like." **Ask:** How does this explain the meaning of the term? *(It means taking on a culture like that of other people.)* OL

Answers and Additional Support

R1 Many immigrants, including women and children, worked in **sweatshops** in the garment industry. These were dark, crowded workshops where workers made clothing. The work was repetitious and hazardous, the pay low, and the hours long.

Pauline Newman, who later became an official in the International Ladies' Garment Workers Union, worked in a New York sweatshop as a child. She recalled:

C **"During most of the year we youngsters worked overtime until 9 p.m. every night except Fridays and Saturdays. No, we did not get additional pay for overtime. At this point it is worth recording the [generosity] of the Triangle Waist Co. by giving us a piece of apple pie for supper instead of additional pay!"**

—Pauline Newman, Letter to Michael and Hugh Owens

How Did Immigrants Adjust? Once they had moved to the United States, immigrants had to adjust to life in a new land. In their new homes, immigrants tried to preserve some **aspects** of their own cultures. At the same time, most wanted to **assimilate** (uh • SIH • muh • LAYT), or become part of the American culture. These two desires sometimes came into conflict. R2

History Makers

Immigration Stations

The first stop for millions of immigrants was Ellis Island. About 12 million people passed through the Ellis Island immigration center between 1892 and 1954. The main building was reopened in 1990 as the Ellis Island Museum of Immigration. Located a short distance north of the Statue of Liberty in New York Harbor, Ellis Island stands as a memorial to the traditions of freedom and opportunity in America.

Hundreds of thousands of immigrants from Japan and China arrived on the West Coast during the late 1800s and early 1900s. In 1910 an immigration station was opened on Angel Island near San Francisco, California, to accommodate Asian immigrants.

▼ Immigrants arriving at Ellis Island

Immigrants at Angel Island ▶

History Makers

Angel Island is the largest island in San Francisco Bay. Between 1910 and 1940, hundreds of thousands of immigrants were processed there, including people from India, Japan, Korea, Mexico, the Philippines, Portugal, and Russia. Many immigrants carved poems into the walls of the barracks, expressing their fears and hopes during the long days of uncertainty while they awaited entry. Today, Angel Island is a state park, and the immigration station is a museum. Several buildings are still standing. A barracks museum has exhibits as well as a reproduction of the living areas and of an interrogation room.

Picturing **History**

In the cities, immigrants lived in neighborhoods that were often separated into ethnic groups. ***How did immigrants try to adjust to their lives in the United States?***

R Many immigrant parents continued to speak their native languages. Their children spoke English at school and with friends, but they also spoke their native language at home. On the other hand, the grandchildren of many immigrants spoke only English.

The role of immigrant women also changed in the United States, where women generally had more freedom than women in European and Asian countries. New lifestyles conflicted with traditional ways and sometimes caused family friction.

Where Did Immigrants Settle? Most of the new immigrants were from rural areas. Because they lacked the money to buy farmland in America, however, they often settled in industrial cities. With little or no education, they usually worked as unskilled laborers.

History Online

Student Web Activity Visit ca.hss.glencoe.com and click on *Chapter 17—Student Web Activities* for an activity on immigration.

Relatives who had already immigrated to the United States helped new arrivals get settled, and people of the same ethnic group naturally tended to form communities. As a result neighborhoods of Jewish, Italian, Polish, Chinese, and other groups quickly developed in New York, Chicago, San Francisco, and other large cities. The immigrants sought to re-create some of the life they had left behind. The communities they established revolved around a number of traditional institutions. Most important were the houses of worship—the churches and synagogues—where worship was conducted and holidays were celebrated as they had been in their homelands. Priests and rabbis often acted as community leaders. C

The immigrants published newspapers in their native languages, opened stores and theaters, and organized social clubs. Ethnic communities and institutions helped the immigrants preserve their cultural heritage.

Reading Check **Identify** What is assimilation?

R Reading Strategy

Scaffolding—Identifying the Main Idea and Supporting Details **Ask:** How did living in a new country change the immigrants' family life? *(The language spoken at home changed to English with the younger generations; women had more freedom in America; many traditions could not be kept up.)* **OL** **CA HI3.**

This READING SKILL was introduced in Chapter 2.

C Critical Thinking

Making Generalizations **Ask:** Why would immigrants try to re-create traditional institutions in their new land? *(Students may suggest they did so to have some familiar and comfortable things in their lives; to preserve their cultural heritage.)* Discuss how cultural heritage is a source of pride and helps give a person a sense of identity. **OL** **CA HR3.**

History Online

Objectives and answers to the student activity can be found in the Web Activity Lesson Plan feature at ca.hss.glencoe.com.

Reading Check

Answer: adjusting to and becoming part of a new culture

Resources for page 745

Geography and History Activity 17

Picturing **History**

Today many Americans enjoy eating at ethnic restaurants and taking part in the traditional holiday celebrations of different cultures.

Answer: by trying to assimilate as well as maintaining some culture traditions

C1 Critical Thinking

Comparing and Contrasting Ask: During what earlier periods in U. S. history had people feared immigrants? *(during the Adams presidency, leading to the Alien and Sedition Acts; in the middle 1800s, leading to the Know-Nothing Party)* OL CA HI1.

R Reading Strategy

Using Context Clues Ask: Whom did the *nativist* movement try to protect? *(native-born Americans)* OL

C2 Critical Thinking

Analyzing Information Ask: What group was treated most harshly by the laws? *(the Chinese)* How did the Japanese avoid similar treatment? *(by agreeing to limit immigration)* OL

Answers and Additional Support

US8.12.7 Identify the new sources of large-scale immigration and the contributions of immigrants to the building of cities and the economy; explain the ways in which new social and economic patterns encouraged assimilation of newcomers into the mainstream amidst growing cultural diversity; and discuss the new wave of nativism.

Nativist Movement

C1 **Main Idea** **Many native-born Americans resented the immigrants and pushed for laws to control their numbers.**

Reading Connection Have you ever been forced to share something you wanted to keep to yourself? How did that make you feel? Read to find out how some Americans felt about all the new immigrants who were pouring into the United States.

Assimilation was also slowed by the attitudes of many native-born Americans. Although employers were happy to hire immigrant workers at low wages, some American-born workers resented the immigrants. These Americans feared that the immigrants would take away their jobs or drive down everyone's wages by accepting lower pay.

Ethnic, religious, and racial differences contributed to tensions between Americans and the new immigrants. Some Americans argued that the new immigrants—with their foreign languages, unfamiliar religions, and distinctive customs—did not fit into American society.

People found it easy to blame immigrants for increasing crime, unemployment, and other problems. **Nativists** (NAY•tuh•vihsts) had opposed immigration earlier in the 1800s. Nativism gained strength in the late 1800s. Calls for restrictions on immigration mounted. R

What Laws Limited Immigration? Lawmakers responded quickly to the tide of anti-immigrant feeling. In 1882 Congress passed the first law to limit immigration—the Chinese Exclusion Act. This law prohibited Chinese workers from entering the United States for 10 years. Congress extended the law in 1892 and again in 1902. C2

In 1907 the federal government and Japan came to a "gentleman's agreement." The Japanese agreed to limit the number of immigrants to the United States, and the Americans pledged fair treatment for Japanese Americans who were already in the United States.

Analyzing *Political Cartoons*

In this cartoon, the female figure Columbia, representing the United States, turns away unwanted immigrants, such as criminals and those with radical political beliefs. ***Why did some American-born workers resent the immigrants?***

746

More Skill Practice

Visual Literacy Tell students to examine the cartoon. **Ask:** What details convey why the immigrants are viewed as undesirable? *(the ugly figures with an ape-like gait; the scroll; the knives; the way the figures come out of underground holes)* OL CA 8LS1.9

Analyzing *Political Cartoons*

Answer: American workers were afraid immigrants would take away their jobs and drive down their wages.

Other legislation affected immigrants from all nations. An 1882 law made each immigrant pay a tax and also barred criminals from entering the country. In 1897 Congress passed a bill requiring immigrants to be able to read and write in some language. Although President Cleveland vetoed the bill as unfair, Congress later passed the Immigration Act of 1917, which included a similar literacy requirement.

Support for Immigrants Despite some anti-immigrant sentiment, many Americans—including **Grace Abbott** and **Julia Clifford Lathrop,** who helped found the Immigrants' Protective League—spoke out in support of immigration. These Americans recognized that the United States was a nation of immigrants and that the newcomers made lasting contributions to their new society.

Immigrants' Contributions The new immigrants supplied the country's growing industries with the workers that were necessary for economic growth. At the same time, the new immigrants and their children—like the old immigrants before them—helped shape American life. They gave the nation its major religious groups—Protestants, Catholics, and Jews. As they became part of the society around them, they enriched that society with the customs, cultures, language, and literature of their homelands. U

The effects of immigration were most visible in the cities, with their fast-growing ethnic neighborhoods. The flow of immigrants was one of the factors that transformed America's cities in the late 1800s and the early 1900s.

Reading Check **Explain** What was the nativist movement?

History Online
Study Central Need help understanding the immigrant experience? Visit ca.hss.glencoe.com and click on Study Central.

Section 1 Review

Reading Summary

Review the Main Ideas

- In the late 1800s, many of the immigrants who arrived in America came from southern and eastern Europe, rather than western and northern Europe.
- Many new immigrants to America settled in ethnic neighborhoods and found work in low-paying and sometimes dangerous workshops known as sweatshops.
- Americans who were members of the nativist movement called for laws to limit immigration.

What Did You Learn?

1. What was the difference between "old" and "new" immigration?
2. Which two cities were the points of entry into America for most immigrants?

Critical Thinking

3. **Analyze** Re-create the diagram below. List reasons people left their home countries (pushed) and came to the United States (pulled). CA H12.

Pushed to Emigrate	Pulled to Immigrate

4. **Conclude** Why do you think some Americans blamed the "new" immigrants for many of society's problems? CA HR5.
5. **The Big Ideas** What were some of the cultural differences that immigrants had to adjust to in the United States? Explain the concept of assimilation and its effect on families and American culture. CA HI3.
6. **Reading** **Visual Literacy** Select one of the photographs that appear in Section 1 and write a paragraph in which you describe the scene, as well as why the author included the image with the text. Include a title for the paragraph. CA 8LS1.9

SECTION 1 REVIEW ANSWERS

Review questions reinforce content standard US12.7.

1. Old—from northern, western Europe; spoke English; Protestant; New—from southern and eastern Europe, Asia, and Mexico; did not speak English; had other religions
2. New York and San Francisco
3. Push: economic problems, discrimination, persecution; Pull: saw the U.S. as a land of plenty, including jobs
4. Immigrants were willing to work for little money and had different cultures.
5. **The Big Ideas** Answers should reflect text information.
6. **Reading** Answers should address the questions in Get Ready to Read.

U Universal Access

Special Education To help students remember the points on this page, review the Big Idea "Immigration leads to the economic development of an area with varying consequences." Then help them list the major contributions immigrants made to American society. *(helped develop the economy; gave country different religions; enriched American culture)* Encourage students to give examples of each. OL

ASSESS

Resources for page 747

Use these resources to assess student mastery of section content.

Section Quiz 17–1

Interactive Tutor Self-Assessment CD-ROM

Reading Check

Answer: a movement by native-born Americans to keep immigrants out of the United States

History Online

Study Central provides summaries, interactive games, and online graphic organizers to help students review section content.

CLOSE

Questioning **Ask:** Why is the United States called "a nation of immigrants"? *(Most Americans either came or are descended from people who came from another country.)* OL

FOCUS

Remind students of the conditions American workers were working under. Discuss why labor unions were formed.

TEACH

R1 Reading Strategy

Scaffolding—Recognizing Bias **Ask:** What attitude does the writer of the Real Estate Circular express towards Chinese immigrants? *(looks down on them)* What words and phrases convey this attitude? *("suffering," "slaves," and "make them live decently")* OL

This READING SKILL was introduced in Chapter 5.

R2 Reading Strategy

Activating Prior Knowledge **Ask:** Why would labor unions support the Chinese Exclusion Act? How might immigrant workers pose a threat to American workers? *(The Act would limit the number of immigrant workers, making more jobs available to American workers; Employers could replace American workers with cheaper immigrant labor or force Americans to accept lower wages.)* BL

Answers and Additional Support

You Decide . . .

US8.12.7 Identify the new sources of large-scale immigration and the contributions of immigrants to the building of cities and the economy; explain the ways in which new social and economic patterns encouraged assimilation of newcomers into the mainstream amidst growing cultural diversity; and discuss the new wave of nativism.

Should Immigration Be Limited?

Immigrants struggled to find their place in American society. They changed American society with customs from their cultures. Many Americans resisted these changes and warned against further immigration. Read to find out how Americans viewed new immigrants.

Yes

The Chinese come for a season only; and, while they give their labor, they do not [spend the money they earn] in the country. They do not come to settle or make homes. . . . To compare the Chinese with even the lowest white laborers is, therefore, absurd. R1

Our best interests are suffering of these Asiatic slaves; we are trying to make them live decently while here, and to discourage their arrival in such numbers as to drive white laborers out of the country. . . .

—San Francisco Real Estate Circular, September 1874

The Chinese Exclusion Act of 1882 reflected the widespread hostility against immigrant workers. The law halted immigration of Chinese workers and gained wide support from American labor unions. R2

Preamble. Whereas, in the opinion of the Government of the United States the coming of Chinese laborers to this country endangers the good order of certain localities within the territory thereof: Therefore,

Be it enacted by the Senate and House of Representatives of the United States of America in Congress assembled, That . . . until the expiration of 10 years next after the passage of this act, the coming of Chinese laborers to the United States be, and the same is hereby, suspended; and during such suspension it shall not be lawful for any Chinese laborer to come, or, . . . to remain within the United States.

—1882 Chinese Exclusion Act
47th Congress, 1st Session, 1882

◀ Immigrants from China

748

Extending the Content

Chinese Citizens The children of Chinese-Americans who had been born in the United States could not be excluded because they were American citizens. Some Chinese men purchased false documents that identified them as the children of U.S. citizens. These "paper sons" had to learn everything they could about the family and homes of the people with whom they claimed to be related to pass exams given by immigration officers at Angel Island.

No

Author, traveler, and artist Constance Gordon-Cumming wrote about discrimination against Chinese immigrants.

[It is unbelievable that legislation against Chinese immigrants could have arisen] among a people whose national existence is based on the Declaration of Independence, and the assumption of liberty and equality of all men, without distinction of race or colour....

That [laws] so utterly un-American could have been suffered to pass, appears so extraordinary. . . .

—from *California As I Saw It, 1849–1900*

R

Attorney Louis Marshall was a consistent champion of the rights of immigrants to the United States.

U

In common with all other immigrants, those who have come from the countries sought to be tabooed [forbidden] have been industrious, and law-abiding and have made valuable contributions to our industrial, commercial and social development. . . .

C

To say that they are not assimilable argues ignorance. The facts show that they adopt American standards of living and that they are permeated [filled] with the spirit of our institutions. It is said that they speak foreign languages, but in those foreign languages they are taught to love our Government. . . .

—Attorney Louis Marshall Speaks Out Against Limiting Immigration, 1924

▲ Louis Marshall

You Be The Historian

DBQ Document-Based Questions

1. What did the writer from San Francisco fear? CA HR5.
2. What did Louis Marshall claim about the immigrants' contributions? CA HR3.
3. What facts does Marshall use to support his view that the newcomers are "assimilable"? CA HR2.

You Decide . . .

R Reading Strategy

Scaffolding—Predicting After reading the excerpts in favor of restricting immigration, and before reading Louis Marshall's piece, ask students to predict the points Marshall is likely to argue against. Tell students to base their predictions not only on what they read on page 748, but also on what they learned in Section 1. OL

This READING SKILL was introduced in Chapter 16.

C Critical Thinking

Comparing and Contrasting Ask: How does Marshall's opinion of immigrants compare with the opinion expressed in paragraph 2 of the Real Estate Circular? *(Marshall says that immigrants are already decent, hard-working people. They do not have to be made to "live decently.")* OL CA HR5.

U Universal Access

English Learners Pair English learners with students that have strong English skills. Have the strong English speaker read the first paragraph aloud to model pronunciation. Then have the English learner read the paragraph aloud. Together students should write a one sentence summary of the paragraph. Then have students do the same with the second paragraph. EL

ASSESS/CLOSE

Have students answer the You Be The Historian questions. Then discuss the questions that every new wave of immigration raises for a society. OL

You Be The Historian

1. The Chinese workers would force American laborers to seek work in other countries.
2. Immigrants have contributed to the industrial, commercial, and social development of the United States.
3. They adopt American standards of living and the spirit of American institutions and are taught to love American government.

FOCUS

BELLRINGER
SKILLBUILDER ACTIVITY

Project **Daily Focus Skills Transparency 17–2** and have students answer the question.

Guide to Reading

Preteaching Vocabulary: Have students look up the meaning of each content vocabulary term in the Glossary and then write the definition.

Answers to Graphic: Overcrowded tenements; Sanitation problems; Threat of fire; Disease; Crime

Unpacking the Standards
After reading the section, students will be able to:

- Describe how the United States became urbanized.
- Explain the differences between the way the rich and the poor lived.
- Identify the problems faced by cities and the attempts to solve them.

Section 2 Moving to the City

History Social Science Standards

US8.12 Students analyze the transformation of the American economy and the changing social and political conditions in the United States in response to the Industrial Revolution.

Guide to Reading

Looking Back, Looking Ahead
You learned that millions of new immigrants arrived in the United States in the late 1800s and early 1900s. All of these new people led to tremendous growth and change in America's cities.

Focusing on the Main Ideas
- As Americans crowded into cities, strong contrasts emerged between the lives of the rich and the poor. *(page 751)*
- America's rapidly growing cities faced many problems. *(page 753)*
- As cities grew, Americans created new styles of buildings and improved forms of transportation. *(page 754)*

Locating Places
Central Park

Meeting People
Jane Addams
Elisha Otis
William LeBaron Jenney
Louis Sullivan
Frederick Law Olmsted (OHM•stehd)

Content Vocabulary
tenement (TEH•nuh•muhnt)
slum
suburb
Gilded Age (GIHL•duhd)
settlement house (SEH•tuhl•muhnt)

Academic Vocabulary
accommodate (uh•KAH•muh•DAYT)
professional (pruh•FEH•shuh•nuhl)

Reading Strategy
Analyzing Information As you study Section 2, re-create the diagram below and list three serious problems facing American cities in the late 1800s.

Urban problems

NATIONAL GEOGRAPHIC Where & When?

- **1870**
- **1873** *The Gilded Age* is published
- **1880**
- **1883** The Brooklyn Bridge opens
- **1884** First skyscraper constructed in Chicago
- **1889** Jane Addams founds Hull House
- **1890**

SECTION RESOURCES

Print Material
- Reproducible Lesson Plan 17–2*
- Daily Lesson and Discussion Notes 17–2
- Guided Reading Activity 17–2
- Reading Essentials and Study Guide 17–2
- Active Reading Note-Taking Guide 17–2
- Section Quiz 17–2

Transparencies
- Daily Focus Skills Transparency 17–2
- Section Graphic Organizer Transparency 17–2
- California Standards Practice Transparencies

Technology
- Interactive Tutor Self-Assessment CD-ROM
- Exam*View*® Pro Testmaker CD-ROM
- Presentation Plus! CD-ROM

*Available on TeacherWorks™

US8.12.5 Examine the location and effects of urbanization, renewed immigration, and industrialization (e.g., the effects on social fabrics of cities, wealth and economic opportunity, the conservation movement).

Growth of Cities

U **Main Idea** **As Americans crowded into cities, strong contrasts emerged between the lives of the rich and the poor.**

Reading Connection Do you live in a city, in a suburb, or in a rural area? Read to find out the changes that all three places underwent in the late 1800s and early 1900s.

An American Story

A train pulling into Chicago in 1884 carried a young passenger named Hamlin Garland. For Garland, who had grown up on a farm, the big city was a bewildering sight. Garland later became famous for his stories about the Midwest. In one novel, he described his feeling of dismay when he first saw Chicago. "The mere thought of a million people stunned my imagination." Garland wondered, "How can so many people find a living in one place?"

Why Did Urban Areas Grow? American cities grew rapidly after the Civil War. In 1870 one American in four lived in cities with 2,500 or more people. By 1910 nearly half of the American population were city dwellers. The United States was changing from a rural to an urban nation.

Immigrants played an enormous part in the growth of cities. In major urban centers such as New York, Detroit, and Chicago, immigrants and their children made up 80 percent or more of the population by 1900. Native-born Americans also contributed to urban growth. Americans moved in huge numbers from farming areas to cities, looking for jobs.

C Industrialization had also changed work on farms. New machinery produced crops, using fewer farmworkers. In addition, women in rural areas no longer had to make clothing and household goods. These items, made by machine, could now be bought in stores or from catalogs. Freed from such chores, many women left farms to look for jobs in the cities.

African Americans also migrated to cities in large numbers. Most African Americans lived in the rural South. Many began moving to Southern cities in search of jobs and to escape debt, injustice, or discrimination. After 1914 a large number of African Americans moved to Northern cities, which offered more jobs in industry and manufacturing than Southern cities did. Many African Americans also hoped to find less discrimination and violence in the North.

Transportation and Resources America's expanding railroad network fed the growth of the cities. R Railroads helped people move to the cities, and they transported the raw materials for industry. Trains carried cattle to Chicago and Kansas City, making these cities great meatpacking centers.

Some cities flourished because of nearby resources. Pittsburgh developed rapidly as a center for iron and steel manufacturing because both iron ore and coal—to fuel the industry's huge furnaces—were found in the area.

Urban and Rural Population Growth, 1860–1900

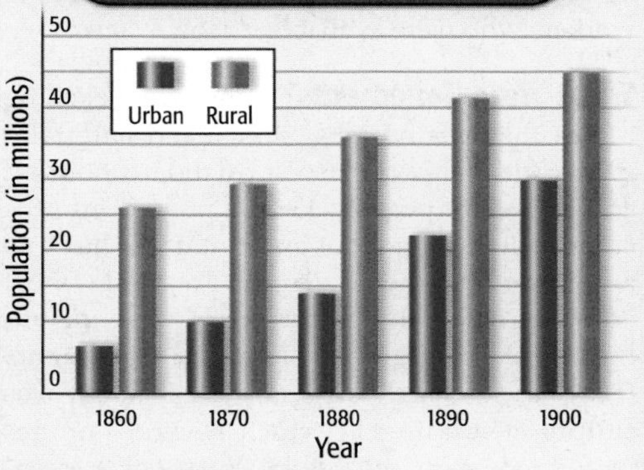

Source: *Historical Statistics of the United States.*

Understanding Graphs

The gap between the urban and rural populations narrowed in the late 1800s.

Compare About how many more people lived in urban areas in 1900 than in 1860?

TEACH

U Universal Access

Visual/Spatial Organize students into groups of five to create a video or slide show about city life in the late 1800s, using images from the textbook, Internet, and library. Ask groups to choose one of the following topics: transportation, housing, social problems, social services, and architecture. Have each group share its work with the class. OL CA 8LS1.9

Review The Big Idea

Review the Big Idea for this section: "Immigration influences a nation's or region's economy and society." Discuss how immigrants were most of the cheap labor force that helped industry grow but also ended up in inadequate housing. OL

C Critical Thinking

Determining Cause and Effect **Ask:** Why did people move from farms to cities? *(Farm jobs were replaced by machinery; items once made by women at home were now purchased.)* Why did African Americans move to cities? *(to find good jobs and to escape debt, injustice, and discrimination)* OL CA HI1. CA HI2.

R Reading Strategy

Identifying the Main Idea and Supporting Details After reading this subsection, **ask:** What factors helped cities to grow? *(transportation, natural resources, a large pool of workers)* Tell students to give examples of each. OL

More Skill Practice

Historical and Social Sciences Analysis Skill Have students brainstorm features that make rural and urban areas different from each other. To get them started, have students contrast different types of technology, but explore other differences as well. OL CA HI2.

Understanding Graphs

Answer: about 24 million more

Ask: In which year was the difference between rural and urban population the greatest? *(1880)*

R1 Reading Strategy

Academic Vocabulary
Ask students to use the word *accommodate* in a sentence. OL

C Critical Thinking

Comparing and Contrasting **Ask:** How did middle class, suburban houses compare with tenements? *(suburban houses were built for single families, not many; they had both hot and cold water, not just a shared, cold tap; indoor plumbing; and electricity)* OL

R2 Reading Strategy

Identifying the Main Idea and Supporting Details
Ask: Who lived the "gilded life" during the Gilded Age? *(the very rich)* In what way were their lives "gilded"? *(They lived in extreme luxury and spent huge amounts of money on their own pleasure.)* OL CA HR3.

Reading Check

Answer: Tenements were located in run-down neighborhoods. Few had running hot water or bathtubs, and most were overcrowded and dirty.

Answers and Additional Support

Picturing **History**

In 1900 New York City's East Side was crowded with new immigrants. ***What were some other major urban centers in 1900?***

Seaports such as New York and San Francisco developed as American trade with the rest of the world increased. In addition, the immigrant population of these cities provided a large pool of workers who were available for low wages.

What Were Tenements? Cities were exciting places that offered jobs, stores, and entertainment. But there was also substandard housing and desperate poverty. People poured into the cities faster than housing could be built to **accommodate** them. In the biggest, most crowded cities, the poorest residents—including most immigrants—lived in **tenements** (TEH • nuh • muhnts). Originally a tenement was simply a building in which several families rented rooms. By the late 1800s, however, a tenement had come to mean an apartment building in the **slums**—poor, run-down urban neighborhoods.

Tenements had many small, dark rooms. Three, four, or more people lived in each room. Usually several families had to share a cold-water tap and a toilet. Few tenement houses had hot water or bathtubs. A government inspector wrote of the "filthy and rotten tenements" of the Chicago slums in 1896, where children filled "every nook, eating and sleeping in every windowsill, pouring in and out of every door."

How Did the Middle Class Live? The cities also had a growing middle class. The middle class included the families of **professional** people such as doctors, lawyers, and ministers. Some managers and salaried office clerks also became part of the middle class.

The middle class enjoyed a comfortable life. Many families moved from cities to the **suburbs,** residential areas that sprang up outside of city centers as a result of improvements in transportation. There they lived in houses with hot water, indoor toilets, and—by 1900—electricity. Middle-class families might have one or two servants and the leisure time to enjoy music, art, and literature.

What Was the Gilded Age? At the top of the economic and social ladder stood the very rich. The wealthy lived very different lives from most Americans. They built enormous mansions in the cities and huge estates in the country. Some homes, such as those of J.P. Morgan and Henry Clay Frick in New York City, are now museums.

In these mansions, the rich lived lives of extreme luxury, throwing enormous parties and dinners. One party at a New York mansion had more than 1,000 guests and was estimated to have cost $75,000 for food and entertainment, which is equal to about $1.3 million today.

Mark Twain and Charles Dudley Warner published a novel in 1873 called *The Gilded Age.* The name—which refers to something covered with a thin layer of gold—became associated with America in the late 1800s. The **Gilded Age** (GIHL • duhd) suggested both the extravagant wealth of the time and the terrible poverty that lay underneath.

Reading Check **Describe** Why was tenement living difficult?

More Skill Practice

Connecting Have students use all four terms on this page—*tenements, slums, suburbs, Gilded Age*—in just two sentences. OL

Picturing **History**

Answer: Chicago, Detroit, Kansas City, Pittsburg, San Francisco

US8.12.5 Examine the location and effects of urbanization, renewed immigration, and industrialization (e.g., the effects on social fabrics of cities, wealth and economic opportunity, the conservation movement).

Cities in Crisis

Main Idea **America's rapidly growing cities faced many problems.**

Reading Connection What sort of problems do cities face today? Read to find out about the problems that arose as America's cities grew.

The rapid growth of the cities produced serious problems. The terrible overcrowding in tenement districts created sanitation and health problems. Garbage and horse manure accumulated in city streets, and the sewers could not handle the flow of human waste. Filth created a breeding ground for diseases, which spread rapidly through the crowded districts.

Fires were an ever-present threat. About 18,000 buildings were destroyed and 100,000 Chicagoans lost their homes in the Chicago fire of 1871. Two years later, Boston experienced a devastating fire.

Health and Crime Problems In a poor Chicago neighborhood in 1900, babies often died of whooping cough, diphtheria, or measles before their first birthday. A section of New York was called the "lung block" because so many residents had tuberculosis.

In an effort to control disease, New York City began to screen schoolchildren for contagious diseases and to provide visiting nurses to mothers with young children. The city also established public health clinics for those who could not pay for medical care.

The poverty in the cities often led to increased crime. Orphaned and homeless children sometimes resorted to picking pockets and other minor crimes to survive. Gangs roaming the poor neighborhoods committed more serious crimes. Writer Jacob Riis reported:

> **"The gang is the ripe fruit of tenement-house growth. It was born there."**
>
> —Jacob Riis, *How the Other Half Lives*

Seeking Solutions The problems of the cities did not go unnoticed. Many dedicated people worked to improve urban life and help the poor. Religious groups aided the poor. Some religious orders helped the poor in orphanages, prisons, and hospitals. Organizations such as the YMCA (Young Men's Christian Association) and YWCA (Young Women's Christian Association) offered recreation centers where city youngsters could meet and play.

The poor also received assistance from establishments called **settlement houses** (SEH•tuhl•muhnt). The settlement house movement had spread to the United States from Britain. Located in poor neighborhoods, settlement houses provided medical care, playgrounds, nurseries, and libraries as well as classes in English, music, and arts and crafts. Settlement workers—mostly women—also tried to get better police protection, garbage removal, and public parks for poor districts.

One of the most famous settlement houses was Chicago's Hull House, founded by **Jane Addams** in 1889. Addams paid all the expenses from her own income, until the activities at Hull House grew beyond her means. She then turned to the public to raise funds. Addams explained the purpose of Hull House:

> **"We were ready to perform the humblest neighborhood services. We were asked to wash the new-born babies, and to prepare the dead for burial, to nurse the sick, and to 'mind the children.'"**
>
> —Jane Addams, *Twenty Years at Hull House*

Reading Check **Explain** What purpose did settlement houses serve?

C Critical Thinking

Determining Cause and Effect Ask: How did urban poverty lead to crime? *(Children and youths committed crimes to get money to live on.)* OL CA HI2.

U Universal Access

Below Grade Level Organize students into small groups to create a three-column table illustrating social problems, solutions, and alternatives. Ask groups to identify in the first column the social problems described in this section. In the second column, students should describe the solutions that were used. Students should explain alternative solutions in the third column. BL CA HI1.

R Reading Strategy

Understanding Vocabulary Point out to students that the term *settlement house* is explained through examples. Tell them that this is a technique they can use in their own writing. **Ask:** What services did settlement houses provide? *(medical care, playgrounds, child care, libraries, and lessons in English, music, and arts and crafts; they also pushed for public services and helped families)* OL

Reading Check

Answer: They provided medical care, playgrounds, nurseries, libraries, and classes in various subjects.

More Skill Practice

Historical and Social Sciences Analysis Skill Have students draw a cause-and-effect chain of the problems that followed from the initial problem of overcrowding. *(overcrowding led to excessive garbage, which led to disease, which led to high infant mortality)* OL CA HI2.

Did You Know?

In the 1870s, some people thought that typing was too strenuous and complicated for women. As a result, most secretaries were men. To help working-class women, the Young Women's Christian Association (YWCA) offered shorthand and typing classes for women because stenography was a well-paying job.

W Writing Support

Narrative Writing Have students write a letter in the voice of an immigrant describing what living in a city is like to relatives on a farm in his or her native country. AL CA 8WA2.1

R Reading Strategy

Setting a Purpose **Ask:** What will you learn about in the subsection "The Changing City"? *(how cities grew and changed to accommodate growth by building skyscrapers, new types of transportation, and parks)* OL CA HI3.

C Critical Thinking

Making Inferences **Ask:** Why were iron supports necessary for building skyscrapers? *(A very tall building needs very strong supports to stay up.)* To reinforce the idea tell students to imagine a child building a tower with blocks and how the tower becomes shaky after it reaches a certain height. OL

Resources for page 754

American Art and Architecture Transparencies 22 and 24

US8.12.5 Examine the location and effects of urbanization, renewed immigration, and industrialization (e.g., the effects on social fabrics of cities, wealth and economic opportunity, the conservation movement).

The Changing City

Main Idea **As cities grew, Americans created new styles of buildings and improved forms of transportation.**

Reading Connection Have you ever admired the towering skyscrapers in a large city and wondered when the first tall buildings were made? Read to find out about the first skyscrapers and other advances that occurred in American cities.

Urban growth led to important new developments. In the late 1800s, cities saw the introduction of a new type of building, new kinds of public transportation, and public parks.

Building Up—Not Out Because of the limited space in cities, imaginative architects began building upward rather than outward. In the 1860s architects started to use iron frames to strengthen the walls of buildings. Iron supports—together with the safety elevator that **Elisha Otis** invented in 1852—made taller buildings possible.

In 1884 **William LeBaron Jenney** constructed a 10-story office building in Chicago. Supported by an iron-and-steel frame, it was the world's first skyscraper. Architect **Louis Sullivan** gave style to the skyscraper. "It must be every inch a proud and soaring thing, rising in sheer exultation," he said. Sullivan and his colleagues changed the face of America's cities.

Picturing History

The Woolworth Building was designed and built to be the tallest building in the world. ***Where was the first skyscraper built, and how tall was it?***

Answers and Additional Support

Picturing History

The Woolworth empire began in 1879 when Frank Winfield Woolworth opened his first successful 5-cent store in Lancaster, Pennsylvania. By 1911, Woolworth owned hundreds of stores. In 1913, President Woodrow Wilson pressed a button to turn on 5,000 lights in New York's new Woolworth Building. Taking three years to build, the "Cathedral of Commerce" was the tallest building in the world until 1930, when the Chrysler Building, 1,048 feet (319 m) high, became the tallest. Just one year later, the Empire State Building, at 1,250 feet (381 m), left the other two behind.

Answer: in Chicago; 10 stories high

Picturing **History**

Pedestrians stroll across a walkway on the Brooklyn Bridge in New York City. ***How did the new bridges in New York City and St. Louis improve transportation?***

Soon architects were designing even taller structures. New York's Woolworth Building, completed in 1913, soared an incredible 55 stories—792 feet (241 m) high. People called the building the Cathedral of Commerce.

R1 **What New Designs Appeared in Cities?** Some people looked to reshape the urban landscape. A group known as the "City Beautiful" movement believed city dwellers should be able to enjoy the beauties of nature. **Frederick Law Olmsted** (OHM•stehd), a leader in this movement, designed New York's **Central Park** as well as several parks in Boston.

R2 In 1892 and 1893, Chicago hosted a World's Fair on fairgrounds designed by Olmsted. The World's Fair revealed that American architecture was dynamic and original. The best architects thoroughly understood European styles U and adapted them for modern use. The firm of McKim, Mead, and White used the Italian Renaissance style in its design for the Boston Public Library. Another architect, Henry Richardson, adapted styles from ancient Rome in his designs for churches, libraries, and even department stores.

New Forms of Transportation As cities grew, people needed new means of transportation. Author Mark Twain complained in 1867 that

> **"[New York] is too large. You cannot accomplish anything . . . without devoting a whole day to it. . . . The distances are too great."** R3
>
> **—Mark Twain, San Francisco** ***Alta California***

Streetcars, which horses pulled on tracks, provided public transportation at the time. Horses were slow, however, and left piles of manure. In 1873 San Francisco began construction of cable-car lines. A large underground cable powered by a motor at one end of the rail line moved passengers along.

R1 Reading Strategy

Scaffolding—Questioning
Ask: How did the "City Beautiful" movement enable city people to enjoy nature? *(by building parks)* BL

This READING SKILL was introduced in Chapter 9.

R2 Reading Strategy

Scaffolding—Academic Vocabulary The word *dynamic* was introduced in Chapter 15, Section 4. Ask students to list synonyms for the word. OL

U Universal Access

Advanced Learners Have students bring in pictures of buildings designed by McKim, Mead, and White and by Henry Richardson. Ask students to show the pictures to the class and explain how they resemble Renaissance and Roman styles. Have them refer to the architectural characteristics from earlier periods. AL

R3 Reading Strategy

Reading Primary Sources
Ask: According to Mark Twain, what transportation problems did large cities have? *(It took too long to get from one place to another.)* What was the reason? *(Cities were too large, and horse-drawn trolleys were slow.)* OL

Picturing **History**

The Brooklyn Bridge took fourteen years to build, and was the longest suspension bridge of its time. Techniques pioneered in its construction are still used in building such bridges.
Answer: They linked sections of cities.

R Reading Strategy

Determining Importance
Ask: How did bridges improve communications in cities? *(They connected separate sections and gave easy access to them.)* OL

ASSESS

Resources for page 756

Use these resources to assess student mastery of section content.

- Section Quiz 17–2
- Interactive Tutor Self-Assessment CD-ROM

Reading Check
Answer: cable cars, trolley cars, subways

History Online
Study Central provides summaries, interactive games, and online graphic organizers to help students review section content.

CLOSE

Determining Importance
Ask students to choose the technological development they think had the most impact on the growth of American cities and explain why it did. OL

In 1888 Richmond, Virginia, pioneered the use of the trolley car, a motorized train that was powered by electricity supplied through overhead cables. By the turn of the century, the trolley was everywhere. In 1897 Boston opened the nation's first subway, or underground railway. In 1904 New York City opened the first section of what was to become the largest subway system in the world.

Another improvement in transportation was street paving. During most of the 1800s, city streets remained poorly paved. Many streets were nothing more than sand and gravel. Other cities used wood blocks, brick, or cobblestone, all of which were bumpy, noisy, and hard to repair. The growing use of asphalt—a by-product of petroleum refining—beginning in the 1890s made city streets smoother and quieter.

Building Bridges R Bridge construction also improved urban transportation. Many American cities were divided or bounded by rivers. Using new construction technology, architects and engineers designed huge steel bridges to link sections of cities. The 520-foot (156-m) Eads Bridge across the Mississippi River in St. Louis opened in 1873. Ten years later New York's majestic Brooklyn Bridge, 1,600 feet (488 m) long, connected Manhattan and Brooklyn. Both bridges remain in use today.

The new forms of transportation not only helped people travel within the cities, but they also helped the cities grow. Middle-class suburbs developed along train or trolley lines stretching away from city centers. People who moved out of the city centers could easily travel downtown to work or shop.

The increase in immigration and the growth of the cities went hand in hand with other changes in American life. Education, culture, and recreation were changing too.

Reading Check **Summarize** What new forms of urban transportation were developed?

History Online
Study Central Need help understanding the growth of American cities? Visit ca.hss.glencoe.com and click on Study Central.

Section 2 Review

Reading Summary

Review the Main Ideas

- Both native-born Americans and immigrants flocked to the cities looking for jobs.
- Disease, fire, and crime were major problems faced by America's cities.
- Skyscrapers and parks, along with streetcars and paved roads, became part of America's cityscapes.

What Did You Learn?

1. Who founded Hull House?
2. Who invented the safety elevator?

Critical Thinking

3. **Summarizing Information** Re-create the diagram below and describe three efforts made to improve living conditions in the cities. CA HR3.

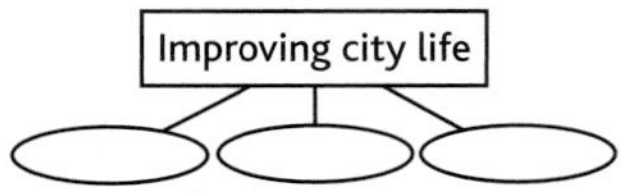

4. **Analyze** How did the efforts of religious groups help those living in poverty? CA HI2.
5. **Summarize** Describe the differences in everyday life for the poor, middle-class, and wealthy in America's cities. CA HI2.
6. **The Big Ideas** Describe the relationship between improvements in transportation and the growth of cities and suburbs. CA CS3.
7. **Analysis** **Linking Past to Present** Write an essay that describes efforts to enhance urban life during this period. How do those initiatives continue to affect city life today? CA HI3. CA 8WA2.3

SECTION 2 REVIEW ANSWERS

Review questions reinforce content standard US8.12.

1. Jane Addams
2. Elisha Otis
3. Settlement houses; Creation of parks; New styles of architecture; Improved transportation
4. by working in orphanages, prisons, and hospitals and building recreational centers
5. Answers will vary but should discuss varying living conditions.
6. The Big Ideas Answers will vary but should discuss the effects of trolley cars, subways, steel bridges, cable cars, and paved streets.
7. Reading Answers will vary but should discuss changes in social services, transportation, and urban design.

Section 3

A Changing Culture

Guide to Reading

Looking Back, Looking Ahead

You learned that America's population boomed and its cities grew rapidly in the late 1800s and early 1900s. Elements of American culture—including education, the arts, and leisure activities—also changed during this period.

Focusing on the Main Ideas

- The expanding education system provided opportunities for Americans and new immigrants. *(page 758)*
- Reading for learning and pleasure grew more popular as education and leisure time increased for Americans. *(page 761)*
- American art, music, and leisure time activities continued to develop their own distinct style. *(page 762)*

Meeting People

John Dewey
Booker T. Washington
George Washington Carver
Joseph Pulitzer (PU • luht • suhr)
William Randolph Hearst (HUHRST)
Thomas Edison

Locating Places

Tuskegee Institute

Content Vocabulary

land-grant college
yellow journalism
realism (REE • uh • LIH • zuhm)
regionalism (REE • juh • nuhl • IZUHM)
ragtime
vaudeville (VAHD • vihl)

Academic Vocabulary

benefit (BEH • nuh • FIHT)
isolate (EYE • suh • LAYT)
ethnic

Reading Strategy

Classifying Information As you study Section 3, re-create the diagram below and describe the achievements of the persons listed.

	Achievements
John Dewey	
George Washington Carver	
Mary Cassatt	
Scott Joplin	

History Social Science Standards

US8.12 Students analyze the transformation of the American economy and the changing social and political conditions in the United States in response to the Industrial Revolution.

NATIONAL GEOGRAPHIC Who & When?

1860 — 1875 — 1890

The Ohio State University

1862 Morrill Act provides funds for colleges

Carlisle student

1879 Carlisle Indian Industrial School is founded

1881 Tuskegee Institute opens

Booker T. Washington

FOCUS

Bellringer
Skillbuilder Activity

Project **Daily Focus Skills Transparency 17–3** and have students answer the question.

Guide to Reading

Preteaching Vocabulary: Use the Vocabulary PuzzleMaker CD ROM to create crossword and word search puzzles.

Answers to Graphic: Dewey: Emphasized relevancy in education; Carver: Transformed agriculture in the South; Cassatt: Important French Impressionist painter; Joplin: Well-known ragtime composer

Unpacking the Standards

After reading the section, students will be able to:

- Describe how the educational system changed.
- Explain how widespread literacy made newspapers and books more popular.
- Identify American artistic styles and some artists and musicians of the period.
- Explain how increased leisure time led to the growth of recreational activities.

SECTION RESOURCES

Print Material
- Reproducible Lesson Plan 17–3*
- Daily Lesson and Discussion Notes 17–3
- Guided Reading Activity 17–3
- Reading Essentials and Study Guide 17–3
- Active Reading Note-Taking Guide 17–3
- Section Quiz 17–3

Transparencies
- Daily Focus Skills Transparency 17–3
- Section Graphic Organizer Transparency 17–3
- California Standards Practice Transparencies

Technology
- Interactive Tutor Self-Assessment CD-ROM
- Exam*View*® Pro Testmaker CD-ROM
- Presentation Plus! CD-ROM

*Available on TeacherWorks™

TEACH

C1 Critical Thinking

Making Inferences Ask: Why did immigrants consider education a "treasure"? *(It would give them a chance for better jobs and easier lives.)* What impression did the father's taking the children to school make on Mary Antin? *(It emphasized how important education was.)* OL

C2 Critical Thinking

Identifying Central Issues Ask: Why is an educated population necessary for a nation to progress? *(Students may say that people need education so they can recognize and solve a nation's problems, develop and use new technologies, write and interpret laws, and establish and run businesses.)* OL

Answers and Additional Support

US8.12.7 Identify the new sources of large-scale immigration and the contributions of immigrants to the building of cities and the economy; explain the ways in which new social and economic patterns encouraged assimilation of newcomers into the mainstream amidst growing cultural diversity; and discuss the new wave of nativism.

Expanding Education

Main Idea **The expanding education system provided opportunities for Americans and new immigrants.**

Reading Connection Today, laws require that all children attend school. Did you know that it was not always that way? Read to find out about the changes that occurred in education in the late 1800s and early 1900s.

An American Story

Mary Antin, a young girl who came to the United States from Russia in 1894, never forgot her first day of school.

> **"Father himself conducted us to school. He would not have delegated that mission to the President of the United States. . . . [Education was] the essence of American opportunity, the treasure that no thief could touch, not even misfortune or poverty. . . . The doors stood open for every one of us."**
>
> —Mary Antin, *The Promised Land*

C1

How Did Enrollment Change? Most Americans in 1865 had attended school for an average of only four years. Government and business leaders and reformers believed that for the nation to progress, the people needed more schooling. Toward the end of the 1800s, the "treasure" of education became more widely available to Americans.

C2

By 1914 most states required children to have at least some schooling. More than 80 percent of all children between the ages of 5 and 17 were enrolled in elementary and secondary schools.

Public Schools The expansion of public education was particularly notable in high schools. The number of public high schools increased from 100 in 1860 to 6,000 in 1900, and to 12,000 in 1914. Despite this huge increase, however, many teenagers did not attend high school. Boys often went to work to help their families instead of attending school. The majority of high school students were girls.

The Way It Was

School Days

On the Bus
Students line up for a ride to school in Fresno, California. Few schools were lucky enough to have their own buses in the early 1900s. Not until 1939 were national standards for school buses adopted, including the color "school-bus yellow" to promote visibility and safety.

758

The Way It Was

In the early 1900s, children in rural areas attended school when they could be spared from doing farm work, between harvest and planting times. Today, school calendars in most of the United States are still built around the needs of an agrarian society, although some school districts now have year-round schooling. Have students discuss the advantages and disadvantages of having school year-round.

The **benefits** of a public school education were not shared equally by everyone. In the South, many African Americans received little or no education. In many parts of the country, African American children had no choice but to attend segregated elementary and secondary schools.

What Was Progressive Education? Around 1900 a new philosophy of education emerged in the United States. Supporters of this "progressive education" wanted to shape students' characters and teach them good citizenship as well as facts. They also believed children should learn through the use of hands-on activities. These ideas had the greatest effect in elementary schools.

John Dewey, the leading spokesperson for progressive education, criticized schools for overemphasizing memorization of information. Instead, Dewey argued, schools should relate learning to the interests, problems, and concerns of students.

Crossing Guard
A New York City police officer guides students on their way to school in 1899. By the early 1900s, the police provided this service in many communities.

Writing
By 1900, the Palmer method of penmanship was taught everywhere. In the Palmer method, some capital letters were no longer written separately, and entire words could be completed before the pen was lifted to cross a "t" or dot an "i." Writing sets included ink bottles like this one. Its double covers prevented evaporation and protected against leakage.

Bookmobile
Librarians attempted to provide reading material to rural communities. Here, a traveling library makes book deliveries in Washington County, Maryland.

Elementary Students
The classroom was the primary place where immigrant children learned American ways.

The Classroom
Students observe an experiment and take notes during science class in 1900.

R1 Reading Strategy

Identifying the Main Idea and Supporting Details
Ask: What groups did not get to take full advantage of public education? Why? *(Boys in particular often went to work and did not attend high school. African Americans did not always have schools available.)* BL

R2 Reading Strategy

Academic Vocabulary Tell students that the word *benefit* can be used as a noun and as a verb. Have students write a sentence using *benefit* as both parts of speech. OL

C Critical Thinking

Comparing and Contrasting Ask students to reread the subsection "What Was Progressive Education?" Then have them write an essay comparing and contrasting progressive education with the philosophy of education followed in their school today. Remind them to write their essays with a coherent thesis and a well-supported conclusion. AL CA 8WS1.1

U Universal Access

Special Education Help students identify which pointers connect each picture with its caption. Explore what additional information the image teaches about the topic discussed in the caption. OL CA 8LS1.9

More Skill Practice

Historical and Social Sciences Analysis Skill Ask: Does public education today continue to teach good citizenship? If so, how? *(teaching about the Constitution, the structure of government, civil rights, elections, and current events; encouraging students to stay informed and get involved in community concerns)* OL CA HI3.

R Reading Strategy

Understanding Vocabulary
Ask: What is a *grant?* *(a gift)* Talk about how *land-grant colleges* resulted from gifts of land. OL

C1 Critical Thinking

Determining Cause and Effect **Ask:** What impact did the establishment of new colleges in the 1800s have on women's lives? *(By the 1890s, almost 40 percent of college students were women, which allowed some to train for professions previously closed to them.)* OL CA HI2.

C2 Critical Thinking

Predicting Consequences
Ask: How would isolating Native American students from their culture affect them? *(Students may suggest it would encourage them to assimilate into American culture more quickly or make them feel homesick and out of place.)* OL CA HI1.

Reading Check
Answer: All were women's colleges.

Answers and Additional Support

How Did Higher Education Change?

Colleges and universities also changed and expanded. An 1862 law called the Morrill Act gave the states large amounts of federal land that could be sold to raise money for education. R The states used these funds to start dozens of schools called **land-grant colleges.** Wealthy individuals also established and supported colleges and universities. Some schools were named for the donors—for example, Cornell University for Ezra Cornell and Stanford University for Leland Stanford.

In 1865 only a handful of American colleges admitted women. The new land-grant schools admitted women students, as did new C1 women's colleges—Vassar, Smith, Wellesley, and Bryn Mawr—founded in the late 1800s. By 1890 women could attend a wide range of schools, and by 1910 almost 40 percent of all American college students were women.

Some new colleges, such as Hampton Institute in Virginia, provided higher education for African Americans and Native Americans. Howard University in Washington, D.C., founded shortly after the Civil War, had a largely African American student body. By the early 1870s, Howard offered degrees in theology, medicine, law, and agriculture. Prominent graduates of Howard include Thurgood Marshall, who later became a justice of the Supreme Court, writer Toni Morrison, and political scientist Ralph Bunche, the first African American to win the Nobel Peace Prize.

▲ Students in classroom at Tuskegee Institute

One Hampton Institute student, **Booker T. Washington,** became an educator. In 1881 Washington founded the **Tuskegee Institute** in Alabama to train teachers and to provide practical education for African Americans. As a result of his work, Washington became influential in business and politics.

In 1896 scientist **George Washington Carver** joined the Tuskegee faculty. His research transformed agricultural development in the South. From the peanut, which was formerly of little use, Carver developed hundreds of products, including plastics and synthetic rubber.

▲ These two photographs of a young Navajo, Tom Torlino, show how his appearance changed a short time after he entered the Carlisle Indian School.

Schools for Native Americans Reservation schools and boarding schools also opened to train Native Americans for jobs. The Carlisle Indian Industrial School in Pennsylvania was founded in 1879, and similar schools opened in the West. Although these schools provided C2 Native Americans with training for jobs in industry, they also **isolated** Native Americans from their tribal traditions. Sometimes, boarding schools were located hundreds of miles away from a student's family.

Reading Check **Compare** What did the colleges Bryn Mawr, Vassar, and Smith have in common?

Did You Know?

In 1974, Congress established the Tuskegee Institute National Historic Site, which includes the George Washington Carver Museum. The Tuskegee Institute became Tuskegee University in 1985. Its schools include agriculture and home economics; arts and sciences; education; engineering and architecture; and veterinary medicine.

US8.12.7 Identify the new sources of large-scale immigration and the contributions of immigrants to the building of cities and the economy; explain the ways in which new social and economic patterns encouraged assimilation of newcomers into the mainstream amidst growing cultural diversity; and discuss the new wave of nativism.

A Nation of Readers

Main Idea **Reading for learning and pleasure grew more popular as education and leisure time increased for Americans.**

Reading Connection Do you read a newspaper every day? Read to find out about the growth of daily newspapers in America's large cities.

As opportunities for education grew, a growing number of Americans became interested in reading. Public libraries opened across the nation, mainly through the efforts of Andrew Carnegie. In 1881 the wealthy steel industrialist had made an extraordinary announcement. He pledged to build a public library in any city that would agree to pay its operating costs. In the next 30 years, Carnegie donated more than $30 million to found more than 2,000 libraries throughout the world.

Spreading the News Technological advances in printing, paper making, and communications made it possible to publish daily papers for large numbers of readers. The growing cities provided readers for the newspapers.

In 1883 **Joseph Pulitzer** (PU • luht • suhr) purchased the New York *World* and created a new kind of newspaper. The paper grabbed attention with illustrations, cartoons, and sensational stories with huge, shocking headlines, such as "ANOTHER MURDERER TO HANG." The *World* soon built up its circulation to more than one million readers every day.

William Randolph Hearst's (HUHRST) New York *Morning Journal* became even more successful than the *World*, attracting readers by exaggerating the dramatic or gruesome aspects of stories. This style of sensational writing became known as **yellow journalism**—a name that came from the paper's popular comic strip, "The Yellow Kid."

Newspapers published by **ethnic** groups and people of color thrived as well. By 1900, six daily Jewish-language newspapers were printed in New York City. African Americans started more than 1,000 newspapers between 1865 and 1900.

More magazines took advantage of printing improvements and mass circulation techniques to reach a national market. Between 1865 and 1900, the number of magazines in the United States rose from about 700 to 5,000. Some magazines of that era, such as *Ladies' Home Journal*, are still published today.

How Did Literature Change? Many writers of the era explored new themes and subjects. Their approach to literature was called **realism** (REE • uh • LIH • zuhm) because it dealt with the lives of people. Related to realism was **regionalism** (REE • juh • nuhl • IZUHM), writing that focused on a particular region of the country.

Mark Twain was a realist and a regionalist. Many of his books, including *The Adventures of Huckleberry Finn* and *The Adventures of Tom Sawyer*, are set along the Mississippi River, where Twain grew up.

Stephen Crane wrote about city slums in *Maggie* and about the Civil War in *The Red Badge of Courage*. In books such as *The Call of the Wild* and *The Sea Wolf*, Jack London portrayed the lives of miners and hunters in the far Northwest. Edith Wharton described the joys and sorrows of upper-class Easterners in *The House of Mirth* and *The Age of Innocence*.

Paul Laurence Dunbar, the son of former slaves, wrote poetry and novels that used the dialects and folktales of Southern African Americans. Dunbar was one of the first African American writers to gain fame worldwide.

Inexpensive paperback books appeared for the first time in the late 1800s. Many paperbacks featured lively adventure tales or stories of athletic boys and girls.

Horatio Alger wrote a successful series of young adult books with such titles as *Work and Win* and *Luck and Pluck*. Based on the idea that hard work and honesty brought success, Alger's books sold millions of copies.

Reading Check **Explain** What is regionalism?

More Skill Practice

Historical and Social Sciences Analysis Skill Organize students into small groups to create a magazine that would appeal to the national public in the late 1800s. Have groups choose their target market, the type of magazine to meet that target market's needs, and the title of the magazine. Encourage students to include a variety of elements, such as feature articles, interviews, fictional stories, illustrations, and advertisements. AL CA HR5.

U Universal Access

English Learners People's names and other proper nouns may be difficult for English learners to read since they are not recurring words. Model the pronunciation of the names of people and institutions that appear in Section 3. Have students read them back to you and help them understand any errors they make. EL

C1 Critical Thinking

Drawing Conclusions Distribute a newspaper page to each student. Ask them to compare the quality of the paper and print of the newspaper with those of their textbook. Discuss why people make books with more lasting materials than newspapers. Explore how the quality of materials affects the cost of production and why it is necessary to keep down the cost of printing newspapers. OL CA HI6.

R Reading Strategy

Using Word Parts Point out the suffix *-ism* in the terms *yellow journalism*, *realism*, and *regionalism*. Explain that it tells the reader that the word is a noun. **Ask:** What other words do you know that end in *-ism*? *(patriotism, criticism)* OL

C2 Critical Thinking

Making Generalizations **Ask:** Why were regionalist writers also realists? *(To create a convincing portrait of a place, regionalists had to give recognizable details about the place and its people.)* OL

Reading Check

Answer: In literature, it is writing that focuses on a particular region or area of the country.

Review The Big Idea

Review the Big Idea for this section: "As a society matures, a distinctive culture can develop." Have students list the major cultural areas (newspapers, fiction, painting, music, and leisure activities) and the characteristics that made them American. OL

R Reading Strategy

Understanding Vocabulary
Explain to students that it was its complex rhythm or "ragged time" that gave *ragtime* its name. OL

Resources for page 761

- American Art and Architecture Transparency 20
- American Art and Architecture Transparency 23
- American Music: Hits Through History, "Maple Leaf Rag"

Answers and Additional Support

US8.12.7 Identify the new sources of large-scale immigration and the contributions of immigrants to the building of cities and the economy; explain the ways in which new social and economic patterns encouraged assimilation of newcomers into the mainstream amidst growing cultural diversity; and discuss the new wave of nativism.

Art, Music, and Leisure

Main Idea **American art, music, and leisure time activities continued to develop their own distinct style.**

Reading Connection Can you imagine the United States without baseball or football? What about without jazz music? Read to find out about the activities and art forms that took hold in America in the late 1800s.

For most of the 1800s, the work of American artists and musicians reflected a European influence. After the Civil War, Americans began to develop a distinctively American style.

What Did American Artists Paint? Some American painters pursued realist themes. Thomas Eakins painted the human anatomy and surgical operations. One of Eakins's students, Henry Tanner, depicted warm family scenes of African Americans in the South. Frederic Remington portrayed the American West, focusing on subjects such as cowhands and Native Americans. Winslow Homer was one of America's greatest artists. Homer painted Southern farmers, Adirondack campers, and stormy sea scenes. Although Homer died in 1910, his work remains popular with collectors and museum visitors. James Whistler's *Arrangement in Grey and Black,* commonly known as *Whistler's Mother,* is one of the best-known American paintings. Mary Cassatt was influential in the French Impressionist school of painting. Impressionists tried to capture the play of light, color, and patterns as they made immediate impressions on the senses.

History *Through Art*

Girls with Lobster **by Winslow Homer**
Homer painted scenes of people enjoying the New Jersey and New England seashores.
What themes did many American painters represent in their works?

Music in America More distinctively American kinds of music were also becoming popular. Bandleader John Philip Sousa composed many rousing marches, including "The Stars and Stripes Forever." African American musicians in New Orleans in the late 1800s developed an entirely new kind of music—jazz. Jazz combined elements of work songs, gospel music, spirituals, and African rhythms. Related to jazz was ragtime music. For about 20 years, beginning around the turn of the century, **ragtime**—with its complex rhythms—was the dominant force in popular music. One of the best-known ragtime composers is Scott Joplin. He wrote "Maple Leaf Rag" and many other well-known works. R

The symphony orchestras of New York, Boston, and Philadelphia—all founded before 1900—were among the world's finest. Great singers and conductors came from all over the world to perform at New York's Metropolitan Opera House.

Leisure Time Although sweatshop workers labored long hours for six or even seven days a week, middle-class people and even some factory workers enjoyed increasing amounts of leisure time.

Unlike round-the-clock farmwork, professional and industrial jobs gave people hours and even days of free time. Americans developed new forms of recreation.

History *Through Art*

Winslow Homer is the era's foremost realist. During the 1860s and 1870s, he painted scenes from American life. In the 1880s and 1890s, he turned to dramatic images of the power of the sea and the smallness of humanity.

Answer: realistic themes about people, places, and events

More Skill Practice

Historical and Social Sciences Analysis Skill **Ask:** Why did city people enjoy more leisure time than farmers? *(Urban workers generally work for a set number of hours and then go home. Farmers have to care for animals day and night and perform many other tasks when necessary, not according to the clock.)* OL CA HI2.

A favorite leisure-time activity for many people was watching and following sports. Baseball became the most popular spectator sport in America. By the turn of the century, both the National and American Leagues had been founded—each made up of teams from major cities. Another popular spectator sport was football, which developed from the English game of rugby. By the 1890s, college games were drawing huge crowds.

C Basketball, invented by Dr. James Naismith of Springfield, Massachusetts, also became popular. Naismith developed the game in the 1890s as an indoor winter sport for his YMCA physical education classes. Considered the only major sport that is completely American in origin, basketball soon spread to other countries.

Americans not only watched but also participated in sports. Tennis and golf were enjoyed by the wealthy, usually in exclusive private clubs. Bicycling grew in popularity after the "safety" bicycle was developed. These new bicycles used air-filled rubber tires instead of metal-rimmed wheels.

Large cities had many theaters. Plays performed ranged from serious dramas by Shakespeare to **vaudeville** (VAHD•vihl) shows, R which were variety shows with dancing, singing, comedy, and magic acts. Tickets to vaudeville shows were inexpensive, making them very popular. The circus also attracted large crowds. In 1910 the United States had about 80 traveling circuses.

Thomas Edison invented "moving pictures" in the 1880s. The "movies" soon became enormously popular. Some theaters, called nickelodeons, charged five cents to see short films. The nickelodeons were the beginning of today's film industry.

Reading Check **Describe** What elements made up jazz music?

History Online
Study Central Need help understanding changes in American culture? Visit ca.hss.glencoe.com and click on Study Central.

Section 3 Review

Reading Summary

Review the Main Ideas

- In the late 1800s and early 1900s, the number of public schools in the United States increased greatly, and the number of colleges for women and African Americans also grew.
- Newspaper and magazine readership increased greatly, and a number of American writers explored new themes.
- Distinctive styles of American art and music developed, and watching professional sports became a favorite leisure time activity.

What Did You Learn?

1. Describe the new philosophy of education that emerged around 1900.
2. What was yellow journalism?

Critical Thinking

3. **Summarizing Information** Re-create the diagram below and describe the work of each of these writers. CA HR3

Writer	Description of work
Horatio Alger	
Stephen Crane	
Edith Wharton	

4. **The Big Ideas** Explain the correlation between leisure time and the development of the arts. CA HI2.
5. **Analyze** What did supporters of progressive education emphasize? What did they criticize in existing models of education? CA HI1.
6. **Creative Writing** Write a letter to Andrew Carnegie persuading him to establish a public library in your community. Describe the advantages of locating the library in your area and the benefits citizens would receive from his grant. CA 8WA2.1

C Critical Thinking

Analyzing Information
Ask: How did new technologies contribute to leisure activities? *(Technologies enabled the spread of some activities, like bicycling, and created new ones, like motion pictures.)* OL CA HI3.

R Reading Strategy

Understanding Vocabulary
Tell students that the term *vaudeville* comes from *Vau de Vire*, a valley in Normandy, France, known for its lively music. OL

ASSESS

Resources for page 763

Use these resources to assess student mastery of section content.

- Section Quiz 17–3
- Interactive Tutor Self-Assessment CD-ROM

Reading Check
Answer: elements from work songs, gospel music, spirituals, and African rhythms

History Online
Study Central provides summaries, interactive games, and online graphic organizers to help students review section content.

CLOSE

Drawing Conclusions
Discuss which cultural areas have had the greatest influence on American society. OL

SECTION 3 REVIEW ANSWERS

Review questions reinforce content standard US8.12.

1. progressive education; aimed to shape character, teach citizenship
2. sensational writing that exaggerated dramatic, gruesome aspects of stories
3. Alger: Wrote books for young adults about hard work leading to success; Crane: Described Civil War and poverty in cities; Wharton: Described life among upper-class Easterners
4. **The Big Ideas** With more free time, Americans could support the arts.
5. Answers should reflect text information.
6. Answers should list benefits of having books available to people.

FOCUS

BELLRINGER
SKILLBUILDER ACTIVITY

Project **Daily Focus Skills Transparency 17–4** and have students answer the question.

Guide to Reading

Preteaching Vocabulary:
Have students create a word search using the content vocabulary terms.

Answers to Graphic:
Government: Civil service reform, new forms of city government; Business: Antitrust laws, regulation of industries; Voting: primaries, initiative, referendum, recall, Seventeenth Amendment

Unpacking the Standards

After reading the section, students will be able to:

- Explain how Americans fought corruption in government and business.
- Identify the activists who exposed corruption.
- Describe laws giving people more voice in government.
- Explain how women obtained the right to vote.

Section 4

The Progressive Movement

Guide to Reading

History Social Science Standards

US8.12 Students analyze the transformation of the American economy and the changing social and political conditions in the United States in response to the Industrial Revolution.

Looking Back, Looking Ahead

You learned that America's businesses and cities grew rapidly in the late 1800s. Such rapid growth allowed corruption in business and government to spread.

Focusing on the Main Ideas

- Americans took action against corruption in business and government. *(page 765)*
- New calls for reform were aided by writers who exposed government and business corruption. *(page 767)*
- In the early 1900s, more people received the right to vote, and the government began to regulate industry. *(page 769)*

Meeting People

William M. Tweed
Jacob Riis (REES)
Eugene V. Debs
Lincoln Steffens
Ida Tarbell
Upton Sinclair (sihn • KLEHR)
Robert La Follette (luh FAH • luht)
Theodore Roosevelt

Content Vocabulary

political machine
trust
oligopoly (AH • lih • GAH • puh • lee)
muckraker (MUHK • RAYK • uhr)
primary
initiative (ih • NIH • shuh • tiv)
referendum (REH • fuh • REHN • duhm)
recall
laissez-faire (LEH • ZAY • FEHR)
conservation

Academic Vocabulary

underlie
inspect

Reading Strategy

Organizing Information As you read Section 4, re-create the diagram below and list reforms for each category.

Reforms		
Government	Business	Voting

NATIONAL GEOGRAPHIC Who & When?

1900 — 1910 — 1920

Theodore Roosevelt

1901 Roosevelt becomes president

1904 Ida Tarbell publishes history of Standard Oil

Ida Tarbell

1912 Congress passes the Seventeenth Amendment

1920 Women vote in presidential election for first time

SECTION RESOURCES

Print Material
- Reproducible Lesson Plan 17–4*
- Daily Lesson and Discussion Notes 17–4
- Guided Reading Activity 17–4
- Reading Essentials and Study Guide 17–4
- Active Reading Note-Taking Guide 17–4
- Section Quiz 17–4

Transparencies
- Daily Focus Skills Transparency 17–4
- Section Graphic Organizer Transparency 17–4
- California Standards Practice Transparencies

Technology
- Interactive Tutor Self-Assessment CD-ROM
- Exam*View*® Pro Testmaker CD-ROM
- Presentation Plus! CD-ROM

*Available on TeacherWorks™

US8.12.6 Discuss child labor, working conditions, and laissez-faire policies toward big business and examine the labor movement, including its leaders (e.g., Samuel Gompers), its demand for collective bargaining, and its strikes and protests over labor conditions.

Call for Reform

Main Idea **Americans took action against corruption in business and government.**

Reading Connection What would you think if the members of a school sports team who paid the coach the most money got to be the starting players? Read to find out how reformers worked to prevent unqualified and dishonest people from receiving important government jobs.

Many Americans called for reform in the late 1800s. The reformers, called progressives, had many different goals. These progressive reformers focused on urban problems, government, and business. They claimed that government and big business were taking advantage of the American people rather than serving them.

Fighting Corruption **Political machines**—powerful organizations linked to political parties—controlled local government in many cities. In each ward, or political district within a city, a machine representative controlled jobs and services. This representative was the political boss. A political boss was often a citizen's closest link to local government. Although they did help people, many bosses were dishonest.

Corrupt politicians found numerous ways to make money. They accepted bribes from tenement landlords in return for overlooking violations of city housing codes. They received campaign contributions from contractors hoping to do business with the city. They also accepted kickbacks. A kickback is an arrangement in which contractors padded the amount of their bill for city work and paid, or "kicked back," a percentage of that amount to the bosses.

Some politicians used their knowledge of city business for personal profit. One of the most corrupt city bosses, **William M. Tweed,** known as Boss Tweed, headed New York City's Democratic political machine in the 1860s and 1870s. Boss Tweed led a network of city officials called the Tweed ring.

A Boss Tweed B Peter Sweeny C Richard Connelly D Mayor A. Oakley Hall

Analyzing Political Cartoons

The Tweed Ring Boss Tweed and New York City officials are shown pointing to one another in response to the question "Who stole the people's money?" On Tweed's right, a man holds a hat labeled "Chairs," a reference to the $179,000 New York City paid for 40 chairs and 3 tables. Other contractors and cheats—their names on their coats—complete the "ring."
How did political bosses gain votes for their parties?

TEACH

U Universal Access

English Learners Students whose native languages are not read from left to right may have trouble following the English text or get fatigued doing so for an extended period. Have students read the text under "Call for Reform." Encourage them to track the lines of text with their finger or place a blank index card under the line they are reading. **EL**

Review The Big Idea

Review the Big Idea for this section: "Reactions to social injustice can lead to reform movements." Point out that Progressivism was a reform movement that arose to make progress or improvements. Explain that many of the problems it tried to solve were urban problems. **OL**

R Reading Strategy

Understanding Vocabulary Ask a volunteer to define the term *political machine*, and explore the connotations of the word *machine*. Discuss how machines are impersonal, can work indefinitely, and are powerful. **OL**

C Critical Thinking

Drawing Conclusions
Ask: What jobs would a boss control? *(jobs in the civil service, hospitals, schools, fire and police departments)* How could a boss use city services to control the people in his district? *(by giving or taking away services as rewards or punishments)* **OL** **CA HI1.**

Analyzing Political Cartoons

Thomas Nast (1840–1902), the cartoonist who drew the Tweed Ring, helped bring Boss Tweed to justice. Although Tweed fled to Spain, authorities reportedly used one of Nast's cartoons to identify and capture him there in 1876. Nast also popularized the Democratic donkey and created the Republican elephant.

Answer: The bosses did favors for people in exchange for their votes for the bosses' political parties.

R1 Reading Strategy

Understanding Vocabulary
Ask: How was the spoils system bad for a city? *(Unqualified and dishonest people got hired.)* OL CA HI2.

R2 Reading Strategy

Understanding Vocabulary Ask students to restate the meanings of the terms *trusts* and *oligopoly* in their own words. OL CA 8RW1.3

C1 Critical Thinking

Drawing Conclusions Show students a Monopoly board and discuss how owning all of one property group benefits the owner. Explain that preventing such results in real life was the purpose of antitrust laws. OL CA HI2.

C2 Critical Thinking

Determining Cause and Effect Ask: Why did Congress require railroads to publish their rates? *(so they could not trick or overcharge customers)* OL

Reading Check
Answer: They thought high tariffs led to higher prices.

Answers and Additional Support

Picturing History
Small businesses and farmers often had to pay high rates to the railroads to ship their goods to market. ***What did the Interstate Commerce Act do?***

The Tweed Ring controlled the police, courts, and some newspapers. Political cartoonist Thomas Nast exposed the Tweed ring's operations in his cartoons for *Harper's Weekly*. Tweed was convicted and sentenced to prison.

To break the power of political bosses, reformers founded organizations such as the National Municipal League in Philadelphia. These groups worked to make city governments more honest and efficient.

What Was the Spoils System? The spoils system—rewarding political supporters with jobs and favors—had been common practice since the time of Andrew Jackson. Also called patronage, the system existed at all levels of government and led to numerous abuses. Many who received government jobs were not qualified. Some were dishonest. R1

A number of presidents, including Rutherford B. Hayes (1877–1881) and James Garfield (1881), wanted to change the spoils system. Hayes's efforts received little support, and Garfield was assassinated by an unsuccessful office seeker before he could launch his reforms.

When Vice President Chester A. Arthur succeeded Garfield, he tried to end the spoils system. In 1883 Congress passed the Pendleton Act, which established the Civil Service Commission to set up competitive examinations for federal jobs.

Controlling Business During the late 1800s, many Americans came to believe that **trusts,** or combinations of companies, were becoming too large. They believed these trusts had too much control over the economy and the government. This public concern led to new laws.

In 1890 Congress passed the Sherman Antitrust Act, the first federal law to control trusts and monopolies. Supporters of the law hoped it would keep trusts from limiting competition. R2 During the 1890s, however, the government rarely used the Sherman Act to curb business. C1 Instead, it applied the act against labor unions, claiming that union strikes interfered with trade. Not until the early 1900s did the government win cases against trusts by using the Sherman Act.

Reining in the Railroads The railroads functioned as an **oligopoly** (AH • lih • GAH • puh • lee)—a market structure in which a few large companies control the prices of the industry. In 1887 Congress passed the Interstate Commerce Act, which required railroads to charge "reasonable C2 and just" rates and to publish those rates. The act also created the Interstate Commerce Commission (ICC) to supervise the railroad industry.

Lowering Tariffs Reformers also wanted to lower tariffs. Many people believed that high tariffs led to higher prices for goods. In 1890 the Republicans raised tariffs sharply to protect American businesses from international competition. Voters showed their opposition to high tariffs by sending many Democrats to Congress. Grover Cleveland, who became president in 1893, also supported lower tariffs.

Reading Check **Explain** Why did many people want lower tariffs?

Did You Know?

Garfield's assassin was Charles J. Guiteau, a frustrated patronage seeker. The assassination was probably the single most powerful symbol of the need for the reforms finally achieved by the Pendleton Act.

Picturing History

Ask: What kind of competition was there in the railroad industry? *(limited because it was an oligopoly)* OL

Answer: supervised the railroad industry

US8.12.6 Discuss child labor, working conditions, and laissez-faire policies toward big business and examine the labor movement, including its leaders (e.g., Samuel Gompers), its demand for collective bargaining, and its strikes and protests over labor conditions.

R1 The New Reformers

Main Idea **New calls for reform were aided by writers who exposed government and business corruption.**

Reading Connection Have you ever watched the investigative reporters on your local television news shows? What sorts of problems do they report on? Read to find out about the investigative reporters who wrote about problems in government and business in the early 1900s.

An American Story

Newspaper reporter **Jacob Riis** (REES) shocked Americans with exposés of living conditions in large cities. With words and powerful photographs, Riis vividly portrayed immigrant life in New York City's crowded tenements.

C1 **"We used to go in the small hours of the morning into the worst tenements to count noses and see if the law against overcrowding was violated, and the sights I saw there gripped my heart until I felt that I must tell of them, or burst."**

—Jacob Riis, *The Making of an American*

Socialists and Progressives In the early 1900s, new ideas for correcting injustice and solving social problems emerged among American reformers. Socialism and progressivism were two such ideas.

U Socialists believed a nation's resources and major industries should be owned and operated by the government on behalf of all the people—not by individuals and private companies for their own profit. **Eugene V. Debs** helped found the American Socialist Party in 1898. Under Debs's leadership, the party won some support in the early 1900s. Debs ran for president five times but never received more than 6 percent of the popular vote.

During the same period, progressives brought new energy to the reform movement. Like the socialists, many progressives were alarmed by the concentration of wealth and power in the hands of a few. Progressives rejected the socialist idea of government ownership of industries. Instead, they supported government efforts to regulate industry.

They also sought to reform government, to make it more efficient and better able to resist the influence of powerful business interests. Progressives also believed that society had an obligation to protect and help all its members. Many progressive reforms were meant to help those who lacked wealth and influence.

Who Were the Muckrakers? Journalists aided the reformers by exposing injustices and corruption. Investigative reporters wrote stories that brought problems to the attention of the public—and gained readers. These journalists were called **muckrakers** (MUHK•RAYK•uhrz) because they "raked" (exposed) the "muck" (dirt and corruption) **underlying** society. R2

One of the most effective muckrakers, **Lincoln Steffens,** reported for *McClure's Magazine*. Steffens's articles exposed corrupt machine politics in New York, Chicago, and other cities. **Ida Tarbell,** also writing for *McClure's,* described the unfair practices of the oil trust. Her articles led to public pressure for more government control over big business. In her 1904 book *The History of the Standard Oil Company,* she warned of the giant corporation's power. C2

In his novel *The Jungle,* published in 1906, **Upton Sinclair** (sihn•KLEHR) described the horrors of the meatpacking industry in Chicago. His vivid descriptions shocked Americans and helped persuade Congress to pass the Meat Inspection Act in 1906. That same year, Congress also passed the Pure Food and Drug Act, requiring accurate labeling of food and medicine and banning the sale of harmful food.

Reading Check **Identify** Who wrote about unfair practices in the oil industry?

More Skill Practice

Historical and Social Sciences Analysis Skill Organize the class into small groups, and have groups make a chart about the reforms discussed in Section 4. Groups should do additional research as needed. Charts should provide information on the problems, the specific reforms set in place to solve them, the reformers involved, and the success of the reforms. Discuss the information different groups gave for the same problems. OL CA HI3.

R1 Reading Strategy

Scaffolding—Previewing Have students read the title of the subsection, the Main Idea, and the boldface headings. Then ask them what "The New Reformers" will be about. BL

This READING SKILL was introduced in Chapter 1.

C1 Critical Thinking

Analyzing Primary Sources **Ask:** Why did Riis and his coworkers check the tenements for overcrowding during the early morning? *(To get an accurate idea of how many people actually lived in the same place, they went when everyone was likely to be home.)* OL

U Universal Access

Below Grade Level Have students make a Venn diagram, showing the similarities and differences between socialists and progressives. BL

R2 Reading Strategy

Understanding Vocabulary Review the definition of *muckraker* and ask students to list antonyms. OL

C2 Critical Thinking

Drawing Conclusions **Ask:** Why did muckrakers' articles and books capture public attention? *(muckrakers wrote about issues that affected the finances and health of people or that were clearly social injustices.)* OL

Reading Check

Answer: Ida Tarbell

Resources for page 767

Primary Source Reading 17

Biography

TEACH

R1 Reading Strategy

Setting a Purpose Remind students that the quotation on page 767 was by Jacob Riis. **Ask:** Who do you think Jacob Riis was? *(a reformer)* Why are you being asked to read his biography? *(Students may say to learn more about what motivated reformers.)* OL

R2 Reading Strategy

Identifying the Main Idea and Supporting Details
Ask: What experiences convinced Riis that the poor were not to blame for their situation? *(having lived in poverty himself and going into poor areas of New York City as a reporter)* BL CA HR3.

C Critical Thinking

Drawing Conclusions
Ask: Why weren't Riis's readers aware of the plight of the poor before he brought it to their attention? *(Students may say that magazine readers were largely middle class people who lived and worked in nicer neighborhoods and did not see how the poor lived.)* OL CA HR5.

Answers and Additional Support

Biography

US8.12 Students analyze the transformation of the American economy and the changing social and political conditions in the United States in response to the Industrial Revolution.

JACOB RIIS R1

1849–1914

Jacob Riis came to the United States from Denmark when he was 21. Riis lived in poverty for many years and often made police lodging houses his temporary home. In 1873 Riis began to work as a reporter and photographer for New York City newspapers. In addition to his own experience with R2 poverty, Riis's job allowed him to further witness the poverty in which many lived in New York City.

Riis strongly believed that the poor were not to blame for their situation and felt that something should be done to help them. He realized he could use his newspaper stories to focus attention on the needs of the poor. Riis published many articles about the living conditions in the poorer sections of the city. These articles were accompanied by his photographs or illustrations, which brought to life the circumstances in which the city's inhabitants lived and worked. In 1890 Riis wrote *How the Other Half Lives.* By taking pictures of the tenements, Riis was able to bring the terrible conditions of the slums to the attention of readers. His book helped establish housing codes to prevent the worst abuses. C

"The poor we shall always have with us, but the slum we need not have."
—**Jacob Riis, *Battle with the Slum***

When Theodore Roosevelt became the city's police commissioner, he asked Riis to present a reform program. Through Riis's efforts, many playgrounds and parks were established in the city. Riis helped make others aware of the problems many urban Americans faced in their daily lives. He was later known as one of the first muckraking journalists, a group of people whose articles and photographs exposed corruption and social problems in American life. Riis served as an example of what individuals could do to lessen these problems.

Then and Now

Are photographs still a powerful means of exposing corruption and injustice? Explain.

Then and Now

Theodore Roosevelt called Jacob Riis the "best American I ever knew." In *How the Other Half Lives,* Riis described the squalid living conditions, the lack of ventilation and light, and the poor sanitation of the tenements. Among the changes that resulted from his work were a window in each apartment and an airshaft in the stairway of every building.

Answer: Students may say that photographs continue to let people see for themselves what the writer is describing. They can also be shot or altered so as to emphasize the point.

US8.12.5 Examine the location and effects of urbanization, renewed immigration, and industrialization (e.g., the effects on social fabrics of cities, wealth and economic opportunity, the conservation movement).

Expanding Democracy

Main Idea **In the early 1900s, more people received the right to vote, and the government began to regulate industry.**

Reading Connection Do you consider protecting public parks and the environment to be an important issue? Read to find out about one of the first American presidents to be concerned with the environment.

In the early 1900s, progressives backed a number of reforms designed to increase the people's direct control of the government. **Robert La Follette** (luh FAH • luht), known as "Fighting Bob," led Wisconsin's reform-minded Republicans. La Follette's greatest achievement was reforming the state electoral system. Candidates for general elections in Wisconsin had been chosen at state conventions run by party bosses. La Follette introduced a direct **primary** election, allowing the state's voters to choose their party's candidates. Reformers in other states copied this "Wisconsin idea."

What Was the Oregon System? The state of Oregon also made important changes in the political process to give voters more power. The reforms in Oregon included a direct primary election and the initiative, the referendum, and the recall.

The **initiative** (ih • NIH • shuh • tiv) allowed citizens to place a measure or issue on the ballot in a state election. The **referendum** (REH • fuh • REHN • duhm) gave voters the opportunity to accept or reject measures that the state legislature enacted. The **recall** enabled voters to remove unsatisfactory elected officials from their jobs. These reforms were called the Oregon System. Other western states soon adopted the reforms.

Picturing **History**

Before the passage of the Nineteenth Amendment, many women campaigned for the right to vote. ***Which was the first state to allow women to vote?***

769

Picturing **History**

Women generally enjoyed more rights in Western states than in other parts of the country. They could own and run ranches and farms, for example. Western women were also the first to win the right to vote. The first eleven states to grant woman suffrage were in the West: Wyoming (1869), Utah (1870), Colorado (1893), Idaho (1896), Washington (1910), California (1911), Oregon (1912), Kansas (1912), Arizona (1912), and Nevada (1914), Montana (1914).

Answer: Wyoming

R1 Reading Strategy

Skimming Have students read the main idea and headings and skim the text on this page. Then ask them to list the progressive reforms that expanded people's voting rights. *(primary elections, initiative, referendum, recall, direct election of senators)* OL

R2 Reading Strategy

Understanding Vocabulary Remind students that the word *primary* means "first." Explain that the primary election comes before the general election. **Ask:** What other expressions do you know that have the word primary in them? *(primary school)* OL

R3 Reading Strategy

Understanding Vocabulary Model how to read aloud expository text, giving emphasis to the vocabulary words, by reading the paragraphs under the heading "What Was the Oregon System?" OL

C1 Critical Thinking

Analyzing Information **Ask:** How does the initiative give citizens a direct voice in government? *(It allows them to suggest laws themselves.)* Why would voters want that power? *(Legislators may be unwilling to suggest certain laws for fear of displeasing some voters.)* OL

C2 Critical Thinking

Drawing Conclusions **Ask:** How do referendum and recall give voters some control over legislators? *(Voters can accept or reject what their legislators want to do and even get rid of the elected officials themselves.)* OL

W Writing Support

Research Reports Writing Have students conduct research about the lives and views of a prominent suffragist of the period, such as Carrie Chapman Catt or Alice Paul. Have students give an oral presentation in which they explain the suffragist's ideas. OL CA 8LS1.3.

Review The Big Idea

Review the Big Idea for this section: "Reactions to social injustice can lead to reform movements." Discuss why the passing of the Fifteenth Amendment energized the suffragist movement. *(It showed reformers that they could make a difference; it highlighted the injustice of denying civil rights to women who had fought for the rights of others.)* OL CA HI3.

C Critical Thinking

Determining Cause and Effect Ask: Why was Roosevelt able to get the Justice Department to apply the Sherman Antitrust Act as it was originally intended? *(As president, Roosevelt could direct the department to follow his policies.)* OL CA HI2.

Answers and Additional Support

◀ Theodore Roosevelt board game

McKinley/Roosevelt ▶ glass canteen, 1900

The Seventeenth Amendment Progressives also changed the way U.S. senators are elected. The Constitution had given state legislatures the responsibility for choosing senators, but party bosses and business interests often controlled the selection process. Progressives wanted to give the people an opportunity to vote for their senators directly. Support for this idea grew. In 1912 Congress passed the Seventeenth Amendment to the Constitution to provide for the direct election of senators. Ratified in 1913, the amendment gave the people a voice in selecting their representatives. *(See page 264 for the text of the Seventeenth Amendment.)*

The Fight for Suffrage At the Seneca Falls Convention in 1848, women had called for the right to vote. After the Civil War, Congress passed the Fifteenth Amendment, giving voting rights to freed men—but not to women. Some leading abolitionists became suffragists, men and women who fought for woman suffrage, or women's right to vote. The suffragists won their early victories in the West. First as a territory in 1869 and then as a state in 1890, Wyoming led the nation in giving women the vote. Between 1910 and 1913, six other states adopted woman suffrage. By 1919 women could vote in at least some elections in most of the 48 states.

In 1919 Congress voted in favor of the Nineteenth Amendment, which allowed woman suffrage. The amendment was ratified in 1920, in time for women to vote in that year's presidential election. For the first time, American women were able to participate in the election of their national leaders.

"Trustbuster" in the White House President William McKinley, elected in 1900, was assassinated less than a year later. Suddenly, 42-year-old **Theodore Roosevelt,** the Republican vice president, took over the top office and became the youngest president in the nation's history. When Roosevelt moved into the White House in 1901, he brought progressivism with him.

President McKinley had favored big business, but President Roosevelt was known to support business regulation and other progressive reforms. In 1902 Roosevelt ordered the Justice Department to take legal action against certain trusts that had violated the Sherman Antitrust Act. His first target was the Northern Securities Company, a railroad monopoly formed by financiers J.P. Morgan and James J. Hill to control transportation in the Northwest. The Supreme Court finally decided that Northern Securities had illegally limited trade and ordered the trust to be taken apart.

During the rest of Roosevelt's term as president, he obtained a total of 25 indictments (legal charges) against trusts in the beef, oil, and tobacco industries. Although hailed as a trustbuster, Roosevelt did not want to break up all trusts. As he saw it, trusts should be regulated, not destroyed.

Roosevelt ran for the presidency in 1904, promising the people a Square Deal—fair and equal treatment for all. He was elected with more than 57 percent of the popular vote.

More Skill Practice

Historical and Social Sciences Analysis Skill In 1902, during a strike by the United Mine Workers, Theodore Roosevelt forced coal companies to agree to arbitration to settle the dispute with the union. Mine workers won a pay increase and fewer hours, but not recognition of their union. Have students research this and other labor disputes in which President Roosevelt was involved. Then have students make a poster that summarizes their findings and draws conclusions about Roosevelt's views on business and labor unions. OL CA HI1.

Roosevelt's Policies Roosevelt's "Square Deal" called for a considerable amount of government regulation of business. This contrasted with an attitude toward business that dated back to the presidency of Thomas Jefferson, which was summed up in the phrase **laissez-faire** (LEH • ZAY FEHR). This French term generally means "let people do as they choose."

R1 R2 Roosevelt introduced a new era of government regulation. He supported the Meat Inspection and Pure Food and Drug Acts; these acts gave the Department of Agriculture and the Food and Drug Administration the power to visit businesses and **inspect** their products.

Why Was Conservation Important? Roosevelt held a lifelong enthusiasm for the great outdoors and the wilderness. He believed in the need for **conservation,** the protection and preservation of natural resources. As president, Roosevelt took steps to conserve the country's forests, mineral deposits, and water resources. In 1905 he proposed the creation of the U.S. Forest Service. He pressured Congress to set aside millions of acres of national forests and created the nation's first wildlife sanctuaries. Roosevelt also formed the National Conservation Commission, which produced the first survey of the country's natural resources.

Roosevelt has been called America's first environmental president. While he made conservation an important public issue, Roosevelt also recognized the need for economic growth and development. He tried to strike a balance between business interests and protection of the environment and conservation.

Reading Check **Identify** What reform allowed voters to place a measure on the ballot?

History Online
Study Central Need help understanding the Progressive Movement? Visit ca.hss.glencoe.com and click on Study Central.

Section 4 Review

Reading Summary

Review the Main Ideas

- Americans became angered by corrupt politicians who made money illegally and by large trusts, which began to control the economy and the government.
- Socialists and progressives wanted the government to more tightly control business practices, and reforming journalists exposed injustices and corruption in business.
- Changes led to more political control for common citizens, and the government began to regulate industry and conserve the environment.

What Did You Learn?

1. Explain how the Civil Service Commission helped eliminate the spoils system.
2. What industry did Upton Sinclair describe in his book *The Jungle*?

Critical Thinking

3. **Organizing Information** Re-create the diagram below and show how the Seventeenth Amendment reformed the political process. CA HI3.

Seventeenth Amendment	
Policy before	Policy after

4. **Compare and Contrast** Write a paragraph comparing socialist and progressive views on industry.
5. **Analyze** Examine the political cartoon on page 765. Why are the individuals pointing to someone else? What statement is cartoonist Thomas Nast making about the extent of political corruption in New York City? CA HR4.
6. **The Big Ideas** Write an essay summarizing the role of muckrakers in the reform movement. How would the reform movement have been different if the press were controlled by the government instead of being free? CA 8WA2.3

SECTION 4 REVIEW ANSWERS

Review questions reinforce content standard US8.12.

1. It established competitive exams for applicants to show their ability to do a job.
2. meatpacking industry
3. Before: senators chosen by state legislatures often controlled by party bosses, business interests; After: senators chosen by citizens through direct elections
4. Answers should reflect text information.
5. Each is trying to blame someone else for stealing. Nast suggests that corruption is found throughout the government.
6. **The Big Ideas** Answers will vary but should give reasons.

R1 Reading Strategy

Understanding Vocabulary Review the definitions of *laissez-faire* and *conservation*, and ask students for examples from U.S. history when the government has followed both of these practices. OL CA 8RW1.3

R2 Reading Strategy

Academic Vocabulary Discuss with students the need to inspect food products. OL

ASSESS

Resources for page 771

Use these resources to assess student mastery of section content.

- Biography Activity 17A
- Economics and History Activity 17
- Section Quiz 17–4
- Interactive Tutor Self-Assessment CD-ROM

Reading Check

Answer: the initiative

History Online

Study Central provides summaries, interactive games, and online graphic organizers to help students review section content.

CLOSE

Determining Importance Review the political and business reforms discussed in this section. Have students name the reform they consider the most important in each category and explain why they think so. OL CA HI2.

FOCUS

History–Social Science Standards

The following standard is covered on pages 772–773.

US8.12.5 Students examine the location and effects of urbanization, renewed immigration, and industrialization (e.g., the effects on social fabrics of cities, wealth, and economic opportunity, the conservation movement).

TEACH

C1 Critical Thinking

Making Inferences
Ask: Why do you think the government changed the name of Mount McKinley National Park to Denali National Park? *(Possible answer: out of respect for Native American tradition)* **OL**

C2 Critical Thinking

Making Generalizations
Ask: Why did Americans' view about natural areas change in the 1800s? *(Colonists and pioneers would see nature and wildlife differently than the people of later times.)* **OL** **CA HI5.**

Answers and Additional Support

NATIONAL GEOGRAPHIC

GEOGRAPHY & HISTORY

WILD WONDERS

GRIZZLY BEARS, WOLVES, MOOSE, CARIBOU, DALL'S SHEEP and many other animals roam Alaska's Denali National Park and Preserve. Larger than Massachusetts, the six-million-acre park includes the highest mountain in North America.

C1 The Alaskan wilderness area set aside as Mount McKinley National Park in 1917 was renamed Denali in 1980 when Congress tripled the size of the park. Denali was the peak's Native American name, meaning "the High One."

C2 The idea of setting aside areas of natural beauty and historic importance for the benefit of the people dates back to the mid-1800s. Before then, Americans had viewed wild places either as obstacles or as a source of natural resources for people to use.

The conservation movement gained popularity in the early 1900s when President Theodore Roosevelt and other conservationists urged Americans to protect natural resources.

Today conservation continues to be an important issue. Although many of us enjoy visiting national parks such as Denali, the parks also serve as refuges for wildlife. Scientists study the plants and animals so that they can protect them. With 430 species of flowering plants, 37 species of mammals, and 156 species of birds, Denali is one of America's great areas of unspoiled wilderness.

LEARNING from GEOGRAPHY

1. **Which peaks are higher than 15,000 feet?**
2. **Do you think it is necessary for the government to aid environmental programs? Explain.**

LEARNING from GEOGRAPHY

Answers:

1. Mt. Foraker and Mt. McKinley (Denali)
2. Accept all reasonable answers, such as conservation has become increasingly important as people have learned more about the importance of preserving ecosystems and endangered species. Also, as increasing population and development have taken away large amounts of land, people have become more interested as a nation in preserving wild and scenic places.

US8.12.5 Examine the location and effects of urbanization, renewed immigration, and industrialization (e.g., the effects on social fabric of cities, wealth and economic opportunity, the conservation movement).

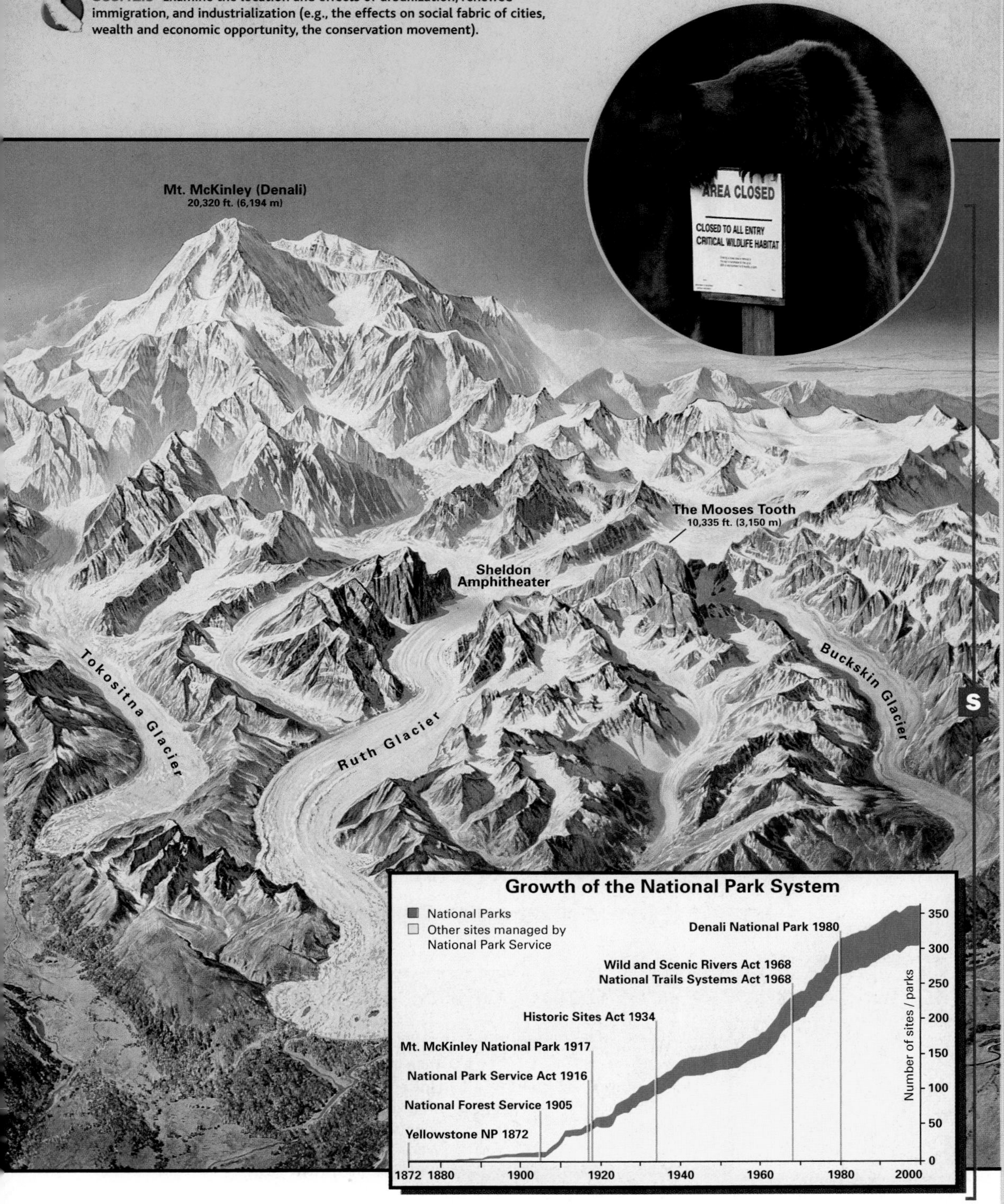

NATIONAL GEOGRAPHIC

GEOGRAPHY & HISTORY

S Skill Practice

Using Geography Skills Tell students to look closely at the map. **Ask:** What glacier extends south from the Sheldon Amphitheater? *(Ruth Glacier)* How many peaks does Denali have? *(two)* Tell students that the shorter northern peak is 19,470 feet (5,934 meters) high and has a sheer drop on the north side. OL CA CS3.

ASSESS

Have students answer the **Learning from Geography** questions.

NGS ONLINE

Access National Geographic's Web site for current events, atlas updates, activities, links, interactive features, and archive at www.nationalgeographic.com

CLOSE

Determining Cause and Effect In recent years, there has been resistance on the part of some people to adding new territory to the national park and national wildlife refuge systems. Ask students to explain why some interests might take this position. OL CA HI2.

EXTENDING THE CONTENT

National Parks The National Park System started in 1872, with the creation of the first national park, Yellowstone. National parks protect areas of scenic beauty, places of historic or cultural interest, or specific environments and wildlife populations. The National Park System today has more than 350 units, including national parks, monuments, historic sites, seashores, recreation areas, and trails. Delaware is the only state that does not have a national park unit.

FOCUS

BELLRINGER
SKILLBUILDER ACTIVITY

Project **Daily Focus Skills Transparency 17–5** and have students answer the question.

Guide to Reading

Preteaching Vocabulary: Explain the meaning of the content vocabulary words and ask students to write an analogy with each one.

Answers to Graphic: Roosevelt Corollary: U.S. has right to intervene in Latin America; Dollar Diplomacy: link business interests and diplomacy; Moral Diplomacy: foreign policy should be based on moral principles

Unpacking the Standards

After reading the section, students will be able to:

- Describe how U.S. power abroad grew.
- Explain how ethnic and religious minorities were discriminated against.
- Describe the actions minority groups took to win equality.

Section 5 A Changing Nation

History Social Science Standards

US8.12 Students analyze the transformation of the American economy and the changing social and political conditions in the United States in response to the Industrial Revolution.

Guide to Reading

Looking Back, Looking Ahead

You learned that American reformers attempted to reduce corruption in business and government. At the same time, Americans wanted to expand their power and trade around the world.

Focusing on the Main Ideas

- The United States demonstrated its power in areas such as Latin America and the Pacific. *(page 775)*
- Many ethnic and religious minorities in America faced discrimination and even violence. *(page 778)*
- Minority groups in the United States sought to end discrimination and gain equal rights. *(page 780)*

Locating Places

Alaska
Hawaiian Islands
Cuba
Guam
Philippines
Panama

Content Vocabulary

isthmus (IHS • muhs)
discrimination (dihs • KRIH • muh • NAY • shuhn)
ward
barrio (BAHR • ee • OH)

Academic Vocabulary

reject
modify (MAH • duh • FY)
bias (BY • uhs)

Reading Strategy

Analyzing Information As you study Section 5, re-create the diagram below and describe the policies listed.

	Description
Roosevelt Corollary	
Dollar Diplomacy	
Moral Diplomacy	

NATIONAL GEOGRAPHIC Where & When?

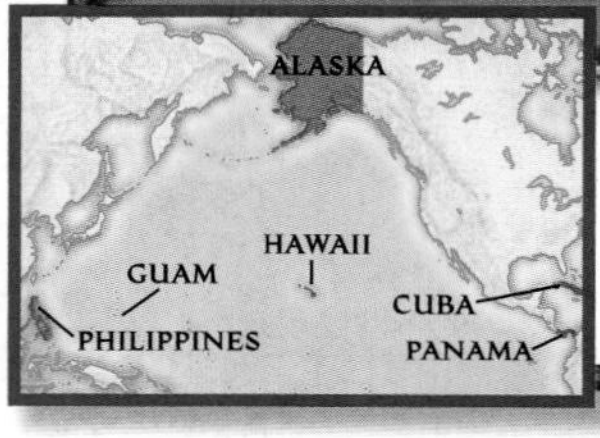

1865 — 1890 — 1915

1867 United States buys Alaska territory

1898 United States annexes Hawaii; Spanish-American War

1914 Panama Canal completed

SECTION RESOURCES

Print Material
- Reproducible Lesson Plan 17–5*
- Daily Lesson and Discussion Notes 17–5
- Guided Reading Activity 17–5
- Reading Essentials and Study Guide 17–5
- Active Reading Note-Taking Guide 17–5
- Section Quiz 17–5

Transparencies
- Daily Focus Skills Transparency 17–5
- Section Graphic Organizer Transparency 17–5
- California Standards Practice Transparencies

Technology
- Interactive Tutor Self-Assessment CD-ROM
- Exam*View*® Pro Testmaker CD-ROM
- Presentation Plus! CD-ROM

*Available on TeacherWorks™

US8.12 Students analyze the transformation of the American economy and the changing social and political conditions in the United States in response to the Industrial Revolution.

American Foreign Policy

R **Main Idea** **The United States demonstrated its power in areas such as Latin America and the Pacific.**

Reading Connection Have you ever wondered how the United States came to include places such as Alaska and Hawaii which are so far from the continental states? Read to find out how the United States expanded its power around the world.

An American Story

In the late 1800s and early 1900s, Americans looked beyond their borders and yearned for an empire. Merchants desired overseas markets, and adventurers wanted another frontier to conquer. Senator Albert Beveridge voiced the feelings of many when he proclaimed in 1900:

> C **"The Philippines are ours forever. . . . And just beyond the Philippines are China's illimitable markets. We will not retreat from either. . . . The Pacific is our ocean."**
>
> —Albert Beveridge, "In Support of an American Empire"

Goals of Foreign Policy When President George Washington published his Farewell Address in 1796, he advised Americans to increase trade with other countries but to have "as little political connection as possible." Above all else, he warned Americans to "steer clear of permanent alliances with any portion of the foreign world." These principles guided American foreign policy for about 100 years. However, various people interpreted Washington's words in different ways. Some believed he meant that the United States should follow a policy of isolationism, or noninvolvement, in world affairs. Others believed that Washington supported trade with other countries and was not calling for complete isolation from the world.

How Did the United States Expand? Soon after the Civil War, some American leaders began to push for the United States to expand beyond its borders. They believed that acquiring new territories would increase trade and allow the United States to become a world power. In 1867 Secretary of State William Seward negotiated the purchase of **Alaska,** which was Russian territory at the time. At first, many people ridiculed Alaska as "Seward's Ice Box." The discovery of gold there later proved the value of the region's natural resources.

In 1898, during the presidency of William McKinley, the United States annexed—took control of—the **Hawaiian Islands.** The islands provided a base for the American navy. From Hawaii the United States could oversee its trade in Japan and China.

That same year, the United States went to war with Spain. The American press had aroused intense anger by reporting the brutal way that Spain crushed a rebellion in **Cuba.** Almost immediately, fighting extended to Spanish colonies in the Pacific Ocean as well as in Cuba. When the Spanish-American War ended, not only did Cuba gain its independence, but the United States also gained **Guam** and the **Philippines.** U

Although about 400 American soldiers died fighting in the war, more than 2,000 died of diseases such as yellow fever, malaria, and other diseases contracted in the tropical climate. The African Americans who served faced the additional burden of discrimination. Serving in segregated units, African Americans battled alongside the Cuban rebel army, in which black and white troops fought as equals.

American Interest in Latin America Since colonial times, the United States had carried on a flourishing trade with Latin America, including the Caribbean region. Fear of European influence in the region was a factor that led to the Monroe Doctrine in 1823, when President James Monroe warned European nations not to attempt to establish new colonies in North or South America.

TEACH

R Reading Strategy

Outlining Have students outline the subsection on American Foreign Policy as a study aid. Tell them to use the boldface headings as the Roman numeral entries; the topic sentence of each paragraph as the capital letter entries; and the supporting details for the Arabic numeral entries. OL

C Critical Thinking

Analyzing Primary Sources
Ask: How is Senator Beveridge's remark reminiscent of the attitude of European countries towards their colonies in the Americas? *(Like colonial European officials and businessmen, Beveridge felt that a strong country could use less powerful countries as markets.)* OL CA HI3.

U Universal Access

Auditory/Musical Tell students that the late 1800s and early 1900s saw a rise in patriotic feeling in the United States. This feeling found expression in the music of "march king" John Philip Sousa, whose works include "The Stars and Stripes Forever"; "The Liberty Bell"; and "Semper Fidelis," which became the Marine Corps march. Ask students to write words to an appropriate-sounding melody summarizing how the United States expanded into another part of the world. Have them sing or cite their lyrics to the class. OL CA 8SA2.5

More Skill Practice

Historical and Social Sciences Analysis Skill Have pairs of students research the places that became American possessions in the second half of the 1800s, including Alaska, Hawaii, Guam, the Philippines, Puerto Rico, and any other places shown on the map on page 776. Tell the pairs to give an oral presentation summarizing the history of the place, describing the culture of the people who lived there, and explaining how the United States gained control over it. Have students use maps, time lines and other visual aids in their presentation. If the resources are available, you could ask them to put together a slide presentation. OL CA HR3. CA 8SA2.3

Review The Big Idea

Review the Big Idea for this section: "Political ideas and major events shape how people form governments." **Ask:** How did events in Venezuela and the Dominican Republic help shape the foreign policy of the United States? *(Problems in each country created a potential for European intervention, so President Roosevelt took action first.)* **OL**

R Reading Strategy

Evaluating Ask: How did the Roosevelt Corollary differ from the Monroe Doctrine? *(The Monroe doctrine sought to keep Europe from intervening in the Americas; the Roosevelt Corollary claimed the right of the United States to intervene in Latin America.)* **OL**

C Critical Thinking

Predicting Consequences Have students write a short essay predicting how the United States might be different today if it had not expanded in the late 1800s, but had remained neutral in world conflicts and within its existing boundaries. **OL** **CA 8WS1.1**

Answers and Additional Support

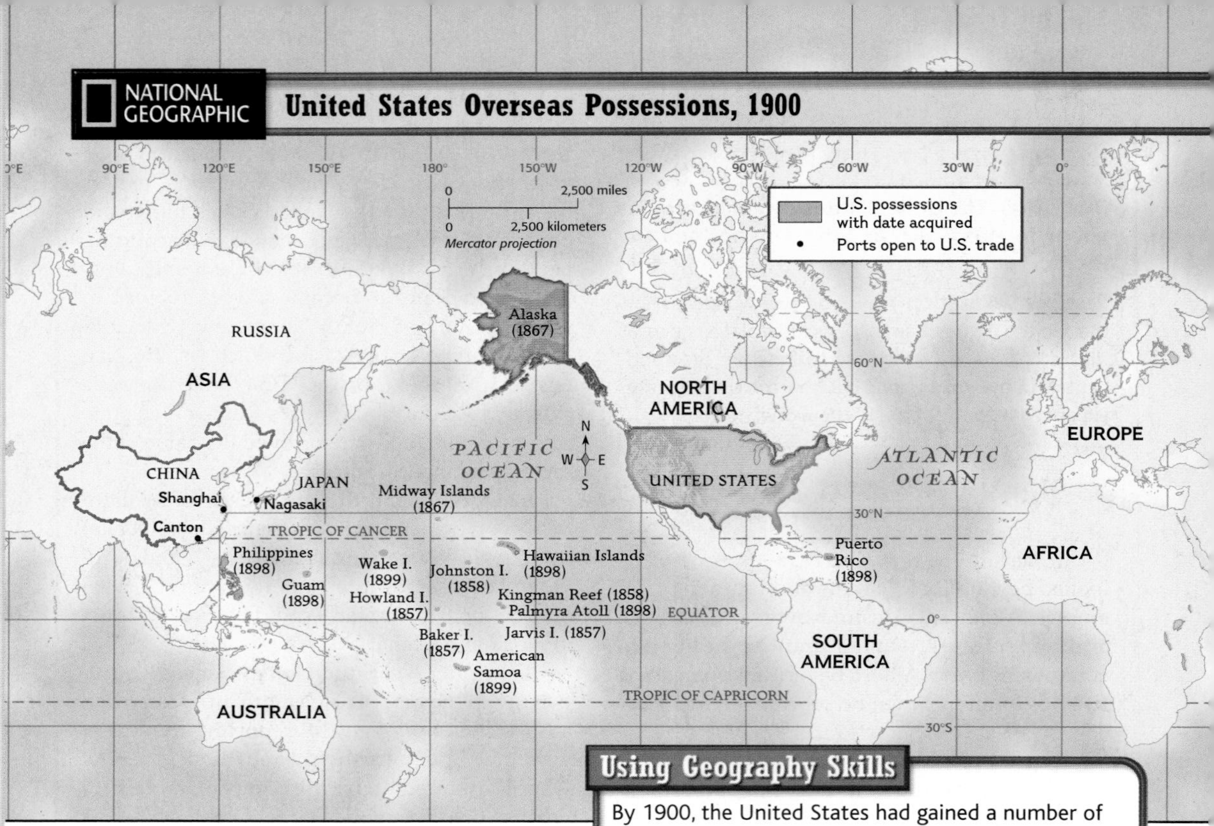

Using Geography Skills

By 1900, the United States had gained a number of possessions in the Pacific.

1. **Location** Locate Puerto Rico, Guam, and the Philippines. Which of these is farthest from the continental United States?
2. **Analyze** When were the Hawaiian Islands acquired?

Theodore Roosevelt, who became President after McKinley's assassination in 1901, worried that instability in the Caribbean region would lead European powers to intervene. In 1902 Venezuela and the Dominican Republic were deeply in debt to European nations. Roosevelt was concerned that European powers would step in to protect their financial interests there.

The president responded to these incidents in 1904 by asserting America's right to act as a "policeman" in Latin America, intervening "however reluctantly . . . in cases of wrongdoing." This policy, known as the Roosevelt Corollary, was an addition to the Monroe Doctrine. Up to that time, the United States had used the Monroe Doctrine only to prevent European intervention in Latin America. Under the Roosevelt Corollary, the United States now claimed the right to intervene in the affairs of Latin American nations whenever those nations seemed unstable. Roosevelt liked to proclaim "Speak softly, but carry a big stick." He meant that he preferred peace, but that he would use force when necessary. Roosevelt put his "big stick" to use to advance U.S. interests in Panama.

The Panama Canal For years the United States and other countries had wanted to build a canal across Central America to connect the Atlantic and Pacific Oceans. An ideal location for such a canal was across the **isthmus** (IHS • muhs) of **Panama.** An isthmus is a narrow strip of land that connects two larger landmasses—in this case, North and South America. Colombia, however, controlled Panama, and the Colombian legislature **rejected** the United States's offer to buy a strip of land across the isthmus.

Using Geography Skills

Alaska and Hawaii became states in 1959. The Philippines gained full independence on July 4, 1946, after having been a commonwealth for 11 years. Guam became a self-governing territory in 1968 and has been in negotiations with Congress for commonwealth status since 1987. Guamanians are U.S. citizens. Puerto Rico has been a commonwealth since 1952, and its people are U.S. citizens also.

Answers:

1. The Philippines
2. 1898

To obtain the canal site, Roosevelt helped organize a revolt in Panama in 1903. With the help of American marines, the Panamanian rebels overthrew their Colombian rulers and set up their own government. The United States and the new government of Panama quickly signed a canal treaty. For $10 million plus an annual fee, Panama granted Americans control of a strip across the isthmus. Finished in 1914, the Panama Canal ranks as one of the great engineering works of all time.

Taft and Wilson Theodore Roosevelt thought of American power mostly in military terms. His successor in the White House, William Howard Taft, took a different view. Taft hoped to **modify** American foreign policy. He believed that American investments would bring stability to troubled areas of the world, as well as profit and power to the United States, without the need for force. Taft's approach was known as dollar diplomacy.

Elected in 1912, the new president, Woodrow Wilson said he wanted to promote democracy and further the cause of world peace. This new policy was called "moral diplomacy" because its purpose was to help other countries.

The Mexican Revolution From 1884 to 1911, a dictator named Porfirio Díaz, ruled Mexico. A few wealthy landowners dominated Mexican society. Most of the Mexican people were poor and owned no land. In 1911 Francisco Madero, a reformer who called for constitutional government and land reform, forced Díaz from power. Reform came slowly, however, and rebel groups fought against Madero's forces. Madero was captured and murdered and Venustiano Carranza, whose forces had acquired arms from the United States, became Mexico's president.

When the U.S. government came out openly in support of Carranza, rebel leader Pancho Villa retaliated by raiding U.S. border towns, most notably Columbus, New Mexico. American troops under General John J. Pershing crossed the border into Mexico and pursued Villa but were unsuccessful.

The Mexican Revolution had been the first major effort in Latin America to overturn the system of large estates in the hands of the few and raise the living standards for the Mexican people. Out of the revolution emerged historic social and economic reform. The revolution also was responsible for the first big wave of immigration from Mexico to the United States. More than 1 million refugees entered the United States. They influenced the culture and contributed to the economic and political development of the Southwest in particular and the nation as a whole.

Reading Check **Explain** On what principles did Wilson base his foreign policy?

History *Through Art*

***Work Trains, Miraflores* by Alson Skinner Clark**
This painting shows the building of the Panama Canal. The stamp commemorates the canal's 25th anniversary. ***What role did the United States play in the independence of Panama?***

S Skill Practice

Using Geography Skills Have students look closely at the map on page 776. Discuss the challenges the United States faced trying to supply and stay connected with troops and other personnel in both the Pacific and the Caribbean. **Ask:** How would the Panama Canal aid in maintaining and running all these possessions? *(make it faster to transport people and supplies between the east and west coasts; between the West Coast and the Caribbean; and between the East Coast and the Pacific)* OL CA CS3.

R1 Reading Strategy

Scaffolding—Visualizing Write the word *isthmus* on the board and show students where the Isthmus of Panama is on a large map. Explain that the narrowness of this region was why this route was chosen for the canal. OL

This READING SKILL was introduced in Chapter 10.

R2 Reading Strategy

Academic Vocabulary Ask students to describe how President Taft hoped to modify foreign policy. OL

C Critical Thinking

Determining Cause and Effect **Ask:** How can economic investment in a country be a form of diplomacy? *(Large businesses that employ many people, own land, and pay taxes can influence government policies in that country.)* OL CA HI2.

Reading Check

Answer: desire to promote peace and democracy

History *Through Art*

Alson Skinner Clark (1876–1949), an American impressionist, studied in Paris and then in New York.

Answer: The United States helped organize and finance the Panamanian rebels and sent Marines to help them gain independence from Colombia.

Resources for page 777

Biography Activity 17B

R1 Reading Strategy

Connecting Analyze the difference between discrimination and prejudice—a judgment formed without a factual basis. Point out that prejudice can lead to discrimination. OL CA 8RW 1.3.

R2 Reading Strategy

Monitoring Ask: Why were eastern European Jews more discriminated against than other European groups? *(Jews seemed different from most Americans because they were not Christian.)* OL

S Skill Practice

Visual Literacy Ask: In what years was more than 10 percent of the population foreign born? *(1900, 1910, 1920, 1930, 2000)* What was the percentage of non-European foreign born in 1900? *(15.1%)* What was that percentage in 2000? *(84.7%)* OL

US8.12.7 Identify the new sources of large-scale immigration and the contributions of immigrants to the building of cities and the economy; explain the ways in which new social and economic patterns encouraged assimilation of newcomers into the mainstream amidst growing cultural diversity; and discuss the new wave of nativism.

Facing Prejudice at Home

Main Idea **Many ethnic and religious minorities in America faced discrimination and even violence.**

Reading Connection What might it have been like to travel thousands of miles to a new land, hoping to start a new, successful life, only to be told that you could go only to certain schools or hold certain low-paying jobs? Read to learn about the discrimination faced by some new immigrants to the United States around the turn of the century.

During the 1800s the overwhelming majority of Americans were white and Protestant and had been born in the United States. Many Americans believed that the United States should remain a white, Protestant nation. Nonwhite, non-Protestant, and nonnative residents often faced **discrimination** (dihs • KRIH • muh • NAY • shuhn)—unequal treatment because of their race, religion, ethnic background, or place of birth. The government rarely interfered with this discrimination.

Anti-Semitism Many Jewish immigrants came to the United States to escape prejudice in their homelands. Some of them found the same anti-Semitic attitudes in America. Landlords, employers, and schools discriminated against Jewish immigrants. Eastern European Jews faced prejudice both as Jews and as eastern Europeans, whom many Americans regarded as more foreign than western Europeans.

Anti-Catholicism Catholics also faced discrimination because of their religion. America's largely Protestant population feared that Catholic immigrants threatened the "American" way of life. Anti-Catholic Iowans formed the American Protective Association (APA) in 1887.

MORE ABOUT...

Immigration

Immigration rose during the period of rapid industrialization at the turn of the century. Then, immigration decreased when Congress imposed immigration restrictions. Towards the end of the century, a dramatic increase took place after the restrictions were relaxed.

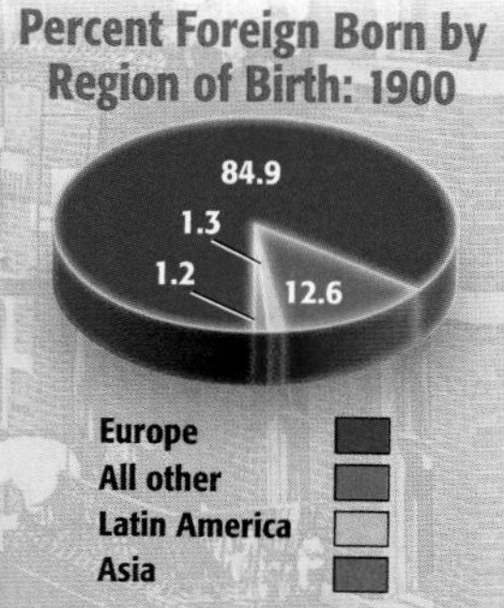

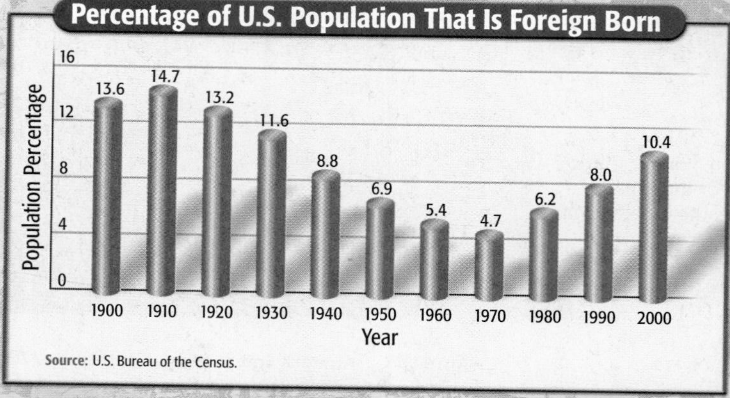

Answers and Additional Support

MORE ABOUT...

Visual Literacy Prejudice against Catholic and Jewish immigrants, as well as other groups such as the Chinese and Japanese, who began to arrive in larger numbers in the late 1800s, led to selective legal restrictions on immigration between 1924 and 1965. The Immigration Act of 1965 eliminated restrictions based on race and ethnicity and set the stage for a new wave of immigration, primarily from Latin America, Asia, and Africa south of the Sahara in the late twentieth century. Have students examine the bar graph. **Ask:** What has been the general trend in the percentage of foreign-born American population between 1900 and 2000? *(The percentage decreased steadily from 1910 through 1970, then began to increase.)* OL CA HI3.

Picturing History

A Ku Klux Klan pamphlet (right) promotes the Klan's hate campaign. Meanwhile, opponents of lynching called for an end to racial murders. ***What two groups experienced the terror of lynching?***

By the mid-1890s, the APA claimed a membership of two million, mostly in the West. Among other activities, the APA spread rumors that Catholics were preparing to take over the country.

What Were Anti-Asian Policies? Discrimination was also based on race. In California and other Western states, Asians struggled against prejudice and resentment. White Americans claimed that Chinese immigrants, who worked for lower wages, took away jobs. Congress passed the Chinese Exclusion Act in 1882 to prevent Chinese immigrants from entering the United States.

America's westward expansion created opportunities for thousands of Japanese immigrants who came to the United States to work as railroad or farm laborers. Like the Chinese who had come before them, Japanese immigrants encountered prejudice. California would not allow them to become citizens. In 1906 in San Francisco, the school board tried to make Japanese children attend a separate school for Asians until President Roosevelt stepped in to prevent such segregation.

Roosevelt yielded to a rising tide of anti-Japanese feeling, however, and authorized the Gentlemen's Agreement with Japan in 1907. This agreement restricted Japanese immigration to the United States, but it did not bring an end to anti-Japanese feeling. In 1913 California made it illegal for Japanese immigrants to buy land. Other Western states passed similar laws.

Discrimination Against African Americans

Four-fifths of the nation's African Americans lived in the South. Most worked as rural sharecroppers or in low-paying jobs in the cities. They were separated from white society in their own neighborhoods, schools, parks, restaurants, theaters, and even cemeteries. In 1896 the Supreme Court legalized segregation in the case of *Plessy* v. *Ferguson,* which recognized "separate but equal" facilities.

The Ku Klux Klan, which had terrorized African Americans during Reconstruction, was reborn in Georgia in 1915. The new Klan wanted to restore white, Protestant America. The Klan lashed out against minorities—Catholics, Jews, and immigrants, as well as African Americans.

R1 Reading Strategy

Identifying the Main Idea and Supporting Details
Ask: What are examples of government policies that discriminated against Asians? *(Chinese Exclusion Act; California did not allow Japanese immigrants to become citizens and attempted to put Asian children in segregated schools; Gentlemen's Agreement)* BL

C1 Critical Thinking

Making Inferences Ask: What actions by President Roosevelt show that he was conflicted about the treatment of Japanese immigrants? *(He stopped the segregation of Japanese children but authorized the Gentlemen's Agreement.)* BL

R2 Reading Strategy

Using Word Parts Tell students to look at the parts of the word *sharecropper*. Explain that sharecroppers worked someone else's land and received a share of their crop in payment. Note that sharecroppers could barely survive on what they made. OL

C2 Critical Thinking

Drawing Conclusions Ask: What practices were legalized by the ***Plessy*** v ***Ferguson*** decision? *(segregation of African Americans into separate neighborhoods, schools, and public facilities)* Why was this decision unjust? *(Once African Americans were separated from whites, it was easy to direct public funds to benefit whites, allowing inferior public services and facilities to exist for African Americans.)* OL
CA HI4.

Did You Know?

The Chinese often called the United States Mei Kwok ("the Beautiful Land") or Gum Shan ("the Land of the Golden Mountains"). Today San Francisco has the largest Chinese population of any North American city.

Picturing History

The revived Klan was most active from 1915 until 1924. By 1925, newspaper reports of Klan activities caused a decline in membership.

Answer: African Americans and Chinese immigrants

C Critical Thinking

Comparing and Contrasting Organize the class into pairs and assign each pair one of the following roles: Progressive reformer, political boss, trade union member, woman Asian immigrant, Catholic immigrant, Jewish immigrant. Ask pairs to present the concerns of their group about civil rights and then debate each other from the point of view of their group. Finally, have the class discuss the merits of the different arguments. OL

R Reading Strategy

Connecting Ask: How is Booker T. Washington's belief that economic power was the way for African Americans to get social equality similar to President Taft's policy of dollar diplomacy? *(Both men believed that economic power was the key to political power.)* OL

Reading Check

Answer: *Plessy* v. *Ferguson*

Answers and Additional Support

US8.12.7 Identify the new sources of large-scale immigration and the contributions of immigrants to the building of cities and the economy; explain the ways in which new social and economic patterns encouraged assimilation of newcomers into the mainstream amidst growing cultural diversity; and discuss the new wave of nativism.

Racial Violence People who lost their jobs during the economic depressions of 1893 and 1907 sometimes unleashed their anger against African Americans and other minorities. More than 2,600 African Americans were lynched between 1886 and 1916, mostly in the South. Lynchings were also used to terrorize Chinese immigrants in the West.

Racial violence also occurred in the North, however. A 1908 riot in Springfield, Illinois, Abraham Lincoln's hometown, shocked the nation. A false accusation by a white woman led to the lynching of two African Americans, and dozens more were injured. No one was ever punished for these violent crimes.

Ida B. Wells, the editor of an African American newspaper in Memphis, Tennessee, was forced to leave town after publishing the names of people involved in a lynching. The incident started Wells on a national crusade to stop lynching. Although Congress rejected an anti-lynching bill, the number of lynchings decreased significantly in the 1900s due in great part to activists such as Wells.

Progressivism and Prejudice In the late 1800s and the early 1900s, many Americans held **biased** views. They believed that white, male, native-born Americans had the right to make decisions for all of society.

Most of the progressive reformers came from the middle and upper classes. They saw themselves as moral leaders working to improve the lives of people less fortunate than themselves. Nevertheless, the reforms they supported often discriminated against one group as they tried to help another group.

Trade unions often prohibited African Americans, women, and immigrants from joining. Skilled laborers, these unions argued, could obtain better working conditions for themselves if they did not demand improved conditions for all workers. In spite of these problems, progressive reforms did succeed in improving conditions for many Americans.

Reading Check **Identify** What Supreme Court decision legalized segregation?

Struggle for Equal Opportunity

Main Idea **Minority groups in the United States sought to end discrimination and gain equal rights.**

Reading Connection Have you ever joined a group that worked toward a common cause? Read to find out how some people formed groups to work to end discrimination.

Booker T. Washington, who founded the Tuskegee Institute, believed that if African Americans gained economic power, they would be in a better position to demand equality. Washington founded the National Negro Business League to promote business development among African Americans. In Washington's autobiography, *Up from Slavery,* he counseled African Americans to work patiently toward equality. Washington argued that equality would be achieved when African Americans gained the education and skills to become valuable members of their community.

Other African Americans had different ideas about attaining equality. W.E.B. Du Bois (doo • BAWIHS), an educator and activist, believed that gaining and using the right to vote would best help African Americans succeed. He helped found the National Association for the Advancement of Colored People (NAACP) in 1909. Some African Americans thought that they would be better off in separate societies, either in the United States or in Africa. They founded organizations to establish African American towns and promoted a back-to-Africa movement. These movements were not popular, however.

During the early 1900s, African Americans achieved success in a variety of professions. Chemist George Washington Carver, director of agricultural research at Tuskegee Institute, helped improve the economy of the South through his discoveries of plant products. Maggie Lena founded the St. Luke Penny Savings Bank in Richmond, Virginia. She was the first American woman to serve as a bank president.

Did You Know?

Ida B. Wells, the editor of an African American newspaper in Memphis, Tennessee, was forced to leave town after publishing the names of people involved in a lynching. The incident started Wells on a national crusade against that practice. In her 1895 book, *A Red Record*, Wells showed that lynching was used primarily against African Americans who had become prosperous or who competed with white businesses. "Can you remain silent and inactive when such things are done in your own community and country?" she wrote.

Biography

US8.12 Students analyze the transformation of the American economy and the changing social and political conditions in the United States in response to the Industrial Revolution.

BOOKER T. WASHINGTON
1856–1915

C

W.E.B. DU BOIS
1868–1963

▲ Booker T. Washington

In the late 1800s and early 1900s, two of the most important African American leaders were Booker T. Washington and W.E.B. Du Bois. Both men had the same goals, but they took different approaches to reaching those goals.

Washington was born into slavery. Later, he attended an industrial school and went on to become a teacher. As a teacher, he developed his own theories about education, which led him to found the Tuskegee Institute.

Washington became an influential leader who advised presidents and governors. He gained support because he was willing—temporarily—to compromise on political rights for African Americans. In return, Washington wanted support for African R American schools, economic gains, and an end to violence against African Americans.

W.E.B. Du Bois, the first African American to receive a doctorate degree from Harvard, refused to accept racial inequality. Du Bois helped start the Niagara Movement in 1905 to fight against racial discrimination and demand full political rights and responsibilities for African Americans. Later, Du Bois joined others to form the National Association for the Advancement of Colored People (NAACP). This group today remains a force in the efforts to gain legal and economic equality for African Americans. Du Bois rejected Washington's emphasis on job skills and argued that the right to vote was the way to end racial inequality, stop lynching, and gain better schools. "The power of the ballot we need in sheer self-defense," he said, "else what shall save us from a second slavery?" S

◀ W.E.B. Du Bois

Then and Now

Why did Washington and Du Bois take the stands they did? Which leaders today have taken stands for equal rights for all?

Then and Now

'ashington and Du Bois had different points of view about the best way to solve the problems cing African Americans. Washington wanted to focus on economic development and Du Bois ı political rights. Accept all reasonable answers about current leaders.

Biography

C Critical Thinking

Comparing and Contrasting Have the class brainstorm reasons to support the positions of both leaders and list them in separate columns on the board. Then discuss whether one approach seems better than the other. Students will probably conclude that the two approaches were not mutually exclusive. OL CA HR5.

S Skill Practice

Analyzing Primary Sources **Ask:** Why does Du Bois think African Americans needed the right to vote for "self-defense"? *(to elect legislators who would protect their civil rights)* Why does he speak of "a second slavery"? *(The rights of African Americans had eroded since Reconstruction and more losses could turn the situation of black Americans into virtual slavery.)* OL CA HR4.

R Reading Strategy

Analyzing Text Structure **Ask:** How is the information in this Biography page organized? *(as a contrast essay that contrasts Washington's views and Du Bois's views)* Explain that this is one of two ways to organize a comparison or contrast essay. In longer essays in which both subjects address the same issues, it is more effective to go issue by issue, showing what both subjects think about each problem. **Ask:** Why would that be more effective in a longer essay? *(makes it easier for the reader to follow)* OL

S Skill Practice

Historical and Social Sciences Analysis Skill

Ask: How did Native Americans deal with the loss of their cultures? *(Some formed the Society of American Indians to improve Native American life and sensitize whites. Others thought Indians should assimilate into white society.)* OL CA HI2.

R1 Reading Strategy

Using Context Clues

Review the meaning of wards. **Ask:** Who is usually under the guardianship of another? *(children)* What relationship did the United States government try to establish with Native Americans? *(parent-child relationship)* How would Native Americans feel about that? *(Students will probably say they would not be very happy.)* OL

R2 Reading Strategy

Understanding Vocabulary

Tell students that *barrio* is the Spanish word for neighborhood. OL

Native Americans Seek Justice The federal government's efforts to assimilate Native Americans into white society threatened to break down traditional native cultures. In 1910–1911 Native American leaders from around the country formed the Society of American Indians to seek justice for Native Americans, to improve their living conditions, and to educate white Americans about different Native American cultures. Some leaders believed that Native Americans should leave the reservations and make their own way in white society.

Primary Sources

George Washington Carver

In his studies in botany and agriculture at the Tuskegee Institute, George Washington Carver made a number of amazing discoveries. He found dozens of new uses for plants such as the peanut and sweet potato. A teacher for nearly 50 years, Carver taught his students, often the children of formerly enslaved people, to conserve land and resources.

> The primary idea in all of my work was to help the farmer and fill the poor man's empty dinner pail. . . . My idea is to help the "man farthest down," this is why I have made every process just as simply as I could to put it within his reach.
>
> —George Washington Carver

DBQ Document-Based Question

What was Carver's purpose in much of his work? How did he do this?

Surprisingly, at the time the Fourteenth Amendment was passed, Native Americans, who were considered **wards,** or persons under the legal guardianship of the U.S. government, were not granted citizenship under the amendment. In 1924 Congress reversed this ruling by granting citizenship to all Native Americans who did not possess it.

Mexican Americans Work Together Immigrants from Mexico had long come to the United States as laborers, especially in the West and Southwest. Like the Japanese and other immigrant groups, Mexican Americans encountered discrimination and violence. Relying on themselves to solve their problems, they formed *mutualistas*—self-defense associations—to raise money for insurance and legal help. One of the first *mutualistas* was the Alianza Hispano Americo (Hispanic American Alliance), formed in Tucson, Arizona, in 1894. In labor camps and Mexican neighborhoods called **barrios** (BAHR•ee•OHS), *mutualistas* worked to end overcrowding, poor sanitation, and inadequate public services.

César Chávez Organizes Mexican Workers From the early 1900s on, some efforts were made to organize farmworkers but with little success. In the 1960s, however, César Chávez (CHAH•vehz), born in 1927, finally began making real headway in organizing the workers in the California vineyards and lettuce fields. In 1962 he organized farmworkers into the organization called the United Farm Workers (UFW) and started a five-year strike against California grape growers to force them to recognize the union. The UFW organized a nationwide boycott of table grapes. Sympathetic priests, civic groups, and students aided Chávez in his efforts. In 1965 he launched a strike that led to a nationwide boycott of produce not bearing the label of the United Farm Workers. In 1970, the strikers finally won, and the strike ended in a pact with the growers. By 1975 Chávez and the strikers had convinced the California legislature to pass a bill that gave farmworkers the same rights held by union members elsewhere.

Answers and Additional Support

Primary Sources

Answer: Carver aimed to help poor people make a living. He made his processes as simple as possible so all could afford to use them.

Did You Know?

Mexican Americans were a mixed group. Some had been settled for generations in areas that became part of the United States after the war with Mexico. Others came after 1909 to find work in the Southwest and California and to escape the turmoil of the Mexican Revolution.

Changes and Challenges By 1914 the United States had changed tremendously. Its population had grown and become more urban than rural. The nation had become industrialized, and people traveled by train, automobile, and even airplane.

While the United States had used its power to establish a limited empire in far-off lands, it had steered clear of Europe's arguments and wars. However, the conflict that was growing in Europe by 1914 would develop into a war that would entangle much of the world. Once the United States became involved, its position in the world would change forever.

Looking to the Future Then, as now, Americans approached the future as a free nation committed to the truths expressed in the Declaration of Independence. The Declaration protects the rights of the American people and states that the purpose of government is to protect these rights:

> **"We hold these truths to be self-evident, that all men are created equal, that they are endowed by their Creator with certain unalienable Rights, that among these are Life, Liberty and the pursuit of Happiness. That to secure these rights, Governments are instituted among Men, deriving their just powers from the consent of the governed . . . ."**

Reading Check **Describe** What were *mutualistas?*

History Online
Study Central Need help understanding the struggle for equal opportunity? Visit ca.hss.glencoe.com and click on Study Central.

Section 5 Review

Reading Summary
Review the Main Ideas
- The United States pursued an increasingly international role, especially in Latin America and the Pacific.
- Discrimination and violence were painful, pressing issues for many groups and often went unaddressed by the federal government.
- Minority groups developed strategies for working together to end racial and social discrimination.

What Did You Learn?
1. What was the significance of the Panama Canal?
2. How did the Supreme Court legalize segregation?

Critical Thinking
3. **Summarizing Information** Re-create the diagram below to describe how different minority groups worked toward equality and change. CA HR3.

	Describe
African Americans	
Native Americans	
Mexican Americans	

4. The Big Ideas Explain the United States's interest in Latin America. CA CS1.
5. **Describe** What was the impact of African Americans who pioneered new means for achieving equality? Write a paragraph that includes references to Booker T. Washington, George Washington Carver, and Maggie Lena. CA 8WS1.1
6. **Linking Past to Present** Summarize the plight of Mexican farmworkers during this period and the impact of César Chávez later in the century. What was the lasting legacy of his work? CA HI3.

ASSESS

Resources for page 783

Use these resources to assess student mastery of section content.

Section Quiz 17–5

Interactive Tutor Self-Assessment CD-ROM

Reading Check
Answer: self-defense associations that raised money for insurance and legal help

History Online
Study Central provides summaries, interactive games, and online graphic organizers to help students review section content.

CLOSE

Summarizing Discuss how specific people and organizations addressed the need for reform. OL

SECTION 5 REVIEW ANSWERS

Review questions reinforce content standard US8.12.

1. connected the Atlantic and Pacific oceans
2. in its ruling *Plessy* v *Ferguson.*
3. Answers should reflect text information.
4. The Big Ideas U.S. had extensive trade with Latin America.
5. Washington pushed for education and business development; Carver pursued agricultural research to help farmers; Lena founded a savings bank.
6. Answers should reflect information in the chapter.

FOCUS

Have different students read aloud the Verbatim quotations and explore how they reflect the themes of business, foreign policy, immigration, and the growth of cities discussed in Chapter 17.

TEACH

R Reading Strategy

Scaffolding—Evaluating Text Ask: What were Booker T. Washington's aims at Tuskegee? *(to use the building of school facilities as a means of teaching the most advanced techniques and methods; to have students give back to the school; to teach students to take pride in their work)* OL

This READING SKILL was introduced in Chapter 13.

C Critical Thinking

Making Inferences Ask: How fast do you think cars traveled? *(not fast if someone could walk in front)* OL

Answers and Additional Support

STEP BACK IN TIME

What—and who—were people talking about? What did they eat? What did they do for fun? These two pages will give you some clues to everyday life in the U.S. as you step back in time with TIME Notebook.

Profile

BOOKER T. WASHINGTON *Teaching industrial training as a means to success, in 1881 Washington founded the Tuskegee Institute in Alabama. Here is an excerpt from his autobiography,* Up From Slavery.

FROM THE VERY BEGINNING, AT TUSKEGEE, I was determined to have the students do not only the agricultural and domestic work, but to have them erect their own buildings. My plan was to have them, while performing this service, taught the latest and best methods of labour, so that the school would not only get the benefit of their efforts, but the R students themselves would be taught to see not only utility in labour, but beauty and dignity. . . . My plan was not to teach them to work in the old way, but to show them how to make the forces of nature—air, water, steam, electricity, horse-power—assist them in their labour.

Booker T. Washington

VERBATIM

WHAT PEOPLE ARE SAYING

"If you pick up a starving dog and make him prosperous, he will not bite you. This is the principal difference between a dog and a man."

MARK TWAIN, *author of* The Adventures of Tom Sawyer

"Speak softly and carry a big stick; you will go far."

PRESIDENT TEDDY ROOSEVELT, *proposing action when asked how the United States will deal with its new far-flung colonies in 1901*

"Give me your tired, your poor, your huddled masses yearning to breathe free."

WORDS BY EMMA LAZARUS, *engraved on the Statue of Liberty in 1903*

"Mountains! Look at them!"

EDWARD CORSI, *10-year-old Italian immigrant on spotting the high-rise buildings in New York City for the first time in 1907*

It's The Law

Two laws were passed in 1902 to deal with the automobile.

1. Tennessee demands all drivers give the public a week's notice before they start any trip.
2. C Vermont states an adult waving a red flag has to walk in front of any moving automobile.

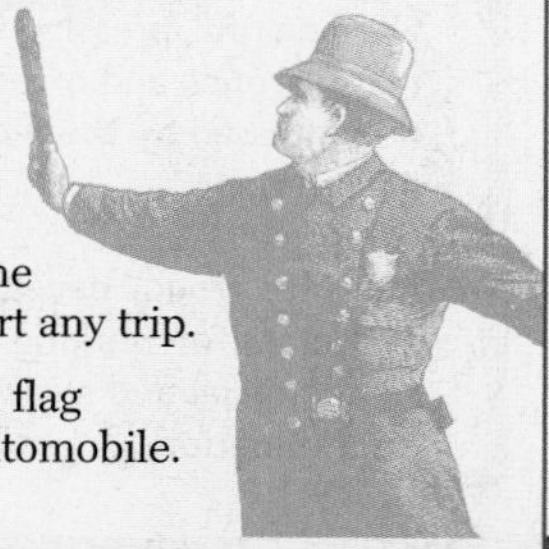

EXTENDING THE CONTENT

The Tuskegee Institute When Booker T. Washington established Tuskegee Institute in 1881, classes met in an old, rented church, and there was little money to pay for teachers or supplies. Within a few weeks, Washington had raised enough to buy an old plantation to house the school. The first students learned skills such as carpentry by building the classrooms and dormitories and learned farming by raising food eaten at the school. As the school's reputation grew, Washington was able to recruit more students and better teachers. Today, the campus of Tuskegee University has about 5,000 acres and more than 70 buildings.

TIME NOTEBOOK

MILESTONES

EVENTS AND PEOPLE OF THE TIME

Annie Oakley

SIGNED UP. Sharpshooter **ANNIE OAKLEY** to Buffalo Bill's Wild West Show in 1885.

FLEW. 19-year-old Cromwell Dixon over the Continental Divide in 1911 in a biplane. At age 14, Dixon was building **DIRIGIBLES** (sausage-shaped balloons), including a model that could be pedaled through the air like a bicycle. Dixon later traveled around the country, flying at state fairs.

AMERICAN SCENE

Average Life Spans in 1900

S

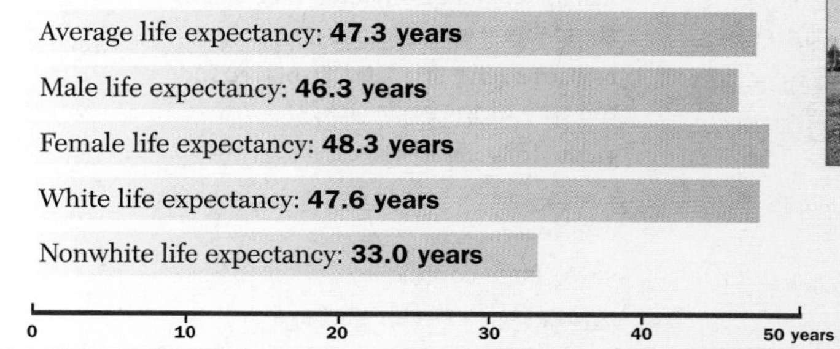

TRANSPORTATION

Take a Ride in My Car!

Here's what one magazine from the early 1900s recommends you carry in your car at all times:

- **1** Efficient tire pump
- **1** Strong two-gallon can extra gasoline
- **1** Sheet fine sandpaper
- **1** Small, short-handled axe
- **1** Ball asbestos cord
- **4** Half-pound cans of meat or fish
- **2** Pounds sweet chocolate

NUMBERS

U.S. AT THE TIME

12¢ Price of a dozen eggs in 1910

$12 Price of a sewing machine in 1900

$12 Lowest price for a steamship ticket from Italy to America in 1905

$12 Average weekly salary (seven-day weeks/12-hour days) for arriving immigrants in 1907

Wright brothers

12 seconds Air time of Wright brothers' first flight in 1903

1.2 million Approximate number of immigrants who entered the U.S. in 1907

395,000 Approximate number of immigrants in 1908 who gave up on America and returned home

50¢ Price of cheapest seat at baseball's first World Series in 1903

785

S Skill Practice

Visual Literacy Ask: What was the difference between the life expectancy of men and women in 1900? *(Women lived two years longer than men.)* What was the difference between white and nonwhite life expectancy compared to the American average? *(Whites lived 0.3 years more than the average; nonwhites lived 14.3 years less than the average.)* Why do you think nonwhite life expectancy was so much lower? *(Students may say that nonwhites were poorer and had less access to healthcare and good nutrition.)* OL

ASSESS

Ask students to write a paragraph characterizing the period. Tell them to draw conclusions based on what they know from studying Chapter 17 and the information in this TIME Notebook and to use the facts on these pages as examples.

CLOSE

Ask students if they expect the life expectancy for Americans today is higher than it was in this period and why. OL

History Online

Visit the TIME Web site at www.time.com for up-to-date news, weekly magazine articles, editorials, online polls, and an archive of past magazine and Web articles.

FOCUS

History–Social Science Standards

The following standards are covered on pages 786–787.

US8.12 Students analyze the transformation of the American economy and the changing social and political conditions in the United States in response to the Industrial Revolution.

R Reading Strategy

Reading Primary Sources
Ask: What problems does Addams identify? *(dirty streets, poor schools, lack of sanitation, poor street lighting, poor paving)* **OL**

U Universal Access

English Learners Ask: What does Addams mean in saying they had to keep "furniture from the clutches of the installment store"? *(They made sure that furniture stores did not reclaim furniture on which people had missed an installment payment.)* **EL**

Answers and Additional Support

Analyzing Primary Sources

US8.12 Students analyze the transformation of the American economy and the changing social and political conditions in the United States in response to the Industrial Revolution.

A Time of Change

The United States changed in the late 1800s and early 1900s. Cities grew as people poured into them, looking for work. In addition, reformers investigated the practices of big business.

Read the passages on pages 786 and 787 and answer the questions that follow.

Jane Addams with immigrant children at Hull House in Chicago ▶

Reader's Dictionary

initiative (ih • NIH • shuh • tiv): the first action in a process

ward: an area of a city

sanitary (SA • nuh • TEHR • ee): having to do with cleanliness

foul (FAUL): very dirty

bewildered (bih • WIHL • duhrd): confused

clutches: strong hold of claws

interpretation (ihn • TUHR • pruh • TAY • shuhn): explanation done in an understandable way

asylums (uh • SY • luhms): places for the care of the poor, sick, and insane

gash: long, deep cut

contagion (kuhn • TAY • juhn): spreading of disease

vats: large containers

refuse (REH • FYOOS): garbage

Hull House

In her book, Twenty Years at Hull-House, *Jane Addams describes the area of the city where Hull House is located.*

The policy of the public authorities of never taking an **initiative,** and always waiting to be urged to do their duty, is obviously fatal in a neighborhood where there is little initiative among the citizens. The idea underlying our self-government breaks down in such a **ward.** The streets are **R** inexpressibly dirty, the number of schools inadequate, **sanitary** legislation unenforced, the street lighting bad, the paving miserable and altogether lacking in the alleys and smaller streets, and the stables **foul** beyond description. Hundreds of houses are unconnected with the street sewer.

Addams also explains how settlement houses help disadvantaged people.

We early found ourselves spending many hours in efforts to secure support for deserted women, insurance for **bewildered** widows, damages for injured operators, furniture from the **clutches** of the installment store. **U** The Settlement is valuable as an information and **interpretation** bureau.

EXTENDING THE CONTENT

Muckracking Novels Upton Sinclair wrote several other muckracking novels. He took on such topics as fad diets, working conditions in coal mines, Henry Ford, and the Teapot Dome scandal. One book was even an exposé of the publishing industry. In a two-volume book, Sinclair explored the Sacco and Vanzetti case. Sinclair ran for state office in California several times as a Socialist and, running as a Democrat, lost the election for governor in that state in 1935.

It constantly acts between the various institutions of the city and the people for whose benefit these institutions were erected. The hospitals, the county agencies, and State **asylums** are often but vague rumors to the people who need them most. Another function of the Settlement to its neighborhood resembles that of the big brother whose mere presence on the playground protects the little one from bullies.

—from *Twenty Years at Hull-House with Autobiographical Notes*

The Jungle

Upton Sinclair writes about the meatpacking industry in his novel The Jungle.

R [Mikolas] is a beef-boner, and that is a dangerous trade, especially when you are on piecework and trying to earn a bride. Your hands are slippery, and your knife is slippery, C and you are toiling like mad, when somebody happens to speak to you, or you strike a bone. Then your hand slips up on the blade, and there is a fearful **gash**. And that would not be so bad, only for the deadly **contagion.** The cut may heal, but you never can tell. Twice now; within the last three years, Mikolas has been lying at home with blood poisoning—once for three months and once for nearly seven. The last time, too, he lost his job, and that meant six weeks more of standing at the doors of the packing houses, at six o'clock on bitter winter mornings.

One character, Antanas, has a new job. He must mop up the chemicals used on the meat.

[T]he beef had lain in **vats** full of chemicals, and men with great forks speared it out and dumped it into trucks, to be taken to the cooking room. When they had speared out all they could reach, they emptied the vat on the floor, and then with shovels scraped up the balance and dumped it into the truck. This floor was filthy, yet they set Antanas with his mop slopping the "pickle" into a hole that connected with a sink, where it was caught and used over again forever; and if that were not enough, there was a trap [bend] in the pipe, where all the scraps of meat and odds and ends of **refuse** were caught, and every few days it was the old man's task to clean these out, and shovel their contents into one of the trucks with the rest of the meat!

—from *The Jungle*

◀ A famous muckraking book

DBQ Document-Based Questions

Hull House

1. Why was the area around Hull House in such bad condition?
2. What did Addams mean by comparing the settlement house to a "big brother"?

The Jungle

3. Write three adjectives that describe the working conditions of Mikolas and Antanas.
4. How would you feel about eating meat that comes from a company like the one where Antanas is working? Why?

Read to Write

5. In these writings, Addams reports on social conditions and Sinclair reports on working conditions. Do you think these works were intended to inform or spark reform, or both? How do you think readers responded to these writings? How do you think government officials responded? CA HR3.

R Reading Strategy

Monitoring Ask: What does Sinclair mean by the phrase "trying to earn a bride"? *(Answers may include earning enough money to get married.)* OL CA HR4

C Critical Thinking

Analyzing Primary Sources Why does Sinclair write "you" and "your" in this passage instead of referring to Mikolas? What is the effect? *(to put the reader in the position of the worker; the reader feels more outrage)* OL CA 8RL3.6

ASSESS

Have students answer the Document-Based Questions.

CLOSE

Identifying Central Issues
Have students suggest steps they would take if they were legislators in the Progressive era and had read these accounts. OL

DBQ Document-Based Questions

1. Neither local government officials nor the people took any initiative to do anything.
2. The Settlement protected the people of the neighborhood.
3. Adjectives might include words like dangerous, disgusting, grueling.
4. Students are likely to express no interest in eating such meat because of the unhealthful conditions in the plant.
5. Students are likely to say that both writers aimed to spur reform and that the work is so dramatic that government officials were likely to act.

CHAPTER 17 Assessment

Resources for pages 788–789

Use these resources to review, assess, or reteach the chapter.

- Active Reading Note-Taking Guide, Chapter 17
- Chapter 17 Reading Essentials and Study Guide
- Chapter 17 Tests, Forms A and B
- Standards Assessment, Forms A and B
- California Standards Practice Workbook
- Succeeding on the California History-Social Science Standards CD-ROM
- MindJogger Videoquiz
- Interactive Tutor Self-Assessment CD-ROM

Review Content Vocabulary

1. Paragraphs will vary but should reflect how the vocabulary words are related.

Review the Main Ideas

4. finding work
5. to stop immigration
6. development of cable cars, trolley cars, paved streets, and bridges
7. substandard apartment buildings in the slums, or poor neighborhoods.
8. state colleges funded by the sale of land the federal government had given to the states
9. Thomas Edison
10. rewarding political supporters with jobs and favors, also known as patronage
11. proposed the U.S. Forest Service; pressured Congress to create national forests and wildlife sanctuaries; and formed the National Conservation Commission
12. purchased Alaska; annexed Hawaii; gained Guam and the Philippines from Spain after the Spanish-American War
13. Whites rioted after a white woman falsely accused two African Americans. The two were lynched and dozens more were injured.

Critical Thinking

14. because they spoke languages other than English, had different customs, were not Protestant, or were of a different race; minority groups formed organizations, took legal action, taught whites about their culture and created businesses
15. Taft wanted to use American investment abroad as a way of influencing politics in other countries. Wilson wanted U.S. foreign

Chapter 17 Assessment

Standard US8.12

Review Content Vocabulary

For each of the pairs of terms below, write a sentence or short paragraph showing how the two are related.

1. emigrate, ethnic groups
2. slum, settlement house
3. trust, oligopoly

Review the Main Ideas

Section 1 • The New Immigrants

4. What was an immigrant's greatest challenge upon arriving in the United States?
5. What was the goal of the nativist movement?

Section 2 • Moving to the City

6. What were some important advances in transportation?
7. What were tenements and slums?

Section 3 • A Changing Culture

8. What was a land-grant college?
9. Who invented moving pictures?

Section 4 • The Progressive Movement

10. What was the spoils system?
11. What did President Roosevelt do to protect the environment?

Section 5 • A Changing Nation

12. How did the United States expand its territorial interests in the Pacific?
13. What was the Springfield riot of 1908?

Critical Thinking

14. **Explain** Why were minority groups discriminated against during this period? How did these groups respond? CA HI2.
15. **Compare and Contrast** How did Presidents Taft and Wilson differ in their views on international relations? CA HR3.
16. **Cause and Effect** Re-create the diagram below. Describe three ways newcomers to America tried to preserve their culture. CA HI2.

Preserving cultural heritage → ( ) ( ) ( )

17. **Analyze** Why did leisure time develop for some Americans? How did that affect American culture? CA HI3.

Geography Skills

Study the map below and answer the following questions. CA CS3.

NATIONAL GEOGRAPHIC **The Panama Canal**

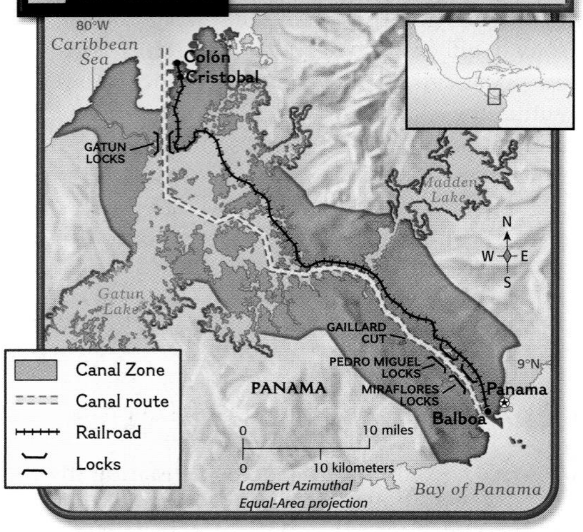

18. **Location** What bodies of water are shown on the map of the Panama Canal?
19. **Movement** Besides the canal, what other form of transportation is shown here?

History Online
Self-Check Quiz Visit ca.hss.glencoe.com to prepare for the Chapter 17 test.

Read to Write

20. **The Big Ideas** **Describe** Write an essay that describes the challenges that urban life posed around the turn of the century. Identify and describe efforts made by reformers to improve the quality of life of poor city dwellers. CA 8WS1.1

21. **Using Your FOLDABLES** Use the information you listed in your foldable to create a brief study guide for the chapter. For each section, your study guide should include at least five questions that focus on the main ideas. CA 8RC2.0

Using Academic Vocabulary

A suffix is a syllable placed after a base word to form a new word. For example, *-less* means "without." *Hopeless* means "without hope." Other suffixes are *-al*, *-able*, *-ary*, *-ion*, and *-ism*. For each of the academic vocabulary words, add a suffix to create a new word.

22. inspect
23. isolate
24. process

Linking Past and Present

25. **Organizing Information** Search the Internet to find three groups that work to protect the environment or our national parks. Write an essay that describes each group's efforts and connects their work to President Roosevelt's passion for the outdoors. CA HI3.

Building Citizenship

26. **Working for Equality** With a partner check your local newspaper and magazines to identify instances of discrimination in your community. Together, generate a list of ideas that you think would help eliminate the prejudice and inequality that you read about. CA HI3.

Reviewing Skills

27. **Review READING SKILL** **Visual Literacy** Choose two photographs from this chapter and write an essay describing the significance of those images in illustrating the content of the chapter. CA 8RC2.0 CA 8LS1.9

28. **Review ANALYSIS SKILL** **Economic Performance** Contrast Roosevelt's "Square Deal" with laissez-faire policy. Identify the economic benefits and weaknesses in both approaches to government regulation of business. CA HI6.

Standards Practice

Read the passage below and answer the following question.

> Between 1860 and 1900 American urban areas grew twice as fast as the total population. Chicago, which in the 1830s had been a frontier town with a few hundred residents, became a vast metropolis. New York became the second-largest city in the world. During the same span of years, the populations of Boston, Baltimore, and Philadelphia also grew rapidly.

29 **The main idea of the passage is best expressed as:**

A New York City grew rapidly.
B Only cities in the northeastern United States grew rapidly.
C The population of urban America grew at a very fast rate during this era.
D Rural growth continued, but not as quickly as urban growth.

CHAPTER 17 Assessment

21. Using Your FOLDABLES Study guides should include questions that focus on the main ideas of each section.

Using Academic Vocabulary

22. inspection
23. isolation
24. processor

Linking Past and Present

25. Essays will vary but should connect the organization to Roosevelt's interests.

Building Citizenship

26. Examples of discrimination and sources will vary.

Reviewing Skills

27. Review READING SKILL Answers will vary but should explain how the photographs relate to chapter content.

28. Review ANALYSIS SKILL Answers will vary but should discuss the benefits and weaknesses of both policies.

Standards Practice

29. C

Bonus Question

Ask: Who were the two most influential African American leaders of the late 1800s and early 1900s? *(Booker T. Washington and W.E.B. Du Bois)* OL

policy to be guided by moral principles.

16. Any three: established houses of worship, newspapers in native languages, stores that sold traditional products, theaters, social organizations
17. Professional and industrial jobs in cities gave people some regular time off work. Many people had time to read, go to the theater, and watch and participate in sports.

Geography Skills

18. Caribbean Sea, Gatun Lake, Madden Lake, Bay of Panama
19. railroads

Read to Write

20. The Big Ideas Answers will vary but should reflect text information.

History Online

Have students visit the Web site at ca.hss.glencoe.com to review Chapter 17 and take the Self-Check Quiz.

FOCUS

Reviewing Unit Objectives

Having studied this unit, students should be able to

- Describe the impact of railroads on settlement and on economic growth.
- Explain how businesses changed and grew and why some had great power.
- Discuss the impact of immigration in this period and the efforts made to help immigrants adapt to American culture and to keep some groups from entering the country.
- Describe the groups that moved to settle areas in the West and the impact of those movements on the land and people already there.
- Identify ways that cities changed, the problems that arose from these changes, and attempts to fix those problems.
- Explain how the United States took a greater role in the world.

TEACH

Have students brainstorm words that they think describe this period in American history. OL

Unit Review Activity

To help students review the unit objectives, have them explain how each of the following developments is an example of "reshaping the nation": westward expansion, industrialization, labor movements, immigration, urbanization, and Progressivism. OL

Unit 6 REVIEW

Reshaping the Nation

After the Civil War, the United States experienced many changes. The frontier ceased to exist. The United States became an industrial nation with overseas possessions. Immigrants poured into the country. Progressives worked to reform government and control big business.

	Chapter 15: The Western Frontier	Chapter 16: The Growth of Industry	Chapter 17: America Enters a New Century
When	• 1858–1896	• 1865–1914	• 1865–1920
Where	• Abilene and Dodge City, Kansas • Cheyenne, Wyoming • Pikes Peak • Virginia City, Nevada • Promontory Summit, Utah • Great Plains • Oklahoma • Dakota Territory • Arizona	• Menlo Park, New Jersey • Detroit, Michigan • Titusville, Pennsylvania • Cleveland, Ohio • Pittsburgh, Pennsylvania • Chicago, Illinois • Homestead, Pennsylvania	• New York City (Ellis Island) • San Francisco (Angel Island) • Chicago, Illinois • Kansas City, Kansas • Pittsburgh, Pennsylvania • Hawaii • Latin America • Philippine Islands

Cattle branding iron

Panama Canal brochure

END-OF-UNIT RESOURCES

Use these resources to review and assess unit material.

- Step Into American History Activities
- Cumulative Assessment Activities
- Reading Essentials and Study Guide
- California Standards Practice Workbook
- Interactive Tutor Self-Assessment CD-ROM
- Exam*View*® Pro Testmaker CD-ROM
- Succeeding on the California History–Social Science Standards CD-ROM

	Chapter 15: The Western Frontier	Chapter 16: The Growth of Industry	Chapter 17: America Enters a New Century
Major Events	• **1859** Silver discovered in Nevada • **1860s–mid-1880s** Cattle Kingdom • **1862** Homestead Act • **1867** Reservation policy • **1869** Transcontinental railroad completed • **1876** Battle of the Little Bighorn • **1889** Oklahoma Land Rush • **1890** Populist Party • **1890** Frontier no longer exists • **1890** Wounded Knee	• **1869** Knights of Labor • **1870s** Steel mills open in Ohio and Pennsylvania • **1870** Standard Oil Company • **1876** Telephone • **1879** Electric lightbulb • **1880s** Railroads adopt standard gauge track • **1881** AFL forms • **1890** Sherman Antitrust Act • **1892** Homestead Strike • **1908** Model T Ford	• **Late 1800s** Realist themes in art and literature • **1882** Chinese Exclusion Act • **1884** First skyscraper • **1887** Interstate Commerce Act • **1896** *Plessy* v. *Ferguson* • **1898** Spanish-American War • **1907** 1.3 million immigrants arrive in America • **1910** Half of Americans live in cities • **1914** Panama Canal completed • **1920** Women gain right to vote
Some Important People	• Henry Comstock • Crazy Horse • Sitting Bull • George Custer • Geronimo • Helen Hunt Jackson • Grover Cleveland • William Jennings Bryan • William McKinley	• Cornelius Vanderbilt • Leland Stanford • Alexander Graham Bell • Thomas Edison • Henry Ford • John D. Rockefeller • Andrew Carnegie • Samuel Gompers	• Jane Addams • Booker T. Washington • Joseph Pulitzer • Jacob Riis • Eugene V. Debs • Ida Tarbell • Upton Sinclair • Robert La Follette • Theodore Roosevelt • César Chávez
How do these events and ideas affect our lives today?	• The settling of the Plains led to America's position as a major agricultural producer.	• America's inventors and industrialists helped make the country the economic power that it is today.	• The muckrakers began a long tradition of investigative journalism in America.
What was happening in California at this time?	• **1872** Modoc War is last armed resistance by California's Native Americans	• **1861** First transcontinental telegraph line is completed	• **1870** *Ward* v. *Flood* keeps African Americans out of white schools

Sioux Buffalo Shield ▶

Andrew Carnegie ▶

◀ *Book on ranching*

Unit 6 Review

ASSESS/CLOSE

Unit Wrap-Up Activity

Free-Form Mapping With free-form mapping, students create their own text representations.

1. Organize students into groups of four. Each group should have markers and a large sheet of paper. Group members must decide on the important ideas in the unit and organize a way of presenting those ideas on paper in words, pictures, and diagrams.
2. Explain to students that there is no one correct way to map the unit. The only criterion is to represent main ideas and their interrelationships. Encourage students to use words, pictures, phrases, circles, squares, or whatever creative endeavor they feel best portrays their analysis of the unit content.
3. Have each group share its map with the class and discuss the ideas found on them. OL

PROFESSIONAL DEVELOPMENT: DESIGNING WEBQUESTS

Use these resources for help developing webquests.

- Brooks, D. W., D.E. Nolan, and S.M. Gallagher. *Web-Teaching: A Guide to Designing Interactive Teaching for the World Wide Web* (Second Edition). Kluwer Academic/Plenum Publishers, 2001.
- Callison, Daniel. *Key Words, Concepts, and Methods for Information Age Instruction: A Guide to Teaching Information Inquiry.* LMS Associates (2003).
- Dodge, Bernie. "FOCUS: Five Rules for Writing a Great WebQuest." *Learning & Leading with Technology,* 28(8) (2001).
- Starr, Linda. "Creating a WebQuest: It's Easier Than You Think," *Education World* (2003).

FOCUS

Have students suggest events that they have read about that affect Americans' lives today. Have volunteers mention the event and outline its impact. Write their suggestions on the board. After students have identified five or six key events, poll the class to determine which they think is most important.

More About the Photo

The telephone was an invention of the late 1800s. Within little more than two decades, the country had more than one million phone lines. The cell phone, invented in the late 1900s, spread far more rapidly. In little more than one decade, more than 75 million Americans subscribed to a cell phone service.

ASSESS

The Big Ideas

As you begin teaching this section, use these questions and activities to focus on the Big Ideas.

A Changing Nation in a Changing World

Ask: What major international conflicts have taken place in your lifetime? How have they affected Americans' lives? *(Students may mention September 11, 2001, and the war on terrorism.)* After students discuss the issue, explain that they will learn about some of the major conflicts of the twentieth century and the changes that resulted from them. OL

Connections to Today

Why It's Important

As you studied this text, you learned about how our nation's government, economy, and society first developed and began to change. In **Connections to Today,** *you will read about how those past changes affect your life today. By learning how things were, you will better understand how things are.*

As you read **Connections to Today,** *think about:*

- How have things changed over time?
- Why did these changes occur?
- As a citizen in a democracy, how can I influence events?
- How can I participate in public life?

Major Events: 1900 to the Present

	1900	1915	1930	1945
U.S. Events		1917 U.S. enters World War I; 1920 Women win right to vote	1929 Stock market crash triggers Great Depression	1941 U.S. enters World War II
California Events	1906 San Francisco earthquake	1914 Construction of Hetch Hetchy Dam begins	1932 Unemployment reaches 28 percent; 1937 Golden Gate Bridge completed	
World Events	1910 Mexican Revolution	1914 World War I begins	1939 World War II begins in Europe	1948 Berlin Airlift

792 Connections to Today

A Changing Society

Ask: What groups had full political rights when the nation was formed? *(Students should recall that generally only white male property owners could vote when the United States began.)* What groups have those rights today? *(Citizens over 18 from any group all have voting rights.)* OL

The Big Ideas

A Changing Nation in a Changing World *Page 794*

The nation's history has been shaped by significant individuals, groups, ideas, events, eras, and developments. Throughout the twentieth century and into the twenty-first century, one theme remained constant—change. Breakthroughs in science and technology have been as much a part of life as conflict and political and social change.

A Changing Society *Page 798*

Reactions to social injustice can lead to reform movements. In the past, discrimination caused most ethnic and racial groups to lag behind the white majority in jobs, income, and education. Read to find out what advances were made in the twentieth and twenty-first centuries.

New Roles, New Faces *Page 806*

The free-enterprise economy of the United States is consistent with the nation's history of rights and freedoms. Economic changes have eliminated certain kinds of jobs and created others. As jobs in all fields become more high tech and demanding, workers need to be better prepared and better educated.

Rights and Responsibilities *Page 812*

Citizen participation is essential to the foundation and preservation of the U.S. political system. When the founders, in the Declaration of Independence, stated that all people are created equal and all have the right to life, liberty, and the pursuit of happiness, they were stating the ideals of the American dream.

1960 | 1975 | 1990 | 2005

- **1955** Salk develops polio vaccine
- **1961** Berlin Wall built
- **1962** César Chávez organizes National Farm Workers
- **1965** U.S. combat troops arrive in Vietnam
- **1974** President Nixon resigns
- **1984** 23rd Olympics held in Los Angeles
- **1991** Soviet Union collapses
- **1993** European Union launched
- **1998** President Clinton impeached
- **2001** Terrorist attacks destroy World Trade Center and damage Pentagon
- **2003** Arnold Schwarzenegger elected governor
- **2003** Saddam Hussein overthrown in Iraq

Connections to Today

New Roles, New Faces

Ask: What economic changes took place in the 1800s? *(Students should recall that in this period, manufacturing became a much more important part of the economy.)* Explain that in this section, they will learn about how the economy changed in the 1900s. **OL**

Rights and Responsibilities

Ask: What do you think are the most important responsibilities that American citizens have? *(Answers may include such duties as voting, taking part in political processes, paying taxes, serving on juries, or defending the country.)* Explain that in this section, students will learn about how people and groups exercised their rights and responsibilities as American citizens. **OL**

History Online

Go to ca.hss.glencoe.com for student activities, lesson plans, and links to additional Web resources about the 1900s and early 2000s.

Connections to Today

FOCUS

Ask: What does the phrase "Turning Points" mean? *(momentous events that bring about deep and profound change)* What "turning points" in American history have you read about up until this point? *(Answers may include the European age of exploration, the American Revolution, the Louisiana Purchase, the Civil War, Reconstruction, and others.)* OL

TEACH

R Reading Strategy

Analyzing Text Structure Explain that in this section, each subsection begins with a summary outlining the major trends that will be described. **Ask:** What can you expect to read in the text that follows? *(The text will fill in details about these broad trends.)* OL

C Critical Thinking

Drawing Conclusions **Ask:** In what ways was World War I a "turning point"? *(It changed the way of life in Europe forever; empires collapsed; new nations emerged; it marked the end of a long era of peace.)* OL

Answers and Additional Support

A Changing Nation in a Changing World

▼ World War I recruitment poster

▲ The automobile became a vital part of American lives in the 1920s.

Turning Points, 1914–1950

R *From 1914 to 1950, the United States played a major role in shaping world affairs. The world plunged into two world wars in which the United States took part. After World War II, the democratic United States and the communist Soviet Union competed for influence in the world.*

"The War to End All Wars"

C In 1914 tensions in Europe sparked a world war. It was known as the Great War, the "war to end all wars," and later World War I. The conflict involved more nations, used more technological weapons, and resulted in more deaths than any previous war. The United States entered the war in 1917 and helped Britain and France defeat Germany and its allies. The war led to the collapse of empires and the rise of new nations.

From Boom to Bust

After World War I, Americans were tired of war and world responsibilities. They turned inward to look after their own affairs. People called the 1920s the Jazz Age—partly because of jazz, but also because of the restlessness and carefree mood of the time. The U.S. economy grew, and many Americans prospered. However, the strong economy faltered. By the end of the 1920s, thousands of Americans were jobless, and many farmers had lost their land. The Great Depression, triggered by the Stock Market Crash of 1929, endangered the nation's economic system. It soon spread throughout the rest of the industrialized world.

Around the World and at Home, 1900–1950

1900 — 1910 — 1920

- **1904** Russo-Japanese War
- **1910** Mexican Revolution begins
- **1914** World War I begins
- **1920** Women win right to vote

More Skill Practice

Visual Literacy Have students look at the poster titled "Spirit of 1917." **Ask:** What major world event does this poster relate to? *(Students should connect the title to the year the U.S. entered World War I.)* Why was it probably created? *(Students should infer that it is a recruiting poster.)* OL CA 8LS1.9

Did You Know?

The unemployment rate hit an all-time high in 1933 when 24.9 percent of nonfarm workers were without jobs—essentially a quarter of the workforce. Just 11 years later, manpower needs in World War II dropped the rate to 1.2 percent.

A Global Struggle

The worldwide depression aided the rise of dictatorships in Europe and Japan. These governments aggressively sought to expand their territories. World War II began when Germany invaded Poland. Britain and France responded by declaring war on Germany. In 1941 the Soviet Union joined the conflict when Germany invaded its territory. The United States entered the war later that year after Japan bombed the U.S. naval base at Pearl Harbor, Hawaii.

World War II, the most destructive war in history, resulted in the deaths of more than 40 million people. More than half of them were civilians, including about 6 million Jews and many others in the Holocaust.

At the end of the war, the United States emerged as one of the strongest nations in the world and the sole possessor of a powerful weapon—the atomic bomb.

Democracy Versus Communism

The democratic United States and the communist Soviet Union emerged from World War II as the two most powerful nations, struggling for world leadership. This rivalry became known as the Cold War because, although great tensions divided them, the two countries did not actually go to war with each other. Each side tried to gain allies and prove that its system of government—democracy or communism—was better than the other.

The Cold War turned "hot," however, when Communist North Korean soldiers invaded South Korea. United Nations troops led by the United States became involved in the conflict. The Communist Chinese came to the aid of their North Korean ally. The two sides finally agreed to stop fighting. They accepted an armistice line that divided Korea along the existing battlefront.

▲ The attack on Pearl Harbor drew the United States into World War II.

Review

1. What factors made World Wars I and II different from earlier wars?
2. Why were the 1920s called the Jazz Age? What happened to the U.S. economy at the end of this period?
3. Who was at odds during the Cold War?

1930 — 1940 — 1950

- **1929** Stock market crashes, triggering Great Depression
- **1939** World War II begins in Europe
- **1945** Germany and Japan surrender; World War II ends
- **1950** North Korea invades South Korea

Connections to Today

S Skill Practice

Historical and Social Sciences Analysis Skill
Ask: How would you describe a dictator? *(Students may say that a dictator is a leader who has absolute power and who does not let people have much freedom.)* OL CA HI3.

W Writing Support

Research Reports Writing Have students research and report on one aspect of World War II as it relates to the United States, such as the attack on Pearl Harbor; the mobilization of the country's effort; the Holocaust; the decision to use the atomic bomb; or key battles. OL CA 8WA2.3

U Universal Access

English Learners Explain that in the phrase "Cold War" and "turned 'hot,'" the words about temperature are being used figuratively and not literally. **Ask:** If the two countries did not actually fight, why was the rivalry called a war? *(Students may say that the word signals how bitter their relations were.)* OL

Review Answers

1. Students might mention the worldwide scope of both wars and the use of technology that made them both so destructive.
2. because of the restlessness and carefree mood of the time; the Great Depression began, leading to widespread job loss
3. the democratic United States and the communist Soviet Union

Connections to Today

U Universal Access

Logical/Mathematical Have students explain what 250-percent growth means. *(Students should explain that for every dollar of output in 1945, the economy produced $250 in 1960.)* OL

C Critical Thinking

Making Inferences Ask: What impact do you think the building boom in the suburbs would have on the nation's cities? *(Students may infer that the cities would lose population, as people moved to the suburbs, and that their housing would get older, since most new construction was outside the cities.)* OL CA HI2.

R Reading Strategy

Activating Prior Knowledge Have students give examples of cases they have read about earlier in the textbook in which groups were denied their rights. *(Students might mention slavery or the failure of the government to ensure African Americans' rights after the Civil War; harsh treatment of Native Americans; and other examples.)* OL

A Changing Nation in a Changing World

▼ After World War II, more Americans owned cars and homes than ever before.

▲ More than 200,000 people joined the March on Washington in August 1963 to call for civil rights legislation.

Modern America, 1950 to the Present

From the 1950s to the 1980s, the United States struggled with communism abroad and advanced civil rights at home. Americans prospered, and American culture spread around the globe. In the early 1990s, the Soviet Union collapsed, bringing the Cold War to an end. Meanwhile, new technologies and a changing population transformed America in new ways. Entering the new century, Americans responded to the global spread of terrorism by looking for fresh ways to preserve and protect their ideals in a changing world.

America in the 1950s

After years of "going without" during the Great Depression and World War II, Americans hungered for new cars, electronics, appliances, and gadgets. During the 1950s, the American economy began to grow rapidly and steadily. Between 1945 and 1960, the total value of goods and services produced in the United States increased about 250 percent. During the 1950s, 85 percent of new home construction took place in the suburbs—neighborhoods developed just outside of a city.

The Struggle for Civil Rights

In the 1950s, a tide of protest began to rise in America against deeply rooted attitudes of racism and discrimination. This campaign for equality gained momentum in the 1960s. African Americans, women, Hispanic Americans, and Native Americans became more active in seeking equal rights. Leaders such as Martin Luther King, Jr., and César Chávez developed peaceful methods of protest to realize this goal. Although the civil rights movement could not overcome all the obstacles that stood in the way of full equality, it achieved some stunning successes.

Around the World and at Home, 1950–Present

1950 — 1960 — 1970

- **1954** Polio vaccine given to school children
- **1963** March on Washington rallies support for civil rights
- **1973** U.S. ends involvement in Vietnam

Answers and Additional Support

More Skill Practice

Historical and Social Sciences Analysis Skill Ask: What major industry helped spur the economy in the late 1800s? Why? *(railroads; because growth of railroads created demand for the output of other industries)* Point out that the auto industry had a similar effect on the country in the 1900s. OL

Search for Stability

S R The Vietnam conflict—an effort to defeat communism in Southeast Asia—left scars on America. More than 58,000 U.S. troops died in Vietnam, and thousands more were wounded. The people of Southeast Asia also paid a price for war in Vietnam. Two million Vietnamese and uncounted Cambodians and Laotians were killed. Their villages and towns lay in ruins.

Dramatic change marked the period of the 1960s and 1970s. Faith in government was shaken by presidential scandal. Yet the American system of constitutional government worked and survived. The nation had responsibilities as a world power, faced conflict with the communist world, and carried out ventures in outer space. All of these tasks demanded that the nation learn new ways of carrying out its role in the world. Still, Americans tried to adjust to changes in ways that would assure the future of their democracy.

The attacks of September 11, 2001, shocked Americans, but also united them.

Toward a New Century

The 1980s and 1990s saw the dawn of a new era. With the collapse of communism in Europe, the Cold War came to an end. Relations between East and West changed dramatically. Meanwhile, after centuries of conflict, European nations began to unite economically and politically in the European Union. Worldwide pressure led to the end of apartheid—government-sponsored segregation—and the rise of a multiracial democratic government in South Africa.

At home, new advances in technology, medicine, and industry transformed the American economy. As the United States entered a new century, new challenges emerged. The terrorist attacks on New York City and Washington, D.C. began a new war against global terrorism, as well as renewed commitment to supporting freedom, equality, and democracy in America and abroad. C

Review

1. Why did the United States fight a war in Vietnam?
2. What event changed East-West relations beginning in the late 1980s?
3. What new challenge did the United States and the world face at the beginning of the new century?

1980	1990	2000

- **1989** Communism crumbles in Eastern Europe
- **1990** Allies launch Operation Desert Storm in Iraq
- **2001** Terrorists attack New York City and Washington, D.C.
- **2003** U.S. invades Iraq

S Skill Practice

Visual Literacy Have students conduct research to find the number of American casualties in each war in the nation's history and create a graph displaying their findings. OL CA 8LS1.9

R Reading Strategy

Activating Prior Knowledge **Ask:** What part of the United States suffered similar devastation in a war? *(the South in the Civil War)* OL

C Critical Thinking

Identifying Central Issues Ask students to explain why terrorism is a problem and have them suggest steps the nation should take to reduce the threat of terrorism. OL

ASSESS/CLOSE

Assign students the Review questions at the bottom of the page. Then have them write a brief paragraph stating which "turning point" that took place from 1950 to the present was the most important and explain why. OL

Review Answers

1. in an effort to defeat communism in Southeast Asia
2. collapse of communism, which led to end of the Cold War
3. terrorism

Connections to Today

FOCUS

Have students examine the time line at the bottom of these two pages. **Ask:** What kinds of issues do you think this section will discuss? *(Students may say food and drug safety, labor issues, health issues such as alcohol, women's rights, and economic issues.)* OL

TEACH

R Reading Strategy

Organizing Information Suggest that students take notes on this material and subsequent pages by creating a three-column chart with the headings *Problem*, *Reform*, and *Result*. BL

C Critical Thinking

Comparing and Contrasting Ask students to think back to their study of the late 1800s and early 1900s and identify other ways in which that period was different from today. Have volunteers offer their ideas. Then have a class discussion on the similarities between that period and modern times. OL CA HI3.

Answers and Additional Support

A Changing Society

▲ Young boys working in a Georgia mill, early 1900s

The Beginnings of Reform

The spirit of reform gained strength in the late 1800s and thrived during the early 1900s. The reformers were confident in their ability to improve government and the quality of life.

Problems in American Society

At the beginning of the 1900s, the United States was a different country than it is today. The vision described in the Declaration of Independence—that all are created equal and possess certain unalienable rights—remained a dream for many Americans. Women could not vote. Laws in many parts of the country enforced racial segregation. People with disabilities were often unable to enjoy the same range of opportunities as other people. Government did little to protect citizens from dangerous medicines, contaminated food, and unfair business practices. There was little concern that our country's air, water, and natural areas were at risk of being polluted or destroyed.

Equal Rights and Reform, 1900–1950

1900 · 1910 · 1920

- **1906** Pure Food and Drug Act passed
- **1916** Keating-Owen Child Labor Act passed
- **1919** Eighteenth Amendment prohibits alcohol
- **1920** Women vote in national election for the first time

More Skill Practice

Visual Literacy Have students examine the photograph. **Ask:** Does this work look safe or dangerous? Why? *(Students will probably say that the children seem to be in a dangerous position because they are standing on top of the machines. They could fall or have their clothes tangled in the equipment and get hurt.)* OL

▲ Women march for suffrage in New York City in 1920.

Progressive Reforms

Early in the century, reformers known as Progressives gained influence in local, state, and national government. Progressives believed that government should take a more active role in improving people's lives and solving society's problems.

Some Progressives took aim at political corruption, urban poverty, child labor, or questionable business practices. Others wanted to reform government itself to make it more able to deal with the nation's challenges. Still others wanted to ban the sale and consumption of alcohol. A quarter-century of Progressive reforms left their mark on the nation. As a result, Americans began to look to the government to protect their interests.

Review

1. What impact did Progressive policies have on how Americans perceived their government?
2. Explain the effect of Progressive reforms on the lives of Americans.
3. What reforms would you like to see enacted today? What could you do to make that possible?

1930 — 1940 — 1950

- **1929** Great Depression begins
- **1935** Social Security Act adopted
- **1938** Fair Labor Standards Act passed
- **1944** GI Bill enacted

C Critical Thinking

Drawing Conclusions Have students examine the photograph. **Ask:** Based on this photograph, what other country do you think had women campaign for the right to vote? Why do you say so? *(England; because the second sign from the right talks about a leader of English suffragettes)* OL

S Skill Practice

Historical and Social Sciences Analysis Skill
Ask: What philosophy of government views its role differently than Progressives did? *(laissez-faire)* OL CA HI3.

W Writing Support

Persuasive Writing Tell students to take the role of a citizen in the early 1900s. Point out that while Progressives wanted to expand the role of government, others disagreed, believing that government should not interfere with business by passing safety or labor laws. Have students choose which position they agree with and write a letter to the editor of a newspaper explaining how a larger role for government does or does not fit into the framework of the U.S. Constitution. OL CA 8WA2.5

Review Answers

1. Due to the work of Progressives, Americans began to look to the government to protect their interests.
2. Progressives worked for change in politics, poverty, child labor, and business practices, among other areas.
3. Students' answers will vary but should include steps that can be taken to fix the problem.

S Skill Practice

Historical and Social Sciences Analysis Skill

Ask: Which amendment aimed to grant equal rights to African Americans? *(Fourteenth)* OL

W Writing Support

Research Reports Writing

Organize students into groups and have each group choose a civil rights organization, such as the NAACP or the Urban League. Have the groups conduct research into the organization, focusing on three areas: why and how it was founded; its important achievements; and its goals and strategies today. The groups should report their findings to the class. OL CA 8SA2.3

C Critical Thinking

Predicting Consequences

Ask: How would African American soldiers who fought for the nation in war feel when returning home and facing segregation? *(Students should note that they would probably feel frustrated and angry.)* Why? *(because they put their lives on the line for a country that denied them their rights)* OL

Answers and Additional Support

The Struggle for Equal Rights

Reformers addressed a number of issues in the 1900s, and some of the most difficult struggles were those faced by African Americans and other ethnic groups. Their battles for equal rights led to major changes in American society.

▲ Separate drinking facilities for African Americans and whites

African Americans Face Discrimination

S Although amendments to the Constitution guaranteed rights to all Americans, African American and other groups still did not enjoy civil rights, or the rights of full citizenship and equality under the law. In the early 1900s, African Americans routinely faced discrimination. Laws in the South limited their right to vote. Laws in many parts of the nation barred African Americans from attending the same schools as white students. African Americans had to ride in the back of buses, sit in separate sections of restaurants and theaters, and stay in separate hotels. The social separation of races was known as segregation.

W African Americans began to campaign actively for civil rights in the 1900s. In 1909 a group of African Americans and whites founded the National Association for the Advancement of Colored People (NAACP). That group sought to end discrimination through legal means. C After African Americans fought with American forces in both world wars, the call for equal rights grew even stronger. A major victory in the struggle for civil rights occurred in 1948 when President Harry S. Truman issued an executive order that ended racial segregation in the armed forces.

The Equal Rights Movement, 1900–1970

1900 — 1910 — 1920 — 1930

- **1909** NAACP formed
- **1917** African Americans serve as officers during World War I
- **1930s** President Roosevelt appoints 45 African Americans to serve in New Deal agencies

Did You Know?

Segregation was not practiced exclusively in the South. Northern states and cities had laws creating separate facilities for African Americans and whites.

The Civil Rights Era

The landmark 1954 Supreme Court decision *Brown* v. *Board of Education* ruled that segregated schools were unconstitutional. Schools began to desegregate, but the move faced great opposition in some parts of the country. A year later, a young minister led a successful boycott of the segregated Montgomery, Alabama, bus system. His name was Martin Luther King, Jr., and he would become the nation's most important civil rights leader. African Americans and whites protested against segregated facilities in restaurants, at bus and train stations, and in other areas. In many parts of the country, especially the South, the protesters were met with anger and violence.

Voter Registration Before and After the Voting Rights Act

- 7% of African American adults registered to vote in Mississippi in 1964 before passage of the Voting Rights Act of 1965
- 67% of African American adults in Mississippi registered to vote in 1969
- 70% of white adults registered to vote nationwide in 1964
- 90% of white adults registered to vote nationwide in 1969

Source: TIME.

◀ Forcing civil rights protesters to stop their marches, 1963

The Federal Government Takes a Role

Over time, more and more Americans grew sympathetic to the demands for equal rights. The federal government became an ally, passing and enforcing important new laws. These included the Civil Rights Act of 1964 and the Voting Rights Act of 1965. Presidents John F. Kennedy and Lyndon Johnson expressed sympathy for expanding and safeguarding civil rights.

Review

1. How did President Truman demonstrate important leadership for the movement for equality for all people?
2. Who would become the nation's most important civil rights leader?

1940 — 1950 — 1960 — 1970

- **1948** President Truman orders desegregation of U.S. military
- **1954** *Brown* v. *Board of Education*
- **1964** Civil Rights Act passed
- **1965** Voting Rights Act passed

C Critical Thinking

Drawing Conclusions Have students study the chart. **Ask:** Would you say that the Voting Rights Act was a success? Why or why not? *(Students are likely to say that it was a success because the percentage of registered voters—among both African Americans and whites—increased after the law was passed.)* OL

S Skill Practice

Historical and Social Sciences Analysis Skill Ask students to create a presentation on the civil rights movement of the 1950s and 1960s, highlighting its achievements. Students' presentations could take the form of a time line, a collage, or a computerized slide presentation. Ask students to share their presentations with the class. OL

W Writing Support

Research Reports Writing Have students research and report on the events leading to the passage of either the Civil Rights Act of 1964 or the Voting Rights Act of 1965. Students should present their findings in a written report. AL

Review Answers

1. by ending racial discrimination in the armed forces
2. Martin Luther King, Jr.

C1 Critical Thinking

Analyzing Information
Ask: As a group, how do Hispanic Americans differ from African Americans? *(They have different cultural backgrounds because they originally came from different countries.)* OL
CA 8WA2.3

S Skill Practice

Visual Literacy **Ask:** What happened at Wounded Knee in 1890? *(Army troops fired on Native Americans, killing nearly 200 men, women, and children.)* Why would Native Americans fighting for their rights in the 1970s remember that event? *(Students may suggest they would remember it as a symbol of the injustice done to Native Americans over the years.)* OL CA HI3.

C2 Critical Thinking

Comparing and Contrasting Have students conduct research to compare the way African American groups, like the NAACP, have used the courts to gain civil rights and how Native Americans have done so. Students should report their findings in a brief essay. OL CA 8WA2.3

Answers and Additional Support

A Changing Society

▲ The American Indian Movement protested civil rights violations.

Other Civil Rights Challenges

African Americans were not the only group in American society to face discrimination and inequality. Hispanics, Native Americans, and others also had to struggle to gain equal rights in the 1900s.

Hispanic Americans Seek Equal Rights

Other groups soon followed African Americans in demanding equal rights. The nation's Hispanic population grew rapidly during the 1960s. Including people of Mexican, Puerto Rican, Cuban, and other backgrounds, Hispanics often faced discrimination and had to cope with limited access to housing, education, and employment.

Many Mexican Americans, the largest Hispanic group, worked on large farms in western states. These farmworkers earned little pay and received few benefits. In the mid-1960s, César Chávez and Dolores Huerta successfully organized the United Farm Workers union in California to fight for better working conditions. Another group, La Raza Unida, organized voters in the Southwest and West.

Native Americans Struggle

Like other groups in the 1950s and 1960s, Native Americans suffered from discrimination in housing, employment, and health care. They, too, began to organize to combat racism and rebuild cultural identity. The American Indian Movement (AIM) led protests, which sometimes turned violent. Working through the federal courts, Native Americans won decisions that helped them establish their economic independence.

Ethnic Groups and Equal Rights

1960 — 1970

- **1963** March on Washington for Equal Rights
- **1966** United Farm Workers formed by César Chávez and Dolores Huerta
- **1970** *La Raza Unida* formed by Jose Angel Gutierrez

More Skill Practice

Using Geography Skills Have students conduct research using the most recent census to find the percentage of Hispanic Americans in each state. Students should create a map of the United States showing their findings. Suggest that they identify population ranges that can be grouped together, such as under 5 percent, 5.1–10 percent, and so on. AL

A More Aggressive Approach

W Most civil rights protesters followed the nonviolent teachings of Martin Luther King, Jr., and other leaders. Others, however, felt that violent opposition should be met with more aggressive methods. Leaders like Malcolm X and Stokely Carmichael endorsed an idea called Black Power, through which African Americans would build economic, political, and cultural strength. Frustration with the slow pace of improvement led to deadly riots in black neighborhoods of some large cities.

Entering a New Century

By the year 2000, America's ethnic and racial groups had achieved some remarkable successes. African Americans, Hispanics, and Asian Americans held thousands of elected offices throughout the nation. Business and educational leadership grew more diverse as well.

As the 2000s began, the United States had an increasingly diverse population. Hispanic Americans became the fastest growing ethnic group in the country, growing from 22.4 million in 1990 to 35.3 million in 2000. Increased immigration from Latin America, Asia, and Africa also had an impact on the country's population. For the first time since the early 1930s, one out of every ten Americans was foreign-born.

C America has become increasingly appreciative of its multicultural heritage and respectful of diversity. Yet economic, social, and political challenges remain, and much still needs to be done.

Population of the United States by Race and Hispanic/Latino Origin

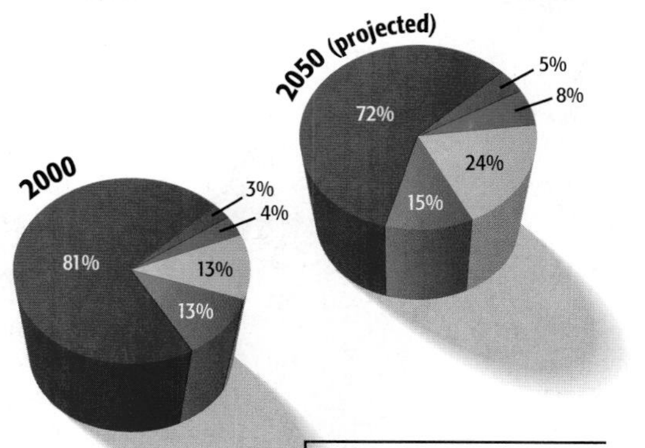

- White
- Black
- Hispanic (may be of any race)
- Asian
- All Others (Native American, Alaskan Native, Hawaiian, Pacific Islander)

Source: *U.S. Census Bureau, Census 2000 Brief*, March 2001, and National Population Estimates.

Review

1. What did Chávez and Huerta do to aid Hispanic farmworkers?
2. How did the methods of Malcolm X and Stokely Carmichael differ from those of Martin Luther King, Jr.?
3. What challenges to civil rights still exist today? What could you do to make a difference?

1980 — 1990 — 2000

1974 Congressional act makes bilingual education available to Hispanic youth

1990 Antonia C. Novello becomes the first female and first Hispanic Surgeon General of the United States

2004 National Museum of the American Indian opens in Washington, D.C.

W Writing Support

Narrative Writing Have students research and report on the life of one of the leaders discussed here. OL CA 8WA2.1

C Critical Thinking

Identifying Central Issues Discuss with students the issues of diversity and tolerance. **Ask:** How is diversity a benefit to the nation? How does tolerance promote diversity? What can individual Americans do to promote tolerance? OL

S Skill Practice

Reading a Time Line Have students use this and the other time lines in the section "A Changing Society" to create time lines focused on the history of one of four minority groups—African Americans, Hispanic Americans, Native Americans, or women. Students should add illustrations and other events to their time lines and present them to the class. OL CA CS2.

Review Answers

1. organized the United Farm Workers union in California to fight for better working conditions
2. They thought the violent opposition to the civil rights movement should be answered with more aggressive methods.
3. Students' answers will vary but should include ideas about how they can contribute to solving the problems they identify.

R Reading Strategy

Activating Prior Knowledge **Ask:** With what other group did participation in war efforts lead to a push for equality? *(African Americans)* OL

C Critical Thinking

Determining Cause and Effect **Ask:** How would access ramps make getting into buildings easier for some people? *(easier for people in wheelchairs to go up or down stairs)* How does closed captioning of television programs help some people? *(helps those with hearing difficulty)* OL

S Skill Practice

Reading a Time Line Direct students' attention to the time line. **Ask:** Which entry reflects growing religious diversity in the United States? Why? *(the 1916 entry; because a mosque is a Muslim house of worship)* OL

Answers and Additional Support

A Changing Society

Jeannette Rankin (above) was the first woman elected to the U.S. Congress (1917). In 2004 Kathleen Blanco (right) became the first woman governor of Louisiana.

▲ Demonstrators urging equal access for people with disabilities

Into the Mainstream

The 1900s saw important advances in the status of women and people with disabilities. Another significant movement, with roots in the Progressive era, was environmentalism. As multiculturalism became more valued, religious distinctions were increasingly respected as well.

Women: Second-Class Citizens No More

Women pursued equal rights long before the 1900s. Early pioneers like Susan B. Anthony, Elizabeth Cady Stanton, and Lucretia Mott demanded suffrage, or voting rights. Women finally gained the right to vote in 1920, when the Nineteenth Amendment to the U.S. Constitution was approved. R During the world wars, many women went to work outside the home. They began to demand the same rights and treatment as men. In the 1960s, women pressed for better educational opportunities, workplace equality and flexibility, and easier access to health care under the leadership of groups like the National Organization for Women (NOW). An Equal Rights Amendment (ERA) passed in both houses of Congress in 1972 but was never ratified by enough states to become law.

Gaining Access for All Americans

Like women, people with disabilities often could not fully participate in American life. In 1990 the Americans with Disabilities Act (ADA) outlawed discrimination against people with physical or mental disabilities. Access ramps were added to buildings, and closed-caption TV programs became common. C

S Protecting All Americans, 1890–Present

1890 — 1905 — 1920 — 1935

- **1890** Women have right to vote in Wyoming
- **1905** U.S. Forest Service created
- **1916** Mosque established in Detroit, Michigan
- **1920** Women gain right to vote nationally

Did You Know?

Jeannette Rankin was a devoted pacifist. In 1917, she joined 48 other members of Congress to vote against the declaration of war that placed the United States in World War I. After nearly two decades of absence from the House, she was re-elected to Congress in 1940 on the basis of her campaign to keep the United States out of the war. The next year, she was the only member of Congress to vote against the declaration of war against Japan. She cast that vote knowing that it would probably cost her re-election.

Rise of Environmentalism

Activists in the 1960s and 1970s turned their attention to another challenge: protecting the earth's resources. Environmentalism was not new. Leaders such as Theodore Roosevelt and John Muir had warned Americans of the need to protect natural places. Groups like the Sierra Club (founded in 1892) and the U.S. Forest Service (created in 1905) worked to protect natural areas. A landmark 1962 book by Rachel Carson, *Silent Spring*, sounded an alarm about pesticides that grew into the environmental movement. Soon, the federal government, through its new Environmental Protection Agency (EPA) and laws like the Wilderness, Clean Air, and Endangered Species Acts, took on the responsibility of safeguarding the environment.

Religious Diversity

One of the founding ideals of the United States was religious tolerance. As more people immigrated to the United States, the variety of religious beliefs also grew. Today, almost every religion has followers in the United States. In the period following the terrorist attacks on New York and Washington, D.C. in 2001, Americans wanted to show their respect for all religious faiths. This marked a time of great national unity and mutual tolerance. Annually, the president recognizes January 16 as Religious Freedom Day to commemorate the passage of the 1786 Virginia Statute for Religious Freedom, written by Thomas Jefferson.

Religious Membership in the United States*

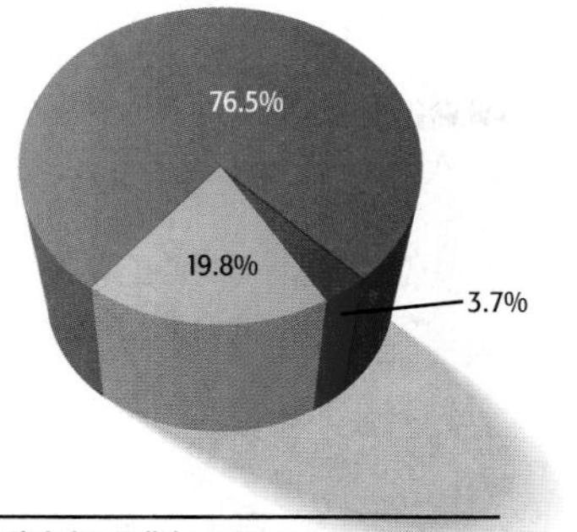

● Christian Religious Groups– more than 159 million, including:	
Catholic	50.9 million
Baptist	33.8 million
Methodist/Wesleyan	14.2 million
Lutheran	9.6 million
Presbyterian	5.6 million
Pentecostal/Charismatic	4.4 million
Episcopalian/Anglican	3.5 million
● Other Religious Groups– more than 7.7 million, including:	
Jewish	2.8 million
Muslim/Islamic	1.1 million
Buddhist	1.0 million
● Other/No religion specified	

* Based on adult population

Source: *American Religious Identification Survey,* 2001; The Graduate Center of the City University of New York.

Review

1. What did the Americans With Disabilities Act accomplish?
2. What government agency was created to protect the environment?
3. What can you do to safeguard religious liberty?

1950 · 1965 · 1980 · 1995

1962 *Silent Spring* published by Rachel Carson

1970 Environmental Protection Agency formed

1981 Sandra Day O'Connor is first woman appointed to U.S. Supreme Court

C Critical Thinking

Comparing and Contrasting Ask: How did the early environmental movement of the Sierra Club and the Forest Service differ from the movement of the 1960s and 1970s? *(The early movement focused on preserving natural areas. The later movement aimed to clean up pollution.)* OL

W Writing Support

Summary Writing Have students investigate one of the laws mentioned here and write a brief report summarizing the reason it was passed, the chief provisions of the law, and the effect the law has had. AL

CA 8WA2.3

S Skill Practice

Historical and Social Sciences Analysis Skill
Ask: Why do Americans enjoy freedom of religion? *(It is guaranteed in the First Amendment to the Constitution.)* OL CA HI3.

ASSESS/CLOSE

Assign students the Review questions at the bottom of the page. Then have them write a summary of the changes that have affected American society since 1900. OL

Review Answers

1. outlawed discrimination against people with physical or mental disabilities
2. Environmental Protection Agency
3. Students' answers will vary but should reflect contributions that individuals can make.

Connections to Today

FOCUS

Ask: How would you describe the American economy today? *(Students might say it is very diverse, with many different industries.)* OL

TEACH

S Skill Practice

Historical and Social Sciences Analysis Skill

Ask: Which part of the economy is being compared in the sentence about the United States, Britain, and Germany? *(only manufacturing)* What part of the economy is being compared in the sentence about the United States and China? *(the entire economies)* OL

R Reading Strategy

Activating Prior Knowledge Have students explain how the assembly line helped mass production. *(by dividing a complex manufacturing process into several distinct steps)* OL

New Roles, New Faces

Poverty in the United States: Total Number and Rate

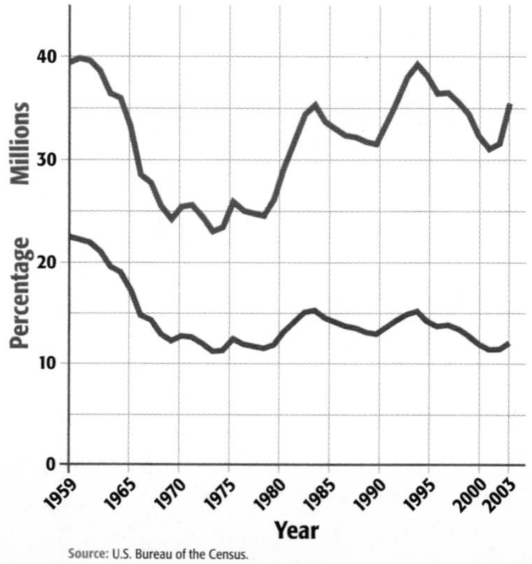

Source: U.S. Bureau of the Census.

Economic Growth

S *Manufacturing in the United States increased greatly in the late 1800s. During this period, the American economy changed from one that was primarily agricultural to one based on industry. The country's economy continued to grow tremendously in the 1900s.*

An Industrial Powerhouse

Around the beginning of the 1900s, the United States surpassed Great Britain and Germany to become the world's leading industrial nation. By the end of the century, the U.S. economy had expanded so much that it was almost twice as large as the world's second largest, China's.

Mass production was the key to the growth of America's industrial might. This form of large-scale manufacturing increased supply and lowered costs to consumers. Thanks to Henry Ford's assembly line, automobiles became affordable for millions of consumers. His ideas were quickly put into place in other industries. R

Depression and War

The production of consumer goods; heavy manufacturing; and processing of natural resources such as coal, iron, and oil grew at a rapid pace in the early 1900s. However, the Great Depression of the 1930s handcuffed the U.S. economy for a decade. Industrial production and agriculture fell steeply. Then in the early 1940s, manufacturing rebounded to supply the military during World War II.

An Expanding and Changing Economy, 1900–Present

1900 — 1915 — 1930 — 1945

- **1908** Ford's Model T is sold to the public
- **1912** Department of Labor created
- **1929** Stock market crash triggers Great Depression
- **1938** Fair Labor Standards Act passed
- **1941** U.S. enters World War II; economic growth surges

Answers and Additional Support

More About the Photo

The top photograph, taken by Dorothea Lange, is one of the most famous photos of the Great Depression. Lange was trained as a teacher but became interested in photography and had her own studio by the time she was 23. In 1935, the state of California hired her to take pictures of migrant workers. This picture was part of a series of pictures she took from 1935 to 1939 for the Farm Security Administration, many of which focused on the suffering of Dust Bowl families.

High-Tech Revolution R

The 1950s and 1960s saw continued growth in the U.S. economy. In the 1970s, the nation faced economic roadblocks, such as high inflation, unemployment, and increased energy costs. By the 1980s, a new element had emerged to recharge America's economy—technology. Centered in California, the technology revolution transformed the infrastructure of business. Advances in computers, communications, and other high-tech fields led the U.S. economy—and society—into the next century. C

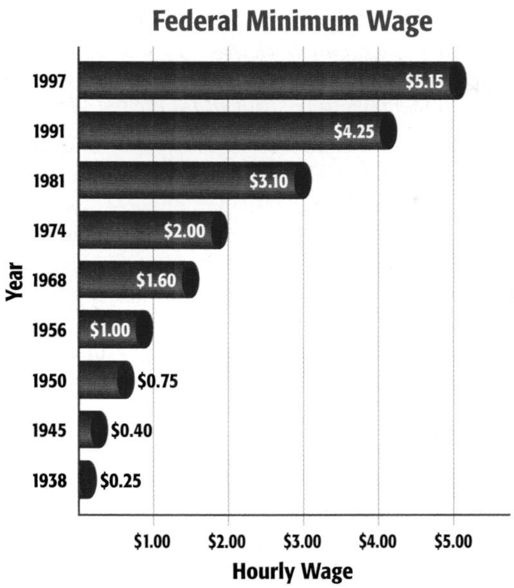

Source: http://usgovinfo.about.com/library/blminwage.htm

S

The Income Gap Remains

Not all Americans have benefited from the expanding economy. Although the middle class has grown over the century, millions of people remain in poverty. The federal poverty level in 2003 was set at an income of $18,810 for a family of four. One in eight Americans, or 12.5 percent, lived at or below the poverty level. (See graph on page 806.) African Americans and children were more likely than others to be living in poverty.

One way the federal government has chosen to deal with poverty is the minimum wage. Since 1938, the government has required employers to pay a minimum hourly wage. (See graph above.) Today, younger workers may be paid less than minimum wage for their first 90 days on the job.

◀ During the Great Depression, many Americans could not find work.

Review

1. What was the technology revolution?
2. About how many Americans live at or below the federal poverty level?
3. Why has American industry changed so much over the past century?

1960	1975	1990	2005

- **1970s** Oil embargo and inflation hurt U.S. economy
- **1975** First personal computers are sold
- **1994** NAFTA creates huge free trade zone

Connections to Today

R Reading Strategy

Using Context Clues Ask: What is meant by the term *high-tech?* *(Industries that use advanced technologies, such as computers and communications.)* OL

C Critical Thinking

Drawing Conclusions Ask: Why is the change to high-tech industries called a revolution? *(Students should note that these industries radically changed how business was done.)* What other revolutions related to the nation's economy can you identify? *(the Industrial Revolution of the 1800s)* OL

S Skill Practice

Visual Literacy Have students study the graph. **Ask:** What does the graph show? *(the minimum wage at different years)* Why are only certain years shown? *(Students might infer that the years shown are the years that the minimum wage changed.)* In which year did the minimum wage go up the most? By how much did it rise? *(1991; by $1.15)* OL

Review Answers

1. a movement that transformed the infrastructure of business
2. about 35 million in 2003
3. Students may say the economy changed as technology changed.

C1 Critical Thinking

Comparing and Contrasting **Ask:** How would working in a factory differ from working on a farm? *(Answers might include indoor work rather than outdoor work; being less affected by weather; working in the midst of more noise and harsher conditions; working with more people.)* OL

U Universal Access

English Learners Explain that the phrases *blue collar* and *white collar* stem from the workers' traditional clothing. Factory workers often wore blue work shirts; male office workers wore white shirts and ties. OL

C2 Critical Thinking

Analyzing Information Challenge students to give examples of service jobs. *(Answers might include teachers, sales clerks, restaurant workers, police officers and firefighters, and so on.)* OL

Answers and Additional Support

New Roles, New Faces

Changing Nature of Work

As the American economy changed, so did the way the people of the United States worked. In the 1900s, the types of jobs held by most workers shifted from jobs that created goods to positions that offered services.

Moving to the Cities

At the beginning of the 1900s, many people were still moving from farms to the rapidly growing cities. Improved farm machinery made it possible to grow more crops using fewer workers. The higher wages paid in the cities also attracted workers. Many of those moving to the cities found work in newly opened factories. These workers became known as blue collar workers. Others found jobs in offices, schools, stores, and other nonfactory settings and were called white collar workers. By 1920 more than half of all Americans lived in towns or cities.

The Service Economy

Another significant change that took place during the twentieth century was the shift from manufacturing jobs to service industry jobs. Service jobs are those that provide services to people and businesses. They include banking and insurance, communications, retail sales, health care, education, and government. Today, most of the total economic activity of California and much of the United States is made up of this type of business.

▼ America's workforce is diverse with jobs in many different fields.

Changing Nature of Work, 1900–Present

1900 | 1915 | 1930 | 1945

- **1907** Henry Ford pioneers assembly line production
- **1929** Thousands lose their jobs in the Great Depression
- **1940** 40-hour work-week set

Did You Know?

The number of farms dropped only slightly in the first half of the 1900s from 5.7 million in 1900 to 5.4 million in 1950. By 1997, though, the nation had only 1.9 million farms—but farms were much more productive than in earlier years.

Number of Employees in Selected Professions, 1910 and 2002

R

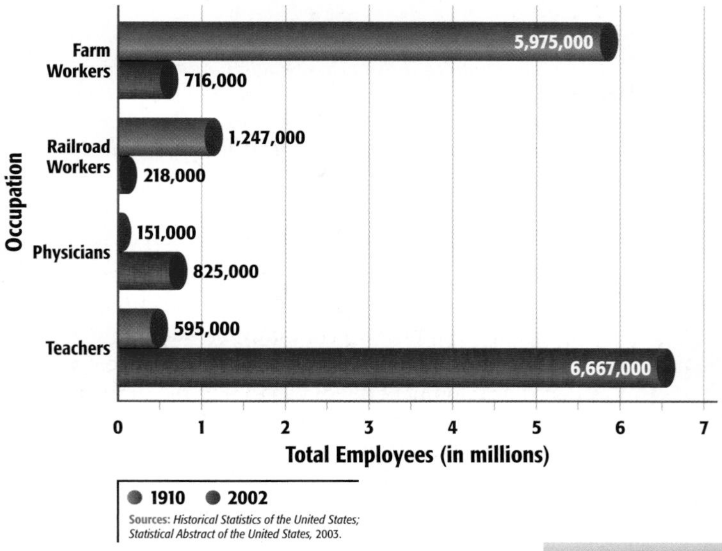

▼ World War II created opportunities for women.

S1

Women Enter the Work Force

During the last century, many women entered the full-time workforce during economic boom times and especially during the two world wars. Often, these women would have to give up their jobs in order to make room for men needing work. Beginning in the 1960s, the women's liberation movement created a broader understanding of women's roles in the workplace. Many more women entered the working world, and they began to rise into positions that had not been possible before. Still, women generally earn less than men in the same profession. Today women are free to pursue their dreams in education, career, and family in ways that would have been hard to imagine in the past. W

Review

1. What is the difference between jobs in manufacturing and in the service industry?
2. Why did so many people leave farming as a way of life?

S2

1960 — 1975 — 1990 — 2005

- **1956** White-collar workers outnumber blue-collar workers for the first time
- **1970** About 86 million people are in the U.S. workforce
- **1999** About 140 million people are in the U.S. workforce
- **2003** Women make up about 47% of the workforce

Connections to Today

R Reading Strategy

Reading Maps, Graphs, and Charts **Ask:** Which two professions were the most important in 1910? *(farm and railroad workers)* Which were most important in 2002? *(physicians and teachers)* What trends does this graph illustrate? *(the shifts away from farm and industrial work to service work)* OL

W Writing Support

Expository Writing Have students take the role of a woman transferred from the early 1900s to today. Ask them to write a story or essay describing the changes that the woman would see in women's lives and what she would think of those changes. OL CA HI3.

S1 Skill Practice

Visual Literacy **Ask:** What does the phrase "We can't win without them" mean? *(Women's work is vital to the war effort.)* OL CA 8LS1.9

S2 Skill Practice

Reading a Time Line **Ask:** What is significant about the entry for 1956? *(It shows the year that the service part of the economy became larger, at least in terms of the workforce, than the manufacturing sector)* OL

Review Answers

1. Manufacturing jobs are in factories, where workers make things. Service jobs include those in banking and insurance, communications, retail sales, healthcare, education, and government.
2. Improved farm machinery made it possible to grow more crops using fewer workers.

Connections to Today

R Reading Strategy

Scaffolding—Identifying the Main Idea and Supporting Details **Ask:** What details on this page support the idea that high school enrollment increased since 1900? *(Students should point to the graph showing a dramatic rise in the percentage of 14 to 17 year olds enrolled in high school. They may cite the figure of 53 million students, but that figure does not specify high school students and there is no comparison figure for 1900 to prove that the number is higher.)* OL

This READING SKILL was introduced in Chapter 2.

W Writing Support

Persuasive Writing Have students write an essay explaining how learning geography, history, or science will help prepare today's students for their roles as workers and citizens. OL CA 8WA2.5

C Critical Thinking

Predicting Consequences Discuss with students how they think computers will change education in the future. OL

Answers and Additional Support

New Roles, New Faces

Changes in Education

The changes in American society and the economy also led to changes in education in the United States. Americans realized that success in an increasingly industrial and technological society required a higher level of education for all citizens.

Increases in School Enrollment

By 1900, the United States achieved the goal of providing public elementary education to all children. At that time, however, only a small number of teenagers went on to high school or college. One major development in education was the dramatic rise in high school and college enrollment. Today, about 53 million students are enrolled in the nation's public and private schools. Another 15.3 million attend colleges and universities. R

High School Enrollment

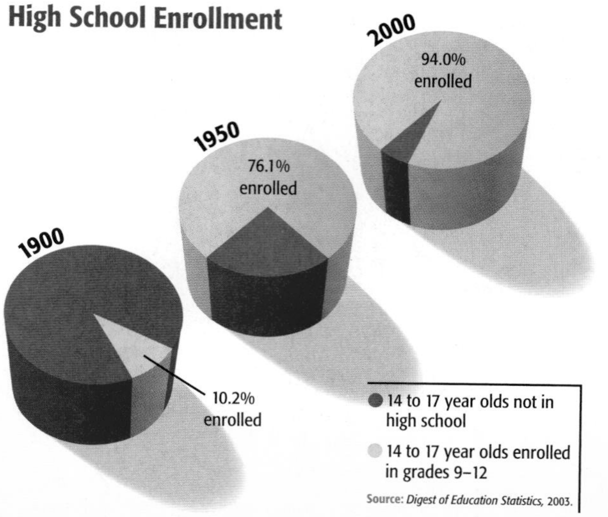

Source: *Digest of Education Statistics*, 2003.

Changes in the Classroom

The early 1900s brought far-reaching changes to public school education in the United States. Most students studied only reading, writing, and arithmetic. In the 1900s, schools became less formal and emphasized a well-rounded education that was able to meet the needs of individual children. Subjects were broadened to include geography, history, and science. W

By 2000, technological advances promised more breakthroughs in education. Computers were increasingly common in schools. Technology made it possible for students to have access to more information than ever before. Students became empowered to learn on their own as well as in the classroom. C

Changing Nature of Education, 1900–Present

1900 | 1915 | 1930 | 1945

1900 16.9 million children in U.S. public and private schools

1917 Smith-Hughes Act passed, providing federal funds for high school vocational education

More Skill Practice

Visual Literacy Have students compare the two classrooms shown. **Ask:** How are they similar? How are they different? *(Similarities—both include teacher, students, and board; Differences—more formal dress in older picture; fewer students for the teacher in the more recent picture)* OL

Education and Government

Public education in the United States has historically been the responsibility of state and local governments. The federal government has expanded its role in education since the mid-1900s. It worked to ensure that every state provides equal educational opportunities for all citizens. In the mid-1950s, the U.S. Supreme Court ruled that public schools segregated by race were "inherently unequal" and ordered desegregation of schools. This ruling led to other measures to ensure equal educational opportunities for women, people with disabilities, and people who do not speak English.

Government has provided large amounts of money for education. This trend started after World War II, when Congress began granting funds to armed forces veterans to attend colleges and other schools. In the 1960s, Congress began passing laws to aid local schools and to improve the education of children from low-income families.

Since the 1980s, government leaders have worked to raise educational standards. In 2001 the No Child Left Behind Act introduced new federal requirements for student testing and measures for holding schools accountable for student progress.

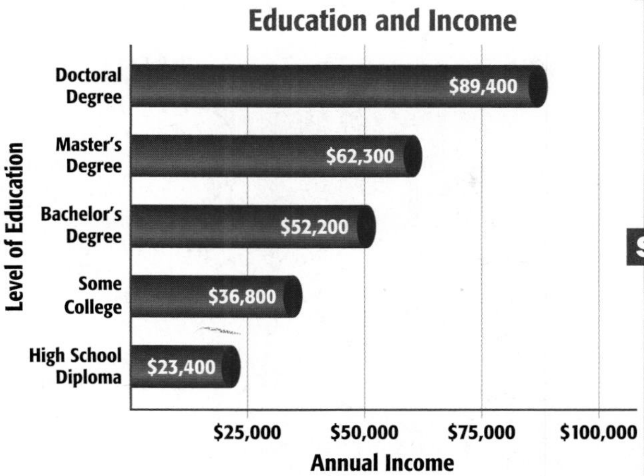

Source: National Center for Education Statistics.

Education and Income

As more Americans enrolled in schools during the twentieth century, education became a powerful social and economic force. Most Americans now expect schools to provide children with skills, values, and behaviors that will help them become responsible and productive citizens. Statistics show that people with a higher level of education make more money than those with less education.

Review

1. How did the classes taught in schools change in the 1900s?
2. How has the federal government increased its role in education?
3. Do you think the educational system prepares a person well for a role in society today? Explain.

1960 — 1975 — 1990 — 2005

- **1954** U.S. Supreme Court declares segregated schools unconstitutional
- **1979** Congress establishes the U.S. Department of Education
- **2001** No Child Left Behind Act passes

R Reading Strategy

Activating Prior Knowledge **Ask:** What movement saw other advances in people's rights, along with the end to segregated schools? *(civil rights movement)* OL

S Skill Practice

Visual Literacy Have students examine the graph. **Ask:** What level of education generates an income twice the amount of that earned by someone with a high school diploma? *(bachelor's degree)* OL

C Critical Thinking

Drawing Conclusions **Ask:** How can people benefit by increasing their education? *(People with more education tend to make more money.)* OL

ASSESS/CLOSE

Assign students the Review questions at the bottom of the page. Then have them explain how technological changes have impacted the working world or education. OL

Review Answers

1. New subjects, such as geography, history, and science, were added to the curriculum.
2. by working to ensure that every state provided equal educational opportunities to all citizens, by increasing funding, by improving the education of children from low-income families, and by raising educational standards
3. Students' answers should be supported by reasons.

Connections to Today

FOCUS

Ask: What are taxes? Why do governments need to collect taxes? *(payments that citizens make to the government; they need the revenues from taxes to fund their spending)* OL

TEACH

R Reading Strategy

Monitoring Ask: How did the power of the federal government change in 1913? *(It gained the power to levy income taxes.)* Did that change the power of state governments as well? *(no; only the federal government)* OL

S Skill Practice

Historical and Social Sciences Analysis Skill
Ask: What are some examples of fees that governments charge? *(fees for driver's licenses, or for hunting or fishing; tolls on highways or bridges)* OL

U Universal Access

Below Grade Level Explain to students how tax withholding works. BL

Answers and Additional Support

Rights and Responsibilities

Our System of Taxation

It is the combination of rights and responsibilities that characterizes what it means to be a citizen of a free and democratic society. As citizens, we are free to exercise our rights. In return, we are expected to fulfill certain responsibilities. One of a citizen's responsibilities is paying his or her fair share of taxes.

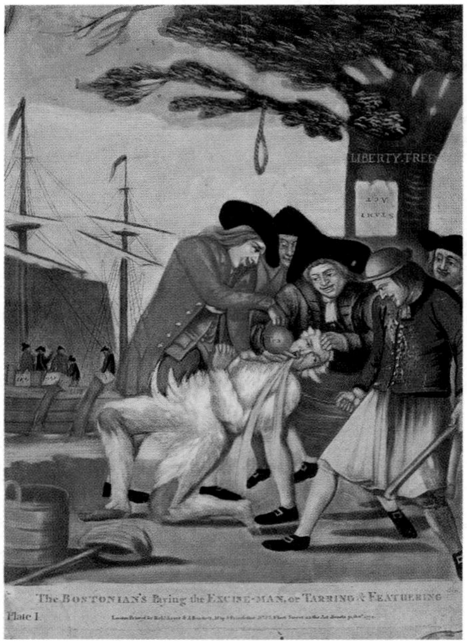

▲ American colonists protested against British taxes.

Paying Taxes

Taxes have been with us since the founding of our nation. British taxes that the colonists considered unfair were major causes of the American Revolution. Until the beginning of the 1900s, taxes were relatively low, as was government spending. Then, in 1913 the Sixteenth Amendment to the Constitution was passed. It allowed the federal government to tax the incomes of individuals and businesses. Since that time, income tax rates have gone up and down. This kind of tax, however, has been the government's primary way to get money to pay for its programs. U R

How Do Governments Pay for Their Programs?

S Governments collect other kinds of taxes and fees as well. Social Security and Medicare taxes pay for retirement and medical benefits for older people. Most states, including California, use a sales tax to earn money. Real estate property taxes usually help pay for local schools. Excise taxes are special taxes that are attached to specific items. Tariffs are a kind of tax paid by foreign companies on goods they export to the United States. Poll taxes are taxes people pay to vote. These were made illegal in 1964 by the passage of the Twenty-fourth Amendment.

Taxation, 1900–Present

1900 — 1915 — 1930 — 1945

- **1913** Sixteenth Amendment gives U.S. government the power to tax incomes
- **1935** Tax levied on employers and workers to fund Social Security

More Skill Practice

Historical and Social Sciences Analysis Skill Have students research the percentage of government revenues generated by different kinds of taxes for the federal government and their state and create graphs showing their results. AL

Principles of Taxation W

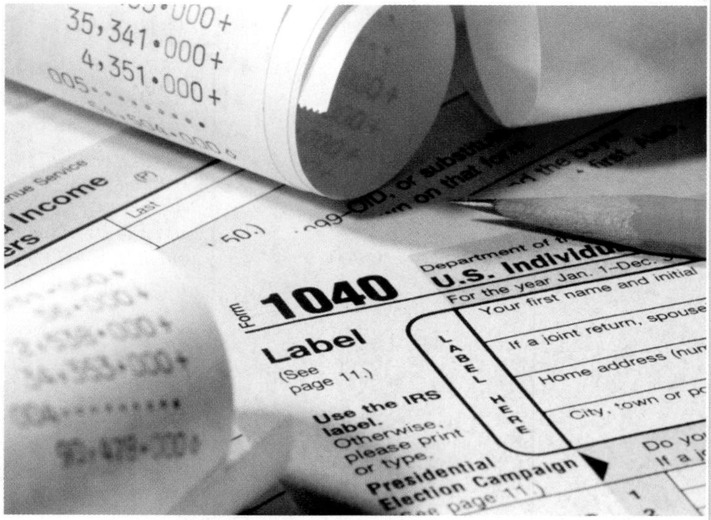

Taxes are usually justified according to one of two major principles. Under the *benefits-received principle,* those who use a particular government service should support it with taxes in proportion to the benefit they receive. Those who do not use a service do not pay taxes for it. A gasoline tax to pay for highway construction and repair is based on the benefits-received principle. Frequent users of the highways often buy more gasoline and, therefore, pay more in gasoline taxes. S

Under the *ability-to-pay principle,* those with higher incomes pay more taxes than those with lower incomes, regardless of the number of government services they use. For example, in most cities all property owners, even those without school-aged children, must pay property taxes to support the local school system. Property taxes are calculated as a percentage of the value of a person's home. Thus, wealthier people pay more property taxes. R

The "Tax Revolt"

By the 1970s, many Americans had come to resent the taxes they had to pay for expensive government programs. Led by California, voters rebelled against high taxes. In 1978 voters in the state approved Proposition 13. The referendum greatly reduced property taxes. As a result, state government programs were also reduced. Antitax movements quickly sprang up in other states. Conservatives argued that government had become too big, and tax cuts were instituted by the states and the federal government. C

Review

1. What are poll taxes? Are they still part of voting today?
2. What was Proposition 13? What effect did it have on California and the nation?
3. What is the relationship between paying taxes and effective citizenship?

1960 | 1975 | 1990 | 2005

- **1978** California approves Proposition 13
- **1986** Tax Reform Act of 1986 reduced the number and level of tax rates
- **2004** President Bush signs $136 billion Corporate Tax Cut Bill

Connections to Today

S Skill Practice

Historical and Social Sciences Analysis Skill Explain that the federal income tax is graduated, with people who earn less paying a smaller percentage of their incomes. **Ask:** Which of these two principles does this demonstrate? *(ability to pay principle)* OL

W Writing Support

Persuasive Writing Have students write a paragraph explaining which of these principles of taxation they think is more fair and why. OL CA 8WA2.5

R Reading Strategy

Inferring **Ask:** What principle of taxation is shown by exempting people without school-age children from property taxes? *(the benefits-received principle)* OL

C Critical Thinking

Making Inferences **Ask:** What area of government spending was likely to increase greatly when property taxes were cut? Why? *(spending on education; because property taxes were used to support public schools)* OL

Review Answers

1. taxes people have to pay to vote; they are not a part of voting today because they are illegal
2. a referendum that greatly reduced property taxes in California; it led to lower property taxes and less state spending and promoted similar movements in other states
3. Paying taxes is one way that citizens meet their responsibilities.

R Reading Strategy

Connecting Have students give examples of laws at the local, state, and national levels. *(Examples will vary but might include local laws such as traffic safety laws or public health laws; state laws such as highway speed limits or education standards; and federal laws such as minimum wage laws and national security laws.)* OL

S Skill Practice

Historical and Social Sciences Analysis Skill
Ask: What are some examples of rights that people have? *(Students might mention the right to free speech, the right to vote, the right to equal protection under the law, and other rights guaranteed by the Constitution.)* OL

W Writing Support

Expository Writing Have students work in groups to write public service announcements encouraging people to serve on juries. Ask the groups to present their announcements to the class. OL

Answers and Additional Support

Rights and Responsibilities

Obeying Our Laws

Another responsibility of citizens is to obey the law. City, state, and federal laws are made by legislators who are elected by the voters. These laws are designed for special purposes—to help people get along, to prevent accidents, to see that resources are used fairly, and so on. In a democracy like ours, people have an ethical obligation to obey laws made by the people they choose to govern them. If we do not obey the law, then governments cannot maintain order or protect our health, safety, and property.

▲ The United States Congress, made up of the Senate (above) and the House of Representatives, makes our nation's laws.

Supporting Our Legal System

The Declaration of Independence states that "all men are created equal." This democratic ideal of equality means that all people are entitled to equal rights and treatment before the law. As citizens of a democracy, Americans also have a number of legal responsibilities. By fulfilling them, we ensure that our legal system works as it should and that our legal rights are protected.

A government's ability to enforce laws depends on people's willingness to obey the laws and to cooperate with law-enforcement authorities. The effectiveness of law-enforcement officials often depends on people's willingness to become involved and tell what they know about a crime. Serving on a jury and testifying in court are important responsibilities. The legal right to a jury trial can be effective only if people are willing to serve on juries and appear in court.

Americans must work peacefully to change unfair, outdated laws. This might involve gathering voters' signatures on petitions to place an issue on the ballot for a vote or asking legislatures to change the law.

Laws and Policies, 1900 to the Present

1900 — 1915 — 1930 — 1945

- **1909** NAACP founded to advance African American rights
- **1934** Indian Reorganization Act restores traditional tribal government
- **1948** President Truman orders end to segregation in the armed forces

More Skill Practice

Historical and Social Sciences Analysis Skill **Ask:** What document sets forth and protects Americans' individual rights? *(the Constitution)* OL

Respect Others' Rights

C To enjoy your rights to the fullest, you must be prepared to respect other people's rights as well. For example, if you own a dog, you have an obligation to keep it from becoming a nuisance to your neighbors. If you are in the library, you should not interfere with anyone's right to work quietly.

Citizens also have a responsibility to show respect for public property and for the property of others. Some people might claim that "no one gets hurt" when they litter in a park or paint graffiti on a school wall, yet such public property belongs to all of us, and we all pay if it is damaged.

R Vandalism and littering are actually more than disrespectful acts; they are crimes. Indeed, many of our laws have been enacted to encourage people to respect others' rights. If you have a party that gets out of hand, for example, you could be arrested for disturbing the peace.

Equal Rights for All

During the 1950s and 1960s, laws helped expand rights for many more Americans. One of the most important was the Supreme Court's 1954 ruling that "separate but equal" segregated schools were unconstitutional. In the decade that followed, the Court also made rulings that gave people accused of crimes certain rights, made the drawing of electoral districts more fair, and clarified a person's right to free speech. Two of the most influential laws of the 1960s were the Civil Rights Act of 1964 and the Voting Act of 1965. The first gave the federal government the power to fight racial discrimination. The second made it illegal to prevent any voter from voting.

The table on this page lists these and other landmark laws of recent decades.

Landmark Acts of the Civil Rights Movement

W

- ***Brown* v. *Board of Education of Topeka, Kansas,* 1954**
  Supreme Court rules segregated schools unconstitutional
- **Civil Rights Act of 1957**
  Congress sets up commission on civil rights and creates a division of civil rights in Justice Department
- **Equal Pay Act of 1963**
  Bans wage discrimination based on race, gender, religion, or national origin
- **Civil Rights Act of 1964**
  Strenghtens Fourteenth Amendment protections; bans discrimination in employment, voting, and public accommodations
- **Voting Rights Act of 1965**
  Empowers federal government to intervene in voter registration discrimination
- **Open Housing Act of 1968**
  Prevents people who are selling or renting homes from using certain forms of discrimination
- **Equal Employment Opportunity Act of 1972**
  Provides that businesses receiving federal funds must have affirmative action programs to increase number of female and minority employees
- **Americans With Disabilities Act of 1990**
  Bans discrimination in employment, transportation, public accommodations, and telecommunications against persons with physical or mental disabilities

Review

1. How can citizens show support for our legal system?
2. What did the Civil Rights Act of 1964 give to the federal government?
3. Why it is important for citizens in a democracy to obey its laws?

1960 | 1975 | 1990 | 2005

1962 César Chávez founds NFWA in Fresno, California

1968 Congress passes Indian Civil Rights Act

1990 Americans With Disabilities Act becomes law

Connections to Today

C Critical Thinking

Synthesizing Write the phrase "My rights end where yours begin" on the board. Have students discuss what the phrase means. OL

R Reading Strategy

Monitoring Have students give examples of other laws that encourage people to respect the rights of others. *(They may mention no trespassing laws or laws against theft.)* OL

W Writing Support

Research Reports Writing Ask students to choose one of the landmark acts listed in the table and prepare a written report outlining why it was passed and what effect it had. AL

Review Answers

1. by obeying laws and cooperating with law enforcement officials; by serving on juries and testifying in court; by working peacefully to change unfair or outdated laws
2. the power to fight racial discrimination
3. to ensure that the legal system works as it is supposed to and that legal rights are protected

Connections to Today

S Skill Practice

Historical and Social Sciences Analysis Skill Organize students into groups and have each student in the group ask three to five adults what voting means to them. Have the groups pool the answers they received and work together on a presentation summarizing those findings. After the groups make their presentations, discuss the answers. OL

W Writing Support

Expository Writing Have students learn how to register to vote in their state and summarize the steps. OL CA 8WA2.1

C Critical Thinking

Making Inferences Point out that some people vote by absentee ballots. **Ask:** What do you think that means? *(Students should infer that this method is used by people who will not be at home on election day.)* OL

Answers and Additional Support

Rights and Responsibilities

▲ The efforts of suffragists like Alice Paul (above) ensured the right to vote for all Americans.

Voting

Voting is an important right of American citizenship. Without it, citizens would not be able to choose the people who will run their government. Voting is also a major responsibility. Those who do not vote are failing to carry out a civic responsibility. They are also handing over their share of political power to voters whose views they may oppose. President Franklin Roosevelt reminded Americans of the importance of voting when he said, "Let us never forget that government is ourselves. The ultimate rulers of our democracy . . . are the voters of this country." S

A Precious Right

The U.S. Constitution states that no state may deny the right to vote because of race, color, gender, or age—if the person is at least 18 years old. People who have been convicted of serious crimes are the most common exception to the general rules. To be eligible to vote, a person must be at least 18 years old, a resident of the state for a specific period of time, and a citizen of the United States. In most states, you must also be registered to vote. W

Why People Don't Vote

C Despite the fact that voting gives Americans a chance to participate in their government, not every person who is eligible to vote actually votes. Some citizens do not vote because they do not meet state voting requirements, or they have not reregistered after changing residences. Other Americans do not think that any of the candidates represent their feelings on issues, or they think that their vote will not make a difference. Another reason is apathy, or lack of interest. Ironically, changes in the twentieth century have made it possible for more Americans to cast ballots than ever before.

Voter and Citizen Participation, 1900–Present

1900 — 1915 — 1930 — 1945

1914 Women have right to vote in 11 states

1920 Nineteenth Amendment grants women right to vote

Did You Know?

One woman—named Charlotte Woodward—who had attended the Seneca Falls Convention back in 1848 was still alive when the Nineteenth Amendment was ratified and women won the right to vote. Woodward voted in the presidential election of 1920.

A Century of Progress

Beginning with the Nineteenth Amendment, which gave women the right to vote in 1920, new laws and court decisions have increased the number of voters. In 1964 the Twenty-fourth Amendment made poll taxes illegal. The next year, the landmark Voting Rights Act took registration out of the hands of local authorities, who often discriminated against African Americans. Within a year, more than 250,000 new black voters had registered. Helped by these new voters, the number of African American office-holders in the South increased from about 100 in 1965 to more than 500,000 in 1990.

Another large group of Americans received the vote in 1971. The Twenty-sixth Amendment lowered the voting age to 18 from 21. Typically, young voters, ages 18 to 24, have the lowest rates of participation of any age group. However, in the 2004 presidential election, 10.5 million under-25 voters voted, compared to 8.7 million in 2000, raising the turnout rate to 42.3 percent from 36.5 percent.

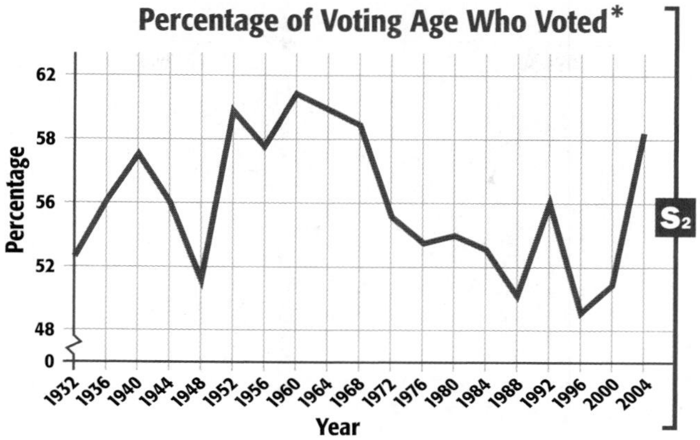

* Presidential elections

Source: Federal Election Commission; *Congressional Research Service reports.*

Why Your Vote Counts

The best way to prepare to vote is to stay informed about candidates and public issues. Newspapers, TV, radio, news magazines, and the Internet carry useful information. Other good sources include the *Voter's Information Bulletin;* the League of Women Voters; literature distributed by each political party; and information distributed by interest groups such as the American Conservative Union or the AFL-CIO Committee on Political Education. As you read about candidates and the issues they support, though, read carefully to separate facts from opinions. Everyone has different reasons for supporting particular candidates.

Review

1. What did the Twenty-Sixth Amendment do?
2. How have laws protecting the right to vote changed in the past century?
3. Why is voting a vital civic responsibility?

1960 — 1975 — 1990 — 2005

- **1964** Civil Rights Act passes
- **1971** Twenty-sixth Amendment lowers voting age to 18
- **2004** 120 million Americans—60 percent of all eligible voters—vote in the presidential election

Connections to Today

S1 Skill Practice

Historical and Social Sciences Analysis Skill
Ask: Why did the federal government take voter registration out of the hands of local people in the 1960s? *(Local officials often discriminated against African Americans.)* OL

S2 Skill Practice

Visual Literacy Have students examine the graph. **Ask:** What trend is evident in the last two elections? *(the percentage of people of voting age who voted has increased)* OL

C Critical Thinking

Analyzing Information
Ask: What kind of information can voters get from each of these different types of sources? *(Students might mention such information as candidates' positions on different issues, their plans for the future, the people or groups who endorse them, and so on.)* Which source is preferable? *(Students may say that the most preferable source is one that offers the candidates' ideas without bias.)*

Review Answers

1. lowered the voting age from 21 to 18
2. They made it possible for more Americans to vote.
3. Students may say it is a responsibility because the government's power derives from the people.

C Critical Thinking

Analyzing Information
Ask: Why are the values that all Americans share called core values? *(because they are fundamental to American life)* OL

W Writing Support

Expository Writing Have students identify the belief they would add and write an essay defining it and giving examples of how it is demonstrated in American life. OL CA 8WA2.1

S Skill Practice

Historical and Social Sciences Analysis Skill
Point to the second fact in the chart. **Ask:** Why do schools require service learning? *(Students may say they do so to encourage good citizenship and to help students gain skills and experience.)* Should more schools do so? *(Answers will vary but should be supported by reasons.)* OL

Answers and Additional Support

Shared Beliefs

The United States is a diverse country. Many different racial, ethnic, and religious groups live together peacefully. People with such varied backgrounds can succeed as a nation only when they share core values and respect the rights and beliefs of others.

Our Beliefs Unite Americans

C What are the core beliefs that Americans share? Any list would include:

- a respect for the rights of each individual to equal treatment under the law, as described in the Constitution
- an appreciation of the cultural contributions of all the nation's people
- A respect for self-determination and an appreciation for community
- an awareness that it is each citizen's responsibility to participate thoughtfully in civic life

W What beliefs would you add to this list?

Service Learning Facts S

- 73% of America's 60 million young people believe they can make a difference in their communities
- 20% of California's school districts have community or service learning requirements
- Teenagers volunteer 2.4 billion hours annually
- Teenage service is worth $34.4 billion to the U.S. economy

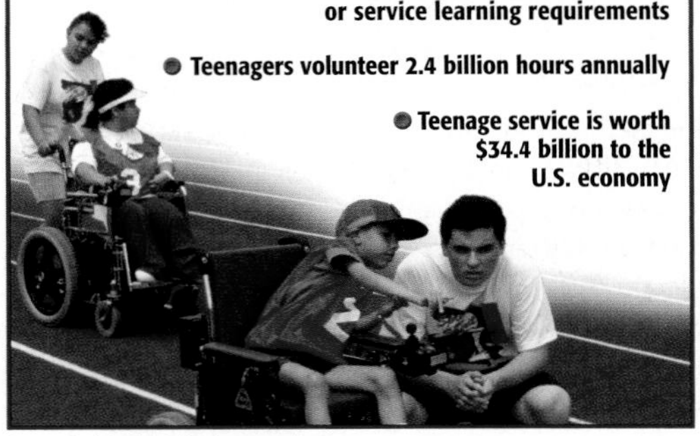

Source: *Youth Services California*, www.yscal.org

What Is Effective Citizenship?

A key part of being an effective citizen is taking an active role in your community. You make a difference by engaging in community service where your efforts are needed, valued, and respected. Service learning is one way you can help your community. As you read, think about these questions: What exactly is service learning? Why should I participate? How do I get involved?

More Skill Practice

Historical and Social Sciences Analysis Skill Invite to class a person—preferably a teen—who does volunteer work such as tutoring, elder care, hospital work, or any other community-oriented work. Ask the guest to describe his or her experiences, how he or she became involved, and how he or she benefits from the experience. Have students develop questions for the person in advance of the visit and set aside some time for them to ask those questions. OL

What Is Service Learning?

Performing important tasks that meet real community needs forms the basis of service learning. Service learning projects can be organized as a partnership between your school and your community. **R** Examples of these projects are refurbishing parks, teaching younger children to read, and sharing your time with nursing home residents. Service learning requires an investment of your time as well as your talents. **C** You and your team play an active role in planning the project and deciding how to use your skills and talents to complete your tasks.

Volunteer Opportunities

- ✓ Read to an elderly person
- ✓ Collect litter in your school yard
- ✓ Recycle at home
- ✓ Circulate a petition
- ✓ Put up a poster announcing Earth Day
- ✓ Bring groceries to a shut in

Why Should I Participate?

You can make a difference. Share your knowledge and skills to help others in your school and community. You will cultivate new knowledge and develop new skills. A well-planned project gives you opportunities to practice your rights and responsibilities as a citizen. You take part in setting the goals of the project. You decide what you will do and how you will do it. An effective service learning project also provides time to share your thoughts about the service experience with others.

When you take part in your community and civic life, you not only help others, you also protect your rights. **S** Supreme Court Justice Learned Hand expressed this view during an "I Am An American Day" celebration in 1944. His words are just as true today:

"Liberty lies in the hearts of men and women; when it dies there, no Constitution, no court, can even do much to help it."

How Do I Get Involved?

Many students are already taking part in service learning. National organizations such as AmeriCorps and Learn and Serve America are always looking for volunteers. Forty-eight states are administering service learning programs through their state education agencies, and at least 64 percent of all public schools had students participating in community service activities recognized by the schools. By exploring the needs of your community, you can plan and organize your own service learning project.

Review

1. What is service learning?
2. Why should you get involved in your community?
3. How could your community be positively impacted by increased participation by its citizens?

Connections to Today

TEACH

R Reading Strategy

Analyzing Information **Ask:** What are some examples of service learning projects? *(caring for parks, tutoring younger children, sharing time with nursing home residents)* OL

C Critical Thinking

Making Inferences **Ask:** What kinds of skills can people gain from service learning? *(Answers will vary but could include learning how to plan and organize work; learning how to teach; learning how to work cooperatively with others.)* OL

S Skill Practice

Analyzing Primary Sources **Ask:** What does Justice Hand mean? *(Students may say that Hand means that what keeps liberty alive is the spirit of the American people.)* OL

ASSESS/CLOSE

Assign students the Review questions at the bottom of the page. Then have them explain how citizens' rights and responsibilities are connected. OL

Review Answers

1. performing important tasks that meet real community needs within the framework of a partnership between a school and its community
2. Each person can make a difference toward building a better community.
3. Students should give examples of improvements that can make life in a community better.

Using an Appendix

Explain to students that an Appendix is additional material found at the end of the book. Have students look at the table of contents on page 820. Ask students to identify the materials found in the Appendix.

Review the descriptions of each Appendix item from the information on page 821. After students have read the descriptions of each item, have them turn to the page where this item is found, using the page number references from the table of contents. Ask students to describe what information is found on the pages and how it can help them as they read their textbooks.

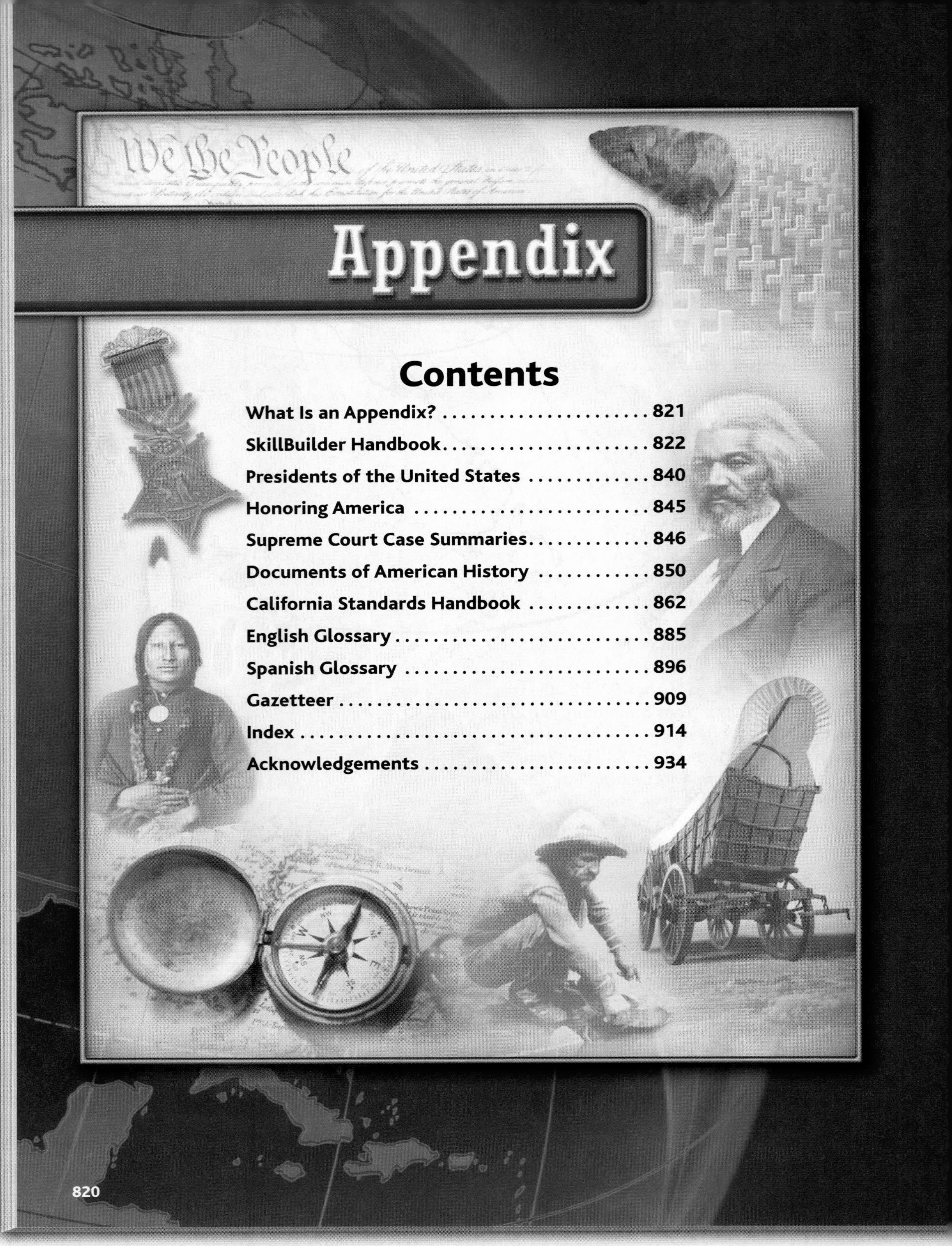

Appendix

Contents

What Is an Appendix? 821
SkillBuilder Handbook 822
Presidents of the United States 840
Honoring America 845
Supreme Court Case Summaries 846
Documents of American History 850
California Standards Handbook 862
English Glossary 885
Spanish Glossary 896
Gazetteer 909
Index 914
Acknowledgements 934

820

What Is an Appendix?

An appendix is the additional material you often find at the end of books. The following information will help you learn how to use the Appendix in **Discovering Our Past: The American Journey to World War I.**

SkillBuilder Handbook
The **SkillBuilder Handbook** offers you information and practice using critical thinking and social studies skills. Mastering these skills will help you in all your courses.

Presidents of the United States
In this resource you will find information of interest on each of the nation's **presidents.**

Supreme Court Case Summaries
The **Supreme Court Case Summaries** discuss important Supreme Court cases. The summaries are listed in alphabetical order and include a summary of the facts of the case and its impact.

Documents of American History
This collection contains some of the most important writings in American history. Each **document** begins with an introduction that describes the author and places the selection within its historical context.

California Standards Handbook
Take time to review what you have learned in this book by using the **California Standards Handbook.** The handbook lists all the content standards listed in each chapter and challenges you with a question about each.

Glossary
A **glossary** is a list of important or difficult terms found in a textbook. Since words sometimes have other meanings, you may wish to consult a dictionary to find other uses for the term. The glossary gives a definition of each term as it is used in the book. The glossary also includes page numbers telling you where in the textbook the term is used.

Spanish Glossary
A **Spanish glossary** contains everything that an English glossary does, but it is in Spanish.

Gazetteer
A **gazetteer** (GA • **zuh** • **TIHR**) is a geographical dictionary. It lists some of the largest countries, cities, and several important geographic features. Each entry also includes a page number telling where this place is mentioned in this book.

Index
An **index** is an alphabetical listing that includes the subjects of the book and the page numbers where those subjects can be found. The index in this book also lets you know that certain pages contain maps, graphs, photos, or paintings about the subject.

Acknowledgements and Photo Credits
This section lists literary credits and/or photo credits for the book. You can look at this section to find out where the publisher of this textbook obtained the permission to use excerpts from other books or a photograph.

Test Yourself

Use the Appendix to answer these questions.

1. Who was the sixth president of the United States?
2. What was the Supreme Court's decision in *Marbury* v. *Madison*?
3. What was the purpose of issuing the Seneca Falls Declaration?
4. California standard US8.9.2 deals with the ending of slavery in early state constitutions. Where does this textbook discuss that topic?
5. What does the expression "favorite son" mean?

Appendix

Have students complete the Test Yourself questions on page 821. As students answer the questions, ask them to identify where in the Appendix they found the answers.

Ask students to write on a sheet of paper five questions similar to those on page 821, with the answers written on the back of the paper. Have students exchange their questions with another student. Students should answer the questions using the Appendix and identify where they found each answer.

Have students review different books to see what other types of information can be included in an Appendix. Tell students to use the Appendix throughout their study of the textbook.

Test Yourself Answers

1. John Quincy Adams was the sixth president of the United States.
2. The Supreme Court ruled that it has the final say on what the Constitution means and the Court defined its right to determine whether a law violated the Constitution.
3. The purpose was to call for suffrage, educational, and economic opportunities for women.
4. chapter 3, section 2
5. It refers to a candidate who receives the backing of his home state rather than the national party.

Introduction

The following **SkillBuilder Handbook** offers students the opportunity to practice critical thinking skills and research skills. Students can benefit in several ways from completing the lessons. First, being equipped with these skills makes students' reading more meaningful. Second, the lessons give students practice in using skills they will need to successfully complete the section and chapter assessments included in the text. Finally, the lessons help prepare students for standardized test taking since many of these skills are assessed on standardized tests.

The lessons are written to be used at any point in the text and in any order you choose. They also can be revisited as you review lessons for students who need extra practice.

SkillBuilder Handbook

Contents

Taking Notes and Outlining 823
Reading a Time Line 824
Understanding the Parts of a Map 825
Understanding Cause and Effect 826
Making Comparisons 827
Drawing Inferences and Conclusions 828
Predicting Consequences 829
Sequencing and Categorizing Information 830
Writing a Paragraph 831
Analyzing Information 832
Distinguishing Fact from Opinion 833
Recognizing Bias 834
Analyzing Library and Research Resources 835
Analyzing Primary Source Documents ... 836
Interpreting a Political Cartoon 837
Analyzing News Media 838
Recognizing Economic Indicators 839

Taking Notes and Outlining

Why Learn This Skill?

One of the best ways to remember something is to write it down. Taking notes—writing down information in a brief and orderly form—not only helps you remember, but it also makes your studying easier.

1 Learning the Skill

There are several styles of note taking, but all explain and put information in a logical order. As you read, identify and summarize the main ideas and details that support them and write them in your notes. Paraphrase, or state in your own words, the information rather than copying it directly from the text. Using note cards or developing a personal "shorthand"—using symbols to represent words—can help.

You may also find it helpful to create an outline when taking notes. When outlining written material, first read the material to identify the main ideas. In textbooks, section headings provide clues to main topics. Then identify the subheadings. Place supporting details under the appropriate heading. The basic pattern for outlines is as follows:

Main Topic
- I. First idea or item
  - A. First detail
    - 1. Subdetail
    - 2. Subdetail
  - B. Second detail
- II. Second idea or item
  - A. First detail
  - B. Second detail
    - 1. Subdetail
    - 2. Subdetail
- III. Third idea or item, and so forth

2 Practicing the Skill

Look back at Chapter 6, Section 2. Take notes about the section and use these notes to create an outline of the main ideas, as shown at the bottom of the left column.

3 Applying the Skill

Scan a local newspaper for a short editorial or article about your local government. Take notes by using shorthand or by creating an outline. Summarize the article, using only your notes.

TEACH

R1 Reading Strategy

Modeling Help students practice taking notes by modeling how to paraphrase the sentences in the first paragraph under the heading "Learning the Skill." Then have students practice on the second paragraph. **OL**

R2 Reading Strategy

Analyzing Text Structure Have students turn to page 312, the first page of Chapter 6, Section 2. **Ask:** What is the main topic of this section? *(the Louisiana Purchase)* Then have them look at page 313 and **ask:** What would be the first idea or item that you would write with the first roman numeral? *(Western Territory)* How do you know this is the topic? *(It is the first subheading of the section.)* **OL**

Resources for page 823

Glencoe Skillbuilder Interactive Workbook CD-ROM, Level 1

Answers and Additional Support

Practicing the Skill Answers

Students' outlines should reflect the information in Chapter 6, Section 2.

Applying the Skill Have students submit their outlines as well as their summaries, to ensure that they completed both parts of the assignment. You may wish to ask them to supply a copy of the original article as well, to check the accuracy of their outlines and summaries.

TEACH

C Critical Thinking

Making Inferences Explain that a time line is like a ruler used to measure distance. **Ask:** Why do the intervals need to be evenly spaced? *(to make it more accurate and easier to compare the position of items on the line)* OL CA CS2.

S Skill Practice

Reading a Time Line **Ask:** What event on the time line below is related to Magellan's being named to lead a Spanish expedition to sail around the world? *(1517: Offers services to king of Spain)* OL CA CS2.

Reading a Time Line

Why Learn this Skill?

Knowing the relationship of time to events is important in studying history. A time line is a visual way to show the flow of dates and events. On most time lines, years are evenly spaced. For example, a time line showing 1,000 years might be divided into ten 100-year sections. Each event on a time line appears beside the date when the event took place.

1 Learning the Skill

To read a time line, follow these steps:

- Find the dates on the opposite ends of the time line to know the time span. Also note the intervals between dates on the time line.
- Study the order of events.
- Analyze relationships among events or look for trends.

◀ Magellan

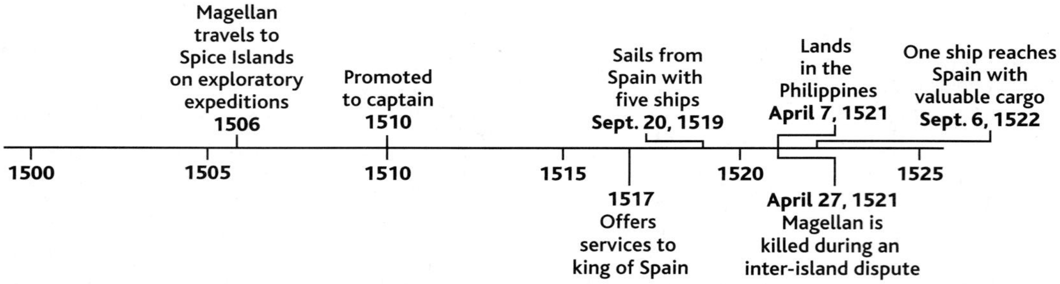

2 Practicing the Skill

Analyze the time line about Magellan, which is at the bottom of the page. Use the time line to answer the questions below.

1. What time span is represented?
2. How many years does each of the sections represent?
3. Did Magellan's voyage to the Spice Islands occur before or after his voyage to the Philippines?
4. How long did it take for Magellan's men to go around the world?

3 Applying the Skill

List 10 key events that have occurred in your life and the dates on which these events occurred. Write the events in chronological order on a time line.

Answers and Additional Support

Practicing the Skill Answers

1. 1500 to 1525; 25 years
2. 5 years
3. before
4. almost three years

Applying the Skill Students' time lines should include 10 dates from their lives, placed in the correct sequence. Their time lines should also include clear start and end dates and regular intervals.

Understanding the Parts of a Map

Why Learn This Skill?

Maps can direct you down the street or around the world. There are as many different kinds of maps as there are uses for them. Being able to read a map begins with learning about its parts.

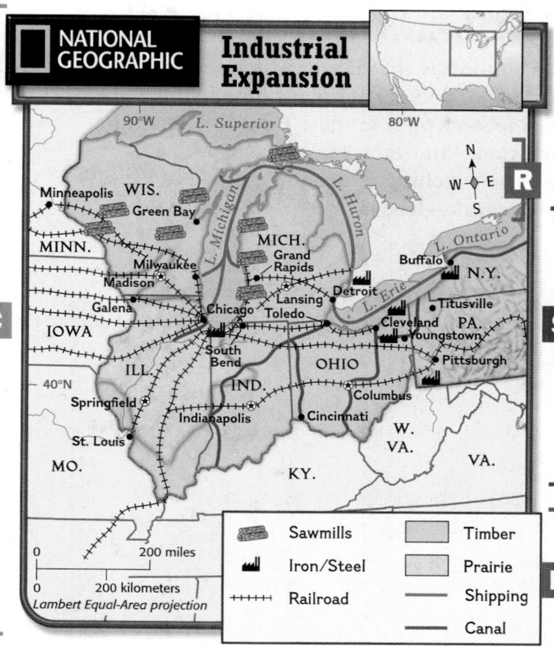

1 Learning the Skill

Maps usually include a key, a compass rose, and a scale bar. The map key explains the meaning of special colors, symbols, and lines used on the map.

After reading the map key, look for the compass rose. It is the direction marker that shows the cardinal directions of north, south, east, and west.

A measuring line, often called a scale bar, helps you estimate distance on a map. The map's scale tells you what distance on the earth is represented by the measurement on the scale bar. For example, 1 inch (2.54 cm) on the map may represent 100 miles (160.9 km) on the earth.

2 Practicing the Skill

The map on this page shows industrial expansion in the late 1800s. Look at the parts of this map, and then answer the questions that follow.

1. What information is given in the key?
2. Which states have the most sawmills?
3. What direction would you travel from Springfield, Illinois, to Columbus, Ohio?
4. About how many miles is the route from Pittsburgh to Chicago?

3 Applying the Skill

Picture a mental image of your house or room. Draw a map showing the location of various areas. Include a map key explaining any symbols or colors you use. Also include a scale bar explaining the size of your map compared to the real area. Finally, add a compass rose and title to your map.

SkillBuilder Handbook

TEACH

C Critical Thinking

Making Inferences Ask: Why are the parts of a map often located in the corners? *(to keep them out of the way of the main map information)* OL

R Reading Strategy

Reading Maps, Graphs, and Charts Have students locate the compass rose, the key, and the scale in the map on this page. *(compass rose—upper right corner; scale—lower left corner; key—lower right corner)* OL

S Skill Practice

Using Geography Skills What other symbols are used on this map that are not explained in the key? *(dots for cities, open circles with stars inside for state capitals, thick lines for state boundaries, thin blue lines for rivers)* OL

Resources for page 825

Glencoe Skillbuilder Interactive Workbook CD-ROM, Level 1

Answers and Additional Support

Practicing the Skill Answers

1. Symbols for sawmills, iron/steel centers, railroads, shipping routes, and canals and colors used for timber land and prairies.
2. Michigan and Wisconsin
3. east
4. about 400 miles

Applying the Skill Students' maps should include the following features: a key explaining symbols and colors used, a scale bar, a compass rose and title.

TEACH

C Critical Thinking

Analyzing Information **Ask:** Will you always find a cause-and-effect relationship between two events or more events? Why or why not? *(Some events are unconnected and so there would be no cause-and-effect relationship between them.)* OL CA HI2.

R Reading Strategy

Questioning Point students' to the second guideline. **Ask:** Would these questions be most likely to identify causes or effects? Why? *(causes; because they look for things that happened before the event that will explain what led to it)* What about the fourth guideline—would questions like this one be most likely to identify causes or effects? Why? *(effects; because they will lead to identifying the results)* OL CA HI2.

W Writing Support

Expository Writing Have students write a paragraph summarizing the cause-and-effect relationships shown in the chart, using at least two of the "clue words" mentioned. OL

Answers and Additional Support

Understanding Cause and Effect

Why Learn This Skill?

You know that if you watch television instead of completing your homework you will receive poor grades. This is an example of a cause-and-effect relationship. The cause—watching television instead of doing homework—leads to an effect—poor grades.

Causes and Effects of the Slave Trade

Causes

- Southerners need to grow cash crops, such as cotton and tobacco.
- European demand for cotton and tobacco increases.
- Growing cotton and tobacco requires large labor force.

Effects

- African Americans are robbed of basic human rights.
- Population of enslaved African Americans grows.
- Slavery creates feelings of injustice and plants seeds of regional conflict.

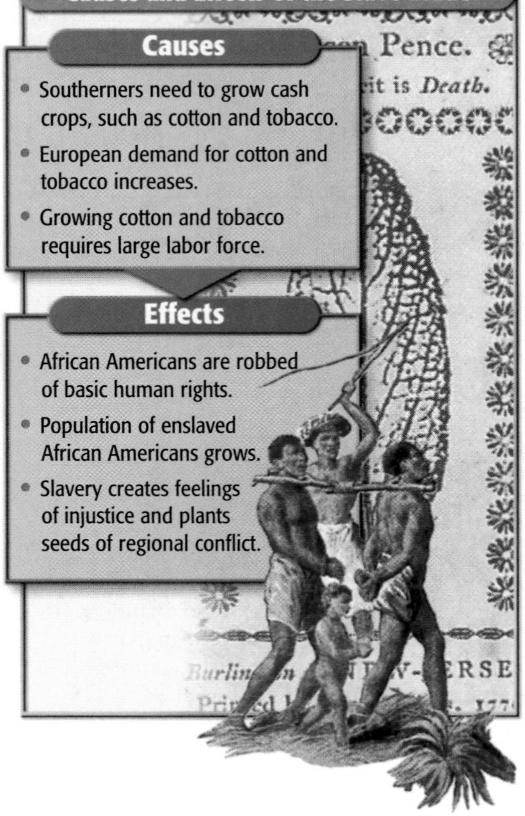

1 Learning the Skill

A *cause* is any person, event, or condition that makes something happen. What happens as a result is known as an *effect*.

These guidelines will help you identify cause and effect.

- Identify two or more events.
- Ask questions about why events occur.
- Look for "clue words" that alert you to cause and effect, such as *because, led to, brought about, produced,* and *therefore.*
- Identify the outcome of events.

2 Practicing the Skill

Study the cause-and-effect chart about the slave trade on this page. Think about the guidelines listed. Then answer the questions below.

1. What were some causes of the development of slavery in the South?
2. What were some of the short-term, or immediate, effects of enslaving Africans?
3. Read the second cause and second effect on the chart. How might these events be related?

3 Applying the Skill

Read an account of a recent event or chain of events in your community newspaper. Determine at least one cause and one effect of that event. Show the cause-and-effect relationship in a chart.

Practicing the Skill Answers

1. Southerners' need to grow cash crops; increased demand for cotton and tobacco; need for large labor force to grow these crops.
2. African Americans were robbed of basic human rights and the population of enslaved African Americans grew.
3. Increased demand for cotton and tobacco led Southerners to want more slaves so they could grow more cotton and tobacco.

Applying the Skill Students' charts might be similar to the one on the page.

Making Comparisons

Why Learn This Skill?

Suppose you want to buy a portable compact disc (CD) player, and you must choose among three models. You would probably compare characteristics of the three models, such as price, sound quality, and size to figure out which model is best for you. When you study American history, you often compare people or events from one time period with those from a different time period.

1 Learning the Skill

When making comparisons, you examine two or more groups, situations, events, or documents. Then you identify similarities and differences. For example, the chart on this page compares two documents, specifically the powers each gave the federal government.

When making comparisons, you first decide what items will be compared and determine which characteristics you will use to compare them. Then you identify similarities and differences in these characteristics.

Powers of the Federal Government

	Articles of Confederation	United States Constitution
Declare war; make peace	✔	✔
Coin money	✔	✔
Manage foreign affairs	✔	✔
Establish a postal system	✔	✔
Impose taxes		✔
Regulate trade		✔
Organize a court system		✔
Call state militias for service		✔
Protect copyrights		✔
Take other necessary actions to run the federal government		✔

2 Practicing the Skill

Analyze the information on the chart on this page. Then answer the following questions.

1. What items are being compared?
2. Which document allowed the government to use state militias?
3. Which document allowed the government to regulate trade?
4. In what ways are the two documents different?
5. In what ways are the two documents similar?

3 Applying the Skill

On the editorial page of your local newspaper, find two letters to the editor that express different viewpoints on the same issue. Read the letters and identify the similarities and differences between the two points of view.

SkillBuilder Handbook

TEACH

C Critical Thinking

Making Inferences Have students brainstorm some things that historians might want to compare. *(nations, regions, leaders, important events, cultures, methods of government, and so on)* OL

R Reading Strategy

Activating Prior Knowledge Write the words *cat* and *dog* on the board. Ask students to name ways the two animals are similar. *(Both are mammals, have fur and four legs, and are popular pets.)* Then have students identify differences. *(Cats meow, dogs bark; cats climb trees, dogs do not; cats are felines, dogs are canines; cats are often solitary, dogs like to live in packs or with people.)* Point out to students that the skill of making comparisons includes identifying how things are alike *and* different from one another. OL

Resources for page 827

Glencoe Skillbuilder Interactive Workbook CD-ROM, Level 1

Answers and Additional Support

Practicing the Skill Answers

1. the Articles of Confederation and the U.S. Constitution
2. U.S. Constitution
3. U.S. Constitution
4. the U.S. Constitution gave more powers to the federal government
5. both gave four key powers to the federal government

Applying the Skill Invite students to present their findings in either a chart like the one on this page or in a paragraph.

TEACH

R Reading Strategy

Inferring Share this scenario with students: You walk into your home's living room late at night. The TV is on, and your sister is asleep on the couch. There is popcorn all over the floor. **Ask:** What do you think happened? *(Your sister fell asleep watching TV, and the popcorn spilled onto the floor.)* Explain that students have just drawn a conclusion based on several inferences based on evidence. Tell them that they will use the same skills when they read about events in history. OL

C Critical Thinking

Analyzing Information
Ask: How would a person's understanding of human nature help him or her in making inferences? *(Students may suggest that understanding human nature will help them make more accurate inferences about how people will react to new situations.)* OL

SkillBuilder Handbook

Drawing Inferences and Conclusions

Why Learn This Skill?

Have you ever heard someone say, "You can't judge him on face value"? It means that people, things you see, or things you read might not be as they appear to be. There might be a double or hidden meaning to what you see or hear.

1 Learning the Skill

R To infer means to evaluate information and arrive at a conclusion. Inferences are ideas that are not directly stated. Making inferences involves reading between the lines to interpret what you are reading. You must then use your own knowledge and common sense to draw a conclusion.

C Use the following steps to help you draw inferences and make conclusions:

- Read carefully for stated facts and ideas.
- Apply related information that you may already know to make inferences.
- Use your knowledge and insight to develop conclusions about these facts.

James Madison

2 Practicing the Skill

Read the passage below and answer the questions that follow.

> Quite often the British would lie in wait for American ships outside an American harbor. This happened in June 1807 off the coast of Virginia. A British warship, the *Leopard*, intercepted the American vessel *Chesapeake* and demanded to search it for British deserters. When the captain of the *Chesapeake* refused, the British opened fire, killing 3, wounding 18, and crippling the American ship.
>
> As news of the attack spread, Americans reacted with an anti-British fury not seen since the Revolutionary War. Secretary of State James Madison called the attack an outrage.

1. What facts are given in the passage?
2. What can you infer about James Madison's political policy regarding Britain?
3. Knowing what you know about this period in America's past, what conclusions can you draw about how this incident relates to British and U.S. relations?

3 Applying the Skill

Choose a poem, or a quote found in a newspaper, that you think has more than one meaning. Share your selection with a classmate. Ask your classmate to infer the hidden meaning.

Answers and Additional Support

Practicing the Skill Answers

1. British ships would wait for American ships, stop them, and search for deserters. The *Chesapeake* incident angered many Americans.
2. Students should note that Madison probably took a harsh approach to Britain after the incident.
3. Students should be able to conclude that the incident strained relations.

Applying the Skill Students' inferences should be well reasoned.

Predicting Consequences

Why Learn This Skill?

Did you ever wish you could see into the future? Predicting future events is very difficult. You can, however, develop skills that will help you identify the logical consequences of decisions or actions.

1 Learning the Skill

As you read in your book, think about what might come next. What you think will happen is your prediction. What happens as a result of an event is called a consequence.

Follow these steps to help you accurately predict consequences.

- Review what you already know by listing facts, events, and people's responses. The list will help you recall events and how they affected people.
- R1 Ask yourself what prior knowledge you have about the events that are described.
- Use your knowledge and observations of similar situations. In other words, ask yourself, "What were the consequences of a similar decision or action that occurred in the past?"
- Map out all possible consequences or outcomes. Analyze each of the potential consequences by asking, "How likely is it that this will occur?"

2 Practicing the Skill

R2 Read the paragraphs at the top of the next column. They are about the first presidency under the new Constitution. Then answer the questions that follow.

The new United States government faced many challenges during Washington's presidency. To limit the growing debt, Alexander Hamilton proposed the repayment of bonds issued during the American Revolution, the creation of a national bank, and the imposition of taxes on whiskey and other merchandise.

Each of these proposals encountered opposition. Southern states had amassed less debt during the war than Northern states. The Southern states felt that they would be paying more than their share to help end the debt. Many Americans feared that the creation of a national bank would take power away from state governments and make the rich wealthier. The tax on whiskey caused problems for farmers who lived by bartering and could not pay a monetary tax. While Washington and Hamilton were able to compromise with the opposition on most of these proposals, discontent still existed among many in the new United States.

1. Predict what you think is most likely to occur between discontented Americans and the government.
2. Explain why you made the prediction that you did.

3 Applying the Skill

Read newspapers for articles about an event that affects your community. Make an educated prediction about what will happen. Explain your reasoning.

SkillBuilder Handbook

SkillBuilder Handbook

TEACH

R1 Reading Strategy

Activating Prior Knowledge Ask students what they think would happen if they watch a movie the evening before an important test instead of studying. *(Students are likely to predict that they will perform less well on the test than they would have done if they had studied.)* **Why do they think this outcome is likely? On what factors are they basing their predictions?** *(prior experience, experiences of others, common sense)* OL

R2 Reading Strategy

Predicting Have students read the first paragraph from a section in their textbooks. Ask them to think about what might happen next. Then have them read the following paragraphs to see if their predictions are true. OL CA HI3.

Resources for page 829

Glencoe Skillbuilder Interactive Workbook CD-ROM, Level 1

Answers and Additional Support

Practicing the Skill Answers

1. Students may say that the people who represent those discontented Americans would probably work to get compromises more favorable to their position.
2. Students should explain the reasoning behind their predictions.

Applying the Skill Students' responses should include a prediction and the rationale for it.

TEACH

R1 Reading Strategy

Activating Prior Knowledge To show the importance of proper sequencing, write the following three steps on the board:

- Put two slices of bread together.
- Place slices of ham and cheese on one slice.
- Put lettuce and tomatoes on the other slice.

Ask students to explain the problem with this sequence. *(The slices should not be put together until the ham, cheese, lettuce, and tomatoes are already in place.)* OL

R2 Reading Strategy

Categorizing Information Ask students to categorize their favorite musical groups and singers. Suggest that they include such categories as pop, rock, rap, jazz, country, and others. Point out that some performers may fit into more than one category and that the same is true when categorizing historical information.

Answers and Additional Support

Sequencing and Categorizing Information

Why Learn This Skill?

Sequencing is placing facts in the order in which they happened. Categorizing means grouping information by related facts and ideas. Both help you organize large quantities of information.

1 Learning the Skill

Follow these steps to learn sequencing and categorizing skills.

R1
- When sequencing look for dates or clue words that describe chronological order: *in 2004, the late 1900s, first, then, finally, after,* and so on.
- Sequencing can be seen in time lines or graphs where information covers several years.

R2
- To put information in categories, look for topics and facts that can be grouped together with similar characteristics. If the information is about farming, one category might be *tools of farming*.
- List these categories, or characteristics, as the headings on a chart.
- As you read, look for details and fill them in under the proper categories on the chart.

Immigrants from China and Japan arrived in the late 1800s.

2 Practicing the Skill

Read the passages below and then answer the questions that follow.

- Before 1865 most immigrants to the United States—except for the enslaved—came from northern and western Europe.
- In the mid-1880s the pattern of immigration started to change. Large groups of "new" immigrants arrived from eastern and southern Europe.
- By 1907 only about 20 percent of immigrants came from northern and western Europe, while 80 percent came from southern and eastern Europe.
- After 1900 immigration from Mexico also increased. In addition many people came to the United States from China and Japan.

1. What information can be organized by sequencing?
2. What categories could you use to organize the information in the above list? What facts could be placed under each category?

3 Applying the Skill

Look at the Geographic Dictionary on pages 46–47. Record terms that would fit into the category "bodies of water." Also, find two newspaper articles about a local issue. Sequence or categorize the information in a chart.

Practicing the Skill Answers

1. The information connected to dates.
2. national origin of immigrants before 1865 and after the mid-1880s; before 1865, most immigrants came from northern and western Europe; after the mid-1880s, 80 percent of immigrants came from southern and western Europe and the number from Mexico, China, and Japan rose

Applying the Skill From the Geographical Dictionary, students should identify the following terms: bay, channel, glacier, lake, ocean, river, sea, strait, and tributary. Their charts should show either sequencing or categorizing.

Writing a Paragraph

Why Learn This Skill?

Paragraphs are the building blocks of an essay or other composition. Each paragraph is a unit—a group of sentences about a single topic or idea.

1 Learning the Skill

Most well-written paragraphs share four characteristics.

W
1. First, a paragraph expresses one main idea or is about one subject. A topic sentence states that main idea. The topic sentence may be located at the beginning, the middle, or the end of a paragraph.
2. Second, the rest of the sentences in a paragraph support the main idea. The main idea may be developed by facts, examples, and reasons.
3. Third, the sentences are arranged in a logical order.

R
4. Fourth, transitional words link sentences within the paragraph. These words can also link one paragraph with the next. Examples include *next, then, finally, also, because, however*, and *as a result*.

2 Practicing the Skill

Use the following sentences to build a paragraph containing a topic sentence and other sentences that give supporting details. Put the sentences in a logical order and add transitional words if you need to. Underline your topic sentence.

- Many such women became role models.
- Women also gained more free time as technology made housework easier.
- Their responsibilities at home lessened as families became smaller, more children spent the day at school, and men worked away from home.
- The situation of middle-class women changed during the late 1800s.
- Many more middle-class women were gaining higher education.
- These changes created the "new women"—a popular term for educated, up-to-date women who pursued interests outside of their homes.
- Many leaders of the urban reform movement were middle-class women.

3 Applying the Skill

Choose a topic concerning the Progressive Movement and write a paragraph about it. Then rewrite the paragraph with its sentences out of order. Exchange papers with a classmate. Have him or her find the topic sentence.

A suffragist ▶ asking for the right to vote

SkillBuilder Handbook

TEACH

W Writing Support

Expository Writing Tell students to find a paragraph in the textbook and identify its topic sentence. Then have them rewrite the paragraph two times putting the topic sentence in two other locations. For instance, if the topic sentence is the first sentence in the paragraph, they should rewrite it once putting the topic sentence in the middle and once putting it at the end. OL

R Reading Strategy

Analyzing Text Structure Tell students to think of all the text under the heading "Learning the Skill" as one paragraph. **Ask:** What four transitional words are used in this paragraph? *(first, second, third, fourth)* OL

Resources for page 831

Glencoe Skillbuilder Interactive Workbook CD-ROM, Level 1

Answers and Additional Support

Practicing the Skill Answers

Students should identify the sentence containing the information "The situation of middle-class women changed during the late 1800s" as the topic sentence.

Applying the Skill If students' partners cannot correctly identify the topic sentence, have students revise their paragraphs and then give them to the other student to be checked again.

TEACH

C1 Critical Thinking

Drawing Conclusions **Ask:** How does knowing the meaning and intent of a writer or speaker help you in trying to understand and use what you read or hear? *(This information helps interpret the reliability of what one reads and hears.)* OL

S Skill Practice

Historical and Social Sciences Analysis Skill
Ask: Why is reliability important? *(Reliable information is more trustworthy and the inferences one draws or conclusions one reaches from reliable information are more likely to be valid.)* OL

C2 Critical Thinking

Identifying Central Issues
Ask: What if you find information that contradicts something you already know? What should you do? *(Students may say that they will believe the source they think most reliable or that they should investigate further to try to find out which information is correct.)* OL

Answers and Additional Support

Analyzing Information

Why Learn This Skill?

Have you ever heard someone say, "Don't believe everything you read"? To be an informed citizen, you have to analyze information carefully as you read to make sure you understand the meaning and the intent of the writer. C1

1 Learning the Skill

Follow these steps to learn how to analyze.

- Identify the subject or topic of the information.
- How is the information organized? What are the main points?
- S Think about how reliable the source of the information is.
- C2 Summarize the information in your own words. Does the information agree with or contradict something you already know?

Kit Carson

2 Practicing the Skill

Read the paragraph below that is from a Public Broadcasting System biography of Kit Carson. Then answer the questions that follow.

As was the case with many white trappers, Carson became somewhat integrated into the Indian world; he traveled and lived extensively among Indians, and his first two wives were Arapahoe and Cheyenne women. Carson was evidently unusual among trappers, however, for his self-restraint and temperate lifestyle. "Clean as a hound's tooth," according to one acquaintance, and a man whose "word was as sure as the sun comin' up." He was noted for an unassuming manner and implacable [firm] courage.

1. Was the information easy to understand? Explain.
2. Consider the source of the information. Does that make it seem more valid or less valid? Why?
3. Summarize the paragraph in a sentence of your own.
4. What is the main point of the paragraph?

3 Applying the Skill

Choose an article from a news magazine. Read it and analyze the information. Answer questions 1–4 as they apply to the article.

Practicing the Skill Answers

1. yes; because it was clearly written in accessible language
2. Answers should be supported by reasons.
3. Possible answer: "Kit Carson was similar to many trappers in mixing easily with the Indian world but his upright character commanded respect."
4. Students may say that the main point is that Carson was similar to and different from most white trappers.

Applying the Skill You may wish to have students submit the article along with their answers so you can check their analyses.

Distinguishing Fact From Opinion

Why Learn This Skill?

Suppose a friend says, "Our school's basketball team is awesome. That's a fact." Actually, it is not a fact; it is an opinion. Knowing how to tell the difference between a fact and an opinion can help you analyze the accuracy of political claims, advertisements, and many other kinds of statements.

1 Learning the Skill

C A fact answers a specific question such as: What happened? Who did it? When and where did it happen? Why did it happen? Statements of fact can be checked for accuracy and proven.

An opinion, on the other hand, expresses beliefs, feelings, and judgments. Although it may reflect someone's thoughts, it is not possible to prove or disprove it.

An opinion often begins with phrases such as *I believe, I think, probably, it seems to me,* or *in my opinion.* It often contains words such as *might, could, should,* and *ought* and superlatives such as *best, worst,* and *greatest.* Judgment words that express approval or disapproval—such as *good, bad, poor,* and *satisfactory*—also usually indicate an opinion.

To distinguish between a fact and an opinion, ask yourself these questions:

- Does this statement give specific information about an event?
- Can I check the accuracy of this statement?
- Does this statement express someone's feelings, beliefs, or judgment?
- Does the statement include phrases such as *I believe,* superlatives, or judgment words?

2 Practicing the Skill

Read each numbered statement below. Tell whether each is a fact or an opinion, and explain how you arrived at your answer.

1. Paul Revere rode to Lexington with the news that the British soldiers were coming.
2. The British were the most feared soldiers in the world at that time.
3. The Daughters of Liberty opposed the Tea Act of 1773.
4. The Boston Tea Party raiders should have sunk the tea ships.
5. George III was a foolish king.

▲ Paul Revere's Ride

3 Applying the Skill

Analyze 10 advertisements. List the topics of each and at least three facts and three opinions presented in the ads.

TEACH

R Reading Strategy

Activating Prior Knowledge Point out that students are confronted with facts and opinions every day in the media. **Ask:** Where would you look for opinions? *(advertisements; record, movie, or book reviews; editorials or columns in newspapers or magazines, web logs on the Internet)* Where would you look for facts? *(news and sports stories, weather reports of the previous day, stock market reports)* OL

C Critical Thinking

Drawing Conclusions Ask: Would you categorize statements about events that happened on particular dates or involved particular people or groups as facts or opinions? *(facts)* OL

Resources for page 833

Glencoe Skillbuilder Interactive Workbook CD-ROM, Level 1

Answers and Additional Support

Practicing the Skill Answers

Facts—numbers 1 and 3; opinions—numbers 2, 4, and 5

Applying the Skill Students might point to such items as the product's or service's name, the price, and special features as facts and claims about the product's or service's effectiveness or merits as opinions. Remind them that images as well as words can convey facts and opinions.

TEACH

C1 Critical Thinking

Analyzing Information
Ask: Is this paragraph saying that it is wrong to have opinions? If not, what is the point of the paragraph? *(The paragraph is not warning against having opinions but against allowing opinions to cloud one's judgment.)* OL

S Skill Practice

Visual Literacy Point out that images can show bias as well. Pictures of a leader looking tired and haggard communicate a different message than photos of the same person striding with confidence or speaking forcefully to a crowd. Have students find a picture in the textbook and analyze it for bias. OL CA 8LS1.9

C2 Critical Thinking

Comparing and Contrasting Distribute copies of two reviews of the same movie, book, television show, or music CD. After students have read both, ask them what biases are revealed in the reviews. Have them identify words and sentences that reveal those biases. OL

Answers and Additional Support

Recognizing Bias

Why Learn This Skill?

Cats make better pets than dogs. If you say this, then you are stating a bias. A bias is a prejudice. It can prevent you from looking at a situation in a reasonable or truthful way. Recognizing bias will help you judge the accuracy of what you read.

1 Learning the Skill

Each of us has feelings and ideas that affect our point of view. Our opinions, or biases, influence how we interpret events. Therefore, an idea that is stated as a fact may really be only an opinion. There are several clues to look for in order to recognize an author's bias.

- Identify the author and examine his or her views and possible reasons for writing the material.
- Look for language that reflects an emotion or opinion—words such as *all, never, best, worst, might,* or *should.*
- Examine the writing for imbalances—discussing only one viewpoint and failing to provide equal coverage for other possible viewpoints.

William McKinley

2 Practicing the Skill

In the excerpt below, President William McKinley explains his decision to annex—add to U.S. territories—the Philippines. Read the excerpt. Answer the questions that follow.

> I walked the floor of the White House night after night until midnight; and I am not ashamed to tell you gentlemen, that I went down on my knees and prayed [to] Almighty God for light and guidance more than one night. And one night late it came to me this way—I don't know how it was, but it came. . . . [T]hat there was nothing left for us to do but to take them all, and to educate the Filipinos, and uplift and civilize and Christianize them, and by God's grace do the very best we could by them, as our fellow-men for whom Christ also died. . . , and the next morning I sent for the chief engineer of the War Department (our map-maker), and I told him to put the Philippines on the map of the United States. . . , and there they will stay while I am President!

1. Imperialism consists of the actions one nation takes to control a weaker nation. Is McKinley stating a pro- or anti-imperialist bias? Which statements indicate bias?
2. What is the main reason McKinley wants to annex the Philippines?
3. What might people today think of this speech?

3 Applying the Skill

Look through the letters to the editor in your local newspaper. Write a short report analyzing one of the letters for evidence of bias.

Practicing the Skill Answers

1. pro-imperialist bias; statements include the idea that the people of the Philippines needed to be educated, uplifted, civilized, and Christianized and that the Philippines would remain part of the United States as long as he was president
2. to improve the lives of the Filipinos
3. Students might say that they would view McKinley as arrogant for thinking he had the right to impose American culture on the Filipinos.

Applying the Skill Encourage students to submit the letter along with their analysis.

Analyzing Library and Research Resources

Why Learn This Skill?

Imagine that your teacher has sent you to the library to write a report on the history of the Civil War. Knowing how to choose good sources for your research will help you save time in the library and write a better report.

1 Learning the Skill

Not all sources will be useful for your report on the Civil War. Even some sources that involve topics about the Civil War will not always provide the information you want. In analyzing sources for your research project, choose items that are nonfiction and that contain the most information about your topic.

When choosing research resources ask yourself these questions:

- Is the information up-to-date?
- Does the index have several pages listed for the topic?
- Is the resource written in a way that is easy to understand?
- Are there helpful illustrations and photos?

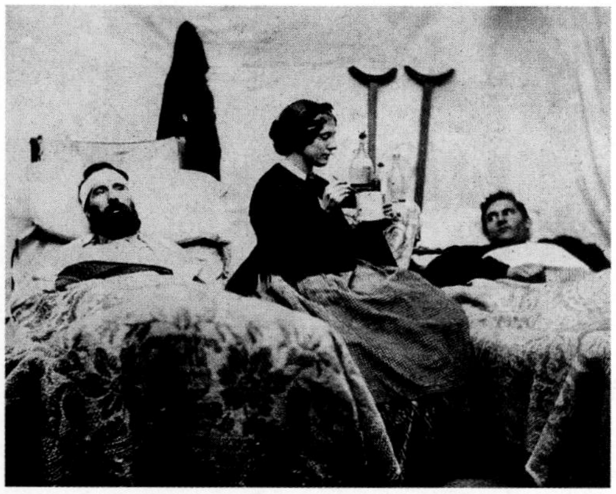

◀ **Women made dramatic contributions to the Civil War by acting as nurses to the wounded.**

2 Practicing the Skill

Look at the following list of sources. Which would be most helpful in writing a report on the Civil War? Explain your choices.

1. A biographical dictionary of U.S. presidents
2. A history of America's Civil Rights Struggle
3. A photographic essay of the Civil War
4. A history of the United States from 1492–1900
5. The "C" volume of an encyclopedia
6. A history of the Republican Party in America
7. A historical atlas of the United States
8. A children's storybook about America in the 1800s
9. A book on the rise and fall of the South
10. A history of United States economic policy

3 Applying the Skill

Go to your local library or use the Internet to create a bibliography of sources you might use to write a report on the Civil War. List at least five sources.

TEACH

U Universal Access

Below Grade Level Ask: What are examples of works that are nonfiction? *(histories, biographies)* What are examples of works that are fiction? *(novels, short stories)* OL

C Critical Thinking

Making Inferences Ask: What does having several pages listed for the topic tell you about the book? *(that it has more or less information about the topic)* What other parts of the book could you use to make this judgment? *(the table of contents)* OL

R Reading Strategy

Reading Secondary Sources Ask: How could you answer this question about a source? *(Students may say that they could read a few paragraphs or a couple pages of text to judge the source's readability.)* OL

Answers and Additional Support

Practicing the Skill Answers

Students should indicate that the most helpful sources would be numbers 3 and 9, though they might also get some information from 1, 4, 5, 6, and 7.

Applying the Skill Encourage students to evaluate each source to identify the topics it would cover and how extensive and reliable its information is.

TEACH

S Skill Practice

Visual Literacy Remind students that images can be primary sources as well, if they were created in a past time. Have them identify five images from the textbook that are primary sources. OL

R Reading Strategy

Activating Prior Knowledge Have students skim the textbook for primary source quotes. Call on volunteers to read some examples aloud. Discuss how the source helps bring to life the time period in which it was written. OL

Answers and Additional Support

Analyzing Primary Source Documents

Why Learn This Skill?

Historians determine what happened in the past by combing through bits of evidence to reconstruct events. These pieces of evidence are called primary sources. They are often first-person accounts from someone who saw or lived through what is being described. Examining primary sources can help you understand history.

1 Learning the Skill

S Primary sources are records of events made by the people who witnessed them. They include letters, diaries, photographs and pictures, news articles, and legal documents.

To analyze primary sources, follow these steps:

R
- Identify when and where the document was written.
- Read the document for its content and try to answer the five "W" questions:

  Who is it about?
  What is it about?
  When did it happen?
  Where did it happen?
  Why did it happen?
- Identify the author's opinions.

▲ Choctaw forced from their land

2 Practicing the Skill

The primary source that follows comes from Speckled Snake, an elder of the Creek Nation, in 1829. He was more than 100 years old at the time he said these words. Read the quote, then answer the questions that follow.

> Brothers! I have listened to many talks from our Great Father. When he first came over the wide waters, he was but a little man.... But when the white man had warmed himself before the Indians' fire and filled himself with their hominy, he became very large. With a step he bestrode the mountains and his feet covered the plains and the valleys. His hand grasped the eastern and the western sea, and his head rested on the moon. Then he became our Great Father. Brothers, I have listened to a great many talks from our Great Father. But they always began and ended in this—"Get a little further; you are too near me."

1. What events is Speckled Snake describing?
2. Who was affected by these events?
3. What is Speckled Snake's general feeling toward the white man?

3 Applying the Skill

Find a primary source from your past—a photograph, a report card, an old newspaper clipping, or your first baseball card. Bring this source to class and explain what it shows about that time in your life.

Practicing the Skill Answers

1. Students should respond that he is describing the coming of white settlers and treaties between whites and Native Americans.
2. Native Americans
3. Students may say that he feels betrayed or pushed around.

Applying the Skill Encourage students to respond on the level of their interests or likes and dislikes but not to reveal personal information.

Interpreting a Political Cartoon

Why Learn This Skill?

You have probably heard the saying, "A picture is worth a thousand words." For more than 200 years, political cartoonists have drawn pictures to present their opinions about a person or event. Learning to interpret political cartoons can help you understand issues of both the past and present.

1 Learning the Skill

Political cartoons state opinions about particular subjects. To illustrate those opinions, cartoonists provide clues, using several different techniques. They often exaggerate a person's physical features or appearance in a special effect called caricature. A caricature can be positive or negative, depending on the artist's point of view.

Cartoonists often use symbols to represent something else. The bald eagle is often shown in political cartoons as a symbol of the United States. Sometimes cartoonists help readers interpret their message by adding labels or captions.

To interpret a political cartoon, follow these steps:

- Read the caption and any other words printed in the cartoon.
- Analyze each element in the cartoon.
- Identify the clues: What is happening in the cartoon? Who or what is represented by each part of the drawing? Are there any symbols? To whom or what do they refer?
- Study all these elements to decide the point the cartoonist is making.

2 Practicing the Skill

Study the cartoon below and read the information about Jim Crow laws on pages 647–648. Then answer the following questions.

1. Are the white people in the cartoon friendly or unfriendly toward the African American? Explain.
2. What does the sign "POLLS" tell you about where the people are?
3. Who are the people represented in the cartoon?
4. What message do you think the cartoonist is trying to send?

3 Applying the Skill

Bring to class a copy of a political cartoon from a recent newspaper or magazine. Explain the cartoonist's point and the tools used to express it.

TEACH

C Critical Thinking

Recognizing Bias Point out that during wartime, cartoonists sometimes draw soldiers from enemy nations in inhuman ways. **Ask:** Why would they do so? *(to make the enemy soldiers seem more hateful or threatening)* OL

R Reading Strategy

Activating Prior Knowledge **Ask:** What other symbols might cartoonists use to represent the United States? *(Students might mention the flag, the Capitol building, or the Statue of Liberty.)* OL CA 8LS1.9

U Universal Access

Visual/Spatial Encourage artistic students to draw their own political cartoons on an important contemporary issue. Ask them to share their cartoons with the class and have other students interpret them. OL CA 8LS1.9

Answers and Additional Support

Practicing the Skill Answers

1. unfriendly; they look angrily at the African American and are holding weapons
2. at a location where voting will take place
3. The man standing represents African American freedmen after the Civil War. The people on the right represent white Southerners, including the Ku Klux Klan. They are preventing the freedman from voting.
4. that white Southerners blocked the rights of African Americans

Applying the Skill You may wish to bring several cartoons and let students work in groups to practice the skill.

TEACH

S Skill Practice

Historical and Social Sciences Analysis Skill
Ask: What sources of news information do you consider reliable? Why? Discuss students responses. If possible, encourage them to bring to class examples of biased and unbiased reporting. OL

C Critical Thinking

Making Inferences Write the words *who*, *what*, *where*, *when*, *how*, and *why* on the board. Point out that reporters are trained to deliver information that answers these six questions when they write a news story. **Ask:** Which question represents interpretation? *(why)* OL

Analyzing News Media

Why Learn This Skill?

Every citizen needs to be aware of current issues and events to make good decisions when exercising citizenship rights.

1 Learning the Skill

To get an accurate profile of current events, you must learn to think critically about the news. The steps below will help you think critically.

- First, think about the source of the news story. Reports that reveal sources are more reliable than those that do not. If you know the sources, you can evaluate them. Can all facts be verified?
- S Many news stories also interpret events. Such analyses may reflect a reporter's biases. Look for biases as you read or listen to news stories. C
- Ask yourself whether the news is even-handed and thorough. Is it reported on the scene or secondhand? Does it represent both sides of an issue? The more sources cited for a fact, the more reliable it usually is.

◀ Alexander Graham Bell makes the first phone call.

2 Practicing the Skill

Below is an excerpt from an 1891 *New York Times* newspaper article. The article states that the Bell Company did not renew a patent on their telephone.

Read the excerpt below and answer the questions that follow.

> THE TELEPHONE MONOPOLY
>
> It is incredible that the Fifty-second Congress will pass an act to authorize the Bell Company to bleed for another seventeen years the public that has enriched the proprietors of that monopoly for nearly that period. . . . But behind the company and the Congress there is the long-suffering public, . . . [it] will unquestionably take a lively interest in killing off members who dare to support the pretensions of this arrogant and rapacious [greedy] monopoly."

1. What point is the article trying to make?
2. Does the article reflect bias or strong opinion? Explain.

3 Applying the Skill

Think of an issue in your community on which public opinion is divided. Read newspaper features and editorials about the issue and listen to television reports. What biases can you identify? Which reports are the most reliable?

Answers and Additional Support

Practicing the Skill Answers

1. that it is unfair for the Bell Company to enjoy a monopoly on phone service
2. Students should conclude that the article reflects strong bias, evident from the use of such words as *bleed*, *arrogant*, and *rapacious*.

Applying the Skill Encourage students to continue investigating news sources until they can identify at least one with an evident bias. Remind them that all biases are not related to political issues; for instance, there could be bias in favor of a local team in a sports report.

Recognizing Economic Indicators

Why Learn This Skill?

Every day, business and government leaders are faced with the challenge of trying to predict what will happen to the economy in the coming months and years. To help these leaders in making decisions economists have developed ways to measure an economy's performance. These are called economic indicators. U

1 Learning the Skill

Economic indicators are statistics, or numbers, that tell how well the economy is doing and how well the economy is going to do in the future. They include the number of jobless, the rate at which prices rise over a period of time, and the amount of goods and services that are produced and sold. Each month, the U.S. Department of Commerce gathers data for 78 economic indicators. They cover all aspects of the state of the United States economy. The chart at the right lists some common terms for economic indicators that you may have read about or heard mentioned.

▲ **Stock prices often rise and fall based on the news from economic indicators.**

2 Practicing the Skill

Start an Economics Handbook. Using a dictionary, look up each economic term listed on this chart. Write a definition for each term in your Economics Handbook.

Economic Indicators

Term	Definition
Federal Reserve Bank	
Gross National Product (GNP)	
Depression	
Recession	
Inflation	
Import	
Export	
Interest Rates	
Consumer Index	
Federal Deficit	
Capital	
Stock Market	

3 Applying the Skill

At the library or on the Internet, find information about the current economic state of the United States. Using the terms that you have defined, write a few brief paragraphs describing the current economy.

TEACH

U Universal Access

English Learners Explain that these factors are called *indicators* because they *indicate*, or suggest, economic trends. OL

S Skill Practice

Historical and Social Sciences Analysis Skill Explain that all economic indicators do not always point to the same trends. For instance, unemployment may be low, which usually suggests a strong economy, but overall wages may be low, which indicates that workers are having difficult times. **Ask:** **What could economists do with conflicting statistics in evaluating an economy's performance?** *(Students may say they would see how many statistics point in an overall positive or negative direction.)* OL CA HI6.

Resources for page 839

Glencoe Skillbuilder Interactive Workbook CD-ROM, Level 1

Answers and Additional Support

Practicing the Skill Answers

Federal Reserve Bank: part of national banking system; *GNP:* total value of goods and services a country produces: *depression:* severe economic slowdown; *recession:* mild economic slowdown; *inflation:* generally rising prices; *import:* good brought into a country; *export:* good sold to another country; *interest rates:* cost of borrowing money; *consumer index:* index measuring consumer prices; *federal deficit:* amount government must borrow to meet expenditures; *capital:* money invested in businesses; *stock market:* market where shares of ownerships in corporations are bought and sold

Applying the Skill Paragraphs should employ some of the terms students learned.

Presidents of the United States

In this resource you will find portraits of the individuals who served as presidents of the United States, along with their occupations, political party affiliations, and other interesting facts.

***The Republican Party during this period developed into today's Democratic Party. Today's Republican Party originated in 1854.*

1 George Washington

1789–1797
Lived: 1732–1799
Born in: Virginia
Elected from: Virginia
Occupations: Soldier, Planter
Party: None
Vice President: John Adams

2 John Adams

1797–1801
Lived: 1735–1826
Born in: Massachusetts
Elected from: Massachusetts
Occupations: Teacher, Lawyer
Party: Federalist
Vice President: Thomas Jefferson

3 Thomas Jefferson

1801–1809
Lived: 1743–1826
Born in: Virginia
Elected from: Virginia
Occupations: Planter, Lawyer
Party: Republican**
Vice Presidents: Aaron Burr, George Clinton

4 James Madison

1809–1817
Lived: 1751–1836
Born in: Virginia
Elected from: Virginia
Occupation: Planter
Party: Republican**
Vice Presidents: George Clinton, Elbridge Gerry

5 James Monroe

1817–1825
Lived: 1758–1831
Born in: Virginia
Elected from: Virginia
Occupation: Lawyer
Party: Republican**
Vice President: Daniel D. Tompkins

6 John Quincy Adams

1825–1829
Lived: 1767–1848
Born in: Massachusetts
Elected from: Massachusetts
Occupation: Lawyer
Party: Republican**
Vice President: John C. Calhoun

7 Andrew Jackson

1829–1837
Lived: 1767–1845
Born in: South Carolina
Elected from: Tennessee
Occupations: Lawyer, Soldier
Party: Democratic
Vice Presidents: John C. Calhoun, Martin Van Buren

8 Martin Van Buren

1837–1841
Lived: 1782–1862
Born in: New York
Elected from: New York
Occupation: Lawyer
Party: Democratic
Vice President: Richard M. Johnson

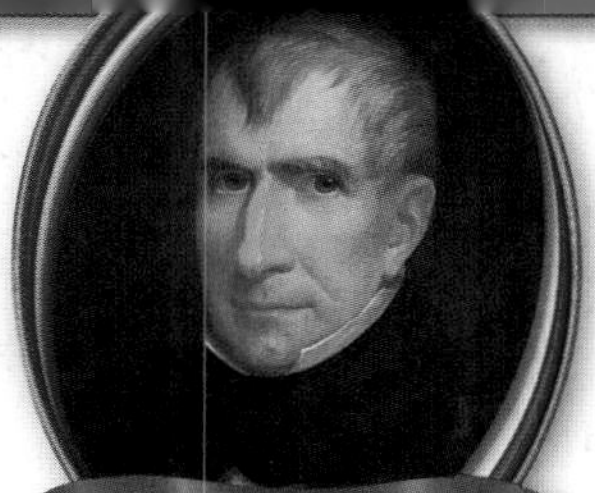

9 William H. Harrsion

1841
Lived: 1773–1841
Born in: Virginia
Elected from: Ohio
Occupations: Soldier, Planter
Party: Whig
Vice President: John Tyler

10 John Tyler

1841–1845
Lived: 1790–1862
Born in: Virginia
Elected as V.P. from: Virginia; Succeeded Harrison
Occupation: Lawyer
Party: Whig
Vice President: None

11 James K. Polk

1845–1849
Lived: 1795–1849
Born in: North Carolina
Elected from: Tennessee
Occupation: Lawyer
Party: Democratic
Vice President: George M. Dallas

12 Zachary Taylor

1849–1850
Lived: 1784–1850
Born in: Virginia
Elected from: Louisiana
Occupation: Soldier
Party: Whig
Vice President: Millard Fillmore

13 Millard Fillmore

1850–1853
Lived: 1800–1874
Born in: New York
Elected as V.P. from: New York; Succeeded Taylor
Occupation: Lawyer
Party: Whig
Vice President: None

14 Franklin Pierce

1853–1857
Lived: 1804–1869
Born in: New Hampshire
Elected from: New Hampshire
Occupation: Lawyer
Party: Democratic
Vice President: William R. King

15 James Buchanan

1857–1861
Lived: 1791–1868
Born in: Pennsylvania
Elected from: Pennsylvania
Occupation: Lawyer
Party: Democratic
Vice President: John C. Breckinridge

16 Abraham Lincoln

1861–1865
Lived: 1809–1865
Born in: Kentucky
Elected from: Illinois
Occupation: Lawyer
Party: Republican
Vice Presidents: Hannibal Hamlin, Andrew Johnson

17 Andrew Johnson
1865–1869
Lived: 1808–1875
Born in: North Carolina
Elected as V.P. from: Tennessee; Succeeded Lincoln
Occupation: Tailor
Party: Republican
Vice President: None

18 Ulysses S. Grant
1869–1877
Lived: 1822–1885
Born in: Ohio
Elected from: Illinois
Occupations: Farmer, Soldier
Party: Republican
Vice Presidents: Schuyler Colfax, Henry Wilson

19 Rutherford B. Hayes
1877–1881
Lived: 1822–1893
Born in: Ohio
Elected from: Ohio
Occupation: Lawyer
Party: Republican
Vice President: William A. Wheeler

20 James A. Garfield
1881
Lived: 1831–1881
Born in: Ohio
Elected from: Ohio
Occupations: Laborer, Professor
Party: Republican
Vice President: Chester A. Arthur

21 Chester A. Arthur
1881–1885
Lived: 1830–1886
Born in: Vermont
Elected as V.P. from: New York; Succeeded Garfield
Occupations: Teacher, Lawyer
Party: Republican
Vice President: None

22 Grover Cleveland
1885–1889
Lived: 1837–1908
Born in: New Jersey
Elected from: New York
Occupation: Lawyer
Party: Democratic
Vice President: Thomas A. Hendricks

23 Benjamin Harrison
1889–1893
Lived: 1833–1901
Born in: Ohio
Elected from: Indiana
Occupation: Lawyer
Party: Republican
Vice President: Levi P. Morton

24 Grover Cleveland
1893–1897
Lived: 1837–1908
Born in: New Jersey
Elected from: New York
Occupation: Lawyer
Party: Democratic
Vice President: Adlai E. Stevenson

25 William McKinley
1897–1901
Lived: 1843–1901
Born in: Ohio
Elected from: Ohio
Occupations: Teacher, Lawyer
Party: Republican
Vice Presidents: Garret Hobart, Theodore Roosevelt

26 Theodore Roosevelt
1901–1909
Lived: 1858–1919
Born in: New York
Elected as V.P. from: New York; Succeeded McKinley
Occupations: Historian, Rancher
Party: Republican
Vice President: Charles W. Fairbanks

27 William H. Taft
1909–1913
Lived: 1857–1930
Born in: Ohio
Elected from: Ohio
Occupation: Lawyer
Party: Republican
Vice President: James S. Sherman

28 Woodrow Wilson
1913–1921
Lived: 1856–1924
Born in: Virginia
Elected from: New Jersey
Occupation: College Professor
Party: Democratic
Vice President: Thomas R. Marshall

29 Warren G. Harding
1921–1923
Lived: 1865–1923
Born in: Ohio
Elected from: Ohio
Occupations: Newspaper Editor, Publisher
Party: Republican
Vice President: Calvin Coolidge

30 Calvin Coolidge
1923–1929
Lived: 1872–1933
Born in: Vermont
Elected as V.P. from: Massachusetts; Succeeded Harding
Occupation: Lawyer
Party: Republican
Vice President: Charles G. Dawes

31 Herbert C. Hoover
1929–1933
Lived: 1874–1964
Born in: Iowa
Elected from: California
Occupation: Engineer
Party: Republican
Vice President: Charles Curtis

32 Franklin D. Roosevelt
1933–1945
Lived: 1882–1945
Born in: New York
Elected from: New York
Occupation: Lawyer
Party: Democratic
Vice Presidents: John N. Garner, Henry A. Wallace, Harry S. Truman

33 Harry S. Truman
1945–1953
Lived: 1884–1972
Born in: Missouri
Elected as V.P. from: Missouri; Succeeded Roosevelt
Occupations: Clerk, Farmer
Party: Democratic
Vice President: Alben W. Barkley

34 Dwight D. Eisenhower
1953–1961
Lived: 1890–1969
Born in: Texas
Elected from: New York
Occupation: Soldier
Party: Republican
Vice President: Richard M. Nixon

35 John F. Kennedy

1961–1963
Lived: 1917–1963
Born in: Massachusetts
Elected from: Massachusetts
Occupations: Author, Reporter
Party: Democratic
Vice President: Lyndon B. Johnson

36 Lyndon B. Johnson

1963–1969
Lived: 1908–1973
Born in: Texas
Elected as V.P. from: Texas; Succeeded Kennedy
Occupation: Teacher
Party: Democratic
Vice President: Hubert H. Humphrey

37 Richard M. Nixon

1969–1974
Lived: 1913–1994
Born in: California
Elected from: New York
Occupation: Lawyer
Party: Republican
Vice Presidents: Spiro T. Agnew, Gerald R. Ford

38 Gerald R. Ford

1974–1977
Lived: 1913–
Born in: Nebraska; Appointed as V.P. upon Agnew's resignation; Succeeded Nixon
Occupation: Lawyer
Party: Republican
Vice President: Nelson A. Rockefeller

39 James E. Carter, Jr.

1977–1981
Lived: 1924–
Born in: Georgia
Elected from: Georgia
Occupations: Business, Farmer
Party: Democratic
Vice President: Walter F. Mondale

40 Ronald W. Reagan

1981–1989
Lived: 1911–2004
Born in: Illinois
Elected from: California
Occupations: Actor, Lecturer
Party: Republican
Vice President: George H.W. Bush

41 George H. W. Bush

1989–1993
Lived: 1924–
Born in: Massachusetts
Elected from: Texas
Occupation: Business
Party: Republican
Vice President: J. Danforth Quayle

42 William J. Clinton

1993–2001
Lived: 1946–
Born in: Arkansas
Elected from: Arkansas
Occupation: Lawyer
Party: Democratic
Vice President: Albert Gore, Jr.

43 George W. Bush

2001–
Lived: 1946–
Born in: Connecticut
Elected from: Texas
Occupation: Business
Party: Republican
Vice President: Richard B. Cheney

Honoring America

★ For Americans, the flag has always had a special meaning. It is a symbol of our nation's freedom and democracy. ★

Flag Etiquette

Over the years, Americans have developed rules and customs concerning the use and display of the flag. One of the most important things every American should remember is to treat the flag with respect.

- The flag should be raised and lowered by hand and displayed only from sunrise to sunset. On special occasions, the flag may be displayed at night, but it should be illuminated.
- The flag may be displayed on all days, weather permitting, particularly on national and state holidays and on historic and special occasions.
- No flag may be flown above the American flag or to the right of it at the same height.
- The flag should never touch the ground or floor beneath it.
- The flag may be flown at half-staff by order of the president, usually to mourn the death of a public official.
- The flag may be flown upside down only to signal distress.
- The flag should never be carried flat or horizontally, but always carried aloft and free.
- When the flag becomes old and tattered, it should be destroyed by burning. According to an approved custom, the Union (stars on blue field) is first cut from the flag; then the two pieces, which no longer form a flag, are burned.

★ ★ ★ ★ ★ ★ ★ ★

The American's Creed

I believe in the United States of America as a Government of the people, by the people, for the people, whose just powers are derived from the consent of the governed; a democracy in a republic; a sovereign Nation of many sovereign States; a perfect union, one and inseparable; established upon those principles of freedom, equality, justice, and humanity for which American patriots sacrificed their lives and fortunes.

I therefore believe it is my duty to my Country to love it; to support its Constitution; to obey its laws; to respect its flag, and to defend it against all enemies.

The Pledge of Allegiance

I pledge allegiance to the Flag of the United States of America and to the Republic for which it stands, one Nation under God, indivisible, with liberty and justice for all.

Supreme Court Case Summaries

The following summaries give details about important Supreme Court cases.

Brown v. Board of Education (1954)

In *Brown* v. *Board of Education of Topeka, Kansas,* the Supreme Court overruled *Plessy* v. *Ferguson* (1896) making the separate-but-equal doctrine in public schools unconstitutional. The Supreme Court rejected the idea that truly equal but separate schools for African American and white students would be constitutional. The Court explained that the Fourteenth Amendment's requirement that all persons be guaranteed equal protection of the law is not met simply by ensuring that African American and white schools "have been equalized…with respect to buildings, curricula, qualifications and salaries, and other tangible factors."

The Court then ruled that racial segregation in public schools violates the Equal Protection Clause of the Constitution because it is inherently unequal. In other words, nothing can make racially segregated public schools equal under the Constitution because the very fact of separation marks the separated race as inferior. In practical terms, the Court's decision in this case has been extended beyond public education to virtually all public accommodations and activities.

Dred Scott v. Sandford (1857)

Dred Scott was taken by slaveholder John Sandford to the free state of Illinois and to the Wisconsin Territory, which had also banned slavery. Later they returned to a slave state, Missouri. Several years later, Scott sued for his freedom under the Missouri legal principle of "once free, always free." In other words, under state law enslaved people were entitled to freedom if they had lived in a free state at any time.

Dred Scott

Missouri courts ruled against Scott, but he appealed the case all the way to the United States Supreme Court.

The Supreme Court decided this case before the Fourteenth Amendment was added to the Constitution. (The Fourteenth Amendment provides that anyone born or naturalized in the United States is a citizen of the nation and of his or her state of residence.) The court held that enslaved African Americans were property, not citizens, and thus had no rights under the Constitution. The decision also declared that it was unconstitutional to prohibit slavery in the territories. Many people in the North were outraged by the decision, which moved the nation closer to civil war.

Gibbons v. Ogden (1824)

Thomas Gibbons had a federal license to operate a steamboat along the coast, but he did not have a license from the state of New York to travel on New York waters. He wanted to run a steamboat line between Manhattan and New Jersey that would compete with Aaron Ogden's company. Ogden had a New York license. Gibbons sued for the freedom to use his federal license to compete against Ogden on New York waters.

Gibbons won the case. The Supreme Court made it clear that the authority of Congress to regulate interstate commerce (among states) includes the authority to regulate intrastate commerce (within a single state) that bears on, or relates to, interstate commerce.

Before this decision, it was thought that the Constitution would permit a state to close its borders to interstate commercial activity—which, in effect, would stop such activity in its tracks. This case says that a state can regulate purely internal commercial activity, but only Congress can regulate commercial activity that has both intrastate and interstate dimensions.

Gideon v. *Wainwright* (1963)

After being accused of robbery, Clarence Gideon defended himself in a Florida court because the judge in the case refused to appoint a free lawyer. The jury found Gideon guilty. Eventually, Gideon appealed his conviction to the United States Supreme Court, claiming that by failing to appoint a lawyer the lower court had violated his rights under the Sixth and Fourteenth Amendments.

The Supreme Court agreed with Gideon. In *Gideon* v. *Wainwright* the Supreme Court held for the first time that poor defendants in criminal cases have the right to a state-paid attorney under the Sixth Amendment. The rule announced in this case has been refined to apply whenever the defendant, if convicted, can be sentenced to more than six months in jail or prison.

Korematsu v. *United States* (1944)

After the Japanese bombing of Pearl Harbor in 1941, thousands of Japanese Americans on the West Coast were forced to abandon their homes and businesses, and they were moved to internment camps in California, Idaho, Utah, Arizona, Wyoming, Colorado, and Arkansas. The prison-like camps offered poor food and cramped quarters.

In 1983 Fred Korematsu (center) won a reversal of his conviction.

The Supreme Court's decision in *Korematsu* v. *United States* supported the authority of the federal government to move Japanese Americans, many of whom were citizens, from designated military areas that included almost the entire West Coast. The government defended the so-called exclusion orders as a necessary response to Japan's attack on Pearl Harbor. Only after his reelection in 1944 did President Franklin Roosevelt rescind the evacuation orders, and by the end of 1945 the camps were closed.

Marbury v. *Madison* (1803)

During his last days in office, President John Adams, a Federalist, appointed William Marbury and several other men as judges. This action angered the incoming Democratic-Republican president Thomas Jefferson. Jefferson then ordered James Madison, his secretary of state, not to deliver the commissions, thus blocking the appointments. William Marbury sued. He asked the Supreme Court to order Madison to deliver the commission that would make him a judge.

The Court ruled against Marbury, but more importantly, the decision in this case established one of the most significant principles of American constitutional law. The Supreme Court held that it is the Court itself that has the final say on what the Constitution means. This right is known as judicial review. It is also the Supreme Court that has the final say in whether or not an act of government—legislative or executive at the federal, state, or local level—violates the Constitution.

McCulloch v. *Maryland* (1819)

Following the War of 1812, the United States experienced years of high inflation and general economic turmoil. In an attempt to stabilize the economy, the United States Congress chartered a Second Bank of the United States in 1816. Maryland and several other states, however, opposed the competition that the new national bank created and passed state laws taxing its branches.

In 1818, James McCulloch, head of the Baltimore branch of the Second Bank of the United States, refused to pay the tax to the state of Maryland. The case worked its way through the Maryland state courts all the way to the United States Supreme Court.

The Supreme Court declared the Maryland tax unconstitutional and void. More importantly, the decision established the foundation for expanded Congressional authority. The Court held that the necessary and proper clause of the Constitution allows Congress to do more than the Constitution expressly states it may do. The decision allows Congress to enact nearly any law that will help it achieve any of its constitutional duties. For example, Congress has the express authority to regulate interstate commerce. The necessary and proper clause permits Congress to do so in ways not actually specified in the Constitution.

Miranda v. *Arizona* (1966)

In 1963, police in Arizona arrested Ernesto Miranda for kidnapping. The court found Miranda guilty on the basis of a signed confession. The police admitted that neither before nor during the questioning had Miranda been advised of his right to consult with an attorney before answering any questions or of his right to have an attorney present during the interrogation.

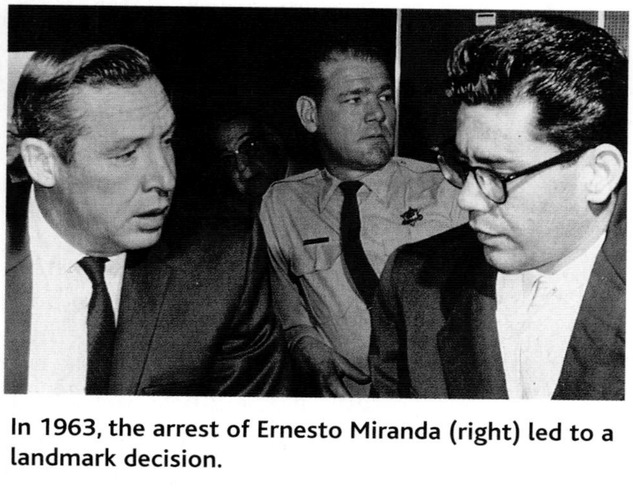

In 1963, the arrest of Ernesto Miranda (right) led to a landmark decision.

Miranda appealed his conviction, claiming that police had violated his right against self-incrimination under the Fifth Amendment by not informing him of his legal rights during the questioning.

Miranda won the case. The Supreme Court held that a person in police custody cannot be questioned unless told that he or she has: 1) the right to remain silent, 2) the right to an attorney (at government expense if the accused is unable to pay), and 3) that anything the person says after stating that he or she understands these rights can be used as evidence of guilt at trial. These rights have come to be called the Miranda warning. They are intended to ensure that an accused person in custody will not unknowingly give up the Fifth Amendment's protection against self-incrimination.

New York Times Company v. *United States* (1971)

In June 1971, the *New York Times* published its first installment of the "Pentagon Papers," a classified document about government actions in the Vietnam War era. The secret document had been leaked to the *Times* by antiwar activist Daniel Ellsberg, who had previously worked in national security for the government. President Richard Nixon went to court to block further publication of the Pentagon Papers. The *New York Times* appealed to the Supreme Court to allow it to continue publishing without government interference.

The Supreme Court's ruling in this case upheld earlier decisions that established the doctrine of prior restraint. This doctrine protects the press (broadly defined as radio and television, newspapers, filmmakers and distributors, etc.) from government attempts to block publication. Except in extraordinary circumstances, the press must be allowed to publish.

Supreme Court Cases

Plessy v. *Ferguson* (1896)

In the late 1800s, railroad companies in Louisiana were required by state law to provide "separate-but-equal" cars for white and African American passengers. In 1890 a group of citizens in New Orleans selected Homer Plessy to challenge that law. In 1892, Plessy boarded a whites-only car and refused to move. He was arrested. Plessy appealed to the Supreme Court, arguing that the Louisiana separate-but-equal law violated his right to equal protection under the Fourteenth Amendment.

Homer Plessy lost the case. The Plessy decision upheld the separate-but-equal doctrine used by Southern states to perpetuate segregation following the Civil War. The court ruled that the Fourteenth Amendment's equal protection clause required only equal public facilities for the two races, not equal access to the same facilities. This decision was overruled in 1954 by *Brown* v. *Board of Education of Topeka, Kansas* (discussed previously).

Roe v. *Wade* (1973)

Roe v. *Wade* challenged restrictive abortion laws in both Texas and Georgia. The suit was brought in the name of Jane Roe, an alias used to protect the privacy of the plaintiff.

In this decision, the Supreme Court ruled that females have a constitutional right under various provisions of the Constitution—most notably, the due process clause—to decide whether or not to terminate a pregnancy. The Supreme Court's decision in this case was the most significant in a long line of decisions over a period of 50 years that recognized a constitutional right of privacy, even though the word *privacy* is not found in the Constitution.

United States v. *Nixon* (1974)

In the early 1970s, President Nixon was named an unindicted coconspirator in the criminal investigation that arose in the aftermath of a break-in at the offices of the Democratic Party in Washington, D.C. A federal judge had ordered President Nixon to turn over tapes of conversations he had with his advisers about the break-in. Nixon resisted the order, claiming that the conversations were entitled to absolute confidentiality by Article II of the Constitution.

The decision in this case made it clear that the president is not above the law. The Supreme Court held that only those presidential conversations and communications that relate to performing the duties of the office of president are confidential and protected from a judicial order of disclosure. The Court ordered Nixon to give up the tapes, which revealed evidence linking the president to the conspiracy to obstruct justice. He resigned from office shortly thereafter.

Worcester v. *Georgia* (1832)

State officials in Georgia wanted to remove the Cherokees from land that had been guaranteed to them in treaties. Samuel Worcester was a Congregational missionary who worked with the Cherokee people. He was arrested for failure to have a license that the state required to live in Cherokee country and for refusing to obey an order from the Georgia militia to leave Cherokee lands. Worcester then sued the state of Georgia. He claimed that Georgia had no legal authority on Cherokee land because the United States government recognized the Cherokee in Georgia as a separate nation.

The Supreme Court agreed with Worcester by a vote of 5 to 1. Chief Justice John Marshall wrote the majority opinion which said that Native American nations were a distinct people with the right to have independent political communities and that only the federal government had authority over matters that involved the Cherokee.

President Andrew Jackson supported Georgia's efforts to remove the Cherokee to Indian Territory and refused to enforce the court's ruling. After the ruling Jackson remarked, "John Marshall has made his decision. Now let him enforce it."

The Magna Carta

The Magna Carta, signed by King John in 1215, marked a decisive step forward in the development of constitutional government in England. Later, it became a model for colonists who carried the Magna Carta's guarantees of legal and political rights to America.

1. . . . [T]hat the English Church shall be free, and shall have its rights undiminished, and its liberties unimpaired. . . . we have also granted, for us and our heirs for ever, all the liberties written out below, to have and to keep for them and their heirs, of us and our heirs:

39. No free man shall be seized or imprisoned, or stripped of his rights or possessions, or outlawed or exiled, or deprived of his standing in any other way, nor will we proceed with force against him, or send others to do so, except by the lawful judgement of his equals or by the law of the land.

40. To no one will we sell, to no one deny or delay right or justice.

41. All merchants may enter or leave England unharmed and without fear, and may stay or travel within it, by land or water, for purposes of trade, free from all illegal exactions, in accordance with ancient and lawful customs. This, however, does not apply in time of war to merchants from a country that is at war with us.

42. In future it shall be lawful for any man to leave and return to our kingdom unharmed and without fear, by land or water, preserving his allegiance to us, except in time of war, for some short period, for the common benefit of the realm.

60. All these customs and liberties that we have granted shall be observed in our kingdom in so far as concerns our own relations with our subjects. Let all men of our kingdom, whether clergy or laymen, observe them similarly in their relations with their own men.

63. . . . Both we and the barons have sworn that all this shall be observed in good faith and without deceit. Witness the abovementioned people and many others. Given by our hand in the meadow that is called Runnymede, between Windsor and Staines, on the fifteenth day of June in the seventeenth year of our reign.

◀ **Illuminated manuscript, Middle Ages**

The Mayflower Compact

On November 21, 1620, 41 colonists aboard the Mayflower drafted this agreement. The Mayflower Compact was the first plan of self-government enacted in the English colonies.

IN The Name of God, Amen. We, whose names are underwritten, the Loyal Subjects of our dread Sovereign Lord King James, by the Grace of God, of Great Britain, France, and Ireland, King, Defender of the Faith, &c. Having undertaken for the Glory of God, and Advancement of the Christian Faith, and the Honour of our King and Country, a Voyage to plant the first colony in the northern Parts of Virginia; Do by these Presents, solemnly and mutually in the Presence of God and one another, covenant and combine ourselves together into a civil Body Politick, for our better Ordering and Preservation, and Furtherance of the Ends aforesaid: And by Virtue hereof do enact, constitute, and frame, such just and equal Laws, Ordinances, Acts, Constitutions, and Offices, from time to time, as shall be thought most meet and convenient for the general Good of the Colony; unto which we promise all due Submission and Obedience. In Witness whereof we have hereunto subscribed our names at Cape Cod the eleventh of November, in the Reign of our Sovereign Lord King James of England, France, and Ireland, the eighteenth and of Scotland, the fifty-fourth. Anno Domini, 1620

The Federalist, No. 10

James Madison wrote several articles supporting ratification of the Constitution. Below, Madison argues for the idea of a federal republic.

By a faction, I understand a number of citizens . . . who are united and actuated by some common impulse . . . adversed to the rights of other citizens. . . .

The inference to which we are brought is, that the CAUSES of faction cannot be removed, and that relief is only to be sought in the means of controlling its EFFECTS. . . .

A republic, by which I mean a government in which the scheme of representation takes place, . . . promises the cure for which we are seeking. . . .

The two great points of difference between a democracy and a republic are: first, the delegation of the government, in the latter, to a small number of citizens elected by the rest; secondly, the greater number of citizens, and greater sphere of country, over which the latter may be extended.

▲ **James Madison**

The effect of the first difference is . . . to refine and enlarge the public views, by passing them through the medium of a chosen body of citizens, whose wisdom may best discern the true interest of their country, and whose patriotism and love of justice will be least likely to sacrifice it to temporary or partial considerations.

Documents

Washington's Farewell Address

At the end of his second term as president, George Washington spoke of the dangers facing the young nation. He warned against the dangers of political parties and sectionalism, and he advised the nation against permanent alliances with other nations.

Citizens by birth or choice of a common country, that country has a right to concentrate your affections. The name of American, which belongs to you, in your national capacity, must always exalt the just pride of patriotism more than any appellation derived from local discriminations. With slight shades of difference, you have the same religion, manners, habits, and political principles. You have in a common cause fought and triumphed together. . . .

In contemplating the causes which may disturb our Union, it occurs as matter of serious concern that any ground should have been furnished for characterizing parties by *geographical* discriminations. . . .

No alliances, however strict between the parts, can be an adequate substitute. They must inevitably experience the infractions and interruptions which all alliances in all times have experienced. . . .

▲ **George Washington**

The great rule of conduct for us, in regard to foreign nations, is in extending our commercial relations to have with them as little *political* connection as possible. . . .

. . . I anticipate with pleasing expectations that retreat in which I promise myself to realize . . . the sweet enjoyment of partaking, in the midst of my fellow citizens, the benign influence of good laws under a free government, the ever favorite object of my heart, and the happy reward, as I trust, of our mutual cares, labors, and dangers.

The Star-Spangled Banner

During the British bombardment of Fort McHenry during the War of 1812, a young Baltimore lawyer named Francis Scott Key was inspired by the sight to write the words to "The Star-Spangled Banner." Although it became popular immediately, it was not until 1931 that Congress officially declared this song our national anthem.

O! say can you see by the dawn's early light,
What so proudly we hail'd at the twilight's last gleaming;
Whose broad stripes and bright stars, through the perilous fight,
O'er the ramparts we watch'd were so gallantly streaming;
And the rockets' red glare, the bombs bursting in air,
Gave proof through the night that our flag was still there;
O! say does that star-spangled banner yet wave,
O'er the land of the free, and the home of the brave.

Documents

The Monroe Doctrine

In an 1823 address to Congress, President James Monroe proclaimed the Monroe Doctrine. Designed to end European influence in the Western Hemisphere, it became a cornerstone of United States foreign policy.

With the existing colonies or dependencies of any European power we have not interfered and shall not interfere. But with the governments who have declared their independence and maintained it, and whose independence we have, on great consideration and on just principles, acknowledged, we could not view any interposition for the purpose of oppressing them, or controlling in any other manner their destiny, by any European power in any other light than as the manifestation of an unfriendly disposition toward the United States. . . .

▲ James Monroe

Our policy in regard to Europe, which was adopted at an early stage of the wars which have so long agitated that quarter of the globe, nevertheless remains the same, which is not to interfere in the internal concerns of any of its powers; to consider the government de facto as the legitimate government for us; to cultivate friendly relations with it, and to preserve those relations by a frank, firm, and manly policy, meeting in all instances the just claims of every power, submitting to injuries from none.

The Memorial of the Cherokee Nation

The Indian Removal Act of 1830 called for moving Native Americans west of the Mississippi River. Cherokee leaders protested the policy.

We are aware, that some persons suppose it will be for our advantage to remove beyond the Mississippi. We think otherwise. Our people universally think otherwise. . . .

We wish to remain on the land of our fathers. We have a perfect and original right to remain without interruption or molestation. The treaties with us, and laws of the United States made in pursuance of treaties, guaranty our residence and our privileges, and secure us against intruders. Our only request is, that these treaties may be fulfilled, and these laws executed. . . .

. . . We have been called a poor, ignorant, and degraded people. We certainly are not rich; nor have we ever boasted of our knowledge, or our moral or intellectual elevation. But there is not a man within our limits so ignorant as not to know that he has a right to live on the land of his fathers, in the possession of his immemorial privileges, and that this right has been acknowledged and guaranteed by the United States; nor is there a man so degraded as not to feel a keen sense of injury, on being deprived of this right and driven into exile.

▲ Beaded shoulder bag, Cherokee people

Documents

The Seneca Falls Declaration

One of the first documents to express the desire for equal rights for women is the Declaration of Sentiments and Resolutions, issued in 1848 at the Seneca Falls Convention in Seneca Falls, New York. Led by Lucretia Mott and Elizabeth Cady Stanton, the delegates adopted a set of resolutions that called for woman suffrage and opportunities for women in employment and education. Excerpts from the Declaration follow.

When, in the course of human events, it becomes necessary for one portion of the family of man to assume among the people of the earth a position different from that which they have hitherto occupied, but one to which the laws of nature and of nature's God entitle them, a decent respect to the opinions of mankind requires that they should declare the causes that impel them to such a course.

We hold these truths to be self-evident: that all men and women are created equal; that they are endowed by their Creator with certain inalienable rights; that among these are life, liberty, and the pursuit of happiness; that to secure these rights governments are instituted, deriving their just powers from the consent of the governed. Whenever any form of government becomes destructive of these ends, it is the right of those who suffer from it to refuse allegiance to it, and to insist upon the institution of a new government, laying its foundation on such principles, and organizing its powers in such form as to them shall seem most likely to effect their safety and happiness. Prudence, indeed, will dictate that governments long established should not be changed for light and transient causes; . . . But when a long train of abuses and usurpations, pursuing invariably the same object, evinces a design to reduce them under absolute despotism, it is their duty to throw off such government, and to provide new guards for their future security. . . .

The history of mankind is a history of repeated injuries and usurpations on the part of man toward woman, having in direct object the establishment of an absolute tyranny over her. To prove this, let facts be submitted to a candid world. . . .

Now, in view of this entire disfranchisement of one-half the people of this country, their social and religious degradation,—in view of the unjust laws above mentioned, and because women do feel themselves aggrieved, oppressed, and fraudulently deprived of their most sacred rights, we insist that they have immediate admission to all the rights and privileges which belong to them as citizens of these United States.

▲ **Elizabeth Cady Stanton**

Documents

The Emancipation Proclamation

On January 1, 1863, President Abraham Lincoln issued the Emancipation Proclamation, which freed all enslaved people in states under Confederate control. The Proclamation was a step toward the Thirteenth Amendment (1865), which ended slavery in all of the United States.

That on the 1st day of January, in the year of our Lord [1863], all persons held as slaves within any state or designated part of a state, the people whereof shall then be in rebellion against the United States, shall be then, thenceforward, and forever free; and the Executive Government of the United States, including the military and naval authority thereof, will recognize and maintain the freedom of such persons, and will do no act or acts to repress such persons, or any of them, in any efforts they may make for their actual freedom.

That the Executive will, on the 1st day of January aforesaid, by proclamation, designate the states and parts of states, if any, in which the people thereof, respectively, shall then be in rebellion against the United States; and the fact that any state, or the people thereof, shall on that day be, in good faith, represented in the Congress of the United States by members chosen thereto at elections wherein a majority of the qualified voters of such state shall have participated, shall, in the absence of strong countervailing testimony, be deemed conclusive evidence that such state, and the people thereof, are not then in rebellion against the United States. . . .

And by virtue of the power, and for the purpose aforesaid, I do order and declare that all persons held as slaves within said designated states, and parts of states, are, and henceforward shall be free; and that the Executive Government of the United States, including the military and naval authorities thereof, will recognize and maintain the freedom of said persons.

And I hereby enjoin upon the people so declared to be free to abstain from all violence, unless in necessary self-defense; and I recommend to them that, in all cases when allowed, they labor faithfully for reasonable wages.

And I further declare and make known, that such persons of suitable condition, will be received into the armed service of the United States. . . .

And upon this act, sincerely believed to be an act of justice, warranted by the Constitution, upon military necessity, I invoke the considerate judgement of mankind, and the gracious favor of Almighty God.

▲ Abraham Lincoln

Members of the 4th Infantry ▶

Documents

The Gettysburg Address

On November 19, 1863, President Abraham Lincoln gave a short speech at the dedication of a national cemetery at Gettysburg. His simple yet eloquent words expressed his hopes for a nation divided by civil war.

Four score and seven years ago our fathers brought forth on this continent, a new nation, conceived in Liberty, and dedicated to the proposition that all men are created equal.

Now we are engaged in a great civil war, testing whether that nation or any nation so conceived and so dedicated, can long endure. We are met on a great battle–field of that war. We have come to dedicate a portion of that field, as a final resting place for those who here gave their lives that that nation might live. It is altogether fitting and proper that we should do this.

But, in a larger sense, we can not dedicate—we can not consecrate—we can not hallow—this ground. The brave men, living and dead, who struggled here, have consecrated it, far above our poor power to add or detract. The world will little note, nor long remember what we say here, but it can never forget what they did here. It is for us the living, rather, to be dedicated here to the unfinished work which they who fought here have thus far so nobly advanced. It is rather for us to be here dedicated to the great task remaining before us—that from these honored dead we take increased devotion to that cause for which they gave the last full measure of devotion—that we here highly resolve that these dead shall not have died in vain—that this nation, under God, shall have a new birth of freedom—and that government of the people, by the people, for the people, shall not perish from the earth.

Soldier's kit, Civil War ▼

▲ Gettysburg Memorial

I Will Fight No More

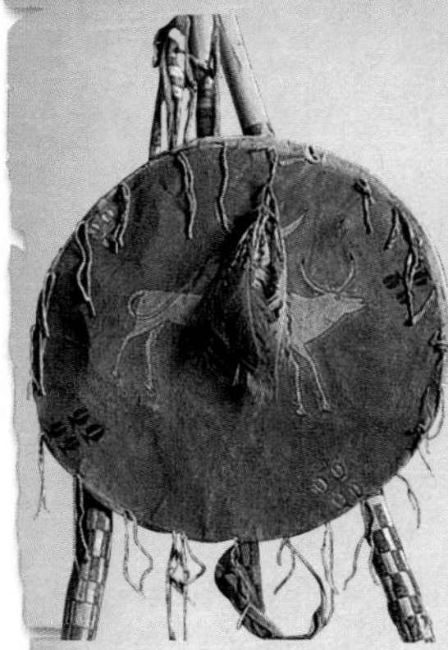

Shield made of buffalo hide

In 1877 the Nez Perce fought the government's attempt to move them to a smaller reservation. After a remarkable attempt to escape to Canada, Chief Joseph realized that resistance was hopeless and advised his people to surrender.

Tell General Howard I know his heart. What he told me before, I have it in my heart. I am tired of fighting. . . . The old men are all dead. It is the young men who say yes or no. He who led on the young men is dead. It is cold, and we have no blankets; the little children are freezing to death. My people, some of them, have run away to the hills, and have no blankets, no food. No one knows where they are—perhaps freezing to death. I want to have time to look for my children, and see how many of them I can find. Maybe I shall find them among the dead. Hear me, my chiefs! I am tired; my heart is sick and sad. From where the sun now stands I will fight no more forever.

The Pledge of Allegiance

In 1892 the nation celebrated the 400th anniversary of Columbus's landing in America. In connection with this celebration, Francis Bellamy, a magazine editor, wrote and published the Pledge of Allegiance. The words "under God" were added by Congress in 1954 at the urging of President Dwight D. Eisenhower.

I pledge allegiance to the flag of the United States of America and to the Republic for which it stands, one nation under God, indivisible, with liberty and justice for all.

Students in a New York City school recite the Pledge of Allegiance.

The American's Creed

William Tyler Page of Friendship Heights, Maryland, wrote The American's Creed. This statement of political faith summarizes the true meaning of freedom available to all Americans. The U.S. House of Representatives adopted the creed on behalf of the American people on April 3, 1918.

I believe in the United States of America as a Government of the people, by the people, for the people; whose just powers are derived from the consent of the governed; a democracy in a republic; a sovereign Nation of many sovereign States; a perfect union, one and inseparable; established upon those principles of freedom, equality, justice, and humanity for which American patriots sacrificed their lives and fortunes.

I therefore believe it is my duty to my Country to love it; to support its Constitution; to obey its laws; to respect its flag; and to defend it against all enemies.

The Fourteen Points

On January 8, 1918, President Woodrow Wilson went before Congress to offer a statement of aims called the Fourteen Points. Wilson's plan called for freedom of the seas in peace and war, an end to secret alliances, and equal trading rights for all countries. The excerpt that follows is taken from the President's message.

We entered this war because violations of right had occurred which touched us to the quick and made the life of our own people impossible unless they were corrected and the world secure once for all against their recurrence. What we demand in this war, therefore, is nothing peculiar to ourselves. It is that the world be made fit and safe to live in; and particularly that it be made safe for every peace-loving nation which, like our own, wishes to live its own life, determine its own institutions, be assured of justice and fair dealing by the other peoples of the world as against force and selfish aggression. All the peoples of the world are in effect partners in this interest, and for our own part we see very clearly that unless justice be done to others it will not be done to us. The programme of the world's peace, therefore, is our programme; and that programme, the only possible programme, as we see it, is this:

I. Open covenants of peace, openly arrived at, after which there shall be no private international understandings of any kind but diplomacy shall proceed always frankly and in the public view.

II. Absolute freedom of navigation upon the seas, outside territorial waters, alike in peace and in war, except as the seas may be closed in whole or in part by international action for the enforcement of international covenants.

XIV. A general association of nations must be formed under specific covenants for the purpose of affording mutual guarantees of political independence and territorial integrity to great and small states alike.

Brown v. Board of Education

On May 17, 1954, the Supreme Court ruled in Brown *v.* Board of Education of Topeka, Kansas, *that racial segregation in public schools was unconstitutional. This decision provided the legal basis for court challenges to segregation in every aspect of American life.*

The plaintiffs contend that segregated public schools are not "equal" and cannot be made "equal," and that hence they are deprived of the equal protection of the laws. Because of the obvious importance of the question presented, the Court took jurisdiction. . . .

Our decision, therefore, cannot turn on merely a comparison of these tangible factors in the Negro and white schools involved in each of the cases. We must look instead to the effect of segregation itself on public education.

In approaching this problem, we cannot turn the clock back to 1868, when the Amendment was adopted, or even to 1896, when *Plessy* v. *Ferguson* was written. We must consider public education in the light of its full development and its present place in American life throughout the Nation. Only in this way can it be determined if segregation in public schools deprives these plaintiffs of the equal protection of the laws.

Today, education is perhaps the most important function of state and local governments. Compulsory school attendance laws and the great expenditures for education both demonstrate our recognition of the importance of education to our democratic society. . . . In these days, it is doubtful that any child may reasonably be expected to succeed in life if he is denied the opportunity of an education. Such an opportunity, where the state has undertaken to provide it, is a right which must be made available to all on equal terms.

We come then to the question presented: Does segregation of children in public schools solely on the basis of race, even though the physical facilities and other "tangible" factors may be equal, deprive the children of the minority group of equal educational opportunities? We believe that it does. . . .

. . . We conclude that, in the field of public education, the doctrine of "separate but equal" has no place. Separate educational facilities are inherently unequal. Therefore, we hold that the plaintiffs and others similarly situated for whom the actions have been brought are, by reason of the segregation complained of, deprived of the equal protection of the laws guaranteed by the Fourteenth Amendment.

▲ Troops escort students to newly integrated school.

Documents

John F. Kennedy's Inaugural Address

President Kennedy's Inaugural Address on January 20, 1961, set the tone for his administration. In his address he stirred the nation by calling for "a grand and global alliance" to fight tyranny, poverty, disease, and war.

We observe today not a victory of party but a celebration of freedom—symbolizing an end as well as a beginning—signifying renewal as well as change. For I have sworn before you and Almighty God the same solemn oath our forebears prescribed nearly a century and three-quarters ago.

The world is very different now. For man holds in his mortal hands the power to abolish all forms of human poverty and all forms of human life. And yet the same revolutionary beliefs for which our forebears fought are still at issue around the globe—the belief that the rights of man come not from the generosity of the state but from the hand of God.

We dare not forget today that we are the heirs of that first revolution. Let the word go forth from this time and place, to friend and foe alike, that the torch has been passed to a new generation of Americans—born in this century, tempered by war, disciplined by a hard and bitter peace, proud of our ancient heritage—and unwilling to witness or permit the slow undoing of those human rights to which this nation has always been committed, and to which we are committed today at home and around the world.

Let every nation know, whether it wishes us well or ill, that we shall pay any price, bear any burden, meet any hardship, support any friend, oppose any foe to assure the survival and the success of liberty.

This much we pledge—and more.

To those old allies whose cultural and spiritual origins we share, we pledge the loyalty of faithful friends. United, there is little we cannot do in a host of cooperative ventures. Divided, there is little we can do. . . .

Let us never negotiate out of fear. But let us never fear to negotiate.

Let both sides explore what problems unite us instead of belaboring those problems which divide us. . . .

Let both sides seek to invoke the wonders of science instead of its terrors. Together let us explore the stars, conquer the deserts, eradicate disease, tap the ocean depths, and encourage the arts and commerce. . . .

And so, my fellow Americans: ask not what your country can do for you—ask what you can do for your country.

My fellow citizens of the world: ask not what America will do for you, but what together we can do for the freedom of man.

◀ **President Kennedy speaking at his inauguration**

Documents

I Have a Dream

On August 28, 1963, while Congress debated wide-ranging civil rights legislation, Dr. Martin Luther King, Jr., led more than 200,000 people in a march on Washington, D.C. On the steps of the Lincoln Memorial he gave a stirring speech in which he eloquently spoke of his dreams for African Americans and for the United States. Excerpts of the speech follow.

There are those who are asking the devotees of civil rights, "When will you be satisfied?"

We can never be satisfied as long as the Negro is the victim of the unspeakable horrors of police brutality. . . .

We cannot be satisfied as long as the Negro's basic mobility is from a smaller ghetto to a larger one.

We can never be satisfied as long as a Negro in Mississippi cannot vote and a Negro in New York believes he has nothing for which to vote. . . .

I say to you today, my friends, that in spite of the difficulties and frustrations of the moment I still have a dream. It is a dream deeply rooted in the American dream.

I have a dream that one day this nation will rise up and live out the true meaning of its creed: "We hold these truths to be self-evident, that all men are created equal."

▲ Dr. Martin Luther King, Jr.

I have a dream that one day on the red hills of Georgia the sons of former slaves and the sons of former slave-owners will be able to sit down together at the table of brotherhood.

I have a dream that one day even the state of Mississippi, a desert state sweltering with the heat of injustice and oppression, will be transformed into an oasis of freedom and justice.

I have a dream that my four little children will one day live in a nation where they will not be judged by the color of their skin but by the content of their character. . . .

When we let freedom ring, when we let it ring from every village and every hamlet, from every state and every city, we will be able to speed up that day when all of God's children, black men and white men, Jews and Gentiles, Protestants and Catholics, will be able to join hands and sing in the words of the old Negro spiritual: "Free at last! Free at last! Thank God Almighty, we are free at last!"

◀ The March on Washington

Documents

Review

California Standards Handbook

Grade 8

Dear Student and Family,

After you complete each chapter, take time to review what you have learned by using this handbook. The Standards Handbook lists all of the California History–Social Science content standards covered in each chapter of the book. In addition, a brief review of the content and page numbers where the content can be found are included. Test your knowledge of each major standard by answering the questions that appear in each of the red boxes.

Remember, the importance of the knowledge and skills you gain this year will extend well beyond your classroom. After all, you learn about American history not simply to know names and dates, but to become a well-informed citizen of the United States and the world.

Contents

Standard US8.1 863
Standard US8.2 864
Standard US8.3 866
Standard US8.4 868
Standard US8.5 869
Standard US8.6 870
Standard US8.7 872
Standard US8.8 873
Standard US8.9 875
Standard US8.10 877
Standard US8.11 879
Standard US8.12 881
Answer Key 884

US8.1

What Is the Standard?	Where Can I Find It?
US8.1 Students understand the major events preceding the founding of the nation and relate their significance to the development of American constitutional democracy.	**Chapter 2** covers Standard 8.1, including the beginnings of self-government in America, England's policies towards the colonies, the Declaration of Independence, and the American Revolution.
US8.1.1 Describe the relationship between the moral and political ideas of the Great Awakening and the development of revolutionary fervor.	**Chapter 2, Section 2** The Great Awakening expanded religious freedom and unified colonists from varying regions. **(Review pages 128–129.)**
US8.1.2 Analyze the philosophy of government expressed in the Declaration of Independence, with an emphasis on government as a means of securing individual rights (e.g., key phrases such as "all men are created equal, that they are endowed by their Creator with certain unalienable Rights").	**Chapter 2, Section 4** The Declaration of Independence sets forth ideas of individual rights and limited government. **(Review pages 152, 155, 164–167.)**
US8.1.3 Analyze how the American Revolution affected other nations, especially France.	**Chapter 2, Section 4** The American Revolution influenced similar movements in France, Saint Domingue, and other places. **(Review page 157.)**
US8.1.4 Describe the nation's blend of civic republicanism, classical liberal principles, and English parliamentary traditions.	**Chapter 2, Section 1** Many American colonies were created out of the desire for freedom of religion. **(Review pages 120–124.)** **Chapter 2, Sections 1 and 2** Many of the colonies experimented successfully with self-government. **(Review pages 119–124, 130–131, 132–133.)** **Chapter 2, Section 3** New taxes and the attempt by Great Britain to strengthen control over the colonies led colonists to rebel and declare independence. **(Review pages 135–141.)**

Standards Practice

1 The Great Awakening was important because it

A alerted colonists to the need for freedom from taxation without representation.

B was part of the Declaration of Independence.

C strengthened English control over the colonies.

D contributed to the expansion of religious freedom and helped unify colonists.

US8.2

What Is the Standard?	Where Can I Find It?
US8.2 Students analyze the political principles underlying the U.S. Constitution and compare the enumerated and implied powers of the federal government.	**Chapters 2, 3, and 4** discuss the development of a constitutional democracy and how the United States Constitution reflects the values, goals, and history of the society that created it.
US8.2.1 Discuss the significance of the Magna Carta, the English Bill of Rights, and the Mayflower Compact.	**Chapter 2, Sections 1 and 2** The Mayflower Compact followed English political tradition. **(Review pages 120, 133.)** **Chapter 2, Section 2 and Chapter 3, Section 3** The political ideals of American leaders were based on English democratic thought. **(Review pages 132–133, 203, 850.)**
US8.2.2 Analyze the Articles of Confederation and the Constitution and the success of each in implementing the ideals of the Declaration of Independence.	**Chapter 3, Sections 1, 2, and 3** Both the Articles of Confederation and the Constitution created systems of representative government. **(Review pages 180–185, 194–201, 206–207.)** **Chapter 4, Section 1** Many of the Constitution's goals and major principles are directly related to the Declaration of Independence. **(Review pages 219–223.)**
US8.2.3 Evaluate the major debates that occurred during the development of the Constitution and their ultimate resolutions in such areas as shared power among institutions, divided state-federal power, slavery, the rights of individuals and states (later addressed by the addition of the Bill of Rights), and the status of American Indian nations under the commerce clause.	**Chapter 3, Sections 2 and 3** The framers of the Constitution met in Philadelphia in 1787 and discussed the creation of the new government, debating issues that would have a significant impact on the nation. **(Review pages 197–201, 204–207.)**
US8.2.4 Describe the political philosophy underpinning the Constitution as specified in the *Federalist Papers* (authored by James Madison, Alexander Hamilton, and John Jay) and the role of such leaders as Madison, George Washington, Roger Sherman, Gouverneur Morris, and James Wilson in the writing and ratification of the Constitution.	**Chapter 3, Section 2** Some leaders called for the protection of personal liberties through a Bill of Rights and sought to balance power between the states and the federal government. **(Review pages 197–201.)** **Chapter 3, Section 3** In order to explain and defend the principles of the newly drafted Constitution, Madison, Hamilton, and Jay wrote *The Federalist Papers*. **(Review pages 206–207, 208–209.)**

US8.2 *cont.*

What Is the Standard?	Where Can I Find It?
US8.2.5 Understand the significance of Jefferson's Statute for Religious Freedom as a forerunner of the First Amendment and the origins, purpose, and differing views of the founding fathers on the issue of separation of church and state.	**Chapter 4, Section 3** Jefferson's statute suggested a rigid separation between church and state and declared that a person could not be persecuted because of religious beliefs. Both ideas were fundamental to the creation of the First Amendment. **(Review page 235.)**
US8.2.6 Enumerate the powers of government set forth in the Constitution and the fundamental liberties ensured by the Bill of Rights.	**Chapter 4, Sections 1, 2, and 3** The Constitution is considered the ultimate source regarding the powers of the federal government. It was amended soon after its acceptance to include a Bill of Rights which provides for important individual freedoms. **(Review pages 223–225, 227–233, 235–236.)**
US8.2.7 Describe the principles of federalism, dual sovereignty, separation of powers, checks and balances, the nature and purpose of majority rule, and the ways in which the American idea of constitutionalism preserves individual rights.	**Chapter 4, Section 1** The principles found in the Constitution were the Framers' solutions to the problems posed by a representative government. The principles ensure that the power of the government rests in the hands of the people and that no part of government grows too strong. **(Review pages 221–225.)**

Standards Practice

1 What did the Bill of Rights accomplish?

A It freed enslaved people.
B It defined the separation of powers between the state and federal governments.
C It safeguarded individual rights and liberties.
D It explained guidelines for voting.

2 The system in which the power to govern is shared between the national government and the states is called

A popular sovereignty.
B federalism.
C domestic tranquility.
D the Bill of Rights.

US8.3

What Is the Standard?	Where Can I Find It?
US8.3 **Students understand the foundation of the American political system and the ways in which citizens participate in it.**	**Chapters 3, 4, and 5** cover Standard US8.3, including an analysis of the transformation from a colonial government to a republic, and the role of citizens in government.
US8.3.1 **Analyze the principles and concepts codified in state constitutions between 1777 and 1781 that created the context out of which American political institutions and ideas developed.**	**Chapter 3, Section 1** Soon after the Declaration of Independence was signed, colonial leaders began preparing state constitutions to replace colonial charters, establishing a political framework for the new Republic. **(Review page 179.)**
US8.3.2 **Explain how the ordinances of 1785 and 1787 privatized national resources and transferred federally owned lands into private holdings, townships, and states.**	**Chapter 3, Section 1** The Confederation Congress passed laws regarding surveying and organizing new territory. The Congress set policies that allowed new territories to become states in the Union. **(Review pages 181–183.)**
US8.3.3 **Enumerate the advantages of a common market among the states as foreseen in and protected by the Constitution's clauses on interstate commerce, common coinage, and full-faith and credit.**	**Chapter 4, Section 1** The United States became a large common market in which trade barriers between the states were eliminated, and individual states were prohibited from acting as separate nations. **(Review page 219.)**
US8.3.4 **Understand how the conflicts between Thomas Jefferson and Alexander Hamilton resulted in the emergence of two political parties (e.g., view of foreign policy, Alien and Sedition Acts, economic policy, National Bank, funding and assumption of the revolutionary debt).**	**Chapter 5, Section 1** Jefferson and Hamilton were members of George Washington's cabinet and were influential leaders of their time. **(Review pages 280–284.)** **Chapter 5, Section 3** Their ideas about the role of government reflected differences among Americans and contributed to the rise of the first political parties. **(Review pages 291–293.)**
US8.3.5 **Know the significance of the domestic resistance movements and ways in which the central government responded to such movements (e.g., Shays' Rebellion, the Whiskey Rebellion).**	**Chapter 3, Section 2 and Chapter 5, Section 2** Domestic uprisings challenged leaders in the young Republic to demonstrate that the federal government could control unrest and prevent violence. **(Review pages 194–195, 286.)**

US8.3 *cont.*

What Is the Standard?	Where Can I Find It?
US8.3.6 **Describe the basic law-making process and how the Constitution provides numerous opportunities for citizens to participate in the political process and to monitor and influence government (e.g., function of elections, political parties, interest groups).**	**Chapter 4, Section 2** The legislative branch is responsible for making laws, and thousands of bills are introduced in Congress each year. **(Review pages 227–228.)** **Chapter 4, Section 3** Citizens are expected to carry out certain duties and responsibilities to help ensure a good government and to protect their basic rights. **(Review pages 236–239.)**
US8.3.7 **Understand the functions and responsibilities of a free press.**	**Chapter 4, Section 3** Freedom of the press in America owes its origins in part to John Peter Zenger. **(Review pages 240–241.)** **Chapter 4, Section 3** The First Amendment protects freedom of the press. **(Review pages 240–241.)**

Standards Practice

1 Why were the ordinances of 1785 and 1787 important?

A They returned land to Native Americans.
B They transferred federally owned lands into private holdings.
C They provided for a national bank.
D They established a system of common coinage.

2 Alexander Hamilton was the leader of the political party known as the

A Republicans.
B Patriots.
C Federalists.
D Constitutionalists.

3 Shays's Rebellion was in protest to

A the transfer of lands to Canada.
B the call for a Constitutional Convention.
C northern laws that ended slavery.
D taxes and debts faced by farmers.

US8.4

What Is the Standard?	Where Can I Find It?
US8.4 Students analyze the aspirations and ideals of the people of the new nation.	**Chapters 5 and 6** cover the early years of the Republic. New policies were developed and the United States grew in size, while daily life reflected uniquely American qualities. Additional information can be found in **Chapter 10.**
US8.4.1 Describe the country's physical landscapes, political divisions, and territorial expansion during the terms of the first four presidents.	**Chapter 5, Section 3** Political parties developed and influenced national policy. **(Review pages 291–297.)** **Chapter 6, Sections 2 and 3** America's landscape encouraged settlement, agriculture, and industry, while the Louisiana Purchase extended the territory of the United States westward to the Rocky Mountains. **(Review pages 313–317, 326–327.)**
US8.4.2 Explain the policy significance of famous speeches (e.g., Washington's Farewell Address, Jefferson's 1801 Inaugural Address, John Q. Adams' Fourth of July 1821 Address).	**Chapter 5, Section 2 and Chapter 6, Section 1** Through important speeches, leaders, including Washington, Jefferson, and John Quincy Adams, influenced views on foreign policy and the power of the federal government. **(Review pages 289, 307, 331.)**
US8.4.3 Analyze the rise of capitalism and the economic problems and conflicts that accompanied it (e.g., Jackson's opposition to the National Bank; early decisions of the U.S. Supreme Court that reinforced the sanctity of contracts and a capitalist economic system of law).	**Chapters 6, Section 1 and Chapter 10, Section 3** While the Supreme Court had ruled in favor of the National Bank, as well as other measures in support of a capitalist economic system, some politicians, such as Andrew Jackson, fought against the Bank. **(Review pages 310–311, 459–460.)**
US8.4.4 Discuss daily life, including traditions in art, music, and literature, of early national America (e.g., through writings by Washington Irving, James Fenimore Cooper).	**Chapter 6, Section 3** In the early Republic, daily life for Americans varied by region, and Americans began to develop their own forms of literature, music, and architecture. **(Review pages 321–329.)**

Standards Practice

1 What river provided the eastern boundary of the Louisiana Purchase?

A Missouri River
B Columbia River
C Mississippi River
D Rio Grande River

US8.5

What Is the Standard?	Where Can I Find It?
US8.5 Students analyze U.S. foreign policy in the early Republic.	**Chapter 7** covers Standard US8.5 and explores how the United States met challenges in trade, foreign relations, and war in the early 1800s.
US8.5.1 Understand the political and economic causes and consequences of the War of 1812 and know the major battles, leaders, and events that led to a final peace.	**Chapter 7, Sections 1, 2, and 3** The United States was drawn into the conflict between Britain and France, eventually leading to war with Britain. Hard-fought battles on land and sea resulted in a victory for the United States and a new wave of American nationalism. **(Review pages 341–345, 354–359, 363–365, 368–369.)**
US8.5.2 Know the changing boundaries of the United States and describe the relationships the country had with its neighbors (current Mexico and Canada) and Europe, including the influence of the Monroe Doctrine, and how those relationships influenced westward expansion and the Mexican-American War.	**Chapter 7, Section 3** In the first half of the 1800s, the United States gained territory through war and treaties with other nations. The Monroe Doctrine was an attempt to limit European interventions in the Americas. **(Review pages 363–367.)**
US8.5.3 Outline the major treaties with American Indian nations during the administrations of the first four presidents and the varying outcomes of those treaties.	**Chapter 7, Section 1** As white Americans settled in Native American territories, conflict continued to develop between the two peoples. Treaties were made, but were often set aside or ignored. **(Review page 343.)**

Standards Practice

1 What did the Adams-Onís Treaty accomplish?

A It established the border between the United States and Canada.

B It ended the War of 1812.

C It established new trade relations with Spain.

D It resolved territorial disputes between Spain and the United States.

US8.6

What Is the Standard?	Where Can I Find It?
US8.6 Students analyze the divergent paths of the American people from 1800 to the mid-1800s and the challenges they faced, with emphasis on the Northeast.	**Chapter 8** covers Standard US8.6, and describes major developments in immigration, transportation, and industrialization in the United States.
US8.6.1 **Discuss the influence of industrialization and technological developments on the region, including human modification of the landscape and how physical geography shaped human actions (e.g., growth of cities, deforestation, farming, mineral extraction).**	**Chapter 8, Section 1** As new technology emerged in manufacturing, the economy of the Northeast became increasingly industrial. At the same time, cities developed along transportation routes like rivers and newly built roads. **(Review pages 383–387.)** **Chapter 8, Section 1** Americans used the natural resources at their disposal to provide for their families or create new industry. **(Review page 383.)**
US8.6.2 **Outline the physical obstacles to and the economic and political factors involved in building a network of roads, canals, and railroads (e.g., Henry Clay's American System).**	**Chapter 8, Section 2** In the early 1800s, leaders in the northeast promoted internal improvements, such as the building of the National Road and a canal system, to help the development of trade and industry. The invention of the steam engine and the railroad led to a revolution in transportation. **(Review pages 389–394.)**
US8.6.3 **List the reasons for the wave of immigration from Northern Europe to the United States and describe the growth in the number, size, and spatial arrangements of cities (e.g., Irish immigrants and the Great Irish Famine).**	**Chapter 8, Section 3** Many people from northern Europe migrated to the Northeast United States because of economic or political unrest in their home countries. Both the development of cities and the culture of the Northeast were affected by these newcomers. **(Review pages 398–401.)**
US8.6.4 **Study the lives of black Americans who gained freedom in the North and founded schools and churches to advance their rights and communities.**	**Chapter 8, Section 3** As slavery died out in the Northeast, African Americans tried to realize the ideals of freedom and developed institutions that reflected their needs and interests. **(Review page 397.)**

US8.6 *cont.*

What Is the Standard?	Where Can I Find It?
US8.6.5 Trace the development of the American education system from its earliest roots, including the roles of religious and private schools and Horace Mann's campaign for free public education and its assimilating role in American culture.	**Chapter 8, Section 4** Education played an increasingly important role in the young Republic and took on many different forms, including new colleges and schools for students with disabilities. **(Review page 405.)**
US8.6.6 Examine the women's suffrage movement (e.g., biographies, writings, and speeches of Elizabeth Cady Stanton, Margaret Fuller, Lucretia Mott, Susan B. Anthony).	**Chapter 8, Section 5** Women were eager to share in the ideals of the Declaration of Independence, and a movement to give women the right to vote developed. Women also made gains in education and in their legal rights related to marriage and family. **(Review pages 409–413.)**
US8.6.7 Identify common themes in American art as well as transcendentalism and individualism (e.g., writings about and by Ralph Waldo Emerson, Henry David Thoreau, Herman Melville, Louisa May Alcott, Nathaniel Hawthorne, Henry Wadsworth Longfellow).	**Chapter 8, Section 4** As American identity evolved, themes in art, writing, and music became distinctive. American authors created and explored new themes like transcendentalism and individualism. **(Review pages 406–407.)**

Standards Practice

1 What was the relationship between the Irish potato famine and the United States in the mid-1800s?

A The famine created a devastating shortage of food, causing more than 1.5 million Irish immigrants to come to the United States.
B The famine limited trade between the United States and Ireland.
C The famine caused a revolt among Irish in New York City.
D The famine inspired new farming technology in the United States.

2 Henry David Thoreau and Ralph Waldo Emerson belonged to a group of writers known as the

A Fundamentalists.
B Constitutionalists.
C Federalists.
D Transcendentalists.

US8.7

What Is the Standard?	Where Can I Find It?
US8.7 Students analyze the divergent paths of the American people in the South from 1800 to the mid-1800s and the challenges they faced.	**Chapter 9** covers Standard US8.7 as it explores the distinctive elements of the South's economy and culture, as well as the institution of slavery.
US8.7.1 Describe the development of the agrarian economy in the South, identify the locations of the cotton-producing states, and discuss the significance of cotton and the cotton gin.	**Chapter 9, Section 1** The production of cotton defined large-scale Southern agriculture, especially in the Deep South, while small independent farmers grew varied crops. **(Review pages 423–425.)**
US8.7.2 Trace the origins and development of slavery; its effects on black Americans and on the region's political, social, religious, economic, and cultural development; and identify the strategies that were tried to both overturn and preserve it (e.g., through the writings and historical documents on Nat Turner, Denmark Vesey).	**Chapter 9, Section 3** Slavery had an immense impact on the lives and culture of African Americans, and others, in the South. Enslaved people resisted slavery in a number of ways, including rebellions. **(Review pages 433–437.)**
US8.7.3 Examine the characteristics of white southern society and how the physical environment influenced events and conditions prior to the Civil War.	**Chapter 9, Section 1** The culture of white Southerners was primarily defined by small tenant farming or plantation farming. Cities were generally smaller than in the North, and industry played a much smaller role in the Southern economy. **(Review pages 423–431.)**
US8.7.4 Compare the lives of and opportunities for free blacks in the North with those of free blacks in the South.	**Chapter 9, Section 3** Free African Americans faced prejudice and discrimination in both the North and the South. **(Review page 430.)**

Standards Practice

1 The cotton gin was invented by Eli Whitney in 1793. How did the new technology change cotton production?

A It led to agricultural growth in the North.

B It contributed to the industrialization of the South.

C It dramatically increased the amount of cotton that could be processed.

D It reduced dependence on slave labor.

US8.8

What Is the Standard?	Where Can I Find It?
US8.8 Students analyze the divergent paths of the American people in the West from 1800 to the mid-1800s and the challenges they faced.	**Chapters 10 and 11** cover Standard US8.8 as they trace the development of the American West as a region with political, geographic, and cultural impact on the United States as a whole. Additional information can be found in **Chapter 15.**
US8.8.1 Discuss the election of Andrew Jackson as president in 1828, the importance of Jacksonian democracy, and his actions as president (e.g., the spoils system, veto of the National Bank, policy of Indian removal, opposition to the Supreme Court).	**Chapter 10, Sections 1 and 3** Andrew Jackson promised "equal protection and equal rights" to all, and a spirit of equality spread through American politics and government. His opposition to the National Bank was seen as supportive of the common people, rather than the wealthy. **(Review pages 447–448, 459–460.)** **Chapter 10, Section 2** Despite a Supreme Court ruling to the contrary, Jackson pursued a policy of Indian Removal to open lands for white settlement and to ensure security on the frontier. **(Review pages 453–457, 463.)**
US8.8.2 Describe the purpose, challenges, and economic incentives associated with westward expansion, including the concept of Manifest Destiny (e.g., the Lewis and Clark expedition, accounts of the removal of Indians, the Cherokees' "Trail of Tears," settlement of the Great Plains) and the territorial acquisitions that spanned numerous decades.	**Chapter 11, Section 1** Once the United States reached an agreement to gain control of the Oregon Country, American settlers streamed to the Far West despite many difficulties. Soon Americans came to believe that they should occupy the entire continent. **(Review pages 471–475.)**
US8.8.3 Describe the role of pioneer women and the new status that western women achieved (e.g., Laura Ingalls Wilder, Annie Bidwell; slave women gaining freedom in the West; Wyoming granting suffrage to women in 1869).	**Chapter 11, Section 4** Annie Bidwell, a California pioneer, dedicated her life to social and agricultural reform. **(Review page 502.)** **Chapter 15, Section 2** On the frontier, women enjoyed new freedoms and became farmers, business owners, and community leaders. **(Review pages 676–679.)**
US8.8.4 Examine the importance of the great rivers and the struggle over water rights.	**Chapter 11, Section 2** As settlers moved into the American West, rivers were an important resource for transportation, irrigation, and eventually energy production. **(Review pages 488–489.)**

US8.8 *cont.*

What Is the Standard?	Where Can I Find It?
US8.8.5 Discuss Mexican settlements and their locations, cultural traditions, attitudes toward slavery, land-grant system, and economies.	**Chapter 11, Section 3** Following Mexico's independence from Spain, Spanish missions in the Southwest were abolished and an economy based on large ranches developed. **(Review pages 492–494.)**
US8.8.6 Describe the Texas War for Independence and the Mexican-American War, including territorial settlements, the aftermath of the wars, and the effects the wars had on the lives of Americans, including Mexican Americans today.	**Chapter 11, Section 2** Settlers in Texas fought for independence from Mexico and created a new nation before becoming a state in the Union. **(Review pages 481–487.)** **Chapter 11, Section 3** The Mexican-American War resolved territorial disputes between the United States and Mexico and resulted in America's acquisition of additional territories, including California. **(Review pages 491–497.)**

Standards Practice

1 The Treaty of Guadalupe Hidalgo of 1848 is significant because

A Mexico gave up all claims to Texas, California, and New Mexico.
B it ended the Texas War for Independence.
C it created a new trade relationship between the United States and Mexico.
D Spain gave up all claims to Florida.

2 The slogan "Fifty-four Forty or Fight" referred to which of the following territories?

A Texas
B Oregon
C Florida
D California

3 Relations between Mexico and the United States were strained because the United States insisted that the Texas-Mexico border was the

A Nueces River.
B Pacific Ocean.
C Mississippi River.
D Rio Grande.

US8.9

What Is the Standard?	Where Can I Find It?
US8.9 Students analyze the early and steady attempts to abolish slavery and to realize the ideals of the Declaration of Independence.	**Chapter 12** covers the efforts to ban or limit slavery as the United States expanded in the early 1800s. Additional information can be found in **Chapters 3, 6, 8, and 9.**
US8.9.1 Describe the leaders of the movement (e.g., John Quincy Adams and his proposed constitutional amendment, John Brown and the armed resistance, Harriet Tubman and the Underground Railroad, Benjamin Franklin, Theodore Weld, William Lloyd Garrison, Frederick Douglass).	**Chapter 12, Section 1** The courageous leadership of many people gave the abolition movement increasing power and effectiveness. For example, William Lloyd Garrison stimulated the growth of the antislavery movement. The most widely known African American abolitionists were Frederick Douglass and Harriet Tubman. **(Review pages 529–534.)**
US8.9.2 Discuss the abolition of slavery in early state constitutions.	**Chapter 3, Section 2** Between 1783 and 1804, states, such as Connecticut, Rhode Island, New York, and New Jersey, passed laws that gradually ended slavery. **(Review pages 195–196.)**
US8.9.3 Describe the significance of the Northwest Ordinance in education and in the banning of slavery in new states north of the Ohio River.	**Chapter 3, Section 1** The Northwest Ordinance outlawed slavery in territory north of the Ohio River, marking the United States' first attempt to make slavery illegal. **(Review page 182.)** **Chapter 6, Section 3** Education was a vital part of a healthy democracy, and it was provided for in the Northwest Ordinance. **(Review page 321.)**
US8.9.4 Discuss the importance of the slavery issue as raised by the annexation of Texas and California's admission to the union as a free state under the Compromise of 1850.	**Chapter 12, Section 2** Pro-slavery leaders wanted to preserve their balance of power in Congress and resisted the admission of new states where slavery would not be legal. Political disagreement was often heated and divisive. **(Review pages 539–542.)**

US8.9 *cont.*

What Is the Standard?	Where Can I Find It?
US8.9.5 Analyze the significance of the States' Rights Doctrine, the Missouri Compromise (1820), the Wilmot Proviso (1846), the Compromise of 1850, Henry Clay's role in the Missouri Compromise and the Compromise of 1850, the Kansas-Nebraska Act (1854), the *Dred Scott* v. *Sandford* decision (1857), and the Lincoln-Douglas debates (1858).	**Chapter 12, Section 2** The possible spread of slavery into the West was an issue that repeatedly divided the nation. The South affirmed states' rights, while political decisions, such as the Missouri Compromise, the Wilmot Proviso, and the Compromise of 1850, were proposed or implemented to deal with the spread of slavery. **(Review pages 536, 539–542.)** **Chapter 12, Section 3** The Kansas-Nebraska Act resulted from another dispute over slavery in Congress. **(Review page 544.)** **Chapter 12, Section 4** The Supreme Court's decision in the *Dred Scott* case and the Lincoln-Douglas debates called attention to the issue of slavery as the nation moved to the brink of conflict. **(Review pages 549–553.)**
US8.9.6 Describe the lives of free blacks and the laws that limited their freedom and economic opportunities.	**Chapter 8, Section 3 and Chapter 12, Section 4** In the North, free African Americans were barred from schools and public facilities; some African Americans, however, were successful in the business world. **(Review pages 397, 551.)** **Chapter 9, Section 2** Cities allowed free African Americans in the South to form their own communities, but laws limited their rights. **(Review page 430.)**

Standards Practice

1 Which abolition leader escaped slavery in Maryland and settled in the North?

A David Walker
B Frederick Douglass
C William Lloyd Garrison
D Angelina Grimké

2 What principle did the Supreme Court establish in the *Dred Scott* decision?

A It made the sale of slaves illegal.
B It ruled slavery illegal west of the Mississippi River.
C It declared that slaves were not people and therefore could be legally traded as property.
D It set a profit limit on the sale of slaves.

US8.10

What Is the Standard?	Where Can I Find It?
US8.10 Students analyze the multiple causes, key events, and complex consequences of the Civil War.	**Chapters 12 and 13** cover the Civil War, including the road to war, the political and constitutional crisis of secession, the slavery debate, and the impact of the war on daily life in both the North and South.
US8.10.1 Compare the conflicting interpretations of state and federal authority as emphasized in the speeches and writings of statesmen such as Daniel Webster and John C. Calhoun.	**Chapter 12, Section 2** Daniel Webster declared that the federal government was sovereign and supported a strong Union, while John C. Calhoun was a champion of states' rights. **(Review pages 537–538.)**
US8.10.2 Trace the boundaries constituting the North and the South, the geographical differences between the two regions, and the differences between agrarians and industrialists.	**Chapter 13, Section 1** The North and South were distinct regions with marked differences in economy, transportation, and geography. The North had a larger population and more industry and resources. The South remained largely agricultural. **(Review pages 571–573.)**
US8.10.3 Identify the constitutional issues posed by the doctrine of nullification and secession and the earliest origins of that doctrine.	**Chapter 12, Section 2** After the Constitution's ratification, different leaders threatened to reject federal laws or leave the Union, for example, in the Virginia and Kentucky Resolutions, the Hartford Convention, and the tariff controversy. **(Review pages 537–538.)** **Chapter 12, Section 5** Some Southerners justified secession based on the contract theory of the Constitution. **(Review page 556.)**
US8.10.4 Discuss Abraham Lincoln's presidency and his significant writings and speeches and their relationship to the Declaration of Independence, such as his "House Divided" speech (1858), Gettysburg Address (1863), Emancipation Proclamation (1863), and inaugural addresses (1861 and 1865).	**Chapter 12, Section 4** Lincoln expressed concern about the morality of slavery and emphasized the need to preserve the Union in his "House Divided" speech. **(Review pages 552–553.)** **Chapter 12, Section 5 and Chapter 13, Section 5** Lincoln articulated his ideals of freedom and unity in his two inaugural addresses. **(Review pages 557, 560, 610.)** **Chapter 13, Sections 3 and 5** In 1863, Lincoln made significant statements about freedom in the Emancipation Proclamation and the Gettysburg Address. **(Review pages 592–594, 607.)**

US8.10 *cont.*

What Is the Standard?	Where Can I Find It?
US8.10.5 Study the views and lives of leaders (e.g., Ulysses S. Grant, Jefferson Davis, Robert E. Lee) and soldiers on both sides of the war, including those of black soldiers and regiments.	**Chapter 12, Section 5 and Chapter 13, Section 1** Confederate President Jefferson Davis believed in states' rights. **(Review pages 561, 573.)** **Chapter 13, Sections 2 and 5** Battlefield decisions by Ulysses S. Grant changed the course of the war for the North. **(Review pages 579, 606–611.)** **Chapter 13, Sections 1, 2, and 5** Robert E. Lee was an effective Confederate general, but he could not lead his armies to ultimate victory. **(Review pages 574, 580–583, 605–606, 610–611.)** **Chapter 13, Section 3** In both the North and South, soldiers suffered terrible hardships. Black soldiers were kept from battle early in the war, but eventually were an important part of the Union army. **(Review pages 592–593, 595–596.)**
US8.10.6 Describe critical developments and events in the war, including the major battles, geographical advantages and obstacles, technological advances, and General Lee's surrender at Appomattox.	**Chapter 13, Sections 1 and 5** Although both the North and South had advantages and disadvantages, the North was in a better overall position to fight the Civil War. Aggressive offensives by the Union finally resulted in the Confederacy surrendering at Appomattox. **(Review pages 572–573, 605–613.)**
US8.10.7 Explain how the war affected combatants, civilians, the physical environment, and future warfare.	**Chapter 13, Sections 1 to 5** The Civil War became a "total war" that affected soldiers and civilians alike. **(Review pages 574, 582, 595–596, 598–601, 609–610.)** **Chapter 13, Sections 2 and 5** The use of new technology made the Civil War one of the first of the modern wars. The Civil War had a devastating effect on the countryside—for example, Sherman's march across Georgia. **(Review pages 578–579, 609–610.)**

Standards Practice

1 Who was the leader of the Confederate Army during the Civil War?

A Thomas "Stonewall" Jackson
B Jefferson Davis
C Robert E. Lee
D Ulysses S. Grant

2 Why was the Battle of Vicksburg an important turning point in the Civil War?

A The Confederacy surrendered.
B Confederacy captured Pennsylvania.
C The North gained control of Virginia.
D It split the South in two.

US8.11

What Is the Standard?	Where Can I Find It?
US8.11 Students analyze the character and lasting consequences of Reconstruction.	**Chapter 14** covers the aftermath of the Civil War in different regions of the country. Additional information can be found in **Chapters 15 and 17.**
US8.11.1 List the original aims of Reconstruction and describe its effects on the political and social structures of different regions.	**Chapter 14, Sections 1 and 2** The plan for Reconstruction developed by the Radical Republicans was much harsher than that proposed by Lincoln. Johnson's opposition to Radical Reconstruction led to his impeachment. **(Review pages 625–628, 631–634.)** **Chapter 14, Section 3** Reconstruction policies enabled African Americans and anti-Confederate groups to serve in Southern governments. New schools were built in the South for African Americans. **(Review pages 636–639.)**
US8.11.2 Identify the push-pull factors in the movement of former slaves to the cities in the North and to the West and their differing experiences in those regions (e.g., the experiences of Buffalo Soldiers).	**Chapter 14, Section 4; Chapter 15, Section 2; and Chapter 17, Section 2** Some African Americans left the restrictions of the South to settle or serve as soldiers on the western frontier. Others migrated from the South to seek economic opportunities in Northern cities. **(Review pages 641, 676–677, 751.)**
US8.11.3 Understand the effects of the Freedmen's Bureau and the restrictions placed on the rights and opportunities of freedmen, including racial segregation and "Jim Crow" laws.	**Chapter 14, Section 1** During the Reconstruction period, the Freedmen's Bureau brought food, clothing, medical services, and education to former enslaved persons. **(Review page 626.)** **Chapter 14, Sections 2 and 4** As Reconstruction lost its effectiveness, new legal and cultural barriers were erected against freedoms for black Americans. **(Review pages 630, 647–649.)**
US8.11.4 Trace the rise of the Ku Klux Klan and describe the Klan's effects.	**Chapter 14, Sections 3 and 4** Some Southerners used violence to undermine freedom for African Americans. The KKK carried out acts of terror to keep African Americans from exercising their rights. **(Review pages 638, 648.)**

US8.11 *cont.*

What Is the Standard? → Where Can I Find It?

US8.11.5 Understand the Thirteenth, Fourteenth, and Fifteenth Amendments to the Constitution and analyze their connection to Reconstruction.

Chapter 14, Sections 1 and 2 Through the Thirteenth, Fourteenth, and Fifteenth Amendments, Republican leaders in Congress sought to extend and protect the rights of African Americans. **(Review pages 628, 631, 634.)**

Standards Practice

1 How could former Confederate States reenter the Union under the Reconstruction Act of 1867?

A through a majority vote of the population

B by ratifying the Fourteenth Amendment and submitting a new state constitution for approval by Congress

C by giving freed slaves the right to vote

D by signing an oath of loyalty

2 What did the Fifteenth Amendment do?

A It forbade states from denying the vote on the basis of race.

B It gave citizenship to formerly enslaved African Americans.

C It ended slavery in the United States.

D It gave the right to vote to former Confederates.

3 Northern whites who settled in the South and supported Republican policies were known as

A sharecroppers.

B segregationists.

C carpetbaggers.

D Redeemers.

US8.12

What Is the Standard?	Where Can I Find It?
US8.12 Students analyze the transformation of the American economy and the changing social and political conditions in the United States in response to the Industrial Revolution.	**Chapters 15, 16, and 17** discuss the impact of the Industrial Revolution on ranching, farming, manufacturing, urbanization, and settling the West.
US8.12.1 Trace patterns of agricultural and industrial development as they relate to climate, use of natural resources, markets, and trade and locate such development on a map.	**Chapter 15, Sections 1 and 2** New discoveries of gold and silver brought miners to the West. Cattle raised on the open range in Texas were driven north to railroad lines and shipped to eastern markets. The Homestead Act brought farmers to the West. **(Review pages 667–671, 673–679.)** **Chapter 16, Sections 1, 2, 3** After the Civil War, railroads brought about the faster transport of goods and people. The American economy shifted from agriculture to industry as the nation realized it had the necessary materials for growth. A map on page 710 shows major railroads and mining centers. **(Review pages 707–711, 717, 719–723.)** **Chapter 17, Section 4** During the early 1900s, the federal government began to regulate America's growing industry. **(Review pages 766, 770–771.)**
US8.12.2 Identify the reasons for the development of federal Indian policy and the wars with American Indians and their relationship to agricultural development and industrialization.	**Chapter 15, Section 3** White settlement of the West led to conflict with and forced changes on Native Americans. The federal government set up policies to protect the agricultural and mining interests of settlers and to relocate Native Americans. **(Review pages 685–692.)**
US8.12.3 Explain how states and the federal government encouraged business expansion through tariffs, banking, land grants, and subsidies.	**Chapter 15, Section 1** Government grants to the railroad companies included land for tracks and strips of land along railways. Cash subsidies from local governments also helped the growth of railroads. **(Review pages 669–670.)** **Chapter 17, Section 4** The federal government passed high tariffs that protected industries from foreign competition but led to higher prices for goods. **(Review page 766.)**

US8.12 *cont.*

What Is the Standard?	Where Can I Find It?
US8.12.4 Discuss entrepreneurs, industrialists, and bankers in politics, commerce, and industry (e.g., Andrew Carnegie, John D. Rockefeller, Leland Stanford).	**Chapter 16, Sections 1 and 3** Business leaders, such as Carnegie, Rockefeller, and Stanford, gained control of various industries and turned them into successful businesses. **(Review pages 708, 720–723.)**
US8.12.5 Examine the location and effects of urbanization, renewed immigration, and industrialization (e.g., the effects on social fabric of cities, wealth and economic opportunity, the conservation movement).	**Chapter 17, Sections 1, 2, and 4** During the late 1800s and early 1900s, large numbers of immigrants came to America in search of jobs and settled in neighborhoods in large urban areas. As city populations rose, cities faced health and crime problems and a growing gap between the rich and poor. Urban growth saw the introduction of new buildings, more public transportation, and city parks. Conservation also became an important issue. **(Review pages 741–747, 751–756, 771–773.)**
US8.12.6 Discuss child labor, working conditions, and laissez-faire policies toward big business and examine the labor movement, including its leaders (e.g., Samuel Gompers), its demand for collective bargaining, and its strikes and protests over labor conditions.	**Chapter 16, Section 4** Industrial workers labored long hours for low pay, often in unsafe conditions. Because government favored big business, workers formed labor unions to advance their interests. Union strikes sometimes turned violent. **(Review pages 725–729, 730–731.)** **Chapter 17, Section 4** Reformers sought to improve working conditions and control big business. **(Review pages 765–768.)**
US8.12.7 Identify the sources of large-scale immigration and the contributions of immigrants to the building of cities and the economy; explain the ways in which new social and economic patterns encouraged assimilation of newcomers into the mainstream amidst growing cultural diversity; and discuss the new wave of nativism.	**Chapter 17, Sections 1 and 3** Immigrants who arrived in America came from many different countries. They often settled in urban ethnic neighborhoods and contributed their labor and cultures. Schools helped to bring immigrant children into the mainstream. Americans in the nativist movement called for laws to limit immigration. **(Review pages 741–749, 758–763.)**
US8.12.8 Identify the characteristics and impact of Grangerism and Populism.	**Chapter 15, Section 4** When crop prices fell in the late 1800s, farmers formed the Grange to protect their interests. In the 1890s the Populist Party developed to represent the views of farmers and common people. Although the party did not last long, Populists got many new laws passed. **(Review pages 694–697.)**

US8.12 *cont.*

What Is the Standard? → Where Can I Find It?

US8.12.9 Name the significant inventors and their inventions and identify how they improved the quality of life (e.g., Thomas Edison, Alexander Graham Bell, Orville and Wilbur Wright).

Chapter 16, Section 2 The electric lightbulb (Edison), the telephone (Bell), and the airplane (the Wright brothers) were among the new inventions that changed the lives of Americans during the late 1800s and early 1900s. **(Review pages 713–717.)**

Standards Practice

1 Why did Great Plains farmers have to use new methods and tools?

A Factories were far away, and farmers had to fend for themselves.
B The Great Plains were dry and had a tough layer of sod.
C The Mississippi River often flooded vast areas of the Great Plains.
D Labor strikes in the East blocked the shipment of goods westward.

2 What factor was most likely to inspire migration to urban centers in the late 1800s?

A affordable housing
B libraries and museums
C employment opportunities
D education

3 Poor, run-down neighborhoods in urban areas are known as

A suburbs.
B settlements.
C subways.
D slums.

California Standards Handbook Answer Key

The answers to the California Standards Handbook presented on the previous pages are listed below. Use this answer key to check your understanding of the material covered in your grade 8 social studies course.

US8.1
page 863

1 D

US8.2
page 865

1 C
2 B

US8.3
page 867

1 B
2 C
3 D

US8.4
page 868

1 C

US8.5
page 869

1 D

US8.6
page 871

1 A
2 D

US8.7
page 872

1 C

US8.8
page 874

1 A
2 B
3 D

US8.9
page 876

1 B
2 C

US8.10
page 878

1 C
2 D

US8.11
page 880

1 B
2 A
3 C

US8.12
page 883

1 B
2 C
3 D

Glossary

This glossary includes all the yellow highlighted and boldfaced vocabulary words from your text. Content vocabulary (those words highlighted in yellow in your text) are words that relate to history content. Academic vocabulary (those words **boldfaced** in your text) are words that will help you understand all of your school subjects. Academic vocabulary is shown here with an asterisk (*).

A

* **abandon** to give up completely or desert (p. 578)

abolitionist a person who strongly favors doing away with slavery (p. 529)

abstain to not take part in some activity, such as voting (p. 542)

* **access** a way or means of approach (p. 471)

* **accommodate** make suitable for or to provide help (p. 752)

* **accompany** to attend as a companion (p. 296)

* **achieve** to reach an aim or goal (p. 691)

* **acquire** obtain or take possession of something (p. 676)

* **adapt** to fit a new situation (p. 128)

* **adequate** enough to satisfy a particular requirement (p. 201)

* **aid** to provide with help (p. 626)

alien an immigrant living in a country in which he or she is not a citizen (p. 295)

amendment an addition to a formal document such as the Constitution (p. 223)

amnesty the granting of pardon to a large number of persons; protection from prosecution for an illegal act (p. 625)

annex to add a territory to one's own territory (p. 486)

* **annual** occurs once a year (p. 472)

* **anticipate** to look forward to (p. 224)

Antifederalists individuals who opposed ratification of the Constitution (p. 206)

* **approach** a way to deal with an issue (p. 625)

appropriate to set something aside for a particular purpose, especially funds (p. 227)

* **area** part of a country (p. 594)

arsenal a storage place for weapons and ammunition (p. 553)

article a part of a document, such as the Constitution, that deals with a single subject (p. 204)

* **aspect** a certain way something appears or may be regarded (p. 744)

* **assemble** to collect in one place or group together (p. 354)

assembly line a production system with machines and workers arranged so that each person performs an assigned task again and again as the item passes before him or her (p. 717)

* **assign** to be given a specific role or responsibility (p. 296)

assimilate to absorb a group into the culture of a larger population (p. 744)

* **assist** giving help when needed (p. 91)

* **assume** to take on a special quality or responsibility (p. 231)

astrolabe an instrument used by sailors to observe positions of stars (p. 83)

* **authority** power of influence over others (p. 180)

* **available** easy or possible to obtain (p. 322)

B

barrio a Spanish-speaking neighborhood in a city, especially in the southwest U.S. (p. 782)

* **benefit** something that does good to a person or thing (p. 759)

* **bias** an attitude that always favors one way of feeling or acting over another (p. 780)

bicameral consisting of two houses, or chambers, especially in a legislature (p. 179)

black codes laws passed in the South just after the Civil War aimed at controlling freedmen and enabling plantation owners to exploit African American workers (p. 630)

blockade cut off an area by means of troops or warships to stop supplies or people from coming in or going out; to close off a country's ports (p. 573)

Glossary

bond a note issued by the government, which promises to pay off a loan with interest (p. 281)

boomtown a community experiencing a sudden growth in business or population (pp. 503, 668)

border ruffians Missourians who traveled in armed groups to vote in Kansas's election during the mid-1850s (p. 546)

border states the states between the North and the South that were divided over whether to stay in the Union or join the Confederacy (pp. 555, 571)

bounty money given as a reward, such as to encourage enlistment in the army (p. 602)

boycott to refuse to buy items from a particular country (p. 136)

brand a symbol burned into an animal's hide to show ownership (p. 673)

***brief** not very long (p. 636)

bullion gold or silver in the form of bars (p. 94)

bureaucracy system in which nonelected officials carry out laws and policies (p. 449)

burgesses elected representatives to an assembly (p. 119)

C

cabinet a group of advisers to the president (p. 280)

Californios Mexicans who lived in California (p. 496)

canal an artificial waterway (p. 392)

capital money for investment (pp. 383, 424)

capitalism an economic system based on private property and free enterprise (pp. 91, 383)

carpetbaggers name given to Northern whites who moved South after the Civil War and supported the Republicans (p. 638)

cash crop farm crop raised to be sold for money (pp. 126, 646)

casualty a military person killed, wounded, or captured (p. 579)

caucus a meeting held by a political party to choose their party's candidate for president or decide policy (pp. 293, 449)

cede to give up by treaty (p. 497)

census official count of a population (p. 389)

***challenge** a demanding task (p. 154)

charter a document that gives the holder the right to organize settlements in an area (p. 119)

charter colony colony established by a group of settlers who had been given a formal document allowing them to settle (p. 130)

checks and balances the system in which each branch of government has a check on the other two branches so that no one branch becomes too powerful (p. 205)

circumnavigate to sail around the world (p. 85)

citizen a person who owes loyalty to and is entitled to the protection of a state or nation (p. 236)

civil war conflict between opposing groups of citizens of the same country (p. 547)

coeducation the teaching of male and female students together (p. 410)

***collapse** to fall down suddenly (p. 542)

collective bargaining discussion between an employer and union representatives of workers over wages, hours, and working conditions (p. 727)

colony a settlement of people living in a new territory but controlled by their home country (p. 95)

Columbian Exchange exchange of goods, ideas, and people between Europe and the Americas (p. 95)

commission a group of persons directed to perform some duty (p. 643)

***commit** to perform an action (p. 648)

***communicate** to transmit information, thought, or feeling so it is received and understood (p. 434)

***community** a group of people with common interests, especially when living together (p. 501)

compromise agreement between two or more sides in which each side gives up some of what it wants (p. 199)

***concentrate** giving most attention to one central idea (p. 386)

***concept** principle or idea (p. 491)

***conclude** to come to a final decision (p. 345)

concurrent powers powers shared by the states and the federal government (p. 222)

***conduct** manage or control the direction of relations between two or more parties (p. 205)

Conestoga wagon sturdy vehicle topped with white canvas and used by pioneers to move west (p. 313)

confederation a voluntary association of independent states (p. 180)

***confirm** to support or agree to (p. 280)

***conflict** a disagreement or struggle (p. 329)

conquistador Spanish explorer in the Americas in the 1500s (p. 86)

conservation the protection and preservation of natural resources (p. 771)

***consist** made up of (p. 354)

consolidation the practice of combining separate companies into one (p. 707)

***constant** happening a lot or all the time (p. 433)

constituents people that members of Congress represent (p. 227)

constitution a formal plan of government (p. 121)

***contract** an agreement between people (p. 103)

***contrary** the exact opposite (p. 327)

***contrast** showing the difference between two things when they are compared (p. 292)

***contribute** help to cause an event or situation (p. 460)

***controversy** a lot of disagreement or argument about something, usually because it affects something or someone (p. 537)

***convert** change from one to another (p. 710)

***convince** make a person believe by arguing or showing facts (p. 136)

***cooperate** to work with others to get a task done (p. 221)

cooperative store where farmers bought products from each other; an enterprise owned and operated by those who use its services (p. 694)

corporation a business in which investors own shares (p. 719)

***correspond** to communicate by letters (p. 137)

corruption dishonest or illegal actions (p. 638)

cotton gin a machine that removed seeds from cotton fiber (pp. 384, 423)

court-martial to try by a military court (p. 365)

covenant a formal agreement, or promise, between two or more people (p. 99)

***create** to make or produce (p. 638)

credit a form of loan; ability to buy goods based on future payment (p. 429)

***culture** a way of life of a group of people who share similar beliefs and customs (p. 81)

***currency** money (p. 194)

D

***debate** a verbal argument (p. 536)

debtor person or country that owes money (p. 124)

***decline** to become less in value (p. 695)

decree an order given by one in authority (p. 482)

demilitarize to remove armed forces from an area (p. 363)

***demonstrate** show by examples (p. 365)

***deny** refuse to accept (p. 626)

depression a period of low economic activity and widespread unemployment (pp. 194, 460)

***derive** the origin of something, such as a word, from which another has developed (p. 674)

***design** the creation of something according to a plan (p. 83)

***despite** without taking any notice of or being influenced by (p. 686)

***device** an object or machine which has been invented to fulfill a particular purpose (p. 713)

***devote** to use space, area, or time for a particular purpose (p. 492)

***diminish** to be reduced in size or importance (p. 238)

disarmament removal of weapons (p. 363)

discrimination unfair treatment of a group; unequal treatment because of a person's race, religion, ethnic background, or place of birth (pp. 397, 778)

dissenter person who disagrees with or opposes established views (p. 121)

***distinct** clearly different from one another (p. 291)

***distribute** to divide among several or many (p. 599)

diversity variety or difference (p. 123)

dividend a stockholder's share of a company's profits, usually as a cash payment (p. 719)

***document** an important paper (p. 103)

***dominate** having great influence over all others (p. 636)

draft the selection of persons for military service (p. 602)

Glossary

dry farming a way of farming dry land in which seeds are planted deep in the ground where there is some moisture (p. 678)

due process of law idea that the government must follow procedures established by law and guaranteed by the Constitution (p. 235)

* **dynamic** to be energetic and forceful in presentation (p. 697)

E

* **economy** the money system of a country, region, or community (p. 359)

* **eliminate** to remove or get rid of (p. 645)

emancipate to free from slavery (p. 594)

embargo an order prohibiting trade with another country (p. 340)

emigrant a person who leaves a country or region to live elsewhere (p. 474)

emigrate to leave one's homeland to live elsewhere (p. 742)

empresario a person who arranged for the settlement of land in Texas during the 1800s (p. 481)

* **enable** to make possible (p. 634)

encomienda system of rewarding conquistadors with tracts of land and the right to tax and demand labor from Native Americans who lived on the land (p. 88)

* **encounter** an unexpected meeting (p. 580)

* **enforce** to make people obey a law or to accept a new situation (p. 641)

Enlightenment movement during the 1700s that spread the idea that knowledge, reason, and science could improve society (p. 203)

* **enormous** very big (p. 313)

* **ensure** to make sure or certain (p. 309)

entrenched occupying a strong defensive position (p. 605)

entrepreneur someone who starts their own business (p. 93)

enumerated powers powers belonging only to the federal government (p. 222)

* **environment** the combination of the soil, climate and living things that influence the survival of a plant, animal, or human being (p. 239)

* **equip** to supply with necessary tools to work properly (p. 390)

* **establish** to set up (p. 363)

* **ethnic** relating to a large group of people classed according to common racial, national, or cultural origin or background (p. 761)

ethnic group a minority that speaks a different language or follows different customs than the majority of people in a country (p. 742)

* **evaluate** judge the quality or amount (p. 580)

* **eventual** happening or existing at a later time or at the end, especially after a lot of effort or problems (p. 555)

* **exceed** to go beyond the limits (p. 430)

executive branch the branch of government, headed by the president, that carries out the nation's laws and policies (p. 205)

* **expand** open up or spread out in terms of size, number or amount (p. 386)

* **exploit** to use unfairly for one's own advantage (p. 641)

* **export** to sell goods abroad (p. 95)

* **extract** to remove (p. 667)

F

factory system system bringing manufacturing steps together in one place to increase efficiency (p. 385)

famine an extreme shortage of food (p. 398)

favorite son candidate that receives the backing of his home state rather than of the national party (p. 447)

* **federal** national government (p. 453)

federalism the sharing of power between federal and state governments (pp. 204, 222)

Federalists supporters of the Constitution (p. 206)

* **finance** providing funds or capital (p. 91)

fixed costs regular expenses such as housing or maintaining equipment that remain about the same year after year (p. 429)

* **focus** to concentrate on a central point (p. 405)

forty-niners people who went to California during the gold rush of 1849 (p. 501)

* **found** establish (p. 403)

free enterprise the freedom of private businesses to operate competitively for profit with minimal government regulation (p. 383)

free silver the unlimited production of silver coins (p. 696)

freedman a person freed from slavery (p. 626)

frigate warship (p. 355)

fugitive runaway or trying to run away (p. 541)

* **function** to work or serve towards a particular goal (p. 221)

* **fund** a sum of money saved, collected, or provided for a particular purpose (p. 93)

G

* **generation** individuals born and living at the same time (p. 314)

Gilded Age the name associated with America in the late 1800s, referring to the extravagant wealth of a few and the terrible poverty that lay underneath (p. 752)

* **goal** an aim or purpose (p. 413)

grandfather clause a clause that allowed individuals who did not pass the literacy test to vote if their fathers or grandfathers had voted before Reconstruction began; an exception to a law based on preexisting circumstances (p. 648)

* **grant** giving consent or permission (p. 122)

* **guarantee** a promise that some condition will be fulfilled (p. 341)

guerrilla tactics referring to surprise attacks or raids rather than organized warfare (p. 455)

guerrilla warfare a hit-and-run technique used in fighting a war; fighting by small bands of warriors using tactics such as sudden ambushes (p. 156)

H

habeas corpus a legal order for an inquiry to determine whether a person has been lawfully imprisoned (p. 600)

homestead to acquire a piece of U.S. public land by living on and cultivating it (p. 676)

horizontal integration the combining of competing firms into one corporation (p. 720)

I

impeach to formally charge a public official with misconduct in office (pp. 227, 633)

implied powers powers not specifically mentioned in the Constitution (pp. 224, 292)

import to buy goods from foreign markets (p. 136)

impressment forcing people into service, as in the navy (pp. 288, 339)

indentured servant laborer who agreed to work without pay for a certain period of time in exchange for passage to America (p. 126)

Industrial Revolution the change from an agrarian society to one based on industry which began in Great Britain and spread to the United States around 1800 (p. 383)

* **inevitable** impossible to avoid (p. 546)

inflation a continuous rise in the price of goods and services (p. 603)

initiative the right of citizens to place a measure or issue before the voters or the legislature for approval (p. 769)

injunction a court order to stop an action, such as a strike (p. 729)

* **inspect** to examine closely (p. 771)

integrate to end separation of different races and bring into equal membership in society (p. 638)

interchangeable parts uniform pieces that can be made in large quantities to replace other identical pieces (p. 385)

* **interpret** explain the meaning (p. 179)

* **intervene** to come between (p. 229)

* **invest** to commit money in order to receive a profit (p. 719)

* **involve** to contain or include (p. 236)

ironclad armored naval vessel (p. 578)

* **isolate** to set or keep apart from others (p. 760)

* **issue** a matter that is in dispute between two or more parties (p. 450)

isthmus a narrow strip of land connecting two larger land areas (p. 776)

* **item** a good or a product (p. 504)

J

* **job** duty or work done for pay (p. 725)

joint occupation the possession and settling of an area shared by two or more countries (p. 471)

Glossary

joint-stock company a company in which investors buy stock in the company in return for a share of its future profits (p. 93)

judicial branch the branch of government, including the federal court system, that interprets the nation's laws (p. 205)

judicial review the right of the Supreme Court to determine if a law violates the Constitution (pp. 225, 309)

***justify** having a good reason for choosing a particular side (p. 556)

L

***labor** to work for wages, such as in production of goods and services (p. 725)

laissez-faire policy that government should interfere as little as possible in the nation's economy (pp. 307, 460, 771)

land-grant college originally, an agricultural college established as a result of the 1862 Morrill Act that gave states large amounts of federal land that could be sold to raise money for education (p. 760)

landslide an overwhelming victory (p. 448)

legislative branch the branch of government that makes the nation's laws (p. 204)

***levy** an imposed tax required to pay off a country, region, or district's loan or debt (p. 194)

literacy test a method used to prevent African Americans from voting by requiring prospective voters to read and write at a specified level (p. 647)

lock in a canal, an enclosure with gates at each end used in raising or lowering boats as they pass from level to level (p. 392)

lode a mass or strip of ore sandwiched between layers of rock (p. 667)

Loyalists American colonists who remained loyal to Britain and opposed the war for independence (p. 153)

lynching putting to death a person by the illegal action of a mob (p. 648)

M

***maintain** to keep up (p. 286)

***major** to be great in size, number, or length (p. 105)

Manifest Destiny the idea popular in the United States during the 1800s that the country must expand its boundaries to the Pacific (p. 474)

***manual** done by hand (p. 399)

manumission the freeing of some enslaved persons (p. 196)

martyr a person who sacrifices his or her life for a principle or cause (p. 553)

mass production the production of large quantities of goods using machinery and often an assembly line (p. 717)

Mayflower Compact a formal document, written in 1620, that provided law and order to the Plymouth colony (p. 120)

mercantilism the theory that a state's or nation's power depended on its wealth (p. 94)

merger the combining of two or more businesses into one (p. 722)

***migrate** to move from one country to another (p. 329)

***military** armed forces (p. 124)

militia a group of civilians trained to fight in emergencies (p. 139)

***ministry** the office, duties or work of a minister (p. 413)

minutemen companies of civilian soldiers who boasted that they were ready to fight on a minute's notice (p. 140)

mission religious settlement (p. 88)

***modify** to make changes (p. 777)

***monitor** to observe for a special purpose (p. 227)

monopoly total control of a type of industry by one person or one company (p. 720)

mountain man a frontiersman living in the wilderness, as in the Rocky Mountains (p. 472)

muckraker a journalist who uncovers abuses and corruption in a society (p. 767)

mudslinging attempt to ruin an opponent's reputation with insults (p. 447)

N

national debt the amount of money a national government owes to other governments or its people (p. 281)

National Grange the first farmers' organization in the United States (p. 694)

nationalism loyalty to a nation and promotion of its interests above all others (pp. 321, 345)

nativist a person who favors those born in his country and is opposed to immigrants (pp. 401, 746)

naturalization to grant full citizenship to a foreigner (p. 236)

***network** a system of connected parts (p. 711)

neutral taking no side in a conflict (p. 153)

neutral rights the right to sail the seas and not take sides in a war (p. 339)

neutrality a position of not taking sides in a conflict (p. 288)

***nevertheless** despite what has just been said or referred to (p. 606)

nomadic moving from place to place with no permanent home (p. 686)

normal school a two-year school for training high school graduates as teachers (p. 405)

Northwest Passage water route to Asia through North America sought by European explorers (p. 88)

***notion** an idea or concept (p. 529)

nullify to cancel or make ineffective (pp. 296, 450, 537)

O

***obtain** to gain (p. 669)

***obvious** easily found, seen or understood (p. 573)

***occupy** to take possession of (pp. 157, 326)

***occur** to happen (p. 603)

offensive position of attacking or the attack itself (p. 573)

oligopoly a market structure in which a few large companies control the prices of the industry (p. 766)

open range land not fenced or divided into lots (p. 673)

ordinance a law or regulation (p. 181)

ore a mineral mined for the valuable substance it contains, such as silver (p. 667)

***outcome** result (p. 605)

override to overturn or defeat, as a bill proposed in Congress (p. 630)

overseer person who supervises a large operation or its workers (pp. 127, 430)

P

***participate** to take part in something that others are doing (p. 194)

partisan favoring one side of an issue (p. 291)

patent a document that gives an inventor the sole legal right to an invention for a period of time (p. 384)

Patriots American colonists who were determined to fight the British until American independence was won (p. 153)

***percent** one unit of 100 (p. 386)

***period** length of time (p. 625)

persecute to treat someone harshly because of that person's beliefs or differences (p. 122)

petition a formal request (p. 150)

philanthropy charitable acts or gifts of money to benefit the community (p. 722)

philosophe French for "philosopher"; during the Enlightenment thinkers, such as writers, teachers, journalists, and observers of society (p. 105)

philosophy a set of beliefs or ideas related to a particular system of cultural values (p. 307)

planter large landowner (p. 326)

plurality largest single share (p. 447)

***policy** a plan or course of action (p. 367)

political machine an organization linked to a political party that often controlled local government (p. 765)

poll tax a tax of a fixed amount per person that had to be paid before the person could vote (p. 647)

pool a group sharing in some activity, for example, among railroad barons who made secret agreements and set rates among themselves (p. 711)

popular sovereignty political theory that government is subject to the will of the people (pp. 179, 222); before the Civil War, the idea that people living in a territory had the right to decide by voting if slavery would be allowed there (p. 544)

Populist Party U.S. political party formed in 1892 representing mainly farmers, favoring free coinage of silver and government control of railroads and other monopolies (p. 695)

***pose** to put forth; to present (p. 504)

preamble the introduction to a formal document, especially the Constitution (pp. 152, 219)

precedent a tradition (p. 279)

***predominant** greater in importance, strength, influence, or authority (p. 424)

prejudice an unfair opinion not based on facts (p. 397)

presidio Spanish fort in the Americas built to protect mission settlements (p. 88)

***primary** the main or most important (p. 573); an election in which voters choose their party's candidate (p. 769)

***principle** a basic truth that other theories are based on (p. 130)

privateer armed private ship (p. 355)

***process** a continuing action or series of actions (p. 743)

***professional** engaging in a given activity as a source of support or as a career (p. 752)

***prohibit** to forbid (p. 633)

***promote** to encourage or contribute to the growth of an idea (p. 203)

proportional to be the same as or corresponding to (p. 199)

proprietary colony colony run by individuals or groups to whom land was granted (p. 130)

***prospect** the idea of something that will or might happen in the future (p. 580)

protective tariff tariff that raises the price of goods from other countries (p. 537)

***publication** printed material offered for distribution or sale (p. 530)

***publish** preparing printed material for public display or sale (p. 407)

pueblo home or community of homes built by Native Americans (p. 88)

***purchase** to buy (p. 429)

***pursue** strive to gain or accomplish a goal (p. 102)

R

radical extreme (p. 625)

ragtime a type of music with a strong rhythm and a lively melody with accented notes, which was popular in early 1900s (p. 762)

ranchero Mexican ranch owner (p. 492)

rancho huge properties for raising livestock set up by Mexican settlers in California (p. 492)

***range** series of mountain peaks (p. 501)

ratify to give official approval to (pp. 181, 206, 594)

realism an approach to literature, art, and theater that shows things as they really are (p. 761)

rebate discount or return of part of a payment (p. 710)

Rebel Confederate soldier, so called because of opposition to the established government (p. 574)

recall the right that enables voters to remove unsatisfactory elected officials from office (p. 769)

reconciliation settling by agreement or coming together again (p. 641)

Reconstruction the reorganization and rebuilding of the former Confederate states after the Civil War (p. 625)

referendum the practice of letting voters accept or reject measures proposed by the legislature (p. 769)

***region** an area, division, or district (p. 638)

regionalism in art or literature, the practice of focusing on a particular region of the country (p. 761)

***register** a written record or list of items (p. 743)

***regulate** to govern by rules or laws (p. 199)

***reinforce** to provide an army with more soldiers or weapons to make it stronger (p. 577)

***reject** to refuse to grant or consider (p. 776)

relocate to force a person or group of people to move (p. 453)

***reluctance** an unwillingness to act (p. 593)

***remove** take away or dismiss (p. 453)

Renaissance a period of intellectual and artistic creativity, c. 1300–1600 (p. 102)

rendezvous a meeting (p. 472)

repeal to cancel an act or law (p. 136)

republicanism favoring a republic, or representative democracy, as the best form of government (p. 222)

* **require** to have a need for (p. 307)

reservation an area of public lands set aside for Native Americans (p. 687)

reserved powers powers retained by the states (p. 222)

resolution a formal expression of opinion (p. 139)

* **resolve** to clear up any unsettled matters (p. 341)

* **resource** a useful or valuable possession (p. 719)

* **restrict** to place under limits (p. 550)

* **reveal** to allow something to be seen that, until then, had been unknown or hidden (p. 544)

* **revenue** incoming money (p. 284)

revival a series of meetings conducted by a preacher to arouse religious emotions (p. 403)

right of deposit Americans reached an agreement with Spain that would allow free navigation along the Mississippi River (p. 185)

* **role** a function assigned or taken on (p. 447)

* **route** an established course of travel (p. 472)

royal colony colony run by a governor and a council appointed by the king or queen (p. 130)

rule of law in ancient Roman law, everyone should be treated equally (p. 99)

S

scalawags name given by former Confederates to Southern whites who supported Republican Reconstruction of the South (p. 638)

scientific method an orderly way of collecting and analyzing evidence (p. 105)

secede to leave or withdraw (pp. 316, 450, 541)

secession withdrawal from the Union (p. 556)

sectionalism loyalty to a region (p. 536)

* **secure** guarding from danger or loss (p. 155)

sedition activities aimed at weakening established government (p. 295)

segregation the separation or isolation of a race, class, or group (p. 648)

settlement house institution located in a poor neighborhood that provided numerous community services such as medical care, child care, libraries, and classes in English (p. 753)

sharecropping system of farming in which a farmer works land for an owner who provides equipment and seeds and receives a share of the crop (p. 639)

shareholder a person who invests in a corporation by buying stock and is a partial owner (p. 719)

* **shift** to change from one place or position to another (p. 396)

* **significant** having a major effect on something (p. 308)

* **similar** having common qualities (p. 484)

slave code the laws passed in the Southern states that controlled and restricted enslaved people (p. 434)

slum poor, crowded, and run-down urban neighborhoods (p. 752)

smuggling trading illegally with other nations (p. 136)

sodbuster a name given to the Plains farmer (p. 678)

* **sole** being the only one (p. 474)

sovereignty supreme power (p. 180)

speculator person who risks money in order to make a large profit (p. 282)

spiritual an African American religious folk song (p. 433)

spoils system practice of handing out government jobs to supporters; replacing government employees with the winning candidate's supporters (p. 449)

standard gauge the uniform width of 4 feet, 8.5 inches for railroad tracks, adopted during the 1880s (p. 709)

states' rights rights and powers independent of the federal government that are reserved for the states by the Constitution; the belief that states' rights supersede federal rights and law (pp. 296, 556)

* **status** position or rank in relation to others (p. 482)

steerage cramped quarters on a ship's lower decks for passengers paying the lowest fares (p. 742)

stock shares of ownership a company sells in its business which often carry voting power (p. 719)

***strategy** a careful plan or method of action (p. 341)

strike a stopping of work by workers to force an employer to meet demands (p. 397)

strikebreaker person hired to replace a striking worker in order to break up a strike (p. 727)

***structure** an arrangement of parts (p. 279)

subsidy grant of money from the government to a person or a company for an action intended to benefit the public (p. 669)

subsistence farming farming in which only enough food to feed one's family is produced (p. 126)

***substitute** a person or thing that takes the place of another (p. 602)

suburbs residential areas that sprang up close to or surrounding cities as a result of improvements in transportation (p. 752)

***sufficient** enough to achieve a goal or fulfill a need (p. 573)

suffrage the right to vote (pp. 409, 449)

***sum** describe or express briefly the important facts about something or someone (p. 425)

***survive** to remain alive despite hardships and trauma (p. 119)

sweatshop a shop or factory where workers work long hours at low wages under unhealthy conditions (pp. 725, 744)

***symbol** a letter, character, or sign used instead of words (p. 461)

T

tariff a tax on imports or exports (pp. 282, 450)

***technique** the method or skill used in accomplishing a goal (p. 156)

***technology** the application of scientific discoveries to practical use (pp. 82, 384, 710)

Tejano a Mexican who claims Texas as his home (p. 481)

temperance the use of little or no alcoholic drink (p. 403)

tenant farmer farmer who works land owned by another and pays rent either in cash or crops (p. 428)

tenement a building in which several families rent rooms or apartments, often with little sanitation or safety (p. 752)

theology the study of religion and religious beliefs (p. 101)

***theory** an idea that is the starting point for argument or investigation (p. 556)

toleration the acceptance of different beliefs (p. 121)

***topic** a subject that is discussed, written about, or studied (p. 552)

total war war on all aspects of the enemy's life (p. 609)

trade union organization of workers with the same trade or skill (pp. 397, 726)

transcendentalist any of a group of New England writers who stressed the relationship between human beings and nature, spiritual things over material things, and the importance of the individual conscience (p. 406)

transcontinental extending across a continent (p. 670)

***transmit** transfer from one person or place to another (p. 713)

***transport** carrying from one place to another (p. 286)

triangular trade a trade route that exchanged goods between the West Indies, the American colonies, and West Africa (p. 126)

tribute money paid for protection (p. 339)

trust a combination of firms or corporations formed by a legal agreement, especially to reduce competition (pp. 720, 766)

turnpike a road that one must pay to use; the money is used to pay for the road (p. 389)

U

***ultimate** the final or extreme result (p. 279)

unconstitutional not agreeing or consistent with the Constitution (p. 282)

Underground Railroad a system that helped enslaved African Americans follow a network of escape routes out of the South to freedom in the North (p. 534)

***underlie** to be the support or basis of (p. 767)

undertake take on as a duty (p. 389)

***unify** to unite or bring together (p. 713)

***unique** being the only one of its kind (p. 325)

utopia community based on a vision of a perfect society sought by reformers (p. 403)

V

vaquero Hispanic ranch hand (p. 674)

vaudeville stage entertainment made up of various acts, such as dancing, singing, comedy, and magic shows (p. 763)

vertical integration the combining of companies that supply equipment and services needed for a particular industry (p. 721)

veto to reject a bill and prevent it from becoming a law (p. 459)

vigilantes people who take the law into their own hands (pp. 504, 668)

***violate** to do harm or damage (p. 136)

***vision** the intellectual ability to think or plan ahead (p. 505)

W

ward a person under the guardianship of the U.S. government (p. 782)

War Hawks Republicans during Madison's presidency who pressed for war with Britain (p. 343)

Y

Yankee Union soldier (p. 574)

yellow journalism writing which exaggerates sensational, dramatic, and gruesome events to attract readers, named for stories that were popular during the late 1800s (p. 761)

yeoman Southern owner of a small farm who did not have enslaved people (p. 428)

Spanish Glossary

This glossary includes all the yellow highlighted and boldfaced vocabulary words from your text. Content vocabulary (those words highlighted in yellow in your text) are words that relate to history content. Academic vocabulary (those words **boldfaced** in your text) are words that will help you understand all of your school subjects. Academic vocabulary is shown with an asterisk (*).

A

***abandon / abandoner** renunciar o dejar un lugar o a una persona (p. 578)

abolitionist / abolicionista una persona que favorece firmemente suprimir la esclavitud (p. 529)

abstain / abstenerse no tomar parte de una actividad, como de votar (p. 542)

***access / acceso** modo de acercarse o entrada (p. 471)

***accommodate / acomodar** hacer ajustes o proporcionar ayuda (p. 743)

***accompany / acompañar** servir de acompañante (p. 296)

***achieve / lograr** alcanzar un objetivo o meta (p. 691)

***acquire / adquirir** obtener o tomar posesión de algo (p. 676)

***adapt / adaptar** ajustar a una nueva situación (p. 128)

***adequate / adecuado** lo suficiente para satisfacer un requisito en particular (p. 201)

***aid / ayudar** dar asistencia o socorrer (p. 626)

alien / extranjero una persona inmigrante que vive en un país en el cual no es ciudadano (p. 295)

amendment / enmienda una adición a un documento formal tal como la Constitución (p. 223)

amnesty / amnistía el otorgar perdón a un número grande de personas; la protección del proceso a causa de una acción ilegal (p. 625)

annex / anexar añadir un territorio a su propio territorio (p. 486)

***annual / anual** que sucede una vez al año (p. 472)

***anticipate / prever** esperar que algo suceda (p. 224)

Antifederalists / antifederalistas personas que estaban en contra de que se ratificara la Constitución (p. 206)

***approach / enfoque** método de resolver un asunto (p. 625)

appropriate / destinar apartar para un propósito en particular, dicho especialmente de fondos (p. 227)

***area / área** parte de un país (p. 594)

arsenal / arsenal un lugar para el almacenaje de armas y municiones (p. 553)

article / artículo una parte de un documento tal como la Constitución que trata de un solo tema (p. 204)

***aspect / aspecto** manera en que algo luce o en que se puede ver (p. 743)

***assemble / reunir** acumular en un sitio o agrupar (p. 354)

assembly line / línea de montaje un sistema de producción arreglado con máquinas y trabajadores para que cada persona haga vez tras vez su trabajo designado mientras el artículo pasa por en frente de él (p. 717)

***assign / asignar** dar un trabajo o responsabilidad en particular a alguien (p. 296)

assimilate / asimilar introducir a un grupo dentro de la cultura de una población más grande (p. 744)

***assist / asistir** dar ayuda (p. 91)

***assume / asumir** adoptar una cualidad especial o responsabilidad nueva (p. 231)

astrolabe / astrolabio un instrumento usado por los marineros para observar las posiciones de las estrellas (p. 83)

***authority / autoridad** poder o influencia sobre otras personas (p. 180)

***available / disponible** fácil o posible de conseguir (p. 322)

B

barrio / barrio una vecindad hispanoparlante de una ciudad, especialmente en el sudoeste de EE.UU. (p. 782)

***benefit / beneficio** algo que le hace el bien a alguien o algo (p. 759)

***bias / parcialidad** actitud que siempre favorece el mismo modo de pensar o actuar (p. 780)

bicameral / bicameral que consiste de dos cámaras, especialmente dicho en una legislatura (p. 179)

black codes / códigos negros leyes establecidas en el Sur al terminar la Guerra Civil para controlar a los libertos y permitir a los dueños de plantaciones la explotación de los trabajadores afroamericanos (p. 630)

blockade / bloqueo el cerrar un área por medio de tropas o de buques de guerra para prohibir el entrar y el salir de abastos y de personas; cerrar los puertos de un país (p. 573)

bond / bono una obligación hecha por el gobierno la cual promete pagar un préstamo con interés (p. 281)

boomtown / pueblo en bonanza una comunidad experimentando un auge repentino de comercio o población (pp. 503, 668)

border ruffians / rufianes fronterizos hombres de Missouri que viajaban en grupos armados a votar en la elección de Kansas a mediados de los años 1850 (p. 546)

border states / estados fronterizos los estados entre el Norte y el Sur que fueron divididos sobre el problema de quedarse en la Unión o de unirse a la Confederación (pp. 555, 571)

bounty / gratificación dinero dado como recompensa, como para animar el alistamiento en el ejército (p. 602)

boycott / boicotear rehusar comprar artículos de un país en particular (p. 136)

brand / marca a fuego un símbolo quemado en la piel de un animal para mostrar título de propiedad (p. 673)

***brief / breve** no muy largo (p. 636)

bullion / lingotes barras de oro o plata (p. 94)

bureaucracy / burocracia sistema en el cual oficiales no elegidos administran las leyes y políticas (p. 449)

burgesses / burgueses representantes elegidos para una asamblea (p. 119)

C

cabinet / gabinete un grupo de consejeros al presidente (p. 280)

Californios / californios mexicanos que vivían en California (p. 496)

canal / canal vía artificial de agua (p. 392)

capital / capital dinero para inversión (pp. 383, 424)

capitalism / capitalismo un sistema económico basado en la propiedad particular y la empresa libre (pp. 91, 383)

carpetbaggers / carpetbaggers nombre dado a los blancos norteños que se trasladaban al Sur después de la guerra y apoyaban a los republicanos (p. 638)

cash crop / cultivo comercial cosecha cultivada para vender por dinero (pp. 126, 646)

casualty / baja un miliciano muerto, herido, o capturado (p. 579)

caucus / junta electoral una reunión llevada a cabo por un partido político para escoger el candidato a la presidencia de su partido o para decidir políticas (pp. 293, 449)

cede / ceder abandonar por tratado (p. 497)

census / censo registro oficial de una población (p. 389)

***challenge / reto** desafío o tarea muy difícil (p. 154)

charter / carta de privilegio un documento que otorga los derechos de organizar establecimientos en una área (p. 119)

charter colony / colonia a carta colonia establecida por un grupo de colonizadores a quienes se les había dado un documento formal permitiéndoles colonizar (p. 130)

checks and balances / inspecciones y balances el sistema en el cual cada rama de gobierno refrena las otras dos ramas para que ninguna rama vuelva a ser demasiado poderosa (p. 205)

circumnavigate / circunnavegar navegar alrededor del mundo (p. 85)

citizen / ciudadano una persona que debe ser leal y tiene derecho a la protección de un estado o nación (p. 236)

civil war / guerra civil conflicto entre grupos opuestos de ciudadanos del mismo país (p. 547)

coeducation / coeducación la enseñanza conjunta de estudiantes hombres y mujeres (p. 410)

***collapse / derrumbarse** caer o venirse abajo de pronto (p. 542)

collective bargaining / negociaciones colectivas discusión entre el empresario y los representantes sindicales de los trabajadores sobre salario, horas, y condiciones del taller (p. 727)

colony / colonia asentamiento de personas en un nuevo territorio controlado por su país nativo (p. 95)

Columbian Exchange / Cambio Colombiano el cambio de productos, ideas, y personas entre Europa y las Américas (p. 95)

commission / comisión un grupo de personas dirigidas a hacer algún deber (p. 643)

***commit / cometer** llevar a cabo un acto (p. 648)

***communicate / comunicar** transmitir información, pensamientos o sentimientos de manera que se entiendan y comprendan (p. 434)

***community / comunidad** grupo de personas con intereses en común, especialmente cuando viven en la misma localidad (p. 501)

compromise / compromiso un acuerdo entre dos o más partidos en el cual cada partido abandona algo de lo que quiere (p. 199)

***concentrate / concentrarse** fijar la atención en una idea central (p. 386)

***concept / concepto** principio o idea (p. 491)

***conclude / concluir** llegar a una decisión final (p. 345)

concurrent powers / poderes concurrentes poderes compartidos por los estados y el gobierno federal (p. 222)

***conduct / conducir** dirigir o controlar las relaciones entre dos o más personas o grupos (p. 205)

Conestoga wagon / conestoga vehículo firme cubierto de lona blanca usado por los pioneros para moverse hacia el oeste (p. 313)

confederation / confederación asociación voluntaria de estados independientes (p. 180)

***confirm / confirmar** apoyar o consentir (p. 280)

***conflict / conflicto** desacuerdo o lucha (p. 329)

conquistador / conquistador explorador español en las Américas en los años 1500 (p. 86)

conservation / conservación la protección y preservación de recursos naturales (p. 771)

***consist / consistir** estar compuesto de (p. 354)

consolidation / consolidación la práctica de juntar compañías particulares en una (p. 707)

***constant / constante** que ocurre a menudo o todo el tiempo (p. 433)

constituents / constituyentes personas representadas por miembros del Congreso (p. 227)

constitution / constitución un plan formal de gobierno (p. 121)

***contract / contrato** acuerdo entre personas (p. 103)

***contrary / contrario** lo opuesto (p. 327)

***contrast / contrastar** mostrar las diferencias entre dos cosas que se comparan (p. 292)

***contribute / contribuir** ayudar a causar un suceso o situación (p. 460)

***controversy / controversia** gran desacuerdo o discusión sobre algo, generalmente porque afecta o les importa a muchas personas (p. 537)

***convert / convertir** cambiar una cosa en otra (p. 710)

***convince / convencer** hacer que alguien crea algo por medio de razones o hechos (p. 136)

***cooperate / cooperar** trabajar con otros para completar una tarea (p. 221)

cooperative / cooperativa una tienda donde los granjeros compraban productos uno al otro; una empresa poseída y operada por los que usan sus servicios (p. 694)

corporation / sociedad anónima un grupo autorizado por ley a montar una actividad pero con los derechos y deberes de una persona particular (p. 719)

***correspond / corresponder** comunicarse por cartas (p. 137)

corruption / corrupción acciones deshonestas o ilegales (p. 638)

cotton gin / despepitadora de algodón una máquina que sacaba las semillas de las fibras de algodón (pp. 384, 423)

court-martial / formar un consejo de guerra ser enjuiciado por una corte militar (p. 365)

Spanish Glossary

covenant / pacto acuerdo formal o promesa entre dos o más personas (p. 99)

***create / crear** hacer o producir (p. 638)

credit / crédito una forma de préstamo; la capacidad de comprar productos basada en pagos futuros (p. 429)

***culture / cultura** la manera de vivir de un grupo de personas que tienen en común sus creencias y costumbres (p. 81)

***currency / moneda** dinero (p. 194)

D

***debate / debate** discusión oral (p. 536)

debtor / deudor persona o país que debe dinero (p. 124)

***decline / decaer** perder valor (p. 695)

decree / decreto una orden o decisión dada por alguien de autoridad (p. 482)

demilitarize / desmilitarizar quitar las fuerzas armadas de un área (p. 363)

***demonstrate / demostrar** enseñar por medio de ejemplos (p. 365)

***deny / negar** no aceptar algo (p. 626)

depression / depresión un período de poca actividad económica y de desempleo extenso (pp. 194, 460)

***derive / derivarse** venir de algo, como una palabra que se ha formado de otra (p. 674)

***design / diseño** creación de un producto de acuerdo con un plan (p. 83)

***despite / a pesar de** sin tomar algo en cuenta o sin ser influido por algo (p. 686)

***device / dispositivo** invento o aparato (p. 713)

***devote / dedicar** usar un espacio, área o período de tiempo para un propósito (p. 492)

***diminish / disminuir** empequeñecer (p. 238)

disarmament / desarme eliminación de las armas (p. 363)

discrimination / discriminación trato injusto de un grupo; trato parcial a causa de la raza, la religión, los antecedentes étnicos, o lugar de nacimiento de alguién (pp. 397, 778)

dissenter / disidente persona que no esta de acuerdo con u opínese a opiniones establecidas (p. 121)

***distinct / bien diferenciados** totalmente distintos (p. 291)

***distribute / distribuir** dividir entre varios o muchos (p. 599)

diversity / diversidad variedad o diferencia (p. 123)

dividend / dividendo cheque que se paga a los accionistas, por lo general trimestralmente, representa una porción de las ganancias de la corporación (p. 719)

***document / documento** escrito importante (p. 103)

***dominate / dominar** tener gran influencia sobre todos los demás (p. 636)

draft / reclutamiento la selección de personas a servicio militar requirido (p. 602)

dry farming / agricultura seca una manera de cultivar tierra seca en la cual las semillas se plantan al fondo de la tierra donde hay un poco de humedad (p. 678)

due process of law / proceso justo de ley idea de que el gobierno debe de seguir los procesos establecidos por ley y garantizados por la Constitución (p. 235)

***dynamic / dinámico** tener mucho carácter y energía (p. 697)

E

***economy / economía** sistema monetario de un país, región o comunidad (p. 359)

***eliminate / eliminar** quitar o deshacerse de algo (p. 645)

emancipate / emancipar liberar de la esclavitud (p. 594)

embargo / embargo una orden que prohibe el comercio con otro país (p. 340)

emigrant / emigrante una persona que sale de un país o una región para vivir en otras partes (p. 474)

emigrate / emigrar dejar su patria para vivir en otras partes (p. 742)

***empresario* / empresario** una persona que arregló la coloización de tierra en Texas durante los años 1800 (p. 481)

***enable / posibilitar** hacer posible; permitir que algo suceda (p. 634)

***encomienda* / encomienda** sistema de recompensar a los conquistadores con extensiones de tierra y el derecho de recaudar impuestos y exigir mano de obra a los Nativos Americanos que vivían en la tierra (p. 88)

***encounter / encuentro casual** hallarse con otras personas inesperadamente (p. 580)

***enforce / hacer respetar** hacer que la gente obedezca la ley o que acepte una nueva situación (p. 641)

Enlightenment / Siglo de las Luces movimiento durante los años 1700 que propagaba la idea de que el conocimiento, la razón, y la ciencia podrían mejorar la sociedad (p. 203)

***enormous / enorme** muy grande (p. 313)

***ensure / asegurar** confirmar o cerciorarse de algo (p. 309)

entrenched / atrincherado que ocupa una fuerte posición defensiva (p. 605)

entrepreneur / empresario alguien que empieza su propio negocio (p. 93)

enumerated powers / poderes enumerados poderes que pertenecen solamente al gobierno federal (p. 222)

***environment / medio ambiente** combinación de suelo, clima y seres vivos que influyen en la habilidad para sobrevivir de una planta, animal o ser humano (p. 239)

***equip / equipar** proporcionar los materiales necesarios para hacer un trabajo (p. 390)

***establish / establecer** fundar, instalar o abrir (p. 363)

***ethnic / étnico** adjetivo relativo a un grupo grande de personas clasificadas según orígenes o antecedentes raciales, nacionales o culturales comunes (p. 761)

ethnic group / grupo étnico una minoría que habla un idioma diferente o que sigue costumbres diferentes que la mayoría de la gente de un país (p. 742)

***evaluate / evaluar** juzgar sobre la calidad o cantidad de algo (p. 580)

***eventual / mucho después** que sucede al pasar bastante tiempo o finalmente, en general después de mucho trabajo o muchos problemas (p. 555)

***exceed / exceder** sobrepasar los límites (p. 430)

executive branch / rama ejecutiva la rama de gobierno, dirigida por el presidente, que administra las leyes y la política de una nación (p. 205)

***expand / expandir** abrirse o ensancharse; aumentar en tamaño, número o cantidad (p. 386)

***exploit / explotar** usar de manera injusta para ventaja propia (p. 641)

***export / exportar** vender bienes en el extranjero (p. 95)

***extract / extraer** sacar (p. 667)

F

factory system / sistema de fábrica sistema que junta en un solo lugar las categorías de fabricación para aumentar la eficiencia (p. 385)

famine / hambre una escasez extrema de comida (p. 398)

favorite son / hijo favorito candidato que recibe el apoyo de su estado natal en lugar del partido nacional (p. 447)

***federal / federal** gobierno nacional (p. 453)

federalism / federalismo el compartir el poder entre el gobierno federal y los gobiernos estatales (pp. 204, 222)

Federalists / federalistas apoyadores de la Constitución (p. 206)

***finance / financiar** proporcionar fondos o capital (p. 91)

fixed costs / costos fijos gastos regulares tal como de vivienda o mantenimiento de equipo que se quedan casi iguales año tras año (p. 429)

***focus / concentrarse** fijar la atención y reflexionar sobre una idea central (p. 405)

forty-niners / forty-niners personas que fueron a California durante la fiebre del oro en 1849 (p. 501)

***found / fundar** establecer (p. 403)

free enterprise / libre comercio la libertad de empresas privadas para operarse competetivamente para ganancias con la mínima regulación gubernamental (p. 383)

free silver / plata libre la producción sin límite de monedas de plata (p. 696)

freedman / liberto una persona liberada de la esclavitud (p. 626)

frigate / fragata buque de guerra (p. 355)

fugitive / fugitivo evadido que trata de huir (p. 541)

Spanish Glossary

***function / funcionar** trabajar o servir para alcanzar una meta (p. 221)

***fund / fondo** cantidad de dinero ahorrada, colectada o proporcionada para algún propósito (p. 93)

G

***generation / generación** personas que nacen y viven durante los mismos años (p. 314)

Gilded Age / la Época Dorada el nombre asociado con América al final de los años 1800, referente a la gran riqueza de los tiempos y la terrible pobreza que estaba debajo (p. 752)

***goal / meta** objetivo o propósito (p. 413)

grandfather clause / cláusula de abuelo una cláusula que permitía votar a las personas que no aprobaron el examen de alfabetismo si sus padres o sus abuelos habían votado antes de que empezó la Reconstrucción; una excepción a una ley basada en circunstancias preexistentes (p. 648)

***grant / conceder** dar el consentimiento o permiso (p. 122)

***guarantee / garantía** compromiso que se va a cumplir una condición (p. 341)

guerrilla tactics / tácticas de guerrilla referente a ataques sorpresas o incursiones en lugar de la guerra organizada (p. 455)

guerrilla warfare / contienda a guerrilleros una técnica de tirar y darse a la huída usada en combates de guerra (p. 156)

H

habeas corpus / hábeas corpus una orden legal para una encuesta para determinar si una persona ha sido encarcelada legalmente (p. 600)

homestead / homestead adquirir una pieza de tierra pública de EE.UU. por medio de vivir en ella y cultivarla (p. 676)

horizontal integration / integración horizontal la asociación de firmas competitivas en una sociedad anónima (p. 720)

I

impeach / acusar acusación formal a un oficial público de mala conducta en la oficina (pp. 227, 633)

implied powers / poderes implícitos poderes no mencionados específicamente en la Constitución (pp. 224, 292)

import / importar comprar bienes de mercados extranjeros (p. 136)

impressment / requisición captura de marineros para forzarlos a servir en una marina extranjera (pp. 288, 339)

indentured servant / sirviente contratado trabajador que consiente trabajar sin pago durante un cierto período de tiempo a cambio del pasaje a América (p. 126)

Industrial Revolution / Revolución Industrial el cambio de una sociedad agraria en una basada en la industria que empezó en la Gran Bretaña y se promulgó a los Estados Unidos alrededor del año 1800 (p. 383)

***inevitable / inevitable** que no se puede impedir o escapar (p. 546)

inflation / inflación aumento contínuo del precio de productos y servicios (p. 603)

initiative / iniciativa el derecho de los ciudadanos de poner una medida o tema ante los votantes o la legislatura para aprobación (p. 769)

injunction / amonestación una orden judicial para terminar una acción, tal como una huelga (p. 729)

***inspect / inspeccionar** examinar con cuidado (p. 771)

integrate / integrar suprimir la segregación de las razas diferentes e introducir a membrecía igual y común en la sociedad (p. 638)

interchangeable parts / partes intercambiables piezas uniformes que pueden ser hechas en grandes cantidades para reemplazar otras piezas idénticas (p. 385)

***interpret / interpretar** explicar el significado (p. 179)

***intervene / intervenir** ponerse entre dos cosas (p. 229)

***invest / invertir** gastar dinero en un negocio para sacar ganancias (p. 719)

***involve / envolver** contener, involucrar o incluir (p. 236)

ironclad / acorazado buque armado (p. 578)

***isolate / aislar** separar o mantener separado de otros (p. 760)

***issue / tema** un tema que se disputa entre dos o más partidos (p. 450)

isthmus / istmo una faja estrecha de tierra que conecta dos áreas de tierra más grandes (p. 776)

***item / artículo** una mercancía o producto (p. 504)

J

***job / trabajo** deber o labor por la cual se recibe pago (p. 725)

joint occupation / ocupación en común la posesión y colonización de un área como esfuerzo compartido por dos o más países (p. 471)

joint-stock company / compañía por acciones una compañía en la cual los inversionistas compran acciones de la compañia a cambio de una porción de las ganancias en el futuro (p. 93)

judicial branch / rama judicial la rama de gobierno, incluyendo el sistema de tribunales federales, que interpreta las leyes de una nación (p. 205)

judicial review / repaso judicial el derecho del Tribunal Supremo para determinar si una ley viola la Constitución (pp. 225, 309)

***justify / justificar** tener buenas razones para escoger un bando (p. 556)

L

***labor / laborar** trabajar por un sueldo, como en la producción de bienes y servicios (p. 725)

laissez-faire / laissez-faire la creencia de que el gobierno no debe de involucrarse en los asuntos comerciales y económicos del país (pp. 307, 460, 771)

land-grant college / colegio de tierras donadas originalmente, un colegio agrícola establecido como resultado del Decreto Morrill de 1862 que dio a los estados, grandes cantidades de tierras federales que podrían ser vendidas para recaudar dinero para la educación (p. 760)

landslide / victoria arrolladora una victoria abrumadora (p. 448)

legislative branch / rama legislativa la rama de gobierno que redacta las leyes de una nación (p. 204)

***levy / gravamen** impuesto que un país, región o distrito cobra para pagar un préstamo o deuda (p. 194)

literacy test / examen de alfabetismo un método usado para prohibir a los afroamericanos a votar por requerir a presuntos votantes que pudieran leer y escribir a niveles especificados (p. 647)

lock / esclusa en un canal un recinto con puertas en cada extremo y usado para levantar y bajar los buques mientras pasan de un nivel al otro (p. 392)

lode / filón una faja o venero de mena intercalada entre estratos de piedra (p. 667)

Loyalists / lealistas colonizadores americanos que quedaron leales a la Bretaña y se opusieron a la guerra para la independencia (p. 153)

lynching / linchamiento matar a una persona a través de la acción ilegal de una muchedumbre airada (p. 648)

M

***maintain / mantener** continuar o sostener (p. 286)

***major / mayor** importancia que tiene gran tamaño, número o longitud (p. 105)

Manifest Destiny / Destino Manifiesto la idea popular en los Estados Unidos durante los años 1800 de que el país debería de extender sus fronteras hasta el Pacífico (p. 474)

***manual / manual** hecho a mano (p. 399)

manumission / manumisión el liberar a unas personas esclavizadas (p. 196)

martyr / mártir una persona que sacrifica su vida por un principio o una causa (p. 553)

mass production / fabricación en serie la producción de grandes cantidades de productos usando máquinas y muchas veces una línea de montaje (p. 717)

Mayflower Compact / Convenio del Mayflower un documento formal escrito en 1620 que proporcionó leyes para el mantenimiento del orden público en la colonia de Plymouth (p. 120)

mercantilism / mercantilismo idea de que el poder de una nación dependía de ampliar su comercio y aumentar sus reservas de oro (p. 94)

merger / fusión de empresas la asociación de dos o más negocios en uno (p. 722)

***migrate / migrar** mudarse de un país a otro (p. 329)

***military / militares** las fuerzas armadas (p. 124)

militia / milicia un grupo de civiles entrenados para luchar durante emergencias (p. 139)

Spanish Glossary

***ministry / clerecía** oficio, deberes y labores de un pastor (p. 413)

minutemen / *minutemen* compañías de soldados civiles que se jactaban de que podrían estar listos para tomar armas en sólo un minuto (p. 140)

mission / misión una comunidad religiosa (p. 88)

***modify / modificar** hacer cambios (p. 777)

***monitor / observar** seguir de cerca con un propósito en particular (p. 227)

monopoly / monopolio control total de una industria por una persona o una compañía (p. 720)

mountain man / hombre montañés colonizador que vivía en el monte, como en las Montañas Rocosas (p. 472)

muckraker / expositor de corrupción periodista que descubre abusos y corrupción en una sociedad (p. 767)

mudslinging / detractar intentar arruinar la reputación de un adversario con insultos (p. 447)

N

national debt / deuda nacional la cantidad de dinero que un gobierno debe a otros gobiernos o a su pueblo (p. 281)

National Grange / Granja Nacional la primera organización de granjeros de los Estados Unidos (p. 694)

nationalism / nacionalismo lealtad a una nación y promoción de sus intereses sobre todos los demás (pp. 321, 345)

nativist / nativista una persona que favorece a los nacidos en su patria y se opone a los inmigrantes (pp. 401, 746)

naturalization / naturalización el otorgar la plena ciudadanía a un extranjero (p. 236)

***network / red sistema** de partes conectadas (p. 711)

neutral / neutral que no toma partido a ninguna persona ni a ningún país en un conflicto (p. 153)

neutral rights / derechos neutrales el derecho para navegar en el mar sin tomar partido en una guerra (p. 339)

neutrality / neutralidad una posición de no tomar partido en un conflicto (p. 288)

***nevertheless / no obstante** sin embargo (p. 606)

nomadic / nómada que se mueve de un lugar a otro sin hogar permanente (p. 686)

normal school / escuela normal una escuela con programa de dos años para entrenar a los graduados de preparatoria para ser maestros (p. 405)

Northwest Passage / Paso Noroeste ruta acuática para Asia por América del Norte buscada por exploradores europeos (p. 88)

***notion / noción** idea o concepto (p. 529)

nullify / anular cancelar o hacer sin efecto (pp. 296, 450, 537)

O

***obtain / obtener** conseguir (p. 669)

***obvious / obvio** fácil de ver, comprender o hallar (p. 573)

***occupy / ocupar** tomar posesión de (pp. 157, 326)

***occur / ocurrir** suceder (p. 603)

offensive / ofensiva la posición de atacar o el mismo ataque (p. 573)

oligopoly / oligopolio mercado en que hay pocos productores y cada uno afecta pero no controla el mercado (p. 766)

open range / terreno abierto tierra sin cercas ni dividida en solares (p. 673)

ordinance / ordenanza una ley o regulación (p. 181)

ore / mena un mineral minado por la sustancia valorable que contiene, tal como plata (p. 667)

***outcome / resultado** efecto, consecuencias, o producto (p. 605)

override / vencer rechazar o derrotar, como un proyecto de ley propuesto en el Congreso (p. 630)

overseer / capataz persona que supervisa una operación grande o a sus trabajadores (pp. 127, 430)

P

***participate / participar** tomar parte en una actividad con otras personas (p. 194)

partisan / partidario a favor de una parte de un asunto (p. 291)

patent / patente un documento que da al inventor el derecho exclusivo legal de una invención durante un período de tiempo (p. 384)

Patriots / patriotas colonizadores americanos que estaban determinados para luchar en contra de los británicos hasta que se ganara la independencia americana (p. 153)

***percent / por ciento** una parte de 100 (p. 386)

***period / período** cantidad de tiempo (p. 625)

persecute / perseguir tratar cruelmente a alguien a causa de sus creencias o diferencias (p. 122)

petition / petición una solicitud formal (p. 150)

philanthropy / filantropía acciones caritativas o donaciones de dinero para beneficiar a la comunidad (p. 722)

philosophe / filósofo palabra francesa; durante el Siglo de las Luces, se aplicaba a intelectuales, como escritores, maestros, periodistas y observadores de la sociedad (p. 105)

philosophy / filosofía conjunto de creencias o ideas relacionadas con un sistema de valores culturales (p. 307)

planter / hacendado dueño de muchas tierras (p. 326)

plurality / pluralidad el mayor número de individuos (p. 447)

***policy / política** plan o instrucciones para lo que se va a hacer (p. 367)

political machine / máquina política una organización aliada con un partido político que muchas veces controlaba el gobierno local (p. 765)

poll tax / impuesto de capitación un impuesto de una cantidad fija por cada persona que tenía que ser pagada antes de que pudiera votar la persona (p. 647)

pool / consorcio un grupo compartiendo de una actividad, por ejemplo, entre barones ferrocarrileros que hacían acuerdos secretos y fijaban tipos entre ellos mismos (p. 711)

popular sovereignty / soberanía popular la teoría política de que el gobierno está sujeto a la voluntad del pueblo (pp. 179, 222); antes de la Guerra Civil, la idea de que la gente que vivía en un territorio tenía el derecho de decidir por votar si allí sería permitida la esclavitud (p. 544)

Populist Party / Partido Populista partido político de los EE.UU. formado en 1892 que representaba principalmente a los granjeros, que favorecía la acuñación libre de plata y el control gubernamental de ferrocarriles y otros monopolios (p. 695)

***pose / presentar** plantear; causar (p. 504)

preamble / preámbulo la introducción de un documento formal, especialmente la Constitución (pp. 152, 219)

precedent / precedente una tradición (p. 279)

***predominant / predominante** que tiene mayor importancia, fuerza, influencia o autoridad (p. 424)

prejudice / prejuicio una opinión injusta no basada en los hechos (p. 397)

presidio / presidio un fuerte español en las Américas construido para proteger las colonias misioneras (p. 88)

***primary / primario** el principal o más importante (p. 573); **elección preliminar** una elección en la cual los votantes escogen al candidato de su partido (p. 769)

***principle / principio** una verdad fundamental en que se basan otras teorías (p. 130)

privateer / buque corsario buque armado privado (p. 355)

***process / proceso** una acción continua o serie de acciones (p. 743)

***professional / profesional** que participa en una actividad para su manutención o como carrera (p. 752)

***prohibit / prohibir** vedar o no permitir (p. 633)

***promote / promover** alentar o contribuir a la diseminación de una idea (p. 203)

proportional / proporcional que son iguales o que corresponden (p. 199)

proprietary colony / colonia propietaria colonia dirigida por personas o grupos a quienes se les había otorgado la tierra (p. 130)

***prospect / perspectivas** posibilidad de que algo suceda en el futuro (p. 580)

protective tariff / arancel tarifa que sube el precio de productos de otros países (p. 537)

***publication / publicación** material impreso que se ofrece para distribución o venta (p. 530)

***publish / publicar** preparar materiales impresos para exhibición pública o venta (p. 407)

Spanish Glossary

pueblo / pueblo una casa o una comunidad de casas cons-truidas por Nativos Americanos (p. 88)

***purchase / comprar** obtener por dinero (p. 429)

***pursue / afanarse** luchar para alcanzar una meta (p. 102)

R

radical / radical extremo (p. 625)

ragtime / ragtime una clase de música con un ritmo fuerte y una melodía animada con notas acentuadas que era popular al principio del siglo (p. 762)

ranchero / ranchero dueño de rancho mexicano (p. 492)

rancho / rancho propiedades grandísimas para producir ganado establecidas por colonizadores mexicanos en California (p. 492)

***range / cordillera** serie de montañas (p. 501)

ratify / ratificar dar aprobación oficial para (pp. 181, 206, 594)

realism / realismo una perspectiva de literatura, arte, y teatro que representa las cosas tal como son (p. 761)

rebate / rebaja descuento o devolución de una porción de un pago (p. 710)

Rebel / rebelde soldado confederado, así nombrado a causa de su oposición al gobierno establecido (p. 574)

recall / elección de revocación el derecho que permite a los votantes que despidan de la oficina a los oficiales elegidos que son inadecuados (p. 769)

reconciliation / reconciliación arreglar por acuerdo o por reunirse de nuevo (p. 641)

Reconstruction / Reconstrucción la reorganización y la reconstrucción de los anteriores estados confederados después de la Guerra Civil (p. 625)

referendum / referéndum la práctica de permitir a los votantes que acepten o rechazen medidas propuestas por la legislatura (p. 769)

***region / región** un área, división o distrito (p. 638)

regionalism / regionalismo en arte o literatura, la práctica de enfocar en una región en particular del país (p. 761)

***register / registro** escrito con informes o datos; lista de datos (p. 743)

***regulate / regular** gobernar de acuerdo con reglas o leyes (p. 199)

***reinforce / reforzar** dar más soldados o armas a un ejército para hacerlo más fuerte (p. 577)

***reject / rechazar** negarse a dar o a considerar (p. 776)

relocate / reubicar forzar a una persona o a un grupo de personas a trasladarse (p. 453)

***reluctance / renuencia** desagrado o mala gana de hacer algo (p. 593)

***remove / quitar** sacar, despedir, retirar (p. 453)

Renaissance / Renacimiento un período de creatividad intelectual y artística, alrededor de los años 1300–1600 (p. 102)

rendezvous / rendezvous una reunión (p. 472)

repeal / revocar cancelar un decreto o ley (p. 136)

republicanism / republicanismo que favorece una república, o sea una democracia representativa, como la mejor forma de gobierno (p. 222)

***require / requerir** necesitar (p. 307)

reservation / reservación un área de tierra pública apartada para los Nativos Americanos (p. 687)

reserved powers / poderes reservados poderes retenidos por los estados (p. 222)

resolution / resolución una expresión formal de opinion (p. 139)

***resolve / resolver** solucionar un asunto (p. 341)

***resource / recurso** un bien muy útil o valioso (p. 719)

***restrict / restringir** limitar (p. 550)

***reveal / revelar** descubrir algo que hasta entonces estaba escondido o se desconocía (p. 544)

***revenue / ingresos** entrada de dinero (p. 284)

revival / renacimiento religioso una serie de reuniones dirigidas por un predicador para animar emociones religiosas (p. 403)

right of deposit / derecho de depositar Estados Unidos llegó a un acuerdo con España que le permitía navegar libremente por el río Mississippi (p. 185)

***role / papel** función dada a una persona o de la cual se hace cargo (p. 447)

***route / ruta** camino establecido (p. 472)

royal colony / colonia real colonia administrada por un gobernador y un consejo nombrados por el rey o reina (p. 130)

rule of law / imperio de la ley de acuerdo con la antigua ley romana, todos debían ser tratados con igualdad (p. 99)

S

scalawags / scalawags nombre dado por los confederados anteriores a los blancos sureños que apoyaban la Reconstrucción republicana del Sur (p. 638)

scientific method / método científico manera ordenada de recopilar y analizar pruebas (p. 105)

secede / separarse abandonar o retirar (pp. 316, 450, 541)

secession / secesión retiro de la Unión (p. 556)

sectionalism / regionalismo lealtad a una región (p. 536)

***secure / salvaguardar** proteger contra el peligro o la pérdida (p. 155)

sedition / sedición actividades con el propósito de debilitar un gobierno establecido (p. 295)

segregation / segregación la separación o aislamiento de una raza, una clase, o un grupo (p. 648)

settlement house / casa de beneficencia institución colocada en una vecindad pobre que proveía numerosos servicios a la comunidad tal como cuidado médico, cuidado de niños, bibliotecas, y clases de inglés (p. 753)

sharecropping / aparcería sistema de agricultura en el cual un granjero labra la tierra para un dueño que provee equipo y semillas y recibe una porción de la cosecha (p. 639)

shareholder / accionista una persona que invierte en una sociedad anónima por comprar acciones y que es un dueño parcial (p. 719)

***shift / mover** cambiar una cosa de lugar o posición (p. 396)

***significant / importante** significativo; que tiene un efecto profundo en algo (p. 308)

***similar / similar** semejante o parecido; con las mismas cualidades (p. 484)

slave code / código de esclavos las leyes aprobadas en los estados sureños que controlaban y restringían a la gente esclavizada (p. 434)

slum / barrio bajo vecindad pobre, superpoblada, y de de vecindades ruinosas (p. 752)

smuggling / contrabandear cambiar ilegalmente con otras naciones (p. 136)

sodbuster / rompedor de césped nombre dado al granjero de las Llanuras (p. 678)

***sole / solo** sin otra cosa o sin compañía (p. 474)

sovereignty / soberanía poder supremo (p. 180)

speculator / especulador persona que arriesga dinero para hacer una ganancia grande (p. 282)

spiritual / espiritual una canción popular religiosa afroamericana (p. 433)

spoils system / sistema de despojos la práctica de dar puestos gubernamentales a los partidarios; reemplazar a los empleados del gobierno con los partidarios del candidato victorioso (p. 449)

standard gauge / medida normal la anchura uniforme de 4 pies, 8.5 pulgadas de las vías ferroviarias, adoptada durante los años 1880 (p. 709)

states' rights / derechos estatales derechos y poderes independientes del gobierno federal que son reservados a los estados por la Constitución (pp. 296, 556)

***status / status** posición o categoría con relación a las demás personas (p. 482)

steerage / entrepuente los cuarteles apretados de las cubiertas bajas de un barco para los pasajeros que pagan los pasajes más bajos (p. 742)

stock / acciones valores de propiedad de comercio que vende una compañía que llevan muchas veces el poder de votar (p. 719)

***strategy / estrategia** plan detallado o método de proceder (p. 341)

strike / huelga un paro de trabajo por los trabajadores para forzar al empresario a satisfacer demandas (p. 397)

strikebreaker / esquirol una persona contratada para reemplazar a un huelguista para suprimir una huelga (p. 727)

***structure / estructura** disposición de las partes de algo (p. 279)

subsidy / subsidio donación de dinero del gobierno a una persona o una compañía para una acción con el propósito de beneficiar al público (p. 669)

Spanish Glossary

subsistence farming / agricultura para subsistencia labranza que produce solamente la comida que se necesita para dar de comer a la familia del trabajador (p. 126)

***substitute / sustituto** persona o cosa que reemplaza a otra (p. 602)

suburbs / suburbios áreas residenciales que brotaron cerca de o alrededor de ciudades como resultado de mejoramientos de transportación (p. 752)

***sufficient / suficiente** bastante para alcanzar una meta o satisfacer una necesidad (p. 573)

suffrage / sufragio el derecho al voto (pp. 409, 449)

***sum / resumir** describir o expresar en breve los datos importantes sobre un tema (p. 425)

***survive / sobrevivir** mantenerse vivo a pesar de dificultades y traumas (p. 119)

sweatshop / fábrica-opresora un taller o fábrica donde se explota a los trabajadores, trabajándolos muchas horas por poco pago y en condiciones malsanas (pp. 725, 744)

***symbol / símbolo** letra, carácter o signo que se usa en vez de palabras (p. 461)

T

tariff / tarifa impuesto sobre productos importados o exportados (pp. 282, 450)

***technique / técnica** método o destreza que se usa para lograr una meta (p. 156)

***technology / tecnología** el uso de conocimientos científicos para propósitos prácticos (pp. 82, 384, 710)

***Tejano* / tejano** un mexicano que reclama Texas como su patria (p. 481)

temperance / templanza el uso de poca o de ninguna bebida alcohólica (p. 403)

tenant farmer / granjero arrendatario un granjero que labra la tierra de otro dueño y paga renta ya sea con la cosecha o al contado (p. 428)

tenement / casa de vecindad un edificio en el cual varias familias alquilan cuartos o apartamentos, a menudo con pocas medidas sanitarias o seguridad (p. 752)

theology / teología el estudio de la religión y las creencias religiosas (p.101)

***theory / teoría** idea que sirve de punto de partida para una discusión o investigación (p. 556)

toleration / tolerancia el aceptar creencias diferentes (p. 121)

***topic / tema** materia bajo estudio y discusión, y sobre la cual se escribe (p. 552)

total war / guerra total la guerra en todo aspecto de la vida del enemigo (p. 609)

trade union / gremio una organización de artesanos con el mismo oficio o destreza (pp. 397, 726)

transcendentalist / transcendentalista uno de un grupo de escritores de Nueva Inglaterra que acentuaban la relación entre los seres humanos y la naturaleza, asuntos espirituales sobre asuntos materiales, y la importancia de la conciencia particular (p. 406)

transcontinental / transcontinental que se extiende a través del continente (p. 670)

***transmit / transmitir** pasar de una persona o sitio a otro (p. 713)

***transport / transportar** llevar de un lugar a otro (p. 286)

triangular trade / trato triangular una ruta de comercio para cambiar productos entre las Antillas, las colonias americanas, y África del Oeste (p. 126)

tribute / tributo dinero pagado para protección (p. 339)

trust / cártel una combinación de firmas o sociedades anónimas formada por un acuerdo legal, especialmente para reducir la competición (pp. 720, 766)

turnpike / autopista una carretera que uno debe de pagar para usar; el dinero se usa para pagar el costo de la carretera (p. 389)

U

***ultimate / último** resultado final o supremo (p. 279)

unconstitutional / anticonstitucional no de acuerdo ni consistente con la Constitución (p. 282)

Underground Railroad / Ferrocarril Subterráneo un sistema que ayudó a los afroamericanos esclavizados a seguir una red de rutas de escape afuera del Sur hacia la libertad del Norte (p. 534)

underlie / subyacer estar por debajo, o servir de base o apoyo (p. 767)

undertake / emprender asumir una responsabilidad (p. 386)

***unify / unificar** unir o reunir (p. 713)

***unique / único** solo en su clase; sin igual (p. 325)

utopia / utopía una comunidad basada en una visión de la sociedad perfecta buscada por los reformistas (p. 403)

V

vaquero / vaquero trabajador ranchero hispánico (p. 674)

vaudeville / teatro de variedades entretenimiento compuesto de varios actos, tal como baile, canción, comedia, y espectáculos de mágica (p. 763)

vertical integration / integración vertical la asociación de compañías que abastecen con equipo y servicios necesarios para una industria particular (p. 721)

veto / vetar rechazar un proyecto de ley y prevenir que vuelva a ser una ley (p. 459)

vigilantes / vigilantes gente que toman la ley en sus propias manos (pp. 504, 668)

***violate / violar** romper la ley o hacer daño (p. 136)

***vision / visión** habilidad para pensar en el futuro y planear de antemano (p. 505)

W

ward / pupilo persona bajo la tutela del gobierno de Estados Unidos (p. 782)

War Hawks / halcones de guerra republicanos durante la presidencia de Madison que insistían en la guerra con la Bretaña (p. 343)

Y

Yankee / yanqui soldado de la Unión (p. 574)

yellow journalism / periodismo amarillista escritura que exageraba acontecimientos sensacionales, dramáticos, y repulsivos para atraer a los lectores, citando historias que fueron populares durante los fines de los años 1800 (p. 761)

yeoman / terrateniente menor dueño sureño de una granja pequeña que no tenía esclavos (p. 428)

Gazetteer

A Gazetteer (GA • zuh • TIHR) *is a geographic index or dictionary. It shows latitude and longitude for cities and certain other places. Latitude and longitude are shown in this way: 48°N 2°E, or 48 degrees north latitude and two degrees east longitude. This Gazetteer lists most of the world's largest independent countries, their capitals, and several important geographic features. The page numbers tell where each entry can be found in this book.*

A

Abilene City in Kansas (39°N/97°W) 673

Africa Continent of the Eastern Hemisphere south of the Mediterranean Sea and adjoining Asia on its northeastern border 27, 87, 96, 100, 558, 776

Alabama State in the southeastern United States; 22nd state to enter the Union 31, 644

Alamo Texas mission captured by Mexican forces in 1836 (29°N/98°W) 483, 485

Alaska State in the United States, located in northwestern North America 26, 31, 32, 776

Albany Capital of New York State located in the Hudson Valley; site where Albany Congress proposed first formal plan to unite the 13 colonies (42°N/74°W) 390

Angel Island Island in San Francisco, California; served as an immigrant processing center (37°N/122°W) 743

Annapolis Capital city of Maryland (39°N/76°W) 31

Antietam Civil War battle site in western Maryland (40°N/78°W) 614

Appalachian Mountains Chief mountain system in eastern North America extending from Quebec and New Brunswick to central Alabama 33, 122, 135

Appomattox Court House Site in central Virginia where Confederate forces surrendered, ending the Civil War (37°N/78°W) 610

Argentina Country in South America 26

Arizona State in the southwestern United States; 48th state to enter the Union 30

Arkansas State in the south central U.S.; acquired as part of Louisiana Purchase 31, 558, 606, 632

Asia Continent of the Eastern Hemisphere forming a single landmass with Europe 26, 776

Asia Minor The peninsula forming western boundary of Asia between the Black Sea and Mediterranean Sea and bordering on the Aegean Sea to form the greater part of Turkey 100

Atlanta Capital of Georgia located in the northwest central part of the state (34°N/84°W) 33

Atlantic Ocean Ocean separating North and South America from Europe and Africa 26, 33, 87, 96, 119, 135, 156

Augusta Capital city of Maine (44°N/69°W) 31

Austin Capital city of Texas (30°N/97°W) 31

Australia Continent and country southeast of Asia 27, 776

B

Baltimore City on the Chesapeake Bay in central Maryland (39°N/76°W) 122

Barbary Coast North coast of Africa between Morocco and Tunisia 339

Baton Rouge Capital city of Louisiana (30°N/91°W) 31

Birmingham City in north central Alabama; scene of several civil rights protests (33°N/87°W) 721

Bismarck Capital city of North Dakota (47°N/101°W) 31

Black Hills Mountains in southwestern South Dakota; site of conflict between the Sioux and white settlers during 1870s 688

Boise Capital city of Idaho (43°N/116°W) 30

Boston Capital of Massachusetts located in the eastern part of the state; founded by English Puritans in 1630 (42°N/71°W) 122

Brazil Country in South America 26

Bull Run Site of two Civil War battles in northern Virginia; also called Manassas (39°N/77°W) 577

C

California State in the western United States; attracted thousands of miners during gold rush of 1849 30, 558, 644

Canada Country in northern North America 26, 31, 32–33

Cape of Good Hope Southern tip of Africa (34°S/18°E) 84

Caribbean Sea Tropical sea in the Western Hemisphere 29

Carson City Capital city of Nevada (39°N/120°W) 30

Caspian Sea Inland salt lake between Europe and Asia 100

Central America Area of North America between Mexico and South America (11°N/87°W) 29

Central Park A municipal park located on Manhattan Island in New York City; designed by Frederick Law Olmsted 755

Chancellorsville Virginia site of 1863 Confederate victory (38°N/78°W) 605, 606

Charleston (SC) City in South Carolina on the Atlantic coast; original name Charles Town (33°N/80°W) 122, 156

Charleston (WV) Capital city of West Virginia (38°N/81°W) 31

Chattanooga City in southwest Tennessee; grew into a center for trade in the South (35°N/85°W) 430

Cheyenne City in southeast Wyoming; became an important rail station for cattle drives (41°N/105°W) 673

Chile South American country (35°S/72°W) 26

China Country in eastern Asia; mainland (People's Republic of China) under Communist control since 1949 27, 776

Cincinnati City in southern Ohio on the Ohio River; grew as a result of increasing steamship traffic during the mid-1800s (39°N/84°W) 387, 390

Cleveland City in northern Ohio on Lake Erie (41°N/81°W) 533

Colombia Country in South America 26

Colorado State in the western United States 30, 644

Colorado River River that flows from the Colorado Rockies to the Gulf of California 32, 316

Columbia Capital of South Carolina; became a center for trade in the South (34°N/81°W) 430

Columbia River River flowing through southwest Canada and northwestern United States into the Pacific Ocean 32

Columbus Capital city of Ohio (40°N/83°W) 31

Concord (MA) Village northwest of Boston, Massachusetts; site of early battle of the American Revolution (42°N/71°W) 140

Concord (NH) Capital city of New Hampshire (43°N/71°W) 31

Connecticut State in the northeastern United States; one of the original 13 states 31, 121, 355, 558, 606

Cuba Country in the West Indies, North America 29, 775

D

Dakota Territory Included North and South Dakota, most of Wyoming and Montana; this land was created by Congress as Indian Territory 687

Delaware State in the northeastern United States; one of the original 13 states (38°N/75°W) 122, 355, 558, 606

Delaware River River flowing through eastern U.S.; empties into the Delaware Bay 390

Denver Capital city of Colorado (39°N/105°W) 31

Des Moines Capital city of Iowa (41°N/93°W) 31

Detroit City in southeastern Michigan; site of significant battles during the French and Indian War and the War of 1812 (42°N/83°W) 31, 355

Dodge City Kansas cattle town during the 19th century (37°N/100°W) 673

Dominican Republic Country in the West Indies on the eastern part of Hispaniola Island 29

Dover Capital city of Delaware (39°N/75°W) 31

E

Ellis Island Island in upper New York Bay; served as immigrant station from 1892–1954 (41°N/74°W) 743

England Division of the United Kingdom of Great Britain and Northern Ireland 87

Europe Continent of the northern part of the Eastern Hemisphere between Asia and the Atlantic Ocean 26, 87, 96, 776

F

Fallen Timbers Site in northwestern Ohio of General Anthony Wayne's victory over Native Americans in 1794 (42°N/84°W) 287

Florida State in the southeastern United States 31, 558

Fort Sumter Union fort during the Civil War located on island near Charleston, South Carolina; site of first military engagement of Civil War (33°N/80°W) 558

France Country in western Europe 30, 87

Frankfort Capital city of Kentucky (38°N/85°W) 31

Fredericksburg City and Civil War battle site in northeast Virginia (38°N/77°W) 605

Freeport City in northern Illinois; site of 1858 Lincoln-Douglas campaign debate (42°N/89°W) 552

G

Gadsden Purchase Portion of present-day Arizona and New Mexico; area purchased from Mexico in 1853 34, 497

Gaul Ancient country of Europe 100

Genoa Important seaport city in northwest Italy (44°N/10°E) 94

Georgia State in the southeastern United States 31, 119, 355, 558, 632

Gettysburg City and Civil War battle site in south central Pennsylvania; site where Lincoln delivered the Gettysburg Address (40°N/77°W) 605

Great Britain Kingdom in west Europe comprised of England, Scotland, and Wales 100

Great Lakes Chain of five lakes—Superior, Erie, Michigan, Ontario, and Huron—in central North America 33

Great Plains Flat grassland in the central United States 30

Great Salt Lake Lake in northern Utah with no outlet and strongly saline waters (41°N/112°W) 31, 506

Greece Country in southeastern Europe 100

Guam Unincorporated U.S. territory 775, 776

Guatemala Country in Central America, south of Mexico 29

Gulf of Mexico Gulf on the southeast coast of North America 33, 117

H

Haiti Country on Hispaniola Island in the West Indies 29

Harpers Ferry Town in northern West Virginia on the Potomac River (39°N/77°W) 553

Harrisburg Capital city of Pennsylvania (40°N/77°W) 31

Hartford Capital city of Connecticut (41°N/72°W) 31

Hawaii State in the United States located in the Pacific Ocean 31, 776

Hawaiian Islands Chain of volcanic and coral islands in north central Pacific Ocean; comprised of eight major islands and 114 minor islands 775, 776

Helena Capital city of Montana (46°N/112°W) 31

Hispaniola Island in the West Indies in North America (17°N/73°W) 29

Homestead City in southwest Pennsylvania; the location of Andrew Carnegie's steel plant where workers went on strike in 1892 (40°N/80°W) 729

Honolulu Capital city of Hawaii (21°N/158°W) 30

Hudson Bay Large bay in northern Canada (60°N/85°W) 29, 89, 135

Hudson River River flowing through New York State 390

I

Idaho State in the northwestern U.S.; ranks among top states in silver production 30

Illinois State in the north central United States; one of the states formed from the Northwest Territory 31, 558, 644

Indian Territory Land reserved by the United States government for Native Americans, now the state of Oklahoma 316, 454

Indiana State in the north central United States; one of the states formed from the Northwest Territory 31, 644

Indianapolis Capital city of Indiana (39°N/86°W) 31

Indonesia Country in Southeast Asia 27

Iowa State in the north central U.S. acquired as part of the Louisiana Purchase 31, 35, 558

Italy Country in southern Europe along the Mediterranean 26, 100

J

Jackson Capital city of Mississippi (32°N/90°W) 430

Jamestown First permanent English settlement in North America; located in southeastern Virginia (37°N/77°W) 122

Japan Island country in eastern Asia 27

Jefferson City Capital city of Missouri (38°N/92°W) 31

Judea The south division of Palestine under Persian, Greek, and Roman rule, succeeding the kingdom of Judah 100

Juneau Capital city of Alaska (58°N/134°W) 30

K

Kansas State in the central United States; fighting over slavery issue in 1850s gave territory the name "Bleeding Kansas" 31, 558, 644

Kentucky State in the south central United States; border state that sided with the Union during the Civil War 31, 558, 644

L

Lake Erie One of the five Great Lakes between Canada and the U.S. (42°N/81°W) 33, 355

Lake Huron One of the five Great Lakes between Canada and the U.S. (45°N/82°W) 33, 355

Lake Michigan One of the five Great Lakes between Canada and the U.S. (43°N/87°W) 33, 355

Lake Ontario The smallest of the five Great Lakes (43°N/79°W) 33, 355

Lake Superior The largest of the five Great Lakes (48°N/89°W) 33, 355

Latin America Central and South America; settled by Spain and Portugal 26

Lexington Revolutionary War battle site in eastern Massachusetts; site of first clash between colonists and British, April 19, 1775 (42°N/71°W) 140

Lincoln Capital city of Nebraska (41°N/97°W) 31

Little Bighorn River River south of Montana; where Sioux and Cheyenne warriors defeated the United States army 688

Little Rock Capital of Arkansas located in the center of the state; site of 1957 conflict over public school integration (35°N/92°W) 533

Los Angeles City along Pacific coast in southern California; industrial, financial, and trade center of western United States (34°N/118°W) 670

Louisiana State in the south central United States 31, 119, 606

Louisiana Territory Region of west central United States between the Mississippi River and the Rocky Mountains purchased from France in 1803 35, 135, 313, 316, 558, 606

Louisville City in north central Kentucky (38°N/86°W) 387

Lowell City in Massachusetts (43°N/71°W) 385

M

Maine State in the northeastern United States; 23rd state to enter the Union 31, 122, 558, 644

Mali Country in Western Africa 26

Manhattan Island Island at northeast end of New York Bay; part of New York City between Hudson and East rivers (44°N/76°W) 117

Maryland State in the eastern United States; one of the original 13 states 35, 122, 355, 387, 558, 606

Massachusetts State in the northeastern United States; one of the original 13 states 121, 122, 140, 558, 606

Mediterranean Sea Sea between Europe and Africa 27, 100

Memphis Tennessee city on the Mississippi River near the Mississippi border (37°N/90°W) 429

Mexican Cession Territory gained by the United States after war with Mexico in 1848 497

Mexico Country in North America south of the United States 26, 30–31, 32, 485, 495

Mexico City Capital and most populous city of Mexico (19°N/99°W) 26

Michigan State in the north central United States; one of the states formed in the Northwest Territory 31

Minnesota State in the north central United States; fur trade, good soil, and lumber attracted early settlers 31, 558, 644

Mississippi State in the southeastern United States; became English territory after French and Indian War 31, 558, 606, 644

Mississippi River River flowing through the United States from Minnesota to the Gulf of Mexico; explored by French in 1600s 33, 117

Missouri State in the south central U.S.; petition for statehood resulted in sectional conflict and the Missouri Compromise 31

Missouri River River flowing through the United States from the Rocky Mountains to the Mississippi River near St. Louis 31, 315, 316, 491

Mobile Commercial seaport in southwest Alabama; exported cotton, coal and agricultural products (31°N/88°W) 429

Mobile Bay Boundary of southwest Alabama and the Gulf of Mexico; the Union controlled this area in 1864 609

Montana State in the northwestern United States; cattle industry grew during 1850s 31, 644

Montgomery Capital of Alabama located in the central part of the state; site of 1955 bus boycott to protest segregation (32°N/86°W) 430

N

Nashville Capital of Tennessee located in the north central part of the state (36°N/87°W) 533

National Road Road from Baltimore, Maryland, to Vandalia, Illinois 389

Nebraska State in the central United States 31, 644

Netherlands Country in northwestern Europe 27, 87

Nevada State in the western United States 30, 644

New Amsterdam Town founded on Manhattan Island by Dutch settlers in 1625; renamed New York by British settlers (41°N/74°W) 117

New England Region in northeastern United States 33

New France French land claims stretching from Quebec to Louisiana 117, 119

New Hampshire State in the northeastern United States; one of the original 13 states 122, 558, 606

New Haven Coastal city in Connecticut; settled by Puritans in 1638 (41°N/73°W) 122

New Jersey State in the northeastern United States; one of the original 13 states 122, 355, 558, 606

New Mexico State in the southwestern United States; ceded to the United States by Mexico in 1848 31, 117

New Netherland Dutch Hudson River colony 117

New Orleans City in Louisiana in the Mississippi Delta (30°N/90°W) 289, 313, 316, 429

New Spain Part of Spain's empire in the Western Hemisphere 35, 119

New York State in the northeastern United States; one of the original 13 states 31, 117, 122, 387, 558, 606, 644

New York City City in southeastern New York State at the mouth of the Hudson River; first capital of nation (41°N/74°W) 117, 122

Newfoundland Province in eastern Canada (48°N/56°W) 29, 87, 119

Norfolk City in southeastern Virignia; Confederate forces seized a naval shipyard and rebuilt the *Merrimack* and renamed it *Virginia* (37°N/76°W) 578

North America Continent in the northern part of the Western Hemisphere between the Atlantic and Pacific oceans 26, 87, 96, 776

North Carolina State in the southeastern United States; one of the original 13 states 119, 122, 355, 558, 606, 632

North Dakota State in the north central U.S.; Congress created Dakota Territory in 1861 31

North Sea Arm of the Atlantic Ocean and east of Great Britain 100

Northwest Territory Territory north of the Ohio River and east of the Mississippi River 34, 183

O

Ohio State in the north central United States; first state in the Northwest Territory 31, 341, 389, 644

Ohio River River flowing from Allegheny and Monongahela rivers in western Pennsylvania into the Mississippi River 33, 355, 386

Oklahoma State in the south central United States; Five Civilized Tribes moved to territory in the period 1830–1842 31, 689

Oklahoma City Capital city of Oklahoma (35°N/98°W) 31

Olympia Capital city of Washington (47°N/123°W) 30

Omaha City in east Nebraska where the Populist Party held their presidential convention in 1892 (41°N/96°W) 696, 670

Oregon State in the northwestern United States; adopted woman suffrage in 1912 30, 558, 644

Oregon Country Area that is now Oregon, Idaho, Washington state, and parts of western Montana and Wyoming 363

Oregon Trail Pioneer trail from Independence, Missouri, to the Oregon Territory 474

P

Pacific Ocean World's largest ocean, located between Asia and the Americas 26–27, 31, 87, 119, 776

Panama Country in the southern part of Central America, occupying the Isthmus of Panama 29, 776

Panama Canal Canal built across the Isthmus of Panama through Panama to connect the Caribbean Sea and the Pacific Ocean (9°N/80°W) 776–777

Pawtucket City in north Rhode Island; location where Samuel Slater opened a cotton mill (42°N/71°W) 385

Pennsylvania State in the northeastern United States 31, 122, 558, 606, 644

Peru Country in South America, south of Ecuador and Colombia 26, 86

Petersburg City in southeastern Virginia; an important railroad city that the Union seized for nine months (37°N/78°W) 608

Philadelphia City in eastern Pennsylvania on the Delaware River; Declaration of Independence and the Constitution both adopted in city's Independence Hall (40°N/75°W) 122, 726

Philippines Island country in southeast Asia 27, 776

Phoenix Capital city of Arizona (33°N/112°W) 30

Pierre Capital city of South Dakota (44°N/100°W) 31

Pikes Peak Mountain in Rocky Mountains in central Colorado 316

Pittsburgh City in western Pennsylvania; one of the great steelmaking centers of the world (40°N/80°W) 387

Plymouth Town in eastern Massachusetts; first successful English colony in New England (42°N/71°W) 120, 122

Portsmouth Seaport city in southeast New Hampshire (43°N/71°W) 122

Portugal Country in southwestern Europe 26, 87

Potomac River River flowing from West Virginia into Chesapeake Bay 307, 390

Princeton City in west central New Jersey (40°N/75°W) 153

Promontory Summit Site where two sets of the transcontinental railroad connected 670

Providence Capital of Rhode Island; site of first English settlement in Rhode Island (42°N/71°W) 31, 122, 670

Puerto Rico United States commonwealth in the West Indies 29

Q

Quebec City in Canada, capital of Quebec Province, on the St. Lawrence River; first settlement in New France (47°N/71°W) 117

R

Raleigh Capital city of North Carolina (36°N/79°W) 31

Rhode Island State in the northeastern United States; one of the original 13 states 31, 121, 355, 558, 606

Richmond Capital of Virginia located in the central part of the state; capital of the Confederacy during the Civil War (38°N/78°W) 31

Rio Grande River between the United States and Mexico in North America; forms the boundary between Texas and Mexico 32

Roanoke Island off the coast of present-day North Carolina that was site of early British colonizing efforts (36°N/77°W) 119

Rocky Mountains Mountain range in western United States and Canada in North America 32

Rome City in Italy; one of the most ancient of the European civilizations; developed a republic form of government 99

Russia Name of republic; former empire of eastern Europe and northern Asia coinciding with Soviet Union 27, 776

S

Sacramento Capital of California located in the north central part of the state (38°N/121°W) 670

Salem Capital city of Oregon (45°N/123°W) 30

Salt Lake City Capital of Utah located in the northern part of the state; founded by Mormons in 1847 (41°N/112°W) 474

Gazetteer

San Antonio City in south central Texas (29°N/98°W) 483

San Diego City in southern California (33°N/117°W) 118

San Francisco City in northern California on the Pacific coast (38°N/122°W) 503

San Juan Capital city of Puerto Rico (18°N/66°W) 31

Santa Fe Capital of New Mexico located in the north central part of the state (36°N/106°W) 117, 491, 495

Santa Fe Trail Cattle trail from Independence, Missouri, to Santa Fe, New Mexico 491

Saratoga Revolutionary War battle site in the Hudson Valley of eastern New York State (43°N/74°W) 154

Savannah City in far eastern Georgia (32°N/81°W) 429

Scandinavia Region of north Europe encompassing Denmark, Norway, and Sweden 87

Seattle Washington city bordered by Puget Sound and Lake Washington (47°N/122°W) 30

Sedalia City in Missouri; the nearest trail point for Texas cattle ranchers (39°N/93°W) 673

Seneca Falls Town in New York State; site of women's rights convention in 1848 (43°N/77°W) 409

Shiloh Site of 1862 Union victory in Tennessee (35°N/88°W) 579

South America Continent in the southern part of the Western Hemisphere lying between the Atlantic and Pacific oceans 26, 119, 776

South Carolina State in the southeastern United States; one of the original 13 states 122, 355, 556, 558, 606, 632

South Dakota State in the north central United States; acquired through the Louisiana Purchase 31

Spain Country in southwestern Europe 26, 87, 100

Springfield Capital city of Illinois (40°N/90°W) 31

St. Augustine City in northeastern Florida on the Atlantic coast; oldest permanent existing European settlement in North America, founded in 1565 (30°N/81°W) 117

St. Louis City in Missouri; the invention of the steamboat played an important role in the growth of this city (39°N/90°W) 31, 390

St. Paul Capital city of Minnesota (45°N/93°W) 31

Switzerland European country in the Alps 27

Syria Ancient country in Asia at the eastern end of the Mediterranean Sea 100

T

Tallahassee Capital city of Florida (30°N/84°W) 31

Tennessee State in the south central United States; first state readmitted to the Union after the Civil War 31, 558, 606, 644

Tenochtitlán Aztec capital at the site of present-day Mexico City (19°N/99°W) 86

Texas State in the south central United States; Mexican colony that became a republic before joining the United States 31, 485, 495, 558, 606, 632

Topeka Capital city of Kansas (39°N/96°W) 31

Toronto City in Canada on Lake Ontario; capital of the province of Ontario (44°N/79°W) 26

Trenton Capital of New Jersey located on the Delaware River in the central part of the state; site of Revolutionary War battle in December 1776 (40°N/75°W) 153

U

Union of Soviet Socialist Republics See Soviet Union.

United States Country in central North America; fourth largest country in the world in both area and population 26, 495, 776

Utah State in the western United States; settled by Mormons in 1840s 30

V

Valley Forge Revolutionary War winter camp northwest of Philadelphia (40°N/75°W) 154

Vandalia City in south central Illinois; the National Road reached here (39°N/89°W) 389

Venezuela South American country on the Caribbean Sea 26

Venice Important seaport city in northeast Italy 94

Vermont State in the northeastern United States; 14th state to enter the Union 606

Vicksburg City and Civil War battle site in western Mississippi on the Mississippi River (32°N/91°W) 606

Virginia State in the eastern United States; colony of first permanent English settlement in the Americas 31, 120, 122, 340, 355, 558, 606, 632

Virginia City City in west Nevada; became a Comstock boomtown during the gold and silver strikes of 1859 (39°N/120°W) 668

W

Waltham City in northeast Massachusetts; Francis Cabot Lowell opened a textile plant in 1814 (42°N/71°W) 385

Washington State in the northwestern United States; territory reached by Lewis and Clark in 1805 30

Washington, D.C. Capital of the United States located on the Potomac River at its confluence with the Anacostia River, between Maryland and Virginia coinciding with the District of Columbia (39°N/77°W) 31, 282, 307

West Indies Islands in the Caribbean Sea, between North America and South America (19°N/79°W) 29

West Virginia State in the east central United States 31

Willamette Valley Valley of the Willamette River in western Oregon 474

Williamsburg City in southeastern Virginia (37°N/77°W) 122

Wisconsin State in the north central United States; passed first state unemployment compensation act, 1932 31, 558

Wounded Knee Site of massacre of Native Americans by soldiers in southern South Dakota in 1890 and of American Indian Movement protest in 1973 (43°N/102°W) 689, 692

Wyoming State in the western United States; territory provided women the right to vote, 1869 31

Y

Yorktown Town in southeastern Virginia and site of final battle of Revolutionary War (37°N/76°W) 156

Index

Italicized page numbers refer to illustrations. The following abbreviations are used in the index: c = chart or graph, ctn = cartoon, m = map, p = photograph or picture, ptg = painting, q = quote.

A

Abbott, E. C., 673
Abbott, Grace, 747
Abilene, Kansas, 673, 675
ability-to-pay principle, 813
abolition movement, 195–196, 529; African Americans in, 529, 531–32; changes in, 530; early, 195–96, *m244*, 529; Garrison as member of, 562; Grimké sisters in, 412, *p412*; newspapers in, 530, 531, 532, 562; *Uncle Tom's Cabin* and, 407; women in, 530
absolute location, 42, *p42*, 54
absolutism, 103
accused persons, rights of, 260
Act of Toleration (1649), 123
Adams, Abigail, 155, *q155*, 293, 294, *p294*, 307, 363
Adams, Andy, 698
Adams, John, *p250*, 294, *p294*, *q297*, 840, *p840*; administration of, 293, 295–97; as colonial leader, 139, 155; as delegate to Second Continental Congress, 150, 152, 197, 294; in election of 1796, 238, 293; in election of 1800, 297, 307; midnight judges and, 308–9; problems with Britain and, 184; Treaty of Paris (1783) and, 156; as vice president, 279, 280
Adams, John Quincy, 363, *p531*, 840, *p840*; abolition of slavery and, 531, *q531;* in election of 1824, 447, *c447*; in election of 1828, 447–48; Fourth of July address of, *q331*; Manifest Destiny and, 474; as president, 447; as secretary of state, 363, 365, 367; slavery issue and, 536; western settlement and, 471
Adams, Samuel, 137, *q138*; as delegate to Second Continental Congress, 150
Adams-Onís Treaty (1819), 365, 471
Addams, Jane, 753, *p753*, *q753*, 786–87
adding machines, 714
The Adventures of Huckleberry Finn **(Twain),** 761
The Adventures of Tom Sawyer **(Twain),** 761
AFL-CIO Committee on Political Education, 817
Africa: back-to, movement, 780; Barbary pirates in North, 339; Portuguese explorations of, 84
African Americans, 563; in abolition movement, 529, 531–32; as Buffalo Soldiers, 676, 677, *p677*; citizenship for, 651; civil rights movement and, 404, 780, 796, *p796*, *p800*, 800–801; in Civil War, 574, 575; as cowhands, 674, 675; discrimination against, 397, 779, *p800*, 800–801; education for, 233, 397, 405, 409, 638, 651, 759, 760; Emancipation Proclamation and, 592–94, *q594*; Farmers' Alliance for, 695; free, 195–96, 327, 429, 430; Freedmen's Bureau and, 626; in government, 636, *p636*; inventions by, 715; Jim Crow laws and, 647, 648; Ku Klux Klan and, 638, 642; lynchings of, 648; migration of, 641, 751; music of, 327, 762; newspapers for, 397, 761; under Reconstruction, 648; religion of, 322; suffrage for, 696, 770; in the Underground Railroad, 533–34; in unions, 731; violence against, 648; voting rights for, 264, 397, 647–48; in workforce, 397, *p397*
The Age of Innocence **(Wharton),** 761
agrarianism, 538–39
agriculture: cash crops in, 119, 126, 326, 646; of Native Americans, 95–96; in the South, 1850–1890, *g645*; in the West, 386. *See also* farmers; farming
Agriculture, U.S. Department of, 771
airplanes, first flight of, 714, *p714–15*
Alabama: Civil War in, 579; readmission to union, 632; removal of Native Americans from, 453; secession of, 556; statehood for, 393, 426
Alamo, defense of, 483–84
Alaska: Denali National Park and Preserve in, 772, *p772–73*; purchase of, from Russia, 499, 775; statehood for, 499
Albany Plan of Union, 135
Albuquerque, New Mexico, 88
alcohol, temperance movement and, 403, 410, 502
Aldrich, Bess Streeter, 680
Alexandria, Virginia, Civil War medical care in, *p582*
Alger, Horatio, 761
Alien and Sedition Acts (1798), *c295*, 295–96
Allen, Macon B., 397
Allen, Richard, 196, *p196*
almanacs, colonial, 129
alphabet, Cherokee, 453, *p453*
amendments, 223, 258, 260–69. *See also specific amendments*
American AntiSlavery Society, 439, 530, 637
American colonies, *m119*; British colonial policies toward, 130–31, 136; Carolinas as, 123–24; colonial protests in, 137–38; Connecticut as, 121; Delaware as, 121, 122; education in, 129; English heritage in, 133; Georgia as, 124; growth of, 126–27; Maryland as, 123; Massachusetts as, 121; national origin of colonists in, *m162*; Native Americans and, 119, 123; New Jersey as, 121, 122; New York as, 121, 122; Pennsylvania as, 121, 122; Plymouth as, 120; religious freedom in, 121, 123; resistance in, 131, 136–37; Rhode Island as, 121; Roanoke as, 119; self-government in, 130; Virginia as, 119, 123
American Colonization Society, 529
American Conservative Union, 817
American Federation of Labor, 727
American Fur Company, 472
American Indian Movement (AIM), 802
American Notes **(Dickens),** 415
American Party, 401, 549
American Protective Association, 778
American Railway Association, 709
American Railway Union, 729
American Revolution: African Americans in, 155, *p155*; allies in, 154–55; American victory in, 156–57; British in, 153; early battles in, *m140*, 140–41, 153–54; effects of, 156; end of, 156; home front in, 155; loyalists in, 153, 159, *p159*; naval battles in, 155; patriots in, 153, 156, 158; preparing for, 140; in the South, 156, *m156*; in the west, 155
American Samoa, representation of, in House of Representatives, 227
American's Creed, 845, 858

American Slavery As It Is **(Grimké, Grimké and Weld),** 439, 530
American Socialist Party, 767
The American Spelling Book **(Webster),** 321, *p321*
Americans With Disabilities Act (1990), 804
American System, 389
American Tobacco Company, 646
AmeriCorps, 819
Ames, Nathaniel, 135
Amherst College, 413
amnesty, offering of, after Civil War, 625
Amnesty Act (1872), 642
amusements: in 1800s, 762–63; in western settlement, 394
Anaconda Plan, 608, *m608*
Anderson, Joseph Reid, 426
Anderson, Robert, 558
Andrews, Sidney, *q652*
Angel Island, 743, 744, *p744*
Anglican Church, 120, 123
Anthony, Susan B., 410, 502, 804
anti-Catholicism, 778
Antietam, Battle of, 582–83, 593, 594, 598, 601, *m614–15*, 615
Antifederalists, 206–7, 209
Antin, Mary, 758
anti-Semitism, 778
antislavery movement. *See* abolition movement
antitax movement, 813
antitrust movement, 723, 766, 770–71
Apache people, 481
Apache wars, 689
Appalachian Mountains, 135, 328
appeals courts, 230
Appomattox Court House, 611; Lee's surrender at, 610, *p610*, 611, 612
Aquinas, Thomas, 101
Arapaho people, 687, 688
archaeologists, 49, *p49*; dating finds of, 50–51
architecture: in early 1800s, 325, *p325*; skyscrapers in, *p754*, 754–55
Arizona: mining in, 668; San Carlos reservation in, 689; settlement of, 366, 491; statehood for, 499
Arkansas: Civil War in, 606; readmission to union, 632; Reconstruction in, 625; secession of, 559, 571; statehood for, 426
Arkwright, Richard, 385
arms, right to bear, 260
army: continental, 150, 153, 154; in early 1800s, 354; Native Americans and, 688–89,690, 691
Arouet, François-Marie, 105
art: in the 1800s, 325, 762; western settlement and, *p361*
Arthur, Chester A., 842, *p842*; spoils system and, 766
Articles of Confederation, 180, 204; call for change, 194, 196–97; comparison to Constitution, U.S., *c206*; weaknesses under, 181, *c181*, 183, 194–96, 219
Ashmun Institute, 405
assembly, freedom of, 260
assembly line, 717, 806
Astor, John Jacob, 472
astrolabe, 83, *p83*
Atahualpa, 86
Athens, 99
Atlanta, Georgia, 609; in Civil War, 608, *p612*; life in, 430
Atlanta University, 626, 638
atlas, 58; historical, 58
attorney general, 280
Attucks, Crispus, 137
Auld, Sophia, 637
Austin, Stephen F., 481–82
automation, 731
automobiles, 713, 785, *p785*, *p796*; impact of, 716–17; invention of, *p794*
Aztec, 86; Spanish and, 109, *p109*; stone calendar of, *p50*

B

back-to-Africa movement, 780
Bacon, Francis, 105
Bagley, Sarah G., 397
Bahamas, 84
Baker, David, 91
Balmes, Kathy, 507
Baltimore, Maryland, 426; growth of, 387, 400; population in, 430; strikes in, 727; in War of 1812, 358
banking: changes in, 93; growth of, 91; role of, in economic growth, 719
Bank of the United States: Hamilton's proposal for, 282; Jackson and, 459, *q459*, *ctn460*
"Barbara Frietchie" (Whittier), 617
Barbary Coast states, 339
Barbary pirates, 339
barbed wire, 675, 679
barrios, 782
Barton, Clara, 600, 601, *q601*, *p601*
baseball, 763
basketball, 763
Battle of Monmouth, *ptg154*
Battle of North Point, *ptg358*
"Battle of Stonington," 368
Baumfree, Isabella, 532
bayonet rule, 641
Bear Flag Republic, 496
Becknell, William, 491
Beckwourth, Jim, 472, *p472*
Beecher, Catherine, 412
Beef Bonanza **(Brisbin),** *p675*
Bell, Alexander Graham, 713, 716
Bell, John, 555
Bell Telephone Company, 713
benefits-received principle, 813
Bessemer, Henry, 646, 721
Bessemer process, 646
Bethel Church Resolution, 196
Beveridge, Albert, 775, *q775*
bias, 63
bicameral legislature, 179
bicycling, 763
Biddle, Nicholas, *p449*, 459
Bidwell, Annie, 502, *p502*
Bidwell, John, 502, *q502*, *p502*
bill, passage of, 228, *c229*
Bill of Rights, 179, 198, 201, 207, 222, 223, *c223*, 260–61, 281; English, 103, 106, 107, 152, 179, 203. *See also specific amendments*
Bingham, George Caleb, 325
Birmingham, Alabama, steel production in, 721
black codes, challenges to, 630
Black Hawk, 455, *p457*
Black Hills, 688
Black Kettle, 688
Black Power, 803
blacksmith, *p383*
Blackwell, Elizabeth, 411, *p411*, 413
Blanco, Kathleen, *p804*
blockade in Civil War, 573, 578, 603
blue collar workers, 808
Blue Jacket, 287, 343, *q343*, *p343*
blue jeans, 503
Blümmer, August, 398
Bolívar, Simón, 366
Bologna, university in, 101
Bonaparte, Napoleon, 313, 341
Bonhomme Richard **(ship),** 155
bookmobiles, *p759*
boomtowns, 503; growth of, 668, *p668*; women in, 668
Booth, John Wilkes, 612, 626
border states in Civil War, 571–72
Boston, Massachusetts, 121; celebration in, following ratification of Constitution, 207, 279; 1873 fire in, 753; growth of, 327, 387; music in, 762; painting of harbor, *ptg400*; public library in, 755; subway in, 756
Boston Massacre, 137, *p137*

Boston Tea Party, 138, *q138, p138*
Bowie, Jim, 483, 484
Boyd, Belle, 600
Boyd, Henry, 397
Bozeman Trail, 688
Brady, Mathew, 602
branding, 673
Brazil: independence of, 366; Portuguese in, 97
Breckinridge, John C., 555
Breed's Hill, 150
bridge construction, *p755,* 756
Bridger, Jim, 472
Brisbin, General, *p675*
British East India Company, 138
Brooklyn Bridge, *p755,* 756
Brooks, Preston, 547
Brown, Albert, 556
Brown, John, 547, 549; execution of, 553; raid on Harpers Ferry, 553, 555
Brown, Linda, 233, *p233,* 651, *p651*
***Brown* v. *Board of Education*,** 233, 651, 801, 846, 859
Bruce, Blanche K., 636
Bryan, Vincent, *q713*
Bryan, William Jennings, in election of 1896, 696–97
Bryant, William Cullen, 325
Bryn Mawr College, 760
Buchanan, James, 841, *p841*; in election of 1856, 549; secession of the South and, 557
Buckner, Simon, 579
Buffalo, New York: Erie Canal and, 392; growth of, 398
buffalo, threats to, 686, 691
Buffalo Bill, 686
Buffalo Soldiers, 676, 677, *p677*
bullion, 94, *p94*
Bull Run: First Battle of, 577, 579, 600; Second Battle of, 581
Bunche, Ralph, 760
Bunker Hill, 150
Bunyan, Paul, legend of, 448
Burbank, J. Maze, *ptg322*
Burgoyne, John, 154
Burnaby, Andrew, 126
Burnet, David G., 485
Burnett, Peter H., 504
Burns, Anthony, 533
Burnside, Ambrose, 583, 605
Burr, Aaron: duel with Hamilton, 283, 317; in election of 1796, 293; in election of 1800, 283, 307; Jefferson and, 317; as vice president, 317
Burrough, William, 714
Burton, Henry, 493
Bush, George H. W., 844, *p844*
Bush, George W., 844, *p844*; terrorism and, 236, *q236*
business: laissez-faire philosophy in, 771. *See also* corporations
Butler, Andrew P., 547

C

Cabeza de Vaca, Álvar Núñez, 87
cabinet, 230; of George Washington, 279–80, 291; of Thomas Jefferson, 308
Cabot, John, *m87,* 88
Cabral, Pedro Alvares, 84, *m87*
Cairo, Illinois, 579
calendars, 50, *p50*
Calhoun, John C., 344, *p344,* 345, *p449, p537, p541*; in election of 1828, 448; nullification and, 451; as secretary of war, 365; tariff of 1828 and, 537–38; Wilmot Proviso and, 540
California: annexation of, 496–97; as Bear Flag Republic, 496; Constitution for, 504; economy in, 505; forty-niners in, 501; gold rush in, 501, 504, 505, *p540,* 667; life in, 503; Manifest Destiny and, 494; Mexican territory of, 491; population in, 505; Proposition 13 in, 813; railroads and, 707; settlement of, 366, 539, 540; Spanish culture in, 492; statehood for, 499, 505, 541; state seal of, *p498*; suffrage in, 504; U.S. offer to purchase from Mexico, 494; women's rights in, 413
California Land Act (1851), 493, 501
Californios, 496, 501
***The Call of the Wild* (London),** 761
Calvert, Cecilius, 123
Calvert, George, 123
Calvin, John, 102–3
Canada: conflicts with Britain over border with, 364; flight of Nez Perce to, 689; French settlements and, 117; War of 1812 in, 354–55
canals, 392–93, *p392–93,* 394
Cape of Good Hope, 84
capital: as factor of production, 719; raising, 719
capitalism, 94, 383; development of, 91
Capitol, *p274,* 282, *p282*
caravel, 83
cardinal directions, 43
Carlisle Indian Industrial School, 760
Carmichael, Stokely, 803
Carnegie, Andrew, 721, *p721,* 729, 761; philanthropy of, 722
Carnegie Foundation for the Advancement of Teaching, 722
Carnegie Hall, 722
Carnegie Steel Company, 722
Carolinas: colony of, 123–24. *See also* North Carolina; South Carolina
carpetbaggers, 638
Carson, Kit, 472, 496, 832, *p832*
Carson, Rachel, 805
Carter, Dennis Malone, *ptg154*
Carter, James, *q360*
Carter, Jr., James E., 844, *p844*
Cartier, Jacques, *m87,* 89
cartographers, 82
Carver, George Washington, 760, 780, 782, *p782, q782*
Cary, Mary Ann Shadd, 411, *p411*
cash crops, 119, 126, 326, 646
Cass, Lewis, 540
Cassatt, Mary, 762
Castillo, Bernal Díaz de, 109
Castle Garden, 743
Catholics: immigration and, 400, 742; rise of Protestantism and, 102
Catlin, George, 325, *ptg361*
cattle drives, 673–74, *q698;* dangers on, 674–75; Spanish influences on, 674
Cattle Kingdom, 673–75, *m700;* end of, 675
cattle ranching, 671, *p673,* 673–75; as big business, 675; conflict with farming, 675
caucus in political process, 449
cause-and-effect chain, 64–65
causes, 65
Cavalier, René-Robert, 117
Cayuse people, 473–74
Cemetery Ridge, 605
census: of 1790, 389. *See also* population
Central Pacific Railroad, 670, 707, 708
century, 52
***A Century of Dishonor* (Jackson),** 691
chain stores, 717
Champlain, Samuel de, 117
Chancellorsville, Virginia, 605
Charles I, King of England, 103, 120, 123
Charles II, King of England, 122, 123
Charleston, South Carolina, 426, *p620;* celebration in, following ratification of Constitution, 279; in Civil War, 596; growth of, 327; life in, 429; plantations near, *p418;* schools in, 431

Charles Town, 156
charter, 119
charter colonies, 130
Charter of Liberties, 122
Chattanooga, Tennessee, 607, 608; life in, 430
Chávez, César Estrada, 728, *p728*, *q730*, *p730*, 731, 782, 796, 802
Chávez, Helen Fabela, 728
checks and balances, 205, *c221*, 223, *c228*
Cherokee people: acceptance of Christianity, 329; Jackson and, 485; removal of, to Oklahoma, *m454*, 453–54; treaties with, 343; western settlement and, 329
***Chesapeake* (American vessel),** 340
Chesnut, Mary, *q599*, *q625*
Cheyenne, Wyoming, 673
Cheyenne people, 687, 688
Chicago, Illinois: 1871 fire in, 753; growth of, 398; Hull House in, 753, 786–87; immigrants in, 745, 751; meatpacking industry in, 751, 767; slums in, 752; steel production in, 721; strikes in, 727; World's Fair in, 755
Chicago, University of, 722
Chickasaw people: removal of, to Oklahoma, 453, *m454*; treaties with, 343
child labor, 396, 725, *p725*, 733, *p798*
children, First Amendment protection of, 241
Chile, independence for, 367
Chinese: as cowhands, 675; discrimination against, 515, *p515*, 708; immigration of, 746, 748, *p748*, 779; in railroad construction, 670–71
Chinese Exclusion Act (1882), 746, 748, 779
***Chisholm* v. *Georgia*,** 261
Chivington, John, 688
Choctaw people, removal of, to Oklahoma, 453, *m454*
cholera, 387
Christianity, 99, 100, 805; for African Americans, 322; spread of, *m100*, 102; teaching of, to Native Americans, 117, 118, 329
chronology, 53
Cincinnati, Ohio, growth of, 387, 390, 398
circuit courts, 230
circumnavigate, 85
cities: changing, *p754*, 754–56, *p755*; crime in, 753; ethnic neighborhoods in, 745, *p745*, 747; fire as threat to, 387; growth of, 387, 398, *g751*, 751–52; health problems in, 753; immigrants in, 751; living conditions in, 387; middle class in, 752; settlement houses in, 753; tenements in, 752, 767, 768; transportation in, 755–56. *See also* towns; *specific cities*
citizenship, 236–37, 650–51; for African Americans, 651; rights and responsibilities of, 234–39, 263
City Beautiful movement, 755
civic republicanism, 238
civil disobedience, 404, 406
"Civil Disobedience" (Thoreau), 403, 404
Civil Rights Act (1964), 801, 815
civil rights movement, 404, 796, *p796*, *p800*, 800–801
Civil Service Commission, 766
Civil War, 547, *m609*; African Americans in, 574, 594–96, *p595*; Anaconda Plan in, 608, *m608*; arms and strategy in, 573, *p577*, 581; blockade of South in, 573, 578, 603; casualties in, 579; comparison of North and South in, 571–72, *c572*; costs of, *g608*; destruction of South in, *p620*, 625; draft in, 602; early battles in, 577, 579–83, *m581*; economy and, 603, 613; final battles in, 607–8, 609, 610; home front in, 616; medical care in, 600, 601; military leaders in, 573, 574, 577, 579, 580, 605, 606, 607; naval battles in, *p578*, 578–79; North in, 595; opposition to, 600; results of, 613, 616; soldiers in, *p571*, 574–75, 598, *p598*, *p599*, 600, *g593*; South in, 581, 595, 599–600; spies in, 600; start of, 558–59; technology in, 578; turning points in, 605–7, *m606*; volunteers in, 577; in the West, 579; women in, 599–600
Civil War amendments, 262–64
Clark, Alson Skinner, painting by, *ptg777*
Clark, George Rogers, 155
Clark, William, 315, 319, 321, 330, 471
Clay, Henry, 344, *p344*, 345, *p449*, 487, *p536*, *p541*; American System of, 389; debate over slavery and, 541; in election of 1824, 447, *c447*; in election of 1832, 459–60; in election of 1844, 461; Missouri Compromise and, 536–37; national bank and, 459; Oregon issue and, 475; tariffs and, 451
***Clermont* (steamboat),** 390, *p390*, 391
Cleveland, Grover, 842, *p842*; in election of 1892, 696; in election of 1896, 696–97; labor relations and, 729; tariffs and, 766
Cleveland, Ohio, steel production in, 721
Clinton, De Witt, 392
Clinton, George, 317
Clinton, William J. (Bill), 634, 844, *p844*
coal industry, 709, 725
Cody, William, 686
coeducation, 410
Cold Harbor, Battle of, 608
Cold War, 795
collective bargaining, 727
colleges and universities: for African Americans, 405, 760; first, in North America, 129; land-grant, 760; in mid 1800s, 405; in the Middle Ages, 101; for Native Americans, 760; for women, 405, 409, 412, 413, 760. *See also* education
colonial legislatures, development of, 107
colonial trade, 126, 131
colony, 95
Colorado: exploration and settlement of, 316, 366, 688; statehood for, 499, 668
Colorado River, 488–89
Colorado River Basin, 488
Colored Farmers' National Alliance, 695
Columbia, South Carolina: in Civil War, 652; life in, 430
Columbian Exchange, 95–96, *m96*
Columbia River, 488, 489; exploration of, 471
Columbus, Christopher, *ptg79*, 81, *p84*, 84–85, *m87*, 108, *p108*, *q108*, *p108*
Comanche people, 481, 686, 687
commerce clause, 225, 252
Commercial Revolution, 91
committee of correspondence, 137–38
common market, 219
***Common Sense* (Paine),** 150, 158, 159
communications, advances in, 713
communism, democracy versus, 795
community service, 818–19
compass, 82, *p82*
Compromise of 1850, 499, 542, 544, *m546*
Compromise of 1877, 644
computers, 810
Comstock, Henry, 667
Comstock Lode, *p667*, 667–68
Concord, Massachusetts, *p112*, 140, *m140*, 141
"The Concord Hymn" (Emerson), 141
concurrent powers, 222, *c222*

Index

Index

Conestoga wagons, 313, 314, *p314*
confederation, 180; weakness of, 185
Congress, U.S., 204–5; before and after Reconstruction, *m654*; under Articles of Confederation, 180, 181; Brooks-Sumner incident in, 547; creation of time zones, 671; first, 279–80; mail delivery and, 394; patent laws of, 384; powers of, under Constitution, 205; representation in, 263; restraint on salaries in, 269; role of, 227–28. *See also* House of Representatives, U.S.; Senate, U.S.
congressional elections, of 1866, 631
Connecticut: colony of, 121; industry in, 383
conquistadors, Spanish, 86
conservation, 771, 772, *p772*
constitution, 121
***Constitution* (frigate),** 355, 360
Constitution, U.S., 106, 248–69; amending, 224, *c224*, 258; checks and balances in, 205; citizenship and, 650–51; commerce clause in, 225, 310–11; comparison to Articles of Confederation, *c206*; elastic clause in, 224; executive branch in, 205, 225, 254–56; Federalist versus Democratic-Republican view of, 292; influences on, 203; interpretation of, 224–25, 292; judicial branch in, 205, 225, 256–57; legislative branch in, 204–5, 224–25, 249–54; national supremacy in, 259; opposition to, 243; Preamble to, 152, 219, 249; principles of, 219, *c221*, 221–22; ratification of, 201, 206, 208–9, 259; relations among the states in, 257–58; silence of, on territorial acquisition, 314
Constitutional Convention (1787), 197, 198, 199–200; delegates at, 197, 201, 203, 219, 220; Great Compromise at, 199; New Jersey Plan at, 199; slavery as issue at, 529; Three-Fifths Compromise at, 200; Virginia Plan at, 199
Constitutional Union Party, 555
constitutions, state, 179
Continental Army under Washington, 150, 153, 154
Continental Congress, First, 139–40
Continental Congress, Second, 150, 151, 155, 180; delegates to, 150, 152, 197, 294; national debt under, 281
contour lines, 44
contour map, 44
contracts, sanctity of, 311
Convention of 1818, 363, 364
Conyngham, D.P., *q571*
Coolidge, Calvin, 843, *p843*
Cooper, James Fenimore, 323, 324, *p324*
cooperatives, 694–95
Copernicus, Nicolaus, 105
Copley, John Singleton, *ptg142*
copper, mining for, 668
Copperheads, 600
corduroy roads, 389
Corinth, Mississippi, in Civil War, 579
Cornell, Ezra, 760
Cornell University, 760
corn huskings, 394
Cornish, Samuel, 397, 531
Coronado, Francisco Vásquez de, 87
corporations, 719; government regulation of, 723; growth of, 719
corruption: fighting urban, *p765*, 765–66; Reconstruction and, 638; under Ulysses S. Grant, 641, 643, *ctn641*
Corsi, Edward, *q784*
Cortés, Hernán, 86, 109
cottage industry, 93
cotton gin, 423, 424, *p424*, 438
cotton production, 384; in the South, 423, *m425*, *c425*, 429
covenant, 99
cowhands, 665, *p665*, 674, *p674*, 675
cow towns, 675; railroads and, 673
Crane, Stephen, 761
Crazy Horse, 688
credibility, 63
Creek people: removal of, to Oklahoma, 453, *m454*; treaties with, 343; western settlement and, 329
Creek Wars (1813–1814), 485
Crèvecoeur, J. Hector St. John, 211
crime: in cities, 753; vigilantes and, 504, 668
Crittenden, John, 556, 574
Crocker, Charles, 708, *p708*
Crocker Art Museum, 708
Crockett, Davy, 474–75, 481, *p481*, 483, 484; legend of, 448
crossing guard, *p759*
***Crossing the Panther's Path* (Alder),** 346
Crusades, 81
Cuba, Spanish-American War and, 775
culture, African American, 433
Cummings, Kate, 600
Cushing, William, 179
Custer, George, 688

D

Dade, Francis, 455
da Gama, Vasco, 84
Dakota Territory: Indian reservations in, 687; settlement of, 676
dame schools, 321
***Dartmouth College* v. *Woodward*,** 311
Darwin, Charles, 722–23
da Verrazano, Giovanni, *m87*, 88
da Vinci, Leonardo, 92
Davis, Jefferson, *p561*, 582; capture of, 612; Inaugural Address of, *q561*; as president of the Confederacy, 556, 559, 561, 573, 602
Dawes, William, 140
Dawes Act (1887), 691, 692
De Anza, Juan Bautista, 492
debates: Lincoln-Douglas, *p552*, 552–53; Webster-Hayne, 450
Debs, Eugene V., 729, 767
debt, after American Revolution, 184
debtors, settlement of Georgia by, 124
De Burton, María Amparo Ruiz, 493, *p493*
decades, 52
Declaration of Independence, 106, 157, 164–67, 179, 221, 235, 321, 409, 783, *q783*, 793, 798, 814; drafting, 151, 152, 180
Declaration of Sentiments and Resolutions, 409
Declaratory Act (1766), 136
***The Deerslayer* (Cooper),** 323
De la Guerra, Pablo, 504, *p504*
Delaware: in Civil War, 573; colony of, 121, 122
democracy: versus communism, 795; direct, 133; expanding, 769–71
Democratic Party: in election of 1844, 475; in election of 1860, 555; in election of 1868, 634; in election of 1892, 696; in election of 1896, 696–97
Democratic-Republican Party, 238; in election of 1828, 447–48; views of, *c292*, 292–93
Denali National Park and Preserve, 772, *m772–73*
De Portolá, Gaspar, 492
depression: of 1837, 460; post American Revolution, 194
Deseret, 506
De Soto, Hernando, 87
Detroit, Michigan: growth of, 398; immigrants in, 751; steel production in, 721
Dewey, John, 759

De Zavala, Lorenzo, 485
Dias, Bartholomeu, 84
Díaz, Porfirio, 777
Dickens, Charles, 415
Dickinson, Emily, 407, *q407*
Dickinson, Susanna, 484
Diderot, Denis, 105
diphtheria, 753
direct democracy, 133
dirigibles, 785
discrimination, 651; against African Americans, 397, 779, *p800*, 800–801; on cattle drives, 675; against the Chinese, *p514*, 515, 708; against immigrants, 400, 778–79
disease: acquisition of, fighting Spanish-American War, 775; in cities, 753; impact on Native Americans, 86, 473; in late 1700s, 387. *See also* medical care
District of Columbia: presidential electors for, 267; representation of, in House of Representatives, 227; slavery in, 541. *See also* Washington, D.C.
Dix, Dorothea, 405, 600
Dixon, Cromwell, 785
DNA analysis, 51
Dodge, Grenville, 671
Dodge City, Kansas, 673, 675
Dominican Republic, U.S. involvement in, 776
Doubleday, Abner, 559
Doughty, Thomas, 325
Douglas, Stephen A., 542, 544, 552; debate with Lincoln, *p552*, 552–53; in election of 1860, 555
Douglass, Frederick, 437, 496, 529, 532, *p592*, *q592*, 636, 637, *p637*, *q637*, 653, *p653*
draft, 238; in Civil War, 602; in 1813, 369
Drake, Sir Francis, 89
***Dred Scott* v. *Sandford*,** 549–50, 555, 651, 846
Driscoll (union sergeant), 571
dry farming, 678–79
Du Bois, W. E. B., 649, *p649*, 780, 781, *p781*
due process of law, 235
Duke, James, 646
Dunbar, Paul Laurence, 761
Dutch. *See* Netherlands
Dutch East India Company, 93, 96

E

Eads Bridge, 756
Eakins, Thomas, 762
Eastern Hemisphere, 41, *p41*
East India Company, 96
Eastman, George, 714, 716
economic indicators, 67, 839, *c839*, *p839*
economics, history and, 67
economy: after the American Revolution, 183–84; Civil War and, 603, 613; Hamilton's plan for, 281–82; impact of mining on, 668; laissez-faire, 460, 771; in Northeast, 383, 386–87; railroads and, 707, 708, 709–11; role of banks in growth of; service, 808; Supreme Court and, 310–11
Edison, Thomas, 714–15, 716, 763
education: for African Americans, 233, 397, 405, 409, 651, 759, 760; changes in, 760, 810; in early 1800s, 321–22; in English colonies, 129; expansion of public, 758–59; Freedmen's Bureau and, 626; government and, 811; for immigrants, 779; income and, 811, *c811*; for Native Americans, 691, 699, 760–61; one-room schoolhouses in, 406, *p406*; progressive, 759; reforms for, 405; school enrollment, *c810*; in the South, 431; for women, 405, 412, 760. *See also* colleges and universities
Edwards, Gus, *q713*
Edwards, Jonathan, 115, *p115*
effects, 65
Eighteenth Amendment, 265
eighteen-year-olds, voting rights for, 269
Eighth Amendment, *c223*, 261
Eisenhower, Dwight D., 843, *p843*
elastic clause, 224
***El Camino Real*,** 492
election(s): of 1796, 293, *m300*; of 1800, 283, 297, 307; of 1804, 317, 339; of 1808, 340; of 1824, 447, *c447*; of 1828, 447–48, *m464*; of 1832, 449, 459–60; of 1840, 460, 461; of 1844, 461, 475; of 1848, 540; of 1856, 549; of 1860, 555, *m564*; of 1864, 609; of 1868, 634; of 1872, 641–42; of 1876, 643–644, *m644*; of 1892, 696; of 1896, 696–97; of 2004, 817
Electoral College, 280; in election of 1800, 307
electric lights, 713
elevation, 44
Eleventh Amendment, 261
Elizabeth I of England, 89, 103
Ellis Island, 743, 744, *p744*
Emancipation Proclamation, 592–94, *q592–94*, 855
Embargo Act (1807), 340
Emerson, Ralph Waldo, 141, 403, 406, 553
emigration: African American, to Liberia, 529
***empresarios*,** 481
***encomienda*,** 88
***Encyclopedia*,** 106
England: exploration by, *m87*, 88; Parliament in, 103, 107; rise of monarchies in, 82; trade rivalry with Spain, 89. *See also* American colonies; Great Britain
English, Samuel J., *q577*
English Bill of Rights, 103, 106, 107, 152, 179, 203
Enlightenment, 105–6, 129, 203
entrepreneurs, 93
enumerated powers, 222, *c222*
environmentalism, 805
Environmental Protection Agency (EPA), 805
Equal Rights Amendment, 804
Equator, 41, 42, *p42*
Equiano, Olaudah, 127
Era of Good Feelings, 363
Erie Canal: building, 392–93; travel on, 415, *p415*
ethnic neighborhoods, life in, 745, *p745*, 747
Europe, heritage of, 99–103
events, dating of, 50
executive branch, 106, 205, 225, 229–30; in checks and balances, *c228*; in U.S. Constitution, 254–56. *See also* president
Executive Office of the President (EOP), 230
Exodusters, 676
***Ex parte Milligan*,** 231

F

factories, 384, *p384*, 385; Irish workers in, 399; working conditions in, 396, *p396*
factors of production, 719
facts versus opinions, 60–61
Fair Labor Standards Act (1938), 731
Falconer, John Mackie, painting by, *ptg397*
Fallen Timbers, Battle of, 287
fall line, 423, *p423*
families: farm, 678; laws for, 413; middle-class, 752; slave, 433
farmers: organizing by, 694–95; Populist Party and, *p695*, 695–96; United Farm Workers for Mexican, 728, 731, 782, 802; Whiskey Rebellion and, 286. *See also* agriculture; farming
Farmers' Alliances, 695
farming, 671; conflict with cattle ranching, 675; dry, 678–79; on the Great Plains, 676, *p678*, 678–79; in New England, 383; in the North, 326; share-cropping in, 639;

Index

in the South, 428; subsistence, 126. *See also* agriculture; farmers
Farragut, David, 579, 609
Federal Communications Commission (FCC), 241
federal court system, 230–31, *c231*
federalism, 204, *c221*, 222
The Federalist Papers, 206, *q208*, 208; *Number 10*, 242–43, 851; *Number 51*, 198; *Number 70*, 208
Federalist Party, 206–7, 208, 238, 317; in election of 1800, 297, 307; in election of 1808, 340; opposition to Louisiana Purchase, 316; views of, *c292*, 292–93; weakening of, at end of War of 1812, 359
federal system, 204–5, *c222*
Fetterman, William J., 688
Fetterman Massacre, 688
Field, Cyrus, 713
Fifteenth Amendment, 264, 634, 637, 655, 770
Fifth Amendment, *c223*, 235, 260, 550
54th Massachusetts, 596
"Fifty-four Forty or Fight," 474–75
Fillmore, Millard, 542, 841, *p841*; in election of 1856, 549; as president, 542
Finney, Charles, 403, *q403*, *p403*
fire: Triangle Shirtwaist Company, 727; as urban threat, 387
First African Methodist Episcopal Church, 551
First Amendment, *c223*, 235, 240–41, 260
Fisk University, 626
Fitch, John, 390
Five Civilized Tribes, 453, 457
flag: etiquette for, 845; first, 200
Fletcher* v. *Peck, 311
Florence, 92
Florida: Ponce de León's discovery of, 86–87; readmission to union, 632; removal of Native Americans from, 453; secession of, 556; Seminole wars in, 455, 456; Spanish control of, 117, 124
folk remedies, 195, *p195*
Food and Drug Administration, 771
Force Act, 451
Ford, Gerald R., 268, 844, *p844*
Ford, Henry, 716–17, 806
Ford's Theater, 626
Fort Donelson, 579
Forten, Charlotte, 626, 627, *p627*, *q627*
Fort Henry, 579
Fort Leavenworth, Kansas, 677
Fort Lyon, 688
Fort McHenry, 356, 358, *p368*
Fort Niagara, *p334*
Fort Ross, 471
Fort Sumter, 558–59, 571
Foster, Stephen C., 325
Fourteen Points, 858
Fourteenth Amendment, 235, 263–64, 631, 632, 650, 651, 731, 782
Fourth Amendment, *c223*, 260
France: Civil War and, 573; as colonial ally in American Revolution, 155, 156; colonial rivalry with Great Britain, 135, 339; control of Louisiana Territory by, 313; Emancipation Proclamation and, 594; explorations by, *m87*, 88–89; foreign relations with, in late 1800s, 295–97; fur traders and, 117, *p117*; rise of monarchies in, 82; settlements in North America, 117; XYZ affair and, 293
Franklin, Benjamin, 104, 151, *p151*, 159, 199, 201; as author of *Poor Richard's Almanack*, 151, 161; as colonial leader, 107; on Constitutional Convention, 224; as delegate to Constitutional Convention, 197, 203, 219; as delegate to Second Continental Congress, 150, 152; inventions of, 129; Treaty of Paris and, 156
Franklin, William, 159
Free American Society, 196
free blacks, 327, 434
Freedmen's Bank, 639
Freedmen's Bureau, 626, 638
Freedom's Journal, 397, 531
free enterprise, 383
Freeport Doctrine, 552
Free-Soil Party, 540
Frémont, John C., 494, 496, *p496*; in election of 1856, 549
French and Indian War, 135, 136
French Revolution, 157, 288, 295
Freneau, Philip, 291
Frick, Henry Clay, 752
Frobisher, Martin, *m87*
Fuggers family, 91
Fugitive Slave Act (1850), 533–34, 544, 545, 556
fugitive slaves, 437, 541
full faith and credit, 219
Fuller, Margaret, 406
Fulton, Robert, 390, 391, *p391*
Fundamental Orders of Connecticut, 121
fur trade, 472

G

Gadsden Purchase, 497
Gage, Sir Thomas, 140
gag orders, 241
Galilei, Galileo, 105
Gallatin, Albert, 476, *p476*, *q476*; as secretary of the treasury, 308
Gallaudet, Thomas, 405
Gálvez, Bernardo de, 155
Gandhi, Mohandas, 404
Garfield, James A., 842, *p842*; assassination of, 766; spoils system and, 766
Garland, Hamlin, 751
Garrison, William Lloyd, 529, 530, *p530*, 531, 562
Gast, John, painting by, *ptg477*
Gates, Horatio, 154
Gay, Martha, 471
Geary, John, 547
general purpose maps, 44, *m44*
General Trade Union of New York, 397
Genêt Edmond, 288
Geneva College, 413
Genoa, 82, 94
geography: essential elements of, 39–40, 57; terminology for, 46–47; themes in, 40, 54–57; uses of, 40
George III, King, *p138*, 140, 150, 205
Georgia: colony of, 124; poll tax in, 648; readmission to union, 632; removal of Native Americans from, 453–54, *m454*; secession of, 556
Germantown Protest, 160
Germany, immigration from, 399–400, *p741*
Geronimo, 689
Gerry, Elbridge, as delegate at Constitutional Convention, 201
Gettysburg, Battle of, *p566*, 605, 606, 607, *m618*
Gettysburg Address, 607, *q607*, 856
Gettysburg Memorial, *p856*
Ghent, Treaty of (1814), 358
Ghost Dance, 692
Gibbons* v. *Ogden, 309, 311, 846
Gideon* v. *Wainwright, 261, 847
Gilded Age, 752
***The Gilded Age* (Twain and Warner),** 752
Glorious Revolution, 103, 132–33
gold, mining for, 667, 668, 669
gold rush in California, 501, 503, 504, 505, 667
golf, 763
Goliad, 485
Gompers, Samuel, 727
Gonzales, 483, 484
Gordon-Cumming, Constance, *q749*

government: education and, 811; grants to railroads, 669–70; labor and, 730–31; representative, 107, 130, 132; self-, 119, 130
Grady, Henry, 646
grandfather clauses, 648
Grand Peak, 316
Grange, 694–95
Grant, Ulysses S., *q579*, 842, *p842*; as Civil War general, 579, 606, 607, 608, 609, 610, 611, *p611*; corruption under, 641, 643, *ctn641*; in election of 1868, 634; in election of 1872, 641; presidency of, 641; surrender of Lee to, 610, *p610*, 611, 612
grasshoppers, Great Plains farming and, 678
Gray, Robert, 471
Great Awakening, 115; 128–29; Second, 403, 412, 414
Great Britain: in American Revolution, 141, 153, 156; Civil War and, 573, 583; claims to Oregon, 471–72, 474; colonial policies of, 130–31, 136; colonial rivalry with France, 135; early problems with, 184; Emancipation Proclamation and, 594; foreign relations with, 363–64; impressment of U.S. sailors, 339–40; Industrial Revolution in, 383, 385; Jay's Treaty with, 288; navy of, 339–40; Parliament in, 130; war between France and, 339; War of 1812 and, 345. *See also* England
Great Compromise, 199
Great Depression, 794–95, 806
Great Northern Railroad, 707
Great Plains: farming on, 676, *p678*, 678–79; settlement of, 711
Great Salt Lake, 506
Great Seal, 299
Greece, 99
Greek philosophy, 99
Greek Revival style of architecture, 325
Greeley, Horace, in election of 1872, 641–42
Greene, Catherine, 424
Greenhow, Rose O'Neal, 600
Greenville, Treaty of (1795), 287, 343
Gregg, Josiah, 491
Gregg, William, 426
Griffin, John Strother, 551
Grimké, Angelina, 412, 439, 530
Grimké, Sarah, 412, *p412*, *q412*, 439, 530
Griswold, Roger, *ctn296*
Gruber, John, *q360*
Grundy, Felix, 368
Guadalupe Hidalgo, Treaty of (1848), 493, 497, 499, 501
Guam: acquisition of, 775; representation of, in House of Representatives, 227
***Guerriére* (frigate),** 355
guerrilla warfare, 156

H

habeas corpus, 600
Haiti, 157
Hamilton, Alexander, 196, 206, *p208*, *q208*, 238, *q277*, *p277*, 283, *q283*, *p283*; as author of *The Federalist Papers*, 242, 283; duel with Burr, 284, 317; economic plan of, 281–82, 284; as Federalist, 208; Jefferson, Thomas and, 283, 284; opposition to plan of, 281–82; ratification of Constitution and, 207; as secretary of the treasury, 280, 281, 286, 291
Hampton Institute, 760
Hancock, John, 140
Hand, Learned, 236, *q236*
Harding, Warren G., 843, *p843*
Harlan, John Marshall, *q650*
Harpers Ferry, raid on, 553, 555
Harrison, Benjamin, 842, *p842*
Harrison, William Henry, *p346*, 354, 486, 841, *p841*; death of, 461; in election of 1840, 461; as governor of Indiana, 342; Tecumseh and, 342
Hartford Convention, 359, 537
Hartford School for the Deaf, 405
Harvard College, 129
Hatfield convention, 194
Hawaii: annexation of, 775; statehood for, 499
Hawley, Joseph, 139
Hayes, Benjamin, 551
Hayes, Rutherford B., 842, *p842*; in election of 1876, 643, *m644*; Inaugural Address of, *q644*; presidency of, 644; spoils system and, 766
Haymarket Square strike, 727
Hayne, Robert, 538; debate with Webster, Daniel, 450
Hearst, William Randolph, 761
hemispheres, 41, *p41*
Henry, E. L., painting by, *ptg571*
Henry, John, 732–33; legend of, 448, *p448*
Henry, Patrick, 139, *q139*, *q209*; as delegate to Second Continental Congress, 150
Henry, Prince of Portugal, 84
Henry VIII, King of England, 103
Henson, Josiah, 439
Hidalgo, Miguel, 366, *p366*
Hill, James J., 707, 770
***His First Vote*,** *ptg631*
Hispanics: in Civil War, 575; as cowhands, 674, 675; equal rights for, 802; labor union for, 728, 731
historians: making sense of the past, 64–67; thinking like, 61, 63, 65, 67; tools of, 48–71; work of, 60–63
historical atlas, 58
historical maps, *m58*, 58–59, *m59*
historical routes, 59, *m59*
history: different interpretations of, 66–67; economics and, 67; error and chance in, 66; geography and, 54–57; interpreting, 64; periods of, 52; providing setting, 64
***The History of the Standard Oil Company* (Tarbell),** 767
***H.L. Hunley* (submarine),** 578
Hobbes, Thomas, 103
holding companies, 722
Holocaust, 795
Homer, Winslow, 762; painting by, *ptg762*
Homestead Act (1862), 676
homesteading, 676
Homestead Strike, 729
Hooker, Joseph, *q582*, 605
Hooker, Thomas, 121
Hoover, Herbert, 843, *p843*
Hopkins, Mark, 708
horizontal integration, 720
horses, Native Americans and, 95
Horseshoe Bend, Battle of, 355, 448
House of Burgesses in Virginia, 119, 123, 133
***The House of Mirth* (Wharton),** 761
House of Representatives, U.S., 204–5, 227; African Americans in, 636; committees of, 227–28; in election of 1800, 307; in election of 1824, 447; role of, in impeachment, 227, 633. *See also* Congress, U.S.; Senate, U.S.
Houston, Sam, 485, 486, *p487*, 544
Howard University, 626, 760
Howe, Samuel Gridley, 405
***How the Other Half Lives* (Riis),** 768
Hudson, Henry, *m87*, 89
Hudson Bay, 89
Hudson River, 89, 117
Hudson River School of painting, *p323*, 325
Huerta, Dolores, 802
Hull, William, 354
Hull House, 753, 786–87

human/environmental interaction, 40, 55
human systems, 40
Huntington, Collis P., 707, 708
Huntington Library and Art Gallery, 708
hypothesis, 105

I

Idaho, statehood for, 668
"I Have a Dream" speech, 861
Illinois: lifestyle in, 394; statehood for, 182, 393, 499
immigrants: adjustments for, 744; contributions of, 747; discrimination against, 400, 778–79; education for, *p743*, 779; entering U.S., 743; in Great Plains, *p705*; in homesteading, 676; identifying the new, 741–42; journey of, to U.S., 742; role of women, 745; settlement of, 745, *p745*; support for, 747; work for, 743–44, 746
Immigrants' Protective League, 747
immigration: Chinese, 746, 748, *p748*, 779; German, 399–400, *p741*; growth of, 756; impact of, 400; Irish, 398–99; Italian, 741, 742; Japanese, 746, 779; of Jews, 399, 742; limitations on, 746–49; in mid 1800s, 398–400, *g399*; Nativist movement and, 400, 746–47; opposition to, 400–401; prejudice faced by, 401; reasons for, 398, 400, 742; sources of U.S., *g399*, *g778*
Immigration Act (1917), 747
impeachment, 227; of Andrew Johnson, 633
implied powers, 224, 292
impressment, 288, 339–40, 358
Inca Empire, 86
income, education and, 811
income gap, 807
income taxes, 264
indentured servants, 126
Independence Hall, *p174*, 197
independent agencies, 230
Indiana: statehood for, 182, 393, 499; women's rights in, 413
Indian Peace Commission, 687
Indian Removal Act (1830), 453, 456
indigo, 126
individual rights, *c221*, 223
Indonesia, 96
industrialization, 539, 751, *m825*
Industrial Revolution, 383, 384, 385; impact on economic roles of men and women, 411
industry: coal, 709, 725; growth of, in Northeast, 383–85; iron, 646; lumber, 709; oil, 720; shoe, 715; in the South, 424–26; steel, 646, 709, 721–22
Inerius, 101
inflation in Civil War, 603
Inglis, Charles, 159, *q159*
initiative, 769
injunctions, 729, 730
integration: horizontal, 720; vertical, 721–22
interchangeable parts, 385
interest groups, 239
The Interesting Narrative of the Life of Olaudah Equiano, 127
Interior, U.S. Department of, 230
International Ladies' Garment Workers Union, 727, 744
interstate commerce, 311
Interstate Commerce Act (1887), 766
Interstate Commerce Commission, 766
inventions: of African Americans, 715; of automobile, 716–17; in communication, 713, 714; cotton production and, 423, 424, *p424*, 438; Edison and, 714–15
Ireland: immigration from, 398–99; potato crop in, 398
ironclads, in Civil War, 578, *p578*
iron industry, 646
Irving, Washington, 322–23, 324, *p324*
Isabella, Queen of Spain, 84, *p84*
Islam, 81; influence of, 101; spread of, 100. *See also* Muslims
Italy, immigration from, 741
"I Will Fight No More," 690, 857

J

Jackson, Andrew, *p449*, 840, *p840*; administration of, 448–55, 457–59; annexation of Texas and, 486; Bank of the United States and, 459, *q459*, *ctn460*; cartoon of, *ctn450*; Cherokee people and, 485; in election of 1824, 447, *c447*; in election of 1828, 447–48; in election of 1832, 459–60; Inauguration of, 448, 462; invasion of Spanish East Florida by, 364; Native American removal and, 453–54, *m454*, 463; nullification and, 451; popularity of, 448; spoils system and, 449, 766; tariffs and, 450; in War of 1812, 355, 359, 448
Jackson, Helen Hunt, 691
Jackson, Mississippi, life in, 430
Jackson, Thomas (Stonewall), 577, 605, 615
James I, King of England, 103, 119, 120
James II, King of England, 132
Jamestown, 119, 133
Janney, Eli H., 710
Japanese: immigration of, 746, 779; unfair treatment of, 708
Jay, John, 139, 184, 206, 231, 288; as Chief Justice, 281; as Federalist, 209, 283; Treaty of Paris (1783) and, 156
Jay's Treaty, 288, 293
jazz, 762
Jazz Age, 794
Jefferson, Thomas, 104, *q132*, *p132*, 225, 238, 240, *q277*, *p277*, *q293*, *q321*, 805, 840, *p840*; agrarianism and, 538–39; as architect, *p302*, 325, *p325*; as author of Declaration of Independence, 150, 152, *p152*; as author of *The Virginia Statute for Religious Freedom*, *q235*; as author of Virginia Resolution, 537; cabinet of, 308; as colonial leader, 107; on creation of national bank, 282; as delegate to Second Continental Congress, 150, 197; in election of 1796, 293; in election of 1800, 283, 297, 307; in election of 1804, 317, 339; foreign policy under, 339–40; on Fulton, 391; Hamilton, Alexander and, 283, 284; inauguration of, 307; laissez-faire philosophy of, 771; Louisiana Purchase and, 313–16; policies of, 152, 308; as secretary of state, 280, 291; on Shays's Rebellion, 195; slavery issue and, 536; as vice president, 293
Jenney, William LeBaron, 754
Jesus of Nazareth, 81, 100
Jews: contributions of, 99–100; as financiers, 93; Holocaust and, 795; immigration of, 399, 742
Jim Crow Laws, 647, 648, 651
John, King of England, 106, *p106*, 132
John II, King of Portugal, 84
Johnson, Andrew, 842, *p842*; administration of, 613, 628, 630; impeachment of, 633, 642, *p642*; Reconstruction under, 628, 630–31
Johnson, Lyndon B., 844, *p844*
joint-stock companies, 93, 119
Joliet, Louis, 117
Jones, Absalom, 196, *p196*
Jones, John Paul, 155

Jones, Mary Harris, 727, 728, *p728*
Joplin, Scott, 762
Jordan, Barbara, 225, *q225*
Joseph, Chief, 689, 690, *p690*, 857
journalism: muckrakers in, 767; yellow, 761. *See also* newspapers; press
Judah, Theodore, 708
Judaism, *p99*, 99–100
judicial branch, 106, 205, 225, 230–31, *c231*, 233; in checks and balances, *c228*; under Jefferson, 308–9; in U.S. Constitution, 256–57. *See also* Supreme Court, U.S.
judicial review, 225, 231, 233, 309, 311
Judiciary Act (1789), 230, 281
Judiciary Act (1801), 308–9
***The Jungle* (Sinclair),** 767, 787

K

Kansas: bleeding, 547; conflict over slavery in, 546–47; settlement of, 366, 544
Kansas City, Kansas, as meatpacking center, 751
Kansas-Nebraska Act (1854), 544, *m546*, 549
Kansas Pacific Railroad, 686
Kearney, Stephen Watts, 496, 497
Keith, Harold, 584
Keller, Helen, 411, *p411*
Kelly, William, 646
Kennedy, John F., 844, *p844*; civil rights and, 801; Inaugural Address of, 860, *p860*
Kentucky: in Civil War, 571–72; schools in, 431; statehood for, 393, 498
Kentucky Resolution, 296–97, 450, 537, 538
Key, Francis Scott, 356, 358, 852
***A Key to Uncle Tom's Cabin; Presenting the Original Facts and Documents Upon Which It Is Based* (Stowe),** 545
Khan, Kublai, 81, *p81*
kickbacks, 765
King, Martin Luther, Jr., 404, *p404*, 796, 801, 803, *p861*; "I Have a Dream" speech of, 861
King, Rufus, in election of 1804, 317
Kino, Eusebio, 117
Kiowa people, 457, 481, 687
Kitty Hawk, first airplane flight at, 714, *p714–15*
Knight, Amelia Stewart, *q473*
Knights of Labor, 726–27
Know-Nothing Party, 401, 549
Knox, Henry, as secretary of war, 280
Kodak camera, 714, 716, *p716*
Korean War, 795
***Korematsu* v. *United States*,** 847
Kosciusko, Thaddeus, 155
Ku Klux Klan, 638, 642, 779, *p779*
Kunstler, Mort, painting by, *ptg670*

L

labor, as factor of production, 719
labor movement: government and, 730–31; Mexican Americans in, 782; strikes in, 397, 727, 729
labor unions: African Americans in, 731; efforts to organizing first, 397; formation of, 726–27; Hispanics in, 728, 731; women in, 727, 728, 731
***Ladies' Home Journal*,** 761
Lafayette, Marquis de, 155
La Flesche, Susette, 411, *p411*
La Follette, Robert, 769
La Huelga, 728
laissez-faire, 307, 460, 771
Lake Champlain, in War of 1812, 358
Lake Erie, 354, 392
Lakota people, 687
Lame-Duck Amendment, 265
land, as factor of production, 719
land-grant colleges, 760
Land Law of 1851, 501
land speculation, 691
Langdon, John, 279
***A Lantern in Her Hand* (Aldrich),** 680–83
La Raza Unida, 802
Larcom, Lucy, 385
La Salle, Sieur de, 117
Las Casas, Bartolomé de, 88, 97
***The Last of the Mohicans* (Cooper),** 323
Lathrop, Julia Clifford, 747
Latimer, Lewis Howard, 715, 716, *p716*
Latin America: British trade with, 340; independence movement in, 366–67; Monroe Doctrine and, 367, 775, 776, 853; U.S. interests in, 775–76
Latin language, 101
latitude, 42, *p42*
"Law of the River" (1922), 489
laws: family, 413; functions of, 237; stages of bill becoming, 228, *c229*
Lazarus, Emma, 742, *q784*
Leadville, Colorado, *p668*
League of Women Voters, 817
Learn and Serve America, 819
***The Leatherstocking Tales* (Cooper),** 324
***Leaves of Grass* (Whitman),** 407
Lee, Richard Henry, 139
Lee, Robert E.: as Civil War general, 557, 574, 580, 581, 582, 583, 595, 598, 605, 606, 608, 610, 611, *p611*, 615; surrender of, at Appomattox, 610, *p610*, 611, 612
"The Legend of Sleepy Hollow" (Irving), 322–23, 324
legislative branch, 106, 204–5, 224–25, 227–28; in checks and balances, *c228*; in U.S. Constitution, 249–54. *See also* Congress, U.S.; House of Representatives, U.S.; Senate, U.S.
legislatures, colonial, 130
Lena, Maggie, 780
***Leopard* (British warship),** 340
***Letters from an American Farmer* (Crèvecoeur),** 211
Leutze, Emanuel, *ptg153*
***Leviathan* (Hobbes),** 103
Lewis, Meriwether, 315, 319, 321, 330–31, 471
Lexington, Massachusetts, 140, *m140*, 141
Libby, Willard Frank, 51
Liberal Republicans, 644; Reconstruction and, 641
***The Liberator*,** 530, 531, 562
Liberia, African American emigration to, 529
Liberty Party, 540
libraries: bookmobiles and, *p759*; in Boston, 755; public, 761
***Life on the Sea Islands* (Forten),** 627
lifespans, average, *c785*
lightbulbs, 715, 716, *p716*
limited government, 130, 132, *c221*, 222
Lincoln, Abraham, 552, *p560*, *q592*, *q600*, 841, *p841*, *p855*; assassination of, 612, 626, 637; in Civil War, 558–59, 572–73, 577, 580, 583; as Congressman, 496; debate with Douglas, *p552*, 552–53; in election of 1860, 555; in election of 1864, 609; Emancipation Proclamation of, 592–94, 855; *Ex parte Milligan* and, 231; feelings on slavery, 593; First Inaugural Address of, 557, *q557*, *q560*; Fort Sumter and, 558; funeral carriage of, *p643*; Gettysburg Address of, 607, *q607*, 856; House Divided Address, 552, *q552*; Reconstruction plan of, 625–26, 642; Second Inaugural Address of, 626, *q642*

Index

Index

Lincoln, Mary Todd, 574
Lindneux, Robert, painting by, *ptg455*
literacy, 761
literacy test, 647–48
literature: of early 1800s, 322–24; in late 1800s, 761; in mid 1800s, 407; transcendentalists in, 406
littering, 815
Little Bighorn, Battle of, 688–89
Livingston, Robert, 313, 314, 390
location, 39, 54–55; absolute, 42, *p42*, 54; relative, 55
***Lochner* v. *New York*,** 731
Locke, John, 103, 104, *q104*, *p104*, 107, 152, 203, *p203*, 537
London Bridge, 91
London, Jack, 761
Lone Star Republic, 486
Long Drive, 673–74
Longfellow, Henry Wadsworth, 142, 407
longhorns, 673
longitude, 42, *p42*
Los Angeles, California, Southern Pacific Railroad and, 670
Lost Colony, 119
Louisiana: Civil War in, 606; readmission to union, 632; Reconstruction in, 625; secession of, 556
Louisiana Purchase, *m316*, 364; Lewis and Clark exploration of, 315, *m318*, 319, *q330–31*
Louisiana Territory, 313
Louisville, Kentucky: growth of, 387, 398; schools in, 431
Louis XIV, King of France, 117
Love, Nat, *p673*
Lowell, Francis Cabot, 385
Lowell factory, 384, *p384*, 385, 396; women in, 385, *p385*
Lowell Female Labor Reform Organization, 397
Loyalists, 153, 159, *p159*, 184
***Luck and Pluck* (Alger),** 761
lumber industry, 709
Lunt, Dolly Sumner, 616
Luther, Martin, 102, *p102*
Lynch, John, *q645*
lynchings, 648, 780
Lyon, Mary, 405, 413
Lyon, Matthew, 296, *ctn296*

M

MADD, 239
Madero, Francisco, 777
Madison, Dolley, 356, 357, *p357*; letter to her sister Anna Cutts, 357
Madison, James, 104, 196, 198, *p198*, *q198*, 199, 203, 238, *p248*, 840, *p840*, *p851*; as author of Kentucky Resolution, 537; as author of *The Federalist Papers,* 242, 283; Bill of Rights and, 281; as colonial leader, 107; on creation of national bank, 282; as delegate to Constitutional Convention, 197, 198, 220; draft proposal of, 369; in election of 1808, 340; as Federalist, 206, 208; foreign policy under, 341, 343; on Fulton, 391; ratification of Constitution and, 207; as secretary of state, 308, 309, 340; War Hawks and, 343; War of 1812 and, 345
magazines, technology in printing, 761
Magellan, Ferdinand, 85
Magna Carta (1215), 106, *p106*, 107, 132, 152, 179, 203, 850, *p850*
mail order businesses, 717
Maine: slavery and, 536; statehood for, 498
malaria, 96, 775
Malcolm X, 803
Manassas Junction, 577
Manhattan Island, 117
Manifest Destiny, 474, 475, 487, 491, 499; California and, 494; justification of, 476–77; War with Mexico and, 495–97
Mann, Horace, 405
manumission, 196
maps: compass rose on, 43, *p43*; contour, 44; general purpose, 44; historical, *m58*, 58–59, *m59*; improvements in, 82; map key for, 43, *p43*; parts of, 43; physical, 44, *m44*; political, 44, *m44*, 58; scale for, 43, *p43*; special purpose, 45, *m45*; thematic, 58
Marbury, William, 309
***Marbury* v. *Madison*,** 225, 231, 232, 309, 311, 847
March on Washington, *p796*, *p861*
Marco Polo, 81, *p81*
Marcy, William, 494
Maria, Henrietta, 123
Martineau, Harriet, 313
Marquette, Jacques, 117
Marshall, James, 501
Marshall, John, 225, 231, 232, *p232*, 310, *q310*; administration of oath to Jackson by, 462; as Chief Justice, 309, 310–11, 453
Marshall, Louis, 749, *p749*
Marshall, Thurgood, 760
Maryland: in Civil War, 572, 573, 582–83, 598; colony of, 123
Mary of Orange, Queen of England, 103, 132
Mason, Bridget, 549, 551, *p551*, *q551*
Mason, George, 201, *p209*, *q209*, 243
Mason-Dixon line, 549
Massachusetts, 120; colony of, 121; education in, 322; end of slavery in, 179; industry in, 383; population in, 431
Massachusetts Antislavery Society, 532
mass media, 240
mass production, 717, 806
Matzeliger, Jan E., 715
***Mayflower*,** *p120*, 133
Mayflower Compact, 120, 133, *p133*, 851
McClellan, George B., 574, 577, 580, 581, 582, 583, 615
***McClure's Magazine*,** 767
McCormick Harvester Company, 729
McCoy, Elijah, 715
***McCulloch* v. *Maryland*,** 309, 459, 847–48
***McGuffey Readers*,** *p406*
McKinley, William, 842, *p842*; annexation of Hawaii, 775; annexation of Philippines, *q834*, *p834*; antitrust legislation under, 770; assassination of, 776; in election of 1896, 697
Meade, George, 605
measles, 96, 753
Meat Inspection Act (1906), 767, 771
Mechoopda people, 502
medical care: in cities, 753; in Civil War, 600, 601; folk remedies in, 195, *p195*; women in, 413. *See also* disease
Medicare taxes, 812
Medici, Lorenzo de', 92, *q92*, *p92*
Medici family, 91, 92
Medici Library, 92
Meek, Joe, 472
Memorial of the Cherokee Nation, 853
Mennonites, 160; opposition to slavery, 127
mercantilism, 94–95, 131
mergers, 722, 723
***Merrimack* (ironclad),** 578
Mexican Americans, organization of, 782
Mexican Cession, 497
Mexican Revolution, 777
Mexico: boundaries between U.S. and, *m488–89*; conflict with, 365; Cortés exploration of, 86; independence from Spain, 365; revolution, 777; Texas independence from, 482–84, *m485*; war with, *m495*, 495–97, 514; western settlement and, 365
Mexico City, capture of, 497
Michelangelo, 92
Michigan, statehood for, 182, 499
Middle Ages: rise of nations in, 82; ship

navigation in, *p82*, 83, *p83*, 84; technological advances in, 82, *p82*; trade in, 81, 82
middle class, 752, 756
Middle Colonies, 121–22, 129; Great Awakening in, 128–29; growth of, 126; industries in, 126
Middle East, centers of trade in, 82
Middle Passage, 127
migration: of African Americans, 641, 751; forced, of Native Americans, 329, 453–54, *m454*, *p455*, 463, *p463*
Milan, 92
militia, 140
Milwaukee, Wisconsin, growth of, 398
Milwaukee College for Women, 412
minimum wage, 807, *c807*
mining: booms and busts in, 668; for copper, 668; for gold, 501, 503, 504, 505, 667, 668, 669; impact on economy, 668; for silver, 667, 668, 669
Minnesota: clashes between Native Americans and settlers in, 687; railroads and, 707; settlement of, 676; statehood for, 499
Minutemen, 140, 141
***Miranda* v. *Arizona*,** 848
missions, 88, 473–74; Spanish, 118, 492
Mississippi: Civil War in, 579; removal of Native Americans from, 453; secession of, 556; statehood for, 393, 426; women's rights in, 413
Mississippi River, 135; in goods transport, 184–85
Missouri: slavery in, 536; statehood for, 393
Missouri Compromise, 536, 544, 550, 556
Missouri Pacific Railroad, 673
Missouri River, 315
Mitchell, Maria, 411, *p411*
Mobile, Alabama: life in, 429, 431
Mobile Bay, 609
Mohawk people, 699
monarchs, 132
money: under Articles of Confederation, 183–84, *p184*; paper, *p459*
***Monitor* (ironclad),** 578
monopoly, 720
Monroe, James, 840, *p840*, *p853*; Era of Good Feelings and, 363; foreign policy under, 363–64, 775; Inaugural Address of, 363; Louisiana Purchase and, 314
Monroe Doctrine, 367, 775, 853; Roosevelt Corollary to, 776
Montana, mining in, 668
Monterey, as capital of California, *p494*
Montesquieu, Charles de, 106, 203, 204
Montezuma, 86, *p109*
Montgomery, Alabama, life in, 430
Montgomery Ward, 717
Monticello, *p302*, 325
Moore, Annie, 743
Morehouse College, 638
Morgan, J. Pierpont, 722, 752, 770
Mormons, 514; settlement of, in Utah, 505–6
Mormon Trail, *p505*
Morrill Act (1862), 760
Morris, Gouverneur, 220, *p220*; as delegate to Constitutional Convention, 197, 219
Morris, Robert, 184
Morrison, Toni, 760
Morse, Samuel, 713
Morse Code, 713
Moses, 99
motion picture projector, 715
Mott, Lucretia, 409, 410, *p410*, 804
mountain men, 472, *p472*, 496
Mount Holyoke Female Seminary, 405, 413
Mount McKinley National Park, 772
Mount Vernon, 289
movement, 56
muckrakers, 767
mudslinging in election of 1828, 447
Muhammad, 100
Muir, John, 805
music: in the 1800s, 325, 762; jazz, 794; slavery and, 327; spirituals as, 433–34, 563, *q563*
Muslims, 81, 100, *c805*; crusades and, 81. *See also* Islam
***mutualistas*,** 782

N

Naismith, James, 763
Napoleon, 314, 358
***Narrative of the Life of Frederick Douglass, an American Slave*,** 637
Nast, Thomas, political cartoons by, 766
National Archives, *p214*
National Association for the Advancement of Colored People (NAACP), 780, 781, 800
National Association of Manufacturers, 239
National Conservation Commission, 771
national debt, post Revolution, 281
National Grange, 694–95
nationalism, 321, 345, 359
National Labor Relations Board, 731
***National Labor Relations Board* v. *Jones & Laughlin Steel Corporation*,** 731
National Municipal League, 766
National Negro Business League, 780
National Organization for Women (NOW), 804
national parks: in Alaska, 772, *p772–73*; growth of, *g773*
National Republican Party: in election of 1824, 447; in election of 1828, 447–48
National Road, 389
National Supremacy, 259
Native Americans, 88; agriculture of, 95–96; attack on Whitman mission, 473–74; changing culture for, 691; Columbian Exchange and, 95–96, *m96*; and commerce clause, 252; Dawes Act and, 691, 692; education for, 691, 699, 760; English colonies and, 119, 123; equal rights for, 802, *p802*; forced migration of, 329; impact of disease on, 86, 473; justice for, 782; Penn and, 122; population of, *g686*; relocation of, to Oklahoma, 453–54, *p454*, *m454*, 463, *p463*; remedies used, 195, *p195*; Spanish and, 86, 117, 118; treaties with, 341, 343; to acquire land from, 669; unfair treatment of, 708; western settlement and, 287, *p287*, *m287*, 329, 455, 457, 679, *m686*, 686–89, *p687*, *p688*, *m689*
nativism, 401, 746–47
naturalization, 236, 650
natural laws, 101, 104, 105
natural rights, 103, 152
natural selection, 722
***Nautilus* (submarine),** 391
Navigation Acts, 131
Navstar Global Positioning System, 83, *p83*
navy: annexation of California and, 496–97; in early 1800s, 339
Navy Department, establishment of, 295
Nebraska, settlement of, 544
Netherlands: explorations by, *m87*, 89; settlements of, 117, 121; trade efforts by, 93
Neugin, Rebecca, *p463*
neutral rights, 339
Nevada: settlement of, 366, 491; statehood for, 499
New Amsterdam, 122
New Deal, 731
New England: colonies in, 121, 126; factories in, 385; farming in, 383; geographic location of, 383; Great Awakening in, 128–29; industry in,

383; shipbuilding in, 126; towns in, 237

New England Antislavery Society, 530

Newfoundland, 88–89

New France, 117, *m119*

New Hampshire: constitution of, 179; industry in, 383; ratification of Constitution, 207

New Harmony, Indiana, founding of, 403

New Jersey: colony of, 121, 122

New Jersey Plan, 199

Newman, Pauline, 744

New Mexico: mining in, 668; settlement of, 366, 491, 539, 540; statehood for, 499, 541; U.S. offer to purchase from Mexico, 494

New Netherlands, 117, 122

New Orleans, Louisiana, 313, 426, 448; in Civil War, 579; growth of, 327, 400; life in, 429; music in, 762; population in, 430; trade with, 185, 288; in War of 1812, 359

newspapers: African American, 397, 761; colonial, 129; technological advances in, 761; War with Mexico and, 496. *See also* journalism; press

Newton, Sir Isaac, 104, 105

New York (state), 117; celebration in, following ratification of Constitution, 207, 279; German settlers in, 400; settlement of, 121, 122; women's rights in, 413

New York Central Railroad, 707

New York City: Brooklyn Bridge in, *p755*, 756; as capital, 279, 282; Central Park in, 755; draft protest in, 602; growth of, 126, 327, 387, 398; immigrants in, *p741*, 742, 745, 751; music in, 762; as seaport, 752; skyscrapers in, *p754*, 755; strikes in, 397, 727; subway in, 756; tenements in, 767; terrorist attacks on, 236, *p797*, 797; Tweed Ring in, *p765*, 765–66

New York *Morning Journal*, 761

***New York Times Company v. United States*,** 848

New York *World*, 761

Nez Perce people, 689, 690

Niagara Movement, 781

nickelodeons, 763

***Niña* (ship),** 84

Nineteenth Amendment, 265, *p769*, 770, 804, 817

Ninth Amendment, *c223*, 236, 261

Nixon, Richard M., 844, *p844*

No Child Left Behind Act, 811

nominating convention, in political process, 449

normal schools, 405

North: city life in, 327; in Civil War, 571–73, *g572*; life in the early 1800s, 326

North Africa, Barbary pirates in, 339

North Carolina, 124; Democratic Party in, 642; population in, 431; ratification of Constitution and, 207; readmission to union, 632; schools in, 431; secession of, 559, 571. *See also* Carolinas

North Dakota, statehood for, 668

Northeast: economy in, 383, 386–87; farms in, 386; growth of industry in, *p383*, 383–85

Northern Confederacy, 316; failure of, 317

Northern Hemisphere, 41, *p41*

Northern Securities Company, 770

***North Star*,** 532

Northup, Solomon, 434, *p434*

Northwest Ordinance (1787), 181–82, 185, 321, 499, 550

Northwest Passage, 88

Northwest Territory, *m177*, 182, *m183*; settlement of, 313

Nueces River, 495

nullification, 296, 450, 451, 537; ordinance of, 537–38

Nullification Act (1832), 451

O

Oakley, Annie, 785, *p785*

Oberlin College, 405, 409

Oglethorpe, James, 124

Ohio: settlement of, 394; statehood for, 182, 341, 389, 393, 499

oil industry, 720

Oklahoma: Indian reservations in, 687; removal of Cherokees to, *m454*, 453–54; settlement of, 366, 679

Oklahoma land rush, 679

Old Senate Chamber, *p204*

oligopoly, 766

Olive Branch Petition, 150

Olmsted, Frederick Law, 755

Olney, Richard, 729

Omaha, Nebraska, building of transcontinental railroad and, 670

Oneida people, 210; treaties with, 343

opinions, facts versus, 60–61

Ordinance of 1785, 181, 182

Oregon: settlement of, 363–64, 471, *p473*, 473–75, *m474*; statehood for, 541

Oregon System, 769

Oregon Trail, 473, *p473*, 474, 494, 501, 514

Osage people, 457, 686

Osceola, 455, 456, *q456*, *p456*

O'Sullivan, John, 474, 477, *q477*

Otis, Elisha, 754

Otis, James, 136

Owen, Robert, 403

P

Paine, Thomas, 150, 158, *p158*

Palmer method of penmanship, 759

Panama Canal, *m788*; building, 776–77

Panic of 1837, 459

Panic of 1873, 727

paper money, *p459*

parallels, 42, *p42*

Parker, John, 141

Parkman, Francis, 514

patents, 384

Paterson, William, 199

Patriots, 153, 156, 198

patronage, 766

***Paul Revere*,** *ptg142*

"Paul Revere's Ride" (Longfellow), 142–47

Pawtucket, Rhode Island, cotton mill in, 385

Peace Democrats, 600

Peale, Charles Willson, painting by, *ptg211*

Pearl Harbor, Japanese invasion of, 795, *p795*

Peffer, William A., 694

Pendleton Act (1883), 766

Peninsular Campaign, 580

Penn, William, 122, *q160*

Pennsylvania: Civil War in, 606; colony of, 121, 122; as English colony, 121, 122; German settlers in, 400; growth of, 160; voting rights in, 397; women's rights in, 413

Pennsylvania Railroad, 721

Pennsylvania, University of, 151

people, powers reserved to, 261

People's Party of the U.S.A., 695

people with disabilities, reforms in education for, 405

periods: of history, 52

Perkins, Jacob, 384

Perkins Institute, 405

Perry, Oliver Hazard, 354

Pershing, John J., 777

Peru: independence for, 366; Pizarro's exploration of, 86

Petersburg, Virginia, siege of, 608, 610

petition, freedom of, 260
***Philadelphia* (U.S. warship),** 339
Philadelphia, Pennsylvania, *p197;* as capital, 282; celebration in, following ratification of Constitution, 207, 279; colonial, 122; Constitutional Convention in, 197, 199–200; education in, 322; First Continental Congress in, 139; growth of, 126, 327, 398; music in, 762; National Municipal League in, 766; Second Continental Congress in, 150; yellow fever epidemic in, 387
Philadelphia Female Anti-Slavery Society, 409
philanthrophy, 708, 722
Philip II of Spain, 89
Philippines, Spanish-American War and, 775
philosophe, 105
phonographs, 715, 716, *p716*
photography in Civil War, 602
physical maps, 44, *m44*
physical systems, 39
Pickens, Francis, 558
Pickett, George, 606
Pierce, Franklin, 841, *p841;* as president, 544, 546
Pike, Zebulon, 316
Pikes Peak, 316, 667
Pilgrims, 120, 133
Pinckney, Charles: in election of 1796, 293; in election of 1800, 307; in election of 1804, 317; in election of 1808, 340
Pinckney, Thomas, 288
Pinckney's Treaty, 288
***Pinta* (ship),** 84, 108
pioneers, amusements of, 394
pirates, Barbary, 339
Pisa, 82
Pitcairn, John, 141
Pitcher, Molly, 154, *ptg154*
Pittsburgh, Pennsylvania: growth of, 387, 389, 398, 751; as steel capital, 721; strikes in, 727; work for immigrants in, 743
Pittsburg Landing, in Civil War, 579
Pizarro, Francisco, 86
places, 39, 55
plantations, *p418;* life on, 386; in the South, 126–27, 326, 429–30
Plattsburgh, in War of 1812, 358
Pledge of Allegiance, 845, 857
***Plessy* v. *Ferguson*,** 233, 648, 651, 779, 849
Poe, Edgar Allan, 407
point of view, 63
political machines, 765–66
political maps, 44, *m44*, 58
political parties, 239; emergence of first, 291–92; roots of two party system, 238. *See also specific parties*
Polk, James K., 487, 494, 539, 841, *p841;* in election of 1844, 461, 475; Manifest Destiny and, 475; War with Mexico and, 495–96, 514
poll taxes, 647, 812, 817; abolition of, 268
Polo, Marco, 81, *ptg81*
polygamy, 506
Ponce de León, Juan, 86
Pony Express, 478
pools, railroad, 711
***Poor Richard's Almanack* (Franklin),** 151, 161
Pope, John, 580–81
popular sovereignty, 179, *c221*, 222, 544
population: in California, 505; in 1820, *m386*, *g386;* foreign born, *g778;* Native American, *g686;* in 1900, *m734;* railroads in redistribution of, 711
Populist Party, *p695*, 695–96; in election of 1892, 696; in election of 1896, 696–97; legacy of, 697
Port Hudson, 606
Port Royal Experiment, 627
Portugal: explorations of, 84, *m87;* improved ship design in, 83; monarchy in, 82; slave trade and, 97
postmaster general, 280
poverty level, *c806*, 807
Powderly, Terence V., 726
Powell, Colin, 677
power loom, 384
Powhatan Confederation, 123
Preamble of the U.S. Constitution, 219, 220, 249
prejudice. *See* discrimination
Prescott, William, 150
president: appointments of, 280; disability and succession of, 268–69; election of, 262; powers of, 225; roles of, 229–30; succession of, 266. *See also* executive branch; *specific presidents*
presidential electors, change in selection of, 449
presidential terms: limit on, 267; number of, 291
presidio, 88
press: colonial, 129; freedom of, 240–41, 260. *See also* journalism; newspapers
Prevost, George, 358
primary elections, 697, 769
primary sources, 62
Prime Meridian, 41, 42
Princeton, in American Revolution, 153
Pringle, Catherine Sager, *q473*
prisoners, reforms for treatment of, 405
privateers, 355
Proclamation of 1763, *m135*, 135–36
Proclamation of Neutrality (1793), 288
progressive education, 759
progressive reforms, 799
progressives, 765, 767, 770
Prohibition, 265; repeal of, 266
Promontory Summit, 670
property taxes, 812, 813
Prophet, 342
Prophetstown, 342, 343
proprietary colonies, 130
Prosser, Gabriel, 435
Protestantism, rise of, 102
public schools, 758–59. *See also* education
pueblos, 88
Puerto Rico, representation of, in House of Representatives, 227
Pulaski, Casimir, 155
Pulitzer, Joseph, 761
Pullman, George M., 710, 729
Pullman Strike, 729
Pun Chi, 515
Pure Food and Drug Act (1906), 767, 771
Puritans, 103, 120, 121
push-pull factors, 641

Q

Quadruple Alliance, 367
Quakers: opposition to slavery, 127, 195; in reform movements, 409; settlement of, in Pennsylvania, 122
quinine, 195, *p195*

R

racial violence, 780
Radical Reconstruction, 626, 627, 631–33
radiocarbon dating, *p49*, 51
ragtime, 762
railroads: cattle drives and, 673–74; Chinese laborers on, 670; competition and, 710–11; cow towns and, 673; economic growth and, 707, 708, 709–11; effects of, 671; expansion of, 707; formation of corporations and, 719; government control of, 766; government subsidies to, 669–70; growth of cities and, 751; impact of, 707, 711; improving, 709; industrial development and, 646; before 1900, *m710;* in the South, 426; technology and, 710; transcontinental, 669–71, 707; in western settlement, 676
Raleigh, Sir Walter, 119
ranchos, 492

Index

Randolph, Edmund, 199; as attorney general, 280; as delegate to Constitutional Convention, 197, 201; ratification of Constitution and, 207
Randolph, John, 641
range wars, 675
Rankin, Jeannette, *p804*
ratification, of U.S. Constitution, 207, 259
Reagan, Ronald W., 844, *p844*
realism, 761
Rebels, 574
recall, 769
Reconstruction, 613; Congress before and after, *c654*; corruption and, 638; end of, 641–44, 647; impact of, 648–49; under Johnson, 628; Johnson's plan for, 628, 630–31; Lincoln's plan for, 625; military districts in, *m632*; primary sources on, 652–53; Radical, 626, 631–33; readmission of states to union, 632; resistance to, 638; South after, 645–46, *g645*; South in, 636, 638–39
Reconstruction Act (1867), 632
***The Red Badge of Courage* (Crane),** 761
Red Cloud, 686, 687
Redeemers, 645
referendum, 769
reform movements: for the disabled, 405; in education, 405; for Native Americans, 691; in temperance, 403, 410, 502; in women's rights, 409–13, 410
regionalism, 761
regions, 39, 57
relevance, 61
religion: of African Americans, 322, 433–34; Second Great Awakening in, 322, 403, 412, 414
Religious Camp Meeting, *ptg322, ptg414*
religious diversity, 805, *c805*
religious freedom, 260; in English colonies, 121, 123, *q235*
religious toleration, 121
Remington, Frederic, 762
Renaissance, 92, 102
rendezvous, 472
representative government, 107, 130, 132
republic, 203
republicanism, *c221*, 222
Republican Party: domination of South, 636; in election of 1800, 307; in election of 1804, 317; in election of 1808, 340; in election of 1856, 549; in election of 1860, 555; in election of 1868, 634; in election of 1896, 697; formation of, 549; as War Hawks, 343
reservations, 687, 689
reserved powers, 222, *c222*
Revels, Hiram, 636, *p636*
Revere, Paul, 140
Rhode Island: Articles of Confederation and, 184; colony of, 121; industry in, 383; ratification of Constitution and, 207; voting rights in, 397
rice, 126
Richardson, Henry, 755
Richmond, Virginia: as Confederate capital, 571, 573, 580; fall of, in Civil War, 610; trolley car system in, 756
***Rifles for Watie* (Keith),** 584–89
right of deposit, 185
Riis, Jacob, *q753*, 767, *q767*, 768, p768
Rio Grande, 495
"Rip Van Winkle" (Irving), 322, 324
rivers, water rights, *m488–89*, 488–89
river travel, 389, 390, *p390*, 391
roads: building of first, 389; paving, 756
Roanoke, 119
Rockefeller, John D., 720, 723; philanthrophy of, 722
Rockefeller Institute for Medical Research, 722
***Roe* v. *Wade*,** 849
Rolfe, John, 119
Rome, 99
Roosevelt, Franklin D., 816, 843, *p843*; labor and, 731; terms of office, 291
Roosevelt, Theodore, *q784*, 805, 843, *p843*; antitrust legislation under, 770; conservation under, 771; foreign policy under, 776, 777; immigration policy under, 779; as New York City police commissioner, 768; square deal under, 770–71
Roosevelt Corollary, 776
Ross, Betsy, 200
Ross, John, *p463*
Rousseau, Jean-Jacques, 106
royal colonies, 124, 130
Royal Observatory, 42
rule of law, 99, 100
Rumsey, James, 390
runaway slaves, 533–34
rural areas, population in, *g751*
Rush-Bagot Treaty (1817), 363
Russell, Charles, painting by, *ptg674*
Russia: claims to Oregon, 471; purchase of Alaska from, 499
Russwurm, John, 397, 531
rustlers, 674

S

Sacagawea, 315
Sacramento, California: building of transcontinental railroad and, 670; capital building in, *p498*; discovery of gold near, 501
Sacramento River, 488–89
Sagoyewatha, 360, *p360*
St. Augustine, Florida, 86, 88, *ptg88*, 117; growth of, 400
St. Clair, Arthur, 287
Saint Domingue, 157
St. Lawrence River, 89
St. Louis, Missouri, 315; growth of, 390, 398
St. Luke Penny Savings Bank, 780
Salmon, Robert, painting by, *ptg400*
Sampson, Deborah, 154
San Antonio, Texas, 88, 483
Sand Creek, 688
San Diego, 88, 118
San Francisco, California: *m54*; cable-car lines in, 755; before gold rush, p540; growth of, 503; immigrants in, 745; as seaport, 752
San Francisco Art Institute, 708
San Gabriel Mission, 492
San Jacinto, Battle of, 485–86, *p486*
San Joaquin River, 488–89
San Martin, José de, 366
San Salvador, 85
Santa Anna, Antonio López de, 482, 483, 484, 485, 486
Santa Barbara, mission, 76
Santa Fe, New Mexico, 117; settlement of, 491
Santa Fe Trail, 491, *p491*, 496, 501
***Santa María* (ship),** 84
Santo Domingo, 313
Saratoga, Battle of, 154
Sauk and Fox people, resistance of, 455
Savannah, Georgia, 156; in Civil War, 609; growth of, 327; life in, 429
scalawags, 638
scale bar, 43
scholasticism, development of, 101
school busing, *p758*
scientific method, 105
Scotland, 130
Scott, Dred, 549–50, 651, 846
Scott, Winfield, 497; Trail of Tears and, 454
Sears Roebuck, 717
***The Sea Wolf* (London),** 761
secession, 450, 541; of South, 556, *m558*

Second Amendment, *c223*, 260
secondary sources, 62
Second Continental Congress, 150, 151, 155, 180
Second Daughter **(Walter),** 186–91
Second Great Awakening, 322, 403, 412, 414
secret ballot, 697
sectionalism, 536, 538
Sedalia, Missouri, 673
segregation, 233, 397, 648
Seguín, Juan, 483
self-government: in English colonies, 130; in Virginia, 119
Seminole people: in Florida, 364, 456; removal of, to Oklahoma, 453, *m454*; resistance of, 455
Senate, U.S., 204–5, 227; African Americans in, 636; approval of Louisiana Purchase by, 314; in approval of presidential appointments, 280; committees of, 227–28; role of, in impeachment, 227, 633; in U.S. Constitution, 250–52. *See also* Congress, U.S.; House of Representatives, U.S.
Senators, direct election of, 264, 697, 770
Seneca Falls Convention (1848), 409, 410–11, 770
Seneca Falls Declaration, 854
separate but equal facilities, 779, 815
separation of powers, 106, *c221*, 223
Separatists, 120
September 11, 2001, terrorist attacks on, 236, *p797*, 797
Sequoyah, 329, 453, *p453*
Serapis **(ship),** 155
Serra, Junípero, 117, 118, *q118*, *p118*, 492
service economy, 808
service learning, 818–19, *c818*
settlement houses, 753
Seven Cities of Gold, 87
Seven Days' Battles, 580
Seventeenth Amendment, 264, 697, 770
Seventh Amendment, *c223*, 261
Seward, William, 775
Seymour, Horatio, in election of 1868, 634
Shaler, William, *q330*
sharecropping, 639, 646
Shawnee people, western settlement and, 329
Shays, Daniel, 195
Shays's Rebellion, *p194*, 194–95, 207, 221, 286
Sherman, Roger, 199
Sherman, William Tecumseh, 574, 575, *p575*, 607, 608, 609, *p616*
Sherman Antitrust Act (1890), 723, 730, 766, 770
shield laws, 241
Shiloh, Battle of, 579, 598, 600
Shinbone Peak, 503
shipbuilding, 83, 126
shoe industry, 715
Sholes, Christopher, 714
Sierra Club, 239, 805
Sierra Nevada Range, 501
Silent Spring **(Carson),** 805
silver: as issue for the Populist Party, 696; mining for, 667, 668, 669
Sinclair, Upton, 767, 787
Sioux people, 686, 688, 692
Sitting Bull, 688, 692
Sixteenth Amendment, 264, 697, 812
Sixth Amendment, *c223*, 261
The Sketch Book **(Irving),** 322, 324
skyscrapers, *p754*, 754–55
Slater, Samuel, 385
slave(s), *p435*; African traditions of, 127; culture of, 433; emancipation of 1780–1804, *m244*; family life of, 433; fugitive, 437, 541; life of, 435, 439, *p439*; religion of, 433–34; runaway, 533–34, 534; spirituals of, 433–34
slave codes, 127, 434–35
slave revolts, 434–35, 437; under Toussaint, 313
slave runaways, 437
slavery: abolition of, 244, 262; criticism of, 127; division in country over, 401; end of, in Massachusetts, 179; as issue, in American Revolution, 155; new states and, 499; prohibition against, in Northwest Territory, 182; in the South, 127, 326–27; Three-Fifths Compromise and, 199–200
slave trade, 200–201, 433; abolishment of, 541; beginnings of, 97
Slidell, John, 495
Sloat, John, 496, 497
smallpox, 86, 96
Smith, Adam, 94, *q94*
Smith, Jedediah, 472, 492
Smith, John, 119
Smith, Joseph, 506
Smith, Mrs. Samuel Harrison, on Jackson's inauguration, 462
Smith, Robert, 551
Smith College, 760
smuggling, 131, 136
social contract, 103, 106
The Social Contract **(Rousseau),** 106
social Darwinism, 722–23
socialists, 767
Social Security, 812
Society of American Indians, 782
sodbusters, *p678*, 678–79
sod houses, 678, *p678*
Sojourner Truth, 532, *p532*
sooners, 679
Sorenson, Charles, 716
sources: credibility of, 63; examination of, 62; primary, 62; secondary, 62
Sousa, John Philip, 762
South: after Reconstruction, 645–46, *g645*; American Revolution in, 156, *m156*; in Civil War, 571–73, *g572*; cotton production in, 423, *m425*, *c425*, 426; destruction of, in Civil War, *q616*, 625; economy of, 426; education in, 431; industry in, 424–26; life in the, 428–31; opposition to tariffs, 284, 450; plantations in, 126–27, 326, 386, *p418*, 429–30; population in, *c428*, *m440*; Reconstruction in, 636, 638–39; Republican domination of, 636; secession of, 556–57, *m558*; slavery in the, 127, 326–27; transportation in, 426
South Carolina, 124; nullification and, 538; readmission to union, 632; secession of, 556. *See also* Carolinas
South Dakota, statehood for, 668
Southern Alliance, 695
Southern Hemisphere, 41, *p41*
Southern Pacific Railroad, 670
sovereignty, 180
Spain: as colonial ally in American Revolution, 155; control of Florida by, 117, 124; control of Louisiana Territory by, 313; early exploration of, 84–87, *m87*, 108; early problems with, 184–85; foreign relations with, 364; Hispanic heritage of, 88; missions of, 117, 118; in California, 492; Native Americans and, 88, 97; Pinckney's Treaty with, 288; rise of monarchies in, 82; settlements in North America, 88, 117; slave trade and, 97; trade rivalry with England, 89; western settlement and, 491
Spanish-American War, 775
Spanish Armada, 89
Spanish conquistadors, 86
Spanish East Florida, 364
Spanish galleon, 85, *p85*
Spanish language, 88
special-purpose maps, 45, *m45*
speech, freedom of, 260

Index

spies, in Civil War, 600
spinning jenny, 384
***The Spirit of Laws* (Montesquieu),** 106, 203
spirituals, 433–34, 563, *q563*
spoils system, 449, 766
sports, for the pioneers, 394
Spotsylvania, Battle of, 608
Springfield, Illinois, race riot in, 780
***The Squatter and the Don* (Burton),** 493
stagecoaches, 669
Stamp Act (1765), 136, 137; repeal of, 136
Stamp Act Congress, 136
standard gauge, adoption of, by railroads, 709
Standard Oil of New Jersey, 722
Standard Oil of Ohio, 720, *ctn720*
Stanford, Leland, 671, 707, 708, *p708*, 760
Stanford University, 708, 760
Stanton, Edwin, as secretary of war, 633
Stanton, Elizabeth Cady, 409, 410, 804, *p854*
"The Star-Spangled Banner," 356, 358, 852
State, U.S. Department of, 230, 279
state constitutions, 179
states: admission of new, 498–99; powers reserved to, 261; relations among, in U.S. Constitution, 257–58; suits against, 261. *See also specific states*
state sovereignty, 450
states' rights, 556; as cause of Civil War, 573; doctrine of, 296–97, 538
Statue of Liberty, 742
steamboats, 390, *p390*, 391, 392, 393
steam locomotives, 669, *p669*
steel industry, 646, 709; growth of, 721–22
Steffens, Lincoln, 767
Stevens, Thaddeus, *q625*, *p625*, 626, 641
Stewart, Amelia, 478
Stockbridge, treaty, 343
Stock Market Crash of 1929, 794
Stone, Kate, 574
Stone, Lucy, *p409*
Stone, William, 574
storage battery, 715
Stowe, Harriet Beecher, 407, 544, 545, *p545*
Strauss, Levi, 478, 503
streetcars, 755–56
strikes, 397; Haymarket Square, 727; major, 729; Pullman, 729
Stuart, James E. B. (J.E.B.), 580
Stuart, Robert, 472
submarines, 391; in Civil War, 578
subsistence farming, 126
suburbs, 752; middle-class, 756
suffrage. *See* voting rights
Sugar Act (1764), 136
Sullivan, Louis, 754
Sumner, Charles, 547, 633
supporting evidence, 61
supremacy clause in Constitution, 259
Supreme Court, U.S., 205, 230–31; economy and, 310–11; under John Jay, 281; under John Marshall, 309, 310–11, 453; judicial review and, 309, 311; justices of, *p205*; under Roger Taney, 550, 651
Supreme Court, U.S., cases: *Brown* v. *Board of Education*, 233, 651, 801, 846, 859; *Chisholm* v. *Georgia*, 261; *Dartmouth College* v. *Woodward*, 311; *Dred Scott* v. *Sandford*, 549–50, 555, 651, 846; *Ex parte Milligan*, 231; *Fletcher* v. *Peck*, 311; *Gibbons* v. *Ogden*, 309, 311, 846; *Gideon* v. *Wainwright*, 261, 847; *Korematsu* v. *United States*, 847; *Marbury* v. *Madison*, 225, 231, 232, 309, 311, 847; *McCulloch* v. *Maryland*, 309, 459, 847–48; *Miranda* v. *Arizona*, 848; *New York Times Company* v. *United States*, 848; *Plessy* v. *Ferguson*, 233, 648, 651, 779, 849; *Roe* v. *Wade*, 849; *United States* v. *Nixon*, 849; *Woodruff* v. *North Bloomfied*, 502; *Worcester* v. *Georgia*, 453, 459, 849
Sutter, John, 494, 501, 502
sweatshops, 725, 733; work for immigrants in, 744
Swift, Gustavus, 710
symbols, 200
systems of government, 179

T

Taft, William Howard, 843, *p843*; foreign policy under, 777
Taino, *m110*
Talleyrand, Charles de, 293, 314
Taney, Roger B., 550, 651
Tanner, Henry, 762
Tarbell, Ida, 767
tariffs, 95, 282, 450, 537, 766, 812; of abominations, 450; opposition to, 284; protests of, in the South, 450
taxes, 812–13; in Hamilton's economic program, 284; income, 264; Medicare, 812; poll, 268, 647, 812, 817; property, 812, 813
Taylor, Zachary, 841, *p841*; in election of 1848, 540; illness and death of, 542; as president, 541; in War with Mexico, 495–96
Tea Act (1773), 138
technology: in Civil War, 578; computers and, 810; economy and, 807; in the Middle Ages, 82, *p82*; in printing, 761; railroad, 710–11
Tecumseh, 341–42, *q342*, *p342*, 343, 346, *p347*, 354
***Tejanos*,** 481
telegraphs, 713, 715
telephones, 713, 715, 716, *p716*
temperance movement, 403, 410, 502
tenant farmers in the South, 428
Ten Commandments, 99–100
tenements, 752, 767, 768
Tennessee: Civil War in, 579, 580, 613; Reconstruction in, 625; secession of, 559, 571, 628; statehood for, 393, 498
tennis, 763
Tenochtitlán, 86, *p109*
Ten Percent Plan, 625
Tenskwatawa, 342
Tenth Amendment, 222, *c223*, 261, 281, 537
Tenure of Office Act (1867), 633
Texas: Alamo defense and, 481, 483–84; annexation of, 486, 495, 539; Civil War in, 606; independence from Mexico, 482–84, *m485*; as Lone Star Republic, 486; open range in, 673; secession of, 556; settlement of, 366, 481–82; statehood for, 487, 499, 539; U.S. claims to Spanish, 365
Texas Declaration of Independence, 484–85
Thames, Battle of the, 354
Thames River, 91
"Thanatopsis" (Bryant), 325
thematic maps, 58
theology, 101
thermoluminescence dating, 51
Third Amendment, *c223*, 260
Thirteenth Amendment, 262, 594, 628, 631
Thompson, J. Edgar, Steel Works, 721
Thoreau, Henry David, 403, 404, *p404*, 406
Three-Fifths Compromise, 200
***Thunder on the Sierra* (Balmes),** 507–12
Tilden, Samuel J., 633; in election of 1876, 643, *m644*
time: links across, 68–71; measuring, *p50*, 50–51; organizing, 52–53
time line, 53, *p53*, 824
time zones, 709, *m709*, 711; creation of, 671

Tippecanoe, Battle of, 343, 461
tobacco, 96, 119, 123, 126, 646
Todd, John, Jr., 357
Tompkins, Sally, 600
Torah, 99
Torlino, Tom, *p760*
Toussaint-Louverture, 157, 313
town meetings, 133, 237, *p237*
towns: boom, 503, 668, *p668*; cow, 673, 675; in New England, 237. *See also* cities
Townshend Acts (1767), 136, 137
township, 183, *m183*
trade: with British, 194; colonial, 96, 126, 131; in early 1800s, 341; Embargo Act (1807) and, 340; imports and exports, 1800–1820, *c340*; in Middle Ages, 81; in Middle East, 82; slave, 97, 200–201, 433; triangular, 126
trade unions, 726, 780
Trail of Tears, 454, *m454*, *p455*
transcendentalists, 406
transcontinental railroads, 669–71, 707
transformers, 715
transportation: advances in, 716–17; in the South, 426. *See also* specific types of
travel: in cities, 755–56; for immigrants, 742; in western settlement, 389–90, 392–94
***Travels* (Polo),** 81
Travis, William, 483, 484
Treasury, U.S. Department of, 279
***A Treatise on Domestic Economy* (Beecher),** 412
Treaty of Paris (1783), 156, 184, 293
Tredegar Iron Works, 426
Trenton, New Jersey, in American Revolution, 153
trial by jury, 238, 261
Triangle Shirtwaist Company fire, 727
triangular trade, 126
Trinity College, 405
Troiani, Don, *ptg358*
trolley cars, 756
Troy Female Seminary, 413
Truman, Harry S., 800, 843, *p843*
trusts, 720, 766
tuberculosis, 753
Tubman, Harriet, 436, *q436*, *p436*, 437, 534, 595, 600
Tucson, Arizona, 88
Turner, Nat, 435
turnpikes, 389
Tuscarora people, treaties with, 343
Tuskegee Institute, 760, *p760*, 780, 782, 784
Twain, Mark, 752, *q755*, 761, *q784*
Tweed, William M., *p765*, 765–66
Tweed Ring, *p765*, 765–66
Twelfth Amendment, 255, 262, 307, 447
***Twelve Years a Slave* (Northup),** 434
Twentieth Amendment, 265–66
Twenty-fifth Amendment, 268–69
Twenty-first Amendment, 266
Twenty-fourth Amendment, 268, 812, 817
Twenty-second Amendment, 265–66
Twenty-seventh Amendment, 269
Twenty-sixth Amendment, 235, 269, 817
Twenty-third Amendment, 267
two-party system, 238
***Two Treatises of Civil Government* (Locke),** 103, 104
Tyler, John, 266, 486, 841, *p841*; administration of, 461; in election of 1840, 461
typewriters, 714

U

***Uncle Tom's Cabin* (Stowe),** 407, 544, 545
Underground Railroad, 436, 437, *m533*, 533–34, 595
Union Pacific Company, 670, 707
United Farm Workers, 728, 731, 782, 802
United Kingdom, 130
United Nations, 795
United States, *m488–89*; district courts in, 230; expansion of, 775; overseas possessions of, *m776*
U.S. Forest Service, 771, 805
U.S. Post Office, 230, 717
United States Steel Corporation, 722
***United States* v. *Nixon*,** 849
***Up from Slavery* (Washington),** 780
Upson, Theodore, 574, 616
Utah: railroads and, 707; settlement of, 366, 491, 505–6; statehood for, 499, 541
utopias, 403

V

Vaca, Álvar Núñez Cabeza de, 87
Valley Forge, 154
Van Buren, Martin, 486, 841, *p841*; administration of, 460; in election of 1836, 460; election of 1844 and, 475; in election of 1848, 540; national bank and, 459; as vice president, 459
Vandalia, Illinois, 389
vandalism, 815
Vanderbilt, Cornelius, 707
van Leeuwenhoek, Anton, 99
***vaqueros*,** 88, *p492*, 497, 674
Vassar College, 760
vaudeville, 763
vegetation, 44
Velázquez, Loretta, Janeta, 600
Venezuela, U.S. involvement in, 776
Venice, 82, 92, 94
Veracruz, 497
Vermont: industry in, 383; lifestyle in, 394; statehood for, 393, 498
vertical integration, 721–22
Vesey, Denmark, 435
Vespucci, Amerigo, *m87*
veto, use of, by president, 228
vice president: election of, 262; succession of, 266
Vicksburg, Mississippi, Battle of, 606, 607
Vietnam War, 797
vigilantes, 504, 668
Villa, Pancho, 777
violence: in boomtowns, 668; racial, 780
Virginia, 119; colony of, 123; Democratic Party in, 642; House of Burgesses in, 119, 123, 133; manumission of slavery in, 196; population in, 431; ratification of Constitution, 207; secession of, 559, 571; self-government in, 119
Virginia, University of, 325, *p325*
Virginia City, Nevada, 668
Virginia Company, 119, 123, 133
Virginia Plan, 199
Virginia Resolution, 296–97, 450, 537, 538
Virginia Statute for Religious Freedom, 235, *q235*, 805
Virgin Islands, representation of, in House of Representatives, 227
Voltaire, 105
von Steuben, Friedrich, 155
voting rights, 238, 816–17; for African Americans, 264, 397, 647–48, 696, 770; in California, 504; for eighteen year olds, 235, 269; property ownership and, 448–49; for white men, 179; for women, 265, 409, 410, *p769*, 770, p799
Voting Rights Act (1965), 801, 815, 817

Index

Index

W

Waddel, Moses, 431
Wade-Davis Bill (1864), 626
Wagner Act (1935), 731
wagon trains, 669
Walker, David, 531
Walker, James, painting by, *ptg492*
Walker, Quock, 179
Waltham, Massachusetts, cotton mill in, 385
Ward, Mary A., *q577*
War Department, 279–80
War Hawks, 343, 344, 345, 359
Warner, Charles Dudley, 752
War of 1812, 353–59, *m355*, 389, 391, 448, 537; attack on Washington, D.C. in, 356, 357; Baltimore in, 358; declaration of war in, 345; end of, 358–59; Native Americans in, 354–55; naval battles in, 354–55, 358
Warren, Mercy Otis, 206, *q206*, 209
Washington (state): railroads and, 707; statehood for, 667
Washington, Booker T., 760, 780, 781, *p781*, 784, *p784*
Washington, D.C.: *m332*, attack on, in War of 1812, 356; as capital, 282, 307; in 1800, 308, *p308*. *See also* District of Columbia
Washington, George, 139, 196, *p280*, *p286*, *p291*, *q360*, 840, *p840*, *p852*; cabinet of, 279–80, 291; as commanding general in war with France, 295; as Continental Army general, 150, 153, 154, *ptg153*; Farewell Address of, 289, *q289*, 775, 852; as first president, *p255*, 279–82, 284; foreign policy under, 288–89, 367, 775; letter to James McHenry, 185; ratification of Constitution and, 207; at Second Continental Congress, 150, 196, 199; on Shays's Rebellion, 195; terms of office and, 291; use of veto by, 228; Whiskey Rebellion and, 286
Washington Crossing the Delaware, *ptg153*
water, as resource, *m488–89*, 488–89
water frame, 384
Watson, Tom, in election of 1896, 697
Wayne, Anthony, 287
***The Wealth of Nations* (Smith),** 94
Weaver, James B., in election of 1892, 696
Webster, Daniel, *p541*, 541–42; debate with Hayne, Robert, 450; national bank and, 459; nullification and, 538
Webster, Noah, 321
Weld, Theodore, 439, 530
Wellesley College, 760
Wells, Ida B., 780
Wesleyan College, 405
West, American Revolution in, 155
Western Hempisphere, 41, *p41*
western settlement, 313, *m316*, 393–94, 499; California in, 492–97, 504–5; cattle ranching in, 671, *p673*, 673–75; farming in, 286, 386, 676, *p678*, 678–79, 694; land policies and, 181; land use in 1890, *m676*; life during, 328, 698–99; mining in, 501, 667–68; mountain men in, 472, *p472*; Native Americans in, 287, *m287*, *p287*, 329, 455, 457, 679, *m686*, 686–89, *p687*, *p688*, *m689*; New Mexico Territory in, 491; Oregon in, 471, *p473*, 473–75, *m474*; Proclamation of 1763 and, *m135*, 135–36; Texas in, 481–87, *m485*; travel in, 328, 389–90, 392–94, 491, 669–71; Utah in, 505–6
Western Union Telegraph Company, 713
West Indies, 97; slaves in, 126
Westinghouse, George, 710, 715
Wharton, Edith, 761
Whig Party: disintegration of, 549; in election of 1836, 459; in election of 1840, 460, 461; in election of 1844, 461; in election of 1848, 540; Oregon issue and, 475
Whirling Thunder, *p457*
Whiskey Rebellion, 286
Whistler, James, 762
white collar workers, 808
Whitefield, George, 128–29, *p129*
White House, 307, *p442*
Whitman, Marcus, 473
Whitman, Narcissa, 473
Whitman, Walt, 407
Whitman mission, 473–74
Whitney, Eli, 384, 385, 423, 424, *p424*, 438, *p438*
Whittier, John Greenleaf, 407, 617
whooping cough, 753
Wilder, Laura Ingalls, 699
Wilderness, Battle of, 608
Willard, Emma Hart, 412
William and Mary College, 129
William of Orange, 103, 132
Williams, Roger, 121
Willington, South Carolina, schools in, 431
Wilmot, David, 539
Wilmot Proviso, 539, 540
Wilson, James, 208, *q208;* as delegate to Constitutional Convention, 197
Wilson, Woodrow, 843, *p843*; foreign policy under, 777; Fourteen Points of, 858
Winnemucca, Sarah, 691, *p691*
Winthrop, John, 121
Wisconsin: statehood for, 182, 499; women's rights in, 413
Wisconsin idea, 769
women: in abolition movement, 530; at the Alamo, 484; in all wars, 154, *p154*; in American Revolution, 154, *p154*; in Civil War, 599–600; education for, 405, 409, 412, 760; efforts to organize workplace by, 397; in factories, 385, *p385*; in homesteading, 676; as immigrants, 745; in labor unions, 727, 728, 731; life on Southern plantations, 429; in literature, 407; in medicine, 413; role of, in the home, 412; in rural areas, 751; as settlement workers, 753; suffrage for, 265, 409, 410, *p769*, 770, *p799;* in workforce, *p396*, 397, 725, 809
Woman's Christian Temperance Union, 502
women's rights movement, 409–13, *p769*, *p799*; progress in, 411
Wood, Thomas Waterman, *ptg631*
***Woodruff* v. *North Bloomfield*,** 502
Woods, Granville, 715
Woolworth, F. W., five-and-ten-cent stores, 717
Woolworth Building, *p754*, 755
***Worcester* v. *Georgia*,** 453, 459, 849
work: changing nature of, 808; conditions of, 725; for immigrants, 743–44, 746
***Work and Win* (Alger),** 761
work day, length of, 396, 697
workforce: African Americans in, 397, *p397*; blue collar workers in, 808; children in, 396, 725, *p725*, 733, *p798*; selected professions, *c809;* white collar workers in, 808; women in, *p396*, 397, 725, 809
World's Fair in Chicago, 755
World War I, 794; freedom of the press during, 241; recruitment poster for, *p794*
World War II, 795, *p795*
Wounded Knee, 692
Wovoka, 692

Wright, Orville, 714
Wright, Wilbur, 714
Wyoming: settlement of, 366; women's suffrage in, 770

X

XYZ affair, 293

Y

Yale College, 129
Yancey, Charles, 321
Yankees, 574
yellow fever, 387, 775
yellow journalism, 761
YMCA (Young Men's Christian Association), 753
York (Clark's servant), 315
Yorktown, Virginia, British surrender at, 156
You Bet, 503
Young, Brigham, 506
Young, Charles M., *p677*
***Young Man in White Apron* (Falconer),** *ptg397*
YWCA (Young Women's Christian Association), 753

Z

Zenger, John Peter, *p240,* 241

One-Stop Internet Resources

This textbook contains one-stop Internet resources for teachers, students, and parents. Log on to ca.hss.glencoe.com for more information. Online study tools include Study Central, Chapter Overviews, ePuzzles and Games, Self-Check Quizzes, Vocabulary e-Flashcards, and Multi-Language Glossaries. Online research tools include Student Web Activities, Current Events, Beyond the Textbook Features, Web Resources, and State Resources. Especially for teachers, Glencoe offers an online Teacher Forum and Web Activity Lesson Plans. The interactive online student edition includes the complete Interactive Student Edition along with textbook updates.

Acknowledgements

Text

186 From *Second Daughter: The Story of a Slave Girl* by Mildred Pitts Walter. Copyright © 1996 by Mildred Pitts Walter. Reprinted by permission of Scholastic Inc. **346** Excerpt from *Crossing the Panther's Path* by Elizabeth Adler. Copyright © 2002 by Elizabeth Adler. Reprinted by permission of Farrar, Straus & Giroux, LLC. **507** From *Thunder on the Sierra*, by Kathy Balmes. Copyright © 2001 by Kathy Balmes. Reprinted by permission of Silver Moon Press, New York. **584** From *Rifles for Watie*, by Harold Keith. Text copyright © 1957 by Harold Keith. Used by permission of HarperCollins Publishers. **680** Excerpt from *A Lantern in Her Hand*, by Bess Streeter Aldrich. Copyright 1928 by D. Appleton & Company, renewed © 1956 by Mary Aldrich Beechner, Robert Streeter Beechner, Charles S. Aldrich, and James Whitson Aldrich. Used by permission of Penguin Group (USA) Inc.

Glencoe would like to acknowledge the artists and agencies who participated in illustrating this program: American Artists Rep., Inc.; The Artifact Group; John Brewster Creative Services; Mapping Specialists, Ltd.; Morgan-Cain & Associates; Studio Inklink; WildLife Art Ltd.

Photo Credits

vi Royalty-Free/CORBIS; **vii** (tl)Fort Ticonderoga Museum, (tr)Lexington Historical Society, Lexington, MA, (br)Copyright 1996, Virginia Historical Society, Lora Robins Collection of Virginia Art; **viii** (tr)Henry Groskinsky/Timepix, (br)Manassas National Battlefield Park/Larry Shere; **ix** Courtesy Ford Motor Company; **xi** (l)Stock Montage, (r)Chester County Historical Society, West Chester, PA; **xii** Fraunces Tavern Museum, New York City; **xiii** Jacob A. Riss Collection, Museum of the City of New York; **CA0–CA1** Royalty-Free/CORBIS; **CA2–CA3** Getty Images; **CA4–CA5 CA6–CA7** Royalty-Free/CORBIS; **CA8–CA9 CA10–CA11 CA12–CA13** Getty Images; **CA20** John Elk III./Lonely Planet Images, Inc.; **CA35** Royalty-Free/CORBIS; **38** Getty Images; **39** (bl)Rober Landau/CORBIS, Getty Images; **40** Getty Images; **48** (l)Comstock Images, (c)AP/Worldwide Photos, (r)Getty Images; **49** (t)Ron Sheridan/Ancient Art & Architecture Collection, (cl)Katie Deits/Index Stock Imagery, (b)Photo Researchers, Inc.; **50** (t)Scala/Art Resource, NY, (b) Nimatallah/Art Resource, NY; **51** (l)Michel Zabe/Museo Templo Mayor, (r)Kunsthistorisches Museum, Wien oder KHM, Wien; **52** (t)National Portrait Gallery, Smithsonian Institution/Art Resource, NY, (c)Henry Groskinsky, (bl)Mark Burnett, (br)Library of Congress; **54** NASA; **55** (l)Courtesy Denver Public Library Western History Department, (c)Huntington Library/SuperStock, (r)Henry Groskinsky; **56 59 60 62** Getty Images; **57** H. Armstrong Roberts; **60** (t)Will Hart/PhotoEdit, (bl)Massachusetts Historic Royal Palaces, (bc)The Shelburne Museum, (br)Charles & Josette Lenars/CORBIS; **61** (l)Bettmann/CORBIS, (r)Getty Images; **62** (t)Wenham Museum, (bl) Missouri Historical Society, St. Louis, (bc) Thomas Gilcrease Institute of American Art, Tulsa, OK, (br)Collection of David J. & Janice L. Frent; **63** Bettmann/CORBIS; **64** (l)St. Louis Art Museum, St. Louis, Missouri, USA/SuperStock, (r)Bettmann/CORBIS; **65** (l)Private Collection/Picture Research Consultants, (c)New York Historical Society, (r)The Saint Louis Art Museum. Gift of Bank of America; **66** (t)Richard A. Cooke/CORBIS, (b)The City of Plainfield, NJ; **68** (cw from top)Photograph Courtesy Peabody Essex Museum, SuperStock, H. ARMSTRONG ROBERTS, Pablo San Juan/CORBIS, Morgan-Cain, Tim Flach/Getty Images; **69** (cw from top)Dennis Brack/Black Star, Ted Spiegel/CORBIS, (cl)Fraunces Tavern Museum, (br)Stock Montage; **70** (cw from top)California State Library, Levi Strauss & Company, Bettmann/CORBIS, Larry Lee Photography/CORBIS, EyeWire Images; **71** (tl)Flip Schulke/Black Star, (tr)Collection of Cheekwood Museum of Art, (cl)Library of Congress, (cr)Picture Research Consultants, (bl)Bettmann/CORBIS, (br)Arthur Schatz/TimePix, Nashville, Tennessee; **72** (t)U.S. Architect of the Capitol, (bl)Scala/Art Resource, (br)Bettmann/CORBIS; **73** (bl)The Pilgrim Society, (bc)National Portrait Gallery, (br)Bettmann/CORBIS; **74** (t)Charles & Josette Lenars/CORBIS, (c)Giraudon/Art Resource, NY, (bl)Scala/Art Resource, NY, (bcl)National Portrait Gallery, (bcr)Historical Picture Collection/Stock Montage, (br)Mary Evans Picture Library; **74–75** (bkgd)Worldsat International Inc. 2004, All Rights Reserved; **75** (t)Jamestown Foundation, (c)Francis G. Mayer/CORBIS, (bl)Independence National Historical Park, (bcl)White House Historical Association, (br)Stock Montage, (bcr)National Portrait Gallery, Smithsonian Institution/Art Resource, NY; **76–77** William S. Helsel/Getty Images; **79** U.S. Architect of the Capitol; **81** (l)Hulton Archive, (r)The Bodleian Library, Oxford, Ms. Bodl. 264, fol.219R; **82** (l)National Museum of American History, Smithsonian Institution, Behring Center, (r)Photograph Courtesy Peabody Essex Museum; **83** (l)National Maritime Museum, (r)CORBIS; **84** Giraudon/Art Resource, NY; **85** Doug Martin; **88** Florida State Archives; **91** Bibliotheque Nationale, Paris; **92** Scala/Art Resource, NY; **93** Réunion des Musées Nationaux/Art Resource, NY; **94** Jack Fields/CORBIS; **99** The Jewish Museum, NY/Art Resource; **101** Archivo Iconografico, S.A./CORBIS; **102** SuperStock; **104** National Portrait Gallery, London, copyright Snark/Art Resource, NY; **106** Stock Montage; **108** The City of Plainfield, NJ; **109** 1997 Suzanne-Murphy-Larronde; **112–113** Owaki-Kulla/CORBIS; **115** Yale University Art Gallery, Bequest of Eugene Phelps Edwards; **117** Bettmann/CORBIS; **118** Robert Holmes/CORBIS; **123** Gibbes Museum of Art/Carolina Art Association; **125** (bl)National Museum of American History/Smithsonian Institution, (br)Bettmann/CORBIS; **127** file photo; **128** (bkgd)Getty, Yale University Art Gallery, Bequest of Eugene Phelps Edwards; **129** National Portrait Gallery, London/SuperStock; **130** Patrick Henry Before the Virginia House of Burgesses (1851) by Peter F. Rothermel. Red Hill, The Patrick Henry National Memorial, Brookneal, VA; **132** White House Historical Association; **133** Bettmann/CORBIS; **136** (tr)Courtesy of the Massachusetts Historical Society, (bl)file photo; **137** (bl)Library of Congress, (br)Kevin Fleming/CORBIS; **138** (tl)The Royal Collection © 2003 Her Majesty Queen Elizabeth II, (t)DAR Museum on loan from Boston Tea Party Chapter, (bl)Stock Montage, (br)Courtesy American Antiquarian Society; **139** Photograph Courtesy Peabody Essex Museum; **142** Museum of Fine Arts, Boston. Gift of Joseph W. Revere, William B. Revere, and Edward H.R. Revere; **148** (tl cl br)Doug Martin, (cr)file photo; **151** (tr)National Portrait Gallery, Smithsonian Institution/Art Resources, NY, (bl)Yale University Art Gallery; **152** Copyright 1996, Virginia Historical Society, Lora Robins Collection of Virginia Art; **153** Bettmann/CORBIS; **154** (tr)Bill Gentile/CORBIS, (bl)Fraunces Tavern Museum, New York City; **155** William T. Ranney, MARION CROSSING THE PEDEE, 1850, o/c, 1983.126; Amon Carter Museum, Fort Worth, Texas; **158 159 160** Bettmann/CORBIS; **161** Stapleton Collection/CORBIS; **165** Francis G. Mayer/CORBIS; **167** Bettmann/CORBIS; **168** (bl)Photograph Courtesy Peabody Essex Museum, (br)Courtesy Pilgrim Society, Plymouth, MA; **169** (c)Hulton-Deutsch Collection/CORBIS, (cr)Fort Ticonderoga Museum, (cl)Lexington Historical Society, Lexington, MA, (br)Bettmann/CORBIS; **170** (t)Library of Congress; **171** (tl)Bettmann/CORBIS, (tr)Charles E. Rotkin/CORBIS, (b)CORBIS; **172** (t)file photo, (c)Bettmann/CORBIS, (cr)Burstein Collection/CORBIS, (bl)Moorland Spingarn Research Center, Howard University, (bcl)Delaware Art Museum, Wilmington. Gift of Absalom Jones School, Wilmington, (br)Yale University Art Gallery, gift of Roger Sherman White, B.A. 1859; **172–173** (bkgd)Worldsat International Inc. 2004, All Rights Reserved; **173** (t)SuperStock, (tcr)Mary Evans Picture Library, (c)David R. Frazie, (bl)Bettmann/CORBIS, (bcl)Museum of Fine Arts, Boston; Bequest of Winslow Warren, (br)Getty Images; **174–175** SuperStock; **180** Picture Research Consultants; **181** (b)Minute Man National Historic Park/Rob Huntley for Chromographics; **184** Chicago Historical Society; **192** Doug Martin; **194** Bettmann/CORBIS; **195** Gallo Images/CORBIS; **196** (tr)Moorland Spingarn Research Center, Howard University, (bl)Delaware Art Museum, Wilmington. Gift of Absalom Jones School, Wilmington; **197** Independence National Historic Park; **198** Burstein Collection/CORBIS; **200** (l)Francis G. Mayer/CORBIS, (r)Joseph Sohm; Visions of America/CORBIS; **203** National Portrait Gallery, London, copyright Snark/Art Resource, NY; **204** Fred Maroon/Smithsonian Institution; **205** Richard Strauss, Smithsonian Institution/The Supreme Court Historical Society; **208** Stock Montage; **209** Bettmann/CORBIS; **210** Library of Congress/American Antiquarian Society; **211** Collection of The New York Historical Society; **214–215** Elliot Teel Photography; **217** Jeff Greenberg/Photo Edit; **218** (l) Bettmann/CORBIS, (r)White House Historical Association; **219** David Young-Wolff/Photo Edit; **220** Mary Evans Picture Library; **226** (l) Francis G. Mayer/CORBIS, (c) White House Historical Association (r)Getty Images; **227 229** Courtesy U.S. Congress; **231** Richard T. Nowitz/CORBIS; **232** Getty Images; **233** Carl Iwaski/TimePix/Getty Images; **234 235** White House Historical Association; **237** (l)North Wind/North Wind Picture Archives, (r) Jeff Greenberg/Photo Edit; **240** (t)Getty Images, (b) Bettmann/CORBIS; **241** Glenn Martin/Denver Post/Wide World Photos; **242** The Pierpont Morgan Library/Art Resource, NY; **243** (t)Burstein Collection/CORBIS, (b) Bettmann/CORBIS; **246** (t)Bettmann/CORBIS, (bl)Picture Research Consultant, (br)Courtesy U.S. Congress; **247** (t)Carl Iwaski/TimePix/Getty Images, (bl)Burstein Collection/CORBIS, (br)Mary Evans Picture Library; **248** (bkgd)Wes Thompson/The Stock Market/CORBIS, (l)Library of Congress; **250** White House Historical Association; **251** Courtesy U.S. Senate; **252** Bettmann/CORBIS; **254** Boltin Picture Library; **255** White House Historical Association; **262** Joseph Sohm; ChromoShom Inc./CORBIS; **266** Bettmann/CORBIS; **267** Nathan Benn/CORBIS; **268** TimePix; **269** Sandy Schaeffer/TimePix; **270** (t)Frank & Marie-Therese Wood Print Collection, Alexandria, VA, (bl)AKG London, (br)Giraudon/Art Resource, NY; **271** (t)North Wind Picture Archives, (bl)Michael T. Sedman/CORBIS, (br)Royalty Free/CORBIS; **272** (t)Chicago Historical Society, (c)North Wind Picture Archive, (bl)Archivo Iconografico, S.A./CORBIS, (bcl)White House Historical Association, (bcr)Bettmann/CORBIS, (br)E.S. Paxson,"Lewis and Clark at Three Forks," Courtesy of the Montana Historical Society, photograph by Don Beaty; **272–273** (bkgd)Worldsat International Inc. 2004, All Rights Reserved; **273** (t)Western American Prints, (c)Don Troiani, www.historicalartprints.com, (bl bcl)Bettmann/CORBIS, (br)Stock Montage, (bcr)Greenville County Museum of Art; **274–275** Royalty-

Free/CORBIS; **277** Stock Montage; **278** (l r)White House Historical Association, (c)Yale University Art Gallery; **279** Frank & Marie-Therese Wood Print Collection, Alexandria, VA; **280** (l)General Washington on a White Charger, Gift of Edgar William & Bernie Chrysler Garbisch, Image © 2004 Board of Trustees, National Gallery of Art, Washington D.C., (r)Fred Prouser/Reuters/CORBIS; **282** David R. Frazier; **283** Archivo Iconografico, S.A./CORBIS; **286** Courtesy Winterthur Museum; **287** Chicago Historical Society; **291** Museum of the City of New York/CORBIS; **292** Stock Montage; **294** (tr)Stock Montage, (bl)Bettmann/CORBIS; **296** Stock Montage; **298** Bettmann/CORBIS; **299** file photo; **302–303** Joe Sohm/Alamy Images; **305** Stock Montage; **306** (l)White House Historical Association, (r)Duke University Archives; **308** White House Historical Association; **310** Getty Images; **311** Museum of the City of New York/CORBIS; **312** Western American Prints; **314** Brown Brothers; **315** Bettmann/CORBIS; **318** Bates Littlehales, (t)From Curtis's Botanical Magazine, 1863, photo by Volkmar Wentzel, (bl)E.S. Paxson, "Lewis and Clark at Three Forks," Courtesy of the Montana Historical Society, photograph by Don Beaty; **319** (t)Western American Prints, (b)Kevin C. Chadwick; **321** Beinecke Rare Book and Manuscript Library, Yale University; **322** Old Dartmouth Historical Society/New Bedford Whaling Museum; **323** The Wadsworth Atheneum Museum of Art, Hartford, CT. Purchased from the Artist before 1850; **324** Bettmann/CORBIS; **325** Angelo Hornak, CORBIS; **326 327** Getty Images; **328** North Wind/North Wind Picture Archives; **330** Thomas Gilcrease Institute; **331** Missouri Historical Society, St. Louis; **334–335** Mark E. Gibson/CORBIS; **337 340** CORBIS; **342** (Tecumseh) Field Museum of Natural History; **343** Lorence Bjorklund; **344** (tr)Greenville County Museum of Art, (bl)New York Historical Society; **352** Doug Martin; **354** Library of Congress; **357** Stock Montage; **358** Don Troiani, www.historicalartprints.com; **360** (tr)Hulton Getty, (c)TIME Inc. Picture Collection, (bl)Bettmann/CORBIS; **361** (t)National Gallery of Art, (b)NY Public Library/TIME Picture Collection; **364** (l)Library of Congress, (r)Collection of the Boston Public Library, Print Division; **366** file photo; **368** Smithsonian Institution; **369** Brown Brothers; **372** (t)H. Armstrong Roberts, (bl)National Museum of American History, Smithsonian Institution, Behring Center, (br)Western American Prints; **373** (t)Missouri Historical Society, St. Louis, (r)(Tecumseh)Field Museum of Natural History, (b)Michael T. Sedman/CORBIS; **374** (t)New York Historical Society, (cl)Smithsonian Institution, (cr)HOLT-ATHERTON SPECIAL COLLECTIONS, UNIVERSITY OF THE PACIFIC LIBRARIES, (b)Bettmann/CORBIS; **375** (t)Chicago Historical Society, (c)California State Library, (b)Harper's Weekly/CORBIS; **376** (t)Joseph Sohm; Chromosohm Inc./CORBIS, (c)SuperStock, (bl)Bettmann/CORBIS, (bcl bcr)National Portrait Gallery, Smithsonian Institution/Art Resource, NY, (br)Stock Montage; **376–377** (bkgd)Worldsat International Inc. 2004, All Rights Reserved; **377** (t)Steve Vidler/SuperStock, (c)Robert Holmes/CORBIS, (bl)White House Historical Association, (bcl)Stock Montage, (bcr)Smithsonian American Art Museum, Washington, DC/Art Resource, NY, (br)file photo; **378–379** David Muench/CORBIS; **381** (l r)Bettmann/CORBIS; **382** (l)Bettmann/CORBIS, (r)Getty Images; **383** Bettmann/CORBIS; **384** Aaron Haupt; **385** Lewis Hine/Museum of Photography at George Eastman House; **388** (l)SuperStock, (c)Stock Montage; **391** Stock Montage; **392** Joseph Sohm; Chromosohm Inc./CORBIS; **395** Howard University; **396** Jack Naylor; **397** Museum of Fine Arts, Boston; Gift of Maxim Karolik **398** National Park Service Collection; **399** (bkgd)(Detail) The Bay and Harbor of New York c. 1953–1855 Samuel B. Waugh (1814–1885) Watercolor on canvas, 99 1/5 X 198 1/4 Gift of Mrs. Robert L. Littlejohn, Museum of the City of New York, 33.169, (inset)Courtesy of The Bostonian Society/Old State House; **400** United States Naval Academy Museum; **402** (c)CORBIS, (r)National Portrait Gallery, Smithsonian Institution/Art Resource, NY; **403** Bettmann/CORBIS; **404** (t)National Portrait Gallery, Smithsonian Institution, Washington, DC/Art Resource, (b)Time Life Pictures/Getty Images; **406** (bl)Brown Brothers, (br)FPG/Getty Images; **408** (r)Chicago Historical Society; **408** (l)Mount Holyoke College Art Museum, South Hadley,Massachusetts; **409** Bettmann/CORBIS; **410** (l)Chicago Historical Society, (r)Meserve-Kunhardt Collection, courtesy Picture History, Mt. Kisco, NY; **411** (tl)Courtesy of Maria Mitchell Association, (tr)National Archives of Canada, (bl)Bettmann/CORBIS, (bc)Hulton Archive, (br)Nebraska State Historical Society Photograph Collections; **412** Robert Jackson; **414** (t)Library of Congress, (b)Old Dartmouth Historical Society/New Bedford Whaling Museum; **418–419** Bob Krist/CORBIS; **421** The J. Paul Getty Museum; **422** Smithsonian Institution; **423** James Randklev/CORBIS; **424** Bettmann/CORBIS, (r)Smithsonian Institution; **428** Jan Butchofsky-Houser/CORBIS; **429** The J. Paul Getty Museum; **430** Bettmann/CORBIS; **432** (l)Picture Research Consultants, (r)Stock Montage; **434** Trustees of the Boston Public Library; **435** (bkgd)Photo Researchers, (tr)John Deere Museum, (c)Adam Woolfitt/CORBIS (bl)Courtesy of The Charleston Museum, Charleston, South Carolina, (br)Valentine Museum; **436** Stock Montage; **438** Bettmann/CORBIS; **439** Photo Researchers; **442–443** Peter Gridley/Getty Images; **442** (l)White House Historical Association, (c)SuperStock, (r)National Portrait Gallery, Smithsonian Institution/Art Resource, NY; **445** Bettmann/CORBIS; **446** White House Historical Association; **447** New York Historical Society; **448** Pat & Chuck Blackley; **449** Library Company of Philadelphia; **450** North Wind Picture Archive; **452** (l)Smithsonian American Art Museum, Washington, DC/Art Resource, NY, (r)SuperStock; **453** Stock Montage; **455** SuperStock; **456** Smithsonian American Art Museum, Washington, DC/Art Resource, NY; **457** Thomas Gilcrease Institute of American Art, Tulsa, OK; **458** (l)Bettmann/CORBIS, (r)National Portrait Gallery, Smithsonian Institution/Art Resource, NY; **459** Bettmann/CORBIS; **460** New York Historical Society; **462** CORBIS; **463** Archives and Manuscripts Division of the Oklahoma Historical Society; **466–467** Steve Vidler/SuperStock; **468** Hulton Archive/Getty Images; **470** (l)Mongerson-Wunderlich Gallery, Chicago, (r)White House Historical Association; **471** Hulton Archive/Getty Images; **472** (l)Joel W. Rogers/CORBIS, (r)Bettmann/CORBIS; **473** (t)Mongerson-Wunderlich Gallery, Chicago, (b)Henry Groskinsky/Timepix; **476** National Portrait Gallery, Smithsonian Institution/Art Resource, NY; **477** Library of Congress, Prints & Photographs Division; **478** (l)Brown Brothers, (r)Bettmann/CORBIS; **479** (br)Northwind Picture Archives, (r)Brown Brothers, (bl)Chicago Historical Society/Photo Researchers Inc.; **480** (l)Texas Department of Highways and Public Transportation, (r)Texas State Library and Archives Commission; **481** (l)Center for American History/Barker Collection/UT-Austin, (r)Texas State Library and Archives Commission; **482–483** (bkgd)Friends of the Governor's Mansion, Austin; **484** Susanna Dickinson by Harry Anthony DeYoung. Alamo Collection. Photograph courtesy the Daughters of the Republic of Texas Library. CT97.9.; **485** Texas State Library and Archives Commission; **486** (l)Texas State Library and Archives Commission, photo by Eric Beggs, (r)San Jacinto Museum History Association; **488** (tr)Jim Corwin/Index Stock Imagery, (bl)Royalty-Free/CORBIS; **489** CORBIS; **490** (l)Chicago Historical Society, (r)California State Library; **491** (tl)Robert Holmes/CORBIS; **492** Thomas Gilcrease Institute of American Art, Tulsa, OK; **493** Arte Publico Press Archives; **494** Courtesy The Bancroft Library, University of California, Berkeley; **496** (l)file photo, (r)California State Library; **498** (l)Gerald French/CORBIS, (r)In house file; **499** Alaska Division of Tourism; **500** (l)Courtesy Wells Fargo Bank, (r)California State Capitol; **501** Courtesy The Oakland Museum; **502** Courtesy The Bancroft Library University of California, Berkeley; **503** (l)Levi Strauss & Company, (r)Syracuse Newspapers/The Image Works; **504** (t)Royalty-Free/CORBIS, (l)Courtesy The Bancroft Library University of California, Berkeley, (r)Monterey Public Library, California History Room Archives; **505** Courtesy Museum of Art, Brigham Young University; **513** Doug Martin; **514** Courtesy Denver Public Library Western History Collection; **515** Bettmann/CORBIS; **518** (t)Henry Groskinsky, (bl)American Antiquarian Society, (br)Collection of David J. and Janice L. Frent; **519** (t)New York Historical Society, (c)Stock Montage, (b)Courtesy The Oakland Museum; **520** (tr)CORBIS, (br)Courtesy of the United States Naval Academy Museum; **521** (tl)Michigan Capitol Committee, photography by Peter Glendinning, (tr)Museum of the Confederacy, (c)CORBIS, (b)Image Select/Art Resource, NY; **522** (l)Bettmann/CORBIS, (c)Thad Samuels Abell II/Getty Images, (bl)Chester County Historical Society, West Chester, PA, (bcl)Collection of William Gladstone, (bcr)Missouri Historical Society, St. Louis, (br)Courtesy Chicago Historical Society; **522–533** (bkgd)Worldsat International Inc. 2004, All Rights Reserved; **523** (t)Joseph Sohm; ChromoSohm Inc./CORBIS, (c)Lee Snider/Photo Images/CORBIS, (bl)National Archives, (bcl)CORBIS, (bcr)FPG, (br)White House Historical Association; **524–525** William A. Bake/CORBIS; **527** Getty Images; **530** Peabody Essex Museum/Mark Sexton; **531** CORBIS; **532** Collection of William Gladstone; **536** New York Historical Society; **537** Bettmann/CORBIS; **538** file photo; **539** The Corcoran Gallery of Art/CORBIS; **540** Gianni Dagli Orti/CORBIS; **541** New York Public Library, print division.; **544** Bettmann/CORBIS; **545** Schlesinger Library, Radcliffe Institute, Harvard University; **548** (l)White House Historical Association, (c)Missouri Historical Society, St. Louis, (r)National Portrait Gallery, Smithsonian Institution; **550** (t)The Supreme Court of the United States Office of the Curator, #1991.402.2, (b)Library of Congress; **551** The Miriam Matthews Collection; **552** Courtesy Illinois State Historical Library; **555** Chicago Historical Society; **557** Bettmann/CORBIS; **560 561** CORBIS; **562** Massachusetts Historical Society/Picture Research Consultants; **563** Bettmann/CORBIS; **560** (cl)Doug Martin; **565–566** Thad Samuels Abell II/Getty Images; **566** (tl)Museum of the Confederacy, (bl)Michigan Capitol Committee, photography by Peter Glendinning, (r)Getty Images; **569** Museum of the Confederacy; **570** Seventh Regiment Fund, New York City; **572–573** (bkgd)Getty Images; **574** Kean E. Wilcox Collection; **575** Royalty Free/CORBIS; **577** Manassas National Battlefield Park/Larry Sherer; **578** Getty Images; **580** (l)Michigan Capitol Committee, photography by Peter Glendinning, (r)Museum of the Confederacy; **582** Medford Historical Society Collection/CORBIS; **590** Doug Martin; **591** (l)Getty Images, (r)McLellan Lincoln Collection, The John Hay Library, Brown University/John Miller; **592 593** Getty Images; **595** file photo; **597** Kean E. Wilcox Collection; **598** (bkgd)Getty Images, (t)Museum of the Confederacy; **599** Library of Congress; **601** Hulton Archive/Getty Images; **602** (l)Brown Brothers, (c)file photo, (r)CORBIS; **607** Lester Lefkowitz/CORBIS; **610** Northwind Picture Archives; **611** (tr)Washington & Lee University, Virginia, (bl)Bettmann/CORBIS; **612** National Archives; **616** Medford Historical Society Collection/CORBIS; **617** Museum of the Confederacy; **620** (tl)Time Life Books, from the series Civil War/Edward Owen, (bl)Illinois State Historical Library, (bc)Bettmann/CORBIS; **620–621** CORBIS; **623** Photographic History Collection, National Museum of American History, Smithsonian Institution, negative number 86-11374; **624** (l)National Museum of American History, Smithsonian Institution, Behring Center, (r)North Wind Picture Archive; **625** Thaddeus Stevens by Edward Dalton, The Library of the Union League of Philadelphia photo by Rick Echelmeyer; **627** Howard University; **629** White House Historical Association; **630** Chicago Historical Society; **631** Collection of Cheekwood Museum of Art, Nashville, Tennessee; **633** Bettmann/CORBIS; **635 636** CORBIS; **637** Chester County Historical Society, West Chester, PA; **639** Photographic History Collection, National Museum of American History, Smithsonian Institution, negative number 86-11374.; **640** White House Historical Association; **641** Stock Montage; **642** (c)file photo; **642–643** (bkgd)CORBIS; **643** (r)Bettmann/CORBIS; **646** Pembroke Herbert/Picture Research Consultants; **647** Amistad Foundation/Wadsworth Atheneum; **648** The Museum of American Political Life, University of Hartford; **649** Brown Brothers; **650** Bettmann/CORBIS; **651** Carl Iwaski/TimePix/Getty Images; **652** Cook Collection/Valentine Museum; **653** Library of Congress/CORBIS; **656** (tl tr)Museum of the Confederacy, (bl)Frank & Marie-Therese Wood Print Collection, Alexandria, VA, (br)Getty Images; **657** (t)Illinois State Historical Library, (c)Chicago Historical Society, (b)Getty Images; **658** (t)Stanford University Museum of Art, (c)Getty Images, (bl)Museo Civico Modigliana, Italy/Dagli Orti/Art Archive, (br)Mary Evans Picture Library; **659** (t)Library of Congress, (c)Ted Streshinsky/CORBIS, (b)Brown Brothers; **660** (t)Wolfgang Kaehler/CORBIS, (cl)Stock Montage, (cr)Worldsat International Inc. 2004, All Rights Reserved, (bl)National Anthropological Archives, Smithsonian Institution (neg. #2906), (bcl)CORBIS, (bcr)Bettmann/CORBIS, (br)Jane Addams Memorial Collection (JAMC neg. 1003), The University Library, University of Illinois at Chicago; **660–661** (bkgd)Worldsat International Inc. 2004, All Rights Reserved; **661** (t)CORBIS, (cl)Worldsat International Inc. 2004, All Rights Reserved, (cr)Bettmann/CORBIS, (bl)Oscar White/CORBIS, (bcl)Archive Photo, (bcr)Oscar B. Willis/The Schomburg Center for Research in Black Culture, New York Public Library, (br)The Schomburg Center for Research in Black Culture, New York Public Library; **662** (l)Library of Congress, (r)Collection of David J. & Janice L. Frent; **662–663** Wyoming Division of Cultural Resources; **665** Photograph from the book The Life and Adventures of Nat Love by himself/Rare Book and Manuscripts, Special Collections Library, Duke University, Durham, North Carolina; **667** CORBIS; **668** Colorado Historical Society; **669** (l)Brown Brothers, (r)L. Berger/SuperStock; **670** From the original painting by Mort Kunstler, The Race, Mort Kunstler, Inc.; **673** Photograph from the book The Life and Adventures of Nat Love by himself/Rare Book and Manuscripts, Special Collections Library, Duke University, Durham, North Carolina; **674** Thomas Gilcrease Institute of American Art, Tulsa, OK; **675** Yale Collection of Western Americana, Beinecke Rare Book & Manuscript Library; **677** United States Military Museum, West Point; **678** (l)Nebraska State Historical Society Photograph Collections, (r)Montana Historical Society, Helena; **684** Doug Martin; **686** Smithsonian American Art Museum, Washington, DC/Art Resource, NY; **687** Courtesy, National Museum of the American Indian, Smithsonian Institution (20/6563). Photo by Carmelo Guadagno.; **688** Denver Public Library, Western History Collection; **690** Bettmann/CORBIS; **691** National Portrait Gallery, Smithsonian Institution/Art Resource, NY; **693** (l)Collection of David J. & Janice L. Frent, (r)White House Historical Association; **694** New York Historical Society; **695** Kansas State Historical Society; **696** AP/Wide World Photos; **698** Amon Carter Museum, Fort Worth, Texas; **699** file photo; **702–703** Huntington Library/SuperStock; **702** (l)Courtesy Rockefeller Archive Center, (r)Photo by Dane Penland, National Air and Space Museum, Smithsonian Institution (SI 79-764); **705** Kansas Collection, Spencer Research Library, University of Kansas Libraries; **707** Michael Masslan Historic Photographs/CORBIS; **708** Getty Images; **712** (l)Electricity Collections, National Museum of American History, Smithsonian Institution, (r)Courtesy Ford Motor Company; **714–715** Brown Brothers; **716** (tl)Electricity Collections, National Museum of American History, Smithsonian Institution, (tc)Picture Research Consultants, (tr)The Queens Borough Public Library, Long Island Division, Latimer Family Papers, (bl)Picture Research Consultants, (br)Courtesy George Eastman House; **718** (l)Courtesy Rockefeller Archive Center, (r)National Portrait Gallery/Smithsonian Institution/Art Resource, NY; **720** Library of Congress; **721** (l)National Portrait Gallery/Smithsonian Institution/Art Resource, NY, (r)National Park Service; **722** Courtesy Rockefeller Archive Center; **724** (l)The George Meany Memorial Archives, (r)Library of Congress; **725** Library of Congress; **726** Fine Arts Museums of San Francisco, Gift of Mr. and Mrs. John D. Rockefeller 3rd 1979.7.4 zz; **728** Bettmann/CORBIS; **730** Time Life Pictures/Getty Images; **731** North Wind/North Wind Picture Archives; **732 733** CORBIS; **736–737** Charles O'Rear/CORBIS; **736** (l)Bettmann/CORBIS, (r)Brown Brothers; **738** CORBIS; **739** Picture Research Consultants; **741** Library of Congress; **743** Jacob A. Riis Collection, Museum of the City of New York; **744** (t)National Archives, (b)Brown Brothers; **745** Bettmann/CORBIS; **746** Picture Research Consultants; **748** Rykoff Collection/CORBIS; **749** Austrian Archives/CORBIS; **752** Orchard Films; **753** Jane Addams Memorial Collection (JAMC neg. 1003), The University Library, University of Illinois at Chicago; **754** Brown Brothers; **755** CORBIS; **757** (l)Doug Martin, (c)Courtesy, National Museum of the American Indian, Smithsonian Institution (N36122/3), (r)Harris Ewing; **758** Library of Congress; **759** (bc br)Bettmann/CORBIS, (others)Library of Congress; **760** (t)CORBIS, (bl)Courtesy, National Museum of the American Indian, Smithsonian Institution, (br)Courtesy, National Museum of the American Indian, Smithsonian Institution (N36122/3).; **762** Winslow Homer American, 1836–1910. Girls with Lobster, 1873. Watercolor and gouache over graphite, 24.2 X 32.9 cm. (c) The Cleveland Museum of Art, 2002. Purchase from the J. H. Wade Fund, 1943.660; **764** (l)White House Historical Association, (r)The Ida M. Tarbell Collection, Pelletier Library, Allegheny College; **765** Library of Congress; **766** CORBIS; **768** file photo; **769** Bettmann/CORBIS; **770** Collection of David J. & Janice L. Frent; **772** Daniel J. Cox/naturalexposures.com; **773** Robin Brandt; **777** (l)Leonard de Selva/CORBIS, (r)Private Collection/courtesy R.H. Love Galleries, Chicago; **779** (l)Bettmann/CORBIS, (r)Private Collection; **781** (t)Oscar White/CORBIS, (b)The Schomburg Center for Research in Black Culture, New York Public Library; **782** CORBIS; **784** (bl)Harris Ewing; **785** (tr)Schenectady Museum/Hall of Electrical History Foundation/CORBIS, (others)Bettmann/CORBIS; **786** Underwood & Underwood/CORBIS; **787** Library of Congress; **790** (t)Brown Brothers, (bl)Bob Mullenix, (br)Picture Research Consultants; **791** (t)Courtesy, National Museum of the American Indian, Smithsonian Institution (20/6563). Photo by Carmelo Guadagno., (c)National Portrait Gallery/Smithsonian Insitiution/Art Resource, NY, (b)Yale Collection of Western Americana, Beinecke Rare Book & Manuscript Library; **792** Underwood Archives/Index Stock Imagery; **793** Getty Images; **794** (t)Franklin D. Roosevelt Library, (b)Library of Congress; **795** (t)National Archives, (b)US Army; **796** (t)Robert Reiff/MagicLight Productions, (b)Flip Schulke/Black Star; **797** (t)Mike Segar/Reuters/TimePix, (b)Thomas E. Franklin/Bergen Record/SABA/CORBIS; **798** Bettmann/CORBIS; **799** Underwood & Underwood/CORBIS; **800** Library of Congress; **801** Charles Moore/Black Star; **802** (t)AP/Wide World Photos, (b)Collection of David J. & Janice L. Frent; **804** (t)CORBIS, (c)A.J. SISCO/CORBIS, (b)Bruce Kliewe/Index Stock; **806** (t)Library of Congress; **807** Detroit Publishing Company; **808** Rob Lewine/The Stock Market; **809** (t)Swim Ink/CORBIS, (b)US Air Force Museum; **810** (t)Bettmann/CORBIS, (b)Getty Images; **812** Christie's Images; **813** Getty Images; **814** Official Senate Photo/CNP/Getty Images; **816** (t)Schlesinger Library, Radcliffe Institute, Harvard University, (b)Joe Raedle/Newsmakers; **817** (l)Bob Daemmrich, (r)AP/Wide World Photos; **818** (t)Tony Freeman/PhotoEdit, (b)James Shaffer/PhotoEdit; **819** Royalty Free/CORBIS; **820** (tl)Picture Research Consultants, (tr)Peter Turnley/CORBIS, (tcr)file photo, (cl)SuperStock, (cr bcl)Getty (bcr)Brown Brothers, (br)Courtesy Smithsonian Institution, NMAH/Transportation; **823** MAK I; **824** Maritime Museum, Seville/Artephot/Oronoz; **826** file photo; **828** White House Historical Association; **830** National Archives; **831 832** Bettmann/CORBIS; **833** Geoffrey Clements/CORBIS; **834** Library of Congress; **835** US Army Military History Institute; **836** Choctaw Removal, 1966. Valjean McCarty Hessing, Choctaw, B. 1934. Watercolor on paper, Museum purchase, The Philbrook Museum of Art, Tulsa, Oklahoma., 1967.24; **837** The Museum of American Political Life, University of Hartford; **838** Tim Flach/Getty Images, (l)North Wind Picture Archives, (r)Electricity Collections, National Museum of American History, Smithsonian Institution; **840 841 842 843** White House Historical Association; **844** (br)Official White House Photo by Eric Draper, (bcr)White House Historical Association (White House Collection, 6196), (others)White House Historical Association; **845** (bkgd)Getty Images, (tl)CORBIS; **846** Missouri Historical Society, St. Louis; **847 848** Bettmann/CORBIS; **850** North Wind Picture Archive; **851 852** Bettmann/CORBIS; **853** (t)Bettmann/CORBIS, (b)Courtesy, National Museum of the American Indian, Smithsonian Institution (20/1843). Photo by Carmelo Guadagno.; **854** National Portrait Gallery, Smithsonian Institution/Art Resource, NY; **855** (t)National Portrait Gallery, Smithsonian Institution/Art Resource, NY, (b)Mark Burnett; **856** (l)file photo, (r)Mark Burnett; **857** (t)Denver Art Museum, (b)Bettmann/CORBIS; **859** UPI/Bettmann/CORBIS; **860** Bettmann/CORBIS; **861** Flip Schulke/Black Star.